Collins

SCRABBLE®

WORDS

2005

Collins

SCRABBLE®

WORDS
2005

Collins

An Imprint of HarperCollins*Publishers*

first edition 2004

© HarperCollins Publishers 2004

HarperCollins Publishers
Westerhill Road, Bishopbriggs, Glasgow G64 2QT
Great Britain

www.collins.co.uk

Collins® is a registered trademark of
HarperCollins Publishers Limited

SCRABBLE® is a registered trademark of
J. W. Spear & Sons Ltd., a subsidiary of Mattel, Inc.
© 2004 Mattel, Inc.

ISBN 0-00-719019-0

A catalogue record for this book is available
from the British Library

This book is set in CollinsFedra, a typeface specially
created for Collins dictionaries by Peter Bil'ak.

Project Manager
Morven Dooner

Editor
Justin Crozier

Publishing Manager
Elaine Higgleton

Computing Support
Thomas Callan

Collins Corpus Programmer
Nigel Rochford

Typesetting
Wordcraft

Printed and bound in Great Britain
by Clays Ltd, St Ives plc

Introduction

Collins Scrabble Words – Every Word Counts

Collins Scrabble Words, the new Scrabble authority, is the most extensive Scrabble word list ever published. The list includes over 260,000 words, which have been carefully selected from over two billion words of world English held in the Collins collection of word sources and corpora, including *Collins English Dictionary*.

Collins Scrabble Words includes words and their inflected forms of up to and including 15 letters in length, all of which are allowable in Scrabble and should give players more flexibility in their games than ever before. It's an invaluable adjudication tool for everyone playing in English.

Words not listed include those spelt with an initial capital letter, abbreviations, prefixes and suffixes, and words requiring apostrophes and hyphens, none of which are allowed in Scrabble.

Accents

As English-language Scrabble tiles are not accented, no accents are shown in *Collins Scrabble Words*.

Word Order

Collins Scrabble Words is an alphabetical word list: therefore any inflected forms of a base word are given in alphabetical order, and not after the base form, as in many dictionaries.

Offensive Terms

There may be words in *Collins Scrabble Words* that most or some players might consider taboo or offensive. We strongly recommend that players check meanings and suitability for general use in *Collins English Dictionary*.

A

AA
AAH
AAHED
AAHING
AAHS
AAL
AALII
AALIIS
AALS
AARDVARK
AARDVARKS
AARDWOLF
AARDWOLVES
AARGH
AARRGH
AARRGHH
AAS
AASVOGEL
AASVOGELS
AB
ABA
ABAC
ABACA
ABACAS
ABACI
ABACK
ABACS
ABACTERIAL
ABACTINAL
ABACTINALLY
ABACTOR
ABACTORS
ABACUS
ABACUSES
ABAFT
ABAKA
ABAKAS
ABALONE
ABALONES
ABAMP
ABAMPERE
ABAMPERES
ABAMPS
ABAND
ABANDED
ABANDING
ABANDON
ABANDONED
ABANDONEDLY
ABANDONEE
ABANDONEES

ABANDONER
ABANDONERS
ABANDONING
ABANDONMENT
ABANDONMENTS
ABANDONS
ABANDS
ABAPICAL
ABAS
ABASE
ABASED
ABASEDLY
ABASEMENT
ABASEMENTS
ABASER
ABASERS
ABASES
ABASH
ABASHED
ABASHEDLY
ABASHES
ABASHING
ABASHLESS
ABASHMENT
ABASHMENTS
ABASIA
ABASIAS
ABASING
ABASK
ABATABLE
ABATE
ABATED
ABATEMENT
ABATEMENTS
ABATER
ABATERS
ABATES
ABATING
ABATIS
ABATISES
ABATOR
ABATORS
ABATTIS
ABATTISES
ABATTOIR
ABATTOIRS
ABATTU
ABATURE
ABATURES
ABAXIAL
ABAXILE

ABAYA
ABAYAS
ABB
ABBA
ABBACIES
ABBACY
ABBAS
ABBATIAL
ABBE
ABBED
ABBES
ABBESS
ABBESSES
ABBEY
ABBEYS
ABBOT
ABBOTCIES
ABBOTCY
ABBOTS
ABBOTSHIP
ABBOTSHIPS
ABBREVIATE
ABBREVIATED
ABBREVIATES
ABBREVIATING
ABBREVIATION
ABBREVIATIONS
ABBREVIATOR
ABBREVIATORS
ABBREVIATORY
ABBREVIATURE
ABBREVIATURES
ABBS
ABCEE
ABCEES
ABCOULOMB
ABCOULOMBS
ABDABS
ABDICABLE
ABDICANT
ABDICATE
ABDICATED
ABDICATES
ABDICATING
ABDICATION
ABDICATIONS
ABDICATIVE
ABDICATIVENESS
ABDICATOR
ABDICATORS
ABDOMEN

ABDOMENS
ABDOMINA
ABDOMINAL
ABDOMINALLY
ABDOMINOUS
ABDUCE
ABDUCED
ABDUCENS
ABDUCENT
ABDUCENTES
ABDUCES
ABDUCING
ABDUCT
ABDUCTED
ABDUCTEE
ABDUCTEES
ABDUCTING
ABDUCTION
ABDUCTIONS
ABDUCTOR
ABDUCTORES
ABDUCTORS
ABDUCTS
ABEAM
ABEAR
ABEARING
ABEARS
ABECEDARIAN
ABECEDARIANS
ABED
ABEIGH
ABELE
ABELES
ABELIA
ABELIAN
ABELIAS
ABELMOSK
ABELMOSKS
ABERDEVINE
ABERDEVINES
ABERNETHIES
ABERNETHY
ABERRANCE
ABERRANCES
ABERRANCIES
ABERRANCY
ABERRANT
ABERRANTLY
ABERRANTS
ABERRATE
ABERRATED

ABERRATES
ABERRATING
ABERRATION
ABERRATIONAL
ABERRATIONS
ABESSIVE
ABESSIVES
ABET
ABETMENT
ABETMENTS
ABETS
ABETTAL
ABETTALS
ABETTED
ABETTER
ABETTERS
ABETTING
ABETTOR
ABETTORS
ABEYANCE
ABEYANCES
ABEYANCIES
ABEYANCY
ABEYANT
ABFARAD
ABFARADS
ABHENRIES
ABHENRY
ABHENRYS
ABHOMINABLE
ABHOR
ABHORRED
ABHORRENCE
ABHORRENCES
ABHORRENCIES
ABHORRENCY
ABHORRENT
ABHORRENTLY
ABHORRER
ABHORRERS
ABHORRING
ABHORRINGS
ABHORS
ABID
ABIDANCE
ABIDANCES
ABIDDEN
ABIDE
ABIDED
ABIDER
ABIDERS
ABIDES
ABIDING
ABIDINGLY
ABIDINGS
ABIES

ABIETIC
ABIGAIL
ABIGAILS
ABILITIES
ABILITY
ABIOGENESES
ABIOGENESIS
ABIOGENETIC
ABIOGENETICALLY
ABIOGENIC
ABIOGENICALLY
ABIOGENIST
ABIOGENISTS
ABIOLOGICAL
ABIOSES
ABIOSIS
ABIOTIC
ABIOTICALLY
ABIRRITANT
ABIRRITANTS
ABIRRITATE
ABIRRITATED
ABIRRITATES
ABIRRITATING
ABIRRITATION
ABIRRITATIONAL
ABITURIENT
ABITURIENTS
ABJECT
ABJECTED
ABJECTING
ABJECTION
ABJECTIONS
ABJECTLY
ABJECTNESS
ABJECTNESSES
ABJECTS
ABJOINT
ABJOINTED
ABJOINTING
ABJOINTS
ABJUNCTION
ABJUNCTIONS
ABJURATION
ABJURATIONS
ABJURE
ABJURED
ABJURER
ABJURERS
ABJURES
ABJURING
ABLACTATION
ABLACTATIONS
ABLATE
ABLATED
ABLATES

ABLATING
ABLATION
ABLATIONS
ABLATITIOUS
ABLATIVAL
ABLATIVE
ABLATIVELY
ABLATIVES
ABLATOR
ABLATORS
ABLAUT
ABLAUTS
ABLAZE
ABLE
ABLED
ABLEGATE
ABLEGATES
ABLEISM
ABLEISMS
ABLEIST
ABLER
ABLES
ABLEST
ABLET
ABLETS
ABLING
ABLINGS
ABLINS
ABLOOM
ABLOW
ABLUENT
ABLUENTS
ABLUSH
ABLUTED
ABLUTION
ABLUTIONARY
ABLUTIONS
ABLUTOMANE
ABLUTOMANES
ABLY
ABMHO
ABMHOS
ABNEGATE
ABNEGATED
ABNEGATES
ABNEGATING
ABNEGATION
ABNEGATIONS
ABNEGATOR
ABNEGATORS
ABNORMAL
ABNORMALISM
ABNORMALISMS
ABNORMALITIES
ABNORMALITY
ABNORMALLY

ABNORMALS
ABNORMITIES
ABNORMITY
ABNORMOUS
ABO
ABOARD
ABODE
ABODED
ABODEMENT
ABODEMENTS
ABODES
ABODING
ABOHM
ABOHMS
ABOIDEAU
ABOIDEAUS
ABOIDEAUX
ABOIL
ABOITEAU
ABOITEAUS
ABOITEAUX
ABOLISH
ABOLISHABLE
ABOLISHED
ABOLISHER
ABOLISHERS
ABOLISHES
ABOLISHING
ABOLISHMENT
ABOLISHMENTS
ABOLITION
ABOLITIONAL
ABOLITIONARY
ABOLITIONISM
ABOLITIONISMS
ABOLITIONIST
ABOLITIONISTS
ABOLITIONS
ABOLLA
ABOLLAE
ABOLLAS
ABOMA
ABOMAS
ABOMASA
ABOMASAL
ABOMASI
ABOMASUM
ABOMASUS
ABOMASUSES
ABOMINABLE
ABOMINABLENESS
ABOMINABLY
ABOMINATE
ABOMINATED
ABOMINATES
ABOMINATING

ABOMINATION
ABOMINATIONS
ABOMINATOR
ABOMINATORS
ABONDANCE
ABONDANCES
ABONNEMENT
ABONNEMENTS
ABOON
ABORAL
ABORALLY
ABORD
ABORDED
ABORDING
ABORDS
ABORE
ABORIGEN
ABORIGENS
ABORIGIN
ABORIGINAL
ABORIGINALISM
ABORIGINALISMS
ABORIGINALITIES
ABORIGINALITY
ABORIGINALLY
ABORIGINALS
ABORIGINE
ABORIGINES
ABORIGINS
ABORNE
ABORNING
ABORT
ABORTED
ABORTEE
ABORTEES
ABORTER
ABORTERS
ABORTICIDE
ABORTICIDES
ABORTIFACIENT
ABORTIFACIENTS
ABORTING
ABORTION
ABORTIONAL
ABORTIONIST
ABORTIONISTS
ABORTIONS
ABORTIVE
ABORTIVELY
ABORTIVENESS
ABORTIVENESSES
ABORTS
ABORTUARIES
ABORTUARY
ABOS
ABOUGHT

ABOULIA
ABOULIAS
ABOULIC
ABOUND
ABOUNDED
ABOUNDING
ABOUNDS
ABOUT
ABOUTS
ABOVE
ABOVEBOARD
ABOVEGROUND
ABOVES
ABRACADABRA
ABRACADABRAS
ABRACHIA
ABRACHIAS
ABRADABLE
ABRADANT
ABRADANTS
ABRADE
ABRADED
ABRADER
ABRADERS
ABRADES
ABRADING
ABRAID
ABRAIDED
ABRAIDING
ABRAIDS
ABRAM
ABRANCHIAL
ABRANCHIATE
ABRASAX
ABRASION
ABRASIONS
ABRASIVE
ABRASIVELY
ABRASIVENESS
ABRASIVENESSES
ABRASIVES
ABRAXAS
ABRAXASES
ABRAY
ABRAYED
ABRAYING
ABRAYS
ABRAZO
ABRAZOS
ABREACT
ABREACTED
ABREACTING
ABREACTION
ABREACTIONS
ABREACTIVE
ABREACTS

ABREAST
ABREGE
ABREGES
ABRI
ABRICOCK
ABRICOCKS
ABRIDGABLE
ABRIDGE
ABRIDGEABLE
ABRIDGED
ABRIDGEMENT
ABRIDGEMENTS
ABRIDGER
ABRIDGERS
ABRIDGES
ABRIDGING
ABRIDGMENT
ABRIDGMENTS
ABRIM
ABRIN
ABRINS
ABRIS
ABROACH
ABROAD
ABROADS
ABROGATE
ABROGATED
ABROGATES
ABROGATING
ABROGATION
ABROGATIONS
ABROGATIVE
ABROGATOR
ABROGATORS
ABROOKE
ABROOKED
ABROOKES
ABROOKING
ABROSIA
ABROSIAS
ABRUPT
ABRUPTER
ABRUPTEST
ABRUPTION
ABRUPTIONS
ABRUPTLY
ABRUPTNESS
ABRUPTNESSES
ABRUPTS
ABS
ABSCESS
ABSCESSED
ABSCESSES
ABSCESSING
ABSCIND
ABSCINDED

ABSCINDING
ABSCINDS
ABSCISE
ABSCISED
ABSCISES
ABSCISIN
ABSCISING
ABSCISINS
ABSCISS
ABSCISSA
ABSCISSAE
ABSCISSAS
ABSCISSE
ABSCISSES
ABSCISSIN
ABSCISSINS
ABSCISSION
ABSCISSIONS
ABSCOND
ABSCONDED
ABSCONDENCE
ABSCONDENCES
ABSCONDER
ABSCONDERS
ABSCONDING
ABSCONDS
ABSEIL
ABSEILED
ABSEILING
ABSEILINGS
ABSEILS
ABSENCE
ABSENCES
ABSENT
ABSENTED
ABSENTEE
ABSENTEEISM
ABSENTEEISMS
ABSENTEES
ABSENTER
ABSENTERS
ABSENTING
ABSENTLY
ABSENTMINDED
ABSENTMINDEDLY
ABSENTS
ABSEY
ABSEYS
ABSINTH
ABSINTHE
ABSINTHES
ABSINTHIATED
ABSINTHISM
ABSINTHISMS
ABSINTHS
ABSIT

ABSITS
ABSOLUTE
ABSOLUTELY
ABSOLUTENESS
ABSOLUTENESSES
ABSOLUTER
ABSOLUTES
ABSOLUTEST
ABSOLUTION
ABSOLUTIONS
ABSOLUTISM
ABSOLUTISMS
ABSOLUTIST
ABSOLUTISTIC
ABSOLUTISTS
ABSOLUTIVE
ABSOLUTIZE
ABSOLUTIZED
ABSOLUTIZES
ABSOLUTIZING
ABSOLUTORY
ABSOLVABILITY
ABSOLVABLE
ABSOLVABLY
ABSOLVE
ABSOLVED
ABSOLVER
ABSOLVERS
ABSOLVES
ABSOLVING
ABSOLVITOR
ABSOLVITORS
ABSONANT
ABSORB
ABSORBABILITIES
ABSORBABILITY
ABSORBABLE
ABSORBANCE
ABSORBANCES
ABSORBANCIES
ABSORBANCY
ABSORBANT
ABSORBANTS
ABSORBATE
ABSORBATES
ABSORBED
ABSORBEDLY
ABSORBEFACIENT
ABSORBEFACIENTS
ABSORBENCIES
ABSORBENCY
ABSORBENT
ABSORBENTS
ABSORBER
ABSORBERS
ABSORBING

ABSORBINGLY
ABSORBS
ABSORPTANCE
ABSORPTANCES
ABSORPTIOMETER
ABSORPTIOMETERS
ABSORPTION
ABSORPTIONS
ABSORPTIVE
ABSORPTIVENESS
ABSORPTIVITIES
ABSORPTIVITY
ABSQUATULATE
ABSQUATULATED
ABSQUATULATES
ABSQUATULATING
ABSTAIN
ABSTAINED
ABSTAINER
ABSTAINERS
ABSTAINING
ABSTAINS
ABSTEMIOUS
ABSTEMIOUSLY
ABSTEMIOUSNESS
ABSTENTION
ABSTENTIONISM
ABSTENTIONISMS
ABSTENTIONIST
ABSTENTIONISTS
ABSTENTIONS
ABSTENTIOUS
ABSTERGE
ABSTERGED
ABSTERGENT
ABSTERGENTS
ABSTERGES
ABSTERGING
ABSTERSION
ABSTERSIONS
ABSTERSIVE
ABSTERSIVES
ABSTINENCE
ABSTINENCES
ABSTINENCIES
ABSTINENCY
ABSTINENT
ABSTINENTLY
ABSTRACT
ABSTRACTABLE
ABSTRACTED
ABSTRACTEDLY
ABSTRACTEDNESS
ABSTRACTER
ABSTRACTERS
ABSTRACTEST

ABSTRACTING
ABSTRACTION
ABSTRACTIONAL
ABSTRACTIONISM
ABSTRACTIONISMS
ABSTRACTIONIST
ABSTRACTIONISTS
ABSTRACTIONS
ABSTRACTIVE
ABSTRACTIVELY
ABSTRACTIVES
ABSTRACTLY
ABSTRACTNESS
ABSTRACTNESSES
ABSTRACTOR
ABSTRACTORS
ABSTRACTS
ABSTRICT
ABSTRICTED
ABSTRICTING
ABSTRICTION
ABSTRICTIONS
ABSTRICTS
ABSTRUSE
ABSTRUSELY
ABSTRUSENESS
ABSTRUSENESSES
ABSTRUSER
ABSTRUSEST
ABSTRUSITIES
ABSTRUSITY
ABSURD
ABSURDER
ABSURDEST
ABSURDISM
ABSURDISMS
ABSURDIST
ABSURDISTS
ABSURDITIES
ABSURDITY
ABSURDLY
ABSURDNESS
ABSURDNESSES
ABSURDS
ABTHANE
ABTHANES
ABUBBLE
ABUILDING
ABULIA
ABULIAS
ABULIC
ABUNA
ABUNAS
ABUNDANCE
ABUNDANCES
ABUNDANCIES

ABUNDANCY
ABUNDANT
ABUNDANTLY
ABUNE
ABURST
ABUSABLE
ABUSAGE
ABUSAGES
ABUSE
ABUSED
ABUSER
ABUSERS
ABUSES
ABUSING
ABUSION
ABUSIONS
ABUSIVE
ABUSIVELY
ABUSIVENESS
ABUSIVENESSES
ABUT
ABUTILON
ABUTILONS
ABUTMENT
ABUTMENTS
ABUTS
ABUTTAL
ABUTTALS
ABUTTED
ABUTTER
ABUTTERS
ABUTTING
ABUZZ
ABVOLT
ABVOLTS
ABWATT
ABWATTS
ABY
ABYE
ABYEING
ABYES
ABYING
ABYS
ABYSM
ABYSMAL
ABYSMALLY
ABYSMS
ABYSS
ABYSSAL
ABYSSES
ABYSSOPELAGIC
ACACIA
ACACIAS
ACADEME
ACADEMES
ACADEMIA

ACADEMIAS
ACADEMIC
ACADEMICAL
ACADEMICALISM
ACADEMICALISMS
ACADEMICALLY
ACADEMICALS
ACADEMICIAN
ACADEMICIANS
ACADEMICISM
ACADEMICISMS
ACADEMICS
ACADEMIES
ACADEMISM
ACADEMISMS
ACADEMIST
ACADEMISTS
ACADEMY
ACAJOU
ACAJOUS
ACALCULIA
ACALEPH
ACALEPHAE
ACALEPHAN
ACALEPHANS
ACALEPHE
ACALEPHES
ACALEPHS
ACANACEOUS
ACANTH
ACANTHA
ACANTHACEOUS
ACANTHAS
ACANTHI
ACANTHIN
ACANTHINE
ACANTHINS
ACANTHOCEPHALAN
ACANTHOID
ACANTHOUS
ACANTHS
ACANTHUS
ACANTHUSES
ACAPNIA
ACAPNIAS
ACARI
ACARIAN
ACARIASES
ACARIASIS
ACARICIDAL
ACARICIDE
ACARICIDES
ACARID
ACARIDAN
ACARIDANS
ACARIDEAN

ACARIDEANS
ACARIDIAN
ACARIDIANS
ACARIDOMATIA
ACARIDOMATIUM
ACARIDS
ACARINE
ACARINES
ACARODOMATIA
ACARODOMATIUM
ACAROID
ACAROLOGIES
ACAROLOGIST
ACAROLOGISTS
ACAROLOGY
ACAROPHILIES
ACAROPHILY
ACARPELLOUS
ACARPELOUS
ACARPOUS
ACARUS
ACATALECTIC
ACATALECTICS
ACATALEPSIES
ACATALEPSY
ACATALEPTIC
ACATALEPTICS
ACATAMATHESIA
ACATAMATHESIAS
ACATER
ACATERS
ACATES
ACATOUR
ACATOURS
ACAUDAL
ACAUDATE
ACAULESCENT
ACAULINE
ACAULOSE
ACAULOUS
ACCABLE
ACCEDE
ACCEDED
ACCEDENCE
ACCEDENCES
ACCEDER
ACCEDERS
ACCEDES
ACCEDING
ACCELERABILITY
ACCELERABLE
ACCELERANDO
ACCELERANDOS
ACCELERANT
ACCELERANTS
ACCELERATE

ACCELERATED
ACCELERATES
ACCELERATING
ACCELERATINGLY
ACCELERATION
ACCELERATIONS
ACCELERATIVE
ACCELERATOR
ACCELERATORS
ACCELERATORY
ACCELEROMETER
ACCELEROMETERS
ACCEND
ACCENDED
ACCENDING
ACCENDS
ACCENSION
ACCENSIONS
ACCENT
ACCENTED
ACCENTING
ACCENTLESS
ACCENTOR
ACCENTORS
ACCENTS
ACCENTUAL
ACCENTUALITIES
ACCENTUALITY
ACCENTUALLY
ACCENTUATE
ACCENTUATED
ACCENTUATES
ACCENTUATING
ACCENTUATION
ACCENTUATIONS
ACCEPT
ACCEPTABILITIES
ACCEPTABILITY
ACCEPTABLE
ACCEPTABLENESS
ACCEPTABLY
ACCEPTANCE
ACCEPTANCES
ACCEPTANCIES
ACCEPTANCY
ACCEPTANT
ACCEPTANTS
ACCEPTATION
ACCEPTATIONS
ACCEPTED
ACCEPTEDLY
ACCEPTEE
ACCEPTEES
ACCEPTER
ACCEPTERS
ACCEPTILATION

ACCEPTILATIONS
ACCEPTING
ACCEPTINGLY
ACCEPTINGNESS
ACCEPTINGNESSES
ACCEPTIVE
ACCEPTIVITIES
ACCEPTIVITY
ACCEPTOR
ACCEPTORS
ACCEPTS
ACCESS
ACCESSARIES
ACCESSARILY
ACCESSARINESS
ACCESSARY
ACCESSED
ACCESSES
ACCESSIBILITIES
ACCESSIBILITY
ACCESSIBLE
ACCESSIBLENESS
ACCESSIBLY
ACCESSING
ACCESSION
ACCESSIONAL
ACCESSIONED
ACCESSIONING
ACCESSIONS
ACCESSORIAL
ACCESSORIES
ACCESSORII
ACCESSORILY
ACCESSORINESS
ACCESSORISE
ACCESSORISED
ACCESSORISES
ACCESSORISING
ACCESSORIUS
ACCESSORIZE
ACCESSORIZED
ACCESSORIZES
ACCESSORIZING
ACCESSORY
ACCIACCATURA
ACCIACCATURAS
ACCIACCATURE
ACCIDENCE
ACCIDENCES
ACCIDENT
ACCIDENTAL
ACCIDENTALISM
ACCIDENTALISMS
ACCIDENTALITIES
ACCIDENTALITY
ACCIDENTALLY

ACCIDENTALNESS
ACCIDENTALS
ACCIDENTED
ACCIDENTLY
ACCIDENTOLOGIST
ACCIDENTOLOGY
ACCIDENTS
ACCIDIA
ACCIDIAS
ACCIDIE
ACCIDIES
ACCINGE
ACCINGED
ACCINGES
ACCINGING
ACCIPITER
ACCIPITERS
ACCIPITRAL
ACCIPITRINE
ACCIPITRINES
ACCITE
ACCITED
ACCITES
ACCITING
ACCLAIM
ACCLAIMED
ACCLAIMER
ACCLAIMERS
ACCLAIMING
ACCLAIMS
ACCLAMATION
ACCLAMATIONS
ACCLAMATORY
ACCLIMATABILITY
ACCLIMATABLE
ACCLIMATATION
ACCLIMATATIONS
ACCLIMATE
ACCLIMATED
ACCLIMATES
ACCLIMATING
ACCLIMATION
ACCLIMATIONS
ACCLIMATISABLE
ACCLIMATISATION
ACCLIMATISE
ACCLIMATISED
ACCLIMATISER
ACCLIMATISERS
ACCLIMATISES
ACCLIMATISING
ACCLIMATIZABLE
ACCLIMATIZATION
ACCLIMATIZE
ACCLIMATIZED
ACCLIMATIZER

ACCLIMATIZERS
ACCLIMATIZES
ACCLIMATIZING
ACCLIVITIES
ACCLIVITOUS
ACCLIVITY
ACCLIVOUS
ACCLOY
ACCLOYED
ACCLOYING
ACCLOYS
ACCOAST
ACCOASTED
ACCOASTING
ACCOASTS
ACCOIED
ACCOIL
ACCOILS
ACCOLADE
ACCOLADES
ACCOMMODABLE
ACCOMMODATE
ACCOMMODATED
ACCOMMODATES
ACCOMMODATING
ACCOMMODATINGLY
ACCOMMODATION
ACCOMMODATIONAL
ACCOMMODATIONS
ACCOMMODATIVE
ACCOMMODATOR
ACCOMMODATORS
ACCOMPANIED
ACCOMPANIER
ACCOMPANIERS
ACCOMPANIES
ACCOMPANIMENT
ACCOMPANIMENTS
ACCOMPANIST
ACCOMPANISTS
ACCOMPANY
ACCOMPANYING
ACCOMPANYIST
ACCOMPANYISTS
ACCOMPLICE
ACCOMPLICES
ACCOMPLISH
ACCOMPLISHABLE
ACCOMPLISHED
ACCOMPLISHER
ACCOMPLISHERS
ACCOMPLISHES
ACCOMPLISHING
ACCOMPLISHMENT
ACCOMPLISHMENTS
ACCOMPT

ACCOMPTABLE
ACCOMPTANT
ACCOMPTANTS
ACCOMPTED
ACCOMPTING
ACCOMPTS
ACCORAGE
ACCORAGED
ACCORAGES
ACCORAGING
ACCORD
ACCORDABLE
ACCORDANCE
ACCORDANCES
ACCORDANCIES
ACCORDANCY
ACCORDANT
ACCORDANTLY
ACCORDED
ACCORDER
ACCORDERS
ACCORDING
ACCORDINGLY
ACCORDION
ACCORDIONIST
ACCORDIONISTS
ACCORDIONS
ACCORDS
ACCOST
ACCOSTABLE
ACCOSTED
ACCOSTING
ACCOSTS
ACCOUCHEMENT
ACCOUCHEMENTS
ACCOUCHEUR
ACCOUCHEURS
ACCOUCHEUSE
ACCOUCHEUSES
ACCOUNT
ACCOUNTABILITY
ACCOUNTABLE
ACCOUNTABLENESS
ACCOUNTABLY
ACCOUNTANCIES
ACCOUNTANCY
ACCOUNTANT
ACCOUNTANTS
ACCOUNTANTSHIP
ACCOUNTANTSHIPS
ACCOUNTED
ACCOUNTING
ACCOUNTINGS
ACCOUNTS
ACCOUPLEMENT
ACCOUPLEMENTS

ACCOURAGE
ACCOURAGED
ACCOURAGES
ACCOURAGING
ACCOURT
ACCOURTED
ACCOURTING
ACCOURTS
ACCOUSTREMENT
ACCOUSTREMENTS
ACCOUTER
ACCOUTERED
ACCOUTERING
ACCOUTERMENT
ACCOUTERMENTS
ACCOUTERS
ACCOUTRE
ACCOUTRED
ACCOUTREMENT
ACCOUTREMENTS
ACCOUTRES
ACCOUTRING
ACCOY
ACCOYED
ACCOYING
ACCOYLD
ACCOYS
ACCREDIT
ACCREDITABLE
ACCREDITATION
ACCREDITATIONS
ACCREDITED
ACCREDITING
ACCREDITS
ACCRESCENCE
ACCRESCENCES
ACCRESCENT
ACCRETE
ACCRETED
ACCRETES
ACCRETING
ACCRETION
ACCRETIONARY
ACCRETIONS
ACCRETIVE
ACCREW
ACCREWED
ACCREWING
ACCREWS
ACCROIDES
ACCRUABLE
ACCRUAL
ACCRUALS
ACCRUE
ACCRUED
ACCRUEMENT

ACCRUEMENTS
ACCRUES
ACCRUING
ACCUBATION
ACCUBATIONS
ACCULTURAL
ACCULTURATE
ACCULTURATED
ACCULTURATES
ACCULTURATING
ACCULTURATION
ACCULTURATIONAL
ACCULTURATIONS
ACCULTURATIVE
ACCUMBENCIES
ACCUMBENCY
ACCUMBENT
ACCUMULABILITY
ACCUMULABLE
ACCUMULATE
ACCUMULATED
ACCUMULATES
ACCUMULATING
ACCUMULATION
ACCUMULATIONS
ACCUMULATIVE
ACCUMULATIVELY
ACCUMULATOR
ACCUMULATORS
ACCURACIES
ACCURACY
ACCURATE
ACCURATELY
ACCURATENESS
ACCURATENESSES
ACCURSE
ACCURSED
ACCURSEDLY
ACCURSEDNESS
ACCURSEDNESSES
ACCURSES
ACCURSING
ACCURST
ACCUSABLE
ACCUSAL
ACCUSALS
ACCUSANT
ACCUSANTS
ACCUSATION
ACCUSATIONS
ACCUSATIVAL
ACCUSATIVE
ACCUSATIVELY
ACCUSATIVES
ACCUSATORIAL
ACCUSATORY

ACCUSE
ACCUSED
ACCUSEMENT
ACCUSEMENTS
ACCUSER
ACCUSERS
ACCUSES
ACCUSING
ACCUSINGLY
ACCUSTOM
ACCUSTOMARY
ACCUSTOMATION
ACCUSTOMATIONS
ACCUSTOMED
ACCUSTOMEDNESS
ACCUSTOMING
ACCUSTOMS
ACCUSTREMENT
ACCUSTREMENTS
ACE
ACED
ACEDIA
ACEDIAS
ACELDAMA
ACELDAMAS
ACELLULAR
ACENTRIC
ACEPHALOUS
ACEQUIA
ACEQUIAS
ACER
ACERACEOUS
ACERATE
ACERATED
ACERB
ACERBATE
ACERBATED
ACERBATES
ACERBATING
ACERBER
ACERBEST
ACERBIC
ACERBICALLY
ACERBITIES
ACERBITY
ACEROLA
ACEROLAS
ACEROSE
ACEROUS
ACERS
ACERVATE
ACERVATELY
ACERVATION
ACERVATIONS
ACERVULI
ACERVULUS

ACES
ACESCENCE
ACESCENCES
ACESCENCIES
ACESCENCY
ACESCENT
ACESCENTS
ACETA
ACETABULA
ACETABULAR
ACETABULUM
ACETABULUMS
ACETAL
ACETALDEHYDE
ACETALDEHYDES
ACETALS
ACETAMID
ACETAMIDE
ACETAMIDES
ACETAMIDS
ACETAMINOPHEN
ACETAMINOPHENS
ACETANILID
ACETANILIDE
ACETANILIDES
ACETANILIDS
ACETATE
ACETATED
ACETATES
ACETAZOLAMIDE
ACETAZOLAMIDES
ACETIC
ACETIFICATION
ACETIFICATIONS
ACETIFIED
ACETIFIER
ACETIFIERS
ACETIFIES
ACETIFY
ACETIFYING
ACETIN
ACETINS
ACETOMETER
ACETOMETERS
ACETOMETRIC
ACETOMETRY
ACETONAEMIA
ACETONE
ACETONEMIA
ACETONES
ACETONIC
ACETONITRILE
ACETONITRILES
ACETONURIA
ACETOPHENETIDIN
ACETOSE

ACETOUS
ACETOXYL
ACETOXYLS
ACETUM
ACETYL
ACETYLATE
ACETYLATED
ACETYLATES
ACETYLATING
ACETYLATION
ACETYLATIONS
ACETYLATIVE
ACETYLCHOLINE
ACETYLCHOLINES
ACETYLENE
ACETYLENES
ACETYLENIC
ACETYLIC
ACETYLIDE
ACETYLIDES
ACETYLS
ACETYLSALICYLIC
ACH
ACHAENIA
ACHAENIUM
ACHAENIUMS
ACHAENOCARP
ACHAENOCARPS
ACHAGE
ACHAGES
ACHALASIA
ACHALASIAS
ACHARNE
ACHARYA
ACHARYAS
ACHATES
ACHE
ACHED
ACHENE
ACHENES
ACHENIA
ACHENIAL
ACHENIUM
ACHENIUMS
ACHES
ACHIER
ACHIEST
ACHIEVABLE
ACHIEVE
ACHIEVED
ACHIEVEMENT
ACHIEVEMENTS
ACHIEVER
ACHIEVERS
ACHIEVES
ACHIEVING

ACHILLEA
ACHILLEAS
ACHIMENES
ACHIMENESES
ACHINESS
ACHINESSES
ACHING
ACHINGLY
ACHINGS
ACHIOTE
ACHIOTES
ACHKAN
ACHKANS
ACHLAMYDEOUS
ACHLORHYDRIA
ACHLORHYDRIAS
ACHLORHYDRIC
ACHOLIA
ACHOLIAS
ACHONDRITE
ACHONDRITES
ACHONDRITIC
ACHONDROPLASIA
ACHONDROPLASIAS
ACHONDROPLASTIC
ACHOO
ACHROMAT
ACHROMATIC
ACHROMATICALLY
ACHROMATICITIES
ACHROMATICITY
ACHROMATIN
ACHROMATINS
ACHROMATISATION
ACHROMATISE
ACHROMATISED
ACHROMATISES
ACHROMATISING
ACHROMATISM
ACHROMATISMS
ACHROMATIZATION
ACHROMATIZE
ACHROMATIZED
ACHROMATIZES
ACHROMATIZING
ACHROMATOPSIA
ACHROMATOPSIAS
ACHROMATOUS
ACHROMATS
ACHROMIC
ACHROMOUS
ACHY
ACICULA
ACICULAE
ACICULAR
ACICULAS

ACICULATE
ACICULATED
ACICULUM
ACICULUMS
ACID
ACIDANTHERA
ACIDANTHERAS
ACIDEMIA
ACIDEMIAS
ACIDER
ACIDEST
ACIDFREAK
ACIDFREAKS
ACIDHEAD
ACIDHEADS
ACIDIC
ACIDIER
ACIDIEST
ACIDIFIABLE
ACIDIFICATION
ACIDIFICATIONS
ACIDIFIED
ACIDIFIER
ACIDIFIERS
ACIDIFIES
ACIDIFY
ACIDIFYING
ACIDIMETER
ACIDIMETERS
ACIDIMETRIC
ACIDIMETRICAL
ACIDIMETRICALLY
ACIDIMETRIES
ACIDIMETRY
ACIDITIES
ACIDITY
ACIDLY
ACIDNESS
ACIDNESSES
ACIDOMETER
ACIDOMETERS
ACIDOPHIL
ACIDOPHILE
ACIDOPHILES
ACIDOPHILIC
ACIDOPHILOUS
ACIDOPHILS
ACIDOPHILUS
ACIDOPHILUSES
ACIDOSES
ACIDOSIS
ACIDOTIC
ACIDS
ACIDULATE
ACIDULATED
ACIDULATES

ACIDULATING
ACIDULATION
ACIDULATIONS
ACIDULENT
ACIDULOUS
ACIDURIA
ACIDURIAS
ACIDY
ACIERAGE
ACIERAGES
ACIERATE
ACIERATED
ACIERATES
ACIERATING
ACIERATION
ACIERATIONS
ACIFORM
ACINACEOUS
ACINACIFORM
ACINAR
ACING
ACINI
ACINIC
ACINIFORM
ACINOSE
ACINOUS
ACINUS
ACKEE
ACKEES
ACKER
ACKERS
ACKNEW
ACKNOW
ACKNOWING
ACKNOWLEDGE
ACKNOWLEDGEABLE
ACKNOWLEDGEABLY
ACKNOWLEDGED
ACKNOWLEDGEDLY
ACKNOWLEDGEMENT
ACKNOWLEDGER
ACKNOWLEDGERS
ACKNOWLEDGES
ACKNOWLEDGING
ACKNOWLEDGMENT
ACKNOWLEDGMENTS
ACKNOWN
ACKNOWNE
ACKNOWS
ACLINIC
ACMATIC
ACME
ACMES
ACMIC
ACMITE
ACMITES

ACNE
ACNED
ACNES
ACNODAL
ACNODALLY
ACNODE
ACNODES
ACOCK
ACOELOMATE
ACOELOMATES
ACOEMETI
ACOLD
ACOLOUTHIC
ACOLOUTHITE
ACOLOUTHITES
ACOLOUTHOS
ACOLOUTHOSES
ACOLUTHIC
ACOLYTE
ACOLYTES
ACOLYTH
ACOLYTHS
ACONITE
ACONITES
ACONITIC
ACONITINE
ACONITINES
ACONITUM
ACONITUMS
ACORN
ACORNED
ACORNS
ACOSMISM
ACOSMISMS
ACOSMIST
ACOSMISTS
ACOTYLEDON
ACOTYLEDONOUS
ACOTYLEDONS
ACOUCHI
ACOUCHIES
ACOUCHIS
ACOUCHY
ACOUSTIC
ACOUSTICAL
ACOUSTICALLY
ACOUSTICIAN
ACOUSTICIANS
ACOUSTICS
ACQUAINT
ACQUAINTANCE
ACQUAINTANCES
ACQUAINTED
ACQUAINTING
ACQUAINTS
ACQUEST

ACQUESTS
ACQUIESCE
ACQUIESCED
ACQUIESCENCE
ACQUIESCENCES
ACQUIESCENT
ACQUIESCENTLY
ACQUIESCENTS
ACQUIESCES
ACQUIESCING
ACQUIESCINGLY
ACQUIGHT
ACQUIGHTING
ACQUIGHTS
ACQUIRABILITIES
ACQUIRABILITY
ACQUIRABLE
ACQUIRAL
ACQUIRALS
ACQUIRE
ACQUIRED
ACQUIREMENT
ACQUIREMENTS
ACQUIRER
ACQUIRERS
ACQUIRES
ACQUIRING
ACQUISITION
ACQUISITIONAL
ACQUISITIONS
ACQUISITIVE
ACQUISITIVELY
ACQUISITIVENESS
ACQUISITOR
ACQUISITORS
ACQUIST
ACQUISTS
ACQUIT
ACQUITE
ACQUITES
ACQUITING
ACQUITMENT
ACQUITMENTS
ACQUITS
ACQUITTAL
ACQUITTALS
ACQUITTANCE
ACQUITTANCED
ACQUITTANCES
ACQUITTANCING
ACQUITTED
ACQUITTER
ACQUITTERS
ACQUITTING
ACRASIA
ACRASIAS

ACRASIN
ACRASINS
ACRATIC
ACRAWL
ACRE
ACREAGE
ACREAGES
ACRED
ACRES
ACRID
ACRIDER
ACRIDEST
ACRIDIN
ACRIDINE
ACRIDINES
ACRIDINS
ACRIDITIES
ACRIDITY
ACRIDLY
ACRIDNESS
ACRIDNESSES
ACRIFLAVIN
ACRIFLAVINE
ACRIFLAVINES
ACRIFLAVINS
ACRIMONIES
ACRIMONIOUS
ACRIMONIOUSLY
ACRIMONIOUSNESS
ACRIMONY
ACRITARCH
ACRITARCHS
ACROAMATIC
ACROAMATICAL
ACROBAT
ACROBATIC
ACROBATICALLY
ACROBATICS
ACROBATISM
ACROBATISMS
ACROBATS
ACROCARPOUS
ACROCENTRIC
ACROCENTRICS
ACROCYANOSES
ACROCYANOSIS
ACRODONT
ACRODONTS
ACRODROME
ACRODROMOUS
ACROGEN
ACROGENIC
ACROGENOUS
ACROGENOUSLY
ACROGENS
ACROLECT

ACROLECTS
ACROLEIN
ACROLEINS
ACROLITH
ACROLITHIC
ACROLITHS
ACROMEGALIC
ACROMEGALICS
ACROMEGALIES
ACROMEGALY
ACROMIA
ACROMIAL
ACROMION
ACRONIC
ACRONICAL
ACRONICALLY
ACRONYCAL
ACRONYCALLY
ACRONYCHAL
ACRONYCHALLY
ACRONYM
ACRONYMANIA
ACRONYMANIAS
ACRONYMIC
ACRONYMICALLY
ACRONYMOUS
ACRONYMS
ACROPARESTHESIA
ACROPETAL
ACROPETALLY
ACROPHOBE
ACROPHOBES
ACROPHOBIA
ACROPHOBIAS
ACROPHOBIC
ACROPHONETIC
ACROPHONIC
ACROPHONIES
ACROPHONY
ACROPOLIS
ACROPOLISES
ACROSOMAL
ACROSOME
ACROSOMES
ACROSPIRE
ACROSPIRES
ACROSS
ACROSTIC
ACROSTICAL
ACROSTICALLY
ACROSTICS
ACROTER
ACROTERIA
ACROTERIAL
ACROTERION
ACROTERIUM

ACROTERIUMS
ACROTERS
ACROTIC
ACROTISM
ACROTISMS
ACRYLAMIDE
ACRYLAMIDES
ACRYLATE
ACRYLATES
ACRYLIC
ACRYLICS
ACRYLONITRILE
ACRYLONITRILES
ACRYLYL
ACT
ACTA
ACTABILITIES
ACTABILITY
ACTABLE
ACTANT
ACTANTS
ACTED
ACTIN
ACTINAL
ACTINALLY
ACTING
ACTINGS
ACTINIA
ACTINIAE
ACTINIAN
ACTINIANS
ACTINIAS
ACTINIC
ACTINICALLY
ACTINIDE
ACTINIDES
ACTINIFORM
ACTINISM
ACTINISMS
ACTINIUM
ACTINIUMS
ACTINOBACILLI
ACTINOBACILLUS
ACTINOBIOLOGY
ACTINOCHEMISTRY
ACTINOID
ACTINOIDS
ACTINOLITE
ACTINOLITES
ACTINOMERE
ACTINOMERES
ACTINOMETER
ACTINOMETERS
ACTINOMETRIC
ACTINOMETRICAL
ACTINOMETRIES

ACTINOMETRY
ACTINOMORPHIC
ACTINOMORPHIES
ACTINOMORPHISM
ACTINOMORPHOUS
ACTINOMORPHY
ACTINOMYCES
ACTINOMYCETE
ACTINOMYCETES
ACTINOMYCETOUS
ACTINOMYCIN
ACTINOMYCINS
ACTINOMYCOSES
ACTINOMYCOSIS
ACTINOMYCOTIC
ACTINON
ACTINONS
ACTINOPOD
ACTINOPODS
ACTINOTHERAPIES
ACTINOTHERAPY
ACTINOURANIUM
ACTINOZOAN
ACTINOZOANS
ACTINS
ACTION
ACTIONABLE
ACTIONABLY
ACTIONED
ACTIONER
ACTIONERS
ACTIONING
ACTIONIST
ACTIONISTS
ACTIONLESS
ACTIONS
ACTIVATE
ACTIVATED
ACTIVATES
ACTIVATING
ACTIVATION
ACTIVATIONS
ACTIVATOR
ACTIVATORS
ACTIVE
ACTIVELY
ACTIVENESS
ACTIVENESSES
ACTIVES
ACTIVISM
ACTIVISMS
ACTIVIST
ACTIVISTIC
ACTIVISTS
ACTIVITIES
ACTIVITY

ACTIVIZE
ACTIVIZED
ACTIVIZES
ACTIVIZING
ACTOMYOSIN
ACTOMYOSINS
ACTON
ACTONS
ACTOR
ACTORISH
ACTORS
ACTRESS
ACTRESSES
ACTRESSY
ACTS
ACTUAL
ACTUALISATION
ACTUALISATIONS
ACTUALISE
ACTUALISED
ACTUALISES
ACTUALISING
ACTUALIST
ACTUALISTS
ACTUALITE
ACTUALITES
ACTUALITIES
ACTUALITY
ACTUALIZATION
ACTUALIZATIONS
ACTUALIZE
ACTUALIZED
ACTUALIZES
ACTUALIZING
ACTUALLY
ACTUALS
ACTUARIAL
ACTUARIALLY
ACTUARIES
ACTUARY
ACTUATE
ACTUATED
ACTUATES
ACTUATING
ACTUATION
ACTUATIONS
ACTUATOR
ACTUATORS
ACTURE
ACTURES
ACUATE
ACUITIES
ACUITY
ACULEATE
ACULEATED
ACULEI

ACULEUS
ACULEUSES
ACUMEN
ACUMENS
ACUMINATE
ACUMINATED
ACUMINATES
ACUMINATING
ACUMINATION
ACUMINATIONS
ACUMINOUS
ACUPOINT
ACUPOINTS
ACUPRESSURE
ACUPRESSURES
ACUPUNCTURAL
ACUPUNCTURE
ACUPUNCTURES
ACUPUNCTURIST
ACUPUNCTURISTS
ACUSHLA
ACUSHLAS
ACUTANCE
ACUTANCES
ACUTE
ACUTELY
ACUTENESS
ACUTENESSES
ACUTER
ACUTES
ACUTEST
ACYCLIC
ACYCLOVIR
ACYCLOVIRS
ACYL
ACYLATE
ACYLATED
ACYLATES
ACYLATING
ACYLATION
ACYLATIONS
ACYLOIN
ACYLOINS
ACYLS
AD
ADACTYLOUS
ADAGE
ADAGES
ADAGIAL
ADAGIO
ADAGIOS
ADAMANCE
ADAMANCES
ADAMANCIES
ADAMANCY
ADAMANT

ADAMANTEAN
ADAMANTINE
ADAMANTLY
ADAMANTS
ADAMSITE
ADAMSITES
ADAPT
ADAPTABILITIES
ADAPTABILITY
ADAPTABLE
ADAPTABLENESS
ADAPTABLENESSES
ADAPTATION
ADAPTATIONAL
ADAPTATIONALLY
ADAPTATIONS
ADAPTATIVE
ADAPTED
ADAPTEDNESS
ADAPTEDNESSES
ADAPTER
ADAPTERS
ADAPTING
ADAPTION
ADAPTIONS
ADAPTIVE
ADAPTIVELY
ADAPTIVENESS
ADAPTIVENESSES
ADAPTIVITIES
ADAPTIVITY
ADAPTOR
ADAPTORS
ADAPTS
ADAW
ADAWED
ADAWING
ADAWS
ADAXIAL
ADAYS
ADD
ADDABLE
ADDAX
ADDAXES
ADDEBTED
ADDED
ADDEDLY
ADDEEM
ADDEEMED
ADDEEMING
ADDEEMS
ADDEND
ADDENDA
ADDENDS
ADDENDUM
ADDER

ADDERS
ADDERSTONE
ADDERSTONES
ADDERWORT
ADDERWORTS
ADDIBLE
ADDICT
ADDICTED
ADDICTEDNESS
ADDICTEDNESSES
ADDICTING
ADDICTION
ADDICTIONS
ADDICTIVE
ADDICTS
ADDIES
ADDING
ADDIO
ADDIOS
ADDITAMENT
ADDITAMENTS
ADDITION
ADDITIONAL
ADDITIONALITY
ADDITIONALLY
ADDITIONS
ADDITITIOUS
ADDITIVE
ADDITIVELY
ADDITIVES
ADDITIVITIES
ADDITIVITY
ADDITORY
ADDLE
ADDLED
ADDLEMENT
ADDLEMENTS
ADDLEPATED
ADDLES
ADDLING
ADDOOM
ADDOOMED
ADDOOMING
ADDOOMS
ADDORSED
ADDRESS
ADDRESSABILITY
ADDRESSABLE
ADDRESSED
ADDRESSEE
ADDRESSEES
ADDRESSER
ADDRESSERS
ADDRESSES
ADDRESSING
ADDRESSOR

ADDRESSORS
ADDREST
ADDS
ADDUCE
ADDUCEABLE
ADDUCEABLY
ADDUCED
ADDUCENT
ADDUCER
ADDUCERS
ADDUCES
ADDUCIBLE
ADDUCING
ADDUCT
ADDUCTED
ADDUCTING
ADDUCTION
ADDUCTIONS
ADDUCTIVE
ADDUCTOR
ADDUCTORS
ADDUCTS
ADDY
ADEEM
ADEEMED
ADEEMING
ADEEMS
ADELANTADO
ADELANTADOS
ADEMPTION
ADEMPTIONS
ADENECTOMIES
ADENECTOMY
ADENINE
ADENINES
ADENITIS
ADENITISES
ADENOCARCINOMA
ADENOCARCINOMAS
ADENOHYPOPHYSES
ADENOHYPOPHYSIS
ADENOID
ADENOIDAL
ADENOIDECTOMIES
ADENOIDECTOMY
ADENOIDS
ADENOMA
ADENOMAS
ADENOMATA
ADENOMATOUS
ADENOPATHIC
ADENOPATHY
ADENOSES
ADENOSINE
ADENOSINES
ADENOSIS

ADENOVIRAL
ADENOVIRUS
ADENOVIRUSES
ADENYL
ADENYLIC
ADENYLS
ADEPT
ADEPTER
ADEPTEST
ADEPTLY
ADEPTNESS
ADEPTNESSES
ADEPTS
ADEQUACIES
ADEQUACY
ADEQUATE
ADEQUATELY
ADEQUATENESS
ADEQUATENESSES
ADEQUATIVE
ADERMIN
ADERMINS
ADESPOTA
ADESSIVE
ADESSIVES
ADHAN
ADHARMA
ADHARMAS
ADHERE
ADHERED
ADHERENCE
ADHERENCES
ADHEREND
ADHERENDS
ADHERENT
ADHERENTLY
ADHERENTS
ADHERER
ADHERERS
ADHERES
ADHERING
ADHESION
ADHESIONAL
ADHESIONS
ADHESIVE
ADHESIVELY
ADHESIVENESS
ADHESIVENESSES
ADHESIVES
ADHIBIT
ADHIBITED
ADHIBITING
ADHIBITION
ADHIBITIONS
ADHIBITS
ADHOCRACIES

ADHOCRACY
ADIABATIC
ADIABATICALLY
ADIABATICS
ADIACTINIC
ADIAPHORA
ADIAPHORISM
ADIAPHORISMS
ADIAPHORIST
ADIAPHORISTIC
ADIAPHORISTS
ADIAPHORON
ADIAPHOROUS
ADIATHERMANCIES
ADIATHERMANCY
ADIATHERMANOUS
ADIATHERMIC
ADIEU
ADIEUS
ADIEUX
ADIOS
ADIPIC
ADIPOCERE
ADIPOCERES
ADIPOCEROUS
ADIPOCYTE
ADIPOCYTES
ADIPOSE
ADIPOSES
ADIPOSIS
ADIPOSITIES
ADIPOSITY
ADIPOUS
ADIPSIA
ADIT
ADITS
ADJACENCIES
ADJACENCY
ADJACENT
ADJACENTLY
ADJACENTS
ADJECTIVAL
ADJECTIVALLY
ADJECTIVE
ADJECTIVELY
ADJECTIVES
ADJIGO
ADJIGOS
ADJOIN
ADJOINED
ADJOINING
ADJOINS
ADJOINT
ADJOINTS
ADJOURN
ADJOURNED

ADJOURNING
ADJOURNMENT
ADJOURNMENTS
ADJOURNS
ADJUDGE
ADJUDGED
ADJUDGEMENT
ADJUDGEMENTS
ADJUDGES
ADJUDGING
ADJUDGMENT
ADJUDGMENTS
ADJUDICATE
ADJUDICATED
ADJUDICATES
ADJUDICATING
ADJUDICATION
ADJUDICATIONS
ADJUDICATIVE
ADJUDICATOR
ADJUDICATORS
ADJUDICATORY
ADJUNCT
ADJUNCTION
ADJUNCTIONS
ADJUNCTIVE
ADJUNCTIVELY
ADJUNCTLY
ADJUNCTS
ADJURATION
ADJURATIONS
ADJURATORY
ADJURE
ADJURED
ADJURER
ADJURERS
ADJURES
ADJURING
ADJUROR
ADJURORS
ADJUST
ADJUSTABILITIES
ADJUSTABILITY
ADJUSTABLE
ADJUSTABLY
ADJUSTED
ADJUSTER
ADJUSTERS
ADJUSTING
ADJUSTIVE
ADJUSTMENT
ADJUSTMENTAL
ADJUSTMENTS
ADJUSTOR
ADJUSTORS
ADJUSTS

ADJUTAGE
ADJUTAGES
ADJUTANCIES
ADJUTANCY
ADJUTANT
ADJUTANTS
ADJUVANCIES
ADJUVANCY
ADJUVANT
ADJUVANTS
ADLAND
ADLANDS
ADMAN
ADMASS
ADMASSES
ADMEASURE
ADMEASURED
ADMEASUREMENT
ADMEASUREMENTS
ADMEASURES
ADMEASURING
ADMEN
ADMIN
ADMINICLE
ADMINICLES
ADMINICULAR
ADMINICULATE
ADMINICULATED
ADMINICULATES
ADMINICULATING
ADMINISTER
ADMINISTERED
ADMINISTERING
ADMINISTERS
ADMINISTRABLE
ADMINISTRANT
ADMINISTRANTS
ADMINISTRATE
ADMINISTRATED
ADMINISTRATES
ADMINISTRATING
ADMINISTRATION
ADMINISTRATIONS
ADMINISTRATIVE
ADMINISTRATOR
ADMINISTRATORS
ADMINISTRATRIX
ADMINS
ADMIRABILITIES
ADMIRABILITY
ADMIRABLE
ADMIRABLENESS
ADMIRABLENESSES
ADMIRABLY
ADMIRAL
ADMIRALS

ADMIRALSHIP
ADMIRALSHIPS
ADMIRALTIES
ADMIRALTY
ADMIRANCE
ADMIRANCES
ADMIRATION
ADMIRATIONS
ADMIRATIVE
ADMIRAUNCE
ADMIRAUNCES
ADMIRE
ADMIRED
ADMIRER
ADMIRERS
ADMIRES
ADMIRING
ADMIRINGLY
ADMISSIBILITIES
ADMISSIBILITY
ADMISSIBLE
ADMISSIBLENESS
ADMISSION
ADMISSIONS
ADMISSIVE
ADMIT
ADMITS
ADMITTABLE
ADMITTANCE
ADMITTANCES
ADMITTED
ADMITTEDLY
ADMITTER
ADMITTERS
ADMITTING
ADMIX
ADMIXED
ADMIXES
ADMIXING
ADMIXT
ADMIXTURE
ADMIXTURES
ADMONISH
ADMONISHED
ADMONISHER
ADMONISHERS
ADMONISHES
ADMONISHING
ADMONISHINGLY
ADMONISHMENT
ADMONISHMENTS
ADMONITION
ADMONITIONS
ADMONITIVE
ADMONITOR
ADMONITORILY

ADMONITORS
ADMONITORY
ADNASCENT
ADNATE
ADNATION
ADNATIONS
ADNEXA
ADNEXAL
ADNOMINAL
ADNOMINALLY
ADNOMINALS
ADNOUN
ADNOUNS
ADO
ADOBE
ADOBELIKE
ADOBES
ADOBO
ADOBOS
ADOLESCENCE
ADOLESCENCES
ADOLESCENT
ADOLESCENTLY
ADOLESCENTS
ADONIS
ADONISE
ADONISED
ADONISES
ADONISING
ADONIZE
ADONIZED
ADONIZES
ADONIZING
ADOORS
ADOPT
ADOPTABILITIES
ADOPTABILITY
ADOPTABLE
ADOPTED
ADOPTEE
ADOPTEES
ADOPTER
ADOPTERS
ADOPTIANISM
ADOPTIANISMS
ADOPTIANIST
ADOPTIANISTS
ADOPTING
ADOPTION
ADOPTIONISM
ADOPTIONISMS
ADOPTIONIST
ADOPTIONISTS
ADOPTIONS
ADOPTIOUS
ADOPTIVE

ADOPTIVELY
ADOPTS
ADORABILITIES
ADORABILITY
ADORABLE
ADORABLENESS
ADORABLENESSES
ADORABLY
ADORATION
ADORATIONS
ADORE
ADORED
ADORER
ADORERS
ADORES
ADORING
ADORINGLY
ADORN
ADORNED
ADORNER
ADORNERS
ADORNING
ADORNMENT
ADORNMENTS
ADORNS
ADOS
ADOWN
ADOZE
ADPRESS
ADPRESSED
ADPRESSES
ADPRESSING
ADRAD
ADREAD
ADREADED
ADREADING
ADREADS
ADRED
ADRENAL
ADRENALECTOMIES
ADRENALECTOMY
ADRENALIN
ADRENALINE
ADRENALINES
ADRENALINS
ADRENALISED
ADRENALISER
ADRENALISERS
ADRENALISES
ADRENALISING
ADRENALIZED
ADRENALS
ADRENERGIC
ADRENERGICALLY
ADRENOCHROME
ADRENOCHROMES

ADRENOCORTICAL
ADRIAMYCIN
ADRIAMYCINS
ADRIFT
ADROIT
ADROITER
ADROITEST
ADROITLY
ADROITNESS
ADROITNESSES
ADRY
ADS
ADSCITITIOUS
ADSCITITIOUSLY
ADSCRIPT
ADSCRIPTION
ADSCRIPTIONS
ADSCRIPTS
ADSORB
ADSORBABILITIES
ADSORBABILITY
ADSORBABLE
ADSORBATE
ADSORBATES
ADSORBED
ADSORBENT
ADSORBENTS
ADSORBER
ADSORBERS
ADSORBING
ADSORBS
ADSORPTION
ADSORPTIONS
ADSORPTIVE
ADSUKI
ADSUM
ADUKI
ADULARESCENCE
ADULARESCENT
ADULARIA
ADULARIAS
ADULATE
ADULATED
ADULATES
ADULATING
ADULATION
ADULATIONS
ADULATOR
ADULATORS
ADULATORY
ADULT
ADULTERANT
ADULTERANTS
ADULTERATE
ADULTERATED
ADULTERATES

ADULTERATING
ADULTERATION
ADULTERATIONS
ADULTERATOR
ADULTERATORS
ADULTERER
ADULTERERS
ADULTERESS
ADULTERESSES
ADULTERIES
ADULTERINE
ADULTERINES
ADULTERISE
ADULTERISED
ADULTERISES
ADULTERISING
ADULTERIZE
ADULTERIZED
ADULTERIZES
ADULTERIZING
ADULTEROUS
ADULTEROUSLY
ADULTERY
ADULTESE
ADULTHOOD
ADULTHOODS
ADULTLIKE
ADULTLY
ADULTNESS
ADULTNESSES
ADULTS
ADUMBRAL
ADUMBRATE
ADUMBRATED
ADUMBRATES
ADUMBRATING
ADUMBRATION
ADUMBRATIONS
ADUMBRATIVE
ADUMBRATIVELY
ADUNC
ADUNCATE
ADUNCATED
ADUNCITIES
ADUNCITY
ADUNCOUS
ADUST
ADUSTED
ADUSTING
ADUSTS
ADVANCE
ADVANCED
ADVANCEMENT
ADVANCEMENTS
ADVANCER
ADVANCERS

ADVANCES
ADVANCING
ADVANCINGLY
ADVANTAGE
ADVANTAGEABLE
ADVANTAGED
ADVANTAGEOUS
ADVANTAGEOUSLY
ADVANTAGES
ADVANTAGING
ADVECT
ADVECTED
ADVECTING
ADVECTION
ADVECTIONS
ADVECTIVE
ADVECTS
ADVENE
ADVENED
ADVENES
ADVENING
ADVENT
ADVENTITIA
ADVENTITIAL
ADVENTITIAS
ADVENTITIOUS
ADVENTITIOUSLY
ADVENTIVE
ADVENTIVES
ADVENTS
ADVENTURE
ADVENTURED
ADVENTUREFUL
ADVENTURER
ADVENTURERS
ADVENTURES
ADVENTURESOME
ADVENTURESS
ADVENTURESSES
ADVENTURING
ADVENTURISM
ADVENTURISMS
ADVENTURIST
ADVENTURISTIC
ADVENTURISTS
ADVENTUROUS
ADVENTUROUSLY
ADVENTUROUSNESS
ADVERB
ADVERBIAL
ADVERBIALISE
ADVERBIALISED
ADVERBIALISES
ADVERBIALISING
ADVERBIALIZE
ADVERBIALIZED

ADVERBIALIZES
ADVERBIALIZING
ADVERBIALLY
ADVERBIALS
ADVERBS
ADVERSARIA
ADVERSARIAL
ADVERSARIES
ADVERSARINESS
ADVERSARINESSES
ADVERSARY
ADVERSATIVE
ADVERSATIVELY
ADVERSATIVES
ADVERSE
ADVERSELY
ADVERSENESS
ADVERSENESSES
ADVERSER
ADVERSEST
ADVERSITIES
ADVERSITY
ADVERT
ADVERTED
ADVERTENCE
ADVERTENCES
ADVERTENCIES
ADVERTENCY
ADVERTENT
ADVERTENTLY
ADVERTING
ADVERTISE
ADVERTISED
ADVERTISEMENT
ADVERTISEMENTS
ADVERTISER
ADVERTISERS
ADVERTISES
ADVERTISING
ADVERTISINGS
ADVERTIZE
ADVERTIZED
ADVERTIZEMENT
ADVERTIZEMENTS
ADVERTIZER
ADVERTIZERS
ADVERTIZES
ADVERTIZING
ADVERTORIAL
ADVERTORIALS
ADVERTS
ADVEW
ADVEWED
ADVEWING
ADVEWS
ADVICE

ADVICEFUL
ADVICES
ADVISABILITIES
ADVISABILITY
ADVISABLE
ADVISABLENESS
ADVISABLENESSES
ADVISABLY
ADVISATORY
ADVISE
ADVISED
ADVISEDLY
ADVISEDNESS
ADVISEDNESSES
ADVISEE
ADVISEES
ADVISEMENT
ADVISEMENTS
ADVISER
ADVISERS
ADVISERSHIP
ADVISERSHIPS
ADVISES
ADVISING
ADVISINGS
ADVISOR
ADVISORATE
ADVISORATES
ADVISORIES
ADVISORS
ADVISORY
ADVOCAAT
ADVOCAATS
ADVOCACIES
ADVOCACY
ADVOCATE
ADVOCATED
ADVOCATES
ADVOCATING
ADVOCATION
ADVOCATIONS
ADVOCATIVE
ADVOCATOR
ADVOCATORS
ADVOCATORY
ADVOUTRER
ADVOUTRERS
ADVOUTRIES
ADVOUTRY
ADVOWSON
ADVOWSONS
ADWARD
ADWARDED
ADWARDING
ADWARDS
ADYNAMIA

ADYNAMIAS
ADYNAMIC
ADYTA
ADYTUM
ADZ
ADZE
ADZES
ADZUKI
ADZUKIS
AE
AECIA
AECIAL
AECIDIA
AECIDIAL
AECIDIOSPORE
AECIDIOSPORES
AECIDIUM
AECIDOSPORE
AECIDOSPORES
AECIOSPORE
AECIOSPORES
AECIUM
AEDES
AEDESES
AEDICULE
AEDICULES
AEDILE
AEDILES
AEDILESHIP
AEDILESHIPS
AEDINE
AEFALD
AEFAULD
AEGIRINE
AEGIRINES
AEGIRITE
AEGIRITES
AEGIS
AEGISES
AEGLOGUE
AEGLOGUES
AEGROTAT
AEGROTATS
AEMULE
AEMULED
AEMULES
AEMULING
AENEOUS
AENEUS
AEOLIAN
AEOLIPILE
AEOLIPILES
AEOLIPYLE
AEOLIPYLES
AEOLOTROPIC
AEOLOTROPIES

AEOLOTROPY
AEON
AEONIAN
AEONIC
AEONS
AEPYORNIS
AEPYORNISES
AEQUORIN
AEQUORINS
AERATE
AERATED
AERATES
AERATING
AERATION
AERATIONS
AERATOR
AERATORS
AERENCHYMA
AERENCHYMAS
AERENCHYMATOUS
AERIAL
AERIALIST
AERIALISTS
AERIALITIES
AERIALITY
AERIALLY
AERIALS
AERIE
AERIED
AERIER
AERIES
AERIEST
AERIFICATION
AERIFICATIONS
AERIFIED
AERIFIES
AERIFORM
AERIFY
AERIFYING
AERILY
AERO
AEROACOUSTICS
AEROBALLISTICS
AEROBATIC
AEROBATICS
AEROBE
AEROBES
AEROBIA
AEROBIC
AEROBICALLY
AEROBICIST
AEROBICISTS
AEROBICIZE
AEROBICIZED
AEROBICIZES
AEROBICIZING

AEROBICS
AEROBIOLOGICAL
AEROBIOLOGIES
AEROBIOLOGIST
AEROBIOLOGISTS
AEROBIOLOGY
AEROBIONT
AEROBIONTS
AEROBIOSES
AEROBIOSIS
AEROBIOTIC
AEROBIOTICALLY
AEROBIUM
AEROBOMB
AEROBOMBS
AEROBRAKE
AEROBRAKED
AEROBRAKES
AEROBRAKING
AEROBRAKINGS
AEROBUS
AEROBUSES
AEROBUSSES
AERODART
AERODARTS
AERODONETICAL
AERODONETICALLY
AERODONETICS
AERODROME
AERODROMES
AERODUCT
AERODUCTS
AERODYNAMIC
AERODYNAMICAL
AERODYNAMICALLY
AERODYNAMICIST
AERODYNAMICISTS
AERODYNAMICS
AERODYNE
AERODYNES
AEROELASTIC
AEROELASTICIAN
AEROELASTICIANS
AEROELASTICITY
AEROEMBOLISM
AEROEMBOLISMS
AEROFOIL
AEROFOILS
AEROGEL
AEROGELS
AEROGENERATOR
AEROGENERATORS
AEROGRAM
AEROGRAMME
AEROGRAMMES
AEROGRAMS

AEROGRAPH
AEROGRAPHIES
AEROGRAPHS
AEROGRAPHY
AEROHYDROPLANE
AEROHYDROPLANES
AEROLITE
AEROLITES
AEROLITH
AEROLITHOLOGIES
AEROLITHOLOGY
AEROLITHS
AEROLITIC
AEROLOGIC
AEROLOGICAL
AEROLOGICALLY
AEROLOGIES
AEROLOGIST
AEROLOGISTS
AEROLOGY
AEROMAGNETIC
AEROMANCIES
AEROMANCY
AEROMECHANIC
AEROMECHANICAL
AEROMECHANICS
AEROMEDICAL
AEROMEDICINE
AEROMEDICINES
AEROMETER
AEROMETERS
AEROMETRIC
AEROMETRIES
AEROMETRY
AEROMOTOR
AEROMOTORS
AERONAUT
AERONAUTIC
AERONAUTICAL
AERONAUTICALLY
AERONAUTICS
AERONAUTS
AERONEUROSES
AERONEUROSIS
AERONOMER
AERONOMERS
AERONOMIC
AERONOMICAL
AERONOMIES
AERONOMIST
AERONOMISTS
AERONOMY
AEROPAUSE
AEROPAUSES
AEROPHAGIA
AEROPHAGY

AEROPHOBE
AEROPHOBES
AEROPHOBIA
AEROPHOBIAS
AEROPHOBIC
AEROPHONE
AEROPHONES
AEROPHYTE
AEROPHYTES
AEROPLANE
AEROPLANES
AEROPLANKTON
AEROPLANKTONS
AEROS
AEROSAT
AEROSATS
AEROSHELL
AEROSHELLS
AEROSIDERITE
AEROSIDERITES
AEROSOL
AEROSOLIZATION
AEROSOLIZATIONS
AEROSOLIZE
AEROSOLIZED
AEROSOLIZES
AEROSOLIZING
AEROSOLS
AEROSPACE
AEROSPACES
AEROSPHERE
AEROSPHERES
AEROSTAT
AEROSTATIC
AEROSTATICAL
AEROSTATICS
AEROSTATION
AEROSTATIONS
AEROSTATS
AEROSTRUCTURAL
AEROSTRUCTURE
AEROSTRUCTURES
AEROTACTIC
AEROTAXES
AEROTAXIS
AEROTONE
AEROTONES
AEROTRAIN
AEROTRAINS
AEROTROPIC
AEROTROPISM
AEROTROPISMS
AERUGINOUS
AERUGO
AERUGOS
AERY

AESC
AESCES
AESCULIN
AESCULINS
AESIR
AESTHESES
AESTHESIA
AESTHESIAS
AESTHESIOGEN
AESTHESIOGENIC
AESTHESIOGENS
AESTHESIS
AESTHETE
AESTHETES
AESTHETIC
AESTHETICAL
AESTHETICALLY
AESTHETICIAN
AESTHETICIANS
AESTHETICISE
AESTHETICISED
AESTHETICISES
AESTHETICISING
AESTHETICISM
AESTHETICISMS
AESTHETICIST
AESTHETICISTS
AESTHETICIZE
AESTHETICIZED
AESTHETICIZES
AESTHETICIZING
AESTHETICS
AESTIVAL
AESTIVATE
AESTIVATED
AESTIVATES
AESTIVATING
AESTIVATION
AESTIVATIONS
AESTIVATOR
AESTIVATORS
AETHER
AETHEREAL
AETHEREALITY
AETHEREALLY
AETHERIC
AETHERS
AETHRIOSCOPE
AETHRIOSCOPES
AETIOLOGICAL
AETIOLOGICALLY
AETIOLOGIES
AETIOLOGIST
AETIOLOGISTS
AETIOLOGY
AFALD

AFAR
AFARA
AFARAS
AFARS
AFAWLD
AFEAR
AFEARD
AFEARED
AFEARING
AFEARS
AFEBRILE
AFF
AFFABILITIES
AFFABILITY
AFFABLE
AFFABLY
AFFAIR
AFFAIRE
AFFAIRES
AFFAIRS
AFFEAR
AFFEARD
AFFEARE
AFFEARED
AFFEARES
AFFEARING
AFFEARS
AFFECT
AFFECTABILITIES
AFFECTABILITY
AFFECTABLE
AFFECTATION
AFFECTATIONS
AFFECTED
AFFECTEDLY
AFFECTEDNESS
AFFECTEDNESSES
AFFECTER
AFFECTERS
AFFECTING
AFFECTINGLY
AFFECTION
AFFECTIONAL
AFFECTIONALLY
AFFECTIONATE
AFFECTIONATELY
AFFECTIONED
AFFECTIONING
AFFECTIONLESS
AFFECTIONS
AFFECTIVE
AFFECTIVELY
AFFECTIVENESS
AFFECTIVITIES
AFFECTIVITY
AFFECTLESS

AFFECTLESSNESS
AFFECTS
AFFEER
AFFEERED
AFFEERING
AFFEERMENT
AFFEERMENTS
AFFEERS
AFFENPINSCHER
AFFENPINSCHERS
AFFERENT
AFFERENTLY
AFFERENTS
AFFETTUOSO
AFFETTUOSOS
AFFIANCE
AFFIANCED
AFFIANCES
AFFIANCING
AFFIANT
AFFIANTS
AFFICHE
AFFICHES
AFFICIONADO
AFFICIONADOS
AFFIDAVIT
AFFIDAVITS
AFFIED
AFFIES
AFFILIABLE
AFFILIATE
AFFILIATED
AFFILIATES
AFFILIATING
AFFILIATION
AFFILIATIONS
AFFINAL
AFFINE
AFFINED
AFFINELY
AFFINES
AFFINITIES
AFFINITIVE
AFFINITY
AFFIRM
AFFIRMABLE
AFFIRMANCE
AFFIRMANCES
AFFIRMANT
AFFIRMANTS
AFFIRMATION
AFFIRMATIONS
AFFIRMATIVE
AFFIRMATIVELY
AFFIRMATIVES
AFFIRMATORY

AFFIRMED
AFFIRMER
AFFIRMERS
AFFIRMING
AFFIRMINGLY
AFFIRMS
AFFIX
AFFIXABLE
AFFIXAL
AFFIXATION
AFFIXATIONS
AFFIXED
AFFIXER
AFFIXERS
AFFIXES
AFFIXIAL
AFFIXING
AFFIXMENT
AFFIXMENTS
AFFIXTURE
AFFIXTURES
AFFLATED
AFFLATION
AFFLATIONS
AFFLATUS
AFFLATUSES
AFFLICT
AFFLICTED
AFFLICTING
AFFLICTINGS
AFFLICTION
AFFLICTIONS
AFFLICTIVE
AFFLICTIVELY
AFFLICTS
AFFLUENCE
AFFLUENCES
AFFLUENCIES
AFFLUENCY
AFFLUENT
AFFLUENTIAL
AFFLUENTIALS
AFFLUENTLY
AFFLUENTNESS
AFFLUENTNESSES
AFFLUENTS
AFFLUENZA
AFFLUENZAS
AFFLUX
AFFLUXES
AFFLUXION
AFFLUXIONS
AFFOORD
AFFOORDED
AFFOORDING
AFFOORDS

AFFORCE
AFFORCED
AFFORCEMENT
AFFORCEMENTS
AFFORCES
AFFORCING
AFFORD
AFFORDABILITIES
AFFORDABILITY
AFFORDABLE
AFFORDABLY
AFFORDED
AFFORDING
AFFORDS
AFFOREST
AFFORESTABLE
AFFORESTATION
AFFORESTATIONS
AFFORESTED
AFFORESTING
AFFORESTS
AFFRANCHISE
AFFRANCHISED
AFFRANCHISEMENT
AFFRANCHISES
AFFRANCHISING
AFFRAP
AFFRAPPED
AFFRAPPING
AFFRAPS
AFFRAY
AFFRAYED
AFFRAYER
AFFRAYERS
AFFRAYING
AFFRAYS
AFFREIGHTMENT
AFFREIGHTMENTS
AFFRENDED
AFFRET
AFFRETS
AFFRICATE
AFFRICATED
AFFRICATES
AFFRICATION
AFFRICATIONS
AFFRICATIVE
AFFRICATIVES
AFFRIGHT
AFFRIGHTED
AFFRIGHTEDLY
AFFRIGHTEN
AFFRIGHTENED
AFFRIGHTENING
AFFRIGHTENS
AFFRIGHTFUL

AFFRIGHTING
AFFRIGHTMENT
AFFRIGHTMENTS
AFFRIGHTS
AFFRONT
AFFRONTE
AFFRONTED
AFFRONTEE
AFFRONTING
AFFRONTINGLY
AFFRONTINGS
AFFRONTIVE
AFFRONTS
AFFUSION
AFFUSIONS
AFFY
AFFYDE
AFFYING
AFGHAN
AFGHANI
AFGHANIS
AFGHANS
AFICIONADA
AFICIONADAS
AFICIONADO
AFICIONADOS
AFIELD
AFIRE
AFLAJ
AFLAME
AFLATOXIN
AFLATOXINS
AFLOAT
AFLUTTER
AFOOT
AFORE
AFOREHAND
AFOREMENTIONED
AFORESAID
AFORETHOUGHT
AFORETHOUGHTS
AFORETIME
AFOUL
AFRAID
AFREET
AFREETS
AFRESH
AFRIT
AFRITS
AFRO
AFRONT
AFRORMOSIA
AFRORMOSIAS
AFROS
AFT
AFTER

AFTERBIRTH
AFTERBIRTHS
AFTERBODIES
AFTERBODY
AFTERBRAIN
AFTERBRAINS
AFTERBURNER
AFTERBURNERS
AFTERBURNING
AFTERBURNINGS
AFTERCARE
AFTERCARES
AFTERCLAP
AFTERCLAPS
AFTERDAMP
AFTERDECK
AFTERDECKS
AFTEREFFECT
AFTEREFFECTS
AFTEREYE
AFTEREYED
AFTEREYEING
AFTEREYES
AFTEREYING
AFTERGAME
AFTERGAMES
AFTERGLOW
AFTERGLOWS
AFTERGRASS
AFTERGRASSES
AFTERGROWTH
AFTERGROWTHS
AFTERHEAT
AFTERHEATS
AFTERIMAGE
AFTERIMAGES
AFTERINGS
AFTERLIFE
AFTERLIVES
AFTERMARKET
AFTERMARKETS
AFTERMATH
AFTERMATHS
AFTERMOST
AFTERNOON
AFTERNOONS
AFTERPAINS
AFTERPEAK
AFTERPEAKS
AFTERPIECE
AFTERPIECES
AFTERS
AFTERSALES
AFTERSENSATION
AFTERSENSATIONS
AFTERSHAFT

AFTERSHAFTS
AFTERSHAVE
AFTERSHAVES
AFTERSHOCK
AFTERSHOCKS
AFTERSHOW
AFTERSHOWS
AFTERSUN
AFTERSUNS
AFTERSUPPER
AFTERSUPPERS
AFTERSWARM
AFTERSWARMS
AFTERTASTE
AFTERTASTES
AFTERTAX
AFTERTHOUGHT
AFTERTHOUGHTS
AFTERTIME
AFTERTIMES
AFTERWARD
AFTERWARDS
AFTERWORD
AFTERWORDS
AFTERWORLD
AFTERWORLDS
AFTMOST
AFTOSA
AFTOSAS
AG
AGA
AGACANT
AGACANTE
AGACERIE
AGACERIES
AGAIN
AGAINST
AGALACTIA
AGALACTIAS
AGALLOCH
AGALLOCHS
AGALMATOLITE
AGALMATOLITES
AGALWOOD
AGALWOODS
AGAMA
AGAMAS
AGAMETE
AGAMETES
AGAMI
AGAMIC
AGAMICALLY
AGAMID
AGAMIDS
AGAMIS
AGAMOGENESES

AGAMOGENESIS
AGAMOGENETIC
AGAMOGONIES
AGAMOGONY
AGAMOID
AGAMOIDS
AGAMONT
AGAMONTS
AGAMOSPERMIES
AGAMOSPERMY
AGAMOUS
AGAPAE
AGAPAI
AGAPANTHUS
AGAPANTHUSES
AGAPE
AGAPEIC
AGAR
AGARIC
AGARICACEOUS
AGARICS
AGAROSE
AGAROSES
AGARS
AGAS
AGAST
AGATE
AGATES
AGATEWARE
AGATEWARES
AGATHODAIMON
AGATHODAIMONS
AGATIZE
AGATIZED
AGATIZES
AGATIZING
AGATOID
AGAVE
AGAVES
AGAZE
AGAZED
AGE
AGED
AGEDLY
AGEDNESS
AGEDNESSES
AGEE
AGEING
AGEINGS
AGEISM
AGEISMS
AGEIST
AGEISTS
AGELAST
AGELASTIC
AGELASTS

AGELESS
AGELESSLY
AGELESSNESS
AGELESSNESSES
AGELONG
AGEN
AGENCIES
AGENCY
AGENDA
AGENDALESS
AGENDAS
AGENDUM
AGENDUMS
AGENE
AGENES
AGENESES
AGENESIA
AGENESIAS
AGENESIS
AGENETIC
AGENIZE
AGENIZED
AGENIZES
AGENIZING
AGENT
AGENTED
AGENTIAL
AGENTIALLY
AGENTIALS
AGENTING
AGENTINGS
AGENTIVE
AGENTIVES
AGENTIVITIES
AGENTIVITY
AGENTRIES
AGENTRY
AGENTS
AGER
AGERATUM
AGERATUMS
AGERS
AGES
AGEUSIA
AGGADIC
AGGER
AGGERS
AGGIE
AGGIES
AGGIORNAMENTI
AGGIORNAMENTO
AGGIORNAMENTOS
AGGLOMERATE
AGGLOMERATED
AGGLOMERATES
AGGLOMERATING

AGGLOMERATION
AGGLOMERATIONS
AGGLOMERATIVE
AGGLUTINABILITY
AGGLUTINABLE
AGGLUTINANT
AGGLUTINANTS
AGGLUTINATE
AGGLUTINATED
AGGLUTINATES
AGGLUTINATING
AGGLUTINATION
AGGLUTINATIONS
AGGLUTINATIVE
AGGLUTININ
AGGLUTININS
AGGLUTINOGEN
AGGLUTINOGENIC
AGGLUTINOGENS
AGGRACE
AGGRACED
AGGRACES
AGGRACING
AGGRADATION
AGGRADATIONS
AGGRADE
AGGRADED
AGGRADES
AGGRADING
AGGRANDISE
AGGRANDISED
AGGRANDISEMENT
AGGRANDISEMENTS
AGGRANDISER
AGGRANDISERS
AGGRANDISES
AGGRANDISING
AGGRANDIZE
AGGRANDIZED
AGGRANDIZEMENT
AGGRANDIZEMENTS
AGGRANDIZER
AGGRANDIZERS
AGGRANDIZES
AGGRANDIZING
AGGRATE
AGGRATED
AGGRATES
AGGRATING
AGGRAVATE
AGGRAVATED
AGGRAVATES
AGGRAVATING
AGGRAVATINGLY
AGGRAVATION
AGGRAVATIONS

AGGREGATE
AGGREGATED
AGGREGATELY
AGGREGATENESS
AGGREGATENESSES
AGGREGATES
AGGREGATING
AGGREGATION
AGGREGATIONAL
AGGREGATIONS
AGGREGATIVE
AGGREGATIVELY
AGGREGATOR
AGGREGATORS
AGGRESS
AGGRESSED
AGGRESSES
AGGRESSING
AGGRESSION
AGGRESSIONS
AGGRESSIVE
AGGRESSIVELY
AGGRESSIVENESS
AGGRESSIVITIES
AGGRESSIVITY
AGGRESSOR
AGGRESSORS
AGGRI
AGGRIEVE
AGGRIEVED
AGGRIEVEDLY
AGGRIEVEMENT
AGGRIEVEMENTS
AGGRIEVES
AGGRIEVING
AGGRO
AGGROS
AGGRY
AGHA
AGHAS
AGHAST
AGILA
AGILAS
AGILE
AGILELY
AGILER
AGILEST
AGILITIES
AGILITY
AGIN
AGING
AGINGS
AGINNER
AGINNERS
AGIO
AGIOS

AGIOTAGE
AGIOTAGES
AGISM
AGISMS
AGIST
AGISTED
AGISTER
AGISTERS
AGISTING
AGISTMENT
AGISTMENTS
AGISTOR
AGISTORS
AGISTS
AGITABLE
AGITATE
AGITATED
AGITATEDLY
AGITATES
AGITATING
AGITATION
AGITATIONAL
AGITATIONS
AGITATIVE
AGITATO
AGITATOR
AGITATORS
AGITPOP
AGITPROP
AGITPROPS
AGLARE
AGLEAM
AGLEE
AGLET
AGLETS
AGLEY
AGLIMMER
AGLITTER
AGLOO
AGLOOS
AGLOSSAL
AGLOSSATE
AGLOSSIA
AGLOW
AGLU
AGLUS
AGLY
AGLYCON
AGLYCONE
AGLYCONES
AGLYCONS
AGMA
AGMAS
AGMINATE
AGNAIL
AGNAILS

AGNAME
AGNAMED
AGNAMES
AGNATE
AGNATES
AGNATHAN
AGNATHANS
AGNATHOUS
AGNATIC
AGNATICAL
AGNATICALLY
AGNATION
AGNATIONS
AGNISE
AGNISED
AGNISES
AGNISING
AGNIZE
AGNIZED
AGNIZES
AGNIZING
AGNOIOLOGICAL
AGNOIOLOGICALLY
AGNOIOLOGY
AGNOMEN
AGNOMENS
AGNOMINA
AGNOMINAL
AGNOSIA
AGNOSIAS
AGNOSIC
AGNOSTIC
AGNOSTICISM
AGNOSTICISMS
AGNOSTICS
AGO
AGOG
AGOGE
AGOGES
AGOGIC
AGOGICS
AGOING
AGON
AGONAL
AGONE
AGONES
AGONIC
AGONIES
AGONISE
AGONISED
AGONISEDLY
AGONISES
AGONISING
AGONISINGLY
AGONIST
AGONISTES

AGONISTIC
AGONISTICAL
AGONISTICALLY
AGONISTICS
AGONISTS
AGONIZE
AGONIZED
AGONIZEDLY
AGONIZES
AGONIZING
AGONIZINGLY
AGONOTHETES
AGONS
AGONY
AGOOD
AGORA
AGORAE
AGORAPHOBE
AGORAPHOBES
AGORAPHOBIA
AGORAPHOBIAS
AGORAPHOBIC
AGORAPHOBICS
AGORAS
AGOROT
AGOROTH
AGOUTA
AGOUTAS
AGOUTI
AGOUTIES
AGOUTIS
AGOUTY
AGRAFE
AGRAFES
AGRAFFE
AGRAFFES
AGRANULOCYTE
AGRANULOCYTES
AGRANULOCYTOSES
AGRANULOCYTOSIS
AGRANULOSES
AGRANULOSIS
AGRAPHA
AGRAPHIA
AGRAPHIAS
AGRAPHIC
AGRAPHON
AGRARIAN
AGRARIANISM
AGRARIANISMS
AGRARIANS
AGRASTE
AGRAVIC
AGREE
AGREEABILITIES
AGREEABILITY

AGREEABLE
AGREEABLENESS
AGREEABLENESSES
AGREEABLY
AGREED
AGREEING
AGREEMENT
AGREEMENTS
AGREES
AGREGATION
AGREGATIONS
AGREGE
AGREGES
AGREMENS
AGREMENT
AGREMENTS
AGRESTAL
AGRESTIAL
AGRESTIC
AGRIA
AGRIAS
AGRIBUSINESS
AGRIBUSINESSES
AGRIBUSINESSMAN
AGRIBUSINESSMEN
AGRICHEMICAL
AGRICHEMICALS
AGRICULTURAL
AGRICULTURALIST
AGRICULTURALLY
AGRICULTURE
AGRICULTURES
AGRICULTURIST
AGRICULTURISTS
AGRIMONIES
AGRIMONY
AGRIN
AGRIOLOGIES
AGRIOLOGY
AGRIPRODUCT
AGRIPRODUCTS
AGRISE
AGRISED
AGRISES
AGRISING
AGRIZE
AGRIZED
AGRIZES
AGRIZING
AGROBIOLOGICAL
AGROBIOLOGIES
AGROBIOLOGIST
AGROBIOLOGISTS
AGROBIOLOGY
AGROBUSINESS
AGROBUSINESSES

AGROCHEMICAL
AGROCHEMICALS
AGROFORESTER
AGROFORESTERS
AGROFORESTRIES
AGROFORESTRY
AGROINDUSTRIAL
AGROINDUSTRIES
AGROINDUSTRY
AGROLOGICAL
AGROLOGIES
AGROLOGIST
AGROLOGISTS
AGROLOGY
AGRONOMIAL
AGRONOMIC
AGRONOMICAL
AGRONOMICALLY
AGRONOMICS
AGRONOMIES
AGRONOMIST
AGRONOMISTS
AGRONOMY
AGROSTEMMA
AGROSTEMMAS
AGROSTOLOGICAL
AGROSTOLOGIES
AGROSTOLOGIST
AGROSTOLOGISTS
AGROSTOLOGY
AGROTERRORISM
AGROTERRORIST
AGROTERRORISTS
AGROUND
AGRYPNIA
AGRYPNIAS
AGRYPNOPTICAL
AGRYPNOPTICALLY
AGRYPNOTIC
AGRYPNOTICS
AGRYZE
AGRYZED
AGRYZES
AGRYZING
AGTERSKOT
AGTERSKOTS
AGUACATE
AGUACATES
AGUARDIENTE
AGUARDIENTES
AGUE
AGUED
AGUELIKE
AGUES
AGUEWEED
AGUEWEEDS

AGUISE
AGUISED
AGUISES
AGUISH
AGUISHLY
AGUISING
AGUIZE
AGUIZED
AGUIZES
AGUIZING
AGUTI
AGUTIS
AH
AHA
AHCHOO
AHEAD
AHEAP
AHED
AHEIGHT
AHEM
AHEMERAL
AHEMERALLY
AHENT
AHIGH
AHIMSA
AHIMSAS
AHIND
AHING
AHINT
AHISTORIC
AHISTORICAL
AHOLD
AHOLDS
AHORSE
AHORSEBACK
AHOY
AHS
AHULL
AHUNGERED
AHUNGRY
AI
AIA
AIAS
AIBLINS
AICHMOPHOBIA
AICHMOPHOBIAS
AID
AIDANCE
AIDANCES
AIDANT
AIDE
AIDED
AIDER
AIDERS
AIDES
AIDFUL

AIDING
AIDLESS
AIDMAN
AIDMEN
AIDOI
AIDOS
AIDS
AIERIES
AIERY
AIGA
AIGLET
AIGLETS
AIGRET
AIGRETS
AIGRETTE
AIGRETTES
AIGUILLE
AIGUILLES
AIGUILLETTE
AIGUILLETTES
AIKIDO
AIKIDOS
AIKONA
AIL
AILANTHUS
AILANTHUSES
AILANTO
AILANTOS
AILED
AILERON
AILERONS
AILETTE
AILETTES
AILING
AILMENT
AILMENTS
AILOUROPHILE
AILOUROPHILES
AILOUROPHILIA
AILOUROPHILIAS
AILOUROPHILIC
AILOUROPHOBE
AILOUROPHOBES
AILOUROPHOBIA
AILOUROPHOBIAS
AILOUROPHOBIC
AILS
AILUROPHILE
AILUROPHILES
AILUROPHILIA
AILUROPHILIAS
AILUROPHILIC
AILUROPHOBE
AILUROPHOBES
AILUROPHOBIA
AILUROPHOBIAS

AILUROPHOBIC
AIM
AIMED
AIMER
AIMERS
AIMFUL
AIMFULLY
AIMING
AIMLESS
AIMLESSLY
AIMLESSNESS
AIMLESSNESSES
AIMS
AIN
AINE
AINEE
AING
AINGA
AINGAS
AINS
AINSELL
AINSELLS
AIOLI
AIOLIS
AIR
AIRBASE
AIRBASES
AIRBOAT
AIRBOATS
AIRBORNE
AIRBOUND
AIRBRICK
AIRBRICKS
AIRBRUSH
AIRBRUSHED
AIRBRUSHES
AIRBRUSHING
AIRBURST
AIRBURSTS
AIRBUS
AIRBUSES
AIRBUSSES
AIRCHECK
AIRCHECKS
AIRCOACH
AIRCOACHES
AIRCRAFT
AIRCRAFTMAN
AIRCRAFTMEN
AIRCRAFTSMAN
AIRCRAFTSMEN
AIRCRAFTSWOMAN
AIRCRAFTSWOMEN
AIRCRAFTWOMAN
AIRCRAFTWOMEN
AIRCREW

AIRCREWS
AIRDATE
AIRDATES
AIRDRAWN
AIRDROME
AIRDROMES
AIRDROP
AIRDROPPED
AIRDROPPING
AIRDROPS
AIRED
AIRER
AIRERS
AIREST
AIRFARE
AIRFARES
AIRFIELD
AIRFIELDS
AIRFLOW
AIRFLOWS
AIRFOIL
AIRFOILS
AIRFRAME
AIRFRAMES
AIRFREIGHT
AIRFREIGHTED
AIRFREIGHTING
AIRFREIGHTS
AIRGAP
AIRGAPS
AIRGLOW
AIRGLOWS
AIRGRAPH
AIRGRAPHS
AIRHEAD
AIRHEADED
AIRHEADS
AIRHOLE
AIRHOLES
AIRIER
AIRIEST
AIRILY
AIRINESS
AIRINESSES
AIRING
AIRINGS
AIRLESS
AIRLESSNESS
AIRLESSNESSES
AIRLIFT
AIRLIFTED
AIRLIFTING
AIRLIFTS
AIRLIKE
AIRLINE
AIRLINER

AIRLINERS
AIRLINES
AIRLOCK
AIRLOCKS
AIRMAIL
AIRMAILED
AIRMAILING
AIRMAILS
AIRMAN
AIRMANSHIP
AIRMANSHIPS
AIRMEN
AIRMOBILE
AIRN
AIRNED
AIRNING
AIRNS
AIRPARK
AIRPARKS
AIRPLANE
AIRPLANES
AIRPLAY
AIRPLAYS
AIRPORT
AIRPORTS
AIRPOST
AIRPOSTS
AIRPOWER
AIRPOWERS
AIRPROOF
AIRPROOFED
AIRPROOFING
AIRPROOFS
AIRS
AIRSCAPE
AIRSCAPES
AIRSCREW
AIRSCREWS
AIRSHAFT
AIRSHAFTS
AIRSHED
AIRSHEDS
AIRSHIP
AIRSHIPS
AIRSHOW
AIRSHOWS
AIRSICK
AIRSICKNESS
AIRSICKNESSES
AIRSIDE
AIRSIDES
AIRSPACE
AIRSPACES
AIRSPEED
AIRSPEEDS
AIRSTOP

AIRSTOPS
AIRSTREAM
AIRSTREAMS
AIRSTRIP
AIRSTRIPS
AIRT
AIRTED
AIRTH
AIRTHED
AIRTHING
AIRTHS
AIRTIGHT
AIRTIGHTNESS
AIRTIGHTNESSES
AIRTIME
AIRTIMES
AIRTING
AIRTS
AIRWARD
AIRWARDS
AIRWAVE
AIRWAVES
AIRWAY
AIRWAYS
AIRWISE
AIRWOMAN
AIRWOMEN
AIRWORTHINESS
AIRWORTHINESSES
AIRWORTHY
AIRY
AIS
AISLE
AISLED
AISLELESS
AISLES
AISLEWAY
AISLEWAYS
AISLING
AISLINGS
AIT
AITCH
AITCHBONE
AITCHBONES
AITCHES
AITS
AITU
AITUS
AIVER
AIVERS
AIZLE
AIZLES
AJAR
AJEE
AJIVA
AJIVAS

AJOWAN
AJOWANS
AJUGA
AJUGAS
AJUTAGE
AJUTAGES
AJWAN
AJWANS
AKARYOTE
AKARYOTES
AKARYOTIC
AKE
AKEAKE
AKEAKES
AKED
AKEDAH
AKEDAHS
AKEE
AKEES
AKELA
AKELAS
AKENE
AKENES
AKENIAL
AKES
AKHARA
AKHARAS
AKIMBO
AKIN
AKINESES
AKINESIA
AKINESIAS
AKINESIS
AKING
AKITA
AKITAS
AKKAS
AKOLOUTHOS
AKOLOUTHOSES
AKOLUTHOS
AKOLUTHOSES
AKRASIA
AKRATIC
AKVAVIT
AKVAVITS
AL
ALA
ALAAP
ALAAPS
ALABAMINE
ALABAMINES
ALABANDINE
ALABANDINES
ALABANDITE
ALABANDITES
ALABASTER

ALABASTERS
ALABASTRINE
ALABLASTER
ALABLASTERS
ALACK
ALACKADAY
ALACRITIES
ALACRITOUS
ALACRITY
ALAE
ALAIMENT
ALAIMENTS
ALALAGMOI
ALALAGMOS
ALALIA
ALALIAS
ALAMEDA
ALAMEDAS
ALAMO
ALAMODE
ALAMODES
ALAMORT
ALAMOS
ALAN
ALAND
ALANDS
ALANE
ALANG
ALANGS
ALANIN
ALANINE
ALANINES
ALANINS
ALANNAH
ALANNAHS
ALANS
ALANT
ALANTS
ALANYL
ALANYLS
ALAP
ALAPA
ALAPAS
ALAPS
ALAR
ALARM
ALARMED
ALARMEDLY
ALARMING
ALARMINGLY
ALARMISM
ALARMISMS
ALARMIST
ALARMISTS
ALARMS
ALARUM

ALARUMED
ALARUMING
ALARUMS
ALARY
ALAS
ALASKA
ALASKAS
ALASTOR
ALASTORS
ALASTRIM
ALASTRIMS
ALATE
ALATED
ALATES
ALATION
ALATIONS
ALAY
ALAYED
ALAYING
ALAYS
ALB
ALBA
ALBACORE
ALBACORES
ALBARELLI
ALBARELLO
ALBARELLOS
ALBAS
ALBATA
ALBATAS
ALBATROSS
ALBATROSSES
ALBE
ALBEDO
ALBEDOES
ALBEDOS
ALBEE
ALBEIT
ALBERGHI
ALBERGO
ALBERT
ALBERTITE
ALBERTITES
ALBERTS
ALBESCENCE
ALBESCENCES
ALBESCENT
ALBESPINE
ALBESPINES
ALBESPYNE
ALBESPYNES
ALBICORE
ALBICORES
ALBINAL
ALBINESS
ALBINESSES

ALBINIC
ALBINISM
ALBINISMS
ALBINISTIC
ALBINO
ALBINOISM
ALBINOISMS
ALBINOS
ALBINOTIC
ALBITE
ALBITES
ALBITIC
ALBITISE
ALBITISED
ALBITISES
ALBITISING
ALBITIZE
ALBITIZED
ALBITIZES
ALBITIZING
ALBIZIA
ALBIZIAS
ALBIZZIA
ALBIZZIAS
ALBRICIAS
ALBS
ALBUGINEOUS
ALBUGO
ALBUGOS
ALBUM
ALBUMBLATT
ALBUMBLATTS
ALBUMEN
ALBUMENISE
ALBUMENISED
ALBUMENISES
ALBUMENISING
ALBUMENIZE
ALBUMENIZED
ALBUMENIZES
ALBUMENIZING
ALBUMENS
ALBUMIN
ALBUMINATE
ALBUMINATES
ALBUMINISE
ALBUMINISED
ALBUMINISES
ALBUMINISING
ALBUMINIZE
ALBUMINIZED
ALBUMINIZES
ALBUMINIZING
ALBUMINOID
ALBUMINOIDS
ALBUMINOUS

ALBUMINS
ALBUMINURIA
ALBUMINURIAS
ALBUMINURIC
ALBUMOSE
ALBUMOSES
ALBUMS
ALBURNOUS
ALBURNUM
ALBURNUMS
ALCADE
ALCADES
ALCAHEST
ALCAHESTS
ALCAIC
ALCAICERIA
ALCAICERIAS
ALCAICS
ALCAIDE
ALCAIDES
ALCALDE
ALCALDES
ALCARRAZA
ALCARRAZAS
ALCATRAS
ALCATRASES
ALCAYDE
ALCAYDES
ALCAZAR
ALCAZARS
ALCHEMIC
ALCHEMICAL
ALCHEMICALLY
ALCHEMIES
ALCHEMISE
ALCHEMISED
ALCHEMISES
ALCHEMISING
ALCHEMIST
ALCHEMISTIC
ALCHEMISTICAL
ALCHEMISTS
ALCHEMIZE
ALCHEMIZED
ALCHEMIZES
ALCHEMIZING
ALCHEMY
ALCHERA
ALCHERAS
ALCHERINGA
ALCHERINGAS
ALCHYMIES
ALCHYMY
ALCID
ALCIDINE
ALCIDS

ALCO
ALCOHOL
ALCOHOLIC
ALCOHOLICALLY
ALCOHOLICITY
ALCOHOLICS
ALCOHOLISATION
ALCOHOLISATIONS
ALCOHOLISE
ALCOHOLISED
ALCOHOLISES
ALCOHOLISING
ALCOHOLISM
ALCOHOLISMS
ALCOHOLIZATION
ALCOHOLIZATIONS
ALCOHOLIZE
ALCOHOLIZED
ALCOHOLIZES
ALCOHOLIZING
ALCOHOLOMETER
ALCOHOLOMETERS
ALCOHOLOMETRIES
ALCOHOLOMETRY
ALCOHOLS
ALCOOL
ALCOOLS
ALCOPOP
ALCOPOPS
ALCORZA
ALCORZAS
ALCOS
ALCOVE
ALCOVED
ALCOVES
ALCYONARIAN
ALCYONARIANS
ALDEA
ALDEAS
ALDEHYDE
ALDEHYDES
ALDEHYDIC
ALDER
ALDERFLIES
ALDERFLY
ALDERMAN
ALDERMANIC
ALDERMANITIES
ALDERMANITY
ALDERMANLIKE
ALDERMANLY
ALDERMANRIES
ALDERMANRY
ALDERMANSHIP
ALDERMANSHIPS
ALDERMEN

ALDERN
ALDERS
ALDERWOMAN
ALDERWOMEN
ALDODIA
ALDOHEXOSE
ALDOHEXOSES
ALDOL
ALDOLASE
ALDOLASES
ALDOLIZATION
ALDOLIZATIONS
ALDOLS
ALDOPENTOSE
ALDOPENTOSES
ALDOSE
ALDOSES
ALDOSTERONE
ALDOSTERONES
ALDOSTERONISM
ALDOSTERONISMS
ALDOXIME
ALDOXIMES
ALDRIN
ALDRINS
ALE
ALEATORIC
ALEATORIES
ALEATORY
ALEBENCH
ALEBENCHES
ALEC
ALECITHAL
ALECITHALLY
ALECK
ALECKS
ALECOST
ALECOSTS
ALECS
ALECTRYON
ALECTRYONS
ALEE
ALEF
ALEFS
ALEFT
ALEGAR
ALEGARS
ALEGGE
ALEGGEAUNCE
ALEGGEAUNCES
ALEGGED
ALEGGES
ALEGGING
ALEHOUSE
ALEHOUSES
ALEMBIC

ALEMBICATED
ALEMBICATION
ALEMBICATIONS
ALEMBICS
ALEMBROTH
ALEMBROTHS
ALENCON
ALENCONS
ALENGTH
ALEPH
ALEPHS
ALEPINE
ALEPINES
ALERCE
ALERCES
ALERION
ALERIONS
ALERT
ALERTED
ALERTER
ALERTEST
ALERTING
ALERTLY
ALERTNESS
ALERTNESSES
ALERTS
ALES
ALETHIC
ALEURON
ALEURONE
ALEURONES
ALEURONS
ALEVIN
ALEVINS
ALEW
ALEWASHED
ALEWIFE
ALEWIVES
ALEWS
ALEXANDER
ALEXANDERS
ALEXANDERSES
ALEXANDRINE
ALEXANDRINES
ALEXANDRITE
ALEXANDRITES
ALEXIA
ALEXIAS
ALEXIC
ALEXIN
ALEXINE
ALEXINES
ALEXINIC
ALEXINS
ALEXIPHARMAKON
ALEXIPHARMAKONS

ALEXIPHARMIC
ALEXIPHARMICS
ALEYE
ALEYED
ALEYES
ALEYING
ALF
ALFA
ALFAKI
ALFAKIS
ALFALFA
ALFALFAS
ALFAQUI
ALFAQUIN
ALFAQUINS
ALFAQUIS
ALFAS
ALFERECES
ALFEREZ
ALFILARIA
ALFILARIAS
ALFILERIA
ALFILERIAS
ALFORJA
ALFORJAS
ALFRESCO
ALFS
ALGA
ALGAE
ALGAECIDE
ALGAECIDES
ALGAL
ALGAROBA
ALGAROBAS
ALGARROBA
ALGARROBAS
ALGARROBO
ALGARROBOS
ALGAS
ALGATE
ALGATES
ALGEBRA
ALGEBRAIC
ALGEBRAICAL
ALGEBRAICALLY
ALGEBRAIST
ALGEBRAISTS
ALGEBRAS
ALGERINE
ALGERINES
ALGESES
ALGESIA
ALGESIAS
ALGESIC
ALGESIS
ALGETIC

ALGICIDAL
ALGICIDE
ALGICIDES
ALGID
ALGIDITIES
ALGIDITY
ALGIN
ALGINATE
ALGINATES
ALGINIC
ALGINS
ALGOID
ALGOLAGNIA
ALGOLAGNIAC
ALGOLAGNIACS
ALGOLAGNIAS
ALGOLAGNIC
ALGOLAGNICALLY
ALGOLAGNIST
ALGOLAGNISTS
ALGOLOGICAL
ALGOLOGICALLY
ALGOLOGIES
ALGOLOGIST
ALGOLOGISTS
ALGOLOGY
ALGOMETER
ALGOMETERS
ALGOMETRICAL
ALGOMETRICALLY
ALGOMETRY
ALGOPHOBIA
ALGOPHOBIAS
ALGOR
ALGORISM
ALGORISMIC
ALGORISMICALLY
ALGORISMS
ALGORITHM
ALGORITHMIC
ALGORITHMICALLY
ALGORITHMS
ALGORS
ALGUACIL
ALGUACILS
ALGUAZIL
ALGUAZILS
ALGUM
ALGUMS
ALIAS
ALIASES
ALIASING
ALIASINGS
ALIBI
ALIBIED
ALIBIES

ALIBIING
ALIBIS
ALIBLE
ALICANT
ALICANTS
ALICYCLIC
ALIDAD
ALIDADE
ALIDADES
ALIDADS
ALIEN
ALIENABILITIES
ALIENABILITY
ALIENABLE
ALIENAGE
ALIENAGES
ALIENATE
ALIENATED
ALIENATES
ALIENATING
ALIENATION
ALIENATIONS
ALIENATOR
ALIENATORS
ALIENED
ALIENEE
ALIENEES
ALIENER
ALIENERS
ALIENING
ALIENISM
ALIENISMS
ALIENIST
ALIENISTS
ALIENLY
ALIENNESS
ALIENNESSES
ALIENOR
ALIENORS
ALIENS
ALIF
ALIFORM
ALIFS
ALIGARTA
ALIGARTAS
ALIGHT
ALIGHTED
ALIGHTING
ALIGHTMENT
ALIGHTMENTS
ALIGHTS
ALIGN
ALIGNED
ALIGNER
ALIGNERS
ALIGNING

ALIGNMENT
ALIGNMENTS
ALIGNS
ALIKE
ALIKENESS
ALIKENESSES
ALIMENT
ALIMENTAL
ALIMENTARY
ALIMENTATION
ALIMENTATIONS
ALIMENTATIVE
ALIMENTED
ALIMENTING
ALIMENTIVENESS
ALIMENTS
ALIMONIES
ALIMONY
ALINE
ALINEATION
ALINEATIONS
ALINED
ALINEMENT
ALINEMENTS
ALINER
ALINERS
ALINES
ALINING
ALIPED
ALIPEDS
ALIPHATIC
ALIQUANT
ALIQUOT
ALIQUOTS
ALISMA
ALISMACEOUS
ALISMAS
ALISON
ALISONS
ALIST
ALIT
ALITERACIES
ALITERACY
ALITERATE
ALITERATES
ALIUNDE
ALIVE
ALIVENESS
ALIVENESSES
ALIYA
ALIYAH
ALIYAHS
ALIYAS
ALIYOS
ALIYOT
ALIYOTH

ALIZARI
ALIZARIN
ALIZARINE
ALIZARINES
ALIZARINS
ALIZARIS
ALKAHEST
ALKAHESTIC
ALKAHESTS
ALKALESCENCE
ALKALESCENCES
ALKALESCENCIES
ALKALESCENCY
ALKALESCENT
ALKALI
ALKALIC
ALKALIES
ALKALIFIED
ALKALIFIES
ALKALIFY
ALKALIFYING
ALKALIMETER
ALKALIMETERS
ALKALIMETRIC
ALKALIMETRIES
ALKALIMETRY
ALKALIN
ALKALINE
ALKALINISE
ALKALINISED
ALKALINISES
ALKALINISING
ALKALINITIES
ALKALINITY
ALKALINIZATION
ALKALINIZATIONS
ALKALINIZE
ALKALINIZED
ALKALINIZES
ALKALINIZING
ALKALIS
ALKALISABILITY
ALKALISABLE
ALKALISE
ALKALISED
ALKALISES
ALKALISING
ALKALIZABILITY
ALKALIZABLE
ALKALIZE
ALKALIZED
ALKALIZES
ALKALIZING
ALKALOID
ALKALOIDAL
ALKALOIDS

ALKALOSES
ALKALOSIS
ALKALOTIC
ALKANE
ALKANES
ALKANET
ALKANETS
ALKANNIN
ALKANNINS
ALKENE
ALKENES
ALKIE
ALKIES
ALKINE
ALKINES
ALKO
ALKOS
ALKOXIDE
ALKOXIDES
ALKOXY
ALKY
ALKYD
ALKYDS
ALKYL
ALKYLATE
ALKYLATED
ALKYLATES
ALKYLATING
ALKYLATION
ALKYLATIONS
ALKYLIC
ALKYLS
ALKYNE
ALKYNES
ALL
ALLANITE
ALLANITES
ALLANTOIC
ALLANTOID
ALLANTOIDAL
ALLANTOIDES
ALLANTOIDS
ALLANTOIN
ALLANTOINS
ALLANTOIS
ALLANTOISES
ALLARGANDO
ALLATIVE
ALLATIVES
ALLAY
ALLAYED
ALLAYER
ALLAYERS
ALLAYING
ALLAYINGS
ALLAYMENT

ALLAYMENTS
ALLAYS
ALLCOMERS
ALLEDGE
ALLEDGED
ALLEDGES
ALLEDGING
ALLEE
ALLEES
ALLEGATION
ALLEGATIONS
ALLEGE
ALLEGEANCE
ALLEGEANCES
ALLEGED
ALLEGEDLY
ALLEGER
ALLEGERS
ALLEGES
ALLEGGE
ALLEGGED
ALLEGGES
ALLEGGING
ALLEGIANCE
ALLEGIANCES
ALLEGIANT
ALLEGING
ALLEGORIC
ALLEGORICAL
ALLEGORICALLY
ALLEGORICALNESS
ALLEGORIES
ALLEGORISATION
ALLEGORISATIONS
ALLEGORISE
ALLEGORISED
ALLEGORISER
ALLEGORISERS
ALLEGORISES
ALLEGORISING
ALLEGORIST
ALLEGORISTS
ALLEGORIZATION
ALLEGORIZATIONS
ALLEGORIZE
ALLEGORIZED
ALLEGORIZER
ALLEGORIZERS
ALLEGORIZES
ALLEGORIZING
ALLEGORY
ALLEGRETTO
ALLEGRETTOS
ALLEGRO
ALLEGROS
ALLEL

ALLELE
ALLELES
ALLELIC
ALLELISM
ALLELISMS
ALLELOMORPH
ALLELOMORPHIC
ALLELOMORPHISM
ALLELOMORPHISMS
ALLELOMORPHS
ALLELOPATHIC
ALLELOPATHIES
ALLELOPATHY
ALLELS
ALLELUIA
ALLELUIAH
ALLELUIAHS
ALLELUIAS
ALLEMANDE
ALLEMANDES
ALLENARLY
ALLERGEN
ALLERGENIC
ALLERGENICITIES
ALLERGENICITY
ALLERGENS
ALLERGIC
ALLERGICS
ALLERGIES
ALLERGIN
ALLERGINS
ALLERGIST
ALLERGISTS
ALLERGY
ALLERION
ALLERIONS
ALLETHRIN
ALLETHRINS
ALLEVIATE
ALLEVIATED
ALLEVIATES
ALLEVIATING
ALLEVIATION
ALLEVIATIONS
ALLEVIATIVE
ALLEVIATOR
ALLEVIATORS
ALLEVIATORY
ALLEY
ALLEYCAT
ALLEYCATS
ALLEYED
ALLEYS
ALLEYWAY
ALLEYWAYS
ALLHALLOND

ALLHALLOWN
ALLHEAL
ALLHEALS
ALLIABLE
ALLIACEOUS
ALLIANCE
ALLIANCES
ALLICE
ALLICES
ALLICHOLIES
ALLICHOLY
ALLICIN
ALLICINS
ALLIED
ALLIES
ALLIGARTA
ALLIGARTAS
ALLIGATE
ALLIGATED
ALLIGATES
ALLIGATING
ALLIGATION
ALLIGATIONS
ALLIGATOR
ALLIGATORS
ALLINEATION
ALLINEATIONS
ALLIS
ALLISES
ALLITERATE
ALLITERATED
ALLITERATES
ALLITERATING
ALLITERATION
ALLITERATIONS
ALLITERATIVE
ALLITERATIVELY
ALLIUM
ALLIUMS
ALLNESS
ALLNESSES
ALLNIGHT
ALLNIGHTER
ALLNIGHTERS
ALLOANTIBODIES
ALLOANTIBODY
ALLOANTIGEN
ALLOANTIGENS
ALLOBAR
ALLOBARS
ALLOCABLE
ALLOCARPIES
ALLOCARPY
ALLOCATABLE
ALLOCATE
ALLOCATED

ALLOCATES
ALLOCATING
ALLOCATION
ALLOCATIONS
ALLOCATOR
ALLOCATORS
ALLOCHEIRIA
ALLOCHEIRIAS
ALLOCHIRIA
ALLOCHIRIAS
ALLOCHTHONOUS
ALLOCUTION
ALLOCUTIONS
ALLOD
ALLODIA
ALLODIAL
ALLODIUM
ALLODIUMS
ALLODS
ALLOGAMIES
ALLOGAMOUS
ALLOGAMY
ALLOGENEIC
ALLOGENIC
ALLOGRAFT
ALLOGRAFTED
ALLOGRAFTING
ALLOGRAFTS
ALLOGRAPH
ALLOGRAPHIC
ALLOGRAPHS
ALLOIOSTROPHOS
ALLOMERIC
ALLOMERISM
ALLOMERISMS
ALLOMEROUS
ALLOMETRIC
ALLOMETRIES
ALLOMETRY
ALLOMONE
ALLOMONES
ALLOMORPH
ALLOMORPHIC
ALLOMORPHISM
ALLOMORPHISMS
ALLOMORPHS
ALLONGE
ALLONGES
ALLONS
ALLONYM
ALLONYMOUS
ALLONYMS
ALLOPATH
ALLOPATHIC
ALLOPATHICALLY
ALLOPATHIES

ALLOPATHIST
ALLOPATHISTS
ALLOPATHS
ALLOPATHY
ALLOPATRIC
ALLOPATRICALLY
ALLOPATRIES
ALLOPATRY
ALLOPHANE
ALLOPHANES
ALLOPHONE
ALLOPHONES
ALLOPHONIC
ALLOPLASM
ALLOPLASMIC
ALLOPLASMS
ALLOPLASTIC
ALLOPOLYPLOID
ALLOPOLYPLOIDS
ALLOPOLYPLOIDY
ALLOPURINOL
ALLOPURINOLS
ALLOSAUR
ALLOSAURS
ALLOSAURUS
ALLOSAURUSES
ALLOSTERIC
ALLOSTERICALLY
ALLOSTERIES
ALLOSTERY
ALLOT
ALLOTETRAPLOID
ALLOTETRAPLOIDS
ALLOTETRAPLOIDY
ALLOTHEISM
ALLOTHEISMS
ALLOTMENT
ALLOTMENTS
ALLOTRIOMORPHIC
ALLOTROPE
ALLOTROPES
ALLOTROPIC
ALLOTROPICALLY
ALLOTROPIES
ALLOTROPISM
ALLOTROPISMS
ALLOTROPOUS
ALLOTROPY
ALLOTS
ALLOTTED
ALLOTTEE
ALLOTTEES
ALLOTTER
ALLOTTERIES
ALLOTTERS
ALLOTTERY

ALLOTTING
ALLOTYPE
ALLOTYPES
ALLOTYPIC
ALLOTYPICALLY
ALLOTYPIES
ALLOTYPY
ALLOVER
ALLOVERS
ALLOW
ALLOWABILITIES
ALLOWABILITY
ALLOWABLE
ALLOWABLENESS
ALLOWABLENESSES
ALLOWABLY
ALLOWANCE
ALLOWANCED
ALLOWANCES
ALLOWANCING
ALLOWED
ALLOWEDLY
ALLOWING
ALLOWS
ALLOXAN
ALLOXANS
ALLOY
ALLOYED
ALLOYING
ALLOYS
ALLOZYME
ALLOZYMES
ALLS
ALLSEED
ALLSEEDS
ALLSORTS
ALLSPICE
ALLSPICES
ALLUDE
ALLUDED
ALLUDES
ALLUDING
ALLURE
ALLURED
ALLUREMENT
ALLUREMENTS
ALLURER
ALLURERS
ALLURES
ALLURING
ALLURINGLY
ALLUSION
ALLUSIONS
ALLUSIVE
ALLUSIVELY
ALLUSIVENESS

ALLUSIVENESSES
ALLUVIA
ALLUVIAL
ALLUVIALS
ALLUVION
ALLUVIONS
ALLUVIUM
ALLUVIUMS
ALLY
ALLYCHOLLIES
ALLYCHOLLY
ALLYING
ALLYL
ALLYLIC
ALLYLS
ALLYOU
ALMA
ALMACANTAR
ALMACANTARS
ALMAGEST
ALMAGESTS
ALMAH
ALMAHS
ALMAIN
ALMAINS
ALMANAC
ALMANACK
ALMANACKS
ALMANACS
ALMANDINE
ALMANDINES
ALMANDITE
ALMANDITES
ALMAS
ALME
ALMEH
ALMEHS
ALMEMAR
ALMEMARS
ALMERIES
ALMERY
ALMES
ALMIGHTILY
ALMIGHTINESS
ALMIGHTINESSES
ALMIGHTY
ALMIRAH
ALMIRAHS
ALMNER
ALMNERS
ALMOND
ALMONDS
ALMONER
ALMONERS
ALMONRIES
ALMONRY

ALMOST
ALMOUS
ALMS
ALMSGIVER
ALMSGIVERS
ALMSGIVING
ALMSGIVINGS
ALMSHOUSE
ALMSHOUSES
ALMSMAN
ALMSMEN
ALMSWOMAN
ALMSWOMEN
ALMUCANTAR
ALMUCANTARS
ALMUCE
ALMUCES
ALMUD
ALMUDE
ALMUDES
ALMUDS
ALMUG
ALMUGS
ALNAGE
ALNAGER
ALNAGERS
ALNAGES
ALNICO
ALNICOES
ALOD
ALODIA
ALODIAL
ALODIUM
ALODIUMS
ALODS
ALOE
ALOED
ALOES
ALOETIC
ALOETICS
ALOFT
ALOGIA
ALOGIAS
ALOGICAL
ALOGICALLY
ALOHA
ALOHAS
ALOIN
ALOINS
ALONE
ALONELY
ALONENESS
ALONENESSES
ALONG
ALONGSHORE
ALONGSHOREMAN

ALONGSHOREMEN
ALONGSIDE
ALONGST
ALOOF
ALOOFLY
ALOOFNESS
ALOOFNESSES
ALOPECIA
ALOPECIAS
ALOPECIC
ALOPECOID
ALOUD
ALOW
ALOWE
ALP
ALPACA
ALPACAS
ALPACCA
ALPACCAS
ALPARGATA
ALPARGATAS
ALPEEN
ALPEENS
ALPENGLOW
ALPENGLOWS
ALPENHORN
ALPENHORNS
ALPENSTOCK
ALPENSTOCKS
ALPESTRINE
ALPHA
ALPHABET
ALPHABETARIAN
ALPHABETARIANS
ALPHABETED
ALPHABETIC
ALPHABETICAL
ALPHABETICALLY
ALPHABETIFORM
ALPHABETING
ALPHABETISATION
ALPHABETISE
ALPHABETISED
ALPHABETISER
ALPHABETISERS
ALPHABETISES
ALPHABETISING
ALPHABETIZATION
ALPHABETIZE
ALPHABETIZED
ALPHABETIZER
ALPHABETIZERS
ALPHABETIZES
ALPHABETIZING
ALPHABETS
ALPHAMERIC

ALPHAMERICAL
ALPHAMERICALLY
ALPHAMETIC
ALPHAMETICS
ALPHANUMERIC
ALPHANUMERICAL
ALPHANUMERICS
ALPHAS
ALPHASORT
ALPHASORTED
ALPHASORTING
ALPHASORTS
ALPHORN
ALPHORNS
ALPHOSIS
ALPHOSISES
ALPHYL
ALPHYLS
ALPINE
ALPINELY
ALPINES
ALPINISM
ALPINISMS
ALPINIST
ALPINISTS
ALPS
ALREADY
ALRIGHT
ALS
ALSIKE
ALSIKES
ALSO
ALSOON
ALSOONE
ALSTROEMERIA
ALSTROEMERIAS
ALT
ALTALTISSIMO
ALTALTISSIMOS
ALTAR
ALTARAGE
ALTARAGES
ALTARPIECE
ALTARPIECES
ALTARS
ALTARWISE
ALTAZIMUTH
ALTAZIMUTHS
ALTER
ALTERABILITIES
ALTERABILITY
ALTERABLE
ALTERABLY
ALTERANT
ALTERANTS
ALTERATION

ALTERATIONS
ALTERATIVE
ALTERATIVES
ALTERCATE
ALTERCATED
ALTERCATES
ALTERCATING
ALTERCATION
ALTERCATIONS
ALTERCATIVE
ALTERED
ALTERER
ALTERERS
ALTERING
ALTERITIES
ALTERITY
ALTERN
ALTERNANCE
ALTERNANCES
ALTERNANT
ALTERNANTS
ALTERNAT
ALTERNATE
ALTERNATED
ALTERNATELY
ALTERNATES
ALTERNATIM
ALTERNATING
ALTERNATION
ALTERNATIONS
ALTERNATIVE
ALTERNATIVELY
ALTERNATIVENESS
ALTERNATIVES
ALTERNATOR
ALTERNATORS
ALTERNATS
ALTERNE
ALTERNES
ALTERS
ALTESSE
ALTESSES
ALTEZA
ALTEZAS
ALTEZZA
ALTEZZAS
ALTHAEA
ALTHAEAS
ALTHEA
ALTHEAS
ALTHO
ALTHORN
ALTHORNS
ALTHOUGH
ALTIMETER
ALTIMETERS

ALTIMETRICAL
ALTIMETRICALLY
ALTIMETRIES
ALTIMETRY
ALTIPLANO
ALTIPLANOS
ALTISONANT
ALTISSIMO
ALTITONANT
ALTITUDE
ALTITUDES
ALTITUDINAL
ALTITUDINARIAN
ALTITUDINARIANS
ALTITUDINOUS
ALTO
ALTOCUMULI
ALTOCUMULUS
ALTOGETHER
ALTOGETHERS
ALTOIST
ALTOISTS
ALTOS
ALTOSTRATI
ALTOSTRATUS
ALTRICES
ALTRICIAL
ALTRICIALS
ALTRUISM
ALTRUISMS
ALTRUIST
ALTRUISTIC
ALTRUISTICALLY
ALTRUISTS
ALTS
ALUDEL
ALUDELS
ALULA
ALULAE
ALULAR
ALUM
ALUMIN
ALUMINA
ALUMINAS
ALUMINATE
ALUMINATES
ALUMINE
ALUMINES
ALUMINIC
ALUMINIFEROUS
ALUMINISE
ALUMINISED
ALUMINISES
ALUMINISING
ALUMINIUM
ALUMINIUMS

ALUMINIZE
ALUMINIZED
ALUMINIZES
ALUMINIZING
ALUMINOSILICATE
ALUMINOSITY
ALUMINOTHERMIC
ALUMINOTHERMY
ALUMINOUS
ALUMINS
ALUMINUM
ALUMINUMS
ALUMISH
ALUMIUM
ALUMIUMS
ALUMNA
ALUMNAE
ALUMNI
ALUMNUS
ALUMROOT
ALUMROOTS
ALUMS
ALUNITE
ALUNITES
ALURE
ALURES
ALVEARIES
ALVEARY
ALVEATED
ALVEOLAR
ALVEOLARLY
ALVEOLARS
ALVEOLATE
ALVEOLATION
ALVEOLATIONS
ALVEOLE
ALVEOLES
ALVEOLI
ALVEOLITIS
ALVEOLITISES
ALVEOLUS
ALVINE
ALWAY
ALWAYS
ALYCOMPAINE
ALYCOMPAINES
ALYSSUM
ALYSSUMS
AM
AMA
AMABILE
AMABOKOBOKO
AMADAVAT
AMADAVATS
AMADODA
AMADOU

AMADOUS
AMAH
AMAHS
AMAIN
AMAKWEREKWERE
AMALGAM
AMALGAMATE
AMALGAMATED
AMALGAMATES
AMALGAMATING
AMALGAMATION
AMALGAMATIONS
AMALGAMATIVE
AMALGAMATOR
AMALGAMATORS
AMALGAMS
AMANDINE
AMANDINES
AMANDLA
AMANITA
AMANITAS
AMANITIN
AMANITINS
AMANTADINE
AMANTADINES
AMANUENSES
AMANUENSIS
AMANUENSISES
AMARACUS
AMARACUSES
AMARANT
AMARANTACEOUS
AMARANTH
AMARANTHACEOUS
AMARANTHINE
AMARANTHS
AMARANTIN
AMARANTINE
AMARANTS
AMARELLE
AMARELLES
AMARETTI
AMARETTO
AMARETTOS
AMARNA
AMARYLLID
AMARYLLIDACEOUS
AMARYLLIDS
AMARYLLIS
AMARYLLISES
AMAS
AMASS
AMASSABLE
AMASSED
AMASSER
AMASSERS

AMASSES
AMASSING
AMASSMENT
AMASSMENTS
AMATE
AMATED
AMATES
AMATEUR
AMATEURISH
AMATEURISHLY
AMATEURISHNESS
AMATEURISM
AMATEURISMS
AMATEURS
AMATEURSHIP
AMATEURSHIPS
AMATING
AMATION
AMATIONS
AMATIVE
AMATIVELY
AMATIVENESS
AMATIVENESSES
AMATOL
AMATOLS
AMATORIAL
AMATORIALLY
AMATORIAN
AMATORIOUS
AMATORY
AMAUROSES
AMAUROSIS
AMAUROTIC
AMAUT
AMAUTS
AMAZE
AMAZED
AMAZEDLY
AMAZEDNESS
AMAZEDNESSES
AMAZEMENT
AMAZEMENTS
AMAZES
AMAZING
AMAZINGLY
AMAZON
AMAZONIAN
AMAZONITE
AMAZONITES
AMAZONS
AMAZONSTONE
AMAZONSTONES
AMBACH
AMBACHES
AMBAGE
AMBAGES

AMBAGIOUS
AMBAGITORY
AMBAN
AMBANS
AMBARI
AMBARIES
AMBARIS
AMBARY
AMBASSADOR
AMBASSADORIAL
AMBASSADORS
AMBASSADORSHIP
AMBASSADORSHIPS
AMBASSADRESS
AMBASSADRESSES
AMBASSAGE
AMBASSAGES
AMBASSIES
AMBASSY
AMBATCH
AMBATCHES
AMBEER
AMBEERS
AMBER
AMBERED
AMBERGRIS
AMBERGRISES
AMBERIES
AMBERINA
AMBERINAS
AMBERITE
AMBERITES
AMBERJACK
AMBERJACKS
AMBEROID
AMBEROIDS
AMBEROUS
AMBERS
AMBERY
AMBIANCE
AMBIANCES
AMBIDENTATE
AMBIDEXTER
AMBIDEXTERITIES
AMBIDEXTERITY
AMBIDEXTEROUS
AMBIDEXTERS
AMBIDEXTROUS
AMBIDEXTROUSLY
AMBIENCE
AMBIENCES
AMBIENT
AMBIENTS
AMBIGUITIES
AMBIGUITY
AMBIGUOUS

AMBIGUOUSLY
AMBIGUOUSNESS
AMBIGUOUSNESSES
AMBILATERAL
AMBIOPHONIC
AMBIOPHONICALLY
AMBIOPHONIES
AMBIOPHONY
AMBIPOLAR
AMBIPOLARITY
AMBISEXUAL
AMBISEXUALITIES
AMBISEXUALITY
AMBISEXUALS
AMBISONICS
AMBIT
AMBITION
AMBITIONED
AMBITIONING
AMBITIONLESS
AMBITIONS
AMBITIOUS
AMBITIOUSLY
AMBITIOUSNESS
AMBITIOUSNESSES
AMBITS
AMBITTY
AMBIVALENCE
AMBIVALENCES
AMBIVALENCIES
AMBIVALENCY
AMBIVALENT
AMBIVALENTLY
AMBIVERSION
AMBIVERSIONS
AMBIVERT
AMBIVERTS
AMBLE
AMBLED
AMBLER
AMBLERS
AMBLES
AMBLING
AMBLINGS
AMBLYGONITE
AMBLYGONITES
AMBLYOPIA
AMBLYOPIAS
AMBLYOPIC
AMBO
AMBOCEPTOR
AMBOCEPTORS
AMBOINA
AMBOINAS
AMBONES
AMBOS

AMBOSEXUAL
AMBOYNA
AMBOYNAS
AMBRIES
AMBROID
AMBROIDS
AMBROSIA
AMBROSIAL
AMBROSIALLY
AMBROSIAN
AMBROSIAS
AMBROTYPE
AMBROTYPES
AMBRY
AMBSACE
AMBSACES
AMBULACRA
AMBULACRAL
AMBULACRUM
AMBULANCE
AMBULANCEMAN
AMBULANCEMEN
AMBULANCES
AMBULANCEWOMAN
AMBULANCEWOMEN
AMBULANT
AMBULANTS
AMBULATE
AMBULATED
AMBULATES
AMBULATING
AMBULATION
AMBULATIONS
AMBULATOR
AMBULATORIES
AMBULATORILY
AMBULATORS
AMBULATORY
AMBUSCADE
AMBUSCADED
AMBUSCADER
AMBUSCADERS
AMBUSCADES
AMBUSCADING
AMBUSCADO
AMBUSCADOES
AMBUSCADOS
AMBUSH
AMBUSHED
AMBUSHER
AMBUSHERS
AMBUSHES
AMBUSHING
AMBUSHMENT
AMBUSHMENTS
AMEARST

AMEBA
AMEBAE
AMEBAN
AMEBAS
AMEBEAN
AMEBIASES
AMEBIASIS
AMEBIC
AMEBOCYTE
AMEBOCYTES
AMEBOID
AMEER
AMEERATE
AMEERATES
AMEERS
AMEIOSES
AMEIOSIS
AMELCORN
AMELCORNS
AMELIA
AMELIAS
AMELIORABLE
AMELIORABLY
AMELIORANT
AMELIORANTS
AMELIORATE
AMELIORATED
AMELIORATES
AMELIORATING
AMELIORATION
AMELIORATIONS
AMELIORATIVE
AMELIORATOR
AMELIORATORS
AMELIORATORY
AMELLIBRANCH
AMELOBLAST
AMELOBLASTS
AMELOGENESIS
AMELOGENETIC
AMEN
AMENABILITIES
AMENABILITY
AMENABLE
AMENABLENESS
AMENABLENESSES
AMENABLY
AMENAGE
AMENAGED
AMENAGES
AMENAGING
AMENAUNCE
AMENAUNCES
AMEND
AMENDABLE
AMENDATORY

AMENDE
AMENDED
AMENDER
AMENDERS
AMENDES
AMENDING
AMENDMENT
AMENDMENTS
AMENDS
AMENE
AMENED
AMENING
AMENITIES
AMENITY
AMENORRHEA
AMENORRHEAS
AMENORRHEIC
AMENORRHOEA
AMENORRHOEAS
AMENS
AMENT
AMENTA
AMENTACEOUS
AMENTAL
AMENTIA
AMENTIAS
AMENTIFEROUS
AMENTS
AMENTUM
AMERCE
AMERCEABLE
AMERCED
AMERCEMENT
AMERCEMENTS
AMERCER
AMERCERS
AMERCES
AMERCIABLE
AMERCIAMENT
AMERCIAMENTS
AMERCING
AMERICIUM
AMERICIUMS
AMESACE
AMESACES
AMETABOLIC
AMETABOLISM
AMETABOLISMS
AMETABOLOUS
AMETHYST
AMETHYSTINE
AMETHYSTS
AMETROPIA
AMETROPIAS
AMETROPIC
AMI

AMIA	AMINE	AMMINES	AMNESICS
AMIABILITIES	AMINES	AMMINO	AMNESTIC
AMIABILITY	AMINIC	AMMIRAL	AMNESTIED
AMIABLE	AMINITIES	AMMIRALS	AMNESTIES
AMIABLENESS	AMINITY	AMMO	AMNESTY
AMIABLENESSES	AMINO	AMMOCETE	AMNESTYING
AMIABLY	AMINOACIDURIA	AMMOCETES	AMNIA
AMIANTHINE	AMINOACIDURIAS	AMMOCOETE	AMNIC
AMIANTHOID	AMINOBENZOIC	AMMON	AMNIO
AMIANTHOIDAL	AMINOBENZOICS	AMMONAL	AMNIOCENTESES
AMIANTHUS	AMINOBUTENE	AMMONALS	AMNIOCENTESIS
AMIANTHUSES	AMINOBUTENES	AMMONATE	AMNION
AMIANTUS	AMINOPEPTIDASE	AMMONATES	AMNIONIC
AMIANTUSES	AMINOPEPTIDASES	AMMONIA	AMNIONS
AMIAS	AMINOPHENAZONE	AMMONIAC	AMNIOS
AMICABILITIES	AMINOPHENAZONES	AMMONIACAL	AMNIOTE
AMICABILITY	AMINOPHENOL	AMMONIACS	AMNIOTES
AMICABLE	AMINOPHENOLS	AMMONIACUM	AMNIOTIC
AMICABLENESS	AMINOPHYLLINE	AMMONIACUMS	AMNIOTOMIES
AMICABLENESSES	AMINOPHYLLINES	AMMONIAS	AMNIOTOMY
AMICABLY	AMINOPTERIN	AMMONIATE	AMOBARBITAL
AMICE	AMINOPTERINS	AMMONIATED	AMOBARBITALS
AMICES	AMINOPYRINE	AMMONIATES	AMOEBA
AMICI	AMINOPYRINES	AMMONIATING	AMOEBAE
AMICUS	AMINS	AMMONIATION	AMOEBAEAN
AMID	AMIR	AMMONIATIONS	AMOEBAN
AMIDASE	AMIRATE	AMMONIC	AMOEBAS
AMIDASES	AMIRATES	AMMONICAL	AMOEBEAN
AMIDE	AMIRS	AMMONICALLY	AMOEBIASES
AMIDES	AMIS	AMMONIFICATION	AMOEBIASIS
AMIDIC	AMISES	AMMONIFICATIONS	AMOEBIC
AMIDIN	AMISS	AMMONIFIED	AMOEBIFORM
AMIDINE	AMISSES	AMMONIFIES	AMOEBOCYTE
AMIDINES	AMISSIBILITIES	AMMONIFY	AMOEBOCYTES
AMIDINS	AMISSIBILITY	AMMONIFYING	AMOEBOID
AMIDMOST	AMISSIBLE	AMMONITE	AMOK
AMIDO	AMISSING	AMMONITES	AMOKS
AMIDOGEN	AMITIES	AMMONITIC	AMOLE
AMIDOGENS	AMITOSES	AMMONIUM	AMOLES
AMIDOL	AMITOSIS	AMMONIUMS	AMOMUM
AMIDOLS	AMITOTIC	AMMONO	AMOMUMS
AMIDONE	AMITOTICALLY	AMMONOID	AMONG
AMIDONES	AMITRIPTYLINE	AMMONOIDS	AMONGST
AMIDS	AMITRIPTYLINES	AMMONOLYSIS	AMONTILLADO
AMIDSHIP	AMITROLE	AMMONS	AMONTILLADOS
AMIDSHIPS	AMITROLES	AMMOPHILOUS	AMOOVE
AMIDST	AMITRYPTYLINE	AMMOS	AMOOVED
AMIE	AMITRYPTYLINES	AMMUNITION	AMOOVES
AMIES	AMITY	AMMUNITIONED	AMOOVING
AMIGA	AMLA	AMMUNITIONING	AMORAL
AMIGAS	AMLAS	AMMUNITIONS	AMORALISM
AMIGO	AMMAN	AMNESIA	AMORALISMS
AMIGOS	AMMANS	AMNESIAC	AMORALIST
AMILDAR	AMMETER	AMNESIACS	AMORALISTS
AMILDARS	AMMETERS	AMNESIAS	AMORALITIES
AMIN	AMMINE	AMNESIC	AMORALITY

AMORALLY
AMORANCE
AMORANCES
AMORANT
AMORCE
AMORCES
AMORET
AMORETS
AMORETTI
AMORETTO
AMORETTOS
AMORINI
AMORINO
AMORISM
AMORISMS
AMORIST
AMORISTIC
AMORISTS
AMORNINGS
AMOROSA
AMOROSAS
AMOROSITIES
AMOROSITY
AMOROSO
AMOROSOS
AMOROUS
AMOROUSLY
AMOROUSNESS
AMOROUSNESSES
AMORPHISM
AMORPHISMS
AMORPHOUS
AMORPHOUSLY
AMORPHOUSNESS
AMORPHOUSNESSES
AMORT
AMORTISABLE
AMORTISATION
AMORTISATIONS
AMORTISE
AMORTISED
AMORTISEMENT
AMORTISEMENTS
AMORTISES
AMORTISING
AMORTIZABLE
AMORTIZATION
AMORTIZATIONS
AMORTIZE
AMORTIZED
AMORTIZEMENT
AMORTIZEMENTS
AMORTIZES
AMORTIZING
AMOSITE
AMOSITES

AMOTION
AMOTIONS
AMOUNT
AMOUNTED
AMOUNTING
AMOUNTS
AMOUR
AMOURETTE
AMOURETTES
AMOURS
AMOVE
AMOVED
AMOVES
AMOVING
AMOWT
AMOWTS
AMOXICILLIN
AMOXICILLINS
AMOXYCILLIN
AMOXYCILLINS
AMP
AMPASSIES
AMPASSY
AMPELOGRAPHIES
AMPELOGRAPHY
AMPELOPSES
AMPELOPSIS
AMPERAGE
AMPERAGES
AMPERE
AMPERES
AMPEROMETRIC
AMPERSAND
AMPERSANDS
AMPERZAND
AMPERZANDS
AMPHETAMINE
AMPHETAMINES
AMPHIARTHROSES
AMPHIARTHROSIS
AMPHIASTER
AMPHIASTERS
AMPHIBIA
AMPHIBIAN
AMPHIBIANS
AMPHIBIOTIC
AMPHIBIOTICALLY
AMPHIBIOUS
AMPHIBIOUSLY
AMPHIBIOUSNESS
AMPHIBLASTIC
AMPHIBLASTULA
AMPHIBOLE
AMPHIBOLES
AMPHIBOLIC
AMPHIBOLIES

AMPHIBOLITE
AMPHIBOLITES
AMPHIBOLOGICAL
AMPHIBOLOGIES
AMPHIBOLOGY
AMPHIBOLOUS
AMPHIBOLY
AMPHIBRACH
AMPHIBRACHIC
AMPHIBRACHS
AMPHICHROIC
AMPHICHROICALLY
AMPHICHROMATIC
AMPHICHROMATISM
AMPHICOELOUS
AMPHICTYON
AMPHICTYONIC
AMPHICTYONIES
AMPHICTYONS
AMPHICTYONY
AMPHIDENTATE
AMPHIDIPLOID
AMPHIDIPLOIDIES
AMPHIDIPLOIDS
AMPHIDIPLOIDY
AMPHIGASTRIA
AMPHIGASTRIUM
AMPHIGORIC
AMPHIGORICALLY
AMPHIGORIES
AMPHIGORY
AMPHIGOURI
AMPHIGOURIS
AMPHIMACER
AMPHIMACERS
AMPHIMICTIC
AMPHIMIXES
AMPHIMIXIS
AMPHIOXES
AMPHIOXI
AMPHIOXUS
AMPHIOXUSES
AMPHIPATH
AMPHIPATHIC
AMPHIPATHS
AMPHIPHILE
AMPHIPHILES
AMPHIPHILIC
AMPHIPLOID
AMPHIPLOIDIES
AMPHIPLOIDS
AMPHIPLOIDY
AMPHIPOD
AMPHIPODOUS
AMPHIPODS
AMPHIPROSTYLAR

AMPHIPROSTYLE
AMPHIPROSTYLES
AMPHIPROTIC
AMPHISBAENA
AMPHISBAENAE
AMPHISBAENAS
AMPHISBAENIC
AMPHISCIAN
AMPHISCIANS
AMPHISTOMATAL
AMPHISTOMATALLY
AMPHISTOMATIC
AMPHISTOMOUS
AMPHISTYLAR
AMPHISTYLARS
AMPHITHEATER
AMPHITHEATERS
AMPHITHEATRAL
AMPHITHEATRE
AMPHITHEATRES
AMPHITHEATRIC
AMPHITHEATRICAL
AMPHITHECIA
AMPHITHECIUM
AMPHITRICHA
AMPHITRICHOUS
AMPHITROPOUS
AMPHOLYTE
AMPHOLYTES
AMPHORA
AMPHORAE
AMPHORAL
AMPHORAS
AMPHORIC
AMPHOTERIC
AMPICILLIN
AMPICILLINS
AMPLE
AMPLENESS
AMPLENESSES
AMPLER
AMPLEST
AMPLEXICAUL
AMPLEXUS
AMPLEXUSES
AMPLIATION
AMPLIATIONS
AMPLIATIVE
AMPLIDYNE
AMPLIDYNES
AMPLIFIABLE
AMPLIFICATION
AMPLIFICATIONS
AMPLIFIED
AMPLIFIER
AMPLIFIERS

AMPLIFIES
AMPLIFY
AMPLIFYING
AMPLITUDE
AMPLITUDES
AMPLOSOME
AMPLOSOMES
AMPLY
AMPOULE
AMPOULES
AMPS
AMPUL
AMPULE
AMPULES
AMPULLA
AMPULLACEAL
AMPULLACEOUS
AMPULLAE
AMPULLAR
AMPULLARY
AMPULLOSITIES
AMPULLOSITY
AMPULS
AMPUTATE
AMPUTATED
AMPUTATES
AMPUTATING
AMPUTATION
AMPUTATIONS
AMPUTATOR
AMPUTATORS
AMPUTEE
AMPUTEES
AMREETA
AMREETAS
AMRIT
AMRITA
AMRITAS
AMRITATTVA
AMRITATTVAS
AMRITS
AMTMAN
AMTMANS
AMTRAC
AMTRACK
AMTRACKS
AMTRACS
AMU
AMUCK
AMUCKS
AMULET
AMULETIC
AMULETS
AMUS
AMUSABLE
AMUSE

AMUSEABLE
AMUSED
AMUSEDLY
AMUSEMENT
AMUSEMENTS
AMUSER
AMUSERS
AMUSES
AMUSETTE
AMUSETTES
AMUSIA
AMUSIAS
AMUSING
AMUSINGLY
AMUSINGNESS
AMUSINGNESSES
AMUSIVE
AMUSIVENESS
AMUSIVENESSES
AMYGDAL
AMYGDALA
AMYGDALACEOUS
AMYGDALAE
AMYGDALAS
AMYGDALATE
AMYGDALE
AMYGDALES
AMYGDALIN
AMYGDALINE
AMYGDALINS
AMYGDALOID
AMYGDALOIDAL
AMYGDALOIDS
AMYGDALS
AMYGDULE
AMYGDULES
AMYL
AMYLACEOUS
AMYLASE
AMYLASES
AMYLENE
AMYLENES
AMYLIC
AMYLOGEN
AMYLOGENS
AMYLOID
AMYLOIDAL
AMYLOIDOSES
AMYLOIDOSIS
AMYLOIDS
AMYLOLYSES
AMYLOLYSIS
AMYLOLYTIC
AMYLOPECTIN
AMYLOPECTINS
AMYLOPLAST

AMYLOPLASTS
AMYLOPSIN
AMYLOPSINS
AMYLOSE
AMYLOSES
AMYLS
AMYLUM
AMYLUMS
AMYOTONIA
AMYOTONIAS
AMYOTROPHIC
AMYOTROPHIES
AMYOTROPHY
AMYTAL
AMYTALS
AN
ANA
ANABAENA
ANABAENAS
ANABANTID
ANABANTIDS
ANABAPTISE
ANABAPTISED
ANABAPTISES
ANABAPTISING
ANABAPTISM
ANABAPTISMS
ANABAPTIST
ANABAPTISTIC
ANABAPTISTS
ANABAPTIZE
ANABAPTIZED
ANABAPTIZES
ANABAPTIZING
ANABAS
ANABASES
ANABASIS
ANABATIC
ANABIOSES
ANABIOSIS
ANABIOTIC
ANABLEPS
ANABLEPSES
ANABOLIC
ANABOLISM
ANABOLISMS
ANABOLITE
ANABOLITES
ANABOLITIC
ANABRANCH
ANABRANCHES
ANACARDIACEOUS
ANACARDIUM
ANACARDIUMS
ANACATHARSES
ANACATHARSIS

ANACATHARTIC
ANACATHARTICS
ANACHARIS
ANACHARISES
ANACHORISM
ANACHORISMS
ANACHRONIC
ANACHRONICAL
ANACHRONICALLY
ANACHRONISM
ANACHRONISMS
ANACHRONISTIC
ANACHRONOUS
ANACHRONOUSLY
ANACLASTIC
ANACLINAL
ANACLINALLY
ANACLISIS
ANACLITIC
ANACOLUTHA
ANACOLUTHIA
ANACOLUTHIAS
ANACOLUTHIC
ANACOLUTHICALLY
ANACOLUTHON
ANACOLUTHONS
ANACONDA
ANACONDAS
ANACOUSTIC
ANACOUSTICALLY
ANACREONTIC
ANACREONTICALLY
ANACREONTICS
ANACRUSES
ANACRUSIS
ANACRUSTIC
ANADEM
ANADEMS
ANADIPLOSES
ANADIPLOSIS
ANADROMOUS
ANADYOMENE
ANAEMIA
ANAEMIAS
ANAEMIC
ANAEROBE
ANAEROBES
ANAEROBIA
ANAEROBIC
ANAEROBICALLY
ANAEROBIONT
ANAEROBIONTS
ANAEROBIOSES
ANAEROBIOSIS
ANAEROBIOTIC
ANAEROBIUM

ANAESTHESES
ANAESTHESIA
ANAESTHESIAS
ANAESTHESIOLOGY
ANAESTHESIS
ANAESTHETIC
ANAESTHETICALLY
ANAESTHETICS
ANAESTHETISE
ANAESTHETISED
ANAESTHETISES
ANAESTHETISING
ANAESTHETIST
ANAESTHETISTS
ANAESTHETIZE
ANAESTHETIZED
ANAESTHETIZES
ANAESTHETIZING
ANAGENESES
ANAGENESIS
ANAGLYPH
ANAGLYPHIC
ANAGLYPHICAL
ANAGLYPHICALLY
ANAGLYPHS
ANAGLYPHY
ANAGLYPTIC
ANAGLYPTICAL
ANAGNORISES
ANAGNORISIS
ANAGOGE
ANAGOGES
ANAGOGIC
ANAGOGICAL
ANAGOGICALLY
ANAGOGIES
ANAGOGY
ANAGRAM
ANAGRAMMATIC
ANAGRAMMATICAL
ANAGRAMMATISE
ANAGRAMMATISED
ANAGRAMMATISES
ANAGRAMMATISING
ANAGRAMMATISM
ANAGRAMMATISMS
ANAGRAMMATIST
ANAGRAMMATISTS
ANAGRAMMATIZE
ANAGRAMMATIZED
ANAGRAMMATIZES
ANAGRAMMATIZING
ANAGRAMMED
ANAGRAMMER
ANAGRAMMERS
ANAGRAMMING

ANAGRAMS
ANAL
ANALCIME
ANALCIMES
ANALCITE
ANALCITES
ANALECTA
ANALECTIC
ANALECTS
ANALEMMA
ANALEMMAS
ANALEMMATA
ANALEMMATIC
ANALEPTIC
ANALEPTICS
ANALGESIA
ANALGESIAS
ANALGESIC
ANALGESICS
ANALGETIC
ANALGETICS
ANALGIA
ANALGIAS
ANALITIES
ANALITY
ANALLY
ANALOG
ANALOGA
ANALOGIC
ANALOGICAL
ANALOGICALLY
ANALOGIES
ANALOGISE
ANALOGISED
ANALOGISES
ANALOGISING
ANALOGIST
ANALOGISTS
ANALOGIZE
ANALOGIZED
ANALOGIZES
ANALOGIZING
ANALOGON
ANALOGONS
ANALOGOUS
ANALOGOUSLY
ANALOGOUSNESS
ANALOGOUSNESSES
ANALOGS
ANALOGUE
ANALOGUES
ANALOGY
ANALPHABET
ANALPHABETE
ANALPHABETES
ANALPHABETIC

ANALPHABETICS
ANALPHABETISM
ANALPHABETISMS
ANALPHABETS
ANALYSABLE
ANALYSAND
ANALYSANDS
ANALYSATION
ANALYSATIONS
ANALYSE
ANALYSED
ANALYSER
ANALYSERS
ANALYSES
ANALYSING
ANALYSIS
ANALYST
ANALYSTS
ANALYTIC
ANALYTICAL
ANALYTICALLY
ANALYTICITIES
ANALYTICITY
ANALYTICS
ANALYZABILITIES
ANALYZABILITY
ANALYZABLE
ANALYZATION
ANALYZATIONS
ANALYZE
ANALYZED
ANALYZER
ANALYZERS
ANALYZES
ANALYZING
ANAMNESES
ANAMNESIS
ANAMNESTIC
ANAMNESTICALLY
ANAMNIOTE
ANAMNIOTES
ANAMNIOTIC
ANAMORPHIC
ANAMORPHISM
ANAMORPHISMS
ANAMORPHOSCOPE
ANAMORPHOSCOPES
ANAMORPHOSES
ANAMORPHOSIS
ANAMORPHOUS
ANAN
ANANA
ANANAS
ANANASES
ANANDAMIDE
ANANDAMIDES

ANANDROUS
ANANKE
ANANKES
ANANTHOUS
ANAPAEST
ANAPAESTIC
ANAPAESTICAL
ANAPAESTS
ANAPEST
ANAPESTIC
ANAPESTICS
ANAPESTS
ANAPHASE
ANAPHASES
ANAPHASIC
ANAPHOR
ANAPHORA
ANAPHORAL
ANAPHORAS
ANAPHORESES
ANAPHORESIS
ANAPHORIC
ANAPHORICAL
ANAPHORICALLY
ANAPHORS
ANAPHRODISIA
ANAPHRODISIAC
ANAPHRODISIACS
ANAPHYLACTIC
ANAPHYLACTOID
ANAPHYLAXES
ANAPHYLAXIES
ANAPHYLAXIS
ANAPHYLAXY
ANAPLASIA
ANAPLASIAS
ANAPLASMOSES
ANAPLASMOSIS
ANAPLASTIC
ANAPLASTIES
ANAPLASTY
ANAPLEROSES
ANAPLEROSIS
ANAPLEROTIC
ANAPTYCTIC
ANAPTYCTICAL
ANAPTYCTICALLY
ANAPTYXES
ANAPTYXIS
ANARCH
ANARCHAL
ANARCHIAL
ANARCHIC
ANARCHICAL
ANARCHICALLY
ANARCHIES

ANARCHISE
ANARCHISED
ANARCHISES
ANARCHISING
ANARCHISM
ANARCHISMS
ANARCHIST
ANARCHISTIC
ANARCHISTS
ANARCHIZE
ANARCHIZED
ANARCHIZES
ANARCHIZING
ANARCHS
ANARCHY
ANARTHRIA
ANARTHROUS
ANARTHROUSLY
ANARTHROUSNESS
ANAS
ANASARCA
ANASARCAS
ANASARCOUS
ANASTASES
ANASTASIS
ANASTATIC
ANASTIGMAT
ANASTIGMATIC
ANASTIGMATISM
ANASTIGMATISMS
ANASTIGMATS
ANASTOMOSE
ANASTOMOSED
ANASTOMOSES
ANASTOMOSING
ANASTOMOSIS
ANASTOMOTIC
ANASTROPHE
ANASTROPHES
ANATA
ANATAMAN
ANATASE
ANATASES
ANATHEMA
ANATHEMAS
ANATHEMATA
ANATHEMATICAL
ANATHEMATISE
ANATHEMATISED
ANATHEMATISES
ANATHEMATISING
ANATHEMATIZE
ANATHEMATIZED
ANATHEMATIZES
ANATHEMATIZING
ANATMAN

ANATOMIC
ANATOMICAL
ANATOMICALLY
ANATOMIES
ANATOMISATION
ANATOMISATIONS
ANATOMISE
ANATOMISED
ANATOMISER
ANATOMISERS
ANATOMISES
ANATOMISING
ANATOMIST
ANATOMISTS
ANATOMIZATION
ANATOMIZATIONS
ANATOMIZE
ANATOMIZED
ANATOMIZER
ANATOMIZERS
ANATOMIZES
ANATOMIZING
ANATOMY
ANATOXIN
ANATOXINS
ANATROPIES
ANATROPOUS
ANATROPY
ANATTA
ANATTAS
ANATTO
ANATTOS
ANAXIAL
ANBURIES
ANBURY
ANCE
ANCESTOR
ANCESTORED
ANCESTORIAL
ANCESTORING
ANCESTORS
ANCESTRAL
ANCESTRALLY
ANCESTRESS
ANCESTRESSES
ANCESTRIES
ANCESTRY
ANCHOR
ANCHORAGE
ANCHORAGES
ANCHORED
ANCHORESS
ANCHORESSES
ANCHORET
ANCHORETIC
ANCHORETICAL

ANCHORETS
ANCHORETTE
ANCHORETTES
ANCHORING
ANCHORITE
ANCHORITES
ANCHORITIC
ANCHORITICAL
ANCHORITICALLY
ANCHORLESS
ANCHORMAN
ANCHORMEN
ANCHORPEOPLE
ANCHORPERSON
ANCHORPERSONS
ANCHORS
ANCHORWOMAN
ANCHORWOMEN
ANCHOVETA
ANCHOVETAS
ANCHOVETTA
ANCHOVETTAS
ANCHOVIES
ANCHOVY
ANCHUSA
ANCHUSAS
ANCHUSIN
ANCHUSINS
ANCHYLOSE
ANCHYLOSED
ANCHYLOSES
ANCHYLOSING
ANCHYLOSIS
ANCHYLOTIC
ANCHYLOTICALLY
ANCIENT
ANCIENTER
ANCIENTEST
ANCIENTLY
ANCIENTNESS
ANCIENTNESSES
ANCIENTRIES
ANCIENTRY
ANCIENTS
ANCILE
ANCILIA
ANCILLA
ANCILLAE
ANCILLARIES
ANCILLARY
ANCILLAS
ANCIPITAL
ANCIPITOUS
ANCLE
ANCLES
ANCOME

ANCOMES
ANCON
ANCONAL
ANCONE
ANCONEAL
ANCONES
ANCONOID
ANCORA
ANCRESS
ANCRESSES
ANCYLOSTOMIASES
ANCYLOSTOMIASIS
AND
ANDALUSITE
ANDALUSITES
ANDANTE
ANDANTES
ANDANTINO
ANDANTINOS
ANDESINE
ANDESINES
ANDESITE
ANDESITES
ANDESITIC
ANDESYTE
ANDESYTES
ANDIRON
ANDIRONS
ANDOUILLE
ANDOUILLES
ANDOUILLETTE
ANDOUILLETTES
ANDRADITE
ANDRADITES
ANDROCENTRIC
ANDROCENTRISM
ANDROCEPHALOUS
ANDROCLINIA
ANDROCLINIUM
ANDRODIOECIOUS
ANDRODIOECISM
ANDRODIOECISMS
ANDROECIA
ANDROECIAL
ANDROECIUM
ANDROECIUMS
ANDROGEN
ANDROGENESES
ANDROGENESIS
ANDROGENETIC
ANDROGENIC
ANDROGENOUS
ANDROGENS
ANDROGYNE
ANDROGYNES
ANDROGYNIES

ANDROGYNOPHORE ANELASTIC ANEROIDS ANGEKKOKS
ANDROGYNOPHORES ANELASTICITIES ANES ANGEKOK
ANDROGYNOUS ANELASTICITY ANESTHESIA ANGEKOKS
ANDROGYNY ANELE ANESTHESIAS ANGEL
ANDROID ANELED ANESTHESIOLOGY ANGELED
ANDROIDS ANELES ANESTHETIC ANGELFISH
ANDROLOGIES ANELING ANESTHETICALLY ANGELFISHES
ANDROLOGIST ANEMIA ANESTHETICS ANGELHOOD
ANDROLOGISTS ANEMIAS ANESTHETIST ANGELHOODS
ANDROLOGY ANEMIC ANESTHETISTS ANGELIC
ANDROMEDA ANEMICALLY ANESTHETIZATION ANGELICA
ANDROMEDAS ANEMOCHORE ANESTHETIZE ANGELICAL
ANDROMEDOTOXIN ANEMOCHORES ANESTHETIZED ANGELICALLY
ANDROMEDOTOXINS ANEMOCHOROUS ANESTHETIZES ANGELICAS
ANDROMONOECIOUS ANEMOGRAM ANESTHETIZING ANGELING
ANDROMONOECISM ANEMOGRAMS ANESTRA ANGELOLATRIES
ANDROMONOECISMS ANEMOGRAPH ANESTRI ANGELOLATRY
ANDROPAUSE ANEMOGRAPHIC ANESTROUS ANGELOLOGIES
ANDROPAUSES ANEMOGRAPHIES ANESTRUM ANGELOLOGIST
ANDROPHORE ANEMOGRAPHS ANESTRUS ANGELOLOGISTS
ANDROPHORES ANEMOGRAPHY ANETHOL ANGELOLOGY
ANDROSPHINGES ANEMOLOGIES ANETHOLE ANGELOPHANIES
ANDROSPHINX ANEMOLOGY ANETHOLES ANGELOPHANY
ANDROSPHINXES ANEMOMETER ANETHOLS ANGELS
ANDROSTERONE ANEMOMETERS ANETIC ANGELUS
ANDROSTERONES ANEMOMETRIC ANEUPLOID ANGELUSES
ANDS ANEMOMETRICAL ANEUPLOIDIES ANGER
ANDVILE ANEMOMETRIES ANEUPLOIDS ANGERED
ANDVILES ANEMOMETRY ANEUPLOIDY ANGERING
ANE ANEMONE ANEURIN ANGERLESS
ANEAR ANEMONES ANEURINS ANGERLY
ANEARED ANEMOPHILIES ANEURISM ANGERS
ANEARING ANEMOPHILOUS ANEURISMAL ANGICO
ANEARS ANEMOPHILY ANEURISMALLY ANGICOS
ANEATH ANEMOPHOBIA ANEURISMATIC ANGINA
ANECDOTA ANEMOPHOBIAS ANEURISMS ANGINAL
ANECDOTAGE ANEMOSCOPE ANEURYSM ANGINAS
ANECDOTAGES ANEMOSCOPES ANEURYSMAL ANGINOSE
ANECDOTAL ANEMOSCOPIC ANEURYSMALLY ANGINOUS
ANECDOTALISM ANEMOSCOPICALLY ANEURYSMATIC ANGIOCARPOUS
ANECDOTALISMS ANEMOSES ANEURYSMS ANGIOGENESES
ANECDOTALIST ANEMOSIS ANEW ANGIOGENESIS
ANECDOTALISTS ANENCEPHALIA ANFRACTUOSITIES ANGIOGENIC
ANECDOTALLY ANENCEPHALIAS ANFRACTUOSITY ANGIOGRAM
ANECDOTE ANENCEPHALIC ANFRACTUOUS ANGIOGRAMS
ANECDOTES ANENCEPHALIES ANGA ANGIOGRAPHIC
ANECDOTIC ANENCEPHALY ANGAKOK ANGIOGRAPHIES
ANECDOTICAL ANENST ANGAKOKS ANGIOGRAPHY
ANECDOTICALLY ANENT ANGARIA ANGIOLOGICAL
ANECDOTIST ANERGIA ANGARIAS ANGIOLOGICALLY
ANECDOTISTS ANERGIAS ANGARIES ANGIOLOGY
ANECDYSIS ANERGIC ANGARY ANGIOMA
ANECHOIC ANERGIES ANGAS ANGIOMAS
ANECTOTISTS ANERGY ANGASHORE ANGIOMATA
ANELACE ANERLY ANGASHORES ANGIOMATOUS
ANELACES ANEROID ANGEKKOK ANGIOPLASTIES

35

ANGIOPLASTY
ANGIOSARCOMA
ANGIOSARCOMAS
ANGIOSARCOMATA
ANGIOSPERM
ANGIOSPERMAL
ANGIOSPERMOUS
ANGIOSPERMS
ANGIOSTOMATOUS
ANGIOSTOMOUS
ANGIOTENSIN
ANGIOTENSINS
ANGKLUNG
ANGKLUNGS
ANGLE
ANGLEBERRIES
ANGLEBERRY
ANGLED
ANGLEDOZER
ANGLEDOZERS
ANGLEDUG
ANGLEDUGS
ANGLEPOD
ANGLEPODS
ANGLER
ANGLERFISH
ANGLERFISHES
ANGLERS
ANGLES
ANGLESITE
ANGLESITES
ANGLETWITCH
ANGLETWITCHES
ANGLEWISE
ANGLEWORM
ANGLEWORMS
ANGLICE
ANGLICISATION
ANGLICISATIONS
ANGLICISE
ANGLICISED
ANGLICISES
ANGLICISING
ANGLICISM
ANGLICISMS
ANGLICIST
ANGLICISTS
ANGLICIZATION
ANGLICIZATIONS
ANGLICIZE
ANGLICIZED
ANGLICIZES
ANGLICIZING
ANGLIFIED
ANGLIFIES
ANGLIFY

ANGLIFYING
ANGLING
ANGLINGS
ANGLIST
ANGLISTICS
ANGLISTS
ANGLOMANIA
ANGLOMANIAC
ANGLOMANIACS
ANGLOMANIAS
ANGLOPHIL
ANGLOPHILE
ANGLOPHILES
ANGLOPHILIA
ANGLOPHILIAS
ANGLOPHILIC
ANGLOPHILS
ANGLOPHOBE
ANGLOPHOBES
ANGLOPHOBIA
ANGLOPHOBIAC
ANGLOPHOBIAS
ANGLOPHOBIC
ANGLOPHONE
ANGLOPHONES
ANGLOPHONIC
ANGOLA
ANGOPHORA
ANGOPHORAS
ANGORA
ANGORAS
ANGOSTURA
ANGRIER
ANGRIES
ANGRIEST
ANGRILY
ANGRINESS
ANGRINESSES
ANGRY
ANGST
ANGSTIER
ANGSTIEST
ANGSTROM
ANGSTROMS
ANGSTS
ANGSTY
ANGUIFAUNA
ANGUIFAUNAS
ANGUIFORM
ANGUILLIFORM
ANGUINE
ANGUIPED
ANGUIPEDE
ANGUISH
ANGUISHED
ANGUISHES

ANGUISHING
ANGULAR
ANGULARITIES
ANGULARITY
ANGULARLY
ANGULARNESS
ANGULATE
ANGULATED
ANGULATES
ANGULATING
ANGULATION
ANGULATIONS
ANGULOSE
ANGULOUS
ANGUSTIFOLIATE
ANGUSTIROSTRATE
ANGWANTIBO
ANGWANTIBOS
ANHARMONIC
ANHEDONIA
ANHEDONIAS
ANHEDONIC
ANHEDRAL
ANHELATION
ANHELATIONS
ANHIDROSIS
ANHIDROTIC
ANHIDROTICALLY
ANHIDROTICS
ANHINGA
ANHINGAS
ANHUNGERED
ANHUNGRED
ANHYDRIDE
ANHYDRIDES
ANHYDRITE
ANHYDRITES
ANHYDROUS
ANI
ANICCA
ANICONIC
ANICONISM
ANICONISMS
ANICONIST
ANICONISTS
ANICUT
ANICUTS
ANIDROSIS
ANIGH
ANIGHT
ANIL
ANILE
ANILIN
ANILINCTUS
ANILINCTUSES
ANILINE

ANILINES
ANILINGUS
ANILINGUSES
ANILINS
ANILITIES
ANILITY
ANILS
ANIMA
ANIMADVERSION
ANIMADVERSIONS
ANIMADVERT
ANIMADVERTED
ANIMADVERTER
ANIMADVERTERS
ANIMADVERTING
ANIMADVERTS
ANIMAL
ANIMALCULA
ANIMALCULAR
ANIMALCULE
ANIMALCULES
ANIMALCULISM
ANIMALCULISMS
ANIMALCULIST
ANIMALCULISTS
ANIMALCULUM
ANIMALIC
ANIMALIER
ANIMALIERS
ANIMALISATION
ANIMALISATIONS
ANIMALISE
ANIMALISED
ANIMALISES
ANIMALISING
ANIMALISM
ANIMALISMS
ANIMALIST
ANIMALISTIC
ANIMALISTS
ANIMALITIES
ANIMALITY
ANIMALIZATION
ANIMALIZATIONS
ANIMALIZE
ANIMALIZED
ANIMALIZES
ANIMALIZING
ANIMALLIKE
ANIMALLY
ANIMALS
ANIMAS
ANIMATE
ANIMATED
ANIMATEDLY
ANIMATELY

ANIMATENESS
ANIMATENESSES
ANIMATER
ANIMATERS
ANIMATES
ANIMATIC
ANIMATICS
ANIMATING
ANIMATINGLY
ANIMATION
ANIMATIONS
ANIMATISM
ANIMATISMS
ANIMATO
ANIMATOR
ANIMATORS
ANIMATRONIC
ANIMATRONICALLY
ANIMATRONICS
ANIME
ANIMES
ANIMI
ANIMIS
ANIMISM
ANIMISMS
ANIMIST
ANIMISTIC
ANIMISTS
ANIMOSITIES
ANIMOSITY
ANIMUS
ANIMUSES
ANION
ANIONIC
ANIONS
ANIS
ANISE
ANISEED
ANISEEDS
ANISEIKONIA
ANISEIKONIAS
ANISEIKONIC
ANISES
ANISETTE
ANISETTES
ANISIC
ANISOCERCAL
ANISODACTYL
ANISODACTYLOUS
ANISODACTYLS
ANISOGAMIES
ANISOGAMOUS
ANISOGAMY
ANISOLE
ANISOLES
ANISOMERIC

ANISOMEROUS
ANISOMETRIC
ANISOMETRICALLY
ANISOMETROPIA
ANISOMETROPIAS
ANISOMETROPIC
ANISOMORPHIC
ANISOPHYLLOUS
ANISOPHYLLY
ANISOTROPIC
ANISOTROPICALLY
ANISOTROPIES
ANISOTROPISM
ANISOTROPISMS
ANISOTROPY
ANKER
ANKERITE
ANKERITES
ANKERS
ANKH
ANKHS
ANKLE
ANKLEBONE
ANKLEBONES
ANKLED
ANKLES
ANKLET
ANKLETS
ANKLING
ANKLONG
ANKLONGS
ANKLUNG
ANKLUNGS
ANKUS
ANKUSES
ANKUSH
ANKUSHES
ANKYLOSAUR
ANKYLOSAURS
ANKYLOSAURUS
ANKYLOSAURUSES
ANKYLOSE
ANKYLOSED
ANKYLOSES
ANKYLOSING
ANKYLOSIS
ANKYLOSTOMIASES
ANKYLOSTOMIASIS
ANKYLOTIC
ANLACE
ANLACES
ANLAGE
ANLAGEN
ANLAGES
ANLAS
ANLASES

ANN
ANNA
ANNABERGITE
ANNABERGITES
ANNAL
ANNALISE
ANNALISED
ANNALISES
ANNALISING
ANNALIST
ANNALISTIC
ANNALISTS
ANNALIZE
ANNALIZED
ANNALIZES
ANNALIZING
ANNALS
ANNAS
ANNAT
ANNATES
ANNATS
ANNATTA
ANNATTAS
ANNATTO
ANNATTOS
ANNEAL
ANNEALED
ANNEALER
ANNEALERS
ANNEALING
ANNEALINGS
ANNEALS
ANNECTENT
ANNELID
ANNELIDAN
ANNELIDANS
ANNELIDS
ANNEX
ANNEXABLE
ANNEXABLY
ANNEXATION
ANNEXATIONAL
ANNEXATIONISM
ANNEXATIONIST
ANNEXATIONISTS
ANNEXATIONS
ANNEXE
ANNEXED
ANNEXES
ANNEXING
ANNEXION
ANNEXIONS
ANNEXMENT
ANNEXMENTS
ANNEXURE
ANNEXURES

ANNICUT
ANNICUTS
ANNIHILABLE
ANNIHILATE
ANNIHILATED
ANNIHILATES
ANNIHILATING
ANNIHILATION
ANNIHILATIONISM
ANNIHILATIONS
ANNIHILATIVE
ANNIHILATOR
ANNIHILATORS
ANNIHILATORY
ANNIVERSARIES
ANNIVERSARY
ANNO
ANNOTATABLE
ANNOTATE
ANNOTATED
ANNOTATES
ANNOTATING
ANNOTATION
ANNOTATIONS
ANNOTATIVE
ANNOTATOR
ANNOTATORS
ANNOUNCE
ANNOUNCED
ANNOUNCEMENT
ANNOUNCEMENTS
ANNOUNCER
ANNOUNCERS
ANNOUNCES
ANNOUNCING
ANNOY
ANNOYANCE
ANNOYANCES
ANNOYED
ANNOYER
ANNOYERS
ANNOYING
ANNOYINGLY
ANNOYS
ANNS
ANNUAL
ANNUALISE
ANNUALISED
ANNUALISES
ANNUALISING
ANNUALIZE
ANNUALIZED
ANNUALIZES
ANNUALIZING
ANNUALLY
ANNUALS

ANNUITANT
ANNUITANTS
ANNUITIES
ANNUITY
ANNUL
ANNULAR
ANNULARITIES
ANNULARITY
ANNULARLY
ANNULARS
ANNULATE
ANNULATED
ANNULATES
ANNULATION
ANNULATIONS
ANNULET
ANNULETS
ANNULI
ANNULLABLE
ANNULLED
ANNULLING
ANNULMENT
ANNULMENTS
ANNULOSE
ANNULS
ANNULUS
ANNULUSES
ANNUNCIATE
ANNUNCIATED
ANNUNCIATES
ANNUNCIATING
ANNUNCIATION
ANNUNCIATIONS
ANNUNCIATIVE
ANNUNCIATOR
ANNUNCIATORS
ANNUNCIATORY
ANNUNTIATE
ANNUNTIATED
ANNUNTIATES
ANNUNTIATING
ANOA
ANOAS
ANOBIID
ANOBIIDS
ANODAL
ANODALLY
ANODE
ANODES
ANODIC
ANODICALLY
ANODISE
ANODISED
ANODISES
ANODISING
ANODIZATION

ANODIZATIONS
ANODIZE
ANODIZED
ANODIZES
ANODIZING
ANODONTIA
ANODYNE
ANODYNES
ANODYNIC
ANOESES
ANOESIS
ANOESTRA
ANOESTRI
ANOESTROUS
ANOESTRUM
ANOESTRUS
ANOETIC
ANOINT
ANOINTED
ANOINTER
ANOINTERS
ANOINTING
ANOINTMENT
ANOINTMENTS
ANOINTS
ANOLE
ANOLES
ANOLYTE
ANOLYTES
ANOMALIES
ANOMALISTIC
ANOMALISTICAL
ANOMALISTICALLY
ANOMALOUS
ANOMALOUSLY
ANOMALOUSNESS
ANOMALOUSNESSES
ANOMALY
ANOMIC
ANOMIE
ANOMIES
ANOMY
ANON
ANONACEOUS
ANONYM
ANONYMA
ANONYMAS
ANONYMISE
ANONYMISED
ANONYMISES
ANONYMISING
ANONYMITIES
ANONYMITY
ANONYMIZE
ANONYMIZED
ANONYMIZES

ANONYMIZING
ANONYMOUS
ANONYMOUSLY
ANONYMOUSNESS
ANONYMOUSNESSES
ANONYMS
ANOOPSIA
ANOOPSIAS
ANOPHELES
ANOPHELINE
ANOPHELINES
ANOPIA
ANOPIAS
ANOPSIA
ANOPSIAS
ANORAK
ANORAKS
ANORECTAL
ANORECTIC
ANORECTICS
ANORETIC
ANORETICS
ANOREXIA
ANOREXIAS
ANOREXIC
ANOREXICS
ANOREXIES
ANOREXIGENIC
ANOREXY
ANORTHIC
ANORTHITE
ANORTHITES
ANORTHITIC
ANORTHOSITE
ANORTHOSITES
ANORTHOSITIC
ANOSMATIC
ANOSMATICS
ANOSMIA
ANOSMIAS
ANOSMIC
ANOTHER
ANOTHERGUESS
ANOUGH
ANOUROUS
ANOVULANT
ANOVULANTS
ANOVULAR
ANOVULATORY
ANOW
ANOXAEMIA
ANOXAEMIC
ANOXEMIA
ANOXEMIAS
ANOXEMIC
ANOXIA

ANOXIAS
ANOXIC
ANSA
ANSAE
ANSATE
ANSATED
ANSERINE
ANSERINES
ANSEROUS
ANSWER
ANSWERABILITIES
ANSWERABILITY
ANSWERABLE
ANSWERABLENESS
ANSWERABLY
ANSWERED
ANSWERER
ANSWERERS
ANSWERING
ANSWERLESS
ANSWERPHONE
ANSWERPHONES
ANSWERS
ANT
ANTA
ANTACID
ANTACIDS
ANTAE
ANTAGONISABLE
ANTAGONISATION
ANTAGONISATIONS
ANTAGONISE
ANTAGONISED
ANTAGONISES
ANTAGONISING
ANTAGONISM
ANTAGONISMS
ANTAGONIST
ANTAGONISTIC
ANTAGONISTS
ANTAGONIZABLE
ANTAGONIZATION
ANTAGONIZATIONS
ANTAGONIZE
ANTAGONIZED
ANTAGONIZES
ANTAGONIZING
ANTALGIC
ANTALGICS
ANTALKALI
ANTALKALIES
ANTALKALINE
ANTALKALINES
ANTALKALIS
ANTAPHRODISIAC
ANTAPHRODISIACS

ANTAR
ANTARA
ANTARAS
ANTARCTIC
ANTARS
ANTARTHRITIC
ANTARTHRITICS
ANTAS
ANTASTHMATIC
ANTASTHMATICS
ANTBEAR
ANTBEARS
ANTBIRD
ANTBIRDS
ANTE
ANTEATER
ANTEATERS
ANTEBELLUM
ANTECEDE
ANTECEDED
ANTECEDENCE
ANTECEDENCES
ANTECEDENT
ANTECEDENTLY
ANTECEDENTS
ANTECEDES
ANTECEDING
ANTECESSOR
ANTECESSORS
ANTECHAMBER
ANTECHAMBERS
ANTECHAPEL
ANTECHAPELS
ANTECHOIR
ANTECHOIRS
ANTED
ANTEDATE
ANTEDATED
ANTEDATES
ANTEDATING
ANTEDILUVIAL
ANTEDILUVIALLY
ANTEDILUVIAN
ANTEDILUVIANS
ANTEED
ANTEFIX
ANTEFIXA
ANTEFIXAE
ANTEFIXAL
ANTEFIXES
ANTEING
ANTELOPE
ANTELOPES
ANTELUCAN
ANTEMERIDIAN
ANTEMORTEM

ANTEMUNDANE
ANTENATAL
ANTENATALLY
ANTENATALS
ANTENATI
ANTENNA
ANTENNAE
ANTENNAL
ANTENNARY
ANTENNAS
ANTENNIFEROUS
ANTENNIFORM
ANTENNULAR
ANTENNULE
ANTENNULES
ANTENUPTIAL
ANTEORBITAL
ANTEPAST
ANTEPASTS
ANTEPENDIA
ANTEPENDIUM
ANTEPENDIUMS
ANTEPENULT
ANTEPENULTIMA
ANTEPENULTIMAS
ANTEPENULTIMATE
ANTEPENULTS
ANTEPOSITION
ANTEPOSITIONS
ANTEPRANDIAL
ANTERIOR
ANTERIORITIES
ANTERIORITY
ANTERIORLY
ANTEROGRADE
ANTEROOM
ANTEROOMS
ANTES
ANTETYPE
ANTETYPES
ANTEVERSION
ANTEVERSIONS
ANTEVERT
ANTEVERTED
ANTEVERTING
ANTEVERTS
ANTHELIA
ANTHELICES
ANTHELION
ANTHELIONS
ANTHELIX
ANTHELIXES
ANTHELMINTHIC
ANTHELMINTHICS
ANTHELMINTIC
ANTHELMINTICS

ANTHEM
ANTHEMED
ANTHEMIA
ANTHEMIC
ANTHEMING
ANTHEMION
ANTHEMS
ANTHEMWISE
ANTHER
ANTHERAL
ANTHERID
ANTHERIDIA
ANTHERIDIAL
ANTHERIDIUM
ANTHERIDS
ANTHEROZOID
ANTHEROZOIDS
ANTHEROZOOID
ANTHEROZOOIDS
ANTHERS
ANTHERSMUT
ANTHERSMUTS
ANTHESES
ANTHESIS
ANTHILL
ANTHILLS
ANTHOCARP
ANTHOCARPOUS
ANTHOCARPS
ANTHOCHLORE
ANTHOCHLORES
ANTHOCYAN
ANTHOCYANIN
ANTHOCYANINS
ANTHOCYANS
ANTHODIA
ANTHODIUM
ANTHOID
ANTHOLOGICAL
ANTHOLOGIES
ANTHOLOGISE
ANTHOLOGISED
ANTHOLOGISES
ANTHOLOGISING
ANTHOLOGIST
ANTHOLOGISTS
ANTHOLOGIZE
ANTHOLOGIZED
ANTHOLOGIZER
ANTHOLOGIZERS
ANTHOLOGIZES
ANTHOLOGIZING
ANTHOLOGY
ANTHOMANIA
ANTHOMANIAC
ANTHOMANIACS

ANTHOMANIAS
ANTHOPHILOUS
ANTHOPHORE
ANTHOPHORES
ANTHOPHYLLITE
ANTHOPHYLLITES
ANTHOTAXY
ANTHOXANTHIN
ANTHOXANTHINS
ANTHOZOAN
ANTHOZOANS
ANTHRACENE
ANTHRACENES
ANTHRACES
ANTHRACIC
ANTHRACITE
ANTHRACITES
ANTHRACITIC
ANTHRACNOSE
ANTHRACNOSES
ANTHRACOID
ANTHRACOSES
ANTHRACOSIS
ANTHRANILATE
ANTHRANILATES
ANTHRAQUINONE
ANTHRAQUINONES
ANTHRAX
ANTHRAXES
ANTHROPIC
ANTHROPICAL
ANTHROPOBIOLOGY
ANTHROPOCENTRIC
ANTHROPOGENESES
ANTHROPOGENESIS
ANTHROPOGENETIC
ANTHROPOGENIC
ANTHROPOGENIES
ANTHROPOGENY
ANTHROPOGONIES
ANTHROPOGONY
ANTHROPOGRAPHY
ANTHROPOID
ANTHROPOIDAL
ANTHROPOIDS
ANTHROPOLATRIES
ANTHROPOLATRY
ANTHROPOLOGICAL
ANTHROPOLOGIES
ANTHROPOLOGIST
ANTHROPOLOGISTS
ANTHROPOLOGY
ANTHROPOMETRIC
ANTHROPOMETRIES
ANTHROPOMETRIST
ANTHROPOMETRY

ANTHROPOMORPH
ANTHROPOMORPHIC
ANTHROPOMORPHS
ANTHROPOPATHIC
ANTHROPOPATHIES
ANTHROPOPATHISM
ANTHROPOPATHY
ANTHROPOPHAGI
ANTHROPOPHAGIC
ANTHROPOPHAGIES
ANTHROPOPHAGITE
ANTHROPOPHAGOUS
ANTHROPOPHAGUS
ANTHROPOPHAGY
ANTHROPOPHOBIA
ANTHROPOPHOBIAS
ANTHROPOPHOBIC
ANTHROPOPHOBICS
ANTHROPOPHUISM
ANTHROPOPHUISMS
ANTHROPOPHYTE
ANTHROPOPHYTES
ANTHROPOPSYCHIC
ANTHROPOSOPHIC
ANTHROPOSOPHIES
ANTHROPOSOPHIST
ANTHROPOSOPHY
ANTHROPOTOMIES
ANTHROPOTOMY
ANTHURIUM
ANTHURIUMS
ANTI
ANTIABORTION
ANTIABORTIONIST
ANTIACADEMIC
ANTIADITIS
ANTIADITISES
ANTIAGGRESSION
ANTIAGING
ANTIAIR
ANTIAIRCRAFT
ANTIAIRCRAFTS
ANTIALCOHOL
ANTIALCOHOLISM
ANTIALIEN
ANTIALLERGENIC
ANTIANEMIA
ANTIANXIETY
ANTIAPARTHEID
ANTIAPHRODISIAC
ANTIAR
ANTIARIN
ANTIARINS
ANTIARRHYTHMIC
ANTIARRHYTHMICS
ANTIARS

ANTIARTHRITIC
ANTIARTHRITICS
ANTIARTHRITIS
ANTIASTHMA
ANTIASTHMATIC
ANTIASTHMATICS
ANTIATOM
ANTIATOMS
ANTIAUTHORITY
ANTIAUXIN
ANTIAUXINS
ANTIBACCHII
ANTIBACCHIUS
ANTIBACKLASH
ANTIBACTERIAL
ANTIBACTERIALS
ANTIBALLISTIC
ANTIBARBARUS
ANTIBARBARUSES
ANTIBARYON
ANTIBARYONS
ANTIBIAS
ANTIBIBLICAL
ANTIBIBLICALLY
ANTIBILIOUS
ANTIBILLBOARD
ANTIBIOSES
ANTIBIOSIS
ANTIBIOTIC
ANTIBIOTICALLY
ANTIBIOTICS
ANTIBLACK
ANTIBLACKISM
ANTIBLACKISMS
ANTIBODIES
ANTIBODY
ANTIBOSS
ANTIBOURGEOIS
ANTIBOYCOTT
ANTIBUG
ANTIBURGLAR
ANTIBURGLARY
ANTIBUSINESS
ANTIBUSING
ANTIC
ANTICAKING
ANTICAL
ANTICALLY
ANTICANCER
ANTICAPITALISM
ANTICAPITALISMS
ANTICAPITALIST
ANTICAPITALISTS
ANTICAR
ANTICARCINOGEN
ANTICARCINOGENS

ANTICARIES
ANTICATALYST
ANTICATALYSTS
ANTICATHODE
ANTICATHODES
ANTICATHOLIC
ANTICELLULITE
ANTICENSORSHIP
ANTICENSORSHIPS
ANTICHLOR
ANTICHLORISTIC
ANTICHLORS
ANTICHOICE
ANTICHOICER
ANTICHOICERS
ANTICHOLESTEROL
ANTICHOLINERGIC
ANTICHRISTIAN
ANTICHRISTIANLY
ANTICHTHONES
ANTICHURCH
ANTICIGARETTE
ANTICIPANT
ANTICIPANTS
ANTICIPATABLE
ANTICIPATE
ANTICIPATED
ANTICIPATES
ANTICIPATING
ANTICIPATION
ANTICIPATIONS
ANTICIPATIVE
ANTICIPATIVELY
ANTICIPATOR
ANTICIPATORILY
ANTICIPATORS
ANTICIPATORY
ANTICITY
ANTICIVIC
ANTICIVISM
ANTICIVISMS
ANTICIZE
ANTICIZED
ANTICIZES
ANTICIZING
ANTICK
ANTICKE
ANTICKED
ANTICKING
ANTICKS
ANTICLASSICAL
ANTICLASTIC
ANTICLASTICALLY
ANTICLERICAL
ANTICLERICALISM
ANTICLERICALS

ANTICLIMACTIC
ANTICLIMACTICAL
ANTICLIMAX
ANTICLIMAXES
ANTICLINAL
ANTICLINALS
ANTICLINE
ANTICLINES
ANTICLING
ANTICLINORIA
ANTICLINORIUM
ANTICLINORIUMS
ANTICLOCKWISE
ANTICLOTTING
ANTICLY
ANTICOAGULANT
ANTICOAGULANTS
ANTICOAGULATING
ANTICODON
ANTICODONS
ANTICOINCIDENCE
ANTICOLD
ANTICOLLISION
ANTICOLONIAL
ANTICOLONIALISM
ANTICOLONIALIST
ANTICOMMERCIAL
ANTICOMMUNISM
ANTICOMMUNISMS
ANTICOMMUNIST
ANTICOMMUNISTS
ANTICOMPETITIVE
ANTICONSUMER
ANTICONVULSANT
ANTICONVULSANTS
ANTICONVULSIVE
ANTICONVULSIVES
ANTICORPORATE
ANTICORROSION
ANTICORROSIVE
ANTICORROSIVES
ANTICORRUPTION
ANTICOUS
ANTICRACK
ANTICREATIVE
ANTICRIME
ANTICRUELTY
ANTICS
ANTICULT
ANTICULTURAL
ANTICYCLONE
ANTICYCLONES
ANTICYCLONIC
ANTIDANDRUFF
ANTIDAZZLE
ANTIDEFAMATION

ANTIDEMOCRATIC
ANTIDEPRESSANT
ANTIDEPRESSANTS
ANTIDEPRESSION
ANTIDERIVATIVE
ANTIDERIVATIVES
ANTIDESICCANT
ANTIDESICCANTS
ANTIDEVELOPMENT
ANTIDIABETIC
ANTIDIARRHEAL
ANTIDIARRHEALS
ANTIDILUTION
ANTIDIURETIC
ANTIDIURETICS
ANTIDOGMATIC
ANTIDORA
ANTIDOTAL
ANTIDOTALLY
ANTIDOTE
ANTIDOTED
ANTIDOTES
ANTIDOTING
ANTIDRAFT
ANTIDROMIC
ANTIDROMICALLY
ANTIDRUG
ANTIDUMPING
ANTIDUNE
ANTIDUNES
ANTIECONOMIC
ANTIEDUCATIONAL
ANTIEGALITARIAN
ANTIELECTRON
ANTIELECTRONS
ANTIELITE
ANTIELITISM
ANTIELITISMS
ANTIELITIST
ANTIEMETIC
ANTIEMETICS
ANTIENT
ANTIENTROPIC
ANTIENTS
ANTIEPILEPSY
ANTIEPILEPTIC
ANTIEPILEPTICS
ANTIEROTIC
ANTIESTROGEN
ANTIESTROGENS
ANTIEVOLUTION
ANTIFACTION
ANTIFACTIONS
ANTIFAMILY
ANTIFASCISM
ANTIFASCISMS

ANTIFASCIST
ANTIFASCISTS
ANTIFASHION
ANTIFASHIONABLE
ANTIFASHIONS
ANTIFAT
ANTIFATIGUE
ANTIFEBRILE
ANTIFEBRILES
ANTIFEMALE
ANTIFEMININE
ANTIFEMINISM
ANTIFEMINISMS
ANTIFEMINIST
ANTIFEMINISTS
ANTIFERROMAGNET
ANTIFERTILITY
ANTIFILIBUSTER
ANTIFLU
ANTIFOAM
ANTIFOAMING
ANTIFOGGING
ANTIFORECLOSURE
ANTIFOREIGN
ANTIFOREIGNER
ANTIFORMALIST
ANTIFOULING
ANTIFOULINGS
ANTIFRAUD
ANTIFREEZE
ANTIFREEZES
ANTIFRICTION
ANTIFUNGAL
ANTIFUNGALS
ANTIFUR
ANTIGAMBLING
ANTIGAY
ANTIGEN
ANTIGENE
ANTIGENES
ANTIGENIC
ANTIGENICALLY
ANTIGENICITIES
ANTIGENICITY
ANTIGENS
ANTIGLARE
ANTIGLOBULIN
ANTIGLOBULINS
ANTIGOVERNMENT
ANTIGRAVITIES
ANTIGRAVITY
ANTIGROPELOES
ANTIGROPELOS
ANTIGROWTH
ANTIGUERRILLA
ANTIGUN

ANTIHALATION
ANTIHALATIONS
ANTIHELICES
ANTIHELIX
ANTIHELIXES
ANTIHELMINTHIC
ANTIHERO
ANTIHEROES
ANTIHEROIC
ANTIHEROINE
ANTIHEROINES
ANTIHERPES
ANTIHIJACK
ANTIHISTAMINE
ANTIHISTAMINES
ANTIHISTAMINIC
ANTIHISTAMINICS
ANTIHISTORICAL
ANTIHOMOSEXUAL
ANTIHUMAN
ANTIHUMANISM
ANTIHUMANISMS
ANTIHUMANIST
ANTIHUMANISTIC
ANTIHUMANISTS
ANTIHUNTER
ANTIHUNTING
ANTIHYDROGEN
ANTIHYSTERIC
ANTIHYSTERICS
ANTIJACOBIN
ANTIJACOBINS
ANTIJAM
ANTIJAMMING
ANTIJAMMINGS
ANTIKICKBACK
ANTIKING
ANTIKINGS
ANTIKNOCK
ANTIKNOCKS
ANTILABOR
ANTILABOUR
ANTILEAK
ANTILEFT
ANTILEGOMENA
ANTILEPROSY
ANTILEPTON
ANTILEPTONS
ANTILEUKEMIC
ANTILIBERAL
ANTILIBERALISM
ANTILIBERALISMS
ANTILIBERALS
ANTILIBERTARIAN
ANTILIFE
ANTILITERATE

ANTILITTER
ANTILITTERING
ANTILITURGICAL
ANTILOCK
ANTILOG
ANTILOGARITHM
ANTILOGARITHMIC
ANTILOGARITHMS
ANTILOGICAL
ANTILOGIES
ANTILOGOUS
ANTILOGS
ANTILOGY
ANTILOPINE
ANTILYNCHING
ANTIMACASSAR
ANTIMACASSARS
ANTIMACHO
ANTIMAGNETIC
ANTIMALARIA
ANTIMALARIAL
ANTIMALARIALS
ANTIMALE
ANTIMAN
ANTIMANAGEMENT
ANTIMARIJUANA
ANTIMARKET
ANTIMASK
ANTIMASKS
ANTIMASQUE
ANTIMASQUES
ANTIMATERIALISM
ANTIMATERIALIST
ANTIMATTER
ANTIMATTERS
ANTIMECHANIST
ANTIMECHANISTS
ANTIMERE
ANTIMERES
ANTIMERGER
ANTIMERIC
ANTIMERICALLY
ANTIMERISM
ANTIMETABOLE
ANTIMETABOLES
ANTIMETABOLIC
ANTIMETABOLITE
ANTIMETABOLITES
ANTIMETATHESES
ANTIMETATHESIS
ANTIMICROBIAL
ANTIMICROBIALS
ANTIMILITARISM
ANTIMILITARISMS
ANTIMILITARIST
ANTIMILITARISTS

ANTIMILITARY	ANTINEUTRINO	ANTIPATHOGENIC	ANTIPOPES
ANTIMISSILE	ANTINEUTRINOS	ANTIPATHOGENS	ANTIPOPULAR
ANTIMISSILES	ANTINEUTRON	ANTIPATHY	ANTIPORN
ANTIMITOTIC	ANTINEUTRONS	ANTIPERIODIC	ANTIPORNOGRAPHY
ANTIMITOTICS	ANTING	ANTIPERIODICS	ANTIPOT
ANTIMNEMONIC	ANTINGS	ANTIPERISTALSES	ANTIPOVERTY
ANTIMNEMONICS	ANTINODAL	ANTIPERISTALSIS	ANTIPREDATOR
ANTIMODERN	ANTINODE	ANTIPERISTALTIC	ANTIPRESS
ANTIMODERNIST	ANTINODES	ANTIPERISTASES	ANTIPROGRESSIVE
ANTIMODERNISTS	ANTINOISE	ANTIPERISTASIS	ANTIPROHIBITION
ANTIMONARCHICAL	ANTINOMIAN	ANTIPERSONNEL	ANTIPROTON
ANTIMONARCHIST	ANTINOMIANISM	ANTIPERSPIRANT	ANTIPROTONS
ANTIMONARCHISTS	ANTINOMIANISMS	ANTIPERSPIRANTS	ANTIPRURITIC
ANTIMONATE	ANTINOMIANS	ANTIPESTICIDE	ANTIPRURITICS
ANTIMONATES	ANTINOMIC	ANTIPETALOUS	ANTIPSYCHIATRIC
ANTIMONIAL	ANTINOMICAL	ANTIPHLOGISTIC	ANTIPSYCHIATRY
ANTIMONIALS	ANTINOMICALLY	ANTIPHLOGISTICS	ANTIPSYCHOTIC
ANTIMONIATE	ANTINOMIES	ANTIPHON	ANTIPSYCHOTICS
ANTIMONIATES	ANTINOMY	ANTIPHONAL	ANTIPURITAN
ANTIMONIC	ANTINOVEL	ANTIPHONALLY	ANTIPURITANS
ANTIMONIDE	ANTINOVELIST	ANTIPHONALS	ANTIPYIC
ANTIMONIDES	ANTINOVELISTS	ANTIPHONARIES	ANTIPYICS
ANTIMONIES	ANTINOVELS	ANTIPHONARY	ANTIPYRESES
ANTIMONIOUS	ANTINUCLEAR	ANTIPHONER	ANTIPYRESIS
ANTIMONITE	ANTINUCLEARIST	ANTIPHONERS	ANTIPYRETIC
ANTIMONITES	ANTINUCLEARISTS	ANTIPHONIC	ANTIPYRETICS
ANTIMONOPOLIST	ANTINUCLEON	ANTIPHONICAL	ANTIPYRINE
ANTIMONOPOLISTS	ANTINUCLEONS	ANTIPHONICALLY	ANTIPYRINES
ANTIMONOPOLY	ANTINUKE	ANTIPHONIES	ANTIQUARIAN
ANTIMONOUS	ANTIOBESITY	ANTIPHONS	ANTIQUARIANISM
ANTIMONY	ANTIOBSCENITY	ANTIPHONY	ANTIQUARIANISMS
ANTIMONYL	ANTIODONTALGIC	ANTIPHRASES	ANTIQUARIANS
ANTIMONYLS	ANTIODONTALGICS	ANTIPHRASIS	ANTIQUARIES
ANTIMOSQUITO	ANTIOXIDANT	ANTIPHRASTIC	ANTIQUARK
ANTIMUON	ANTIOXIDANTS	ANTIPHRASTICAL	ANTIQUARKS
ANTIMUONS	ANTIOZONANT	ANTIPILL	ANTIQUARY
ANTIMUSICAL	ANTIOZONANTS	ANTIPIRACY	ANTIQUATE
ANTIMUTAGEN	ANTIPACIFIST	ANTIPLAGUE	ANTIQUATED
ANTIMUTAGENS	ANTIPACIFISTS	ANTIPLAQUE	ANTIQUATEDNESS
ANTIMYCIN	ANTIPAPAL	ANTIPLEASURE	ANTIQUATES
ANTIMYCINS	ANTIPARALLEL	ANTIPOACHING	ANTIQUATING
ANTIMYCOTIC	ANTIPARALLELS	ANTIPODAL	ANTIQUATION
ANTIMYCOTICS	ANTIPARASITIC	ANTIPODALS	ANTIQUATIONS
ANTINARCOTIC	ANTIPARTICLE	ANTIPODE	ANTIQUE
ANTINARCOTICS	ANTIPARTICLES	ANTIPODEAN	ANTIQUED
ANTINARRATIVE	ANTIPARTY	ANTIPODEANS	ANTIQUELY
ANTINARRATIVES	ANTIPASTI	ANTIPODES	ANTIQUENESS
ANTINATIONAL	ANTIPASTO	ANTIPOETIC	ANTIQUENESSES
ANTINATIONALIST	ANTIPASTOS	ANTIPOLE	ANTIQUER
ANTINATURAL	ANTIPATHETIC	ANTIPOLES	ANTIQUERS
ANTINATURE	ANTIPATHETICAL	ANTIPOLICE	ANTIQUES
ANTINAUSEA	ANTIPATHIC	ANTIPOLITICAL	ANTIQUEY
ANTINEOPLASTIC	ANTIPATHIES	ANTIPOLITICS	ANTIQUING
ANTINEPHRITIC	ANTIPATHIST	ANTIPOLLUTION	ANTIQUITARIAN
ANTINEPHRITICS	ANTIPATHISTS	ANTIPOLLUTIONS	ANTIQUITARIANS
ANTINEPOTISM	ANTIPATHOGEN	ANTIPOPE	ANTIQUITIES

ANTIQUITY
ANTIRABIES
ANTIRACHITIC
ANTIRACHITICS
ANTIRACISM
ANTIRACISMS
ANTIRACIST
ANTIRACISTS
ANTIRADAR
ANTIRADICAL
ANTIRADICALISM
ANTIRADICALISMS
ANTIRAPE
ANTIRATIONAL
ANTIRATIONALISM
ANTIRATIONALIST
ANTIRATIONALITY
ANTIREALISM
ANTIREALISMS
ANTIREALIST
ANTIREALISTS
ANTIRECESSION
ANTIRED
ANTIREFLECTION
ANTIREFLECTIVE
ANTIREFORM
ANTIREGULATORY
ANTIREJECTION
ANTIRELIGION
ANTIRELIGIOUS
ANTIREPUBLICAN
ANTIREPUBLICANS
ANTIRHEUMATIC
ANTIRHEUMATICS
ANTIRIOT
ANTIRITUALISM
ANTIRITUALISMS
ANTIROCK
ANTIROLL
ANTIROMANTIC
ANTIROMANTICISM
ANTIROMANTICS
ANTIROYALIST
ANTIROYALISTS
ANTIRRHINUM
ANTIRRHINUMS
ANTIRUST
ANTIRUSTS
ANTIS
ANTISAG
ANTISATELLITE
ANTISCIAN
ANTISCIANS
ANTISCIENCE
ANTISCIENCES
ANTISCIENTIFIC

ANTISCORBUTIC
ANTISCORBUTICS
ANTISCRIPTURAL
ANTISECRECY
ANTISEGREGATION
ANTISEIZURE
ANTISENSE
ANTISENTIMENTAL
ANTISEPALOUS
ANTISEPARATIST
ANTISEPARATISTS
ANTISEPSES
ANTISEPSIS
ANTISEPTIC
ANTISEPTICALLY
ANTISEPTICISE
ANTISEPTICISED
ANTISEPTICISES
ANTISEPTICISING
ANTISEPTICISM
ANTISEPTICISMS
ANTISEPTICIZE
ANTISEPTICIZED
ANTISEPTICIZES
ANTISEPTICIZING
ANTISEPTICS
ANTISERA
ANTISERUM
ANTISERUMS
ANTISEX
ANTISEXIST
ANTISEXISTS
ANTISEXUAL
ANTISEXUALITIES
ANTISEXUALITY
ANTISHARK
ANTISHIP
ANTISHOCK
ANTISHOPLIFTING
ANTISKID
ANTISLAVERY
ANTISLEEP
ANTISLIP
ANTISMOG
ANTISMOKE
ANTISMOKER
ANTISMOKERS
ANTISMOKING
ANTISMUGGLING
ANTISMUT
ANTISNOB
ANTISOCIAL
ANTISOCIALISM
ANTISOCIALISMS
ANTISOCIALIST
ANTISOCIALISTS

ANTISOCIALITIES
ANTISOCIALITY
ANTISOCIALLY
ANTISOLAR
ANTISPASMODIC
ANTISPASMODICS
ANTISPAST
ANTISPASTIC
ANTISPASTS
ANTISPECULATION
ANTISPECULATIVE
ANTISPENDING
ANTISPIRITUAL
ANTISTAT
ANTISTATE
ANTISTATIC
ANTISTATICS
ANTISTATS
ANTISTICK
ANTISTORIES
ANTISTORY
ANTISTRESS
ANTISTRIKE
ANTISTROPHE
ANTISTROPHES
ANTISTROPHIC
ANTISTROPHON
ANTISTROPHONS
ANTISTUDENT
ANTISUBMARINE
ANTISUBSIDY
ANTISUBVERSION
ANTISUBVERSIVE
ANTISUICIDE
ANTISYMMETRIC
ANTISYPHILITIC
ANTISYPHILITICS
ANTISYZYGIES
ANTISYZYGY
ANTITAKEOVER
ANTITANK
ANTITARNISH
ANTITARNISHING
ANTITAX
ANTITECHNOLOGY
ANTITERRORISM
ANTITERRORISMS
ANTITERRORIST
ANTITERRORISTS
ANTITHALIAN
ANTITHEFT
ANTITHEISM
ANTITHEISMS
ANTITHEIST
ANTITHEISTIC
ANTITHEISTS

ANTITHEORETICAL
ANTITHESES
ANTITHESIS
ANTITHET
ANTITHETIC
ANTITHETICAL
ANTITHETICALLY
ANTITHETS
ANTITHROMBIN
ANTITHROMBINS
ANTITHYROID
ANTITOBACCO
ANTITOXIC
ANTITOXIN
ANTITOXINS
ANTITRADE
ANTITRADES
ANTITRADITIONAL
ANTITRAGI
ANTITRAGUS
ANTITRANSPIRANT
ANTITRINITARIAN
ANTITRUST
ANTITRUSTER
ANTITRUSTERS
ANTITUBERCULAR
ANTITUBERCULOUS
ANTITUMOR
ANTITUMORAL
ANTITUSSIVE
ANTITUSSIVES
ANTITYPAL
ANTITYPE
ANTITYPES
ANTITYPHOID
ANTITYPIC
ANTITYPICAL
ANTITYPICALLY
ANTIULCER
ANTIUNION
ANTIUNIVERSITY
ANTIURBAN
ANTIVENENE
ANTIVENENES
ANTIVENIN
ANTIVENINS
ANTIVIOLENCE
ANTIVIRAL
ANTIVIRUS
ANTIVITAMIN
ANTIVITAMINS
ANTIVIVISECTION
ANTIWAR
ANTIWEAR
ANTIWEED
ANTIWELFARE

ANTIWHALING	ANVILING	APADANAS	APERIENTS
ANTIWHITE	ANVILLED	APAGE	APERIES
ANTIWOMAN	ANVILLING	APAGOGE	APERIODIC
ANTIWORLD	ANVILS	APAGOGES	APERIODICALLY
ANTIWORLDLY	ANVILTOP	APAGOGIC	APERIODICITIES
ANTIWORLDS	ANVILTOPS	APAGOGICAL	APERIODICITY
ANTIWRINKLE	ANXIETIES	APAGOGICALLY	APERITIF
ANTLER	ANXIETY	APAID	APERITIFS
ANTLERED	ANXIOLYTIC	APANAGE	APERITIVE
ANTLERS	ANXIOLYTICS	APANAGED	APERITIVES
ANTLIA	ANXIOUS	APANAGES	APERS
ANTLIAE	ANXIOUSLY	APAREJO	APERT
ANTLIATE	ANXIOUSNESS	APAREJOS	APERTNESS
ANTLIKE	ANXIOUSNESSES	APART	APERTNESSES
ANTLION	ANY	APARTHEID	APERTURE
ANTLIONS	ANYBODIES	APARTHEIDS	APERTURES
ANTONINIANUS	ANYBODY	APARTMENT	APERY
ANTONINIANUSES	ANYHOW	APARTMENTAL	APES
ANTONOMASIA	ANYMORE	APARTMENTS	APETALIES
ANTONOMASIAS	ANYONE	APARTNESS	APETALOUS
ANTONOMASTIC	ANYONES	APARTNESSES	APETALY
ANTONYM	ANYPLACE	APATETIC	APEX
ANTONYMIC	ANYROAD	APATHATON	APEXES
ANTONYMIES	ANYTHING	APATHATONS	APFELSTRUDEL
ANTONYMOUS	ANYTHINGARIAN	APATHETIC	APFELSTRUDELS
ANTONYMS	ANYTHINGARIANS	APATHETICAL	APGAR
ANTONYMY	ANYTHINGS	APATHETICALLY	APHAERESES
ANTRA	ANYTIME	APATHIES	APHAERESIS
ANTRAL	ANYWAY	APATHY	APHAERETIC
ANTRE	ANYWAYS	APATITE	APHAGIA
ANTRES	ANYWHEN	APATITES	APHAGIAS
ANTRORSE	ANYWHERE	APATOSAURUS	APHAKIA
ANTRORSELY	ANYWHERES	APATOSAURUSES	APHANIPTEROUS
ANTRUM	ANYWHITHER	APAY	APHANITE
ANTRUMS	ANYWISE	APAYD	APHANITES
ANTS	ANZIANI	APAYING	APHANITIC
ANTSIER	AORIST	APAYS	APHASIA
ANTSIEST	AORISTIC	APE	APHASIAC
ANTSY	AORISTICALLY	APEAK	APHASIACS
ANTWACKIE	AORISTS	APED	APHASIAS
ANUCLEATE	AORTA	APEDOM	APHASIC
ANUCLEATED	AORTAE	APEDOMS	APHASICS
ANURAL	AORTAL	APEEK	APHELANDRA
ANURAN	AORTAS	APEHOOD	APHELANDRAS
ANURANS	AORTIC	APEHOODS	APHELIA
ANURESES	AORTITIS	APELIKE	APHELIAN
ANURESIS	AORTITISES	APEMAN	APHELION
ANURETIC	AORTOGRAPHIC	APEMEN	APHELIONS
ANURIA	AORTOGRAPHIES	APEPSIA	APHELIOTROPIC
ANURIAS	AORTOGRAPHY	APEPSIAS	APHELIOTROPISM
ANURIC	AOUDAD	APEPSIES	APHELIOTROPISMS
ANUROUS	AOUDADS	APEPSY	APHERESES
ANUS	APACE	APER	APHERESIS
ANUSES	APACHE	APERCU	APHERETIC
ANVIL	APACHES	APERCUS	APHERETICALLY
ANVILED	APADANA	APERIENT	APHESES

APHESIS
APHETIC
APHETICALLY
APHETISE
APHETISED
APHETISES
APHETISING
APHETIZE
APHETIZED
APHETIZES
APHETIZING
APHICIDE
APHICIDES
APHID
APHIDES
APHIDIAN
APHIDIANS
APHIDICIDE
APHIDICIDES
APHIDIOUS
APHIDS
APHIS
APHOLATE
APHOLATES
APHONIA
APHONIAS
APHONIC
APHONICS
APHONIES
APHONOUS
APHONY
APHORISE
APHORISED
APHORISER
APHORISERS
APHORISES
APHORISING
APHORISM
APHORISMS
APHORIST
APHORISTIC
APHORISTICALLY
APHORISTS
APHORIZE
APHORIZED
APHORIZER
APHORIZERS
APHORIZES
APHORIZING
APHOTIC
APHRODISIA
APHRODISIAC
APHRODISIACAL
APHRODISIACS
APHRODISIAS
APHTHA

APHTHAE
APHTHOUS
APHYLLIES
APHYLLOUS
APHYLLY
APIAN
APIARIAN
APIARIANS
APIARIES
APIARIST
APIARISTS
APIARY
APICAL
APICALLY
APICALS
APICES
APICIAN
APICULATE
APICULI
APICULTURAL
APICULTURE
APICULTURES
APICULTURIST
APICULTURISTS
APICULUS
APIECE
APIMANIA
APIMANIAS
APING
APIOL
APIOLOGIES
APIOLOGY
APIOLS
APISH
APISHLY
APISHNESS
APISHNESSES
APISM
APISMS
APITHERAPIES
APITHERAPY
APIVOROUS
APLACENTAL
APLANAT
APLANATIC
APLANATICALLY
APLANATISM
APLANATISMS
APLANATS
APLANETIC
APLANETICALLY
APLANOGAMETE
APLANOGAMETES
APLANOSPORE
APLANOSPORES
APLASIA

APLASIAS
APLASTIC
APLENTY
APLITE
APLITES
APLITIC
APLOMB
APLOMBS
APLUSTRE
APLUSTRES
APNEA
APNEAL
APNEAS
APNEIC
APNEUSIS
APNEUSTIC
APNEUSTICALLY
APNOEA
APNOEAL
APNOEAS
APNOEIC
APOAPSIDES
APOAPSIS
APOCALYPSE
APOCALYPSES
APOCALYPTIC
APOCALYPTICAL
APOCALYPTICALLY
APOCALYPTICISM
APOCALYPTICISMS
APOCALYPTISM
APOCALYPTISMS
APOCALYPTIST
APOCALYPTISTS
APOCARP
APOCARPIES
APOCARPOUS
APOCARPS
APOCARPY
APOCATASTASES
APOCATASTASIS
APOCHROMAT
APOCHROMATIC
APOCHROMATISM
APOCHROMATISMS
APOCHROMATS
APOCOPATE
APOCOPATED
APOCOPATES
APOCOPATING
APOCOPATION
APOCOPATIONS
APOCOPE
APOCOPES
APOCOPIC
APOCRINE

APOCRYPHA
APOCRYPHAL
APOCRYPHALLY
APOCRYPHALNESS
APOCRYPHON
APOCYNACEOUS
APOCYNTHION
APOCYNTHIONS
APOD
APODAL
APODE
APODEICTIC
APODEICTICAL
APODEICTICALLY
APODES
APODICTIC
APODICTICAL
APODICTICALLY
APODOSES
APODOSIS
APODOUS
APODS
APODYTERIUM
APODYTERIUMS
APOENZYME
APOENZYMES
APOGAEIC
APOGAMIC
APOGAMIES
APOGAMOUS
APOGAMOUSLY
APOGAMY
APOGEAL
APOGEAN
APOGEE
APOGEES
APOGEIC
APOGEOTROPIC
APOGEOTROPISM
APOGEOTROPISMS
APOGRAPH
APOGRAPHS
APOLAUSTIC
APOLAUSTICS
APOLIPOPROTEIN
APOLIPOPROTEINS
APOLITICAL
APOLITICALITIES
APOLITICALITY
APOLITICALLY
APOLITICISM
APOLITICISMS
APOLLO
APOLLONICON
APOLLONICONS
APOLLOS

APOLOG
APOLOGAL
APOLOGETIC
APOLOGETICAL
APOLOGETICALLY
APOLOGETICS
APOLOGIA
APOLOGIAE
APOLOGIAS
APOLOGIES
APOLOGISE
APOLOGISED
APOLOGISER
APOLOGISERS
APOLOGISES
APOLOGISING
APOLOGIST
APOLOGISTS
APOLOGIZE
APOLOGIZED
APOLOGIZER
APOLOGIZERS
APOLOGIZES
APOLOGIZING
APOLOGS
APOLOGUE
APOLOGUES
APOLOGY
APOLUNE
APOLUNES
APOMICT
APOMICTIC
APOMICTICAL
APOMICTICALLY
APOMICTS
APOMIXES
APOMIXIS
APOMORPHIA
APOMORPHIAS
APOMORPHINE
APOMORPHINES
APONEUROSES
APONEUROSIS
APONEUROTIC
APOOP
APOPEMPTIC
APOPEMPTICS
APOPHASES
APOPHASIS
APOPHATIC
APOPHLEGMATIC
APOPHLEGMATICS
APOPHONIES
APOPHONY
APOPHTHEGM
APOPHTHEGMATIC

APOPHTHEGMATISE
APOPHTHEGMATIST
APOPHTHEGMATIZE
APOPHTHEGMS
APOPHYGE
APOPHYGES
APOPHYLLITE
APOPHYLLITES
APOPHYSATE
APOPHYSEAL
APOPHYSES
APOPHYSIAL
APOPHYSIS
APOPLAST
APOPLASTS
APOPLECTIC
APOPLECTICAL
APOPLECTICALLY
APOPLECTICS
APOPLEX
APOPLEXED
APOPLEXES
APOPLEXIES
APOPLEXING
APOPLEXY
APOPROTEIN
APOPROTEINS
APOPTOSES
APOPTOSIS
APOPTOTIC
APORETIC
APORETICALLY
APORIA
APORIAS
APORT
APOSEMATIC
APOSEMATICALLY
APOSIOPESES
APOSIOPESIS
APOSIOPETIC
APOSITIA
APOSITIAS
APOSITIC
APOSPORIES
APOSPOROUS
APOSPORY
APOSTACIES
APOSTACY
APOSTASIES
APOSTASY
APOSTATE
APOSTATES
APOSTATIC
APOSTATICAL
APOSTATISE
APOSTATISED

APOSTATISES
APOSTATISING
APOSTATIZE
APOSTATIZED
APOSTATIZES
APOSTATIZING
APOSTIL
APOSTILLE
APOSTILLES
APOSTILS
APOSTLE
APOSTLES
APOSTLESHIP
APOSTLESHIPS
APOSTOLATE
APOSTOLATES
APOSTOLIC
APOSTOLICAL
APOSTOLICALLY
APOSTOLICISM
APOSTOLICISMS
APOSTOLICITIES
APOSTOLICITY
APOSTOLISE
APOSTOLISED
APOSTOLISES
APOSTOLISING
APOSTOLIZE
APOSTOLIZED
APOSTOLIZES
APOSTOLIZING
APOSTROPHE
APOSTROPHES
APOSTROPHIC
APOSTROPHISE
APOSTROPHISED
APOSTROPHISES
APOSTROPHISING
APOSTROPHIZE
APOSTROPHIZED
APOSTROPHIZES
APOSTROPHIZING
APOSTROPHUS
APOSTROPHUSES
APOTHECARIES
APOTHECARY
APOTHECE
APOTHECES
APOTHECIA
APOTHECIAL
APOTHECIUM
APOTHEGM
APOTHEGMATIC
APOTHEGMATICAL
APOTHEGMATISE
APOTHEGMATISED

APOTHEGMATISES
APOTHEGMATISING
APOTHEGMATIST
APOTHEGMATISTS
APOTHEGMATIZE
APOTHEGMATIZED
APOTHEGMATIZES
APOTHEGMATIZING
APOTHEGMS
APOTHEM
APOTHEMS
APOTHEOSES
APOTHEOSIS
APOTHEOSISE
APOTHEOSISED
APOTHEOSISES
APOTHEOSISING
APOTHEOSIZE
APOTHEOSIZED
APOTHEOSIZES
APOTHEOSIZING
APOTROPAIC
APOTROPAICALLY
APOTROPAISM
APOTROPAISMS
APOTROPOUS
APOZEM
APOZEMS
APP
APPAID
APPAIR
APPAIRED
APPAIRING
APPAIRS
APPAL
APPALL
APPALLED
APPALLING
APPALLINGLY
APPALLS
APPALS
APPALTI
APPALTO
APPANAGE
APPANAGED
APPANAGES
APPARAT
APPARATCHIK
APPARATCHIKI
APPARATCHIKS
APPARATS
APPARATUS
APPARATUSES
APPAREL
APPARELED
APPARELING

APPARELLED
APPARELLING
APPARELMENT
APPARELMENTS
APPARELS
APPARENCIES
APPARENCY
APPARENT
APPARENTLY
APPARENTNESS
APPARENTNESSES
APPARENTS
APPARITION
APPARITIONAL
APPARITIONS
APPARITOR
APPARITORS
APPARTEMENT
APPARTEMENTS
APPASSIONATO
APPAY
APPAYD
APPAYING
APPAYS
APPEACH
APPEACHED
APPEACHES
APPEACHING
APPEACHMENT
APPEACHMENTS
APPEAL
APPEALABILITIES
APPEALABILITY
APPEALABLE
APPEALED
APPEALER
APPEALERS
APPEALING
APPEALINGLY
APPEALINGNESS
APPEALINGNESSES
APPEALS
APPEAR
APPEARANCE
APPEARANCES
APPEARED
APPEARER
APPEARERS
APPEARING
APPEARS
APPEASABLE
APPEASE
APPEASED
APPEASEMENT
APPEASEMENTS
APPEASER

APPEASERS
APPEASES
APPEASING
APPEASINGLY
APPEL
APPELLANT
APPELLANTS
APPELLATE
APPELLATION
APPELLATIONAL
APPELLATIONS
APPELLATIVE
APPELLATIVELY
APPELLATIVES
APPELLEE
APPELLEES
APPELLOR
APPELLORS
APPELS
APPEND
APPENDAGE
APPENDAGES
APPENDANT
APPENDANTS
APPENDECTOMIES
APPENDECTOMY
APPENDED
APPENDICECTOMY
APPENDICES
APPENDICITIS
APPENDICITISES
APPENDICLE
APPENDICLES
APPENDICULAR
APPENDICULARIAN
APPENDICULATE
APPENDING
APPENDIX
APPENDIXES
APPENDS
APPERCEIVE
APPERCEIVED
APPERCEIVES
APPERCEIVING
APPERCEPTION
APPERCEPTIONS
APPERCEPTIVE
APPERCIPIENT
APPERIL
APPERILL
APPERILLS
APPERILS
APPERTAIN
APPERTAINANCE
APPERTAINANCES
APPERTAINED

APPERTAINING
APPERTAINMENT
APPERTAINMENTS
APPERTAINS
APPERTINENT
APPERTINENTS
APPESTAT
APPESTATS
APPETEEZEMENTS
APPETENCE
APPETENCES
APPETENCIES
APPETENCY
APPETENT
APPETIBLE
APPETISE
APPETISED
APPETISEMENT
APPETISEMENTS
APPETISER
APPETISERS
APPETISES
APPETISING
APPETISINGLY
APPETITE
APPETITES
APPETITION
APPETITIONS
APPETITIVE
APPETIZE
APPETIZED
APPETIZER
APPETIZERS
APPETIZES
APPETIZING
APPETIZINGLY
APPLAUD
APPLAUDABLE
APPLAUDABLY
APPLAUDED
APPLAUDER
APPLAUDERS
APPLAUDING
APPLAUDINGLY
APPLAUDS
APPLAUSE
APPLAUSES
APPLAUSIVE
APPLAUSIVELY
APPLE
APPLECART
APPLECARTS
APPLEDRAIN
APPLEDRAINS
APPLEJACK
APPLEJACKS

APPLERINGIE
APPLERINGIES
APPLES
APPLESAUCE
APPLESAUCES
APPLESNITS
APPLET
APPLETS
APPLEY
APPLEYNESS
APPLIABLE
APPLIANCE
APPLIANCES
APPLICABILITIES
APPLICABILITY
APPLICABLE
APPLICABLENESS
APPLICABLY
APPLICANT
APPLICANTS
APPLICATE
APPLICATION
APPLICATIONS
APPLICATIVE
APPLICATIVELY
APPLICATOR
APPLICATORS
APPLICATORY
APPLIED
APPLIER
APPLIERS
APPLIES
APPLIQUE
APPLIQUED
APPLIQUEING
APPLIQUES
APPLY
APPLYING
APPOGGIATURA
APPOGGIATURAS
APPOGGIATURE
APPOINT
APPOINTED
APPOINTEE
APPOINTEES
APPOINTER
APPOINTERS
APPOINTING
APPOINTIVE
APPOINTMENT
APPOINTMENTS
APPOINTOR
APPOINTORS
APPOINTS
APPORT
APPORTION

APPORTIONABLE
APPORTIONED
APPORTIONER
APPORTIONERS
APPORTIONING
APPORTIONMENT
APPORTIONMENTS
APPORTIONS
APPORTS
APPOSABLE
APPOSABLY
APPOSE
APPOSED
APPOSER
APPOSERS
APPOSES
APPOSING
APPOSITE
APPOSITELY
APPOSITENESS
APPOSITENESSES
APPOSITION
APPOSITIONAL
APPOSITIONS
APPOSITIVE
APPOSITIVELY
APPOSITIVES
APPRAISABLE
APPRAISAL
APPRAISALS
APPRAISE
APPRAISED
APPRAISEE
APPRAISEES
APPRAISEMENT
APPRAISEMENTS
APPRAISER
APPRAISERS
APPRAISES
APPRAISING
APPRAISINGLY
APPRAISIVE
APPRAISIVELY
APPRECIABLE
APPRECIABLY
APPRECIATE
APPRECIATED
APPRECIATES
APPRECIATING
APPRECIATION
APPRECIATIONS
APPRECIATIVE
APPRECIATIVELY
APPRECIATOR
APPRECIATORILY
APPRECIATORS

APPRECIATORY
APPREHEND
APPREHENDED
APPREHENDING
APPREHENDS
APPREHENSIBLE
APPREHENSIBLY
APPREHENSION
APPREHENSIONS
APPREHENSIVE
APPREHENSIVELY
APPRENTICE
APPRENTICED
APPRENTICEHOOD
APPRENTICEHOODS
APPRENTICEMENT
APPRENTICEMENTS
APPRENTICES
APPRENTICESHIP
APPRENTICESHIPS
APPRENTICING
APPRESS
APPRESSED
APPRESSES
APPRESSING
APPRESSORIA
APPRESSORIUM
APPRISE
APPRISED
APPRISER
APPRISERS
APPRISES
APPRISING
APPRISINGS
APPRIZE
APPRIZED
APPRIZER
APPRIZERS
APPRIZES
APPRIZING
APPRIZINGS
APPROACH
APPROACHABILITY
APPROACHABLE
APPROACHED
APPROACHES
APPROACHING
APPROBATE
APPROBATED
APPROBATES
APPROBATING
APPROBATION
APPROBATIONS
APPROBATIVE
APPROBATORY
APPROOF

APPROOFS
APPROPINQUATE
APPROPINQUATED
APPROPINQUATES
APPROPINQUATING
APPROPINQUATION
APPROPINQUE
APPROPINQUED
APPROPINQUES
APPROPINQUING
APPROPINQUITIES
APPROPINQUITY
APPROPRIABLE
APPROPRIACY
APPROPRIATE
APPROPRIATED
APPROPRIATELY
APPROPRIATENESS
APPROPRIATES
APPROPRIATING
APPROPRIATION
APPROPRIATIONS
APPROPRIATIVE
APPROPRIATOR
APPROPRIATORS
APPROVABLE
APPROVABLY
APPROVAL
APPROVALS
APPROVANCE
APPROVANCES
APPROVE
APPROVED
APPROVER
APPROVERS
APPROVES
APPROVING
APPROVINGLY
APPROXIMAL
APPROXIMATE
APPROXIMATED
APPROXIMATELY
APPROXIMATES
APPROXIMATING
APPROXIMATION
APPROXIMATIONS
APPROXIMATIVE
APPUI
APPUIED
APPUIS
APPULSE
APPULSES
APPULSIVE
APPULSIVELY
APPULSIVENESS
APPURTENANCE

APPURTENANCES
APPURTENANT
APPURTENANTS
APPUY
APPUYED
APPUYING
APPUYS
APRACTIC
APRAXIA
APRAXIAS
APRAXIC
APRES
APRICATE
APRICATED
APRICATES
APRICATING
APRICATION
APRICATIONS
APRICOCK
APRICOCKS
APRICOT
APRICOTS
APRIORISM
APRIORISMS
APRIORIST
APRIORISTS
APRIORITIES
APRIORITY
APRON
APRONED
APRONFUL
APRONFULS
APRONING
APRONS
APROPOS
APROTIC
APSARAS
APSARASES
APSE
APSES
APSIDAL
APSIDES
APSIDIOLE
APSIDIOLES
APSIS
APT
APTED
APTER
APTERAL
APTERIA
APTERISM
APTERISMS
APTERIUM
APTEROUS
APTERYGIAL
APTERYX

APTERYXES
APTEST
APTING
APTITUDE
APTITUDES
APTITUDINAL
APTITUDINALLY
APTLY
APTNESS
APTNESSES
APTOTE
APTOTES
APTOTIC
APTS
APYRASE
APYRASES
APYRETIC
APYREXIA
APYREXIAS
AQUA
AQUABATIC
AQUABATICS
AQUABOARD
AQUABOARDS
AQUACADE
AQUACADES
AQUACULTURAL
AQUACULTURE
AQUACULTURES
AQUACULTURIST
AQUACULTURISTS
AQUADROME
AQUADROMES
AQUAE
AQUAEROBICALLY
AQUAEROBICIST
AQUAEROBICISTS
AQUAEROBICS
AQUAFER
AQUAFERS
AQUAFORTIS
AQUAFORTISES
AQUAFORTIST
AQUAFORTISTS
AQUALEATHER
AQUALEATHERS
AQUALUNG
AQUALUNGS
AQUAMANALE
AQUAMANALES
AQUAMANILE
AQUAMANILES
AQUAMARINE
AQUAMARINES
AQUANAUT
AQUANAUTICS

AQUANAUTS
AQUAPHOBE
AQUAPHOBES
AQUAPHOBIA
AQUAPHOBIAS
AQUAPHOBIC
AQUAPHOBICS
AQUAPLANE
AQUAPLANED
AQUAPLANER
AQUAPLANERS
AQUAPLANES
AQUAPLANING
AQUAPLANINGS
AQUAPORIN
AQUARELLE
AQUARELLES
AQUARELLIST
AQUARELLISTS
AQUARIA
AQUARIAL
AQUARIAN
AQUARIANS
AQUARIIST
AQUARIISTS
AQUARIST
AQUARISTS
AQUARIUM
AQUARIUMS
AQUAROBIC
AQUAROBICS
AQUAS
AQUASHOW
AQUASHOWS
AQUATIC
AQUATICALLY
AQUATICS
AQUATINT
AQUATINTA
AQUATINTAS
AQUATINTED
AQUATINTER
AQUATINTERS
AQUATINTING
AQUATINTIST
AQUATINTISTS
AQUATINTS
AQUATONE
AQUATONES
AQUAVIT
AQUAVITS
AQUEDUCT
AQUEDUCTS
AQUEOUS
AQUICULTURAL
AQUICULTURALLY

AQUICULTURE
AQUICULTURES
AQUICULTURIST
AQUICULTURISTS
AQUIFER
AQUIFEROUS
AQUIFERS
AQUIFOLIACEOUS
AQUILEGIA
AQUILEGIAS
AQUILINE
AQUILINITIES
AQUILINITY
AQUILON
AQUILONS
AQUIVER
AR
ARABA
ARABAS
ARABESK
ARABESKS
ARABESQUE
ARABESQUED
ARABESQUES
ARABIC
ARABICA
ARABICAS
ARABICIZATION
ARABICIZATIONS
ARABICIZE
ARABICIZED
ARABICIZES
ARABICIZING
ARABILITIES
ARABILITY
ARABIN
ARABINOSE
ARABINOSES
ARABINOSIDE
ARABINOSIDES
ARABINS
ARABIS
ARABISATION
ARABISATIONS
ARABISE
ARABISED
ARABISES
ARABISING
ARABIZATION
ARABIZATIONS
ARABIZE
ARABIZED
ARABIZES
ARABIZING
ARABLE
ARABLES

ARACEOUS
ARACHIDONIC
ARACHIS
ARACHISES
ARACHNID
ARACHNIDAN
ARACHNIDANS
ARACHNIDS
ARACHNOID
ARACHNOIDAL
ARACHNOIDITIS
ARACHNOIDITISES
ARACHNOIDS
ARACHNOLOGICAL
ARACHNOLOGIES
ARACHNOLOGIST
ARACHNOLOGISTS
ARACHNOLOGY
ARACHNOPHOBE
ARACHNOPHOBES
ARACHNOPHOBIA
ARACHNOPHOBIAS
ARAEOMETER
ARAEOMETERS
ARAEOMETRIC
ARAEOMETRICAL
ARAEOMETRIES
ARAEOMETRY
ARAEOSTYLE
ARAEOSTYLES
ARAEOSYSTYLE
ARAEOSYSTYLES
ARAGONITE
ARAGONITES
ARAGONITIC
ARAISE
ARAISED
ARAISES
ARAISING
ARAK
ARAKS
ARALIA
ARALIACEOUS
ARALIAS
ARAME
ARAMES
ARAMID
ARAMIDS
ARANEID
ARANEIDS
ARANEOUS
ARAPAIMA
ARAPAIMAS
ARAPONGA
ARAPONGAS
ARAPUNGA

ARAPUNGAS
ARAR
ARAROBA
ARAROBAS
ARARS
ARAUCARIA
ARAUCARIAN
ARAUCARIAS
ARAYSE
ARAYSED
ARAYSES
ARAYSING
ARB
ARBA
ARBALEST
ARBALESTER
ARBALESTERS
ARBALESTS
ARBALIST
ARBALISTER
ARBALISTERS
ARBALISTS
ARBAS
ARBELEST
ARBELESTS
ARBITER
ARBITERS
ARBITRABLE
ARBITRAGE
ARBITRAGED
ARBITRAGER
ARBITRAGERS
ARBITRAGES
ARBITRAGEUR
ARBITRAGEURS
ARBITRAGING
ARBITRAL
ARBITRAMENT
ARBITRAMENTS
ARBITRARIES
ARBITRARILY
ARBITRARINESS
ARBITRARINESSES
ARBITRARY
ARBITRATE
ARBITRATED
ARBITRATES
ARBITRATING
ARBITRATION
ARBITRATIONAL
ARBITRATIONS
ARBITRATIVE
ARBITRATOR
ARBITRATORS
ARBITRATRIX
ARBITRATRIXES

ARBITREMENT
ARBITREMENTS
ARBITRESS
ARBITRESSES
ARBITRIUM
ARBITRIUMS
ARBLAST
ARBLASTER
ARBLASTERS
ARBLASTS
ARBOR
ARBORACEOUS
ARBOREAL
ARBOREALLY
ARBORED
ARBOREOUS
ARBORES
ARBORESCENCE
ARBORESCENCES
ARBORESCENT
ARBORET
ARBORETA
ARBORETS
ARBORETUM
ARBORETUMS
ARBORICULTURAL
ARBORICULTURE
ARBORICULTURES
ARBORICULTURIST
ARBORISATION
ARBORISATIONS
ARBORIST
ARBORISTS
ARBORIZATION
ARBORIZATIONS
ARBORIZE
ARBORIZED
ARBORIZES
ARBORIZING
ARBOROUS
ARBORS
ARBORVITAE
ARBORVITAES
ARBOUR
ARBOURED
ARBOURS
ARBOVIRUS
ARBOVIRUSES
ARBS
ARBUSCLE
ARBUSCLES
ARBUTE
ARBUTEAN
ARBUTES
ARBUTUS
ARBUTUSES

ARC
ARCADE
ARCADED
ARCADES
ARCADIA
ARCADIAN
ARCADIANS
ARCADIAS
ARCADING
ARCADINGS
ARCANA
ARCANAS
ARCANE
ARCANELY
ARCANENESS
ARCANENESSES
ARCANIST
ARCANISTS
ARCANUM
ARCANUMS
ARCATURE
ARCATURES
ARCCOS
ARCCOSES
ARCCOSINE
ARCCOSINES
ARCED
ARCH
ARCHAEBACTERIA
ARCHAEBACTERIUM
ARCHAEI
ARCHAEOBOTANIST
ARCHAEOBOTANY
ARCHAEOLOGICAL
ARCHAEOLOGIES
ARCHAEOLOGIST
ARCHAEOLOGISTS
ARCHAEOLOGY
ARCHAEOMETRIC
ARCHAEOMETRIES
ARCHAEOMETRIST
ARCHAEOMETRISTS
ARCHAEOMETRY
ARCHAEOPTERYX
ARCHAEOPTERYXES
ARCHAEORNIS
ARCHAEOZOOLOGY
ARCHAEUS
ARCHAIC
ARCHAICALLY
ARCHAICISM
ARCHAICISMS
ARCHAISE
ARCHAISED
ARCHAISER
ARCHAISERS

ARCHAISES
ARCHAISING
ARCHAISM
ARCHAISMS
ARCHAIST
ARCHAISTIC
ARCHAISTS
ARCHAIZE
ARCHAIZED
ARCHAIZER
ARCHAIZERS
ARCHAIZES
ARCHAIZING
ARCHANGEL
ARCHANGELIC
ARCHANGELS
ARCHBISHOP
ARCHBISHOPRIC
ARCHBISHOPRICS
ARCHBISHOPS
ARCHDEACON
ARCHDEACONRIES
ARCHDEACONRY
ARCHDEACONS
ARCHDIOCESAN
ARCHDIOCESE
ARCHDIOCESES
ARCHDUCAL
ARCHDUCHESS
ARCHDUCHESSES
ARCHDUCHIES
ARCHDUCHY
ARCHDUKE
ARCHDUKEDOM
ARCHDUKEDOMS
ARCHDUKES
ARCHED
ARCHEGONIA
ARCHEGONIAL
ARCHEGONIATE
ARCHEGONIATES
ARCHEGONIUM
ARCHEI
ARCHENEMIES
ARCHENEMY
ARCHENTERA
ARCHENTERIC
ARCHENTERON
ARCHENTERONS
ARCHEOASTRONOMY
ARCHEOBOTANICAL
ARCHEOBOTANIST
ARCHEOBOTANISTS
ARCHEOBOTANY
ARCHEOLOGICAL
ARCHEOLOGICALLY

ARCHEOLOGIES
ARCHEOLOGIST
ARCHEOLOGISTS
ARCHEOLOGY
ARCHEOMAGNETIC
ARCHEOMAGNETISM
ARCHEOMETRIES
ARCHEOMETRY
ARCHEOZOOLOGIST
ARCHEOZOOLOGY
ARCHER
ARCHERESS
ARCHERESSES
ARCHERFISH
ARCHERFISHES
ARCHERIES
ARCHERS
ARCHERY
ARCHES
ARCHESPORE
ARCHESPORES
ARCHESPORIA
ARCHESPORIAL
ARCHESPORIUM
ARCHEST
ARCHETYPAL
ARCHETYPALLY
ARCHETYPE
ARCHETYPES
ARCHETYPICAL
ARCHETYPICALLY
ARCHEUS
ARCHFIEND
ARCHFIENDS
ARCHGENETHLIAC
ARCHGENETHLIACS
ARCHICARP
ARCHICARPS
ARCHIDIACONAL
ARCHIDIACONATE
ARCHIDIACONATES
ARCHIEPISCOPACY
ARCHIEPISCOPAL
ARCHIEPISCOPATE
ARCHIL
ARCHILOWE
ARCHILOWES
ARCHILS
ARCHIMAGE
ARCHIMAGES
ARCHIMANDRITE
ARCHIMANDRITES
ARCHINE
ARCHINES
ARCHING
ARCHINGS

ARCHIPELAGIAN
ARCHIPELAGIANS
ARCHIPELAGIC
ARCHIPELAGO
ARCHIPELAGOES
ARCHIPELAGOS
ARCHIPHONEME
ARCHIPHONEMES
ARCHIPLASM
ARCHIPLASMIC
ARCHITECT
ARCHITECTED
ARCHITECTING
ARCHITECTONIC
ARCHITECTONICS
ARCHITECTS
ARCHITECTURAL
ARCHITECTURALLY
ARCHITECTURE
ARCHITECTURES
ARCHITRAVE
ARCHITRAVED
ARCHITRAVES
ARCHITYPE
ARCHITYPES
ARCHIVAL
ARCHIVE
ARCHIVED
ARCHIVES
ARCHIVING
ARCHIVIST
ARCHIVISTS
ARCHIVOLT
ARCHIVOLTS
ARCHLET
ARCHLETS
ARCHLUTE
ARCHLUTES
ARCHLY
ARCHNESS
ARCHNESSES
ARCHOLOGIES
ARCHOLOGY
ARCHON
ARCHONS
ARCHONSHIP
ARCHONSHIPS
ARCHONTATE
ARCHONTATES
ARCHONTIC
ARCHOPLASM
ARCHOPLASMIC
ARCHOSAUR
ARCHOSAURIAN
ARCHOSAURS
ARCHPRIEST

ARCHPRIESTHOOD
ARCHPRIESTHOODS
ARCHPRIESTS
ARCHPRIESTSHIP
ARCHPRIESTSHIPS
ARCHWAY
ARCHWAYS
ARCHWISE
ARCIFORM
ARCING
ARCINGS
ARCKED
ARCKING
ARCKINGS
ARCO
ARCOGRAPH
ARCOGRAPHS
ARCOLOGIES
ARCOLOGY
ARCS
ARCSECOND
ARCSECONDS
ARCSIN
ARCSINE
ARCSINES
ARCSINS
ARCTAN
ARCTANGENT
ARCTANGENTS
ARCTANS
ARCTIC
ARCTICALLY
ARCTICS
ARCTIID
ARCTIIDS
ARCTOID
ARCTOPHIL
ARCTOPHILE
ARCTOPHILES
ARCTOPHILIA
ARCTOPHILIAS
ARCTOPHILIES
ARCTOPHILIST
ARCTOPHILISTS
ARCTOPHILS
ARCTOPHILY
ARCUATE
ARCUATED
ARCUATELY
ARCUATION
ARCUATIONS
ARCUBALIST
ARCUBALISTS
ARCUS
ARCUSES
ARD

ARDEB
ARDEBS
ARDENCIES
ARDENCY
ARDENT
ARDENTLY
ARDOR
ARDORS
ARDOUR
ARDOURS
ARDRI
ARDRIGH
ARDRIGHS
ARDRIS
ARDS
ARDUOUS
ARDUOUSLY
ARDUOUSNESS
ARDUOUSNESSES
ARE
AREA
AREACH
AREACHED
AREACHES
AREACHING
AREAD
AREADING
AREADS
AREAE
AREAL
AREALLY
AREAR
AREAS
AREAWAY
AREAWAYS
ARECA
ARECAS
ARECOLINE
ARECOLINES
ARED
AREDD
AREDE
AREDES
AREDING
AREFACTION
AREFACTIONS
AREFIED
AREFIES
AREFY
AREFYING
AREG
AREIC
ARENA
ARENACEOUS
ARENAS
ARENATION

ARENATIONS
ARENE
ARENES
ARENICOLOUS
ARENITE
ARENITES
ARENITIC
ARENOSE
ARENOUS
AREOCENTRIC
AREOGRAPHIC
AREOGRAPHIES
AREOGRAPHY
AREOLA
AREOLAE
AREOLAR
AREOLAS
AREOLATE
AREOLATED
AREOLATION
AREOLATIONS
AREOLE
AREOLES
AREOLOGIES
AREOLOGY
AREOMETER
AREOMETERS
AREOSTYLE
AREOSTYLES
AREOSYSTILE
AREOSYSTILES
ARERE
ARES
ARET
ARETE
ARETES
ARETHUSA
ARETHUSAS
ARETS
ARETT
ARETTED
ARETTING
ARETTS
AREW
ARF
ARFS
ARFVEDSONITE
ARFVEDSONITES
ARGAL
ARGALA
ARGALAS
ARGALI
ARGALIS
ARGALS
ARGAN
ARGAND

ARGANDS
ARGANS
ARGEMONE
ARGEMONES
ARGENT
ARGENTAL
ARGENTIC
ARGENTIFEROUS
ARGENTINE
ARGENTINES
ARGENTITE
ARGENTITES
ARGENTOUS
ARGENTS
ARGENTUM
ARGENTUMS
ARGHAN
ARGHANS
ARGIL
ARGILLACEOUS
ARGILLIFEROUS
ARGILLITE
ARGILLITES
ARGILLITIC
ARGILS
ARGINASE
ARGINASES
ARGININE
ARGININES
ARGLE
ARGLED
ARGLES
ARGLING
ARGOL
ARGOLS
ARGON
ARGONAUT
ARGONAUTIC
ARGONAUTS
ARGONON
ARGONONS
ARGONS
ARGOSIES
ARGOSY
ARGOT
ARGOTIC
ARGOTS
ARGUABLE
ARGUABLY
ARGUE
ARGUED
ARGUER
ARGUERS
ARGUES
ARGUFIED
ARGUFIER

ARGUFIERS
ARGUFIES
ARGUFY
ARGUFYING
ARGUING
ARGULI
ARGULUS
ARGUMENT
ARGUMENTA
ARGUMENTATION
ARGUMENTATIONS
ARGUMENTATIVE
ARGUMENTATIVELY
ARGUMENTIVE
ARGUMENTS
ARGUMENTUM
ARGUMENTUMS
ARGUS
ARGUSES
ARGUTE
ARGUTELY
ARGUTENESS
ARGUTENESSES
ARGYLE
ARGYLES
ARGYLL
ARGYLLS
ARGYRIA
ARGYRIAS
ARGYRITE
ARGYRITES
ARGYRODITE
ARGYRODITES
ARHAT
ARHATS
ARHATSHIP
ARHATSHIPS
ARHYTHMIA
ARHYTHMIAS
ARHYTHMIC
ARIA
ARIAS
ARIBOFLAVINOSES
ARIBOFLAVINOSIS
ARID
ARIDER
ARIDEST
ARIDITIES
ARIDITY
ARIDLY
ARIDNESS
ARIDNESSES
ARIEL
ARIELS
ARIETTA
ARIETTAS

ARIETTE
ARIETTES
ARIGHT
ARIKI
ARIKIS
ARIL
ARILED
ARILLARY
ARILLATE
ARILLATED
ARILLI
ARILLODE
ARILLODES
ARILLOID
ARILLUS
ARILS
ARIOSE
ARIOSI
ARIOSO
ARIOSOS
ARIOT
ARIPPLE
ARIS
ARISE
ARISEN
ARISES
ARISH
ARISHES
ARISING
ARISTA
ARISTAE
ARISTAS
ARISTATE
ARISTO
ARISTOCRACIES
ARISTOCRACY
ARISTOCRAT
ARISTOCRATIC
ARISTOCRATICAL
ARISTOCRATISM
ARISTOCRATISMS
ARISTOCRATS
ARISTOLOCHIA
ARISTOLOCHIAS
ARISTOLOGIES
ARISTOLOGY
ARISTOS
ARISTOTLE
ARISTOTLES
ARITHMETIC
ARITHMETICAL
ARITHMETICALLY
ARITHMETICIAN
ARITHMETICIANS
ARITHMETICS
ARITHMOMANIA

ARITHMOMANIAS
ARITHMOMETER
ARITHMOMETERS
ARITHMOPHOBIA
ARITHMOPHOBIAS
ARK
ARKED
ARKING
ARKITE
ARKITES
ARKOSE
ARKOSES
ARKOSIC
ARKS
ARLE
ARLED
ARLES
ARLING
ARM
ARMADA
ARMADAS
ARMADILLO
ARMADILLOS
ARMAGNAC
ARMAGNACS
ARMAMENT
ARMAMENTARIA
ARMAMENTARIUM
ARMAMENTARIUMS
ARMAMENTS
ARMATURE
ARMATURED
ARMATURES
ARMATURING
ARMBAND
ARMBANDS
ARMCHAIR
ARMCHAIRS
ARMED
ARMER
ARMERIA
ARMERS
ARMET
ARMETS
ARMFUL
ARMFULS
ARMGAUNT
ARMHOLE
ARMHOLES
ARMIES
ARMIGER
ARMIGERAL
ARMIGERO
ARMIGEROS
ARMIGEROUS
ARMIGERS

ARMIL
ARMILLA
ARMILLAE
ARMILLARIA
ARMILLARIAS
ARMILLARY
ARMILLAS
ARMILS
ARMING
ARMINGS
ARMIPOTENCE
ARMIPOTENCES
ARMIPOTENT
ARMISTICE
ARMISTICES
ARMLESS
ARMLET
ARMLETS
ARMLIKE
ARMLOAD
ARMLOADS
ARMLOCK
ARMLOCKED
ARMLOCKING
ARMLOCKS
ARMOIRE
ARMOIRES
ARMONICA
ARMONICAS
ARMOR
ARMORED
ARMORER
ARMORERS
ARMORIAL
ARMORIALLY
ARMORIALS
ARMORIES
ARMORING
ARMORIST
ARMORISTS
ARMORLESS
ARMORS
ARMORY
ARMOUR
ARMOURED
ARMOURER
ARMOURERS
ARMOURIES
ARMOURING
ARMOURLESS
ARMOURS
ARMOURY
ARMOZEEN
ARMOZEENS
ARMOZINE
ARMOZINES

ARMPIT
ARMPITS
ARMREST
ARMRESTS
ARMS
ARMSFUL
ARMURE
ARMURES
ARMY
ARMYWORM
ARMYWORMS
ARNA
ARNAS
ARNATTO
ARNATTOS
ARNICA
ARNICAS
ARNOTTO
ARNOTTOS
ARNUT
ARNUTS
AROBA
AROBAS
AROHA
AROID
AROIDS
AROINT
AROINTED
AROINTING
AROINTS
AROLLA
AROLLAS
AROMA
AROMAS
AROMATHERAPIES
AROMATHERAPIST
AROMATHERAPISTS
AROMATHERAPY
AROMATIC
AROMATICALLY
AROMATICITIES
AROMATICITY
AROMATICS
AROMATISATION
AROMATISATIONS
AROMATISE
AROMATISED
AROMATISES
AROMATISING
AROMATIZATION
AROMATIZATIONS
AROMATIZE
AROMATIZED
AROMATIZES
AROMATIZING
AROSE

AROUND
AROUSAL
AROUSALS
AROUSE
AROUSED
AROUSER
AROUSERS
AROUSES
AROUSING
AROW
AROYNT
AROYNTED
AROYNTING
AROYNTS
ARPA
ARPEGGIATE
ARPEGGIATED
ARPEGGIATES
ARPEGGIATING
ARPEGGIATION
ARPEGGIATIONS
ARPEGGIO
ARPEGGIONE
ARPEGGIONES
ARPEGGIOS
ARPEN
ARPENS
ARPENT
ARPENTS
ARPILLERA
ARPILLERAS
ARQUEBUS
ARQUEBUSADE
ARQUEBUSADES
ARQUEBUSES
ARQUEBUSIER
ARQUEBUSIERS
ARRACACHA
ARRACACHAS
ARRACK
ARRACKS
ARRAGONITE
ARRAGONITES
ARRAH
ARRAIGN
ARRAIGNED
ARRAIGNER
ARRAIGNERS
ARRAIGNING
ARRAIGNINGS
ARRAIGNMENT
ARRAIGNMENTS
ARRAIGNS
ARRANGE
ARRANGEABILITY
ARRANGEABLE

ARRANGED
ARRANGEMENT
ARRANGEMENTS
ARRANGER
ARRANGERS
ARRANGES
ARRANGING
ARRANT
ARRANTLY
ARRAS
ARRASED
ARRASENE
ARRASENES
ARRASES
ARRAUGHT
ARRAY
ARRAYAL
ARRAYALS
ARRAYED
ARRAYER
ARRAYERS
ARRAYING
ARRAYMENT
ARRAYMENTS
ARRAYS
ARREAR
ARREARAGE
ARREARAGES
ARREARS
ARRECT
ARREEDE
ARREEDES
ARREEDING
ARREST
ARRESTABLE
ARRESTANT
ARRESTANTS
ARRESTATION
ARRESTATIONS
ARRESTED
ARRESTEE
ARRESTEES
ARRESTER
ARRESTERS
ARRESTING
ARRESTINGLY
ARRESTIVE
ARRESTMENT
ARRESTMENTS
ARRESTOR
ARRESTORS
ARRESTS
ARRET
ARRETS
ARRHENOTOKIES
ARRHENOTOKY

ARRHIZAL
ARRHYTHMIA
ARRHYTHMIAS
ARRHYTHMIC
ARRIAGE
ARRIAGES
ARRIDE
ARRIDED
ARRIDES
ARRIDING
ARRIERE
ARRIERO
ARRIEROS
ARRIS
ARRISES
ARRISH
ARRISHES
ARRIVAL
ARRIVALS
ARRIVANCE
ARRIVANCES
ARRIVANCIES
ARRIVANCY
ARRIVE
ARRIVED
ARRIVEDERCI
ARRIVER
ARRIVERS
ARRIVES
ARRIVING
ARRIVISME
ARRIVISMES
ARRIVISTE
ARRIVISTES
ARROBA
ARROBAS
ARROGANCE
ARROGANCES
ARROGANT
ARROGANTLY
ARROGATE
ARROGATED
ARROGATES
ARROGATING
ARROGATION
ARROGATIONS
ARROGATIVE
ARROGATIVELY
ARROGATOR
ARROGATORS
ARRONDISSEMENT
ARRONDISSEMENTS
ARROW
ARROWED
ARROWGRASS
ARROWGRASSES

ARROWHEAD
ARROWHEADS
ARROWING
ARROWROOT
ARROWROOTS
ARROWS
ARROWWOOD
ARROWWOODS
ARROWWORM
ARROWWORMS
ARROWY
ARROYO
ARROYOS
ARS
ARSE
ARSED
ARSEHOLE
ARSEHOLES
ARSENAL
ARSENALS
ARSENATE
ARSENATES
ARSENIATE
ARSENIATES
ARSENIC
ARSENICAL
ARSENICALS
ARSENICS
ARSENIDE
ARSENIDES
ARSENIOUS
ARSENITE
ARSENITES
ARSENO
ARSENOPYRITE
ARSENOPYRITES
ARSENOUS
ARSES
ARSEY
ARSHEEN
ARSHEENS
ARSHIN
ARSHINE
ARSHINES
ARSHINS
ARSIER
ARSIEST
ARSINE
ARSINES
ARSING
ARSINO
ARSIS
ARSMETRICKS
ARSON
ARSONIST
ARSONISTS

ARSONITE
ARSONITES
ARSONOUS
ARSONS
ARSPHENAMINE
ARSPHENAMINES
ART
ARTAL
ARTEFACT
ARTEFACTS
ARTEFACTUAL
ARTEL
ARTELS
ARTEMISIA
ARTEMISIAS
ARTEMISININ
ARTEMISININS
ARTERIAL
ARTERIALISATION
ARTERIALISE
ARTERIALISED
ARTERIALISES
ARTERIALISING
ARTERIALIZATION
ARTERIALIZE
ARTERIALIZED
ARTERIALIZES
ARTERIALIZING
ARTERIALLY
ARTERIALS
ARTERIES
ARTERIOGRAM
ARTERIOGRAMS
ARTERIOGRAPHIC
ARTERIOGRAPHIES
ARTERIOGRAPHY
ARTERIOLAR
ARTERIOLE
ARTERIOLES
ARTERIOTOMIES
ARTERIOTOMY
ARTERIOVENOUS
ARTERITIDES
ARTERITIS
ARTERITISES
ARTERY
ARTESIAN
ARTFUL
ARTFULLY
ARTFULNESS
ARTFULNESSES
ARTHRALGIA
ARTHRALGIAS
ARTHRALGIC
ARTHRECTOMIES
ARTHRECTOMY

ARTHRITIC
ARTHRITICALLY
ARTHRITICS
ARTHRITIDES
ARTHRITIS
ARTHRITISES
ARTHRODESES
ARTHRODESIS
ARTHRODIA
ARTHRODIAE
ARTHRODIAL
ARTHROGRAPHER
ARTHROGRAPHERS
ARTHROGRAPHIES
ARTHROGRAPHY
ARTHROMERE
ARTHROMERES
ARTHROMERIC
ARTHROPATHIES
ARTHROPATHY
ARTHROPLASTIES
ARTHROPLASTY
ARTHROPOD
ARTHROPODAL
ARTHROPODAN
ARTHROPODOUS
ARTHROPODS
ARTHROSCOPE
ARTHROSCOPES
ARTHROSCOPIC
ARTHROSCOPIES
ARTHROSCOPY
ARTHROSES
ARTHROSIS
ARTHROSPORE
ARTHROSPORES
ARTHROSPORIC
ARTHROSPOROUS
ARTI
ARTIC
ARTICHOKE
ARTICHOKES
ARTICLE
ARTICLED
ARTICLES
ARTICLING
ARTICS
ARTICULABLE
ARTICULACIES
ARTICULACY
ARTICULAR
ARTICULATE
ARTICULATED
ARTICULATELY
ARTICULATENESS
ARTICULATES

ARTICULATING
ARTICULATION
ARTICULATIONS
ARTICULATIVE
ARTICULATOR
ARTICULATORS
ARTICULATORY
ARTIER
ARTIES
ARTIEST
ARTIFACT
ARTIFACTS
ARTIFACTUAL
ARTIFICE
ARTIFICER
ARTIFICERS
ARTIFICES
ARTIFICIAL
ARTIFICIALISE
ARTIFICIALISED
ARTIFICIALISES
ARTIFICIALISING
ARTIFICIALITIES
ARTIFICIALITY
ARTIFICIALIZE
ARTIFICIALIZED
ARTIFICIALIZES
ARTIFICIALIZING
ARTIFICIALLY
ARTIFICIALNESS
ARTILLERIES
ARTILLERIST
ARTILLERISTS
ARTILLERY
ARTILLERYMAN
ARTILLERYMEN
ARTILY
ARTINESS
ARTINESSES
ARTIODACTYL
ARTIODACTYLOUS
ARTIODACTYLS
ARTISAN
ARTISANAL
ARTISANS
ARTISANSHIP
ARTISANSHIPS
ARTIST
ARTISTE
ARTISTES
ARTISTIC
ARTISTICAL
ARTISTICALLY
ARTISTRIES
ARTISTRY
ARTISTS

ARTLESS
ARTLESSLY
ARTLESSNESS
ARTLESSNESSES
ARTOCARPUS
ARTOCARPUSES
ARTS
ARTSIER
ARTSIES
ARTSIEST
ARTSMAN
ARTSMEN
ARTSY
ARTWORK
ARTWORKS
ARTY
ARUGOLA
ARUGOLAS
ARUGULA
ARUGULAS
ARUM
ARUMS
ARUNDINACEOUS
ARUSPEX
ARUSPICES
ARVAL
ARVICOLE
ARVICOLES
ARVICOLINE
ARVO
ARVOS
ARY
ARYBALLOID
ARYBALLOS
ARYBALLOSES
ARYL
ARYLS
ARYTAENOID
ARYTAENOIDS
ARYTENOID
ARYTENOIDAL
ARYTENOIDS
ARYTHMIA
ARYTHMIAS
ARYTHMIC
AS
ASAFETIDA
ASAFETIDAS
ASAFOETIDA
ASAFOETIDAS
ASANA
ASANAS
ASAR
ASARABACCA
ASARABACCAS
ASARUM

ASARUMS
ASBESTIC
ASBESTIFORM
ASBESTINE
ASBESTOS
ASBESTOSES
ASBESTOSIS
ASBESTOUS
ASBESTUS
ASBESTUSES
ASCARIASES
ASCARIASIS
ASCARID
ASCARIDES
ASCARIDS
ASCARIS
ASCAUNT
ASCEND
ASCENDABLE
ASCENDANCE
ASCENDANCES
ASCENDANCIES
ASCENDANCY
ASCENDANT
ASCENDANTLY
ASCENDANTS
ASCENDED
ASCENDENCE
ASCENDENCES
ASCENDENCIES
ASCENDENCY
ASCENDENT
ASCENDENTS
ASCENDER
ASCENDERS
ASCENDEUR
ASCENDEURS
ASCENDIBLE
ASCENDING
ASCENDS
ASCENSION
ASCENSIONAL
ASCENSIONIST
ASCENSIONISTS
ASCENSIONS
ASCENSIVE
ASCENT
ASCENTS
ASCERTAIN
ASCERTAINABLE
ASCERTAINABLY
ASCERTAINED
ASCERTAINING
ASCERTAINMENT
ASCERTAINMENTS
ASCERTAINS

ASCESES
ASCESIS
ASCETIC
ASCETICAL
ASCETICALLY
ASCETICISM
ASCETICISMS
ASCETICS
ASCI
ASCIAN
ASCIANS
ASCIDIA
ASCIDIAN
ASCIDIANS
ASCIDIUM
ASCITES
ASCITIC
ASCITICAL
ASCITITIOUS
ASCLEPIAD
ASCLEPIADACEOUS
ASCLEPIADS
ASCLEPIAS
ASCLEPIASES
ASCOCARP
ASCOCARPIC
ASCOCARPS
ASCOGONIA
ASCOGONIUM
ASCOMYCETE
ASCOMYCETES
ASCOMYCETOUS
ASCONCE
ASCORBATE
ASCORBATES
ASCORBIC
ASCOSPORE
ASCOSPORES
ASCOSPORIC
ASCOT
ASCOTS
ASCRIBABLE
ASCRIBE
ASCRIBED
ASCRIBES
ASCRIBING
ASCRIPTION
ASCRIPTIONS
ASCRIPTIVE
ASCUS
ASDIC
ASDICS
ASEA
ASEISMIC
ASEITIES
ASEITY

ASEPALOUS
ASEPSES
ASEPSIS
ASEPTATE
ASEPTIC
ASEPTICALLY
ASEPTICISE
ASEPTICISED
ASEPTICISES
ASEPTICISING
ASEPTICISM
ASEPTICISMS
ASEPTICIZE
ASEPTICIZED
ASEPTICIZES
ASEPTICIZING
ASEPTICS
ASEXUAL
ASEXUALITIES
ASEXUALITY
ASEXUALLY
ASH
ASHAKE
ASHAME
ASHAMED
ASHAMEDLY
ASHAMEDNESS
ASHAMEDNESSES
ASHAMES
ASHAMING
ASHCAN
ASHCANS
ASHED
ASHEN
ASHERIES
ASHERY
ASHES
ASHET
ASHETS
ASHFALL
ASHFALLS
ASHIER
ASHIEST
ASHINE
ASHINESS
ASHINESSES
ASHING
ASHIVER
ASHKEY
ASHKEYS
ASHLAR
ASHLARED
ASHLARING
ASHLARINGS
ASHLARS
ASHLER

ASHLERED
ASHLERING
ASHLERINGS
ASHLERS
ASHLESS
ASHMAN
ASHMEN
ASHORE
ASHPLANT
ASHPLANTS
ASHRAF
ASHRAM
ASHRAMA
ASHRAMAS
ASHRAMITE
ASHRAMITES
ASHRAMS
ASHTRAY
ASHTRAYS
ASHY
ASIAGI
ASIAGO
ASIDE
ASIDES
ASINICO
ASINICOS
ASININE
ASININELY
ASININITIES
ASININITY
ASK
ASKANCE
ASKANCED
ASKANCES
ASKANCING
ASKANT
ASKANTED
ASKANTING
ASKANTS
ASKARI
ASKARIS
ASKED
ASKER
ASKERS
ASKESES
ASKESIS
ASKEW
ASKEWNESS
ASKEWNESSES
ASKING
ASKINGS
ASKLENT
ASKOI
ASKOS
ASKS
ASLAKE

ASLAKED
ASLAKES
ASLAKING
ASLANT
ASLEEP
ASLOPE
ASMEAR
ASMOULDER
ASOCIAL
ASP
ASPARAGINASE
ASPARAGINASES
ASPARAGINE
ASPARAGINES
ASPARAGUS
ASPARAGUSES
ASPARKLE
ASPARTAME
ASPARTAMES
ASPARTATE
ASPARTATES
ASPARTIC
ASPECT
ASPECTABLE
ASPECTED
ASPECTING
ASPECTS
ASPECTUAL
ASPEN
ASPENDICITIS
ASPENS
ASPER
ASPERATE
ASPERATED
ASPERATES
ASPERATING
ASPERGATION
ASPERGATIONS
ASPERGE
ASPERGED
ASPERGER
ASPERGERS
ASPERGES
ASPERGILL
ASPERGILLA
ASPERGILLI
ASPERGILLOSES
ASPERGILLOSIS
ASPERGILLS
ASPERGILLUM
ASPERGILLUMS
ASPERGILLUS
ASPERGING
ASPERITIES
ASPERITY
ASPERMIA

ASPERMIC
ASPEROUS
ASPERS
ASPERSE
ASPERSED
ASPERSER
ASPERSERS
ASPERSES
ASPERSING
ASPERSION
ASPERSIONS
ASPERSIVE
ASPERSIVELY
ASPERSIVENESS
ASPERSOIR
ASPERSOIRS
ASPERSOR
ASPERSORIA
ASPERSORIES
ASPERSORIUM
ASPERSORIUMS
ASPERSORS
ASPERSORY
ASPHALT
ASPHALTED
ASPHALTER
ASPHALTERS
ASPHALTIC
ASPHALTING
ASPHALTITE
ASPHALTITES
ASPHALTS
ASPHALTUM
ASPHALTUMS
ASPHERIC
ASPHERICAL
ASPHETERISE
ASPHETERISED
ASPHETERISES
ASPHETERISING
ASPHETERISM
ASPHETERISMS
ASPHETERIZE
ASPHETERIZED
ASPHETERIZES
ASPHETERIZING
ASPHODEL
ASPHODELS
ASPHYXIA
ASPHYXIAL
ASPHYXIANT
ASPHYXIANTS
ASPHYXIAS
ASPHYXIATE
ASPHYXIATED
ASPHYXIATES

ASPHYXIATING
ASPHYXIATION
ASPHYXIATIONS
ASPHYXIATOR
ASPHYXIATORS
ASPHYXIES
ASPHYXY
ASPIC
ASPICK
ASPICKS
ASPICS
ASPIDIA
ASPIDIOID
ASPIDISTRA
ASPIDISTRAS
ASPIDIUM
ASPINE
ASPINES
ASPIRANT
ASPIRANTS
ASPIRATA
ASPIRATAE
ASPIRATE
ASPIRATED
ASPIRATES
ASPIRATING
ASPIRATION
ASPIRATIONAL
ASPIRATIONS
ASPIRATOR
ASPIRATORS
ASPIRATORY
ASPIRE
ASPIRED
ASPIRER
ASPIRERS
ASPIRES
ASPIRIN
ASPIRING
ASPIRINGLY
ASPIRINGNESS
ASPIRINGNESSES
ASPIRINS
ASPIS
ASPISES
ASPISH
ASPLANCHNIC
ASPLENIUM
ASPLENIUMS
ASPORT
ASPORTATION
ASPORTATIONS
ASPORTED
ASPORTING
ASPORTS
ASPOUT

ASPRAWL
ASPREAD
ASPRO
ASPROS
ASPROUT
ASPS
ASQUAT
ASQUINT
ASRAMA
ASRAMAS
ASS
ASSAFETIDA
ASSAFETIDAS
ASSAFOETIDA
ASSAFOETIDAS
ASSAGAI
ASSAGAIED
ASSAGAIING
ASSAGAIS
ASSAI
ASSAIL
ASSAILABLE
ASSAILANT
ASSAILANTS
ASSAILED
ASSAILER
ASSAILERS
ASSAILING
ASSAILMENT
ASSAILMENTS
ASSAILS
ASSAIS
ASSAM
ASSAMS
ASSART
ASSARTED
ASSARTING
ASSARTS
ASSASSIN
ASSASSINATE
ASSASSINATED
ASSASSINATES
ASSASSINATING
ASSASSINATION
ASSASSINATIONS
ASSASSINATOR
ASSASSINATORS
ASSASSINS
ASSAULT
ASSAULTED
ASSAULTER
ASSAULTERS
ASSAULTING
ASSAULTIVE
ASSAULTIVELY
ASSAULTIVENESS

ASSAULTS
ASSAY
ASSAYABLE
ASSAYED
ASSAYER
ASSAYERS
ASSAYING
ASSAYINGS
ASSAYS
ASSEGAAI
ASSEGAAIED
ASSEGAAIING
ASSEGAAIS
ASSEGAI
ASSEGAIED
ASSEGAIING
ASSEGAIS
ASSEMBLAGE
ASSEMBLAGES
ASSEMBLAGIST
ASSEMBLAGISTS
ASSEMBLANCE
ASSEMBLANCES
ASSEMBLAUNCE
ASSEMBLAUNCES
ASSEMBLE
ASSEMBLED
ASSEMBLER
ASSEMBLERS
ASSEMBLES
ASSEMBLIES
ASSEMBLING
ASSEMBLY
ASSEMBLYMAN
ASSEMBLYMEN
ASSEMBLYWOMAN
ASSEMBLYWOMEN
ASSENT
ASSENTANEOUS
ASSENTATION
ASSENTATIONS
ASSENTATOR
ASSENTATORS
ASSENTED
ASSENTER
ASSENTERS
ASSENTIENT
ASSENTIENTS
ASSENTING
ASSENTINGLY
ASSENTIVE
ASSENTIVENESS
ASSENTIVENESSES
ASSENTOR
ASSENTORS
ASSENTS

ASSERT
ASSERTABLE
ASSERTED
ASSERTEDLY
ASSERTER
ASSERTERS
ASSERTIBILITY
ASSERTIBLE
ASSERTING
ASSERTION
ASSERTIONS
ASSERTIVE
ASSERTIVELY
ASSERTIVENESS
ASSERTIVENESSES
ASSERTOR
ASSERTORIC
ASSERTORICALLY
ASSERTORS
ASSERTORY
ASSERTS
ASSES
ASSESS
ASSESSABLE
ASSESSED
ASSESSES
ASSESSING
ASSESSMENT
ASSESSMENTS
ASSESSOR
ASSESSORIAL
ASSESSORS
ASSESSORSHIP
ASSESSORSHIPS
ASSET
ASSETS
ASSEVER
ASSEVERATE
ASSEVERATED
ASSEVERATES
ASSEVERATING
ASSEVERATINGLY
ASSEVERATION
ASSEVERATIONS
ASSEVERATIVE
ASSEVERED
ASSEVERING
ASSEVERS
ASSEZ
ASSHOLE
ASSHOLES
ASSIBILATE
ASSIBILATED
ASSIBILATES
ASSIBILATING
ASSIBILATION

ASSIBILATIONS
ASSIDUITIES
ASSIDUITY
ASSIDUOUS
ASSIDUOUSLY
ASSIDUOUSNESS
ASSIDUOUSNESSES
ASSIEGE
ASSIEGED
ASSIEGES
ASSIEGING
ASSIENTO
ASSIENTOS
ASSIGN
ASSIGNABILITIES
ASSIGNABILITY
ASSIGNABLE
ASSIGNABLY
ASSIGNAT
ASSIGNATION
ASSIGNATIONS
ASSIGNATS
ASSIGNED
ASSIGNEE
ASSIGNEES
ASSIGNER
ASSIGNERS
ASSIGNING
ASSIGNMENT
ASSIGNMENTS
ASSIGNOR
ASSIGNORS
ASSIGNS
ASSIMILABILITY
ASSIMILABLE
ASSIMILABLY
ASSIMILATE
ASSIMILATED
ASSIMILATES
ASSIMILATING
ASSIMILATION
ASSIMILATIONISM
ASSIMILATIONIST
ASSIMILATIONS
ASSIMILATIVE
ASSIMILATIVELY
ASSIMILATOR
ASSIMILATORS
ASSIMILATORY
ASSIST
ASSISTANCE
ASSISTANCES
ASSISTANT
ASSISTANTS
ASSISTANTSHIP
ASSISTANTSHIPS

ASSISTED
ASSISTER
ASSISTERS
ASSISTING
ASSISTIVE
ASSISTIVENESS
ASSISTOR
ASSISTORS
ASSISTS
ASSIZE
ASSIZED
ASSIZER
ASSIZERS
ASSIZES
ASSIZING
ASSLIKE
ASSOCIABILITIES
ASSOCIABILITY
ASSOCIABLE
ASSOCIATE
ASSOCIATED
ASSOCIATES
ASSOCIATESHIP
ASSOCIATESHIPS
ASSOCIATING
ASSOCIATION
ASSOCIATIONAL
ASSOCIATIONISM
ASSOCIATIONISMS
ASSOCIATIONIST
ASSOCIATIONISTS
ASSOCIATIONS
ASSOCIATIVE
ASSOCIATIVELY
ASSOCIATIVITIES
ASSOCIATIVITY
ASSOCIATOR
ASSOCIATORICAL
ASSOCIATORS
ASSOCIATORY
ASSOIL
ASSOILED
ASSOILING
ASSOILMENT
ASSOILMENTS
ASSOILS
ASSOILZIE
ASSOILZIED
ASSOILZIEING
ASSOILZIES
ASSONANCE
ASSONANCES
ASSONANT
ASSONANTAL
ASSONANTS
ASSONATE

ASSONATED
ASSONATES
ASSONATING
ASSORT
ASSORTATIVE
ASSORTATIVELY
ASSORTED
ASSORTEDNESS
ASSORTEDNESSES
ASSORTER
ASSORTERS
ASSORTING
ASSORTIVE
ASSORTIVENESS
ASSORTMENT
ASSORTMENTS
ASSORTS
ASSOT
ASSOTS
ASSOTT
ASSOTTED
ASSOTTING
ASSUAGE
ASSUAGED
ASSUAGEMENT
ASSUAGEMENTS
ASSUAGER
ASSUAGERS
ASSUAGES
ASSUAGING
ASSUAGINGS
ASSUASIVE
ASSUBJUGATE
ASSUBJUGATED
ASSUBJUGATES
ASSUBJUGATING
ASSUEFACTION
ASSUEFACTIONS
ASSUETUDE
ASSUETUDES
ASSUMABILITIES
ASSUMABILITY
ASSUMABLE
ASSUMABLY
ASSUME
ASSUMED
ASSUMEDLY
ASSUMER
ASSUMERS
ASSUMES
ASSUMING
ASSUMINGLY
ASSUMINGS
ASSUMPSIT
ASSUMPSITS
ASSUMPTION

ASSUMPTIONS
ASSUMPTIVE
ASSUMPTIVELY
ASSURABLE
ASSURANCE
ASSURANCES
ASSURE
ASSURED
ASSUREDLY
ASSUREDNESS
ASSUREDNESSES
ASSUREDS
ASSURER
ASSURERS
ASSURES
ASSURGENCIES
ASSURGENCY
ASSURGENT
ASSURING
ASSUROR
ASSURORS
ASSWAGE
ASSWAGED
ASSWAGES
ASSWAGING
ASSYTHMENT
ASSYTHMENTS
ASTABLE
ASTACOLOGIES
ASTACOLOGIST
ASTACOLOGISTS
ASTACOLOGY
ASTARBOARD
ASTARE
ASTART
ASTARTED
ASTARTING
ASTARTS
ASTASIA
ASTASIAS
ASTASTIDES
ASTATIC
ASTATICALLY
ASTATICISM
ASTATIDE
ASTATINE
ASTATINES
ASTATKI
ASTATKIS
ASTEISM
ASTEISMS
ASTELIC
ASTELIES
ASTELY
ASTER
ASTEREOGNOSIS

ASTERIA
ASTERIAS
ASTERIATED
ASTERID
ASTERIDIAN
ASTERIDIANS
ASTERIDS
ASTERISK
ASTERISKED
ASTERISKING
ASTERISKLESS
ASTERISKS
ASTERISM
ASTERISMS
ASTERN
ASTERNAL
ASTEROID
ASTEROIDAL
ASTEROIDEAN
ASTEROIDEANS
ASTEROIDS
ASTERS
ASTERT
ASTERTED
ASTERTING
ASTERTS
ASTHENIA
ASTHENIAS
ASTHENIC
ASTHENICS
ASTHENIES
ASTHENOPIA
ASTHENOPIC
ASTHENOSPHERE
ASTHENOSPHERES
ASTHENOSPHERIC
ASTHENY
ASTHMA
ASTHMAS
ASTHMATIC
ASTHMATICAL
ASTHMATICALLY
ASTHMATICS
ASTHORE
ASTHORES
ASTICHOUS
ASTIGMATIC
ASTIGMATICALLY
ASTIGMATICS
ASTIGMATISM
ASTIGMATISMS
ASTIGMIA
ASTIGMIAS
ASTILBE
ASTILBES
ASTIR

ASTOMATOUS
ASTOMOUS
ASTONE
ASTONED
ASTONES
ASTONIED
ASTONIES
ASTONING
ASTONISH
ASTONISHED
ASTONISHES
ASTONISHING
ASTONISHINGLY
ASTONISHMENT
ASTONISHMENTS
ASTONY
ASTONYING
ASTOOP
ASTOUND
ASTOUNDED
ASTOUNDING
ASTOUNDINGLY
ASTOUNDMENT
ASTOUNDMENTS
ASTOUNDS
ASTRADDLE
ASTRAGAL
ASTRAGALI
ASTRAGALS
ASTRAGALUS
ASTRAGALUSES
ASTRAKHAN
ASTRAKHANS
ASTRAL
ASTRALLY
ASTRALS
ASTRAND
ASTRANTIA
ASTRANTIAS
ASTRAPHOBIA
ASTRAPHOBIAS
ASTRAPHOBIC
ASTRAPOPHOBIA
ASTRAPOPHOBIAS
ASTRAY
ASTRICT
ASTRICTED
ASTRICTING
ASTRICTION
ASTRICTIONS
ASTRICTIVE
ASTRICTIVELY
ASTRICTIVENESS
ASTRICTS
ASTRIDE
ASTRINGE

ASTRINGED
ASTRINGENCE
ASTRINGENCIES
ASTRINGENCY
ASTRINGENT
ASTRINGENTLY
ASTRINGENTS
ASTRINGER
ASTRINGERS
ASTRINGES
ASTRINGING
ASTROBIOLOGIES
ASTROBIOLOGIST
ASTROBIOLOGISTS
ASTROBIOLOGY
ASTROBLEME
ASTROBLEMES
ASTROBOTANICAL
ASTROBOTANIST
ASTROBOTANISTS
ASTROBOTANY
ASTROCHEMISTRY
ASTROCOMPASS
ASTROCOMPASSES
ASTROCYTE
ASTROCYTES
ASTROCYTIC
ASTROCYTOMA
ASTROCYTOMAS
ASTROCYTOMATA
ASTRODOME
ASTRODOMES
ASTRODYNAMICIST
ASTRODYNAMICS
ASTROFELL
ASTROFELLS
ASTROGEOLOGIES
ASTROGEOLOGIST
ASTROGEOLOGISTS
ASTROGEOLOGY
ASTROHATCH
ASTROHATCHES
ASTROID
ASTROIDS
ASTROLABE
ASTROLABES
ASTROLATRIES
ASTROLATRY
ASTROLOGER
ASTROLOGERS
ASTROLOGIC
ASTROLOGICAL
ASTROLOGICALLY
ASTROLOGIES
ASTROLOGIST
ASTROLOGISTS

ASTROLOGY
ASTROMETRIC
ASTROMETRICAL
ASTROMETRICALLY
ASTROMETRIES
ASTROMETRY
ASTRONAUT
ASTRONAUTIC
ASTRONAUTICAL
ASTRONAUTICALLY
ASTRONAUTICS
ASTRONAUTS
ASTRONAVIGATION
ASTRONAVIGATOR
ASTRONAVIGATORS
ASTRONOMER
ASTRONOMERS
ASTRONOMIC
ASTRONOMICAL
ASTRONOMICALLY
ASTRONOMIES
ASTRONOMISE
ASTRONOMISED
ASTRONOMISES
ASTRONOMISING
ASTRONOMIZE
ASTRONOMIZED
ASTRONOMIZES
ASTRONOMIZING
ASTRONOMY
ASTROPHEL
ASTROPHELS
ASTROPHOBIA
ASTROPHOBIC
ASTROPHOTOGRAPH
ASTROPHYSICAL
ASTROPHYSICALLY
ASTROPHYSICIST
ASTROPHYSICISTS
ASTROPHYSICS
ASTROSPHERE
ASTROSPHERES
ASTROTOURIST
ASTROTOURISTS
ASTRUT
ASTUCIOUS
ASTUCIOUSLY
ASTUCITIES
ASTUCITY
ASTUN
ASTUNNED
ASTUNNING
ASTUNS
ASTUTE
ASTUTELY
ASTUTENESS

ASTUTENESSES
ASTUTER
ASTUTEST
ASTYLAR
ASUDDEN
ASUNDER
ASWARM
ASWAY
ASWIM
ASWING
ASWIRL
ASWOON
ASYLA
ASYLLABIC
ASYLLABICALLY
ASYLUM
ASYLUMS
ASYMMETRIC
ASYMMETRICAL
ASYMMETRICALLY
ASYMMETRIES
ASYMMETRY
ASYMPTOMATIC
ASYMPTOTE
ASYMPTOTES
ASYMPTOTIC
ASYMPTOTICAL
ASYMPTOTICALLY
ASYNAPSES
ASYNAPSIS
ASYNARTETE
ASYNARTETES
ASYNARTETIC
ASYNCHRONIES
ASYNCHRONISM
ASYNCHRONISMS
ASYNCHRONOUS
ASYNCHRONOUSLY
ASYNCHRONY
ASYNDETA
ASYNDETIC
ASYNDETICALLY
ASYNDETON
ASYNDETONS
ASYNERGIA
ASYNERGIAS
ASYNERGIES
ASYNERGY
ASYNTACTIC
ASYSTOLE
ASYSTOLES
ASYSTOLIC
ASYSTOLICALLY
ASYSTOLISM
ASYSTOLISMS
AT

ATABAL
ATABALS
ATABEG
ATABEGS
ATABEK
ATABEKS
ATABRIN
ATABRINS
ATACAMITE
ATACAMITES
ATACTIC
ATAGHAN
ATAGHANS
ATALAYA
ATALAYAS
ATAMAN
ATAMANS
ATAMASCO
ATAMASCOS
ATAP
ATAPS
ATARACTIC
ATARACTICS
ATARAXIA
ATARAXIAS
ATARAXIC
ATARAXICS
ATARAXIES
ATARAXY
ATAVIC
ATAVISM
ATAVISMS
ATAVIST
ATAVISTIC
ATAVISTICALLY
ATAVISTS
ATAXIA
ATAXIAS
ATAXIC
ATAXICS
ATAXIES
ATAXY
ATCHIEVE
ATCHIEVED
ATCHIEVES
ATCHIEVING
ATE
ATEBRIN
ATEBRINS
ATECHNIC
ATELECTASES
ATELECTASIS
ATELECTATIC
ATELEIOSES
ATELEIOSIS
ATELIC

ATELIER
ATELIERS
ATEMOYA
ATEMOYAS
ATEMPORAL
ATES
ATHAME
ATHAMES
ATHANASIES
ATHANASY
ATHANOR
ATHANORS
ATHEISE
ATHEISED
ATHEISES
ATHEISING
ATHEISM
ATHEISMS
ATHEIST
ATHEISTIC
ATHEISTICAL
ATHEISTICALLY
ATHEISTS
ATHEIZE
ATHEIZED
ATHEIZES
ATHEIZING
ATHELING
ATHELINGS
ATHEMATIC
ATHEMATICALLY
ATHENAEUM
ATHENAEUMS
ATHENEUM
ATHENEUMS
ATHEOLOGICAL
ATHEOLOGIES
ATHEOLOGY
ATHEORETICAL
ATHEOUS
ATHERINE
ATHERINES
ATHERMANCIES
ATHERMANCY
ATHERMANOUS
ATHEROGENESES
ATHEROGENESIS
ATHEROGENIC
ATHEROMA
ATHEROMAS
ATHEROMATA
ATHEROMATOUS
ATHEROSCLEROSES
ATHEROSCLEROSIS
ATHEROSCLEROTIC
ATHETESES

ATHETESIS
ATHETISE
ATHETISED
ATHETISES
ATHETISING
ATHETIZE
ATHETIZED
ATHETIZES
ATHETIZING
ATHETOID
ATHETOSES
ATHETOSIC
ATHETOSIS
ATHETOTIC
ATHIRST
ATHLETA
ATHLETAS
ATHLETE
ATHLETES
ATHLETIC
ATHLETICALLY
ATHLETICISM
ATHLETICISMS
ATHLETICS
ATHODYD
ATHODYDS
ATHRILL
ATHROB
ATHROCYTE
ATHROCYTES
ATHROCYTOSES
ATHROCYTOSIS
ATHWART
ATHWARTSHIP
ATHWARTSHIPS
ATIGI
ATIGIS
ATILT
ATIMIES
ATIMY
ATINGLE
ATISHOO
ATISHOOS
ATLANTES
ATLAS
ATLASES
ATLATL
ATLATLS
ATMA
ATMAN
ATMANS
ATMAS
ATMOLOGIES
ATMOLOGIST
ATMOLOGISTS
ATMOLOGY

ATMOLYSE
ATMOLYSED
ATMOLYSES
ATMOLYSING
ATMOLYSIS
ATMOLYZE
ATMOLYZED
ATMOLYZES
ATMOLYZING
ATMOMETER
ATMOMETERS
ATMOMETRICAL
ATMOMETRICALLY
ATMOMETRY
ATMOSPHERE
ATMOSPHERED
ATMOSPHERES
ATMOSPHERIC
ATMOSPHERICAL
ATMOSPHERICALLY
ATMOSPHERICS
ATOC
ATOCIA
ATOCIAS
ATOCS
ATOK
ATOKAL
ATOKE
ATOKES
ATOKOUS
ATOKS
ATOLL
ATOLLS
ATOM
ATOMIC
ATOMICAL
ATOMICALLY
ATOMICITIES
ATOMICITY
ATOMICS
ATOMIES
ATOMISATION
ATOMISATIONS
ATOMISE
ATOMISED
ATOMISER
ATOMISERS
ATOMISES
ATOMISING
ATOMISM
ATOMISMS
ATOMIST
ATOMISTIC
ATOMISTICAL
ATOMISTICALLY
ATOMISTS

ATOMIZATION
ATOMIZATIONS
ATOMIZE
ATOMIZED
ATOMIZER
ATOMIZERS
ATOMIZES
ATOMIZING
ATOMS
ATOMY
ATONABLE
ATONAL
ATONALISM
ATONALISMS
ATONALIST
ATONALISTS
ATONALITIES
ATONALITY
ATONALLY
ATONE
ATONEABLE
ATONED
ATONEMENT
ATONEMENTS
ATONER
ATONERS
ATONES
ATONIC
ATONICITIES
ATONICITY
ATONICS
ATONIES
ATONING
ATONINGLY
ATONY
ATOP
ATOPIC
ATOPIES
ATOPY
ATRABILIAR
ATRABILIOUS
ATRABILIOUSNESS
ATRACURIUM
ATRACURIUMS
ATRAMENT
ATRAMENTAL
ATRAMENTOUS
ATRAMENTS
ATRAZINE
ATRAZINES
ATREMBLE
ATRESIA
ATRESIAS
ATRIA
ATRIAL
ATRIP

ATRIUM
ATRIUMS
ATROCIOUS
ATROCIOUSLY
ATROCIOUSNESS
ATROCIOUSNESSES
ATROCITIES
ATROCITY
ATROPHIA
ATROPHIAS
ATROPHIC
ATROPHIED
ATROPHIES
ATROPHY
ATROPHYING
ATROPIA
ATROPIAS
ATROPIN
ATROPINE
ATROPINES
ATROPINS
ATROPISM
ATROPISMS
ATROPOUS
ATT
ATTABOY
ATTACH
ATTACHABLE
ATTACHE
ATTACHED
ATTACHER
ATTACHERS
ATTACHES
ATTACHING
ATTACHMENT
ATTACHMENTS
ATTACK
ATTACKABLE
ATTACKED
ATTACKER
ATTACKERS
ATTACKING
ATTACKMAN
ATTACKMEN
ATTACKS
ATTAIN
ATTAINABILITIES
ATTAINABILITY
ATTAINABLE
ATTAINABLENESS
ATTAINDER
ATTAINDERS
ATTAINED
ATTAINER
ATTAINERS
ATTAINING

ATTAINMENT	ATTENTIONS	ATTITUDINISERS	ATTRACTS
ATTAINMENTS	ATTENTIVE	ATTITUDINISES	ATTRAHENS
ATTAINS	ATTENTIVELY	ATTITUDINISING	ATTRAHENT
ATTAINT	ATTENTIVENESS	ATTITUDINISINGS	ATTRAHENTS
ATTAINTED	ATTENTIVENESSES	ATTITUDINIZE	ATTRAP
ATTAINTING	ATTENTS	ATTITUDINIZED	ATTRAPPED
ATTAINTMENT	ATTENUANT	ATTITUDINIZER	ATTRAPPING
ATTAINTMENTS	ATTENUANTS	ATTITUDINIZERS	ATTRAPS
ATTAINTS	ATTENUATE	ATTITUDINIZES	ATTRIBUTABLE
ATTAINTURE	ATTENUATED	ATTITUDINIZING	ATTRIBUTE
ATTAINTURES	ATTENUATES	ATTITUDINIZINGS	ATTRIBUTED
ATTAP	ATTENUATING	ATTOLASER	ATTRIBUTER
ATTAPS	ATTENUATION	ATTOLASERS	ATTRIBUTERS
ATTAR	ATTENUATIONS	ATTOLLENS	ATTRIBUTES
ATTARS	ATTENUATOR	ATTOLLENT	ATTRIBUTING
ATTASK	ATTENUATORS	ATTOLLENTS	ATTRIBUTION
ATTASKED	ATTERCOP	ATTONCE	ATTRIBUTIONAL
ATTASKING	ATTERCOPS	ATTONE	ATTRIBUTIONS
ATTASKS	ATTEST	ATTONES	ATTRIBUTIVE
ATTASKT	ATTESTABLE	ATTOPHYSICS	ATTRIBUTIVELY
ATTEMPER	ATTESTANT	ATTORN	ATTRIBUTIVENESS
ATTEMPERED	ATTESTANTS	ATTORNED	ATTRIBUTIVES
ATTEMPERING	ATTESTATION	ATTORNEY	ATTRIBUTOR
ATTEMPERMENT	ATTESTATIONS	ATTORNEYDOM	ATTRIBUTORS
ATTEMPERS	ATTESTATIVE	ATTORNEYDOMS	ATTRIST
ATTEMPT	ATTESTATOR	ATTORNEYED	ATTRISTED
ATTEMPTABILITY	ATTESTATORS	ATTORNEYING	ATTRISTING
ATTEMPTABLE	ATTESTED	ATTORNEYISM	ATTRISTS
ATTEMPTED	ATTESTER	ATTORNEYISMS	ATTRIT
ATTEMPTER	ATTESTERS	ATTORNEYS	ATTRITE
ATTEMPTERS	ATTESTING	ATTORNEYSHIP	ATTRITED
ATTEMPTING	ATTESTOR	ATTORNEYSHIPS	ATTRITES
ATTEMPTS	ATTESTORS	ATTORNING	ATTRITING
ATTEND	ATTESTS	ATTORNMENT	ATTRITION
ATTENDANCE	ATTIC	ATTORNMENTS	ATTRITIONAL
ATTENDANCES	ATTICISM	ATTORNS	ATTRITIONS
ATTENDANCIES	ATTICISMS	ATTRACT	ATTRITIVE
ATTENDANCY	ATTICIST	ATTRACTABLE	ATTRITIVELY
ATTENDANT	ATTICISTS	ATTRACTANCE	ATTRITS
ATTENDANTS	ATTICS	ATTRACTANCES	ATTRITTED
ATTENDED	ATTIRE	ATTRACTANCIES	ATTRITTING
ATTENDEE	ATTIRED	ATTRACTANCY	ATTUENT
ATTENDEES	ATTIREMENT	ATTRACTANT	ATTUITE
ATTENDEMENT	ATTIREMENTS	ATTRACTANTS	ATTUITED
ATTENDEMENTS	ATTIRES	ATTRACTED	ATTUITES
ATTENDER	ATTIRING	ATTRACTER	ATTUITING
ATTENDERS	ATTIRINGS	ATTRACTERS	ATTUITION
ATTENDING	ATTITUDE	ATTRACTING	ATTUITIONAL
ATTENDMENT	ATTITUDES	ATTRACTINGLY	ATTUITIONS
ATTENDMENTS	ATTITUDINAL	ATTRACTION	ATTUITIVE
ATTENDS	ATTITUDINALLY	ATTRACTIONS	ATTUITIVELY
ATTENT	ATTITUDINARIAN	ATTRACTIVE	ATTUNE
ATTENTAT	ATTITUDINARIANS	ATTRACTIVELY	ATTUNED
ATTENTATS	ATTITUDINISE	ATTRACTIVENESS	ATTUNEMENT
ATTENTION	ATTITUDINISED	ATTRACTOR	ATTUNEMENTS
ATTENTIONAL	ATTITUDINISER	ATTRACTORS	ATTUNES

ATTUNING
ATUA
ATUAS
ATWAIN
ATWEEL
ATWEEN
ATWITTER
ATWIXT
ATYPIC
ATYPICAL
ATYPICALITIES
ATYPICALITY
ATYPICALLY
AUBADE
AUBADES
AUBERGE
AUBERGES
AUBERGINE
AUBERGINES
AUBERGISTE
AUBERGISTES
AUBRETIA
AUBRETIAS
AUBRIETA
AUBRIETAS
AUBRIETIA
AUBRIETIAS
AUBURN
AUBURNS
AUCEPS
AUCEPSES
AUCTION
AUCTIONARY
AUCTIONED
AUCTIONEER
AUCTIONEERED
AUCTIONEERING
AUCTIONEERS
AUCTIONING
AUCTIONS
AUCTORIAL
AUCUBA
AUCUBAS
AUDACIOUS
AUDACIOUSLY
AUDACIOUSNESS
AUDACIOUSNESSES
AUDACITIES
AUDACITY
AUDAD
AUDADS
AUDIAL
AUDIBILITIES
AUDIBILITY
AUDIBLE
AUDIBLENESS

AUDIBLENESSES
AUDIBLES
AUDIBLY
AUDIENCE
AUDIENCES
AUDIENCIA
AUDIENCIAS
AUDIENT
AUDIENTS
AUDILE
AUDILES
AUDING
AUDINGS
AUDIO
AUDIOCASSETTE
AUDIOCASSETTES
AUDIOGENIC
AUDIOGRAM
AUDIOGRAMS
AUDIOGRAPH
AUDIOGRAPHS
AUDIOLOGIC
AUDIOLOGICAL
AUDIOLOGICALLY
AUDIOLOGIES
AUDIOLOGIST
AUDIOLOGISTS
AUDIOLOGY
AUDIOMETER
AUDIOMETERS
AUDIOMETRIC
AUDIOMETRICALLY
AUDIOMETRICIAN
AUDIOMETRICIANS
AUDIOMETRIES
AUDIOMETRIST
AUDIOMETRISTS
AUDIOMETRY
AUDIOPHIL
AUDIOPHILE
AUDIOPHILES
AUDIOPHILS
AUDIOS
AUDIOTAPE
AUDIOTAPES
AUDIOTYPING
AUDIOTYPINGS
AUDIOTYPIST
AUDIOTYPISTS
AUDIOVISUAL
AUDIOVISUALLY
AUDIOVISUALS
AUDIPHONE
AUDIPHONES
AUDIT
AUDITABLE

AUDITED
AUDITING
AUDITION
AUDITIONED
AUDITIONER
AUDITIONERS
AUDITIONING
AUDITIONS
AUDITIVE
AUDITIVES
AUDITOR
AUDITORIA
AUDITORIAL
AUDITORIALS
AUDITORIES
AUDITORILY
AUDITORIUM
AUDITORIUMS
AUDITORS
AUDITORSHIP
AUDITORSHIPS
AUDITORY
AUDITRESS
AUDITRESSES
AUDITS
AUE
AUF
AUFGABE
AUFGABES
AUFS
AUGEND
AUGENDS
AUGER
AUGERS
AUGHT
AUGHTS
AUGITE
AUGITES
AUGITIC
AUGMENT
AUGMENTABLE
AUGMENTATION
AUGMENTATIONS
AUGMENTATIVE
AUGMENTATIVELY
AUGMENTATIVES
AUGMENTED
AUGMENTER
AUGMENTERS
AUGMENTING
AUGMENTOR
AUGMENTORS
AUGMENTS
AUGUR
AUGURAL
AUGURED

AUGURER
AUGURERS
AUGURIES
AUGURING
AUGURS
AUGURSHIP
AUGURSHIPS
AUGURY
AUGUST
AUGUSTE
AUGUSTER
AUGUSTES
AUGUSTEST
AUGUSTLY
AUGUSTNESS
AUGUSTNESSES
AUGUSTS
AUK
AUKLET
AUKLETS
AUKS
AULA
AULARIAN
AULARIANS
AULAS
AULD
AULDER
AULDEST
AULIC
AULNAGE
AULNAGER
AULNAGERS
AULNAGES
AULOI
AULOS
AUMAIL
AUMAILED
AUMAILING
AUMAILS
AUMBRIES
AUMBRY
AUMIL
AUMILS
AUNE
AUNES
AUNT
AUNTER
AUNTERS
AUNTHOOD
AUNTHOODS
AUNTIE
AUNTIES
AUNTLIER
AUNTLIEST
AUNTLIKE
AUNTLY

AUNTS
AUNTY
AURA
AURAE
AURAL
AURALLY
AURAR
AURAS
AURATE
AURATED
AURATES
AUREATE
AUREATELY
AUREATENESS
AUREI
AUREITIES
AUREITY
AURELIA
AURELIAN
AURELIANS
AURELIAS
AUREOLA
AUREOLAE
AUREOLAS
AUREOLE
AUREOLED
AUREOLES
AUREOLING
AURES
AUREUS
AURIC
AURICLE
AURICLED
AURICLES
AURICULA
AURICULAE
AURICULAR
AURICULARLY
AURICULARS
AURICULAS
AURICULATE
AURICULATED
AURICULATELY
AURIFEROUS
AURIFIED
AURIFIES
AURIFORM
AURIFY
AURIFYING
AURIS
AURISCOPE
AURISCOPES
AURISCOPIC
AURISCOPICALLY
AURIST
AURISTS

AUROCHS
AUROCHSES
AURORA
AURORAE
AURORAL
AURORALLY
AURORAS
AUROREAN
AUROUS
AURUM
AURUMS
AUSCULTATE
AUSCULTATED
AUSCULTATES
AUSCULTATING
AUSCULTATION
AUSCULTATIONS
AUSCULTATIVE
AUSCULTATIVELY
AUSCULTATOR
AUSCULTATORS
AUSCULTATORY
AUSFORM
AUSFORMED
AUSFORMING
AUSFORMS
AUSLANDER
AUSLANDERS
AUSPEX
AUSPICATE
AUSPICATED
AUSPICATES
AUSPICATING
AUSPICE
AUSPICES
AUSPICIOUS
AUSPICIOUSLY
AUSPICIOUSNESS
AUSTENITE
AUSTENITES
AUSTENITIC
AUSTERE
AUSTERELY
AUSTERENESS
AUSTERENESSES
AUSTERER
AUSTEREST
AUSTERITIES
AUSTERITY
AUSTRAL
AUSTRALES
AUSTRALITE
AUSTRALITES
AUSTRALS
AUSTRINGER
AUSTRINGERS

AUSUBO
AUSUBOS
AUTACOID
AUTACOIDS
AUTARCHIC
AUTARCHICAL
AUTARCHIES
AUTARCHIST
AUTARCHISTS
AUTARCHY
AUTARKIC
AUTARKICAL
AUTARKIES
AUTARKIST
AUTARKISTS
AUTARKY
AUTECIOUS
AUTECISM
AUTECISMS
AUTECOLOGIC
AUTECOLOGICAL
AUTECOLOGIES
AUTECOLOGY
AUTEUR
AUTEURIST
AUTEURISTS
AUTEURS
AUTHENTIC
AUTHENTICAL
AUTHENTICALLY
AUTHENTICATE
AUTHENTICATED
AUTHENTICATES
AUTHENTICATING
AUTHENTICATION
AUTHENTICATIONS
AUTHENTICATOR
AUTHENTICATORS
AUTHENTICITIES
AUTHENTICITY
AUTHIGENIC
AUTHIGENICALLY
AUTHOR
AUTHORCRAFT
AUTHORCRAFTS
AUTHORED
AUTHORESS
AUTHORESSES
AUTHORIAL
AUTHORING
AUTHORINGS
AUTHORISABLE
AUTHORISATION
AUTHORISATIONS
AUTHORISE
AUTHORISED

AUTHORISER
AUTHORISERS
AUTHORISES
AUTHORISH
AUTHORISING
AUTHORISM
AUTHORISMS
AUTHORITARIAN
AUTHORITARIANS
AUTHORITATIVE
AUTHORITATIVELY
AUTHORITIES
AUTHORITY
AUTHORIZABLE
AUTHORIZATION
AUTHORIZATIONS
AUTHORIZE
AUTHORIZED
AUTHORIZER
AUTHORIZERS
AUTHORIZES
AUTHORIZING
AUTHORLESS
AUTHORS
AUTHORSHIP
AUTHORSHIPS
AUTISM
AUTISMS
AUTISTIC
AUTISTICALLY
AUTISTICS
AUTO
AUTOALLOGAMOUS
AUTOALLOGAMY
AUTOANTIBODIES
AUTOANTIBODY
AUTOBAHN
AUTOBAHNEN
AUTOBAHNS
AUTOBIOGRAPHER
AUTOBIOGRAPHERS
AUTOBIOGRAPHIC
AUTOBIOGRAPHIES
AUTOBIOGRAPHY
AUTOBUS
AUTOBUSES
AUTOBUSSES
AUTOCADE
AUTOCADES
AUTOCAR
AUTOCARP
AUTOCARPS
AUTOCARS
AUTOCATALYSE
AUTOCATALYSED
AUTOCATALYSES

AUTOCATALYSING
AUTOCATALYSIS
AUTOCATALYTIC
AUTOCATALYZE
AUTOCATALYZED
AUTOCATALYZES
AUTOCATALYZING
AUTOCEPHALIC
AUTOCEPHALICS
AUTOCEPHALIES
AUTOCEPHALOUS
AUTOCEPHALY
AUTOCHANGER
AUTOCHANGERS
AUTOCHTHON
AUTOCHTHONAL
AUTOCHTHONALLY
AUTOCHTHONES
AUTOCHTHONIC
AUTOCHTHONIES
AUTOCHTHONISM
AUTOCHTHONISMS
AUTOCHTHONOUS
AUTOCHTHONOUSLY
AUTOCHTHONS
AUTOCHTHONY
AUTOCIDAL
AUTOCIDALLY
AUTOCLAVE
AUTOCLAVED
AUTOCLAVES
AUTOCLAVING
AUTOCOID
AUTOCOIDS
AUTOCOPROPHAGY
AUTOCORRELATION
AUTOCRACIES
AUTOCRACY
AUTOCRAT
AUTOCRATIC
AUTOCRATICAL
AUTOCRATICALLY
AUTOCRATS
AUTOCRIME
AUTOCRIMES
AUTOCRITIQUE
AUTOCRITIQUES
AUTOCROSS
AUTOCROSSES
AUTOCUE
AUTOCUES
AUTOCUTIE
AUTOCUTIES
AUTOCYCLE
AUTOCYCLES
AUTODESTRUCT

AUTODESTRUCTED
AUTODESTRUCTING
AUTODESTRUCTIVE
AUTODESTRUCTS
AUTODIDACT
AUTODIDACTIC
AUTODIDACTICISM
AUTODIDACTS
AUTODYNE
AUTODYNES
AUTOECIOUS
AUTOECIOUSLY
AUTOECISM
AUTOECISMS
AUTOED
AUTOEROTIC
AUTOEROTICISM
AUTOEROTICISMS
AUTOEROTISM
AUTOEROTISMS
AUTOEXPOSURE
AUTOEXPOSURES
AUTOFLARE
AUTOFLARES
AUTOFOCUS
AUTOFOCUSES
AUTOGAMIC
AUTOGAMIES
AUTOGAMOUS
AUTOGAMY
AUTOGENESES
AUTOGENESIS
AUTOGENETIC
AUTOGENETICALLY
AUTOGENIC
AUTOGENICS
AUTOGENIES
AUTOGENOUS
AUTOGENOUSLY
AUTOGENY
AUTOGIRO
AUTOGIROS
AUTOGRAFT
AUTOGRAFTED
AUTOGRAFTING
AUTOGRAFTS
AUTOGRAPH
AUTOGRAPHED
AUTOGRAPHIC
AUTOGRAPHICAL
AUTOGRAPHICALLY
AUTOGRAPHIES
AUTOGRAPHING
AUTOGRAPHS
AUTOGRAPHY
AUTOGRAVURE

AUTOGRAVURES
AUTOGUIDE
AUTOGUIDES
AUTOGYRO
AUTOGYROS
AUTOHARP
AUTOHARPS
AUTOHYPNOSES
AUTOHYPNOSIS
AUTOHYPNOTIC
AUTOICOUS
AUTOIMMUNE
AUTOIMMUNITIES
AUTOIMMUNITY
AUTOINFECTION
AUTOINFECTIONS
AUTOING
AUTOINOCULATION
AUTOINOCULATORY
AUTOIONISATION
AUTOIONISATIONS
AUTOIONIZATION
AUTOIONIZATIONS
AUTOJUMBLE
AUTOJUMBLES
AUTOKINESES
AUTOKINESIS
AUTOKINETIC
AUTOLATRIES
AUTOLATRY
AUTOLOADING
AUTOLOGIES
AUTOLOGOUS
AUTOLOGY
AUTOLYSATE
AUTOLYSATES
AUTOLYSE
AUTOLYSED
AUTOLYSES
AUTOLYSIN
AUTOLYSING
AUTOLYSINS
AUTOLYSIS
AUTOLYTIC
AUTOLYZATE
AUTOLYZATES
AUTOLYZE
AUTOLYZED
AUTOLYZES
AUTOLYZING
AUTOMAKER
AUTOMAKERS
AUTOMAN
AUTOMAT
AUTOMATA
AUTOMATABLE

AUTOMATE
AUTOMATED
AUTOMATES
AUTOMATIC
AUTOMATICAL
AUTOMATICALLY
AUTOMATICITIES
AUTOMATICITY
AUTOMATICS
AUTOMATING
AUTOMATION
AUTOMATIONS
AUTOMATISATION
AUTOMATISATIONS
AUTOMATISE
AUTOMATISED
AUTOMATISES
AUTOMATISING
AUTOMATISM
AUTOMATISMS
AUTOMATIST
AUTOMATISTS
AUTOMATIZATION
AUTOMATIZATIONS
AUTOMATIZE
AUTOMATIZED
AUTOMATIZES
AUTOMATIZING
AUTOMATON
AUTOMATONS
AUTOMATOUS
AUTOMATS
AUTOMEN
AUTOMETER
AUTOMETERS
AUTOMETRICALLY
AUTOMOBILE
AUTOMOBILED
AUTOMOBILES
AUTOMOBILIA
AUTOMOBILING
AUTOMOBILISM
AUTOMOBILISMS
AUTOMOBILIST
AUTOMOBILISTS
AUTOMOBILITIES
AUTOMOBILITY
AUTOMORPHIC
AUTOMORPHICALLY
AUTOMORPHISM
AUTOMORPHISMS
AUTOMOTIVE
AUTONOMIC
AUTONOMICAL
AUTONOMICALLY
AUTONOMICS

AUTONOMIES
AUTONOMIST
AUTONOMISTS
AUTONOMOUS
AUTONOMOUSLY
AUTONOMY
AUTONYM
AUTONYMS
AUTOPHAGIA
AUTOPHAGIAS
AUTOPHAGIES
AUTOPHAGOUS
AUTOPHAGY
AUTOPHANOUS
AUTOPHOBIA
AUTOPHOBIAS
AUTOPHOBIES
AUTOPHOBY
AUTOPHONIES
AUTOPHONY
AUTOPHYTE
AUTOPHYTES
AUTOPHYTIC
AUTOPHYTICALLY
AUTOPILOT
AUTOPILOTS
AUTOPISTA
AUTOPISTAS
AUTOPLASTIC
AUTOPLASTIES
AUTOPLASTY
AUTOPOINT
AUTOPOINTS
AUTOPOLYPLOID
AUTOPOLYPLOIDS
AUTOPOLYPLOIDY
AUTOPSIA
AUTOPSIAS
AUTOPSIC
AUTOPSIED
AUTOPSIES
AUTOPSY
AUTOPSYING
AUTOPTIC
AUTOPTICAL
AUTOPTICALLY
AUTOPUT
AUTOPUTS
AUTORADIOGRAM
AUTORADIOGRAMS
AUTORADIOGRAPH
AUTORADIOGRAPHS
AUTORADIOGRAPHY
AUTORICKSHAW
AUTORICKSHAWS
AUTOROTATE

AUTOROTATED
AUTOROTATES
AUTOROTATING
AUTOROTATION
AUTOROTATIONS
AUTOROUTE
AUTOROUTES
AUTOS
AUTOSCHEDIASM
AUTOSCHEDIASMS
AUTOSCHEDIASTIC
AUTOSCHEDIAZE
AUTOSCHEDIAZED
AUTOSCHEDIAZES
AUTOSCHEDIAZING
AUTOSCOPIC
AUTOSCOPIES
AUTOSCOPY
AUTOSEXING
AUTOSOMAL
AUTOSOMALLY
AUTOSOME
AUTOSOMES
AUTOSPORE
AUTOSPORES
AUTOSPORIC
AUTOSTABILITY
AUTOSTABLE
AUTOSTRADA
AUTOSTRADAS
AUTOSTRADE
AUTOSUGGEST
AUTOSUGGESTED
AUTOSUGGESTING
AUTOSUGGESTION
AUTOSUGGESTIONS
AUTOSUGGESTIVE
AUTOSUGGESTS
AUTOTELIC
AUTOTELLER
AUTOTELLERS
AUTOTETRAPLOID
AUTOTETRAPLOIDS
AUTOTETRAPLOIDY
AUTOTHEISM
AUTOTHEISMS
AUTOTHEIST
AUTOTHEISTS
AUTOTIMER
AUTOTIMERS
AUTOTOMIC
AUTOTOMICALLY
AUTOTOMIES
AUTOTOMISE
AUTOTOMISED
AUTOTOMISES

AUTOTOMISING
AUTOTOMIZE
AUTOTOMIZED
AUTOTOMIZES
AUTOTOMIZING
AUTOTOMOUS
AUTOTOMY
AUTOTOXAEMIA
AUTOTOXEMIA
AUTOTOXEMIC
AUTOTOXIC
AUTOTOXICALLY
AUTOTOXIN
AUTOTOXINS
AUTOTRANSFORMER
AUTOTRANSFUSION
AUTOTROPH
AUTOTROPHIC
AUTOTROPHICALLY
AUTOTROPHIES
AUTOTROPHS
AUTOTROPHY
AUTOTYPE
AUTOTYPED
AUTOTYPES
AUTOTYPIC
AUTOTYPICALLY
AUTOTYPIES
AUTOTYPING
AUTOTYPOGRAPHY
AUTOTYPY
AUTOVAC
AUTOVACS
AUTOWINDER
AUTOWINDERS
AUTOWORKER
AUTOWORKERS
AUTOXICITY
AUTOXIDATION
AUTOXIDATIONS
AUTUMN
AUTUMNAL
AUTUMNALLY
AUTUMNS
AUTUMNY
AUTUNITE
AUTUNITES
AUXANOMETER
AUXANOMETERS
AUXESES
AUXESIS
AUXETIC
AUXETICS
AUXILIAR
AUXILIARIES
AUXILIARS

AUXILIARY
AUXIN
AUXINIC
AUXINS
AUXOCHROME
AUXOCHROMES
AUXOCYTE
AUXOCYTES
AUXOCYTIC
AUXOMETER
AUXOMETERS
AUXOSPORE
AUXOSPORES
AUXOSPORIC
AUXOTONIC
AUXOTONICALLY
AUXOTROPH
AUXOTROPHIC
AUXOTROPHIES
AUXOTROPHS
AUXOTROPHY
AVA
AVADAVAT
AVADAVATS
AVAIL
AVAILABILITIES
AVAILABILITY
AVAILABLE
AVAILABLENESS
AVAILABLENESSES
AVAILABLY
AVAILE
AVAILED
AVAILES
AVAILFUL
AVAILING
AVAILINGLY
AVAILS
AVAL
AVALANCHE
AVALANCHED
AVALANCHES
AVALANCHING
AVALE
AVALED
AVALES
AVALING
AVANT
AVANTI
AVANTIST
AVANTISTS
AVANTURINE
AVANTURINES
AVARICE
AVARICES
AVARICIOUS

AVARICIOUSLY
AVARICIOUSNESS
AVAS
AVASCULAR
AVASCULARITIES
AVASCULARITY
AVAST
AVATAR
AVATARS
AVAUNT
AVAUNTED
AVAUNTING
AVAUNTS
AVE
AVEL
AVELLAN
AVELLANE
AVELS
AVENACEOUS
AVENGE
AVENGED
AVENGEFUL
AVENGEMENT
AVENGEMENTS
AVENGER
AVENGERESS
AVENGERESSES
AVENGERS
AVENGES
AVENGING
AVENIR
AVENIRS
AVENS
AVENSES
AVENTAIL
AVENTAILE
AVENTAILES
AVENTAILS
AVENTRE
AVENTRED
AVENTRES
AVENTRING
AVENTURE
AVENTURES
AVENTURIN
AVENTURINE
AVENTURINES
AVENTURINS
AVENUE
AVENUES
AVER
AVERAGE
AVERAGED
AVERAGELY
AVERAGENESS
AVERAGENESSES

AVERAGES
AVERAGING
AVERMENT
AVERMENTS
AVERRED
AVERRING
AVERRUNCATE
AVERRUNCATED
AVERRUNCATES
AVERRUNCATING
AVERRUNCATION
AVERRUNCATIONS
AVERRUNCATOR
AVERRUNCATORS
AVERS
AVERSE
AVERSELY
AVERSENESS
AVERSENESSES
AVERSION
AVERSIONS
AVERSIVE
AVERSIVELY
AVERSIVENESS
AVERSIVENESSES
AVERT
AVERTABLE
AVERTED
AVERTEDLY
AVERTIBLE
AVERTIMENT
AVERTIMENTS
AVERTING
AVERTS
AVES
AVGAS
AVGASES
AVGASSES
AVGOLEMONO
AVGOLEMONOS
AVIAN
AVIANIZE
AVIANIZED
AVIANIZES
AVIANIZING
AVIANS
AVIARIES
AVIARIST
AVIARISTS
AVIARY
AVIATE
AVIATED
AVIATES
AVIATING
AVIATION
AVIATIONS

AVIATOR
AVIATORS
AVIATRESS
AVIATRESSES
AVIATRICES
AVIATRIX
AVIATRIXES
AVICULAR
AVICULTURE
AVICULTURES
AVICULTURIST
AVICULTURISTS
AVID
AVIDER
AVIDEST
AVIDIN
AVIDINS
AVIDITIES
AVIDITY
AVIDLY
AVIDNESS
AVIDNESSES
AVIETTE
AVIETTES
AVIFAUNA
AVIFAUNAE
AVIFAUNAL
AVIFAUNAS
AVIFORM
AVIGATOR
AVIGATORS
AVINE
AVION
AVIONIC
AVIONICS
AVIONS
AVIRULENT
AVISANDUM
AVISANDUMS
AVISE
AVISED
AVISEMENT
AVISEMENTS
AVISES
AVISING
AVISO
AVISOS
AVITAL
AVITAMINOSES
AVITAMINOSIS
AVITAMINOTIC
AVIZANDUM
AVIZANDUMS
AVIZE
AVIZED
AVIZEFULL

AVIZES
AVIZING
AVO
AVOCADO
AVOCADOES
AVOCADOS
AVOCATION
AVOCATIONAL
AVOCATIONALLY
AVOCATIONS
AVOCET
AVOCETS
AVODIRE
AVODIRES
AVOID
AVOIDABLE
AVOIDABLY
AVOIDANCE
AVOIDANCES
AVOIDANT
AVOIDANTS
AVOIDED
AVOIDER
AVOIDERS
AVOIDING
AVOIDS
AVOIRDUPOIS
AVOIRDUPOISES
AVOISION
AVOISIONS
AVOS
AVOSET
AVOSETS
AVOUCH
AVOUCHABLE
AVOUCHED
AVOUCHER
AVOUCHERS
AVOUCHES
AVOUCHING
AVOUCHMENT
AVOUCHMENTS
AVOURE
AVOURES
AVOUTERER
AVOUTERERS
AVOUTRER
AVOUTRERS
AVOUTRIES
AVOUTRY
AVOW
AVOWABLE
AVOWABLENESS
AVOWABLENESSES
AVOWABLY
AVOWAL

AVOWALS
AVOWED
AVOWEDLY
AVOWER
AVOWERS
AVOWING
AVOWRIES
AVOWRY
AVOWS
AVOYER
AVOYERS
AVRUGA
AVULSE
AVULSED
AVULSES
AVULSING
AVULSION
AVULSIONS
AVUNCULAR
AVUNCULARITIES
AVUNCULARITY
AVUNCULARLY
AVUNCULATE
AVUNCULATION
AVVOGADORES
AVYZE
AVYZED
AVYZES
AVYZING
AW
AWA
AWAHTOS
AWAIT
AWAITED
AWAITER
AWAITERS
AWAITING
AWAITS
AWAKE
AWAKED
AWAKEN
AWAKENED
AWAKENER
AWAKENERS
AWAKENING
AWAKENINGS
AWAKENS
AWAKES
AWAKING
AWAKINGS
AWANTING
AWARD
AWARDABLE
AWARDED
AWARDEE
AWARDEES

AWARDER
AWARDERS
AWARDING
AWARDS
AWARE
AWARENESS
AWARENESSES
AWARER
AWAREST
AWARN
AWARNED
AWARNING
AWARNS
AWASH
AWATCH
AWATO
AWAVE
AWAY
AWAYDAY
AWAYDAYS
AWAYES
AWAYNESS
AWAYNESSES
AWAYS
AWDL
AWDLS
AWE
AWEARIED
AWEARY
AWEATHER
AWED
AWEE
AWEEL
AWEIGH
AWEING
AWELESS
AWELESSNESS
AWELESSNESSES
AWES
AWESOME
AWESOMELY
AWESOMENESS
AWESOMENESSES
AWESTRICKEN
AWESTRIKE
AWESTRIKES
AWESTRIKING
AWESTRUCK
AWETO
AWETOS
AWFUL
AWFULLER
AWFULLEST
AWFULLY
AWFULNESS
AWFULNESSES

AWHAPE
AWHAPED
AWHAPES
AWHAPING
AWHATO
AWHEEL
AWHEELS
AWHETO
AWHILE
AWHIRL
AWING
AWKWARD
AWKWARDER
AWKWARDEST
AWKWARDISH
AWKWARDLY
AWKWARDNESS
AWKWARDNESSES
AWL
AWLBIRD
AWLBIRDS
AWLESS
AWLS
AWLWORT
AWLWORTS
AWMOUS
AWMRIE
AWMRIES
AWMRY
AWN
AWNED
AWNER
AWNERS
AWNIER
AWNIEST
AWNING
AWNINGED
AWNINGS
AWNLESS
AWNS
AWNY
AWOKE
AWOKEN
AWOL
AWOLS
AWORK
AWRACK
AWRONG
AWRY
AWSOME
AX
AXAL
AXE
AXEBIRD
AXEBIRDS
AXED

AXEL
AXELS
AXEMAN
AXEMEN
AXENIC
AXENICALLY
AXEROPHTHOL
AXEROPHTHOLS
AXES
AXIAL
AXIALITIES
AXIALITY
AXIALLY
AXIL
AXILE
AXILEMMA
AXILEMMAS
AXILLA
AXILLAE
AXILLAR
AXILLARIES
AXILLARS
AXILLARY
AXILLAS
AXILS
AXING
AXINITE
AXINITES
AXINOMANCIES
AXINOMANCY
AXIOLOGICAL
AXIOLOGICALLY
AXIOLOGIES
AXIOLOGIST
AXIOLOGISTS
AXIOLOGY
AXIOM
AXIOMATIC
AXIOMATICAL
AXIOMATICALLY
AXIOMATICS
AXIOMATISATION
AXIOMATISATIONS
AXIOMATIZATION
AXIOMATIZATIONS
AXIOMATIZE
AXIOMATIZED
AXIOMATIZES
AXIOMATIZING
AXIOMS
AXION
AXIONS
AXIS
AXISED
AXISES
AXISYMMETRIC

AXISYMMETRICAL
AXISYMMETRIES
AXISYMMETRY
AXITE
AXITES
AXLE
AXLED
AXLES
AXLETREE
AXLETREES
AXLIKE
AXMAN
AXMEN
AXOID
AXOIDS
AXOLEMMA
AXOLEMMAS
AXOLOTL
AXOLOTLS
AXON
AXONAL
AXONE
AXONEMAL
AXONEME
AXONEMES
AXONES
AXONIC
AXONOMETRIC
AXONOMETRICAL
AXONOMETRICALLY
AXONOMETRY
AXONS
AXOPLASM
AXOPLASMIC
AXOPLASMS
AXSEED
AXSEEDS
AY
AYAH
AYAHS
AYAHUASCA
AYAHUASCAS
AYAHUASCO
AYAHUASCOS
AYATOLLAH
AYATOLLAHS
AYE
AYELP
AYENBITE
AYENBITES
AYES
AYGRE
AYIN
AYINS
AYONT
AYRE

AYRES
AYRIE
AYRIES
AYS
AYU
AYUNTAMIENTO
AYUNTAMIENTOS
AYURVEDA
AYURVEDAS
AYURVEDIC
AYUS
AYWORD
AYWORDS
AZALEA
AZALEAS
AZAN
AZANS
AZATHIOPRINE
AZATHIOPRINES
AZEDARACH
AZEDARACHS
AZEOTROPE
AZEOTROPES
AZEOTROPIC
AZERTY
AZIDE
AZIDES
AZIDO
AZIDOTHYMIDINE
AZIDOTHYMIDINES
AZIMUTH
AZIMUTHAL
AZIMUTHALLY
AZIMUTHS
AZINE
AZINES
AZIONE
AZIONES
AZLON
AZLONS
AZO
AZOBENZENE
AZOBENZENES
AZOIC
AZOLE
AZOLES
AZOLLA
AZOLLAS
AZON
AZONAL
AZONIC
AZONS
AZOOSPERMIA
AZOOSPERMIAS
AZOOSPERMIC
AZOOSPERMISM

AZOTAEMIA
AZOTAEMIC
AZOTE
AZOTED
AZOTEMIA
AZOTEMIAS
AZOTEMIC
AZOTES
AZOTH
AZOTHS
AZOTIC
AZOTISE
AZOTISED
AZOTISES
AZOTISING
AZOTIZE
AZOTIZED
AZOTIZES
AZOTIZING
AZOTOBACTER
AZOTOBACTERS
AZOTOUS
AZOTURIA
AZOTURIAS
AZULEJO
AZULEJOS
AZURE
AZUREAN
AZURES
AZURINE
AZURINES
AZURITE
AZURITES
AZURN
AZURY
AZYGIES
AZYGOS
AZYGOSES
AZYGOSPORE
AZYGOSPORES
AZYGOSPORIC
AZYGOUS
AZYGY
AZYM
AZYME
AZYMES
AZYMITE
AZYMITES
AZYMOUS
AZYMS

B

BA
BAA
BAAED
BAAING
BAAINGS
BAAL
BAALEBATIM
BAALEBOS
BAALIM
BAALISM
BAALISMS
BAALS
BAAS
BAASES
BAASKAAP
BAASKAAPS
BAASKAP
BAASSKAP
BAASSKAPS
BABA
BABACO
BABACOOTE
BABACOOTES
BABACOS
BABALAS
BABAS
BABASSU
BABASSUS
BABBITT
BABBITTED
BABBITTING
BABBITTS
BABBLATIVE
BABBLE
BABBLED
BABBLEMENT
BABBLEMENTS
BABBLER
BABBLERS
BABBLES
BABBLIER
BABBLIEST
BABBLING
BABBLINGS
BABBLY
BABE
BABEL
BABELDOM
BABELDOMS
BABELESQUE
BABELISH

BABELISM
BABELISMS
BABELS
BABES
BABESIA
BABESIAS
BABESIASES
BABESIASIS
BABESIOSES
BABESIOSIS
BABICHE
BABICHES
BABIED
BABIER
BABIES
BABIEST
BABINGTONITE
BABINGTONITES
BABIROUSSA
BABIROUSSAS
BABIRUSA
BABIRUSAS
BABIRUSSA
BABIRUSSAS
BABKA
BABKAS
BABLAH
BABLAHS
BABOO
BABOOL
BABOOLS
BABOON
BABOONERIES
BABOONERY
BABOONISH
BABOONS
BABOOS
BABOOSH
BABOOSHES
BABOUCHE
BABOUCHES
BABU
BABUCHE
BABUCHES
BABUDOM
BABUDOMS
BABUISM
BABUISMS
BABUL
BABULS
BABUS

BABUSHKA
BABUSHKAS
BABY
BABYFOOD
BABYFOODS
BABYHOOD
BABYHOODS
BABYING
BABYISH
BAC
BACALAO
BACALAOS
BACCA
BACCAE
BACCALAUREAN
BACCALAUREATE
BACCALAUREATES
BACCARA
BACCARAS
BACCARAT
BACCARATS
BACCARE
BACCAS
BACCATE
BACCATED
BACCHANAL
BACCHANALIA
BACCHANALIAN
BACCHANALIANISM
BACCHANALIANS
BACCHANALS
BACCHANT
BACCHANTE
BACCHANTES
BACCHANTS
BACCHIAC
BACCHIAN
BACCHIC
BACCHII
BACCHIUS
BACCIES
BACCIFEROUS
BACCIFORM
BACCIVOROUS
BACCO
BACCOES
BACCOS
BACCY
BACH
BACHARACH
BACHARACHS

BACHED
BACHELOR
BACHELORDOM
BACHELORDOMS
BACHELORETTE
BACHELORETTES
BACHELORHOOD
BACHELORHOODS
BACHELORISM
BACHELORISMS
BACHELORS
BACHELORSHIP
BACHELORSHIPS
BACHES
BACHING
BACHS
BACILLAEMIA
BACILLAEMIAS
BACILLAR
BACILLARY
BACILLEMIA
BACILLEMIAS
BACILLI
BACILLICIDE
BACILLICIDES
BACILLIFORM
BACILLURIA
BACILLURIC
BACILLUS
BACITRACIN
BACITRACINS
BACK
BACKACHE
BACKACHES
BACKARE
BACKBAND
BACKBANDS
BACKBEAT
BACKBEATS
BACKBENCH
BACKBENCHER
BACKBENCHERS
BACKBENCHES
BACKBEND
BACKBENDS
BACKBIT
BACKBITE
BACKBITER
BACKBITERS
BACKBITES
BACKBITING

BACKBITINGS
BACKBITTEN
BACKBLOCK
BACKBLOCKER
BACKBLOCKERS
BACKBLOCKS
BACKBOARD
BACKBOARDS
BACKBOND
BACKBONDS
BACKBONE
BACKBONED
BACKBONELESS
BACKBONES
BACKBREAKER
BACKBREAKERS
BACKBREAKING
BACKBURN
BACKBURNED
BACKBURNING
BACKBURNS
BACKCAST
BACKCASTS
BACKCHAT
BACKCHATS
BACKCHATTED
BACKCHATTING
BACKCLOTH
BACKCLOTHS
BACKCOMB
BACKCOMBED
BACKCOMBING
BACKCOMBS
BACKCOUNTRIES
BACKCOUNTRY
BACKCOURT
BACKCOURTMAN
BACKCOURTMEN
BACKCOURTS
BACKCROSS
BACKCROSSED
BACKCROSSES
BACKCROSSING
BACKDATE
BACKDATED
BACKDATES
BACKDATING
BACKDOOR
BACKDOWN
BACKDOWNS
BACKDROP
BACKDROPPED
BACKDROPPING
BACKDROPS
BACKDROPT
BACKED

BACKER
BACKERS
BACKET
BACKETS
BACKFALL
BACKFALLS
BACKFIELD
BACKFIELDS
BACKFILE
BACKFILES
BACKFILL
BACKFILLED
BACKFILLING
BACKFILLS
BACKFIRE
BACKFIRED
BACKFIRES
BACKFIRING
BACKFISCH
BACKFISCHES
BACKFIT
BACKFITS
BACKFITTED
BACKFITTING
BACKFITTINGS
BACKFLOW
BACKFLOWS
BACKGAMMON
BACKGAMMONED
BACKGAMMONING
BACKGAMMONS
BACKGROUND
BACKGROUNDED
BACKGROUNDER
BACKGROUNDERS
BACKGROUNDING
BACKGROUNDS
BACKHAND
BACKHANDED
BACKHANDEDLY
BACKHANDEDNESS
BACKHANDER
BACKHANDERS
BACKHANDING
BACKHANDS
BACKHAUL
BACKHAULED
BACKHAULING
BACKHAULS
BACKHOE
BACKHOES
BACKHOUSE
BACKHOUSES
BACKIE
BACKIES
BACKING

BACKINGS
BACKLAND
BACKLANDS
BACKLASH
BACKLASHED
BACKLASHER
BACKLASHERS
BACKLASHES
BACKLASHING
BACKLESS
BACKLIFT
BACKLIFTS
BACKLIGHT
BACKLIGHTED
BACKLIGHTING
BACKLIGHTS
BACKLIST
BACKLISTED
BACKLISTING
BACKLISTS
BACKLIT
BACKLOG
BACKLOGGED
BACKLOGGING
BACKLOGS
BACKLOT
BACKLOTS
BACKMARKER
BACKMARKERS
BACKMOST
BACKOUT
BACKOUTS
BACKPACK
BACKPACKED
BACKPACKER
BACKPACKERS
BACKPACKING
BACKPACKINGS
BACKPACKS
BACKPAY
BACKPAYS
BACKPEDAL
BACKPEDALED
BACKPEDALING
BACKPEDALLED
BACKPEDALLING
BACKPEDALS
BACKPIECE
BACKPIECES
BACKRA
BACKRAS
BACKREST
BACKRESTS
BACKROOM
BACKRUSH
BACKRUSHES

BACKS
BACKSAW
BACKSAWS
BACKSCATTER
BACKSCATTERED
BACKSCATTERING
BACKSCATTERINGS
BACKSCATTERS
BACKSCRATCH
BACKSCRATCHED
BACKSCRATCHER
BACKSCRATCHERS
BACKSCRATCHES
BACKSCRATCHING
BACKSCRATCHINGS
BACKSEAT
BACKSEATS
BACKSET
BACKSETS
BACKSEY
BACKSEYS
BACKSHEESH
BACKSHEESHED
BACKSHEESHES
BACKSHEESHING
BACKSHISH
BACKSHISHED
BACKSHISHES
BACKSHISHING
BACKSIDE
BACKSIDES
BACKSIGHT
BACKSIGHTS
BACKSLAP
BACKSLAPPED
BACKSLAPPER
BACKSLAPPERS
BACKSLAPPING
BACKSLAPS
BACKSLASH
BACKSLASHES
BACKSLID
BACKSLIDDEN
BACKSLIDE
BACKSLIDER
BACKSLIDERS
BACKSLIDES
BACKSLIDING
BACKSLIDINGS
BACKSPACE
BACKSPACED
BACKSPACER
BACKSPACERS
BACKSPACES
BACKSPACING
BACKSPEER

BACKSPEERED
BACKSPEERING
BACKSPEERS
BACKSPEIR
BACKSPEIRED
BACKSPEIRING
BACKSPEIRS
BACKSPIN
BACKSPINS
BACKSPLASH
BACKSPLASHES
BACKSTAB
BACKSTABBED
BACKSTABBER
BACKSTABBERS
BACKSTABBING
BACKSTABBINGS
BACKSTABS
BACKSTAGE
BACKSTAIR
BACKSTAIRS
BACKSTALL
BACKSTALLS
BACKSTARTING
BACKSTAY
BACKSTAYS
BACKSTITCH
BACKSTITCHED
BACKSTITCHES
BACKSTITCHING
BACKSTOP
BACKSTOPPED
BACKSTOPPING
BACKSTOPS
BACKSTREET
BACKSTREETS
BACKSTRETCH
BACKSTRETCHES
BACKSTROKE
BACKSTROKES
BACKSWEPT
BACKSWING
BACKSWINGS
BACKSWORD
BACKSWORDMAN
BACKSWORDMEN
BACKSWORDS
BACKSWORDSMAN
BACKSWORDSMEN
BACKTRACK
BACKTRACKED
BACKTRACKING
BACKTRACKINGS
BACKTRACKS
BACKUP
BACKUPS

BACKVELD
BACKVELDER
BACKVELDERS
BACKVELDS
BACKWARD
BACKWARDATION
BACKWARDATIONS
BACKWARDLY
BACKWARDNESS
BACKWARDNESSES
BACKWARDS
BACKWASH
BACKWASHED
BACKWASHES
BACKWASHING
BACKWATER
BACKWATERS
BACKWOOD
BACKWOODS
BACKWOODSMAN
BACKWOODSMEN
BACKWOODSY
BACKWORD
BACKWORDS
BACKWORK
BACKWORKER
BACKWORKERS
BACKWORKS
BACKWRAP
BACKWRAPS
BACKYARD
BACKYARDS
BACLAVA
BACLAVAS
BACON
BACONER
BACONERS
BACONS
BACS
BACTERAEMIA
BACTERAEMIAS
BACTEREMIA
BACTEREMIAS
BACTEREMIC
BACTERIA
BACTERIAL
BACTERIALLY
BACTERIAN
BACTERIAS
BACTERIC
BACTERICIDAL
BACTERICIDALLY
BACTERICIDE
BACTERICIDES
BACTERIN
BACTERINS

BACTERIOCIN
BACTERIOCINS
BACTERIOID
BACTERIOIDS
BACTERIOLOGIC
BACTERIOLOGICAL
BACTERIOLOGIES
BACTERIOLOGIST
BACTERIOLOGISTS
BACTERIOLOGY
BACTERIOLYSES
BACTERIOLYSIN
BACTERIOLYSINS
BACTERIOLYSIS
BACTERIOLYTIC
BACTERIOPHAGE
BACTERIOPHAGES
BACTERIOPHAGIC
BACTERIOPHAGIES
BACTERIOPHAGOUS
BACTERIOPHAGY
BACTERIOSES
BACTERIOSIS
BACTERIOSTASES
BACTERIOSTASIS
BACTERIOSTAT
BACTERIOSTATIC
BACTERIOSTATS
BACTERIOTOXIC
BACTERIOTOXIN
BACTERIOTOXINS
BACTERISE
BACTERISED
BACTERISES
BACTERISING
BACTERIUM
BACTERIURIA
BACTERIURIAS
BACTERIZATION
BACTERIZATIONS
BACTERIZE
BACTERIZED
BACTERIZES
BACTERIZING
BACTEROID
BACTEROIDS
BACTERURIA
BACULA
BACULIFORM
BACULINE
BACULITE
BACULITES
BACULOVIRUS
BACULOVIRUSES
BACULUM
BACULUMS

BAD
BADASS
BADASSED
BADASSES
BADDELEYITE
BADDELEYITES
BADDER
BADDERLOCK
BADDERLOCKS
BADDEST
BADDIE
BADDIES
BADDISH
BADDY
BADE
BADGE
BADGED
BADGER
BADGERED
BADGERING
BADGERLY
BADGERS
BADGES
BADGING
BADINAGE
BADINAGED
BADINAGES
BADINAGING
BADINERIE
BADINERIES
BADIOUS
BADLAND
BADLANDS
BADLY
BADMAN
BADMASH
BADMASHES
BADMEN
BADMINTON
BADMINTONS
BADMOUTH
BADMOUTHED
BADMOUTHING
BADMOUTHS
BADNESS
BADNESSES
BADS
BAEL
BAELS
BAETYL
BAETYLS
BAFF
BAFFED
BAFFIES
BAFFING
BAFFLE

BAFFLED
BAFFLEGAB
BAFFLEGABS
BAFFLEMENT
BAFFLEMENTS
BAFFLER
BAFFLERS
BAFFLES
BAFFLING
BAFFLINGLY
BAFFS
BAFFY
BAFT
BAFTS
BAG
BAGARRE
BAGARRES
BAGASS
BAGASSE
BAGASSES
BAGASSOSES
BAGASSOSIS
BAGATELLE
BAGATELLES
BAGEL
BAGELS
BAGFUL
BAGFULS
BAGGAGE
BAGGAGES
BAGGED
BAGGER
BAGGERS
BAGGIE
BAGGIER
BAGGIES
BAGGIEST
BAGGILY
BAGGINESS
BAGGINESSES
BAGGING
BAGGINGS
BAGGIT
BAGGITS
BAGGY
BAGH
BAGHOUSE
BAGHOUSES
BAGHS
BAGIE
BAGIES
BAGLESS
BAGLESSNESS
BAGMAN
BAGMEN
BAGNETTE

BAGNETTES
BAGNIO
BAGNIOS
BAGPIPE
BAGPIPER
BAGPIPERS
BAGPIPES
BAGPIPING
BAGPIPINGS
BAGS
BAGSFUL
BAGSWINGER
BAGSWINGERS
BAGUET
BAGUETS
BAGUETTE
BAGUETTES
BAGUIO
BAGUIOS
BAGWASH
BAGWASHES
BAGWIG
BAGWIGS
BAGWORM
BAGWORMS
BAH
BAHADA
BAHADAS
BAHADUR
BAHADURS
BAHT
BAHTS
BAHUT
BAHUTS
BAHUVRIHI
BAHUVRIHIS
BAIDARKA
BAIDARKAS
BAIGNOIRE
BAIGNOIRES
BAIL
BAILABLE
BAILBOND
BAILBONDS
BAILED
BAILEE
BAILEES
BAILER
BAILERS
BAILEY
BAILEYS
BAILIE
BAILIES
BAILIESHIP
BAILIESHIPS
BAILIFF

BAILIFFS
BAILIFFSHIP
BAILIFFSHIPS
BAILING
BAILIWICK
BAILIWICKS
BAILLI
BAILLIAGE
BAILLIAGES
BAILLIE
BAILLIES
BAILLIESHIP
BAILLIESHIPS
BAILLIS
BAILMENT
BAILMENTS
BAILOR
BAILORS
BAILOUT
BAILOUTS
BAILS
BAILSMAN
BAILSMEN
BAININ
BAININS
BAINITE
BAINITES
BAIRN
BAIRNISH
BAIRNLIER
BAIRNLIEST
BAIRNLIKE
BAIRNLY
BAIRNS
BAISEMAIN
BAISEMAINS
BAIT
BAITED
BAITER
BAITERS
BAITFISH
BAITFISHES
BAITH
BAITING
BAITINGS
BAITS
BAIZA
BAIZAS
BAIZE
BAIZED
BAIZES
BAIZING
BAJADA
BAJADAS
BAJAN
BAJANS

BAJRA
BAJRAS
BAJREE
BAJREES
BAJRI
BAJRIS
BAJU
BAJUS
BAKE
BAKEAPPLE
BAKEAPPLES
BAKEBOARD
BAKEBOARDS
BAKED
BAKEHOUSE
BAKEHOUSES
BAKEMEAT
BAKEMEATS
BAKEN
BAKER
BAKERIES
BAKERS
BAKERY
BAKES
BAKESHOP
BAKESHOPS
BAKESTONE
BAKESTONES
BAKEWARE
BAKEWARES
BAKHSHISH
BAKHSHISHED
BAKHSHISHES
BAKHSHISHING
BAKING
BAKINGS
BAKKIE
BAKKIES
BAKLAVA
BAKLAVAS
BAKLAWA
BAKLAWAS
BAKRA
BAKRAS
BAKSHEESH
BAKSHEESHED
BAKSHEESHES
BAKSHEESHING
BAKSHISH
BAKSHISHED
BAKSHISHES
BAKSHISHING
BAL
BALACLAVA
BALACLAVAS
BALADIN

BALADINE	BALDING	BALKIER	BALLBREAKINGLY
BALADINES	BALDISH	BALKIEST	BALLCARRIER
BALADINS	BALDLY	BALKILY	BALLCARRIERS
BALALAIKA	BALDMONEY	BALKINESS	BALLCLAY
BALALAIKAS	BALDMONEYS	BALKINESSES	BALLCLAYS
BALANCE	BALDMONIES	BALKING	BALLCOCK
BALANCEABILITY	BALDNESS	BALKINGLY	BALLCOCKS
BALANCEABLE	BALDNESSES	BALKINGS	BALLED
BALANCED	BALDPATE	BALKLINE	BALLER
BALANCER	BALDPATED	BALKLINES	BALLERINA
BALANCERS	BALDPATES	BALKS	BALLERINAS
BALANCES	BALDRIC	BALKY	BALLERINE
BALANCING	BALDRICK	BALL	BALLERS
BALANITIS	BALDRICKS	BALLABILE	BALLET
BALANITISES	BALDRICS	BALLABILES	BALLETED
BALAS	BALDS	BALLABILI	BALLETIC
BALASES	BALDY	BALLAD	BALLETICALLY
BALATA	BALE	BALLADE	BALLETING
BALATAS	BALECTION	BALLADED	BALLETOMANE
BALBOA	BALECTIONS	BALLADEER	BALLETOMANES
BALBOAS	BALED	BALLADEERED	BALLETOMANIA
BALBRIGGAN	BALEEN	BALLADEERING	BALLETOMANIAS
BALBRIGGANS	BALEENS	BALLADEERS	BALLETS
BALBUTIENT	BALEFIRE	BALLADES	BALLFLOWER
BALCONET	BALEFIRES	BALLADIC	BALLFLOWERS
BALCONETS	BALEFUL	BALLADIN	BALLGAME
BALCONETTE	BALEFULLY	BALLADINE	BALLGAMES
BALCONETTES	BALEFULNESS	BALLADINES	BALLHANDLING
BALCONIED	BALEFULNESSES	BALLADING	BALLHANDLINGS
BALCONIES	BALER	BALLADINS	BALLHAWK
BALCONY	BALERS	BALLADIST	BALLHAWKS
BALD	BALES	BALLADISTS	BALLICATTER
BALDACHIN	BALIBUNTAL	BALLADMONGER	BALLIES
BALDACHINO	BALIBUNTALS	BALLADMONGERS	BALLING
BALDACHINOS	BALING	BALLADRIES	BALLINGS
BALDACHINS	BALISAUR	BALLADRY	BALLISTA
BALDAQUIN	BALISAURS	BALLADS	BALLISTAE
BALDAQUINS	BALISTA	BALLAN	BALLISTAS
BALDED	BALISTAE	BALLANS	BALLISTIC
BALDER	BALISTAS	BALLANT	BALLISTICALLY
BALDERDASH	BALK	BALLANTED	BALLISTICS
BALDERDASHES	BALKANISATION	BALLANTING	BALLISTITE
BALDERLOCKS	BALKANISATIONS	BALLANTS	BALLISTITES
BALDERLOCKSES	BALKANISE	BALLANWRASSE	BALLISTOSPORE
BALDEST	BALKANISED	BALLANWRASSES	BALLISTOSPORES
BALDFACED	BALKANISES	BALLAST	BALLISTOSPORIC
BALDFACEDNESS	BALKANISING	BALLASTED	BALLIUM
BALDHEAD	BALKANIZATION	BALLASTING	BALLIUMS
BALDHEADED	BALKANIZATIONS	BALLASTS	BALLOCKS
BALDHEADEDNESS	BALKANIZE	BALLAT	BALLOCKSED
BALDHEADS	BALKANIZED	BALLATED	BALLOCKSES
BALDICOOT	BALKANIZES	BALLATING	BALLOCKSING
BALDICOOTS	BALKANIZING	BALLATS	BALLON
BALDIER	BALKED	BALLBREAKER	BALLONET
BALDIES	BALKER	BALLBREAKERS	BALLONETS
BALDIEST	BALKERS	BALLBREAKING	BALLONNE

BALLONNES
BALLONS
BALLOON
BALLOONED
BALLOONING
BALLOONINGS
BALLOONIST
BALLOONISTS
BALLOONS
BALLOT
BALLOTED
BALLOTEE
BALLOTEES
BALLOTER
BALLOTERS
BALLOTING
BALLOTINI
BALLOTINO
BALLOTS
BALLOTTEMENT
BALLOTTEMENTS
BALLOW
BALLOWS
BALLPARK
BALLPARKS
BALLPLAYER
BALLPLAYERS
BALLPOINT
BALLPOINTS
BALLROOM
BALLROOMS
BALLS
BALLSIER
BALLSIEST
BALLSINESS
BALLSINESSES
BALLSY
BALLUP
BALLUPS
BALLUTE
BALLUTES
BALLY
BALLYHOO
BALLYHOOED
BALLYHOOING
BALLYHOOS
BALLYRAG
BALLYRAGGED
BALLYRAGGING
BALLYRAGS
BALM
BALMACAAN
BALMACAANS
BALMED
BALMIER
BALMIEST

BALMILY
BALMINESS
BALMINESSES
BALMING
BALMLIKE
BALMORAL
BALMORALITIES
BALMORALITY
BALMORALS
BALMS
BALMY
BALNEAL
BALNEARIES
BALNEARY
BALNEATION
BALNEATIONS
BALNEOLOGICAL
BALNEOLOGICALLY
BALNEOLOGIES
BALNEOLOGIST
BALNEOLOGISTS
BALNEOLOGY
BALNEOTHERAPIES
BALNEOTHERAPY
BALONEY
BALONEYS
BALOO
BALOOS
BALS
BALSA
BALSAM
BALSAMED
BALSAMIC
BALSAMIFEROUS
BALSAMINACEOUS
BALSAMING
BALSAMS
BALSAMY
BALSAS
BALSAWOOD
BALSAWOODS
BALTHASAR
BALTHASARS
BALTHAZAR
BALTHAZARS
BALTI
BALTIS
BALU
BALUN
BALUNS
BALUS
BALUSTER
BALUSTERED
BALUSTERS
BALUSTRADE
BALUSTRADED

BALUSTRADES
BALZARINE
BALZARINES
BAM
BAMBI
BAMBINI
BAMBINO
BAMBINOS
BAMBIS
BAMBOO
BAMBOOS
BAMBOOZLE
BAMBOOZLED
BAMBOOZLEMENT
BAMBOOZLEMENTS
BAMBOOZLER
BAMBOOZLERS
BAMBOOZLES
BAMBOOZLING
BAMMED
BAMMER
BAMMERS
BAMMING
BAMPOT
BAMPOTS
BAMS
BAN
BANAK
BANAKS
BANAL
BANALER
BANALEST
BANALISATION
BANALISATIONS
BANALISE
BANALISED
BANALISES
BANALISING
BANALITIES
BANALITY
BANALIZATION
BANALIZATIONS
BANALIZE
BANALIZED
BANALIZES
BANALIZING
BANALLY
BANANA
BANANAS
BANAUSIAN
BANAUSIC
BANC
BANCASSURANCE
BANCASSURANCES
BANCASSURER
BANCASSURERS

BANCO
BANCOS
BANCS
BAND
BANDA
BANDAGE
BANDAGED
BANDAGER
BANDAGERS
BANDAGES
BANDAGING
BANDALORE
BANDALORES
BANDANA
BANDANAS
BANDANNA
BANDANNAS
BANDAR
BANDARS
BANDAS
BANDBOX
BANDBOXES
BANDBRAKE
BANDBRAKES
BANDEAU
BANDEAUS
BANDEAUX
BANDED
BANDEIRANTE
BANDEIRANTES
BANDELET
BANDELETS
BANDELIER
BANDELIERS
BANDER
BANDERILLA
BANDERILLAS
BANDERILLERO
BANDERILLEROS
BANDEROL
BANDEROLE
BANDEROLES
BANDEROLS
BANDERS
BANDERSNATCH
BANDERSNATCHES
BANDH
BANDHS
BANDICOOT
BANDICOOTED
BANDICOOTING
BANDICOOTS
BANDIED
BANDIER
BANDIES
BANDIEST

BANDING
BANDINGS
BANDIT
BANDITRIES
BANDITRY
BANDITS
BANDITTI
BANDITTIS
BANDLEADER
BANDLEADERS
BANDMASTER
BANDMASTERS
BANDOBAST
BANDOBASTS
BANDOBUST
BANDOBUSTS
BANDOG
BANDOGS
BANDOLEER
BANDOLEERED
BANDOLEERS
BANDOLEON
BANDOLEONS
BANDOLERO
BANDOLEROS
BANDOLIER
BANDOLIERED
BANDOLIERS
BANDOLINE
BANDOLINED
BANDOLINES
BANDOLINING
BANDONEON
BANDONEONS
BANDONION
BANDONIONS
BANDOOK
BANDOOKS
BANDORA
BANDORAS
BANDORE
BANDORES
BANDROL
BANDROLS
BANDS
BANDSMAN
BANDSMEN
BANDSPREADER
BANDSPREADERS
BANDSPREADING
BANDSTAND
BANDSTANDS
BANDSTER
BANDSTERS
BANDURA
BANDURAS

BANDWAGON
BANDWAGONS
BANDWIDTH
BANDWIDTHS
BANDY
BANDYING
BANDYINGS
BANDYMAN
BANDYMEN
BANE
BANEBERRIES
BANEBERRY
BANED
BANEFUL
BANEFULLY
BANEFULNESS
BANEFULNESSES
BANES
BANG
BANGALAY
BANGALAYS
BANGALOW
BANGALOWS
BANGED
BANGER
BANGERS
BANGING
BANGINGS
BANGKOK
BANGKOKS
BANGLE
BANGLED
BANGLES
BANGS
BANGSRING
BANGSRINGS
BANGSTER
BANGSTERS
BANGTAIL
BANGTAILS
BANI
BANIA
BANIAN
BANIANS
BANIAS
BANING
BANISH
BANISHED
BANISHER
BANISHERS
BANISHES
BANISHING
BANISHMENT
BANISHMENTS
BANISTER
BANISTERED

BANISTERS
BANJAX
BANJAXED
BANJAXES
BANJAXING
BANJO
BANJOES
BANJOIST
BANJOISTS
BANJOS
BANJULELE
BANJULELES
BANK
BANKABILITIES
BANKABILITY
BANKABLE
BANKBOOK
BANKBOOKS
BANKCARD
BANKCARDS
BANKED
BANKER
BANKERLY
BANKERS
BANKET
BANKETS
BANKING
BANKINGS
BANKNOTE
BANKNOTES
BANKROLL
BANKROLLED
BANKROLLER
BANKROLLERS
BANKROLLING
BANKROLLS
BANKRUPT
BANKRUPTCIES
BANKRUPTCY
BANKRUPTED
BANKRUPTING
BANKRUPTS
BANKS
BANKSIA
BANKSIAS
BANKSIDE
BANKSIDES
BANKSMAN
BANKSMEN
BANLIEUE
BANLIEUES
BANNED
BANNER
BANNERALL
BANNERALLS
BANNERED

BANNERET
BANNERETS
BANNERETTE
BANNERETTES
BANNERING
BANNEROL
BANNEROLS
BANNERS
BANNET
BANNETS
BANNING
BANNISTER
BANNISTERS
BANNOCK
BANNOCKS
BANNS
BANOFFEE
BANOFFEES
BANOFFI
BANOFFIS
BANQUET
BANQUETED
BANQUETEER
BANQUETEERS
BANQUETER
BANQUETERS
BANQUETING
BANQUETINGS
BANQUETS
BANQUETTE
BANQUETTES
BANS
BANSELA
BANSELAS
BANSHEE
BANSHEES
BANSHIE
BANSHIES
BANT
BANTAM
BANTAMS
BANTAMWEIGHT
BANTAMWEIGHTS
BANTED
BANTENG
BANTENGS
BANTER
BANTERED
BANTERER
BANTERERS
BANTERING
BANTERINGLY
BANTERINGS
BANTERS
BANTIES
BANTING

BANTINGISM
BANTINGISMS
BANTINGS
BANTLING
BANTLINGS
BANTS
BANTU
BANTUS
BANTY
BANXRING
BANXRINGS
BANYAN
BANYANS
BANZAI
BANZAIS
BAOBAB
BAOBABS
BAP
BAPHOMETIC
BAPS
BAPTISE
BAPTISED
BAPTISES
BAPTISIA
BAPTISIAS
BAPTISING
BAPTISM
BAPTISMAL
BAPTISMALLY
BAPTISMS
BAPTIST
BAPTISTERIES
BAPTISTERY
BAPTISTRIES
BAPTISTRY
BAPTISTS
BAPTIZE
BAPTIZED
BAPTIZER
BAPTIZERS
BAPTIZES
BAPTIZING
BAPU
BAPUS
BAR
BARACAN
BARACANS
BARACHOIS
BARAESTHESIA
BARAGOUIN
BARAGOUINS
BARASINGA
BARASINGAS
BARASINGHA
BARASINGHAS
BARATHEA

BARATHEAS
BARATHRUM
BARATHRUMS
BARAZA
BARAZAS
BARB
BARBAL
BARBARESQUE
BARBARIAN
BARBARIANISM
BARBARIANISMS
BARBARIANS
BARBARIC
BARBARICALLY
BARBARISATION
BARBARISATIONS
BARBARISE
BARBARISED
BARBARISES
BARBARISING
BARBARISM
BARBARISMS
BARBARITIES
BARBARITY
BARBARIZATION
BARBARIZATIONS
BARBARIZE
BARBARIZED
BARBARIZES
BARBARIZING
BARBAROUS
BARBAROUSLY
BARBAROUSNESS
BARBAROUSNESSES
BARBASCO
BARBASCOES
BARBASCOS
BARBASTEL
BARBASTELLE
BARBASTELLES
BARBASTELS
BARBATE
BARBATED
BARBE
BARBECUE
BARBECUED
BARBECUER
BARBECUERS
BARBECUES
BARBECUING
BARBED
BARBEL
BARBELL
BARBELLATE
BARBELLS
BARBELS

BARBEQUE
BARBEQUED
BARBEQUES
BARBEQUING
BARBER
BARBERED
BARBERING
BARBERRIES
BARBERRY
BARBERS
BARBERSHOP
BARBERSHOPS
BARBES
BARBET
BARBETS
BARBETTE
BARBETTES
BARBICAN
BARBICANS
BARBICEL
BARBICELS
BARBIE
BARBIES
BARBING
BARBITAL
BARBITALS
BARBITONE
BARBITONES
BARBITURATE
BARBITURATES
BARBITURIC
BARBLESS
BARBOLA
BARBOLAS
BARBOTINE
BARBOTINES
BARBS
BARBULE
BARBULES
BARBUT
BARBUTS
BARBWIRE
BARBWIRES
BARBY
BARCA
BARCAROLE
BARCAROLES
BARCAROLLE
BARCAROLLES
BARCAS
BARCHAN
BARCHANE
BARCHANES
BARCHANS
BARD
BARDASH

BARDASHES
BARDE
BARDED
BARDES
BARDIC
BARDIE
BARDIER
BARDIES
BARDIEST
BARDING
BARDLING
BARDLINGS
BARDO
BARDOLATER
BARDOLATERS
BARDOLATRIES
BARDOLATROUS
BARDOLATRY
BARDOS
BARDS
BARDSHIP
BARDSHIPS
BARDY
BARE
BAREBACK
BAREBACKED
BAREBOAT
BAREBOATS
BAREBONE
BAREBONES
BARED
BAREFACED
BAREFACEDLY
BAREFACEDNESS
BAREFACEDNESSES
BAREFIT
BAREFOOT
BAREFOOTED
BAREGE
BAREGES
BAREGINE
BAREGINES
BAREHANDED
BAREHEAD
BAREHEADED
BARELEGGED
BARELY
BARENESS
BARENESSES
BARER
BARES
BARESARK
BARESARKS
BAREST
BARESTHESIA
BARF

BARFED
BARFING
BARFLIES
BARFLY
BARFS
BARFUL
BARGAIN
BARGAINED
BARGAINER
BARGAINERS
BARGAINING
BARGAININGS
BARGAINS
BARGANDER
BARGANDERS
BARGE
BARGEBOARD
BARGEBOARDS
BARGED
BARGEE
BARGEES
BARGEESE
BARGELLO
BARGELLOS
BARGEMAN
BARGEMASTER
BARGEMASTERS
BARGEMEN
BARGEPOLE
BARGEPOLES
BARGES
BARGEST
BARGESTS
BARGHAISTS
BARGHEST
BARGHESTS
BARGING
BARGOOSE
BARGUEST
BARGUESTS
BARHOP
BARHOPPED
BARHOPPING
BARHOPS
BARIC
BARILLA
BARILLAS
BARING
BARISH
BARISTA
BARISTAS
BARISTI
BARITE
BARITES
BARITONAL
BARITONE

BARITONES
BARIUM
BARIUMS
BARK
BARKAN
BARKANS
BARKANTINE
BARKANTINES
BARKED
BARKEEP
BARKEEPER
BARKEEPERS
BARKEEPS
BARKEN
BARKENED
BARKENING
BARKENS
BARKENTINE
BARKENTINES
BARKER
BARKERS
BARKHAN
BARKHANS
BARKIER
BARKIEST
BARKING
BARKLESS
BARKS
BARKY
BARLEDUC
BARLEDUCS
BARLESS
BARLEY
BARLEYCORN
BARLEYCORNS
BARLEYS
BARLOW
BARLOWS
BARM
BARMAID
BARMAIDS
BARMAN
BARMBRACK
BARMBRACKS
BARMEN
BARMIE
BARMIER
BARMIEST
BARMINESS
BARMINESSES
BARMITSVAH
BARMITSVAHS
BARMITZVAH
BARMITZVAHS
BARMKIN
BARMKINS

BARMS
BARMY
BARN
BARNACLE
BARNACLED
BARNACLES
BARNBRACK
BARNBRACKS
BARNED
BARNET
BARNETS
BARNEY
BARNEYED
BARNEYING
BARNEYS
BARNIER
BARNIEST
BARNING
BARNLIKE
BARNS
BARNSBREAKING
BARNSBREAKINGS
BARNSTORM
BARNSTORMED
BARNSTORMER
BARNSTORMERS
BARNSTORMING
BARNSTORMINGS
BARNSTORMS
BARNY
BARNYARD
BARNYARDS
BARO
BAROCCO
BAROCCOS
BAROCEPTOR
BAROCEPTORS
BAROCK
BAROCKS
BARODYNAMICS
BAROGNOSIS
BAROGNOSTIC
BAROGRAM
BAROGRAMS
BAROGRAPH
BAROGRAPHIC
BAROGRAPHS
BAROMETER
BAROMETERS
BAROMETRIC
BAROMETRICAL
BAROMETRICALLY
BAROMETRIES
BAROMETRY
BAROMETZ
BAROMETZES

BARON
BARONAGE
BARONAGES
BARONESS
BARONESSES
BARONET
BARONETAGE
BARONETAGES
BARONETCIES
BARONETCY
BARONETESS
BARONETESSES
BARONETICAL
BARONETS
BARONG
BARONGS
BARONIAL
BARONIES
BARONNE
BARONNES
BARONS
BARONY
BAROPHILE
BAROPHILES
BAROPHILIC
BAROPHORESIS
BAROQUE
BAROQUELY
BAROQUES
BARORECEPTOR
BARORECEPTORS
BAROSCOPE
BAROSCOPES
BAROSCOPIC
BAROSCOPICALLY
BAROSTAT
BAROSTATS
BAROUCHE
BAROUCHES
BARP
BARPERSON
BARPERSONS
BARPS
BARQUANTINE
BARQUANTINES
BARQUE
BARQUENTINE
BARQUENTINES
BARQUES
BARQUETTE
BARQUETTES
BARRA
BARRABLE
BARRACAN
BARRACANS
BARRACE

BARRACES
BARRACK
BARRACKED
BARRACKER
BARRACKERS
BARRACKING
BARRACKINGS
BARRACKS
BARRACOON
BARRACOONS
BARRACOOTA
BARRACOOTAS
BARRACOUTA
BARRACOUTAS
BARRACUDA
BARRACUDAS
BARRAGE
BARRAGED
BARRAGES
BARRAGING
BARRAMUNDA
BARRAMUNDAS
BARRAMUNDI
BARRAMUNDIES
BARRAMUNDIS
BARRANCA
BARRANCAS
BARRANCO
BARRANCOS
BARRAT
BARRATER
BARRATERS
BARRATOR
BARRATORS
BARRATRIES
BARRATROUS
BARRATROUSLY
BARRATRY
BARRATS
BARRE
BARRED
BARREED
BARREFULL
BARREING
BARREL
BARRELAGE
BARRELAGES
BARRELED
BARRELFUL
BARRELFULS
BARRELHEAD
BARRELHEADS
BARRELHOUSE
BARRELHOUSES
BARRELING
BARRELLED

BARRELLING
BARRELS
BARRELSFUL
BARREN
BARRENER
BARRENEST
BARRENLY
BARRENNESS
BARRENNESSES
BARRENS
BARRENWORT
BARRENWORTS
BARRES
BARRET
BARRETOR
BARRETORS
BARRETRIES
BARRETROUS
BARRETROUSLY
BARRETRY
BARRETS
BARRETTE
BARRETTER
BARRETTERS
BARRETTES
BARRICADE
BARRICADED
BARRICADER
BARRICADERS
BARRICADES
BARRICADING
BARRICADO
BARRICADOED
BARRICADOES
BARRICADOING
BARRICADOS
BARRICO
BARRICOES
BARRICOS
BARRIE
BARRIER
BARRIERED
BARRIERING
BARRIERS
BARRIES
BARRING
BARRINGS
BARRIO
BARRIOS
BARRISTER
BARRISTERIAL
BARRISTERS
BARRISTERSHIP
BARRISTERSHIPS
BARRO
BARROOM

BARROOMS
BARROW
BARROWFUL
BARROWFULS
BARROWS
BARRULET
BARRULETS
BARRY
BARS
BARSTOOL
BARSTOOLS
BARTEND
BARTENDED
BARTENDER
BARTENDERS
BARTENDING
BARTENDS
BARTER
BARTERED
BARTERER
BARTERERS
BARTERING
BARTERS
BARTISAN
BARTISANS
BARTIZAN
BARTIZANED
BARTIZANS
BARTON
BARTONS
BARTSIA
BARTSIAS
BARWARE
BARWARES
BARWOOD
BARWOODS
BARYCENTRE
BARYCENTRES
BARYCENTRIC
BARYE
BARYES
BARYON
BARYONIC
BARYONS
BARYSPHERE
BARYSPHERES
BARYTA
BARYTAS
BARYTE
BARYTES
BARYTIC
BARYTON
BARYTONE
BARYTONES
BARYTONS
BAS

BASAL
BASALLY
BASALT
BASALTES
BASALTIC
BASALTS
BASALTWARE
BASAN
BASANITE
BASANITES
BASANS
BASCINET
BASCINETS
BASCULE
BASCULES
BASE
BASEBALL
BASEBALLER
BASEBALLERS
BASEBALLS
BASEBAND
BASEBANDS
BASEBOARD
BASEBOARDS
BASEBORN
BASEBURNER
BASEBURNERS
BASED
BASELARD
BASELARDS
BASELESS
BASELESSLY
BASELESSNESS
BASELESSNESSES
BASELINE
BASELINER
BASELINERS
BASELINES
BASELY
BASEMAN
BASEMEN
BASEMENT
BASEMENTLESS
BASEMENTS
BASENESS
BASENESSES
BASENJI
BASENJIS
BASEPLATE
BASEPLATES
BASER
BASERUNNER
BASERUNNERS
BASERUNNING
BASERUNNINGS
BASES

BASEST
BASH
BASHAW
BASHAWISM
BASHAWISMS
BASHAWS
BASHAWSHIP
BASHAWSHIPS
BASHED
BASHER
BASHERS
BASHES
BASHFUL
BASHFULLY
BASHFULNESS
BASHFULNESSES
BASHIBAZOUK
BASHIBAZOUKS
BASHING
BASHINGS
BASHLESS
BASHLIK
BASHLIKS
BASHLYK
BASHLYKS
BASHO
BASIC
BASICALLY
BASICITIES
BASICITY
BASICRANIAL
BASICRANIALLY
BASICS
BASIDIA
BASIDIAL
BASIDIOCARP
BASIDIOCARPS
BASIDIOMYCETE
BASIDIOMYCETES
BASIDIOMYCETOUS
BASIDIOSPORE
BASIDIOSPORES
BASIDIOSPOROUS
BASIDIUM
BASIFICATION
BASIFICATIONS
BASIFIED
BASIFIER
BASIFIERS
BASIFIES
BASIFIXED
BASIFUGAL
BASIFY
BASIFYING
BASIL
BASILAR

BASILARY
BASILIC
BASILICA
BASILICAE
BASILICAL
BASILICAN
BASILICAS
BASILICON
BASILICONS
BASILISK
BASILISKS
BASILS
BASIN
BASINAL
BASINED
BASINET
BASINETS
BASINFUL
BASINFULS
BASING
BASINS
BASION
BASIONS
BASIPETAL
BASIPETALLY
BASIS
BASK
BASKED
BASKET
BASKETBALL
BASKETBALLS
BASKETFUL
BASKETFULS
BASKETLIKE
BASKETRIES
BASKETRY
BASKETS
BASKETSFUL
BASKETWEAVE
BASKETWEAVER
BASKETWEAVERS
BASKETWEAVES
BASKETWORK
BASKETWORKS
BASKING
BASKS
BASMATI
BASMATIS
BASMITZVAH
BASMITZVAHS
BASNET
BASNETS
BASOCHE
BASOCHES
BASON
BASONS

BASOPHIL
BASOPHILE
BASOPHILES
BASOPHILIA
BASOPHILIAS
BASOPHILIC
BASOPHILS
BASQUE
BASQUED
BASQUES
BASQUINE
BASQUINES
BASS
BASSE
BASSED
BASSER
BASSES
BASSEST
BASSET
BASSETED
BASSETING
BASSETS
BASSETT
BASSETTED
BASSETTING
BASSETTS
BASSI
BASSIER
BASSIEST
BASSINET
BASSINETS
BASSING
BASSIST
BASSISTS
BASSLY
BASSNESS
BASSNESSES
BASSO
BASSOON
BASSOONIST
BASSOONISTS
BASSOONS
BASSOS
BASSWOOD
BASSWOODS
BASSY
BAST
BASTA
BASTARD
BASTARDIES
BASTARDISATION
BASTARDISATIONS
BASTARDISE
BASTARDISED
BASTARDISES
BASTARDISING

BASTARDISM
BASTARDISMS
BASTARDIZATION
BASTARDIZATIONS
BASTARDIZE
BASTARDIZED
BASTARDIZES
BASTARDIZING
BASTARDLY
BASTARDRY
BASTARDS
BASTARDY
BASTE
BASTED
BASTER
BASTERS
BASTES
BASTI
BASTIDE
BASTIDES
BASTILE
BASTILES
BASTILLE
BASTILLES
BASTINADE
BASTINADED
BASTINADES
BASTINADING
BASTINADO
BASTINADOED
BASTINADOES
BASTINADOING
BASTING
BASTINGS
BASTION
BASTIONED
BASTIONS
BASTIS
BASTLE
BASTLES
BASTNAESITE
BASTNAESITES
BASTNASITE
BASTNASITES
BASTO
BASTOS
BASTS
BASUCO
BASUCOS
BAT
BATABLE
BATATA
BATATAS
BATAVIA
BATAVIAS
BATBOY

BATBOYS
BATCH
BATCHED
BATCHER
BATCHERS
BATCHES
BATCHING
BATCHINGS
BATE
BATEAU
BATEAUX
BATED
BATELESS
BATELEUR
BATELEURS
BATEMENT
BATEMENTS
BATES
BATFISH
BATFISHES
BATFOWL
BATFOWLED
BATFOWLER
BATFOWLERS
BATFOWLING
BATFOWLINGS
BATFOWLS
BATH
BATHCUBE
BATHCUBES
BATHE
BATHED
BATHER
BATHERS
BATHES
BATHETIC
BATHETICALLY
BATHHOUSE
BATHHOUSES
BATHING
BATHLESS
BATHMAT
BATHMATS
BATHMIC
BATHMISM
BATHMISMS
BATHMITSVAHS
BATHMITZVAH
BATHMITZVAHS
BATHMIZVAHS
BATHOCHROME
BATHOCHROMES
BATHOCHROMIC
BATHOLITE
BATHOLITES
BATHOLITH

BATHOLITHIC
BATHOLITHS
BATHOLITIC
BATHOMETER
BATHOMETERS
BATHOMETRIC
BATHOMETRICALLY
BATHOMETRY
BATHOPHILE
BATHOPHILES
BATHOPHILOUS
BATHOPHOBIA
BATHOPHOBIAS
BATHORSE
BATHORSES
BATHOS
BATHOSES
BATHROBE
BATHROBES
BATHROOM
BATHROOMS
BATHS
BATHTUB
BATHTUBS
BATHWATER
BATHWATERS
BATHYAL
BATHYBIUS
BATHYBIUSES
BATHYGRAPHICAL
BATHYLIMNETIC
BATHYLITE
BATHYLITES
BATHYLITH
BATHYLITHIC
BATHYLITHS
BATHYLITIC
BATHYMETER
BATHYMETERS
BATHYMETRIC
BATHYMETRICAL
BATHYMETRICALLY
BATHYMETRIES
BATHYMETRY
BATHYPELAGIC
BATHYSCAPE
BATHYSCAPES
BATHYSCAPH
BATHYSCAPHE
BATHYSCAPHES
BATHYSCAPHS
BATHYSPHERE
BATHYSPHERES
BATIK
BATIKS
BATING

BATISTE
BATISTES
BATLER
BATLERS
BATLET
BATLETS
BATLIKE
BATMAN
BATMEN
BATMITZVAH
BATMITZVAHS
BATOLOGICAL
BATOLOGIES
BATOLOGIST
BATOLOGISTS
BATOLOGY
BATON
BATONED
BATONING
BATONS
BATOON
BATOONED
BATOONING
BATOONS
BATRACHIA
BATRACHIAN
BATRACHIANS
BATRACHOPHOBIA
BATRACHOPHOBIAS
BATRACHOPHOBIC
BATS
BATSMAN
BATSMANSHIP
BATSMANSHIPS
BATSMEN
BATSWING
BATSWOMAN
BATSWOMEN
BATT
BATTA
BATTAILOUS
BATTALIA
BATTALIAS
BATTALION
BATTALIONS
BATTAS
BATTEAU
BATTEAUX
BATTED
BATTEL
BATTELED
BATTELER
BATTELERS
BATTELING
BATTELLED
BATTELLING

BATTELS
BATTEMENT
BATTEMENTS
BATTEN
BATTENED
BATTENER
BATTENERS
BATTENING
BATTENINGS
BATTENS
BATTER
BATTERED
BATTERER
BATTERERS
BATTERIE
BATTERIES
BATTERING
BATTERINGS
BATTERO
BATTEROS
BATTERS
BATTERY
BATTIER
BATTIEST
BATTIK
BATTIKS
BATTILL
BATTILLED
BATTILLING
BATTILLS
BATTINESS
BATTINESSES
BATTING
BATTINGS
BATTLE
BATTLEBUS
BATTLEBUSES
BATTLEBUSSES
BATTLED
BATTLEDOOR
BATTLEDOORS
BATTLEDORE
BATTLEDORED
BATTLEDORES
BATTLEDORING
BATTLEDRESS
BATTLEDRESSES
BATTLEFIELD
BATTLEFIELDS
BATTLEFRONT
BATTLEFRONTS
BATTLEGROUND
BATTLEGROUNDS
BATTLEMENT
BATTLEMENTED
BATTLEMENTS

BATTLEPIECE
BATTLEPIECES
BATTLEPLANE
BATTLEPLANES
BATTLER
BATTLERS
BATTLES
BATTLESHIP
BATTLESHIPS
BATTLEWAGON
BATTLEWAGONS
BATTLING
BATTOLOGICAL
BATTOLOGIES
BATTOLOGY
BATTS
BATTU
BATTUE
BATTUES
BATTUTA
BATTUTAS
BATTY
BATWING
BATWOMAN
BATWOMEN
BAUBEE
BAUBEES
BAUBLE
BAUBLES
BAUBLING
BAUCHLE
BAUCHLED
BAUCHLES
BAUCHLING
BAUD
BAUDEKIN
BAUDEKINS
BAUDIKIN
BAUDIKINS
BAUDRIC
BAUDRICK
BAUDRICKE
BAUDRICKES
BAUDRICKS
BAUDRICS
BAUDRONS
BAUDRONSES
BAUDS
BAUERA
BAUERAS
BAUHINIA
BAUHINIAS
BAUK
BAUKED
BAUKING
BAUKS

BAULK
BAULKED
BAULKER
BAULKERS
BAULKIER
BAULKIEST
BAULKILY
BAULKINESS
BAULKING
BAULKS
BAULKY
BAUR
BAURS
BAUSOND
BAUXITE
BAUXITES
BAUXITIC
BAVARDAGE
BAVARDAGES
BAVAROIS
BAVIN
BAVINS
BAWBEE
BAWBEES
BAWBLE
BAWBLES
BAWCOCK
BAWCOCKS
BAWD
BAWDIER
BAWDIES
BAWDIEST
BAWDILY
BAWDINESS
BAWDINESSES
BAWDKIN
BAWDKINS
BAWDRIC
BAWDRICS
BAWDRIES
BAWDRY
BAWDS
BAWDY
BAWDYHOUSE
BAWDYHOUSES
BAWL
BAWLED
BAWLER
BAWLERS
BAWLEY
BAWLEYS
BAWLING
BAWLINGS
BAWLS
BAWN
BAWNEEN

BAWNEENS
BAWNS
BAWR
BAWRS
BAWSUNT
BAWTIE
BAWTIES
BAWTY
BAXTER
BAXTERS
BAY
BAYADEER
BAYADEERS
BAYADERE
BAYADERES
BAYAMO
BAYAMOS
BAYARD
BAYARDS
BAYBERRIES
BAYBERRY
BAYE
BAYED
BAYES
BAYING
BAYLE
BAYLES
BAYMAN
BAYMEN
BAYONET
BAYONETED
BAYONETING
BAYONETS
BAYONETTED
BAYONETTING
BAYOU
BAYOUS
BAYS
BAYT
BAYTED
BAYTING
BAYTS
BAYWOOD
BAYWOODS
BAZAAR
BAZAARS
BAZAR
BAZARS
BAZAZZ
BAZAZZES
BAZOO
BAZOOKA
BAZOOKAS
BAZOOMS
BAZOOS
BAZOUKI

BAZOUKIS
BDELLIUM
BDELLIUMS
BE
BEACH
BEACHBOY
BEACHBOYS
BEACHCOMB
BEACHCOMBED
BEACHCOMBER
BEACHCOMBERS
BEACHCOMBING
BEACHCOMBINGS
BEACHCOMBS
BEACHED
BEACHES
BEACHFRONT
BEACHFRONTS
BEACHGOER
BEACHGOERS
BEACHHEAD
BEACHHEADS
BEACHIE
BEACHIER
BEACHIES
BEACHIEST
BEACHING
BEACHSIDE
BEACHWEAR
BEACHY
BEACON
BEACONED
BEACONING
BEACONS
BEAD
BEADBLAST
BEADBLASTED
BEADBLASTER
BEADBLASTERS
BEADBLASTING
BEADBLASTS
BEADED
BEADIER
BEADIEST
BEADILY
BEADINESS
BEADING
BEADINGS
BEADLE
BEADLEDOM
BEADLEDOMS
BEADLEHOOD
BEADLEHOODS
BEADLES
BEADLESHIP
BEADLESHIPS

BEADLIKE
BEADMAN
BEADMEN
BEADROLL
BEADROLLS
BEADS
BEADSMAN
BEADSMEN
BEADSWOMAN
BEADSWOMEN
BEADWORK
BEADWORKS
BEADY
BEAGLE
BEAGLED
BEAGLER
BEAGLERS
BEAGLES
BEAGLING
BEAGLINGS
BEAK
BEAKED
BEAKER
BEAKERS
BEAKIER
BEAKIEST
BEAKLESS
BEAKLIKE
BEAKS
BEAKY
BEAM
BEAMED
BEAMER
BEAMERS
BEAMIER
BEAMIEST
BEAMILY
BEAMINESS
BEAMINESSES
BEAMING
BEAMINGLY
BEAMINGS
BEAMISH
BEAMISHLY
BEAMLESS
BEAMLET
BEAMLETS
BEAMLIKE
BEAMS
BEAMY
BEAN
BEANBAG
BEANBAGS
BEANBALL
BEANBALLS
BEANED

BEANERIES
BEANERY
BEANFEAST
BEANFEASTS
BEANIE
BEANIES
BEANING
BEANLIKE
BEANO
BEANOS
BEANPOLE
BEANPOLES
BEANS
BEANSTALK
BEANSTALKS
BEANY
BEAR
BEARABILITIES
BEARABILITY
BEARABLE
BEARABLENESS
BEARABLENESSES
BEARABLY
BEARBAITING
BEARBAITINGS
BEARBERRIES
BEARBERRY
BEARBINE
BEARBINES
BEARCAT
BEARCATS
BEARD
BEARDED
BEARDEDNESS
BEARDEDNESSES
BEARDIE
BEARDIES
BEARDING
BEARDLESS
BEARDLESSNESS
BEARDS
BEARDTONGUE
BEARDTONGUES
BEARE
BEARED
BEARER
BEARERS
BEARES
BEARHUG
BEARHUGS
BEARING
BEARINGS
BEARISH
BEARISHLY
BEARISHNESS
BEARISHNESSES

BEARLIKE
BEARNAISE
BEARNAISES
BEARS
BEARSKIN
BEARSKINS
BEARWARD
BEARWARDS
BEARWOOD
BEARWOODS
BEAST
BEASTHOOD
BEASTHOODS
BEASTIE
BEASTIES
BEASTILY
BEASTINGS
BEASTLIER
BEASTLIEST
BEASTLIKE
BEASTLINESS
BEASTLINESSES
BEASTLY
BEASTOID
BEASTOIDS
BEASTS
BEAT
BEATABLE
BEATBOX
BEATBOXES
BEATEN
BEATER
BEATERS
BEATH
BEATHED
BEATHING
BEATHS
BEATIER
BEATIEST
BEATIFIC
BEATIFICAL
BEATIFICALLY
BEATIFICATION
BEATIFICATIONS
BEATIFIED
BEATIFIES
BEATIFY
BEATIFYING
BEATING
BEATINGS
BEATITUDE
BEATITUDES
BEATLESS
BEATNIK
BEATNIKS
BEATS

BEATY
BEAU
BEAUCOUP
BEAUFET
BEAUFETS
BEAUFFET
BEAUFFETS
BEAUFIN
BEAUFINS
BEAUISH
BEAUJOLAIS
BEAUMONTAGE
BEAUMONTAGES
BEAUMONTAGUE
BEAUMONTAGUES
BEAUS
BEAUT
BEAUTEOUS
BEAUTEOUSLY
BEAUTEOUSNESS
BEAUTEOUSNESSES
BEAUTICIAN
BEAUTICIANS
BEAUTIED
BEAUTIES
BEAUTIFICATION
BEAUTIFICATIONS
BEAUTIFIED
BEAUTIFIER
BEAUTIFIERS
BEAUTIFIES
BEAUTIFUL
BEAUTIFULLY
BEAUTIFULNESS
BEAUTIFULNESSES
BEAUTIFY
BEAUTIFYING
BEAUTS
BEAUTY
BEAUTYING
BEAUX
BEAUXITE
BEAUXITES
BEAVER
BEAVERBOARD
BEAVERBOARDS
BEAVERED
BEAVERIES
BEAVERING
BEAVERS
BEAVERY
BEBEERINE
BEBEERINES
BEBEERU
BEBEERUS
BEBLOOD

BEBLOODED
BEBLOODING
BEBLOODS
BEBLUBBERED
BEBOP
BEBOPPED
BEBOPPER
BEBOPPERS
BEBOPPING
BEBOPS
BEBUNG
BEBUNGS
BECALL
BECALLED
BECALLING
BECALLS
BECALM
BECALMED
BECALMING
BECALMS
BECAME
BECAP
BECAPPED
BECAPPING
BECAPS
BECARPET
BECARPETED
BECARPETING
BECARPETS
BECASSE
BECASSES
BECAUSE
BECCACCIA
BECCACCIAS
BECCAFICO
BECCAFICOS
BECHALK
BECHALKED
BECHALKING
BECHALKS
BECHAMEL
BECHAMELS
BECHANCE
BECHANCED
BECHANCES
BECHANCING
BECHARM
BECHARMED
BECHARMING
BECHARMS
BECK
BECKE
BECKED
BECKES
BECKET
BECKETS

BECKING
BECKON
BECKONED
BECKONER
BECKONERS
BECKONING
BECKONS
BECKS
BECLAMOR
BECLAMORED
BECLAMORING
BECLAMORS
BECLASP
BECLASPED
BECLASPING
BECLASPS
BECLOAK
BECLOAKED
BECLOAKING
BECLOAKS
BECLOG
BECLOGGED
BECLOGGING
BECLOGS
BECLOTHE
BECLOTHED
BECLOTHES
BECLOTHING
BECLOUD
BECLOUDED
BECLOUDING
BECLOUDS
BECLOWN
BECLOWNED
BECLOWNING
BECLOWNS
BECOME
BECOMES
BECOMING
BECOMINGLY
BECOMINGNESS
BECOMINGNESSES
BECOMINGS
BECOWARD
BECOWARDED
BECOWARDING
BECOWARDS
BECQUEREL
BECQUERELS
BECRAWL
BECRAWLED
BECRAWLING
BECRAWLS
BECRIME
BECRIMED
BECRIMES

BECRIMING
BECROWD
BECROWDED
BECROWDING
BECROWDS
BECRUST
BECRUSTED
BECRUSTING
BECRUSTS
BECUDGEL
BECUDGELED
BECUDGELING
BECUDGELLED
BECUDGELLING
BECUDGELS
BECURL
BECURLED
BECURLING
BECURLS
BECURSE
BECURSED
BECURSES
BECURSING
BECURST
BED
BEDABBLE
BEDABBLED
BEDABBLES
BEDABBLING
BEDAD
BEDAGGLE
BEDAGGLED
BEDAGGLES
BEDAGGLING
BEDAMN
BEDAMNED
BEDAMNING
BEDAMNS
BEDARKEN
BEDARKENED
BEDARKENING
BEDARKENS
BEDASH
BEDASHED
BEDASHES
BEDASHING
BEDAUB
BEDAUBED
BEDAUBING
BEDAUBS
BEDAWIN
BEDAWINS
BEDAZE
BEDAZED
BEDAZES
BEDAZING

BEDAZZLE
BEDAZZLED
BEDAZZLEMENT
BEDAZZLEMENTS
BEDAZZLES
BEDAZZLING
BEDBUG
BEDBUGS
BEDCHAIR
BEDCHAIRS
BEDCHAMBER
BEDCHAMBERS
BEDCLOTHES
BEDCOVER
BEDCOVERING
BEDCOVERINGS
BEDCOVERS
BEDDABLE
BEDDED
BEDDER
BEDDERS
BEDDING
BEDDINGS
BEDE
BEDEAFEN
BEDEAFENED
BEDEAFENING
BEDEAFENS
BEDECK
BEDECKED
BEDECKING
BEDECKS
BEDEGUAR
BEDEGUARS
BEDEL
BEDELL
BEDELLS
BEDELLSHIP
BEDELLSHIPS
BEDELS
BEDELSHIP
BEDELSHIPS
BEDEMAN
BEDEMEN
BEDERAL
BEDERALS
BEDES
BEDESMAN
BEDESMEN
BEDEVIL
BEDEVILED
BEDEVILING
BEDEVILLED
BEDEVILLING
BEDEVILMENT
BEDEVILMENTS

BEDEVILS
BEDEW
BEDEWED
BEDEWING
BEDEWS
BEDFAST
BEDFELLOW
BEDFELLOWS
BEDFRAME
BEDFRAMES
BEDGOWN
BEDGOWNS
BEDIAPER
BEDIAPERED
BEDIAPERING
BEDIAPERS
BEDIDE
BEDIGHT
BEDIGHTED
BEDIGHTING
BEDIGHTS
BEDIM
BEDIMMED
BEDIMMING
BEDIMMINGS
BEDIMPLE
BEDIMPLED
BEDIMPLES
BEDIMPLING
BEDIMS
BEDIRTIED
BEDIRTIES
BEDIRTY
BEDIRTYING
BEDIZEN
BEDIZENED
BEDIZENING
BEDIZENMENT
BEDIZENMENTS
BEDIZENS
BEDLAM
BEDLAMISM
BEDLAMISMS
BEDLAMITE
BEDLAMITES
BEDLAMP
BEDLAMPS
BEDLAMS
BEDLESS
BEDLIKE
BEDMAKER
BEDMAKERS
BEDMATE
BEDMATES
BEDOTTED
BEDOUIN

BEDOUINS
BEDPAN
BEDPANS
BEDPLATE
BEDPLATES
BEDPOST
BEDPOSTS
BEDPRESSER
BEDPRESSERS
BEDQUILT
BEDQUILTS
BEDRAGGLE
BEDRAGGLED
BEDRAGGLES
BEDRAGGLING
BEDRAIL
BEDRAILS
BEDRAL
BEDRALS
BEDRAPE
BEDRAPED
BEDRAPES
BEDRAPING
BEDRENCH
BEDRENCHED
BEDRENCHES
BEDRENCHING
BEDRID
BEDRIDDEN
BEDRIGHT
BEDRIGHTS
BEDRIVEL
BEDRIVELED
BEDRIVELING
BEDRIVELLED
BEDRIVELLING
BEDRIVELS
BEDROCK
BEDROCKS
BEDROLL
BEDROLLS
BEDROOM
BEDROOMED
BEDROOMS
BEDROP
BEDROPPED
BEDROPPING
BEDROPS
BEDROPT
BEDRUG
BEDRUGGED
BEDRUGGING
BEDRUGS
BEDS
BEDSHEET
BEDSHEETS

BEDSIDE
BEDSIDES
BEDSIT
BEDSITS
BEDSITTER
BEDSITTERS
BEDSITTING
BEDSOCKS
BEDSONIA
BEDSONIAS
BEDSORE
BEDSORES
BEDSPREAD
BEDSPREADS
BEDSPRING
BEDSPRINGS
BEDSTAND
BEDSTANDS
BEDSTEAD
BEDSTEADS
BEDSTRAW
BEDSTRAWS
BEDTICK
BEDTICKS
BEDTIME
BEDTIMES
BEDU
BEDUCK
BEDUCKED
BEDUCKING
BEDUCKS
BEDUIN
BEDUINS
BEDUMB
BEDUMBED
BEDUMBING
BEDUMBS
BEDUNCE
BEDUNCED
BEDUNCES
BEDUNCING
BEDUNG
BEDUNGED
BEDUNGING
BEDUNGS
BEDUST
BEDUSTED
BEDUSTING
BEDUSTS
BEDWARD
BEDWARDS
BEDWARF
BEDWARFED
BEDWARFING
BEDWARFS
BEDWARMER

BEDWARMERS
BEDYDE
BEDYE
BEDYED
BEDYEING
BEDYES
BEE
BEEBEE
BEEBEES
BEEBREAD
BEEBREADS
BEECH
BEECHDROPS
BEECHEN
BEECHES
BEECHIER
BEECHIEST
BEECHNUT
BEECHNUTS
BEECHY
BEEF
BEEFALO
BEEFALOES
BEEFALOS
BEEFBURGER
BEEFBURGERS
BEEFCAKE
BEEFCAKES
BEEFEATER
BEEFEATERS
BEEFED
BEEFIER
BEEFIEST
BEEFILY
BEEFINESS
BEEFING
BEEFLESS
BEEFS
BEEFSTEAK
BEEFSTEAKS
BEEFWOOD
BEEFWOODS
BEEFY
BEEGAH
BEEGAHS
BEEHIVE
BEEHIVES
BEEKEEPER
BEEKEEPERS
BEEKEEPING
BEEKEEPINGS
BEELIKE
BEELINE
BEELINED
BEELINES
BEELINING

BEEN
BEENAH
BEENAHS
BEENTO
BEENTOS
BEEP
BEEPED
BEEPER
BEEPERS
BEEPING
BEEPS
BEER
BEERAGE
BEERAGES
BEERHALL
BEERHALLS
BEERIER
BEERIEST
BEERILY
BEERINESS
BEERINESSES
BEERS
BEERY
BEES
BEESOME
BEESTINGS
BEESWAX
BEESWAXED
BEESWAXES
BEESWAXING
BEESWING
BEESWINGED
BEESWINGS
BEET
BEETED
BEETFLIES
BEETFLY
BEETING
BEETLE
BEETLEBRAIN
BEETLEBRAINED
BEETLEBRAINS
BEETLED
BEETLEHEAD
BEETLEHEADED
BEETLEHEADS
BEETLER
BEETLERS
BEETLES
BEETLING
BEETMASTER
BEETMASTERS
BEETMISTER
BEETMISTERS
BEETROOT
BEETROOTS

BEETS
BEEVES
BEEYARD
BEEYARDS
BEEZER
BEEZERS
BEFALL
BEFALLEN
BEFALLING
BEFALLS
BEFANA
BEFANAS
BEFELD
BEFELL
BEFFANA
BEFFANAS
BEFINGER
BEFINGERED
BEFINGERING
BEFINGERS
BEFINNED
BEFIT
BEFITS
BEFITTED
BEFITTING
BEFITTINGLY
BEFLAG
BEFLAGGED
BEFLAGGING
BEFLAGS
BEFLEA
BEFLEAED
BEFLEAING
BEFLEAS
BEFLECK
BEFLECKED
BEFLECKING
BEFLECKS
BEFLOWER
BEFLOWERED
BEFLOWERING
BEFLOWERS
BEFLUM
BEFLUMMED
BEFLUMMING
BEFLUMS
BEFOAM
BEFOAMED
BEFOAMING
BEFOAMS
BEFOG
BEFOGGED
BEFOGGING
BEFOGS
BEFOOL
BEFOOLED

BEFOOLING
BEFOOLS
BEFORE
BEFOREHAND
BEFORETIME
BEFORTUNE
BEFORTUNED
BEFORTUNES
BEFORTUNING
BEFOUL
BEFOULED
BEFOULER
BEFOULERS
BEFOULING
BEFOULMENT
BEFOULMENTS
BEFOULS
BEFRET
BEFRETS
BEFRETTED
BEFRETTING
BEFRIEND
BEFRIENDED
BEFRIENDER
BEFRIENDERS
BEFRIENDING
BEFRIENDS
BEFRINGE
BEFRINGED
BEFRINGES
BEFRINGING
BEFUDDLE
BEFUDDLED
BEFUDDLEMENT
BEFUDDLEMENTS
BEFUDDLES
BEFUDDLING
BEG
BEGAD
BEGALL
BEGALLED
BEGALLING
BEGALLS
BEGAN
BEGAR
BEGARS
BEGAT
BEGAZE
BEGAZED
BEGAZES
BEGAZING
BEGEM
BEGEMMED
BEGEMMING
BEGEMS
BEGET

BEGETS
BEGETTER
BEGETTERS
BEGETTING
BEGGAR
BEGGARDOM
BEGGARDOMS
BEGGARED
BEGGARHOOD
BEGGARIES
BEGGARING
BEGGARLINESS
BEGGARLINESSES
BEGGARLY
BEGGARS
BEGGARWEED
BEGGARWEEDS
BEGGARY
BEGGED
BEGGING
BEGGINGLY
BEGGINGS
BEGHARD
BEGHARDS
BEGIFT
BEGIFTED
BEGIFTING
BEGIFTS
BEGILD
BEGILDED
BEGILDING
BEGILDS
BEGILT
BEGIN
BEGINNE
BEGINNER
BEGINNERS
BEGINNES
BEGINNING
BEGINNINGLESS
BEGINNINGS
BEGINS
BEGIRD
BEGIRDED
BEGIRDING
BEGIRDLE
BEGIRDLED
BEGIRDLES
BEGIRDLING
BEGIRDS
BEGIRT
BEGLAD
BEGLADDED
BEGLADDING
BEGLADS
BEGLAMOR

BEGLAMORED
BEGLAMORING
BEGLAMORS
BEGLAMOUR
BEGLAMOURED
BEGLAMOURING
BEGLAMOURS
BEGLERBEG
BEGLERBEGS
BEGLOOM
BEGLOOMED
BEGLOOMING
BEGLOOMS
BEGNAW
BEGNAWED
BEGNAWING
BEGNAWS
BEGO
BEGOES
BEGOING
BEGONE
BEGONIA
BEGONIAS
BEGORAH
BEGORED
BEGORRA
BEGORRAH
BEGOT
BEGOTTEN
BEGRIM
BEGRIME
BEGRIMED
BEGRIMES
BEGRIMING
BEGRIMMED
BEGRIMMING
BEGRIMS
BEGROAN
BEGROANED
BEGROANING
BEGROANS
BEGRUDGE
BEGRUDGED
BEGRUDGES
BEGRUDGING
BEGRUDGINGLY
BEGS
BEGUILE
BEGUILED
BEGUILEMENT
BEGUILEMENTS
BEGUILER
BEGUILERS
BEGUILES
BEGUILING
BEGUILINGLY

BEGUIN
BEGUINAGE
BEGUINAGES
BEGUINE
BEGUINES
BEGUINS
BEGULF
BEGULFED
BEGULFING
BEGULFS
BEGUM
BEGUMS
BEGUN
BEGUNK
BEGUNKED
BEGUNKING
BEGUNKS
BEHALF
BEHALVES
BEHAPPEN
BEHAPPENED
BEHAPPENING
BEHAPPENS
BEHATTED
BEHAVE
BEHAVED
BEHAVER
BEHAVERS
BEHAVES
BEHAVING
BEHAVIOR
BEHAVIORAL
BEHAVIORALLY
BEHAVIORISM
BEHAVIORISMS
BEHAVIORIST
BEHAVIORISTIC
BEHAVIORISTS
BEHAVIORS
BEHAVIOUR
BEHAVIOURAL
BEHAVIOURALLY
BEHAVIOURISM
BEHAVIOURISMS
BEHAVIOURIST
BEHAVIOURISTIC
BEHAVIOURISTS
BEHAVIOURS
BEHEAD
BEHEADAL
BEHEADALS
BEHEADED
BEHEADING
BEHEADINGS
BEHEADS
BEHELD

BEHEMOTH
BEHEMOTHS
BEHEST
BEHESTS
BEHIGHT
BEHIGHTING
BEHIGHTS
BEHIND
BEHINDHAND
BEHINDS
BEHOLD
BEHOLDEN
BEHOLDER
BEHOLDERS
BEHOLDING
BEHOLDINGS
BEHOLDS
BEHOOF
BEHOOFS
BEHOOVE
BEHOOVED
BEHOOVES
BEHOOVING
BEHOTE
BEHOTES
BEHOTING
BEHOVE
BEHOVED
BEHOVEFUL
BEHOVELY
BEHOVES
BEHOVING
BEHOWL
BEHOWLED
BEHOWLING
BEHOWLS
BEIGE
BEIGEL
BEIGELS
BEIGES
BEIGNET
BEIGNETS
BEIGY
BEIN
BEING
BEINGLESS
BEINGNESS
BEINGNESSES
BEINGS
BEINKED
BEINNESS
BEINNESSES
BEJABBERS
BEJABERS
BEJADE
BEJADED

BEJADES
BEJADING
BEJANT
BEJANTS
BEJEEZUS
BEJESUIT
BEJESUITED
BEJESUITING
BEJESUITS
BEJESUS
BEJEWEL
BEJEWELED
BEJEWELING
BEJEWELLED
BEJEWELLING
BEJEWELS
BEJUMBLE
BEJUMBLED
BEJUMBLES
BEJUMBLING
BEKAH
BEKAHS
BEKISS
BEKISSED
BEKISSES
BEKISSING
BEKNAVE
BEKNAVED
BEKNAVES
BEKNAVING
BEKNIGHT
BEKNIGHTED
BEKNIGHTING
BEKNIGHTS
BEKNOT
BEKNOTS
BEKNOTTED
BEKNOTTING
BEKNOWN
BEL
BELABOR
BELABORED
BELABORING
BELABORS
BELABOUR
BELABOURED
BELABOURING
BELABOURS
BELACE
BELACED
BELACES
BELACING
BELADIED
BELADIES
BELADY
BELADYING

BELAH
BELAHS
BELAMIES
BELAMOURE
BELAMOURES
BELAMY
BELAR
BELARS
BELATE
BELATED
BELATEDLY
BELATEDNESS
BELATEDNESSES
BELATES
BELATING
BELAUD
BELAUDED
BELAUDING
BELAUDS
BELAY
BELAYED
BELAYING
BELAYS
BELCH
BELCHED
BELCHER
BELCHERS
BELCHES
BELCHING
BELDAM
BELDAME
BELDAMES
BELDAMS
BELEAGUER
BELEAGUERED
BELEAGUERING
BELEAGUERMENT
BELEAGUERMENTS
BELEAGUERS
BELEAP
BELEAPED
BELEAPING
BELEAPS
BELEAPT
BELEE
BELEED
BELEEING
BELEES
BELEMNITE
BELEMNITES
BELEMNOID
BELEMNOIDS
BELFRIED
BELFRIES
BELFRY
BELGA

BELGARD
BELGARDS
BELGAS
BELIE
BELIED
BELIEF
BELIEFLESS
BELIEFS
BELIER
BELIERS
BELIES
BELIEVABILITIES
BELIEVABILITY
BELIEVABLE
BELIEVABLY
BELIEVE
BELIEVED
BELIEVER
BELIEVERS
BELIEVES
BELIEVING
BELIEVINGLY
BELIKE
BELIQUOR
BELIQUORED
BELIQUORING
BELIQUORS
BELITTLE
BELITTLED
BELITTLEMENT
BELITTLEMENTS
BELITTLER
BELITTLERS
BELITTLES
BELITTLING
BELITTLINGLY
BELIVE
BELL
BELLADONNA
BELLADONNAS
BELLAMOURE
BELLAMOURES
BELLARMINE
BELLARMINES
BELLBIND
BELLBINDS
BELLBIRD
BELLBIRDS
BELLBOY
BELLBOYS
BELLCOTE
BELLCOTES
BELLE
BELLED
BELLEEK
BELLEEKS

BELLES
BELLETER
BELLETERS
BELLETRISM
BELLETRISMS
BELLETRIST
BELLETRISTIC
BELLETRISTICAL
BELLETRISTS
BELLETTRIST
BELLETTRISTS
BELLFLOWER
BELLFLOWERS
BELLFOUNDER
BELLFOUNDERS
BELLFOUNDRIES
BELLFOUNDRY
BELLHANGER
BELLHANGERS
BELLHOP
BELLHOPS
BELLIBONE
BELLIBONES
BELLICOSE
BELLICOSELY
BELLICOSITIES
BELLICOSITY
BELLIED
BELLIES
BELLIGERATI
BELLIGERATIS
BELLIGERENCE
BELLIGERENCES
BELLIGERENCIES
BELLIGERENCY
BELLIGERENT
BELLIGERENTLY
BELLIGERENTS
BELLING
BELLMAN
BELLMEN
BELLOCK
BELLOCKED
BELLOCKING
BELLOCKS
BELLOW
BELLOWED
BELLOWER
BELLOWERS
BELLOWING
BELLOWS
BELLPULL
BELLPULLS
BELLPUSH
BELLPUSHES
BELLS

BELLWETHER
BELLWETHERS
BELLWORT
BELLWORTS
BELLY
BELLYACHE
BELLYACHED
BELLYACHER
BELLYACHERS
BELLYACHES
BELLYACHING
BELLYBAND
BELLYBANDS
BELLYBUTTON
BELLYBUTTONS
BELLYFUL
BELLYFULS
BELLYING
BELLYINGS
BELOMANCIES
BELOMANCY
BELONG
BELONGED
BELONGER
BELONGERS
BELONGING
BELONGINGNESS
BELONGINGNESSES
BELONGINGS
BELONGS
BELOVE
BELOVED
BELOVEDS
BELOVES
BELOVING
BELOW
BELOWDECKS
BELOWGROUND
BELOWS
BELOWSTAIRS
BELS
BELSHAZZAR
BELSHAZZARS
BELT
BELTCOURSE
BELTCOURSES
BELTED
BELTER
BELTERS
BELTING
BELTINGS
BELTLESS
BELTLINE
BELTLINES
BELTMAN
BELTMEN

BELTS
BELTWAY
BELTWAYS
BELUGA
BELUGAS
BELVEDERE
BELVEDERES
BELYING
BEMA
BEMAD
BEMADAM
BEMADAMED
BEMADAMING
BEMADAMS
BEMADDED
BEMADDEN
BEMADDENED
BEMADDENING
BEMADDENS
BEMADDING
BEMADS
BEMAS
BEMATA
BEMAUL
BEMAULED
BEMAULING
BEMAULS
BEMAZED
BEMBEX
BEMBEXES
BEMBIX
BEMBIXES
BEMEAN
BEMEANED
BEMEANING
BEMEANS
BEMEANT
BEMEDAL
BEMEDALED
BEMEDALLED
BEMEDALLING
BEMEDALS
BEMETE
BEMETED
BEMETES
BEMETING
BEMINGLE
BEMINGLED
BEMINGLES
BEMINGLING
BEMIRE
BEMIRED
BEMIRES
BEMIRING
BEMIST
BEMISTED

BEMISTING
BEMISTS
BEMIX
BEMIXED
BEMIXES
BEMIXING
BEMIXT
BEMOAN
BEMOANED
BEMOANER
BEMOANERS
BEMOANING
BEMOANINGS
BEMOANS
BEMOCK
BEMOCKED
BEMOCKING
BEMOCKS
BEMOIL
BEMOILED
BEMOILING
BEMOILS
BEMONSTER
BEMONSTERED
BEMONSTERING
BEMONSTERS
BEMOUTH
BEMOUTHED
BEMOUTHING
BEMOUTHS
BEMUD
BEMUDDED
BEMUDDING
BEMUDDLE
BEMUDDLED
BEMUDDLES
BEMUDDLING
BEMUDS
BEMUFFLE
BEMUFFLED
BEMUFFLES
BEMUFFLING
BEMURMUR
BEMURMURED
BEMURMURING
BEMURMURS
BEMUSE
BEMUSED
BEMUSEDLY
BEMUSEMENT
BEMUSEMENTS
BEMUSES
BEMUSING
BEMUZZLE
BEMUZZLED
BEMUZZLES

BEMUZZLING
BEN
BENAME
BENAMED
BENAMES
BENAMING
BENCH
BENCHED
BENCHER
BENCHERS
BENCHERSHIP
BENCHERSHIPS
BENCHES
BENCHIER
BENCHIEST
BENCHING
BENCHLAND
BENCHLANDS
BENCHMARK
BENCHMARKING
BENCHMARKINGS
BENCHMARKS
BENCHWARMER
BENCHWARMERS
BENCHY
BEND
BENDABLE
BENDAY
BENDAYED
BENDAYING
BENDAYS
BENDED
BENDEE
BENDEES
BENDER
BENDERS
BENDIER
BENDIEST
BENDING
BENDINGLY
BENDINGS
BENDLET
BENDLETS
BENDS
BENDWAYS
BENDWISE
BENDY
BENDYS
BENE
BENEATH
BENEDICITE
BENEDICITES
BENEDICK
BENEDICKS
BENEDICT
BENEDICTION

BENEDICTIONAL
BENEDICTIONS
BENEDICTIVE
BENEDICTORY
BENEDICTS
BENEDIGHT
BENEFACT
BENEFACTED
BENEFACTING
BENEFACTION
BENEFACTIONS
BENEFACTOR
BENEFACTORS
BENEFACTORY
BENEFACTRESS
BENEFACTRESSES
BENEFACTS
BENEFIC
BENEFICE
BENEFICED
BENEFICENCE
BENEFICENCES
BENEFICENT
BENEFICENTIAL
BENEFICENTLY
BENEFICES
BENEFICIAL
BENEFICIALLY
BENEFICIALNESS
BENEFICIALS
BENEFICIARIES
BENEFICIARY
BENEFICIATE
BENEFICIATED
BENEFICIATES
BENEFICIATING
BENEFICIATION
BENEFICIATIONS
BENEFICING
BENEFIT
BENEFITED
BENEFITER
BENEFITERS
BENEFITING
BENEFITS
BENEFITTED
BENEFITTING
BENEMPT
BENEMPTED
BENEPLACITO
BENES
BENET
BENETS
BENETTED
BENETTING
BENEVOLENCE

BENEVOLENCES
BENEVOLENT
BENEVOLENTLY
BENEVOLENTNESS
BENGALINE
BENGALINES
BENI
BENIGHT
BENIGHTED
BENIGHTEDLY
BENIGHTEDNESS
BENIGHTEDNESSES
BENIGHTEN
BENIGHTENED
BENIGHTENING
BENIGHTENINGS
BENIGHTENS
BENIGHTER
BENIGHTERS
BENIGHTING
BENIGHTINGS
BENIGHTMENT
BENIGHTMENTS
BENIGHTS
BENIGN
BENIGNANCIES
BENIGNANCY
BENIGNANT
BENIGNANTLY
BENIGNER
BENIGNEST
BENIGNITIES
BENIGNITY
BENIGNLY
BENIS
BENISEED
BENISEEDS
BENISON
BENISONS
BENITIER
BENITIERS
BENJ
BENJAMIN
BENJAMINS
BENJES
BENNE
BENNES
BENNET
BENNETS
BENNI
BENNIES
BENNIS
BENNY
BENOMYL
BENOMYLS
BENS

BENT
BENTHAL
BENTHIC
BENTHOAL
BENTHON
BENTHONIC
BENTHOPELAGIC
BENTHOS
BENTHOSCOPE
BENTHOSCOPES
BENTHOSES
BENTIER
BENTIEST
BENTO
BENTONITE
BENTONITES
BENTONITIC
BENTOS
BENTS
BENTWOOD
BENTWOODS
BENTY
BENUMB
BENUMBED
BENUMBEDNESS
BENUMBEDNESSES
BENUMBING
BENUMBINGLY
BENUMBMENT
BENUMBMENTS
BENUMBS
BENZAL
BENZALDEHYDE
BENZALDEHYDES
BENZALS
BENZANTHRACENE
BENZANTHRACENES
BENZENE
BENZENECARBONYL
BENZENES
BENZENOID
BENZIDIN
BENZIDINE
BENZIDINES
BENZIDINS
BENZIL
BENZILS
BENZIMIDAZOLE
BENZIMIDAZOLES
BENZIN
BENZINE
BENZINES
BENZINS
BENZOAPYRENE
BENZOAPYRENES
BENZOATE

BENZOATES
BENZOCAINE
BENZOCAINES
BENZODIAZEPINE
BENZODIAZEPINES
BENZOFURAN
BENZOFURANS
BENZOIC
BENZOIN
BENZOINS
BENZOL
BENZOLE
BENZOLES
BENZOLINE
BENZOLINES
BENZOLS
BENZOPHENONE
BENZOPHENONES
BENZOQUINONE
BENZOYL
BENZOYLS
BENZPYRENE
BENZPYRENES
BENZYL
BENZYLIC
BENZYLIDINE
BENZYLIDINES
BENZYLS
BEPAINT
BEPAINTED
BEPAINTING
BEPAINTS
BEPAT
BEPATCHED
BEPATS
BEPATTED
BEPATTING
BEPEARL
BEPEARLED
BEPEARLING
BEPEARLS
BEPELT
BEPELTED
BEPELTING
BEPELTS
BEPEPPER
BEPEPPERED
BEPEPPERING
BEPEPPERS
BEPESTER
BEPESTERED
BEPESTERING
BEPESTERS
BEPIMPLE
BEPIMPLED
BEPIMPLES

BEPIMPLING
BEPITIED
BEPITIES
BEPITY
BEPITYING
BEPLASTER
BEPLASTERED
BEPLASTERING
BEPLASTERS
BEPLUMED
BEPOMMEL
BEPOMMELLED
BEPOMMELLING
BEPOMMELS
BEPOWDER
BEPOWDERED
BEPOWDERING
BEPOWDERS
BEPRAISE
BEPRAISED
BEPRAISES
BEPRAISING
BEPROSE
BEPROSED
BEPROSES
BEPROSING
BEPUFF
BEPUFFED
BEPUFFING
BEPUFFS
BEQUEATH
BEQUEATHABLE
BEQUEATHAL
BEQUEATHALS
BEQUEATHED
BEQUEATHER
BEQUEATHERS
BEQUEATHING
BEQUEATHMENT
BEQUEATHMENTS
BEQUEATHS
BEQUEST
BEQUESTS
BERAKE
BERAKED
BERAKES
BERAKING
BERASCAL
BERASCALED
BERASCALING
BERASCALS
BERATE
BERATED
BERATES
BERATING
BERAY

BERAYED
BERAYING
BERAYS
BERBERE
BERBERIDACEOUS
BERBERIN
BERBERINE
BERBERINES
BERBERINS
BERBERIS
BERBERISES
BERBICE
BERBICES
BERCEAU
BERCEAUX
BERCEUSE
BERCEUSES
BERDACHE
BERDACHES
BERDASH
BERDASHES
BERE
BEREAVE
BEREAVED
BEREAVEMENT
BEREAVEMENTS
BEREAVEN
BEREAVER
BEREAVERS
BEREAVES
BEREAVING
BEREFT
BERES
BERET
BERETS
BERETTA
BERETTAS
BERG
BERGAMA
BERGAMAS
BERGAMASK
BERGAMASKS
BERGAMOT
BERGAMOTS
BERGANDER
BERGANDERS
BERGEN
BERGENIA
BERGENIAS
BERGENS
BERGERE
BERGERES
BERGFALL
BERGFALLS
BERGHAAN
BERGHAANS

BERGMEHL
BERGMEHLS
BERGOMASK
BERGOMASKS
BERGS
BERGSCHRUND
BERGSCHRUNDS
BERGYLT
BERGYLTS
BERHYME
BERHYMED
BERHYMES
BERHYMING
BERIBBONED
BERIBERI
BERIBERIS
BERIMBAU
BERIMBAUS
BERIME
BERIMED
BERIMES
BERIMING
BERINGED
BERK
BERKELIUM
BERKELIUMS
BERKO
BERKS
BERLEY
BERLEYED
BERLEYING
BERLEYS
BERLIN
BERLINE
BERLINES
BERLINS
BERM
BERME
BERMES
BERMS
BERMUDAS
BERNICLE
BERNICLES
BEROB
BEROBBED
BEROBBING
BEROBED
BEROBS
BEROUGED
BERRET
BERRETS
BERRETTA
BERRETTAS
BERRIED
BERRIES
BERRIGAN

BERRIGANS
BERRY
BERRYING
BERRYINGS
BERRYLIKE
BERSAGLIERE
BERSAGLIERI
BERSEEM
BERSEEMS
BERSERK
BERSERKER
BERSERKERS
BERSERKLY
BERSERKS
BERTH
BERTHA
BERTHAGE
BERTHAGES
BERTHAS
BERTHE
BERTHED
BERTHES
BERTHING
BERTHS
BERTILLONAGE
BERTILLONAGES
BERYL
BERYLINE
BERYLLIA
BERYLLIAS
BERYLLIOSES
BERYLLIOSIS
BERYLLIUM
BERYLLIUMS
BERYLS
BESAINT
BESAINTED
BESAINTING
BESAINTS
BESANG
BESAT
BESAW
BESCATTER
BESCATTERED
BESCATTERING
BESCATTERS
BESCORCH
BESCORCHED
BESCORCHES
BESCORCHING
BESCOUR
BESCOURED
BESCOURING
BESCOURS
BESCRAWL
BESCRAWLED

BESCRAWLING
BESCRAWLS
BESCREEN
BESCREENED
BESCREENING
BESCREENS
BESCRIBBLE
BESCRIBBLED
BESCRIBBLES
BESCRIBBLING
BESEE
BESEECH
BESEECHED
BESEECHER
BESEECHERS
BESEECHES
BESEECHING
BESEECHINGLY
BESEECHINGNESS
BESEECHINGS
BESEEING
BESEEKE
BESEEKES
BESEEKING
BESEEM
BESEEMED
BESEEMING
BESEEMINGLY
BESEEMINGNESS
BESEEMINGNESSES
BESEEMINGS
BESEEMLY
BESEEMS
BESEEN
BESEES
BESET
BESETMENT
BESETMENTS
BESETS
BESETTER
BESETTERS
BESETTING
BESHADOW
BESHADOWED
BESHADOWING
BESHADOWS
BESHAME
BESHAMED
BESHAMES
BESHAMING
BESHINE
BESHINES
BESHINING
BESHIVER
BESHIVERED
BESHIVERING

BESHIVERS
BESHONE
BESHOUT
BESHOUTED
BESHOUTING
BESHOUTS
BESHREW
BESHREWED
BESHREWING
BESHREWS
BESHROUD
BESHROUDED
BESHROUDING
BESHROUDS
BESIDE
BESIDES
BESIEGE
BESIEGED
BESIEGEMENT
BESIEGEMENTS
BESIEGER
BESIEGERS
BESIEGES
BESIEGING
BESIEGINGLY
BESIEGINGS
BESIGH
BESIGHED
BESIGHING
BESIGHS
BESING
BESINGING
BESINGS
BESIT
BESITS
BESITTING
BESLAVE
BESLAVED
BESLAVER
BESLAVERED
BESLAVERING
BESLAVERS
BESLAVES
BESLAVING
BESLIME
BESLIMED
BESLIMES
BESLIMING
BESLOBBER
BESLOBBERED
BESLOBBERING
BESLOBBERS
BESLUBBER
BESLUBBERED
BESLUBBERING
BESLUBBERS

BESMEAR
BESMEARED
BESMEARING
BESMEARS
BESMILE
BESMILED
BESMILES
BESMILING
BESMIRCH
BESMIRCHED
BESMIRCHES
BESMIRCHING
BESMOKE
BESMOKED
BESMOKES
BESMOKING
BESMOOTH
BESMOOTHED
BESMOOTHING
BESMOOTHS
BESMUDGE
BESMUDGED
BESMUDGES
BESMUDGING
BESMUT
BESMUTCH
BESMUTCHED
BESMUTCHES
BESMUTCHING
BESMUTS
BESMUTTED
BESMUTTING
BESNOW
BESNOWED
BESNOWING
BESNOWS
BESOGNIO
BESOGNIOS
BESOIN
BESOINS
BESOM
BESOMED
BESOMING
BESOMS
BESONIAN
BESONIANS
BESOOTHE
BESOOTHED
BESOOTHES
BESOOTHING
BESORT
BESORTED
BESORTING
BESORTS
BESOT
BESOTS

BESOTTED
BESOTTEDLY
BESOTTEDNESS
BESOTTEDNESSES
BESOTTING
BESOUGHT
BESOULED
BESPAKE
BESPANGLE
BESPANGLED
BESPANGLES
BESPANGLING
BESPAT
BESPATE
BESPATTER
BESPATTERED
BESPATTERING
BESPATTERS
BESPEAK
BESPEAKING
BESPEAKS
BESPECKLE
BESPECKLED
BESPECKLES
BESPECKLING
BESPECTACLED
BESPED
BESPEED
BESPEEDING
BESPEEDS
BESPICE
BESPICED
BESPICES
BESPICING
BESPIT
BESPITS
BESPITTING
BESPOKE
BESPOKEN
BESPORT
BESPORTED
BESPORTING
BESPORTS
BESPOT
BESPOTS
BESPOTTED
BESPOTTEDNESS
BESPOTTEDNESSES
BESPOTTING
BESPOUSE
BESPOUSED
BESPOUSES
BESPOUSING
BESPOUT
BESPOUTED
BESPOUTING

BESPOUTS
BESPREAD
BESPREADING
BESPREADS
BESPRENT
BESPRINKLE
BESPRINKLED
BESPRINKLES
BESPRINKLING
BEST
BESTAD
BESTADDE
BESTAIN
BESTAINED
BESTAINING
BESTAINS
BESTAR
BESTARRED
BESTARRING
BESTARS
BESTEAD
BESTEADED
BESTEADING
BESTEADS
BESTED
BESTIAL
BESTIALISE
BESTIALISED
BESTIALISES
BESTIALISING
BESTIALISM
BESTIALISMS
BESTIALITIES
BESTIALITY
BESTIALIZE
BESTIALIZED
BESTIALIZES
BESTIALIZING
BESTIALLY
BESTIALS
BESTIARIES
BESTIARY
BESTICK
BESTICKING
BESTICKS
BESTILL
BESTILLED
BESTILLING
BESTILLS
BESTING
BESTIR
BESTIRRED
BESTIRRING
BESTIRS
BESTORM
BESTORMED

BESTORMING
BESTORMS
BESTOW
BESTOWAL
BESTOWALS
BESTOWED
BESTOWER
BESTOWERS
BESTOWING
BESTOWMENT
BESTOWMENTS
BESTOWS
BESTRADDLE
BESTRADDLED
BESTRADDLES
BESTRADDLING
BESTRAUGHT
BESTREAK
BESTREAKED
BESTREAKING
BESTREAKS
BESTREW
BESTREWED
BESTREWING
BESTREWN
BESTREWS
BESTRID
BESTRIDABLE
BESTRIDDEN
BESTRIDE
BESTRIDES
BESTRIDING
BESTRODE
BESTROW
BESTROWED
BESTROWING
BESTROWN
BESTROWS
BESTS
BESTSELLER
BESTSELLERDOM
BESTSELLERDOMS
BESTSELLERS
BESTSELLING
BESTUCK
BESTUD
BESTUDDED
BESTUDDING
BESTUDS
BESUITED
BESUNG
BESWARM
BESWARMED
BESWARMING
BESWARMS
BET

BETA
BETACAROTENE
BETACISM
BETACISMS
BETACYANIN
BETACYANINS
BETAINE
BETAINES
BETAKE
BETAKEN
BETAKES
BETAKING
BETAS
BETATOPIC
BETATRON
BETATRONS
BETATTER
BETATTERED
BETATTERING
BETATTERS
BETAXED
BETE
BETED
BETEEM
BETEEME
BETEEMED
BETEEMES
BETEEMING
BETEEMS
BETEL
BETELNUT
BETELNUTS
BETELS
BETES
BETH
BETHANK
BETHANKED
BETHANKING
BETHANKIT
BETHANKITS
BETHANKS
BETHEL
BETHELS
BETHESDA
BETHESDAS
BETHINK
BETHINKING
BETHINKS
BETHORN
BETHORNED
BETHORNING
BETHORNS
BETHOUGHT
BETHRALL
BETHRALLED
BETHRALLING

BETHRALLS
BETHS
BETHUMB
BETHUMBED
BETHUMBING
BETHUMBS
BETHUMP
BETHUMPED
BETHUMPING
BETHUMPS
BETHWACK
BETHWACKED
BETHWACKING
BETHWACKS
BETID
BETIDE
BETIDED
BETIDES
BETIDING
BETIGHT
BETIME
BETIMED
BETIMES
BETIMING
BETING
BETISE
BETISES
BETITLE
BETITLED
BETITLES
BETITLING
BETOIL
BETOILED
BETOILING
BETOILS
BETOKEN
BETOKENED
BETOKENING
BETOKENS
BETON
BETONIES
BETONS
BETONY
BETOOK
BETOSS
BETOSSED
BETOSSES
BETOSSING
BETRAY
BETRAYAL
BETRAYALS
BETRAYED
BETRAYER
BETRAYERS
BETRAYING
BETRAYS

BETREAD
BETREADING
BETREADS
BETRIM
BETRIMMED
BETRIMMING
BETRIMS
BETROD
BETRODDEN
BETROTH
BETROTHAL
BETROTHALS
BETROTHED
BETROTHEDS
BETROTHING
BETROTHMENT
BETROTHMENTS
BETROTHS
BETS
BETTA
BETTAS
BETTED
BETTER
BETTERED
BETTERING
BETTERINGS
BETTERMENT
BETTERMENTS
BETTERMOST
BETTERNESS
BETTERNESSES
BETTERS
BETTIES
BETTING
BETTINGS
BETTONG
BETTONGS
BETTOR
BETTORS
BETTY
BETULACEOUS
BETUMBLED
BETWEEN
BETWEENBRAIN
BETWEENBRAINS
BETWEENITIES
BETWEENITY
BETWEENNESS
BETWEENNESSES
BETWEENS
BETWEENTIME
BETWEENTIMES
BETWEENWHILES
BETWIXT
BEUNCLED
BEURRE

BEURRES
BEVATRON
BEVATRONS
BEVEL
BEVELED
BEVELER
BEVELERS
BEVELING
BEVELLED
BEVELLER
BEVELLERS
BEVELLING
BEVELLINGS
BEVELMENT
BEVELMENTS
BEVELS
BEVER
BEVERAGE
BEVERAGES
BEVERS
BEVIES
BEVOMIT
BEVOMITED
BEVOMITING
BEVOMITS
BEVOR
BEVORS
BEVUE
BEVUES
BEVVIED
BEVVIES
BEVVY
BEVVYING
BEVY
BEWAIL
BEWAILED
BEWAILER
BEWAILERS
BEWAILING
BEWAILINGLY
BEWAILINGS
BEWAILS
BEWARE
BEWARED
BEWARES
BEWARING
BEWEARIED
BEWEARIES
BEWEARY
BEWEARYING
BEWEEP
BEWEEPING
BEWEEPS
BEWELTERED
BEWENT
BEWEPT

BEWET
BEWETS
BEWETTED
BEWETTING
BEWHISKERED
BEWHORE
BEWHORED
BEWHORES
BEWHORING
BEWIG
BEWIGGED
BEWIGGING
BEWIGS
BEWILDER
BEWILDERED
BEWILDEREDLY
BEWILDEREDNESS
BEWILDERING
BEWILDERINGLY
BEWILDERMENT
BEWILDERMENTS
BEWILDERS
BEWINGED
BEWITCH
BEWITCHED
BEWITCHERIES
BEWITCHERY
BEWITCHES
BEWITCHING
BEWITCHINGLY
BEWITCHMENT
BEWITCHMENTS
BEWORM
BEWORMED
BEWORMING
BEWORMS
BEWORRIED
BEWORRIES
BEWORRY
BEWORRYING
BEWRAP
BEWRAPPED
BEWRAPPING
BEWRAPS
BEWRAPT
BEWRAY
BEWRAYED
BEWRAYER
BEWRAYERS
BEWRAYING
BEWRAYS
BEY
BEYLIC
BEYLICS
BEYLIK
BEYLIKS

BEYOND
BEYONDS
BEYS
BEZ
BEZANT
BEZANTS
BEZAZZ
BEZAZZES
BEZEL
BEZELS
BEZES
BEZIL
BEZILS
BEZIQUE
BEZIQUES
BEZOAR
BEZOARDIC
BEZOARS
BEZONIAN
BEZONIANS
BEZZANT
BEZZANTS
BEZZAZZ
BEZZLE
BEZZLED
BEZZLES
BEZZLING
BHAGEE
BHAGEES
BHAJAN
BHAJANS
BHAJEE
BHAJEES
BHAJI
BHAJIS
BHAKTA
BHAKTAS
BHAKTI
BHAKTIS
BHANG
BHANGRA
BHANGRAS
BHANGS
BHARAL
BHARALS
BHAVAN
BHAVANS
BHAWAN
BHAWANS
BHEESTIE
BHEESTIES
BHEESTY
BHEL
BHELS
BHIKHU
BHIKHUS

BHIKKHUNI
BHIKKHUNIES
BHINDI
BHINDIS
BHISHTI
BHISHTIES
BHISTEE
BHISTEES
BHISTI
BHISTIE
BHISTIES
BHISTIS
BHOOT
BHOOTS
BHUT
BHUTS
BI
BIACETYL
BIACETYLS
BIALI
BIALIS
BIALY
BIALYS
BIANNUAL
BIANNUALLY
BIANNUALS
BIANNULATE
BIAS
BIASED
BIASEDLY
BIASES
BIASING
BIASINGS
BIASNESS
BIASNESSES
BIASSED
BIASSES
BIASSING
BIATHLETE
BIATHLETES
BIATHLON
BIATHLONS
BIAURICULAR
BIAURICULATE
BIAXAL
BIAXIAL
BIAXIALLY
BIB
BIBACIOUS
BIBASIC
BIBATION
BIBATIONS
BIBB
BIBBED
BIBBER
BIBBERIES

BIBBERS
BIBBERY
BIBBING
BIBBLE
BIBBLES
BIBBS
BIBCOCK
BIBCOCKS
BIBELOT
BIBELOTS
BIBLE
BIBLES
BIBLESS
BIBLICAL
BIBLICALLY
BIBLICISM
BIBLICISMS
BIBLICIST
BIBLICISTS
BIBLIKE
BIBLIOGRAPHER
BIBLIOGRAPHERS
BIBLIOGRAPHIC
BIBLIOGRAPHICAL
BIBLIOGRAPHIES
BIBLIOGRAPHY
BIBLIOLATER
BIBLIOLATERS
BIBLIOLATRIES
BIBLIOLATRIST
BIBLIOLATRISTS
BIBLIOLATROUS
BIBLIOLATRY
BIBLIOLOGICAL
BIBLIOLOGIES
BIBLIOLOGIST
BIBLIOLOGISTS
BIBLIOLOGY
BIBLIOMANCIES
BIBLIOMANCY
BIBLIOMANE
BIBLIOMANES
BIBLIOMANIA
BIBLIOMANIAC
BIBLIOMANIACAL
BIBLIOMANIACS
BIBLIOMANIAS
BIBLIOPEGIC
BIBLIOPEGIES
BIBLIOPEGIST
BIBLIOPEGISTS
BIBLIOPEGY
BIBLIOPHAGIST
BIBLIOPHAGISTS
BIBLIOPHIL
BIBLIOPHILE

BIBLIOPHILES
BIBLIOPHILIC
BIBLIOPHILIES
BIBLIOPHILISM
BIBLIOPHILISMS
BIBLIOPHILIST
BIBLIOPHILISTIC
BIBLIOPHILISTS
BIBLIOPHILS
BIBLIOPHILY
BIBLIOPHOBIA
BIBLIOPHOBIAS
BIBLIOPOLE
BIBLIOPOLES
BIBLIOPOLIC
BIBLIOPOLICAL
BIBLIOPOLIES
BIBLIOPOLIST
BIBLIOPOLISTS
BIBLIOPOLY
BIBLIOTHECA
BIBLIOTHECAE
BIBLIOTHECAL
BIBLIOTHECARIES
BIBLIOTHECARY
BIBLIOTHECAS
BIBLIOTHERAPIES
BIBLIOTHERAPY
BIBLIOTIC
BIBLIOTICS
BIBLIOTIST
BIBLIOTISTS
BIBLIST
BIBLISTS
BIBS
BIBULOUS
BIBULOUSLY
BIBULOUSNESS
BIBULOUSNESSES
BICAMERAL
BICAMERALISM
BICAMERALISMS
BICAMERALIST
BICAMERALISTS
BICAPSULAR
BICARB
BICARBONATE
BICARBONATES
BICARBS
BICARPELLARY
BICAUDAL
BICCIES
BICCY
BICE
BICENTENARIES
BICENTENARY

BICENTENNIAL
BICENTENNIALS
BICEPHALOUS
BICEPS
BICEPSES
BICES
BICHLORIDE
BICHLORIDES
BICHORD
BICHROMATE
BICHROMATED
BICHROMATES
BICHROME
BICIPITAL
BICKER
BICKERED
BICKERER
BICKERERS
BICKERING
BICKERINGS
BICKERS
BICKIE
BICKIES
BICOASTAL
BICOLLATERAL
BICOLOR
BICOLORED
BICOLORS
BICOLOUR
BICOLOURED
BICOLOURS
BICOMPONENT
BICONCAVE
BICONCAVITIES
BICONCAVITY
BICONDITIONAL
BICONDITIONALS
BICONVEX
BICONVEXITIES
BICONVEXITY
BICORN
BICORNATE
BICORNATES
BICORNE
BICORNES
BICORNS
BICORNUATE
BICORNUATES
BICORPORATE
BICRON
BICRONS
BICULTURAL
BICULTURALISM
BICULTURALISMS
BICUSPID
BICUSPIDATE

BICUSPIDATES
BICUSPIDS
BICYCLE
BICYCLED
BICYCLER
BICYCLERS
BICYCLES
BICYCLIC
BICYCLICAL
BICYCLICALLY
BICYCLING
BICYCLIST
BICYCLISTS
BID
BIDARKA
BIDARKAS
BIDARKEE
BIDARKEES
BIDDABILITIES
BIDDABILITY
BIDDABLE
BIDDABLENESS
BIDDABLENESSES
BIDDABLY
BIDDEN
BIDDER
BIDDERS
BIDDIES
BIDDING
BIDDINGS
BIDDY
BIDE
BIDED
BIDENT
BIDENTAL
BIDENTALS
BIDENTATE
BIDENTATED
BIDENTS
BIDER
BIDERS
BIDES
BIDET
BIDETS
BIDIALECTAL
BIDIALECTALISM
BIDIALECTALISMS
BIDING
BIDINGS
BIDIRECTIONAL
BIDIRECTIONALLY
BIDON
BIDONS
BIDONVILLE
BIDONVILLES
BIDS

BIELD
BIELDED
BIELDIER
BIELDIEST
BIELDING
BIELDS
BIELDY
BIEN
BIENNALE
BIENNALES
BIENNIA
BIENNIAL
BIENNIALLY
BIENNIALS
BIENNIUM
BIENNIUMS
BIENSEANCE
BIENSEANCES
BIER
BIERKELLER
BIERKELLERS
BIERS
BIESTINGS
BIFACE
BIFACES
BIFACIAL
BIFACIALLY
BIFARIOUS
BIFARIOUSLY
BIFF
BIFFED
BIFFER
BIFFERS
BIFFIES
BIFFIN
BIFFING
BIFFINS
BIFFO
BIFFS
BIFFY
BIFID
BIFIDITIES
BIFIDITY
BIFIDLY
BIFILAR
BIFILARLY
BIFLAGELLATE
BIFLEX
BIFOCAL
BIFOCALS
BIFOLD
BIFOLIATE
BIFOLIOLATE
BIFORATE
BIFORKED
BIFORM

BIFORMED
BIFTER
BIFTERS
BIFUNCTIONAL
BIFURCATE
BIFURCATED
BIFURCATES
BIFURCATING
BIFURCATION
BIFURCATIONS
BIG
BIGA
BIGAE
BIGAMIES
BIGAMIST
BIGAMISTS
BIGAMOUS
BIGAMOUSLY
BIGAMY
BIGARADE
BIGARADES
BIGAROON
BIGAROONS
BIGARREAU
BIGARREAUS
BIGEMINAL
BIGEMINIES
BIGEMINY
BIGENER
BIGENERIC
BIGENERS
BIGEYE
BIGEYES
BIGFEET
BIGFOOT
BIGFOOTS
BIGG
BIGGED
BIGGER
BIGGEST
BIGGETY
BIGGIE
BIGGIES
BIGGIN
BIGGING
BIGGINGS
BIGGINS
BIGGISH
BIGGITY
BIGGON
BIGGONS
BIGGS
BIGGY
BIGHA
BIGHAS
BIGHEAD

BIGHEADED
BIGHEADEDLY
BIGHEADEDNESS
BIGHEADS
BIGHEARTED
BIGHEARTEDLY
BIGHEARTEDNESS
BIGHORN
BIGHORNS
BIGHT
BIGHTED
BIGHTING
BIGHTS
BIGLY
BIGMOUTH
BIGMOUTHED
BIGMOUTHS
BIGNESS
BIGNESSES
BIGNONIA
BIGNONIACEOUS
BIGNONIAS
BIGOT
BIGOTED
BIGOTEDLY
BIGOTRIES
BIGOTRY
BIGOTS
BIGS
BIGUANIDE
BIGUANIDES
BIGWIG
BIGWIGS
BIHOURLY
BIJECTION
BIJECTIONS
BIJECTIVE
BIJOU
BIJOUS
BIJOUTERIE
BIJOUTERIES
BIJOUX
BIJUGATE
BIJUGOUS
BIJWONER
BIJWONERS
BIKE
BIKED
BIKER
BIKERS
BIKES
BIKEWAY
BIKEWAYS
BIKIE
BIKIES
BIKING

BIKINGS
BIKINI
BIKINIED
BIKINIS
BILABIAL
BILABIALS
BILABIATE
BILANDER
BILANDERS
BILATERAL
BILATERALISM
BILATERALISMS
BILATERALLY
BILAYER
BILAYERS
BILBERRIES
BILBERRY
BILBIES
BILBO
BILBOA
BILBOAS
BILBOES
BILBOS
BILBY
BILDUNGSROMAN
BILDUNGSROMANS
BILE
BILECTION
BILECTIONS
BILED
BILES
BILESTONE
BILESTONES
BILGE
BILGED
BILGES
BILGEWATER
BILGEWATERS
BILGIER
BILGIEST
BILGING
BILGY
BILHARZIA
BILHARZIAL
BILHARZIAS
BILHARZIASES
BILHARZIASIS
BILHARZIOSES
BILHARZIOSIS
BILIAN
BILIANS
BILIARIES
BILIARY
BILIMBI
BILIMBING
BILIMBINGS

BILIMBIS
BILINEAR
BILING
BILINGUAL
BILINGUALISM
BILINGUALISMS
BILINGUALLY
BILINGUALS
BILINGUIST
BILINGUISTS
BILIOUS
BILIOUSLY
BILIOUSNESS
BILIOUSNESSES
BILIRUBIN
BILIRUBINS
BILITERAL
BILIVERDIN
BILIVERDINS
BILK
BILKED
BILKER
BILKERS
BILKING
BILKS
BILL
BILLABLE
BILLABONG
BILLABONGS
BILLBOARD
BILLBOARDED
BILLBOARDING
BILLBOARDS
BILLBOOK
BILLBOOKS
BILLBUG
BILLBUGS
BILLED
BILLER
BILLERS
BILLET
BILLETED
BILLETEE
BILLETEES
BILLETER
BILLETERS
BILLETING
BILLETS
BILLFISH
BILLFISHES
BILLFOLD
BILLFOLDS
BILLHEAD
BILLHEADS
BILLHOOK
BILLHOOKS

BILLIARD
BILLIARDS
BILLIE
BILLIES
BILLING
BILLINGS
BILLINGSGATE
BILLINGSGATES
BILLION
BILLIONAIRE
BILLIONAIRES
BILLIONS
BILLIONTH
BILLIONTHS
BILLMAN
BILLMEN
BILLON
BILLONS
BILLOW
BILLOWED
BILLOWIER
BILLOWIEST
BILLOWINESS
BILLOWING
BILLOWS
BILLOWY
BILLPOSTED
BILLPOSTER
BILLPOSTERS
BILLPOSTING
BILLPOSTS
BILLS
BILLSTICKER
BILLSTICKERS
BILLSTICKING
BILLY
BILLYBOY
BILLYBOYS
BILLYCAN
BILLYCANS
BILLYCOCK
BILLYCOCKS
BILLYO
BILLYOH
BILOBAR
BILOBATE
BILOBED
BILOBULAR
BILOCATION
BILOCATIONS
BILOCULAR
BILOCULATELY
BILSTED
BILSTEDS
BILTONG
BILTONGS

BIMA
BIMAH
BIMAHS
BIMANAL
BIMANOUS
BIMANUAL
BIMANUALLY
BIMAS
BIMBASHI
BIMBASHIS
BIMBETTE
BIMBETTES
BIMBO
BIMBOES
BIMBOS
BIMENSAL
BIMESTER
BIMESTERS
BIMESTRIAL
BIMESTRIALLY
BIMETAL
BIMETALLIC
BIMETALLICS
BIMETALLISM
BIMETALLISMS
BIMETALLIST
BIMETALLISTIC
BIMETALLISTS
BIMETALS
BIMETHYL
BIMETHYLS
BIMILLENARIES
BIMILLENARY
BIMILLENNIA
BIMILLENNIAL
BIMILLENNIALS
BIMILLENNIUM
BIMILLENNIUMS
BIMODAL
BIMODALITIES
BIMODALITY
BIMOLECULAR
BIMOLECULARLY
BIMONTHLIES
BIMONTHLY
BIMORPH
BIMORPHEMIC
BIMORPHS
BIN
BINAL
BINARIES
BINARY
BINATE
BINATELY
BINATIONAL
BINAURAL

BINAURALLY
BIND
BINDABLE
BINDER
BINDERIES
BINDERS
BINDERY
BINDHI
BINDHIS
BINDI
BINDING
BINDINGLY
BINDINGNESS
BINDINGNESSES
BINDINGS
BINDIS
BINDLE
BINDLES
BINDS
BINDWEED
BINDWEEDS
BINE
BINERVATE
BINES
BING
BINGE
BINGED
BINGEING
BINGER
BINGERS
BINGES
BINGEY
BINGEYS
BINGHI
BINGHIS
BINGIES
BINGING
BINGLE
BINGLED
BINGLES
BINGLING
BINGO
BINGOS
BINGS
BINGY
BINIOU
BINIOUS
BINIT
BINITS
BINK
BINKS
BINMAN
BINMEN
BINNACLE
BINNACLES
BINNED

BINNING
BINOCLE
BINOCLES
BINOCS
BINOCULAR
BINOCULARITIES
BINOCULARITY
BINOCULARLY
BINOCULARS
BINOMIAL
BINOMIALLY
BINOMIALS
BINOMINAL
BINOMINALS
BINOVULAR
BINOVULARLY
BINS
BINT
BINTS
BINTURONG
BINTURONGS
BINUCLEAR
BINUCLEARS
BINUCLEATE
BINUCLEATED
BIO
BIOACCUMULATE
BIOACCUMULATED
BIOACCUMULATES
BIOACCUMULATING
BIOACOUSTICS
BIOACTIVE
BIOACTIVITIES
BIOACTIVITY
BIOAERATION
BIOAERONAUTICAL
BIOAERONAUTICS
BIOASSAY
BIOASSAYED
BIOASSAYING
BIOASSAYS
BIOASTRONAUTICS
BIOAVAILABILITY
BIOAVAILABLE
BIOBLAST
BIOBLASTS
BIOCATALYST
BIOCATALYSTS
BIOCATALYTIC
BIOCELLATE
BIOCENOLOGICAL
BIOCENOLOGY
BIOCENOSES
BIOCENOSIS
BIOCENOTIC
BIOCENOTICALLY

BIOCHEMICAL
BIOCHEMICALLY
BIOCHEMICALS
BIOCHEMIST
BIOCHEMISTRIES
BIOCHEMISTRY
BIOCHEMISTS
BIOCHIP
BIOCHIPS
BIOCIDAL
BIOCIDE
BIOCIDES
BIOCLASTIC
BIOCLEAN
BIOCLIMATIC
BIOCLIMATOLOGY
BIOCOENOLOGIES
BIOCOENOLOGY
BIOCOENOSES
BIOCOENOSIS
BIOCOENOTIC
BIOCOMPATIBLE
BIOCONTROL
BIOCONTROLS
BIOCONVERSION
BIOCONVERSIONS
BIOCYCLE
BIOCYCLES
BIODATA
BIODEGRADABLE
BIODEGRADATION
BIODEGRADATIONS
BIODEGRADE
BIODEGRADED
BIODEGRADES
BIODEGRADING
BIODESTRUCTIBLE
BIODIESEL
BIODIESELS
BIODIVERSITIES
BIODIVERSITY
BIODOT
BIODOTS
BIODYNAMIC
BIODYNAMICAL
BIODYNAMICALLY
BIODYNAMICS
BIOECOLOGICAL
BIOECOLOGICALLY
BIOECOLOGIES
BIOECOLOGIST
BIOECOLOGISTS
BIOECOLOGY
BIOELECTRIC
BIOELECTRICAL
BIOELECTRICALLY

BIOELECTRICITY
BIOENERGETIC
BIOENERGETICS
BIOENGINEER
BIOENGINEERED
BIOENGINEERING
BIOENGINEERINGS
BIOENGINEERS
BIOETHIC
BIOETHICAL
BIOETHICIST
BIOETHICISTS
BIOETHICS
BIOFACT
BIOFACTS
BIOFEEDBACK
BIOFEEDBACKS
BIOFLAVONOID
BIOFLAVONOIDS
BIOFOULING
BIOFOULINGS
BIOFUEL
BIOFUELS
BIOG
BIOGAS
BIOGASES
BIOGASSES
BIOGEN
BIOGENESES
BIOGENESIS
BIOGENETIC
BIOGENETICAL
BIOGENETICALLY
BIOGENIC
BIOGENIES
BIOGENOUS
BIOGENS
BIOGENY
BIOGEOCHEMICAL
BIOGEOCHEMICALS
BIOGEOCHEMISTRY
BIOGEOGRAPHER
BIOGEOGRAPHERS
BIOGEOGRAPHIC
BIOGEOGRAPHICAL
BIOGEOGRAPHIES
BIOGEOGRAPHY
BIOGRAPH
BIOGRAPHED
BIOGRAPHEE
BIOGRAPHEES
BIOGRAPHER
BIOGRAPHERS
BIOGRAPHIC
BIOGRAPHICAL
BIOGRAPHICALLY

BIOGRAPHIES
BIOGRAPHING
BIOGRAPHISE
BIOGRAPHISED
BIOGRAPHISES
BIOGRAPHISING
BIOGRAPHIZE
BIOGRAPHIZED
BIOGRAPHIZES
BIOGRAPHIZING
BIOGRAPHS
BIOGRAPHY
BIOGS
BIOHAZARD
BIOHAZARDOUS
BIOHAZARDS
BIOHERM
BIOHERMS
BIOINFORMATICS
BIOLOGIC
BIOLOGICAL
BIOLOGICALLY
BIOLOGICALS
BIOLOGICS
BIOLOGIES
BIOLOGISM
BIOLOGISMS
BIOLOGIST
BIOLOGISTIC
BIOLOGISTS
BIOLOGY
BIOLUMINESCENCE
BIOLUMINESCENT
BIOLYSES
BIOLYSIS
BIOLYTIC
BIOMAGNETICS
BIOMARKER
BIOMARKERS
BIOMASS
BIOMASSES
BIOMATERIAL
BIOMATERIALS
BIOMATHEMATICAL
BIOMATHEMATICS
BIOME
BIOMECHANICAL
BIOMECHANICALLY
BIOMECHANICS
BIOMEDICAL
BIOMEDICINE
BIOMEDICINES
BIOMES
BIOMETEOROLOGY
BIOMETRIC
BIOMETRICAL

BIOMETRICALLY
BIOMETRICIAN
BIOMETRICIANS
BIOMETRICS
BIOMETRIES
BIOMETRY
BIOMIMETIC
BIOMIMETICS
BIOMIMICRIES
BIOMIMICRY
BIOMINING
BIOMININGS
BIOMOLECULAR
BIOMOLECULE
BIOMOLECULES
BIOMORPH
BIOMORPHIC
BIOMORPHS
BIONIC
BIONICS
BIONOMIC
BIONOMICALLY
BIONOMICS
BIONOMIES
BIONOMIST
BIONOMISTS
BIONOMY
BIONT
BIONTIC
BIONTS
BIOPARENT
BIOPARENTS
BIOPHILIA
BIOPHILIAC
BIOPHILIACS
BIOPHOR
BIOPHORE
BIOPHORES
BIOPHORS
BIOPHYSICAL
BIOPHYSICALITY
BIOPHYSICALLY
BIOPHYSICIST
BIOPHYSICISTS
BIOPHYSICS
BIOPIC
BIOPICS
BIOPIRACY
BIOPIRATE
BIOPIRATES
BIOPLASM
BIOPLASMIC
BIOPLASMS
BIOPLAST
BIOPLASTS
BIOPOIESES

BIOPOIESIS
BIOPOLYMER
BIOPOLYMERS
BIOPROSPECTING
BIOPROSPECTOR
BIOPROSPECTORS
BIOPSIC
BIOPSIED
BIOPSIES
BIOPSY
BIOPSYCHOLOGIES
BIOPSYCHOLOGY
BIOPSYING
BIOPTIC
BIOREACTOR
BIOREACTORS
BIOREAGENT
BIOREAGENTS
BIOREGIONAL
BIOREGIONALISM
BIOREGIONALISMS
BIOREGIONALIST
BIOREGIONALISTS
BIOREMEDIATION
BIOREMEDIATIONS
BIORHYTHM
BIORHYTHMIC
BIORHYTHMICALLY
BIORHYTHMICS
BIORHYTHMS
BIOS
BIOSAFETIES
BIOSAFETY
BIOSATELLITE
BIOSATELLITES
BIOSCIENCE
BIOSCIENCES
BIOSCIENTIFIC
BIOSCIENTIST
BIOSCIENTISTS
BIOSCOPE
BIOSCOPES
BIOSCOPIES
BIOSCOPY
BIOSENSOR
BIOSENSORS
BIOSOCIAL
BIOSOCIALLY
BIOSPHERE
BIOSPHERES
BIOSPHERIC
BIOSTABLE
BIOSTATIC
BIOSTATICALLY
BIOSTATICS
BIOSTATISTICAL

BIOSTATISTICIAN
BIOSTATISTICS
BIOSTRATIGRAPHY
BIOSTROME
BIOSTROMES
BIOSURGEON
BIOSURGEONS
BIOSURGERY
BIOSYNTHESES
BIOSYNTHESIS
BIOSYNTHETIC
BIOSYSTEMATIC
BIOSYSTEMATICS
BIOSYSTEMATIST
BIOSYSTEMATISTS
BIOTA
BIOTAS
BIOTECH
BIOTECHNICAL
BIOTECHNOLOGIES
BIOTECHNOLOGIST
BIOTECHNOLOGY
BIOTECHS
BIOTELEMETRIC
BIOTELEMETRIES
BIOTELEMETRY
BIOTIC
BIOTICAL
BIOTICALLY
BIOTICS
BIOTIN
BIOTINS
BIOTITE
BIOTITES
BIOTITIC
BIOTOPE
BIOTOPES
BIOTOXIN
BIOTOXINS
BIOTRON
BIOTRONS
BIOTROPH
BIOTROPHS
BIOTURBATION
BIOTURBATIONS
BIOTYPE
BIOTYPES
BIOTYPIC
BIOVULAR
BIOWEAPON
BIOWEAPONRY
BIOWEAPONS
BIPACK
BIPACKS
BIPARENTAL
BIPARENTALLY

BIPARIETAL
BIPARIETALLY
BIPAROUS
BIPARTED
BIPARTISAN
BIPARTISANISM
BIPARTISANISMS
BIPARTISANSHIP
BIPARTISANSHIPS
BIPARTITE
BIPARTITELY
BIPARTITION
BIPARTITIONS
BIPARTY
BIPED
BIPEDAL
BIPEDALISM
BIPEDALISMS
BIPEDALITIES
BIPEDALITY
BIPEDALLY
BIPEDS
BIPETALOUS
BIPHASIC
BIPHENYL
BIPHENYLS
BIPINNARIA
BIPINNARIAS
BIPINNATE
BIPINNATELY
BIPLANE
BIPLANES
BIPOD
BIPODS
BIPOLAR
BIPOLARITIES
BIPOLARITY
BIPOLARIZATION
BIPOLARIZATIONS
BIPOLARIZE
BIPOLARIZED
BIPOLARIZES
BIPOLARIZING
BIPRISM
BIPRISMS
BIPROPELLANT
BIPROPELLANTS
BIPYRAMID
BIPYRAMIDAL
BIPYRAMIDS
BIQUADRATE
BIQUADRATES
BIQUADRATIC
BIQUADRATICS
BIQUARTERLIES
BIQUARTERLY

BIQUINTILE
BIQUINTILES
BIRACIAL
BIRACIALISM
BIRACIALISMS
BIRACIALLY
BIRADIAL
BIRAMOSE
BIRAMOUS
BIRCH
BIRCHED
BIRCHEN
BIRCHES
BIRCHING
BIRD
BIRDBATH
BIRDBATHS
BIRDBRAIN
BIRDBRAINED
BIRDBRAINS
BIRDCAGE
BIRDCAGES
BIRDCALL
BIRDCALLS
BIRDED
BIRDER
BIRDERS
BIRDFARM
BIRDFARMS
BIRDHOUSE
BIRDHOUSES
BIRDIE
BIRDIED
BIRDIEING
BIRDIES
BIRDING
BIRDINGS
BIRDLIKE
BIRDLIME
BIRDLIMED
BIRDLIMES
BIRDLIMING
BIRDMAN
BIRDMEN
BIRDS
BIRDSEED
BIRDSEEDS
BIRDSEYE
BIRDSEYES
BIRDSHOT
BIRDSHOTS
BIRDSONG
BIRDSONGS
BIRDWATCHER
BIRDWATCHERS
BIRDWING

BIRDWINGS
BIREFRINGENCE
BIREFRINGENCES
BIREFRINGENT
BIREME
BIREMES
BIRETTA
BIRETTAS
BIRIANI
BIRIANIS
BIRIYANI
BIRIYANIS
BIRK
BIRKEN
BIRKIE
BIRKIER
BIRKIES
BIRKIEST
BIRKS
BIRL
BIRLE
BIRLED
BIRLER
BIRLERS
BIRLES
BIRLIEMAN
BIRLIEMEN
BIRLING
BIRLINGS
BIRLINN
BIRLINNS
BIRLS
BIROSTRATE
BIRR
BIRRED
BIRRETTA
BIRRETTAS
BIRRING
BIRROTCH
BIRRS
BIRSE
BIRSES
BIRSIER
BIRSIEST
BIRSLE
BIRSLED
BIRSLES
BIRSLING
BIRSY
BIRTH
BIRTHDAY
BIRTHDAYS
BIRTHDOM
BIRTHDOMS
BIRTHED
BIRTHING

BIRTHINGS
BIRTHMARK
BIRTHMARKS
BIRTHNIGHT
BIRTHNIGHTS
BIRTHPLACE
BIRTHPLACES
BIRTHRATE
BIRTHRATES
BIRTHRIGHT
BIRTHRIGHTS
BIRTHROOT
BIRTHROOTS
BIRTHS
BIRTHSTONE
BIRTHSTONES
BIRTHWORT
BIRTHWORTS
BIRYANI
BIRYANIS
BIS
BISCACHA
BISCACHAS
BISCUIT
BISCUITS
BISCUITY
BISE
BISECT
BISECTED
BISECTING
BISECTION
BISECTIONAL
BISECTIONALLY
BISECTIONS
BISECTOR
BISECTORS
BISECTRICES
BISECTRIX
BISECTS
BISERIAL
BISERIATE
BISERIATELY
BISERRATE
BISES
BISEXUAL
BISEXUALISM
BISEXUALITIES
BISEXUALITY
BISEXUALLY
BISEXUALS
BISH
BISHES
BISHOP
BISHOPBIRD
BISHOPBIRDS
BISHOPDOM

BISHOPDOMS
BISHOPED
BISHOPESS
BISHOPESSES
BISHOPING
BISHOPRIC
BISHOPRICS
BISHOPS
BISHOPWEED
BISHOPWEEDS
BISK
BISKS
BISMAR
BISMARS
BISMILLAH
BISMUTH
BISMUTHAL
BISMUTHIC
BISMUTHINITE
BISMUTHOUS
BISMUTHS
BISNAGA
BISNAGAS
BISOCIATION
BISOCIATIONS
BISOCIATIVE
BISON
BISONS
BISONTINE
BISPHOSPHONATE
BISPHOSPHONATES
BISQUE
BISQUES
BISSEXTILE
BISSEXTILES
BISSON
BIST
BISTABLE
BISTABLES
BISTATE
BISTER
BISTERED
BISTERS
BISTORT
BISTORTS
BISTOURIES
BISTOURY
BISTRE
BISTRED
BISTRES
BISTRO
BISTROIC
BISTROS
BISULCATE
BISULFATE
BISULFATES

BISULFIDE	BITSTOCK	BITTURS	BIYEARLY
BISULFIDES	BITSTOCKS	BITTY	BIZ
BISULFITE	BITSY	BITUMED	BIZARRE
BISULFITES	BITT	BITUMEN	BIZARRELY
BISULPHATE	BITTACLE	BITUMENS	BIZARRENESS
BISULPHATES	BITTACLES	BITUMINATE	BIZARRENESSES
BISULPHIDE	BITTE	BITUMINATED	BIZARRERIE
BISULPHIDES	BITTED	BITUMINATES	BIZARRERIES
BISULPHITE	BITTEN	BITUMINATING	BIZARRES
BISULPHITES	BITTER	BITUMINISATION	BIZAZZ
BISYMMETRIC	BITTERBARK	BITUMINISATIONS	BIZAZZES
BISYMMETRICAL	BITTERBARKS	BITUMINISE	BIZCACHA
BISYMMETRICALLY	BITTERBRUSH	BITUMINISED	BIZCACHAS
BISYMMETRY	BITTERBRUSHES	BITUMINISES	BIZE
BIT	BITTERCRESS	BITUMINISING	BIZES
BITABLE	BITTERCRESSES	BITUMINIZATION	BIZNAGA
BITARTRATE	BITTERED	BITUMINIZATIONS	BIZNAGAS
BITARTRATES	BITTERER	BITUMINIZE	BIZONAL
BITCH	BITTEREST	BITUMINIZED	BIZONE
BITCHED	BITTERING	BITUMINIZES	BIZONES
BITCHERIES	BITTERISH	BITUMINIZING	BIZZES
BITCHERY	BITTERLING	BITUMINOUS	BIZZIES
BITCHES	BITTERLINGS	BIUNIQUE	BIZZO
BITCHFEST	BITTERLY	BIUNIQUENESS	BIZZOS
BITCHFESTS	BITTERN	BIUNIQUENESSES	BIZZY
BITCHIER	BITTERNESS	BIVALENCE	BLAB
BITCHIEST	BITTERNESSES	BIVALENCES	BLABBED
BITCHILY	BITTERNS	BIVALENCIES	BLABBER
BITCHINESS	BITTERNUT	BIVALENCY	BLABBERED
BITCHINESSES	BITTERNUTS	BIVALENT	BLABBERING
BITCHING	BITTERROOT	BIVALENTS	BLABBERMOUTH
BITCHY	BITTERROOTS	BIVALVATE	BLABBERMOUTHS
BITE	BITTERS	BIVALVE	BLABBERS
BITEABLE	BITTERSWEET	BIVALVED	BLABBING
BITER	BITTERSWEETLY	BIVALVES	BLABBINGS
BITERS	BITTERSWEETNESS	BIVALVULAR	BLABBY
BITES	BITTERSWEETS	BIVARIANT	BLABS
BITESIZE	BITTERWEED	BIVARIANTS	BLACK
BITEWING	BITTERWEEDS	BIVARIATE	BLACKAMOOR
BITEWINGS	BITTERWOOD	BIVARIATES	BLACKAMOORS
BITING	BITTERWOODS	BIVIA	BLACKBALL
BITINGLY	BITTIE	BIVINYL	BLACKBALLED
BITINGS	BITTIER	BIVINYLS	BLACKBALLING
BITLESS	BITTIES	BIVIOUS	BLACKBALLINGS
BITMAP	BITTIEST	BIVIUM	BLACKBALLS
BITMAPS	BITTINESS	BIVOUAC	BLACKBAND
BITO	BITTING	BIVOUACKED	BLACKBANDS
BITONAL	BITTINGS	BIVOUACKING	BLACKBERRIED
BITONALITIES	BITTOCK	BIVOUACKS	BLACKBERRIES
BITONALITY	BITTOCKS	BIVOUACS	BLACKBERRY
BITOS	BITTOR	BIVVIED	BLACKBERRYING
BITS	BITTORS	BIVVIES	BLACKBERRYINGS
BITSER	BITTOUR	BIVVY	BLACKBIRD
BITSERS	BITTOURS	BIVVYING	BLACKBIRDED
BITSIER	BITTS	BIWEEKLIES	BLACKBIRDER
BITSIEST	BITTUR	BIWEEKLY	BLACKBIRDERS

BLACKBIRDING
BLACKBIRDINGS
BLACKBIRDS
BLACKBOARD
BLACKBOARDS
BLACKBODIES
BLACKBODY
BLACKBOY
BLACKBOYS
BLACKBUCK
BLACKBUCKS
BLACKBUTT
BLACKBUTTS
BLACKCAP
BLACKCAPS
BLACKCOCK
BLACKCOCKS
BLACKCURRANT
BLACKCURRANTS
BLACKDAMP
BLACKDAMPS
BLACKED
BLACKEN
BLACKENED
BLACKENER
BLACKENERS
BLACKENING
BLACKENINGS
BLACKENS
BLACKER
BLACKEST
BLACKFACE
BLACKFACED
BLACKFACES
BLACKFIN
BLACKFINS
BLACKFISH
BLACKFISHES
BLACKFLIES
BLACKFLY
BLACKGAME
BLACKGAMES
BLACKGUARD
BLACKGUARDED
BLACKGUARDING
BLACKGUARDISM
BLACKGUARDISMS
BLACKGUARDLY
BLACKGUARDS
BLACKGUM
BLACKGUMS
BLACKHANDER
BLACKHANDERS
BLACKHEAD
BLACKHEADED
BLACKHEADS

BLACKHEART
BLACKHEARTS
BLACKING
BLACKINGS
BLACKISH
BLACKISHLY
BLACKJACK
BLACKJACKED
BLACKJACKING
BLACKJACKS
BLACKLAND
BLACKLANDS
BLACKLEAD
BLACKLEADS
BLACKLEG
BLACKLEGGED
BLACKLEGGING
BLACKLEGS
BLACKLIST
BLACKLISTED
BLACKLISTER
BLACKLISTERS
BLACKLISTING
BLACKLISTINGS
BLACKLISTS
BLACKLY
BLACKMAIL
BLACKMAILED
BLACKMAILER
BLACKMAILERS
BLACKMAILING
BLACKMAILS
BLACKNESS
BLACKNESSES
BLACKOUT
BLACKOUTS
BLACKPOLL
BLACKPOLLS
BLACKS
BLACKSMITH
BLACKSMITHING
BLACKSMITHINGS
BLACKSMITHS
BLACKSNAKE
BLACKSNAKES
BLACKSTRAP
BLACKTAIL
BLACKTAILS
BLACKTHORN
BLACKTHORNS
BLACKTOP
BLACKTOPPED
BLACKTOPPING
BLACKTOPS
BLACKWASH
BLACKWASHES

BLACKWATER
BLACKWATERS
BLACKWOOD
BLACKWOODS
BLAD
BLADDED
BLADDER
BLADDERED
BLADDERLIKE
BLADDERNOSE
BLADDERNOSES
BLADDERNUT
BLADDERNUTS
BLADDERS
BLADDERWORT
BLADDERWORTS
BLADDERWRACK
BLADDERWRACKS
BLADDERY
BLADDING
BLADE
BLADED
BLADELIKE
BLADES
BLADEWORK
BLADEWORKS
BLADING
BLADS
BLAE
BLAEBERRIES
BLAEBERRY
BLAER
BLAES
BLAEST
BLAG
BLAGGED
BLAGGER
BLAGGERS
BLAGGING
BLAGS
BLAGUE
BLAGUER
BLAGUERS
BLAGUES
BLAGUEUR
BLAGUEURS
BLAH
BLAHED
BLAHING
BLAHS
BLAIN
BLAINS
BLAISE
BLAIZE
BLAM
BLAMABLE

BLAMABLENESS
BLAMABLENESSES
BLAMABLY
BLAME
BLAMEABLE
BLAMEABLENESS
BLAMEABLENESSES
BLAMEABLY
BLAMED
BLAMEFUL
BLAMEFULLY
BLAMEFULNESS
BLAMEFULNESSES
BLAMELESS
BLAMELESSLY
BLAMELESSNESS
BLAMELESSNESSES
BLAMER
BLAMERS
BLAMES
BLAMEWORTHINESS
BLAMEWORTHY
BLAMING
BLAMS
BLANCH
BLANCHED
BLANCHER
BLANCHERS
BLANCHES
BLANCHING
BLANCHISSEUSE
BLANCHISSEUSES
BLANCMANGE
BLANCMANGES
BLANCO
BLANCOED
BLANCOING
BLANCOS
BLAND
BLANDER
BLANDEST
BLANDISH
BLANDISHED
BLANDISHER
BLANDISHERS
BLANDISHES
BLANDISHING
BLANDISHMENT
BLANDISHMENTS
BLANDLY
BLANDNESS
BLANDNESSES
BLANDS
BLANK
BLANKED
BLANKER

BLANKEST	BLASTEMA	BLASTOSPORES	BLAZER
BLANKET	BLASTEMAL	BLASTS	BLAZERED
BLANKETED	BLASTEMAS	BLASTULA	BLAZERS
BLANKETFLOWER	BLASTEMATA	BLASTULAE	BLAZES
BLANKETFLOWERS	BLASTEMATIC	BLASTULAR	BLAZING
BLANKETIES	BLASTEMIC	BLASTULAS	BLAZINGLY
BLANKETING	BLASTEMICALLY	BLASTULATION	BLAZON
BLANKETINGS	BLASTER	BLASTULATIONS	BLAZONED
BLANKETLIKE	BLASTERS	BLASTY	BLAZONER
BLANKETS	BLASTIE	BLAT	BLAZONERS
BLANKETWEED	BLASTIER	BLATANCIES	BLAZONING
BLANKETWEEDS	BLASTIES	BLATANCY	BLAZONINGS
BLANKETY	BLASTIEST	BLATANT	BLAZONRIES
BLANKIES	BLASTING	BLATANTLY	BLAZONRY
BLANKING	BLASTINGS	BLATE	BLAZONS
BLANKINGS	BLASTMENT	BLATER	BLEACH
BLANKLY	BLASTMENTS	BLATEST	BLEACHABLE
BLANKNESS	BLASTOCHYLE	BLATHER	BLEACHED
BLANKNESSES	BLASTOCHYLES	BLATHERED	BLEACHER
BLANKS	BLASTOCOEL	BLATHERER	BLEACHERIES
BLANKY	BLASTOCOELE	BLATHERERS	BLEACHERITE
BLANQUET	BLASTOCOELES	BLATHERING	BLEACHERITES
BLANQUETS	BLASTOCOELIC	BLATHERS	BLEACHERS
BLANQUETTE	BLASTOCOELS	BLATHERSKITE	BLEACHERY
BLANQUETTES	BLASTOCYST	BLATHERSKITES	BLEACHES
BLARE	BLASTOCYSTS	BLATS	BLEACHING
BLARED	BLASTODERM	BLATT	BLEACHINGS
BLARES	BLASTODERMIC	BLATTANT	BLEAK
BLARING	BLASTODERMS	BLATTED	BLEAKER
BLARNEY	BLASTODISC	BLATTER	BLEAKEST
BLARNEYED	BLASTODISCS	BLATTERED	BLEAKISH
BLARNEYING	BLASTOFF	BLATTERING	BLEAKLY
BLARNEYS	BLASTOFFS	BLATTERS	BLEAKNESS
BLART	BLASTOGENESES	BLATTING	BLEAKNESSES
BLARTED	BLASTOGENESIS	BLATTS	BLEAKS
BLARTING	BLASTOGENETIC	BLAUBOK	BLEAKY
BLARTS	BLASTOGENIC	BLAUBOKS	BLEAR
BLASE	BLASTOID	BLAUD	BLEARED
BLASH	BLASTOIDS	BLAUDED	BLEARER
BLASHES	BLASTOMA	BLAUDING	BLEAREST
BLASHIER	BLASTOMAS	BLAUDS	BLEAREYED
BLASHIEST	BLASTOMATA	BLAW	BLEARIER
BLASHY	BLASTOMERE	BLAWED	BLEARIEST
BLASPHEME	BLASTOMERES	BLAWING	BLEARILY
BLASPHEMED	BLASTOMERIC	BLAWN	BLEARINESS
BLASPHEMER	BLASTOMYCOSES	BLAWORT	BLEARINESSES
BLASPHEMERS	BLASTOMYCOSIS	BLAWORTS	BLEARING
BLASPHEMES	BLASTOPOR	BLAWS	BLEARS
BLASPHEMIES	BLASTOPORAL	BLAXPLOITATION	BLEARY
BLASPHEMING	BLASTOPORE	BLAXPLOITATIONS	BLEAT
BLASPHEMOUS	BLASTOPORES	BLAXPLOITATIVE	BLEATED
BLASPHEMOUSLY	BLASTOPORIC	BLAXSPLOITATION	BLEATER
BLASPHEMOUSNESS	BLASTOPORS	BLAY	BLEATERS
BLASPHEMY	BLASTOSPHERE	BLAYS	BLEATING
BLAST	BLASTOSPHERES	BLAZE	BLEATINGS
BLASTED	BLASTOSPORE	BLAZED	BLEATS

BLEB
BLEBBY
BLEBS
BLED
BLEE
BLEED
BLEEDER
BLEEDERS
BLEEDING
BLEEDINGS
BLEEDS
BLEEP
BLEEPED
BLEEPER
BLEEPERS
BLEEPING
BLEEPS
BLEES
BLELLUM
BLELLUMS
BLEMISH
BLEMISHED
BLEMISHES
BLEMISHING
BLEMISHMENT
BLEMISHMENTS
BLENCH
BLENCHED
BLENCHER
BLENCHERS
BLENCHES
BLENCHING
BLEND
BLENDE
BLENDED
BLENDER
BLENDERS
BLENDES
BLENDING
BLENDINGS
BLENDS
BLENNIES
BLENNIOID
BLENNIOIDS
BLENNORRHEA
BLENNORRHEAS
BLENNORRHOEA
BLENNORRHOEAS
BLENNY
BLENT
BLEPHARISM
BLEPHARISMS
BLEPHARITIC
BLEPHARITIS
BLEPHARITISES
BLEPHAROPLAST

BLEPHAROPLASTS
BLEPHAROPLASTY
BLEPHAROSPASM
BLEPHAROSPASMS
BLERT
BLERTS
BLESBOK
BLESBOKS
BLESBUCK
BLESBUCKS
BLESS
BLESSED
BLESSEDER
BLESSEDEST
BLESSEDLY
BLESSEDNESS
BLESSEDNESSES
BLESSER
BLESSERS
BLESSES
BLESSING
BLESSINGS
BLEST
BLET
BLETHER
BLETHERANSKATES
BLETHERATION
BLETHERATIONS
BLETHERED
BLETHERER
BLETHERERS
BLETHERING
BLETHERINGS
BLETHERS
BLETHERSKATE
BLETHERSKATES
BLETS
BLETTED
BLETTING
BLEUATRE
BLEW
BLEWART
BLEWARTS
BLEWITS
BLEWITSES
BLEY
BLEYS
BLIGHT
BLIGHTED
BLIGHTER
BLIGHTERS
BLIGHTIES
BLIGHTING
BLIGHTINGLY
BLIGHTINGS
BLIGHTS

BLIGHTY
BLIMBING
BLIMBINGS
BLIMEY
BLIMP
BLIMPISH
BLIMPISHLY
BLIMPISHNESS
BLIMPISHNESSES
BLIMPS
BLIMY
BLIN
BLIND
BLINDAGE
BLINDAGES
BLINDED
BLINDER
BLINDERS
BLINDEST
BLINDFISH
BLINDFISHES
BLINDFOLD
BLINDFOLDED
BLINDFOLDING
BLINDFOLDS
BLINDING
BLINDINGLY
BLINDINGS
BLINDLESS
BLINDLY
BLINDNESS
BLINDNESSES
BLINDS
BLINDSIDE
BLINDSIDED
BLINDSIDES
BLINDSIDING
BLINDSIGHT
BLINDSTOREY
BLINDSTOREYS
BLINDSTORIES
BLINDSTORY
BLINDWORM
BLINDWORMS
BLING
BLINI
BLINIS
BLINK
BLINKARD
BLINKARDS
BLINKED
BLINKER
BLINKERED
BLINKERING
BLINKERS
BLINKING

BLINKS
BLINNED
BLINNING
BLINS
BLINTZ
BLINTZE
BLINTZES
BLINY
BLIP
BLIPPED
BLIPPING
BLIPS
BLIPVERT
BLIPVERTS
BLISS
BLISSED
BLISSES
BLISSFUL
BLISSFULLY
BLISSFULNESS
BLISSFULNESSES
BLISSING
BLISSLESS
BLIST
BLISTER
BLISTERED
BLISTERIER
BLISTERIEST
BLISTERING
BLISTERINGLY
BLISTERS
BLISTERY
BLITE
BLITES
BLITHE
BLITHELY
BLITHENESS
BLITHENESSES
BLITHER
BLITHERED
BLITHERING
BLITHERS
BLITHESOME
BLITHESOMELY
BLITHESOMENESS
BLITHEST
BLITZ
BLITZED
BLITZES
BLITZING
BLITZKRIEG
BLITZKRIEGS
BLIVE
BLIZZARD
BLIZZARDLY
BLIZZARDS

BLIZZARDY
BLOAT
BLOATED
BLOATEDNESS
BLOATEDNESSES
BLOATER
BLOATERS
BLOATING
BLOATINGS
BLOATS
BLOATWARE
BLOATWARES
BLOB
BLOBBED
BLOBBIER
BLOBBIEST
BLOBBING
BLOBBY
BLOBS
BLOC
BLOCK
BLOCKADE
BLOCKADED
BLOCKADER
BLOCKADERS
BLOCKADES
BLOCKADING
BLOCKAGE
BLOCKAGES
BLOCKBOARD
BLOCKBOARDS
BLOCKBUSTER
BLOCKBUSTERS
BLOCKBUSTING
BLOCKBUSTINGS
BLOCKED
BLOCKER
BLOCKERS
BLOCKHEAD
BLOCKHEADED
BLOCKHEADEDLY
BLOCKHEADEDNESS
BLOCKHEADS
BLOCKHOLE
BLOCKHOLES
BLOCKHOUSE
BLOCKHOUSES
BLOCKIE
BLOCKIER
BLOCKIEST
BLOCKING
BLOCKINGS
BLOCKISH
BLOCKISHLY
BLOCKISHNESS
BLOCKS

BLOCKWORK
BLOCKWORKS
BLOCKY
BLOCS
BLOG
BLOGGED
BLOGGING
BLOGS
BLOKE
BLOKEDOM
BLOKEDOMS
BLOKEISH
BLOKEISHNESS
BLOKES
BLOKEY
BLOKIER
BLOKIEST
BLOKISH
BLOKISHNESS
BLONCKET
BLOND
BLONDE
BLONDENESS
BLONDER
BLONDES
BLONDEST
BLONDING
BLONDINGS
BLONDISH
BLONDNESS
BLONDS
BLOOD
BLOODBATH
BLOODBATHS
BLOODCURDLING
BLOODCURDLINGLY
BLOODED
BLOODFIN
BLOODFINS
BLOODGUILT
BLOODGUILTINESS
BLOODGUILTS
BLOODGUILTY
BLOODHEAT
BLOODHEATS
BLOODHOUND
BLOODHOUNDS
BLOODHOUSE
BLOODHOUSES
BLOODIED
BLOODIER
BLOODIES
BLOODIEST
BLOODILY
BLOODINESS
BLOODINESSES

BLOODING
BLOODINGS
BLOODLESS
BLOODLESSLY
BLOODLESSNESS
BLOODLESSNESSES
BLOODLETTER
BLOODLETTERS
BLOODLETTING
BLOODLETTINGS
BLOODLINE
BLOODLINES
BLOODLUST
BLOODLUSTS
BLOODMOBILE
BLOODMOBILES
BLOODRED
BLOODROOT
BLOODROOTS
BLOODS
BLOODSHED
BLOODSHEDS
BLOODSHOT
BLOODSTAIN
BLOODSTAINED
BLOODSTAINS
BLOODSTOCK
BLOODSTOCKS
BLOODSTONE
BLOODSTONES
BLOODSTREAM
BLOODSTREAMS
BLOODSUCKER
BLOODSUCKERS
BLOODSUCKING
BLOODTHIRSTIER
BLOODTHIRSTIEST
BLOODTHIRSTILY
BLOODTHIRSTY
BLOODWOOD
BLOODWOODS
BLOODWORM
BLOODWORMS
BLOODY
BLOODYING
BLOOEY
BLOOIE
BLOOM
BLOOMED
BLOOMER
BLOOMERIES
BLOOMERS
BLOOMERY
BLOOMIER
BLOOMIEST
BLOOMING

BLOOMLESS
BLOOMS
BLOOMY
BLOOP
BLOOPED
BLOOPER
BLOOPERS
BLOOPING
BLOOPS
BLOOSME
BLOOSMED
BLOOSMES
BLOOSMING
BLORE
BLORES
BLOSSOM
BLOSSOMED
BLOSSOMING
BLOSSOMINGS
BLOSSOMLESS
BLOSSOMS
BLOSSOMY
BLOT
BLOTCH
BLOTCHED
BLOTCHES
BLOTCHIER
BLOTCHIEST
BLOTCHILY
BLOTCHINESS
BLOTCHINESSES
BLOTCHING
BLOTCHINGS
BLOTCHY
BLOTLESS
BLOTS
BLOTTED
BLOTTER
BLOTTERS
BLOTTESQUE
BLOTTESQUES
BLOTTIER
BLOTTIEST
BLOTTING
BLOTTINGS
BLOTTO
BLOTTY
BLOUBOK
BLOUBOKS
BLOUSE
BLOUSED
BLOUSES
BLOUSIER
BLOUSIEST
BLOUSILY
BLOUSING

BLOUSON
BLOUSONS
BLOUSY
BLOVIATE
BLOVIATED
BLOVIATES
BLOVIATING
BLOVIATION
BLOVIATIONS
BLOW
BLOWBACK
BLOWBACKS
BLOWBALL
BLOWBALLS
BLOWBY
BLOWBYS
BLOWDOWN
BLOWDOWNS
BLOWED
BLOWER
BLOWERS
BLOWFISH
BLOWFISHES
BLOWFLIES
BLOWFLY
BLOWGUN
BLOWGUNS
BLOWHARD
BLOWHARDS
BLOWHOLE
BLOWHOLES
BLOWIE
BLOWIER
BLOWIES
BLOWIEST
BLOWING
BLOWJOB
BLOWJOBS
BLOWLAMP
BLOWLAMPS
BLOWN
BLOWOFF
BLOWOFFS
BLOWOUT
BLOWOUTS
BLOWPIPE
BLOWPIPES
BLOWS
BLOWSE
BLOWSED
BLOWSES
BLOWSIER
BLOWSIEST
BLOWSILY
BLOWSINESS
BLOWSY

BLOWTORCH
BLOWTORCHES
BLOWTUBE
BLOWTUBES
BLOWUP
BLOWUPS
BLOWY
BLOWZE
BLOWZED
BLOWZES
BLOWZIER
BLOWZIEST
BLOWZILY
BLOWZINESS
BLOWZY
BLUB
BLUBBED
BLUBBER
BLUBBERED
BLUBBERER
BLUBBERERS
BLUBBERING
BLUBBERS
BLUBBERY
BLUBBING
BLUBS
BLUCHER
BLUCHERS
BLUDE
BLUDES
BLUDGE
BLUDGED
BLUDGEON
BLUDGEONED
BLUDGEONER
BLUDGEONERS
BLUDGEONING
BLUDGEONS
BLUDGER
BLUDGERS
BLUDGES
BLUDGING
BLUDIE
BLUDIER
BLUDIEST
BLUDY
BLUE
BLUEBACK
BLUEBACKS
BLUEBALL
BLUEBALLS
BLUEBEARD
BLUEBEARDS
BLUEBEAT
BLUEBELL
BLUEBELLS

BLUEBERRIES
BLUEBERRY
BLUEBILL
BLUEBILLS
BLUEBIRD
BLUEBIRDS
BLUEBONNET
BLUEBONNETS
BLUEBOOK
BLUEBOOKS
BLUEBOTTLE
BLUEBOTTLES
BLUEBREAST
BLUEBREASTS
BLUEBUCK
BLUEBUCKS
BLUEBUSH
BLUEBUSHES
BLUECAP
BLUECAPS
BLUECOAT
BLUECOATS
BLUED
BLUEFIN
BLUEFINS
BLUEFISH
BLUEFISHES
BLUEGILL
BLUEGILLS
BLUEGOWN
BLUEGOWNS
BLUEGRASS
BLUEGRASSES
BLUEGUM
BLUEGUMS
BLUEHEAD
BLUEHEADS
BLUEING
BLUEINGS
BLUEISH
BLUEISHNESS
BLUEJACK
BLUEJACKET
BLUEJACKETS
BLUEJACKS
BLUEJAY
BLUEJAYS
BLUELINE
BLUELINES
BLUELY
BLUENESS
BLUENESSES
BLUENOSE
BLUENOSES
BLUEPOINT
BLUEPOINTS

BLUEPRINT
BLUEPRINTED
BLUEPRINTING
BLUEPRINTS
BLUER
BLUES
BLUESHIFT
BLUESHIFTED
BLUESHIFTS
BLUESIER
BLUESIEST
BLUESMAN
BLUESMEN
BLUEST
BLUESTEM
BLUESTEMS
BLUESTOCKING
BLUESTOCKINGS
BLUESTONE
BLUESTONES
BLUESY
BLUET
BLUETHROAT
BLUETHROATS
BLUETICK
BLUETICKS
BLUETIT
BLUETITS
BLUETONGUE
BLUETONGUES
BLUETS
BLUETTE
BLUETTES
BLUEWEED
BLUEWEEDS
BLUEWING
BLUEWINGS
BLUEWOOD
BLUEWOODS
BLUEY
BLUEYS
BLUFF
BLUFFED
BLUFFER
BLUFFERS
BLUFFEST
BLUFFING
BLUFFLY
BLUFFNESS
BLUFFNESSES
BLUFFS
BLUGGIER
BLUGGIEST
BLUGGY
BLUID
BLUIDIER

BLUIDIEST
BLUIDS
BLUIDY
BLUIER
BLUIEST
BLUING
BLUINGS
BLUISH
BLUISHNESS
BLUISHNESSES
BLUME
BLUMED
BLUMES
BLUMING
BLUNDER
BLUNDERBUSS
BLUNDERBUSSES
BLUNDERED
BLUNDERER
BLUNDERERS
BLUNDERING
BLUNDERINGLY
BLUNDERINGS
BLUNDERS
BLUNGE
BLUNGED
BLUNGER
BLUNGERS
BLUNGES
BLUNGING
BLUNK
BLUNKED
BLUNKER
BLUNKERS
BLUNKING
BLUNKS
BLUNT
BLUNTED
BLUNTER
BLUNTEST
BLUNTING
BLUNTISH
BLUNTLY
BLUNTNESS
BLUNTNESSES
BLUNTS
BLUR
BLURB
BLURBED
BLURBING
BLURBS
BLURRED
BLURREDLY
BLURREDNESS
BLURRIER
BLURRIEST

BLURRILY
BLURRINESS
BLURRINESSES
BLURRING
BLURRINGLY
BLURRY
BLURS
BLURT
BLURTED
BLURTER
BLURTERS
BLURTING
BLURTINGS
BLURTS
BLUSH
BLUSHED
BLUSHER
BLUSHERS
BLUSHES
BLUSHET
BLUSHETS
BLUSHFUL
BLUSHING
BLUSHINGLY
BLUSHINGS
BLUSHLESS
BLUSHLESSLY
BLUSTER
BLUSTERED
BLUSTERER
BLUSTERERS
BLUSTERIER
BLUSTERIEST
BLUSTERING
BLUSTERINGLY
BLUSTERINGS
BLUSTEROUS
BLUSTEROUSLY
BLUSTERS
BLUSTERY
BLUSTROUS
BLUTWURST
BLUTWURSTS
BLYPE
BLYPES
BO
BOA
BOAB
BOABS
BOAK
BOAKED
BOAKING
BOAKS
BOAR
BOARD
BOARDABILITY

BOARDABLE
BOARDED
BOARDER
BOARDERS
BOARDING
BOARDINGHOUSE
BOARDINGHOUSES
BOARDINGS
BOARDLIKE
BOARDMAN
BOARDMEN
BOARDROOM
BOARDROOMS
BOARDS
BOARDSAILING
BOARDSAILINGS
BOARDSAILOR
BOARDSAILORS
BOARDWALK
BOARDWALKS
BOARFISH
BOARFISHES
BOARISH
BOARISHLY
BOARISHNESS
BOARS
BOART
BOARTS
BOAS
BOAST
BOASTED
BOASTER
BOASTERS
BOASTFUL
BOASTFULLY
BOASTFULNESS
BOASTFULNESSES
BOASTING
BOASTINGLY
BOASTINGS
BOASTLESS
BOASTS
BOAT
BOATABLE
BOATBILL
BOATBILLS
BOATBUILDER
BOATBUILDERS
BOATBUILDING
BOATBUILDINGS
BOATED
BOATEL
BOATELS
BOATER
BOATERS
BOATFUL

BOATFULS
BOATHOOK
BOATHOOKS
BOATHOUSE
BOATHOUSES
BOATIE
BOATIES
BOATING
BOATINGS
BOATLIKE
BOATLOAD
BOATLOADS
BOATMAN
BOATMEN
BOATS
BOATSMAN
BOATSMEN
BOATSWAIN
BOATSWAINS
BOATTAIL
BOATTAILS
BOATYARD
BOATYARDS
BOB
BOBA
BOBAC
BOBACS
BOBAK
BOBAKS
BOBAS
BOBBED
BOBBEJAAN
BOBBEJAANS
BOBBER
BOBBERIES
BOBBERS
BOBBERY
BOBBIES
BOBBIN
BOBBINET
BOBBINETS
BOBBING
BOBBINS
BOBBISH
BOBBITT
BOBBITTED
BOBBITTING
BOBBITTS
BOBBLE
BOBBLED
BOBBLES
BOBBLIER
BOBBLIEST
BOBBLING
BOBBLY
BOBBY

BOBBYSOCK
BOBBYSOCKS
BOBBYSOXER
BOBBYSOXERS
BOBCAT
BOBCATS
BOBECHE
BOBECHES
BOBFLOAT
BOBFLOATS
BOBLET
BOBLETS
BOBOL
BOBOLINK
BOBOLINKS
BOBOLLED
BOBOLLING
BOBOLS
BOBOTIE
BOBOTIES
BOBOWLER
BOBOWLERS
BOBS
BOBSLED
BOBSLEDDED
BOBSLEDDER
BOBSLEDDERS
BOBSLEDDING
BOBSLEDDINGS
BOBSLEDS
BOBSLEIGH
BOBSLEIGHED
BOBSLEIGHING
BOBSLEIGHS
BOBSTAY
BOBSTAYS
BOBTAIL
BOBTAILED
BOBTAILING
BOBTAILS
BOBWEIGHT
BOBWEIGHTS
BOBWHEEL
BOBWHEELS
BOBWHITE
BOBWHITES
BOBWIG
BOBWIGS
BOCACCIO
BOCACCIOS
BOCAGE
BOCAGES
BOCCA
BOCCAS
BOCCE
BOCCES

BOCCI
BOCCIA
BOCCIAS
BOCCIE
BOCCIES
BOCCIS
BOCHE
BOCHES
BOCK
BOCKED
BOCKEDY
BOCKING
BOCKS
BOD
BODACH
BODACHS
BODACIOUS
BODACIOUSLY
BODDHISATTVA
BODDHISATTVAS
BODDLE
BODDLES
BODE
BODED
BODEFUL
BODEGA
BODEGAS
BODEGUERO
BODEGUEROS
BODEMENT
BODEMENTS
BODES
BODGE
BODGED
BODGER
BODGERS
BODGES
BODGIE
BODGIER
BODGIES
BODGIEST
BODGING
BODHISATTVA
BODHISATTVAS
BODHRAN
BODHRANS
BODICE
BODICES
BODIED
BODIES
BODIKIN
BODIKINS
BODILESS
BODILY
BODING
BODINGLY

BODINGS
BODKIN
BODKINS
BODLE
BODLES
BODRAG
BODRAGS
BODS
BODY
BODYBOARD
BODYBOARDED
BODYBOARDING
BODYBOARDS
BODYBUILDER
BODYBUILDERS
BODYBUILDING
BODYBUILDINGS
BODYCHECK
BODYCHECKED
BODYCHECKING
BODYCHECKS
BODYGUARD
BODYGUARDS
BODYING
BODYLINE
BODYLINES
BODYSHELL
BODYSHELLS
BODYSUIT
BODYSUITS
BODYSURF
BODYSURFED
BODYSURFER
BODYSURFERS
BODYSURFING
BODYSURFS
BODYWORK
BODYWORKER
BODYWORKERS
BODYWORKS
BOEHMITE
BOEHMITES
BOERBUL
BOERBULS
BOEREMUSIEK
BOEREWORS
BOEREWORSES
BOERPERD
BOERPERDE
BOET
BOETS
BOEUF
BOFF
BOFFED
BOFFIN
BOFFING

BOFFINS
BOFFO
BOFFOLA
BOFFOLAS
BOFFOS
BOFFS
BOG
BOGAN
BOGANS
BOGART
BOGARTED
BOGARTING
BOGARTS
BOGBEAN
BOGBEANS
BOGEY
BOGEYED
BOGEYING
BOGEYISM
BOGEYISMS
BOGEYMAN
BOGEYMEN
BOGEYS
BOGGARD
BOGGARDS
BOGGART
BOGGARTS
BOGGED
BOGGER
BOGGERS
BOGGIER
BOGGIEST
BOGGINESS
BOGGINESSES
BOGGING
BOGGISH
BOGGLE
BOGGLED
BOGGLER
BOGGLERS
BOGGLES
BOGGLING
BOGGY
BOGIE
BOGIED
BOGIEING
BOGIES
BOGLAND
BOGLANDS
BOGLE
BOGLES
BOGMAN
BOGMEN
BOGOAK
BOGOAKS
BOGONG

BOGONGS
BOGS
BOGTROTTER
BOGTROTTERS
BOGTROTTING
BOGTROTTINGS
BOGUS
BOGUSLY
BOGUSNESS
BOGWOOD
BOGWOODS
BOGY
BOGYISM
BOGYISMS
BOGYMAN
BOGYMEN
BOH
BOHEA
BOHEAS
BOHEMIA
BOHEMIAN
BOHEMIANISM
BOHEMIANISMS
BOHEMIANS
BOHEMIAS
BOHO
BOHRIUM
BOHS
BOHUNK
BOHUNKS
BOIL
BOILABLE
BOILED
BOILER
BOILERIES
BOILERMAKER
BOILERMAKERS
BOILERPLATE
BOILERPLATES
BOILERS
BOILERSUIT
BOILERSUITS
BOILERY
BOILING
BOILINGS
BOILOFF
BOILOFFS
BOILOVER
BOILOVERS
BOILS
BOING
BOINGED
BOINGING
BOINGS
BOINK
BOINKED

BOINKING
BOINKS
BOISERIE
BOISERIES
BOISTEROUS
BOISTEROUSLY
BOISTEROUSNESS
BOITE
BOITES
BOK
BOKE
BOKED
BOKES
BOKING
BOKMAKIERIE
BOKMAKIERIES
BOKO
BOKOS
BOKS
BOLA
BOLAR
BOLAS
BOLASES
BOLD
BOLDEN
BOLDENED
BOLDENING
BOLDENS
BOLDER
BOLDEST
BOLDFACE
BOLDFACED
BOLDFACES
BOLDFACING
BOLDLY
BOLDNESS
BOLDNESSES
BOLDS
BOLE
BOLECTION
BOLECTIONS
BOLERO
BOLEROS
BOLES
BOLETE
BOLETES
BOLETI
BOLETUS
BOLETUSES
BOLIDE
BOLIDES
BOLINE
BOLINES
BOLIVAR
BOLIVARES
BOLIVARS

BOLIVIA
BOLIVIANO
BOLIVIANOS
BOLIVIAS
BOLIX
BOLIXED
BOLIXES
BOLIXING
BOLL
BOLLARD
BOLLARDS
BOLLED
BOLLEN
BOLLETRIE
BOLLETRIES
BOLLING
BOLLIX
BOLLIXED
BOLLIXES
BOLLIXING
BOLLOCK
BOLLOCKED
BOLLOCKING
BOLLOCKINGS
BOLLOCKS
BOLLOCKSED
BOLLOCKSES
BOLLOCKSING
BOLLOX
BOLLOXED
BOLLOXES
BOLLOXING
BOLLS
BOLLWORM
BOLLWORMS
BOLO
BOLOGNA
BOLOGNAS
BOLOMETER
BOLOMETERS
BOLOMETRIC
BOLOMETRICALLY
BOLOMETRIES
BOLOMETRY
BOLONEY
BOLONEYS
BOLOS
BOLSHEVIK
BOLSHEVIKS
BOLSHEVISE
BOLSHEVISED
BOLSHEVISES
BOLSHEVISING
BOLSHEVISM
BOLSHEVISMS
BOLSHEVIST

BOLSHEVISTS
BOLSHEVIZE
BOLSHEVIZED
BOLSHEVIZES
BOLSHEVIZING
BOLSHIE
BOLSHIER
BOLSHIES
BOLSHIEST
BOLSHY
BOLSON
BOLSONS
BOLSTER
BOLSTERED
BOLSTERER
BOLSTERERS
BOLSTERING
BOLSTERINGS
BOLSTERS
BOLT
BOLTED
BOLTER
BOLTERS
BOLTHEAD
BOLTHEADS
BOLTHOLE
BOLTHOLES
BOLTING
BOLTINGS
BOLTONIA
BOLTONIAS
BOLTROPE
BOLTROPES
BOLTS
BOLUS
BOLUSES
BOMA
BOMAS
BOMB
BOMBACACEOUS
BOMBARD
BOMBARDE
BOMBARDED
BOMBARDES
BOMBARDIER
BOMBARDIERS
BOMBARDING
BOMBARDMENT
BOMBARDMENTS
BOMBARDON
BOMBARDONS
BOMBARDS
BOMBASINE
BOMBASINES
BOMBAST
BOMBASTED

BOMBASTIC
BOMBASTICALLY
BOMBASTING
BOMBASTS
BOMBAX
BOMBAXES
BOMBAZINE
BOMBAZINES
BOMBE
BOMBED
BOMBER
BOMBERS
BOMBES
BOMBESIN
BOMBESINS
BOMBILATE
BOMBILATED
BOMBILATES
BOMBILATING
BOMBILATION
BOMBILATIONS
BOMBINATE
BOMBINATED
BOMBINATES
BOMBINATING
BOMBINATION
BOMBINATIONS
BOMBING
BOMBINGS
BOMBLET
BOMBLETS
BOMBLOAD
BOMBLOADS
BOMBO
BOMBORA
BOMBORAS
BOMBOS
BOMBPROOF
BOMBS
BOMBSHELL
BOMBSHELLS
BOMBSIGHT
BOMBSIGHTS
BOMBSITE
BOMBSITES
BOMBYCID
BOMBYCIDS
BOMBYX
BOMBYXES
BON
BONA
BONACI
BONACIS
BONAMANI
BONAMANO
BONAMIA

BONAMIAS
BONAMIASES
BONAMIASIS
BONANZA
BONANZAS
BONASSUS
BONASSUSES
BONASUS
BONASUSES
BONBON
BONBONNIERE
BONBONNIERES
BONBONS
BONCE
BONCES
BOND
BONDABLE
BONDAGE
BONDAGER
BONDAGERS
BONDAGES
BONDED
BONDER
BONDERS
BONDHOLDER
BONDHOLDERS
BONDING
BONDINGS
BONDMAID
BONDMAIDS
BONDMAN
BONDMANSHIP
BONDMANSHIPS
BONDMEN
BONDS
BONDSERVANT
BONDSERVANTS
BONDSMAN
BONDSMEN
BONDSTONE
BONDSTONES
BONDSWOMAN
BONDSWOMEN
BONDUC
BONDUCS
BONDWOMAN
BONDWOMEN
BONE
BONEBLACK
BONED
BONEFISH
BONEFISHES
BONEFISHING
BONEFISHINGS
BONEHEAD
BONEHEADED

BONEHEADEDNESS
BONEHEADS
BONELESS
BONEMEAL
BONEMEALS
BONER
BONERS
BONES
BONESET
BONESETS
BONESETTER
BONESETTERS
BONESHAKER
BONESHAKERS
BONEY
BONEYARD
BONEYARDS
BONFIRE
BONFIRES
BONG
BONGED
BONGING
BONGO
BONGOES
BONGOIST
BONGOISTS
BONGOS
BONGRACE
BONGRACES
BONGS
BONHAM
BONHAMS
BONHOMIE
BONHOMIES
BONHOMMIE
BONHOMMIES
BONHOMOUS
BONIBELL
BONIBELLS
BONIE
BONIER
BONIEST
BONIFACE
BONIFACES
BONILASSE
BONILASSES
BONINESS
BONINESSES
BONING
BONINGS
BONISM
BONISMS
BONIST
BONISTS
BONITA
BONITAS

BONITO
BONITOES
BONITOS
BONJOUR
BONK
BONKBUSTER
BONKBUSTERS
BONKED
BONKERS
BONKING
BONKINGS
BONKS
BONNE
BONNES
BONNET
BONNETED
BONNETING
BONNETS
BONNIBELL
BONNIBELLS
BONNIE
BONNIER
BONNIES
BONNIEST
BONNILASSES
BONNILY
BONNINESS
BONNINESSES
BONNOCK
BONNOCKS
BONNY
BONNYCLABBER
BONNYCLABBERS
BONOBO
BONOBOS
BONSAI
BONSAIS
BONSELA
BONSELAS
BONSELLA
BONSELLAS
BONSOIR
BONSPELL
BONSPELLS
BONSPIEL
BONSPIELS
BONTEBOK
BONTEBOKS
BONUS
BONUSES
BONXIE
BONXIES
BONY
BONZA
BONZE
BONZER

BONZES
BOO
BOOB
BOOBED
BOOBHEAD
BOOBHEADED
BOOBHEADS
BOOBIALLA
BOOBIALLAS
BOOBIE
BOOBIES
BOOBING
BOOBISH
BOOBOISIE
BOOBOISIES
BOOBOO
BOOBOOK
BOOBOOKS
BOOBOOS
BOOBS
BOOBY
BOOBYISH
BOOBYISM
BOOBYISMS
BOODIE
BOODIED
BOODIES
BOODLE
BOODLED
BOODLER
BOODLERS
BOODLES
BOODLING
BOODY
BOODYING
BOOED
BOOFHEAD
BOOFHEADS
BOOFIER
BOOFIEST
BOOFY
BOOGER
BOOGERMAN
BOOGERMEN
BOOGERS
BOOGEY
BOOGEYED
BOOGEYING
BOOGEYMAN
BOOGEYMEN
BOOGEYS
BOOGIE
BOOGIED
BOOGIEING
BOOGIES
BOOGY

BOOGYING
BOOGYMAN
BOOGYMEN
BOOH
BOOHAI
BOOHAIS
BOOHED
BOOHING
BOOHOO
BOOHOOED
BOOHOOING
BOOHOOS
BOOHS
BOOING
BOOK
BOOKABLE
BOOKBINDER
BOOKBINDERIES
BOOKBINDERS
BOOKBINDERY
BOOKBINDING
BOOKBINDINGS
BOOKCASE
BOOKCASES
BOOKED
BOOKEND
BOOKENDS
BOOKER
BOOKERS
BOOKFUL
BOOKFULS
BOOKIE
BOOKIER
BOOKIES
BOOKIEST
BOOKING
BOOKINGS
BOOKISH
BOOKISHLY
BOOKISHNESS
BOOKISHNESSES
BOOKKEEPER
BOOKKEEPERS
BOOKKEEPING
BOOKKEEPINGS
BOOKLAND
BOOKLANDS
BOOKLESS
BOOKLET
BOOKLETS
BOOKLICE
BOOKLIGHT
BOOKLIGHTS
BOOKLORE
BOOKLORES
BOOKLOUSE

BOOKMAKER
BOOKMAKERS
BOOKMAKING
BOOKMAKINGS
BOOKMAN
BOOKMARK
BOOKMARKER
BOOKMARKERS
BOOKMARKS
BOOKMEN
BOOKMOBILE
BOOKMOBILES
BOOKPLATE
BOOKPLATES
BOOKRACK
BOOKRACKS
BOOKREST
BOOKRESTS
BOOKS
BOOKSELLER
BOOKSELLERS
BOOKSELLING
BOOKSELLINGS
BOOKSHELF
BOOKSHELVES
BOOKSHOP
BOOKSHOPS
BOOKSIE
BOOKSIER
BOOKSIEST
BOOKSTALL
BOOKSTALLS
BOOKSTAND
BOOKSTANDS
BOOKSTORE
BOOKSTORES
BOOKSY
BOOKWORK
BOOKWORKS
BOOKWORM
BOOKWORMS
BOOKY
BOOL
BOOLED
BOOLING
BOOLS
BOOM
BOOMBOX
BOOMBOXES
BOOMED
BOOMER
BOOMERANG
BOOMERANGED
BOOMERANGING
BOOMERANGS
BOOMERS

BOOMIER
BOOMIEST
BOOMING
BOOMINGS
BOOMKIN
BOOMKINS
BOOMLET
BOOMLETS
BOOMS
BOOMSLANG
BOOMSLANGS
BOOMTOWN
BOOMTOWNS
BOOMY
BOON
BOONDOCK
BOONDOCKS
BOONDOGGLE
BOONDOGGLED
BOONDOGGLER
BOONDOGGLERS
BOONDOGGLES
BOONDOGGLING
BOONG
BOONGA
BOONGARIES
BOONGARY
BOONGAS
BOONGS
BOONIES
BOONS
BOOR
BOORD
BOORDE
BOORDES
BOORDS
BOORISH
BOORISHLY
BOORISHNESS
BOORISHNESSES
BOORKA
BOORKAS
BOORS
BOORTREE
BOORTREES
BOOS
BOOSE
BOOSED
BOOSES
BOOSHIT
BOOSING
BOOST
BOOSTED
BOOSTER
BOOSTERISH
BOOSTERISM

BOOSTERISMS
BOOSTERS
BOOSTING
BOOSTS
BOOT
BOOTABLE
BOOTBLACK
BOOTBLACKS
BOOTED
BOOTEE
BOOTEES
BOOTERIES
BOOTERY
BOOTH
BOOTHOSE
BOOTHS
BOOTIE
BOOTIES
BOOTIKIN
BOOTIKINS
BOOTING
BOOTJACK
BOOTJACKS
BOOTLACE
BOOTLACES
BOOTLAST
BOOTLASTS
BOOTLEG
BOOTLEGGED
BOOTLEGGER
BOOTLEGGERS
BOOTLEGGING
BOOTLEGGINGS
BOOTLEGS
BOOTLESS
BOOTLESSLY
BOOTLESSNESS
BOOTLESSNESSES
BOOTLICK
BOOTLICKED
BOOTLICKER
BOOTLICKERS
BOOTLICKING
BOOTLICKINGS
BOOTLICKS
BOOTLOADER
BOOTLOADERS
BOOTMAKER
BOOTMAKERS
BOOTMAKING
BOOTMAKINGS
BOOTS
BOOTSTRAP
BOOTSTRAPPED
BOOTSTRAPPING
BOOTSTRAPS

BOOTY
BOOTYLICIOUS
BOOTYLICIOUSLY
BOOZE
BOOZED
BOOZER
BOOZERS
BOOZES
BOOZEY
BOOZIER
BOOZIEST
BOOZILY
BOOZINESS
BOOZINESSES
BOOZING
BOOZY
BOP
BOPEEP
BOPEEPS
BOPPED
BOPPER
BOPPERS
BOPPING
BOPS
BOR
BORA
BORACES
BORACHIO
BORACHIOS
BORACIC
BORACITE
BORACITES
BORAGE
BORAGES
BORAGINACEOUS
BORAK
BORAKS
BORAL
BORALS
BORANE
BORANES
BORAS
BORATE
BORATED
BORATES
BORATING
BORAX
BORAXES
BORAZON
BORAZONS
BORBORYGMAL
BORBORYGMALLY
BORBORYGMI
BORBORYGMIC
BORBORYGMUS
BORBORYGMUSES

BORD
BORDAR
BORDARS
BORDE
BORDEAUX
BORDEL
BORDELLO
BORDELLOS
BORDELS
BORDER
BORDEREAU
BORDEREAUX
BORDERED
BORDERER
BORDERERS
BORDERING
BORDERLAND
BORDERLANDS
BORDERLESS
BORDERLINE
BORDERLINES
BORDERS
BORDES
BORDRAGING
BORDRAGINGS
BORDS
BORDURE
BORDURES
BORE
BOREAL
BORECOLE
BORECOLES
BORED
BOREDOM
BOREDOMS
BOREE
BOREEN
BOREENS
BOREES
BOREHOLE
BOREHOLES
BOREL
BORER
BORERS
BORES
BORESCOPE
BORESCOPES
BORESOME
BORGHETTO
BORGHETTOS
BORGO
BORGOS
BORIC
BORIDE
BORIDES
BORING

BORINGLY
BORINGNESS
BORINGNESSES
BORINGS
BORLOTTI
BORLOTTO
BORM
BORMED
BORMING
BORMS
BORN
BORNE
BORNEOL
BORNEOLS
BORNITE
BORNITES
BOROHYDRIDE
BOROHYDRIDES
BORON
BORONIA
BORONIAS
BORONIC
BORONS
BOROSILICATE
BOROSILICATES
BOROUGH
BOROUGHS
BORREL
BORRELL
BORROW
BORROWED
BORROWER
BORROWERS
BORROWING
BORROWINGS
BORROWS
BORS
BORSCH
BORSCHES
BORSCHT
BORSCHTS
BORSH
BORSHCH
BORSHCHES
BORSHES
BORSHT
BORSHTS
BORSIC
BORSTAL
BORSTALL
BORSTALLS
BORSTALS
BORT
BORTIER
BORTIEST
BORTS

BORTSCH
BORTSCHES
BORTY
BORTZ
BORTZES
BORZOI
BORZOIS
BOS
BOSBERAAD
BOSBERAADS
BOSBOK
BOSBOKS
BOSCAGE
BOSCAGES
BOSCHBOK
BOSCHBOKS
BOSCHE
BOSCHES
BOSCHVARK
BOSCHVARKS
BOSCHVELD
BOSCHVELDS
BOSH
BOSHBOK
BOSHBOKS
BOSHES
BOSHTA
BOSHTER
BOSHVARK
BOSHVARKS
BOSK
BOSKAGE
BOSKAGES
BOSKER
BOSKET
BOSKETS
BOSKIER
BOSKIEST
BOSKINESS
BOSKINESSES
BOSKS
BOSKY
BOSOM
BOSOMED
BOSOMIER
BOSOMIEST
BOSOMING
BOSOMS
BOSOMY
BOSON
BOSONS
BOSQUE
BOSQUES
BOSQUET
BOSQUETS
BOSS

BOSSBOY
BOSSBOYS
BOSSDOM
BOSSDOMS
BOSSED
BOSSER
BOSSES
BOSSEST
BOSSET
BOSSETS
BOSSIER
BOSSIES
BOSSIEST
BOSSILY
BOSSINESS
BOSSINESSES
BOSSING
BOSSISM
BOSSISMS
BOSSY
BOSSYBOOTS
BOSTANGI
BOSTANGIS
BOSTHOON
BOSTHOONS
BOSTON
BOSTONS
BOSTRYX
BOSTRYXES
BOSUN
BOSUNS
BOT
BOTA
BOTANIC
BOTANICA
BOTANICAL
BOTANICALLY
BOTANICALS
BOTANICAS
BOTANICS
BOTANIES
BOTANISE
BOTANISED
BOTANISES
BOTANISING
BOTANIST
BOTANISTS
BOTANIZE
BOTANIZED
BOTANIZES
BOTANIZING
BOTANOMANCIES
BOTANOMANCY
BOTANY
BOTARGO
BOTARGOES

BOTARGOS
BOTAS
BOTCH
BOTCHED
BOTCHER
BOTCHERIES
BOTCHERS
BOTCHERY
BOTCHES
BOTCHIER
BOTCHIEST
BOTCHILY
BOTCHINESS
BOTCHING
BOTCHINGS
BOTCHY
BOTEL
BOTELS
BOTFLIES
BOTFLY
BOTH
BOTHAN
BOTHANS
BOTHER
BOTHERATION
BOTHERATIONS
BOTHERED
BOTHERING
BOTHERS
BOTHERSOME
BOTHIE
BOTHIES
BOTHOLE
BOTHOLES
BOTHRIA
BOTHRIUM
BOTHRIUMS
BOTHY
BOTHYMAN
BOTHYMEN
BOTONE
BOTONEE
BOTONNEE
BOTRYOID
BOTRYOIDAL
BOTRYOSE
BOTRYTIS
BOTRYTISES
BOTS
BOTT
BOTTE
BOTTED
BOTTEGA
BOTTEGAS
BOTTES
BOTTIES

BOTTINE
BOTTINES
BOTTING
BOTTLE
BOTTLEBRUSH
BOTTLEBRUSHES
BOTTLED
BOTTLEFUL
BOTTLEFULS
BOTTLENECK
BOTTLENECKED
BOTTLENECKING
BOTTLENECKS
BOTTLENOSE
BOTTLENOSES
BOTTLER
BOTTLERS
BOTTLES
BOTTLING
BOTTLINGS
BOTTOM
BOTTOMED
BOTTOMER
BOTTOMERS
BOTTOMING
BOTTOMLAND
BOTTOMLANDS
BOTTOMLESS
BOTTOMLESSLY
BOTTOMLESSNESS
BOTTOMMOST
BOTTOMNESS
BOTTOMNESSES
BOTTOMRIES
BOTTOMRY
BOTTOMS
BOTTOMSET
BOTTONY
BOTTS
BOTTY
BOTULIN
BOTULINAL
BOTULINS
BOTULINUM
BOTULINUMS
BOTULINUS
BOTULINUSES
BOTULISM
BOTULISMS
BOUBOU
BOUBOUS
BOUCHE
BOUCHEE
BOUCHEES
BOUCHES
BOUCLE

BOUCLEE
BOUCLEES
BOUCLES
BOUDERIE
BOUDERIES
BOUDIN
BOUDINS
BOUDOIR
BOUDOIRS
BOUFFANT
BOUFFANTS
BOUFFE
BOUFFES
BOUGAINVILIA
BOUGAINVILIAS
BOUGAINVILLAEA
BOUGAINVILLAEAS
BOUGAINVILLEA
BOUGAINVILLEAS
BOUGE
BOUGED
BOUGES
BOUGET
BOUGETS
BOUGH
BOUGHED
BOUGHPOT
BOUGHPOTS
BOUGHS
BOUGHT
BOUGHTEN
BOUGHTS
BOUGIE
BOUGIES
BOUGING
BOUILLABAISSE
BOUILLABAISSES
BOUILLI
BOUILLIS
BOUILLON
BOUILLONS
BOUILLOTTE
BOUILLOTTES
BOUK
BOUKS
BOULDER
BOULDERED
BOULDERING
BOULDERS
BOULDERY
BOULE
BOULES
BOULEVARD
BOULEVARDIER
BOULEVARDIERS
BOULEVARDS

BOULEVERSEMENT
BOULEVERSEMENTS
BOULLE
BOULLES
BOULLEWORK
BOULT
BOULTED
BOULTER
BOULTERS
BOULTING
BOULTINGS
BOULTS
BOUN
BOUNCE
BOUNCED
BOUNCER
BOUNCERS
BOUNCES
BOUNCIER
BOUNCIEST
BOUNCILY
BOUNCINESS
BOUNCINESSES
BOUNCING
BOUNCINGLY
BOUNCY
BOUND
BOUNDARIES
BOUNDARY
BOUNDED
BOUNDEDNESS
BOUNDEDNESSES
BOUNDEN
BOUNDER
BOUNDERISH
BOUNDERS
BOUNDING
BOUNDLESS
BOUNDLESSLY
BOUNDLESSNESS
BOUNDLESSNESSES
BOUNDS
BOUNED
BOUNING
BOUNS
BOUNTEOUS
BOUNTEOUSLY
BOUNTEOUSNESS
BOUNTEOUSNESSES
BOUNTIED
BOUNTIES
BOUNTIFUL
BOUNTIFULLY
BOUNTIFULNESS
BOUNTIFULNESSES
BOUNTREE

BOUNTREES
BOUNTY
BOUNTYHED
BOUNTYHEDS
BOUQUET
BOUQUETIERE
BOUQUETIERES
BOUQUETS
BOURASQUE
BOURASQUES
BOURBON
BOURBONISM
BOURBONISMS
BOURBONS
BOURD
BOURDER
BOURDERS
BOURDON
BOURDONS
BOURDS
BOURG
BOURGEOIS
BOURGEOISE
BOURGEOISES
BOURGEOISIE
BOURGEOISIES
BOURGEOISIFIED
BOURGEOISIFIES
BOURGEOISIFY
BOURGEOISIFYING
BOURGEON
BOURGEONED
BOURGEONING
BOURGEONS
BOURGS
BOURGUIGNON
BOURGUIGNONNE
BOURKHA
BOURKHAS
BOURLAW
BOURLAWS
BOURN
BOURNE
BOURNES
BOURNS
BOURREE
BOURREES
BOURRIDE
BOURRIDES
BOURSE
BOURSES
BOURSIER
BOURSIERS
BOURTREE
BOURTREES
BOUSE

BOUSED
BOUSES
BOUSIER
BOUSIEST
BOUSING
BOUSINGKENS
BOUSOUKI
BOUSOUKIA
BOUSOUKIS
BOUSTROPHEDON
BOUSTROPHEDONIC
BOUSTROPHEDONS
BOUSY
BOUT
BOUTADE
BOUTADES
BOUTIQUE
BOUTIQUES
BOUTON
BOUTONNE
BOUTONNEE
BOUTONNIERE
BOUTONNIERES
BOUTONS
BOUTS
BOUVIER
BOUVIERS
BOUZOUKI
BOUZOUKIA
BOUZOUKIS
BOVATE
BOVATES
BOVID
BOVIDS
BOVINE
BOVINELY
BOVINES
BOVINITIES
BOVINITY
BOVVER
BOVVERS
BOW
BOWAT
BOWATS
BOWBENT
BOWDLERISATION
BOWDLERISATIONS
BOWDLERISE
BOWDLERISED
BOWDLERISER
BOWDLERISERS
BOWDLERISES
BOWDLERISING
BOWDLERISM
BOWDLERISMS
BOWDLERIZATION

BOWDLERIZATIONS
BOWDLERIZE
BOWDLERIZED
BOWDLERIZER
BOWDLERIZERS
BOWDLERIZES
BOWDLERIZING
BOWED
BOWEL
BOWELED
BOWELING
BOWELLED
BOWELLESS
BOWELLING
BOWELS
BOWER
BOWERBIRD
BOWERBIRDS
BOWERED
BOWERIES
BOWERING
BOWERS
BOWERWOMAN
BOWERWOMEN
BOWERY
BOWES
BOWET
BOWETS
BOWFIN
BOWFINS
BOWFRONT
BOWGET
BOWGETS
BOWHEAD
BOWHEADS
BOWIE
BOWIES
BOWING
BOWINGLY
BOWINGS
BOWKNOT
BOWKNOTS
BOWL
BOWLDER
BOWLDERS
BOWLED
BOWLEG
BOWLEGGED
BOWLEGS
BOWLER
BOWLERS
BOWLESS
BOWLFUL
BOWLFULS
BOWLIKE
BOWLINE

BOWLINES
BOWLING
BOWLINGS
BOWLLIKE
BOWLS
BOWMAN
BOWMEN
BOWNE
BOWNED
BOWNES
BOWNING
BOWPOT
BOWPOTS
BOWR
BOWRS
BOWS
BOWSAW
BOWSAWS
BOWSE
BOWSED
BOWSER
BOWSERS
BOWSES
BOWSHOT
BOWSHOTS
BOWSIE
BOWSIES
BOWSING
BOWSPRIT
BOWSPRITS
BOWSTRING
BOWSTRINGED
BOWSTRINGING
BOWSTRINGS
BOWSTRUNG
BOWWOW
BOWWOWED
BOWWOWING
BOWWOWS
BOWYANG
BOWYANGS
BOWYER
BOWYERS
BOX
BOXBERRIES
BOXBERRY
BOXBOARD
BOXBOARDS
BOXCAR
BOXCARS
BOXED
BOXEN
BOXER
BOXERCISE
BOXERCISES
BOXERS

BOXES
BOXFISH
BOXFISHES
BOXFUL
BOXFULS
BOXHAUL
BOXHAULED
BOXHAULING
BOXHAULS
BOXIER
BOXIEST
BOXINESS
BOXINESSES
BOXING
BOXINGS
BOXKEEPER
BOXKEEPERS
BOXLIKE
BOXROOM
BOXROOMS
BOXTHORN
BOXTHORNS
BOXWALLAH
BOXWALLAHS
BOXWOOD
BOXWOODS
BOXY
BOY
BOYAR
BOYARD
BOYARDS
BOYARISM
BOYARISMS
BOYARS
BOYAU
BOYAUX
BOYCHICK
BOYCHICKS
BOYCHIK
BOYCHIKS
BOYCOTT
BOYCOTTED
BOYCOTTER
BOYCOTTERS
BOYCOTTING
BOYCOTTS
BOYED
BOYF
BOYFRIEND
BOYFRIENDS
BOYFS
BOYG
BOYGS
BOYHOOD
BOYHOODS
BOYING

BOYISH
BOYISHLY
BOYISHNESS
BOYISHNESSES
BOYLA
BOYLAS
BOYO
BOYOS
BOYS
BOYSENBERRIES
BOYSENBERRY
BOYSIER
BOYSIEST
BOYSY
BOZO
BOZOS
BOZZETTI
BOZZETTO
BRA
BRAAI
BRAAIED
BRAAIING
BRAAIS
BRAAIVLEIS
BRAAIVLEISES
BRAATA
BRAATAS
BRAATASES
BRABBLE
BRABBLED
BRABBLEMENT
BRABBLEMENTS
BRABBLER
BRABBLERS
BRABBLES
BRABBLING
BRACCATE
BRACCIA
BRACCIO
BRACE
BRACED
BRACELET
BRACELETS
BRACER
BRACERO
BRACEROS
BRACERS
BRACES
BRACH
BRACHAH
BRACHES
BRACHET
BRACHETS
BRACHIA
BRACHIAL
BRACHIALS

BRACHIATE
BRACHIATED
BRACHIATES
BRACHIATING
BRACHIATION
BRACHIATIONS
BRACHIATOR
BRACHIATORS
BRACHIOCEPHALIC
BRACHIOPOD
BRACHIOPODS
BRACHIOSAURUS
BRACHIOSAURUSES
BRACHISTOCHRONE
BRACHIUM
BRACHS
BRACHYAXIS
BRACHYCEPHAL
BRACHYCEPHALIC
BRACHYCEPHALICS
BRACHYCEPHALIES
BRACHYCEPHALISM
BRACHYCEPHALOUS
BRACHYCEPHALS
BRACHYCEPHALY
BRACHYCEROUS
BRACHYDACTYL
BRACHYDACTYLIC
BRACHYDACTYLIES
BRACHYDACTYLISM
BRACHYDACTYLOUS
BRACHYDACTYLY
BRACHYDIAGONAL
BRACHYDIAGONALS
BRACHYDOME
BRACHYDOMES
BRACHYDONTS
BRACHYGRAPHIES
BRACHYGRAPHY
BRACHYLOGIES
BRACHYLOGOUS
BRACHYLOGY
BRACHYODONT
BRACHYPINAKOIDS
BRACHYPRISM
BRACHYPRISMS
BRACHYPTERISM
BRACHYPTEROUS
BRACHYURAL
BRACHYURAN
BRACHYURANS
BRACHYUROUS
BRACING
BRACINGLY
BRACINGS
BRACIOLA

BRACIOLAS
BRACIOLE
BRACIOLES
BRACK
BRACKEN
BRACKENS
BRACKET
BRACKETED
BRACKETING
BRACKETINGS
BRACKETS
BRACKISH
BRACKISHNESS
BRACKISHNESSES
BRACKS
BRACONID
BRACONIDS
BRACT
BRACTEAL
BRACTEATE
BRACTEATES
BRACTED
BRACTEOLATE
BRACTEOLE
BRACTEOLES
BRACTLESS
BRACTLET
BRACTLETS
BRACTS
BRAD
BRADAWL
BRADAWLS
BRADDED
BRADDING
BRADOON
BRADOONS
BRADS
BRADYCARDIA
BRADYCARDIAC
BRADYCARDIACS
BRADYCARDIAS
BRADYKINESIA
BRADYKINESIAC
BRADYKINESIACS
BRADYKININ
BRADYKININS
BRADYPEPTIC
BRADYPEPTICS
BRADYSEISM
BRADYSEISMS
BRAE
BRAEHEID
BRAEHEIDS
BRAES
BRAG
BRAGADISME

BRAGADISMES
BRAGGADOCIO
BRAGGADOCIOS
BRAGGADOCIOUS
BRAGGART
BRAGGARTISM
BRAGGARTISMS
BRAGGARTLY
BRAGGARTS
BRAGGED
BRAGGER
BRAGGERS
BRAGGEST
BRAGGIER
BRAGGIEST
BRAGGING
BRAGGINGLY
BRAGGINGS
BRAGGY
BRAGLY
BRAGS
BRAHMA
BRAHMAS
BRAID
BRAIDE
BRAIDED
BRAIDER
BRAIDERS
BRAIDEST
BRAIDING
BRAIDINGS
BRAIDS
BRAIL
BRAILED
BRAILING
BRAILLE
BRAILLED
BRAILLER
BRAILLERS
BRAILLES
BRAILLEWRITER
BRAILLEWRITERS
BRAILLING
BRAILLIST
BRAILLISTS
BRAILS
BRAIN
BRAINBOX
BRAINBOXES
BRAINCASE
BRAINCASES
BRAINCHILD
BRAINCHILDREN
BRAINDEAD
BRAINDEADS
BRAINED

BRAINIAC
BRAINIACS
BRAINIER
BRAINIEST
BRAINILY
BRAININESS
BRAININESSES
BRAINING
BRAINISH
BRAINLESS
BRAINLESSLY
BRAINLESSNESS
BRAINLESSNESSES
BRAINPAN
BRAINPANS
BRAINPOWER
BRAINPOWERS
BRAINS
BRAINSICK
BRAINSICKLY
BRAINSICKNESS
BRAINSICKNESSES
BRAINSTEM
BRAINSTEMS
BRAINSTORM
BRAINSTORMED
BRAINSTORMER
BRAINSTORMERS
BRAINSTORMING
BRAINSTORMINGS
BRAINSTORMS
BRAINTEASER
BRAINTEASERS
BRAINWASH
BRAINWASHED
BRAINWASHER
BRAINWASHERS
BRAINWASHES
BRAINWASHING
BRAINWASHINGS
BRAINWAVE
BRAINWAVES
BRAINY
BRAIRD
BRAIRDED
BRAIRDING
BRAIRDS
BRAISE
BRAISED
BRAISES
BRAISING
BRAIZE
BRAIZES
BRAK
BRAKE
BRAKEAGE

BRAKEAGES
BRAKED
BRAKELESS
BRAKEMAN
BRAKEMEN
BRAKES
BRAKESMAN
BRAKESMEN
BRAKIER
BRAKIEST
BRAKING
BRAKY
BRALESS
BRAMBLE
BRAMBLED
BRAMBLES
BRAMBLIER
BRAMBLIEST
BRAMBLING
BRAMBLINGS
BRAMBLY
BRAME
BRAMES
BRAN
BRANCARD
BRANCARDS
BRANCH
BRANCHED
BRANCHER
BRANCHERIES
BRANCHERS
BRANCHERY
BRANCHES
BRANCHIA
BRANCHIAE
BRANCHIAL
BRANCHIATE
BRANCHIER
BRANCHIEST
BRANCHING
BRANCHINGS
BRANCHIOPOD
BRANCHIOPODS
BRANCHIOSTEGAL
BRANCHLESS
BRANCHLET
BRANCHLETS
BRANCHLIKE
BRANCHLINE
BRANCHLINES
BRANCHY
BRAND
BRANDADE
BRANDADES
BRANDED
BRANDER

BRANDERED
BRANDERING
BRANDERS
BRANDIED
BRANDIES
BRANDING
BRANDISE
BRANDISES
BRANDISH
BRANDISHED
BRANDISHER
BRANDISHERS
BRANDISHES
BRANDISHING
BRANDLING
BRANDLINGS
BRANDRETH
BRANDRETHS
BRANDS
BRANDY
BRANDYING
BRANFULNESS
BRANFULNESSES
BRANGLE
BRANGLED
BRANGLES
BRANGLING
BRANGLINGS
BRANK
BRANKED
BRANKIER
BRANKIEST
BRANKING
BRANKS
BRANKURSINE
BRANKURSINES
BRANKY
BRANLE
BRANLES
BRANNED
BRANNER
BRANNERS
BRANNIER
BRANNIEST
BRANNIGAN
BRANNIGANS
BRANNING
BRANNY
BRANS
BRANSLE
BRANSLES
BRANT
BRANTAIL
BRANTAILS
BRANTLE
BRANTLES

BRANTS
BRAS
BRASCO
BRASCOS
BRASERO
BRASEROS
BRASES
BRASH
BRASHED
BRASHER
BRASHES
BRASHEST
BRASHIER
BRASHIEST
BRASHINESS
BRASHING
BRASHLY
BRASHNESS
BRASHNESSES
BRASHY
BRASIER
BRASIERS
BRASIL
BRASILEIN
BRASILIN
BRASILINS
BRASILS
BRASS
BRASSAGE
BRASSAGES
BRASSARD
BRASSARDS
BRASSART
BRASSARTS
BRASSBOUND
BRASSED
BRASSERIE
BRASSERIES
BRASSES
BRASSET
BRASSETS
BRASSFOUNDER
BRASSFOUNDERS
BRASSFOUNDING
BRASSFOUNDINGS
BRASSICA
BRASSICACEOUS
BRASSICAS
BRASSIE
BRASSIER
BRASSIERE
BRASSIERES
BRASSIES
BRASSIEST
BRASSILY
BRASSINESS

BRASSINESSES
BRASSING
BRASSISH
BRASSY
BRAST
BRASTING
BRASTS
BRAT
BRATCHET
BRATCHETS
BRATLING
BRATLINGS
BRATPACK
BRATPACKER
BRATPACKERS
BRATPACKS
BRATS
BRATTICE
BRATTICED
BRATTICES
BRATTICING
BRATTICINGS
BRATTIER
BRATTIEST
BRATTINESS
BRATTINESSES
BRATTISH
BRATTISHED
BRATTISHES
BRATTISHING
BRATTISHINGS
BRATTLE
BRATTLED
BRATTLES
BRATTLING
BRATTLINGS
BRATTY
BRATWURST
BRATWURSTS
BRAUNCH
BRAUNCHED
BRAUNCHES
BRAUNCHING
BRAUNITE
BRAUNITES
BRAUNSCHWEIGER
BRAUNSCHWEIGERS
BRAVA
BRAVADO
BRAVADOED
BRAVADOES
BRAVADOING
BRAVADOS
BRAVAS
BRAVE
BRAVED

BRAVELY
BRAVENESS
BRAVER
BRAVERIES
BRAVERS
BRAVERY
BRAVES
BRAVEST
BRAVI
BRAVING
BRAVISSIMA
BRAVISSIMO
BRAVO
BRAVOED
BRAVOES
BRAVOING
BRAVOS
BRAVURA
BRAVURAS
BRAVURE
BRAW
BRAWER
BRAWEST
BRAWL
BRAWLED
BRAWLER
BRAWLERS
BRAWLIE
BRAWLIER
BRAWLIEST
BRAWLING
BRAWLINGS
BRAWLS
BRAWLY
BRAWN
BRAWNED
BRAWNIER
BRAWNIEST
BRAWNILY
BRAWNINESS
BRAWNINESSES
BRAWNS
BRAWNY
BRAWS
BRAXIES
BRAXY
BRAY
BRAYED
BRAYER
BRAYERS
BRAYING
BRAYS
BRAZA
BRAZAS
BRAZE
BRAZED

BRAZELESS
BRAZEN
BRAZENED
BRAZENING
BRAZENLY
BRAZENNESS
BRAZENNESSES
BRAZENRIES
BRAZENRY
BRAZENS
BRAZER
BRAZERS
BRAZES
BRAZIER
BRAZIERIES
BRAZIERS
BRAZIERY
BRAZIL
BRAZILEIN
BRAZILEINS
BRAZILIN
BRAZILINS
BRAZILS
BRAZILWOOD
BRAZILWOODS
BRAZING
BREACH
BREACHED
BREACHER
BREACHERS
BREACHES
BREACHING
BREAD
BREADBASKET
BREADBASKETS
BREADBERRIES
BREADBERRY
BREADBOARD
BREADBOARDED
BREADBOARDING
BREADBOARDS
BREADBOX
BREADBOXES
BREADCRUMB
BREADCRUMBED
BREADCRUMBING
BREADCRUMBS
BREADED
BREADFRUIT
BREADFRUITS
BREADHEAD
BREADHEADS
BREADING
BREADLINE
BREADLINES
BREADNUT

BREADNUTS
BREADROOM
BREADROOMS
BREADROOT
BREADROOTS
BREADS
BREADSTUFF
BREADSTUFFS
BREADTH
BREADTHS
BREADTHWAYS
BREADTHWISE
BREADWINNER
BREADWINNERS
BREADWINNING
BREADWINNINGS
BREADY
BREAK
BREAKABLE
BREAKABLENESS
BREAKABLENESSES
BREAKABLES
BREAKAGE
BREAKAGES
BREAKAWAY
BREAKAWAYS
BREAKBACK
BREAKBEAT
BREAKBEATS
BREAKBONE
BREAKDANCE
BREAKDANCED
BREAKDANCER
BREAKDANCERS
BREAKDANCES
BREAKDANCING
BREAKDANCINGS
BREAKDOWN
BREAKDOWNS
BREAKER
BREAKERS
BREAKEVEN
BREAKEVENS
BREAKFAST
BREAKFASTED
BREAKFASTER
BREAKFASTERS
BREAKFASTING
BREAKFASTS
BREAKFRONT
BREAKFRONTS
BREAKING
BREAKINGS
BREAKNECK
BREAKOFF
BREAKOFFS

BREAKOUT
BREAKOUTS
BREAKPOINT
BREAKPOINTS
BREAKS
BREAKTHROUGH
BREAKTHROUGHS
BREAKTIME
BREAKTIMES
BREAKUP
BREAKUPS
BREAKWATER
BREAKWATERS
BREAM
BREAMED
BREAMING
BREAMS
BREARE
BREARES
BREASKIT
BREASKITS
BREAST
BREASTBONE
BREASTBONES
BREASTED
BREASTING
BREASTPIN
BREASTPINS
BREASTPLATE
BREASTPLATES
BREASTPLOUGH
BREASTPLOUGHS
BREASTRAIL
BREASTRAILS
BREASTS
BREASTSTROKE
BREASTSTROKER
BREASTSTROKERS
BREASTSTROKES
BREASTSUMMER
BREASTSUMMERS
BREASTWORK
BREASTWORKS
BREATH
BREATHABILITIES
BREATHABILITY
BREATHABLE
BREATHALYSE
BREATHALYSED
BREATHALYSER
BREATHALYSERS
BREATHALYSES
BREATHALYSING
BREATHALYZE
BREATHALYZED
BREATHALYZER

BREATHALYZERS
BREATHALYZES
BREATHALYZING
BREATHARIAN
BREATHARIANS
BREATHE
BREATHED
BREATHER
BREATHERS
BREATHES
BREATHFUL
BREATHIER
BREATHIEST
BREATHILY
BREATHINESS
BREATHINESSES
BREATHING
BREATHINGS
BREATHLESS
BREATHLESSLY
BREATHLESSNESS
BREATHS
BREATHTAKING
BREATHTAKINGLY
BREATHY
BRECCIA
BRECCIAL
BRECCIAS
BRECCIATE
BRECCIATED
BRECCIATES
BRECCIATING
BRECCIATION
BRECCIATIONS
BRECHAM
BRECHAMS
BRECHAN
BRECHANS
BRED
BREDE
BREDED
BREDES
BREDIE
BREDIES
BREDING
BREE
BREECH
BREECHBLOCK
BREECHBLOCKS
BREECHCLOTH
BREECHCLOTHS
BREECHCLOUT
BREECHCLOUTS
BREECHED
BREECHES
BREECHING

BREECHINGS
BREECHLESS
BREECHLOADER
BREECHLOADERS
BREED
BREEDER
BREEDERS
BREEDING
BREEDINGS
BREEDS
BREEKS
BREEM
BREENGE
BREENGED
BREENGER
BREENGERS
BREENGES
BREENGING
BREER
BREERED
BREERING
BREERS
BREES
BREESE
BREESES
BREEST
BREESTS
BREEZE
BREEZED
BREEZELESS
BREEZES
BREEZEWAY
BREEZEWAYS
BREEZIER
BREEZIEST
BREEZILY
BREEZINESS
BREEZINESSES
BREEZING
BREEZY
BREGMA
BREGMATA
BREGMATE
BREGMATIC
BREHON
BREHONS
BREI
BREID
BREIDS
BREIING
BREINGE
BREINGED
BREINGES
BREINGING
BREIS
BREIST

BREISTS
BREKKIES
BREKKY
BRELOQUE
BRELOQUES
BREME
BREMSSTRAHLUNG
BREMSSTRAHLUNGS
BREN
BRENNE
BRENNES
BRENNING
BRENS
BRENT
BRENTER
BRENTEST
BRENTS
BRER
BRERE
BRERES
BRERS
BRESSUMMER
BRESSUMMERS
BRETASCHE
BRETASCHES
BRETESSE
BRETESSES
BRETHREN
BRETON
BRETONS
BRETTICE
BRETTICED
BRETTICES
BRETTICING
BREUNNERITE
BREVE
BREVES
BREVET
BREVETCIES
BREVETCY
BREVETE
BREVETED
BREVETING
BREVETS
BREVETTED
BREVETTING
BREVIARIES
BREVIARY
BREVIATE
BREVIATES
BREVIER
BREVIERS
BREVIPENNATE
BREVIS
BREVISES
BREVITIES

BREVITY
BREW
BREWAGE
BREWAGES
BREWED
BREWER
BREWERIES
BREWERS
BREWERY
BREWING
BREWINGS
BREWIS
BREWISES
BREWMASTER
BREWMASTERS
BREWPUB
BREWPUBS
BREWS
BREWSTER
BREWSTERS
BREY
BREYED
BREYING
BREYS
BRIAR
BRIARD
BRIARDS
BRIARED
BRIARROOT
BRIARS
BRIARWOOD
BRIARY
BRIBABLE
BRIBE
BRIBEABILITY
BRIBEABLE
BRIBED
BRIBEE
BRIBEES
BRIBER
BRIBERIES
BRIBERS
BRIBERY
BRIBES
BRIBING
BRICABRAC
BRICABRACS
BRICHT
BRICHTER
BRICHTEST
BRICK
BRICKBAT
BRICKBATS
BRICKCLAY
BRICKCLAYS
BRICKEARTH

BRICKEARTHS
BRICKED
BRICKEN
BRICKFIELD
BRICKFIELDER
BRICKFIELDERS
BRICKFIELDS
BRICKIE
BRICKIER
BRICKIES
BRICKIEST
BRICKING
BRICKINGS
BRICKLAYER
BRICKLAYERS
BRICKLAYING
BRICKLAYINGS
BRICKLE
BRICKLENESS
BRICKLES
BRICKMAKER
BRICKMAKERS
BRICKMAKING
BRICKMAKINGS
BRICKS
BRICKSHAPED
BRICKWALL
BRICKWALLS
BRICKWORK
BRICKWORKS
BRICKY
BRICKYARD
BRICKYARDS
BRICOLAGE
BRICOLAGES
BRICOLE
BRICOLES
BRIDAL
BRIDALLY
BRIDALS
BRIDE
BRIDECAKE
BRIDECAKES
BRIDED
BRIDEGROOM
BRIDEGROOMS
BRIDEMAID
BRIDEMAIDEN
BRIDEMAIDENS
BRIDEMAIDS
BRIDEMAN
BRIDEMEN
BRIDES
BRIDESMAID
BRIDESMAIDS
BRIDESMAN

BRIDESMEN
BRIDEWEALTH
BRIDEWEALTHS
BRIDEWELL
BRIDEWELLS
BRIDGABLE
BRIDGE
BRIDGEABLE
BRIDGEBOARD
BRIDGEBOARDS
BRIDGED
BRIDGEHEAD
BRIDGEHEADS
BRIDGELESS
BRIDGES
BRIDGEWORK
BRIDGEWORKS
BRIDGING
BRIDGINGS
BRIDIE
BRIDIES
BRIDING
BRIDLE
BRIDLED
BRIDLER
BRIDLERS
BRIDLES
BRIDLEWISE
BRIDLING
BRIDOON
BRIDOONS
BRIE
BRIEF
BRIEFCASE
BRIEFCASES
BRIEFED
BRIEFER
BRIEFERS
BRIEFEST
BRIEFING
BRIEFINGS
BRIEFLESS
BRIEFLY
BRIEFNESS
BRIEFNESSES
BRIEFS
BRIER
BRIERED
BRIERIER
BRIERIEST
BRIERROOT
BRIERS
BRIERWOOD
BRIERY
BRIES
BRIG

BRIGADE
BRIGADED
BRIGADES
BRIGADIER
BRIGADIERS
BRIGADING
BRIGALOW
BRIGALOWS
BRIGAND
BRIGANDAGE
BRIGANDAGES
BRIGANDINE
BRIGANDINES
BRIGANDRIES
BRIGANDRY
BRIGANDS
BRIGANTINE
BRIGANTINES
BRIGHT
BRIGHTEN
BRIGHTENED
BRIGHTENER
BRIGHTENERS
BRIGHTENING
BRIGHTENS
BRIGHTER
BRIGHTEST
BRIGHTLY
BRIGHTNESS
BRIGHTNESSES
BRIGHTS
BRIGHTSOME
BRIGHTWORK
BRIGHTWORKS
BRIGS
BRIGUE
BRIGUED
BRIGUES
BRIGUING
BRIGUINGS
BRIK
BRIKS
BRILL
BRILLER
BRILLEST
BRILLIANCE
BRILLIANCES
BRILLIANCIES
BRILLIANCY
BRILLIANT
BRILLIANTE
BRILLIANTED
BRILLIANTES
BRILLIANTINE
BRILLIANTINES
BRILLIANTING

BRILLIANTLY
BRILLIANTNESS
BRILLIANTNESSES
BRILLIANTS
BRILLS
BRIM
BRIMFUL
BRIMFULL
BRIMFULLNESS
BRIMFULLNESSES
BRIMFULNESS
BRIMFULNESSES
BRIMING
BRIMINGS
BRIMLESS
BRIMMED
BRIMMER
BRIMMERS
BRIMMING
BRIMS
BRIMSTONE
BRIMSTONES
BRIMSTONY
BRIN
BRINDED
BRINDISI
BRINDISIS
BRINDLE
BRINDLED
BRINDLES
BRINE
BRINED
BRINELLED
BRINELLING
BRINER
BRINERS
BRINES
BRING
BRINGDOWN
BRINGDOWNS
BRINGER
BRINGERS
BRINGING
BRINGINGS
BRINGS
BRINIER
BRINIES
BRINIEST
BRININESS
BRININESSES
BRINING
BRINISH
BRINJAL
BRINJALS
BRINJARRIES
BRINJARRY

BRINK
BRINKMAN
BRINKMANSHIP
BRINKMANSHIPS
BRINKMEN
BRINKS
BRINKSMANSHIP
BRINKSMANSHIPS
BRINNIES
BRINNY
BRINS
BRINY
BRIO
BRIOCHE
BRIOCHES
BRIOLETTE
BRIOLETTES
BRIONIES
BRIONY
BRIOS
BRIQUET
BRIQUETED
BRIQUETING
BRIQUETS
BRIQUETTE
BRIQUETTED
BRIQUETTES
BRIQUETTING
BRIS
BRISANCE
BRISANCES
BRISANT
BRISE
BRISES
BRISK
BRISKED
BRISKEN
BRISKENED
BRISKENING
BRISKENS
BRISKER
BRISKEST
BRISKET
BRISKETS
BRISKING
BRISKISH
BRISKLY
BRISKNESS
BRISKNESSES
BRISKS
BRISKY
BRISLING
BRISLINGS
BRISSES
BRISTLE
BRISTLECONE

BRISTLECONES
BRISTLED
BRISTLELIKE
BRISTLES
BRISTLETAIL
BRISTLETAILS
BRISTLIER
BRISTLIEST
BRISTLINESS
BRISTLINESSES
BRISTLING
BRISTLY
BRISTOL
BRISTOLS
BRISURE
BRISURES
BRIT
BRITCHES
BRITH
BRITHS
BRITS
BRITSCHKA
BRITSCHKAS
BRITSKA
BRITSKAS
BRITT
BRITTLE
BRITTLED
BRITTLELY
BRITTLENESS
BRITTLENESSES
BRITTLER
BRITTLES
BRITTLEST
BRITTLING
BRITTLY
BRITTS
BRITZKA
BRITZKAS
BRITZSKA
BRITZSKAS
BRIZE
BRIZES
BRO
BROACH
BROACHED
BROACHER
BROACHERS
BROACHES
BROACHING
BROAD
BROADAX
BROADAXE
BROADAXES
BROADBAND
BROADBILL

BROADBILLS
BROADBRIM
BROADBRIMS
BROADBRUSH
BROADCAST
BROADCASTED
BROADCASTER
BROADCASTERS
BROADCASTING
BROADCASTINGS
BROADCASTS
BROADCLOTH
BROADCLOTHS
BROADEN
BROADENED
BROADENING
BROADENS
BROADER
BROADEST
BROADISH
BROADLEAF
BROADLEAVES
BROADLOOM
BROADLOOMS
BROADLY
BROADMINDED
BROADMINDEDLY
BROADMINDEDNESS
BROADNESS
BROADNESSES
BROADPIECE
BROADPIECES
BROADS
BROADSCALE
BROADSHEET
BROADSHEETS
BROADSIDE
BROADSIDED
BROADSIDES
BROADSIDING
BROADSWORD
BROADSWORDS
BROADTAIL
BROADTAILS
BROADWAY
BROADWAYS
BROADWISE
BROBDINGNAGIAN
BROCADE
BROCADED
BROCADES
BROCADING
BROCAGE
BROCAGES
BROCARD
BROCARDS

BROCATEL
BROCATELLE
BROCATELLES
BROCATELS
BROCCOLI
BROCCOLIS
BROCH
BROCHAN
BROCHANS
BROCHE
BROCHED
BROCHES
BROCHETTE
BROCHETTES
BROCHING
BROCHO
BROCHS
BROCHURE
BROCHURES
BROCK
BROCKAGE
BROCKAGES
BROCKED
BROCKET
BROCKETS
BROCKIT
BROCKRAM
BROCKRAMS
BROCKS
BROCOLI
BROCOLIS
BROD
BRODDED
BRODDING
BRODDLE
BRODDLED
BRODDLES
BRODDLING
BRODEKIN
BRODEKINS
BRODKIN
BRODKINS
BRODS
BROEKIES
BROG
BROGAN
BROGANS
BROGGED
BROGGING
BROGH
BROGHS
BROGS
BROGUE
BROGUEISH
BROGUERIES
BROGUERY

BROGUES
BROGUISH
BROIDER
BROIDERED
BROIDERER
BROIDERERS
BROIDERIES
BROIDERING
BROIDERINGS
BROIDERS
BROIDERY
BROIL
BROILED
BROILER
BROILERS
BROILING
BROILS
BROKAGE
BROKAGES
BROKE
BROKED
BROKEN
BROKENHEARTED
BROKENHEARTEDLY
BROKENLY
BROKENNESS
BROKENNESSES
BROKER
BROKERAGE
BROKERAGES
BROKERED
BROKERIES
BROKERING
BROKERINGS
BROKERS
BROKERY
BROKES
BROKING
BROKINGS
BROLGA
BROLGAS
BROLLIES
BROLLY
BROMAL
BROMALS
BROMATE
BROMATED
BROMATES
BROMATING
BROME
BROMEGRASS
BROMEGRASSES
BROMELAIN
BROMELAINS
BROMELIA
BROMELIACEOUS

BROMELIAD
BROMELIADS
BROMELIAS
BROMELIN
BROMELINS
BROMEOSIN
BROMES
BROMHIDROSES
BROMHIDROSIS
BROMIC
BROMID
BROMIDE
BROMIDES
BROMIDIC
BROMIDROSES
BROMIDROSIS
BROMIDS
BROMIN
BROMINATE
BROMINATED
BROMINATES
BROMINATING
BROMINATION
BROMINATIONS
BROMINE
BROMINES
BROMINISM
BROMINISMS
BROMINS
BROMISM
BROMISMS
BROMIZE
BROMIZED
BROMIZES
BROMIZING
BROMMER
BROMMERS
BROMO
BROMOCRIPTINE
BROMOCRIPTINES
BROMOFORM
BROMOFORMS
BROMOS
BROMOURACIL
BROMOURACILS
BRONC
BRONCHI
BRONCHIA
BRONCHIAL
BRONCHIALLY
BRONCHIECTASES
BRONCHIECTASIS
BRONCHIOLAR
BRONCHIOLE
BRONCHIOLES
BRONCHIOLITIC

BRONCHIOLITICS
BRONCHIOLITIS
BRONCHITIC
BRONCHITICS
BRONCHITIS
BRONCHITISES
BRONCHIUM
BRONCHO
BRONCHODILATOR
BRONCHODILATORS
BRONCHOGENIC
BRONCHOGRAPHIES
BRONCHOGRAPHY
BRONCHOS
BRONCHOSCOPE
BRONCHOSCOPES
BRONCHOSCOPIC
BRONCHOSCOPICAL
BRONCHOSCOPIES
BRONCHOSCOPIST
BRONCHOSCOPISTS
BRONCHOSCOPY
BRONCHOSPASM
BRONCHOSPASMS
BRONCHOSPASTIC
BRONCHUS
BRONCO
BRONCOBUSTER
BRONCOBUSTERS
BRONCOS
BRONCS
BROND
BRONDS
BRONDYRON
BRONDYRONS
BRONTOSAUR
BRONTOSAURS
BRONTOSAURUS
BRONTOSAURUSES
BRONZE
BRONZED
BRONZEN
BRONZER
BRONZERS
BRONZES
BRONZIER
BRONZIEST
BRONZIFIED
BRONZIFIES
BRONZIFY
BRONZIFYING
BRONZING
BRONZINGS
BRONZITE
BRONZITES
BRONZY

BROO
BROOCH
BROOCHED
BROOCHES
BROOCHING
BROOD
BROODED
BROODER
BROODERS
BROODIER
BROODIEST
BROODILY
BROODINESS
BROODINESSES
BROODING
BROODINGLY
BROODINGS
BROODMARE
BROODMARES
BROODS
BROODY
BROOK
BROOKABLE
BROOKED
BROOKIE
BROOKIES
BROOKING
BROOKITE
BROOKITES
BROOKLET
BROOKLETS
BROOKLIME
BROOKLIMES
BROOKS
BROOKWEED
BROOKWEEDS
BROOL
BROOLS
BROOM
BROOMBALL
BROOMBALLER
BROOMBALLERS
BROOMBALLS
BROOMCORN
BROOMCORNS
BROOMED
BROOMIE
BROOMIER
BROOMIES
BROOMIEST
BROOMING
BROOMRAPE
BROOMRAPES
BROOMS
BROOMSTAFF
BROOMSTAFFS

BROOMSTICK
BROOMSTICKS
BROOMY
BROOS
BROOSE
BROOSES
BROS
BROSE
BROSES
BROSY
BROTH
BROTHEL
BROTHELS
BROTHER
BROTHERED
BROTHERHOOD
BROTHERHOODS
BROTHERING
BROTHERLIKE
BROTHERLINESS
BROTHERLINESSES
BROTHERLY
BROTHERS
BROTHS
BROTHY
BROUGH
BROUGHAM
BROUGHAMS
BROUGHS
BROUGHT
BROUGHTA
BROUGHTAS
BROUGHTASES
BROUHAHA
BROUHAHAS
BROUZE
BROUZES
BROW
BROWBAND
BROWBANDS
BROWBEAT
BROWBEATEN
BROWBEATER
BROWBEATERS
BROWBEATING
BROWBEATINGS
BROWBEATS
BROWED
BROWLESS
BROWN
BROWNED
BROWNER
BROWNEST
BROWNFIELD
BROWNFIELDS
BROWNIE

BROWNIER
BROWNIES
BROWNIEST
BROWNING
BROWNINGS
BROWNISH
BROWNNESS
BROWNNESSES
BROWNNOSE
BROWNNOSED
BROWNNOSER
BROWNNOSERS
BROWNNOSES
BROWNNOSING
BROWNOUT
BROWNOUTS
BROWNS
BROWNSHIRT
BROWNSHIRTS
BROWNSTONE
BROWNSTONES
BROWNY
BROWRIDGE
BROWRIDGES
BROWS
BROWSE
BROWSED
BROWSER
BROWSERS
BROWSES
BROWSIER
BROWSIEST
BROWSING
BROWSINGS
BROWST
BROWSTS
BROWSY
BRR
BRRR
BRUCELLA
BRUCELLAE
BRUCELLAS
BRUCELLOSES
BRUCELLOSIS
BRUCHID
BRUCHIDS
BRUCIN
BRUCINE
BRUCINES
BRUCINS
BRUCITE
BRUCITES
BRUCKLE
BRUGH
BRUGHS
BRUGMANSIA

BRUGMANSIAN
BRUHAHA
BRUHAHAS
BRUILZIE
BRUILZIES
BRUIN
BRUINS
BRUISE
BRUISED
BRUISER
BRUISERS
BRUISES
BRUISING
BRUISINGS
BRUIT
BRUITED
BRUITER
BRUITERS
BRUITING
BRUITS
BRULE
BRULOT
BRULOTS
BRULYIE
BRULYIES
BRULZIE
BRULZIES
BRUMAL
BRUMBIES
BRUMBY
BRUME
BRUMES
BRUMMAGEM
BRUMMAGEMS
BRUMMER
BRUMMERS
BRUMOUS
BRUNCH
BRUNCHED
BRUNCHES
BRUNCHING
BRUNET
BRUNETS
BRUNETTE
BRUNETTES
BRUNIZEM
BRUNIZEMS
BRUNT
BRUNTED
BRUNTING
BRUNTS
BRUSCHETTA
BRUSCHETTAS
BRUSCHETTE
BRUSH
BRUSHABILITIES

BRUSHABILITY
BRUSHBACK
BRUSHBACKS
BRUSHED
BRUSHER
BRUSHERS
BRUSHES
BRUSHFIRE
BRUSHIER
BRUSHIEST
BRUSHING
BRUSHINGS
BRUSHLAND
BRUSHLANDS
BRUSHLIKE
BRUSHMARK
BRUSHMARKS
BRUSHOFF
BRUSHOFFS
BRUSHUP
BRUSHUPS
BRUSHWHEEL
BRUSHWHEELS
BRUSHWOOD
BRUSHWOODS
BRUSHWORK
BRUSHWORKS
BRUSHY
BRUSK
BRUSKER
BRUSKEST
BRUSQUE
BRUSQUELY
BRUSQUENESS
BRUSQUENESSES
BRUSQUER
BRUSQUERIE
BRUSQUERIES
BRUSQUEST
BRUSSEN
BRUST
BRUSTING
BRUSTS
BRUT
BRUTAL
BRUTALISATION
BRUTALISATIONS
BRUTALISE
BRUTALISED
BRUTALISES
BRUTALISING
BRUTALISM
BRUTALISMS
BRUTALIST
BRUTALISTS
BRUTALITIES

BRUTALITY
BRUTALIZATION
BRUTALIZATIONS
BRUTALIZE
BRUTALIZED
BRUTALIZES
BRUTALIZING
BRUTALLY
BRUTE
BRUTED
BRUTELIKE
BRUTELY
BRUTENESS
BRUTENESSES
BRUTER
BRUTERS
BRUTES
BRUTIFIED
BRUTIFIES
BRUTIFY
BRUTIFYING
BRUTING
BRUTINGS
BRUTISH
BRUTISHLY
BRUTISHNESS
BRUTISHNESSES
BRUTISM
BRUTISMS
BRUXISM
BRUXISMS
BRYOLOGICAL
BRYOLOGIES
BRYOLOGIST
BRYOLOGISTS
BRYOLOGY
BRYONIES
BRYONY
BRYOPHYLLUM
BRYOPHYLLUMS
BRYOPHYTE
BRYOPHYTES
BRYOPHYTIC
BRYOZOAN
BRYOZOANS
BUAT
BUATS
BUAZE
BUAZES
BUB
BUBA
BUBAL
BUBALE
BUBALES
BUBALINE
BUBALIS

BUBALISES
BUBALS
BUBAS
BUBBIES
BUBBLE
BUBBLED
BUBBLEGUM
BUBBLEGUMS
BUBBLEHEAD
BUBBLEHEADED
BUBBLEHEADS
BUBBLER
BUBBLERS
BUBBLES
BUBBLIER
BUBBLIES
BUBBLIEST
BUBBLING
BUBBLY
BUBBY
BUBINGA
BUBINGAS
BUBO
BUBOED
BUBOES
BUBONIC
BUBONOCELE
BUBONOCELES
BUBS
BUBU
BUBUKLE
BUBUKLES
BUBUS
BUCCAL
BUCCALLY
BUCCANEER
BUCCANEERED
BUCCANEERING
BUCCANEERINGS
BUCCANEERISH
BUCCANEERS
BUCCANIER
BUCCANIERED
BUCCANIERING
BUCCANIERS
BUCCINA
BUCCINAS
BUCCINATOR
BUCCINATORS
BUCCINATORY
BUCELLAS
BUCELLASES
BUCENTAUR
BUCENTAURS
BUCHU
BUCHUS

BUCK
BUCKAROO
BUCKAROOS
BUCKAYRO
BUCKAYROS
BUCKBEAN
BUCKBEANS
BUCKBOARD
BUCKBOARDS
BUCKED
BUCKEEN
BUCKEENS
BUCKER
BUCKEROO
BUCKEROOS
BUCKERS
BUCKET
BUCKETED
BUCKETFUL
BUCKETFULS
BUCKETING
BUCKETINGS
BUCKETS
BUCKETSFUL
BUCKEYE
BUCKEYES
BUCKHORN
BUCKHORNS
BUCKHOUND
BUCKHOUNDS
BUCKIE
BUCKIES
BUCKING
BUCKINGS
BUCKISH
BUCKISHLY
BUCKISHNESS
BUCKJUMPER
BUCKJUMPERS
BUCKJUMPING
BUCKLE
BUCKLED
BUCKLER
BUCKLERED
BUCKLERING
BUCKLERS
BUCKLES
BUCKLING
BUCKLINGS
BUCKO
BUCKOES
BUCKRA
BUCKRAKE
BUCKRAKES
BUCKRAM
BUCKRAMED

BUCKRAMING
BUCKRAMS
BUCKRAS
BUCKS
BUCKSAW
BUCKSAWS
BUCKSHEE
BUCKSHEES
BUCKSHISH
BUCKSHISHED
BUCKSHISHES
BUCKSHISHING
BUCKSHOT
BUCKSHOTS
BUCKSKIN
BUCKSKINNED
BUCKSKINS
BUCKSOM
BUCKTAIL
BUCKTAILS
BUCKTEETH
BUCKTHORN
BUCKTHORNS
BUCKTOOTH
BUCKTOOTHED
BUCKU
BUCKUS
BUCKWHEAT
BUCKWHEATS
BUCKYBALL
BUCKYBALLS
BUCKYTUBE
BUCKYTUBES
BUCOLIC
BUCOLICAL
BUCOLICALLY
BUCOLICS
BUD
BUDDED
BUDDER
BUDDERS
BUDDHA
BUDDHAS
BUDDIED
BUDDIER
BUDDIES
BUDDIEST
BUDDING
BUDDINGS
BUDDLE
BUDDLED
BUDDLEIA
BUDDLEIAS
BUDDLES
BUDDLING
BUDDY

BUDDYING
BUDGE
BUDGED
BUDGER
BUDGEREE
BUDGERIGAR
BUDGERIGARS
BUDGERO
BUDGEROS
BUDGEROW
BUDGEROWS
BUDGERS
BUDGES
BUDGET
BUDGETARY
BUDGETED
BUDGETEER
BUDGETEERS
BUDGETER
BUDGETERS
BUDGETING
BUDGETS
BUDGIE
BUDGIES
BUDGING
BUDLESS
BUDLIKE
BUDMASH
BUDMASHES
BUDO
BUDOS
BUDS
BUDWORM
BUDWORMS
BUFF
BUFFA
BUFFABLE
BUFFALO
BUFFALOBERRIES
BUFFALOBERRY
BUFFALOED
BUFFALOES
BUFFALOFISH
BUFFALOFISHES
BUFFALOING
BUFFALOS
BUFFE
BUFFED
BUFFER
BUFFERED
BUFFERING
BUFFERS
BUFFET
BUFFETED
BUFFETER
BUFFETERS

BUFFETING
BUFFETINGS
BUFFETS
BUFFI
BUFFIER
BUFFIEST
BUFFING
BUFFINGS
BUFFLEHEAD
BUFFLEHEADS
BUFFO
BUFFOON
BUFFOONERIES
BUFFOONERY
BUFFOONISH
BUFFOONS
BUFFOS
BUFFS
BUFFY
BUFO
BUFOS
BUFOTALIN
BUFOTENINE
BUFOTENINES
BUG
BUGABOO
BUGABOOS
BUGBANE
BUGBANES
BUGBEAR
BUGBEARS
BUGEYE
BUGEYES
BUGGAN
BUGGANE
BUGGANES
BUGGANS
BUGGED
BUGGER
BUGGERED
BUGGERIES
BUGGERING
BUGGERS
BUGGERY
BUGGIER
BUGGIES
BUGGIEST
BUGGIN
BUGGINESS
BUGGING
BUGGINGS
BUGGINS
BUGGY
BUGHOUSE
BUGHOUSES
BUGLE

BUGLED
BUGLER
BUGLERS
BUGLES
BUGLET
BUGLETS
BUGLEWEED
BUGLEWEEDS
BUGLING
BUGLOSS
BUGLOSSES
BUGONG
BUGONGS
BUGS
BUGSEED
BUGSEEDS
BUGSHA
BUGSHAS
BUGWORT
BUGWORTS
BUHL
BUHLS
BUHLWORK
BUHLWORKS
BUHR
BUHRS
BUHRSTONE
BUHRSTONES
BUIBUI
BUIBUIS
BUIK
BUIKS
BUILD
BUILDABLE
BUILDED
BUILDER
BUILDERS
BUILDING
BUILDINGS
BUILDS
BUILDUP
BUILDUPS
BUILT
BUIRDLIER
BUIRDLIEST
BUIRDLY
BUIST
BUISTED
BUISTING
BUISTS
BUKE
BUKES
BUKSHEE
BUKSHEES
BUKSHI
BUKSHIS

BULB
BULBAR
BULBED
BULBEL
BULBELS
BULBIFEROUS
BULBIL
BULBILS
BULBING
BULBLET
BULBLETS
BULBOSITIES
BULBOSITY
BULBOUS
BULBOUSLY
BULBOUSNESS
BULBOUSNESSES
BULBS
BULBUL
BULBULS
BULGE
BULGED
BULGER
BULGERS
BULGES
BULGHUR
BULGHURS
BULGIER
BULGIEST
BULGINE
BULGINES
BULGINESS
BULGINESSES
BULGING
BULGINGLY
BULGUR
BULGURS
BULGY
BULIMIA
BULIMIAC
BULIMIAS
BULIMIC
BULIMICS
BULIMIES
BULIMUS
BULIMUSES
BULIMY
BULK
BULKAGE
BULKAGES
BULKED
BULKER
BULKERS
BULKHEAD
BULKHEADS
BULKIER

BULKIEST
BULKILY
BULKINESS
BULKINESSES
BULKING
BULKS
BULKY
BULL
BULLA
BULLACE
BULLACES
BULLAE
BULLARIES
BULLARY
BULLATE
BULLBAITING
BULLBAITINGS
BULLBAR
BULLBARS
BULLBAT
BULLBATS
BULLDOG
BULLDOGGED
BULLDOGGER
BULLDOGGERS
BULLDOGGING
BULLDOGGINGS
BULLDOGS
BULLDOZE
BULLDOZED
BULLDOZER
BULLDOZERS
BULLDOZES
BULLDOZING
BULLDUST
BULLDUSTS
BULLED
BULLER
BULLERED
BULLERING
BULLERS
BULLET
BULLETED
BULLETIN
BULLETINED
BULLETING
BULLETINING
BULLETINS
BULLETPROOF
BULLETPROOFED
BULLETPROOFING
BULLETPROOFS
BULLETRIE
BULLETRIES
BULLETS
BULLETWOOD

BULLFIGHT
BULLFIGHTER
BULLFIGHTERS
BULLFIGHTING
BULLFIGHTINGS
BULLFIGHTS
BULLFINCH
BULLFINCHES
BULLFROG
BULLFROGS
BULLGINE
BULLGINES
BULLHEAD
BULLHEADED
BULLHEADEDLY
BULLHEADEDNESS
BULLHEADS
BULLHORN
BULLHORNS
BULLIED
BULLIER
BULLIES
BULLIEST
BULLING
BULLINGS
BULLION
BULLIONIST
BULLIONISTS
BULLIONS
BULLISH
BULLISHLY
BULLISHNESS
BULLISHNESSES
BULLMASTIFF
BULLMASTIFFS
BULLNECK
BULLNECKED
BULLNECKS
BULLNOSE
BULLNOSES
BULLOCK
BULLOCKED
BULLOCKIES
BULLOCKING
BULLOCKS
BULLOCKY
BULLOUS
BULLPEN
BULLPENS
BULLPOUT
BULLPOUTS
BULLRING
BULLRINGS
BULLROARER
BULLROARERS
BULLRUSH

BULLRUSHES
BULLS
BULLSHIT
BULLSHITS
BULLSHITTED
BULLSHITTER
BULLSHITTERS
BULLSHITTING
BULLSHITTINGS
BULLSHOT
BULLSHOTS
BULLTERRIER
BULLTERRIERS
BULLWADDIE
BULLWADDY
BULLWEED
BULLWEEDS
BULLWHACK
BULLWHACKED
BULLWHACKING
BULLWHACKS
BULLWHIP
BULLWHIPPED
BULLWHIPPING
BULLWHIPS
BULLY
BULLYBOY
BULLYBOYS
BULLYING
BULLYISM
BULLYISMS
BULLYRAG
BULLYRAGGED
BULLYRAGGING
BULLYRAGS
BULNBULN
BULNBULNS
BULRUSH
BULRUSHES
BULRUSHY
BULSE
BULSES
BULWADDEE
BULWADDY
BULWARK
BULWARKED
BULWARKING
BULWARKS
BUM
BUMALO
BUMALOTI
BUMALOTIS
BUMBAG
BUMBAGS
BUMBAILIFF
BUMBAILIFFS

BUMBAZE
BUMBAZED
BUMBAZES
BUMBAZING
BUMBERSHOOT
BUMBERSHOOTS
BUMBLE
BUMBLEBEE
BUMBLEBEES
BUMBLED
BUMBLEDOM
BUMBLER
BUMBLERS
BUMBLES
BUMBLING
BUMBLINGLY
BUMBLINGS
BUMBO
BUMBOAT
BUMBOATS
BUMBOS
BUMF
BUMFLUFF
BUMFREEZER
BUMFREEZERS
BUMFS
BUMKIN
BUMKINS
BUMMALO
BUMMALOTI
BUMMALOTIS
BUMMAREE
BUMMAREES
BUMMED
BUMMEL
BUMMELS
BUMMER
BUMMERS
BUMMEST
BUMMING
BUMMLE
BUMMLED
BUMMLES
BUMMLING
BUMMOCK
BUMMOCKS
BUMP
BUMPED
BUMPER
BUMPERED
BUMPERING
BUMPERS
BUMPH
BUMPHS
BUMPIER
BUMPIEST

BUMPILY
BUMPINESS
BUMPINESSES
BUMPING
BUMPINGS
BUMPKIN
BUMPKINISH
BUMPKINLY
BUMPKINS
BUMPOLOGIES
BUMPOLOGY
BUMPS
BUMPSADAISY
BUMPTIOUS
BUMPTIOUSLY
BUMPTIOUSNESS
BUMPTIOUSNESSES
BUMPY
BUMS
BUMSTERS
BUMSUCKER
BUMSUCKERS
BUMSUCKING
BUMSUCKINGS
BUN
BUNA
BUNAS
BUNCE
BUNCED
BUNCES
BUNCH
BUNCHBERRIES
BUNCHBERRY
BUNCHED
BUNCHES
BUNCHGRASS
BUNCHGRASSES
BUNCHIER
BUNCHIEST
BUNCHILY
BUNCHINESS
BUNCHINESSES
BUNCHING
BUNCHINGS
BUNCHY
BUNCING
BUNCO
BUNCOED
BUNCOING
BUNCOMBE
BUNCOMBES
BUNCOS
BUND
BUNDED
BUNDH
BUNDHS

BUNDIES
BUNDING
BUNDIST
BUNDISTS
BUNDLE
BUNDLED
BUNDLER
BUNDLERS
BUNDLES
BUNDLING
BUNDLINGS
BUNDOBUST
BUNDOBUSTS
BUNDOOK
BUNDOOKS
BUNDS
BUNDT
BUNDTS
BUNDU
BUNDUS
BUNDWALL
BUNDWALLS
BUNDY
BUNFIGHT
BUNFIGHTS
BUNG
BUNGALOID
BUNGALOIDS
BUNGALOW
BUNGALOWS
BUNGED
BUNGEE
BUNGEES
BUNGER
BUNGERS
BUNGEY
BUNGEYS
BUNGHOLE
BUNGHOLES
BUNGIE
BUNGIES
BUNGING
BUNGLE
BUNGLED
BUNGLER
BUNGLERS
BUNGLES
BUNGLESOME
BUNGLING
BUNGLINGLY
BUNGLINGS
BUNGS
BUNGWALL
BUNGWALLS
BUNGY
BUNIA

BUNIAS
BUNION
BUNIONS
BUNJE
BUNJEE
BUNJEES
BUNJES
BUNJIE
BUNJIES
BUNJY
BUNK
BUNKED
BUNKER
BUNKERED
BUNKERING
BUNKERS
BUNKHOUSE
BUNKHOUSES
BUNKING
BUNKMATE
BUNKMATES
BUNKO
BUNKOED
BUNKOING
BUNKOS
BUNKS
BUNKUM
BUNKUMS
BUNN
BUNNET
BUNNETS
BUNNIA
BUNNIAS
BUNNIES
BUNNS
BUNNY
BUNODONT
BUNRAKU
BUNRAKUS
BUNS
BUNSEN
BUNSENS
BUNT
BUNTAL
BUNTALS
BUNTED
BUNTER
BUNTERS
BUNTIER
BUNTIEST
BUNTING
BUNTINGS
BUNTLINE
BUNTLINES
BUNTS
BUNTY

BUNYA
BUNYAS
BUNYIP
BUNYIPS
BUONAMANO
BUOY
BUOYAGE
BUOYAGES
BUOYANCE
BUOYANCES
BUOYANCIES
BUOYANCY
BUOYANT
BUOYANTLY
BUOYANTNESS
BUOYANTNESSES
BUOYED
BUOYING
BUOYS
BUPIVACAINE
BUPLEVER
BUPLEVERS
BUPPIE
BUPPIES
BUPPY
BUPRENORPHINE
BUPRESTID
BUPRESTIDS
BUQSHA
BUQSHAS
BUR
BURA
BURAN
BURANS
BURAS
BURBLE
BURBLED
BURBLER
BURBLERS
BURBLES
BURBLIER
BURBLIEST
BURBLING
BURBLINGS
BURBLY
BURBOT
BURBOTS
BURBS
BURD
BURDASH
BURDASHES
BURDEN
BURDENED
BURDENER
BURDENERS
BURDENING

BURDENOUS
BURDENS
BURDENSOME
BURDIE
BURDIES
BURDIZZO
BURDIZZOS
BURDOCK
BURDOCKS
BURDS
BUREAU
BUREAUCRACIES
BUREAUCRACY
BUREAUCRAT
BUREAUCRATESE
BUREAUCRATESES
BUREAUCRATIC
BUREAUCRATISE
BUREAUCRATISED
BUREAUCRATISES
BUREAUCRATISING
BUREAUCRATISM
BUREAUCRATISMS
BUREAUCRATIST
BUREAUCRATISTS
BUREAUCRATIZE
BUREAUCRATIZED
BUREAUCRATIZES
BUREAUCRATIZING
BUREAUCRATS
BUREAUS
BUREAUX
BURET
BURETS
BURETTE
BURETTES
BURG
BURGAGE
BURGAGES
BURGANET
BURGANETS
BURGEE
BURGEES
BURGEON
BURGEONED
BURGEONING
BURGEONS
BURGER
BURGERS
BURGESS
BURGESSES
BURGH
BURGHAL
BURGHER
BURGHERS
BURGHS

BURGHUL
BURGHULS
BURGLAR
BURGLARED
BURGLARIES
BURGLARING
BURGLARIOUS
BURGLARIOUSLY
BURGLARISE
BURGLARISED
BURGLARISES
BURGLARISING
BURGLARIZE
BURGLARIZED
BURGLARIZES
BURGLARIZING
BURGLARPROOF
BURGLARS
BURGLARY
BURGLE
BURGLED
BURGLES
BURGLING
BURGOMASTER
BURGOMASTERS
BURGONET
BURGONETS
BURGOO
BURGOOS
BURGOUT
BURGOUTS
BURGRAVE
BURGRAVES
BURGS
BURGUNDIES
BURGUNDY
BURHEL
BURHELS
BURIAL
BURIALS
BURIED
BURIER
BURIERS
BURIES
BURIN
BURINIST
BURINISTS
BURINS
BURITI
BURITIS
BURK
BURKA
BURKAS
BURKE
BURKED
BURKER

BURKERS
BURKES
BURKING
BURKITE
BURKITES
BURKS
BURL
BURLADERO
BURLADEROS
BURLAP
BURLAPS
BURLED
BURLER
BURLERS
BURLESK
BURLESKS
BURLESQUE
BURLESQUED
BURLESQUELY
BURLESQUER
BURLESQUERS
BURLESQUES
BURLESQUING
BURLETTA
BURLETTAS
BURLEY
BURLEYCUE
BURLEYCUES
BURLEYED
BURLEYING
BURLEYS
BURLIER
BURLIEST
BURLILY
BURLINESS
BURLINESSES
BURLING
BURLS
BURLY
BURN
BURNABLE
BURNABLES
BURNED
BURNER
BURNERS
BURNET
BURNETS
BURNETTISE
BURNETTISED
BURNETTISES
BURNETTISING
BURNETTIZE
BURNETTIZED
BURNETTIZES
BURNETTIZING
BURNIE

BURNIES
BURNING
BURNINGLY
BURNINGS
BURNISH
BURNISHABLE
BURNISHED
BURNISHER
BURNISHERS
BURNISHES
BURNISHING
BURNISHINGS
BURNISHMENT
BURNISHMENTS
BURNOOSE
BURNOOSED
BURNOOSES
BURNOUS
BURNOUSE
BURNOUSED
BURNOUSES
BURNOUT
BURNOUTS
BURNS
BURNSIDE
BURNSIDES
BURNT
BUROO
BUROOS
BURP
BURPED
BURPING
BURPS
BURQA
BURQAS
BURR
BURRAMUNDI
BURRAMUNDIS
BURRAMYS
BURRAMYSES
BURRAWANG
BURRAWANGS
BURRED
BURREL
BURRELL
BURRELLS
BURRELS
BURRER
BURRERS
BURRHEL
BURRHELS
BURRIER
BURRIEST
BURRING
BURRITO
BURRITOS

BURRO
BURROS
BURROW
BURROWED
BURROWER
BURROWERS
BURROWING
BURROWS
BURROWSTOWN
BURROWSTOWNS
BURRS
BURRSTONE
BURRSTONES
BURRY
BURS
BURSA
BURSAE
BURSAL
BURSAR
BURSARIAL
BURSARIES
BURSARS
BURSARSHIP
BURSARSHIPS
BURSARY
BURSAS
BURSATE
BURSE
BURSEED
BURSEEDS
BURSERA
BURSERACEOUS
BURSES
BURSICON
BURSICULATE
BURSIFORM
BURSITIS
BURSITISES
BURST
BURSTED
BURSTEN
BURSTER
BURSTERS
BURSTING
BURSTONE
BURSTONES
BURSTS
BURTHEN
BURTHENED
BURTHENING
BURTHENS
BURTHENSOME
BURTHENSOMELY
BURTON
BURTONS
BURWEED

BURWEEDS
BURY
BURYING
BUS
BUSBAR
BUSBARS
BUSBIES
BUSBOY
BUSBOYS
BUSBY
BUSED
BUSERA
BUSERAS
BUSES
BUSGIRL
BUSGIRLS
BUSH
BUSHBABIES
BUSHBABY
BUSHBASHING
BUSHBUCK
BUSHBUCKS
BUSHCRAFT
BUSHCRAFTS
BUSHED
BUSHEL
BUSHELED
BUSHELER
BUSHELERS
BUSHELING
BUSHELLED
BUSHELLER
BUSHELLERS
BUSHELLING
BUSHELLINGS
BUSHELMAN
BUSHELMEN
BUSHELS
BUSHELWOMAN
BUSHELWOMEN
BUSHER
BUSHERS
BUSHES
BUSHFIRE
BUSHFIRES
BUSHFLIES
BUSHFLY
BUSHGOAT
BUSHGOATS
BUSHHAMMER
BUSHHAMMERS
BUSHIDO
BUSHIDOS
BUSHIE
BUSHIER
BUSHIES

BUSHIEST
BUSHILY
BUSHINESS
BUSHINESSES
BUSHING
BUSHINGS
BUSHLAND
BUSHLANDS
BUSHLESS
BUSHLIKE
BUSHMAN
BUSHMANSHIP
BUSHMANSHIPS
BUSHMASTER
BUSHMASTERS
BUSHMEAT
BUSHMEN
BUSHPIG
BUSHPIGS
BUSHRANGER
BUSHRANGERS
BUSHRANGING
BUSHRANGINGS
BUSHTIT
BUSHTITS
BUSHVELD
BUSHVELDS
BUSHWA
BUSHWAH
BUSHWAHS
BUSHWALK
BUSHWALKED
BUSHWALKER
BUSHWALKERS
BUSHWALKING
BUSHWALKINGS
BUSHWALKS
BUSHWAS
BUSHWHACK
BUSHWHACKED
BUSHWHACKER
BUSHWHACKERS
BUSHWHACKING
BUSHWHACKINGS
BUSHWHACKS
BUSHWOMAN
BUSHWOMEN
BUSHY
BUSIED
BUSIER
BUSIES
BUSIEST
BUSILY
BUSINESS
BUSINESSES
BUSINESSLIKE

BUSINESSMAN
BUSINESSMEN
BUSINESSPEOPLE
BUSINESSPERSON
BUSINESSPERSONS
BUSINESSWOMAN
BUSINESSWOMEN
BUSINESSY
BUSING
BUSINGS
BUSK
BUSKED
BUSKER
BUSKERS
BUSKET
BUSKETS
BUSKIN
BUSKINED
BUSKING
BUSKINGS
BUSKINS
BUSKS
BUSKY
BUSLOAD
BUSLOADS
BUSMAN
BUSMEN
BUSS
BUSSED
BUSSES
BUSSING
BUSSINGS
BUSSU
BUSSUS
BUST
BUSTARD
BUSTARDS
BUSTED
BUSTEE
BUSTEES
BUSTER
BUSTERS
BUSTI
BUSTIC
BUSTICS
BUSTIER
BUSTIERS
BUSTIEST
BUSTING
BUSTINGS
BUSTIS
BUSTLE
BUSTLED
BUSTLER
BUSTLERS
BUSTLES

BUSTLINE
BUSTLINES
BUSTLING
BUSTLINGLY
BUSTS
BUSTY
BUSULFAN
BUSULFANS
BUSUUTI
BUSUUTIS
BUSY
BUSYBODIED
BUSYBODIES
BUSYBODY
BUSYBODYING
BUSYING
BUSYNESS
BUSYNESSES
BUSYWORK
BUSYWORKS
BUT
BUTADIENE
BUTADIENES
BUTANE
BUTANES
BUTANOL
BUTANOLS
BUTANONE
BUTANONES
BUTAT
BUTATS
BUTCH
BUTCHER
BUTCHERBIRD
BUTCHERBIRDS
BUTCHERED
BUTCHERIES
BUTCHERING
BUTCHERINGS
BUTCHERLY
BUTCHERS
BUTCHERY
BUTCHES
BUTCHEST
BUTCHING
BUTCHINGS
BUTE
BUTENE
BUTENEDIOIC
BUTENES
BUTEO
BUTEOS
BUTES
BUTLE
BUTLED
BUTLER

BUTLERAGE
BUTLERAGES
BUTLERED
BUTLERIES
BUTLERING
BUTLERS
BUTLERSHIP
BUTLERSHIPS
BUTLERY
BUTLES
BUTLING
BUTMENT
BUTMENTS
BUTS
BUTSUDAN
BUTSUDANS
BUTT
BUTTALS
BUTTE
BUTTED
BUTTER
BUTTERBALL
BUTTERBALLS
BUTTERBUR
BUTTERBURS
BUTTERCUP
BUTTERCUPS
BUTTERDOCK
BUTTERDOCKS
BUTTERED
BUTTERFAT
BUTTERFATS
BUTTERFINGERED
BUTTERFINGERS
BUTTERFISH
BUTTERFISHES
BUTTERFLIED
BUTTERFLIES
BUTTERFLY
BUTTERFLYER
BUTTERFLYERS
BUTTERFLYING
BUTTERIER
BUTTERIES
BUTTERIEST
BUTTERINE
BUTTERINES
BUTTERINESS
BUTTERINESSES
BUTTERING
BUTTERLESS
BUTTERMILK
BUTTERMILKS
BUTTERNUT
BUTTERNUTS
BUTTERS

BUTTERSCOTCH
BUTTERSCOTCHES
BUTTERWEED
BUTTERWEEDS
BUTTERWORT
BUTTERWORTS
BUTTERY
BUTTES
BUTTIES
BUTTING
BUTTINSKI
BUTTINSKIES
BUTTINSKY
BUTTLE
BUTTLED
BUTTLES
BUTTLING
BUTTOCK
BUTTOCKED
BUTTOCKING
BUTTOCKS
BUTTON
BUTTONBALL
BUTTONBALLS
BUTTONBUSH
BUTTONBUSHES
BUTTONED
BUTTONER
BUTTONERS
BUTTONHELD
BUTTONHOLD
BUTTONHOLDING
BUTTONHOLDS
BUTTONHOLE
BUTTONHOLED
BUTTONHOLER
BUTTONHOLERS
BUTTONHOLES
BUTTONHOLING
BUTTONHOOK
BUTTONHOOKED
BUTTONHOOKING
BUTTONHOOKS
BUTTONING
BUTTONLESS
BUTTONMOULD
BUTTONMOULDS
BUTTONS
BUTTONWOOD
BUTTONWOODS
BUTTONY
BUTTRESS
BUTTRESSED
BUTTRESSES
BUTTRESSING
BUTTS

BUTTSTOCK
BUTTSTOCKS
BUTTY
BUTTYMAN
BUTTYMEN
BUTUT
BUTUTS
BUTYL
BUTYLATE
BUTYLATED
BUTYLATES
BUTYLATING
BUTYLATION
BUTYLATIONS
BUTYLENE
BUTYLENES
BUTYLS
BUTYRACEOUS
BUTYRAL
BUTYRALDEHYDE
BUTYRALDEHYDES
BUTYRALS
BUTYRATE
BUTYRATES
BUTYRIC
BUTYRIN
BUTYRINS
BUTYROPHENONE
BUTYROPHENONES
BUTYROUS
BUTYRYL
BUTYRYLS
BUVETTE
BUVETTES
BUXOM
BUXOMER
BUXOMEST
BUXOMLY
BUXOMNESS
BUXOMNESSES
BUY
BUYABLE
BUYABLES
BUYBACK
BUYBACKS
BUYER
BUYERS
BUYING
BUYOUT
BUYOUTS
BUYS
BUZKASHI
BUZUKI
BUZUKIA
BUZUKIS
BUZZ

BUZZARD
BUZZARDS
BUZZED
BUZZER
BUZZERS
BUZZES
BUZZIER
BUZZIEST
BUZZING
BUZZINGLY
BUZZINGS
BUZZWIG
BUZZWIGS
BUZZWORD
BUZZWORDS
BUZZY
BWANA
BWANAS
BWAZI
BWAZIS
BY
BYCATCH
BYCATCHES
BYCOKET
BYCOKETS
BYDE
BYDED
BYDES
BYDING
BYE
BYELAW
BYELAWS
BYES
BYGONE
BYGONES
BYKE
BYKED
BYKES
BYKING
BYLANDER
BYLANDERS
BYLANE
BYLANES
BYLAW
BYLAWS
BYLINE
BYLINED
BYLINER
BYLINERS
BYLINES
BYLINING
BYLIVE
BYNAME
BYNAMES
BYNEMPT
BYPASS

BYPASSED
BYPASSES
BYPASSING
BYPAST
BYPATH
BYPATHS
BYPLACE
BYPLACES
BYPLAY
BYPLAYS
BYRE
BYREMAN
BYREMEN
BYRES
BYREWOMAN
BYREWOMEN
BYRL
BYRLADY
BYRLAKIN
BYRLAW
BYRLAWS
BYRLED
BYRLING
BYRLS
BYRNIE
BYRNIES
BYROAD
BYROADS
BYROOM
BYROOMS
BYS
BYSSACEOUS
BYSSAL
BYSSI
BYSSINE
BYSSINOSES
BYSSINOSIS
BYSSOID
BYSSUS
BYSSUSES
BYSTANDER
BYSTANDERS
BYSTREET
BYSTREETS
BYTALK
BYTALKS
BYTE
BYTES
BYTOWNITE
BYTOWNITES
BYWAY
BYWAYS
BYWONER
BYWONERS
BYWORD
BYWORDS

BYWORK
BYWORKS
BYZANT
BYZANTINE
BYZANTS

C

CAA
CAAED
CAAING
CAAS
CAATINGA
CAATINGAS
CAB
CABA
CABAL
CABALA
CABALAS
CABALETTA
CABALETTAS
CABALETTE
CABALISM
CABALISMS
CABALIST
CABALISTIC
CABALISTICAL
CABALISTS
CABALLED
CABALLER
CABALLERO
CABALLEROS
CABALLERS
CABALLINE
CABALLING
CABALS
CABANA
CABANAS
CABARET
CABARETS
CABAS
CABBAGE
CABBAGED
CABBAGES
CABBAGETOWN
CABBAGETOWNS
CABBAGEWORM
CABBAGEWORMS
CABBAGING
CABBAGY
CABBALA
CABBALAH
CABBALAHS
CABBALAS
CABBALISM
CABBALISMS
CABBALIST
CABBALISTIC
CABBALISTICAL

CABBALISTS
CABBED
CABBIE
CABBIES
CABBING
CABBY
CABDRIVER
CABDRIVERS
CABER
CABERNET
CABERNETS
CABERS
CABESTRO
CABESTROS
CABEZON
CABEZONE
CABEZONES
CABEZONS
CABILDO
CABILDOS
CABIN
CABINED
CABINET
CABINETMAKER
CABINETMAKERS
CABINETMAKING
CABINETMAKINGS
CABINETRIES
CABINETRY
CABINETS
CABINETWORK
CABINETWORKS
CABINING
CABINS
CABLE
CABLED
CABLEGRAM
CABLEGRAMS
CABLES
CABLET
CABLETS
CABLEVISION
CABLEVISIONS
CABLEWAY
CABLEWAYS
CABLING
CABLINGS
CABMAN
CABMEN
CABOB
CABOBBED

CABOBBING
CABOBS
CABOC
CABOCEER
CABOCEERS
CABOCHED
CABOCHON
CABOCHONS
CABOCS
CABOMBA
CABOMBAS
CABOODLE
CABOODLES
CABOOSE
CABOOSES
CABOSHED
CABOTAGE
CABOTAGES
CABOVER
CABRE
CABRESTA
CABRESTAS
CABRESTO
CABRESTOS
CABRETTA
CABRETTAS
CABRIE
CABRIES
CABRILLA
CABRILLAS
CABRIOLE
CABRIOLES
CABRIOLET
CABRIOLETS
CABRIT
CABRITS
CABS
CABSTAND
CABSTANDS
CACA
CACAFOGO
CACAFOGOS
CACAFUEGO
CACAFUEGOS
CACAO
CACAOS
CACAS
CACCIATORA
CACCIATORE
CACHAEMIA
CACHAEMIAS

CACHAEMIC
CACHALOT
CACHALOTS
CACHE
CACHECTIC
CACHECTICAL
CACHED
CACHEPOT
CACHEPOTS
CACHES
CACHET
CACHETED
CACHETING
CACHETS
CACHEXIA
CACHEXIAS
CACHEXIC
CACHEXIES
CACHEXY
CACHING
CACHINNATE
CACHINNATED
CACHINNATES
CACHINNATING
CACHINNATION
CACHINNATIONS
CACHINNATORY
CACHOLONG
CACHOLONGS
CACHOLOT
CACHOLOTS
CACHOU
CACHOUS
CACHUCHA
CACHUCHAS
CACIQUE
CACIQUES
CACIQUISM
CACIQUISMS
CACKERMANDER
CACKERMANDERS
CACKIER
CACKIEST
CACKLE
CACKLED
CACKLER
CACKLERS
CACKLES
CACKLING
CACKY
CACODAEMON

CACODAEMONS
CACODEMON
CACODEMONIC
CACODEMONS
CACODOXIES
CACODOXY
CACODYL
CACODYLIC
CACODYLS
CACOEPIES
CACOEPISTIC
CACOEPY
CACOETHES
CACOETHIC
CACOETHICALLY
CACOGASTRIC
CACOGENESIS
CACOGENIC
CACOGENICITY
CACOGENICS
CACOGRAPHER
CACOGRAPHERS
CACOGRAPHIC
CACOGRAPHICAL
CACOGRAPHIES
CACOGRAPHY
CACOLET
CACOLETS
CACOLOGIES
CACOLOGY
CACOMISTLE
CACOMISTLES
CACOMIXL
CACOMIXLE
CACOMIXLES
CACOMIXLS
CACOON
CACOONS
CACOPHONIC
CACOPHONICAL
CACOPHONICALLY
CACOPHONIES
CACOPHONIOUS
CACOPHONOUS
CACOPHONOUSLY
CACOPHONY
CACOTOPIA
CACOTOPIAN
CACOTOPIAS
CACOTROPHIES
CACOTROPHY
CACTACEOUS
CACTI
CACTIFORM
CACTOBLASTIS
CACTOID

CACTUS
CACTUSES
CACUMEN
CACUMINA
CACUMINAL
CACUMINALS
CACUMINOUS
CAD
CADAGA
CADAGAS
CADAGI
CADAGIS
CADASTER
CADASTERS
CADASTRAL
CADASTRALLY
CADASTRE
CADASTRES
CADAVER
CADAVERIC
CADAVERINE
CADAVERINES
CADAVEROUS
CADAVEROUSLY
CADAVEROUSNESS
CADAVERS
CADDICE
CADDICES
CADDIE
CADDIED
CADDIES
CADDIS
CADDISES
CADDISH
CADDISHLY
CADDISHNESS
CADDISHNESSES
CADDISWORM
CADDISWORMS
CADDY
CADDYING
CADDYSS
CADDYSSES
CADE
CADEAU
CADEAUX
CADEE
CADEES
CADELLE
CADELLES
CADENCE
CADENCED
CADENCES
CADENCIES
CADENCING
CADENCY

CADENT
CADENTIAL
CADENZA
CADENZAS
CADES
CADET
CADETS
CADETSHIP
CADETSHIPS
CADGE
CADGED
CADGER
CADGERS
CADGES
CADGIER
CADGIEST
CADGING
CADGY
CADI
CADIE
CADIES
CADIS
CADMIC
CADMIUM
CADMIUMS
CADRANS
CADRANSES
CADRE
CADRES
CADS
CADUAC
CADUACS
CADUCEAN
CADUCEI
CADUCEUS
CADUCITIES
CADUCITY
CADUCOUS
CAECA
CAECAL
CAECALLY
CAECILIAN
CAECILIANS
CAECITIS
CAECITISES
CAECUM
CAENOGENESES
CAENOGENESIS
CAENOGENETIC
CAEOMA
CAEOMAS
CAERULE
CAERULEAN
CAESALPINOID
CAESALPINOIDS
CAESAR

CAESAREAN
CAESAREANS
CAESARIAN
CAESARIANS
CAESAROPAPISM
CAESAROPAPISMS
CAESARS
CAESE
CAESIOUS
CAESIUM
CAESIUMS
CAESPITOSE
CAESPITOSELY
CAESTUS
CAESTUSES
CAESURA
CAESURAE
CAESURAL
CAESURAS
CAESURIC
CAFARD
CAFARDS
CAFE
CAFES
CAFETERIA
CAFETERIAS
CAFETIERE
CAFETIERES
CAFETORIUM
CAFETORIUMS
CAFF
CAFFEIN
CAFFEINATED
CAFFEINE
CAFFEINES
CAFFEINISM
CAFFEINISMS
CAFFEINS
CAFFEISM
CAFFEISMS
CAFFILA
CAFFILAS
CAFFS
CAFILA
CAFILAS
CAFTAN
CAFTANS
CAG
CAGANER
CAGANERS
CAGE
CAGEBIRD
CAGEBIRDS
CAGED
CAGEFUL
CAGEFULS

CAGELING
CAGELINGS
CAGER
CAGERS
CAGES
CAGEWORK
CAGEWORKS
CAGEY
CAGEYNESS
CAGEYNESSES
CAGIER
CAGIEST
CAGILY
CAGINESS
CAGINESSES
CAGING
CAGMAG
CAGMAGGED
CAGMAGGING
CAGMAGS
CAGOT
CAGOTS
CAGOUL
CAGOULE
CAGOULES
CAGOULS
CAGS
CAGY
CAGYNESS
CAGYNESSES
CAHIER
CAHIERS
CAHOOT
CAHOOTS
CAHOW
CAHOWS
CAID
CAIDS
CAILLACH
CAILLACHS
CAILLE
CAILLEACH
CAILLEACHS
CAILLES
CAILLIACH
CAILLIACHS
CAIMAC
CAIMACAM
CAIMACAMS
CAIMACS
CAIMAN
CAIMANS
CAIN
CAINOGENESES
CAINOGENESIS
CAINOGENETIC

CAINS
CAIQUE
CAIQUES
CAIRD
CAIRDS
CAIRN
CAIRNED
CAIRNGORM
CAIRNGORMS
CAIRNS
CAIRNY
CAISSON
CAISSONS
CAITIFF
CAITIFFS
CAITIVE
CAITIVES
CAJAPUT
CAJAPUTS
CAJEPUT
CAJEPUTS
CAJOLE
CAJOLED
CAJOLEMENT
CAJOLEMENTS
CAJOLER
CAJOLERIES
CAJOLERS
CAJOLERY
CAJOLES
CAJOLING
CAJOLINGLY
CAJON
CAJONES
CAJUN
CAJUPUT
CAJUPUTS
CAKE
CAKED
CAKES
CAKEWALK
CAKEWALKED
CAKEWALKER
CAKEWALKERS
CAKEWALKING
CAKEWALKS
CAKEY
CAKIER
CAKIEST
CAKING
CAKINGS
CAKY
CALABASH
CALABASHES
CALABOGUS
CALABOOSE

CALABOOSES
CALABRESE
CALABRESES
CALADIUM
CALADIUMS
CALALOO
CALALU
CALAMANCO
CALAMANCOES
CALAMANCOS
CALAMANDER
CALAMANDERS
CALAMAR
CALAMARI
CALAMARIES
CALAMARIS
CALAMARS
CALAMARY
CALAMI
CALAMINE
CALAMINED
CALAMINES
CALAMINING
CALAMINT
CALAMINTS
CALAMITE
CALAMITES
CALAMITIES
CALAMITOUS
CALAMITOUSLY
CALAMITOUSNESS
CALAMITY
CALAMONDIN
CALAMONDINS
CALAMUS
CALANDO
CALANDRIA
CALANDRIAS
CALANTHE
CALANTHES
CALASH
CALASHES
CALATHEA
CALATHEAS
CALATHI
CALATHOS
CALATHUS
CALAVANCE
CALAVANCES
CALAVERITE
CALCANEA
CALCANEAL
CALCANEAN
CALCANEI
CALCANEUM
CALCANEUS

CALCAR
CALCARATE
CALCAREOUS
CALCAREOUSLY
CALCARIA
CALCARIFEROUS
CALCARIFORM
CALCARINE
CALCARS
CALCEAMENTA
CALCEAMENTUM
CALCEATE
CALCEATED
CALCEATES
CALCEATING
CALCED
CALCEDONIES
CALCEDONIO
CALCEDONIOS
CALCEDONY
CALCEIFORM
CALCEOLARIA
CALCEOLARIAS
CALCEOLATE
CALCES
CALCIC
CALCICOLE
CALCICOLES
CALCICOLOUS
CALCIFEROL
CALCIFEROLS
CALCIFEROUS
CALCIFIC
CALCIFICATION
CALCIFICATIONS
CALCIFIED
CALCIFIES
CALCIFUGAL
CALCIFUGE
CALCIFUGES
CALCIFUGOUS
CALCIFY
CALCIFYING
CALCIGEROUS
CALCIMINE
CALCIMINED
CALCIMINES
CALCIMINING
CALCINABLE
CALCINATION
CALCINATIONS
CALCINE
CALCINED
CALCINES
CALCINING
CALCINOSES

CALCINOSIS
CALCITE
CALCITES
CALCITIC
CALCITONIN
CALCITONINS
CALCIUM
CALCIUMS
CALCRETE
CALCRETES
CALCSINTER
CALCSPAR
CALCSPARS
CALCTUFA
CALCTUFAS
CALCTUFF
CALCTUFFS
CALCULABILITY
CALCULABLE
CALCULABLY
CALCULAR
CALCULARY
CALCULATE
CALCULATED
CALCULATEDLY
CALCULATEDNESS
CALCULATES
CALCULATING
CALCULATINGLY
CALCULATION
CALCULATIONAL
CALCULATIONS
CALCULATIVE
CALCULATOR
CALCULATORS
CALCULI
CALCULOSE
CALCULOUS
CALCULUS
CALCULUSES
CALDARIA
CALDARIUM
CALDERA
CALDERAS
CALDRON
CALDRONS
CALECHE
CALECHES
CALEFACIENT
CALEFACIENTS
CALEFACTION
CALEFACTIONS
CALEFACTIVE
CALEFACTOR
CALEFACTORIES
CALEFACTORS

CALEFACTORY
CALEFIED
CALEFIES
CALEFY
CALEFYING
CALEMBOUR
CALEMBOURS
CALENDAL
CALENDAR
CALENDARED
CALENDARER
CALENDARERS
CALENDARING
CALENDARISATION
CALENDARISE
CALENDARISED
CALENDARISES
CALENDARISING
CALENDARIST
CALENDARISTS
CALENDARIZATION
CALENDARIZE
CALENDARIZED
CALENDARIZES
CALENDARIZING
CALENDARS
CALENDER
CALENDERED
CALENDERER
CALENDERERS
CALENDERING
CALENDERINGS
CALENDERS
CALENDRER
CALENDRERS
CALENDRIC
CALENDRICAL
CALENDRIES
CALENDRY
CALENDS
CALENDULA
CALENDULAS
CALENTURE
CALENTURES
CALESA
CALESAS
CALESCENCE
CALESCENCES
CALF
CALFDOZER
CALFDOZERS
CALFLESS
CALFLICK
CALFLICKS
CALFLIKE
CALFS

CALFSKIN
CALFSKINS
CALIATOUR
CALIATOURS
CALIBER
CALIBERED
CALIBERS
CALIBRATE
CALIBRATED
CALIBRATER
CALIBRATERS
CALIBRATES
CALIBRATING
CALIBRATION
CALIBRATIONS
CALIBRATOR
CALIBRATORS
CALIBRE
CALIBRED
CALIBRES
CALICES
CALICHE
CALICHES
CALICLE
CALICLES
CALICO
CALICOES
CALICOS
CALICULAR
CALID
CALIDITIES
CALIDITY
CALIF
CALIFATE
CALIFATES
CALIFONT
CALIFONTS
CALIFORNIUM
CALIFORNIUMS
CALIFS
CALIGINOSITIES
CALIGINOSITY
CALIGINOUS
CALIGO
CALIGOES
CALIGOS
CALIMA
CALIMAS
CALIOLOGIES
CALIOLOGY
CALIPASH
CALIPASHES
CALIPEE
CALIPEES
CALIPER
CALIPERED

CALIPERING
CALIPERS
CALIPH
CALIPHAL
CALIPHATE
CALIPHATES
CALIPHS
CALISAYA
CALISAYAS
CALISTHENIC
CALISTHENICS
CALIVER
CALIVERS
CALIX
CALK
CALKED
CALKER
CALKERS
CALKIN
CALKING
CALKINNED
CALKINNING
CALKINS
CALKS
CALL
CALLA
CALLABLE
CALLAIS
CALLALOO
CALLALOOS
CALLAN
CALLANS
CALLANT
CALLANTS
CALLAS
CALLBACK
CALLBACKS
CALLBOY
CALLBOYS
CALLED
CALLER
CALLERS
CALLET
CALLETS
CALLIATURES
CALLID
CALLIDITIES
CALLIDITY
CALLIGRAM
CALLIGRAMME
CALLIGRAMMES
CALLIGRAMS
CALLIGRAPHER
CALLIGRAPHERS
CALLIGRAPHIC
CALLIGRAPHICAL

CALLIGRAPHIES
CALLIGRAPHIST
CALLIGRAPHISTS
CALLIGRAPHY
CALLING
CALLINGS
CALLIOPE
CALLIOPES
CALLIOPSIS
CALLIPASH
CALLIPASHES
CALLIPEE
CALLIPEES
CALLIPER
CALLIPERED
CALLIPERING
CALLIPERS
CALLIPYGEAN
CALLIPYGIAN
CALLIPYGOUS
CALLISTEMON
CALLISTEMONS
CALLISTHENIC
CALLISTHENICS
CALLITHUMP
CALLITHUMPIAN
CALLITHUMPS
CALLOP
CALLOPS
CALLOSE
CALLOSES
CALLOSITIES
CALLOSITY
CALLOUS
CALLOUSED
CALLOUSES
CALLOUSING
CALLOUSLY
CALLOUSNESS
CALLOUSNESSES
CALLOW
CALLOWER
CALLOWEST
CALLOWNESS
CALLOWNESSES
CALLOWS
CALLS
CALLUNA
CALLUNAS
CALLUS
CALLUSED
CALLUSES
CALLUSING
CALM
CALMANT
CALMANTS

CALMATIVE
CALMATIVES
CALMED
CALMER
CALMEST
CALMIER
CALMIEST
CALMING
CALMLY
CALMNESS
CALMNESSES
CALMODULIN
CALMODULINS
CALMS
CALMSTONE
CALMSTONES
CALMY
CALO
CALOMEL
CALOMELS
CALORESCENCE
CALORESCENCES
CALORESCENT
CALORIC
CALORICALLY
CALORICITIES
CALORICITY
CALORICS
CALORIE
CALORIES
CALORIFIC
CALORIFICALLY
CALORIFICATION
CALORIFICATIONS
CALORIFIER
CALORIFIERS
CALORIMETER
CALORIMETERS
CALORIMETRIC
CALORIMETRICAL
CALORIMETRIES
CALORIMETRY
CALORIST
CALORISTS
CALORIZE
CALORIZED
CALORIZES
CALORIZING
CALORY
CALOTTE
CALOTTES
CALOTYPE
CALOTYPES
CALOTYPIST
CALOTYPISTS
CALOYER

CALOYERS
CALP
CALPA
CALPAC
CALPACK
CALPACKS
CALPACS
CALPAS
CALPS
CALQUE
CALQUED
CALQUES
CALQUING
CALTHA
CALTHAS
CALTHROP
CALTHROPS
CALTRAP
CALTRAPS
CALTROP
CALTROPS
CALUMBA
CALUMBAS
CALUMET
CALUMETS
CALUMNIABLE
CALUMNIATE
CALUMNIATED
CALUMNIATES
CALUMNIATING
CALUMNIATION
CALUMNIATIONS
CALUMNIATOR
CALUMNIATORS
CALUMNIATORY
CALUMNIES
CALUMNIOUS
CALUMNIOUSLY
CALUMNY
CALUTRON
CALUTRONS
CALVADOS
CALVADOSES
CALVARIA
CALVARIAS
CALVARIES
CALVARIUM
CALVARY
CALVE
CALVED
CALVER
CALVERED
CALVERING
CALVERS
CALVES
CALVING

CALVITIES
CALX
CALXES
CALYCANTHEMIES
CALYCANTHEMY
CALYCANTHUS
CALYCANTHUSES
CALYCATE
CALYCEAL
CALYCES
CALYCIFORM
CALYCINAL
CALYCINE
CALYCLE
CALYCLED
CALYCLES
CALYCOID
CALYCOIDEOUS
CALYCULAR
CALYCULATE
CALYCULE
CALYCULES
CALYCULI
CALYCULUS
CALYPSO
CALYPSOES
CALYPSONIAN
CALYPSONIANS
CALYPSOS
CALYPTER
CALYPTERA
CALYPTERAS
CALYPTERS
CALYPTRA
CALYPTRAS
CALYPTRATE
CALYPTROGEN
CALYPTROGENS
CALYX
CALYXES
CALZONE
CALZONES
CALZONI
CAM
CAMA
CAMAIEU
CAMAIEUX
CAMAIL
CAMAILED
CAMAILS
CAMAN
CAMANACHD
CAMANACHDS
CAMANS
CAMARADERIE
CAMARADERIES

CAMARILLA
CAMARILLAS
CAMARON
CAMARONS
CAMAS
CAMASES
CAMASH
CAMASHES
CAMASS
CAMASSES
CAMBER
CAMBERED
CAMBERING
CAMBERINGS
CAMBERS
CAMBIA
CAMBIAL
CAMBIFORM
CAMBISM
CAMBISMS
CAMBIST
CAMBISTRIES
CAMBISTRY
CAMBISTS
CAMBIUM
CAMBIUMS
CAMBOGE
CAMBOGES
CAMBOGIA
CAMBOGIAS
CAMBOOSE
CAMBOOSES
CAMBREL
CAMBRELS
CAMBRIC
CAMBRICS
CAMCORDER
CAMCORDERS
CAME
CAMEL
CAMELBACK
CAMELBACKS
CAMELEER
CAMELEERS
CAMELEON
CAMELEONS
CAMELEOPARD
CAMELEOPARDS
CAMELIA
CAMELIAS
CAMELID
CAMELIDS
CAMELINE
CAMELINES
CAMELISH
CAMELLIA

CAMELLIAS
CAMELOID
CAMELOIDS
CAMELOPARD
CAMELOPARDS
CAMELOT
CAMELOTS
CAMELRIES
CAMELRY
CAMELS
CAMEO
CAMEOED
CAMEOING
CAMEOS
CAMERA
CAMERAE
CAMERAL
CAMERAMAN
CAMERAMEN
CAMERAPERSON
CAMERAPERSONS
CAMERAS
CAMERATED
CAMERATION
CAMERATIONS
CAMERAWOMAN
CAMERAWOMEN
CAMERAWORK
CAMERAWORKS
CAMERLENGO
CAMERLENGOS
CAMERLINGO
CAMERLINGOS
CAMES
CAMESE
CAMESES
CAMIKNICKERS
CAMIKNICKS
CAMION
CAMIONS
CAMIS
CAMISA
CAMISADE
CAMISADES
CAMISADO
CAMISADOES
CAMISADOS
CAMISAS
CAMISE
CAMISES
CAMISIA
CAMISIAS
CAMISOLE
CAMISOLES
CAMLET
CAMLETS

CAMMED
CAMMING
CAMO
CAMOGIE
CAMOGIES
CAMOMILE
CAMOMILES
CAMOODI
CAMOODIS
CAMORRA
CAMORRAS
CAMORRISTA
CAMORRISTI
CAMOTE
CAMOTES
CAMOUFLAGE
CAMOUFLAGEABLE
CAMOUFLAGED
CAMOUFLAGES
CAMOUFLAGIC
CAMOUFLAGING
CAMOUFLET
CAMOUFLETS
CAMOUFLEUR
CAMOUFLEURS
CAMP
CAMPAGNA
CAMPAGNAS
CAMPAGNE
CAMPAIGN
CAMPAIGNED
CAMPAIGNER
CAMPAIGNERS
CAMPAIGNING
CAMPAIGNS
CAMPANA
CAMPANAS
CAMPANERO
CAMPANEROS
CAMPANIFORM
CAMPANILE
CAMPANILES
CAMPANILI
CAMPANIST
CAMPANISTS
CAMPANOLOGER
CAMPANOLOGERS
CAMPANOLOGICAL
CAMPANOLOGIES
CAMPANOLOGIST
CAMPANOLOGISTS
CAMPANOLOGY
CAMPANULA
CAMPANULACEOUS
CAMPANULAR
CAMPANULAS

CAMPANULATE
CAMPCRAFT
CAMPCRAFTS
CAMPEADOR
CAMPEADORS
CAMPED
CAMPER
CAMPERS
CAMPESINO
CAMPESINOS
CAMPEST
CAMPESTRAL
CAMPESTRIAN
CAMPFIRE
CAMPFIRES
CAMPGROUND
CAMPGROUNDS
CAMPHANE
CAMPHANES
CAMPHENE
CAMPHENES
CAMPHINE
CAMPHINES
CAMPHIRE
CAMPHIRES
CAMPHOL
CAMPHOLS
CAMPHOR
CAMPHORACEOUS
CAMPHORATE
CAMPHORATED
CAMPHORATES
CAMPHORATING
CAMPHORIC
CAMPHORS
CAMPI
CAMPIER
CAMPIEST
CAMPILY
CAMPIMETRIC
CAMPIMETRY
CAMPINESS
CAMPINESSES
CAMPING
CAMPINGS
CAMPION
CAMPIONS
CAMPLE
CAMPLED
CAMPLES
CAMPLING
CAMPLY
CAMPNESS
CAMPNESSES
CAMPO
CAMPODEID

CAMPODEIDS
CAMPODEIFORM
CAMPONG
CAMPONGS
CAMPOREE
CAMPOREES
CAMPOS
CAMPS
CAMPSITE
CAMPSITES
CAMPUS
CAMPUSED
CAMPUSES
CAMPUSING
CAMPY
CAMPYLOBACTER
CAMPYLOBACTERS
CAMPYLOTROPOUS
CAMS
CAMSHAFT
CAMSHAFTS
CAMSHO
CAMSHOCH
CAMSTAIRY
CAMSTANE
CAMSTANES
CAMSTEARY
CAMSTEERIE
CAMSTONE
CAMSTONES
CAMUS
CAMUSES
CAMWOOD
CAMWOODS
CAN
CANADA
CANADAS
CANAIGRE
CANAIGRES
CANAILLE
CANAILLES
CANAKIN
CANAKINS
CANAL
CANALED
CANALICULAR
CANALICULATE
CANALICULATED
CANALICULI
CANALICULUS
CANALING
CANALISATION
CANALISATIONS
CANALISE
CANALISED
CANALISES

CANALISING
CANALIZATION
CANALIZATIONS
CANALIZE
CANALIZED
CANALIZES
CANALIZING
CANALLED
CANALLER
CANALLERS
CANALLING
CANALS
CANAPE
CANAPES
CANARD
CANARDS
CANARIED
CANARIES
CANARY
CANARYING
CANASTA
CANASTAS
CANASTER
CANASTERS
CANBANK
CANBANKS
CANCAN
CANCANS
CANCEL
CANCELABLE
CANCELATION
CANCELATIONS
CANCELED
CANCELEER
CANCELEERED
CANCELEERING
CANCELEERS
CANCELER
CANCELERS
CANCELIER
CANCELIERED
CANCELIERING
CANCELIERS
CANCELING
CANCELLABLE
CANCELLARIAL
CANCELLARIAN
CANCELLARIATES
CANCELLATE
CANCELLATED
CANCELLATION
CANCELLATIONS
CANCELLED
CANCELLER
CANCELLERS
CANCELLI

CANCELLING
CANCELLOUS
CANCELS
CANCER
CANCERATE
CANCERATED
CANCERATES
CANCERATING
CANCERATION
CANCERATIONS
CANCEROPHOBIA
CANCEROPHOBIAS
CANCEROUS
CANCEROUSLY
CANCERPHOBIA
CANCERPHOBIAS
CANCERS
CANCHA
CANCHAS
CANCIONERO
CANCIONEROS
CANCRIFORM
CANCRINE
CANCRIZANS
CANCROID
CANCROIDS
CANDELA
CANDELABRA
CANDELABRAS
CANDELABRUM
CANDELABRUMS
CANDELAS
CANDELILLA
CANDELILLAS
CANDENT
CANDESCENCE
CANDESCENCES
CANDESCENT
CANDESCENTLY
CANDID
CANDIDA
CANDIDACIES
CANDIDACY
CANDIDAL
CANDIDAS
CANDIDATE
CANDIDATES
CANDIDATESHIP
CANDIDATESHIPS
CANDIDATURE
CANDIDATURES
CANDIDER
CANDIDEST
CANDIDIASES
CANDIDIASIS
CANDIDLY

CANDIDNESS
CANDIDNESSES
CANDIDS
CANDIE
CANDIED
CANDIES
CANDLE
CANDLEBERRIES
CANDLEBERRY
CANDLED
CANDLEFISH
CANDLEFISHES
CANDLEHOLDER
CANDLEHOLDERS
CANDLELIGHT
CANDLELIGHTED
CANDLELIGHTER
CANDLELIGHTERS
CANDLELIGHTS
CANDLELIT
CANDLENUT
CANDLENUTS
CANDLEPIN
CANDLEPINS
CANDLEPOWER
CANDLEPOWERS
CANDLER
CANDLERS
CANDLES
CANDLESNUFFER
CANDLESNUFFERS
CANDLESTICK
CANDLESTICKS
CANDLEWICK
CANDLEWICKS
CANDLEWOOD
CANDLEWOODS
CANDLING
CANDOCK
CANDOCKS
CANDOR
CANDORS
CANDOUR
CANDOURS
CANDY
CANDYFLOSS
CANDYFLOSSES
CANDYING
CANDYTUFT
CANDYTUFTS
CANE
CANEBRAKE
CANEBRAKES
CANED
CANEFRUIT
CANEFRUITS

CANEH
CANEHS
CANELLA
CANELLAS
CANELLINI
CANEPHOR
CANEPHORA
CANEPHORAS
CANEPHORE
CANEPHORES
CANEPHORS
CANEPHORUS
CANEPHORUSES
CANER
CANERS
CANES
CANESCENCE
CANESCENCES
CANESCENT
CANEWARE
CANEWARES
CANFIELD
CANFIELDS
CANFUL
CANFULS
CANG
CANGLE
CANGLED
CANGLES
CANGLING
CANGS
CANGUE
CANGUES
CANICULAR
CANID
CANIDS
CANIER
CANIEST
CANIKIN
CANIKINS
CANINE
CANINES
CANING
CANINGS
CANINITIES
CANINITY
CANISTER
CANISTERED
CANISTERING
CANISTERISATION
CANISTERISE
CANISTERISED
CANISTERISES
CANISTERISING
CANISTERIZATION
CANISTERIZE

CANISTERIZED
CANISTERIZES
CANISTERIZING
CANISTERS
CANITIES
CANKER
CANKERED
CANKEREDLY
CANKEREDNESS
CANKEREDNESSES
CANKERING
CANKEROUS
CANKERS
CANKERWORM
CANKERWORMS
CANKERY
CANN
CANNA
CANNABIC
CANNABIN
CANNABINOID
CANNABINOIDS
CANNABINOL
CANNABINOLS
CANNABINS
CANNABIS
CANNABISES
CANNACH
CANNACHS
CANNAE
CANNAS
CANNED
CANNEL
CANNELLINI
CANNELLONI
CANNELON
CANNELONI
CANNELONS
CANNELS
CANNELURE
CANNELURES
CANNER
CANNERIES
CANNERS
CANNERY
CANNIBAL
CANNIBALISATION
CANNIBALISE
CANNIBALISED
CANNIBALISES
CANNIBALISING
CANNIBALISM
CANNIBALISMS
CANNIBALISTIC
CANNIBALIZATION
CANNIBALIZE

CANNIBALIZED
CANNIBALIZES
CANNIBALIZING
CANNIBALLY
CANNIBALS
CANNIE
CANNIER
CANNIEST
CANNIKIN
CANNIKINS
CANNILY
CANNINESS
CANNINESSES
CANNING
CANNINGS
CANNISTER
CANNISTERS
CANNOLI
CANNON
CANNONADE
CANNONADED
CANNONADES
CANNONADING
CANNONBALL
CANNONBALLED
CANNONBALLING
CANNONBALLS
CANNONED
CANNONEER
CANNONEERS
CANNONIER
CANNONIERS
CANNONING
CANNONRIES
CANNONRY
CANNONS
CANNOT
CANNS
CANNULA
CANNULAE
CANNULAR
CANNULAS
CANNULATE
CANNULATED
CANNULATES
CANNULATING
CANNULATION
CANNULATIONS
CANNY
CANOE
CANOEABLE
CANOED
CANOEING
CANOEINGS
CANOEIST
CANOEISTS

CANOES
CANOEWOOD
CANOEWOODS
CANOLA
CANON
CANONESS
CANONESSES
CANONIC
CANONICAL
CANONICALLY
CANONICALS
CANONICATE
CANONICATES
CANONICITIES
CANONICITY
CANONISATION
CANONISATIONS
CANONISE
CANONISED
CANONISES
CANONISING
CANONIST
CANONISTIC
CANONISTS
CANONIZATION
CANONIZATIONS
CANONIZE
CANONIZED
CANONIZES
CANONIZING
CANONRIES
CANONRY
CANONS
CANOODLE
CANOODLED
CANOODLER
CANOODLERS
CANOODLES
CANOODLING
CANOPHILIA
CANOPHILIAS
CANOPHILIST
CANOPHILISTS
CANOPHOBIA
CANOPHOBIAS
CANOPIED
CANOPIES
CANOPY
CANOPYING
CANOROUS
CANOROUSLY
CANOROUSNESS
CANOROUSNESSES
CANS
CANSFUL
CANSO

CANSOS
CANST
CANSTICK
CANSTICKS
CANT
CANTABANK
CANTABANKS
CANTABILE
CANTABILES
CANTALA
CANTALAS
CANTALOUP
CANTALOUPE
CANTALOUPES
CANTALOUPS
CANTANKEROUS
CANTANKEROUSLY
CANTAR
CANTARS
CANTATA
CANTATAS
CANTATE
CANTATES
CANTATRICE
CANTATRICES
CANTATRICI
CANTDOG
CANTDOGS
CANTED
CANTEEN
CANTEENS
CANTER
CANTERBURIES
CANTERBURY
CANTERBURYS
CANTERED
CANTERING
CANTERS
CANTEST
CANTHAL
CANTHARI
CANTHARID
CANTHARIDAL
CANTHARIDES
CANTHARIDIAN
CANTHARIDIC
CANTHARIDIN
CANTHARIDINE
CANTHARIDINES
CANTHARIDINS
CANTHARIDS
CANTHARIS
CANTHARUS
CANTHAXANTHIN
CANTHAXANTHINE
CANTHAXANTHINES

CANTHAXANTHINS
CANTHI
CANTHOOK
CANTHOOKS
CANTHUS
CANTIC
CANTICLE
CANTICLES
CANTICO
CANTICOED
CANTICOING
CANTICOS
CANTICOY
CANTICOYED
CANTICOYING
CANTICOYS
CANTICUM
CANTICUMS
CANTIER
CANTIEST
CANTILENA
CANTILENAS
CANTILEVER
CANTILEVERED
CANTILEVERING
CANTILEVERS
CANTILLATE
CANTILLATED
CANTILLATES
CANTILLATING
CANTILLATION
CANTILLATIONS
CANTILLATORY
CANTILY
CANTINA
CANTINAS
CANTINESS
CANTINESSES
CANTING
CANTINGLY
CANTINGS
CANTION
CANTIONS
CANTLE
CANTLED
CANTLES
CANTLET
CANTLETS
CANTLING
CANTO
CANTON
CANTONAL
CANTONED
CANTONING
CANTONISATION
CANTONISATIONS

CANTONISE
CANTONISED
CANTONISES
CANTONISING
CANTONIZATION
CANTONIZATIONS
CANTONIZE
CANTONIZED
CANTONIZES
CANTONIZING
CANTONMENT
CANTONMENTS
CANTONS
CANTOR
CANTORIAL
CANTORIS
CANTORS
CANTOS
CANTRAIP
CANTRAIPS
CANTRAP
CANTRAPS
CANTRED
CANTREDS
CANTREF
CANTREFS
CANTRIP
CANTRIPS
CANTS
CANTUS
CANTY
CANULA
CANULAE
CANULAR
CANULARLY
CANULAS
CANULATE
CANULATED
CANULATES
CANULATING
CANULATION
CANULATIONS
CANVAS
CANVASBACK
CANVASBACKS
CANVASED
CANVASER
CANVASERS
CANVASES
CANVASING
CANVASLIKE
CANVASS
CANVASSED
CANVASSER
CANVASSERS
CANVASSES

CANVASSING
CANY
CANYON
CANYONS
CANZONA
CANZONAS
CANZONE
CANZONES
CANZONET
CANZONETS
CANZONETTA
CANZONETTAS
CANZONETTE
CANZONI
CAOUTCHOUC
CAOUTCHOUCS
CAP
CAPA
CAPABILITIES
CAPABILITY
CAPABLE
CAPABLENESS
CAPABLENESSES
CAPABLER
CAPABLEST
CAPABLY
CAPACIOUS
CAPACIOUSLY
CAPACIOUSNESS
CAPACIOUSNESSES
CAPACITANCE
CAPACITANCES
CAPACITATE
CAPACITATED
CAPACITATES
CAPACITATING
CAPACITATION
CAPACITATIONS
CAPACITIES
CAPACITIVE
CAPACITIVELY
CAPACITOR
CAPACITORS
CAPACITY
CAPARISON
CAPARISONED
CAPARISONING
CAPARISONS
CAPAS
CAPE
CAPED
CAPELAN
CAPELANS
CAPELET
CAPELETS
CAPELIN

CAPELINE
CAPELINES
CAPELINS
CAPELLET
CAPELLETS
CAPELLINE
CAPELLINES
CAPELLMEISTER
CAPELLMEISTERS
CAPER
CAPERCAILLIE
CAPERCAILLIES
CAPERCAILZIE
CAPERCAILZIES
CAPERED
CAPERER
CAPERERS
CAPERING
CAPERINGLY
CAPERNOITED
CAPERNOITIE
CAPERNOITIES
CAPERNOITY
CAPERS
CAPES
CAPESKIN
CAPESKINS
CAPEWORK
CAPEWORKS
CAPFUL
CAPFULS
CAPH
CAPHS
CAPI
CAPIAS
CAPIASES
CAPILLACEOUS
CAPILLAIRE
CAPILLAIRES
CAPILLARIES
CAPILLARITIES
CAPILLARITY
CAPILLARY
CAPILLITIA
CAPILLITIUM
CAPILLITIUMS
CAPING
CAPITA
CAPITAL
CAPITALISATION
CAPITALISATIONS
CAPITALISE
CAPITALISED
CAPITALISES
CAPITALISING
CAPITALISM

CAPITALISMS
CAPITALIST
CAPITALISTIC
CAPITALISTS
CAPITALIZATION
CAPITALIZATIONS
CAPITALIZE
CAPITALIZED
CAPITALIZES
CAPITALIZING
CAPITALLY
CAPITALS
CAPITAN
CAPITANI
CAPITANO
CAPITANOS
CAPITANS
CAPITATE
CAPITATION
CAPITATIONS
CAPITATIVE
CAPITATIVENESS
CAPITAYN
CAPITAYNS
CAPITELLA
CAPITELLUM
CAPITOL
CAPITOLIAN
CAPITOLINE
CAPITOLS
CAPITULA
CAPITULANT
CAPITULANTS
CAPITULAR
CAPITULARIES
CAPITULARLY
CAPITULARS
CAPITULARY
CAPITULATE
CAPITULATED
CAPITULATES
CAPITULATING
CAPITULATION
CAPITULATIONS
CAPITULATOR
CAPITULATORS
CAPITULATORY
CAPITULUM
CAPIZ
CAPIZES
CAPLE
CAPLES
CAPLESS
CAPLET
CAPLETS
CAPLIN

CAPLINS
CAPMAKER
CAPMAKERS
CAPNOMANCIES
CAPNOMANCY
CAPO
CAPOCCHIA
CAPOCCHIAS
CAPODASTRO
CAPODASTROS
CAPOEIRA
CAPOEIRAS
CAPON
CAPONATA
CAPONATAS
CAPONIER
CAPONIERE
CAPONIERES
CAPONIERS
CAPONISE
CAPONISED
CAPONISES
CAPONISING
CAPONIZE
CAPONIZED
CAPONIZES
CAPONIZING
CAPONS
CAPORAL
CAPORALS
CAPOS
CAPOT
CAPOTASTO
CAPOTASTOS
CAPOTE
CAPOTES
CAPOTS
CAPOTTED
CAPOTTING
CAPOUCH
CAPOUCHES
CAPPARIDACEOUS
CAPPED
CAPPELLETTI
CAPPER
CAPPERNOITIES
CAPPERS
CAPPIE
CAPPIES
CAPPING
CAPPINGS
CAPPUCCINO
CAPPUCCINOS
CAPRATE
CAPRATES
CAPREOLATE

CAPRIC
CAPRICCI
CAPRICCIO
CAPRICCIOS
CAPRICCIOSO
CAPRICE
CAPRICES
CAPRICIOUS
CAPRICIOUSLY
CAPRICIOUSNESS
CAPRID
CAPRIDS
CAPRIFICATION
CAPRIFICATIONS
CAPRIFIED
CAPRIFIES
CAPRIFIG
CAPRIFIGS
CAPRIFOIL
CAPRIFOILS
CAPRIFOLE
CAPRIFOLES
CAPRIFOLIACEOUS
CAPRIFORM
CAPRIFY
CAPRIFYING
CAPRINE
CAPRIOLE
CAPRIOLED
CAPRIOLES
CAPRIOLING
CAPRIS
CAPROATE
CAPROATES
CAPROCK
CAPROCKS
CAPROIC
CAPROLACTAM
CAPROLACTAMS
CAPRYLATE
CAPRYLATES
CAPRYLIC
CAPS
CAPSAICIN
CAPSAICINS
CAPSICIN
CAPSICINS
CAPSICUM
CAPSICUMS
CAPSID
CAPSIDAL
CAPSIDS
CAPSIZABLE
CAPSIZAL
CAPSIZALS
CAPSIZE

CAPSIZED
CAPSIZES
CAPSIZING
CAPSOMER
CAPSOMERE
CAPSOMERES
CAPSOMERS
CAPSTAN
CAPSTANS
CAPSTONE
CAPSTONES
CAPSULAR
CAPSULARY
CAPSULATE
CAPSULATED
CAPSULATION
CAPSULATIONS
CAPSULATORY
CAPSULE
CAPSULED
CAPSULES
CAPSULING
CAPSULISE
CAPSULISED
CAPSULISES
CAPSULISING
CAPSULIZE
CAPSULIZED
CAPSULIZES
CAPSULIZING
CAPTAIN
CAPTAINCIES
CAPTAINCY
CAPTAINED
CAPTAINING
CAPTAINRIES
CAPTAINRY
CAPTAINS
CAPTAINSHIP
CAPTAINSHIPS
CAPTAN
CAPTANS
CAPTION
CAPTIONED
CAPTIONING
CAPTIONLESS
CAPTIONS
CAPTIOUS
CAPTIOUSLY
CAPTIOUSNESS
CAPTIOUSNESSES
CAPTIVANCE
CAPTIVANCES
CAPTIVATE
CAPTIVATED
CAPTIVATES

CAPTIVATING
CAPTIVATINGLY
CAPTIVATION
CAPTIVATIONS
CAPTIVATOR
CAPTIVATORS
CAPTIVAUNCES
CAPTIVE
CAPTIVED
CAPTIVES
CAPTIVING
CAPTIVITIES
CAPTIVITY
CAPTOPRIL
CAPTOPRILS
CAPTOR
CAPTORS
CAPTURE
CAPTURED
CAPTURER
CAPTURERS
CAPTURES
CAPTURING
CAPUCCIO
CAPUCCIOS
CAPUCHE
CAPUCHED
CAPUCHES
CAPUCHIN
CAPUCHINS
CAPUERA
CAPUERAS
CAPUL
CAPULS
CAPUT
CAPYBARA
CAPYBARAS
CAR
CARABAO
CARABAOS
CARABID
CARABIDS
CARABIN
CARABINE
CARABINEER
CARABINEERS
CARABINER
CARABINERO
CARABINEROS
CARABINERS
CARABINES
CARABINIER
CARABINIERE
CARABINIERI
CARABINIERS
CARABINS

CARACAL
CARACALS
CARACARA
CARACARAS
CARACK
CARACKS
CARACOL
CARACOLE
CARACOLED
CARACOLES
CARACOLING
CARACOLLED
CARACOLLING
CARACOLS
CARACT
CARACTS
CARACUL
CARACULS
CARAFE
CARAFES
CARAGANA
CARAGANAS
CARAGEEN
CARAGEENAN
CARAGEENANS
CARAGEENS
CARAMBA
CARAMBOLA
CARAMBOLAS
CARAMBOLE
CARAMBOLED
CARAMBOLES
CARAMBOLING
CARAMEL
CARAMELISATION
CARAMELISATIONS
CARAMELISE
CARAMELISED
CARAMELISES
CARAMELISING
CARAMELIZATION
CARAMELIZATIONS
CARAMELIZE
CARAMELIZED
CARAMELIZES
CARAMELIZING
CARAMELLED
CARAMELLING
CARAMELS
CARANGID
CARANGIDS
CARANGOID
CARANGOIDS
CARANNA
CARANNAS
CARAP

CARAPACE
CARAPACES
CARAPACIAL
CARAPAX
CARAPAXES
CARAPS
CARASSOW
CARASSOWS
CARAT
CARATE
CARATES
CARATS
CARAUNA
CARAUNAS
CARAVAN
CARAVANCE
CARAVANCES
CARAVANED
CARAVANEER
CARAVANEERS
CARAVANER
CARAVANERS
CARAVANETTE
CARAVANETTES
CARAVANING
CARAVANNED
CARAVANNER
CARAVANNERS
CARAVANNING
CARAVANS
CARAVANSARAI
CARAVANSARAIS
CARAVANSARIES
CARAVANSARY
CARAVANSERAI
CARAVANSERAIS
CARAVEL
CARAVELS
CARAWAY
CARAWAYS
CARB
CARBACHOL
CARBACHOLS
CARBAMATE
CARBAMATES
CARBAMAZEPINE
CARBAMIC
CARBAMIDE
CARBAMIDES
CARBAMIDINE
CARBAMINO
CARBAMYL
CARBAMYLS
CARBANION
CARBANIONS
CARBARN

CARBARNS
CARBARYL
CARBARYLS
CARBAZOLE
CARBAZOLES
CARBEEN
CARBEENS
CARBENE
CARBENES
CARBIDE
CARBIDES
CARBIES
CARBIMAZOLE
CARBINE
CARBINEER
CARBINEERS
CARBINES
CARBINIER
CARBINIERS
CARBINOL
CARBINOLS
CARBO
CARBOCYCLIC
CARBOHYDRASE
CARBOHYDRASES
CARBOHYDRATE
CARBOHYDRATES
CARBOLATED
CARBOLATES
CARBOLATING
CARBOLATION
CARBOLIC
CARBOLICS
CARBOLISATION
CARBOLISE
CARBOLISED
CARBOLISES
CARBOLISING
CARBOLIZATION
CARBOLIZE
CARBOLIZED
CARBOLIZES
CARBOLIZING
CARBON
CARBONACEOUS
CARBONADE
CARBONADES
CARBONADO
CARBONADOED
CARBONADOES
CARBONADOING
CARBONADOS
CARBONARA
CARBONARAS
CARBONATE
CARBONATED

CARBONATES
CARBONATING
CARBONATION
CARBONATIONS
CARBONATITE
CARBONATITES
CARBONETTE
CARBONETTES
CARBONIC
CARBONIFEROUS
CARBONISATION
CARBONISATIONS
CARBONISE
CARBONISED
CARBONISER
CARBONISERS
CARBONISES
CARBONISING
CARBONIUM
CARBONIZATION
CARBONIZATIONS
CARBONIZE
CARBONIZED
CARBONIZER
CARBONIZERS
CARBONIZES
CARBONIZING
CARBONLESS
CARBONNADE
CARBONNADES
CARBONOUS
CARBONS
CARBONYL
CARBONYLATE
CARBONYLATED
CARBONYLATES
CARBONYLATING
CARBONYLATION
CARBONYLATIONS
CARBONYLIC
CARBONYLS
CARBORA
CARBORAS
CARBOS
CARBOXYL
CARBOXYLASE
CARBOXYLASES
CARBOXYLATE
CARBOXYLATED
CARBOXYLATES
CARBOXYLATING
CARBOXYLATION
CARBOXYLATIONS
CARBOXYLIC
CARBOXYLS
CARBOY

CARBOYED
CARBOYS
CARBS
CARBUNCLE
CARBUNCLED
CARBUNCLES
CARBUNCULAR
CARBURATE
CARBURATED
CARBURATES
CARBURATING
CARBURATION
CARBURATIONS
CARBURET
CARBURETED
CARBURETER
CARBURETERS
CARBURETING
CARBURETION
CARBURETIONS
CARBURETOR
CARBURETORS
CARBURETS
CARBURETTED
CARBURETTER
CARBURETTERS
CARBURETTING
CARBURETTOR
CARBURETTORS
CARBURISATION
CARBURISATIONS
CARBURISE
CARBURISED
CARBURISES
CARBURISING
CARBURIZATION
CARBURIZATIONS
CARBURIZE
CARBURIZED
CARBURIZES
CARBURIZING
CARBY
CARBYLAMINE
CARBYLAMINES
CARCAJOU
CARCAJOUS
CARCAKE
CARCAKES
CARCANET
CARCANETS
CARCASE
CARCASED
CARCASES
CARCASING
CARCASS
CARCASSED

CARCASSES
CARCASSING
CARCEL
CARCELS
CARCERAL
CARCINOGEN
CARCINOGENESES
CARCINOGENESIS
CARCINOGENIC
CARCINOGENICITY
CARCINOGENS
CARCINOID
CARCINOIDS
CARCINOLOGICAL
CARCINOLOGIES
CARCINOLOGIST
CARCINOLOGISTS
CARCINOLOGY
CARCINOMA
CARCINOMAS
CARCINOMATA
CARCINOMATOID
CARCINOMATOSES
CARCINOMATOSIS
CARCINOMATOUS
CARCINOSARCOMA
CARCINOSARCOMAS
CARCINOSES
CARCINOSIS
CARD
CARDAMINE
CARDAMINES
CARDAMOM
CARDAMOMS
CARDAMON
CARDAMONS
CARDAMUM
CARDAMUMS
CARDAN
CARDANS
CARDBOARD
CARDBOARDS
CARDBOARDY
CARDCASE
CARDCASES
CARDCASTLE
CARDCASTLES
CARDECU
CARDECUE
CARDECUES
CARDECUS
CARDED
CARDER
CARDERS
CARDHOLDER
CARDHOLDERS

CARDI
CARDIA
CARDIAC
CARDIACAL
CARDIACS
CARDIAE
CARDIALGIA
CARDIALGIAS
CARDIALGIC
CARDIALGIES
CARDIALGY
CARDIAS
CARDIE
CARDIES
CARDIGAN
CARDIGANED
CARDIGANS
CARDINAL
CARDINALATE
CARDINALATES
CARDINALATIAL
CARDINALITIAL
CARDINALITIES
CARDINALITY
CARDINALLY
CARDINALS
CARDINALSHIP
CARDINALSHIPS
CARDING
CARDINGS
CARDIOCENTESES
CARDIOCENTESIS
CARDIOGENIC
CARDIOGRAM
CARDIOGRAMS
CARDIOGRAPH
CARDIOGRAPHER
CARDIOGRAPHERS
CARDIOGRAPHIC
CARDIOGRAPHICAL
CARDIOGRAPHIES
CARDIOGRAPHS
CARDIOGRAPHY
CARDIOID
CARDIOIDS
CARDIOLOGICAL
CARDIOLOGIES
CARDIOLOGIST
CARDIOLOGISTS
CARDIOLOGY
CARDIOMEGALIES
CARDIOMEGALY
CARDIOMOTOR
CARDIOMYOPATHY
CARDIOPATHIES
CARDIOPATHY

CARDIOPLEGIA
CARDIOPLEGIAL
CARDIOPLEGIAS
CARDIOPULMONARY
CARDIOTHORACIC
CARDIOTONIC
CARDIOTONICS
CARDIOVASCULAR
CARDIS
CARDITIC
CARDITIS
CARDITISES
CARDOON
CARDOONS
CARDOPHAGI
CARDOPHAGUS
CARDPHONE
CARDPHONES
CARDPLAYER
CARDPLAYERS
CARDPUNCH
CARDPUNCHES
CARDS
CARDSHARP
CARDSHARPER
CARDSHARPERS
CARDSHARPING
CARDSHARPS
CARDUACEOUS
CARDUUS
CARDUUSES
CARDY
CARE
CARED
CAREEN
CAREENAGE
CAREENAGES
CAREENED
CAREENER
CAREENERS
CAREENING
CAREENS
CAREER
CAREERED
CAREERER
CAREERERS
CAREERING
CAREERISM
CAREERISMS
CAREERIST
CAREERISTS
CAREERS
CAREFREE
CAREFREENESS
CAREFUL
CAREFULLER

CAREFULLEST
CAREFULLY
CAREFULNESS
CAREFULNESSES
CAREGIVER
CAREGIVERS
CAREGIVING
CAREGIVINGS
CARELESS
CARELESSLY
CARELESSNESS
CARELESSNESSES
CARELINE
CARELINES
CAREME
CAREMES
CARER
CARERS
CARES
CARESS
CARESSED
CARESSER
CARESSERS
CARESSES
CARESSING
CARESSINGLY
CARESSINGS
CARESSIVE
CARESSIVELY
CARET
CARETAKE
CARETAKEN
CARETAKER
CARETAKERS
CARETAKES
CARETAKING
CARETAKINGS
CARETOOK
CARETS
CAREWORKER
CAREWORKERS
CAREWORN
CAREX
CARFARE
CARFARES
CARFAX
CARFAXES
CARFOX
CARFOXES
CARFUFFLE
CARFUFFLED
CARFUFFLES
CARFUFFLING
CARFUL
CARFULS
CARGEESE

CARGO
CARGOED
CARGOES
CARGOING
CARGOOSE
CARGOS
CARHOP
CARHOPS
CARIACOU
CARIACOUS
CARIAMA
CARIAMAS
CARIBE
CARIBES
CARIBOU
CARIBOUS
CARICATURA
CARICATURAL
CARICATURAS
CARICATURE
CARICATURED
CARICATURES
CARICATURING
CARICATURIST
CARICATURISTS
CARICES
CARIED
CARIERE
CARIERES
CARIES
CARILLON
CARILLONED
CARILLONING
CARILLONIST
CARILLONISTS
CARILLONNED
CARILLONNEUR
CARILLONNEURS
CARILLONNING
CARILLONS
CARINA
CARINAE
CARINAL
CARINAS
CARINATE
CARINATED
CARING
CARIOCA
CARIOCAS
CARIOGENIC
CARIOLE
CARIOLES
CARIOSE
CARIOSITY
CARIOUS
CARIOUSNESS

CARITAS	CARNALISM	CARNIVOROUS	CAROUSED
CARITASES	CARNALISMS	CARNIVOROUSLY	CAROUSEL
CARITATES	CARNALIST	CARNIVOROUSNESS	CAROUSELS
CARJACK	CARNALISTS	CARNOSE	CAROUSER
CARJACKED	CARNALITIES	CARNOSITIES	CAROUSERS
CARJACKER	CARNALITY	CARNOSITY	CAROUSES
CARJACKERS	CARNALIZE	CARNOTITE	CAROUSING
CARJACKING	CARNALIZED	CARNOTITES	CAROUSINGLY
CARJACKINGS	CARNALIZES	CARNS	CARP
CARJACKS	CARNALIZING	CARNY	CARPACCIO
CARJACOU	CARNALLED	CARNYING	CARPACCIOS
CARJACOUS	CARNALLING	CAROACH	CARPAL
CARK	CARNALLITE	CAROACHES	CARPALE
CARKED	CARNALLITES	CAROB	CARPALES
CARKING	CARNALLY	CAROBS	CARPALIA
CARKS	CARNALS	CAROCH	CARPALS
CARL	CARNAPTIOUS	CAROCHE	CARPARK
CARLE	CARNAROLI	CAROCHES	CARPARKS
CARLES	CARNASSIAL	CAROL	CARPED
CARLESS	CARNASSIALS	CAROLED	CARPEL
CARLIN	CARNATION	CAROLER	CARPELLARY
CARLINE	CARNATIONED	CAROLERS	CARPELLATE
CARLINES	CARNATIONS	CAROLI	CARPELLATES
CARLING	CARNAUBA	CAROLING	CARPELS
CARLINGS	CARNAUBAS	CAROLINGS	CARPENTARIA
CARLINS	CARNELIAN	CAROLLED	CARPENTARIAS
CARLISH	CARNELIANS	CAROLLER	CARPENTER
CARLOAD	CARNEOUS	CAROLLERS	CARPENTERED
CARLOADS	CARNET	CAROLLING	CARPENTERING
CARLOCK	CARNETS	CAROLLINGS	CARPENTERS
CARLOCKS	CARNEY	CAROLS	CARPENTRIES
CARLOT	CARNEYED	CAROLUS	CARPENTRY
CARLOTS	CARNEYING	CAROLUSES	CARPER
CARLS	CARNEYS	CAROM	CARPERS
CARMAGNOLE	CARNIE	CAROMED	CARPET
CARMAGNOLES	CARNIED	CAROMEL	CARPETBAG
CARMAKER	CARNIER	CAROMELLED	CARPETBAGGER
CARMAKERS	CARNIES	CAROMELLING	CARPETBAGGERIES
CARMAN	CARNIEST	CAROMELS	CARPETBAGGERS
CARMELITE	CARNIFEX	CAROMING	CARPETBAGGERY
CARMELITES	CARNIFEXES	CAROMS	CARPETBAGGING
CARMEN	CARNIFICATION	CAROTENE	CARPETBAGS
CARMINATIVE	CARNIFICATIONS	CAROTENES	CARPETED
CARMINATIVES	CARNIFICIAL	CAROTENOID	CARPETING
CARMINE	CARNIFIED	CAROTENOIDS	CARPETINGS
CARMINES	CARNIFIES	CAROTID	CARPETMONGER
CARN	CARNIFY	CAROTIDAL	CARPETMONGERS
CARNAGE	CARNIFYING	CAROTIDALLY	CARPETS
CARNAGES	CARNITINE	CAROTIDS	CARPETWEED
CARNAHUBA	CARNITINES	CAROTIN	CARPETWEEDS
CARNAHUBAS	CARNIVAL	CAROTINOID	CARPHOLOGIES
CARNAL	CARNIVALESQUE	CAROTINOIDS	CARPHOLOGY
CARNALISE	CARNIVALS	CAROTINS	CARPI
CARNALISED	CARNIVORA	CAROUSAL	CARPING
CARNALISES	CARNIVORE	CAROUSALS	CARPINGLY
CARNALISING	CARNIVORES	CAROUSE	CARPINGS

CARPOGONIA
CARPOGONIAL
CARPOGONIUM
CARPOLOGICAL
CARPOLOGICALLY
CARPOLOGIES
CARPOLOGIST
CARPOLOGISTS
CARPOLOGY
CARPOMETACARPI
CARPOMETACARPUS
CARPOOL
CARPOOLED
CARPOOLER
CARPOOLERS
CARPOOLING
CARPOOLS
CARPOPHAGOUS
CARPOPHORE
CARPOPHORES
CARPORT
CARPORTS
CARPOSPORE
CARPOSPORES
CARPS
CARPUS
CARR
CARRACK
CARRACKS
CARRACT
CARRACTS
CARRAGEEN
CARRAGEENAN
CARRAGEENANS
CARRAGEENIN
CARRAGEENINS
CARRAGEENS
CARRAGHEEN
CARRAGHEENAN
CARRAGHEENANS
CARRAGHEENIN
CARRAGHEENINS
CARRAGHEENS
CARRAT
CARRATS
CARRAWAY
CARRAWAYS
CARRECT
CARRECTS
CARREFOUR
CARREFOURS
CARREL
CARRELL
CARRELLS
CARRELS
CARRIAGE

CARRIAGEABLE
CARRIAGES
CARRIAGEWAY
CARRIAGEWAYS
CARRICK
CARRICKS
CARRIED
CARRIER
CARRIERS
CARRIES
CARRIOLE
CARRIOLES
CARRION
CARRIONS
CARRITCH
CARRITCHES
CARRIWITCHET
CARRIWITCHETS
CARROCH
CARROCHES
CARROM
CARROMED
CARROMING
CARROMS
CARRON
CARRONADE
CARRONADES
CARROT
CARROTIER
CARROTIEST
CARROTIN
CARROTINS
CARROTS
CARROTTOP
CARROTTOPPED
CARROTTOPS
CARROTY
CARROUSEL
CARROUSELS
CARRS
CARRY
CARRYALL
CARRYALLS
CARRYBACK
CARRYBACKS
CARRYCOT
CARRYCOTS
CARRYFORWARD
CARRYFORWARDS
CARRYING
CARRYON
CARRYONS
CARRYOUT
CARRYOUTS
CARRYOVER
CARRYOVERS

CARRYTALE
CARRYTALES
CARS
CARSE
CARSES
CARSEY
CARSEYS
CARSICK
CARSICKNESS
CART
CARTA
CARTABLE
CARTAGE
CARTAGES
CARTAS
CARTE
CARTED
CARTEL
CARTELISATION
CARTELISATIONS
CARTELISE
CARTELISED
CARTELISES
CARTELISING
CARTELISM
CARTELISMS
CARTELIST
CARTELISTS
CARTELIZATION
CARTELIZATIONS
CARTELIZE
CARTELIZED
CARTELIZES
CARTELIZING
CARTELS
CARTER
CARTERS
CARTES
CARTFUL
CARTFULS
CARTHAMINE
CARTHAMINES
CARTHORSE
CARTHORSES
CARTILAGE
CARTILAGES
CARTILAGINOUS
CARTING
CARTLOAD
CARTLOADS
CARTOGRAM
CARTOGRAMS
CARTOGRAPHER
CARTOGRAPHERS
CARTOGRAPHIC
CARTOGRAPHICAL

CARTOGRAPHIES
CARTOGRAPHY
CARTOLOGICAL
CARTOLOGIES
CARTOLOGY
CARTOMANCIES
CARTOMANCY
CARTON
CARTONAGE
CARTONAGES
CARTONED
CARTONING
CARTONNAGE
CARTONNAGES
CARTONS
CARTOON
CARTOONED
CARTOONING
CARTOONINGS
CARTOONISH
CARTOONISHLY
CARTOONIST
CARTOONISTS
CARTOONLIKE
CARTOONS
CARTOONY
CARTOP
CARTOPHILE
CARTOPHILES
CARTOPHILIC
CARTOPHILIES
CARTOPHILIST
CARTOPHILISTS
CARTOPHILY
CARTOPPER
CARTOPPERS
CARTOUCH
CARTOUCHE
CARTOUCHES
CARTRIDGE
CARTRIDGES
CARTROAD
CARTROADS
CARTS
CARTULARIES
CARTULARY
CARTWAY
CARTWAYS
CARTWHEEL
CARTWHEELED
CARTWHEELER
CARTWHEELERS
CARTWHEELING
CARTWHEELS
CARTWRIGHT
CARTWRIGHTS

CARUCAGE
CARUCAGES
CARUCATE
CARUCATES
CARUNCLE
CARUNCLES
CARUNCULAR
CARUNCULATE
CARUNCULATED
CARUNCULOUS
CARVACROL
CARVACROLS
CARVE
CARVED
CARVEL
CARVELS
CARVEN
CARVER
CARVERIES
CARVERS
CARVERY
CARVES
CARVIES
CARVING
CARVINGS
CARVY
CARWASH
CARWASHES
CARYATIC
CARYATID
CARYATIDAL
CARYATIDEAN
CARYATIDES
CARYATIDIC
CARYATIDS
CARYOPSES
CARYOPSIDES
CARYOPSIS
CARYOPTERIS
CARYOPTERISES
CARYOTIN
CARYOTINS
CARZEY
CARZEYS
CASA
CASABA
CASABAS
CASAS
CASAVA
CASAVAS
CASBAH
CASBAHS
CASCABEL
CASCABELS
CASCABLE
CASCABLES

CASCADE
CASCADED
CASCADES
CASCADING
CASCADURA
CASCADURAS
CASCARA
CASCARAS
CASCARILLA
CASCARILLAS
CASCHROM
CASCHROMS
CASCO
CASCOS
CASE
CASEASE
CASEASES
CASEATE
CASEATED
CASEATES
CASEATING
CASEATION
CASEATIONS
CASEBEARER
CASEBEARERS
CASEBOOK
CASEBOOKS
CASEBOUND
CASEBOUNDS
CASED
CASEFIED
CASEFIES
CASEFY
CASEFYING
CASEIC
CASEIN
CASEINATE
CASEINATES
CASEINOGEN
CASEINS
CASELOAD
CASELOADS
CASEMAKER
CASEMAKERS
CASEMAN
CASEMATE
CASEMATED
CASEMATES
CASEMEN
CASEMENT
CASEMENTED
CASEMENTS
CASEOSE
CASEOSES
CASEOUS
CASERN

CASERNE
CASERNES
CASERNS
CASES
CASETTE
CASETTES
CASEWORK
CASEWORKER
CASEWORKERS
CASEWORKS
CASEWORM
CASEWORMS
CASH
CASHABLE
CASHAW
CASHAWS
CASHBACK
CASHBACKS
CASHBOOK
CASHBOOKS
CASHBOX
CASHBOXES
CASHED
CASHES
CASHEW
CASHEWS
CASHIER
CASHIERED
CASHIERER
CASHIERERS
CASHIERING
CASHIERINGS
CASHIERMENT
CASHIERMENTS
CASHIERS
CASHING
CASHLESS
CASHMERE
CASHMERES
CASHOO
CASHOOS
CASHPOINT
CASHPOINTS
CASIMERE
CASIMERES
CASIMIRE
CASIMIRES
CASING
CASINGHEAD
CASINGHEADS
CASINGS
CASINI
CASINO
CASINOS
CASITA
CASITAS

CASK
CASKED
CASKET
CASKETED
CASKETING
CASKETS
CASKING
CASKS
CASKSTAND
CASKSTANDS
CASKY
CASQUE
CASQUED
CASQUES
CASSABA
CASSABAS
CASSAREEP
CASSAREEPS
CASSARIPES
CASSATA
CASSATAS
CASSATION
CASSATIONS
CASSAVA
CASSAVAS
CASSEROLE
CASSEROLED
CASSEROLES
CASSEROLING
CASSETTE
CASSETTES
CASSIA
CASSIAS
CASSIMERE
CASSIMERES
CASSINGLE
CASSINGLES
CASSINO
CASSINOS
CASSIOPEIUM
CASSIOPEIUMS
CASSIS
CASSISES
CASSITERITE
CASSITERITES
CASSOCK
CASSOCKED
CASSOCKS
CASSOLETTE
CASSOLETTES
CASSONADE
CASSONADES
CASSONE
CASSONES
CASSOULET
CASSOULETS

CASSOWARIES
CASSOWARY
CASSPIR
CASSPIRS
CASSUMUNAR
CASSUMUNARS
CAST
CASTABILITIES
CASTABILITY
CASTABLE
CASTANET
CASTANETS
CASTANOSPERMINE
CASTAWAY
CASTAWAYS
CASTE
CASTED
CASTEISM
CASTEISMS
CASTELESS
CASTELLA
CASTELLAN
CASTELLANIES
CASTELLANS
CASTELLANY
CASTELLATED
CASTELLATION
CASTELLATIONS
CASTELLUM
CASTELLUMS
CASTER
CASTERS
CASTES
CASTIGATE
CASTIGATED
CASTIGATES
CASTIGATING
CASTIGATION
CASTIGATIONS
CASTIGATOR
CASTIGATORS
CASTIGATORY
CASTING
CASTINGS
CASTLE
CASTLED
CASTLES
CASTLING
CASTOCK
CASTOCKS
CASTOFF
CASTOFFS
CASTOR
CASTOREUM
CASTOREUMS
CASTORIES

CASTORS
CASTORY
CASTRAL
CASTRAMETATION
CASTRAMETATIONS
CASTRATE
CASTRATED
CASTRATES
CASTRATI
CASTRATING
CASTRATION
CASTRATIONS
CASTRATO
CASTRATOR
CASTRATORS
CASTRATORY
CASTRATOS
CASTS
CASUAL
CASUALISATION
CASUALISATIONS
CASUALISE
CASUALISED
CASUALISES
CASUALISING
CASUALISM
CASUALISMS
CASUALIZATION
CASUALIZATIONS
CASUALIZE
CASUALIZED
CASUALIZES
CASUALIZING
CASUALLY
CASUALNESS
CASUALNESSES
CASUALS
CASUALTIES
CASUALTY
CASUARINA
CASUARINAS
CASUIST
CASUISTIC
CASUISTICAL
CASUISTICALLY
CASUISTRIES
CASUISTRY
CASUISTS
CASUS
CAT
CATABASES
CATABASIS
CATABATIC
CATABATICALLY
CATABOLIC
CATABOLICALLY

CATABOLISM
CATABOLISMS
CATABOLITE
CATABOLITES
CATABOLIZE
CATABOLIZED
CATABOLIZES
CATABOLIZING
CATACAUSTIC
CATACAUSTICS
CATACHRESES
CATACHRESIS
CATACHRESTIC
CATACHRESTICAL
CATACLASES
CATACLASIS
CATACLASM
CATACLASMIC
CATACLASMS
CATACLASTIC
CATACLASTICALLY
CATACLINAL
CATACLINALLY
CATACLYSM
CATACLYSMAL
CATACLYSMIC
CATACLYSMICALLY
CATACLYSMS
CATACOMB
CATACOMBS
CATACOUSTICS
CATACUMBAL
CATADIOPTRIC
CATADIOPTRICAL
CATADROMOUS
CATAFALCO
CATAFALCOES
CATAFALQUE
CATAFALQUES
CATALASE
CATALASES
CATALATIC
CATALECTIC
CATALECTICS
CATALEPSIES
CATALEPSY
CATALEPTIC
CATALEPTICALLY
CATALEPTICS
CATALEXES
CATALEXIS
CATALLACTIC
CATALLACTICALLY
CATALLACTICS
CATALO
CATALOES

CATALOG
CATALOGED
CATALOGER
CATALOGERS
CATALOGING
CATALOGIZE
CATALOGIZED
CATALOGIZES
CATALOGIZING
CATALOGS
CATALOGUE
CATALOGUED
CATALOGUER
CATALOGUERS
CATALOGUES
CATALOGUING
CATALOGUISE
CATALOGUISED
CATALOGUISES
CATALOGUISING
CATALOGUIST
CATALOGUISTS
CATALOGUIZE
CATALOGUIZED
CATALOGUIZES
CATALOGUIZING
CATALOS
CATALPA
CATALPAS
CATALYSE
CATALYSED
CATALYSER
CATALYSERS
CATALYSES
CATALYSING
CATALYSIS
CATALYST
CATALYSTS
CATALYTIC
CATALYTICAL
CATALYTICALLY
CATALYZE
CATALYZED
CATALYZER
CATALYZERS
CATALYZES
CATALYZING
CATAMARAN
CATAMARANS
CATAMENIA
CATAMENIAL
CATAMITE
CATAMITES
CATAMOUNT
CATAMOUNTAIN
CATAMOUNTAINS

CATAMOUNTS
CATANANCHE
CATANANCHES
CATAPAN
CATAPANS
CATAPHONIC
CATAPHONICS
CATAPHORA
CATAPHORAS
CATAPHORESES
CATAPHORESIS
CATAPHORETIC
CATAPHORIC
CATAPHRACT
CATAPHRACTIC
CATAPHRACTS
CATAPHYLL
CATAPHYLLARY
CATAPHYLLS
CATAPHYSICAL
CATAPLASIA
CATAPLASM
CATAPLASMS
CATAPLASTIC
CATAPLASTICALLY
CATAPLECTIC
CATAPLEXIES
CATAPLEXY
CATAPULT
CATAPULTED
CATAPULTIC
CATAPULTIER
CATAPULTIERS
CATAPULTING
CATAPULTS
CATARACT
CATARACTOUS
CATARACTS
CATARHINE
CATARRH
CATARRHAL
CATARRHALLY
CATARRHINE
CATARRHINES
CATARRHOUS
CATARRHS
CATASTA
CATASTAS
CATASTASES
CATASTASIS
CATASTROPHE
CATASTROPHES
CATASTROPHIC
CATASTROPHISM
CATASTROPHISMS
CATASTROPHIST

CATASTROPHISTS
CATATONIA
CATATONIAS
CATATONIC
CATATONICALLY
CATATONICS
CATATONIES
CATATONY
CATAWBA
CATAWBAS
CATBIRD
CATBIRDS
CATBOAT
CATBOATS
CATBRIER
CATBRIERS
CATCALL
CATCALLED
CATCALLER
CATCALLERS
CATCALLING
CATCALLS
CATCH
CATCHABLE
CATCHALL
CATCHALLS
CATCHED
CATCHEN
CATCHER
CATCHERS
CATCHES
CATCHFLIES
CATCHFLY
CATCHIER
CATCHIEST
CATCHINESS
CATCHING
CATCHINGS
CATCHMENT
CATCHMENTS
CATCHPENNIES
CATCHPENNY
CATCHPHRASE
CATCHPHRASES
CATCHPOLE
CATCHPOLES
CATCHPOLL
CATCHPOLLS
CATCHT
CATCHUP
CATCHUPS
CATCHWATER
CATCHWATERS
CATCHWEED
CATCHWEEDS
CATCHWEIGHT

CATCHWEIGHTS
CATCHWORD
CATCHWORDS
CATCHY
CATCLAW
CATCLAWS
CATE
CATECHESES
CATECHESIS
CATECHETIC
CATECHETICAL
CATECHETICALLY
CATECHETICS
CATECHIN
CATECHINS
CATECHISATION
CATECHISATIONS
CATECHISE
CATECHISED
CATECHISER
CATECHISERS
CATECHISES
CATECHISING
CATECHISINGS
CATECHISM
CATECHISMAL
CATECHISMS
CATECHIST
CATECHISTIC
CATECHISTICAL
CATECHISTICALLY
CATECHISTS
CATECHIZATION
CATECHIZATIONS
CATECHIZE
CATECHIZED
CATECHIZER
CATECHIZERS
CATECHIZES
CATECHIZING
CATECHIZINGS
CATECHOL
CATECHOLAMINE
CATECHOLAMINES
CATECHOLS
CATECHU
CATECHUMEN
CATECHUMENAL
CATECHUMENALS
CATECHUMENATE
CATECHUMENATES
CATECHUMENICAL
CATECHUMENISM
CATECHUMENISMS
CATECHUMENS
CATECHUMENSHIP

CATECHUMENSHIPS
CATECHUS
CATEGOREMATIC
CATEGORIAL
CATEGORIALLY
CATEGORIC
CATEGORICAL
CATEGORICALLY
CATEGORICALNESS
CATEGORIES
CATEGORISATION
CATEGORISATIONS
CATEGORISE
CATEGORISED
CATEGORISES
CATEGORISING
CATEGORIST
CATEGORISTS
CATEGORIZATION
CATEGORIZATIONS
CATEGORIZE
CATEGORIZED
CATEGORIZES
CATEGORIZING
CATEGORY
CATELOG
CATELOGS
CATENA
CATENACCIO
CATENAE
CATENANE
CATENANES
CATENARIAN
CATENARIES
CATENARY
CATENAS
CATENATE
CATENATED
CATENATES
CATENATING
CATENATION
CATENATIONS
CATENOID
CATENOIDS
CATENULATE
CATENULATION
CATENULATIONS
CATER
CATERAN
CATERANS
CATERCORNER
CATERCORNERED
CATERED
CATERER
CATERERS
CATERESS

CATERESSES
CATERING
CATERINGS
CATERPILLAR
CATERPILLARS
CATERS
CATERWAUL
CATERWAULED
CATERWAULER
CATERWAULERS
CATERWAULING
CATERWAULINGS
CATERWAULS
CATES
CATFACE
CATFACES
CATFACING
CATFACINGS
CATFALL
CATFALLS
CATFIGHT
CATFIGHTS
CATFISH
CATFISHES
CATGUT
CATGUTS
CATHARISE
CATHARISED
CATHARISES
CATHARISING
CATHARIZE
CATHARIZED
CATHARIZES
CATHARIZING
CATHARSES
CATHARSIS
CATHARTIC
CATHARTICAL
CATHARTICALLY
CATHARTICS
CATHEAD
CATHEADS
CATHECT
CATHECTED
CATHECTIC
CATHECTING
CATHECTS
CATHEDRA
CATHEDRAE
CATHEDRAL
CATHEDRALS
CATHEDRAS
CATHEDRATIC
CATHEPSIN
CATHEPSINS
CATHETER

CATHETERISATION
CATHETERISE
CATHETERISED
CATHETERISES
CATHETERISING
CATHETERISM
CATHETERISMS
CATHETERIZATION
CATHETERIZE
CATHETERIZED
CATHETERIZES
CATHETERIZING
CATHETERS
CATHETOMETER
CATHETOMETERS
CATHETUS
CATHETUSES
CATHEXES
CATHEXIS
CATHIODERMIE
CATHIODERMIES
CATHISMA
CATHISMAS
CATHODAL
CATHODALLY
CATHODE
CATHODES
CATHODIC
CATHODICAL
CATHODICALLY
CATHODOGRAPH
CATHODOGRAPHER
CATHODOGRAPHERS
CATHODOGRAPHIES
CATHODOGRAPHS
CATHODOGRAPHY
CATHOLE
CATHOLES
CATHOLIC
CATHOLICALLY
CATHOLICATE
CATHOLICATES
CATHOLICISATION
CATHOLICISE
CATHOLICISED
CATHOLICISES
CATHOLICISING
CATHOLICISM
CATHOLICISMS
CATHOLICITIES
CATHOLICITY
CATHOLICIZATION
CATHOLICIZE
CATHOLICIZED
CATHOLICIZES
CATHOLICIZING

CATHOLICLY
CATHOLICOI
CATHOLICON
CATHOLICONS
CATHOLICOS
CATHOLICOSES
CATHOLICS
CATHOLYTE
CATHOLYTES
CATHOOD
CATHOODS
CATHOUSE
CATHOUSES
CATILINARIAN
CATION
CATIONIC
CATIONICALLY
CATIONS
CATKIN
CATKINS
CATLIKE
CATLIN
CATLING
CATLINGS
CATLINS
CATMINT
CATMINTS
CATNAP
CATNAPER
CATNAPERS
CATNAPPED
CATNAPPER
CATNAPPERS
CATNAPPING
CATNAPS
CATNEP
CATNEPS
CATNIP
CATNIPS
CATOLYTE
CATOLYTES
CATOPTRIC
CATOPTRICAL
CATOPTRICALLY
CATOPTRICS
CATRIGGED
CATS
CATSKIN
CATSKINS
CATSPAW
CATSPAWS
CATSUIT
CATSUITS
CATSUP
CATSUPS
CATTABU

CATTABUS
CATTAIL
CATTAILS
CATTALO
CATTALOES
CATTALOS
CATTED
CATTERIES
CATTERY
CATTIE
CATTIER
CATTIES
CATTIEST
CATTILY
CATTINESS
CATTINESSES
CATTING
CATTISH
CATTISHLY
CATTISHNESS
CATTISHNESSES
CATTLE
CATTLEMAN
CATTLEMEN
CATTLEYA
CATTLEYAS
CATTY
CATWALK
CATWALKS
CATWORKS
CATWORM
CATWORMS
CAUCHEMAR
CAUCHEMARS
CAUCUS
CAUCUSED
CAUCUSES
CAUCUSING
CAUCUSSED
CAUCUSSES
CAUCUSSING
CAUDA
CAUDAD
CAUDAL
CAUDALLY
CAUDAS
CAUDATE
CAUDATED
CAUDATES
CAUDATION
CAUDATIONS
CAUDEX
CAUDEXES
CAUDICES
CAUDICLE
CAUDICLES

CAUDILLISMO
CAUDILLISMOS
CAUDILLO
CAUDILLOS
CAUDLE
CAUDLED
CAUDLES
CAUDLING
CAUDRON
CAUDRONS
CAUF
CAUGHT
CAUK
CAUKER
CAUKERS
CAUKS
CAUL
CAULD
CAULDER
CAULDEST
CAULDRIFE
CAULDRON
CAULDRONS
CAULDS
CAULES
CAULESCENT
CAULICLE
CAULICLES
CAULICOLOUS
CAULICULI
CAULICULUS
CAULICULUSES
CAULIFLORIES
CAULIFLOROUS
CAULIFLOROUSLY
CAULIFLORY
CAULIFLOWER
CAULIFLOWERET
CAULIFLOWERETS
CAULIFLOWERS
CAULIFORM
CAULIGENOUS
CAULINARY
CAULINE
CAULIS
CAULK
CAULKED
CAULKER
CAULKERS
CAULKING
CAULKINGS
CAULKS
CAULOME
CAULOMES
CAULS
CAUM

CAUMED
CAUMING
CAUMS
CAUMSTONE
CAUMSTONES
CAUP
CAUPS
CAUSA
CAUSABILITY
CAUSABLE
CAUSAE
CAUSAL
CAUSALGIA
CAUSALGIAS
CAUSALGIC
CAUSALITIES
CAUSALITY
CAUSALLY
CAUSALS
CAUSATION
CAUSATIONAL
CAUSATIONALLY
CAUSATIONISM
CAUSATIONISMS
CAUSATIONIST
CAUSATIONISTS
CAUSATIONS
CAUSATIVE
CAUSATIVELY
CAUSATIVENESS
CAUSATIVES
CAUSE
CAUSED
CAUSELESS
CAUSELESSLY
CAUSELESSNESS
CAUSELESSNESSES
CAUSEN
CAUSER
CAUSERIE
CAUSERIES
CAUSERS
CAUSES
CAUSEWAY
CAUSEWAYED
CAUSEWAYING
CAUSEWAYS
CAUSEY
CAUSEYED
CAUSEYS
CAUSING
CAUSTIC
CAUSTICAL
CAUSTICALLY
CAUSTICITIES
CAUSTICITY

CAUSTICNESS
CAUSTICNESSES
CAUSTICS
CAUTEL
CAUTELOUS
CAUTELS
CAUTER
CAUTERANT
CAUTERANTS
CAUTERIES
CAUTERISATION
CAUTERISATIONS
CAUTERISE
CAUTERISED
CAUTERISES
CAUTERISING
CAUTERISM
CAUTERISMS
CAUTERIZATION
CAUTERIZATIONS
CAUTERIZE
CAUTERIZED
CAUTERIZES
CAUTERIZING
CAUTERS
CAUTERY
CAUTION
CAUTIONARY
CAUTIONED
CAUTIONER
CAUTIONERS
CAUTIONING
CAUTIONRIES
CAUTIONRY
CAUTIONS
CAUTIOUS
CAUTIOUSLY
CAUTIOUSNESS
CAUTIOUSNESSES
CAUVES
CAVA
CAVALCADE
CAVALCADED
CAVALCADES
CAVALCADING
CAVALERO
CAVALEROS
CAVALETTI
CAVALIER
CAVALIERED
CAVALIERING
CAVALIERISH
CAVALIERISM
CAVALIERISMS
CAVALIERLY
CAVALIERS

CAVALLA
CAVALLAS
CAVALLETTI
CAVALLIES
CAVALLY
CAVALRIES
CAVALRY
CAVALRYMAN
CAVALRYMEN
CAVASS
CAVASSES
CAVATINA
CAVATINAS
CAVATINE
CAVE
CAVEAT
CAVEATED
CAVEATING
CAVEATOR
CAVEATORS
CAVEATS
CAVED
CAVEFISH
CAVEFISHES
CAVEL
CAVELIKE
CAVELS
CAVEMAN
CAVEMEN
CAVENDISH
CAVENDISHES
CAVER
CAVERN
CAVERNED
CAVERNICOLOUS
CAVERNING
CAVERNOUS
CAVERNOUSLY
CAVERNS
CAVERNULOUS
CAVERS
CAVES
CAVESSON
CAVESSONS
CAVETTI
CAVETTO
CAVETTOS
CAVIAR
CAVIARE
CAVIARES
CAVIARIE
CAVIARIES
CAVIARS
CAVICORN
CAVICORNS
CAVIE

CAVIER
CAVIERS
CAVIES
CAVIL
CAVILED
CAVILER
CAVILERS
CAVILING
CAVILLATION
CAVILLATIONS
CAVILLED
CAVILLER
CAVILLERS
CAVILLING
CAVILLINGS
CAVILS
CAVING
CAVINGS
CAVITARY
CAVITATE
CAVITATED
CAVITATES
CAVITATING
CAVITATION
CAVITATIONS
CAVITIED
CAVITIES
CAVITY
CAVORT
CAVORTED
CAVORTER
CAVORTERS
CAVORTING
CAVORTS
CAVY
CAW
CAWED
CAWING
CAWINGS
CAWK
CAWKER
CAWKERS
CAWKS
CAWS
CAXON
CAXONS
CAY
CAYENNE
CAYENNED
CAYENNES
CAYMAN
CAYMANS
CAYS
CAYUSE
CAYUSES
CAZ

CAZIQUE
CAZIQUES
CEANOTHUS
CEANOTHUSES
CEAS
CEASE
CEASED
CEASELESS
CEASELESSLY
CEASELESSNESS
CEASELESSNESSES
CEASES
CEASING
CEASINGS
CEAZE
CEAZED
CEAZES
CEAZING
CEBADILLA
CEBADILLAS
CEBID
CEBIDS
CEBOID
CEBOIDS
CECA
CECAL
CECALLY
CECILS
CECITIES
CECITIS
CECITISES
CECITY
CECROPIA
CECROPIAS
CECUM
CECUTIENCIES
CECUTIENCY
CEDAR
CEDARBIRD
CEDARBIRDS
CEDARED
CEDARN
CEDARS
CEDARWOOD
CEDARWOODS
CEDE
CEDED
CEDER
CEDERS
CEDES
CEDI
CEDILLA
CEDILLAS
CEDING
CEDIS
CEDRATE

CEDRATES
CEDRINE
CEDULA
CEDULAS
CEE
CEES
CEIBA
CEIBAS
CEIL
CEILED
CEILER
CEILERS
CEILI
CEILIDH
CEILIDHS
CEILING
CEILINGED
CEILINGS
CEILIS
CEILOMETER
CEILOMETERS
CEILS
CEINTURE
CEINTURES
CEL
CELADON
CELADONS
CELANDINE
CELANDINES
CELEB
CELEBRANT
CELEBRANTS
CELEBRATE
CELEBRATED
CELEBRATEDNESS
CELEBRATES
CELEBRATING
CELEBRATION
CELEBRATIONS
CELEBRATIVE
CELEBRATIVELY
CELEBRATOR
CELEBRATORS
CELEBRATORY
CELEBRITIES
CELEBRITY
CELEBS
CELERIAC
CELERIACS
CELERIES
CELERITIES
CELERITY
CELERY
CELESTA
CELESTAS
CELESTE

CELESTES
CELESTIAL
CELESTIALLY
CELESTIALS
CELESTINE
CELESTINES
CELESTITE
CELESTITES
CELIAC
CELIACS
CELIBACIES
CELIBACY
CELIBATARIAN
CELIBATE
CELIBATES
CELL
CELLA
CELLAE
CELLAR
CELLARAGE
CELLARAGES
CELLARED
CELLARER
CELLARERS
CELLARET
CELLARETS
CELLARETTE
CELLARETTES
CELLARING
CELLARIST
CELLARISTS
CELLARMAN
CELLARMEN
CELLAROUS
CELLARS
CELLED
CELLENTANI
CELLENTANO
CELLI
CELLIFEROUS
CELLING
CELLIST
CELLISTS
CELLMATE
CELLMATES
CELLO
CELLOBIOSE
CELLOBIOSES
CELLOIDIN
CELLOIDINS
CELLOPHANE
CELLOPHANES
CELLOS
CELLOSE
CELLOSES
CELLPHONE

CELLPHONES
CELLS
CELLULAR
CELLULARITIES
CELLULARITY
CELLULASE
CELLULASES
CELLULATED
CELLULE
CELLULES
CELLULIFEROUS
CELLULITE
CELLULITES
CELLULITIS
CELLULITISES
CELLULOID
CELLULOIDS
CELLULOLYTIC
CELLULOSE
CELLULOSES
CELLULOSIC
CELLULOSICS
CELLULOUS
CELOM
CELOMATA
CELOMIC
CELOMICALLY
CELOMS
CELOSIA
CELOSIAS
CELS
CELSITUDE
CELSITUDES
CELT
CELTS
CEMBALI
CEMBALIST
CEMBALISTS
CEMBALO
CEMBALOS
CEMBRA
CEMBRAS
CEMENT
CEMENTA
CEMENTATION
CEMENTATIONS
CEMENTATORY
CEMENTED
CEMENTER
CEMENTERS
CEMENTING
CEMENTITE
CEMENTITES
CEMENTITIOUS
CEMENTS
CEMENTUM

CEMETERIES
CEMETERY
CEMITARE
CEMITARES
CENACLE
CENACLES
CENDRE
CENESTHESES
CENESTHESIA
CENESTHESIAS
CENESTHESIS
CENESTHETIC
CENOBITE
CENOBITES
CENOBITIC
CENOBITICAL
CENOBITICALLY
CENOGENESES
CENOGENESIS
CENOGENETIC
CENOGENETICALLY
CENOSPECIES
CENOTAPH
CENOTAPHIC
CENOTAPHS
CENOTE
CENOTES
CENS
CENSE
CENSED
CENSER
CENSERS
CENSES
CENSING
CENSOR
CENSORABLE
CENSORED
CENSORIAL
CENSORIAN
CENSORING
CENSORIOUS
CENSORIOUSLY
CENSORIOUSNESS
CENSORS
CENSORSHIP
CENSORSHIPS
CENSUAL
CENSURABILITY
CENSURABLE
CENSURABLENESS
CENSURABLY
CENSURE
CENSURED
CENSURER
CENSURERS
CENSURES

CENSURING
CENSUS
CENSUSED
CENSUSES
CENSUSING
CENT
CENTAGE
CENTAGES
CENTAI
CENTAL
CENTALS
CENTARE
CENTARES
CENTAS
CENTAUR
CENTAUREA
CENTAUREAS
CENTAURIAN
CENTAURIES
CENTAURS
CENTAURY
CENTAVO
CENTAVOS
CENTENARIAN
CENTENARIANISM
CENTENARIANISMS
CENTENARIANS
CENTENARIES
CENTENARY
CENTENIER
CENTENIERS
CENTENNIAL
CENTENNIALLY
CENTENNIALS
CENTER
CENTERBOARD
CENTERBOARDS
CENTERED
CENTEREDNESS
CENTEREDNESSES
CENTERFOLD
CENTERFOLDS
CENTERING
CENTERINGS
CENTERLESS
CENTERLINE
CENTERLINES
CENTERPIECE
CENTERPIECES
CENTERS
CENTESES
CENTESIMAL
CENTESIMALLY
CENTESIMALS
CENTESIMI
CENTESIMO

CENTESIMOS
CENTESIS
CENTIARE
CENTIARES
CENTIGRADE
CENTIGRAM
CENTIGRAMME
CENTIGRAMMES
CENTIGRAMS
CENTILE
CENTILES
CENTILITER
CENTILITERS
CENTILITRE
CENTILITRES
CENTILLION
CENTILLIONS
CENTILLIONTH
CENTILLIONTHS
CENTIME
CENTIMES
CENTIMETER
CENTIMETERS
CENTIMETRE
CENTIMETRES
CENTIMETRIC
CENTIMO
CENTIMORGAN
CENTIMORGANS
CENTIMOS
CENTINEL
CENTINELL
CENTINELLS
CENTINELS
CENTIPEDE
CENTIPEDES
CENTIPOISE
CENTIPOISES
CENTNER
CENTNERS
CENTO
CENTOIST
CENTOISTS
CENTONATE
CENTONEL
CENTONELL
CENTONELLS
CENTONELS
CENTONES
CENTONIST
CENTONISTS
CENTOS
CENTRA
CENTRAL
CENTRALER
CENTRALEST

CENTRALISATION
CENTRALISATIONS
CENTRALISE
CENTRALISED
CENTRALISER
CENTRALISERS
CENTRALISES
CENTRALISING
CENTRALISM
CENTRALISMS
CENTRALIST
CENTRALISTIC
CENTRALISTS
CENTRALITIES
CENTRALITY
CENTRALIZATION
CENTRALIZATIONS
CENTRALIZE
CENTRALIZED
CENTRALIZER
CENTRALIZERS
CENTRALIZES
CENTRALIZING
CENTRALLY
CENTRALS
CENTRE
CENTREBOARD
CENTREBOARDS
CENTRED
CENTREFOLD
CENTREFOLDS
CENTREING
CENTREINGS
CENTRELINE
CENTRELINES
CENTREPIECE
CENTREPIECES
CENTRES
CENTREX
CENTREXES
CENTRIC
CENTRICAL
CENTRICALLY
CENTRICALNESS
CENTRICALNESSES
CENTRICITIES
CENTRICITY
CENTRIES
CENTRIFUGAL
CENTRIFUGALISE
CENTRIFUGALISED
CENTRIFUGALISES
CENTRIFUGALIZE
CENTRIFUGALIZED
CENTRIFUGALIZES
CENTRIFUGALLY

CENTRIFUGALS
CENTRIFUGATION
CENTRIFUGATIONS
CENTRIFUGE
CENTRIFUGED
CENTRIFUGENCE
CENTRIFUGENCES
CENTRIFUGES
CENTRIFUGING
CENTRING
CENTRINGS
CENTRIOLE
CENTRIOLES
CENTRIPETAL
CENTRIPETALISM
CENTRIPETALISMS
CENTRIPETALLY
CENTRISM
CENTRISMS
CENTRIST
CENTRISTS
CENTROBARIC
CENTROCLINAL
CENTRODE
CENTRODES
CENTROID
CENTROIDAL
CENTROIDS
CENTROLECITHAL
CENTROMERE
CENTROMERES
CENTROMERIC
CENTROSOME
CENTROSOMES
CENTROSOMIC
CENTROSPHERE
CENTROSPHERES
CENTROSYMMETRIC
CENTRUM
CENTRUMS
CENTRY
CENTS
CENTUM
CENTUMS
CENTUMVIR
CENTUMVIRATE
CENTUMVIRATES
CENTUMVIRI
CENTUPLE
CENTUPLED
CENTUPLES
CENTUPLICATE
CENTUPLICATED
CENTUPLICATES
CENTUPLICATING
CENTUPLICATION

CENTUPLICATIONS
CENTUPLING
CENTURIAL
CENTURIATION
CENTURIATIONS
CENTURIATOR
CENTURIATORS
CENTURIES
CENTURION
CENTURIONS
CENTURY
CEORL
CEORLISH
CEORLS
CEP
CEPACEOUS
CEPE
CEPES
CEPHALAD
CEPHALAGRA
CEPHALAGRAS
CEPHALALGIA
CEPHALALGIAS
CEPHALALGIC
CEPHALATE
CEPHALEXIN
CEPHALEXINS
CEPHALIC
CEPHALICALLY
CEPHALICS
CEPHALIN
CEPHALINS
CEPHALISATION
CEPHALISATIONS
CEPHALITIS
CEPHALITISES
CEPHALIZATION
CEPHALIZATIONS
CEPHALOCELE
CEPHALOCELES
CEPHALOCHORDATE
CEPHALOMETER
CEPHALOMETERS
CEPHALOMETRIC
CEPHALOMETRIES
CEPHALOMETRY
CEPHALOPOD
CEPHALOPODAN
CEPHALOPODANS
CEPHALOPODIC
CEPHALOPODOUS
CEPHALOPODS
CEPHALORIDINE
CEPHALORIDINES
CEPHALOSPORIN
CEPHALOSPORINS

CEPHALOTHIN
CEPHALOTHINS
CEPHALOTHORACES
CEPHALOTHORACIC
CEPHALOTHORAX
CEPHALOTHORAXES
CEPHALOTOMIES
CEPHALOTOMY
CEPHALOUS
CEPHEID
CEPHEIDS
CEPS
CERACEOUS
CERAMAL
CERAMALS
CERAMIC
CERAMICIST
CERAMICISTS
CERAMICS
CERAMIDE
CERAMIDES
CERAMIST
CERAMISTS
CERAMOGRAPHIES
CERAMOGRAPHY
CERARGYRITE
CERARGYRITES
CERASIN
CERASINS
CERASTES
CERASTIUM
CERASTIUMS
CERATE
CERATED
CERATES
CERATIN
CERATINS
CERATITIS
CERATITISES
CERATODUS
CERATODUSES
CERATOID
CERATOPSIAN
CERATOPSIANS
CERATOPSID
CERATOPSIDS
CERBEREAN
CERBERIAN
CERCAL
CERCARIA
CERCARIAE
CERCARIAL
CERCARIAN
CERCARIANS
CERCARIAS
CERCI

CERCIS
CERCISES
CERCOPITHECID
CERCOPITHECIDS
CERCOPITHECOID
CERCOPITHECOIDS
CERCUS
CERE
CEREAL
CEREALIST
CEREALISTS
CEREALS
CEREBELLA
CEREBELLAR
CEREBELLIC
CEREBELLOUS
CEREBELLUM
CEREBELLUMS
CEREBRA
CEREBRAL
CEREBRALISM
CEREBRALISMS
CEREBRALIST
CEREBRALISTS
CEREBRALLY
CEREBRALS
CEREBRATE
CEREBRATED
CEREBRATES
CEREBRATING
CEREBRATION
CEREBRATIONS
CEREBRIC
CEREBRIFORM
CEREBRITIS
CEREBRITISES
CEREBROID
CEREBROIDS
CEREBROSIDE
CEREBROSIDES
CEREBROSPINAL
CEREBROTONIA
CEREBROTONIAS
CEREBROTONIC
CEREBROVASCULAR
CEREBRUM
CEREBRUMS
CERECLOTH
CERECLOTHS
CERED
CEREMENT
CEREMENTS
CEREMONIAL
CEREMONIALISM
CEREMONIALISMS
CEREMONIALIST

CEREMONIALISTS
CEREMONIALLY
CEREMONIALS
CEREMONIES
CEREMONIOUS
CEREMONIOUSLY
CEREMONIOUSNESS
CEREMONY
CEREOUS
CERES
CERESIN
CERESINE
CERESINES
CERESINS
CEREUS
CEREUSES
CERGE
CERGES
CERIA
CERIAS
CERIC
CERIFEROUS
CERING
CERIPH
CERIPHS
CERISE
CERISES
CERITE
CERITES
CERIUM
CERIUMS
CERMET
CERMETS
CERNE
CERNED
CERNES
CERNING
CERNUOUS
CERO
CEROGRAPH
CEROGRAPHIC
CEROGRAPHICAL
CEROGRAPHIES
CEROGRAPHIST
CEROGRAPHISTS
CEROGRAPHS
CEROGRAPHY
CEROMANCIES
CEROMANCY
CEROON
CEROONS
CEROPLASTIC
CEROPLASTICS
CEROS
CEROTIC
CEROTYPE

CEROTYPES
CEROUS
CERRIAL
CERRIS
CERRISES
CERT
CERTAIN
CERTAINER
CERTAINEST
CERTAINLY
CERTAINTIES
CERTAINTY
CERTES
CERTIFIABLE
CERTIFIABLY
CERTIFICATE
CERTIFICATED
CERTIFICATES
CERTIFICATING
CERTIFICATION
CERTIFICATIONS
CERTIFICATORIES
CERTIFICATORY
CERTIFIED
CERTIFIER
CERTIFIERS
CERTIFIES
CERTIFY
CERTIFYING
CERTIORARI
CERTIORARIS
CERTITUDE
CERTITUDES
CERTS
CERULE
CERULEAN
CERULEANS
CERULEIN
CERULEINS
CERULEOUS
CERULOPLASMIN
CERULOPLASMINS
CERUMEN
CERUMENS
CERUMINOUS
CERUSE
CERUSES
CERUSITE
CERUSITES
CERUSSITE
CERUSSITES
CERVELAS
CERVELASES
CERVELAT
CERVELATS
CERVENA

CERVENAS
CERVICAL
CERVICES
CERVICITIS
CERVICITISES
CERVICOGRAPHIES
CERVICOGRAPHY
CERVICUM
CERVICUMS
CERVID
CERVIDS
CERVINE
CERVIX
CERVIXES
CESAREAN
CESAREANS
CESAREVICH
CESAREVICHES
CESAREVITCH
CESAREVITCHES
CESAREVNA
CESAREVNAS
CESAREWICH
CESAREWICHES
CESAREWITCH
CESAREWITCHES
CESARIAN
CESARIANS
CESIOUS
CESIUM
CESIUMS
CESPITOSE
CESPITOSELY
CESS
CESSATION
CESSATIONS
CESSE
CESSED
CESSER
CESSERS
CESSES
CESSING
CESSION
CESSIONARIES
CESSIONARY
CESSIONS
CESSPIT
CESSPITS
CESSPOOL
CESSPOOLS
CESTA
CESTAS
CESTI
CESTODE
CESTODES
CESTOI

CESTOID
CESTOIDEAN
CESTOIDEANS
CESTOIDS
CESTOS
CESTOSES
CESTUI
CESTUIS
CESTUS
CESTUSES
CESURA
CESURAE
CESURAL
CESURAS
CESURE
CESURES
CETACEAN
CETACEANS
CETACEOUS
CETANE
CETANES
CETE
CETEOSAURUS
CETEOSAURUSES
CETERACH
CETERACHS
CETES
CETOLOGICAL
CETOLOGICALLY
CETOLOGIES
CETOLOGIST
CETOLOGISTS
CETOLOGY
CETRIMIDE
CETYL
CETYLS
CETYWALL
CETYWALLS
CEVADILLA
CEVADILLAS
CEVAPCICI
CEVICHE
CEVICHES
CEYLANITE
CEYLANITES
CEYLONITE
CEYLONITES
CH
CHA
CHABAZITE
CHABAZITES
CHABLIS
CHABOUK
CHABOUKS
CHABUK
CHABUKS

CHACE
CHACED
CHACES
CHACING
CHACK
CHACKED
CHACKING
CHACKS
CHACMA
CHACMAS
CHACO
CHACOES
CHACONNE
CHACONNES
CHACOS
CHAD
CHADAR
CHADARIM
CHADARS
CHADDAR
CHADDARS
CHADDOR
CHADDORS
CHADLESS
CHADO
CHADOR
CHADORS
CHADRI
CHADS
CHAEBOL
CHAEBOLS
CHAENOMELES
CHAENOMELESES
CHAETA
CHAETAE
CHAETAL
CHAETIFEROUS
CHAETODON
CHAETODONS
CHAETOGNATH
CHAETOGNATHS
CHAETOPOD
CHAETOPODS
CHAFE
CHAFED
CHAFER
CHAFERS
CHAFES
CHAFF
CHAFFED
CHAFFER
CHAFFERED
CHAFFERER
CHAFFERERS
CHAFFERIES
CHAFFERING

CHAFFERS
CHAFFERY
CHAFFIER
CHAFFIEST
CHAFFINCH
CHAFFINCHES
CHAFFING
CHAFFINGLY
CHAFFINGS
CHAFFRON
CHAFFRONS
CHAFFS
CHAFFY
CHAFING
CHAFT
CHAFTS
CHAGAN
CHAGANS
CHAGRIN
CHAGRINED
CHAGRINING
CHAGRINNED
CHAGRINNING
CHAGRINS
CHAI
CHAIN
CHAINBRAKE
CHAINBRAKES
CHAINE
CHAINED
CHAINES
CHAINING
CHAINLESS
CHAINLET
CHAINLETS
CHAINMAN
CHAINMEN
CHAINPLATE
CHAINPLATES
CHAINS
CHAINSAW
CHAINSAWED
CHAINSAWING
CHAINSAWS
CHAINSHOT
CHAINSHOTS
CHAINSTITCH
CHAINSTITCHES
CHAINWHEEL
CHAINWHEELS
CHAINWORK
CHAINWORKS
CHAIR
CHAIRBORNE
CHAIRBOUND
CHAIRDAYS

CHAIRED
CHAIRING
CHAIRLIFT
CHAIRLIFTS
CHAIRMAN
CHAIRMANED
CHAIRMANING
CHAIRMANNED
CHAIRMANNING
CHAIRMANS
CHAIRMANSHIP
CHAIRMANSHIPS
CHAIRMEN
CHAIRPERSON
CHAIRPERSONS
CHAIRS
CHAIRWOMAN
CHAIRWOMEN
CHAIS
CHAISE
CHAISELESS
CHAISES
CHAKALAKA
CHAKALAKAS
CHAKRA
CHAKRAS
CHAL
CHALAH
CHALAHS
CHALAN
CHALANED
CHALANING
CHALANS
CHALAZA
CHALAZAE
CHALAZAL
CHALAZAS
CHALAZIA
CHALAZION
CHALAZIONS
CHALAZOGAMIC
CHALAZOGAMIES
CHALAZOGAMY
CHALCANTHITE
CHALCANTHITES
CHALCEDONIC
CHALCEDONIES
CHALCEDONY
CHALCEDONYX
CHALCEDONYXES
CHALCID
CHALCIDS
CHALCOCITE
CHALCOCITES
CHALCOGEN
CHALCOGENIDE

CHALCOGENIDES
CHALCOGENS
CHALCOGRAPHER
CHALCOGRAPHERS
CHALCOGRAPHIC
CHALCOGRAPHICAL
CHALCOGRAPHIES
CHALCOGRAPHIST
CHALCOGRAPHISTS
CHALCOGRAPHY
CHALCOLITHIC
CHALCOPYRITE
CHALCOPYRITES
CHALDER
CHALDERS
CHALDRON
CHALDRONS
CHALEH
CHALEHS
CHALET
CHALETS
CHALICE
CHALICED
CHALICES
CHALICOTHERE
CHALICOTHERES
CHALK
CHALKBOARD
CHALKBOARDS
CHALKED
CHALKFACE
CHALKFACES
CHALKIER
CHALKIEST
CHALKINESS
CHALKINESSES
CHALKING
CHALKLIKE
CHALKPIT
CHALKPITS
CHALKS
CHALKSTONE
CHALKSTONES
CHALKY
CHALLA
CHALLAH
CHALLAHS
CHALLAN
CHALLANED
CHALLANING
CHALLANS
CHALLAS
CHALLENGE
CHALLENGEABLE
CHALLENGED
CHALLENGER

CHALLENGERS
CHALLENGES
CHALLENGING
CHALLENGINGLY
CHALLIE
CHALLIES
CHALLIS
CHALLISES
CHALLOT
CHALLOTH
CHALLY
CHALONE
CHALONES
CHALONIC
CHALOT
CHALOTH
CHALS
CHALUMEAU
CHALUMEAUX
CHALUTZ
CHALUTZES
CHALUTZIM
CHALYBEAN
CHALYBEATE
CHALYBEATES
CHALYBITE
CHALYBITES
CHAM
CHAMADE
CHAMADES
CHAMAELEON
CHAMAELEONS
CHAMAEPHYTE
CHAMAEPHYTES
CHAMBER
CHAMBERED
CHAMBERER
CHAMBERERS
CHAMBERHAND
CHAMBERHANDS
CHAMBERING
CHAMBERINGS
CHAMBERLAIN
CHAMBERLAINS
CHAMBERLAINSHIP
CHAMBERMAID
CHAMBERMAIDS
CHAMBERPOT
CHAMBERPOTS
CHAMBERS
CHAMBRANLE
CHAMBRANLES
CHAMBRAY
CHAMBRAYS
CHAMBRE
CHAMELEON

CHAMELEONIC
CHAMELEONLIKE
CHAMELEONS
CHAMELOT
CHAMELOTS
CHAMETZ
CHAMFER
CHAMFERED
CHAMFERER
CHAMFERERS
CHAMFERING
CHAMFERS
CHAMFRAIN
CHAMFRAINS
CHAMFRON
CHAMFRONS
CHAMISAL
CHAMISALS
CHAMISE
CHAMISES
CHAMISO
CHAMISOS
CHAMLET
CHAMLETS
CHAMMIED
CHAMMIES
CHAMMY
CHAMMYING
CHAMOIS
CHAMOISED
CHAMOISES
CHAMOISING
CHAMOIX
CHAMOMILE
CHAMOMILES
CHAMP
CHAMPAC
CHAMPACS
CHAMPAGNE
CHAMPAGNES
CHAMPAIGN
CHAMPAIGNS
CHAMPAK
CHAMPAKS
CHAMPART
CHAMPARTS
CHAMPED
CHAMPER
CHAMPERS
CHAMPERTIES
CHAMPERTOUS
CHAMPERTY
CHAMPIGNON
CHAMPIGNONS
CHAMPING
CHAMPION

CHAMPIONED
CHAMPIONESS
CHAMPIONESSES
CHAMPIONING
CHAMPIONS
CHAMPIONSHIP
CHAMPIONSHIPS
CHAMPLEVE
CHAMPLEVES
CHAMPS
CHAMPY
CHAMS
CHANCE
CHANCED
CHANCEFUL
CHANCEL
CHANCELESS
CHANCELLERIES
CHANCELLERY
CHANCELLOR
CHANCELLORIES
CHANCELLORS
CHANCELLORSHIP
CHANCELLORSHIPS
CHANCELLORY
CHANCELS
CHANCER
CHANCERIES
CHANCERS
CHANCERY
CHANCES
CHANCEY
CHANCIER
CHANCIEST
CHANCILY
CHANCINESS
CHANCINESSES
CHANCING
CHANCRE
CHANCRES
CHANCROID
CHANCROIDAL
CHANCROIDS
CHANCROUS
CHANCY
CHANDELIER
CHANDELIERED
CHANDELIERS
CHANDELLE
CHANDELLED
CHANDELLES
CHANDELLING
CHANDLER
CHANDLERIES
CHANDLERING
CHANDLERINGS

CHANDLERLY
CHANDLERS
CHANDLERY
CHANFRON
CHANFRONS
CHANG
CHANGE
CHANGEABILITIES
CHANGEABILITY
CHANGEABLE
CHANGEABLENESS
CHANGEABLY
CHANGED
CHANGEFUL
CHANGEFULLY
CHANGEFULNESS
CHANGEFULNESSES
CHANGELESS
CHANGELESSLY
CHANGELESSNESS
CHANGELING
CHANGELINGS
CHANGEOVER
CHANGEOVERS
CHANGER
CHANGEROUND
CHANGEROUNDS
CHANGERS
CHANGES
CHANGING
CHANGS
CHANK
CHANKS
CHANNEL
CHANNELED
CHANNELER
CHANNELERS
CHANNELING
CHANNELISE
CHANNELISED
CHANNELISES
CHANNELISING
CHANNELIZATION
CHANNELIZATIONS
CHANNELIZE
CHANNELIZED
CHANNELIZES
CHANNELIZING
CHANNELLED
CHANNELLER
CHANNELLERS
CHANNELLING
CHANNELS
CHANNER
CHANNERS
CHANOYO

CHANOYU
CHANOYUS
CHANSON
CHANSONETTE
CHANSONETTES
CHANSONNIER
CHANSONNIERS
CHANSONS
CHANT
CHANTAGE
CHANTAGES
CHANTARELLE
CHANTARELLES
CHANTECLER
CHANTECLERS
CHANTED
CHANTER
CHANTERELLE
CHANTERELLES
CHANTERS
CHANTEUSE
CHANTEUSES
CHANTEY
CHANTEYS
CHANTICLEER
CHANTICLEERS
CHANTIE
CHANTIES
CHANTING
CHANTINGLY
CHANTOR
CHANTORS
CHANTRESS
CHANTRESSES
CHANTRIES
CHANTRY
CHANTS
CHANTY
CHANUKIAH
CHAO
CHAOLOGIES
CHAOLOGIST
CHAOLOGISTS
CHAOLOGY
CHAOS
CHAOSES
CHAOTIC
CHAOTICALLY
CHAP
CHAPARAJOS
CHAPAREJOS
CHAPARRAL
CHAPARRALS
CHAPATI
CHAPATIES
CHAPATIS

CHAPATTI
CHAPATTIES
CHAPATTIS
CHAPBOOK
CHAPBOOKS
CHAPE
CHAPEAU
CHAPEAUS
CHAPEAUX
CHAPEL
CHAPELESS
CHAPELRIES
CHAPELRY
CHAPELS
CHAPERON
CHAPERONAGE
CHAPERONAGES
CHAPERONE
CHAPERONED
CHAPERONES
CHAPERONING
CHAPERONS
CHAPES
CHAPESS
CHAPESSES
CHAPFALLEN
CHAPITER
CHAPITERS
CHAPKA
CHAPKAS
CHAPLAIN
CHAPLAINCIES
CHAPLAINCY
CHAPLAINRIES
CHAPLAINRY
CHAPLAINS
CHAPLAINSHIP
CHAPLAINSHIPS
CHAPLESS
CHAPLET
CHAPLETED
CHAPLETS
CHAPMAN
CHAPMANSHIP
CHAPMEN
CHAPPAL
CHAPPALS
CHAPPATI
CHAPPATIS
CHAPPED
CHAPPESS
CHAPPESSES
CHAPPIE
CHAPPIER
CHAPPIES
CHAPPIEST

CHAPPING
CHAPPY
CHAPRASSI
CHAPRASSIES
CHAPRASSIS
CHAPS
CHAPSTICK
CHAPSTICKS
CHAPT
CHAPTALISATION
CHAPTALISATIONS
CHAPTALISE
CHAPTALISED
CHAPTALISES
CHAPTALISING
CHAPTALIZATION
CHAPTALIZATIONS
CHAPTALIZE
CHAPTALIZED
CHAPTALIZES
CHAPTALIZING
CHAPTER
CHAPTERED
CHAPTERHOUSE
CHAPTERHOUSES
CHAPTERING
CHAPTERS
CHAPTREL
CHAPTRELS
CHAQUETA
CHAQUETAS
CHAR
CHARA
CHARABANC
CHARABANCS
CHARACID
CHARACIDS
CHARACIN
CHARACINOID
CHARACINS
CHARACT
CHARACTER
CHARACTERED
CHARACTERFUL
CHARACTERIES
CHARACTERING
CHARACTERISABLE
CHARACTERISE
CHARACTERISED
CHARACTERISER
CHARACTERISERS
CHARACTERISES
CHARACTERISING
CHARACTERISM
CHARACTERISMS
CHARACTERISTIC

CHARACTERISTICS
CHARACTERIZABLE
CHARACTERIZE
CHARACTERIZED
CHARACTERIZER
CHARACTERIZERS
CHARACTERIZES
CHARACTERIZING
CHARACTERLESS
CHARACTEROLOGY
CHARACTERS
CHARACTERY
CHARACTS
CHARADE
CHARADES
CHARANGA
CHARANGO
CHARANGOS
CHARAS
CHARASES
CHARBROIL
CHARBROILED
CHARBROILER
CHARBROILERS
CHARBROILING
CHARBROILS
CHARCOAL
CHARCOALED
CHARCOALING
CHARCOALS
CHARCUTERIE
CHARCUTERIES
CHARD
CHARDONNAY
CHARDONNAYS
CHARDS
CHARE
CHARED
CHARES
CHARET
CHARETS
CHARGE
CHARGEABILITY
CHARGEABLE
CHARGEABLENESS
CHARGEABLY
CHARGED
CHARGEFUL
CHARGEHAND
CHARGEHANDS
CHARGELESS
CHARGENURSE
CHARGENURSES
CHARGER
CHARGERS
CHARGES

CHARGESHEET
CHARGESHEETS
CHARGING
CHARGRILL
CHARGRILLED
CHARGRILLING
CHARGRILLS
CHARIDEE
CHARIDEES
CHARIER
CHARIEST
CHARILY
CHARINESS
CHARINESSES
CHARING
CHARIOT
CHARIOTED
CHARIOTEER
CHARIOTEERED
CHARIOTEERING
CHARIOTEERS
CHARIOTING
CHARIOTS
CHARISM
CHARISMA
CHARISMAS
CHARISMATA
CHARISMATIC
CHARISMATICS
CHARISMS
CHARITABLE
CHARITABLENESS
CHARITABLY
CHARITIES
CHARITY
CHARIVARI
CHARIVARIS
CHARK
CHARKA
CHARKAS
CHARKED
CHARKHA
CHARKHAS
CHARKING
CHARKS
CHARLADIES
CHARLADY
CHARLATAN
CHARLATANIC
CHARLATANICAL
CHARLATANISM
CHARLATANISMS
CHARLATANISTIC
CHARLATANRIES
CHARLATANRY
CHARLATANS

CHARLESTON
CHARLESTONED
CHARLESTONING
CHARLESTONS
CHARLEY
CHARLEYS
CHARLIE
CHARLIES
CHARLOCK
CHARLOCKS
CHARLOTTE
CHARLOTTES
CHARM
CHARMED
CHARMER
CHARMERS
CHARMEUSE
CHARMEUSES
CHARMFUL
CHARMING
CHARMINGER
CHARMINGEST
CHARMINGLY
CHARMLESS
CHARMLESSLY
CHARMS
CHARNECO
CHARNECOS
CHARNEL
CHARNELS
CHAROSET
CHAROSETH
CHAROSETHS
CHAROSETS
CHARPAI
CHARPAIS
CHARPIE
CHARPIES
CHARPOY
CHARPOYS
CHARQUI
CHARQUID
CHARQUIS
CHARR
CHARRED
CHARRIER
CHARRIEST
CHARRING
CHARRO
CHARROS
CHARRS
CHARRY
CHARS
CHART
CHARTA
CHARTABILITY

CHARTABLE
CHARTABLY
CHARTACEOUS
CHARTAS
CHARTED
CHARTER
CHARTERAGE
CHARTERAGES
CHARTERED
CHARTERER
CHARTERERS
CHARTERING
CHARTERPARTIES
CHARTERPARTY
CHARTERS
CHARTHOUSE
CHARTHOUSES
CHARTING
CHARTISM
CHARTISMS
CHARTIST
CHARTISTS
CHARTLESS
CHARTOGRAPHER
CHARTOGRAPHERS
CHARTOGRAPHIC
CHARTOGRAPHICAL
CHARTOGRAPHIES
CHARTOGRAPHY
CHARTREUSE
CHARTREUSES
CHARTS
CHARTULARIES
CHARTULARY
CHARVER
CHARVERS
CHARWOMAN
CHARWOMEN
CHARY
CHAS
CHASE
CHASEABLE
CHASED
CHASEPORT
CHASEPORTS
CHASER
CHASERS
CHASES
CHASING
CHASINGS
CHASM
CHASMAL
CHASMED
CHASMIC
CHASMIER
CHASMIEST

CHASMOGAMIC
CHASMOGAMIES
CHASMOGAMOUS
CHASMOGAMOUSLY
CHASMOGAMY
CHASMS
CHASMY
CHASSE
CHASSED
CHASSEED
CHASSEING
CHASSEPOT
CHASSEPOTS
CHASSES
CHASSEUR
CHASSEURS
CHASSIS
CHASTE
CHASTELY
CHASTEN
CHASTENED
CHASTENER
CHASTENERS
CHASTENESS
CHASTENESSES
CHASTENING
CHASTENINGLY
CHASTENMENT
CHASTENMENTS
CHASTENS
CHASTER
CHASTEST
CHASTISABLE
CHASTISE
CHASTISED
CHASTISEMENT
CHASTISEMENTS
CHASTISER
CHASTISERS
CHASTISES
CHASTISING
CHASTITIES
CHASTITY
CHASUBLE
CHASUBLES
CHAT
CHATBOT
CHATBOTS
CHATCHKA
CHATCHKAS
CHATCHKE
CHATCHKES
CHATEAU
CHATEAUBRIAND
CHATEAUBRIANDS
CHATEAUS

CHATEAUX
CHATELAIN
CHATELAINE
CHATELAINES
CHATELAINS
CHATLINE
CHATLINES
CHATON
CHATONS
CHATOYANCE
CHATOYANCES
CHATOYANCIES
CHATOYANCY
CHATOYANT
CHATOYANTS
CHATROOM
CHATROOMS
CHATS
CHATTA
CHATTAS
CHATTED
CHATTEL
CHATTELS
CHATTER
CHATTERATI
CHATTERATO
CHATTERBOX
CHATTERBOXES
CHATTERED
CHATTERER
CHATTERERS
CHATTERING
CHATTERINGS
CHATTERS
CHATTERY
CHATTI
CHATTIER
CHATTIES
CHATTIEST
CHATTILY
CHATTINESS
CHATTINESSES
CHATTING
CHATTIS
CHATTY
CHAUDFROID
CHAUDFROIDS
CHAUFE
CHAUFED
CHAUFER
CHAUFERS
CHAUFES
CHAUFF
CHAUFFED
CHAUFFER
CHAUFFERS

CHAUFFEUR
CHAUFFEURED
CHAUFFEURING
CHAUFFEURS
CHAUFFEUSE
CHAUFFEUSED
CHAUFFEUSES
CHAUFFEUSING
CHAUFFING
CHAUFFS
CHAUFING
CHAULMOOGRA
CHAULMOOGRAS
CHAULMUGRA
CHAULMUGRAS
CHAUMER
CHAUMERS
CHAUNCE
CHAUNCED
CHAUNCES
CHAUNCING
CHAUNGE
CHAUNGED
CHAUNGES
CHAUNGING
CHAUNT
CHAUNTED
CHAUNTER
CHAUNTERS
CHAUNTING
CHAUNTRESS
CHAUNTRESSES
CHAUNTRIES
CHAUNTRY
CHAUNTS
CHAUSSES
CHAUSSURE
CHAUSSURES
CHAUTAUQUA
CHAUTAUQUAS
CHAUVIN
CHAUVINISM
CHAUVINISMS
CHAUVINIST
CHAUVINISTIC
CHAUVINISTS
CHAUVINS
CHAVE
CHAVENDER
CHAVENDERS
CHAW
CHAWBACON
CHAWBACONS
CHAWDRON
CHAWDRONS
CHAWED

CHAWER
CHAWERS
CHAWING
CHAWK
CHAWKS
CHAWS
CHAY
CHAYA
CHAYAS
CHAYOTE
CHAYOTES
CHAYROOT
CHAYROOTS
CHAYS
CHAZAN
CHAZANIM
CHAZANS
CHAZZAN
CHAZZANIM
CHAZZANS
CHAZZEN
CHAZZENIM
CHAZZENS
CHE
CHEAP
CHEAPEN
CHEAPENED
CHEAPENER
CHEAPENERS
CHEAPENING
CHEAPENS
CHEAPER
CHEAPEST
CHEAPIE
CHEAPIES
CHEAPISH
CHEAPISHLY
CHEAPJACK
CHEAPJACKS
CHEAPLY
CHEAPNESS
CHEAPNESSES
CHEAPO
CHEAPOS
CHEAPS
CHEAPSKATE
CHEAPSKATES
CHEAPY
CHEAT
CHEATABILITY
CHEATABLE
CHEATED
CHEATER
CHEATERIES
CHEATERS
CHEATERY

CHEATING
CHEATINGLY
CHEATINGS
CHEATS
CHEBEC
CHEBECS
CHECHAKO
CHECHAKOES
CHECHAKOS
CHECHAQUAS
CHECHAQUO
CHECHAQUOS
CHECHIA
CHECHIAS
CHECK
CHECKABLE
CHECKBOOK
CHECKBOOKS
CHECKCLERKS
CHECKED
CHECKER
CHECKERBERRIES
CHECKERBERRY
CHECKERBLOOM
CHECKERBLOOMS
CHECKERBOARD
CHECKERBOARDS
CHECKERED
CHECKERING
CHECKERS
CHECKING
CHECKLATON
CHECKLATONS
CHECKLESS
CHECKLIST
CHECKLISTS
CHECKMARK
CHECKMARKED
CHECKMARKING
CHECKMARKS
CHECKMATE
CHECKMATED
CHECKMATES
CHECKMATING
CHECKOFF
CHECKOFFS
CHECKOUT
CHECKOUTS
CHECKPOINT
CHECKPOINTS
CHECKRAIL
CHECKRAILS
CHECKREIN
CHECKREINS
CHECKROOM
CHECKROOMS

CHECKROW
CHECKROWED
CHECKROWING
CHECKROWS
CHECKS
CHECKSUM
CHECKSUMS
CHECKUP
CHECKUPS
CHECKWEIGHER
CHECKWEIGHERS
CHECKY
CHEDDAR
CHEDDARS
CHEDDITE
CHEDDITES
CHEDER
CHEDERS
CHEDITE
CHEDITES
CHEECHAKO
CHEECHAKOES
CHEECHAKOS
CHEECHALKO
CHEECHALKOES
CHEECHALKOS
CHEEK
CHEEKBONE
CHEEKBONES
CHEEKED
CHEEKFUL
CHEEKFULS
CHEEKIER
CHEEKIEST
CHEEKILY
CHEEKINESS
CHEEKINESSES
CHEEKING
CHEEKLESS
CHEEKLESSNESS
CHEEKPIECE
CHEEKPIECES
CHEEKPOUCH
CHEEKPOUCHES
CHEEKS
CHEEKTEETH
CHEEKTOOTH
CHEEKY
CHEEP
CHEEPED
CHEEPER
CHEEPERS
CHEEPING
CHEEPS
CHEER
CHEERED

CHEERER
CHEERERS
CHEERFUL
CHEERFULLER
CHEERFULLEST
CHEERFULLY
CHEERFULNESS
CHEERFULNESSES
CHEERIER
CHEERIEST
CHEERILY
CHEERINESS
CHEERINESSES
CHEERING
CHEERINGLY
CHEERIO
CHEERIOS
CHEERISHNESS
CHEERISHNESSES
CHEERLEAD
CHEERLEADER
CHEERLEADERS
CHEERLEADING
CHEERLEADS
CHEERLED
CHEERLESS
CHEERLESSLY
CHEERLESSNESS
CHEERLESSNESSES
CHEERLY
CHEERO
CHEEROS
CHEERS
CHEERY
CHEESE
CHEESEBOARD
CHEESEBOARDS
CHEESEBURGER
CHEESEBURGERS
CHEESECAKE
CHEESECAKES
CHEESECLOTH
CHEESECLOTHS
CHEESECUTTER
CHEESECUTTERS
CHEESED
CHEESEHOPPERS
CHEESEMITE
CHEESEMITES
CHEESEMONGER
CHEESEMONGERS
CHEESEPARER
CHEESEPARERS
CHEESEPARING
CHEESEPARINGS
CHEESEPRESS

CHEESEPRESSES
CHEESES
CHEESETASTER
CHEESETASTERS
CHEESEVAT
CHEESEVATS
CHEESEWIRE
CHEESEWIRES
CHEESEWOOD
CHEESEWOODS
CHEESEWRING
CHEESEWRINGS
CHEESIER
CHEESIEST
CHEESILY
CHEESINESS
CHEESINESSES
CHEESING
CHEESY
CHEETAH
CHEETAHS
CHEEWINK
CHEEWINKS
CHEF
CHEFDOM
CHEFDOMS
CHEFFED
CHEFFING
CHEFS
CHEGOE
CHEGOES
CHEILITIS
CHEILITISES
CHEKA
CHEKAS
CHEKIST
CHEKISTS
CHELA
CHELAE
CHELAS
CHELASHIP
CHELASHIPS
CHELATABLE
CHELATE
CHELATED
CHELATES
CHELATING
CHELATION
CHELATIONS
CHELATOR
CHELATORS
CHELICERA
CHELICERAE
CHELICERAL
CHELICERATE
CHELICERATES

CHELIFEROUS
CHELIFORM
CHELIPED
CHELIPEDS
CHELLUP
CHELLUPS
CHELOID
CHELOIDAL
CHELOIDS
CHELONE
CHELONES
CHELONIAN
CHELONIANS
CHELP
CHELPED
CHELPING
CHELPS
CHELUVIATION
CHELUVIATIONS
CHEMAUTOTROPH
CHEMAUTOTROPHIC
CHEMAUTOTROPHS
CHEMIATRIC
CHEMIC
CHEMICAL
CHEMICALLY
CHEMICALS
CHEMICKED
CHEMICKING
CHEMICS
CHEMIOSMOSIS
CHEMIOSMOTIC
CHEMISE
CHEMISES
CHEMISETTE
CHEMISETTES
CHEMISM
CHEMISMS
CHEMISORB
CHEMISORBED
CHEMISORBING
CHEMISORBS
CHEMISORPTION
CHEMISORPTIONS
CHEMIST
CHEMISTRIES
CHEMISTRY
CHEMISTS
CHEMITYPE
CHEMITYPES
CHEMITYPIES
CHEMITYPY
CHEMMIES
CHEMMY
CHEMO
CHEMOATTRACTANT

CHEMOAUTOTROPH
CHEMOAUTOTROPHS
CHEMOAUTOTROPHY
CHEMOAUTROPH
CHEMOAUTROPHS
CHEMOCEPTOR
CHEMOCEPTORS
CHEMOKINESIS
CHEMOKINETIC
CHEMOLITHOTROPH
CHEMONASTIES
CHEMONASTY
CHEMOPSYCHIATRY
CHEMORECEPTION
CHEMORECEPTIONS
CHEMORECEPTIVE
CHEMORECEPTOR
CHEMORECEPTORS
CHEMOS
CHEMOSMOSIS
CHEMOSMOTIC
CHEMOSORB
CHEMOSORBED
CHEMOSORBING
CHEMOSORBS
CHEMOSPHERE
CHEMOSPHERES
CHEMOSPHERIC
CHEMOSTAT
CHEMOSTATS
CHEMOSURGERIES
CHEMOSURGERY
CHEMOSURGICAL
CHEMOSYNTHESES
CHEMOSYNTHESIS
CHEMOSYNTHETIC
CHEMOTACTIC
CHEMOTACTICALLY
CHEMOTAXES
CHEMOTAXIS
CHEMOTAXONOMIC
CHEMOTAXONOMIES
CHEMOTAXONOMIST
CHEMOTAXONOMY
CHEMOTHERAPIES
CHEMOTHERAPIST
CHEMOTHERAPISTS
CHEMOTHERAPY
CHEMOTROPIC
CHEMOTROPICALLY
CHEMOTROPISM
CHEMOTROPISMS
CHEMPADUK
CHEMPADUKS
CHEMURGIC
CHEMURGICAL

CHEMURGIES
CHEMURGY
CHENAR
CHENARS
CHENET
CHENETS
CHENILLE
CHENILLES
CHENIX
CHENIXES
CHENOPOD
CHENOPODIACEOUS
CHENOPODS
CHEONGSAM
CHEONGSAMS
CHEQUE
CHEQUEBOOK
CHEQUEBOOKS
CHEQUER
CHEQUERBOARD
CHEQUERBOARDS
CHEQUERED
CHEQUERING
CHEQUERS
CHEQUERWISE
CHEQUERWORK
CHEQUERWORKS
CHEQUES
CHEQUY
CHER
CHERALITE
CHERALITES
CHERE
CHERIMOYA
CHERIMOYAS
CHERIMOYER
CHERIMOYERS
CHERISH
CHERISHABLE
CHERISHED
CHERISHER
CHERISHERS
CHERISHES
CHERISHING
CHERISHINGLY
CHERISHMENT
CHERISHMENTS
CHERNOZEM
CHERNOZEMIC
CHERNOZEMS
CHEROOT
CHEROOTS
CHERRIED
CHERRIER
CHERRIES
CHERRIEST

CHERRY
CHERRYING
CHERRYLIKE
CHERRYSTONE
CHERRYSTONES
CHERSONESE
CHERSONESES
CHERT
CHERTIER
CHERTIEST
CHERTS
CHERTY
CHERUB
CHERUBIC
CHERUBICAL
CHERUBICALLY
CHERUBIM
CHERUBIMIC
CHERUBIMS
CHERUBIN
CHERUBINS
CHERUBLIKE
CHERUBS
CHERUP
CHERUPED
CHERUPING
CHERUPS
CHERVIL
CHERVILS
CHERVONETS
CHESIL
CHESILS
CHESNUT
CHESNUTS
CHESS
CHESSBOARD
CHESSBOARDS
CHESSEL
CHESSELS
CHESSES
CHESSMAN
CHESSMEN
CHESSPIECE
CHESSPIECES
CHESSYLITE
CHESSYLITES
CHEST
CHESTED
CHESTERFIELD
CHESTERFIELDS
CHESTFUL
CHESTFULS
CHESTIER
CHESTIEST
CHESTINESS
CHESTING

CHESTNUT	CHEW	CHIBOUQUE	CHICKWEEDS
CHESTNUTS	CHEWABLE	CHIBOUQUES	CHICLE
CHESTS	CHEWED	CHIC	CHICLES
CHESTY	CHEWER	CHICA	CHICLY
CHETAH	CHEWERS	CHICALOTE	CHICNESS
CHETAHS	CHEWET	CHICALOTES	CHICNESSES
CHETH	CHEWETS	CHICANA	CHICO
CHETHS	CHEWIE	CHICANAS	CHICON
CHETNIK	CHEWIER	CHICANE	CHICONS
CHETNIKS	CHEWIES	CHICANED	CHICORIES
CHETRUM	CHEWIEST	CHICANER	CHICORY
CHETRUMS	CHEWING	CHICANERIES	CHICOS
CHEVAL	CHEWINK	CHICANERS	CHICS
CHEVALET	CHEWINKS	CHICANERY	CHID
CHEVALETS	CHEWS	CHICANES	CHIDDEN
CHEVALIER	CHEWY	CHICANING	CHIDE
CHEVALIERS	CHEZ	CHICANINGS	CHIDED
CHEVALS	CHI	CHICANO	CHIDER
CHEVELURE	CHIA	CHICANOS	CHIDERS
CHEVELURES	CHIACK	CHICAS	CHIDES
CHEVEN	CHIACKED	CHICCORIES	CHIDING
CHEVENS	CHIACKING	CHICCORY	CHIDINGLY
CHEVEREL	CHIACKINGS	CHICER	CHIDINGS
CHEVERELS	CHIACKS	CHICEST	CHIDLINGS
CHEVERIL	CHIANTI	CHICH	CHIEF
CHEVERILS	CHIANTIS	CHICHA	CHIEFDOM
CHEVERON	CHIAO	CHICHAS	CHIEFDOMS
CHEVERONS	CHIAREZZA	CHICHES	CHIEFER
CHEVERYE	CHIAREZZE	CHICHI	CHIEFERIES
CHEVERYES	CHIAROSCURISM	CHICHIS	CHIEFERY
CHEVESAILE	CHIAROSCURIST	CHICK	CHIEFESS
CHEVESAILES	CHIAROSCURISTS	CHICKABIDDIES	CHIEFESSES
CHEVET	CHIAROSCURO	CHICKABIDDY	CHIEFEST
CHEVETS	CHIAROSCUROS	CHICKADEE	CHIEFLESS
CHEVIED	CHIAS	CHICKADEES	CHIEFLING
CHEVIES	CHIASM	CHICKAREE	CHIEFLINGS
CHEVILLE	CHIASMA	CHICKAREES	CHIEFLY
CHEVILLES	CHIASMAL	CHICKEE	CHIEFRIES
CHEVIN	CHIASMAS	CHICKEES	CHIEFRY
CHEVINS	CHIASMATA	CHICKEN	CHIEFS
CHEVIOT	CHIASMATIC	CHICKENED	CHIEFSHIP
CHEVIOTS	CHIASMI	CHICKENHEARTED	CHIEFSHIPS
CHEVISANCE	CHIASMIC	CHICKENING	CHIEFTAIN
CHEVISANCES	CHIASMS	CHICKENPOX	CHIEFTAINCIES
CHEVRE	CHIASMUS	CHICKENPOXES	CHIEFTAINCY
CHEVRES	CHIASTIC	CHICKENS	CHIEFTAINESS
CHEVRETTE	CHIASTOLITE	CHICKENSHIT	CHIEFTAINESSES
CHEVRETTES	CHIASTOLITES	CHICKENSHITS	CHIEFTAINRIES
CHEVRON	CHIAUS	CHICKLING	CHIEFTAINRY
CHEVRONED	CHIAUSED	CHICKLINGS	CHIEFTAINS
CHEVRONS	CHIAUSES	CHICKORIES	CHIEFTAINSHIP
CHEVRONY	CHIAUSING	CHICKORY	CHIEFTAINSHIPS
CHEVROTAIN	CHIBOL	CHICKPEA	CHIEL
CHEVROTAINS	CHIBOLS	CHICKPEAS	CHIELD
CHEVY	CHIBOUK	CHICKS	CHIELDS
CHEVYING	CHIBOUKS	CHICKWEED	CHIELS

CHIFFCHAFF
CHIFFCHAFFS
CHIFFON
CHIFFONADE
CHIFFONADES
CHIFFONIER
CHIFFONIERS
CHIFFONNIER
CHIFFONNIERS
CHIFFONS
CHIFFONY
CHIFFOROBE
CHIFFOROBES
CHIGETAI
CHIGETAIS
CHIGGER
CHIGGERS
CHIGNON
CHIGNONED
CHIGNONS
CHIGOE
CHIGOES
CHIGRE
CHIGRES
CHIHUAHUA
CHIHUAHUAS
CHIK
CHIKARA
CHIKARAS
CHIKHOR
CHIKHORS
CHIKOR
CHIKORS
CHIKS
CHILBLAIN
CHILBLAINED
CHILBLAINS
CHILD
CHILDBEARING
CHILDBEARINGS
CHILDBED
CHILDBEDS
CHILDBIRTH
CHILDBIRTHS
CHILDCARE
CHILDCROWING
CHILDCROWINGS
CHILDE
CHILDED
CHILDER
CHILDERMAS
CHILDERMASES
CHILDES
CHILDHOOD
CHILDHOODS
CHILDING

CHILDISH
CHILDISHLY
CHILDISHNESS
CHILDISHNESSES
CHILDLESS
CHILDLESSNESS
CHILDLESSNESSES
CHILDLIER
CHILDLIEST
CHILDLIKE
CHILDLIKENESS
CHILDLIKENESSES
CHILDLY
CHILDMINDER
CHILDMINDERS
CHILDNESS
CHILDNESSES
CHILDPROOF
CHILDREN
CHILDS
CHILE
CHILES
CHILI
CHILIAD
CHILIADAL
CHILIADIC
CHILIADS
CHILIAGON
CHILIAGONS
CHILIAHEDRON
CHILIAHEDRONS
CHILIARCH
CHILIARCHIES
CHILIARCHS
CHILIARCHY
CHILIASM
CHILIASMS
CHILIAST
CHILIASTIC
CHILIASTS
CHILIDOG
CHILIDOGS
CHILIES
CHILIOI
CHILIOIS
CHILIS
CHILL
CHILLADA
CHILLADAS
CHILLED
CHILLER
CHILLERS
CHILLEST
CHILLI
CHILLIER
CHILLIES

CHILLIEST
CHILLILY
CHILLINESS
CHILLINESSES
CHILLING
CHILLINGLY
CHILLINGS
CHILLIS
CHILLNESS
CHILLNESSES
CHILLS
CHILLUM
CHILLUMS
CHILLY
CHILOPOD
CHILOPODAN
CHILOPODANS
CHILOPODOUS
CHILOPODS
CHIMAERA
CHIMAERAS
CHIMAERIC
CHIMAERISM
CHIMAERISMS
CHIMAR
CHIMARS
CHIMB
CHIMBLEY
CHIMBLEYS
CHIMBLIES
CHIMBLY
CHIMBS
CHIME
CHIMED
CHIMER
CHIMERA
CHIMERAS
CHIMERE
CHIMERES
CHIMERIC
CHIMERICAL
CHIMERICALLY
CHIMERICALNESS
CHIMERID
CHIMERIDS
CHIMERISM
CHIMERISMS
CHIMERS
CHIMES
CHIMICHANGA
CHIMICHANGAS
CHIMING
CHIMLA
CHIMLAS
CHIMLEY
CHIMLEYS

CHIMNEY
CHIMNEYBOARD
CHIMNEYBOARDS
CHIMNEYBREAST
CHIMNEYBREASTS
CHIMNEYED
CHIMNEYING
CHIMNEYLIKE
CHIMNEYPIECE
CHIMNEYPIECES
CHIMNEYPOT
CHIMNEYPOTS
CHIMNEYS
CHIMO
CHIMP
CHIMPANZEE
CHIMPANZEES
CHIMPS
CHIN
CHINA
CHINABERRIES
CHINABERRY
CHINACHINA
CHINACHINAS
CHINAMPA
CHINAMPAS
CHINAR
CHINAROOT
CHINAROOTS
CHINARS
CHINAS
CHINAWARE
CHINAWARES
CHINBONE
CHINBONES
CHINCAPIN
CHINCAPINS
CHINCH
CHINCHERINCHEE
CHINCHERINCHEES
CHINCHES
CHINCHIER
CHINCHIEST
CHINCHILLA
CHINCHILLAS
CHINCHY
CHINCOUGH
CHINCOUGHS
CHINDIT
CHINDITS
CHINE
CHINED
CHINES
CHINESE
CHINING
CHINK

CHINKAPIN
CHINKAPINS
CHINKARA
CHINKARAS
CHINKED
CHINKERINCHEE
CHINKERINCHEES
CHINKIE
CHINKIER
CHINKIES
CHINKIEST
CHINKING
CHINKS
CHINKY
CHINLESS
CHINNED
CHINNING
CHINO
CHINOISERIE
CHINOISERIES
CHINONE
CHINONES
CHINOOK
CHINOOKS
CHINOS
CHINOVNIK
CHINOVNIKS
CHINQUAPIN
CHINQUAPINS
CHINS
CHINSTRAP
CHINSTRAPS
CHINTS
CHINTSES
CHINTZ
CHINTZES
CHINTZIER
CHINTZIEST
CHINTZY
CHINWAG
CHINWAGGED
CHINWAGGING
CHINWAGS
CHIONODOXA
CHIONODOXAS
CHIP
CHIPBOARD
CHIPBOARDS
CHIPMUCK
CHIPMUCKS
CHIPMUNK
CHIPMUNKS
CHIPOCHIA
CHIPOCHIAS
CHIPOLATA
CHIPOLATAS

CHIPPED
CHIPPER
CHIPPERED
CHIPPERING
CHIPPERS
CHIPPIE
CHIPPIER
CHIPPIES
CHIPPIEST
CHIPPING
CHIPPINGS
CHIPPY
CHIPS
CHIPSET
CHIPSETS
CHIQUICHIQUI
CHIQUICHIQUIS
CHIRAGRA
CHIRAGRAS
CHIRAGRIC
CHIRAGRICAL
CHIRAL
CHIRALITIES
CHIRALITY
CHIRIMOYA
CHIRIMOYAS
CHIRK
CHIRKED
CHIRKER
CHIRKEST
CHIRKING
CHIRKS
CHIRL
CHIRLED
CHIRLING
CHIRLS
CHIRM
CHIRMED
CHIRMING
CHIRMS
CHIRO
CHIROGNOMIES
CHIROGNOMY
CHIROGRAPH
CHIROGRAPHER
CHIROGRAPHERS
CHIROGRAPHIC
CHIROGRAPHICAL
CHIROGRAPHIES
CHIROGRAPHIST
CHIROGRAPHISTS
CHIROGRAPHS
CHIROGRAPHY
CHIROLOGIES
CHIROLOGIST
CHIROLOGISTS

CHIROLOGY
CHIROMANCER
CHIROMANCERS
CHIROMANCIES
CHIROMANCY
CHIROMANTIC
CHIROMANTICAL
CHIRONOMERS
CHIRONOMIC
CHIRONOMID
CHIRONOMIDS
CHIRONOMIES
CHIRONOMY
CHIROPODIAL
CHIROPODIES
CHIROPODIST
CHIROPODISTS
CHIROPODY
CHIROPRACTIC
CHIROPRACTICS
CHIROPRACTOR
CHIROPRACTORS
CHIROPTER
CHIROPTERAN
CHIROPTERANS
CHIROPTEROUS
CHIROPTERS
CHIROS
CHIRP
CHIRPED
CHIRPER
CHIRPERS
CHIRPIER
CHIRPIEST
CHIRPILY
CHIRPINESS
CHIRPINESSES
CHIRPING
CHIRPS
CHIRPY
CHIRR
CHIRRE
CHIRRED
CHIRRES
CHIRRING
CHIRRS
CHIRRUP
CHIRRUPED
CHIRRUPER
CHIRRUPERS
CHIRRUPING
CHIRRUPPED
CHIRRUPPING
CHIRRUPS
CHIRRUPY
CHIRT

CHIRTED
CHIRTING
CHIRTS
CHIRU
CHIRURGEON
CHIRURGEONLY
CHIRURGEONS
CHIRURGERIES
CHIRURGERY
CHIRURGICAL
CHIRUS
CHIS
CHISEL
CHISELED
CHISELER
CHISELERS
CHISELING
CHISELLED
CHISELLER
CHISELLERS
CHISELLING
CHISELLINGS
CHISELS
CHIT
CHITAL
CHITALS
CHITARRONE
CHITARRONI
CHITCHAT
CHITCHATS
CHITCHATTED
CHITCHATTING
CHITIN
CHITINOID
CHITINOUS
CHITINS
CHITLIN
CHITLING
CHITLINGS
CHITLINS
CHITON
CHITONS
CHITOSAN
CHITOSANS
CHITS
CHITTAGONG
CHITTAGONGS
CHITTED
CHITTER
CHITTERED
CHITTERING
CHITTERINGS
CHITTERLING
CHITTERLINGS
CHITTERS
CHITTIER

CHITTIES
CHITTIEST
CHITTING
CHITTY
CHIV
CHIVALRIC
CHIVALRIES
CHIVALROUS
CHIVALROUSLY
CHIVALROUSNESS
CHIVALRY
CHIVAREE
CHIVAREED
CHIVAREEING
CHIVAREES
CHIVARI
CHIVARIED
CHIVARIES
CHIVARIING
CHIVE
CHIVED
CHIVES
CHIVIED
CHIVIES
CHIVING
CHIVS
CHIVVED
CHIVVIED
CHIVVIES
CHIVVING
CHIVVY
CHIVVYING
CHIVY
CHIVYING
CHIYOGAMI
CHIYOGAMIS
CHIZ
CHIZZ
CHIZZED
CHIZZES
CHIZZING
CHLAMYDATE
CHLAMYDEOUS
CHLAMYDES
CHLAMYDIA
CHLAMYDIAE
CHLAMYDIAL
CHLAMYDIAS
CHLAMYDOMONAS
CHLAMYDOSPORE
CHLAMYDOSPORES
CHLAMYS
CHLAMYSES
CHLOANTHITE
CHLOANTHITES
CHLOASMA

CHLOASMATA
CHLORACETIC
CHLORACNE
CHLORACNES
CHLORAL
CHLORALISM
CHLORALISMS
CHLORALOSE
CHLORALOSED
CHLORALOSES
CHLORALS
CHLORAMBUCIL
CHLORAMBUCILS
CHLORAMINE
CHLORAMINES
CHLORAMPHENICOL
CHLORARGYRITE
CHLORARGYRITES
CHLORATE
CHLORATES
CHLORDAN
CHLORDANE
CHLORDANES
CHLORDANS
CHLORELLA
CHLORELLAS
CHLORENCHYMA
CHLORENCHYMAS
CHLORHEXIDINE
CHLORIC
CHLORID
CHLORIDATE
CHLORIDATED
CHLORIDATES
CHLORIDATING
CHLORIDE
CHLORIDES
CHLORIDIC
CHLORIDISE
CHLORIDISED
CHLORIDISES
CHLORIDISING
CHLORIDIZE
CHLORIDIZED
CHLORIDIZES
CHLORIDIZING
CHLORIDS
CHLORIMETER
CHLORIMETERS
CHLORIMETRIC
CHLORIMETRIES
CHLORIMETRY
CHLORIN
CHLORINATE
CHLORINATED
CHLORINATES

CHLORINATING
CHLORINATION
CHLORINATIONS
CHLORINATOR
CHLORINATORS
CHLORINE
CHLORINES
CHLORINISE
CHLORINISED
CHLORINISES
CHLORINISING
CHLORINITIES
CHLORINITY
CHLORINIZE
CHLORINIZED
CHLORINIZES
CHLORINIZING
CHLORINS
CHLORITE
CHLORITES
CHLORITIC
CHLORITISATION
CHLORITISATIONS
CHLORITIZATION
CHLORITIZATIONS
CHLOROACETIC
CHLOROARGYRITE
CHLOROBENZENE
CHLOROBENZENES
CHLOROBROMIDE
CHLOROBROMIDES
CHLOROCRUORIN
CHLOROCRUORINS
CHLORODYNE
CHLORODYNES
CHLOROFORM
CHLOROFORMED
CHLOROFORMER
CHLOROFORMERS
CHLOROFORMING
CHLOROFORMIST
CHLOROFORMISTS
CHLOROFORMS
CHLOROHYDRIN
CHLOROHYDRINS
CHLOROMETER
CHLOROMETERS
CHLOROMETHANE
CHLOROMETRIC
CHLOROMETRIES
CHLOROMETRY
CHLOROPHYL
CHLOROPHYLL
CHLOROPHYLLOID
CHLOROPHYLLOUS
CHLOROPHYLLS

CHLOROPHYLS
CHLOROPHYTUM
CHLOROPHYTUMS
CHLOROPICRIN
CHLOROPICRINS
CHLOROPLAST
CHLOROPLASTAL
CHLOROPLASTIC
CHLOROPLASTS
CHLOROPRENE
CHLOROPRENES
CHLOROQUIN
CHLOROQUINE
CHLOROQUINES
CHLOROQUINS
CHLOROSES
CHLOROSIS
CHLOROTHIAZIDE
CHLOROTHIAZIDES
CHLOROTIC
CHLOROUS
CHLORPICRIN
CHLORPROMAZINE
CHLORPROMAZINES
CHLORPROPAMIDE
CHLORPROPAMIDES
CHLORTHALIDONE
CHOANA
CHOANAE
CHOANOCYTE
CHOANOCYTES
CHOBDAR
CHOBDARS
CHOC
CHOCAHOLIC
CHOCAHOLICS
CHOCCIER
CHOCCIES
CHOCCIEST
CHOCCY
CHOCHO
CHOCHOS
CHOCK
CHOCKABLOCK
CHOCKED
CHOCKER
CHOCKFUL
CHOCKING
CHOCKO
CHOCKOS
CHOCKS
CHOCKSTONE
CHOCKSTONES
CHOCO
CHOCOHOLIC
CHOCOHOLICS

CHOCOLATE
CHOCOLATES
CHOCOLATEY
CHOCOLATIER
CHOCOLATIERS
CHOCOLATIEST
CHOCOLATY
CHOCOS
CHOCS
CHOCTAW
CHOCTAWS
CHODE
CHOENIX
CHOENIXES
CHOG
CHOICE
CHOICEFUL
CHOICELY
CHOICENESS
CHOICENESSES
CHOICER
CHOICES
CHOICEST
CHOIR
CHOIRBOY
CHOIRBOYS
CHOIRED
CHOIRGIRL
CHOIRGIRLS
CHOIRING
CHOIRLIKE
CHOIRMAN
CHOIRMASTER
CHOIRMASTERS
CHOIRMEN
CHOIRS
CHOIRSCREEN
CHOIRSCREENS
CHOIRSTALLS
CHOKE
CHOKEABILITY
CHOKEABLE
CHOKEBERRIES
CHOKEBERRY
CHOKEBORE
CHOKEBORES
CHOKECHERRIES
CHOKECHERRY
CHOKECOIL
CHOKECOILS
CHOKED
CHOKEDAMP
CHOKEDAMPS
CHOKER
CHOKERS
CHOKES

CHOKEY
CHOKEYS
CHOKIDAR
CHOKIDARS
CHOKIER
CHOKIES
CHOKIEST
CHOKING
CHOKINGLY
CHOKO
CHOKOS
CHOKRA
CHOKRAS
CHOKRI
CHOKRIS
CHOKY
CHOLAEMIA
CHOLAEMIAS
CHOLAEMIC
CHOLAGOGIC
CHOLAGOGUE
CHOLAGOGUES
CHOLANGIOGRAM
CHOLANGIOGRAMS
CHOLANGIOGRAPHY
CHOLATE
CHOLATES
CHOLECALCIFEROL
CHOLECYST
CHOLECYSTECTOMY
CHOLECYSTITIS
CHOLECYSTITISES
CHOLECYSTOKININ
CHOLECYSTOSTOMY
CHOLECYSTOTOMY
CHOLECYSTS
CHOLELITH
CHOLELITHIASES
CHOLELITHIASIS
CHOLELITHS
CHOLEMIA
CHOLEMIAS
CHOLENT
CHOLENTS
CHOLER
CHOLERA
CHOLERAIC
CHOLERAS
CHOLERIC
CHOLERICALLY
CHOLERICLY
CHOLEROID
CHOLERS
CHOLESTASES
CHOLESTASIS
CHOLESTATIC

CHOLESTERIC
CHOLESTERIN
CHOLESTERINS
CHOLESTEROL
CHOLESTEROLEMIA
CHOLESTEROLS
CHOLESTYRAMINE
CHOLESTYRAMINES
CHOLI
CHOLIAMB
CHOLIAMBIC
CHOLIAMBICS
CHOLIAMBS
CHOLIC
CHOLINE
CHOLINERGIC
CHOLINERGICALLY
CHOLINES
CHOLINESTERASE
CHOLINESTERASES
CHOLIS
CHOLLA
CHOLLAS
CHOLLERS
CHOLO
CHOLOS
CHOLTRIES
CHOLTRY
CHOMA
CHOMETZ
CHOMOPHYTE
CHOMOPHYTES
CHOMP
CHOMPED
CHOMPER
CHOMPERS
CHOMPING
CHOMPS
CHON
CHONDRAL
CHONDRE
CHONDRES
CHONDRI
CHONDRICHTHYAN
CHONDRICHTHYANS
CHONDRIFICATION
CHONDRIFIED
CHONDRIFIES
CHONDRIFY
CHONDRIFYING
CHONDRIN
CHONDRINS
CHONDRIOSOMAL
CHONDRIOSOME
CHONDRIOSOMES
CHONDRITE

CHONDRITES
CHONDRITIC
CHONDRITIS
CHONDRITISES
CHONDROBLAST
CHONDROBLASTS
CHONDROCRANIA
CHONDROCRANIUM
CHONDROCRANIUMS
CHONDROGENESES
CHONDROGENESIS
CHONDROID
CHONDROITIN
CHONDROITINS
CHONDROMA
CHONDROMAS
CHONDROMATA
CHONDROMATOSES
CHONDROMATOSIS
CHONDROMATOUS
CHONDROPHORINE
CHONDROPHORINES
CHONDROSKELETON
CHONDROSTIANS
CHONDRULE
CHONDRULES
CHONDRUS
CHONS
CHOOF
CHOOFED
CHOOFING
CHOOFS
CHOOK
CHOOKED
CHOOKIE
CHOOKIES
CHOOKING
CHOOKS
CHOOM
CHOOMS
CHOOSE
CHOOSER
CHOOSERS
CHOOSES
CHOOSEY
CHOOSIER
CHOOSIEST
CHOOSING
CHOOSY
CHOP
CHOPFALLEN
CHOPHOUSE
CHOPHOUSES
CHOPIN
CHOPINE
CHOPINES

CHOPINS
CHOPLOGIC
CHOPLOGICS
CHOPPED
CHOPPER
CHOPPERED
CHOPPERING
CHOPPERS
CHOPPIER
CHOPPIEST
CHOPPILY
CHOPPINESS
CHOPPINESSES
CHOPPING
CHOPPINGS
CHOPPY
CHOPS
CHOPSTICK
CHOPSTICKS
CHORAGI
CHORAGIC
CHORAGUS
CHORAGUSES
CHORAL
CHORALE
CHORALES
CHORALIST
CHORALISTS
CHORALLY
CHORALS
CHORD
CHORDA
CHORDAE
CHORDAL
CHORDAMESODERM
CHORDAMESODERMS
CHORDATE
CHORDATES
CHORDED
CHORDEE
CHORDEES
CHORDING
CHORDINGS
CHORDOPHONE
CHORDOPHONES
CHORDOPHONIC
CHORDOTOMIES
CHORDOTOMY
CHORDS
CHORDWISE
CHORE
CHOREA
CHOREAL
CHOREAS
CHORED
CHOREE

CHOREES
CHOREGI
CHOREGIC
CHOREGRAPH
CHOREGRAPHED
CHOREGRAPHER
CHOREGRAPHERS
CHOREGRAPHIC
CHOREGRAPHIES
CHOREGRAPHING
CHOREGRAPHS
CHOREGRAPHY
CHOREGUS
CHOREGUSES
CHOREIC
CHOREIFORM
CHOREMAN
CHOREMEN
CHOREODRAMA
CHOREODRAMAS
CHOREOGRAPH
CHOREOGRAPHED
CHOREOGRAPHER
CHOREOGRAPHERS
CHOREOGRAPHIC
CHOREOGRAPHIES
CHOREOGRAPHING
CHOREOGRAPHS
CHOREOGRAPHY
CHOREOID
CHOREOLOGIES
CHOREOLOGIST
CHOREOLOGISTS
CHOREOLOGY
CHOREPISCOPAL
CHORES
CHOREUS
CHOREUSES
CHORIA
CHORIAL
CHORIAMB
CHORIAMBI
CHORIAMBIC
CHORIAMBICS
CHORIAMBS
CHORIAMBUS
CHORIAMBUSES
CHORIC
CHORINE
CHORINES
CHORING
CHORIOALLANTOIC
CHORIOALLANTOIS
CHORIOCARCINOMA
CHORIOID
CHORIOIDS

CHORION
CHORIONIC
CHORIONS
CHORISATION
CHORISATIONS
CHORISES
CHORISIS
CHORISM
CHORISMS
CHORIST
CHORISTER
CHORISTERS
CHORISTS
CHORIZATION
CHORIZATIONS
CHORIZO
CHORIZONT
CHORIZONTIST
CHORIZONTISTS
CHORIZONTS
CHORIZOS
CHOROGRAPHER
CHOROGRAPHERS
CHOROGRAPHIC
CHOROGRAPHICAL
CHOROGRAPHIES
CHOROGRAPHY
CHOROID
CHOROIDAL
CHOROIDITIS
CHOROIDITISES
CHOROIDS
CHOROLOGICAL
CHOROLOGIES
CHOROLOGIST
CHOROLOGISTS
CHOROLOGY
CHOROPLETH
CHOROPLETHS
CHORRIE
CHORRIES
CHORTLE
CHORTLED
CHORTLER
CHORTLERS
CHORTLES
CHORTLING
CHORUS
CHORUSED
CHORUSES
CHORUSING
CHORUSMASTER
CHORUSMASTERS
CHORUSSED
CHORUSSES
CHORUSSING

CHOSE
CHOSEN
CHOSES
CHOTA
CHOTT
CHOTTS
CHOU
CHOUCROUTE
CHOUCROUTES
CHOUGH
CHOUGHS
CHOULTRIES
CHOULTRY
CHOUNTER
CHOUNTERED
CHOUNTERING
CHOUNTERS
CHOUSE
CHOUSED
CHOUSER
CHOUSERS
CHOUSES
CHOUSH
CHOUSHES
CHOUSING
CHOUT
CHOUTS
CHOUX
CHOW
CHOWCHOW
CHOWCHOWS
CHOWDER
CHOWDERED
CHOWDERHEAD
CHOWDERHEADED
CHOWDERHEADS
CHOWDERING
CHOWDERS
CHOWED
CHOWHOUND
CHOWHOUNDS
CHOWING
CHOWK
CHOWKIDAR
CHOWKIDARS
CHOWKS
CHOWRI
CHOWRIES
CHOWRIS
CHOWRY
CHOWS
CHOWSE
CHOWSED
CHOWSES
CHOWSING
CHOWTIME

CHOWTIMES
CHREMATIST
CHREMATISTIC
CHREMATISTICS
CHREMATISTS
CHRESARD
CHRESARDS
CHRESTOMATHIC
CHRESTOMATHICAL
CHRESTOMATHIES
CHRESTOMATHY
CHRISM
CHRISMA
CHRISMAL
CHRISMALS
CHRISMATION
CHRISMATIONS
CHRISMATORIES
CHRISMATORY
CHRISMON
CHRISMONS
CHRISMS
CHRISOM
CHRISOMS
CHRISTCROSS
CHRISTCROSSES
CHRISTEN
CHRISTENED
CHRISTENER
CHRISTENERS
CHRISTENING
CHRISTENINGS
CHRISTENS
CHRISTIANIA
CHRISTIANIAS
CHRISTIANISE
CHRISTIANISED
CHRISTIANISER
CHRISTIANISERS
CHRISTIANISES
CHRISTIANISING
CHRISTIANIZE
CHRISTIANIZED
CHRISTIANIZER
CHRISTIANIZERS
CHRISTIANIZES
CHRISTIANIZING
CHRISTIANLY
CHRISTIE
CHRISTIES
CHRISTINGLE
CHRISTINGLES
CHRISTOM
CHRISTOMS
CHRISTOPHANIES
CHRISTOPHANY

CHRISTY
CHROMA
CHROMAFFIN
CHROMAKEY
CHROMAKEYS
CHROMAS
CHROMATE
CHROMATES
CHROMATIC
CHROMATICALLY
CHROMATICISM
CHROMATICISMS
CHROMATICITIES
CHROMATICITY
CHROMATICNESS
CHROMATICS
CHROMATID
CHROMATIDS
CHROMATIN
CHROMATINIC
CHROMATINS
CHROMATIST
CHROMATISTS
CHROMATOGRAM
CHROMATOGRAMS
CHROMATOGRAPH
CHROMATOGRAPHED
CHROMATOGRAPHER
CHROMATOGRAPHIC
CHROMATOGRAPHS
CHROMATOGRAPHY
CHROMATOID
CHROMATOIDS
CHROMATOLOGICAL
CHROMATOLOGIST
CHROMATOLOGISTS
CHROMATOLOGY
CHROMATOLYSES
CHROMATOLYSIS
CHROMATOLYTIC
CHROMATOPHORE
CHROMATOPHORES
CHROMATOPHORIC
CHROMATOPHOROUS
CHROMATOPSIA
CHROMATOPSIAS
CHROMATOSPHERE
CHROMATOSPHERES
CHROMATYPE
CHROMATYPES
CHROME
CHROMED
CHROMEL
CHROMELS
CHROMENE
CHROMENES

CHROMES
CHROMIC
CHROMIDE
CHROMIDES
CHROMIDIA
CHROMIDIUM
CHROMINANCE
CHROMINANCES
CHROMING
CHROMINGS
CHROMITE
CHROMITES
CHROMIUM
CHROMIUMS
CHROMIZE
CHROMIZED
CHROMIZES
CHROMIZING
CHROMO
CHROMOCENTER
CHROMOCENTERS
CHROMODYNAMICS
CHROMOGEN
CHROMOGENIC
CHROMOGENS
CHROMOGRAM
CHROMOGRAMS
CHROMOMERE
CHROMOMERES
CHROMOMERIC
CHROMONEMA
CHROMONEMAL
CHROMONEMATA
CHROMONEMATIC
CHROMONEMIC
CHROMOPHIL
CHROMOPHILIC
CHROMOPHOBE
CHROMOPHONIC
CHROMOPHORE
CHROMOPHORES
CHROMOPHORIC
CHROMOPHOROUS
CHROMOPLAST
CHROMOPLASTS
CHROMOPROTEIN
CHROMOPROTEINS
CHROMOS
CHROMOSCOPE
CHROMOSCOPES
CHROMOSOMAL
CHROMOSOMALLY
CHROMOSOME
CHROMOSOMES
CHROMOSPHERE
CHROMOSPHERES

CHROMOSPHERIC
CHROMOTHERAPIES
CHROMOTHERAPY
CHROMOTYPE
CHROMOTYPES
CHROMOUS
CHROMOXYLOGRAPH
CHROMYL
CHROMYLS
CHRONAXIE
CHRONAXIES
CHRONAXY
CHRONIC
CHRONICAL
CHRONICALLY
CHRONICITIES
CHRONICITY
CHRONICLE
CHRONICLED
CHRONICLER
CHRONICLERS
CHRONICLES
CHRONICLING
CHRONICS
CHRONOBIOLOGIC
CHRONOBIOLOGIES
CHRONOBIOLOGIST
CHRONOBIOLOGY
CHRONOGRAM
CHRONOGRAMMATIC
CHRONOGRAMS
CHRONOGRAPH
CHRONOGRAPHER
CHRONOGRAPHERS
CHRONOGRAPHIC
CHRONOGRAPHIES
CHRONOGRAPHS
CHRONOGRAPHY
CHRONOLOGER
CHRONOLOGERS
CHRONOLOGIC
CHRONOLOGICAL
CHRONOLOGICALLY
CHRONOLOGIES
CHRONOLOGISE
CHRONOLOGISED
CHRONOLOGISES
CHRONOLOGISING
CHRONOLOGIST
CHRONOLOGISTS
CHRONOLOGIZE
CHRONOLOGIZED
CHRONOLOGIZES
CHRONOLOGIZING
CHRONOLOGY
CHRONOMETER

CHRONOMETERS
CHRONOMETRIC
CHRONOMETRICAL
CHRONOMETRIES
CHRONOMETRY
CHRONON
CHRONONS
CHRONOSCOPE
CHRONOSCOPES
CHRONOSCOPIC
CHRONOTHERAPIES
CHRONOTHERAPY
CHRONOTRON
CHRONOTRONS
CHRYSALID
CHRYSALIDAL
CHRYSALIDES
CHRYSALIDS
CHRYSALIS
CHRYSALISES
CHRYSANTH
CHRYSANTHEMUM
CHRYSANTHEMUMS
CHRYSANTHS
CHRYSAROBIN
CHRYSAROBINS
CHRYSOBERYL
CHRYSOBERYLS
CHRYSOCOLLA
CHRYSOCOLLAS
CHRYSOCRACIES
CHRYSOCRACY
CHRYSOLITE
CHRYSOLITES
CHRYSOLITIC
CHRYSOLITICALLY
CHRYSOMELID
CHRYSOMELIDS
CHRYSOPHAN
CHRYSOPHANS
CHRYSOPHILITE
CHRYSOPHILITES
CHRYSOPHYTE
CHRYSOPHYTES
CHRYSOPRASE
CHRYSOPRASES
CHRYSOTILE
CHRYSOTILES
CHTHONIAN
CHTHONIC
CHUB
CHUBASCO
CHUBASCOS
CHUBBIER
CHUBBIEST
CHUBBILY

CHUBBINESS
CHUBBINESSES
CHUBBY
CHUBS
CHUCK
CHUCKAWALLA
CHUCKAWALLAS
CHUCKED
CHUCKER
CHUCKHOLE
CHUCKHOLES
CHUCKIE
CHUCKIES
CHUCKING
CHUCKLE
CHUCKLED
CHUCKLEHEAD
CHUCKLEHEADED
CHUCKLEHEADS
CHUCKLER
CHUCKLERS
CHUCKLES
CHUCKLESOME
CHUCKLING
CHUCKLINGLY
CHUCKLINGS
CHUCKS
CHUCKWALLA
CHUCKWALLAS
CHUCKY
CHUDDAH
CHUDDAHS
CHUDDAR
CHUDDARS
CHUDDER
CHUDDERS
CHUDDIES
CHUDDY
CHUFA
CHUFAS
CHUFF
CHUFFED
CHUFFER
CHUFFEST
CHUFFIE
CHUFFIER
CHUFFIEST
CHUFFINESS
CHUFFINESSES
CHUFFING
CHUFFS
CHUFFY
CHUG
CHUGALUG
CHUGALUGGED
CHUGALUGGING

CHUGALUGS
CHUGGED
CHUGGER
CHUGGERS
CHUGGING
CHUGS
CHUKAR
CHUKARS
CHUKKA
CHUKKAR
CHUKKARS
CHUKKAS
CHUKKER
CHUKKERS
CHUKOR
CHUKORS
CHUM
CHUMASH
CHUMLEY
CHUMLEYS
CHUMMAGE
CHUMMAGES
CHUMMED
CHUMMIER
CHUMMIES
CHUMMIEST
CHUMMILY
CHUMMINESS
CHUMMINESSES
CHUMMING
CHUMMY
CHUMP
CHUMPED
CHUMPING
CHUMPINGS
CHUMPS
CHUMS
CHUMSHIP
CHUMSHIPS
CHUNDER
CHUNDERED
CHUNDERING
CHUNDEROUS
CHUNDERS
CHUNK
CHUNKED
CHUNKIER
CHUNKIEST
CHUNKILY
CHUNKINESS
CHUNKING
CHUNKINGS
CHUNKS
CHUNKY
CHUNNEL
CHUNNELS

CHUNNER
CHUNNERED
CHUNNERING
CHUNNERS
CHUNTER
CHUNTERED
CHUNTERING
CHUNTERS
CHUPATI
CHUPATIS
CHUPATTI
CHUPATTIES
CHUPATTIS
CHUPATTY
CHUPPAH
CHUPPAHS
CHUPRASSIES
CHUPRASSY
CHURCH
CHURCHED
CHURCHES
CHURCHGOER
CHURCHGOERS
CHURCHGOING
CHURCHGOINGS
CHURCHIANITIES
CHURCHIANITY
CHURCHIER
CHURCHIEST
CHURCHING
CHURCHINGS
CHURCHISM
CHURCHISMS
CHURCHLESS
CHURCHLIER
CHURCHLIEST
CHURCHLINESS
CHURCHLINESSES
CHURCHLY
CHURCHMAN
CHURCHMANLY
CHURCHMANSHIP
CHURCHMANSHIPS
CHURCHMEN
CHURCHPEOPLE
CHURCHWARD
CHURCHWARDEN
CHURCHWARDENS
CHURCHWARDS
CHURCHWAY
CHURCHWAYS
CHURCHWOMAN
CHURCHWOMEN
CHURCHY
CHURCHYARD
CHURCHYARDS

CHURIDARS
CHURINGA
CHURINGAS
CHURL
CHURLISH
CHURLISHLY
CHURLISHNESS
CHURLISHNESSES
CHURLS
CHURN
CHURNED
CHURNER
CHURNERS
CHURNING
CHURNINGS
CHURNMILK
CHURNMILKS
CHURNS
CHURR
CHURRED
CHURRIGUERESCO
CHURRIGUERESQUE
CHURRING
CHURRS
CHURRUS
CHURRUSES
CHUSE
CHUSES
CHUSING
CHUT
CHUTE
CHUTED
CHUTES
CHUTING
CHUTIST
CHUTISTS
CHUTNEE
CHUTNEES
CHUTNEY
CHUTNEYS
CHUTTIE
CHUTTIES
CHUTTY
CHUTZPA
CHUTZPAH
CHUTZPAHS
CHUTZPAS
CHYACK
CHYACKED
CHYACKING
CHYACKS
CHYLACEOUS
CHYLDE
CHYLE
CHYLES
CHYLIFEROUS

CHYLIFICATION
CHYLIFICATIONS
CHYLIFIED
CHYLIFIES
CHYLIFY
CHYLIFYING
CHYLOMICRON
CHYLOMICRONS
CHYLOUS
CHYLURIA
CHYLURIAS
CHYME
CHYMES
CHYMIC
CHYMICS
CHYMIFEROUS
CHYMIFICATION
CHYMIFICATIONS
CHYMIFIED
CHYMIFIES
CHYMIFY
CHYMIFYING
CHYMIST
CHYMISTRIES
CHYMISTRY
CHYMISTS
CHYMOSIN
CHYMOSINS
CHYMOTRYPSIN
CHYMOTRYPSINS
CHYMOTRYPTIC
CHYMOUS
CHYND
CHYPRE
CHYPRES
CIABATTA
CIABATTAS
CIABATTE
CIAO
CIAOS
CIBACHROME
CIBACHROMES
CIBATION
CIBATIONS
CIBOL
CIBOLS
CIBORIA
CIBORIUM
CIBOULE
CIBOULES
CICADA
CICADAE
CICADAS
CICADELLID
CICADELLIDS
CICALA

CICALAS
CICALE
CICATRICE
CICATRICES
CICATRICHULES
CICATRICIAL
CICATRICLE
CICATRICLES
CICATRICOSE
CICATRICULA
CICATRICULAS
CICATRISANT
CICATRISANTS
CICATRISATION
CICATRISATIONS
CICATRISE
CICATRISED
CICATRISER
CICATRISERS
CICATRISES
CICATRISING
CICATRIX
CICATRIXES
CICATRIZANT
CICATRIZANTS
CICATRIZATION
CICATRIZATIONS
CICATRIZE
CICATRIZED
CICATRIZER
CICATRIZERS
CICATRIZES
CICATRIZING
CICELIES
CICELY
CICERO
CICERONE
CICERONED
CICERONEING
CICERONES
CICERONI
CICEROS
CICHLID
CICHLIDAE
CICHLIDS
CICHLOID
CICHORACEOUS
CICINNUS
CICINNUSES
CICISBEI
CICISBEISM
CICISBEISMS
CICISBEO
CICISBEOS
CICLATON
CICLATONS

CICLATOUN
CICLATOUNS
CICLOSPORIN
CICLOSPORINS
CICOREE
CICOREES
CICUTA
CICUTAS
CICUTINE
CID
CIDARIS
CIDARISES
CIDE
CIDED
CIDER
CIDERKIN
CIDERKINS
CIDERS
CIDERY
CIDES
CIDING
CIDS
CIEL
CIELED
CIELING
CIELINGS
CIELS
CIERGE
CIERGES
CIG
CIGAR
CIGARET
CIGARETS
CIGARETTE
CIGARETTES
CIGARILLO
CIGARILLOS
CIGARS
CIGGIE
CIGGIES
CIGGY
CIGS
CIGUATERA
CIGUATERAS
CILANTRO
CILANTROS
CILIA
CILIARY
CILIATE
CILIATED
CILIATES
CILIATION
CILIATIONS
CILICE
CILICES
CILICIOUS

CILIOLATE
CILIUM
CILL
CILLS
CIMAR
CIMARS
CIMBALOM
CIMBALOMS
CIMELIA
CIMETIDINE
CIMETIDINES
CIMEX
CIMICES
CIMIER
CIMIERS
CIMINITE
CIMINITES
CIMOLITE
CIMOLITES
CINCH
CINCHED
CINCHES
CINCHING
CINCHINGS
CINCHONA
CINCHONACEOUS
CINCHONAS
CINCHONIC
CINCHONIDINE
CINCHONINE
CINCHONINES
CINCHONINIC
CINCHONISATION
CINCHONISATIONS
CINCHONISE
CINCHONISED
CINCHONISES
CINCHONISING
CINCHONISM
CINCHONISMS
CINCHONIZATION
CINCHONIZATIONS
CINCHONIZE
CINCHONIZED
CINCHONIZES
CINCHONIZING
CINCINNATE
CINCINNUS
CINCINNUSES
CINCT
CINCTURE
CINCTURED
CINCTURES
CINCTURING
CINDER
CINDERED

CINDERING
CINDERS
CINDERY
CINE
CINEANGIOGRAPHY
CINEAST
CINEASTE
CINEASTES
CINEASTS
CINEMA
CINEMAGOER
CINEMAGOERS
CINEMAS
CINEMATHEQUE
CINEMATHEQUES
CINEMATIC
CINEMATICALLY
CINEMATIZE
CINEMATIZED
CINEMATIZES
CINEMATIZING
CINEMATOGRAPH
CINEMATOGRAPHED
CINEMATOGRAPHER
CINEMATOGRAPHIC
CINEMATOGRAPHS
CINEMATOGRAPHY
CINEMICROGRAPHY
CINEOL
CINEOLE
CINEOLES
CINEOLS
CINEPHILE
CINEPHILES
CINEPLEX
CINEPLEXES
CINERAMIC
CINERARIA
CINERARIAS
CINERARIUM
CINERARY
CINERATION
CINERATIONS
CINERATOR
CINERATORS
CINEREA
CINEREAL
CINEREAS
CINEREOUS
CINERIN
CINERINS
CINERITIOUS
CINES
CINGULA
CINGULATE
CINGULATED

CINGULUM
CINNABAR
CINNABARIC
CINNABARINE
CINNABARS
CINNAMIC
CINNAMON
CINNAMONIC
CINNAMONS
CINNAMYL
CINNAMYLS
CINNARIZINE
CINNARIZINES
CINQUAIN
CINQUAINS
CINQUE
CINQUECENTIST
CINQUECENTISTS
CINQUECENTO
CINQUECENTOS
CINQUEFOIL
CINQUEFOILS
CINQUES
CION
CIONS
CIOPPINO
CIOPPINOS
CIPHER
CIPHERED
CIPHERING
CIPHERINGS
CIPHERS
CIPHERTEXT
CIPHERTEXTS
CIPHONIES
CIPHONY
CIPOLIN
CIPOLINS
CIPOLLINO
CIPOLLINOS
CIPPI
CIPPUS
CIPROFLOXACIN
CIRCA
CIRCADIAN
CIRCAR
CIRCARS
CIRCASSIAN
CIRCASSIANS
CIRCASSIENNE
CIRCASSIENNES
CIRCENSIAL
CIRCENSIAN
CIRCINATE
CIRCINATELY
CIRCITER

CIRCLE
CIRCLED
CIRCLER
CIRCLERS
CIRCLES
CIRCLET
CIRCLETS
CIRCLING
CIRCLINGS
CIRCLIP
CIRCLIPS
CIRCS
CIRCUIT
CIRCUITAL
CIRCUITED
CIRCUITEER
CIRCUITEERS
CIRCUITIES
CIRCUITING
CIRCUITOUS
CIRCUITOUSLY
CIRCUITOUSNESS
CIRCUITRIES
CIRCUITRY
CIRCUITS
CIRCUITY
CIRCULABLE
CIRCULAR
CIRCULARISATION
CIRCULARISE
CIRCULARISED
CIRCULARISER
CIRCULARISERS
CIRCULARISES
CIRCULARISING
CIRCULARITIES
CIRCULARITY
CIRCULARIZATION
CIRCULARIZE
CIRCULARIZED
CIRCULARIZER
CIRCULARIZERS
CIRCULARIZES
CIRCULARIZING
CIRCULARLY
CIRCULARNESS
CIRCULARNESSES
CIRCULARS
CIRCULATABLE
CIRCULATE
CIRCULATED
CIRCULATES
CIRCULATING
CIRCULATINGS
CIRCULATION
CIRCULATIONS

CIRCULATIVE
CIRCULATOR
CIRCULATORS
CIRCULATORY
CIRCUMAMBAGES
CIRCUMAMBAGIOUS
CIRCUMAMBIENCE
CIRCUMAMBIENCES
CIRCUMAMBIENCY
CIRCUMAMBIENT
CIRCUMAMBIENTLY
CIRCUMAMBULATE
CIRCUMAMBULATED
CIRCUMAMBULATES
CIRCUMAMBULATOR
CIRCUMBENDIBUS
CIRCUMCENTER
CIRCUMCENTERS
CIRCUMCENTRE
CIRCUMCENTRES
CIRCUMCIRCLE
CIRCUMCIRCLES
CIRCUMCISE
CIRCUMCISED
CIRCUMCISER
CIRCUMCISERS
CIRCUMCISES
CIRCUMCISING
CIRCUMCISION
CIRCUMCISIONS
CIRCUMDUCE
CIRCUMDUCED
CIRCUMDUCES
CIRCUMDUCING
CIRCUMDUCT
CIRCUMDUCTED
CIRCUMDUCTING
CIRCUMDUCTION
CIRCUMDUCTIONS
CIRCUMDUCTORY
CIRCUMDUCTS
CIRCUMFERENCE
CIRCUMFERENCES
CIRCUMFERENTIAL
CIRCUMFERENTOR
CIRCUMFERENTORS
CIRCUMFLECT
CIRCUMFLECTED
CIRCUMFLECTING
CIRCUMFLECTS
CIRCUMFLEX
CIRCUMFLEXES
CIRCUMFLEXION
CIRCUMFLEXIONS
CIRCUMFLUENCE
CIRCUMFLUENCES

CIRCUMFLUENT
CIRCUMFLUOUS
CIRCUMFORANEAN
CIRCUMFORANEOUS
CIRCUMFUSE
CIRCUMFUSED
CIRCUMFUSES
CIRCUMFUSILE
CIRCUMFUSING
CIRCUMFUSION
CIRCUMFUSIONS
CIRCUMGYRATE
CIRCUMGYRATED
CIRCUMGYRATES
CIRCUMGYRATING
CIRCUMGYRATION
CIRCUMGYRATIONS
CIRCUMGYRATORY
CIRCUMINCESSION
CIRCUMINSESSION
CIRCUMJACENCIES
CIRCUMJACENCY
CIRCUMJACENT
CIRCUMLITTORAL
CIRCUMLOCUTE
CIRCUMLOCUTED
CIRCUMLOCUTES
CIRCUMLOCUTING
CIRCUMLOCUTION
CIRCUMLOCUTIONS
CIRCUMLOCUTORY
CIRCUMLUNAR
CIRCUMMURE
CIRCUMMURED
CIRCUMMURES
CIRCUMMURING
CIRCUMNAVIGABLE
CIRCUMNAVIGATE
CIRCUMNAVIGATED
CIRCUMNAVIGATES
CIRCUMNAVIGATOR
CIRCUMNUTATE
CIRCUMNUTATED
CIRCUMNUTATES
CIRCUMNUTATING
CIRCUMNUTATION
CIRCUMNUTATIONS
CIRCUMNUTATORY
CIRCUMPOLAR
CIRCUMPOSE
CIRCUMPOSED
CIRCUMPOSES
CIRCUMPOSING
CIRCUMPOSITION
CIRCUMPOSITIONS
CIRCUMSCISSILE

CIRCUMSCRIBABLE
CIRCUMSCRIBE
CIRCUMSCRIBED
CIRCUMSCRIBER
CIRCUMSCRIBERS
CIRCUMSCRIBES
CIRCUMSCRIBING
CIRCUMSCRIPTION
CIRCUMSCRIPTIVE
CIRCUMSOLAR
CIRCUMSPECT
CIRCUMSPECTION
CIRCUMSPECTIONS
CIRCUMSPECTIVE
CIRCUMSPECTLY
CIRCUMSPECTNESS
CIRCUMSTANCE
CIRCUMSTANCED
CIRCUMSTANCES
CIRCUMSTANCING
CIRCUMSTANTIAL
CIRCUMSTANTIALS
CIRCUMSTANTIATE
CIRCUMSTELLAR
CIRCUMVALLATE
CIRCUMVALLATED
CIRCUMVALLATES
CIRCUMVALLATING
CIRCUMVALLATION
CIRCUMVENT
CIRCUMVENTED
CIRCUMVENTER
CIRCUMVENTERS
CIRCUMVENTING
CIRCUMVENTION
CIRCUMVENTIONS
CIRCUMVENTIVE
CIRCUMVENTOR
CIRCUMVENTORS
CIRCUMVENTS
CIRCUMVOLUTION
CIRCUMVOLUTIONS
CIRCUMVOLUTORY
CIRCUMVOLVE
CIRCUMVOLVED
CIRCUMVOLVES
CIRCUMVOLVING
CIRCUS
CIRCUSES
CIRCUSSY
CIRCUSY
CIRE
CIRES
CIRL
CIRLS
CIRQUE

CIRQUES
CIRRATE
CIRRHIPEDES
CIRRHOPODS
CIRRHOSED
CIRRHOSES
CIRRHOSING
CIRRHOSIS
CIRRHOTIC
CIRRHOTICS
CIRRI
CIRRIFORM
CIRRIGRADE
CIRRIPED
CIRRIPEDE
CIRRIPEDES
CIRRIPEDS
CIRROCUMULI
CIRROCUMULUS
CIRROSE
CIRROSTRATI
CIRROSTRATIVE
CIRROSTRATUS
CIRROUS
CIRRUS
CIRSOID
CIS
CISALPINE
CISCO
CISCOES
CISCOS
CISELEUR
CISELEURS
CISELURE
CISELURES
CISLUNAR
CISMONTANE
CISPADANE
CISPLATIN
CISPLATINS
CISPONTINE
CISSIER
CISSIES
CISSIEST
CISSIFIED
CISSING
CISSOID
CISSOIDS
CISSUS
CISSUSES
CISSY
CIST
CISTACEOUS
CISTED
CISTERN
CISTERNA

CISTERNAE
CISTERNAL
CISTERNS
CISTIC
CISTRON
CISTRONIC
CISTRONS
CISTS
CISTUS
CISTUSES
CISTVAEN
CISTVAENS
CIT
CITABLE
CITADEL
CITADELS
CITAL
CITALS
CITATION
CITATIONAL
CITATIONS
CITATOR
CITATORS
CITATORY
CITE
CITEABLE
CITED
CITER
CITERS
CITES
CITESS
CITESSES
CITHARA
CITHARAS
CITHARIST
CITHARISTIC
CITHARISTS
CITHER
CITHERN
CITHERNS
CITHERS
CITHREN
CITHRENS
CITIED
CITIES
CITIFICATION
CITIFICATIONS
CITIFIED
CITIFIES
CITIFY
CITIFYING
CITIGRADE
CITING
CITIZEN
CITIZENESS
CITIZENESSES

CITIZENISE
CITIZENISED
CITIZENISES
CITIZENISING
CITIZENIZE
CITIZENIZED
CITIZENIZES
CITIZENIZING
CITIZENLY
CITIZENRIES
CITIZENRY
CITIZENS
CITIZENSHIP
CITIZENSHIPS
CITO
CITOLA
CITOLAS
CITOLE
CITOLES
CITRAL
CITRALS
CITRANGE
CITRANGES
CITRATE
CITRATED
CITRATES
CITREOUS
CITRIC
CITRICULTURE
CITRICULTURES
CITRICULTURIST
CITRICULTURISTS
CITRIN
CITRINE
CITRINES
CITRININ
CITRININS
CITRINS
CITRON
CITRONELLA
CITRONELLAL
CITRONELLALS
CITRONELLAS
CITRONELLOL
CITRONELLOLS
CITRONS
CITROUS
CITRULLINE
CITRULLINES
CITRUS
CITRUSES
CITRUSSY
CITRUSY
CITS
CITTERN
CITTERNS

CITY
CITYFICATION
CITYFICATIONS
CITYFIED
CITYFIES
CITYFY
CITYFYING
CITYSCAPE
CITYSCAPES
CITYWARD
CITYWIDE
CIVE
CIVES
CIVET
CIVETS
CIVIC
CIVICALLY
CIVICISM
CIVICISMS
CIVICS
CIVIE
CIVIES
CIVIL
CIVILIAN
CIVILIANISE
CIVILIANISED
CIVILIANISES
CIVILIANISING
CIVILIANIZATION
CIVILIANIZE
CIVILIANIZED
CIVILIANIZES
CIVILIANIZING
CIVILIANS
CIVILISABLE
CIVILISATION
CIVILISATIONS
CIVILISE
CIVILISED
CIVILISER
CIVILISERS
CIVILISES
CIVILISING
CIVILIST
CIVILISTS
CIVILITIES
CIVILITY
CIVILIZABLE
CIVILIZATION
CIVILIZATIONAL
CIVILIZATIONS
CIVILIZE
CIVILIZED
CIVILIZER
CIVILIZERS
CIVILIZES

CIVILIZING
CIVILLY
CIVILNESS
CIVISM
CIVISMS
CIVVIES
CIVVY
CIZERS
CLABBER
CLABBERED
CLABBERING
CLABBERS
CLACH
CLACHAN
CLACHANS
CLACHS
CLACK
CLACKBOX
CLACKBOXES
CLACKDISH
CLACKDISHES
CLACKED
CLACKER
CLACKERS
CLACKING
CLACKS
CLAD
CLADDED
CLADDER
CLADDERS
CLADDING
CLADDINGS
CLADE
CLADES
CLADISM
CLADISMS
CLADIST
CLADISTIC
CLADISTICALLY
CLADISTICS
CLADISTS
CLADOCERAN
CLADOCERANS
CLADODE
CLADODES
CLADODIAL
CLADOGENESES
CLADOGENESIS
CLADOGENETIC
CLADOGRAM
CLADOGRAMS
CLADOPHYLL
CLADOPHYLLS
CLADOSPORIA
CLADOSPORIUM
CLADOSPORIUMS

CLADS
CLAES
CLAG
CLAGGED
CLAGGIER
CLAGGIEST
CLAGGING
CLAGGY
CLAGS
CLAIM
CLAIMABLE
CLAIMANT
CLAIMANTS
CLAIMED
CLAIMER
CLAIMERS
CLAIMING
CLAIMS
CLAIRAUDIENCE
CLAIRAUDIENCES
CLAIRAUDIENT
CLAIRAUDIENTLY
CLAIRAUDIENTS
CLAIRCOLLE
CLAIRCOLLES
CLAIRSCHACH
CLAIRSCHACHS
CLAIRVOYANCE
CLAIRVOYANCES
CLAIRVOYANCIES
CLAIRVOYANCY
CLAIRVOYANT
CLAIRVOYANTLY
CLAIRVOYANTS
CLAM
CLAMANCIES
CLAMANCY
CLAMANT
CLAMANTLY
CLAMATORIAL
CLAMBAKE
CLAMBAKES
CLAMBE
CLAMBER
CLAMBERED
CLAMBERER
CLAMBERERS
CLAMBERING
CLAMBERS
CLAME
CLAMES
CLAMJAMFRIES
CLAMJAMFRY
CLAMJAMPHRIE
CLAMJAMPHRIES
CLAMMED

CLAMMER
CLAMMERS
CLAMMIER
CLAMMIEST
CLAMMILY
CLAMMINESS
CLAMMINESSES
CLAMMING
CLAMMY
CLAMOR
CLAMORED
CLAMORER
CLAMORERS
CLAMORING
CLAMOROUS
CLAMOROUSLY
CLAMOROUSNESS
CLAMOROUSNESSES
CLAMORS
CLAMOUR
CLAMOURED
CLAMOURER
CLAMOURERS
CLAMOURING
CLAMOURS
CLAMP
CLAMPDOWN
CLAMPDOWNS
CLAMPED
CLAMPER
CLAMPERED
CLAMPERING
CLAMPERS
CLAMPING
CLAMPS
CLAMS
CLAMSHELL
CLAMSHELLS
CLAMWORM
CLAMWORMS
CLAN
CLANDESTINE
CLANDESTINELY
CLANDESTINENESS
CLANDESTINITIES
CLANDESTINITY
CLANG
CLANGBOX
CLANGBOXES
CLANGED
CLANGER
CLANGERS
CLANGING
CLANGINGS
CLANGOR
CLANGORED

CLANGORING
CLANGOROUS
CLANGOROUSLY
CLANGORS
CLANGOUR
CLANGOURED
CLANGOURING
CLANGOURS
CLANGS
CLANJAMFRAY
CLANJAMFRAYS
CLANK
CLANKED
CLANKING
CLANKINGLY
CLANKINGS
CLANKS
CLANNISH
CLANNISHLY
CLANNISHNESS
CLANNISHNESSES
CLANS
CLANSHIP
CLANSHIPS
CLANSMAN
CLANSMEN
CLANSWOMAN
CLANSWOMEN
CLAP
CLAPBOARD
CLAPBOARDED
CLAPBOARDING
CLAPBOARDS
CLAPBREAD
CLAPBREADS
CLAPDISH
CLAPDISHES
CLAPNET
CLAPNETS
CLAPOMETER
CLAPOMETERS
CLAPPED
CLAPPER
CLAPPERBOARD
CLAPPERBOARDS
CLAPPERBOY
CLAPPERBOYS
CLAPPERCLAW
CLAPPERCLAWED
CLAPPERCLAWER
CLAPPERCLAWERS
CLAPPERCLAWING
CLAPPERCLAWS
CLAPPERED
CLAPPERING
CLAPPERINGS

CLAPPERS
CLAPPING
CLAPPINGS
CLAPS
CLAPT
CLAPTRAP
CLAPTRAPPERIES
CLAPTRAPPERY
CLAPTRAPS
CLAQUE
CLAQUER
CLAQUERS
CLAQUES
CLAQUEUR
CLAQUEURS
CLARABELLA
CLARABELLAS
CLARAIN
CLARAINS
CLARENCE
CLARENCES
CLARENDON
CLARENDONS
CLARET
CLARETED
CLARETING
CLARETS
CLARIBELLA
CLARIBELLAS
CLARICHORD
CLARICHORDS
CLARIES
CLARIFICATION
CLARIFICATIONS
CLARIFIED
CLARIFIER
CLARIFIERS
CLARIFIES
CLARIFY
CLARIFYING
CLARINET
CLARINETIST
CLARINETISTS
CLARINETS
CLARINETTIST
CLARINETTISTS
CLARINI
CLARINO
CLARINOS
CLARION
CLARIONED
CLARIONET
CLARIONETS
CLARIONING
CLARIONS
CLARITIES

CLARITY
CLARKIA
CLARKIAS
CLARO
CLAROES
CLAROS
CLARSACH
CLARSACHS
CLART
CLARTED
CLARTHEAD
CLARTHEADS
CLARTIER
CLARTIEST
CLARTING
CLARTS
CLARTY
CLARY
CLASH
CLASHED
CLASHER
CLASHERS
CLASHES
CLASHING
CLASHINGLY
CLASHINGS
CLASP
CLASPED
CLASPER
CLASPERS
CLASPING
CLASPINGS
CLASPS
CLASPT
CLASS
CLASSABLE
CLASSED
CLASSER
CLASSERS
CLASSES
CLASSIBLE
CLASSIC
CLASSICAL
CLASSICALISM
CLASSICALISMS
CLASSICALIST
CLASSICALISTS
CLASSICALITIES
CLASSICALITY
CLASSICALLY
CLASSICALNESS
CLASSICALNESSES
CLASSICISE
CLASSICISED
CLASSICISES
CLASSICISING

CLASSICISM
CLASSICISMS
CLASSICIST
CLASSICISTIC
CLASSICISTS
CLASSICIZE
CLASSICIZED
CLASSICIZES
CLASSICIZING
CLASSICO
CLASSICS
CLASSIER
CLASSIEST
CLASSIFIABLE
CLASSIFIC
CLASSIFICATION
CLASSIFICATIONS
CLASSIFICATORY
CLASSIFIED
CLASSIFIER
CLASSIFIERS
CLASSIFIES
CLASSIFY
CLASSIFYING
CLASSILY
CLASSINESS
CLASSINESSES
CLASSING
CLASSIS
CLASSISM
CLASSISMS
CLASSIST
CLASSISTS
CLASSLESS
CLASSLESSNESS
CLASSLESSNESSES
CLASSMAN
CLASSMATE
CLASSMATES
CLASSMEN
CLASSROOM
CLASSROOMS
CLASSY
CLAST
CLASTIC
CLASTICS
CLASTS
CLAT
CLATCH
CLATCHED
CLATCHES
CLATCHING
CLATHRATE
CLATHRATES
CLATS
CLATTED

CLATTER
CLATTERED
CLATTERER
CLATTERERS
CLATTERING
CLATTERINGLY
CLATTERS
CLATTERY
CLATTING
CLAUCHT
CLAUCHTED
CLAUCHTING
CLAUCHTS
CLAUDICATION
CLAUDICATIONS
CLAUGHT
CLAUGHTED
CLAUGHTING
CLAUGHTS
CLAUSAL
CLAUSE
CLAUSES
CLAUSTRA
CLAUSTRAL
CLAUSTRATION
CLAUSTRATIONS
CLAUSTROPHOBE
CLAUSTROPHOBES
CLAUSTROPHOBIA
CLAUSTROPHOBIAS
CLAUSTROPHOBIC
CLAUSTRUM
CLAUSULA
CLAUSULAE
CLAUSULAR
CLAUT
CLAUTED
CLAUTING
CLAUTS
CLAVATE
CLAVATED
CLAVATELY
CLAVATION
CLAVATIONS
CLAVE
CLAVECIN
CLAVECINIST
CLAVECINISTS
CLAVECINS
CLAVER
CLAVERED
CLAVERING
CLAVERS
CLAVES
CLAVI
CLAVICEMBALO

CLAVICEMBALOS
CLAVICHORD
CLAVICHORDIST
CLAVICHORDISTS
CLAVICHORDS
CLAVICLE
CLAVICLES
CLAVICORN
CLAVICORNS
CLAVICULA
CLAVICULAE
CLAVICULAR
CLAVICULATE
CLAVICYTHERIA
CLAVICYTHERIUM
CLAVIE
CLAVIER
CLAVIERIST
CLAVIERISTIC
CLAVIERISTS
CLAVIERS
CLAVIES
CLAVIFORM
CLAVIGER
CLAVIGEROUS
CLAVIGERS
CLAVIS
CLAVULATE
CLAVUS
CLAW
CLAWBACK
CLAWBACKS
CLAWED
CLAWER
CLAWERS
CLAWHAMMER
CLAWING
CLAWLESS
CLAWLIKE
CLAWS
CLAXON
CLAXONS
CLAY
CLAYBANK
CLAYBANKS
CLAYED
CLAYEY
CLAYIER
CLAYIEST
CLAYING
CLAYISH
CLAYLIKE
CLAYMATION
CLAYMATIONS
CLAYMORE
CLAYMORES

CLAYPAN
CLAYPANS
CLAYS
CLAYSTONE
CLAYSTONES
CLAYTONIA
CLAYTONIAS
CLAYWARE
CLAYWARES
CLEAN
CLEANABILITIES
CLEANABILITY
CLEANABLE
CLEANED
CLEANER
CLEANERS
CLEANEST
CLEANHANDED
CLEANING
CLEANINGS
CLEANLIER
CLEANLIEST
CLEANLILY
CLEANLINESS
CLEANLINESSES
CLEANLY
CLEANNESS
CLEANNESSES
CLEANS
CLEANSABLE
CLEANSE
CLEANSED
CLEANSER
CLEANSERS
CLEANSES
CLEANSING
CLEANSINGS
CLEANSKIN
CLEANSKINS
CLEANUP
CLEANUPS
CLEAR
CLEARABLE
CLEARAGE
CLEARAGES
CLEARANCE
CLEARANCES
CLEARCOLE
CLEARCOLED
CLEARCOLES
CLEARCOLING
CLEARED
CLEARER
CLEARERS
CLEAREST
CLEARHEADED

CLEARHEADEDLY
CLEARHEADEDNESS
CLEARING
CLEARINGHOUSE
CLEARINGHOUSES
CLEARINGS
CLEARLY
CLEARNESS
CLEARNESSES
CLEARS
CLEARSKIN
CLEARSKINS
CLEARSTORIED
CLEARSTORIES
CLEARSTORY
CLEARWAY
CLEARWAYS
CLEARWING
CLEARWINGS
CLEAT
CLEATED
CLEATING
CLEATS
CLEAVABILITY
CLEAVABLE
CLEAVABLENESS
CLEAVABLENESSES
CLEAVAGE
CLEAVAGES
CLEAVE
CLEAVED
CLEAVER
CLEAVERS
CLEAVES
CLEAVING
CLEAVINGS
CLECHE
CLECK
CLECKED
CLECKIER
CLECKIEST
CLECKING
CLECKINGS
CLECKS
CLECKY
CLEEK
CLEEKED
CLEEKING
CLEEKIT
CLEEKS
CLEEP
CLEEPED
CLEEPING
CLEEPS
CLEEVE
CLEEVES

CLEF
CLEFS
CLEFT
CLEFTED
CLEFTING
CLEFTS
CLEG
CLEGS
CLEIDOIC
CLEIK
CLEIKS
CLEISTOGAMIC
CLEISTOGAMIES
CLEISTOGAMOUS
CLEISTOGAMOUSLY
CLEISTOGAMY
CLEITHRAL
CLEM
CLEMATIS
CLEMATISES
CLEMENCIES
CLEMENCY
CLEMENT
CLEMENTINE
CLEMENTINES
CLEMENTLY
CLEMMED
CLEMMING
CLEMS
CLENBUTEROL
CLENBUTEROLS
CLENCH
CLENCHED
CLENCHER
CLENCHERS
CLENCHES
CLENCHING
CLEOME
CLEOMES
CLEOPATRA
CLEOPATRAS
CLEPE
CLEPED
CLEPES
CLEPING
CLEPSYDRA
CLEPSYDRAE
CLEPSYDRAS
CLEPT
CLEPTOMANIA
CLEPTOMANIAC
CLEPTOMANIACAL
CLEPTOMANIACS
CLEPTOMANIAS
CLERECOLES
CLERESTORIED

CLERESTORIES
CLERESTORY
CLERGIABLE
CLERGIES
CLERGY
CLERGYABLE
CLERGYMAN
CLERGYMEN
CLERGYWOMAN
CLERGYWOMEN
CLERIC
CLERICAL
CLERICALISM
CLERICALISMS
CLERICALIST
CLERICALISTS
CLERICALLY
CLERICALS
CLERICATE
CLERICATES
CLERICITIES
CLERICITY
CLERICS
CLERID
CLERIDS
CLERIHEW
CLERIHEWS
CLERISIES
CLERISY
CLERK
CLERKDOM
CLERKDOMS
CLERKED
CLERKESS
CLERKESSES
CLERKING
CLERKISH
CLERKLIER
CLERKLIEST
CLERKLIKE
CLERKLINESS
CLERKLING
CLERKLINGS
CLERKLY
CLERKS
CLERKSHIP
CLERKSHIPS
CLEROMANCIES
CLEROMANCY
CLERUCH
CLERUCHIA
CLERUCHIAL
CLERUCHIAS
CLERUCHIES
CLERUCHS
CLERUCHY

CLEUCH
CLEUCHS
CLEUGH
CLEUGHS
CLEVE
CLEVEITE
CLEVEITES
CLEVER
CLEVERALITIES
CLEVERALITY
CLEVERDICK
CLEVERDICKS
CLEVERER
CLEVEREST
CLEVERISH
CLEVERLY
CLEVERNESS
CLEVERNESSES
CLEVES
CLEVIS
CLEVISES
CLEW
CLEWED
CLEWING
CLEWS
CLIANTHUS
CLIANTHUSES
CLICHE
CLICHED
CLICHEED
CLICHES
CLICK
CLICKABILITY
CLICKABLE
CLICKABLY
CLICKED
CLICKER
CLICKERS
CLICKET
CLICKETED
CLICKETING
CLICKETS
CLICKING
CLICKINGS
CLICKS
CLICKSTREAM
CLICKSTREAMS
CLIED
CLIENT
CLIENTAGE
CLIENTAGES
CLIENTAL
CLIENTELE
CLIENTELES
CLIENTLESS
CLIENTS

CLIENTSHIP
CLIENTSHIPS
CLIES
CLIFF
CLIFFED
CLIFFHANG
CLIFFHANGER
CLIFFHANGERS
CLIFFHANGING
CLIFFHANGINGS
CLIFFHANGS
CLIFFHUNG
CLIFFIER
CLIFFIEST
CLIFFS
CLIFFY
CLIFT
CLIFTED
CLIFTIER
CLIFTIEST
CLIFTS
CLIFTY
CLIMACTERIC
CLIMACTERICAL
CLIMACTERICALLY
CLIMACTERICS
CLIMACTIC
CLIMACTICAL
CLIMACTICALLY
CLIMATAL
CLIMATE
CLIMATED
CLIMATES
CLIMATIC
CLIMATICAL
CLIMATICALLY
CLIMATING
CLIMATISE
CLIMATISED
CLIMATISES
CLIMATISING
CLIMATIZE
CLIMATIZED
CLIMATIZES
CLIMATIZING
CLIMATOGRAPHIES
CLIMATOGRAPHY
CLIMATOLOGIC
CLIMATOLOGICAL
CLIMATOLOGIES
CLIMATOLOGIST
CLIMATOLOGISTS
CLIMATOLOGY
CLIMATURE
CLIMATURES
CLIMAX

CLIMAXED
CLIMAXES
CLIMAXING
CLIMAXLESS
CLIMB
CLIMBABLE
CLIMBED
CLIMBER
CLIMBERS
CLIMBING
CLIMBINGS
CLIMBS
CLIME
CLIMES
CLINAL
CLINALLY
CLINAMEN
CLINAMENS
CLINANDRIA
CLINANDRIUM
CLINCH
CLINCHED
CLINCHER
CLINCHERS
CLINCHES
CLINCHING
CLINCHINGLY
CLINDAMYCIN
CLINDAMYCINS
CLINE
CLINES
CLING
CLINGED
CLINGER
CLINGERS
CLINGFILM
CLINGFILMS
CLINGFISH
CLINGFISHES
CLINGIER
CLINGIEST
CLINGINESS
CLINGINESSES
CLINGING
CLINGINGLY
CLINGINGNESS
CLINGS
CLINGSTONE
CLINGSTONES
CLINGY
CLINIC
CLINICAL
CLINICALLY
CLINICALNESS
CLINICIAN
CLINICIANS

CLINICS
CLINIQUE
CLINIQUES
CLINK
CLINKED
CLINKER
CLINKERED
CLINKERING
CLINKERS
CLINKING
CLINKS
CLINKSTONE
CLINKSTONES
CLINOAXES
CLINOAXIS
CLINOCHLORE
CLINOCHLORES
CLINODIAGONAL
CLINODIAGONALS
CLINOMETER
CLINOMETERS
CLINOMETRIC
CLINOMETRICAL
CLINOMETRICALLY
CLINOMETRIES
CLINOMETRY
CLINOPINACOID
CLINOPINACOIDS
CLINOPINAKOIDS
CLINOPYROXENE
CLINOPYROXENES
CLINOSTAT
CLINOSTATS
CLINQUANT
CLINQUANTS
CLINT
CLINTONIA
CLINTONIAS
CLINTS
CLIOMETRIC
CLIOMETRICAL
CLIOMETRICALLY
CLIOMETRICIAN
CLIOMETRICIANS
CLIOMETRICS
CLIP
CLIPART
CLIPARTS
CLIPBOARD
CLIPBOARDS
CLIPE
CLIPED
CLIPES
CLIPING
CLIPPABLE
CLIPPED

CLIPPER
CLIPPERS
CLIPPIE
CLIPPIES
CLIPPING
CLIPPINGS
CLIPS
CLIPSHEAR
CLIPSHEARS
CLIPSHEET
CLIPSHEETS
CLIPT
CLIQUE
CLIQUED
CLIQUES
CLIQUEY
CLIQUIER
CLIQUIEST
CLIQUINESS
CLIQUINESSES
CLIQUING
CLIQUISH
CLIQUISHLY
CLIQUISHNESS
CLIQUISHNESSES
CLIQUISM
CLIQUISMS
CLIQUY
CLISHMACLAVER
CLISHMACLAVERS
CLISTOGAMIES
CLITELLA
CLITELLAR
CLITELLUM
CLITHRAL
CLITIC
CLITICS
CLITORAL
CLITORECTOMIES
CLITORECTOMY
CLITORIC
CLITORIDECTOMY
CLITORIDES
CLITORIS
CLITORISES
CLITTER
CLITTERED
CLITTERING
CLITTERS
CLIVERS
CLIVIA
CLIVIAS
CLOACA
CLOACAE
CLOACAL
CLOACALINE

CLOACAS
CLOACINAL
CLOACITIS
CLOAK
CLOAKED
CLOAKING
CLOAKROOM
CLOAKROOMS
CLOAKS
CLOAM
CLOAMS
CLOBBER
CLOBBERED
CLOBBERING
CLOBBERS
CLOCHARD
CLOCHARDS
CLOCHE
CLOCHES
CLOCK
CLOCKED
CLOCKER
CLOCKERS
CLOCKING
CLOCKINGS
CLOCKLIKE
CLOCKMAKER
CLOCKMAKERS
CLOCKS
CLOCKWISE
CLOCKWORK
CLOCKWORKS
CLOD
CLODDED
CLODDIER
CLODDIEST
CLODDING
CLODDISH
CLODDISHLY
CLODDISHNESS
CLODDISHNESSES
CLODDY
CLODHOPPER
CLODHOPPERS
CLODHOPPING
CLODLY
CLODPATE
CLODPATED
CLODPATES
CLODPOLE
CLODPOLES
CLODPOLL
CLODPOLLS
CLODS
CLOFF
CLOFFS

CLOFIBRATE
CLOFIBRATES
CLOG
CLOGDANCE
CLOGDANCES
CLOGGED
CLOGGER
CLOGGERS
CLOGGIER
CLOGGIEST
CLOGGINESS
CLOGGINESSES
CLOGGING
CLOGGY
CLOGS
CLOISON
CLOISONNAGE
CLOISONNAGES
CLOISONNE
CLOISONNES
CLOISONS
CLOISTER
CLOISTERED
CLOISTERER
CLOISTERERS
CLOISTERING
CLOISTERS
CLOISTRAL
CLOISTRESS
CLOISTRESSES
CLOKE
CLOKED
CLOKES
CLOKING
CLOMB
CLOMIPHENE
CLOMIPHENES
CLOMP
CLOMPED
CLOMPING
CLOMPS
CLON
CLONAL
CLONALLY
CLONAZEPAM
CLONAZEPAMS
CLONE
CLONED
CLONER
CLONERS
CLONES
CLONIC
CLONICITIES
CLONICITY
CLONIDINE
CLONIDINES

CLONING
CLONINGS
CLONISM
CLONISMS
CLONK
CLONKED
CLONKING
CLONKS
CLONS
CLONUS
CLONUSES
CLOOP
CLOOPS
CLOOT
CLOOTS
CLOP
CLOPPED
CLOPPING
CLOPS
CLOQUE
CLOQUES
CLOSABLE
CLOSE
CLOSEABLE
CLOSED
CLOSEDOWN
CLOSEDOWNS
CLOSEFISTED
CLOSEHEAD
CLOSEHEADS
CLOSELY
CLOSEMOUTHED
CLOSENESS
CLOSENESSES
CLOSEOUT
CLOSEOUTS
CLOSER
CLOSERS
CLOSES
CLOSEST
CLOSESTOOL
CLOSESTOOLS
CLOSET
CLOSETED
CLOSETFUL
CLOSETFULS
CLOSETING
CLOSETS
CLOSING
CLOSINGS
CLOSTRIDIA
CLOSTRIDIAL
CLOSTRIDIAN
CLOSTRIDIUM
CLOSTRIDIUMS
CLOSURE

CLOSURED
CLOSURES
CLOSURING
CLOT
CLOTBUR
CLOTBURS
CLOTE
CLOTEBURS
CLOTES
CLOTH
CLOTHBOUND
CLOTHE
CLOTHED
CLOTHES
CLOTHESHORSE
CLOTHESHORSES
CLOTHESLINE
CLOTHESLINED
CLOTHESLINES
CLOTHESLINING
CLOTHESPIN
CLOTHESPINS
CLOTHESPRESS
CLOTHESPRESSES
CLOTHIER
CLOTHIERS
CLOTHING
CLOTHINGS
CLOTHS
CLOTPOLL
CLOTPOLLS
CLOTS
CLOTTED
CLOTTER
CLOTTERED
CLOTTERING
CLOTTERS
CLOTTIER
CLOTTIEST
CLOTTINESS
CLOTTINESSES
CLOTTING
CLOTTINGS
CLOTTISH
CLOTTISHLY
CLOTTISHNESS
CLOTTY
CLOTURE
CLOTURED
CLOTURES
CLOTURING
CLOU
CLOUD
CLOUDAGE
CLOUDAGES
CLOUDBERRIES

CLOUDBERRY
CLOUDBURST
CLOUDBURSTS
CLOUDED
CLOUDIER
CLOUDIEST
CLOUDILY
CLOUDINESS
CLOUDINESSES
CLOUDING
CLOUDINGS
CLOUDLAND
CLOUDLANDS
CLOUDLESS
CLOUDLESSLY
CLOUDLESSNESS
CLOUDLESSNESSES
CLOUDLET
CLOUDLETS
CLOUDLIKE
CLOUDS
CLOUDSCAPE
CLOUDSCAPES
CLOUDTOWN
CLOUDTOWNS
CLOUDY
CLOUGH
CLOUGHS
CLOUR
CLOURED
CLOURING
CLOURS
CLOUS
CLOUT
CLOUTED
CLOUTER
CLOUTERLY
CLOUTERS
CLOUTING
CLOUTS
CLOVE
CLOVEN
CLOVEPINK
CLOVEPINKS
CLOVER
CLOVERED
CLOVERGRASS
CLOVERGRASSES
CLOVERLEAF
CLOVERLEAFS
CLOVERLEAVES
CLOVERS
CLOVERY
CLOVES
CLOVIS
CLOVISES

CLOW
CLOWDER
CLOWDERS
CLOWN
CLOWNED
CLOWNERIES
CLOWNERY
CLOWNING
CLOWNINGS
CLOWNISH
CLOWNISHLY
CLOWNISHNESS
CLOWNISHNESSES
CLOWNS
CLOWS
CLOXACILLIN
CLOXACILLINS
CLOY
CLOYE
CLOYED
CLOYEDNESS
CLOYES
CLOYING
CLOYINGLY
CLOYINGNESS
CLOYLESS
CLOYMENT
CLOYMENTS
CLOYS
CLOYSOME
CLOZE
CLOZES
CLUB
CLUBABILITIES
CLUBABILITY
CLUBABLE
CLUBBABILITIES
CLUBBABILITY
CLUBBABLE
CLUBBED
CLUBBER
CLUBBERS
CLUBBIER
CLUBBIEST
CLUBBILY
CLUBBINESS
CLUBBINESSES
CLUBBING
CLUBBINGS
CLUBBISH
CLUBBISM
CLUBBISMS
CLUBBIST
CLUBBISTS
CLUBBY
CLUBFEET

CLUBFOOT
CLUBFOOTED
CLUBHAND
CLUBHANDS
CLUBHAUL
CLUBHAULED
CLUBHAULING
CLUBHAULS
CLUBHOUSE
CLUBHOUSES
CLUBLAND
CLUBLANDS
CLUBMAN
CLUBMANSHIP
CLUBMANSHIPS
CLUBMASTER
CLUBMASTERS
CLUBMEN
CLUBROOM
CLUBROOMS
CLUBROOT
CLUBROOTS
CLUBRUSH
CLUBRUSHES
CLUBS
CLUBWOMAN
CLUBWOMEN
CLUCK
CLUCKED
CLUCKIER
CLUCKIEST
CLUCKING
CLUCKS
CLUCKY
CLUDGIE
CLUDGIES
CLUE
CLUED
CLUEING
CLUELESS
CLUES
CLUING
CLUMBER
CLUMBERS
CLUMP
CLUMPED
CLUMPER
CLUMPERS
CLUMPIER
CLUMPIEST
CLUMPINESS
CLUMPINESSES
CLUMPING
CLUMPISH
CLUMPLIKE
CLUMPS

CLUMPY
CLUMSIER
CLUMSIEST
CLUMSILY
CLUMSINESS
CLUMSINESSES
CLUMSY
CLUNCH
CLUNCHES
CLUNG
CLUNK
CLUNKED
CLUNKER
CLUNKERS
CLUNKIER
CLUNKIEST
CLUNKING
CLUNKS
CLUNKY
CLUPEID
CLUPEIDS
CLUPEOID
CLUPEOIDS
CLUSIA
CLUSIAS
CLUSTER
CLUSTERED
CLUSTERING
CLUSTERINGLY
CLUSTERS
CLUSTERY
CLUTCH
CLUTCHED
CLUTCHES
CLUTCHING
CLUTCHY
CLUTTER
CLUTTERED
CLUTTERING
CLUTTERS
CLUTTERY
CLY
CLYING
CLYPE
CLYPEAL
CLYPEATE
CLYPED
CLYPEI
CLYPEIFORM
CLYPES
CLYPEUS
CLYPING
CLYSTER
CLYSTERS
CNEMIAL
CNEMIS

CNEMISES
CNIDA
CNIDAE
CNIDARIAN
CNIDARIANS
CNIDOBLAST
CNIDOBLASTS
COACERVATE
COACERVATED
COACERVATES
COACERVATING
COACERVATION
COACERVATIONS
COACH
COACHABLE
COACHBUILDER
COACHBUILDERS
COACHBUILDING
COACHBUILDINGS
COACHBUILT
COACHDOG
COACHDOGS
COACHED
COACHEE
COACHEES
COACHER
COACHERS
COACHES
COACHIES
COACHING
COACHINGS
COACHLINE
COACHLINES
COACHLOAD
COACHLOADS
COACHMAN
COACHMEN
COACHWHIP
COACHWHIPS
COACHWOOD
COACHWOODS
COACHWORK
COACHWORKS
COACHY
COACT
COACTED
COACTING
COACTION
COACTIONS
COACTIVE
COACTIVELY
COACTIVITIES
COACTIVITY
COACTOR
COACTORS
COACTS

COADAPTATION
COADAPTATIONS
COADAPTED
COADJACENCIES
COADJACENCY
COADJACENT
COADJUTANT
COADJUTANTS
COADJUTOR
COADJUTORS
COADJUTORSHIP
COADJUTORSHIPS
COADJUTRESS
COADJUTRESSES
COADJUTRICES
COADJUTRIX
COADJUTRIXES
COADMIRE
COADMIRED
COADMIRES
COADMIRING
COADMIT
COADMITS
COADMITTED
COADMITTING
COADUNATE
COADUNATED
COADUNATES
COADUNATING
COADUNATION
COADUNATIONS
COADUNATIVE
COAEVAL
COAEVALS
COAGENCIES
COAGENCY
COAGENT
COAGENTS
COAGULA
COAGULABILITIES
COAGULABILITY
COAGULABLE
COAGULANT
COAGULANTS
COAGULASE
COAGULASES
COAGULATE
COAGULATED
COAGULATES
COAGULATING
COAGULATION
COAGULATIONS
COAGULATIVE
COAGULATOR
COAGULATORS
COAGULATORY

COAGULUM
COAGULUMS
COAITA
COAITAS
COAL
COALA
COALAS
COALBALL
COALBALLS
COALBIN
COALBINS
COALBOX
COALBOXES
COALED
COALER
COALERS
COALESCE
COALESCED
COALESCENCE
COALESCENCES
COALESCENT
COALESCES
COALESCING
COALFACE
COALFACES
COALFIELD
COALFIELDS
COALFISH
COALFISHES
COALHOLE
COALHOLES
COALHOUSE
COALHOUSES
COALIER
COALIEST
COALIFICATION
COALIFICATIONS
COALIFIED
COALIFIES
COALIFY
COALIFYING
COALING
COALISE
COALISED
COALISES
COALISING
COALITION
COALITIONAL
COALITIONER
COALITIONERS
COALITIONISM
COALITIONISMS
COALITIONIST
COALITIONISTS
COALITIONS
COALIZE

COALIZED
COALIZES
COALIZING
COALLESS
COALMAN
COALMASTER
COALMASTERS
COALMEN
COALMINE
COALMINER
COALMINERS
COALMINES
COALPIT
COALPITS
COALS
COALSACK
COALSACKS
COALSHED
COALSHEDS
COALTAR
COALTARS
COALY
COALYARD
COALYARDS
COAMING
COAMINGS
COANCHOR
COANCHORED
COANCHORING
COANCHORS
COANNEX
COANNEXED
COANNEXES
COANNEXING
COAPPEAR
COAPPEARED
COAPPEARING
COAPPEARS
COAPT
COAPTATION
COAPTATIONS
COAPTED
COAPTING
COAPTS
COARB
COARBS
COARCTATE
COARCTATED
COARCTATES
COARCTATING
COARCTATION
COARCTATIONS
COARSE
COARSELY
COARSEN
COARSENED

COARSENESS
COARSENESSES
COARSENING
COARSENS
COARSER
COARSEST
COARSISH
COASSIST
COASSISTED
COASSISTING
COASSISTS
COASSUME
COASSUMED
COASSUMES
COASSUMING
COAST
COASTAL
COASTALLY
COASTED
COASTER
COASTERS
COASTGUARD
COASTGUARDMAN
COASTGUARDMEN
COASTGUARDS
COASTGUARDSMAN
COASTGUARDSMEN
COASTING
COASTINGS
COASTLAND
COASTLANDS
COASTLINE
COASTLINES
COASTS
COASTWARD
COASTWARDS
COASTWISE
COAT
COATDRESS
COATDRESSES
COATE
COATED
COATEE
COATEES
COATER
COATERS
COATES
COATI
COATIMUNDI
COATIMUNDIS
COATING
COATINGS
COATIS
COATLESS
COATRACK
COATRACKS

COATROOM
COATROOMS
COATS
COATSTAND
COATSTANDS
COATTAIL
COATTAILS
COATTEND
COATTENDED
COATTENDING
COATTENDS
COATTEST
COATTESTED
COATTESTING
COATTESTS
COAUTHOR
COAUTHORED
COAUTHORING
COAUTHORS
COAUTHORSHIP
COAUTHORSHIPS
COAX
COAXAL
COAXED
COAXER
COAXERS
COAXES
COAXIAL
COAXIALLY
COAXING
COAXINGLY
COB
COBAEA
COBAEAS
COBALAMIN
COBALAMINS
COBALT
COBALTIC
COBALTIFEROUS
COBALTINE
COBALTINES
COBALTITE
COBALTITES
COBALTOUS
COBALTS
COBB
COBBED
COBBER
COBBERS
COBBIER
COBBIEST
COBBING
COBBLE
COBBLED
COBBLER
COBBLERIES

COBBLERS
COBBLERY
COBBLES
COBBLESTONE
COBBLESTONED
COBBLESTONES
COBBLESTONING
COBBLING
COBBLINGS
COBBS
COBBY
COBELLIGERENT
COBELLIGERENTS
COBIA
COBIAS
COBLE
COBLES
COBLOAF
COBLOAVES
COBNUT
COBNUTS
COBRA
COBRAS
COBRIC
COBRIFORM
COBS
COBURG
COBURGS
COBWEB
COBWEBBED
COBWEBBERIES
COBWEBBERY
COBWEBBIER
COBWEBBIEST
COBWEBBING
COBWEBBY
COBWEBS
COBZA
COBZAS
COCA
COCAIN
COCAINE
COCAINES
COCAINISATION
COCAINISATIONS
COCAINISE
COCAINISED
COCAINISES
COCAINISING
COCAINISM
COCAINISMS
COCAINIST
COCAINISTS
COCAINIZATION
COCAINIZATIONS
COCAINIZE

COCAINIZED
COCAINIZES
COCAINIZING
COCAINS
COCAPTAIN
COCAPTAINED
COCAPTAINING
COCAPTAINS
COCARBOXYLASE
COCARBOXYLASES
COCARCINOGEN
COCARCINOGENIC
COCARCINOGENS
COCAS
COCATALYST
COCATALYSTS
COCCAL
COCCI
COCCIC
COCCID
COCCIDIA
COCCIDIOSES
COCCIDIOSIS
COCCIDIOSTAT
COCCIDIOSTATS
COCCIDIUM
COCCIDS
COCCIFEROUS
COCCINEOUS
COCCO
COCCOID
COCCOIDS
COCCOLITE
COCCOLITES
COCCOLITH
COCCOLITHS
COCCOS
COCCOUS
COCCUS
COCCYGEAL
COCCYGES
COCCYGIAN
COCCYX
COCCYXES
COCH
COCHAIR
COCHAIRED
COCHAIRING
COCHAIRMAN
COCHAIRMEN
COCHAIRPERSON
COCHAIRPERSONS
COCHAIRS
COCHAIRWOMAN
COCHAIRWOMEN
COCHAMPION

COCHAMPIONS
COCHES
COCHIN
COCHINEAL
COCHINEALS
COCHINS
COCHLEA
COCHLEAE
COCHLEAR
COCHLEARE
COCHLEARES
COCHLEARIFORM
COCHLEARS
COCHLEAS
COCHLEATE
COCHLEATED
COCINERA
COCINERAS
COCK
COCKABULLIES
COCKABULLY
COCKADE
COCKADED
COCKADES
COCKALEEKIE
COCKALEEKIES
COCKALORUM
COCKALORUMS
COCKAMAMIE
COCKAMAMY
COCKAPOO
COCKAPOOS
COCKATEEL
COCKATEELS
COCKATIEL
COCKATIELS
COCKATOO
COCKATOOS
COCKATRICE
COCKATRICES
COCKBILL
COCKBILLED
COCKBILLING
COCKBILLS
COCKBIRD
COCKBIRDS
COCKBOAT
COCKBOATS
COCKCHAFER
COCKCHAFERS
COCKCROW
COCKCROWING
COCKCROWINGS
COCKCROWS
COCKED
COCKER

COCKERED
COCKEREL
COCKERELS
COCKERING
COCKERNONIES
COCKERNONY
COCKERS
COCKET
COCKETS
COCKEYE
COCKEYED
COCKEYEDLY
COCKEYEDNESS
COCKEYEDNESSES
COCKEYES
COCKFIGHT
COCKFIGHTING
COCKFIGHTINGS
COCKFIGHTS
COCKHORSE
COCKHORSES
COCKIELEEKIE
COCKIELEEKIES
COCKIER
COCKIES
COCKIEST
COCKILY
COCKINESS
COCKINESSES
COCKING
COCKISH
COCKLAIRDS
COCKLE
COCKLEBOAT
COCKLEBOATS
COCKLEBUR
COCKLEBURS
COCKLED
COCKLEERT
COCKLEERTS
COCKLEMAN
COCKLEMEN
COCKLES
COCKLESHELL
COCKLESHELLS
COCKLIKE
COCKLING
COCKLOFT
COCKLOFTS
COCKMATCH
COCKMATCHES
COCKNEY
COCKNEYDOM
COCKNEYDOMS
COCKNEYFICATION
COCKNEYFIED

COCKNEYFIES
COCKNEYFY
COCKNEYFYING
COCKNEYISH
COCKNEYISM
COCKNEYISMS
COCKNEYS
COCKNIFICATION
COCKNIFICATIONS
COCKNIFIED
COCKNIFIES
COCKNIFY
COCKNIFYING
COCKPIT
COCKPITS
COCKROACH
COCKROACHES
COCKS
COCKSCOMB
COCKSCOMBS
COCKSFOOT
COCKSFOOTS
COCKSHIES
COCKSHOT
COCKSHOTS
COCKSHUT
COCKSHUTS
COCKSHY
COCKSIER
COCKSIEST
COCKSINESS
COCKSINESSES
COCKSPUR
COCKSPURS
COCKSUCKER
COCKSUCKERS
COCKSURE
COCKSURELY
COCKSURENESS
COCKSURENESSES
COCKSWAIN
COCKSWAINED
COCKSWAINING
COCKSWAINS
COCKSY
COCKTAIL
COCKTAILED
COCKTAILING
COCKTAILS
COCKTEASER
COCKTEASERS
COCKTHROWING
COCKTHROWINGS
COCKUP
COCKUPS
COCKY

COCKYLEEKIES
COCKYLEEKY
COCO
COCOA
COCOANUT
COCOANUTS
COCOAS
COCOBOLA
COCOBOLAS
COCOBOLO
COCOBOLOS
COCOMAT
COCOMATS
COCOMPOSER
COCOMPOSERS
COCONSCIOUS
COCONSCIOUSES
COCONSCIOUSNESS
COCONSPIRATOR
COCONSPIRATORS
COCONUT
COCONUTS
COCOON
COCOONED
COCOONERIES
COCOONERY
COCOONING
COCOONINGS
COCOONS
COCOPAN
COCOPANS
COCOPLUM
COCOPLUMS
COCOS
COCOTTE
COCOTTES
COCOUNSEL
COCOUNSELED
COCOUNSELING
COCOUNSELLED
COCOUNSELLING
COCOUNSELS
COCOYAM
COCOYAMS
COCREATE
COCREATED
COCREATES
COCREATING
COCREATOR
COCREATORS
COCTILE
COCTION
COCTIONS
COCULTIVATE
COCULTIVATED
COCULTIVATES

COCULTIVATING
COCULTIVATION
COCULTIVATIONS
COCULTURE
COCULTURED
COCULTURES
COCULTURING
COCURATOR
COCURATORS
COCURRICULAR
COCUSWOOD
COCUSWOODS
COD
CODA
CODABLE
CODAS
CODDED
CODDER
CODDERS
CODDING
CODDLE
CODDLED
CODDLER
CODDLERS
CODDLES
CODDLING
CODE
CODEBOOK
CODEBOOKS
CODEBTOR
CODEBTORS
CODEC
CODECLINATION
CODECLINATIONS
CODECS
CODED
CODEFENDANT
CODEFENDANTS
CODEIA
CODEIAS
CODEIN
CODEINA
CODEINAS
CODEINE
CODEINES
CODEINS
CODELESS
CODEN
CODENAME
CODENAMES
CODENS
CODEPENDENCE
CODEPENDENCES
CODEPENDENCIES
CODEPENDENCY
CODEPENDENT

CODEPENDENTS
CODER
CODERIVE
CODERIVED
CODERIVES
CODERIVING
CODERS
CODES
CODESIGN
CODESIGNED
CODESIGNING
CODESIGNS
CODETERMINATION
CODETTA
CODETTAS
CODEVELOP
CODEVELOPED
CODEVELOPER
CODEVELOPERS
CODEVELOPING
CODEVELOPS
CODEWORD
CODEWORDS
CODEX
CODFISH
CODFISHES
CODGER
CODGERS
CODICES
CODICIL
CODICILLARY
CODICILS
CODICOLOGICAL
CODICOLOGIES
CODICOLOGY
CODIFIABILITIES
CODIFIABILITY
CODIFICATION
CODIFICATIONS
CODIFIED
CODIFIER
CODIFIERS
CODIFIES
CODIFY
CODIFYING
CODILLA
CODILLAS
CODILLE
CODILLES
CODING
CODINGS
CODIRECT
CODIRECTED
CODIRECTING
CODIRECTION
CODIRECTIONS

CODIRECTOR
CODIRECTORS
CODIRECTS
CODISCOVER
CODISCOVERED
CODISCOVERER
CODISCOVERERS
CODISCOVERING
CODISCOVERS
CODIST
CODISTS
CODLIN
CODLING
CODLINGS
CODLINS
CODOLOGICAL
CODOLOGICALLY
CODOLOGY
CODOMAIN
CODOMAINS
CODOMINANCE
CODOMINANT
CODOMINANTLY
CODOMINANTS
CODON
CODONS
CODPIECE
CODPIECES
CODRIVE
CODRIVEN
CODRIVER
CODRIVERS
CODRIVES
CODRIVING
CODROVE
CODS
CODSWALLOP
CODSWALLOPS
COED
COEDIT
COEDITED
COEDITING
COEDITOR
COEDITORS
COEDITS
COEDS
COEDUCATION
COEDUCATIONAL
COEDUCATIONALLY
COEDUCATIONS
COEFFECT
COEFFECTS
COEFFICIENT
COEFFICIENTS
COEHORN
COEHORNS

COELACANTH
COELACANTHIC
COELACANTHS
COELANAGLYPHIC
COELENTERA
COELENTERATE
COELENTERATES
COELENTERIC
COELENTERON
COELIAC
COELIACS
COELOM
COELOMATA
COELOMATE
COELOMATES
COELOMATIC
COELOME
COELOMES
COELOMIC
COELOMS
COELOSTAT
COELOSTATS
COELUROSAUR
COELUROSAURS
COEMBODIED
COEMBODIES
COEMBODY
COEMBODYING
COEMPLOY
COEMPLOYED
COEMPLOYING
COEMPLOYS
COEMPT
COEMPTED
COEMPTING
COEMPTION
COEMPTIONS
COEMPTS
COENACLE
COENACLES
COENACT
COENACTED
COENACTING
COENACTS
COENAESTHESES
COENAESTHESIA
COENAESTHESIAS
COENAESTHESIS
COENAMOR
COENAMORED
COENAMORING
COENAMORS
COENDURE
COENDURED
COENDURES
COENDURING

COENENCHYMA
COENENCHYMAS
COENESTHESIA
COENESTHESIS
COENESTHETIC
COENOBIA
COENOBITE
COENOBITES
COENOBITIC
COENOBITICAL
COENOBITISM
COENOBITISMS
COENOBIUM
COENOCYTE
COENOCYTES
COENOCYTIC
COENOSARC
COENOSARCS
COENOSPECIES
COENOSTEUM
COENOSTEUMS
COENURE
COENURES
COENURI
COENURUS
COENZYMATIC
COENZYMATICALLY
COENZYME
COENZYMES
COEQUAL
COEQUALITIES
COEQUALITY
COEQUALLY
COEQUALNESS
COEQUALS
COEQUATE
COEQUATED
COEQUATES
COEQUATING
COERCE
COERCED
COERCER
COERCERS
COERCES
COERCIBLE
COERCIBLY
COERCIMETER
COERCIMETERS
COERCING
COERCION
COERCIONIST
COERCIONISTS
COERCIONS
COERCIVE
COERCIVELY
COERCIVENESS

COERCIVENESSES
COERCIVITIES
COERCIVITY
COERECT
COERECTED
COERECTING
COERECTS
COESITE
COESITES
COESSENTIAL
COESSENTIALITY
COESSENTIALLY
COESSENTIALNESS
COETANEOUS
COETANEOUSLY
COETANEOUSNESS
COETERNAL
COETERNALLY
COETERNITIES
COETERNITY
COEVAL
COEVALITIES
COEVALITY
COEVALLY
COEVALS
COEVOLUTION
COEVOLUTIONARY
COEVOLUTIONS
COEVOLVE
COEVOLVED
COEVOLVES
COEVOLVING
COEXECUTOR
COEXECUTORS
COEXECUTRICES
COEXECUTRIX
COEXERT
COEXERTED
COEXERTING
COEXERTS
COEXIST
COEXISTED
COEXISTENCE
COEXISTENCES
COEXISTENT
COEXISTING
COEXISTS
COEXTEND
COEXTENDED
COEXTENDING
COEXTENDS
COEXTENSION
COEXTENSIONS
COEXTENSIVE
COEXTENSIVELY
COFACTOR

COFACTORS
COFAVORITE
COFAVORITES
COFEATURE
COFEATURED
COFEATURES
COFEATURING
COFF
COFFED
COFFEE
COFFEEHOUSE
COFFEEHOUSES
COFFEEMAKER
COFFEEMAKERS
COFFEEPOT
COFFEEPOTS
COFFEES
COFFER
COFFERDAM
COFFERDAMS
COFFERED
COFFERING
COFFERS
COFFIN
COFFINED
COFFING
COFFINING
COFFINITE
COFFINITES
COFFINS
COFFLE
COFFLED
COFFLES
COFFLING
COFFRET
COFFRETS
COFFS
COFINANCE
COFINANCED
COFINANCES
COFINANCING
COFOUND
COFOUNDED
COFOUNDER
COFOUNDERS
COFOUNDING
COFOUNDS
COFT
COFUNCTION
COFUNCTIONS
COG
COGENCE
COGENCES
COGENCIES
COGENCY
COGENER

COGENERATION
COGENERATIONS
COGENERATOR
COGENERATORS
COGENERS
COGENT
COGENTLY
COGGED
COGGER
COGGERS
COGGIE
COGGIES
COGGING
COGGINGS
COGGLE
COGGLED
COGGLES
COGGLIER
COGGLIEST
COGGLING
COGGLY
COGIE
COGIES
COGITABLE
COGITATE
COGITATED
COGITATES
COGITATING
COGITATINGLY
COGITATION
COGITATIONS
COGITATIVE
COGITATIVELY
COGITATIVENESS
COGITATOR
COGITATORS
COGITO
COGITOS
COGNAC
COGNACS
COGNATE
COGNATELY
COGNATENESS
COGNATENESSES
COGNATES
COGNATION
COGNATIONS
COGNISABLE
COGNISABLY
COGNISANCE
COGNISANCES
COGNISANT
COGNISE
COGNISED
COGNISES
COGNISING

COGNITION
COGNITIONAL
COGNITIONS
COGNITIVE
COGNITIVELY
COGNITIVISM
COGNITIVISTIC
COGNITIVITIES
COGNITIVITY
COGNIZABLE
COGNIZABLY
COGNIZANCE
COGNIZANCES
COGNIZANT
COGNIZE
COGNIZED
COGNIZER
COGNIZERS
COGNIZES
COGNIZING
COGNOMEN
COGNOMENS
COGNOMINA
COGNOMINAL
COGNOMINALLY
COGNOMINATE
COGNOMINATED
COGNOMINATES
COGNOMINATING
COGNOMINATION
COGNOMINATIONS
COGNOSCE
COGNOSCED
COGNOSCENTE
COGNOSCENTI
COGNOSCES
COGNOSCIBLE
COGNOSCING
COGNOVIT
COGNOVITS
COGON
COGONS
COGS
COGUE
COGUES
COGWAY
COGWAYS
COGWHEEL
COGWHEELS
COHAB
COHABIT
COHABITANT
COHABITANTS
COHABITATION
COHABITATIONS
COHABITED

COHABITEE
COHABITEES
COHABITER
COHABITERS
COHABITING
COHABITOR
COHABITORS
COHABITS
COHABS
COHEAD
COHEADED
COHEADING
COHEADS
COHEIR
COHEIRESS
COHEIRESSES
COHEIRS
COHERE
COHERED
COHERENCE
COHERENCES
COHERENCIES
COHERENCY
COHERENT
COHERENTLY
COHERER
COHERERS
COHERES
COHERING
COHERITOR
COHERITORS
COHESIBILITIES
COHESIBILITY
COHESIBLE
COHESION
COHESIONLESS
COHESIONS
COHESIVE
COHESIVELY
COHESIVENESS
COHESIVENESSES
COHIBIT
COHIBITED
COHIBITING
COHIBITION
COHIBITIONS
COHIBITIVE
COHIBITS
COHO
COHOBATE
COHOBATED
COHOBATES
COHOBATING
COHOE
COHOES
COHOG

COHOGS
COHOLDER
COHOLDERS
COHOMOLOGICAL
COHOMOLOGIES
COHOMOLOGY
COHORN
COHORNS
COHORT
COHORTATIVE
COHORTATIVES
COHORTS
COHOS
COHOSH
COHOSHES
COHOST
COHOSTED
COHOSTESS
COHOSTESSED
COHOSTESSES
COHOSTESSING
COHOSTING
COHOSTS
COHUNE
COHUNES
COHYPONYM
COHYPONYMS
COIF
COIFED
COIFFE
COIFFED
COIFFES
COIFFEUR
COIFFEURS
COIFFEUSE
COIFFEUSES
COIFFING
COIFFURE
COIFFURED
COIFFURES
COIFFURING
COIFING
COIFS
COIGN
COIGNE
COIGNED
COIGNES
COIGNING
COIGNS
COIL
COILABILITIES
COILABILITY
COILED
COILER
COILERS
COILING

COILS
COIN
COINABLE
COINAGE
COINAGES
COINCIDE
COINCIDED
COINCIDENCE
COINCIDENCES
COINCIDENCIES
COINCIDENCY
COINCIDENT
COINCIDENTAL
COINCIDENTALLY
COINCIDENTLY
COINCIDES
COINCIDING
COINED
COINER
COINERS
COINFER
COINFERRED
COINFERRING
COINFERS
COINHERE
COINHERED
COINHERENCE
COINHERENCES
COINHERES
COINHERING
COINHERITANCE
COINHERITANCES
COINHERITOR
COINHERITORS
COINING
COININGS
COINMATE
COINMATES
COINS
COINSTANTANEITY
COINSTANTANEOUS
COINSURANCE
COINSURANCES
COINSURE
COINSURED
COINSURER
COINSURERS
COINSURES
COINSURING
COINTER
COINTERRED
COINTERRING
COINTERS
COINVENT
COINVENTED
COINVENTING

COINVENTOR
COINVENTORS
COINVENTS
COINVESTIGATOR
COINVESTIGATORS
COINVESTOR
COINVESTORS
COIR
COIRS
COISTREL
COISTRELS
COISTRIL
COISTRILS
COIT
COITAL
COITALLY
COITION
COITIONAL
COITIONS
COITS
COITUS
COITUSES
COJOIN
COJOINED
COJOINING
COJOINS
COJONES
COKE
COKED
COKEHEAD
COKEHEADS
COKERNUT
COKERNUTS
COKES
COKESES
COKIER
COKIEST
COKING
COKULORIS
COKULORISES
COKY
COL
COLA
COLANDER
COLANDERS
COLAS
COLATITUDE
COLATITUDES
COLCANNON
COLCANNONS
COLCHICA
COLCHICINE
COLCHICINES
COLCHICUM
COLCHICUMS
COLCOTHAR

COLCOTHARS
COLD
COLDBLOOD
COLDBLOODS
COLDCOCK
COLDCOCKED
COLDCOCKING
COLDCOCKS
COLDER
COLDEST
COLDHEARTED
COLDHEARTEDLY
COLDHEARTEDNESS
COLDHOUSE
COLDHOUSES
COLDIE
COLDIES
COLDISH
COLDLY
COLDNESS
COLDNESSES
COLDS
COLE
COLEAD
COLEADER
COLEADERS
COLEADING
COLEADS
COLECTOMIES
COLECTOMY
COLED
COLEMANITE
COLEMANITES
COLEOPTER
COLEOPTERA
COLEOPTERAL
COLEOPTERAN
COLEOPTERANS
COLEOPTERIST
COLEOPTERISTS
COLEOPTERON
COLEOPTERONS
COLEOPTEROUS
COLEOPTERS
COLEOPTILE
COLEOPTILES
COLEORHIZA
COLEORHIZAE
COLEORHIZAS
COLEORRHIZA
COLEORRHIZAS
COLES
COLESEED
COLESEEDS
COLESLAW
COLESLAWS

COLESSEE
COLESSEES
COLESSOR
COLESSORS
COLESTIPOL
COLETIT
COLETITS
COLEUS
COLEUSES
COLEWORT
COLEWORTS
COLEY
COLEYS
COLIBRI
COLIBRIS
COLIC
COLICIN
COLICINE
COLICINES
COLICINS
COLICKIER
COLICKIEST
COLICKY
COLICROOT
COLICROOTS
COLICS
COLICWEED
COLICWEEDS
COLIES
COLIFORM
COLIFORMS
COLIN
COLINEAR
COLINEARITIES
COLINEARITY
COLINS
COLIPHAGE
COLIPHAGES
COLISEUM
COLISEUMS
COLISTIN
COLISTINS
COLITIC
COLITIS
COLITISES
COLL
COLLABORATE
COLLABORATED
COLLABORATES
COLLABORATING
COLLABORATION
COLLABORATIONS
COLLABORATIVE
COLLABORATIVELY
COLLABORATIVES
COLLABORATOR

COLLABORATORS
COLLAGE
COLLAGED
COLLAGEN
COLLAGENASE
COLLAGENASES
COLLAGENIC
COLLAGENOUS
COLLAGENS
COLLAGES
COLLAGING
COLLAGIST
COLLAGISTS
COLLAPSABILITY
COLLAPSABLE
COLLAPSAR
COLLAPSARS
COLLAPSE
COLLAPSED
COLLAPSES
COLLAPSIBILITY
COLLAPSIBLE
COLLAPSING
COLLAR
COLLARBONE
COLLARBONES
COLLARD
COLLARDS
COLLARED
COLLARET
COLLARETS
COLLARETTE
COLLARETTES
COLLARING
COLLARLESS
COLLARS
COLLATABLE
COLLATE
COLLATED
COLLATERAL
COLLATERALITIES
COLLATERALITY
COLLATERALIZE
COLLATERALIZED
COLLATERALIZES
COLLATERALIZING
COLLATERALLY
COLLATERALS
COLLATES
COLLATING
COLLATION
COLLATIONS
COLLATIVE
COLLATOR
COLLATORS
COLLEAGUE

COLLEAGUED
COLLEAGUES
COLLEAGUESHIP
COLLEAGUESHIPS
COLLEAGUING
COLLECT
COLLECTABLE
COLLECTABLES
COLLECTANEA
COLLECTED
COLLECTEDLY
COLLECTEDNESS
COLLECTEDNESSES
COLLECTIBLE
COLLECTIBLES
COLLECTING
COLLECTINGS
COLLECTION
COLLECTIONS
COLLECTIVE
COLLECTIVELY
COLLECTIVENESS
COLLECTIVES
COLLECTIVISE
COLLECTIVISED
COLLECTIVISES
COLLECTIVISING
COLLECTIVISM
COLLECTIVISMS
COLLECTIVIST
COLLECTIVISTIC
COLLECTIVISTS
COLLECTIVITIES
COLLECTIVITY
COLLECTIVIZE
COLLECTIVIZED
COLLECTIVIZES
COLLECTIVIZING
COLLECTOR
COLLECTORATE
COLLECTORATES
COLLECTORS
COLLECTORSHIP
COLLECTORSHIPS
COLLECTS
COLLED
COLLEEN
COLLEENS
COLLEGE
COLLEGER
COLLEGERS
COLLEGES
COLLEGIA
COLLEGIAL
COLLEGIALISM
COLLEGIALISMS

COLLEGIALITIES
COLLEGIALITY
COLLEGIALLY
COLLEGIAN
COLLEGIANER
COLLEGIANERS
COLLEGIANS
COLLEGIATE
COLLEGIATELY
COLLEGIATES
COLLEGIUM
COLLEGIUMS
COLLEMBOLAN
COLLEMBOLANS
COLLEMBOLOUS
COLLENCHYMA
COLLENCHYMAS
COLLENCHYMATA
COLLENCHYMATOUS
COLLET
COLLETED
COLLETERIAL
COLLETING
COLLETS
COLLICULI
COLLICULUS
COLLICULUSES
COLLIDE
COLLIDED
COLLIDER
COLLIDERS
COLLIDES
COLLIDING
COLLIE
COLLIED
COLLIER
COLLIERIES
COLLIERS
COLLIERY
COLLIES
COLLIESHANGIE
COLLIESHANGIES
COLLIEST
COLLIGATE
COLLIGATED
COLLIGATES
COLLIGATING
COLLIGATION
COLLIGATIONS
COLLIGATIVE
COLLIMATE
COLLIMATED
COLLIMATES
COLLIMATING
COLLIMATION
COLLIMATIONS

COLLIMATOR
COLLIMATORS
COLLINEAR
COLLINEARITIES
COLLINEARITY
COLLINEARLY
COLLING
COLLINGS
COLLINS
COLLINSES
COLLINSIA
COLLIQUABLE
COLLIQUANT
COLLIQUATE
COLLIQUATED
COLLIQUATES
COLLIQUATING
COLLIQUATION
COLLIQUATIONS
COLLIQUATIVE
COLLIQUESCENCES
COLLISION
COLLISIONAL
COLLISIONALLY
COLLISIONS
COLLOCATE
COLLOCATED
COLLOCATES
COLLOCATING
COLLOCATION
COLLOCATIONAL
COLLOCATIONS
COLLOCUTOR
COLLOCUTORS
COLLOCUTORY
COLLODION
COLLODIONS
COLLODIUM
COLLOGUE
COLLOGUED
COLLOGUES
COLLOGUING
COLLOID
COLLOIDAL
COLLOIDALITY
COLLOIDALLY
COLLOIDS
COLLOP
COLLOPS
COLLOQUE
COLLOQUED
COLLOQUES
COLLOQUIA
COLLOQUIAL
COLLOQUIALISM
COLLOQUIALISMS

COLLOQUIALIST
COLLOQUIALISTS
COLLOQUIALITIES
COLLOQUIALITY
COLLOQUIALLY
COLLOQUIALNESS
COLLOQUIALS
COLLOQUIED
COLLOQUIES
COLLOQUING
COLLOQUISE
COLLOQUISED
COLLOQUISES
COLLOQUISING
COLLOQUIST
COLLOQUISTS
COLLOQUIUM
COLLOQUIUMS
COLLOQUIZE
COLLOQUIZED
COLLOQUIZES
COLLOQUIZING
COLLOQUY
COLLOQUYING
COLLOTYPE
COLLOTYPES
COLLOTYPIC
COLLS
COLLUCTATION
COLLUCTATIONS
COLLUDE
COLLUDED
COLLUDER
COLLUDERS
COLLUDES
COLLUDING
COLLUSION
COLLUSIONS
COLLUSIVE
COLLUSIVELY
COLLUVIA
COLLUVIAL
COLLUVIES
COLLUVIUM
COLLUVIUMS
COLLY
COLLYING
COLLYRIA
COLLYRIUM
COLLYRIUMS
COLLYWOBBLES
COLOBI
COLOBID
COLOBOMA
COLOBOMAS
COLOBOMATA

COLOBUS
COLOBUSES
COLOCATE
COLOCATED
COLOCATES
COLOCATING
COLOCYNTH
COLOCYNTHS
COLOG
COLOGARITHM
COLOGARITHMS
COLOGNE
COLOGNED
COLOGNES
COLOGS
COLON
COLONE
COLONEL
COLONELCIES
COLONELCY
COLONELLING
COLONELLINGS
COLONELS
COLONELSHIP
COLONELSHIPS
COLONES
COLONI
COLONIAL
COLONIALISM
COLONIALISMS
COLONIALIST
COLONIALISTIC
COLONIALISTS
COLONIALIZE
COLONIALIZED
COLONIALIZES
COLONIALIZING
COLONIALLY
COLONIALNESS
COLONIALNESSES
COLONIALS
COLONIC
COLONICS
COLONIES
COLONISABLE
COLONISATION
COLONISATIONS
COLONISE
COLONISED
COLONISER
COLONISERS
COLONISES
COLONISING
COLONIST
COLONISTS
COLONITIS

COLONITISES
COLONIZABLE
COLONIZATION
COLONIZATIONIST
COLONIZATIONS
COLONIZE
COLONIZED
COLONIZER
COLONIZERS
COLONIZES
COLONIZING
COLONNADE
COLONNADED
COLONNADES
COLONOSCOPE
COLONOSCOPES
COLONOSCOPIES
COLONOSCOPY
COLONS
COLONUS
COLONY
COLOPHON
COLOPHONIES
COLOPHONS
COLOPHONY
COLOQUINTIDA
COLOQUINTIDAS
COLOR
COLORABLE
COLORABLY
COLORADO
COLORANT
COLORANTS
COLORATION
COLORATIONS
COLORATURA
COLORATURAS
COLORATURE
COLORATURES
COLORBRED
COLORECTAL
COLORED
COLOREDS
COLORER
COLORERS
COLORFAST
COLORFASTNESS
COLORFASTNESSES
COLORFUL
COLORFULLY
COLORFULNESS
COLORFULNESSES
COLORIFIC
COLORIMETER
COLORIMETERS
COLORIMETRIC

COLORIMETRICAL
COLORIMETRIES
COLORIMETRY
COLORING
COLORINGS
COLORISM
COLORISMS
COLORIST
COLORISTIC
COLORISTICALLY
COLORISTS
COLORIZATION
COLORIZATIONS
COLORIZE
COLORIZED
COLORIZES
COLORIZING
COLORLESS
COLORLESSLY
COLORLESSNESS
COLORLESSNESSES
COLORMAN
COLORMEN
COLORPOINT
COLORPOINTS
COLORS
COLORY
COLOSSAL
COLOSSALLY
COLOSSEUM
COLOSSEUMS
COLOSSI
COLOSSUS
COLOSSUSES
COLOSTOMIES
COLOSTOMY
COLOSTRAL
COLOSTRIC
COLOSTROUS
COLOSTRUM
COLOSTRUMS
COLOTOMIES
COLOTOMY
COLOUR
COLOURABILITY
COLOURABLE
COLOURABLENESS
COLOURABLY
COLOURANT
COLOURANTS
COLOURATION
COLOURATIONS
COLOURED
COLOUREDS
COLOURER
COLOURERS

COLOURFAST
COLOURFASTNESS
COLOURFUL
COLOURFULLY
COLOURFULNESS
COLOURING
COLOURINGS
COLOURISATION
COLOURISATIONS
COLOURISE
COLOURISED
COLOURISES
COLOURISING
COLOURIST
COLOURISTIC
COLOURISTICALLY
COLOURISTS
COLOURIZATION
COLOURIZATIONS
COLOURIZE
COLOURIZED
COLOURIZES
COLOURIZING
COLOURLESS
COLOURLESSLY
COLOURLESSNESS
COLOURMAN
COLOURMEN
COLOURPOINT
COLOURPOINTS
COLOURS
COLOURWASH
COLOURWASHED
COLOURWASHES
COLOURWASHING
COLOURWAY
COLOURWAYS
COLOURY
COLPITIS
COLPITISES
COLPORTAGE
COLPORTAGES
COLPORTEUR
COLPORTEURS
COLPOSCOPE
COLPOSCOPES
COLPOSCOPICAL
COLPOSCOPICALLY
COLPOSCOPIES
COLPOSCOPY
COLPOTOMIES
COLPOTOMY
COLS
COLT
COLTAN
COLTED

COLTER
COLTERS
COLTING
COLTISH
COLTISHLY
COLTISHNESS
COLTISHNESSES
COLTS
COLTSFOOT
COLTSFOOTS
COLTWOOD
COLTWOODS
COLUBRIAD
COLUBRIADS
COLUBRID
COLUBRIDS
COLUBRIFORM
COLUBRINE
COLUGO
COLUGOS
COLUMBARIA
COLUMBARIES
COLUMBARIUM
COLUMBARY
COLUMBATE
COLUMBATES
COLUMBIC
COLUMBINE
COLUMBINES
COLUMBITE
COLUMBITES
COLUMBIUM
COLUMBIUMS
COLUMBOUS
COLUMEL
COLUMELLA
COLUMELLAE
COLUMELLAR
COLUMELS
COLUMN
COLUMNAL
COLUMNAR
COLUMNARITIES
COLUMNARITY
COLUMNATED
COLUMNED
COLUMNIATED
COLUMNIATION
COLUMNIATIONS
COLUMNIST
COLUMNISTIC
COLUMNISTS
COLUMNS
COLURE
COLURES
COLY

COLZA
COLZAS
COMA
COMADE
COMAE
COMAKE
COMAKER
COMAKERS
COMAKES
COMAKING
COMAL
COMANAGE
COMANAGED
COMANAGEMENT
COMANAGEMENTS
COMANAGER
COMANAGERS
COMANAGES
COMANAGING
COMANCHERO
COMANCHEROS
COMARB
COMARBS
COMART
COMARTS
COMAS
COMATE
COMATES
COMATIC
COMATIK
COMATIKS
COMATOSE
COMATOSELY
COMATULA
COMATULAE
COMATULID
COMATULIDS
COMB
COMBAT
COMBATABLE
COMBATANT
COMBATANTS
COMBATED
COMBATER
COMBATERS
COMBATING
COMBATIVE
COMBATIVELY
COMBATIVENESS
COMBATIVENESSES
COMBATS
COMBATTED
COMBATTING
COMBE
COMBED
COMBER

COMBERS
COMBES
COMBI
COMBIER
COMBIES
COMBIEST
COMBINABILITIES
COMBINABILITY
COMBINABLE
COMBINATE
COMBINATION
COMBINATIONAL
COMBINATIONS
COMBINATIVE
COMBINATORIAL
COMBINATORIALLY
COMBINATORICS
COMBINATORY
COMBINE
COMBINED
COMBINER
COMBINERS
COMBINES
COMBING
COMBINGS
COMBINING
COMBIS
COMBLE
COMBLES
COMBLESS
COMBLIKE
COMBO
COMBOS
COMBRETUM
COMBRETUMS
COMBS
COMBURGESS
COMBURGESSES
COMBUST
COMBUSTED
COMBUSTIBILITY
COMBUSTIBLE
COMBUSTIBLENESS
COMBUSTIBLES
COMBUSTIBLY
COMBUSTING
COMBUSTION
COMBUSTIONS
COMBUSTIOUS
COMBUSTIVE
COMBUSTIVES
COMBUSTOR
COMBUSTORS
COMBUSTS
COMBWISE
COMBY

COME
COMEBACK
COMEBACKS
COMEDDLE
COMEDDLED
COMEDDLES
COMEDDLING
COMEDIAN
COMEDIANS
COMEDIC
COMEDICALLY
COMEDIENNE
COMEDIENNES
COMEDIES
COMEDIETTA
COMEDIETTAS
COMEDO
COMEDOGENIC
COMEDONES
COMEDOS
COMEDOWN
COMEDOWNS
COMEDY
COMELIER
COMELIEST
COMELILY
COMELINESS
COMELINESSES
COMELY
COMEMBER
COMEMBERS
COMEOVER
COMEOVERS
COMER
COMERS
COMES
COMESTIBLE
COMESTIBLES
COMET
COMETARY
COMETH
COMETHER
COMETHERS
COMETIC
COMETOGRAPHIES
COMETOGRAPHY
COMETOLOGIES
COMETOLOGY
COMETS
COMEUPPANCE
COMEUPPANCES
COMFIER
COMFIEST
COMFIT
COMFITS
COMFITURE

COMFITURES
COMFORT
COMFORTABLE
COMFORTABLENESS
COMFORTABLY
COMFORTED
COMFORTER
COMFORTERS
COMFORTING
COMFORTINGLY
COMFORTLESS
COMFORTLESSLY
COMFORTLESSNESS
COMFORTS
COMFREY
COMFREYS
COMFY
COMIC
COMICAL
COMICALITIES
COMICALITY
COMICALLY
COMICALNESS
COMICALNESSES
COMICE
COMICES
COMICS
COMING
COMINGLE
COMINGLED
COMINGLES
COMINGLING
COMINGS
COMIQUE
COMIQUES
COMITADJI
COMITADJIS
COMITAL
COMITATIVE
COMITATIVES
COMITATUS
COMITATUSES
COMITIA
COMITIAL
COMITIAS
COMITIES
COMITY
COMIX
COMMA
COMMAND
COMMANDABLE
COMMANDANT
COMMANDANTS
COMMANDANTSHIP
COMMANDANTSHIPS
COMMANDED

COMMANDEER
COMMANDEERED
COMMANDEERING
COMMANDEERS
COMMANDER
COMMANDERIES
COMMANDERS
COMMANDERSHIP
COMMANDERSHIPS
COMMANDERY
COMMANDING
COMMANDINGLY
COMMANDMENT
COMMANDMENTS
COMMANDO
COMMANDOES
COMMANDOS
COMMANDS
COMMAS
COMMATA
COMMEASURABLE
COMMEASURE
COMMEASURED
COMMEASURES
COMMEASURING
COMMEMORABLE
COMMEMORATE
COMMEMORATED
COMMEMORATES
COMMEMORATING
COMMEMORATION
COMMEMORATIONAL
COMMEMORATIONS
COMMEMORATIVE
COMMEMORATIVELY
COMMEMORATIVES
COMMEMORATOR
COMMEMORATORS
COMMEMORATORY
COMMENCE
COMMENCED
COMMENCEMENT
COMMENCEMENTS
COMMENCER
COMMENCERS
COMMENCES
COMMENCING
COMMEND
COMMENDABLE
COMMENDABLENESS
COMMENDABLY
COMMENDAM
COMMENDAMS
COMMENDATION
COMMENDATIONS
COMMENDATOR

COMMENDATORS
COMMENDATORY
COMMENDED
COMMENDER
COMMENDERS
COMMENDING
COMMENDS
COMMENSAL
COMMENSALISM
COMMENSALISMS
COMMENSALITIES
COMMENSALITY
COMMENSALLY
COMMENSALS
COMMENSURABLE
COMMENSURABLY
COMMENSURATE
COMMENSURATELY
COMMENSURATION
COMMENSURATIONS
COMMENT
COMMENTARIAL
COMMENTARIAT
COMMENTARIATS
COMMENTARIES
COMMENTARY
COMMENTATE
COMMENTATED
COMMENTATES
COMMENTATING
COMMENTATION
COMMENTATIONS
COMMENTATOR
COMMENTATORIAL
COMMENTATORS
COMMENTED
COMMENTER
COMMENTERS
COMMENTING
COMMENTOR
COMMENTORS
COMMENTS
COMMER
COMMERCE
COMMERCED
COMMERCES
COMMERCIAL
COMMERCIALESE
COMMERCIALESES
COMMERCIALISE
COMMERCIALISED
COMMERCIALISES
COMMERCIALISING
COMMERCIALISM
COMMERCIALISMS
COMMERCIALIST

COMMERCIALISTIC
COMMERCIALISTS
COMMERCIALITIES
COMMERCIALITY
COMMERCIALIZE
COMMERCIALIZED
COMMERCIALIZES
COMMERCIALIZING
COMMERCIALLY
COMMERCIALS
COMMERCING
COMMERE
COMMERES
COMMERGE
COMMERGED
COMMERGES
COMMERGING
COMMERS
COMMIE
COMMIES
COMMINATE
COMMINATED
COMMINATES
COMMINATING
COMMINATION
COMMINATIONS
COMMINATIVE
COMMINATORY
COMMINGLE
COMMINGLED
COMMINGLES
COMMINGLING
COMMINUTE
COMMINUTED
COMMINUTES
COMMINUTING
COMMINUTION
COMMINUTIONS
COMMIS
COMMISERABLE
COMMISERATE
COMMISERATED
COMMISERATES
COMMISERATING
COMMISERATINGLY
COMMISERATION
COMMISERATIONS
COMMISERATIVE
COMMISERATIVELY
COMMISERATOR
COMMISERATORS
COMMISSAIRE
COMMISSAIRES
COMMISSAR
COMMISSARIAL
COMMISSARIAT

COMMISSARIATS
COMMISSARIES
COMMISSARS
COMMISSARY
COMMISSARYSHIP
COMMISSARYSHIPS
COMMISSION
COMMISSIONAIRE
COMMISSIONAIRES
COMMISSIONAL
COMMISSIONARY
COMMISSIONED
COMMISSIONER
COMMISSIONERS
COMMISSIONING
COMMISSIONS
COMMISSURAL
COMMISSURE
COMMISSURES
COMMIT
COMMITMENT
COMMITMENTS
COMMITS
COMMITTABLE
COMMITTAL
COMMITTALS
COMMITTED
COMMITTEE
COMMITTEEMAN
COMMITTEEMEN
COMMITTEES
COMMITTEESHIP
COMMITTEESHIPS
COMMITTEEWOMAN
COMMITTEEWOMEN
COMMITTER
COMMITTERS
COMMITTING
COMMIX
COMMIXED
COMMIXES
COMMIXING
COMMIXT
COMMIXTION
COMMIXTIONS
COMMIXTURE
COMMIXTURES
COMMO
COMMODE
COMMODES
COMMODIFICATION
COMMODIFIED
COMMODIFIES
COMMODIFY
COMMODIFYING
COMMODIOUS

COMMODIOUSLY
COMMODIOUSNESS
COMMODITIES
COMMODITY
COMMODO
COMMODORE
COMMODORES
COMMON
COMMONABLE
COMMONAGE
COMMONAGES
COMMONALITIES
COMMONALITY
COMMONALTIES
COMMONALTY
COMMONED
COMMONER
COMMONERS
COMMONEST
COMMONEY
COMMONEYS
COMMONHOLD
COMMONHOLDS
COMMONING
COMMONINGS
COMMONLY
COMMONNESS
COMMONNESSES
COMMONPLACE
COMMONPLACED
COMMONPLACENESS
COMMONPLACES
COMMONPLACING
COMMONS
COMMONSENSE
COMMONSENSIBLE
COMMONSENSICAL
COMMONWEAL
COMMONWEALS
COMMONWEALTH
COMMONWEALTHS
COMMORANT
COMMORANTS
COMMORIENTES
COMMOS
COMMOT
COMMOTE
COMMOTES
COMMOTION
COMMOTIONAL
COMMOTIONS
COMMOTS
COMMOVE
COMMOVED
COMMOVES
COMMOVING

COMMS
COMMUNAL
COMMUNALISATION
COMMUNALISE
COMMUNALISED
COMMUNALISER
COMMUNALISERS
COMMUNALISES
COMMUNALISING
COMMUNALISM
COMMUNALISMS
COMMUNALIST
COMMUNALISTIC
COMMUNALISTS
COMMUNALITIES
COMMUNALITY
COMMUNALIZATION
COMMUNALIZE
COMMUNALIZED
COMMUNALIZER
COMMUNALIZERS
COMMUNALIZES
COMMUNALIZING
COMMUNALLY
COMMUNARD
COMMUNARDS
COMMUNAUTAIRE
COMMUNAUTAIRES
COMMUNE
COMMUNED
COMMUNES
COMMUNICABILITY
COMMUNICABLE
COMMUNICABLY
COMMUNICANT
COMMUNICANTS
COMMUNICATE
COMMUNICATED
COMMUNICATEE
COMMUNICATEES
COMMUNICATES
COMMUNICATING
COMMUNICATION
COMMUNICATIONAL
COMMUNICATIONS
COMMUNICATIVE
COMMUNICATIVELY
COMMUNICATOR
COMMUNICATORS
COMMUNICATORY
COMMUNING
COMMUNINGS
COMMUNION
COMMUNIONAL
COMMUNIONALLY
COMMUNIONS

COMMUNIQUE
COMMUNIQUES
COMMUNISATION
COMMUNISATIONS
COMMUNISE
COMMUNISED
COMMUNISES
COMMUNISING
COMMUNISM
COMMUNISMS
COMMUNIST
COMMUNISTIC
COMMUNISTICALLY
COMMUNISTS
COMMUNITAIRE
COMMUNITAIRES
COMMUNITARIAN
COMMUNITARIANS
COMMUNITIES
COMMUNITY
COMMUNIZATION
COMMUNIZATIONS
COMMUNIZE
COMMUNIZED
COMMUNIZES
COMMUNIZING
COMMUTABILITIES
COMMUTABILITY
COMMUTABLE
COMMUTABLENESS
COMMUTATE
COMMUTATED
COMMUTATES
COMMUTATING
COMMUTATION
COMMUTATIONS
COMMUTATIVE
COMMUTATIVELY
COMMUTATIVITIES
COMMUTATIVITY
COMMUTATOR
COMMUTATORS
COMMUTE
COMMUTED
COMMUTER
COMMUTERS
COMMUTES
COMMUTING
COMMUTUAL
COMMY
COMODO
COMONOMER
COMONOMERS
COMOSE
COMOUS
COMP

COMPACT
COMPACTED
COMPACTEDLY
COMPACTEDNESS
COMPACTEDNESSES
COMPACTER
COMPACTERS
COMPACTEST
COMPACTIBLE
COMPACTIFIED
COMPACTIFIES
COMPACTIFY
COMPACTIFYING
COMPACTING
COMPACTION
COMPACTIONS
COMPACTLY
COMPACTNESS
COMPACTNESSES
COMPACTOR
COMPACTORS
COMPACTS
COMPACTURE
COMPACTURES
COMPADRE
COMPADRES
COMPAGE
COMPAGES
COMPAGINATE
COMPAGINATED
COMPAGINATES
COMPAGINATING
COMPAGINATION
COMPAGINATIONS
COMPAND
COMPANDED
COMPANDER
COMPANDERS
COMPANDING
COMPANDOR
COMPANDORS
COMPANDS
COMPANIABLE
COMPANIED
COMPANIES
COMPANING
COMPANION
COMPANIONABLE
COMPANIONABLY
COMPANIONATE
COMPANIONED
COMPANIONHOOD
COMPANIONHOODS
COMPANIONING
COMPANIONLESS
COMPANIONS

COMPANIONSHIP
COMPANIONSHIPS
COMPANIONWAY
COMPANIONWAYS
COMPANY
COMPANYING
COMPARABILITIES
COMPARABILITY
COMPARABLE
COMPARABLENESS
COMPARABLY
COMPARATIST
COMPARATISTS
COMPARATIVE
COMPARATIVELY
COMPARATIVENESS
COMPARATIVES
COMPARATIVIST
COMPARATIVISTS
COMPARATOR
COMPARATORS
COMPARE
COMPARED
COMPARER
COMPARERS
COMPARES
COMPARING
COMPARISON
COMPARISONS
COMPART
COMPARTED
COMPARTING
COMPARTMENT
COMPARTMENTAL
COMPARTMENTALLY
COMPARTMENTED
COMPARTMENTING
COMPARTMENTS
COMPARTS
COMPASS
COMPASSABLE
COMPASSED
COMPASSES
COMPASSING
COMPASSINGS
COMPASSION
COMPASSIONABLE
COMPASSIONATE
COMPASSIONATED
COMPASSIONATELY
COMPASSIONATES
COMPASSIONATING
COMPASSIONED
COMPASSIONING
COMPASSIONLESS
COMPASSIONS

COMPAST
COMPATIBILITIES
COMPATIBILITY
COMPATIBLE
COMPATIBLENESS
COMPATIBLES
COMPATIBLY
COMPATRIOT
COMPATRIOTIC
COMPATRIOTISM
COMPATRIOTISMS
COMPATRIOTS
COMPEAR
COMPEARANCE
COMPEARANCES
COMPEARANT
COMPEARANTS
COMPEARED
COMPEARING
COMPEARS
COMPED
COMPEER
COMPEERED
COMPEERING
COMPEERS
COMPEL
COMPELLABLE
COMPELLABLY
COMPELLATION
COMPELLATIONS
COMPELLATIVE
COMPELLATIVES
COMPELLED
COMPELLER
COMPELLERS
COMPELLING
COMPELLINGLY
COMPELS
COMPEND
COMPENDIA
COMPENDIOUS
COMPENDIOUSLY
COMPENDIOUSNESS
COMPENDIUM
COMPENDIUMS
COMPENDS
COMPENSABILITY
COMPENSABLE
COMPENSATE
COMPENSATED
COMPENSATES
COMPENSATING
COMPENSATION
COMPENSATIONAL
COMPENSATIONS
COMPENSATIVE

COMPENSATOR
COMPENSATORS
COMPENSATORY
COMPER
COMPERE
COMPERED
COMPERES
COMPERING
COMPERS
COMPESCE
COMPESCED
COMPESCES
COMPESCING
COMPETE
COMPETED
COMPETENCE
COMPETENCES
COMPETENCIES
COMPETENCY
COMPETENT
COMPETENTLY
COMPETENTNESS
COMPETES
COMPETING
COMPETITION
COMPETITIONS
COMPETITIVE
COMPETITIVELY
COMPETITIVENESS
COMPETITOR
COMPETITORS
COMPILATION
COMPILATIONS
COMPILATOR
COMPILATORS
COMPILATORY
COMPILE
COMPILED
COMPILEMENT
COMPILEMENTS
COMPILER
COMPILERS
COMPILES
COMPILING
COMPING
COMPINGS
COMPITAL
COMPLACENCE
COMPLACENCES
COMPLACENCIES
COMPLACENCY
COMPLACENT
COMPLACENTLY
COMPLAIN
COMPLAINANT
COMPLAINANTS

COMPLAINED
COMPLAINER
COMPLAINERS
COMPLAINING
COMPLAININGLY
COMPLAININGS
COMPLAINS
COMPLAINT
COMPLAINTS
COMPLAISANCE
COMPLAISANCES
COMPLAISANT
COMPLAISANTLY
COMPLANATE
COMPLANATION
COMPLANATIONS
COMPLEAT
COMPLECT
COMPLECTED
COMPLECTING
COMPLECTS
COMPLEMENT
COMPLEMENTAL
COMPLEMENTALLY
COMPLEMENTARIES
COMPLEMENTARILY
COMPLEMENTARITY
COMPLEMENTARY
COMPLEMENTATION
COMPLEMENTED
COMPLEMENTING
COMPLEMENTIZER
COMPLEMENTIZERS
COMPLEMENTS
COMPLETABLE
COMPLETE
COMPLETED
COMPLETELY
COMPLETENESS
COMPLETENESSES
COMPLETER
COMPLETERS
COMPLETES
COMPLETEST
COMPLETING
COMPLETION
COMPLETIONS
COMPLETIST
COMPLETISTS
COMPLETIVE
COMPLETORY
COMPLEX
COMPLEXATION
COMPLEXATIONS
COMPLEXED
COMPLEXEDNESS

COMPLEXEDNESSES
COMPLEXER
COMPLEXES
COMPLEXEST
COMPLEXIFIED
COMPLEXIFIES
COMPLEXIFY
COMPLEXIFYING
COMPLEXING
COMPLEXION
COMPLEXIONAL
COMPLEXIONED
COMPLEXIONLESS
COMPLEXIONS
COMPLEXITIES
COMPLEXITY
COMPLEXLY
COMPLEXNESS
COMPLEXNESSES
COMPLEXOMETRIC
COMPLEXONE
COMPLEXONES
COMPLEXUS
COMPLEXUSES
COMPLIABLE
COMPLIABLENESS
COMPLIABLY
COMPLIANCE
COMPLIANCES
COMPLIANCIES
COMPLIANCY
COMPLIANT
COMPLIANTLY
COMPLIANTNESS
COMPLICACIES
COMPLICACY
COMPLICANT
COMPLICATE
COMPLICATED
COMPLICATEDLY
COMPLICATEDNESS
COMPLICATES
COMPLICATING
COMPLICATION
COMPLICATIONS
COMPLICATIVE
COMPLICE
COMPLICES
COMPLICIT
COMPLICITIES
COMPLICITOUS
COMPLICITY
COMPLIED
COMPLIER
COMPLIERS
COMPLIES

COMPLIMENT
COMPLIMENTAL
COMPLIMENTARILY
COMPLIMENTARY
COMPLIMENTED
COMPLIMENTER
COMPLIMENTERS
COMPLIMENTING
COMPLIMENTS
COMPLIN
COMPLINE
COMPLINES
COMPLINS
COMPLISH
COMPLISHED
COMPLISHES
COMPLISHING
COMPLOT
COMPLOTS
COMPLOTTED
COMPLOTTER
COMPLOTTERS
COMPLOTTING
COMPLUVIA
COMPLUVIUM
COMPLUVIUMS
COMPLY
COMPLYING
COMPO
COMPONE
COMPONENCIES
COMPONENCY
COMPONENT
COMPONENTAL
COMPONENTIAL
COMPONENTS
COMPONY
COMPORT
COMPORTANCE
COMPORTANCES
COMPORTED
COMPORTING
COMPORTMENT
COMPORTMENTS
COMPORTS
COMPOS
COMPOSE
COMPOSED
COMPOSEDLY
COMPOSEDNESS
COMPOSEDNESSES
COMPOSER
COMPOSERS
COMPOSES
COMPOSING
COMPOSITE

COMPOSITED
COMPOSITELY
COMPOSITENESS
COMPOSITENESSES
COMPOSITES
COMPOSITING
COMPOSITION
COMPOSITIONAL
COMPOSITIONALLY
COMPOSITIONS
COMPOSITIVE
COMPOSITOR
COMPOSITORIAL
COMPOSITORIALLY
COMPOSITORS
COMPOSITOUS
COMPOSSIBILITY
COMPOSSIBLE
COMPOST
COMPOSTABLE
COMPOSTED
COMPOSTER
COMPOSTERS
COMPOSTING
COMPOSTS
COMPOSTURE
COMPOSTURED
COMPOSTURES
COMPOSTURING
COMPOSURE
COMPOSURES
COMPOT
COMPOTATION
COMPOTATIONS
COMPOTATIONSHIP
COMPOTATOR
COMPOTATORS
COMPOTATORY
COMPOTE
COMPOTES
COMPOTIER
COMPOTIERS
COMPOTS
COMPOUND
COMPOUNDABLE
COMPOUNDED
COMPOUNDER
COMPOUNDERS
COMPOUNDING
COMPOUNDS
COMPRADOR
COMPRADORE
COMPRADORES
COMPRADORS
COMPREHEND
COMPREHENDED

COMPREHENDIBLE
COMPREHENDING
COMPREHENDS
COMPREHENSIBLE
COMPREHENSIBLY
COMPREHENSION
COMPREHENSIONS
COMPREHENSIVE
COMPREHENSIVELY
COMPREHENSIVES
COMPREHENSIVISE
COMPREHENSIVIZE
COMPRESS
COMPRESSED
COMPRESSEDLY
COMPRESSES
COMPRESSIBILITY
COMPRESSIBLE
COMPRESSIBLY
COMPRESSING
COMPRESSION
COMPRESSIONAL
COMPRESSIONS
COMPRESSIVE
COMPRESSIVELY
COMPRESSOR
COMPRESSORS
COMPRESSURE
COMPRESSURES
COMPRIMARIO
COMPRIMARIOS
COMPRINT
COMPRINTED
COMPRINTING
COMPRINTS
COMPRISABLE
COMPRISAL
COMPRISALS
COMPRISE
COMPRISED
COMPRISES
COMPRISING
COMPRIZE
COMPRIZED
COMPRIZES
COMPRIZING
COMPROMISE
COMPROMISED
COMPROMISER
COMPROMISERS
COMPROMISES
COMPROMISING
COMPROMISINGLY
COMPROVINCIAL
COMPS
COMPT

COMPTABLE
COMPTED
COMPTER
COMPTERS
COMPTIBLE
COMPTING
COMPTROLL
COMPTROLLED
COMPTROLLER
COMPTROLLERS
COMPTROLLERSHIP
COMPTROLLING
COMPTROLLS
COMPTS
COMPULSATIVE
COMPULSATORY
COMPULSE
COMPULSED
COMPULSES
COMPULSING
COMPULSION
COMPULSIONIST
COMPULSIONISTS
COMPULSIONS
COMPULSITOR
COMPULSITORS
COMPULSIVE
COMPULSIVELY
COMPULSIVENESS
COMPULSIVES
COMPULSIVITIES
COMPULSIVITY
COMPULSORIES
COMPULSORILY
COMPULSORINESS
COMPULSORY
COMPUNCTION
COMPUNCTIONS
COMPUNCTIOUS
COMPUNCTIOUSLY
COMPURGATION
COMPURGATIONS
COMPURGATOR
COMPURGATORIAL
COMPURGATORS
COMPURGATORY
COMPURSION
COMPURSIONS
COMPUTABILITIES
COMPUTABILITY
COMPUTABLE
COMPUTANT
COMPUTANTS
COMPUTATION
COMPUTATIONAL
COMPUTATIONALLY

COMPUTATIONS
COMPUTATIVE
COMPUTATOR
COMPUTATORS
COMPUTE
COMPUTED
COMPUTER
COMPUTERATE
COMPUTERDOM
COMPUTERDOMS
COMPUTERESE
COMPUTERESES
COMPUTERISATION
COMPUTERISE
COMPUTERISED
COMPUTERISES
COMPUTERISING
COMPUTERIST
COMPUTERISTS
COMPUTERIZABLE
COMPUTERIZATION
COMPUTERIZE
COMPUTERIZED
COMPUTERIZES
COMPUTERIZING
COMPUTERLESS
COMPUTERLIKE
COMPUTERNIK
COMPUTERNIKS
COMPUTERPHOBE
COMPUTERPHOBES
COMPUTERPHOBIA
COMPUTERPHOBIAS
COMPUTERPHOBIC
COMPUTERS
COMPUTES
COMPUTING
COMPUTIST
COMPUTISTS
COMRADE
COMRADELINESS
COMRADELINESSES
COMRADELY
COMRADERIES
COMRADERY
COMRADES
COMRADESHIP
COMRADESHIPS
COMS
COMSAT
COMSATS
COMSTOCKER
COMSTOCKERIES
COMSTOCKERS
COMSTOCKERY
COMSTOCKISM

COMSTOCKISMS
COMSYMP
COMSYMPS
COMTE
COMTES
COMUS
COMUSES
CON
CONACRE
CONACRED
CONACREISM
CONACREISMS
CONACRES
CONACRING
CONARIA
CONARIAL
CONARIUM
CONATION
CONATIONAL
CONATIONALLY
CONATIONS
CONATIVE
CONATUS
CONCANAVALIN
CONCANAVALINS
CONCATENATE
CONCATENATED
CONCATENATES
CONCATENATING
CONCATENATION
CONCATENATIONS
CONCAUSE
CONCAUSES
CONCAVE
CONCAVED
CONCAVELY
CONCAVENESS
CONCAVES
CONCAVING
CONCAVITIES
CONCAVITY
CONCEAL
CONCEALABLE
CONCEALED
CONCEALER
CONCEALERS
CONCEALING
CONCEALINGLY
CONCEALMENT
CONCEALMENTS
CONCEALS
CONCEDE
CONCEDED
CONCEDEDLY
CONCEDER
CONCEDERS

CONCEDES
CONCEDING
CONCEDO
CONCEIT
CONCEITED
CONCEITEDLY
CONCEITEDNESS
CONCEITEDNESSES
CONCEITFUL
CONCEITING
CONCEITLESS
CONCEITS
CONCEITY
CONCEIVABILITY
CONCEIVABLE
CONCEIVABLENESS
CONCEIVABLY
CONCEIVE
CONCEIVED
CONCEIVER
CONCEIVERS
CONCEIVES
CONCEIVING
CONCELEBRANT
CONCELEBRANTS
CONCELEBRATE
CONCELEBRATED
CONCELEBRATES
CONCELEBRATING
CONCELEBRATION
CONCELEBRATIONS
CONCENT
CONCENTER
CONCENTERED
CONCENTERING
CONCENTERS
CONCENTRATE
CONCENTRATED
CONCENTRATEDLY
CONCENTRATES
CONCENTRATING
CONCENTRATION
CONCENTRATIONS
CONCENTRATIVE
CONCENTRATIVELY
CONCENTRATOR
CONCENTRATORS
CONCENTRE
CONCENTRED
CONCENTRES
CONCENTRIC
CONCENTRICAL
CONCENTRICALLY
CONCENTRICITIES
CONCENTRICITY
CONCENTRING

CONCENTS
CONCENTUS
CONCEPT
CONCEPTACLE
CONCEPTACLES
CONCEPTI
CONCEPTION
CONCEPTIONAL
CONCEPTIONS
CONCEPTIOUS
CONCEPTIVE
CONCEPTS
CONCEPTUAL
CONCEPTUALISE
CONCEPTUALISED
CONCEPTUALISES
CONCEPTUALISING
CONCEPTUALISM
CONCEPTUALISMS
CONCEPTUALIST
CONCEPTUALISTIC
CONCEPTUALISTS
CONCEPTUALITIES
CONCEPTUALITY
CONCEPTUALIZE
CONCEPTUALIZED
CONCEPTUALIZER
CONCEPTUALIZERS
CONCEPTUALIZES
CONCEPTUALIZING
CONCEPTUALLY
CONCEPTUS
CONCEPTUSES
CONCERN
CONCERNANCIES
CONCERNANCY
CONCERNED
CONCERNEDLY
CONCERNEDNESS
CONCERNEDNESSES
CONCERNING
CONCERNMENT
CONCERNMENTS
CONCERNS
CONCERT
CONCERTANTE
CONCERTANTES
CONCERTANTI
CONCERTED
CONCERTEDLY
CONCERTEDNESS
CONCERTEDNESSES
CONCERTGOER
CONCERTGOERS
CONCERTGOING
CONCERTGOINGS

CONCERTI
CONCERTINA
CONCERTINAED
CONCERTINAING
CONCERTINAS
CONCERTING
CONCERTINI
CONCERTINIST
CONCERTINISTS
CONCERTINO
CONCERTINOS
CONCERTISE
CONCERTISED
CONCERTISES
CONCERTISING
CONCERTIZE
CONCERTIZED
CONCERTIZES
CONCERTIZING
CONCERTMASTER
CONCERTMASTERS
CONCERTMEISTER
CONCERTMEISTERS
CONCERTO
CONCERTOS
CONCERTS
CONCERTSTUCK
CONCERTSTUCKS
CONCESSIBLE
CONCESSION
CONCESSIONAIRE
CONCESSIONAIRES
CONCESSIONAL
CONCESSIONARIES
CONCESSIONARY
CONCESSIONER
CONCESSIONERS
CONCESSIONIST
CONCESSIONISTS
CONCESSIONNAIRE
CONCESSIONS
CONCESSIVE
CONCESSIVELY
CONCETTI
CONCETTISM
CONCETTISMS
CONCETTIST
CONCETTISTS
CONCETTO
CONCH
CONCHA
CONCHAE
CONCHAL
CONCHATE
CONCHE
CONCHED

CONCHES
CONCHIE
CONCHIES
CONCHIFEROUS
CONCHIFORM
CONCHIGLIE
CONCHING
CONCHIOLIN
CONCHIOLINS
CONCHITIS
CONCHITISES
CONCHOID
CONCHOIDAL
CONCHOIDALLY
CONCHOIDS
CONCHOLOGICAL
CONCHOLOGIES
CONCHOLOGIST
CONCHOLOGISTS
CONCHOLOGY
CONCHS
CONCHY
CONCIERGE
CONCIERGES
CONCILIABLE
CONCILIAR
CONCILIARLY
CONCILIARY
CONCILIATE
CONCILIATED
CONCILIATES
CONCILIATING
CONCILIATION
CONCILIATIONS
CONCILIATIVE
CONCILIATOR
CONCILIATORILY
CONCILIATORS
CONCILIATORY
CONCINNITIES
CONCINNITY
CONCINNOUS
CONCIPIENCIES
CONCIPIENCY
CONCIPIENT
CONCISE
CONCISED
CONCISELY
CONCISENESS
CONCISENESSES
CONCISER
CONCISES
CONCISEST
CONCISING
CONCISION
CONCISIONS

CONCLAMATION
CONCLAMATIONS
CONCLAVE
CONCLAVES
CONCLAVIST
CONCLAVISTS
CONCLUDE
CONCLUDED
CONCLUDER
CONCLUDERS
CONCLUDES
CONCLUDING
CONCLUSION
CONCLUSIONARY
CONCLUSIONS
CONCLUSIVE
CONCLUSIVELY
CONCLUSIVENESS
CONCLUSORY
CONCOCT
CONCOCTED
CONCOCTER
CONCOCTERS
CONCOCTING
CONCOCTION
CONCOCTIONS
CONCOCTIVE
CONCOCTOR
CONCOCTORS
CONCOCTS
CONCOLOR
CONCOLORATE
CONCOLOROUS
CONCOMITANCE
CONCOMITANCES
CONCOMITANCIES
CONCOMITANCY
CONCOMITANT
CONCOMITANTLY
CONCOMITANTS
CONCORD
CONCORDANCE
CONCORDANCES
CONCORDANT
CONCORDANTLY
CONCORDAT
CONCORDATS
CONCORDED
CONCORDIAL
CONCORDING
CONCORDS
CONCORPORATE
CONCORPORATED
CONCORPORATES
CONCORPORATING
CONCOURS

CONCOURSE
CONCOURSES
CONCREATE
CONCREATED
CONCREATES
CONCREATING
CONCREMATION
CONCREMATIONS
CONCRESCENCE
CONCRESCENCES
CONCRESCENT
CONCRETE
CONCRETED
CONCRETELY
CONCRETENESS
CONCRETENESSES
CONCRETES
CONCRETING
CONCRETION
CONCRETIONARY
CONCRETIONS
CONCRETISATION
CONCRETISATIONS
CONCRETISE
CONCRETISED
CONCRETISES
CONCRETISING
CONCRETISM
CONCRETISMS
CONCRETIST
CONCRETISTS
CONCRETIVE
CONCRETIVELY
CONCRETIZATION
CONCRETIZATIONS
CONCRETIZE
CONCRETIZED
CONCRETIZES
CONCRETIZING
CONCREW
CONCREWED
CONCREWING
CONCREWS
CONCUBINAGE
CONCUBINAGES
CONCUBINARY
CONCUBINE
CONCUBINES
CONCUBITANCIES
CONCUBITANCY
CONCUBITANT
CONCUBITANTS
CONCUPIES
CONCUPISCENCE
CONCUPISCENCES
CONCUPISCENT

CONCUPISCIBLE
CONCUPY
CONCUR
CONCURRED
CONCURRENCE
CONCURRENCES
CONCURRENCIES
CONCURRENCY
CONCURRENT
CONCURRENTLY
CONCURRENTS
CONCURRING
CONCURRINGLY
CONCURS
CONCUSS
CONCUSSED
CONCUSSES
CONCUSSING
CONCUSSION
CONCUSSIONS
CONCUSSIVE
CONCYCLIC
CONCYCLICALLY
COND
CONDEMN
CONDEMNABLE
CONDEMNABLY
CONDEMNATION
CONDEMNATIONS
CONDEMNATORY
CONDEMNED
CONDEMNER
CONDEMNERS
CONDEMNING
CONDEMNINGLY
CONDEMNOR
CONDEMNORS
CONDEMNS
CONDENSABILITY
CONDENSABLE
CONDENSATE
CONDENSATED
CONDENSATES
CONDENSATING
CONDENSATION
CONDENSATIONAL
CONDENSATIONS
CONDENSE
CONDENSED
CONDENSER
CONDENSERIES
CONDENSERS
CONDENSERY
CONDENSES
CONDENSIBILITY
CONDENSIBLE

CONDENSING
CONDER
CONDERS
CONDESCEND
CONDESCENDED
CONDESCENDENCE
CONDESCENDENCES
CONDESCENDING
CONDESCENDINGLY
CONDESCENDS
CONDESCENSION
CONDESCENSIONS
CONDIDDLE
CONDIDDLED
CONDIDDLES
CONDIDDLING
CONDIE
CONDIES
CONDIGN
CONDIGNLY
CONDIGNNESS
CONDIGNNESSES
CONDIMENT
CONDIMENTAL
CONDIMENTED
CONDIMENTING
CONDIMENTS
CONDISCIPLE
CONDISCIPLES
CONDITION
CONDITIONABLE
CONDITIONAL
CONDITIONALITY
CONDITIONALLY
CONDITIONALS
CONDITIONATE
CONDITIONATED
CONDITIONATES
CONDITIONATING
CONDITIONED
CONDITIONER
CONDITIONERS
CONDITIONING
CONDITIONINGS
CONDITIONS
CONDO
CONDOES
CONDOLATORY
CONDOLE
CONDOLED
CONDOLEMENT
CONDOLEMENTS
CONDOLENCE
CONDOLENCES
CONDOLENT
CONDOLER

CONDOLERS
CONDOLES
CONDOLING
CONDOLINGLY
CONDOM
CONDOMINIUM
CONDOMINIUMS
CONDOMS
CONDONABLE
CONDONATION
CONDONATIONS
CONDONE
CONDONED
CONDONER
CONDONERS
CONDONES
CONDONING
CONDOR
CONDORES
CONDORS
CONDOS
CONDOTTIERE
CONDOTTIERI
CONDUCE
CONDUCED
CONDUCEMENT
CONDUCEMENTS
CONDUCER
CONDUCERS
CONDUCES
CONDUCIBLE
CONDUCING
CONDUCINGLY
CONDUCIVE
CONDUCIVENESS
CONDUCIVENESSES
CONDUCT
CONDUCTANCE
CONDUCTANCES
CONDUCTED
CONDUCTI
CONDUCTIBILITY
CONDUCTIBLE
CONDUCTIMETRIC
CONDUCTING
CONDUCTIOMETRIC
CONDUCTION
CONDUCTIONAL
CONDUCTIONS
CONDUCTIVE
CONDUCTIVELY
CONDUCTIVITIES
CONDUCTIVITY
CONDUCTOMETRIC
CONDUCTOR
CONDUCTORIAL

CONDUCTORS
CONDUCTORSHIP
CONDUCTORSHIPS
CONDUCTRESS
CONDUCTRESSES
CONDUCTS
CONDUCTUS
CONDUIT
CONDUITS
CONDUPLICATE
CONDUPLICATION
CONDUPLICATIONS
CONDYLAR
CONDYLE
CONDYLES
CONDYLOID
CONDYLOMA
CONDYLOMAS
CONDYLOMATA
CONDYLOMATOUS
CONE
CONED
CONEFLOWER
CONEFLOWERS
CONELRAD
CONELRADS
CONENOSE
CONENOSES
CONEPATE
CONEPATES
CONEPATL
CONEPATLS
CONES
CONEY
CONEYS
CONF
CONFAB
CONFABBED
CONFABBING
CONFABS
CONFABULAR
CONFABULATE
CONFABULATED
CONFABULATES
CONFABULATING
CONFABULATION
CONFABULATIONS
CONFABULATOR
CONFABULATORS
CONFABULATORY
CONFARREATE
CONFARREATION
CONFARREATIONS
CONFECT
CONFECTED
CONFECTING

CONFECTION
CONFECTIONARIES
CONFECTIONARY
CONFECTIONER
CONFECTIONERIES
CONFECTIONERS
CONFECTIONERY
CONFECTIONS
CONFECTS
CONFEDERACIES
CONFEDERACY
CONFEDERAL
CONFEDERATE
CONFEDERATED
CONFEDERATES
CONFEDERATING
CONFEDERATION
CONFEDERATIONS
CONFEDERATIVE
CONFER
CONFEREE
CONFEREES
CONFERENCE
CONFERENCES
CONFERENCIER
CONFERENCIERS
CONFERENCING
CONFERENCINGS
CONFERENTIAL
CONFERMENT
CONFERMENTS
CONFERRABLE
CONFERRAL
CONFERRALS
CONFERRED
CONFERREE
CONFERREES
CONFERRENCE
CONFERRENCES
CONFERRER
CONFERRERS
CONFERRING
CONFERS
CONFERVA
CONFERVAE
CONFERVAL
CONFERVAS
CONFERVOID
CONFERVOIDS
CONFESS
CONFESSABLE
CONFESSANT
CONFESSANTS
CONFESSED
CONFESSEDLY
CONFESSES

CONFESSING
CONFESSION
CONFESSIONAL
CONFESSIONALISM
CONFESSIONALIST
CONFESSIONALLY
CONFESSIONALS
CONFESSIONARIES
CONFESSIONARY
CONFESSIONS
CONFESSOR
CONFESSORESS
CONFESSORESSES
CONFESSORS
CONFESSORSHIP
CONFESSORSHIPS
CONFEST
CONFESTLY
CONFETTI
CONFETTO
CONFIDANT
CONFIDANTE
CONFIDANTES
CONFIDANTS
CONFIDE
CONFIDED
CONFIDENCE
CONFIDENCES
CONFIDENCIES
CONFIDENCY
CONFIDENT
CONFIDENTIAL
CONFIDENTIALITY
CONFIDENTIALLY
CONFIDENTLY
CONFIDENTS
CONFIDER
CONFIDERS
CONFIDES
CONFIDING
CONFIDINGLY
CONFIDINGNESS
CONFIDINGNESSES
CONFIGURATE
CONFIGURATED
CONFIGURATES
CONFIGURATING
CONFIGURATION
CONFIGURATIONAL
CONFIGURATIONS
CONFIGURATIVE
CONFIGURE
CONFIGURED
CONFIGURES
CONFIGURING
CONFINABLE

CONFINE
CONFINEABLE
CONFINED
CONFINEDLY
CONFINEDNESS
CONFINELESS
CONFINEMENT
CONFINEMENTS
CONFINER
CONFINERS
CONFINES
CONFINING
CONFIRM
CONFIRMABILITY
CONFIRMABLE
CONFIRMAND
CONFIRMANDS
CONFIRMATION
CONFIRMATIONAL
CONFIRMATIONS
CONFIRMATIVE
CONFIRMATOR
CONFIRMATORS
CONFIRMATORY
CONFIRMED
CONFIRMEDLY
CONFIRMEDNESS
CONFIRMEDNESSES
CONFIRMEE
CONFIRMEES
CONFIRMER
CONFIRMERS
CONFIRMING
CONFIRMINGS
CONFIRMOR
CONFIRMORS
CONFIRMS
CONFISCABLE
CONFISCATABLE
CONFISCATE
CONFISCATED
CONFISCATES
CONFISCATING
CONFISCATION
CONFISCATIONS
CONFISCATOR
CONFISCATORS
CONFISCATORY
CONFISERIE
CONFISERIES
CONFISEUR
CONFISEURS
CONFIT
CONFITEOR
CONFITEORS
CONFITS

CONFITURE
CONFITURES
CONFIX
CONFIXED
CONFIXES
CONFIXING
CONFLAGRANT
CONFLAGRATE
CONFLAGRATED
CONFLAGRATES
CONFLAGRATING
CONFLAGRATION
CONFLAGRATIONS
CONFLAGRATIVE
CONFLATE
CONFLATED
CONFLATES
CONFLATING
CONFLATION
CONFLATIONS
CONFLICT
CONFLICTED
CONFLICTFUL
CONFLICTING
CONFLICTINGLY
CONFLICTION
CONFLICTIONS
CONFLICTIVE
CONFLICTORY
CONFLICTS
CONFLICTUAL
CONFLUENCE
CONFLUENCES
CONFLUENT
CONFLUENTLY
CONFLUENTS
CONFLUX
CONFLUXES
CONFOCAL
CONFOCALLY
CONFORM
CONFORMABILITY
CONFORMABLE
CONFORMABLENESS
CONFORMABLY
CONFORMAL
CONFORMANCE
CONFORMANCES
CONFORMATION
CONFORMATIONAL
CONFORMATIONS
CONFORMED
CONFORMER
CONFORMERS
CONFORMING
CONFORMINGLY

CONFORMISM
CONFORMISMS
CONFORMIST
CONFORMISTS
CONFORMITIES
CONFORMITY
CONFORMS
CONFOUND
CONFOUNDABLE
CONFOUNDED
CONFOUNDEDLY
CONFOUNDEDNESS
CONFOUNDER
CONFOUNDERS
CONFOUNDING
CONFOUNDINGLY
CONFOUNDS
CONFRATERNAL
CONFRATERNALLY
CONFRATERNITIES
CONFRATERNITY
CONFRERE
CONFRERES
CONFRERIE
CONFRERIES
CONFRONT
CONFRONTAL
CONFRONTALS
CONFRONTATION
CONFRONTATIONAL
CONFRONTATIONS
CONFRONTE
CONFRONTED
CONFRONTER
CONFRONTERS
CONFRONTING
CONFRONTMENT
CONFRONTMENTS
CONFRONTS
CONFS
CONFUSABILITY
CONFUSABLE
CONFUSABLES
CONFUSE
CONFUSED
CONFUSEDLY
CONFUSEDNESS
CONFUSEDNESSES
CONFUSES
CONFUSIBLE
CONFUSIBLES
CONFUSING
CONFUSINGLY
CONFUSION
CONFUSIONAL
CONFUSIONS

CONFUTABLE
CONFUTATION
CONFUTATIONS
CONFUTATIVE
CONFUTE
CONFUTED
CONFUTEMENT
CONFUTEMENTS
CONFUTER
CONFUTERS
CONFUTES
CONFUTING
CONGA
CONGAED
CONGAING
CONGAS
CONGE
CONGEAL
CONGEALABLE
CONGEALABLENESS
CONGEALED
CONGEALER
CONGEALERS
CONGEALING
CONGEALMENT
CONGEALMENTS
CONGEALS
CONGED
CONGEE
CONGEED
CONGEEING
CONGEES
CONGEING
CONGELATION
CONGELATIONS
CONGENER
CONGENERIC
CONGENERICAL
CONGENERICS
CONGENEROUS
CONGENERS
CONGENETIC
CONGENIAL
CONGENIALITIES
CONGENIALITY
CONGENIALLY
CONGENIALNESS
CONGENIC
CONGENITAL
CONGENITALLY
CONGENITALNESS
CONGER
CONGERIES
CONGERS
CONGES
CONGEST

CONGESTED
CONGESTIBLE
CONGESTING
CONGESTION
CONGESTIONS
CONGESTIVE
CONGESTS
CONGIARIES
CONGIARY
CONGII
CONGIUS
CONGLOBATE
CONGLOBATED
CONGLOBATES
CONGLOBATING
CONGLOBATION
CONGLOBATIONS
CONGLOBE
CONGLOBED
CONGLOBES
CONGLOBING
CONGLOBULATE
CONGLOBULATED
CONGLOBULATES
CONGLOBULATING
CONGLOBULATION
CONGLOBULATIONS
CONGLOMERATE
CONGLOMERATED
CONGLOMERATES
CONGLOMERATEUR
CONGLOMERATEURS
CONGLOMERATIC
CONGLOMERATING
CONGLOMERATION
CONGLOMERATIONS
CONGLOMERATIVE
CONGLOMERATOR
CONGLOMERATORS
CONGLUTINANT
CONGLUTINATE
CONGLUTINATED
CONGLUTINATES
CONGLUTINATING
CONGLUTINATION
CONGLUTINATIONS
CONGLUTINATIVE
CONGLUTINATOR
CONGLUTINATORS
CONGO
CONGOES
CONGOS
CONGOU
CONGOUS
CONGRATS
CONGRATTERS

CONGRATULABLE
CONGRATULANT
CONGRATULANTS
CONGRATULATE
CONGRATULATED
CONGRATULATES
CONGRATULATING
CONGRATULATION
CONGRATULATIONS
CONGRATULATIVE
CONGRATULATOR
CONGRATULATORS
CONGRATULATORY
CONGREE
CONGREED
CONGREEING
CONGREES
CONGREET
CONGREETED
CONGREETING
CONGREETS
CONGREGANT
CONGREGANTS
CONGREGATE
CONGREGATED
CONGREGATES
CONGREGATING
CONGREGATION
CONGREGATIONAL
CONGREGATIONS
CONGREGATIVE
CONGREGATOR
CONGREGATORS
CONGRESS
CONGRESSED
CONGRESSES
CONGRESSING
CONGRESSIONAL
CONGRESSIONALLY
CONGRESSMAN
CONGRESSMEN
CONGRESSPEOPLE
CONGRESSPERSON
CONGRESSPERSONS
CONGRESSWOMAN
CONGRESSWOMEN
CONGRUE
CONGRUED
CONGRUENCE
CONGRUENCES
CONGRUENCIES
CONGRUENCY
CONGRUENT
CONGRUENTLY
CONGRUES
CONGRUING

CONGRUITIES
CONGRUITY
CONGRUOUS
CONGRUOUSLY
CONGRUOUSNESS
CONGRUOUSNESSES
CONI
CONIA
CONIAS
CONIC
CONICAL
CONICALLY
CONICINE
CONICITIES
CONICITY
CONICS
CONIDIA
CONIDIAL
CONIDIAN
CONIDIOPHORE
CONIDIOPHORES
CONIDIOPHOROUS
CONIDIOSPORE
CONIDIOSPORES
CONIDIUM
CONIES
CONIFER
CONIFEROUS
CONIFERS
CONIFORM
CONIINE
CONIINES
CONIMA
CONIMAS
CONIN
CONINE
CONINES
CONING
CONINS
CONIOLOGICAL
CONIOLOGICALLY
CONIOLOGY
CONIOSES
CONIOSIS
CONIROSTRAL
CONIUM
CONIUMS
CONJECT
CONJECTED
CONJECTING
CONJECTS
CONJECTURABLE
CONJECTURABLY
CONJECTURAL
CONJECTURALLY
CONJECTURE

CONJECTURED
CONJECTURER
CONJECTURERS
CONJECTURES
CONJECTURING
CONJEE
CONJEED
CONJEEING
CONJEES
CONJOIN
CONJOINED
CONJOINER
CONJOINERS
CONJOINING
CONJOINS
CONJOINT
CONJOINTLY
CONJUGABLE
CONJUGABLY
CONJUGAL
CONJUGALITIES
CONJUGALITY
CONJUGALLY
CONJUGANT
CONJUGANTS
CONJUGATE
CONJUGATED
CONJUGATELY
CONJUGATENESS
CONJUGATENESSES
CONJUGATES
CONJUGATING
CONJUGATINGS
CONJUGATION
CONJUGATIONAL
CONJUGATIONALLY
CONJUGATIONS
CONJUGATIVE
CONJUGATOR
CONJUGATORS
CONJUNCT
CONJUNCTION
CONJUNCTIONAL
CONJUNCTIONALLY
CONJUNCTIONS
CONJUNCTIVA
CONJUNCTIVAE
CONJUNCTIVAL
CONJUNCTIVAS
CONJUNCTIVE
CONJUNCTIVELY
CONJUNCTIVENESS
CONJUNCTIVES
CONJUNCTIVITIS
CONJUNCTLY
CONJUNCTS

CONJUNCTURAL
CONJUNCTURALLY
CONJUNCTURE
CONJUNCTURES
CONJURATION
CONJURATIONS
CONJURATOR
CONJURATORS
CONJURE
CONJURED
CONJUREMENT
CONJUREMENTS
CONJURER
CONJURERS
CONJURES
CONJURIES
CONJURING
CONJURINGS
CONJUROR
CONJURORS
CONJURY
CONK
CONKED
CONKER
CONKERS
CONKIER
CONKIEST
CONKING
CONKS
CONKY
CONN
CONNASCENCE
CONNASCENCES
CONNASCENCIES
CONNASCENCY
CONNASCENT
CONNATE
CONNATELY
CONNATENESS
CONNATION
CONNATIONS
CONNATURAL
CONNATURALISE
CONNATURALISED
CONNATURALISES
CONNATURALISING
CONNATURALITIES
CONNATURALITY
CONNATURALIZE
CONNATURALIZED
CONNATURALIZES
CONNATURALIZING
CONNATURALLY
CONNATURALNESS
CONNATURE
CONNATURES

CONNE
CONNECT
CONNECTABLE
CONNECTED
CONNECTEDLY
CONNECTEDNESS
CONNECTEDNESSES
CONNECTER
CONNECTERS
CONNECTIBLE
CONNECTING
CONNECTION
CONNECTIONAL
CONNECTIONISM
CONNECTIONISMS
CONNECTIONS
CONNECTIVE
CONNECTIVELY
CONNECTIVES
CONNECTIVITIES
CONNECTIVITY
CONNECTOR
CONNECTORS
CONNECTS
CONNED
CONNER
CONNERS
CONNES
CONNEXION
CONNEXIONAL
CONNEXIONALLY
CONNEXIONS
CONNEXIVE
CONNING
CONNINGS
CONNIPTION
CONNIPTIONS
CONNIVANCE
CONNIVANCES
CONNIVANCIES
CONNIVANCY
CONNIVE
CONNIVED
CONNIVENCE
CONNIVENCES
CONNIVENCIES
CONNIVENCY
CONNIVENT
CONNIVENTLY
CONNIVER
CONNIVERS
CONNIVES
CONNIVING
CONNIVINGLY
CONNOISSEUR
CONNOISSEURS

CONNOISSEURSHIP
CONNOTATE
CONNOTATED
CONNOTATES
CONNOTATING
CONNOTATION
CONNOTATIONAL
CONNOTATIONS
CONNOTATIVE
CONNOTATIVELY
CONNOTE
CONNOTED
CONNOTES
CONNOTING
CONNOTIVE
CONNOTIVELY
CONNS
CONNUBIAL
CONNUBIALISM
CONNUBIALISMS
CONNUBIALITIES
CONNUBIALITY
CONNUBIALLY
CONNUMERATE
CONNUMERATED
CONNUMERATES
CONNUMERATING
CONNUMERATION
CONNUMERATIONS
CONODONT
CONODONTS
CONOID
CONOIDAL
CONOIDALLY
CONOIDIC
CONOIDICAL
CONOIDS
CONOMINEE
CONOMINEES
CONOSCENTE
CONOSCENTI
CONQUER
CONQUERABLE
CONQUERABLENESS
CONQUERED
CONQUERESS
CONQUERESSES
CONQUERING
CONQUERINGLY
CONQUEROR
CONQUERORS
CONQUERS
CONQUEST
CONQUESTS
CONQUIAN
CONQUIANS

CONQUISTADOR
CONQUISTADORES
CONQUISTADORS
CONS
CONSANGUINE
CONSANGUINEOUS
CONSANGUINITIES
CONSANGUINITY
CONSCIENCE
CONSCIENCELESS
CONSCIENCES
CONSCIENT
CONSCIENTIOUS
CONSCIENTIOUSLY
CONSCIENTISE
CONSCIENTISED
CONSCIENTISES
CONSCIENTISING
CONSCIENTIZE
CONSCIENTIZED
CONSCIENTIZES
CONSCIENTIZING
CONSCIONABLE
CONSCIONABLY
CONSCIOUS
CONSCIOUSES
CONSCIOUSLY
CONSCIOUSNESS
CONSCIOUSNESSES
CONSCRIBE
CONSCRIBED
CONSCRIBES
CONSCRIBING
CONSCRIPT
CONSCRIPTED
CONSCRIPTING
CONSCRIPTION
CONSCRIPTIONAL
CONSCRIPTIONIST
CONSCRIPTIONS
CONSCRIPTS
CONSECRATE
CONSECRATED
CONSECRATEDNESS
CONSECRATES
CONSECRATING
CONSECRATION
CONSECRATIONS
CONSECRATIVE
CONSECRATOR
CONSECRATORS
CONSECRATORY
CONSECTANEOUS
CONSECTARIES
CONSECTARY
CONSECUTION

CONSECUTIONS
CONSECUTIVE
CONSECUTIVELY
CONSECUTIVENESS
CONSEIL
CONSEILS
CONSENESCENCE
CONSENESCENCES
CONSENESCENCIES
CONSENESCENCY
CONSENSION
CONSENSIONS
CONSENSUAL
CONSENSUALLY
CONSENSUS
CONSENSUSES
CONSENT
CONSENTANEITIES
CONSENTANEITY
CONSENTANEOUS
CONSENTANEOUSLY
CONSENTED
CONSENTER
CONSENTERS
CONSENTIENCE
CONSENTIENCES
CONSENTIENT
CONSENTING
CONSENTINGLY
CONSENTS
CONSEQUENCE
CONSEQUENCED
CONSEQUENCES
CONSEQUENCING
CONSEQUENT
CONSEQUENTIAL
CONSEQUENTIALLY
CONSEQUENTLY
CONSEQUENTS
CONSERVABLE
CONSERVANCIES
CONSERVANCY
CONSERVANT
CONSERVATION
CONSERVATIONAL
CONSERVATIONIST
CONSERVATIONS
CONSERVATISM
CONSERVATISMS
CONSERVATIVE
CONSERVATIVELY
CONSERVATIVES
CONSERVATIZE
CONSERVATIZED
CONSERVATIZES
CONSERVATIZING

CONSERVATOIRE
CONSERVATOIRES
CONSERVATOR
CONSERVATORIA
CONSERVATORIAL
CONSERVATORIES
CONSERVATORIUM
CONSERVATORIUMS
CONSERVATORS
CONSERVATORSHIP
CONSERVATORY
CONSERVATRICES
CONSERVATRIX
CONSERVATRIXES
CONSERVE
CONSERVED
CONSERVER
CONSERVERS
CONSERVES
CONSERVING
CONSIDER
CONSIDERABLE
CONSIDERABLES
CONSIDERABLY
CONSIDERANCE
CONSIDERANCES
CONSIDERATE
CONSIDERATELY
CONSIDERATENESS
CONSIDERATION
CONSIDERATIONS
CONSIDERATIVE
CONSIDERATIVELY
CONSIDERED
CONSIDERER
CONSIDERERS
CONSIDERING
CONSIDERINGLY
CONSIDERS
CONSIGLIERE
CONSIGLIERI
CONSIGN
CONSIGNABLE
CONSIGNATION
CONSIGNATIONS
CONSIGNATORIES
CONSIGNATORY
CONSIGNED
CONSIGNEE
CONSIGNEES
CONSIGNER
CONSIGNERS
CONSIGNIFIED
CONSIGNIFIES
CONSIGNIFY
CONSIGNIFYING

CONSIGNING
CONSIGNMENT
CONSIGNMENTS
CONSIGNOR
CONSIGNORS
CONSIGNS
CONSILIENCE
CONSILIENCES
CONSILIENT
CONSIMILAR
CONSIMILARITIES
CONSIMILARITY
CONSIMILITIES
CONSIMILITUDE
CONSIMILITUDES
CONSIMILITY
CONSIST
CONSISTED
CONSISTENCE
CONSISTENCES
CONSISTENCIES
CONSISTENCY
CONSISTENT
CONSISTENTLY
CONSISTING
CONSISTORIAL
CONSISTORIAN
CONSISTORIES
CONSISTORY
CONSISTS
CONSOCIATE
CONSOCIATED
CONSOCIATES
CONSOCIATING
CONSOCIATION
CONSOCIATIONAL
CONSOCIATIONS
CONSOCIES
CONSOL
CONSOLABLE
CONSOLATE
CONSOLATED
CONSOLATES
CONSOLATING
CONSOLATION
CONSOLATIONS
CONSOLATORIES
CONSOLATORY
CONSOLATRICES
CONSOLATRIX
CONSOLATRIXES
CONSOLE
CONSOLED
CONSOLEMENT
CONSOLEMENTS
CONSOLER

CONSOLERS
CONSOLES
CONSOLIDATE
CONSOLIDATED
CONSOLIDATES
CONSOLIDATING
CONSOLIDATION
CONSOLIDATIONS
CONSOLIDATIVE
CONSOLIDATOR
CONSOLIDATORS
CONSOLING
CONSOLINGLY
CONSOLS
CONSOLUTE
CONSOMME
CONSOMMES
CONSONANCE
CONSONANCES
CONSONANCIES
CONSONANCY
CONSONANT
CONSONANTAL
CONSONANTALLY
CONSONANTLY
CONSONANTS
CONSONOUS
CONSORT
CONSORTABLE
CONSORTED
CONSORTER
CONSORTERS
CONSORTIA
CONSORTIAL
CONSORTIALLY
CONSORTING
CONSORTISM
CONSORTISMS
CONSORTIUM
CONSORTIUMS
CONSORTS
CONSPECIFIC
CONSPECIFICS
CONSPECTUITIES
CONSPECTUITY
CONSPECTUS
CONSPECTUSES
CONSPICUITIES
CONSPICUITY
CONSPICUOUS
CONSPICUOUSLY
CONSPICUOUSNESS
CONSPIRACIES
CONSPIRACY
CONSPIRANT
CONSPIRATION

CONSPIRATIONAL
CONSPIRATIONS
CONSPIRATOR
CONSPIRATORIAL
CONSPIRATORS
CONSPIRATORY
CONSPIRATRESS
CONSPIRATRESSES
CONSPIRE
CONSPIRED
CONSPIRER
CONSPIRERS
CONSPIRES
CONSPIRING
CONSPIRINGLY
CONSPURCATION
CONSPURCATIONS
CONSTABLE
CONSTABLES
CONSTABLESHIP
CONSTABLESHIPS
CONSTABLEWICK
CONSTABLEWICKS
CONSTABULARIES
CONSTABULARY
CONSTANCIES
CONSTANCY
CONSTANT
CONSTANTAN
CONSTANTANS
CONSTANTLY
CONSTANTS
CONSTATATION
CONSTATATIONS
CONSTATE
CONSTATED
CONSTATES
CONSTATING
CONSTATIVE
CONSTATIVES
CONSTELLATE
CONSTELLATED
CONSTELLATES
CONSTELLATING
CONSTELLATION
CONSTELLATIONAL
CONSTELLATIONS
CONSTELLATORY
CONSTER
CONSTERED
CONSTERING
CONSTERNATE
CONSTERNATED
CONSTERNATES
CONSTERNATING
CONSTERNATION

CONSTERNATIONS
CONSTERS
CONSTIPATE
CONSTIPATED
CONSTIPATES
CONSTIPATING
CONSTIPATION
CONSTIPATIONS
CONSTITUENCIES
CONSTITUENCY
CONSTITUENT
CONSTITUENTLY
CONSTITUENTS
CONSTITUTE
CONSTITUTED
CONSTITUTER
CONSTITUTERS
CONSTITUTES
CONSTITUTING
CONSTITUTION
CONSTITUTIONAL
CONSTITUTIONALS
CONSTITUTIONIST
CONSTITUTIONS
CONSTITUTIVE
CONSTITUTIVELY
CONSTITUTOR
CONSTITUTORS
CONSTRAIN
CONSTRAINABLE
CONSTRAINED
CONSTRAINEDLY
CONSTRAINER
CONSTRAINERS
CONSTRAINING
CONSTRAINS
CONSTRAINT
CONSTRAINTS
CONSTRICT
CONSTRICTED
CONSTRICTING
CONSTRICTION
CONSTRICTIONS
CONSTRICTIVE
CONSTRICTIVELY
CONSTRICTOR
CONSTRICTORS
CONSTRICTS
CONSTRINGE
CONSTRINGED
CONSTRINGENCE
CONSTRINGENCIES
CONSTRINGENCY
CONSTRINGENT
CONSTRINGES
CONSTRINGING

CONSTRUABILITY
CONSTRUABLE
CONSTRUCT
CONSTRUCTABLE
CONSTRUCTED
CONSTRUCTER
CONSTRUCTERS
CONSTRUCTIBLE
CONSTRUCTING
CONSTRUCTION
CONSTRUCTIONAL
CONSTRUCTIONISM
CONSTRUCTIONIST
CONSTRUCTIONS
CONSTRUCTIVE
CONSTRUCTIVELY
CONSTRUCTIVISM
CONSTRUCTIVISMS
CONSTRUCTIVIST
CONSTRUCTIVISTS
CONSTRUCTOR
CONSTRUCTORS
CONSTRUCTS
CONSTRUCTURE
CONSTRUCTURES
CONSTRUE
CONSTRUED
CONSTRUER
CONSTRUERS
CONSTRUES
CONSTRUING
CONSTUPRATE
CONSTUPRATED
CONSTUPRATES
CONSTUPRATING
CONSTUPRATION
CONSTUPRATIONS
CONSUBSIST
CONSUBSISTED
CONSUBSISTING
CONSUBSISTS
CONSUBSTANTIAL
CONSUBSTANTIATE
CONSUETUDE
CONSUETUDES
CONSUETUDINARY
CONSUL
CONSULAGE
CONSULAGES
CONSULAR
CONSULARS
CONSULATE
CONSULATES
CONSULS
CONSULSHIP
CONSULSHIPS

CONSULT
CONSULTA
CONSULTABLE
CONSULTANCIES
CONSULTANCY
CONSULTANT
CONSULTANTS
CONSULTANTSHIP
CONSULTANTSHIPS
CONSULTAS
CONSULTATION
CONSULTATIONS
CONSULTATIVE
CONSULTATIVELY
CONSULTATORY
CONSULTED
CONSULTEE
CONSULTEES
CONSULTER
CONSULTERS
CONSULTING
CONSULTIVE
CONSULTOR
CONSULTORS
CONSULTORY
CONSULTS
CONSUMABLE
CONSUMABLES
CONSUME
CONSUMED
CONSUMEDLY
CONSUMER
CONSUMERISM
CONSUMERISMS
CONSUMERIST
CONSUMERISTIC
CONSUMERISTS
CONSUMERS
CONSUMERSHIP
CONSUMERSHIPS
CONSUMES
CONSUMING
CONSUMINGLY
CONSUMINGS
CONSUMMATE
CONSUMMATED
CONSUMMATELY
CONSUMMATES
CONSUMMATING
CONSUMMATION
CONSUMMATIONS
CONSUMMATIVE
CONSUMMATOR
CONSUMMATORS
CONSUMMATORY
CONSUMPT

CONSUMPTION
CONSUMPTIONS
CONSUMPTIVE
CONSUMPTIVELY
CONSUMPTIVENESS
CONSUMPTIVES
CONSUMPTIVITIES
CONSUMPTIVITY
CONSUMPTS
CONTABESCENCE
CONTABESCENCES
CONTABESCENT
CONTACT
CONTACTABLE
CONTACTED
CONTACTING
CONTACTOR
CONTACTORS
CONTACTS
CONTACTUAL
CONTACTUALLY
CONTADINA
CONTADINAS
CONTADINE
CONTADINI
CONTADINO
CONTAGIA
CONTAGION
CONTAGIONIST
CONTAGIONISTS
CONTAGIONS
CONTAGIOUS
CONTAGIOUSLY
CONTAGIOUSNESS
CONTAGIUM
CONTAIN
CONTAINABLE
CONTAINED
CONTAINER
CONTAINERBOARD
CONTAINERBOARDS
CONTAINERISE
CONTAINERISED
CONTAINERISES
CONTAINERISING
CONTAINERIZE
CONTAINERIZED
CONTAINERIZES
CONTAINERIZING
CONTAINERLESS
CONTAINERPORT
CONTAINERPORTS
CONTAINERS
CONTAINERSHIP
CONTAINERSHIPS
CONTAINING

CONTAINMENT
CONTAINMENTS
CONTAINS
CONTAMINABLE
CONTAMINANT
CONTAMINANTS
CONTAMINATE
CONTAMINATED
CONTAMINATES
CONTAMINATING
CONTAMINATION
CONTAMINATIONS
CONTAMINATIVE
CONTAMINATOR
CONTAMINATORS
CONTANGO
CONTANGOED
CONTANGOES
CONTANGOING
CONTANGOS
CONTE
CONTECK
CONTECKS
CONTEMN
CONTEMNED
CONTEMNER
CONTEMNERS
CONTEMNIBLE
CONTEMNIBLY
CONTEMNING
CONTEMNOR
CONTEMNORS
CONTEMNS
CONTEMPER
CONTEMPERATION
CONTEMPERATIONS
CONTEMPERATURE
CONTEMPERATURES
CONTEMPERED
CONTEMPERING
CONTEMPERS
CONTEMPLABLE
CONTEMPLANT
CONTEMPLANTS
CONTEMPLATE
CONTEMPLATED
CONTEMPLATES
CONTEMPLATING
CONTEMPLATION
CONTEMPLATIONS
CONTEMPLATIST
CONTEMPLATISTS
CONTEMPLATIVE
CONTEMPLATIVELY
CONTEMPLATIVES
CONTEMPLATOR

CONTEMPLATORS
CONTEMPORANEAN
CONTEMPORANEANS
CONTEMPORANEITY
CONTEMPORANEOUS
CONTEMPORARIES
CONTEMPORARILY
CONTEMPORARY
CONTEMPORISE
CONTEMPORISED
CONTEMPORISES
CONTEMPORISING
CONTEMPORIZE
CONTEMPORIZED
CONTEMPORIZES
CONTEMPORIZING
CONTEMPT
CONTEMPTIBILITY
CONTEMPTIBLE
CONTEMPTIBLY
CONTEMPTS
CONTEMPTUOUS
CONTEMPTUOUSLY
CONTEND
CONTENDED
CONTENDENT
CONTENDENTS
CONTENDER
CONTENDERS
CONTENDING
CONTENDINGLY
CONTENDINGS
CONTENDS
CONTENEMENT
CONTENEMENTS
CONTENT
CONTENTATION
CONTENTATIONS
CONTENTED
CONTENTEDLY
CONTENTEDNESS
CONTENTEDNESSES
CONTENTING
CONTENTION
CONTENTIONS
CONTENTIOUS
CONTENTIOUSLY
CONTENTIOUSNESS
CONTENTLESS
CONTENTLY
CONTENTMENT
CONTENTMENTS
CONTENTS
CONTERMINAL
CONTERMINALLY
CONTERMINANT

CONTERMINATE	CONTINENTALIST	CONTORNOS	CONTRACTILE
CONTERMINOUS	CONTINENTALISTS	CONTORT	CONTRACTILITIES
CONTERMINOUSLY	CONTINENTALLY	CONTORTED	CONTRACTILITY
CONTES	CONTINENTALS	CONTORTEDLY	CONTRACTING
CONTESSA	CONTINENTLY	CONTORTEDNESS	CONTRACTION
CONTESSAS	CONTINENTS	CONTORTING	CONTRACTIONAL
CONTESSERATION	CONTINGENCE	CONTORTION	CONTRACTIONARY
CONTESSERATIONS	CONTINGENCES	CONTORTIONAL	CONTRACTIONS
CONTEST	CONTINGENCIES	CONTORTIONATE	CONTRACTIVE
CONTESTABILITY	CONTINGENCY	CONTORTIONED	CONTRACTIVELY
CONTESTABLE	CONTINGENT	CONTORTIONISM	CONTRACTIVENESS
CONTESTABLENESS	CONTINGENTLY	CONTORTIONISMS	CONTRACTOR
CONTESTABLY	CONTINGENTS	CONTORTIONIST	CONTRACTORS
CONTESTANT	CONTINUA	CONTORTIONISTIC	CONTRACTS
CONTESTANTS	CONTINUABLE	CONTORTIONISTS	CONTRACTUAL
CONTESTATION	CONTINUAL	CONTORTIONS	CONTRACTUALLY
CONTESTATIONS	CONTINUALITY	CONTORTIVE	CONTRACTURAL
CONTESTED	CONTINUALLY	CONTORTS	CONTRACTURE
CONTESTER	CONTINUALNESS	CONTOS	CONTRACTURES
CONTESTERS	CONTINUANCE	CONTOUR	CONTRACYCLICAL
CONTESTING	CONTINUANCES	CONTOURED	CONTRADANCE
CONTESTINGLY	CONTINUANT	CONTOURING	CONTRADANCES
CONTESTS	CONTINUANTS	CONTOURS	CONTRADICT
CONTEXT	CONTINUATE	CONTRA	CONTRADICTABLE
CONTEXTLESS	CONTINUATION	CONTRABAND	CONTRADICTED
CONTEXTS	CONTINUATIONS	CONTRABANDISM	CONTRADICTER
CONTEXTUAL	CONTINUATIVE	CONTRABANDISMS	CONTRADICTERS
CONTEXTUALISE	CONTINUATIVELY	CONTRABANDIST	CONTRADICTING
CONTEXTUALISED	CONTINUATIVES	CONTRABANDISTS	CONTRADICTION
CONTEXTUALISES	CONTINUATOR	CONTRABANDS	CONTRADICTIONS
CONTEXTUALISING	CONTINUATORS	CONTRABASS	CONTRADICTIOUS
CONTEXTUALIZE	CONTINUE	CONTRABASSES	CONTRADICTIVE
CONTEXTUALIZED	CONTINUED	CONTRABASSI	CONTRADICTIVELY
CONTEXTUALIZES	CONTINUEDLY	CONTRABASSIST	CONTRADICTOR
CONTEXTUALIZING	CONTINUEDNESS	CONTRABASSISTS	CONTRADICTORIES
CONTEXTUALLY	CONTINUEDNESSES	CONTRABASSO	CONTRADICTORILY
CONTEXTURAL	CONTINUER	CONTRABASSOON	CONTRADICTORS
CONTEXTURALLY	CONTINUERS	CONTRABASSOONS	CONTRADICTORY
CONTEXTURE	CONTINUES	CONTRABASSOS	CONTRADICTS
CONTEXTURES	CONTINUING	CONTRABBASSI	CONTRAFAGOTTO
CONTICENT	CONTINUINGLY	CONTRABBASSO	CONTRAFAGOTTOS
CONTIGNATION	CONTINUITIES	CONTRABBASSOS	CONTRAFLOW
CONTIGNATIONS	CONTINUITY	CONTRACEPTION	CONTRAFLOWS
CONTIGUITIES	CONTINUO	CONTRACEPTIONS	CONTRAGESTION
CONTIGUITY	CONTINUOS	CONTRACEPTIVE	CONTRAGESTIONS
CONTIGUOUS	CONTINUOUS	CONTRACEPTIVES	CONTRAGESTIVE
CONTIGUOUSLY	CONTINUOUSLY	CONTRACLOCKWISE	CONTRAGESTIVES
CONTIGUOUSNESS	CONTINUOUSNESS	CONTRACT	CONTRAHENT
CONTINENCE	CONTINUUM	CONTRACTABILITY	CONTRAHENTS
CONTINENCES	CONTINUUMS	CONTRACTABLE	CONTRAIL
CONTINENCIES	CONTLINE	CONTRACTED	CONTRAILS
CONTINENCY	CONTLINES	CONTRACTEDLY	CONTRAINDICANT
CONTINENT	CONTO	CONTRACTEDNESS	CONTRAINDICANTS
CONTINENTAL	CONTORNIATE	CONTRACTIBILITY	CONTRAINDICATE
CONTINENTALISM	CONTORNIATES	CONTRACTIBLE	CONTRAINDICATED
CONTINENTALISMS	CONTORNO	CONTRACTIBLY	CONTRAINDICATES

CONTRAIR
CONTRALATERAL
CONTRALTI
CONTRALTO
CONTRALTOS
CONTRANATANT
CONTRAOCTAVE
CONTRAOCTAVES
CONTRAPLEX
CONTRAPOSITION
CONTRAPOSITIONS
CONTRAPOSITIVE
CONTRAPOSITIVES
CONTRAPPOSTO
CONTRAPPOSTOS
CONTRAPROP
CONTRAPROPELLER
CONTRAPROPS
CONTRAPTION
CONTRAPTIONS
CONTRAPUNTAL
CONTRAPUNTALIST
CONTRAPUNTALLY
CONTRAPUNTIST
CONTRAPUNTISTS
CONTRARIAN
CONTRARIANS
CONTRARIED
CONTRARIES
CONTRARIETIES
CONTRARIETY
CONTRARILY
CONTRARINESS
CONTRARINESSES
CONTRARIOUS
CONTRARIOUSLY
CONTRARIOUSNESS
CONTRARIWISE
CONTRARY
CONTRARYING
CONTRAS
CONTRAST
CONTRASTABLE
CONTRASTABLY
CONTRASTED
CONTRASTING
CONTRASTIVE
CONTRASTIVELY
CONTRASTS
CONTRASTY
CONTRAT
CONTRATE
CONTRATERRENE
CONTRATS
CONTRAVALLATION
CONTRAVENE

CONTRAVENED
CONTRAVENER
CONTRAVENERS
CONTRAVENES
CONTRAVENING
CONTRAVENTION
CONTRAVENTIONS
CONTRAYERVA
CONTRAYERVAS
CONTRECOUP
CONTRECOUPS
CONTREDANCE
CONTREDANCES
CONTREDANSE
CONTREDANSES
CONTRETEMPS
CONTRIBUTABLE
CONTRIBUTARIES
CONTRIBUTARY
CONTRIBUTE
CONTRIBUTED
CONTRIBUTES
CONTRIBUTING
CONTRIBUTION
CONTRIBUTIONS
CONTRIBUTIVE
CONTRIBUTIVELY
CONTRIBUTOR
CONTRIBUTORIES
CONTRIBUTORS
CONTRIBUTORY
CONTRIST
CONTRISTATION
CONTRISTATIONS
CONTRISTED
CONTRISTING
CONTRISTS
CONTRITE
CONTRITELY
CONTRITENESS
CONTRITENESSES
CONTRITION
CONTRITIONS
CONTRITURATE
CONTRITURATED
CONTRITURATES
CONTRITURATING
CONTRIVABLE
CONTRIVANCE
CONTRIVANCES
CONTRIVE
CONTRIVED
CONTRIVEMENT
CONTRIVEMENTS
CONTRIVER
CONTRIVERS

CONTRIVES
CONTRIVING
CONTROL
CONTROLE
CONTROLLABILITY
CONTROLLABLE
CONTROLLABLY
CONTROLLED
CONTROLLER
CONTROLLERS
CONTROLLERSHIP
CONTROLLERSHIPS
CONTROLLING
CONTROLMENT
CONTROLMENTS
CONTROLS
CONTROUL
CONTROULED
CONTROULING
CONTROULS
CONTROVERSE
CONTROVERSES
CONTROVERSIAL
CONTROVERSIALLY
CONTROVERSIES
CONTROVERSY
CONTROVERT
CONTROVERTED
CONTROVERTER
CONTROVERTERS
CONTROVERTIBLE
CONTROVERTIBLY
CONTROVERTING
CONTROVERTIST
CONTROVERTISTS
CONTROVERTS
CONTUBERNAL
CONTUMACIES
CONTUMACIOUS
CONTUMACIOUSLY
CONTUMACITIES
CONTUMACITY
CONTUMACY
CONTUMELIES
CONTUMELIOUS
CONTUMELIOUSLY
CONTUMELY
CONTUND
CONTUNDED
CONTUNDING
CONTUNDS
CONTUSE
CONTUSED
CONTUSES
CONTUSING
CONTUSION

CONTUSIONED
CONTUSIONS
CONTUSIVE
CONUNDRUM
CONUNDRUMS
CONURBAN
CONURBATION
CONURBATIONS
CONURBIA
CONURBIAS
CONURE
CONURES
CONUS
CONVALESCE
CONVALESCED
CONVALESCENCE
CONVALESCENCES
CONVALESCENCIES
CONVALESCENCY
CONVALESCENT
CONVALESCENTLY
CONVALESCENTS
CONVALESCES
CONVALESCING
CONVECT
CONVECTED
CONVECTING
CONVECTION
CONVECTIONAL
CONVECTIONS
CONVECTIVE
CONVECTOR
CONVECTORS
CONVECTS
CONVENABLE
CONVENANCE
CONVENANCES
CONVENE
CONVENED
CONVENER
CONVENERS
CONVENERSHIP
CONVENERSHIPS
CONVENES
CONVENIENCE
CONVENIENCES
CONVENIENCIES
CONVENIENCY
CONVENIENT
CONVENIENTLY
CONVENING
CONVENOR
CONVENORS
CONVENORSHIP
CONVENORSHIPS
CONVENT

CONVENTED
CONVENTICLE
CONVENTICLED
CONVENTICLER
CONVENTICLERS
CONVENTICLES
CONVENTICLING
CONVENTING
CONVENTION
CONVENTIONAL
CONVENTIONALISE
CONVENTIONALISM
CONVENTIONALIST
CONVENTIONALITY
CONVENTIONALIZE
CONVENTIONALLY
CONVENTIONALS
CONVENTIONARY
CONVENTIONEER
CONVENTIONEERS
CONVENTIONER
CONVENTIONERS
CONVENTIONIST
CONVENTIONISTS
CONVENTIONS
CONVENTS
CONVENTUAL
CONVENTUALLY
CONVENTUALS
CONVERGE
CONVERGED
CONVERGENCE
CONVERGENCES
CONVERGENCIES
CONVERGENCY
CONVERGENT
CONVERGES
CONVERGING
CONVERSABLE
CONVERSABLENESS
CONVERSABLY
CONVERSANCE
CONVERSANCES
CONVERSANCIES
CONVERSANCY
CONVERSANT
CONVERSANTLY
CONVERSATION
CONVERSATIONAL
CONVERSATIONISM
CONVERSATIONIST
CONVERSATIONS
CONVERSATIVE
CONVERSAZIONE
CONVERSAZIONES
CONVERSAZIONI

CONVERSE
CONVERSED
CONVERSELY
CONVERSER
CONVERSERS
CONVERSES
CONVERSING
CONVERSION
CONVERSIONAL
CONVERSIONARY
CONVERSIONS
CONVERT
CONVERTAPLANE
CONVERTAPLANES
CONVERTED
CONVERTEND
CONVERTENDS
CONVERTER
CONVERTERS
CONVERTIBILITY
CONVERTIBLE
CONVERTIBLENESS
CONVERTIBLES
CONVERTIBLY
CONVERTING
CONVERTIPLANE
CONVERTIPLANES
CONVERTITE
CONVERTITES
CONVERTIVE
CONVERTIVELY
CONVERTIVENESS
CONVERTOPLANE
CONVERTOPLANES
CONVERTOR
CONVERTORS
CONVERTS
CONVEX
CONVEXED
CONVEXEDLY
CONVEXES
CONVEXING
CONVEXITIES
CONVEXITY
CONVEXLY
CONVEXNESS
CONVEXNESSES
CONVEY
CONVEYABLE
CONVEYAL
CONVEYALS
CONVEYANCE
CONVEYANCER
CONVEYANCERS
CONVEYANCES
CONVEYANCING

CONVEYANCINGS
CONVEYED
CONVEYER
CONVEYERS
CONVEYING
CONVEYOR
CONVEYORISE
CONVEYORISED
CONVEYORISES
CONVEYORISING
CONVEYORIZATION
CONVEYORIZE
CONVEYORIZED
CONVEYORIZES
CONVEYORIZING
CONVEYORS
CONVEYS
CONVICINITIES
CONVICINITY
CONVICT
CONVICTABLE
CONVICTABLY
CONVICTED
CONVICTIBLE
CONVICTIBLY
CONVICTING
CONVICTION
CONVICTIONAL
CONVICTIONALLY
CONVICTIONS
CONVICTISM
CONVICTISMS
CONVICTIVE
CONVICTIVELY
CONVICTS
CONVINCE
CONVINCED
CONVINCEMENT
CONVINCEMENTS
CONVINCER
CONVINCERS
CONVINCES
CONVINCIBLE
CONVINCING
CONVINCINGLY
CONVINCINGNESS
CONVIVE
CONVIVED
CONVIVES
CONVIVIAL
CONVIVIALIST
CONVIVIALISTS
CONVIVIALITIES
CONVIVIALITY
CONVIVIALLY
CONVIVING

CONVO
CONVOCATE
CONVOCATED
CONVOCATES
CONVOCATING
CONVOCATION
CONVOCATIONAL
CONVOCATIONIST
CONVOCATIONISTS
CONVOCATIONS
CONVOCATIVE
CONVOCATIVELY
CONVOCATOR
CONVOCATORS
CONVOKE
CONVOKED
CONVOKER
CONVOKERS
CONVOKES
CONVOKING
CONVOLUTE
CONVOLUTED
CONVOLUTEDLY
CONVOLUTEDNESS
CONVOLUTELY
CONVOLUTES
CONVOLUTING
CONVOLUTION
CONVOLUTIONAL
CONVOLUTIONALLY
CONVOLUTIONARY
CONVOLUTIONS
CONVOLVE
CONVOLVED
CONVOLVES
CONVOLVING
CONVOLVULACEOUS
CONVOLVULI
CONVOLVULUS
CONVOLVULUSES
CONVOS
CONVOY
CONVOYED
CONVOYING
CONVOYS
CONVULSANT
CONVULSANTS
CONVULSE
CONVULSED
CONVULSES
CONVULSIBLE
CONVULSING
CONVULSION
CONVULSIONAL
CONVULSIONARIES
CONVULSIONARY

CONVULSIONIST
CONVULSIONISTS
CONVULSIONS
CONVULSIVE
CONVULSIVELY
CONVULSIVENESS
CONY
COO
COOCH
COOCHES
COOCOO
COOED
COOEE
COOEED
COOEEING
COOEES
COOER
COOERS
COOEY
COOEYED
COOEYING
COOEYS
COOF
COOFS
COOING
COOINGLY
COOINGS
COOK
COOKABLE
COOKBOOK
COOKBOOKS
COOKED
COOKER
COOKERIES
COOKERS
COOKERY
COOKEY
COOKEYS
COOKHOUSE
COOKHOUSES
COOKIE
COOKIES
COOKING
COOKINGS
COOKLESS
COOKMAID
COOKMAIDS
COOKOUT
COOKOUTS
COOKROOM
COOKROOMS
COOKS
COOKSHACK
COOKSHACKS
COOKSHOP
COOKSHOPS

COOKSTOVE
COOKSTOVES
COOKTOP
COOKTOPS
COOKWARE
COOKWARES
COOKY
COOL
COOLABAH
COOLABAHS
COOLAMON
COOLAMONS
COOLANT
COOLANTS
COOLDOWN
COOLDOWNS
COOLED
COOLER
COOLERS
COOLEST
COOLHEADED
COOLHOUSE
COOLHOUSES
COOLIBAH
COOLIBAHS
COOLIBAR
COOLIBARS
COOLIE
COOLIES
COOLING
COOLINGLY
COOLINGNESS
COOLISH
COOLLY
COOLNESS
COOLNESSES
COOLS
COOLTH
COOLTHS
COOLY
COOM
COOMB
COOMBE
COOMBES
COOMBS
COOMCEILED
COOMED
COOMIER
COOMIEST
COOMING
COOMS
COOMY
COON
COONCAN
COONCANS
COONDOG

COONDOGS
COONHOUND
COONHOUNDS
COONS
COONSKIN
COONSKINS
COONTIE
COONTIES
COONTY
COOP
COOPED
COOPER
COOPERAGE
COOPERAGES
COOPERATE
COOPERATED
COOPERATES
COOPERATING
COOPERATION
COOPERATIONIST
COOPERATIONISTS
COOPERATIONS
COOPERATIVE
COOPERATIVELY
COOPERATIVENESS
COOPERATIVES
COOPERATIVITY
COOPERATOR
COOPERATORS
COOPERED
COOPERIES
COOPERING
COOPERINGS
COOPERS
COOPERY
COOPING
COOPS
COOPT
COOPTATION
COOPTATIONS
COOPTATIVE
COOPTED
COOPTING
COOPTION
COOPTIONS
COOPTS
COORDINAL
COORDINANCE
COORDINANCES
COORDINATE
COORDINATED
COORDINATELY
COORDINATENESS
COORDINATES
COORDINATING
COORDINATION

COORDINATIONS
COORDINATIVE
COORDINATOR
COORDINATORS
COORIE
COORIED
COORIEING
COORIES
COOS
COOSEN
COOSENED
COOSENING
COOSENS
COOSER
COOSERS
COOSIN
COOSINED
COOSINING
COOSINS
COOST
COOT
COOTCH
COOTCHED
COOTCHES
COOTCHING
COOTER
COOTERS
COOTIE
COOTIES
COOTIKIN
COOTIKINS
COOTS
COP
COPACETIC
COPAIBA
COPAIBAS
COPAIVA
COPAIVAS
COPAL
COPALM
COPALMS
COPALS
COPARCENARIES
COPARCENARY
COPARCENER
COPARCENERIES
COPARCENERS
COPARCENERY
COPARCENY
COPARENT
COPARENTS
COPARTNER
COPARTNERED
COPARTNERIES
COPARTNERING
COPARTNERS

COPARTNERSHIP
COPARTNERSHIPS
COPARTNERY
COPASETIC
COPASTOR
COPASTORS
COPATAINE
COPATRIOT
COPATRIOTS
COPATRON
COPATRONS
COPE
COPECK
COPECKS
COPED
COPEMATE
COPEMATES
COPEN
COPENS
COPEPOD
COPEPODS
COPER
COPERED
COPERING
COPERS
COPES
COPESETIC
COPESETTIC
COPESTONE
COPESTONES
COPIED
COPIER
COPIERS
COPIES
COPIHUE
COPIHUES
COPILOT
COPILOTS
COPING
COPINGS
COPINGSTONE
COPINGSTONES
COPIOUS
COPIOUSLY
COPIOUSNESS
COPIOUSNESSES
COPITA
COPITAS
COPLANAR
COPLANARITIES
COPLANARITY
COPLOT
COPLOTS
COPLOTTED
COPLOTTING
COPOLYMER

COPOLYMERIC
COPOLYMERISE
COPOLYMERISED
COPOLYMERISES
COPOLYMERISING
COPOLYMERIZE
COPOLYMERIZED
COPOLYMERIZES
COPOLYMERIZING
COPOLYMERS
COPPED
COPPER
COPPERAH
COPPERAHS
COPPERAS
COPPERASES
COPPERED
COPPERHEAD
COPPERHEADS
COPPERING
COPPERINGS
COPPERISH
COPPERPLATE
COPPERPLATES
COPPERS
COPPERSKIN
COPPERSKINS
COPPERSMITH
COPPERSMITHS
COPPERWORK
COPPERWORKS
COPPERWORM
COPPERWORMS
COPPERY
COPPICE
COPPICED
COPPICES
COPPICING
COPPICINGS
COPPIES
COPPIN
COPPING
COPPINS
COPPLE
COPPLES
COPPRA
COPPRAS
COPPY
COPRA
COPRAH
COPRAHS
COPRAS
COPREMIA
COPREMIAS
COPREMIC
COPRESENCE

COPRESENCES
COPRESENT
COPRESENTED
COPRESENTING
COPRESENTS
COPRESIDENT
COPRESIDENTS
COPRINCE
COPRINCES
COPRINCIPAL
COPRINCIPALS
COPRISONER
COPRISONERS
COPROCESSING
COPROCESSOR
COPROCESSORS
COPRODUCE
COPRODUCED
COPRODUCER
COPRODUCERS
COPRODUCES
COPRODUCING
COPRODUCT
COPRODUCTION
COPRODUCTIONS
COPRODUCTS
COPROLALIA
COPROLALIAC
COPROLALIAS
COPROLITE
COPROLITES
COPROLITH
COPROLITHS
COPROLITIC
COPROLOGIES
COPROLOGY
COPROMOTER
COPROMOTERS
COPROPHAGAN
COPROPHAGANS
COPROPHAGIC
COPROPHAGIES
COPROPHAGIST
COPROPHAGISTS
COPROPHAGOUS
COPROPHAGY
COPROPHILIA
COPROPHILIAC
COPROPHILIACS
COPROPHILIAS
COPROPHILIC
COPROPHILICALLY
COPROPHILOUS
COPROPRIETOR
COPROPRIETORS
COPROSMA

COPROSMAS
COPROSPERITIES
COPROSPERITY
COPROSTEROL
COPROSTEROLS
COPROZOIC
COPS
COPSE
COPSED
COPSES
COPSEWOOD
COPSEWOODS
COPSHOP
COPSHOPS
COPSIER
COPSIEST
COPSING
COPSY
COPTER
COPTERS
COPUBLISH
COPUBLISHED
COPUBLISHER
COPUBLISHERS
COPUBLISHES
COPUBLISHING
COPULA
COPULAE
COPULAR
COPULAS
COPULATE
COPULATED
COPULATES
COPULATING
COPULATION
COPULATIONS
COPULATIVE
COPULATIVELY
COPULATIVES
COPULATORY
COPURIFIED
COPURIFIES
COPURIFY
COPURIFYING
COPY
COPYBOOK
COPYBOOKS
COPYBOY
COPYBOYS
COPYCAT
COPYCATS
COPYCATTED
COPYCATTING
COPYDESK
COPYDESKS
COPYEDIT

COPYEDITED
COPYEDITING
COPYEDITS
COPYGRAPH
COPYGRAPHS
COPYHOLD
COPYHOLDER
COPYHOLDERS
COPYHOLDS
COPYING
COPYISM
COPYISMS
COPYIST
COPYISTS
COPYREAD
COPYREADER
COPYREADERS
COPYREADING
COPYREADINGS
COPYREADS
COPYRIGHT
COPYRIGHTABLE
COPYRIGHTED
COPYRIGHTER
COPYRIGHTERS
COPYRIGHTING
COPYRIGHTS
COPYTAKER
COPYTAKERS
COPYWRITER
COPYWRITERS
COPYWRITING
COQUELICOT
COQUELICOTS
COQUET
COQUETRIES
COQUETRY
COQUETS
COQUETTE
COQUETTED
COQUETTES
COQUETTING
COQUETTISH
COQUETTISHLY
COQUETTISHNESS
COQUILLA
COQUILLAS
COQUILLE
COQUILLES
COQUIMBITE
COQUIMBITES
COQUINA
COQUINAS
COQUITO
COQUITOS
COR

CORACIIFORM
CORACLE
CORACLES
CORACOID
CORACOIDS
CORADICATE
CORAGGIO
CORAGGIOS
CORAL
CORALBELLS
CORALBERRIES
CORALBERRY
CORALLA
CORALLACEOUS
CORALLIFEROUS
CORALLIFORM
CORALLIGENOUS
CORALLINE
CORALLINES
CORALLITE
CORALLITES
CORALLOID
CORALLOIDAL
CORALLUM
CORALROOT
CORALROOTS
CORALS
CORALWORT
CORALWORTS
CORAM
CORAMINE
CORAMINES
CORANACH
CORANACHS
CORANTO
CORANTOES
CORANTOS
CORBAN
CORBANS
CORBE
CORBEAU
CORBEAUS
CORBEIL
CORBEILLE
CORBEILLES
CORBEILS
CORBEL
CORBELED
CORBELING
CORBELINGS
CORBELLED
CORBELLING
CORBELLINGS
CORBELS
CORBES
CORBICULA

CORBICULAE
CORBICULATE
CORBIE
CORBIES
CORBINA
CORBINAS
CORBY
CORCASS
CORCASSES
CORD
CORDAGE
CORDAGES
CORDATE
CORDATELY
CORDECTOMIES
CORDECTOMY
CORDED
CORDELLE
CORDELLED
CORDELLES
CORDELLING
CORDER
CORDERS
CORDGRASS
CORDGRASSES
CORDIAL
CORDIALISE
CORDIALISED
CORDIALISES
CORDIALISING
CORDIALITIES
CORDIALITY
CORDIALIZE
CORDIALIZED
CORDIALIZES
CORDIALIZING
CORDIALLY
CORDIALNESS
CORDIALNESSES
CORDIALS
CORDIERITE
CORDIERITES
CORDIFORM
CORDILLERA
CORDILLERAN
CORDILLERAS
CORDINER
CORDINERS
CORDING
CORDINGS
CORDITE
CORDITES
CORDLESS
CORDLIKE
CORDOBA
CORDOBAS

CORDOCENTESES
CORDOCENTESIS
CORDON
CORDONED
CORDONING
CORDONS
CORDOTOMIES
CORDOTOMY
CORDOVAN
CORDOVANS
CORDS
CORDUROY
CORDUROYED
CORDUROYING
CORDUROYS
CORDWAIN
CORDWAINER
CORDWAINERIES
CORDWAINERS
CORDWAINERY
CORDWAINS
CORDWOOD
CORDWOODS
CORDYLINE
CORDYLINES
CORE
CORECIPIENT
CORECIPIENTS
CORED
COREDEEM
COREDEEMED
COREDEEMING
COREDEEMS
COREFERENTIAL
COREGENT
COREGENTS
COREGONINE
COREIGN
COREIGNS
CORELATE
CORELATED
CORELATES
CORELATING
CORELATION
CORELATIONS
CORELATIVE
CORELATIVES
CORELESS
CORELIGIONIST
CORELIGIONISTS
CORELLA
CORELLAS
COREMIA
COREMIUM
COREOPSIS
COREOPSISES

COREPRESSOR
COREPRESSORS
COREQUISITE
COREQUISITES
CORER
CORERS
CORES
CORESEARCHER
CORESEARCHERS
CORESIDENT
CORESIDENTIAL
CORESIDENTS
CORESPONDENT
CORESPONDENTS
COREY
COREYS
CORF
CORFHOUSE
CORFHOUSES
CORGI
CORGIS
CORIA
CORIACEOUS
CORIANDER
CORIANDERS
CORIES
CORING
CORINTHIANISE
CORINTHIANISED
CORINTHIANISES
CORINTHIANISING
CORINTHIANIZE
CORINTHIANIZED
CORINTHIANIZES
CORINTHIANIZING
CORIOUS
CORIUM
CORIUMS
CORIVAL
CORIVALLED
CORIVALLING
CORIVALRIES
CORIVALRY
CORIVALS
CORIVALSHIP
CORIVALSHIPS
CORIXID
CORIXIDS
CORK
CORKAGE
CORKAGES
CORKBOARD
CORKBOARDS
CORKBORER
CORKBORERS
CORKED

CORKER
CORKERS
CORKIER
CORKIEST
CORKINESS
CORKINESSES
CORKING
CORKIR
CORKIRS
CORKLIKE
CORKS
CORKSCREW
CORKSCREWED
CORKSCREWING
CORKSCREWS
CORKTREE
CORKTREES
CORKWING
CORKWINGS
CORKWOOD
CORKWOODS
CORKY
CORM
CORMEL
CORMELS
CORMIDIA
CORMIDIUM
CORMLIKE
CORMOID
CORMOPHYTE
CORMOPHYTES
CORMOPHYTIC
CORMORANT
CORMORANTS
CORMOUS
CORMS
CORMUS
CORMUSES
CORN
CORNACEOUS
CORNACRE
CORNACRES
CORNAGE
CORNAGES
CORNBALL
CORNBALLS
CORNBORER
CORNBORERS
CORNBRAKES
CORNBRANDIES
CORNBRASH
CORNBRASHES
CORNBREAD
CORNBREADS
CORNCAKE
CORNCAKES

CORNCOB
CORNCOBS
CORNCOCKLE
CORNCOCKLES
CORNCRAKE
CORNCRAKES
CORNCRIB
CORNCRIBS
CORNEA
CORNEAE
CORNEAL
CORNEAS
CORNED
CORNEL
CORNELIAN
CORNELIANS
CORNELS
CORNEMUSE
CORNEMUSES
CORNEOUS
CORNER
CORNERBACK
CORNERBACKS
CORNERED
CORNERING
CORNERMAN
CORNERMEN
CORNERS
CORNERSTONE
CORNERSTONES
CORNERWAYS
CORNERWISE
CORNET
CORNETCIES
CORNETCY
CORNETIST
CORNETISTS
CORNETS
CORNETT
CORNETTI
CORNETTINO
CORNETTINOS
CORNETTIST
CORNETTISTS
CORNETTO
CORNETTS
CORNFED
CORNFIELD
CORNFIELDS
CORNFLAG
CORNFLAGS
CORNFLAKE
CORNFLAKES
CORNFLIES
CORNFLOUR
CORNFLOURS

CORNFLOWER
CORNFLOWERS
CORNFLY
CORNHUSK
CORNHUSKER
CORNHUSKERS
CORNHUSKING
CORNHUSKINGS
CORNHUSKS
CORNI
CORNICE
CORNICED
CORNICES
CORNICHE
CORNICHES
CORNICHON
CORNICHONS
CORNICING
CORNICLE
CORNICLES
CORNICULA
CORNICULATE
CORNICULUM
CORNICULUMS
CORNIER
CORNIEST
CORNIFEROUS
CORNIFIC
CORNIFICATION
CORNIFICATIONS
CORNIFORM
CORNIGEROUS
CORNILY
CORNINESS
CORNINESSES
CORNING
CORNIST
CORNISTS
CORNLAND
CORNLANDS
CORNLOFT
CORNLOFTS
CORNMEAL
CORNMEALS
CORNMILL
CORNMILLS
CORNMOTH
CORNMOTHS
CORNO
CORNOPEAN
CORNOPEANS
CORNPIPE
CORNPIPES
CORNPONE
CORNPONES
CORNRENT

CORNRENTS
CORNROW
CORNROWED
CORNROWING
CORNROWS
CORNS
CORNSTALK
CORNSTALKS
CORNSTARCH
CORNSTARCHES
CORNSTONE
CORNSTONES
CORNU
CORNUA
CORNUAL
CORNUCOPIA
CORNUCOPIAN
CORNUCOPIAS
CORNUS
CORNUSES
CORNUTE
CORNUTED
CORNUTES
CORNUTING
CORNUTO
CORNUTOS
CORNWORM
CORNWORMS
CORNY
COROCORE
COROCORES
COROCORO
COROCOROS
CORODIES
CORODY
COROLLA
COROLLACEOUS
COROLLARIES
COROLLARY
COROLLAS
COROLLATE
COROLLIFLORAL
COROLLIFLOROUS
COROLLIFORM
COROLLINE
COROMANDEL
COROMANDELS
CORONA
CORONACH
CORONACHS
CORONAE
CORONAGRAPH
CORONAGRAPHS
CORONAL
CORONALS
CORONARIES

CORONARY
CORONAS
CORONATE
CORONATED
CORONATES
CORONATING
CORONATION
CORONATIONS
CORONEL
CORONELS
CORONER
CORONERS
CORONERSHIP
CORONERSHIPS
CORONET
CORONETED
CORONETS
CORONIS
CORONISES
CORONIUM
CORONIUMS
CORONOGRAPH
CORONOGRAPHS
CORONOID
COROTATE
COROTATED
COROTATES
COROTATING
COROTATION
COROTATIONS
COROZO
COROZOS
CORPORA
CORPORAL
CORPORALE
CORPORALES
CORPORALITIES
CORPORALITY
CORPORALLY
CORPORALS
CORPORALSHIP
CORPORALSHIPS
CORPORAS
CORPORASES
CORPORATE
CORPORATELY
CORPORATENESS
CORPORATENESSES
CORPORATION
CORPORATIONS
CORPORATISATION
CORPORATISE
CORPORATISED
CORPORATISES
CORPORATISING
CORPORATISM

CORPORATISMS
CORPORATIST
CORPORATISTS
CORPORATIVE
CORPORATIVISM
CORPORATIVISMS
CORPORATIZATION
CORPORATIZE
CORPORATIZED
CORPORATIZES
CORPORATIZING
CORPORATOR
CORPORATORS
CORPOREAL
CORPOREALISE
CORPOREALISED
CORPOREALISES
CORPOREALISING
CORPOREALISM
CORPOREALISMS
CORPOREALIST
CORPOREALISTS
CORPOREALITIES
CORPOREALITY
CORPOREALIZE
CORPOREALIZED
CORPOREALIZES
CORPOREALIZING
CORPOREALLY
CORPOREALNESS
CORPOREALNESSES
CORPOREITIES
CORPOREITY
CORPORIFICATION
CORPORIFIED
CORPORIFIES
CORPORIFY
CORPORIFYING
CORPOSANT
CORPOSANTS
CORPS
CORPSE
CORPSED
CORPSES
CORPSING
CORPSMAN
CORPSMEN
CORPULENCE
CORPULENCES
CORPULENCIES
CORPULENCY
CORPULENT
CORPULENTLY
CORPUS
CORPUSCLE
CORPUSCLES

CORPUSCULAR
CORPUSCULARIAN
CORPUSCULARIANS
CORPUSCULARITY
CORPUSCULE
CORPUSCULES
CORRADE
CORRADED
CORRADES
CORRADING
CORRAL
CORRALLED
CORRALLING
CORRALS
CORRASION
CORRASIONS
CORRASIVE
CORREA
CORREAS
CORRECT
CORRECTABLE
CORRECTED
CORRECTER
CORRECTEST
CORRECTIBLE
CORRECTING
CORRECTION
CORRECTIONAL
CORRECTIONER
CORRECTIONERS
CORRECTIONS
CORRECTITUDE
CORRECTITUDES
CORRECTIVE
CORRECTIVELY
CORRECTIVES
CORRECTLY
CORRECTNESS
CORRECTNESSES
CORRECTOR
CORRECTORS
CORRECTORY
CORRECTS
CORREGIDOR
CORREGIDORS
CORRELATABLE
CORRELATE
CORRELATED
CORRELATES
CORRELATING
CORRELATION
CORRELATIONAL
CORRELATIONS
CORRELATIVE
CORRELATIVELY
CORRELATIVENESS

CORRELATIVES
CORRELATIVITIES
CORRELATIVITY
CORRELATOR
CORRELATORS
CORRELIGIONIST
CORRELIGIONISTS
CORREPTION
CORREPTIONS
CORRESPOND
CORRESPONDED
CORRESPONDENCE
CORRESPONDENCES
CORRESPONDENCY
CORRESPONDENT
CORRESPONDENTLY
CORRESPONDENTS
CORRESPONDING
CORRESPONDINGLY
CORRESPONDS
CORRESPONSIVE
CORRIDA
CORRIDAS
CORRIDOR
CORRIDORS
CORRIE
CORRIES
CORRIGENDA
CORRIGENDUM
CORRIGENT
CORRIGENTS
CORRIGIBILITIES
CORRIGIBILITY
CORRIGIBLE
CORRIGIBLENESS
CORRIGIBLY
CORRIVAL
CORRIVALLED
CORRIVALLING
CORRIVALRIES
CORRIVALRY
CORRIVALS
CORRIVALSHIP
CORRIVALSHIPS
CORROBORABLE
CORROBORANT
CORROBORANTS
CORROBORATE
CORROBORATED
CORROBORATES
CORROBORATING
CORROBORATION
CORROBORATIONS
CORROBORATIVE
CORROBORATIVELY
CORROBORATIVES

CORROBORATOR
CORROBORATORS
CORROBORATORY
CORROBOREE
CORROBOREED
CORROBOREEING
CORROBOREES
CORRODANT
CORRODANTS
CORRODE
CORRODED
CORRODENT
CORRODENTS
CORRODER
CORRODERS
CORRODES
CORRODIBILITY
CORRODIBLE
CORRODIES
CORRODING
CORRODY
CORROSIBILITIES
CORROSIBILITY
CORROSIBLE
CORROSION
CORROSIONS
CORROSIVE
CORROSIVELY
CORROSIVENESS
CORROSIVENESSES
CORROSIVES
CORRUGATE
CORRUGATED
CORRUGATES
CORRUGATING
CORRUGATION
CORRUGATIONS
CORRUGATOR
CORRUGATORS
CORRUPT
CORRUPTED
CORRUPTER
CORRUPTERS
CORRUPTEST
CORRUPTIBILITY
CORRUPTIBLE
CORRUPTIBLENESS
CORRUPTIBLY
CORRUPTING
CORRUPTION
CORRUPTIONIST
CORRUPTIONISTS
CORRUPTIONS
CORRUPTIVE
CORRUPTIVELY
CORRUPTLY

CORRUPTNESS
CORRUPTNESSES
CORRUPTOR
CORRUPTORS
CORRUPTS
CORS
CORSAC
CORSACS
CORSAGE
CORSAGES
CORSAIR
CORSAIRS
CORSE
CORSELET
CORSELETS
CORSELETTE
CORSELETTES
CORSES
CORSET
CORSETED
CORSETIER
CORSETIERE
CORSETIERES
CORSETIERS
CORSETING
CORSETRIES
CORSETRY
CORSETS
CORSEY
CORSEYS
CORSIVE
CORSIVES
CORSLET
CORSLETED
CORSLETS
CORSNED
CORSNEDS
CORSO
CORSOS
CORTEGE
CORTEGES
CORTEX
CORTEXES
CORTICAL
CORTICALLY
CORTICATE
CORTICATED
CORTICATION
CORTICES
CORTICOID
CORTICOIDS
CORTICOLOUS
CORTICOSTEROID
CORTICOSTEROIDS
CORTICOSTERONE
CORTICOSTERONES

CORTICOTROPHIC
CORTICOTROPHIN
CORTICOTROPHINS
CORTICOTROPIC
CORTICOTROPIN
CORTICOTROPINS
CORTILE
CORTILI
CORTIN
CORTINS
CORTISOL
CORTISOLS
CORTISONE
CORTISONES
CORULER
CORULERS
CORUNDUM
CORUNDUMS
CORUSCANT
CORUSCATE
CORUSCATED
CORUSCATES
CORUSCATING
CORUSCATION
CORUSCATIONS
CORVEE
CORVEES
CORVES
CORVET
CORVETED
CORVETING
CORVETS
CORVETTE
CORVETTED
CORVETTES
CORVETTING
CORVID
CORVIDS
CORVINA
CORVINAS
CORVINE
CORVUS
CORVUSES
CORY
CORYBANT
CORYBANTES
CORYBANTIC
CORYBANTISM
CORYBANTISMS
CORYBANTS
CORYDALINE
CORYDALINES
CORYDALIS
CORYDALISES
CORYLOPSES
CORYLOPSIS

CORYLUS
CORYLUSES
CORYMB
CORYMBED
CORYMBOSE
CORYMBOSELY
CORYMBOUS
CORYMBS
CORYNEBACTERIA
CORYNEBACTERIAL
CORYNEBACTERIUM
CORYNEFORM
CORYPHAEI
CORYPHAEUS
CORYPHE
CORYPHEE
CORYPHEES
CORYPHENE
CORYPHENES
CORYPHES
CORYZA
CORYZAL
CORYZAS
COS
COSCINOMANCIES
COSCINOMANCY
COSCRIPT
COSCRIPTED
COSCRIPTING
COSCRIPTS
COSE
COSEC
COSECANT
COSECANTS
COSECH
COSECHS
COSECS
COSED
COSEISMAL
COSEISMALS
COSEISMIC
COSEISMICS
COSENTIENT
COSES
COSET
COSETS
COSEY
COSEYS
COSH
COSHED
COSHER
COSHERED
COSHERER
COSHERERS
COSHERIES
COSHERING

COSHERINGS
COSHERS
COSHERY
COSHES
COSHING
COSIE
COSIED
COSIER
COSIERS
COSIES
COSIEST
COSIGN
COSIGNATORIES
COSIGNATORY
COSIGNED
COSIGNER
COSIGNERS
COSIGNIFICATIVE
COSIGNING
COSIGNS
COSILY
COSINE
COSINES
COSINESS
COSINESSES
COSING
COSMEA
COSMEAS
COSMECEUTICAL
COSMECEUTICALS
COSMESES
COSMESIS
COSMETIC
COSMETICAL
COSMETICALLY
COSMETICIAN
COSMETICIANS
COSMETICISE
COSMETICISED
COSMETICISES
COSMETICISING
COSMETICISM
COSMETICISMS
COSMETICIZE
COSMETICIZED
COSMETICIZES
COSMETICIZING
COSMETICOLOGY
COSMETICS
COSMETOLOGIES
COSMETOLOGIST
COSMETOLOGISTS
COSMETOLOGY
COSMIC
COSMICAL
COSMICALLY

COSMIN
COSMINE
COSMISM
COSMISMS
COSMIST
COSMISTS
COSMOCHEMICAL
COSMOCHEMIST
COSMOCHEMISTRY
COSMOCHEMISTS
COSMOCRAT
COSMOCRATIC
COSMOCRATS
COSMODROME
COSMODROMES
COSMOGENIC
COSMOGENIES
COSMOGENY
COSMOGONAL
COSMOGONALLY
COSMOGONIC
COSMOGONICAL
COSMOGONIES
COSMOGONIST
COSMOGONISTS
COSMOGONY
COSMOGRAPHER
COSMOGRAPHERS
COSMOGRAPHIC
COSMOGRAPHICAL
COSMOGRAPHIES
COSMOGRAPHIST
COSMOGRAPHISTS
COSMOGRAPHY
COSMOID
COSMOLATRIES
COSMOLATRY
COSMOLOGIC
COSMOLOGICAL
COSMOLOGICALLY
COSMOLOGIES
COSMOLOGIST
COSMOLOGISTS
COSMOLOGY
COSMONAUT
COSMONAUTICS
COSMONAUTS
COSMOPLASTIC
COSMOPOLIS
COSMOPOLISES
COSMOPOLITAN
COSMOPOLITANISM
COSMOPOLITANS
COSMOPOLITE
COSMOPOLITES
COSMOPOLITIC

COSMOPOLITICAL
COSMOPOLITICS
COSMOPOLITISM
COSMOPOLITISMS
COSMORAMA
COSMORAMAS
COSMORAMIC
COSMOS
COSMOSES
COSMOSPHERE
COSMOSPHERES
COSMOTHEISM
COSMOTHEISMS
COSMOTHETIC
COSMOTHETICAL
COSMOTRON
COSMOTRONS
COSPHERED
COSPONSOR
COSPONSORED
COSPONSORING
COSPONSORS
COSPONSORSHIP
COSPONSORSHIPS
COSS
COSSACK
COSSACKS
COSSES
COSSET
COSSETED
COSSETING
COSSETS
COSSIE
COSSIES
COST
COSTA
COSTAE
COSTAL
COSTALGIA
COSTALGIAS
COSTALS
COSTAR
COSTARD
COSTARDMONGER
COSTARDMONGERS
COSTARDS
COSTARRED
COSTARRING
COSTARS
COSTATE
COSTATED
COSTE
COSTEAN
COSTEANED
COSTEANING
COSTEANINGS

COSTEANS
COSTED
COSTER
COSTERMONGER
COSTERMONGERS
COSTERS
COSTES
COSTING
COSTIVE
COSTIVELY
COSTIVENESS
COSTIVENESSES
COSTLESS
COSTLESSLY
COSTLIER
COSTLIEST
COSTLINESS
COSTLINESSES
COSTLY
COSTMARIES
COSTMARY
COSTOTOMIES
COSTOTOMY
COSTREL
COSTRELS
COSTS
COSTUME
COSTUMED
COSTUMER
COSTUMERIES
COSTUMERS
COSTUMERY
COSTUMES
COSTUMEY
COSTUMIER
COSTUMIERS
COSTUMING
COSTUS
COSTUSES
COSURFACTANT
COSURFACTANTS
COSY
COSYING
COT
COTAN
COTANGENT
COTANGENTIAL
COTANGENTIALLY
COTANGENTS
COTANS
COTE
COTEAU
COTEAUX
COTED
COTELETTE
COTELETTES

COTELINE
COTELINES
COTEMPORANEOUS
COTEMPORARIES
COTEMPORARY
COTENANCIES
COTENANCY
COTENANT
COTENANTS
COTERIE
COTERIES
COTERMINOUS
COTERMINOUSLY
COTES
COTH
COTHS
COTHURN
COTHURNI
COTHURNS
COTHURNUS
COTICULAR
COTIDAL
COTILLION
COTILLIONS
COTILLON
COTILLONS
COTING
COTINGA
COTINGAS
COTISE
COTISED
COTISES
COTISING
COTLAND
COTLANDS
COTONEASTER
COTONEASTERS
COTQUEAN
COTQUEANS
COTRANSDUCE
COTRANSDUCED
COTRANSDUCES
COTRANSDUCING
COTRANSDUCTION
COTRANSDUCTIONS
COTRANSFER
COTRANSFERS
COTRANSPORT
COTRANSPORTED
COTRANSPORTING
COTRANSPORTS
COTRUSTEE
COTRUSTEES
COTS
COTT
COTTA

COTTABUS
COTTABUSES
COTTAE
COTTAGE
COTTAGED
COTTAGER
COTTAGERS
COTTAGES
COTTAGEY
COTTAGING
COTTAGINGS
COTTAR
COTTARS
COTTAS
COTTED
COTTER
COTTERED
COTTERING
COTTERLESS
COTTERS
COTTID
COTTIDS
COTTIER
COTTIERISM
COTTIERISMS
COTTIERS
COTTING
COTTISE
COTTISED
COTTISES
COTTISING
COTTOID
COTTON
COTTONADE
COTTONADES
COTTONED
COTTONING
COTTONMOUTH
COTTONMOUTHS
COTTONOCRACIES
COTTONOCRACY
COTTONS
COTTONSEED
COTTONSEEDS
COTTONTAIL
COTTONTAILS
COTTONWEED
COTTONWEEDS
COTTONWOOD
COTTONWOODS
COTTONY
COTTOWN
COTTOWNS
COTTS
COTTUS
COTTUSES

COTWAL
COTWALS
COTYLAE
COTYLE
COTYLEDON
COTYLEDONAL
COTYLEDONARY
COTYLEDONOID
COTYLEDONOUS
COTYLEDONS
COTYLES
COTYLIFORM
COTYLOID
COTYLOIDAL
COTYLOIDALS
COTYLOIDS
COTYLOSAUR
COTYLOSAURS
COTYPE
COTYPES
COUCAL
COUCALS
COUCH
COUCHANT
COUCHE
COUCHED
COUCHEE
COUCHEES
COUCHER
COUCHERS
COUCHES
COUCHETTE
COUCHETTES
COUCHING
COUCHINGS
COUDE
COUGAN
COUGANS
COUGAR
COUGARS
COUGH
COUGHED
COUGHER
COUGHERS
COUGHING
COUGHINGS
COUGHS
COUGUAR
COUGUARS
COULD
COULDEST
COULDST
COULEE
COULEES
COULIBIACA
COULIBIACAS

COULIS
COULISES
COULISSE
COULISSES
COULOIR
COULOIRS
COULOMB
COULOMBIC
COULOMBMETER
COULOMBMETERS
COULOMBS
COULOMETER
COULOMETERS
COULOMETRIC
COULOMETRICALLY
COULOMETRIES
COULOMETRY
COULTER
COULTERS
COUMARIC
COUMARILIC
COUMARIN
COUMARINS
COUMARONE
COUMAROU
COUMAROUS
COUNCIL
COUNCILLOR
COUNCILLORS
COUNCILLORSHIP
COUNCILLORSHIPS
COUNCILMAN
COUNCILMANIC
COUNCILMEN
COUNCILOR
COUNCILORS
COUNCILORSHIP
COUNCILORSHIPS
COUNCILS
COUNCILWOMAN
COUNCILWOMEN
COUNSEL
COUNSELABLE
COUNSELED
COUNSELEE
COUNSELEES
COUNSELING
COUNSELINGS
COUNSELLABLE
COUNSELLED
COUNSELLING
COUNSELLINGS
COUNSELLOR
COUNSELLORS
COUNSELLORSHIP
COUNSELLORSHIPS

COUNSELOR
COUNSELORS
COUNSELORSHIP
COUNSELORSHIPS
COUNSELS
COUNT
COUNTABILITIES
COUNTABILITY
COUNTABLE
COUNTABLY
COUNTBACK
COUNTBACKS
COUNTDOWN
COUNTDOWNS
COUNTED
COUNTENANCE
COUNTENANCED
COUNTENANCER
COUNTENANCERS
COUNTENANCES
COUNTENANCING
COUNTER
COUNTERACT
COUNTERACTED
COUNTERACTING
COUNTERACTION
COUNTERACTIONS
COUNTERACTIVE
COUNTERACTIVELY
COUNTERACTS
COUNTERAGENT
COUNTERAGENTS
COUNTERARGUE
COUNTERARGUED
COUNTERARGUES
COUNTERARGUING
COUNTERARGUMENT
COUNTERASSAULT
COUNTERASSAULTS
COUNTERATTACK
COUNTERATTACKED
COUNTERATTACKER
COUNTERATTACKS
COUNTERBALANCE
COUNTERBALANCED
COUNTERBALANCES
COUNTERBASE
COUNTERBASES
COUNTERBID
COUNTERBIDDER
COUNTERBIDDERS
COUNTERBIDS
COUNTERBLAST
COUNTERBLASTS
COUNTERBLOCKADE
COUNTERBLOW

COUNTERBLOWS
COUNTERBLUFF
COUNTERBLUFFS
COUNTERBOND
COUNTERBONDS
COUNTERBORE
COUNTERBORED
COUNTERBORES
COUNTERBORING
COUNTERBRACE
COUNTERBRACED
COUNTERBRACES
COUNTERBRACING
COUNTERBUFF
COUNTERBUFFED
COUNTERBUFFING
COUNTERBUFFS
COUNTERCAMPAIGN
COUNTERCHANGE
COUNTERCHANGED
COUNTERCHANGES
COUNTERCHANGING
COUNTERCHARGE
COUNTERCHARGED
COUNTERCHARGES
COUNTERCHARGING
COUNTERCHARM
COUNTERCHARMED
COUNTERCHARMING
COUNTERCHARMS
COUNTERCHECK
COUNTERCHECKED
COUNTERCHECKING
COUNTERCHECKS
COUNTERCLAIM
COUNTERCLAIMANS
COUNTERCLAIMANT
COUNTERCLAIMED
COUNTERCLAIMING
COUNTERCLAIMS
COUNTERCOUP
COUNTERCOUPS
COUNTERCRIES
COUNTERCRY
COUNTERCULTURAL
COUNTERCULTURE
COUNTERCULTURES
COUNTERCURRENT
COUNTERCURRENTS
COUNTERCYCLICAL
COUNTERDEMAND
COUNTERDEMANDS
COUNTERDRAW
COUNTERDRAWING
COUNTERDRAWN
COUNTERDRAWS

COUNTERDREW
COUNTERED
COUNTEREFFORT
COUNTEREFFORTS
COUNTEREVIDENCE
COUNTEREXAMPLE
COUNTEREXAMPLES
COUNTERFACTUAL
COUNTERFACTUALS
COUNTERFECT
COUNTERFEISANCE
COUNTERFEIT
COUNTERFEITED
COUNTERFEITER
COUNTERFEITERS
COUNTERFEITING
COUNTERFEITLY
COUNTERFEITS
COUNTERFESAUNCE
COUNTERFIRE
COUNTERFIRES
COUNTERFLOW
COUNTERFLOWS
COUNTERFOIL
COUNTERFOILS
COUNTERFORCE
COUNTERFORCES
COUNTERFORT
COUNTERFORTS
COUNTERGLOW
COUNTERGLOWS
COUNTERGUERILLA
COUNTERIMAGE
COUNTERIMAGES
COUNTERING
COUNTERINSTANCE
COUNTERION
COUNTERIONS
COUNTERIRRITANT
COUNTERLIGHT
COUNTERLIGHTS
COUNTERMAN
COUNTERMAND
COUNTERMANDABLE
COUNTERMANDED
COUNTERMANDING
COUNTERMANDS
COUNTERMARCH
COUNTERMARCHED
COUNTERMARCHES
COUNTERMARCHING
COUNTERMARK
COUNTERMARKS
COUNTERMEASURE
COUNTERMEASURES
COUNTERMELODIES

COUNTERMELODY
COUNTERMEMO
COUNTERMEMOS
COUNTERMEN
COUNTERMINE
COUNTERMINED
COUNTERMINES
COUNTERMINING
COUNTERMOTION
COUNTERMOTIONS
COUNTERMOVE
COUNTERMOVED
COUNTERMOVEMENT
COUNTERMOVES
COUNTERMOVING
COUNTERMURE
COUNTERMURED
COUNTERMURES
COUNTERMURING
COUNTERMYTH
COUNTERMYTHS
COUNTEROFFER
COUNTEROFFERS
COUNTERORDER
COUNTERORDERED
COUNTERORDERING
COUNTERORDERS
COUNTERPACE
COUNTERPACES
COUNTERPANE
COUNTERPANES
COUNTERPART
COUNTERPARTIES
COUNTERPARTS
COUNTERPARTY
COUNTERPEISE
COUNTERPEISED
COUNTERPEISES
COUNTERPEISING
COUNTERPETITION
COUNTERPICKET
COUNTERPICKETED
COUNTERPICKETS
COUNTERPLAN
COUNTERPLANS
COUNTERPLAY
COUNTERPLAYER
COUNTERPLAYERS
COUNTERPLAYS
COUNTERPLEA
COUNTERPLEAD
COUNTERPLEADED
COUNTERPLEADING
COUNTERPLEADS
COUNTERPLEAS
COUNTERPLED

COUNTERPLOT
COUNTERPLOTS
COUNTERPLOTTED
COUNTERPLOTTING
COUNTERPLOY
COUNTERPLOYS
COUNTERPOINT
COUNTERPOINTED
COUNTERPOINTING
COUNTERPOINTS
COUNTERPOISE
COUNTERPOISED
COUNTERPOISES
COUNTERPOISING
COUNTERPOSE
COUNTERPOSED
COUNTERPOSES
COUNTERPOSING
COUNTERPOWER
COUNTERPOWERS
COUNTERPRESSURE
COUNTERPROJECT
COUNTERPROJECTS
COUNTERPROOF
COUNTERPROOFS
COUNTERPROPOSAL
COUNTERPROTEST
COUNTERPROTESTS
COUNTERPUNCH
COUNTERPUNCHED
COUNTERPUNCHER
COUNTERPUNCHERS
COUNTERPUNCHES
COUNTERPUNCHING
COUNTERQUESTION
COUNTERRAID
COUNTERRAIDS
COUNTERRALLIED
COUNTERRALLIES
COUNTERRALLY
COUNTERRALLYING
COUNTERREACTION
COUNTERREFORM
COUNTERREFORMER
COUNTERREFORMS
COUNTERRESPONSE
COUNTERS
COUNTERSANK
COUNTERSCARP
COUNTERSCARPS
COUNTERSEAL
COUNTERSEALED
COUNTERSEALING
COUNTERSEALS
COUNTERSHADING
COUNTERSHADINGS

COUNTERSHAFT
COUNTERSHAFTS
COUNTERSHOT
COUNTERSHOTS
COUNTERSIGN
COUNTERSIGNED
COUNTERSIGNING
COUNTERSIGNS
COUNTERSINK
COUNTERSINKING
COUNTERSINKS
COUNTERSNIPER
COUNTERSNIPERS
COUNTERSPELL
COUNTERSPELLS
COUNTERSPIES
COUNTERSPY
COUNTERSPYING
COUNTERSPYINGS
COUNTERSTAIN
COUNTERSTAINED
COUNTERSTAINING
COUNTERSTAINS
COUNTERSTATE
COUNTERSTATED
COUNTERSTATES
COUNTERSTATING
COUNTERSTEP
COUNTERSTEPS
COUNTERSTRATEGY
COUNTERSTREAM
COUNTERSTREAMS
COUNTERSTRICKEN
COUNTERSTRIKE
COUNTERSTRIKES
COUNTERSTRIKING
COUNTERSTROKE
COUNTERSTROKES
COUNTERSTRUCK
COUNTERSTYLE
COUNTERSTYLES
COUNTERSUBJECT
COUNTERSUBJECTS
COUNTERSUE
COUNTERSUED
COUNTERSUES
COUNTERSUING
COUNTERSUIT
COUNTERSUITS
COUNTERSUNK
COUNTERTACTIC
COUNTERTACTICS
COUNTERTENDENCY
COUNTERTENOR
COUNTERTENORS
COUNTERTERROR

COUNTERTERRORS
COUNTERTHREAT
COUNTERTHREATS
COUNTERTHRUST
COUNTERTHRUSTS
COUNTERTOP
COUNTERTOPS
COUNTERTRADE
COUNTERTRADED
COUNTERTRADES
COUNTERTRADING
COUNTERTREND
COUNTERTRENDS
COUNTERTYPE
COUNTERTYPES
COUNTERVAIL
COUNTERVAILABLE
COUNTERVAILED
COUNTERVAILING
COUNTERVAILS
COUNTERVIEW
COUNTERVIEWS
COUNTERVIOLENCE
COUNTERWEIGH
COUNTERWEIGHED
COUNTERWEIGHING
COUNTERWEIGHS
COUNTERWEIGHT
COUNTERWEIGHTED
COUNTERWEIGHTS
COUNTERWORD
COUNTERWORDS
COUNTERWORK
COUNTERWORKED
COUNTERWORKER
COUNTERWORKERS
COUNTERWORKING
COUNTERWORKS
COUNTERWORLD
COUNTERWORLDS
COUNTESS
COUNTESSES
COUNTIAN
COUNTIANS
COUNTIES
COUNTING
COUNTINGHOUSE
COUNTINGHOUSES
COUNTLESS
COUNTLESSLY
COUNTLINE
COUNTLINES
COUNTRIES
COUNTRIFIED
COUNTROL
COUNTROLLED

COUNTROLLING
COUNTROLS
COUNTRY
COUNTRYFIED
COUNTRYISH
COUNTRYMAN
COUNTRYMEN
COUNTRYSEAT
COUNTRYSEATS
COUNTRYSIDE
COUNTRYSIDES
COUNTRYWIDE
COUNTRYWOMAN
COUNTRYWOMEN
COUNTS
COUNTSHIP
COUNTSHIPS
COUNTY
COUP
COUPE
COUPED
COUPEE
COUPEES
COUPER
COUPERS
COUPES
COUPING
COUPLE
COUPLED
COUPLEDOM
COUPLEDOMS
COUPLEMENT
COUPLEMENTS
COUPLER
COUPLERS
COUPLES
COUPLET
COUPLETS
COUPLING
COUPLINGS
COUPON
COUPONING
COUPONINGS
COUPONS
COUPS
COUPURE
COUPURES
COUR
COURAGE
COURAGEFUL
COURAGEOUS
COURAGEOUSLY
COURAGEOUSNESS
COURAGES
COURANT
COURANTE

COURANTES
COURANTO
COURANTOES
COURANTOS
COURANTS
COURB
COURBARIL
COURBARILS
COURBED
COURBETTE
COURBETTES
COURBING
COURBS
COURD
COURE
COURED
COURES
COURGETTE
COURGETTES
COURIE
COURIED
COURIEING
COURIER
COURIERS
COURIES
COURING
COURLAN
COURLANS
COURS
COURSE
COURSEBOOK
COURSEBOOKS
COURSED
COURSER
COURSERS
COURSES
COURSEWARE
COURSEWARES
COURSEWORK
COURSEWORKS
COURSING
COURSINGS
COURT
COURTCRAFT
COURTCRAFTS
COURTED
COURTEOUS
COURTEOUSLY
COURTEOUSNESS
COURTEOUSNESSES
COURTER
COURTERS
COURTESAN
COURTESANS
COURTESIED
COURTESIES

COURTESY
COURTESYING
COURTEZAN
COURTEZANS
COURTHOUSE
COURTHOUSES
COURTIER
COURTIERISM
COURTIERISMS
COURTIERLIKE
COURTIERLY
COURTIERS
COURTING
COURTINGS
COURTLET
COURTLETS
COURTLIER
COURTLIEST
COURTLIKE
COURTLINESS
COURTLINESSES
COURTLING
COURTLINGS
COURTLY
COURTMARTIALLED
COURTROOM
COURTROOMS
COURTS
COURTSHIP
COURTSHIPS
COURTSIDE
COURTSIDES
COURTYARD
COURTYARDS
COUSCOUS
COUSCOUSES
COUSCOUSOU
COUSCOUSOUS
COUSIN
COUSINAGE
COUSINAGES
COUSINHOOD
COUSINHOODS
COUSINLY
COUSINRIES
COUSINRY
COUSINS
COUSINSHIP
COUSINSHIPS
COUTEAU
COUTEAUX
COUTER
COUTERS
COUTH
COUTHER
COUTHEST

COUTHIE
COUTHIER
COUTHIEST
COUTHS
COUTHY
COUTIL
COUTILLE
COUTILLES
COUTILS
COUTURE
COUTURES
COUTURIER
COUTURIERE
COUTURIERES
COUTURIERS
COUVADE
COUVADES
COUVERT
COUVERTS
COVALENCE
COVALENCES
COVALENCIES
COVALENCY
COVALENT
COVALENTLY
COVARIANCE
COVARIANCES
COVARIANT
COVARIANTS
COVARIATION
COVARIATIONS
COVARIED
COVARIES
COVARY
COVARYING
COVE
COVED
COVELET
COVELETS
COVELLINE
COVELLINES
COVELLITE
COVELLITES
COVEN
COVENANT
COVENANTAL
COVENANTALLY
COVENANTED
COVENANTEE
COVENANTEES
COVENANTER
COVENANTERS
COVENANTING
COVENANTOR
COVENANTORS
COVENANTS

COVENS
COVENT
COVENTS
COVER
COVERABLE
COVERAGE
COVERAGES
COVERALL
COVERALLED
COVERALLS
COVERED
COVERER
COVERERS
COVERING
COVERINGS
COVERLESS
COVERLET
COVERLETS
COVERLID
COVERLIDS
COVERMOUNT
COVERMOUNTS
COVERS
COVERSED
COVERSLIP
COVERSLIPS
COVERT
COVERTLY
COVERTNESS
COVERTNESSES
COVERTS
COVERTURE
COVERTURES
COVERUP
COVERUPS
COVES
COVET
COVETABLE
COVETED
COVETER
COVETERS
COVETING
COVETINGLY
COVETISE
COVETISES
COVETIVENESS
COVETIVENESSES
COVETOUS
COVETOUSLY
COVETOUSNESS
COVETOUSNESSES
COVETS
COVEY
COVEYS
COVIN
COVING

COVINGS
COVINOUS
COVINS
COVYNE
COVYNES
COW
COWABUNGA
COWAGE
COWAGES
COWAL
COWALS
COWAN
COWANS
COWARD
COWARDED
COWARDICE
COWARDICES
COWARDING
COWARDLINESS
COWARDLINESSES
COWARDLY
COWARDREES
COWARDRIES
COWARDRY
COWARDS
COWARDSHIP
COWARDSHIPS
COWBANE
COWBANES
COWBELL
COWBELLS
COWBERRIES
COWBERRY
COWBIND
COWBINDS
COWBIRD
COWBIRDS
COWBOY
COWBOYS
COWCATCHER
COWCATCHERS
COWED
COWEDLY
COWER
COWERED
COWERING
COWERINGLY
COWERS
COWFEEDER
COWFEEDERS
COWFETERIA
COWFETERIAS
COWFISH
COWFISHES
COWFLAP
COWFLAPS

COWFLOP
COWFLOPS
COWGIRL
COWGIRLS
COWGRASS
COWGRASSES
COWHAGE
COWHAGES
COWHAND
COWHANDS
COWHEARD
COWHEARDS
COWHEEL
COWHEELS
COWHERB
COWHERBS
COWHERD
COWHERDS
COWHIDE
COWHIDED
COWHIDES
COWHIDING
COWHOUSE
COWHOUSES
COWIER
COWIEST
COWING
COWINNER
COWINNERS
COWISH
COWITCH
COWITCHES
COWK
COWKED
COWKING
COWKS
COWL
COWLED
COWLICK
COWLICKS
COWLING
COWLINGS
COWLS
COWLSTAFF
COWLSTAFFS
COWLSTAVES
COWMAN
COWMEN
COWORKER
COWORKERS
COWP
COWPAT
COWPATS
COWPEA
COWPEAS
COWPED

COWPIE
COWPIES
COWPING
COWPLOP
COWPLOPS
COWPOKE
COWPOKES
COWPOX
COWPOXES
COWPS
COWPUNCHER
COWPUNCHERS
COWRIE
COWRIES
COWRITE
COWRITES
COWRITING
COWRITTEN
COWROTE
COWRY
COWS
COWSHED
COWSHEDS
COWSKIN
COWSKINS
COWSLIP
COWSLIPS
COWTREE
COWTREES
COWY
COX
COXA
COXAE
COXAL
COXALGIA
COXALGIAS
COXALGIC
COXALGIES
COXALGY
COXCOMB
COXCOMBIC
COXCOMBICAL
COXCOMBICALITY
COXCOMBICALLY
COXCOMBRIES
COXCOMBRY
COXCOMBS
COXCOMICAL
COXED
COXES
COXIER
COXIEST
COXINESS
COXINESSES
COXING
COXITIDES

COXITIS
COXLESS
COXSWAIN
COXSWAINED
COXSWAINING
COXSWAINS
COXY
COY
COYDOG
COYDOGS
COYED
COYER
COYEST
COYING
COYISH
COYISHLY
COYISHNESS
COYISHNESSES
COYLY
COYNESS
COYNESSES
COYOTE
COYOTES
COYOTILLO
COYOTILLOS
COYPOU
COYPOUS
COYPU
COYPUS
COYS
COYSTREL
COYSTRELS
COYSTRIL
COYSTRILS
COZ
COZE
COZED
COZEN
COZENAGE
COZENAGES
COZENED
COZENER
COZENERS
COZENING
COZENS
COZES
COZEY
COZEYS
COZIE
COZIED
COZIER
COZIERS
COZIES
COZIEST
COZILY
COZINESS

COZINESSES
COZING
COZY
COZYING
COZZES
CRAAL
CRAALED
CRAALING
CRAALS
CRAB
CRABBED
CRABBEDLY
CRABBEDNESS
CRABBEDNESSES
CRABBER
CRABBERS
CRABBIER
CRABBIEST
CRABBILY
CRABBINESS
CRABBINESSES
CRABBING
CRABBY
CRABGRASS
CRABGRASSES
CRABLIKE
CRABMEAT
CRABMEATS
CRABS
CRABSTICK
CRABSTICKS
CRABWISE
CRABWOOD
CRABWOODS
CRACK
CRACKAJACK
CRACKAJACKS
CRACKBACK
CRACKBACKS
CRACKBRAIN
CRACKBRAINED
CRACKBRAINS
CRACKDOWN
CRACKDOWNS
CRACKED
CRACKER
CRACKERJACK
CRACKERJACKS
CRACKERS
CRACKET
CRACKETS
CRACKHEAD
CRACKHEADS
CRACKING
CRACKINGS
CRACKJAW

CRACKJAWS
CRACKLE
CRACKLED
CRACKLES
CRACKLEWARE
CRACKLEWARES
CRACKLIER
CRACKLIEST
CRACKLING
CRACKLINGS
CRACKLY
CRACKNEL
CRACKNELS
CRACKPOT
CRACKPOTS
CRACKS
CRACKSMAN
CRACKSMEN
CRACKUP
CRACKUPS
CRACKY
CRACOVIENNE
CRACOVIENNES
CRACOWE
CRACOWES
CRADLE
CRADLED
CRADLER
CRADLERS
CRADLES
CRADLESONG
CRADLESONGS
CRADLEWALKS
CRADLING
CRADLINGS
CRAFT
CRAFTED
CRAFTIER
CRAFTIEST
CRAFTILY
CRAFTINESS
CRAFTINESSES
CRAFTING
CRAFTLESS
CRAFTMANSHIP
CRAFTMANSHIPS
CRAFTS
CRAFTSMAN
CRAFTSMANLIKE
CRAFTSMANLY
CRAFTSMANSHIP
CRAFTSMANSHIPS
CRAFTSMEN
CRAFTSPEOPLE
CRAFTSPERSON
CRAFTSPERSONS

CRAFTSWOMAN
CRAFTSWOMEN
CRAFTWORK
CRAFTWORKS
CRAFTY
CRAG
CRAGFAST
CRAGGED
CRAGGEDNESS
CRAGGEDNESSES
CRAGGIER
CRAGGIEST
CRAGGILY
CRAGGINESS
CRAGGINESSES
CRAGGY
CRAGS
CRAGSMAN
CRAGSMEN
CRAIC
CRAIG
CRAIGFLUKES
CRAIGS
CRAKE
CRAKEBERRIES
CRAKEBERRY
CRAKED
CRAKES
CRAKING
CRAM
CRAMBE
CRAMBES
CRAMBO
CRAMBOCLINK
CRAMBOCLINKS
CRAMBOES
CRAMBOS
CRAME
CRAMES
CRAMESIES
CRAMESY
CRAMMABLE
CRAMMED
CRAMMER
CRAMMERS
CRAMMING
CRAMOISIE
CRAMOISIES
CRAMOISY
CRAMP
CRAMPBARK
CRAMPBARKS
CRAMPED
CRAMPER
CRAMPERS
CRAMPET

CRAMPETS
CRAMPIER
CRAMPIEST
CRAMPING
CRAMPIT
CRAMPITS
CRAMPON
CRAMPONED
CRAMPONING
CRAMPONS
CRAMPOON
CRAMPOONS
CRAMPS
CRAMPY
CRAMS
CRAN
CRANAGE
CRANAGES
CRANBERRIES
CRANBERRY
CRANCH
CRANCHED
CRANCHES
CRANCHING
CRANE
CRANED
CRANEFLIES
CRANEFLY
CRANES
CRANESBILL
CRANESBILLS
CRANIA
CRANIAL
CRANIALLY
CRANIATE
CRANIATES
CRANIECTOMIES
CRANIECTOMY
CRANING
CRANIOCEREBRAL
CRANIOFACIAL
CRANIOGNOMIES
CRANIOGNOMY
CRANIOLOGICAL
CRANIOLOGICALLY
CRANIOLOGIES
CRANIOLOGIST
CRANIOLOGISTS
CRANIOLOGY
CRANIOMETER
CRANIOMETERS
CRANIOMETRIC
CRANIOMETRICAL
CRANIOMETRIES
CRANIOMETRIST
CRANIOMETRISTS

CRANIOMETRY
CRANIOPAGUS
CRANIOSACRAL
CRANIOSCOPIES
CRANIOSCOPIST
CRANIOSCOPISTS
CRANIOSCOPY
CRANIOTOMIES
CRANIOTOMY
CRANIUM
CRANIUMS
CRANK
CRANKCASE
CRANKCASES
CRANKED
CRANKER
CRANKEST
CRANKHANDLE
CRANKHANDLES
CRANKIER
CRANKIEST
CRANKILY
CRANKINESS
CRANKINESSES
CRANKING
CRANKISH
CRANKLE
CRANKLED
CRANKLES
CRANKLING
CRANKLY
CRANKNESS
CRANKNESSES
CRANKOUS
CRANKPIN
CRANKPINS
CRANKS
CRANKSHAFT
CRANKSHAFTS
CRANKY
CRANNIED
CRANNIES
CRANNOG
CRANNOGE
CRANNOGES
CRANNOGS
CRANNY
CRANNYING
CRANREUCH
CRANREUCHS
CRANS
CRANTS
CRANTSES
CRAP
CRAPAUD
CRAPAUDS

CRAPE
CRAPED
CRAPEHANGER
CRAPEHANGERS
CRAPEHANGINGS
CRAPES
CRAPIER
CRAPIEST
CRAPING
CRAPLE
CRAPLES
CRAPOLA
CRAPPED
CRAPPER
CRAPPERS
CRAPPIE
CRAPPIER
CRAPPIES
CRAPPIEST
CRAPPING
CRAPPY
CRAPS
CRAPSHOOT
CRAPSHOOTER
CRAPSHOOTERS
CRAPSHOOTS
CRAPULENCE
CRAPULENCES
CRAPULENT
CRAPULENTLY
CRAPULOSITIES
CRAPULOSITY
CRAPULOUS
CRAPULOUSLY
CRAPULOUSNESS
CRAPY
CRAQUELURE
CRAQUELURES
CRARE
CRARES
CRASES
CRASH
CRASHED
CRASHER
CRASHERS
CRASHES
CRASHING
CRASHINGLY
CRASHLAND
CRASHLANDED
CRASHLANDING
CRASHLANDS
CRASHPAD
CRASHPADS
CRASHWORTHINESS
CRASHWORTHY

CRASIS
CRASS
CRASSAMENTUM
CRASSER
CRASSEST
CRASSITUDE
CRASSITUDES
CRASSLY
CRASSNESS
CRASSNESSES
CRASSULACEAN
CRASSULACEOUS
CRATCH
CRATCHES
CRATE
CRATED
CRATEFUL
CRATEFULS
CRATER
CRATERED
CRATERIFORM
CRATERING
CRATERLESS
CRATERLET
CRATERLETS
CRATERLIKE
CRATEROUS
CRATERS
CRATES
CRATING
CRATON
CRATONIC
CRATONS
CRATUR
CRATURS
CRAUNCH
CRAUNCHABLE
CRAUNCHED
CRAUNCHES
CRAUNCHIER
CRAUNCHIEST
CRAUNCHINESS
CRAUNCHING
CRAUNCHY
CRAVAT
CRAVATS
CRAVATTED
CRAVATTING
CRAVE
CRAVED
CRAVEN
CRAVENED
CRAVENING
CRAVENLY
CRAVENNESS
CRAVENNESSES

CRAVENS
CRAVER
CRAVERS
CRAVES
CRAVING
CRAVINGS
CRAW
CRAWDAD
CRAWDADS
CRAWFISH
CRAWFISHED
CRAWFISHES
CRAWFISHING
CRAWL
CRAWLED
CRAWLER
CRAWLERS
CRAWLIER
CRAWLIEST
CRAWLING
CRAWLINGLY
CRAWLINGS
CRAWLS
CRAWLWAY
CRAWLWAYS
CRAWLY
CRAWS
CRAY
CRAYER
CRAYERS
CRAYFISH
CRAYFISHES
CRAYON
CRAYONED
CRAYONING
CRAYONIST
CRAYONISTS
CRAYONS
CRAYS
CRAYTHUR
CRAYTHURS
CRAZE
CRAZED
CRAZES
CRAZIER
CRAZIES
CRAZIEST
CRAZILY
CRAZINESS
CRAZINESSES
CRAZING
CRAZY
CRAZYWEED
CRAZYWEEDS
CREACH
CREACHS

CREAGH
CREAGHS
CREAK
CREAKED
CREAKIER
CREAKIEST
CREAKILY
CREAKINESS
CREAKINESSES
CREAKING
CREAKINGLY
CREAKS
CREAKY
CREAM
CREAMCUPS
CREAMED
CREAMER
CREAMERIES
CREAMERS
CREAMERY
CREAMIER
CREAMIEST
CREAMILY
CREAMINESS
CREAMINESSES
CREAMING
CREAMLAID
CREAMLIKE
CREAMS
CREAMWARE
CREAMWARES
CREAMWOVE
CREAMY
CREANCE
CREANCES
CREANT
CREASE
CREASED
CREASELESS
CREASER
CREASERS
CREASES
CREASIER
CREASIEST
CREASING
CREASOTE
CREASOTED
CREASOTES
CREASOTING
CREASY
CREATABLE
CREATE
CREATED
CREATES
CREATIANISM
CREATIANISMS

CREATIC
CREATIN
CREATINE
CREATINES
CREATING
CREATININE
CREATININES
CREATINS
CREATION
CREATIONAL
CREATIONISM
CREATIONISMS
CREATIONIST
CREATIONISTIC
CREATIONISTS
CREATIONS
CREATIVE
CREATIVELY
CREATIVENESS
CREATIVENESSES
CREATIVES
CREATIVITIES
CREATIVITY
CREATOR
CREATORS
CREATORSHIP
CREATORSHIPS
CREATRESS
CREATRESSES
CREATRIX
CREATRIXES
CREATURAL
CREATURE
CREATUREHOOD
CREATUREHOODS
CREATURELINESS
CREATURELY
CREATURES
CREATURESHIP
CREATURESHIPS
CRECHE
CRECHES
CRED
CREDAL
CREDENCE
CREDENCES
CREDENDA
CREDENDUM
CREDENT
CREDENTIAL
CREDENTIALED
CREDENTIALING
CREDENTIALISM
CREDENTIALISMS
CREDENTIALLED
CREDENTIALLING

CREDENTIALS
CREDENZA
CREDENZAS
CREDIBILITIES
CREDIBILITY
CREDIBLE
CREDIBLENESS
CREDIBLENESSES
CREDIBLY
CREDIT
CREDITABILITIES
CREDITABILITY
CREDITABLE
CREDITABLENESS
CREDITABLY
CREDITED
CREDITING
CREDITLESS
CREDITOR
CREDITORS
CREDITS
CREDITWORTHY
CREDO
CREDOS
CREDS
CREDULITIES
CREDULITY
CREDULOUS
CREDULOUSLY
CREDULOUSNESS
CREDULOUSNESSES
CREE
CREED
CREEDAL
CREEDS
CREEING
CREEK
CREEKIER
CREEKIEST
CREEKS
CREEKY
CREEL
CREELED
CREELING
CREELS
CREEP
CREEPAGE
CREEPAGES
CREEPER
CREEPERED
CREEPERS
CREEPIE
CREEPIER
CREEPIES
CREEPIEST
CREEPILY

CREEPINESS
CREEPINESSES
CREEPING
CREEPINGLY
CREEPMOUSE
CREEPS
CREEPY
CREES
CREESE
CREESED
CREESES
CREESH
CREESHED
CREESHES
CREESHIER
CREESHIEST
CREESHING
CREESHY
CREESING
CREMAILLERE
CREMAILLERES
CREMAINS
CREMASTER
CREMASTERS
CREMATE
CREMATED
CREMATES
CREMATING
CREMATION
CREMATIONISM
CREMATIONIST
CREMATIONISTS
CREMATIONS
CREMATOR
CREMATORIA
CREMATORIAL
CREMATORIES
CREMATORIUM
CREMATORIUMS
CREMATORS
CREMATORY
CREME
CREMES
CREMOCARP
CREMOCARPS
CREMONA
CREMONAS
CREMOR
CREMORNE
CREMORNES
CREMORS
CREMOSIN
CREMSIN
CRENA
CRENAS
CRENATE

CRENATED
CRENATELY
CRENATION
CRENATIONS
CRENATURE
CRENATURES
CRENEL
CRENELATE
CRENELATED
CRENELATES
CRENELATING
CRENELATION
CRENELATIONS
CRENELED
CRENELING
CRENELLATE
CRENELLATED
CRENELLATES
CRENELLATING
CRENELLATION
CRENELLATIONS
CRENELLE
CRENELLED
CRENELLES
CRENELLING
CRENELS
CRENULATE
CRENULATED
CRENULATION
CRENULATIONS
CREODONT
CREODONTS
CREOLE
CREOLES
CREOLIAN
CREOLIANS
CREOLISATION
CREOLISATIONS
CREOLISE
CREOLISED
CREOLISES
CREOLISING
CREOLIST
CREOLISTS
CREOLIZATION
CREOLIZATIONS
CREOLIZE
CREOLIZED
CREOLIZES
CREOLIZING
CREOPHAGOUS
CREOPHAGY
CREOSOL
CREOSOLS
CREOSOTE
CREOSOTED

CREOSOTES
CREOSOTIC
CREOSOTING
CREPANCE
CREPANCES
CREPE
CREPED
CREPEHANGER
CREPEHANGERS
CREPEHANGING
CREPEHANGINGS
CREPERIE
CREPERIES
CREPES
CREPEY
CREPIER
CREPIEST
CREPINESS
CREPINESSES
CREPING
CREPITANT
CREPITATE
CREPITATED
CREPITATES
CREPITATING
CREPITATION
CREPITATIONS
CREPITATIVE
CREPITUS
CREPITUSES
CREPOLINE
CREPOLINES
CREPON
CREPONS
CREPT
CREPUSCLE
CREPUSCLES
CREPUSCULAR
CREPUSCULE
CREPUSCULES
CREPUSCULOUS
CREPY
CRESCENDI
CRESCENDO
CRESCENDOED
CRESCENDOES
CRESCENDOING
CRESCENDOS
CRESCENT
CRESCENTADE
CRESCENTADES
CRESCENTED
CRESCENTIC
CRESCENTS
CRESCIVE
CRESCIVELY

CRESCOGRAPH
CRESCOGRAPHS
CRESOL
CRESOLS
CRESS
CRESSES
CRESSET
CRESSETS
CREST
CRESTAL
CRESTED
CRESTFALLEN
CRESTFALLENLY
CRESTFALLENNESS
CRESTING
CRESTINGS
CRESTLESS
CRESTON
CRESTONS
CRESTS
CRESYL
CRESYLIC
CRESYLS
CRETACEOUS
CRETACEOUSES
CRETACEOUSLY
CRETIC
CRETICS
CRETIN
CRETINISE
CRETINISED
CRETINISES
CRETINISING
CRETINISM
CRETINISMS
CRETINIZE
CRETINIZED
CRETINIZES
CRETINIZING
CRETINOID
CRETINOIDS
CRETINOUS
CRETINS
CRETISM
CRETISMS
CRETONNE
CRETONNES
CREUTZER
CREUTZERS
CREVALLE
CREVALLES
CREVASSE
CREVASSED
CREVASSES
CREVASSING
CREVETTE

CREVETTES
CREVICE
CREVICED
CREVICES
CREW
CREWE
CREWED
CREWEL
CREWELIST
CREWELISTS
CREWELLED
CREWELLERIES
CREWELLERY
CREWELLING
CREWELS
CREWELWORK
CREWELWORKS
CREWES
CREWING
CREWLESS
CREWMAN
CREWMATE
CREWMATES
CREWMEN
CREWNECK
CREWNECKS
CREWS
CRIANT
CRIB
CRIBBAGE
CRIBBAGES
CRIBBED
CRIBBER
CRIBBERS
CRIBBING
CRIBBINGS
CRIBBLE
CRIBBLED
CRIBBLES
CRIBBLING
CRIBELLA
CRIBELLAR
CRIBELLUM
CRIBLE
CRIBRATE
CRIBRATION
CRIBRATIONS
CRIBRIFORM
CRIBROSE
CRIBROUS
CRIBS
CRIBWORK
CRIBWORKS
CRICETID
CRICETIDS
CRICK

CRICKED
CRICKET
CRICKETED
CRICKETER
CRICKETERS
CRICKETING
CRICKETINGS
CRICKETS
CRICKEY
CRICKING
CRICKS
CRICKY
CRICOID
CRICOIDS
CRIED
CRIER
CRIERS
CRIES
CRIKEY
CRIM
CRIME
CRIMED
CRIMEFUL
CRIMELESS
CRIMEN
CRIMES
CRIMEWAVE
CRIMEWAVES
CRIMINA
CRIMINAL
CRIMINALESE
CRIMINALESES
CRIMINALISATION
CRIMINALISE
CRIMINALISED
CRIMINALISES
CRIMINALISING
CRIMINALIST
CRIMINALISTICS
CRIMINALISTS
CRIMINALITIES
CRIMINALITY
CRIMINALIZATION
CRIMINALIZE
CRIMINALIZED
CRIMINALIZES
CRIMINALIZING
CRIMINALLY
CRIMINALS
CRIMINATE
CRIMINATED
CRIMINATES
CRIMINATING
CRIMINATION
CRIMINATIONS
CRIMINATIVE

CRIMINATOR
CRIMINATORS
CRIMINATORY
CRIMINE
CRIMING
CRIMINI
CRIMINOGENIC
CRIMINOLOGIC
CRIMINOLOGICAL
CRIMINOLOGIES
CRIMINOLOGIST
CRIMINOLOGISTS
CRIMINOLOGY
CRIMINOUS
CRIMINOUSNESS
CRIMINOUSNESSES
CRIMMER
CRIMMERS
CRIMP
CRIMPED
CRIMPER
CRIMPERS
CRIMPIER
CRIMPIEST
CRIMPING
CRIMPLE
CRIMPLED
CRIMPLES
CRIMPLING
CRIMPS
CRIMPY
CRIMS
CRIMSON
CRIMSONED
CRIMSONING
CRIMSONNESS
CRIMSONS
CRINAL
CRINATE
CRINATED
CRINE
CRINED
CRINES
CRINGE
CRINGED
CRINGELING
CRINGELINGS
CRINGER
CRINGERS
CRINGES
CRINGEWORTHY
CRINGING
CRINGINGLY
CRINGINGS
CRINGLE
CRINGLES

CRINICULTURAL
CRINIGEROUS
CRINING
CRINITE
CRINITES
CRINKLE
CRINKLED
CRINKLEROOT
CRINKLEROOTS
CRINKLES
CRINKLIER
CRINKLIES
CRINKLIEST
CRINKLING
CRINKLY
CRINOID
CRINOIDAL
CRINOIDEAN
CRINOIDEANS
CRINOIDS
CRINOLETTE
CRINOLETTES
CRINOLINE
CRINOLINED
CRINOLINES
CRINOSE
CRINUM
CRINUMS
CRIOLLO
CRIOLLOS
CRIOS
CRIPE
CRIPES
CRIPPLE
CRIPPLED
CRIPPLEDOM
CRIPPLEDOMS
CRIPPLER
CRIPPLERS
CRIPPLES
CRIPPLEWARE
CRIPPLEWARES
CRIPPLING
CRIPPLINGLY
CRIPPLINGS
CRIS
CRISE
CRISES
CRISIC
CRISIS
CRISP
CRISPATE
CRISPATED
CRISPATION
CRISPATIONS
CRISPATURE

CRISPATURES
CRISPBREAD
CRISPBREADS
CRISPED
CRISPEN
CRISPENED
CRISPENING
CRISPENS
CRISPER
CRISPERS
CRISPEST
CRISPIER
CRISPIEST
CRISPILY
CRISPIN
CRISPINESS
CRISPINESSES
CRISPING
CRISPINS
CRISPLY
CRISPNESS
CRISPNESSES
CRISPS
CRISPY
CRISSA
CRISSAL
CRISSCROSS
CRISSCROSSED
CRISSCROSSES
CRISSCROSSING
CRISSUM
CRISTA
CRISTAE
CRISTATE
CRISTATED
CRISTIFORM
CRISTOBALITE
CRISTOBALITES
CRIT
CRITERIA
CRITERION
CRITERIONS
CRITERIUM
CRITERIUMS
CRITH
CRITHIDIAL
CRITHOMANCIES
CRITHOMANCY
CRITHS
CRITIC
CRITICAL
CRITICALITIES
CRITICALITY
CRITICALLY
CRITICALNESS
CRITICALNESSES

CRITICASTER
CRITICASTERS
CRITICISABLE
CRITICISE
CRITICISED
CRITICISER
CRITICISERS
CRITICISES
CRITICISING
CRITICISINGLY
CRITICISM
CRITICISMS
CRITICIZABLE
CRITICIZE
CRITICIZED
CRITICIZER
CRITICIZERS
CRITICIZES
CRITICIZING
CRITICIZINGLY
CRITICS
CRITIQUE
CRITIQUED
CRITIQUES
CRITIQUING
CRITS
CRITTER
CRITTERS
CRITTUR
CRITTURS
CRIVENS
CRIVVENS
CROAK
CROAKED
CROAKER
CROAKERS
CROAKIER
CROAKIEST
CROAKILY
CROAKINESS
CROAKING
CROAKINGS
CROAKS
CROAKY
CROC
CROCEATE
CROCEIN
CROCEINE
CROCEINES
CROCEINS
CROCEOUS
CROCHE
CROCHES
CROCHET
CROCHETED
CROCHETER

CROCHETERS
CROCHETING
CROCHETINGS
CROCHETS
CROCI
CROCIDOLITE
CROCIDOLITES
CROCINE
CROCK
CROCKED
CROCKERIES
CROCKERY
CROCKET
CROCKETED
CROCKETS
CROCKING
CROCKS
CROCODILE
CROCODILES
CROCODILIAN
CROCODILIANS
CROCOISITE
CROCOISITES
CROCOITE
CROCOITES
CROCOSMIA
CROCOSMIAS
CROCS
CROCUS
CROCUSES
CROFT
CROFTER
CROFTERS
CROFTING
CROFTINGS
CROFTS
CROG
CROGGED
CROGGIES
CROGGING
CROGGY
CROISSANT
CROISSANTS
CROJIK
CROJIKS
CROMACK
CROMACKS
CROMB
CROMBEC
CROMBECS
CROMBED
CROMBING
CROMBS
CROME
CROMED
CROMES

CROMING
CROMLECH
CROMLECHS
CROMORNA
CROMORNAS
CROMORNE
CROMORNES
CRONE
CRONES
CRONET
CRONETS
CRONIES
CRONK
CRONKER
CRONKEST
CRONY
CRONYISM
CRONYISMS
CROODLE
CROODLED
CROODLES
CROODLING
CROOK
CROOKBACK
CROOKBACKED
CROOKBACKS
CROOKED
CROOKEDER
CROOKEDEST
CROOKEDLY
CROOKEDNESS
CROOKEDNESSES
CROOKER
CROOKERIES
CROOKERY
CROOKEST
CROOKING
CROOKNECK
CROOKNECKS
CROOKS
CROOL
CROOLED
CROOLING
CROOLS
CROON
CROONED
CROONER
CROONERS
CROONING
CROONINGS
CROONS
CROOVE
CROOVES
CROP
CROPBOUND
CROPDUSTER

CROPDUSTERS
CROPFUL
CROPFULL
CROPFULS
CROPLAND
CROPLANDS
CROPLESS
CROPPED
CROPPER
CROPPERS
CROPPIE
CROPPIES
CROPPING
CROPPINGS
CROPPY
CROPS
CROPSICK
CROQUANTE
CROQUANTES
CROQUET
CROQUETED
CROQUETING
CROQUETS
CROQUETTE
CROQUETTES
CROQUIGNOLE
CROQUIGNOLES
CROQUIS
CRORE
CRORES
CROSIER
CROSIERED
CROSIERS
CROSS
CROSSABILITIES
CROSSABILITY
CROSSABLE
CROSSANDRA
CROSSANDRAS
CROSSARM
CROSSARMS
CROSSBAND
CROSSBANDED
CROSSBANDING
CROSSBANDINGS
CROSSBANDS
CROSSBAR
CROSSBARRED
CROSSBARRING
CROSSBARS
CROSSBEAM
CROSSBEAMS
CROSSBEARER
CROSSBEARERS
CROSSBENCH
CROSSBENCHER

CROSSBENCHERS
CROSSBENCHES
CROSSBILL
CROSSBILLS
CROSSBIRTH
CROSSBIRTHS
CROSSBIT
CROSSBITE
CROSSBITES
CROSSBITING
CROSSBITTEN
CROSSBONES
CROSSBOW
CROSSBOWER
CROSSBOWERS
CROSSBOWMAN
CROSSBOWMEN
CROSSBOWS
CROSSBRED
CROSSBREDS
CROSSBREED
CROSSBREEDING
CROSSBREEDINGS
CROSSBREEDS
CROSSBUCK
CROSSBUCKS
CROSSCHECK
CROSSCHECKED
CROSSCHECKING
CROSSCHECKS
CROSSCLAIM
CROSSCLAIMS
CROSSCOURT
CROSSCURRENT
CROSSCURRENTS
CROSSCUT
CROSSCUTS
CROSSCUTTING
CROSSCUTTINGS
CROSSE
CROSSED
CROSSER
CROSSERS
CROSSES
CROSSEST
CROSSETTE
CROSSETTES
CROSSFALL
CROSSFALLS
CROSSFIELD
CROSSFIRE
CROSSFIRES
CROSSFISH
CROSSFISHES
CROSSHAIR
CROSSHAIRS

CROSSHATCH
CROSSHATCHED
CROSSHATCHES
CROSSHATCHING
CROSSHEAD
CROSSHEADS
CROSSING
CROSSINGS
CROSSISH
CROSSJACK
CROSSJACKS
CROSSLET
CROSSLETS
CROSSLIGHT
CROSSLIGHTS
CROSSLINGUISTIC
CROSSLY
CROSSNESS
CROSSNESSES
CROSSOPTERYGIAN
CROSSOVER
CROSSOVERS
CROSSPATCH
CROSSPATCHES
CROSSPIECE
CROSSPIECES
CROSSROAD
CROSSROADS
CROSSRUFF
CROSSRUFFED
CROSSRUFFING
CROSSRUFFS
CROSSTALK
CROSSTIE
CROSSTIES
CROSSTOWN
CROSSTREE
CROSSTREES
CROSSWALK
CROSSWALKS
CROSSWAY
CROSSWAYS
CROSSWIND
CROSSWINDS
CROSSWISE
CROSSWORD
CROSSWORDS
CROSSWORT
CROSSWORTS
CROST
CROSTINI
CROSTINIS
CROTAL
CROTALA
CROTALARIA
CROTALARIAS

CROTALINE
CROTALISM
CROTALISMS
CROTALS
CROTALUM
CROTCH
CROTCHED
CROTCHES
CROTCHET
CROTCHETED
CROTCHETEER
CROTCHETEERS
CROTCHETIER
CROTCHETIEST
CROTCHETINESS
CROTCHETINESSES
CROTCHETS
CROTCHETY
CROTON
CROTONIC
CROTONS
CROTTLE
CROTTLES
CROUCH
CROUCHED
CROUCHES
CROUCHING
CROUP
CROUPADE
CROUPADES
CROUPE
CROUPED
CROUPER
CROUPERS
CROUPES
CROUPIER
CROUPIERS
CROUPIEST
CROUPILY
CROUPINESS
CROUPINESSES
CROUPING
CROUPON
CROUPONS
CROUPOUS
CROUPS
CROUPY
CROUSE
CROUSELY
CROUSTADE
CROUSTADES
CROUT
CROUTE
CROUTES
CROUTON
CROUTONS

CROUTS
CROW
CROWBAR
CROWBARRED
CROWBARRING
CROWBARS
CROWBERRIES
CROWBERRY
CROWBOOT
CROWBOOTS
CROWD
CROWDED
CROWDEDLY
CROWDEDNESS
CROWDEDNESSES
CROWDER
CROWDERS
CROWDIE
CROWDIES
CROWDING
CROWDS
CROWDY
CROWEA
CROWED
CROWER
CROWERS
CROWFEET
CROWFOOT
CROWFOOTS
CROWING
CROWINGLY
CROWKEEPER
CROWKEEPERS
CROWN
CROWNED
CROWNER
CROWNERS
CROWNET
CROWNETS
CROWNING
CROWNINGS
CROWNLAND
CROWNLESS
CROWNLET
CROWNLETS
CROWNPIECE
CROWNPIECES
CROWNS
CROWNWORK
CROWNWORKS
CROWS
CROWSTEP
CROWSTEPPED
CROWSTEPS
CROZE
CROZER

CROZERS
CROZES
CROZIER
CROZIERS
CROZZLED
CROZZLES
CROZZLING
CRU
CRUBEEN
CRUBEENS
CRUCES
CRUCIAL
CRUCIALLY
CRUCIAN
CRUCIANS
CRUCIATE
CRUCIATELY
CRUCIBLE
CRUCIBLES
CRUCIFER
CRUCIFEROUS
CRUCIFERS
CRUCIFIED
CRUCIFIER
CRUCIFIERS
CRUCIFIES
CRUCIFIX
CRUCIFIXES
CRUCIFIXION
CRUCIFIXIONS
CRUCIFORM
CRUCIFORMLY
CRUCIFORMS
CRUCIFY
CRUCIFYING
CRUCIVERBAL
CRUCIVERBALISM
CRUCIVERBALISMS
CRUCIVERBALIST
CRUCIVERBALISTS
CRUCK
CRUCKS
CRUD
CRUDDED
CRUDDIER
CRUDDIEST
CRUDDING
CRUDDLE
CRUDDLED
CRUDDLES
CRUDDLING
CRUDDY
CRUDE
CRUDELY
CRUDENESS
CRUDENESSES

CRUDER
CRUDES
CRUDEST
CRUDITES
CRUDITIES
CRUDITY
CRUDS
CRUDY
CRUE
CRUEL
CRUELER
CRUELEST
CRUELLER
CRUELLEST
CRUELLS
CRUELLY
CRUELNESS
CRUELNESSES
CRUELS
CRUELTIES
CRUELTY
CRUES
CRUET
CRUETS
CRUISE
CRUISED
CRUISER
CRUISERS
CRUISERWEIGHT
CRUISERWEIGHTS
CRUISES
CRUISEWAY
CRUISEWAYS
CRUISEWEAR
CRUISEWEARS
CRUISIE
CRUISIES
CRUISING
CRUISINGS
CRUIVE
CRUIVES
CRUIZIE
CRUIZIES
CRULLER
CRULLERS
CRUMB
CRUMBCLOTH
CRUMBCLOTHS
CRUMBED
CRUMBER
CRUMBERS
CRUMBIER
CRUMBIEST
CRUMBING
CRUMBLE
CRUMBLED

CRUMBLES
CRUMBLIER
CRUMBLIES
CRUMBLIEST
CRUMBLINESS
CRUMBLINESSES
CRUMBLING
CRUMBLINGS
CRUMBLY
CRUMBS
CRUMBUM
CRUMBUMS
CRUMBY
CRUMEN
CRUMENAL
CRUMENALS
CRUMENS
CRUMHORN
CRUMHORNS
CRUMMACK
CRUMMACKS
CRUMMIE
CRUMMIER
CRUMMIES
CRUMMIEST
CRUMMINESS
CRUMMINESSES
CRUMMOCK
CRUMMOCKS
CRUMMY
CRUMP
CRUMPED
CRUMPER
CRUMPEST
CRUMPET
CRUMPETS
CRUMPIER
CRUMPIEST
CRUMPING
CRUMPLE
CRUMPLED
CRUMPLES
CRUMPLIER
CRUMPLIEST
CRUMPLING
CRUMPLINGS
CRUMPLY
CRUMPS
CRUMPY
CRUNCH
CRUNCHABLE
CRUNCHED
CRUNCHER
CRUNCHERS
CRUNCHES
CRUNCHIE

CRUNCHIER
CRUNCHIES
CRUNCHIEST
CRUNCHILY
CRUNCHINESS
CRUNCHINESSES
CRUNCHING
CRUNCHY
CRUNKLE
CRUNKLED
CRUNKLES
CRUNKLING
CRUNODAL
CRUNODE
CRUNODES
CRUOR
CRUORES
CRUORS
CRUPPER
CRUPPERS
CRURA
CRURAL
CRUS
CRUSADE
CRUSADED
CRUSADER
CRUSADERS
CRUSADES
CRUSADING
CRUSADO
CRUSADOES
CRUSADOS
CRUSE
CRUSES
CRUSET
CRUSETS
CRUSH
CRUSHABILITY
CRUSHABLE
CRUSHED
CRUSHER
CRUSHERS
CRUSHES
CRUSHING
CRUSHINGLY
CRUSHPROOF
CRUSIAN
CRUSIANS
CRUSIE
CRUSIES
CRUSILY
CRUST
CRUSTA
CRUSTACEA
CRUSTACEAN
CRUSTACEANS

CRUSTACEOUS
CRUSTAE
CRUSTAL
CRUSTATE
CRUSTATED
CRUSTATION
CRUSTATIONS
CRUSTED
CRUSTIER
CRUSTIES
CRUSTIEST
CRUSTILY
CRUSTINESS
CRUSTINESSES
CRUSTING
CRUSTLESS
CRUSTOSE
CRUSTS
CRUSTY
CRUSY
CRUTCH
CRUTCHED
CRUTCHES
CRUTCHING
CRUTCHINGS
CRUVE
CRUVES
CRUX
CRUXES
CRUZADO
CRUZADOES
CRUZADOS
CRUZEIRO
CRUZEIROS
CRUZIE
CRUZIES
CRWTH
CRWTHS
CRY
CRYBABIES
CRYBABY
CRYING
CRYINGLY
CRYINGS
CRYMOTHERAPIES
CRYMOTHERAPY
CRYOBIOLOGICAL
CRYOBIOLOGIES
CRYOBIOLOGIST
CRYOBIOLOGISTS
CRYOBIOLOGY
CRYOCABLE
CRYOCABLES
CRYOCONITE
CRYOCONITES
CRYOGEN

CRYOGENIC
CRYOGENICALLY
CRYOGENICS
CRYOGENIES
CRYOGENS
CRYOGENY
CRYOGLOBULIN
CRYOGLOBULINS
CRYOHYDRATE
CRYOHYDRATES
CRYOLITE
CRYOLITES
CRYOMETER
CRYOMETERS
CRYOMETRIC
CRYOMETRY
CRYONIC
CRYONICS
CRYOPHILIC
CRYOPHORUS
CRYOPHORUSES
CRYOPHYSICS
CRYOPHYTE
CRYOPHYTES
CRYOPLANKTON
CRYOPRECIPITATE
CRYOPRESERVE
CRYOPRESERVED
CRYOPRESERVES
CRYOPRESERVING
CRYOPROBE
CRYOPROBES
CRYOPROTECTANT
CRYOPROTECTANTS
CRYOPROTECTIVE
CRYOSCOPE
CRYOSCOPES
CRYOSCOPIC
CRYOSCOPIES
CRYOSCOPY
CRYOSTAT
CRYOSTATIC
CRYOSTATS
CRYOSURGEON
CRYOSURGEONS
CRYOSURGERIES
CRYOSURGERY
CRYOSURGICAL
CRYOTHERAPIES
CRYOTHERAPY
CRYOTRON
CRYOTRONS
CRYPT
CRYPTADIA
CRYPTAESTHESIA
CRYPTAESTHESIAS

CRYPTAESTHETIC
CRYPTAL
CRYPTANALYSES
CRYPTANALYSIS
CRYPTANALYST
CRYPTANALYSTS
CRYPTANALYTIC
CRYPTANALYTICAL
CRYPTARITHM
CRYPTARITHMS
CRYPTESTHESIA
CRYPTESTHESIAS
CRYPTIC
CRYPTICAL
CRYPTICALLY
CRYPTO
CRYPTOBIONT
CRYPTOBIONTS
CRYPTOBIOSIS
CRYPTOBIOTIC
CRYPTOCLASTIC
CRYPTOCOCCAL
CRYPTOCOCCI
CRYPTOCOCCOSES
CRYPTOCOCCOSIS
CRYPTOCOCCUS
CRYPTOGAM
CRYPTOGAMIAN
CRYPTOGAMIC
CRYPTOGAMIES
CRYPTOGAMIST
CRYPTOGAMISTS
CRYPTOGAMOUS
CRYPTOGAMS
CRYPTOGAMY
CRYPTOGENIC
CRYPTOGRAM
CRYPTOGRAMS
CRYPTOGRAPH
CRYPTOGRAPHER
CRYPTOGRAPHERS
CRYPTOGRAPHIC
CRYPTOGRAPHICAL
CRYPTOGRAPHIES
CRYPTOGRAPHIST
CRYPTOGRAPHISTS
CRYPTOGRAPHS
CRYPTOGRAPHY
CRYPTOLOGIC
CRYPTOLOGICAL
CRYPTOLOGIES
CRYPTOLOGIST
CRYPTOLOGISTS
CRYPTOLOGY
CRYPTOMERIA
CRYPTOMERIAS

CRYPTOMETER
CRYPTOMETERS
CRYPTOMNESIA
CRYPTOMNESIAS
CRYPTOMNESIC
CRYPTON
CRYPTONS
CRYPTONYM
CRYPTONYMOUS
CRYPTONYMS
CRYPTOPHYTE
CRYPTOPHYTES
CRYPTOPHYTIC
CRYPTORCHID
CRYPTORCHIDISM
CRYPTORCHIDISMS
CRYPTORCHIDS
CRYPTORCHISM
CRYPTORCHISMS
CRYPTOS
CRYPTOSPORIDIA
CRYPTOSPORIDIUM
CRYPTOZOIC
CRYPTOZOITE
CRYPTOZOITES
CRYPTOZOOLOGIES
CRYPTOZOOLOGIST
CRYPTOZOOLOGY
CRYPTS
CRYSTAL
CRYSTALISABLE
CRYSTALISATION
CRYSTALISATIONS
CRYSTALISE
CRYSTALISED
CRYSTALISER
CRYSTALISERS
CRYSTALISES
CRYSTALISING
CRYSTALIZABLE
CRYSTALIZATION
CRYSTALIZATIONS
CRYSTALIZE
CRYSTALIZED
CRYSTALIZER
CRYSTALIZERS
CRYSTALIZES
CRYSTALIZING
CRYSTALL
CRYSTALLINE
CRYSTALLINES
CRYSTALLINITIES
CRYSTALLINITY
CRYSTALLISABLE
CRYSTALLISATION
CRYSTALLISE

CRYSTALLISED
CRYSTALLISER
CRYSTALLISERS
CRYSTALLISES
CRYSTALLISING
CRYSTALLISM
CRYSTALLITE
CRYSTALLITES
CRYSTALLITIC
CRYSTALLITIS
CRYSTALLITISES
CRYSTALLIZABLE
CRYSTALLIZATION
CRYSTALLIZE
CRYSTALLIZED
CRYSTALLIZER
CRYSTALLIZERS
CRYSTALLIZES
CRYSTALLIZING
CRYSTALLOGRAPHY
CRYSTALLOID
CRYSTALLOIDAL
CRYSTALLOIDS
CRYSTALLOMANCY
CRYSTALS
CSARDAS
CSARDASES
CTENE
CTENES
CTENIDIA
CTENIDIUM
CTENIFORM
CTENOID
CTENOPHORAN
CTENOPHORANS
CTENOPHORE
CTENOPHORES
CUADRILLA
CUADRILLAS
CUB
CUBAGE
CUBAGES
CUBANE
CUBATURE
CUBATURES
CUBBED
CUBBIES
CUBBING
CUBBINGS
CUBBISH
CUBBISHLY
CUBBY
CUBBYHOLE
CUBBYHOLES
CUBE
CUBEB

CUBEBS
CUBED
CUBER
CUBERS
CUBES
CUBHOOD
CUBHOODS
CUBIC
CUBICA
CUBICAL
CUBICALLY
CUBICALNESS
CUBICALNESSES
CUBICAS
CUBICITIES
CUBICITY
CUBICLE
CUBICLES
CUBICLY
CUBICS
CUBICULA
CUBICULUM
CUBIFORM
CUBING
CUBISM
CUBISMS
CUBIST
CUBISTIC
CUBISTICALLY
CUBISTS
CUBIT
CUBITAL
CUBITS
CUBITUS
CUBITUSES
CUBLESS
CUBOID
CUBOIDAL
CUBOIDS
CUBS
CUCKING
CUCKOLD
CUCKOLDED
CUCKOLDING
CUCKOLDISE
CUCKOLDISED
CUCKOLDISES
CUCKOLDISING
CUCKOLDIZE
CUCKOLDIZED
CUCKOLDIZES
CUCKOLDIZING
CUCKOLDLY
CUCKOLDOM
CUCKOLDOMS
CUCKOLDRIES

CUCKOLDRY
CUCKOLDS
CUCKOO
CUCKOOED
CUCKOOFLOWER
CUCKOOFLOWERS
CUCKOOING
CUCKOOPINT
CUCKOOPINTS
CUCKOOS
CUCULIFORM
CUCULIFORMS
CUCULLATE
CUCULLATED
CUCULLATELY
CUCUMBER
CUCUMBERS
CUCUMIFORM
CUCURBIT
CUCURBITACEOUS
CUCURBITAL
CUCURBITS
CUD
CUDBEAR
CUDBEARS
CUDDEEHIHS
CUDDEN
CUDDENS
CUDDIE
CUDDIES
CUDDIN
CUDDINS
CUDDLE
CUDDLED
CUDDLER
CUDDLERS
CUDDLES
CUDDLESOME
CUDDLIER
CUDDLIEST
CUDDLING
CUDDLY
CUDDY
CUDGEL
CUDGELED
CUDGELER
CUDGELERS
CUDGELING
CUDGELLED
CUDGELLER
CUDGELLERS
CUDGELLING
CUDGELLINGS
CUDGELS
CUDGERIE
CUDGERIES

CUDS
CUDWEED
CUDWEEDS
CUE
CUED
CUEING
CUEIST
CUEISTS
CUES
CUESTA
CUESTAS
CUFF
CUFFED
CUFFIN
CUFFING
CUFFINS
CUFFLE
CUFFLED
CUFFLES
CUFFLESS
CUFFLING
CUFFO
CUFFS
CUFFUFFLE
CUFFUFFLES
CUIF
CUIFS
CUING
CUIRASS
CUIRASSED
CUIRASSES
CUIRASSIER
CUIRASSIERS
CUIRASSING
CUISH
CUISHES
CUISINE
CUISINES
CUISINIER
CUISINIERS
CUISSE
CUISSER
CUISSERS
CUISSES
CUIT
CUITER
CUITERED
CUITERING
CUITERS
CUITIKIN
CUITIKINS
CUITS
CUITTLE
CUITTLED
CUITTLES
CUITTLING

CUKE
CUKES
CULCH
CULCHES
CULCHIE
CULCHIES
CULET
CULETS
CULEX
CULICES
CULICID
CULICIDS
CULICIFORM
CULICINE
CULICINES
CULINARIAN
CULINARIANS
CULINARILY
CULINARY
CULL
CULLAY
CULLAYS
CULLED
CULLENDER
CULLENDERS
CULLER
CULLERS
CULLET
CULLETS
CULLIED
CULLIES
CULLING
CULLINGS
CULLION
CULLIONLY
CULLIONS
CULLIS
CULLISES
CULLS
CULLY
CULLYING
CULLYISM
CULLYISMS
CULM
CULMED
CULMEN
CULMENS
CULMIFEROUS
CULMINANT
CULMINATE
CULMINATED
CULMINATES
CULMINATING
CULMINATION
CULMINATIONS
CULMING

CULMS
CULOTTE
CULOTTES
CULPA
CULPABILITIES
CULPABILITY
CULPABLE
CULPABLENESS
CULPABLENESSES
CULPABLY
CULPAE
CULPATORY
CULPRIT
CULPRITS
CULT
CULTCH
CULTCHES
CULTER
CULTERS
CULTI
CULTIC
CULTIER
CULTIEST
CULTIGEN
CULTIGENS
CULTISH
CULTISHLY
CULTISHNESS
CULTISHNESSES
CULTISM
CULTISMS
CULTIST
CULTISTS
CULTIVABILITIES
CULTIVABILITY
CULTIVABLE
CULTIVAR
CULTIVARS
CULTIVATABLE
CULTIVATE
CULTIVATED
CULTIVATES
CULTIVATING
CULTIVATION
CULTIVATIONS
CULTIVATOR
CULTIVATORS
CULTLIKE
CULTRATE
CULTRATED
CULTRIFORM
CULTS
CULTURABLE
CULTURAL
CULTURALLY
CULTURATI

CULTURE
CULTURED
CULTURELESS
CULTURES
CULTURING
CULTURIST
CULTURISTS
CULTUS
CULTUSES
CULTY
CULVER
CULVERIN
CULVERINEER
CULVERINEERS
CULVERINS
CULVERS
CULVERT
CULVERTAGE
CULVERTAGES
CULVERTAILED
CULVERTS
CUM
CUMACEAN
CUMACEANS
CUMARIC
CUMARIN
CUMARINS
CUMARONE
CUMBENT
CUMBER
CUMBERBUND
CUMBERBUNDS
CUMBERED
CUMBERER
CUMBERERS
CUMBERING
CUMBERLESS
CUMBERMENT
CUMBERMENTS
CUMBERS
CUMBERSOME
CUMBERSOMELY
CUMBERSOMENESS
CUMBRANCE
CUMBRANCES
CUMBROUS
CUMBROUSLY
CUMBROUSNESS
CUMBROUSNESSES
CUMBUNGI
CUMEC
CUMECS
CUMIN
CUMINS
CUMMER
CUMMERBUND

CUMMERBUNDS
CUMMERS
CUMMIN
CUMMINGTONITE
CUMMINGTONITES
CUMMINS
CUMQUAT
CUMQUATS
CUMSHAW
CUMSHAWS
CUMULATE
CUMULATED
CUMULATELY
CUMULATES
CUMULATING
CUMULATION
CUMULATIONS
CUMULATIVE
CUMULATIVELY
CUMULATIVENESS
CUMULET
CUMULETS
CUMULI
CUMULIFORM
CUMULOCIRRI
CUMULOCIRRUS
CUMULONIMBI
CUMULONIMBUS
CUMULONIMBUSES
CUMULOSE
CUMULOSTRATI
CUMULOSTRATUS
CUMULOUS
CUMULUS
CUNABULA
CUNCTATION
CUNCTATIONS
CUNCTATIOUS
CUNCTATIVE
CUNCTATOR
CUNCTATORS
CUNCTATORY
CUNDIES
CUNDUM
CUNDUMS
CUNDY
CUNEAL
CUNEATE
CUNEATED
CUNEATELY
CUNEATIC
CUNEIFORM
CUNEIFORMS
CUNETTE
CUNETTES
CUNEUS

CUNIFORM
CUNIFORMS
CUNJEVOI
CUNJEVOIS
CUNNER
CUNNERS
CUNNILINCTUS
CUNNILINCTUSES
CUNNILINGUS
CUNNILINGUSES
CUNNING
CUNNINGER
CUNNINGEST
CUNNINGLY
CUNNINGNESS
CUNNINGNESSES
CUNNINGS
CUNT
CUNTS
CUP
CUPBEARER
CUPBEARERS
CUPBOARD
CUPBOARDED
CUPBOARDING
CUPBOARDS
CUPCAKE
CUPCAKES
CUPEL
CUPELED
CUPELER
CUPELERS
CUPELING
CUPELLATION
CUPELLATIONS
CUPELLED
CUPELLER
CUPELLERS
CUPELLING
CUPELS
CUPFUL
CUPFULS
CUPGALL
CUPGALLS
CUPHEAD
CUPHEADS
CUPID
CUPIDINOUS
CUPIDITIES
CUPIDITY
CUPIDS
CUPLIKE
CUPMAN
CUPMEN
CUPOLA
CUPOLAED

CUPOLAING
CUPOLAR
CUPOLAS
CUPOLATED
CUPPA
CUPPAS
CUPPED
CUPPER
CUPPERS
CUPPIER
CUPPIEST
CUPPING
CUPPINGS
CUPPY
CUPRAMMONIUM
CUPRAMMONIUMS
CUPREOUS
CUPRESSUS
CUPRESSUSES
CUPRIC
CUPRIFEROUS
CUPRITE
CUPRITES
CUPRONICKEL
CUPRONICKELS
CUPROUS
CUPRUM
CUPRUMS
CUPS
CUPSFUL
CUPULA
CUPULAE
CUPULAI
CUPULAR
CUPULATE
CUPULE
CUPULES
CUPULIFEROUS
CUR
CURABILITIES
CURABILITY
CURABLE
CURABLENESS
CURABLENESSES
CURABLY
CURACAO
CURACAOS
CURACIES
CURACOA
CURACOAS
CURACY
CURAGH
CURAGHS
CURARA
CURARAS
CURARE

CURARES
CURARI
CURARINE
CURARINES
CURARIS
CURARISATION
CURARISATIONS
CURARISE
CURARISED
CURARISES
CURARISING
CURARIZATION
CURARIZATIONS
CURARIZE
CURARIZED
CURARIZES
CURARIZING
CURASSOW
CURASSOWS
CURAT
CURATE
CURATED
CURATES
CURATESHIP
CURATESHIPS
CURATING
CURATIVE
CURATIVELY
CURATIVENESS
CURATIVES
CURATOR
CURATORIAL
CURATORS
CURATORSHIP
CURATORSHIPS
CURATORY
CURATRIX
CURATRIXES
CURATS
CURB
CURBABLE
CURBED
CURBER
CURBERS
CURBING
CURBINGS
CURBLESS
CURBS
CURBSIDE
CURBSIDES
CURBSTONE
CURBSTONES
CURCH
CURCHEF
CURCHEFS
CURCHES

CURCULIO
CURCULIOS
CURCUMA
CURCUMAS
CURCUMIN
CURCUMINE
CURCUMINES
CURCUMINS
CURD
CURDED
CURDIER
CURDIEST
CURDINESS
CURDINESSES
CURDING
CURDLE
CURDLED
CURDLER
CURDLERS
CURDLES
CURDLING
CURDS
CURDY
CURE
CURED
CURELESS
CURER
CURERS
CURES
CURET
CURETS
CURETTAGE
CURETTAGES
CURETTE
CURETTED
CURETTEMENT
CURETTEMENTS
CURETTES
CURETTING
CURF
CURFEW
CURFEWS
CURFS
CURFUFFLE
CURFUFFLED
CURFUFFLES
CURFUFFLING
CURIA
CURIAE
CURIAL
CURIALISM
CURIALISMS
CURIALIST
CURIALISTIC
CURIALISTS
CURIAS

CURIE
CURIES
CURIET
CURIETHERAPIES
CURIETHERAPY
CURIETS
CURING
CURIO
CURIOS
CURIOSA
CURIOSITIES
CURIOSITY
CURIOUS
CURIOUSER
CURIOUSEST
CURIOUSLY
CURIOUSNESS
CURIOUSNESSES
CURITE
CURITES
CURIUM
CURIUMS
CURL
CURLED
CURLER
CURLERS
CURLEW
CURLEWS
CURLI
CURLICUE
CURLICUED
CURLICUES
CURLICUING
CURLIER
CURLIEST
CURLIEWURLIE
CURLIEWURLIES
CURLILY
CURLINESS
CURLINESSES
CURLING
CURLINGS
CURLPAPER
CURLPAPERS
CURLS
CURLY
CURLYCUE
CURLYCUES
CURMUDGEON
CURMUDGEONLY
CURMUDGEONS
CURMURRING
CURMURRINGS
CURN
CURNEY
CURNIER

CURNIEST
CURNS
CURNY
CURPEL
CURPELS
CURR
CURRACH
CURRACHS
CURRAGH
CURRAGHS
CURRAJONG
CURRAJONGS
CURRAN
CURRANS
CURRANT
CURRANTIER
CURRANTIEST
CURRANTS
CURRANTY
CURRAWONG
CURRAWONGS
CURRED
CURRENCIES
CURRENCY
CURRENT
CURRENTLY
CURRENTNESS
CURRENTNESSES
CURRENTS
CURRICLE
CURRICLES
CURRICULA
CURRICULAR
CURRICULUM
CURRICULUMS
CURRIE
CURRIED
CURRIER
CURRIERIES
CURRIERS
CURRIERY
CURRIES
CURRING
CURRISH
CURRISHLY
CURRISHNESS
CURRISHNESSES
CURRS
CURRY
CURRYCOMB
CURRYCOMBED
CURRYCOMBING
CURRYCOMBS
CURRYING
CURRYINGS
CURS

CURSAL
CURSE
CURSED
CURSEDER
CURSEDEST
CURSEDLY
CURSEDNESS
CURSEDNESSES
CURSELARIE
CURSENARY
CURSER
CURSERS
CURSES
CURSI
CURSING
CURSINGS
CURSITOR
CURSITORS
CURSITORY
CURSIVE
CURSIVELY
CURSIVENESS
CURSIVENESSES
CURSIVES
CURSOR
CURSORARY
CURSORES
CURSORIAL
CURSORILY
CURSORINESS
CURSORINESSES
CURSORS
CURSORY
CURST
CURSTNESS
CURSTNESSES
CURSUS
CURT
CURTAIL
CURTAILED
CURTAILER
CURTAILERS
CURTAILING
CURTAILMENT
CURTAILMENTS
CURTAILS
CURTAIN
CURTAINED
CURTAINING
CURTAINLESS
CURTAINS
CURTAL
CURTALAX
CURTALAXE
CURTALAXES
CURTALS

CURTANA
CURTANAS
CURTATE
CURTATION
CURTATIONS
CURTAXE
CURTAXES
CURTER
CURTESIES
CURTEST
CURTESY
CURTILAGE
CURTILAGES
CURTLY
CURTNESS
CURTNESSES
CURTSEY
CURTSEYED
CURTSEYING
CURTSEYS
CURTSIED
CURTSIES
CURTSY
CURTSYING
CURULE
CURVACEOUS
CURVACEOUSLY
CURVACIOUS
CURVATE
CURVATED
CURVATION
CURVATIONS
CURVATIVE
CURVATURE
CURVATURES
CURVE
CURVEBALL
CURVEBALLED
CURVEBALLING
CURVEBALLS
CURVED
CURVEDLY
CURVEDNESS
CURVES
CURVESOME
CURVET
CURVETED
CURVETING
CURVETS
CURVETTED
CURVETTING
CURVEY
CURVICAUDATE
CURVICOSTATE
CURVIER
CURVIEST

CURVIFOLIATE
CURVIFORM
CURVILINEAL
CURVILINEAR
CURVILINEARITY
CURVILINEARLY
CURVING
CURVIROSTRAL
CURVITAL
CURVITIES
CURVITY
CURVY
CUSCUS
CUSCUSES
CUSEC
CUSECS
CUSH
CUSHAT
CUSHATS
CUSHAW
CUSHAWS
CUSHES
CUSHIE
CUSHIER
CUSHIES
CUSHIEST
CUSHILY
CUSHION
CUSHIONED
CUSHIONET
CUSHIONETS
CUSHIONING
CUSHIONLESS
CUSHIONS
CUSHIONY
CUSHTY
CUSHY
CUSK
CUSKS
CUSP
CUSPATE
CUSPATED
CUSPED
CUSPID
CUSPIDAL
CUSPIDATE
CUSPIDATED
CUSPIDATION
CUSPIDATIONS
CUSPIDES
CUSPIDOR
CUSPIDORE
CUSPIDORES
CUSPIDORS
CUSPIDS
CUSPIS

CUSPS
CUSS
CUSSED
CUSSEDLY
CUSSEDNESS
CUSSEDNESSES
CUSSER
CUSSERS
CUSSES
CUSSING
CUSSO
CUSSOS
CUSSWORD
CUSSWORDS
CUSTARD
CUSTARDS
CUSTARDY
CUSTOCK
CUSTOCKS
CUSTODE
CUSTODES
CUSTODIAL
CUSTODIAN
CUSTODIANS
CUSTODIANSHIP
CUSTODIANSHIPS
CUSTODIER
CUSTODIERS
CUSTODIES
CUSTODY
CUSTOM
CUSTOMABLE
CUSTOMARIES
CUSTOMARILY
CUSTOMARINESS
CUSTOMARINESSES
CUSTOMARY
CUSTOMED
CUSTOMER
CUSTOMERS
CUSTOMHOUSE
CUSTOMHOUSES
CUSTOMISATION
CUSTOMISATIONS
CUSTOMISE
CUSTOMISED
CUSTOMISES
CUSTOMISING
CUSTOMIZATION
CUSTOMIZATIONS
CUSTOMIZE
CUSTOMIZED
CUSTOMIZER
CUSTOMIZERS
CUSTOMIZES
CUSTOMIZING

CUSTOMS
CUSTOMSHOUSE
CUSTOMSHOUSES
CUSTOS
CUSTREL
CUSTRELS
CUSTUMAL
CUSTUMALS
CUSTUMARIES
CUSTUMARY
CUT
CUTABILITIES
CUTABILITY
CUTANEOUS
CUTANEOUSLY
CUTAWAY
CUTAWAYS
CUTBACK
CUTBACKS
CUTBANK
CUTBANKS
CUTCH
CUTCHA
CUTCHERIES
CUTCHERRIES
CUTCHERRY
CUTCHERY
CUTCHES
CUTDOWN
CUTDOWNS
CUTE
CUTELY
CUTENESS
CUTENESSES
CUTER
CUTES
CUTESIE
CUTESIER
CUTESIEST
CUTEST
CUTESY
CUTEY
CUTEYS
CUTGLASS
CUTGRASS
CUTGRASSES
CUTICLE
CUTICLES
CUTICULA
CUTICULAE
CUTICULAR
CUTIE
CUTIES
CUTIKIN
CUTIKINS
CUTIN

CUTINISATION
CUTINISATIONS
CUTINISE
CUTINISED
CUTINISES
CUTINISING
CUTINIZATION
CUTINIZATIONS
CUTINIZE
CUTINIZED
CUTINIZES
CUTINIZING
CUTINS
CUTIS
CUTISES
CUTLAS
CUTLASES
CUTLASS
CUTLASSES
CUTLER
CUTLERIES
CUTLERS
CUTLERY
CUTLET
CUTLETS
CUTLINE
CUTLINES
CUTOFF
CUTOFFS
CUTOUT
CUTOUTS
CUTOVER
CUTOVERS
CUTPURSE
CUTPURSES
CUTS
CUTTABLE
CUTTAGE
CUTTAGES
CUTTER
CUTTERS
CUTTHROAT
CUTTHROATS
CUTTIER
CUTTIES
CUTTIEST
CUTTING
CUTTINGLY
CUTTINGS
CUTTLE
CUTTLEBONE
CUTTLEBONES
CUTTLED
CUTTLEFISH
CUTTLEFISHES
CUTTLES

CUTTLING
CUTTO
CUTTOE
CUTTOES
CUTTY
CUTUP
CUTUPS
CUTWATER
CUTWATERS
CUTWORK
CUTWORKS
CUTWORM
CUTWORMS
CUVEE
CUVEES
CUVETTE
CUVETTES
CUZ
CUZZES
CWM
CWMS
CWTCH
CWTCHED
CWTCHES
CWTCHING
CYAN
CYANAMID
CYANAMIDE
CYANAMIDES
CYANAMIDS
CYANATE
CYANATES
CYANIC
CYANID
CYANIDATION
CYANIDATIONS
CYANIDE
CYANIDED
CYANIDES
CYANIDING
CYANIDINGS
CYANIDS
CYANIN
CYANINE
CYANINES
CYANINS
CYANISE
CYANISED
CYANISES
CYANISING
CYANITE
CYANITES
CYANITIC
CYANIZE
CYANIZED
CYANIZES

CYANIZING
CYANO
CYANOACETYLENE
CYANOACETYLENES
CYANOACRYLATE
CYANOACRYLATES
CYANOBACTERIA
CYANOBACTERIUM
CYANOCOBALAMIN
CYANOCOBALAMINE
CYANOCOBALAMINS
CYANOETHYLATE
CYANOETHYLATED
CYANOETHYLATES
CYANOETHYLATING
CYANOETHYLATION
CYANOGEN
CYANOGENAMIDE
CYANOGENESES
CYANOGENESIS
CYANOGENETIC
CYANOGENIC
CYANOGENS
CYANOHYDRIN
CYANOHYDRINS
CYANOMETER
CYANOMETERS
CYANOPHYTE
CYANOPHYTES
CYANOSED
CYANOSES
CYANOSIS
CYANOTIC
CYANOTYPE
CYANOTYPES
CYANS
CYANURET
CYANURETS
CYATHI
CYATHIA
CYATHIFORM
CYATHIUM
CYATHUS
CYBERCAFE
CYBERCAFES
CYBERCRIME
CYBERCRIMES
CYBERNATE
CYBERNATED
CYBERNATES
CYBERNATING
CYBERNATION
CYBERNATIONS
CYBERNETIC
CYBERNETICAL
CYBERNETICALLY

CYBERNETICIAN
CYBERNETICIANS
CYBERNETICIST
CYBERNETICISTS
CYBERNETICS
CYBERPET
CYBERPETS
CYBERPHOBIA
CYBERPHOBIAS
CYBERPHOBIC
CYBERPHOBICALLY
CYBERPHOBICS
CYBERPUNK
CYBERPUNKS
CYBERSEX
CYBERSEXES
CYBERSPACE
CYBERSPACES
CYBERSQUATTING
CYBERTERRORISM
CYBERWAR
CYBERWARS
CYBORG
CYBORGS
CYBRID
CYBRIDS
CYCAD
CYCADACEOUS
CYCADEOID
CYCADEOIDS
CYCADOPHYTE
CYCADOPHYTES
CYCADS
CYCAS
CYCASES
CYCASIN
CYCASINS
CYCLAMATE
CYCLAMATES
CYCLAMEN
CYCLAMENS
CYCLANDELATE
CYCLANDELATES
CYCLANTHACEOUS
CYCLASE
CYCLASES
CYCLAZOCINE
CYCLAZOCINES
CYCLE
CYCLECAR
CYCLECARS
CYCLED
CYCLER
CYCLERIES
CYCLERS
CYCLERY

CYCLES
CYCLEWAY
CYCLEWAYS
CYCLIC
CYCLICAL
CYCLICALITIES
CYCLICALITY
CYCLICALLY
CYCLICALS
CYCLICISM
CYCLICISMS
CYCLICITIES
CYCLICITY
CYCLICLY
CYCLING
CYCLINGS
CYCLIST
CYCLISTS
CYCLITOL
CYCLITOLS
CYCLIZATION
CYCLIZATIONS
CYCLIZE
CYCLIZED
CYCLIZES
CYCLIZINE
CYCLIZINES
CYCLIZING
CYCLO
CYCLOADDITION
CYCLOADDITIONS
CYCLOALIPHATIC
CYCLOALKANE
CYCLOALKANES
CYCLOBARBITONE
CYCLOBARBITONES
CYCLODEXTRIN
CYCLODEXTRINS
CYCLODIALYSES
CYCLODIALYSIS
CYCLODIENE
CYCLODIENES
CYCLOGENESES
CYCLOGENESIS
CYCLOGIRO
CYCLOGIROS
CYCLOGRAPH
CYCLOGRAPHIC
CYCLOGRAPHS
CYCLOHEXANE
CYCLOHEXANES
CYCLOHEXANONE
CYCLOHEXANONES
CYCLOHEXIMIDE
CYCLOHEXIMIDES
CYCLOHEXYLAMINE

CYCLOID
CYCLOIDAL
CYCLOIDALLY
CYCLOIDIAN
CYCLOIDIANS
CYCLOIDS
CYCLOLITH
CYCLOLITHS
CYCLOMETER
CYCLOMETERS
CYCLOMETRICAL
CYCLOMETRY
CYCLONAL
CYCLONE
CYCLONES
CYCLONIC
CYCLONICAL
CYCLONICALLY
CYCLONITE
CYCLONITES
CYCLOOLEFIN
CYCLOOLEFINIC
CYCLOOLEFINS
CYCLOPAEDIA
CYCLOPAEDIAS
CYCLOPAEDIC
CYCLOPAEDIST
CYCLOPAEDISTS
CYCLOPARAFFIN
CYCLOPARAFFINS
CYCLOPEAN
CYCLOPEDIA
CYCLOPEDIAS
CYCLOPEDIC
CYCLOPEDIST
CYCLOPEDISTS
CYCLOPENTADIENE
CYCLOPENTANE
CYCLOPENTOLATE
CYCLOPENTOLATES
CYCLOPES
CYCLOPIAN
CYCLOPIC
CYCLOPLEGIA
CYCLOPLEGIAS
CYCLOPLEGIC
CYCLOPLEGICS
CYCLOPROPANE
CYCLOPROPANES
CYCLOPS
CYCLORAMA
CYCLORAMAS
CYCLORAMIC
CYCLOS
CYCLOSERINE
CYCLOSERINES

CYCLOSES
CYCLOSIS
CYCLOSPERMOUS
CYCLOSPORIN
CYCLOSPORINE
CYCLOSPORINES
CYCLOSTOMATE
CYCLOSTOMATOUS
CYCLOSTOME
CYCLOSTOMES
CYCLOSTOMOUS
CYCLOSTYLE
CYCLOSTYLED
CYCLOSTYLES
CYCLOSTYLING
CYCLOTHYME
CYCLOTHYMES
CYCLOTHYMIA
CYCLOTHYMIAC
CYCLOTHYMIACS
CYCLOTHYMIAS
CYCLOTHYMIC
CYCLOTHYMICS
CYCLOTOMIC
CYCLOTRON
CYCLOTRONS
CYCLUS
CYCLUSES
CYDER
CYDERS
CYESES
CYESIS
CYGNET
CYGNETS
CYLICES
CYLINDER
CYLINDERED
CYLINDERING
CYLINDERS
CYLINDRACEOUS
CYLINDRIC
CYLINDRICAL
CYLINDRICALITY
CYLINDRICALLY
CYLINDRICALNESS
CYLINDRICITIES
CYLINDRICITY
CYLINDRIFORM
CYLINDRITE
CYLINDRITES
CYLINDROID
CYLINDROIDS
CYLIX
CYMA
CYMAE
CYMAGRAPH

CYMAGRAPHS
CYMAR
CYMARS
CYMAS
CYMATIA
CYMATICS
CYMATIUM
CYMBAL
CYMBALEER
CYMBALEERS
CYMBALER
CYMBALERS
CYMBALIST
CYMBALISTS
CYMBALO
CYMBALOES
CYMBALOM
CYMBALOMS
CYMBALOS
CYMBALS
CYMBIDIA
CYMBIDIUM
CYMBIDIUMS
CYMBIFORM
CYMBLING
CYMBLINGS
CYME
CYMENE
CYMENES
CYMES
CYMIFEROUS
CYMLIN
CYMLING
CYMLINGS
CYMLINS
CYMOGENE
CYMOGENES
CYMOGRAPH
CYMOGRAPHIC
CYMOGRAPHS
CYMOID
CYMOL
CYMOLS
CYMOPHANE
CYMOPHANES
CYMOPHANOUS
CYMOSE
CYMOSELY
CYMOTRICHIES
CYMOTRICHOUS
CYMOTRICHY
CYMOUS
CYNANCHE
CYNANCHES
CYNEGETIC
CYNGHANEDD

CYNGHANEDDS
CYNIC
CYNICAL
CYNICALLY
CYNICALNESS
CYNICALNESSES
CYNICISM
CYNICISMS
CYNICS
CYNODONT
CYNOMOLGI
CYNOMOLGUS
CYNOPHILIA
CYNOPHILIAS
CYNOPHILIST
CYNOPHILISTS
CYNOPHOBIA
CYNOPHOBIAS
CYNOPODOUS
CYNOSURAL
CYNOSURE
CYNOSURES
CYPERACEOUS
CYPHER
CYPHERED
CYPHERING
CYPHERS
CYPRES
CYPRESES
CYPRESS
CYPRESSES
CYPRIAN
CYPRIANS
CYPRID
CYPRIDES
CYPRIDS
CYPRINE
CYPRINID
CYPRINIDS
CYPRINODONT
CYPRINODONTS
CYPRINOID
CYPRINOIDS
CYPRIPEDIA
CYPRIPEDIUM
CYPRIPEDIUMS
CYPRIS
CYPROHEPTADINE
CYPROHEPTADINES
CYPROTERONE
CYPROTERONES
CYPRUS
CYPRUSES
CYPSELA
CYPSELAE
CYST

CYSTEAMINE
CYSTEAMINES
CYSTECTOMIES
CYSTECTOMY
CYSTEIN
CYSTEINE
CYSTEINES
CYSTEINIC
CYSTEINS
CYSTIC
CYSTICERCI
CYSTICERCOID
CYSTICERCOIDS
CYSTICERCOSES
CYSTICERCOSIS
CYSTICERCUS
CYSTID
CYSTIDEAN
CYSTIDEANS
CYSTIDS
CYSTIFORM
CYSTINE
CYSTINES
CYSTINOSES
CYSTINOSIS
CYSTINURIA
CYSTINURIAS
CYSTITIDES
CYSTITIS
CYSTITISES
CYSTOCARP
CYSTOCARPIC
CYSTOCARPS
CYSTOCELE
CYSTOCELES
CYSTOGENOUS
CYSTOGRAPHER
CYSTOGRAPHERS
CYSTOGRAPHIC
CYSTOGRAPHY
CYSTOID
CYSTOIDS
CYSTOLITH
CYSTOLITHIASES
CYSTOLITHIASIS
CYSTOLITHS
CYSTOSCOPE
CYSTOSCOPES
CYSTOSCOPIC
CYSTOSCOPIES
CYSTOSCOPY
CYSTOSTOMIES
CYSTOSTOMY
CYSTOTOMIES
CYSTOTOMY
CYSTS

CYTASE
CYTASES
CYTASTER
CYTASTERS
CYTE
CYTES
CYTIDINE
CYTIDINES
CYTIDYLIC
CYTISI
CYTISINE
CYTISINES
CYTISUS
CYTOCHALASIN
CYTOCHALASINS
CYTOCHEMICAL
CYTOCHEMISTRIES
CYTOCHEMISTRY
CYTOCHROME
CYTOCHROMES
CYTODE
CYTODES
CYTODIAGNOSES
CYTODIAGNOSIS
CYTOGENESES
CYTOGENESIS
CYTOGENETIC
CYTOGENETICAL
CYTOGENETICALLY
CYTOGENETICIST
CYTOGENETICISTS
CYTOGENETICS
CYTOGENIES
CYTOGENY
CYTOID
CYTOKINE
CYTOKINES
CYTOKINESES
CYTOKINESIS
CYTOKINETIC
CYTOKININ
CYTOKININS
CYTOLOGIC
CYTOLOGICAL
CYTOLOGICALLY
CYTOLOGIES
CYTOLOGIST
CYTOLOGISTS
CYTOLOGY
CYTOLYSES
CYTOLYSIN
CYTOLYSINS
CYTOLYSIS
CYTOLYTIC
CYTOMEGALIC
CYTOMEGALOVIRUS

CYTOMEMBRANE
CYTOMEMBRANES
CYTOMETER
CYTOMETERS
CYTOMETRIC
CYTOMETRIES
CYTOMETRY
CYTON
CYTONS
CYTOPATHIC
CYTOPATHOGENIC
CYTOPATHOLOGIES
CYTOPATHOLOGY
CYTOPENIA
CYTOPENIAS
CYTOPHILIC
CYTOPHOTOMETRIC
CYTOPHOTOMETRY
CYTOPLASM
CYTOPLASMIC
CYTOPLASMICALLY
CYTOPLASMS
CYTOPLAST
CYTOPLASTIC
CYTOPLASTS
CYTOSINE
CYTOSINES
CYTOSKELETAL
CYTOSKELETON
CYTOSKELETONS
CYTOSOL
CYTOSOLIC
CYTOSOLS
CYTOSOME
CYTOSOMES
CYTOSTATIC
CYTOSTATICALLY
CYTOSTATICS
CYTOTAXIS
CYTOTAXONOMIC
CYTOTAXONOMIES
CYTOTAXONOMIST
CYTOTAXONOMISTS
CYTOTAXONOMY
CYTOTECHNOLOGY
CYTOTOXIC
CYTOTOXICITIES
CYTOTOXICITY
CYTOTOXIN
CYTOTOXINS
CZAPKA
CZAPKAS
CZAR
CZARDAS
CZARDASES
CZARDOM

CZARDOMS
CZAREVICH
CZAREVICHES
CZAREVITCH
CZAREVITCHES
CZAREVNA
CZAREVNAS
CZARINA
CZARINAS
CZARISM
CZARISMS
CZARIST
CZARISTS
CZARITSA
CZARITSAS
CZARITZA
CZARITZAS
CZARS

D

DA
DAB
DABBED
DABBER
DABBERS
DABBING
DABBITIES
DABBITY
DABBLE
DABBLED
DABBLER
DABBLERS
DABBLES
DABBLING
DABBLINGLY
DABBLINGS
DABCHICK
DABCHICKS
DABS
DABSTER
DABSTERS
DACE
DACES
DACHA
DACHAS
DACHSHUND
DACHSHUNDS
DACITE
DACITES
DACK
DACKER
DACKERED
DACKERING
DACKERS
DACKS
DACOIT
DACOITAGE
DACOITAGES
DACOITIES
DACOITS
DACOITY
DACTYL
DACTYLAR
DACTYLI
DACTYLIC
DACTYLICALLY
DACTYLICS
DACTYLIOGRAPHY
DACTYLIOLOGIES
DACTYLIOLOGY
DACTYLIOMANCIES

DACTYLIOMANCY
DACTYLIST
DACTYLISTS
DACTYLOGRAM
DACTYLOGRAMS
DACTYLOGRAPHER
DACTYLOGRAPHERS
DACTYLOGRAPHIC
DACTYLOGRAPHIES
DACTYLOGRAPHY
DACTYLOLOGIES
DACTYLOLOGY
DACTYLOSCOPIES
DACTYLOSCOPY
DACTYLS
DACTYLUS
DAD
DADA
DADAH
DADAISM
DADAISMS
DADAIST
DADAISTIC
DADAISTS
DADAS
DADDED
DADDIES
DADDING
DADDLE
DADDLED
DADDLES
DADDLING
DADDOCK
DADDOCKS
DADDY
DADO
DADOED
DADOES
DADOING
DADOS
DADS
DAE
DAED
DAEDAL
DAEDALIAN
DAEDALIC
DAEING
DAEMON
DAEMONIC
DAEMONS
DAES

DAFF
DAFFADOWNDILLY
DAFFED
DAFFIER
DAFFIES
DAFFIEST
DAFFILY
DAFFING
DAFFINGS
DAFFODIL
DAFFODILLIES
DAFFODILLY
DAFFODILS
DAFFS
DAFFY
DAFT
DAFTAR
DAFTARS
DAFTER
DAFTEST
DAFTIE
DAFTIES
DAFTLY
DAFTNESS
DAFTNESSES
DAG
DAGABA
DAGABAS
DAGGA
DAGGAS
DAGGED
DAGGER
DAGGERBOARD
DAGGERBOARDS
DAGGERED
DAGGERING
DAGGERLIKE
DAGGERS
DAGGIER
DAGGIEST
DAGGING
DAGGINGS
DAGGLE
DAGGLED
DAGGLES
DAGGLING
DAGGY
DAGLOCK
DAGLOCKS
DAGO
DAGOBA

DAGOBAS
DAGOES
DAGOS
DAGS
DAGUERREAN
DAGUERREOTYPE
DAGUERREOTYPED
DAGUERREOTYPER
DAGUERREOTYPERS
DAGUERREOTYPES
DAGUERREOTYPIES
DAGUERREOTYPING
DAGUERREOTYPIST
DAGUERREOTYPY
DAGWOOD
DAGWOODS
DAH
DAHABEAH
DAHABEAHS
DAHABEEAH
DAHABEEAHS
DAHABEEYAH
DAHABEEYAHS
DAHABIAH
DAHABIAHS
DAHABIEH
DAHABIEHS
DAHABIYA
DAHABIYAH
DAHABIYAHS
DAHABIYAS
DAHABIYEH
DAHABIYEHS
DAHL
DAHLIA
DAHLIAS
DAHLS
DAHOON
DAHOONS
DAHS
DAIDLE
DAIDLED
DAIDLES
DAIDLING
DAIKER
DAIKERED
DAIKERING
DAIKERS
DAIKON
DAIKONS
DAILIES

DAILINESS
DAILINESSES
DAILY
DAIMEN
DAIMIO
DAIMIOS
DAIMOKU
DAIMOKUS
DAIMON
DAIMONES
DAIMONIC
DAIMONS
DAIMYO
DAIMYOS
DAINE
DAINED
DAINES
DAINING
DAINT
DAINTIER
DAINTIES
DAINTIEST
DAINTILY
DAINTINESS
DAINTINESSES
DAINTY
DAIQUIRI
DAIQUIRIS
DAIRIES
DAIRY
DAIRYING
DAIRYINGS
DAIRYMAID
DAIRYMAIDS
DAIRYMAN
DAIRYMEN
DAIS
DAISES
DAISHIKI
DAISHIKIS
DAISIED
DAISIES
DAISY
DAISYCUTTER
DAISYCUTTERS
DAISYWHEEL
DAISYWHEELS
DAK
DAKER
DAKERED
DAKERHEN
DAKERHENS
DAKERING
DAKERS
DAKOIT
DAKOITI

DAKOITIES
DAKOITIS
DAKOITS
DAKOITY
DAKS
DAL
DALAPON
DALAPONS
DALASI
DALASIS
DALE
DALED
DALEDH
DALEDHS
DALEDS
DALES
DALESMAN
DALESMEN
DALETH
DALETHS
DALGYTE
DALGYTES
DALI
DALIS
DALLE
DALLES
DALLIANCE
DALLIANCES
DALLIED
DALLIER
DALLIERS
DALLIES
DALLOP
DALLOPS
DALLY
DALLYING
DALMAHOY
DALMAHOYS
DALMATIAN
DALMATIANS
DALMATIC
DALMATICS
DALS
DALT
DALTON
DALTONIC
DALTONISM
DALTONISMS
DALTONS
DALTS
DAM
DAMAGE
DAMAGEABILITIES
DAMAGEABILITY
DAMAGEABLE
DAMAGED

DAMAGER
DAMAGERS
DAMAGES
DAMAGING
DAMAGINGLY
DAMAN
DAMANS
DAMAR
DAMARS
DAMASCEENED
DAMASCEENES
DAMASCEENING
DAMASCENE
DAMASCENED
DAMASCENES
DAMASCENING
DAMASCENINGS
DAMASK
DAMASKED
DAMASKEEN
DAMASKEENED
DAMASKEENING
DAMASKEENS
DAMASKIN
DAMASKINED
DAMASKING
DAMASKINING
DAMASKINS
DAMASKS
DAMASQUIN
DAMASQUINED
DAMASQUINING
DAMASQUINS
DAMASSIN
DAMASSINS
DAMBOARD
DAMBOARDS
DAMBROD
DAMBRODS
DAME
DAMES
DAMEWORT
DAMEWORTS
DAMFOOL
DAMINOZIDE
DAMINOZIDES
DAMMAR
DAMMARS
DAMME
DAMMED
DAMMER
DAMMERS
DAMMING
DAMMIT
DAMN
DAMNABILITIES

DAMNABILITY
DAMNABLE
DAMNABLENESS
DAMNABLENESSES
DAMNABLY
DAMNATION
DAMNATIONS
DAMNATORY
DAMNDEST
DAMNDESTS
DAMNED
DAMNEDER
DAMNEDEST
DAMNEDESTS
DAMNER
DAMNERS
DAMNIFICATION
DAMNIFICATIONS
DAMNIFIED
DAMNIFIES
DAMNIFY
DAMNIFYING
DAMNING
DAMNINGLY
DAMNS
DAMOISEL
DAMOISELLE
DAMOISELLES
DAMOISELS
DAMOSEL
DAMOSELS
DAMOZEL
DAMOZELS
DAMP
DAMPCOURSE
DAMPCOURSES
DAMPED
DAMPEN
DAMPENED
DAMPENER
DAMPENERS
DAMPENING
DAMPENS
DAMPER
DAMPERS
DAMPEST
DAMPIER
DAMPIEST
DAMPING
DAMPINGS
DAMPISH
DAMPISHNESS
DAMPISHNESSES
DAMPLY
DAMPNESS
DAMPNESSES

DAMPS
DAMPY
DAMS
DAMSEL
DAMSELFISH
DAMSELFISHES
DAMSELFLIES
DAMSELFLY
DAMSELS
DAMSON
DAMSONS
DAN
DANCE
DANCEABLE
DANCED
DANCEHALL
DANCEHALLS
DANCER
DANCERS
DANCES
DANCETTE
DANCETTEE
DANCETTES
DANCETTY
DANCEY
DANCIER
DANCIEST
DANCING
DANCINGS
DANDELION
DANDELIONS
DANDER
DANDERED
DANDERING
DANDERS
DANDIACAL
DANDIER
DANDIES
DANDIEST
DANDIFICATION
DANDIFICATIONS
DANDIFIED
DANDIFIES
DANDIFY
DANDIFYING
DANDILY
DANDIPRAT
DANDIPRATS
DANDLE
DANDLED
DANDLER
DANDLERS
DANDLES
DANDLING
DANDRIFF
DANDRIFFS

DANDRUFF
DANDRUFFS
DANDRUFFY
DANDY
DANDYFUNK
DANDYFUNKS
DANDYISH
DANDYISHLY
DANDYISM
DANDYISMS
DANDYPRAT
DANDYPRATS
DANEGELD
DANEGELDS
DANEGELT
DANEGELTS
DANELAGH
DANELAGHS
DANELAW
DANELAWS
DANEWEED
DANEWEEDS
DANEWORT
DANEWORTS
DANG
DANGED
DANGER
DANGERED
DANGERING
DANGERLESS
DANGEROUS
DANGEROUSLY
DANGEROUSNESS
DANGEROUSNESSES
DANGERS
DANGING
DANGLE
DANGLED
DANGLER
DANGLERS
DANGLES
DANGLIER
DANGLIEST
DANGLING
DANGLINGLY
DANGLINGS
DANGLY
DANGS
DANIO
DANIOS
DANISH
DANK
DANKER
DANKEST
DANKISH
DANKLY

DANKNESS
DANKNESSES
DANKS
DANNEBROG
DANNEBROGS
DANNIES
DANNY
DANS
DANSEUR
DANSEURS
DANSEUSE
DANSEUSES
DANT
DANTED
DANTHONIA
DANTHONIAS
DANTING
DANTON
DANTONED
DANTONING
DANTONS
DANTS
DAP
DAPHNE
DAPHNES
DAPHNIA
DAPHNIAS
DAPHNID
DAPHNIDS
DAPPED
DAPPER
DAPPERER
DAPPEREST
DAPPERLING
DAPPERLINGS
DAPPERLY
DAPPERNESS
DAPPERNESSES
DAPPERS
DAPPING
DAPPLE
DAPPLED
DAPPLES
DAPPLING
DAPS
DAPSONE
DAPSONES
DAQUIRI
DAQUIRIS
DARAF
DARAFS
DARB
DARBIES
DARBS
DARCIES
DARCY

DARCYS
DARE
DARED
DAREDEVIL
DAREDEVILRIES
DAREDEVILRY
DAREDEVILS
DAREDEVILTRIES
DAREDEVILTRY
DAREFUL
DARER
DARERS
DARES
DARESAY
DARG
DARGA
DARGAH
DARGAHS
DARGAS
DARGLE
DARGLES
DARGS
DARI
DARIC
DARICS
DARING
DARINGLY
DARINGNESS
DARINGNESSES
DARINGS
DARIOLE
DARIOLES
DARIS
DARK
DARKED
DARKEN
DARKENED
DARKENER
DARKENERS
DARKENING
DARKENS
DARKER
DARKEST
DARKEY
DARKEYS
DARKIE
DARKIES
DARKING
DARKISH
DARKLE
DARKLED
DARKLES
DARKLIER
DARKLIEST
DARKLING
DARKLINGS

DARKLY
DARKMANS
DARKNESS
DARKNESSES
DARKROOM
DARKROOMS
DARKS
DARKSOME
DARKY
DARLING
DARLINGLY
DARLINGNESS
DARLINGNESSES
DARLINGS
DARN
DARNDEST
DARNDESTS
DARNED
DARNEDER
DARNEDEST
DARNEL
DARNELS
DARNER
DARNERS
DARNING
DARNINGS
DARNS
DAROGHA
DAROGHAS
DARRAIGN
DARRAIGNE
DARRAIGNED
DARRAIGNES
DARRAIGNING
DARRAIGNMENT
DARRAIGNMENTS
DARRAIGNS
DARRAIN
DARRAINE
DARRAINED
DARRAINES
DARRAINING
DARRAINS
DARRAYN
DARRAYNED
DARRAYNING
DARRAYNS
DARRE
DARRED
DARRES
DARRING
DARSHAN
DARSHANS
DART
DARTBOARD
DARTBOARDS

DARTED
DARTER
DARTERS
DARTING
DARTINGLY
DARTLE
DARTLED
DARTLES
DARTLING
DARTRE
DARTRES
DARTROUS
DARTS
DARZI
DARZIS
DAS
DASH
DASHBOARD
DASHBOARDS
DASHED
DASHEEN
DASHEENS
DASHEKI
DASHEKIS
DASHER
DASHERS
DASHES
DASHI
DASHIER
DASHIEST
DASHIKI
DASHIKIS
DASHING
DASHINGLY
DASHIS
DASHPOT
DASHPOTS
DASHY
DASSIE
DASSIES
DASTARD
DASTARDIES
DASTARDLINESS
DASTARDLINESSES
DASTARDLY
DASTARDNESS
DASTARDNESSES
DASTARDS
DASTARDY
DASYPAEDAL
DASYPHYLLOUS
DASYPOD
DASYPODS
DASYURE
DASYURES
DATA

DATABANK
DATABANKS
DATABASE
DATABASES
DATABLE
DATABUS
DATABUSES
DATABUSSES
DATACOMMS
DATAFLOW
DATAFLOWS
DATAGLOVE
DATAGLOVES
DATAL
DATALLER
DATALLERS
DATALS
DATAMATION
DATAMATIONS
DATARIA
DATARIAS
DATARIES
DATARY
DATCHA
DATCHAS
DATE
DATEABLE
DATED
DATEDLY
DATEDNESS
DATEDNESSES
DATELESS
DATELINE
DATELINED
DATELINES
DATELINING
DATER
DATERS
DATES
DATING
DATINGS
DATIVAL
DATIVE
DATIVELY
DATIVES
DATO
DATOLITE
DATOLITES
DATOS
DATTO
DATTOS
DATUM
DATUMS
DATURA
DATURAS
DATURIC

DATURINE
DATURINES
DAUB
DAUBE
DAUBED
DAUBER
DAUBERIES
DAUBERS
DAUBERY
DAUBES
DAUBIER
DAUBIEST
DAUBING
DAUBINGS
DAUBRIES
DAUBRY
DAUBS
DAUBY
DAUD
DAUDED
DAUDING
DAUDS
DAUGHTER
DAUGHTERHOOD
DAUGHTERLESS
DAUGHTERLINESS
DAUGHTERLING
DAUGHTERLINGS
DAUGHTERLY
DAUGHTERS
DAULT
DAULTS
DAUNDER
DAUNDERED
DAUNDERING
DAUNDERS
DAUNER
DAUNERED
DAUNERING
DAUNERS
DAUNOMYCIN
DAUNOMYCINS
DAUNORUBICIN
DAUNORUBICINS
DAUNT
DAUNTED
DAUNTER
DAUNTERS
DAUNTING
DAUNTINGLY
DAUNTLESS
DAUNTLESSLY
DAUNTLESSNESS
DAUNTLESSNESSES
DAUNTON
DAUNTONED

DAUNTONING
DAUNTONS
DAUNTS
DAUPHIN
DAUPHINE
DAUPHINES
DAUPHINESS
DAUPHINESSES
DAUPHINS
DAUR
DAURED
DAURING
DAURS
DAUT
DAUTED
DAUTIE
DAUTIES
DAUTING
DAUTS
DAVEN
DAVENED
DAVENING
DAVENNED
DAVENNING
DAVENPORT
DAVENPORTS
DAVENS
DAVIDIA
DAVIDIAS
DAVIES
DAVIT
DAVITS
DAVY
DAW
DAWBAKE
DAWBAKES
DAWBRIES
DAWBRY
DAWCOCK
DAWCOCKS
DAWD
DAWDED
DAWDING
DAWDLE
DAWDLED
DAWDLER
DAWDLERS
DAWDLES
DAWDLING
DAWDLINGLY
DAWDS
DAWED
DAWEN
DAWING
DAWISH
DAWK

DAWKS
DAWN
DAWNED
DAWNER
DAWNERED
DAWNERING
DAWNERS
DAWNEY
DAWNING
DAWNINGS
DAWNLIKE
DAWNS
DAWS
DAWSONITE
DAWSONITES
DAWT
DAWTED
DAWTIE
DAWTIES
DAWTING
DAWTS
DAY
DAYAN
DAYANS
DAYBED
DAYBEDS
DAYBOOK
DAYBOOKS
DAYBOY
DAYBOYS
DAYBREAK
DAYBREAKS
DAYCARE
DAYCENTRE
DAYCENTRES
DAYCH
DAYCHED
DAYCHES
DAYCHING
DAYDREAM
DAYDREAMED
DAYDREAMER
DAYDREAMERS
DAYDREAMING
DAYDREAMLIKE
DAYDREAMS
DAYDREAMT
DAYDREAMY
DAYFLIES
DAYFLOWER
DAYFLOWERS
DAYFLY
DAYGLO
DAYGLOW
DAYGLOWS
DAYLIGHT

DAYLIGHTED
DAYLIGHTING
DAYLIGHTINGS
DAYLIGHTS
DAYLILIES
DAYLILY
DAYLIT
DAYLONG
DAYMARE
DAYMARES
DAYMARK
DAYMARKS
DAYNT
DAYROOM
DAYROOMS
DAYS
DAYSACK
DAYSACKS
DAYSHELL
DAYSHELLS
DAYSIDE
DAYSIDES
DAYSMAN
DAYSMEN
DAYSPRING
DAYSPRINGS
DAYSTAR
DAYSTARS
DAYTALE
DAYTALER
DAYTALERS
DAYTALES
DAYTIME
DAYTIMES
DAYWORK
DAYWORKS
DAZE
DAZED
DAZEDLY
DAZEDNESS
DAZEDNESSES
DAZER
DAZERS
DAZES
DAZING
DAZZLE
DAZZLED
DAZZLEMENT
DAZZLEMENTS
DAZZLER
DAZZLERS
DAZZLES
DAZZLING
DAZZLINGLY
DAZZLINGS
DE

DEACIDIFICATION
DEACIDIFIED
DEACIDIFIES
DEACIDIFY
DEACIDIFYING
DEACON
DEACONED
DEACONESS
DEACONESSES
DEACONHOOD
DEACONHOODS
DEACONING
DEACONRIES
DEACONRY
DEACONS
DEACONSHIP
DEACONSHIPS
DEACTIVATE
DEACTIVATED
DEACTIVATES
DEACTIVATING
DEACTIVATION
DEACTIVATIONS
DEACTIVATOR
DEACTIVATORS
DEAD
DEADBEAT
DEADBEATS
DEADBOLT
DEADBOLTS
DEADBOY
DEADBOYS
DEADED
DEADEN
DEADENED
DEADENER
DEADENERS
DEADENING
DEADENINGLY
DEADENINGS
DEADENS
DEADER
DEADERS
DEADEST
DEADEYE
DEADEYES
DEADFALL
DEADFALLS
DEADHEAD
DEADHEADED
DEADHEADING
DEADHEADS
DEADHOUSE
DEADHOUSES
DEADING
DEADLIER

DEADLIEST
DEADLIFT
DEADLIFTED
DEADLIFTING
DEADLIFTS
DEADLIGHT
DEADLIGHTS
DEADLINE
DEADLINES
DEADLINESS
DEADLINESSES
DEADLOCK
DEADLOCKED
DEADLOCKING
DEADLOCKS
DEADLY
DEADMAN
DEADMEN
DEADNESS
DEADNESSES
DEADPAN
DEADPANNED
DEADPANNER
DEADPANNERS
DEADPANNING
DEADPANS
DEADS
DEADSTOCK
DEADSTOCKS
DEADSTROKE
DEADWEIGHT
DEADWEIGHTS
DEADWOOD
DEADWOODS
DEAERATE
DEAERATED
DEAERATES
DEAERATING
DEAERATION
DEAERATIONS
DEAERATOR
DEAERATORS
DEAF
DEAFBLIND
DEAFEN
DEAFENED
DEAFENING
DEAFENINGLY
DEAFENINGS
DEAFENS
DEAFER
DEAFEST
DEAFISH
DEAFLY
DEAFNESS
DEAFNESSES

DEAIR
DEAIRED
DEAIRING
DEAIRS
DEAL
DEALATE
DEALATED
DEALATES
DEALATION
DEALATIONS
DEALBATE
DEALBATION
DEALBATIONS
DEALER
DEALERS
DEALERSHIP
DEALERSHIPS
DEALFISH
DEALFISHES
DEALING
DEALINGS
DEALS
DEALT
DEAMBULATORIES
DEAMBULATORY
DEAMINASE
DEAMINASES
DEAMINATE
DEAMINATED
DEAMINATES
DEAMINATING
DEAMINATION
DEAMINATIONS
DEAMINISATION
DEAMINISATIONS
DEAMINISE
DEAMINISED
DEAMINISES
DEAMINISING
DEAMINIZATION
DEAMINIZATIONS
DEAMINIZE
DEAMINIZED
DEAMINIZES
DEAMINIZING
DEAN
DEANED
DEANER
DEANERIES
DEANERS
DEANERY
DEANING
DEANS
DEANSHIP
DEANSHIPS
DEAR

DEARBOUGHT
DEARE
DEARED
DEARER
DEARES
DEAREST
DEARIE
DEARIES
DEARING
DEARLING
DEARLINGS
DEARLY
DEARN
DEARNESS
DEARNESSES
DEARNFUL
DEARNLY
DEARNS
DEARS
DEARTH
DEARTHS
DEARTICULATE
DEARTICULATED
DEARTICULATES
DEARTICULATING
DEARY
DEASH
DEASHED
DEASHES
DEASHING
DEASIL
DEASILS
DEASIUL
DEASIULS
DEASOIL
DEASOILS
DEASPIRATE
DEASPIRATED
DEASPIRATES
DEASPIRATING
DEASPIRATION
DEASPIRATIONS
DEATH
DEATHBED
DEATHBEDS
DEATHBLOW
DEATHBLOWS
DEATHCUP
DEATHCUPS
DEATHFUL
DEATHIER
DEATHIEST
DEATHLESS
DEATHLESSLY
DEATHLESSNESS
DEATHLESSNESSES

DEATHLIER
DEATHLIEST
DEATHLIKE
DEATHLINESS
DEATHLINESSES
DEATHLY
DEATHS
DEATHSMAN
DEATHSMEN
DEATHTRAP
DEATHTRAPS
DEATHWARD
DEATHWARDS
DEATHWATCH
DEATHWATCHES
DEATHY
DEATTRIBUTE
DEATTRIBUTED
DEATTRIBUTES
DEATTRIBUTING
DEAVE
DEAVED
DEAVES
DEAVING
DEAW
DEAWIE
DEAWS
DEAWY
DEB
DEBACLE
DEBACLES
DEBAG
DEBAGGED
DEBAGGING
DEBAGGINGS
DEBAGS
DEBAR
DEBARCATION
DEBARCATIONS
DEBARK
DEBARKATION
DEBARKATIONS
DEBARKED
DEBARKING
DEBARKS
DEBARMENT
DEBARMENTS
DEBARRASS
DEBARRASSED
DEBARRASSES
DEBARRASSING
DEBARRED
DEBARRING
DEBARS
DEBASE
DEBASED

DEBASEDNESS
DEBASEDNESSES
DEBASEMENT
DEBASEMENTS
DEBASER
DEBASERS
DEBASES
DEBASING
DEBASINGLY
DEBATABLE
DEBATE
DEBATEABLE
DEBATED
DEBATEFUL
DEBATEMENT
DEBATEMENTS
DEBATER
DEBATERS
DEBATES
DEBATING
DEBATINGLY
DEBAUCH
DEBAUCHED
DEBAUCHEDLY
DEBAUCHEDNESS
DEBAUCHEDNESSES
DEBAUCHEE
DEBAUCHEES
DEBAUCHER
DEBAUCHERIES
DEBAUCHERS
DEBAUCHERY
DEBAUCHES
DEBAUCHING
DEBAUCHMENT
DEBAUCHMENTS
DEBBIER
DEBBIES
DEBBIEST
DEBBY
DEBE
DEBEAK
DEBEAKED
DEBEAKING
DEBEAKS
DEBEL
DEBELLED
DEBELLING
DEBELS
DEBENTURE
DEBENTURED
DEBENTURES
DEBES
DEBILE
DEBILITATE
DEBILITATED

DEBILITATES
DEBILITATING
DEBILITATION
DEBILITATIONS
DEBILITATIVE
DEBILITIES
DEBILITY
DEBIT
DEBITED
DEBITING
DEBITOR
DEBITORS
DEBITS
DEBONAIR
DEBONAIRLY
DEBONAIRNESS
DEBONAIRNESSES
DEBONE
DEBONED
DEBONER
DEBONERS
DEBONES
DEBONING
DEBONNAIRE
DEBOSH
DEBOSHED
DEBOSHES
DEBOSHING
DEBOSS
DEBOSSED
DEBOSSES
DEBOSSING
DEBOUCH
DEBOUCHE
DEBOUCHED
DEBOUCHES
DEBOUCHING
DEBOUCHMENT
DEBOUCHMENTS
DEBOUCHURE
DEBOUCHURES
DEBRIDE
DEBRIDED
DEBRIDEMENT
DEBRIDEMENTS
DEBRIDES
DEBRIDING
DEBRIEF
DEBRIEFED
DEBRIEFING
DEBRIEFINGS
DEBRIEFS
DEBRIS
DEBRUISE
DEBRUISED
DEBRUISES

DEBRUISING
DEBS
DEBT
DEBTED
DEBTEE
DEBTEES
DEBTLESS
DEBTOR
DEBTORS
DEBTS
DEBUD
DEBUDDED
DEBUDDING
DEBUDS
DEBUG
DEBUGGED
DEBUGGER
DEBUGGERS
DEBUGGING
DEBUGS
DEBUNK
DEBUNKED
DEBUNKER
DEBUNKERS
DEBUNKING
DEBUNKS
DEBURR
DEBURRED
DEBURRING
DEBURRS
DEBUS
DEBUSED
DEBUSES
DEBUSING
DEBUSSED
DEBUSSES
DEBUSSING
DEBUT
DEBUTANT
DEBUTANTE
DEBUTANTES
DEBUTANTS
DEBUTED
DEBUTING
DEBUTS
DEBYE
DEBYES
DECACHORD
DECACHORDS
DECAD
DECADAL
DECADE
DECADENCE
DECADENCES
DECADENCIES
DECADENCY

DECADENT
DECADENTLY
DECADENTS
DECADES
DECADS
DECAF
DECAFF
DECAFFEINATE
DECAFFEINATED
DECAFFEINATES
DECAFFEINATING
DECAFFS
DECAFS
DECAGON
DECAGONAL
DECAGONALLY
DECAGONS
DECAGRAM
DECAGRAMME
DECAGRAMMES
DECAGRAMS
DECAGYNIAN
DECAGYNOUS
DECAHEDRA
DECAHEDRAL
DECAHEDRON
DECAHEDRONS
DECAL
DECALCIFICATION
DECALCIFIED
DECALCIFIER
DECALCIFIERS
DECALCIFIES
DECALCIFY
DECALCIFYING
DECALCOMANIA
DECALCOMANIAS
DECALED
DECALESCENCE
DECALESCENCES
DECALESCENT
DECALING
DECALITER
DECALITERS
DECALITRE
DECALITRES
DECALLED
DECALLING
DECALOG
DECALOGIST
DECALOGISTS
DECALOGS
DECALOGUE
DECALOGUES
DECALS
DECAMERONIC

DECAMEROUS
DECAMETER
DECAMETERS
DECAMETHONIUM
DECAMETHONIUMS
DECAMETRE
DECAMETRES
DECAMETRIC
DECAMP
DECAMPED
DECAMPING
DECAMPMENT
DECAMPMENTS
DECAMPS
DECANAL
DECANALLY
DECANDRIAN
DECANDROUS
DECANE
DECANEDIOIC
DECANES
DECANI
DECANICALLY
DECANOIC
DECANT
DECANTATE
DECANTATED
DECANTATES
DECANTATING
DECANTATION
DECANTATIONS
DECANTED
DECANTER
DECANTERS
DECANTING
DECANTS
DECAPITALISE
DECAPITALISED
DECAPITALISES
DECAPITALISING
DECAPITALIZE
DECAPITALIZED
DECAPITALIZES
DECAPITALIZING
DECAPITATE
DECAPITATED
DECAPITATES
DECAPITATING
DECAPITATION
DECAPITATIONS
DECAPITATOR
DECAPITATORS
DECAPOD
DECAPODAL
DECAPODAN
DECAPODANS

DECAPODOUS
DECAPODS
DECAPSULATE
DECAPSULATED
DECAPSULATES
DECAPSULATING
DECAPSULATION
DECARB
DECARBED
DECARBING
DECARBONATE
DECARBONATED
DECARBONATES
DECARBONATING
DECARBONATION
DECARBONATIONS
DECARBONATOR
DECARBONATORS
DECARBONISATION
DECARBONISE
DECARBONISED
DECARBONISER
DECARBONISERS
DECARBONISES
DECARBONISING
DECARBONIZATION
DECARBONIZE
DECARBONIZED
DECARBONIZER
DECARBONIZERS
DECARBONIZES
DECARBONIZING
DECARBOXYLASE
DECARBOXYLASES
DECARBOXYLATE
DECARBOXYLATED
DECARBOXYLATES
DECARBOXYLATING
DECARBOXYLATION
DECARBS
DECARBURATION
DECARBURATIONS
DECARBURISATION
DECARBURISE
DECARBURISED
DECARBURISES
DECARBURISING
DECARBURIZATION
DECARBURIZE
DECARBURIZED
DECARBURIZES
DECARBURIZING
DECARE
DECARES
DECASTERE
DECASTERES

DECASTICH
DECASTICHS
DECASTYLE
DECASTYLES
DECASUALIZATION
DECASYLLABIC
DECASYLLABICS
DECASYLLABLE
DECASYLLABLES
DECATHLETE
DECATHLETES
DECATHLON
DECATHLONS
DECAUDATE
DECAUDATED
DECAUDATES
DECAUDATING
DECAY
DECAYABLE
DECAYED
DECAYER
DECAYERS
DECAYING
DECAYS
DECCIE
DECCIES
DECEASE
DECEASED
DECEASES
DECEASING
DECEDENT
DECEDENTS
DECEIT
DECEITFUL
DECEITFULLY
DECEITFULNESS
DECEITFULNESSES
DECEITS
DECEIVABILITIES
DECEIVABILITY
DECEIVABLE
DECEIVABLENESS
DECEIVABLY
DECEIVE
DECEIVED
DECEIVER
DECEIVERS
DECEIVES
DECEIVING
DECEIVINGLY
DECELERATE
DECELERATED
DECELERATES
DECELERATING
DECELERATION
DECELERATIONS

DECELERATOR
DECELERATORS
DECELEROMETER
DECELEROMETERS
DECEMVIR
DECEMVIRAL
DECEMVIRATE
DECEMVIRATES
DECEMVIRI
DECEMVIRS
DECENARIES
DECENARY
DECENCIES
DECENCY
DECENNARIES
DECENNARY
DECENNIA
DECENNIAL
DECENNIALLY
DECENNIALS
DECENNIUM
DECENNIUMS
DECENNOVAL
DECENT
DECENTER
DECENTERED
DECENTERING
DECENTERS
DECENTEST
DECENTLY
DECENTNESS
DECENTRALISE
DECENTRALISED
DECENTRALISES
DECENTRALISING
DECENTRALIST
DECENTRALISTS
DECENTRALIZE
DECENTRALIZED
DECENTRALIZES
DECENTRALIZING
DECENTRE
DECENTRED
DECENTRES
DECENTRING
DECEPTIBILITIES
DECEPTIBILITY
DECEPTIBLE
DECEPTION
DECEPTIONAL
DECEPTIONS
DECEPTIOUS
DECEPTIVE
DECEPTIVELY
DECEPTIVENESS
DECEPTIVENESSES

DECEPTORY
DECEREBRATE
DECEREBRATED
DECEREBRATES
DECEREBRATING
DECEREBRATION
DECEREBRATIONS
DECEREBRISE
DECEREBRISED
DECEREBRISES
DECEREBRISING
DECEREBRIZE
DECEREBRIZED
DECEREBRIZES
DECEREBRIZING
DECERN
DECERNED
DECERNING
DECERNS
DECERTIFICATION
DECERTIFIED
DECERTIFIES
DECERTIFY
DECERTIFYING
DECESSION
DECESSIONS
DECHEANCE
DECHEANCES
DECHLORINATE
DECHLORINATED
DECHLORINATES
DECHLORINATING
DECHLORINATION
DECHLORINATIONS
DECHRISTIANISE
DECHRISTIANISED
DECHRISTIANISES
DECHRISTIANIZE
DECHRISTIANIZED
DECHRISTIANIZES
DECIARE
DECIARES
DECIBEL
DECIBELS
DECIDABILITIES
DECIDABILITY
DECIDABLE
DECIDE
DECIDED
DECIDEDLY
DECIDEDNESS
DECIDEDNESSES
DECIDER
DECIDERS
DECIDES
DECIDING

DECIDUA
DECIDUAE
DECIDUAL
DECIDUAS
DECIDUATE
DECIDUOUS
DECIDUOUSLY
DECIDUOUSNESS
DECIDUOUSNESSES
DECIGRAM
DECIGRAMME
DECIGRAMMES
DECIGRAMS
DECILE
DECILES
DECILITER
DECILITERS
DECILITRE
DECILITRES
DECILLION
DECILLIONS
DECILLIONTH
DECILLIONTHS
DECIMAL
DECIMALISATION
DECIMALISATIONS
DECIMALISE
DECIMALISED
DECIMALISES
DECIMALISING
DECIMALISM
DECIMALISMS
DECIMALIST
DECIMALISTS
DECIMALIZATION
DECIMALIZATIONS
DECIMALIZE
DECIMALIZED
DECIMALIZES
DECIMALIZING
DECIMALLY
DECIMALS
DECIMATE
DECIMATED
DECIMATES
DECIMATING
DECIMATION
DECIMATIONS
DECIMATOR
DECIMATORS
DECIME
DECIMES
DECIMETER
DECIMETERS
DECIMETRE
DECIMETRES

DECIMETRIC
DECIMETRICALLY
DECINORMAL
DECIPHER
DECIPHERABILITY
DECIPHERABLE
DECIPHERED
DECIPHERER
DECIPHERERS
DECIPHERING
DECIPHERMENT
DECIPHERMENTS
DECIPHERS
DECISION
DECISIONAL
DECISIONED
DECISIONING
DECISIONS
DECISIVE
DECISIVELY
DECISIVENESS
DECISIVENESSES
DECISORY
DECISTERE
DECISTERES
DECITIZENISE
DECITIZENISED
DECITIZENISES
DECITIZENISING
DECITIZENIZE
DECITIZENIZED
DECITIZENIZES
DECITIZENIZING
DECIVILISE
DECIVILISED
DECIVILISES
DECIVILISING
DECIVILIZE
DECIVILIZED
DECIVILIZES
DECIVILIZING
DECK
DECKCHAIR
DECKCHAIRS
DECKED
DECKEL
DECKELS
DECKER
DECKERS
DECKHAND
DECKHANDS
DECKHOUSE
DECKHOUSES
DECKING
DECKINGS
DECKLE

DECKLED
DECKLES
DECKO
DECKOED
DECKOING
DECKOS
DECKS
DECLAIM
DECLAIMANT
DECLAIMANTS
DECLAIMED
DECLAIMER
DECLAIMERS
DECLAIMING
DECLAIMINGS
DECLAIMS
DECLAMATION
DECLAMATIONS
DECLAMATORILY
DECLAMATORY
DECLARABLE
DECLARANT
DECLARANTS
DECLARATION
DECLARATIONS
DECLARATIVE
DECLARATIVELY
DECLARATOR
DECLARATORILY
DECLARATORS
DECLARATORY
DECLARE
DECLARED
DECLAREDLY
DECLARER
DECLARERS
DECLARES
DECLARING
DECLASS
DECLASSE
DECLASSED
DECLASSEE
DECLASSES
DECLASSIFIABLE
DECLASSIFIED
DECLASSIFIES
DECLASSIFY
DECLASSIFYING
DECLASSING
DECLAW
DECLAWED
DECLAWING
DECLAWS
DECLENSION
DECLENSIONAL
DECLENSIONALLY

DECLENSIONS
DECLINABLE
DECLINAL
DECLINANT
DECLINATE
DECLINATION
DECLINATIONAL
DECLINATIONS
DECLINATOR
DECLINATORS
DECLINATORY
DECLINATURE
DECLINATURES
DECLINE
DECLINED
DECLINER
DECLINERS
DECLINES
DECLINING
DECLINOMETER
DECLINOMETERS
DECLIVITIES
DECLIVITOUS
DECLIVITY
DECLIVOUS
DECLUTCH
DECLUTCHED
DECLUTCHES
DECLUTCHING
DECLUTTER
DECLUTTERED
DECLUTTERING
DECLUTTERS
DECO
DECOCT
DECOCTED
DECOCTIBLE
DECOCTING
DECOCTION
DECOCTIONS
DECOCTIVE
DECOCTS
DECOCTURE
DECOCTURES
DECODE
DECODED
DECODER
DECODERS
DECODES
DECODING
DECOHERER
DECOHERERS
DECOKE
DECOKED
DECOKES
DECOKING

DECOLLATE
DECOLLATED
DECOLLATES
DECOLLATING
DECOLLATION
DECOLLATIONS
DECOLLATOR
DECOLLATORS
DECOLLETAGE
DECOLLETAGES
DECOLLETE
DECOLLETES
DECOLONISATION
DECOLONISATIONS
DECOLONISE
DECOLONISED
DECOLONISES
DECOLONISING
DECOLONIZATION
DECOLONIZATIONS
DECOLONIZE
DECOLONIZED
DECOLONIZES
DECOLONIZING
DECOLOR
DECOLORANT
DECOLORANTS
DECOLORATE
DECOLORATED
DECOLORATES
DECOLORATING
DECOLORATION
DECOLORATIONS
DECOLORED
DECOLORING
DECOLORISATION
DECOLORISATIONS
DECOLORISE
DECOLORISED
DECOLORISES
DECOLORISING
DECOLORIZATION
DECOLORIZATIONS
DECOLORIZE
DECOLORIZED
DECOLORIZER
DECOLORIZERS
DECOLORIZES
DECOLORIZING
DECOLORS
DECOLOUR
DECOLOURED
DECOLOURING
DECOLOURISATION
DECOLOURISE
DECOLOURISED

DECOLOURISES
DECOLOURISING
DECOLOURIZATION
DECOLOURIZE
DECOLOURIZED
DECOLOURIZES
DECOLOURIZING
DECOLOURS
DECOMMISSION
DECOMMISSIONED
DECOMMISSIONER
DECOMMISSIONERS
DECOMMISSIONING
DECOMMISSIONS
DECOMMIT
DECOMPENSATE
DECOMPENSATED
DECOMPENSATES
DECOMPENSATING
DECOMPENSATION
DECOMPENSATIONS
DECOMPLEX
DECOMPOSABILITY
DECOMPOSABLE
DECOMPOSE
DECOMPOSED
DECOMPOSER
DECOMPOSERS
DECOMPOSES
DECOMPOSING
DECOMPOSITE
DECOMPOSITION
DECOMPOSITIONS
DECOMPOUND
DECOMPOUNDABLE
DECOMPOUNDED
DECOMPOUNDING
DECOMPOUNDS
DECOMPRESS
DECOMPRESSED
DECOMPRESSES
DECOMPRESSING
DECOMPRESSION
DECOMPRESSIONS
DECOMPRESSIVE
DECOMPRESSOR
DECOMPRESSORS
DECONCENTRATE
DECONCENTRATED
DECONCENTRATES
DECONCENTRATING
DECONCENTRATION
DECONDITION
DECONDITIONED
DECONDITIONING
DECONDITIONS

DECONGEST
DECONGESTANT
DECONGESTANTS
DECONGESTED
DECONGESTING
DECONGESTION
DECONGESTIONS
DECONGESTIVE
DECONGESTS
DECONSECRATE
DECONSECRATED
DECONSECRATES
DECONSECRATING
DECONSECRATION
DECONSECRATIONS
DECONSTRUCT
DECONSTRUCTED
DECONSTRUCTING
DECONSTRUCTION
DECONSTRUCTIONS
DECONSTRUCTIVE
DECONSTRUCTOR
DECONSTRUCTORS
DECONSTRUCTS
DECONTAMINANT
DECONTAMINANTS
DECONTAMINATE
DECONTAMINATED
DECONTAMINATES
DECONTAMINATING
DECONTAMINATION
DECONTAMINATIVE
DECONTAMINATOR
DECONTAMINATORS
DECONTROL
DECONTROLLED
DECONTROLLING
DECONTROLS
DECOR
DECORATE
DECORATED
DECORATES
DECORATING
DECORATION
DECORATIONS
DECORATIVE
DECORATIVELY
DECORATIVENESS
DECORATOR
DECORATORS
DECOROUS
DECOROUSLY
DECOROUSNESS
DECOROUSNESSES
DECORS
DECORTICATE

DECORTICATED
DECORTICATES
DECORTICATING
DECORTICATION
DECORTICATIONS
DECORTICATOR
DECORTICATORS
DECORUM
DECORUMS
DECOS
DECOUPAGE
DECOUPAGED
DECOUPAGES
DECOUPAGING
DECOUPLE
DECOUPLED
DECOUPLES
DECOUPLING
DECOUPLINGS
DECOY
DECOYED
DECOYER
DECOYERS
DECOYING
DECOYS
DECRASSIFIED
DECRASSIFIES
DECRASSIFY
DECRASSIFYING
DECREASE
DECREASED
DECREASES
DECREASING
DECREASINGLY
DECREE
DECREEABLE
DECREED
DECREEING
DECREER
DECREERS
DECREES
DECREET
DECREETS
DECREMENT
DECREMENTAL
DECREMENTED
DECREMENTING
DECREMENTS
DECREPIT
DECREPITATE
DECREPITATED
DECREPITATES
DECREPITATING
DECREPITATION
DECREPITATIONS
DECREPITLY

DECREPITNESS
DECREPITNESSES
DECREPITUDE
DECREPITUDES
DECRESCENCE
DECRESCENCES
DECRESCENDO
DECRESCENDOS
DECRESCENT
DECRETAL
DECRETALIST
DECRETALISTS
DECRETALS
DECRETIST
DECRETISTS
DECRETIVE
DECRETORY
DECREW
DECREWED
DECREWING
DECREWS
DECRIAL
DECRIALS
DECRIED
DECRIER
DECRIERS
DECRIES
DECRIMINALISE
DECRIMINALISED
DECRIMINALISES
DECRIMINALISING
DECRIMINALIZE
DECRIMINALIZED
DECRIMINALIZES
DECRIMINALIZING
DECROWN
DECROWNED
DECROWNING
DECROWNS
DECRUSTATION
DECRUSTATIONS
DECRY
DECRYING
DECRYPT
DECRYPTED
DECRYPTING
DECRYPTION
DECRYPTIONS
DECRYPTS
DECTET
DECTETS
DECUBITAL
DECUBITI
DECUBITUS
DECUMAN
DECUMANS

DECUMBENCE
DECUMBENCES
DECUMBENCIES
DECUMBENCY
DECUMBENT
DECUMBENTLY
DECUMBITURE
DECUMBITURES
DECUPLE
DECUPLED
DECUPLES
DECUPLING
DECURIA
DECURIAS
DECURIES
DECURION
DECURIONATE
DECURIONATES
DECURIONS
DECURRENCIES
DECURRENCY
DECURRENT
DECURRENTLY
DECURSION
DECURSIONS
DECURSIVE
DECURSIVELY
DECURVATION
DECURVATIONS
DECURVE
DECURVED
DECURVES
DECURVING
DECURY
DECUSSATE
DECUSSATED
DECUSSATELY
DECUSSATES
DECUSSATING
DECUSSATION
DECUSSATIONS
DEDAL
DEDALIAN
DEDANS
DEDICANT
DEDICANTS
DEDICATE
DEDICATED
DEDICATEDLY
DEDICATEE
DEDICATEES
DEDICATES
DEDICATING
DEDICATION
DEDICATIONAL
DEDICATIONS

DEDICATIVE
DEDICATOR
DEDICATORIAL
DEDICATORS
DEDICATORY
DEDIFFERENTIATE
DEDIMUS
DEDIMUSES
DEDRAMATISE
DEDRAMATISED
DEDRAMATISES
DEDRAMATISING
DEDRAMATIZE
DEDRAMATIZED
DEDRAMATIZES
DEDRAMATIZING
DEDUCE
DEDUCED
DEDUCEMENT
DEDUCEMENTS
DEDUCES
DEDUCIBILITIES
DEDUCIBILITY
DEDUCIBLE
DEDUCIBLENESS
DEDUCIBLENESSES
DEDUCING
DEDUCT
DEDUCTED
DEDUCTIBILITIES
DEDUCTIBILITY
DEDUCTIBLE
DEDUCTIBLES
DEDUCTING
DEDUCTION
DEDUCTIONS
DEDUCTIVE
DEDUCTIVELY
DEDUCTS
DEE
DEED
DEEDED
DEEDER
DEEDEST
DEEDFUL
DEEDIER
DEEDIEST
DEEDILY
DEEDING
DEEDLESS
DEEDS
DEEDY
DEEING
DEEJAY
DEEJAYED
DEEJAYING

DEEJAYS
DEEK
DEEM
DEEMED
DEEMING
DEEMS
DEEMSTER
DEEMSTERS
DEEMSTERSHIP
DEEMSTERSHIPS
DEEN
DEENS
DEEP
DEEPEN
DEEPENED
DEEPENER
DEEPENERS
DEEPENING
DEEPENS
DEEPER
DEEPEST
DEEPFELT
DEEPFREEZE
DEEPFREEZES
DEEPIE
DEEPIES
DEEPLY
DEEPMOST
DEEPNESS
DEEPNESSES
DEEPS
DEEPWATER
DEEPWATERMAN
DEEPWATERMEN
DEER
DEERBERRIES
DEERBERRY
DEERE
DEERFLIES
DEERFLY
DEERGRASS
DEERGRASSES
DEERHORN
DEERHORNS
DEERHOUND
DEERHOUNDS
DEERLET
DEERLETS
DEERLIKE
DEERS
DEERSKIN
DEERSKINS
DEERSTALKER
DEERSTALKERS
DEERSTALKING
DEERSTALKINGS

DEERWEED
DEERWEEDS
DEERYARD
DEERYARDS
DEES
DEET
DEETS
DEEV
DEEVE
DEEVED
DEEVES
DEEVING
DEEVS
DEEWAN
DEEWANS
DEF
DEFACE
DEFACEABLE
DEFACED
DEFACEMENT
DEFACEMENTS
DEFACER
DEFACERS
DEFACES
DEFACING
DEFACINGLY
DEFAECATE
DEFAECATED
DEFAECATES
DEFAECATING
DEFAECATION
DEFAECATIONS
DEFAECATOR
DEFAECATORS
DEFALCATE
DEFALCATED
DEFALCATES
DEFALCATING
DEFALCATION
DEFALCATIONS
DEFALCATOR
DEFALCATORS
DEFAMATION
DEFAMATIONS
DEFAMATORILY
DEFAMATORY
DEFAME
DEFAMED
DEFAMER
DEFAMERS
DEFAMES
DEFAMING
DEFAMINGS
DEFANG
DEFANGED
DEFANGING

DEFANGS
DEFAST
DEFASTE
DEFAT
DEFATS
DEFATTED
DEFATTING
DEFAULT
DEFAULTED
DEFAULTER
DEFAULTERS
DEFAULTING
DEFAULTS
DEFEASANCE
DEFEASANCED
DEFEASANCES
DEFEASIBILITIES
DEFEASIBILITY
DEFEASIBLE
DEFEASIBLENESS
DEFEAT
DEFEATED
DEFEATER
DEFEATERS
DEFEATING
DEFEATISM
DEFEATISMS
DEFEATIST
DEFEATISTS
DEFEATS
DEFEATURE
DEFEATURED
DEFEATURES
DEFEATURING
DEFECATE
DEFECATED
DEFECATES
DEFECATING
DEFECATION
DEFECATIONS
DEFECATOR
DEFECATORS
DEFECT
DEFECTED
DEFECTIBILITIES
DEFECTIBILITY
DEFECTIBLE
DEFECTING
DEFECTION
DEFECTIONIST
DEFECTIONISTS
DEFECTIONS
DEFECTIVE
DEFECTIVELY
DEFECTIVENESS
DEFECTIVENESSES

DEFECTIVES
DEFECTOR
DEFECTORS
DEFECTS
DEFEMINIZATION
DEFEMINIZATIONS
DEFEMINIZE
DEFEMINIZED
DEFEMINIZES
DEFEMINIZING
DEFENCE
DEFENCED
DEFENCELESS
DEFENCELESSLY
DEFENCELESSNESS
DEFENCEMAN
DEFENCEMEN
DEFENCES
DEFEND
DEFENDABLE
DEFENDANT
DEFENDANTS
DEFENDED
DEFENDER
DEFENDERS
DEFENDING
DEFENDS
DEFENESTRATE
DEFENESTRATED
DEFENESTRATES
DEFENESTRATING
DEFENESTRATION
DEFENESTRATIONS
DEFENSATIVE
DEFENSATIVES
DEFENSE
DEFENSED
DEFENSELESS
DEFENSELESSLY
DEFENSELESSNESS
DEFENSEMAN
DEFENSEMEN
DEFENSES
DEFENSIBILITIES
DEFENSIBILITY
DEFENSIBLE
DEFENSIBLENESS
DEFENSIBLY
DEFENSING
DEFENSIVE
DEFENSIVELY
DEFENSIVENESS
DEFENSIVENESSES
DEFENSIVES
DEFER
DEFERABLE

DEFERENCE
DEFERENCES
DEFERENT
DEFERENTIAL
DEFERENTIALLY
DEFERENTS
DEFERMENT
DEFERMENTS
DEFERRABLE
DEFERRABLES
DEFERRAL
DEFERRALS
DEFERRED
DEFERRER
DEFERRERS
DEFERRING
DEFERS
DEFERVESCENCE
DEFERVESCENCES
DEFERVESCENCIES
DEFERVESCENCY
DEFEUDALISE
DEFEUDALISED
DEFEUDALISES
DEFEUDALISING
DEFEUDALIZE
DEFEUDALIZED
DEFEUDALIZES
DEFEUDALIZING
DEFFER
DEFFEST
DEFFLY
DEFFO
DEFI
DEFIANCE
DEFIANCES
DEFIANT
DEFIANTLY
DEFIANTNESS
DEFIANTNESSES
DEFIBRILLATE
DEFIBRILLATED
DEFIBRILLATES
DEFIBRILLATING
DEFIBRILLATION
DEFIBRILLATIONS
DEFIBRILLATOR
DEFIBRILLATORS
DEFIBRINATE
DEFIBRINATED
DEFIBRINATES
DEFIBRINATING
DEFIBRINATION
DEFIBRINATIONS
DEFIBRINISED
DEFIBRINISES

DEFIBRINISING
DEFIBRINIZE
DEFIBRINIZED
DEFIBRINIZES
DEFIBRINIZING
DEFICIENCE
DEFICIENCES
DEFICIENCIES
DEFICIENCY
DEFICIENT
DEFICIENTLY
DEFICIENTNESS
DEFICIENTNESSES
DEFICIENTS
DEFICIT
DEFICITS
DEFIED
DEFIER
DEFIERS
DEFIES
DEFILADE
DEFILADED
DEFILADES
DEFILADING
DEFILE
DEFILED
DEFILEMENT
DEFILEMENTS
DEFILER
DEFILERS
DEFILES
DEFILIATION
DEFILIATIONS
DEFILING
DEFINABILITIES
DEFINABILITY
DEFINABLE
DEFINABLY
DEFINE
DEFINED
DEFINEMENT
DEFINEMENTS
DEFINER
DEFINERS
DEFINES
DEFINIENDA
DEFINIENDUM
DEFINIENS
DEFINIENTIA
DEFINING
DEFINITE
DEFINITELY
DEFINITENESS
DEFINITENESSES
DEFINITION
DEFINITIONAL

DEFINITIONS
DEFINITIVE
DEFINITIVELY
DEFINITIVENESS
DEFINITIVES
DEFINITIZE
DEFINITIZED
DEFINITIZES
DEFINITIZING
DEFINITUDE
DEFINITUDES
DEFIS
DEFLAGRABILITY
DEFLAGRABLE
DEFLAGRATE
DEFLAGRATED
DEFLAGRATES
DEFLAGRATING
DEFLAGRATION
DEFLAGRATIONS
DEFLAGRATOR
DEFLAGRATORS
DEFLATE
DEFLATED
DEFLATER
DEFLATERS
DEFLATES
DEFLATING
DEFLATION
DEFLATIONARY
DEFLATIONIST
DEFLATIONISTS
DEFLATIONS
DEFLATOR
DEFLATORS
DEFLEA
DEFLEAED
DEFLEAING
DEFLEAS
DEFLECT
DEFLECTABLE
DEFLECTED
DEFLECTING
DEFLECTION
DEFLECTIONAL
DEFLECTIONS
DEFLECTIVE
DEFLECTOR
DEFLECTORS
DEFLECTS
DEFLEX
DEFLEXED
DEFLEXES
DEFLEXING
DEFLEXION
DEFLEXIONAL

DEFLEXIONS
DEFLEXURE
DEFLEXURES
DEFLOCCULANT
DEFLOCCULANTS
DEFLOCCULATE
DEFLOCCULATED
DEFLOCCULATES
DEFLOCCULATING
DEFLOCCULATION
DEFLOCCULATIONS
DEFLORATE
DEFLORATED
DEFLORATES
DEFLORATING
DEFLORATION
DEFLORATIONS
DEFLOWER
DEFLOWERED
DEFLOWERER
DEFLOWERERS
DEFLOWERING
DEFLOWERS
DEFLUENT
DEFLUXION
DEFLUXIONS
DEFOAM
DEFOAMED
DEFOAMER
DEFOAMERS
DEFOAMING
DEFOAMS
DEFOCUS
DEFOCUSED
DEFOCUSES
DEFOCUSING
DEFOCUSSED
DEFOCUSSES
DEFOCUSSING
DEFOG
DEFOGGED
DEFOGGER
DEFOGGERS
DEFOGGING
DEFOGS
DEFOLIANT
DEFOLIANTS
DEFOLIATE
DEFOLIATED
DEFOLIATES
DEFOLIATING
DEFOLIATION
DEFOLIATIONS
DEFOLIATOR
DEFOLIATORS
DEFORCE

DEFORCED
DEFORCEMENT
DEFORCEMENTS
DEFORCES
DEFORCIANT
DEFORCIANTS
DEFORCIATION
DEFORCIATIONS
DEFORCING
DEFOREST
DEFORESTATION
DEFORESTATIONS
DEFORESTED
DEFORESTER
DEFORESTERS
DEFORESTING
DEFORESTS
DEFORM
DEFORMABILITIES
DEFORMABILITY
DEFORMABLE
DEFORMALIZE
DEFORMALIZED
DEFORMALIZES
DEFORMALIZING
DEFORMATION
DEFORMATIONAL
DEFORMATIONS
DEFORMATIVE
DEFORMED
DEFORMEDLY
DEFORMEDNESS
DEFORMEDNESSES
DEFORMER
DEFORMERS
DEFORMING
DEFORMITIES
DEFORMITY
DEFORMS
DEFOUL
DEFOULED
DEFOULING
DEFOULS
DEFRAG
DEFRAGGED
DEFRAGGING
DEFRAGMENT
DEFRAGMENTED
DEFRAGMENTING
DEFRAGMENTS
DEFRAGS
DEFRAUD
DEFRAUDATION
DEFRAUDATIONS
DEFRAUDED
DEFRAUDER

DEFRAUDERS
DEFRAUDING
DEFRAUDMENT
DEFRAUDMENTS
DEFRAUDS
DEFRAY
DEFRAYABLE
DEFRAYAL
DEFRAYALS
DEFRAYED
DEFRAYER
DEFRAYERS
DEFRAYING
DEFRAYMENT
DEFRAYMENTS
DEFRAYS
DEFREEZE
DEFREEZES
DEFREEZING
DEFROCK
DEFROCKED
DEFROCKING
DEFROCKS
DEFROST
DEFROSTED
DEFROSTER
DEFROSTERS
DEFROSTING
DEFROSTS
DEFROZE
DEFROZEN
DEFT
DEFTER
DEFTEST
DEFTLY
DEFTNESS
DEFTNESSES
DEFUNCT
DEFUNCTION
DEFUNCTIONS
DEFUNCTIVE
DEFUNCTNESS
DEFUNCTS
DEFUND
DEFUNDED
DEFUNDING
DEFUNDS
DEFUSE
DEFUSED
DEFUSES
DEFUSING
DEFUZE
DEFUZED
DEFUZES
DEFUZING
DEFY

DEFYING
DEGAGE
DEGAME
DEGAMES
DEGAMI
DEGAMIS
DEGARNISH
DEGARNISHED
DEGARNISHES
DEGARNISHING
DEGAS
DEGASES
DEGASSED
DEGASSER
DEGASSERS
DEGASSES
DEGASSING
DEGAUSS
DEGAUSSED
DEGAUSSER
DEGAUSSERS
DEGAUSSES
DEGAUSSING
DEGEARING
DEGENDER
DEGENDERED
DEGENDERING
DEGENDERS
DEGENERACIES
DEGENERACY
DEGENERATE
DEGENERATED
DEGENERATELY
DEGENERATENESS
DEGENERATES
DEGENERATING
DEGENERATION
DEGENERATIONIST
DEGENERATIONS
DEGENERATIVE
DEGENEROUS
DEGERM
DEGERMED
DEGERMING
DEGERMS
DEGGED
DEGGING
DEGLACIATED
DEGLACIATION
DEGLACIATIONS
DEGLAMORIZATION
DEGLAMORIZE
DEGLAMORIZED
DEGLAMORIZES
DEGLAMORIZING
DEGLAZE

DEGLAZED
DEGLAZES
DEGLAZING
DEGLUTINATE
DEGLUTINATED
DEGLUTINATES
DEGLUTINATING
DEGLUTINATION
DEGLUTINATIONS
DEGLUTITION
DEGLUTITIONS
DEGLUTITIVE
DEGLUTITORY
DEGOUT
DEGOUTS
DEGRADABILITIES
DEGRADABILITY
DEGRADABLE
DEGRADATION
DEGRADATIONS
DEGRADATIVE
DEGRADE
DEGRADED
DEGRADEDLY
DEGRADER
DEGRADERS
DEGRADES
DEGRADING
DEGRADINGLY
DEGRADINGNESS
DEGRANULATION
DEGRANULATIONS
DEGRAS
DEGREASANT
DEGREASANTS
DEGREASE
DEGREASED
DEGREASER
DEGREASERS
DEGREASES
DEGREASING
DEGREE
DEGREED
DEGREELESS
DEGREES
DEGRESSION
DEGRESSIONS
DEGRESSIVE
DEGRESSIVELY
DEGRINGOLADE
DEGRINGOLADED
DEGRINGOLADES
DEGRINGOLADING
DEGRINGOLER
DEGRINGOLERED
DEGRINGOLERING

DEGRINGOLERS
DEGS
DEGUM
DEGUMMED
DEGUMMING
DEGUMS
DEGUST
DEGUSTATE
DEGUSTATED
DEGUSTATES
DEGUSTATING
DEGUSTATION
DEGUSTATIONS
DEGUSTATORY
DEGUSTED
DEGUSTING
DEGUSTS
DEHISCE
DEHISCED
DEHISCENCE
DEHISCENCES
DEHISCENT
DEHISCES
DEHISCING
DEHORN
DEHORNED
DEHORNER
DEHORNERS
DEHORNING
DEHORNS
DEHORT
DEHORTATION
DEHORTATIONS
DEHORTATIVE
DEHORTATORY
DEHORTED
DEHORTER
DEHORTERS
DEHORTING
DEHORTS
DEHUMANISATION
DEHUMANISE
DEHUMANISED
DEHUMANISES
DEHUMANISING
DEHUMANIZATION
DEHUMANIZATIONS
DEHUMANIZE
DEHUMANIZED
DEHUMANIZES
DEHUMANIZING
DEHUMIDIFIED
DEHUMIDIFIER
DEHUMIDIFIERS
DEHUMIDIFIES
DEHUMIDIFY

DEHUMIDIFYING
DEHYDRATE
DEHYDRATED
DEHYDRATER
DEHYDRATERS
DEHYDRATES
DEHYDRATING
DEHYDRATION
DEHYDRATIONS
DEHYDRATOR
DEHYDRATORS
DEHYDROGENASE
DEHYDROGENASES
DEHYDROGENATE
DEHYDROGENATED
DEHYDROGENATES
DEHYDROGENATING
DEHYDROGENATION
DEHYDROGENISE
DEHYDROGENISED
DEHYDROGENISES
DEHYDROGENISING
DEHYDROGENIZE
DEHYDROGENIZED
DEHYDROGENIZES
DEHYDROGENIZING
DEHYDRORETINOL
DEHYDRORETINOLS
DEHYPNOTISATION
DEHYPNOTISE
DEHYPNOTISED
DEHYPNOTISES
DEHYPNOTISING
DEHYPNOTIZATION
DEHYPNOTIZE
DEHYPNOTIZED
DEHYPNOTIZES
DEHYPNOTIZING
DEI
DEICE
DEICED
DEICER
DEICERS
DEICES
DEICIDAL
DEICIDE
DEICIDES
DEICING
DEICTIC
DEICTICALLY
DEICTICS
DEID
DEIDER
DEIDEST
DEIDS
DEIF

DEIFER
DEIFEST
DEIFIC
DEIFICAL
DEIFICATION
DEIFICATIONS
DEIFIED
DEIFIER
DEIFIERS
DEIFIES
DEIFORM
DEIFY
DEIFYING
DEIGN
DEIGNED
DEIGNING
DEIGNS
DEIL
DEILS
DEINDEX
DEINDEXED
DEINDEXES
DEINDEXING
DEINDIVIDUATION
DEINDUSTRIALISE
DEINDUSTRIALIZE
DEINONYCHUS
DEINONYCHUSES
DEINOSAUR
DEINOSAURS
DEINOTHERE
DEINOTHERES
DEINOTHERIUM
DEINOTHERIUMS
DEIONISATION
DEIONISATIONS
DEIONIZATION
DEIONIZATIONS
DEIONIZE
DEIONIZED
DEIONIZER
DEIONIZERS
DEIONIZES
DEIONIZING
DEIPAROUS
DEIPNOSOPHIST
DEIPNOSOPHISTS
DEISEAL
DEISEALS
DEISHEAL
DEISHEALS
DEISM
DEISMS
DEIST
DEISTIC
DEISTICAL

DEISTICALLY
DEISTS
DEITIES
DEITY
DEIXES
DEIXIS
DEIXISES
DEJECT
DEJECTA
DEJECTED
DEJECTEDLY
DEJECTEDNESS
DEJECTEDNESSES
DEJECTING
DEJECTION
DEJECTIONS
DEJECTORY
DEJECTS
DEJEUNE
DEJEUNER
DEJEUNERS
DEJEUNES
DEKAGRAM
DEKAGRAMS
DEKALITER
DEKALITERS
DEKALOGIES
DEKALOGY
DEKAMETER
DEKAMETERS
DEKAMETRIC
DEKARE
DEKARES
DEKE
DEKED
DEKES
DEKING
DEKKO
DEKKOED
DEKKOING
DEKKOS
DEL
DELAINE
DELAINES
DELAMINATE
DELAMINATED
DELAMINATES
DELAMINATING
DELAMINATION
DELAMINATIONS
DELAPSE
DELAPSED
DELAPSES
DELAPSING
DELAPSION
DELAPSIONS

DELASSEMENT
DELASSEMENTS
DELATE
DELATED
DELATES
DELATING
DELATION
DELATIONS
DELATOR
DELATORS
DELAY
DELAYED
DELAYER
DELAYERING
DELAYERINGS
DELAYERS
DELAYING
DELAYINGLY
DELAYS
DELE
DELEAD
DELEADED
DELEADING
DELEADS
DELEAVE
DELEAVED
DELEAVES
DELEAVING
DELEBLE
DELECTABILITIES
DELECTABILITY
DELECTABLE
DELECTABLENESS
DELECTABLES
DELECTABLY
DELECTATION
DELECTATIONS
DELED
DELEGABLE
DELEGACIES
DELEGACY
DELEGATE
DELEGATED
DELEGATEE
DELEGATEES
DELEGATES
DELEGATING
DELEGATION
DELEGATIONS
DELEGATOR
DELEGATORS
DELEGITIMATION
DELEGITIMATIONS
DELEGITIMISE
DELEGITIMIZE
DELEING

DELENDA
DELES
DELETE
DELETED
DELETERIOUS
DELETERIOUSLY
DELETERIOUSNESS
DELETES
DELETING
DELETION
DELETIONS
DELETIVE
DELETORY
DELF
DELFS
DELFT
DELFTS
DELFTWARE
DELFTWARES
DELI
DELIBATE
DELIBATED
DELIBATES
DELIBATING
DELIBATION
DELIBATIONS
DELIBERATE
DELIBERATED
DELIBERATELY
DELIBERATENESS
DELIBERATES
DELIBERATING
DELIBERATION
DELIBERATIONS
DELIBERATIVE
DELIBERATIVELY
DELIBERATOR
DELIBERATORS
DELIBLE
DELICACIES
DELICACY
DELICATE
DELICATELY
DELICATENESS
DELICATENESSES
DELICATES
DELICATESSEN
DELICATESSENS
DELICE
DELICES
DELICIOUS
DELICIOUSLY
DELICIOUSNESS
DELICIOUSNESSES
DELICT
DELICTS

DELIGATION
DELIGATIONS
DELIGHT
DELIGHTED
DELIGHTEDLY
DELIGHTEDNESS
DELIGHTEDNESSES
DELIGHTER
DELIGHTERS
DELIGHTFUL
DELIGHTFULLY
DELIGHTFULNESS
DELIGHTING
DELIGHTLESS
DELIGHTS
DELIGHTSOME
DELIME
DELIMED
DELIMES
DELIMING
DELIMIT
DELIMITATE
DELIMITATED
DELIMITATES
DELIMITATING
DELIMITATION
DELIMITATIONS
DELIMITATIVE
DELIMITED
DELIMITER
DELIMITERS
DELIMITING
DELIMITS
DELINEABLE
DELINEATE
DELINEATED
DELINEATES
DELINEATING
DELINEATION
DELINEATIONS
DELINEATIVE
DELINEATOR
DELINEATORS
DELINEAVIT
DELINQUENCIES
DELINQUENCY
DELINQUENT
DELINQUENTLY
DELINQUENTS
DELIQUESCE
DELIQUESCED
DELIQUESCENCE
DELIQUESCENCES
DELIQUESCENT
DELIQUESCES
DELIQUESCING

DELIQUIUM
DELIQUIUMS
DELIRATION
DELIRATIONS
DELIRIA
DELIRIANT
DELIRIFACIENT
DELIRIFACIENTS
DELIRIOUS
DELIRIOUSLY
DELIRIOUSNESS
DELIRIOUSNESSES
DELIRIUM
DELIRIUMS
DELIS
DELIST
DELISTED
DELISTING
DELISTS
DELITESCENCE
DELITESCENCES
DELITESCENT
DELIVER
DELIVERABILITY
DELIVERABLE
DELIVERANCE
DELIVERANCES
DELIVERED
DELIVERER
DELIVERERS
DELIVERIES
DELIVERING
DELIVERLY
DELIVERS
DELIVERY
DELIVERYMAN
DELIVERYMEN
DELL
DELLIES
DELLS
DELLY
DELO
DELOCALISATION
DELOCALISE
DELOCALISED
DELOCALISES
DELOCALISING
DELOCALIZATION
DELOCALIZATIONS
DELOCALIZE
DELOCALIZED
DELOCALIZES
DELOCALIZING
DELOPE
DELOPED
DELOPES

DELOPING
DELOS
DELOUSE
DELOUSED
DELOUSER
DELOUSERS
DELOUSES
DELOUSING
DELPH
DELPHIC
DELPHICALLY
DELPHIN
DELPHINIA
DELPHINIUM
DELPHINIUMS
DELPHINOID
DELPHS
DELS
DELT
DELTA
DELTAIC
DELTAS
DELTIC
DELTIOLOGIES
DELTIOLOGIST
DELTIOLOGISTS
DELTIOLOGY
DELTOID
DELTOIDEI
DELTOIDEUS
DELTOIDS
DELTS
DELUBRUM
DELUBRUMS
DELUDABLE
DELUDE
DELUDED
DELUDER
DELUDERS
DELUDES
DELUDING
DELUDINGLY
DELUGE
DELUGED
DELUGES
DELUGING
DELUNDUNG
DELUNDUNGS
DELUSION
DELUSIONAL
DELUSIONARY
DELUSIONIST
DELUSIONISTS
DELUSIONS
DELUSIVE
DELUSIVELY

DELUSIVENESS
DELUSIVENESSES
DELUSORY
DELUSTER
DELUSTERED
DELUSTERING
DELUSTERS
DELUSTRANT
DELUSTRANTS
DELUXE
DELVE
DELVED
DELVER
DELVERS
DELVES
DELVING
DEMAGNETISATION
DEMAGNETISE
DEMAGNETISED
DEMAGNETISER
DEMAGNETISERS
DEMAGNETISES
DEMAGNETISING
DEMAGNETIZATION
DEMAGNETIZE
DEMAGNETIZED
DEMAGNETIZER
DEMAGNETIZERS
DEMAGNETIZES
DEMAGNETIZING
DEMAGOG
DEMAGOGED
DEMAGOGIC
DEMAGOGICAL
DEMAGOGICALLY
DEMAGOGIES
DEMAGOGING
DEMAGOGISM
DEMAGOGISMS
DEMAGOGS
DEMAGOGUE
DEMAGOGUED
DEMAGOGUERIES
DEMAGOGUERY
DEMAGOGUES
DEMAGOGUING
DEMAGOGUISM
DEMAGOGUISMS
DEMAGOGY
DEMAIN
DEMAINE
DEMAINES
DEMAINS
DEMAN
DEMAND
DEMANDABLE

DEMANDANT
DEMANDANTS
DEMANDED
DEMANDER
DEMANDERS
DEMANDING
DEMANDINGLY
DEMANDINGNESS
DEMANDINGNESSES
DEMANDS
DEMANNED
DEMANNING
DEMANNINGS
DEMANS
DEMANTOID
DEMANTOIDS
DEMARCATE
DEMARCATED
DEMARCATES
DEMARCATING
DEMARCATION
DEMARCATIONS
DEMARCATOR
DEMARCATORS
DEMARCHE
DEMARCHES
DEMARK
DEMARKATION
DEMARKATIONS
DEMARKED
DEMARKET
DEMARKETED
DEMARKETING
DEMARKETS
DEMARKING
DEMARKS
DEMAST
DEMASTED
DEMASTING
DEMASTS
DEMATERIALISE
DEMATERIALISED
DEMATERIALISES
DEMATERIALISING
DEMATERIALIZE
DEMATERIALIZED
DEMATERIALIZES
DEMATERIALIZING
DEMAYNE
DEMAYNES
DEME
DEMEAN
DEMEANE
DEMEANED
DEMEANES
DEMEANING

DEMEANOR
DEMEANORS
DEMEANOUR
DEMEANOURS
DEMEANS
DEMEASNURE
DEMEASNURES
DEMENT
DEMENTATE
DEMENTATED
DEMENTATES
DEMENTATING
DEMENTED
DEMENTEDLY
DEMENTEDNESS
DEMENTEDNESSES
DEMENTI
DEMENTIA
DEMENTIAL
DEMENTIAS
DEMENTING
DEMENTIS
DEMENTS
DEMERARA
DEMERARAS
DEMERGE
DEMERGED
DEMERGER
DEMERGERED
DEMERGERING
DEMERGERS
DEMERGES
DEMERGING
DEMERIT
DEMERITED
DEMERITING
DEMERITORIOUS
DEMERITORIOUSLY
DEMERITS
DEMERSAL
DEMERSE
DEMERSED
DEMERSES
DEMERSING
DEMERSION
DEMERSIONS
DEMES
DEMESNE
DEMESNES
DEMETON
DEMETONS
DEMIBASTION
DEMIBASTIONS
DEMIC
DEMICANTON
DEMICANTONS

DEMIES
DEMIGOD
DEMIGODDESS
DEMIGODDESSES
DEMIGODS
DEMIGRATION
DEMIGRATIONS
DEMIJOHN
DEMIJOHNS
DEMILITARISE
DEMILITARISED
DEMILITARISES
DEMILITARISING
DEMILITARIZE
DEMILITARIZED
DEMILITARIZES
DEMILITARIZING
DEMILUNE
DEMILUNES
DEMIMONDAINE
DEMIMONDAINES
DEMIMONDE
DEMIMONDES
DEMINERALISE
DEMINERALISED
DEMINERALISES
DEMINERALISING
DEMINERALIZE
DEMINERALIZED
DEMINERALIZER
DEMINERALIZERS
DEMINERALIZES
DEMINERALIZING
DEMIPIQUE
DEMIPIQUES
DEMIRELIEF
DEMIRELIEFS
DEMIREP
DEMIREPDOM
DEMIREPDOMS
DEMIREPS
DEMISABLE
DEMISE
DEMISED
DEMISEMIQUAVER
DEMISEMIQUAVERS
DEMISES
DEMISING
DEMISS
DEMISSION
DEMISSIONS
DEMISSIVE
DEMISSLY
DEMIST
DEMISTED
DEMISTER

DEMISTERS
DEMISTING
DEMISTS
DEMIT
DEMITASSE
DEMITASSES
DEMITS
DEMITTED
DEMITTING
DEMIURGE
DEMIURGEOUS
DEMIURGES
DEMIURGIC
DEMIURGICAL
DEMIURGICALLY
DEMIURGUS
DEMIURGUSES
DEMIVEG
DEMIVIERGE
DEMIVIERGES
DEMIVOLT
DEMIVOLTE
DEMIVOLTES
DEMIVOLTS
DEMIWORLD
DEMIWORLDS
DEMO
DEMOB
DEMOBBED
DEMOBBING
DEMOBILISATION
DEMOBILISATIONS
DEMOBILISE
DEMOBILISED
DEMOBILISES
DEMOBILISING
DEMOBILIZATION
DEMOBILIZATIONS
DEMOBILIZE
DEMOBILIZED
DEMOBILIZES
DEMOBILIZING
DEMOBS
DEMOCRACIES
DEMOCRACY
DEMOCRAT
DEMOCRATIC
DEMOCRATICAL
DEMOCRATICALLY
DEMOCRATIES
DEMOCRATIFIABLE
DEMOCRATISATION
DEMOCRATISE
DEMOCRATISED
DEMOCRATISES
DEMOCRATISING

DEMOCRATIST
DEMOCRATISTS
DEMOCRATIZATION
DEMOCRATIZE
DEMOCRATIZED
DEMOCRATIZER
DEMOCRATIZERS
DEMOCRATIZES
DEMOCRATIZING
DEMOCRATS
DEMOCRATY
DEMODE
DEMODED
DEMODULATE
DEMODULATED
DEMODULATES
DEMODULATING
DEMODULATION
DEMODULATIONS
DEMODULATOR
DEMODULATORS
DEMOGRAPHER
DEMOGRAPHERS
DEMOGRAPHIC
DEMOGRAPHICAL
DEMOGRAPHICALLY
DEMOGRAPHICS
DEMOGRAPHIES
DEMOGRAPHIST
DEMOGRAPHISTS
DEMOGRAPHY
DEMOISELLE
DEMOISELLES
DEMOLISH
DEMOLISHED
DEMOLISHER
DEMOLISHERS
DEMOLISHES
DEMOLISHING
DEMOLISHMENT
DEMOLISHMENTS
DEMOLITION
DEMOLITIONIST
DEMOLITIONISTS
DEMOLITIONS
DEMOLOGIES
DEMOLOGY
DEMON
DEMONESS
DEMONESSES
DEMONETARISE
DEMONETARISED
DEMONETARISES
DEMONETARISING
DEMONETARIZE
DEMONETARIZED

DEMONETARIZES
DEMONETARIZING
DEMONETISATION
DEMONETISATIONS
DEMONETISE
DEMONETISED
DEMONETISES
DEMONETISING
DEMONETIZATION
DEMONETIZATIONS
DEMONETIZE
DEMONETIZED
DEMONETIZES
DEMONETIZING
DEMONIAC
DEMONIACAL
DEMONIACALLY
DEMONIACISM
DEMONIACISMS
DEMONIACS
DEMONIAN
DEMONIANISM
DEMONIANISMS
DEMONIC
DEMONICAL
DEMONICALLY
DEMONISE
DEMONISED
DEMONISES
DEMONISING
DEMONISM
DEMONISMS
DEMONIST
DEMONISTS
DEMONIZATION
DEMONIZATIONS
DEMONIZE
DEMONIZED
DEMONIZES
DEMONIZING
DEMONOCRACIES
DEMONOCRACY
DEMONOLATER
DEMONOLATERS
DEMONOLATRIES
DEMONOLATRY
DEMONOLOGIC
DEMONOLOGICAL
DEMONOLOGIES
DEMONOLOGIST
DEMONOLOGISTS
DEMONOLOGY
DEMONOMANIA
DEMONOMANIAS
DEMONRIES
DEMONRY

DEMONS
DEMONSTRABILITY
DEMONSTRABLE
DEMONSTRABLY
DEMONSTRATE
DEMONSTRATED
DEMONSTRATES
DEMONSTRATING
DEMONSTRATION
DEMONSTRATIONAL
DEMONSTRATIONS
DEMONSTRATIVE
DEMONSTRATIVELY
DEMONSTRATIVES
DEMONSTRATOR
DEMONSTRATORS
DEMONSTRATORY
DEMORALISATION
DEMORALISATIONS
DEMORALISE
DEMORALISED
DEMORALISER
DEMORALISERS
DEMORALISES
DEMORALISING
DEMORALIZATION
DEMORALIZATIONS
DEMORALIZE
DEMORALIZED
DEMORALIZER
DEMORALIZERS
DEMORALIZES
DEMORALIZING
DEMORALIZINGLY
DEMOS
DEMOSES
DEMOTE
DEMOTED
DEMOTES
DEMOTIC
DEMOTICIST
DEMOTICISTS
DEMOTICS
DEMOTING
DEMOTION
DEMOTIONS
DEMOTIST
DEMOTISTS
DEMOTIVATE
DEMOTIVATED
DEMOTIVATES
DEMOTIVATING
DEMOUNT
DEMOUNTABLE
DEMOUNTED
DEMOUNTING

DEMOUNTS
DEMPSTER
DEMPSTERS
DEMPT
DEMULCENT
DEMULCENTS
DEMULSIFICATION
DEMULSIFIED
DEMULSIFIER
DEMULSIFIERS
DEMULSIFIES
DEMULSIFY
DEMULSIFYING
DEMULTIPLEXER
DEMULTIPLEXERS
DEMUR
DEMURE
DEMURED
DEMURELY
DEMURENESS
DEMURENESSES
DEMURER
DEMURES
DEMUREST
DEMURING
DEMURRABLE
DEMURRAGE
DEMURRAGES
DEMURRAL
DEMURRALS
DEMURRED
DEMURRER
DEMURRERS
DEMURRING
DEMURS
DEMUTUALISATION
DEMUTUALISE
DEMUTUALISED
DEMUTUALISES
DEMUTUALISING
DEMUTUALIZATION
DEMUTUALIZE
DEMUTUALIZED
DEMUTUALIZES
DEMUTUALIZING
DEMY
DEMYELINATE
DEMYELINATED
DEMYELINATES
DEMYELINATING
DEMYELINATION
DEMYELINATIONS
DEMYSHIP
DEMYSHIPS
DEMYSTIFICATION
DEMYSTIFIED

DEMYSTIFIES
DEMYSTIFY
DEMYSTIFYING
DEMYTHOLOGISE
DEMYTHOLOGISED
DEMYTHOLOGISES
DEMYTHOLOGISING
DEMYTHOLOGIZE
DEMYTHOLOGIZED
DEMYTHOLOGIZER
DEMYTHOLOGIZERS
DEMYTHOLOGIZES
DEMYTHOLOGIZING
DEN
DENAR
DENARIES
DENARII
DENARIUS
DENARS
DENARY
DENATIONALISE
DENATIONALISED
DENATIONALISES
DENATIONALISING
DENATIONALIZE
DENATIONALIZED
DENATIONALIZES
DENATIONALIZING
DENATURALISE
DENATURALISED
DENATURALISES
DENATURALISING
DENATURALIZE
DENATURALIZED
DENATURALIZES
DENATURALIZING
DENATURANT
DENATURANTS
DENATURATION
DENATURATIONS
DENATURE
DENATURED
DENATURES
DENATURING
DENATURISE
DENATURISED
DENATURISES
DENATURISING
DENATURIZE
DENATURIZED
DENATURIZES
DENATURIZING
DENAY
DENAYED
DENAYING
DENAYS

DENAZIFICATION
DENAZIFICATIONS
DENAZIFIED
DENAZIFIES
DENAZIFY
DENAZIFYING
DENDRACHATE
DENDRACHATES
DENDRIFORM
DENDRITE
DENDRITES
DENDRITIC
DENDRITICAL
DENDRITICALLY
DENDROBIUM
DENDROBIUMS
DENDROGLYPH
DENDROGLYPHS
DENDROGRAM
DENDROGRAMS
DENDROID
DENDROIDAL
DENDROLATRIES
DENDROLATRY
DENDROLOGIC
DENDROLOGICAL
DENDROLOGIES
DENDROLOGIST
DENDROLOGISTS
DENDROLOGOUS
DENDROLOGY
DENDROMETER
DENDROMETERS
DENDRON
DENDRONS
DENDROPHIS
DENDROPHISES
DENE
DENEGATION
DENEGATIONS
DENERVATE
DENERVATED
DENERVATES
DENERVATING
DENERVATION
DENERVATIONS
DENES
DENET
DENETS
DENETTED
DENETTING
DENGUE
DENGUES
DENI
DENIABILITIES
DENIABILITY

DENIABLE
DENIABLY
DENIAL
DENIALS
DENIED
DENIER
DENIERS
DENIES
DENIGRATE
DENIGRATED
DENIGRATES
DENIGRATING
DENIGRATION
DENIGRATIONS
DENIGRATIVE
DENIGRATOR
DENIGRATORS
DENIGRATORY
DENIM
DENIMS
DENITRATE
DENITRATED
DENITRATES
DENITRATING
DENITRATION
DENITRATIONS
DENITRIFICATION
DENITRIFICATOR
DENITRIFICATORS
DENITRIFIED
DENITRIFIER
DENITRIFIERS
DENITRIFIES
DENITRIFY
DENITRIFYING
DENIZATION
DENIZATIONS
DENIZEN
DENIZENED
DENIZENING
DENIZENNED
DENIZENNING
DENIZENS
DENIZENSHIP
DENIZENSHIPS
DENNED
DENNET
DENNETS
DENNING
DENOMINABLE
DENOMINAL
DENOMINATE
DENOMINATED
DENOMINATES
DENOMINATING
DENOMINATION

DENOMINATIONAL
DENOMINATIONS
DENOMINATIVE
DENOMINATIVELY
DENOMINATIVES
DENOMINATOR
DENOMINATORS
DENOTABLE
DENOTATE
DENOTATED
DENOTATES
DENOTATING
DENOTATION
DENOTATIONS
DENOTATIVE
DENOTATIVELY
DENOTE
DENOTED
DENOTEMENT
DENOTEMENTS
DENOTES
DENOTING
DENOTIVE
DENOUEMENT
DENOUEMENTS
DENOUNCE
DENOUNCED
DENOUNCEMENT
DENOUNCEMENTS
DENOUNCER
DENOUNCERS
DENOUNCES
DENOUNCING
DENS
DENSE
DENSELY
DENSENESS
DENSENESSES
DENSER
DENSEST
DENSIFICATION
DENSIFICATIONS
DENSIFIED
DENSIFIER
DENSIFIERS
DENSIFIES
DENSIFY
DENSIFYING
DENSIMETER
DENSIMETERS
DENSIMETRIC
DENSIMETRIES
DENSIMETRY
DENSITIES
DENSITOMETER
DENSITOMETERS

DENSITOMETRIC
DENSITOMETRIES
DENSITOMETRY
DENSITY
DENT
DENTAL
DENTALIA
DENTALIUM
DENTALIUMS
DENTALLY
DENTALS
DENTARIA
DENTARIAS
DENTARIES
DENTARY
DENTATE
DENTATED
DENTATELY
DENTATION
DENTATIONS
DENTED
DENTEL
DENTELLE
DENTELLES
DENTELS
DENTEX
DENTEXES
DENTICLE
DENTICLES
DENTICULATE
DENTICULATED
DENTICULATELY
DENTICULATION
DENTICULATIONS
DENTIFORM
DENTIFRICE
DENTIFRICES
DENTIGEROUS
DENTIL
DENTILABIAL
DENTILED
DENTILINGUAL
DENTILINGUALS
DENTILS
DENTIN
DENTINAL
DENTINE
DENTINES
DENTING
DENTINS
DENTIROSTRAL
DENTIST
DENTISTRIES
DENTISTRY
DENTISTS
DENTITION

DENTITIONS
DENTOID
DENTS
DENTULOUS
DENTURAL
DENTURE
DENTURES
DENTURIST
DENTURISTS
DENUCLEARISE
DENUCLEARISED
DENUCLEARISES
DENUCLEARISING
DENUCLEARIZE
DENUCLEARIZED
DENUCLEARIZES
DENUCLEARIZING
DENUDATE
DENUDATED
DENUDATES
DENUDATING
DENUDATION
DENUDATIONS
DENUDE
DENUDED
DENUDEMENT
DENUDEMENTS
DENUDER
DENUDERS
DENUDES
DENUDING
DENUMERABILITY
DENUMERABLE
DENUMERABLY
DENUNCIATE
DENUNCIATED
DENUNCIATES
DENUNCIATING
DENUNCIATION
DENUNCIATIONS
DENUNCIATIVE
DENUNCIATOR
DENUNCIATORS
DENUNCIATORY
DENY
DENYING
DENYINGLY
DEOBSTRUENT
DEOBSTRUENTS
DEODAND
DEODANDS
DEODAR
DEODARA
DEODARAS
DEODARS
DEODATE

DEODATES
DEODORANT
DEODORANTS
DEODORISATION
DEODORISATIONS
DEODORISE
DEODORISED
DEODORISER
DEODORISERS
DEODORISES
DEODORISING
DEODORIZATION
DEODORIZATIONS
DEODORIZE
DEODORIZED
DEODORIZER
DEODORIZERS
DEODORIZES
DEODORIZING
DEONTIC
DEONTICS
DEONTOLOGICAL
DEONTOLOGIES
DEONTOLOGIST
DEONTOLOGISTS
DEONTOLOGY
DEOPPILATE
DEOPPILATED
DEOPPILATES
DEOPPILATING
DEOPPILATION
DEOPPILATIONS
DEOPPILATIVE
DEORBIT
DEORBITED
DEORBITING
DEORBITS
DEOXIDATE
DEOXIDATED
DEOXIDATES
DEOXIDATING
DEOXIDATION
DEOXIDATIONS
DEOXIDISATION
DEOXIDISATIONS
DEOXIDISE
DEOXIDISED
DEOXIDISER
DEOXIDISERS
DEOXIDISES
DEOXIDISING
DEOXIDIZATION
DEOXIDIZATIONS
DEOXIDIZE
DEOXIDIZED
DEOXIDIZER

DEOXIDIZERS
DEOXIDIZES
DEOXIDIZING
DEOXY
DEOXYCORTONE
DEOXYCORTONES
DEOXYGENATE
DEOXYGENATED
DEOXYGENATES
DEOXYGENATING
DEOXYGENATION
DEOXYGENATIONS
DEOXYGENISE
DEOXYGENISED
DEOXYGENISES
DEOXYGENISING
DEOXYGENIZE
DEOXYGENIZED
DEOXYGENIZES
DEOXYGENIZING
DEOXYRIBOSE
DEOXYRIBOSES
DEPAINT
DEPAINTED
DEPAINTING
DEPAINTS
DEPANNEUR
DEPANNEURS
DEPART
DEPARTED
DEPARTEE
DEPARTEES
DEPARTEMENT
DEPARTEMENTS
DEPARTER
DEPARTERS
DEPARTING
DEPARTINGS
DEPARTMENT
DEPARTMENTAL
DEPARTMENTALISE
DEPARTMENTALISM
DEPARTMENTALIZE
DEPARTMENTALLY
DEPARTMENTS
DEPARTS
DEPARTURE
DEPARTURES
DEPASTURE
DEPASTURED
DEPASTURES
DEPASTURING
DEPAUPERATE
DEPAUPERATED
DEPAUPERATES
DEPAUPERATING

DEPAUPERISE
DEPAUPERISED
DEPAUPERISES
DEPAUPERISING
DEPAUPERIZE
DEPAUPERIZED
DEPAUPERIZES
DEPAUPERIZING
DEPECHE
DEPECHES
DEPEINCT
DEPEINCTED
DEPEINCTING
DEPEINCTS
DEPEND
DEPENDABILITIES
DEPENDABILITY
DEPENDABLE
DEPENDABLENESS
DEPENDABLY
DEPENDACIES
DEPENDANCE
DEPENDANCES
DEPENDANCIES
DEPENDANCY
DEPENDANT
DEPENDANTS
DEPENDED
DEPENDENCE
DEPENDENCES
DEPENDENCIES
DEPENDENCY
DEPENDENT
DEPENDENTLY
DEPENDENTS
DEPENDING
DEPENDINGLY
DEPENDS
DEPERM
DEPERMED
DEPERMING
DEPERMS
DEPERSONALISE
DEPERSONALISED
DEPERSONALISES
DEPERSONALISING
DEPERSONALIZE
DEPERSONALIZED
DEPERSONALIZES
DEPERSONALIZING
DEPHLEGMATE
DEPHLEGMATED
DEPHLEGMATES
DEPHLEGMATING
DEPHLEGMATION
DEPHLEGMATIONS

DEPHLEGMATOR
DEPHLEGMATORS
DEPHLOGISTICATE
DEPHOSPHORYLATE
DEPICT
DEPICTED
DEPICTER
DEPICTERS
DEPICTING
DEPICTION
DEPICTIONS
DEPICTIVE
DEPICTOR
DEPICTORS
DEPICTS
DEPICTURE
DEPICTURED
DEPICTURES
DEPICTURING
DEPIGMENTATION
DEPIGMENTATIONS
DEPILATE
DEPILATED
DEPILATES
DEPILATING
DEPILATION
DEPILATIONS
DEPILATOR
DEPILATORIES
DEPILATORS
DEPILATORY
DEPLANE
DEPLANED
DEPLANES
DEPLANING
DEPLETABLE
DEPLETE
DEPLETED
DEPLETES
DEPLETING
DEPLETION
DEPLETIONS
DEPLETIVE
DEPLETORY
DEPLORABILITIES
DEPLORABILITY
DEPLORABLE
DEPLORABLENESS
DEPLORABLY
DEPLORATION
DEPLORATIONS
DEPLORE
DEPLORED
DEPLORER
DEPLORERS
DEPLORES

DEPLORING
DEPLORINGLY
DEPLOY
DEPLOYABLE
DEPLOYED
DEPLOYING
DEPLOYMENT
DEPLOYMENTS
DEPLOYS
DEPLUMATION
DEPLUMATIONS
DEPLUME
DEPLUMED
DEPLUMES
DEPLUMING
DEPOLARISATION
DEPOLARISATIONS
DEPOLARISE
DEPOLARISED
DEPOLARISER
DEPOLARISERS
DEPOLARISES
DEPOLARISING
DEPOLARIZATION
DEPOLARIZATIONS
DEPOLARIZE
DEPOLARIZED
DEPOLARIZER
DEPOLARIZERS
DEPOLARIZES
DEPOLARIZING
DEPOLISH
DEPOLISHED
DEPOLISHES
DEPOLISHING
DEPOLITICISE
DEPOLITICISED
DEPOLITICISES
DEPOLITICISING
DEPOLITICIZE
DEPOLITICIZED
DEPOLITICIZES
DEPOLITICIZING
DEPOLYMERISE
DEPOLYMERISED
DEPOLYMERISES
DEPOLYMERISING
DEPOLYMERIZE
DEPOLYMERIZED
DEPOLYMERIZES
DEPOLYMERIZING
DEPONE
DEPONED
DEPONENT
DEPONENTS
DEPONES

DEPONING
DEPOPULATE
DEPOPULATED
DEPOPULATES
DEPOPULATING
DEPOPULATION
DEPOPULATIONS
DEPOPULATOR
DEPOPULATORS
DEPORT
DEPORTABLE
DEPORTATION
DEPORTATIONS
DEPORTED
DEPORTEE
DEPORTEES
DEPORTING
DEPORTMENT
DEPORTMENTS
DEPORTS
DEPOSABLE
DEPOSAL
DEPOSALS
DEPOSE
DEPOSED
DEPOSER
DEPOSERS
DEPOSES
DEPOSING
DEPOSIT
DEPOSITARIES
DEPOSITARY
DEPOSITATION
DEPOSITATIONS
DEPOSITED
DEPOSITING
DEPOSITION
DEPOSITIONAL
DEPOSITIONS
DEPOSITIVE
DEPOSITOR
DEPOSITORIES
DEPOSITORS
DEPOSITORY
DEPOSITS
DEPOT
DEPOTS
DEPRAVATION
DEPRAVATIONS
DEPRAVE
DEPRAVED
DEPRAVEDLY
DEPRAVEDNESS
DEPRAVEDNESSES
DEPRAVEMENT
DEPRAVEMENTS

DEPRAVER
DEPRAVERS
DEPRAVES
DEPRAVING
DEPRAVINGLY
DEPRAVITIES
DEPRAVITY
DEPRECABLE
DEPRECATE
DEPRECATED
DEPRECATES
DEPRECATING
DEPRECATINGLY
DEPRECATION
DEPRECATIONS
DEPRECATIVE
DEPRECATIVELY
DEPRECATOR
DEPRECATORILY
DEPRECATORS
DEPRECATORY
DEPRECIABLE
DEPRECIATE
DEPRECIATED
DEPRECIATES
DEPRECIATING
DEPRECIATINGLY
DEPRECIATION
DEPRECIATIONS
DEPRECIATIVE
DEPRECIATOR
DEPRECIATORS
DEPRECIATORY
DEPREDATE
DEPREDATED
DEPREDATES
DEPREDATING
DEPREDATION
DEPREDATIONS
DEPREDATOR
DEPREDATORS
DEPREDATORY
DEPREHEND
DEPREHENDED
DEPREHENDING
DEPREHENDS
DEPRESS
DEPRESSANT
DEPRESSANTS
DEPRESSED
DEPRESSES
DEPRESSIBLE
DEPRESSING
DEPRESSINGLY
DEPRESSION
DEPRESSIONS

DEPRESSIVE
DEPRESSIVELY
DEPRESSIVENESS
DEPRESSIVES
DEPRESSOMOTOR
DEPRESSOMOTORS
DEPRESSOR
DEPRESSORS
DEPRESSURISE
DEPRESSURISED
DEPRESSURISES
DEPRESSURISING
DEPRESSURIZE
DEPRESSURIZED
DEPRESSURIZES
DEPRESSURIZING
DEPRIVABLE
DEPRIVAL
DEPRIVALS
DEPRIVATION
DEPRIVATIONS
DEPRIVATIVE
DEPRIVE
DEPRIVED
DEPRIVEMENT
DEPRIVEMENTS
DEPRIVER
DEPRIVERS
DEPRIVES
DEPRIVING
DEPROGRAM
DEPROGRAMED
DEPROGRAMING
DEPROGRAMME
DEPROGRAMMED
DEPROGRAMMER
DEPROGRAMMERS
DEPROGRAMMES
DEPROGRAMMING
DEPROGRAMS
DEPSIDE
DEPSIDES
DEPTH
DEPTHLESS
DEPTHS
DEPURANT
DEPURANTS
DEPURATE
DEPURATED
DEPURATES
DEPURATING
DEPURATION
DEPURATIONS
DEPURATIVE
DEPURATIVES
DEPURATOR

DEPURATORS
DEPURATORY
DEPUTATION
DEPUTATIONS
DEPUTE
DEPUTED
DEPUTES
DEPUTIES
DEPUTING
DEPUTISE
DEPUTISED
DEPUTISES
DEPUTISING
DEPUTIZATION
DEPUTIZATIONS
DEPUTIZE
DEPUTIZED
DEPUTIZES
DEPUTIZING
DEPUTY
DERACIALISE
DERACIALISED
DERACIALISES
DERACIALISING
DERACIALIZE
DERACIALIZED
DERACIALIZES
DERACIALIZING
DERACINATE
DERACINATED
DERACINATES
DERACINATING
DERACINATION
DERACINATIONS
DERACINE
DERAIGN
DERAIGNED
DERAIGNING
DERAIGNMENT
DERAIGNMENTS
DERAIGNS
DERAIL
DERAILED
DERAILER
DERAILERS
DERAILING
DERAILLEUR
DERAILLEURS
DERAILMENT
DERAILMENTS
DERAILS
DERANGE
DERANGED
DERANGEMENT
DERANGEMENTS
DERANGES

DERANGING
DERAT
DERATE
DERATED
DERATES
DERATING
DERATINGS
DERATION
DERATIONED
DERATIONING
DERATIONS
DERATS
DERATTED
DERATTING
DERAY
DERAYED
DERAYING
DERAYS
DERBIES
DERBY
DERE
DEREALIZATION
DEREALIZATIONS
DERECOGNISE
DERECOGNISED
DERECOGNISES
DERECOGNISING
DERECOGNITION
DERECOGNITIONS
DERECOGNIZE
DERECOGNIZED
DERECOGNIZES
DERECOGNIZING
DERED
DEREGISTER
DEREGISTERED
DEREGISTERING
DEREGISTERS
DEREGISTRATION
DEREGISTRATIONS
DEREGULATE
DEREGULATED
DEREGULATES
DEREGULATING
DEREGULATION
DEREGULATIONS
DEREGULATOR
DEREGULATORS
DEREGULATORY
DERELICT
DERELICTION
DERELICTIONS
DERELICTS
DERELIGIONISE
DERELIGIONISED
DERELIGIONISES

DERELIGIONISING
DERELIGIONIZE
DERELIGIONIZED
DERELIGIONIZES
DERELIGIONIZING
DEREPRESS
DEREPRESSED
DEREPRESSES
DEREPRESSING
DEREPRESSION
DEREPRESSIONS
DEREQUISITION
DEREQUISITIONED
DEREQUISITIONS
DERES
DERESTRICT
DERESTRICTED
DERESTRICTING
DERESTRICTION
DERESTRICTIONS
DERESTRICTS
DERHAM
DERHAMS
DERIDE
DERIDED
DERIDER
DERIDERS
DERIDES
DERIDING
DERIDINGLY
DERIG
DERIGGED
DERIGGING
DERIGS
DERING
DERINGER
DERINGERS
DERISIBLE
DERISION
DERISIONS
DERISIVE
DERISIVELY
DERISIVENESS
DERISIVENESSES
DERISORY
DERIVABLE
DERIVABLY
DERIVATE
DERIVATES
DERIVATION
DERIVATIONAL
DERIVATIONIST
DERIVATIONISTS
DERIVATIONS
DERIVATIVE
DERIVATIVELY

DERIVATIVENESS
DERIVATIVES
DERIVATIZATION
DERIVATIZATIONS
DERIVATIZE
DERIVATIZED
DERIVATIZES
DERIVATIZING
DERIVE
DERIVED
DERIVER
DERIVERS
DERIVES
DERIVING
DERM
DERMA
DERMABRASION
DERMABRASIONS
DERMAL
DERMAPTERAN
DERMAPTERANS
DERMAS
DERMATIC
DERMATITIS
DERMATITISES
DERMATOGEN
DERMATOGENS
DERMATOGLYPHIC
DERMATOGLYPHICS
DERMATOGRAPHIA
DERMATOGRAPHIAS
DERMATOGRAPHIC
DERMATOGRAPHIES
DERMATOGRAPHY
DERMATOID
DERMATOLOGIC
DERMATOLOGICAL
DERMATOLOGIES
DERMATOLOGIST
DERMATOLOGISTS
DERMATOLOGY
DERMATOMAL
DERMATOME
DERMATOMES
DERMATOMIC
DERMATOMICALLY
DERMATOMYOSITIS
DERMATOPHYTE
DERMATOPHYTES
DERMATOPHYTIC
DERMATOPHYTOSIS
DERMATOPLASTIC
DERMATOPLASTIES
DERMATOPLASTY
DERMATOSES
DERMATOSIS

DERMESTID
DERMESTIDS
DERMIC
DERMIS
DERMISES
DERMOGRAPHIES
DERMOGRAPHY
DERMOID
DERMOIDS
DERMS
DERN
DERNFUL
DERNIER
DERNLY
DERNS
DERO
DEROGATE
DEROGATED
DEROGATELY
DEROGATES
DEROGATING
DEROGATION
DEROGATIONS
DEROGATIVE
DEROGATIVELY
DEROGATORILY
DEROGATORINESS
DEROGATORY
DEROS
DERRICK
DERRICKED
DERRICKING
DERRICKS
DERRIERE
DERRIERES
DERRIES
DERRINGER
DERRINGERS
DERRIS
DERRISES
DERRO
DERROS
DERRY
DERTH
DERTHS
DERV
DERVISH
DERVISHES
DERVS
DESACRALISATION
DESACRALISE
DESACRALISED
DESACRALISES
DESACRALISING
DESACRALIZATION
DESACRALIZE

DESACRALIZED
DESACRALIZES
DESACRALIZING
DESAGREMENT
DESAGREMENTS
DESALINATE
DESALINATED
DESALINATES
DESALINATING
DESALINATION
DESALINATIONS
DESALINATOR
DESALINATORS
DESALINISATION
DESALINISATIONS
DESALINISE
DESALINISED
DESALINISES
DESALINISING
DESALINIZATION
DESALINIZATIONS
DESALINIZE
DESALINIZED
DESALINIZES
DESALINIZING
DESALT
DESALTED
DESALTER
DESALTERS
DESALTING
DESALTINGS
DESALTS
DESAND
DESANDED
DESANDING
DESANDS
DESATURATION
DESATURATIONS
DESCALE
DESCALED
DESCALES
DESCALING
DESCANT
DESCANTED
DESCANTER
DESCANTERS
DESCANTING
DESCANTS
DESCEND
DESCENDABLE
DESCENDANT
DESCENDANTS
DESCENDED
DESCENDENT
DESCENDENTS
DESCENDER

DESCENDERS
DESCENDEUR
DESCENDEURS
DESCENDIBLE
DESCENDING
DESCENDINGS
DESCENDS
DESCENSION
DESCENSIONAL
DESCENSIONS
DESCENT
DESCENTS
DESCHOOL
DESCHOOLED
DESCHOOLER
DESCHOOLERS
DESCHOOLING
DESCHOOLINGS
DESCHOOLS
DESCRAMBLE
DESCRAMBLED
DESCRAMBLER
DESCRAMBLERS
DESCRAMBLES
DESCRAMBLING
DESCRIBABLE
DESCRIBE
DESCRIBED
DESCRIBER
DESCRIBERS
DESCRIBES
DESCRIBING
DESCRIED
DESCRIER
DESCRIERS
DESCRIES
DESCRIPTION
DESCRIPTIONS
DESCRIPTIVE
DESCRIPTIVELY
DESCRIPTIVENESS
DESCRIPTIVISM
DESCRIPTIVISMS
DESCRIPTIVIST
DESCRIPTIVISTS
DESCRIPTOR
DESCRIPTORS
DESCRIVE
DESCRIVED
DESCRIVES
DESCRIVING
DESCRY
DESCRYING
DESECRATE
DESECRATED
DESECRATER

DESECRATERS
DESECRATES
DESECRATING
DESECRATION
DESECRATIONS
DESECRATOR
DESECRATORS
DESEGREGATE
DESEGREGATED
DESEGREGATES
DESEGREGATING
DESEGREGATION
DESEGREGATIONS
DESELECT
DESELECTED
DESELECTING
DESELECTION
DESELECTIONS
DESELECTS
DESENSITISATION
DESENSITISE
DESENSITISED
DESENSITISER
DESENSITISERS
DESENSITISES
DESENSITISING
DESENSITIZATION
DESENSITIZE
DESENSITIZED
DESENSITIZER
DESENSITIZERS
DESENSITIZES
DESENSITIZING
DESERPIDINE
DESERPIDINES
DESERT
DESERTED
DESERTER
DESERTERS
DESERTIC
DESERTIFICATION
DESERTING
DESERTION
DESERTIONS
DESERTISATION
DESERTISATIONS
DESERTIZATION
DESERTIZATIONS
DESERTLESS
DESERTS
DESERVE
DESERVED
DESERVEDLY
DESERVEDNESS
DESERVEDNESSES
DESERVER

DESERVERS
DESERVES
DESERVING
DESERVINGLY
DESERVINGNESS
DESERVINGS
DESEX
DESEXED
DESEXES
DESEXING
DESEXUALISATION
DESEXUALISE
DESEXUALISED
DESEXUALISES
DESEXUALISING
DESEXUALIZATION
DESEXUALIZE
DESEXUALIZED
DESEXUALIZES
DESEXUALIZING
DESHABILLE
DESHABILLES
DESICCANT
DESICCANTS
DESICCATE
DESICCATED
DESICCATES
DESICCATING
DESICCATION
DESICCATIONS
DESICCATIVE
DESICCATIVES
DESICCATOR
DESICCATORS
DESIDERATA
DESIDERATE
DESIDERATED
DESIDERATES
DESIDERATING
DESIDERATION
DESIDERATIONS
DESIDERATIVE
DESIDERATIVES
DESIDERATUM
DESIDERIUM
DESIDERIUMS
DESIGN
DESIGNABLE
DESIGNATE
DESIGNATED
DESIGNATES
DESIGNATING
DESIGNATION
DESIGNATIONS
DESIGNATIVE
DESIGNATOR

DESIGNATORS
DESIGNATORY
DESIGNED
DESIGNEDLY
DESIGNEE
DESIGNEES
DESIGNER
DESIGNERS
DESIGNFUL
DESIGNING
DESIGNINGLY
DESIGNINGS
DESIGNLESS
DESIGNMENT
DESIGNMENTS
DESIGNS
DESILVER
DESILVERED
DESILVERING
DESILVERISATION
DESILVERISE
DESILVERISED
DESILVERISES
DESILVERISING
DESILVERIZATION
DESILVERIZE
DESILVERIZED
DESILVERIZES
DESILVERIZING
DESILVERS
DESINE
DESINED
DESINENCE
DESINENCES
DESINENT
DESINENTIAL
DESINES
DESINING
DESIPIENCE
DESIPIENCES
DESIPIENT
DESIPRAMINE
DESIPRAMINES
DESIRABILITIES
DESIRABILITY
DESIRABLE
DESIRABLENESS
DESIRABLENESSES
DESIRABLES
DESIRABLY
DESIRE
DESIRED
DESIRELESS
DESIRER
DESIRERS
DESIRES

DESIRING
DESIROUS
DESIROUSLY
DESIROUSNESS
DESIROUSNESSES
DESIST
DESISTANCE
DESISTANCES
DESISTED
DESISTENCE
DESISTENCES
DESISTING
DESISTS
DESK
DESKBOUND
DESKFAST
DESKFASTS
DESKILL
DESKILLED
DESKILLING
DESKILLS
DESKMAN
DESKMEN
DESKS
DESKTOP
DESKTOPS
DESMAN
DESMANS
DESMID
DESMIDIAN
DESMIDS
DESMINE
DESMINES
DESMODIUM
DESMODIUMS
DESMODROMIC
DESMOID
DESMOIDS
DESMOSOMAL
DESMOSOME
DESMOSOMES
DESNOOD
DESNOODED
DESNOODING
DESNOODS
DESOBLIGEANTE
DESOBLIGEANTES
DESOEUVRE
DESOLATE
DESOLATED
DESOLATELY
DESOLATENESS
DESOLATENESSES
DESOLATER
DESOLATERS
DESOLATES

DESOLATING
DESOLATINGLY
DESOLATION
DESOLATIONS
DESOLATOR
DESOLATORS
DESOLATORY
DESORB
DESORBED
DESORBING
DESORBS
DESORIENTE
DESORPTION
DESORPTIONS
DESOXY
DESOXYRIBOSE
DESPAIR
DESPAIRED
DESPAIRER
DESPAIRERS
DESPAIRFUL
DESPAIRING
DESPAIRINGLY
DESPAIRS
DESPATCH
DESPATCHED
DESPATCHER
DESPATCHERS
DESPATCHES
DESPATCHING
DESPERADO
DESPERADOES
DESPERADOS
DESPERATE
DESPERATELY
DESPERATENESS
DESPERATENESSES
DESPERATION
DESPERATIONS
DESPICABILITIES
DESPICABILITY
DESPICABLE
DESPICABLENESS
DESPICABLY
DESPIGHT
DESPIGHTS
DESPIRITUALIZE
DESPIRITUALIZED
DESPIRITUALIZES
DESPISABLE
DESPISAL
DESPISALS
DESPISE
DESPISED
DESPISEDNESS
DESPISEDNESSES

DESPISEMENT
DESPISEMENTS
DESPISER
DESPISERS
DESPISES
DESPISING
DESPITE
DESPITED
DESPITEFUL
DESPITEFULLY
DESPITEFULNESS
DESPITEOUS
DESPITEOUSLY
DESPITES
DESPITING
DESPOIL
DESPOILED
DESPOILER
DESPOILERS
DESPOILING
DESPOILMENT
DESPOILMENTS
DESPOILS
DESPOLIATION
DESPOLIATIONS
DESPOND
DESPONDED
DESPONDENCE
DESPONDENCES
DESPONDENCIES
DESPONDENCY
DESPONDENT
DESPONDENTLY
DESPONDING
DESPONDINGLY
DESPONDINGS
DESPONDS
DESPOT
DESPOTAT
DESPOTATE
DESPOTATES
DESPOTATS
DESPOTIC
DESPOTICAL
DESPOTICALLY
DESPOTICALNESS
DESPOTISM
DESPOTISMS
DESPOTOCRACIES
DESPOTOCRACY
DESPOTS
DESPUMATE
DESPUMATED
DESPUMATES
DESPUMATING
DESPUMATION

DESPUMATIONS
DESQUAMATE
DESQUAMATED
DESQUAMATES
DESQUAMATING
DESQUAMATION
DESQUAMATIONS
DESQUAMATIVE
DESQUAMATORY
DESSE
DESSERT
DESSERTS
DESSERTSPOON
DESSERTSPOONFUL
DESSERTSPOONS
DESSES
DESSIATINE
DESSIATINES
DESSIGNMENT
DESSIGNMENTS
DESSYATINE
DESSYATINES
DESTABILISATION
DESTABILISE
DESTABILISED
DESTABILISER
DESTABILISERS
DESTABILISES
DESTABILISING
DESTABILIZATION
DESTABILIZE
DESTABILIZED
DESTABILIZER
DESTABILIZERS
DESTABILIZES
DESTABILIZING
DESTAIN
DESTAINED
DESTAINING
DESTAINS
DESTEMPER
DESTEMPERED
DESTEMPERING
DESTEMPERS
DESTINATE
DESTINATED
DESTINATES
DESTINATING
DESTINATION
DESTINATIONS
DESTINE
DESTINED
DESTINES
DESTINIES
DESTINING
DESTINY

DESTITUTE
DESTITUTED
DESTITUTENESS
DESTITUTENESSES
DESTITUTES
DESTITUTING
DESTITUTION
DESTITUTIONS
DESTOCK
DESTOCKED
DESTOCKING
DESTOCKS
DESTRIER
DESTRIERS
DESTROY
DESTROYABLE
DESTROYED
DESTROYER
DESTROYERS
DESTROYING
DESTROYS
DESTRUCT
DESTRUCTED
DESTRUCTIBILITY
DESTRUCTIBLE
DESTRUCTING
DESTRUCTION
DESTRUCTIONAL
DESTRUCTIONIST
DESTRUCTIONISTS
DESTRUCTIONS
DESTRUCTIVE
DESTRUCTIVELY
DESTRUCTIVENESS
DESTRUCTIVES
DESTRUCTIVIST
DESTRUCTIVISTS
DESTRUCTIVITIES
DESTRUCTIVITY
DESTRUCTO
DESTRUCTOES
DESTRUCTOR
DESTRUCTORS
DESTRUCTOS
DESTRUCTS
DESUETUDE
DESUETUDES
DESUGAR
DESUGARED
DESUGARING
DESUGARS
DESULFUR
DESULFURED
DESULFURING
DESULFURIZATION
DESULFURIZE

DESULFURIZED
DESULFURIZES
DESULFURIZING
DESULFURS
DESULPHUR
DESULPHURATE
DESULPHURATED
DESULPHURATES
DESULPHURATING
DESULPHURATION
DESULPHURATIONS
DESULPHURED
DESULPHURING
DESULPHURISE
DESULPHURISED
DESULPHURISER
DESULPHURISERS
DESULPHURISES
DESULPHURISING
DESULPHURIZE
DESULPHURIZED
DESULPHURIZER
DESULPHURIZERS
DESULPHURIZES
DESULPHURIZING
DESULPHURS
DESULTORILY
DESULTORINESS
DESULTORINESSES
DESULTORY
DESYATIN
DESYATINS
DESYNE
DESYNED
DESYNES
DESYNING
DETACH
DETACHABILITIES
DETACHABILITY
DETACHABLE
DETACHABLY
DETACHED
DETACHEDLY
DETACHEDNESS
DETACHEDNESSES
DETACHER
DETACHERS
DETACHES
DETACHING
DETACHMENT
DETACHMENTS
DETAIL
DETAILED
DETAILEDLY
DETAILEDNESS
DETAILEDNESSES

DETAILER
DETAILERS
DETAILING
DETAILS
DETAIN
DETAINABLE
DETAINED
DETAINEE
DETAINEES
DETAINER
DETAINERS
DETAINING
DETAINMENT
DETAINMENTS
DETAINS
DETASSEL
DETASSELED
DETASSELING
DETASSELLED
DETASSELLING
DETASSELS
DETECT
DETECTABILITIES
DETECTABILITY
DETECTABLE
DETECTED
DETECTER
DETECTERS
DETECTIBLE
DETECTING
DETECTION
DETECTIONS
DETECTIVE
DETECTIVELIKE
DETECTIVES
DETECTIVIST
DETECTIVISTS
DETECTOPHONE
DETECTOPHONES
DETECTOR
DETECTORIST
DETECTORISTS
DETECTORS
DETECTS
DETENT
DETENTE
DETENTES
DETENTION
DETENTIONS
DETENTS
DETENU
DETENUE
DETENUES
DETENUS
DETER
DETERGE

DETERGED
DETERGENCE
DETERGENCES
DETERGENCIES
DETERGENCY
DETERGENT
DETERGENTS
DETERGER
DETERGERS
DETERGES
DETERGING
DETERIORATE
DETERIORATED
DETERIORATES
DETERIORATING
DETERIORATION
DETERIORATIONS
DETERIORATIVE
DETERIORISM
DETERIORISMS
DETERIORITIES
DETERIORITY
DETERMENT
DETERMENTS
DETERMINABILITY
DETERMINABLE
DETERMINABLY
DETERMINACIES
DETERMINACY
DETERMINANT
DETERMINANTAL
DETERMINANTS
DETERMINATE
DETERMINATED
DETERMINATELY
DETERMINATENESS
DETERMINATES
DETERMINATING
DETERMINATION
DETERMINATIONS
DETERMINATIVE
DETERMINATIVELY
DETERMINATIVES
DETERMINATOR
DETERMINATORS
DETERMINE
DETERMINED
DETERMINEDLY
DETERMINEDNESS
DETERMINER
DETERMINERS
DETERMINES
DETERMINING
DETERMINISM
DETERMINISMS
DETERMINIST

DETERMINISTIC
DETERMINISTS
DETERRABILITIES
DETERRABILITY
DETERRABLE
DETERRED
DETERRENCE
DETERRENCES
DETERRENT
DETERRENTLY
DETERRENTS
DETERRER
DETERRERS
DETERRING
DETERS
DETERSION
DETERSIONS
DETERSIVE
DETERSIVES
DETEST
DETESTABILITIES
DETESTABILITY
DETESTABLE
DETESTABLENESS
DETESTABLY
DETESTATION
DETESTATIONS
DETESTED
DETESTER
DETESTERS
DETESTING
DETESTS
DETHRONE
DETHRONED
DETHRONEMENT
DETHRONEMENTS
DETHRONER
DETHRONERS
DETHRONES
DETHRONING
DETHRONINGS
DETICK
DETICKED
DETICKER
DETICKERS
DETICKING
DETICKS
DETINUE
DETINUES
DETONABILITIES
DETONABILITY
DETONABLE
DETONATABLE
DETONATE
DETONATED
DETONATES

DETONATING
DETONATION
DETONATIONS
DETONATIVE
DETONATOR
DETONATORS
DETORSION
DETORSIONS
DETORT
DETORTED
DETORTING
DETORTION
DETORTIONS
DETORTS
DETOUR
DETOURED
DETOURING
DETOURS
DETOX
DETOXED
DETOXES
DETOXICANT
DETOXICANTS
DETOXICATE
DETOXICATED
DETOXICATES
DETOXICATING
DETOXICATION
DETOXICATIONS
DETOXIFICATION
DETOXIFICATIONS
DETOXIFIED
DETOXIFIES
DETOXIFY
DETOXIFYING
DETOXING
DETRACT
DETRACTED
DETRACTING
DETRACTINGLY
DETRACTINGS
DETRACTION
DETRACTIONS
DETRACTIVE
DETRACTIVELY
DETRACTOR
DETRACTORS
DETRACTORY
DETRACTRESS
DETRACTRESSES
DETRACTS
DETRAIN
DETRAINED
DETRAINING
DETRAINMENT
DETRAINMENTS

DETRAINS
DETRAQUE
DETRAQUEE
DETRAQUEES
DETRAQUES
DETRIBALISATION
DETRIBALISE
DETRIBALISED
DETRIBALISES
DETRIBALISING
DETRIBALIZATION
DETRIBALIZE
DETRIBALIZED
DETRIBALIZES
DETRIBALIZING
DETRIMENT
DETRIMENTAL
DETRIMENTALLY
DETRIMENTALS
DETRIMENTS
DETRITAL
DETRITION
DETRITIONS
DETRITOVORE
DETRITOVORES
DETRITUS
DETRUDE
DETRUDED
DETRUDES
DETRUDING
DETRUNCATE
DETRUNCATED
DETRUNCATES
DETRUNCATING
DETRUNCATION
DETRUNCATIONS
DETRUSION
DETRUSIONS
DETUMESCENCE
DETUMESCENCES
DETUMESCENT
DETUNE
DETUNED
DETUNES
DETUNING
DEUCE
DEUCED
DEUCEDLY
DEUCES
DEUCING
DEUDDARN
DEUDDARNS
DEUS
DEUTERAGONIST
DEUTERAGONISTS
DEUTERANOMALIES

DEUTERANOMALOUS
DEUTERANOMALY
DEUTERANOPE
DEUTERANOPES
DEUTERANOPIA
DEUTERANOPIAS
DEUTERANOPIC
DEUTERATE
DEUTERATED
DEUTERATES
DEUTERATING
DEUTERATION
DEUTERATIONS
DEUTERIC
DEUTERIDE
DEUTERIDES
DEUTERIUM
DEUTERIUMS
DEUTEROGAMIES
DEUTEROGAMIST
DEUTEROGAMISTS
DEUTEROGAMY
DEUTERON
DEUTERONS
DEUTEROPLASM
DEUTEROPLASMS
DEUTEROSCOPIC
DEUTEROSCOPIES
DEUTEROSCOPY
DEUTEROSTOME
DEUTEROSTOMES
DEUTEROTOKIES
DEUTEROTOKY
DEUTON
DEUTONS
DEUTOPLASM
DEUTOPLASMIC
DEUTOPLASMS
DEUTOPLASTIC
DEUTOPLASTICITY
DEUTZIA
DEUTZIAS
DEV
DEVA
DEVALL
DEVALLED
DEVALLING
DEVALLS
DEVALORISATION
DEVALORISATIONS
DEVALORISE
DEVALORISED
DEVALORISES
DEVALORISING
DEVALORIZATION
DEVALORIZATIONS

DEVALORIZE
DEVALORIZED
DEVALORIZES
DEVALORIZING
DEVALUATE
DEVALUATED
DEVALUATES
DEVALUATING
DEVALUATION
DEVALUATIONS
DEVALUE
DEVALUED
DEVALUES
DEVALUING
DEVANAGARI
DEVANAGARIS
DEVAS
DEVASTATE
DEVASTATED
DEVASTATES
DEVASTATING
DEVASTATINGLY
DEVASTATION
DEVASTATIONS
DEVASTATIVE
DEVASTATOR
DEVASTATORS
DEVASTAVIT
DEVASTAVITS
DEVEIN
DEVEINED
DEVEINING
DEVEINS
DEVEL
DEVELED
DEVELING
DEVELLED
DEVELLING
DEVELOP
DEVELOPABLE
DEVELOPE
DEVELOPED
DEVELOPER
DEVELOPERS
DEVELOPES
DEVELOPING
DEVELOPMENT
DEVELOPMENTAL
DEVELOPMENTALLY
DEVELOPMENTS
DEVELOPS
DEVELS
DEVERBAL
DEVERBATIVE
DEVERBATIVES
DEVEST

DEVESTED
DEVESTING
DEVESTS
DEVIANCE
DEVIANCES
DEVIANCIES
DEVIANCY
DEVIANT
DEVIANTS
DEVIATE
DEVIATED
DEVIATES
DEVIATING
DEVIATION
DEVIATIONISM
DEVIATIONISMS
DEVIATIONIST
DEVIATIONISTS
DEVIATIONS
DEVIATOR
DEVIATORS
DEVIATORY
DEVICE
DEVICEFUL
DEVICES
DEVIL
DEVILDOM
DEVILDOMS
DEVILED
DEVILESS
DEVILESSES
DEVILET
DEVILETS
DEVILFISH
DEVILFISHES
DEVILING
DEVILINGS
DEVILISH
DEVILISHLY
DEVILISHNESS
DEVILISHNESSES
DEVILISM
DEVILISMS
DEVILKIN
DEVILKINS
DEVILLED
DEVILLING
DEVILMENT
DEVILMENTS
DEVILRIES
DEVILRY
DEVILS
DEVILSHIP
DEVILSHIPS
DEVILTRIES
DEVILTRY

DEVILWOOD
DEVILWOODS
DEVIOUS
DEVIOUSLY
DEVIOUSNESS
DEVIOUSNESSES
DEVISABLE
DEVISAL
DEVISALS
DEVISE
DEVISED
DEVISEE
DEVISEES
DEVISER
DEVISERS
DEVISES
DEVISING
DEVISOR
DEVISORS
DEVITALISATION
DEVITALISATIONS
DEVITALISE
DEVITALISED
DEVITALISES
DEVITALISING
DEVITALIZATION
DEVITALIZATIONS
DEVITALIZE
DEVITALIZED
DEVITALIZES
DEVITALIZING
DEVITRIFICATION
DEVITRIFIED
DEVITRIFIES
DEVITRIFY
DEVITRIFYING
DEVLING
DEVLINGS
DEVOCALISE
DEVOCALISED
DEVOCALISES
DEVOCALISING
DEVOCALIZE
DEVOCALIZED
DEVOCALIZES
DEVOCALIZING
DEVOICE
DEVOICED
DEVOICES
DEVOICING
DEVOID
DEVOIR
DEVOIRS
DEVOLUTION
DEVOLUTIONARY
DEVOLUTIONIST

DEVOLUTIONISTS
DEVOLUTIONS
DEVOLVE
DEVOLVED
DEVOLVEMENT
DEVOLVEMENTS
DEVOLVES
DEVOLVING
DEVON
DEVONPORT
DEVONPORTS
DEVONS
DEVORE
DEVORES
DEVOT
DEVOTE
DEVOTED
DEVOTEDLY
DEVOTEDNESS
DEVOTEDNESSES
DEVOTEE
DEVOTEES
DEVOTEMENT
DEVOTEMENTS
DEVOTES
DEVOTING
DEVOTION
DEVOTIONAL
DEVOTIONALIST
DEVOTIONALISTS
DEVOTIONALITIES
DEVOTIONALITY
DEVOTIONALLY
DEVOTIONALNESS
DEVOTIONALS
DEVOTIONIST
DEVOTIONISTS
DEVOTIONS
DEVOTS
DEVOUR
DEVOURED
DEVOURER
DEVOURERS
DEVOURING
DEVOURINGLY
DEVOURMENT
DEVOURMENTS
DEVOURS
DEVOUT
DEVOUTER
DEVOUTEST
DEVOUTLY
DEVOUTNESS
DEVOUTNESSES
DEVS
DEVVEL

DEVVELLED
DEVVELLING
DEVVELS
DEW
DEWAN
DEWANI
DEWANIS
DEWANNIES
DEWANNY
DEWANS
DEWAR
DEWARS
DEWATER
DEWATERED
DEWATERER
DEWATERERS
DEWATERING
DEWATERINGS
DEWATERS
DEWAX
DEWAXED
DEWAXES
DEWAXING
DEWBERRIES
DEWBERRY
DEWCLAW
DEWCLAWED
DEWCLAWS
DEWDROP
DEWDROPS
DEWED
DEWFALL
DEWFALLS
DEWFULL
DEWIER
DEWIEST
DEWILY
DEWINESS
DEWINESSES
DEWING
DEWITT
DEWITTED
DEWITTING
DEWITTS
DEWLAP
DEWLAPPED
DEWLAPS
DEWLAPT
DEWLESS
DEWOOL
DEWOOLED
DEWOOLING
DEWOOLS
DEWORM
DEWORMED
DEWORMER

DEWORMERS
DEWORMING
DEWORMS
DEWPOINT
DEWPOINTS
DEWS
DEWY
DEX
DEXAMETHASONE
DEXAMETHASONES
DEXAMPHETAMINE
DEXAMPHETAMINES
DEXES
DEXIE
DEXIES
DEXIOTROPIC
DEXTER
DEXTERITIES
DEXTERITY
DEXTEROUS
DEXTEROUSLY
DEXTEROUSNESS
DEXTEROUSNESSES
DEXTERS
DEXTERWISE
DEXTRAL
DEXTRALITIES
DEXTRALITY
DEXTRALLY
DEXTRAN
DEXTRANASE
DEXTRANASES
DEXTRANS
DEXTRIN
DEXTRINE
DEXTRINES
DEXTRINS
DEXTRO
DEXTROCARDIA
DEXTROCARDIAC
DEXTROCARDIACS
DEXTROCARDIAS
DEXTROGLUCOSE
DEXTROGYRATE
DEXTROGYRE
DEXTROROTARY
DEXTROROTATION
DEXTROROTATIONS
DEXTROROTATORY
DEXTRORSAL
DEXTRORSE
DEXTRORSELY
DEXTROSE
DEXTROSES
DEXTROUS
DEXTROUSLY

DEXTROUSNESS	DHUTIS	DIACHYLUMS	DIAGNOSTICAL
DEXTROUSNESSES	DI	DIACID	DIAGNOSTICALLY
DEXY	DIABASE	DIACIDIC	DIAGNOSTICIAN
DEY	DIABASES	DIACIDS	DIAGNOSTICIANS
DEYS	DIABASIC	DIACODION	DIAGNOSTICS
DEZINC	DIABETES	DIACODIONS	DIAGOMETER
DEZINCED	DIABETIC	DIACODIUM	DIAGOMETERS
DEZINCING	DIABETICAL	DIACODIUMS	DIAGONAL
DEZINCKED	DIABETICS	DIACONAL	DIAGONALIZABLE
DEZINCKING	DIABETOGENIC	DIACONATE	DIAGONALIZATION
DEZINCS	DIABETOLOGIST	DIACONATES	DIAGONALIZE
DHAK	DIABETOLOGISTS	DIACONICON	DIAGONALIZED
DHAKS	DIABLE	DIACONICONS	DIAGONALIZES
DHAL	DIABLERIE	DIACOUSTIC	DIAGONALIZING
DHALS	DIABLERIES	DIACOUSTICS	DIAGONALLY
DHAMMA	DIABLERY	DIACRITIC	DIAGONALS
DHANSAK	DIABLES	DIACRITICAL	DIAGRAM
DHANSAKS	DIABOLIC	DIACRITICALLY	DIAGRAMED
DHARMA	DIABOLICAL	DIACRITICS	DIAGRAMING
DHARMAS	DIABOLICALLY	DIACT	DIAGRAMMABLE
DHARMIC	DIABOLICALNESS	DIACTINAL	DIAGRAMMATIC
DHARMSALA	DIABOLISE	DIACTINE	DIAGRAMMATICAL
DHARMSALAS	DIABOLISED	DIACTINIC	DIAGRAMMED
DHARMSHALA	DIABOLISES	DIACTINISM	DIAGRAMMING
DHARMSHALAS	DIABOLISING	DIADELPHOUS	DIAGRAMS
DHARNA	DIABOLISM	DIADEM	DIAGRAPH
DHARNAS	DIABOLISMS	DIADEMED	DIAGRAPHIC
DHOBI	DIABOLIST	DIADEMING	DIAGRAPHS
DHOBIS	DIABOLISTS	DIADEMS	DIAGRID
DHOL	DIABOLIZE	DIADOCHI	DIAGRIDS
DHOLE	DIABOLIZED	DIADOCHIES	DIAHELIOTROPIC
DHOLES	DIABOLIZES	DIADOCHY	DIAHELIOTROPISM
DHOLL	DIABOLIZING	DIADROM	DIAKINESES
DHOLLS	DIABOLO	DIADROMOUS	DIAKINESIS
DHOLS	DIABOLOGIES	DIADROMS	DIAL
DHOOLIES	DIABOLOGY	DIAERESES	DIALECT
DHOOLY	DIABOLOLOGIES	DIAERESIS	DIALECTAL
DHOORA	DIABOLOLOGY	DIAERETIC	DIALECTALLY
DHOORAS	DIABOLOS	DIAGENESES	DIALECTIC
DHOOTI	DIACATHOLICON	DIAGENESIS	DIALECTICAL
DHOOTIE	DIACATHOLICONS	DIAGENETIC	DIALECTICALLY
DHOOTIES	DIACAUSTIC	DIAGENETICALLY	DIALECTICIAN
DHOOTIS	DIACAUSTICS	DIAGEOTROPIC	DIALECTICIANS
DHOTI	DIACETYL	DIAGEOTROPISM	DIALECTICISM
DHOTIS	DIACETYLS	DIAGEOTROPISMS	DIALECTICISMS
DHOURRA	DIACHRONIC	DIAGLYPH	DIALECTICS
DHOURRAS	DIACHRONICALLY	DIAGLYPHS	DIALECTOLOGICAL
DHOW	DIACHRONIES	DIAGNOSABILITY	DIALECTOLOGIES
DHOWS	DIACHRONISM	DIAGNOSABLE	DIALECTOLOGIST
DHURNA	DIACHRONISMS	DIAGNOSE	DIALECTOLOGISTS
DHURNAS	DIACHRONISTIC	DIAGNOSEABLE	DIALECTOLOGY
DHURRA	DIACHRONOUS	DIAGNOSED	DIALECTS
DHURRAS	DIACHRONY	DIAGNOSES	DIALED
DHURRIE	DIACHYLON	DIAGNOSING	DIALER
DHURRIES	DIACHYLONS	DIAGNOSIS	DIALERS
DHUTI	DIACHYLUM	DIAGNOSTIC	DIALING

DIALINGS
DIALIST
DIALISTS
DIALLAGE
DIALLAGES
DIALLAGIC
DIALLAGOID
DIALLED
DIALLEL
DIALLER
DIALLERS
DIALLING
DIALLINGS
DIALLIST
DIALLISTS
DIALOG
DIALOGED
DIALOGER
DIALOGERS
DIALOGGED
DIALOGGING
DIALOGIC
DIALOGICAL
DIALOGICALLY
DIALOGING
DIALOGISE
DIALOGISED
DIALOGISES
DIALOGISING
DIALOGISM
DIALOGIST
DIALOGISTIC
DIALOGISTICAL
DIALOGISTS
DIALOGITE
DIALOGITES
DIALOGIZE
DIALOGIZED
DIALOGIZES
DIALOGIZING
DIALOGS
DIALOGUE
DIALOGUED
DIALOGUER
DIALOGUERS
DIALOGUES
DIALOGUING
DIALS
DIALYPETALOUS
DIALYSABILITY
DIALYSABLE
DIALYSATE
DIALYSATES
DIALYSATION
DIALYSE
DIALYSED

DIALYSER
DIALYSERS
DIALYSES
DIALYSING
DIALYSIS
DIALYTIC
DIALYTICALLY
DIALYZABILITY
DIALYZABLE
DIALYZATE
DIALYZATES
DIALYZATION
DIALYZE
DIALYZED
DIALYZER
DIALYZERS
DIALYZES
DIALYZING
DIAMAGNET
DIAMAGNETIC
DIAMAGNETICALLY
DIAMAGNETISM
DIAMAGNETISMS
DIAMAGNETS
DIAMANTE
DIAMANTES
DIAMANTIFEROUS
DIAMANTINE
DIAMETER
DIAMETERS
DIAMETRAL
DIAMETRALLY
DIAMETRIC
DIAMETRICAL
DIAMETRICALLY
DIAMIDE
DIAMIDES
DIAMIN
DIAMINE
DIAMINES
DIAMINS
DIAMOND
DIAMONDBACK
DIAMONDBACKS
DIAMONDED
DIAMONDIFEROUS
DIAMONDING
DIAMONDS
DIAMORPHINE
DIAMORPHINES
DIAMYL
DIANDRIES
DIANDROUS
DIANDRY
DIANODAL
DIANOETIC

DIANOIA
DIANTHUS
DIANTHUSES
DIAPASE
DIAPASES
DIAPASON
DIAPASONAL
DIAPASONIC
DIAPASONS
DIAPAUSE
DIAPAUSED
DIAPAUSES
DIAPAUSING
DIAPEDESES
DIAPEDESIS
DIAPEDETIC
DIAPENTE
DIAPENTES
DIAPER
DIAPERED
DIAPERING
DIAPERINGS
DIAPERS
DIAPHANEITIES
DIAPHANEITY
DIAPHANOMETER
DIAPHANOMETERS
DIAPHANOUS
DIAPHANOUSLY
DIAPHANOUSNESS
DIAPHONE
DIAPHONES
DIAPHONIC
DIAPHONICALLY
DIAPHONIES
DIAPHONY
DIAPHORASE
DIAPHORASES
DIAPHORESES
DIAPHORESIS
DIAPHORETIC
DIAPHORETICS
DIAPHOTOTROPIC
DIAPHOTOTROPIES
DIAPHOTOTROPISM
DIAPHRAGM
DIAPHRAGMAL
DIAPHRAGMATIC
DIAPHRAGMATITIS
DIAPHRAGMS
DIAPHYSEAL
DIAPHYSES
DIAPHYSIAL
DIAPHYSIS
DIAPIR
DIAPIRIC

DIAPIRISM
DIAPIRISMS
DIAPIRS
DIAPOPHYSES
DIAPOPHYSIAL
DIAPOPHYSIS
DIAPOSITIVE
DIAPOSITIVES
DIAPSID
DIAPYESES
DIAPYESIS
DIAPYETIC
DIAPYETICS
DIARCH
DIARCHAL
DIARCHIC
DIARCHICAL
DIARCHICALLY
DIARCHIES
DIARCHY
DIARIAL
DIARIAN
DIARIES
DIARISE
DIARISED
DIARISES
DIARISING
DIARIST
DIARISTS
DIARIZE
DIARIZED
DIARIZES
DIARIZING
DIARRHEA
DIARRHEAL
DIARRHEAS
DIARRHEIC
DIARRHETIC
DIARRHOEA
DIARRHOEAL
DIARRHOEAS
DIARRHOEIC
DIARTHRODIAL
DIARTHROSES
DIARTHROSIS
DIARY
DIASCOPE
DIASCOPES
DIASCORDIUM
DIASCORDIUMS
DIASKEUAST
DIASKEUASTS
DIASPORA
DIASPORAS
DIASPORE
DIASPORES

DIASTALSES
DIASTALSIS
DIASTALTIC
DIASTASE
DIASTASES
DIASTASIC
DIASTASIS
DIASTATIC
DIASTEM
DIASTEMA
DIASTEMATA
DIASTEMATIC
DIASTEMS
DIASTER
DIASTEREOISOMER
DIASTEREOMER
DIASTEREOMERIC
DIASTEREOMERS
DIASTERS
DIASTOLE
DIASTOLES
DIASTOLIC
DIASTRAL
DIASTROPHIC
DIASTROPHICALLY
DIASTROPHISM
DIASTROPHISMS
DIASTYLE
DIASTYLES
DIATESSARON
DIATESSARONS
DIATHERMACIES
DIATHERMACY
DIATHERMAL
DIATHERMANCIES
DIATHERMANCY
DIATHERMANEITY
DIATHERMANOUS
DIATHERMIA
DIATHERMIC
DIATHERMIES
DIATHERMOUS
DIATHERMY
DIATHESES
DIATHESIS
DIATHETIC
DIATOM
DIATOMACEOUS
DIATOMIC
DIATOMICITY
DIATOMIST
DIATOMISTS
DIATOMITE
DIATOMITES
DIATOMS
DIATONIC

DIATONICALLY
DIATONICISM
DIATRETUM
DIATRETUMS
DIATRIBE
DIATRIBES
DIATRIBIST
DIATRIBISTS
DIATRON
DIATRONS
DIATROPIC
DIATROPISM
DIATROPISMS
DIAXON
DIAXONS
DIAZEPAM
DIAZEPAMS
DIAZEUCTIC
DIAZEUXES
DIAZEUXIS
DIAZIN
DIAZINE
DIAZINES
DIAZINON
DIAZINONS
DIAZINS
DIAZO
DIAZOES
DIAZOLE
DIAZOLES
DIAZOMETHANE
DIAZONIUM
DIAZONIUMS
DIAZOS
DIAZOTISATION
DIAZOTISATIONS
DIAZOTISE
DIAZOTISED
DIAZOTISES
DIAZOTISING
DIAZOTIZATION
DIAZOTIZATIONS
DIAZOTIZE
DIAZOTIZED
DIAZOTIZES
DIAZOTIZING
DIB
DIBASIC
DIBASICITY
DIBBED
DIBBER
DIBBERED
DIBBERING
DIBBERS
DIBBING
DIBBLE

DIBBLED
DIBBLER
DIBBLERS
DIBBLES
DIBBLING
DIBBS
DIBBUK
DIBBUKIM
DIBBUKKIM
DIBBUKS
DIBENZOFURAN
DIBENZOFURANS
DIBRANCHIATE
DIBRANCHIATES
DIBROMIDE
DIBROMIDES
DIBS
DIBUTYL
DICACIOUS
DICACITIES
DICACITY
DICACODYL
DICARBOXYLIC
DICARPELLARY
DICAST
DICASTERIES
DICASTERY
DICASTIC
DICASTS
DICE
DICED
DICENTRA
DICENTRAS
DICENTRIC
DICENTRICS
DICEPHALISM
DICEPHALOUS
DICER
DICERS
DICES
DICEY
DICH
DICHASIA
DICHASIAL
DICHASIALLY
DICHASIUM
DICHLAMYDEOUS
DICHLORIDE
DICHLORIDES
DICHLOROBENZENE
DICHLOROETHANE
DICHLOROETHANES
DICHLOROMETHANE
DICHLORVOS
DICHLORVOSES
DICHOGAMIC

DICHOGAMIES
DICHOGAMOUS
DICHOGAMY
DICHONDRA
DICHONDRAS
DICHOPTIC
DICHOPTICALLY
DICHORD
DICHORDS
DICHOTIC
DICHOTICALLY
DICHOTOMIC
DICHOTOMIES
DICHOTOMISATION
DICHOTOMISE
DICHOTOMISED
DICHOTOMISES
DICHOTOMISING
DICHOTOMIST
DICHOTOMISTS
DICHOTOMIZATION
DICHOTOMIZE
DICHOTOMIZED
DICHOTOMIZES
DICHOTOMIZING
DICHOTOMOUS
DICHOTOMOUSLY
DICHOTOMOUSNESS
DICHOTOMY
DICHROIC
DICHROISCOPE
DICHROISCOPES
DICHROISCOPIC
DICHROISM
DICHROISMS
DICHROITE
DICHROITES
DICHROITIC
DICHROMAT
DICHROMATE
DICHROMATES
DICHROMATIC
DICHROMATICISM
DICHROMATICS
DICHROMATISM
DICHROMATISMS
DICHROMATS
DICHROMIC
DICHROMISM
DICHROMISMS
DICHROOSCOPE
DICHROOSCOPES
DICHROOSCOPIC
DICHROSCOPE
DICHROSCOPES
DICHROSCOPIC

DICHT
DICHTED
DICHTING
DICHTS
DICIER
DICIEST
DICING
DICINGS
DICK
DICKCISSEL
DICKCISSELS
DICKED
DICKENS
DICKENSES
DICKER
DICKERED
DICKERING
DICKERS
DICKEY
DICKEYBIRD
DICKEYBIRDS
DICKEYS
DICKHEAD
DICKHEADS
DICKIE
DICKIER
DICKIES
DICKIEST
DICKING
DICKS
DICKTIER
DICKTIEST
DICKTY
DICKY
DICKYBIRD
DICKYBIRDS
DICLINIES
DICLINISM
DICLINISMS
DICLINOUS
DICLINY
DICOT
DICOTS
DICOTYL
DICOTYLEDON
DICOTYLEDONOUS
DICOTYLEDONS
DICOTYLS
DICOUMARIN
DICOUMARINS
DICOUMAROL
DICOUMAROLS
DICROTAL
DICROTIC
DICROTISM
DICROTISMS

DICROTOUS
DICT
DICTA
DICTATE
DICTATED
DICTATES
DICTATING
DICTATION
DICTATIONAL
DICTATIONALLY
DICTATIONS
DICTATOR
DICTATORIAL
DICTATORIALLY
DICTATORIALNESS
DICTATORS
DICTATORSHIP
DICTATORSHIPS
DICTATORY
DICTATRESS
DICTATRESSES
DICTATRICES
DICTATRIX
DICTATRIXES
DICTATURE
DICTATURES
DICTED
DICTIER
DICTIEST
DICTING
DICTION
DICTIONAL
DICTIONALLY
DICTIONARIES
DICTIONARY
DICTIONS
DICTS
DICTUM
DICTUMS
DICTY
DICTYOGEN
DICTYOGENS
DICTYOPTERAN
DICTYOPTERANS
DICTYOSOME
DICTYOSOMES
DICTYOSTELE
DICTYOSTELES
DICUMAROL
DICUMAROLS
DICYCLIC
DICYCLIES
DICYCLY
DICYNODONT
DICYNODONTS
DID

DIDACT
DIDACTIC
DIDACTICAL
DIDACTICALLY
DIDACTICISM
DIDACTICISMS
DIDACTICS
DIDACTS
DIDACTYL
DIDACTYLISM
DIDACTYLOUS
DIDACTYLS
DIDAKAI
DIDAKAIS
DIDAKEI
DIDAKEIS
DIDAPPER
DIDAPPERS
DIDASCALIC
DIDDER
DIDDERED
DIDDERING
DIDDERS
DIDDICOY
DIDDICOYS
DIDDIER
DIDDIES
DIDDIEST
DIDDLE
DIDDLED
DIDDLER
DIDDLERS
DIDDLES
DIDDLEY
DIDDLEYS
DIDDLIES
DIDDLING
DIDDLY
DIDDY
DIDELPHIAN
DIDELPHIC
DIDELPHID
DIDELPHIDS
DIDELPHINE
DIDELPHOUS
DIDGERIDOO
DIDGERIDOOS
DIDICOI
DIDICOIS
DIDICOY
DIDICOYS
DIDIE
DIDIES
DIDJERIDOO
DIDJERIDOOS
DIDO

DIDOES
DIDOS
DIDRACHM
DIDRACHMA
DIDRACHMAS
DIDRACHMS
DIDST
DIDY
DIDYMIUM
DIDYMIUMS
DIDYMOUS
DIDYNAMIAN
DIDYNAMIES
DIDYNAMOUS
DIDYNAMY
DIE
DIEB
DIEBACK
DIEBACKS
DIEBS
DIECIOUS
DIECIOUSLY
DIECIOUSNESS
DIED
DIEDRAL
DIEDRALS
DIEDRE
DIEDRES
DIEFFENBACHIA
DIEFFENBACHIAS
DIEGESES
DIEGESIS
DIEHARD
DIEHARDS
DIEING
DIEL
DIELDRIN
DIELDRINS
DIELECTRIC
DIELECTRICALLY
DIELECTRICS
DIELYTRA
DIELYTRAS
DIEMAKER
DIEMAKERS
DIENCEPHALA
DIENCEPHALIC
DIENCEPHALON
DIENCEPHALONS
DIENE
DIENES
DIERESES
DIERESIS
DIERETIC
DIES
DIESEL

DIESELED
DIESELING
DIESELINGS
DIESELISATION
DIESELISATIONS
DIESELISE
DIESELISED
DIESELISES
DIESELISING
DIESELIZATION
DIESELIZATIONS
DIESELIZE
DIESELIZED
DIESELIZES
DIESELIZING
DIESELS
DIESES
DIESIS
DIESTER
DIESTERS
DIESTOCK
DIESTOCKS
DIESTROUS
DIESTRUM
DIESTRUMS
DIESTRUS
DIESTRUSES
DIET
DIETARIAN
DIETARIANS
DIETARIES
DIETARILY
DIETARY
DIETED
DIETER
DIETERS
DIETETIC
DIETETICAL
DIETETICALLY
DIETETICS
DIETHER
DIETHERS
DIETHYL
DIETHYLAMINE
DIETHYLAMINES
DIETHYLENE
DIETICIAN
DIETICIANS
DIETINE
DIETINES
DIETING
DIETIST
DIETISTS
DIETITIAN
DIETITIANS
DIETS

DIFFARREATION
DIFFARREATIONS
DIFFER
DIFFERED
DIFFERENCE
DIFFERENCED
DIFFERENCES
DIFFERENCIED
DIFFERENCIES
DIFFERENCING
DIFFERENCY
DIFFERENCYING
DIFFERENT
DIFFERENTIA
DIFFERENTIABLE
DIFFERENTIAE
DIFFERENTIAL
DIFFERENTIALLY
DIFFERENTIALS
DIFFERENTIATE
DIFFERENTIATED
DIFFERENTIATES
DIFFERENTIATING
DIFFERENTIATION
DIFFERENTIATOR
DIFFERENTIATORS
DIFFERENTLY
DIFFERENTNESS
DIFFERENTNESSES
DIFFERING
DIFFERS
DIFFICILE
DIFFICULT
DIFFICULTIES
DIFFICULTLY
DIFFICULTY
DIFFIDENCE
DIFFIDENCES
DIFFIDENT
DIFFIDENTLY
DIFFLUENT
DIFFORM
DIFFORMITIES
DIFFORMITY
DIFFRACT
DIFFRACTED
DIFFRACTING
DIFFRACTION
DIFFRACTIONS
DIFFRACTIVE
DIFFRACTIVELY
DIFFRACTIVENESS
DIFFRACTOMETER
DIFFRACTOMETERS
DIFFRACTOMETRIC
DIFFRACTOMETRY

DIFFRACTS
DIFFRANGIBILITY
DIFFRANGIBLE
DIFFUSE
DIFFUSED
DIFFUSEDLY
DIFFUSEDNESS
DIFFUSEDNESSES
DIFFUSELY
DIFFUSENESS
DIFFUSENESSES
DIFFUSER
DIFFUSERS
DIFFUSES
DIFFUSIBILITIES
DIFFUSIBILITY
DIFFUSIBLE
DIFFUSIBLENESS
DIFFUSING
DIFFUSION
DIFFUSIONAL
DIFFUSIONISM
DIFFUSIONISMS
DIFFUSIONIST
DIFFUSIONISTS
DIFFUSIONS
DIFFUSIVE
DIFFUSIVELY
DIFFUSIVENESS
DIFFUSIVENESSES
DIFFUSIVITIES
DIFFUSIVITY
DIFFUSOR
DIFFUSORS
DIFUNCTIONAL
DIFUNCTIONALS
DIG
DIGAMIES
DIGAMIST
DIGAMISTS
DIGAMMA
DIGAMMAS
DIGAMOUS
DIGAMY
DIGASTRIC
DIGASTRICS
DIGENESES
DIGENESIS
DIGENETIC
DIGERATI
DIGERATO
DIGEST
DIGESTANT
DIGESTANTS
DIGESTED
DIGESTEDLY

DIGESTER
DIGESTERS
DIGESTIBILITIES
DIGESTIBILITY
DIGESTIBLE
DIGESTIBLENESS
DIGESTIBLY
DIGESTIF
DIGESTIFS
DIGESTING
DIGESTION
DIGESTIONAL
DIGESTIONALLY
DIGESTIONS
DIGESTIVE
DIGESTIVELY
DIGESTIVES
DIGESTOR
DIGESTORS
DIGESTS
DIGGABLE
DIGGED
DIGGER
DIGGERS
DIGGING
DIGGINGS
DIGHT
DIGHTED
DIGHTING
DIGHTS
DIGIT
DIGITAL
DIGITALIN
DIGITALINS
DIGITALIS
DIGITALISATION
DIGITALISATIONS
DIGITALISE
DIGITALISED
DIGITALISES
DIGITALISING
DIGITALISM
DIGITALIZATION
DIGITALIZATIONS
DIGITALIZE
DIGITALIZED
DIGITALIZES
DIGITALIZING
DIGITALLY
DIGITALS
DIGITATE
DIGITATED
DIGITATELY
DIGITATION
DIGITATIONS
DIGITIFORM

DIGITIGRADE
DIGITIGRADES
DIGITISATION
DIGITISATIONS
DIGITISE
DIGITISED
DIGITISER
DIGITISERS
DIGITISES
DIGITISING
DIGITIZATION
DIGITIZATIONS
DIGITIZE
DIGITIZED
DIGITIZER
DIGITIZERS
DIGITIZES
DIGITIZING
DIGITONIN
DIGITONINS
DIGITORIUM
DIGITORIUMS
DIGITOXIGENIN
DIGITOXIGENINS
DIGITOXIN
DIGITOXINS
DIGITRON
DIGITRONS
DIGITS
DIGITULE
DIGITULES
DIGLADIATE
DIGLADIATED
DIGLADIATES
DIGLADIATING
DIGLADIATION
DIGLADIATIONS
DIGLADIATOR
DIGLADIATORS
DIGLOSSIA
DIGLOSSIAN
DIGLOT
DIGLOTS
DIGLOTTIC
DIGLYCERIDE
DIGLYCERIDES
DIGLYPH
DIGLYPHS
DIGNIFICATION
DIGNIFICATIONS
DIGNIFIED
DIGNIFIEDLY
DIGNIFIEDNESS
DIGNIFIES
DIGNIFY
DIGNIFYING

DIGNITARIES
DIGNITARY
DIGNITIES
DIGNITY
DIGONAL
DIGONEUTIC
DIGONEUTISM
DIGOXIN
DIGOXINS
DIGRAPH
DIGRAPHIC
DIGRAPHICALLY
DIGRAPHS
DIGRESS
DIGRESSED
DIGRESSER
DIGRESSERS
DIGRESSES
DIGRESSING
DIGRESSION
DIGRESSIONAL
DIGRESSIONARY
DIGRESSIONS
DIGRESSIVE
DIGRESSIVELY
DIGRESSIVENESS
DIGS
DIGYNIAN
DIGYNOUS
DIHEDRA
DIHEDRAL
DIHEDRALS
DIHEDRON
DIHEDRONS
DIHYBRID
DIHYBRIDISM
DIHYBRIDS
DIHYDRIC
DIJUDICATE
DIJUDICATED
DIJUDICATES
DIJUDICATING
DIJUDICATION
DIJUDICATIONS
DIKA
DIKAS
DIKAST
DIKASTS
DIKDIK
DIKDIKS
DIKE
DIKED
DIKER
DIKERS
DIKES
DIKEY

DIKIER
DIKIEST
DIKING
DIKKOP
DIKKOPS
DIKTAT
DIKTATS
DILACERATE
DILACERATED
DILACERATES
DILACERATING
DILACERATION
DILACERATIONS
DILAPIDATE
DILAPIDATED
DILAPIDATES
DILAPIDATING
DILAPIDATION
DILAPIDATIONS
DILAPIDATOR
DILAPIDATORS
DILATABILITIES
DILATABILITY
DILATABLE
DILATABLENESS
DILATANCIES
DILATANCY
DILATANT
DILATANTS
DILATATE
DILATATION
DILATATIONAL
DILATATIONS
DILATATOR
DILATATORS
DILATE
DILATED
DILATER
DILATERS
DILATES
DILATING
DILATION
DILATIONS
DILATIVE
DILATOMETER
DILATOMETERS
DILATOMETRIC
DILATOMETRIES
DILATOMETRY
DILATOR
DILATORILY
DILATORINESS
DILATORINESSES
DILATORS
DILATORY
DILDO

DILDOE
DILDOES
DILDOS
DILEMMA
DILEMMAS
DILEMMATIC
DILEMMIC
DILETTANTE
DILETTANTEISH
DILETTANTEISM
DILETTANTEISMS
DILETTANTES
DILETTANTI
DILETTANTISH
DILETTANTISM
DILETTANTISMS
DILIGENCE
DILIGENCES
DILIGENT
DILIGENTLY
DILL
DILLED
DILLI
DILLIER
DILLIES
DILLIEST
DILLING
DILLINGS
DILLIS
DILLS
DILLY
DILLYDALLIED
DILLYDALLIES
DILLYDALLY
DILLYDALLYING
DILUCIDATE
DILUCIDATED
DILUCIDATES
DILUCIDATING
DILUCIDATION
DILUCIDATIONS
DILUENT
DILUENTS
DILUTABLE
DILUTABLES
DILUTE
DILUTED
DILUTEE
DILUTEES
DILUTENESS
DILUTENESSES
DILUTER
DILUTERS
DILUTES
DILUTING
DILUTION

DILUTIONARY
DILUTIONS
DILUTIVE
DILUTOR
DILUTORS
DILUVIA
DILUVIAL
DILUVIALISM
DILUVIALISMS
DILUVIALIST
DILUVIALISTS
DILUVIAN
DILUVION
DILUVIONS
DILUVIUM
DILUVIUMS
DIM
DIMBLE
DIMBLES
DIME
DIMENHYDRINATE
DIMENHYDRINATES
DIMENSION
DIMENSIONAL
DIMENSIONALITY
DIMENSIONALLY
DIMENSIONED
DIMENSIONING
DIMENSIONLESS
DIMENSIONS
DIMER
DIMERCAPROL
DIMERCAPROLS
DIMERIC
DIMERISATION
DIMERISATIONS
DIMERISE
DIMERISED
DIMERISES
DIMERISING
DIMERISM
DIMERISMS
DIMERIZATION
DIMERIZATIONS
DIMERIZE
DIMERIZED
DIMERIZES
DIMERIZING
DIMEROUS
DIMERS
DIMES
DIMETER
DIMETERS
DIMETHOATE
DIMETHOATES
DIMETHYL

DIMETHYLAMINE
DIMETHYLAMINES
DIMETHYLANILINE
DIMETHYLS
DIMETRIC
DIMIDIATE
DIMIDIATED
DIMIDIATES
DIMIDIATING
DIMIDIATION
DIMIDIATIONS
DIMINISH
DIMINISHABLE
DIMINISHED
DIMINISHES
DIMINISHING
DIMINISHINGLY
DIMINISHINGS
DIMINISHMENT
DIMINISHMENTS
DIMINUENDO
DIMINUENDOES
DIMINUENDOS
DIMINUTION
DIMINUTIONS
DIMINUTIVAL
DIMINUTIVE
DIMINUTIVELY
DIMINUTIVENESS
DIMINUTIVES
DIMISSORY
DIMITIES
DIMITY
DIMLY
DIMMABLE
DIMMED
DIMMER
DIMMERS
DIMMEST
DIMMING
DIMMISH
DIMNESS
DIMNESSES
DIMORPH
DIMORPHIC
DIMORPHISM
DIMORPHISMS
DIMORPHOUS
DIMORPHS
DIMOUT
DIMOUTS
DIMPLE
DIMPLED
DIMPLEMENT
DIMPLEMENTS
DIMPLES

DIMPLIER
DIMPLIEST
DIMPLING
DIMPLY
DIMPSY
DIMS
DIMWIT
DIMWITS
DIMYARIAN
DIN
DINANDERIE
DINANDERIES
DINAR
DINARCHIES
DINARCHY
DINARS
DINDLE
DINDLED
DINDLES
DINDLING
DINE
DINED
DINER
DINERIC
DINERO
DINEROS
DINERS
DINES
DINETTE
DINETTES
DINFUL
DING
DINGBAT
DINGBATS
DINGDONG
DINGDONGED
DINGDONGING
DINGDONGS
DINGE
DINGED
DINGER
DINGERS
DINGES
DINGESES
DINGEY
DINGEYS
DINGHIES
DINGHY
DINGIER
DINGIES
DINGIEST
DINGILY
DINGINESS
DINGINESSES
DINGING
DINGLE

DINGLEBERRIES
DINGLEBERRY
DINGLES
DINGO
DINGOED
DINGOES
DINGOING
DINGS
DINGUS
DINGUSES
DINGY
DINIC
DINICS
DINING
DINITRO
DINITROBENZENE
DINITROBENZENES
DINITROGEN
DINITROPHENOL
DINITROPHENOLS
DINK
DINKED
DINKER
DINKEST
DINKEY
DINKEYS
DINKIE
DINKIER
DINKIES
DINKIEST
DINKING
DINKLY
DINKS
DINKUM
DINKUMS
DINKY
DINMONT
DINMONTS
DINNA
DINNED
DINNER
DINNERED
DINNERING
DINNERLESS
DINNERS
DINNERTIME
DINNERTIMES
DINNERWARE
DINNERWARES
DINNING
DINNLE
DINNLED
DINNLES
DINNLING
DINO
DINOCERAS

DINOCERASES
DINOFLAGELLATE
DINOFLAGELLATES
DINOMANIA
DINOMANIAS
DINOS
DINOSAUR
DINOSAURIAN
DINOSAURIC
DINOSAURS
DINOTHERE
DINOTHERES
DINOTHERIUM
DINOTHERIUMS
DINOTURBATION
DINOTURBATIONS
DINS
DINT
DINTED
DINTING
DINTLESS
DINTS
DINUCLEOTIDE
DINUCLEOTIDES
DIOBOL
DIOBOLON
DIOBOLONS
DIOBOLS
DIOCESAN
DIOCESANS
DIOCESE
DIOCESES
DIODE
DIODES
DIOECIES
DIOECIOUS
DIOECIOUSLY
DIOECIOUSNESS
DIOECISM
DIOECISMS
DIOECY
DIOESTRUS
DIOESTRUSES
DIOICOUS
DIOICOUSLY
DIOICOUSNESS
DIOL
DIOLEFIN
DIOLEFINS
DIOLS
DIOPHYSITE
DIOPHYSITES
DIOPSIDE
DIOPSIDES
DIOPSIDIC
DIOPTASE

DIOPTASES
DIOPTER
DIOPTERS
DIOPTOMETER
DIOPTOMETERS
DIOPTOMETRIC
DIOPTOMETRY
DIOPTRAL
DIOPTRATE
DIOPTRE
DIOPTRES
DIOPTRIC
DIOPTRICAL
DIOPTRICALLY
DIOPTRICS
DIORAMA
DIORAMAS
DIORAMIC
DIORISM
DIORISMS
DIORISTIC
DIORISTICAL
DIORISTICALLY
DIORITE
DIORITES
DIORITIC
DIORTHOSES
DIORTHOSIS
DIORTHOTIC
DIOSCOREACEOUS
DIOSGENIN
DIOSGENINS
DIOTA
DIOTAS
DIOTHELETES
DIOTHELETIC
DIOTHELETICAL
DIOTHELISMS
DIOTHELITES
DIOXAN
DIOXANE
DIOXANES
DIOXANS
DIOXID
DIOXIDE
DIOXIDES
DIOXIDS
DIOXIN
DIOXINS
DIP
DIPCHICK
DIPCHICKS
DIPEPTIDASE
DIPEPTIDASES
DIPEPTIDE
DIPEPTIDES

DIPETALOUS
DIPHASE
DIPHASIC
DIPHENHYDRAMINE
DIPHENYL
DIPHENYLAMINE
DIPHENYLAMINES
DIPHENYLENIMINE
DIPHENYLKETONE
DIPHENYLS
DIPHONE
DIPHONES
DIPHOSGENE
DIPHOSGENES
DIPHOSPHATE
DIPHOSPHATES
DIPHTHERIA
DIPHTHERIAL
DIPHTHERIAS
DIPHTHERIC
DIPHTHERITIC
DIPHTHERITIS
DIPHTHERITISES
DIPHTHEROID
DIPHTHEROIDS
DIPHTHONG
DIPHTHONGAL
DIPHTHONGALLY
DIPHTHONGIC
DIPHTHONGISE
DIPHTHONGISED
DIPHTHONGISES
DIPHTHONGISING
DIPHTHONGIZE
DIPHTHONGIZED
DIPHTHONGIZES
DIPHTHONGIZING
DIPHTHONGS
DIPHYCERCAL
DIPHYLETIC
DIPHYLLOUS
DIPHYODONT
DIPHYODONTS
DIPHYSITE
DIPHYSITES
DIPHYSITISM
DIPHYSITISMS
DIPLEGIA
DIPLEGIAS
DIPLEGIC
DIPLEGICS
DIPLEIDOSCOPE
DIPLEIDOSCOPES
DIPLEX
DIPLEXER
DIPLEXERS

DIPLOBIONT
DIPLOBIONTIC
DIPLOBIONTS
DIPLOBLASTIC
DIPLOCARDIAC
DIPLOCOCCAL
DIPLOCOCCI
DIPLOCOCCIC
DIPLOCOCCUS
DIPLODOCUS
DIPLODOCUSES
DIPLOE
DIPLOES
DIPLOGEN
DIPLOGENESES
DIPLOGENESIS
DIPLOGENS
DIPLOIC
DIPLOID
DIPLOIDIC
DIPLOIDIES
DIPLOIDS
DIPLOIDY
DIPLOMA
DIPLOMACIES
DIPLOMACY
DIPLOMAED
DIPLOMAING
DIPLOMAS
DIPLOMAT
DIPLOMATA
DIPLOMATE
DIPLOMATED
DIPLOMATES
DIPLOMATESE
DIPLOMATESES
DIPLOMATIC
DIPLOMATICAL
DIPLOMATICALLY
DIPLOMATICS
DIPLOMATING
DIPLOMATISE
DIPLOMATISED
DIPLOMATISES
DIPLOMATISING
DIPLOMATIST
DIPLOMATISTS
DIPLOMATIZE
DIPLOMATIZED
DIPLOMATIZES
DIPLOMATIZING
DIPLOMATOLOGIES
DIPLOMATOLOGY
DIPLOMATS
DIPLON
DIPLONEMA

DIPLONS
DIPLONT
DIPLONTIC
DIPLONTS
DIPLOPHASE
DIPLOPHASES
DIPLOPIA
DIPLOPIAS
DIPLOPIC
DIPLOPOD
DIPLOPODS
DIPLOSES
DIPLOSIS
DIPLOSTEMONOUS
DIPLOTENE
DIPLOTENES
DIPLOZOA
DIPLOZOIC
DIPLOZOON
DIPNET
DIPNETS
DIPNETTED
DIPNETTING
DIPNOAN
DIPNOANS
DIPNOOUS
DIPODIC
DIPODIES
DIPODY
DIPOLAR
DIPOLE
DIPOLES
DIPPABLE
DIPPED
DIPPER
DIPPERFUL
DIPPERFULS
DIPPERS
DIPPIER
DIPPIEST
DIPPING
DIPPINGS
DIPPY
DIPRIONIDIAN
DIPROPELLANT
DIPROPELLANTS
DIPROTODON
DIPROTODONS
DIPROTODONT
DIPROTODONTID
DIPROTODONTIDS
DIPROTODONTS
DIPS
DIPSADES
DIPSAS
DIPSO

DIPSOMANIA
DIPSOMANIAC
DIPSOMANIACAL
DIPSOMANIACS
DIPSOMANIAS
DIPSOS
DIPSTICK
DIPSTICKS
DIPT
DIPTERA
DIPTERAL
DIPTERAN
DIPTERANS
DIPTERAS
DIPTERIST
DIPTERISTS
DIPTEROCARP
DIPTEROCARPOUS
DIPTEROCARPS
DIPTEROI
DIPTERON
DIPTERONS
DIPTEROS
DIPTEROSES
DIPTEROUS
DIPTYCA
DIPTYCAS
DIPTYCH
DIPTYCHS
DIQUAT
DIQUATS
DIRDAM
DIRDAMS
DIRDUM
DIRDUMS
DIRE
DIRECT
DIRECTED
DIRECTEDNESS
DIRECTEDNESSES
DIRECTER
DIRECTEST
DIRECTING
DIRECTION
DIRECTIONAL
DIRECTIONALITY
DIRECTIONLESS
DIRECTIONS
DIRECTIVE
DIRECTIVES
DIRECTIVITIES
DIRECTIVITY
DIRECTLY
DIRECTNESS
DIRECTNESSES
DIRECTOR

DIRECTORATE
DIRECTORATES
DIRECTORIAL
DIRECTORIALLY
DIRECTORIES
DIRECTORS
DIRECTORSHIP
DIRECTORSHIPS
DIRECTORY
DIRECTRESS
DIRECTRESSES
DIRECTRICE
DIRECTRICES
DIRECTRIX
DIRECTRIXES
DIRECTS
DIREFUL
DIREFULLY
DIREFULNESS
DIREFULNESSES
DIRELY
DIREMPT
DIREMPTED
DIREMPTING
DIREMPTION
DIREMPTIONS
DIREMPTS
DIRENESS
DIRENESSES
DIRER
DIREST
DIRGE
DIRGEFUL
DIRGELIKE
DIRGES
DIRHAM
DIRHAMS
DIRHEM
DIRHEMS
DIRIGE
DIRIGENT
DIRIGES
DIRIGIBILITY
DIRIGIBLE
DIRIGIBLES
DIRIGISM
DIRIGISME
DIRIGISMES
DIRIGISMS
DIRIGISTE
DIRIMENT
DIRK
DIRKE
DIRKED
DIRKES
DIRKING

DIRKS
DIRL
DIRLED
DIRLING
DIRLS
DIRNDL
DIRNDLS
DIRT
DIRTBAG
DIRTBAGS
DIRTED
DIRTIED
DIRTIER
DIRTIES
DIRTIEST
DIRTILY
DIRTINESS
DIRTINESSES
DIRTING
DIRTS
DIRTY
DIRTYING
DIS
DISA
DISABILITIES
DISABILITY
DISABLE
DISABLED
DISABLEMENT
DISABLEMENTS
DISABLES
DISABLING
DISABUSAL
DISABUSALS
DISABUSE
DISABUSED
DISABUSES
DISABUSING
DISACCHARID
DISACCHARIDASE
DISACCHARIDASES
DISACCHARIDE
DISACCHARIDES
DISACCHARIDS
DISACCOMMODATE
DISACCOMMODATED
DISACCOMMODATES
DISACCORD
DISACCORDANT
DISACCORDED
DISACCORDING
DISACCORDS
DISACCREDIT
DISACCREDITED
DISACCREDITING
DISACCREDITS

DISACCUSTOM
DISACCUSTOMED
DISACCUSTOMING
DISACCUSTOMS
DISACKNOWLEDGE
DISACKNOWLEDGED
DISACKNOWLEDGES
DISADORN
DISADORNED
DISADORNING
DISADORNS
DISADVANCE
DISADVANCED
DISADVANCES
DISADVANCING
DISADVANTAGE
DISADVANTAGED
DISADVANTAGEOUS
DISADVANTAGES
DISADVANTAGING
DISADVENTURE
DISADVENTURES
DISADVENTUROUS
DISAFFECT
DISAFFECTED
DISAFFECTEDLY
DISAFFECTEDNESS
DISAFFECTING
DISAFFECTION
DISAFFECTIONATE
DISAFFECTIONS
DISAFFECTS
DISAFFILIATE
DISAFFILIATED
DISAFFILIATES
DISAFFILIATING
DISAFFILIATION
DISAFFILIATIONS
DISAFFIRM
DISAFFIRMANCE
DISAFFIRMANCES
DISAFFIRMATION
DISAFFIRMATIONS
DISAFFIRMED
DISAFFIRMING
DISAFFIRMS
DISAFFOREST
DISAFFORESTED
DISAFFORESTING
DISAFFORESTMENT
DISAFFORESTS
DISAGGREGATE
DISAGGREGATED
DISAGGREGATES
DISAGGREGATING
DISAGGREGATION

DISAGGREGATIONS
DISAGGREGATIVE
DISAGREE
DISAGREEABILITY
DISAGREEABLE
DISAGREEABLES
DISAGREEABLY
DISAGREED
DISAGREEING
DISAGREEMENT
DISAGREEMENTS
DISAGREES
DISALLIED
DISALLIES
DISALLOW
DISALLOWABLE
DISALLOWANCE
DISALLOWANCES
DISALLOWED
DISALLOWING
DISALLOWS
DISALLY
DISALLYING
DISAMBIGUATE
DISAMBIGUATED
DISAMBIGUATES
DISAMBIGUATING
DISAMBIGUATION
DISAMBIGUATIONS
DISAMENITIES
DISAMENITY
DISANALOGIES
DISANALOGOUS
DISANALOGY
DISANCHOR
DISANCHORED
DISANCHORING
DISANCHORS
DISANIMATE
DISANIMATED
DISANIMATES
DISANIMATING
DISANNEX
DISANNEXED
DISANNEXES
DISANNEXING
DISANNUL
DISANNULLED
DISANNULLER
DISANNULLERS
DISANNULLING
DISANNULLINGS
DISANNULMENT
DISANNULMENTS
DISANNULS
DISANOINT

DISANOINTED
DISANOINTING
DISANOINTS
DISAPPAREL
DISAPPARELLED
DISAPPARELLING
DISAPPARELS
DISAPPEAR
DISAPPEARANCE
DISAPPEARANCES
DISAPPEARED
DISAPPEARING
DISAPPEARS
DISAPPLICATION
DISAPPLICATIONS
DISAPPLIED
DISAPPLIES
DISAPPLY
DISAPPLYING
DISAPPOINT
DISAPPOINTED
DISAPPOINTEDLY
DISAPPOINTING
DISAPPOINTINGLY
DISAPPOINTMENT
DISAPPOINTMENTS
DISAPPOINTS
DISAPPROBATION
DISAPPROBATIONS
DISAPPROBATIVE
DISAPPROBATORY
DISAPPROPRIATE
DISAPPROPRIATED
DISAPPROPRIATES
DISAPPROVAL
DISAPPROVALS
DISAPPROVE
DISAPPROVED
DISAPPROVER
DISAPPROVERS
DISAPPROVES
DISAPPROVING
DISAPPROVINGLY
DISARM
DISARMAMENT
DISARMAMENTS
DISARMED
DISARMER
DISARMERS
DISARMING
DISARMINGLY
DISARMS
DISARRANGE
DISARRANGED
DISARRANGEMENT
DISARRANGEMENTS

DISARRANGES
DISARRANGING
DISARRAY
DISARRAYED
DISARRAYING
DISARRAYS
DISARTICULATE
DISARTICULATED
DISARTICULATES
DISARTICULATING
DISARTICULATION
DISARTICULATOR
DISARTICULATORS
DISAS
DISASSEMBLE
DISASSEMBLED
DISASSEMBLER
DISASSEMBLERS
DISASSEMBLES
DISASSEMBLIES
DISASSEMBLING
DISASSEMBLY
DISASSIMILATE
DISASSIMILATED
DISASSIMILATES
DISASSIMILATING
DISASSIMILATION
DISASSIMILATIVE
DISASSOCIATE
DISASSOCIATED
DISASSOCIATES
DISASSOCIATING
DISASSOCIATION
DISASSOCIATIONS
DISASTER
DISASTERS
DISASTROUS
DISASTROUSLY
DISATTIRE
DISATTIRED
DISATTIRES
DISATTIRING
DISATTRIBUTION
DISATTRIBUTIONS
DISATTUNE
DISATTUNED
DISATTUNES
DISATTUNING
DISAUTHORISE
DISAUTHORISED
DISAUTHORISES
DISAUTHORISING
DISAUTHORIZE
DISAUTHORIZED
DISAUTHORIZES
DISAUTHORIZING

DISAVAUNCE
DISAVAUNCED
DISAVAUNCES
DISAVAUNCING
DISAVENTURE
DISAVENTURES
DISAVOUCH
DISAVOUCHED
DISAVOUCHES
DISAVOUCHING
DISAVOW
DISAVOWABLE
DISAVOWAL
DISAVOWALS
DISAVOWED
DISAVOWEDLY
DISAVOWER
DISAVOWERS
DISAVOWING
DISAVOWS
DISBAND
DISBANDED
DISBANDING
DISBANDMENT
DISBANDMENTS
DISBANDS
DISBAR
DISBARK
DISBARKED
DISBARKING
DISBARKS
DISBARMENT
DISBARMENTS
DISBARRED
DISBARRING
DISBARS
DISBELIEF
DISBELIEFS
DISBELIEVE
DISBELIEVED
DISBELIEVER
DISBELIEVERS
DISBELIEVES
DISBELIEVING
DISBELIEVINGLY
DISBENCH
DISBENCHED
DISBENCHES
DISBENCHING
DISBENEFIT
DISBENEFITS
DISBODIED
DISBOSOM
DISBOSOMED
DISBOSOMING
DISBOSOMS

DISBOUND
DISBOWEL
DISBOWELED
DISBOWELING
DISBOWELLED
DISBOWELLING
DISBOWELS
DISBRANCH
DISBRANCHED
DISBRANCHES
DISBRANCHING
DISBUD
DISBUDDED
DISBUDDING
DISBUDS
DISBURDEN
DISBURDENED
DISBURDENING
DISBURDENMENT
DISBURDENMENTS
DISBURDENS
DISBURSABLE
DISBURSAL
DISBURSALS
DISBURSE
DISBURSED
DISBURSEMENT
DISBURSEMENTS
DISBURSER
DISBURSERS
DISBURSES
DISBURSING
DISBURTHEN
DISBURTHENED
DISBURTHENING
DISBURTHENS
DISC
DISCAGE
DISCAGED
DISCAGES
DISCAGING
DISCAL
DISCALCEATE
DISCALCEATES
DISCALCED
DISCANDERING
DISCANDERINGS
DISCANDIE
DISCANDIED
DISCANDIES
DISCANDY
DISCANDYING
DISCANDYINGS
DISCANT
DISCANTED
DISCANTER

DISCANTERS
DISCANTING
DISCANTS
DISCAPACITATE
DISCAPACITATED
DISCAPACITATES
DISCAPACITATING
DISCARD
DISCARDABLE
DISCARDED
DISCARDER
DISCARDERS
DISCARDING
DISCARDMENT
DISCARDMENTS
DISCARDS
DISCARNATE
DISCASE
DISCASED
DISCASES
DISCASING
DISCED
DISCEPT
DISCEPTATION
DISCEPTATIONS
DISCEPTATOR
DISCEPTATORS
DISCEPTED
DISCEPTING
DISCEPTS
DISCERN
DISCERNABILITY
DISCERNABLE
DISCERNABLY
DISCERNED
DISCERNER
DISCERNERS
DISCERNIBLE
DISCERNIBLY
DISCERNING
DISCERNINGLY
DISCERNMENT
DISCERNMENTS
DISCERNS
DISCERP
DISCERPED
DISCERPIBILITY
DISCERPIBLE
DISCERPING
DISCERPS
DISCERPTIBLE
DISCERPTION
DISCERPTIONS
DISCERPTIVE
DISCHARGE
DISCHARGEABLE

DISCHARGED
DISCHARGEE
DISCHARGEES
DISCHARGER
DISCHARGERS
DISCHARGES
DISCHARGING
DISCHUFFED
DISCHURCH
DISCHURCHED
DISCHURCHES
DISCHURCHING
DISCI
DISCIDE
DISCIDED
DISCIDES
DISCIDING
DISCIFORM
DISCINCT
DISCING
DISCIPLE
DISCIPLED
DISCIPLES
DISCIPLESHIP
DISCIPLESHIPS
DISCIPLINABLE
DISCIPLINAL
DISCIPLINANT
DISCIPLINANTS
DISCIPLINARIAN
DISCIPLINARIANS
DISCIPLINARILY
DISCIPLINARITY
DISCIPLINARIUM
DISCIPLINARIUMS
DISCIPLINARY
DISCIPLINE
DISCIPLINED
DISCIPLINER
DISCIPLINERS
DISCIPLINES
DISCIPLING
DISCIPLINING
DISCIPULAR
DISCISSION
DISCISSIONS
DISCLAIM
DISCLAIMED
DISCLAIMER
DISCLAIMERS
DISCLAIMING
DISCLAIMS
DISCLAMATION
DISCLAMATIONS
DISCLIKE
DISCLIMAX

DISCLIMAXES
DISCLOSE
DISCLOSED
DISCLOSER
DISCLOSERS
DISCLOSES
DISCLOSING
DISCLOST
DISCLOSURE
DISCLOSURES
DISCO
DISCOBOLI
DISCOBOLOS
DISCOBOLUS
DISCOBOLUSES
DISCOED
DISCOER
DISCOERS
DISCOGRAPHER
DISCOGRAPHERS
DISCOGRAPHIC
DISCOGRAPHICAL
DISCOGRAPHIES
DISCOGRAPHY
DISCOID
DISCOIDAL
DISCOIDS
DISCOING
DISCOLOGICAL
DISCOLOGICALLY
DISCOLOGIST
DISCOLOGISTS
DISCOLOGY
DISCOLOR
DISCOLORATION
DISCOLORATIONS
DISCOLORED
DISCOLORING
DISCOLORMENT
DISCOLORMENTS
DISCOLORS
DISCOLOUR
DISCOLOURATION
DISCOLOURATIONS
DISCOLOURED
DISCOLOURING
DISCOLOURMENT
DISCOLOURMENTS
DISCOLOURS
DISCOMBOBERATE
DISCOMBOBERATED
DISCOMBOBERATES
DISCOMBOBULATE
DISCOMBOBULATED
DISCOMBOBULATES
DISCOMEDUSAN

DISCOMEDUSANS
DISCOMFIT
DISCOMFITED
DISCOMFITER
DISCOMFITERS
DISCOMFITING
DISCOMFITS
DISCOMFITURE
DISCOMFITURES
DISCOMFORT
DISCOMFORTABLE
DISCOMFORTED
DISCOMFORTING
DISCOMFORTS
DISCOMMEND
DISCOMMENDABLE
DISCOMMENDATION
DISCOMMENDED
DISCOMMENDING
DISCOMMENDS
DISCOMMISSION
DISCOMMISSIONED
DISCOMMISSIONS
DISCOMMODE
DISCOMMODED
DISCOMMODES
DISCOMMODING
DISCOMMODIOUS
DISCOMMODIOUSLY
DISCOMMODITIES
DISCOMMODITY
DISCOMMON
DISCOMMONED
DISCOMMONING
DISCOMMONS
DISCOMMUNITIES
DISCOMMUNITY
DISCOMPOSE
DISCOMPOSED
DISCOMPOSEDLY
DISCOMPOSEDNESS
DISCOMPOSES
DISCOMPOSING
DISCOMPOSINGLY
DISCOMPOSURE
DISCOMPOSURES
DISCOMYCETE
DISCOMYCETES
DISCOMYCETOUS
DISCONCERT
DISCONCERTED
DISCONCERTEDLY
DISCONCERTING
DISCONCERTINGLY
DISCONCERTION
DISCONCERTIONS

DISCONCERTMENT
DISCONCERTMENTS
DISCONCERTS
DISCONFIRM
DISCONFIRMATION
DISCONFIRMED
DISCONFIRMING
DISCONFIRMS
DISCONFORMABLE
DISCONFORMITIES
DISCONFORMITY
DISCONNECT
DISCONNECTED
DISCONNECTEDLY
DISCONNECTER
DISCONNECTERS
DISCONNECTING
DISCONNECTION
DISCONNECTIONS
DISCONNECTIVE
DISCONNECTIVITY
DISCONNECTS
DISCONNEXION
DISCONNEXIONS
DISCONSENT
DISCONSENTED
DISCONSENTING
DISCONSENTS
DISCONSIDER
DISCONSIDERED
DISCONSIDERING
DISCONSIDERS
DISCONSOLATE
DISCONSOLATELY
DISCONSOLATION
DISCONSOLATIONS
DISCONTENT
DISCONTENTED
DISCONTENTEDLY
DISCONTENTFUL
DISCONTENTING
DISCONTENTMENT
DISCONTENTMENTS
DISCONTENTS
DISCONTIGUITIES
DISCONTIGUITY
DISCONTIGUOUS
DISCONTINUANCE
DISCONTINUANCES
DISCONTINUATION
DISCONTINUE
DISCONTINUED
DISCONTINUER
DISCONTINUERS
DISCONTINUES
DISCONTINUING

DISCONTINUITIES
DISCONTINUITY
DISCONTINUOUS
DISCONTINUOUSLY
DISCOPHIL
DISCOPHILE
DISCOPHILES
DISCOPHILS
DISCOPHORAN
DISCOPHORANS
DISCOPHOROUS
DISCORD
DISCORDANCE
DISCORDANCES
DISCORDANCIES
DISCORDANCY
DISCORDANT
DISCORDANTLY
DISCORDED
DISCORDFUL
DISCORDING
DISCORDS
DISCORPORATE
DISCOS
DISCOTHEQUE
DISCOTHEQUES
DISCOUNSEL
DISCOUNSELLED
DISCOUNSELLING
DISCOUNSELS
DISCOUNT
DISCOUNTABLE
DISCOUNTED
DISCOUNTENANCE
DISCOUNTENANCED
DISCOUNTENANCES
DISCOUNTER
DISCOUNTERS
DISCOUNTING
DISCOUNTS
DISCOURAGE
DISCOURAGEABLE
DISCOURAGED
DISCOURAGEMENT
DISCOURAGEMENTS
DISCOURAGER
DISCOURAGERS
DISCOURAGES
DISCOURAGING
DISCOURAGINGLY
DISCOURAGINGS
DISCOURE
DISCOURED
DISCOURES
DISCOURING
DISCOURSAL

DISCOURSE
DISCOURSED
DISCOURSER
DISCOURSERS
DISCOURSES
DISCOURSING
DISCOURSIVE
DISCOURTEISE
DISCOURTEOUS
DISCOURTEOUSLY
DISCOURTESIES
DISCOURTESY
DISCOVER
DISCOVERABLE
DISCOVERED
DISCOVERER
DISCOVERERS
DISCOVERIES
DISCOVERING
DISCOVERS
DISCOVERT
DISCOVERTURE
DISCOVERTURES
DISCOVERY
DISCREDIT
DISCREDITABLE
DISCREDITABLY
DISCREDITED
DISCREDITING
DISCREDITS
DISCREET
DISCREETER
DISCREETEST
DISCREETLY
DISCREETNESS
DISCREETNESSES
DISCREPANCE
DISCREPANCES
DISCREPANCIES
DISCREPANCY
DISCREPANT
DISCREPANTLY
DISCRETE
DISCRETELY
DISCRETENESS
DISCRETENESSES
DISCRETER
DISCRETEST
DISCRETION
DISCRETIONAL
DISCRETIONALLY
DISCRETIONARILY
DISCRETIONARY
DISCRETIONS
DISCRETIVE
DISCRETIVELY

DISCRIMINABLE
DISCRIMINABLY
DISCRIMINANT
DISCRIMINANTS
DISCRIMINATE
DISCRIMINATED
DISCRIMINATELY
DISCRIMINATES
DISCRIMINATING
DISCRIMINATION
DISCRIMINATIONS
DISCRIMINATIVE
DISCRIMINATOR
DISCRIMINATORS
DISCRIMINATORY
DISCROWN
DISCROWNED
DISCROWNING
DISCROWNS
DISCS
DISCULPATE
DISCULPATED
DISCULPATES
DISCULPATING
DISCUMBER
DISCUMBERED
DISCUMBERING
DISCUMBERS
DISCURE
DISCURED
DISCURES
DISCURING
DISCURSION
DISCURSIONS
DISCURSIST
DISCURSISTS
DISCURSIVE
DISCURSIVELY
DISCURSIVENESS
DISCURSORY
DISCURSUS
DISCURSUSES
DISCUS
DISCUSES
DISCUSS
DISCUSSABLE
DISCUSSANT
DISCUSSANTS
DISCUSSED
DISCUSSER
DISCUSSERS
DISCUSSES
DISCUSSIBLE
DISCUSSING
DISCUSSION
DISCUSSIONAL

DISCUSSIONALLY
DISCUSSIONS
DISCUSSIVE
DISCUTIENT
DISCUTIENTS
DISDAIN
DISDAINED
DISDAINFUL
DISDAINFULLY
DISDAINFULNESS
DISDAINING
DISDAINS
DISEASE
DISEASED
DISEASEDNESS
DISEASEDNESSES
DISEASEFUL
DISEASES
DISEASING
DISECONOMIES
DISECONOMY
DISED
DISEDGE
DISEDGED
DISEDGES
DISEDGING
DISEMBARK
DISEMBARKATION
DISEMBARKATIONS
DISEMBARKED
DISEMBARKING
DISEMBARKMENT
DISEMBARKMENTS
DISEMBARKS
DISEMBARRASS
DISEMBARRASSED
DISEMBARRASSES
DISEMBARRASSING
DISEMBELLISH
DISEMBELLISHED
DISEMBELLISHES
DISEMBELLISHING
DISEMBITTER
DISEMBITTERED
DISEMBITTERING
DISEMBITTERS
DISEMBODIED
DISEMBODIES
DISEMBODIMENT
DISEMBODIMENTS
DISEMBODY
DISEMBODYING
DISEMBOGUE
DISEMBOGUED
DISEMBOGUEMENT
DISEMBOGUEMENTS

DISEMBOGUES
DISEMBOGUING
DISEMBOSOM
DISEMBOSOMED
DISEMBOSOMING
DISEMBOSOMS
DISEMBOWEL
DISEMBOWELED
DISEMBOWELING
DISEMBOWELLED
DISEMBOWELLING
DISEMBOWELMENT
DISEMBOWELMENTS
DISEMBOWELS
DISEMBRANGLE
DISEMBRANGLED
DISEMBRANGLES
DISEMBRANGLING
DISEMBROIL
DISEMBROILED
DISEMBROILING
DISEMBROILS
DISEMBURDEN
DISEMBURDENED
DISEMBURDENING
DISEMBURDENS
DISEMPLOY
DISEMPLOYED
DISEMPLOYING
DISEMPLOYMENT
DISEMPLOYMENTS
DISEMPLOYS
DISEMPOWER
DISEMPOWERED
DISEMPOWERING
DISEMPOWERMENT
DISEMPOWERMENTS
DISEMPOWERS
DISENABLE
DISENABLED
DISENABLEMENT
DISENABLES
DISENABLING
DISENCHAIN
DISENCHAINED
DISENCHAINING
DISENCHAINS
DISENCHANT
DISENCHANTED
DISENCHANTER
DISENCHANTERS
DISENCHANTING
DISENCHANTINGLY
DISENCHANTMENT
DISENCHANTMENTS
DISENCHANTRESS

DISENCHANTS
DISENCLOSE
DISENCLOSED
DISENCLOSES
DISENCLOSING
DISENCUMBER
DISENCUMBERED
DISENCUMBERING
DISENCUMBERMENT
DISENCUMBERS
DISENCUMBRANCE
DISENCUMBRANCES
DISENDOW
DISENDOWED
DISENDOWER
DISENDOWERS
DISENDOWING
DISENDOWMENT
DISENDOWMENTS
DISENDOWS
DISENFRANCHISE
DISENFRANCHISED
DISENFRANCHISES
DISENGAGE
DISENGAGED
DISENGAGEDNESS
DISENGAGEMENT
DISENGAGEMENTS
DISENGAGES
DISENGAGING
DISENNOBLE
DISENNOBLED
DISENNOBLES
DISENNOBLING
DISENROL
DISENROLLED
DISENROLLING
DISENROLS
DISENSHROUD
DISENSHROUDED
DISENSHROUDING
DISENSHROUDS
DISENSLAVE
DISENSLAVED
DISENSLAVES
DISENSLAVING
DISENTAIL
DISENTAILED
DISENTAILING
DISENTAILMENT
DISENTAILMENTS
DISENTAILS
DISENTANGLE
DISENTANGLED
DISENTANGLEMENT
DISENTANGLES

DISENTANGLING
DISENTHRAL
DISENTHRALL
DISENTHRALLED
DISENTHRALLING
DISENTHRALLMENT
DISENTHRALLS
DISENTHRALMENT
DISENTHRALMENTS
DISENTHRALS
DISENTHRONE
DISENTHRONED
DISENTHRONES
DISENTHRONING
DISENTITLE
DISENTITLED
DISENTITLES
DISENTITLING
DISENTOMB
DISENTOMBED
DISENTOMBING
DISENTOMBS
DISENTRAIL
DISENTRAILED
DISENTRAILING
DISENTRAILS
DISENTRAIN
DISENTRAINED
DISENTRAINING
DISENTRAINMENT
DISENTRAINMENTS
DISENTRAINS
DISENTRANCE
DISENTRANCED
DISENTRANCEMENT
DISENTRANCES
DISENTRANCING
DISENTRAYLE
DISENTRAYLED
DISENTRAYLES
DISENTRAYLING
DISENTWINE
DISENTWINED
DISENTWINES
DISENTWINING
DISENVELOP
DISENVELOPED
DISENVELOPING
DISENVELOPS
DISENVIRON
DISENVIRONED
DISENVIRONING
DISENVIRONS
DISEPALOUS
DISEQUILIBRATE
DISEQUILIBRATED

DISEQUILIBRATES
DISEQUILIBRIA
DISEQUILIBRIUM
DISEQUILIBRIUMS
DISES
DISESPOUSE
DISESPOUSED
DISESPOUSES
DISESPOUSING
DISESTABLISH
DISESTABLISHED
DISESTABLISHES
DISESTABLISHING
DISESTEEM
DISESTEEMED
DISESTEEMING
DISESTEEMS
DISESTIMATION
DISESTIMATIONS
DISEUR
DISEURS
DISEUSE
DISEUSES
DISFAME
DISFAMES
DISFAVOR
DISFAVORED
DISFAVORING
DISFAVORS
DISFAVOUR
DISFAVOURED
DISFAVOURER
DISFAVOURERS
DISFAVOURING
DISFAVOURS
DISFEATURE
DISFEATURED
DISFEATUREMENT
DISFEATUREMENTS
DISFEATURES
DISFEATURING
DISFELLOWSHIP
DISFELLOWSHIPS
DISFIGURATION
DISFIGURATIONS
DISFIGURE
DISFIGURED
DISFIGUREMENT
DISFIGUREMENTS
DISFIGURER
DISFIGURERS
DISFIGURES
DISFIGURING
DISFLESH
DISFLESHED
DISFLESHES

DISFLESHING
DISFLUENCIES
DISFLUENCY
DISFLUENT
DISFOREST
DISFORESTATION
DISFORESTED
DISFORESTING
DISFORESTS
DISFORM
DISFORMED
DISFORMING
DISFORMS
DISFRANCHISE
DISFRANCHISED
DISFRANCHISES
DISFRANCHISING
DISFROCK
DISFROCKED
DISFROCKING
DISFROCKS
DISFUNCTION
DISFUNCTIONS
DISFURNISH
DISFURNISHED
DISFURNISHES
DISFURNISHING
DISFURNISHMENT
DISFURNISHMENTS
DISGARNISH
DISGARNISHED
DISGARNISHES
DISGARNISHING
DISGARRISON
DISGARRISONED
DISGARRISONING
DISGARRISONS
DISGAVEL
DISGAVELLED
DISGAVELLING
DISGAVELS
DISGEST
DISGESTED
DISGESTING
DISGESTION
DISGESTIONS
DISGESTS
DISGLORIFIED
DISGLORIFIES
DISGLORIFY
DISGLORIFYING
DISGODDED
DISGORGE
DISGORGED
DISGORGEMENT
DISGORGEMENTS

DISGORGER
DISGORGERS
DISGORGES
DISGORGING
DISGOSPELLING
DISGOWN
DISGOWNED
DISGOWNING
DISGOWNS
DISGRACE
DISGRACED
DISGRACEFUL
DISGRACEFULLY
DISGRACEFULNESS
DISGRACER
DISGRACERS
DISGRACES
DISGRACING
DISGRACIOUS
DISGRADATION
DISGRADATIONS
DISGRADE
DISGRADED
DISGRADES
DISGRADING
DISGREGATION
DISGREGATIONS
DISGRUNTLE
DISGRUNTLED
DISGRUNTLEMENT
DISGRUNTLEMENTS
DISGRUNTLES
DISGRUNTLING
DISGUISABLE
DISGUISE
DISGUISED
DISGUISEDLY
DISGUISEDNESS
DISGUISEDNESSES
DISGUISELESS
DISGUISEMENT
DISGUISEMENTS
DISGUISER
DISGUISERS
DISGUISES
DISGUISING
DISGUISINGS
DISGUST
DISGUSTED
DISGUSTEDLY
DISGUSTEDNESS
DISGUSTEDNESSES
DISGUSTFUL
DISGUSTFULLY
DISGUSTFULNESS
DISGUSTING

DISGUSTINGLY
DISGUSTINGNESS
DISGUSTS
DISH
DISHABILITATE
DISHABILITATED
DISHABILITATES
DISHABILITATING
DISHABILITATION
DISHABILLE
DISHABILLES
DISHABIT
DISHABITED
DISHABITING
DISHABITS
DISHABLE
DISHABLED
DISHABLES
DISHABLING
DISHALLOW
DISHALLOWED
DISHALLOWING
DISHALLOWS
DISHARMONIC
DISHARMONIES
DISHARMONIOUS
DISHARMONIOUSLY
DISHARMONISE
DISHARMONISED
DISHARMONISES
DISHARMONISING
DISHARMONIZE
DISHARMONIZED
DISHARMONIZES
DISHARMONIZING
DISHARMONY
DISHCLOTH
DISHCLOTHS
DISHCLOUT
DISHCLOUTS
DISHEARTEN
DISHEARTENED
DISHEARTENING
DISHEARTENINGLY
DISHEARTENMENT
DISHEARTENMENTS
DISHEARTENS
DISHED
DISHELM
DISHELMED
DISHELMING
DISHELMS
DISHERISON
DISHERISONS
DISHERIT
DISHERITED

DISHERITING
DISHERITOR
DISHERITORS
DISHERITS
DISHES
DISHEVEL
DISHEVELED
DISHEVELING
DISHEVELLED
DISHEVELLING
DISHEVELMENT
DISHEVELMENTS
DISHEVELS
DISHFUL
DISHFULS
DISHIER
DISHIEST
DISHING
DISHINGS
DISHLIKE
DISHOME
DISHOMED
DISHOMES
DISHOMING
DISHONEST
DISHONESTIES
DISHONESTLY
DISHONESTY
DISHONOR
DISHONORABLE
DISHONORABLY
DISHONORARY
DISHONORED
DISHONORER
DISHONORERS
DISHONORING
DISHONORS
DISHONOUR
DISHONOURABLE
DISHONOURABLY
DISHONOURED
DISHONOURER
DISHONOURERS
DISHONOURING
DISHONOURS
DISHORN
DISHORNED
DISHORNING
DISHORNS
DISHORSE
DISHORSED
DISHORSES
DISHORSING
DISHOUSE
DISHOUSED
DISHOUSES

DISHOUSING
DISHPAN
DISHPANS
DISHRAG
DISHRAGS
DISHTOWEL
DISHTOWELS
DISHUMOUR
DISHUMOURED
DISHUMOURING
DISHUMOURS
DISHWARE
DISHWARES
DISHWASHER
DISHWASHERS
DISHWATER
DISHWATERS
DISHY
DISILLUDE
DISILLUDED
DISILLUDES
DISILLUDING
DISILLUMINATE
DISILLUMINATED
DISILLUMINATES
DISILLUMINATING
DISILLUSION
DISILLUSIONARY
DISILLUSIONED
DISILLUSIONING
DISILLUSIONISE
DISILLUSIONISED
DISILLUSIONISES
DISILLUSIONIZE
DISILLUSIONIZED
DISILLUSIONIZES
DISILLUSIONMENT
DISILLUSIONS
DISILLUSIVE
DISIMAGINE
DISIMAGINED
DISIMAGINES
DISIMAGINING
DISIMMURE
DISIMMURED
DISIMMURES
DISIMMURING
DISIMPASSIONED
DISIMPRISON
DISIMPRISONED
DISIMPRISONING
DISIMPRISONMENT
DISIMPRISONS
DISIMPROVE
DISIMPROVED
DISIMPROVES

DISIMPROVING
DISINCARCERATE
DISINCARCERATED
DISINCARCERATES
DISINCENTIVE
DISINCENTIVES
DISINCLINATION
DISINCLINATIONS
DISINCLINE
DISINCLINED
DISINCLINES
DISINCLINING
DISINCLOSE
DISINCLOSED
DISINCLOSES
DISINCLOSING
DISINCORPORATE
DISINCORPORATED
DISINCORPORATES
DISINFECT
DISINFECTANT
DISINFECTANTS
DISINFECTED
DISINFECTING
DISINFECTION
DISINFECTIONS
DISINFECTOR
DISINFECTORS
DISINFECTS
DISINFEST
DISINFESTANT
DISINFESTANTS
DISINFESTATION
DISINFESTATIONS
DISINFESTED
DISINFESTING
DISINFESTS
DISINFLATION
DISINFLATIONARY
DISINFLATIONS
DISINFORMATION
DISINFORMATIONS
DISING
DISINGENUITIES
DISINGENUITY
DISINGENUOUS
DISINGENUOUSLY
DISINHERISON
DISINHERISONS
DISINHERIT
DISINHERITANCE
DISINHERITANCES
DISINHERITED
DISINHERITING
DISINHERITS
DISINHIBIT

DISINHIBITED
DISINHIBITING
DISINHIBITION
DISINHIBITIONS
DISINHIBITORY
DISINHIBITS
DISINHUME
DISINHUMED
DISINHUMES
DISINHUMING
DISINTEGRABLE
DISINTEGRATE
DISINTEGRATED
DISINTEGRATES
DISINTEGRATING
DISINTEGRATION
DISINTEGRATIONS
DISINTEGRATIVE
DISINTEGRATOR
DISINTEGRATORS
DISINTER
DISINTEREST
DISINTERESTED
DISINTERESTEDLY
DISINTERESTING
DISINTERESTS
DISINTERMENT
DISINTERMENTS
DISINTERRED
DISINTERRING
DISINTERS
DISINTHRAL
DISINTHRALLED
DISINTHRALLING
DISINTHRALS
DISINTOXICATE
DISINTOXICATED
DISINTOXICATES
DISINTOXICATING
DISINTOXICATION
DISINTRICATE
DISINTRICATED
DISINTRICATES
DISINTRICATING
DISINURE
DISINURED
DISINURES
DISINURING
DISINVEST
DISINVESTED
DISINVESTING
DISINVESTITURE
DISINVESTITURES
DISINVESTMENT
DISINVESTMENTS
DISINVESTS

DISINVIGORATE
DISINVIGORATED
DISINVIGORATES
DISINVIGORATING
DISINVITE
DISINVITED
DISINVITES
DISINVITING
DISINVOLVE
DISINVOLVED
DISINVOLVES
DISINVOLVING
DISJASKIT
DISJECT
DISJECTED
DISJECTING
DISJECTION
DISJECTIONS
DISJECTS
DISJOIN
DISJOINABLE
DISJOINED
DISJOINING
DISJOINS
DISJOINT
DISJOINTED
DISJOINTEDLY
DISJOINTEDNESS
DISJOINTING
DISJOINTS
DISJUNCT
DISJUNCTION
DISJUNCTIONS
DISJUNCTIVE
DISJUNCTIVELY
DISJUNCTIVES
DISJUNCTOR
DISJUNCTORS
DISJUNCTS
DISJUNCTURE
DISJUNCTURES
DISJUNE
DISJUNES
DISK
DISKED
DISKETTE
DISKETTES
DISKING
DISKLESS
DISKLIKE
DISKS
DISLEAF
DISLEAFED
DISLEAFING
DISLEAFS
DISLEAL

DISLEAVE
DISLEAVED
DISLEAVES
DISLEAVING
DISLIKABLE
DISLIKE
DISLIKEABLE
DISLIKED
DISLIKEFUL
DISLIKEN
DISLIKENED
DISLIKENESS
DISLIKENESSES
DISLIKENING
DISLIKENS
DISLIKER
DISLIKERS
DISLIKES
DISLIKING
DISLIMB
DISLIMBED
DISLIMBING
DISLIMBS
DISLIMN
DISLIMNED
DISLIMNING
DISLIMNS
DISLINK
DISLINKED
DISLINKING
DISLINKS
DISLOAD
DISLOADED
DISLOADING
DISLOADS
DISLOCATE
DISLOCATED
DISLOCATEDLY
DISLOCATES
DISLOCATING
DISLOCATION
DISLOCATIONS
DISLODGE
DISLODGED
DISLODGEMENT
DISLODGEMENTS
DISLODGES
DISLODGING
DISLODGMENT
DISLODGMENTS
DISLOIGN
DISLOIGNED
DISLOIGNING
DISLOIGNS
DISLOYAL
DISLOYALLY

DISLOYALTIES
DISLOYALTY
DISLUSTRE
DISLUSTRED
DISLUSTRES
DISLUSTRING
DISMAL
DISMALER
DISMALEST
DISMALITIES
DISMALITY
DISMALLER
DISMALLEST
DISMALLY
DISMALNESS
DISMALNESSES
DISMALS
DISMAN
DISMANNED
DISMANNING
DISMANS
DISMANTLE
DISMANTLED
DISMANTLEMENT
DISMANTLEMENTS
DISMANTLER
DISMANTLERS
DISMANTLES
DISMANTLING
DISMASK
DISMASKED
DISMASKING
DISMASKS
DISMAST
DISMASTED
DISMASTING
DISMASTMENT
DISMASTMENTS
DISMASTS
DISMAY
DISMAYD
DISMAYED
DISMAYEDNESS
DISMAYEDNESSES
DISMAYFUL
DISMAYFULLY
DISMAYING
DISMAYINGLY
DISMAYL
DISMAYLED
DISMAYLING
DISMAYLS
DISMAYS
DISME
DISMEMBER
DISMEMBERED

DISMEMBERER
DISMEMBERERS
DISMEMBERING
DISMEMBERMENT
DISMEMBERMENTS
DISMEMBERS
DISMES
DISMISS
DISMISSAL
DISMISSALS
DISMISSED
DISMISSES
DISMISSIBLE
DISMISSING
DISMISSION
DISMISSIONS
DISMISSIVE
DISMISSIVELY
DISMISSORY
DISMODED
DISMOUNT
DISMOUNTABLE
DISMOUNTED
DISMOUNTING
DISMOUNTS
DISMUTATION
DISMUTATIONS
DISNATURALISE
DISNATURALISED
DISNATURALISES
DISNATURALISING
DISNATURALIZE
DISNATURALIZED
DISNATURALIZES
DISNATURALIZING
DISNATURED
DISNEST
DISNESTED
DISNESTING
DISNESTS
DISOBEDIENCE
DISOBEDIENCES
DISOBEDIENT
DISOBEDIENTLY
DISOBEY
DISOBEYED
DISOBEYER
DISOBEYERS
DISOBEYING
DISOBEYS
DISOBLIGATION
DISOBLIGATIONS
DISOBLIGATORY
DISOBLIGE
DISOBLIGED
DISOBLIGEMENT

DISOBLIGEMENTS
DISOBLIGES
DISOBLIGING
DISOBLIGINGLY
DISOBLIGINGNESS
DISOMIC
DISOMIES
DISOMY
DISOPERATION
DISOPERATIONS
DISORBED
DISORDER
DISORDERED
DISORDEREDLY
DISORDEREDNESS
DISORDERING
DISORDERLIES
DISORDERLINESS
DISORDERLY
DISORDERS
DISORDINATE
DISORDINATELY
DISORGANIC
DISORGANISATION
DISORGANISE
DISORGANISED
DISORGANISER
DISORGANISERS
DISORGANISES
DISORGANISING
DISORGANIZATION
DISORGANIZE
DISORGANIZED
DISORGANIZER
DISORGANIZERS
DISORGANIZES
DISORGANIZING
DISORIENT
DISORIENTATE
DISORIENTATED
DISORIENTATES
DISORIENTATING
DISORIENTATION
DISORIENTATIONS
DISORIENTED
DISORIENTING
DISORIENTS
DISOWN
DISOWNED
DISOWNER
DISOWNERS
DISOWNING
DISOWNMENT
DISOWNMENTS
DISOWNS
DISPACE

DISPACED
DISPACES
DISPACING
DISPARAGE
DISPARAGED
DISPARAGEMENT
DISPARAGEMENTS
DISPARAGER
DISPARAGERS
DISPARAGES
DISPARAGING
DISPARAGINGLY
DISPARATE
DISPARATELY
DISPARATENESS
DISPARATENESSES
DISPARATES
DISPARITIES
DISPARITY
DISPARK
DISPARKED
DISPARKING
DISPARKS
DISPART
DISPARTED
DISPARTING
DISPARTS
DISPASSION
DISPASSIONATE
DISPASSIONATELY
DISPASSIONS
DISPATCH
DISPATCHED
DISPATCHER
DISPATCHERS
DISPATCHES
DISPATCHFUL
DISPATCHING
DISPATHIES
DISPATHY
DISPAUPER
DISPAUPERED
DISPAUPERING
DISPAUPERISE
DISPAUPERISED
DISPAUPERISES
DISPAUPERISING
DISPAUPERIZE
DISPAUPERIZED
DISPAUPERIZES
DISPAUPERIZING
DISPAUPERS
DISPEACE
DISPEACES
DISPEL
DISPELLED

DISPELLER
DISPELLERS
DISPELLING
DISPELS
DISPENCE
DISPENCED
DISPENCES
DISPENCING
DISPEND
DISPENDED
DISPENDING
DISPENDS
DISPENSABILITY
DISPENSABLE
DISPENSABLENESS
DISPENSABLY
DISPENSARIES
DISPENSARY
DISPENSATION
DISPENSATIONAL
DISPENSATIONS
DISPENSATIVE
DISPENSATIVELY
DISPENSATOR
DISPENSATORIES
DISPENSATORILY
DISPENSATORS
DISPENSATORY
DISPENSE
DISPENSED
DISPENSER
DISPENSERS
DISPENSES
DISPENSING
DISPEOPLE
DISPEOPLED
DISPEOPLES
DISPEOPLING
DISPERMOUS
DISPERSAL
DISPERSALS
DISPERSANT
DISPERSANTS
DISPERSE
DISPERSED
DISPERSEDLY
DISPERSEDNESS
DISPERSEDNESSES
DISPERSER
DISPERSERS
DISPERSES
DISPERSIBLE
DISPERSING
DISPERSION
DISPERSIONS
DISPERSIVE

DISPERSIVELY
DISPERSIVENESS
DISPERSOID
DISPERSOIDS
DISPIRIT
DISPIRITED
DISPIRITEDLY
DISPIRITEDNESS
DISPIRITING
DISPIRITINGLY
DISPIRITMENT
DISPIRITMENTS
DISPIRITS
DISPITEOUS
DISPITEOUSLY
DISPITEOUSNESS
DISPLACE
DISPLACEABLE
DISPLACED
DISPLACEMENT
DISPLACEMENTS
DISPLACER
DISPLACERS
DISPLACES
DISPLACING
DISPLANT
DISPLANTATION
DISPLANTATIONS
DISPLANTED
DISPLANTING
DISPLANTS
DISPLAY
DISPLAYABLE
DISPLAYED
DISPLAYER
DISPLAYERS
DISPLAYING
DISPLAYS
DISPLE
DISPLEASANCE
DISPLEASANCES
DISPLEASANT
DISPLEASE
DISPLEASED
DISPLEASEDLY
DISPLEASEDNESS
DISPLEASES
DISPLEASING
DISPLEASINGLY
DISPLEASINGNESS
DISPLEASURE
DISPLEASURED
DISPLEASURES
DISPLEASURING
DISPLED
DISPLENISH

DISPLENISHED
DISPLENISHES
DISPLENISHING
DISPLENISHMENT
DISPLENISHMENTS
DISPLES
DISPLING
DISPLODE
DISPLODED
DISPLODES
DISPLODING
DISPLOSION
DISPLOSIONS
DISPLUME
DISPLUMED
DISPLUMES
DISPLUMING
DISPONDAIC
DISPONDEE
DISPONDEES
DISPONE
DISPONED
DISPONEE
DISPONEES
DISPONER
DISPONERS
DISPONES
DISPONGE
DISPONGED
DISPONGES
DISPONGING
DISPONING
DISPORT
DISPORTED
DISPORTING
DISPORTMENT
DISPORTMENTS
DISPORTS
DISPOSABILITIES
DISPOSABILITY
DISPOSABLE
DISPOSABLENESS
DISPOSABLES
DISPOSAL
DISPOSALS
DISPOSE
DISPOSED
DISPOSEDLY
DISPOSER
DISPOSERS
DISPOSES
DISPOSIBILITIES
DISPOSIBILITY
DISPOSING
DISPOSINGLY
DISPOSINGS

DISPOSITION
DISPOSITIONAL
DISPOSITIONED
DISPOSITIONS
DISPOSITIVE
DISPOSITIVELY
DISPOSITOR
DISPOSITORS
DISPOSSESS
DISPOSSESSED
DISPOSSESSES
DISPOSSESSING
DISPOSSESSION
DISPOSSESSIONS
DISPOSSESSOR
DISPOSSESSORS
DISPOSSESSORY
DISPOST
DISPOSTED
DISPOSTING
DISPOSTS
DISPOSURE
DISPOSURES
DISPRAD
DISPRAISE
DISPRAISED
DISPRAISER
DISPRAISERS
DISPRAISES
DISPRAISING
DISPRAISINGLY
DISPREAD
DISPREADING
DISPREADS
DISPRED
DISPREDDEN
DISPREDDING
DISPREDS
DISPRINCED
DISPRISON
DISPRISONED
DISPRISONING
DISPRISONS
DISPRIVACIED
DISPRIVILEGE
DISPRIVILEGED
DISPRIVILEGES
DISPRIVILEGING
DISPRIZE
DISPRIZED
DISPRIZES
DISPRIZING
DISPROFESS
DISPROFESSED
DISPROFESSES
DISPROFESSING

DISPROFIT
DISPROFITS
DISPROOF
DISPROOFS
DISPROOVE
DISPROOVED
DISPROOVES
DISPROOVING
DISPROPERTIED
DISPROPERTIES
DISPROPERTY
DISPROPERTYING
DISPROPORTION
DISPROPORTIONAL
DISPROPORTIONED
DISPROPORTIONS
DISPROPRIATE
DISPROPRIATED
DISPROPRIATES
DISPROPRIATING
DISPROVABLE
DISPROVAL
DISPROVALS
DISPROVE
DISPROVED
DISPROVEN
DISPROVES
DISPROVIDE
DISPROVIDED
DISPROVIDES
DISPROVIDING
DISPROVING
DISPUNGE
DISPUNGED
DISPUNGES
DISPUNGING
DISPURSE
DISPURSED
DISPURSES
DISPURSING
DISPURVEY
DISPURVEYANCE
DISPURVEYANCES
DISPURVEYED
DISPURVEYING
DISPURVEYS
DISPUTABILITIES
DISPUTABILITY
DISPUTABLE
DISPUTABLENESS
DISPUTABLY
DISPUTANT
DISPUTANTS
DISPUTATION
DISPUTATIONS
DISPUTATIOUS

DISPUTATIOUSLY
DISPUTATIVE
DISPUTATIVELY
DISPUTATIVENESS
DISPUTE
DISPUTED
DISPUTER
DISPUTERS
DISPUTES
DISPUTING
DISQUALIFIABLE
DISQUALIFIED
DISQUALIFIER
DISQUALIFIERS
DISQUALIFIES
DISQUALIFY
DISQUALIFYING
DISQUANTITIED
DISQUANTITIES
DISQUANTITY
DISQUANTITYING
DISQUIET
DISQUIETED
DISQUIETEDLY
DISQUIETEDNESS
DISQUIETEN
DISQUIETENED
DISQUIETENING
DISQUIETENS
DISQUIETFUL
DISQUIETING
DISQUIETINGLY
DISQUIETIVE
DISQUIETLY
DISQUIETNESS
DISQUIETNESSES
DISQUIETOUS
DISQUIETS
DISQUIETUDE
DISQUIETUDES
DISQUISITION
DISQUISITIONAL
DISQUISITIONARY
DISQUISITIONS
DISQUISITIVE
DISQUISITORY
DISRANK
DISRANKED
DISRANKING
DISRANKS
DISRATE
DISRATED
DISRATES
DISRATING
DISREGARD
DISREGARDED

DISREGARDER
DISREGARDERS
DISREGARDFUL
DISREGARDFULLY
DISREGARDING
DISREGARDS
DISRELATED
DISRELATION
DISRELATIONS
DISRELISH
DISRELISHED
DISRELISHES
DISRELISHING
DISREMEMBER
DISREMEMBERED
DISREMEMBERING
DISREMEMBERS
DISREPAIR
DISREPAIRS
DISREPUTABILITY
DISREPUTABLE
DISREPUTABLY
DISREPUTATION
DISREPUTATIONS
DISREPUTE
DISREPUTES
DISRESPECT
DISRESPECTABLE
DISRESPECTED
DISRESPECTFUL
DISRESPECTFULLY
DISRESPECTING
DISRESPECTS
DISROBE
DISROBED
DISROBEMENT
DISROBEMENTS
DISROBER
DISROBERS
DISROBES
DISROBING
DISROOT
DISROOTED
DISROOTING
DISROOTS
DISRUPT
DISRUPTED
DISRUPTER
DISRUPTERS
DISRUPTING
DISRUPTION
DISRUPTIONS
DISRUPTIVE
DISRUPTIVELY
DISRUPTIVENESS
DISRUPTOR

DISRUPTORS
DISRUPTS
DISS
DISSATISFACTION
DISSATISFACTORY
DISSATISFIED
DISSATISFIEDLY
DISSATISFIES
DISSATISFY
DISSATISFYING
DISSAVE
DISSAVED
DISSAVES
DISSAVING
DISSAVINGS
DISSEAT
DISSEATED
DISSEATING
DISSEATS
DISSECT
DISSECTED
DISSECTIBLE
DISSECTING
DISSECTINGS
DISSECTION
DISSECTIONS
DISSECTIVE
DISSECTOR
DISSECTORS
DISSECTS
DISSED
DISSEISE
DISSEISED
DISSEISES
DISSEISIN
DISSEISING
DISSEISINS
DISSEISOR
DISSEISORS
DISSEIZE
DISSEIZED
DISSEIZES
DISSEIZIN
DISSEIZING
DISSEIZINS
DISSEIZOR
DISSEIZORS
DISSELBOOM
DISSELBOOMS
DISSEMBLANCE
DISSEMBLANCES
DISSEMBLE
DISSEMBLED
DISSEMBLER
DISSEMBLERS
DISSEMBLES

DISSEMBLIES
DISSEMBLING
DISSEMBLINGLY
DISSEMBLINGS
DISSEMBLY
DISSEMINATE
DISSEMINATED
DISSEMINATES
DISSEMINATING
DISSEMINATION
DISSEMINATIONS
DISSEMINATIVE
DISSEMINATOR
DISSEMINATORS
DISSEMINULE
DISSEMINULES
DISSENSION
DISSENSIONS
DISSENSUS
DISSENSUSES
DISSENT
DISSENTED
DISSENTER
DISSENTERISH
DISSENTERISM
DISSENTERISMS
DISSENTERS
DISSENTIENCE
DISSENTIENCY
DISSENTIENT
DISSENTIENTLY
DISSENTIENTS
DISSENTING
DISSENTINGLY
DISSENTION
DISSENTIONS
DISSENTIOUS
DISSENTS
DISSEPIMENT
DISSEPIMENTAL
DISSEPIMENTS
DISSERT
DISSERTATE
DISSERTATED
DISSERTATES
DISSERTATING
DISSERTATION
DISSERTATIONAL
DISSERTATIONIST
DISSERTATIONS
DISSERTATIVE
DISSERTATOR
DISSERTATORS
DISSERTED
DISSERTING
DISSERTS

DISSERVE
DISSERVED
DISSERVES
DISSERVICE
DISSERVICEABLE
DISSERVICES
DISSERVING
DISSES
DISSEVER
DISSEVERANCE
DISSEVERANCES
DISSEVERATION
DISSEVERATIONS
DISSEVERED
DISSEVERING
DISSEVERMENT
DISSEVERMENTS
DISSEVERS
DISSHEATHE
DISSHEATHED
DISSHEATHES
DISSHEATHING
DISSHIVER
DISSHIVERED
DISSHIVERING
DISSHIVERS
DISSIDENCE
DISSIDENCES
DISSIDENT
DISSIDENTLY
DISSIDENTS
DISSIGHT
DISSIGHTS
DISSILIENCE
DISSILIENCES
DISSILIENT
DISSIMILAR
DISSIMILARITIES
DISSIMILARITY
DISSIMILARLY
DISSIMILARS
DISSIMILATE
DISSIMILATED
DISSIMILATES
DISSIMILATING
DISSIMILATION
DISSIMILATIONS
DISSIMILATIVE
DISSIMILATIVELY
DISSIMILATORY
DISSIMILE
DISSIMILES
DISSIMILITUDE
DISSIMILITUDES
DISSIMULATE
DISSIMULATED

DISSIMULATES
DISSIMULATING
DISSIMULATION
DISSIMULATIONS
DISSIMULATIVE
DISSIMULATOR
DISSIMULATORS
DISSING
DISSIPABLE
DISSIPATE
DISSIPATED
DISSIPATEDLY
DISSIPATEDNESS
DISSIPATER
DISSIPATERS
DISSIPATES
DISSIPATING
DISSIPATION
DISSIPATIONS
DISSIPATIVE
DISSIPATOR
DISSIPATORS
DISSOCIABILITY
DISSOCIABLE
DISSOCIABLENESS
DISSOCIABLY
DISSOCIAL
DISSOCIALISE
DISSOCIALISED
DISSOCIALISES
DISSOCIALISING
DISSOCIALITIES
DISSOCIALITY
DISSOCIALIZE
DISSOCIALIZED
DISSOCIALIZES
DISSOCIALIZING
DISSOCIATE
DISSOCIATED
DISSOCIATES
DISSOCIATING
DISSOCIATION
DISSOCIATIONS
DISSOCIATIVE
DISSOLUBILITIES
DISSOLUBILITY
DISSOLUBLE
DISSOLUBLENESS
DISSOLUTE
DISSOLUTELY
DISSOLUTENESS
DISSOLUTENESSES
DISSOLUTES
DISSOLUTION
DISSOLUTIONISM
DISSOLUTIONISMS

DISSOLUTIONIST
DISSOLUTIONISTS
DISSOLUTIONS
DISSOLUTIVE
DISSOLVABILITY
DISSOLVABLE
DISSOLVABLENESS
DISSOLVE
DISSOLVED
DISSOLVENT
DISSOLVENTS
DISSOLVER
DISSOLVERS
DISSOLVES
DISSOLVING
DISSOLVINGS
DISSONANCE
DISSONANCES
DISSONANCIES
DISSONANCY
DISSONANT
DISSONANTLY
DISSUADABLE
DISSUADE
DISSUADED
DISSUADER
DISSUADERS
DISSUADES
DISSUADING
DISSUASION
DISSUASIONS
DISSUASIVE
DISSUASIVELY
DISSUASIVENESS
DISSUASIVES
DISSUASORIES
DISSUASORY
DISSUNDER
DISSUNDERED
DISSUNDERING
DISSUNDERS
DISSYLLABIC
DISSYLLABICALLY
DISSYLLABLE
DISSYLLABLES
DISSYMMETRIC
DISSYMMETRICAL
DISSYMMETRIES
DISSYMMETRY
DISTAFF
DISTAFFS
DISTAIN
DISTAINED
DISTAINING
DISTAINS
DISTAL

DISTALLY
DISTANCE
DISTANCED
DISTANCELESS
DISTANCES
DISTANCING
DISTANT
DISTANTLY
DISTANTNESS
DISTANTNESSES
DISTASTE
DISTASTED
DISTASTEFUL
DISTASTEFULLY
DISTASTEFULNESS
DISTASTES
DISTASTING
DISTAVES
DISTELFINK
DISTELFINKS
DISTEMPER
DISTEMPERATE
DISTEMPERATURE
DISTEMPERATURES
DISTEMPERED
DISTEMPERING
DISTEMPERS
DISTEND
DISTENDED
DISTENDER
DISTENDERS
DISTENDING
DISTENDS
DISTENSIBILITY
DISTENSIBLE
DISTENSILE
DISTENSION
DISTENSIONS
DISTENSIVE
DISTENT
DISTENTION
DISTENTIONS
DISTHENE
DISTHENES
DISTHRONE
DISTHRONED
DISTHRONES
DISTHRONING
DISTHRONIZE
DISTHRONIZED
DISTHRONIZES
DISTHRONIZING
DISTICH
DISTICHAL
DISTICHOUS
DISTICHOUSLY

DISTICHS
DISTIL
DISTILL
DISTILLABLE
DISTILLAND
DISTILLANDS
DISTILLATE
DISTILLATES
DISTILLATION
DISTILLATIONS
DISTILLATORY
DISTILLED
DISTILLER
DISTILLERIES
DISTILLERS
DISTILLERY
DISTILLING
DISTILLINGS
DISTILLMENT
DISTILLMENTS
DISTILLS
DISTILMENT
DISTILMENTS
DISTILS
DISTINCT
DISTINCTER
DISTINCTEST
DISTINCTION
DISTINCTIONS
DISTINCTIVE
DISTINCTIVELY
DISTINCTIVENESS
DISTINCTIVES
DISTINCTLY
DISTINCTNESS
DISTINCTNESSES
DISTINCTURE
DISTINCTURES
DISTINGUE
DISTINGUEE
DISTINGUISH
DISTINGUISHABLE
DISTINGUISHABLY
DISTINGUISHED
DISTINGUISHER
DISTINGUISHERS
DISTINGUISHES
DISTINGUISHING
DISTINGUISHMENT
DISTOME
DISTOMES
DISTORT
DISTORTED
DISTORTEDLY
DISTORTEDNESS
DISTORTER

DISTORTERS
DISTORTING
DISTORTION
DISTORTIONAL
DISTORTIONS
DISTORTIVE
DISTORTS
DISTRACT
DISTRACTABLE
DISTRACTED
DISTRACTEDLY
DISTRACTEDNESS
DISTRACTER
DISTRACTERS
DISTRACTIBILITY
DISTRACTIBLE
DISTRACTING
DISTRACTINGLY
DISTRACTION
DISTRACTIONS
DISTRACTIVE
DISTRACTIVELY
DISTRACTS
DISTRAIL
DISTRAILS
DISTRAIN
DISTRAINABLE
DISTRAINED
DISTRAINEE
DISTRAINEES
DISTRAINER
DISTRAINERS
DISTRAINING
DISTRAINMENT
DISTRAINMENTS
DISTRAINOR
DISTRAINORS
DISTRAINS
DISTRAINT
DISTRAINTS
DISTRAIT
DISTRAITE
DISTRAUGHT
DISTRAUGHTLY
DISTRESS
DISTRESSED
DISTRESSER
DISTRESSERS
DISTRESSES
DISTRESSFUL
DISTRESSFULLY
DISTRESSFULNESS
DISTRESSING
DISTRESSINGLY
DISTRIBUEND
DISTRIBUENDS

DISTRIBUTABLE
DISTRIBUTARIES
DISTRIBUTARY
DISTRIBUTE
DISTRIBUTED
DISTRIBUTEE
DISTRIBUTEES
DISTRIBUTER
DISTRIBUTERS
DISTRIBUTES
DISTRIBUTING
DISTRIBUTION
DISTRIBUTIONAL
DISTRIBUTIONS
DISTRIBUTIVE
DISTRIBUTIVELY
DISTRIBUTIVES
DISTRIBUTIVITY
DISTRIBUTOR
DISTRIBUTORS
DISTRICT
DISTRICTED
DISTRICTING
DISTRICTS
DISTRINGAS
DISTRINGASES
DISTRIX
DISTROUBLE
DISTROUBLED
DISTROUBLES
DISTROUBLING
DISTRUST
DISTRUSTED
DISTRUSTER
DISTRUSTERS
DISTRUSTFUL
DISTRUSTFULLY
DISTRUSTFULNESS
DISTRUSTING
DISTRUSTLESS
DISTRUSTS
DISTUNE
DISTUNED
DISTUNES
DISTUNING
DISTURB
DISTURBANCE
DISTURBANCES
DISTURBANT
DISTURBANTS
DISTURBATIVE
DISTURBED
DISTURBER
DISTURBERS
DISTURBING
DISTURBINGLY

DISTURBS
DISTYLE
DISTYLES
DISUBSTITUTED
DISULFID
DISULFIDE
DISULFIDES
DISULFIDS
DISULFIRAM
DISULFIRAMS
DISULFOTON
DISULFOTONS
DISULPHATE
DISULPHATES
DISULPHIDE
DISULPHIDES
DISULPHURET
DISULPHURETS
DISULPHURIC
DISUNION
DISUNIONIST
DISUNIONISTS
DISUNIONS
DISUNITE
DISUNITED
DISUNITER
DISUNITERS
DISUNITES
DISUNITIES
DISUNITING
DISUNITY
DISUSAGE
DISUSAGES
DISUSE
DISUSED
DISUSES
DISUSING
DISUTILITIES
DISUTILITY
DISVALUE
DISVALUED
DISVALUES
DISVALUING
DISVOUCH
DISVOUCHED
DISVOUCHES
DISVOUCHING
DISWORSHIP
DISWORSHIPS
DISYLLABIC
DISYLLABIFIED
DISYLLABIFIES
DISYLLABIFY
DISYLLABIFYING
DISYLLABISM
DISYLLABISMS

DISYLLABLE
DISYLLABLES
DISYOKE
DISYOKED
DISYOKES
DISYOKING
DIT
DITA
DITAL
DITALS
DITAS
DITCH
DITCHDIGGER
DITCHDIGGERS
DITCHED
DITCHER
DITCHERS
DITCHES
DITCHING
DITCHLESS
DITCHWATER
DITE
DITED
DITES
DITHECAL
DITHECOUS
DITHEISM
DITHEISMS
DITHEIST
DITHEISTIC
DITHEISTICAL
DITHEISTS
DITHELETE
DITHELETES
DITHELETIC
DITHELETICAL
DITHELETISM
DITHELETISMS
DITHELISMS
DITHELITISMS
DITHER
DITHERED
DITHERER
DITHERERS
DITHERIER
DITHERIEST
DITHERING
DITHERS
DITHERY
DITHIOCARBAMATE
DITHIOL
DITHIONATE
DITHIONATES
DITHIONITE
DITHIONITES
DITHIONOUS

DITHYRAMB
DITHYRAMBIC
DITHYRAMBICALLY
DITHYRAMBIST
DITHYRAMBISTS
DITHYRAMBS
DITING
DITOKOUS
DITONE
DITONES
DITRANSITIVE
DITRANSITIVES
DITRIGLYPH
DITRIGLYPHIC
DITRIGLYPHS
DITROCHEAN
DITROCHEE
DITROCHEES
DITS
DITSIER
DITSIEST
DITSY
DITT
DITTANDER
DITTANDERS
DITTANIES
DITTANY
DITTAY
DITTAYS
DITTED
DITTIED
DITTIES
DITTING
DITTIT
DITTO
DITTOED
DITTOGRAPHIC
DITTOGRAPHIES
DITTOGRAPHY
DITTOING
DITTOLOGIES
DITTOLOGY
DITTOS
DITTS
DITTY
DITTYING
DITZ
DITZES
DITZIER
DITZIEST
DITZY
DIURESES
DIURESIS
DIURETIC
DIURETICALLY
DIURETICALNESS

DIURETICS
DIURNAL
DIURNALIST
DIURNALISTS
DIURNALLY
DIURNALS
DIURON
DIURONS
DIUTURNAL
DIUTURNITIES
DIUTURNITY
DIV
DIVA
DIVAGATE
DIVAGATED
DIVAGATES
DIVAGATING
DIVAGATION
DIVAGATIONS
DIVALENCIES
DIVALENCY
DIVALENT
DIVALENTS
DIVAN
DIVANS
DIVARICATE
DIVARICATED
DIVARICATELY
DIVARICATES
DIVARICATING
DIVARICATINGLY
DIVARICATION
DIVARICATIONS
DIVARICATOR
DIVARICATORS
DIVAS
DIVE
DIVEBOMB
DIVEBOMBED
DIVEBOMBING
DIVEBOMBS
DIVED
DIVELLENT
DIVELLICATE
DIVELLICATED
DIVELLICATES
DIVELLICATING
DIVER
DIVERGE
DIVERGED
DIVERGEMENT
DIVERGEMENTS
DIVERGENCE
DIVERGENCES
DIVERGENCIES
DIVERGENCY

DIVERGENT
DIVERGENTLY
DIVERGES
DIVERGING
DIVERGINGLY
DIVERS
DIVERSE
DIVERSED
DIVERSELY
DIVERSENESS
DIVERSENESSES
DIVERSES
DIVERSIFIABLE
DIVERSIFICATION
DIVERSIFIED
DIVERSIFIER
DIVERSIFIERS
DIVERSIFIES
DIVERSIFORM
DIVERSIFY
DIVERSIFYING
DIVERSING
DIVERSION
DIVERSIONAL
DIVERSIONALLY
DIVERSIONARY
DIVERSIONIST
DIVERSIONISTS
DIVERSIONS
DIVERSITIES
DIVERSITY
DIVERSLY
DIVERT
DIVERTED
DIVERTER
DIVERTERS
DIVERTIBILITIES
DIVERTIBILITY
DIVERTIBLE
DIVERTICULA
DIVERTICULAR
DIVERTICULATE
DIVERTICULATED
DIVERTICULITIS
DIVERTICULOSES
DIVERTICULOSIS
DIVERTICULUM
DIVERTIMENTI
DIVERTIMENTO
DIVERTIMENTOS
DIVERTING
DIVERTINGLY
DIVERTISEMENT
DIVERTISEMENTS
DIVERTISSEMENT
DIVERTISSEMENTS

DIVERTIVE
DIVERTS
DIVES
DIVEST
DIVESTED
DIVESTIBLE
DIVESTING
DIVESTITURE
DIVESTITURES
DIVESTMENT
DIVESTMENTS
DIVESTS
DIVESTURE
DIVESTURES
DIVI
DIVIDABLE
DIVIDANT
DIVIDE
DIVIDED
DIVIDEDLY
DIVIDEDNESS
DIVIDEDNESSES
DIVIDEND
DIVIDENDLESS
DIVIDENDS
DIVIDER
DIVIDERS
DIVIDES
DIVIDING
DIVIDINGS
DIVIDIVI
DIVIDIVIS
DIVIDUAL
DIVIDUOUS
DIVINABLE
DIVINATION
DIVINATIONS
DIVINATOR
DIVINATORS
DIVINATORY
DIVINE
DIVINED
DIVINELY
DIVINENESS
DIVINENESSES
DIVINER
DIVINERESS
DIVINERESSES
DIVINERS
DIVINES
DIVINEST
DIVING
DIVINGS
DIVINIFIED
DIVINIFIES
DIVINIFY

DIVINIFYING
DIVINING
DIVINISATION
DIVINISE
DIVINISED
DIVINISES
DIVINISING
DIVINITIES
DIVINITY
DIVINIZATION
DIVINIZE
DIVINIZED
DIVINIZES
DIVINIZING
DIVIS
DIVISIBILITIES
DIVISIBILITY
DIVISIBLE
DIVISIBLENESS
DIVISIBLENESSES
DIVISIBLY
DIVISIM
DIVISION
DIVISIONAL
DIVISIONALLY
DIVISIONARY
DIVISIONISM
DIVISIONISMS
DIVISIONIST
DIVISIONISTS
DIVISIONS
DIVISIVE
DIVISIVELY
DIVISIVENESS
DIVISIVENESSES
DIVISOR
DIVISORS
DIVORCE
DIVORCEABLE
DIVORCED
DIVORCEE
DIVORCEES
DIVORCEMENT
DIVORCEMENTS
DIVORCER
DIVORCERS
DIVORCES
DIVORCING
DIVORCIVE
DIVOT
DIVOTS
DIVS
DIVULGATE
DIVULGATED
DIVULGATER
DIVULGATERS

DIVULGATES
DIVULGATING
DIVULGATION
DIVULGATIONS
DIVULGATOR
DIVULGATORS
DIVULGE
DIVULGED
DIVULGEMENT
DIVULGEMENTS
DIVULGENCE
DIVULGENCES
DIVULGER
DIVULGERS
DIVULGES
DIVULGING
DIVULSION
DIVULSIONS
DIVULSIVE
DIVVIED
DIVVIES
DIVVY
DIVVYING
DIWAN
DIWANS
DIXI
DIXIE
DIXIES
DIXIT
DIXITS
DIXY
DIZAIN
DIZAINS
DIZEN
DIZENED
DIZENING
DIZENMENT
DIZENMENTS
DIZENS
DIZYGOTIC
DIZYGOUS
DIZZARD
DIZZARDS
DIZZIED
DIZZIER
DIZZIES
DIZZIEST
DIZZILY
DIZZINESS
DIZZINESSES
DIZZY
DIZZYING
DIZZYINGLY
DJEBEL
DJEBELS
DJELLABA

DJELLABAH
DJELLABAHS
DJELLABAS
DJEMBE
DJIBBAH
DJIBBAHS
DJIN
DJINN
DJINNI
DJINNS
DJINNY
DJINS
DO
DOAB
DOABLE
DOABS
DOAT
DOATED
DOATER
DOATERS
DOATING
DOATINGS
DOATS
DOB
DOBBED
DOBBER
DOBBERS
DOBBIE
DOBBIES
DOBBIN
DOBBING
DOBBINS
DOBBY
DOBCHICK
DOBCHICKS
DOBHASH
DOBHASHES
DOBIE
DOBIES
DOBLA
DOBLAS
DOBLON
DOBLONES
DOBLONS
DOBRA
DOBRAS
DOBS
DOBSON
DOBSONFLIES
DOBSONFLY
DOBSONS
DOBY
DOC
DOCENT
DOCENTS
DOCENTSHIP

DOCENTSHIPS
DOCETIC
DOCHMIAC
DOCHMIACAL
DOCHMII
DOCHMIUS
DOCHMIUSES
DOCHT
DOCIBILITIES
DOCIBILITY
DOCIBLE
DOCIBLENESS
DOCIBLENESSES
DOCILE
DOCILELY
DOCILER
DOCILEST
DOCILITIES
DOCILITY
DOCIMASIES
DOCIMASTIC
DOCIMASY
DOCIMOLOGIES
DOCIMOLOGY
DOCK
DOCKAGE
DOCKAGES
DOCKED
DOCKEN
DOCKENS
DOCKER
DOCKERS
DOCKET
DOCKETED
DOCKETING
DOCKETS
DOCKHAND
DOCKHANDS
DOCKING
DOCKINGS
DOCKISATION
DOCKISATIONS
DOCKISE
DOCKISED
DOCKISES
DOCKISING
DOCKIZATION
DOCKIZATIONS
DOCKIZE
DOCKIZED
DOCKIZES
DOCKIZING
DOCKLAND
DOCKLANDS
DOCKMASTER
DOCKMASTERS

DOCKS
DOCKSIDE
DOCKSIDES
DOCKWORKER
DOCKWORKERS
DOCKYARD
DOCKYARDS
DOCO
DOCOS
DOCQUET
DOCQUETED
DOCQUETING
DOCQUETS
DOCS
DOCTOR
DOCTORAL
DOCTORAND
DOCTORANDS
DOCTORATE
DOCTORATED
DOCTORATES
DOCTORATING
DOCTORED
DOCTORESS
DOCTORESSES
DOCTORIAL
DOCTORING
DOCTORLESS
DOCTORLY
DOCTORS
DOCTORSHIP
DOCTORSHIPS
DOCTRESS
DOCTRESSES
DOCTRINAIRE
DOCTRINAIRES
DOCTRINAIRISM
DOCTRINAIRISMS
DOCTRINAL
DOCTRINALITIES
DOCTRINALITY
DOCTRINALLY
DOCTRINARIAN
DOCTRINARIANISM
DOCTRINARIANS
DOCTRINARISM
DOCTRINE
DOCTRINES
DOCTRINISM
DOCTRINIST
DOCTRINISTS
DOCUDRAMA
DOCUDRAMAS
DOCUMENT
DOCUMENTABLE
DOCUMENTAL

DOCUMENTALIST
DOCUMENTALISTS
DOCUMENTARIAN
DOCUMENTARIANS
DOCUMENTARIES
DOCUMENTARILY
DOCUMENTARISE
DOCUMENTARISED
DOCUMENTARISES
DOCUMENTARISING
DOCUMENTARIST
DOCUMENTARISTS
DOCUMENTARIZE
DOCUMENTARIZED
DOCUMENTARIZES
DOCUMENTARIZING
DOCUMENTARY
DOCUMENTATION
DOCUMENTATIONAL
DOCUMENTATIONS
DOCUMENTED
DOCUMENTER
DOCUMENTERS
DOCUMENTING
DOCUMENTS
DOD
DODDARD
DODDED
DODDER
DODDERED
DODDERER
DODDERERS
DODDERIER
DODDERIEST
DODDERING
DODDERS
DODDERY
DODDIER
DODDIES
DODDIEST
DODDING
DODDIPOLL
DODDIPOLLS
DODDLE
DODDLES
DODDY
DODDYPOLL
DODDYPOLLS
DODECAGON
DODECAGONAL
DODECAGONS
DODECAGYNIAN
DODECAGYNOUS
DODECAHEDRA
DODECAHEDRAL
DODECAHEDRON

DODECAHEDRONS
DODECANDROUS
DODECANOIC
DODECAPHONIC
DODECAPHONIES
DODECAPHONISM
DODECAPHONISMS
DODECAPHONIST
DODECAPHONISTS
DODECAPHONY
DODECASTYLE
DODECASTYLES
DODECASYLLABIC
DODECASYLLABLE
DODECASYLLABLES
DODGE
DODGEBALL
DODGEBALLS
DODGED
DODGEM
DODGEMS
DODGER
DODGERIES
DODGERS
DODGERY
DODGES
DODGIER
DODGIEST
DODGINESS
DODGINESSES
DODGING
DODGINGS
DODGY
DODKIN
DODKINS
DODMAN
DODMANS
DODO
DODOES
DODOISM
DODOISMS
DODOS
DODS
DOE
DOEK
DOEKS
DOEN
DOER
DOERS
DOES
DOESKIN
DOESKINS
DOEST
DOETH
DOFF
DOFFED

DOFFER
DOFFERS
DOFFING
DOFFS
DOG
DOGARESSA
DOGARESSAS
DOGATE
DOGATES
DOGBANE
DOGBANES
DOGBERRIES
DOGBERRY
DOGBERRYISM
DOGBOLT
DOGBOLTS
DOGCART
DOGCARTS
DOGCATCHER
DOGCATCHERS
DOGDAYS
DOGDOM
DOGDOMS
DOGE
DOGEAR
DOGEARED
DOGEARING
DOGEARS
DOGEATE
DOGEATES
DOGEDOM
DOGEDOMS
DOGES
DOGESHIP
DOGESHIPS
DOGEY
DOGEYS
DOGFACE
DOGFACES
DOGFIGHT
DOGFIGHTING
DOGFIGHTS
DOGFISH
DOGFISHES
DOGFOUGHT
DOGFOX
DOGFOXES
DOGGED
DOGGEDER
DOGGEDEST
DOGGEDLY
DOGGEDNESS
DOGGEDNESSES
DOGGER
DOGGEREL
DOGGERELS

DOGGERIES
DOGGERMAN
DOGGERMEN
DOGGERS
DOGGERY
DOGGESS
DOGGESSES
DOGGIE
DOGGIER
DOGGIES
DOGGIEST
DOGGINESS
DOGGINESSES
DOGGING
DOGGINGS
DOGGISH
DOGGISHLY
DOGGISHNESS
DOGGISHNESSES
DOGGO
DOGGONE
DOGGONED
DOGGONEDER
DOGGONEDEST
DOGGONER
DOGGONES
DOGGONEST
DOGGONING
DOGGREL
DOGGRELS
DOGGY
DOGHOLE
DOGHOLES
DOGHOUSE
DOGHOUSES
DOGIE
DOGIES
DOGLEG
DOGLEGGED
DOGLEGGING
DOGLEGS
DOGLIKE
DOGMA
DOGMAN
DOGMAS
DOGMATA
DOGMATIC
DOGMATICAL
DOGMATICALLY
DOGMATICALNESS
DOGMATICS
DOGMATISATION
DOGMATISATIONS
DOGMATISE
DOGMATISED
DOGMATISER

DOGMATISERS
DOGMATISES
DOGMATISING
DOGMATISM
DOGMATISMS
DOGMATIST
DOGMATISTS
DOGMATIZATION
DOGMATIZATIONS
DOGMATIZE
DOGMATIZED
DOGMATIZER
DOGMATIZERS
DOGMATIZES
DOGMATIZING
DOGMATOLOGIES
DOGMATOLOGY
DOGMATORY
DOGMEN
DOGNAP
DOGNAPED
DOGNAPER
DOGNAPERS
DOGNAPING
DOGNAPPED
DOGNAPPER
DOGNAPPERS
DOGNAPPING
DOGNAPS
DOGREL
DOGS
DOGSBODIED
DOGSBODIES
DOGSBODY
DOGSBODYING
DOGSHIP
DOGSHIPS
DOGSHORES
DOGSKIN
DOGSKINS
DOGSLED
DOGSLEDDED
DOGSLEDDER
DOGSLEDDERS
DOGSLEDDING
DOGSLEDS
DOGSLEEP
DOGSLEEPS
DOGTEETH
DOGTOOTH
DOGTOWN
DOGTOWNS
DOGTROT
DOGTROTS
DOGTROTTED
DOGTROTTING

DOGVANE
DOGVANES
DOGWATCH
DOGWATCHES
DOGWOOD
DOGWOODS
DOGY
DOH
DOHS
DOHYO
DOHYOS
DOILED
DOILIES
DOILT
DOILTER
DOILTEST
DOILY
DOING
DOINGS
DOIT
DOITED
DOITIT
DOITKIN
DOITKINS
DOITS
DOJO
DOJOS
DOL
DOLABRATE
DOLABRATES
DOLABRIFORM
DOLCE
DOLCELATTE
DOLCELATTES
DOLCEMENTE
DOLCES
DOLCI
DOLDRUMS
DOLE
DOLED
DOLEFUL
DOLEFULLER
DOLEFULLEST
DOLEFULLY
DOLEFULNESS
DOLEFULNESSES
DOLENT
DOLENTE
DOLERITE
DOLERITES
DOLERITIC
DOLES
DOLESOME
DOLESOMELY
DOLIA
DOLICHOCEPHAL

DOLICHOCEPHALIC
DOLICHOCEPHALS
DOLICHOCEPHALY
DOLICHOS
DOLICHOSAURUS
DOLICHOSAURUSES
DOLICHOSES
DOLICHURI
DOLICHURUS
DOLICHURUSES
DOLINA
DOLINAS
DOLINE
DOLINES
DOLING
DOLIUM
DOLL
DOLLAR
DOLLARBIRD
DOLLARBIRDS
DOLLARED
DOLLARFISH
DOLLARFISHES
DOLLARISATION
DOLLARISATIONS
DOLLARIZATION
DOLLARIZATIONS
DOLLARLESS
DOLLAROCRACIES
DOLLAROCRACY
DOLLARS
DOLLARSHIP
DOLLARSHIPS
DOLLDOM
DOLLDOMS
DOLLED
DOLLHOOD
DOLLHOODS
DOLLHOUSE
DOLLHOUSES
DOLLIED
DOLLIER
DOLLIERS
DOLLIES
DOLLINESS
DOLLINESSES
DOLLING
DOLLISH
DOLLISHLY
DOLLISHNESS
DOLLISHNESSES
DOLLOP
DOLLOPED
DOLLOPING
DOLLOPS
DOLLS

DOLLY
DOLLYING
DOLMA
DOLMADES
DOLMAN
DOLMANS
DOLMAS
DOLMEN
DOLMENS
DOLOMITE
DOLOMITES
DOLOMITIC
DOLOMITISATION
DOLOMITISATIONS
DOLOMITISE
DOLOMITISED
DOLOMITISES
DOLOMITISING
DOLOMITIZATION
DOLOMITIZATIONS
DOLOMITIZE
DOLOMITIZED
DOLOMITIZES
DOLOMITIZING
DOLOR
DOLORIFEROUS
DOLORIFIC
DOLORIMETRIC
DOLORIMETRY
DOLOROSO
DOLOROUS
DOLOROUSLY
DOLOROUSNESS
DOLOROUSNESSES
DOLORS
DOLOS
DOLOSSE
DOLOSTONE
DOLOSTONES
DOLOUR
DOLOURS
DOLPHIN
DOLPHINARIA
DOLPHINARIUM
DOLPHINARIUMS
DOLPHINET
DOLPHINETS
DOLPHINFISH
DOLPHINFISHES
DOLPHINS
DOLS
DOLT
DOLTISH
DOLTISHLY
DOLTISHNESS
DOLTISHNESSES

DOLTS
DOM
DOMAIN
DOMAINAL
DOMAINS
DOMAL
DOMANIAL
DOMATIA
DOMATIUM
DOME
DOMED
DOMELIKE
DOMES
DOMESDAY
DOMESDAYS
DOMESTIC
DOMESTICABLE
DOMESTICAL
DOMESTICALLY
DOMESTICATE
DOMESTICATED
DOMESTICATES
DOMESTICATING
DOMESTICATION
DOMESTICATIONS
DOMESTICATIVE
DOMESTICATOR
DOMESTICATORS
DOMESTICISE
DOMESTICISED
DOMESTICISES
DOMESTICISING
DOMESTICITIES
DOMESTICITY
DOMESTICIZE
DOMESTICIZED
DOMESTICIZES
DOMESTICIZING
DOMESTICS
DOMETT
DOMETTS
DOMIC
DOMICAL
DOMICIL
DOMICILE
DOMICILED
DOMICILES
DOMICILIARY
DOMICILIATE
DOMICILIATED
DOMICILIATES
DOMICILIATING
DOMICILIATION
DOMICILIATIONS
DOMICILING
DOMICILS

DOMIER
DOMIEST
DOMINANCE
DOMINANCES
DOMINANCIES
DOMINANCY
DOMINANT
DOMINANTLY
DOMINANTS
DOMINATE
DOMINATED
DOMINATES
DOMINATING
DOMINATINGLY
DOMINATION
DOMINATIONS
DOMINATIVE
DOMINATOR
DOMINATORS
DOMINATRICES
DOMINATRIX
DOMINATRIXES
DOMINE
DOMINEE
DOMINEER
DOMINEERED
DOMINEERING
DOMINEERINGLY
DOMINEERINGNESS
DOMINEERS
DOMINEES
DOMINES
DOMING
DOMINICAL
DOMINICK
DOMINICKER
DOMINICKERS
DOMINICKS
DOMINIE
DOMINIES
DOMINION
DOMINIONS
DOMINIQUE
DOMINIQUES
DOMINIUM
DOMINIUMS
DOMINO
DOMINOES
DOMINOS
DOMKOP
DOMKOPS
DOMS
DOMY
DON
DONA
DONAH

DONAHS
DONARIES
DONARY
DONAS
DONATARIES
DONATARY
DONATE
DONATED
DONATES
DONATING
DONATION
DONATIONS
DONATISM
DONATISMS
DONATISTIC
DONATISTICAL
DONATIVE
DONATIVES
DONATOR
DONATORIES
DONATORS
DONATORY
DONDER
DONDERED
DONDERING
DONDERS
DONE
DONEE
DONEES
DONENESS
DONENESSES
DONG
DONGA
DONGAS
DONGED
DONGING
DONGLE
DONGLES
DONGOLA
DONGOLAS
DONGS
DONING
DONINGS
DONJON
DONJONS
DONKEY
DONKEYS
DONKEYWORK
DONKEYWORKS
DONKO
DONKOS
DONNA
DONNARD
DONNART
DONNAS
DONNAT

DONNATS
DONNE
DONNED
DONNEE
DONNEES
DONNERD
DONNERED
DONNERT
DONNES
DONNICKER
DONNICKERS
DONNIES
DONNIKER
DONNIKERS
DONNING
DONNISH
DONNISHLY
DONNISHNESS
DONNISHNESSES
DONNISM
DONNISMS
DONNOT
DONNOTS
DONNY
DONNYBROOK
DONNYBROOKS
DONOR
DONORS
DONORSHIP
DONORSHIPS
DONS
DONSHIP
DONSHIPS
DONSIE
DONSIER
DONSIEST
DONSY
DONUT
DONUTS
DONUTTED
DONUTTING
DONZEL
DONZELS
DOO
DOOB
DOOBS
DOOCOT
DOOCOTS
DOODAD
DOODADS
DOODAH
DOODAHS
DOODLE
DOODLEBUG
DOODLEBUGS
DOODLED

DOODLER
DOODLERS
DOODLES
DOODLING
DOOFER
DOOFERS
DOOFUS
DOOFUSES
DOOHICKEY
DOOHICKEYS
DOOHICKIES
DOOK
DOOKED
DOOKET
DOOKETS
DOOKING
DOOKS
DOOL
DOOLALLY
DOOLAN
DOOLANS
DOOLE
DOOLEE
DOOLEES
DOOLES
DOOLIE
DOOLIES
DOOLS
DOOLY
DOOM
DOOMED
DOOMFUL
DOOMFULLY
DOOMIER
DOOMIEST
DOOMILY
DOOMING
DOOMS
DOOMSAYER
DOOMSAYERS
DOOMSAYING
DOOMSAYINGS
DOOMSDAY
DOOMSDAYER
DOOMSDAYERS
DOOMSDAYS
DOOMSMAN
DOOMSMEN
DOOMSTER
DOOMSTERS
DOOMWATCH
DOOMWATCHED
DOOMWATCHER
DOOMWATCHERS
DOOMWATCHES
DOOMWATCHING

DOOMWATCHINGS
DOOMY
DOON
DOONA
DOONAS
DOOR
DOORBELL
DOORBELLS
DOORCASE
DOORCASES
DOORFRAME
DOORFRAMES
DOORJAMB
DOORJAMBS
DOORKEEPER
DOORKEEPERS
DOORKNOB
DOORKNOBS
DOORKNOCK
DOORKNOCKED
DOORKNOCKER
DOORKNOCKERS
DOORKNOCKING
DOORKNOCKS
DOORLESS
DOORMAN
DOORMAT
DOORMATS
DOORMEN
DOORN
DOORNAIL
DOORNAILS
DOORNS
DOORPLATE
DOORPLATES
DOORPOST
DOORPOSTS
DOORS
DOORSILL
DOORSILLS
DOORSMAN
DOORSMEN
DOORSTEP
DOORSTEPPED
DOORSTEPPER
DOORSTEPPERS
DOORSTEPPING
DOORSTEPPINGS
DOORSTEPS
DOORSTONE
DOORSTONES
DOORSTOP
DOORSTOPS
DOORWAY
DOORWAYS
DOORYARD

DOORYARDS
DOOS
DOOZER
DOOZERS
DOOZIE
DOOZIES
DOOZY
DOP
DOPA
DOPAMINE
DOPAMINERGIC
DOPAMINES
DOPANT
DOPANTS
DOPAS
DOPATTA
DOPATTAS
DOPE
DOPED
DOPEHEAD
DOPEHEADS
DOPER
DOPERS
DOPES
DOPESTER
DOPESTERS
DOPEY
DOPIER
DOPIEST
DOPILY
DOPINESS
DOPINESSES
DOPING
DOPINGS
DOPPED
DOPPELGANGER
DOPPELGANGERS
DOPPER
DOPPERS
DOPPIE
DOPPIES
DOPPING
DOPPINGS
DOPPIO
DOPPIOS
DOPPLERITE
DOPPLERITES
DOPS
DOPY
DOR
DORAD
DORADO
DORADOS
DORADS
DORB
DORBA

DORBAS
DORBS
DORBUG
DORBUGS
DORE
DOREE
DOREES
DORHAWK
DORHAWKS
DORIDOID
DORIDOIDS
DORIES
DORIS
DORISE
DORISED
DORISES
DORISING
DORIZE
DORIZED
DORIZES
DORIZING
DORK
DORKIER
DORKIEST
DORKS
DORKY
DORLACH
DORLACHS
DORM
DORMANCIES
DORMANCY
DORMANT
DORMANTS
DORMER
DORMERS
DORMICE
DORMIE
DORMIENT
DORMIN
DORMINS
DORMITION
DORMITIONS
DORMITIVE
DORMITIVES
DORMITORIES
DORMITORY
DORMOUSE
DORMS
DORMY
DORNECK
DORNECKS
DORNICK
DORNICKS
DORNOCK
DORNOCKS
DORONICUM

DORONICUMS
DORP
DORPER
DORPERS
DORPS
DORR
DORRED
DORRING
DORRS
DORS
DORSA
DORSAD
DORSAL
DORSALLY
DORSALS
DORSE
DORSEL
DORSELS
DORSER
DORSERS
DORSES
DORSIBRANCHIATE
DORSIFEROUS
DORSIFIXED
DORSIFLEX
DORSIFLEXION
DORSIFLEXIONS
DORSIGRADE
DORSIVENTRAL
DORSIVENTRALITY
DORSIVENTRALLY
DORSOLATERAL
DORSOLUMBAR
DORSOVENTRAL
DORSOVENTRALITY
DORSOVENTRALLY
DORSUM
DORT
DORTED
DORTER
DORTERS
DORTIER
DORTIEST
DORTINESS
DORTING
DORTOUR
DORTOURS
DORTS
DORTY
DORY
DOS
DOSAGE
DOSAGES
DOSE
DOSED
DOSEH

DOSEHS
DOSEMETER
DOSEMETERS
DOSER
DOSERS
DOSES
DOSH
DOSHES
DOSIMETER
DOSIMETERS
DOSIMETRIC
DOSIMETRICIAN
DOSIMETRICIANS
DOSIMETRIES
DOSIMETRIST
DOSIMETRISTS
DOSIMETRY
DOSING
DOSIOLOGIES
DOSIOLOGY
DOSOLOGIES
DOSOLOGY
DOSS
DOSSAL
DOSSALS
DOSSED
DOSSEL
DOSSELS
DOSSER
DOSSERET
DOSSERETS
DOSSERS
DOSSES
DOSSHOUSE
DOSSHOUSES
DOSSIER
DOSSIERS
DOSSIL
DOSSILS
DOSSING
DOST
DOT
DOTAGE
DOTAGES
DOTAL
DOTANT
DOTANTS
DOTARD
DOTARDLY
DOTARDS
DOTATION
DOTATIONS
DOTCOM
DOTCOMMER
DOTCOMS
DOTE

DOTED
DOTER
DOTERS
DOTES
DOTH
DOTIER
DOTIEST
DOTING
DOTINGLY
DOTINGS
DOTISH
DOTS
DOTTED
DOTTEL
DOTTELS
DOTTER
DOTTEREL
DOTTERELS
DOTTERS
DOTTIER
DOTTIEST
DOTTILY
DOTTINESS
DOTTINESSES
DOTTING
DOTTIPOLLS
DOTTLE
DOTTLED
DOTTLER
DOTTLES
DOTTLEST
DOTTREL
DOTTRELS
DOTTY
DOTY
DOUANE
DOUANES
DOUANIER
DOUANIERS
DOUAR
DOUARS
DOUBLE
DOUBLED
DOUBLEHEADER
DOUBLEHEADERS
DOUBLENESS
DOUBLENESSES
DOUBLER
DOUBLERS
DOUBLES
DOUBLESPEAK
DOUBLESPEAKER
DOUBLESPEAKERS
DOUBLESPEAKS
DOUBLET
DOUBLETHINK

DOUBLETHINKS
DOUBLETON
DOUBLETONS
DOUBLETREE
DOUBLETREES
DOUBLETS
DOUBLING
DOUBLINGS
DOUBLOON
DOUBLOONS
DOUBLURE
DOUBLURES
DOUBLY
DOUBT
DOUBTABILITY
DOUBTABLE
DOUBTABLY
DOUBTED
DOUBTER
DOUBTERS
DOUBTFUL
DOUBTFULLY
DOUBTFULNESS
DOUBTFULNESSES
DOUBTFULS
DOUBTING
DOUBTINGLY
DOUBTINGS
DOUBTLESS
DOUBTLESSLY
DOUBTLESSNESS
DOUBTLESSNESSES
DOUBTS
DOUC
DOUCE
DOUCELY
DOUCENESS
DOUCENESSES
DOUCEPERE
DOUCEPERES
DOUCER
DOUCEST
DOUCET
DOUCETS
DOUCEUR
DOUCEURS
DOUCHE
DOUCHED
DOUCHES
DOUCHING
DOUCINE
DOUCINES
DOUCS
DOUGH
DOUGHBOY
DOUGHBOYS

DOUGHFACE
DOUGHFACED
DOUGHFACES
DOUGHIER
DOUGHIEST
DOUGHINESS
DOUGHINESSES
DOUGHLIKE
DOUGHNUT
DOUGHNUTLIKE
DOUGHNUTS
DOUGHNUTTED
DOUGHNUTTING
DOUGHNUTTINGS
DOUGHS
DOUGHT
DOUGHTIER
DOUGHTIEST
DOUGHTILY
DOUGHTINESS
DOUGHTINESSES
DOUGHTY
DOUGHY
DOUK
DOUKED
DOUKING
DOUKS
DOULA
DOULAS
DOULEIA
DOULEIAS
DOULOCRACIES
DOULOCRACY
DOUM
DOUMA
DOUMAS
DOUMS
DOUN
DOUP
DOUPIONI
DOUPIONIS
DOUPS
DOUR
DOURA
DOURAH
DOURAHS
DOURAS
DOURER
DOUREST
DOURINE
DOURINES
DOURLY
DOURNESS
DOURNESSES
DOUROUCOULI
DOUROUCOULIS

DOUSE
DOUSED
DOUSER
DOUSERS
DOUSES
DOUSING
DOUT
DOUTED
DOUTER
DOUTERS
DOUTING
DOUTS
DOUX
DOUZEPER
DOUZEPERS
DOVE
DOVECOT
DOVECOTE
DOVECOTES
DOVECOTS
DOVED
DOVEISH
DOVEISHNESS
DOVEISHNESSES
DOVEKEY
DOVEKEYS
DOVEKIE
DOVEKIES
DOVELET
DOVELETS
DOVELIKE
DOVEN
DOVENED
DOVENING
DOVENS
DOVER
DOVERED
DOVERING
DOVERS
DOVES
DOVETAIL
DOVETAILED
DOVETAILING
DOVETAILINGS
DOVETAILS
DOVIE
DOVIER
DOVIEST
DOVING
DOVISH
DOVISHNESS
DOVISHNESSES
DOW
DOWABLE
DOWAGER
DOWAGERS

DOWAR
DOWARS
DOWD
DOWDIER
DOWDIES
DOWDIEST
DOWDILY
DOWDINESS
DOWDINESSES
DOWDS
DOWDY
DOWDYISH
DOWDYISM
DOWDYISMS
DOWED
DOWEL
DOWELED
DOWELING
DOWELLED
DOWELLING
DOWELLINGS
DOWELS
DOWER
DOWERED
DOWERIES
DOWERING
DOWERLESS
DOWERS
DOWERY
DOWF
DOWFNESS
DOWFNESSES
DOWIE
DOWIER
DOWIEST
DOWING
DOWITCHER
DOWITCHERS
DOWL
DOWLAS
DOWLASES
DOWLE
DOWLES
DOWLIER
DOWLIEST
DOWLNE
DOWLNES
DOWLNEY
DOWLS
DOWLY
DOWN
DOWNA
DOWNBEAT
DOWNBEATS
DOWNBOW
DOWNBOWS

DOWNBURST
DOWNBURSTS
DOWNCAST
DOWNCASTS
DOWNCOME
DOWNCOMER
DOWNCOMERS
DOWNCOMES
DOWNCOURT
DOWNDRAFT
DOWNDRAFTS
DOWNDRAUGHT
DOWNDRAUGHTS
DOWNED
DOWNER
DOWNERS
DOWNFALL
DOWNFALLEN
DOWNFALLS
DOWNFIELD
DOWNFLOW
DOWNFLOWS
DOWNFORCE
DOWNFORCES
DOWNGRADE
DOWNGRADED
DOWNGRADES
DOWNGRADING
DOWNHAUL
DOWNHAULS
DOWNHEARTED
DOWNHEARTEDLY
DOWNHEARTEDNESS
DOWNHILL
DOWNHILLER
DOWNHILLERS
DOWNHILLS
DOWNHOLE
DOWNHOME
DOWNIER
DOWNIEST
DOWNINESS
DOWNINESSES
DOWNING
DOWNLAND
DOWNLANDS
DOWNLIFTING
DOWNLIGHTER
DOWNLIGHTERS
DOWNLINK
DOWNLINKS
DOWNLOAD
DOWNLOADABLE
DOWNLOADED
DOWNLOADING
DOWNLOADS

DOWNLOOKED
DOWNMOST
DOWNPIPE
DOWNPIPES
DOWNPLAY
DOWNPLAYED
DOWNPLAYING
DOWNPLAYS
DOWNPOUR
DOWNPOURS
DOWNRANGE
DOWNRIGHT
DOWNRIGHTLY
DOWNRIGHTNESS
DOWNRIGHTNESSES
DOWNRIVER
DOWNRUSH
DOWNRUSHES
DOWNS
DOWNSCALE
DOWNSCALED
DOWNSCALES
DOWNSCALING
DOWNSHIFT
DOWNSHIFTED
DOWNSHIFTING
DOWNSHIFTINGS
DOWNSHIFTS
DOWNSIDE
DOWNSIDES
DOWNSIZE
DOWNSIZED
DOWNSIZES
DOWNSIZING
DOWNSLIDE
DOWNSLIDES
DOWNSLOPE
DOWNSPOUT
DOWNSPOUTS
DOWNSTAGE
DOWNSTAGES
DOWNSTAIR
DOWNSTAIRS
DOWNSTAIRSES
DOWNSTATE
DOWNSTATER
DOWNSTATERS
DOWNSTATES
DOWNSTREAM
DOWNSTROKE
DOWNSTROKES
DOWNSWING
DOWNSWINGS
DOWNTHROW
DOWNTHROWS
DOWNTICK

DOWNTICKS
DOWNTIME
DOWNTIMES
DOWNTOWN
DOWNTOWNER
DOWNTOWNERS
DOWNTOWNS
DOWNTREND
DOWNTRENDS
DOWNTROD
DOWNTRODDEN
DOWNTURN
DOWNTURNED
DOWNTURNS
DOWNWARD
DOWNWARDLY
DOWNWARDNESS
DOWNWARDNESSES
DOWNWARDS
DOWNWASH
DOWNWASHES
DOWNWIND
DOWNY
DOWP
DOWPS
DOWRIES
DOWRY
DOWS
DOWSABEL
DOWSABELS
DOWSE
DOWSED
DOWSER
DOWSERS
DOWSES
DOWSET
DOWSETS
DOWSING
DOWT
DOWTS
DOWY
DOXASTIC
DOXASTICALLY
DOXIE
DOXIES
DOXOGRAPHER
DOXOGRAPHERS
DOXOGRAPHIC
DOXOGRAPHIES
DOXOGRAPHY
DOXOLOGICAL
DOXOLOGICALLY
DOXOLOGIES
DOXOLOGY
DOXORUBICIN
DOXORUBICINS

DOXY
DOXYCYCLINE
DOXYCYCLINES
DOY
DOYEN
DOYENNE
DOYENNES
DOYENS
DOYLEY
DOYLEYS
DOYLIES
DOYLY
DOYS
DOZE
DOZED
DOZEN
DOZENED
DOZENING
DOZENS
DOZENTH
DOZENTHS
DOZER
DOZERS
DOZES
DOZIER
DOZIEST
DOZILY
DOZINESS
DOZINESSES
DOZING
DOZINGS
DOZY
DRAB
DRABBED
DRABBER
DRABBERS
DRABBEST
DRABBET
DRABBETS
DRABBIER
DRABBIEST
DRABBINESS
DRABBINESSES
DRABBING
DRABBISH
DRABBLE
DRABBLED
DRABBLER
DRABBLERS
DRABBLES
DRABBLING
DRABBLINGS
DRABBY
DRABETTES
DRABLER
DRABLERS

DRABLY
DRABNESS
DRABNESSES
DRABS
DRAC
DRACAENA
DRACAENAS
DRACHM
DRACHMA
DRACHMAE
DRACHMAI
DRACHMAS
DRACHMS
DRACK
DRACO
DRACONE
DRACONES
DRACONIAN
DRACONIC
DRACONICALLY
DRACONISM
DRACONISMS
DRACONITES
DRACONTIASES
DRACONTIASIS
DRACONTIC
DRACOS
DRACUNCULUS
DRACUNCULUSES
DRAD
DRAFF
DRAFFIER
DRAFFIEST
DRAFFISH
DRAFFS
DRAFFY
DRAFT
DRAFTABLE
DRAFTED
DRAFTEE
DRAFTEES
DRAFTER
DRAFTERS
DRAFTIER
DRAFTIEST
DRAFTILY
DRAFTINESS
DRAFTINESSES
DRAFTING
DRAFTINGS
DRAFTS
DRAFTSMAN
DRAFTSMANSHIP
DRAFTSMANSHIPS
DRAFTSMEN
DRAFTSPERSON

DRAFTSPERSONS
DRAFTSWOMAN
DRAFTSWOMEN
DRAFTY
DRAG
DRAGEE
DRAGEES
DRAGGED
DRAGGER
DRAGGERS
DRAGGIER
DRAGGIEST
DRAGGING
DRAGGINGLY
DRAGGLE
DRAGGLED
DRAGGLES
DRAGGLETAILED
DRAGGLING
DRAGGY
DRAGHOUND
DRAGHOUNDS
DRAGLINE
DRAGLINES
DRAGNET
DRAGNETS
DRAGOMAN
DRAGOMANS
DRAGOMEN
DRAGON
DRAGONESS
DRAGONESSES
DRAGONET
DRAGONETS
DRAGONFLIES
DRAGONFLY
DRAGONHEAD
DRAGONHEADS
DRAGONISE
DRAGONISED
DRAGONISES
DRAGONISH
DRAGONISING
DRAGONISM
DRAGONISMS
DRAGONIZE
DRAGONIZED
DRAGONIZES
DRAGONIZING
DRAGONLIKE
DRAGONNADE
DRAGONNADED
DRAGONNADES
DRAGONNADING
DRAGONNE
DRAGONROOT

DRAGONROOTS
DRAGONS
DRAGOON
DRAGOONAGE
DRAGOONED
DRAGOONING
DRAGOONS
DRAGROPE
DRAGROPES
DRAGS
DRAGSMAN
DRAGSMEN
DRAGSTER
DRAGSTERS
DRAIL
DRAILED
DRAILING
DRAILS
DRAIN
DRAINABLE
DRAINAGE
DRAINAGES
DRAINED
DRAINER
DRAINERS
DRAINING
DRAINLAYER
DRAINLAYERS
DRAINPIPE
DRAINPIPES
DRAINS
DRAISENE
DRAISENES
DRAISINE
DRAISINES
DRAKE
DRAKES
DRAKESTONE
DRAKESTONES
DRAM
DRAMA
DRAMAS
DRAMATIC
DRAMATICAL
DRAMATICALLY
DRAMATICISM
DRAMATICISMS
DRAMATICS
DRAMATISABLE
DRAMATISATION
DRAMATISATIONS
DRAMATISE
DRAMATISED
DRAMATISER
DRAMATISERS
DRAMATISES

DRAMATISING
DRAMATIST
DRAMATISTS
DRAMATIZABLE
DRAMATIZATION
DRAMATIZATIONS
DRAMATIZE
DRAMATIZED
DRAMATIZER
DRAMATIZERS
DRAMATIZES
DRAMATIZING
DRAMATURG
DRAMATURGE
DRAMATURGES
DRAMATURGIC
DRAMATURGICAL
DRAMATURGICALLY
DRAMATURGIES
DRAMATURGIST
DRAMATURGISTS
DRAMATURGS
DRAMATURGY
DRAMEDIES
DRAMEDY
DRAMMACH
DRAMMACHS
DRAMMED
DRAMMING
DRAMMOCK
DRAMMOCKS
DRAMS
DRAMSHOP
DRAMSHOPS
DRANGWAY
DRANGWAYS
DRANK
DRANT
DRANTED
DRANTING
DRANTS
DRAP
DRAPABILITIES
DRAPABILITY
DRAPABLE
DRAPE
DRAPEABILITIES
DRAPEABILITY
DRAPEABLE
DRAPED
DRAPER
DRAPERIED
DRAPERIES
DRAPERS
DRAPERY
DRAPERYING

DRAPES
DRAPET
DRAPETS
DRAPEY
DRAPIER
DRAPIERS
DRAPING
DRAPPED
DRAPPIE
DRAPPIES
DRAPPING
DRAPPY
DRAPS
DRASTIC
DRASTICALLY
DRASTICS
DRAT
DRATCHELL
DRATCHELLS
DRATS
DRATTED
DRATTING
DRAUGHT
DRAUGHTBOARD
DRAUGHTBOARDS
DRAUGHTED
DRAUGHTER
DRAUGHTERS
DRAUGHTIER
DRAUGHTIEST
DRAUGHTILY
DRAUGHTINESS
DRAUGHTINESSES
DRAUGHTING
DRAUGHTMAN
DRAUGHTMEN
DRAUGHTS
DRAUGHTSMAN
DRAUGHTSMANSHIP
DRAUGHTSMEN
DRAUGHTSWOMAN
DRAUGHTSWOMEN
DRAUGHTY
DRAUNT
DRAUNTED
DRAUNTING
DRAUNTS
DRAVE
DRAW
DRAWABLE
DRAWBACK
DRAWBACKS
DRAWBAR
DRAWBARS
DRAWBORE
DRAWBORES

DRAWBRIDGE
DRAWBRIDGES
DRAWDOWN
DRAWDOWNS
DRAWEE
DRAWEES
DRAWER
DRAWERFUL
DRAWERFULS
DRAWERS
DRAWING
DRAWINGS
DRAWKNIFE
DRAWKNIVES
DRAWL
DRAWLED
DRAWLER
DRAWLERS
DRAWLIER
DRAWLIEST
DRAWLING
DRAWLINGLY
DRAWLINGNESS
DRAWLINGNESSES
DRAWLS
DRAWLY
DRAWN
DRAWNWORK
DRAWNWORKS
DRAWPLATE
DRAWPLATES
DRAWS
DRAWSHAVE
DRAWSHAVES
DRAWSTRING
DRAWSTRINGS
DRAWTUBE
DRAWTUBES
DRAY
DRAYAGE
DRAYAGES
DRAYED
DRAYHORSE
DRAYHORSES
DRAYING
DRAYMAN
DRAYMEN
DRAYS
DRAZEL
DRAZELS
DREAD
DREADED
DREADER
DREADERS
DREADFUL
DREADFULLY

DREADFULNESS
DREADFULNESSES
DREADFULS
DREADING
DREADLESS
DREADLESSLY
DREADLESSNESS
DREADLESSNESSES
DREADLOCK
DREADLOCKS
DREADLY
DREADNAUGHT
DREADNAUGHTS
DREADNOUGHT
DREADNOUGHTS
DREADS
DREAM
DREAMBOAT
DREAMBOATS
DREAMED
DREAMER
DREAMERIES
DREAMERS
DREAMERY
DREAMFUL
DREAMFULLY
DREAMFULNESS
DREAMFULNESSES
DREAMHOLE
DREAMHOLES
DREAMIER
DREAMIEST
DREAMILY
DREAMINESS
DREAMINESSES
DREAMING
DREAMINGLY
DREAMINGS
DREAMLAND
DREAMLANDS
DREAMLESS
DREAMLESSLY
DREAMLESSNESS
DREAMLESSNESSES
DREAMLIKE
DREAMS
DREAMT
DREAMTIME
DREAMTIMES
DREAMWHILE
DREAMWHILES
DREAMWORLD
DREAMWORLDS
DREAMY
DREAR
DREARE

DREARER
DREARES
DREAREST
DREARIER
DREARIES
DREARIEST
DREARIHEAD
DREARIHEADS
DREARIHOOD
DREARIHOODS
DREARILY
DREARIMENT
DREARIMENTS
DREARINESS
DREARINESSES
DREARING
DREARINGS
DREARISOME
DREARS
DREARY
DRECK
DRECKIER
DRECKIEST
DRECKS
DRECKSILL
DRECKSILLS
DRECKY
DREDGE
DREDGED
DREDGER
DREDGERS
DREDGES
DREDGING
DREDGINGS
DREE
DREED
DREEING
DREES
DREG
DREGGIER
DREGGIEST
DREGGINESS
DREGGINESSES
DREGGISH
DREGGY
DREGS
DREICH
DREICHER
DREICHEST
DREIDEL
DREIDELS
DREIDL
DREIDLS
DREIGH
DREIKANTER
DREIKANTERS

DREK
DREKS
DRENCH
DRENCHED
DRENCHER
DRENCHERS
DRENCHES
DRENCHING
DRENCHINGS
DRENT
DREPANID
DREPANIDS
DREPANIUM
DREPANIUMS
DRERE
DRERES
DRERIHEAD
DRERIHEADS
DRESS
DRESSAGE
DRESSAGES
DRESSED
DRESSER
DRESSERS
DRESSES
DRESSGUARD
DRESSGUARDS
DRESSIER
DRESSIEST
DRESSILY
DRESSINESS
DRESSINESSES
DRESSING
DRESSINGS
DRESSMADE
DRESSMAKE
DRESSMAKER
DRESSMAKERS
DRESSMAKES
DRESSMAKING
DRESSMAKINGS
DRESSY
DREST
DREVILL
DREVILLS
DREW
DREY
DREYS
DRIB
DRIBBED
DRIBBER
DRIBBERS
DRIBBING
DRIBBLE
DRIBBLED
DRIBBLER

DRIBBLERS
DRIBBLES
DRIBBLET
DRIBBLETS
DRIBBLIER
DRIBBLIEST
DRIBBLING
DRIBBLY
DRIBLET
DRIBLETS
DRIBS
DRICE
DRICES
DRICKSIE
DRICKSIER
DRICKSIEST
DRIED
DRIEGH
DRIER
DRIERS
DRIES
DRIEST
DRIFT
DRIFTAGE
DRIFTAGES
DRIFTED
DRIFTER
DRIFTERS
DRIFTIER
DRIFTIEST
DRIFTING
DRIFTINGLY
DRIFTLESS
DRIFTPIN
DRIFTPINS
DRIFTS
DRIFTWOOD
DRIFTWOODS
DRIFTY
DRILL
DRILLABILITIES
DRILLABILITY
DRILLABLE
DRILLED
DRILLER
DRILLERS
DRILLING
DRILLINGS
DRILLMASTER
DRILLMASTERS
DRILLS
DRILLSHIP
DRILLSHIPS
DRILLSTOCK
DRILLSTOCKS
DRILY

DRINK
DRINKABILITIES
DRINKABILITY
DRINKABLE
DRINKABLENESS
DRINKABLENESSES
DRINKABLES
DRINKER
DRINKERS
DRINKING
DRINKINGS
DRINKS
DRIP
DRIPLESS
DRIPPED
DRIPPER
DRIPPERS
DRIPPIER
DRIPPIEST
DRIPPING
DRIPPINGS
DRIPPY
DRIPS
DRIPSTONE
DRIPSTONES
DRIPT
DRISHEEN
DRISHEENS
DRIVABILITIES
DRIVABILITY
DRIVABLE
DRIVE
DRIVEABILITIES
DRIVEABILITY
DRIVEABLE
DRIVEL
DRIVELED
DRIVELER
DRIVELERS
DRIVELINE
DRIVELINES
DRIVELING
DRIVELLED
DRIVELLER
DRIVELLERS
DRIVELLING
DRIVELS
DRIVEN
DRIVENNESS
DRIVENNESSES
DRIVER
DRIVERLESS
DRIVERS
DRIVES
DRIVESHAFT
DRIVESHAFTS

DRIVETHROUGH
DRIVETHROUGHS
DRIVETRAIN
DRIVETRAINS
DRIVEWAY
DRIVEWAYS
DRIVING
DRIVINGS
DRIZZLE
DRIZZLED
DRIZZLES
DRIZZLIER
DRIZZLIEST
DRIZZLING
DRIZZLINGLY
DRIZZLY
DROGER
DROGERS
DROGHER
DROGHERS
DROGUE
DROGUES
DROGUET
DROGUETS
DROICH
DROICHIER
DROICHIEST
DROICHS
DROIL
DROILED
DROILING
DROILS
DROIT
DROITS
DROLE
DROLER
DROLES
DROLEST
DROLL
DROLLED
DROLLER
DROLLERIES
DROLLERY
DROLLEST
DROLLING
DROLLINGS
DROLLISH
DROLLNESS
DROLLNESSES
DROLLS
DROLLY
DROME
DROMEDARE
DROMEDARES
DROMEDARIES
DROMEDARY

DROMES
DROMIC
DROMICAL
DROMOI
DROMON
DROMOND
DROMONDS
DROMONS
DROMOPHOBIA
DROMOPHOBIAS
DROMOS
DRONE
DRONED
DRONER
DRONERS
DRONES
DRONGO
DRONGOES
DRONGOS
DRONIER
DRONIEST
DRONING
DRONINGLY
DRONISH
DRONISHLY
DRONISHNESS
DRONISHNESSES
DRONY
DROOB
DROOBS
DROOG
DROOGISH
DROOGS
DROOK
DROOKED
DROOKING
DROOKINGS
DROOKIT
DROOKS
DROOL
DROOLED
DROOLING
DROOLS
DROOME
DROOMES
DROOP
DROOPED
DROOPIER
DROOPIEST
DROOPILY
DROOPINESS
DROOPINESSES
DROOPING
DROOPINGLY
DROOPS
DROOPY

DROP
DROPFLIES
DROPFLY
DROPHEAD
DROPHEADS
DROPKICK
DROPKICKER
DROPKICKERS
DROPKICKS
DROPLET
DROPLETS
DROPLIGHT
DROPLIGHTS
DROPOUT
DROPOUTS
DROPPABLE
DROPPED
DROPPER
DROPPERFUL
DROPPERFULS
DROPPERS
DROPPERSFUL
DROPPING
DROPPINGS
DROPPLE
DROPPLES
DROPS
DROPSHOT
DROPSHOTS
DROPSICAL
DROPSICALLY
DROPSIED
DROPSIES
DROPSONDE
DROPSONDES
DROPSTONE
DROPSTONES
DROPSY
DROPT
DROPWISE
DROPWORT
DROPWORTS
DROSERA
DROSERACEOUS
DROSERAS
DROSHKIES
DROSHKY
DROSKIES
DROSKY
DROSOMETER
DROSOMETERS
DROSOPHILA
DROSOPHILAE
DROSOPHILAS
DROSS
DROSSES

DROSSIER
DROSSIEST
DROSSINESS
DROSSINESSES
DROSSY
DROSTDIES
DROSTDY
DROSTDYS
DROUGHT
DROUGHTIER
DROUGHTIEST
DROUGHTINESS
DROUGHTINESSES
DROUGHTS
DROUGHTY
DROUK
DROUKED
DROUKING
DROUKINGS
DROUKIT
DROUKS
DROUTH
DROUTHIER
DROUTHIEST
DROUTHINESS
DROUTHINESSES
DROUTHS
DROUTHY
DROVE
DROVED
DROVER
DROVERS
DROVES
DROVING
DROVINGS
DROW
DROWN
DROWND
DROWNDED
DROWNDING
DROWNDS
DROWNED
DROWNER
DROWNERS
DROWNING
DROWNINGS
DROWNS
DROWS
DROWSE
DROWSED
DROWSES
DROWSIER
DROWSIEST
DROWSIHEAD
DROWSIHEADS
DROWSIHED

DROWSIHEDS
DROWSILY
DROWSINESS
DROWSINESSES
DROWSING
DROWSY
DRUB
DRUBBED
DRUBBER
DRUBBERS
DRUBBING
DRUBBINGS
DRUBS
DRUCKEN
DRUCKENNESS
DRUCKENNESSES
DRUDGE
DRUDGED
DRUDGER
DRUDGERIES
DRUDGERS
DRUDGERY
DRUDGES
DRUDGING
DRUDGINGLY
DRUDGISM
DRUDGISMS
DRUG
DRUGGED
DRUGGER
DRUGGERS
DRUGGET
DRUGGETS
DRUGGIE
DRUGGIER
DRUGGIES
DRUGGIEST
DRUGGING
DRUGGIST
DRUGGISTS
DRUGGY
DRUGLORD
DRUGLORDS
DRUGMAKER
DRUGMAKERS
DRUGS
DRUGSTORE
DRUGSTORES
DRUID
DRUIDESS
DRUIDESSES
DRUIDIC
DRUIDICAL
DRUIDISM
DRUIDISMS
DRUIDS

DRUM
DRUMBEAT
DRUMBEATER
DRUMBEATERS
DRUMBEATING
DRUMBEATINGS
DRUMBEATS
DRUMBLE
DRUMBLED
DRUMBLEDORS
DRUMBLEDRANE
DRUMBLEDRANES
DRUMBLES
DRUMBLING
DRUMFIRE
DRUMFIRES
DRUMFISH
DRUMFISHES
DRUMHEAD
DRUMHEADS
DRUMLIER
DRUMLIEST
DRUMLIKE
DRUMLIN
DRUMLINS
DRUMLY
DRUMMED
DRUMMER
DRUMMERS
DRUMMIES
DRUMMING
DRUMMOCK
DRUMMOCKS
DRUMMY
DRUMROLL
DRUMROLLS
DRUMS
DRUMSTICK
DRUMSTICKS
DRUNK
DRUNKARD
DRUNKARDS
DRUNKATHON
DRUNKATHONS
DRUNKEN
DRUNKENLY
DRUNKENNESS
DRUNKENNESSES
DRUNKER
DRUNKEST
DRUNKOMETER
DRUNKOMETERS
DRUNKS
DRUPACEOUS
DRUPE
DRUPEL

DRUPELET
DRUPELETS
DRUPELS
DRUPES
DRUSE
DRUSES
DRUSIER
DRUSIEST
DRUSY
DRUTHERS
DRUXIER
DRUXIEST
DRUXY
DRY
DRYABLE
DRYAD
DRYADES
DRYADIC
DRYADS
DRYASDUST
DRYASDUSTS
DRYBEAT
DRYBEATEN
DRYBEATING
DRYBEATS
DRYER
DRYERS
DRYEST
DRYING
DRYINGS
DRYISH
DRYLAND
DRYLOT
DRYLOTS
DRYLY
DRYMOUTH
DRYMOUTHS
DRYNESS
DRYNESSES
DRYOPITHECINE
DRYOPITHECINES
DRYPOINT
DRYPOINTS
DRYS
DRYSALTER
DRYSALTERIES
DRYSALTERS
DRYSALTERY
DRYSTONE
DRYWALL
DRYWALLS
DSO
DSOBO
DSOBOS
DSOMO
DSOMOS

DSOS
DUAD
DUADS
DUAL
DUALATHON
DUALATHONS
DUALIN
DUALINS
DUALISM
DUALISMS
DUALIST
DUALISTIC
DUALISTICALLY
DUALISTS
DUALITIES
DUALITY
DUALIZE
DUALIZED
DUALIZES
DUALIZING
DUALLED
DUALLING
DUALLY
DUALS
DUAN
DUANS
DUAR
DUARCHIES
DUARCHY
DUARS
DUATHLON
DUATHLONS
DUB
DUBBED
DUBBER
DUBBERS
DUBBIN
DUBBING
DUBBINGS
DUBBINS
DUBBO
DUBBOS
DUBIETIES
DUBIETY
DUBIOSITIES
DUBIOSITY
DUBIOUS
DUBIOUSLY
DUBIOUSNESS
DUBIOUSNESSES
DUBITABLE
DUBITABLY
DUBITANCIES
DUBITANCY
DUBITATE
DUBITATED

DUBITATES
DUBITATING
DUBITATION
DUBITATIONS
DUBITATIVE
DUBITATIVELY
DUBNIUM
DUBONNET
DUBONNETS
DUBS
DUCAL
DUCALLY
DUCAT
DUCATOON
DUCATOONS
DUCATS
DUCDAME
DUCE
DUCES
DUCHESS
DUCHESSE
DUCHESSED
DUCHESSES
DUCHESSING
DUCHIES
DUCHY
DUCI
DUCK
DUCKBILL
DUCKBILLS
DUCKBOARD
DUCKBOARDS
DUCKED
DUCKER
DUCKERS
DUCKFOOT
DUCKIE
DUCKIER
DUCKIES
DUCKIEST
DUCKING
DUCKINGS
DUCKLING
DUCKLINGS
DUCKMOLE
DUCKMOLES
DUCKPIN
DUCKPINS
DUCKS
DUCKSHOVE
DUCKSHOVED
DUCKSHOVER
DUCKSHOVERS
DUCKSHOVES
DUCKSHOVING
DUCKTAIL

DUCKTAILS
DUCKWALK
DUCKWALKED
DUCKWALKING
DUCKWALKS
DUCKWEED
DUCKWEEDS
DUCKY
DUCT
DUCTAL
DUCTED
DUCTILE
DUCTILELY
DUCTILENESS
DUCTILENESSES
DUCTILITIES
DUCTILITY
DUCTING
DUCTINGS
DUCTLESS
DUCTS
DUCTULE
DUCTULES
DUCTWORK
DUCTWORKS
DUD
DUDDER
DUDDERIES
DUDDERS
DUDDERY
DUDDIE
DUDDIER
DUDDIEST
DUDDY
DUDE
DUDED
DUDEEN
DUDEENS
DUDES
DUDGEON
DUDGEONS
DUDHEEN
DUDHEENS
DUDING
DUDISH
DUDISHLY
DUDISM
DUDISMS
DUDS
DUE
DUECENTO
DUECENTOS
DUED
DUEFUL
DUEL
DUELED

DUELER
DUELERS
DUELING
DUELIST
DUELISTS
DUELLED
DUELLER
DUELLERS
DUELLI
DUELLING
DUELLINGS
DUELLIST
DUELLISTS
DUELLO
DUELLOS
DUELS
DUELSOME
DUENDE
DUENDES
DUENESS
DUENESSES
DUENNA
DUENNAS
DUENNASHIP
DUENNASHIPS
DUES
DUET
DUETS
DUETT
DUETTED
DUETTI
DUETTING
DUETTINO
DUETTINOS
DUETTIST
DUETTISTS
DUETTO
DUETTOS
DUETTS
DUFF
DUFFED
DUFFEL
DUFFELS
DUFFER
DUFFERDOM
DUFFERDOMS
DUFFERISM
DUFFERISMS
DUFFERS
DUFFEST
DUFFING
DUFFINGS
DUFFLE
DUFFLES
DUFFS
DUG

DUGITE
DUGITES
DUGONG
DUGONGS
DUGOUT
DUGOUTS
DUGS
DUH
DUHKHA
DUI
DUIKER
DUIKERBOK
DUIKERBOKS
DUIKERS
DUING
DUIT
DUITS
DUKA
DUKAS
DUKE
DUKED
DUKEDOM
DUKEDOMS
DUKELING
DUKELINGS
DUKERIES
DUKERY
DUKES
DUKESHIP
DUKESHIPS
DUKING
DUKKA
DUKKAH
DUKKERIPEN
DUKKERIPENS
DUKKHA
DULCAMARA
DULCAMARAS
DULCET
DULCETLY
DULCETNESS
DULCETS
DULCIAN
DULCIANA
DULCIANAS
DULCIANS
DULCIFICATION
DULCIFICATIONS
DULCIFIED
DULCIFIES
DULCIFLUOUS
DULCIFY
DULCIFYING
DULCILOQUIES
DULCILOQUY
DULCIMER

DULCIMERS
DULCIMORE
DULCIMORES
DULCINEA
DULCINEAS
DULCITE
DULCITES
DULCITOL
DULCITOLS
DULCITUDE
DULCITUDES
DULCOSE
DULCOSES
DULE
DULES
DULIA
DULIAS
DULL
DULLARD
DULLARDS
DULLED
DULLER
DULLEST
DULLIER
DULLIEST
DULLING
DULLISH
DULLISHLY
DULLNESS
DULLNESSES
DULLS
DULLSVILLE
DULLSVILLES
DULLY
DULNESS
DULNESSES
DULOCRACIES
DULOCRACY
DULOSES
DULOSIS
DULOTIC
DULSE
DULSES
DULY
DUMA
DUMAIST
DUMAISTS
DUMAS
DUMB
DUMBBELL
DUMBBELLS
DUMBCANE
DUMBCANES
DUMBED
DUMBER
DUMBEST

DUMBFOUND
DUMBFOUNDED
DUMBFOUNDER
DUMBFOUNDERED
DUMBFOUNDERING
DUMBFOUNDERS
DUMBFOUNDING
DUMBFOUNDS
DUMBHEAD
DUMBHEADS
DUMBING
DUMBLEDORE
DUMBLEDORES
DUMBLY
DUMBNESS
DUMBNESSES
DUMBO
DUMBOS
DUMBS
DUMBSTRICKEN
DUMBSTRUCK
DUMBWAITER
DUMBWAITERS
DUMDUM
DUMDUMS
DUMELA
DUMFOUND
DUMFOUNDED
DUMFOUNDER
DUMFOUNDERED
DUMFOUNDERING
DUMFOUNDERS
DUMFOUNDING
DUMFOUNDS
DUMKA
DUMKY
DUMMELHEAD
DUMMELHEADS
DUMMERER
DUMMERERS
DUMMIED
DUMMIER
DUMMIES
DUMMIEST
DUMMINESS
DUMMINESSES
DUMMKOPF
DUMMKOPFS
DUMMY
DUMMYING
DUMORTIERITE
DUMORTIERITES
DUMOSE
DUMOSITIES
DUMOSITY
DUMOUS

DUMP
DUMPBIN
DUMPBINS
DUMPCART
DUMPCARTS
DUMPED
DUMPER
DUMPERS
DUMPIER
DUMPIES
DUMPIEST
DUMPILY
DUMPINESS
DUMPINESSES
DUMPING
DUMPINGS
DUMPISH
DUMPISHLY
DUMPISHNESS
DUMPISHNESSES
DUMPLE
DUMPLED
DUMPLES
DUMPLING
DUMPLINGS
DUMPS
DUMPSTER
DUMPSTERS
DUMPY
DUN
DUNAM
DUNAMS
DUNCE
DUNCEDOM
DUNCEDOMS
DUNCELIKE
DUNCERIES
DUNCERY
DUNCES
DUNCH
DUNCHED
DUNCHES
DUNCHING
DUNCICAL
DUNCISH
DUNDER
DUNDERFUNK
DUNDERFUNKS
DUNDERHEAD
DUNDERHEADED
DUNDERHEADISM
DUNDERHEADISMS
DUNDERHEADS
DUNDERPATE
DUNDERPATES
DUNDERS

DUNDREARIES
DUNE
DUNELAND
DUNELANDS
DUNELIKE
DUNES
DUNG
DUNGAREE
DUNGAREES
DUNGAS
DUNGED
DUNGEON
DUNGEONED
DUNGEONER
DUNGEONERS
DUNGEONING
DUNGEONS
DUNGER
DUNGERS
DUNGHILL
DUNGHILLS
DUNGIER
DUNGIEST
DUNGING
DUNGMERE
DUNGMERES
DUNGS
DUNGY
DUNIEWASSAL
DUNIEWASSALS
DUNITE
DUNITES
DUNITIC
DUNIWASSAL
DUNIWASSALS
DUNK
DUNKED
DUNKER
DUNKERS
DUNKING
DUNKS
DUNLIN
DUNLINS
DUNNAGE
DUNNAGES
DUNNAKIN
DUNNAKINS
DUNNART
DUNNARTS
DUNNED
DUNNER
DUNNESS
DUNNESSES
DUNNEST
DUNNIER
DUNNIES

DUNNIEST
DUNNIEWASSALS
DUNNING
DUNNINGS
DUNNISH
DUNNITE
DUNNITES
DUNNO
DUNNOCK
DUNNOCKS
DUNNY
DUNS
DUNSH
DUNSHED
DUNSHES
DUNSHING
DUNT
DUNTED
DUNTING
DUNTS
DUO
DUOBINARY
DUODECENNIAL
DUODECILLION
DUODECILLIONS
DUODECIMAL
DUODECIMALLY
DUODECIMALS
DUODECIMO
DUODECIMOS
DUODENA
DUODENAL
DUODENARY
DUODENECTOMIES
DUODENECTOMY
DUODENITIS
DUODENITISES
DUODENUM
DUODENUMS
DUOLOG
DUOLOGS
DUOLOGUE
DUOLOGUES
DUOMI
DUOMO
DUOMOS
DUOPOLIES
DUOPOLISTIC
DUOPOLY
DUOPSONIES
DUOPSONY
DUOS
DUOTONE
DUOTONES
DUP
DUPABILITIES

DUPABILITY
DUPABLE
DUPATTA
DUPATTAS
DUPE
DUPED
DUPER
DUPERIES
DUPERS
DUPERY
DUPES
DUPING
DUPION
DUPIONS
DUPLE
DUPLET
DUPLETS
DUPLEX
DUPLEXED
DUPLEXER
DUPLEXERS
DUPLEXES
DUPLEXING
DUPLEXITIES
DUPLEXITY
DUPLICABILITY
DUPLICABLE
DUPLICAND
DUPLICANDS
DUPLICATE
DUPLICATED
DUPLICATELY
DUPLICATES
DUPLICATING
DUPLICATION
DUPLICATIONS
DUPLICATIVE
DUPLICATOR
DUPLICATORS
DUPLICATURE
DUPLICATURES
DUPLICIDENT
DUPLICITIES
DUPLICITOUS
DUPLICITOUSLY
DUPLICITY
DUPLIED
DUPLIES
DUPLY
DUPLYING
DUPONDII
DUPONDIUS
DUPPED
DUPPIES
DUPPING
DUPPY

DUPS
DURA
DURABILITIES
DURABILITY
DURABLE
DURABLENESS
DURABLENESSES
DURABLES
DURABLY
DURAL
DURALS
DURALUMIN
DURALUMINIUM
DURALUMINIUMS
DURALUMINS
DURAMEN
DURAMENS
DURANCE
DURANCES
DURANT
DURANTS
DURAS
DURATION
DURATIONAL
DURATIONS
DURATIVE
DURATIVES
DURBAR
DURBARS
DURCHKOMPONIERT
DURDUM
DURDUMS
DURE
DURED
DUREFUL
DURES
DURESS
DURESSE
DURESSES
DURGAH
DURGAHS
DURGAN
DURGANS
DURGIER
DURGIEST
DURGY
DURIAN
DURIANS
DURICRUST
DURICRUSTS
DURING
DURION
DURIONS
DURMAST
DURMASTS
DURN

DURNDEST
DURNED
DURNEDER
DURNEDEST
DURNING
DURNS
DURO
DUROC
DUROCS
DUROMETER
DUROMETERS
DUROS
DUROY
DUROYS
DURR
DURRA
DURRAS
DURRIE
DURRIES
DURRS
DURRY
DURST
DURUKULI
DURUKULIS
DURUM
DURUMS
DURZI
DURZIS
DUSH
DUSHED
DUSHES
DUSHING
DUSK
DUSKED
DUSKEN
DUSKENED
DUSKENING
DUSKENS
DUSKER
DUSKEST
DUSKIER
DUSKIEST
DUSKILY
DUSKINESS
DUSKINESSES
DUSKING
DUSKISH
DUSKISHLY
DUSKISHNESS
DUSKISHNESSES
DUSKLY
DUSKNESS
DUSKNESSES
DUSKS
DUSKY
DUST

DUSTBIN
DUSTBINS
DUSTCART
DUSTCARTS
DUSTCOVER
DUSTCOVERS
DUSTED
DUSTER
DUSTERS
DUSTHEAP
DUSTHEAPS
DUSTIER
DUSTIEST
DUSTILY
DUSTINESS
DUSTINESSES
DUSTING
DUSTINGS
DUSTLESS
DUSTLIKE
DUSTMAN
DUSTMEN
DUSTOFF
DUSTOFFS
DUSTPAN
DUSTPANS
DUSTPROOF
DUSTRAG
DUSTRAGS
DUSTS
DUSTSHEET
DUSTSHEETS
DUSTUP
DUSTUPS
DUSTY
DUTCH
DUTCHES
DUTCHMAN
DUTCHMEN
DUTEOUS
DUTEOUSLY
DUTEOUSNESS
DUTEOUSNESSES
DUTIABILITY
DUTIABLE
DUTIED
DUTIES
DUTIFUL
DUTIFULLY
DUTIFULNESS
DUTIFULNESSES
DUTY
DUUMVIR
DUUMVIRAL
DUUMVIRATE
DUUMVIRATES

DUUMVIRI
DUUMVIRS
DUVET
DUVETINE
DUVETINES
DUVETS
DUVETYN
DUVETYNE
DUVETYNES
DUVETYNS
DUX
DUXELLES
DUXES
DUYKER
DUYKERS
DVANDVA
DVANDVAS
DVORNIK
DVORNIKS
DWAAL
DWALE
DWALES
DWALM
DWALMED
DWALMING
DWALMS
DWAM
DWAMMED
DWAMMING
DWAMS
DWANG
DWANGS
DWARF
DWARFED
DWARFER
DWARFEST
DWARFING
DWARFISH
DWARFISHLY
DWARFISHNESS
DWARFISHNESSES
DWARFISM
DWARFISMS
DWARFLIKE
DWARFNESS
DWARFNESSES
DWARFS
DWARVES
DWAUM
DWAUMED
DWAUMING
DWAUMS
DWEEB
DWEEBIER
DWEEBIEST
DWEEBS

DWEEBY
DWELL
DWELLED
DWELLER
DWELLERS
DWELLING
DWELLINGS
DWELLS
DWELT
DWILE
DWILES
DWINDLE
DWINDLED
DWINDLEMENT
DWINDLEMENTS
DWINDLES
DWINDLING
DWINE
DWINED
DWINES
DWINING
DYABLE
DYAD
DYADIC
DYADICALLY
DYADICS
DYADS
DYARCHAL
DYARCHIC
DYARCHICAL
DYARCHIES
DYARCHY
DYBBUK
DYBBUKIM
DYBBUKKIM
DYBBUKS
DYE
DYEABILITIES
DYEABILITY
DYEABLE
DYED
DYEING
DYEINGS
DYELINE
DYELINES
DYER
DYERS
DYES
DYESTER
DYESTERS
DYESTUFF
DYESTUFFS
DYEWEED
DYEWEEDS
DYEWOOD
DYEWOODS

DYING
DYINGLY
DYINGNESS
DYINGNESSES
DYINGS
DYKE
DYKED
DYKES
DYKEY
DYKIER
DYKIEST
DYKING
DYNAMETER
DYNAMETERS
DYNAMIC
DYNAMICAL
DYNAMICALLY
DYNAMICIST
DYNAMICISTS
DYNAMICS
DYNAMISE
DYNAMISED
DYNAMISES
DYNAMISING
DYNAMISM
DYNAMISMS
DYNAMIST
DYNAMISTIC
DYNAMISTS
DYNAMITARD
DYNAMITARDS
DYNAMITE
DYNAMITED
DYNAMITER
DYNAMITERS
DYNAMITES
DYNAMITIC
DYNAMITING
DYNAMIZE
DYNAMIZED
DYNAMIZES
DYNAMIZING
DYNAMO
DYNAMOELECTRIC
DYNAMOGENESES
DYNAMOGENESIS
DYNAMOGENIES
DYNAMOGENY
DYNAMOGRAPH
DYNAMOGRAPHS
DYNAMOMETER
DYNAMOMETERS
DYNAMOMETRIC
DYNAMOMETRICAL
DYNAMOMETRIES
DYNAMOMETRY

DYNAMOS
DYNAMOTOR
DYNAMOTORS
DYNAST
DYNASTIC
DYNASTICAL
DYNASTICALLY
DYNASTIES
DYNASTS
DYNASTY
DYNATRON
DYNATRONS
DYNE
DYNEIN
DYNEL
DYNELS
DYNES
DYNODE
DYNODES
DYOPHYSITE
DYOPHYSITES
DYOTHELETE
DYOTHELETES
DYOTHELETIC
DYOTHELETICAL
DYOTHELETISM
DYOTHELETISMS
DYOTHELISM
DYOTHELISMS
DYOTHELITE
DYOTHELITES
DYOTHELITIC
DYOTHELITICAL
DYSAESTHESIA
DYSAESTHESIAS
DYSAESTHETIC
DYSARTHRIA
DYSARTHRIAS
DYSCALCULIA
DYSCALCULIC
DYSCALCULICS
DYSCHROA
DYSCHROAS
DYSCHROIA
DYSCHROIAS
DYSCRASIA
DYSCRASIAS
DYSCRASITE
DYSCRASITES
DYSENTERIC
DYSENTERIES
DYSENTERY
DYSFUNCTION
DYSFUNCTIONAL
DYSFUNCTIONS
DYSGENESES

DYSGENESIS
DYSGENIC
DYSGENICS
DYSGRAPHIA
DYSGRAPHIAS
DYSGRAPHIC
DYSHARMONIC
DYSKINESIA
DYSKINESIAS
DYSKINETIC
DYSLALIA
DYSLALIC
DYSLALICS
DYSLECTIC
DYSLECTICS
DYSLEXIA
DYSLEXIAS
DYSLEXIC
DYSLEXICS
DYSLOGIES
DYSLOGISTIC
DYSLOGISTICALLY
DYSLOGY
DYSMELIA
DYSMELIAS
DYSMELIC
DYSMENORRHEA
DYSMENORRHEAL
DYSMENORRHEAS
DYSMENORRHEIC
DYSMENORRHOEA
DYSMENORRHOEAL
DYSMENORRHOEAS
DYSMENORRHOEIC
DYSMORPHOPHOBIA
DYSODIL
DYSODILE
DYSODILES
DYSODILS
DYSODYLE
DYSODYLES
DYSPAREUNIA
DYSPAREUNIAS
DYSPATHETIC
DYSPATHIES
DYSPATHY
DYSPEPSIA
DYSPEPSIAS
DYSPEPSIES
DYSPEPSY
DYSPEPTIC
DYSPEPTICAL
DYSPEPTICALLY
DYSPEPTICALS
DYSPEPTICS
DYSPHAGIA

DYSPHAGIAS
DYSPHAGIC
DYSPHAGIES
DYSPHAGY
DYSPHASIA
DYSPHASIAS
DYSPHASIC
DYSPHASICS
DYSPHEMISM
DYSPHEMISMS
DYSPHEMISTIC
DYSPHONIA
DYSPHONIAS
DYSPHONIC
DYSPHORIA
DYSPHORIAS
DYSPHORIC
DYSPLASIA
DYSPLASIAS
DYSPLASTIC
DYSPNEA
DYSPNEAL
DYSPNEAS
DYSPNEIC
DYSPNOEA
DYSPNOEAL
DYSPNOEAS
DYSPNOEIC
DYSPNOIC
DYSPRAXIA
DYSPRAXIAS
DYSPROSIUM
DYSPROSIUMS
DYSRHYTHMIA
DYSRHYTHMIAS
DYSRHYTHMIC
DYSSNERGIC
DYSSYNERGIA
DYSTAXIA
DYSTAXIAS
DYSTECTIC
DYSTELEOLOGICAL
DYSTELEOLOGIES
DYSTELEOLOGIST
DYSTELEOLOGISTS
DYSTELEOLOGY
DYSTHESIA
DYSTHESIAS
DYSTHETIC
DYSTHYMIA
DYSTHYMIAC
DYSTHYMIACS
DYSTHYMIAS
DYSTHYMIC
DYSTOCIA
DYSTOCIAL

DYSTOCIAS
DYSTONIA
DYSTONIAS
DYSTONIC
DYSTOPIA
DYSTOPIAN
DYSTOPIANS
DYSTOPIAS
DYSTOSOCIALLY
DYSTROPHIA
DYSTROPHIAS
DYSTROPHIC
DYSTROPHIES
DYSTROPHIN
DYSTROPHINS
DYSTROPHY
DYSURIA
DYSURIAS
DYSURIC
DYSURIES
DYSURY
DYTISCID
DYTISCIDS
DYVOUR
DYVOURIES
DYVOURS
DYVOURY
DZEREN
DZERENS
DZHO
DZHOS
DZIGGETAI
DZIGGETAIS
DZO
DZOS

E

EA
EACH
EACHWHERE
EADISH
EADISHES
EAGER
EAGERER
EAGEREST
EAGERLY
EAGERNESS
EAGERNESSES
EAGERS
EAGLE
EAGLEHAWK
EAGLEHAWKS
EAGLES
EAGLESTONE
EAGLESTONES
EAGLET
EAGLETS
EAGLEWOOD
EAGLEWOODS
EAGRE
EAGRES
EALDORMAN
EALDORMEN
EALE
EALES
EAN
EANED
EANING
EANLING
EANLINGS
EANS
EAR
EARACHE
EARACHES
EARBALL
EARBALLS
EARBASH
EARBASHED
EARBASHER
EARBASHERS
EARBASHES
EARBASHING
EARBASHINGS
EARBOB
EARBOBS
EARCON
EARCONS
EARD

EARDED
EARDING
EARDROP
EARDROPS
EARDRUM
EARDRUMS
EARDS
EARED
EARFLAP
EARFLAPS
EARFUL
EARFULS
EARING
EARINGS
EARL
EARLAP
EARLAPS
EARLDOM
EARLDOMS
EARLESS
EARLIER
EARLIERISE
EARLIERISED
EARLIERISES
EARLIERISING
EARLIERIZE
EARLIERIZED
EARLIERIZES
EARLIERIZING
EARLIES
EARLIEST
EARLIKE
EARLINESS
EARLINESSES
EARLOBE
EARLOBES
EARLOCK
EARLOCKS
EARLS
EARLSHIP
EARLSHIPS
EARLY
EARLYWOOD
EARLYWOODS
EARMARK
EARMARKED
EARMARKING
EARMARKS
EARMUFF
EARMUFFS
EARN

EARNED
EARNER
EARNERS
EARNEST
EARNESTLY
EARNESTNESS
EARNESTNESSES
EARNESTS
EARNING
EARNINGS
EARNS
EARPHONE
EARPHONES
EARPICK
EARPICKS
EARPIECE
EARPIECES
EARPLUG
EARPLUGS
EARRING
EARRINGS
EARS
EARSHOT
EARSHOTS
EARSPLITTING
EARST
EARSTONE
EARSTONES
EARTH
EARTHBORN
EARTHBOUND
EARTHED
EARTHEN
EARTHENWARE
EARTHENWARES
EARTHFALL
EARTHFALLS
EARTHFAST
EARTHFLAX
EARTHFLAXES
EARTHIER
EARTHIEST
EARTHILY
EARTHINESS
EARTHINESSES
EARTHING
EARTHLIER
EARTHLIES
EARTHLIEST
EARTHLIGHT
EARTHLIGHTS

EARTHLIKE
EARTHLINESS
EARTHLINESSES
EARTHLING
EARTHLINGS
EARTHLY
EARTHMAN
EARTHMEN
EARTHMOVER
EARTHMOVERS
EARTHMOVING
EARTHMOVINGS
EARTHNUT
EARTHNUTS
EARTHPEA
EARTHPEAS
EARTHQUAKE
EARTHQUAKED
EARTHQUAKES
EARTHQUAKING
EARTHRISE
EARTHRISES
EARTHS
EARTHSET
EARTHSETS
EARTHSHAKER
EARTHSHAKERS
EARTHSHAKING
EARTHSHAKINGLY
EARTHSHATTERING
EARTHSHINE
EARTHSHINES
EARTHSTAR
EARTHSTARS
EARTHWARD
EARTHWARDS
EARTHWAX
EARTHWAXES
EARTHWOLF
EARTHWOLVES
EARTHWOMAN
EARTHWOMEN
EARTHWORK
EARTHWORKS
EARTHWORM
EARTHWORMS
EARTHY
EARWAX
EARWAXES
EARWIG
EARWIGGED

EARWIGGING	EASTMOST	EBENEZERS	EBULLIOSCOPE
EARWIGGINGS	EASTS	EBENISTE	EBULLIOSCOPES
EARWIGGY	EASTWARD	EBENISTES	EBULLIOSCOPIC
EARWIGS	EASTWARDLY	EBIONISE	EBULLIOSCOPICAL
EARWITNESS	EASTWARDS	EBIONISED	EBULLIOSCOPIES
EARWITNESSES	EASY	EBIONISES	EBULLIOSCOPY
EARWORM	EASYGOING	EBIONISING	EBULLITION
EARWORMS	EASYGOINGNESS	EBIONISM	EBULLITIONS
EAS	EASYGOINGNESSES	EBIONISMS	EBURNATION
EASE	EASYING	EBIONITIC	EBURNATIONS
EASED	EAT	EBIONITISM	EBURNEAN
EASEFUL	EATABLE	EBIONITISMS	EBURNEOUS
EASEFULLY	EATABLES	EBIONIZE	EBURNIFICATION
EASEFULNESS	EATAGE	EBIONIZED	EBURNIFICATIONS
EASEL	EATAGES	EBIONIZES	ECAD
EASELESS	EATCHE	EBIONIZING	ECADS
EASELS	EATCHES	EBON	ECARDINATE
EASEMENT	EATEN	EBONICS	ECARINATE
EASEMENTS	EATER	EBONIES	ECARTE
EASER	EATERIE	EBONISE	ECARTES
EASERS	EATERIES	EBONISED	ECAUDATE
EASES	EATERS	EBONISES	ECBLASTESES
EASIED	EATERY	EBONISING	ECBLASTESIS
EASIER	EATH	EBONIST	ECBOLE
EASIES	EATHE	EBONISTS	ECBOLES
EASIEST	EATHLY	EBONITE	ECBOLIC
EASILY	EATING	EBONITES	ECBOLICS
EASINESS	EATINGS	EBONIZE	ECCALEOBION
EASINESSES	EATS	EBONIZED	ECCALEOBIONS
EASING	EAU	EBONIZES	ECCE
EASLE	EAUS	EBONIZING	ECCENTRIC
EASLES	EAUX	EBONS	ECCENTRICAL
EASSEL	EAVE	EBONY	ECCENTRICALLY
EASSELWARD	EAVED	EBOULEMENT	ECCENTRICITIES
EASSIL	EAVES	EBOULEMENTS	ECCENTRICITY
EAST	EAVESDRIP	EBRACTEATE	ECCENTRICS
EASTBOUND	EAVESDRIPS	EBRACTEOLATE	ECCHYMOSED
EASTED	EAVESDROP	EBRIATE	ECCHYMOSES
EASTER	EAVESDROPPED	EBRIATED	ECCHYMOSIS
EASTERLIES	EAVESDROPPER	EBRIETIES	ECCHYMOTIC
EASTERLING	EAVESDROPPERS	EBRIETY	ECCLESIA
EASTERLINGS	EAVESDROPPING	EBRILLADE	ECCLESIAE
EASTERLY	EAVESDROPPINGS	EBRILLADES	ECCLESIAL
EASTERMOST	EAVESDROPS	EBRIOSE	ECCLESIARCH
EASTERN	EBAUCHE	EBRIOSITIES	ECCLESIARCHS
EASTERNER	EBAUCHES	EBRIOSITY	ECCLESIAST
EASTERNERS	EBB	EBULLIENCE	ECCLESIASTIC
EASTERNMOST	EBBED	EBULLIENCES	ECCLESIASTICAL
EASTERS	EBBET	EBULLIENCIES	ECCLESIASTICISM
EASTING	EBBETS	EBULLIENCY	ECCLESIASTICS
EASTINGS	EBBING	EBULLIENT	ECCLESIASTS
EASTLAND	EBBLESS	EBULLIENTLY	ECCLESIOLATER
EASTLIN	EBBS	EBULLIOMETER	ECCLESIOLATERS
EASTLING	EBBTIDE	EBULLIOMETERS	ECCLESIOLATRIES
EASTLINGS	EBBTIDES	EBULLIOMETRIC	ECCLESIOLATRY
EASTLINS	EBENEZER	EBULLIOMETRY	ECCLESIOLOGICAL

309

ECCLESIOLOGIES
ECCLESIOLOGIST
ECCLESIOLOGISTS
ECCLESIOLOGY
ECCO
ECCOPROTIC
ECCOPROTICS
ECCREMOCARPUS
ECCREMOCARPUSES
ECCRINE
ECCRINOLOGIES
ECCRINOLOGY
ECCRISES
ECCRISIS
ECCRITIC
ECCRITICS
ECDEMIC
ECDEMICALLY
ECDYSES
ECDYSIAL
ECDYSIAST
ECDYSIASTS
ECDYSIS
ECDYSON
ECDYSONE
ECDYSONES
ECDYSONS
ECESIS
ECESISES
ECH
ECHAPPE
ECHAPPES
ECHARD
ECHARDS
ECHE
ECHED
ECHELLE
ECHELLES
ECHELON
ECHELONED
ECHELONING
ECHELONS
ECHES
ECHEVERIA
ECHEVERIAS
ECHIDNA
ECHIDNAE
ECHIDNAS
ECHIDNINE
ECHIDNINES
ECHINACEA
ECHINATE
ECHINATED
ECHING
ECHINI
ECHINOCOCCI

ECHINOCOCCOSES
ECHINOCOCCOSIS
ECHINOCOCCUS
ECHINODERM
ECHINODERMAL
ECHINODERMATOUS
ECHINODERMS
ECHINOID
ECHINOIDS
ECHINUS
ECHINUSES
ECHIUM
ECHIUMS
ECHIUROID
ECHIUROIDS
ECHO
ECHOCARDIOGRAM
ECHOCARDIOGRAMS
ECHOED
ECHOER
ECHOERS
ECHOES
ECHOEY
ECHOGRAM
ECHOGRAMS
ECHOGRAPHIC
ECHOGRAPHICALLY
ECHOGRAPHIES
ECHOGRAPHY
ECHOIC
ECHOING
ECHOISE
ECHOISED
ECHOISES
ECHOISING
ECHOISM
ECHOISMS
ECHOIST
ECHOISTS
ECHOIZE
ECHOIZED
ECHOIZES
ECHOIZING
ECHOLALIA
ECHOLALIAS
ECHOLALIC
ECHOLESS
ECHOLOCATION
ECHOLOCATIONS
ECHOPRAXIA
ECHOPRAXIAS
ECHOPRAXIS
ECHOS
ECHOVIRUS
ECHOVIRUSES
ECHT

ECLAIR
ECLAIRCISSEMENT
ECLAIRS
ECLAMPSIA
ECLAMPSIAS
ECLAMPSIES
ECLAMPSY
ECLAMPTIC
ECLAT
ECLATS
ECLECTIC
ECLECTICALLY
ECLECTICISM
ECLECTICISMS
ECLECTICS
ECLIPSE
ECLIPSED
ECLIPSER
ECLIPSERS
ECLIPSES
ECLIPSING
ECLIPSIS
ECLIPSISES
ECLIPTIC
ECLIPTICALLY
ECLIPTICS
ECLOGITE
ECLOGITES
ECLOGUE
ECLOGUES
ECLOSE
ECLOSED
ECLOSES
ECLOSING
ECLOSION
ECLOSIONS
ECO
ECOCATASTROPHE
ECOCATASTROPHES
ECOCENTRIC
ECOCENTRICALLY
ECOCENTRICS
ECOCIDAL
ECOCIDE
ECOCIDES
ECOCLIMATE
ECOCLIMATES
ECOD
ECOFEMINISM
ECOFEMINISMS
ECOFEMINIST
ECOFEMINISTS
ECOFREAK
ECOFREAKS
ECOFRIENDLY
ECOLOGIC

ECOLOGICAL
ECOLOGICALLY
ECOLOGIES
ECOLOGIST
ECOLOGISTS
ECOLOGY
ECOMMERCE
ECOMMERCIAL
ECOMMERCIALLY
ECONOBOX
ECONOBOXES
ECONOMETRIC
ECONOMETRICAL
ECONOMETRICALLY
ECONOMETRICIAN
ECONOMETRICIANS
ECONOMETRICS
ECONOMETRIST
ECONOMETRISTS
ECONOMIC
ECONOMICAL
ECONOMICALLY
ECONOMICS
ECONOMIES
ECONOMISATION
ECONOMISATIONS
ECONOMISE
ECONOMISED
ECONOMISER
ECONOMISERS
ECONOMISES
ECONOMISING
ECONOMISM
ECONOMISMS
ECONOMIST
ECONOMISTIC
ECONOMISTICALLY
ECONOMISTS
ECONOMIZATION
ECONOMIZATIONS
ECONOMIZE
ECONOMIZED
ECONOMIZER
ECONOMIZERS
ECONOMIZES
ECONOMIZING
ECONOMY
ECONUT
ECONUTS
ECOPHOBIA
ECOPHOBIAS
ECOPHYSIOLOGIES
ECOPHYSIOLOGY
ECORCHE
ECORCHES
ECOREGION

ECOREGIONAL
ECOREGIONALLY
ECOREGIONS
ECOSPECIES
ECOSPECIFIC
ECOSPECIFICALLY
ECOSPHERE
ECOSPHERES
ECOSSAISE
ECOSSAISES
ECOSTATE
ECOSYSTEM
ECOSYSTEMS
ECOTERRORISM
ECOTERRORISMS
ECOTERRORIST
ECOTERRORISTS
ECOTONAL
ECOTONE
ECOTONES
ECOTOURISM
ECOTOURISMS
ECOTOURIST
ECOTOURISTS
ECOTOXIC
ECOTOXICOLOGIES
ECOTOXICOLOGIST
ECOTOXICOLOGY
ECOTYPE
ECOTYPES
ECOTYPIC
ECOTYPICALLY
ECPHONESES
ECPHONESIS
ECPHRACTIC
ECPHRACTICS
ECRASEUR
ECRASEURS
ECRITOIRE
ECRITOIRES
ECRU
ECRUS
ECSTASES
ECSTASIED
ECSTASIES
ECSTASIS
ECSTASISE
ECSTASISED
ECSTASISES
ECSTASISING
ECSTASIZE
ECSTASIZED
ECSTASIZES
ECSTASIZING
ECSTASY
ECSTASYING

ECSTATIC
ECSTATICALLY
ECSTATICS
ECTASES
ECTASIA
ECTASIS
ECTATIC
ECTHLIPSES
ECTHLIPSIS
ECTHYMA
ECTHYMAS
ECTHYMATA
ECTOBLAST
ECTOBLASTIC
ECTOBLASTS
ECTOCRINE
ECTOCRINES
ECTODERM
ECTODERMAL
ECTODERMIC
ECTODERMS
ECTOENZYME
ECTOENZYMES
ECTOGENESES
ECTOGENESIS
ECTOGENETIC
ECTOGENIC
ECTOGENICALLY
ECTOGENIES
ECTOGENOUS
ECTOGENY
ECTOMERE
ECTOMERES
ECTOMERIC
ECTOMORPH
ECTOMORPHIC
ECTOMORPHIES
ECTOMORPHS
ECTOMORPHY
ECTOMYCORRHIZA
ECTOPARASITE
ECTOPARASITES
ECTOPARASITIC
ECTOPHYTE
ECTOPHYTES
ECTOPHYTIC
ECTOPIA
ECTOPIAS
ECTOPIC
ECTOPICALLY
ECTOPIES
ECTOPLASM
ECTOPLASMIC
ECTOPLASMS
ECTOPLASTIC
ECTOPROCT

ECTOPROCTS
ECTOPY
ECTOSARC
ECTOSARCOUS
ECTOSARCS
ECTOTHERM
ECTOTHERMIC
ECTOTHERMS
ECTOTROPHIC
ECTOZOA
ECTOZOAN
ECTOZOANS
ECTOZOIC
ECTOZOON
ECTROPIC
ECTROPION
ECTROPIONS
ECTROPIUM
ECTROPIUMS
ECTYPAL
ECTYPE
ECTYPES
ECTYPOGRAPHIES
ECTYPOGRAPHY
ECU
ECUELLE
ECUELLES
ECUMENIC
ECUMENICAL
ECUMENICALISM
ECUMENICALISMS
ECUMENICALLY
ECUMENICISM
ECUMENICISMS
ECUMENICIST
ECUMENICISTS
ECUMENICITIES
ECUMENICITY
ECUMENICS
ECUMENISM
ECUMENISMS
ECUMENIST
ECUMENISTS
ECURIE
ECURIES
ECUS
ECZEMA
ECZEMAS
ECZEMATOUS
ED
EDACIOUS
EDACIOUSLY
EDACIOUSNESS
EDACIOUSNESSES
EDACITIES
EDACITY

EDAPHIC
EDAPHICALLY
EDAPHOLOGIES
EDAPHOLOGY
EDDIED
EDDIES
EDDISH
EDDISHES
EDDO
EDDOES
EDDY
EDDYING
EDELWEISS
EDELWEISSES
EDEMA
EDEMAS
EDEMATA
EDEMATOSE
EDEMATOUS
EDENIC
EDENTAL
EDENTATE
EDENTATES
EDENTULATE
EDENTULOUS
EDGE
EDGEBONE
EDGEBONES
EDGED
EDGELESS
EDGER
EDGERS
EDGES
EDGEWAYS
EDGEWISE
EDGIER
EDGIEST
EDGILY
EDGINESS
EDGINESSES
EDGING
EDGINGS
EDGY
EDH
EDHS
EDIBILITIES
EDIBILITY
EDIBLE
EDIBLENESS
EDIBLENESSES
EDIBLES
EDICT
EDICTAL
EDICTALLY
EDICTS
EDIFICATION

EDIFICATIONS
EDIFICATORY
EDIFICE
EDIFICES
EDIFICIAL
EDIFIED
EDIFIER
EDIFIERS
EDIFIES
EDIFY
EDIFYING
EDIFYINGLY
EDILE
EDILES
EDIT
EDITABLE
EDITED
EDITING
EDITION
EDITIONS
EDITOR
EDITORIAL
EDITORIALISE
EDITORIALISED
EDITORIALISER
EDITORIALISERS
EDITORIALISES
EDITORIALISING
EDITORIALIST
EDITORIALISTS
EDITORIALIZE
EDITORIALIZED
EDITORIALIZER
EDITORIALIZERS
EDITORIALIZES
EDITORIALIZING
EDITORIALLY
EDITORIALS
EDITORS
EDITORSHIP
EDITORSHIPS
EDITRESS
EDITRESSES
EDITS
EDRIOPHTHALMIAN
EDRIOPHTHALMIC
EDRIOPHTHALMOUS
EDS
EDUCABILITIES
EDUCABILITY
EDUCABLE
EDUCABLES
EDUCATABILITIES
EDUCATABILITY
EDUCATABLE
EDUCATABLY

EDUCATE
EDUCATED
EDUCATEDNESS
EDUCATEDNESSES
EDUCATES
EDUCATING
EDUCATION
EDUCATIONAL
EDUCATIONALIST
EDUCATIONALISTS
EDUCATIONALLY
EDUCATIONESE
EDUCATIONESES
EDUCATIONIST
EDUCATIONISTS
EDUCATIONS
EDUCATIVE
EDUCATOR
EDUCATORS
EDUCATORY
EDUCE
EDUCED
EDUCEMENT
EDUCEMENTS
EDUCES
EDUCIBLE
EDUCING
EDUCT
EDUCTION
EDUCTIONS
EDUCTIVE
EDUCTOR
EDUCTORS
EDUCTS
EDULCORANT
EDULCORATE
EDULCORATED
EDULCORATES
EDULCORATING
EDULCORATION
EDULCORATIONS
EDULCORATIVE
EDULCORATOR
EDULCORATORS
EDUSKUNTA
EDUSKUNTAS
EDUTAINMENT
EDUTAINMENTS
EE
EECH
EECHED
EECHES
EECHING
EEJIT
EEJITS
EEK

EEL
EELFARE
EELFARES
EELGRASS
EELGRASSES
EELIER
EELIEST
EELLIKE
EELPOUT
EELPOUTS
EELS
EELWORM
EELWORMS
EELWRACK
EELWRACKS
EELY
EEN
EERIE
EERIER
EERIEST
EERILY
EERINESS
EERINESSES
EERY
EEVEN
EEVENS
EEVN
EEVNING
EEVNINGS
EEVNS
EF
EFF
EFFABLE
EFFACE
EFFACEABLE
EFFACED
EFFACEMENT
EFFACEMENTS
EFFACER
EFFACERS
EFFACES
EFFACING
EFFECT
EFFECTED
EFFECTER
EFFECTERS
EFFECTIBLE
EFFECTING
EFFECTIVE
EFFECTIVELY
EFFECTIVENESS
EFFECTIVENESSES
EFFECTIVES
EFFECTIVITIES
EFFECTIVITY
EFFECTLESS

EFFECTOR
EFFECTORS
EFFECTS
EFFECTUAL
EFFECTUALITIES
EFFECTUALITY
EFFECTUALLY
EFFECTUALNESS
EFFECTUALNESSES
EFFECTUATE
EFFECTUATED
EFFECTUATES
EFFECTUATING
EFFECTUATION
EFFECTUATIONS
EFFED
EFFEIR
EFFEIRED
EFFEIRING
EFFEIRS
EFFEMINACIES
EFFEMINACY
EFFEMINATE
EFFEMINATED
EFFEMINATELY
EFFEMINATENESS
EFFEMINATES
EFFEMINATING
EFFEMINISE
EFFEMINISED
EFFEMINISES
EFFEMINISING
EFFEMINIZE
EFFEMINIZED
EFFEMINIZES
EFFEMINIZING
EFFENDI
EFFENDIS
EFFERE
EFFERED
EFFERENCE
EFFERENCES
EFFERENT
EFFERENTLY
EFFERENTS
EFFERES
EFFERING
EFFERVESCE
EFFERVESCED
EFFERVESCENCE
EFFERVESCENCES
EFFERVESCENCIES
EFFERVESCENCY
EFFERVESCENT
EFFERVESCENTLY
EFFERVESCES

EFFERVESCIBLE
EFFERVESCING
EFFERVESCINGLY
EFFETE
EFFETELY
EFFETENESS
EFFETENESSES
EFFICACIES
EFFICACIOUS
EFFICACIOUSLY
EFFICACIOUSNESS
EFFICACITIES
EFFICACITY
EFFICACY
EFFICIENCE
EFFICIENCES
EFFICIENCIES
EFFICIENCY
EFFICIENT
EFFICIENTLY
EFFICIENTS
EFFIERCE
EFFIERCED
EFFIERCES
EFFIERCING
EFFIGIAL
EFFIGIES
EFFIGURATE
EFFIGURATION
EFFIGURATIONS
EFFIGY
EFFING
EFFINGS
EFFLEURAGE
EFFLEURAGED
EFFLEURAGES
EFFLEURAGING
EFFLORESCE
EFFLORESCED
EFFLORESCENCE
EFFLORESCENCES
EFFLORESCENT
EFFLORESCES
EFFLORESCING
EFFLUENCE
EFFLUENCES
EFFLUENT
EFFLUENTS
EFFLUVIA
EFFLUVIAL
EFFLUVIUM
EFFLUVIUMS
EFFLUX
EFFLUXES
EFFLUXION
EFFLUXIONS

EFFORCE
EFFORCED
EFFORCES
EFFORCING
EFFORT
EFFORTFUL
EFFORTFULLY
EFFORTFULNESS
EFFORTFULNESSES
EFFORTLESS
EFFORTLESSLY
EFFORTLESSNESS
EFFORTS
EFFRAIDE
EFFRAY
EFFRAYS
EFFRONTERIES
EFFRONTERY
EFFS
EFFULGE
EFFULGED
EFFULGENCE
EFFULGENCES
EFFULGENT
EFFULGENTLY
EFFULGES
EFFULGING
EFFUSE
EFFUSED
EFFUSES
EFFUSING
EFFUSIOMETER
EFFUSIOMETERS
EFFUSION
EFFUSIONS
EFFUSIVE
EFFUSIVELY
EFFUSIVENESS
EFFUSIVENESSES
EFS
EFT
EFTEST
EFTS
EFTSOON
EFTSOONS
EGAD
EGADS
EGAL
EGALITARIAN
EGALITARIANISM
EGALITARIANISMS
EGALITARIANS
EGALITE
EGALITES
EGALITIES
EGALITY

EGALLY
EGAREMENT
EGAREMENTS
EGENCE
EGENCES
EGENCIES
EGENCY
EGER
EGERS
EGEST
EGESTA
EGESTED
EGESTING
EGESTION
EGESTIONS
EGESTIVE
EGESTS
EGG
EGGAR
EGGARS
EGGBEATER
EGGBEATERS
EGGCUP
EGGCUPS
EGGED
EGGER
EGGERIES
EGGERS
EGGERY
EGGHEAD
EGGHEADED
EGGHEADEDNESS
EGGHEADEDNESSES
EGGHEADS
EGGIER
EGGIEST
EGGING
EGGLER
EGGLERS
EGGLESS
EGGMASS
EGGMASSES
EGGNOG
EGGNOGS
EGGPLANT
EGGPLANTS
EGGS
EGGSHELL
EGGSHELLS
EGGWASH
EGGWASHES
EGGWHISK
EGGWHISKS
EGGY
EGIS
EGISES

EGLANDULAR
EGLANDULOSE
EGLANTINE
EGLANTINES
EGLATERE
EGLATERES
EGLOMISE
EGMA
EGMAS
EGO
EGOCENTRIC
EGOCENTRICALLY
EGOCENTRICITIES
EGOCENTRICITY
EGOCENTRICS
EGOCENTRISM
EGOCENTRISMS
EGOISM
EGOISMS
EGOIST
EGOISTIC
EGOISTICAL
EGOISTICALLY
EGOISTS
EGOITIES
EGOITY
EGOLESS
EGOMANIA
EGOMANIAC
EGOMANIACAL
EGOMANIACALLY
EGOMANIACS
EGOMANIAS
EGOS
EGOTHEISM
EGOTHEISMS
EGOTISE
EGOTISED
EGOTISES
EGOTISING
EGOTISM
EGOTISMS
EGOTIST
EGOTISTIC
EGOTISTICAL
EGOTISTICALLY
EGOTISTS
EGOTIZE
EGOTIZED
EGOTIZES
EGOTIZING
EGREGIOUS
EGREGIOUSLY
EGREGIOUSNESS
EGREGIOUSNESSES
EGRESS

EGRESSED
EGRESSES
EGRESSING
EGRESSION
EGRESSIONS
EGRET
EGRETS
EGURGITATE
EGURGITATED
EGURGITATES
EGURGITATING
EGYPTIAN
EGYPTIANS
EH
EHED
EHING
EHS
EICOSANOID
EICOSANOIDS
EIDE
EIDENT
EIDER
EIDERDOWN
EIDERDOWNS
EIDERS
EIDETIC
EIDETICALLY
EIDETICS
EIDOGRAPH
EIDOGRAPHS
EIDOLA
EIDOLIC
EIDOLON
EIDOLONS
EIDOS
EIGEN
EIGENFREQUENCY
EIGENFUNCTION
EIGENFUNCTIONS
EIGENMODE
EIGENMODES
EIGENTONE
EIGENTONES
EIGENVALUE
EIGENVALUES
EIGENVECTOR
EIGENVECTORS
EIGHT
EIGHTEEN
EIGHTEENMO
EIGHTEENMOS
EIGHTEENS
EIGHTEENTH
EIGHTEENTHLY
EIGHTEENTHS
EIGHTFOIL

EIGHTFOILS
EIGHTFOLD
EIGHTFOOT
EIGHTH
EIGHTHLY
EIGHTHS
EIGHTIES
EIGHTIETH
EIGHTIETHS
EIGHTPENCE
EIGHTPENCES
EIGHTPENNY
EIGHTS
EIGHTSCORE
EIGHTSCORES
EIGHTSMAN
EIGHTSMEN
EIGHTSOME
EIGHTSOMES
EIGHTVO
EIGHTVOS
EIGHTY
EIGNE
EIK
EIKED
EIKING
EIKON
EIKONES
EIKONS
EIKS
EILD
EILDING
EILDINGS
EILDS
EINA
EINE
EINKORN
EINKORNS
EINSTEIN
EINSTEINIUM
EINSTEINIUMS
EINSTEINS
EIRACK
EIRACKS
EIRENIC
EIRENICAL
EIRENICALLY
EIRENICON
EIRENICONS
EISEGESES
EISEGESIS
EISEL
EISELL
EISELLS
EISELS
EISTEDDFOD

EISTEDDFODAU
EISTEDDFODIC
EISTEDDFODS
EISWEIN
EISWEINS
EITHER
EJACULATE
EJACULATED
EJACULATES
EJACULATING
EJACULATION
EJACULATIONS
EJACULATIVE
EJACULATOR
EJACULATORS
EJACULATORY
EJECT
EJECTA
EJECTABLE
EJECTAMENTA
EJECTED
EJECTING
EJECTION
EJECTIONS
EJECTIVE
EJECTIVELY
EJECTIVES
EJECTIVITY
EJECTMENT
EJECTMENTS
EJECTOR
EJECTORS
EJECTS
EKE
EKED
EKES
EKING
EKISTIC
EKISTICAL
EKISTICALLY
EKISTICIAN
EKISTICIANS
EKISTICS
EKKA
EKKAS
EKLOGITE
EKLOGITES
EKPHRASES
EKPHRASIS
EKPWELE
EKPWELES
EKTEXINE
EKTEXINES
EKUELE
EL
ELABORATE

ELABORATED
ELABORATELY
ELABORATENESS
ELABORATENESSES
ELABORATES
ELABORATING
ELABORATION
ELABORATIONS
ELABORATIVE
ELABORATOR
ELABORATORIES
ELABORATORS
ELABORATORY
ELAEOLITE
ELAEOLITES
ELAEOPTENE
ELAEOPTENES
ELAIN
ELAINS
ELAIOSOME
ELAIOSOMES
ELAN
ELANCE
ELANCED
ELANCES
ELANCING
ELAND
ELANDS
ELANET
ELANETS
ELANS
ELAPHINE
ELAPID
ELAPIDS
ELAPINE
ELAPSE
ELAPSED
ELAPSES
ELAPSING
ELASMOBRANCH
ELASMOBRANCHES
ELASMOBRANCHS
ELASMOSAUR
ELASMOSAURS
ELASTANCE
ELASTANCES
ELASTANE
ELASTANES
ELASTASE
ELASTASES
ELASTIC
ELASTICALLY
ELASTICATE
ELASTICATED
ELASTICATES
ELASTICATING

ELASTICATION
ELASTICISE
ELASTICISED
ELASTICISES
ELASTICISING
ELASTICITIES
ELASTICITY
ELASTICIZE
ELASTICIZED
ELASTICIZES
ELASTICIZING
ELASTICNESS
ELASTICNESSES
ELASTICS
ELASTIN
ELASTINS
ELASTIVITY
ELASTOMER
ELASTOMERIC
ELASTOMERS
ELATE
ELATED
ELATEDLY
ELATEDNESS
ELATEDNESSES
ELATER
ELATERID
ELATERIDS
ELATERIN
ELATERINS
ELATERITE
ELATERITES
ELATERIUM
ELATERIUMS
ELATERS
ELATES
ELATING
ELATION
ELATIONS
ELATIVE
ELATIVES
ELBOW
ELBOWED
ELBOWING
ELBOWROOM
ELBOWROOMS
ELBOWS
ELCHEE
ELCHEES
ELCHI
ELCHIS
ELD
ELDER
ELDERBERRIES
ELDERBERRY
ELDERLIES

ELDERLINESS
ELDERLINESSES
ELDERLY
ELDERS
ELDERSHIP
ELDERSHIPS
ELDEST
ELDIN
ELDING
ELDINGS
ELDINS
ELDORADO
ELDRESS
ELDRESSES
ELDRICH
ELDRITCH
ELDS
ELECAMPANE
ELECAMPANES
ELECT
ELECTABILITIES
ELECTABILITY
ELECTABLE
ELECTED
ELECTEE
ELECTEES
ELECTING
ELECTION
ELECTIONEER
ELECTIONEERED
ELECTIONEERER
ELECTIONEERERS
ELECTIONEERING
ELECTIONEERINGS
ELECTIONEERS
ELECTIONS
ELECTIVE
ELECTIVELY
ELECTIVENESS
ELECTIVENESSES
ELECTIVES
ELECTIVITIES
ELECTIVITY
ELECTOR
ELECTORAL
ELECTORALLY
ELECTORATE
ELECTORATES
ELECTORESS
ELECTORESSES
ELECTORIAL
ELECTORS
ELECTORSHIP
ELECTORSHIPS
ELECTRESS
ELECTRESSES

ELECTRET
ELECTRETS
ELECTRIC
ELECTRICAL
ELECTRICALLY
ELECTRICIAN
ELECTRICIANS
ELECTRICITIES
ELECTRICITY
ELECTRICS
ELECTRIFIABLE
ELECTRIFICATION
ELECTRIFIED
ELECTRIFIER
ELECTRIFIERS
ELECTRIFIES
ELECTRIFY
ELECTRIFYING
ELECTRISATION
ELECTRISATIONS
ELECTRISE
ELECTRISED
ELECTRISES
ELECTRISING
ELECTRIZATION
ELECTRIZATIONS
ELECTRIZE
ELECTRIZED
ELECTRIZES
ELECTRIZING
ELECTRO
ELECTROACOUSTIC
ELECTROANALYSES
ELECTROANALYSIS
ELECTROANALYTIC
ELECTROBIOLOGY
ELECTROCAUTERY
ELECTROCEMENT
ELECTROCEMENTS
ELECTROCHEMIC
ELECTROCHEMICAL
ELECTROCHEMIST
ELECTROCHEMISTS
ELECTROCLASH
ELECTROCULTURE
ELECTROCULTURES
ELECTROCUTE
ELECTROCUTED
ELECTROCUTES
ELECTROCUTING
ELECTROCUTION
ELECTROCUTIONS
ELECTROCYTE
ELECTROCYTES
ELECTRODE
ELECTRODEPOSIT

ELECTRODEPOSITS
ELECTRODERMAL
ELECTRODES
ELECTRODIALYSES
ELECTRODIALYSIS
ELECTRODIALYTIC
ELECTRODYNAMIC
ELECTRODYNAMICS
ELECTROED
ELECTROFISHING
ELECTROFISHINGS
ELECTROFLUOR
ELECTROFLUORS
ELECTROFORM
ELECTROFORMED
ELECTROFORMING
ELECTROFORMINGS
ELECTROFORMS
ELECTROGEN
ELECTROGENESES
ELECTROGENESIS
ELECTROGENIC
ELECTROGENS
ELECTROGILDING
ELECTROGILDINGS
ELECTROGRAM
ELECTROGRAMS
ELECTROGRAPH
ELECTROGRAPHIC
ELECTROGRAPHIES
ELECTROGRAPHS
ELECTROGRAPHY
ELECTROING
ELECTROJET
ELECTROJETS
ELECTROKINETIC
ELECTROKINETICS
ELECTROLESS
ELECTROLIER
ELECTROLIERS
ELECTROLOGIES
ELECTROLOGIST
ELECTROLOGISTS
ELECTROLOGY
ELECTROLYSATION
ELECTROLYSE
ELECTROLYSED
ELECTROLYSER
ELECTROLYSERS
ELECTROLYSES
ELECTROLYSING
ELECTROLYSIS
ELECTROLYTE
ELECTROLYTES
ELECTROLYTIC
ELECTROLYTICS

ELECTROLYZATION
ELECTROLYZE
ELECTROLYZED
ELECTROLYZER
ELECTROLYZERS
ELECTROLYZES
ELECTROLYZING
ELECTROMAGNET
ELECTROMAGNETIC
ELECTROMAGNETS
ELECTROMER
ELECTROMERIC
ELECTROMERISM
ELECTROMERISMS
ELECTROMERS
ELECTROMETER
ELECTROMETERS
ELECTROMETRIC
ELECTROMETRICAL
ELECTROMETRIES
ELECTROMETRY
ELECTROMOTANCE
ELECTROMOTANCES
ELECTROMOTIVE
ELECTROMOTOR
ELECTROMOTORS
ELECTROMYOGRAM
ELECTROMYOGRAMS
ELECTROMYOGRAPH
ELECTRON
ELECTRONEGATIVE
ELECTRONIC
ELECTRONICA
ELECTRONICALLY
ELECTRONICAS
ELECTRONICS
ELECTRONS
ELECTRONVOLT
ELECTRONVOLTS
ELECTROOSMOSES
ELECTROOSMOSIS
ELECTROOSMOTIC
ELECTROPHILE
ELECTROPHILES
ELECTROPHILIC
ELECTROPHONE
ELECTROPHONES
ELECTROPHONIC
ELECTROPHORESE
ELECTROPHORESED
ELECTROPHORESES
ELECTROPHORESIS
ELECTROPHORETIC
ELECTROPHORI
ELECTROPHORUS
ELECTROPHORUSES

ELECTROPLATE
ELECTROPLATED
ELECTROPLATER
ELECTROPLATERS
ELECTROPLATES
ELECTROPLATING
ELECTROPLATINGS
ELECTROPOLAR
ELECTROPOSITIVE
ELECTRORECEPTOR
ELECTRORHEOLOGY
ELECTROS
ELECTROSCOPE
ELECTROSCOPES
ELECTROSCOPIC
ELECTROSHOCK
ELECTROSHOCKS
ELECTROSONDE
ELECTROSONDES
ELECTROSTATIC
ELECTROSTATICS
ELECTROSURGERY
ELECTROSURGICAL
ELECTROTECHNICS
ELECTROTHERAPY
ELECTROTHERMAL
ELECTROTHERMIC
ELECTROTHERMICS
ELECTROTHERMIES
ELECTROTHERMY
ELECTROTINT
ELECTROTINTS
ELECTROTONIC
ELECTROTONUS
ELECTROTONUSES
ELECTROTYPE
ELECTROTYPED
ELECTROTYPER
ELECTROTYPERS
ELECTROTYPES
ELECTROTYPIC
ELECTROTYPIES
ELECTROTYPING
ELECTROTYPIST
ELECTROTYPISTS
ELECTROTYPY
ELECTROVALENCE
ELECTROVALENCES
ELECTROVALENCY
ELECTROVALENT
ELECTROVALENTLY
ELECTROWEAK
ELECTROWINNING
ELECTROWINNINGS
ELECTRUM
ELECTRUMS

ELECTS
ELECTUARIES
ELECTUARY
ELEDOISIN
ELEDOISINS
ELEEMOSYNARY
ELEGANCE
ELEGANCES
ELEGANCIES
ELEGANCY
ELEGANT
ELEGANTLY
ELEGIAC
ELEGIACAL
ELEGIACALLY
ELEGIACS
ELEGIAST
ELEGIASTS
ELEGIES
ELEGISE
ELEGISED
ELEGISES
ELEGISING
ELEGIST
ELEGISTS
ELEGIT
ELEGITS
ELEGIZE
ELEGIZED
ELEGIZES
ELEGIZING
ELEGY
ELEMENT
ELEMENTAL
ELEMENTALISM
ELEMENTALISMS
ELEMENTALLY
ELEMENTALS
ELEMENTARILY
ELEMENTARINESS
ELEMENTARY
ELEMENTS
ELEMI
ELEMIS
ELENCH
ELENCHI
ELENCHIC
ELENCHS
ELENCHUS
ELENCTIC
ELEOPTENE
ELEOPTENES
ELEPHANT
ELEPHANTIASES
ELEPHANTIASIC
ELEPHANTIASIS

ELEPHANTINE
ELEPHANTOID
ELEPHANTS
ELEUTHERARCH
ELEUTHERARCHS
ELEUTHERI
ELEUTHERIAN
ELEUTHEROCOCCI
ELEUTHEROCOCCUS
ELEUTHERODACTYL
ELEUTHEROMANIA
ELEUTHEROMANIAS
ELEUTHEROPHOBIA
ELEUTHEROPHOBIC
ELEVATE
ELEVATED
ELEVATEDS
ELEVATES
ELEVATING
ELEVATION
ELEVATIONAL
ELEVATIONALLY
ELEVATIONS
ELEVATOR
ELEVATORS
ELEVATORY
ELEVEN
ELEVENS
ELEVENSES
ELEVENTH
ELEVENTHLY
ELEVENTHS
ELEVON
ELEVONS
ELF
ELFED
ELFHOOD
ELFHOODS
ELFIN
ELFING
ELFINS
ELFISH
ELFISHLY
ELFISHNESS
ELFLAND
ELFLANDS
ELFLIKE
ELFLOCK
ELFLOCKS
ELFS
ELHI
ELIAD
ELIADS
ELICHE
ELICIT
ELICITABLE

ELICITATION
ELICITATIONS
ELICITED
ELICITING
ELICITOR
ELICITORS
ELICITS
ELIDE
ELIDED
ELIDES
ELIDIBLE
ELIDING
ELIGIBILITIES
ELIGIBILITY
ELIGIBLE
ELIGIBLES
ELIGIBLY
ELIMINABILITY
ELIMINABLE
ELIMINANT
ELIMINANTS
ELIMINATE
ELIMINATED
ELIMINATES
ELIMINATING
ELIMINATION
ELIMINATIONS
ELIMINATIVE
ELIMINATOR
ELIMINATORS
ELIMINATORY
ELINT
ELINTS
ELISION
ELISIONS
ELITE
ELITES
ELITISM
ELITISMS
ELITIST
ELITISTS
ELIXIR
ELIXIRS
ELK
ELKHOUND
ELKHOUNDS
ELKS
ELL
ELLAGIC
ELLIPSE
ELLIPSES
ELLIPSIS
ELLIPSOGRAPH
ELLIPSOGRAPHS
ELLIPSOID
ELLIPSOIDAL

ELLIPSOIDS
ELLIPTIC
ELLIPTICAL
ELLIPTICALLY
ELLIPTICALNESS
ELLIPTICALS
ELLIPTICITIES
ELLIPTICITY
ELLOPS
ELLOPSES
ELLS
ELLWAND
ELLWANDS
ELM
ELMEN
ELMIER
ELMIEST
ELMS
ELMWOOD
ELMWOODS
ELMY
ELOCUTE
ELOCUTED
ELOCUTES
ELOCUTING
ELOCUTION
ELOCUTIONARY
ELOCUTIONIST
ELOCUTIONISTS
ELOCUTIONS
ELOCUTORY
ELODEA
ELODEAS
ELOGE
ELOGES
ELOGIES
ELOGIST
ELOGISTS
ELOGIUM
ELOGIUMS
ELOGY
ELOIGN
ELOIGNED
ELOIGNER
ELOIGNERS
ELOIGNING
ELOIGNMENT
ELOIGNMENTS
ELOIGNS
ELOIN
ELOINED
ELOINER
ELOINERS
ELOINING
ELOINMENT
ELOINMENTS

ELOINS
ELONGATE
ELONGATED
ELONGATES
ELONGATING
ELONGATION
ELONGATIONS
ELOPE
ELOPED
ELOPEMENT
ELOPEMENTS
ELOPER
ELOPERS
ELOPES
ELOPING
ELOPS
ELOPSES
ELOQUENCE
ELOQUENCES
ELOQUENT
ELOQUENTLY
ELPEE
ELPEES
ELS
ELSE
ELSEWHERE
ELSEWHITHER
ELSEWISE
ELSHIN
ELSHINS
ELSIN
ELSINS
ELT
ELTCHI
ELTCHIS
ELTS
ELUANT
ELUANTS
ELUATE
ELUATES
ELUCIDATE
ELUCIDATED
ELUCIDATES
ELUCIDATING
ELUCIDATION
ELUCIDATIONS
ELUCIDATIVE
ELUCIDATOR
ELUCIDATORS
ELUCIDATORY
ELUCUBRATE
ELUCUBRATED
ELUCUBRATES
ELUCUBRATING
ELUCUBRATION
ELUCUBRATIONS

ELUDE
ELUDED
ELUDER
ELUDERS
ELUDES
ELUDIBLE
ELUDING
ELUENT
ELUENTS
ELUSION
ELUSIONS
ELUSIVE
ELUSIVELY
ELUSIVENESS
ELUSIVENESSES
ELUSORINESS
ELUSORINESSES
ELUSORY
ELUTE
ELUTED
ELUTES
ELUTING
ELUTION
ELUTIONS
ELUTOR
ELUTORS
ELUTRIATE
ELUTRIATED
ELUTRIATES
ELUTRIATING
ELUTRIATION
ELUTRIATIONS
ELUTRIATOR
ELUTRIATORS
ELUVIA
ELUVIAL
ELUVIATE
ELUVIATED
ELUVIATES
ELUVIATING
ELUVIATION
ELUVIATIONS
ELUVIUM
ELUVIUMS
ELVAN
ELVANITE
ELVANITES
ELVANS
ELVER
ELVERS
ELVES
ELVISH
ELVISHLY
ELVISHNESS
ELYSIAN
ELYTRA

ELYTRAL	EMASCULATES	EMBARKMENTS	EMBELLISH
ELYTRIFORM	EMASCULATING	EMBARKS	EMBELLISHED
ELYTRIGEROUS	EMASCULATION	EMBARQUEMENT	EMBELLISHER
ELYTROID	EMASCULATIONS	EMBARQUEMENTS	EMBELLISHERS
ELYTRON	EMASCULATIVE	EMBARRASS	EMBELLISHES
ELYTROUS	EMASCULATOR	EMBARRASSABLE	EMBELLISHING
ELYTRUM	EMASCULATORS	EMBARRASSED	EMBELLISHINGLY
EM	EMASCULATORY	EMBARRASSEDLY	EMBELLISHMENT
EMACIATE	EMBACE	EMBARRASSES	EMBELLISHMENTS
EMACIATED	EMBACES	EMBARRASSING	EMBER
EMACIATES	EMBACING	EMBARRASSINGLY	EMBERS
EMACIATING	EMBAIL	EMBARRASSMENT	EMBEZZLE
EMACIATION	EMBAILED	EMBARRASSMENTS	EMBEZZLED
EMACIATIONS	EMBAILING	EMBARRED	EMBEZZLEMENT
EMAIL	EMBAILS	EMBARRING	EMBEZZLEMENTS
EMAILED	EMBALE	EMBARRINGS	EMBEZZLER
EMAILING	EMBALED	EMBARS	EMBEZZLERS
EMAILS	EMBALES	EMBASE	EMBEZZLES
EMALANGENI	EMBALING	EMBASED	EMBEZZLING
EMANANT	EMBALL	EMBASEMENT	EMBITTER
EMANATE	EMBALLED	EMBASEMENTS	EMBITTERED
EMANATED	EMBALLING	EMBASES	EMBITTERER
EMANATES	EMBALLINGS	EMBASING	EMBITTERERS
EMANATING	EMBALLS	EMBASSADE	EMBITTERING
EMANATION	EMBALM	EMBASSADES	EMBITTERINGS
EMANATIONAL	EMBALMED	EMBASSADOR	EMBITTERMENT
EMANATIONS	EMBALMER	EMBASSADORS	EMBITTERMENTS
EMANATIST	EMBALMERS	EMBASSAGE	EMBITTERS
EMANATISTS	EMBALMING	EMBASSAGES	EMBLAZE
EMANATIVE	EMBALMINGS	EMBASSIES	EMBLAZED
EMANATOR	EMBALMMENT	EMBASSY	EMBLAZER
EMANATORS	EMBALMMENTS	EMBASTE	EMBLAZERS
EMANATORY	EMBALMS	EMBATHE	EMBLAZES
EMANCIPATE	EMBANK	EMBATHED	EMBLAZING
EMANCIPATED	EMBANKED	EMBATHES	EMBLAZON
EMANCIPATES	EMBANKER	EMBATHING	EMBLAZONED
EMANCIPATING	EMBANKERS	EMBATTLE	EMBLAZONER
EMANCIPATION	EMBANKING	EMBATTLED	EMBLAZONERS
EMANCIPATIONIST	EMBANKMENT	EMBATTLEMENT	EMBLAZONING
EMANCIPATIONS	EMBANKMENTS	EMBATTLEMENTS	EMBLAZONMENT
EMANCIPATIVE	EMBANKS	EMBATTLES	EMBLAZONMENTS
EMANCIPATIVELY	EMBAR	EMBATTLING	EMBLAZONRIES
EMANCIPATOR	EMBARCADERO	EMBAY	EMBLAZONRY
EMANCIPATORS	EMBARCADEROS	EMBAYED	EMBLAZONS
EMANCIPATORY	EMBARCATION	EMBAYING	EMBLEM
EMANCIPIST	EMBARCATIONS	EMBAYLD	EMBLEMA
EMANCIPISTS	EMBARGO	EMBAYMENT	EMBLEMATA
EMARGINATE	EMBARGOED	EMBAYMENTS	EMBLEMATIC
EMARGINATED	EMBARGOES	EMBAYS	EMBLEMATICAL
EMARGINATELY	EMBARGOING	EMBED	EMBLEMATICALLY
EMARGINATES	EMBARK	EMBEDDED	EMBLEMATISE
EMARGINATING	EMBARKATION	EMBEDDING	EMBLEMATISED
EMARGINATION	EMBARKATIONS	EMBEDDINGS	EMBLEMATISES
EMARGINATIONS	EMBARKED	EMBEDMENT	EMBLEMATISING
EMASCULATE	EMBARKING	EMBEDMENTS	EMBLEMATIST
EMASCULATED	EMBARKMENT	EMBEDS	EMBLEMATISTS

EMBLEMATIZE
EMBLEMATIZED
EMBLEMATIZES
EMBLEMATIZING
EMBLEMED
EMBLEMENTS
EMBLEMING
EMBLEMISE
EMBLEMISED
EMBLEMISES
EMBLEMISING
EMBLEMIZE
EMBLEMIZED
EMBLEMIZES
EMBLEMIZING
EMBLEMS
EMBLIC
EMBLICS
EMBLOOM
EMBLOOMED
EMBLOOMING
EMBLOOMS
EMBLOSSOM
EMBLOSSOMED
EMBLOSSOMING
EMBLOSSOMS
EMBODIED
EMBODIER
EMBODIERS
EMBODIES
EMBODIMENT
EMBODIMENTS
EMBODY
EMBODYING
EMBOG
EMBOGGED
EMBOGGING
EMBOGS
EMBOGUE
EMBOGUED
EMBOGUES
EMBOGUING
EMBOIL
EMBOILED
EMBOILING
EMBOILS
EMBOITEMENT
EMBOITEMENTS
EMBOLDEN
EMBOLDENED
EMBOLDENER
EMBOLDENERS
EMBOLDENING
EMBOLDENS
EMBOLECTOMIES
EMBOLECTOMY

EMBOLI
EMBOLIC
EMBOLIES
EMBOLISATION
EMBOLISATIONS
EMBOLISE
EMBOLISED
EMBOLISES
EMBOLISING
EMBOLISM
EMBOLISMAL
EMBOLISMIC
EMBOLISMS
EMBOLIZATION
EMBOLIZATIONS
EMBOLIZE
EMBOLIZED
EMBOLIZES
EMBOLIZING
EMBOLUS
EMBOLUSES
EMBOLY
EMBONPOINT
EMBONPOINTS
EMBORDER
EMBORDERED
EMBORDERING
EMBORDERS
EMBOSCATA
EMBOSCATAS
EMBOSK
EMBOSKED
EMBOSKING
EMBOSKS
EMBOSOM
EMBOSOMED
EMBOSOMING
EMBOSOMS
EMBOSS
EMBOSSABLE
EMBOSSED
EMBOSSER
EMBOSSERS
EMBOSSES
EMBOSSING
EMBOSSMENT
EMBOSSMENTS
EMBOST
EMBOTHRIUM
EMBOTHRIUMS
EMBOUCHURE
EMBOUCHURES
EMBOUND
EMBOUNDED
EMBOUNDING
EMBOUNDS

EMBOURGEOISE
EMBOURGEOISED
EMBOURGEOISES
EMBOURGEOISING
EMBOW
EMBOWED
EMBOWEL
EMBOWELED
EMBOWELING
EMBOWELLED
EMBOWELLING
EMBOWELMENT
EMBOWELMENTS
EMBOWELS
EMBOWER
EMBOWERED
EMBOWERING
EMBOWERMENT
EMBOWERMENTS
EMBOWERS
EMBOWING
EMBOWMENT
EMBOWMENTS
EMBOWS
EMBOX
EMBOXED
EMBOXES
EMBOXING
EMBRACE
EMBRACEABLE
EMBRACED
EMBRACEMENT
EMBRACEMENTS
EMBRACEOR
EMBRACEORS
EMBRACER
EMBRACERIES
EMBRACERS
EMBRACERY
EMBRACES
EMBRACING
EMBRACINGLY
EMBRACINGNESS
EMBRACINGNESSES
EMBRACIVE
EMBRAID
EMBRAIDED
EMBRAIDING
EMBRAIDS
EMBRANCHMENT
EMBRANCHMENTS
EMBRANGLE
EMBRANGLED
EMBRANGLEMENT
EMBRANGLEMENTS
EMBRANGLES

EMBRANGLING
EMBRASOR
EMBRASORS
EMBRASURE
EMBRASURED
EMBRASURES
EMBRAVE
EMBRAVED
EMBRAVES
EMBRAVING
EMBRAZURE
EMBRAZURES
EMBREAD
EMBREADED
EMBREADING
EMBREADS
EMBREATHE
EMBREATHED
EMBREATHES
EMBREATHING
EMBREWED
EMBREWES
EMBREWING
EMBRITTLE
EMBRITTLED
EMBRITTLEMENT
EMBRITTLEMENTS
EMBRITTLES
EMBRITTLING
EMBROCATE
EMBROCATED
EMBROCATES
EMBROCATING
EMBROCATION
EMBROCATIONS
EMBROGLIO
EMBROGLIOS
EMBROIDER
EMBROIDERED
EMBROIDERER
EMBROIDERERS
EMBROIDERIES
EMBROIDERING
EMBROIDERS
EMBROIDERY
EMBROIL
EMBROILED
EMBROILER
EMBROILERS
EMBROILING
EMBROILMENT
EMBROILMENTS
EMBROILS
EMBROWN
EMBROWNED
EMBROWNING

EMBROWNS
EMBRUE
EMBRUED
EMBRUEMENT
EMBRUEMENTS
EMBRUES
EMBRUING
EMBRUTE
EMBRUTED
EMBRUTES
EMBRUTING
EMBRYECTOMIES
EMBRYECTOMY
EMBRYO
EMBRYOGENESES
EMBRYOGENESIS
EMBRYOGENETIC
EMBRYOGENIC
EMBRYOGENIES
EMBRYOGENY
EMBRYOID
EMBRYOIDS
EMBRYOLOGIC
EMBRYOLOGICAL
EMBRYOLOGICALLY
EMBRYOLOGIES
EMBRYOLOGIST
EMBRYOLOGISTS
EMBRYOLOGY
EMBRYON
EMBRYONAL
EMBRYONATE
EMBRYONATED
EMBRYONIC
EMBRYONICALLY
EMBRYONS
EMBRYOPHYTE
EMBRYOPHYTES
EMBRYOS
EMBRYOTIC
EMBRYOTOMIES
EMBRYOTOMY
EMBRYULCIA
EMBRYULCIAS
EMBUS
EMBUSED
EMBUSES
EMBUSIED
EMBUSIES
EMBUSING
EMBUSQUE
EMBUSQUES
EMBUSSED
EMBUSSES
EMBUSSING
EMBUSY

EMBUSYING
EMCEE
EMCEED
EMCEEING
EMCEES
EME
EMEER
EMEERATE
EMEERATES
EMEERS
EMEND
EMENDABLE
EMENDALS
EMENDATE
EMENDATED
EMENDATES
EMENDATING
EMENDATION
EMENDATIONS
EMENDATOR
EMENDATORS
EMENDATORY
EMENDED
EMENDER
EMENDERS
EMENDING
EMENDS
EMERALD
EMERALDS
EMERAUDE
EMERAUDES
EMERGE
EMERGED
EMERGENCE
EMERGENCES
EMERGENCIES
EMERGENCY
EMERGENT
EMERGENTLY
EMERGENTS
EMERGES
EMERGING
EMERIED
EMERIES
EMERITA
EMERITAE
EMERITI
EMERITUS
EMEROD
EMERODS
EMEROID
EMEROIDS
EMERSED
EMERSION
EMERSIONS
EMERY

EMERYING
EMES
EMESES
EMESIS
EMETIC
EMETICAL
EMETICALLY
EMETICS
EMETIN
EMETINE
EMETINES
EMETINS
EMETOPHOBIA
EMETOPHOBIAS
EMEU
EMEUS
EMEUTE
EMEUTES
EMF
EMFS
EMIC
EMICANT
EMICATE
EMICATED
EMICATES
EMICATING
EMICATION
EMICATIONS
EMICTION
EMICTIONS
EMICTORY
EMIGRANT
EMIGRANTS
EMIGRATE
EMIGRATED
EMIGRATES
EMIGRATING
EMIGRATION
EMIGRATIONAL
EMIGRATIONIST
EMIGRATIONISTS
EMIGRATIONS
EMIGRATORY
EMIGRE
EMIGRES
EMINENCE
EMINENCES
EMINENCIES
EMINENCY
EMINENT
EMINENTIAL
EMINENTLY
EMIR
EMIRATE
EMIRATES
EMIRS

EMISSARIES
EMISSARY
EMISSILE
EMISSION
EMISSIONS
EMISSIVE
EMISSIVITIES
EMISSIVITY
EMIT
EMITS
EMITTANCE
EMITTANCES
EMITTED
EMITTER
EMITTERS
EMITTING
EMMA
EMMARBLE
EMMARBLED
EMMARBLES
EMMARBLING
EMMAS
EMMENAGOGIC
EMMENAGOGUE
EMMENAGOGUES
EMMENOLOGIES
EMMENOLOGY
EMMER
EMMERS
EMMESH
EMMESHED
EMMESHES
EMMESHING
EMMET
EMMETROPE
EMMETROPES
EMMETROPIA
EMMETROPIAS
EMMETROPIC
EMMETS
EMMEW
EMMEWED
EMMEWING
EMMEWS
EMMOVE
EMMOVED
EMMOVES
EMMOVING
EMODIN
EMODINS
EMOLLESCENCE
EMOLLESCENCES
EMOLLIATE
EMOLLIATED
EMOLLIATES
EMOLLIATING

EMOLLIENCE
EMOLLIENT
EMOLLIENTS
EMOLLITION
EMOLLITIONS
EMOLUMENT
EMOLUMENTAL
EMOLUMENTARY
EMOLUMENTS
EMONG
EMONGES
EMONGEST
EMONGST
EMOTE
EMOTED
EMOTER
EMOTERS
EMOTES
EMOTICON
EMOTICONS
EMOTING
EMOTION
EMOTIONABLE
EMOTIONAL
EMOTIONALISE
EMOTIONALISED
EMOTIONALISES
EMOTIONALISING
EMOTIONALISM
EMOTIONALISMS
EMOTIONALIST
EMOTIONALISTIC
EMOTIONALISTS
EMOTIONALITIES
EMOTIONALITY
EMOTIONALIZE
EMOTIONALIZED
EMOTIONALIZES
EMOTIONALIZING
EMOTIONALLY
EMOTIONLESS
EMOTIONLESSLY
EMOTIONLESSNESS
EMOTIONS
EMOTIVE
EMOTIVELY
EMOTIVENESS
EMOTIVISM
EMOTIVISMS
EMOTIVITIES
EMOTIVITY
EMOVE
EMOVED
EMOVES
EMOVING
EMPACKET

EMPACKETED
EMPACKETING
EMPACKETS
EMPAESTIC
EMPAIRE
EMPAIRED
EMPAIRES
EMPAIRING
EMPALE
EMPALED
EMPALEMENT
EMPALEMENTS
EMPALER
EMPALERS
EMPALES
EMPALING
EMPANADA
EMPANADAS
EMPANEL
EMPANELED
EMPANELING
EMPANELLED
EMPANELLING
EMPANELMENT
EMPANELMENTS
EMPANELS
EMPANOPLIED
EMPANOPLIES
EMPANOPLY
EMPANOPLYING
EMPARADISE
EMPARADISED
EMPARADISES
EMPARADISING
EMPARE
EMPARED
EMPARES
EMPARING
EMPARL
EMPARLAUNCE
EMPARLAUNCES
EMPARLED
EMPARLING
EMPARLS
EMPART
EMPARTED
EMPARTING
EMPARTS
EMPASSIONATE
EMPASSIONED
EMPATHETIC
EMPATHETICALLY
EMPATHIC
EMPATHICALLY
EMPATHIES
EMPATHISE

EMPATHISED
EMPATHISES
EMPATHISING
EMPATHIST
EMPATHISTS
EMPATHIZE
EMPATHIZED
EMPATHIZES
EMPATHIZING
EMPATHY
EMPATRON
EMPATRONED
EMPATRONING
EMPATRONS
EMPAYRE
EMPAYRED
EMPAYRES
EMPAYRING
EMPEACH
EMPEACHED
EMPEACHES
EMPEACHING
EMPENNAGE
EMPENNAGES
EMPEOPLE
EMPEOPLED
EMPEOPLES
EMPEOPLING
EMPERCE
EMPERCED
EMPERCES
EMPERCING
EMPERIES
EMPERISE
EMPERISED
EMPERISES
EMPERISH
EMPERISHED
EMPERISHES
EMPERISHING
EMPERISING
EMPERIZE
EMPERIZED
EMPERIZES
EMPERIZING
EMPEROR
EMPERORS
EMPERORSHIP
EMPERORSHIPS
EMPERY
EMPHASES
EMPHASIS
EMPHASISE
EMPHASISED
EMPHASISES
EMPHASISING

EMPHASIZE
EMPHASIZED
EMPHASIZES
EMPHASIZING
EMPHATIC
EMPHATICAL
EMPHATICALLY
EMPHATICALNESS
EMPHATICS
EMPHLYSES
EMPHLYSIS
EMPHRACTIC
EMPHRACTICS
EMPHYSEMA
EMPHYSEMAS
EMPHYSEMATOUS
EMPHYSEMIC
EMPHYSEMICS
EMPHYTEUSES
EMPHYTEUSIS
EMPHYTEUTIC
EMPIECEMENT
EMPIECEMENTS
EMPIERCE
EMPIERCED
EMPIERCES
EMPIERCING
EMPIGHT
EMPIRE
EMPIRES
EMPIRIC
EMPIRICAL
EMPIRICALLY
EMPIRICALNESS
EMPIRICISM
EMPIRICISMS
EMPIRICIST
EMPIRICISTS
EMPIRICS
EMPIRICUTIC
EMPLACE
EMPLACED
EMPLACEMENT
EMPLACEMENTS
EMPLACES
EMPLACING
EMPLANE
EMPLANED
EMPLANES
EMPLANING
EMPLASTER
EMPLASTERED
EMPLASTERING
EMPLASTERS
EMPLASTIC
EMPLASTICS

EMPLASTRON	EMPOWER	EMPYREUMATA	EMULSIONISING
EMPLASTRONS	EMPOWERED	EMPYREUMATIC	EMULSIONIZE
EMPLASTRUM	EMPOWERING	EMPYREUMATICAL	EMULSIONIZED
EMPLASTRUMS	EMPOWERMENT	EMPYREUMATISE	EMULSIONIZES
EMPLEACH	EMPOWERMENTS	EMPYREUMATISED	EMULSIONIZING
EMPLEACHED	EMPOWERS	EMPYREUMATISES	EMULSIONS
EMPLEACHES	EMPRESS	EMPYREUMATISING	EMULSIVE
EMPLEACHING	EMPRESSE	EMPYREUMATIZE	EMULSOID
EMPLECTON	EMPRESSEMENT	EMPYREUMATIZED	EMULSOIDAL
EMPLECTONS	EMPRESSEMENTS	EMPYREUMATIZES	EMULSOIDS
EMPLECTUM	EMPRESSES	EMPYREUMATIZING	EMULSOR
EMPLECTUMS	EMPRISE	EMS	EMULSORS
EMPLONGE	EMPRISES	EMU	EMUNCTION
EMPLONGED	EMPRIZE	EMULATE	EMUNCTIONS
EMPLONGES	EMPRIZES	EMULATED	EMUNCTORIES
EMPLONGING	EMPT	EMULATES	EMUNCTORY
EMPLOY	EMPTED	EMULATING	EMUNGE
EMPLOYABILITIES	EMPTIABLE	EMULATION	EMUNGED
EMPLOYABILITY	EMPTIED	EMULATIONS	EMUNGES
EMPLOYABLE	EMPTIER	EMULATIVE	EMUNGING
EMPLOYABLES	EMPTIERS	EMULATIVELY	EMURE
EMPLOYE	EMPTIES	EMULATOR	EMURED
EMPLOYED	EMPTIEST	EMULATORS	EMURES
EMPLOYEE	EMPTILY	EMULATRESS	EMURING
EMPLOYEES	EMPTINESS	EMULATRESSES	EMUS
EMPLOYER	EMPTINESSES	EMULE	EMYD
EMPLOYERS	EMPTING	EMULED	EMYDE
EMPLOYES	EMPTINGS	EMULES	EMYDES
EMPLOYING	EMPTINS	EMULGE	EMYDS
EMPLOYMENT	EMPTION	EMULGED	EMYS
EMPLOYMENTS	EMPTIONAL	EMULGENCE	EN
EMPLOYS	EMPTIONS	EMULGENCES	ENABLE
EMPLUME	EMPTS	EMULGENT	ENABLED
EMPLUMED	EMPTY	EMULGES	ENABLEMENT
EMPLUMES	EMPTYING	EMULGING	ENABLEMENTS
EMPLUMING	EMPTYINGS	EMULING	ENABLER
EMPOISON	EMPTYSES	EMULOUS	ENABLERS
EMPOISONED	EMPTYSIS	EMULOUSLY	ENABLES
EMPOISONING	EMPURPLE	EMULOUSNESS	ENABLING
EMPOISONMENT	EMPURPLED	EMULOUSNESSES	ENACT
EMPOISONMENTS	EMPURPLES	EMULSIBLE	ENACTABLE
EMPOISONS	EMPURPLING	EMULSIFIABLE	ENACTED
EMPOLDER	EMPUSA	EMULSIFICATION	ENACTING
EMPOLDERED	EMPUSAS	EMULSIFICATIONS	ENACTION
EMPOLDERING	EMPUSE	EMULSIFIED	ENACTIONS
EMPOLDERS	EMPUSES	EMULSIFIER	ENACTIVE
EMPORIA	EMPYEMA	EMULSIFIERS	ENACTMENT
EMPORIUM	EMPYEMAS	EMULSIFIES	ENACTMENTS
EMPORIUMS	EMPYEMATA	EMULSIFY	ENACTOR
EMPOVERISH	EMPYEMIC	EMULSIFYING	ENACTORS
EMPOVERISHED	EMPYESES	EMULSIN	ENACTORY
EMPOVERISHER	EMPYESIS	EMULSINS	ENACTS
EMPOVERISHERS	EMPYREAL	EMULSION	ENACTURE
EMPOVERISHES	EMPYREAN	EMULSIONISE	ENACTURES
EMPOVERISHING	EMPYREANS	EMULSIONISED	ENALAPRIL
EMPOVERISHMENT	EMPYREUMA	EMULSIONISES	ENALAPRILS

ENALLAGE
ENALLAGES
ENAMEL
ENAMELED
ENAMELER
ENAMELERS
ENAMELING
ENAMELIST
ENAMELISTS
ENAMELLED
ENAMELLER
ENAMELLERS
ENAMELLING
ENAMELLINGS
ENAMELLIST
ENAMELLISTS
ENAMELS
ENAMELWARE
ENAMELWARES
ENAMELWORK
ENAMINE
ENAMINES
ENAMOR
ENAMORADO
ENAMORADOS
ENAMORED
ENAMORING
ENAMORS
ENAMOUR
ENAMOURED
ENAMOURING
ENAMOURS
ENANTIODROMIA
ENANTIODROMIAS
ENANTIODROMIC
ENANTIOMER
ENANTIOMERIC
ENANTIOMERS
ENANTIOMORPH
ENANTIOMORPHIC
ENANTIOMORPHIES
ENANTIOMORPHISM
ENANTIOMORPHOUS
ENANTIOMORPHS
ENANTIOMORPHY
ENANTIOPATHIES
ENANTIOPATHY
ENANTIOSES
ENANTIOSIS
ENANTIOSTYLIES
ENANTIOSTYLOUS
ENANTIOSTYLY
ENANTIOTROPIC
ENANTIOTROPIES
ENANTIOTROPY
ENARCH

ENARCHED
ENARCHES
ENARCHING
ENARM
ENARMED
ENARMING
ENARMS
ENARRATION
ENARRATIONS
ENARTHRODIAL
ENARTHROSES
ENARTHROSIS
ENATE
ENATES
ENATIC
ENATION
ENATIONS
ENAUNTER
ENCAENIA
ENCAENIAS
ENCAGE
ENCAGED
ENCAGES
ENCAGING
ENCALM
ENCALMED
ENCALMING
ENCALMS
ENCAMP
ENCAMPED
ENCAMPING
ENCAMPMENT
ENCAMPMENTS
ENCAMPS
ENCANTHIS
ENCANTHISES
ENCAPSULATE
ENCAPSULATED
ENCAPSULATER
ENCAPSULATERS
ENCAPSULATES
ENCAPSULATING
ENCAPSULATION
ENCAPSULATIONS
ENCAPSULE
ENCAPSULED
ENCAPSULES
ENCAPSULING
ENCARNALISE
ENCARNALISED
ENCARNALISES
ENCARNALISING
ENCARNALIZE
ENCARNALIZED
ENCARNALIZES
ENCARNALIZING

ENCARPUS
ENCARPUSES
ENCASE
ENCASED
ENCASEMENT
ENCASEMENTS
ENCASES
ENCASH
ENCASHABLE
ENCASHED
ENCASHES
ENCASHING
ENCASHMENT
ENCASHMENTS
ENCASING
ENCASTRE
ENCAUSTIC
ENCAUSTICALLY
ENCAUSTICS
ENCAVE
ENCAVED
ENCAVES
ENCAVING
ENCEINTE
ENCEINTES
ENCEPHALA
ENCEPHALALGIA
ENCEPHALIC
ENCEPHALIN
ENCEPHALINE
ENCEPHALINES
ENCEPHALINS
ENCEPHALITIC
ENCEPHALITIDES
ENCEPHALITIS
ENCEPHALITISES
ENCEPHALITOGEN
ENCEPHALITOGENS
ENCEPHALOCELE
ENCEPHALOCELES
ENCEPHALOGRAM
ENCEPHALOGRAMS
ENCEPHALOGRAPH
ENCEPHALOGRAPHS
ENCEPHALOGRAPHY
ENCEPHALOID
ENCEPHALOMA
ENCEPHALOMAS
ENCEPHALOMATA
ENCEPHALON
ENCEPHALONS
ENCEPHALOPATHIC
ENCEPHALOPATHY
ENCEPHALOTOMIES
ENCEPHALOTOMY
ENCEPHALOUS

ENCHAFE
ENCHAFED
ENCHAFES
ENCHAFING
ENCHAIN
ENCHAINED
ENCHAINING
ENCHAINMENT
ENCHAINMENTS
ENCHAINS
ENCHANT
ENCHANTED
ENCHANTER
ENCHANTERS
ENCHANTING
ENCHANTINGLY
ENCHANTMENT
ENCHANTMENTS
ENCHANTRESS
ENCHANTRESSES
ENCHANTS
ENCHARGE
ENCHARGED
ENCHARGES
ENCHARGING
ENCHARM
ENCHARMED
ENCHARMING
ENCHARMS
ENCHASE
ENCHASED
ENCHASER
ENCHASERS
ENCHASES
ENCHASING
ENCHEASON
ENCHEASONS
ENCHEER
ENCHEERED
ENCHEERING
ENCHEERS
ENCHEIRIDION
ENCHEIRIDIONS
ENCHILADA
ENCHILADAS
ENCHIRIDIA
ENCHIRIDION
ENCHIRIDIONS
ENCHONDROMA
ENCHONDROMAS
ENCHONDROMATA
ENCHONDROMATOUS
ENCHORIAL
ENCHORIC
ENCIERRO
ENCIERROS

ENCINA
ENCINAL
ENCINAS
ENCINCTURE
ENCINCTURED
ENCINCTURES
ENCINCTURING
ENCIPHER
ENCIPHERED
ENCIPHERER
ENCIPHERERS
ENCIPHERING
ENCIPHERMENT
ENCIPHERMENTS
ENCIPHERS
ENCIRCLE
ENCIRCLED
ENCIRCLEMENT
ENCIRCLEMENTS
ENCIRCLES
ENCIRCLING
ENCIRCLINGS
ENCLASP
ENCLASPED
ENCLASPING
ENCLASPS
ENCLAVE
ENCLAVED
ENCLAVES
ENCLAVING
ENCLISES
ENCLISIS
ENCLITIC
ENCLITICALLY
ENCLITICS
ENCLOISTER
ENCLOISTERED
ENCLOISTERING
ENCLOISTERS
ENCLOSABLE
ENCLOSABLY
ENCLOSE
ENCLOSED
ENCLOSER
ENCLOSERS
ENCLOSES
ENCLOSING
ENCLOSURE
ENCLOSURES
ENCLOTHE
ENCLOTHED
ENCLOTHES
ENCLOTHING
ENCLOUD
ENCLOUDED
ENCLOUDING

ENCLOUDS
ENCODE
ENCODED
ENCODEMENT
ENCODEMENTS
ENCODER
ENCODERS
ENCODES
ENCODING
ENCOIGNURE
ENCOIGNURES
ENCOLOUR
ENCOLOURED
ENCOLOURING
ENCOLOURS
ENCOLPION
ENCOLPIONS
ENCOLPIUM
ENCOLPIUMS
ENCOLURE
ENCOLURES
ENCOMENDERO
ENCOMENDEROS
ENCOMIA
ENCOMIAST
ENCOMIASTIC
ENCOMIASTICAL
ENCOMIASTICALLY
ENCOMIASTS
ENCOMIENDA
ENCOMIENDAS
ENCOMION
ENCOMIUM
ENCOMIUMS
ENCOMPASS
ENCOMPASSED
ENCOMPASSES
ENCOMPASSING
ENCOMPASSMENT
ENCOMPASSMENTS
ENCOPRESES
ENCOPRESIS
ENCOPRETIC
ENCORE
ENCORED
ENCORES
ENCORING
ENCOUNTER
ENCOUNTERED
ENCOUNTERER
ENCOUNTERERS
ENCOUNTERING
ENCOUNTERS
ENCOURAGE
ENCOURAGED
ENCOURAGEMENT

ENCOURAGEMENTS
ENCOURAGER
ENCOURAGERS
ENCOURAGES
ENCOURAGING
ENCOURAGINGLY
ENCOURAGINGS
ENCRADLE
ENCRADLED
ENCRADLES
ENCRADLING
ENCRATIES
ENCRATY
ENCREASE
ENCREASED
ENCREASES
ENCREASING
ENCRIMSON
ENCRIMSONED
ENCRIMSONING
ENCRIMSONS
ENCRINAL
ENCRINIC
ENCRINITAL
ENCRINITE
ENCRINITES
ENCRINITIC
ENCROACH
ENCROACHED
ENCROACHER
ENCROACHERS
ENCROACHES
ENCROACHING
ENCROACHINGLY
ENCROACHMENT
ENCROACHMENTS
ENCRUST
ENCRUSTATION
ENCRUSTATIONS
ENCRUSTED
ENCRUSTING
ENCRUSTMENT
ENCRUSTMENTS
ENCRUSTS
ENCRYPT
ENCRYPTED
ENCRYPTING
ENCRYPTION
ENCRYPTIONS
ENCRYPTS
ENCULTURATE
ENCULTURATED
ENCULTURATES
ENCULTURATING
ENCULTURATION
ENCULTURATIONS

ENCULTURATIVE
ENCUMBER
ENCUMBERED
ENCUMBERING
ENCUMBERINGLY
ENCUMBERMENT
ENCUMBERMENTS
ENCUMBERS
ENCUMBRANCE
ENCUMBRANCER
ENCUMBRANCERS
ENCUMBRANCES
ENCURTAIN
ENCURTAINED
ENCURTAINING
ENCURTAINS
ENCYCLIC
ENCYCLICAL
ENCYCLICALS
ENCYCLICS
ENCYCLOPAEDIA
ENCYCLOPAEDIAS
ENCYCLOPAEDIC
ENCYCLOPAEDISM
ENCYCLOPAEDIST
ENCYCLOPAEDISTS
ENCYCLOPEDIA
ENCYCLOPEDIAN
ENCYCLOPEDIAS
ENCYCLOPEDIC
ENCYCLOPEDICAL
ENCYCLOPEDISM
ENCYCLOPEDISMS
ENCYCLOPEDIST
ENCYCLOPEDISTS
ENCYST
ENCYSTATION
ENCYSTATIONS
ENCYSTED
ENCYSTING
ENCYSTMENT
ENCYSTMENTS
ENCYSTS
END
ENDAMAGE
ENDAMAGED
ENDAMAGEMENT
ENDAMAGEMENTS
ENDAMAGES
ENDAMAGING
ENDAMEBA
ENDAMEBAE
ENDAMEBAS
ENDAMOEBA
ENDAMOEBAE
ENDAMOEBAS

ENDANGER
ENDANGERED
ENDANGERER
ENDANGERERS
ENDANGERING
ENDANGERMENT
ENDANGERMENTS
ENDANGERS
ENDARCH
ENDARCHIES
ENDARCHY
ENDART
ENDARTED
ENDARTERECTOMY
ENDARTING
ENDARTS
ENDBRAIN
ENDBRAINS
ENDEAR
ENDEARED
ENDEARING
ENDEARINGLY
ENDEARINGNESS
ENDEARINGNESSES
ENDEARMENT
ENDEARMENTS
ENDEARS
ENDEAVOR
ENDEAVORED
ENDEAVORER
ENDEAVORERS
ENDEAVORING
ENDEAVORS
ENDEAVOUR
ENDEAVOURED
ENDEAVOURER
ENDEAVOURERS
ENDEAVOURING
ENDEAVOURMENT
ENDEAVOURMENTS
ENDEAVOURS
ENDECAGON
ENDECAGONS
ENDED
ENDEICTIC
ENDEIXES
ENDEIXIS
ENDEIXISES
ENDEMIAL
ENDEMIC
ENDEMICAL
ENDEMICALLY
ENDEMICITIES
ENDEMICITY
ENDEMICS
ENDEMIOLOGIES

ENDEMIOLOGY
ENDEMISM
ENDEMISMS
ENDENIZEN
ENDENIZENED
ENDENIZENING
ENDENIZENS
ENDER
ENDERGONIC
ENDERMATIC
ENDERMIC
ENDERMICAL
ENDERON
ENDERONS
ENDERS
ENDEW
ENDEWED
ENDEWING
ENDEWS
ENDEXINE
ENDEXINES
ENDGAME
ENDGAMES
ENDING
ENDINGS
ENDIRON
ENDIRONS
ENDITE
ENDITED
ENDITES
ENDITING
ENDIVE
ENDIVES
ENDLANG
ENDLEAF
ENDLEAVES
ENDLESS
ENDLESSLY
ENDLESSNESS
ENDLESSNESSES
ENDLONG
ENDMOST
ENDNOTE
ENDNOTES
ENDOBIOTIC
ENDOBLAST
ENDOBLASTIC
ENDOBLASTS
ENDOCARDIA
ENDOCARDIAC
ENDOCARDIAL
ENDOCARDITIC
ENDOCARDITIS
ENDOCARDITISES
ENDOCARDIUM
ENDOCARP

ENDOCARPAL
ENDOCARPIC
ENDOCARPS
ENDOCAST
ENDOCASTS
ENDOCENTRIC
ENDOCENTRICALLY
ENDOCHONDRAL
ENDOCHYLOUS
ENDOCRANIA
ENDOCRANIAL
ENDOCRANIALLY
ENDOCRANIUM
ENDOCRINAL
ENDOCRINE
ENDOCRINES
ENDOCRINIC
ENDOCRINOLOGIC
ENDOCRINOLOGIES
ENDOCRINOLOGIST
ENDOCRINOLOGY
ENDOCRINOPATHIC
ENDOCRINOPATHY
ENDOCRINOUS
ENDOCRITIC
ENDOCUTICLE
ENDOCUTICLES
ENDOCYTOSES
ENDOCYTOSIS
ENDOCYTOTIC
ENDODERM
ENDODERMAL
ENDODERMIC
ENDODERMIS
ENDODERMISES
ENDODERMS
ENDODONTAL
ENDODONTIC
ENDODONTICALLY
ENDODONTICS
ENDODONTIST
ENDODONTISTS
ENDODYNE
ENDOENZYME
ENDOENZYMES
ENDOERGIC
ENDOGAMIC
ENDOGAMIES
ENDOGAMOUS
ENDOGAMY
ENDOGEN
ENDOGENIC
ENDOGENIES
ENDOGENOUS
ENDOGENOUSLY
ENDOGENS

ENDOGENY
ENDOLITHIC
ENDOLYMPH
ENDOLYMPHATIC
ENDOLYMPHS
ENDOMETRIA
ENDOMETRIAL
ENDOMETRIOSES
ENDOMETRIOSIS
ENDOMETRITIS
ENDOMETRITISES
ENDOMETRIUM
ENDOMITOSES
ENDOMITOSIS
ENDOMITOTIC
ENDOMIXES
ENDOMIXIS
ENDOMIXISES
ENDOMORPH
ENDOMORPHIC
ENDOMORPHIES
ENDOMORPHISM
ENDOMORPHISMS
ENDOMORPHS
ENDOMORPHY
ENDONEURIAL
ENDONEURIALLY
ENDONEURIUM
ENDONUCLEASE
ENDONUCLEASES
ENDONUCLEOLYTIC
ENDOPARASITE
ENDOPARASITES
ENDOPARASITIC
ENDOPARASITISM
ENDOPARASITISMS
ENDOPEPTIDASE
ENDOPEPTIDASES
ENDOPEROXIDE
ENDOPEROXIDES
ENDOPHAGIES
ENDOPHAGOUS
ENDOPHAGY
ENDOPHYLLOUS
ENDOPHYTE
ENDOPHYTES
ENDOPHYTIC
ENDOPHYTICALLY
ENDOPLASM
ENDOPLASMIC
ENDOPLASMS
ENDOPLASTIC
ENDOPLEURA
ENDOPLEURAS
ENDOPOD
ENDOPODITE

ENDOPODITES
ENDOPODS
ENDOPOLYPLOID
ENDOPOLYPLOIDY
ENDORADIOSONDE
ENDORADIOSONDES
ENDORHIZAL
ENDORPHIN
ENDORPHINS
ENDORSABLE
ENDORSE
ENDORSED
ENDORSEE
ENDORSEES
ENDORSEMENT
ENDORSEMENTS
ENDORSER
ENDORSERS
ENDORSES
ENDORSING
ENDORSOR
ENDORSORS
ENDOSARC
ENDOSARCS
ENDOSCOPE
ENDOSCOPES
ENDOSCOPIC
ENDOSCOPICALLY
ENDOSCOPIES
ENDOSCOPIST
ENDOSCOPISTS
ENDOSCOPY
ENDOSKELETAL
ENDOSKELETON
ENDOSKELETONS
ENDOSMOMETER
ENDOSMOMETERS
ENDOSMOMETRIC
ENDOSMOS
ENDOSMOSE
ENDOSMOSES
ENDOSMOSIS
ENDOSMOTIC
ENDOSMOTICALLY
ENDOSOME
ENDOSOMES
ENDOSPERM
ENDOSPERMIC
ENDOSPERMS
ENDOSPORE
ENDOSPORES
ENDOSPOROUS
ENDOSS
ENDOSSED
ENDOSSES
ENDOSSING

ENDOSTEA
ENDOSTEAL
ENDOSTEALLY
ENDOSTEUM
ENDOSTOSES
ENDOSTOSIS
ENDOSTYLE
ENDOSTYLES
ENDOSULFAN
ENDOSULFANS
ENDOSYMBIONT
ENDOSYMBIONTS
ENDOSYMBIOSES
ENDOSYMBIOSIS
ENDOSYMBIOTIC
ENDOTHECIA
ENDOTHECIAL
ENDOTHECIUM
ENDOTHELIA
ENDOTHELIAL
ENDOTHELIOID
ENDOTHELIOMA
ENDOTHELIOMAS
ENDOTHELIOMATA
ENDOTHELIUM
ENDOTHERM
ENDOTHERMAL
ENDOTHERMALLY
ENDOTHERMIC
ENDOTHERMICALLY
ENDOTHERMIES
ENDOTHERMISM
ENDOTHERMS
ENDOTHERMY
ENDOTOXIC
ENDOTOXIN
ENDOTOXINS
ENDOTRACHEAL
ENDOTROPHIC
ENDOW
ENDOWED
ENDOWER
ENDOWERS
ENDOWING
ENDOWMENT
ENDOWMENTS
ENDOWS
ENDOZOA
ENDOZOIC
ENDOZOON
ENDPAPER
ENDPAPERS
ENDPLATE
ENDPLATES
ENDPLAY
ENDPLAYED

ENDPLAYING
ENDPLAYS
ENDPOINT
ENDPOINTS
ENDRIN
ENDRINS
ENDS
ENDSHIP
ENDSHIPS
ENDUE
ENDUED
ENDUES
ENDUING
ENDUNGEON
ENDUNGEONED
ENDUNGEONING
ENDUNGEONS
ENDURABILITY
ENDURABLE
ENDURABLENESS
ENDURABLENESSES
ENDURABLY
ENDURANCE
ENDURANCES
ENDURE
ENDURED
ENDURER
ENDURERS
ENDURES
ENDURING
ENDURINGLY
ENDURINGNESS
ENDURINGNESSES
ENDURO
ENDUROS
ENDWAYS
ENDWISE
ENDYSIS
ENE
ENEMA
ENEMAS
ENEMATA
ENEMIES
ENEMY
ENERGETIC
ENERGETICAL
ENERGETICALLY
ENERGETICS
ENERGIC
ENERGID
ENERGIDS
ENERGIES
ENERGISE
ENERGISED
ENERGISER
ENERGISERS

ENERGISES
ENERGISING
ENERGIZATION
ENERGIZATIONS
ENERGIZE
ENERGIZED
ENERGIZER
ENERGIZERS
ENERGIZES
ENERGIZING
ENERGUMEN
ENERGUMENS
ENERGY
ENERVATE
ENERVATED
ENERVATES
ENERVATING
ENERVATION
ENERVATIONS
ENERVATIVE
ENERVATOR
ENERVATORS
ENERVE
ENERVED
ENERVES
ENERVING
ENES
ENEW
ENEWED
ENEWING
ENEWS
ENFACE
ENFACED
ENFACEMENT
ENFACEMENTS
ENFACES
ENFACING
ENFANT
ENFANTS
ENFEEBLE
ENFEEBLED
ENFEEBLEMENT
ENFEEBLEMENTS
ENFEEBLER
ENFEEBLERS
ENFEEBLES
ENFEEBLING
ENFELON
ENFELONED
ENFELONING
ENFELONS
ENFEOFF
ENFEOFFED
ENFEOFFING
ENFEOFFMENT
ENFEOFFMENTS

ENFEOFFS
ENFESTED
ENFESTERED
ENFETTER
ENFETTERED
ENFETTERING
ENFETTERS
ENFEVER
ENFEVERED
ENFEVERING
ENFEVERS
ENFIERCE
ENFIERCED
ENFIERCES
ENFIERCING
ENFILADE
ENFILADED
ENFILADES
ENFILADING
ENFILED
ENFIRE
ENFIRED
ENFIRES
ENFIRING
ENFIX
ENFIXED
ENFIXES
ENFIXING
ENFLAME
ENFLAMED
ENFLAMES
ENFLAMING
ENFLESH
ENFLESHED
ENFLESHES
ENFLESHING
ENFLEURAGE
ENFLEURAGES
ENFLOWER
ENFLOWERED
ENFLOWERING
ENFLOWERS
ENFOLD
ENFOLDED
ENFOLDER
ENFOLDERS
ENFOLDING
ENFOLDMENT
ENFOLDMENTS
ENFOLDS
ENFORCE
ENFORCEABILITY
ENFORCEABLE
ENFORCED
ENFORCEDLY
ENFORCEMENT

ENFORCEMENTS
ENFORCER
ENFORCERS
ENFORCES
ENFORCING
ENFOREST
ENFORESTED
ENFORESTING
ENFORESTS
ENFORM
ENFORMED
ENFORMING
ENFORMS
ENFOULDERED
ENFRAME
ENFRAMED
ENFRAMEMENT
ENFRAMEMENTS
ENFRAMES
ENFRAMING
ENFRANCHISE
ENFRANCHISED
ENFRANCHISEMENT
ENFRANCHISER
ENFRANCHISERS
ENFRANCHISES
ENFRANCHISING
ENFREE
ENFREED
ENFREEDOM
ENFREEDOMED
ENFREEDOMING
ENFREEDOMS
ENFREEING
ENFREES
ENFREEZE
ENFREEZES
ENFREEZING
ENFROSEN
ENFROZE
ENFROZEN
ENG
ENGAGE
ENGAGED
ENGAGEDLY
ENGAGEE
ENGAGEMENT
ENGAGEMENTS
ENGAGER
ENGAGERS
ENGAGES
ENGAGING
ENGAGINGLY
ENGAGINGNESS
ENGAGINGNESSES
ENGAOL

ENGAOLED
ENGAOLING
ENGAOLS
ENGARLAND
ENGARLANDED
ENGARLANDING
ENGARLANDS
ENGARRISON
ENGARRISONED
ENGARRISONING
ENGARRISONS
ENGENDER
ENGENDERED
ENGENDERER
ENGENDERERS
ENGENDERING
ENGENDERMENT
ENGENDERMENTS
ENGENDERS
ENGENDRURE
ENGENDRURES
ENGENDURE
ENGENDURES
ENGILD
ENGILDED
ENGILDING
ENGILDS
ENGILT
ENGINE
ENGINED
ENGINEER
ENGINEERED
ENGINEERING
ENGINEERINGS
ENGINEERS
ENGINER
ENGINERIES
ENGINERS
ENGINERY
ENGINES
ENGINING
ENGINOUS
ENGIRD
ENGIRDED
ENGIRDING
ENGIRDLE
ENGIRDLED
ENGIRDLES
ENGIRDLING
ENGIRDS
ENGIRT
ENGISCOPE
ENGISCOPES
ENGLACIAL
ENGLACIALLY
ENGLISH

ENGLISHED
ENGLISHES
ENGLISHING
ENGLOBE
ENGLOBED
ENGLOBES
ENGLOBING
ENGLOOM
ENGLOOMED
ENGLOOMING
ENGLOOMS
ENGLUT
ENGLUTS
ENGLUTTED
ENGLUTTING
ENGOBE
ENGOBES
ENGORE
ENGORED
ENGORES
ENGORGE
ENGORGED
ENGORGEMENT
ENGORGEMENTS
ENGORGES
ENGORGING
ENGORING
ENGOUEMENT
ENGOUEMENTS
ENGOULED
ENGOUMENT
ENGOUMENTS
ENGRACE
ENGRACED
ENGRACES
ENGRACING
ENGRAFF
ENGRAFFED
ENGRAFFING
ENGRAFFS
ENGRAFT
ENGRAFTATION
ENGRAFTATIONS
ENGRAFTED
ENGRAFTING
ENGRAFTMENT
ENGRAFTMENTS
ENGRAFTS
ENGRAIL
ENGRAILED
ENGRAILING
ENGRAILMENT
ENGRAILMENTS
ENGRAILS
ENGRAIN
ENGRAINED

ENGRAINEDLY
ENGRAINEDNESS
ENGRAINER
ENGRAINERS
ENGRAINING
ENGRAINS
ENGRAM
ENGRAMMA
ENGRAMMAS
ENGRAMMATIC
ENGRAMME
ENGRAMMES
ENGRAMMIC
ENGRAMS
ENGRASP
ENGRASPED
ENGRASPING
ENGRASPS
ENGRAVE
ENGRAVED
ENGRAVEN
ENGRAVER
ENGRAVERIES
ENGRAVERS
ENGRAVERY
ENGRAVES
ENGRAVING
ENGRAVINGS
ENGRENAGE
ENGRENAGES
ENGRIEVE
ENGRIEVED
ENGRIEVES
ENGRIEVING
ENGROOVE
ENGROOVED
ENGROOVES
ENGROOVING
ENGROSS
ENGROSSED
ENGROSSEDLY
ENGROSSER
ENGROSSERS
ENGROSSES
ENGROSSING
ENGROSSINGLY
ENGROSSMENT
ENGROSSMENTS
ENGS
ENGUARD
ENGUARDED
ENGUARDING
ENGUARDS
ENGULF
ENGULFED
ENGULFING

ENGULFMENT
ENGULFMENTS
ENGULFS
ENGULPH
ENGULPHED
ENGULPHING
ENGULPHS
ENGYSCOPE
ENGYSCOPES
ENHALO
ENHALOED
ENHALOES
ENHALOING
ENHALOS
ENHANCE
ENHANCED
ENHANCEMENT
ENHANCEMENTS
ENHANCER
ENHANCERS
ENHANCES
ENHANCING
ENHANCIVE
ENHARMONIC
ENHARMONICAL
ENHARMONICALLY
ENHEARSE
ENHEARSED
ENHEARSES
ENHEARSING
ENHEARTEN
ENHEARTENED
ENHEARTENING
ENHEARTENS
ENHUNGER
ENHUNGERED
ENHUNGERING
ENHUNGERS
ENHYDRITE
ENHYDRITES
ENHYDRITIC
ENHYDROS
ENHYDROSES
ENHYDROUS
ENHYPOSTASIA
ENHYPOSTASIAS
ENHYPOSTATIC
ENHYPOSTATISE
ENHYPOSTATISED
ENHYPOSTATISES
ENHYPOSTATISING
ENHYPOSTATIZE
ENHYPOSTATIZED
ENHYPOSTATIZES
ENHYPOSTATIZING
ENIAC

ENIACS
ENIGMA
ENIGMAS
ENIGMATA
ENIGMATIC
ENIGMATICAL
ENIGMATICALLY
ENIGMATISE
ENIGMATISED
ENIGMATISES
ENIGMATISING
ENIGMATIST
ENIGMATISTS
ENIGMATIZE
ENIGMATIZED
ENIGMATIZES
ENIGMATIZING
ENIGMATOGRAPHY
ENISLE
ENISLED
ENISLES
ENISLING
ENJAMB
ENJAMBED
ENJAMBEMENT
ENJAMBEMENTS
ENJAMBING
ENJAMBMENT
ENJAMBMENTS
ENJAMBS
ENJOIN
ENJOINED
ENJOINER
ENJOINERS
ENJOINING
ENJOINMENT
ENJOINMENTS
ENJOINS
ENJOY
ENJOYABLE
ENJOYABLENESS
ENJOYABLENESSES
ENJOYABLY
ENJOYED
ENJOYER
ENJOYERS
ENJOYING
ENJOYMENT
ENJOYMENTS
ENJOYS
ENKEPHALIN
ENKEPHALINE
ENKEPHALINES
ENKEPHALINS
ENKERNEL
ENKERNELLED

ENKERNELLING
ENKERNELS
ENKINDLE
ENKINDLED
ENKINDLER
ENKINDLERS
ENKINDLES
ENKINDLING
ENLACE
ENLACED
ENLACEMENT
ENLACEMENTS
ENLACES
ENLACING
ENLARD
ENLARDED
ENLARDING
ENLARDS
ENLARGE
ENLARGEABLE
ENLARGED
ENLARGEDLY
ENLARGEDNESS
ENLARGEDNESSES
ENLARGEMENT
ENLARGEMENTS
ENLARGEN
ENLARGENED
ENLARGENING
ENLARGENS
ENLARGER
ENLARGERS
ENLARGES
ENLARGING
ENLEVE
ENLEVEMENT
ENLEVEMENTS
ENLIGHT
ENLIGHTED
ENLIGHTEN
ENLIGHTENED
ENLIGHTENER
ENLIGHTENERS
ENLIGHTENING
ENLIGHTENMENT
ENLIGHTENMENTS
ENLIGHTENS
ENLIGHTING
ENLIGHTS
ENLINK
ENLINKED
ENLINKING
ENLINKS
ENLIST
ENLISTED
ENLISTEE

ENLISTEES
ENLISTER
ENLISTERS
ENLISTING
ENLISTMENT
ENLISTMENTS
ENLISTS
ENLIT
ENLIVEN
ENLIVENED
ENLIVENER
ENLIVENERS
ENLIVENING
ENLIVENMENT
ENLIVENMENTS
ENLIVENS
ENLOCK
ENLOCKED
ENLOCKING
ENLOCKS
ENLUMINE
ENLUMINED
ENLUMINES
ENLUMINING
ENMESH
ENMESHED
ENMESHES
ENMESHING
ENMESHMENT
ENMESHMENTS
ENMEW
ENMEWED
ENMEWING
ENMEWS
ENMITIES
ENMITY
ENMOSSED
ENMOVE
ENMOVED
ENMOVES
ENMOVING
ENNAGE
ENNAGES
ENNEAD
ENNEADIC
ENNEADS
ENNEAGON
ENNEAGONAL
ENNEAGONS
ENNEAHEDRA
ENNEAHEDRAL
ENNEAHEDRON
ENNEAHEDRONS
ENNEANDRIAN
ENNEANDROUS
ENNEASTYLE

ENNOBLE
ENNOBLED
ENNOBLEMENT
ENNOBLEMENTS
ENNOBLER
ENNOBLERS
ENNOBLES
ENNOBLING
ENNOG
ENNOGS
ENNUI
ENNUIED
ENNUIS
ENNUYE
ENNUYED
ENNUYEE
ENNUYING
ENODAL
ENOKI
ENOKIDAKE
ENOKIDAKES
ENOKIS
ENOL
ENOLASE
ENOLASES
ENOLIC
ENOLOGICAL
ENOLOGIES
ENOLOGIST
ENOLOGISTS
ENOLOGY
ENOLS
ENOMOTIES
ENOMOTY
ENORM
ENORMITIES
ENORMITY
ENORMOUS
ENORMOUSLY
ENORMOUSNESS
ENORMOUSNESSES
ENOSES
ENOSIS
ENOSISES
ENOUGH
ENOUGHS
ENOUNCE
ENOUNCED
ENOUNCEMENT
ENOUNCEMENTS
ENOUNCES
ENOUNCING
ENOW
ENOWS
ENPHYTOTIC
ENPLANE

ENPLANED
ENPLANES
ENPLANING
ENPRINT
ENPRINTS
ENQUIRATION
ENQUIRATIONS
ENQUIRE
ENQUIRED
ENQUIRER
ENQUIRERS
ENQUIRES
ENQUIRIES
ENQUIRING
ENQUIRY
ENRACE
ENRACED
ENRACES
ENRACING
ENRAGE
ENRAGED
ENRAGEDLY
ENRAGEMENT
ENRAGEMENTS
ENRAGES
ENRAGING
ENRANCKLED
ENRANCKLES
ENRANCKLING
ENRANGE
ENRANGED
ENRANGES
ENRANGING
ENRANK
ENRANKED
ENRANKING
ENRANKS
ENRAPT
ENRAPTURE
ENRAPTURED
ENRAPTURES
ENRAPTURING
ENRAUNGE
ENRAUNGED
ENRAUNGES
ENRAUNGING
ENRAVISH
ENRAVISHED
ENRAVISHES
ENRAVISHING
ENREGIMENT
ENREGIMENTED
ENREGIMENTING
ENREGIMENTS
ENREGISTER
ENREGISTERED

ENREGISTERING
ENREGISTERS
ENRHEUM
ENRHEUMED
ENRHEUMING
ENRHEUMS
ENRICH
ENRICHED
ENRICHER
ENRICHERS
ENRICHES
ENRICHING
ENRICHMENT
ENRICHMENTS
ENRIDGED
ENRING
ENRINGED
ENRINGING
ENRINGS
ENRIVEN
ENROBE
ENROBED
ENROBER
ENROBERS
ENROBES
ENROBING
ENROL
ENROLL
ENROLLED
ENROLLEE
ENROLLEES
ENROLLER
ENROLLERS
ENROLLING
ENROLLMENT
ENROLLMENTS
ENROLLS
ENROLMENT
ENROLMENTS
ENROLS
ENROOT
ENROOTED
ENROOTING
ENROOTS
ENROUGH
ENROUGHED
ENROUGHING
ENROUGHS
ENROUND
ENROUNDED
ENROUNDING
ENROUNDS
ENS
ENSAMPLE
ENSAMPLED
ENSAMPLES

ENSAMPLING
ENSANGUINATED
ENSANGUINE
ENSANGUINED
ENSANGUINES
ENSANGUINING
ENSATE
ENSCHEDULE
ENSCHEDULED
ENSCHEDULES
ENSCHEDULING
ENSCONCE
ENSCONCED
ENSCONCES
ENSCONCING
ENSCROLL
ENSCROLLED
ENSCROLLING
ENSCROLLS
ENSEAL
ENSEALED
ENSEALING
ENSEALS
ENSEAM
ENSEAMED
ENSEAMING
ENSEAMS
ENSEAR
ENSEARED
ENSEARING
ENSEARS
ENSEMBLE
ENSEMBLES
ENSEPULCHRE
ENSEPULCHRED
ENSEPULCHRES
ENSEPULCHRING
ENSERF
ENSERFED
ENSERFING
ENSERFMENT
ENSERFMENTS
ENSERFS
ENSEW
ENSEWED
ENSEWING
ENSEWS
ENSHEATH
ENSHEATHE
ENSHEATHED
ENSHEATHES
ENSHEATHING
ENSHEATHS
ENSHELL
ENSHELLED
ENSHELLING

ENSHELLS
ENSHELTER
ENSHELTERED
ENSHELTERING
ENSHELTERS
ENSHIELD
ENSHIELDED
ENSHIELDING
ENSHIELDS
ENSHRINE
ENSHRINED
ENSHRINEE
ENSHRINEES
ENSHRINEMENT
ENSHRINEMENTS
ENSHRINES
ENSHRINING
ENSHROUD
ENSHROUDED
ENSHROUDING
ENSHROUDS
ENSIFORM
ENSIGN
ENSIGNCIES
ENSIGNCY
ENSIGNED
ENSIGNING
ENSIGNS
ENSIGNSHIP
ENSIGNSHIPS
ENSILABILITIES
ENSILABILITY
ENSILAGE
ENSILAGED
ENSILAGEING
ENSILAGES
ENSILAGING
ENSILE
ENSILED
ENSILES
ENSILING
ENSKIED
ENSKIES
ENSKY
ENSKYED
ENSKYING
ENSLAVE
ENSLAVED
ENSLAVEMENT
ENSLAVEMENTS
ENSLAVER
ENSLAVERS
ENSLAVES
ENSLAVING
ENSNARE
ENSNARED

ENSNAREMENT
ENSNAREMENTS
ENSNARER
ENSNARERS
ENSNARES
ENSNARING
ENSNARL
ENSNARLED
ENSNARLING
ENSNARLS
ENSORCEL
ENSORCELED
ENSORCELING
ENSORCELL
ENSORCELLED
ENSORCELLING
ENSORCELLMENT
ENSORCELLMENTS
ENSORCELLS
ENSORCELS
ENSOUL
ENSOULED
ENSOULING
ENSOULMENT
ENSOULMENTS
ENSOULS
ENSPHERE
ENSPHERED
ENSPHERES
ENSPHERING
ENSTAMP
ENSTAMPED
ENSTAMPING
ENSTAMPS
ENSTATITE
ENSTATITES
ENSTEEP
ENSTEEPED
ENSTEEPING
ENSTEEPS
ENSTRUCTURED
ENSTYLE
ENSTYLED
ENSTYLES
ENSTYLING
ENSUE
ENSUED
ENSUES
ENSUING
ENSURE
ENSURED
ENSURER
ENSURERS
ENSURES
ENSURING
ENSWATHE

ENSWATHED
ENSWATHEMENT
ENSWATHEMENTS
ENSWATHES
ENSWATHING
ENSWEEP
ENSWEEPING
ENSWEEPS
ENSWEPT
ENTABLATURE
ENTABLATURES
ENTABLEMENT
ENTABLEMENTS
ENTAIL
ENTAILED
ENTAILER
ENTAILERS
ENTAILING
ENTAILMENT
ENTAILMENTS
ENTAILS
ENTAME
ENTAMEBA
ENTAMEBAE
ENTAMEBAS
ENTAMED
ENTAMES
ENTAMING
ENTAMOEBA
ENTAMOEBAE
ENTAMOEBAS
ENTANGLE
ENTANGLED
ENTANGLEMENT
ENTANGLEMENTS
ENTANGLER
ENTANGLERS
ENTANGLES
ENTANGLING
ENTASES
ENTASIA
ENTASIAS
ENTASIS
ENTASTIC
ENTAYLE
ENTAYLED
ENTAYLES
ENTAYLING
ENTELECHIES
ENTELECHY
ENTELLUS
ENTELLUSES
ENTENDER
ENTENDERED
ENTENDERING
ENTENDERS

ENTENTE
ENTENTES
ENTER
ENTERA
ENTERABLE
ENTERAL
ENTERALLY
ENTERATE
ENTERCHAUNGE
ENTERCHAUNGED
ENTERCHAUNGES
ENTERCHAUNGING
ENTERDEALE
ENTERDEALED
ENTERDEALES
ENTERDEALING
ENTERECTOMIES
ENTERECTOMY
ENTERED
ENTERER
ENTERERS
ENTERIC
ENTERICS
ENTERING
ENTERINGS
ENTERITIDES
ENTERITIS
ENTERITISES
ENTEROBACTERIA
ENTEROBACTERIAL
ENTEROBACTERIUM
ENTEROBIASES
ENTEROBIASIS
ENTEROCELE
ENTEROCELES
ENTEROCENTESES
ENTEROCENTESIS
ENTEROCOCCAL
ENTEROCOCCI
ENTEROCOCCUS
ENTEROCOEL
ENTEROCOELE
ENTEROCOELES
ENTEROCOELIC
ENTEROCOELOUS
ENTEROCOELS
ENTEROCOLITIS
ENTEROCOLITISES
ENTEROGASTRONE
ENTEROGASTRONES
ENTEROKINASE
ENTEROKINASES
ENTEROLITH
ENTEROLITHS
ENTERON
ENTERONS

ENTEROPATHIES
ENTEROPATHY
ENTEROPNEUST
ENTEROPNEUSTAL
ENTEROPNEUSTS
ENTEROPTOSES
ENTEROPTOSIS
ENTEROSTOMAL
ENTEROSTOMIES
ENTEROSTOMY
ENTEROTOMIES
ENTEROTOMY
ENTEROTOXIN
ENTEROTOXINS
ENTEROVIRAL
ENTEROVIRUS
ENTEROVIRUSES
ENTERPRISE
ENTERPRISED
ENTERPRISER
ENTERPRISERS
ENTERPRISES
ENTERPRISING
ENTERPRISINGLY
ENTERS
ENTERTAIN
ENTERTAINED
ENTERTAINER
ENTERTAINERS
ENTERTAINING
ENTERTAININGLY
ENTERTAININGS
ENTERTAINMENT
ENTERTAINMENTS
ENTERTAINS
ENTERTAKE
ENTERTAKEN
ENTERTAKES
ENTERTAKING
ENTERTISSUED
ENTERTOOK
ENTETE
ENTETEE
ENTHALPIES
ENTHALPY
ENTHETIC
ENTHRAL
ENTHRALDOM
ENTHRALDOMS
ENTHRALL
ENTHRALLED
ENTHRALLER
ENTHRALLERS
ENTHRALLING
ENTHRALLMENT
ENTHRALLMENTS

ENTHRALLS
ENTHRALMENT
ENTHRALMENTS
ENTHRALS
ENTHRONE
ENTHRONED
ENTHRONEMENT
ENTHRONEMENTS
ENTHRONES
ENTHRONING
ENTHRONISATION
ENTHRONISATIONS
ENTHRONISE
ENTHRONISED
ENTHRONISES
ENTHRONISING
ENTHRONIZATION
ENTHRONIZATIONS
ENTHRONIZE
ENTHRONIZED
ENTHRONIZES
ENTHRONIZING
ENTHUSE
ENTHUSED
ENTHUSES
ENTHUSIASM
ENTHUSIASMS
ENTHUSIAST
ENTHUSIASTIC
ENTHUSIASTICAL
ENTHUSIASTS
ENTHUSING
ENTHYMEMATIC
ENTHYMEMATICAL
ENTHYMEME
ENTHYMEMES
ENTIA
ENTICE
ENTICEABLE
ENTICED
ENTICEMENT
ENTICEMENTS
ENTICER
ENTICERS
ENTICES
ENTICING
ENTICINGLY
ENTICINGNESS
ENTICINGS
ENTIRE
ENTIRELY
ENTIRENESS
ENTIRENESSES
ENTIRES
ENTIRETIES
ENTIRETY

ENTITATIVE
ENTITIES
ENTITLE
ENTITLED
ENTITLEMENT
ENTITLEMENTS
ENTITLES
ENTITLING
ENTITY
ENTOBLAST
ENTOBLASTIC
ENTOBLASTS
ENTODERM
ENTODERMAL
ENTODERMIC
ENTODERMS
ENTOIL
ENTOILED
ENTOILING
ENTOILMENT
ENTOILMENTS
ENTOILS
ENTOMB
ENTOMBED
ENTOMBING
ENTOMBMENT
ENTOMBMENTS
ENTOMBS
ENTOMIC
ENTOMOFAUNA
ENTOMOFAUNAE
ENTOMOFAUNAS
ENTOMOLOGIC
ENTOMOLOGICAL
ENTOMOLOGICALLY
ENTOMOLOGIES
ENTOMOLOGISE
ENTOMOLOGISED
ENTOMOLOGISES
ENTOMOLOGISING
ENTOMOLOGIST
ENTOMOLOGISTS
ENTOMOLOGIZE
ENTOMOLOGIZED
ENTOMOLOGIZES
ENTOMOLOGIZING
ENTOMOLOGY
ENTOMOPHAGIES
ENTOMOPHAGOUS
ENTOMOPHAGY
ENTOMOPHILIES
ENTOMOPHILOUS
ENTOMOPHILY
ENTOMOSTRACA
ENTOMOSTRACAN
ENTOMOSTRACANS

ENTOMOSTRACOUS
ENTOPHYTAL
ENTOPHYTE
ENTOPHYTES
ENTOPHYTIC
ENTOPHYTOUS
ENTOPIC
ENTOPLASTRA
ENTOPLASTRAL
ENTOPLASTRON
ENTOPROCT
ENTOPROCTS
ENTOPTIC
ENTOPTICS
ENTOTIC
ENTOURAGE
ENTOURAGES
ENTOZOA
ENTOZOAL
ENTOZOAN
ENTOZOANS
ENTOZOIC
ENTOZOON
ENTRAIL
ENTRAILED
ENTRAILING
ENTRAILS
ENTRAIN
ENTRAINED
ENTRAINEMENT
ENTRAINEMENTS
ENTRAINER
ENTRAINERS
ENTRAINING
ENTRAINMENT
ENTRAINMENTS
ENTRAINS
ENTRALL
ENTRALLES
ENTRAMMEL
ENTRAMMELLED
ENTRAMMELLING
ENTRAMMELS
ENTRANCE
ENTRANCED
ENTRANCEMENT
ENTRANCEMENTS
ENTRANCES
ENTRANCEWAY
ENTRANCEWAYS
ENTRANCING
ENTRANT
ENTRANTS
ENTRAP
ENTRAPMENT
ENTRAPMENTS

ENTRAPPED
ENTRAPPER
ENTRAPPERS
ENTRAPPING
ENTRAPS
ENTREASURE
ENTREASURED
ENTREASURES
ENTREASURING
ENTREAT
ENTREATABLE
ENTREATED
ENTREATIES
ENTREATING
ENTREATINGLY
ENTREATIVE
ENTREATMENT
ENTREATMENTS
ENTREATS
ENTREATY
ENTRECHAT
ENTRECHATS
ENTRECOTE
ENTRECOTES
ENTREE
ENTREES
ENTREMES
ENTREMESSES
ENTREMETS
ENTRENCH
ENTRENCHED
ENTRENCHER
ENTRENCHERS
ENTRENCHES
ENTRENCHING
ENTRENCHMENT
ENTRENCHMENTS
ENTREPOT
ENTREPOTS
ENTREPRENEUR
ENTREPRENEURIAL
ENTREPRENEURS
ENTREPRENEUSE
ENTREPRENEUSES
ENTRESOL
ENTRESOLS
ENTREZ
ENTRIES
ENTRISM
ENTRISMS
ENTRIST
ENTRISTS
ENTROLD
ENTROPIC
ENTROPICALLY
ENTROPIES

ENTROPION
ENTROPIONS
ENTROPIUM
ENTROPIUMS
ENTROPY
ENTRUST
ENTRUSTED
ENTRUSTING
ENTRUSTMENT
ENTRUSTMENTS
ENTRUSTS
ENTRY
ENTRYISM
ENTRYISMS
ENTRYIST
ENTRYISTS
ENTRYWAY
ENTRYWAYS
ENTWINE
ENTWINED
ENTWINEMENT
ENTWINEMENTS
ENTWINES
ENTWINING
ENTWIST
ENTWISTED
ENTWISTING
ENTWISTS
ENUCLEATE
ENUCLEATED
ENUCLEATES
ENUCLEATING
ENUCLEATION
ENUCLEATIONS
ENUMERABILITIES
ENUMERABILITY
ENUMERABLE
ENUMERATE
ENUMERATED
ENUMERATES
ENUMERATING
ENUMERATION
ENUMERATIONS
ENUMERATIVE
ENUMERATOR
ENUMERATORS
ENUNCIABLE
ENUNCIATE
ENUNCIATED
ENUNCIATES
ENUNCIATING
ENUNCIATION
ENUNCIATIONS
ENUNCIATIVE
ENUNCIATIVELY
ENUNCIATOR

ENUNCIATORS
ENUNCIATORY
ENURE
ENURED
ENUREDNESS
ENUREDNESSES
ENUREMENT
ENUREMENTS
ENURES
ENURESES
ENURESIS
ENURESISES
ENURETIC
ENURETICS
ENURING
ENVASSAL
ENVASSALLED
ENVASSALLING
ENVASSALS
ENVAULT
ENVAULTED
ENVAULTING
ENVAULTS
ENVEIGLE
ENVEIGLED
ENVEIGLES
ENVEIGLING
ENVELOP
ENVELOPE
ENVELOPED
ENVELOPES
ENVELOPING
ENVELOPMENT
ENVELOPMENTS
ENVELOPS
ENVENOM
ENVENOMED
ENVENOMING
ENVENOMIZATION
ENVENOMIZATIONS
ENVENOMS
ENVERMEIL
ENVERMEILED
ENVERMEILING
ENVERMEILS
ENVIABLE
ENVIABLENESS
ENVIABLENESSES
ENVIABLY
ENVIED
ENVIER
ENVIERS
ENVIES
ENVIOUS
ENVIOUSLY
ENVIOUSNESS

ENVIOUSNESSES
ENVIRO
ENVIRON
ENVIRONED
ENVIRONICS
ENVIRONING
ENVIRONMENT
ENVIRONMENTAL
ENVIRONMENTALLY
ENVIRONMENTS
ENVIRONS
ENVIROS
ENVISAGE
ENVISAGED
ENVISAGEMENT
ENVISAGEMENTS
ENVISAGES
ENVISAGING
ENVISION
ENVISIONED
ENVISIONING
ENVISIONS
ENVOI
ENVOIS
ENVOY
ENVOYS
ENVOYSHIP
ENVOYSHIPS
ENVY
ENVYING
ENVYINGLY
ENVYINGS
ENWALL
ENWALLED
ENWALLING
ENWALLOW
ENWALLOWED
ENWALLOWING
ENWALLOWS
ENWALLS
ENWHEEL
ENWHEELED
ENWHEELING
ENWHEELS
ENWIND
ENWINDING
ENWINDS
ENWOMB
ENWOMBED
ENWOMBING
ENWOMBS
ENWOUND
ENWRAP
ENWRAPMENT
ENWRAPMENTS
ENWRAPPED

ENWRAPPING
ENWRAPPINGS
ENWRAPS
ENWREATH
ENWREATHE
ENWREATHED
ENWREATHES
ENWREATHING
ENWREATHS
ENZIAN
ENZIANS
ENZONE
ENZONED
ENZONES
ENZONING
ENZOOTIC
ENZOOTICALLY
ENZOOTICS
ENZYM
ENZYMATIC
ENZYMATICALLY
ENZYME
ENZYMES
ENZYMIC
ENZYMICALLY
ENZYMOLOGICAL
ENZYMOLOGICALLY
ENZYMOLOGIES
ENZYMOLOGIST
ENZYMOLOGISTS
ENZYMOLOGY
ENZYMOLYSIS
ENZYMOLYTIC
ENZYMS
EOAN
EOBIONT
EOBIONTS
EOHIPPUS
EOHIPPUSES
EOLIAN
EOLIENNE
EOLIENNES
EOLIPILE
EOLIPILES
EOLITH
EOLITHIC
EOLITHS
EOLOPILE
EOLOPILES
EON
EONIAN
EONISM
EONISMS
EONS
EORL
EORLS

EOSIN
EOSINE
EOSINES
EOSINIC
EOSINOPHIL
EOSINOPHILE
EOSINOPHILES
EOSINOPHILIA
EOSINOPHILIAS
EOSINOPHILIC
EOSINOPHILOUS
EOSINOPHILS
EOSINS
EOTHEN
EPACRID
EPACRIDS
EPACRIS
EPACRISES
EPACT
EPACTS
EPAENETIC
EPAGOGE
EPAGOGES
EPAGOGIC
EPAGOMENAL
EPANADIPLOSES
EPANADIPLOSIS
EPANALEPSES
EPANALEPSIS
EPANALEPTIC
EPANAPHORA
EPANAPHORAL
EPANAPHORAS
EPANODOS
EPANODOSES
EPANORTHOSES
EPANORTHOSIS
EPANORTHOTIC
EPARCH
EPARCHATE
EPARCHATES
EPARCHIAL
EPARCHIES
EPARCHS
EPARCHY
EPATANT
EPAULE
EPAULEMENT
EPAULEMENTS
EPAULES
EPAULET
EPAULETS
EPAULETTE
EPAULETTED
EPAULETTES
EPAXIAL

EPAZOTE
EPAZOTES
EPEDAPHIC
EPEE
EPEEIST
EPEEISTS
EPEES
EPEIRA
EPEIRAS
EPEIRIC
EPEIRID
EPEIRIDS
EPEIROGENESES
EPEIROGENESIS
EPEIROGENETIC
EPEIROGENIC
EPEIROGENICALLY
EPEIROGENIES
EPEIROGENY
EPENCEPHALA
EPENCEPHALIC
EPENCEPHALON
EPENCEPHALONS
EPENDYMA
EPENDYMAL
EPENDYMALLY
EPENDYMAS
EPENTHESES
EPENTHESIS
EPENTHETIC
EPEOLATRIES
EPEOLATRY
EPERDU
EPERDUE
EPERGNE
EPERGNES
EPEXEGESES
EPEXEGESIS
EPEXEGETIC
EPEXEGETICAL
EPEXEGETICALLY
EPHA
EPHAH
EPHAHS
EPHAS
EPHEBE
EPHEBES
EPHEBI
EPHEBIC
EPHEBOI
EPHEBOPHILIA
EPHEBOPHILIAS
EPHEBOS
EPHEBUS
EPHEDRA
EPHEDRAS

EPHEDRIN
EPHEDRINE
EPHEDRINES
EPHEDRINS
EPHELIDES
EPHELIS
EPHEMERA
EPHEMERAE
EPHEMERAL
EPHEMERALITIES
EPHEMERALITY
EPHEMERALLY
EPHEMERALNESS
EPHEMERALS
EPHEMERAS
EPHEMERID
EPHEMERIDES
EPHEMERIDS
EPHEMERIS
EPHEMERIST
EPHEMERISTS
EPHEMERON
EPHEMERONS
EPHEMEROPTERAN
EPHEMEROPTERANS
EPHEMEROUS
EPHIALTES
EPHOD
EPHODS
EPHOR
EPHORAL
EPHORALTIES
EPHORALTY
EPHORATE
EPHORATES
EPHORI
EPHORS
EPIBIOSIS
EPIBIOTIC
EPIBIOTICALLY
EPIBLAST
EPIBLASTIC
EPIBLASTS
EPIBLEM
EPIBLEMS
EPIBOLIC
EPIBOLIES
EPIBOLY
EPIC
EPICAL
EPICALLY
EPICALYCES
EPICALYX
EPICALYXES
EPICANTHI
EPICANTHIC

EPICANTHUS
EPICARDIA
EPICARDIAC
EPICARDIAL
EPICARDIUM
EPICARP
EPICARPS
EPICEDE
EPICEDES
EPICEDIA
EPICEDIAL
EPICEDIAN
EPICEDIUM
EPICENE
EPICENES
EPICENISM
EPICENISMS
EPICENTER
EPICENTERS
EPICENTRAL
EPICENTRE
EPICENTRES
EPICHEIREMA
EPICHEIREMAS
EPICHLOROHYDRIN
EPICIER
EPICIERS
EPICISM
EPICISMS
EPICIST
EPICISTS
EPICLESES
EPICLESIS
EPICLIKE
EPICONDYLE
EPICONDYLES
EPICONDYLITIS
EPICONDYLITISES
EPICONTINENTAL
EPICOTYL
EPICOTYLS
EPICRISES
EPICRISIS
EPICRITIC
EPICS
EPICURE
EPICUREAN
EPICUREANISM
EPICUREANISMS
EPICUREANS
EPICURES
EPICURISE
EPICURISED
EPICURISES
EPICURISING
EPICURISM

EPICURISMS
EPICURIZE
EPICURIZED
EPICURIZES
EPICURIZING
EPICUTICLE
EPICUTICLES
EPICUTICULAR
EPICYCLE
EPICYCLES
EPICYCLIC
EPICYCLICAL
EPICYCLOID
EPICYCLOIDAL
EPICYCLOIDS
EPIDEICTIC
EPIDEICTICAL
EPIDEMIC
EPIDEMICAL
EPIDEMICALLY
EPIDEMICITIES
EPIDEMICITY
EPIDEMICS
EPIDEMIOLOGIC
EPIDEMIOLOGICAL
EPIDEMIOLOGIES
EPIDEMIOLOGIST
EPIDEMIOLOGISTS
EPIDEMIOLOGY
EPIDENDRONES
EPIDENDRUM
EPIDENDRUMS
EPIDERM
EPIDERMAL
EPIDERMIC
EPIDERMIS
EPIDERMISES
EPIDERMOID
EPIDERMS
EPIDIASCOPE
EPIDIASCOPES
EPIDICTIC
EPIDIDYMAL
EPIDIDYMIDES
EPIDIDYMIS
EPIDIDYMITIS
EPIDIDYMITISES
EPIDIORITE
EPIDIORITES
EPIDOSITE
EPIDOSITES
EPIDOTE
EPIDOTES
EPIDOTIC
EPIDOTISATION
EPIDOTISATIONS

EPIDOTISED
EPIDOTIZATION
EPIDOTIZATIONS
EPIDOTIZED
EPIDURAL
EPIDURALS
EPIFAUNA
EPIFAUNAE
EPIFAUNAL
EPIFAUNAS
EPIFOCAL
EPIGAEAL
EPIGAEAN
EPIGAEOUS
EPIGAMIC
EPIGASTRIA
EPIGASTRIAL
EPIGASTRIC
EPIGASTRIUM
EPIGEAL
EPIGEAN
EPIGEIC
EPIGENE
EPIGENESES
EPIGENESIS
EPIGENESIST
EPIGENESISTS
EPIGENETIC
EPIGENETICALLY
EPIGENETICIST
EPIGENETICISTS
EPIGENETICS
EPIGENIC
EPIGENIST
EPIGENISTS
EPIGENOUS
EPIGENOUSLY
EPIGEOUS
EPIGLOTTAL
EPIGLOTTIC
EPIGLOTTIDES
EPIGLOTTIS
EPIGLOTTISES
EPIGNATH
EPIGNATHOUS
EPIGNATHS
EPIGON
EPIGONE
EPIGONES
EPIGONI
EPIGONIC
EPIGONISM
EPIGONISMS
EPIGONOUS
EPIGONS
EPIGONUS

EPIGRAM	EPILOBIUMS	EPINICIAN	EPISCOPACIES
EPIGRAMMATIC	EPILOG	EPINICION	EPISCOPACY
EPIGRAMMATICAL	EPILOGIC	EPINICIONS	EPISCOPAL
EPIGRAMMATISE	EPILOGISE	EPINIKIAN	EPISCOPALIAN
EPIGRAMMATISED	EPILOGISED	EPINIKION	EPISCOPALIANISM
EPIGRAMMATISES	EPILOGISES	EPINIKIONS	EPISCOPALIANS
EPIGRAMMATISING	EPILOGISING	EPINOSIC	EPISCOPALISM
EPIGRAMMATISM	EPILOGIST	EPIPELAGIC	EPISCOPALISMS
EPIGRAMMATISMS	EPILOGISTIC	EPIPETALOUS	EPISCOPALLY
EPIGRAMMATIST	EPILOGISTS	EPIPHANIC	EPISCOPANT
EPIGRAMMATISTS	EPILOGIZE	EPIPHANIES	EPISCOPANTS
EPIGRAMMATIZE	EPILOGIZED	EPIPHANOUS	EPISCOPATE
EPIGRAMMATIZED	EPILOGIZES	EPIPHANY	EPISCOPATED
EPIGRAMMATIZER	EPILOGIZING	EPIPHENOMENA	EPISCOPATES
EPIGRAMMATIZERS	EPILOGS	EPIPHENOMENAL	EPISCOPATING
EPIGRAMMATIZES	EPILOGUE	EPIPHENOMENALLY	EPISCOPE
EPIGRAMMATIZING	EPILOGUED	EPIPHENOMENON	EPISCOPES
EPIGRAMS	EPILOGUES	EPIPHONEMA	EPISCOPIES
EPIGRAPH	EPILOGUING	EPIPHONEMAS	EPISCOPISE
EPIGRAPHED	EPILOGUISE	EPIPHRAGM	EPISCOPISED
EPIGRAPHER	EPILOGUISED	EPIPHRAGMS	EPISCOPISES
EPIGRAPHERS	EPILOGUISES	EPIPHYLLOUS	EPISCOPISING
EPIGRAPHIC	EPILOGUISING	EPIPHYSEAL	EPISCOPIZE
EPIGRAPHICAL	EPILOGUIZE	EPIPHYSES	EPISCOPIZED
EPIGRAPHICALLY	EPILOGUIZED	EPIPHYSIAL	EPISCOPIZES
EPIGRAPHIES	EPILOGUIZES	EPIPHYSIS	EPISCOPIZING
EPIGRAPHING	EPILOGUIZING	EPIPHYTAL	EPISCOPY
EPIGRAPHIST	EPIMELETIC	EPIPHYTE	EPISEMATIC
EPIGRAPHISTS	EPIMER	EPIPHYTES	EPISEMON
EPIGRAPHS	EPIMERASE	EPIPHYTIC	EPISEMONS
EPIGRAPHY	EPIMERASES	EPIPHYTICAL	EPISEPALOUS
EPIGYNIES	EPIMERE	EPIPHYTICALLY	EPISIOTOMIES
EPIGYNOUS	EPIMERES	EPIPHYTISM	EPISIOTOMY
EPIGYNY	EPIMERIC	EPIPHYTISMS	EPISODAL
EPILATE	EPIMERISM	EPIPHYTOLOGIES	EPISODE
EPILATED	EPIMERS	EPIPHYTOLOGY	EPISODES
EPILATES	EPIMORPHIC	EPIPHYTOTIC	EPISODIAL
EPILATING	EPIMORPHICALLY	EPIPHYTOTICS	EPISODIC
EPILATION	EPIMORPHOSIS	EPIPLASTRA	EPISODICAL
EPILATIONS	EPIMORPHS	EPIPLASTRAL	EPISODICALLY
EPILATOR	EPIMYSIA	EPIPLASTRON	EPISOMAL
EPILATORS	EPIMYSIUM	EPIPLOIC	EPISOMALLY
EPILEPSIES	EPINAOI	EPIPLOON	EPISOME
EPILEPSY	EPINAOS	EPIPLOONS	EPISOMES
EPILEPTIC	EPINASTIC	EPIPOLIC	EPISPASTIC
EPILEPTICAL	EPINASTICALLY	EPIPOLISM	EPISPASTICS
EPILEPTICALLY	EPINASTIES	EPIPOLISMS	EPISPERM
EPILEPTICS	EPINASTY	EPIROGENETIC	EPISPERMS
EPILEPTIFORM	EPINEPHRIN	EPIROGENIC	EPISPORE
EPILEPTOGENIC	EPINEPHRINE	EPIROGENICALLY	EPISPORES
EPILEPTOID	EPINEPHRINES	EPIROGENY	EPISTASES
EPILIMNION	EPINEPHRINS	EPIRRHEMA	EPISTASIES
EPILIMNIONS	EPINEURAL	EPIRRHEMAS	EPISTASIS
EPILITHIC	EPINEURIAL	EPIRRHEMATIC	EPISTASY
EPILITHS	EPINEURIUM	EPISCIA	EPISTATIC
EPILOBIUM	EPINEURIUMS	EPISCIAS	EPISTAXES

EPISTAXIS
EPISTAXISES
EPISTEMIC
EPISTEMICALLY
EPISTEMICS
EPISTEMOLOGICAL
EPISTEMOLOGIES
EPISTEMOLOGIST
EPISTEMOLOGISTS
EPISTEMOLOGY
EPISTERNA
EPISTERNAL
EPISTERNUM
EPISTERNUMS
EPISTILBITE
EPISTILBITES
EPISTLE
EPISTLED
EPISTLER
EPISTLERS
EPISTLES
EPISTLING
EPISTOLARIAN
EPISTOLARIANS
EPISTOLARIES
EPISTOLARY
EPISTOLATORY
EPISTOLER
EPISTOLERS
EPISTOLET
EPISTOLETS
EPISTOLIC
EPISTOLICAL
EPISTOLISE
EPISTOLISED
EPISTOLISES
EPISTOLISING
EPISTOLIST
EPISTOLISTS
EPISTOLIZE
EPISTOLIZED
EPISTOLIZES
EPISTOLIZING
EPISTOLOGRAPHY
EPISTOME
EPISTOMES
EPISTROPHE
EPISTROPHES
EPISTYLE
EPISTYLES
EPITAPH
EPITAPHED
EPITAPHER
EPITAPHERS
EPITAPHIAL
EPITAPHIAN

EPITAPHIC
EPITAPHING
EPITAPHIST
EPITAPHISTS
EPITAPHS
EPITASES
EPITASIS
EPITAXIAL
EPITAXIALLY
EPITAXIC
EPITAXIES
EPITAXIS
EPITAXY
EPITHALAMIA
EPITHALAMIC
EPITHALAMION
EPITHALAMIUM
EPITHALAMIUMS
EPITHECA
EPITHECAE
EPITHELIA
EPITHELIAL
EPITHELIALIZE
EPITHELIALIZED
EPITHELIALIZES
EPITHELIALIZING
EPITHELIOID
EPITHELIOMA
EPITHELIOMAS
EPITHELIOMATA
EPITHELIOMATOUS
EPITHELIUM
EPITHELIUMS
EPITHELIZATION
EPITHELIZATIONS
EPITHELIZE
EPITHELIZED
EPITHELIZES
EPITHELIZING
EPITHEM
EPITHEMA
EPITHEMATA
EPITHEMS
EPITHERMAL
EPITHESES
EPITHESIS
EPITHET
EPITHETED
EPITHETIC
EPITHETICAL
EPITHETING
EPITHETON
EPITHETONS
EPITHETS
EPITHYMETIC
EPITOME

EPITOMES
EPITOMIC
EPITOMICAL
EPITOMISATION
EPITOMISATIONS
EPITOMISE
EPITOMISED
EPITOMISER
EPITOMISERS
EPITOMISES
EPITOMISING
EPITOMIST
EPITOMISTS
EPITOMIZATION
EPITOMIZATIONS
EPITOMIZE
EPITOMIZED
EPITOMIZER
EPITOMIZERS
EPITOMIZES
EPITOMIZING
EPITONIC
EPITOPE
EPITOPES
EPITRACHELION
EPITRACHELIONS
EPITRITE
EPITRITES
EPITROCHOID
EPITROCHOIDS
EPIZEUXES
EPIZEUXIS
EPIZEUXISES
EPIZOA
EPIZOAN
EPIZOANS
EPIZOIC
EPIZOISM
EPIZOISMS
EPIZOITE
EPIZOITES
EPIZOON
EPIZOOTIC
EPIZOOTICALLY
EPIZOOTICS
EPIZOOTIES
EPIZOOTIOLOGIC
EPIZOOTIOLOGIES
EPIZOOTIOLOGY
EPIZOOTY
EPOCH
EPOCHA
EPOCHAL
EPOCHALLY
EPOCHAS
EPOCHS

EPODE
EPODES
EPODIC
EPONYCHIUM
EPONYCHIUMS
EPONYM
EPONYMIC
EPONYMIES
EPONYMOUS
EPONYMOUSLY
EPONYMS
EPONYMY
EPOPEE
EPOPEES
EPOPOEIA
EPOPOEIAS
EPOPT
EPOPTS
EPOS
EPOSES
EPOXIDATION
EPOXIDATIONS
EPOXIDE
EPOXIDES
EPOXIDIZE
EPOXIDIZED
EPOXIDIZES
EPOXIDIZING
EPOXIED
EPOXIES
EPOXY
EPOXYED
EPOXYING
EPRIS
EPRISE
EPROM
EPROMS
EPROUVETTE
EPROUVETTES
EPSILON
EPSILONIC
EPSILONS
EPSOMITE
EPSOMITES
EPUISE
EPUISEE
EPULARY
EPULATION
EPULATIONS
EPULIDES
EPULIS
EPULISES
EPULOTIC
EPULOTICS
EPURATE
EPURATED

EPURATES
EPURATING
EPURATION
EPURATIONS
EPYLLIA
EPYLLION
EPYLLIONS
EQUABILITIES
EQUABILITY
EQUABLE
EQUABLENESS
EQUABLENESSES
EQUABLY
EQUAL
EQUALED
EQUALI
EQUALING
EQUALISATION
EQUALISATIONS
EQUALISE
EQUALISED
EQUALISER
EQUALISERS
EQUALISES
EQUALISING
EQUALITARIAN
EQUALITARIANISM
EQUALITARIANS
EQUALITIES
EQUALITY
EQUALIZATION
EQUALIZATIONS
EQUALIZE
EQUALIZED
EQUALIZER
EQUALIZERS
EQUALIZES
EQUALIZING
EQUALLED
EQUALLING
EQUALLY
EQUALNESS
EQUALNESSES
EQUALS
EQUANIMITIES
EQUANIMITY
EQUANIMOUS
EQUANIMOUSLY
EQUANT
EQUANTS
EQUATABILITY
EQUATABLE
EQUATABLY
EQUATE
EQUATED
EQUATES

EQUATING
EQUATION
EQUATIONAL
EQUATIONALLY
EQUATIONS
EQUATOR
EQUATORIAL
EQUATORIALLY
EQUATORIALS
EQUATORS
EQUATORWARD
EQUERRIES
EQUERRY
EQUESTRIAN
EQUESTRIANISM
EQUESTRIANISMS
EQUESTRIANS
EQUESTRIENNE
EQUESTRIENNES
EQUIANGULAR
EQUIANGULARITY
EQUIBALANCE
EQUIBALANCED
EQUIBALANCES
EQUIBALANCING
EQUICALORIC
EQUID
EQUIDIFFERENT
EQUIDISTANCE
EQUIDISTANCES
EQUIDISTANT
EQUIDISTANTLY
EQUIDS
EQUILATERAL
EQUILATERALLY
EQUILATERALS
EQUILIBRANT
EQUILIBRANTS
EQUILIBRATE
EQUILIBRATED
EQUILIBRATES
EQUILIBRATING
EQUILIBRATION
EQUILIBRATIONS
EQUILIBRATOR
EQUILIBRATORS
EQUILIBRATORY
EQUILIBRIA
EQUILIBRIST
EQUILIBRISTIC
EQUILIBRISTS
EQUILIBRITIES
EQUILIBRITY
EQUILIBRIUM
EQUILIBRIUMS
EQUIMOLAR

EQUIMOLECULAR
EQUIMOLECULARLY
EQUIMULTIPLE
EQUIMULTIPLES
EQUINAL
EQUINE
EQUINELY
EQUINES
EQUINIA
EQUINIAS
EQUINITIES
EQUINITY
EQUINOCTIAL
EQUINOCTIALLY
EQUINOCTIALS
EQUINOX
EQUINOXES
EQUINUMEROUS
EQUINUMEROUSLY
EQUIP
EQUIPAGE
EQUIPAGED
EQUIPAGES
EQUIPAGING
EQUIPARATE
EQUIPARATED
EQUIPARATES
EQUIPARATING
EQUIPARATION
EQUIPARATIONS
EQUIPARTITION
EQUIPARTITIONS
EQUIPE
EQUIPES
EQUIPMENT
EQUIPMENTS
EQUIPOISE
EQUIPOISED
EQUIPOISES
EQUIPOISING
EQUIPOLLENCE
EQUIPOLLENCES
EQUIPOLLENCIES
EQUIPOLLENCY
EQUIPOLLENT
EQUIPOLLENTLY
EQUIPOLLENTS
EQUIPONDERANCE
EQUIPONDERANCES
EQUIPONDERANCY
EQUIPONDERANT
EQUIPONDERATE
EQUIPONDERATED
EQUIPONDERATES
EQUIPONDERATING
EQUIPOTENT

EQUIPOTENTIAL
EQUIPPED
EQUIPPER
EQUIPPERS
EQUIPPING
EQUIPROBABILITY
EQUIPROBABLE
EQUIPS
EQUISETA
EQUISETACEOUS
EQUISETIC
EQUISETIFORM
EQUISETUM
EQUISETUMS
EQUITABILITIES
EQUITABILITY
EQUITABLE
EQUITABLENESS
EQUITABLENESSES
EQUITABLY
EQUITANT
EQUITATION
EQUITATIONS
EQUITES
EQUITIES
EQUITY
EQUIVALENCE
EQUIVALENCES
EQUIVALENCIES
EQUIVALENCY
EQUIVALENT
EQUIVALENTLY
EQUIVALENTS
EQUIVALVE
EQUIVOCAL
EQUIVOCALITIES
EQUIVOCALITY
EQUIVOCALLY
EQUIVOCALNESS
EQUIVOCALNESSES
EQUIVOCATE
EQUIVOCATED
EQUIVOCATES
EQUIVOCATING
EQUIVOCATINGLY
EQUIVOCATION
EQUIVOCATIONS
EQUIVOCATOR
EQUIVOCATORS
EQUIVOCATORY
EQUIVOKE
EQUIVOKES
EQUIVOQUE
EQUIVOQUES
ER
ERA

ERADIATE
ERADIATED
ERADIATES
ERADIATING
ERADIATION
ERADIATIONS
ERADICABLE
ERADICABLY
ERADICATE
ERADICATED
ERADICATES
ERADICATING
ERADICATION
ERADICATIONS
ERADICATIVE
ERADICATOR
ERADICATORS
ERAS
ERASABILITIES
ERASABILITY
ERASABLE
ERASE
ERASED
ERASEMENT
ERASEMENTS
ERASER
ERASERS
ERASES
ERASING
ERASION
ERASIONS
ERASURE
ERASURES
ERATHEM
ERATHEMS
ERBIA
ERBIAS
ERBIUM
ERBIUMS
ERE
ERECT
ERECTABLE
ERECTED
ERECTER
ERECTERS
ERECTILE
ERECTILITIES
ERECTILITY
ERECTING
ERECTION
ERECTIONS
ERECTIVE
ERECTLY
ERECTNESS
ERECTNESSES
ERECTOR

ERECTORS
ERECTS
ERED
ERELONG
EREMACAUSES
EREMACAUSIS
EREMIC
EREMITAL
EREMITE
EREMITES
EREMITIC
EREMITICAL
EREMITISM
EREMITISMS
EREMURI
EREMURUS
ERENOW
EREPSIN
EREPSINS
ERES
ERETHIC
ERETHISM
ERETHISMIC
ERETHISMS
ERETHISTIC
ERETHITIC
EREV
EREVS
EREWHILE
EREWHILES
ERF
ERG
ERGASTIC
ERGASTOPLASM
ERGASTOPLASMIC
ERGASTOPLASMS
ERGATANDROMORPH
ERGATANER
ERGATANERS
ERGATE
ERGATES
ERGATIVE
ERGATIVES
ERGATIVITIES
ERGATIVITY
ERGATOCRACIES
ERGATOCRACY
ERGATOGYNE
ERGATOGYNES
ERGATOID
ERGATOMORPH
ERGATOMORPHIC
ERGATOMORPHS
ERGO
ERGODIC
ERGODICITIES

ERGODICITY
ERGOGRAM
ERGOGRAMS
ERGOGRAPH
ERGOGRAPHS
ERGOMANIA
ERGOMANIAC
ERGOMANIACS
ERGOMANIAS
ERGOMETER
ERGOMETERS
ERGOMETRIC
ERGON
ERGONOMIC
ERGONOMICALLY
ERGONOMICS
ERGONOMIST
ERGONOMISTS
ERGONOVINE
ERGONOVINES
ERGONS
ERGOPHOBIA
ERGOPHOBIAS
ERGOSTEROL
ERGOSTEROLS
ERGOT
ERGOTAMINE
ERGOTAMINES
ERGOTIC
ERGOTISE
ERGOTISED
ERGOTISES
ERGOTISING
ERGOTISM
ERGOTISMS
ERGOTIZE
ERGOTIZED
ERGOTIZES
ERGOTIZING
ERGOTS
ERGS
ERIACH
ERIACHS
ERIC
ERICA
ERICACEOUS
ERICAS
ERICK
ERICKS
ERICOID
ERICS
ERIGERON
ERIGERONS
ERINACEOUS
ERING
ERINGO

ERINGOES
ERINGOS
ERINITE
ERINITES
ERINUS
ERIOMETER
ERIOMETERS
ERIONITE
ERIONITES
ERIOPHOROUS
ERIOPHORUM
ERIOPHORUMS
ERIOPHYID
ERIOPHYIDS
ERIOSTEMON
ERIOSTEMONS
ERISTIC
ERISTICAL
ERISTICALLY
ERISTICS
ERK
ERKS
ERLANG
ERLANGS
ERLKING
ERLKINGS
ERMELIN
ERMELINS
ERMINE
ERMINED
ERMINES
ERN
ERNE
ERNED
ERNES
ERNING
ERNS
ERODE
ERODED
ERODENT
ERODENTS
ERODES
ERODIBILITIES
ERODIBILITY
ERODIBLE
ERODING
ERODIUM
ERODIUMS
EROGENEITY
EROGENIC
EROGENOUS
EROS
EROSE
EROSELY
EROSES
EROSIBLE

EROSION
EROSIONAL
EROSIONALLY
EROSIONS
EROSIVE
EROSIVENESS
EROSIVENESSES
EROSIVITIES
EROSIVITY
EROSTRATE
EROTEMA
EROTEMAS
EROTEME
EROTEMES
EROTESES
EROTESIS
EROTETIC
EROTIC
EROTICA
EROTICAL
EROTICALLY
EROTICISATION
EROTICISATIONS
EROTICISE
EROTICISED
EROTICISES
EROTICISING
EROTICISM
EROTICISMS
EROTICIST
EROTICISTS
EROTICIZATION
EROTICIZATIONS
EROTICIZE
EROTICIZED
EROTICIZES
EROTICIZING
EROTICS
EROTISM
EROTISMS
EROTIZATION
EROTIZATIONS
EROTIZE
EROTIZED
EROTIZES
EROTIZING
EROTOGENIC
EROTOGENOUS
EROTOLOGICAL
EROTOLOGICALLY
EROTOLOGIST
EROTOLOGISTS
EROTOLOGY
EROTOMANIA
EROTOMANIAC
EROTOMANIACS

EROTOMANIAS
EROTOPHOBIA
EROTOPHOBIAS
ERR
ERRABLE
ERRANCIES
ERRANCY
ERRAND
ERRANDS
ERRANT
ERRANTLY
ERRANTRIES
ERRANTRY
ERRANTS
ERRATA
ERRATAS
ERRATIC
ERRATICAL
ERRATICALLY
ERRATICISM
ERRATICISMS
ERRATICS
ERRATUM
ERRED
ERRHINE
ERRHINES
ERRING
ERRINGLY
ERRINGS
ERRONEOUS
ERRONEOUSLY
ERRONEOUSNESS
ERRONEOUSNESSES
ERROR
ERRORIST
ERRORISTS
ERRORLESS
ERRORS
ERRS
ERS
ERSATZ
ERSATZES
ERSES
ERST
ERSTWHILE
ERUBESCENCE
ERUBESCENCES
ERUBESCENCIES
ERUBESCENCY
ERUBESCENT
ERUBESCITE
ERUBESCITES
ERUCIFORM
ERUCT
ERUCTATE
ERUCTATED

ERUCTATES
ERUCTATING
ERUCTATION
ERUCTATIONS
ERUCTATIVE
ERUCTED
ERUCTING
ERUCTS
ERUDITE
ERUDITELY
ERUDITENESS
ERUDITES
ERUDITION
ERUDITIONS
ERUGO
ERUGOS
ERUMPENT
ERUPT
ERUPTED
ERUPTIBLE
ERUPTING
ERUPTION
ERUPTIONAL
ERUPTIONS
ERUPTIVE
ERUPTIVELY
ERUPTIVENESS
ERUPTIVENESSES
ERUPTIVES
ERUPTIVITIES
ERUPTIVITY
ERUPTS
ERUV
ERUVS
ERVALENTA
ERVALENTAS
ERVEN
ERVIL
ERVILS
ERYNGIUM
ERYNGIUMS
ERYNGO
ERYNGOES
ERYNGOS
ERYSIPELAS
ERYSIPELASES
ERYSIPELATOUS
ERYSIPELOID
ERYSIPELOIDS
ERYTHEMA
ERYTHEMAL
ERYTHEMAS
ERYTHEMATIC
ERYTHEMATOUS
ERYTHORBATE
ERYTHORBATES

ERYTHRAEMIA
ERYTHREMIA
ERYTHREMIAS
ERYTHRINA
ERYTHRINAS
ERYTHRISM
ERYTHRISMAL
ERYTHRISMS
ERYTHRISTIC
ERYTHRITE
ERYTHRITES
ERYTHRITIC
ERYTHRITOL
ERYTHROBLAST
ERYTHROBLASTIC
ERYTHROBLASTS
ERYTHROCYTE
ERYTHROCYTES
ERYTHROCYTIC
ERYTHROID
ERYTHROMELALGIA
ERYTHROMELALGIC
ERYTHROMYCIN
ERYTHROMYCINS
ERYTHRON
ERYTHRONIUM
ERYTHRONIUMS
ERYTHRONS
ERYTHROPENIA
ERYTHROPENIAS
ERYTHROPHOBIA
ERYTHROPHOBIAS
ERYTHROPOIESES
ERYTHROPOIESIS
ERYTHROPOIETIC
ERYTHROPOIETIN
ERYTHROPOIETINS
ERYTHROPSIA
ERYTHROPSIC
ERYTHROSIN
ERYTHROSINE
ERYTHROSINES
ERYTHROSINS
ES
ESCADRILLE
ESCADRILLES
ESCALADE
ESCALADED
ESCALADER
ESCALADERS
ESCALADES
ESCALADING
ESCALADO
ESCALADOES
ESCALATE
ESCALATED

ESCALATES
ESCALATING
ESCALATION
ESCALATIONS
ESCALATOR
ESCALATORS
ESCALATORY
ESCALIER
ESCALIERS
ESCALLONIA
ESCALLONIAS
ESCALLOP
ESCALLOPED
ESCALLOPING
ESCALLOPS
ESCALOP
ESCALOPE
ESCALOPED
ESCALOPES
ESCALOPING
ESCALOPS
ESCAMOTAGE
ESCAMOTAGES
ESCAPABLE
ESCAPADE
ESCAPADES
ESCAPADO
ESCAPADOES
ESCAPE
ESCAPED
ESCAPEE
ESCAPEES
ESCAPELESS
ESCAPEMENT
ESCAPEMENTS
ESCAPER
ESCAPERS
ESCAPES
ESCAPING
ESCAPISM
ESCAPISMS
ESCAPIST
ESCAPISTS
ESCAPOLOGIES
ESCAPOLOGIST
ESCAPOLOGISTS
ESCAPOLOGY
ESCAR
ESCARGOT
ESCARGOTS
ESCARMOUCHE
ESCARMOUCHES
ESCAROLE
ESCAROLES
ESCARP
ESCARPED

ESCARPING
ESCARPMENT
ESCARPMENTS
ESCARPS
ESCARS
ESCHALOT
ESCHALOTS
ESCHAR
ESCHAROTIC
ESCHAROTICS
ESCHARS
ESCHATOLOGIC
ESCHATOLOGICAL
ESCHATOLOGIES
ESCHATOLOGIST
ESCHATOLOGISTS
ESCHATOLOGY
ESCHEAT
ESCHEATABLE
ESCHEATAGE
ESCHEATAGES
ESCHEATED
ESCHEATING
ESCHEATMENT
ESCHEATMENTS
ESCHEATOR
ESCHEATORS
ESCHEATS
ESCHEW
ESCHEWAL
ESCHEWALS
ESCHEWED
ESCHEWER
ESCHEWERS
ESCHEWING
ESCHEWS
ESCHSCHOLTZIA
ESCHSCHOLTZIAS
ESCHSCHOLZIA
ESCHSCHOLZIAS
ESCLANDRE
ESCLANDRES
ESCOLAR
ESCOLARS
ESCOPETTE
ESCOPETTES
ESCORT
ESCORTAGE
ESCORTAGES
ESCORTED
ESCORTING
ESCORTS
ESCOT
ESCOTED
ESCOTING
ESCOTS

ESCOTTED
ESCOTTING
ESCRIBANO
ESCRIBANOS
ESCRIBE
ESCRIBED
ESCRIBES
ESCRIBING
ESCRITOIRE
ESCRITOIRES
ESCRITORIAL
ESCROC
ESCROCS
ESCROL
ESCROLL
ESCROLLS
ESCROLS
ESCROW
ESCROWED
ESCROWING
ESCROWS
ESCUAGE
ESCUAGES
ESCUDO
ESCUDOS
ESCULENT
ESCULENTS
ESCUTCHEON
ESCUTCHEONED
ESCUTCHEONS
ESEMPLASIES
ESEMPLASTIC
ESEMPLASY
ESERINE
ESERINES
ESES
ESILE
ESILES
ESKAR
ESKARS
ESKER
ESKERS
ESKIES
ESKY
ESLOIN
ESLOINED
ESLOINING
ESLOINS
ESLOYNE
ESLOYNED
ESLOYNES
ESLOYNING
ESNE
ESNECIES
ESNECY
ESNES

ESOPHAGEAL
ESOPHAGI
ESOPHAGOSCOPE
ESOPHAGOSCOPIC
ESOPHAGUS
ESOPHAGUSES
ESOTERIC
ESOTERICA
ESOTERICALLY
ESOTERICISM
ESOTERICISMS
ESOTERICIST
ESOTERICISTS
ESOTERIES
ESOTERISM
ESOTERISMS
ESOTERY
ESPADA
ESPADAS
ESPADRILLE
ESPADRILLES
ESPAGNOLE
ESPAGNOLES
ESPAGNOLETTE
ESPAGNOLETTES
ESPALIER
ESPALIERED
ESPALIERING
ESPALIERS
ESPANOL
ESPANOLES
ESPARTO
ESPARTOS
ESPECIAL
ESPECIALLY
ESPERANCE
ESPERANCES
ESPIAL
ESPIALS
ESPIED
ESPIEGLE
ESPIEGLERIE
ESPIEGLERIES
ESPIER
ESPIERS
ESPIES
ESPIONAGE
ESPIONAGES
ESPLANADE
ESPLANADES
ESPOUSAL
ESPOUSALS
ESPOUSE
ESPOUSED
ESPOUSER
ESPOUSERS

ESPOUSES
ESPOUSING
ESPRESSIVO
ESPRESSO
ESPRESSOS
ESPRIT
ESPRITS
ESPUMOSO
ESPUMOSOS
ESPY
ESPYING
ESQUIRE
ESQUIRED
ESQUIRES
ESQUIRESS
ESQUIRESSES
ESQUIRING
ESQUISSE
ESQUISSES
ESS
ESSAY
ESSAYED
ESSAYER
ESSAYERS
ESSAYETTE
ESSAYETTES
ESSAYING
ESSAYISH
ESSAYIST
ESSAYISTIC
ESSAYISTS
ESSAYS
ESSE
ESSENCE
ESSENCES
ESSENTIAL
ESSENTIALISM
ESSENTIALISMS
ESSENTIALIST
ESSENTIALISTS
ESSENTIALITIES
ESSENTIALITY
ESSENTIALIZE
ESSENTIALIZED
ESSENTIALIZES
ESSENTIALIZING
ESSENTIALLY
ESSENTIALNESS
ESSENTIALNESSES
ESSENTIALS
ESSES
ESSIVE
ESSIVES
ESSOIN
ESSOINER
ESSOINERS

ESSOINS
ESSONITE
ESSONITES
ESSOYNE
ESSOYNES
EST
ESTABLISH
ESTABLISHABLE
ESTABLISHED
ESTABLISHER
ESTABLISHERS
ESTABLISHES
ESTABLISHING
ESTABLISHMENT
ESTABLISHMENTS
ESTACADE
ESTACADES
ESTAFETTE
ESTAFETTES
ESTAMINET
ESTAMINETS
ESTANCIA
ESTANCIAS
ESTANCIERO
ESTANCIEROS
ESTATE
ESTATED
ESTATES
ESTATESMAN
ESTATESMEN
ESTATING
ESTEEM
ESTEEMED
ESTEEMING
ESTEEMS
ESTER
ESTERASE
ESTERASES
ESTERIFICATION
ESTERIFICATIONS
ESTERIFIED
ESTERIFIES
ESTERIFY
ESTERIFYING
ESTERS
ESTHESES
ESTHESIA
ESTHESIAS
ESTHESIOGEN
ESTHESIOGENS
ESTHESIS
ESTHESISES
ESTHETE
ESTHETES
ESTHETIC
ESTHETICAL

ESTHETICALLY
ESTHETICIAN
ESTHETICIANS
ESTHETICISM
ESTHETICISMS
ESTHETICS
ESTIMABLE
ESTIMABLENESS
ESTIMABLENESSES
ESTIMABLY
ESTIMATE
ESTIMATED
ESTIMATES
ESTIMATING
ESTIMATION
ESTIMATIONS
ESTIMATIVE
ESTIMATOR
ESTIMATORS
ESTIPULATE
ESTIVAL
ESTIVATE
ESTIVATED
ESTIVATES
ESTIVATING
ESTIVATION
ESTIVATIONS
ESTIVATOR
ESTIVATORS
ESTOC
ESTOCS
ESTOILE
ESTOILES
ESTOP
ESTOPPAGE
ESTOPPAGES
ESTOPPED
ESTOPPEL
ESTOPPELS
ESTOPPING
ESTOPS
ESTOVER
ESTOVERS
ESTRADE
ESTRADES
ESTRADIOL
ESTRADIOLS
ESTRAGON
ESTRAGONS
ESTRAL
ESTRALS
ESTRAMAZONES
ESTRANGE
ESTRANGED
ESTRANGEDNESS
ESTRANGEDNESSES

ESTRANGELO
ESTRANGELOS
ESTRANGEMENT
ESTRANGEMENTS
ESTRANGER
ESTRANGERS
ESTRANGES
ESTRANGHELO
ESTRANGHELOS
ESTRANGING
ESTRAPADE
ESTRAPADES
ESTRAY
ESTRAYED
ESTRAYING
ESTRAYS
ESTREAT
ESTREATED
ESTREATING
ESTREATS
ESTREPE
ESTREPED
ESTREPEMENT
ESTREPEMENTS
ESTREPES
ESTREPING
ESTRICH
ESTRICHES
ESTRIDGE
ESTRIDGES
ESTRILDID
ESTRILDIDS
ESTRIN
ESTRINS
ESTRIOL
ESTRIOLS
ESTRO
ESTROGEN
ESTROGENIC
ESTROGENICALLY
ESTROGENS
ESTRONE
ESTRONES
ESTROS
ESTROUS
ESTRUAL
ESTRUM
ESTRUMS
ESTRUS
ESTRUSES
ESTS
ESTUARIAL
ESTUARIAN
ESTUARIES
ESTUARINE
ESTUARY

ESURIENCE
ESURIENCES
ESURIENCIES
ESURIENCY
ESURIENT
ESURIENTLY
ET
ETA
ETACISM
ETACISMS
ETAERIO
ETAERIOS
ETAGE
ETAGERE
ETAGERES
ETAGES
ETALAGE
ETALAGES
ETALON
ETALONS
ETAMIN
ETAMINE
ETAMINES
ETAMINS
ETAPE
ETAPES
ETAS
ETAT
ETATISM
ETATISME
ETATISMES
ETATISMS
ETATIST
ETATISTE
ETATISTES
ETATS
ETCETERA
ETCETERAS
ETCH
ETCHANT
ETCHANTS
ETCHED
ETCHER
ETCHERS
ETCHES
ETCHING
ETCHINGS
ETEN
ETENS
ETEPIMELETIC
ETERNAL
ETERNALISATION
ETERNALISATIONS
ETERNALISE
ETERNALISED
ETERNALISES

ETERNALISING
ETERNALIST
ETERNALISTS
ETERNALITY
ETERNALIZATION
ETERNALIZATIONS
ETERNALIZE
ETERNALIZED
ETERNALIZES
ETERNALIZING
ETERNALLY
ETERNALNESS
ETERNALNESSES
ETERNALS
ETERNE
ETERNISATION
ETERNISATIONS
ETERNISE
ETERNISED
ETERNISES
ETERNISING
ETERNITIES
ETERNITY
ETERNIZATION
ETERNIZATIONS
ETERNIZE
ETERNIZED
ETERNIZES
ETERNIZING
ETESIAN
ETESIANS
ETH
ETHAL
ETHALS
ETHAMBUTOL
ETHAMBUTOLS
ETHANAL
ETHANE
ETHANEDIOIC
ETHANEDIOL
ETHANES
ETHANOATE
ETHANOATES
ETHANOIC
ETHANOL
ETHANOLAMINE
ETHANOLAMINES
ETHANOLS
ETHANOYL
ETHE
ETHENE
ETHENES
ETHEPHON
ETHEPHONS
ETHER
ETHERCAP

ETHERCAPS
ETHEREAL
ETHEREALISATION
ETHEREALISE
ETHEREALISED
ETHEREALISES
ETHEREALISING
ETHEREALITIES
ETHEREALITY
ETHEREALIZATION
ETHEREALIZE
ETHEREALIZED
ETHEREALIZES
ETHEREALIZING
ETHEREALLY
ETHEREALNESS
ETHEREALNESSES
ETHEREOUS
ETHERIAL
ETHERIC
ETHERICAL
ETHERIFICATION
ETHERIFICATIONS
ETHERIFIED
ETHERIFIES
ETHERIFY
ETHERIFYING
ETHERION
ETHERIONS
ETHERISATION
ETHERISATIONS
ETHERISE
ETHERISED
ETHERISER
ETHERISERS
ETHERISES
ETHERISH
ETHERISING
ETHERISM
ETHERISMS
ETHERIST
ETHERISTS
ETHERIZATION
ETHERIZATIONS
ETHERIZE
ETHERIZED
ETHERIZER
ETHERIZERS
ETHERIZES
ETHERIZING
ETHEROMANIA
ETHEROMANIAC
ETHEROMANIACS
ETHEROMANIAS
ETHERS
ETHIC

ETHICAL
ETHICALITIES
ETHICALITY
ETHICALLY
ETHICALNESS
ETHICALNESSES
ETHICALS
ETHICIAN
ETHICIANS
ETHICISE
ETHICISED
ETHICISES
ETHICISING
ETHICISM
ETHICISMS
ETHICIST
ETHICISTS
ETHICIZE
ETHICIZED
ETHICIZES
ETHICIZING
ETHICS
ETHINYL
ETHINYLS
ETHION
ETHIONAMIDE
ETHIONAMIDES
ETHIONINE
ETHIONINES
ETHIONS
ETHIOPS
ETHIOPSES
ETHMOID
ETHMOIDAL
ETHMOIDS
ETHNARCH
ETHNARCHIES
ETHNARCHS
ETHNARCHY
ETHNIC
ETHNICAL
ETHNICALLY
ETHNICISM
ETHNICISMS
ETHNICITIES
ETHNICITY
ETHNICS
ETHNOBIOLOGICAL
ETHNOBIOLOGIST
ETHNOBIOLOGISTS
ETHNOBIOLOGY
ETHNOBOTANICAL
ETHNOBOTANIES
ETHNOBOTANIST
ETHNOBOTANISTS
ETHNOBOTANY

ETHNOCENTRIC
ETHNOCENTRICITY
ETHNOCENTRISM
ETHNOCENTRISMS
ETHNOCIDE
ETHNOCIDES
ETHNOGENIC
ETHNOGENICALLY
ETHNOGENIST
ETHNOGENISTS
ETHNOGENY
ETHNOGRAPHER
ETHNOGRAPHERS
ETHNOGRAPHIC
ETHNOGRAPHICA
ETHNOGRAPHICAL
ETHNOGRAPHIES
ETHNOGRAPHY
ETHNOHISTORIAN
ETHNOHISTORIANS
ETHNOHISTORIC
ETHNOHISTORICAL
ETHNOHISTORIES
ETHNOHISTORY
ETHNOLINGUIST
ETHNOLINGUISTIC
ETHNOLINGUISTS
ETHNOLOGIC
ETHNOLOGICAL
ETHNOLOGICALLY
ETHNOLOGIES
ETHNOLOGIST
ETHNOLOGISTS
ETHNOLOGY
ETHNOMUSICOLOGY
ETHNOS
ETHNOSCIENCE
ETHNOSCIENCES
ETHNOSES
ETHOLOGIC
ETHOLOGICAL
ETHOLOGICALLY
ETHOLOGIES
ETHOLOGIST
ETHOLOGISTS
ETHOLOGY
ETHONONE
ETHONONES
ETHOS
ETHOSES
ETHOXIDE
ETHOXIDES
ETHOXIES
ETHOXY
ETHOXYETHANE
ETHOXYL

ETHOXYLS
ETHS
ETHYL
ETHYLAMINE
ETHYLAMINES
ETHYLATE
ETHYLATED
ETHYLATES
ETHYLATING
ETHYLATION
ETHYLATIONS
ETHYLBENZENE
ETHYLBENZENES
ETHYLENE
ETHYLENES
ETHYLENIC
ETHYLIC
ETHYLS
ETHYNE
ETHYNES
ETHYNYL
ETHYNYLS
ETIC
ETIOLATE
ETIOLATED
ETIOLATES
ETIOLATING
ETIOLATION
ETIOLATIONS
ETIOLIN
ETIOLINS
ETIOLOGIC
ETIOLOGICAL
ETIOLOGICALLY
ETIOLOGIES
ETIOLOGIST
ETIOLOGISTS
ETIOLOGY
ETIQUETTE
ETIQUETTES
ETNA
ETNAS
ETOILE
ETOILES
ETONOGESTREL
ETOUFFEE
ETOUFFEES
ETOURDERIE
ETOURDERIES
ETOURDI
ETOURDIE
ETRANGER
ETRANGERE
ETRANGERES
ETRANGERS
ETRENNE

ETRENNES
ETRIER
ETRIERS
ETTERCAP
ETTERCAPS
ETTIN
ETTINS
ETTLE
ETTLED
ETTLES
ETTLING
ETUDE
ETUDES
ETUI
ETUIS
ETWEE
ETWEES
ETYMA
ETYMIC
ETYMOLOGICA
ETYMOLOGICAL
ETYMOLOGICALLY
ETYMOLOGICON
ETYMOLOGICUM
ETYMOLOGIES
ETYMOLOGISE
ETYMOLOGISED
ETYMOLOGISES
ETYMOLOGISING
ETYMOLOGIST
ETYMOLOGISTS
ETYMOLOGIZE
ETYMOLOGIZED
ETYMOLOGIZES
ETYMOLOGIZING
ETYMOLOGY
ETYMON
ETYMONS
ETYPIC
ETYPICAL
EUBACTERIA
EUBACTERIUM
EUCAIN
EUCAINE
EUCAINES
EUCAINS
EUCALYPT
EUCALYPTI
EUCALYPTOL
EUCALYPTOLE
EUCALYPTOLES
EUCALYPTOLS
EUCALYPTS
EUCALYPTUS
EUCALYPTUSES
EUCARYON

EUCARYONS
EUCARYOT
EUCARYOTE
EUCARYOTES
EUCARYOTIC
EUCARYOTS
EUCHARIS
EUCHARISES
EUCHARISTIC
EUCHARISTICAL
EUCHLORIC
EUCHLORIN
EUCHLORINE
EUCHLORINES
EUCHOLOGIA
EUCHOLOGIES
EUCHOLOGION
EUCHOLOGY
EUCHRE
EUCHRED
EUCHRES
EUCHRING
EUCHROMATIC
EUCHROMATIN
EUCHROMATINS
EUCLASE
EUCLASES
EUCLIDEAN
EUCLIDIAN
EUCRITE
EUCRITES
EUCRITIC
EUCRYPHIA
EUCRYPHIAS
EUCYCLIC
EUDAEMON
EUDAEMONIA
EUDAEMONIAS
EUDAEMONIC
EUDAEMONICS
EUDAEMONIES
EUDAEMONISM
EUDAEMONISMS
EUDAEMONIST
EUDAEMONISTIC
EUDAEMONISTICAL
EUDAEMONISTS
EUDAEMONS
EUDAEMONY
EUDAIMONISM
EUDAIMONISMS
EUDEMON
EUDEMONIA
EUDEMONIC
EUDEMONICS
EUDEMONISM

EUDEMONISMS
EUDEMONIST
EUDEMONISTIC
EUDEMONISTICAL
EUDEMONISTS
EUDEMONS
EUDIALYTE
EUDIALYTES
EUDICOTYLEDON
EUDICOTYLEDONS
EUDIOMETER
EUDIOMETERS
EUDIOMETRIC
EUDIOMETRICAL
EUDIOMETRICALLY
EUDIOMETRY
EUGARIE
EUGARIES
EUGE
EUGENECIST
EUGENECISTS
EUGENIA
EUGENIAS
EUGENIC
EUGENICALLY
EUGENICIST
EUGENICISTS
EUGENICS
EUGENISM
EUGENISMS
EUGENIST
EUGENISTS
EUGENOL
EUGENOLS
EUGEOSYNCLINAL
EUGEOSYNCLINE
EUGEOSYNCLINES
EUGH
EUGHEN
EUGHS
EUGLENA
EUGLENAS
EUGLENOID
EUGLENOIDS
EUGLOBULIN
EUGLOBULINS
EUHARMONIC
EUHEMERISE
EUHEMERISED
EUHEMERISES
EUHEMERISING
EUHEMERISM
EUHEMERISMS
EUHEMERIST
EUHEMERISTIC
EUHEMERISTS

EUHEMERIZE
EUHEMERIZED
EUHEMERIZES
EUHEMERIZING
EUK
EUKARYON
EUKARYONS
EUKARYOT
EUKARYOTE
EUKARYOTES
EUKARYOTIC
EUKARYOTS
EUKED
EUKING
EUKS
EULACHAN
EULACHANS
EULACHON
EULACHONS
EULOGIA
EULOGIAE
EULOGIAS
EULOGIES
EULOGISE
EULOGISED
EULOGISER
EULOGISERS
EULOGISES
EULOGISING
EULOGIST
EULOGISTIC
EULOGISTICAL
EULOGISTICALLY
EULOGISTS
EULOGIUM
EULOGIUMS
EULOGIZE
EULOGIZED
EULOGIZER
EULOGIZERS
EULOGIZES
EULOGIZING
EULOGY
EUMELANIN
EUMELANINS
EUMERISM
EUMERISMS
EUMONG
EUMONGS
EUMUNG
EUMUNGS
EUNUCH
EUNUCHISE
EUNUCHISED
EUNUCHISES
EUNUCHISING

EUNUCHISM
EUNUCHISMS
EUNUCHIZE
EUNUCHIZED
EUNUCHIZES
EUNUCHIZING
EUNUCHOID
EUNUCHOIDISM
EUNUCHOIDISMS
EUNUCHOIDS
EUNUCHS
EUOI
EUONYMIN
EUONYMINS
EUONYMUS
EUONYMUSES
EUOUAE
EUOUAES
EUPAD
EUPADS
EUPATORIUM
EUPATORIUMS
EUPATRID
EUPATRIDAE
EUPATRIDS
EUPEPSIA
EUPEPSIAS
EUPEPSIES
EUPEPSY
EUPEPTIC
EUPEPTICITIES
EUPEPTICITY
EUPHAUSIACEAN
EUPHAUSIACEANS
EUPHAUSID
EUPHAUSIDS
EUPHAUSIID
EUPHAUSIIDS
EUPHEMISE
EUPHEMISED
EUPHEMISER
EUPHEMISERS
EUPHEMISES
EUPHEMISING
EUPHEMISM
EUPHEMISMS
EUPHEMIST
EUPHEMISTIC
EUPHEMISTICALLY
EUPHEMISTS
EUPHEMIZE
EUPHEMIZED
EUPHEMIZER
EUPHEMIZERS
EUPHEMIZES
EUPHEMIZING

EUPHENIC
EUPHENICS
EUPHOBIA
EUPHOBIAS
EUPHON
EUPHONIA
EUPHONIAS
EUPHONIC
EUPHONICAL
EUPHONICALLY
EUPHONIES
EUPHONIOUS
EUPHONIOUSLY
EUPHONIOUSNESS
EUPHONISE
EUPHONISED
EUPHONISES
EUPHONISING
EUPHONISM
EUPHONISMS
EUPHONIUM
EUPHONIUMS
EUPHONIZE
EUPHONIZED
EUPHONIZES
EUPHONIZING
EUPHONS
EUPHONY
EUPHORBIA
EUPHORBIACEOUS
EUPHORBIAS
EUPHORBIUM
EUPHORBIUMS
EUPHORIA
EUPHORIANT
EUPHORIANTS
EUPHORIAS
EUPHORIC
EUPHORICALLY
EUPHORIES
EUPHORY
EUPHOTIC
EUPHRASIES
EUPHRASY
EUPHROE
EUPHROES
EUPHUISE
EUPHUISED
EUPHUISES
EUPHUISING
EUPHUISM
EUPHUISMS
EUPHUIST
EUPHUISTIC
EUPHUISTICAL
EUPHUISTICALLY

EUPHUISTS	EUROPEANIZING	EUTHANASIAST	EVADIBLE
EUPHUIZE	EUROPIUM	EUTHANASIASTS	EVADING
EUPHUIZED	EUROPIUMS	EUTHANASIC	EVADINGLY
EUPHUIZES	EUROS	EUTHANASIES	EVAGATION
EUPHUIZING	EUROTERMINAL	EUTHANASY	EVAGATIONS
EUPLASTIC	EUROTERMINALS	EUTHANATIZE	EVAGINATE
EUPLOID	EURYBATH	EUTHANATIZED	EVAGINATED
EUPLOIDIES	EURYBATHIC	EUTHANATIZES	EVAGINATES
EUPLOIDS	EURYBATHS	EUTHANATIZING	EVAGINATING
EUPLOIDY	EURYHALINE	EUTHANIZE	EVAGINATION
EUPNEA	EURYOKIES	EUTHANIZED	EVAGINATIONS
EUPNEAS	EURYOKY	EUTHANIZES	EVALUATE
EUPNEIC	EURYPTERID	EUTHANIZING	EVALUATED
EUPNOEA	EURYPTERIDS	EUTHENICS	EVALUATES
EUPNOEAS	EURYPTEROID	EUTHENIST	EVALUATING
EUPNOEIC	EURYPTEROIDS	EUTHENISTS	EVALUATION
EUREKA	EURYTHERM	EUTHERIAN	EVALUATIONS
EUREKAS	EURYTHERMAL	EUTHERIANS	EVALUATIVE
EURHYTHMIC	EURYTHERMIC	EUTHYMIA	EVALUATOR
EURHYTHMICAL	EURYTHERMOUS	EUTHYMIC	EVALUATORS
EURHYTHMICS	EURYTHERMS	EUTHYMICS	EVANESCE
EURHYTHMIES	EURYTHMIC	EUTHYROID	EVANESCED
EURHYTHMIST	EURYTHMICAL	EUTRAPELIA	EVANESCENCE
EURHYTHMISTS	EURYTHMICALLY	EUTRAPELIAS	EVANESCENCES
EURHYTHMY	EURYTHMICS	EUTRAPELIES	EVANESCENT
EURIPI	EURYTHMIES	EUTRAPELY	EVANESCENTLY
EURIPUS	EURYTHMY	EUTROPHIC	EVANESCES
EURIPUSES	EURYTOPIC	EUTROPHICATION	EVANESCING
EURO	EUSOL	EUTROPHICATIONS	EVANGEL
EUROBOND	EUSOLS	EUTROPHIES	EVANGELIAR
EUROBONDS	EUSPORANGIATE	EUTROPHY	EVANGELIARIES
EUROCHEQUE	EUSTACIES	EUTROPIC	EVANGELIARION
EUROCHEQUES	EUSTACY	EUTROPIES	EVANGELIARIONS
EUROCRAT	EUSTASIES	EUTROPOUS	EVANGELIARIUM
EUROCRATS	EUSTASY	EUTROPY	EVANGELIARIUMS
EUROCREEP	EUSTATIC	EUXENITE	EVANGELIARS
EUROCURRENCIES	EUSTATICALLY	EUXENITES	EVANGELIARY
EUROCURRENCY	EUSTELE	EVACUANT	EVANGELIC
EURODEPOSIT	EUSTELES	EVACUANTS	EVANGELICAL
EURODEPOSITS	EUSTYLE	EVACUATE	EVANGELICALISM
EURODOLLAR	EUSTYLES	EVACUATED	EVANGELICALISMS
EURODOLLARS	EUTAXIA	EVACUATES	EVANGELICALLY
EUROKIES	EUTAXIC	EVACUATING	EVANGELICALNESS
EUROKOUS	EUTAXIES	EVACUATION	EVANGELICALS
EUROKY	EUTAXITE	EVACUATIONS	EVANGELICISM
EUROMARKET	EUTAXITES	EVACUATIVE	EVANGELICISMS
EUROMARKETS	EUTAXITIC	EVACUATOR	EVANGELIES
EURONOTE	EUTAXY	EVACUATORS	EVANGELISATION
EURONOTES	EUTECTIC	EVACUEE	EVANGELISATIONS
EUROPEANISE	EUTECTICS	EVACUEES	EVANGELISE
EUROPEANISED	EUTECTOID	EVADABLE	EVANGELISED
EUROPEANISES	EUTECTOIDS	EVADE	EVANGELISER
EUROPEANISING	EUTEXIA	EVADED	EVANGELISERS
EUROPEANIZE	EUTEXIAS	EVADER	EVANGELISES
EUROPEANIZED	EUTHANASIA	EVADERS	EVANGELISING
EUROPEANIZES	EUTHANASIAS	EVADES	EVANGELISM

EVANGELISMS
EVANGELIST
EVANGELISTARIES
EVANGELISTARION
EVANGELISTARY
EVANGELISTIC
EVANGELISTS
EVANGELIZATION
EVANGELIZATIONS
EVANGELIZE
EVANGELIZED
EVANGELIZER
EVANGELIZERS
EVANGELIZES
EVANGELIZING
EVANGELS
EVANGELY
EVANISH
EVANISHED
EVANISHES
EVANISHING
EVANISHMENT
EVANISHMENTS
EVANITION
EVANITIONS
EVAPORABILITIES
EVAPORABILITY
EVAPORABLE
EVAPORATE
EVAPORATED
EVAPORATES
EVAPORATING
EVAPORATION
EVAPORATIONS
EVAPORATIVE
EVAPORATOR
EVAPORATORS
EVAPORIMETER
EVAPORIMETERS
EVAPORITE
EVAPORITES
EVAPORITIC
EVAPOROGRAPH
EVAPOROGRAPHS
EVAPOROMETER
EVAPOROMETERS
EVASIBLE
EVASION
EVASIONS
EVASIVE
EVASIVELY
EVASIVENESS
EVASIVENESSES
EVE
EVECTION
EVECTIONAL

EVECTIONS
EVEJAR
EVEJARS
EVEN
EVENED
EVENEMENT
EVENEMENTS
EVENER
EVENERS
EVENEST
EVENFALL
EVENFALLS
EVENHANDED
EVENHANDEDLY
EVENHANDEDNESS
EVENING
EVENINGS
EVENLY
EVENNESS
EVENNESSES
EVENS
EVENSONG
EVENSONGS
EVENT
EVENTED
EVENTER
EVENTERS
EVENTFUL
EVENTFULLY
EVENTFULNESS
EVENTFULNESSES
EVENTIDE
EVENTIDES
EVENTING
EVENTINGS
EVENTISE
EVENTIZE
EVENTLESS
EVENTRATE
EVENTRATED
EVENTRATES
EVENTRATING
EVENTRATION
EVENTRATIONS
EVENTS
EVENTUAL
EVENTUALISE
EVENTUALISED
EVENTUALISES
EVENTUALISING
EVENTUALITIES
EVENTUALITY
EVENTUALIZE
EVENTUALIZED
EVENTUALIZES
EVENTUALIZING

EVENTUALLY
EVENTUATE
EVENTUATED
EVENTUATES
EVENTUATING
EVENTUATION
EVENTUATIONS
EVER
EVERBLOOMING
EVERDURING
EVERGLADE
EVERGLADES
EVERGREEN
EVERGREENS
EVERLASTING
EVERLASTINGLY
EVERLASTINGNESS
EVERLASTINGS
EVERMORE
EVERNET
EVERSIBLE
EVERSION
EVERSIONS
EVERT
EVERTED
EVERTING
EVERTOR
EVERTORS
EVERTS
EVERY
EVERYBODY
EVERYDAY
EVERYDAYNESS
EVERYDAYNESSES
EVERYDAYS
EVERYMAN
EVERYMEN
EVERYONE
EVERYPLACE
EVERYTHING
EVERYWAY
EVERYWHEN
EVERYWHENCE
EVERYWHERE
EVERYWHITHER
EVERYWOMAN
EVERYWOMEN
EVES
EVET
EVETS
EVHOE
EVICT
EVICTED
EVICTEE
EVICTEES
EVICTING

EVICTION
EVICTIONS
EVICTOR
EVICTORS
EVICTS
EVIDENCE
EVIDENCED
EVIDENCES
EVIDENCING
EVIDENT
EVIDENTIAL
EVIDENTIALLY
EVIDENTIARY
EVIDENTLY
EVIDENTS
EVIL
EVILDOER
EVILDOERS
EVILDOING
EVILDOINGS
EVILER
EVILEST
EVILLER
EVILLEST
EVILLY
EVILNESS
EVILNESSES
EVILS
EVINCE
EVINCED
EVINCEMENT
EVINCEMENTS
EVINCES
EVINCIBLE
EVINCIBLY
EVINCING
EVINCIVE
EVIRATE
EVIRATED
EVIRATES
EVIRATING
EVISCERATE
EVISCERATED
EVISCERATES
EVISCERATING
EVISCERATION
EVISCERATIONS
EVISCERATOR
EVISCERATORS
EVITABLE
EVITATE
EVITATED
EVITATES
EVITATING
EVITATION
EVITATIONS

EVITE
EVITED
EVITERNAL
EVITERNALLY
EVITERNITIES
EVITERNITY
EVITES
EVITING
EVO
EVOCABLE
EVOCATE
EVOCATED
EVOCATES
EVOCATING
EVOCATION
EVOCATIONS
EVOCATIVE
EVOCATIVELY
EVOCATIVENESS
EVOCATIVENESSES
EVOCATOR
EVOCATORS
EVOCATORY
EVOE
EVOHE
EVOKE
EVOKED
EVOKER
EVOKERS
EVOKES
EVOKING
EVOLUE
EVOLUES
EVOLUTE
EVOLUTED
EVOLUTES
EVOLUTING
EVOLUTION
EVOLUTIONAL
EVOLUTIONARILY
EVOLUTIONARY
EVOLUTIONISM
EVOLUTIONISMS
EVOLUTIONIST
EVOLUTIONISTIC
EVOLUTIONISTS
EVOLUTIONS
EVOLUTIVE
EVOLVABLE
EVOLVE
EVOLVED
EVOLVEMENT
EVOLVEMENTS
EVOLVENT
EVOLVER
EVOLVERS

EVOLVES
EVOLVING
EVONYMUS
EVONYMUSES
EVOVAE
EVOVAES
EVULGATE
EVULGATED
EVULGATES
EVULGATING
EVULSE
EVULSED
EVULSES
EVULSING
EVULSION
EVULSIONS
EVZONE
EVZONES
EWE
EWER
EWERS
EWES
EWEST
EWFTES
EWGHEN
EWHOW
EWK
EWKED
EWKING
EWKS
EWT
EWTS
EX
EXACERBATE
EXACERBATED
EXACERBATES
EXACERBATING
EXACERBATION
EXACERBATIONS
EXACERBESCENCE
EXACERBESCENCES
EXACT
EXACTA
EXACTABLE
EXACTAS
EXACTED
EXACTER
EXACTERS
EXACTEST
EXACTING
EXACTINGLY
EXACTINGNESS
EXACTINGNESSES
EXACTION
EXACTIONS
EXACTITUDE

EXACTITUDES
EXACTLY
EXACTMENT
EXACTMENTS
EXACTNESS
EXACTNESSES
EXACTOR
EXACTORS
EXACTRESS
EXACTRESSES
EXACTS
EXACUM
EXACUMS
EXAGGERATE
EXAGGERATED
EXAGGERATEDLY
EXAGGERATEDNESS
EXAGGERATES
EXAGGERATING
EXAGGERATINGLY
EXAGGERATION
EXAGGERATIONS
EXAGGERATIVE
EXAGGERATOR
EXAGGERATORS
EXAGGERATORY
EXALBUMINOUS
EXALT
EXALTATION
EXALTATIONS
EXALTED
EXALTEDLY
EXALTEDNESS
EXALTEDNESSES
EXALTER
EXALTERS
EXALTING
EXALTS
EXAM
EXAMEN
EXAMENS
EXAMINABILITIES
EXAMINABILITY
EXAMINABLE
EXAMINANT
EXAMINANTS
EXAMINATE
EXAMINATES
EXAMINATION
EXAMINATIONAL
EXAMINATIONS
EXAMINATOR
EXAMINATORS
EXAMINE
EXAMINED
EXAMINEE

EXAMINEES
EXAMINER
EXAMINERS
EXAMINERSHIP
EXAMINERSHIPS
EXAMINES
EXAMINING
EXAMPLAR
EXAMPLARS
EXAMPLE
EXAMPLED
EXAMPLES
EXAMPLING
EXAMS
EXANIMATE
EXANIMATION
EXANIMATIONS
EXANTHEM
EXANTHEMA
EXANTHEMAS
EXANTHEMATA
EXANTHEMATIC
EXANTHEMATOUS
EXANTHEMS
EXARATE
EXARATION
EXARATIONS
EXARCH
EXARCHAL
EXARCHATE
EXARCHATES
EXARCHIES
EXARCHIST
EXARCHISTS
EXARCHS
EXARCHY
EXASPERATE
EXASPERATED
EXASPERATEDLY
EXASPERATER
EXASPERATERS
EXASPERATES
EXASPERATING
EXASPERATINGLY
EXASPERATION
EXASPERATIONS
EXASPERATIVE
EXASPERATOR
EXASPERATORS
EXCAMB
EXCAMBED
EXCAMBING
EXCAMBION
EXCAMBIONS
EXCAMBIUM
EXCAMBIUMS

EXCAMBS
EXCARNATE
EXCARNATED
EXCARNATES
EXCARNATING
EXCARNATION
EXCARNATIONS
EXCAUDATE
EXCAVATE
EXCAVATED
EXCAVATES
EXCAVATING
EXCAVATION
EXCAVATIONAL
EXCAVATIONS
EXCAVATOR
EXCAVATORS
EXCEED
EXCEEDABLE
EXCEEDABLY
EXCEEDED
EXCEEDER
EXCEEDERS
EXCEEDING
EXCEEDINGLY
EXCEEDS
EXCEL
EXCELLED
EXCELLENCE
EXCELLENCES
EXCELLENCIES
EXCELLENCY
EXCELLENT
EXCELLENTLY
EXCELLING
EXCELS
EXCELSIOR
EXCELSIORS
EXCENTRIC
EXCENTRICS
EXCEPT
EXCEPTANT
EXCEPTANTS
EXCEPTED
EXCEPTING
EXCEPTION
EXCEPTIONABLE
EXCEPTIONABLY
EXCEPTIONAL
EXCEPTIONALISM
EXCEPTIONALISMS
EXCEPTIONALITY
EXCEPTIONALLY
EXCEPTIONALNESS
EXCEPTIONALS
EXCEPTIONS

EXCEPTIOUS
EXCEPTIVE
EXCEPTLESS
EXCEPTOR
EXCEPTORS
EXCEPTS
EXCERPT
EXCERPTA
EXCERPTED
EXCERPTER
EXCERPTERS
EXCERPTIBLE
EXCERPTING
EXCERPTINGS
EXCERPTION
EXCERPTIONS
EXCERPTOR
EXCERPTORS
EXCERPTS
EXCERPTUM
EXCESS
EXCESSED
EXCESSES
EXCESSING
EXCESSIVE
EXCESSIVELY
EXCESSIVENESS
EXCESSIVENESSES
EXCHANGE
EXCHANGEABILITY
EXCHANGEABLE
EXCHANGEABLY
EXCHANGED
EXCHANGER
EXCHANGERS
EXCHANGES
EXCHANGING
EXCHEAT
EXCHEATS
EXCHEQUER
EXCHEQUERED
EXCHEQUERING
EXCHEQUERS
EXCIDE
EXCIDED
EXCIDES
EXCIDING
EXCIMER
EXCIMERS
EXCIPIENT
EXCIPIENTS
EXCIPLE
EXCIPLES
EXCISABLE
EXCISE
EXCISED

EXCISEMAN
EXCISEMEN
EXCISES
EXCISING
EXCISION
EXCISIONAL
EXCISIONS
EXCITABILITIES
EXCITABILITY
EXCITABLE
EXCITABLENESS
EXCITABLENESSES
EXCITABLY
EXCITANCIES
EXCITANCY
EXCITANT
EXCITANTS
EXCITATION
EXCITATIONS
EXCITATIVE
EXCITATORY
EXCITE
EXCITED
EXCITEDLY
EXCITEDNESS
EXCITEDNESSES
EXCITEMENT
EXCITEMENTS
EXCITER
EXCITERS
EXCITES
EXCITING
EXCITINGLY
EXCITON
EXCITONIC
EXCITONS
EXCITOR
EXCITORS
EXCLAIM
EXCLAIMED
EXCLAIMER
EXCLAIMERS
EXCLAIMING
EXCLAIMS
EXCLAMATION
EXCLAMATIONAL
EXCLAMATIONS
EXCLAMATIVE
EXCLAMATORILY
EXCLAMATORY
EXCLAUSTRATION
EXCLAUSTRATIONS
EXCLAVE
EXCLAVES
EXCLOSURE
EXCLOSURES

EXCLUDABILITIES
EXCLUDABILITY
EXCLUDABLE
EXCLUDE
EXCLUDED
EXCLUDEE
EXCLUDEES
EXCLUDER
EXCLUDERS
EXCLUDES
EXCLUDIBLE
EXCLUDING
EXCLUSION
EXCLUSIONARY
EXCLUSIONISM
EXCLUSIONISMS
EXCLUSIONIST
EXCLUSIONISTS
EXCLUSIONS
EXCLUSIVE
EXCLUSIVELY
EXCLUSIVENESS
EXCLUSIVENESSES
EXCLUSIVES
EXCLUSIVISM
EXCLUSIVISMS
EXCLUSIVIST
EXCLUSIVISTS
EXCLUSIVITIES
EXCLUSIVITY
EXCLUSORY
EXCOGITABLE
EXCOGITABLY
EXCOGITATE
EXCOGITATED
EXCOGITATES
EXCOGITATING
EXCOGITATION
EXCOGITATIONS
EXCOGITATIVE
EXCOGITATOR
EXCOGITATORS
EXCOMMUNICABLE
EXCOMMUNICATE
EXCOMMUNICATED
EXCOMMUNICATES
EXCOMMUNICATING
EXCOMMUNICATION
EXCOMMUNICATIVE
EXCOMMUNICATOR
EXCOMMUNICATORS
EXCOMMUNICATORY
EXCOMMUNION
EXCOMMUNIONS
EXCORIATE
EXCORIATED

EXCORIATES	EXCURSED	EXECUTABLE	EXEMPLARINESS
EXCORIATING	EXCURSES	EXECUTANCIES	EXEMPLARINESSES
EXCORIATION	EXCURSING	EXECUTANCY	EXEMPLARITIES
EXCORIATIONS	EXCURSION	EXECUTANT	EXEMPLARITY
EXCORTICATE	EXCURSIONED	EXECUTANTS	EXEMPLARS
EXCORTICATED	EXCURSIONING	EXECUTARY	EXEMPLARY
EXCORTICATES	EXCURSIONISE	EXECUTE	EXEMPLE
EXCORTICATING	EXCURSIONISED	EXECUTED	EXEMPLES
EXCORTICATION	EXCURSIONISES	EXECUTER	EXEMPLIFIABLE
EXCORTICATIONS	EXCURSIONISING	EXECUTERS	EXEMPLIFICATION
EXCREMENT	EXCURSIONIST	EXECUTES	EXEMPLIFICATIVE
EXCREMENTA	EXCURSIONISTS	EXECUTING	EXEMPLIFIED
EXCREMENTAL	EXCURSIONIZE	EXECUTION	EXEMPLIFIER
EXCREMENTITIAL	EXCURSIONIZED	EXECUTIONER	EXEMPLIFIERS
EXCREMENTITIOUS	EXCURSIONIZES	EXECUTIONERS	EXEMPLIFIES
EXCREMENTS	EXCURSIONIZING	EXECUTIONS	EXEMPLIFY
EXCREMENTUM	EXCURSIONS	EXECUTIVE	EXEMPLIFYING
EXCRESCENCE	EXCURSIVE	EXECUTIVELY	EXEMPLUM
EXCRESCENCES	EXCURSIVELY	EXECUTIVES	EXEMPT
EXCRESCENCIES	EXCURSIVENESS	EXECUTOR	EXEMPTED
EXCRESCENCY	EXCURSIVENESSES	EXECUTORIAL	EXEMPTING
EXCRESCENT	EXCURSUS	EXECUTORS	EXEMPTION·
EXCRESCENTIAL	EXCURSUSES	EXECUTORSHIP	EXEMPTIONS
EXCRESCENTLY	EXCUSABLE	EXECUTORSHIPS	EXEMPTS
EXCRETA	EXCUSABLENESS	EXECUTORY	EXENTERATE
EXCRETAL	EXCUSABLENESSES	EXECUTRESS	EXENTERATED
EXCRETE	EXCUSABLY	EXECUTRESSES	EXENTERATES
EXCRETED	EXCUSAL	EXECUTRICES	EXENTERATING
EXCRETER	EXCUSALS	EXECUTRIES	EXENTERATION
EXCRETERS	EXCUSATORY	EXECUTRIX	EXENTERATIONS
EXCRETES	EXCUSE	EXECUTRIXES	EXEQUATUR
EXCRETING	EXCUSED	EXECUTRY	EXEQUATURS
EXCRETION	EXCUSER	EXEDRA	EXEQUIAL
EXCRETIONS	EXCUSERS	EXEDRAE	EXEQUIES
EXCRETIVE	EXCUSES	EXEDRAS	EXEQUY
EXCRETORIES	EXCUSING	EXEEM	EXERCISABLE
EXCRETORY	EXCUSIVE	EXEEMED	EXERCISE
EXCRUCIATE	EXEAT	EXEEMING	EXERCISED
EXCRUCIATED	EXEATS	EXEEMS	EXERCISER
EXCRUCIATES	EXEC	EXEGESES	EXERCISERS
EXCRUCIATING	EXECRABLE	EXEGESIS	EXERCISES
EXCRUCIATINGLY	EXECRABLENESS	EXEGETE	EXERCISING
EXCRUCIATION	EXECRABLENESSES	EXEGETES	EXERCITATION
EXCRUCIATIONS	EXECRABLY	EXEGETIC	EXERCITATIONS
EXCUBANT	EXECRATE	EXEGETICAL	EXERGONIC
EXCUDIT	EXECRATED	EXEGETICALLY	EXERGUAL
EXCULPABLE	EXECRATES	EXEGETICS	EXERGUE
EXCULPATE	EXECRATING	EXEGETIST	EXERGUES
EXCULPATED	EXECRATION	EXEGETISTS	EXERT
EXCULPATES	EXECRATIONS	EXEME	EXERTED
EXCULPATING	EXECRATIVE	EXEMED	EXERTING
EXCULPATION	EXECRATIVELY	EXEMES	EXERTION
EXCULPATIONS	EXECRATOR	EXEMING	EXERTIONS
EXCULPATORY	EXECRATORS	EXEMPLA	EXERTIVE
EXCURRENT	EXECRATORY	EXEMPLAR	EXERTS
EXCURSE	EXECS	EXEMPLARILY	EXES

EXEUNT
EXFOLIATE
EXFOLIATED
EXFOLIATES
EXFOLIATING
EXFOLIATION
EXFOLIATIONS
EXFOLIATIVE
EXFOLIATOR
EXFOLIATORS
EXHALABLE
EXHALANT
EXHALANTS
EXHALATION
EXHALATIONS
EXHALE
EXHALED
EXHALENT
EXHALENTS
EXHALES
EXHALING
EXHAUST
EXHAUSTED
EXHAUSTER
EXHAUSTERS
EXHAUSTIBILITY
EXHAUSTIBLE
EXHAUSTING
EXHAUSTION
EXHAUSTIONS
EXHAUSTIVE
EXHAUSTIVELY
EXHAUSTIVENESS
EXHAUSTIVITIES
EXHAUSTIVITY
EXHAUSTLESS
EXHAUSTLESSLY
EXHAUSTLESSNESS
EXHAUSTS
EXHEDRA
EXHEDRAE
EXHEREDATE
EXHEREDATED
EXHEREDATES
EXHEREDATING
EXHEREDATION
EXHEREDATIONS
EXHIBIT
EXHIBITED
EXHIBITER
EXHIBITERS
EXHIBITING
EXHIBITION
EXHIBITIONER
EXHIBITIONERS
EXHIBITIONISM

EXHIBITIONISMS
EXHIBITIONIST
EXHIBITIONISTIC
EXHIBITIONISTS
EXHIBITIONS
EXHIBITIVE
EXHIBITIVELY
EXHIBITOR
EXHIBITORS
EXHIBITORY
EXHIBITS
EXHILARANT
EXHILARANTS
EXHILARATE
EXHILARATED
EXHILARATES
EXHILARATING
EXHILARATINGLY
EXHILARATION
EXHILARATIONS
EXHILARATIVE
EXHILARATOR
EXHILARATORS
EXHILARATORY
EXHORT
EXHORTATION
EXHORTATIONS
EXHORTATIVE
EXHORTATORY
EXHORTED
EXHORTER
EXHORTERS
EXHORTING
EXHORTS
EXHUMATE
EXHUMATED
EXHUMATES
EXHUMATING
EXHUMATION
EXHUMATIONS
EXHUME
EXHUMED
EXHUMER
EXHUMERS
EXHUMES
EXHUMING
EXIES
EXIGEANT
EXIGEANTE
EXIGENCE
EXIGENCES
EXIGENCIES
EXIGENCY
EXIGENT
EXIGENTLY
EXIGENTS

EXIGIBLE
EXIGUITIES
EXIGUITY
EXIGUOUS
EXIGUOUSLY
EXIGUOUSNESS
EXIGUOUSNESSES
EXILE
EXILED
EXILEMENT
EXILEMENTS
EXILES
EXILIAN
EXILIC
EXILING
EXILITIES
EXILITY
EXIMIOUS
EXIMIOUSLY
EXINE
EXINES
EXIST
EXISTED
EXISTENCE
EXISTENCES
EXISTENT
EXISTENTIAL
EXISTENTIALISM
EXISTENTIALISMS
EXISTENTIALIST
EXISTENTIALISTS
EXISTENTIALLY
EXISTENTS
EXISTING
EXISTS
EXIT
EXITANCE
EXITANCES
EXITED
EXITING
EXITLESS
EXITS
EXO
EXOBIOLOGICAL
EXOBIOLOGIES
EXOBIOLOGIST
EXOBIOLOGISTS
EXOBIOLOGY
EXOCARP
EXOCARPS
EXOCENTRIC
EXOCRINE
EXOCRINES
EXOCUTICLE
EXOCUTICLES
EXOCYCLIC

EXOCYTOSES
EXOCYTOSIS
EXOCYTOTIC
EXODE
EXODERM
EXODERMAL
EXODERMIS
EXODERMISES
EXODERMS
EXODES
EXODIC
EXODIST
EXODISTS
EXODOI
EXODONTIA
EXODONTIAS
EXODONTICS
EXODONTIST
EXODONTISTS
EXODOS
EXODUS
EXODUSES
EXOENZYME
EXOENZYMES
EXOERGIC
EXOERYTHROCYTIC
EXOGAMIC
EXOGAMIES
EXOGAMOUS
EXOGAMY
EXOGEN
EXOGENETIC
EXOGENOUS
EXOGENOUSLY
EXOGENS
EXOMION
EXOMIONS
EXOMIS
EXOMISES
EXON
EXONERATE
EXONERATED
EXONERATES
EXONERATING
EXONERATION
EXONERATIONS
EXONERATIVE
EXONERATOR
EXONERATORS
EXONIC
EXONS
EXONUCLEASE
EXONUCLEASES
EXONUMIA
EXONYM
EXONYMS

EXOPARASITE
EXOPARASITES
EXOPARASITIC
EXOPEPTIDASE
EXOPEPTIDASES
EXOPHAGIES
EXOPHAGOUS
EXOPHAGY
EXOPHORIA
EXOPHORIC
EXOPHORICS
EXOPHTHALMIA
EXOPHTHALMIAS
EXOPHTHALMIC
EXOPHTHALMOS
EXOPHTHALMOSES
EXOPHTHALMUS
EXOPHTHALMUSES
EXOPLANET
EXOPLANETS
EXOPLASM
EXOPLASMS
EXOPOD
EXOPODITE
EXOPODITES
EXOPODITIC
EXOPODS
EXORABILITIES
EXORABILITY
EXORABLE
EXORATION
EXORATIONS
EXORBITANCE
EXORBITANCES
EXORBITANCIES
EXORBITANCY
EXORBITANT
EXORBITANTLY
EXORBITATE
EXORBITATED
EXORBITATES
EXORBITATING
EXORCISE
EXORCISED
EXORCISER
EXORCISERS
EXORCISES
EXORCISING
EXORCISM
EXORCISMS
EXORCIST
EXORCISTIC
EXORCISTICAL
EXORCISTS
EXORCIZE
EXORCIZED

EXORCIZER
EXORCIZERS
EXORCIZES
EXORCIZING
EXORDIA
EXORDIAL
EXORDIUM
EXORDIUMS
EXOSKELETAL
EXOSKELETON
EXOSKELETONS
EXOSMIC
EXOSMOSE
EXOSMOSES
EXOSMOSIS
EXOSMOTIC
EXOSPHERE
EXOSPHERES
EXOSPHERIC
EXOSPHERICAL
EXOSPORAL
EXOSPORE
EXOSPORES
EXOSPOROUS
EXOSTOSES
EXOSTOSIS
EXOTERIC
EXOTERICAL
EXOTERICALLY
EXOTERICISM
EXOTERICISMS
EXOTHERMAL
EXOTHERMALLY
EXOTHERMIC
EXOTHERMICALLY
EXOTHERMICITIES
EXOTHERMICITY
EXOTIC
EXOTICA
EXOTICALLY
EXOTICISM
EXOTICISMS
EXOTICNESS
EXOTICNESSES
EXOTICS
EXOTISM
EXOTISMS
EXOTOXIC
EXOTOXIN
EXOTOXINS
EXPAND
EXPANDABILITIES
EXPANDABILITY
EXPANDABLE
EXPANDED
EXPANDER

EXPANDERS
EXPANDING
EXPANDOR
EXPANDORS
EXPANDS
EXPANSE
EXPANSES
EXPANSIBILITIES
EXPANSIBILITY
EXPANSIBLE
EXPANSIBLY
EXPANSILE
EXPANSION
EXPANSIONAL
EXPANSIONARY
EXPANSIONISM
EXPANSIONISMS
EXPANSIONIST
EXPANSIONISTIC
EXPANSIONISTS
EXPANSIONS
EXPANSIVE
EXPANSIVELY
EXPANSIVENESS
EXPANSIVENESSES
EXPANSIVITIES
EXPANSIVITY
EXPAT
EXPATIATE
EXPATIATED
EXPATIATES
EXPATIATING
EXPATIATION
EXPATIATIONS
EXPATIATIVE
EXPATIATOR
EXPATIATORS
EXPATIATORY
EXPATRIATE
EXPATRIATED
EXPATRIATES
EXPATRIATING
EXPATRIATION
EXPATRIATIONS
EXPATRIATISM
EXPATRIATISMS
EXPATS
EXPECT
EXPECTABLE
EXPECTABLY
EXPECTANCE
EXPECTANCES
EXPECTANCIES
EXPECTANCY
EXPECTANT
EXPECTANTLY

EXPECTANTS
EXPECTATION
EXPECTATIONAL
EXPECTATIONS
EXPECTATIVE
EXPECTATIVES
EXPECTED
EXPECTEDLY
EXPECTEDNESS
EXPECTEDNESSES
EXPECTER
EXPECTERS
EXPECTING
EXPECTINGLY
EXPECTINGS
EXPECTORANT
EXPECTORANTS
EXPECTORATE
EXPECTORATED
EXPECTORATES
EXPECTORATING
EXPECTORATION
EXPECTORATIONS
EXPECTORATIVE
EXPECTORATOR
EXPECTORATORS
EXPECTS
EXPEDIENCE
EXPEDIENCES
EXPEDIENCIES
EXPEDIENCY
EXPEDIENT
EXPEDIENTIAL
EXPEDIENTIALLY
EXPEDIENTLY
EXPEDIENTS
EXPEDITATE
EXPEDITATED
EXPEDITATES
EXPEDITATING
EXPEDITATION
EXPEDITATIONS
EXPEDITE
EXPEDITED
EXPEDITELY
EXPEDITER
EXPEDITERS
EXPEDITES
EXPEDITING
EXPEDITION
EXPEDITIONARY
EXPEDITIONS
EXPEDITIOUS
EXPEDITIOUSLY
EXPEDITIOUSNESS
EXPEDITIVE

EXPEDITOR
EXPEDITORS
EXPEL
EXPELLABLE
EXPELLANT
EXPELLANTS
EXPELLED
EXPELLEE
EXPELLEES
EXPELLENT
EXPELLENTS
EXPELLER
EXPELLERS
EXPELLING
EXPELS
EXPEND
EXPENDABILITIES
EXPENDABILITY
EXPENDABLE
EXPENDABLES
EXPENDED
EXPENDER
EXPENDERS
EXPENDING
EXPENDITURE
EXPENDITURES
EXPENDS
EXPENSE
EXPENSED
EXPENSES
EXPENSING
EXPENSIVE
EXPENSIVELY
EXPENSIVENESS
EXPENSIVENESSES
EXPERIENCE
EXPERIENCEABLE
EXPERIENCEABLY
EXPERIENCED
EXPERIENCELESS
EXPERIENCER
EXPERIENCERS
EXPERIENCES
EXPERIENCING
EXPERIENTIAL
EXPERIENTIALISM
EXPERIENTIALIST
EXPERIENTIALLY
EXPERIMENT
EXPERIMENTAL
EXPERIMENTALISE
EXPERIMENTALISM
EXPERIMENTALIST
EXPERIMENTALIZE
EXPERIMENTALLY
EXPERIMENTATION

EXPERIMENTATIVE
EXPERIMENTED
EXPERIMENTER
EXPERIMENTERS
EXPERIMENTING
EXPERIMENTIST
EXPERIMENTISTS
EXPERIMENTS
EXPERT
EXPERTED
EXPERTING
EXPERTISE
EXPERTISED
EXPERTISES
EXPERTISING
EXPERTISM
EXPERTISMS
EXPERTIZE
EXPERTIZED
EXPERTIZES
EXPERTIZING
EXPERTLY
EXPERTNESS
EXPERTNESSES
EXPERTS
EXPIABLE
EXPIATE
EXPIATED
EXPIATES
EXPIATING
EXPIATION
EXPIATIONS
EXPIATOR
EXPIATORS
EXPIATORY
EXPIRABLE
EXPIRANT
EXPIRANTS
EXPIRATION
EXPIRATIONS
EXPIRATORY
EXPIRE
EXPIRED
EXPIRER
EXPIRERS
EXPIRES
EXPIRIES
EXPIRING
EXPIRY
EXPISCATE
EXPISCATED
EXPISCATES
EXPISCATING
EXPISCATION
EXPISCATIONS
EXPISCATORY

EXPLAIN
EXPLAINABLE
EXPLAINED
EXPLAINER
EXPLAINERS
EXPLAINING
EXPLAINS
EXPLANATION
EXPLANATIONS
EXPLANATIVE
EXPLANATIVELY
EXPLANATORILY
EXPLANATORY
EXPLANT
EXPLANTATION
EXPLANTATIONS
EXPLANTED
EXPLANTING
EXPLANTS
EXPLETIVE
EXPLETIVELY
EXPLETIVES
EXPLETORY
EXPLICABLE
EXPLICABLY
EXPLICATE
EXPLICATED
EXPLICATES
EXPLICATING
EXPLICATION
EXPLICATIONS
EXPLICATIVE
EXPLICATIVELY
EXPLICATOR
EXPLICATORS
EXPLICATORY
EXPLICIT
EXPLICITLY
EXPLICITNESS
EXPLICITNESSES
EXPLICITS
EXPLODE
EXPLODED
EXPLODER
EXPLODERS
EXPLODES
EXPLODING
EXPLOIT
EXPLOITABLE
EXPLOITAGE
EXPLOITAGES
EXPLOITATION
EXPLOITATIONS
EXPLOITATIVE
EXPLOITATIVELY
EXPLOITED

EXPLOITER
EXPLOITERS
EXPLOITING
EXPLOITIVE
EXPLOITS
EXPLORATION
EXPLORATIONAL
EXPLORATIONIST
EXPLORATIONISTS
EXPLORATIONS
EXPLORATIVE
EXPLORATIVELY
EXPLORATORY
EXPLORE
EXPLORED
EXPLORER
EXPLORERS
EXPLORES
EXPLORING
EXPLOSIBLE
EXPLOSION
EXPLOSIONS
EXPLOSIVE
EXPLOSIVELY
EXPLOSIVENESS
EXPLOSIVENESSES
EXPLOSIVES
EXPO
EXPONENT
EXPONENTIAL
EXPONENTIALLY
EXPONENTIALS
EXPONENTIATION
EXPONENTIATIONS
EXPONENTS
EXPONIBLE
EXPORT
EXPORTABILITIES
EXPORTABILITY
EXPORTABLE
EXPORTATION
EXPORTATIONS
EXPORTED
EXPORTER
EXPORTERS
EXPORTING
EXPORTS
EXPOS
EXPOSABLE
EXPOSAL
EXPOSALS
EXPOSE
EXPOSED
EXPOSEDNESS
EXPOSEDNESSES
EXPOSER

EXPOSERS
EXPOSES
EXPOSING
EXPOSIT
EXPOSITED
EXPOSITING
EXPOSITION
EXPOSITIONAL
EXPOSITIONS
EXPOSITIVE
EXPOSITIVELY
EXPOSITOR
EXPOSITORILY
EXPOSITORS
EXPOSITORY
EXPOSITRESS
EXPOSITRESSES
EXPOSITS
EXPOSTULATE
EXPOSTULATED
EXPOSTULATES
EXPOSTULATING
EXPOSTULATINGLY
EXPOSTULATION
EXPOSTULATIONS
EXPOSTULATIVE
EXPOSTULATOR
EXPOSTULATORS
EXPOSTULATORY
EXPOSTURE
EXPOSTURES
EXPOSURE
EXPOSURES
EXPOUND
EXPOUNDED
EXPOUNDER
EXPOUNDERS
EXPOUNDING
EXPOUNDS
EXPRESS
EXPRESSAGE
EXPRESSAGES
EXPRESSED
EXPRESSER
EXPRESSERS
EXPRESSES
EXPRESSIBLE
EXPRESSING
EXPRESSION
EXPRESSIONAL
EXPRESSIONISM
EXPRESSIONISMS
EXPRESSIONIST
EXPRESSIONISTIC
EXPRESSIONISTS
EXPRESSIONLESS

EXPRESSIONS
EXPRESSIVE
EXPRESSIVELY
EXPRESSIVENESS
EXPRESSIVITIES
EXPRESSIVITY
EXPRESSLY
EXPRESSMAN
EXPRESSMEN
EXPRESSNESS
EXPRESSNESSES
EXPRESSO
EXPRESSOS
EXPRESSURE
EXPRESSURES
EXPRESSWAY
EXPRESSWAYS
EXPROBRATE
EXPROBRATED
EXPROBRATES
EXPROBRATING
EXPROBRATION
EXPROBRATIONS
EXPROBRATIVE
EXPROBRATORY
EXPROMISSION
EXPROMISSIONS
EXPROMISSOR
EXPROMISSORS
EXPROPRIABLE
EXPROPRIATE
EXPROPRIATED
EXPROPRIATES
EXPROPRIATING
EXPROPRIATION
EXPROPRIATIONS
EXPROPRIATOR
EXPROPRIATORS
EXPUGN
EXPUGNABLE
EXPUGNATION
EXPUGNATIONS
EXPUGNED
EXPUGNING
EXPUGNS
EXPULSE
EXPULSED
EXPULSES
EXPULSING
EXPULSION
EXPULSIONS
EXPULSIVE
EXPUNCT
EXPUNCTED
EXPUNCTING
EXPUNCTION

EXPUNCTIONS
EXPUNCTS
EXPUNGE
EXPUNGED
EXPUNGER
EXPUNGERS
EXPUNGES
EXPUNGING
EXPURGATE
EXPURGATED
EXPURGATES
EXPURGATING
EXPURGATION
EXPURGATIONS
EXPURGATOR
EXPURGATORIAL
EXPURGATORS
EXPURGATORY
EXPURGE
EXPURGED
EXPURGES
EXPURGING
EXQUISITE
EXQUISITELY
EXQUISITENESS
EXQUISITENESSES
EXQUISITES
EXSANGUINATE
EXSANGUINATED
EXSANGUINATES
EXSANGUINATING
EXSANGUINATION
EXSANGUINATIONS
EXSANGUINE
EXSANGUINED
EXSANGUINEOUS
EXSANGUINITIES
EXSANGUINITY
EXSANGUINOUS
EXSCIND
EXSCINDED
EXSCINDING
EXSCINDS
EXSECANT
EXSECANTS
EXSECT
EXSECTED
EXSECTING
EXSECTION
EXSECTIONS
EXSECTS
EXSERT
EXSERTED
EXSERTILE
EXSERTING
EXSERTION

EXSERTIONS
EXSERTS
EXSICCANT
EXSICCATE
EXSICCATED
EXSICCATES
EXSICCATING
EXSICCATION
EXSICCATIONS
EXSICCATIVE
EXSICCATOR
EXSICCATORS
EXSOLUTION
EXSOLUTIONS
EXSTIPULATE
EXSTROPHIES
EXSTROPHY
EXSUCCOUS
EXSUFFLATE
EXSUFFLATED
EXSUFFLATES
EXSUFFLATING
EXSUFFLATION
EXSUFFLATIONS
EXSUFFLICATE
EXTANT
EXTASIES
EXTASY
EXTATIC
EXTEMPORAL
EXTEMPORALLY
EXTEMPORANEITY
EXTEMPORANEOUS
EXTEMPORARILY
EXTEMPORARINESS
EXTEMPORARY
EXTEMPORE
EXTEMPORES
EXTEMPORISATION
EXTEMPORISE
EXTEMPORISED
EXTEMPORISER
EXTEMPORISERS
EXTEMPORISES
EXTEMPORISING
EXTEMPORIZATION
EXTEMPORIZE
EXTEMPORIZED
EXTEMPORIZER
EXTEMPORIZERS
EXTEMPORIZES
EXTEMPORIZING
EXTEND
EXTENDABILITIES
EXTENDABILITY
EXTENDABLE

EXTENDANT
EXTENDED
EXTENDEDLY
EXTENDEDNESS
EXTENDEDNESSES
EXTENDER
EXTENDERS
EXTENDIBILITIES
EXTENDIBILITY
EXTENDIBLE
EXTENDING
EXTENDS
EXTENSE
EXTENSIBILITIES
EXTENSIBILITY
EXTENSIBLE
EXTENSIBLENESS
EXTENSIFICATION
EXTENSILE
EXTENSIMETER
EXTENSIMETERS
EXTENSION
EXTENSIONAL
EXTENSIONALISM
EXTENSIONALISMS
EXTENSIONALITY
EXTENSIONALLY
EXTENSIONIST
EXTENSIONISTS
EXTENSIONS
EXTENSITIES
EXTENSITY
EXTENSIVE
EXTENSIVELY
EXTENSIVENESS
EXTENSIVENESSES
EXTENSIVIZATION
EXTENSOMETER
EXTENSOMETERS
EXTENSOR
EXTENSORS
EXTENT
EXTENTS
EXTENUATE
EXTENUATED
EXTENUATES
EXTENUATING
EXTENUATINGLY
EXTENUATINGS
EXTENUATION
EXTENUATIONS
EXTENUATIVE
EXTENUATOR
EXTENUATORS
EXTENUATORY
EXTERIOR

EXTERIORISATION
EXTERIORISE
EXTERIORISED
EXTERIORISES
EXTERIORISING
EXTERIORITIES
EXTERIORITY
EXTERIORIZATION
EXTERIORIZE
EXTERIORIZED
EXTERIORIZES
EXTERIORIZING
EXTERIORLY
EXTERIORS
EXTERMINABLE
EXTERMINATE
EXTERMINATED
EXTERMINATES
EXTERMINATING
EXTERMINATION
EXTERMINATIONS
EXTERMINATIVE
EXTERMINATOR
EXTERMINATORS
EXTERMINATORY
EXTERMINE
EXTERMINED
EXTERMINES
EXTERMINING
EXTERN
EXTERNAL
EXTERNALISATION
EXTERNALISE
EXTERNALISED
EXTERNALISES
EXTERNALISING
EXTERNALISM
EXTERNALISMS
EXTERNALIST
EXTERNALISTS
EXTERNALITIES
EXTERNALITY
EXTERNALIZATION
EXTERNALIZE
EXTERNALIZED
EXTERNALIZES
EXTERNALIZING
EXTERNALLY
EXTERNALS
EXTERNAT
EXTERNATS
EXTERNE
EXTERNES
EXTERNS
EXTERNSHIP
EXTERNSHIPS

EXTEROCEPTIVE
EXTEROCEPTOR
EXTEROCEPTORS
EXTERRITORIAL
EXTERRITORIALLY
EXTINCT
EXTINCTED
EXTINCTING
EXTINCTION
EXTINCTIONS
EXTINCTIVE
EXTINCTS
EXTINCTURE
EXTINCTURES
EXTINE
EXTINES
EXTINGUISH
EXTINGUISHABLE
EXTINGUISHANT
EXTINGUISHANTS
EXTINGUISHED
EXTINGUISHER
EXTINGUISHERS
EXTINGUISHES
EXTINGUISHING
EXTINGUISHMENT
EXTINGUISHMENTS
EXTIRP
EXTIRPABLE
EXTIRPATE
EXTIRPATED
EXTIRPATES
EXTIRPATING
EXTIRPATION
EXTIRPATIONS
EXTIRPATIVE
EXTIRPATOR
EXTIRPATORS
EXTIRPATORY
EXTIRPED
EXTIRPING
EXTIRPS
EXTOL
EXTOLD
EXTOLL
EXTOLLED
EXTOLLER
EXTOLLERS
EXTOLLING
EXTOLLINGLY
EXTOLLS
EXTOLMENT
EXTOLMENTS
EXTOLS
EXTORSIVE
EXTORSIVELY

EXTORT
EXTORTED
EXTORTER
EXTORTERS
EXTORTING
EXTORTION
EXTORTIONARY
EXTORTIONATE
EXTORTIONATELY
EXTORTIONER
EXTORTIONERS
EXTORTIONIST
EXTORTIONISTS
EXTORTIONS
EXTORTIVE
EXTORTS
EXTRA
EXTRACANONICAL
EXTRACELLULAR
EXTRACELLULARLY
EXTRACORPOREAL
EXTRACRANIAL
EXTRACT
EXTRACTABILITY
EXTRACTABLE
EXTRACTANT
EXTRACTANTS
EXTRACTED
EXTRACTIBLE
EXTRACTING
EXTRACTION
EXTRACTIONS
EXTRACTIVE
EXTRACTIVELY
EXTRACTIVES
EXTRACTOR
EXTRACTORS
EXTRACTS
EXTRACURRICULAR
EXTRADITABLE
EXTRADITE
EXTRADITED
EXTRADITES
EXTRADITING
EXTRADITION
EXTRADITIONS
EXTRADOS
EXTRADOSES
EXTRADOTAL
EXTRADURAL
EXTRADURALLY
EXTRADURALS
EXTRAEMBRYONIC
EXTRAFLORAL
EXTRAFORANEOUS
EXTRAGALACTIC

EXTRAHEPATIC
EXTRAIT
EXTRAITS
EXTRAJUDICIAL
EXTRAJUDICIALLY
EXTRALEGAL
EXTRALEGALLY
EXTRALIMITAL
EXTRALIMITARY
EXTRALINGUISTIC
EXTRALITERARY
EXTRALITIES
EXTRALITY
EXTRALOGICAL
EXTRAMARITAL
EXTRAMETRICAL
EXTRAMUNDANE
EXTRAMURAL
EXTRAMURALLY
EXTRAMUSICAL
EXTRANEITIES
EXTRANEITY
EXTRANEOUS
EXTRANEOUSLY
EXTRANEOUSNESS
EXTRANET
EXTRANETS
EXTRANUCLEAR
EXTRAORDINAIRE
EXTRAORDINARIES
EXTRAORDINARILY
EXTRAORDINARY
EXTRAPOLATE
EXTRAPOLATED
EXTRAPOLATES
EXTRAPOLATING
EXTRAPOLATION
EXTRAPOLATIONS
EXTRAPOLATIVE
EXTRAPOLATOR
EXTRAPOLATORS
EXTRAPOLATORY
EXTRAPOSE
EXTRAPOSED
EXTRAPOSES
EXTRAPOSING
EXTRAPOSITION
EXTRAPOSITIONS
EXTRAPYRAMIDAL
EXTRAS
EXTRASENSORY
EXTRASOLAR
EXTRASYSTOLE
EXTRASYSTOLES
EXTRATEXTUAL
EXTRATROPICAL

EXTRAUGHT
EXTRAUTERINE
EXTRAVAGANCE
EXTRAVAGANCES
EXTRAVAGANCIES
EXTRAVAGANCY
EXTRAVAGANT
EXTRAVAGANTLY
EXTRAVAGANZA
EXTRAVAGANZAS
EXTRAVAGATE
EXTRAVAGATED
EXTRAVAGATES
EXTRAVAGATING
EXTRAVAGATION
EXTRAVAGATIONS
EXTRAVASATE
EXTRAVASATED
EXTRAVASATES
EXTRAVASATING
EXTRAVASATION
EXTRAVASATIONS
EXTRAVASCULAR
EXTRAVEHICULAR
EXTRAVERSION
EXTRAVERSIONS
EXTRAVERSIVE
EXTRAVERSIVELY
EXTRAVERT
EXTRAVERTED
EXTRAVERTING
EXTRAVERTS
EXTREAT
EXTREATS
EXTREMA
EXTREMAL
EXTREMALS
EXTREME
EXTREMELY
EXTREMENESS
EXTREMENESSES
EXTREMER
EXTREMES
EXTREMEST
EXTREMISM
EXTREMISMS
EXTREMIST
EXTREMISTS
EXTREMITIES
EXTREMITY
EXTREMUM
EXTRICABLE
EXTRICATE
EXTRICATED
EXTRICATES
EXTRICATING

EXTRICATION
EXTRICATIONS
EXTRINSIC
EXTRINSICAL
EXTRINSICALITY
EXTRINSICALLY
EXTRORSAL
EXTRORSE
EXTROVERSION
EXTROVERSIONS
EXTROVERSIVE
EXTROVERSIVELY
EXTROVERT
EXTROVERTED
EXTROVERTING
EXTROVERTS
EXTRUDABILITIES
EXTRUDABILITY
EXTRUDABLE
EXTRUDE
EXTRUDED
EXTRUDER
EXTRUDERS
EXTRUDES
EXTRUDING
EXTRUSIBLE
EXTRUSION
EXTRUSIONS
EXTRUSIVE
EXTRUSORY
EXTUBATE
EXTUBATED
EXTUBATES
EXTUBATING
EXUBERANCE
EXUBERANCES
EXUBERANCIES
EXUBERANCY
EXUBERANT
EXUBERANTLY
EXUBERATE
EXUBERATED
EXUBERATES
EXUBERATING
EXUDATE
EXUDATES
EXUDATION
EXUDATIONS
EXUDATIVE
EXUDE
EXUDED
EXUDES
EXUDING
EXUL
EXULCERATE
EXULCERATED

EXULCERATES
EXULCERATING
EXULCERATION
EXULCERATIONS
EXULS
EXULT
EXULTANCE
EXULTANCES
EXULTANCIES
EXULTANCY
EXULTANT
EXULTANTLY
EXULTATION
EXULTATIONS
EXULTED
EXULTING
EXULTINGLY
EXULTS
EXURB
EXURBAN
EXURBANITE
EXURBANITES
EXURBIA
EXURBIAS
EXURBS
EXUVIA
EXUVIAE
EXUVIAL
EXUVIATE
EXUVIATED
EXUVIATES
EXUVIATING
EXUVIATION
EXUVIATIONS
EXUVIUM
EYALET
EYALETS
EYAS
EYASES
EYE
EYEABLE
EYEBALL
EYEBALLED
EYEBALLING
EYEBALLS
EYEBANK
EYEBANKS
EYEBAR
EYEBATH
EYEBATHS
EYEBEAM
EYEBEAMS
EYEBLACK
EYEBOLT
EYEBOLTS

EYEBRIGHT
EYEBRIGHTS
EYEBROW
EYEBROWED
EYEBROWING
EYEBROWLESS
EYEBROWS
EYECUP
EYECUPS
EYED
EYEDNESS
EYEDNESSES
EYEDROPPER
EYEDROPPERS
EYEDROPS
EYEFUL
EYEFULS
EYEGLASS
EYEGLASSES
EYEHOLE
EYEHOLES
EYEHOOK
EYEHOOKS
EYEING
EYELASH
EYELASHES
EYELESS
EYELET
EYELETED
EYELETEER
EYELETEERS
EYELETING
EYELETS
EYELETTED
EYELETTING
EYELEVEL
EYELIAD
EYELIADS
EYELID
EYELIDS
EYELIKE
EYELINER
EYELINERS
EYEN
EYEPIECE
EYEPIECES
EYEPOINT
EYEPOINTS
EYEPOPPER
EYEPOPPERS
EYER
EYERS
EYES
EYESHADE
EYESHADES
EYESHADOW

EYESHADOWS
EYESHOT
EYESHOTS
EYESIGHT
EYESIGHTS
EYESOME
EYESORE
EYESORES
EYESPOT
EYESPOTS
EYESTALK
EYESTALKS
EYESTONE
EYESTONES
EYESTRAIN
EYESTRAINS
EYESTRINGS
EYETEETH
EYETOOTH
EYEWASH
EYEWASHES
EYEWATER
EYEWATERS
EYEWEAR
EYEWINK
EYEWINKS
EYEWITNESS
EYEWITNESSES
EYING
EYLIAD
EYLIADS
EYNE
EYOT
EYOTS
EYRA
EYRAS
EYRE
EYRES
EYRIE
EYRIES
EYRIR
EYRY

F

FA
FAA
FAAED
FAAING
FAAS
FAB
FABACEOUS
FABBER
FABBEST
FABLE
FABLED
FABLER
FABLERS
FABLES
FABLIAU
FABLIAUX
FABLING
FABLINGS
FABRIC
FABRICANT
FABRICANTS
FABRICATE
FABRICATED
FABRICATES
FABRICATING
FABRICATION
FABRICATIONS
FABRICATIVE
FABRICATOR
FABRICATORS
FABRICKED
FABRICKING
FABRICS
FABULAR
FABULISE
FABULISED
FABULISES
FABULISING
FABULIST
FABULISTIC
FABULISTS
FABULIZE
FABULIZED
FABULIZES
FABULIZING
FABULOSITIES
FABULOSITY
FABULOUS
FABULOUSLY
FABULOUSNESS
FABULOUSNESSES

FABURDEN
FABURDENS
FACADE
FACADES
FACE
FACEABLE
FACEBAR
FACEBARS
FACECLOTH
FACECLOTHS
FACED
FACEDOWN
FACELESS
FACELESSNESS
FACELESSNESSES
FACEMAIL
FACEMAN
FACEMEN
FACEPLATE
FACEPLATES
FACEPRINT
FACEPRINTED
FACEPRINTING
FACEPRINTS
FACER
FACERS
FACES
FACET
FACETE
FACETED
FACETELY
FACETIAE
FACETING
FACETIOUS
FACETIOUSLY
FACETIOUSNESS
FACETIOUSNESSES
FACETS
FACETTED
FACETTING
FACEUP
FACEWORKER
FACEWORKERS
FACIA
FACIAE
FACIAL
FACIALLY
FACIALS
FACIAS
FACIEND
FACIENDS

FACIES
FACILE
FACILELY
FACILENESS
FACILENESSES
FACILITATE
FACILITATED
FACILITATES
FACILITATING
FACILITATION
FACILITATIONS
FACILITATIVE
FACILITATOR
FACILITATORS
FACILITATORY
FACILITIES
FACILITY
FACINERIOUS
FACING
FACINGS
FACINOROUS
FACINOROUSNESS
FACONNE
FACONNES
FACSIMILE
FACSIMILED
FACSIMILEING
FACSIMILES
FACSIMILIST
FACSIMILISTS
FACT
FACTFUL
FACTICE
FACTICES
FACTICITIES
FACTICITY
FACTION
FACTIONAL
FACTIONALISM
FACTIONALISMS
FACTIONALIST
FACTIONALISTS
FACTIONALLY
FACTIONARIES
FACTIONARY
FACTIONIST
FACTIONISTS
FACTIONS
FACTIOUS
FACTIOUSLY
FACTIOUSNESS

FACTIOUSNESSES
FACTIS
FACTISES
FACTITIOUS
FACTITIOUSLY
FACTITIOUSNESS
FACTITIVE
FACTITIVELY
FACTIVE
FACTOID
FACTOIDS
FACTOR
FACTORABILITIES
FACTORABILITY
FACTORABLE
FACTORAGE
FACTORAGES
FACTORED
FACTORIAL
FACTORIALLY
FACTORIALS
FACTORIES
FACTORING
FACTORINGS
FACTORISATION
FACTORISATIONS
FACTORISE
FACTORISED
FACTORISES
FACTORISING
FACTORIZATION
FACTORIZATIONS
FACTORIZE
FACTORIZED
FACTORIZES
FACTORIZING
FACTORS
FACTORSHIP
FACTORSHIPS
FACTORY
FACTORYLIKE
FACTOTUM
FACTOTUMS
FACTS
FACTSHEET
FACTSHEETS
FACTUAL
FACTUALISM
FACTUALISMS
FACTUALIST
FACTUALISTIC

357

FACTUALISTS
FACTUALITIES
FACTUALITY
FACTUALLY
FACTUALNESS
FACTUALNESSES
FACTUM
FACTUMS
FACTURE
FACTURES
FACULA
FACULAE
FACULAR
FACULTATIVE
FACULTATIVELY
FACULTIES
FACULTY
FACUNDITIES
FACUNDITY
FAD
FADABLE
FADAISE
FADAISES
FADDIER
FADDIEST
FADDINESS
FADDINESSES
FADDISH
FADDISHNESS
FADDISHNESSES
FADDISM
FADDISMS
FADDIST
FADDISTS
FADDLE
FADDLED
FADDLES
FADDLING
FADDY
FADE
FADEAWAY
FADEAWAYS
FADED
FADEDLY
FADEDNESS
FADEDNESSES
FADELESS
FADELESSLY
FADER
FADERS
FADES
FADEUR
FADEURS
FADGE
FADGED
FADGES

FADGING
FADIER
FADIEST
FADING
FADINGS
FADO
FADOMETER
FADOMETERS
FADOS
FADS
FADY
FAE
FAECAL
FAECES
FAENA
FAENAS
FAERIE
FAERIES
FAERY
FAFF
FAFFED
FAFFING
FAFFS
FAG
FAGACEOUS
FAGGED
FAGGERIES
FAGGERY
FAGGING
FAGGINGS
FAGGOT
FAGGOTED
FAGGOTING
FAGGOTINGS
FAGGOTRIES
FAGGOTRY
FAGGOTS
FAGGOTY
FAGGY
FAGIN
FAGINS
FAGOT
FAGOTED
FAGOTER
FAGOTERS
FAGOTING
FAGOTINGS
FAGOTS
FAGOTTI
FAGOTTIST
FAGOTTISTS
FAGOTTO
FAGS
FAH
FAHLBAND
FAHLBANDS

FAHLERZ
FAHLERZES
FAHLORE
FAHLORES
FAHS
FAIBLE
FAIBLES
FAIENCE
FAIENCES
FAIK
FAIKED
FAIKES
FAIKING
FAIKS
FAIL
FAILED
FAILING
FAILINGLY
FAILINGS
FAILLE
FAILLES
FAILS
FAILURE
FAILURES
FAIN
FAINE
FAINEANCE
FAINEANCES
FAINEANCIES
FAINEANCY
FAINEANT
FAINEANTISE
FAINEANTISES
FAINEANTS
FAINED
FAINER
FAINES
FAINEST
FAINING
FAINITES
FAINLY
FAINNE
FAINNES
FAINNESS
FAINNESSES
FAINS
FAINT
FAINTED
FAINTER
FAINTERS
FAINTEST
FAINTHEARTED
FAINTHEARTEDLY
FAINTIER
FAINTIEST
FAINTING

FAINTINGLY
FAINTINGS
FAINTISH
FAINTISHNESS
FAINTISHNESSES
FAINTLY
FAINTNESS
FAINTNESSES
FAINTS
FAINTY
FAIR
FAIRED
FAIRER
FAIREST
FAIRFACED
FAIRGROUND
FAIRGROUNDS
FAIRIES
FAIRILY
FAIRING
FAIRINGS
FAIRISH
FAIRISHLY
FAIRLEAD
FAIRLEADER
FAIRLEADERS
FAIRLEADS
FAIRLY
FAIRNESS
FAIRNESSES
FAIRNITICKLES
FAIRNITICLES
FAIRNYTICKLES
FAIRNYTICLES
FAIRS
FAIRWAY
FAIRWAYS
FAIRY
FAIRYDOM
FAIRYDOMS
FAIRYFLOSS
FAIRYFLOSSES
FAIRYHOOD
FAIRYHOODS
FAIRYISM
FAIRYISMS
FAIRYLAND
FAIRYLANDS
FAIRYLIKE
FAIRYTALE
FAIRYTALES
FAITH
FAITHCURE
FAITHCURES
FAITHED
FAITHER

FAITHERS
FAITHFUL
FAITHFULLY
FAITHFULNESS
FAITHFULNESSES
FAITHFULS
FAITHING
FAITHLESS
FAITHLESSLY
FAITHLESSNESS
FAITHLESSNESSES
FAITHS
FAITHWORTHINESS
FAITHWORTHY
FAITOR
FAITORS
FAITOUR
FAITOURS
FAIX
FAJITA
FAJITAS
FAKE
FAKED
FAKEER
FAKEERS
FAKEMENT
FAKEMENTS
FAKER
FAKERIES
FAKERS
FAKERY
FAKES
FAKEY
FAKING
FAKIR
FAKIRISM
FAKIRISMS
FAKIRS
FALAFEL
FALAFELS
FALAJ
FALANGISM
FALANGISMS
FALANGIST
FALANGISTS
FALBALA
FALBALAS
FALCADE
FALCADES
FALCATE
FALCATED
FALCATION
FALCATIONS
FALCES
FALCHION
FALCHIONS

FALCIFORM
FALCON
FALCONER
FALCONERS
FALCONET
FALCONETS
FALCONIFORM
FALCONIFORMS
FALCONINE
FALCONRIES
FALCONRY
FALCONS
FALCULA
FALCULAE
FALCULAS
FALCULATE
FALDAGE
FALDAGES
FALDERAL
FALDERALS
FALDEROL
FALDEROLS
FALDETTA
FALDETTAS
FALDISTORIES
FALDISTORY
FALDSTOOL
FALDSTOOLS
FALL
FALLACIES
FALLACIOUS
FALLACIOUSLY
FALLACIOUSNESS
FALLACY
FALLAL
FALLALERIES
FALLALERY
FALLALS
FALLAWAY
FALLAWAYS
FALLBACK
FALLBACKS
FALLEN
FALLER
FALLERS
FALLFISH
FALLFISHES
FALLIBILISM
FALLIBILISMS
FALLIBILIST
FALLIBILISTS
FALLIBILITIES
FALLIBILITY
FALLIBLE
FALLIBLENESS
FALLIBLY

FALLING
FALLINGS
FALLOFF
FALLOFFS
FALLOUT
FALLOUTS
FALLOW
FALLOWED
FALLOWER
FALLOWEST
FALLOWING
FALLOWNESS
FALLOWNESSES
FALLOWS
FALLS
FALSE
FALSED
FALSEHOOD
FALSEHOODS
FALSELY
FALSENESS
FALSENESSES
FALSER
FALSERS
FALSES
FALSEST
FALSETTO
FALSETTOS
FALSEWORK
FALSEWORKS
FALSIDICAL
FALSIE
FALSIES
FALSIFIABILITY
FALSIFIABLE
FALSIFICATION
FALSIFICATIONS
FALSIFIED
FALSIFIER
FALSIFIERS
FALSIFIES
FALSIFY
FALSIFYING
FALSING
FALSISH
FALSISM
FALSISMS
FALSITIES
FALSITY
FALTBOAT
FALTBOATS
FALTER
FALTERED
FALTERER
FALTERERS
FALTERING

FALTERINGLY
FALTERINGS
FALTERS
FALX
FAME
FAMED
FAMELESS
FAMES
FAMILIAL
FAMILIAR
FAMILIARISATION
FAMILIARISE
FAMILIARISED
FAMILIARISER
FAMILIARISERS
FAMILIARISES
FAMILIARISING
FAMILIARITIES
FAMILIARITY
FAMILIARIZATION
FAMILIARIZE
FAMILIARIZED
FAMILIARIZER
FAMILIARIZERS
FAMILIARIZES
FAMILIARIZING
FAMILIARLY
FAMILIARNESS
FAMILIARNESSES
FAMILIARS
FAMILIES
FAMILISM
FAMILISMS
FAMILISTIC
FAMILLE
FAMILY
FAMINE
FAMINES
FAMING
FAMISH
FAMISHED
FAMISHES
FAMISHING
FAMISHMENT
FAMISHMENTS
FAMOUS
FAMOUSED
FAMOUSES
FAMOUSING
FAMOUSLY
FAMOUSNESS
FAMOUSNESSES
FAMULI
FAMULUS
FAMULUSES
FAN

FANAL
FANALS
FANATIC
FANATICAL
FANATICALLY
FANATICALNESS
FANATICALNESSES
FANATICISE
FANATICISED
FANATICISES
FANATICISING
FANATICISM
FANATICISMS
FANATICIZE
FANATICIZED
FANATICIZES
FANATICIZING
FANATICS
FANBASE
FANBASES
FANCIABLE
FANCIED
FANCIER
FANCIERS
FANCIES
FANCIEST
FANCIFIED
FANCIFIES
FANCIFUL
FANCIFULLY
FANCIFULNESS
FANCIFULNESSES
FANCIFY
FANCIFYING
FANCILESS
FANCILY
FANCINESS
FANCINESSES
FANCY
FANCYING
FANCYWORK
FANCYWORKS
FAND
FANDANGLE
FANDANGLES
FANDANGO
FANDANGOES
FANDANGOS
FANDED
FANDING
FANDOM
FANDOMS
FANDS
FANE
FANEGA
FANEGADA

FANEGADAS
FANEGAS
FANES
FANFARADE
FANFARADES
FANFARE
FANFARED
FANFARES
FANFARING
FANFARON
FANFARONA
FANFARONADE
FANFARONADED
FANFARONADES
FANFARONADING
FANFARONAS
FANFARONS
FANFOLD
FANFOLDED
FANFOLDING
FANFOLDS
FANG
FANGA
FANGAS
FANGED
FANGING
FANGLE
FANGLED
FANGLES
FANGLESS
FANGLIKE
FANGLING
FANGO
FANGOS
FANGS
FANION
FANIONS
FANJET
FANJETS
FANK
FANKLE
FANKLED
FANKLES
FANKLING
FANKS
FANLIGHT
FANLIGHTS
FANLIKE
FANNED
FANNEL
FANNELL
FANNELLS
FANNELS
FANNER
FANNERS
FANNIES

FANNING
FANNINGS
FANNY
FANO
FANON
FANONS
FANOS
FANS
FANTABULOUS
FANTAD
FANTADS
FANTAIL
FANTAILED
FANTAILS
FANTASIA
FANTASIAS
FANTASIE
FANTASIED
FANTASIES
FANTASISE
FANTASISED
FANTASISES
FANTASISING
FANTASIST
FANTASISTS
FANTASIZE
FANTASIZED
FANTASIZER
FANTASIZERS
FANTASIZES
FANTASIZING
FANTASM
FANTASMAL
FANTASMALLY
FANTASMIC
FANTASMICALLY
FANTASMS
FANTASQUE
FANTASQUES
FANTAST
FANTASTIC
FANTASTICAL
FANTASTICALITY
FANTASTICALLY
FANTASTICALNESS
FANTASTICALS
FANTASTICATE
FANTASTICATED
FANTASTICATES
FANTASTICATING
FANTASTICATION
FANTASTICATIONS
FANTASTICISM
FANTASTICISMS
FANTASTICO
FANTASTICOES

FANTASTICS
FANTASTRIES
FANTASTRY
FANTASTS
FANTASY
FANTASYING
FANTASYLAND
FANTASYLANDS
FANTEEG
FANTEEGS
FANTIGUE
FANTIGUES
FANTOCCINI
FANTOD
FANTODS
FANTOM
FANTOMS
FANTOOSH
FANUM
FANUMS
FANWISE
FANWORT
FANWORTS
FANZINE
FANZINES
FAP
FAQIR
FAQIRS
FAQUIR
FAQUIRS
FAR
FARAD
FARADAIC
FARADAY
FARADAYS
FARADIC
FARADISATION
FARADISATIONS
FARADISE
FARADISED
FARADISER
FARADISERS
FARADISES
FARADISING
FARADISM
FARADISMS
FARADIZATION
FARADIZATIONS
FARADIZE
FARADIZED
FARADIZER
FARADIZERS
FARADIZES
FARADIZING
FARADS
FARAND

FARANDINE
FARANDINES
FARANDOLE
FARANDOLES
FARAWAY
FARAWAYNESS
FARAWAYNESSES
FARAWAYS
FARBOROUGH
FARBOROUGHS
FARCE
FARCED
FARCEMEAT
FARCEMEATS
FARCER
FARCERS
FARCES
FARCEUR
FARCEURS
FARCEUSE
FARCEUSES
FARCI
FARCICAL
FARCICALITIES
FARCICALITY
FARCICALLY
FARCICALNESS
FARCIE
FARCIED
FARCIES
FARCIFIED
FARCIFIES
FARCIFY
FARCIFYING
FARCIN
FARCING
FARCINGS
FARCINS
FARCY
FARD
FARDAGE
FARDAGES
FARDED
FARDEL
FARDELS
FARDEN
FARDENS
FARDING
FARDINGS
FARDS
FARE
FARED
FARER
FARERS
FARES
FAREWELL

FAREWELLED
FAREWELLING
FAREWELLS
FARFAL
FARFALS
FARFEL
FARFELS
FARFET
FARFETCHEDNESS
FARINA
FARINACEOUS
FARINAS
FARING
FARINHA
FARINHAS
FARINOSE
FARINOSELY
FARKLEBERRIES
FARKLEBERRY
FARL
FARLE
FARLES
FARLS
FARM
FARMABLE
FARMED
FARMER
FARMERESS
FARMERESSES
FARMERETTE
FARMERETTES
FARMERIES
FARMERS
FARMERY
FARMHAND
FARMHANDS
FARMHOUSE
FARMHOUSES
FARMING
FARMINGS
FARMLAND
FARMLANDS
FARMOST
FARMS
FARMSTEAD
FARMSTEADS
FARMWIFE
FARMWIVES
FARMWORK
FARMWORKER
FARMWORKERS
FARMWORKS
FARMYARD
FARMYARDS
FARNARKEL
FARNARKELS

FARNARKELED
FARNARKELING
FARNESOL
FARNESOLS
FARNESS
FARNESSES
FARO
FAROS
FAROUCHE
FARRAGINOUS
FARRAGO
FARRAGOES
FARRAGOS
FARRAND
FARRANDINE
FARRANDINES
FARRANT
FARRED
FARREN
FARRENS
FARRIER
FARRIERIES
FARRIERS
FARRIERY
FARRING
FARROW
FARROWED
FARROWING
FARROWS
FARRUCA
FARRUCAS
FARS
FARSE
FARSED
FARSEEING
FARSES
FARSIDE
FARSIDES
FARSIGHTED
FARSIGHTEDLY
FARSIGHTEDNESS
FARSING
FART
FARTED
FARTHEL
FARTHELS
FARTHER
FARTHERMORE
FARTHERMOST
FARTHEST
FARTHING
FARTHINGALE
FARTHINGALES
FARTHINGLAND
FARTHINGLANDS
FARTHINGLESS

FARTHINGS
FARTHINGSWORTH
FARTHINGSWORTHS
FARTING
FARTLEK
FARTLEKS
FARTS
FAS
FASCES
FASCI
FASCIA
FASCIAE
FASCIAL
FASCIAS
FASCIATE
FASCIATED
FASCIATELY
FASCIATION
FASCIATIONS
FASCICLE
FASCICLED
FASCICLES
FASCICULAR
FASCICULARLY
FASCICULATE
FASCICULATED
FASCICULATELY
FASCICULATION
FASCICULATIONS
FASCICULE
FASCICULES
FASCICULI
FASCICULUS
FASCIITIS
FASCINATE
FASCINATED
FASCINATEDLY
FASCINATES
FASCINATING
FASCINATINGLY
FASCINATION
FASCINATIONS
FASCINATIVE
FASCINATOR
FASCINATORS
FASCINE
FASCINES
FASCIO
FASCIOLA
FASCIOLAS
FASCIOLE
FASCIOLES
FASCIOLIASES
FASCIOLIASIS
FASCIS
FASCISM

FASCISMI
FASCISMO
FASCISMS
FASCIST
FASCISTA
FASCISTI
FASCISTIC
FASCISTICALLY
FASCISTS
FASH
FASHED
FASHERIES
FASHERY
FASHES
FASHING
FASHION
FASHIONABILITY
FASHIONABLE
FASHIONABLENESS
FASHIONABLES
FASHIONABLY
FASHIONED
FASHIONER
FASHIONERS
FASHIONING
FASHIONIST
FASHIONISTA
FASHIONISTAS
FASHIONISTS
FASHIONMONGER
FASHIONMONGERS
FASHIONMONGING
FASHIONS
FASHIONY
FASHIOUS
FASHIOUSNESS
FASHIOUSNESSES
FAST
FASTBACK
FASTBACKS
FASTBALL
FASTBALLER
FASTBALLERS
FASTBALLS
FASTED
FASTEN
FASTENED
FASTENER
FASTENERS
FASTENING
FASTENINGS
FASTENS
FASTER
FASTERS
FASTEST
FASTI

FASTIDIOUS
FASTIDIOUSLY
FASTIDIOUSNESS
FASTIE
FASTIES
FASTIGIATE
FASTIGIATED
FASTIGIUM
FASTIGIUMS
FASTING
FASTINGS
FASTISH
FASTLY
FASTNESS
FASTNESSES
FASTS
FASTUOUS
FAT
FATAL
FATALISM
FATALISMS
FATALIST
FATALISTIC
FATALISTICALLY
FATALISTS
FATALITIES
FATALITY
FATALLY
FATBACK
FATBACKS
FATBIRD
FATBIRDS
FATBRAINED
FATE
FATED
FATEFUL
FATEFULLY
FATEFULNESS
FATEFULNESSES
FATES
FATHEAD
FATHEADED
FATHEADEDLY
FATHEADEDNESS
FATHEADEDNESSES
FATHEADS
FATHER
FATHERED
FATHERHOOD
FATHERHOODS
FATHERING
FATHERLAND
FATHERLANDS
FATHERLESS
FATHERLESSNESS
FATHERLIKE

FATHERLINESS
FATHERLINESSES
FATHERLY
FATHERS
FATHERSHIP
FATHERSHIPS
FATHOM
FATHOMABLE
FATHOMED
FATHOMER
FATHOMERS
FATHOMETER
FATHOMETERS
FATHOMING
FATHOMLESS
FATHOMLESSLY
FATHOMLESSNESS
FATHOMS
FATIDIC
FATIDICAL
FATIDICALLY
FATIGABILITIES
FATIGABILITY
FATIGABLE
FATIGABLENESS
FATIGABLENESSES
FATIGATE
FATIGATED
FATIGATES
FATIGATING
FATIGUABLE
FATIGUABLENESS
FATIGUE
FATIGUED
FATIGUELESS
FATIGUES
FATIGUING
FATIGUINGLY
FATING
FATISCENCE
FATISCENCES
FATISCENT
FATLESS
FATLIKE
FATLING
FATLINGS
FATLY
FATNESS
FATNESSES
FATS
FATSHEDERA
FATSHEDERAS
FATSIA
FATSIAS
FATSO
FATSOES

FATSOS
FATSTOCK
FATSTOCKS
FATTED
FATTEN
FATTENABLE
FATTENED
FATTENER
FATTENERS
FATTENING
FATTENINGS
FATTENS
FATTER
FATTEST
FATTIER
FATTIES
FATTIEST
FATTILY
FATTINESS
FATTINESSES
FATTING
FATTISH
FATTISM
FATTISMS
FATTIST
FATTISTS
FATTRELS
FATTY
FATUITIES
FATUITOUS
FATUITY
FATUOUS
FATUOUSLY
FATUOUSNESS
FATUOUSNESSES
FATWA
FATWAED
FATWAH
FATWAHED
FATWAHING
FATWAHS
FATWAING
FATWAS
FATWOOD
FATWOODS
FAUBOURG
FAUBOURGS
FAUCAL
FAUCALS
FAUCES
FAUCET
FAUCETS
FAUCHION
FAUCHIONS
FAUCHON
FAUCHONS

FAUCIAL
FAUGH
FAULCHINS
FAULCHION
FAULCHIONS
FAULD
FAULDS
FAULT
FAULTED
FAULTFINDER
FAULTFINDERS
FAULTFINDING
FAULTFINDINGS
FAULTFUL
FAULTIER
FAULTIEST
FAULTILY
FAULTINESS
FAULTINESSES
FAULTING
FAULTLESS
FAULTLESSLY
FAULTLESSNESS
FAULTLESSNESSES
FAULTS
FAULTY
FAUN
FAUNA
FAUNAE
FAUNAL
FAUNALLY
FAUNAS
FAUNIST
FAUNISTIC
FAUNISTICALLY
FAUNISTS
FAUNLIKE
FAUNS
FAUNULA
FAUNULAE
FAUNULE
FAUNULES
FAUR
FAURD
FAURER
FAUREST
FAUSTIAN
FAUT
FAUTED
FAUTEUIL
FAUTEUILS
FAUTING
FAUTOR
FAUTORS
FAUTS
FAUVE

FAUVES
FAUVETTE
FAUVETTES
FAUVISM
FAUVISMS
FAUVIST
FAUVISTS
FAUX
FAUXBOURDON
FAUXBOURDONS
FAVA
FAVAS
FAVE
FAVEL
FAVELA
FAVELAS
FAVELL
FAVELLA
FAVELLAS
FAVEOLATE
FAVER
FAVES
FAVEST
FAVISM
FAVISMS
FAVONIAN
FAVOR
FAVORABLE
FAVORABLENESS
FAVORABLENESSES
FAVORABLY
FAVORED
FAVOREDNESS
FAVOREDNESSES
FAVORER
FAVORERS
FAVORING
FAVORINGLY
FAVORITE
FAVORITES
FAVORITISM
FAVORITISMS
FAVORLESS
FAVORS
FAVOSE
FAVOUR
FAVOURABLE
FAVOURABLENESS
FAVOURABLY
FAVOURED
FAVOUREDNESS
FAVOUREDNESSES
FAVOURER
FAVOURERS
FAVOURING
FAVOURINGLY

FAVOURITE
FAVOURITES
FAVOURITISM
FAVOURITISMS
FAVOURLESS
FAVOURS
FAVOUS
FAVRILE
FAVRILES
FAVUS
FAVUSES
FAW
FAWN
FAWNED
FAWNER
FAWNERS
FAWNIER
FAWNIEST
FAWNING
FAWNINGLY
FAWNINGNESS
FAWNINGNESSES
FAWNINGS
FAWNLIKE
FAWNS
FAWNY
FAWS
FAX
FAXED
FAXES
FAXING
FAY
FAYALITE
FAYALITES
FAYED
FAYENCE
FAYENCES
FAYER
FAYEST
FAYING
FAYNE
FAYNED
FAYNES
FAYNING
FAYRE
FAYRES
FAYS
FAZE
FAZED
FAZENDA
FAZENDAS
FAZENDEIRO
FAZENDEIROS
FAZES
FAZING
FEAGUE

FEAGUED
FEAGUES
FEAGUING
FEAL
FEALED
FEALING
FEALS
FEALTIES
FEALTY
FEAR
FEARE
FEARED
FEARER
FEARERS
FEARES
FEARFUL
FEARFULLER
FEARFULLEST
FEARFULLY
FEARFULNESS
FEARFULNESSES
FEARING
FEARLESS
FEARLESSLY
FEARLESSNESS
FEARLESSNESSES
FEARNAUGHT
FEARNAUGHTS
FEARNOUGHT
FEARNOUGHTS
FEARS
FEARSOME
FEARSOMELY
FEARSOMENESS
FEARSOMENESSES
FEASANCE
FEASANCES
FEASE
FEASED
FEASES
FEASIBILITIES
FEASIBILITY
FEASIBLE
FEASIBLENESS
FEASIBLENESSES
FEASIBLY
FEASING
FEAST
FEASTED
FEASTER
FEASTERS
FEASTFUL
FEASTING
FEASTINGS
FEASTS
FEAT

FEATED
FEATEOUS
FEATEOUSLY
FEATER
FEATEST
FEATHER
FEATHERBED
FEATHERBEDDED
FEATHERBEDDING
FEATHERBEDDINGS
FEATHERBEDS
FEATHERBRAIN
FEATHERBRAINED
FEATHERBRAINS
FEATHERED
FEATHEREDGE
FEATHEREDGED
FEATHEREDGES
FEATHEREDGING
FEATHERHEAD
FEATHERHEADED
FEATHERHEADS
FEATHERIER
FEATHERIEST
FEATHERINESS
FEATHERINESSES
FEATHERING
FEATHERINGS
FEATHERLESS
FEATHERLIGHT
FEATHERS
FEATHERSTITCH
FEATHERSTITCHED
FEATHERSTITCHES
FEATHERWEIGHT
FEATHERWEIGHTS
FEATHERY
FEATING
FEATLIER
FEATLIEST
FEATLINESS
FEATLY
FEATOUS
FEATS
FEATUOUS
FEATURE
FEATURED
FEATURELESS
FEATURELESSNESS
FEATURELY
FEATURES
FEATURETTE
FEATURETTES
FEATURING
FEAZE
FEAZED

FEAZES
FEAZING
FEBLESSE
FEBLESSES
FEBRI
FEBRICITIES
FEBRICITY
FEBRICULA
FEBRICULAS
FEBRICULE
FEBRICULES
FEBRIFACIENT
FEBRIFACIENTS
FEBRIFEROUS
FEBRIFIC
FEBRIFUGAL
FEBRIFUGE
FEBRIFUGES
FEBRILE
FEBRILITIES
FEBRILITY
FECAL
FECES
FECHT
FECHTER
FECHTERS
FECHTING
FECHTS
FECIAL
FECIALS
FECIT
FECK
FECKLESS
FECKLESSLY
FECKLESSNESS
FECKLESSNESSES
FECKLY
FECKS
FECULA
FECULAE
FECULAS
FECULENCE
FECULENCES
FECULENCIES
FECULENCY
FECULENT
FECUND
FECUNDATE
FECUNDATED
FECUNDATES
FECUNDATING
FECUNDATION
FECUNDATIONS
FECUNDATOR
FECUNDATORS
FECUNDATORY

FECUNDITIES
FECUNDITY
FED
FEDARIE
FEDARIES
FEDAYEE
FEDAYEEN
FEDELINI
FEDELINIS
FEDERACIES
FEDERACY
FEDERAL
FEDERALESE
FEDERALESES
FEDERALISATION
FEDERALISATIONS
FEDERALISE
FEDERALISED
FEDERALISES
FEDERALISING
FEDERALISM
FEDERALISMS
FEDERALIST
FEDERALISTIC
FEDERALISTS
FEDERALIZATION
FEDERALIZATIONS
FEDERALIZE
FEDERALIZED
FEDERALIZES
FEDERALIZING
FEDERALLY
FEDERALS
FEDERARIE
FEDERARIES
FEDERARY
FEDERATE
FEDERATED
FEDERATES
FEDERATING
FEDERATION
FEDERATIONS
FEDERATIVE
FEDERATIVELY
FEDORA
FEDORAS
FEDS
FEE
FEEBLE
FEEBLED
FEEBLEMINDED
FEEBLEMINDEDLY
FEEBLENESS
FEEBLENESSES
FEEBLER
FEEBLES

FEEBLEST
FEEBLING
FEEBLISH
FEEBLY
FEED
FEEDABLE
FEEDBACK
FEEDBACKS
FEEDBAG
FEEDBAGS
FEEDBOX
FEEDBOXES
FEEDER
FEEDERS
FEEDHOLE
FEEDHOLES
FEEDING
FEEDINGS
FEEDINGSTUFF
FEEDLOT
FEEDLOTS
FEEDS
FEEDSTOCK
FEEDSTOCKS
FEEDSTUFF
FEEDSTUFFS
FEEDTHROUGH
FEEDTHROUGHS
FEEDWATER
FEEING
FEEL
FEELBAD
FEELBADS
FEELER
FEELERS
FEELESS
FEELGOOD
FEELGOODS
FEELING
FEELINGLESS
FEELINGLY
FEELINGNESS
FEELINGNESSES
FEELINGS
FEELS
FEER
FEERED
FEERIE
FEERIES
FEERIN
FEERING
FEERINGS
FEERINS
FEERS
FEES
FEESE

FEESED	FELDSHER	FELLER	FELT
FEESES	FELDSHERS	FELLERS	FELTED
FEESING	FELDSPAR	FELLEST	FELTER
FEET	FELDSPARS	FELLIES	FELTERED
FEETFIRST	FELDSPATH	FELLING	FELTERING
FEETLESS	FELDSPATHIC	FELLMONGER	FELTERS
FEEZE	FELDSPATHOID	FELLMONGERED	FELTIER
FEEZED	FELDSPATHOIDS	FELLMONGERIES	FELTIEST
FEEZES	FELDSPATHOSE	FELLMONGERING	FELTING
FEEZING	FELDSPATHS	FELLMONGERINGS	FELTINGS
FEG	FELICIA	FELLMONGERS	FELTLIKE
FEGARIES	FELICIAS	FELLMONGERY	FELTS
FEGARY	FELICIFIC	FELLNESS	FELTY
FEGS	FELICITATE	FELLNESSES	FELUCCA
FEH	FELICITATED	FELLOE	FELUCCAS
FEHM	FELICITATES	FELLOES	FELWORT
FEHME	FELICITATING	FELLOW	FELWORTS
FEHMIC	FELICITATION	FELLOWED	FEM
FEHS	FELICITATIONS	FELLOWING	FEMAL
FEIGN	FELICITATOR	FELLOWLY	FEMALE
FEIGNED	FELICITATORS	FELLOWMAN	FEMALENESS
FEIGNEDLY	FELICITER	FELLOWMEN	FEMALENESSES
FEIGNEDNESS	FELICITIES	FELLOWS	FEMALES
FEIGNEDNESSES	FELICITOUS	FELLOWSHIP	FEMALITIES
FEIGNER	FELICITOUSLY	FELLOWSHIPED	FEMALITY
FEIGNERS	FELICITOUSNESS	FELLOWSHIPING	FEMALS
FEIGNING	FELICITY	FELLOWSHIPPED	FEME
FEIGNINGLY	FELID	FELLOWSHIPPING	FEMERALL
FEIGNINGS	FELIDS	FELLOWSHIPS	FEMERALLS
FEIGNS	FELINE	FELLS	FEMES
FEIJOA	FELINELY	FELLWALKER	FEMETARIES
FEIJOAS	FELINENESS	FELLWALKERS	FEMETARY
FEINT	FELINES	FELLY	FEMINACIES
FEINTED	FELINITIES	FELON	FEMINACY
FEINTER	FELINITY	FELONIES	FEMINAL
FEINTEST	FELL	FELONIOUS	FEMINALITIES
FEINTING	FELLA	FELONIOUSLY	FEMINALITY
FEINTS	FELLABLE	FELONIOUSNESS	FEMINEITIES
FEIRIE	FELLAH	FELONIOUSNESSES	FEMINEITY
FEIS	FELLAHEEN	FELONOUS	FEMINIE
FEISEANNA	FELLAHIN	FELONRIES	FEMINILITIES
FEIST	FELLAHS	FELONRY	FEMINILITY
FEISTIER	FELLAS	FELONS	FEMININE
FEISTIEST	FELLATE	FELONY	FEMININELY
FEISTINESS	FELLATED	FELSIC	FEMININENESS
FEISTINESSES	FELLATES	FELSITE	FEMININENESSES
FEISTS	FELLATING	FELSITES	FEMININES
FEISTY	FELLATIO	FELSITIC	FEMININISM
FELAFEL	FELLATION	FELSPAR	FEMININISMS
FELAFELS	FELLATIONS	FELSPARS	FEMININITIES
FELDGRAU	FELLATIOS	FELSPATHIC	FEMININITY
FELDGRAUS	FELLATOR	FELSPATHOID	FEMINISATION
FELDSCHAR	FELLATORS	FELSPATHOIDS	FEMINISATIONS
FELDSCHARS	FELLATRICES	FELSPATHOSE	FEMINISE
FELDSCHER	FELLATRIX	FELSTONE	FEMINISED
FELDSCHERS	FELLED	FELSTONES	FEMINISES

FEMINISING
FEMINISM
FEMINISMS
FEMINIST
FEMINISTIC
FEMINISTS
FEMINITIES
FEMINITY
FEMINIZATION
FEMINIZATIONS
FEMINIZE
FEMINIZED
FEMINIZES
FEMINIZING
FEMITER
FEMITERS
FEMME
FEMMES
FEMMIER
FEMMIEST
FEMMY
FEMORA
FEMORAL
FEMS
FEMTOSECOND
FEMTOSECONDS
FEMUR
FEMURS
FEN
FENAGLE
FENAGLED
FENAGLES
FENAGLING
FENCE
FENCED
FENCELESS
FENCELESSNESS
FENCELESSNESSES
FENCELIKE
FENCER
FENCEROW
FENCEROWS
FENCERS
FENCES
FENCIBLE
FENCIBLES
FENCING
FENCINGS
FEND
FENDED
FENDER
FENDERED
FENDERLESS
FENDERS
FENDIER
FENDIEST

FENDING
FENDS
FENDY
FENESTELLA
FENESTELLAE
FENESTELLAS
FENESTRA
FENESTRAE
FENESTRAL
FENESTRALS
FENESTRAS
FENESTRATE
FENESTRATED
FENESTRATION
FENESTRATIONS
FENI
FENIS
FENITAR
FENITARS
FENKS
FENLAND
FENLANDS
FENMAN
FENMEN
FENNEC
FENNECS
FENNEL
FENNELFLOWER
FENNELS
FENNIER
FENNIES
FENNIEST
FENNISH
FENNY
FENS
FENT
FENTANYL
FENTANYLS
FENTHION
FENTHIONS
FENTS
FENUGREEK
FENUGREEKS
FENURON
FENURONS
FEOD
FEODAL
FEODARIES
FEODARY
FEODS
FEOFF
FEOFFED
FEOFFEE
FEOFFEES
FEOFFER
FEOFFERS

FEOFFING
FEOFFMENT
FEOFFMENTS
FEOFFOR
FEOFFORS
FEOFFS
FER
FERACIOUS
FERACITIES
FERACITY
FERAL
FERALISED
FERALIZED
FERBAM
FERBAMS
FERE
FERER
FERES
FEREST
FERETORIES
FERETORY
FERIA
FERIAE
FERIAL
FERIAS
FERINE
FERITIES
FERITY
FERLIE
FERLIED
FERLIER
FERLIES
FERLIEST
FERLY
FERLYING
FERM
FERMATA
FERMATAS
FERMATE
FERMENT
FERMENTABILITY
FERMENTABLE
FERMENTATION
FERMENTATIONS
FERMENTATIVE
FERMENTATIVELY
FERMENTED
FERMENTER
FERMENTERS
FERMENTESCIBLE
FERMENTING
FERMENTITIOUS
FERMENTIVE
FERMENTOR
FERMENTORS
FERMENTS

FERMI
FERMION
FERMIONS
FERMIS
FERMIUM
FERMIUMS
FERMS
FERN
FERNBIRD
FERNBIRDS
FERNERIES
FERNERY
FERNIER
FERNIEST
FERNING
FERNINGS
FERNITICKLES
FERNITICLES
FERNLESS
FERNLIKE
FERNS
FERNSHAW
FERNSHAWS
FERNTICKLE
FERNTICKLED
FERNTICKLES
FERNTICLE
FERNTICLED
FERNTICLES
FERNY
FERNYTICKLES
FERNYTICLES
FEROCIOUS
FEROCIOUSLY
FEROCIOUSNESS
FEROCIOUSNESSES
FEROCITIES
FEROCITY
FERRANDINE
FERRANDINES
FERRATE
FERRATES
FERREDOXIN
FERREDOXINS
FERREL
FERRELED
FERRELING
FERRELLED
FERRELLING
FERRELS
FERREOUS
FERRET
FERRETED
FERRETER
FERRETERS
FERRETING

FERRETINGS
FERRETS
FERRETY
FERRIAGE
FERRIAGES
FERRIC
FERRICYANIC
FERRICYANIDE
FERRICYANIDES
FERRICYANOGEN
FERRICYANOGENS
FERRIED
FERRIES
FERRIFEROUS
FERRIMAGNET
FERRIMAGNETIC
FERRIMAGNETISM
FERRIMAGNETISMS
FERRIMAGNETS
FERRITE
FERRITES
FERRITIC
FERRITIN
FERRITINS
FERROCENE
FERROCENES
FERROCHROME
FERROCHROMIUM
FERROCONCRETE
FERROCONCRETES
FERROCYANIC
FERROCYANIDE
FERROCYANIDES
FERROCYANOGEN
FERROCYANOGENS
FERROELECTRIC
FERROELECTRICS
FERROGRAMS
FERROGRAPHIES
FERROGRAPHY
FERROMAGNESIAN
FERROMAGNET
FERROMAGNETIC
FERROMAGNETISM
FERROMAGNETISMS
FERROMAGNETS
FERROMANGANESE
FERROMANGANESES
FERROMOLYBDENUM
FERRONICKEL
FERRONIERE
FERRONIERES
FERRONNIERE
FERRONNIERES
FERROPRUSSIATE
FERROPRUSSIATES

FERROSILICON
FERROSILICONS
FERROSOFERRIC
FERROTYPE
FERROTYPES
FERROUS
FERRUGINEOUS
FERRUGINOUS
FERRUGO
FERRUGOS
FERRULE
FERRULED
FERRULES
FERRULING
FERRUM
FERRUMS
FERRY
FERRYBOAT
FERRYBOATS
FERRYING
FERRYMAN
FERRYMEN
FERTILE
FERTILELY
FERTILENESS
FERTILENESSES
FERTILER
FERTILEST
FERTILISABLE
FERTILISATION
FERTILISATIONS
FERTILISE
FERTILISED
FERTILISER
FERTILISERS
FERTILISES
FERTILISING
FERTILITIES
FERTILITY
FERTILIZABLE
FERTILIZATION
FERTILIZATIONS
FERTILIZE
FERTILIZED
FERTILIZER
FERTILIZERS
FERTILIZES
FERTILIZING
FERULA
FERULACEOUS
FERULAE
FERULAS
FERULE
FERULED
FERULES
FERULING

FERVENCIES
FERVENCY
FERVENT
FERVENTER
FERVENTEST
FERVENTLY
FERVENTNESS
FERVESCENT
FERVID
FERVIDER
FERVIDEST
FERVIDITIES
FERVIDITY
FERVIDLY
FERVIDNESS
FERVIDNESSES
FERVOR
FERVOROUS
FERVORS
FERVOUR
FERVOURS
FESCENNINE
FESCUE
FESCUES
FESS
FESSE
FESSED
FESSES
FESSING
FESSWISE
FEST
FESTA
FESTAL
FESTALLY
FESTALS
FESTAS
FESTER
FESTERED
FESTERING
FESTERS
FESTIER
FESTIEST
FESTILOGIES
FESTILOGY
FESTINATE
FESTINATED
FESTINATELY
FESTINATES
FESTINATING
FESTINATION
FESTINATIONS
FESTIVAL
FESTIVALGOER
FESTIVALGOERS
FESTIVALS
FESTIVE

FESTIVELY
FESTIVENESS
FESTIVENESSES
FESTIVITIES
FESTIVITY
FESTIVOUS
FESTOLOGIES
FESTOLOGY
FESTOON
FESTOONED
FESTOONERIES
FESTOONERY
FESTOONING
FESTOONS
FESTS
FESTSCHRIFT
FESTSCHRIFTEN
FESTSCHRIFTS
FESTY
FET
FETA
FETAL
FETAS
FETATION
FETATIONS
FETCH
FETCHED
FETCHER
FETCHERS
FETCHES
FETCHING
FETCHINGLY
FETE
FETED
FETERITA
FETERITAS
FETES
FETIAL
FETIALES
FETIALIS
FETIALS
FETICH
FETICHE
FETICHES
FETICHISE
FETICHISED
FETICHISES
FETICHISING
FETICHISM
FETICHISMS
FETICHIST
FETICHISTIC
FETICHISTS
FETICHIZE
FETICHIZED
FETICHIZES

FETICHIZING
FETICIDAL
FETICIDE
FETICIDES
FETID
FETIDER
FETIDEST
FETIDLY
FETIDNESS
FETIDNESSES
FETING
FETIPAROUS
FETISH
FETISHES
FETISHISE
FETISHISED
FETISHISES
FETISHISING
FETISHISM
FETISHISMS
FETISHIST
FETISHISTIC
FETISHISTICALLY
FETISHISTS
FETISHIZE
FETISHIZED
FETISHIZES
FETISHIZING
FETLOCK
FETLOCKED
FETLOCKS
FETOLOGIES
FETOLOGIST
FETOLOGISTS
FETOLOGY
FETOPROTEIN
FETOPROTEINS
FETOR
FETORS
FETOSCOPE
FETOSCOPES
FETOSCOPIES
FETOSCOPY
FETS
FETT
FETTA
FETTAS
FETTED
FETTER
FETTERED
FETTERER
FETTERERS
FETTERING
FETTERLESS
FETTERLOCK
FETTERLOCKS

FETTERS
FETTING
FETTLE
FETTLED
FETTLER
FETTLERS
FETTLES
FETTLING
FETTLINGS
FETTS
FETTUCCINE
FETTUCCINES
FETTUCCINI
FETTUCINE
FETTUCINES
FETTUCINI
FETTUCINIS
FETUS
FETUSES
FETWA
FETWAS
FEU
FEUAR
FEUARS
FEUD
FEUDAL
FEUDALISATION
FEUDALISATIONS
FEUDALISE
FEUDALISED
FEUDALISES
FEUDALISING
FEUDALISM
FEUDALISMS
FEUDALIST
FEUDALISTIC
FEUDALISTS
FEUDALITIES
FEUDALITY
FEUDALIZATION
FEUDALIZATIONS
FEUDALIZE
FEUDALIZED
FEUDALIZES
FEUDALIZING
FEUDALLY
FEUDARIES
FEUDARY
FEUDATORIES
FEUDATORY
FEUDED
FEUDING
FEUDINGS
FEUDIST
FEUDISTS
FEUDS

FEUED
FEUILLETE
FEUILLETES
FEUILLETON
FEUILLETONISM
FEUILLETONISMS
FEUILLETONIST
FEUILLETONISTIC
FEUILLETONISTS
FEUILLETONS
FEUING
FEUS
FEUTRE
FEUTRED
FEUTRES
FEUTRING
FEVER
FEVERED
FEVERFEW
FEVERFEWS
FEVERING
FEVERISH
FEVERISHLY
FEVERISHNESS
FEVERISHNESSES
FEVERLESS
FEVEROUS
FEVEROUSLY
FEVERS
FEVERWORT
FEVERWORTS
FEW
FEWER
FEWEST
FEWMET
FEWMETS
FEWNESS
FEWNESSES
FEWTER
FEWTERED
FEWTERING
FEWTERS
FEWTRILS
FEY
FEYED
FEYER
FEYEST
FEYING
FEYLY
FEYNESS
FEYNESSES
FEYS
FEZ
FEZES
FEZZED
FEZZES

FIACRE
FIACRES
FIANCAILLES
FIANCE
FIANCEE
FIANCEES
FIANCES
FIANCHETTI
FIANCHETTO
FIANCHETTOED
FIANCHETTOES
FIANCHETTOING
FIANCHETTOS
FIAR
FIARS
FIASCHI
FIASCO
FIASCOES
FIASCOS
FIAT
FIATED
FIATING
FIATS
FIAUNT
FIAUNTS
FIB
FIBBED
FIBBER
FIBBERIES
FIBBERS
FIBBERY
FIBBING
FIBER
FIBERBOARD
FIBERBOARDS
FIBERED
FIBERFILL
FIBERFILLS
FIBERGLASS
FIBERGLASSED
FIBERGLASSES
FIBERGLASSING
FIBERIZATION
FIBERIZATIONS
FIBERIZE
FIBERIZED
FIBERIZES
FIBERIZING
FIBERLESS
FIBERS
FIBERSCOPE
FIBERSCOPES
FIBRANNE
FIBRANNES
FIBRE
FIBREBOARD

FIBREBOARDS
FIBRED
FIBREFILL
FIBREFILLS
FIBREGLASS
FIBREGLASSES
FIBRELESS
FIBREOPTIC
FIBREOPTICALLY
FIBRES
FIBRESCOPE
FIBRESCOPES
FIBRIFORM
FIBRIL
FIBRILAR
FIBRILLA
FIBRILLAE
FIBRILLAR
FIBRILLARY
FIBRILLATE
FIBRILLATED
FIBRILLATES
FIBRILLATING
FIBRILLATION
FIBRILLATIONS
FIBRILLIFORM
FIBRILLIN
FIBRILLINS
FIBRILLOSE
FIBRILLOUS
FIBRILS
FIBRIN
FIBRINOGEN
FIBRINOGENESIS
FIBRINOGENIC
FIBRINOGENOUS
FIBRINOGENS
FIBRINOID
FIBRINOIDS
FIBRINOLYSES
FIBRINOLYSIN
FIBRINOLYSINS
FIBRINOLYSIS
FIBRINOLYTIC
FIBRINOPEPTIDE
FIBRINOPEPTIDES
FIBRINOUS
FIBRINS
FIBRO
FIBROBLAST
FIBROBLASTIC
FIBROBLASTS
FIBROCARTILAGE
FIBROCARTILAGES
FIBROCEMENT
FIBROCEMENTS

FIBROCYSTIC
FIBROCYTE
FIBROCYTES
FIBROID
FIBROIDS
FIBROIN
FIBROINS
FIBROLINE
FIBROLINES
FIBROLITE
FIBROLITES
FIBROMA
FIBROMAS
FIBROMATA
FIBROMATOUS
FIBROMYALGIA
FIBROMYALGIAS
FIBRONECTIN
FIBRONECTINS
FIBROS
FIBROSARCOMA
FIBROSARCOMAS
FIBROSARCOMATA
FIBROSE
FIBROSED
FIBROSES
FIBROSING
FIBROSIS
FIBROSITIS
FIBROSITISES
FIBROTIC
FIBROUS
FIBROUSLY
FIBROUSNESS
FIBROVASCULAR
FIBS
FIBSTER
FIBSTERS
FIBULA
FIBULAE
FIBULAR
FIBULAS
FICE
FICES
FICHE
FICHES
FICHU
FICHUS
FICIN
FICINS
FICKLE
FICKLED
FICKLENESS
FICKLENESSES
FICKLER
FICKLES

FICKLEST
FICKLING
FICKLY
FICO
FICOES
FICOS
FICTILE
FICTION
FICTIONAL
FICTIONALISE
FICTIONALISED
FICTIONALISES
FICTIONALISING
FICTIONALITIES
FICTIONALITY
FICTIONALIZE
FICTIONALIZED
FICTIONALIZES
FICTIONALIZING
FICTIONALLY
FICTIONEER
FICTIONEERING
FICTIONEERINGS
FICTIONEERS
FICTIONIST
FICTIONISTS
FICTIONIZATION
FICTIONIZATIONS
FICTIONIZE
FICTIONIZED
FICTIONIZES
FICTIONIZING
FICTIONS
FICTITIOUS
FICTITIOUSLY
FICTITIOUSNESS
FICTIVE
FICTIVELY
FICTIVENESS
FICTIVENESSES
FICTOR
FICTORS
FICUS
FICUSES
FID
FIDDIOUS
FIDDIOUSED
FIDDIOUSES
FIDDIOUSING
FIDDLE
FIDDLEBACK
FIDDLEBACKS
FIDDLED
FIDDLEDEDEE
FIDDLEDEDEES
FIDDLEDEEDEE

FIDDLEDEEDEES
FIDDLEHEAD
FIDDLEHEADS
FIDDLENECK
FIDDLENECKS
FIDDLER
FIDDLERS
FIDDLES
FIDDLESTICK
FIDDLESTICKS
FIDDLEWOOD
FIDDLEWOODS
FIDDLEY
FIDDLEYS
FIDDLIER
FIDDLIEST
FIDDLING
FIDDLY
FIDEICOMMISSA
FIDEICOMMISSARY
FIDEICOMMISSUM
FIDEISM
FIDEISMS
FIDEIST
FIDEISTIC
FIDEISTS
FIDELITIES
FIDELITY
FIDGE
FIDGED
FIDGES
FIDGET
FIDGETED
FIDGETER
FIDGETERS
FIDGETIER
FIDGETIEST
FIDGETINESS
FIDGETINESSES
FIDGETING
FIDGETINGLY
FIDGETS
FIDGETY
FIDGING
FIDIBUS
FIDIBUSES
FIDO
FIDOS
FIDS
FIDUCIAL
FIDUCIALLY
FIDUCIALS
FIDUCIARIES
FIDUCIARILY
FIDUCIARY
FIE

FIEF
FIEFDOM
FIEFDOMS
FIEFS
FIELD
FIELDBOOTS
FIELDCRAFT
FIELDED
FIELDER
FIELDERS
FIELDFARE
FIELDFARES
FIELDING
FIELDINGS
FIELDMICE
FIELDMOUSE
FIELDPIECE
FIELDPIECES
FIELDS
FIELDSMAN
FIELDSMEN
FIELDSTONE
FIELDSTONES
FIELDSTRIP
FIELDSTRIPPED
FIELDSTRIPPING
FIELDSTRIPS
FIELDVOLE
FIELDVOLES
FIELDWARD
FIELDWARDS
FIELDWORK
FIELDWORKER
FIELDWORKERS
FIELDWORKS
FIEND
FIENDISH
FIENDISHLY
FIENDISHNESS
FIENDISHNESSES
FIENDLIKE
FIENDS
FIENT
FIENTS
FIER
FIERCE
FIERCELY
FIERCENESS
FIERCENESSES
FIERCER
FIERCEST
FIERE
FIERES
FIERIER
FIERIEST
FIERILY

FIERINESS
FIERINESSES
FIERS
FIERY
FIEST
FIESTA
FIESTAS
FIFE
FIFED
FIFER
FIFERS
FIFES
FIFI
FIFING
FIFTEEN
FIFTEENER
FIFTEENERS
FIFTEENS
FIFTEENTH
FIFTEENTHLY
FIFTEENTHS
FIFTH
FIFTHLY
FIFTHS
FIFTIES
FIFTIETH
FIFTIETHS
FIFTY
FIFTYISH
FIG
FIGEATER
FIGEATERS
FIGGED
FIGGERIES
FIGGERY
FIGGING
FIGHT
FIGHTABLE
FIGHTBACK
FIGHTBACKS
FIGHTER
FIGHTERS
FIGHTING
FIGHTINGS
FIGHTS
FIGJAM
FIGJAMS
FIGMENT
FIGMENTS
FIGO
FIGOS
FIGS
FIGULINE
FIGULINES
FIGURABILITIES
FIGURABILITY

FIGURABLE
FIGURAL
FIGURANT
FIGURANTE
FIGURANTES
FIGURANTS
FIGURATE
FIGURATELY
FIGURATION
FIGURATIONS
FIGURATIVE
FIGURATIVELY
FIGURATIVENESS
FIGURE
FIGURED
FIGUREHEAD
FIGUREHEADS
FIGURELESS
FIGURER
FIGURERS
FIGURES
FIGUREWORK
FIGUREWORKS
FIGURINE
FIGURINES
FIGURING
FIGURIST
FIGURISTS
FIGWORT
FIGWORTS
FIKE
FIKED
FIKERIES
FIKERY
FIKES
FIKIER
FIKIEST
FIKING
FIKISH
FIKY
FIL
FILA
FILABEG
FILABEGS
FILACEOUS
FILACER
FILACERS
FILAGREE
FILAGREED
FILAGREEING
FILAGREES
FILAMENT
FILAMENTARY
FILAMENTOUS
FILAMENTS
FILANDER

FILANDERS
FILAR
FILAREE
FILAREES
FILARIA
FILARIAE
FILARIAL
FILARIAN
FILARIAS
FILARIASES
FILARIASIS
FILARIID
FILARIIDS
FILASSE
FILASSES
FILATORIES
FILATORY
FILATURE
FILATURES
FILAZER
FILAZERS
FILBERD
FILBERDS
FILBERT
FILBERTS
FILCH
FILCHED
FILCHER
FILCHERS
FILCHES
FILCHING
FILCHINGLY
FILCHINGS
FILE
FILEABLE
FILECARD
FILECARDS
FILED
FILEFISH
FILEFISHES
FILEMOT
FILEMOTS
FILENAME
FILENAMES
FILER
FILERS
FILES
FILET
FILETED
FILETING
FILETS
FILFOT
FILFOTS
FILIAL
FILIALLY
FILIALNESS

FILIATE
FILIATED
FILIATES
FILIATING
FILIATION
FILIATIONS
FILIBEG
FILIBEGS
FILIBUSTER
FILIBUSTERED
FILIBUSTERER
FILIBUSTERERS
FILIBUSTERING
FILIBUSTERINGS
FILIBUSTERISM
FILIBUSTERISMS
FILIBUSTEROUS
FILIBUSTERS
FILICIDAL
FILICIDALLY
FILICIDE
FILICIDES
FILICINEAN
FILIFORM
FILIGRAIN
FILIGRAINS
FILIGRANE
FILIGRANES
FILIGREE
FILIGREED
FILIGREEING
FILIGREES
FILING
FILINGS
FILIOPIETISTIC
FILIOQUE
FILIOQUES
FILIPENDULOUS
FILISTER
FILISTERS
FILL
FILLAGREE
FILLAGREED
FILLAGREEING
FILLAGREES
FILLE
FILLED
FILLER
FILLERS
FILLES
FILLESTER
FILLESTERS
FILLET
FILLETED
FILLETING
FILLETS

FILLIBEG
FILLIBEGS
FILLIES
FILLING
FILLINGS
FILLIP
FILLIPED
FILLIPEEN
FILLIPEENS
FILLIPING
FILLIPS
FILLISTER
FILLISTERS
FILLO
FILLOS
FILLS
FILLY
FILM
FILMABLE
FILMCARD
FILMCARDS
FILMDOM
FILMDOMS
FILMED
FILMER
FILMERS
FILMGOER
FILMGOERS
FILMIC
FILMICALLY
FILMIER
FILMIEST
FILMILY
FILMINESS
FILMINESSES
FILMING
FILMISH
FILMLAND
FILMLANDS
FILMMAKER
FILMMAKERS
FILMMAKING
FILMMAKINGS
FILMOGRAPHIES
FILMOGRAPHY
FILMS
FILMSET
FILMSETS
FILMSETTER
FILMSETTERS
FILMSETTING
FILMSETTINGS
FILMSTRIP
FILMSTRIPS
FILMY
FILO

FILOPLUME
FILOPLUMES
FILOPODIA
FILOPODIUM
FILOS
FILOSE
FILOSELLE
FILOSELLES
FILOVIRUS
FILOVIRUSES
FILS
FILTER
FILTERABILITIES
FILTERABILITY
FILTERABLE
FILTERABLENESS
FILTERED
FILTERER
FILTERERS
FILTERING
FILTERS
FILTH
FILTHIER
FILTHIEST
FILTHILY
FILTHINESS
FILTHINESSES
FILTHS
FILTHY
FILTRABILITIES
FILTRABILITY
FILTRABLE
FILTRATABLE
FILTRATE
FILTRATED
FILTRATES
FILTRATING
FILTRATION
FILTRATIONS
FILUM
FIMBLE
FIMBLES
FIMBRIA
FIMBRIAE
FIMBRIAL
FIMBRIATE
FIMBRIATED
FIMBRIATES
FIMBRIATING
FIMBRIATION
FIMBRIATIONS
FIMBRILATION
FIMBRILLATE
FIMICOLOUS
FIN
FINABLE

FINABLENESS
FINAGLE
FINAGLED
FINAGLER
FINAGLERS
FINAGLES
FINAGLING
FINAL
FINALE
FINALES
FINALIS
FINALISATION
FINALISATIONS
FINALISE
FINALISED
FINALISES
FINALISING
FINALISM
FINALISMS
FINALIST
FINALISTIC
FINALISTICALLY
FINALISTS
FINALITIES
FINALITY
FINALIZATION
FINALIZATIONS
FINALIZE
FINALIZED
FINALIZES
FINALIZING
FINALLY
FINALS
FINANCE
FINANCED
FINANCES
FINANCIAL
FINANCIALIST
FINANCIALISTS
FINANCIALLY
FINANCIER
FINANCIERED
FINANCIERING
FINANCIERS
FINANCING
FINANCINGS
FINBACK
FINBACKS
FINCH
FINCHED
FINCHES
FIND
FINDABLE
FINDER
FINDERS
FINDING

FINDINGS
FINDRAM
FINDRAMS
FINDS
FINE
FINEABLE
FINEABLENESS
FINED
FINEER
FINEERED
FINEERING
FINEERS
FINEISH
FINELESS
FINELY
FINENESS
FINENESSES
FINER
FINERIES
FINERS
FINERY
FINES
FINESPUN
FINESSE
FINESSED
FINESSER
FINESSERS
FINESSES
FINESSING
FINESSINGS
FINEST
FINFISH
FINFISHES
FINFOOT
FINFOOTS
FINGAN
FINGANS
FINGER
FINGERBOARD
FINGERBOARDS
FINGERBOWL
FINGERBOWLS
FINGERBREADTH
FINGERBREADTHS
FINGERED
FINGERER
FINGERERS
FINGERGLASS
FINGERGLASSES
FINGERGUARD
FINGERGUARDS
FINGERHOLD
FINGERHOLDS
FINGERHOLE
FINGERHOLES
FINGERING

FINGERINGS
FINGERLESS
FINGERLIKE
FINGERLING
FINGERLINGS
FINGERMARK
FINGERMARKS
FINGERNAIL
FINGERNAILS
FINGERPICK
FINGERPICKED
FINGERPICKING
FINGERPICKINGS
FINGERPICKS
FINGERPLATE
FINGERPLATES
FINGERPOST
FINGERPOSTS
FINGERPRINT
FINGERPRINTED
FINGERPRINTING
FINGERPRINTINGS
FINGERPRINTS
FINGERS
FINGERSTALL
FINGERSTALLS
FINGERTIP
FINGERTIPS
FINI
FINIAL
FINIALED
FINIALS
FINICAL
FINICALITIES
FINICALITY
FINICALLY
FINICALNESS
FINICALNESSES
FINICKETIER
FINICKETIEST
FINICKETY
FINICKIER
FINICKIEST
FINICKIN
FINICKINESS
FINICKINESSES
FINICKING
FINICKINGS
FINICKY
FINIKIN
FINIKING
FINING
FININGS
FINIS
FINISES
FINISH

FINISHED
FINISHER
FINISHERS
FINISHES
FINISHING
FINISHINGS
FINITE
FINITELY
FINITENESS
FINITENESSES
FINITES
FINITISM
FINITUDE
FINITUDES
FINJAN
FINJANS
FINK
FINKED
FINKING
FINKS
FINLESS
FINLIKE
FINMARK
FINMARKS
FINNAC
FINNACK
FINNACKS
FINNACS
FINNAN
FINNANS
FINNED
FINNER
FINNERS
FINNESKO
FINNICKIER
FINNICKIEST
FINNICKY
FINNIER
FINNIEST
FINNING
FINNMARK
FINNMARKS
FINNOCHIO
FINNOCHIOS
FINNOCK
FINNOCKS
FINNSKO
FINNY
FINO
FINOCCHIO
FINOCCHIOS
FINOCHIO
FINOCHIOS
FINOS
FINS
FINSKO

FIORD
FIORDS
FIORIN
FIORINS
FIORITURA
FIORITURE
FIPPENCE
FIPPENCES
FIPPLE
FIPPLES
FIQUE
FIQUES
FIR
FIRE
FIREABLE
FIREARM
FIREARMS
FIREBACK
FIREBACKS
FIREBALL
FIREBALLER
FIREBALLERS
FIREBALLING
FIREBALLS
FIREBASE
FIREBASES
FIREBIRD
FIREBIRDS
FIREBOAT
FIREBOATS
FIREBOMB
FIREBOMBED
FIREBOMBING
FIREBOMBS
FIREBOX
FIREBOXES
FIREBRAND
FIREBRANDS
FIREBRAT
FIREBRATS
FIREBREAK
FIREBREAKS
FIREBRICK
FIREBRICKS
FIREBUG
FIREBUGS
FIRECLAY
FIRECLAYS
FIRECRACKER
FIRECRACKERS
FIRECREST
FIRECRESTS
FIRED
FIREDAMP
FIREDAMPS
FIREDOG

FIREDOGS
FIREDRAGON
FIREDRAGONS
FIREDRAKE
FIREDRAKES
FIREFANG
FIREFANGED
FIREFANGING
FIREFANGS
FIREFIGHT
FIREFIGHTER
FIREFIGHTERS
FIREFIGHTING
FIREFIGHTS
FIREFLIES
FIREFLOAT
FIREFLOATS
FIREFLY
FIREGUARD
FIREGUARDS
FIREHALL
FIREHALLS
FIREHOUSE
FIREHOUSES
FIREINESS
FIRELESS
FIRELIGHT
FIRELIGHTER
FIRELIGHTERS
FIRELIGHTS
FIRELIT
FIRELOCK
FIRELOCKS
FIREMAN
FIREMANIC
FIREMARK
FIREMARKS
FIREMEN
FIREPAN
FIREPANS
FIREPINK
FIREPINKS
FIREPLACE
FIREPLACED
FIREPLACES
FIREPLUG
FIREPLUGS
FIREPOT
FIREPOTS
FIREPOWER
FIREPOWERS
FIREPROOF
FIREPROOFED
FIREPROOFING
FIREPROOFINGS
FIREPROOFS

FIRER
FIREROOM
FIREROOMS
FIRERS
FIRES
FIRESCREEN
FIRESCREENS
FIRESHIP
FIRESHIPS
FIRESIDE
FIRESIDES
FIRESTONE
FIRESTONES
FIRESTORM
FIRESTORMS
FIRETHORN
FIRETHORNS
FIRETRAP
FIRETRAPS
FIREWALL
FIREWALLS
FIREWARDEN
FIREWARDENS
FIREWATER
FIREWATERS
FIREWEED
FIREWEEDS
FIREWOMAN
FIREWOMEN
FIREWOOD
FIREWOODS
FIREWORK
FIREWORKS
FIREWORM
FIREWORMS
FIRING
FIRINGS
FIRK
FIRKED
FIRKIN
FIRKING
FIRKINS
FIRKS
FIRLOT
FIRLOTS
FIRM
FIRMAMENT
FIRMAMENTAL
FIRMAMENTS
FIRMAN
FIRMANS
FIRMED
FIRMER
FIRMERS
FIRMEST
FIRMING

FIRMLESS
FIRMLY
FIRMNESS
FIRMNESSES
FIRMS
FIRMWARE
FIRMWARES
FIRN
FIRNS
FIRRIER
FIRRIEST
FIRRING
FIRRINGS
FIRRY
FIRS
FIRST
FIRSTBORN
FIRSTBORNS
FIRSTFRUITS
FIRSTHAND
FIRSTLING
FIRSTLINGS
FIRSTLY
FIRSTS
FIRTH
FIRTHS
FISC
FISCAL
FISCALLY
FISCALS
FISCS
FISGIG
FISGIGS
FISH
FISHABILITIES
FISHABILITY
FISHABLE
FISHBALL
FISHBALLS
FISHBOLT
FISHBOLTS
FISHBONE
FISHBONES
FISHBOWL
FISHBOWLS
FISHBURGER
FISHBURGERS
FISHED
FISHER
FISHERFOLK
FISHERIES
FISHERMAN
FISHERMEN
FISHERS
FISHERWOMAN
FISHERWOMEN

FISHERY
FISHES
FISHEYE
FISHEYES
FISHFINGER
FISHFINGERS
FISHFUL
FISHGIG
FISHGIGS
FISHHOOK
FISHHOOKS
FISHIER
FISHIEST
FISHIFIED
FISHIFIES
FISHIFY
FISHIFYING
FISHILY
FISHINESS
FISHINESSES
FISHING
FISHINGS
FISHLESS
FISHLIKE
FISHLINE
FISHLINES
FISHMEAL
FISHMEALS
FISHMONGER
FISHMONGERS
FISHNET
FISHNETS
FISHPLATE
FISHPLATES
FISHPOLE
FISHPOLES
FISHPOND
FISHPONDS
FISHSKIN
FISHSKINS
FISHTAIL
FISHTAILED
FISHTAILING
FISHTAILS
FISHWAY
FISHWAYS
FISHWIFE
FISHWIVES
FISHWORM
FISHWORMS
FISHY
FISHYBACK
FISHYBACKS
FISK
FISKED
FISKING

FISKS
FISNOMIE
FISNOMIES
FISSATE
FISSICOSTATE
FISSILE
FISSILINGUAL
FISSILITIES
FISSILITY
FISSION
FISSIONABILITY
FISSIONABLE
FISSIONABLES
FISSIONAL
FISSIONED
FISSIONING
FISSIONS
FISSIPALMATE
FISSIPARISM
FISSIPARISMS
FISSIPARITIES
FISSIPARITY
FISSIPAROUS
FISSIPAROUSLY
FISSIPAROUSNESS
FISSIPED
FISSIPEDAL
FISSIPEDE
FISSIPEDES
FISSIPEDS
FISSIROSTRAL
FISSIVE
FISSLE
FISSLED
FISSLES
FISSLING
FISSURE
FISSURED
FISSURES
FISSURING
FIST
FISTED
FISTFIGHT
FISTFIGHTS
FISTFUL
FISTFULS
FISTIANA
FISTIC
FISTICAL
FISTICUFF
FISTICUFFS
FISTIER
FISTIEST
FISTING
FISTMELE
FISTMELES

FISTNOTE
FISTNOTES
FISTS
FISTULA
FISTULAE
FISTULAR
FISTULAS
FISTULATE
FISTULOSE
FISTULOUS
FISTY
FIT
FITCH
FITCHE
FITCHEE
FITCHES
FITCHET
FITCHETS
FITCHEW
FITCHEWS
FITCHY
FITFUL
FITFULLY
FITFULNESS
FITFULNESSES
FITLIER
FITLIEST
FITLY
FITMENT
FITMENTS
FITNESS
FITNESSES
FITS
FITT
FITTABLE
FITTE
FITTED
FITTER
FITTERS
FITTES
FITTEST
FITTING
FITTINGLY
FITTINGNESS
FITTINGNESSES
FITTINGS
FITTS
FIVE
FIVEFINGER
FIVEFINGERS
FIVEFOLD
FIVEPENCE
FIVEPENCES
FIVEPENNY
FIVEPIN
FIVEPINS

FIVER
FIVERS
FIVES
FIX
FIXABLE
FIXATE
FIXATED
FIXATES
FIXATIF
FIXATIFS
FIXATING
FIXATION
FIXATIONS
FIXATIVE
FIXATIVES
FIXATURE
FIXATURES
FIXED
FIXEDLY
FIXEDNESS
FIXEDNESSES
FIXER
FIXERS
FIXES
FIXING
FIXINGS
FIXIT
FIXITIES
FIXITY
FIXIVE
FIXT
FIXTURE
FIXTURELESS
FIXTURES
FIXURE
FIXURES
FIZ
FIZGIG
FIZGIGS
FIZZ
FIZZED
FIZZEN
FIZZENLESS
FIZZENS
FIZZER
FIZZERS
FIZZES
FIZZGIG
FIZZGIGS
FIZZIER
FIZZIEST
FIZZINESS
FIZZING
FIZZINGS
FIZZLE
FIZZLED

FIZZLES
FIZZLING
FIZZY
FJELD
FJELDS
FJORD
FJORDS
FLAB
FLABBERGAST
FLABBERGASTED
FLABBERGASTING
FLABBERGASTS
FLABBIER
FLABBIEST
FLABBILY
FLABBINESS
FLABBINESSES
FLABBY
FLABELLA
FLABELLATE
FLABELLATION
FLABELLATIONS
FLABELLIFORM
FLABELLUM
FLABELLUMS
FLABS
FLACCID
FLACCIDER
FLACCIDEST
FLACCIDITIES
FLACCIDITY
FLACCIDLY
FLACCIDNESS
FLACCIDNESSES
FLACK
FLACKED
FLACKER
FLACKERED
FLACKERIES
FLACKERING
FLACKERS
FLACKERY
FLACKET
FLACKETS
FLACKING
FLACKS
FLACON
FLACONS
FLAFF
FLAFFED
FLAFFER
FLAFFERED
FLAFFERING
FLAFFERS
FLAFFING
FLAFFS

FLAG
FLAGELLA
FLAGELLANT
FLAGELLANTISM
FLAGELLANTISMS
FLAGELLANTS
FLAGELLAR
FLAGELLATE
FLAGELLATED
FLAGELLATES
FLAGELLATING
FLAGELLATION
FLAGELLATIONS
FLAGELLATOR
FLAGELLATORS
FLAGELLATORY
FLAGELLIFEROUS
FLAGELLIFORM
FLAGELLIN
FLAGELLINS
FLAGELLOMANIA
FLAGELLOMANIAC
FLAGELLOMANIACS
FLAGELLOMANIAS
FLAGELLUM
FLAGELLUMS
FLAGEOLET
FLAGEOLETS
FLAGGED
FLAGGER
FLAGGERS
FLAGGIER
FLAGGIEST
FLAGGINESS
FLAGGINESSES
FLAGGING
FLAGGINGLY
FLAGGINGS
FLAGGY
FLAGITATE
FLAGITATED
FLAGITATES
FLAGITATING
FLAGITATION
FLAGITATIONS
FLAGITIOUS
FLAGITIOUSLY
FLAGITIOUSNESS
FLAGLESS
FLAGMAN
FLAGMEN
FLAGON
FLAGONS
FLAGPOLE
FLAGPOLES
FLAGRANCE

FLAGRANCES
FLAGRANCIES
FLAGRANCY
FLAGRANT
FLAGRANTLY
FLAGRANTNESS
FLAGS
FLAGSHIP
FLAGSHIPS
FLAGSTAFF
FLAGSTAFFS
FLAGSTAVES
FLAGSTICK
FLAGSTICKS
FLAGSTONE
FLAGSTONES
FLAIL
FLAILED
FLAILING
FLAILS
FLAIR
FLAIRS
FLAK
FLAKE
FLAKED
FLAKER
FLAKERS
FLAKES
FLAKEY
FLAKIER
FLAKIES
FLAKIEST
FLAKILY
FLAKINESS
FLAKINESSES
FLAKING
FLAKS
FLAKY
FLAM
FLAMBE
FLAMBEAU
FLAMBEAUS
FLAMBEAUX
FLAMBEE
FLAMBEED
FLAMBEEING
FLAMBEES
FLAMBEING
FLAMBES
FLAMBOYANCE
FLAMBOYANCES
FLAMBOYANCIES
FLAMBOYANCY
FLAMBOYANT
FLAMBOYANTE
FLAMBOYANTES

FLAMBOYANTLY
FLAMBOYANTS
FLAME
FLAMED
FLAMELESS
FLAMELET
FLAMELETS
FLAMELIKE
FLAMEN
FLAMENCO
FLAMENCOS
FLAMENS
FLAMEOUT
FLAMEOUTS
FLAMEPROOF
FLAMEPROOFED
FLAMEPROOFER
FLAMEPROOFERS
FLAMEPROOFING
FLAMEPROOFS
FLAMER
FLAMERS
FLAMES
FLAMETHROWER
FLAMETHROWERS
FLAMFEW
FLAMFEWS
FLAMIER
FLAMIEST
FLAMINES
FLAMING
FLAMINGLY
FLAMINGO
FLAMINGOES
FLAMINGOS
FLAMINICAL
FLAMM
FLAMMABILITIES
FLAMMABILITY
FLAMMABLE
FLAMMABLES
FLAMMED
FLAMMIFEROUS
FLAMMING
FLAMMS
FLAMMULATED
FLAMMULATION
FLAMMULATIONS
FLAMMULE
FLAMMULES
FLAMS
FLAMY
FLAN
FLANCARD
FLANCARDS
FLANCH

FLANCHED
FLANCHES
FLANCHING
FLANCHINGS
FLANCONADE
FLANCONADES
FLANERIE
FLANERIES
FLANES
FLANEUR
FLANEURS
FLANGE
FLANGED
FLANGELESS
FLANGER
FLANGERS
FLANGES
FLANGING
FLANK
FLANKED
FLANKEN
FLANKER
FLANKERED
FLANKERING
FLANKERS
FLANKING
FLANKS
FLANNEL
FLANNELBOARD
FLANNELBOARDS
FLANNELED
FLANNELETTE
FLANNELETTES
FLANNELGRAPH
FLANNELGRAPHS
FLANNELING
FLANNELLED
FLANNELLING
FLANNELLY
FLANNELMOUTHED
FLANNELS
FLANNEN
FLANNENS
FLANS
FLAP
FLAPDOODLE
FLAPDOODLES
FLAPJACK
FLAPJACKS
FLAPLESS
FLAPPABLE
FLAPPED
FLAPPER
FLAPPERHOOD
FLAPPERHOODS
FLAPPERISH

FLAPPERS
FLAPPIER
FLAPPIEST
FLAPPING
FLAPPINGS
FLAPPY
FLAPS
FLAPTRACK
FLAPTRACKS
FLARE
FLARED
FLARES
FLARIER
FLARIEST
FLARING
FLARINGLY
FLARY
FLASER
FLASERS
FLASH
FLASHBACK
FLASHBACKED
FLASHBACKING
FLASHBACKS
FLASHBOARD
FLASHBOARDS
FLASHBULB
FLASHBULBS
FLASHCUBE
FLASHCUBES
FLASHED
FLASHER
FLASHERS
FLASHES
FLASHEST
FLASHFORWARD
FLASHFORWARDED
FLASHFORWARDING
FLASHFORWARDS
FLASHGUN
FLASHGUNS
FLASHIER
FLASHIEST
FLASHILY
FLASHINESS
FLASHINESSES
FLASHING
FLASHINGS
FLASHLAMP
FLASHLAMPS
FLASHLIGHT
FLASHLIGHTS
FLASHOVER
FLASHOVERS
FLASHTUBE
FLASHTUBES

FLASHY
FLASK
FLASKET
FLASKETS
FLASKS
FLAT
FLATBACK
FLATBACKS
FLATBED
FLATBEDS
FLATBOAT
FLATBOATS
FLATBREAD
FLATBREADS
FLATCAP
FLATCAPS
FLATCAR
FLATCARS
FLATETTE
FLATETTES
FLATFEET
FLATFISH
FLATFISHES
FLATFOOT
FLATFOOTED
FLATFOOTING
FLATFOOTS
FLATHEAD
FLATHEADS
FLATIRON
FLATIRONS
FLATLAND
FLATLANDER
FLATLANDERS
FLATLANDS
FLATLET
FLATLETS
FLATLINE
FLATLINED
FLATLINER
FLATLINERS
FLATLINES
FLATLING
FLATLINGS
FLATLINING
FLATLONG
FLATLY
FLATMATE
FLATMATES
FLATNESS
FLATNESSES
FLATPACK
FLATPACKS
FLATS
FLATSHARE
FLATSHARES

FLATTED
FLATTEN
FLATTENED
FLATTENER
FLATTENERS
FLATTENING
FLATTENS
FLATTER
FLATTERABLE
FLATTERED
FLATTERER
FLATTERERS
FLATTERIES
FLATTERING
FLATTERINGLY
FLATTEROUS
FLATTEROUSLY
FLATTERS
FLATTERY
FLATTEST
FLATTIE
FLATTIES
FLATTING
FLATTINGS
FLATTISH
FLATTOP
FLATTOPS
FLATTY
FLATULENCE
FLATULENCES
FLATULENCIES
FLATULENCY
FLATULENT
FLATULENTLY
FLATUOUS
FLATUS
FLATUSES
FLATWARE
FLATWARES
FLATWASH
FLATWASHES
FLATWAYS
FLATWISE
FLATWORK
FLATWORKS
FLATWORM
FLATWORMS
FLAUGHT
FLAUGHTED
FLAUGHTER
FLAUGHTERED
FLAUGHTERING
FLAUGHTERS
FLAUGHTING
FLAUGHTS
FLAUNCH

FLAUNCHED
FLAUNCHES
FLAUNCHING
FLAUNCHINGS
FLAUNE
FLAUNES
FLAUNT
FLAUNTED
FLAUNTER
FLAUNTERS
FLAUNTIER
FLAUNTIEST
FLAUNTILY
FLAUNTINESS
FLAUNTING
FLAUNTINGLY
FLAUNTS
FLAUNTY
FLAUTIST
FLAUTISTS
FLAVANOL
FLAVANOLS
FLAVANONE
FLAVANONES
FLAVESCENT
FLAVIN
FLAVINE
FLAVINES
FLAVINS
FLAVIVIRUS
FLAVIVIRUSES
FLAVONE
FLAVONES
FLAVONOID
FLAVONOIDS
FLAVONOL
FLAVONOLS
FLAVOPROTEIN
FLAVOPROTEINS
FLAVOPURPURIN
FLAVOR
FLAVORED
FLAVORER
FLAVORERS
FLAVORFUL
FLAVORFULLY
FLAVORING
FLAVORINGS
FLAVORIST
FLAVORISTS
FLAVORLESS
FLAVOROUS
FLAVORS
FLAVORSOME
FLAVORY
FLAVOUR

FLAVOURED
FLAVOURER
FLAVOURERS
FLAVOURFUL
FLAVOURFULLY
FLAVOURING
FLAVOURINGS
FLAVOURLESS
FLAVOURS
FLAVOURSOME
FLAVOURY
FLAW
FLAWED
FLAWIER
FLAWIEST
FLAWING
FLAWLESS
FLAWLESSLY
FLAWLESSNESS
FLAWLESSNESSES
FLAWN
FLAWNS
FLAWS
FLAWY
FLAX
FLAXEN
FLAXES
FLAXIER
FLAXIEST
FLAXSEED
FLAXSEEDS
FLAXY
FLAY
FLAYED
FLAYER
FLAYERS
FLAYING
FLAYS
FLAYSOME
FLEA
FLEABAG
FLEABAGS
FLEABANE
FLEABANES
FLEABITE
FLEABITES
FLEAHOPPER
FLEAHOPPERS
FLEAM
FLEAMARKET
FLEAMARKETS
FLEAMS
FLEAPIT
FLEAPITS
FLEAS
FLEASOME

FLEAWORT
FLEAWORTS
FLECHE
FLECHES
FLECHETTE
FLECHETTES
FLECK
FLECKED
FLECKER
FLECKERED
FLECKERING
FLECKERS
FLECKING
FLECKLESS
FLECKS
FLECKY
FLECTION
FLECTIONAL
FLECTIONLESS
FLECTIONS
FLED
FLEDGE
FLEDGED
FLEDGELING
FLEDGELINGS
FLEDGES
FLEDGIER
FLEDGIEST
FLEDGING
FLEDGLING
FLEDGLINGS
FLEDGY
FLEE
FLEECE
FLEECED
FLEECELESS
FLEECER
FLEECERS
FLEECES
FLEECH
FLEECHED
FLEECHES
FLEECHING
FLEECHINGS
FLEECHMENT
FLEECHMENTS
FLEECIE
FLEECIER
FLEECIES
FLEECIEST
FLEECILY
FLEECINESS
FLEECING
FLEECY
FLEEIN
FLEEING

FLEER
FLEERED
FLEERER
FLEERERS
FLEERING
FLEERINGLY
FLEERINGS
FLEERS
FLEES
FLEET
FLEETED
FLEETER
FLEETEST
FLEETING
FLEETINGLY
FLEETINGNESS
FLEETINGNESSES
FLEETLY
FLEETNESS
FLEETNESSES
FLEETS
FLEG
FLEGGED
FLEGGING
FLEGS
FLEISHIG
FLEISHIK
FLEME
FLEMES
FLEMING
FLEMISH
FLEMISHED
FLEMISHES
FLEMISHING
FLEMIT
FLENCH
FLENCHED
FLENCHER
FLENCHERS
FLENCHES
FLENCHING
FLENSE
FLENSED
FLENSER
FLENSERS
FLENSES
FLENSING
FLESH
FLESHED
FLESHER
FLESHERS
FLESHES
FLESHHOOD
FLESHHOODS
FLESHIER
FLESHIEST

FLESHINESS
FLESHINESSES
FLESHING
FLESHINGS
FLESHLESS
FLESHLIER
FLESHLIEST
FLESHLINESS
FLESHLINESSES
FLESHLING
FLESHLINGS
FLESHLY
FLESHMENT
FLESHMENTS
FLESHMONGER
FLESHMONGERS
FLESHPOT
FLESHPOTS
FLESHWORM
FLESHWORMS
FLESHY
FLETCH
FLETCHED
FLETCHER
FLETCHERS
FLETCHES
FLETCHING
FLETCHINGS
FLETTON
FLETTONS
FLEURET
FLEURETS
FLEURETTE
FLEURETTES
FLEURON
FLEURONS
FLEURY
FLEW
FLEWED
FLEWS
FLEX
FLEXAGON
FLEXAGONS
FLEXECUTIVE
FLEXECUTIVES
FLEXED
FLEXES
FLEXIBILITIES
FLEXIBILITY
FLEXIBLE
FLEXIBLENESS
FLEXIBLENESSES
FLEXIBLY
FLEXIHOURS
FLEXILE
FLEXING

FLEXION
FLEXIONAL
FLEXIONLESS
FLEXIONS
FLEXITIME
FLEXITIMES
FLEXO
FLEXOGRAPHIC
FLEXOGRAPHIES
FLEXOGRAPHY
FLEXOR
FLEXORS
FLEXTIME
FLEXTIMES
FLEXUOSE
FLEXUOUS
FLEXUOUSLY
FLEXURAL
FLEXURE
FLEXURES
FLEY
FLEYED
FLEYING
FLEYS
FLEYSOME
FLIBBERT
FLIBBERTIGIBBET
FLIBBERTS
FLIC
FLICHTER
FLICHTERED
FLICHTERING
FLICHTERS
FLICK
FLICKED
FLICKER
FLICKERED
FLICKERING
FLICKERINGLY
FLICKERS
FLICKERTAIL
FLICKERTAILS
FLICKERY
FLICKING
FLICKS
FLICS
FLIED
FLIER
FLIERS
FLIES
FLIEST
FLIGHT
FLIGHTED
FLIGHTIER
FLIGHTIEST
FLIGHTILY

FLIGHTINESS
FLIGHTINESSES
FLIGHTING
FLIGHTLESS
FLIGHTS
FLIGHTY
FLIM
FLIMFLAM
FLIMFLAMMED
FLIMFLAMMER
FLIMFLAMMERIES
FLIMFLAMMERS
FLIMFLAMMERY
FLIMFLAMMING
FLIMFLAMS
FLIMP
FLIMPED
FLIMPING
FLIMPS
FLIMSIER
FLIMSIES
FLIMSIEST
FLIMSILY
FLIMSINESS
FLIMSINESSES
FLIMSY
FLINCH
FLINCHED
FLINCHER
FLINCHERS
FLINCHES
FLINCHING
FLINCHINGLY
FLINCHINGS
FLINDER
FLINDERS
FLINDERSIA
FLINDERSIAS
FLING
FLINGER
FLINGERS
FLINGING
FLINGS
FLINKITE
FLINKITES
FLINT
FLINTED
FLINTIER
FLINTIEST
FLINTIFIED
FLINTIFIES
FLINTIFY
FLINTIFYING
FLINTILY
FLINTINESS
FLINTINESSES

FLINTING
FLINTLIKE
FLINTLOCK
FLINTLOCKS
FLINTS
FLINTY
FLIP
FLIPPANCIES
FLIPPANCY
FLIPPANT
FLIPPANTLY
FLIPPANTNESS
FLIPPANTNESSES
FLIPPED
FLIPPER
FLIPPERS
FLIPPEST
FLIPPING
FLIPPY
FLIPS
FLIRT
FLIRTATION
FLIRTATIONS
FLIRTATIOUS
FLIRTATIOUSLY
FLIRTATIOUSNESS
FLIRTED
FLIRTER
FLIRTERS
FLIRTIER
FLIRTIEST
FLIRTING
FLIRTINGLY
FLIRTINGS
FLIRTISH
FLIRTS
FLIRTY
FLISK
FLISKED
FLISKIER
FLISKIEST
FLISKING
FLISKS
FLISKY
FLIT
FLITCH
FLITCHED
FLITCHES
FLITCHING
FLITE
FLITED
FLITES
FLITING
FLITS
FLITT
FLITTED

FLITTER
FLITTERED
FLITTERING
FLITTERMICE
FLITTERMOUSE
FLITTERN
FLITTERNS
FLITTERS
FLITTING
FLITTINGS
FLIVVER
FLIVVERS
FLIX
FLIXED
FLIXES
FLIXING
FLOAT
FLOATABILITY
FLOATABLE
FLOATAGE
FLOATAGES
FLOATANT
FLOATANTS
FLOATATION
FLOATATIONS
FLOATCUT
FLOATED
FLOATEL
FLOATELS
FLOATER
FLOATERS
FLOATIER
FLOATIEST
FLOATING
FLOATINGLY
FLOATINGS
FLOATPLANE
FLOATPLANES
FLOATS
FLOATY
FLOC
FLOCCED
FLOCCI
FLOCCILLATION
FLOCCILLATIONS
FLOCCING
FLOCCOSE
FLOCCULANT
FLOCCULANTS
FLOCCULAR
FLOCCULATE
FLOCCULATED
FLOCCULATES
FLOCCULATING
FLOCCULATION
FLOCCULATIONS

FLOCCULATOR
FLOCCULATORS
FLOCCULE
FLOCCULENCE
FLOCCULENCES
FLOCCULENCY
FLOCCULENT
FLOCCULENTLY
FLOCCULES
FLOCCULI
FLOCCULUS
FLOCCUS
FLOCK
FLOCKED
FLOCKIER
FLOCKIEST
FLOCKING
FLOCKINGS
FLOCKS
FLOCKY
FLOCS
FLOE
FLOES
FLOG
FLOGGED
FLOGGER
FLOGGERS
FLOGGING
FLOGGINGS
FLOGS
FLOKATI
FLOKATIS
FLONG
FLONGS
FLOOD
FLOODABLE
FLOODED
FLOODER
FLOODERS
FLOODGATE
FLOODGATES
FLOODING
FLOODINGS
FLOODLESS
FLOODLIGHT
FLOODLIGHTED
FLOODLIGHTING
FLOODLIGHTINGS
FLOODLIGHTS
FLOODLIT
FLOODMARK
FLOODMARKS
FLOODPLAIN
FLOODPLAINS
FLOODS
FLOODTIDE

FLOODTIDES
FLOODWALL
FLOODWALLS
FLOODWATER
FLOODWATERS
FLOODWAY
FLOODWAYS
FLOOEY
FLOOIE
FLOOR
FLOORAGE
FLOORAGES
FLOORBOARD
FLOORBOARDS
FLOORCLOTH
FLOORCLOTHS
FLOORED
FLOORER
FLOORERS
FLOORHEAD
FLOORHEADS
FLOORING
FLOORINGS
FLOORS
FLOORWALKER
FLOORWALKERS
FLOOSIE
FLOOSIES
FLOOSY
FLOOZIE
FLOOZIES
FLOOZY
FLOP
FLOPHOUSE
FLOPHOUSES
FLOPOVER
FLOPOVERS
FLOPPED
FLOPPER
FLOPPERS
FLOPPIER
FLOPPIES
FLOPPIEST
FLOPPILY
FLOPPINESS
FLOPPINESSES
FLOPPING
FLOPPY
FLOPS
FLOPTICAL
FLOR
FLORA
FLORAE
FLORAL
FLORALLY
FLORALS

FLORAS
FLOREANT
FLOREAT
FLOREATED
FLORENCE
FLORENCES
FLORENTINE
FLORENTINES
FLORESCENCE
FLORESCENCES
FLORESCENT
FLORET
FLORETS
FLORIATED
FLORIATION
FLORIATIONS
FLORIBUNDA
FLORIBUNDAS
FLORICULTURAL
FLORICULTURE
FLORICULTURES
FLORICULTURIST
FLORICULTURISTS
FLORID
FLORIDEAN
FLORIDEANS
FLORIDEOUS
FLORIDER
FLORIDEST
FLORIDITIES
FLORIDITY
FLORIDLY
FLORIDNESS
FLORIDNESSES
FLORIER
FLORIEST
FLORIFEROUS
FLORIFEROUSNESS
FLORIFORM
FLORIGEN
FLORIGENIC
FLORIGENS
FLORILEGIA
FLORILEGIUM
FLORIN
FLORINS
FLORIST
FLORISTIC
FLORISTICALLY
FLORISTICS
FLORISTRIES
FLORISTRY
FLORISTS
FLORS
FLORUIT
FLORUITED

FLORUITING
FLORUITS
FLORULA
FLORULAE
FLORULE
FLORULES
FLORY
FLOSCULAR
FLOSCULE
FLOSCULES
FLOSCULOUS
FLOSH
FLOSHES
FLOSS
FLOSSED
FLOSSES
FLOSSIE
FLOSSIER
FLOSSIES
FLOSSIEST
FLOSSILY
FLOSSING
FLOSSINGS
FLOSSY
FLOTA
FLOTAGE
FLOTAGES
FLOTANT
FLOTAS
FLOTATION
FLOTATIONS
FLOTE
FLOTEL
FLOTELS
FLOTES
FLOTILLA
FLOTILLAS
FLOTSAM
FLOTSAMS
FLOUN
FLOUNCE
FLOUNCED
FLOUNCES
FLOUNCIER
FLOUNCIEST
FLOUNCING
FLOUNCINGS
FLOUNCY
FLOUNDER
FLOUNDERED
FLOUNDERING
FLOUNDERS
FLOUR
FLOURED
FLOURIER
FLOURIEST

FLOURING
FLOURISH
FLOURISHED
FLOURISHER
FLOURISHERS
FLOURISHES
FLOURISHING
FLOURISHINGLY
FLOURISHY
FLOURLESS
FLOURS
FLOURY
FLOUSE
FLOUSED
FLOUSES
FLOUSH
FLOUSHED
FLOUSHES
FLOUSHING
FLOUSING
FLOUT
FLOUTED
FLOUTER
FLOUTERS
FLOUTING
FLOUTINGLY
FLOUTINGSTOCKS
FLOUTS
FLOW
FLOWAGE
FLOWAGES
FLOWCHART
FLOWCHARTING
FLOWCHARTINGS
FLOWCHARTS
FLOWED
FLOWER
FLOWERAGE
FLOWERAGES
FLOWERBED
FLOWERBEDS
FLOWERED
FLOWERER
FLOWERERS
FLOWERET
FLOWERETS
FLOWERETTE
FLOWERETTES
FLOWERFUL
FLOWERIER
FLOWERIEST
FLOWERILY
FLOWERINESS
FLOWERINESSES
FLOWERING
FLOWERINGS

FLOWERLESS
FLOWERLIKE
FLOWERPOT
FLOWERPOTS
FLOWERS
FLOWERY
FLOWIN
FLOWING
FLOWINGLY
FLOWINGNESS
FLOWINGNESSES
FLOWMETER
FLOWMETERS
FLOWN
FLOWS
FLOWSTONE
FLOWSTONES
FLU
FLUATE
FLUATES
FLUB
FLUBBED
FLUBBER
FLUBBERS
FLUBBING
FLUBDUB
FLUBDUBS
FLUBS
FLUCTUANT
FLUCTUATE
FLUCTUATED
FLUCTUATES
FLUCTUATING
FLUCTUATION
FLUCTUATIONAL
FLUCTUATIONS
FLUE
FLUED
FLUEGELHORN
FLUEGELHORNS
FLUELLEN
FLUELLENS
FLUELLIN
FLUELLINS
FLUENCE
FLUENCES
FLUENCIES
FLUENCY
FLUENT
FLUENTLY
FLUENTNESS
FLUENTNESSES
FLUENTS
FLUERIC
FLUERICS
FLUES

FLUEWORK
FLUEWORKS
FLUEY
FLUFF
FLUFFED
FLUFFER
FLUFFERS
FLUFFIER
FLUFFIEST
FLUFFILY
FLUFFINESS
FLUFFINESSES
FLUFFING
FLUFFS
FLUFFY
FLUGEL
FLUGELHORN
FLUGELHORNIST
FLUGELHORNISTS
FLUGELHORNS
FLUGELMAN
FLUGELMEN
FLUGELS
FLUID
FLUIDAL
FLUIDALLY
FLUIDEXTRACT
FLUIDEXTRACTS
FLUIDIC
FLUIDICS
FLUIDIFIED
FLUIDIFIES
FLUIDIFY
FLUIDIFYING
FLUIDISATION
FLUIDISATIONS
FLUIDISE
FLUIDISED
FLUIDISER
FLUIDISERS
FLUIDISES
FLUIDISING
FLUIDITIES
FLUIDITY
FLUIDIZATION
FLUIDIZATIONS
FLUIDIZE
FLUIDIZED
FLUIDIZER
FLUIDIZERS
FLUIDIZES
FLUIDIZING
FLUIDLY
FLUIDNESS
FLUIDNESSES
FLUIDRAM

FLUIDRAMS
FLUIDS
FLUIER
FLUIEST
FLUKE
FLUKED
FLUKES
FLUKEY
FLUKIER
FLUKIEST
FLUKINESS
FLUKING
FLUKY
FLUME
FLUMED
FLUMES
FLUMING
FLUMMERIES
FLUMMERY
FLUMMOX
FLUMMOXED
FLUMMOXES
FLUMMOXING
FLUMP
FLUMPED
FLUMPING
FLUMPS
FLUNG
FLUNITRAZEPAM
FLUNK
FLUNKED
FLUNKER
FLUNKERS
FLUNKEY
FLUNKEYDOM
FLUNKEYDOMS
FLUNKEYISH
FLUNKEYISM
FLUNKEYISMS
FLUNKEYS
FLUNKIES
FLUNKING
FLUNKS
FLUNKY
FLUOR
FLUORAPATITE
FLUORENE
FLUORENES
FLUORESCE
FLUORESCED
FLUORESCEIN
FLUORESCEINE
FLUORESCEINS
FLUORESCENCE
FLUORESCENCES
FLUORESCENT

FLUORESCENTS
FLUORESCER
FLUORESCERS
FLUORESCES
FLUORESCING
FLUORIC
FLUORID
FLUORIDATE
FLUORIDATED
FLUORIDATES
FLUORIDATING
FLUORIDATION
FLUORIDATIONS
FLUORIDE
FLUORIDES
FLUORIDISE
FLUORIDISED
FLUORIDISES
FLUORIDISING
FLUORIDIZE
FLUORIDIZED
FLUORIDIZES
FLUORIDIZING
FLUORIDS
FLUORIMETER
FLUORIMETERS
FLUORIMETRIC
FLUORIMETRIES
FLUORIMETRY
FLUORIN
FLUORINATE
FLUORINATED
FLUORINATES
FLUORINATING
FLUORINATION
FLUORINATIONS
FLUORINE
FLUORINES
FLUORINS
FLUORITE
FLUORITES
FLUOROCARBON
FLUOROCARBONS
FLUOROCHROME
FLUOROCHROMES
FLUOROGRAPHIC
FLUOROGRAPHIES
FLUOROGRAPHY
FLUOROMETER
FLUOROMETERS
FLUOROMETRIC
FLUOROMETRIES
FLUOROMETRY
FLUOROPHORE
FLUOROPHORES
FLUOROSCOPE

FLUOROSCOPED
FLUOROSCOPES
FLUOROSCOPIC
FLUOROSCOPIES
FLUOROSCOPING
FLUOROSCOPIST
FLUOROSCOPISTS
FLUOROSCOPY
FLUOROSES
FLUOROSIS
FLUOROTIC
FLUOROTYPE
FLUOROTYPES
FLUOROURACIL
FLUOROURACILS
FLUORS
FLUORSPAR
FLUORSPARS
FLUOXETINE
FLUOXETINES
FLUPHENAZINE
FLUPHENAZINES
FLURR
FLURRED
FLURRIED
FLURRIES
FLURRING
FLURRS
FLURRY
FLURRYING
FLUS
FLUSH
FLUSHABLE
FLUSHED
FLUSHER
FLUSHERS
FLUSHES
FLUSHEST
FLUSHIER
FLUSHIEST
FLUSHING
FLUSHINGS
FLUSHNESS
FLUSHNESSES
FLUSHWORK
FLUSHY
FLUSTER
FLUSTERED
FLUSTEREDLY
FLUSTERING
FLUSTERMENT
FLUSTERMENTS
FLUSTERS
FLUSTERY
FLUSTRATE
FLUSTRATED

FLUSTRATES
FLUSTRATING
FLUSTRATION
FLUSTRATIONS
FLUTE
FLUTED
FLUTELIKE
FLUTEMOUTH
FLUTEMOUTHS
FLUTER
FLUTERS
FLUTES
FLUTEY
FLUTIER
FLUTIEST
FLUTINA
FLUTINAS
FLUTING
FLUTINGS
FLUTIST
FLUTISTS
FLUTTER
FLUTTERBOARD
FLUTTERBOARDS
FLUTTERED
FLUTTERER
FLUTTERERS
FLUTTERING
FLUTTERINGLY
FLUTTERS
FLUTTERY
FLUTY
FLUVIAL
FLUVIALIST
FLUVIALISTS
FLUVIATIC
FLUVIATILE
FLUVIOMARINE
FLUVOXAMINE
FLUVOXAMINES
FLUX
FLUXED
FLUXES
FLUXGATE
FLUXGATES
FLUXING
FLUXION
FLUXIONAL
FLUXIONALLY
FLUXIONARY
FLUXIONIST
FLUXIONISTS
FLUXIONS
FLUXIVE
FLUXMETER
FLUXMETERS

FLUYT
FLUYTS
FLY
FLYABLE
FLYAWAY
FLYAWAYS
FLYBACK
FLYBACKS
FLYBANE
FLYBANES
FLYBELT
FLYBELTS
FLYBLEW
FLYBLOW
FLYBLOWING
FLYBLOWN
FLYBLOWS
FLYBOAT
FLYBOATS
FLYBOOK
FLYBOOKS
FLYBOY
FLYBOYS
FLYBRIDGE
FLYBRIDGES
FLYBY
FLYBYS
FLYCATCHER
FLYCATCHERS
FLYER
FLYERS
FLYEST
FLYHAND
FLYHANDS
FLYING
FLYINGS
FLYLEAF
FLYLEAVES
FLYLESS
FLYMAKER
FLYMAKERS
FLYMAN
FLYMEN
FLYOFF
FLYOFFS
FLYOVER
FLYOVERS
FLYPAPER
FLYPAPERS
FLYPAST
FLYPASTS
FLYPE
FLYPED
FLYPES
FLYPING
FLYPITCH

FLYPITCHER
FLYPITCHERS
FLYPITCHES
FLYPOSTING
FLYPOSTINGS
FLYSCH
FLYSCHES
FLYSCREEN
FLYSCREENS
FLYSPECK
FLYSPECKED
FLYSPECKING
FLYSPECKS
FLYSTRIKE
FLYSTRIKES
FLYSTRUCK
FLYSWATTER
FLYSWATTERS
FLYTE
FLYTED
FLYTES
FLYTIER
FLYTIERS
FLYTING
FLYTINGS
FLYTRAP
FLYTRAPS
FLYWAY
FLYWAYS
FLYWEIGHT
FLYWEIGHTS
FLYWHEEL
FLYWHEELS
FOAL
FOALED
FOALFOOT
FOALFOOTS
FOALING
FOALS
FOAM
FOAMABLE
FOAMED
FOAMER
FOAMERS
FOAMFLOWER
FOAMFLOWERS
FOAMIER
FOAMIEST
FOAMILY
FOAMINESS
FOAMINESSES
FOAMING
FOAMINGLY
FOAMINGS
FOAMLESS
FOAMLIKE

FOAMS
FOAMY
FOB
FOBBED
FOBBING
FOBS
FOCACCIA
FOCACCIAS
FOCAL
FOCALISATION
FOCALISATIONS
FOCALISE
FOCALISED
FOCALISES
FOCALISING
FOCALIZATION
FOCALIZATIONS
FOCALIZE
FOCALIZED
FOCALIZES
FOCALIZING
FOCALLY
FOCHT
FOCI
FOCIMETER
FOCIMETERS
FOCOMETER
FOCOMETERS
FOCOMETRIC
FOCUS
FOCUSABLE
FOCUSED
FOCUSER
FOCUSERS
FOCUSES
FOCUSING
FOCUSINGS
FOCUSLESS
FOCUSSED
FOCUSSES
FOCUSSING
FODDER
FODDERED
FODDERER
FODDERERS
FODDERING
FODDERINGS
FODDERS
FODGEL
FOE
FOEDARIE
FOEDARIES
FOEDERATI
FOEDERATUS
FOEHN
FOEHNS

FOEMAN
FOEMEN
FOEN
FOES
FOETAL
FOETATION
FOETICIDAL
FOETICIDE
FOETICIDES
FOETID
FOETIDER
FOETIDEST
FOETIDLY
FOETIDNESS
FOETIDNESSES
FOETIPAROUS
FOETOR
FOETORS
FOETOSCOPIES
FOETOSCOPY
FOETUS
FOETUSES
FOG
FOGASH
FOGASHES
FOGBOUND
FOGBOW
FOGBOWS
FOGDOG
FOGDOGS
FOGEY
FOGEYDOM
FOGEYDOMS
FOGEYISH
FOGEYISM
FOGEYISMS
FOGEYS
FOGFRUIT
FOGFRUITS
FOGGAGE
FOGGAGES
FOGGED
FOGGER
FOGGERS
FOGGIER
FOGGIEST
FOGGILY
FOGGINESS
FOGGINESSES
FOGGING
FOGGY
FOGHORN
FOGHORNS
FOGIE
FOGIES
FOGLE

FOGLES
FOGLESS
FOGMAN
FOGMEN
FOGRAM
FOGRAMITE
FOGRAMITES
FOGRAMITIES
FOGRAMITY
FOGRAMS
FOGS
FOGY
FOGYDOM
FOGYDOMS
FOGYISH
FOGYISM
FOGYISMS
FOH
FOHN
FOHNS
FOHS
FOIBLE
FOIBLES
FOID
FOIDS
FOIL
FOILABLE
FOILBORNE
FOILED
FOILING
FOILINGS
FOILS
FOILSMAN
FOILSMEN
FOIN
FOINED
FOINING
FOININGLY
FOINS
FOISON
FOISONLESS
FOISONS
FOIST
FOISTED
FOISTER
FOISTERS
FOISTING
FOISTS
FOLACIN
FOLACINS
FOLATE
FOLATES
FOLD
FOLDABLE
FOLDAWAY
FOLDBACK

FOLDBOAT
FOLDBOATS
FOLDED
FOLDER
FOLDEROL
FOLDEROLS
FOLDERS
FOLDING
FOLDINGS
FOLDOUT
FOLDOUTS
FOLDS
FOLEY
FOLEYS
FOLIA
FOLIACEOUS
FOLIAGE
FOLIAGED
FOLIAGES
FOLIAR
FOLIATE
FOLIATED
FOLIATES
FOLIATING
FOLIATION
FOLIATIONS
FOLIATURE
FOLIATURES
FOLIC
FOLIE
FOLIES
FOLIO
FOLIOED
FOLIOING
FOLIOLATE
FOLIOLE
FOLIOLES
FOLIOLOSE
FOLIOS
FOLIOSE
FOLIOUS
FOLIUM
FOLIUMS
FOLK
FOLKIE
FOLKIES
FOLKISH
FOLKISHNESS
FOLKISHNESSES
FOLKLAND
FOLKLANDS
FOLKLIFE
FOLKLIKE
FOLKLIVES
FOLKLORE
FOLKLORES

FOLKLORIC
FOLKLORISH
FOLKLORIST
FOLKLORISTIC
FOLKLORISTS
FOLKMOOT
FOLKMOOTS
FOLKMOT
FOLKMOTE
FOLKMOTES
FOLKMOTS
FOLKS
FOLKSIER
FOLKSIEST
FOLKSILY
FOLKSINESS
FOLKSINESSES
FOLKSINGER
FOLKSINGERS
FOLKSINGING
FOLKSINGINGS
FOLKSY
FOLKTALE
FOLKTALES
FOLKWAY
FOLKWAYS
FOLKY
FOLLES
FOLLICLE
FOLLICLES
FOLLICULAR
FOLLICULATE
FOLLICULATED
FOLLICULIN
FOLLICULITIS
FOLLICULITISES
FOLLICULOSE
FOLLICULOUS
FOLLIED
FOLLIES
FOLLIS
FOLLOW
FOLLOWABILITY
FOLLOWABLE
FOLLOWED
FOLLOWER
FOLLOWERS
FOLLOWERSHIP
FOLLOWERSHIPS
FOLLOWING
FOLLOWINGS
FOLLOWS
FOLLOWSHIP
FOLLY
FOLLYING
FOMENT

FOMENTATION
FOMENTATIONS
FOMENTED
FOMENTER
FOMENTERS
FOMENTING
FOMENTS
FOMES
FOMITE
FOMITES
FON
FONCTIONNAIRE
FONCTIONNAIRES
FOND
FONDA
FONDANT
FONDANTS
FONDAS
FONDED
FONDER
FONDEST
FONDING
FONDLE
FONDLED
FONDLER
FONDLERS
FONDLES
FONDLING
FONDLINGLY
FONDLINGS
FONDLY
FONDNESS
FONDNESSES
FONDS
FONDU
FONDUE
FONDUES
FONDUS
FONE
FONLY
FONNED
FONNING
FONS
FONT
FONTAL
FONTANEL
FONTANELLE
FONTANELLES
FONTANELS
FONTANGE
FONTANGES
FONTICULI
FONTICULUS
FONTICULUSES
FONTINA
FONTINALIS

FONTINALISES
FONTINAS
FONTLET
FONTLETS
FONTS
FOOBAR
FOOD
FOODFUL
FOODIE
FOODIES
FOODISM
FOODISMS
FOODLESS
FOODLESSNESS
FOODLESSNESSES
FOODS
FOODSTUFF
FOODSTUFFS
FOODWAYS
FOODY
FOOFARAW
FOOFARAWS
FOOL
FOOLED
FOOLERIES
FOOLERY
FOOLFISH
FOOLFISHES
FOOLHARDIER
FOOLHARDIEST
FOOLHARDILY
FOOLHARDINESS
FOOLHARDINESSES
FOOLHARDISE
FOOLHARDISES
FOOLHARDIZE
FOOLHARDIZES
FOOLHARDY
FOOLING
FOOLINGS
FOOLISH
FOOLISHER
FOOLISHEST
FOOLISHLY
FOOLISHNESS
FOOLISHNESSES
FOOLPROOF
FOOLS
FOOLSCAP
FOOLSCAPS
FOOT
FOOTAGE
FOOTAGES
FOOTBALL
FOOTBALLENE
FOOTBALLENES

FOOTBALLER
FOOTBALLERS
FOOTBALLING
FOOTBALLIST
FOOTBALLISTS
FOOTBALLS
FOOTBAR
FOOTBARS
FOOTBATH
FOOTBATHS
FOOTBOARD
FOOTBOARDS
FOOTBOY
FOOTBOYS
FOOTBREADTH
FOOTBREADTHS
FOOTBRIDGE
FOOTBRIDGES
FOOTCLOTH
FOOTCLOTHS
FOOTDRAGGER
FOOTDRAGGERS
FOOTED
FOOTER
FOOTERED
FOOTERING
FOOTERINGLY
FOOTERS
FOOTFALL
FOOTFALLS
FOOTFAULT
FOOTFAULTED
FOOTFAULTING
FOOTFAULTS
FOOTGEAR
FOOTGEARS
FOOTGUARDS
FOOTHILL
FOOTHILLS
FOOTHOLD
FOOTHOLDS
FOOTIE
FOOTIER
FOOTIES
FOOTIEST
FOOTING
FOOTINGS
FOOTLAMBERT
FOOTLAMBERTS
FOOTLE
FOOTLED
FOOTLER
FOOTLERS
FOOTLES
FOOTLESS
FOOTLESSLY

FOOTLESSNESS
FOOTLESSNESSES
FOOTLIGHT
FOOTLIGHTS
FOOTLIKE
FOOTLING
FOOTLINGS
FOOTLOCKER
FOOTLOCKERS
FOOTLOOSE
FOOTMAN
FOOTMARK
FOOTMARKS
FOOTMEN
FOOTMUFF
FOOTMUFFS
FOOTNOTE
FOOTNOTED
FOOTNOTES
FOOTNOTING
FOOTPACE
FOOTPACES
FOOTPAD
FOOTPADS
FOOTPAGE
FOOTPAGES
FOOTPATH
FOOTPATHS
FOOTPLATE
FOOTPLATEMAN
FOOTPLATEMEN
FOOTPLATES
FOOTPLATEWOMAN
FOOTPLATEWOMEN
FOOTPOST
FOOTPOSTS
FOOTPRINT
FOOTPRINTS
FOOTRA
FOOTRACE
FOOTRACES
FOOTRAS
FOOTREST
FOOTRESTS
FOOTROPE
FOOTROPES
FOOTROT
FOOTROTS
FOOTRULE
FOOTRULES
FOOTS
FOOTSIE
FOOTSIES
FOOTSLOG
FOOTSLOGGED
FOOTSLOGGER

FOOTSLOGGERS
FOOTSLOGGING
FOOTSLOGGINGS
FOOTSLOGS
FOOTSORE
FOOTSORENESS
FOOTSORENESSES
FOOTSTALK
FOOTSTALKS
FOOTSTALL
FOOTSTALLS
FOOTSTEP
FOOTSTEPS
FOOTSTOCK
FOOTSTOCKS
FOOTSTONE
FOOTSTONES
FOOTSTOOL
FOOTSTOOLED
FOOTSTOOLS
FOOTSY
FOOTWALL
FOOTWALLS
FOOTWAY
FOOTWAYS
FOOTWEAR
FOOTWEARIED
FOOTWEARINESS
FOOTWEARS
FOOTWEARY
FOOTWELL
FOOTWELLS
FOOTWORK
FOOTWORKS
FOOTWORN
FOOTY
FOOZLE
FOOZLED
FOOZLER
FOOZLERS
FOOZLES
FOOZLING
FOOZLINGS
FOP
FOPLING
FOPLINGS
FOPPED
FOPPERIES
FOPPERY
FOPPING
FOPPISH
FOPPISHLY
FOPPISHNESS
FOPPISHNESSES
FOPS
FOR

FORA
FORAGE
FORAGED
FORAGER
FORAGERS
FORAGES
FORAGING
FORAM
FORAMEN
FORAMENS
FORAMINA
FORAMINAL
FORAMINATED
FORAMINIFER
FORAMINIFERA
FORAMINIFERAL
FORAMINIFERAN
FORAMINIFERANS
FORAMINIFEROUS
FORAMINIFERS
FORAMINOUS
FORAMS
FORANE
FORASMUCH
FORAY
FORAYED
FORAYER
FORAYERS
FORAYING
FORAYS
FORB
FORBAD
FORBADE
FORBEAR
FORBEARANCE
FORBEARANCES
FORBEARANT
FORBEARER
FORBEARERS
FORBEARING
FORBEARINGLY
FORBEARS
FORBID
FORBIDAL
FORBIDALS
FORBIDDAL
FORBIDDALS
FORBIDDANCE
FORBIDDANCES
FORBIDDEN
FORBIDDENLY
FORBIDDER
FORBIDDERS
FORBIDDING
FORBIDDINGLY
FORBIDDINGNESS

FORBIDDINGS
FORBIDS
FORBODE
FORBODED
FORBODES
FORBODING
FORBORE
FORBORNE
FORBS
FORBY
FORBYE
FORCAT
FORCATS
FORCE
FORCEABLE
FORCED
FORCEDLY
FORCEDNESS
FORCEDNESSES
FORCEFUL
FORCEFULLY
FORCEFULNESS
FORCEFULNESSES
FORCELESS
FORCEMEAT
FORCEMEATS
FORCEPS
FORCEPSES
FORCEPSLIKE
FORCER
FORCERS
FORCES
FORCIBILITIES
FORCIBILITY
FORCIBLE
FORCIBLENESS
FORCIBLENESSES
FORCIBLY
FORCING
FORCINGLY
FORCIPATE
FORCIPATED
FORCIPATION
FORCIPATIONS
FORCIPES
FORD
FORDABLE
FORDED
FORDID
FORDING
FORDLESS
FORDO
FORDOES
FORDOING
FORDONE
FORDS

FORE
FOREANENT
FOREARM
FOREARMED
FOREARMING
FOREARMS
FOREBAY
FOREBAYS
FOREBEAR
FOREBEARS
FOREBITT
FOREBITTER
FOREBITTERS
FOREBITTS
FOREBODE
FOREBODED
FOREBODEMENT
FOREBODEMENTS
FOREBODER
FOREBODERS
FOREBODES
FOREBODIES
FOREBODING
FOREBODINGLY
FOREBODINGNESS
FOREBODINGS
FOREBODY
FOREBOOM
FOREBOOMS
FOREBRAIN
FOREBRAINS
FOREBY
FOREBYE
FORECABIN
FORECABINS
FORECADDIE
FORECADDIES
FORECAR
FORECARRIAGE
FORECARRIAGES
FORECARS
FORECAST
FORECASTABLE
FORECASTED
FORECASTER
FORECASTERS
FORECASTING
FORECASTLE
FORECASTLES
FORECASTS
FORECHECK
FORECHECKED
FORECHECKER
FORECHECKERS
FORECHECKING
FORECHECKS

FORECHOSEN
FORECLOSABLE
FORECLOSE
FORECLOSED
FORECLOSES
FORECLOSING
FORECLOSURE
FORECLOSURES
FORECLOTH
FORECLOTHS
FORECOURSE
FORECOURSES
FORECOURT
FORECOURTS
FOREDAMNED
FOREDATE
FOREDATED
FOREDATES
FOREDATING
FOREDECK
FOREDECKS
FOREDID
FOREDO
FOREDOES
FOREDOING
FOREDONE
FOREDOOM
FOREDOOMED
FOREDOOMING
FOREDOOMS
FOREFACE
FOREFACES
FOREFATHER
FOREFATHERLY
FOREFATHERS
FOREFEEL
FOREFEELING
FOREFEELINGLY
FOREFEELS
FOREFEET
FOREFELT
FOREFEND
FOREFENDED
FOREFENDING
FOREFENDS
FOREFINGER
FOREFINGERS
FOREFOOT
FOREFRONT
FOREFRONTS
FOREGATHER
FOREGATHERED
FOREGATHERING
FOREGATHERS
FOREGLEAM
FOREGLEAMS

FOREGO
FOREGOER
FOREGOERS
FOREGOES
FOREGOING
FOREGOINGS
FOREGONE
FOREGONENESS
FOREGONENESSES
FOREGROUND
FOREGROUNDED
FOREGROUNDING
FOREGROUNDS
FOREGUT
FOREGUTS
FOREHAND
FOREHANDED
FOREHANDEDLY
FOREHANDEDNESS
FOREHANDING
FOREHANDS
FOREHEAD
FOREHEADS
FOREHENT
FOREHENTING
FOREHENTS
FOREHOCK
FOREHOCKS
FOREHOOF
FOREHOOFS
FOREHOOVES
FOREIGN
FOREIGNER
FOREIGNERS
FOREIGNISM
FOREIGNISMS
FOREIGNLY
FOREIGNNESS
FOREIGNNESSES
FOREJUDGE
FOREJUDGED
FOREJUDGEMENT
FOREJUDGEMENTS
FOREJUDGES
FOREJUDGING
FOREJUDGMENT
FOREJUDGMENTS
FOREKING
FOREKINGS
FOREKNEW
FOREKNOW
FOREKNOWABLE
FOREKNOWING
FOREKNOWINGLY
FOREKNOWLEDGE
FOREKNOWLEDGES

FOREKNOWN
FOREKNOWS
FOREL
FORELADIES
FORELADY
FORELAID
FORELAIN
FORELAND
FORELANDS
FORELAY
FORELAYING
FORELAYS
FORELEG
FORELEGS
FORELEND
FORELENDING
FORELENDS
FORELENT
FORELIE
FORELIES
FORELIFT
FORELIFTED
FORELIFTING
FORELIFTS
FORELIMB
FORELIMBS
FORELOCK
FORELOCKED
FORELOCKING
FORELOCKS
FORELS
FORELYING
FOREMAN
FOREMANSHIP
FOREMANSHIPS
FOREMAST
FOREMASTMAN
FOREMASTMEN
FOREMASTS
FOREMEAN
FOREMEANING
FOREMEANS
FOREMEANT
FOREMEN
FOREMENTIONED
FOREMILK
FOREMILKS
FOREMOST
FOREMOTHER
FOREMOTHERS
FORENAME
FORENAMED
FORENAMES
FORENIGHT
FORENIGHTS
FORENOON

FORENOONS
FORENSIC
FORENSICALITIES
FORENSICALITY
FORENSICALLY
FORENSICS
FOREORDAIN
FOREORDAINED
FOREORDAINING
FOREORDAINMENT
FOREORDAINMENTS
FOREORDAINS
FOREORDINATION
FOREORDINATIONS
FOREPART
FOREPARTS
FOREPASSED
FOREPAST
FOREPAW
FOREPAWS
FOREPAYMENT
FOREPAYMENTS
FOREPEAK
FOREPEAKS
FOREPLAN
FOREPLANNED
FOREPLANNING
FOREPLANS
FOREPLAY
FOREPLAYS
FOREPOINT
FOREPOINTED
FOREPOINTING
FOREPOINTS
FOREQUARTER
FOREQUARTERS
FORERAN
FORERANK
FORERANKS
FOREREACH
FOREREACHED
FOREREACHES
FOREREACHING
FOREREAD
FOREREADING
FOREREADINGS
FOREREADS
FORERUN
FORERUNNER
FORERUNNERS
FORERUNNING
FORERUNS
FORES
FORESAID
FORESAIL
FORESAILS

FORESAW
FORESAY
FORESAYING
FORESAYS
FORESEE
FORESEEABILITY
FORESEEABLE
FORESEEING
FORESEEINGLY
FORESEEN
FORESEER
FORESEERS
FORESEES
FORESHADOW
FORESHADOWED
FORESHADOWER
FORESHADOWERS
FORESHADOWING
FORESHADOWINGS
FORESHADOWS
FORESHANK
FORESHANKS
FORESHEET
FORESHEETS
FORESHEW
FORESHEWED
FORESHEWING
FORESHEWN
FORESHEWS
FORESHIP
FORESHIPS
FORESHOCK
FORESHOCKS
FORESHORE
FORESHORES
FORESHORTEN
FORESHORTENED
FORESHORTENING
FORESHORTENINGS
FORESHORTENS
FORESHOW
FORESHOWED
FORESHOWING
FORESHOWN
FORESHOWS
FORESIDE
FORESIDES
FORESIGHT
FORESIGHTED
FORESIGHTEDLY
FORESIGHTEDNESS
FORESIGHTFUL
FORESIGHTLESS
FORESIGHTS
FORESIGNIFIED
FORESIGNIFIES

FORESIGNIFY
FORESIGNIFYING
FORESKIN
FORESKINS
FORESKIRT
FORESKIRTS
FORESLACK
FORESLACKED
FORESLACKING
FORESLACKS
FORESLOW
FORESLOWED
FORESLOWING
FORESLOWS
FORESPEAK
FORESPEAKING
FORESPEAKS
FORESPEND
FORESPENDING
FORESPENDS
FORESPENT
FORESPOKE
FORESPOKEN
FOREST
FORESTAGE
FORESTAGES
FORESTAIR
FORESTAIRS
FORESTAL
FORESTALL
FORESTALLED
FORESTALLER
FORESTALLERS
FORESTALLING
FORESTALLINGS
FORESTALLMENT
FORESTALLMENTS
FORESTALLS
FORESTALMENT
FORESTALMENTS
FORESTATION
FORESTATIONS
FORESTAY
FORESTAYS
FORESTAYSAIL
FORESTAYSAILS
FORESTEAL
FORESTED
FORESTER
FORESTERS
FORESTIAL
FORESTINE
FORESTING
FORESTLAND
FORESTLANDS
FORESTLESS

FORESTRIES
FORESTRY
FORESTS
FORESWEAR
FORESWEARING
FORESWEARS
FORESWORE
FORESWORN
FORETASTE
FORETASTED
FORETASTES
FORETASTING
FORETAUGHT
FORETEACH
FORETEACHES
FORETEACHING
FORETEETH
FORETELL
FORETELLER
FORETELLERS
FORETELLING
FORETELLS
FORETHINK
FORETHINKER
FORETHINKERS
FORETHINKING
FORETHINKS
FORETHOUGHT
FORETHOUGHTFUL
FORETHOUGHTS
FORETIME
FORETIMES
FORETOKEN
FORETOKENED
FORETOKENING
FORETOKENINGS
FORETOKENS
FORETOLD
FORETOOTH
FORETOP
FORETOPMAN
FORETOPMAST
FORETOPMASTS
FORETOPMEN
FORETOPS
FORETRIANGLE
FORETRIANGLED
FORETRIANGLES
FOREVER
FOREVERMORE
FOREVERNESS
FOREVERNESSES
FOREVERS
FOREVOUCHED
FOREWARD
FOREWARDS

FOREWARN
FOREWARNED
FOREWARNER
FOREWARNERS
FOREWARNING
FOREWARNINGLY
FOREWARNINGS
FOREWARNS
FOREWEIGH
FOREWEIGHED
FOREWEIGHING
FOREWEIGHS
FOREWENT
FOREWIND
FOREWINDS
FOREWING
FOREWINGS
FOREWOMAN
FOREWOMEN
FOREWORD
FOREWORDS
FOREWORN
FOREX
FOREYARD
FOREYARDS
FORFAIR
FORFAIRED
FORFAIRING
FORFAIRN
FORFAIRS
FORFAITER
FORFAITERS
FORFAITING
FORFAITINGS
FORFAULT
FORFAULTS
FORFEIT
FORFEITABLE
FORFEITED
FORFEITER
FORFEITERS
FORFEITING
FORFEITS
FORFEITURE
FORFEITURES
FORFEND
FORFENDED
FORFENDING
FORFENDS
FORFEUCHEN
FORFEX
FORFEXES
FORFICATE
FORFICULATE
FORFOCHEN
FORFOUGHEN

FORFOUGHTEN
FORGAT
FORGATHER
FORGATHERED
FORGATHERING
FORGATHERS
FORGAVE
FORGE
FORGEABILITIES
FORGEABILITY
FORGEABLE
FORGED
FORGEMAN
FORGEMEN
FORGER
FORGERIES
FORGERS
FORGERY
FORGES
FORGET
FORGETFUL
FORGETFULLY
FORGETFULNESS
FORGETFULNESSES
FORGETIVE
FORGETS
FORGETTABLE
FORGETTER
FORGETTERIES
FORGETTERS
FORGETTERY
FORGETTING
FORGETTINGLY
FORGETTINGS
FORGING
FORGINGS
FORGIVABLE
FORGIVABLY
FORGIVE
FORGIVEN
FORGIVENESS
FORGIVENESSES
FORGIVER
FORGIVERS
FORGIVES
FORGIVING
FORGIVINGLY
FORGIVINGNESS
FORGIVINGNESSES
FORGO
FORGOER
FORGOERS
FORGOES
FORGOING
FORGONE
FORGOT

FORGOTTEN
FORGOTTENNESS
FORGOTTENNESSES
FORHAILE
FORHAILED
FORHAILES
FORHAILING
FORHENT
FORHENTING
FORHENTS
FORHOO
FORHOOED
FORHOOIE
FORHOOIED
FORHOOIEING
FORHOOIES
FORHOOING
FORHOOS
FORHOW
FORHOWED
FORHOWING
FORHOWS
FORINSEC
FORINSECAL
FORINT
FORINTS
FORISFAMILIATE
FORISFAMILIATED
FORISFAMILIATES
FORJASKIT
FORJESKIT
FORJUDGE
FORJUDGED
FORJUDGEMENT
FORJUDGEMENTS
FORJUDGES
FORJUDGING
FORJUDGMENT
FORJUDGMENTS
FORK
FORKBALL
FORKBALLS
FORKED
FORKEDLY
FORKEDNESS
FORKEDNESSES
FORKER
FORKERS
FORKFUL
FORKFULS
FORKHEAD
FORKHEADS
FORKIER
FORKIEST
FORKINESS
FORKINESSES

FORKING
FORKLESS
FORKLIFT
FORKLIFTED
FORKLIFTING
FORKLIFTS
FORKLIKE
FORKS
FORKSFUL
FORKTAIL
FORKTAILS
FORKY
FORLANA
FORLANAS
FORLEND
FORLENDING
FORLENDS
FORLENT
FORLESE
FORLESES
FORLESING
FORLORE
FORLORN
FORLORNER
FORLORNEST
FORLORNLY
FORLORNNESS
FORLORNNESSES
FORLORNS
FORM
FORMABILITIES
FORMABILITY
FORMABLE
FORMAL
FORMALDEHYDE
FORMALDEHYDES
FORMALIN
FORMALINS
FORMALISATION
FORMALISATIONS
FORMALISE
FORMALISED
FORMALISER
FORMALISERS
FORMALISES
FORMALISING
FORMALISM
FORMALISMS
FORMALIST
FORMALISTIC
FORMALISTICAL
FORMALISTICALLY
FORMALISTS
FORMALITER
FORMALITIES
FORMALITY

FORMALIZABLE
FORMALIZATION
FORMALIZATIONS
FORMALIZE
FORMALIZED
FORMALIZER
FORMALIZERS
FORMALIZES
FORMALIZING
FORMALLY
FORMALNESS
FORMALNESSES
FORMALS
FORMAMIDE
FORMAMIDES
FORMANT
FORMANTS
FORMAT
FORMATE
FORMATED
FORMATES
FORMATING
FORMATION
FORMATIONAL
FORMATIONS
FORMATIVE
FORMATIVELY
FORMATIVENESS
FORMATIVES
FORMATS
FORMATTED
FORMATTER
FORMATTERS
FORMATTING
FORME
FORMED
FORMEE
FORMER
FORMERLY
FORMERS
FORMES
FORMFITTING
FORMFUL
FORMIATE
FORMIATES
FORMIC
FORMICANT
FORMICARIA
FORMICARIES
FORMICARIUM
FORMICARY
FORMICATE
FORMICATED
FORMICATES
FORMICATING
FORMICATION

FORMICATIONS
FORMIDABILITIES
FORMIDABILITY
FORMIDABLE
FORMIDABLENESS
FORMIDABLY
FORMING
FORMINGS
FORMLESS
FORMLESSLY
FORMLESSNESS
FORMLESSNESSES
FORMOL
FORMOLS
FORMS
FORMULA
FORMULAE
FORMULAIC
FORMULAICALLY
FORMULAR
FORMULARIES
FORMULARISATION
FORMULARISE
FORMULARISED
FORMULARISER
FORMULARISERS
FORMULARISES
FORMULARISING
FORMULARISTIC
FORMULARIZATION
FORMULARIZE
FORMULARIZED
FORMULARIZER
FORMULARIZERS
FORMULARIZES
FORMULARIZING
FORMULARY
FORMULAS
FORMULATE
FORMULATED
FORMULATES
FORMULATING
FORMULATION
FORMULATIONS
FORMULATOR
FORMULATORS
FORMULISE
FORMULISED
FORMULISES
FORMULISING
FORMULISM
FORMULISMS
FORMULIST
FORMULISTIC
FORMULISTICALLY
FORMULISTS

FORMULIZE
FORMULIZED
FORMULIZES
FORMULIZING
FORMWORK
FORMWORKS
FORMYL
FORMYLS
FORNENST
FORNENT
FORNICAL
FORNICATE
FORNICATED
FORNICATES
FORNICATING
FORNICATION
FORNICATIONS
FORNICATOR
FORNICATORS
FORNICATRESS
FORNICATRESSES
FORNICES
FORNIX
FORPET
FORPETS
FORPINE
FORPINED
FORPINES
FORPINING
FORPIT
FORPITS
FORRAD
FORRADER
FORRARDER
FORRAY
FORRAYED
FORRAYING
FORRAYS
FORREN
FORRIT
FORSAID
FORSAKE
FORSAKEN
FORSAKENLY
FORSAKENNESS
FORSAKENNESSES
FORSAKER
FORSAKERS
FORSAKES
FORSAKING
FORSAKINGS
FORSAY
FORSAYING
FORSAYS
FORSLACK
FORSLACKED

FORSLACKING
FORSLACKS
FORSLOE
FORSLOED
FORSLOEING
FORSLOES
FORSLOW
FORSLOWED
FORSLOWING
FORSLOWS
FORSOOK
FORSOOTH
FORSPEAK
FORSPEAKING
FORSPEAKS
FORSPEND
FORSPENDING
FORSPENDS
FORSPENT
FORSPOKE
FORSPOKEN
FORSTERITE
FORSWATT
FORSWEAR
FORSWEARER
FORSWEARERS
FORSWEARING
FORSWEARS
FORSWINK
FORSWINKED
FORSWINKING
FORSWINKS
FORSWONCK
FORSWORE
FORSWORN
FORSWORNNESS
FORSWORNNESSES
FORSWUNK
FORSYTHIA
FORSYTHIAS
FORT
FORTALICE
FORTALICES
FORTE
FORTED
FORTEPIANIST
FORTEPIANISTS
FORTEPIANO
FORTEPIANOS
FORTES
FORTH
FORTHCAME
FORTHCOME
FORTHCOMES
FORTHCOMING
FORTHCOMINGNESS

FORTHGOING
FORTHGOINGS
FORTHINK
FORTHINKING
FORTHINKS
FORTHOUGHT
FORTHRIGHT
FORTHRIGHTLY
FORTHRIGHTNESS
FORTHRIGHTS
FORTHWITH
FORTHY
FORTIES
FORTIETH
FORTIETHS
FORTIFIABLE
FORTIFICATION
FORTIFICATIONS
FORTIFIED
FORTIFIER
FORTIFIERS
FORTIFIES
FORTIFY
FORTIFYING
FORTIFYINGLY
FORTILAGE
FORTILAGES
FORTING
FORTIS
FORTISSIMI
FORTISSIMO
FORTISSIMOS
FORTISSISSIMO
FORTITUDE
FORTITUDES
FORTITUDINOUS
FORTLET
FORTLETS
FORTNIGHT
FORTNIGHTLIES
FORTNIGHTLY
FORTNIGHTS
FORTRESS
FORTRESSED
FORTRESSES
FORTRESSING
FORTRESSLIKE
FORTS
FORTUITIES
FORTUITISM
FORTUITISMS
FORTUITIST
FORTUITISTS
FORTUITOUS
FORTUITOUSLY
FORTUITOUSNESS

FORTUITY
FORTUNATE
FORTUNATELY
FORTUNATENESS
FORTUNATENESSES
FORTUNE
FORTUNED
FORTUNELESS
FORTUNES
FORTUNING
FORTUNIZE
FORTUNIZED
FORTUNIZES
FORTUNIZING
FORTY
FORTYISH
FORUM
FORUMS
FORWANDER
FORWANDERED
FORWANDERING
FORWANDERS
FORWARD
FORWARDED
FORWARDER
FORWARDERS
FORWARDEST
FORWARDING
FORWARDINGS
FORWARDLY
FORWARDNESS
FORWARDNESSES
FORWARDS
FORWARN
FORWARNED
FORWARNING
FORWARNS
FORWASTE
FORWASTED
FORWASTES
FORWASTING
FORWEARIED
FORWEARIES
FORWEARY
FORWEARYING
FORWENT
FORWHY
FORWORN
FORZA
FORZANDI
FORZANDO
FORZANDOS
FORZATI
FORZATO
FORZATOS
FOSS

FOSSA
FOSSAE
FOSSAS
FOSSATE
FOSSE
FOSSED
FOSSES
FOSSETTE
FOSSETTES
FOSSICK
FOSSICKED
FOSSICKER
FOSSICKERS
FOSSICKING
FOSSICKINGS
FOSSICKS
FOSSIL
FOSSILIFEROUS
FOSSILISABILITY
FOSSILISABLE
FOSSILISATION
FOSSILISATIONS
FOSSILISE
FOSSILISED
FOSSILISES
FOSSILISING
FOSSILIZABILITY
FOSSILIZABLE
FOSSILIZATION
FOSSILIZATIONS
FOSSILIZE
FOSSILIZED
FOSSILIZES
FOSSILIZING
FOSSILS
FOSSOR
FOSSORIAL
FOSSORS
FOSSULA
FOSSULAE
FOSSULATE
FOSTER
FOSTERAGE
FOSTERAGES
FOSTERED
FOSTERER
FOSTERERS
FOSTERING
FOSTERINGLY
FOSTERINGS
FOSTERLING
FOSTERLINGS
FOSTERS
FOSTRESS
FOSTRESSES
FOTHER

FOTHERED
FOTHERGILLA
FOTHERGILLAS
FOTHERING
FOTHERS
FOU
FOUAT
FOUATS
FOUD
FOUDRIE
FOUDRIES
FOUDROYANT
FOUDS
FOUER
FOUEST
FOUET
FOUETS
FOUETTE
FOUETTES
FOUGADE
FOUGADES
FOUGASSE
FOUGASSES
FOUGHT
FOUGHTEN
FOUGHTIER
FOUGHTIEST
FOUGHTY
FOUL
FOULARD
FOULARDS
FOULBROOD
FOULBROODS
FOULDER
FOULDERED
FOULDERING
FOULDERS
FOULE
FOULED
FOULER
FOULES
FOULEST
FOULIE
FOULIES
FOULING
FOULINGS
FOULLY
FOULMART
FOULMARTS
FOULMOUTHED
FOULNESS
FOULNESSES
FOULS
FOUMART
FOUMARTS
FOUND

FOUNDATION
FOUNDATIONAL
FOUNDATIONALLY
FOUNDATIONARY
FOUNDATIONER
FOUNDATIONERS
FOUNDATIONLESS
FOUNDATIONS
FOUNDED
FOUNDER
FOUNDERED
FOUNDERING
FOUNDEROUS
FOUNDERS
FOUNDING
FOUNDINGS
FOUNDLING
FOUNDLINGS
FOUNDRESS
FOUNDRESSES
FOUNDRIES
FOUNDRY
FOUNDS
FOUNT
FOUNTAIN
FOUNTAINED
FOUNTAINHEAD
FOUNTAINHEADS
FOUNTAINING
FOUNTAINLESS
FOUNTAINS
FOUNTFUL
FOUNTS
FOUR
FOURCHEE
FOURCHETTE
FOURCHETTES
FOURDRINIER
FOURDRINIERS
FOURFOLD
FOURFOLDNESS
FOURFOLDNESSES
FOURGON
FOURGONS
FOURPENCE
FOURPENCES
FOURPENNIES
FOURPENNY
FOURPLEX
FOURPLEXES
FOURRAGERE
FOURRAGERES
FOURS
FOURSCORE
FOURSES
FOURSOME

FOURSOMES
FOURSQUARE
FOURSQUARELY
FOURSQUARENESS
FOURTEEN
FOURTEENER
FOURTEENERS
FOURTEENS
FOURTEENTH
FOURTEENTHLY
FOURTEENTHS
FOURTH
FOURTHLY
FOURTHS
FOUS
FOUSSA
FOUSSAS
FOUSTIER
FOUSTIEST
FOUSTY
FOUTER
FOUTERED
FOUTERING
FOUTERS
FOUTH
FOUTHS
FOUTRA
FOUTRAS
FOUTRE
FOUTRED
FOUTRES
FOUTRING
FOVEA
FOVEAE
FOVEAL
FOVEAS
FOVEATE
FOVEATED
FOVEOLA
FOVEOLAE
FOVEOLAR
FOVEOLAS
FOVEOLATE
FOVEOLATED
FOVEOLE
FOVEOLES
FOVEOLET
FOVEOLETS
FOWL
FOWLED
FOWLER
FOWLERS
FOWLING
FOWLINGS
FOWLPOX
FOWLPOXES

FOWLS
FOWTH
FOWTHS
FOX
FOXBERRIES
FOXBERRY
FOXED
FOXES
FOXFIRE
FOXFIRES
FOXFISH
FOXFISHES
FOXGLOVE
FOXGLOVES
FOXHOLE
FOXHOLES
FOXHOUND
FOXHOUNDS
FOXHUNT
FOXHUNTED
FOXHUNTER
FOXHUNTERS
FOXHUNTING
FOXHUNTINGS
FOXHUNTS
FOXIE
FOXIER
FOXIES
FOXIEST
FOXILY
FOXINESS
FOXINESSES
FOXING
FOXINGS
FOXLIKE
FOXSHARK
FOXSHARKS
FOXSHIP
FOXSHIPS
FOXSKIN
FOXSKINS
FOXTAIL
FOXTAILS
FOXTROT
FOXTROTS
FOXTROTTED
FOXTROTTING
FOXY
FOY
FOYBOAT
FOYBOATS
FOYER
FOYERS
FOYLE
FOYLED
FOYLES

FOYLING
FOYNE
FOYNED
FOYNES
FOYNING
FOYS
FOZIER
FOZIEST
FOZINESS
FOZINESSES
FOZY
FRA
FRAB
FRABBED
FRABBING
FRABBIT
FRABJOUS
FRABJOUSLY
FRABS
FRACAS
FRACASES
FRACK
FRACKING
FRACKINGS
FRACT
FRACTAL
FRACTALITIES
FRACTALITY
FRACTALS
FRACTED
FRACTI
FRACTING
FRACTION
FRACTIONAL
FRACTIONALISE
FRACTIONALISED
FRACTIONALISES
FRACTIONALISING
FRACTIONALISM
FRACTIONALISMS
FRACTIONALIST
FRACTIONALISTS
FRACTIONALIZE
FRACTIONALIZED
FRACTIONALIZES
FRACTIONALIZING
FRACTIONALLY
FRACTIONARY
FRACTIONATE
FRACTIONATED
FRACTIONATES
FRACTIONATING
FRACTIONATION
FRACTIONATIONS
FRACTIONATOR
FRACTIONATORS

FRACTIONED
FRACTIONING
FRACTIONISATION
FRACTIONISE
FRACTIONISED
FRACTIONISES
FRACTIONISING
FRACTIONIZATION
FRACTIONIZE
FRACTIONIZED
FRACTIONIZES
FRACTIONIZING
FRACTIONLET
FRACTIONLETS
FRACTIONS
FRACTIOUS
FRACTIOUSLY
FRACTIOUSNESS
FRACTIOUSNESSES
FRACTOCUMULI
FRACTOCUMULUS
FRACTOGRAPHIES
FRACTOGRAPHY
FRACTOSTRATI
FRACTOSTRATUS
FRACTS
FRACTUR
FRACTURABILITY
FRACTURABLE
FRACTURABLENESS
FRACTURAL
FRACTURE
FRACTURED
FRACTURES
FRACTURING
FRACTURS
FRACTUS
FRAE
FRAENA
FRAENUM
FRAENUMS
FRAG
FRAGGED
FRAGGING
FRAGGINGS
FRAGILE
FRAGILELY
FRAGILENESS
FRAGILENESSES
FRAGILER
FRAGILEST
FRAGILITIES
FRAGILITY
FRAGMENT
FRAGMENTAL
FRAGMENTALLY

FRAGMENTARILY
FRAGMENTARINESS
FRAGMENTARY
FRAGMENTATE
FRAGMENTATED
FRAGMENTATES
FRAGMENTATING
FRAGMENTATION
FRAGMENTATIONS
FRAGMENTED
FRAGMENTING
FRAGMENTIZE
FRAGMENTIZED
FRAGMENTIZES
FRAGMENTIZING
FRAGMENTS
FRAGOR
FRAGORS
FRAGRANCE
FRAGRANCED
FRAGRANCES
FRAGRANCIES
FRAGRANCING
FRAGRANCY
FRAGRANT
FRAGRANTLY
FRAGRANTNESS
FRAGRANTNESSES
FRAGS
FRAICHEUR
FRAICHEURS
FRAIL
FRAILER
FRAILEST
FRAILISH
FRAILLY
FRAILNESS
FRAILNESSES
FRAILS
FRAILTEE
FRAILTEES
FRAILTIES
FRAILTY
FRAIM
FRAIMS
FRAISE
FRAISED
FRAISES
FRAISING
FRAKTUR
FRAKTURS
FRAMABLE
FRAMBESIA
FRAMBESIAS
FRAMBOESIA
FRAMBOESIAS

FRAMBOISE
FRAMBOISES
FRAME
FRAMEABLE
FRAMED
FRAMELESS
FRAMELESSLY
FRAMELESSNESS
FRAMER
FRAMERS
FRAMES
FRAMESHIFT
FRAMESHIFTS
FRAMEWORK
FRAMEWORKS
FRAMING
FRAMINGS
FRAMPAL
FRAMPLER
FRAMPLERS
FRAMPOLD
FRANC
FRANCHISE
FRANCHISED
FRANCHISEE
FRANCHISEES
FRANCHISEMENT
FRANCHISEMENTS
FRANCHISER
FRANCHISERS
FRANCHISES
FRANCHISING
FRANCHISOR
FRANCHISORS
FRANCIUM
FRANCIUMS
FRANCO
FRANCOLIN
FRANCOLINS
FRANCOMANIA
FRANCOMANIAS
FRANCOPHIL
FRANCOPHILE
FRANCOPHILES
FRANCOPHILS
FRANCOPHOBE
FRANCOPHOBES
FRANCOPHOBIA
FRANCOPHOBIAS
FRANCOPHONE
FRANCS
FRANGER
FRANGERS
FRANGIBILITIES
FRANGIBILITY
FRANGIBLE

FRANGIBLENESS
FRANGIPANE
FRANGIPANES
FRANGIPANI
FRANGIPANIS
FRANGIPANNI
FRANGLAIS
FRANION
FRANIONS
FRANK
FRANKABLE
FRANKALMOIGN
FRANKALMOIGNS
FRANKED
FRANKER
FRANKERS
FRANKEST
FRANKFURT
FRANKFURTER
FRANKFURTERS
FRANKFURTS
FRANKINCENSE
FRANKINCENSES
FRANKING
FRANKLIN
FRANKLINITE
FRANKLINITES
FRANKLINS
FRANKLY
FRANKNESS
FRANKNESSES
FRANKPLEDGE
FRANKPLEDGES
FRANKS
FRANTIC
FRANTICALLY
FRANTICLY
FRANTICNESS
FRANTICNESSES
FRANZIER
FRANZIEST
FRANZY
FRAP
FRAPE
FRAPPANT
FRAPPE
FRAPPED
FRAPPEE
FRAPPES
FRAPPING
FRAPS
FRAS
FRASCATI
FRASCATIS
FRASS
FRASSES

FRAT
FRATCH
FRATCHES
FRATCHETY
FRATCHIER
FRATCHIEST
FRATCHING
FRATCHY
FRATE
FRATER
FRATERIES
FRATERNAL
FRATERNALISM
FRATERNALISMS
FRATERNALLY
FRATERNISATION
FRATERNISATIONS
FRATERNISE
FRATERNISED
FRATERNISER
FRATERNISERS
FRATERNISES
FRATERNISING
FRATERNITIES
FRATERNITY
FRATERNIZATION
FRATERNIZATIONS
FRATERNIZE
FRATERNIZED
FRATERNIZER
FRATERNIZERS
FRATERNIZES
FRATERNIZING
FRATERS
FRATERY
FRATI
FRATRICIDAL
FRATRICIDE
FRATRICIDES
FRATRIES
FRATRY
FRATS
FRAU
FRAUD
FRAUDFUL
FRAUDFULLY
FRAUDS
FRAUDSMAN
FRAUDSMEN
FRAUDSTER
FRAUDSTERS
FRAUDULENCE
FRAUDULENCES
FRAUDULENCIES
FRAUDULENCY
FRAUDULENT

FRAUDULENTLY
FRAUDULENTNESS
FRAUGHAN
FRAUGHANS
FRAUGHT
FRAUGHTAGE
FRAUGHTAGES
FRAUGHTED
FRAUGHTER
FRAUGHTEST
FRAUGHTING
FRAUGHTS
FRAULEIN
FRAULEINS
FRAUS
FRAUTAGE
FRAUTAGES
FRAWZEY
FRAWZEYS
FRAXINELLA
FRAXINELLAS
FRAY
FRAYED
FRAYING
FRAYINGS
FRAYS
FRAZIL
FRAZILS
FRAZZLE
FRAZZLED
FRAZZLES
FRAZZLING
FREAK
FREAKED
FREAKFUL
FREAKIER
FREAKIEST
FREAKILY
FREAKINESS
FREAKINESSES
FREAKING
FREAKISH
FREAKISHLY
FREAKISHNESS
FREAKISHNESSES
FREAKOUT
FREAKOUTS
FREAKS
FREAKY
FRECKLE
FRECKLED
FRECKLES
FRECKLIER
FRECKLIEST
FRECKLING
FRECKLINGS

FRECKLY
FREDAINE
FREDAINES
FREE
FREEBASE
FREEBASED
FREEBASER
FREEBASERS
FREEBASES
FREEBASING
FREEBEE
FREEBEES
FREEBIE
FREEBIES
FREEBOARD
FREEBOARDS
FREEBOOT
FREEBOOTED
FREEBOOTER
FREEBOOTERIES
FREEBOOTERS
FREEBOOTERY
FREEBOOTIES
FREEBOOTING
FREEBOOTINGS
FREEBOOTS
FREEBOOTY
FREEBORN
FREED
FREEDMAN
FREEDMEN
FREEDOM
FREEDOMS
FREEDWOMAN
FREEDWOMEN
FREEFORM
FREEHAND
FREEHANDED
FREEHANDEDLY
FREEHANDEDNESS
FREEHEARTED
FREEHEARTEDLY
FREEHOLD
FREEHOLDER
FREEHOLDERS
FREEHOLDS
FREEING
FREELANCE
FREELANCED
FREELANCER
FREELANCERS
FREELANCES
FREELANCING
FREELOAD
FREELOADED
FREELOADER

FREELOADERS
FREELOADING
FREELOADINGS
FREELOADS
FREELY
FREEMAN
FREEMARTIN
FREEMARTINS
FREEMASON
FREEMASONIC
FREEMASONRIES
FREEMASONRY
FREEMASONS
FREEMEN
FREENESS
FREENESSES
FREEPHONE
FREEPHONES
FREER
FREERS
FREES
FREESHEET
FREESHEETS
FREESIA
FREESIAS
FREEST
FREESTANDING
FREESTONE
FREESTONES
FREESTYLE
FREESTYLER
FREESTYLERS
FREESTYLES
FREESTYLING
FREET
FREETHINKER
FREETHINKERS
FREETHINKING
FREETHINKINGS
FREETIER
FREETIEST
FREETS
FREETY
FREEWARE
FREEWARES
FREEWAY
FREEWAYS
FREEWHEEL
FREEWHEELED
FREEWHEELER
FREEWHEELERS
FREEWHEELING
FREEWHEELINGLY
FREEWHEELINGS
FREEWHEELS
FREEWILL

FREEWOMAN
FREEWOMEN
FREEWRITING
FREEWRITINGS
FREEZABLE
FREEZE
FREEZER
FREEZERS
FREEZES
FREEZING
FREEZINGLY
FREEZINGS
FREIGHT
FREIGHTAGE
FREIGHTAGES
FREIGHTED
FREIGHTER
FREIGHTERS
FREIGHTING
FREIGHTLESS
FREIGHTLINER
FREIGHTLINERS
FREIGHTS
FREIT
FREITIER
FREITIEST
FREITS
FREITY
FREMD
FREMDS
FREMESCENCE
FREMESCENCES
FREMESCENT
FREMIT
FREMITS
FREMITUS
FREMITUSES
FRENA
FRENCH
FRENCHED
FRENCHES
FRENCHIFICATION
FRENCHIFIED
FRENCHIFIES
FRENCHIFY
FRENCHIFYING
FRENCHING
FRENETIC
FRENETICAL
FRENETICALLY
FRENETICISM
FRENETICISMS
FRENETICNESS
FRENETICS
FRENNE
FRENULA

FRENULUM
FRENULUMS
FRENUM
FRENUMS
FRENZICAL
FRENZIED
FRENZIEDLY
FRENZIES
FRENZILY
FRENZY
FRENZYING
FREON
FREONS
FREQUENCE
FREQUENCES
FREQUENCIES
FREQUENCY
FREQUENT
FREQUENTABLE
FREQUENTATION
FREQUENTATIONS
FREQUENTATIVE
FREQUENTATIVES
FREQUENTED
FREQUENTER
FREQUENTERS
FREQUENTEST
FREQUENTING
FREQUENTLY
FREQUENTNESS
FREQUENTNESSES
FREQUENTS
FRERE
FRERES
FRESCADE
FRESCADES
FRESCO
FRESCOED
FRESCOER
FRESCOERS
FRESCOES
FRESCOING
FRESCOINGS
FRESCOIST
FRESCOISTS
FRESCOS
FRESH
FRESHED
FRESHEN
FRESHENED
FRESHENER
FRESHENERS
FRESHENING
FRESHENS
FRESHER
FRESHERDOM

FRESHERDOMS
FRESHERS
FRESHES
FRESHEST
FRESHET
FRESHETS
FRESHING
FRESHISH
FRESHLY
FRESHMAN
FRESHMANSHIP
FRESHMANSHIPS
FRESHMEN
FRESHNESS
FRESHNESSES
FRESHWATER
FRESHWATERS
FRESNEL
FRESNELS
FRET
FRETBOARD
FRETBOARDS
FRETFUL
FRETFULLY
FRETFULNESS
FRETFULNESSES
FRETLESS
FRETS
FRETSAW
FRETSAWS
FRETSOME
FRETTED
FRETTER
FRETTERS
FRETTIER
FRETTIEST
FRETTING
FRETTINGS
FRETTY
FRETWORK
FRETWORKS
FRIABILITIES
FRIABILITY
FRIABLE
FRIABLENESS
FRIABLENESSES
FRIAND
FRIANDE
FRIANDES
FRIANDS
FRIAR
FRIARBIRD
FRIARBIRDS
FRIARIES
FRIARLY
FRIARS

FRIARY
FRIB
FRIBBLE
FRIBBLED
FRIBBLER
FRIBBLERS
FRIBBLES
FRIBBLING
FRIBBLISH
FRIBS
FRICADEL
FRICADELS
FRICANDEAU
FRICANDEAUS
FRICANDEAUX
FRICANDO
FRICANDOES
FRICASSEE
FRICASSEED
FRICASSEEING
FRICASSEES
FRICATIVE
FRICATIVES
FRICHT
FRICHTED
FRICHTING
FRICHTS
FRICKING
FRICTION
FRICTIONAL
FRICTIONALLY
FRICTIONLESS
FRICTIONLESSLY
FRICTIONS
FRIDGE
FRIDGED
FRIDGES
FRIDGING
FRIED
FRIEDCAKE
FRIEDCAKES
FRIEND
FRIENDED
FRIENDING
FRIENDINGS
FRIENDLESS
FRIENDLESSNESS
FRIENDLIER
FRIENDLIES
FRIENDLIEST
FRIENDLILY
FRIENDLINESS
FRIENDLINESSES
FRIENDLY
FRIENDS
FRIENDSHIP

FRIENDSHIPS
FRIER
FRIERS
FRIES
FRIEZE
FRIEZED
FRIEZELIKE
FRIEZES
FRIEZING
FRIG
FRIGATE
FRIGATES
FRIGATOON
FRIGATOONS
FRIGES
FRIGGED
FRIGGER
FRIGGERS
FRIGGING
FRIGGINGS
FRIGHT
FRIGHTED
FRIGHTEN
FRIGHTENABILITY
FRIGHTENABLE
FRIGHTENED
FRIGHTENER
FRIGHTENERS
FRIGHTENING
FRIGHTENINGLY
FRIGHTENS
FRIGHTFUL
FRIGHTFULLY
FRIGHTFULNESS
FRIGHTFULNESSES
FRIGHTING
FRIGHTS
FRIGHTSOME
FRIGID
FRIGIDARIA
FRIGIDARIUM
FRIGIDER
FRIGIDEST
FRIGIDITIES
FRIGIDITY
FRIGIDLY
FRIGIDNESS
FRIGIDNESSES
FRIGORIFIC
FRIGORIFICO
FRIGORIFICOS
FRIGOT
FRIGOTS
FRIGS
FRIJOL
FRIJOLE

FRIJOLES
FRIKKADEL
FRIKKADELS
FRILL
FRILLED
FRILLER
FRILLERS
FRILLIER
FRILLIES
FRILLIEST
FRILLILY
FRILLINESS
FRILLING
FRILLINGS
FRILLS
FRILLY
FRINGE
FRINGED
FRINGELESS
FRINGES
FRINGIER
FRINGIEST
FRINGILLACEOUS
FRINGILLID
FRINGILLIFORM
FRINGILLINE
FRINGING
FRINGY
FRIPON
FRIPONNERIE
FRIPONNERIES
FRIPONS
FRIPPER
FRIPPERER
FRIPPERERS
FRIPPERIES
FRIPPERS
FRIPPERY
FRIPPET
FRIPPETS
FRIS
FRISE
FRISEE
FRISEES
FRISES
FRISETTE
FRISETTES
FRISEUR
FRISEURS
FRISK
FRISKA
FRISKAS
FRISKED
FRISKER
FRISKERS
FRISKET

FRISKETS
FRISKFUL
FRISKIER
FRISKIEST
FRISKILY
FRISKINESS
FRISKINESSES
FRISKING
FRISKINGLY
FRISKINGS
FRISKS
FRISKY
FRISSON
FRISSONS
FRIST
FRISTED
FRISTING
FRISTS
FRISURE
FRISURES
FRIT
FRITFLIES
FRITFLY
FRITH
FRITHBORH
FRITHBORHS
FRITHGILDS
FRITHS
FRITHSOKEN
FRITHSOKENS
FRITHSTOOL
FRITHSTOOLS
FRITILLARIA
FRITILLARIAS
FRITILLARIES
FRITILLARY
FRITS
FRITT
FRITTATA
FRITTATAS
FRITTED
FRITTER
FRITTERED
FRITTERER
FRITTERERS
FRITTERING
FRITTERS
FRITTING
FRITTS
FRITURE
FRITURES
FRITZ
FRITZES
FRIVOL
FRIVOLED
FRIVOLER

FRIVOLERS
FRIVOLING
FRIVOLITIES
FRIVOLITY
FRIVOLLED
FRIVOLLER
FRIVOLLERS
FRIVOLLING
FRIVOLOUS
FRIVOLOUSLY
FRIVOLOUSNESS
FRIVOLOUSNESSES
FRIVOLS
FRIZ
FRIZE
FRIZED
FRIZER
FRIZERS
FRIZES
FRIZETTE
FRIZETTES
FRIZING
FRIZZ
FRIZZANTE
FRIZZED
FRIZZER
FRIZZERS
FRIZZES
FRIZZIER
FRIZZIEST
FRIZZILY
FRIZZINESS
FRIZZINESSES
FRIZZING
FRIZZLE
FRIZZLED
FRIZZLER
FRIZZLERS
FRIZZLES
FRIZZLIER
FRIZZLIEST
FRIZZLINESS
FRIZZLING
FRIZZLY
FRIZZY
FRO
FROCK
FROCKED
FROCKING
FROCKINGS
FROCKLESS
FROCKS
FROE
FROES
FROG
FROGBIT

FROGBITS
FROGEYE
FROGEYED
FROGEYES
FROGFISH
FROGFISHES
FROGGED
FROGGERIES
FROGGERY
FROGGIER
FROGGIEST
FROGGING
FROGGINGS
FROGGY
FROGHOPPER
FROGHOPPERS
FROGLET
FROGLETS
FROGLIKE
FROGLING
FROGLINGS
FROGMAN
FROGMARCH
FROGMARCHED
FROGMARCHES
FROGMARCHING
FROGMEN
FROGMOUTH
FROGMOUTHS
FROGS
FROGSPAWN
FROGSPAWNS
FROIDEUR
FROIDEURS
FROISE
FROISES
FROLIC
FROLICKED
FROLICKER
FROLICKERS
FROLICKING
FROLICKY
FROLICS
FROLICSOME
FROLICSOMELY
FROLICSOMENESS
FROM
FROMAGE
FROMAGES
FROMENTIES
FROMENTY
FROND
FRONDAGE
FRONDAGES
FRONDED
FRONDENT

FRONDESCENCE
FRONDESCENCES
FRONDESCENT
FRONDEUR
FRONDEURS
FRONDIFEROUS
FRONDLESS
FRONDOSE
FRONDOUS
FRONDS
FRONS
FRONT
FRONTAGE
FRONTAGER
FRONTAGERS
FRONTAGES
FRONTAL
FRONTALITIES
FRONTALITY
FRONTALLY
FRONTALS
FRONTCOURT
FRONTCOURTS
FRONTED
FRONTER
FRONTES
FRONTIER
FRONTIERED
FRONTIERING
FRONTIERS
FRONTIERSMAN
FRONTIERSMEN
FRONTIERSWOMAN
FRONTIERSWOMEN
FRONTING
FRONTISPIECE
FRONTISPIECED
FRONTISPIECES
FRONTISPIECING
FRONTLESS
FRONTLESSLY
FRONTLET
FRONTLETS
FRONTLINE
FRONTMAN
FRONTMEN
FRONTOGENESES
FRONTOGENESIS
FRONTOGENETIC
FRONTOLYSES
FRONTOLYSIS
FRONTON
FRONTONS
FRONTOON
FRONTOONS
FRONTRUNNER

FRONTRUNNERS
FRONTRUNNING
FRONTS
FRONTWARD
FRONTWARDS
FRONTWAYS
FRONTWISE
FRORE
FROREN
FRORN
FRORNE
FRORY
FROSH
FROST
FROSTBIT
FROSTBITE
FROSTBITES
FROSTBITING
FROSTBITINGS
FROSTBITTEN
FROSTBOUND
FROSTED
FROSTEDS
FROSTIER
FROSTIEST
FROSTILY
FROSTINESS
FROSTINESSES
FROSTING
FROSTINGS
FROSTLESS
FROSTLIKE
FROSTS
FROSTWORK
FROSTWORKS
FROSTY
FROTH
FROTHED
FROTHERIES
FROTHERY
FROTHIER
FROTHIEST
FROTHILY
FROTHINESS
FROTHINESSES
FROTHING
FROTHLESS
FROTHS
FROTHY
FROTTAGE
FROTTAGES
FROTTEUR
FROTTEURS
FROUFROU
FROUFROUS
FROUGHIER

FROUGHIEST
FROUGHY
FROUNCE
FROUNCED
FROUNCES
FROUNCING
FROUZIER
FROUZIEST
FROUZILY
FROUZINESS
FROUZY
FROW
FROWARD
FROWARDLY
FROWARDNESS
FROWARDNESSES
FROWARDS
FROWIE
FROWIER
FROWIEST
FROWN
FROWNED
FROWNER
FROWNERS
FROWNING
FROWNINGLY
FROWNS
FROWS
FROWSIER
FROWSIEST
FROWSILY
FROWSINESS
FROWST
FROWSTED
FROWSTER
FROWSTERS
FROWSTIER
FROWSTIEST
FROWSTINESS
FROWSTINESSES
FROWSTING
FROWSTS
FROWSTY
FROWSY
FROWY
FROWZIER
FROWZIEST
FROWZILY
FROWZINESS
FROWZY
FROZE
FROZEN
FROZENLY
FROZENNESS
FROZENNESSES
FRUCTAN

FRUCTANS
FRUCTED
FRUCTIFEROUS
FRUCTIFEROUSLY
FRUCTIFICATION
FRUCTIFICATIONS
FRUCTIFIED
FRUCTIFIER
FRUCTIFIERS
FRUCTIFIES
FRUCTIFY
FRUCTIFYING
FRUCTIVE
FRUCTIVOROUS
FRUCTOSE
FRUCTOSES
FRUCTUARIES
FRUCTUARY
FRUCTUATE
FRUCTUATED
FRUCTUATES
FRUCTUATING
FRUCTUATION
FRUCTUATIONS
FRUCTUOUS
FRUCTUOUSLY
FRUCTUOUSNESS
FRUG
FRUGAL
FRUGALIST
FRUGALISTS
FRUGALITIES
FRUGALITY
FRUGALLY
FRUGALNESS
FRUGGED
FRUGGING
FRUGIFEROUS
FRUGIVORE
FRUGIVORES
FRUGIVOROUS
FRUGS
FRUICT
FRUICTS
FRUIT
FRUITAGE
FRUITAGES
FRUITARIAN
FRUITARIANISM
FRUITARIANS
FRUITCAKE
FRUITCAKED
FRUITCAKES
FRUITED
FRUITER
FRUITERER

FRUITERERS
FRUITERESS
FRUITERESSES
FRUITERIES
FRUITERS
FRUITERY
FRUITFUL
FRUITFULLER
FRUITFULLEST
FRUITFULLY
FRUITFULNESS
FRUITFULNESSES
FRUITIER
FRUITIEST
FRUITILY
FRUITINESS
FRUITINESSES
FRUITING
FRUITINGS
FRUITION
FRUITIONS
FRUITIVE
FRUITLESS
FRUITLESSLY
FRUITLESSNESS
FRUITLESSNESSES
FRUITLET
FRUITLETS
FRUITLIKE
FRUITS
FRUITWOOD
FRUITWOODS
FRUITY
FRUMENTACEOUS
FRUMENTARIOUS
FRUMENTATION
FRUMENTATIONS
FRUMENTIES
FRUMENTY
FRUMP
FRUMPED
FRUMPIER
FRUMPIEST
FRUMPILY
FRUMPINESS
FRUMPING
FRUMPISH
FRUMPISHLY
FRUMPISHNESS
FRUMPLE
FRUMPLED
FRUMPLES
FRUMPLING
FRUMPS
FRUMPY
FRUSEMIDE

FRUSH
FRUSHED
FRUSHES
FRUSHING
FRUST
FRUSTA
FRUSTRATE
FRUSTRATED
FRUSTRATER
FRUSTRATERS
FRUSTRATES
FRUSTRATING
FRUSTRATINGLY
FRUSTRATION
FRUSTRATIONS
FRUSTS
FRUSTULE
FRUSTULES
FRUSTUM
FRUSTUMS
FRUTESCENCE
FRUTESCENT
FRUTEX
FRUTICES
FRUTICOSE
FRUTIFIED
FRUTIFIES
FRUTIFY
FRUTIFYING
FRY
FRYER
FRYERS
FRYING
FRYINGS
FRYPAN
FRYPANS
FUB
FUBAR
FUBBED
FUBBERIES
FUBBERY
FUBBIER
FUBBIEST
FUBBING
FUBBY
FUBS
FUBSIER
FUBSIEST
FUBSY
FUCHSIA
FUCHSIAS
FUCHSIN
FUCHSINE
FUCHSINES
FUCHSINS
FUCHSITE

FUCHSITES
FUCI
FUCIVOROUS
FUCK
FUCKED
FUCKER
FUCKERS
FUCKING
FUCKINGS
FUCKS
FUCKUP
FUCKUPS
FUCKWIT
FUCKWITS
FUCKWITTED
FUCKWITTEDLY
FUCOID
FUCOIDAL
FUCOIDS
FUCOSE
FUCOSES
FUCOUS
FUCOXANTHIN
FUCOXANTHINS
FUCUS
FUCUSED
FUCUSES
FUD
FUDDLE
FUDDLED
FUDDLER
FUDDLERS
FUDDLES
FUDDLING
FUDDLINGS
FUDGE
FUDGED
FUDGES
FUDGING
FUDS
FUEHRER
FUEHRERS
FUEL
FUELED
FUELER
FUELERS
FUELING
FUELLED
FUELLER
FUELLERS
FUELLING
FUELS
FUELWOOD
FUELWOODS
FUERO
FUEROS

FUFF
FUFFED
FUFFIER
FUFFIEST
FUFFING
FUFFS
FUFFY
FUG
FUGACIOUS
FUGACIOUSLY
FUGACIOUSNESS
FUGACIOUSNESSES
FUGACITIES
FUGACITY
FUGAL
FUGALLY
FUGATO
FUGATOS
FUGGED
FUGGIER
FUGGIEST
FUGGILY
FUGGING
FUGGY
FUGHETTA
FUGHETTAS
FUGIE
FUGIES
FUGIO
FUGIOS
FUGITATION
FUGITATIONS
FUGITIVE
FUGITIVELY
FUGITIVENESS
FUGITIVENESSES
FUGITIVES
FUGITOMETER
FUGITOMETERS
FUGITOMETRIC
FUGLE
FUGLED
FUGLEMAN
FUGLEMEN
FUGLES
FUGLING
FUGS
FUGU
FUGUE
FUGUED
FUGUELIKE
FUGUES
FUGUING
FUGUIST
FUGUISTS
FUGUS

FUHRER
FUHRERS
FUJI
FUJIS
FULCRA
FULCRATE
FULCRUM
FULCRUMS
FULFIL
FULFILL
FULFILLED
FULFILLER
FULFILLERS
FULFILLING
FULFILLINGS
FULFILLMENT
FULFILLMENTS
FULFILLS
FULFILMENT
FULFILMENTS
FULFILS
FULGENCIES
FULGENCY
FULGENT
FULGENTLY
FULGID
FULGOR
FULGOROUS
FULGORS
FULGOUR
FULGOURS
FULGURAL
FULGURANT
FULGURATE
FULGURATED
FULGURATES
FULGURATING
FULGURATION
FULGURATIONS
FULGURITE
FULGURITES
FULGUROUS
FULHAM
FULHAMS
FULIGINOSITIES
FULIGINOSITY
FULIGINOUS
FULIGINOUSLY
FULIGINOUSNESS
FULL
FULLAGE
FULLAGES
FULLAM
FULLAMS
FULLAN
FULLANS

FULLBACK
FULLBACKS
FULLED
FULLER
FULLERED
FULLERENE
FULLERENES
FULLERIDE
FULLERIDES
FULLERIES
FULLERING
FULLERITE
FULLERITES
FULLERS
FULLERY
FULLEST
FULLFACE
FULLFACES
FULLING
FULLISH
FULLMOUTHED
FULLNESS
FULLNESSES
FULLS
FULLY
FULMAR
FULMARS
FULMINANT
FULMINANTS
FULMINATE
FULMINATED
FULMINATES
FULMINATING
FULMINATINGLY
FULMINATION
FULMINATIONS
FULMINATOR
FULMINATORS
FULMINATORY
FULMINE
FULMINED
FULMINEOUS
FULMINES
FULMINIC
FULMINING
FULMINOUS
FULNESS
FULNESSES
FULSOME
FULSOMELY
FULSOMENESS
FULSOMENESSES
FULSOMER
FULSOMEST
FULVID
FULVOUS

FUM
FUMADO
FUMADOES
FUMADOS
FUMAGE
FUMAGES
FUMARASE
FUMARASES
FUMARATE
FUMARATES
FUMARIC
FUMAROLE
FUMAROLES
FUMAROLIC
FUMATORIA
FUMATORIES
FUMATORIUM
FUMATORIUMS
FUMATORY
FUMBLE
FUMBLED
FUMBLER
FUMBLERS
FUMBLES
FUMBLING
FUMBLINGLY
FUMBLINGNESS
FUME
FUMED
FUMELESS
FUMELIKE
FUMER
FUMEROLE
FUMEROLES
FUMERS
FUMES
FUMET
FUMETS
FUMETTE
FUMETTES
FUMETTI
FUMETTO
FUMIER
FUMIEST
FUMIGANT
FUMIGANTS
FUMIGATE
FUMIGATED
FUMIGATES
FUMIGATING
FUMIGATION
FUMIGATIONS
FUMIGATOR
FUMIGATORS
FUMIGATORY
FUMING

FUMINGLY
FUMITORIES
FUMITORY
FUMOSITIES
FUMOSITY
FUMOUS
FUMS
FUMULI
FUMULUS
FUMY
FUN
FUNAMBULATE
FUNAMBULATED
FUNAMBULATES
FUNAMBULATING
FUNAMBULATION
FUNAMBULATIONS
FUNAMBULATOR
FUNAMBULATORS
FUNAMBULATORY
FUNAMBULISM
FUNAMBULISMS
FUNAMBULIST
FUNAMBULISTS
FUNBOARD
FUNBOARDS
FUNCTION
FUNCTIONAL
FUNCTIONALISM
FUNCTIONALISMS
FUNCTIONALIST
FUNCTIONALISTIC
FUNCTIONALISTS
FUNCTIONALITIES
FUNCTIONALITY
FUNCTIONALLY
FUNCTIONALS
FUNCTIONARIES
FUNCTIONARY
FUNCTIONATE
FUNCTIONATED
FUNCTIONATES
FUNCTIONATING
FUNCTIONED
FUNCTIONING
FUNCTIONLESS
FUNCTIONS
FUNCTOR
FUNCTORS
FUND
FUNDABLE
FUNDAMENT
FUNDAMENTAL
FUNDAMENTALISM
FUNDAMENTALISMS
FUNDAMENTALIST

FUNDAMENTALISTS
FUNDAMENTALITY
FUNDAMENTALLY
FUNDAMENTALNESS
FUNDAMENTALS
FUNDAMENTS
FUNDED
FUNDER
FUNDERS
FUNDHOLDER
FUNDHOLDERS
FUNDHOLDING
FUNDI
FUNDIC
FUNDIE
FUNDIES
FUNDING
FUNDINGS
FUNDIS
FUNDLESS
FUNDRAISE
FUNDRAISED
FUNDRAISER
FUNDRAISERS
FUNDRAISES
FUNDS
FUNDUS
FUNDY
FUNEBRAL
FUNEBRE
FUNEBRIAL
FUNERAL
FUNERALS
FUNERARY
FUNEREAL
FUNEREALLY
FUNEST
FUNFAIR
FUNFAIRS
FUNG
FUNGAL
FUNGALS
FUNGI
FUNGIBILITIES
FUNGIBILITY
FUNGIBLE
FUNGIBLES
FUNGIC
FUNGICIDAL
FUNGICIDALLY
FUNGICIDE
FUNGICIDES
FUNGIFORM
FUNGISTAT
FUNGISTATIC
FUNGISTATICALLY

FUNGISTATS
FUNGO
FUNGOES
FUNGOID
FUNGOIDAL
FUNGOIDS
FUNGOSITIES
FUNGOSITY
FUNGOUS
FUNGS
FUNGUS
FUNGUSES
FUNICLE
FUNICLES
FUNICULAR
FUNICULARS
FUNICULATE
FUNICULI
FUNICULUS
FUNK
FUNKED
FUNKER
FUNKERS
FUNKHOLE
FUNKHOLES
FUNKIA
FUNKIAS
FUNKIER
FUNKIEST
FUNKINESS
FUNKINESSES
FUNKING
FUNKS
FUNKSTER
FUNKSTERING
FUNKSTERS
FUNKY
FUNNED
FUNNEL
FUNNELED
FUNNELFORM
FUNNELING
FUNNELLED
FUNNELLING
FUNNELS
FUNNER
FUNNEST
FUNNIER
FUNNIES
FUNNIEST
FUNNILY
FUNNINESS
FUNNINESSES
FUNNING
FUNNY
FUNNYMAN

FUNNYMEN
FUNS
FUNSTER
FUNSTERS
FUR
FURACIOUS
FURACIOUSNESS
FURACIOUSNESSES
FURACITIES
FURACITY
FURAL
FURALDEHYDE
FURALS
FURAN
FURANE
FURANES
FURANOSE
FURANOSES
FURANOSIDE
FURANOSIDES
FURANS
FURAZOLIDONE
FURAZOLIDONES
FURBEARER
FURBEARERS
FURBELOW
FURBELOWED
FURBELOWING
FURBELOWS
FURBISH
FURBISHED
FURBISHER
FURBISHERS
FURBISHES
FURBISHING
FURCA
FURCAE
FURCAL
FURCATE
FURCATED
FURCATES
FURCATING
FURCATION
FURCATIONS
FURCIFEROUS
FURCRAEA
FURCRAEAS
FURCULA
FURCULAE
FURCULAR
FURCULUM
FURDER
FUREUR
FUREURS
FURFAIR
FURFAIRS

FURFUR
FURFURACEOUS
FURFURACEOUSLY
FURFURAL
FURFURALDEHYDE
FURFURALDEHYDES
FURFURALS
FURFURAN
FURFURANS
FURFURES
FURFUROL
FURFUROLE
FURFUROLES
FURFUROLS
FURFUROUS
FURFURS
FURIBUND
FURIES
FURIOSITIES
FURIOSITY
FURIOSO
FURIOSOS
FURIOUS
FURIOUSLY
FURIOUSNESS
FURIOUSNESSES
FURL
FURLABLE
FURLANA
FURLANAS
FURLED
FURLER
FURLERS
FURLESS
FURLING
FURLONG
FURLONGS
FURLOUGH
FURLOUGHED
FURLOUGHING
FURLOUGHS
FURLS
FURMENTIES
FURMENTY
FURMETIES
FURMETY
FURMITIES
FURMITY
FURNACE
FURNACED
FURNACES
FURNACING
FURNIMENT
FURNIMENTS
FURNISH
FURNISHED

FURNISHER
FURNISHERS
FURNISHES
FURNISHING
FURNISHINGS
FURNISHMENT
FURNISHMENTS
FURNITURE
FURNITURES
FUROL
FUROLE
FUROLES
FUROLS
FUROR
FURORE
FURORES
FURORS
FUROSEMIDE
FUROSEMIDES
FURPHIES
FURPHY
FURR
FURRED
FURRIER
FURRIERIES
FURRIERS
FURRIERY
FURRIES
FURRIEST
FURRILY
FURRINER
FURRINERS
FURRINESS
FURRINESSES
FURRING
FURRINGS
FURROW
FURROWED
FURROWER
FURROWERS
FURROWING
FURROWLESS
FURROWS
FURROWY
FURRS
FURRY
FURTH
FURTHCOMING
FURTHCOMINGS
FURTHER
FURTHERANCE
FURTHERANCES
FURTHERED
FURTHERER
FURTHERERS

FURTHERING
FURTHERMORE
FURTHERMOST
FURTHERS
FURTHERSOME
FURTHEST
FURTIVE
FURTIVELY
FURTIVENESS
FURTIVENESSES
FURUNCLE
FURUNCLES
FURUNCULAR
FURUNCULOSES
FURUNCULOSIS
FURUNCULOUS
FURY
FURZE
FURZES
FURZIER
FURZIEST
FURZY
FUSAIN
FUSAINS
FUSAROL
FUSAROLE
FUSAROLES
FUSAROLS
FUSC
FUSCOUS
FUSE
FUSED
FUSEE
FUSEES
FUSEL
FUSELAGE
FUSELAGES
FUSELESS
FUSELS
FUSES
FUSHION
FUSHIONLESS
FUSHIONS
FUSIBILITIES
FUSIBILITY
FUSIBLE
FUSIBLENESS
FUSIBLY
FUSIFORM
FUSIL
FUSILE
FUSILEER
FUSILEERS
FUSILIER
FUSILIERS
FUSILLADE

FUSILLADED
FUSILLADES
FUSILLADING
FUSILLATION
FUSILLATIONS
FUSILLI
FUSILLIS
FUSILS
FUSING
FUSION
FUSIONISM
FUSIONISMS
FUSIONIST
FUSIONISTS
FUSIONLESS
FUSIONS
FUSS
FUSSBUDGET
FUSSBUDGETS
FUSSBUDGETY
FUSSED
FUSSER
FUSSERS
FUSSES
FUSSIER
FUSSIEST
FUSSILY
FUSSINESS
FUSSINESSES
FUSSING
FUSSPOT
FUSSPOTS
FUSSY
FUST
FUSTANELLA
FUSTANELLAS
FUSTANELLE
FUSTANELLED
FUSTANELLES
FUSTED
FUSTET
FUSTETS
FUSTIAN
FUSTIANISE
FUSTIANISED
FUSTIANISES
FUSTIANISING
FUSTIANIST
FUSTIANISTS
FUSTIANIZE
FUSTIANIZED
FUSTIANIZES
FUSTIANIZING
FUSTIANS
FUSTIC
FUSTICS

FUSTIER
FUSTIEST
FUSTIGATE
FUSTIGATED
FUSTIGATES
FUSTIGATING
FUSTIGATION
FUSTIGATIONS
FUSTIGATOR
FUSTIGATORS
FUSTIGATORY
FUSTILARIAN
FUSTILARIANS
FUSTILIRIANS
FUSTILLIRIAN
FUSTILLIRIANS
FUSTILUGS
FUSTILY
FUSTINESS
FUSTINESSES
FUSTING
FUSTOC
FUSTOCS
FUSTS
FUSTY
FUSULINID
FUSULINIDS
FUTCHEL
FUTCHELS
FUTHARC
FUTHARCS
FUTHARK
FUTHARKS
FUTHORC
FUTHORCS
FUTHORK
FUTHORKS
FUTILE
FUTILELY
FUTILENESS
FUTILENESSES
FUTILER
FUTILEST
FUTILITARIAN
FUTILITARIANISM
FUTILITARIANS
FUTILITIES
FUTILITY
FUTON
FUTONS
FUTTOCK
FUTTOCKS
FUTURAL
FUTURE
FUTURELESS
FUTURELESSNESS

FUTURES
FUTURISM
FUTURISMS
FUTURIST
FUTURISTIC
FUTURISTICALLY
FUTURISTICS
FUTURISTS
FUTURITIES
FUTURITION
FUTURITIONS
FUTURITY
FUTUROLOGICAL
FUTUROLOGIES
FUTUROLOGIST
FUTUROLOGISTS
FUTUROLOGY
FUTZ
FUTZED
FUTZES
FUTZING
FUZE
FUZED
FUZEE
FUZEES
FUZES
FUZIL
FUZILS
FUZING
FUZZ
FUZZED
FUZZES
FUZZIER
FUZZIEST
FUZZILY
FUZZINESS
FUZZINESSES
FUZZING
FUZZLE
FUZZLED
FUZZLES
FUZZLING
FUZZY
FY
FYCE
FYCES
FYKE
FYKED
FYKES
FYKING
FYLE
FYLES
FYLFOT
FYLFOTS
FYNBOS
FYNBOSES

FYRD
FYRDS
FYTTE
FYTTES

G

GAB
GABAPENTIN
GABAPENTINS
GABARDINE
GABARDINES
GABBARD
GABBARDS
GABBART
GABBARTS
GABBED
GABBER
GABBERS
GABBIER
GABBIEST
GABBING
GABBLE
GABBLED
GABBLEMENT
GABBLEMENTS
GABBLER
GABBLERS
GABBLES
GABBLING
GABBLINGS
GABBRO
GABBROIC
GABBROID
GABBROITIC
GABBROS
GABBY
GABELLE
GABELLED
GABELLER
GABELLERS
GABELLES
GABERDINE
GABERDINES
GABERLUNZIE
GABERLUNZIES
GABFEST
GABFESTS
GABIES
GABION
GABIONADE
GABIONADES
GABIONAGE
GABIONAGES
GABIONED
GABIONNADE
GABIONNADED
GABIONNADES

GABIONS
GABLE
GABLED
GABLES
GABLET
GABLETS
GABLING
GABNASH
GABNASHES
GABOON
GABOONS
GABS
GABY
GAD
GADABOUT
GADABOUTS
GADARENE
GADDED
GADDER
GADDERS
GADDI
GADDING
GADDIS
GADE
GADES
GADFLIES
GADFLY
GADGE
GADGES
GADGET
GADGETEER
GADGETEERS
GADGETRIES
GADGETRY
GADGETS
GADGETY
GADGIE
GADGIES
GADI
GADID
GADIDS
GADIS
GADJE
GADJES
GADLING
GADLINGS
GADOID
GADOIDS
GADOLINIC
GADOLINITE
GADOLINITES

GADOLINIUM
GADOLINIUMS
GADROON
GADROONED
GADROONING
GADROONINGS
GADROONS
GADS
GADSMAN
GADSMEN
GADSO
GADSOS
GADWALL
GADWALLS
GADZOOKERIES
GADZOOKERY
GADZOOKS
GAE
GAED
GAEING
GAELICISE
GAELICISED
GAELICISES
GAELICISING
GAELICISM
GAELICISMS
GAELICIZE
GAELICIZED
GAELICIZES
GAELICIZING
GAEN
GAES
GAFF
GAFFE
GAFFED
GAFFER
GAFFERS
GAFFES
GAFFING
GAFFINGS
GAFFS
GAFFSAIL
GAFFSAILS
GAG
GAGA
GAGAKU
GAGAKUS
GAGE
GAGEABILITY
GAGEABLE
GAGEABLY

GAGED
GAGER
GAGERS
GAGES
GAGGED
GAGGER
GAGGERS
GAGGERY
GAGGING
GAGGLE
GAGGLED
GAGGLES
GAGGLING
GAGGLINGS
GAGING
GAGMAN
GAGMEN
GAGS
GAGSTER
GAGSTERS
GAHNITE
GAHNITES
GAID
GAIDS
GAIETIES
GAIETY
GAIJIN
GAILLARD
GAILLARDE
GAILLARDIA
GAILLARDIAS
GAILY
GAIN
GAINABLE
GAINED
GAINER
GAINERS
GAINEST
GAINFUL
GAINFULLY
GAINFULNESS
GAINFULNESSES
GAINGIVING
GAINGIVINGS
GAINING
GAININGS
GAINLESS
GAINLESSNESS
GAINLESSNESSES
GAINLIER
GAINLIEST

GAINLINESS
GAINLY
GAINS
GAINSAID
GAINSAY
GAINSAYER
GAINSAYERS
GAINSAYING
GAINSAYINGS
GAINSAYS
GAINST
GAINSTRIVE
GAINSTRIVED
GAINSTRIVES
GAINSTRIVING
GAIR
GAIRFOWL
GAIRFOWLS
GAIRS
GAIT
GAITED
GAITER
GAITERLESS
GAITERLESSLY
GAITERLESSNESS
GAITERS
GAITING
GAITS
GAITT
GAITTS
GAJO
GAJOS
GAL
GALA
GALABEA
GALABEAH
GALABEAHS
GALABEAS
GALABIA
GALABIAH
GALABIAHS
GALABIAS
GALABIEH
GALABIEHS
GALABIYA
GALABIYAS
GALACTAGOGUE
GALACTAGOGUES
GALACTIC
GALACTOMETER
GALACTOMETERS
GALACTOMETRIC
GALACTOMETRIES
GALACTOMETRY
GALACTOPHOROUS
GALACTOPOIESIS

GALACTOPOIETIC
GALACTOPOIETICS
GALACTORRHEA
GALACTORRHEAS
GALACTORRHOEA
GALACTORRHOEAS
GALACTOSAEMIA
GALACTOSAEMIAS
GALACTOSAMINE
GALACTOSAMINES
GALACTOSE
GALACTOSEMIA
GALACTOSEMIAS
GALACTOSEMIC
GALACTOSES
GALACTOSIDASE
GALACTOSIDASES
GALACTOSIDE
GALACTOSIDES
GALACTOSYL
GALACTOSYLS
GALAGE
GALAGES
GALAGO
GALAGOS
GALAH
GALAHS
GALANGA
GALANGAL
GALANGALS
GALANGAS
GALANT
GALANTAMINE
GALANTAMINES
GALANTINE
GALANTINES
GALANTY
GALAPAGO
GALAPAGOS
GALAS
GALATEA
GALATEAS
GALAVANT
GALAVANTED
GALAVANTING
GALAVANTS
GALAX
GALAXES
GALAXIES
GALAXY
GALBANUM
GALBANUMS
GALDRAGON
GALDRAGONS
GALE
GALEA

GALEAE
GALEAS
GALEATE
GALEATED
GALEIFORM
GALENA
GALENAS
GALENGALE
GALENGALES
GALENIC
GALENICAL
GALENICALS
GALENITE
GALENITES
GALENOID
GALERE
GALERES
GALES
GALETTE
GALETTES
GALILEE
GALILEES
GALIMATIAS
GALIMATIASES
GALINGALE
GALINGALES
GALIONGEE
GALIONGEES
GALIOT
GALIOTS
GALIPOT
GALIPOTS
GALIVANT
GALIVANTED
GALIVANTING
GALIVANTS
GALL
GALLABEA
GALLABEAH
GALLABEAHS
GALLABEAS
GALLABIA
GALLABIAH
GALLABIAHS
GALLABIAS
GALLABIEH
GALLABIEHS
GALLABIYA
GALLABIYAH
GALLABIYAHS
GALLABIYAS
GALLABIYEH
GALLABIYEHS
GALLAMINE
GALLAMINES
GALLANT

GALLANTED
GALLANTER
GALLANTEST
GALLANTING
GALLANTLY
GALLANTNESS
GALLANTNESSES
GALLANTRIES
GALLANTRY
GALLANTS
GALLATE
GALLATES
GALLBLADDER
GALLBLADDERS
GALLEASS
GALLEASSES
GALLED
GALLEIN
GALLEINS
GALLEON
GALLEONS
GALLERIA
GALLERIAS
GALLERIED
GALLERIES
GALLERIST
GALLERISTIC
GALLERISTS
GALLERY
GALLERYGOER
GALLERYGOERS
GALLERYING
GALLERYITE
GALLERYITES
GALLET
GALLETA
GALLETAS
GALLETED
GALLETING
GALLETS
GALLEY
GALLEYS
GALLFLIES
GALLFLY
GALLIAMBIC
GALLIAMBICS
GALLIARD
GALLIARDISE
GALLIARDISES
GALLIARDS
GALLIASS
GALLIASSES
GALLIC
GALLICAN
GALLICISE
GALLICISED

GALLICISES
GALLICISING
GALLICISM
GALLICISMS
GALLICIZATION
GALLICIZATIONS
GALLICIZE
GALLICIZED
GALLICIZES
GALLICIZING
GALLIED
GALLIES
GALLIGASKINS
GALLIMAUFRIES
GALLIMAUFRY
GALLINACEAN
GALLINACEANS
GALLINACEOUS
GALLINAZO
GALLINAZOS
GALLING
GALLINGLY
GALLINIPPER
GALLINIPPERS
GALLINULE
GALLINULES
GALLIOT
GALLIOTS
GALLIPOT
GALLIPOTS
GALLISE
GALLISED
GALLISES
GALLISING
GALLISISE
GALLISISED
GALLISISES
GALLISISING
GALLISIZE
GALLISIZED
GALLISIZES
GALLISIZING
GALLIUM
GALLIUMS
GALLIVANT
GALLIVANTED
GALLIVANTING
GALLIVANTS
GALLIVAT
GALLIVATS
GALLIWASP
GALLIWASPS
GALLIZE
GALLIZED
GALLIZES
GALLIZING

GALLNUT
GALLNUTS
GALLOCK
GALLOGLASS
GALLOGLASSES
GALLON
GALLONAGE
GALLONAGES
GALLONS
GALLOON
GALLOONED
GALLOONS
GALLOOT
GALLOOTS
GALLOP
GALLOPADE
GALLOPADED
GALLOPADES
GALLOPADING
GALLOPED
GALLOPER
GALLOPERS
GALLOPING
GALLOPS
GALLOUS
GALLOW
GALLOWED
GALLOWGLASS
GALLOWGLASSES
GALLOWING
GALLOWS
GALLOWSES
GALLOWSNESS
GALLOWSNESSES
GALLS
GALLSICKNESS
GALLSICKNESSES
GALLSTONE
GALLSTONES
GALLUMPH
GALLUMPHED
GALLUMPHING
GALLUMPHS
GALLUS
GALLUSED
GALLUSES
GALLY
GALLYGASKINS
GALLYING
GALOCHE
GALOCHED
GALOCHES
GALOCHING
GALOOT
GALOOTS
GALOP

GALOPADE
GALOPADES
GALOPED
GALOPIN
GALOPING
GALOPINS
GALOPPED
GALOPPING
GALOPS
GALORE
GALORES
GALOSH
GALOSHE
GALOSHED
GALOSHES
GALOSHING
GALOWSES
GALRAVAGE
GALRAVAGED
GALRAVAGES
GALRAVAGING
GALRAVITCH
GALRAVITCHED
GALRAVITCHES
GALRAVITCHING
GALS
GALTONIA
GALTONIAS
GALUMPH
GALUMPHED
GALUMPHER
GALUMPHERS
GALUMPHING
GALUMPHS
GALUT
GALUTH
GALUTHS
GALUTS
GALVANIC
GALVANICAL
GALVANICALLY
GALVANISATION
GALVANISATIONS
GALVANISE
GALVANISED
GALVANISER
GALVANISERS
GALVANISES
GALVANISING
GALVANISM
GALVANISMS
GALVANIST
GALVANISTS
GALVANIZATION
GALVANIZATIONS
GALVANIZE

GALVANIZED
GALVANIZER
GALVANIZERS
GALVANIZES
GALVANIZING
GALVANOMETER
GALVANOMETERS
GALVANOMETRIC
GALVANOMETRICAL
GALVANOMETRIES
GALVANOMETRY
GALVANOPLASTIC
GALVANOPLASTIES
GALVANOPLASTY
GALVANOSCOPE
GALVANOSCOPES
GALVANOSCOPIC
GALVANOSCOPIES
GALVANOSCOPY
GALVANOTROPIC
GALVANOTROPISM
GALVANOTROPISMS
GALVO
GALVOS
GALYAC
GALYACS
GALYAK
GALYAKS
GAM
GAMA
GAMAHUCHE
GAMAHUCHED
GAMAHUCHER
GAMAHUCHERS
GAMAHUCHES
GAMAHUCHING
GAMARUCHE
GAMARUCHED
GAMARUCHER
GAMARUCHERS
GAMARUCHES
GAMARUCHING
GAMAS
GAMASH
GAMASHES
GAMAY
GAMAYS
GAMB
GAMBA
GAMBADE
GAMBADES
GAMBADO
GAMBADOED
GAMBADOES
GAMBADOING
GAMBADOS

GAMBAS
GAMBE
GAMBES
GAMBESON
GAMBESONS
GAMBET
GAMBETS
GAMBETTA
GAMBETTAS
GAMBIA
GAMBIAS
GAMBIER
GAMBIERS
GAMBIR
GAMBIRS
GAMBIST
GAMBISTS
GAMBIT
GAMBITED
GAMBITING
GAMBITS
GAMBLE
GAMBLED
GAMBLER
GAMBLERS
GAMBLES
GAMBLING
GAMBLINGS
GAMBO
GAMBOGE
GAMBOGES
GAMBOGIAN
GAMBOGIC
GAMBOL
GAMBOLED
GAMBOLING
GAMBOLLED
GAMBOLLING
GAMBOLS
GAMBOS
GAMBREL
GAMBRELS
GAMBROON
GAMBROONS
GAMBS
GAMBUSIA
GAMBUSIAS
GAME
GAMEBREAKER
GAMEBREAKERS
GAMECOCK
GAMECOCKS
GAMED
GAMEKEEPER
GAMEKEEPERS
GAMEKEEPING

GAMELAN
GAMELANS
GAMELIKE
GAMELY
GAMENESS
GAMENESSES
GAMEPLAY
GAMEPLAYED
GAMEPLAYING
GAMEPLAYS
GAMER
GAMERS
GAMES
GAMESIER
GAMESIEST
GAMESMAN
GAMESMANSHIP
GAMESMANSHIPS
GAMESMEN
GAMESOME
GAMESOMELY
GAMESOMENESS
GAMESOMENESSES
GAMEST
GAMESTER
GAMESTERS
GAMESY
GAMETAL
GAMETANGIA
GAMETANGIAL
GAMETANGIUM
GAMETE
GAMETES
GAMETIC
GAMETICALLY
GAMETOCYTE
GAMETOCYTES
GAMETOGENESES
GAMETOGENESIS
GAMETOGENIC
GAMETOGENICALLY
GAMETOGENOUS
GAMETOGENY
GAMETOPHORE
GAMETOPHORES
GAMETOPHORIC
GAMETOPHYTE
GAMETOPHYTES
GAMETOPHYTIC
GAMEY
GAMIC
GAMIER
GAMIEST
GAMILY
GAMIN
GAMINE

GAMINERIE
GAMINERIES
GAMINES
GAMINESQUE
GAMINESS
GAMINESSES
GAMING
GAMINGS
GAMINS
GAMMA
GAMMADIA
GAMMADION
GAMMAS
GAMMAT
GAMMATIA
GAMMATION
GAMMATS
GAMME
GAMMED
GAMMER
GAMMERS
GAMMERSTANG
GAMMERSTANGS
GAMMES
GAMMIER
GAMMIEST
GAMMING
GAMMOCK
GAMMOCKED
GAMMOCKING
GAMMOCKS
GAMMON
GAMMONED
GAMMONER
GAMMONERS
GAMMONING
GAMMONINGS
GAMMONS
GAMMY
GAMODEME
GAMODEMES
GAMOGENESES
GAMOGENESIS
GAMOGENETIC
GAMOGENETICAL
GAMOGENETICALLY
GAMONE
GAMONES
GAMOPETALOUS
GAMOPHYLLOUS
GAMOSEPALOUS
GAMOTROPIC
GAMOTROPISM
GAMOTROPISMS
GAMP
GAMPISH

GAMPS
GAMS
GAMUT
GAMUTS
GAMY
GAMYNESS
GAMYNESSES
GAN
GANACHE
GANACHES
GANCH
GANCHED
GANCHES
GANCHING
GANDER
GANDERED
GANDERING
GANDERISM
GANDERISMS
GANDERS
GANDY
GANE
GANEF
GANEFS
GANEV
GANEVS
GANG
GANGBANG
GANGBANGED
GANGBANGER
GANGBANGERS
GANGBANGING
GANGBANGS
GANGBOARD
GANGBOARDS
GANGBUSTER
GANGBUSTERS
GANGBUSTING
GANGBUSTINGS
GANGED
GANGER
GANGERS
GANGING
GANGINGS
GANGLAND
GANGLANDS
GANGLIA
GANGLIAL
GANGLIAR
GANGLIATE
GANGLIATED
GANGLIER
GANGLIEST
GANGLIFORM
GANGLING
GANGLION

GANGLIONATED
GANGLIONIC
GANGLIONS
GANGLIOSIDE
GANGLIOSIDES
GANGLY
GANGPLANK
GANGPLANKS
GANGPLOW
GANGPLOWS
GANGREL
GANGRELS
GANGRENE
GANGRENED
GANGRENES
GANGRENING
GANGRENOUS
GANGS
GANGSHAG
GANGSHAGGER
GANGSHAGGERS
GANGSHAGS
GANGSMAN
GANGSMEN
GANGSTA
GANGSTAS
GANGSTER
GANGSTERDOM
GANGSTERDOMS
GANGSTERISH
GANGSTERISM
GANGSTERISMS
GANGSTERLAND
GANGSTERLANDS
GANGSTERS
GANGUE
GANGUES
GANGWAY
GANGWAYS
GANISTER
GANISTERS
GANJA
GANJAH
GANJAHS
GANJAS
GANNED
GANNET
GANNETRIES
GANNETRY
GANNETS
GANNING
GANNISTER
GANNISTERS
GANOF
GANOFS
GANOID

GANOIDS
GANOIN
GANOINE
GANOINES
GANOINS
GANS
GANSEY
GANSEYS
GANT
GANTED
GANTELOPE
GANTELOPES
GANTING
GANTLET
GANTLETED
GANTLETING
GANTLETS
GANTLINE
GANTLINES
GANTLOPE
GANTLOPES
GANTRIES
GANTRY
GANTS
GANYMEDE
GANYMEDES
GAOL
GAOLBIRD
GAOLBIRDS
GAOLBREAK
GAOLBREAKER
GAOLBREAKERS
GAOLBREAKS
GAOLED
GAOLER
GAOLERESS
GAOLERESSES
GAOLERS
GAOLING
GAOLLESS
GAOLS
GAP
GAPE
GAPED
GAPER
GAPERS
GAPES
GAPESEED
GAPESEEDS
GAPEWORM
GAPEWORMS
GAPING
GAPINGLY
GAPINGS
GAPLESS
GAPLESSLY

GAPLESSNESS
GAPO
GAPOS
GAPOSIS
GAPOSISES
GAPPED
GAPPIER
GAPPIEST
GAPPING
GAPPY
GAPS
GAPY
GAR
GARAGE
GARAGED
GARAGEMAN
GARAGEMEN
GARAGES
GARAGING
GARAGINGS
GARAGIST
GARAGISTE
GARAGISTES
GARAGISTS
GARB
GARBAGE
GARBAGEMAN
GARBAGEMEN
GARBAGES
GARBANZO
GARBANZOS
GARBE
GARBED
GARBES
GARBING
GARBLE
GARBLED
GARBLER
GARBLERS
GARBLES
GARBLESS
GARBLING
GARBLINGS
GARBO
GARBOARD
GARBOARDS
GARBOIL
GARBOILS
GARBOLOGIES
GARBOLOGIST
GARBOLOGISTS
GARBOLOGY
GARBOS
GARBS
GARBURE
GARBURES

GARCINIA
GARCINIAS
GARCON
GARCONS
GARDA
GARDAI
GARDANT
GARDANTS
GARDEN
GARDENED
GARDENER
GARDENERS
GARDENFUL
GARDENFULS
GARDENIA
GARDENIAS
GARDENING
GARDENINGS
GARDENLESS
GARDENS
GARDEROBE
GARDEROBES
GARDYLOO
GARDYLOOS
GARE
GAREFOWL
GAREFOWLS
GARFISH
GARFISHES
GARGANEY
GARGANEYS
GARGANTUAN
GARGARISE
GARGARISED
GARGARISES
GARGARISING
GARGARISM
GARGARISMS
GARGARIZE
GARGARIZED
GARGARIZES
GARGARIZING
GARGET
GARGETS
GARGETY
GARGLE
GARGLED
GARGLER
GARGLERS
GARGLES
GARGLING
GARGOYLE
GARGOYLED
GARGOYLES
GARGOYLISM
GARGOYLISMS

GARI
GARIAL
GARIALS
GARIBALDI
GARIBALDIS
GARIGUE
GARIGUES
GARISH
GARISHED
GARISHES
GARISHING
GARISHLY
GARISHNESS
GARISHNESSES
GARJAN
GARJANS
GARLAND
GARLANDAGE
GARLANDAGES
GARLANDED
GARLANDING
GARLANDLESS
GARLANDRIES
GARLANDRY
GARLANDS
GARLIC
GARLICKED
GARLICKIER
GARLICKIEST
GARLICKY
GARLICS
GARMENT
GARMENTED
GARMENTING
GARMENTLESS
GARMENTS
GARMENTURE
GARMENTURES
GARNER
GARNERED
GARNERING
GARNERS
GARNET
GARNETIFEROUS
GARNETS
GARNI
GARNIERITE
GARNIERITES
GARNISH
GARNISHED
GARNISHEE
GARNISHEED
GARNISHEEING
GARNISHEEMENT
GARNISHEEMENTS
GARNISHEES

GARNISHER
GARNISHERS
GARNISHES
GARNISHING
GARNISHINGS
GARNISHMENT
GARNISHMENTS
GARNISHRIES
GARNISHRY
GARNITURE
GARNITURES
GAROTE
GAROTED
GAROTES
GAROTING
GAROTTE
GAROTTED
GAROTTER
GAROTTERS
GAROTTES
GAROTTING
GAROTTINGS
GARPIKE
GARPIKES
GARRAN
GARRANS
GARRE
GARRED
GARRES
GARRET
GARRETED
GARRETEER
GARRETEERS
GARRETS
GARRIGUE
GARRIGUES
GARRING
GARRISON
GARRISONED
GARRISONING
GARRISONS
GARRON
GARRONS
GARROT
GARROTE
GARROTED
GARROTER
GARROTERS
GARROTES
GARROTING
GARROTS
GARROTTE
GARROTTED
GARROTTER
GARROTTERS
GARROTTES

GARROTTING
GARROTTINGS
GARRULITIES
GARRULITY
GARRULOUS
GARRULOUSLY
GARRULOUSNESS
GARRULOUSNESSES
GARRYA
GARRYAS
GARRYOWEN
GARRYOWENS
GARS
GART
GARTER
GARTERED
GARTERING
GARTERS
GARTH
GARTHS
GARUDA
GARUDAS
GARUM
GARUMS
GARVEY
GARVEYS
GARVIE
GARVIES
GARVOCK
GARVOCKS
GAS
GASAHOL
GASAHOLS
GASALIER
GASALIERS
GASBAG
GASBAGGED
GASBAGGING
GASBAGS
GASCON
GASCONADE
GASCONADED
GASCONADER
GASCONADERS
GASCONADES
GASCONADING
GASCONISM
GASCONISMS
GASCONS
GASEITIES
GASEITY
GASELIER
GASELIERS
GASEOUS
GASEOUSNESS
GASEOUSNESSES

GASES
GASFIELD
GASFIELDS
GASH
GASHED
GASHER
GASHES
GASHEST
GASHFUL
GASHING
GASHLINESS
GASHLINESSES
GASHLY
GASHOLDER
GASHOLDERS
GASHOUSE
GASHOUSES
GASIFIABILITY
GASIFIABLE
GASIFICATION
GASIFICATIONS
GASIFIED
GASIFIER
GASIFIERS
GASIFIES
GASIFORM
GASIFY
GASIFYING
GASKET
GASKETS
GASKIN
GASKING
GASKINGS
GASKINS
GASLESS
GASLIGHT
GASLIGHTS
GASLIT
GASMAN
GASMEN
GASOGENE
GASOGENES
GASOHOL
GASOHOLS
GASOLENE
GASOLENES
GASOLIER
GASOLIERS
GASOLINE
GASOLINES
GASOLINIC
GASOMETER
GASOMETERS
GASOMETRIC
GASOMETRICAL
GASOMETRIES

GASOMETRY
GASP
GASPED
GASPER
GASPEREAU
GASPEREAUS
GASPERS
GASPIER
GASPIEST
GASPINESS
GASPINESSES
GASPING
GASPINGLY
GASPINGS
GASPS
GASPY
GASSED
GASSER
GASSERS
GASSES
GASSIER
GASSIEST
GASSILY
GASSINESS
GASSINESSES
GASSING
GASSINGS
GASSY
GAST
GASTED
GASTER
GASTEROPOD
GASTEROPODOUS
GASTEROPODS
GASTERS
GASTFULL
GASTIGHT
GASTIGHTNESS
GASTIGHTNESSES
GASTING
GASTNESS
GASTNESSE
GASTNESSES
GASTRAEA
GASTRAEAS
GASTRAEUM
GASTRAEUMS
GASTRAL
GASTRALGIA
GASTRALGIAS
GASTRALGIC
GASTREA
GASTREAS
GASTRECTOMIES
GASTRECTOMY
GASTRIC

GASTRIN
GASTRINS
GASTRITIC
GASTRITIDES
GASTRITIS
GASTRITISES
GASTROCNEMII
GASTROCNEMIUS
GASTROCOLIC
GASTRODUODENAL
GASTROENTERIC
GASTROENTERITIC
GASTROENTERITIS
GASTROLITH
GASTROLITHS
GASTROLOGER
GASTROLOGERS
GASTROLOGICAL
GASTROLOGIES
GASTROLOGIST
GASTROLOGISTS
GASTROLOGY
GASTROMANCIES
GASTROMANCY
GASTRONOME
GASTRONOMER
GASTRONOMERS
GASTRONOMES
GASTRONOMIC
GASTRONOMICAL
GASTRONOMICALLY
GASTRONOMIES
GASTRONOMIST
GASTRONOMISTS
GASTRONOMY
GASTROPOD
GASTROPODAN
GASTROPODOUS
GASTROPODS
GASTROSCOPE
GASTROSCOPES
GASTROSCOPIC
GASTROSCOPIES
GASTROSCOPIST
GASTROSCOPISTS
GASTROSCOPY
GASTROSOPH
GASTROSOPHER
GASTROSOPHERS
GASTROSOPHIES
GASTROSOPHS
GASTROSOPHY
GASTROSTOMIES
GASTROSTOMY
GASTROTOMIES
GASTROTOMY

GASTROTRICH
GASTROTRICHES
GASTROTRICHS
GASTROVASCULAR
GASTRULA
GASTRULAE
GASTRULAR
GASTRULAS
GASTRULATE
GASTRULATED
GASTRULATES
GASTRULATING
GASTRULATION
GASTRULATIONS
GASTS
GASWORKS
GAT
GATE
GATEAU
GATEAUS
GATEAUX
GATECRASH
GATECRASHED
GATECRASHER
GATECRASHERS
GATECRASHES
GATECRASHING
GATED
GATEFOLD
GATEFOLDS
GATEHOUSE
GATEHOUSES
GATEKEEPER
GATEKEEPERS
GATEKEEPING
GATELEG
GATELESS
GATELIKE
GATEMAN
GATEMEN
GATEPOST
GATEPOSTS
GATES
GATEWAY
GATEWAYS
GATH
GATHER
GATHERABILITY
GATHERABLE
GATHERED
GATHERER
GATHERERS
GATHERING
GATHERINGS
GATHERS
GATHS

GATING
GATINGS
GATOR
GATORS
GATS
GAU
GAUCHE
GAUCHELY
GAUCHENESS
GAUCHENESSES
GAUCHER
GAUCHERIE
GAUCHERIES
GAUCHESCO
GAUCHEST
GAUCHO
GAUCHOS
GAUCIE
GAUCIER
GAUCIEST
GAUCY
GAUD
GAUDEAMUS
GAUDEAMUSES
GAUDED
GAUDERIES
GAUDERY
GAUDGIE
GAUDGIES
GAUDIER
GAUDIES
GAUDIEST
GAUDILY
GAUDINESS
GAUDINESSES
GAUDING
GAUDS
GAUDY
GAUFER
GAUFERS
GAUFFER
GAUFFERED
GAUFFERING
GAUFFERINGS
GAUFFERS
GAUFRE
GAUFRES
GAUGE
GAUGEABILITY
GAUGEABLE
GAUGEABLY
GAUGED
GAUGER
GAUGERS
GAUGES
GAUGING

GAUGINGS
GAUJE
GAUJES
GAULEITER
GAULEITERS
GAULT
GAULTER
GAULTERS
GAULTHERIA
GAULTHERIAS
GAULTS
GAUM
GAUMED
GAUMIER
GAUMIEST
GAUMING
GAUMLESS
GAUMS
GAUMY
GAUN
GAUNCH
GAUNCHED
GAUNCHES
GAUNCHING
GAUNT
GAUNTED
GAUNTER
GAUNTEST
GAUNTING
GAUNTLET
GAUNTLETED
GAUNTLETING
GAUNTLETS
GAUNTLY
GAUNTNESS
GAUNTNESSES
GAUNTREE
GAUNTREES
GAUNTRIES
GAUNTRY
GAUNTS
GAUP
GAUPED
GAUPER
GAUPERS
GAUPING
GAUPS
GAUPUS
GAUPUSES
GAUR
GAURS
GAUS
GAUSS
GAUSSES
GAUSSIAN
GAUSSMETER

GAUSSMETERS
GAUSSMETRIC
GAUSSMETRICALLY
GAUZE
GAUZELIKE
GAUZES
GAUZIER
GAUZIEST
GAUZILY
GAUZINESS
GAUZINESSES
GAUZY
GAVAGE
GAVAGES
GAVE
GAVEL
GAVELED
GAVELING
GAVELKIND
GAVELKINDS
GAVELLED
GAVELLING
GAVELMAN
GAVELMEN
GAVELOCK
GAVELOCKS
GAVELS
GAVIAL
GAVIALS
GAVOT
GAVOTS
GAVOTTE
GAVOTTED
GAVOTTES
GAVOTTING
GAWCIER
GAWCIEST
GAWCY
GAWD
GAWDS
GAWK
GAWKED
GAWKER
GAWKERS
GAWKIER
GAWKIES
GAWKIEST
GAWKIHOOD
GAWKIHOODS
GAWKILY
GAWKINESS
GAWKINESSES
GAWKING
GAWKISH
GAWKISHLY
GAWKISHNESS

GAWKISHNESSES
GAWKS
GAWKY
GAWP
GAWPED
GAWPER
GAWPERS
GAWPING
GAWPS
GAWPUS
GAWPUSES
GAWSIE
GAWSIER
GAWSIEST
GAWSY
GAY
GAYAL
GAYALS
GAYDAR
GAYDARS
GAYER
GAYEST
GAYETIES
GAYETY
GAYLY
GAYNESS
GAYNESSES
GAYS
GAYSOME
GAYWINGS
GAZABO
GAZABOES
GAZABOS
GAZAL
GAZALS
GAZANIA
GAZANIAS
GAZAR
GAZARS
GAZE
GAZEBO
GAZEBOES
GAZEBOS
GAZED
GAZEFUL
GAZEHOUND
GAZEHOUNDS
GAZELLE
GAZELLES
GAZEMENT
GAZEMENTS
GAZER
GAZERS
GAZES
GAZETTE
GAZETTED

GAZETTEER
GAZETTEERED
GAZETTEERING
GAZETTEERISH
GAZETTEERS
GAZETTES
GAZETTING
GAZIER
GAZIEST
GAZING
GAZOGENE
GAZOGENES
GAZON
GAZONS
GAZOO
GAZOOKA
GAZOOKAS
GAZOON
GAZOONS
GAZOOS
GAZPACHO
GAZPACHOS
GAZUMP
GAZUMPED
GAZUMPER
GAZUMPERS
GAZUMPING
GAZUMPS
GAZUNDER
GAZUNDERED
GAZUNDERER
GAZUNDERERS
GAZUNDERING
GAZUNDERS
GAZY
GEAL
GEALED
GEALING
GEALOUS
GEALOUSIES
GEALOUSY
GEALS
GEAN
GEANS
GEANTICLINAL
GEANTICLINE
GEANTICLINES
GEAR
GEARBOX
GEARBOXES
GEARCASE
GEARCASES
GEARCHANGE
GEARCHANGES
GEARE
GEARED

GEARES
GEARING
GEARINGS
GEARLESS
GEARS
GEARSHIFT
GEARSHIFTS
GEARWHEEL
GEARWHEELS
GEASON
GEAT
GEATS
GEBUR
GEBURS
GECK
GECKED
GECKING
GECKO
GECKOES
GECKOS
GECKS
GED
GEDACT
GEDACTS
GEDDIT
GEDECKT
GEDECKTS
GEDS
GEE
GEEBUNG
GEEBUNGS
GEECHEE
GEECHEES
GEED
GEEGAW
GEEGAWS
GEEING
GEEK
GEEKIER
GEEKIEST
GEEKS
GEEKY
GEELBEK
GEELBEKS
GEEP
GEEPOUND
GEEPOUNDS
GEEPS
GEES
GEESE
GEEST
GEESTS
GEEZ
GEEZAH
GEEZAHS
GEEZER

GEEZERS
GEFILTE
GEFUFFLE
GEFUFFLED
GEFUFFLES
GEFUFFLING
GEFULLTE
GEGENSCHEIN
GEGENSCHEINS
GEGGIE
GEGGIES
GEHLENITE
GEHLENITES
GEHLENITIC
GEISHA
GEISHAS
GEIST
GEISTS
GEIT
GEITONOGAMIES
GEITONOGAMOUS
GEITONOGAMY
GEITS
GEL
GELABLE
GELADA
GELADAS
GELANDE
GELANDESPRUNG
GELANDESPRUNGS
GELANT
GELANTS
GELASTIC
GELATE
GELATED
GELATES
GELATI
GELATIN
GELATINATE
GELATINATED
GELATINATES
GELATINATING
GELATINATION
GELATINATIONS
GELATINE
GELATINES
GELATING
GELATINISATION
GELATINISATIONS
GELATINISE
GELATINISED
GELATINISER
GELATINISERS
GELATINISES
GELATINISING
GELATINIZATION

GELATINIZATIONS
GELATINIZE
GELATINIZED
GELATINIZER
GELATINIZERS
GELATINIZES
GELATINIZING
GELATINOID
GELATINOIDS
GELATINOUS
GELATINOUSLY
GELATINOUSNESS
GELATINS
GELATION
GELATIONS
GELATO
GELATOS
GELD
GELDED
GELDER
GELDERS
GELDING
GELDINGS
GELDS
GELEE
GELEES
GELID
GELIDER
GELIDEST
GELIDITIES
GELIDITY
GELIDLY
GELIDNESS
GELIDNESSES
GELIGNITE
GELIGNITES
GELLANT
GELLANTS
GELLED
GELLIES
GELLIFLOWRES
GELLING
GELLY
GELOSIES
GELOSY
GELS
GELSEMIA
GELSEMINE
GELSEMINES
GELSEMININE
GELSEMININES
GELSEMIUM
GELSEMIUMS
GELT
GELTS
GEM

GEMATRIA
GEMATRIAS
GEMCLIP
GEMCLIPS
GEMEINSCHAFT
GEMEINSCHAFTEN
GEMEINSCHAFTS
GEMEL
GEMELS
GEMFIBROZIL
GEMFIBROZILS
GEMFISH
GEMFISHES
GEMINAL
GEMINALLY
GEMINATE
GEMINATED
GEMINATELY
GEMINATENESS
GEMINATES
GEMINATING
GEMINATION
GEMINATIONS
GEMINI
GEMINIES
GEMINOUS
GEMINY
GEMLIKE
GEMMA
GEMMACEOUS
GEMMAE
GEMMAN
GEMMATE
GEMMATED
GEMMATES
GEMMATING
GEMMATION
GEMMATIONS
GEMMATIVE
GEMMED
GEMMEN
GEMMEOUS
GEMMERIES
GEMMERY
GEMMIER
GEMMIEST
GEMMIFEROUS
GEMMILY
GEMMING
GEMMIPAROUS
GEMMIPAROUSLY
GEMMOLOGICAL
GEMMOLOGIES
GEMMOLOGIST
GEMMOLOGISTS
GEMMOLOGY

GEMMULATION
GEMMULATIONS
GEMMULE
GEMMULES
GEMMY
GEMOLOGICAL
GEMOLOGIES
GEMOLOGIST
GEMOLOGISTS
GEMOLOGY
GEMONY
GEMOT
GEMOTE
GEMOTES
GEMOTS
GEMS
GEMSBOK
GEMSBOKS
GEMSBUCK
GEMSBUCKS
GEMSHORN
GEMSHORNS
GEMSTONE
GEMSTONES
GEMUTLICH
GEMUTLICHKEIT
GEMUTLICHKEITS
GEN
GENA
GENAL
GENAPPE
GENAPPES
GENAS
GENDARME
GENDARMERIE
GENDARMERIES
GENDARMERY
GENDARMES
GENDER
GENDERED
GENDERING
GENDERLESS
GENDERS
GENE
GENEALOGIC
GENEALOGICAL
GENEALOGICALLY
GENEALOGIES
GENEALOGISE
GENEALOGISED
GENEALOGISES
GENEALOGISING
GENEALOGIST
GENEALOGISTS
GENEALOGIZE
GENEALOGIZED

GENEALOGIZES
GENEALOGIZING
GENEALOGY
GENECOLOGICALLY
GENECOLOGIES
GENECOLOGY
GENERA
GENERABLE
GENERAL
GENERALATE
GENERALATES
GENERALE
GENERALIA
GENERALISABLE
GENERALISATION
GENERALISATIONS
GENERALISE
GENERALISED
GENERALISER
GENERALISERS
GENERALISES
GENERALISING
GENERALISSIMO
GENERALISSIMOS
GENERALIST
GENERALISTS
GENERALITIES
GENERALITY
GENERALIZABLE
GENERALIZATION
GENERALIZATIONS
GENERALIZE
GENERALIZED
GENERALIZER
GENERALIZERS
GENERALIZES
GENERALIZING
GENERALLED
GENERALLING
GENERALLY
GENERALNESS
GENERALS
GENERALSHIP
GENERALSHIPS
GENERANT
GENERANTS
GENERATE
GENERATED
GENERATES
GENERATING
GENERATION
GENERATIONAL
GENERATIONALLY
GENERATIONISM
GENERATIONISMS
GENERATIONS

GENERATIVE
GENERATOR
GENERATORS
GENERATRICES
GENERATRIX
GENERIC
GENERICAL
GENERICALLY
GENERICNESS
GENERICNESSES
GENERICS
GENEROSITIES
GENEROSITY
GENEROUS
GENEROUSLY
GENEROUSNESS
GENEROUSNESSES
GENES
GENESES
GENESIS
GENET
GENETHLIAC
GENETHLIACAL
GENETHLIACALLY
GENETHLIACON
GENETHLIACONS
GENETHLIACS
GENETHLIALOGIC
GENETHLIALOGIES
GENETHLIALOGY
GENETIC
GENETICAL
GENETICALLY
GENETICIST
GENETICISTS
GENETICS
GENETOTROPHIC
GENETRICES
GENETRIX
GENETRIXES
GENETS
GENETTE
GENETTES
GENEVA
GENEVAS
GENEVRETTE
GENEVRETTES
GENIAL
GENIALISE
GENIALISED
GENIALISES
GENIALISING
GENIALITIES
GENIALITY
GENIALIZE
GENIALIZED

GENIALIZES
GENIALIZING
GENIALLY
GENIALNESS
GENIALNESSES
GENIC
GENICALLY
GENICULAR
GENICULARITY
GENICULATE
GENICULATED
GENICULATELY
GENICULATES
GENICULATING
GENICULATION
GENICULATIONS
GENIE
GENIES
GENII
GENIP
GENIPAP
GENIPAPS
GENIPS
GENISTA
GENISTAS
GENITAL
GENITALIA
GENITALIAL
GENITALIC
GENITALLY
GENITALS
GENITIVAL
GENITIVALLY
GENITIVE
GENITIVELY
GENITIVES
GENITOR
GENITORS
GENITOURINARY
GENITRICES
GENITRIX
GENITRIXES
GENITURE
GENITURES
GENIUS
GENIUSES
GENIZAH
GENIZAHS
GENIZOTH
GENLOCK
GENLOCKS
GENNEL
GENNELS
GENNET
GENNETS
GENNIES

GENNY
GENOA
GENOAS
GENOCIDAL
GENOCIDE
GENOCIDES
GENOISE
GENOISES
GENOM
GENOME
GENOMES
GENOMIC
GENOMICALLY
GENOMICIST
GENOMICS
GENOMS
GENOPHOBIA
GENOPHOBIAS
GENOTYPE
GENOTYPES
GENOTYPIC
GENOTYPICAL
GENOTYPICALLY
GENOTYPICITIES
GENOTYPICITY
GENOUILLERE
GENOUILLERES
GENRE
GENRES
GENRO
GENROS
GENS
GENSDARMES
GENSENG
GENSENGS
GENT
GENTAMICIN
GENTAMICINS
GENTEEL
GENTEELER
GENTEELEST
GENTEELISE
GENTEELISED
GENTEELISES
GENTEELISH
GENTEELISING
GENTEELISM
GENTEELISMS
GENTEELIZE
GENTEELIZED
GENTEELIZES
GENTEELIZING
GENTEELLY
GENTEELNESS
GENTEELNESSES
GENTES

GENTIAN
GENTIANACEOUS
GENTIANELLA
GENTIANELLAS
GENTIANS
GENTIER
GENTIEST
GENTIL
GENTILE
GENTILES
GENTILESSE
GENTILESSES
GENTILHOMME
GENTILIC
GENTILISE
GENTILISED
GENTILISES
GENTILISH
GENTILISING
GENTILISM
GENTILISMS
GENTILITIAL
GENTILITIAN
GENTILITIES
GENTILITIOUS
GENTILITY
GENTILIZE
GENTILIZED
GENTILIZES
GENTILIZING
GENTILSHOMMES
GENTLE
GENTLED
GENTLEFOLK
GENTLEFOLKS
GENTLEHOOD
GENTLEHOODS
GENTLEMAN
GENTLEMANHOOD
GENTLEMANHOODS
GENTLEMANLIKE
GENTLEMANLINESS
GENTLEMANLY
GENTLEMANSHIP
GENTLEMANSHIPS
GENTLEMEN
GENTLENESS
GENTLENESSE
GENTLENESSES
GENTLEPERSON
GENTLEPERSONS
GENTLER
GENTLES
GENTLEST
GENTLEWOMAN
GENTLEWOMANLY

GENTLEWOMEN
GENTLING
GENTLY
GENTOO
GENTOOS
GENTRICE
GENTRICES
GENTRIES
GENTRIFICATION
GENTRIFICATIONS
GENTRIFIED
GENTRIFIER
GENTRIFIERS
GENTRIFIES
GENTRIFY
GENTRIFYING
GENTRY
GENTS
GENTY
GENU
GENUA
GENUFLECT
GENUFLECTED
GENUFLECTING
GENUFLECTION
GENUFLECTIONS
GENUFLECTOR
GENUFLECTORS
GENUFLECTS
GENUFLEXION
GENUFLEXIONS
GENUINE
GENUINELY
GENUINENESS
GENUINENESSES
GENUS
GENUSES
GEO
GEOBOTANIC
GEOBOTANICAL
GEOBOTANIES
GEOBOTANIST
GEOBOTANISTS
GEOBOTANY
GEOCARPIC
GEOCARPIES
GEOCARPY
GEOCENTRIC
GEOCENTRICAL
GEOCENTRICALLY
GEOCENTRICISM
GEOCENTRICISMS
GEOCHEMICAL
GEOCHEMICALLY
GEOCHEMIST
GEOCHEMISTRIES

GEOCHEMISTRY
GEOCHEMISTS
GEOCHRONOLOGIC
GEOCHRONOLOGIES
GEOCHRONOLOGIST
GEOCHRONOLOGY
GEODE
GEODEMOGRAPHICS
GEODES
GEODESIC
GEODESICAL
GEODESICS
GEODESIES
GEODESIST
GEODESISTS
GEODESY
GEODETIC
GEODETICAL
GEODETICALLY
GEODETICS
GEODIC
GEODUCK
GEODUCKS
GEODYNAMIC
GEODYNAMICAL
GEODYNAMICIST
GEODYNAMICISTS
GEODYNAMICS
GEOFACT
GEOFACTS
GEOGENIES
GEOGENY
GEOGNOSES
GEOGNOSIES
GEOGNOSIS
GEOGNOST
GEOGNOSTIC
GEOGNOSTICAL
GEOGNOSTICALLY
GEOGNOSTS
GEOGNOSY
GEOGONIC
GEOGONIES
GEOGONY
GEOGRAPHER
GEOGRAPHERS
GEOGRAPHIC
GEOGRAPHICAL
GEOGRAPHICALLY
GEOGRAPHIES
GEOGRAPHY
GEOHYDROLOGIC
GEOHYDROLOGIES
GEOHYDROLOGIST
GEOHYDROLOGISTS
GEOHYDROLOGY

GEOID
GEOIDAL
GEOIDS
GEOLATRIES
GEOLATRY
GEOLINGUISTICS
GEOLOGER
GEOLOGERS
GEOLOGIAN
GEOLOGIANS
GEOLOGIC
GEOLOGICAL
GEOLOGICALLY
GEOLOGIES
GEOLOGISE
GEOLOGISED
GEOLOGISES
GEOLOGISING
GEOLOGIST
GEOLOGISTS
GEOLOGIZE
GEOLOGIZED
GEOLOGIZES
GEOLOGIZING
GEOLOGY
GEOMAGNETIC
GEOMAGNETICALLY
GEOMAGNETISM
GEOMAGNETISMS
GEOMAGNETIST
GEOMAGNETISTS
GEOMANCER
GEOMANCERS
GEOMANCIES
GEOMANCY
GEOMANT
GEOMANTIC
GEOMANTS
GEOMECHANICALLY
GEOMECHANICS
GEOMEDICAL
GEOMEDICINE
GEOMEDICINES
GEOMETER
GEOMETERS
GEOMETRIC
GEOMETRICAL
GEOMETRICALLY
GEOMETRICIAN
GEOMETRICIANS
GEOMETRICS
GEOMETRID
GEOMETRIDS
GEOMETRIES
GEOMETRISATION
GEOMETRISATIONS

GEOMETRISE
GEOMETRISED
GEOMETRISES
GEOMETRISING
GEOMETRIST
GEOMETRISTS
GEOMETRIZATION
GEOMETRIZATIONS
GEOMETRIZE
GEOMETRIZED
GEOMETRIZES
GEOMETRIZING
GEOMETRY
GEOMORPHIC
GEOMORPHOGENIC
GEOMORPHOGENIES
GEOMORPHOGENIST
GEOMORPHOGENY
GEOMORPHOLOGIC
GEOMORPHOLOGIES
GEOMORPHOLOGIST
GEOMORPHOLOGY
GEOMYOID
GEOPHAGIA
GEOPHAGIC
GEOPHAGIES
GEOPHAGISM
GEOPHAGISMS
GEOPHAGIST
GEOPHAGISTS
GEOPHAGOUS
GEOPHAGY
GEOPHILIC
GEOPHILOUS
GEOPHONE
GEOPHONES
GEOPHYSICAL
GEOPHYSICALLY
GEOPHYSICIST
GEOPHYSICISTS
GEOPHYSICS
GEOPHYTE
GEOPHYTES
GEOPHYTIC
GEOPOLITICAL
GEOPOLITICALLY
GEOPOLITICIAN
GEOPOLITICIANS
GEOPOLITICS
GEOPONIC
GEOPONICAL
GEOPONICS
GEOPRESSURED
GEOPROBE
GEOPROBES
GEORGETTE

GEORGETTES
GEORGIC
GEORGICS
GEOS
GEOSCIENCE
GEOSCIENCES
GEOSCIENTIFIC
GEOSCIENTIST
GEOSCIENTISTS
GEOSPHERE
GEOSPHERES
GEOSTATIC
GEOSTATICS
GEOSTATIONARY
GEOSTRATEGIC
GEOSTRATEGICAL
GEOSTRATEGIES
GEOSTRATEGIST
GEOSTRATEGISTS
GEOSTRATEGY
GEOSTROPHIC
GEOSTROPHICALLY
GEOSYNCHRONOUS
GEOSYNCLINAL
GEOSYNCLINE
GEOSYNCLINES
GEOTACTIC
GEOTACTICAL
GEOTACTICALLY
GEOTAXES
GEOTAXIS
GEOTECHNIC
GEOTECHNICAL
GEOTECHNICS
GEOTECHNOLOGIES
GEOTECHNOLOGY
GEOTECTONIC
GEOTECTONICALLY
GEOTECTONICS
GEOTEXTILE
GEOTEXTILES
GEOTHERM
GEOTHERMAL
GEOTHERMALLY
GEOTHERMIC
GEOTHERMOMETER
GEOTHERMOMETERS
GEOTHERMS
GEOTROPIC
GEOTROPICALLY
GEOTROPISM
GEOTROPISMS
GERAH
GERAHS
GERANIACEOUS
GERANIAL

GERANIALS
GERANIOL
GERANIOLS
GERANIUM
GERANIUMS
GERARDIA
GERARDIAS
GERATOLOGIC
GERATOLOGICAL
GERATOLOGICALLY
GERATOLOGIES
GERATOLOGISTS
GERATOLOGY
GERBE
GERBERA
GERBERAS
GERBES
GERBIL
GERBILLE
GERBILLES
GERBILS
GERE
GERENT
GERENTS
GERENUK
GERENUKS
GERES
GERFALCON
GERFALCONS
GERIATRIC
GERIATRICIAN
GERIATRICIANS
GERIATRICS
GERIATRIST
GERIATRISTS
GERLE
GERLES
GERM
GERMAIN
GERMAINE
GERMAINES
GERMAINS
GERMAN
GERMANDER
GERMANDERS
GERMANE
GERMANELY
GERMANENESS
GERMANENESSES
GERMANIC
GERMANITE
GERMANITES
GERMANIUM
GERMANIUMS
GERMANIZATION
GERMANIZATIONS

GERMANIZE
GERMANIZED
GERMANIZES
GERMANIZING
GERMANOUS
GERMANS
GERMED
GERMEN
GERMENS
GERMFREE
GERMICIDAL
GERMICIDE
GERMICIDES
GERMIER
GERMIEST
GERMIN
GERMINA
GERMINABILITIES
GERMINABILITY
GERMINABLE
GERMINAL
GERMINALLY
GERMINANT
GERMINATE
GERMINATED
GERMINATES
GERMINATING
GERMINATION
GERMINATIONS
GERMINATIVE
GERMINATOR
GERMINATORS
GERMING
GERMINS
GERMPROOF
GERMS
GERMY
GERNE
GERNED
GERNES
GERNING
GERONTIC
GERONTOCRACIES
GERONTOCRACY
GERONTOCRAT
GERONTOCRATIC
GERONTOCRATS
GERONTOLOGIC
GERONTOLOGICAL
GERONTOLOGIES
GERONTOLOGIST
GERONTOLOGISTS
GERONTOLOGY
GERONTOMORPHIC
GERONTOPHIL
GERONTOPHILE

GERONTOPHILES
GERONTOPHILIA
GERONTOPHILIAS
GERONTOPHILS
GERONTOPHOBE
GERONTOPHOBES
GERONTOPHOBIA
GERONTOPHOBIAS
GEROPIGA
GEROPIGAS
GERRYMANDER
GERRYMANDERED
GERRYMANDERER
GERRYMANDERERS
GERRYMANDERING
GERRYMANDERS
GERTCHA
GERUND
GERUNDIAL
GERUNDIVAL
GERUNDIVE
GERUNDIVELY
GERUNDIVENESS
GERUNDIVES
GERUNDS
GESELLSCHAFT
GESELLSCHAFTEN
GESELLSCHAFTS
GESNERIA
GESNERIAD
GESNERIADS
GESNERIAS
GESSAMINE
GESSAMINES
GESSE
GESSED
GESSES
GESSING
GESSO
GESSOED
GESSOES
GESSOS
GEST
GESTALT
GESTALTEN
GESTALTISM
GESTALTISMS
GESTALTIST
GESTALTISTS
GESTALTS
GESTANT
GESTAPO
GESTAPOS
GESTATE
GESTATED
GESTATES

GESTATING
GESTATION
GESTATIONAL
GESTATIONS
GESTATIVE
GESTATORIAL
GESTATORY
GESTE
GESTES
GESTIC
GESTICAL
GESTICULANT
GESTICULATE
GESTICULATED
GESTICULATES
GESTICULATING
GESTICULATION
GESTICULATIONS
GESTICULATIVE
GESTICULATOR
GESTICULATORS
GESTICULATORY
GESTS
GESTURAL
GESTURALLY
GESTURE
GESTURED
GESTURER
GESTURERS
GESTURES
GESTURING
GESUNDHEIT
GET
GETA
GETABLE
GETAS
GETATABLE
GETAWAY
GETAWAYS
GETS
GETTABLE
GETTER
GETTERED
GETTERING
GETTERINGS
GETTERS
GETTING
GETTINGS
GETUP
GETUPS
GEUM
GEUMS
GEWGAW
GEWGAWS
GEWURZTRAMINER
GEWURZTRAMINERS

GEY
GEYAN
GEYER
GEYEST
GEYSER
GEYSERITE
GEYSERITES
GEYSERS
GHARIAL
GHARIALS
GHARRI
GHARRIES
GHARRIS
GHARRY
GHAST
GHASTED
GHASTFUL
GHASTFULLY
GHASTING
GHASTLIER
GHASTLIEST
GHASTLINESS
GHASTLINESSES
GHASTLY
GHASTNESS
GHASTNESSES
GHASTS
GHAT
GHATS
GHAUT
GHAUTS
GHAZAL
GHAZALS
GHAZEL
GHAZELS
GHAZI
GHAZIES
GHAZIS
GHEE
GHEES
GHERAO
GHERAOED
GHERAOES
GHERAOING
GHERAOS
GHERKIN
GHERKINS
GHESSE
GHESSED
GHESSES
GHESSING
GHEST
GHETTO
GHETTOBLASTER
GHETTOBLASTERS
GHETTOBLASTING

GHETTOED
GHETTOES
GHETTOING
GHETTOISATION
GHETTOISATIONS
GHETTOISE
GHETTOISED
GHETTOISES
GHETTOISING
GHETTOIZATION
GHETTOIZATIONS
GHETTOIZE
GHETTOIZED
GHETTOIZES
GHETTOIZING
GHETTOS
GHI
GHIBLI
GHIBLIS
GHILGAI
GHILGAIS
GHILLIE
GHILLIED
GHILLIES
GHILLYING
GHIS
GHOST
GHOSTED
GHOSTIER
GHOSTIEST
GHOSTING
GHOSTINGS
GHOSTLIER
GHOSTLIEST
GHOSTLIKE
GHOSTLINESS
GHOSTLINESSES
GHOSTLY
GHOSTS
GHOSTWRITE
GHOSTWRITER
GHOSTWRITERS
GHOSTWRITES
GHOSTWRITING
GHOSTWRITTEN
GHOSTWROTE
GHOSTY
GHOUL
GHOULIE
GHOULIES
GHOULISH
GHOULISHLY
GHOULISHNESS
GHOULISHNESSES
GHOULS
GHYLL

GHYLLS
GI
GIAMBEUX
GIANT
GIANTESS
GIANTESSES
GIANTHOOD
GIANTHOODS
GIANTISM
GIANTISMS
GIANTLIER
GIANTLIEST
GIANTLIKE
GIANTLY
GIANTRIES
GIANTRY
GIANTS
GIANTSHIP
GIANTSHIPS
GIAOUR
GIAOURS
GIARDIASES
GIARDIASIS
GIB
GIBBED
GIBBER
GIBBERED
GIBBERELLIC
GIBBERELLIN
GIBBERELLINS
GIBBERING
GIBBERISH
GIBBERISHES
GIBBERS
GIBBET
GIBBETED
GIBBETING
GIBBETS
GIBBETTED
GIBBETTING
GIBBING
GIBBON
GIBBONS
GIBBOSE
GIBBOSITIES
GIBBOSITY
GIBBOUS
GIBBOUSLY
GIBBOUSNESS
GIBBOUSNESSES
GIBBSITE
GIBBSITES
GIBE
GIBED
GIBEL
GIBELS

GIBER
GIBERS
GIBES
GIBING
GIBINGLY
GIBLET
GIBLETS
GIBLI
GIBLIS
GIBS
GIBSON
GIBSONS
GIBUS
GIBUSES
GID
GIDDAP
GIDDAY
GIDDAYS
GIDDIED
GIDDIER
GIDDIES
GIDDIEST
GIDDILY
GIDDINESS
GIDDINESSES
GIDDUP
GIDDY
GIDDYAP
GIDDYING
GIDDYUP
GIDGEE
GIDGEES
GIDJEE
GIDJEES
GIDS
GIE
GIED
GIEING
GIEN
GIES
GIF
GIFT
GIFTED
GIFTEDLY
GIFTEDNESS
GIFTEDNESSES
GIFTING
GIFTLESS
GIFTS
GIFTSHOP
GIFTSHOPS
GIFTWARE
GIFTWARES
GIFTWRAP
GIFTWRAPPED
GIFTWRAPPER

GIFTWRAPPING
GIFTWRAPS
GIG
GIGA
GIGABIT
GIGABITS
GIGABYTE
GIGABYTES
GIGAFLOP
GIGAFLOPS
GIGAHERTZ
GIGAHERTZES
GIGANTEAN
GIGANTESQUE
GIGANTIC
GIGANTICALLY
GIGANTICIDE
GIGANTICIDES
GIGANTICNESS
GIGANTISM
GIGANTISMS
GIGANTOLOGIES
GIGANTOLOGY
GIGANTOMACHIA
GIGANTOMACHIAS
GIGANTOMACHIES
GIGANTOMACHY
GIGAS
GIGATON
GIGATONS
GIGAWATT
GIGAWATTS
GIGGED
GIGGING
GIGGIT
GIGGITED
GIGGITING
GIGGITS
GIGGLE
GIGGLED
GIGGLER
GIGGLERS
GIGGLES
GIGGLESOME
GIGGLIER
GIGGLIEST
GIGGLING
GIGGLINGLY
GIGGLINGS
GIGGLY
GIGHE
GIGLET
GIGLETS
GIGLOT
GIGLOTS
GIGMAN

GIGMANITIES
GIGMANITY
GIGMEN
GIGOLO
GIGOLOS
GIGOT
GIGOTS
GIGS
GIGUE
GIGUES
GILA
GILAS
GILBERT
GILBERTS
GILCUP
GILCUPS
GILD
GILDED
GILDEN
GILDER
GILDERS
GILDHALL
GILDHALLS
GILDING
GILDINGS
GILDS
GILDSMAN
GILDSMEN
GILDSWOMAN
GILDSWOMEN
GILET
GILETS
GILGAI
GILGAIS
GILGIE
GILGIES
GILL
GILLAROO
GILLAROOS
GILLED
GILLER
GILLERS
GILLET
GILLETS
GILLFLIRT
GILLFLIRTS
GILLIE
GILLIED
GILLIES
GILLIFLOWER
GILLIFLOWERS
GILLING
GILLION
GILLIONS
GILLNET
GILLNETS

GILLNETTED
GILLNETTER
GILLNETTERS
GILLNETTING
GILLRAVAGED
GILLRAVAGES
GILLRAVAGING
GILLRAVITCHED
GILLRAVITCHES
GILLRAVITCHING
GILLS
GILLY
GILLYFLOWER
GILLYFLOWERS
GILLYING
GILLYVOR
GILLYVORS
GILPEY
GILPEYS
GILPIES
GILPY
GILRAVAGE
GILRAVAGED
GILRAVAGER
GILRAVAGERS
GILRAVAGES
GILRAVAGING
GILRAVITCHED
GILRAVITCHES
GILRAVITCHING
GILSONITE
GILSONITES
GILT
GILTCUP
GILTCUPS
GILTHEAD
GILTHEADS
GILTS
GILTWOOD
GIMBAL
GIMBALED
GIMBALING
GIMBALLED
GIMBALLING
GIMBALS
GIMCRACK
GIMCRACKERIES
GIMCRACKERY
GIMCRACKS
GIMEL
GIMELS
GIMLET
GIMLETED
GIMLETING
GIMLETS
GIMMAL

GIMMALLED
GIMMALS
GIMME
GIMMER
GIMMERS
GIMMES
GIMMICK
GIMMICKED
GIMMICKIER
GIMMICKIEST
GIMMICKING
GIMMICKRIES
GIMMICKRY
GIMMICKS
GIMMICKY
GIMMIE
GIMMIES
GIMMOR
GIMMORS
GIMP
GIMPED
GIMPIER
GIMPIEST
GIMPING
GIMPS
GIMPY
GIN
GING
GINGAL
GINGALL
GINGALLS
GINGALS
GINGE
GINGELEY
GINGELEYS
GINGELI
GINGELIES
GINGELIS
GINGELLI
GINGELLIES
GINGELLIS
GINGELLY
GINGELY
GINGER
GINGERADE
GINGERADES
GINGERBREAD
GINGERBREADED
GINGERBREADS
GINGERBREADY
GINGERED
GINGERING
GINGERLINESS
GINGERLINESSES
GINGERLY
GINGEROUS

GINGERROOT
GINGERROOTS
GINGERS
GINGERSNAP
GINGERSNAPS
GINGERY
GINGHAM
GINGHAMS
GINGILI
GINGILIS
GINGILLI
GINGILLIS
GINGIVA
GINGIVAE
GINGIVAL
GINGIVECTOMIES
GINGIVECTOMY
GINGIVITIS
GINGIVITISES
GINGKO
GINGKOES
GINGLE
GINGLES
GINGLIMOID
GINGLYMI
GINGLYMUS
GINGS
GINHOUSE
GINHOUSES
GINK
GINKGO
GINKGOES
GINKGOS
GINKS
GINN
GINNED
GINNEL
GINNELS
GINNER
GINNERIES
GINNERS
GINNERY
GINNIER
GINNIEST
GINNING
GINNINGS
GINNY
GINORMOUS
GINS
GINSENG
GINSENGS
GINSHOP
GINSHOPS
GIO
GIOCOSO
GIOS

GIP	GIRL	GISMO	GIZZENING
GIPON	GIRLFRIEND	GISMOLOGIES	GIZZENS
GIPONS	GIRLFRIENDS	GISMOLOGY	GIZZES
GIPPED	GIRLHOOD	GISMOS	GJETOST
GIPPER	GIRLHOODS	GISMS	GJETOSTS
GIPPERS	GIRLIE	GIST	GJU
GIPPIES	GIRLIES	GISTS	GJUS
GIPPING	GIRLISH	GIT	GLABELLA
GIPPO	GIRLISHLY	GITANA	GLABELLAE
GIPPOES	GIRLISHNESS	GITANAS	GLABELLAR
GIPPOS	GIRLISHNESSES	GITANO	GLABRATE
GIPPY	GIRLOND	GITANOS	GLABRESCENT
GIPS	GIRLONDS	GITE	GLABROUS
GIPSEN	GIRLS	GITES	GLABROUSLY
GIPSENS	GIRLY	GITS	GLABROUSNESS
GIPSIED	GIRN	GITTARONE	GLACE
GIPSIES	GIRNED	GITTARONES	GLACEED
GIPSY	GIRNEL	GITTARONIST	GLACEING
GIPSYING	GIRNELS	GITTARONISTS	GLACES
GIPSYWORT	GIRNER	GITTERN	GLACIAL
GIPSYWORTS	GIRNERS	GITTERNED	GLACIALIST
GIRAFFE	GIRNIE	GITTERNING	GLACIALISTS
GIRAFFES	GIRNIER	GITTERNS	GLACIALLY
GIRAFFID	GIRNIEST	GITTIN	GLACIALS
GIRAFFINE	GIRNING	GIUST	GLACIATE
GIRAFFISH	GIRNS	GIUSTED	GLACIATED
GIRAFFOID	GIRO	GIUSTING	GLACIATES
GIRANDOLA	GIROLLE	GIUSTO	GLACIATING
GIRANDOLAS	GIROLLES	GIUSTS	GLACIATION
GIRANDOLE	GIRON	GIVABILITY	GLACIATIONS
GIRANDOLES	GIRONIC	GIVABLE	GLACIER
GIRASOL	GIRONNY	GIVE	GLACIERS
GIRASOLE	GIRONS	GIVEABLE	GLACIOLOGIC
GIRASOLES	GIROS	GIVEAWAY	GLACIOLOGICAL
GIRASOLS	GIROSOL	GIVEAWAYS	GLACIOLOGICALLY
GIRD	GIROSOLS	GIVEBACK	GLACIOLOGIES
GIRDED	GIRR	GIVEBACKS	GLACIOLOGIST
GIRDER	GIRRS	GIVED	GLACIOLOGISTS
GIRDERS	GIRSH	GIVEN	GLACIOLOGY
GIRDING	GIRSHES	GIVENNESS	GLACIS
GIRDINGS	GIRT	GIVENNESSES	GLACISES
GIRDLE	GIRTED	GIVENS	GLAD
GIRDLECAKE	GIRTH	GIVER	GLADDED
GIRDLECAKES	GIRTHED	GIVERS	GLADDEN
GIRDLED	GIRTHING	GIVES	GLADDENED
GIRDLER	GIRTHLINE	GIVING	GLADDENER
GIRDLERS	GIRTHLINES	GIVINGS	GLADDENERS
GIRDLES	GIRTHS	GIZMO	GLADDENING
GIRDLESCONE	GIRTING	GIZMOLOGIES	GLADDENINGLY
GIRDLESCONES	GIRTLINE	GIZMOLOGY	GLADDENS
GIRDLESTEAD	GIRTLINES	GIZMOS	GLADDER
GIRDLESTEADS	GIRTS	GIZZ	GLADDEST
GIRDLING	GIS	GIZZARD	GLADDIE
GIRDS	GISARME	GIZZARDS	GLADDIES
GIRKIN	GISARMES	GIZZEN	GLADDING
GIRKINS	GISM	GIZZENED	GLADDON

GLADDONS
GLADE
GLADELIKE
GLADES
GLADFUL
GLADFULNESS
GLADFULNESSES
GLADIATE
GLADIATOR
GLADIATORIAL
GLADIATORIAN
GLADIATORS
GLADIATORSHIP
GLADIATORSHIPS
GLADIATORY
GLADIER
GLADIEST
GLADIOLA
GLADIOLAS
GLADIOLE
GLADIOLES
GLADIOLI
GLADIOLUS
GLADIOLUSES
GLADIUS
GLADIUSES
GLADLIER
GLADLIEST
GLADLY
GLADNESS
GLADNESSES
GLADS
GLADSOME
GLADSOMELY
GLADSOMENESS
GLADSOMENESSES
GLADSOMER
GLADSOMEST
GLADSTONE
GLADSTONES
GLADY
GLAIK
GLAIKET
GLAIKETNESS
GLAIKIT
GLAIKITNESS
GLAIKS
GLAIR
GLAIRE
GLAIRED
GLAIREOUS
GLAIRES
GLAIRIER
GLAIRIEST
GLAIRIN
GLAIRINESS

GLAIRING
GLAIRINS
GLAIRS
GLAIRY
GLAIVE
GLAIVED
GLAIVES
GLAM
GLAMOR
GLAMORED
GLAMORING
GLAMORISATION
GLAMORISATIONS
GLAMORISE
GLAMORISED
GLAMORISER
GLAMORISERS
GLAMORISES
GLAMORISING
GLAMORIZATION
GLAMORIZATIONS
GLAMORIZE
GLAMORIZED
GLAMORIZER
GLAMORIZERS
GLAMORIZES
GLAMORIZING
GLAMOROUS
GLAMOROUSLY
GLAMOROUSNESS
GLAMOROUSNESSES
GLAMORS
GLAMOUR
GLAMOURED
GLAMOURING
GLAMOURIZE
GLAMOURIZED
GLAMOURIZES
GLAMOURIZING
GLAMOURLESS
GLAMOUROUS
GLAMOUROUSLY
GLAMOUROUSNESS
GLAMOURPUSS
GLAMOURPUSSES
GLAMOURS
GLAMS
GLANCE
GLANCED
GLANCER
GLANCERS
GLANCES
GLANCING
GLANCINGLY
GLANCINGS
GLAND

GLANDERED
GLANDEROUS
GLANDERS
GLANDES
GLANDIFEROUS
GLANDIFORM
GLANDLESS
GLANDLIKE
GLANDS
GLANDULAR
GLANDULARLY
GLANDULE
GLANDULES
GLANDULIFEROUS
GLANDULOUS
GLANDULOUSLY
GLANS
GLARE
GLAREAL
GLARED
GLARELESS
GLARELESSLY
GLARELESSNESS
GLAREOUS
GLARES
GLARIER
GLARIEST
GLARING
GLARINGLY
GLARINGNESS
GLARINGNESSES
GLARY
GLASNOST
GLASNOSTIAN
GLASNOSTIC
GLASNOSTS
GLASS
GLASSBLOWER
GLASSBLOWERS
GLASSBLOWING
GLASSBLOWINGS
GLASSED
GLASSEN
GLASSES
GLASSFUL
GLASSFULS
GLASSHOUSE
GLASSHOUSES
GLASSIE
GLASSIER
GLASSIES
GLASSIEST
GLASSIFIED
GLASSIFIES
GLASSIFY
GLASSIFYING

GLASSILY
GLASSINE
GLASSINES
GLASSINESS
GLASSINESSES
GLASSING
GLASSLESS
GLASSLIKE
GLASSMAKER
GLASSMAKERS
GLASSMAKING
GLASSMAKINGS
GLASSMAN
GLASSMEN
GLASSPAPER
GLASSPAPERED
GLASSPAPERING
GLASSPAPERS
GLASSWARE
GLASSWARES
GLASSWORK
GLASSWORKER
GLASSWORKERS
GLASSWORKS
GLASSWORT
GLASSWORTS
GLASSY
GLAUBERITE
GLAUBERITES
GLAUCESCENCE
GLAUCESCENCES
GLAUCESCENT
GLAUCOMA
GLAUCOMAS
GLAUCOMATOUS
GLAUCONITE
GLAUCONITES
GLAUCONITIC
GLAUCOUS
GLAUCOUSLY
GLAUCOUSNESS
GLAUCOUSNESSES
GLAUM
GLAUMED
GLAUMING
GLAUMS
GLAUR
GLAURIER
GLAURIEST
GLAURS
GLAURY
GLAZE
GLAZED
GLAZEN
GLAZER
GLAZERS

GLAZES
GLAZIER
GLAZIERIES
GLAZIERS
GLAZIERY
GLAZIEST
GLAZING
GLAZINGS
GLAZY
GLEAM
GLEAMED
GLEAMER
GLEAMERS
GLEAMIER
GLEAMIEST
GLEAMING
GLEAMINGLY
GLEAMINGS
GLEAMLESS
GLEAMLESSLY
GLEAMS
GLEAMY
GLEAN
GLEANABLE
GLEANED
GLEANER
GLEANERS
GLEANING
GLEANINGS
GLEANS
GLEAVE
GLEAVES
GLEBA
GLEBAE
GLEBE
GLEBES
GLEBOUS
GLEBY
GLED
GLEDE
GLEDES
GLEDGE
GLEDGED
GLEDGES
GLEDGING
GLEDS
GLEE
GLEED
GLEEDS
GLEEFUL
GLEEFULLY
GLEEFULNESS
GLEEFULNESSES
GLEEING
GLEEK
GLEEKED

GLEEKING
GLEEKS
GLEEMAIDEN
GLEEMAIDENS
GLEEMAN
GLEEMEN
GLEENIE
GLEENIES
GLEES
GLEESOME
GLEET
GLEETED
GLEETIER
GLEETIEST
GLEETING
GLEETS
GLEETY
GLEG
GLEGGER
GLEGGEST
GLEGLY
GLEGNESS
GLEGNESSES
GLEI
GLEIS
GLEIZATION
GLEIZATIONS
GLEN
GLENDOVEER
GLENDOVEERS
GLENGARRIES
GLENGARRY
GLENLIKE
GLENOID
GLENOIDAL
GLENOIDS
GLENS
GLENT
GLENTED
GLENTING
GLENTS
GLEY
GLEYED
GLEYING
GLEYINGS
GLEYS
GLIA
GLIADIN
GLIADINE
GLIADINES
GLIADINS
GLIAL
GLIAS
GLIB
GLIBBED
GLIBBER

GLIBBERY
GLIBBEST
GLIBBING
GLIBLY
GLIBNESS
GLIBNESSES
GLIBS
GLID
GLIDDER
GLIDDERY
GLIDDEST
GLIDE
GLIDED
GLIDER
GLIDERS
GLIDES
GLIDING
GLIDINGLY
GLIDINGS
GLIFF
GLIFFING
GLIFFINGS
GLIFFS
GLIFT
GLIFTS
GLIKE
GLIKES
GLIM
GLIME
GLIMED
GLIMES
GLIMING
GLIMMER
GLIMMERED
GLIMMERING
GLIMMERINGLY
GLIMMERINGS
GLIMMERS
GLIMMERY
GLIMPSE
GLIMPSED
GLIMPSER
GLIMPSERS
GLIMPSES
GLIMPSING
GLIMS
GLINT
GLINTED
GLINTING
GLINTS
GLIOBLASTOMA
GLIOBLASTOMAS
GLIOBLASTOMATA
GLIOMA
GLIOMAS
GLIOMATA

GLIOMATOSES
GLIOMATOSIS
GLIOMATOUS
GLIOSES
GLIOSIS
GLISK
GLISKS
GLISSADE
GLISSADED
GLISSADER
GLISSADERS
GLISSADES
GLISSADING
GLISSANDI
GLISSANDO
GLISSANDOS
GLISTEN
GLISTENED
GLISTENING
GLISTENINGLY
GLISTENS
GLISTER
GLISTERED
GLISTERING
GLISTERINGLY
GLISTERS
GLIT
GLITCH
GLITCHES
GLITCHY
GLITS
GLITTER
GLITTERAND
GLITTERATI
GLITTERED
GLITTERIER
GLITTERIEST
GLITTERING
GLITTERINGLY
GLITTERINGS
GLITTERS
GLITTERY
GLITZ
GLITZES
GLITZIER
GLITZIEST
GLITZILY
GLITZINESS
GLITZINESSES
GLITZY
GLOAM
GLOAMING
GLOAMINGS
GLOAMS
GLOAT
GLOATED

GLOATER
GLOATERS
GLOATING
GLOATINGLY
GLOATS
GLOB
GLOBAL
GLOBALISATION
GLOBALISATIONS
GLOBALISE
GLOBALISED
GLOBALISES
GLOBALISING
GLOBALISM
GLOBALISMS
GLOBALIST
GLOBALISTS
GLOBALIZATION
GLOBALIZATIONS
GLOBALIZE
GLOBALIZED
GLOBALIZES
GLOBALIZING
GLOBALLY
GLOBATE
GLOBATED
GLOBBIER
GLOBBIEST
GLOBBY
GLOBE
GLOBED
GLOBEFISH
GLOBEFISHES
GLOBEFLOWER
GLOBEFLOWERS
GLOBELIKE
GLOBES
GLOBETROTTER
GLOBETROTTERS
GLOBETROTTING
GLOBETROTTINGS
GLOBIGERINA
GLOBIGERINAE
GLOBIGERINAS
GLOBIN
GLOBING
GLOBINS
GLOBOID
GLOBOIDS
GLOBOSE
GLOBOSELY
GLOBOSENESS
GLOBOSES
GLOBOSITIES
GLOBOSITY
GLOBOUS

GLOBS
GLOBULAR
GLOBULARITIES
GLOBULARITY
GLOBULARLY
GLOBULARNESS
GLOBULE
GLOBULES
GLOBULET
GLOBULETS
GLOBULIFEROUS
GLOBULIN
GLOBULINS
GLOBULITE
GLOBULITES
GLOBULOUS
GLOBUS
GLOBUSES
GLOBY
GLOCHID
GLOCHIDIA
GLOCHIDIATE
GLOCHIDIUM
GLOCHIDS
GLOCKENSPIEL
GLOCKENSPIELS
GLODE
GLOGG
GLOGGS
GLOIRE
GLOIRES
GLOM
GLOMERA
GLOMERATE
GLOMERATED
GLOMERATES
GLOMERATING
GLOMERATION
GLOMERATIONS
GLOMERULAR
GLOMERULATE
GLOMERULE
GLOMERULES
GLOMERULI
GLOMERULUS
GLOMMED
GLOMMING
GLOMS
GLOMUS
GLONOIN
GLONOINS
GLOOM
GLOOMED
GLOOMFUL
GLOOMFULLY
GLOOMIER

GLOOMIEST
GLOOMILY
GLOOMINESS
GLOOMINESSES
GLOOMING
GLOOMINGS
GLOOMLESS
GLOOMS
GLOOMY
GLOOP
GLOOPED
GLOOPIER
GLOOPIEST
GLOOPING
GLOOPS
GLOOPY
GLOP
GLOPPED
GLOPPING
GLOPPY
GLOPS
GLORIA
GLORIAS
GLORIED
GLORIES
GLORIFIABLE
GLORIFICATION
GLORIFICATIONS
GLORIFIED
GLORIFIER
GLORIFIERS
GLORIFIES
GLORIFY
GLORIFYING
GLORIOLE
GLORIOLES
GLORIOSA
GLORIOSAS
GLORIOUS
GLORIOUSLY
GLORIOUSNESS
GLORIOUSNESSES
GLORY
GLORYING
GLOSS
GLOSSA
GLOSSAE
GLOSSAL
GLOSSARIAL
GLOSSARIALLY
GLOSSARIES
GLOSSARIST
GLOSSARISTS
GLOSSARY
GLOSSAS
GLOSSATOR

GLOSSATORS
GLOSSECTOMIES
GLOSSECTOMY
GLOSSED
GLOSSEME
GLOSSEMES
GLOSSER
GLOSSERS
GLOSSES
GLOSSIER
GLOSSIES
GLOSSIEST
GLOSSILY
GLOSSINA
GLOSSINAS
GLOSSINESS
GLOSSINESSES
GLOSSING
GLOSSINGLY
GLOSSIST
GLOSSISTS
GLOSSITIC
GLOSSITIS
GLOSSITISES
GLOSSLESS
GLOSSLESSNESS
GLOSSODYNIA
GLOSSODYNIAS
GLOSSOGRAPHER
GLOSSOGRAPHERS
GLOSSOGRAPHICAL
GLOSSOGRAPHIES
GLOSSOGRAPHY
GLOSSOLALIA
GLOSSOLALIAS
GLOSSOLALIST
GLOSSOLALISTS
GLOSSOLOGICAL
GLOSSOLOGIES
GLOSSOLOGIST
GLOSSOLOGISTS
GLOSSOLOGY
GLOSSY
GLOST
GLOSTS
GLOTTAL
GLOTTIC
GLOTTIDEAN
GLOTTIDES
GLOTTIS
GLOTTISES
GLOTTOGONIC
GLOTTOLOGIES
GLOTTOLOGY
GLOUT
GLOUTED

GLOUTING
GLOUTS
GLOVE
GLOVED
GLOVELESS
GLOVELESSLY
GLOVELESSNESS
GLOVELIKE
GLOVER
GLOVERS
GLOVES
GLOVING
GLOVINGS
GLOW
GLOWED
GLOWER
GLOWERED
GLOWERING
GLOWERINGLY
GLOWERS
GLOWFLIES
GLOWFLY
GLOWING
GLOWINGLY
GLOWLAMP
GLOWLAMPS
GLOWS
GLOWSTICK
GLOWSTICKS
GLOWWORM
GLOWWORMS
GLOXINIA
GLOXINIAS
GLOZE
GLOZED
GLOZES
GLOZING
GLOZINGS
GLUCAGON
GLUCAGONS
GLUCAN
GLUCANS
GLUCINA
GLUCINAS
GLUCINIC
GLUCINIUM
GLUCINIUMS
GLUCINUM
GLUCINUMS
GLUCOCORTICOID
GLUCOCORTICOIDS
GLUCOKINASE
GLUCOKINASES
GLUCONATE
GLUCONATES
GLUCONEOGENESES

GLUCONEOGENESIS
GLUCONEOGENIC
GLUCOPHORE
GLUCOPHORES
GLUCOPROTEIN
GLUCOPROTEINS
GLUCOSAMINE
GLUCOSAMINES
GLUCOSE
GLUCOSES
GLUCOSIC
GLUCOSIDAL
GLUCOSIDASE
GLUCOSIDASES
GLUCOSIDE
GLUCOSIDES
GLUCOSIDIC
GLUCOSURIA
GLUCOSURIAS
GLUCOSURIC
GLUCURONIDASE
GLUCURONIDASES
GLUCURONIDE
GLUCURONIDES
GLUE
GLUED
GLUEING
GLUELIKE
GLUEPOT
GLUEPOTS
GLUER
GLUERS
GLUES
GLUEY
GLUEYNESS
GLUEYNESSES
GLUG
GLUGGABILITY
GLUGGABLE
GLUGGED
GLUGGING
GLUGS
GLUHWEIN
GLUHWEINS
GLUIER
GLUIEST
GLUILY
GLUING
GLUISH
GLUM
GLUMACEOUS
GLUME
GLUMELIKE
GLUMELLA
GLUMELLAS
GLUMES

GLUMIFEROUS
GLUMLY
GLUMMER
GLUMMEST
GLUMNESS
GLUMNESSES
GLUMPIER
GLUMPIEST
GLUMPILY
GLUMPISH
GLUMPS
GLUMPY
GLUNCH
GLUNCHED
GLUNCHES
GLUNCHING
GLUON
GLUONS
GLUT
GLUTAEAL
GLUTAEI
GLUTAEUS
GLUTAMATE
GLUTAMATES
GLUTAMIC
GLUTAMINASE
GLUTAMINASES
GLUTAMINE
GLUTAMINES
GLUTAMINIC
GLUTARALDEHYDE
GLUTARALDEHYDES
GLUTATHIONE
GLUTATHIONES
GLUTEAL
GLUTEI
GLUTELIN
GLUTELINS
GLUTEN
GLUTENOUS
GLUTENS
GLUTETHIMIDE
GLUTETHIMIDES
GLUTEUS
GLUTINOSITY
GLUTINOUS
GLUTINOUSLY
GLUTINOUSNESS
GLUTS
GLUTTED
GLUTTING
GLUTTINGLY
GLUTTON
GLUTTONIES
GLUTTONISE
GLUTTONISED

GLUTTONISES
GLUTTONISH
GLUTTONISING
GLUTTONIZE
GLUTTONIZED
GLUTTONIZES
GLUTTONIZING
GLUTTONOUS
GLUTTONOUSLY
GLUTTONOUSNESS
GLUTTONS
GLUTTONY
GLYCAN
GLYCANS
GLYCERALDEHYDE
GLYCERALDEHYDES
GLYCERIA
GLYCERIAS
GLYCERIC
GLYCERIDE
GLYCERIDES
GLYCERIDIC
GLYCERIN
GLYCERINATE
GLYCERINATED
GLYCERINATES
GLYCERINATING
GLYCERINE
GLYCERINES
GLYCERINS
GLYCEROL
GLYCEROLS
GLYCERYL
GLYCERYLS
GLYCIN
GLYCINE
GLYCINES
GLYCINS
GLYCOCOLL
GLYCOCOLLS
GLYCOGEN
GLYCOGENESES
GLYCOGENESIS
GLYCOGENETIC
GLYCOGENIC
GLYCOGENOLYSES
GLYCOGENOLYSIS
GLYCOGENOLYTIC
GLYCOGENS
GLYCOL
GLYCOLIC
GLYCOLIPID
GLYCOLIPIDS
GLYCOLLIC
GLYCOLS
GLYCOLYSES

GLYCOLYSIS
GLYCOLYTIC
GLYCONEOGENESIS
GLYCONEOGENETIC
GLYCONIC
GLYCONICS
GLYCOPEPTIDE
GLYCOPEPTIDES
GLYCOPHYTE
GLYCOPHYTES
GLYCOPHYTIC
GLYCOPHYTICALLY
GLYCOPROTEIN
GLYCOPROTEINS
GLYCOSE
GLYCOSES
GLYCOSIDASE
GLYCOSIDASES
GLYCOSIDE
GLYCOSIDES
GLYCOSIDIC
GLYCOSIDICALLY
GLYCOSURIA
GLYCOSURIAS
GLYCOSURIC
GLYCOSYL
GLYCOSYLATE
GLYCOSYLATED
GLYCOSYLATES
GLYCOSYLATING
GLYCOSYLATION
GLYCOSYLATIONS
GLYCOSYLS
GLYCYL
GLYCYLS
GLYOXALINE
GLYOXALINES
GLYPH
GLYPHIC
GLYPHOGRAPH
GLYPHOGRAPHER
GLYPHOGRAPHERS
GLYPHOGRAPHIC
GLYPHOGRAPHICAL
GLYPHOGRAPHIES
GLYPHOGRAPHS
GLYPHOGRAPHY
GLYPHS
GLYPTAL
GLYPTALS
GLYPTIC
GLYPTICS
GLYPTODONT
GLYPTODONTS
GLYPTOGRAPHER
GLYPTOGRAPHERS

GLYPTOGRAPHIC
GLYPTOGRAPHICAL
GLYPTOGRAPHIES
GLYPTOGRAPHY
GLYPTOTHECA
GMELINITE
GMELINITES
GNAPHALIUM
GNAPHALIUMS
GNAR
GNARL
GNARLED
GNARLIER
GNARLIEST
GNARLING
GNARLS
GNARLY
GNARR
GNARRED
GNARRING
GNARRS
GNARS
GNASH
GNASHED
GNASHER
GNASHERS
GNASHES
GNASHING
GNASHINGLY
GNAT
GNATCATCHER
GNATCATCHERS
GNATHAL
GNATHIC
GNATHION
GNATHIONS
GNATHITE
GNATHITES
GNATHONIC
GNATHONICAL
GNATHONICALLY
GNATHOSTOMATOUS
GNATHOSTOME
GNATHOSTOMES
GNATLIKE
GNATLING
GNATLINGS
GNATS
GNATTIER
GNATTIEST
GNATTY
GNAW
GNAWABLE
GNAWED
GNAWER
GNAWERS

GNAWING
GNAWINGLY
GNAWINGS
GNAWN
GNAWS
GNEISS
GNEISSES
GNEISSIC
GNEISSITIC
GNEISSOID
GNEISSOSE
GNETOPHYTE
GNETOPHYTES
GNOCCHI
GNOCCHIS
GNOMAE
GNOME
GNOMELIKE
GNOMES
GNOMIC
GNOMICAL
GNOMICALLY
GNOMISH
GNOMIST
GNOMISTS
GNOMON
GNOMONIC
GNOMONICAL
GNOMONICALLY
GNOMONICS
GNOMONOLOGIES
GNOMONOLOGY
GNOMONS
GNOSEOLOGIES
GNOSEOLOGY
GNOSES
GNOSIOLOGIES
GNOSIOLOGY
GNOSIS
GNOSTIC
GNOSTICAL
GNOSTICALLY
GNOSTICISM
GNOSTICISMS
GNOTOBIOLOGICAL
GNOTOBIOLOGIES
GNOTOBIOLOGY
GNOTOBIOSES
GNOTOBIOSIS
GNOTOBIOTE
GNOTOBIOTES
GNOTOBIOTIC
GNOTOBIOTICALLY
GNOTOBIOTICS
GNOW
GNOWS

GNU
GNUS
GO
GOA
GOAD
GOADED
GOADING
GOADLIKE
GOADS
GOADSMAN
GOADSMEN
GOADSTER
GOADSTERS
GOAF
GOAFS
GOAL
GOALBALL
GOALBALLS
GOALED
GOALIE
GOALIES
GOALING
GOALKEEPER
GOALKEEPERS
GOALKEEPING
GOALKICKER
GOALKICKERS
GOALKICKING
GOALKICKINGS
GOALLESS
GOALMOUTH
GOALMOUTHS
GOALPOST
GOALPOSTS
GOALS
GOALTENDER
GOALTENDERS
GOALTENDING
GOALTENDINGS
GOALWARD
GOANNA
GOANNAS
GOARY
GOAS
GOAT
GOATEE
GOATEED
GOATEES
GOATFISH
GOATFISHES
GOATHERD
GOATHERDS
GOATIER
GOATIEST
GOATISH
GOATISHLY

GOATISHNESS
GOATISHNESSES
GOATLIKE
GOATLING
GOATLINGS
GOATS
GOATSBEARD
GOATSBEARDS
GOATSKIN
GOATSKINS
GOATSUCKER
GOATSUCKERS
GOATWEED
GOATWEEDS
GOATY
GOB
GOBAN
GOBANG
GOBANGS
GOBANS
GOBBED
GOBBELINE
GOBBELINES
GOBBET
GOBBETS
GOBBI
GOBBINESS
GOBBING
GOBBLE
GOBBLED
GOBBLEDEGOOK
GOBBLEDEGOOKS
GOBBLEDYGOOK
GOBBLEDYGOOKS
GOBBLER
GOBBLERS
GOBBLES
GOBBLING
GOBBO
GOBBY
GOBIES
GOBIID
GOBIIDS
GOBIOID
GOBIOIDS
GOBLET
GOBLETS
GOBLIN
GOBLINS
GOBO
GOBOES
GOBONEE
GOBONY
GOBOS
GOBS
GOBSHITE

GOBSHITES
GOBSMACKED
GOBSTOPPER
GOBSTOPPERS
GOBURRA
GOBURRAS
GOBY
GOD
GODCHILD
GODCHILDREN
GODDAM
GODDAMMED
GODDAMMING
GODDAMN
GODDAMNED
GODDAMNING
GODDAMNS
GODDAMS
GODDAUGHTER
GODDAUGHTERS
GODDED
GODDEN
GODDENS
GODDESS
GODDESSES
GODDESSHOOD
GODDING
GODET
GODETIA
GODETIAS
GODETS
GODFATHER
GODFATHERED
GODFATHERING
GODFATHERS
GODFORSAKEN
GODHEAD
GODHEADS
GODHOOD
GODHOODS
GODLESS
GODLESSLY
GODLESSNESS
GODLESSNESSES
GODLIER
GODLIEST
GODLIKE
GODLIKENESS
GODLIKENESSES
GODLILY
GODLINESS
GODLINESSES
GODLING
GODLINGS
GODLY
GODMOTHER

GODMOTHERS
GODOWN
GODOWNS
GODPARENT
GODPARENTS
GODROON
GODROONED
GODROONING
GODROONINGS
GODROONS
GODS
GODSEND
GODSENDS
GODSHIP
GODSHIPS
GODSLOT
GODSLOTS
GODSO
GODSON
GODSONS
GODSOS
GODSPEED
GODSPEEDS
GODSQUAD
GODSQUADS
GODWARD
GODWARDS
GODWIT
GODWITS
GOE
GOEL
GOELS
GOER
GOERS
GOES
GOETHITE
GOETHITES
GOETIC
GOETIES
GOETY
GOEY
GOFER
GOFERS
GOFF
GOFFED
GOFFER
GOFFERED
GOFFERING
GOFFERINGS
GOFFERS
GOFFING
GOFFS
GOGGA
GOGGAS
GOGGLE
GOGGLEBOX

GOGGLEBOXES
GOGGLED
GOGGLER
GOGGLERS
GOGGLES
GOGGLIER
GOGGLIEST
GOGGLINESS
GOGGLING
GOGGLINGLY
GOGGLINGS
GOGGLY
GOGLET
GOGLETS
GOGO
GOGOS
GOHONZON
GOHONZONS
GOIER
GOIEST
GOING
GOINGS
GOITER
GOITERED
GOITERS
GOITRE
GOITRED
GOITRES
GOITROGEN
GOITROGENIC
GOITROGENICITY
GOITROGENS
GOITROUS
GOLCONDA
GOLCONDAS
GOLD
GOLDARN
GOLDARNS
GOLDBRICK
GOLDBRICKED
GOLDBRICKING
GOLDBRICKS
GOLDBUG
GOLDBUGS
GOLDCREST
GOLDCRESTS
GOLDEN
GOLDENBERRIES
GOLDENBERRY
GOLDENED
GOLDENER
GOLDENEST
GOLDENEYE
GOLDENEYES
GOLDENING
GOLDENLY

GOLDENNESS
GOLDENNESSES
GOLDENROD
GOLDENRODS
GOLDENS
GOLDENSEAL
GOLDENSEALS
GOLDER
GOLDEST
GOLDEYE
GOLDEYES
GOLDFIELD
GOLDFIELDS
GOLDFINCH
GOLDFINCHES
GOLDFINNIES
GOLDFINNY
GOLDFISH
GOLDFISHES
GOLDIER
GOLDIEST
GOLDILOCKS
GOLDILOCKSES
GOLDISH
GOLDLESS
GOLDMINER
GOLDMINERS
GOLDS
GOLDSINNIES
GOLDSINNY
GOLDSIZE
GOLDSIZES
GOLDSMITH
GOLDSMITHERIES
GOLDSMITHERY
GOLDSMITHRIES
GOLDSMITHRY
GOLDSMITHS
GOLDSPINK
GOLDSPINKS
GOLDSTICK
GOLDSTICKS
GOLDSTONE
GOLDSTONES
GOLDTAIL
GOLDTAILS
GOLDTHREAD
GOLDTHREADS
GOLDURN
GOLDURNS
GOLDY
GOLE
GOLEM
GOLEMS
GOLES
GOLF

GOLFED
GOLFER
GOLFERS
GOLFIANA
GOLFIANAS
GOLFING
GOLFINGS
GOLFS
GOLGOTHA
GOLGOTHAS
GOLIARD
GOLIARDERIES
GOLIARDERY
GOLIARDIC
GOLIARDIES
GOLIARDS
GOLIARDY
GOLIAS
GOLIASED
GOLIASES
GOLIASING
GOLIATHISED
GOLIATHISES
GOLIATHISING
GOLIATHIZE
GOLIATHIZED
GOLIATHIZES
GOLIATHIZING
GOLLAN
GOLLAND
GOLLANDS
GOLLANS
GOLLAR
GOLLARED
GOLLARING
GOLLARS
GOLLER
GOLLERED
GOLLERING
GOLLERS
GOLLIED
GOLLIER
GOLLIERS
GOLLIES
GOLLIWOG
GOLLIWOGG
GOLLIWOGGS
GOLLIWOGS
GOLLOP
GOLLOPED
GOLLOPER
GOLLOPERS
GOLLOPING
GOLLOPS
GOLLY
GOLLYING

GOLLYWOG
GOLLYWOGS
GOLOMYNKA
GOLOMYNKAS
GOLOPTIOUS
GOLOSH
GOLOSHE
GOLOSHED
GOLOSHES
GOLOSHING
GOLOSHOES
GOLP
GOLPE
GOLPES
GOLPS
GOLUPTIOUS
GOMBEEN
GOMBEENISM
GOMBEENS
GOMBO
GOMBOS
GOMBRO
GOMBROON
GOMBROONS
GOMBROS
GOMERAL
GOMERALS
GOMEREL
GOMERELS
GOMERIL
GOMERILS
GOMOKU
GOMOKUS
GOMPA
GOMPAS
GOMPHOSES
GOMPHOSIS
GOMUTI
GOMUTIS
GOMUTO
GOMUTOS
GON
GONAD
GONADAL
GONADECTOMIES
GONADECTOMIZED
GONADECTOMY
GONADIAL
GONADIC
GONADOTROPHIC
GONADOTROPHIN
GONADOTROPHINS
GONADOTROPIC
GONADOTROPIN
GONADOTROPINS
GONADS

GONDELAY
GONDELAYS
GONDOLA
GONDOLAS
GONDOLIER
GONDOLIERS
GONE
GONEF
GONEFS
GONENESS
GONENESSES
GONER
GONERS
GONFALON
GONFALONIER
GONFALONIERS
GONFALONS
GONFANON
GONFANONS
GONG
GONGED
GONGING
GONGLIKE
GONGORISTIC
GONGS
GONGSTER
GONGSTERS
GONGYO
GONGYOS
GONIA
GONIATITE
GONIATITES
GONIATITOID
GONIATITOIDS
GONIDIA
GONIDIAL
GONIDIC
GONIDIUM
GONIF
GONIFF
GONIFFS
GONIFS
GONIMOBLAST
GONIMOBLASTS
GONIOMETER
GONIOMETERS
GONIOMETRIC
GONIOMETRICAL
GONIOMETRICALLY
GONIOMETRIES
GONIOMETRY
GONION
GONIOSCOPE
GONIOSCOPES
GONIOSCOPIC
GONIOSCOPICALLY

GONIUM
GONK
GONKS
GONNA
GONOCOCCAL
GONOCOCCI
GONOCOCCIC
GONOCOCCOID
GONOCOCCUS
GONOCYTE
GONOCYTES
GONODUCT
GONODUCTS
GONOF
GONOFS
GONOPH
GONOPHORE
GONOPHORES
GONOPHORIC
GONOPHOROUS
GONOPHS
GONOPOD
GONOPODAL
GONOPODS
GONOPORE
GONOPORES
GONORRHEA
GONORRHEAL
GONORRHEAS
GONORRHEIC
GONORRHOEA
GONORRHOEAL
GONORRHOEAS
GONORRHOEIC
GONOSOMAL
GONOSOMALLY
GONOSOME
GONOSOMES
GONS
GONYS
GONYSES
GONZO
GOO
GOOBER
GOOBERS
GOOBIES
GOOBY
GOOD
GOODBY
GOODBYE
GOODBYES
GOODBYS
GOODFACED
GOODFELLOW
GOODFELLOWS
GOODFELLOWSHIP

GOODFELLOWSHIPS
GOODIE
GOODIER
GOODIES
GOODIEST
GOODINESS
GOODINESSES
GOODISH
GOODLIER
GOODLIEST
GOODLIHEAD
GOODLIHEADS
GOODLINESS
GOODLINESSES
GOODLY
GOODLYHEAD
GOODLYHEADS
GOODMAN
GOODMEN
GOODNESS
GOODNESSES
GOODNIGHT
GOODNIGHTS
GOODS
GOODSIRE
GOODSIRES
GOODTIME
GOODWIFE
GOODWILL
GOODWILLED
GOODWILLS
GOODWIVES
GOODY
GOODYEAR
GOODYEARS
GOOEY
GOOEYNESS
GOOEYNESSES
GOOF
GOOFBALL
GOOFBALLS
GOOFED
GOOFIER
GOOFIEST
GOOFILY
GOOFINESS
GOOFINESSES
GOOFING
GOOFS
GOOFY
GOOG
GOOGLE
GOOGLED
GOOGLES
GOOGLIES
GOOGLING

GOOGLY
GOOGOL
GOOGOLPLEX
GOOGOLPLEXES
GOOGOLS
GOOGS
GOOIER
GOOIEST
GOOILY
GOOK
GOOKS
GOOKY
GOOL
GOOLD
GOOLDS
GOOLEY
GOOLEYS
GOOLIE
GOOLIES
GOOLS
GOOLY
GOOMBAH
GOOMBAHS
GOOMBAY
GOOMBAYS
GOON
GOONDA
GOONDAS
GOONEY
GOONEYBIRD
GOONEYBIRDS
GOONEYS
GOONIE
GOONIES
GOONS
GOONY
GOOP
GOOPIER
GOOPIEST
GOOPS
GOOPY
GOOR
GOORAL
GOORALS
GOORIE
GOORIES
GOOROO
GOOROOS
GOORS
GOORY
GOOS
GOOSANDER
GOOSANDERS
GOOSE
GOOSEBERRIES
GOOSEBERRY

GOOSED
GOOSEFISH
GOOSEFISHES
GOOSEFLESH
GOOSEFLESHES
GOOSEFOOT
GOOSEFOOTS
GOOSEGOB
GOOSEGOBS
GOOSEGOG
GOOSEGOGS
GOOSEGRASS
GOOSEGRASSES
GOOSEHERD
GOOSEHERDS
GOOSENECK
GOOSENECKED
GOOSENECKS
GOOSERIES
GOOSERY
GOOSES
GOOSEY
GOOSEYS
GOOSIER
GOOSIES
GOOSIEST
GOOSILY
GOOSINESS
GOOSING
GOOSY
GOPAK
GOPAKS
GOPHER
GOPHERED
GOPHERING
GOPHERS
GOPHERWOOD
GOPHERWOODS
GOPURA
GOPURAM
GOPURAMS
GOPURAS
GOR
GORAL
GORALS
GORAMIES
GORAMY
GORBELLIES
GORBELLY
GORBLIMEY
GORBLIMY
GORCOCK
GORCOCKS
GORCROW
GORCROWS
GORE

GORED
GOREHOUND
GOREHOUNDS
GORES
GORGE
GORGEABLE
GORGED
GORGEDLY
GORGEOUS
GORGEOUSLY
GORGEOUSNESS
GORGEOUSNESSES
GORGER
GORGERIN
GORGERINS
GORGERS
GORGES
GORGET
GORGETED
GORGETS
GORGIA
GORGIAS
GORGING
GORGIO
GORGIOS
GORGON
GORGONEIA
GORGONEION
GORGONIAN
GORGONIANS
GORGONISE
GORGONISED
GORGONISES
GORGONISING
GORGONIZE
GORGONIZED
GORGONIZES
GORGONIZING
GORGONS
GORHEN
GORHENS
GORIER
GORIEST
GORILLA
GORILLAGRAM
GORILLAGRAMS
GORILLAS
GORILLIAN
GORILLINE
GORILLOID
GORILY
GORINESS
GORINESSES
GORING
GORINGS
GORM

GORMAND
GORMANDISE
GORMANDISED
GORMANDISER
GORMANDISERS
GORMANDISES
GORMANDISING
GORMANDISINGS
GORMANDISM
GORMANDISMS
GORMANDIZE
GORMANDIZED
GORMANDIZER
GORMANDIZERS
GORMANDIZES
GORMANDIZING
GORMANDIZINGS
GORMANDS
GORMED
GORMIER
GORMIEST
GORMING
GORMLESS
GORMS
GORMY
GORP
GORPED
GORPING
GORPS
GORSE
GORSEDD
GORSEDDS
GORSES
GORSIER
GORSIEST
GORSOON
GORSOONS
GORSY
GORY
GOS
GOSH
GOSHAWK
GOSHAWKS
GOSHT
GOSHTS
GOSLARITE
GOSLARITES
GOSLET
GOSLETS
GOSLING
GOSLINGS
GOSPEL
GOSPELER
GOSPELERS
GOSPELISE
GOSPELISED

GOSPELISES
GOSPELISING
GOSPELIZE
GOSPELIZED
GOSPELIZES
GOSPELIZING
GOSPELLED
GOSPELLER
GOSPELLERS
GOSPELLING
GOSPELLISED
GOSPELLISES
GOSPELLISING
GOSPELLIZE
GOSPELLIZED
GOSPELLIZES
GOSPELLIZING
GOSPELS
GOSPODA
GOSPODAR
GOSPODARS
GOSPODIN
GOSPORT
GOSPORTS
GOSS
GOSSAMER
GOSSAMERS
GOSSAMERY
GOSSAN
GOSSANS
GOSSE
GOSSED
GOSSES
GOSSIB
GOSSIBS
GOSSING
GOSSIP
GOSSIPED
GOSSIPER
GOSSIPERS
GOSSIPING
GOSSIPINGLY
GOSSIPINGS
GOSSIPMONGER
GOSSIPMONGERS
GOSSIPPED
GOSSIPPING
GOSSIPRIES
GOSSIPRY
GOSSIPS
GOSSIPY
GOSSOON
GOSSOONS
GOSSYPINE
GOSSYPOL
GOSSYPOLS

GOSTER
GOSTERED
GOSTERING
GOSTERS
GOT
GOTHIC
GOTHICALLY
GOTHICISE
GOTHICISED
GOTHICISES
GOTHICISING
GOTHICIZE
GOTHICIZED
GOTHICIZES
GOTHICIZING
GOTHICS
GOTHITE
GOTHITES
GOTTA
GOTTEN
GOUACHE
GOUACHES
GOUGE
GOUGED
GOUGER
GOUGERE
GOUGERES
GOUGERS
GOUGES
GOUGING
GOUJEERS
GOUJON
GOUJONS
GOUK
GOUKS
GOULASH
GOULASHES
GOURA
GOURAMI
GOURAMIES
GOURAMIS
GOURAS
GOURD
GOURDE
GOURDES
GOURDIER
GOURDIEST
GOURDINESS
GOURDINESSES
GOURDLIKE
GOURDS
GOURDY
GOURMAND
GOURMANDISE
GOURMANDISES
GOURMANDISM

GOURMANDISMS
GOURMANDIZE
GOURMANDIZED
GOURMANDIZES
GOURMANDIZING
GOURMANDS
GOURMET
GOURMETS
GOUSTIER
GOUSTIEST
GOUSTROUS
GOUSTY
GOUT
GOUTFLIES
GOUTFLY
GOUTIER
GOUTIEST
GOUTILY
GOUTINESS
GOUTINESSES
GOUTS
GOUTTE
GOUTTES
GOUTWEED
GOUTWEEDS
GOUTWORT
GOUTWORTS
GOUTY
GOUVERNANTE
GOUVERNANTES
GOV
GOVERN
GOVERNABILITY
GOVERNABLE
GOVERNABLENESS
GOVERNALL
GOVERNALLS
GOVERNANCE
GOVERNANCES
GOVERNANTE
GOVERNANTES
GOVERNED
GOVERNESS
GOVERNESSED
GOVERNESSES
GOVERNESSING
GOVERNESSY
GOVERNING
GOVERNMENT
GOVERNMENTAL
GOVERNMENTALISM
GOVERNMENTALIST
GOVERNMENTALIZE
GOVERNMENTALLY
GOVERNMENTESE
GOVERNMENTESES

GOVERNMENTS
GOVERNOR
GOVERNORATE
GOVERNORATES
GOVERNORS
GOVERNORSHIP
GOVERNORSHIPS
GOVERNS
GOVS
GOWAN
GOWANED
GOWANS
GOWANY
GOWD
GOWDER
GOWDEST
GOWDS
GOWDSPINK
GOWDSPINKS
GOWF
GOWFED
GOWFER
GOWFERS
GOWFING
GOWFS
GOWK
GOWKS
GOWL
GOWLAN
GOWLAND
GOWLANDS
GOWLANS
GOWLED
GOWLING
GOWLS
GOWN
GOWNBOY
GOWNBOYS
GOWNED
GOWNING
GOWNMAN
GOWNMEN
GOWNS
GOWNSMAN
GOWNSMEN
GOWPEN
GOWPENFUL
GOWPENFULS
GOWPENS
GOX
GOXES
GOY
GOYIM
GOYISCH
GOYISH
GOYS

GOZZAN
GOZZANS
GRAAL
GRAALS
GRAB
GRABBED
GRABBER
GRABBERS
GRABBIER
GRABBIEST
GRABBING
GRABBLE
GRABBLED
GRABBLER
GRABBLERS
GRABBLES
GRABBLING
GRABBY
GRABEN
GRABENS
GRABS
GRACE
GRACED
GRACEFUL
GRACEFULLER
GRACEFULLEST
GRACEFULLY
GRACEFULNESS
GRACEFULNESSES
GRACELESS
GRACELESSLY
GRACELESSNESS
GRACELESSNESSES
GRACES
GRACILE
GRACILENESS
GRACILENESSES
GRACILES
GRACILIS
GRACILITIES
GRACILITY
GRACING
GRACIOSITIES
GRACIOSITY
GRACIOSO
GRACIOSOS
GRACIOUS
GRACIOUSES
GRACIOUSLY
GRACIOUSNESS
GRACIOUSNESSES
GRACKLE
GRACKLES
GRAD
GRADABILITY
GRADABLE

GRADABLENESS
GRADABLES
GRADATE
GRADATED
GRADATES
GRADATIM
GRADATING
GRADATION
GRADATIONAL
GRADATIONALLY
GRADATIONED
GRADATIONS
GRADATORY
GRADDAN
GRADDANED
GRADDANING
GRADDANS
GRADE
GRADED
GRADELESS
GRADELIER
GRADELIEST
GRADELY
GRADER
GRADERS
GRADES
GRADIENT
GRADIENTER
GRADIENTERS
GRADIENTS
GRADIN
GRADINE
GRADINES
GRADING
GRADINI
GRADINO
GRADINS
GRADIOMETER
GRADIOMETERS
GRADS
GRADUAL
GRADUALISM
GRADUALISMS
GRADUALIST
GRADUALISTIC
GRADUALISTS
GRADUALITIES
GRADUALITY
GRADUALLY
GRADUALNESS
GRADUALNESSES
GRADUALS
GRADUAND
GRADUANDS
GRADUATE
GRADUATED

GRADUATES
GRADUATESHIP
GRADUATESHIPS
GRADUATING
GRADUATION
GRADUATIONS
GRADUATOR
GRADUATORS
GRADUS
GRADUSES
GRAECIZE
GRAECIZED
GRAECIZES
GRAECIZING
GRAFF
GRAFFED
GRAFFING
GRAFFITI
GRAFFITIED
GRAFFITIS
GRAFFITIST
GRAFFITISTS
GRAFFITO
GRAFFS
GRAFT
GRAFTAGE
GRAFTAGES
GRAFTED
GRAFTER
GRAFTERS
GRAFTING
GRAFTINGS
GRAFTS
GRAHAM
GRAHAMS
GRAIL
GRAILE
GRAILES
GRAILS
GRAIN
GRAINAGE
GRAINAGES
GRAINE
GRAINED
GRAINER
GRAINERS
GRAINES
GRAINFIELD
GRAINFIELDS
GRAINIER
GRAINIEST
GRAININESS
GRAININESSES
GRAINING
GRAININGS
GRAINLESS

GRAINLESSLY
GRAINLESSNESS
GRAINS
GRAINY
GRAIP
GRAIPS
GRAITH
GRAITHED
GRAITHING
GRAITHLY
GRAITHS
GRAKLE
GRAKLES
GRALLATORIAL
GRALLOCH
GRALLOCHED
GRALLOCHING
GRALLOCHS
GRAM
GRAMA
GRAMARIES
GRAMARY
GRAMARYE
GRAMARYES
GRAMAS
GRAMASH
GRAMASHES
GRAME
GRAMERCIES
GRAMERCY
GRAMES
GRAMICIDIN
GRAMICIDINS
GRAMINACEOUS
GRAMINEOUS
GRAMINICOLOUS
GRAMINIVOROUS
GRAMINOLOGIST
GRAMINOLOGY
GRAMMA
GRAMMAGE
GRAMMAGES
GRAMMALOGUE
GRAMMALOGUES
GRAMMAR
GRAMMARIAN
GRAMMARIANS
GRAMMARLESS
GRAMMARLESSNESS
GRAMMARS
GRAMMAS
GRAMMATIC
GRAMMATICAL
GRAMMATICALITY
GRAMMATICALLY
GRAMMATICALNESS

GRAMMATICASTER
GRAMMATICASTERS
GRAMMATICISE
GRAMMATICISED
GRAMMATICISES
GRAMMATICISING
GRAMMATICISM
GRAMMATICISMS
GRAMMATICIZE
GRAMMATICIZED
GRAMMATICIZES
GRAMMATICIZING
GRAMMATIST
GRAMMATISTS
GRAMMATOLOGIES
GRAMMATOLOGIST
GRAMMATOLOGISTS
GRAMMATOLOGY
GRAMME
GRAMMES
GRAMOCHE
GRAMOCHES
GRAMOPHONE
GRAMOPHONES
GRAMOPHONIC
GRAMOPHONICALLY
GRAMOPHONIES
GRAMOPHONIST
GRAMOPHONISTS
GRAMOPHONY
GRAMP
GRAMPS
GRAMPUS
GRAMPUSES
GRAMS
GRAN
GRANA
GRANADILLA
GRANADILLAS
GRANARIES
GRANARY
GRAND
GRANDAD
GRANDADDIES
GRANDADDY
GRANDADS
GRANDAM
GRANDAME
GRANDAMES
GRANDAMS
GRANDAUNT
GRANDAUNTS
GRANDBABIES
GRANDBABY
GRANDCHILD
GRANDCHILDREN

GRANDDAD
GRANDDADDIES
GRANDDADDY
GRANDDADS
GRANDDAM
GRANDDAMS
GRANDDAUGHTER
GRANDDAUGHTERS
GRANDE
GRANDEE
GRANDEES
GRANDEESHIP
GRANDEESHIPS
GRANDER
GRANDEST
GRANDEUR
GRANDEURS
GRANDFATHER
GRANDFATHERED
GRANDFATHERING
GRANDFATHERLY
GRANDFATHERS
GRANDIFLORA
GRANDIFLORAS
GRANDILOQUENCE
GRANDILOQUENCES
GRANDILOQUENT
GRANDILOQUENTLY
GRANDILOQUOUS
GRANDIOSE
GRANDIOSELY
GRANDIOSENESS
GRANDIOSENESSES
GRANDIOSITIES
GRANDIOSITY
GRANDIOSO
GRANDKID
GRANDKIDS
GRANDLY
GRANDMA
GRANDMAMA
GRANDMAMAS
GRANDMAMMA
GRANDMAMMAS
GRANDMAS
GRANDMASTER
GRANDMASTERS
GRANDMOTHER
GRANDMOTHERLY
GRANDMOTHERS
GRANDNEPHEW
GRANDNEPHEWS
GRANDNESS
GRANDNESSES
GRANDNIECE
GRANDNIECES

GRANDPA
GRANDPAPA
GRANDPAPAS
GRANDPARENT
GRANDPARENTAL
GRANDPARENTHOOD
GRANDPARENTS
GRANDPAS
GRANDS
GRANDSIR
GRANDSIRE
GRANDSIRES
GRANDSIRS
GRANDSON
GRANDSONS
GRANDSTAND
GRANDSTANDED
GRANDSTANDER
GRANDSTANDERS
GRANDSTANDING
GRANDSTANDS
GRANDSTOOD
GRANDUNCLE
GRANDUNCLES
GRANFER
GRANFERS
GRANGE
GRANGER
GRANGERISATION
GRANGERISATIONS
GRANGERISE
GRANGERISED
GRANGERISER
GRANGERISES
GRANGERISING
GRANGERISM
GRANGERISMS
GRANGERIZATION
GRANGERIZATIONS
GRANGERIZE
GRANGERIZED
GRANGERIZER
GRANGERIZES
GRANGERIZING
GRANGERS
GRANGES
GRANITA
GRANITAS
GRANITE
GRANITELIKE
GRANITES
GRANITEWARE
GRANITEWARES
GRANITIC
GRANITIFICATION
GRANITIFORM

GRANITISATION
GRANITISATIONS
GRANITISE
GRANITISED
GRANITISES
GRANITISING
GRANITITE
GRANITITES
GRANITIZATION
GRANITIZATIONS
GRANITIZE
GRANITIZED
GRANITIZES
GRANITIZING
GRANITOID
GRANIVORE
GRANIVORES
GRANIVOROUS
GRANNAM
GRANNAMS
GRANNIE
GRANNIED
GRANNIEING
GRANNIES
GRANNOM
GRANNOMS
GRANNY
GRANNYING
GRANNYISH
GRANNYISHNESS
GRANODIORITE
GRANODIORITES
GRANODIORITIC
GRANOLA
GRANOLAS
GRANOLITH
GRANOLITHIC
GRANOLITHICS
GRANOPHYRE
GRANOPHYRES
GRANOPHYRIC
GRANS
GRANT
GRANTABLE
GRANTED
GRANTEE
GRANTEES
GRANTER
GRANTERS
GRANTING
GRANTOR
GRANTORS
GRANTS
GRANTSMAN
GRANTSMANSHIP
GRANTSMANSHIPS

GRANTSMEN
GRANULAR
GRANULARITIES
GRANULARITY
GRANULARLY
GRANULARNESS
GRANULARY
GRANULATE
GRANULATED
GRANULATER
GRANULATERS
GRANULATES
GRANULATING
GRANULATION
GRANULATIONS
GRANULATIVE
GRANULATOR
GRANULATORS
GRANULE
GRANULES
GRANULIFEROUS
GRANULIFORM
GRANULITE
GRANULITES
GRANULITIC
GRANULITISATION
GRANULITIZATION
GRANULOCYTE
GRANULOCYTES
GRANULOCYTIC
GRANULOMA
GRANULOMAS
GRANULOMATA
GRANULOMATOUS
GRANULOSE
GRANULOSES
GRANULOSIS
GRANULOUS
GRANUM
GRAPE
GRAPED
GRAPEFRUIT
GRAPEFRUITS
GRAPELESS
GRAPELIKE
GRAPERIES
GRAPERY
GRAPES
GRAPESEED
GRAPESEEDS
GRAPESHOT
GRAPESHOTS
GRAPESTONE
GRAPESTONES
GRAPETREE
GRAPETREES

GRAPEVINE
GRAPEVINES
GRAPEY
GRAPH
GRAPHED
GRAPHEME
GRAPHEMES
GRAPHEMIC
GRAPHEMICALLY
GRAPHEMICS
GRAPHIC
GRAPHICACIES
GRAPHICACY
GRAPHICAL
GRAPHICALLY
GRAPHICALNESS
GRAPHICLY
GRAPHICNESS
GRAPHICNESSES
GRAPHICS
GRAPHING
GRAPHITE
GRAPHITES
GRAPHITIC
GRAPHITISATION
GRAPHITISATIONS
GRAPHITISE
GRAPHITISED
GRAPHITISES
GRAPHITISING
GRAPHITIZABLE
GRAPHITIZATION
GRAPHITIZATIONS
GRAPHITIZE
GRAPHITIZED
GRAPHITIZES
GRAPHITIZING
GRAPHITOID
GRAPHIUM
GRAPHIUMS
GRAPHOLECT
GRAPHOLECTS
GRAPHOLOGIC
GRAPHOLOGICAL
GRAPHOLOGIES
GRAPHOLOGIST
GRAPHOLOGISTS
GRAPHOLOGY
GRAPHOMANIA
GRAPHOMANIAS
GRAPHOMOTOR
GRAPHOPHOBIA
GRAPHOPHOBIAS
GRAPHS
GRAPIER
GRAPIEST

GRAPINESS
GRAPINESSES
GRAPING
GRAPLE
GRAPLEMENT
GRAPLEMENTS
GRAPLES
GRAPLIN
GRAPLINE
GRAPLINES
GRAPLINS
GRAPNEL
GRAPNELS
GRAPPA
GRAPPAS
GRAPPLE
GRAPPLED
GRAPPLER
GRAPPLERS
GRAPPLES
GRAPPLING
GRAPPLINGS
GRAPTOLITE
GRAPTOLITES
GRAPTOLITIC
GRAPY
GRASP
GRASPABLE
GRASPED
GRASPER
GRASPERS
GRASPING
GRASPINGLY
GRASPINGNESS
GRASPINGNESSES
GRASPLESS
GRASPS
GRASS
GRASSED
GRASSER
GRASSERS
GRASSES
GRASSFINCH
GRASSFINCHES
GRASSHOOK
GRASSHOOKS
GRASSHOPPER
GRASSHOPPERS
GRASSIER
GRASSIEST
GRASSILY
GRASSINESS
GRASSINESSES
GRASSING
GRASSINGS
GRASSLAND

GRASSLANDS
GRASSLESS
GRASSLIKE
GRASSQUIT
GRASSQUITS
GRASSROOT
GRASSROOTS
GRASSUM
GRASSUMS
GRASSWRACK
GRASSWRACKS
GRASSY
GRASTE
GRAT
GRATE
GRATED
GRATEFUL
GRATEFULLER
GRATEFULLEST
GRATEFULLY
GRATEFULNESS
GRATEFULNESSES
GRATER
GRATERS
GRATES
GRATICULATION
GRATICULATIONS
GRATICULE
GRATICULES
GRATIFICATION
GRATIFICATIONS
GRATIFIED
GRATIFIER
GRATIFIERS
GRATIFIES
GRATIFY
GRATIFYING
GRATIFYINGLY
GRATILLITIES
GRATILLITY
GRATIN
GRATINATE
GRATINATED
GRATINATES
GRATINATING
GRATINE
GRATINEE
GRATINEED
GRATINEEING
GRATINEES
GRATING
GRATINGLY
GRATINGS
GRATINS
GRATIS
GRATITUDE

GRATITUDES
GRATTOIR
GRATTOIRS
GRATUITIES
GRATUITOUS
GRATUITOUSLY
GRATUITOUSNESS
GRATUITY
GRATULANT
GRATULATE
GRATULATED
GRATULATES
GRATULATING
GRATULATION
GRATULATIONS
GRATULATORY
GRAUNCH
GRAUNCHED
GRAUNCHER
GRAUNCHERS
GRAUNCHES
GRAUNCHING
GRAUPEL
GRAUPELS
GRAV
GRAVADLAX
GRAVADLAXES
GRAVAMEN
GRAVAMENS
GRAVAMINA
GRAVE
GRAVED
GRAVEL
GRAVELED
GRAVELESS
GRAVELING
GRAVELISH
GRAVELLED
GRAVELLING
GRAVELLY
GRAVELS
GRAVELY
GRAVEN
GRAVENESS
GRAVENESSES
GRAVENS
GRAVEOLENT
GRAVER
GRAVERS
GRAVES
GRAVESIDE
GRAVESIDES
GRAVEST
GRAVESTONE
GRAVESTONES
GRAVEYARD

GRAVEYARDS
GRAVID
GRAVIDA
GRAVIDAE
GRAVIDAS
GRAVIDITIES
GRAVIDITY
GRAVIDLY
GRAVIDNESS
GRAVIES
GRAVIMETER
GRAVIMETERS
GRAVIMETRIC
GRAVIMETRICAL
GRAVIMETRICALLY
GRAVIMETRIES
GRAVIMETRY
GRAVING
GRAVINGS
GRAVIPERCEPTION
GRAVIPERCEPTIVE
GRAVITAS
GRAVITASES
GRAVITATE
GRAVITATED
GRAVITATER
GRAVITATERS
GRAVITATES
GRAVITATING
GRAVITATION
GRAVITATIONAL
GRAVITATIONALLY
GRAVITATIONS
GRAVITATIVE
GRAVITIES
GRAVITOMETER
GRAVITOMETERS
GRAVITON
GRAVITONS
GRAVITY
GRAVLAKS
GRAVLAX
GRAVLAXES
GRAVS
GRAVURE
GRAVURES
GRAVY
GRAY
GRAYBACK
GRAYBACKS
GRAYBEARD
GRAYBEARDED
GRAYBEARDS
GRAYED
GRAYER
GRAYEST

GRAYFISH
GRAYFISHES
GRAYFLIES
GRAYFLY
GRAYING
GRAYISH
GRAYLAG
GRAYLAGS
GRAYLE
GRAYLES
GRAYLING
GRAYLINGS
GRAYLY
GRAYMAIL
GRAYMAILS
GRAYNESS
GRAYNESSES
GRAYOUT
GRAYOUTS
GRAYS
GRAYWACKE
GRAYWACKES
GRAZABLE
GRAZE
GRAZEABLE
GRAZED
GRAZER
GRAZERS
GRAZES
GRAZIER
GRAZIERS
GRAZING
GRAZINGLY
GRAZINGS
GRAZIOSO
GREASE
GREASEBALL
GREASEBALLS
GREASEBAND
GREASEBANDS
GREASEBUSH
GREASEBUSHES
GREASED
GREASELESS
GREASEPAINT
GREASEPAINTS
GREASEPROOF
GREASEPROOFS
GREASER
GREASERS
GREASES
GREASEWOOD
GREASEWOODS
GREASIER
GREASIES
GREASIEST

GREASILY
GREASINESS
GREASINESSES
GREASING
GREASY
GREAT
GREATCOAT
GREATCOATED
GREATCOATS
GREATEN
GREATENED
GREATENING
GREATENS
GREATER
GREATEST
GREATESTS
GREATHEARTED
GREATHEARTEDLY
GREATLY
GREATNESS
GREATNESSES
GREATS
GREAVE
GREAVED
GREAVES
GREAVING
GREBE
GREBES
GRECE
GRECES
GRECIAN
GRECIANIZE
GRECIANIZED
GRECIANIZES
GRECIANIZING
GRECIANS
GRECIZE
GRECIZED
GRECIZES
GRECIZING
GRECQUE
GRECQUES
GREE
GREEBO
GREEBOES
GREEBOISH
GREECE
GREECES
GREED
GREEDIER
GREEDIEST
GREEDILY
GREEDINESS
GREEDINESSES
GREEDLESS
GREEDLESSLY

GREEDLESSNESS
GREEDS
GREEDY
GREEGREE
GREEGREES
GREEING
GREEK
GREEKING
GREEKINGS
GREEN
GREENBACK
GREENBACKER
GREENBACKERS
GREENBACKISM
GREENBACKISMS
GREENBACKS
GREENBELT
GREENBELTS
GREENBONE
GREENBONES
GREENBOTTLE
GREENBOTTLES
GREENBRIER
GREENBRIERS
GREENBUG
GREENBUGS
GREENCLOTH
GREENCLOTHS
GREENED
GREENER
GREENERIES
GREENERS
GREENERY
GREENEST
GREENFIELD
GREENFIELDS
GREENFINCH
GREENFINCHES
GREENFLIES
GREENFLY
GREENGAGE
GREENGAGES
GREENGROCER
GREENGROCERIES
GREENGROCERS
GREENGROCERY
GREENHAND
GREENHANDS
GREENHEAD
GREENHEADS
GREENHEART
GREENHEARTS
GREENHORN
GREENHORNS
GREENHOUSE
GREENHOUSES

GREENIE
GREENIER
GREENIES
GREENIEST
GREENING
GREENINGS
GREENISH
GREENISHNESS
GREENISHNESSES
GREENKEEPER
GREENKEEPERS
GREENLET
GREENLETS
GREENLIGHT
GREENLIGHTED
GREENLIGHTING
GREENLIGHTS
GREENLING
GREENLINGS
GREENLY
GREENMAIL
GREENMAILED
GREENMAILER
GREENMAILERS
GREENMAILING
GREENMAILS
GREENNESS
GREENNESSES
GREENOCKITE
GREENOCKITES
GREENROOM
GREENROOMS
GREENS
GREENSAND
GREENSANDS
GREENSHANK
GREENSHANKS
GREENSICK
GREENSICKNESS
GREENSICKNESSES
GREENSKEEPER
GREENSKEEPERS
GREENSOME
GREENSOMES
GREENSPEAK
GREENSPEAKS
GREENSTICK
GREENSTICKS
GREENSTONE
GREENSTONES
GREENSTUFF
GREENSTUFFS
GREENSWARD
GREENSWARDS
GREENTH
GREENTHS

GREENWASH	GREISENISING	GREYBACKS	GRIDING
GREENWASHED	GREISENIZATION	GREYBEARD	GRIDIRON
GREENWASHES	GREISENIZATIONS	GREYBEARDED	GRIDIRONED
GREENWASHING	GREISENIZE	GREYBEARDEDNESS	GRIDIRONING
GREENWAY	GREISENIZED	GREYBEARDS	GRIDIRONS
GREENWAYS	GREISENIZES	GREYED	GRIDLOCK
GREENWEED	GREISENIZING	GREYER	GRIDLOCKED
GREENWEEDS	GREISENS	GREYEST	GRIDLOCKING
GREENWING	GREISLY	GREYHEN	GRIDLOCKS
GREENWINGS	GREMIAL	GREYHENS	GRIDS
GREENWOOD	GREMIALS	GREYHOUND	GRIECE
GREENWOODS	GREMLIN	GREYHOUNDS	GRIECED
GREENY	GREMLINS	GREYING	GRIECES
GREES	GREMMIE	GREYINGS	GRIEF
GREESE	GREMMIES	GREYISH	GRIEFFUL
GREESES	GREMMY	GREYLAG	GRIEFLESS
GREESING	GREMOLATA	GREYLAGS	GRIEFS
GREESINGS	GREMOLATAS	GREYLIST	GRIESIE
GREET	GREN	GREYLISTED	GRIESLY
GREETE	GRENADE	GREYLISTING	GRIESY
GREETED	GRENADES	GREYLISTS	GRIEVANCE
GREETER	GRENADIER	GREYLY	GRIEVANCES
GREETERS	GRENADIERS	GREYNESS	GRIEVANT
GREETES	GRENADILLA	GREYNESSES	GRIEVANTS
GREETING	GRENADILLAS	GREYS	GRIEVE
GREETINGS	GRENADINE	GREYSTONE	GRIEVED
GREETS	GRENADINES	GREYSTONES	GRIEVER
GREFFIER	GRENNED	GREYWACKE	GRIEVERS
GREFFIERS	GRENNING	GREYWACKES	GRIEVES
GREGALE	GRENS	GREYWETHER	GRIEVING
GREGALES	GRENZ	GREYWETHERS	GRIEVINGLY
GREGARIAN	GRENZES	GRIBBLE	GRIEVINGS
GREGARIANISM	GRESE	GRIBBLES	GRIEVOUS
GREGARIANISMS	GRESES	GRICE	GRIEVOUSLY
GREGARINE	GRESSING	GRICER	GRIEVOUSNESS
GREGARINES	GRESSINGS	GRICERS	GRIEVOUSNESSES
GREGARINIAN	GRESSORIAL	GRICES	GRIFF
GREGARIOUS	GRESSORIOUS	GRICING	GRIFFE
GREGARIOUSLY	GREVE	GRICINGS	GRIFFES
GREGARIOUSNESS	GREVES	GRID	GRIFFIN
GREGATIM	GREVILLEA	GRIDDED	GRIFFINISH
GREGE	GREVILLEAS	GRIDDER	GRIFFINISM
GREGO	GREW	GRIDDERS	GRIFFINISMS
GREGOS	GREWED	GRIDDLE	GRIFFINS
GREIGE	GREWHOUND	GRIDDLEBREAD	GRIFFON
GREIGES	GREWHOUNDS	GRIDDLEBREADS	GRIFFONS
GREIN	GREWING	GRIDDLECAKE	GRIFFS
GREINED	GREWS	GRIDDLECAKES	GRIFT
GREINING	GREWSOME	GRIDDLED	GRIFTED
GREINS	GREWSOMER	GRIDDLES	GRIFTER
GREISEN	GREWSOMEST	GRIDDLING	GRIFTERS
GREISENISATION	GREX	GRIDE	GRIFTING
GREISENISATIONS	GREXES	GRIDED	GRIFTS
GREISENISE	GREY	GRIDELIN	GRIG
GREISENISED	GREYBACK	GRIDELINS	GRIGGED
GREISENISES	GREYBACKED	GRIDES	GRIGGING

GRIGRI
GRIGRIS
GRIGS
GRIKE
GRIKES
GRILL
GRILLADE
GRILLADES
GRILLAGE
GRILLAGES
GRILLE
GRILLED
GRILLER
GRILLERS
GRILLES
GRILLING
GRILLINGS
GRILLION
GRILLIONS
GRILLROOM
GRILLROOMS
GRILLS
GRILLSTEAK
GRILLSTEAKS
GRILLWORK
GRILLWORKS
GRILSE
GRILSES
GRIM
GRIMACE
GRIMACED
GRIMACER
GRIMACERS
GRIMACES
GRIMACING
GRIMACINGLY
GRIMALKIN
GRIMALKINS
GRIME
GRIMED
GRIMES
GRIMIER
GRIMIEST
GRIMILY
GRIMINESS
GRIMINESSES
GRIMING
GRIMLY
GRIMMER
GRIMMEST
GRIMNESS
GRIMNESSES
GRIMOIRE
GRIMOIRES
GRIMY
GRIN

GRINCH
GRINCHES
GRIND
GRINDED
GRINDELIA
GRINDELIAS
GRINDER
GRINDERIES
GRINDERS
GRINDERY
GRINDING
GRINDINGLY
GRINDINGS
GRINDS
GRINDSTONE
GRINDSTONES
GRINGO
GRINGOS
GRINNED
GRINNER
GRINNERS
GRINNING
GRINNINGLY
GRINS
GRIOT
GRIOTS
GRIP
GRIPE
GRIPED
GRIPER
GRIPERS
GRIPES
GRIPEY
GRIPIER
GRIPIEST
GRIPING
GRIPINGLY
GRIPLE
GRIPMAN
GRIPMEN
GRIPPE
GRIPPED
GRIPPER
GRIPPERS
GRIPPES
GRIPPIER
GRIPPIEST
GRIPPING
GRIPPINGLY
GRIPPLE
GRIPPLES
GRIPPY
GRIPS
GRIPSACK
GRIPSACKS
GRIPT

GRIPTAPE
GRIPTAPES
GRIPY
GRIS
GRISAILLE
GRISAILLES
GRISE
GRISED
GRISELY
GRISEOFULVIN
GRISEOFULVINS
GRISEOUS
GRISES
GRISETTE
GRISETTES
GRISGRIS
GRISING
GRISKIN
GRISKINS
GRISLED
GRISLIER
GRISLIES
GRISLIEST
GRISLINESS
GRISLINESSES
GRISLY
GRISON
GRISONS
GRIST
GRISTLE
GRISTLES
GRISTLIER
GRISTLIEST
GRISTLINESS
GRISTLINESSES
GRISTLY
GRISTMILL
GRISTMILLS
GRISTS
GRISY
GRIT
GRITH
GRITHS
GRITLESS
GRITS
GRITSTONE
GRITSTONES
GRITTED
GRITTER
GRITTERS
GRITTEST
GRITTIER
GRITTIEST
GRITTILY
GRITTINESS
GRITTINESSES

GRITTING
GRITTY
GRIVATION
GRIVATIONS
GRIVET
GRIVETS
GRIZE
GRIZES
GRIZZLE
GRIZZLED
GRIZZLER
GRIZZLERS
GRIZZLES
GRIZZLIER
GRIZZLIES
GRIZZLIEST
GRIZZLING
GRIZZLY
GROAN
GROANED
GROANER
GROANERS
GROANFUL
GROANING
GROANINGLY
GROANINGS
GROANS
GROAT
GROATS
GROATSWORTH
GROATSWORTHS
GROCER
GROCERIES
GROCERS
GROCERY
GROCETERIA
GROCETERIAS
GROCKLE
GROCKLES
GRODIER
GRODIEST
GRODY
GROG
GROGGED
GROGGERIES
GROGGERY
GROGGIER
GROGGIEST
GROGGILY
GROGGINESS
GROGGINESSES
GROGGING
GROGGY
GROGRAM
GROGRAMS
GROGS

GROGSHOP
GROGSHOPS
GROIN
GROINED
GROINING
GROININGS
GROINS
GROMA
GROMAS
GROMET
GROMETS
GROMMET
GROMMETS
GROMWELL
GROMWELLS
GRONE
GRONED
GRONEFULL
GRONES
GRONING
GROOF
GROOFS
GROOLIER
GROOLIEST
GROOLY
GROOM
GROOMED
GROOMER
GROOMERS
GROOMING
GROOMINGS
GROOMS
GROOMSMAN
GROOMSMEN
GROOVE
GROOVED
GROOVELESS
GROOVELESSNESS
GROOVELIKE
GROOVER
GROOVERS
GROOVES
GROOVIER
GROOVIEST
GROOVING
GROOVY
GROPE
GROPED
GROPER
GROPERS
GROPES
GROPING
GROPINGLY
GROSBEAK
GROSBEAKS
GROSCHEN

GROSCHENS
GROSER
GROSERS
GROSERT
GROSERTS
GROSET
GROSETS
GROSGRAIN
GROSGRAINS
GROSS
GROSSART
GROSSARTS
GROSSED
GROSSER
GROSSERS
GROSSES
GROSSEST
GROSSIERETE
GROSSIERETES
GROSSING
GROSSLY
GROSSNESS
GROSSNESSES
GROSSULAR
GROSSULARITE
GROSSULARITES
GROSSULARS
GROSZ
GROSZE
GROSZY
GROT
GROTESQUE
GROTESQUELY
GROTESQUENESS
GROTESQUENESSES
GROTESQUER
GROTESQUERIE
GROTESQUERIES
GROTESQUERY
GROTESQUES
GROTESQUEST
GROTS
GROTTIER
GROTTIEST
GROTTO
GROTTOES
GROTTOS
GROTTY
GROUCH
GROUCHED
GROUCHES
GROUCHIER
GROUCHIEST
GROUCHILY
GROUCHINESS
GROUCHINESSES

GROUCHING
GROUCHY
GROUF
GROUFS
GROUGH
GROUGHS
GROUND
GROUNDAGE
GROUNDAGES
GROUNDBAIT
GROUNDBAITED
GROUNDBAITING
GROUNDBAITS
GROUNDBREAKER
GROUNDBREAKERS
GROUNDBREAKING
GROUNDBREAKINGS
GROUNDBURST
GROUNDBURSTS
GROUNDED
GROUNDEDLY
GROUNDEN
GROUNDER
GROUNDERS
GROUNDFISH
GROUNDFISHES
GROUNDHOG
GROUNDHOGS
GROUNDING
GROUNDINGS
GROUNDLESS
GROUNDLESSLY
GROUNDLESSNESS
GROUNDLING
GROUNDLINGS
GROUNDMAN
GROUNDMASS
GROUNDMASSES
GROUNDMEN
GROUNDNUT
GROUNDNUTS
GROUNDOUT
GROUNDOUTS
GROUNDPLOT
GROUNDPLOTS
GROUNDPROX
GROUNDPROXES
GROUNDS
GROUNDSEL
GROUNDSELL
GROUNDSELLS
GROUNDSELS
GROUNDSHEET
GROUNDSHEETS
GROUNDSILL
GROUNDSILLS

GROUNDSKEEPER
GROUNDSKEEPERS
GROUNDSMAN
GROUNDSMEN
GROUNDSPEED
GROUNDSPEEDS
GROUNDSWELL
GROUNDSWELLS
GROUNDWATER
GROUNDWATERS
GROUNDWOOD
GROUNDWOODS
GROUNDWORK
GROUNDWORKS
GROUP
GROUPABLE
GROUPAGE
GROUPAGES
GROUPED
GROUPER
GROUPERS
GROUPIE
GROUPIES
GROUPING
GROUPINGS
GROUPIST
GROUPISTS
GROUPLET
GROUPLETS
GROUPOID
GROUPOIDS
GROUPS
GROUPTHINK
GROUPTHINKS
GROUPUSCULE
GROUPUSCULES
GROUPWARE
GROUPWARES
GROUPY
GROUSE
GROUSED
GROUSELIKE
GROUSER
GROUSERS
GROUSES
GROUSEST
GROUSING
GROUT
GROUTED
GROUTER
GROUTERS
GROUTIER
GROUTIEST
GROUTING
GROUTINGS
GROUTS

GROUTY
GROVE
GROVED
GROVEL
GROVELED
GROVELER
GROVELERS
GROVELING
GROVELINGLY
GROVELLED
GROVELLER
GROVELLERS
GROVELLING
GROVELLINGLY
GROVELLINGNESS
GROVELS
GROVES
GROVET
GROVETS
GROW
GROWABLE
GROWER
GROWERS
GROWING
GROWINGLY
GROWINGS
GROWL
GROWLED
GROWLER
GROWLERIES
GROWLERS
GROWLERY
GROWLIER
GROWLIEST
GROWLINESS
GROWLINESSES
GROWLING
GROWLINGLY
GROWLINGS
GROWLS
GROWLY
GROWN
GROWNUP
GROWNUPS
GROWS
GROWTH
GROWTHIER
GROWTHIEST
GROWTHINESS
GROWTHINESSES
GROWTHIST
GROWTHISTS
GROWTHS
GROWTHY
GROYNE
GROYNES

GROZING
GRUB
GRUBBED
GRUBBER
GRUBBERS
GRUBBIER
GRUBBIEST
GRUBBILY
GRUBBINESS
GRUBBINESSES
GRUBBING
GRUBBLE
GRUBBLED
GRUBBLES
GRUBBLING
GRUBBY
GRUBS
GRUBSTAKE
GRUBSTAKED
GRUBSTAKER
GRUBSTAKERS
GRUBSTAKES
GRUBSTAKING
GRUBWORM
GRUBWORMS
GRUDGE
GRUDGED
GRUDGEFUL
GRUDGELESS
GRUDGELESSLY
GRUDGELESSNESS
GRUDGER
GRUDGERS
GRUDGES
GRUDGING
GRUDGINGLY
GRUDGINGS
GRUE
GRUED
GRUEING
GRUEL
GRUELED
GRUELER
GRUELERS
GRUELING
GRUELINGLY
GRUELINGS
GRUELLED
GRUELLER
GRUELLERS
GRUELLING
GRUELLINGS
GRUELS
GRUES
GRUESOME
GRUESOMELY

GRUESOMENESS
GRUESOMENESSES
GRUESOMER
GRUESOMEST
GRUFE
GRUFES
GRUFF
GRUFFED
GRUFFER
GRUFFEST
GRUFFIER
GRUFFIEST
GRUFFILY
GRUFFING
GRUFFISH
GRUFFLY
GRUFFNESS
GRUFFNESSES
GRUFFS
GRUFFY
GRUFTED
GRUGRU
GRUGRUS
GRUIFORM
GRUING
GRUM
GRUMBLE
GRUMBLED
GRUMBLER
GRUMBLERS
GRUMBLES
GRUMBLIER
GRUMBLIEST
GRUMBLING
GRUMBLINGLY
GRUMBLINGS
GRUMBLY
GRUME
GRUMES
GRUMLY
GRUMMER
GRUMMEST
GRUMMET
GRUMMETS
GRUMNESS
GRUMNESSES
GRUMOSE
GRUMOUS
GRUMP
GRUMPED
GRUMPH
GRUMPHED
GRUMPHIE
GRUMPHIES
GRUMPHING
GRUMPHS

GRUMPHY
GRUMPIER
GRUMPIEST
GRUMPILY
GRUMPINESS
GRUMPINESSES
GRUMPING
GRUMPISH
GRUMPISHLY
GRUMPISHNESS
GRUMPS
GRUMPY
GRUNDIES
GRUNGE
GRUNGES
GRUNGIER
GRUNGIEST
GRUNGY
GRUNION
GRUNIONS
GRUNT
GRUNTED
GRUNTER
GRUNTERS
GRUNTING
GRUNTINGLY
GRUNTINGS
GRUNTLE
GRUNTLED
GRUNTLES
GRUNTLING
GRUNTS
GRUPPETTI
GRUPPETTO
GRUSHIE
GRUTCH
GRUTCHED
GRUTCHES
GRUTCHING
GRUTTEN
GRUYERE
GRUYERES
GRYCE
GRYCES
GRYDE
GRYDED
GRYDES
GRYDING
GRYESY
GRYFON
GRYFONS
GRYKE
GRYKES
GRYPE
GRYPES
GRYPHON

GRYPHONS
GRYPT
GRYSBOK
GRYSBOKS
GRYSELY
GRYSIE
GU
GUACAMOLE
GUACAMOLES
GUACHAMOLE
GUACHAMOLES
GUACHARO
GUACHAROES
GUACHAROS
GUACO
GUACOS
GUAIAC
GUAIACOL
GUAIACOLS
GUAIACS
GUAIACUM
GUAIACUMS
GUAIOCUM
GUAIOCUMS
GUAN
GUANA
GUANACO
GUANACOS
GUANAS
GUANASE
GUANASES
GUANAY
GUANAYS
GUANAZOLO
GUANAZOLOS
GUANETHIDINE
GUANETHIDINES
GUANGO
GUANGOS
GUANIDIN
GUANIDINE
GUANIDINES
GUANIDINS
GUANIFEROUS
GUANIN
GUANINE
GUANINES
GUANINS
GUANO
GUANOS
GUANOSINE
GUANOSINES
GUANS
GUANYLIC
GUAR
GUARANA

GUARANAS
GUARANI
GUARANIES
GUARANIS
GUARANTEE
GUARANTEED
GUARANTEEING
GUARANTEES
GUARANTIED
GUARANTIES
GUARANTOR
GUARANTORS
GUARANTY
GUARANTYING
GUARD
GUARDABLE
GUARDAGE
GUARDAGES
GUARDANT
GUARDANTS
GUARDED
GUARDEDLY
GUARDEDNESS
GUARDEDNESSES
GUARDEE
GUARDEES
GUARDER
GUARDERS
GUARDHOUSE
GUARDHOUSES
GUARDIAN
GUARDIANS
GUARDIANSHIP
GUARDIANSHIPS
GUARDING
GUARDLESS
GUARDLIKE
GUARDRAIL
GUARDRAILS
GUARDROOM
GUARDROOMS
GUARDS
GUARDSHIP
GUARDSHIPS
GUARDSMAN
GUARDSMEN
GUARISH
GUARISHED
GUARISHES
GUARISHING
GUARS
GUAVA
GUAVAS
GUAYABERA
GUAYABERAS
GUAYULE

GUAYULES
GUB
GUBBAH
GUBBAHS
GUBBINS
GUBBINSES
GUBERNACULA
GUBERNACULUM
GUBERNATION
GUBERNATIONS
GUBERNATOR
GUBERNATORIAL
GUBERNATORS
GUBERNIYA
GUBERNIYAS
GUBS
GUCK
GUCKIER
GUCKIEST
GUCKS
GUCKY
GUDDLE
GUDDLED
GUDDLES
GUDDLING
GUDE
GUDEMAN
GUDEMEN
GUDES
GUDESIRE
GUDESIRES
GUDEWIFE
GUDEWIVES
GUDGEON
GUDGEONED
GUDGEONING
GUDGEONS
GUE
GUENON
GUENONS
GUERDON
GUERDONED
GUERDONER
GUERDONERS
GUERDONING
GUERDONS
GUEREZA
GUEREZAS
GUERIDON
GUERIDONS
GUERILLA
GUERILLAISM
GUERILLAS
GUERITE
GUERITES

GUERNSEY
GUERNSEYS
GUERRILLA
GUERRILLAISM
GUERRILLAS
GUERRILLERO
GUERRILLEROS
GUES
GUESS
GUESSABLE
GUESSED
GUESSER
GUESSERS
GUESSES
GUESSING
GUESSINGLY
GUESSINGS
GUESSTIMATE
GUESSTIMATED
GUESSTIMATES
GUESSTIMATING
GUESSTIMATION
GUESSWORK
GUESSWORKS
GUEST
GUESTED
GUESTEN
GUESTENED
GUESTENING
GUESTENS
GUESTHOUSE
GUESTHOUSES
GUESTIMATE
GUESTIMATED
GUESTIMATES
GUESTIMATING
GUESTIMATION
GUESTING
GUESTS
GUESTWISE
GUFF
GUFFAW
GUFFAWED
GUFFAWING
GUFFAWS
GUFFIE
GUFFIES
GUFFS
GUGA
GUGAS
GUGGLE
GUGGLED
GUGGLES
GUGGLING
GUGLET
GUGLETS

GUICHET
GUICHETS
GUID
GUIDABLE
GUIDAGE
GUIDAGES
GUIDANCE
GUIDANCES
GUIDE
GUIDEBOOK
GUIDEBOOKS
GUIDED
GUIDELESS
GUIDELINE
GUIDELINES
GUIDEPOST
GUIDEPOSTS
GUIDER
GUIDERS
GUIDES
GUIDESHIP
GUIDESHIPS
GUIDEWAY
GUIDEWAYS
GUIDING
GUIDINGS
GUIDON
GUIDONS
GUIDS
GUIDWILLIE
GUILD
GUILDER
GUILDERS
GUILDHALL
GUILDHALLS
GUILDRIES
GUILDRY
GUILDS
GUILDSHIP
GUILDSHIPS
GUILDSMAN
GUILDSMEN
GUILDSWOMAN
GUILDSWOMEN
GUILE
GUILED
GUILEFUL
GUILEFULLY
GUILEFULNESS
GUILEFULNESSES
GUILELESS
GUILELESSLY
GUILELESSNESS
GUILELESSNESSES
GUILER
GUILERS

GUILES
GUILING
GUILLEMET
GUILLEMETS
GUILLEMOT
GUILLEMOTS
GUILLOCHE
GUILLOCHED
GUILLOCHES
GUILLOCHING
GUILLOTINE
GUILLOTINED
GUILLOTINER
GUILLOTINERS
GUILLOTINES
GUILLOTINING
GUILT
GUILTIER
GUILTIEST
GUILTILY
GUILTINESS
GUILTINESSES
GUILTLESS
GUILTLESSLY
GUILTLESSNESS
GUILTLESSNESSES
GUILTS
GUILTY
GUIMBARD
GUIMBARDS
GUIMP
GUIMPE
GUIMPED
GUIMPES
GUIMPING
GUIMPS
GUINEA
GUINEAS
GUIPURE
GUIPURES
GUIRO
GUIROS
GUISARD
GUISARDS
GUISE
GUISED
GUISER
GUISERS
GUISES
GUISING
GUISINGS
GUITAR
GUITARFISH
GUITARFISHES
GUITARIST
GUITARISTS

GUITARS
GUITGUIT
GUITGUITS
GUIZER
GUIZERS
GUL
GULA
GULAG
GULAGS
GULAR
GULAS
GULCH
GULCHED
GULCHES
GULCHING
GULDEN
GULDENS
GULE
GULES
GULF
GULFED
GULFIER
GULFIEST
GULFING
GULFLIKE
GULFS
GULFWEED
GULFWEEDS
GULFY
GULL
GULLABLE
GULLABLY
GULLED
GULLER
GULLERIES
GULLERS
GULLERY
GULLET
GULLETS
GULLEY
GULLEYED
GULLEYING
GULLEYS
GULLIBILITIES
GULLIBILITY
GULLIBLE
GULLIBLY
GULLIED
GULLIES
GULLING
GULLISH
GULLS
GULLY
GULLYING
GULOSITIES
GULOSITY

GULP
GULPED
GULPER
GULPERS
GULPH
GULPHS
GULPIER
GULPIEST
GULPING
GULPINGLY
GULPS
GULPY
GULS
GULY
GUM
GUMBO
GUMBOIL
GUMBOILS
GUMBOOT
GUMBOOTS
GUMBOS
GUMBOTIL
GUMBOTILS
GUMDROP
GUMDROPS
GUMLANDS
GUMLESS
GUMLIKE
GUMMA
GUMMAS
GUMMATA
GUMMATOUS
GUMMED
GUMMER
GUMMERS
GUMMIER
GUMMIES
GUMMIEST
GUMMIFEROUS
GUMMILY
GUMMINESS
GUMMINESSES
GUMMING
GUMMINGS
GUMMITE
GUMMITES
GUMMOSE
GUMMOSES
GUMMOSIS
GUMMOSITIES
GUMMOSITY
GUMMOUS
GUMMY
GUMNUT
GUMNUTS
GUMP

GUMPED
GUMPHION
GUMPHIONS
GUMPING
GUMPTION
GUMPTIONS
GUMPTIOUS
GUMS
GUMSHIELD
GUMSHIELDS
GUMSHOE
GUMSHOED
GUMSHOEING
GUMSHOES
GUMSUCKER
GUMSUCKERS
GUMTREE
GUMTREES
GUMWEED
GUMWEEDS
GUMWOOD
GUMWOODS
GUN
GUNBOAT
GUNBOATS
GUNCOTTON
GUNCOTTONS
GUNDIES
GUNDOG
GUNDOGS
GUNDY
GUNFIGHT
GUNFIGHTER
GUNFIGHTERS
GUNFIGHTING
GUNFIGHTS
GUNFIRE
GUNFIRES
GUNFLINT
GUNFLINTS
GUNFOUGHT
GUNGE
GUNGED
GUNGES
GUNGIER
GUNGIEST
GUNGINESS
GUNGING
GUNGY
GUNHOUSE
GUNHOUSES
GUNITE
GUNITES
GUNK
GUNKHOLE

GUNKHOLED
GUNKHOLES
GUNKHOLING
GUNKS
GUNKY
GUNLAYER
GUNLAYERS
GUNLESS
GUNLOCK
GUNLOCKS
GUNMAKER
GUNMAKERS
GUNMAN
GUNMANSHIP
GUNMEN
GUNMETAL
GUNMETALS
GUNNAGE
GUNNAGES
GUNNED
GUNNEL
GUNNELS
GUNNEN
GUNNER
GUNNERA
GUNNERAS
GUNNERIES
GUNNERS
GUNNERSHIP
GUNNERY
GUNNIES
GUNNING
GUNNINGS
GUNNY
GUNNYBAG
GUNNYBAGS
GUNNYSACK
GUNNYSACKS
GUNPAPER
GUNPAPERS
GUNPLAY
GUNPLAYS
GUNPOINT
GUNPOINTS
GUNPORT
GUNPORTS
GUNPOWDER
GUNPOWDERS
GUNPOWDERY
GUNROOM
GUNROOMS
GUNRUNNER
GUNRUNNERS
GUNRUNNING
GUNRUNNINGS
GUNS

GUNSEL
GUNSELS
GUNSHIP
GUNSHIPS
GUNSHOT
GUNSHOTS
GUNSLINGER
GUNSLINGERS
GUNSLINGING
GUNSLINGINGS
GUNSMITH
GUNSMITHING
GUNSMITHINGS
GUNSMITHS
GUNSTICK
GUNSTICKS
GUNSTOCK
GUNSTOCKS
GUNSTONE
GUNSTONES
GUNTER
GUNTERS
GUNWALE
GUNWALES
GUNYAH
GUNYAHS
GUP
GUPPIES
GUPPY
GUPS
GUR
GURAMI
GURAMIS
GURDWARA
GURDWARAS
GURGE
GURGED
GURGES
GURGING
GURGITATION
GURGITATIONS
GURGLE
GURGLED
GURGLES
GURGLET
GURGLETS
GURGLING
GURGOYLE
GURGOYLES
GURJUN
GURJUNS
GURL
GURLED
GURLET
GURLETS
GURLIER

GURLIEST
GURLING
GURLS
GURLY
GURN
GURNARD
GURNARDS
GURNED
GURNET
GURNETS
GURNEY
GURNEYS
GURNING
GURNS
GURRAH
GURRAHS
GURRIER
GURRIERS
GURRIES
GURRY
GURS
GURSH
GURSHES
GURU
GURUDOM
GURUDOMS
GURUISM
GURUISMS
GURUS
GURUSHIP
GURUSHIPS
GUS
GUSH
GUSHED
GUSHER
GUSHERS
GUSHES
GUSHIER
GUSHIEST
GUSHILY
GUSHINESS
GUSHINESSES
GUSHING
GUSHINGLY
GUSHY
GUSLA
GUSLAR
GUSLARS
GUSLAS
GUSLE
GUSLES
GUSLI
GUSLIS
GUSSET
GUSSETED
GUSSETING

GUSSETS
GUSSIE
GUSSIED
GUSSIES
GUSSY
GUSSYING
GUST
GUSTABLE
GUSTABLES
GUSTATION
GUSTATIONS
GUSTATIVE
GUSTATORILY
GUSTATORY
GUSTED
GUSTFUL
GUSTIE
GUSTIER
GUSTIEST
GUSTILY
GUSTINESS
GUSTINESSES
GUSTING
GUSTLESS
GUSTO
GUSTOES
GUSTOS
GUSTS
GUSTY
GUT
GUTBUCKET
GUTBUCKETS
GUTCHER
GUTCHERS
GUTFUL
GUTFULS
GUTLESS
GUTLESSNESS
GUTLESSNESSES
GUTLIKE
GUTROT
GUTROTS
GUTS
GUTSED
GUTSER
GUTSERS
GUTSES
GUTSFUL
GUTSFULS
GUTSIER
GUTSIEST
GUTSILY
GUTSINESS
GUTSINESSES
GUTSING
GUTSY

GUTTA
GUTTAE
GUTTAS
GUTTATE
GUTTATED
GUTTATES
GUTTATING
GUTTATION
GUTTATIONS
GUTTED
GUTTER
GUTTERBLOOD
GUTTERBLOODS
GUTTERED
GUTTERING
GUTTERINGS
GUTTERS
GUTTERSNIPE
GUTTERSNIPES
GUTTERSNIPISH
GUTTERY
GUTTIER
GUTTIES
GUTTIEST
GUTTIFEROUS
GUTTING
GUTTLE
GUTTLED
GUTTLER
GUTTLERS
GUTTLES
GUTTLING
GUTTURAL
GUTTURALISATION
GUTTURALISE
GUTTURALISED
GUTTURALISES
GUTTURALISING
GUTTURALISM
GUTTURALISMS
GUTTURALITY
GUTTURALIZATION
GUTTURALIZE
GUTTURALIZED
GUTTURALIZES
GUTTURALIZING
GUTTURALLY
GUTTURALNESS
GUTTURALS
GUTTY
GUTZER
GUTZERS
GUV
GUVS
GUY
GUYED

GUYING
GUYLE
GUYLED
GUYLER
GUYLERS
GUYLES
GUYLINE
GUYLINES
GUYLING
GUYOT
GUYOTS
GUYROPE
GUYROPES
GUYS
GUYSE
GUYSES
GUZZLE
GUZZLED
GUZZLER
GUZZLERS
GUZZLES
GUZZLING
GWEDUC
GWEDUCK
GWEDUCKS
GWEDUCS
GWINIAD
GWINIADS
GWYNIAD
GWYNIADS
GYAL
GYALS
GYBE
GYBED
GYBES
GYBING
GYELD
GYELDS
GYLDEN
GYM
GYMBAL
GYMBALS
GYMKHANA
GYMKHANAS
GYMMAL
GYMMALS
GYMNASIA
GYMNASIAL
GYMNASIARCH
GYMNASIARCHES
GYMNASIARCHS
GYMNASIAST
GYMNASIASTS
GYMNASIC
GYMNASIEN
GYMNASIUM

GYMNASIUMS
GYMNAST
GYMNASTIC
GYMNASTICAL
GYMNASTICALLY
GYMNASTICS
GYMNASTS
GYMNIC
GYMNORHINAL
GYMNOSOPH
GYMNOSOPHIES
GYMNOSOPHIST
GYMNOSOPHISTS
GYMNOSOPHS
GYMNOSOPHY
GYMNOSPERM
GYMNOSPERMIES
GYMNOSPERMOUS
GYMNOSPERMS
GYMNOSPERMY
GYMP
GYMPED
GYMPIE
GYMPIES
GYMPING
GYMPS
GYMS
GYMSLIP
GYMSLIPPED
GYMSLIPS
GYNAE
GYNAECEA
GYNAECEUM
GYNAECEUMS
GYNAECIA
GYNAECIUM
GYNAECOCRACIES
GYNAECOCRACY
GYNAECOCRATIC
GYNAECOID
GYNAECOLOGIC
GYNAECOLOGICAL
GYNAECOLOGIES
GYNAECOLOGIST
GYNAECOLOGISTS
GYNAECOLOGY
GYNAECOMASTIA
GYNAECOMASTIAS
GYNAECOMASTIES
GYNAECOMASTS
GYNAECOMASTY
GYNAES
GYNANDRIES
GYNANDRISM
GYNANDRISMS
GYNANDROMORPH

GYNANDROMORPHIC
GYNANDROMORPHS
GYNANDROMORPHY
GYNANDROUS
GYNANDRY
GYNARCHIES
GYNARCHY
GYNECIA
GYNECIC
GYNECIUM
GYNECOCRACIES
GYNECOCRACY
GYNECOCRATIC
GYNECOID
GYNECOLOGIC
GYNECOLOGICAL
GYNECOLOGIES
GYNECOLOGIST
GYNECOLOGISTS
GYNECOLOGY
GYNECOMASTIA
GYNECOMASTIAS
GYNIATRICS
GYNIATRIES
GYNIATRY
GYNIE
GYNIES
GYNIOLATRIES
GYNIOLATRY
GYNNEY
GYNNEYS
GYNNIES
GYNNY
GYNOCRACIES
GYNOCRACY
GYNOCRATIC
GYNODIOECIOUS
GYNODIOECISM
GYNODIOECISMS
GYNOECIA
GYNOECIUM
GYNOGENESES
GYNOGENESIS
GYNOGENETIC
GYNOMONOECIOUS
GYNOMONOECISM
GYNOMONOECISMS
GYNOPHOBIA
GYNOPHOBIAS
GYNOPHOBIC
GYNOPHOBICS
GYNOPHORE
GYNOPHORES
GYNOPHORIC
GYNOPHORICALLY
GYNOSTEMIA

GYNOSTEMIUM
GYNY
GYOZA
GYOZAS
GYP
GYPLURE
GYPLURES
GYPPED
GYPPER
GYPPERS
GYPPIE
GYPPIES
GYPPING
GYPPO
GYPPOS
GYPPY
GYPS
GYPSEIAN
GYPSEOUS
GYPSIED
GYPSIES
GYPSIFEROUS
GYPSOPHILA
GYPSOPHILAS
GYPSTER
GYPSTERS
GYPSUM
GYPSUMS
GYPSY
GYPSYDOM
GYPSYDOMS
GYPSYING
GYPSYISH
GYPSYISM
GYPSYISMS
GYPSYWORT
GYPSYWORTS
GYRAL
GYRALLY
GYRANT
GYRASE
GYRASES
GYRATE
GYRATED
GYRATES
GYRATING
GYRATION
GYRATIONAL
GYRATIONS
GYRATOR
GYRATORS
GYRATORY
GYRE
GYRED
GYRENE
GYRENES

GYRES
GYRFALCON
GYRFALCONS
GYRI
GYRING
GYRO
GYROCAR
GYROCARS
GYROCOMPASS
GYROCOMPASSES
GYROCOPTER
GYROCOPTERS
GYRODYNE
GYRODYNES
GYROFREQUENCIES
GYROFREQUENCY
GYROIDAL
GYROLITE
GYROLITES
GYROMAGNETIC
GYROMAGNETISM
GYROMAGNETISMS
GYROMANCIES
GYROMANCY
GYRON
GYRONIC
GYRONNY
GYRONS
GYROPLANE
GYROPLANES
GYROS
GYROSCOPE
GYROSCOPES
GYROSCOPIC
GYROSCOPICALLY
GYROSCOPICS
GYROSE
GYROSTABILISER
GYROSTABILISERS
GYROSTABILIZER
GYROSTABILIZERS
GYROSTAT
GYROSTATIC
GYROSTATICALLY
GYROSTATICS
GYROSTATS
GYROUS
GYROVAGUE
GYROVAGUES
GYRUS
GYRUSES
GYTE
GYTES
GYTRASH
GYTRASHES
GYVE

GYVED
GYVES
GYVING

H

HA
HAAF
HAAFS
HAANEPOOT
HAANEPOOTS
HAAR
HAARS
HABANERA
HABANERAS
HABDABS
HABDALAH
HABDALAHS
HABERDASHER
HABERDASHERIES
HABERDASHERS
HABERDASHERY
HABERDINE
HABERDINES
HABERGEON
HABERGEONS
HABILABLE
HABILATORY
HABILE
HABILIMENT
HABILIMENTS
HABILITATE
HABILITATED
HABILITATES
HABILITATING
HABILITATION
HABILITATIONS
HABILITATOR
HABILITATORS
HABIT
HABITABILITIES
HABITABILITY
HABITABLE
HABITABLENESS
HABITABLENESSES
HABITABLY
HABITAN
HABITANS
HABITANT
HABITANTS
HABITAT
HABITATION
HABITATIONAL
HABITATIONS
HABITATS
HABITAUNCE
HABITAUNCES

HABITED
HABITING
HABITS
HABITUAL
HABITUALLY
HABITUALNESS
HABITUALNESSES
HABITUALS
HABITUATE
HABITUATED
HABITUATES
HABITUATING
HABITUATION
HABITUATIONS
HABITUDE
HABITUDES
HABITUDINAL
HABITUE
HABITUES
HABITUS
HABLE
HABOOB
HABOOBS
HABU
HABUS
HACEK
HACEKS
HACENDADO
HACENDADOS
HACHIS
HACHURE
HACHURED
HACHURES
HACHURING
HACIENDA
HACIENDADO
HACIENDADOS
HACIENDAS
HACK
HACKAMORE
HACKAMORES
HACKBERRIES
HACKBERRY
HACKBOLT
HACKBOLTS
HACKBUT
HACKBUTEER
HACKBUTEERS
HACKBUTS
HACKBUTTER
HACKBUTTERS

HACKED
HACKEE
HACKEES
HACKER
HACKERIES
HACKERS
HACKERY
HACKETTE
HACKETTES
HACKIE
HACKIES
HACKING
HACKINGS
HACKLE
HACKLED
HACKLER
HACKLERS
HACKLES
HACKLET
HACKLETS
HACKLIER
HACKLIEST
HACKLING
HACKLY
HACKMAN
HACKMATACK
HACKMATACKS
HACKMEN
HACKNEY
HACKNEYED
HACKNEYING
HACKNEYISM
HACKNEYMAN
HACKNEYMEN
HACKNEYS
HACKS
HACKSAW
HACKSAWED
HACKSAWING
HACKSAWN
HACKSAWS
HACKWORK
HACKWORKS
HACQUETON
HACQUETONS
HAD
HADAL
HADARIM
HADAWAY
HADAWAYS
HADDEN

HADDEST
HADDIE
HADDIES
HADDING
HADDOCK
HADDOCKS
HADE
HADED
HADEDAH
HADEDAHS
HADES
HADING
HADITH
HADITHS
HADJ
HADJEE
HADJEES
HADJES
HADJI
HADJIS
HADROME
HADROMES
HADRON
HADRONIC
HADRONS
HADROSAUR
HADROSAURS
HADROSAURUS
HADROSAURUSES
HADS
HADST
HAE
HAECCEITIES
HAECCEITY
HAED
HAEING
HAEM
HAEMACHROME
HAEMACHROMIC
HAEMACYTOMETER
HAEMACYTOMETERS
HAEMACYTOMETRIC
HAEMAGGLUTINATE
HAEMAGGLUTININ
HAEMAGOGUE
HAEMAGOGUES
HAEMAL
HAEMANGIOMA
HAEMANGIOMAS
HAEMANGIOMATA
HAEMATAL

HAEMATEIN
HAEMATEINS
HAEMATEMESES
HAEMATEMESIS
HAEMATIC
HAEMATICS
HAEMATIN
HAEMATINIC
HAEMATINICS
HAEMATINS
HAEMATITE
HAEMATITES
HAEMATITIC
HAEMATOBLAST
HAEMATOBLASTIC
HAEMATOBLASTS
HAEMATOCELE
HAEMATOCELES
HAEMATOCRIT
HAEMATOCRITS
HAEMATOCRYAL
HAEMATOGENESES
HAEMATOGENESIS
HAEMATOGENETIC
HAEMATOGENIC
HAEMATOGENOUS
HAEMATOID
HAEMATOLOGIC
HAEMATOLOGICAL
HAEMATOLOGIES
HAEMATOLOGIST
HAEMATOLOGISTS
HAEMATOLOGY
HAEMATOLYSES
HAEMATOLYSIS
HAEMATOMA
HAEMATOMAS
HAEMATOMATA
HAEMATOPHAGOUS
HAEMATOPOIESES
HAEMATOPOIESIS
HAEMATOPOIETIC
HAEMATOSES
HAEMATOSIS
HAEMATOTHERMAL
HAEMATOXYLIC
HAEMATOXYLIN
HAEMATOXYLINS
HAEMATOXYLON
HAEMATOXYLONS
HAEMATOZOA
HAEMATOZOON
HAEMATURIA
HAEMATURIAS
HAEMATURIC
HAEMIA

HAEMIC
HAEMIN
HAEMINS
HAEMOCHROME
HAEMOCHROMES
HAEMOCHROMIC
HAEMOCOEL
HAEMOCOELS
HAEMOCONIA
HAEMOCONIAS
HAEMOCYANIN
HAEMOCYANINS
HAEMOCYTE
HAEMOCYTES
HAEMOCYTOMETER
HAEMOCYTOMETERS
HAEMOCYTOMETRIC
HAEMODIALYSES
HAEMODIALYSIS
HAEMOFLAGELLATE
HAEMOGLOBIN
HAEMOGLOBINS
HAEMOGLOBINURIA
HAEMOID
HAEMOLYSES
HAEMOLYSIN
HAEMOLYSINS
HAEMOLYSIS
HAEMOLYTIC
HAEMONIES
HAEMONY
HAEMOPHILE
HAEMOPHILES
HAEMOPHILIA
HAEMOPHILIAC
HAEMOPHILIACS
HAEMOPHILIAS
HAEMOPHILIC
HAEMOPHILIOID
HAEMOPOIESIS
HAEMOPOIETIC
HAEMOPTYSES
HAEMOPTYSIS
HAEMORRHAGE
HAEMORRHAGED
HAEMORRHAGES
HAEMORRHAGIC
HAEMORRHAGING
HAEMORRHOID
HAEMORRHOIDAL
HAEMORRHOIDS
HAEMOSTASES
HAEMOSTASIA
HAEMOSTASIS
HAEMOSTAT
HAEMOSTATIC

HAEMOSTATICS
HAEMOSTATS
HAEMS
HAEN
HAEREDES
HAEREMAI
HAERES
HAES
HAET
HAETS
HAFF
HAFFET
HAFFETS
HAFFIT
HAFFITS
HAFFLIN
HAFFLINS
HAFFS
HAFIS
HAFIZ
HAFIZES
HAFNIUM
HAFNIUMS
HAFT
HAFTARA
HAFTARAH
HAFTARAHS
HAFTARAS
HAFTAROT
HAFTAROTH
HAFTED
HAFTER
HAFTERS
HAFTING
HAFTORAH
HAFTORAHS
HAFTOROT
HAFTOROTH
HAFTS
HAG
HAGADIC
HAGADIST
HAGADISTS
HAGBERRIES
HAGBERRY
HAGBOLT
HAGBOLTS
HAGBORN
HAGBUSH
HAGBUSHES
HAGBUT
HAGBUTEER
HAGBUTEERS
HAGBUTS
HAGBUTTER
HAGBUTTERS

HAGDEN
HAGDENS
HAGDON
HAGDONS
HAGDOWN
HAGDOWNS
HAGFISH
HAGFISHES
HAGG
HAGGADA
HAGGADAH
HAGGADAHS
HAGGADAS
HAGGADIC
HAGGADICAL
HAGGADICALLY
HAGGADIST
HAGGADISTIC
HAGGADISTS
HAGGADOT
HAGGADOTH
HAGGARD
HAGGARDLY
HAGGARDNESS
HAGGARDNESSES
HAGGARDS
HAGGED
HAGGING
HAGGIS
HAGGISES
HAGGISH
HAGGISHLY
HAGGISHNESS
HAGGLE
HAGGLED
HAGGLER
HAGGLERS
HAGGLES
HAGGLING
HAGGS
HAGIARCHIES
HAGIARCHY
HAGIOCRACIES
HAGIOCRACY
HAGIOGRAPHER
HAGIOGRAPHERS
HAGIOGRAPHIC
HAGIOGRAPHICAL
HAGIOGRAPHIES
HAGIOGRAPHIST
HAGIOGRAPHISTS
HAGIOGRAPHY
HAGIOLATER
HAGIOLATERS
HAGIOLATRIES
HAGIOLATROUS

HAGIOLATROUSLY
HAGIOLATRY
HAGIOLOGIC
HAGIOLOGICAL
HAGIOLOGIES
HAGIOLOGIST
HAGIOLOGISTS
HAGIOLOGY
HAGIOSCOPE
HAGIOSCOPES
HAGIOSCOPIC
HAGLET
HAGLETS
HAGLIKE
HAGRIDDEN
HAGRIDE
HAGRIDES
HAGRIDING
HAGRODE
HAGS
HAH
HAHA
HAHAS
HAHNIUM
HAHNIUMS
HAHS
HAICK
HAICKS
HAIDUK
HAIDUKS
HAIK
HAIKA
HAIKAI
HAIKS
HAIKU
HAIL
HAILED
HAILER
HAILERS
HAILIER
HAILIEST
HAILING
HAILS
HAILSHOT
HAILSHOTS
HAILSTONE
HAILSTONES
HAILSTORM
HAILSTORMS
HAILY
HAIN
HAINCH
HAINCHED
HAINCHES
HAINCHING
HAINED

HAINING
HAININGS
HAINS
HAIQUE
HAIQUES
HAIR
HAIRBALL
HAIRBALLS
HAIRBAND
HAIRBANDS
HAIRBELL
HAIRBELLS
HAIRBRAINED
HAIRBRAINEDNESS
HAIRBREADTH
HAIRBREADTHS
HAIRBRUSH
HAIRBRUSHES
HAIRCAP
HAIRCAPS
HAIRCLOTH
HAIRCLOTHS
HAIRCUT
HAIRCUTS
HAIRCUTTER
HAIRCUTTERS
HAIRCUTTING
HAIRCUTTINGS
HAIRDO
HAIRDOS
HAIRDRESSER
HAIRDRESSERS
HAIRDRESSING
HAIRDRESSINGS
HAIRDRIER
HAIRDRIERS
HAIRDRYER
HAIRDRYERS
HAIRED
HAIRGRIP
HAIRGRIPS
HAIRIER
HAIRIEST
HAIRIF
HAIRINESS
HAIRINESSES
HAIRING
HAIRLESS
HAIRLESSNESS
HAIRLESSNESSES
HAIRLIKE
HAIRLINE
HAIRLINES
HAIRLOCK
HAIRLOCKS
HAIRNET

HAIRNETS
HAIRPIECE
HAIRPIECES
HAIRPIN
HAIRPINS
HAIRS
HAIRSBREADTH
HAIRSBREADTHS
HAIRSPLITTER
HAIRSPLITTERS
HAIRSPLITTING
HAIRSPLITTINGS
HAIRSPRAY
HAIRSPRAYS
HAIRSPRING
HAIRSPRINGS
HAIRST
HAIRSTED
HAIRSTING
HAIRSTREAK
HAIRSTREAKS
HAIRSTS
HAIRSTYLE
HAIRSTYLES
HAIRSTYLING
HAIRSTYLINGS
HAIRSTYLIST
HAIRSTYLISTS
HAIRTAIL
HAIRTAILS
HAIRWEAVED
HAIRWEAVES
HAIRWEAVING
HAIRWORK
HAIRWORKS
HAIRWORM
HAIRWORMS
HAIRWOVEN
HAIRY
HAIRYBACK
HAIRYBACKED
HAIRYBACKS
HAITH
HAJ
HAJES
HAJI
HAJIS
HAJJ
HAJJAH
HAJJAHS
HAJJES
HAJJI
HAJJIS
HAKA
HAKAM
HAKAMS

HAKARI
HAKARIS
HAKAS
HAKE
HAKEA
HAKEAS
HAKEEM
HAKEEMS
HAKES
HAKIM
HAKIMS
HALACHA
HALACHAS
HALACHOT
HALAKAH
HALAKAHS
HALAKHA
HALAKHAS
HALAKHOT
HALAKIC
HALAKIST
HALAKISTS
HALAKOTH
HALAL
HALALA
HALALAH
HALALAHS
HALALAS
HALALLED
HALALLING
HALALS
HALATION
HALATIONS
HALAVAH
HALAVAHS
HALAZONE
HALAZONES
HALBERD
HALBERDIER
HALBERDIERS
HALBERDS
HALBERT
HALBERTS
HALCYON
HALCYONIAN
HALCYONIC
HALCYONS
HALE
HALED
HALENESS
HALENESSES
HALER
HALERS
HALERU
HALES
HALEST

HALF
HALFA
HALFAS
HALFBACK
HALFBACKS
HALFBEAK
HALFBEAKS
HALFEN
HALFENDEALE
HALFHEARTED
HALFHEARTEDLY
HALFHEARTEDNESS
HALFLIFE
HALFLIN
HALFLING
HALFLINGS
HALFLINS
HALFLIVES
HALFNESS
HALFNESSES
HALFPACE
HALFPACES
HALFPENCE
HALFPENNIES
HALFPENNY
HALFPENNYWORTH
HALFPENNYWORTHS
HALFS
HALFTIME
HALFTIMES
HALFTONE
HALFTONES
HALFWAY
HALFWIT
HALFWITS
HALFWITTED
HALFWITTEDLY
HALFWITTEDNESS
HALIBUT
HALIBUTS
HALICORE
HALICORES
HALID
HALIDE
HALIDES
HALIDOM
HALIDOME
HALIDOMES
HALIDOMS
HALIDS
HALIEUTIC
HALIEUTICS
HALIMOT
HALIMOTE
HALIMOTES
HALIMOTS

HALING
HALIOTIS
HALIPLANKTON
HALIPLANKTONS
HALITE
HALITES
HALITOSES
HALITOSIS
HALITOTIC
HALITOUS
HALITUS
HALITUSES
HALL
HALLAH
HALLAHS
HALLAL
HALLALI
HALLALIS
HALLALLED
HALLALLING
HALLALOO
HALLALOOS
HALLALS
HALLAN
HALLANS
HALLEFLINTA
HALLEFLINTAS
HALLEL
HALLELS
HALLELUIAH
HALLELUIAHS
HALLELUJAH
HALLELUJAHS
HALLIAN
HALLIANS
HALLIARD
HALLIARDS
HALLING
HALLINGS
HALLION
HALLIONS
HALLMARK
HALLMARKED
HALLMARKING
HALLMARKS
HALLO
HALLOA
HALLOAED
HALLOAING
HALLOAS
HALLOED
HALLOES
HALLOING
HALLOO
HALLOOED
HALLOOING

HALLOOS
HALLOS
HALLOT
HALLOTH
HALLOUMI
HALLOUMIS
HALLOW
HALLOWED
HALLOWEDLY
HALLOWEDNESS
HALLOWER
HALLOWERS
HALLOWING
HALLOWS
HALLOYSITE
HALLOYSITES
HALLS
HALLSTAND
HALLSTANDS
HALLUCES
HALLUCINATE
HALLUCINATED
HALLUCINATES
HALLUCINATING
HALLUCINATION
HALLUCINATIONAL
HALLUCINATIONS
HALLUCINATIVE
HALLUCINATOR
HALLUCINATORS
HALLUCINATORY
HALLUCINOGEN
HALLUCINOGENIC
HALLUCINOGENICS
HALLUCINOGENS
HALLUCINOSES
HALLUCINOSIS
HALLUX
HALLUXES
HALLWAY
HALLWAYS
HALLYON
HALLYONS
HALM
HALMA
HALMAS
HALMS
HALO
HALOBIONT
HALOBIONTIC
HALOBIONTS
HALOBIOTIC
HALOCARBON
HALOCARBONS
HALOCLINE
HALOCLINES

HALOED
HALOES
HALOGEN
HALOGENATE
HALOGENATED
HALOGENATES
HALOGENATING
HALOGENATION
HALOGENATIONS
HALOGENOID
HALOGENOUS
HALOGENS
HALOGETON
HALOGETONS
HALOID
HALOIDS
HALOING
HALOLIKE
HALOMORPHIC
HALON
HALONS
HALOPERIDOL
HALOPERIDOLS
HALOPHILE
HALOPHILES
HALOPHILIC
HALOPHILIES
HALOPHILOUS
HALOPHILY
HALOPHOBE
HALOPHOBES
HALOPHYTE
HALOPHYTES
HALOPHYTIC
HALOPHYTISM
HALOS
HALOSERE
HALOSERES
HALOTHANE
HALOTHANES
HALOUMI
HALOUMIS
HALSE
HALSED
HALSER
HALSERS
HALSES
HALSING
HALT
HALTED
HALTER
HALTERBREAK
HALTERBREAKING
HALTERBREAKS
HALTERBROKE
HALTERBROKEN

HALTERE
HALTERED
HALTERES
HALTERING
HALTERNECK
HALTERNECKED
HALTERNECKS
HALTERS
HALTING
HALTINGLY
HALTINGNESS
HALTINGS
HALTLESS
HALTS
HALUTZ
HALUTZIM
HALVA
HALVAH
HALVAHS
HALVAS
HALVE
HALVED
HALVER
HALVERS
HALVES
HALVING
HALYARD
HALYARDS
HAM
HAMADA
HAMADAS
HAMADRYAD
HAMADRYADES
HAMADRYADS
HAMADRYAS
HAMADRYASES
HAMAL
HAMALS
HAMAMELIDACEOUS
HAMAMELIS
HAMAMELISES
HAMANTASCH
HAMANTASCHEN
HAMARTHRITIS
HAMARTHRITISES
HAMARTIA
HAMARTIAS
HAMARTIOLOGIES
HAMARTIOLOGY
HAMATE
HAMATES
HAMAUL
HAMAULS
HAMBA
HAMBLE
HAMBLED

HAMBLES
HAMBLING
HAMBONE
HAMBONED
HAMBONES
HAMBONING
HAMBURG
HAMBURGER
HAMBURGERS
HAMBURGHER
HAMBURGHERS
HAMBURGS
HAME
HAMED
HAMES
HAMESES
HAMESUCKEN
HAMESUCKENS
HAMEWITH
HAMFATTER
HAMFATTERED
HAMFATTERING
HAMFATTERS
HAMING
HAMLET
HAMLETS
HAMMADA
HAMMADAS
HAMMAL
HAMMALS
HAMMAM
HAMMAMS
HAMMED
HAMMER
HAMMERCLOTH
HAMMERCLOTHS
HAMMERED
HAMMERER
HAMMERERS
HAMMERHEAD
HAMMERHEADED
HAMMERHEADS
HAMMERING
HAMMERINGS
HAMMERKOP
HAMMERKOPS
HAMMERLESS
HAMMERLOCK
HAMMERLOCKS
HAMMERMAN
HAMMERMEN
HAMMERS
HAMMERSTONE
HAMMERSTONES
HAMMERTOE
HAMMERTOES

HAMMIER
HAMMIEST
HAMMILY
HAMMINESS
HAMMINESSES
HAMMING
HAMMOCK
HAMMOCKS
HAMMY
HAMOSE
HAMOUS
HAMPER
HAMPERED
HAMPEREDNESS
HAMPERER
HAMPERERS
HAMPERING
HAMPERS
HAMPSTER
HAMPSTERS
HAMS
HAMSHACKLE
HAMSHACKLED
HAMSHACKLES
HAMSHACKLING
HAMSTER
HAMSTERS
HAMSTRING
HAMSTRINGED
HAMSTRINGING
HAMSTRINGS
HAMSTRUNG
HAMULAR
HAMULATE
HAMULI
HAMULOSE
HAMULOUS
HAMULUS
HAMZA
HAMZAH
HAMZAHS
HAMZAS
HAN
HANAP
HANAPER
HANAPERS
HANAPS
HANCE
HANCES
HANCH
HANCHED
HANCHES
HANCHING
HAND
HANDBAG
HANDBAGGED

HANDBAGGING
HANDBAGGINGS
HANDBAGS
HANDBALL
HANDBALLED
HANDBALLER
HANDBALLERS
HANDBALLING
HANDBALLS
HANDBARROW
HANDBARROWS
HANDBASKET
HANDBASKETS
HANDBELL
HANDBELLS
HANDBILL
HANDBILLS
HANDBLOWN
HANDBOOK
HANDBOOKS
HANDBRAKE
HANDBRAKES
HANDBREADTH
HANDBREADTHS
HANDCAR
HANDCARS
HANDCART
HANDCARTS
HANDCLAP
HANDCLAPS
HANDCLASP
HANDCLASPS
HANDCRAFT
HANDCRAFTED
HANDCRAFTING
HANDCRAFTS
HANDCRAFTSMAN
HANDCRAFTSMEN
HANDCUFF
HANDCUFFED
HANDCUFFING
HANDCUFFS
HANDED
HANDEDNESS
HANDEDNESSES
HANDER
HANDERS
HANDFAST
HANDFASTED
HANDFASTING
HANDFASTINGS
HANDFASTS
HANDFED
HANDFEED
HANDFEEDING
HANDFEEDS

HANDFUL
HANDFULS
HANDGRIP
HANDGRIPS
HANDGUN
HANDGUNS
HANDHELD
HANDHELDS
HANDHOLD
HANDHOLDS
HANDICAP
HANDICAPPED
HANDICAPPER
HANDICAPPERS
HANDICAPPING
HANDICAPS
HANDICRAFT
HANDICRAFTER
HANDICRAFTERS
HANDICRAFTS
HANDICRAFTSMAN
HANDICRAFTSMEN
HANDICUFFS
HANDIER
HANDIEST
HANDILY
HANDINESS
HANDINESSES
HANDING
HANDIWORK
HANDIWORKS
HANDJAR
HANDJARS
HANDKERCHER
HANDKERCHERS
HANDKERCHIEF
HANDKERCHIEFS
HANDKERCHIEVES
HANDLANGER
HANDLANGERS
HANDLE
HANDLEABLE
HANDLEBAR
HANDLEBARS
HANDLED
HANDLELESS
HANDLER
HANDLERS
HANDLES
HANDLESS
HANDLIKE
HANDLING
HANDLINGS
HANDLIST
HANDLISTS
HANDLOOM

HANDLOOMS
HANDMADE
HANDMAID
HANDMAIDEN
HANDMAIDENS
HANDMAIDS
HANDOFF
HANDOFFS
HANDOUT
HANDOUTS
HANDOVER
HANDOVERS
HANDPICK
HANDPICKED
HANDPICKING
HANDPICKS
HANDPLAY
HANDPLAYS
HANDPRESS
HANDPRESSES
HANDPRINT
HANDPRINTS
HANDRAIL
HANDRAILS
HANDS
HANDSAW
HANDSAWS
HANDSBREADTH
HANDSBREADTHS
HANDSEL
HANDSELED
HANDSELING
HANDSELLED
HANDSELLING
HANDSELS
HANDSET
HANDSETS
HANDSEWN
HANDSFUL
HANDSHAKE
HANDSHAKES
HANDSHAKING
HANDSHAKINGS
HANDSOME
HANDSOMELY
HANDSOMENESS
HANDSOMENESSES
HANDSOMER
HANDSOMEST
HANDSPIKE
HANDSPIKES
HANDSPRING
HANDSPRINGS
HANDSTAFF
HANDSTAFFS
HANDSTAND

HANDSTANDS
HANDSTAVES
HANDSTROKE
HANDSTROKES
HANDSTURN
HANDSTURNS
HANDTOWEL
HANDTOWELS
HANDWHEEL
HANDWHEELS
HANDWORK
HANDWORKED
HANDWORKER
HANDWORKERS
HANDWORKS
HANDWOVEN
HANDWRINGER
HANDWRINGERS
HANDWRIT
HANDWRITE
HANDWRITES
HANDWRITING
HANDWRITINGS
HANDWRITTEN
HANDWROTE
HANDWROUGHT
HANDY
HANDYMAN
HANDYMEN
HANDYPERSON
HANDYPERSONS
HANDYWORK
HANDYWORKS
HANEPOOT
HANEPOOTS
HANG
HANGABILITIES
HANGABILITY
HANGABLE
HANGAR
HANGARED
HANGARING
HANGARS
HANGBIRD
HANGBIRDS
HANGDOG
HANGDOGS
HANGED
HANGER
HANGERS
HANGFIRE
HANGFIRES
HANGI
HANGING
HANGINGS
HANGIS

HANGMAN
HANGMEN
HANGNAIL
HANGNAILS
HANGNEST
HANGNESTS
HANGOUT
HANGOUTS
HANGOVER
HANGOVERS
HANGS
HANGTAG
HANGTAGS
HANGUL
HANGUP
HANGUPS
HANIWA
HANJAR
HANJARS
HANK
HANKED
HANKER
HANKERED
HANKERER
HANKERERS
HANKERING
HANKERINGS
HANKERS
HANKIE
HANKIES
HANKING
HANKS
HANKY
HANSA
HANSARDISE
HANSARDISED
HANSARDISES
HANSARDISING
HANSARDIZE
HANSARDIZED
HANSARDIZES
HANSARDIZING
HANSAS
HANSE
HANSEL
HANSELED
HANSELING
HANSELLED
HANSELLING
HANSELS
HANSES
HANSOM
HANSOMS
HANT
HANTAVIRUS
HANTAVIRUSES

HANTED
HANTING
HANTLE
HANTLES
HANTS
HANUKIAH
HANUKIAHS
HANUMAN
HANUMANS
HAO
HAOLE
HAOLES
HAOMA
HAOMAS
HAP
HAPAX
HAPAXANTHIC
HAPAXANTHOUS
HAPAXES
HAPHAZARD
HAPHAZARDLY
HAPHAZARDNESS
HAPHAZARDNESSES
HAPHAZARDRIES
HAPHAZARDRY
HAPHAZARDS
HAPHTARA
HAPHTARAS
HAPHTAROT
HAPHTAROTH
HAPLESS
HAPLESSLY
HAPLESSNESS
HAPLESSNESSES
HAPLITE
HAPLITES
HAPLITIC
HAPLOBIONT
HAPLOBIONTIC
HAPLOBIONTS
HAPLOGRAPHIES
HAPLOGRAPHY
HAPLOID
HAPLOIDIC
HAPLOIDIES
HAPLOIDS
HAPLOIDY
HAPLOLOGIC
HAPLOLOGIES
HAPLOLOGISE
HAPLOLOGISED
HAPLOLOGISES
HAPLOLOGISING
HAPLOLOGY
HAPLONT
HAPLONTIC

HAPLONTS
HAPLOPIA
HAPLOPIAS
HAPLOSES
HAPLOSIS
HAPLOSTEMONOUS
HAPLOTYPE
HAPLOTYPES
HAPLY
HAPPED
HAPPEN
HAPPENCHANCE
HAPPENCHANCES
HAPPENED
HAPPENING
HAPPENINGS
HAPPENS
HAPPENSTANCE
HAPPENSTANCES
HAPPIED
HAPPIER
HAPPIES
HAPPIEST
HAPPILY
HAPPINESS
HAPPINESSES
HAPPING
HAPPY
HAPPYING
HAPS
HAPTEN
HAPTENE
HAPTENES
HAPTENIC
HAPTENS
HAPTERON
HAPTERONS
HAPTIC
HAPTICAL
HAPTICS
HAPTOGLOBIN
HAPTOGLOBINS
HAPTOTROPIC
HAPTOTROPISM
HAPTOTROPISMS
HAPU
HAPUKA
HAPUKAS
HAPUKU
HAPUKUS
HAPUS
HAQUETON
HAQUETONS
HARAM
HARAMBEE
HARAMBEES

HARAMS
HARANGUE
HARANGUED
HARANGUER
HARANGUERS
HARANGUES
HARANGUING
HARASS
HARASSED
HARASSEDLY
HARASSER
HARASSERS
HARASSES
HARASSING
HARASSINGLY
HARASSINGS
HARASSMENT
HARASSMENTS
HARBINGER
HARBINGERED
HARBINGERING
HARBINGERS
HARBOR
HARBORAGE
HARBORAGES
HARBORED
HARBORER
HARBORERS
HARBORFUL
HARBORFULS
HARBORING
HARBORLESS
HARBORMASTER
HARBORMASTERS
HARBORS
HARBORSIDE
HARBOUR
HARBOURAGE
HARBOURAGES
HARBOURED
HARBOURER
HARBOURERS
HARBOURING
HARBOURLESS
HARBOURS
HARD
HARDBACK
HARDBACKED
HARDBACKS
HARDBAG
HARDBAGS
HARDBAKE
HARDBAKES
HARDBALL
HARDBALLS
HARDBEAM

HARDBEAMS
HARDBOARD
HARDBOARDS
HARDBOOT
HARDBOOTS
HARDBOUND
HARDCASE
HARDCORE
HARDCOVER
HARDCOVERS
HARDEDGE
HARDEDGES
HARDEN
HARDENED
HARDENER
HARDENERS
HARDENING
HARDENINGS
HARDENS
HARDER
HARDEST
HARDFACE
HARDFACES
HARDFISTED
HARDGRASS
HARDGRASSES
HARDHACK
HARDHACKS
HARDHANDED
HARDHANDEDNESS
HARDHAT
HARDHATS
HARDHEAD
HARDHEADED
HARDHEADEDLY
HARDHEADEDNESS
HARDHEADS
HARDHEARTED
HARDHEARTEDLY
HARDHEARTEDNESS
HARDIER
HARDIES
HARDIEST
HARDIHEAD
HARDIHEADS
HARDIHOOD
HARDIHOODS
HARDILY
HARDIMENT
HARDIMENTS
HARDINESS
HARDINESSES
HARDINGGRASS
HARDINGGRASSES
HARDISH
HARDLINE

HARDLINER
HARDLINERS
HARDLY
HARDMAN
HARDMOUTHED
HARDNESS
HARDNESSES
HARDNOSE
HARDNOSED
HARDNOSES
HARDOKE
HARDOKES
HARDPAN
HARDPANS
HARDPARTS
HARDROCK
HARDROCKER
HARDROCKERS
HARDROCKING
HARDROCKS
HARDS
HARDSCRABBLE
HARDSET
HARDSHELL
HARDSHIP
HARDSHIPS
HARDSTAND
HARDSTANDING
HARDSTANDINGS
HARDSTANDS
HARDTACK
HARDTACKS
HARDTOP
HARDTOPS
HARDWARE
HARDWAREMAN
HARDWAREMEN
HARDWARES
HARDWIRE
HARDWIRED
HARDWIRES
HARDWIRING
HARDWOOD
HARDWOODS
HARDWORKING
HARDY
HARE
HAREBELL
HAREBELLS
HAREBRAINED
HARED
HAREEM
HAREEMS
HARELD
HARELDS
HARELIKE

HARELIP
HARELIPPED
HARELIPS
HAREM
HAREMS
HARES
HARESTAIL
HARESTAILS
HAREWOOD
HAREWOODS
HARIANA
HARIANAS
HARICOT
HARICOTS
HARIGALDS
HARIGALS
HARIJAN
HARIJANS
HARIM
HARIMS
HARING
HARIOLATE
HARIOLATED
HARIOLATES
HARIOLATING
HARIOLATION
HARIOLATIONS
HARIRA
HARIRAS
HARISH
HARK
HARKED
HARKEN
HARKENED
HARKENER
HARKENERS
HARKENING
HARKENS
HARKING
HARKS
HARL
HARLED
HARLEQUIN
HARLEQUINADE
HARLEQUINADES
HARLEQUINED
HARLEQUINING
HARLEQUINS
HARLING
HARLINGS
HARLOT
HARLOTRIES
HARLOTRY
HARLOTS
HARLS
HARM

HARMALA
HARMALAS
HARMALIN
HARMALINE
HARMALINES
HARMALINS
HARMAN
HARMANS
HARMATTAN
HARMATTANS
HARMDOING
HARMDOINGS
HARMED
HARMEL
HARMELS
HARMER
HARMERS
HARMFUL
HARMFULLY
HARMFULNESS
HARMFULNESSES
HARMIN
HARMINE
HARMINES
HARMING
HARMINS
HARMLESS
HARMLESSLY
HARMLESSNESS
HARMLESSNESSES
HARMOLODIC
HARMOLODICALLY
HARMOLODICS
HARMONIC
HARMONICA
HARMONICAL
HARMONICALLY
HARMONICAS
HARMONICHORD
HARMONICHORDS
HARMONICIST
HARMONICISTS
HARMONICON
HARMONICONS
HARMONICS
HARMONIES
HARMONIOUS
HARMONIOUSLY
HARMONIOUSNESS
HARMONIPHON
HARMONIPHONE
HARMONIPHONES
HARMONIPHONS
HARMONISABLE
HARMONISATION
HARMONISATIONS

HARMONISE
HARMONISED
HARMONISER
HARMONISERS
HARMONISES
HARMONISING
HARMONIST
HARMONISTIC
HARMONISTICALLY
HARMONISTS
HARMONIUM
HARMONIUMIST
HARMONIUMISTS
HARMONIUMS
HARMONIZABLE
HARMONIZATION
HARMONIZATIONS
HARMONIZE
HARMONIZED
HARMONIZER
HARMONIZERS
HARMONIZES
HARMONIZING
HARMONOGRAM
HARMONOGRAMS
HARMONOGRAPH
HARMONOGRAPHS
HARMONOMETER
HARMONOMETERS
HARMONY
HARMOST
HARMOSTIES
HARMOSTS
HARMOSTY
HARMOTOME
HARMOTOMES
HARMS
HARN
HARNESS
HARNESSED
HARNESSER
HARNESSERS
HARNESSES
HARNESSING
HARNESSLESS
HARNS
HARO
HAROS
HAROSET
HAROSETH
HAROSETHS
HAROSETS
HARP
HARPED
HARPER
HARPERS

HARPIES
HARPIN
HARPING
HARPINGS
HARPINS
HARPIST
HARPISTS
HARPOON
HARPOONED
HARPOONEER
HARPOONEERS
HARPOONER
HARPOONERS
HARPOONING
HARPOONS
HARPS
HARPSICHORD
HARPSICHORDIST
HARPSICHORDISTS
HARPSICHORDS
HARPY
HARQUEBUS
HARQUEBUSE
HARQUEBUSES
HARQUEBUSIER
HARQUEBUSIERS
HARQUEBUSS
HARQUEBUSSES
HARRIDAN
HARRIDANS
HARRIED
HARRIER
HARRIERS
HARRIES
HARROW
HARROWED
HARROWER
HARROWERS
HARROWING
HARROWINGLY
HARROWMENT
HARROWMENTS
HARROWS
HARRUMPH
HARRUMPHED
HARRUMPHING
HARRUMPHS
HARRY
HARRYING
HARSH
HARSHEN
HARSHENED
HARSHENING
HARSHENS
HARSHER
HARSHEST

HARSHLY
HARSHNESS
HARSHNESSES
HARSLET
HARSLETS
HART
HARTAL
HARTALS
HARTBEES
HARTBEESES
HARTBEEST
HARTBEESTS
HARTEBEEST
HARTEBEESTS
HARTELY
HARTEN
HARTENED
HARTENING
HARTENS
HARTLESSE
HARTS
HARTSHORN
HARTSHORNS
HARUMPH
HARUMPHED
HARUMPHING
HARUMPHS
HARUSPEX
HARUSPICAL
HARUSPICATE
HARUSPICATED
HARUSPICATES
HARUSPICATING
HARUSPICATION
HARUSPICATIONS
HARUSPICES
HARUSPICIES
HARUSPICY
HARVEST
HARVESTABLE
HARVESTED
HARVESTER
HARVESTERS
HARVESTING
HARVESTINGS
HARVESTLESS
HARVESTMAN
HARVESTMEN
HARVESTS
HARVESTTIME
HARVESTTIMES
HAS
HASENPFEFFER
HASENPFEFFERS
HASH
HASHED

HASHEESH
HASHEESHES
HASHES
HASHHEAD
HASHHEADS
HASHIER
HASHIEST
HASHING
HASHISH
HASHISHES
HASHMARK
HASHMARKS
HASHY
HASK
HASKS
HASLET
HASLETS
HASP
HASPED
HASPING
HASPS
HASSAR
HASSARS
HASSEL
HASSELS
HASSIUM
HASSLE
HASSLED
HASSLES
HASSLING
HASSOCK
HASSOCKS
HASSOCKY
HAST
HASTA
HASTATE
HASTATED
HASTE
HASTED
HASTEFUL
HASTEFULLY
HASTEFULNESS
HASTEN
HASTENED
HASTENER
HASTENERS
HASTENING
HASTENS
HASTES
HASTIER
HASTIEST
HASTILY
HASTINESS
HASTINESSES
HASTING
HASTINGS

HASTY
HAT
HATABLE
HATBAND
HATBANDS
HATBOX
HATBOXES
HATBRUSH
HATBRUSHES
HATCH
HATCHABILITIES
HATCHABILITY
HATCHABLE
HATCHBACK
HATCHBACKS
HATCHECK
HATCHED
HATCHEL
HATCHELED
HATCHELING
HATCHELLED
HATCHELLER
HATCHELLERS
HATCHELLING
HATCHELS
HATCHER
HATCHERIES
HATCHERS
HATCHERY
HATCHES
HATCHET
HATCHETS
HATCHETTITE
HATCHETTITES
HATCHETY
HATCHING
HATCHINGS
HATCHLING
HATCHLINGS
HATCHMENT
HATCHMENTS
HATCHWAY
HATCHWAYS
HATE
HATEABLE
HATED
HATEFUL
HATEFULLY
HATEFULNESS
HATEFULNESSES
HATELESS
HATELESSNESS
HATELESSNESSES
HATER
HATERENT
HATERENTS

HATERS
HATES
HATEWORTHY
HATFUL
HATFULS
HATGUARD
HATGUARDS
HATH
HATHA
HATING
HATLESS
HATLESSNESS
HATLESSNESSES
HATLIKE
HATMAKER
HATMAKERS
HATPEG
HATPEGS
HATPIN
HATPINS
HATRACK
HATRACKS
HATRED
HATREDS
HATS
HATSFUL
HATSTAND
HATSTANDS
HATTED
HATTER
HATTERED
HATTERIA
HATTERIAS
HATTERING
HATTERS
HATTING
HATTINGS
HATTOCK
HATTOCKS
HAUBERGEON
HAUBERGEONED
HAUBERGEONS
HAUBERK
HAUBERKS
HAUBOIS
HAUD
HAUDED
HAUDEN
HAUDER
HAUDERS
HAUDING
HAUDS
HAUF
HAUFS
HAUGH
HAUGHS

HAUGHT
HAUGHTIER
HAUGHTIEST
HAUGHTILY
HAUGHTINESS
HAUGHTINESSES
HAUGHTY
HAUHAU
HAUHAUS
HAUL
HAULAGE
HAULAGES
HAULD
HAULDS
HAULED
HAULER
HAULERS
HAULIER
HAULIERS
HAULING
HAULM
HAULMIER
HAULMIEST
HAULMS
HAULMY
HAULS
HAULST
HAULT
HAULYARD
HAULYARDS
HAUNCH
HAUNCHED
HAUNCHES
HAUNCHING
HAUNT
HAUNTED
HAUNTER
HAUNTERS
HAUNTING
HAUNTINGLY
HAUNTINGS
HAUNTS
HAURIANT
HAURIENT
HAUSE
HAUSED
HAUSEN
HAUSENS
HAUSES
HAUSFRAU
HAUSFRAUEN
HAUSFRAUS
HAUSING
HAUSSMANNISED
HAUSSMANNISES
HAUSSMANNISING

HAUSSMANNIZE
HAUSSMANNIZED
HAUSSMANNIZES
HAUSSMANNIZING
HAUSTELLA
HAUSTELLATE
HAUSTELLUM
HAUSTORIA
HAUSTORIAL
HAUSTORIUM
HAUT
HAUTBOIS
HAUTBOY
HAUTBOYS
HAUTE
HAUTEUR
HAUTEURS
HAUYNE
HAUYNES
HAVARTI
HAVARTIS
HAVDALAH
HAVDALAHS
HAVDOLOH
HAVE
HAVELOCK
HAVELOCKS
HAVEN
HAVENED
HAVENING
HAVENLESS
HAVENLESSNESS
HAVENS
HAVEOUR
HAVEOURS
HAVER
HAVERED
HAVEREL
HAVERELS
HAVERING
HAVERINGS
HAVERS
HAVERSACK
HAVERSACKS
HAVERSINE
HAVERSINES
HAVES
HAVILDAR
HAVILDARS
HAVING
HAVINGS
HAVIOR
HAVIORS
HAVIOUR
HAVIOURS
HAVOC

HAVOCKED
HAVOCKER
HAVOCKERS
HAVOCKING
HAVOCS
HAW
HAWBUCK
HAWBUCKS
HAWED
HAWFINCH
HAWFINCHES
HAWING
HAWK
HAWKBELL
HAWKBELLS
HAWKBILL
HAWKBILLS
HAWKBIT
HAWKBITS
HAWKED
HAWKER
HAWKERS
HAWKEY
HAWKEYED
HAWKEYS
HAWKIE
HAWKIES
HAWKING
HAWKINGS
HAWKISH
HAWKISHLY
HAWKISHNESS
HAWKISHNESSES
HAWKIT
HAWKLIKE
HAWKMOTH
HAWKMOTHS
HAWKNOSE
HAWKNOSES
HAWKS
HAWKSBEARD
HAWKSBEARDS
HAWKSBILL
HAWKSBILLS
HAWKSHAW
HAWKSHAWS
HAWKWEED
HAWKWEEDS
HAWM
HAWMED
HAWMING
HAWMS
HAWS
HAWSE
HAWSED
HAWSEHOLE

HAWSEHOLES
HAWSEPIPE
HAWSEPIPES
HAWSER
HAWSERS
HAWSES
HAWSING
HAWTHORN
HAWTHORNS
HAY
HAYBAND
HAYBANDS
HAYBOX
HAYBOXES
HAYCOCK
HAYCOCKS
HAYED
HAYER
HAYERS
HAYFIELD
HAYFIELDS
HAYFORK
HAYFORKS
HAYING
HAYINGS
HAYLAGE
HAYLAGES
HAYLE
HAYLES
HAYLOFT
HAYLOFTS
HAYMAKER
HAYMAKERS
HAYMAKING
HAYMAKINGS
HAYMOW
HAYMOWS
HAYRACK
HAYRACKS
HAYRICK
HAYRICKS
HAYRIDE
HAYRIDES
HAYS
HAYSEED
HAYSEEDS
HAYSEL
HAYSELS
HAYSTACK
HAYSTACKS
HAYWARD
HAYWARDS
HAYWIRE
HAYWIRES
HAZAN
HAZANIM

HAZANS
HAZARD
HAZARDABLE
HAZARDED
HAZARDING
HAZARDIZE
HAZARDIZES
HAZARDOUS
HAZARDOUSLY
HAZARDOUSNESS
HAZARDOUSNESSES
HAZARDRIES
HAZARDRY
HAZARDS
HAZE
HAZED
HAZEL
HAZELHEN
HAZELHENS
HAZELLY
HAZELNUT
HAZELNUTS
HAZELS
HAZER
HAZERS
HAZES
HAZIER
HAZIEST
HAZILY
HAZINESS
HAZINESSES
HAZING
HAZINGS
HAZY
HAZZAN
HAZZANIM
HAZZANS
HE
HEAD
HEADACHE
HEADACHES
HEADACHEY
HEADACHIER
HEADACHIEST
HEADACHINESS
HEADACHY
HEADAGE
HEADAGES
HEADBAND
HEADBANDS
HEADBANG
HEADBANGED
HEADBANGING
HEADBANGS
HEADBOARD
HEADBOARDS

HEADBOROUGH
HEADBOROUGHS
HEADCASE
HEADCASES
HEADCHAIR
HEADCHAIRS
HEADCHEESE
HEADCHEESES
HEADCLOTH
HEADCLOTHS
HEADDRESS
HEADDRESSES
HEADED
HEADER
HEADERS
HEADFAST
HEADFASTS
HEADFIRST
HEADFISH
HEADFISHES
HEADFOREMOST
HEADFRAME
HEADFRAMES
HEADFUCK
HEADFUCKED
HEADFUCKER
HEADFUCKERS
HEADFUCKING
HEADGATE
HEADGATES
HEADGEAR
HEADGEARS
HEADHUNT
HEADHUNTED
HEADHUNTER
HEADHUNTERS
HEADHUNTING
HEADHUNTINGS
HEADHUNTS
HEADIER
HEADIEST
HEADILY
HEADINESS
HEADINESSES
HEADING
HEADINGS
HEADLAMP
HEADLAMPS
HEADLAND
HEADLANDS
HEADLEASE
HEADLEASES
HEADLESS
HEADLESSNESS
HEADLESSNESSES
HEADLIGHT

HEADLIGHTS
HEADLIKE
HEADLINE
HEADLINED
HEADLINER
HEADLINERS
HEADLINES
HEADLINING
HEADLOCK
HEADLOCKS
HEADLONG
HEADMAN
HEADMARK
HEADMARKS
HEADMASTER
HEADMASTERLY
HEADMASTERS
HEADMASTERSHIP
HEADMASTERSHIPS
HEADMEN
HEADMISTRESS
HEADMISTRESSES
HEADMISTRESSY
HEADMOST
HEADNOTE
HEADNOTES
HEADPEACE
HEADPEACES
HEADPHONE
HEADPHONES
HEADPIECE
HEADPIECES
HEADPIN
HEADPINS
HEADQUARTER
HEADQUARTERED
HEADQUARTERING
HEADQUARTERS
HEADRACE
HEADRACES
HEADRAIL
HEADRAILS
HEADREACH
HEADREACHED
HEADREACHES
HEADREACHING
HEADREST
HEADRESTS
HEADRIG
HEADRIGS
HEADRING
HEADRINGS
HEADROOM
HEADROOMS
HEADROPE
HEADROPES

HEADS
HEADSAIL
HEADSAILS
HEADSCARF
HEADSCARVES
HEADSET
HEADSETS
HEADSHAKE
HEADSHAKES
HEADSHEETS
HEADSHIP
HEADSHIPS
HEADSHOT
HEADSHOTS
HEADSHRINKER
HEADSHRINKERS
HEADSMAN
HEADSMEN
HEADSPACE
HEADSPACES
HEADSPRING
HEADSPRINGS
HEADSQUARE
HEADSQUARES
HEADSTALL
HEADSTALLS
HEADSTAND
HEADSTANDS
HEADSTAY
HEADSTAYS
HEADSTICK
HEADSTICKS
HEADSTOCK
HEADSTOCKS
HEADSTONE
HEADSTONES
HEADSTREAM
HEADSTREAMS
HEADSTRONG
HEADSTRONGER
HEADSTRONGEST
HEADSTRONGLY
HEADSTRONGNESS
HEADWAITER
HEADWAITERS
HEADWARD
HEADWARDLY
HEADWARDS
HEADWATER
HEADWATERS
HEADWAY
HEADWAYS
HEADWIND
HEADWINDS
HEADWORD
HEADWORDS

HEADWORK
HEADWORKER
HEADWORKERS
HEADWORKS
HEADY
HEAL
HEALABLE
HEALD
HEALDED
HEALDING
HEALDS
HEALED
HEALEE
HEALEES
HEALER
HEALERS
HEALING
HEALINGLY
HEALINGS
HEALS
HEALSOME
HEALTH
HEALTHCARE
HEALTHCARES
HEALTHFUL
HEALTHFULLY
HEALTHFULNESS
HEALTHFULNESSES
HEALTHIER
HEALTHIEST
HEALTHILY
HEALTHINESS
HEALTHINESSES
HEALTHISM
HEALTHIST
HEALTHISTIC
HEALTHLESS
HEALTHLESSNESS
HEALTHS
HEALTHSOME
HEALTHY
HEAME
HEAP
HEAPED
HEAPER
HEAPERS
HEAPIER
HEAPIEST
HEAPING
HEAPS
HEAPSTEAD
HEAPSTEADS
HEAPY
HEAR
HEARABLE
HEARD

HEARDS
HEARE
HEARER
HEARERS
HEARES
HEARIE
HEARING
HEARINGS
HEARKEN
HEARKENED
HEARKENER
HEARKENERS
HEARKENING
HEARKENS
HEARS
HEARSAY
HEARSAYS
HEARSE
HEARSED
HEARSES
HEARSIER
HEARSIEST
HEARSING
HEARSY
HEART
HEARTACHE
HEARTACHES
HEARTBEAT
HEARTBEATS
HEARTBREAK
HEARTBREAKER
HEARTBREAKERS
HEARTBREAKING
HEARTBREAKINGLY
HEARTBREAKS
HEARTBROKE
HEARTBROKEN
HEARTBROKENLY
HEARTBROKENNESS
HEARTBURN
HEARTBURNING
HEARTBURNINGS
HEARTBURNS
HEARTED
HEARTEN
HEARTENED
HEARTENING
HEARTENINGLY
HEARTENS
HEARTFELT
HEARTH
HEARTHS
HEARTHSTONE
HEARTHSTONES
HEARTIER
HEARTIES

HEARTIEST
HEARTIKIN
HEARTIKINS
HEARTILY
HEARTINESS
HEARTINESSES
HEARTING
HEARTLAND
HEARTLANDS
HEARTLESS
HEARTLESSLY
HEARTLESSNESS
HEARTLESSNESSES
HEARTLET
HEARTLETS
HEARTLING
HEARTLINGS
HEARTLY
HEARTPEA
HEARTPEAS
HEARTRENDING
HEARTRENDINGLY
HEARTS
HEARTSEASE
HEARTSEASES
HEARTSEED
HEARTSEEDS
HEARTSICK
HEARTSICKNESS
HEARTSICKNESSES
HEARTSOME
HEARTSOMELY
HEARTSOMENESS
HEARTSORE
HEARTSTRING
HEARTSTRINGS
HEARTTHROB
HEARTTHROBS
HEARTWARMING
HEARTWATER
HEARTWATERS
HEARTWOOD
HEARTWOODS
HEARTWORM
HEARTWORMS
HEARTY
HEAST
HEASTE
HEASTES
HEASTS
HEAT
HEATABLE
HEATED
HEATEDLY
HEATEDNESS
HEATER

HEATERS
HEATH
HEATHBERRIES
HEATHBERRY
HEATHBIRD
HEATHBIRDS
HEATHCOCK
HEATHCOCKS
HEATHEN
HEATHENDOM
HEATHENDOMS
HEATHENESSE
HEATHENESSES
HEATHENISE
HEATHENISED
HEATHENISES
HEATHENISH
HEATHENISHLY
HEATHENISHNESS
HEATHENISING
HEATHENISM
HEATHENISMS
HEATHENIZE
HEATHENIZED
HEATHENIZES
HEATHENIZING
HEATHENNESS
HEATHENRIES
HEATHENRY
HEATHENS
HEATHER
HEATHERED
HEATHERIER
HEATHERIEST
HEATHERS
HEATHERY
HEATHFOWL
HEATHFOWLS
HEATHIER
HEATHIEST
HEATHLAND
HEATHLANDS
HEATHLESS
HEATHLIKE
HEATHS
HEATHY
HEATING
HEATINGS
HEATLESS
HEATPROOF
HEATS
HEATSPOT
HEATSPOTS
HEATSTROKE
HEATSTROKES
HEAUME

HEAUMES
HEAVE
HEAVED
HEAVEN
HEAVENLIER
HEAVENLIEST
HEAVENLINESS
HEAVENLINESSES
HEAVENLY
HEAVENS
HEAVENWARD
HEAVENWARDS
HEAVER
HEAVERS
HEAVES
HEAVIER
HEAVIES
HEAVIEST
HEAVILY
HEAVINESS
HEAVINESSES
HEAVING
HEAVINGS
HEAVY
HEAVYHEARTED
HEAVYHEARTEDLY
HEAVYSET
HEAVYWEIGHT
HEAVYWEIGHTS
HEBDOMAD
HEBDOMADAL
HEBDOMADALLY
HEBDOMADAR
HEBDOMADARIES
HEBDOMADARS
HEBDOMADARY
HEBDOMADER
HEBDOMADERS
HEBDOMADS
HEBE
HEBEN
HEBENON
HEBENONS
HEBENS
HEBEPHRENIA
HEBEPHRENIAC
HEBEPHRENIACS
HEBEPHRENIAS
HEBEPHRENIC
HEBEPHRENICS
HEBES
HEBETANT
HEBETATE
HEBETATED
HEBETATES
HEBETATING

HEBETATION
HEBETATIONS
HEBETATIVE
HEBETATOR
HEBETATORS
HEBETIC
HEBETUDE
HEBETUDES
HEBETUDINOUS
HEBONA
HEBONAS
HEBRAIZATION
HEBRAIZATIONS
HEBRAIZE
HEBRAIZED
HEBRAIZES
HEBRAIZING
HECATOMB
HECATOMBS
HECH
HECHT
HECHTING
HECHTS
HECK
HECKELPHONE
HECKELPHONES
HECKLE
HECKLED
HECKLER
HECKLERS
HECKLES
HECKLING
HECKLINGS
HECKS
HECOGENIN
HECOGENINS
HECTARE
HECTARES
HECTIC
HECTICAL
HECTICALLY
HECTICLY
HECTICS
HECTOCOTYLI
HECTOCOTYLUS
HECTOGRAM
HECTOGRAMME
HECTOGRAMMES
HECTOGRAMS
HECTOGRAPH
HECTOGRAPHED
HECTOGRAPHER
HECTOGRAPHIC
HECTOGRAPHING
HECTOGRAPHS
HECTOGRAPHY

HECTOLITER
HECTOLITERS
HECTOLITRE
HECTOLITRES
HECTOMETER
HECTOMETERS
HECTOMETRE
HECTOMETRES
HECTOR
HECTORED
HECTORER
HECTORERS
HECTORING
HECTORINGLY
HECTORINGS
HECTORISM
HECTORISMS
HECTORLY
HECTORS
HECTORSHIP
HECTORSHIPS
HECTOSTERE
HECTOSTERES
HEDDLE
HEDDLED
HEDDLES
HEDDLING
HEDER
HEDERA
HEDERAL
HEDERATED
HEDERS
HEDGE
HEDGEBILL
HEDGEBILLS
HEDGED
HEDGEHOG
HEDGEHOGS
HEDGEHOP
HEDGEHOPPED
HEDGEHOPPER
HEDGEHOPPERS
HEDGEHOPPING
HEDGEHOPPINGS
HEDGEHOPS
HEDGEPIG
HEDGEPIGS
HEDGER
HEDGEROW
HEDGEROWS
HEDGERS
HEDGES
HEDGIER
HEDGIEST
HEDGING
HEDGINGLY

HEDGINGS
HEDGY
HEDONIC
HEDONICALLY
HEDONICS
HEDONISM
HEDONISMS
HEDONIST
HEDONISTIC
HEDONISTICALLY
HEDONISTS
HEDYPHANE
HEDYPHANES
HEED
HEEDED
HEEDER
HEEDERS
HEEDFUL
HEEDFULLY
HEEDFULNESS
HEEDFULNESSES
HEEDINESS
HEEDINESSES
HEEDING
HEEDLESS
HEEDLESSLY
HEEDLESSNESS
HEEDLESSNESSES
HEEDS
HEEDY
HEEHAW
HEEHAWED
HEEHAWING
HEEHAWS
HEEL
HEELBALL
HEELBALLS
HEELED
HEELER
HEELERS
HEELING
HEELINGS
HEELLESS
HEELPIECE
HEELPIECES
HEELPOST
HEELPOSTS
HEELS
HEELTAP
HEELTAPS
HEEZE
HEEZED
HEEZES
HEEZIE
HEEZIES
HEEZING

HEFT
HEFTE
HEFTED
HEFTER
HEFTERS
HEFTIER
HEFTIEST
HEFTILY
HEFTINESS
HEFTINESSES
HEFTING
HEFTS
HEFTY
HEGARI
HEGARIS
HEGEMONIAL
HEGEMONIC
HEGEMONICAL
HEGEMONIES
HEGEMONISM
HEGEMONISMS
HEGEMONIST
HEGEMONISTS
HEGEMONY
HEGIRA
HEGIRAS
HEGUMEN
HEGUMENE
HEGUMENES
HEGUMENIES
HEGUMENOS
HEGUMENOSES
HEGUMENS
HEGUMENY
HEH
HEHS
HEID
HEIDS
HEIFER
HEIFERS
HEIGH
HEIGHT
HEIGHTEN
HEIGHTENED
HEIGHTENER
HEIGHTENERS
HEIGHTENING
HEIGHTENS
HEIGHTH
HEIGHTHS
HEIGHTS
HEIL
HEILED
HEILING
HEILS
HEIMISH

HEINIE
HEINIES
HEINOUS
HEINOUSLY
HEINOUSNESS
HEINOUSNESSES
HEIR
HEIRDOM
HEIRDOMS
HEIRED
HEIRESS
HEIRESSES
HEIRING
HEIRLESS
HEIRLOOM
HEIRLOOMS
HEIRS
HEIRSHIP
HEIRSHIPS
HEISHI
HEIST
HEISTED
HEISTER
HEISTERS
HEISTING
HEISTS
HEITIKI
HEITIKIS
HEJAB
HEJABS
HEJIRA
HEJIRAS
HEJRA
HEJRAS
HEKTARE
HEKTARES
HELCOID
HELD
HELDENTENOR
HELDENTENORS
HELE
HELED
HELENIUM
HELENIUMS
HELES
HELIAC
HELIACAL
HELIACALLY
HELIANTHEMUM
HELIANTHEMUMS
HELIANTHUS
HELIANTHUSES
HELIAST
HELIASTS
HELIBORNE
HELIBUS

HELIBUSES
HELIBUSSES
HELICAL
HELICALLY
HELICES
HELICHRYSUM
HELICHRYSUMS
HELICITIES
HELICITY
HELICLINE
HELICLINES
HELICOGRAPH
HELICOGRAPHS
HELICOID
HELICOIDAL
HELICOIDALLY
HELICOIDS
HELICON
HELICONS
HELICOPT
HELICOPTED
HELICOPTER
HELICOPTERED
HELICOPTERING
HELICOPTERS
HELICOPTING
HELICOPTS
HELICTITE
HELICTITES
HELIDECK
HELIDECKS
HELIDROME
HELIDROMES
HELILIFT
HELILIFTED
HELILIFTING
HELILIFTS
HELIMAN
HELIMEN
HELING
HELIO
HELIOCENTRIC
HELIOCENTRICISM
HELIOCENTRICITY
HELIOCENTRIST
HELIOCHROME
HELIOCHROMES
HELIOCHROMIC
HELIOCHROMIES
HELIOCHROMY
HELIODOR
HELIODORS
HELIOGRAPH
HELIOGRAPHED
HELIOGRAPHER
HELIOGRAPHERS

HELIOGRAPHIC
HELIOGRAPHICAL
HELIOGRAPHIES
HELIOGRAPHING
HELIOGRAPHS
HELIOGRAPHY
HELIOGRAVURE
HELIOGRAVURES
HELIOLATER
HELIOLATERS
HELIOLATRIES
HELIOLATROUS
HELIOLATRY
HELIOLITHIC
HELIOLOGIES
HELIOLOGY
HELIOMETER
HELIOMETERS
HELIOMETRIC
HELIOMETRICAL
HELIOMETRICALLY
HELIOMETRY
HELIOPAUSAL
HELIOPAUSE
HELIOPAUSES
HELIOPHILOUS
HELIOPHOBIC
HELIOPHYTE
HELIOPHYTES
HELIOS
HELIOSCIOPHYTE
HELIOSCIOPHYTES
HELIOSCOPE
HELIOSCOPES
HELIOSCOPIC
HELIOSES
HELIOSIS
HELIOSPHERE
HELIOSPHERES
HELIOSTAT
HELIOSTATIC
HELIOSTATICALLY
HELIOSTATS
HELIOTACTIC
HELIOTAXIS
HELIOTHERAPIES
HELIOTHERAPY
HELIOTROPE
HELIOTROPES
HELIOTROPIC
HELIOTROPICAL
HELIOTROPICALLY
HELIOTROPIES
HELIOTROPIN
HELIOTROPINS
HELIOTROPISM

HELIOTROPISMS
HELIOTROPY
HELIOTYPE
HELIOTYPES
HELIOTYPIC
HELIOTYPIES
HELIOTYPY
HELIOZOAN
HELIOZOANS
HELIOZOIC
HELIPAD
HELIPADS
HELIPILOT
HELIPILOTS
HELIPORT
HELIPORTS
HELISCOOPS
HELISPHERIC
HELISPHERICAL
HELISTOP
HELISTOPS
HELIUM
HELIUMS
HELIX
HELIXES
HELL
HELLACIOUS
HELLACIOUSLY
HELLBENDER
HELLBENDERS
HELLBENT
HELLBOX
HELLBOXES
HELLBROTH
HELLBROTHS
HELLCAT
HELLCATS
HELLDIVER
HELLDIVERS
HELLEBORE
HELLEBORES
HELLEBORINE
HELLEBORINES
HELLED
HELLENISE
HELLENISED
HELLENISES
HELLENISING
HELLENIZATION
HELLENIZATIONS
HELLENIZE
HELLENIZED
HELLENIZES
HELLENIZING
HELLER
HELLERI

HELLERIES
HELLERS
HELLERY
HELLFIRE
HELLFIRES
HELLGRAMITE
HELLGRAMITES
HELLGRAMMITE
HELLGRAMMITES
HELLHOLE
HELLHOLES
HELLHOUND
HELLHOUNDS
HELLICAT
HELLICATS
HELLIER
HELLIERS
HELLING
HELLION
HELLIONS
HELLISH
HELLISHLY
HELLISHNESS
HELLISHNESSES
HELLKITE
HELLKITES
HELLO
HELLOED
HELLOES
HELLOING
HELLOS
HELLOVA
HELLS
HELLUVA
HELLWARD
HELLWARDS
HELM
HELMED
HELMER
HELMERS
HELMET
HELMETED
HELMETING
HELMETLIKE
HELMETS
HELMING
HELMINTH
HELMINTHIASES
HELMINTHIASIS
HELMINTHIC
HELMINTHICS
HELMINTHOID
HELMINTHOLOGIC
HELMINTHOLOGIES
HELMINTHOLOGIST
HELMINTHOLOGY

HELMINTHOUS
HELMINTHS
HELMLESS
HELMS
HELMSMAN
HELMSMANSHIP
HELMSMANSHIPS
HELMSMEN
HELO
HELOPHYTE
HELOPHYTES
HELOPHYTIC
HELOS
HELOT
HELOTAGE
HELOTAGES
HELOTISM
HELOTISMS
HELOTRIES
HELOTRY
HELOTS
HELP
HELPABLE
HELPDESK
HELPDESKS
HELPED
HELPER
HELPERS
HELPFUL
HELPFULLY
HELPFULNESS
HELPFULNESSES
HELPING
HELPINGS
HELPLESS
HELPLESSLY
HELPLESSNESS
HELPLESSNESSES
HELPLINE
HELPLINES
HELPMATE
HELPMATES
HELPMEET
HELPMEETS
HELPS
HELVE
HELVED
HELVES
HELVETIUM
HELVETIUMS
HELVING
HEM
HEMACHROME
HEMACHROMES
HEMACHROMIC
HEMACYTOMETER

HEMACYTOMETERS
HEMAGGLUTINATE
HEMAGGLUTINATED
HEMAGGLUTINATES
HEMAGGLUTININ
HEMAGGLUTININS
HEMAGOG
HEMAGOGS
HEMAGOGUE
HEMAGOGUES
HEMAL
HEMANGIOMA
HEMANGIOMAS
HEMANGIOMATA
HEMATAL
HEMATEIN
HEMATEINS
HEMATEMESIS
HEMATIC
HEMATICS
HEMATIN
HEMATINE
HEMATINES
HEMATINIC
HEMATINICS
HEMATINS
HEMATITE
HEMATITES
HEMATITIC
HEMATOBLAST
HEMATOBLASTIC
HEMATOBLASTS
HEMATOCELE
HEMATOCELES
HEMATOCRIT
HEMATOCRITS
HEMATOCRYAL
HEMATOGENESIS
HEMATOGENETIC
HEMATOGENIC
HEMATOGENICALLY
HEMATOGENOUS
HEMATOID
HEMATOLOGIC
HEMATOLOGICAL
HEMATOLOGIES
HEMATOLOGIST
HEMATOLOGISTS
HEMATOLOGY
HEMATOLYSES
HEMATOLYSIS
HEMATOLYTIC
HEMATOMA
HEMATOMAS
HEMATOMATA
HEMATOPHAGOUS

HEMATOPOIESES
HEMATOPOIESIS
HEMATOPOIETIC
HEMATOPORPHYRIN
HEMATOSES
HEMATOSIS
HEMATOTHERMAL
HEMATOXYLIN
HEMATOXYLINS
HEMATOZOA
HEMATOZOIC
HEMATOZOON
HEMATURIA
HEMATURIAS
HEMATURIC
HEME
HEMELYTRA
HEMELYTRAL
HEMELYTRON
HEMERALOPIA
HEMERALOPIAS
HEMERALOPIC
HEMERALOPICALLY
HEMEROCALLIS
HEMEROCALLISES
HEMERYTHRIN
HEMERYTHRINS
HEMES
HEMIACETAL
HEMIACETALS
HEMIALGIA
HEMIALGIAS
HEMIANOPIA
HEMIANOPIAS
HEMIANOPSIA
HEMIANOPSIAS
HEMIANOPTIC
HEMIC
HEMICELLULOSE
HEMICELLULOSES
HEMICHORDATE
HEMICHORDATES
HEMICRANIA
HEMICRANIAS
HEMICRYPTOPHYTE
HEMICRYSTALLINE
HEMICYCLE
HEMICYCLES
HEMICYCLIC
HEMIELYTRA
HEMIELYTRAL
HEMIELYTRON
HEMIHEDRAL
HEMIHEDRIES
HEMIHEDRISM
HEMIHEDRISMS

HEMIHEDRON
HEMIHEDRONS
HEMIHEDRY
HEMIHYDRATE
HEMIHYDRATED
HEMIHYDRATES
HEMIMETABOLOUS
HEMIMORPHIC
HEMIMORPHISM
HEMIMORPHISMS
HEMIMORPHITE
HEMIMORPHITES
HEMIMORPHY
HEMIN
HEMINA
HEMINAS
HEMINS
HEMIOLA
HEMIOLAS
HEMIOLIA
HEMIOLIAS
HEMIOLIC
HEMIONE
HEMIONES
HEMIONUS
HEMIONUSES
HEMIOPIA
HEMIOPIAS
HEMIOPIC
HEMIOPSIA
HEMIOPSIAS
HEMIPARASITE
HEMIPARASITES
HEMIPARASITIC
HEMIPLEGIA
HEMIPLEGIAS
HEMIPLEGIC
HEMIPLEGICS
HEMIPOD
HEMIPODE
HEMIPODES
HEMIPODS
HEMIPTER
HEMIPTERAL
HEMIPTERAN
HEMIPTERANS
HEMIPTERON
HEMIPTERONS
HEMIPTEROUS
HEMIPTERS
HEMISPACE
HEMISPACES
HEMISPHERE
HEMISPHERES
HEMISPHERIC
HEMISPHERICAL

HEMISPHEROID
HEMISPHEROIDAL
HEMISPHEROIDS
HEMISTICH
HEMISTICHAL
HEMISTICHS
HEMITERPENE
HEMITERPENES
HEMITROPAL
HEMITROPE
HEMITROPES
HEMITROPIC
HEMITROPISM
HEMITROPOUS
HEMITROPY
HEMIZYGOUS
HEMLINE
HEMLINES
HEMLOCK
HEMLOCKS
HEMMED
HEMMER
HEMMERS
HEMMING
HEMOCHROMATOSES
HEMOCHROMATOSIS
HEMOCHROME
HEMOCHROMES
HEMOCHROMIC
HEMOCOEL
HEMOCOELS
HEMOCYANIN
HEMOCYANINS
HEMOCYTE
HEMOCYTES
HEMOCYTOMETER
HEMOCYTOMETERS
HEMODIALYSES
HEMODIALYSIS
HEMODILUTION
HEMODILUTIONS
HEMODYNAMIC
HEMODYNAMICALLY
HEMODYNAMICS
HEMOFLAGELLATE
HEMOFLAGELLATES
HEMOGLOBIN
HEMOGLOBINS
HEMOGLOBINURIA
HEMOGLOBINURIAS
HEMOGLOBINURIC
HEMOID
HEMOLYMPH
HEMOLYMPHS
HEMOLYSES
HEMOLYSIN

HEMOLYSINS
HEMOLYSIS
HEMOLYTIC
HEMOLYZE
HEMOLYZED
HEMOLYZES
HEMOLYZING
HEMOPHILE
HEMOPHILES
HEMOPHILIA
HEMOPHILIAC
HEMOPHILIACS
HEMOPHILIAS
HEMOPHILIC
HEMOPHILICS
HEMOPHILIOID
HEMOPOIESES
HEMOPOIESIS
HEMOPOIETIC
HEMOPROTEIN
HEMOPROTEINS
HEMOPTYSES
HEMOPTYSIS
HEMORRHAGE
HEMORRHAGED
HEMORRHAGES
HEMORRHAGIC
HEMORRHAGING
HEMORRHOID
HEMORRHOIDAL
HEMORRHOIDALS
HEMORRHOIDS
HEMOSIDERIN
HEMOSIDERINS
HEMOSTASES
HEMOSTASIA
HEMOSTASIS
HEMOSTAT
HEMOSTATIC
HEMOSTATICS
HEMOSTATS
HEMP
HEMPEN
HEMPIE
HEMPIER
HEMPIES
HEMPIEST
HEMPLIKE
HEMPS
HEMPSEED
HEMPSEEDS
HEMPWEED
HEMPWEEDS
HEMPY
HEMS
HEMSTITCH

HEMSTITCHED
HEMSTITCHER
HEMSTITCHERS
HEMSTITCHES
HEMSTITCHING
HEN
HENBANE
HENBANES
HENBIT
HENBITS
HENCE
HENCEFORTH
HENCEFORWARD
HENCEFORWARDLY
HENCEFORWARDS
HENCHMAN
HENCHMEN
HENCHPERSON
HENCHPERSONS
HENCHWOMAN
HENCHWOMEN
HENCOOP
HENCOOPS
HEND
HENDECAGON
HENDECAGONAL
HENDECAGONS
HENDECAHEDRA
HENDECAHEDRAL
HENDECAHEDRON
HENDECAHEDRONS
HENDECASYLLABIC
HENDECASYLLABLE
HENDED
HENDIADYS
HENDIADYSES
HENDING
HENDS
HENEQUEN
HENEQUENS
HENEQUIN
HENEQUINS
HENGE
HENGES
HENHOUSE
HENHOUSES
HENIQUEN
HENIQUENS
HENIQUIN
HENIQUINS
HENLIKE
HENNA
HENNAED
HENNAING
HENNAS
HENNED

HENNER
HENNERIES
HENNERS
HENNERY
HENNIER
HENNIES
HENNIEST
HENNIN
HENNING
HENNINS
HENNY
HENOTHEISM
HENOTHEISMS
HENOTHEIST
HENOTHEISTIC
HENOTHEISTS
HENOTIC
HENPECK
HENPECKED
HENPECKERIES
HENPECKERY
HENPECKING
HENPECKS
HENRIES
HENRY
HENRYS
HENS
HENT
HENTED
HENTING
HENTS
HEORTOLOGICAL
HEORTOLOGIES
HEORTOLOGIST
HEORTOLOGISTS
HEORTOLOGY
HEP
HEPAR
HEPARIN
HEPARINIZED
HEPARINOID
HEPARINS
HEPARS
HEPATECTOMIES
HEPATECTOMIZED
HEPATECTOMY
HEPATIC
HEPATICA
HEPATICAE
HEPATICAL
HEPATICAS
HEPATICOLOGICAL
HEPATICOLOGIES
HEPATICOLOGIST
HEPATICOLOGISTS
HEPATICOLOGY

HEPATICS
HEPATISATION
HEPATISATIONS
HEPATISE
HEPATISED
HEPATISES
HEPATISING
HEPATITE
HEPATITES
HEPATITIDES
HEPATITIS
HEPATITISES
HEPATIZATION
HEPATIZATIONS
HEPATIZE
HEPATIZED
HEPATIZES
HEPATIZING
HEPATOCELLULAR
HEPATOCYTE
HEPATOCYTES
HEPATOGENOUS
HEPATOGENOUSLY
HEPATOLOGIES
HEPATOLOGIST
HEPATOLOGISTS
HEPATOLOGY
HEPATOMA
HEPATOMAS
HEPATOMATA
HEPATOMEGALIES
HEPATOMEGALY
HEPATOPANCREAS
HEPATOSCOPIES
HEPATOSCOPY
HEPATOTOXIC
HEPATOTOXICITY
HEPCAT
HEPCATS
HEPHTHEMIMER
HEPHTHEMIMERAL
HEPHTHEMIMERS
HEPPER
HEPPEST
HEPS
HEPSTER
HEPSTERS
HEPT
HEPTACHLOR
HEPTACHLORS
HEPTACHORD
HEPTACHORDS
HEPTAD
HEPTADECANOIC
HEPTADS
HEPTAGLOT

HEPTAGLOTS
HEPTAGON
HEPTAGONAL
HEPTAGONS
HEPTAGYNOUS
HEPTAHEDRA
HEPTAHEDRAL
HEPTAHEDRON
HEPTAHEDRONS
HEPTAMEROUS
HEPTAMETER
HEPTAMETERS
HEPTAMETRICAL
HEPTAMETRICALLY
HEPTANDROUS
HEPTANE
HEPTANES
HEPTANGULAR
HEPTAPODIC
HEPTAPODIES
HEPTAPODY
HEPTARCH
HEPTARCHAL
HEPTARCHALLY
HEPTARCHIC
HEPTARCHIES
HEPTARCHIST
HEPTARCHISTS
HEPTARCHS
HEPTARCHY
HEPTASTICH
HEPTASTICHAL
HEPTASTICHALLY
HEPTASTICHS
HEPTASYLLABIC
HEPTATHLETE
HEPTATHLETES
HEPTATHLON
HEPTATHLONS
HEPTATONIC
HEPTAVALENCY
HEPTAVALENT
HEPTOSE
HEPTOSES
HER
HERALD
HERALDED
HERALDIC
HERALDICALLY
HERALDING
HERALDIST
HERALDISTIC
HERALDISTS
HERALDRIES
HERALDRY
HERALDS

HERALDSHIP
HERALDSHIPS
HERB
HERBACEOUS
HERBACEOUSLY
HERBACEOUSNESS
HERBAGE
HERBAGED
HERBAGES
HERBAL
HERBALISM
HERBALISMS
HERBALIST
HERBALISTS
HERBALS
HERBAR
HERBARIA
HERBARIAL
HERBARIAN
HERBARIANS
HERBARIES
HERBARIUM
HERBARIUMS
HERBARS
HERBARY
HERBED
HERBELET
HERBELETS
HERBICIDAL
HERBICIDALLY
HERBICIDE
HERBICIDES
HERBIER
HERBIEST
HERBIST
HERBISTS
HERBIVORA
HERBIVORE
HERBIVORES
HERBIVORIES
HERBIVOROUS
HERBIVOROUSLY
HERBIVOROUSNESS
HERBIVORY
HERBLESS
HERBLET
HERBLETS
HERBLIKE
HERBORISATION
HERBORISATIONS
HERBORISE
HERBORISED
HERBORISES
HERBORISING
HERBORIST
HERBORISTS

HERBORIZATION
HERBORIZATIONS
HERBORIZE
HERBORIZED
HERBORIZES
HERBORIZING
HERBOSE
HERBOUS
HERBS
HERBY
HERCOGAMIES
HERCOGAMOUS
HERCOGAMY
HERCULEAN
HERCULES
HERCULESES
HERCYNITE
HERCYNITES
HERD
HERDBOY
HERDBOYS
HERDED
HERDEN
HERDENS
HERDER
HERDERS
HERDESS
HERDESSES
HERDIC
HERDICS
HERDING
HERDLIKE
HERDMAN
HERDMEN
HERDS
HERDSMAN
HERDSMEN
HERDWICK
HERDWICKS
HERE
HEREABOUT
HEREABOUTS
HEREAFTER
HEREAFTERS
HEREAT
HEREAWAY
HEREAWAYS
HEREBY
HEREDES
HEREDITABILITY
HEREDITABLE
HEREDITABLY
HEREDITAMENT
HEREDITAMENTS
HEREDITARIAN
HEREDITARIANISM

HEREDITARIANIST
HEREDITARIANS
HEREDITARILY
HEREDITARINESS
HEREDITARY
HEREDITIES
HEREDITIST
HEREDITISTS
HEREDITY
HEREFROM
HEREIN
HEREINABOVE
HEREINAFTER
HEREINBEFORE
HEREINBELOW
HEREINTO
HERENESS
HERENESSES
HEREOF
HEREON
HERES
HERESIARCH
HERESIARCHS
HERESIES
HERESIOGRAPHER
HERESIOGRAPHERS
HERESIOGRAPHIES
HERESIOGRAPHY
HERESIOLOGIES
HERESIOLOGIST
HERESIOLOGISTS
HERESIOLOGY
HERESTHETIC
HERESTHETICIAN
HERESTHETICIANS
HERESY
HERETIC
HERETICAL
HERETICALLY
HERETICATE
HERETICATED
HERETICATES
HERETICATING
HERETICS
HERETO
HERETOFORE
HERETRICES
HERETRIX
HERETRIXES
HEREUNDER
HEREUNTO
HEREUPON
HEREWITH
HERIED
HERIES
HERIOT

457

HERIOTABLE
HERIOTS
HERISSE
HERISSON
HERISSONS
HERITABILITIES
HERITABILITY
HERITABLE
HERITABLY
HERITAGE
HERITAGES
HERITOR
HERITORS
HERITRESS
HERITRESSES
HERITRICES
HERITRIX
HERITRIXES
HERKOGAMIES
HERKOGAMY
HERL
HERLING
HERLINGS
HERLS
HERM
HERMA
HERMAE
HERMAEAN
HERMAI
HERMANDAD
HERMANDADS
HERMAPHRODITE
HERMAPHRODITES
HERMAPHRODITIC
HERMAPHRODITISM
HERMATYPIC
HERMENEUTIC
HERMENEUTICAL
HERMENEUTICALLY
HERMENEUTICS
HERMENEUTIST
HERMENEUTISTS
HERMETIC
HERMETICAL
HERMETICALLY
HERMETICALNESS
HERMETICISM
HERMETICISMS
HERMETICITIES
HERMETICITY
HERMETICS
HERMETISM
HERMETISMS
HERMETIST
HERMETISTS
HERMIT

HERMITAGE
HERMITAGES
HERMITESS
HERMITESSES
HERMITIC
HERMITICAL
HERMITICALLY
HERMITISM
HERMITISMS
HERMITRIES
HERMITRY
HERMITS
HERMS
HERN
HERNIA
HERNIAE
HERNIAL
HERNIAS
HERNIATE
HERNIATED
HERNIATES
HERNIATING
HERNIATION
HERNIATIONS
HERNIORRHAPHIES
HERNIORRHAPHY
HERNIOTOMIES
HERNIOTOMY
HERNS
HERNSHAW
HERNSHAWS
HERO
HEROE
HEROES
HEROIC
HEROICAL
HEROICALLY
HEROICALNESS
HEROICALNESSES
HEROICLY
HEROICNESS
HEROICNESSES
HEROICOMIC
HEROICOMICAL
HEROICS
HEROIN
HEROINE
HEROINES
HEROINISM
HEROINISMS
HEROINS
HEROISE
HEROISED
HEROISES
HEROISING
HEROISM

HEROISMS
HEROIZE
HEROIZED
HEROIZES
HEROIZING
HERON
HERONRIES
HERONRY
HERONS
HERONSEW
HERONSEWS
HERONSHAW
HERONSHAWS
HEROON
HEROONS
HEROS
HEROSHIP
HEROSHIPS
HERPES
HERPESES
HERPESVIRUS
HERPESVIRUSES
HERPETIC
HERPETICS
HERPETOFAUNA
HERPETOFAUNAE
HERPETOFAUNAS
HERPETOID
HERPETOLOGIC
HERPETOLOGICAL
HERPETOLOGIES
HERPETOLOGIST
HERPETOLOGISTS
HERPETOLOGY
HERPTILE
HERRENVOLK
HERRENVOLKS
HERRIED
HERRIES
HERRIMENT
HERRIMENTS
HERRING
HERRINGBONE
HERRINGBONED
HERRINGBONES
HERRINGBONING
HERRINGER
HERRINGERS
HERRINGS
HERRY
HERRYING
HERRYMENT
HERRYMENTS
HERS
HERSALL
HERSALLS

HERSE
HERSED
HERSELF
HERSES
HERSHIP
HERSHIPS
HERSTORIES
HERSTORY
HERTZ
HERTZES
HERY
HERYE
HERYED
HERYES
HERYING
HES
HESITANCE
HESITANCES
HESITANCIES
HESITANCY
HESITANT
HESITANTLY
HESITATE
HESITATED
HESITATER
HESITATERS
HESITATES
HESITATING
HESITATINGLY
HESITATION
HESITATIONS
HESITATIVE
HESITATOR
HESITATORS
HESITATORY
HESP
HESPED
HESPERID
HESPERIDIA
HESPERIDIN
HESPERIDINS
HESPERIDIUM
HESPERIDIUMS
HESPERIDS
HESPING
HESPS
HESSIAN
HESSIANS
HESSITE
HESSITES
HESSONITE
HESSONITES
HEST
HESTERNAL
HESTS
HET

HETAERA
HETAERAE
HETAERAS
HETAERIC
HETAERISM
HETAERISMIC
HETAERISMS
HETAERIST
HETAERISTIC
HETAERISTICALLY
HETAERISTS
HETAIRA
HETAIRAI
HETAIRAS
HETAIRIA
HETAIRIAS
HETAIRIC
HETAIRISM
HETAIRISMIC
HETAIRISMS
HETAIRIST
HETAIRISTIC
HETAIRISTICALLY
HETAIRISTS
HETE
HETERARCHICAL
HETERARCHICALLY
HETERARCHIES
HETERARCHY
HETERAUXESES
HETERAUXESIS
HETERO
HETEROATOM
HETEROATOMS
HETEROAUXIN
HETEROAUXINS
HETEROBLASTIC
HETEROBLASTIES
HETEROBLASTY
HETEROCARPOUS
HETEROCERCAL
HETEROCERCALITY
HETEROCERCIES
HETEROCERCY
HETEROCHROMATIC
HETEROCHROMATIN
HETEROCHROMOUS
HETEROCHRONIC
HETEROCHRONIES
HETEROCHRONISM
HETEROCHRONISMS
HETEROCHRONOUS
HETEROCHRONY
HETEROCLITE
HETEROCLITES
HETEROCLITIC

HETEROCLITOUS
HETEROCONT
HETEROCONTS
HETEROCYCLE
HETEROCYCLES
HETEROCYCLIC
HETEROCYCLICS
HETEROCYST
HETEROCYSTOUS
HETEROCYSTS
HETERODACTYL
HETERODACTYLOUS
HETERODACTYLS
HETERODONT
HETERODOX
HETERODOXIES
HETERODOXY
HETERODUPLEX
HETERODUPLEXES
HETERODYNE
HETERODYNED
HETERODYNES
HETERODYNING
HETEROECIOUS
HETEROECISM
HETEROECISMS
HETEROGAMETE
HETEROGAMETES
HETEROGAMETIC
HETEROGAMETIES
HETEROGAMETY
HETEROGAMIES
HETEROGAMOUS
HETEROGAMY
HETEROGENEITIES
HETEROGENEITY
HETEROGENEOUS
HETEROGENEOUSLY
HETEROGENESES
HETEROGENESIS
HETEROGENETIC
HETEROGENIC
HETEROGENICALLY
HETEROGENIES
HETEROGENOUS
HETEROGENY
HETEROGONIC
HETEROGONIES
HETEROGONOUS
HETEROGONOUSLY
HETEROGONY
HETEROGRAFT
HETEROGRAFTS
HETEROGRAPHIC
HETEROGRAPHICAL
HETEROGRAPHIES

HETEROGRAPHY
HETEROGYNOUS
HETEROGYNOUSLY
HETEROKARYON
HETEROKARYONS
HETEROKARYOSES
HETEROKARYOSIS
HETEROKARYOTIC
HETEROKONT
HETEROKONTAN
HETEROKONTS
HETEROLECITHAL
HETEROLOGIES
HETEROLOGOUS
HETEROLOGOUSLY
HETEROLOGY
HETEROLYSES
HETEROLYSIS
HETEROLYTIC
HETEROMEROUS
HETEROMORPHIC
HETEROMORPHIES
HETEROMORPHISM
HETEROMORPHISMS
HETEROMORPHOUS
HETEROMORPHY
HETERONOMIES
HETERONOMOUS
HETERONOMOUSLY
HETERONOMY
HETERONYM
HETERONYMOUS
HETERONYMOUSLY
HETERONYMS
HETEROOUSIAN
HETEROOUSIANS
HETEROPHIL
HETEROPHILE
HETEROPHONIES
HETEROPHONY
HETEROPHYLLIES
HETEROPHYLLOUS
HETEROPHYLLY
HETEROPHYTE
HETEROPHYTES
HETEROPLASIA
HETEROPLASIAS
HETEROPLASTIC
HETEROPLASTIES
HETEROPLASTY
HETEROPLOID
HETEROPLOIDIES
HETEROPLOIDS
HETEROPLOIDY
HETEROPOD
HETEROPODS

HETEROPOLAR
HETEROPOLARITY
HETEROPTERAN
HETEROPTERANS
HETEROPTEROUS
HETEROS
HETEROSCEDASTIC
HETEROSCIAN
HETEROSCIANS
HETEROSES
HETEROSEXISM
HETEROSEXISMS
HETEROSEXIST
HETEROSEXISTS
HETEROSEXUAL
HETEROSEXUALITY
HETEROSEXUALLY
HETEROSEXUALS
HETEROSIS
HETEROSOCIAL
HETEROSOCIALITY
HETEROSOCIALLY
HETEROSOMATOUS
HETEROSPECIFIC
HETEROSPORIES
HETEROSPOROUS
HETEROSPORY
HETEROSTROPHIC
HETEROSTROPHIES
HETEROSTROPHY
HETEROSTYLED
HETEROSTYLIES
HETEROSTYLISM
HETEROSTYLISMS
HETEROSTYLOUS
HETEROSTYLY
HETEROTACTIC
HETEROTACTOUS
HETEROTAXES
HETEROTAXIA
HETEROTAXIC
HETEROTAXIES
HETEROTAXIS
HETEROTAXY
HETEROTHALLIC
HETEROTHALLIES
HETEROTHALLISM
HETEROTHALLISMS
HETEROTHALLY
HETEROTHERMAL
HETEROTIC
HETEROTOPIA
HETEROTOPIAS
HETEROTOPIC
HETEROTOPOUS
HETEROTOPY

HETEROTROPH
HETEROTROPHIC
HETEROTROPHIES
HETEROTROPHS
HETEROTROPHY
HETEROTYPIC
HETEROTYPICAL
HETEROTYPICALLY
HETEROUSIAN
HETEROUSIANS
HETEROZYGOSES
HETEROZYGOSIS
HETEROZYGOSITY
HETEROZYGOTE
HETEROZYGOTES
HETEROZYGOUS
HETES
HETH
HETHER
HETHERWARD
HETHS
HETING
HETMAN
HETMANATE
HETMANATES
HETMANS
HETMANSHIP
HETMANSHIPS
HETS
HEUCH
HEUCHERA
HEUCHERAS
HEUCHS
HEUGH
HEUGHS
HEULANDITE
HEULANDITES
HEUREKA
HEUREKAS
HEURETIC
HEURETICS
HEURISM
HEURISMS
HEURISTIC
HEURISTICALLY
HEURISTICS
HEVEA
HEVEAS
HEW
HEWABLE
HEWED
HEWER
HEWERS
HEWGH
HEWING
HEWINGS

HEWN
HEWS
HEX
HEXACHLORETHANE
HEXACHLOROPHANE
HEXACHLOROPHENE
HEXACHORD
HEXACHORDS
HEXACOSANOIC
HEXACT
HEXACTINAL
HEXACTINELLID
HEXACTINELLIDS
HEXACTS
HEXAD
HEXADACTYLIC
HEXADACTYLOUS
HEXADE
HEXADECANE
HEXADECANOIC
HEXADECIMAL
HEXADECIMALS
HEXADES
HEXADIC
HEXADS
HEXAEMERIC
HEXAEMERON
HEXAEMERONS
HEXAFOIL
HEXAFOILS
HEXAGLOT
HEXAGON
HEXAGONAL
HEXAGONALLY
HEXAGONS
HEXAGRAM
HEXAGRAMMOID
HEXAGRAMMOIDS
HEXAGRAMS
HEXAGYNIAN
HEXAGYNOUS
HEXAHEDRA
HEXAHEDRAL
HEXAHEDRON
HEXAHEDRONS
HEXAHEMERIC
HEXAHEMERON
HEXAHEMERONS
HEXAHYDRATE
HEXAHYDRATED
HEXAHYDRATES
HEXAMERAL
HEXAMERISM
HEXAMEROUS
HEXAMETER
HEXAMETERS

HEXAMETHONIUM
HEXAMETHONIUMS
HEXAMETRAL
HEXAMETRALLY
HEXAMETRIC
HEXAMETRICAL
HEXAMETRICALLY
HEXAMETRISE
HEXAMETRISED
HEXAMETRISES
HEXAMETRISING
HEXAMETRIST
HEXAMETRISTS
HEXAMETRIZE
HEXAMETRIZED
HEXAMETRIZES
HEXAMETRIZING
HEXAMINE
HEXAMINES
HEXANDRIAN
HEXANDROUS
HEXANE
HEXANES
HEXANGULAR
HEXANGULARLY
HEXANOIC
HEXAPLA
HEXAPLAR
HEXAPLARIAN
HEXAPLARIC
HEXAPLAS
HEXAPLOID
HEXAPLOIDIES
HEXAPLOIDS
HEXAPLOIDY
HEXAPOD
HEXAPODIC
HEXAPODICALLY
HEXAPODIES
HEXAPODS
HEXAPODY
HEXARCH
HEXARCHIES
HEXARCHY
HEXASTICH
HEXASTICHAL
HEXASTICHIC
HEXASTICHICALLY
HEXASTICHON
HEXASTICHONS
HEXASTICHS
HEXASTYLE
HEXASTYLES
HEXATEUCHAL
HEXAVALENCY
HEXAVALENT

HEXED
HEXENE
HEXENES
HEXER
HEXEREI
HEXEREIS
HEXERS
HEXES
HEXING
HEXINGS
HEXOBARBITAL
HEXOBARBITALS
HEXOKINASE
HEXOKINASES
HEXONE
HEXONES
HEXOSAMINIDASE
HEXOSAMINIDASES
HEXOSAN
HEXOSANS
HEXOSE
HEXOSES
HEXYL
HEXYLENE
HEXYLENES
HEXYLRESORCINOL
HEXYLS
HEY
HEYDAY
HEYDAYS
HEYDEY
HEYDEYS
HEYDUCK
HEYDUCKS
HEYED
HEYING
HEYS
HI
HIANT
HIATAL
HIATUS
HIATUSES
HIBACHI
HIBACHIS
HIBAKUSHA
HIBAKUSHAS
HIBERNACLE
HIBERNACLES
HIBERNACULA
HIBERNACULUM
HIBERNAL
HIBERNATE
HIBERNATED
HIBERNATES
HIBERNATING
HIBERNATION

HIBERNATIONS
HIBERNATOR
HIBERNATORS
HIBERNICISE
HIBERNICISED
HIBERNICISES
HIBERNICISING
HIBERNICIZE
HIBERNICIZED
HIBERNICIZES
HIBERNICIZING
HIBERNISATION
HIBERNISATIONS
HIBERNISED
HIBERNISES
HIBERNISING
HIBERNIZATION
HIBERNIZATIONS
HIBERNIZE
HIBERNIZED
HIBERNIZES
HIBERNIZING
HIBISCUS
HIBISCUSES
HIC
HICATEE
HICATEES
HICCATEE
HICCATEES
HICCOUGH
HICCOUGHED
HICCOUGHING
HICCOUGHS
HICCUP
HICCUPED
HICCUPING
HICCUPPED
HICCUPPING
HICCUPS
HICCUPY
HICK
HICKEY
HICKEYS
HICKIES
HICKISH
HICKORIES
HICKORY
HICKS
HICKWALL
HICKWALLS
HICKYMAL
HICKYMALS
HID
HIDABLE
HIDAGE
HIDAGES

HIDALGA
HIDALGAS
HIDALGO
HIDALGOISH
HIDALGOISM
HIDALGOISMS
HIDALGOS
HIDDEN
HIDDENITE
HIDDENITES
HIDDENLY
HIDDENMOST
HIDDENNESS
HIDDENNESSES
HIDDER
HIDDERS
HIDE
HIDEAWAY
HIDEAWAYS
HIDEBOUND
HIDED
HIDELESS
HIDEOSITIES
HIDEOSITY
HIDEOUS
HIDEOUSLY
HIDEOUSNESS
HIDEOUSNESSES
HIDEOUT
HIDEOUTS
HIDER
HIDERS
HIDES
HIDING
HIDINGS
HIDLING
HIDLINGS
HIDLINS
HIDROSES
HIDROSIS
HIDROTIC
HIDROTICS
HIE
HIED
HIEING
HIELAMAN
HIELAMANS
HIELAND
HIEMAL
HIEMS
HIERACIUM
HIERACIUMS
HIERACOSPHINGES
HIERACOSPHINX
HIERACOSPHINXES
HIERARCH

HIERARCHAL
HIERARCHIC
HIERARCHICAL
HIERARCHICALLY
HIERARCHIES
HIERARCHISM
HIERARCHISMS
HIERARCHIZE
HIERARCHIZED
HIERARCHIZES
HIERARCHIZING
HIERARCHS
HIERARCHY
HIERATIC
HIERATICA
HIERATICAL
HIERATICALLY
HIERATICAS
HIEROCRACIES
HIEROCRACY
HIEROCRAT
HIEROCRATIC
HIEROCRATICAL
HIEROCRATS
HIERODULE
HIERODULES
HIERODULIC
HIEROGLYPH
HIEROGLYPHED
HIEROGLYPHIC
HIEROGLYPHICAL
HIEROGLYPHICS
HIEROGLYPHING
HIEROGLYPHIST
HIEROGLYPHISTS
HIEROGLYPHS
HIEROGRAM
HIEROGRAMMAT
HIEROGRAMMATE
HIEROGRAMMATES
HIEROGRAMMATIC
HIEROGRAMMATIST
HIEROGRAMMATS
HIEROGRAMS
HIEROGRAPH
HIEROGRAPHER
HIEROGRAPHERS
HIEROGRAPHIC
HIEROGRAPHICAL
HIEROGRAPHIES
HIEROGRAPHS
HIEROGRAPHY
HIEROLATRIES
HIEROLATRY
HIEROLOGIC
HIEROLOGICAL

HIEROLOGIES
HIEROLOGIST
HIEROLOGISTS
HIEROLOGY
HIEROMANCIES
HIEROMANCY
HIEROPHANT
HIEROPHANTIC
HIEROPHANTS
HIEROPHOBIA
HIEROPHOBIAS
HIEROPHOBIC
HIEROSCOPIES
HIEROSCOPY
HIERURGICAL
HIERURGIES
HIERURGY
HIES
HIFALUTIN
HIGGLE
HIGGLED
HIGGLER
HIGGLERS
HIGGLES
HIGGLING
HIGGLINGS
HIGH
HIGHBALL
HIGHBALLED
HIGHBALLING
HIGHBALLS
HIGHBINDER
HIGHBINDERS
HIGHBORN
HIGHBOY
HIGHBOYS
HIGHBRED
HIGHBROW
HIGHBROWED
HIGHBROWISM
HIGHBROWISMS
HIGHBROWS
HIGHBUSH
HIGHCHAIR
HIGHCHAIRS
HIGHED
HIGHER
HIGHERED
HIGHERING
HIGHERMOST
HIGHERS
HIGHEST
HIGHFALUTIN
HIGHFALUTING
HIGHFALUTINGS
HIGHFALUTINS

HIGHFLIER
HIGHFLIERS
HIGHFLYER
HIGHFLYERS
HIGHING
HIGHISH
HIGHJACK
HIGHJACKED
HIGHJACKER
HIGHJACKERS
HIGHJACKING
HIGHJACKS
HIGHLAND
HIGHLANDER
HIGHLANDERS
HIGHLANDS
HIGHLIFE
HIGHLIFES
HIGHLIGHT
HIGHLIGHTED
HIGHLIGHTER
HIGHLIGHTERS
HIGHLIGHTING
HIGHLIGHTS
HIGHLY
HIGHMAN
HIGHMEN
HIGHMOST
HIGHNESS
HIGHNESSES
HIGHROAD
HIGHROADS
HIGHS
HIGHSPOT
HIGHSPOTS
HIGHT
HIGHTAIL
HIGHTAILED
HIGHTAILING
HIGHTAILS
HIGHTED
HIGHTH
HIGHTHS
HIGHTING
HIGHTS
HIGHVELD
HIGHWAY
HIGHWAYMAN
HIGHWAYMEN
HIGHWAYS
HIGHWROUGHT
HIJAB
HIJABS
HIJACK
HIJACKED
HIJACKER

HIJACKERS
HIJACKING
HIJACKS
HIJINKS
HIJRA
HIJRAH
HIJRAHS
HIJRAS
HIKE
HIKED
HIKER
HIKERS
HIKES
HIKING
HIKOI
HIKOIS
HILA
HILAR
HILARIOUS
HILARIOUSLY
HILARIOUSNESS
HILARIOUSNESSES
HILARITIES
HILARITY
HILCH
HILCHED
HILCHES
HILCHING
HILD
HILDING
HILDINGS
HILI
HILL
HILLBILLIES
HILLBILLY
HILLCREST
HILLCRESTS
HILLED
HILLER
HILLERS
HILLFOLK
HILLFORT
HILLFORTS
HILLIER
HILLIEST
HILLINESS
HILLINESSES
HILLING
HILLMEN
HILLO
HILLOA
HILLOAED
HILLOAING
HILLOAS
HILLOCK
HILLOCKED

HILLOCKS
HILLOCKY
HILLOED
HILLOES
HILLOING
HILLOS
HILLS
HILLSIDE
HILLSIDES
HILLTOP
HILLTOPS
HILLWALKER
HILLWALKERS
HILLWALKING
HILLWALKINGS
HILLY
HILT
HILTED
HILTING
HILTLESS
HILTS
HILUM
HILUS
HILUSES
HIM
HIMATIA
HIMATION
HIMATIONS
HIMBO
HIMBOS
HIMSELF
HIN
HINAU
HINAUS
HIND
HINDBERRIES
HINDBERRY
HINDBRAIN
HINDBRAINS
HINDER
HINDERANCE
HINDERANCES
HINDERED
HINDERER
HINDERERS
HINDERING
HINDERINGLY
HINDERLAND
HINDERLANDS
HINDERLANS
HINDERLINGS
HINDERLINS
HINDERMOST
HINDERS
HINDFEET
HINDFOOT

HINDFOREMOST
HINDGUT
HINDGUTS
HINDHEAD
HINDHEADS
HINDLEG
HINDLEGS
HINDMOST
HINDQUARTER
HINDQUARTERS
HINDRANCE
HINDRANCES
HINDS
HINDSIGHT
HINDSIGHTS
HINDWARD
HINDWING
HINDWINGS
HING
HINGE
HINGED
HINGELESS
HINGELESSLY
HINGELIKE
HINGER
HINGERS
HINGES
HINGING
HINGS
HINNIED
HINNIES
HINNY
HINNYING
HINS
HINT
HINTED
HINTER
HINTERLAND
HINTERLANDS
HINTERS
HINTING
HINTINGLY
HINTINGS
HINTS
HIP
HIPBONE
HIPBONES
HIPLESS
HIPLIKE
HIPLINE
HIPLINES
HIPNESS
HIPNESSES
HIPPARCH
HIPPARCHS
HIPPEASTRUM

HIPPEASTRUMS
HIPPED
HIPPEN
HIPPENS
HIPPER
HIPPEST
HIPPIATRIC
HIPPIATRICS
HIPPIATRIES
HIPPIATRIST
HIPPIATRISTS
HIPPIATRY
HIPPIC
HIPPIE
HIPPIEDOM
HIPPIEDOMS
HIPPIENESS
HIPPIENESSES
HIPPIER
HIPPIES
HIPPIEST
HIPPIN
HIPPINESS
HIPPINESSES
HIPPING
HIPPINGS
HIPPINS
HIPPISH
HIPPO
HIPPOCAMPAL
HIPPOCAMPI
HIPPOCAMPUS
HIPPOCENTAUR
HIPPOCENTAURS
HIPPOCRAS
HIPPOCRASES
HIPPOCREPIAN
HIPPODAME
HIPPODAMES
HIPPODAMIST
HIPPODAMISTS
HIPPODAMOUS
HIPPODROME
HIPPODROMES
HIPPODROMIC
HIPPOGRIFF
HIPPOGRIFFS
HIPPOGRYPH
HIPPOGRYPHS
HIPPOLOGIES
HIPPOLOGIST
HIPPOLOGISTS
HIPPOLOGY
HIPPOMANES
HIPPOPHAGIES
HIPPOPHAGIST

HIPPOPHAGISTS
HIPPOPHAGOUS
HIPPOPHAGY
HIPPOPHILE
HIPPOPHILES
HIPPOPHOBE
HIPPOPHOBES
HIPPOPOTAMI
HIPPOPOTAMIAN
HIPPOPOTAMIC
HIPPOPOTAMUS
HIPPOPOTAMUSES
HIPPOS
HIPPURIC
HIPPURITE
HIPPURITES
HIPPURITIC
HIPPUS
HIPPUSES
HIPPY
HIPPYDOM
HIPPYDOMS
HIPS
HIPSHOT
HIPSTER
HIPSTERISM
HIPSTERISMS
HIPSTERS
HIPT
HIRABLE
HIRAGANA
HIRAGANAS
HIRAGE
HIRAGES
HIRCINE
HIRCOCERVUS
HIRCOCERVUSES
HIRCOSITIES
HIRCOSITY
HIRE
HIREABLE
HIREAGE
HIREAGES
HIRED
HIRELING
HIRELINGS
HIRER
HIRERS
HIRES
HIRING
HIRINGS
HIRLING
HIRLINGS
HIRPLE
HIRPLED
HIRPLES

HIRPLING
HIRRIENT
HIRRIENTS
HIRSEL
HIRSELED
HIRSELING
HIRSELLED
HIRSELLING
HIRSELS
HIRSLE
HIRSLED
HIRSLES
HIRSLING
HIRSTIE
HIRSUTE
HIRSUTENESS
HIRSUTENESSES
HIRSUTISM
HIRSUTISMS
HIRUDIN
HIRUDINEAN
HIRUDINEANS
HIRUDINOID
HIRUDINS
HIRUNDINE
HIS
HISH
HISHED
HISHES
HISHING
HISN
HISPANICISE
HISPANICISED
HISPANICISES
HISPANICISING
HISPANICISM
HISPANICISMS
HISPANICIZE
HISPANICIZED
HISPANICIZES
HISPANICIZING
HISPANIDAD
HISPANIDADS
HISPANIOLISE
HISPANIOLISED
HISPANIOLISES
HISPANIOLISING
HISPANIOLIZE
HISPANIOLIZED
HISPANIOLIZES
HISPANIOLIZING
HISPANISM
HISPANISMS
HISPID
HISPIDITIES
HISPIDITY

HISS
HISSED
HISSELF
HISSER
HISSERS
HISSES
HISSIES
HISSING
HISSINGLY
HISSINGS
HISSY
HIST
HISTAMIN
HISTAMINASE
HISTAMINASES
HISTAMINE
HISTAMINERGIC
HISTAMINES
HISTAMINIC
HISTAMINICALLY
HISTAMINS
HISTED
HISTIDIN
HISTIDINE
HISTIDINES
HISTIDINS
HISTIE
HISTING
HISTIOCYTE
HISTIOCYTES
HISTIOCYTIC
HISTIOID
HISTIOLOGIES
HISTIOLOGY
HISTOBLAST
HISTOBLASTS
HISTOCHEMICAL
HISTOCHEMICALLY
HISTOCHEMIST
HISTOCHEMISTRY
HISTOCHEMISTS
HISTOCOMPATIBLE
HISTOCOMPATIBLY
HISTOGEN
HISTOGENESES
HISTOGENESIS
HISTOGENETIC
HISTOGENIC
HISTOGENICALLY
HISTOGENIES
HISTOGENS
HISTOGENY
HISTOGRAM
HISTOGRAMS
HISTOID
HISTOLOGIC

HISTOLOGICAL
HISTOLOGICALLY
HISTOLOGIES
HISTOLOGIST
HISTOLOGISTS
HISTOLOGY
HISTOLYSES
HISTOLYSIS
HISTOLYTIC
HISTOLYTICALLY
HISTONE
HISTONES
HISTOPATHOLOGIC
HISTOPATHOLOGY
HISTOPHYSIOLOGY
HISTOPLASMOSES
HISTOPLASMOSIS
HISTORIAN
HISTORIANS
HISTORIATED
HISTORIC
HISTORICAL
HISTORICALLY
HISTORICALNESS
HISTORICISE
HISTORICISED
HISTORICISES
HISTORICISING
HISTORICISM
HISTORICISMS
HISTORICIST
HISTORICISTS
HISTORICITIES
HISTORICITY
HISTORICIZE
HISTORICIZED
HISTORICIZES
HISTORICIZING
HISTORIED
HISTORIES
HISTORIETTE
HISTORIETTES
HISTORIFIED
HISTORIFIES
HISTORIFY
HISTORIFYING
HISTORIOGRAPHER
HISTORIOGRAPHIC
HISTORIOGRAPHY
HISTORIOLOGIES
HISTORIOLOGY
HISTORISM
HISTORISMS
HISTORY
HISTORYING
HISTRIO

HISTRION
HISTRIONIC
HISTRIONICAL
HISTRIONICALLY
HISTRIONICALS
HISTRIONICISM
HISTRIONICISMS
HISTRIONICS
HISTRIONISM
HISTRIONISMS
HISTRIONS
HISTRIOS
HISTS
HIT
HITCH
HITCHED
HITCHER
HITCHERS
HITCHES
HITCHHIKE
HITCHHIKED
HITCHHIKER
HITCHHIKERS
HITCHHIKES
HITCHHIKING
HITCHIER
HITCHIEST
HITCHILY
HITCHING
HITCHY
HITHE
HITHER
HITHERED
HITHERING
HITHERMOST
HITHERS
HITHERSIDE
HITHERSIDES
HITHERTO
HITHERWARD
HITHERWARDS
HITHES
HITLESS
HITS
HITTER
HITTERS
HITTING
HIVE
HIVED
HIVELESS
HIVELIKE
HIVER
HIVERS
HIVES
HIVEWARD
HIVEWARDS

HIVING
HIYA
HIZEN
HIZENS
HIZZ
HIZZED
HIZZES
HIZZING
HIZZONER
HIZZONERS
HM
HMM
HO
HOA
HOACTZIN
HOACTZINES
HOACTZINS
HOAED
HOAGIE
HOAGIES
HOAGY
HOAING
HOAR
HOARD
HOARDED
HOARDER
HOARDERS
HOARDING
HOARDINGS
HOARDS
HOARED
HOARFROST
HOARFROSTS
HOARHEAD
HOARHEADS
HOARHOUND
HOARHOUNDS
HOARIER
HOARIEST
HOARILY
HOARINESS
HOARINESSES
HOARING
HOARS
HOARSE
HOARSELY
HOARSEN
HOARSENED
HOARSENESS
HOARSENESSES
HOARSENING
HOARSENS
HOARSER
HOARSEST
HOARY
HOAS

HOAST
HOASTED
HOASTING
HOASTMAN
HOASTMEN
HOASTS
HOATCHING
HOATZIN
HOATZINES
HOATZINS
HOAX
HOAXED
HOAXER
HOAXERS
HOAXES
HOAXING
HOB
HOBBED
HOBBIES
HOBBING
HOBBISH
HOBBIT
HOBBITRIES
HOBBITRY
HOBBITS
HOBBLE
HOBBLEBUSH
HOBBLEBUSHES
HOBBLED
HOBBLEDEHOY
HOBBLEDEHOYDOM
HOBBLEDEHOYDOMS
HOBBLEDEHOYHOOD
HOBBLEDEHOYISH
HOBBLEDEHOYISM
HOBBLEDEHOYISMS
HOBBLEDEHOYS
HOBBLER
HOBBLERS
HOBBLES
HOBBLING
HOBBLINGLY
HOBBLINGS
HOBBY
HOBBYHORSE
HOBBYHORSED
HOBBYHORSES
HOBBYHORSING
HOBBYISM
HOBBYISMS
HOBBYIST
HOBBYISTS
HOBBYLESS
HOBDAY
HOBDAYED
HOBDAYING

HOBDAYS
HOBGOBLIN
HOBGOBLINISM
HOBGOBLINISMS
HOBGOBLINRIES
HOBGOBLINRY
HOBGOBLINS
HOBJOB
HOBJOBBED
HOBJOBBER
HOBJOBBERS
HOBJOBBING
HOBJOBBINGS
HOBJOBS
HOBLIKE
HOBNAIL
HOBNAILED
HOBNAILING
HOBNAILS
HOBNOB
HOBNOBBED
HOBNOBBER
HOBNOBBERS
HOBNOBBING
HOBNOBBY
HOBNOBS
HOBO
HOBODOM
HOBODOMS
HOBOED
HOBOES
HOBOING
HOBOISM
HOBOISMS
HOBOS
HOBS
HOC
HOCHMAGANDIES
HOCHMAGANDY
HOCK
HOCKED
HOCKER
HOCKERS
HOCKEY
HOCKEYS
HOCKING
HOCKLE
HOCKLED
HOCKLES
HOCKLING
HOCKS
HOCKSHOP
HOCKSHOPS
HOCUS
HOCUSED
HOCUSES

HOCUSING
HOCUSSED
HOCUSSES
HOCUSSING
HOD
HODAD
HODADDIES
HODADDY
HODADS
HODDED
HODDEN
HODDENS
HODDIN
HODDING
HODDINS
HODDLE
HODDLED
HODDLES
HODDLING
HODGEPODGE
HODGEPODGES
HODIERNAL
HODJA
HODJAS
HODMAN
HODMANDOD
HODMANDODS
HODMEN
HODOGRAPH
HODOGRAPHIC
HODOGRAPHICALLY
HODOGRAPHS
HODOMETER
HODOMETERS
HODOMETRIES
HODOMETRY
HODOSCOPE
HODOSCOPES
HODS
HOE
HOECAKE
HOECAKES
HOED
HOEDOWN
HOEDOWNS
HOEING
HOELIKE
HOER
HOERS
HOES
HOG
HOGAN
HOGANS
HOGBACK
HOGBACKS
HOGEN

HOGENS
HOGFISH
HOGFISHES
HOGG
HOGGED
HOGGER
HOGGEREL
HOGGERELS
HOGGERIES
HOGGERS
HOGGERY
HOGGET
HOGGETS
HOGGIN
HOGGING
HOGGINGS
HOGGINS
HOGGISH
HOGGISHLY
HOGGISHNESS
HOGGISHNESSES
HOGGS
HOGH
HOGHOOD
HOGHOODS
HOGHS
HOGLIKE
HOGMANAY
HOGMANAYS
HOGMANE
HOGMANES
HOGMENAY
HOGMENAYS
HOGNOSE
HOGNOSED
HOGNOSES
HOGNUT
HOGNUTS
HOGS
HOGSHEAD
HOGSHEADS
HOGTIE
HOGTIED
HOGTIEING
HOGTIES
HOGTYING
HOGWARD
HOGWARDS
HOGWASH
HOGWASHES
HOGWEED
HOGWEEDS
HOH
HOHA
HOHAS
HOHED

HOHING
HOHS
HOI
HOICK
HOICKED
HOICKING
HOICKS
HOICKSED
HOICKSES
HOICKSING
HOIDEN
HOIDENED
HOIDENING
HOIDENISH
HOIDENISHLY
HOIDENISHNESS
HOIDENS
HOIK
HOIKED
HOIKING
HOIKS
HOING
HOISE
HOISED
HOISES
HOISING
HOIST
HOISTED
HOISTER
HOISTERS
HOISTING
HOISTINGS
HOISTMAN
HOISTMEN
HOISTS
HOISTWAY
HOISTWAYS
HOJATOLESLAM
HOJATOLESLAMS
HOJATOLISLAM
HOJATOLISLAMS
HOKE
HOKED
HOKES
HOKEY
HOKEYNESS
HOKEYNESSES
HOKEYPOKEY
HOKEYPOKEYS
HOKI
HOKIER
HOKIEST
HOKILY
HOKINESS
HOKINESSES
HOKING

HOKIS
HOKKU
HOKONUI
HOKONUIS
HOKUM
HOKUMS
HOKYPOKIES
HOKYPOKY
HOLANDRIC
HOLARCHICAL
HOLARCHIES
HOLARCHY
HOLARD
HOLARDS
HOLD
HOLDABLE
HOLDALL
HOLDALLS
HOLDBACK
HOLDBACKS
HOLDEN
HOLDER
HOLDERBAT
HOLDERBATS
HOLDERS
HOLDERSHIP
HOLDERSHIPS
HOLDFAST
HOLDFASTS
HOLDING
HOLDINGS
HOLDOUT
HOLDOUTS
HOLDOVER
HOLDOVERS
HOLDS
HOLDUP
HOLDUPS
HOLE
HOLED
HOLELESS
HOLES
HOLESOM
HOLESOME
HOLEY
HOLEYER
HOLEYEST
HOLIBUT
HOLIBUTS
HOLIDAY
HOLIDAYED
HOLIDAYER
HOLIDAYERS
HOLIDAYING
HOLIDAYMAKER
HOLIDAYMAKERS

HOLIDAYS
HOLIER
HOLIES
HOLIEST
HOLILY
HOLINESS
HOLINESSES
HOLING
HOLINGS
HOLISM
HOLISMS
HOLIST
HOLISTIC
HOLISTICALLY
HOLISTS
HOLK
HOLKED
HOLKING
HOLKS
HOLLA
HOLLAED
HOLLAING
HOLLAND
HOLLANDAISE
HOLLANDAISES
HOLLANDS
HOLLAS
HOLLER
HOLLERED
HOLLERING
HOLLERS
HOLLIDAM
HOLLIDAMS
HOLLIES
HOLLO
HOLLOA
HOLLOAED
HOLLOAING
HOLLOAS
HOLLOED
HOLLOES
HOLLOING
HOLLOO
HOLLOOED
HOLLOOING
HOLLOOS
HOLLOS
HOLLOW
HOLLOWARE
HOLLOWARES
HOLLOWED
HOLLOWER
HOLLOWEST
HOLLOWING
HOLLOWLY
HOLLOWNESS

HOLLOWNESSES
HOLLOWS
HOLLOWWARE
HOLLOWWARES
HOLLY
HOLLYHOCK
HOLLYHOCKS
HOLM
HOLMIA
HOLMIAS
HOLMIC
HOLMIUM
HOLMIUMS
HOLMS
HOLOBENTHIC
HOLOBLASTIC
HOLOBLASTICALLY
HOLOCAUST
HOLOCAUSTAL
HOLOCAUSTIC
HOLOCAUSTS
HOLOCRINE
HOLOCRYSTALLINE
HOLODISCUS
HOLODISCUSES
HOLOENZYME
HOLOENZYMES
HOLOGAMIES
HOLOGAMY
HOLOGRAM
HOLOGRAMS
HOLOGRAPH
HOLOGRAPHED
HOLOGRAPHER
HOLOGRAPHERS
HOLOGRAPHIC
HOLOGRAPHICALLY
HOLOGRAPHIES
HOLOGRAPHING
HOLOGRAPHS
HOLOGRAPHY
HOLOGYNIES
HOLOGYNY
HOLOHEDRA
HOLOHEDRAL
HOLOHEDRISM
HOLOHEDRISMS
HOLOHEDRON
HOLOHEDRONS
HOLOMETABOLIC
HOLOMETABOLISM
HOLOMETABOLISMS
HOLOMETABOLOUS
HOLOMORPHIC
HOLOMORPHICALLY
HOLON

HOLONIC
HOLONICALLY
HOLONS
HOLOPHOTAL
HOLOPHOTE
HOLOPHOTES
HOLOPHRASE
HOLOPHRASES
HOLOPHRASTIC
HOLOPHYTE
HOLOPHYTES
HOLOPHYTIC
HOLOPHYTISM
HOLOPHYTISMS
HOLOPLANKTON
HOLOPLANKTONS
HOLOPTIC
HOLOSTERIC
HOLOTHURIAN
HOLOTHURIANS
HOLOTYPE
HOLOTYPES
HOLOTYPIC
HOLOZOIC
HOLP
HOLPEN
HOLS
HOLSTEIN
HOLSTEINS
HOLSTER
HOLSTERED
HOLSTERS
HOLT
HOLTS
HOLY
HOLYDAM
HOLYDAME
HOLYDAMES
HOLYDAMS
HOLYDAY
HOLYDAYS
HOLYSTONE
HOLYSTONED
HOLYSTONES
HOLYSTONING
HOLYTIDE
HOLYTIDES
HOM
HOMA
HOMAGE
HOMAGED
HOMAGER
HOMAGERS
HOMAGES
HOMAGING
HOMALOGRAPHIC

HOMALOID
HOMALOIDAL
HOMALOIDS
HOMBRE
HOMBRES
HOMBURG
HOMBURGS
HOME
HOMEBODIES
HOMEBODY
HOMEBOUND
HOMEBOY
HOMEBOYS
HOMEBRED
HOMEBREDS
HOMEBUILT
HOMEBUYER
HOMEBUYERS
HOMECOMING
HOMECOMINGS
HOMECRAFT
HOMECRAFTS
HOMED
HOMEFELT
HOMEGIRL
HOMEGIRLISH
HOMEGIRLS
HOMEGIRLY
HOMEGROWN
HOMELAND
HOMELANDS
HOMELESS
HOMELESSNESS
HOMELESSNESSES
HOMELIER
HOMELIEST
HOMELIKE
HOMELILY
HOMELINESS
HOMELINESSES
HOMELY
HOMELYN
HOMELYNS
HOMEMADE
HOMEMAKER
HOMEMAKERS
HOMEMAKING
HOMEMAKINGS
HOMEOBOX
HOMEOBOXES
HOMEOMERIC
HOMEOMERIES
HOMEOMEROUS
HOMEOMERY
HOMEOMORPH
HOMEOMORPHIC

HOMEOMORPHIES
HOMEOMORPHISM
HOMEOMORPHISMS
HOMEOMORPHOUS
HOMEOMORPHS
HOMEOMORPHY
HOMEOPATH
HOMEOPATHIC
HOMEOPATHICALLY
HOMEOPATHIES
HOMEOPATHIST
HOMEOPATHISTS
HOMEOPATHS
HOMEOPATHY
HOMEOSES
HOMEOSIS
HOMEOSTASES
HOMEOSTASIS
HOMEOSTATIC
HOMEOTELEUTON
HOMEOTELEUTONS
HOMEOTHERM
HOMEOTHERMAL
HOMEOTHERMIC
HOMEOTHERMIES
HOMEOTHERMOUS
HOMEOTHERMS
HOMEOTHERMY
HOMEOTIC
HOMEOTYPIC
HOMEOTYPICAL
HOMEOTYPICALLY
HOMEOWNER
HOMEOWNERS
HOMEOWNERSHIP
HOMEPORT
HOMEPORTED
HOMEPORTING
HOMEPORTS
HOMER
HOMERED
HOMERING
HOMEROOM
HOMEROOMS
HOMERS
HOMES
HOMESCHOOL
HOMESCHOOLED
HOMESCHOOLER
HOMESCHOOLERS
HOMESCHOOLING
HOMESCHOOLS
HOMESCREETCH
HOMESCREETCHES
HOMESICK
HOMESICKNESS

HOMESICKNESSES
HOMESITE
HOMESITES
HOMESPUN
HOMESPUNS
HOMESTALL
HOMESTALLS
HOMESTAY
HOMESTAYS
HOMESTEAD
HOMESTEADED
HOMESTEADER
HOMESTEADERS
HOMESTEADING
HOMESTEADINGS
HOMESTEADS
HOMESTRETCH
HOMESTRETCHES
HOMETOWN
HOMETOWNS
HOMEWARD
HOMEWARDS
HOMEWARE
HOMEWARES
HOMEWORK
HOMEWORKER
HOMEWORKERS
HOMEWORKING
HOMEWORKINGS
HOMEWORKS
HOMEY
HOMEYNESS
HOMEYNESSES
HOMICIDAL
HOMICIDALLY
HOMICIDE
HOMICIDES
HOMIE
HOMIER
HOMIES
HOMIEST
HOMILETIC
HOMILETICAL
HOMILETICALLY
HOMILETICS
HOMILIES
HOMILIST
HOMILISTS
HOMILY
HOMINES
HOMINESS
HOMINESSES
HOMING
HOMINGS
HOMINIAN
HOMINIANS

HOMINID
HOMINIDS
HOMINIES
HOMININE
HOMINIZATION
HOMINIZATIONS
HOMINIZE
HOMINIZED
HOMINIZES
HOMINIZING
HOMINOID
HOMINOIDS
HOMINY
HOMME
HOMMES
HOMMOCK
HOMMOCKS
HOMMOS
HOMMOSES
HOMO
HOMOBLASTIC
HOMOBLASTIES
HOMOBLASTY
HOMOCENTRIC
HOMOCENTRICALLY
HOMOCERCAL
HOMOCHLAMYDEOUS
HOMOCHROMATIC
HOMOCHROMATISM
HOMOCHROMIES
HOMOCHROMOUS
HOMOCHROMY
HOMOCYCLIC
HOMOCYSTEINE
HOMOCYSTEINIC
HOMODONT
HOMODYNE
HOMOEOBOX
HOMOEOMERIC
HOMOEOMERIES
HOMOEOMEROUS
HOMOEOMERY
HOMOEOMORPH
HOMOEOMORPHIC
HOMOEOMORPHIES
HOMOEOMORPHISM
HOMOEOMORPHISMS
HOMOEOMORPHOUS
HOMOEOMORPHS
HOMOEOMORPHY
HOMOEOPATH
HOMOEOPATHIC
HOMOEOPATHIES
HOMOEOPATHIST
HOMOEOPATHISTS
HOMOEOPATHS

HOMOEOPATHY
HOMOEOSES
HOMOEOSIS
HOMOEOSTASES
HOMOEOSTASIS
HOMOEOSTATIC
HOMOEOTELEUTON
HOMOEOTELEUTONS
HOMOEOTHERMAL
HOMOEOTHERMIC
HOMOEOTIC
HOMOEOTYPIC
HOMOEOTYPICAL
HOMOEROTIC
HOMOEROTICISM
HOMOEROTICISMS
HOMOEROTISM
HOMOEROTISMS
HOMOGAMETIC
HOMOGAMIC
HOMOGAMIES
HOMOGAMOUS
HOMOGAMY
HOMOGENATE
HOMOGENATES
HOMOGENEITIES
HOMOGENEITY
HOMOGENEOUS
HOMOGENEOUSLY
HOMOGENEOUSNESS
HOMOGENESES
HOMOGENESIS
HOMOGENETIC
HOMOGENETICAL
HOMOGENIES
HOMOGENISATION
HOMOGENISATIONS
HOMOGENISE
HOMOGENISED
HOMOGENISER
HOMOGENISERS
HOMOGENISES
HOMOGENISING
HOMOGENIZATION
HOMOGENIZATIONS
HOMOGENIZE
HOMOGENIZED
HOMOGENIZER
HOMOGENIZERS
HOMOGENIZES
HOMOGENIZING
HOMOGENOUS
HOMOGENY
HOMOGONIES
HOMOGONOUS
HOMOGONOUSLY

HOMOGONY
HOMOGRAFT
HOMOGRAFTS
HOMOGRAPH
HOMOGRAPHIC
HOMOGRAPHS
HOMOIOMEROUS
HOMOIOTHERM
HOMOIOTHERMAL
HOMOIOTHERMIC
HOMOIOTHERMS
HOMOIOTHERMY
HOMOIOUSIAN
HOMOIOUSIANS
HOMOLOG
HOMOLOGATE
HOMOLOGATED
HOMOLOGATES
HOMOLOGATING
HOMOLOGATION
HOMOLOGATIONS
HOMOLOGIC
HOMOLOGICAL
HOMOLOGICALLY
HOMOLOGIES
HOMOLOGISE
HOMOLOGISED
HOMOLOGISER
HOMOLOGISERS
HOMOLOGISES
HOMOLOGISING
HOMOLOGIZE
HOMOLOGIZED
HOMOLOGIZER
HOMOLOGIZERS
HOMOLOGIZES
HOMOLOGIZING
HOMOLOGOUMENA
HOMOLOGOUS
HOMOLOGRAPHIC
HOMOLOGS
HOMOLOGUE
HOMOLOGUES
HOMOLOGUMENA
HOMOLOGY
HOMOLOSINE
HOMOLYSES
HOMOLYSIS
HOMOLYTIC
HOMOMORPH
HOMOMORPHIC
HOMOMORPHICALLY
HOMOMORPHISM
HOMOMORPHISMS
HOMOMORPHOSES
HOMOMORPHOSIS

HOMOMORPHOUS
HOMOMORPHOUSLY
HOMOMORPHS
HOMOMORPHY
HOMONUCLEAR
HOMONYM
HOMONYMIC
HOMONYMIES
HOMONYMITIES
HOMONYMITY
HOMONYMOUS
HOMONYMOUSLY
HOMONYMS
HOMONYMY
HOMOOUSIAN
HOMOOUSIANS
HOMOPHILE
HOMOPHILES
HOMOPHOBE
HOMOPHOBES
HOMOPHOBIA
HOMOPHOBIAS
HOMOPHOBIC
HOMOPHONE
HOMOPHONES
HOMOPHONIC
HOMOPHONICALLY
HOMOPHONIES
HOMOPHONOUS
HOMOPHONY
HOMOPHYLIES
HOMOPHYLLIC
HOMOPHYLY
HOMOPLASIES
HOMOPLASMIES
HOMOPLASMY
HOMOPLASTIC
HOMOPLASTICALLY
HOMOPLASTIES
HOMOPLASTY
HOMOPLASY
HOMOPOLAR
HOMOPOLARITIES
HOMOPOLARITY
HOMOPOLYMER
HOMOPOLYMERIC
HOMOPOLYMERS
HOMOPTERAN
HOMOPTERANS
HOMOPTEROUS
HOMORGANIC
HOMORGANICALLY
HOMOS
HOMOSCEDASTIC
HOMOSEX
HOMOSEXES

HOMOSEXUAL
HOMOSEXUALISM
HOMOSEXUALISMS
HOMOSEXUALIST
HOMOSEXUALISTS
HOMOSEXUALITIES
HOMOSEXUALITY
HOMOSEXUALLY
HOMOSEXUALS
HOMOSOCIAL
HOMOSOCIALITIES
HOMOSOCIALITY
HOMOSPORIES
HOMOSPOROUS
HOMOSPORY
HOMOTAXES
HOMOTAXIAL
HOMOTAXIALLY
HOMOTAXIC
HOMOTAXIS
HOMOTHALLIC
HOMOTHALLIES
HOMOTHALLISM
HOMOTHALLISMS
HOMOTHALLY
HOMOTHERMAL
HOMOTHERMIC
HOMOTHERMOUS
HOMOTHERMY
HOMOTONIC
HOMOTONIES
HOMOTONOUS
HOMOTONY
HOMOTRANSPLANT
HOMOTRANSPLANTS
HOMOTYPAL
HOMOTYPE
HOMOTYPES
HOMOTYPIC
HOMOTYPIES
HOMOTYPY
HOMOUSIAN
HOMOUSIANS
HOMOZYGOSES
HOMOZYGOSIS
HOMOZYGOSITIES
HOMOZYGOSITY
HOMOZYGOTE
HOMOZYGOTES
HOMOZYGOTIC
HOMOZYGOUS
HOMOZYGOUSLY
HOMUNCLE
HOMUNCLES
HOMUNCULAR
HOMUNCULE

HOMUNCULES
HOMUNCULI
HOMUNCULUS
HOMY
HON
HONAN
HONANS
HONCHO
HONCHOED
HONCHOES
HONCHOING
HONCHOS
HOND
HONDA
HONDAS
HONDLE
HONDLED
HONDLES
HONDLING
HONDS
HONE
HONED
HONER
HONERS
HONES
HONEST
HONESTER
HONESTEST
HONESTIES
HONESTLY
HONESTNESS
HONESTY
HONEWORT
HONEWORTS
HONEY
HONEYBEE
HONEYBEES
HONEYBUN
HONEYBUNCH
HONEYBUNCHES
HONEYBUNS
HONEYCOMB
HONEYCOMBED
HONEYCOMBING
HONEYCOMBINGS
HONEYCOMBS
HONEYCREEPER
HONEYCREEPERS
HONEYDEW
HONEYDEWED
HONEYDEWS
HONEYEATER
HONEYEATERS
HONEYED
HONEYEDLY
HONEYEDNESS

HONEYFUL
HONEYGUIDE
HONEYGUIDES
HONEYING
HONEYLESS
HONEYMONTH
HONEYMONTHED
HONEYMONTHING
HONEYMONTHS
HONEYMOON
HONEYMOONED
HONEYMOONER
HONEYMOONERS
HONEYMOONING
HONEYMOONS
HONEYPOT
HONEYPOTS
HONEYS
HONEYSUCKER
HONEYSUCKERS
HONEYSUCKLE
HONEYSUCKLED
HONEYSUCKLES
HONEYTRAP
HONEYTRAPPED
HONEYTRAPPER
HONEYTRAPPERS
HONEYTRAPPING
HONEYTRAPS
HONG
HONGI
HONGING
HONGIS
HONGS
HONIED
HONIEDLY
HONING
HONK
HONKED
HONKER
HONKERS
HONKEY
HONKEYS
HONKIE
HONKIES
HONKING
HONKS
HONKY
HONOR
HONORABILITIES
HONORABILITY
HONORABLE
HONORABLENESS
HONORABLENESSES
HONORABLY
HONORAND

HONORANDS
HONORARIA
HONORARIES
HONORARILY
HONORARIUM
HONORARIUMS
HONORARY
HONORED
HONOREE
HONOREES
HONORER
HONORERS
HONORIFIC
HONORIFICAL
HONORIFICALLY
HONORIFICS
HONORING
HONORLESS
HONORLESSLY
HONORLESSNESS
HONORS
HONOUR
HONOURABLE
HONOURABLENESS
HONOURABLY
HONOURED
HONOURER
HONOURERS
HONOURING
HONOURLESS
HONOURS
HONS
HOO
HOOCH
HOOCHES
HOOD
HOODED
HOODEDNESS
HOODEDNESSES
HOODIA
HOODIAS
HOODIE
HOODIER
HOODIES
HOODIEST
HOODING
HOODLESS
HOODLIKE
HOODLUM
HOODLUMISH
HOODLUMISM
HOODLUMISMS
HOODLUMS
HOODMAN
HOODMEN
HOODOO

HOODOOED
HOODOOING
HOODOOISM
HOODOOISMS
HOODOOS
HOODS
HOODWINK
HOODWINKED
HOODWINKER
HOODWINKERS
HOODWINKING
HOODWINKS
HOODY
HOOEY
HOOEYS
HOOF
HOOFBEAT
HOOFBEATS
HOOFBOUND
HOOFED
HOOFER
HOOFERS
HOOFING
HOOFLESS
HOOFLIKE
HOOFPRINT
HOOFPRINTS
HOOFROT
HOOFROTS
HOOFS
HOOK
HOOKA
HOOKAH
HOOKAHS
HOOKAS
HOOKCHECK
HOOKCHECKS
HOOKED
HOOKEDNESS
HOOKEDNESSES
HOOKER
HOOKERS
HOOKEY
HOOKEYS
HOOKIER
HOOKIES
HOOKIEST
HOOKING
HOOKLESS
HOOKLET
HOOKLETS
HOOKLIKE
HOOKNOSE
HOOKNOSED
HOOKNOSES
HOOKS

HOOKUP
HOOKUPS
HOOKWORM
HOOKWORMS
HOOKY
HOOLACHAN
HOOLACHANS
HOOLEY
HOOLEYS
HOOLICAN
HOOLICANS
HOOLIE
HOOLIER
HOOLIES
HOOLIEST
HOOLIGAN
HOOLIGANISM
HOOLIGANISMS
HOOLIGANS
HOOLOCK
HOOLOCKS
HOOLY
HOON
HOONS
HOOP
HOOPED
HOOPER
HOOPERS
HOOPING
HOOPLA
HOOPLAS
HOOPLESS
HOOPLIKE
HOOPOE
HOOPOES
HOOPOO
HOOPOOS
HOOPS
HOOPSKIRT
HOOPSKIRTS
HOOPSTER
HOOPSTERS
HOORAH
HOORAHED
HOORAHING
HOORAHS
HOORAY
HOORAYED
HOORAYING
HOORAYS
HOORD
HOORDS
HOOROO
HOOSEGOW
HOOSEGOWS
HOOSGOW

HOOSGOWS
HOOSH
HOOSHED
HOOSHES
HOOSHING
HOOT
HOOTANANNIE
HOOTANANNIES
HOOTANANNY
HOOTCH
HOOTCHES
HOOTED
HOOTENANNIE
HOOTENANNIES
HOOTENANNY
HOOTER
HOOTERS
HOOTIER
HOOTIEST
HOOTING
HOOTNANNIE
HOOTNANNIES
HOOTNANNY
HOOTS
HOOTY
HOOVE
HOOVED
HOOVEN
HOOVER
HOOVERED
HOOVERING
HOOVERS
HOOVES
HOOVING
HOP
HOPBIND
HOPBINDS
HOPBINE
HOPBINES
HOPDOG
HOPDOGS
HOPE
HOPED
HOPEFUL
HOPEFULLY
HOPEFULNESS
HOPEFULNESSES
HOPEFULS
HOPELESS
HOPELESSLY
HOPELESSNESS
HOPELESSNESSES
HOPER
HOPERS
HOPES
HOPHEAD

HOPHEADS
HOPING
HOPINGLY
HOPLITE
HOPLITES
HOPLITIC
HOPLOLOGIES
HOPLOLOGIST
HOPLOLOGISTS
HOPLOLOGY
HOPPED
HOPPER
HOPPERCAR
HOPPERCARS
HOPPERS
HOPPIER
HOPPIEST
HOPPING
HOPPINGS
HOPPLE
HOPPLED
HOPPLER
HOPPLERS
HOPPLES
HOPPLING
HOPPY
HOPS
HOPSACK
HOPSACKING
HOPSACKINGS
HOPSACKS
HOPSCOTCH
HOPSCOTCHED
HOPSCOTCHES
HOPSCOTCHING
HOPTOAD
HOPTOADS
HORA
HORAH
HORAHS
HORAL
HORARY
HORAS
HORDE
HORDED
HORDEIN
HORDEINS
HORDEOLA
HORDEOLUM
HORDES
HORDING
HORDOCK
HORDOCKS
HORE
HOREHOUND
HOREHOUNDS

HORI
HORIS
HORIZON
HORIZONAL
HORIZONLESS
HORIZONS
HORIZONTAL
HORIZONTALITIES
HORIZONTALITY
HORIZONTALLY
HORIZONTALNESS
HORIZONTALS
HORKEY
HORKEYS
HORLICKS
HORLICKSES
HORME
HORMES
HORMIC
HORMOGONIA
HORMOGONIUM
HORMONAL
HORMONALLY
HORMONE
HORMONELIKE
HORMONES
HORMONIC
HORN
HORNBEAK
HORNBEAKS
HORNBEAM
HORNBEAMS
HORNBILL
HORNBILLS
HORNBLENDE
HORNBLENDES
HORNBLENDIC
HORNBOOK
HORNBOOKS
HORNBUG
HORNBUGS
HORNED
HORNEDNESS
HORNEDNESSES
HORNER
HORNERS
HORNET
HORNETS
HORNFELS
HORNFUL
HORNFULS
HORNGELD
HORNGELDS
HORNIER
HORNIEST
HORNILY

HORNINESS
HORNINESSES
HORNING
HORNINGS
HORNISH
HORNIST
HORNISTS
HORNITO
HORNITOS
HORNLESS
HORNLESSNESS
HORNLESSNESSES
HORNLET
HORNLETS
HORNLIKE
HORNPIPE
HORNPIPES
HORNPOUT
HORNPOUTS
HORNS
HORNSTONE
HORNSTONES
HORNSWOGGLE
HORNSWOGGLED
HORNSWOGGLES
HORNSWOGGLING
HORNTAIL
HORNTAILS
HORNWORK
HORNWORKS
HORNWORM
HORNWORMS
HORNWORT
HORNWORTS
HORNWRACK
HORNWRACKS
HORNY
HORNYHEAD
HORNYHEADS
HORNYWINK
HORNYWINKS
HOROEKA
HOROEKAS
HOROGRAPHER
HOROGRAPHERS
HOROGRAPHIES
HOROGRAPHY
HOROLOGE
HOROLOGER
HOROLOGERS
HOROLOGES
HOROLOGIA
HOROLOGIC
HOROLOGICAL
HOROLOGIES
HOROLOGION

HOROLOGIST
HOROLOGISTS
HOROLOGIUM
HOROLOGIUMS
HOROLOGY
HOROMETRICAL
HOROMETRIES
HOROMETRY
HOROPITO
HOROPITOS
HOROPTER
HOROSCOPE
HOROSCOPES
HOROSCOPIC
HOROSCOPIES
HOROSCOPIST
HOROSCOPISTS
HOROSCOPY
HORRENDOUS
HORRENDOUSLY
HORRENDOUSNESS
HORRENT
HORRIBLE
HORRIBLENESS
HORRIBLENESSES
HORRIBLES
HORRIBLY
HORRID
HORRIDER
HORRIDEST
HORRIDLY
HORRIDNESS
HORRIDNESSES
HORRIFIC
HORRIFICALLY
HORRIFICATION
HORRIFICATIONS
HORRIFIED
HORRIFIES
HORRIFY
HORRIFYING
HORRIFYINGLY
HORRIPILANT
HORRIPILATE
HORRIPILATED
HORRIPILATES
HORRIPILATING
HORRIPILATION
HORRIPILATIONS
HORRISONANT
HORRISONOUS
HORROR
HORRORS
HORS
HORSE
HORSEBACK

HORSEBACKS
HORSEBEAN
HORSEBEANS
HORSEBOX
HORSEBOXES
HORSECAR
HORSECARS
HORSED
HORSEFEATHERS
HORSEFLESH
HORSEFLESHES
HORSEFLIES
HORSEFLY
HORSEHAIR
HORSEHAIRS
HORSEHIDE
HORSEHIDES
HORSELAUGH
HORSELAUGHS
HORSELEECH
HORSELEECHES
HORSELESS
HORSELIKE
HORSEMAN
HORSEMANSHIP
HORSEMANSHIPS
HORSEMEAT
HORSEMEATS
HORSEMEN
HORSEMINT
HORSEMINTS
HORSEPLAY
HORSEPLAYER
HORSEPLAYERS
HORSEPLAYS
HORSEPOND
HORSEPONDS
HORSEPOWER
HORSEPOWERS
HORSEPOX
HORSEPOXES
HORSERADISH
HORSERADISHES
HORSES
HORSESHIT
HORSESHITS
HORSESHOD
HORSESHOE
HORSESHOED
HORSESHOEING
HORSESHOEINGS
HORSESHOER
HORSESHOERS
HORSESHOES
HORSETAIL
HORSETAILS

HORSEWAY
HORSEWAYS
HORSEWEED
HORSEWEEDS
HORSEWHIP
HORSEWHIPPED
HORSEWHIPPER
HORSEWHIPPERS
HORSEWHIPPING
HORSEWHIPS
HORSEWOMAN
HORSEWOMEN
HORSEY
HORSIER
HORSIEST
HORSILY
HORSINESS
HORSINESSES
HORSING
HORSINGS
HORSON
HORSONS
HORST
HORSTE
HORSTES
HORSTS
HORSY
HORTATION
HORTATIONS
HORTATIVE
HORTATIVELY
HORTATORILY
HORTATORY
HORTICULTURAL
HORTICULTURALLY
HORTICULTURE
HORTICULTURES
HORTICULTURIST
HORTICULTURISTS
HOS
HOSANNA
HOSANNAED
HOSANNAH
HOSANNAING
HOSANNAS
HOSE
HOSED
HOSEL
HOSELS
HOSEMAN
HOSEMEN
HOSEN
HOSEPIPE
HOSEPIPES
HOSER
HOSERS

HOSES
HOSIER
HOSIERIES
HOSIERS
HOSIERY
HOSING
HOSPICE
HOSPICES
HOSPITABLE
HOSPITABLENESS
HOSPITABLY
HOSPITAGE
HOSPITAGES
HOSPITAL
HOSPITALE
HOSPITALER
HOSPITALERS
HOSPITALES
HOSPITALISATION
HOSPITALISE
HOSPITALISED
HOSPITALISES
HOSPITALISING
HOSPITALITIES
HOSPITALITY
HOSPITALIZATION
HOSPITALIZE
HOSPITALIZED
HOSPITALIZES
HOSPITALIZING
HOSPITALLER
HOSPITALLERS
HOSPITALS
HOSPITIA
HOSPITIUM
HOSPODAR
HOSPODARS
HOSS
HOSSES
HOST
HOSTA
HOSTAGE
HOSTAGES
HOSTAS
HOSTED
HOSTEL
HOSTELED
HOSTELER
HOSTELERS
HOSTELING
HOSTELLED
HOSTELLER
HOSTELLERS
HOSTELLING
HOSTELLINGS
HOSTELRIES

HOSTELRY
HOSTELS
HOSTESS
HOSTESSED
HOSTESSES
HOSTESSING
HOSTIE
HOSTIES
HOSTILE
HOSTILELY
HOSTILES
HOSTILITIES
HOSTILITY
HOSTING
HOSTINGS
HOSTLER
HOSTLERS
HOSTLESSE
HOSTLY
HOSTRIES
HOSTRY
HOSTS
HOT
HOTBED
HOTBEDS
HOTBLOOD
HOTBLOODS
HOTBOX
HOTBOXES
HOTCAKE
HOTCAKES
HOTCH
HOTCHED
HOTCHES
HOTCHING
HOTCHPOT
HOTCHPOTCH
HOTCHPOTCHES
HOTCHPOTS
HOTDOG
HOTDOGGED
HOTDOGGER
HOTDOGGERS
HOTDOGGING
HOTDOGS
HOTE
HOTEL
HOTELDOM
HOTELDOMS
HOTELIER
HOTELIERS
HOTELMAN
HOTELMEN
HOTELS
HOTEN
HOTFOOT

HOTFOOTED
HOTFOOTING
HOTFOOTS
HOTHEAD
HOTHEADED
HOTHEADEDLY
HOTHEADEDNESS
HOTHEADEDNESSES
HOTHEADS
HOTHOUSE
HOTHOUSES
HOTLINE
HOTLINES
HOTLY
HOTNESS
HOTNESSES
HOTPLATE
HOTPLATED
HOTPLATES
HOTPOT
HOTPOTS
HOTPRESS
HOTPRESSED
HOTPRESSES
HOTPRESSING
HOTROD
HOTRODS
HOTS
HOTSHOT
HOTSHOTS
HOTSPUR
HOTSPURS
HOTTED
HOTTENTOT
HOTTENTOTS
HOTTER
HOTTERED
HOTTERING
HOTTERS
HOTTEST
HOTTIE
HOTTIES
HOTTING
HOTTINGS
HOTTISH
HOTTY
HOUDAH
HOUDAHS
HOUDAN
HOUDANS
HOUF
HOUFED
HOUFF
HOUFFED
HOUFFING
HOUFFS

HOUFING
HOUFS
HOUGH
HOUGHED
HOUGHING
HOUGHMAGANDIE
HOUGHMAGANDIES
HOUGHS
HOUMMOS
HOUMMOSES
HOUMOUS
HOUMOUSES
HOUMUS
HOUMUSES
HOUND
HOUNDED
HOUNDER
HOUNDERS
HOUNDFISH
HOUNDFISHES
HOUNDING
HOUNDS
HOUNGAN
HOUNGANS
HOUR
HOURGLASS
HOURGLASSES
HOURI
HOURIS
HOURLONG
HOURLY
HOURPLATE
HOURPLATES
HOURS
HOUSE
HOUSEBOAT
HOUSEBOATER
HOUSEBOATERS
HOUSEBOATS
HOUSEBOUND
HOUSEBOY
HOUSEBOYS
HOUSEBREAK
HOUSEBREAKER
HOUSEBREAKERS
HOUSEBREAKING
HOUSEBREAKINGS
HOUSEBREAKS
HOUSEBROKE
HOUSEBROKEN
HOUSECARL
HOUSECARLS
HOUSECLEAN
HOUSECLEANED
HOUSECLEANING
HOUSECLEANINGS

HOUSECLEANS	HOUSEMISTRESS	HOVEA	HOWL
HOUSECOAT	HOUSEMISTRESSES	HOVEAS	HOWLBACK
HOUSECOATS	HOUSEMOTHER	HOVED	HOWLBACKS
HOUSECRAFT	HOUSEMOTHERS	HOVEL	HOWLED
HOUSECRAFTS	HOUSEPAINTER	HOVELED	HOWLER
HOUSED	HOUSEPAINTERS	HOVELING	HOWLERS
HOUSEDRESS	HOUSEPARENT	HOVELLED	HOWLET
HOUSEDRESSES	HOUSEPARENTS	HOVELLER	HOWLETS
HOUSEFATHER	HOUSEPERSON	HOVELLERS	HOWLING
HOUSEFATHERS	HOUSEPERSONS	HOVELLING	HOWLINGLY
HOUSEFLIES	HOUSEPLANT	HOVELS	HOWLINGS
HOUSEFLY	HOUSEPLANTS	HOVEN	HOWLROUND
HOUSEFRONT	HOUSER	HOVER	HOWLROUNDS
HOUSEFRONTS	HOUSEROOM	HOVERCRAFT	HOWLS
HOUSEFUL	HOUSEROOMS	HOVERCRAFTS	HOWRE
HOUSEFULS	HOUSERS	HOVERED	HOWRES
HOUSEGUEST	HOUSES	HOVERER	HOWS
HOUSEGUESTS	HOUSESAT	HOVERERS	HOWSO
HOUSEHOLD	HOUSESIT	HOVERING	HOWSOEVER
HOUSEHOLDER	HOUSESITS	HOVERINGLY	HOWSOMDEVER
HOUSEHOLDERS	HOUSESITTING	HOVERPORT	HOWSOMEVER
HOUSEHOLDERSHIP	HOUSETOP	HOVERPORTS	HOWTOWDIE
HOUSEHOLDS	HOUSETOPS	HOVERS	HOWTOWDIES
HOUSEHUSBAND	HOUSEWARES	HOVERTRAIN	HOWZAT
HOUSEHUSBANDS	HOUSEWARMING	HOVERTRAINS	HOWZIT
HOUSEKEEP	HOUSEWARMINGS	HOVES	HOWZITS
HOUSEKEEPER	HOUSEWIFE	HOVING	HOX
HOUSEKEEPERS	HOUSEWIFELINESS	HOW	HOXED
HOUSEKEEPING	HOUSEWIFELY	HOWBE	HOXES
HOUSEKEEPINGS	HOUSEWIFERIES	HOWBEIT	HOXING
HOUSEKEEPS	HOUSEWIFERY	HOWDAH	HOY
HOUSEKEPT	HOUSEWIFESHIP	HOWDAHS	HOYA
HOUSEL	HOUSEWIFESHIPS	HOWDIE	HOYAS
HOUSELED	HOUSEWIFESKEP	HOWDIED	HOYDEN
HOUSELEEK	HOUSEWIFESKEPS	HOWDIES	HOYDENED
HOUSELEEKS	HOUSEWIFEY	HOWDY	HOYDENHOOD
HOUSELESS	HOUSEWIVES	HOWDYING	HOYDENHOODS
HOUSELESSNESS	HOUSEWORK	HOWE	HOYDENING
HOUSELESSNESSES	HOUSEWORKER	HOWES	HOYDENISH
HOUSELIGHTS	HOUSEWORKERS	HOWEVER	HOYDENISHLY
HOUSELINE	HOUSEWORKING	HOWF	HOYDENISHNESS
HOUSELINED	HOUSEWORKS	HOWFED	HOYDENISM
HOUSELINES	HOUSEY	HOWFF	HOYDENISMS
HOUSELING	HOUSIER	HOWFFED	HOYDENS
HOUSELLED	HOUSIEST	HOWFFING	HOYED
HOUSELLING	HOUSING	HOWFFS	HOYING
HOUSELLINGS	HOUSINGS	HOWFING	HOYLE
HOUSELS	HOUSLING	HOWFS	HOYLES
HOUSEMAID	HOUSTONIA	HOWITZER	HOYS
HOUSEMAIDS	HOUSTONIAS	HOWITZERS	HRYVNA
HOUSEMAN	HOUT	HOWK	HRYVNAS
HOUSEMASTER	HOUTED	HOWKED	HRYVNIA
HOUSEMASTERS	HOUTING	HOWKER	HRYVNIAS
HOUSEMATE	HOUTINGS	HOWKERS	HUANACO
HOUSEMATES	HOUTS	HOWKING	HUANACOS
HOUSEMEN	HOVE	HOWKS	HUAQUERO

473

HUAQUEROS
HUARACHE
HUARACHES
HUARACHO
HUARACHOS
HUB
HUBBIES
HUBBLY
HUBBUB
HUBBUBOO
HUBBUBOOS
HUBBUBS
HUBBY
HUBCAP
HUBCAPS
HUBRIS
HUBRISES
HUBRISTIC
HUBRISTICALLY
HUBS
HUCK
HUCKABACK
HUCKABACKS
HUCKERY
HUCKLE
HUCKLEBERRIES
HUCKLEBERRY
HUCKLEBERRYING
HUCKLEBERRYINGS
HUCKLEBONE
HUCKLEBONES
HUCKLES
HUCKS
HUCKSTER
HUCKSTERAGE
HUCKSTERAGES
HUCKSTERED
HUCKSTERESS
HUCKSTERESSES
HUCKSTERIES
HUCKSTERING
HUCKSTERISM
HUCKSTERISMS
HUCKSTERS
HUCKSTERY
HUCKSTRESS
HUCKSTRESSES
HUDDEN
HUDDLE
HUDDLED
HUDDLER
HUDDLERS
HUDDLES
HUDDLING
HUDDUP
HUDIBRASTIC

HUDIBRASTICALLY
HUDIBRASTICS
HUE
HUED
HUELESS
HUER
HUERS
HUES
HUFF
HUFFED
HUFFIER
HUFFIEST
HUFFILY
HUFFINESS
HUFFINESSES
HUFFING
HUFFISH
HUFFISHLY
HUFFISHNESS
HUFFISHNESSES
HUFFKIN
HUFFKINS
HUFFS
HUFFY
HUG
HUGE
HUGELY
HUGENESS
HUGENESSES
HUGEOUS
HUGEOUSLY
HUGEOUSNESS
HUGEOUSNESSES
HUGER
HUGEST
HUGGABLE
HUGGED
HUGGER
HUGGERMUGGER
HUGGERMUGGERED
HUGGERMUGGERING
HUGGERMUGGERS
HUGGERS
HUGGIER
HUGGIEST
HUGGILY
HUGGING
HUGGY
HUGS
HUGY
HUH
HUHU
HUHUS
HUI
HUIA
HUIAS

HUIC
HUIES
HUIPIL
HUIPILES
HUIPILS
HUIS
HUISACHE
HUISACHES
HUISSIER
HUISSIERS
HUITAIN
HUITAINS
HULA
HULAS
HULE
HULES
HULK
HULKED
HULKIER
HULKIEST
HULKING
HULKS
HULKY
HULL
HULLABALLOO
HULLABALLOOS
HULLABALOO
HULLABALOOS
HULLED
HULLER
HULLERS
HULLIER
HULLIEST
HULLING
HULLO
HULLOA
HULLOAED
HULLOAING
HULLOAS
HULLOED
HULLOES
HULLOING
HULLOS
HULLS
HULLY
HUM
HUMA
HUMAN
HUMANE
HUMANELY
HUMANENESS
HUMANENESSES
HUMANER
HUMANEST
HUMANISATION
HUMANISATIONS

HUMANISE
HUMANISED
HUMANISER
HUMANISERS
HUMANISES
HUMANISING
HUMANISM
HUMANISMS
HUMANIST
HUMANISTIC
HUMANISTICALLY
HUMANISTS
HUMANITARIAN
HUMANITARIANISM
HUMANITARIANIST
HUMANITARIANS
HUMANITIES
HUMANITY
HUMANIZATION
HUMANIZATIONS
HUMANIZE
HUMANIZED
HUMANIZER
HUMANIZERS
HUMANIZES
HUMANIZING
HUMANKIND
HUMANKINDS
HUMANLIKE
HUMANLY
HUMANNESS
HUMANNESSES
HUMANOID
HUMANOIDS
HUMANS
HUMAS
HUMATE
HUMATES
HUMBLE
HUMBLEBEE
HUMBLEBEES
HUMBLED
HUMBLENESS
HUMBLENESSES
HUMBLER
HUMBLERS
HUMBLES
HUMBLESSE
HUMBLESSES
HUMBLEST
HUMBLING
HUMBLINGLY
HUMBLINGS
HUMBLY
HUMBUCKER
HUMBUCKERED

HUMBUCKERS
HUMBUG
HUMBUGGABLE
HUMBUGGED
HUMBUGGER
HUMBUGGERIES
HUMBUGGERS
HUMBUGGERY
HUMBUGGING
HUMBUGS
HUMBUZZ
HUMBUZZES
HUMDINGER
HUMDINGERS
HUMDRUM
HUMDRUMLY
HUMDRUMNESS
HUMDRUMS
HUMDUDGEON
HUMDUDGEONS
HUMECT
HUMECTANT
HUMECTANTS
HUMECTATE
HUMECTATED
HUMECTATES
HUMECTATING
HUMECTATION
HUMECTATIONS
HUMECTED
HUMECTING
HUMECTIVE
HUMECTIVES
HUMECTS
HUMEFIED
HUMEFIES
HUMEFY
HUMEFYING
HUMERAL
HUMERALS
HUMERI
HUMERUS
HUMF
HUMFED
HUMFING
HUMFS
HUMGRUFFIANS
HUMGRUFFIN
HUMGRUFFINS
HUMHUM
HUMHUMS
HUMIC
HUMICOLE
HUMICOLES
HUMICOLOUS
HUMID

HUMIDER
HUMIDEST
HUMIDEX
HUMIDEXES
HUMIDIFICATION
HUMIDIFICATIONS
HUMIDIFIED
HUMIDIFIER
HUMIDIFIERS
HUMIDIFIES
HUMIDIFY
HUMIDIFYING
HUMIDISTAT
HUMIDISTATS
HUMIDITIES
HUMIDITY
HUMIDLY
HUMIDNESS
HUMIDNESSES
HUMIDOR
HUMIDORS
HUMIFICATION
HUMIFICATIONS
HUMIFIED
HUMIFIES
HUMIFY
HUMIFYING
HUMILIANT
HUMILIATE
HUMILIATED
HUMILIATES
HUMILIATING
HUMILIATINGLY
HUMILIATION
HUMILIATIONS
HUMILIATIVE
HUMILIATOR
HUMILIATORS
HUMILIATORY
HUMILITIES
HUMILITY
HUMITE
HUMITES
HUMLIE
HUMLIES
HUMMABLE
HUMMAUM
HUMMAUMS
HUMMED
HUMMEL
HUMMELLED
HUMMELLER
HUMMELLERS
HUMMELLING
HUMMELS
HUMMER

HUMMERS
HUMMING
HUMMINGBIRD
HUMMINGBIRDS
HUMMINGS
HUMMOCK
HUMMOCKED
HUMMOCKING
HUMMOCKS
HUMMOCKY
HUMMUM
HUMMUMS
HUMMUS
HUMMUSES
HUMOGEN
HUMOGENS
HUMONGOUS
HUMOR
HUMORAL
HUMORALISM
HUMORALISMS
HUMORALIST
HUMORALISTS
HUMORALLY
HUMORED
HUMORESK
HUMORESKS
HUMORESQUE
HUMORESQUES
HUMORFUL
HUMORING
HUMORIST
HUMORISTIC
HUMORISTS
HUMORLESS
HUMORLESSLY
HUMORLESSNESS
HUMORLESSNESSES
HUMOROUS
HUMOROUSLY
HUMOROUSNESS
HUMOROUSNESSES
HUMORS
HUMORSOME
HUMORSOMELY
HUMORSOMENESS
HUMOUR
HUMOURED
HUMOURFUL
HUMOURFULLY
HUMOURING
HUMOURLESS
HUMOURLESSLY
HUMOURLESSNESS
HUMOURS
HUMOURSOME

HUMOURSOMENESS
HUMOUS
HUMP
HUMPBACK
HUMPBACKED
HUMPBACKS
HUMPED
HUMPEN
HUMPENS
HUMPER
HUMPERS
HUMPH
HUMPHED
HUMPHING
HUMPHS
HUMPIER
HUMPIES
HUMPIEST
HUMPILY
HUMPINESS
HUMPINESSES
HUMPING
HUMPLESS
HUMPLIKE
HUMPS
HUMPTIES
HUMPTY
HUMPY
HUMS
HUMSTRUM
HUMSTRUMS
HUMUNGOUS
HUMUS
HUMUSES
HUMUSY
HUMVEE
HUMVEES
HUN
HUNCH
HUNCHBACK
HUNCHBACKED
HUNCHBACKS
HUNCHED
HUNCHES
HUNCHING
HUNDRED
HUNDREDER
HUNDREDERS
HUNDREDFOLD
HUNDREDFOLDS
HUNDREDOR
HUNDREDORS
HUNDREDS
HUNDREDTH
HUNDREDTHS
HUNDREDWEIGHT

HUNDREDWEIGHTS
HUNG
HUNGAN
HUNGANS
HUNGER
HUNGERED
HUNGERFUL
HUNGERING
HUNGERINGLY
HUNGERLY
HUNGERS
HUNGOVER
HUNGRIER
HUNGRIEST
HUNGRILY
HUNGRINESS
HUNGRINESSES
HUNGRY
HUNH
HUNK
HUNKER
HUNKERED
HUNKERING
HUNKERS
HUNKIER
HUNKIES
HUNKIEST
HUNKS
HUNKSES
HUNKY
HUNNISH
HUNS
HUNT
HUNTABLE
HUNTAWAY
HUNTAWAYS
HUNTED
HUNTEDLY
HUNTER
HUNTERS
HUNTIEGOWKS
HUNTING
HUNTINGS
HUNTRESS
HUNTRESSES
HUNTS
HUNTSMAN
HUNTSMANSHIP
HUNTSMANSHIPS
HUNTSMEN
HUP
HUPAITHRIC
HUPPAH
HUPPAHS
HUPPED
HUPPING

HUPS
HURCHEON
HURCHEONS
HURDEN
HURDENS
HURDIES
HURDLE
HURDLED
HURDLER
HURDLERS
HURDLES
HURDLING
HURDLINGS
HURDS
HURL
HURLBARROW
HURLBARROWS
HURLBAT
HURLBATS
HURLED
HURLER
HURLERS
HURLEY
HURLEYS
HURLIES
HURLING
HURLINGS
HURLS
HURLY
HURRA
HURRAED
HURRAH
HURRAHED
HURRAHING
HURRAHS
HURRAING
HURRAS
HURRAY
HURRAYED
HURRAYING
HURRAYS
HURRICANE
HURRICANES
HURRICANO
HURRICANOES
HURRIED
HURRIEDLY
HURRIEDNESS
HURRIEDNESSES
HURRIER
HURRIERS
HURRIES
HURRY
HURRYING
HURRYINGLY
HURRYINGS

HURST
HURSTS
HURT
HURTER
HURTERS
HURTFUL
HURTFULLY
HURTFULNESS
HURTFULNESSES
HURTING
HURTLE
HURTLEBERRIES
HURTLEBERRY
HURTLED
HURTLES
HURTLESS
HURTLESSLY
HURTLESSNESS
HURTLESSNESSES
HURTLING
HURTS
HUSBAND
HUSBANDAGE
HUSBANDAGES
HUSBANDED
HUSBANDER
HUSBANDERS
HUSBANDING
HUSBANDLAND
HUSBANDLANDS
HUSBANDLESS
HUSBANDLIKE
HUSBANDLY
HUSBANDMAN
HUSBANDMEN
HUSBANDRIES
HUSBANDRY
HUSBANDS
HUSH
HUSHABIED
HUSHABIES
HUSHABY
HUSHABYING
HUSHED
HUSHEDLY
HUSHER
HUSHERED
HUSHERING
HUSHERS
HUSHES
HUSHFUL
HUSHIER
HUSHIEST
HUSHING
HUSHY
HUSK

HUSKED
HUSKER
HUSKERS
HUSKIER
HUSKIES
HUSKIEST
HUSKILY
HUSKINESS
HUSKINESSES
HUSKING
HUSKINGS
HUSKLIKE
HUSKS
HUSKY
HUSO
HUSOS
HUSS
HUSSAR
HUSSARS
HUSSES
HUSSIES
HUSSIF
HUSSIFS
HUSSY
HUSTINGS
HUSTLE
HUSTLED
HUSTLER
HUSTLERS
HUSTLES
HUSTLING
HUSTLINGS
HUSWIFE
HUSWIFES
HUSWIVES
HUT
HUTCH
HUTCHED
HUTCHES
HUTCHIE
HUTCHIED
HUTCHIES
HUTCHING
HUTIA
HUTIAS
HUTLIKE
HUTMENT
HUTMENTS
HUTS
HUTTED
HUTTING
HUTTINGS
HUTZPA
HUTZPAH
HUTZPAHS
HUTZPAS

HUZOOR
HUZOORS
HUZZA
HUZZAED
HUZZAH
HUZZAHED
HUZZAHING
HUZZAHS
HUZZAING
HUZZAS
HUZZIES
HUZZY
HWAN
HWYL
HWYLS
HYACINE
HYACINES
HYACINTH
HYACINTHINE
HYACINTHS
HYAENA
HYAENAS
HYAENIC
HYALIN
HYALINE
HYALINES
HYALINISATION
HYALINISATIONS
HYALINISE
HYALINISED
HYALINISES
HYALINISING
HYALINIZATION
HYALINIZATIONS
HYALINIZE
HYALINIZED
HYALINIZES
HYALINIZING
HYALINS
HYALITE
HYALITES
HYALOGEN
HYALOGENS
HYALOID
HYALOIDS
HYALOMELAN
HYALOMELANES
HYALOMELANS
HYALONEMA
HYALONEMAS
HYALOPHANE
HYALOPHANES
HYALOPLASM
HYALOPLASMIC
HYALOPLASMS
HYALURONIC

HYALURONIDASE
HYALURONIDASES
HYBRID
HYBRIDISABLE
HYBRIDISATION
HYBRIDISATIONS
HYBRIDISE
HYBRIDISED
HYBRIDISER
HYBRIDISERS
HYBRIDISES
HYBRIDISING
HYBRIDISM
HYBRIDISMS
HYBRIDITIES
HYBRIDITY
HYBRIDIZABLE
HYBRIDIZATION
HYBRIDIZATIONS
HYBRIDIZE
HYBRIDIZED
HYBRIDIZER
HYBRIDIZERS
HYBRIDIZES
HYBRIDIZING
HYBRIDOMA
HYBRIDOMAS
HYBRIDOUS
HYBRIDS
HYBRIS
HYBRISES
HYBRISTIC
HYBRISTICALLY
HYDANTOIN
HYDANTOINS
HYDATHODE
HYDATHODES
HYDATID
HYDATIDIFORM
HYDATIDS
HYDATOID
HYDNOCARPATE
HYDNOCARPATES
HYDNOCARPIC
HYDRA
HYDRACID
HYDRACIDS
HYDRAE
HYDRAEMIA
HYDRAEMIAS
HYDRAGOG
HYDRAGOGS
HYDRAGOGUE
HYDRAGOGUES
HYDRALAZINE
HYDRALAZINES

HYDRANGEA
HYDRANGEAS
HYDRANT
HYDRANTH
HYDRANTHS
HYDRANTS
HYDRARGYRIA
HYDRARGYRIC
HYDRARGYRISM
HYDRARGYRISMS
HYDRARGYRUM
HYDRARGYRUMS
HYDRARTHROSES
HYDRARTHROSIS
HYDRAS
HYDRASE
HYDRASES
HYDRASTINE
HYDRASTINES
HYDRASTININE
HYDRASTININES
HYDRASTIS
HYDRASTISES
HYDRATE
HYDRATED
HYDRATES
HYDRATING
HYDRATION
HYDRATIONS
HYDRATOR
HYDRATORS
HYDRAULIC
HYDRAULICALLY
HYDRAULICKED
HYDRAULICKING
HYDRAULICS
HYDRAZIDE
HYDRAZIDES
HYDRAZINE
HYDRAZINES
HYDRAZOIC
HYDREMIA
HYDREMIAS
HYDRIA
HYDRIAE
HYDRIAS
HYDRIC
HYDRICALLY
HYDRID
HYDRIDE
HYDRIDES
HYDRIDS
HYDRILLA
HYDRILLAS
HYDRIODIC
HYDRO

HYDROACOUSTICS
HYDROBIOLOGICAL
HYDROBIOLOGIES
HYDROBIOLOGIST
HYDROBIOLOGISTS
HYDROBIOLOGY
HYDROBROMIC
HYDROCARBON
HYDROCARBONS
HYDROCELE
HYDROCELES
HYDROCELLULOSE
HYDROCELLULOSES
HYDROCEPHALIC
HYDROCEPHALICS
HYDROCEPHALIES
HYDROCEPHALOID
HYDROCEPHALOUS
HYDROCEPHALUS
HYDROCEPHALUSES
HYDROCEPHALY
HYDROCHLORIC
HYDROCHLORIDE
HYDROCHLORIDES
HYDROCHORE
HYDROCHORES
HYDROCHORIC
HYDROCOLLOID
HYDROCOLLOIDAL
HYDROCOLLOIDS
HYDROCORAL
HYDROCORALLINE
HYDROCORALLINES
HYDROCORALS
HYDROCORTISONE
HYDROCORTISONES
HYDROCRACK
HYDROCRACKED
HYDROCRACKER
HYDROCRACKERS
HYDROCRACKING
HYDROCRACKINGS
HYDROCRACKS
HYDROCYANIC
HYDRODYNAMIC
HYDRODYNAMICAL
HYDRODYNAMICIST
HYDRODYNAMICS
HYDROELASTIC
HYDROELECTRIC
HYDROEXTRACTOR
HYDROEXTRACTORS
HYDROFLUORIC
HYDROFOIL
HYDROFOILS
HYDROFORMING

HYDROFORMINGS
HYDROGEL
HYDROGELS
HYDROGEN
HYDROGENASE
HYDROGENASES
HYDROGENATE
HYDROGENATED
HYDROGENATES
HYDROGENATING
HYDROGENATION
HYDROGENATIONS
HYDROGENATOR
HYDROGENATORS
HYDROGENISATION
HYDROGENISE
HYDROGENISED
HYDROGENISES
HYDROGENISING
HYDROGENIZATION
HYDROGENIZE
HYDROGENIZED
HYDROGENIZES
HYDROGENIZING
HYDROGENOLYSES
HYDROGENOLYSIS
HYDROGENOUS
HYDROGENS
HYDROGEOLOGICAL
HYDROGEOLOGIES
HYDROGEOLOGIST
HYDROGEOLOGISTS
HYDROGEOLOGY
HYDROGRAPH
HYDROGRAPHER
HYDROGRAPHERS
HYDROGRAPHIC
HYDROGRAPHICAL
HYDROGRAPHIES
HYDROGRAPHS
HYDROGRAPHY
HYDROID
HYDROIDS
HYDROKINETIC
HYDROKINETICAL
HYDROKINETICS
HYDROLASE
HYDROLASES
HYDROLOGIC
HYDROLOGICAL
HYDROLOGICALLY
HYDROLOGIES
HYDROLOGIST
HYDROLOGISTS
HYDROLOGY
HYDROLYSABILITY

HYDROLYSABLE
HYDROLYSATE
HYDROLYSATES
HYDROLYSATION
HYDROLYSATIONS
HYDROLYSE
HYDROLYSED
HYDROLYSER
HYDROLYSERS
HYDROLYSES
HYDROLYSING
HYDROLYSIS
HYDROLYTE
HYDROLYTES
HYDROLYTIC
HYDROLYTICALLY
HYDROLYZABLE
HYDROLYZATE
HYDROLYZATES
HYDROLYZATION
HYDROLYZATIONS
HYDROLYZE
HYDROLYZED
HYDROLYZER
HYDROLYZERS
HYDROLYZES
HYDROLYZING
HYDROMA
HYDROMAGNETIC
HYDROMAGNETICS
HYDROMANCER
HYDROMANCERS
HYDROMANCIES
HYDROMANCY
HYDROMANIA
HYDROMANIAS
HYDROMANTIC
HYDROMANTICALLY
HYDROMAS
HYDROMECHANICAL
HYDROMECHANICS
HYDROMEDUSA
HYDROMEDUSAE
HYDROMEDUSAN
HYDROMEDUSANS
HYDROMEDUSAS
HYDROMEDUSOID
HYDROMEDUSOIDS
HYDROMEL
HYDROMELS
HYDROMETALLURGY
HYDROMETEOR
HYDROMETEORS
HYDROMETER
HYDROMETERS
HYDROMETRIC

HYDROMETRICAL
HYDROMETRICALLY
HYDROMETRIES
HYDROMETRY
HYDROMORPHIC
HYDRONAUT
HYDRONAUTS
HYDRONEPHROSES
HYDRONEPHROSIS
HYDRONEPHROTIC
HYDRONIC
HYDRONICALLY
HYDRONIUM
HYDRONIUMS
HYDROPATH
HYDROPATHIC
HYDROPATHICAL
HYDROPATHICALLY
HYDROPATHICS
HYDROPATHIES
HYDROPATHIST
HYDROPATHISTS
HYDROPATHS
HYDROPATHY
HYDROPEROXIDE
HYDROPEROXIDES
HYDROPHANE
HYDROPHANES
HYDROPHANOUS
HYDROPHILE
HYDROPHILES
HYDROPHILIC
HYDROPHILICITY
HYDROPHILIES
HYDROPHILITE
HYDROPHILITES
HYDROPHILOUS
HYDROPHILY
HYDROPHOBIA
HYDROPHOBIAS
HYDROPHOBIC
HYDROPHOBICITY
HYDROPHOBOUS
HYDROPHONE
HYDROPHONES
HYDROPHYTE
HYDROPHYTES
HYDROPHYTIC
HYDROPHYTON
HYDROPHYTONS
HYDROPHYTOUS
HYDROPIC
HYDROPLANE
HYDROPLANED
HYDROPLANES
HYDROPLANING

HYDROPNEUMATIC
HYDROPOLYP
HYDROPOLYPS
HYDROPONIC
HYDROPONICALLY
HYDROPONICS
HYDROPOWER
HYDROPOWERS
HYDROPS
HYDROPSES
HYDROPSIES
HYDROPSY
HYDROPTIC
HYDROPULT
HYDROPULTS
HYDROQUINOL
HYDROQUINOLS
HYDROQUINONE
HYDROQUINONES
HYDROS
HYDROSCOPE
HYDROSCOPES
HYDROSCOPIC
HYDROSCOPICAL
HYDROSCOPICALLY
HYDROSCOPICS
HYDROSERE
HYDROSERES
HYDROSKI
HYDROSKIS
HYDROSOL
HYDROSOLIC
HYDROSOLS
HYDROSOMA
HYDROSOMAL
HYDROSOMATA
HYDROSOMATOUS
HYDROSOME
HYDROSOMES
HYDROSPACE
HYDROSPACES
HYDROSPHERE
HYDROSPHERES
HYDROSPHERIC
HYDROSTAT
HYDROSTATIC
HYDROSTATICAL
HYDROSTATICALLY
HYDROSTATICS
HYDROSTATS
HYDROSULPHATE
HYDROSULPHATES
HYDROSULPHIDE
HYDROSULPHIDES
HYDROSULPHITE
HYDROSULPHITES

HYDROSULPHURIC
HYDROSULPHUROUS
HYDROTACTIC
HYDROTAXES
HYDROTAXIS
HYDROTHECA
HYDROTHECAE
HYDROTHERAPIC
HYDROTHERAPIES
HYDROTHERAPIST
HYDROTHERAPISTS
HYDROTHERAPY
HYDROTHERMAL
HYDROTHERMALLY
HYDROTHORACES
HYDROTHORACIC
HYDROTHORAX
HYDROTHORAXES
HYDROTROPIC
HYDROTROPICALLY
HYDROTROPISM
HYDROTROPISMS
HYDROUS
HYDROVANE
HYDROVANES
HYDROXIDE
HYDROXIDES
HYDROXONIUM
HYDROXY
HYDROXYAPATITE
HYDROXYAPATITES
HYDROXYL
HYDROXYLAMINE
HYDROXYLAMINES
HYDROXYLAPATITE
HYDROXYLASE
HYDROXYLASES
HYDROXYLATE
HYDROXYLATED
HYDROXYLATES
HYDROXYLATING
HYDROXYLATION
HYDROXYLATIONS
HYDROXYLIC
HYDROXYLS
HYDROXYPROLINE
HYDROXYPROLINES
HYDROXYUREA
HYDROXYUREAS
HYDROXYZINE
HYDROXYZINES
HYDROZINCITE
HYDROZINCITES
HYDROZOA
HYDROZOAN
HYDROZOANS

HYDROZOON
HYDYNE
HYDYNES
HYE
HYED
HYEING
HYEN
HYENA
HYENAS
HYENIC
HYENINE
HYENOID
HYENS
HYES
HYETAL
HYETOGRAPH
HYETOGRAPHIC
HYETOGRAPHICAL
HYETOGRAPHIES
HYETOGRAPHS
HYETOGRAPHY
HYETOLOGIES
HYETOLOGY
HYETOMETER
HYETOMETERS
HYETOMETROGRAPH
HYGEIST
HYGEISTS
HYGIEIST
HYGIEISTS
HYGIENE
HYGIENES
HYGIENIC
HYGIENICALLY
HYGIENICS
HYGIENIST
HYGIENISTS
HYGRISTOR
HYGRISTORS
HYGROCHASIES
HYGROCHASTIC
HYGROCHASY
HYGRODEIK
HYGRODEIKS
HYGROGRAPH
HYGROGRAPHIC
HYGROGRAPHICAL
HYGROGRAPHS
HYGROLOGIES
HYGROLOGY
HYGROMA
HYGROMAS
HYGROMETER
HYGROMETERS
HYGROMETRIC
HYGROMETRICAL

HYGROMETRICALLY
HYGROMETRIES
HYGROMETRY
HYGROPHIL
HYGROPHILE
HYGROPHILES
HYGROPHILOUS
HYGROPHOBE
HYGROPHYTE
HYGROPHYTES
HYGROPHYTIC
HYGROSCOPE
HYGROSCOPES
HYGROSCOPIC
HYGROSCOPICAL
HYGROSCOPICALLY
HYGROSCOPICITY
HYGROSTAT
HYGROSTATS
HYING
HYKE
HYKES
HYLA
HYLAS
HYLDING
HYLDINGS
HYLE
HYLEG
HYLEGS
HYLES
HYLIC
HYLICISM
HYLICISMS
HYLICIST
HYLICISTS
HYLISM
HYLISMS
HYLIST
HYLISTS
HYLOBATE
HYLOBATES
HYLOGENESES
HYLOGENESIS
HYLOIST
HYLOISTS
HYLOMORPHIC
HYLOMORPHISM
HYLOMORPHISMS
HYLOPATHISM
HYLOPATHISMS
HYLOPATHIST
HYLOPATHISTS
HYLOPHAGOUS
HYLOPHYTE
HYLOPHYTES
HYLOTHEISM

HYLOTHEISMS
HYLOTHEIST
HYLOTHEISTS
HYLOTOMOUS
HYLOZOIC
HYLOZOICAL
HYLOZOISM
HYLOZOISMS
HYLOZOIST
HYLOZOISTIC
HYLOZOISTICALLY
HYLOZOISTS
HYMEN
HYMENAEAL
HYMENAEAN
HYMENAL
HYMENEAL
HYMENEALLY
HYMENEALS
HYMENEAN
HYMENIA
HYMENIAL
HYMENIUM
HYMENIUMS
HYMENOPHORE
HYMENOPHORES
HYMENOPHOROUS
HYMENOPTERA
HYMENOPTERAN
HYMENOPTERANS
HYMENOPTERON
HYMENOPTERONS
HYMENOPTEROUS
HYMENS
HYMN
HYMNAL
HYMNALS
HYMNARIES
HYMNARY
HYMNBOOK
HYMNBOOKS
HYMNED
HYMNIC
HYMNING
HYMNIST
HYMNISTS
HYMNLESS
HYMNLIKE
HYMNODICAL
HYMNODICALLY
HYMNODIES
HYMNODIST
HYMNODISTS
HYMNODY
HYMNOGRAPHER
HYMNOGRAPHERS

HYMNOGRAPHIES
HYMNOGRAPHY
HYMNOLOGIC
HYMNOLOGICAL
HYMNOLOGICALLY
HYMNOLOGIES
HYMNOLOGIST
HYMNOLOGISTS
HYMNOLOGY
HYMNS
HYNDE
HYNDES
HYOID
HYOIDAL
HYOIDEAN
HYOIDS
HYOPLASTRA
HYOPLASTRAL
HYOPLASTRON
HYOSCINE
HYOSCINES
HYOSCYAMINE
HYOSCYAMINES
HYOSCYAMUS
HYOSCYAMUSES
HYP
HYPABYSSAL
HYPABYSSALLY
HYPAESTHESIA
HYPAESTHESIC
HYPAETHRAL
HYPAETHRON
HYPAETHRONS
HYPALGESIA
HYPALGESIAS
HYPALGESIC
HYPALGIA
HYPALGIAS
HYPALLACTIC
HYPALLAGE
HYPALLAGES
HYPANTHIA
HYPANTHIAL
HYPANTHIUM
HYPATE
HYPATES
HYPE
HYPED
HYPER
HYPERACID
HYPERACIDITIES
HYPERACIDITY
HYPERACTION
HYPERACTIONS
HYPERACTIVE
HYPERACTIVES

HYPERACTIVITIES
HYPERACTIVITY
HYPERACUITIES
HYPERACUITY
HYPERACUSES
HYPERACUSIS
HYPERACUTE
HYPERACUTENESS
HYPERADRENALISM
HYPERAEMIA
HYPERAEMIAS
HYPERAEMIC
HYPERAESTHESIA
HYPERAESTHESIAS
HYPERAESTHESIC
HYPERAESTHETIC
HYPERAGGRESSIVE
HYPERALERT
HYPERALGESIA
HYPERALGESIAS
HYPERALGESIC
HYPERARID
HYPERAROUSAL
HYPERAROUSALS
HYPERAWARE
HYPERAWARENESS
HYPERBARIC
HYPERBARICALLY
HYPERBATIC
HYPERBATICALLY
HYPERBATON
HYPERBATONS
HYPERBOLA
HYPERBOLAE
HYPERBOLAS
HYPERBOLE
HYPERBOLES
HYPERBOLIC
HYPERBOLICAL
HYPERBOLICALLY
HYPERBOLISE
HYPERBOLISED
HYPERBOLISES
HYPERBOLISING
HYPERBOLISM
HYPERBOLISMS
HYPERBOLIST
HYPERBOLISTS
HYPERBOLIZE
HYPERBOLIZED
HYPERBOLIZES
HYPERBOLIZING
HYPERBOLOID
HYPERBOLOIDAL
HYPERBOLOIDS
HYPERBOREAN

HYPERBOREANS
HYPERCALCAEMIA
HYPERCALCAEMIAS
HYPERCALCEMIA
HYPERCALCEMIAS
HYPERCALCEMIC
HYPERCAPNIA
HYPERCAPNIAS
HYPERCAPNIC
HYPERCARBIA
HYPERCARBIC
HYPERCATABOLISM
HYPERCATALECTIC
HYPERCATALEXES
HYPERCATALEXIS
HYPERCAUTIOUS
HYPERCHARGE
HYPERCHARGED
HYPERCHARGES
HYPERCHARGING
HYPERCIVILISED
HYPERCIVILIZED
HYPERCLASSICAL
HYPERCOAGULABLE
HYPERCOLOUR
HYPERCOLOURS
HYPERCOMPLEX
HYPERCONFIDENCE
HYPERCONFIDENT
HYPERCONFORMIST
HYPERCONFORMITY
HYPERCONSCIOUS
HYPERCORRECT
HYPERCORRECTION
HYPERCORRECTLY
HYPERCRITIC
HYPERCRITICAL
HYPERCRITICALLY
HYPERCRITICISE
HYPERCRITICISED
HYPERCRITICISES
HYPERCRITICISM
HYPERCRITICISMS
HYPERCRITICIZE
HYPERCRITICIZED
HYPERCRITICIZES
HYPERCRITICS
HYPERCUBE
HYPERCUBES
HYPERDACTYL
HYPERDACTYLIES
HYPERDACTYLY
HYPERDORIAN
HYPERDULIA
HYPERDULIAS
HYPERDULIC

HYPERDULICAL
HYPEREFFICIENT
HYPERELEGANCE
HYPERELEGANT
HYPERELEGANTLY
HYPEREMESES
HYPEREMESIS
HYPEREMETIC
HYPEREMIA
HYPEREMIAS
HYPEREMIC
HYPEREMOTIONAL
HYPERENDEMIC
HYPERENERGETIC
HYPERENTHUSIASM
HYPERESTHESIA
HYPERESTHESIAS
HYPERESTHETIC
HYPEREUTECTIC
HYPEREUTECTOID
HYPEREXCITABLE
HYPEREXCITED
HYPEREXCITEMENT
HYPEREXCRETION
HYPEREXCRETIONS
HYPEREXTEND
HYPEREXTENDED
HYPEREXTENDING
HYPEREXTENDS
HYPEREXTENSION
HYPEREXTENSIONS
HYPERFASTIDIOUS
HYPERFINE
HYPERFOCAL
HYPERFUNCTION
HYPERFUNCTIONAL
HYPERFUNCTIONS
HYPERGAMIES
HYPERGAMOUS
HYPERGAMY
HYPERGEOMETRIC
HYPERGEOMETRICS
HYPERGLYCAEMIA
HYPERGLYCAEMIAS
HYPERGLYCAEMIC
HYPERGLYCEMIA
HYPERGLYCEMIAS
HYPERGLYCEMIC
HYPERGOL
HYPERGOLIC
HYPERGOLICALLY
HYPERGOLS
HYPERHIDROSES
HYPERHIDROSIS
HYPERICUM
HYPERICUMS

HYPERIDROSES
HYPERIDROSIS
HYPERIMMUNE
HYPERIMMUNIZE
HYPERIMMUNIZED
HYPERIMMUNIZES
HYPERIMMUNIZING
HYPERINFLATED
HYPERINFLATION
HYPERINFLATIONS
HYPERINOSES
HYPERINOSIS
HYPERINOTIC
HYPERINSULINISM
HYPERINTENSE
HYPERINVOLUTION
HYPERIRRITABLE
HYPERKERATOSES
HYPERKERATOSIS
HYPERKERATOTIC
HYPERKINESES
HYPERKINESIA
HYPERKINESIAS
HYPERKINESIS
HYPERKINETIC
HYPERLINK
HYPERLINKS
HYPERLIPEMIA
HYPERLIPEMIAS
HYPERLIPEMIC
HYPERLIPIDAEMIA
HYPERLIPIDAEMIC
HYPERLIPIDEMIA
HYPERLIPIDEMIAS
HYPERLOGICAL
HYPERLOGICALLY
HYPERLYDIAN
HYPERMANIA
HYPERMANIAS
HYPERMANIC
HYPERMARKET
HYPERMARKETS
HYPERMART
HYPERMARTS
HYPERMASCULINE
HYPERMEDIA
HYPERMEDIAS
HYPERMETABOLIC
HYPERMETABOLISM
HYPERMETER
HYPERMETERS
HYPERMETRIC
HYPERMETRICAL
HYPERMETROPIA
HYPERMETROPIAS
HYPERMETROPIC

HYPERMETROPICAL
HYPERMETROPY
HYPERMNESIA
HYPERMNESIAS
HYPERMNESIC
HYPERMOBILITIES
HYPERMOBILITY
HYPERMODERN
HYPERMODERNIST
HYPERMODERNISTS
HYPERMODEST
HYPERMODESTLY
HYPERMODESTY
HYPERMUTABILITY
HYPERMUTABLE
HYPERNATRAEMIA
HYPERNATRAEMIAS
HYPERNORMAL
HYPERNORMALITY
HYPERNORMALLY
HYPERNYM
HYPERNYMIES
HYPERNYMS
HYPERNYMY
HYPERON
HYPERONS
HYPEROPE
HYPEROPES
HYPEROPIA
HYPEROPIAS
HYPEROPIC
HYPEROREXIA
HYPEROREXIC
HYPERORTHODOX
HYPERORTHODOXY
HYPEROSMIA
HYPEROSMIC
HYPEROSTOSES
HYPEROSTOSIS
HYPEROSTOTIC
HYPERPARASITE
HYPERPARASITES
HYPERPARASITIC
HYPERPARASITISM
HYPERPHAGIA
HYPERPHAGIAS
HYPERPHAGIC
HYPERPHRYGIAN
HYPERPHYSICAL
HYPERPHYSICALLY
HYPERPIGMENTED
HYPERPITUITARY
HYPERPLANE
HYPERPLANES
HYPERPLASIA
HYPERPLASIAS

HYPERPLASTIC
HYPERPLOID
HYPERPLOIDIES
HYPERPLOIDS
HYPERPLOIDY
HYPERPNEA
HYPERPNEAS
HYPERPNEIC
HYPERPNOEA
HYPERPOLARIZE
HYPERPOLARIZED
HYPERPOLARIZES
HYPERPOLARIZING
HYPERPOWER
HYPERPOWERFUL
HYPERPOWERS
HYPERPRODUCER
HYPERPRODUCERS
HYPERPRODUCTION
HYPERPROSEXIA
HYPERPURE
HYPERPURISM
HYPERPURIST
HYPERPURISTS
HYPERPYRETIC
HYPERPYREXIA
HYPERPYREXIAL
HYPERPYREXIAS
HYPERRATIONAL
HYPERREACTIVE
HYPERREACTIVITY
HYPERREACTOR
HYPERREACTORS
HYPERREAL
HYPERREALISM
HYPERREALISMS
HYPERREALIST
HYPERREALISTIC
HYPERREALITY
HYPERREALLY
HYPERRESPONSIVE
HYPERROMANTIC
HYPERROMANTICS
HYPERS
HYPERSALINE
HYPERSALINITIES
HYPERSALINITY
HYPERSALIVATION
HYPERSARCOMA
HYPERSARCOMAS
HYPERSARCOMATA
HYPERSARCOSES
HYPERSECRETION
HYPERSECRETIONS
HYPERSENSITISE
HYPERSENSITISED

HYPERSENSITISES
HYPERSENSITIVE
HYPERSENSITIZE
HYPERSENSITIZED
HYPERSENSITIZES
HYPERSENSUAL
HYPERSEXUAL
HYPERSEXUALITY
HYPERSOMNIA
HYPERSOMNIAS
HYPERSOMNOLENCE
HYPERSONIC
HYPERSONICALLY
HYPERSONICS
HYPERSPACE
HYPERSPACES
HYPERSPATIAL
HYPERSPATIALLY
HYPERSTATIC
HYPERSTHENE
HYPERSTHENES
HYPERSTHENIA
HYPERSTHENIAS
HYPERSTHENIC
HYPERSTHENITE
HYPERSTHENITES
HYPERSTIMULATE
HYPERSTIMULATED
HYPERSTIMULATES
HYPERSTRESS
HYPERSTRESSES
HYPERSURFACE
HYPERSURFACES
HYPERTECHNICAL
HYPERTENSE
HYPERTENSION
HYPERTENSIONS
HYPERTENSIVE
HYPERTENSIVES
HYPERTEXT
HYPERTEXTS
HYPERTHERMAL
HYPERTHERMIA
HYPERTHERMIAS
HYPERTHERMIC
HYPERTHERMY
HYPERTHYMIA
HYPERTHYMIAC
HYPERTHYROID
HYPERTHYROIDISM
HYPERTHYROIDS
HYPERTONIA
HYPERTONIAS
HYPERTONIC
HYPERTONICITIES
HYPERTONICITY

HYPERTOXIC
HYPERTOXICALLY
HYPERTOXICITY
HYPERTROPHIC
HYPERTROPHICAL
HYPERTROPHIED
HYPERTROPHIES
HYPERTROPHOUS
HYPERTROPHY
HYPERTROPHYING
HYPERTYPICAL
HYPERURBANISM
HYPERURBANISMS
HYPERURICEMIA
HYPERURICEMIAS
HYPERVELOCITIES
HYPERVELOCITY
HYPERVENTILATE
HYPERVENTILATED
HYPERVENTILATES
HYPERVIGILANCE
HYPERVIGILANCES
HYPERVIGILANT
HYPERVIRULENT
HYPERVISCOSITY
HYPES
HYPESTER
HYPESTERS
HYPESTHESIA
HYPESTHESIC
HYPETHRAL
HYPHA
HYPHAE
HYPHAL
HYPHEMIA
HYPHEMIAS
HYPHEN
HYPHENATE
HYPHENATED
HYPHENATES
HYPHENATING
HYPHENATION
HYPHENATIONS
HYPHENED
HYPHENIC
HYPHENING
HYPHENISATION
HYPHENISATIONS
HYPHENISE
HYPHENISED
HYPHENISES
HYPHENISING
HYPHENISM
HYPHENISMS
HYPHENIZATION
HYPHENIZATIONS

HYPHENIZE
HYPHENIZED
HYPHENIZES
HYPHENIZING
HYPHENLESS
HYPHENS
HYPING
HYPINOSES
HYPINOSIS
HYPNAGOGIC
HYPNIC
HYPNICS
HYPNOANALYSIS
HYPNOANALYST
HYPNOANALYTIC
HYPNOGENESES
HYPNOGENESIS
HYPNOGENETIC
HYPNOGENIC
HYPNOGENIES
HYPNOGENOUS
HYPNOGENY
HYPNOGOGIC
HYPNOID
HYPNOIDAL
HYPNOIDISE
HYPNOIDISED
HYPNOIDISES
HYPNOIDISING
HYPNOIDIZE
HYPNOIDIZED
HYPNOIDIZES
HYPNOIDIZING
HYPNOLOGIC
HYPNOLOGICAL
HYPNOLOGICALLY
HYPNOLOGIES
HYPNOLOGIST
HYPNOLOGISTS
HYPNOLOGY
HYPNONE
HYPNONES
HYPNOPAEDIA
HYPNOPAEDIAS
HYPNOPOMPIC
HYPNOSES
HYPNOSIS
HYPNOTEE
HYPNOTEES
HYPNOTHERAPIES
HYPNOTHERAPIST
HYPNOTHERAPISTS
HYPNOTHERAPY
HYPNOTIC
HYPNOTICALLY
HYPNOTICS

HYPNOTISABILITY
HYPNOTISABLE
HYPNOTISATION
HYPNOTISATIONS
HYPNOTISE
HYPNOTISED
HYPNOTISER
HYPNOTISERS
HYPNOTISES
HYPNOTISING
HYPNOTISM
HYPNOTISMS
HYPNOTIST
HYPNOTISTIC
HYPNOTISTS
HYPNOTIZABILITY
HYPNOTIZABLE
HYPNOTIZATION
HYPNOTIZATIONS
HYPNOTIZE
HYPNOTIZED
HYPNOTIZER
HYPNOTIZERS
HYPNOTIZES
HYPNOTIZING
HYPNOTOID
HYPNUM
HYPNUMS
HYPO
HYPOACID
HYPOACIDITY
HYPOAEOLIAN
HYPOALLERGENIC
HYPOBLAST
HYPOBLASTIC
HYPOBLASTS
HYPOBOLE
HYPOBOLES
HYPOCALCEMIA
HYPOCALCEMIAS
HYPOCALCEMIC
HYPOCAUST
HYPOCAUSTS
HYPOCENTER
HYPOCENTERS
HYPOCENTRAL
HYPOCENTRE
HYPOCENTRES
HYPOCHLORITE
HYPOCHLORITES
HYPOCHLOROUS
HYPOCHONDRIA
HYPOCHONDRIAC
HYPOCHONDRIACAL
HYPOCHONDRIACS
HYPOCHONDRIAS

HYPOCHONDRIASES
HYPOCHONDRIASIS
HYPOCHONDRIASM
HYPOCHONDRIASMS
HYPOCHONDRIAST
HYPOCHONDRIASTS
HYPOCHONDRIUM
HYPOCIST
HYPOCISTS
HYPOCORISM
HYPOCORISMA
HYPOCORISMAS
HYPOCORISMS
HYPOCORISTIC
HYPOCORISTICAL
HYPOCOTYL
HYPOCOTYLOUS
HYPOCOTYLS
HYPOCRISIES
HYPOCRISY
HYPOCRITE
HYPOCRITES
HYPOCRITIC
HYPOCRITICAL
HYPOCRITICALLY
HYPOCRYSTALLINE
HYPOCYCLOID
HYPOCYCLOIDAL
HYPOCYCLOIDS
HYPODERM
HYPODERMA
HYPODERMAL
HYPODERMAS
HYPODERMIC
HYPODERMICALLY
HYPODERMICS
HYPODERMIS
HYPODERMISES
HYPODERMS
HYPODIPLOID
HYPODIPLOIDIES
HYPODIPLOIDY
HYPODORIAN
HYPOED
HYPOEUTECTIC
HYPOEUTECTOID
HYPOGAEA
HYPOGAEAL
HYPOGAEAN
HYPOGAEOUS
HYPOGAEUM
HYPOGASTRIA
HYPOGASTRIC
HYPOGASTRIUM
HYPOGEA
HYPOGEAL

HYPOGEAN
HYPOGENE
HYPOGENIC
HYPOGENICALLY
HYPOGENOUS
HYPOGEOUS
HYPOGEUM
HYPOGLOSSAL
HYPOGLOSSALS
HYPOGLYCAEMIA
HYPOGLYCAEMIAS
HYPOGLYCAEMIC
HYPOGLYCEMIA
HYPOGLYCEMIAS
HYPOGLYCEMIC
HYPOGLYCEMICS
HYPOGNATHISM
HYPOGNATHISMS
HYPOGNATHOUS
HYPOGYNIES
HYPOGYNOUS
HYPOGYNY
HYPOID
HYPOING
HYPOKALEMIA
HYPOKALEMIAS
HYPOKALEMIC
HYPOLIMNIA
HYPOLIMNION
HYPOLIMNIONS
HYPOLYDIAN
HYPOMAGNESAEMIA
HYPOMAGNESEMIA
HYPOMAGNESEMIAS
HYPOMANIA
HYPOMANIAS
HYPOMANIC
HYPOMENORRHEA
HYPOMENORRHEAS
HYPOMENORRHOEA
HYPOMENORRHOEAS
HYPOMIXOLYDIAN
HYPOMORPH
HYPOMORPHIC
HYPOMORPHS
HYPONASTIC
HYPONASTICALLY
HYPONASTIES
HYPONASTY
HYPONATRAEMIA
HYPONATRAEMIC
HYPONEA
HYPONEAS
HYPONITRITE
HYPONITRITES
HYPONITROUS

HYPONOIA
HYPONOIAS
HYPONYM
HYPONYMIES
HYPONYMS
HYPONYMY
HYPOPHARYNGES
HYPOPHARYNX
HYPOPHARYNXES
HYPOPHOSPHATE
HYPOPHOSPHATES
HYPOPHOSPHITE
HYPOPHOSPHITES
HYPOPHOSPHORIC
HYPOPHOSPHOROUS
HYPOPHRYGIAN
HYPOPHYGE
HYPOPHYGES
HYPOPHYSEAL
HYPOPHYSECTOMY
HYPOPHYSES
HYPOPHYSIAL
HYPOPHYSIS
HYPOPITUITARISM
HYPOPITUITARY
HYPOPLASIA
HYPOPLASIAS
HYPOPLASTIC
HYPOPLASTRA
HYPOPLASTRON
HYPOPLASTY
HYPOPLOID
HYPOPLOIDS
HYPOPLOIDY
HYPOPNEA
HYPOPNEAS
HYPOPNOEA
HYPOPYON
HYPOPYONS
HYPOS
HYPOSENSITISE
HYPOSENSITISED
HYPOSENSITISES
HYPOSENSITISING
HYPOSENSITIZE
HYPOSENSITIZED
HYPOSENSITIZES
HYPOSENSITIZING
HYPOSPADIAS
HYPOSPADIASES
HYPOSTASES
HYPOSTASIS
HYPOSTASISATION
HYPOSTASISE
HYPOSTASISED
HYPOSTASISER

HYPOSTASISERS
HYPOSTASISES
HYPOSTASISING
HYPOSTASIZATION
HYPOSTASIZE
HYPOSTASIZED
HYPOSTASIZER
HYPOSTASIZERS
HYPOSTASIZES
HYPOSTASIZING
HYPOSTATIC
HYPOSTATICAL
HYPOSTATICALLY
HYPOSTATISATION
HYPOSTATISE
HYPOSTATISED
HYPOSTATISER
HYPOSTATISERS
HYPOSTATISES
HYPOSTATISING
HYPOSTATIZATION
HYPOSTATIZE
HYPOSTATIZED
HYPOSTATIZER
HYPOSTATIZERS
HYPOSTATIZES
HYPOSTATIZING
HYPOSTHENIA
HYPOSTHENIC
HYPOSTOME
HYPOSTOMES
HYPOSTRESS
HYPOSTRESSES
HYPOSTROPHE
HYPOSTROPHES
HYPOSTYLE
HYPOSTYLES
HYPOSULPHATE
HYPOSULPHATES
HYPOSULPHITE
HYPOSULPHITES
HYPOSULPHURIC
HYPOSULPHUROUS
HYPOTACTIC
HYPOTAXES
HYPOTAXIS
HYPOTENSION
HYPOTENSIONS
HYPOTENSIVE
HYPOTENSIVES
HYPOTENUSE
HYPOTENUSES
HYPOTHALAMI
HYPOTHALAMIC
HYPOTHALAMUS
HYPOTHEC

HYPOTHECA
HYPOTHECAE
HYPOTHECARY
HYPOTHECATE
HYPOTHECATED
HYPOTHECATES
HYPOTHECATING
HYPOTHECATION
HYPOTHECATIONS
HYPOTHECATOR
HYPOTHECATORS
HYPOTHECS
HYPOTHENUSE
HYPOTHENUSES
HYPOTHERMAL
HYPOTHERMIA
HYPOTHERMIAS
HYPOTHERMIC
HYPOTHESES
HYPOTHESIS
HYPOTHESISE
HYPOTHESISED
HYPOTHESISER
HYPOTHESISERS
HYPOTHESISES
HYPOTHESISING
HYPOTHESIST
HYPOTHESISTS
HYPOTHESIZE
HYPOTHESIZED
HYPOTHESIZER
HYPOTHESIZERS
HYPOTHESIZES
HYPOTHESIZING
HYPOTHETIC
HYPOTHETICAL
HYPOTHETICALLY
HYPOTHETISE
HYPOTHETISED
HYPOTHETISES
HYPOTHETISING
HYPOTHETIZE
HYPOTHETIZED
HYPOTHETIZES
HYPOTHETIZING
HYPOTHYMIA
HYPOTHYMIAS
HYPOTHYROID
HYPOTHYROIDISM
HYPOTHYROIDISMS
HYPOTHYROIDS
HYPOTONIA
HYPOTONIAS
HYPOTONIC
HYPOTONICITIES
HYPOTONICITY

HYPOTROCHOID
HYPOTROCHOIDS
HYPOTYPOSES
HYPOTYPOSIS
HYPOVENTILATION
HYPOXAEMIA
HYPOXAEMIAS
HYPOXAEMIC
HYPOXANTHINE
HYPOXANTHINES
HYPOXEMIA
HYPOXEMIAS
HYPOXEMIC
HYPOXIA
HYPOXIAS
HYPOXIC
HYPPED
HYPPING
HYPS
HYPSOCHROME
HYPSOCHROMES
HYPSOCHROMIC
HYPSOGRAPHIC
HYPSOGRAPHICAL
HYPSOGRAPHIES
HYPSOGRAPHY
HYPSOMETER
HYPSOMETERS
HYPSOMETRIC
HYPSOMETRICAL
HYPSOMETRICALLY
HYPSOMETRIES
HYPSOMETRIST
HYPSOMETRISTS
HYPSOMETRY
HYPSOPHOBES
HYPSOPHOBIA
HYPSOPHOBIAS
HYPSOPHYLL
HYPSOPHYLLARY
HYPSOPHYLLS
HYPURAL
HYRACES
HYRACOID
HYRACOIDEAN
HYRACOIDEANS
HYRACOIDS
HYRAX
HYRAXES
HYSON
HYSONS
HYSSOP
HYSSOPS
HYSTERANTHOUS
HYSTERECTOMIES
HYSTERECTOMISE

HYSTERECTOMISED
HYSTERECTOMISES
HYSTERECTOMIZE
HYSTERECTOMIZED
HYSTERECTOMIZES
HYSTERECTOMY
HYSTERESES
HYSTERESIAL
HYSTERESIS
HYSTERETIC
HYSTERETICALLY
HYSTERIA
HYSTERIAS
HYSTERIC
HYSTERICAL
HYSTERICALLY
HYSTERICKY
HYSTERICS
HYSTERITIS
HYSTERITISES
HYSTEROGENIC
HYSTEROGENIES
HYSTEROGENY
HYSTEROID
HYSTEROIDAL
HYSTEROMANIA
HYSTEROMANIAS
HYSTEROTOMIES
HYSTEROTOMY
HYSTRICOMORPH
HYSTRICOMORPHIC
HYSTRICOMORPHS
HYTE
HYTHE
HYTHES

I

IAMB	ICEBOX	ICHOROUS	ICICLED
IAMBI	ICEBOXES	ICHORS	ICICLES
IAMBIC	ICEBREAKER	ICHS	ICIER
IAMBICALLY	ICEBREAKERS	ICHTHIC	ICIEST
IAMBICS	ICEBREAKING	ICHTHYIC	ICILY
IAMBIST	ICECAP	ICHTHYOCOLLA	ICINESS
IAMBISTS	ICECAPS	ICHTHYOCOLLAS	ICINESSES
IAMBOGRAPHER	ICED	ICHTHYODORULITE	ICING
IAMBOGRAPHERS	ICEFALL	ICHTHYOFAUNA	ICINGS
IAMBS	ICEFALLS	ICHTHYOFAUNAE	ICK
IAMBUS	ICEFIELD	ICHTHYOFAUNAL	ICKER
IAMBUSES	ICEFIELDS	ICHTHYOFAUNAS	ICKERS
IANTHINE	ICEHOUSE	ICHTHYOID	ICKIER
IATRIC	ICEHOUSES	ICHTHYOIDAL	ICKIEST
IATRICAL	ICEKHANA	ICHTHYOIDS	ICKILY
IATROCHEMICAL	ICEKHANAS	ICHTHYOLATRIES	ICKINESS
IATROCHEMIST	ICELESS	ICHTHYOLATROUS	ICKINESSES
IATROCHEMISTRY	ICELIKE	ICHTHYOLATRY	ICKLE
IATROCHEMISTS	ICEMAN	ICHTHYOLITE	ICKY
IATROGENIC	ICEMEN	ICHTHYOLITES	ICON
IATROGENICALLY	ICEPACK	ICHTHYOLITIC	ICONES
IATROGENICITIES	ICEPACKS	ICHTHYOLOGIC	ICONIC
IATROGENICITY	ICER	ICHTHYOLOGICAL	ICONICAL
IATROGENIES	ICERS	ICHTHYOLOGIES	ICONICALLY
IATROGENY	ICES	ICHTHYOLOGIST	ICONICITIES
IBERIS	ICESTONE	ICHTHYOLOGISTS	ICONICITY
IBERISES	ICESTONES	ICHTHYOLOGY	ICONIFIED
IBEX	ICEWINE	ICHTHYOPHAGIES	ICONIFIES
IBEXES	ICEWINES	ICHTHYOPHAGIST	ICONIFY
IBICES	ICH	ICHTHYOPHAGISTS	ICONIFYING
IBIDEM	ICHABOD	ICHTHYOPHAGOUS	ICONISE
IBIS	ICHED	ICHTHYOPHAGY	ICONISED
IBISES	ICHES	ICHTHYOPSID	ICONISES
IBOGAINE	ICHING	ICHTHYOPSIDAN	ICONISING
IBOGAINES	ICHNEUMON	ICHTHYOPSIDANS	ICONIZE
IBUPROFEN	ICHNEUMONS	ICHTHYOPSIDS	ICONIZED
IBUPROFENS	ICHNITE	ICHTHYORNIS	ICONIZES
ICE	ICHNITES	ICHTHYORNISES	ICONIZING
ICEBALL	ICHNOFOSSIL	ICHTHYOSAUR	ICONOCLASM
ICEBALLS	ICHNOFOSSILS	ICHTHYOSAURI	ICONOCLASMS
ICEBERG	ICHNOGRAPHIC	ICHTHYOSAURIAN	ICONOCLAST
ICEBERGS	ICHNOGRAPHICAL	ICHTHYOSAURIANS	ICONOCLASTIC
ICEBLINK	ICHNOGRAPHIES	ICHTHYOSAURS	ICONOCLASTS
ICEBLINKS	ICHNOGRAPHY	ICHTHYOSAURUS	ICONOGRAPHER
ICEBOAT	ICHNOLITE	ICHTHYOSAURUSES	ICONOGRAPHERS
ICEBOATER	ICHNOLITES	ICHTHYOSES	ICONOGRAPHIC
ICEBOATERS	ICHNOLOGICAL	ICHTHYOSIS	ICONOGRAPHICAL
ICEBOATING	ICHNOLOGICALLY	ICHTHYOTIC	ICONOGRAPHIES
ICEBOATINGS	ICHNOLOGIES	ICHTHYS	ICONOGRAPHY
ICEBOATS	ICHNOLOGY	ICHTHYSES	ICONOLATER
ICEBOUND	ICHOR	ICICLE	ICONOLATERS

ICONOLATRIES
ICONOLATROUS
ICONOLATRY
ICONOLOGICAL
ICONOLOGIES
ICONOLOGIST
ICONOLOGISTS
ICONOLOGY
ICONOMACHIES
ICONOMACHIST
ICONOMACHISTS
ICONOMACHY
ICONOMATIC
ICONOMATICISM
ICONOMATICISMS
ICONOMETER
ICONOMETERS
ICONOMETRIES
ICONOMETRY
ICONOPHILISM
ICONOPHILISMS
ICONOPHILIST
ICONOPHILISTS
ICONOSCOPE
ICONOSCOPES
ICONOSTAS
ICONOSTASES
ICONOSTASIS
ICONS
ICOSAHEDRA
ICOSAHEDRAL
ICOSAHEDRON
ICOSAHEDRONS
ICOSANDRIAN
ICOSANDROUS
ICOSITETRAHEDRA
ICTAL
ICTERIC
ICTERICAL
ICTERICALS
ICTERICS
ICTERID
ICTERIDS
ICTERINE
ICTERITIOUS
ICTERUS
ICTERUSES
ICTIC
ICTUS
ICTUSES
ICY
ID
IDANT
IDANTS
IDE
IDEA

IDEAED
IDEAL
IDEALESS
IDEALISATION
IDEALISATIONS
IDEALISE
IDEALISED
IDEALISER
IDEALISERS
IDEALISES
IDEALISING
IDEALISM
IDEALISMS
IDEALIST
IDEALISTIC
IDEALISTICALLY
IDEALISTS
IDEALITIES
IDEALITY
IDEALIZATION
IDEALIZATIONS
IDEALIZE
IDEALIZED
IDEALIZER
IDEALIZERS
IDEALIZES
IDEALIZING
IDEALLESS
IDEALLY
IDEALNESS
IDEALOGIES
IDEALOGUE
IDEALOGUES
IDEALOGY
IDEALS
IDEAS
IDEATA
IDEATE
IDEATED
IDEATES
IDEATING
IDEATION
IDEATIONAL
IDEATIONALLY
IDEATIONS
IDEATIVE
IDEATUM
IDEE
IDEES
IDEM
IDEMPOTENCIES
IDEMPOTENCY
IDEMPOTENT
IDEMPOTENTS
IDENT
IDENTIC

IDENTICAL
IDENTICALLY
IDENTICALNESS
IDENTICALNESSES
IDENTIFIABLE
IDENTIFIABLY
IDENTIFICATION
IDENTIFICATIONS
IDENTIFIED
IDENTIFIER
IDENTIFIERS
IDENTIFIES
IDENTIFY
IDENTIFYING
IDENTIKIT
IDENTIKITS
IDENTITIES
IDENTITY
IDEOGRAM
IDEOGRAMIC
IDEOGRAMMATIC
IDEOGRAMMIC
IDEOGRAMS
IDEOGRAPH
IDEOGRAPHIC
IDEOGRAPHICAL
IDEOGRAPHICALLY
IDEOGRAPHIES
IDEOGRAPHS
IDEOGRAPHY
IDEOLOGIC
IDEOLOGICAL
IDEOLOGICALLY
IDEOLOGIES
IDEOLOGIST
IDEOLOGISTS
IDEOLOGIZE
IDEOLOGIZED
IDEOLOGIZES
IDEOLOGIZING
IDEOLOGUE
IDEOLOGUES
IDEOLOGY
IDEOMOTOR
IDEOPHONE
IDEOPHONES
IDEOPRAXIST
IDEOPRAXISTS
IDES
IDIOBLAST
IDIOBLASTIC
IDIOBLASTS
IDIOCIES
IDIOCY
IDIOGLOSSIA
IDIOGLOSSIAS

IDIOGRAM
IDIOGRAMS
IDIOGRAPH
IDIOGRAPHIC
IDIOGRAPHS
IDIOLECT
IDIOLECTAL
IDIOLECTIC
IDIOLECTS
IDIOM
IDIOMATIC
IDIOMATICAL
IDIOMATICALLY
IDIOMATICALNESS
IDIOMATICNESS
IDIOMATICNESSES
IDIOMORPHIC
IDIOMORPHICALLY
IDIOMORPHISM
IDIOMS
IDIOPATHIC
IDIOPATHICALLY
IDIOPATHIES
IDIOPATHY
IDIOPHONE
IDIOPHONES
IDIOPHONIC
IDIOPLASM
IDIOPLASMATIC
IDIOPLASMIC
IDIOPLASMS
IDIORRHYTHMIC
IDIORRHYTHMIC
IDIOSYNCRASIES
IDIOSYNCRASY
IDIOSYNCRATIC
IDIOSYNCRATICAL
IDIOT
IDIOTCIES
IDIOTCY
IDIOTHERMOUS
IDIOTIC
IDIOTICAL
IDIOTICALLY
IDIOTICALNESS
IDIOTICON
IDIOTICONS
IDIOTISH
IDIOTISM
IDIOTISMS
IDIOTS
IDLE
IDLED
IDLEHOOD
IDLEHOODS
IDLENESS

IDLENESSES	IDOLS	IGNITE	IGUANODONS
IDLER	IDOLUM	IGNITED	IHRAM
IDLERS	IDOLUMS	IGNITER	IHRAMS
IDLES	IDONEITIES	IGNITERS	IJTIHAD
IDLESSE	IDONEITY	IGNITES	IJTIHADS
IDLESSES	IDONEOUS	IGNITIBILITIES	IKAN
IDLEST	IDOXURIDINE	IGNITIBILITY	IKAT
IDLING	IDOXURIDINES	IGNITIBLE	IKATS
IDLY	IDS	IGNITING	IKEBANA
IDOCRASE	IDYL	IGNITION	IKEBANAS
IDOCRASES	IDYLIST	IGNITIONS	IKON
IDOL	IDYLISTS	IGNITOR	IKONS
IDOLA	IDYLL	IGNITORS	ILEA
IDOLATER	IDYLLIAN	IGNITRON	ILEAC
IDOLATERS	IDYLLIC	IGNITRONS	ILEAL
IDOLATOR	IDYLLICALLY	IGNOBILITIES	ILEITIDES
IDOLATORS	IDYLLIST	IGNOBILITY	ILEITIS
IDOLATRESS	IDYLLISTS	IGNOBLE	ILEITISES
IDOLATRESSES	IDYLLS	IGNOBLENESS	ILEOSTOMIES
IDOLATRIES	IDYLS	IGNOBLENESSES	ILEOSTOMY
IDOLATRISE	IF	IGNOBLER	ILEUM
IDOLATRISED	IFF	IGNOBLEST	ILEUMS
IDOLATRISER	IFFIER	IGNOBLY	ILEUS
IDOLATRISES	IFFIEST	IGNOMIES	ILEUSES
IDOLATRISING	IFFINESS	IGNOMINIES	ILEX
IDOLATRIZE	IFFINESSES	IGNOMINIOUS	ILEXES
IDOLATRIZED	IFFY	IGNOMINIOUSLY	ILIA
IDOLATRIZER	IFS	IGNOMINIOUSNESS	ILIAC
IDOLATRIZERS	IFTAR	IGNOMINY	ILIACUS
IDOLATRIZES	IGAD	IGNOMY	ILIACUSES
IDOLATRIZING	IGAPO	IGNORABLE	ILIAD
IDOLATROUS	IGAPOS	IGNORAMI	ILIADS
IDOLATROUSLY	IGARAPE	IGNORAMUS	ILIAL
IDOLATROUSNESS	IGARAPES	IGNORAMUSES	ILICES
IDOLATRY	IGLOO	IGNORANCE	ILIUM
IDOLISATION	IGLOOS	IGNORANCES	ILK
IDOLISE	IGLU	IGNORANT	ILKA
IDOLISED	IGLUS	IGNORANTLY	ILKADAY
IDOLISER	IGNARO	IGNORANTNESS	ILKADAYS
IDOLISERS	IGNAROES	IGNORANTNESSES	ILKS
IDOLISES	IGNAROS	IGNORANTS	ILL
IDOLISING	IGNATIA	IGNORATION	ILLAPSE
IDOLISM	IGNATIAS	IGNORATIONS	ILLAPSED
IDOLISMS	IGNEOUS	IGNORE	ILLAPSES
IDOLIST	IGNESCENT	IGNORED	ILLAPSING
IDOLISTS	IGNESCENTS	IGNORER	ILLAQUEABLE
IDOLIZATION	IGNIFIED	IGNORERS	ILLAQUEATE
IDOLIZATIONS	IGNIFIES	IGNORES	ILLAQUEATED
IDOLIZE	IGNIFY	IGNORING	ILLAQUEATES
IDOLIZED	IGNIFYING	IGUANA	ILLAQUEATING
IDOLIZER	IGNIMBRITE	IGUANAS	ILLAQUEATION
IDOLIZERS	IGNIMBRITES	IGUANIAN	ILLAQUEATIONS
IDOLIZES	IGNIPOTENT	IGUANIANS	ILLATION
IDOLIZING	IGNITABILITIES	IGUANID	ILLATIONS
IDOLOCLAST	IGNITABILITY	IGUANIDS	ILLATIVE
IDOLOCLASTS	IGNITABLE	IGUANODON	ILLATIVELY

ILLATIVES
ILLAUDABLE
ILLAUDABLY
ILLEGAL
ILLEGALISATION
ILLEGALISE
ILLEGALISED
ILLEGALISER
ILLEGALISERS
ILLEGALISES
ILLEGALISING
ILLEGALITIES
ILLEGALITY
ILLEGALIZATION
ILLEGALIZATIONS
ILLEGALIZE
ILLEGALIZED
ILLEGALIZES
ILLEGALIZING
ILLEGALLY
ILLEGALS
ILLEGIBILITIES
ILLEGIBILITY
ILLEGIBLE
ILLEGIBLENESS
ILLEGIBLENESSES
ILLEGIBLY
ILLEGITIMACIES
ILLEGITIMACY
ILLEGITIMATE
ILLEGITIMATED
ILLEGITIMATELY
ILLEGITIMATES
ILLEGITIMATING
ILLEGITIMATION
ILLEGITIMATIONS
ILLER
ILLEST
ILLIAD
ILLIADS
ILLIBERAL
ILLIBERALISE
ILLIBERALISED
ILLIBERALISES
ILLIBERALISING
ILLIBERALISM
ILLIBERALISMS
ILLIBERALITIES
ILLIBERALITY
ILLIBERALIZE
ILLIBERALIZED
ILLIBERALIZES
ILLIBERALIZING
ILLIBERALLY
ILLIBERALNESS
ILLIBERALNESSES

ILLICIT
ILLICITLY
ILLICITNESS
ILLICITNESSES
ILLIMITABILITY
ILLIMITABLE
ILLIMITABLENESS
ILLIMITABLY
ILLIMITATION
ILLIMITATIONS
ILLIMITED
ILLINIUM
ILLINIUMS
ILLIPE
ILLIPES
ILLIQUATION
ILLIQUATIONS
ILLIQUID
ILLIQUIDITIES
ILLIQUIDITY
ILLISION
ILLISIONS
ILLITE
ILLITERACIES
ILLITERACY
ILLITERATE
ILLITERATELY
ILLITERATENESS
ILLITERATES
ILLITES
ILLITIC
ILLNESS
ILLNESSES
ILLOCUTION
ILLOCUTIONARY
ILLOCUTIONS
ILLOGIC
ILLOGICAL
ILLOGICALITIES
ILLOGICALITY
ILLOGICALLY
ILLOGICALNESS
ILLOGICALNESSES
ILLOGICS
ILLS
ILLTH
ILLTHS
ILLUDE
ILLUDED
ILLUDES
ILLUDING
ILLUME
ILLUMED
ILLUMES
ILLUMINABLE
ILLUMINANCE

ILLUMINANCES
ILLUMINANT
ILLUMINANTS
ILLUMINATE
ILLUMINATED
ILLUMINATES
ILLUMINATI
ILLUMINATING
ILLUMINATINGLY
ILLUMINATION
ILLUMINATIONAL
ILLUMINATIONS
ILLUMINATIVE
ILLUMINATO
ILLUMINATOR
ILLUMINATORS
ILLUMINE
ILLUMINED
ILLUMINER
ILLUMINERS
ILLUMINES
ILLUMING
ILLUMINING
ILLUMINISM
ILLUMINISMS
ILLUMINIST
ILLUMINISTS
ILLUPI
ILLUPIS
ILLUSION
ILLUSIONAL
ILLUSIONARY
ILLUSIONED
ILLUSIONISM
ILLUSIONISMS
ILLUSIONIST
ILLUSIONISTIC
ILLUSIONISTS
ILLUSIONS
ILLUSIVE
ILLUSIVELY
ILLUSIVENESS
ILLUSIVENESSES
ILLUSORILY
ILLUSORINESS
ILLUSORINESSES
ILLUSORY
ILLUSTRATABLE
ILLUSTRATE
ILLUSTRATED
ILLUSTRATEDS
ILLUSTRATES
ILLUSTRATING
ILLUSTRATION
ILLUSTRATIONAL
ILLUSTRATIONS

ILLUSTRATIVE
ILLUSTRATIVELY
ILLUSTRATOR
ILLUSTRATORS
ILLUSTRATORY
ILLUSTRIOUS
ILLUSTRIOUSLY
ILLUSTRIOUSNESS
ILLUSTRISSIMO
ILLUVIA
ILLUVIAL
ILLUVIATED
ILLUVIATION
ILLUVIATIONS
ILLUVIUM
ILLUVIUMS
ILLY
ILMENITE
ILMENITES
IMAGE
IMAGEABLE
IMAGED
IMAGELESS
IMAGER
IMAGERIES
IMAGERS
IMAGERY
IMAGES
IMAGINABLE
IMAGINABLENESS
IMAGINABLY
IMAGINAL
IMAGINARIES
IMAGINARILY
IMAGINARINESS
IMAGINARINESSES
IMAGINARY
IMAGINATION
IMAGINATIONAL
IMAGINATIONALLY
IMAGINATIONS
IMAGINATIVE
IMAGINATIVELY
IMAGINATIVENESS
IMAGINE
IMAGINED
IMAGINER
IMAGINERS
IMAGINES
IMAGING
IMAGINGS
IMAGINING
IMAGININGS
IMAGINIST
IMAGINISTS
IMAGISM

IMAGISMS	IMBIBER	IMBRICATIONS	IMITATED
IMAGIST	IMBIBERS	IMBRICES	IMITATES
IMAGISTIC	IMBIBES	IMBROCCATA	IMITATING
IMAGISTICALLY	IMBIBING	IMBROCCATAS	IMITATION
IMAGO	IMBIBITION	IMBROGLIO	IMITATIONAL
IMAGOES	IMBIBITIONAL	IMBROGLIOS	IMITATIONALLY
IMAGOS	IMBIBITIONS	IMBROWN	IMITATIONS
IMAM	IMBITTER	IMBROWNED	IMITATIVE
IMAMATE	IMBITTERED	IMBROWNING	IMITATIVELY
IMAMATES	IMBITTERING	IMBROWNS	IMITATIVENESS
IMAMS	IMBITTERS	IMBRUE	IMITATIVENESSES
IMARET	IMBIZO	IMBRUED	IMITATOR
IMARETS	IMBLAZE	IMBRUEMENT	IMITATORS
IMARI	IMBLAZED	IMBRUEMENTS	IMMACULACIES
IMARIS	IMBLAZES	IMBRUES	IMMACULACY
IMAUM	IMBLAZING	IMBRUING	IMMACULATE
IMAUMS	IMBODIED	IMBRUTE	IMMACULATELY
IMBALANCE	IMBODIES	IMBRUTED	IMMACULATENESS
IMBALANCED	IMBODY	IMBRUTES	IMMANACLE
IMBALANCES	IMBODYING	IMBRUTING	IMMANACLED
IMBALM	IMBOLDEN	IMBUE	IMMANACLES
IMBALMED	IMBOLDENED	IMBUED	IMMANACLING
IMBALMER	IMBOLDENING	IMBUEMENT	IMMANATION
IMBALMERS	IMBOLDENS	IMBUES	IMMANATIONS
IMBALMING	IMBORDER	IMBUING	IMMANE
IMBALMS	IMBORDERED	IMBURSE	IMMANELY
IMBAR	IMBORDERING	IMBURSED	IMMANENCE
IMBARK	IMBORDERS	IMBURSES	IMMANENCES
IMBARKED	IMBOSK	IMBURSING	IMMANENCIES
IMBARKING	IMBOSKED	IMID	IMMANENCY
IMBARKS	IMBOSKING	IMIDAZOLE	IMMANENT
IMBARRED	IMBOSKS	IMIDAZOLES	IMMANENTAL
IMBARRING	IMBOSOM	IMIDE	IMMANENTISM
IMBARS	IMBOSOMED	IMIDES	IMMANENTISMS
IMBASE	IMBOSOMING	IMIDIC	IMMANENTIST
IMBASED	IMBOSOMS	IMIDO	IMMANENTISTIC
IMBASES	IMBOSS	IMIDS	IMMANENTISTS
IMBASING	IMBOSSED	IMINAZOLE	IMMANENTLY
IMBATHE	IMBOSSES	IMINAZOLES	IMMANITIES
IMBATHED	IMBOSSING	IMINE	IMMANITY
IMBATHES	IMBOWER	IMINES	IMMANTLE
IMBATHING	IMBOWERED	IMINO	IMMANTLED
IMBECILE	IMBOWERING	IMINOUREA	IMMANTLES
IMBECILELY	IMBOWERS	IMINOUREAS	IMMANTLING
IMBECILES	IMBRANGLE	IMIPRAMINE	IMMARCESCIBLE
IMBECILIC	IMBRANGLED	IMIPRAMINES	IMMARGINATE
IMBECILICALLY	IMBRANGLES	IMITABILITIES	IMMASK
IMBECILITIES	IMBRANGLING	IMITABILITY	IMMASKED
IMBECILITY	IMBRAST	IMITABLE	IMMASKING
IMBED	IMBREX	IMITABLENESS	IMMASKS
IMBEDDED	IMBRICATE	IMITABLENESSES	IMMATERIAL
IMBEDDING	IMBRICATED	IMITANCIES	IMMATERIALISE
IMBEDS	IMBRICATELY	IMITANCY	IMMATERIALISED
IMBIBE	IMBRICATES	IMITANT	IMMATERIALISES
IMBIBED	IMBRICATING	IMITANTS	IMMATERIALISING
	IMBRICATION	IMITATE	IMMATERIALISM

IMMATERIALISMS
IMMATERIALIST
IMMATERIALISTIC
IMMATERIALISTS
IMMATERIALITIES
IMMATERIALITY
IMMATERIALIZE
IMMATERIALIZED
IMMATERIALIZES
IMMATERIALIZING
IMMATERIALLY
IMMATERIALNESS
IMMATURE
IMMATURELY
IMMATURENESS
IMMATURENESSES
IMMATURES
IMMATURITIES
IMMATURITY
IMMEASURABILITY
IMMEASURABLE
IMMEASURABLY
IMMEASURED
IMMEDIACIES
IMMEDIACY
IMMEDIATE
IMMEDIATELY
IMMEDIATENESS
IMMEDIATENESSES
IMMEDIATISM
IMMEDIATISMS
IMMEDICABLE
IMMEDICABLENESS
IMMEDICABLY
IMMEMORIAL
IMMEMORIALLY
IMMENSE
IMMENSELY
IMMENSENESS
IMMENSENESSES
IMMENSER
IMMENSEST
IMMENSITIES
IMMENSITY
IMMENSURABILITY
IMMENSURABLE
IMMERGE
IMMERGED
IMMERGENCE
IMMERGES
IMMERGING
IMMERITOUS
IMMERSE
IMMERSED
IMMERSER
IMMERSERS

IMMERSES
IMMERSIBLE
IMMERSING
IMMERSION
IMMERSIONISM
IMMERSIONISMS
IMMERSIONIST
IMMERSIONISTS
IMMERSIONS
IMMERSIVE
IMMERSIVELY
IMMERSIVENESS
IMMESH
IMMESHED
IMMESHES
IMMESHING
IMMETHODICAL
IMMETHODICALLY
IMMEW
IMMEWED
IMMEWING
IMMEWS
IMMIES
IMMIGRANT
IMMIGRANTS
IMMIGRATE
IMMIGRATED
IMMIGRATES
IMMIGRATING
IMMIGRATION
IMMIGRATIONAL
IMMIGRATIONS
IMMIGRATOR
IMMIGRATORS
IMMIGRATORY
IMMINENCE
IMMINENCES
IMMINENCIES
IMMINENCY
IMMINENT
IMMINENTLY
IMMINENTNESS
IMMINGLE
IMMINGLED
IMMINGLES
IMMINGLING
IMMINUTE
IMMINUTION
IMMINUTIONS
IMMISCIBILITIES
IMMISCIBILITY
IMMISCIBLE
IMMISCIBLY
IMMISERATION
IMMISERATIONS
IMMISERISATION

IMMISERISATIONS
IMMISERISE
IMMISERISED
IMMISERISES
IMMISERISING
IMMISERIZATION
IMMISERIZATIONS
IMMISERIZE
IMMISERIZED
IMMISERIZES
IMMISERIZING
IMMISSION
IMMISSIONS
IMMIT
IMMITIGABILITY
IMMITIGABLE
IMMITIGABLY
IMMITS
IMMITTANCE
IMMITTANCES
IMMITTED
IMMITTING
IMMIX
IMMIXED
IMMIXES
IMMIXING
IMMIXT
IMMIXTURE
IMMIXTURES
IMMOBILE
IMMOBILISATION
IMMOBILISATIONS
IMMOBILISE
IMMOBILISED
IMMOBILISER
IMMOBILISERS
IMMOBILISES
IMMOBILISING
IMMOBILISM
IMMOBILISMS
IMMOBILITIES
IMMOBILITY
IMMOBILIZATION
IMMOBILIZATIONS
IMMOBILIZE
IMMOBILIZED
IMMOBILIZER
IMMOBILIZERS
IMMOBILIZES
IMMOBILIZING
IMMODERACIES
IMMODERACY
IMMODERATE
IMMODERATELY
IMMODERATENESS
IMMODERATION

IMMODERATIONS
IMMODEST
IMMODESTIES
IMMODESTLY
IMMODESTY
IMMOLATE
IMMOLATED
IMMOLATES
IMMOLATING
IMMOLATION
IMMOLATIONS
IMMOLATOR
IMMOLATORS
IMMOMENT
IMMOMENTOUS
IMMORAL
IMMORALISM
IMMORALISMS
IMMORALIST
IMMORALISTS
IMMORALITIES
IMMORALITY
IMMORALLY
IMMORTAL
IMMORTALISATION
IMMORTALISE
IMMORTALISED
IMMORTALISER
IMMORTALISERS
IMMORTALISES
IMMORTALISING
IMMORTALITIES
IMMORTALITY
IMMORTALIZATION
IMMORTALIZE
IMMORTALIZED
IMMORTALIZER
IMMORTALIZERS
IMMORTALIZES
IMMORTALIZING
IMMORTALLY
IMMORTALS
IMMORTELLE
IMMORTELLES
IMMOTILE
IMMOTILITY
IMMOVABILITIES
IMMOVABILITY
IMMOVABLE
IMMOVABLENESS
IMMOVABLENESSES
IMMOVABLES
IMMOVABLY
IMMOVEABILITY
IMMOVEABLE
IMMOVEABLENESS

IMMOVEABLES
IMMOVEABLY
IMMUNE
IMMUNES
IMMUNIFACIENT
IMMUNISATION
IMMUNISATIONS
IMMUNISE
IMMUNISED
IMMUNISER
IMMUNISERS
IMMUNISES
IMMUNISING
IMMUNITIES
IMMUNITY
IMMUNIZATION
IMMUNIZATIONS
IMMUNIZE
IMMUNIZED
IMMUNIZER
IMMUNIZERS
IMMUNIZES
IMMUNIZING
IMMUNOASSAY
IMMUNOASSAYABLE
IMMUNOASSAYED
IMMUNOASSAYIST
IMMUNOASSAYISTS
IMMUNOASSAYS
IMMUNOBLOT
IMMUNOBLOTS
IMMUNOBLOTTING
IMMUNOBLOTTINGS
IMMUNOCHEMICAL
IMMUNOCHEMIST
IMMUNOCHEMISTRY
IMMUNOCHEMISTS
IMMUNOCOMPETENT
IMMUNOCOMPLEX
IMMUNOCOMPLEXES
IMMUNODEFICIENT
IMMUNODIAGNOSES
IMMUNODIAGNOSIS
IMMUNODIFFUSION
IMMUNOGEN
IMMUNOGENESES
IMMUNOGENESIS
IMMUNOGENETIC
IMMUNOGENETICAL
IMMUNOGENETICS
IMMUNOGENIC
IMMUNOGENICALLY
IMMUNOGENICITY
IMMUNOGENS
IMMUNOGLOBULIN
IMMUNOGLOBULINS

IMMUNOLOGIC
IMMUNOLOGICAL
IMMUNOLOGICALLY
IMMUNOLOGIES
IMMUNOLOGIST
IMMUNOLOGISTS
IMMUNOLOGY
IMMUNOMODULATOR
IMMUNOPATHOLOGY
IMMUNOPHORESES
IMMUNOPHORESIS
IMMUNOREACTION
IMMUNOREACTIONS
IMMUNOREACTIVE
IMMUNOSORBENT
IMMUNOSORBENTS
IMMUNOSUPPRESS
IMMUNOTHERAPIES
IMMUNOTHERAPY
IMMUNOTOXIC
IMMUNOTOXIN
IMMUNOTOXINS
IMMURE
IMMURED
IMMUREMENT
IMMUREMENTS
IMMURES
IMMURING
IMMUTABILITIES
IMMUTABILITY
IMMUTABLE
IMMUTABLENESS
IMMUTABLENESSES
IMMUTABLY
IMMY
IMP
IMPACABLE
IMPACT
IMPACTED
IMPACTER
IMPACTERS
IMPACTING
IMPACTION
IMPACTIONS
IMPACTITE
IMPACTITES
IMPACTIVE
IMPACTOR
IMPACTORS
IMPACTS
IMPAINT
IMPAINTED
IMPAINTING
IMPAINTS
IMPAIR
IMPAIRABILITY

IMPAIRABLE
IMPAIRED
IMPAIRER
IMPAIRERS
IMPAIRING
IMPAIRINGS
IMPAIRMENT
IMPAIRMENTS
IMPAIRS
IMPALA
IMPALAS
IMPALE
IMPALED
IMPALEMENT
IMPALEMENTS
IMPALER
IMPALERS
IMPALES
IMPALING
IMPALPABILITIES
IMPALPABILITY
IMPALPABLE
IMPALPABLY
IMPALUDISM
IMPALUDISMS
IMPANATE
IMPANATION
IMPANATIONS
IMPANEL
IMPANELED
IMPANELING
IMPANELLED
IMPANELLING
IMPANELMENT
IMPANELMENTS
IMPANELS
IMPANNEL
IMPANNELLED
IMPANNELLING
IMPANNELS
IMPARADISE
IMPARADISED
IMPARADISES
IMPARADISING
IMPARIDIGITATE
IMPARIPINNATE
IMPARISYLLABIC
IMPARITIES
IMPARITY
IMPARK
IMPARKATION
IMPARKATIONS
IMPARKED
IMPARKING
IMPARKS
IMPARL

IMPARLANCE
IMPARLANCES
IMPARLED
IMPARLING
IMPARLS
IMPART
IMPARTABLE
IMPARTATION
IMPARTATIONS
IMPARTED
IMPARTER
IMPARTERS
IMPARTIAL
IMPARTIALITIES
IMPARTIALITY
IMPARTIALLY
IMPARTIALNESS
IMPARTIALNESSES
IMPARTIBILITIES
IMPARTIBILITY
IMPARTIBLE
IMPARTIBLY
IMPARTING
IMPARTMENT
IMPARTMENTS
IMPARTS
IMPASSABILITIES
IMPASSABILITY
IMPASSABLE
IMPASSABLENESS
IMPASSABLY
IMPASSE
IMPASSES
IMPASSIBILITIES
IMPASSIBILITY
IMPASSIBLE
IMPASSIBLENESS
IMPASSIBLY
IMPASSION
IMPASSIONATE
IMPASSIONED
IMPASSIONEDLY
IMPASSIONEDNESS
IMPASSIONING
IMPASSIONS
IMPASSIVE
IMPASSIVELY
IMPASSIVENESS
IMPASSIVENESSES
IMPASSIVITIES
IMPASSIVITY
IMPASTATION
IMPASTATIONS
IMPASTE
IMPASTED
IMPASTES

IMPASTING
IMPASTO
IMPASTOED
IMPASTOS
IMPATIENCE
IMPATIENCES
IMPATIENS
IMPATIENT
IMPATIENTLY
IMPAVE
IMPAVED
IMPAVES
IMPAVID
IMPAVIDLY
IMPAVING
IMPAWN
IMPAWNED
IMPAWNING
IMPAWNS
IMPEACH
IMPEACHABILITY
IMPEACHABLE
IMPEACHED
IMPEACHER
IMPEACHERS
IMPEACHES
IMPEACHING
IMPEACHMENT
IMPEACHMENTS
IMPEARL
IMPEARLED
IMPEARLING
IMPEARLS
IMPECCABILITIES
IMPECCABILITY
IMPECCABLE
IMPECCABLY
IMPECCANCIES
IMPECCANCY
IMPECCANT
IMPECUNIOSITIES
IMPECUNIOSITY
IMPECUNIOUS
IMPECUNIOUSLY
IMPECUNIOUSNESS
IMPED
IMPEDANCE
IMPEDANCES
IMPEDE
IMPEDED
IMPEDER
IMPEDERS
IMPEDES
IMPEDIMENT
IMPEDIMENTA
IMPEDIMENTAL

IMPEDIMENTARY
IMPEDIMENTS
IMPEDING
IMPEDINGLY
IMPEDITIVE
IMPEDOR
IMPEDORS
IMPEL
IMPELLED
IMPELLENT
IMPELLENTS
IMPELLER
IMPELLERS
IMPELLING
IMPELLOR
IMPELLORS
IMPELS
IMPEND
IMPENDED
IMPENDENCE
IMPENDENCES
IMPENDENCIES
IMPENDENCY
IMPENDENT
IMPENDING
IMPENDS
IMPENETRABILITY
IMPENETRABLE
IMPENETRABLY
IMPENETRATE
IMPENETRATED
IMPENETRATES
IMPENETRATING
IMPENETRATION
IMPENETRATIONS
IMPENITENCE
IMPENITENCES
IMPENITENCIES
IMPENITENCY
IMPENITENT
IMPENITENTLY
IMPENITENTNESS
IMPENITENTS
IMPENNATE
IMPERATIVAL
IMPERATIVE
IMPERATIVELY
IMPERATIVENESS
IMPERATIVES
IMPERATOR
IMPERATORIAL
IMPERATORIALLY
IMPERATORS
IMPERATORSHIP
IMPERATORSHIPS
IMPERCEABLE

IMPERCEIVABLE
IMPERCEPTIBLE
IMPERCEPTIBLY
IMPERCEPTION
IMPERCEPTIVE
IMPERCEPTIVELY
IMPERCEPTIVITY
IMPERCIPIENCE
IMPERCIPIENCES
IMPERCIPIENT
IMPERF
IMPERFECT
IMPERFECTIBLE
IMPERFECTION
IMPERFECTIONS
IMPERFECTIVE
IMPERFECTIVELY
IMPERFECTIVES
IMPERFECTLY
IMPERFECTNESS
IMPERFECTNESSES
IMPERFECTS
IMPERFORABLE
IMPERFORATE
IMPERFORATED
IMPERFORATION
IMPERFORATIONS
IMPERIA
IMPERIAL
IMPERIALISE
IMPERIALISED
IMPERIALISES
IMPERIALISING
IMPERIALISM
IMPERIALISMS
IMPERIALIST
IMPERIALISTIC
IMPERIALISTS
IMPERIALITIES
IMPERIALITY
IMPERIALIZE
IMPERIALIZED
IMPERIALIZES
IMPERIALIZING
IMPERIALLY
IMPERIALNESS
IMPERIALS
IMPERIL
IMPERILED
IMPERILING
IMPERILLED
IMPERILLING
IMPERILMENT
IMPERILMENTS
IMPERILS
IMPERIOUS

IMPERIOUSLY
IMPERIOUSNESS
IMPERIOUSNESSES
IMPERISHABILITY
IMPERISHABLE
IMPERISHABLES
IMPERISHABLY
IMPERIUM
IMPERIUMS
IMPERMANENCE
IMPERMANENCES
IMPERMANENCIES
IMPERMANENCY
IMPERMANENT
IMPERMANENTLY
IMPERMEABILITY
IMPERMEABLE
IMPERMEABLENESS
IMPERMEABLY
IMPERMISSIBLE
IMPERMISSIBLY
IMPERSCRIPTIBLE
IMPERSEVERANT
IMPERSISTENT
IMPERSONAL
IMPERSONALISE
IMPERSONALISED
IMPERSONALISES
IMPERSONALISING
IMPERSONALITIES
IMPERSONALITY
IMPERSONALIZE
IMPERSONALIZED
IMPERSONALIZES
IMPERSONALIZING
IMPERSONALLY
IMPERSONATE
IMPERSONATED
IMPERSONATES
IMPERSONATING
IMPERSONATION
IMPERSONATIONS
IMPERSONATOR
IMPERSONATORS
IMPERTINENCE
IMPERTINENCES
IMPERTINENCIES
IMPERTINENCY
IMPERTINENT
IMPERTINENTLY
IMPERTURBABLE
IMPERTURBABLY
IMPERTURBATION
IMPERTURBATIONS
IMPERVIABILITY
IMPERVIABLE

IMPERVIABLENESS
IMPERVIOUS
IMPERVIOUSLY
IMPERVIOUSNESS
IMPETICOS
IMPETICOSSED
IMPETICOSSES
IMPETICOSSING
IMPETIGINES
IMPETIGINOUS
IMPETIGO
IMPETIGOS
IMPETRATE
IMPETRATED
IMPETRATES
IMPETRATING
IMPETRATION
IMPETRATIONS
IMPETRATIVE
IMPETRATIVELY
IMPETRATOR
IMPETRATORS
IMPETRATORY
IMPETUOSITIES
IMPETUOSITY
IMPETUOUS
IMPETUOUSLY
IMPETUOUSNESS
IMPETUOUSNESSES
IMPETUS
IMPETUSES
IMPHEE
IMPHEES
IMPI
IMPICTURED
IMPIERCEABLE
IMPIES
IMPIETIES
IMPIETY
IMPIGNORATE
IMPIGNORATED
IMPIGNORATES
IMPIGNORATING
IMPIGNORATION
IMPIGNORATIONS
IMPING
IMPINGE
IMPINGED
IMPINGEMENT
IMPINGEMENTS
IMPINGENT
IMPINGER
IMPINGERS
IMPINGES
IMPINGING
IMPINGS

IMPIOUS
IMPIOUSLY
IMPIOUSNESS
IMPIS
IMPISH
IMPISHLY
IMPISHNESS
IMPISHNESSES
IMPLACABILITIES
IMPLACABILITY
IMPLACABLE
IMPLACABLENESS
IMPLACABLY
IMPLACENTAL
IMPLANT
IMPLANTABLE
IMPLANTATION
IMPLANTATIONS
IMPLANTED
IMPLANTER
IMPLANTERS
IMPLANTING
IMPLANTS
IMPLATE
IMPLATED
IMPLATES
IMPLATING
IMPLAUSIBILITY
IMPLAUSIBLE
IMPLAUSIBLENESS
IMPLAUSIBLY
IMPLEACH
IMPLEACHED
IMPLEACHES
IMPLEACHING
IMPLEAD
IMPLEADABLE
IMPLEADED
IMPLEADER
IMPLEADERS
IMPLEADING
IMPLEADS
IMPLEDGE
IMPLEDGED
IMPLEDGES
IMPLEDGING
IMPLEMENT
IMPLEMENTAL
IMPLEMENTATION
IMPLEMENTATIONS
IMPLEMENTED
IMPLEMENTER
IMPLEMENTERS
IMPLEMENTING
IMPLEMENTOR
IMPLEMENTORS

IMPLEMENTS
IMPLETE
IMPLETED
IMPLETES
IMPLETING
IMPLETION
IMPLETIONS
IMPLEX
IMPLEXES
IMPLEXION
IMPLEXIONS
IMPLICATE
IMPLICATED
IMPLICATES
IMPLICATING
IMPLICATION
IMPLICATIONAL
IMPLICATIONALLY
IMPLICATIONS
IMPLICATIVE
IMPLICATIVELY
IMPLICATIVENESS
IMPLICATURE
IMPLICATURES
IMPLICIT
IMPLICITLY
IMPLICITNESS
IMPLICITNESSES
IMPLICITY
IMPLIED
IMPLIEDLY
IMPLIES
IMPLODE
IMPLODED
IMPLODENT
IMPLODENTS
IMPLODES
IMPLODING
IMPLORATION
IMPLORATIONS
IMPLORATOR
IMPLORATORS
IMPLORATORY
IMPLORE
IMPLORED
IMPLORER
IMPLORERS
IMPLORES
IMPLORING
IMPLORINGLY
IMPLOSION
IMPLOSIONS
IMPLOSIVE
IMPLOSIVELY
IMPLOSIVES
IMPLUNGE

IMPLUNGED
IMPLUNGES
IMPLUNGING
IMPLUVIA
IMPLUVIUM
IMPLY
IMPLYING
IMPOCKET
IMPOCKETED
IMPOCKETING
IMPOCKETS
IMPOLDER
IMPOLDERED
IMPOLDERING
IMPOLDERS
IMPOLICIES
IMPOLICY
IMPOLITE
IMPOLITELY
IMPOLITENESS
IMPOLITENESSES
IMPOLITER
IMPOLITEST
IMPOLITIC
IMPOLITICAL
IMPOLITICALLY
IMPOLITICLY
IMPOLITICNESS
IMPOLITICNESSES
IMPONDERABILIA
IMPONDERABILITY
IMPONDERABLE
IMPONDERABLES
IMPONDERABLY
IMPONDEROUS
IMPONE
IMPONED
IMPONENT
IMPONENTS
IMPONES
IMPONING
IMPOROUS
IMPORT
IMPORTABILITY
IMPORTABLE
IMPORTABLENESS
IMPORTANCE
IMPORTANCES
IMPORTANCIES
IMPORTANCY
IMPORTANT
IMPORTANTLY
IMPORTATION
IMPORTATIONS
IMPORTED
IMPORTER

IMPORTERS
IMPORTING
IMPORTS
IMPORTUNACIES
IMPORTUNACY
IMPORTUNATE
IMPORTUNATELY
IMPORTUNATENESS
IMPORTUNE
IMPORTUNED
IMPORTUNELY
IMPORTUNER
IMPORTUNERS
IMPORTUNES
IMPORTUNING
IMPORTUNINGS
IMPORTUNITIES
IMPORTUNITY
IMPOSABLE
IMPOSE
IMPOSED
IMPOSER
IMPOSERS
IMPOSES
IMPOSING
IMPOSINGLY
IMPOSINGNESS
IMPOSINGNESSES
IMPOSITION
IMPOSITIONS
IMPOSSIBILISM
IMPOSSIBILISMS
IMPOSSIBILIST
IMPOSSIBILISTS
IMPOSSIBILITIES
IMPOSSIBILITY
IMPOSSIBLE
IMPOSSIBLENESS
IMPOSSIBLES
IMPOSSIBLY
IMPOST
IMPOSTED
IMPOSTER
IMPOSTERS
IMPOSTHUMATE
IMPOSTHUMATED
IMPOSTHUMATES
IMPOSTHUMATING
IMPOSTHUMATION
IMPOSTHUMATIONS
IMPOSTHUME
IMPOSTHUMED
IMPOSTHUMES
IMPOSTING
IMPOSTOR
IMPOSTOROUS

IMPOSTOROUSLY
IMPOSTORS
IMPOSTROUS
IMPOSTROUSLY
IMPOSTS
IMPOSTUMATE
IMPOSTUMATED
IMPOSTUMATES
IMPOSTUMATING
IMPOSTUMATION
IMPOSTUMATIONS
IMPOSTUME
IMPOSTUMED
IMPOSTUMES
IMPOSTURE
IMPOSTURES
IMPOSTUROUS
IMPOSTUROUSLY
IMPOT
IMPOTENCE
IMPOTENCES
IMPOTENCIES
IMPOTENCY
IMPOTENT
IMPOTENTLY
IMPOTENTNESS
IMPOTENTS
IMPOTS
IMPOUND
IMPOUNDABLE
IMPOUNDAGE
IMPOUNDAGES
IMPOUNDED
IMPOUNDER
IMPOUNDERS
IMPOUNDING
IMPOUNDMENT
IMPOUNDMENTS
IMPOUNDS
IMPOVERISH
IMPOVERISHED
IMPOVERISHER
IMPOVERISHERS
IMPOVERISHES
IMPOVERISHING
IMPOVERISHMENT
IMPOVERISHMENTS
IMPOWER
IMPOWERED
IMPOWERING
IMPOWERS
IMPRACTICABLE
IMPRACTICABLY
IMPRACTICAL
IMPRACTICALITY
IMPRACTICALLY

IMPRACTICALNESS
IMPRECATE
IMPRECATED
IMPRECATES
IMPRECATING
IMPRECATION
IMPRECATIONS
IMPRECATORY
IMPRECISE
IMPRECISELY
IMPRECISENESS
IMPRECISENESSES
IMPRECISION
IMPRECISIONS
IMPREDICATIVE
IMPREDICATIVELY
IMPREGN
IMPREGNABILITY
IMPREGNABLE
IMPREGNABLENESS
IMPREGNABLY
IMPREGNANT
IMPREGNANTS
IMPREGNATABLE
IMPREGNATE
IMPREGNATED
IMPREGNATES
IMPREGNATING
IMPREGNATION
IMPREGNATIONS
IMPREGNATOR
IMPREGNATORS
IMPREGNED
IMPREGNING
IMPREGNS
IMPRESA
IMPRESARI
IMPRESARIO
IMPRESARIOS
IMPRESAS
IMPRESCRIPTIBLE
IMPRESCRIPTIBLY
IMPRESE
IMPRESES
IMPRESS
IMPRESSE
IMPRESSED
IMPRESSER
IMPRESSERS
IMPRESSES
IMPRESSIBILITY
IMPRESSIBLE
IMPRESSING
IMPRESSION
IMPRESSIONABLE
IMPRESSIONAL

IMPRESSIONALLY
IMPRESSIONISM
IMPRESSIONISMS
IMPRESSIONIST
IMPRESSIONISTIC
IMPRESSIONISTS
IMPRESSIONS
IMPRESSIVE
IMPRESSIVELY
IMPRESSIVENESS
IMPRESSMENT
IMPRESSMENTS
IMPRESSURE
IMPRESSURES
IMPREST
IMPRESTS
IMPRIMATUR
IMPRIMATURS
IMPRIMIS
IMPRINT
IMPRINTED
IMPRINTER
IMPRINTERS
IMPRINTING
IMPRINTINGS
IMPRINTS
IMPRISON
IMPRISONABLE
IMPRISONED
IMPRISONER
IMPRISONERS
IMPRISONING
IMPRISONMENT
IMPRISONMENTS
IMPRISONS
IMPROBABILITIES
IMPROBABILITY
IMPROBABLE
IMPROBABLENESS
IMPROBABLY
IMPROBATION
IMPROBATIONS
IMPROBITIES
IMPROBITY
IMPROMPTU
IMPROMPTUS
IMPROPER
IMPROPERLY
IMPROPERNESS
IMPROPERNESSES
IMPROPRIATE
IMPROPRIATED
IMPROPRIATES
IMPROPRIATING
IMPROPRIATION
IMPROPRIATIONS

IMPROPRIATOR
IMPROPRIATORS
IMPROPRIETIES
IMPROPRIETY
IMPROV
IMPROVABILITIES
IMPROVABILITY
IMPROVABLE
IMPROVABLENESS
IMPROVABLY
IMPROVE
IMPROVED
IMPROVEMENT
IMPROVEMENTS
IMPROVER
IMPROVERS
IMPROVES
IMPROVIDENCE
IMPROVIDENCES
IMPROVIDENT
IMPROVIDENTLY
IMPROVING
IMPROVINGLY
IMPROVISATE
IMPROVISATED
IMPROVISATES
IMPROVISATING
IMPROVISATION
IMPROVISATIONAL
IMPROVISATIONS
IMPROVISATOR
IMPROVISATORE
IMPROVISATORES
IMPROVISATORI
IMPROVISATORIAL
IMPROVISATORS
IMPROVISATORY
IMPROVISATRICES
IMPROVISATRIX
IMPROVISATRIXES
IMPROVISE
IMPROVISED
IMPROVISER
IMPROVISERS
IMPROVISES
IMPROVISING
IMPROVISOR
IMPROVISORS
IMPROVS
IMPROVVISATORE
IMPROVVISATORES
IMPROVVISATRICE
IMPRUDENCE
IMPRUDENCES
IMPRUDENT
IMPRUDENTLY

IMPS
IMPSONITE
IMPSONITES
IMPUDENCE
IMPUDENCES
IMPUDENCIES
IMPUDENCY
IMPUDENT
IMPUDENTLY
IMPUDENTNESS
IMPUDICITIES
IMPUDICITY
IMPUGN
IMPUGNABLE
IMPUGNATION
IMPUGNATIONS
IMPUGNED
IMPUGNER
IMPUGNERS
IMPUGNING
IMPUGNMENT
IMPUGNMENTS
IMPUGNS
IMPUISSANCE
IMPUISSANCES
IMPUISSANT
IMPULSE
IMPULSED
IMPULSES
IMPULSING
IMPULSION
IMPULSIONS
IMPULSIVE
IMPULSIVELY
IMPULSIVENESS
IMPULSIVENESSES
IMPULSIVITIES
IMPULSIVITY
IMPUNDULU
IMPUNDULUS
IMPUNITIES
IMPUNITY
IMPURE
IMPURELY
IMPURENESS
IMPURENESSES
IMPURER
IMPUREST
IMPURITIES
IMPURITY
IMPURPLE
IMPURPLED
IMPURPLES
IMPURPLING
IMPUTABILITIES
IMPUTABILITY

IMPUTABLE
IMPUTABLENESS
IMPUTABLENESSES
IMPUTABLY
IMPUTATION
IMPUTATIONS
IMPUTATIVE
IMPUTATIVELY
IMPUTE
IMPUTED
IMPUTER
IMPUTERS
IMPUTES
IMPUTING
IMSHI
IMSHY
IN
INABILITIES
INABILITY
INABSTINENCE
INABSTINENCES
INACCESSIBILITY
INACCESSIBLE
INACCESSIBLY
INACCURACIES
INACCURACY
INACCURATE
INACCURATELY
INACCURATENESS
INACTION
INACTIONS
INACTIVATE
INACTIVATED
INACTIVATES
INACTIVATING
INACTIVATION
INACTIVATIONS
INACTIVE
INACTIVELY
INACTIVENESS
INACTIVITIES
INACTIVITY
INADAPTABLE
INADAPTATION
INADAPTATIONS
INADAPTIVE
INADEQUACIES
INADEQUACY
INADEQUATE
INADEQUATELY
INADEQUATENESS
INADEQUATES
INADMISSIBILITY
INADMISSIBLE
INADMISSIBLY
INADVERTENCE

INADVERTENCES
INADVERTENCIES
INADVERTENCY
INADVERTENT
INADVERTENTLY
INADVISABILITY
INADVISABLE
INADVISABLENESS
INADVISABLY
INAIDABLE
INALIENABILITY
INALIENABLE
INALIENABLENESS
INALIENABLY
INALTERABILITY
INALTERABLE
INALTERABLENESS
INALTERABLY
INAMORATA
INAMORATAS
INAMORATO
INAMORATOS
INANE
INANELY
INANENESS
INANENESSES
INANER
INANES
INANEST
INANGA
INANGAS
INANIMATE
INANIMATELY
INANIMATENESS
INANIMATENESSES
INANIMATION
INANIMATIONS
INANITIES
INANITION
INANITIONS
INANITY
INAPPARENT
INAPPARENTLY
INAPPEASABLE
INAPPELLABLE
INAPPETENCE
INAPPETENCES
INAPPETENCIES
INAPPETENCY
INAPPETENT
INAPPLICABILITY
INAPPLICABLE
INAPPLICABLY
INAPPOSITE
INAPPOSITELY
INAPPOSITENESS

INAPPRECIABLE	INAUGURATED	INCANDESCE	INCARDINATE
INAPPRECIABLY	INAUGURATES	INCANDESCED	INCARDINATED
INAPPRECIATION	INAUGURATING	INCANDESCENCE	INCARDINATES
INAPPRECIATIONS	INAUGURATION	INCANDESCENCES	INCARDINATING
INAPPRECIATIVE	INAUGURATIONS	INCANDESCENCIES	INCARDINATION
INAPPREHENSIBLE	INAUGURATOR	INCANDESCENCY	INCARDINATIONS
INAPPREHENSION	INAUGURATORS	INCANDESCENT	INCARNADINE
INAPPREHENSIONS	INAUGURATORY	INCANDESCENTLY	INCARNADINED
INAPPREHENSIVE	INAURATE	INCANDESCENTS	INCARNADINES
INAPPROACHABLE	INAUSPICIOUS	INCANDESCES	INCARNADINING
INAPPROACHABLY	INAUSPICIOUSLY	INCANDESCING	INCARNATE
INAPPROPRIATE	INAUTHENTIC	INCANT	INCARNATED
INAPPROPRIATELY	INAUTHENTICITY	INCANTATION	INCARNATES
INAPT	INBEING	INCANTATIONAL	INCARNATING
INAPTITUDE	INBEINGS	INCANTATIONS	INCARNATION
INAPTITUDES	INBENT	INCANTATOR	INCARNATIONS
INAPTLY	INBOARD	INCANTATORS	INCARVILLEA
INAPTNESS	INBOARDS	INCANTATORY	INCARVILLEAS
INAPTNESSES	INBORN	INCANTED	INCASE
INARABLE	INBOUND	INCANTING	INCASED
INARCH	INBOUNDED	INCANTS	INCASEMENT
INARCHED	INBOUNDING	INCAPABILITIES	INCASEMENTS
INARCHES	INBOUNDS	INCAPABILITY	INCASES
INARCHING	INBREAK	INCAPABLE	INCASING
INARGUABLE	INBREAKS	INCAPABLENESS	INCATENATION
INARGUABLY	INBREATHE	INCAPABLENESSES	INCATENATIONS
INARM	INBREATHED	INCAPABLES	INCAUTION
INARMED	INBREATHES	INCAPABLY	INCAUTIONS
INARMING	INBREATHING	INCAPACIOUS	INCAUTIOUS
INARMS	INBRED	INCAPACIOUSNESS	INCAUTIOUSLY
INARTICULACIES	INBREDS	INCAPACITANT	INCAUTIOUSNESS
INARTICULACY	INBREED	INCAPACITANTS	INCAVE
INARTICULATE	INBREEDING	INCAPACITATE	INCAVED
INARTICULATELY	INBREEDINGS	INCAPACITATED	INCAVES
INARTICULATES	INBREEDS	INCAPACITATES	INCAVI
INARTICULATION	INBRING	INCAPACITATING	INCAVING
INARTICULATIONS	INBRINGING	INCAPACITATION	INCAVO
INARTIFICIAL	INBRINGINGS	INCAPACITATIONS	INCEDE
INARTIFICIALLY	INBRINGS	INCAPACITIES	INCEDED
INARTISTIC	INBROUGHT	INCAPACITY	INCEDES
INARTISTICALLY	INBUILT	INCAPSULATE	INCEDING
INASMUCH	INBURNING	INCAPSULATED	INCEDINGLY
INATTENTION	INBURST	INCAPSULATES	INCENDIARIES
INATTENTIONS	INBURSTS	INCAPSULATING	INCENDIARISM
INATTENTIVE	INBY	INCAPSULATION	INCENDIARISMS
INATTENTIVELY	INBYE	INCAPSULATIONS	INCENDIARY
INATTENTIVENESS	INCAGE	INCAPSULATOR	INCENDIVITIES
INAUDIBILITIES	INCAGED	INCAPSULATORS	INCENDIVITY
INAUDIBILITY	INCAGES	INCARCERATE	INCENSATION
INAUDIBLE	INCAGING	INCARCERATED	INCENSATIONS
INAUDIBLENESS	INCALCULABILITY	INCARCERATES	INCENSE
INAUDIBLENESSES	INCALCULABLE	INCARCERATING	INCENSED
INAUDIBLY	INCALCULABLY	INCARCERATION	INCENSEMENT
INAUGURAL	INCALESCENCE	INCARCERATIONS	INCENSEMENTS
INAUGURALS	INCALESCENCES	INCARCERATOR	INCENSER
INAUGURATE	INCALESCENT	INCARCERATORS	INCENSERS

INCENSES
INCENSING
INCENSOR
INCENSORIES
INCENSORS
INCENSORY
INCENTER
INCENTERS
INCENTIVE
INCENTIVELY
INCENTIVES
INCENTIVISATION
INCENTIVISE
INCENTIVISED
INCENTIVISES
INCENTIVISING
INCENTIVIZATION
INCENTIVIZE
INCENTIVIZED
INCENTIVIZES
INCENTIVIZING
INCENTRE
INCENTRES
INCEPT
INCEPTED
INCEPTING
INCEPTION
INCEPTIONS
INCEPTIVE
INCEPTIVELY
INCEPTIVES
INCEPTOR
INCEPTORS
INCEPTS
INCERTAIN
INCERTAINTIES
INCERTAINTY
INCERTITUDE
INCERTITUDES
INCESSANCIES
INCESSANCY
INCESSANT
INCESSANTLY
INCESSANTNESS
INCESSANTNESSES
INCEST
INCESTS
INCESTUOUS
INCESTUOUSLY
INCESTUOUSNESS
INCH
INCHARITABLE
INCHASE
INCHASED
INCHASES
INCHASING

INCHED
INCHES
INCHING
INCHMEAL
INCHOATE
INCHOATED
INCHOATELY
INCHOATENESS
INCHOATENESSES
INCHOATES
INCHOATING
INCHOATION
INCHOATIONS
INCHOATIVE
INCHOATIVELY
INCHOATIVES
INCHPIN
INCHPINS
INCHWORM
INCHWORMS
INCIDENCE
INCIDENCES
INCIDENT
INCIDENTAL
INCIDENTALLY
INCIDENTALNESS
INCIDENTALS
INCIDENTS
INCINERATE
INCINERATED
INCINERATES
INCINERATING
INCINERATION
INCINERATIONS
INCINERATOR
INCINERATORS
INCIPIENCE
INCIPIENCES
INCIPIENCIES
INCIPIENCY
INCIPIENT
INCIPIENTLY
INCIPIT
INCIPITS
INCISAL
INCISE
INCISED
INCISES
INCISIFORM
INCISING
INCISION
INCISIONS
INCISIVE
INCISIVELY
INCISIVENESS
INCISIVENESSES

INCISOR
INCISORIAL
INCISORS
INCISORY
INCISURAL
INCISURE
INCISURES
INCITANT
INCITANTS
INCITATION
INCITATIONS
INCITATIVE
INCITATIVES
INCITE
INCITED
INCITEMENT
INCITEMENTS
INCITER
INCITERS
INCITES
INCITING
INCITINGLY
INCIVIL
INCIVILITIES
INCIVILITY
INCIVISM
INCIVISMS
INCLASP
INCLASPED
INCLASPING
INCLASPS
INCLE
INCLEMENCIES
INCLEMENCY
INCLEMENT
INCLEMENTLY
INCLEMENTNESS
INCLES
INCLINABLE
INCLINABLENESS
INCLINATION
INCLINATIONAL
INCLINATIONS
INCLINATORIA
INCLINATORIUM
INCLINATORY
INCLINE
INCLINED
INCLINER
INCLINERS
INCLINES
INCLINING
INCLININGS
INCLINOMETER
INCLINOMETERS
INCLIP

INCLIPPED
INCLIPPING
INCLIPS
INCLOSABLE
INCLOSE
INCLOSED
INCLOSER
INCLOSERS
INCLOSES
INCLOSING
INCLOSURE
INCLOSURES
INCLUDABLE
INCLUDE
INCLUDED
INCLUDEDLY
INCLUDEDNESS
INCLUDES
INCLUDIBLE
INCLUDING
INCLUSION
INCLUSIONS
INCLUSIVE
INCLUSIVELY
INCLUSIVENESS
INCLUSIVENESSES
INCLUSIVITY
INCOAGULABLE
INCOERCIBLE
INCOG
INCOGITABILITY
INCOGITABLE
INCOGITANCIES
INCOGITANCY
INCOGITANT
INCOGITATIVE
INCOGNISABLE
INCOGNISANCE
INCOGNISANCES
INCOGNISANT
INCOGNITA
INCOGNITAS
INCOGNITO
INCOGNITOS
INCOGNIZABLE
INCOGNIZANCE
INCOGNIZANCES
INCOGNIZANT
INCOGS
INCOHERENCE
INCOHERENCES
INCOHERENCIES
INCOHERENCY
INCOHERENT
INCOHERENTLY
INCOHERENTNESS

INCOMBUSTIBLE	INCOMPOSSIBLE	INCONSISTENCES	INCORPORABLE
INCOMBUSTIBLES	INCOMPREHENSION	INCONSISTENCIES	INCORPORAL
INCOMBUSTIBLY	INCOMPREHENSIVE	INCONSISTENCY	INCORPORALL
INCOME	INCOMPRESSIBLE	INCONSISTENT	INCORPORATE
INCOMER	INCOMPRESSIBLY	INCONSISTENTLY	INCORPORATED
INCOMERS	INCOMPUTABILITY	INCONSOLABILITY	INCORPORATES
INCOMES	INCOMPUTABLE	INCONSOLABLE	INCORPORATING
INCOMING	INCOMPUTABLY	INCONSOLABLY	INCORPORATION
INCOMINGS	INCOMUNICADO	INCONSONANCE	INCORPORATIONS
INCOMMENSURABLE	INCONCEIVABLE	INCONSONANCES	INCORPORATIVE
INCOMMENSURABLY	INCONCEIVABLES	INCONSONANT	INCORPORATOR
INCOMMENSURATE	INCONCEIVABLY	INCONSONANTLY	INCORPORATORS
INCOMMISCIBLE	INCONCINNITIES	INCONSONANTNESS	INCORPOREAL
INCOMMODE	INCONCINNITY	INCONSPICUOUS	INCORPOREALITY
INCOMMODED	INCONCINNOUS	INCONSPICUOUSLY	INCORPOREALLY
INCOMMODES	INCONCLUSION	INCONSTANCIES	INCORPOREITIES
INCOMMODING	INCONCLUSIONS	INCONSTANCY	INCORPOREITY
INCOMMODIOUS	INCONCLUSIVE	INCONSTANT	INCORPSE
INCOMMODIOUSLY	INCONCLUSIVELY	INCONSTANTLY	INCORPSED
INCOMMODITIES	INCONDENSABLE	INCONSTRUABLE	INCORPSES
INCOMMODITY	INCONDENSIBLE	INCONSUMABLE	INCORPSING
INCOMMUNICABLE	INCONDITE	INCONSUMABLY	INCORRECT
INCOMMUNICABLY	INCONDITELY	INCONTESTABLE	INCORRECTLY
INCOMMUNICADO	INCONFORMITIES	INCONTESTABLY	INCORRECTNESS
INCOMMUNICATIVE	INCONFORMITY	INCONTIGUOUS	INCORRECTNESSES
INCOMMUTABILITY	INCONGRUENCE	INCONTIGUOUSLY	INCORRIGIBILITY
INCOMMUTABLE	INCONGRUENCES	INCONTINENCE	INCORRIGIBLE
INCOMMUTABLY	INCONGRUENT	INCONTINENCES	INCORRIGIBLES
INCOMPARABILITY	INCONGRUENTLY	INCONTINENCIES	INCORRIGIBLY
INCOMPARABLE	INCONGRUITIES	INCONTINENCY	INCORRODIBLE
INCOMPARABLY	INCONGRUITY	INCONTINENT	INCORROSIBLE
INCOMPARED	INCONGRUOUS	INCONTINENTLY	INCORRUPT
INCOMPATIBILITY	INCONGRUOUSLY	INCONTROLLABLE	INCORRUPTED
INCOMPATIBLE	INCONGRUOUSNESS	INCONTROLLABLY	INCORRUPTIBLE
INCOMPATIBLES	INCONIE	INCONVENIENCE	INCORRUPTIBLES
INCOMPATIBLY	INCONNU	INCONVENIENCED	INCORRUPTIBLY
INCOMPETENCE	INCONNUE	INCONVENIENCES	INCORRUPTION
INCOMPETENCES	INCONNUES	INCONVENIENCIES	INCORRUPTIONS
INCOMPETENCIES	INCONNUS	INCONVENIENCING	INCORRUPTIVE
INCOMPETENCY	INCONSCIENT	INCONVENIENCY	INCORRUPTLY
INCOMPETENT	INCONSCIENTLY	INCONVENIENT	INCORRUPTNESS
INCOMPETENTLY	INCONSCIONABLE	INCONVENIENTLY	INCORRUPTNESSES
INCOMPETENTS	INCONSCIOUS	INCONVERSABLE	INCRASSATE
INCOMPLETE	INCONSECUTIVE	INCONVERSANT	INCRASSATED
INCOMPLETELY	INCONSECUTIVELY	INCONVERTIBLE	INCRASSATES
INCOMPLETENESS	INCONSEQUENCE	INCONVERTIBLY	INCRASSATING
INCOMPLETION	INCONSEQUENCES	INCONVINCIBLE	INCRASSATION
INCOMPLETIONS	INCONSEQUENT	INCONVINCIBLY	INCRASSATIONS
INCOMPLIANCE	INCONSEQUENTIAL	INCONY	INCRASSATIVE
INCOMPLIANCES	INCONSEQUENTLY	INCOORDINATE	INCREASABLE
INCOMPLIANCIES	INCONSIDERABLE	INCOORDINATION	INCREASE
INCOMPLIANCY	INCONSIDERABLY	INCOORDINATIONS	INCREASED
INCOMPLIANT	INCONSIDERATE	INCORONATE	INCREASEDLY
INCOMPLIANTLY	INCONSIDERATELY	INCORONATED	INCREASEFUL
INCOMPOSED	INCONSIDERATION	INCORONATION	INCREASER
INCOMPOSITE	INCONSISTENCE	INCORONATIONS	INCREASERS

INCREASES
INCREASING
INCREASINGLY
INCREASINGS
INCREATE
INCREATELY
INCREDIBILITIES
INCREDIBILITY
INCREDIBLE
INCREDIBLENESS
INCREDIBLY
INCREDULITIES
INCREDULITY
INCREDULOUS
INCREDULOUSLY
INCREDULOUSNESS
INCREMATE
INCREMATED
INCREMATES
INCREMATING
INCREMATION
INCREMATIONS
INCREMENT
INCREMENTAL
INCREMENTALISM
INCREMENTALISMS
INCREMENTALIST
INCREMENTALISTS
INCREMENTALLY
INCREMENTALS
INCREMENTED
INCREMENTING
INCREMENTS
INCRESCENT
INCRETION
INCRETIONARY
INCRETIONS
INCRETORY
INCRIMINATE
INCRIMINATED
INCRIMINATES
INCRIMINATING
INCRIMINATION
INCRIMINATIONS
INCRIMINATOR
INCRIMINATORS
INCRIMINATORY
INCROSS
INCROSSBRED
INCROSSBREDS
INCROSSBREED
INCROSSBREEDING
INCROSSBREEDS
INCROSSED
INCROSSES
INCROSSING

INCRUST
INCRUSTANT
INCRUSTANTS
INCRUSTATION
INCRUSTATIONS
INCRUSTED
INCRUSTING
INCRUSTS
INCUBATE
INCUBATED
INCUBATES
INCUBATING
INCUBATION
INCUBATIONAL
INCUBATIONALLY
INCUBATIONS
INCUBATIVE
INCUBATOR
INCUBATORS
INCUBATORY
INCUBI
INCUBOUS
INCUBUS
INCUBUSES
INCUDAL
INCUDATE
INCUDES
INCULCATE
INCULCATED
INCULCATES
INCULCATING
INCULCATION
INCULCATIONS
INCULCATIVE
INCULCATOR
INCULCATORS
INCULCATORY
INCULPABILITY
INCULPABLE
INCULPABLENESS
INCULPABLY
INCULPATE
INCULPATED
INCULPATES
INCULPATING
INCULPATION
INCULPATIONS
INCULPATIVE
INCULPATORY
INCULT
INCUMBENCIES
INCUMBENCY
INCUMBENT
INCUMBENTLY
INCUMBENTS
INCUMBER

INCUMBERED
INCUMBERING
INCUMBERINGLY
INCUMBERS
INCUMBRANCE
INCUMBRANCES
INCUNABLE
INCUNABLES
INCUNABULA
INCUNABULAR
INCUNABULIST
INCUNABULISTS
INCUNABULUM
INCUR
INCURABILITIES
INCURABILITY
INCURABLE
INCURABLENESS
INCURABLENESSES
INCURABLES
INCURABLY
INCURIOSITIES
INCURIOSITY
INCURIOUS
INCURIOUSLY
INCURIOUSNESS
INCURIOUSNESSES
INCURRABLE
INCURRED
INCURRENCE
INCURRENCES
INCURRENT
INCURRING
INCURS
INCURSION
INCURSIONS
INCURSIVE
INCURVATE
INCURVATED
INCURVATES
INCURVATING
INCURVATION
INCURVATIONS
INCURVATURE
INCURVATURES
INCURVE
INCURVED
INCURVES
INCURVING
INCURVITIES
INCURVITY
INCUS
INCUSE
INCUSED
INCUSES
INCUSING

INCUT
INDABA
INDABAS
INDAGATE
INDAGATED
INDAGATES
INDAGATING
INDAGATION
INDAGATIONS
INDAGATIVE
INDAGATOR
INDAGATORS
INDAGATORY
INDAMIN
INDAMINE
INDAMINES
INDAMINS
INDAPAMIDE
INDAPAMIDES
INDART
INDARTED
INDARTING
INDARTS
INDEBTED
INDEBTEDNESS
INDEBTEDNESSES
INDECENCIES
INDECENCY
INDECENT
INDECENTER
INDECENTEST
INDECENTLY
INDECIDUATE
INDECIDUOUS
INDECIPHERABLE
INDECIPHERABLES
INDECIPHERABLY
INDECISION
INDECISIONS
INDECISIVE
INDECISIVELY
INDECISIVENESS
INDECLINABLE
INDECLINABLY
INDECOMPOSABLE
INDECOROUS
INDECOROUSLY
INDECOROUSNESS
INDECORUM
INDECORUMS
INDEED
INDEFATIGABLE
INDEFATIGABLY
INDEFEASIBILITY
INDEFEASIBLE
INDEFEASIBLY

INDEFECTIBILITY
INDEFECTIBLE
INDEFECTIBLY
INDEFENSIBILITY
INDEFENSIBLE
INDEFENSIBLY
INDEFINABILITY
INDEFINABLE
INDEFINABLENESS
INDEFINABLES
INDEFINABLY
INDEFINITE
INDEFINITELY
INDEFINITENESS
INDEFINITES
INDEHISCENCE
INDEHISCENCES
INDEHISCENT
INDELIBILITIES
INDELIBILITY
INDELIBLE
INDELIBLENESS
INDELIBLENESSES
INDELIBLY
INDELICACIES
INDELICACY
INDELICATE
INDELICATELY
INDELICATENESS
INDEMNIFICATION
INDEMNIFIED
INDEMNIFIER
INDEMNIFIERS
INDEMNIFIES
INDEMNIFY
INDEMNIFYING
INDEMNITIES
INDEMNITY
INDEMONSTRABLE
INDEMONSTRABLY
INDENE
INDENES
INDENT
INDENTATION
INDENTATIONS
INDENTED
INDENTER
INDENTERS
INDENTING
INDENTION
INDENTIONS
INDENTOR
INDENTORS
INDENTS
INDENTURE
INDENTURED

INDENTURES
INDENTURESHIP
INDENTURESHIPS
INDENTURING
INDEPENDENCE
INDEPENDENCES
INDEPENDENCIES
INDEPENDENCY
INDEPENDENT
INDEPENDENTLY
INDEPENDENTS
INDESCRIBABLE
INDESCRIBABLES
INDESCRIBABLY
INDESIGNATE
INDESTRUCTIBLE
INDESTRUCTIBLY
INDETECTABLE
INDETECTIBLE
INDETERMINABLE
INDETERMINABLY
INDETERMINACIES
INDETERMINACY
INDETERMINATE
INDETERMINATELY
INDETERMINATION
INDETERMINED
INDETERMINISM
INDETERMINISMS
INDETERMINIST
INDETERMINISTIC
INDETERMINISTS
INDEVOUT
INDEW
INDEWED
INDEWING
INDEWS
INDEX
INDEXAL
INDEXATION
INDEXATIONS
INDEXED
INDEXER
INDEXERS
INDEXES
INDEXICAL
INDEXICALS
INDEXING
INDEXINGS
INDEXLESS
INDEXTERITIES
INDEXTERITY
INDICAN
INDICANS
INDICANT
INDICANTS

INDICATABILITY
INDICATABLE
INDICATE
INDICATED
INDICATES
INDICATING
INDICATION
INDICATIONAL
INDICATIONS
INDICATIVE
INDICATIVELY
INDICATIVES
INDICATOR
INDICATORS
INDICATORY
INDICES
INDICIA
INDICIAL
INDICIAS
INDICIUM
INDICIUMS
INDICOLITE
INDICOLITES
INDICT
INDICTABLE
INDICTABLY
INDICTED
INDICTEE
INDICTEES
INDICTER
INDICTERS
INDICTING
INDICTION
INDICTIONAL
INDICTIONS
INDICTMENT
INDICTMENTS
INDICTOR
INDICTORS
INDICTS
INDIE
INDIES
INDIFFERENCE
INDIFFERENCES
INDIFFERENCIES
INDIFFERENCY
INDIFFERENT
INDIFFERENTISM
INDIFFERENTISMS
INDIFFERENTIST
INDIFFERENTISTS
INDIFFERENTLY
INDIFFERENTS
INDIGEN
INDIGENCE
INDIGENCES

INDIGENCIES
INDIGENCY
INDIGENE
INDIGENES
INDIGENISATION
INDIGENISATIONS
INDIGENISE
INDIGENISED
INDIGENISES
INDIGENISING
INDIGENITIES
INDIGENITY
INDIGENIZATION
INDIGENIZATIONS
INDIGENIZE
INDIGENIZED
INDIGENIZES
INDIGENIZING
INDIGENOUS
INDIGENOUSLY
INDIGENOUSNESS
INDIGENS
INDIGENT
INDIGENTLY
INDIGENTS
INDIGEST
INDIGESTED
INDIGESTIBILITY
INDIGESTIBLE
INDIGESTIBLES
INDIGESTIBLY
INDIGESTION
INDIGESTIONS
INDIGESTIVE
INDIGESTS
INDIGN
INDIGNANCE
INDIGNANCES
INDIGNANT
INDIGNANTLY
INDIGNATION
INDIGNATIONS
INDIGNIFIED
INDIGNIFIES
INDIGNIFY
INDIGNIFYING
INDIGNITIES
INDIGNITY
INDIGNLY
INDIGO
INDIGOES
INDIGOID
INDIGOIDS
INDIGOLITE
INDIGOLITES
INDIGOS

INDIGOTIC
INDIGOTIN
INDIGOTINS
INDIRECT
INDIRECTION
INDIRECTIONS
INDIRECTLY
INDIRECTNESS
INDIRECTNESSES
INDIRUBIN
INDIRUBINS
INDISCERNIBLE
INDISCERNIBLY
INDISCERPTIBLE
INDISCIPLINABLE
INDISCIPLINE
INDISCIPLINED
INDISCIPLINES
INDISCOVERABLE
INDISCREET
INDISCREETLY
INDISCREETNESS
INDISCRETE
INDISCRETELY
INDISCRETENESS
INDISCRETION
INDISCRETIONARY
INDISCRETIONS
INDISCRIMINATE
INDISPENSABLE
INDISPENSABLES
INDISPENSABLY
INDISPOSE
INDISPOSED
INDISPOSEDNESS
INDISPOSES
INDISPOSING
INDISPOSITION
INDISPOSITIONS
INDISPUTABILITY
INDISPUTABLE
INDISPUTABLY
INDISSOCIABLE
INDISSOCIABLY
INDISSOLUBILITY
INDISSOLUBLE
INDISSOLUBLY
INDISSOLVABLE
INDISSUADABLE
INDISSUADABLY
INDISTINCT
INDISTINCTION
INDISTINCTIONS
INDISTINCTIVE
INDISTINCTIVELY
INDISTINCTLY

INDISTINCTNESS
INDISTRIBUTABLE
INDITE
INDITED
INDITEMENT
INDITEMENTS
INDITER
INDITERS
INDITES
INDITING
INDIUM
INDIUMS
INDIVERTIBILITY
INDIVERTIBLE
INDIVERTIBLY
INDIVIDABLE
INDIVIDUA
INDIVIDUAL
INDIVIDUALISE
INDIVIDUALISED
INDIVIDUALISER
INDIVIDUALISERS
INDIVIDUALISES
INDIVIDUALISING
INDIVIDUALISM
INDIVIDUALISMS
INDIVIDUALIST
INDIVIDUALISTIC
INDIVIDUALISTS
INDIVIDUALITIES
INDIVIDUALITY
INDIVIDUALIZE
INDIVIDUALIZED
INDIVIDUALIZER
INDIVIDUALIZERS
INDIVIDUALIZES
INDIVIDUALIZING
INDIVIDUALLY
INDIVIDUALS
INDIVIDUATE
INDIVIDUATED
INDIVIDUATES
INDIVIDUATING
INDIVIDUATION
INDIVIDUATIONS
INDIVIDUATOR
INDIVIDUATORS
INDIVIDUUM
INDIVISIBILITY
INDIVISIBLE
INDIVISIBLENESS
INDIVISIBLES
INDIVISIBLY
INDOCIBLE
INDOCILE
INDOCILITIES

INDOCILITY
INDOCTRINATE
INDOCTRINATED
INDOCTRINATES
INDOCTRINATING
INDOCTRINATION
INDOCTRINATIONS
INDOCTRINATOR
INDOCTRINATORS
INDOL
INDOLE
INDOLEACETIC
INDOLEBUTYRIC
INDOLENCE
INDOLENCES
INDOLENCIES
INDOLENCY
INDOLENT
INDOLENTLY
INDOLES
INDOLS
INDOMETHACIN
INDOMETHACINS
INDOMITABILITY
INDOMITABLE
INDOMITABLENESS
INDOMITABLY
INDOOR
INDOORS
INDOPHENOL
INDOPHENOLS
INDORSABILITY
INDORSABLE
INDORSE
INDORSED
INDORSEE
INDORSEES
INDORSEMENT
INDORSEMENTS
INDORSER
INDORSERS
INDORSES
INDORSING
INDORSOR
INDORSORS
INDOW
INDOWED
INDOWING
INDOWS
INDOXYL
INDOXYLS
INDRAFT
INDRAFTS
INDRAUGHT
INDRAUGHTS
INDRAWN

INDRENCH
INDRENCHED
INDRENCHES
INDRENCHING
INDRI
INDRIS
INDRISES
INDUBIOUS
INDUBITABILITY
INDUBITABLE
INDUBITABLENESS
INDUBITABLY
INDUCE
INDUCED
INDUCEMENT
INDUCEMENTS
INDUCER
INDUCERS
INDUCES
INDUCIAE
INDUCIBILITIES
INDUCIBILITY
INDUCIBLE
INDUCING
INDUCT
INDUCTANCE
INDUCTANCES
INDUCTED
INDUCTEE
INDUCTEES
INDUCTILE
INDUCTILITIES
INDUCTILITY
INDUCTING
INDUCTION
INDUCTIONAL
INDUCTIONS
INDUCTIVE
INDUCTIVELY
INDUCTIVENESS
INDUCTIVITIES
INDUCTIVITY
INDUCTOR
INDUCTORS
INDUCTS
INDUE
INDUED
INDUES
INDUING
INDULGE
INDULGED
INDULGENCE
INDULGENCED
INDULGENCES
INDULGENCIES
INDULGENCING

INDULGENCY
INDULGENT
INDULGENTLY
INDULGER
INDULGERS
INDULGES
INDULGING
INDULGINGLY
INDULIN
INDULINE
INDULINES
INDULINS
INDULT
INDULTS
INDUMENTA
INDUMENTUM
INDUMENTUMS
INDUNA
INDUNAS
INDUPLICATE
INDUPLICATED
INDUPLICATION
INDUPLICATIONS
INDURATE
INDURATED
INDURATES
INDURATING
INDURATION
INDURATIONS
INDURATIVE
INDUSIA
INDUSIAL
INDUSIATE
INDUSIUM
INDUSTRIAL
INDUSTRIALISE
INDUSTRIALISED
INDUSTRIALISES
INDUSTRIALISING
INDUSTRIALISM
INDUSTRIALISMS
INDUSTRIALIST
INDUSTRIALISTS
INDUSTRIALIZE
INDUSTRIALIZED
INDUSTRIALIZES
INDUSTRIALIZING
INDUSTRIALLY
INDUSTRIALS
INDUSTRIES
INDUSTRIOUS
INDUSTRIOUSLY
INDUSTRIOUSNESS
INDUSTRY
INDUSTRYWIDE
INDUVIAE

INDUVIAL
INDUVIATE
INDWELL
INDWELLER
INDWELLERS
INDWELLING
INDWELLINGS
INDWELLS
INDWELT
INEARTH
INEARTHED
INEARTHING
INEARTHS
INEBRIANT
INEBRIANTS
INEBRIATE
INEBRIATED
INEBRIATES
INEBRIATING
INEBRIATION
INEBRIATIONS
INEBRIETIES
INEBRIETY
INEBRIOUS
INEDIBILITIES
INEDIBILITY
INEDIBLE
INEDITA
INEDITED
INEDUCABILITIES
INEDUCABILITY
INEDUCABLE
INEFFABILITIES
INEFFABILITY
INEFFABLE
INEFFABLENESS
INEFFABLENESSES
INEFFABLY
INEFFACEABILITY
INEFFACEABLE
INEFFACEABLY
INEFFECTIVE
INEFFECTIVELY
INEFFECTIVENESS
INEFFECTUAL
INEFFECTUALITY
INEFFECTUALLY
INEFFECTUALNESS
INEFFICACIES
INEFFICACIOUS
INEFFICACIOUSLY
INEFFICACITY
INEFFICACY
INEFFICIENCIES
INEFFICIENCY
INEFFICIENT

INEFFICIENTLY
INEFFICIENTS
INEGALITARIAN
INELABORATE
INELABORATELY
INELASTIC
INELASTICALLY
INELASTICITIES
INELASTICITY
INELEGANCE
INELEGANCES
INELEGANCIES
INELEGANCY
INELEGANT
INELEGANTLY
INELIGIBILITIES
INELIGIBILITY
INELIGIBLE
INELIGIBLENESS
INELIGIBLES
INELIGIBLY
INELOQUENCE
INELOQUENCES
INELOQUENT
INELOQUENTLY
INELUCTABILITY
INELUCTABLE
INELUCTABLY
INELUDIBILITY
INELUDIBLE
INELUDIBLY
INENARRABLE
INEPT
INEPTER
INEPTEST
INEPTITUDE
INEPTITUDES
INEPTLY
INEPTNESS
INEPTNESSES
INEQUABLE
INEQUALITIES
INEQUALITY
INEQUATION
INEQUATIONS
INEQUIPOTENT
INEQUITABLE
INEQUITABLENESS
INEQUITABLY
INEQUITIES
INEQUITY
INEQUIVALVE
INEQUIVALVED
INERADICABILITY
INERADICABLE
INERADICABLY

INERASABLE
INERASABLY
INERASIBLE
INERASIBLY
INERM
INERMOUS
INERRABILITIES
INERRABILITY
INERRABLE
INERRABLENESS
INERRABLENESSES
INERRABLY
INERRANCIES
INERRANCY
INERRANT
INERT
INERTER
INERTEST
INERTIA
INERTIAE
INERTIAL
INERTIALLY
INERTIAS
INERTLY
INERTNESS
INERTNESSES
INERTS
INERUDITE
INESCAPABLE
INESCAPABLY
INESCULENT
INESCUTCHEON
INESCUTCHEONS
INESSENTIAL
INESSENTIALITY
INESSENTIALNESS
INESSENTIALS
INESSIVE
INESSIVES
INESTIMABILITY
INESTIMABLE
INESTIMABLENESS
INESTIMABLY
INEVITABILITIES
INEVITABILITY
INEVITABLE
INEVITABLENESS
INEVITABLY
INEXACT
INEXACTITUDE
INEXACTITUDES
INEXACTLY
INEXACTNESS
INEXACTNESSES
INEXCITABLE
INEXCUSABILITY

INEXCUSABLE
INEXCUSABLENESS
INEXCUSABLY
INEXECRABLE
INEXECUTABLE
INEXECUTION
INEXECUTIONS
INEXHAUSTED
INEXHAUSTIBLE
INEXHAUSTIBLY
INEXHAUSTIVE
INEXISTANT
INEXISTENCE
INEXISTENCES
INEXISTENCY
INEXISTENT
INEXORABILITIES
INEXORABILITY
INEXORABLE
INEXORABLENESS
INEXORABLY
INEXPANSIBLE
INEXPECTANCIES
INEXPECTANCY
INEXPECTANT
INEXPECTATION
INEXPECTATIONS
INEXPEDIENCE
INEXPEDIENCES
INEXPEDIENCIES
INEXPEDIENCY
INEXPEDIENT
INEXPEDIENTLY
INEXPENSIVE
INEXPENSIVELY
INEXPENSIVENESS
INEXPERIENCE
INEXPERIENCED
INEXPERIENCES
INEXPERT
INEXPERTLY
INEXPERTNESS
INEXPERTNESSES
INEXPERTS
INEXPIABLE
INEXPIABLENESS
INEXPIABLY
INEXPLAINABLE
INEXPLAINABLES
INEXPLAINABLY
INEXPLICABILITY
INEXPLICABLE
INEXPLICABLY
INEXPLICIT
INEXPLICITLY
INEXPLICITNESS

INEXPRESSIBLE
INEXPRESSIBLES
INEXPRESSIBLY
INEXPRESSIVE
INEXPRESSIVELY
INEXPUGNABILITY
INEXPUGNABLE
INEXPUGNABLY
INEXPUNGIBLE
INEXTENDED
INEXTENSIBILITY
INEXTENSIBLE
INEXTENSION
INEXTENSIONS
INEXTIRPABLE
INEXTRICABILITY
INEXTRICABLE
INEXTRICABLY
INFALL
INFALLIBILISM
INFALLIBILISMS
INFALLIBILIST
INFALLIBILISTS
INFALLIBILITIES
INFALLIBILITY
INFALLIBLE
INFALLIBLENESS
INFALLIBLES
INFALLIBLY
INFALLING
INFALLS
INFAME
INFAMED
INFAMES
INFAMIES
INFAMING
INFAMISE
INFAMISED
INFAMISES
INFAMISING
INFAMIZE
INFAMIZED
INFAMIZES
INFAMIZING
INFAMONISED
INFAMONISES
INFAMONISING
INFAMONIZE
INFAMONIZED
INFAMONIZES
INFAMONIZING
INFAMOUS
INFAMOUSLY
INFAMOUSNESS
INFAMY
INFANCIES

INFANCY
INFANGTHIEF
INFANGTHIEFS
INFANT
INFANTA
INFANTAS
INFANTE
INFANTES
INFANTHOOD
INFANTHOODS
INFANTICIDAL
INFANTICIDE
INFANTICIDES
INFANTILE
INFANTILISM
INFANTILISMS
INFANTILITIES
INFANTILITY
INFANTILIZATION
INFANTILIZE
INFANTILIZED
INFANTILIZES
INFANTILIZING
INFANTINE
INFANTIVORE
INFANTIVOROUS
INFANTIVOROUSLY
INFANTRIES
INFANTRY
INFANTRYMAN
INFANTRYMEN
INFANTS
INFARCT
INFARCTED
INFARCTION
INFARCTIONS
INFARCTS
INFARE
INFARES
INFATUATE
INFATUATED
INFATUATEDLY
INFATUATEDNESS
INFATUATES
INFATUATING
INFATUATION
INFATUATIONS
INFAUNA
INFAUNAE
INFAUNAL
INFAUNAS
INFAUST
INFEASIBILITIES
INFEASIBILITY
INFEASIBLE
INFEASIBLENESS

INFECT
INFECTED
INFECTER
INFECTERS
INFECTING
INFECTION
INFECTIONS
INFECTIOUS
INFECTIOUSLY
INFECTIOUSNESS
INFECTIVE
INFECTIVELY
INFECTIVENESS
INFECTIVENESSES
INFECTIVITIES
INFECTIVITY
INFECTOR
INFECTORS
INFECTS
INFECUND
INFECUNDITIES
INFECUNDITY
INFEFT
INFEFTED
INFEFTING
INFEFTMENT
INFEFTMENTS
INFEFTS
INFELICITIES
INFELICITOUS
INFELICITOUSLY
INFELICITY
INFELT
INFEOFF
INFEOFFED
INFEOFFING
INFEOFFS
INFER
INFERABLE
INFERABLY
INFERE
INFERENCE
INFERENCES
INFERENCING
INFERENTIAL
INFERENTIALLY
INFERIAE
INFERIBLE
INFERIOR
INFERIORITIES
INFERIORITY
INFERIORLY
INFERIORS
INFERNAL
INFERNALITIES
INFERNALITY

INFERNALLY
INFERNO
INFERNOS
INFERRABLE
INFERRED
INFERRER
INFERRERS
INFERRIBLE
INFERRING
INFERS
INFERTILE
INFERTILELY
INFERTILITIES
INFERTILITY
INFEST
INFESTANT
INFESTANTS
INFESTATION
INFESTATIONS
INFESTED
INFESTER
INFESTERS
INFESTING
INFESTS
INFEUDATION
INFEUDATIONS
INFIBULATE
INFIBULATED
INFIBULATES
INFIBULATING
INFIBULATION
INFIBULATIONS
INFICETE
INFIDEL
INFIDELITIES
INFIDELITY
INFIDELS
INFIELD
INFIELDER
INFIELDERS
INFIELDS
INFIELDSMAN
INFIELDSMEN
INFIGHT
INFIGHTER
INFIGHTERS
INFIGHTING
INFIGHTINGS
INFIGHTS
INFILL
INFILLED
INFILLING
INFILLINGS
INFILLS
INFILTRATE
INFILTRATED

INFILTRATES
INFILTRATING
INFILTRATION
INFILTRATIONS
INFILTRATIVE
INFILTRATOR
INFILTRATORS
INFIMA
INFIMUM
INFIMUMS
INFINITANT
INFINITARY
INFINITATE
INFINITATED
INFINITATES
INFINITATING
INFINITE
INFINITELY
INFINITENESS
INFINITENESSES
INFINITES
INFINITESIMAL
INFINITESIMALLY
INFINITESIMALS
INFINITIES
INFINITIVAL
INFINITIVALLY
INFINITIVE
INFINITIVELY
INFINITIVES
INFINITUDE
INFINITUDES
INFINITY
INFIRM
INFIRMARER
INFIRMARERS
INFIRMARIAN
INFIRMARIANS
INFIRMARIES
INFIRMARY
INFIRMED
INFIRMER
INFIRMEST
INFIRMING
INFIRMITIES
INFIRMITY
INFIRMLY
INFIRMNESS
INFIRMNESSES
INFIRMS
INFIX
INFIXATION
INFIXATIONS
INFIXED
INFIXES
INFIXING

INFIXION
INFIXIONS
INFLAMABLE
INFLAME
INFLAMED
INFLAMER
INFLAMERS
INFLAMES
INFLAMING
INFLAMINGLY
INFLAMMABILITY
INFLAMMABLE
INFLAMMABLENESS
INFLAMMABLES
INFLAMMABLY
INFLAMMATION
INFLAMMATIONS
INFLAMMATORILY
INFLAMMATORY
INFLATABLE
INFLATABLES
INFLATE
INFLATED
INFLATEDLY
INFLATEDNESS
INFLATER
INFLATERS
INFLATES
INFLATING
INFLATINGLY
INFLATION
INFLATIONARY
INFLATIONISM
INFLATIONISMS
INFLATIONIST
INFLATIONISTS
INFLATIONS
INFLATIVE
INFLATOR
INFLATORS
INFLATUS
INFLATUSES
INFLECT
INFLECTABLE
INFLECTED
INFLECTEDLY
INFLECTEDNESS
INFLECTING
INFLECTION
INFLECTIONAL
INFLECTIONALLY
INFLECTIONLESS
INFLECTIONS
INFLECTIVE
INFLECTOR
INFLECTORS

INFLECTS
INFLEXED
INFLEXIBILITIES
INFLEXIBILITY
INFLEXIBLE
INFLEXIBLENESS
INFLEXIBLY
INFLEXION
INFLEXIONAL
INFLEXIONALLY
INFLEXIONLESS
INFLEXIONS
INFLEXURE
INFLEXURES
INFLICT
INFLICTABLE
INFLICTED
INFLICTER
INFLICTERS
INFLICTING
INFLICTION
INFLICTIONS
INFLICTIVE
INFLICTOR
INFLICTORS
INFLICTS
INFLIGHT
INFLORESCENCE
INFLORESCENCES
INFLORESCENT
INFLOW
INFLOWING
INFLOWINGS
INFLOWS
INFLUENCE
INFLUENCEABLE
INFLUENCED
INFLUENCER
INFLUENCERS
INFLUENCES
INFLUENCING
INFLUENT
INFLUENTIAL
INFLUENTIALLY
INFLUENTIALS
INFLUENTS
INFLUENZA
INFLUENZAL
INFLUENZAS
INFLUX
INFLUXES
INFLUXION
INFLUXIONS
INFO
INFOBAHN
INFOBAHNS

INFOLD
INFOLDED
INFOLDER
INFOLDERS
INFOLDING
INFOLDMENT
INFOLDMENTS
INFOLDS
INFOMANIA
INFOMANIAS
INFOMERCIAL
INFOMERCIALS
INFOPRENEURIAL
INFORCE
INFORCED
INFORCES
INFORCING
INFORM
INFORMABLE
INFORMABLY
INFORMAL
INFORMALITIES
INFORMALITY
INFORMALLY
INFORMANT
INFORMANTS
INFORMATICIAN
INFORMATICIANS
INFORMATICS
INFORMATION
INFORMATIONAL
INFORMATIONALLY
INFORMATIONS
INFORMATIVE
INFORMATIVELY
INFORMATIVENESS
INFORMATORILY
INFORMATORY
INFORMED
INFORMEDLY
INFORMER
INFORMERS
INFORMIDABLE
INFORMING
INFORMINGLY
INFORMINGNESS
INFORMS
INFORTUNE
INFORTUNES
INFOS
INFOSPHERE
INFOSPHERES
INFOTAINMENT
INFOTAINMENTS
INFOUGHT
INFRA

INFRACOSTAL
INFRACT
INFRACTED
INFRACTING
INFRACTION
INFRACTIONS
INFRACTOR
INFRACTORS
INFRACTS
INFRAGRANT
INFRAHUMAN
INFRAHUMANS
INFRALAPSARIAN
INFRALAPSARIANS
INFRAMAXILLARY
INFRANGIBILITY
INFRANGIBLE
INFRANGIBLENESS
INFRANGIBLY
INFRAORBITAL
INFRAPOSED
INFRAPOSITION
INFRAPOSITIONS
INFRARED
INFRAREDS
INFRASONIC
INFRASOUND
INFRASOUNDS
INFRASPECIFIC
INFRASTRUCTURAL
INFRASTRUCTURE
INFRASTRUCTURES
INFREQUENCE
INFREQUENCES
INFREQUENCIES
INFREQUENCY
INFREQUENT
INFREQUENTLY
INFRINGE
INFRINGED
INFRINGEMENT
INFRINGEMENTS
INFRINGER
INFRINGERS
INFRINGES
INFRINGING
INFRUCTUOUS
INFRUCTUOUSLY
INFRUGAL
INFULA
INFULAE
INFUNDIBULA
INFUNDIBULAR
INFUNDIBULATE
INFUNDIBULIFORM
INFUNDIBULUM

INFURIATE
INFURIATED
INFURIATELY
INFURIATES
INFURIATING
INFURIATINGLY
INFURIATION
INFURIATIONS
INFUSCATE
INFUSCATED
INFUSE
INFUSED
INFUSER
INFUSERS
INFUSES
INFUSIBILITIES
INFUSIBILITY
INFUSIBLE
INFUSIBLENESS
INFUSIBLENESSES
INFUSING
INFUSION
INFUSIONISM
INFUSIONIST
INFUSIONISTS
INFUSIONS
INFUSIVE
INFUSORIA
INFUSORIAL
INFUSORIAN
INFUSORIANS
INFUSORY
INGAN
INGANS
INGATE
INGATES
INGATHER
INGATHERED
INGATHERER
INGATHERERS
INGATHERING
INGATHERINGS
INGATHERS
INGEMINATE
INGEMINATED
INGEMINATES
INGEMINATING
INGEMINATION
INGEMINATIONS
INGENER
INGENERATE
INGENERATED
INGENERATES
INGENERATING
INGENERATION
INGENERATIONS

INGENERS
INGENIOUS
INGENIOUSLY
INGENIOUSNESS
INGENIOUSNESSES
INGENIUM
INGENIUMS
INGENU
INGENUE
INGENUES
INGENUITIES
INGENUITY
INGENUOUS
INGENUOUSLY
INGENUOUSNESS
INGENUOUSNESSES
INGENUS
INGEST
INGESTA
INGESTED
INGESTIBLE
INGESTING
INGESTION
INGESTIONS
INGESTIVE
INGESTS
INGINE
INGINES
INGLE
INGLENEUK
INGLENEUKS
INGLENOOK
INGLENOOKS
INGLES
INGLOBE
INGLOBED
INGLOBES
INGLOBING
INGLORIOUS
INGLORIOUSLY
INGLORIOUSNESS
INGLUVIAL
INGLUVIES
INGO
INGOES
INGOING
INGOINGS
INGOS
INGOT
INGOTED
INGOTING
INGOTS
INGRAFT
INGRAFTATION
INGRAFTATIONS
INGRAFTED

INGRAFTING
INGRAFTMENT
INGRAFTMENTS
INGRAFTS
INGRAIN
INGRAINED
INGRAINEDLY
INGRAINEDNESS
INGRAINING
INGRAINS
INGRAM
INGRATE
INGRATEFUL
INGRATELY
INGRATES
INGRATIATE
INGRATIATED
INGRATIATES
INGRATIATING
INGRATIATINGLY
INGRATIATION
INGRATIATIONS
INGRATIATORY
INGRATITUDE
INGRATITUDES
INGRAVESCENCE
INGRAVESCENT
INGRAVESCENTLY
INGREDIENT
INGREDIENTS
INGRESS
INGRESSES
INGRESSION
INGRESSIONS
INGRESSIVE
INGRESSIVENESS
INGRESSIVES
INGROOVE
INGROOVED
INGROOVES
INGROOVING
INGROSS
INGROSSED
INGROSSES
INGROSSING
INGROUP
INGROUPS
INGROWING
INGROWN
INGROWNNESS
INGROWNNESSES
INGROWTH
INGROWTHS
INGRUM
INGUINAL
INGULF

INGULFED
INGULFING
INGULFMENT
INGULFMENTS
INGULFS
INGULPH
INGULPHED
INGULPHING
INGULPHS
INGURGITATE
INGURGITATED
INGURGITATES
INGURGITATING
INGURGITATION
INGURGITATIONS
INHABIT
INHABITABILITY
INHABITABLE
INHABITABLENESS
INHABITANCE
INHABITANCES
INHABITANCIES
INHABITANCY
INHABITANT
INHABITANTS
INHABITATION
INHABITATIONS
INHABITED
INHABITER
INHABITERS
INHABITING
INHABITIVENESS
INHABITOR
INHABITORS
INHABITRESS
INHABITRESSES
INHABITS
INHALANT
INHALANTS
INHALATION
INHALATIONAL
INHALATIONS
INHALATOR
INHALATORIUM
INHALATORIUMS
INHALATORS
INHALE
INHALED
INHALER
INHALERS
INHALES
INHALING
INHARMONIC
INHARMONICAL
INHARMONICITIES
INHARMONICITY

INHARMONIES
INHARMONIOUS
INHARMONIOUSLY
INHARMONY
INHAUL
INHAULER
INHAULERS
INHAULS
INHAUST
INHAUSTED
INHAUSTING
INHAUSTS
INHEARSE
INHEARSED
INHEARSES
INHEARSING
INHERCE
INHERCED
INHERCES
INHERCING
INHERE
INHERED
INHERENCE
INHERENCES
INHERENCIES
INHERENCY
INHERENT
INHERENTLY
INHERES
INHERING
INHERIT
INHERITABILITY
INHERITABLE
INHERITABLENESS
INHERITABLY
INHERITANCE
INHERITANCES
INHERITED
INHERITING
INHERITOR
INHERITORS
INHERITRESS
INHERITRESSES
INHERITRICES
INHERITRIX
INHERITRIXES
INHERITS
INHESION
INHESIONS
INHIBIN
INHIBINS
INHIBIT
INHIBITABLE
INHIBITED
INHIBITER
INHIBITERS

INHIBITING
INHIBITION
INHIBITIONS
INHIBITIVE
INHIBITOR
INHIBITORS
INHIBITORY
INHIBITS
INHOLDER
INHOLDERS
INHOLDING
INHOLDINGS
INHOMOGENEITIES
INHOMOGENEITY
INHOMOGENEOUS
INHOOP
INHOOPED
INHOOPING
INHOOPS
INHOSPITABLE
INHOSPITABLY
INHOSPITALITIES
INHOSPITALITY
INHUMAN
INHUMANE
INHUMANELY
INHUMANITIES
INHUMANITY
INHUMANLY
INHUMANNESS
INHUMANNESSES
INHUMATE
INHUMATED
INHUMATES
INHUMATING
INHUMATION
INHUMATIONS
INHUME
INHUMED
INHUMER
INHUMERS
INHUMES
INHUMING
INIA
INIMICAL
INIMICALITIES
INIMICALITY
INIMICALLY
INIMICALNESS
INIMICALNESSES
INIMICITIOUS
INIMITABILITIES
INIMITABILITY
INIMITABLE
INIMITABLENESS
INIMITABLY

INION	INJECT	INKED	INLOCKING
INIONS	INJECTABLE	INKER	INLOCKS
INIQUITIES	INJECTABLES	INKERS	INLY
INIQUITOUS	INJECTANT	INKHOLDER	INLYING
INIQUITOUSLY	INJECTANTS	INKHOLDERS	INMARRIAGE
INIQUITOUSNESS	INJECTED	INKHORN	INMARRIAGES
INIQUITY	INJECTING	INKHORNS	INMATE
INISLE	INJECTION	INKIER	INMATES
INISLED	INJECTIONS	INKIEST	INMESH
INISLES	INJECTIVE	INKINESS	INMESHED
INISLING	INJECTOR	INKINESSES	INMESHES
INITIAL	INJECTORS	INKING	INMESHING
INITIALED	INJECTS	INKJET	IMMIGRANT
INITIALER	INJELLIED	INKLE	INMIGRANTS
INITIALERS	INJELLIES	INKLED	INMOST
INITIALING	INJELLY	INKLES	INN
INITIALISATION	INJELLYING	INKLESS	INNARDS
INITIALISATIONS	INJERA	INKLIKE	INNATE
INITIALISE	INJERAS	INKLING	INNATELY
INITIALISED	INJOINT	INKLINGS	INNATENESS
INITIALISES	INJOINTED	INKPOT	INNATENESSES
INITIALISING	INJOINTING	INKPOTS	INNATIVE
INITIALISM	INJOINTS	INKS	INNAVIGABLE
INITIALISMS	INJUDICIAL	INKSPOT	INNAVIGABLY
INITIALIZATION	INJUDICIALLY	INKSPOTS	INNED
INITIALIZATIONS	INJUDICIOUS	INKSTAND	INNER
INITIALIZE	INJUDICIOUSLY	INKSTANDS	INNERLY
INITIALIZED	INJUDICIOUSNESS	INKSTONE	INNERMOST
INITIALIZES	INJUNCT	INKSTONES	INNERMOSTS
INITIALIZING	INJUNCTED	INKWELL	INNERNESS
INITIALLED	INJUNCTING	INKWELLS	INNERS
INITIALLER	INJUNCTION	INKWOOD	INNERSOLE
INITIALLERS	INJUNCTIONS	INKWOODS	INNERSOLES
INITIALLING	INJUNCTIVE	INKY	INNERSPRING
INITIALLY	INJUNCTIVELY	INLACE	INNERVATE
INITIALNESS	INJUNCTS	INLACED	INNERVATED
INITIALNESSES	INJURABLE	INLACES	INNERVATES
INITIALS	INJURE	INLACING	INNERVATING
INITIATE	INJURED	INLAID	INNERVATION
INITIATED	INJURER	INLAND	INNERVATIONS
INITIATES	INJURERS	INLANDER	INNERVE
INITIATING	INJURES	INLANDERS	INNERVED
INITIATION	INJURIES	INLANDS	INNERVES
INITIATIONS	INJURING	INLAY	INNERVING
INITIATIVE	INJURIOUS	INLAYER	INNERWEAR
INITIATIVELY	INJURIOUSLY	INLAYERS	INNERWEARS
INITIATIVES	INJURIOUSNESS	INLAYING	INNING
INITIATOR	INJURIOUSNESSES	INLAYINGS	INNINGS
INITIATORIES	INJURY	INLAYS	INNKEEPER
INITIATORS	INJUSTICE	INLET	INNKEEPERS
INITIATORY	INJUSTICES	INLETS	INNLESS
INITIATRESS	INK	INLETTING	INNOCENCE
INITIATRESSES	INKBERRIES	INLIER	INNOCENCES
INITIATRICES	INKBERRY	INLIERS	INNOCENCIES
INITIATRIX	INKBLOT	INLOCK	INNOCENCY
INITIATRIXES	INKBLOTS	INLOCKED	INNOCENT

INNOCENTER
INNOCENTEST
INNOCENTLY
INNOCENTS
INNOCUITIES
INNOCUITY
INNOCUOUS
INNOCUOUSLY
INNOCUOUSNESS
INNOCUOUSNESSES
INNOMINABLE
INNOMINABLES
INNOMINATE
INNOVATE
INNOVATED
INNOVATES
INNOVATING
INNOVATION
INNOVATIONAL
INNOVATIONIST
INNOVATIONISTS
INNOVATIONS
INNOVATIVE
INNOVATIVELY
INNOVATIVENESS
INNOVATOR
INNOVATORS
INNOVATORY
INNOXIOUS
INNOXIOUSLY
INNOXIOUSNESS
INNOXIOUSNESSES
INNS
INNUENDO
INNUENDOED
INNUENDOES
INNUENDOING
INNUENDOS
INNUMERABILITY
INNUMERABLE
INNUMERABLENESS
INNUMERABLY
INNUMERACIES
INNUMERACY
INNUMERATE
INNUMERATES
INNUMEROUS
INNUTRIENT
INNUTRITION
INNUTRITIONS
INNUTRITIOUS
INNYARD
INNYARDS
INOBEDIENCE
INOBEDIENCES
INOBEDIENT

INOBEDIENTLY
INOBSERVABLE
INOBSERVANCE
INOBSERVANCES
INOBSERVANT
INOBSERVANTLY
INOBSERVATION
INOBSERVATIONS
INOBTRUSIVE
INOBTRUSIVELY
INOBTRUSIVENESS
INOCCUPATION
INOCCUPATIONS
INOCULA
INOCULABILITIES
INOCULABILITY
INOCULABLE
INOCULANT
INOCULANTS
INOCULATE
INOCULATED
INOCULATES
INOCULATING
INOCULATION
INOCULATIONS
INOCULATIVE
INOCULATOR
INOCULATORS
INOCULATORY
INOCULUM
INOCULUMS
INODOROUS
INODOROUSLY
INODOROUSNESS
INODOROUSNESSES
INOFFENSIVE
INOFFENSIVELY
INOFFENSIVENESS
INOFFICIOUS
INOFFICIOUSLY
INOFFICIOUSNESS
INOPERABILITIES
INOPERABILITY
INOPERABLE
INOPERABLENESS
INOPERABLY
INOPERATIVE
INOPERATIVENESS
INOPERCULATE
INOPERCULATES
INOPINATE
INOPPORTUNE
INOPPORTUNELY
INOPPORTUNENESS
INOPPORTUNITIES
INOPPORTUNITY

INORB
INORBED
INORBING
INORBS
INORDINACIES
INORDINACY
INORDINATE
INORDINATELY
INORDINATENESS
INORDINATION
INORDINATIONS
INORGANIC
INORGANICALLY
INORGANISATION
INORGANISATIONS
INORGANISED
INORGANIZATION
INORGANIZATIONS
INORGANIZED
INORNATE
INOSCULATE
INOSCULATED
INOSCULATES
INOSCULATING
INOSCULATION
INOSCULATIONS
INOSITE
INOSITES
INOSITOL
INOSITOLS
INOTROPIC
INPATIENT
INPATIENTS
INPAYMENT
INPAYMENTS
INPHASE
INPOUR
INPOURED
INPOURING
INPOURINGS
INPOURS
INPUT
INPUTS
INPUTTED
INPUTTER
INPUTTERS
INPUTTING
INQILAB
INQILABS
INQUERE
INQUERED
INQUERES
INQUERING
INQUEST
INQUESTS
INQUIET

INQUIETED
INQUIETING
INQUIETLY
INQUIETS
INQUIETUDE
INQUIETUDES
INQUILINE
INQUILINES
INQUILINIC
INQUILINICS
INQUILINISM
INQUILINISMS
INQUILINITIES
INQUILINITY
INQUILINOUS
INQUINATE
INQUINATED
INQUINATES
INQUINATING
INQUINATION
INQUINATIONS
INQUIRATION
INQUIRATIONS
INQUIRE
INQUIRED
INQUIRENDO
INQUIRENDOS
INQUIRER
INQUIRERS
INQUIRES
INQUIRIES
INQUIRING
INQUIRINGLY
INQUIRY
INQUISITION
INQUISITIONAL
INQUISITIONIST
INQUISITIONISTS
INQUISITIONS
INQUISITIVE
INQUISITIVELY
INQUISITIVENESS
INQUISITOR
INQUISITORIAL
INQUISITORIALLY
INQUISITORS
INQUISITRESS
INQUISITRESSES
INQUISITURIENT
INQUORATE
INRO
INROAD
INROADS
INRUSH
INRUSHES
INRUSHING

INRUSHINGS
INS
INSALIVATE
INSALIVATED
INSALIVATES
INSALIVATING
INSALIVATION
INSALIVATIONS
INSALUBRIOUS
INSALUBRIOUSLY
INSALUBRITIES
INSALUBRITY
INSALUTARY
INSANE
INSANELY
INSANENESS
INSANENESSES
INSANER
INSANEST
INSANIE
INSANIES
INSANITARINESS
INSANITARY
INSANITATION
INSANITATIONS
INSANITIES
INSANITY
INSATIABILITIES
INSATIABILITY
INSATIABLE
INSATIABLENESS
INSATIABLY
INSATIATE
INSATIATELY
INSATIATENESS
INSATIATENESSES
INSATIETIES
INSATIETY
INSCAPE
INSCAPES
INSCIENCE
INSCIENCES
INSCIENT
INSCONCE
INSCONCED
INSCONCES
INSCONCING
INSCRIBABLE
INSCRIBABLENESS
INSCRIBE
INSCRIBED
INSCRIBER
INSCRIBERS
INSCRIBES
INSCRIBING
INSCRIPTION

INSCRIPTIONAL
INSCRIPTIONS
INSCRIPTIVE
INSCRIPTIVELY
INSCROLL
INSCROLLED
INSCROLLING
INSCROLLS
INSCRUTABILITY
INSCRUTABLE
INSCRUTABLENESS
INSCRUTABLY
INSCULP
INSCULPED
INSCULPING
INSCULPS
INSCULPT
INSCULPTURE
INSCULPTURED
INSCULPTURES
INSCULPTURING
INSEAM
INSEAMED
INSEAMING
INSEAMS
INSECT
INSECTAN
INSECTARIA
INSECTARIES
INSECTARIUM
INSECTARIUMS
INSECTARY
INSECTEAN
INSECTICIDAL
INSECTICIDALLY
INSECTICIDE
INSECTICIDES
INSECTIFORM
INSECTIFUGE
INSECTIFUGES
INSECTILE
INSECTION
INSECTIONS
INSECTIVORE
INSECTIVORES
INSECTIVOROUS
INSECTOLOGIES
INSECTOLOGIST
INSECTOLOGISTS
INSECTOLOGY
INSECTS
INSECURE
INSECURELY
INSECURENESS
INSECURENESSES
INSECURITIES

INSECURITY
INSEEM
INSEEMED
INSEEMING
INSEEMS
INSELBERG
INSELBERGE
INSELBERGS
INSEMINATE
INSEMINATED
INSEMINATES
INSEMINATING
INSEMINATION
INSEMINATIONS
INSEMINATOR
INSEMINATORS
INSENSATE
INSENSATELY
INSENSATENESS
INSENSATENESSES
INSENSIBILITIES
INSENSIBILITY
INSENSIBLE
INSENSIBLENESS
INSENSIBLY
INSENSITIVE
INSENSITIVELY
INSENSITIVENESS
INSENSITIVITIES
INSENSITIVITY
INSENSUOUS
INSENTIENCE
INSENTIENCES
INSENTIENCIES
INSENTIENCY
INSENTIENT
INSEPARABILITY
INSEPARABLE
INSEPARABLENESS
INSEPARABLES
INSEPARABLY
INSEPARATE
INSERT
INSERTABLE
INSERTED
INSERTER
INSERTERS
INSERTING
INSERTION
INSERTIONAL
INSERTIONS
INSERTS
INSESSORIAL
INSET
INSETS
INSETTED

INSETTER
INSETTERS
INSETTING
INSEVERABLE
INSHALLAH
INSHEATH
INSHEATHE
INSHEATHED
INSHEATHES
INSHEATHING
INSHEATHS
INSHELL
INSHELLED
INSHELLING
INSHELLS
INSHELTER
INSHELTERED
INSHELTERING
INSHELTERS
INSHIP
INSHIPPED
INSHIPPING
INSHIPS
INSHORE
INSHRINE
INSHRINED
INSHRINES
INSHRINING
INSIDE
INSIDER
INSIDERS
INSIDES
INSIDIOUS
INSIDIOUSLY
INSIDIOUSNESS
INSIDIOUSNESSES
INSIGHT
INSIGHTFUL
INSIGHTFULLY
INSIGHTS
INSIGNE
INSIGNIA
INSIGNIAS
INSIGNIFICANCE
INSIGNIFICANCES
INSIGNIFICANCY
INSIGNIFICANT
INSIGNIFICANTLY
INSIGNIFICATIVE
INSINCERE
INSINCERELY
INSINCERITIES
INSINCERITY
INSINEW
INSINEWED
INSINEWING

INSINEWS
INSINUATE
INSINUATED
INSINUATES
INSINUATING
INSINUATINGLY
INSINUATION
INSINUATIONS
INSINUATIVE
INSINUATOR
INSINUATORS
INSINUATORY
INSIPID
INSIPIDITIES
INSIPIDITY
INSIPIDLY
INSIPIDNESS
INSIPIDNESSES
INSIPIENCE
INSIPIENCES
INSIPIENT
INSIPIENTLY
INSIST
INSISTED
INSISTENCE
INSISTENCES
INSISTENCIES
INSISTENCY
INSISTENT
INSISTENTLY
INSISTER
INSISTERS
INSISTING
INSISTINGLY
INSISTINGNESS
INSISTS
INSNARE
INSNARED
INSNAREMENT
INSNAREMENTS
INSNARER
INSNARERS
INSNARES
INSNARING
INSOBRIETIES
INSOBRIETY
INSOCIABILITIES
INSOCIABILITY
INSOCIABLE
INSOCIABLY
INSOFAR
INSOLATE
INSOLATED
INSOLATES
INSOLATING
INSOLATION

INSOLATIONS
INSOLE
INSOLENCE
INSOLENCES
INSOLENT
INSOLENTLY
INSOLENTS
INSOLES
INSOLIDITIES
INSOLIDITY
INSOLUBILISE
INSOLUBILISED
INSOLUBILISES
INSOLUBILISING
INSOLUBILITIES
INSOLUBILITY
INSOLUBILIZE
INSOLUBILIZED
INSOLUBILIZES
INSOLUBILIZING
INSOLUBLE
INSOLUBLENESS
INSOLUBLENESSES
INSOLUBLES
INSOLUBLY
INSOLVABILITIES
INSOLVABILITY
INSOLVABLE
INSOLVABLY
INSOLVENCIES
INSOLVENCY
INSOLVENT
INSOLVENTS
INSOMNIA
INSOMNIAC
INSOMNIACS
INSOMNIAS
INSOMNIOUS
INSOMNOLENCE
INSOMNOLENCES
INSOMUCH
INSOOTH
INSOUCIANCE
INSOUCIANCES
INSOUCIANT
INSOUCIANTLY
INSOUL
INSOULED
INSOULING
INSOULMENT
INSOULMENTS
INSOULS
INSPAN
INSPANNED
INSPANNING
INSPANS

INSPECT
INSPECTABLE
INSPECTABLY
INSPECTED
INSPECTING
INSPECTINGLY
INSPECTION
INSPECTIONAL
INSPECTIONS
INSPECTIVE
INSPECTOR
INSPECTORAL
INSPECTORALLY
INSPECTORATE
INSPECTORATES
INSPECTORIAL
INSPECTORS
INSPECTORSHIP
INSPECTORSHIPS
INSPECTS
INSPHERE
INSPHERED
INSPHERES
INSPHERING
INSPIRABLE
INSPIRATION
INSPIRATIONAL
INSPIRATIONALLY
INSPIRATIONISM
INSPIRATIONISMS
INSPIRATIONIST
INSPIRATIONISTS
INSPIRATIONS
INSPIRATIVE
INSPIRATOR
INSPIRATORS
INSPIRATORY
INSPIRE
INSPIRED
INSPIRER
INSPIRERS
INSPIRES
INSPIRING
INSPIRINGLY
INSPIRIT
INSPIRITED
INSPIRITER
INSPIRITERS
INSPIRITING
INSPIRITINGLY
INSPIRITMENT
INSPIRITMENTS
INSPIRITS
INSPISSATE
INSPISSATED
INSPISSATES

INSPISSATING
INSPISSATION
INSPISSATIONS
INSPISSATOR
INSPISSATORS
INSTABILITIES
INSTABILITY
INSTABLE
INSTAL
INSTALL
INSTALLANT
INSTALLANTS
INSTALLATION
INSTALLATIONS
INSTALLED
INSTALLER
INSTALLERS
INSTALLING
INSTALLMENT
INSTALLMENTS
INSTALLS
INSTALMENT
INSTALMENTS
INSTALS
INSTANCE
INSTANCED
INSTANCES
INSTANCIES
INSTANCING
INSTANCY
INSTANT
INSTANTANEITIES
INSTANTANEITY
INSTANTANEOUS
INSTANTANEOUSLY
INSTANTER
INSTANTIAL
INSTANTIATE
INSTANTIATED
INSTANTIATES
INSTANTIATING
INSTANTIATION
INSTANTIATIONS
INSTANTLY
INSTANTNESS
INSTANTNESSES
INSTANTS
INSTAR
INSTARRED
INSTARRING
INSTARS
INSTATE
INSTATED
INSTATEMENT
INSTATEMENTS
INSTATES

INSTATING
INSTAURATION
INSTAURATIONS
INSTAURATOR
INSTAURATORS
INSTEAD
INSTEP
INSTEPS
INSTIGATE
INSTIGATED
INSTIGATES
INSTIGATING
INSTIGATINGLY
INSTIGATION
INSTIGATIONS
INSTIGATIVE
INSTIGATOR
INSTIGATORS
INSTIL
INSTILL
INSTILLATION
INSTILLATIONS
INSTILLED
INSTILLER
INSTILLERS
INSTILLING
INSTILLMENT
INSTILLMENTS
INSTILLS
INSTILMENT
INSTILMENTS
INSTILS
INSTINCT
INSTINCTIVE
INSTINCTIVELY
INSTINCTIVITIES
INSTINCTIVITY
INSTINCTS
INSTINCTUAL
INSTINCTUALLY
INSTITORIAL
INSTITUTE
INSTITUTED
INSTITUTER
INSTITUTERS
INSTITUTES
INSTITUTING
INSTITUTION
INSTITUTIONAL
INSTITUTIONALLY
INSTITUTIONARY
INSTITUTIONS
INSTITUTIST
INSTITUTISTS
INSTITUTIVE
INSTITUTIVELY

INSTITUTOR
INSTITUTORS
INSTREAMING
INSTREAMINGS
INSTRESS
INSTRESSED
INSTRESSES
INSTRESSING
INSTROKE
INSTROKES
INSTRUCT
INSTRUCTED
INSTRUCTIBLE
INSTRUCTING
INSTRUCTION
INSTRUCTIONAL
INSTRUCTIONS
INSTRUCTIVE
INSTRUCTIVELY
INSTRUCTIVENESS
INSTRUCTOR
INSTRUCTORS
INSTRUCTORSHIP
INSTRUCTORSHIPS
INSTRUCTRESS
INSTRUCTRESSES
INSTRUCTS
INSTRUMENT
INSTRUMENTAL
INSTRUMENTALISM
INSTRUMENTALIST
INSTRUMENTALITY
INSTRUMENTALLY
INSTRUMENTALS
INSTRUMENTATION
INSTRUMENTED
INSTRUMENTING
INSTRUMENTS
INSUBJECTION
INSUBJECTIONS
INSUBORDINATE
INSUBORDINATELY
INSUBORDINATES
INSUBORDINATION
INSUBSTANTIAL
INSUBSTANTIALLY
INSUCKEN
INSUFFERABLE
INSUFFERABLY
INSUFFICIENCE
INSUFFICIENCES
INSUFFICIENCIES
INSUFFICIENCY
INSUFFICIENT
INSUFFICIENTLY
INSUFFLATE

INSUFFLATED
INSUFFLATES
INSUFFLATING
INSUFFLATION
INSUFFLATIONS
INSUFFLATOR
INSUFFLATORS
INSULA
INSULAE
INSULANT
INSULANTS
INSULAR
INSULARISM
INSULARISMS
INSULARITIES
INSULARITY
INSULARLY
INSULARS
INSULAS
INSULATE
INSULATED
INSULATES
INSULATING
INSULATION
INSULATIONS
INSULATOR
INSULATORS
INSULIN
INSULINASE
INSULINASES
INSULINS
INSULSE
INSULSITIES
INSULSITY
INSULT
INSULTABLE
INSULTANT
INSULTED
INSULTER
INSULTERS
INSULTING
INSULTINGLY
INSULTMENT
INSULTMENTS
INSULTS
INSUPERABILITY
INSUPERABLE
INSUPERABLENESS
INSUPERABLY
INSUPPORTABLE
INSUPPORTABLY
INSUPPRESSIBLE
INSUPPRESSIBLY
INSURABILITIES
INSURABILITY
INSURABLE

INSURANCE
INSURANCER
INSURANCERS
INSURANCES
INSURANT
INSURANTS
INSURE
INSURED
INSUREDS
INSURER
INSURERS
INSURES
INSURGENCE
INSURGENCES
INSURGENCIES
INSURGENCY
INSURGENT
INSURGENTLY
INSURGENTS
INSURING
INSURMOUNTABLE
INSURMOUNTABLY
INSURRECTION
INSURRECTIONAL
INSURRECTIONARY
INSURRECTIONISM
INSURRECTIONIST
INSURRECTIONS
INSUSCEPTIBLE
INSUSCEPTIBLY
INSUSCEPTIVE
INSUSCEPTIVELY
INSWATHE
INSWATHED
INSWATHES
INSWATHING
INSWEPT
INSWING
INSWINGER
INSWINGERS
INSWINGS
INTACT
INTACTNESS
INTACTNESSES
INTAGLI
INTAGLIATED
INTAGLIO
INTAGLIOED
INTAGLIOING
INTAGLIOS
INTAKE
INTAKES
INTANGIBILITIES
INTANGIBILITY
INTANGIBLE
INTANGIBLENESS

INTANGIBLES
INTANGIBLY
INTARSIA
INTARSIAS
INTEGER
INTEGERS
INTEGRABILITIES
INTEGRABILITY
INTEGRABLE
INTEGRAL
INTEGRALITIES
INTEGRALITY
INTEGRALLY
INTEGRALS
INTEGRAND
INTEGRANDS
INTEGRANT
INTEGRANTS
INTEGRATE
INTEGRATED
INTEGRATES
INTEGRATING
INTEGRATION
INTEGRATIONIST
INTEGRATIONISTS
INTEGRATIONS
INTEGRATIVE
INTEGRATOR
INTEGRATORS
INTEGRITIES
INTEGRITY
INTEGUMENT
INTEGUMENTAL
INTEGUMENTALLY
INTEGUMENTARY
INTEGUMENTS
INTELLECT
INTELLECTED
INTELLECTION
INTELLECTIONS
INTELLECTIVE
INTELLECTIVELY
INTELLECTS
INTELLECTUAL
INTELLECTUALISE
INTELLECTUALISM
INTELLECTUALIST
INTELLECTUALITY
INTELLECTUALIZE
INTELLECTUALLY
INTELLECTUALS
INTELLIGENCE
INTELLIGENCER
INTELLIGENCERS
INTELLIGENCES
INTELLIGENT

INTELLIGENTIAL
INTELLIGENTLY
INTELLIGENTSIA
INTELLIGENTSIAS
INTELLIGENTZIA
INTELLIGENTZIAS
INTELLIGIBILITY
INTELLIGIBLE
INTELLIGIBLY
INTEMERATE
INTEMERATELY
INTEMERATENESS
INTEMPERANCE
INTEMPERANCES
INTEMPERANT
INTEMPERANTS
INTEMPERATE
INTEMPERATELY
INTEMPERATENESS
INTEMPESTIVE
INTEMPESTIVELY
INTEMPESTIVITY
INTENABLE
INTEND
INTENDANCE
INTENDANCES
INTENDANCIES
INTENDANCY
INTENDANT
INTENDANTS
INTENDED
INTENDEDLY
INTENDEDS
INTENDER
INTENDERED
INTENDERING
INTENDERS
INTENDING
INTENDMENT
INTENDMENTS
INTENDS
INTENERATE
INTENERATED
INTENERATES
INTENERATING
INTENERATION
INTENERATIONS
INTENIBLE
INTENSATE
INTENSATED
INTENSATES
INTENSATING
INTENSATIVE
INTENSATIVES
INTENSE
INTENSELY

INTENSENESS
INTENSENESSES
INTENSER
INTENSEST
INTENSIFICATION
INTENSIFIED
INTENSIFIER
INTENSIFIERS
INTENSIFIES
INTENSIFY
INTENSIFYING
INTENSION
INTENSIONAL
INTENSIONALITY
INTENSIONALLY
INTENSIONS
INTENSITIES
INTENSITIVE
INTENSITIVES
INTENSITY
INTENSIVE
INTENSIVELY
INTENSIVENESS
INTENSIVENESSES
INTENSIVES
INTENT
INTENTION
INTENTIONAL
INTENTIONALITY
INTENTIONALLY
INTENTIONED
INTENTIONS
INTENTIVE
INTENTLY
INTENTNESS
INTENTNESSES
INTENTS
INTER
INTERABANG
INTERABANGS
INTERACADEMIC
INTERACT
INTERACTANT
INTERACTANTS
INTERACTED
INTERACTING
INTERACTION
INTERACTIONAL
INTERACTIONISM
INTERACTIONISMS
INTERACTIONIST
INTERACTIONISTS
INTERACTIONS
INTERACTIVE
INTERACTIVELY
INTERACTIVITY

INTERACTS
INTERAGE
INTERAGENCY
INTERALLELIC
INTERALLIED
INTERAMBULACRA
INTERAMBULACRAL
INTERAMBULACRUM
INTERANIMATION
INTERANIMATIONS
INTERANNUAL
INTERATOMIC
INTERBANK
INTERBASIN
INTERBED
INTERBEDDED
INTERBEDDING
INTERBEDDINGS
INTERBEDS
INTERBEHAVIOR
INTERBEHAVIORAL
INTERBEHAVIORS
INTERBLEND
INTERBLENDED
INTERBLENDING
INTERBLENDS
INTERBOROUGH
INTERBRAIN
INTERBRAINS
INTERBRANCH
INTERBRED
INTERBREED
INTERBREEDING
INTERBREEDINGS
INTERBREEDS
INTERBROKER
INTERCALAR
INTERCALARILY
INTERCALARY
INTERCALATE
INTERCALATED
INTERCALATES
INTERCALATING
INTERCALATION
INTERCALATIONS
INTERCALATIVE
INTERCAMPUS
INTERCASTE
INTERCEDE
INTERCEDED
INTERCEDENT
INTERCEDER
INTERCEDERS
INTERCEDES
INTERCEDING
INTERCELL

INTERCELLULAR	INTERCLUSTER	INTERCROPS	INTERDIGITATED
INTERCENSAL	INTERCOASTAL	INTERCROSS	INTERDIGITATES
INTERCEPT	INTERCOLLEGIATE	INTERCROSSED	INTERDIGITATING
INTERCEPTED	INTERCOLLINE	INTERCROSSES	INTERDIGITATION
INTERCEPTER	INTERCOLONIAL	INTERCROSSING	INTERDINE
INTERCEPTERS	INTERCOLONIALLY	INTERCRURAL	INTERDINED
INTERCEPTING	INTERCOLUMNAR	INTERCULTURAL	INTERDINES
INTERCEPTION	INTERCOM	INTERCULTURALLY	INTERDINING
INTERCEPTIONS	INTERCOMMUNAL	INTERCULTURE	INTERDISTRICT
INTERCEPTIVE	INTERCOMMUNE	INTERCURRENCE	INTERDIVISIONAL
INTERCEPTOR	INTERCOMMUNED	INTERCURRENCES	INTERDOMINION
INTERCEPTORS	INTERCOMMUNES	INTERCURRENT	INTERELECTRODE
INTERCEPTS	INTERCOMMUNING	INTERCURRENTLY	INTERELECTRON
INTERCESSION	INTERCOMMUNION	INTERCUT	INTERELECTRONIC
INTERCESSIONAL	INTERCOMMUNIONS	INTERCUTS	INTEREPIDEMIC
INTERCESSIONS	INTERCOMMUNITY	INTERCUTTING	INTERESS
INTERCESSOR	INTERCOMPANY	INTERDASH	INTERESSE
INTERCESSORIAL	INTERCOMPARE	INTERDASHED	INTERESSED
INTERCESSORS	INTERCOMPARED	INTERDASHES	INTERESSES
INTERCESSORY	INTERCOMPARES	INTERDASHING	INTERESSING
INTERCHAIN	INTERCOMPARING	INTERDEAL	INTEREST
INTERCHAINED	INTERCOMPARISON	INTERDEALER	INTERESTED
INTERCHAINING	INTERCOMS	INTERDEALERS	INTERESTEDLY
INTERCHAINS	INTERCONNECT	INTERDEALING	INTERESTEDNESS
INTERCHANGE	INTERCONNECTED	INTERDEALS	INTERESTING
INTERCHANGEABLE	INTERCONNECTING	INTERDEALT	INTERESTINGLY
INTERCHANGEABLY	INTERCONNECTION	INTERDENTAL	INTERESTINGNESS
INTERCHANGED	INTERCONNECTOR	INTERDENTALLY	INTERESTS
INTERCHANGEMENT	INTERCONNECTORS	INTERDEPEND	INTERETHNIC
INTERCHANGER	INTERCONNECTS	INTERDEPENDED	INTERFACE
INTERCHANGERS	INTERCONNEXION	INTERDEPENDENCE	INTERFACED
INTERCHANGES	INTERCONNEXIONS	INTERDEPENDENCY	INTERFACES
INTERCHANGING	INTERCONVERSION	INTERDEPENDENT	INTERFACIAL
INTERCHANNEL	INTERCONVERT	INTERDEPENDING	INTERFACIALLY
INTERCHAPTER	INTERCONVERTED	INTERDEPENDS	INTERFACING
INTERCHAPTERS	INTERCONVERTING	INTERDIALECTAL	INTERFACINGS
INTERCHURCH	INTERCONVERTS	INTERDICT	INTERFACTIONAL
INTERCIPIENT	INTERCOOLED	INTERDICTED	INTERFACULTY
INTERCIPIENTS	INTERCOOLER	INTERDICTING	INTERFAITH
INTERCITY	INTERCOOLERS	INTERDICTION	INTERFAMILIAL
INTERCLAN	INTERCORPORATE	INTERDICTIONS	INTERFAMILY
INTERCLASP	INTERCORRELATE	INTERDICTIVE	INTERFASCICULAR
INTERCLASPED	INTERCORRELATED	INTERDICTIVELY	INTERFEMORAL
INTERCLASPING	INTERCORRELATES	INTERDICTOR	INTERFERE
INTERCLASPS	INTERCORTICAL	INTERDICTORS	INTERFERED
INTERCLASS	INTERCOSTAL	INTERDICTORY	INTERFERENCE
INTERCLAVICLE	INTERCOSTALS	INTERDICTS	INTERFERENCES
INTERCLAVICLES	INTERCOUNTRY	INTERDIFFUSE	INTERFERENTIAL
INTERCLAVICULAR	INTERCOUNTY	INTERDIFFUSED	INTERFERER
INTERCLUB	INTERCOUPLE	INTERDIFFUSES	INTERFERERS
INTERCLUDE	INTERCOURSE	INTERDIFFUSING	INTERFERES
INTERCLUDED	INTERCOURSES	INTERDIFFUSION	INTERFERING
INTERCLUDES	INTERCRATER	INTERDIFFUSIONS	INTERFERINGLY
INTERCLUDING	INTERCROP	INTERDIGITAL	INTERFEROGRAM
INTERCLUSION	INTERCROPPED	INTERDIGITALLY	INTERFEROGRAMS
INTERCLUSIONS	INTERCROPPING	INTERDIGITATE	INTERFEROMETER

INTERFEROMETERS
INTERFEROMETRIC
INTERFEROMETRY
INTERFERON
INTERFERONS
INTERFERTILE
INTERFERTILITY
INTERFIBER
INTERFIBRILLAR
INTERFIBROUS
INTERFILE
INTERFILED
INTERFILES
INTERFILING
INTERFIRM
INTERFLOW
INTERFLOWED
INTERFLOWING
INTERFLOWS
INTERFLUENCE
INTERFLUENCES
INTERFLUENT
INTERFLUOUS
INTERFLUVE
INTERFLUVES
INTERFLUVIAL
INTERFOLD
INTERFOLDED
INTERFOLDING
INTERFOLDS
INTERFOLIATE
INTERFOLIATED
INTERFOLIATES
INTERFOLIATING
INTERFRATERNITY
INTERFRETTED
INTERFRONTAL
INTERFUSE
INTERFUSED
INTERFUSES
INTERFUSING
INTERFUSION
INTERFUSIONS
INTERGALACTIC
INTERGANG
INTERGENERATION
INTERGENERIC
INTERGLACIAL
INTERGLACIALS
INTERGRADATION
INTERGRADATIONS
INTERGRADE
INTERGRADED
INTERGRADES
INTERGRADIENT
INTERGRADIENTS

INTERGRADING
INTERGRAFT
INTERGRAFTED
INTERGRAFTING
INTERGRAFTS
INTERGRANULAR
INTERGREW
INTERGROUP
INTERGROW
INTERGROWING
INTERGROWN
INTERGROWS
INTERGROWTH
INTERGROWTHS
INTERIM
INTERIMS
INTERINDIVIDUAL
INTERINDUSTRY
INTERINFLUENCE
INTERINFLUENCES
INTERINVOLVE
INTERINVOLVED
INTERINVOLVES
INTERINVOLVING
INTERIONIC
INTERIOR
INTERIORISE
INTERIORISED
INTERIORISES
INTERIORISING
INTERIORITIES
INTERIORITY
INTERIORIZATION
INTERIORIZE
INTERIORIZED
INTERIORIZES
INTERIORIZING
INTERIORLY
INTERIORS
INTERISLAND
INTERJACENCIES
INTERJACENCY
INTERJACENT
INTERJACULATE
INTERJACULATED
INTERJACULATES
INTERJACULATING
INTERJACULATORY
INTERJECT
INTERJECTED
INTERJECTING
INTERJECTION
INTERJECTIONAL
INTERJECTIONARY
INTERJECTIONS
INTERJECTOR

INTERJECTORS
INTERJECTORY
INTERJECTS
INTERJECTURAL
INTERJOIN
INTERJOINED
INTERJOINING
INTERJOINS
INTERKINESES
INTERKINESIS
INTERKNIT
INTERKNITS
INTERKNITTED
INTERKNITTING
INTERLACE
INTERLACED
INTERLACEDLY
INTERLACEMENT
INTERLACEMENTS
INTERLACES
INTERLACING
INTERLACUSTRINE
INTERLAID
INTERLAMINAR
INTERLAMINATE
INTERLAMINATED
INTERLAMINATES
INTERLAMINATING
INTERLAMINATION
INTERLAP
INTERLAPPED
INTERLAPPING
INTERLAPS
INTERLARD
INTERLARDED
INTERLARDING
INTERLARDS
INTERLAY
INTERLAYER
INTERLAYERED
INTERLAYERING
INTERLAYERS
INTERLAYING
INTERLAYS
INTERLEAF
INTERLEAVE
INTERLEAVED
INTERLEAVES
INTERLEAVING
INTERLEND
INTERLENDING
INTERLENDS
INTERLENT
INTERLEUKIN
INTERLEUKINS
INTERLIBRARY

INTERLINE
INTERLINEAL
INTERLINEALLY
INTERLINEAR
INTERLINEARLY
INTERLINEARS
INTERLINEATE
INTERLINEATED
INTERLINEATES
INTERLINEATING
INTERLINEATION
INTERLINEATIONS
INTERLINED
INTERLINER
INTERLINERS
INTERLINES
INTERLINGUA
INTERLINGUAL
INTERLINGUALLY
INTERLINGUAS
INTERLINING
INTERLININGS
INTERLINK
INTERLINKED
INTERLINKING
INTERLINKS
INTERLOBULAR
INTERLOCAL
INTERLOCATION
INTERLOCATIONS
INTERLOCK
INTERLOCKED
INTERLOCKER
INTERLOCKERS
INTERLOCKING
INTERLOCKS
INTERLOCUTION
INTERLOCUTIONS
INTERLOCUTOR
INTERLOCUTORILY
INTERLOCUTORS
INTERLOCUTORY
INTERLOCUTRESS
INTERLOCUTRICE
INTERLOCUTRICES
INTERLOCUTRIX
INTERLOCUTRIXES
INTERLOPE
INTERLOPED
INTERLOPER
INTERLOPERS
INTERLOPES
INTERLOPING
INTERLUDE
INTERLUDED
INTERLUDES

INTERLUDIAL
INTERLUDING
INTERLUNAR
INTERLUNARY
INTERLUNATION
INTERLUNATIONS
INTERMALE
INTERMARGINAL
INTERMARRIAGE
INTERMARRIAGES
INTERMARRIED
INTERMARRIES
INTERMARRY
INTERMARRYING
INTERMAXILLA
INTERMAXILLAE
INTERMAXILLARY
INTERMEDDLE
INTERMEDDLED
INTERMEDDLER
INTERMEDDLERS
INTERMEDDLES
INTERMEDDLING
INTERMEDIA
INTERMEDIACIES
INTERMEDIACY
INTERMEDIAL
INTERMEDIARIES
INTERMEDIARY
INTERMEDIATE
INTERMEDIATED
INTERMEDIATELY
INTERMEDIATES
INTERMEDIATING
INTERMEDIATION
INTERMEDIATIONS
INTERMEDIATOR
INTERMEDIATORS
INTERMEDIATORY
INTERMEDIN
INTERMEDINS
INTERMEDIUM
INTERMEDIUMS
INTERMEMBRANE
INTERMENSTRUAL
INTERMENT
INTERMENTS
INTERMESH
INTERMESHED
INTERMESHES
INTERMESHING
INTERMETALLIC
INTERMETALLICS
INTERMEZZI
INTERMEZZO
INTERMEZZOS

INTERMIGRATION
INTERMIGRATIONS
INTERMINABILITY
INTERMINABLE
INTERMINABLY
INTERMINGLE
INTERMINGLED
INTERMINGLEMENT
INTERMINGLES
INTERMINGLING
INTERMINGLINGLY
INTERMISSION
INTERMISSIONS
INTERMISSIVE
INTERMIT
INTERMITOTIC
INTERMITS
INTERMITTED
INTERMITTENCE
INTERMITTENCES
INTERMITTENCIES
INTERMITTENCY
INTERMITTENT
INTERMITTENTLY
INTERMITTER
INTERMITTERS
INTERMITTING
INTERMITTINGLY
INTERMITTOR
INTERMITTORS
INTERMIX
INTERMIXABILITY
INTERMIXABLE
INTERMIXED
INTERMIXES
INTERMIXING
INTERMIXTURE
INTERMIXTURES
INTERMODAL
INTERMODULATION
INTERMOLECULAR
INTERMONT
INTERMONTANE
INTERMOUNTAIN
INTERMUNDANE
INTERMURE
INTERMURED
INTERMURES
INTERMURING
INTERMUSCULAR
INTERMUSCULARLY
INTERN
INTERNAL
INTERNALISATION
INTERNALISE
INTERNALISED

INTERNALISES
INTERNALISING
INTERNALITIES
INTERNALITY
INTERNALIZATION
INTERNALIZE
INTERNALIZED
INTERNALIZES
INTERNALIZING
INTERNALLY
INTERNALNESS
INTERNALS
INTERNATIONAL
INTERNATIONALLY
INTERNATIONALS
INTERNE
INTERNECINE
INTERNECIVE
INTERNED
INTERNEE
INTERNEES
INTERNES
INTERNEURAL
INTERNEURON
INTERNEURONAL
INTERNEURONS
INTERNING
INTERNIST
INTERNISTS
INTERNMENT
INTERNMENTS
INTERNODAL
INTERNODE
INTERNODES
INTERNODIAL
INTERNS
INTERNSHIP
INTERNSHIPS
INTERNUCLEAR
INTERNUCLEON
INTERNUCLEONIC
INTERNUCLEOTIDE
INTERNUNCIAL
INTERNUNCIO
INTERNUNCIOS
INTEROBSERVER
INTEROCEAN
INTEROCEANIC
INTEROCEPTIVE
INTEROCEPTOR
INTEROCEPTORS
INTEROCULAR
INTEROFFICE
INTEROPERABLE
INTEROPERATIVE
INTERORBITAL

INTERORGAN
INTEROSCULANT
INTEROSCULATE
INTEROSCULATED
INTEROSCULATES
INTEROSCULATING
INTEROSCULATION
INTEROSSEAL
INTEROSSEOUS
INTERPAGE
INTERPAGED
INTERPAGES
INTERPAGING
INTERPANDEMIC
INTERPARIETAL
INTERPARISH
INTERPAROCHIAL
INTERPAROXYSMAL
INTERPARTICLE
INTERPARTY
INTERPELLANT
INTERPELLANTS
INTERPELLATE
INTERPELLATED
INTERPELLATES
INTERPELLATING
INTERPELLATION
INTERPELLATIONS
INTERPELLATOR
INTERPELLATORS
INTERPENETRABLE
INTERPENETRANT
INTERPENETRATE
INTERPENETRATED
INTERPENETRATES
INTERPERCEPTUAL
INTERPERMEATE
INTERPERMEATED
INTERPERMEATES
INTERPERMEATING
INTERPERSONAL
INTERPERSONALLY
INTERPETIOLAR
INTERPHALANGEAL
INTERPHASE
INTERPHASES
INTERPHONE
INTERPHONES
INTERPILASTER
INTERPILASTERS
INTERPLAIT
INTERPLAITED
INTERPLAITING
INTERPLAITS
INTERPLANETARY
INTERPLANT

INTERPLANTED
INTERPLANTING
INTERPLANTS
INTERPLAY
INTERPLAYED
INTERPLAYING
INTERPLAYS
INTERPLEAD
INTERPLEADED
INTERPLEADER
INTERPLEADERS
INTERPLEADING
INTERPLEADS
INTERPLED
INTERPLEURAL
INTERPLUVIAL
INTERPOINT
INTERPOLABLE
INTERPOLAR
INTERPOLATE
INTERPOLATED
INTERPOLATER
INTERPOLATERS
INTERPOLATES
INTERPOLATING
INTERPOLATION
INTERPOLATIONS
INTERPOLATIVE
INTERPOLATOR
INTERPOLATORS
INTERPONE
INTERPONED
INTERPONES
INTERPONING
INTERPOPULATION
INTERPOSABILITY
INTERPOSABLE
INTERPOSAL
INTERPOSALS
INTERPOSE
INTERPOSED
INTERPOSER
INTERPOSERS
INTERPOSES
INTERPOSING
INTERPOSITION
INTERPOSITIONS
INTERPRET
INTERPRETABLE
INTERPRETABLY
INTERPRETATE
INTERPRETATED
INTERPRETATES
INTERPRETATING
INTERPRETATION
INTERPRETATIONS

INTERPRETATIVE
INTERPRETED
INTERPRETER
INTERPRETERS
INTERPRETERSHIP
INTERPRETESS
INTERPRETESSES
INTERPRETING
INTERPRETIVE
INTERPRETIVELY
INTERPRETRESS
INTERPRETRESSES
INTERPRETS
INTERPROVINCIAL
INTERPROXIMAL
INTERPSYCHIC
INTERPUNCTION
INTERPUNCTIONS
INTERPUNCTUATE
INTERPUNCTUATED
INTERPUNCTUATES
INTERPUPILLARY
INTERQUARTILE
INTERRACIAL
INTERRACIALLY
INTERRADIAL
INTERRADIALLY
INTERRADII
INTERRADIUS
INTERRADIUSES
INTERRAIL
INTERRAILED
INTERRAILER
INTERRAILERS
INTERRAILING
INTERRAILS
INTERRAMAL
INTERRED
INTERREGAL
INTERREGES
INTERREGIONAL
INTERREGNA
INTERREGNAL
INTERREGNUM
INTERREGNUMS
INTERRELATE
INTERRELATED
INTERRELATEDLY
INTERRELATES
INTERRELATING
INTERRELATION
INTERRELATIONS
INTERRELIGIOUS
INTERRENAL
INTERREX
INTERRING

INTERROBANG
INTERROBANGS
INTERROGABLE
INTERROGANT
INTERROGANTS
INTERROGATE
INTERROGATED
INTERROGATEE
INTERROGATEES
INTERROGATES
INTERROGATING
INTERROGATINGLY
INTERROGATION
INTERROGATIONAL
INTERROGATIONS
INTERROGATIVE
INTERROGATIVELY
INTERROGATIVES
INTERROGATOR
INTERROGATORIES
INTERROGATORILY
INTERROGATORS
INTERROGATORY
INTERROGEE
INTERROGEES
INTERROW
INTERRUPT
INTERRUPTED
INTERRUPTEDLY
INTERRUPTER
INTERRUPTERS
INTERRUPTIBLE
INTERRUPTING
INTERRUPTION
INTERRUPTIONS
INTERRUPTIVE
INTERRUPTIVELY
INTERRUPTOR
INTERRUPTORS
INTERRUPTS
INTERS
INTERSCAPULAR
INTERSCHOLASTIC
INTERSCHOOL
INTERSCRIBE
INTERSCRIBED
INTERSCRIBES
INTERSCRIBING
INTERSECT
INTERSECTED
INTERSECTING
INTERSECTION
INTERSECTIONAL
INTERSECTIONS
INTERSECTS
INTERSEGMENT

INTERSEGMENTAL
INTERSENSORY
INTERSEPTAL
INTERSERT
INTERSERTAL
INTERSERTED
INTERSERTING
INTERSERTS
INTERSERVICE
INTERSESSION
INTERSESSIONS
INTERSEX
INTERSEXES
INTERSEXUAL
INTERSEXUALISM
INTERSEXUALITY
INTERSEXUALLY
INTERSIDEREAL
INTERSOCIETAL
INTERSOCIETY
INTERSPACE
INTERSPACED
INTERSPACES
INTERSPACING
INTERSPATIAL
INTERSPATIALLY
INTERSPECIES
INTERSPECIFIC
INTERSPERSAL
INTERSPERSALS
INTERSPERSE
INTERSPERSED
INTERSPERSEDLY
INTERSPERSES
INTERSPERSING
INTERSPERSION
INTERSPERSIONS
INTERSPINAL
INTERSPINOUS
INTERSTADIAL
INTERSTADIALS
INTERSTAGE
INTERSTATE
INTERSTATES
INTERSTATION
INTERSTELLAR
INTERSTELLARY
INTERSTERILE
INTERSTERILITY
INTERSTICE
INTERSTICES
INTERSTIMULUS
INTERSTITIAL
INTERSTITIALLY
INTERSTITIALS
INTERSTRAIN

INTERSTRAND
INTERSTRATIFIED
INTERSTRATIFIES
INTERSTRATIFY
INTERSUBJECTIVE
INTERSYSTEM
INTERTANGLE
INTERTANGLED
INTERTANGLEMENT
INTERTANGLES
INTERTANGLING
INTERTARSAL
INTERTENTACULAR
INTERTERM
INTERTERMINAL
INTERTEXT
INTERTEXTS
INTERTEXTUAL
INTERTEXTUALITY
INTERTEXTUALLY
INTERTEXTURE
INTERTEXTURES
INTERTIDAL
INTERTIDALLY
INTERTIE
INTERTIES
INTERTILL
INTERTILLAGE
INTERTILLAGES
INTERTILLED
INTERTILLING
INTERTILLS
INTERTISSUED
INTERTRAFFIC
INTERTRAFFICS
INTERTRIAL
INTERTRIBAL
INTERTRIBALLY
INTERTRIGO
INTERTRIGOS
INTERTROOP
INTERTROPICAL
INTERTWINE
INTERTWINED
INTERTWINEMENT
INTERTWINEMENTS
INTERTWINES
INTERTWINING
INTERTWININGLY
INTERTWININGS
INTERTWIST
INTERTWISTED
INTERTWISTING
INTERTWISTINGLY
INTERTWISTS
INTERUNION

INTERUNIONS
INTERUNIT
INTERUNIVERSITY
INTERURBAN
INTERVAL
INTERVALE
INTERVALES
INTERVALLEY
INTERVALLIC
INTERVALLUM
INTERVALLUMS
INTERVALOMETER
INTERVALOMETERS
INTERVALS
INTERVARSITY
INTERVEIN
INTERVEINED
INTERVEINING
INTERVEINS
INTERVENE
INTERVENED
INTERVENER
INTERVENERS
INTERVENES
INTERVENIENT
INTERVENING
INTERVENOR
INTERVENORS
INTERVENTION
INTERVENTIONAL
INTERVENTIONISM
INTERVENTIONIST
INTERVENTIONS
INTERVENTOR
INTERVENTORS
INTERVERTEBRAL
INTERVIEW
INTERVIEWED
INTERVIEWEE
INTERVIEWEES
INTERVIEWER
INTERVIEWERS
INTERVIEWING
INTERVIEWS
INTERVILLAGE
INTERVISIBILITY
INTERVISIBLE
INTERVISITATION
INTERVITAL
INTERVOCALIC
INTERVOLVE
INTERVOLVED
INTERVOLVES
INTERVOLVING
INTERWAR
INTERWEAVE

INTERWEAVED
INTERWEAVEMENT
INTERWEAVEMENTS
INTERWEAVER
INTERWEAVERS
INTERWEAVES
INTERWEAVING
INTERWIND
INTERWINDING
INTERWINDS
INTERWORK
INTERWORKED
INTERWORKING
INTERWORKINGS
INTERWORKS
INTERWOUND
INTERWOVE
INTERWOVEN
INTERWREATHE
INTERWREATHED
INTERWREATHES
INTERWREATHING
INTERWROUGHT
INTERZONAL
INTERZONE
INTERZONES
INTESTACIES
INTESTACY
INTESTATE
INTESTATES
INTESTINAL
INTESTINALLY
INTESTINE
INTESTINES
INTHRAL
INTHRALL
INTHRALLED
INTHRALLING
INTHRALLS
INTHRALS
INTHRONE
INTHRONED
INTHRONES
INTHRONING
INTI
INTIFADA
INTIFADAS
INTIL
INTIMA
INTIMACIES
INTIMACY
INTIMAE
INTIMAL
INTIMAS
INTIMATE
INTIMATED

INTIMATELY
INTIMATENESS
INTIMATENESSES
INTIMATER
INTIMATERS
INTIMATES
INTIMATING
INTIMATION
INTIMATIONS
INTIME
INTIMIDATE
INTIMIDATED
INTIMIDATES
INTIMIDATING
INTIMIDATINGLY
INTIMIDATION
INTIMIDATIONS
INTIMIDATOR
INTIMIDATORS
INTIMIDATORY
INTIMISM
INTIMISMS
INTIMIST
INTIMISTE
INTIMISTES
INTIMISTS
INTIMITIES
INTIMITY
INTINCTION
INTINCTIONS
INTINE
INTINES
INTIRE
INTIS
INTITLE
INTITLED
INTITLES
INTITLING
INTITULE
INTITULED
INTITULES
INTITULING
INTO
INTOED
INTOLERABILITY
INTOLERABLE
INTOLERABLENESS
INTOLERABLY
INTOLERANCE
INTOLERANCES
INTOLERANT
INTOLERANTLY
INTOLERANTNESS
INTOLERANTS
INTOLERATION
INTOLERATIONS

INTOMB
INTOMBED
INTOMBING
INTOMBS
INTONACO
INTONACOS
INTONATE
INTONATED
INTONATES
INTONATING
INTONATION
INTONATIONAL
INTONATIONS
INTONATOR
INTONATORS
INTONE
INTONED
INTONER
INTONERS
INTONES
INTONING
INTONINGLY
INTONINGS
INTORSION
INTORSIONS
INTORT
INTORTED
INTORTING
INTORTION
INTORTIONS
INTORTS
INTOWN
INTOXICABLE
INTOXICANT
INTOXICANTS
INTOXICATE
INTOXICATED
INTOXICATEDLY
INTOXICATES
INTOXICATING
INTOXICATINGLY
INTOXICATION
INTOXICATIONS
INTOXICATIVE
INTOXICATOR
INTOXICATORS
INTOXIMETER
INTOXIMETERS
INTRA
INTRACAPSULAR
INTRACARDIAC
INTRACARDIAL
INTRACARDIALLY
INTRACAVITARY
INTRACELLULAR
INTRACELLULARLY

INTRACEREBRAL
INTRACEREBRALLY
INTRACOMPANY
INTRACRANIAL
INTRACRANIALLY
INTRACTABILITY
INTRACTABLE
INTRACTABLENESS
INTRACTABLY
INTRACUTANEOUS
INTRADA
INTRADAS
INTRADAY
INTRADERMAL
INTRADERMALLY
INTRADERMIC
INTRADERMICALLY
INTRADOS
INTRADOSES
INTRAFALLOPIAN
INTRAFASCICULAR
INTRAGALACTIC
INTRAGENIC
INTRAMEDULLARY
INTRAMERCURIAL
INTRAMOLECULAR
INTRAMUNDANE
INTRAMURAL
INTRAMURALLY
INTRAMUSCULAR
INTRAMUSCULARLY
INTRANASAL
INTRANASALLY
INTRANATIONAL
INTRANET
INTRANETS
INTRANSIGEANCE
INTRANSIGEANCES
INTRANSIGEANT
INTRANSIGEANTLY
INTRANSIGEANTS
INTRANSIGENCE
INTRANSIGENCES
INTRANSIGENCIES
INTRANSIGENCY
INTRANSIGENT
INTRANSIGENTISM
INTRANSIGENTIST
INTRANSIGENTLY
INTRANSIGENTS
INTRANSITIVE
INTRANSITIVELY
INTRANSITIVITY
INTRANSMISSIBLE
INTRANSMUTABLE
INTRANT

INTRANTS
INTRANUCLEAR
INTRAOCULAR
INTRAOCULARLY
INTRAPARIETAL
INTRAPARTUM
INTRAPERITONEAL
INTRAPERSONAL
INTRAPETIOLAR
INTRAPLATE
INTRAPOPULATION
INTRAPRENEUR
INTRAPRENEURIAL
INTRAPRENEURS
INTRAPSYCHIC
INTRASEXUAL
INTRASPECIES
INTRASPECIFIC
INTRASTATE
INTRATELLURIC
INTRATHECAL
INTRATHECALLY
INTRATHORACIC
INTRAUTERINE
INTRAVASATION
INTRAVASATIONS
INTRAVASCULAR
INTRAVASCULARLY
INTRAVENOUS
INTRAVENOUSLY
INTRAVITAL
INTRAVITALLY
INTRAVITAM
INTRAZONAL
INTREAT
INTREATED
INTREATFULL
INTREATING
INTREATINGLY
INTREATMENT
INTREATMENTS
INTREATS
INTRENCH
INTRENCHANT
INTRENCHED
INTRENCHER
INTRENCHERS
INTRENCHES
INTRENCHING
INTRENCHMENT
INTRENCHMENTS
INTREPID
INTREPIDITIES
INTREPIDITY
INTREPIDLY
INTREPIDNESS

INTREPIDNESSES
INTRICACIES
INTRICACY
INTRICATE
INTRICATELY
INTRICATENESS
INTRICATENESSES
INTRIGANT
INTRIGANTE
INTRIGANTES
INTRIGANTS
INTRIGUANT
INTRIGUANTE
INTRIGUANTES
INTRIGUANTS
INTRIGUE
INTRIGUED
INTRIGUER
INTRIGUERS
INTRIGUES
INTRIGUING
INTRIGUINGLY
INTRINCE
INTRINSIC
INTRINSICAL
INTRINSICALITY
INTRINSICALLY
INTRINSICALNESS
INTRINSICATE
INTRO
INTRODUCE
INTRODUCED
INTRODUCER
INTRODUCERS
INTRODUCES
INTRODUCIBLE
INTRODUCING
INTRODUCTION
INTRODUCTIONS
INTRODUCTIVE
INTRODUCTORILY
INTRODUCTORY
INTROFIED
INTROFIES
INTROFY
INTROFYING
INTROGRESSANT
INTROGRESSANTS
INTROGRESSION
INTROGRESSIONS
INTROGRESSIVE
INTROIT
INTROITAL
INTROITALLY
INTROITS
INTROITUS

INTROITUSES
INTROJECT
INTROJECTED
INTROJECTING
INTROJECTION
INTROJECTIONS
INTROJECTIVE
INTROJECTIVELY
INTROJECTS
INTROLD
INTROMISSIBLE
INTROMISSION
INTROMISSIONS
INTROMISSIVE
INTROMIT
INTROMITS
INTROMITTED
INTROMITTENT
INTROMITTER
INTROMITTERS
INTROMITTING
INTRON
INTRONS
INTRORSE
INTRORSELY
INTROS
INTROSPECT
INTROSPECTED
INTROSPECTING
INTROSPECTION
INTROSPECTIONAL
INTROSPECTIONS
INTROSPECTIVE
INTROSPECTIVELY
INTROSPECTS
INTROSUSCEPTION
INTROVERSIBLE
INTROVERSION
INTROVERSIONS
INTROVERSIVE
INTROVERSIVELY
INTROVERT
INTROVERTED
INTROVERTING
INTROVERTIVE
INTROVERTS
INTRUDE
INTRUDED
INTRUDER
INTRUDERS
INTRUDES
INTRUDING
INTRUDINGLY
INTRUSION
INTRUSIONAL
INTRUSIONALLY

INTRUSIONIST
INTRUSIONISTS
INTRUSIONS
INTRUSIVE
INTRUSIVELY
INTRUSIVENESS
INTRUSIVENESSES
INTRUSIVES
INTRUST
INTRUSTED
INTRUSTING
INTRUSTMENT
INTRUSTMENTAL
INTRUSTMENTALLY
INTRUSTMENTS
INTRUSTS
INTUBATE
INTUBATED
INTUBATES
INTUBATING
INTUBATION
INTUBATIONS
INTUIT
INTUITABLE
INTUITED
INTUITING
INTUITION
INTUITIONAL
INTUITIONALISM
INTUITIONALISMS
INTUITIONALIST
INTUITIONALISTS
INTUITIONALLY
INTUITIONISM
INTUITIONISMS
INTUITIONIST
INTUITIONISTS
INTUITIONS
INTUITIVE
INTUITIVELY
INTUITIVENESS
INTUITIVENESSES
INTUITIVISM
INTUITIVISMS
INTUITS
INTUMESCE
INTUMESCED
INTUMESCENCE
INTUMESCENCES
INTUMESCENCIES
INTUMESCENCY
INTUMESCENT
INTUMESCES
INTUMESCING
INTURBIDATE
INTURBIDATED

INTURBIDATES
INTURBIDATING
INTURN
INTURNED
INTURNS
INTUSE
INTUSES
INTUSSUSCEPT
INTUSSUSCEPTED
INTUSSUSCEPTING
INTUSSUSCEPTION
INTUSSUSCEPTIVE
INTUSSUSCEPTS
INTWINE
INTWINED
INTWINEMENT
INTWINEMENTS
INTWINES
INTWINING
INTWIST
INTWISTED
INTWISTING
INTWISTS
INUKSHUK
INUKSHUKS
INULA
INULAS
INULASE
INULASES
INULIN
INULINS
INUMBRATE
INUMBRATED
INUMBRATES
INUMBRATING
INUNCTION
INUNCTIONS
INUNDANT
INUNDATE
INUNDATED
INUNDATES
INUNDATING
INUNDATION
INUNDATIONS
INUNDATOR
INUNDATORS
INUNDATORY
INURBANE
INURBANELY
INURBANITIES
INURBANITY
INURE
INURED
INUREDNESS
INUREDNESSES
INUREMENT

INUREMENTS
INURES
INURING
INURN
INURNED
INURNING
INURNMENT
INURNMENTS
INURNS
INUSITATE
INUSITATION
INUSITATIONS
INUST
INUSTION
INUSTIONS
INUTILE
INUTILELY
INUTILENESS
INUTILITIES
INUTILITY
INUTTERABLE
INVADABILITY
INVADABLE
INVADE
INVADED
INVADER
INVADERS
INVADES
INVADING
INVAGINABILITY
INVAGINABLE
INVAGINATE
INVAGINATED
INVAGINATES
INVAGINATING
INVAGINATION
INVAGINATIONS
INVALID
INVALIDATE
INVALIDATED
INVALIDATES
INVALIDATING
INVALIDATION
INVALIDATIONS
INVALIDATOR
INVALIDATORS
INVALIDED
INVALIDHOOD
INVALIDHOODS
INVALIDING
INVALIDINGS
INVALIDISM
INVALIDISMS
INVALIDITIES
INVALIDITY
INVALIDLY

INVALIDNESS
INVALIDNESSES
INVALIDS
INVALUABLE
INVALUABLENESS
INVALUABLY
INVAR
INVARIABILITIES
INVARIABILITY
INVARIABLE
INVARIABLENESS
INVARIABLES
INVARIABLY
INVARIANCE
INVARIANCES
INVARIANCIES
INVARIANCY
INVARIANT
INVARIANTS
INVARS
INVASION
INVASIONS
INVASIVE
INVASIVENESS
INVASIVENESSES
INVEAGLE
INVEAGLED
INVEAGLES
INVEAGLING
INVECKED
INVECTED
INVECTIVE
INVECTIVELY
INVECTIVENESS
INVECTIVENESSES
INVECTIVES
INVEIGH
INVEIGHED
INVEIGHER
INVEIGHERS
INVEIGHING
INVEIGHS
INVEIGLE
INVEIGLED
INVEIGLEMENT
INVEIGLEMENTS
INVEIGLER
INVEIGLERS
INVEIGLES
INVEIGLING
INVENDIBILITIES
INVENDIBILITY
INVENDIBLE
INVENIT
INVENT
INVENTABLE

INVENTED
INVENTER
INVENTERS
INVENTIBLE
INVENTING
INVENTION
INVENTIONAL
INVENTIONALLY
INVENTIONLESS
INVENTIONS
INVENTIVE
INVENTIVELY
INVENTIVENESS
INVENTIVENESSES
INVENTOR
INVENTORIABLE
INVENTORIAL
INVENTORIALLY
INVENTORIED
INVENTORIES
INVENTORS
INVENTORY
INVENTORYING
INVENTRESS
INVENTRESSES
INVENTS
INVERACITIES
INVERACITY
INVERITIES
INVERITY
INVERNESS
INVERNESSES
INVERSE
INVERSELY
INVERSES
INVERSION
INVERSIONS
INVERSIVE
INVERT
INVERTASE
INVERTASES
INVERTEBRAL
INVERTEBRATE
INVERTEBRATES
INVERTED
INVERTEDLY
INVERTER
INVERTERS
INVERTIBILITY
INVERTIBLE
INVERTIN
INVERTING
INVERTINS
INVERTOR
INVERTORS
INVERTS

INVEST
INVESTABLE
INVESTED
INVESTIBILITY
INVESTIBLE
INVESTIGABLE
INVESTIGATE
INVESTIGATED
INVESTIGATES
INVESTIGATING
INVESTIGATION
INVESTIGATIONAL
INVESTIGATIONS
INVESTIGATIVE
INVESTIGATOR
INVESTIGATORS
INVESTIGATORY
INVESTING
INVESTITIVE
INVESTITURE
INVESTITURES
INVESTMENT
INVESTMENTS
INVESTOR
INVESTORS
INVESTS
INVETERACIES
INVETERACY
INVETERATE
INVETERATELY
INVETERATENESS
INVEXED
INVIABILITIES
INVIABILITY
INVIABLE
INVIABLENESS
INVIABLY
INVIDIOUS
INVIDIOUSLY
INVIDIOUSNESS
INVIDIOUSNESSES
INVIGILATE
INVIGILATED
INVIGILATES
INVIGILATING
INVIGILATION
INVIGILATIONS
INVIGILATOR
INVIGILATORS
INVIGORANT
INVIGORANTS
INVIGORATE
INVIGORATED
INVIGORATES
INVIGORATING
INVIGORATINGLY

INVIGORATION
INVIGORATIONS
INVIGORATIVE
INVIGORATIVELY
INVIGORATOR
INVINCIBILITIES
INVINCIBILITY
INVINCIBLE
INVINCIBLENESS
INVINCIBLY
INVIOLABILITIES
INVIOLABILITY
INVIOLABLE
INVIOLABLENESS
INVIOLABLY
INVIOLACIES
INVIOLACY
INVIOLATE
INVIOLATED
INVIOLATELY
INVIOLATENESS
INVIOLATENESSES
INVIOUS
INVIRILE
INVISCID
INVISIBILITIES
INVISIBILITY
INVISIBLE
INVISIBLENESS
INVISIBLENESSES
INVISIBLES
INVISIBLY
INVITAL
INVITATION
INVITATIONAL
INVITATIONALS
INVITATIONS
INVITATORIES
INVITATORY
INVITE
INVITED
INVITEE
INVITEES
INVITEMENT
INVITEMENTS
INVITER
INVITERS
INVITES
INVITING
INVITINGLY
INVITINGNESS
INVITINGNESSES
INVITINGS
INVOCABLE
INVOCATE

INVOCATED
INVOCATES
INVOCATING
INVOCATION
INVOCATIONAL
INVOCATIONS
INVOCATIVE
INVOCATIVELY
INVOCATIVENESS
INVOCATOR
INVOCATORS
INVOCATORY
INVOICE
INVOICED
INVOICES
INVOICING
INVOKE
INVOKED
INVOKER
INVOKERS
INVOKES
INVOKING
INVOLUCEL
INVOLUCELLA
INVOLUCELLATE
INVOLUCELLATED
INVOLUCELLUM
INVOLUCELS
INVOLUCRA
INVOLUCRAL
INVOLUCRATE
INVOLUCRE
INVOLUCRES
INVOLUCRUM
INVOLUCRUMS
INVOLUNTARILY
INVOLUNTARINESS
INVOLUNTARY
INVOLUTE
INVOLUTED
INVOLUTEDLY
INVOLUTEDNESS
INVOLUTELY
INVOLUTENESS
INVOLUTES
INVOLUTING
INVOLUTION
INVOLUTIONAL
INVOLUTIONS
INVOLVE
INVOLVED
INVOLVEDLY
INVOLVEMENT
INVOLVEMENTS
INVOLVER
INVOLVERS

INVOLVES
INVOLVING
INVULNERABILITY
INVULNERABLE
INVULNERABLY
INVULTUATION
INVULTUATIONS
INWALL
INWALLED
INWALLING
INWALLS
INWARD
INWARDLY
INWARDNESS
INWARDNESSES
INWARDS
INWEAVE
INWEAVED
INWEAVES
INWEAVING
INWICK
INWICKED
INWICKING
INWICKS
INWIND
INWINDING
INWINDS
INWIT
INWITH
INWITS
INWORK
INWORKED
INWORKING
INWORKINGS
INWORKS
INWORN
INWOUND
INWOVE
INWOVEN
INWRAP
INWRAPPED
INWRAPPING
INWRAPS
INWREATHE
INWREATHED
INWREATHES
INWREATHING
INWROUGHT
INYALA
INYALAS
IO
IODATE
IODATED
IODATES
IODATING
IODATION

IODATIONS
IODIC
IODID
IODIDE
IODIDES
IODIDS
IODIN
IODINATE
IODINATED
IODINATES
IODINATING
IODINATION
IODINATIONS
IODINE
IODINES
IODINS
IODISATION
IODISATIONS
IODISE
IODISED
IODISER
IODISERS
IODISES
IODISING
IODISM
IODISMS
IODIZATION
IODIZATIONS
IODIZE
IODIZED
IODIZER
IODIZERS
IODIZES
IODIZING
IODOFORM
IODOFORMS
IODOMETRIC
IODOMETRICAL
IODOMETRICALLY
IODOMETRY
IODOPHILE
IODOPHOR
IODOPHORS
IODOPSIN
IODOPSINS
IODOUS
IODURET
IODURETS
IODYRITE
IODYRITES
IOLITE
IOLITES
ION
IONIC
IONICITIES
IONICITY

IONICS
IONISABILITY
IONISABLE
IONISATION
IONISATIONS
IONISE
IONISED
IONISER
IONISERS
IONISES
IONISING
IONIUM
IONIUMS
IONIZABLE
IONIZATION
IONIZATIONS
IONIZE
IONIZED
IONIZER
IONIZERS
IONIZES
IONIZING
IONOGEN
IONOGENS
IONOMER
IONOMERS
IONONE
IONONES
IONOPAUSE
IONOPAUSES
IONOPHORE
IONOPHORES
IONOPHORESES
IONOPHORESIS
IONOSPHERE
IONOSPHERES
IONOSPHERIC
IONOSPHERICALLY
IONOTROPIES
IONOTROPY
IONS
IONTOPHORESES
IONTOPHORESIS
IONTOPHORETIC
IOS
IOTA
IOTACISM
IOTACISMS
IOTAS
IPECAC
IPECACS
IPECACUANHA
IPECACUANHAS
IPOMOEA
IPOMOEAS
IPPON

IPPONS
IPRATROPIUM
IPRATROPIUMS
IPRINDOLE
IPRINDOLES
IPRONIAZID
IPRONIAZIDS
IPSELATERAL
IPSILATERAL
IPSILATERALLY
IRACUND
IRACUNDITIES
IRACUNDITY
IRACUNDULOUS
IRADE
IRADES
IRASCIBILITIES
IRASCIBILITY
IRASCIBLE
IRASCIBLENESS
IRASCIBLENESSES
IRASCIBLY
IRATE
IRATELY
IRATENESS
IRATENESSES
IRATER
IRATEST
IRE
IRED
IREFUL
IREFULLY
IREFULNESS
IREFULNESSES
IRELESS
IRENIC
IRENICAL
IRENICALLY
IRENICISM
IRENICISMS
IRENICON
IRENICONS
IRENICS
IRENOLOGIES
IRENOLOGY
IRES
IRID
IRIDACEOUS
IRIDAL
IRIDEAL
IRIDECTOMIES
IRIDECTOMY
IRIDES
IRIDESCENCE
IRIDESCENCES
IRIDESCENT

IRIDESCENTLY
IRIDIAL
IRIDIAN
IRIDIC
IRIDISATION
IRIDISATIONS
IRIDISE
IRIDISED
IRIDISES
IRIDISING
IRIDIUM
IRIDIUMS
IRIDIZATION
IRIDIZATIONS
IRIDIZE
IRIDIZED
IRIDIZES
IRIDIZING
IRIDOCYTE
IRIDOCYTES
IRIDOLOGIES
IRIDOLOGIST
IRIDOLOGISTS
IRIDOLOGY
IRIDOSMINE
IRIDOSMINES
IRIDOSMIUM
IRIDOSMIUMS
IRIDOTOMIES
IRIDOTOMY
IRIDS
IRING
IRIS
IRISATE
IRISATED
IRISATES
IRISATING
IRISATION
IRISATIONS
IRISCOPE
IRISCOPES
IRISED
IRISES
IRISING
IRITIC
IRITIS
IRITISES
IRK
IRKED
IRKING
IRKS
IRKSOME
IRKSOMELY
IRKSOMENESS
IRKSOMENESSES
IROKO

IROKOS
IRON
IRONBARK
IRONBARKS
IRONBOUND
IRONCLAD
IRONCLADS
IRONE
IRONED
IRONER
IRONERS
IRONES
IRONFISTED
IRONHANDED
IRONHEARTED
IRONIC
IRONICAL
IRONICALLY
IRONICALNESS
IRONICALNESSES
IRONIER
IRONIES
IRONIEST
IRONING
IRONINGS
IRONISE
IRONISED
IRONISES
IRONISING
IRONIST
IRONISTS
IRONIZE
IRONIZED
IRONIZES
IRONIZING
IRONLESS
IRONLIKE
IRONMASTER
IRONMASTERS
IRONMONGER
IRONMONGERIES
IRONMONGERS
IRONMONGERY
IRONNESS
IRONNESSES
IRONS
IRONSIDE
IRONSIDES
IRONSMITH
IRONSMITHS
IRONSTONE
IRONSTONES
IRONWARE
IRONWARES
IRONWEED
IRONWEEDS

IRONWOOD
IRONWOODS
IRONWORK
IRONWORKER
IRONWORKERS
IRONWORKS
IRONY
IRRADIANCE
IRRADIANCES
IRRADIANCIES
IRRADIANCY
IRRADIANT
IRRADIATE
IRRADIATED
IRRADIATES
IRRADIATING
IRRADIATION
IRRADIATIONS
IRRADIATIVE
IRRADIATOR
IRRADIATORS
IRRADICABLE
IRRADICABLY
IRRADICATE
IRRADICATED
IRRADICATES
IRRADICATING
IRRATIONAL
IRRATIONALISE
IRRATIONALISED
IRRATIONALISES
IRRATIONALISING
IRRATIONALISM
IRRATIONALISMS
IRRATIONALIST
IRRATIONALISTIC
IRRATIONALISTS
IRRATIONALITIES
IRRATIONALITY
IRRATIONALIZE
IRRATIONALIZED
IRRATIONALIZES
IRRATIONALIZING
IRRATIONALLY
IRRATIONALNESS
IRRATIONALS
IRREAL
IRREALISABLE
IRREALITIES
IRREALITY
IRREALIZABLE
IRREBUTTABLE
IRRECEPTIVE
IRRECIPROCAL
IRRECIPROCITIES
IRRECIPROCITY

IRRECLAIMABLE
IRRECLAIMABLY
IRRECOGNISABLE
IRRECOGNITION
IRRECOGNITIONS
IRRECOGNIZABLE
IRRECONCILABLE
IRRECONCILABLES
IRRECONCILABLY
IRRECONCILED
IRRECONCILEMENT
IRRECOVERABLE
IRRECOVERABLY
IRRECUSABLE
IRRECUSABLY
IRREDEEMABILITY
IRREDEEMABLE
IRREDEEMABLES
IRREDEEMABLY
IRREDENTA
IRREDENTAS
IRREDENTISM
IRREDENTISMS
IRREDENTIST
IRREDENTISTS
IRREDUCIBILITY
IRREDUCIBLE
IRREDUCIBLENESS
IRREDUCIBLY
IRREDUCTIBILITY
IRREDUCTION
IRREDUCTIONS
IRREFLECTION
IRREFLECTIONS
IRREFLECTIVE
IRREFLEXION
IRREFLEXIONS
IRREFLEXIVE
IRREFORMABILITY
IRREFORMABLE
IRREFORMABLY
IRREFRAGABILITY
IRREFRAGABLE
IRREFRAGABLY
IRREFRANGIBLE
IRREFRANGIBLY
IRREFUTABILITY
IRREFUTABLE
IRREFUTABLENESS
IRREFUTABLY
IRREGARDLESS
IRREGULAR
IRREGULARITIES
IRREGULARITY
IRREGULARLY
IRREGULARS

IRRELATED
IRRELATION
IRRELATIONS
IRRELATIVE
IRRELATIVELY
IRRELATIVENESS
IRRELEVANCE
IRRELEVANCES
IRRELEVANCIES
IRRELEVANCY
IRRELEVANT
IRRELEVANTLY
IRRELIEVABLE
IRRELIEVABLY
IRRELIGION
IRRELIGIONIST
IRRELIGIONISTS
IRRELIGIONS
IRRELIGIOUS
IRRELIGIOUSLY
IRRELIGIOUSNESS
IRREMEABLE
IRREMEABLY
IRREMEDIABLE
IRREMEDIABLY
IRREMISSIBILITY
IRREMISSIBLE
IRREMISSIBLY
IRREMISSION
IRREMISSIONS
IRREMISSIVE
IRREMOVABILITY
IRREMOVABLE
IRREMOVABLENESS
IRREMOVABLY
IRRENOWNED
IRREPAIRABLE
IRREPARABILITY
IRREPARABLE
IRREPARABLENESS
IRREPARABLY
IRREPEALABILITY
IRREPEALABLE
IRREPEALABLY
IRREPLACEABLE
IRREPLACEABLY
IRREPLEVIABLE
IRREPLEVISABLE
IRREPREHENSIBLE
IRREPREHENSIBLY
IRREPRESSIBLE
IRREPRESSIBLY
IRREPROACHABLE
IRREPROACHABLY
IRREPRODUCIBLE
IRREPROVABLE

IRREPROVABLY
IRRESISTANCE
IRRESISTANCES
IRRESISTIBILITY
IRRESISTIBLE
IRRESISTIBLY
IRRESOLUBILITY
IRRESOLUBLE
IRRESOLUBLY
IRRESOLUTE
IRRESOLUTELY
IRRESOLUTENESS
IRRESOLUTION
IRRESOLUTIONS
IRRESOLVABILITY
IRRESOLVABLE
IRRESOLVABLY
IRRESPECTIVE
IRRESPECTIVELY
IRRESPIRABLE
IRRESPONSIBLE
IRRESPONSIBLES
IRRESPONSIBLY
IRRESPONSIVE
IRRESPONSIVELY
IRRESTRAINABLE
IRRESUSCITABLE
IRRESUSCITABLY
IRRETENTION
IRRETENTIONS
IRRETENTIVE
IRRETENTIVENESS
IRRETRIEVABLE
IRRETRIEVABLY
IRREVERENCE
IRREVERENCES
IRREVERENT
IRREVERENTIAL
IRREVERENTLY
IRREVERSIBILITY
IRREVERSIBLE
IRREVERSIBLY
IRREVOCABILITY
IRREVOCABLE
IRREVOCABLENESS
IRREVOCABLY
IRRIDENTA
IRRIDENTAS
IRRIGABLE
IRRIGATE
IRRIGATED
IRRIGATES
IRRIGATING
IRRIGATION
IRRIGATIONAL
IRRIGATIONS

IRRIGATIVE
IRRIGATOR
IRRIGATORS
IRRIGUOUS
IRRISION
IRRISIONS
IRRISORY
IRRITABILITIES
IRRITABILITY
IRRITABLE
IRRITABLENESS
IRRITABLENESSES
IRRITABLY
IRRITANCIES
IRRITANCY
IRRITANT
IRRITANTS
IRRITATE
IRRITATED
IRRITATES
IRRITATING
IRRITATINGLY
IRRITATION
IRRITATIONS
IRRITATIVE
IRRITATOR
IRRITATORS
IRROTATIONAL
IRRUPT
IRRUPTED
IRRUPTING
IRRUPTION
IRRUPTIONS
IRRUPTIVE
IRRUPTIVELY
IRRUPTS
IS
ISABEL
ISABELLA
ISABELLAS
ISABELLINE
ISABELLINES
ISABELS
ISAGOGE
ISAGOGES
ISAGOGIC
ISAGOGICS
ISALLOBAR
ISALLOBARIC
ISALLOBARS
ISAPOSTOLIC
ISARITHM
ISARITHMS
ISATIN
ISATINE
ISATINES

ISATINIC
ISATINS
ISBA
ISBAS
ISCHAEMIA
ISCHAEMIAS
ISCHAEMIC
ISCHEMIA
ISCHEMIAS
ISCHEMIC
ISCHIA
ISCHIADIC
ISCHIAL
ISCHIATIC
ISCHIUM
ISCHURETIC
ISCHURETICS
ISCHURIA
ISCHURIAS
ISENERGIC
ISENTROPIC
ISENTROPICALLY
ISH
ISHES
ISINGLASS
ISINGLASSES
ISLAND
ISLANDED
ISLANDER
ISLANDERS
ISLANDING
ISLANDS
ISLE
ISLED
ISLELESS
ISLEMAN
ISLEMEN
ISLES
ISLESMAN
ISLESMEN
ISLET
ISLETS
ISLING
ISLOMANE
ISLOMANIA
ISLOMANIAC
ISM
ISMATIC
ISMATICAL
ISMATICALNESS
ISMATICALNESSES
ISMS
ISNA
ISNAE
ISO
ISOAGGLUTININ

ISOAGGLUTININS
ISOALLOXAZINE
ISOALLOXAZINES
ISOAMINILE
ISOAMINILES
ISOAMYL
ISOANTIBODIES
ISOANTIBODY
ISOANTIGEN
ISOANTIGENIC
ISOANTIGENS
ISOBAR
ISOBARE
ISOBARES
ISOBARIC
ISOBARISM
ISOBAROMETRIC
ISOBARS
ISOBASE
ISOBASES
ISOBATH
ISOBATHIC
ISOBATHS
ISOBILATERAL
ISOBRONT
ISOBRONTS
ISOBUTANE
ISOBUTANES
ISOBUTYLENE
ISOBUTYLENES
ISOCALORIC
ISOCARBOXAZID
ISOCARBOXAZIDS
ISOCHASM
ISOCHASMIC
ISOCHASMS
ISOCHEIM
ISOCHEIMAL
ISOCHEIMALS
ISOCHEIMENAL
ISOCHEIMENALS
ISOCHEIMIC
ISOCHEIMS
ISOCHIMAL
ISOCHIMALS
ISOCHIME
ISOCHIMES
ISOCHOR
ISOCHORE
ISOCHORES
ISOCHORIC
ISOCHORS
ISOCHROMATIC
ISOCHROMOSOME
ISOCHROMOSOMES
ISOCHRON

ISOCHRONAL
ISOCHRONALLY
ISOCHRONE
ISOCHRONES
ISOCHRONISE
ISOCHRONISED
ISOCHRONISES
ISOCHRONISING
ISOCHRONISM
ISOCHRONISMS
ISOCHRONIZE
ISOCHRONIZED
ISOCHRONIZES
ISOCHRONIZING
ISOCHRONOUS
ISOCHRONOUSLY
ISOCHRONS
ISOCHROOUS
ISOCLINAL
ISOCLINALS
ISOCLINE
ISOCLINES
ISOCLINIC
ISOCLINICS
ISOCRACIES
ISOCRACY
ISOCRATIC
ISOCRYMAL
ISOCRYMALS
ISOCRYME
ISOCRYMES
ISOCYANATE
ISOCYANATES
ISOCYANIC
ISOCYANIDE
ISOCYANIDES
ISOCYCLIC
ISODIAMETRIC
ISODIAMETRICAL
ISODIAPHERE
ISODIAPHERES
ISODICA
ISODICON
ISODIMORPHIC
ISODIMORPHISM
ISODIMORPHISMS
ISODIMORPHOUS
ISODOMA
ISODOMON
ISODOMONS
ISODOMOUS
ISODOMUM
ISODONT
ISODONTAL
ISODONTALS
ISODONTS

ISODOSE
ISODOSES
ISODYNAMIC
ISODYNAMICS
ISOELECTRIC
ISOELECTRONIC
ISOENZYMATIC
ISOENZYME
ISOENZYMES
ISOENZYMIC
ISOETES
ISOGAMETE
ISOGAMETES
ISOGAMETIC
ISOGAMIC
ISOGAMIES
ISOGAMOUS
ISOGAMY
ISOGENEIC
ISOGENETIC
ISOGENIC
ISOGENIES
ISOGENOUS
ISOGENY
ISOGEOTHERM
ISOGEOTHERMAL
ISOGEOTHERMALS
ISOGEOTHERMIC
ISOGEOTHERMICS
ISOGEOTHERMS
ISOGLOSS
ISOGLOSSAL
ISOGLOSSES
ISOGLOSSIC
ISOGLOTTAL
ISOGLOTTIC
ISOGON
ISOGONAL
ISOGONALS
ISOGONE
ISOGONES
ISOGONIC
ISOGONICS
ISOGONIES
ISOGONS
ISOGONY
ISOGRAFT
ISOGRAFTED
ISOGRAFTING
ISOGRAFTS
ISOGRAM
ISOGRAMS
ISOGRAPH
ISOGRAPHS
ISOGRIV
ISOGRIVS

ISOHEL
ISOHELS
ISOHYDRIC
ISOHYDRICALLY
ISOHYET
ISOHYETAL
ISOHYETALS
ISOHYETS
ISOIMMUNISATION
ISOIMMUNIZATION
ISOKINETIC
ISOKONT
ISOKONTAN
ISOKONTANS
ISOKONTS
ISOLABILITIES
ISOLABILITY
ISOLABLE
ISOLATABLE
ISOLATE
ISOLATED
ISOLATES
ISOLATING
ISOLATION
ISOLATIONISM
ISOLATIONISMS
ISOLATIONIST
ISOLATIONISTS
ISOLATIONS
ISOLATIVE
ISOLATOR
ISOLATORS
ISOLEAD
ISOLEADS
ISOLECITHAL
ISOLECTIC
ISOLEUCINE
ISOLEUCINES
ISOLEX
ISOLEXES
ISOLINE
ISOLINES
ISOLOG
ISOLOGOUS
ISOLOGS
ISOLOGUE
ISOLOGUES
ISOMAGNETIC
ISOMAGNETICS
ISOMER
ISOMERASE
ISOMERASES
ISOMERE
ISOMERES
ISOMERIC
ISOMERISATION

ISOMERISATIONS
ISOMERISE
ISOMERISED
ISOMERISES
ISOMERISING
ISOMERISM
ISOMERISMS
ISOMERIZATION
ISOMERIZATIONS
ISOMERIZE
ISOMERIZED
ISOMERIZES
ISOMERIZING
ISOMEROUS
ISOMERS
ISOMETRIC
ISOMETRICAL
ISOMETRICALLY
ISOMETRICS
ISOMETRIES
ISOMETROPIA
ISOMETRY
ISOMORPH
ISOMORPHIC
ISOMORPHICALLY
ISOMORPHISM
ISOMORPHISMS
ISOMORPHOUS
ISOMORPHS
ISONIAZID
ISONIAZIDE
ISONIAZIDES
ISONIAZIDS
ISONITRILE
ISONITRILES
ISONOME
ISONOMES
ISONOMIC
ISONOMIES
ISONOMOUS
ISONOMY
ISOOCTANE
ISOOCTANES
ISOPACH
ISOPACHS
ISOPACHYTE
ISOPACHYTES
ISOPERIMETER
ISOPERIMETERS
ISOPERIMETRICAL
ISOPERIMETRIES
ISOPERIMETRY
ISOPHONE
ISOPHONES
ISOPHONIC
ISOPHOTAL

ISOPHOTE
ISOPHOTES
ISOPIESTIC
ISOPIESTICALLY
ISOPLETH
ISOPLETHIC
ISOPLETHS
ISOPOD
ISOPODAN
ISOPODANS
ISOPODOUS
ISOPODS
ISOPOLITIES
ISOPOLITY
ISOPRENALINE
ISOPRENALINES
ISOPRENE
ISOPRENES
ISOPRENOID
ISOPROPYL
ISOPROPYLS
ISOPROTERENOL
ISOPROTERENOLS
ISOPTEROUS
ISOPYCNAL
ISOPYCNIC
ISOPYCNICS
ISORHYTHMIC
ISOS
ISOSCELES
ISOSEISMAL
ISOSEISMALS
ISOSEISMIC
ISOSEISMICS
ISOSMOTIC
ISOSMOTICALLY
ISOSPIN
ISOSPINS
ISOSPONDYLOUS
ISOSPORIES
ISOSPOROUS
ISOSPORY
ISOSTASIES
ISOSTASY
ISOSTATIC
ISOSTATICALLY
ISOSTEMONOUS
ISOSTERIC
ISOTACH
ISOTACHS
ISOTACTIC
ISOTENISCOPE
ISOTENISCOPES
ISOTENISCOPY
ISOTHENURIA
ISOTHENURIAS

ISOTHERAL
ISOTHERALS
ISOTHERE
ISOTHERES
ISOTHERM
ISOTHERMAL
ISOTHERMALLY
ISOTHERMALS
ISOTHERMS
ISOTONE
ISOTONES
ISOTONIC
ISOTONICALLY
ISOTONICITIES
ISOTONICITY
ISOTOPE
ISOTOPES
ISOTOPIC
ISOTOPICALLY
ISOTOPIES
ISOTOPY
ISOTRETINOIN
ISOTRETINOINS
ISOTRON
ISOTRONS
ISOTROPIC
ISOTROPICALLY
ISOTROPIES
ISOTROPISM
ISOTROPISMS
ISOTROPOUS
ISOTROPY
ISOTYPE
ISOTYPES
ISOTYPIC
ISOXSUPRINE
ISOXSUPRINES
ISOZYME
ISOZYMES
ISOZYMIC
ISPAGHULA
ISPAGHULAS
ISSEI
ISSEIS
ISSUABLE
ISSUABLY
ISSUANCE
ISSUANCES
ISSUANT
ISSUE
ISSUED
ISSUELESS
ISSUER
ISSUERS
ISSUES
ISSUING

ISTANA
ISTANAS
ISTHMI
ISTHMIAN
ISTHMIANS
ISTHMIC
ISTHMOID
ISTHMUS
ISTHMUSES
ISTLE
ISTLES
IT
ITA
ITACISM
ITACISMS
ITACOLUMITE
ITACOLUMITES
ITACONIC
ITALIANATE
ITALIANATED
ITALIANATES
ITALIANATING
ITALIANISE
ITALIANISED
ITALIANISES
ITALIANISING
ITALIANIZE
ITALIANIZED
ITALIANIZES
ITALIANIZING
ITALIC
ITALICISATION
ITALICISATIONS
ITALICISE
ITALICISED
ITALICISES
ITALICISING
ITALICIZATION
ITALICIZATIONS
ITALICIZE
ITALICIZED
ITALICIZES
ITALICIZING
ITALICS
ITAS
ITCH
ITCHED
ITCHES
ITCHIER
ITCHIEST
ITCHILY
ITCHINESS
ITCHINESSES
ITCHING
ITCHINGS
ITCHWEED

ITCHWEEDS
ITCHY
ITEM
ITEMED
ITEMING
ITEMISATION
ITEMISATIONS
ITEMISE
ITEMISED
ITEMISER
ITEMISERS
ITEMISES
ITEMISING
ITEMIZATION
ITEMIZATIONS
ITEMIZE
ITEMIZED
ITEMIZER
ITEMIZERS
ITEMIZES
ITEMIZING
ITEMS
ITERANCE
ITERANCES
ITERANT
ITERATE
ITERATED
ITERATES
ITERATING
ITERATION
ITERATIONS
ITERATIVE
ITERATIVELY
ITERATIVENESS
ITEROPAROUS
ITEROPAROUSLY
ITERUM
ITHER
ITHYPHALLI
ITHYPHALLIC
ITHYPHALLICALLY
ITHYPHALLICS
ITHYPHALLUS
ITHYPHALLUSES
ITINERACIES
ITINERACY
ITINERANCIES
ITINERANCY
ITINERANT
ITINERANTLY
ITINERANTS
ITINERARIES
ITINERARY
ITINERATE
ITINERATED
ITINERATES

ITINERATING
ITINERATION
ITINERATIONS
ITS
ITSELF
IURE
IVERMECTIN
IVERMECTINS
IVIED
IVIES
IVORIED
IVORIES
IVORIST
IVORISTS
IVORY
IVORYBILL
IVORYBILLS
IVORYWOOD
IVORYWOODS
IVRESSE
IVRESSES
IVY
IVYLIKE
IWI
IWIS
IXIA
IXIAS
IXODIASES
IXODIASIS
IXODID
IXODIDS
IXORA
IXORAS
IXTLE
IXTLES
IZAR
IZARD
IZARDS
IZARS
IZVESTIA
IZVESTIAS
IZVESTIYA
IZVESTIYAS
IZZARD
IZZARDS
IZZAT
IZZATS

J

JAAP
JAAPS
JAB
JABBED
JABBER
JABBERED
JABBERER
JABBERERS
JABBERING
JABBERINGLY
JABBERINGS
JABBERS
JABBERWOCK
JABBERWOCKIES
JABBERWOCKS
JABBERWOCKY
JABBING
JABBINGLY
JABBLE
JABBLED
JABBLES
JABBLING
JABERS
JABIRU
JABIRUS
JABORANDI
JABORANDIS
JABOT
JABOTICABA
JABOTICABAS
JABOTS
JABS
JACAL
JACALES
JACALS
JACAMAR
JACAMARS
JACANA
JACANAS
JACARANDA
JACARANDAS
JACARE
JACARES
JACCHUS
JACCHUSES
JACENT
JACINTH
JACINTHE
JACINTHES
JACINTHS
JACK

JACKAL
JACKALLED
JACKALLING
JACKALS
JACKANAPES
JACKANAPESES
JACKAROO
JACKAROOED
JACKAROOING
JACKAROOS
JACKASS
JACKASSERIES
JACKASSERY
JACKASSES
JACKBOOT
JACKBOOTED
JACKBOOTING
JACKBOOTS
JACKDAW
JACKDAWS
JACKED
JACKEEN
JACKEENS
JACKER
JACKEROO
JACKEROOED
JACKEROOING
JACKEROOS
JACKERS
JACKET
JACKETED
JACKETING
JACKETLESS
JACKETS
JACKFISH
JACKFISHES
JACKFRUIT
JACKFRUITS
JACKHAMMER
JACKHAMMERED
JACKHAMMERING
JACKHAMMERS
JACKIES
JACKING
JACKKNIFE
JACKKNIFED
JACKKNIFES
JACKKNIFING
JACKKNIVES
JACKLEG
JACKLEGS

JACKLIGHT
JACKLIGHTS
JACKMAN
JACKMEN
JACKPOT
JACKPOTS
JACKRABBIT
JACKRABBITS
JACKROLL
JACKROLLED
JACKROLLING
JACKROLLS
JACKS
JACKSCREW
JACKSCREWS
JACKSHAFT
JACKSHAFTS
JACKSIE
JACKSIES
JACKSMELT
JACKSMELTS
JACKSMITH
JACKSMITHS
JACKSNIPE
JACKSNIPES
JACKSTAY
JACKSTAYS
JACKSTONE
JACKSTONES
JACKSTRAW
JACKSTRAWS
JACKSY
JACKY
JACOBIN
JACOBINS
JACOBUS
JACOBUSES
JACONET
JACONETS
JACQUARD
JACQUARDS
JACQUERIE
JACQUERIES
JACTATION
JACTATIONS
JACTITATION
JACTITATIONS
JACULATE
JACULATED
JACULATES
JACULATING

JACULATION
JACULATIONS
JACULATOR
JACULATORS
JACULATORY
JACUZZI
JACUZZIS
JADE
JADED
JADEDLY
JADEDNESS
JADEDNESSES
JADEITE
JADEITES
JADELIKE
JADERIES
JADERY
JADES
JADING
JADISH
JADISHLY
JADISHNESS
JADITIC
JAEGER
JAEGERS
JAFA
JAFAS
JAG
JAGA
JAGAED
JAGAING
JAGAS
JAGER
JAGERS
JAGG
JAGGARIES
JAGGARY
JAGGED
JAGGEDER
JAGGEDEST
JAGGEDLY
JAGGEDNESS
JAGGEDNESSES
JAGGER
JAGGERIES
JAGGERS
JAGGERY
JAGGHERIES
JAGGHERY
JAGGIER
JAGGIEST

JAGGING
JAGGS
JAGGY
JAGHIR
JAGHIRDAR
JAGHIRDARS
JAGHIRE
JAGHIRES
JAGHIRS
JAGIR
JAGIRS
JAGLESS
JAGRA
JAGRAS
JAGS
JAGUAR
JAGUARONDI
JAGUARONDIS
JAGUARS
JAGUARUNDI
JAGUARUNDIS
JAI
JAIL
JAILBAIT
JAILBIRD
JAILBIRDS
JAILBREAK
JAILBREAKS
JAILED
JAILER
JAILERESS
JAILERESSES
JAILERS
JAILHOUSE
JAILHOUSES
JAILING
JAILLESS
JAILOR
JAILORESS
JAILORESSES
JAILORS
JAILS
JAK
JAKE
JAKES
JAKESES
JAKFRUIT
JAKFRUITS
JAKS
JALAP
JALAPENO
JALAPENOS
JALAPIC
JALAPIN
JALAPINS
JALAPS

JALOP
JALOPIES
JALOPPIES
JALOPPY
JALOPS
JALOPY
JALOUSE
JALOUSED
JALOUSES
JALOUSIE
JALOUSIED
JALOUSIES
JALOUSING
JAM
JAMADAR
JAMADARS
JAMAHIRIYA
JAMAHIRIYAS
JAMB
JAMBALAYA
JAMBALAYAS
JAMBART
JAMBARTS
JAMBE
JAMBEAU
JAMBEAUX
JAMBED
JAMBEE
JAMBEES
JAMBER
JAMBERS
JAMBES
JAMBEUX
JAMBIER
JAMBIERS
JAMBING
JAMBIYA
JAMBIYAH
JAMBIYAHS
JAMBIYAS
JAMBO
JAMBOK
JAMBOKKED
JAMBOKKING
JAMBOKS
JAMBOLAN
JAMBOLANA
JAMBOLANAS
JAMBOLANS
JAMBONE
JAMBONES
JAMBOOL
JAMBOOLS
JAMBOREE
JAMBOREES
JAMBOS

JAMBS
JAMBU
JAMBUL
JAMBULS
JAMBUS
JAMDANI
JAMDANIS
JAMES
JAMESES
JAMJAR
JAMJARS
JAMMED
JAMMER
JAMMERS
JAMMIER
JAMMIES
JAMMIEST
JAMMING
JAMMY
JAMPAN
JAMPANEE
JAMPANEES
JAMPANI
JAMPANIS
JAMPANS
JAMPOT
JAMPOTS
JAMS
JANDAL
JANDALS
JANE
JANES
JANGLE
JANGLED
JANGLER
JANGLERS
JANGLES
JANGLIER
JANGLIEST
JANGLING
JANGLINGS
JANGLY
JANIFORM
JANISARIES
JANISARY
JANISSARIES
JANISSARY
JANITOR
JANITORIAL
JANITORS
JANITORSHIP
JANITORSHIPS
JANITRESS
JANITRESSES
JANITRIX
JANITRIXES

JANIZAR
JANIZARIAN
JANIZARIES
JANIZARS
JANIZARY
JANKER
JANKERS
JANN
JANNIED
JANNOCK
JANNOCKS
JANNS
JANNY
JANNYING
JANOLA
JANSKY
JANSKYS
JANTEE
JANTIER
JANTIES
JANTIEST
JANTY
JAP
JAPAN
JAPANIZE
JAPANIZED
JAPANIZES
JAPANIZING
JAPANNED
JAPANNER
JAPANNERS
JAPANNING
JAPANS
JAPE
JAPED
JAPER
JAPERIES
JAPERS
JAPERY
JAPES
JAPING
JAPINGLY
JAPINGS
JAPONAISERIE
JAPONAISERIES
JAPONICA
JAPONICAS
JAPPED
JAPPING
JAPS
JAR
JARARACA
JARARACAS
JARARAKA
JARARAKAS
JARDINIERE

JARDINIERES
JARFUL
JARFULS
JARGON
JARGONED
JARGONEER
JARGONEERS
JARGONEL
JARGONELLE
JARGONELLES
JARGONELS
JARGONING
JARGONISATION
JARGONISATIONS
JARGONISE
JARGONISED
JARGONISES
JARGONISH
JARGONISING
JARGONIST
JARGONISTIC
JARGONISTS
JARGONIZATION
JARGONIZATIONS
JARGONIZE
JARGONIZED
JARGONIZES
JARGONIZING
JARGONS
JARGOON
JARGOONS
JARHEAD
JARHEADS
JARINA
JARINAS
JARK
JARKMAN
JARKMEN
JARKS
JARL
JARLDOM
JARLDOMS
JARLS
JAROOL
JAROOLS
JAROSITE
JAROSITES
JAROVIZE
JAROVIZED
JAROVIZES
JAROVIZING
JARP
JARPED
JARPING
JARPS
JARRAH

JARRAHS
JARRED
JARRING
JARRINGLY
JARRINGS
JARS
JARSFUL
JARTA
JARTAS
JARUL
JARULS
JARVEY
JARVEYS
JARVIE
JARVIES
JASEY
JASEYS
JASIES
JASMIN
JASMINE
JASMINES
JASMINS
JASP
JASPE
JASPER
JASPERISE
JASPERISED
JASPERISES
JASPERISING
JASPERIZE
JASPERIZED
JASPERIZES
JASPERIZING
JASPEROUS
JASPERS
JASPERWARE
JASPERWARES
JASPERY
JASPES
JASPIDEAN
JASPIDEOUS
JASPIS
JASPISES
JASPS
JASS
JASSES
JASSID
JASSIDS
JASY
JATAKA
JATAKAS
JATO
JATOS
JAUK
JAUKED
JAUKING

JAUKS
JAUNCE
JAUNCED
JAUNCES
JAUNCING
JAUNDICE
JAUNDICED
JAUNDICES
JAUNDICING
JAUNSE
JAUNSED
JAUNSES
JAUNSING
JAUNT
JAUNTED
JAUNTEE
JAUNTIE
JAUNTIER
JAUNTIES
JAUNTIEST
JAUNTILY
JAUNTINESS
JAUNTINESSES
JAUNTING
JAUNTINGLY
JAUNTS
JAUNTY
JAUP
JAUPED
JAUPING
JAUPS
JAVA
JAVAS
JAVEL
JAVELIN
JAVELINA
JAVELINAS
JAVELINED
JAVELINING
JAVELINS
JAVELS
JAW
JAWAN
JAWANS
JAWARI
JAWARIS
JAWBATION
JAWBATIONS
JAWBONE
JAWBONED
JAWBONER
JAWBONERS
JAWBONES
JAWBONING
JAWBONINGS
JAWBOX

JAWBOXES
JAWBREAKER
JAWBREAKERS
JAWBREAKING
JAWBREAKINGLY
JAWBREAKINGS
JAWCRUSHER
JAWCRUSHERS
JAWCRUSHING
JAWCRUSHINGLY
JAWDROPPINGLY
JAWED
JAWFALL
JAWFALLS
JAWHOLE
JAWHOLES
JAWING
JAWINGS
JAWLIKE
JAWLINE
JAWLINES
JAWS
JAXIE
JAXIES
JAXY
JAY
JAYBIRD
JAYBIRDS
JAYGEE
JAYGEES
JAYHAWKER
JAYHAWKERS
JAYS
JAYVEE
JAYVEES
JAYWALK
JAYWALKED
JAYWALKER
JAYWALKERS
JAYWALKING
JAYWALKINGS
JAYWALKS
JAZERANT
JAZERANTS
JAZIES
JAZY
JAZZ
JAZZED
JAZZER
JAZZERS
JAZZES
JAZZIER
JAZZIEST
JAZZILY
JAZZINESS
JAZZINESSES

JAZZING
JAZZLIKE
JAZZMAN
JAZZMEN
JAZZY
JEALOUS
JEALOUSE
JEALOUSED
JEALOUSES
JEALOUSHOOD
JEALOUSHOODS
JEALOUSIES
JEALOUSING
JEALOUSLY
JEALOUSNESS
JEALOUSNESSES
JEALOUSY
JEAN
JEANETTE
JEANETTES
JEANS
JEAT
JEATS
JEBEL
JEBELS
JEE
JEED
JEEING
JEEL
JEELED
JEELIE
JEELIED
JEELIEING
JEELIES
JEELING
JEELS
JEELY
JEELYING
JEEP
JEEPED
JEEPERS
JEEPING
JEEPNEY
JEEPNEYS
JEEPS
JEER
JEERED
JEERER
JEERERS
JEERING
JEERINGLY
JEERINGS
JEERS
JEES
JEEZ
JEFE

JEFES
JEFF
JEFFED
JEFFING
JEFFS
JEHAD
JEHADS
JEHU
JEHUS
JEISTIECOR
JEISTIECORS
JEJUNA
JEJUNAL
JEJUNE
JEJUNELY
JEJUNENESS
JEJUNENESSES
JEJUNITIES
JEJUNITY
JEJUNOSTOMAL
JEJUNOSTOMIES
JEJUNOSTOMY
JEJUNUM
JEJUNUMS
JELAB
JELABS
JELL
JELLABA
JELLABAH
JELLABAHED
JELLABAHS
JELLABAS
JELLED
JELLIED
JELLIES
JELLIFICATION
JELLIFICATIONS
JELLIFIED
JELLIFIES
JELLIFY
JELLIFYING
JELLING
JELLO
JELLOS
JELLS
JELLY
JELLYBEAN
JELLYBEANS
JELLYFISH
JELLYFISHES
JELLYGRAPH
JELLYGRAPHED
JELLYGRAPHING
JELLYGRAPHS
JELLYING
JELLYLIKE

JELUTONG
JELUTONGS
JEMADAR
JEMADARS
JEMBE
JEMBES
JEMIDAR
JEMIDARS
JEMIMA
JEMIMAS
JEMMIED
JEMMIER
JEMMIES
JEMMIEST
JEMMINESS
JEMMINESSES
JEMMY
JEMMYING
JENNET
JENNETING
JENNETINGS
JENNETS
JENNIES
JENNY
JEOFAIL
JEOFAILS
JEON
JEOPARD
JEOPARDED
JEOPARDER
JEOPARDERS
JEOPARDIED
JEOPARDIES
JEOPARDING
JEOPARDISE
JEOPARDISED
JEOPARDISES
JEOPARDISING
JEOPARDIZE
JEOPARDIZED
JEOPARDIZES
JEOPARDIZING
JEOPARDOUS
JEOPARDOUSLY
JEOPARDS
JEOPARDY
JEOPARDYING
JEQUERITIES
JEQUERITY
JEQUIRITIES
JEQUIRITY
JERBIL
JERBILS
JERBOA
JERBOAS
JEREED

JEREEDS
JEREMIAD
JEREMIADS
JEREPIGO
JEREPIGOS
JERFALCON
JERFALCONS
JERID
JERIDS
JERK
JERKED
JERKER
JERKERS
JERKIER
JERKIES
JERKIEST
JERKILY
JERKIN
JERKINESS
JERKINESSES
JERKING
JERKINGS
JERKINHEAD
JERKINHEADS
JERKINS
JERKS
JERKWATER
JERKWATERS
JERKY
JEROBOAM
JEROBOAMS
JERQUE
JERQUED
JERQUER
JERQUERS
JERQUES
JERQUING
JERQUINGS
JERREED
JERREEDS
JERRICAN
JERRICANS
JERRID
JERRIDS
JERRIES
JERRY
JERRYCAN
JERRYCANS
JERRYMANDER
JERRYMANDERED
JERRYMANDERING
JERRYMANDERS
JERSEY
JERSEYED
JERSEYS
JESS

JESSAMIES
JESSAMINE
JESSAMINES
JESSAMY
JESSANT
JESSE
JESSED
JESSERANT
JESSERANTS
JESSES
JESSIE
JESSIES
JESSING
JEST
JESTBOOK
JESTBOOKS
JESTED
JESTEE
JESTEES
JESTER
JESTERS
JESTFUL
JESTING
JESTINGLY
JESTINGS
JESTS
JESUIT
JESUITIC
JESUITICAL
JESUITICALLY
JESUITISM
JESUITISMS
JESUITRIES
JESUITRY
JESUITS
JESUS
JET
JETBEAD
JETBEADS
JETE
JETES
JETFOIL
JETFOILS
JETLIKE
JETLINER
JETLINERS
JETON
JETONS
JETPLANE
JETPLANES
JETPORT
JETPORTS
JETS
JETSAM
JETSAMS
JETSOM

JETSOMS
JETSON
JETSONS
JETSTREAM
JETSTREAMS
JETTATURA
JETTATURAS
JETTED
JETTIED
JETTIER
JETTIES
JETTIEST
JETTINESS
JETTINESSES
JETTING
JETTISON
JETTISONABLE
JETTISONED
JETTISONING
JETTISONS
JETTON
JETTONS
JETTY
JETTYING
JEU
JEUNE
JEUX
JEW
JEWED
JEWEL
JEWELED
JEWELER
JEWELERS
JEWELFISH
JEWELFISHES
JEWELING
JEWELLED
JEWELLER
JEWELLERIES
JEWELLERS
JEWELLERY
JEWELLIKE
JEWELLING
JEWELRIES
JEWELRY
JEWELS
JEWELWEED
JEWELWEEDS
JEWFISH
JEWFISHES
JEWIE
JEWIES
JEWING
JEWS
JEZAIL
JEZAILS

JEZEBEL
JEZEBELS
JHALA
JHALAS
JHATKA
JIAO
JIAOS
JIB
JIBB
JIBBAH
JIBBAHS
JIBBED
JIBBER
JIBBERED
JIBBERING
JIBBERS
JIBBING
JIBBINGS
JIBBONS
JIBBOOM
JIBBOOMS
JIBBS
JIBE
JIBED
JIBER
JIBERS
JIBES
JIBING
JIBINGLY
JIBS
JICAMA
JICAMAS
JICKAJOG
JICKAJOGGED
JICKAJOGGING
JICKAJOGS
JIFF
JIFFIES
JIFFS
JIFFY
JIG
JIGABOO
JIGABOOS
JIGAJIG
JIGAJIGGED
JIGAJIGGING
JIGAJIGS
JIGAJOG
JIGAJOGGED
JIGAJOGGING
JIGAJOGS
JIGAMAREE
JIGAMAREES
JIGGED
JIGGER
JIGGERED

JIGGERING
JIGGERMAST
JIGGERMASTS
JIGGERS
JIGGIER
JIGGIEST
JIGGING
JIGGINGS
JIGGISH
JIGGLE
JIGGLED
JIGGLES
JIGGLIER
JIGGLIEST
JIGGLING
JIGGLY
JIGGUMBOB
JIGGUMBOBS
JIGGY
JIGJIG
JIGJIGGED
JIGJIGGING
JIGJIGS
JIGOT
JIGOTS
JIGS
JIGSAW
JIGSAWED
JIGSAWING
JIGSAWN
JIGSAWS
JIHAD
JIHADS
JILBAB
JILBABS
JILGIE
JILGIES
JILL
JILLAROO
JILLAROOS
JILLET
JILLETS
JILLFLIRT
JILLFLIRTS
JILLION
JILLIONS
JILLIONTH
JILLS
JILT
JILTED
JILTER
JILTERS
JILTING
JILTS
JIMCRACK
JIMCRACKS

JIMINY
JIMJAM
JIMJAMS
JIMMIED
JIMMIES
JIMMINY
JIMMY
JIMMYING
JIMP
JIMPER
JIMPEST
JIMPIER
JIMPIEST
JIMPLY
JIMPNESS
JIMPNESSES
JIMPY
JIMSON
JIMSONWEED
JIMSONWEEDS
JIN
JINGAL
JINGALL
JINGALLS
JINGALS
JINGBANG
JINGBANGS
JINGKO
JINGKOES
JINGLE
JINGLED
JINGLER
JINGLERS
JINGLES
JINGLET
JINGLETS
JINGLIER
JINGLIEST
JINGLING
JINGLY
JINGO
JINGOES
JINGOISH
JINGOISM
JINGOISMS
JINGOIST
JINGOISTIC
JINGOISTICALLY
JINGOISTS
JINJILI
JINJILIS
JINK
JINKED
JINKER
JINKERS
JINKING

JINKS
JINN
JINNEE
JINNI
JINNS
JINRICKSHA
JINRICKSHAS
JINRICKSHAW
JINRICKSHAWS
JINRIKISHA
JINRIKISHAS
JINRIKSHA
JINRIKSHAS
JINS
JINX
JINXED
JINXES
JINXING
JIPIJAPA
JIPIJAPAS
JIPYAPA
JIPYAPAS
JIRBLE
JIRBLED
JIRBLES
JIRBLING
JIRD
JIRDS
JIRGA
JIRGAS
JIRKINET
JIRKINETS
JISM
JISMS
JISSOM
JISSOMS
JITNEY
JITNEYS
JITTER
JITTERBUG
JITTERBUGGED
JITTERBUGGING
JITTERBUGS
JITTERED
JITTERIER
JITTERIEST
JITTERINESS
JITTERINESSES
JITTERING
JITTERS
JITTERY
JIUJITSU
JIUJITSUS
JIUJUTSU
JIUJUTSUS
JIVE

JIVEASS
JIVED
JIVER
JIVERS
JIVES
JIVEY
JIVIER
JIVIEST
JIVING
JIZ
JIZZ
JIZZES
JNANA
JNANAS
JO
JOANNA
JOANNAS
JOANNES
JOANNESES
JOB
JOBATION
JOBATIONS
JOBBED
JOBBER
JOBBERIES
JOBBERS
JOBBERY
JOBBIE
JOBBIES
JOBBING
JOBBINGS
JOBCENTRE
JOBCENTRES
JOBE
JOBED
JOBERNOWL
JOBERNOWLS
JOBES
JOBHOLDER
JOBHOLDERS
JOBING
JOBLESS
JOBLESSNESS
JOBLESSNESSES
JOBNAME
JOBNAMES
JOBS
JOBSHARE
JOBSHARES
JOBSWORTH
JOBSWORTHS
JOCK
JOCKETTE
JOCKETTES
JOCKEY
JOCKEYED

JOCKEYING
JOCKEYISM
JOCKEYISMS
JOCKEYS
JOCKEYSHIP
JOCKEYSHIPS
JOCKNEY
JOCKNEYS
JOCKO
JOCKOS
JOCKS
JOCKSTRAP
JOCKSTRAPS
JOCKTELEG
JOCKTELEGS
JOCO
JOCOSE
JOCOSELY
JOCOSENESS
JOCOSENESSES
JOCOSERIOUS
JOCOSITIES
JOCOSITY
JOCULAR
JOCULARITIES
JOCULARITY
JOCULARLY
JOCULATOR
JOCULATORS
JOCUND
JOCUNDITIES
JOCUNDITY
JOCUNDLY
JOCUNDNESS
JOCUNDNESSES
JODEL
JODELLED
JODELLING
JODELS
JODHPUR
JODHPURS
JOE
JOES
JOEY
JOEYS
JOG
JOGGED
JOGGER
JOGGERS
JOGGING
JOGGINGS
JOGGLE
JOGGLED
JOGGLER
JOGGLERS
JOGGLES

JOGGLING
JOGPANTS
JOGS
JOGTROT
JOGTROTS
JOHANNES
JOHANNESES
JOHN
JOHNBOAT
JOHNBOATS
JOHNNIE
JOHNNIES
JOHNNY
JOHNNYCAKE
JOHNNYCAKES
JOHNS
JOHNSONGRASS
JOHNSONGRASSES
JOIN
JOINABLE
JOINDER
JOINDERS
JOINED
JOINER
JOINERIES
JOINERS
JOINERY
JOINING
JOININGS
JOINS
JOINT
JOINTED
JOINTEDLY
JOINTEDNESS
JOINTEDNESSES
JOINTER
JOINTERS
JOINTING
JOINTLESS
JOINTLY
JOINTNESS
JOINTNESSES
JOINTRESS
JOINTRESSES
JOINTS
JOINTURE
JOINTURED
JOINTURES
JOINTURESS
JOINTURESSES
JOINTURING
JOINTWORM
JOINTWORMS
JOIST
JOISTED
JOISTING

JOISTS
JOJOBA
JOJOBAS
JOKE
JOKED
JOKER
JOKERS
JOKES
JOKESMITH
JOKESMITHS
JOKESOME
JOKESTER
JOKESTERS
JOKEY
JOKIER
JOKIEST
JOKILY
JOKINESS
JOKINESSES
JOKING
JOKINGLY
JOKOL
JOKY
JOL
JOLE
JOLED
JOLES
JOLING
JOLL
JOLLED
JOLLEY
JOLLEYER
JOLLEYERS
JOLLEYING
JOLLEYINGS
JOLLEYS
JOLLIED
JOLLIER
JOLLIES
JOLLIEST
JOLLIFICATION
JOLLIFICATIONS
JOLLIFIED
JOLLIFIES
JOLLIFY
JOLLIFYING
JOLLILY
JOLLIMENT
JOLLIMENTS
JOLLINESS
JOLLINESSES
JOLLING
JOLLITIES
JOLLITY
JOLLOP
JOLLOPS

JOLLS
JOLLY
JOLLYBOAT
JOLLYBOATS
JOLLYER
JOLLYERS
JOLLYHEAD
JOLLYHEADS
JOLLYING
JOLLYINGS
JOLS
JOLT
JOLTED
JOLTER
JOLTERHEAD
JOLTERHEADS
JOLTERS
JOLTHEAD
JOLTHEADS
JOLTIER
JOLTIEST
JOLTILY
JOLTING
JOLTINGLY
JOLTS
JOLTY
JOMO
JOMOS
JONCANOE
JONCANOES
JONES
JONESES
JONG
JONGLEUR
JONGLEURS
JONNOCK
JONQUIL
JONQUILS
JONTIES
JONTY
JOOK
JOOKED
JOOKERIES
JOOKERY
JOOKING
JOOKS
JOR
JORAM
JORAMS
JORDAN
JORDANS
JORDELOO
JORDELOOS
JORS
JORUM
JORUMS

JOSEPH
JOSEPHINITE
JOSEPHINITES
JOSEPHS
JOSH
JOSHED
JOSHER
JOSHERS
JOSHES
JOSHING
JOSKIN
JOSKINS
JOSS
JOSSER
JOSSERS
JOSSES
JOSTLE
JOSTLED
JOSTLEMENT
JOSTLEMENTS
JOSTLER
JOSTLERS
JOSTLES
JOSTLING
JOSTLINGS
JOT
JOTA
JOTAS
JOTS
JOTTED
JOTTER
JOTTERS
JOTTING
JOTTINGS
JOTTY
JOTUN
JOTUNN
JOTUNNS
JOTUNS
JOUAL
JOUALS
JOUGS
JOUISANCE
JOUISANCES
JOUK
JOUKED
JOUKERIES
JOUKERY
JOUKING
JOUKS
JOULE
JOULED
JOULES
JOULING
JOUNCE
JOUNCED

JOUNCES
JOUNCIER
JOUNCIEST
JOUNCING
JOUNCY
JOUR
JOURNAL
JOURNALESE
JOURNALESES
JOURNALISATION
JOURNALISATIONS
JOURNALISE
JOURNALISED
JOURNALISER
JOURNALISERS
JOURNALISES
JOURNALISING
JOURNALISM
JOURNALISMS
JOURNALIST
JOURNALISTIC
JOURNALISTS
JOURNALIZATION
JOURNALIZATIONS
JOURNALIZE
JOURNALIZED
JOURNALIZER
JOURNALIZERS
JOURNALIZES
JOURNALIZING
JOURNALLED
JOURNALLING
JOURNALS
JOURNEY
JOURNEYED
JOURNEYER
JOURNEYERS
JOURNEYING
JOURNEYMAN
JOURNEYMEN
JOURNEYS
JOURNEYWORK
JOURNEYWORKS
JOURNO
JOURNOS
JOURS
JOUST
JOUSTED
JOUSTER
JOUSTERS
JOUSTING
JOUSTS
JOUYSAUNCES
JOVIAL
JOVIALITIES
JOVIALITY

JOVIALLY
JOVIALNESS
JOVIALNESSES
JOVIALTIES
JOVIALTY
JOVYSAUNCES
JOW
JOWAR
JOWARI
JOWARIS
JOWARS
JOWED
JOWING
JOWL
JOWLED
JOWLER
JOWLERS
JOWLIER
JOWLIEST
JOWLING
JOWLS
JOWLY
JOWS
JOY
JOYANCE
JOYANCES
JOYED
JOYFUL
JOYFULLER
JOYFULLEST
JOYFULLY
JOYFULNESS
JOYFULNESSES
JOYING
JOYLESS
JOYLESSLY
JOYLESSNESS
JOYLESSNESSES
JOYOUS
JOYOUSLY
JOYOUSNESS
JOYOUSNESSES
JOYPOP
JOYPOPPED
JOYPOPPER
JOYPOPPERS
JOYPOPPING
JOYPOPS
JOYRIDDEN
JOYRIDE
JOYRIDER
JOYRIDERS
JOYRIDES
JOYRIDING
JOYRIDINGS
JOYRODE

JOYS
JOYSTICK
JOYSTICKS
JUBA
JUBAS
JUBATE
JUBBAH
JUBBAHS
JUBE
JUBES
JUBHAH
JUBHAHS
JUBILANCE
JUBILANCES
JUBILANCIES
JUBILANCY
JUBILANT
JUBILANTLY
JUBILARIAN
JUBILARIANS
JUBILATE
JUBILATED
JUBILATES
JUBILATING
JUBILATION
JUBILATIONS
JUBILE
JUBILEE
JUBILEES
JUBILES
JUD
JUDAS
JUDASES
JUDDER
JUDDERED
JUDDERING
JUDDERS
JUDGE
JUDGEABILITY
JUDGEABLE
JUDGEABLY
JUDGED
JUDGELESS
JUDGELESSLY
JUDGELESSNESS
JUDGELIKE
JUDGEMENT
JUDGEMENTAL
JUDGEMENTS
JUDGER
JUDGERS
JUDGES
JUDGESHIP
JUDGESHIPS
JUDGING
JUDGINGLY

JUDGMATIC
JUDGMATICAL
JUDGMATICALLY
JUDGMENT
JUDGMENTAL
JUDGMENTALLY
JUDGMENTS
JUDICABLE
JUDICATION
JUDICATIONS
JUDICATIVE
JUDICATOR
JUDICATORIAL
JUDICATORIALLY
JUDICATORIES
JUDICATORS
JUDICATORY
JUDICATURE
JUDICATURES
JUDICIAL
JUDICIALLY
JUDICIARIES
JUDICIARY
JUDICIOUS
JUDICIOUSLY
JUDICIOUSNESS
JUDICIOUSNESSES
JUDIES
JUDO
JUDOGI
JUDOGIS
JUDOIST
JUDOISTS
JUDOKA
JUDOKAS
JUDOS
JUDS
JUDY
JUG
JUGA
JUGAL
JUGALS
JUGATE
JUGFUL
JUGFULS
JUGGED
JUGGERNAUT
JUGGERNAUTS
JUGGING
JUGGINGS
JUGGINS
JUGGINSES
JUGGLE
JUGGLED
JUGGLER
JUGGLERIES

JUGGLERS
JUGGLERY
JUGGLES
JUGGLING
JUGGLINGLY
JUGGLINGS
JUGHEAD
JUGHEADS
JUGLANDACEOUS
JUGLET
JUGLETS
JUGS
JUGSFUL
JUGULA
JUGULAR
JUGULARS
JUGULATE
JUGULATED
JUGULATES
JUGULATING
JUGULATION
JUGULATIONS
JUGULUM
JUGUM
JUGUMS
JUICE
JUICED
JUICEHEAD
JUICEHEADS
JUICELESS
JUICER
JUICERS
JUICES
JUICIER
JUICIEST
JUICILY
JUICINESS
JUICINESSES
JUICING
JUICY
JUJITSU
JUJITSUS
JUJU
JUJUBE
JUJUBES
JUJUISM
JUJUISMS
JUJUIST
JUJUISTS
JUJUS
JUJUTSU
JUJUTSUS
JUKE
JUKEBOX
JUKEBOXES
JUKED

JUKES
JUKING
JUKSKEI
JUKSKEIS
JULEP
JULEPS
JULIENNE
JULIENNED
JULIENNES
JULIENNING
JUMAR
JUMARED
JUMARING
JUMARRED
JUMARRING
JUMARS
JUMART
JUMARTS
JUMBAL
JUMBALS
JUMBIE
JUMBIES
JUMBLE
JUMBLED
JUMBLER
JUMBLERS
JUMBLES
JUMBLIER
JUMBLIEST
JUMBLING
JUMBLINGLY
JUMBLY
JUMBO
JUMBOISE
JUMBOISED
JUMBOISES
JUMBOISING
JUMBOIZE
JUMBOIZED
JUMBOIZES
JUMBOIZING
JUMBOS
JUMBUCK
JUMBUCKS
JUMBY
JUMELLE
JUMELLES
JUMHOURIYA
JUMHOURIYAS
JUMP
JUMPABLE
JUMPED
JUMPER
JUMPERS
JUMPIER
JUMPIEST

JUMPILY
JUMPINESS
JUMPINESSES
JUMPING
JUMPINGLY
JUMPINGNESS
JUMPOFF
JUMPOFFS
JUMPS
JUMPSUIT
JUMPSUITS
JUMPY
JUN
JUNCACEOUS
JUNCATE
JUNCATES
JUNCO
JUNCOES
JUNCOS
JUNCTION
JUNCTIONAL
JUNCTIONS
JUNCTURAL
JUNCTURE
JUNCTURES
JUNCUS
JUNCUSES
JUNEATING
JUNEATINGS
JUNGLE
JUNGLED
JUNGLELIKE
JUNGLES
JUNGLI
JUNGLIER
JUNGLIEST
JUNGLIS
JUNGLIST
JUNGLISTS
JUNGLY
JUNIOR
JUNIORATE
JUNIORATES
JUNIORITIES
JUNIORITY
JUNIORS
JUNIPER
JUNIPERS
JUNK
JUNKANOO
JUNKANOOS
JUNKED
JUNKER
JUNKERS
JUNKET
JUNKETED

JUNKETEER
JUNKETEERS
JUNKETER
JUNKETERS
JUNKETING
JUNKETINGS
JUNKETS
JUNKETTED
JUNKETTER
JUNKETTERS
JUNKETTING
JUNKIE
JUNKIER
JUNKIES
JUNKIEST
JUNKINESS
JUNKINESSES
JUNKING
JUNKMAN
JUNKMEN
JUNKS
JUNKY
JUNKYARD
JUNKYARDS
JUNTA
JUNTAS
JUNTO
JUNTOS
JUPATI
JUPATIS
JUPE
JUPES
JUPON
JUPONS
JURA
JURAL
JURALLY
JURANT
JURANTS
JURAT
JURATORY
JURATS
JURE
JUREL
JURELS
JURIDIC
JURIDICAL
JURIDICALLY
JURIED
JURIES
JURISCONSULT
JURISCONSULTS
JURISDICTION
JURISDICTIONAL
JURISDICTIONS
JURISDICTIVE

JURISPRUDENCE
JURISPRUDENCES
JURISPRUDENT
JURISPRUDENTIAL
JURISPRUDENTS
JURIST
JURISTIC
JURISTICAL
JURISTICALLY
JURISTS
JUROR
JURORS
JURY
JURYING
JURYMAN
JURYMAST
JURYMASTS
JURYMEN
JURYWOMAN
JURYWOMEN
JUS
JUSSIVE
JUSSIVES
JUST
JUSTED
JUSTER
JUSTERS
JUSTEST
JUSTICE
JUSTICER
JUSTICERS
JUSTICES
JUSTICESHIP
JUSTICESHIPS
JUSTICIABILITY
JUSTICIABLE
JUSTICIALISM
JUSTICIALISMS
JUSTICIAR
JUSTICIARIES
JUSTICIARS
JUSTICIARSHIP
JUSTICIARSHIPS
JUSTICIARY
JUSTIFIABILITY
JUSTIFIABLE
JUSTIFIABLENESS
JUSTIFIABLY
JUSTIFICATION
JUSTIFICATIONS
JUSTIFICATIVE
JUSTIFICATOR
JUSTIFICATORS
JUSTIFICATORY
JUSTIFIED
JUSTIFIER

JUSTIFIERS
JUSTIFIES
JUSTIFY
JUSTIFYING
JUSTING
JUSTLE
JUSTLED
JUSTLES
JUSTLING
JUSTLY
JUSTNESS
JUSTNESSES
JUSTS
JUT
JUTE
JUTES
JUTS
JUTTED
JUTTIED
JUTTIES
JUTTING
JUTTINGLY
JUTTY
JUTTYING
JUVE
JUVENAL
JUVENALS
JUVENESCENCE
JUVENESCENCES
JUVENESCENT
JUVENILE
JUVENILELY
JUVENILENESS
JUVENILENESSES
JUVENILES
JUVENILIA
JUVENILITIES
JUVENILITY
JUVES
JUXTAPOSE
JUXTAPOSED
JUXTAPOSES
JUXTAPOSING
JUXTAPOSITION
JUXTAPOSITIONAL
JUXTAPOSITIONS
JYMOLD
JYNX
JYNXES

K

KA
KAAL
KAALER
KAALEST
KAALLY
KAAMA
KAAMAS
KAAS
KAB
KABAB
KABABBED
KABABBING
KABABS
KABADDI
KABADDIS
KABAKA
KABAKAS
KABALA
KABALAS
KABALISM
KABALIST
KABALISTIC
KABALISTICALLY
KABALISTS
KABAR
KABARAGOYA
KABARAGOYAS
KABARS
KABAYA
KABAYAS
KABBALA
KABBALAH
KABBALAHS
KABBALAS
KABBALISM
KABBALIST
KABBALISTIC
KABBALISTICALLY
KABBALISTS
KABELE
KABELES
KABELJOU
KABELJOUS
KABELJOUW
KABELJOUWS
KABIKI
KABIKIS
KABOB
KABOBBED
KABOBBING
KABOBS

KABS
KABUKI
KABUKIS
KACCHA
KACCHAS
KACHA
KACHAHRI
KACHAHRIS
KACHCHA
KACHERI
KACHERIS
KACHINA
KACHINAS
KADAITCHA
KADAITCHAS
KADDISH
KADDISHIM
KADE
KADES
KADI
KADIS
KAE
KAED
KAEING
KAES
KAF
KAFFEEKLATSCH
KAFFEEKLATSCHES
KAFFIR
KAFFIRBOOM
KAFFIRBOOMS
KAFFIRS
KAFFIYEH
KAFFIYEHS
KAFILA
KAFILAS
KAFIR
KAFIRS
KAFS
KAFTAN
KAFTANS
KAGO
KAGOOL
KAGOOLS
KAGOS
KAGOUL
KAGOULE
KAGOULES
KAGOULS
KAGU
KAGUS

KAHAL
KAHALS
KAHAWAI
KAHAWAIS
KAHIKATEA
KAHIKATEAS
KAHUNA
KAHUNAS
KAI
KAIAK
KAIAKED
KAIAKING
KAIAKS
KAID
KAIDS
KAIE
KAIES
KAIF
KAIFS
KAIK
KAIKA
KAIKAI
KAIKAIS
KAIKOMAKO
KAIKOMAKOS
KAIKS
KAIL
KAILS
KAILYAIRD
KAILYAIRDS
KAILYARD
KAILYARDS
KAIM
KAIMAKAM
KAIMAKAMS
KAIMS
KAIN
KAING
KAINGA
KAINGAS
KAINIT
KAINITE
KAINITES
KAINITS
KAINOGENESES
KAINOGENESIS
KAINOGENETIC
KAINS
KAIS
KAISER
KAISERDOM

KAISERDOMS
KAISERIN
KAISERINS
KAISERISM
KAISERISMS
KAISERS
KAISERSHIP
KAISERSHIPS
KAIZEN
KAIZENS
KAJAWAH
KAJAWAHS
KAJEPUT
KAJEPUTS
KAK
KAKA
KAKAPO
KAKAPOS
KAKARIKI
KAKARIKIS
KAKAS
KAKEMONO
KAKEMONOS
KAKI
KAKIEMON
KAKIEMONS
KAKIS
KAKISTOCRACIES
KAKISTOCRACY
KAKKIER
KAKKIEST
KAKKY
KAKODYL
KAKODYLS
KALAM
KALAMDAN
KALAMDANS
KALAMKARI
KALAMKARIS
KALAMS
KALANCHOE
KALANCHOES
KALASHNIKOV
KALASHNIKOVS
KALE
KALEIDOPHONE
KALEIDOPHONES
KALEIDOSCOPE
KALEIDOSCOPES
KALEIDOSCOPIC
KALENDAR

KALENDARED
KALENDARING
KALENDARS
KALENDS
KALES
KALEWIFE
KALEWIVES
KALEYARD
KALEYARDS
KALI
KALIAN
KALIANS
KALIF
KALIFATE
KALIFATES
KALIFS
KALIMBA
KALIMBAS
KALINITE
KALINITES
KALIPH
KALIPHS
KALIS
KALIUM
KALIUMS
KALLIDIN
KALLIDINS
KALLIKREIN
KALLIKREINS
KALLITYPE
KALLITYPES
KALMIA
KALMIAS
KALONG
KALONGS
KALOTYPE
KALOTYPES
KALPA
KALPAK
KALPAKS
KALPAS
KALPIS
KALPISES
KALSOMINE
KALSOMINED
KALSOMINES
KALSOMINING
KALUMPIT
KALUMPITS
KALYPTRA
KALYPTRAS
KAM
KAMA
KAMAAINA
KAMAAINAS
KAMACITE

KAMACITES
KAMAHI
KAMAHIS
KAMALA
KAMALAS
KAMAS
KAME
KAMEES
KAMEESES
KAMEEZ
KAMEEZES
KAMELA
KAMELAS
KAMELAUKION
KAMELAUKIONS
KAMERAD
KAMERADED
KAMERADING
KAMERADS
KAMES
KAMI
KAMICHI
KAMICHIS
KAMIK
KAMIKAZE
KAMIKAZES
KAMIKS
KAMILA
KAMILAROI
KAMILAS
KAMIS
KAMISES
KAMME
KAMPONG
KAMPONGS
KAMSEEN
KAMSEENS
KAMSIN
KAMSINS
KANA
KANAKA
KANAKAS
KANAMYCIN
KANAMYCINS
KANAS
KANBAN
KANBANS
KANDIES
KANDY
KANE
KANEH
KANEHS
KANES
KANG
KANGA
KANGAROO

KANGAROOED
KANGAROOING
KANGAROOS
KANGAS
KANGHA
KANGHAS
KANGS
KANJI
KANJIS
KANS
KANSES
KANT
KANTAR
KANTARS
KANTED
KANTELA
KANTELAS
KANTELE
KANTELES
KANTEN
KANTENS
KANTHA
KANTHAS
KANTIKOY
KANTIKOYED
KANTIKOYING
KANTIKOYS
KANTING
KANTS
KANUKA
KANUKAS
KANZU
KANZUS
KAOLIANG
KAOLIANGS
KAOLIN
KAOLINE
KAOLINES
KAOLINIC
KAOLINISE
KAOLINISED
KAOLINISES
KAOLINISING
KAOLINITE
KAOLINITES
KAOLINITIC
KAOLINIZE
KAOLINIZED
KAOLINIZES
KAOLINIZING
KAOLINOSES
KAOLINOSIS
KAOLINS
KAON
KAONS
KAPA

KAPAS
KAPELLMEISTER
KAPELLMEISTERS
KAPH
KAPHS
KAPOK
KAPOKS
KAPPA
KAPPAS
KAPUT
KAPUTT
KARA
KARABINER
KARABINERS
KARAISM
KARAISMS
KARAIT
KARAITS
KARAKA
KARAKAS
KARAKIA
KARAKIAS
KARAKUL
KARAKULS
KARAMU
KARAMUS
KARANGA
KARANGAS
KARAOKE
KARAOKES
KARAS
KARAT
KARATE
KARATEIST
KARATEISTS
KARATEKA
KARATEKAS
KARATES
KARATS
KARITE
KARITES
KARK
KARKED
KARKING
KARKS
KARMA
KARMAS
KARMIC
KARN
KARNS
KARO
KAROO
KAROOS
KAROS
KAROSHI
KAROSHIS

KAROSS
KAROSSES
KARRI
KARRIS
KARROO
KARROOS
KARSEY
KARSEYS
KARSIES
KARST
KARSTIC
KARSTIFICATION
KARSTIFICATIONS
KARSTIFIED
KARSTIFIES
KARSTIFY
KARSTIFYING
KARSTS
KARSY
KART
KARTER
KARTERS
KARTING
KARTINGS
KARTS
KARYO
KARYOGAMIC
KARYOGAMIES
KARYOGAMY
KARYOGRAM
KARYOGRAMS
KARYOKINESES
KARYOKINESIS
KARYOKINETIC
KARYOLOGIC
KARYOLOGICAL
KARYOLOGIES
KARYOLOGIST
KARYOLOGISTS
KARYOLOGY
KARYOLYMPH
KARYOLYMPHS
KARYOLYSES
KARYOLYSIS
KARYOLYTIC
KARYON
KARYONS
KARYOPLASM
KARYOPLASMIC
KARYOPLASMS
KARYOSOME
KARYOSOMES
KARYOTIN
KARYOTINS
KARYOTYPE
KARYOTYPED

KARYOTYPES
KARYOTYPIC
KARYOTYPICAL
KARYOTYPICALLY
KARYOTYPING
KARZIES
KARZY
KAS
KASBAH
KASBAHS
KASHA
KASHAS
KASHER
KASHERED
KASHERING
KASHERRED
KASHERRING
KASHERS
KASHMIR
KASHMIRS
KASHRUS
KASHRUSES
KASHRUT
KASHRUTH
KASHRUTHS
KASHRUTS
KAT
KATA
KATABASES
KATABASIS
KATABATIC
KATABOLIC
KATABOLICALLY
KATABOLISM
KATABOLISMS
KATABOTHRON
KATABOTHRONS
KATADROMOUS
KATAKANA
KATAKANAS
KATANA
KATANAS
KATAS
KATATHERMOMETER
KATAVOTHRON
KATAVOTHRONS
KATCHINA
KATCHINAS
KATCINA
KATCINAS
KATHAK
KATHAKALI
KATHAKALIS
KATHAKS
KATHAREVOUSA
KATHAREVOUSAS

KATHAROMETER
KATHAROMETERS
KATHARSES
KATHARSIS
KATHODAL
KATHODE
KATHODES
KATHODIC
KATI
KATION
KATIONS
KATIPO
KATIPOS
KATIS
KATORGA
KATORGAS
KATS
KATTI
KATTIS
KATYDID
KATYDIDS
KATZENJAMMER
KATZENJAMMERS
KAUGH
KAUGHS
KAUMATUA
KAUMATUAS
KAUPAPA
KAUPAPAS
KAURI
KAURIES
KAURIS
KAURY
KAVA
KAVAKAVA
KAVAKAVAS
KAVAS
KAVASS
KAVASSES
KAW
KAWA
KAWAKAWA
KAWAKAWAS
KAWANATANGA
KAWATANANGAS
KAWED
KAWING
KAWS
KAY
KAYAK
KAYAKED
KAYAKER
KAYAKERS
KAYAKING
KAYAKINGS
KAYAKS

KAYLE
KAYLES
KAYO
KAYOED
KAYOES
KAYOING
KAYOINGS
KAYOS
KAYS
KAZACHKI
KAZACHOK
KAZATSKI
KAZATSKIES
KAZATSKY
KAZATZKA
KAZATZKAS
KAZI
KAZIS
KAZOO
KAZOOS
KBAR
KBARS
KEA
KEAS
KEASAR
KEASARS
KEAVIE
KEAVIES
KEB
KEBAB
KEBABBED
KEBABBING
KEBABS
KEBAR
KEBARS
KEBBED
KEBBIE
KEBBIES
KEBBING
KEBBOCK
KEBBOCKS
KEBBUCK
KEBBUCKS
KEBELE
KEBELES
KEBLAH
KEBLAHS
KEBOB
KEBOBBED
KEBOBBING
KEBOBS
KEBS
KECK
KECKED
KECKING
KECKLE

KECKLED
KECKLES
KECKLING
KECKLINGS
KECKS
KECKSES
KECKSIES
KECKSY
KED
KEDDAH
KEDDAHS
KEDGE
KEDGED
KEDGER
KEDGEREE
KEDGEREES
KEDGERS
KEDGES
KEDGIER
KEDGIEST
KEDGING
KEDGY
KEDS
KEECH
KEECHES
KEEF
KEEFS
KEEK
KEEKED
KEEKER
KEEKERS
KEEKING
KEEKS
KEEL
KEELAGE
KEELAGES
KEELBOAT
KEELBOATS
KEELED
KEELER
KEELERS
KEELHALE
KEELHALED
KEELHALES
KEELHALING
KEELHAUL
KEELHAULED
KEELHAULING
KEELHAULINGS
KEELHAULS
KEELIE
KEELIES
KEELING
KEELINGS
KEELIVINE
KEELIVINES

KEELLESS
KEELMAN
KEELMEN
KEELS
KEELSON
KEELSONS
KEELYVINE
KEELYVINES
KEEN
KEENED
KEENER
KEENERS
KEENEST
KEENING
KEENINGS
KEENLY
KEENNESS
KEENNESSES
KEENO
KEENOS
KEENS
KEEP
KEEPABLE
KEEPER
KEEPERLESS
KEEPERS
KEEPERSHIP
KEEPERSHIPS
KEEPING
KEEPINGS
KEEPNET
KEEPNETS
KEEPS
KEEPSAKE
KEEPSAKES
KEEPSAKY
KEESHOND
KEESHONDEN
KEESHONDS
KEESTER
KEESTERS
KEET
KEETS
KEEVE
KEEVES
KEF
KEFFEL
KEFFELS
KEFFIYEH
KEFFIYEHS
KEFIR
KEFIRS
KEFS
KEFTEDES
KEFUFFLE
KEFUFFLED

KEFUFFLES
KEFUFFLING
KEG
KEGELER
KEGELERS
KEGLER
KEGLERS
KEGLING
KEGLINGS
KEGS
KEHUA
KEHUAS
KEIGHT
KEIR
KEIRS
KEISTER
KEISTERS
KEITLOA
KEITLOAS
KEKS
KEKSYE
KEKSYES
KELEP
KELEPS
KELIM
KELIMS
KELL
KELLAUT
KELLAUTS
KELLIES
KELLS
KELLY
KELOID
KELOIDAL
KELOIDS
KELP
KELPED
KELPER
KELPERS
KELPIE
KELPIES
KELPING
KELPS
KELPY
KELSON
KELSONS
KELT
KELTER
KELTERS
KELTIE
KELTIES
KELTS
KELTY
KELVIN
KELVINS
KELYPHITIC

KEMB
KEMBED
KEMBING
KEMBLA
KEMBO
KEMBOED
KEMBOING
KEMBOS
KEMBS
KEMP
KEMPED
KEMPER
KEMPERS
KEMPIER
KEMPIEST
KEMPING
KEMPINGS
KEMPLE
KEMPLES
KEMPS
KEMPT
KEMPY
KEN
KENAF
KENAFS
KENCH
KENCHES
KENDO
KENDOS
KENNED
KENNEL
KENNELED
KENNELING
KENNELLED
KENNELLING
KENNELS
KENNER
KENNERS
KENNET
KENNETS
KENNETT
KENNETTED
KENNETTING
KENNETTS
KENNING
KENNINGS
KENO
KENOGENESIS
KENOGENETIC
KENOGENETICALLY
KENOPHOBIA
KENOPHOBIAS
KENOS
KENOSES
KENOSIS
KENOSISES

KENOTIC
KENOTICIST
KENOTICISTS
KENOTRON
KENOTRONS
KENS
KENSPECK
KENSPECKLE
KENT
KENTE
KENTED
KENTES
KENTIA
KENTIAS
KENTING
KENTLEDGE
KENTLEDGES
KENTS
KEP
KEPHALIC
KEPHALICS
KEPHALIN
KEPHALINS
KEPHIR
KEPHIRS
KEPI
KEPIS
KEPPED
KEPPEN
KEPPING
KEPPIT
KEPS
KEPT
KERAMIC
KERAMICS
KERATIN
KERATINISATION
KERATINISATIONS
KERATINISE
KERATINISED
KERATINISES
KERATINISING
KERATINIZATION
KERATINIZATIONS
KERATINIZE
KERATINIZED
KERATINIZES
KERATINIZING
KERATINOPHILIC
KERATINOUS
KERATINS
KERATITIDES
KERATITIS
KERATITISES
KERATOGENOUS
KERATOID

KERATOMA
KERATOMAS
KERATOMATA
KERATOMETER
KERATOMETERS
KERATOPHYRE
KERATOPHYRES
KERATOPLASTIC
KERATOPLASTIES
KERATOPLASTY
KERATOSE
KERATOSES
KERATOSIS
KERATOTIC
KERATOTOMIES
KERATOTOMY
KERAUNOGRAPH
KERAUNOGRAPHS
KERB
KERBAYA
KERBAYAS
KERBED
KERBING
KERBINGS
KERBS
KERBSIDE
KERBSIDES
KERBSTONE
KERBSTONES
KERCHIEF
KERCHIEFED
KERCHIEFING
KERCHIEFS
KERCHIEVES
KERCHOO
KEREL
KERELS
KERERU
KERERUS
KERF
KERFED
KERFING
KERFS
KERFUFFLE
KERFUFFLED
KERFUFFLES
KERFUFFLING
KERKIER
KERKIEST
KERKY
KERMA
KERMAS
KERMES
KERMESITE
KERMESITES
KERMESS

KERMESSE
KERMESSES
KERMIS
KERMISES
KERN
KERNE
KERNED
KERNEL
KERNELED
KERNELING
KERNELLED
KERNELLING
KERNELLY
KERNELS
KERNES
KERNICTERUS
KERNICTERUSES
KERNING
KERNINGS
KERNISH
KERNITE
KERNITES
KERNMANTEL
KERNMANTELS
KERNS
KERO
KEROGEN
KEROGENS
KEROSENE
KEROSENES
KEROSINE
KEROSINES
KERPLUNK
KERPLUNKED
KERPLUNKING
KERPLUNKS
KERRIA
KERRIAS
KERRIES
KERRY
KERSANTITE
KERSANTITES
KERSEY
KERSEYMERE
KERSEYMERES
KERSEYS
KERVE
KERVED
KERVES
KERVING
KERYGMA
KERYGMAS
KERYGMATA
KERYGMATIC
KESAR
KESARS

KESH
KESHES
KEST
KESTING
KESTREL
KESTRELS
KESTS
KET
KETA
KETAMINE
KETAMINES
KETAS
KETCH
KETCHES
KETCHING
KETCHUP
KETCHUPS
KETE
KETENE
KETENES
KETES
KETO
KETOGENESES
KETOGENESIS
KETOGENIC
KETOL
KETOLS
KETONAEMIA
KETONAEMIC
KETONE
KETONEMIA
KETONEMIC
KETONES
KETONIC
KETONURIA
KETONURIAS
KETOSE
KETOSES
KETOSIS
KETOSTEROID
KETOSTEROIDS
KETOTIC
KETOXIME
KETOXIMES
KETS
KETTLE
KETTLEDRUM
KETTLEDRUMMER
KETTLEDRUMMERS
KETTLEDRUMS
KETTLEFUL
KETTLEFULS
KETTLES
KETTLESTITCH
KETTLESTITCHES
KETUBAH

KETUBAHS
KEVEL
KEVELS
KEVIL
KEVILS
KEWL
KEWLER
KEWLEST
KEWPIE
KEWPIES
KEX
KEXES
KEY
KEYBOARD
KEYBOARDED
KEYBOARDER
KEYBOARDERS
KEYBOARDING
KEYBOARDIST
KEYBOARDISTS
KEYBOARDS
KEYBUGLE
KEYBUGLES
KEYBUTTON
KEYBUTTONS
KEYCARD
KEYCARDS
KEYED
KEYHOLE
KEYHOLES
KEYING
KEYLESS
KEYLINE
KEYLINES
KEYNOTE
KEYNOTED
KEYNOTER
KEYNOTERS
KEYNOTES
KEYNOTING
KEYPAD
KEYPADS
KEYPUNCH
KEYPUNCHED
KEYPUNCHER
KEYPUNCHERS
KEYPUNCHES
KEYPUNCHING
KEYS
KEYSET
KEYSETS
KEYSTER
KEYSTERS
KEYSTONE
KEYSTONED
KEYSTONES

KEYSTONING
KEYSTROKE
KEYSTROKED
KEYSTROKES
KEYSTROKING
KEYSTROKINGS
KEYWAY
KEYWAYS
KEYWORD
KEYWORDS
KGOTLA
KGOTLAS
KHADDAR
KHADDARS
KHADI
KHADIS
KHAF
KHAFS
KHAKI
KHAKIS
KHALAT
KHALATS
KHALIF
KHALIFA
KHALIFAH
KHALIFAHS
KHALIFAS
KHALIFAT
KHALIFATE
KHALIFATES
KHALIFATS
KHALIFS
KHAMSEEN
KHAMSEENS
KHAMSIN
KHAMSINS
KHAN
KHANATE
KHANATES
KHANDA
KHANDAS
KHANGA
KHANGAS
KHANJAR
KHANJARS
KHANS
KHANSAMA
KHANSAMAH
KHANSAMAHS
KHANSAMAS
KHANUM
KHANUMS
KHAPH
KHAPHS
KHARIF
KHARIFS

KHAT
KHATS
KHAYA
KHAYAL
KHAYAS
KHAZEN
KHAZENIM
KHAZENS
KHAZI
KHAZIS
KHEDA
KHEDAH
KHEDAHS
KHEDAS
KHEDIVA
KHEDIVAL
KHEDIVAS
KHEDIVATE
KHEDIVATES
KHEDIVE
KHEDIVES
KHEDIVIAL
KHEDIVIATE
KHEDIVIATES
KHET
KHETH
KHETHS
KHETS
KHI
KHIDMUTGAR
KHIDMUTGARS
KHILAFAT
KHILAFATS
KHILAT
KHILATS
KHILIM
KHILIMS
KHIRKAH
KHIRKAHS
KHIS
KHITMUTGAR
KHITMUTGARS
KHODJA
KHODJAS
KHOJA
KHOJAS
KHOR
KHORS
KHOTBAH
KHOTBAHS
KHOTBEH
KHOTBEHS
KHOUM
KHOUMS
KHUD
KHUDS

KHURTA
KHURTAS
KHUSKHUS
KHUSKHUSES
KHUTBAH
KHUTBAHS
KIAAT
KIAATS
KIANG
KIANGS
KIAUGH
KIAUGHS
KIBBE
KIBBEH
KIBBEHS
KIBBES
KIBBI
KIBBIS
KIBBITZ
KIBBITZED
KIBBITZER
KIBBITZERS
KIBBITZES
KIBBITZING
KIBBLE
KIBBLED
KIBBLES
KIBBLING
KIBBUTZ
KIBBUTZIM
KIBBUTZNIK
KIBBUTZNIKS
KIBE
KIBEI
KIBEIS
KIBES
KIBITKA
KIBITKAS
KIBITZ
KIBITZED
KIBITZER
KIBITZERS
KIBITZES
KIBITZING
KIBLA
KIBLAH
KIBLAHS
KIBLAS
KIBOSH
KIBOSHED
KIBOSHES
KIBOSHING
KICK
KICKABLE
KICKBACK
KICKBACKS

KICKBALL
KICKBALLS
KICKBOARD
KICKBOARDS
KICKBOXER
KICKBOXERS
KICKBOXING
KICKBOXINGS
KICKDOWN
KICKDOWNS
KICKED
KICKER
KICKERS
KICKIER
KICKIEST
KICKING
KICKOFF
KICKOFFS
KICKS
KICKSHAW
KICKSHAWS
KICKSHAWSES
KICKSORTER
KICKSORTERS
KICKSTAND
KICKSTANDS
KICKUP
KICKUPS
KICKY
KID
KIDDED
KIDDER
KIDDERS
KIDDIE
KIDDIED
KIDDIER
KIDDIERS
KIDDIES
KIDDIEWINK
KIDDIEWINKIE
KIDDIEWINKIES
KIDDIEWINKS
KIDDING
KIDDINGLY
KIDDISH
KIDDISHLY
KIDDISHNESS
KIDDLE
KIDDLES
KIDDO
KIDDOES
KIDDOS
KIDDUSH
KIDDUSHES
KIDDY
KIDDYING

KIDDYWINK
KIDDYWINKS
KIDEL
KIDELS
KIDGE
KIDGIE
KIDGIER
KIDGIEST
KIDGLOVE
KIDLET
KIDLETS
KIDLIKE
KIDLING
KIDLINGS
KIDNAP
KIDNAPED
KIDNAPEE
KIDNAPEES
KIDNAPER
KIDNAPERS
KIDNAPING
KIDNAPINGS
KIDNAPPED
KIDNAPPEE
KIDNAPPEES
KIDNAPPER
KIDNAPPERS
KIDNAPPING
KIDNAPPINGS
KIDNAPS
KIDNEY
KIDNEYLIKE
KIDNEYS
KIDOLOGIES
KIDOLOGIST
KIDOLOGISTS
KIDOLOGY
KIDS
KIDSKIN
KIDSKINS
KIDSTAKES
KIDULT
KIDULTS
KIDVID
KIDVIDS
KIEF
KIEFS
KIEKIE
KIEKIES
KIELBASA
KIELBASAS
KIELBASI
KIELBASY
KIER
KIERIE
KIERIES

KIERS
KIESELGUHR
KIESELGUHRS
KIESERITE
KIESERITES
KIESTER
KIESTERS
KIEVE
KIEVES
KIF
KIFS
KIGHT
KIGHTS
KIKE
KIKES
KIKOI
KIKOIS
KIKUMON
KIKUMONS
KIKUYU
KIKUYUS
KILD
KILDERKIN
KILDERKINS
KILERG
KILERGS
KILEY
KILEYS
KILIM
KILIMS
KILL
KILLADAR
KILLADARS
KILLAS
KILLASES
KILLCOW
KILLCOWS
KILLCROP
KILLCROPS
KILLDEE
KILLDEER
KILLDEERS
KILLDEES
KILLED
KILLER
KILLERS
KILLICK
KILLICKS
KILLIE
KILLIES
KILLIFISH
KILLIFISHES
KILLIKINICK
KILLIKINICKS
KILLING
KILLINGLY

KILLINGS
KILLJOY
KILLJOYS
KILLOCK
KILLOCKS
KILLOGIE
KILLOGIES
KILLS
KILLUT
KILLUTS
KILN
KILNED
KILNING
KILNS
KILO
KILOBAR
KILOBARS
KILOBASE
KILOBASES
KILOBAUD
KILOBAUDS
KILOBIT
KILOBITS
KILOBYTE
KILOBYTES
KILOCALORIE
KILOCALORIES
KILOCYCLE
KILOCYCLES
KILOGAUSS
KILOGAUSSES
KILOGRAM
KILOGRAMME
KILOGRAMMES
KILOGRAMS
KILOGRAY
KILOGRAYS
KILOHERTZ
KILOHERTZES
KILOJOULE
KILOJOULES
KILOLITER
KILOLITERS
KILOMETER
KILOMETERS
KILOMETRE
KILOMETRES
KILOMETRIC
KILOMETRICAL
KILOMETRICALLY
KILOMOLE
KILOMOLES
KILOPARSEC
KILOPARSECS
KILOPASCAL
KILOPASCALS

KILORAD
KILORADS
KILOS
KILOTON
KILOTONS
KILOVOLT
KILOVOLTS
KILOWATT
KILOWATTS
KILP
KILPS
KILT
KILTED
KILTER
KILTERS
KILTIE
KILTIES
KILTING
KILTINGS
KILTLIKE
KILTS
KILTY
KIMBERLITE
KIMBERLITES
KIMBO
KIMBOED
KIMBOING
KIMBOS
KIMCHEE
KIMCHEES
KIMCHI
KIMCHIS
KIMMER
KIMMERS
KIMONO
KIMONOED
KIMONOS
KIN
KINA
KINAESTHESES
KINAESTHESIA
KINAESTHESIAS
KINAESTHESIS
KINAESTHETIC
KINAKINA
KINAKINAS
KINAS
KINASE
KINASES
KINCHIN
KINCHINS
KINCOB
KINCOBS
KIND
KINDA
KINDED

KINDER
KINDERGARTEN
KINDERGARTENER
KINDERGARTENERS
KINDERGARTENS
KINDERGARTNER
KINDERGARTNERS
KINDERS
KINDERSPIEL
KINDERSPIELS
KINDEST
KINDHEARTED
KINDHEARTEDLY
KINDHEARTEDNESS
KINDIE
KINDIES
KINDING
KINDLE
KINDLED
KINDLER
KINDLERS
KINDLES
KINDLESS
KINDLESSLY
KINDLIER
KINDLIEST
KINDLILY
KINDLINESS
KINDLINESSES
KINDLING
KINDLINGS
KINDLY
KINDNESS
KINDNESSES
KINDRED
KINDREDNESS
KINDREDNESSES
KINDREDS
KINDREDSHIP
KINDREDSHIPS
KINDS
KINDY
KINE
KINEMA
KINEMAS
KINEMATIC
KINEMATICAL
KINEMATICALLY
KINEMATICS
KINEMATOGRAPH
KINEMATOGRAPHER
KINEMATOGRAPHIC
KINEMATOGRAPHS
KINEMATOGRAPHY
KINES
KINESCOPE

KINESCOPED
KINESCOPES
KINESCOPING
KINESES
KINESIATRIC
KINESIATRICS
KINESIC
KINESICS
KINESIOLOGIES
KINESIOLOGIST
KINESIOLOGISTS
KINESIOLOGY
KINESIPATHIC
KINESIPATHIES
KINESIPATHIST
KINESIPATHISTS
KINESIPATHS
KINESIPATHY
KINESIS
KINESITHERAPIES
KINESITHERAPY
KINESTHESES
KINESTHESIA
KINESTHESIAS
KINESTHESIS
KINESTHETIC
KINESTHETICALLY
KINETHEODOLITE
KINETHEODOLITES
KINETIC
KINETICAL
KINETICALLY
KINETICIST
KINETICISTS
KINETICS
KINETIN
KINETINS
KINETOCHORE
KINETOCHORES
KINETOGRAPH
KINETOGRAPHS
KINETONUCLEI
KINETONUCLEUS
KINETONUCLEUSES
KINETOPLAST
KINETOPLASTS
KINETOSCOPE
KINETOSCOPES
KINETOSOME
KINETOSOMES
KINFOLK
KINFOLKS
KING
KINGBIRD
KINGBIRDS
KINGBOLT

KINGBOLTS
KINGCRAFT
KINGCRAFTS
KINGCUP
KINGCUPS
KINGDOM
KINGDOMED
KINGDOMLESS
KINGDOMS
KINGED
KINGFISH
KINGFISHER
KINGFISHERS
KINGFISHES
KINGHOOD
KINGHOODS
KINGING
KINGKLIP
KINGKLIPS
KINGLE
KINGLES
KINGLESS
KINGLET
KINGLETS
KINGLIER
KINGLIEST
KINGLIHOOD
KINGLIHOODS
KINGLIKE
KINGLINESS
KINGLINESSES
KINGLING
KINGLINGS
KINGLY
KINGMAKER
KINGMAKERS
KINGPIN
KINGPINS
KINGPOST
KINGPOSTS
KINGS
KINGSHIP
KINGSHIPS
KINGSIDE
KINGSIDES
KINGWOOD
KINGWOODS
KININ
KININS
KINK
KINKAJOU
KINKAJOUS
KINKED
KINKIER
KINKIEST
KINKILY

KINKINESS
KINKINESSES
KINKING
KINKLE
KINKLES
KINKS
KINKY
KINLESS
KINNIKINIC
KINNIKINICK
KINNIKINICKS
KINNIKINICS
KINNIKINNICK
KINNIKINNICKS
KINO
KINONE
KINONES
KINOS
KINRED
KINREDS
KINS
KINSFOLK
KINSFOLKS
KINSHIP
KINSHIPS
KINSMAN
KINSMEN
KINSWOMAN
KINSWOMEN
KINTLEDGES
KIORE
KIORES
KIOSK
KIOSKS
KIP
KIPE
KIPES
KIPP
KIPPA
KIPPAGE
KIPPAGES
KIPPAS
KIPPED
KIPPEN
KIPPER
KIPPERED
KIPPERER
KIPPERERS
KIPPERING
KIPPERS
KIPPING
KIPPS
KIPS
KIPSKIN
KIPSKINS
KIR

KIRBEH
KIRBEHS
KIRBIED
KIRBIES
KIRBIGRIP
KIRBIGRIPS
KIRBY
KIRBYING
KIRIGAMI
KIRIGAMIS
KIRIMON
KIRIMONS
KIRK
KIRKED
KIRKING
KIRKINGS
KIRKMAN
KIRKMEN
KIRKS
KIRKTON
KIRKTONS
KIRKWARD
KIRKYAIRD
KIRKYAIRDS
KIRKYARD
KIRKYARDS
KIRMESS
KIRMESSES
KIRN
KIRNED
KIRNING
KIRNS
KIRPAN
KIRPANS
KIRRI
KIRRIS
KIRS
KIRSCH
KIRSCHES
KIRSCHWASSER
KIRSCHWASSERS
KIRTAN
KIRTLE
KIRTLED
KIRTLES
KISAN
KISANS
KISH
KISHES
KISHKA
KISHKAS
KISHKE
KISHKES
KISMAT
KISMATS
KISMET

KISMETIC
KISMETS
KISS
KISSABLE
KISSABLY
KISSAGRAM
KISSAGRAMS
KISSED
KISSEL
KISSELS
KISSER
KISSERS
KISSES
KISSING
KISSOGRAM
KISSOGRAMS
KISSY
KIST
KISTED
KISTFUL
KISTFULS
KISTING
KISTS
KISTVAEN
KISTVAENS
KIT
KITBAG
KITBAGS
KITCHEN
KITCHENALIA
KITCHENDOM
KITCHENDOMS
KITCHENED
KITCHENER
KITCHENERS
KITCHENET
KITCHENETS
KITCHENETTE
KITCHENETTES
KITCHENING
KITCHENS
KITCHENWARE
KITCHENWARES
KITE
KITED
KITELIKE
KITENGE
KITENGES
KITER
KITERS
KITES
KITESURFED
KITESURFER
KITESURFERS
KITESURFING
KITESURFS

KITH
KITHARA
KITHARAS
KITHE
KITHED
KITHES
KITHING
KITHS
KITING
KITINGS
KITLING
KITLINGS
KITS
KITSCH
KITSCHES
KITSCHIER
KITSCHIEST
KITSCHILY
KITSCHNESS
KITSCHY
KITTED
KITTEL
KITTELS
KITTEN
KITTENED
KITTENING
KITTENISH
KITTENISHLY
KITTENISHNESS
KITTENISHNESSES
KITTENNED
KITTENNING
KITTENS
KITTENY
KITTIES
KITTING
KITTIWAKE
KITTIWAKES
KITTLE
KITTLED
KITTLER
KITTLES
KITTLEST
KITTLIER
KITTLIEST
KITTLING
KITTLY
KITTUL
KITTULS
KITTY
KIVA
KIVAS
KIWI
KIWIFRUIT
KIWIFRUITS
KIWIS

KIWISPORTS
KLANG
KLANGFARBE
KLANGFARBES
KLANGS
KLATCH
KLATCHES
KLATSCH
KLATSCHES
KLAVERN
KLAVERNS
KLAVIER
KLAVIERS
KLAXON
KLAXONED
KLAXONING
KLAXONS
KLEAGLE
KLEAGLES
KLEBSIELLA
KLEBSIELLAS
KLEINHUISIE
KLEINHUISIES
KLENDUSIC
KLENDUSITIES
KLENDUSITY
KLEPHT
KLEPHTIC
KLEPHTISM
KLEPHTISMS
KLEPHTS
KLEPTOCRACIES
KLEPTOCRACY
KLEPTOCRATIC
KLEPTOMANIA
KLEPTOMANIAC
KLEPTOMANIACS
KLEPTOMANIAS
KLETT
KLETTERSCHUH
KLETTERSCHUHE
KLETTS
KLEZMER
KLEZMORIM
KLIEG
KLIEGS
KLINKER
KLINKERS
KLINOSTAT
KLINOSTATS
KLIPDAS
KLIPDASES
KLIPSPRINGER
KLIPSPRINGERS
KLISTER
KLISTERS

KLONDIKE
KLONDIKED
KLONDIKER
KLONDIKERS
KLONDIKES
KLONDIKING
KLONDYKE
KLONDYKED
KLONDYKER
KLONDYKERS
KLONDYKES
KLONDYKING
KLONG
KLONGS
KLOOCH
KLOOCHES
KLOOCHMAN
KLOOCHMANS
KLOOCHMEN
KLOOF
KLOOFS
KLOOTCH
KLOOTCHES
KLOOTCHMAN
KLOOTCHMANS
KLOOTCHMEN
KLUDGE
KLUDGES
KLUGE
KLUGES
KLUTZ
KLUTZES
KLUTZIER
KLUTZIEST
KLUTZINESS
KLUTZINESSES
KLUTZY
KLYSTRON
KLYSTRONS
KNACK
KNACKED
KNACKER
KNACKERED
KNACKERIES
KNACKERING
KNACKERS
KNACKERY
KNACKIER
KNACKIEST
KNACKINESS
KNACKINESSES
KNACKING
KNACKISH
KNACKS
KNACKWURST
KNACKWURSTS

KNACKY
KNAG
KNAGGIER
KNAGGIEST
KNAGGINESS
KNAGGINESSES
KNAGGY
KNAGS
KNAIDEL
KNAP
KNAPPED
KNAPPER
KNAPPERS
KNAPPING
KNAPPLE
KNAPPLED
KNAPPLES
KNAPPLING
KNAPS
KNAPSACK
KNAPSACKED
KNAPSACKS
KNAPSCAL
KNAPSCALS
KNAPSCULL
KNAPSCULLS
KNAPSKULLS
KNAPWEED
KNAPWEEDS
KNAR
KNARL
KNARLS
KNARRED
KNARRING
KNARRY
KNARS
KNAUR
KNAURS
KNAVE
KNAVERIES
KNAVERY
KNAVES
KNAVESHIP
KNAVESHIPS
KNAVISH
KNAVISHLY
KNAVISHNESS
KNAVISHNESSES
KNAWEL
KNAWELS
KNEAD
KNEADABLE
KNEADED
KNEADER
KNEADERS
KNEADING

KNEADS
KNEE
KNEECAP
KNEECAPPED
KNEECAPPING
KNEECAPPINGS
KNEECAPS
KNEED
KNEEHOLE
KNEEHOLES
KNEEING
KNEEJERK
KNEEJERKISH
KNEEL
KNEELED
KNEELER
KNEELERS
KNEELING
KNEELS
KNEEPAD
KNEEPADS
KNEEPAN
KNEEPANS
KNEES
KNEESOCK
KNEESOCKS
KNEIDEL
KNEIDELS
KNEIDLACH
KNELL
KNELLED
KNELLING
KNELLS
KNELT
KNESSET
KNESSETS
KNEVELL
KNEVELLED
KNEVELLING
KNEVELLS
KNEW
KNICKER
KNICKERBOCKER
KNICKERBOCKERS
KNICKERED
KNICKERS
KNICKKNACK
KNICKKNACKS
KNICKPOINT
KNICKPOINTS
KNICKS
KNIFE
KNIFED
KNIFELESS
KNIFELIKE
KNIFEPOINT

KNIFEPOINTS
KNIFER
KNIFEREST
KNIFERESTS
KNIFERS
KNIFES
KNIFING
KNIFINGS
KNIGHT
KNIGHTAGE
KNIGHTAGES
KNIGHTED
KNIGHTHEAD
KNIGHTHEADS
KNIGHTHOOD
KNIGHTHOODS
KNIGHTING
KNIGHTLESS
KNIGHTLIER
KNIGHTLIEST
KNIGHTLINESS
KNIGHTLINESSES
KNIGHTLY
KNIGHTS
KNIPHOFIA
KNIPHOFIAS
KNISH
KNISHES
KNIT
KNITCH
KNITCHES
KNITS
KNITTABILITY
KNITTABLE
KNITTED
KNITTER
KNITTERS
KNITTING
KNITTINGS
KNITTLE
KNITTLES
KNITWEAR
KNITWEARS
KNIVE
KNIVED
KNIVES
KNIVING
KNOB
KNOBBED
KNOBBER
KNOBBERS
KNOBBIER
KNOBBIEST
KNOBBINESS
KNOBBINESSES
KNOBBING

KNOBBLE
KNOBBLED
KNOBBLES
KNOBBLIER
KNOBBLIEST
KNOBBLING
KNOBBLY
KNOBBY
KNOBHEAD
KNOBHEADED
KNOBHEADS
KNOBKERRIE
KNOBKERRIES
KNOBLIKE
KNOBS
KNOBSTICK
KNOBSTICKS
KNOCK
KNOCKABOUT
KNOCKABOUTS
KNOCKAROUND
KNOCKAROUNDS
KNOCKDOWN
KNOCKDOWNS
KNOCKED
KNOCKER
KNOCKERS
KNOCKING
KNOCKINGS
KNOCKOFF
KNOCKOFFS
KNOCKOUT
KNOCKOUTS
KNOCKS
KNOCKWURST
KNOCKWURSTS
KNOLL
KNOLLED
KNOLLER
KNOLLERS
KNOLLING
KNOLLS
KNOLLY
KNOP
KNOPPED
KNOPS
KNOSP
KNOSPS
KNOT
KNOTGRASS
KNOTGRASSES
KNOTHOLE
KNOTHOLES
KNOTLESS
KNOTLIKE
KNOTS

KNOTTED
KNOTTER
KNOTTERS
KNOTTIER
KNOTTIEST
KNOTTILY
KNOTTINESS
KNOTTINESSES
KNOTTING
KNOTTINGS
KNOTTY
KNOTWEED
KNOTWEEDS
KNOTWORK
KNOTWORKS
KNOUT
KNOUTED
KNOUTING
KNOUTS
KNOW
KNOWABLE
KNOWABLENESS
KNOWABLENESSES
KNOWE
KNOWER
KNOWERS
KNOWES
KNOWHOW
KNOWHOWS
KNOWING
KNOWINGER
KNOWINGEST
KNOWINGLY
KNOWINGNESS
KNOWINGNESSES
KNOWINGS
KNOWLEDGABILITY
KNOWLEDGABLE
KNOWLEDGABLY
KNOWLEDGE
KNOWLEDGEABLE
KNOWLEDGEABLY
KNOWLEDGED
KNOWLEDGES
KNOWLEDGING
KNOWN
KNOWNS
KNOWS
KNUB
KNUBBIER
KNUBBIEST
KNUBBLE
KNUBBLED
KNUBBLES
KNUBBLIER
KNUBBLIEST

KNUBBLING
KNUBBLY
KNUBBY
KNUBS
KNUCKLE
KNUCKLEBALL
KNUCKLEBALLER
KNUCKLEBALLERS
KNUCKLEBALLS
KNUCKLEBONE
KNUCKLEBONES
KNUCKLED
KNUCKLEDUSTER
KNUCKLEDUSTERS
KNUCKLEHEAD
KNUCKLEHEADED
KNUCKLEHEADS
KNUCKLER
KNUCKLERS
KNUCKLES
KNUCKLIER
KNUCKLIEST
KNUCKLING
KNUCKLY
KNUR
KNURL
KNURLED
KNURLIER
KNURLIEST
KNURLING
KNURLINGS
KNURLS
KNURLY
KNURR
KNURRS
KNURS
KNUT
KNUTS
KO
KOA
KOAEA
KOAEAS
KOALA
KOALAS
KOAN
KOANS
KOAS
KOB
KOBAN
KOBANG
KOBANGS
KOBANS
KOBO
KOBOLD
KOBOLDS
KOBS

KOCHIA
KOCHIAS
KOEKSISTER
KOEKSISTERS
KOEL
KOELS
KOFF
KOFFS
KOFTA
KOFTAS
KOFTGAR
KOFTGARI
KOFTGARIS
KOFTGARS
KOFTWORK
KOFTWORKS
KOHA
KOHANGA
KOHAS
KOHEKOHE
KOHEKOHES
KOHL
KOHLRABI
KOHLRABIES
KOHLRABIS
KOHLS
KOI
KOINE
KOINES
KOKAKO
KOKAKOS
KOKANEE
KOKANEES
KOKER
KOKERS
KOKIRI
KOKIRIS
KOKOBEH
KOKOPU
KOKOPUS
KOKOWAI
KOKOWAIS
KOKRA
KOKRAS
KOKUM
KOKUMS
KOLA
KOLACKY
KOLAS
KOLBASI
KOLBASIS
KOLBASSI
KOLBASSIS
KOLHOZ
KOLHOZES
KOLHOZY

KOLINSKI
KOLINSKIES
KOLINSKY
KOLKHOS
KOLKHOSES
KOLKHOSY
KOLKHOZ
KOLKHOZES
KOLKHOZNIK
KOLKHOZNIKI
KOLKHOZNIKS
KOLKHOZY
KOLKOZ
KOLKOZES
KOLKOZY
KOLO
KOLOS
KOMATIK
KOMATIKS
KOMBU
KOMBUS
KOMISSAR
KOMISSARS
KOMITAJI
KOMITAJIS
KOMONDOR
KOMONDOROCK
KOMONDOROK
KOMONDORS
KON
KONAKI
KONAKIS
KONBU
KONBUS
KOND
KONDO
KONDOS
KONEKE
KONEKES
KONFYT
KONFYTS
KONGONI
KONGONIS
KONIMETER
KONIMETERS
KONIOLOGIES
KONIOLOGY
KONISCOPE
KONISCOPES
KONK
KONKED
KONKING
KONKS
KONNING
KONS
KOODOO

KOODOOS
KOOK
KOOKABURRA
KOOKABURRAS
KOOKED
KOOKIE
KOOKIER
KOOKIEST
KOOKINESS
KOOKINESSES
KOOKING
KOOKS
KOOKY
KOOLAH
KOOLAHS
KOORI
KOORIES
KOORIS
KOP
KOPASETIC
KOPECK
KOPECKS
KOPEK
KOPEKS
KOPH
KOPHS
KOPIYKA
KOPIYKAS
KOPJE
KOPJES
KOPPA
KOPPAS
KOPPIE
KOPPIES
KOPS
KOR
KORA
KORAI
KORARI
KORARIS
KORAS
KORAT
KORATS
KORE
KORERO
KOREROS
KORES
KORFBALL
KORFBALLS
KORIMAKO
KORIMAKOS
KORKIR
KORKIRS
KORMA
KORMAS
KORO

KOROMIKO
KOROMIKOS
KORORA
KORORAS
KOROS
KOROWAI
KOROWAIS
KORS
KORU
KORUN
KORUNA
KORUNAS
KORUNY
KORUS
KOS
KOSES
KOSHER
KOSHERED
KOSHERING
KOSHERS
KOSMOS
KOSMOSES
KOSS
KOSSES
KOTAHITANGA
KOTAHITANGAS
KOTARE
KOTARES
KOTO
KOTOS
KOTOW
KOTOWED
KOTOWER
KOTOWERS
KOTOWING
KOTOWS
KOTTABOS
KOTTABOSES
KOTUKU
KOTUKUS
KOTWAL
KOTWALS
KOULAN
KOULANS
KOULIBIACA
KOULIBIACAS
KOUMIS
KOUMISES
KOUMISS
KOUMISSES
KOUMYS
KOUMYSES
KOUMYSS
KOUMYSSES
KOUPREY
KOUPREYS

KOURA
KOURAS
KOURBASH
KOURBASHED
KOURBASHES
KOURBASHING
KOUROI
KOUROS
KOUSKOUS
KOUSKOUSES
KOUSSO
KOUSSOS
KOW
KOWHAI
KOWHAIS
KOWHAIWHAI
KOWHAIWHAIS
KOWS
KOWTOW
KOWTOWED
KOWTOWER
KOWTOWERS
KOWTOWING
KOWTOWS
KRAAL
KRAALED
KRAALING
KRAALS
KRAB
KRABS
KRAFT
KRAFTS
KRAIT
KRAITS
KRAKEN
KRAKENS
KRAKOWIAK
KRAKOWIAKS
KRAMERIA
KRAMERIAS
KRANG
KRANGS
KRANS
KRANSES
KRANTZ
KRANTZES
KRANZ
KRANZES
KRATER
KRATERS
KRAUT
KRAUTS
KREASOTE
KREASOTED
KREASOTES
KREASOTING

KREATINE
KREATINES
KREEP
KREEPS
KREESE
KREESED
KREESES
KREESING
KREMLIN
KREMLINOLOGIES
KREMLINOLOGIST
KREMLINOLOGISTS
KREMLINOLOGY
KREMLINS
KRENG
KRENGS
KREOSOTE
KREOSOTED
KREOSOTES
KREOSOTING
KREPLACH
KREUTZER
KREUTZERS
KREUZER
KREUZERS
KRIEGSPIEL
KRIEGSPIELS
KRIEGSSPIEL
KRIEGSSPIELS
KRILL
KRILLS
KRIMMER
KRIMMERS
KRIS
KRISED
KRISES
KRISING
KROMESKIES
KROMESKY
KRONA
KRONE
KRONEN
KRONER
KRONOR
KRONUR
KROON
KROONI
KROONS
KRUBI
KRUBIS
KRUBUT
KRUBUTS
KRUGERRAND
KRUGERRANDS
KRULLER
KRULLERS

KRUMHORN
KRUMHORNS
KRUMMHOLZ
KRUMMHORN
KRUMMHORNS
KRYOLITE
KRYOLITES
KRYOLITH
KRYOLITHS
KRYOMETER
KRYOMETERS
KRYPSES
KRYPSIS
KRYPTON
KRYPTONS
KRYTRON
KRYTRONS
KSAR
KSARS
KUCCHA
KUCCHAS
KUCHCHA
KUCHEN
KUCHENS
KUDLIK
KUDLIKS
KUDO
KUDOS
KUDOSES
KUDU
KUDUS
KUDZU
KUDZUS
KUE
KUEH
KUES
KUFIYAH
KUFIYAHS
KUGEL
KUGELS
KUIA
KUIAS
KUKRI
KUKRIS
KUKU
KUKUKUMA
KUKUKUMAS
KUKUS
KULA
KULAK
KULAKI
KULAKS
KULAN
KULANS
KULAS
KULFI

KULFIS
KULTUR
KULTURS
KUMARA
KUMARAS
KUMARI
KUMARIS
KUMBALOI
KUMERA
KUMERAS
KUMISS
KUMISSES
KUMITE
KUMMEL
KUMMELS
KUMMERBUND
KUMMERBUNDS
KUMQUAT
KUMQUATS
KUMYS
KUMYSES
KUNA
KUNAS
KUNDALINI
KUNDALINIS
KUNEKUNE
KUNEKUNES
KUNKAR
KUNKARS
KUNKUR
KUNKURS
KUNZITE
KUNZITES
KURBASH
KURBASHED
KURBASHES
KURBASHING
KURCHATOVIUM
KURCHATOVIUMS
KURDAITCHA
KURDAITCHAS
KURFUFFLE
KURFUFFLED
KURFUFFLES
KURFUFFLING
KURGAN
KURGANS
KURI
KURIS
KURRAJONG
KURRAJONGS
KURRE
KURRES
KURSAAL
KURSAALS
KURTA

KURTAS
KURTOSES
KURTOSIS
KURTOSISES
KURU
KURUS
KURVEY
KURVEYED
KURVEYING
KURVEYOR
KURVEYORS
KURVEYS
KUSSO
KUSSOS
KUTCH
KUTCHA
KUTCHES
KUTU
KUTUS
KUVASZ
KUVASZOK
KUZU
KUZUS
KVAS
KVASES
KVASS
KVASSES
KVETCH
KVETCHED
KVETCHER
KVETCHERS
KVETCHES
KVETCHIER
KVETCHIEST
KVETCHING
KVETCHY
KWACHA
KWACHAS
KWAITO
KWANZA
KWANZAS
KWASHIORKOR
KWASHIORKORS
KWELA
KWELAS
KY
KYACK
KYACKS
KYAK
KYAKS
KYANG
KYANGS
KYANISATION
KYANISE
KYANISED
KYANISES

KYANISING
KYANITE
KYANITES
KYANITIC
KYANIZATION
KYANIZE
KYANIZED
KYANIZES
KYANIZING
KYAR
KYARS
KYAT
KYATS
KYBO
KYBOSH
KYBOSHED
KYBOSHES
KYBOSHING
KYDST
KYE
KYLE
KYLES
KYLICES
KYLIE
KYLIES
KYLIKES
KYLIN
KYLINS
KYLIX
KYLLOSES
KYLLOSIS
KYLOE
KYLOES
KYMOGRAM
KYMOGRAMS
KYMOGRAPH
KYMOGRAPHIC
KYMOGRAPHIES
KYMOGRAPHS
KYMOGRAPHY
KYND
KYNDE
KYNDED
KYNDES
KYNDING
KYNDS
KYNE
KYOGEN
KYOGENS
KYPE
KYPES
KYPHOSES
KYPHOSIS
KYPHOTIC
KYRIE
KYRIELLE

KYRIELLES
KYRIES
KYTE
KYTES
KYTHE
KYTHED
KYTHES
KYTHING
KYU
KYUS

L

LA
LAAGER
LAAGERED
LAAGERING
LAAGERS
LAARI
LAARIS
LAB
LABANOTATION
LABANOTATIONS
LABARA
LABARUM
LABARUMS
LABDA
LABDACISM
LABDACISMS
LABDANUM
LABDANUMS
LABDAS
LABEFACTATION
LABEFACTATIONS
LABEFACTION
LABEFACTIONS
LABEL
LABELABLE
LABELED
LABELER
LABELERS
LABELING
LABELLA
LABELLED
LABELLER
LABELLERS
LABELLING
LABELLIST
LABELLOID
LABELLUM
LABELS
LABIA
LABIAL
LABIALISATION
LABIALISATIONS
LABIALISE
LABIALISED
LABIALISES
LABIALISING
LABIALISM
LABIALISMS
LABIALITY
LABIALIZATION
LABIALIZATIONS

LABIALIZE
LABIALIZED
LABIALIZES
LABIALIZING
LABIALLY
LABIALS
LABIATE
LABIATED
LABIATES
LABILE
LABILITIES
LABILITY
LABIODENTAL
LABIODENTALS
LABIONASAL
LABIONASALS
LABIOVELAR
LABIOVELARS
LABIS
LABISES
LABIUM
LABLAB
LABLABS
LABOR
LABORATORIES
LABORATORY
LABORED
LABOREDLY
LABOREDNESS
LABORER
LABORERS
LABORING
LABORINGLY
LABORIOUS
LABORIOUSLY
LABORIOUSNESS
LABORIOUSNESSES
LABORISM
LABORIST
LABORISTS
LABORITE
LABORITES
LABORS
LABORSAVING
LABOUR
LABOURED
LABOUREDLY
LABOUREDNESS
LABOURER
LABOURERS
LABOURING

LABOURINGLY
LABOURISM
LABOURISMS
LABOURIST
LABOURISTS
LABOURS
LABOURSOME
LABRA
LABRADOR
LABRADORESCENT
LABRADORITE
LABRADORITES
LABRADORS
LABRET
LABRETS
LABRID
LABRIDS
LABROID
LABROIDS
LABROSE
LABRUM
LABRUMS
LABRUSCA
LABRYS
LABRYSES
LABS
LABURNUM
LABURNUMS
LABYRINTH
LABYRINTHAL
LABYRINTHIAN
LABYRINTHIC
LABYRINTHICAL
LABYRINTHICALLY
LABYRINTHINE
LABYRINTHITIS
LABYRINTHITISES
LABYRINTHODONT
LABYRINTHODONTS
LABYRINTHS
LAC
LACCOLITE
LACCOLITES
LACCOLITH
LACCOLITHIC
LACCOLITHS
LACCOLITIC
LACE
LACEBARK
LACEBARKS
LACED

LACELESS
LACELIKE
LACER
LACERABILITY
LACERABLE
LACERANT
LACERATE
LACERATED
LACERATES
LACERATING
LACERATION
LACERATIONS
LACERATIVE
LACERS
LACERTIAN
LACERTIANS
LACERTID
LACERTIDS
LACERTILIAN
LACERTILIANS
LACERTINE
LACES
LACET
LACETS
LACEWING
LACEWINGS
LACEWOOD
LACEWOODS
LACEWORK
LACEWORKS
LACEY
LACHES
LACHESES
LACHRYMAL
LACHRYMALS
LACHRYMARIES
LACHRYMARY
LACHRYMATION
LACHRYMATIONS
LACHRYMATOR
LACHRYMATORIES
LACHRYMATORS
LACHRYMATORY
LACHRYMOSE
LACHRYMOSELY
LACHRYMOSITIES
LACHRYMOSITY
LACIER
LACIEST
LACILY
LACINESS

LACINESSES
LACING
LACINGS
LACINIA
LACINIAE
LACINIATE
LACINIATED
LACINIATION
LACINIATIONS
LACK
LACKADAISICAL
LACKADAISICALLY
LACKADAISY
LACKADAY
LACKED
LACKER
LACKERED
LACKERING
LACKERS
LACKEY
LACKEYED
LACKEYING
LACKEYS
LACKING
LACKLAND
LACKLANDS
LACKLUSTER
LACKLUSTERS
LACKLUSTRE
LACKLUSTRES
LACKS
LACMUS
LACMUSES
LACONIC
LACONICAL
LACONICALLY
LACONICISM
LACONICISMS
LACONISM
LACONISMS
LACQUER
LACQUERED
LACQUERER
LACQUERERS
LACQUERING
LACQUERINGS
LACQUERS
LACQUERWARE
LACQUERWARES
LACQUERWORK
LACQUERWORKS
LACQUEY
LACQUEYED
LACQUEYING
LACQUEYS

LACRIMAL
LACRIMALS
LACRIMATION
LACRIMATIONS
LACRIMATOR
LACRIMATORS
LACRIMATORY
LACRIMOSO
LACROSSE
LACROSSES
LACRYMAL
LACRYMALS
LACRYMATOR
LACRYMATORS
LACRYMATORY
LACS
LACTALBUMIN
LACTALBUMINS
LACTAM
LACTAMS
LACTARIAN
LACTARIANS
LACTARY
LACTASE
LACTASES
LACTATE
LACTATED
LACTATES
LACTATING
LACTATION
LACTATIONAL
LACTATIONALLY
LACTATIONS
LACTEAL
LACTEALLY
LACTEALS
LACTEAN
LACTEOUS
LACTESCENCE
LACTESCENCES
LACTESCENT
LACTIC
LACTIFEROUS
LACTIFEROUSNESS
LACTIFIC
LACTIFLUOUS
LACTOBACILLI
LACTOBACILLUS
LACTOFLAVIN
LACTOFLAVINS
LACTOGENIC
LACTOGLOBULIN
LACTOGLOBULINS
LACTOMETER
LACTOMETERS

LACTONE
LACTONES
LACTONIC
LACTOPROTEIN
LACTOPROTEINS
LACTOSCOPE
LACTOSCOPES
LACTOSE
LACTOSES
LACTOSURIA
LACTOVEGETARIAN
LACUNA
LACUNAE
LACUNAL
LACUNAR
LACUNARIA
LACUNARS
LACUNARY
LACUNAS
LACUNATE
LACUNE
LACUNES
LACUNOSE
LACUNOSITY
LACUSTRINE
LACY
LAD
LADANUM
LADANUMS
LADDER
LADDERED
LADDERING
LADDERLIKE
LADDERS
LADDERY
LADDIE
LADDIES
LADDISH
LADDISHNESS
LADDISHNESSES
LADE
LADED
LADEN
LADENED
LADENING
LADENS
LADER
LADERS
LADES
LADETTE
LADETTES
LADIES
LADIESWEAR
LADIESWEARS
LADIFIED

LADIFIES
LADIFY
LADIFYING
LADING
LADINGS
LADINO
LADINOS
LADLE
LADLED
LADLEFUL
LADLEFULS
LADLER
LADLERS
LADLES
LADLING
LADRON
LADRONE
LADRONES
LADRONS
LADS
LADY
LADYBIRD
LADYBIRDS
LADYBOY
LADYBOYS
LADYBUG
LADYBUGS
LADYCOW
LADYCOWS
LADYFIED
LADYFIES
LADYFINGER
LADYFINGERS
LADYFISH
LADYFISHES
LADYFLIES
LADYFLY
LADYFY
LADYFYING
LADYHOOD
LADYHOODS
LADYISH
LADYISM
LADYISMS
LADYKIN
LADYKINS
LADYLIKE
LADYLIKENESS
LADYLOVE
LADYLOVES
LADYPALM
LADYPALMS
LADYSHIP
LADYSHIPS
LAEOTROPIC

LAER
LAERED
LAERING
LAERS
LAESIE
LAETARE
LAETARES
LAETRILE
LAETRILES
LAEVIGATE
LAEVIGATED
LAEVIGATES
LAEVIGATING
LAEVO
LAEVOGYRATE
LAEVOROTARY
LAEVOROTATION
LAEVOROTATIONS
LAEVOROTATORY
LAEVULIN
LAEVULOSE
LAEVULOSES
LAG
LAGAN
LAGANS
LAGENA
LAGENAS
LAGEND
LAGENDS
LAGENIFORM
LAGER
LAGERED
LAGERING
LAGERPHONE
LAGERPHONES
LAGERS
LAGGARD
LAGGARDLY
LAGGARDNESS
LAGGARDNESSES
LAGGARDS
LAGGED
LAGGEN
LAGGENS
LAGGER
LAGGERS
LAGGIN
LAGGING
LAGGINGLY
LAGGINGS
LAGGINS
LAGNAPPE
LAGNAPPES
LAGNIAPPE
LAGNIAPPES

LAGOMORPH
LAGOMORPHIC
LAGOMORPHOUS
LAGOMORPHS
LAGOON
LAGOONAL
LAGOONS
LAGRIMOSO
LAGS
LAGUNA
LAGUNAS
LAGUNE
LAGUNES
LAH
LAHAR
LAHARS
LAHS
LAIC
LAICAL
LAICALLY
LAICH
LAICHS
LAICISATION
LAICISATIONS
LAICISE
LAICISED
LAICISES
LAICISING
LAICISM
LAICISMS
LAICITIES
LAICITY
LAICIZATION
LAICIZATIONS
LAICIZE
LAICIZED
LAICIZES
LAICIZING
LAICS
LAID
LAIDED
LAIDING
LAIDLY
LAIDS
LAIGH
LAIGHER
LAIGHEST
LAIGHS
LAIK
LAIKA
LAIKAS
LAIKED
LAIKER
LAIKERS
LAIKING

LAIKS
LAIN
LAIPSE
LAIPSED
LAIPSING
LAIR
LAIRAGE
LAIRAGES
LAIRD
LAIRDLY
LAIRDS
LAIRDSHIP
LAIRDSHIPS
LAIRED
LAIRIER
LAIRIEST
LAIRING
LAIRISE
LAIRISED
LAIRISES
LAIRISING
LAIRIZE
LAIRIZED
LAIRIZES
LAIRIZING
LAIRS
LAIRY
LAISSE
LAISSES
LAITANCE
LAITANCES
LAITH
LAITHLY
LAITIES
LAITY
LAKE
LAKED
LAKEFRONT
LAKEFRONTS
LAKELAND
LAKELANDS
LAKELET
LAKELETS
LAKELIKE
LAKEPORT
LAKEPORTS
LAKER
LAKERS
LAKES
LAKESHORE
LAKESHORES
LAKESIDE
LAKESIDES
LAKH
LAKHS

LAKIER
LAKIEST
LAKIN
LAKING
LAKINGS
LAKINS
LAKISH
LAKSA
LAKSAS
LAKY
LALANG
LALANGS
LALAPALOOZA
LALAPALOOZAS
LALDIE
LALDIES
LALDY
LALL
LALLAN
LALLAND
LALLANDS
LALLANS
LALLAPALOOZA
LALLAPALOOZAS
LALLATION
LALLATIONS
LALLED
LALLING
LALLINGS
LALLS
LALLYGAG
LALLYGAGGED
LALLYGAGGING
LALLYGAGS
LAM
LAMA
LAMAISTIC
LAMANTIN
LAMANTINS
LAMAS
LAMASERAI
LAMASERAIS
LAMASERIES
LAMASERY
LAMB
LAMBADA
LAMBADAS
LAMBAST
LAMBASTE
LAMBASTED
LAMBASTES
LAMBASTING
LAMBASTS
LAMBDA
LAMBDACISM

LAMBDACISMS
LAMBDAS
LAMBDOID
LAMBDOIDAL
LAMBED
LAMBENCIES
LAMBENCY
LAMBENT
LAMBENTLY
LAMBER
LAMBERS
LAMBERT
LAMBERTS
LAMBIE
LAMBIER
LAMBIES
LAMBIEST
LAMBING
LAMBINGS
LAMBITIVE
LAMBITIVES
LAMBKILL
LAMBKILLS
LAMBKIN
LAMBKINS
LAMBLIKE
LAMBLING
LAMBLINGS
LAMBOYS
LAMBREQUIN
LAMBREQUINS
LAMBS
LAMBSKIN
LAMBSKINS
LAMBY
LAME
LAMEBRAIN
LAMEBRAINED
LAMEBRAINS
LAMED
LAMEDH
LAMEDHS
LAMEDS
LAMELLA
LAMELLAE
LAMELLAR
LAMELLARLY
LAMELLAS
LAMELLATE
LAMELLATED
LAMELLATELY
LAMELLATION
LAMELLATIONS
LAMELLIBRANCH
LAMELLIBRANCHES

LAMELLIBRANCHS
LAMELLICORN
LAMELLICORNS
LAMELLIFORM
LAMELLIROSTRAL
LAMELLIROSTRATE
LAMELLOID
LAMELLOSE
LAMELLOSITIES
LAMELLOSITY
LAMELY
LAMENESS
LAMENESSES
LAMENT
LAMENTABLE
LAMENTABLENESS
LAMENTABLY
LAMENTATION
LAMENTATIONS
LAMENTED
LAMENTEDLY
LAMENTER
LAMENTERS
LAMENTING
LAMENTINGLY
LAMENTINGS
LAMENTS
LAMER
LAMES
LAMEST
LAMETER
LAMETERS
LAMIA
LAMIAE
LAMIAS
LAMIGER
LAMIGERS
LAMINA
LAMINABLE
LAMINAE
LAMINAL
LAMINAR
LAMINARIA
LAMINARIAN
LAMINARIANS
LAMINARIAS
LAMINARIN
LAMINARINS
LAMINARISE
LAMINARISED
LAMINARISES
LAMINARISING
LAMINARIZE
LAMINARIZED
LAMINARIZES

LAMINARIZING
LAMINARY
LAMINAS
LAMINATE
LAMINATED
LAMINATES
LAMINATING
LAMINATION
LAMINATIONS
LAMINATOR
LAMINATORS
LAMINECTOMIES
LAMINECTOMY
LAMING
LAMINGTON
LAMINGTONS
LAMINITIS
LAMINITISES
LAMINOSE
LAMINOUS
LAMISH
LAMISTER
LAMISTERS
LAMITER
LAMITERS
LAMMED
LAMMER
LAMMERGEIER
LAMMERGEIERS
LAMMERGEYER
LAMMERGEYERS
LAMMERS
LAMMIE
LAMMIES
LAMMIGER
LAMMIGERS
LAMMING
LAMMINGS
LAMMY
LAMP
LAMPAD
LAMPADARIES
LAMPADARY
LAMPADEDROMIES
LAMPADEDROMY
LAMPADEPHORIA
LAMPADEPHORIAS
LAMPADIST
LAMPADISTS
LAMPADOMANCIES
LAMPADOMANCY
LAMPADS
LAMPAS
LAMPASES
LAMPASSE

LAMPASSES
LAMPBLACK
LAMPBLACKS
LAMPED
LAMPER
LAMPERN
LAMPERNS
LAMPERS
LAMPERSES
LAMPHOLDER
LAMPHOLDERS
LAMPHOLE
LAMPHOLES
LAMPING
LAMPINGS
LAMPION
LAMPIONS
LAMPLIGHT
LAMPLIGHTER
LAMPLIGHTERS
LAMPLIGHTS
LAMPOON
LAMPOONED
LAMPOONER
LAMPOONERIES
LAMPOONERS
LAMPOONERY
LAMPOONING
LAMPOONIST
LAMPOONISTS
LAMPOONS
LAMPPOST
LAMPPOSTS
LAMPREY
LAMPREYS
LAMPROPHYRE
LAMPROPHYRES
LAMPROPHYRIC
LAMPS
LAMPSHADE
LAMPSHADES
LAMPSHELL
LAMPSHELLS
LAMPUKA
LAMPUKAS
LAMPUKI
LAMPUKIS
LAMPYRID
LAMPYRIDS
LAMS
LAMSTER
LAMSTERS
LANA
LANAI
LANAIS

LANAS
LANATE
LANATED
LANCE
LANCED
LANCEGAY
LANCEGAYS
LANCEJACK
LANCEJACKS
LANCELET
LANCELETS
LANCEOLAR
LANCEOLATE
LANCEOLATED
LANCEOLATELY
LANCER
LANCERS
LANCES
LANCET
LANCETED
LANCETS
LANCEWOOD
LANCEWOODS
LANCH
LANCHED
LANCHES
LANCHING
LANCIERS
LANCIFORM
LANCINATE
LANCINATED
LANCINATES
LANCINATING
LANCINATION
LANCINATIONS
LANCING
LAND
LANDAMMAN
LANDAMMANN
LANDAMMANNS
LANDAMMANS
LANDAU
LANDAULET
LANDAULETS
LANDAULETTE
LANDAULETTES
LANDAUS
LANDDAMNE
LANDDAMNED
LANDDAMNES
LANDDAMNING
LANDDROS
LANDDROSES
LANDDROST
LANDDROSTS

LANDE
LANDED
LANDER
LANDERS
LANDES
LANDFALL
LANDFALLS
LANDFILL
LANDFILLING
LANDFILLINGS
LANDFILLS
LANDFORCE
LANDFORCES
LANDFORM
LANDFORMS
LANDGRAB
LANDGRABS
LANDGRAVATE
LANDGRAVATES
LANDGRAVE
LANDGRAVES
LANDGRAVIATE
LANDGRAVIATES
LANDGRAVINE
LANDGRAVINES
LANDHOLDER
LANDHOLDERS
LANDHOLDING
LANDHOLDINGS
LANDING
LANDINGS
LANDLADIES
LANDLADY
LANDLER
LANDLERS
LANDLESS
LANDLESSNESS
LANDLESSNESSES
LANDLINE
LANDLINES
LANDLOCKED
LANDLOPER
LANDLOPERS
LANDLORD
LANDLORDISM
LANDLORDISMS
LANDLORDS
LANDLUBBER
LANDLUBBERLY
LANDLUBBERS
LANDLUBBING
LANDMAN
LANDMARK
LANDMARKS
LANDMASS

LANDMASSES
LANDMEN
LANDOWNER
LANDOWNERS
LANDOWNERSHIP
LANDOWNERSHIPS
LANDOWNING
LANDOWNINGS
LANDRACE
LANDRACES
LANDRAIL
LANDRAILS
LANDS
LANDSCAPE
LANDSCAPED
LANDSCAPER
LANDSCAPERS
LANDSCAPES
LANDSCAPING
LANDSCAPIST
LANDSCAPISTS
LANDSHARK
LANDSHARKS
LANDSIDE
LANDSIDES
LANDSKIP
LANDSKIPPED
LANDSKIPPING
LANDSKIPS
LANDSKNECHT
LANDSKNECHTS
LANDSLEIT
LANDSLID
LANDSLIDE
LANDSLIDES
LANDSLIDING
LANDSLIP
LANDSLIPS
LANDSMAN
LANDSMEN
LANDWAITER
LANDWAITERS
LANDWARD
LANDWARDS
LANDWIND
LANDWINDS
LANE
LANELY
LANES
LANEWAY
LANEWAYS
LANG
LANGAHA
LANGAHAS
LANGAR

LANGARS
LANGBEINITE
LANGBEINITES
LANGER
LANGEST
LANGLAUF
LANGLAUFER
LANGLAUFERS
LANGLAUFS
LANGLEY
LANGLEYS
LANGOSTINO
LANGOSTINOS
LANGOUSTE
LANGOUSTES
LANGOUSTINE
LANGOUSTINES
LANGRAGE
LANGRAGES
LANGREL
LANGRELS
LANGRIDGE
LANGRIDGES
LANGSHAN
LANGSHANS
LANGSPEL
LANGSPELS
LANGSPIEL
LANGSPIELS
LANGSYNE
LANGSYNES
LANGUAGE
LANGUAGED
LANGUAGELESS
LANGUAGES
LANGUAGING
LANGUE
LANGUED
LANGUES
LANGUESCENT
LANGUET
LANGUETS
LANGUETTE
LANGUETTES
LANGUID
LANGUIDLY
LANGUIDNESS
LANGUIDNESSES
LANGUISH
LANGUISHED
LANGUISHER
LANGUISHERS
LANGUISHES
LANGUISHING
LANGUISHINGLY

LANGUISHINGS
LANGUISHMENT
LANGUISHMENTS
LANGUOR
LANGUOROUS
LANGUOROUSLY
LANGUOROUSNESS
LANGUORS
LANGUR
LANGURS
LANIARD
LANIARDS
LANIARIES
LANIARY
LANIFEROUS
LANIGEROUS
LANITAL
LANITALS
LANK
LANKED
LANKER
LANKEST
LANKIER
LANKIEST
LANKILY
LANKINESS
LANKINESSES
LANKING
LANKLY
LANKNESS
LANKNESSES
LANKS
LANKY
LANNER
LANNERET
LANNERETS
LANNERS
LANOLATED
LANOLIN
LANOLINE
LANOLINES
LANOLINS
LANOSE
LANOSITIES
LANOSITY
LANSQUENET
LANSQUENETS
LANT
LANTANA
LANTANAS
LANTERLOO
LANTERLOOS
LANTERN
LANTERNED
LANTERNING

LANTERNIST
LANTERNISTS
LANTERNS
LANTHANIDE
LANTHANIDES
LANTHANON
LANTHANONS
LANTHANUM
LANTHANUMS
LANTHORN
LANTHORNS
LANTS
LANTSKIP
LANTSKIPS
LANUGINOSE
LANUGINOUS
LANUGINOUSNESS
LANUGO
LANUGOS
LANX
LANYARD
LANYARDS
LANZKNECHT
LANZKNECHTS
LAODICEAN
LAODICEANS
LAP
LAPAROSCOPE
LAPAROSCOPES
LAPAROSCOPIC
LAPAROSCOPIES
LAPAROSCOPIST
LAPAROSCOPISTS
LAPAROSCOPY
LAPAROTOMIES
LAPAROTOMY
LAPBOARD
LAPBOARDS
LAPDOG
LAPDOGS
LAPEL
LAPELED
LAPELLED
LAPELS
LAPFUL
LAPFULS
LAPHELD
LAPIDARIAN
LAPIDARIES
LAPIDARIST
LAPIDARISTS
LAPIDARY
LAPIDATE
LAPIDATED
LAPIDATES

LAPIDATING
LAPIDATION
LAPIDATIONS
LAPIDEOUS
LAPIDES
LAPIDESCENCE
LAPIDESCENCES
LAPIDESCENT
LAPIDICOLOUS
LAPIDIFIC
LAPIDIFICATION
LAPIDIFICATIONS
LAPIDIFIED
LAPIDIFIES
LAPIDIFY
LAPIDIFYING
LAPIDIST
LAPIDISTS
LAPILLI
LAPILLIFORM
LAPILLUS
LAPIN
LAPINS
LAPIS
LAPISES
LAPJE
LAPJES
LAPPED
LAPPEL
LAPPELS
LAPPER
LAPPERED
LAPPERING
LAPPERS
LAPPET
LAPPETED
LAPPETS
LAPPIE
LAPPIES
LAPPING
LAPPINGS
LAPS
LAPSABLE
LAPSANG
LAPSANGS
LAPSE
LAPSED
LAPSER
LAPSERS
LAPSES
LAPSIBLE
LAPSING
LAPSTONE
LAPSTONES
LAPSTRAKE

LAPSTRAKES
LAPSTREAK
LAPSTREAKS
LAPSUS
LAPTOP
LAPTOPS
LAPTRAY
LAPTRAYS
LAPWING
LAPWINGS
LAPWORK
LAPWORKS
LAQUEARIA
LAR
LARBOARD
LARBOARDS
LARCENER
LARCENERS
LARCENIES
LARCENIST
LARCENISTS
LARCENOUS
LARCENOUSLY
LARCENY
LARCH
LARCHEN
LARCHES
LARD
LARDACEOUS
LARDALITE
LARDALITES
LARDED
LARDER
LARDERER
LARDERERS
LARDERS
LARDIER
LARDIEST
LARDING
LARDLIKE
LARDON
LARDONS
LARDOON
LARDOONS
LARDS
LARDY
LARE
LAREE
LAREES
LARES
LARGANDO
LARGE
LARGEHEARTED
LARGELY
LARGEMOUTH

LARGEMOUTHS
LARGEN
LARGENED
LARGENESS
LARGENESSES
LARGENING
LARGENS
LARGER
LARGES
LARGESS
LARGESSE
LARGESSES
LARGEST
LARGHETTO
LARGHETTOS
LARGISH
LARGITION
LARGITIONS
LARGO
LARGOS
LARI
LARIAT
LARIATED
LARIATING
LARIATS
LARINE
LARIS
LARK
LARKED
LARKER
LARKERS
LARKIER
LARKIEST
LARKINESS
LARKINESSES
LARKING
LARKISH
LARKISHNESS
LARKS
LARKSOME
LARKSPUR
LARKSPURS
LARKY
LARMIER
LARMIERS
LARN
LARNAKES
LARNAX
LARNED
LARNEY
LARNEYS
LARNING
LARNS
LAROID
LARRIGAN

LARRIGANS
LARRIKIN
LARRIKINISM
LARRIKINISMS
LARRIKINS
LARRUP
LARRUPED
LARRUPER
LARRUPERS
LARRUPING
LARRUPPED
LARRUPPING
LARRUPS
LARS
LARUM
LARUMS
LARVA
LARVAE
LARVAL
LARVAS
LARVATE
LARVATED
LARVICIDAL
LARVICIDE
LARVICIDES
LARVIFORM
LARVIKITE
LARVIKITES
LARVIPAROUS
LARYNGAL
LARYNGEAL
LARYNGEALLY
LARYNGEALS
LARYNGECTOMEE
LARYNGECTOMEES
LARYNGECTOMIES
LARYNGECTOMIZED
LARYNGECTOMY
LARYNGES
LARYNGISMUS
LARYNGISMUSES
LARYNGITIC
LARYNGITIS
LARYNGITISES
LARYNGOLOGIC
LARYNGOLOGICAL
LARYNGOLOGIES
LARYNGOLOGIST
LARYNGOLOGISTS
LARYNGOLOGY
LARYNGOPHONIES
LARYNGOPHONY
LARYNGOSCOPE
LARYNGOSCOPES
LARYNGOSCOPIC

LARYNGOSCOPIES
LARYNGOSCOPIST
LARYNGOSCOPISTS
LARYNGOSCOPY
LARYNGOSPASM
LARYNGOSPASMS
LARYNGOTOMIES
LARYNGOTOMY
LARYNX
LARYNXES
LAS
LASAGNA
LASAGNAS
LASAGNE
LASAGNES
LASCAR
LASCARS
LASCIVIOUS
LASCIVIOUSLY
LASCIVIOUSNESS
LASE
LASED
LASER
LASERDISC
LASERDISCS
LASERDISK
LASERDISKS
LASERS
LASERWORT
LASERWORTS
LASES
LASH
LASHED
LASHER
LASHERS
LASHES
LASHING
LASHINGLY
LASHINGS
LASHINS
LASHKAR
LASHKARS
LASING
LASINGS
LASKET
LASKETS
LASQUE
LASQUES
LASS
LASSES
LASSI
LASSIE
LASSIES
LASSIS
LASSITUDE

LASSITUDES
LASSLORN
LASSO
LASSOCK
LASSOCKS
LASSOED
LASSOER
LASSOERS
LASSOES
LASSOING
LASSOS
LASSU
LASSUS
LAST
LASTAGE
LASTAGES
LASTED
LASTER
LASTERS
LASTING
LASTINGLY
LASTINGNESS
LASTINGNESSES
LASTINGS
LASTLY
LASTS
LAT
LATAH
LATAKIA
LATAKIAS
LATCH
LATCHED
LATCHES
LATCHET
LATCHETS
LATCHING
LATCHKEY
LATCHKEYS
LATCHSTRING
LATCHSTRINGS
LATE
LATECOMER
LATECOMERS
LATED
LATEEN
LATEENER
LATEENERS
LATEENRIGGED
LATEENS
LATELY
LATEN
LATENCE
LATENCES
LATENCIES
LATENCY

LATENED
LATENESS
LATENESSES
LATENING
LATENS
LATENSIFICATION
LATENT
LATENTLY
LATENTS
LATER
LATERAD
LATERAL
LATERALED
LATERALING
LATERALISATION
LATERALISATIONS
LATERALITIES
LATERALITY
LATERALIZATION
LATERALIZATIONS
LATERALIZE
LATERALIZED
LATERALIZES
LATERALIZING
LATERALLY
LATERALS
LATERIGRADE
LATERISATION
LATERISATIONS
LATERITE
LATERITES
LATERITIC
LATERITIOUS
LATERIZATION
LATERIZATIONS
LATERIZE
LATERIZED
LATERIZES
LATERIZING
LATEROVERSION
LATEROVERSIONS
LATESCENCE
LATESCENCES
LATESCENT
LATEST
LATESTS
LATEWAKE
LATEWAKES
LATEWOOD
LATEWOODS
LATEX
LATEXES
LATH
LATHE
LATHED

LATHEE
LATHEES
LATHEN
LATHER
LATHERED
LATHERER
LATHERERS
LATHERIER
LATHERIEST
LATHERING
LATHERS
LATHERY
LATHES
LATHI
LATHIER
LATHIEST
LATHING
LATHINGS
LATHIS
LATHLIKE
LATHS
LATHWORK
LATHWORKS
LATHY
LATHYRISM
LATHYRISMS
LATHYRITIC
LATHYRUS
LATHYRUSES
LATI
LATICES
LATICIFER
LATICIFEROUS
LATICIFERS
LATICLAVE
LATICLAVES
LATIFONDI
LATIFUNDIA
LATIFUNDIO
LATIFUNDIOS
LATIFUNDIUM
LATIGO
LATIGOES
LATIGOS
LATIMERIA
LATIMERIAS
LATINITIES
LATINITY
LATINIZATION
LATINIZATIONS
LATINIZE
LATINIZED
LATINIZES
LATINIZING
LATINO

LATINOS
LATIROSTRAL
LATISEPTATE
LATISH
LATITANCIES
LATITANCY
LATITANT
LATITAT
LATITATION
LATITATIONS
LATITATS
LATITUDE
LATITUDES
LATITUDINAL
LATITUDINALLY
LATITUDINARIAN
LATITUDINARIANS
LATITUDINOUS
LATKE
LATKES
LATOSOL
LATOSOLIC
LATOSOLS
LATRANT
LATRATION
LATRATIONS
LATRIA
LATRIAS
LATRINE
LATRINES
LATROCINIA
LATROCINIES
LATROCINIUM
LATROCINY
LATRON
LATRONS
LATS
LATTE
LATTEN
LATTENS
LATTER
LATTERLY
LATTERMATH
LATTERMATHS
LATTERMOST
LATTES
LATTICE
LATTICED
LATTICES
LATTICEWORK
LATTICEWORKS
LATTICING
LATTICINI
LATTICINIO
LATTICINO

LATTIN
LATTINS
LATU
LAUAN
LAUANS
LAUCH
LAUCHING
LAUCHS
LAUD
LAUDABILITIES
LAUDABILITY
LAUDABLE
LAUDABLENESS
LAUDABLENESSES
LAUDABLY
LAUDANUM
LAUDANUMS
LAUDATION
LAUDATIONS
LAUDATIVE
LAUDATIVES
LAUDATOR
LAUDATORIES
LAUDATORS
LAUDATORY
LAUDED
LAUDER
LAUDERS
LAUDING
LAUDS
LAUF
LAUFS
LAUGH
LAUGHABLE
LAUGHABLENESS
LAUGHABLENESSES
LAUGHABLY
LAUGHED
LAUGHER
LAUGHERS
LAUGHFUL
LAUGHIER
LAUGHIEST
LAUGHING
LAUGHINGLY
LAUGHINGS
LAUGHINGSTOCK
LAUGHINGSTOCKS
LAUGHS
LAUGHSOME
LAUGHTER
LAUGHTERS
LAUGHWORTHY
LAUGHY
LAUNCE

LAUNCED
LAUNCEGAYE
LAUNCEGAYES
LAUNCES
LAUNCH
LAUNCHED
LAUNCHER
LAUNCHERS
LAUNCHES
LAUNCHING
LAUNCHPAD
LAUNCHPADS
LAUNCING
LAUND
LAUNDER
LAUNDERED
LAUNDERER
LAUNDERERS
LAUNDERETTE
LAUNDERETTES
LAUNDERING
LAUNDERS
LAUNDRESS
LAUNDRESSES
LAUNDRETTE
LAUNDRETTES
LAUNDRIES
LAUNDRY
LAUNDRYMAN
LAUNDRYMEN
LAUNDRYWOMAN
LAUNDRYWOMEN
LAUNDS
LAURA
LAURACEOUS
LAURAE
LAURAS
LAURDALITE
LAURDALITES
LAUREATE
LAUREATED
LAUREATES
LAUREATESHIP
LAUREATESHIPS
LAUREATING
LAUREATION
LAUREATIONS
LAUREL
LAURELED
LAURELING
LAURELLED
LAURELLING
LAURELS
LAURIC
LAURUSTINE

LAURUSTINES
LAURUSTINUS
LAURUSTINUSES
LAURVIKITE
LAURVIKITES
LAURYL
LAUWINE
LAUWINES
LAV
LAVA
LAVABO
LAVABOES
LAVABOS
LAVAFORM
LAVAGE
LAVAGES
LAVALAVA
LAVALAVAS
LAVALIER
LAVALIERE
LAVALIERES
LAVALIERS
LAVALIKE
LAVALLIERE
LAVALLIERES
LAVAS
LAVATERA
LAVATERAS
LAVATION
LAVATIONAL
LAVATIONS
LAVATORIAL
LAVATORIES
LAVATORY
LAVE
LAVED
LAVEER
LAVEERED
LAVEERING
LAVEERS
LAVEMENT
LAVEMENTS
LAVENDER
LAVENDERED
LAVENDERING
LAVENDERS
LAVER
LAVERBREAD
LAVERBREADS
LAVEROCK
LAVEROCKED
LAVEROCKING
LAVEROCKS
LAVERS
LAVES

LAVING
LAVISH
LAVISHED
LAVISHER
LAVISHERS
LAVISHES
LAVISHEST
LAVISHING
LAVISHLY
LAVISHMENT
LAVISHMENTS
LAVISHNESS
LAVISHNESSES
LAVOLT
LAVOLTA
LAVOLTAED
LAVOLTAING
LAVOLTAS
LAVOLTE
LAVOLTED
LAVOLTES
LAVOLTING
LAVOLTS
LAVRA
LAVRAS
LAVROCK
LAVROCKS
LAVS
LAW
LAWBOOK
LAWBOOKS
LAWBREAKER
LAWBREAKERS
LAWBREAKING
LAWBREAKINGS
LAWED
LAWER
LAWEST
LAWFUL
LAWFULLY
LAWFULNESS
LAWFULNESSES
LAWGIVER
LAWGIVERS
LAWGIVING
LAWIN
LAWINE
LAWINES
LAWING
LAWINGS
LAWINS
LAWK
LAWKS
LAWLAND
LAWLANDS

LAWLESS
LAWLESSLY
LAWLESSNESS
LAWLESSNESSES
LAWLIKE
LAWMAKER
LAWMAKERS
LAWMAKING
LAWMAKINGS
LAWMAN
LAWMEN
LAWMONGER
LAWMONGERS
LAWN
LAWNIER
LAWNIEST
LAWNMOWER
LAWNMOWERS
LAWNS
LAWNY
LAWRENCIUM
LAWRENCIUMS
LAWS
LAWSUIT
LAWSUITS
LAWYER
LAWYERED
LAWYERING
LAWYERINGS
LAWYERLIKE
LAWYERLY
LAWYERS
LAX
LAXATION
LAXATIONS
LAXATIVE
LAXATIVENESS
LAXATIVENESSES
LAXATIVES
LAXATOR
LAXATORS
LAXER
LAXES
LAXEST
LAXISM
LAXISMS
LAXIST
LAXISTS
LAXITIES
LAXITY
LAXLY
LAXNESS
LAXNESSES
LAY
LAYABOUT

LAYABOUTS
LAYAWAY
LAYAWAYS
LAYBACK
LAYBACKED
LAYBACKING
LAYBACKS
LAYDEEZ
LAYED
LAYER
LAYERAGE
LAYERAGES
LAYERED
LAYERING
LAYERINGS
LAYERS
LAYETTE
LAYETTES
LAYING
LAYINGS
LAYLOCK
LAYLOCKS
LAYMAN
LAYMEN
LAYOFF
LAYOFFS
LAYOUT
LAYOUTS
LAYOVER
LAYOVERS
LAYPEOPLE
LAYPERSON
LAYPERSONS
LAYS
LAYSHAFT
LAYSHAFTS
LAYSTALL
LAYSTALLS
LAYTIME
LAYTIMES
LAYUP
LAYUPS
LAYWOMAN
LAYWOMEN
LAZAR
LAZARET
LAZARETS
LAZARETTE
LAZARETTES
LAZARETTO
LAZARETTOS
LAZARS
LAZE
LAZED
LAZES

LAZIED
LAZIER
LAZIES
LAZIEST
LAZILY
LAZINESS
LAZINESSES
LAZING
LAZO
LAZOED
LAZOES
LAZOING
LAZOS
LAZULI
LAZULIS
LAZULITE
LAZULITES
LAZURITE
LAZURITES
LAZY
LAZYBONES
LAZYING
LAZYISH
LAZZARONE
LAZZARONI
LAZZI
LAZZO
LEA
LEACH
LEACHABILITIES
LEACHABILITY
LEACHABLE
LEACHATE
LEACHATES
LEACHED
LEACHER
LEACHERS
LEACHES
LEACHIER
LEACHIEST
LEACHING
LEACHINGS
LEACHOUR
LEACHOURS
LEACHTUBS
LEACHY
LEAD
LEADED
LEADEN
LEADENED
LEADENING
LEADENLY
LEADENNESS
LEADENNESSES
LEADENS

LEADER
LEADERBOARD
LEADERBOARDS
LEADERENE
LEADERENES
LEADERETTE
LEADERETTES
LEADERLESS
LEADERS
LEADERSHIP
LEADERSHIPS
LEADIER
LEADIEST
LEADING
LEADINGLY
LEADINGS
LEADLESS
LEADMAN
LEADMEN
LEADOFF
LEADOFFS
LEADPLANT
LEADPLANTS
LEADS
LEADSCREW
LEADSCREWS
LEADSMAN
LEADSMEN
LEADWORK
LEADWORKS
LEADWORT
LEADWORTS
LEADY
LEAF
LEAFAGE
LEAFAGES
LEAFBUD
LEAFBUDS
LEAFCUTTER
LEAFCUTTERS
LEAFED
LEAFERIES
LEAFERY
LEAFHOPPER
LEAFHOPPERS
LEAFIER
LEAFIEST
LEAFINESS
LEAFINESSES
LEAFING
LEAFLESS
LEAFLESSNESS
LEAFLET
LEAFLETED
LEAFLETEER

LEAFLETEERS
LEAFLETER
LEAFLETERS
LEAFLETING
LEAFLETS
LEAFLETTED
LEAFLETTING
LEAFLIKE
LEAFS
LEAFSTALK
LEAFSTALKS
LEAFWORM
LEAFWORMS
LEAFY
LEAGUE
LEAGUED
LEAGUER
LEAGUERED
LEAGUERING
LEAGUERS
LEAGUES
LEAGUING
LEAK
LEAKAGE
LEAKAGES
LEAKED
LEAKER
LEAKERS
LEAKIER
LEAKIEST
LEAKILY
LEAKINESS
LEAKINESSES
LEAKING
LEAKLESS
LEAKPROOF
LEAKS
LEAKY
LEAL
LEALER
LEALEST
LEALLY
LEALTIES
LEALTY
LEAM
LEAMED
LEAMING
LEAMS
LEAN
LEANED
LEANER
LEANERS
LEANEST
LEANING
LEANINGS

LEANLY
LEANNESS
LEANNESSES
LEANS
LEANT
LEANY
LEAP
LEAPED
LEAPER
LEAPEROUS
LEAPERS
LEAPFROG
LEAPFROGGED
LEAPFROGGING
LEAPFROGS
LEAPING
LEAPOROUS
LEAPROUS
LEAPS
LEAPT
LEAR
LEARE
LEARED
LEARES
LEARIER
LEARIEST
LEARINESS
LEARING
LEARN
LEARNABILITIES
LEARNABILITY
LEARNABLE
LEARNED
LEARNEDLY
LEARNEDNESS
LEARNEDNESSES
LEARNER
LEARNERS
LEARNING
LEARNINGS
LEARNS
LEARNT
LEARS
LEARY
LEAS
LEASABLE
LEASE
LEASEBACK
LEASEBACKS
LEASED
LEASEHOLD
LEASEHOLDER
LEASEHOLDERS
LEASEHOLDS
LEASER

LEASERS
LEASES
LEASH
LEASHED
LEASHES
LEASHING
LEASING
LEASINGS
LEASOW
LEASOWE
LEASOWED
LEASOWES
LEASOWING
LEASOWS
LEAST
LEASTAWAYS
LEASTS
LEASTWAYS
LEASTWISE
LEASURE
LEASURES
LEAT
LEATHER
LEATHERBACK
LEATHERBACKS
LEATHERED
LEATHERETTE
LEATHERETTES
LEATHERGOODS
LEATHERHEAD
LEATHERHEADS
LEATHERIER
LEATHERIEST
LEATHERINESS
LEATHERING
LEATHERINGS
LEATHERJACKET
LEATHERJACKETS
LEATHERLEAF
LEATHERLEAVES
LEATHERLIKE
LEATHERN
LEATHERNECK
LEATHERNECKS
LEATHERS
LEATHERWOOD
LEATHERWOODS
LEATHERY
LEATS
LEAVE
LEAVED
LEAVEN
LEAVENED
LEAVENING
LEAVENINGS

LEAVENOUS
LEAVENS
LEAVER
LEAVERS
LEAVES
LEAVIER
LEAVIEST
LEAVING
LEAVINGS
LEAVY
LEAZE
LEAZES
LEBBEK
LEBBEKS
LEBEN
LEBENS
LEBENSRAUM
LEBENSRAUMS
LEBKUCHEN
LECANORA
LECANORAS
LECCY
LECH
LECHAIM
LECHAYIM
LECHAYIMS
LECHED
LECHER
LECHERED
LECHERIES
LECHERING
LECHEROUS
LECHEROUSLY
LECHEROUSNESS
LECHEROUSNESSES
LECHERS
LECHERY
LECHES
LECHING
LECHWE
LECHWES
LECITHIN
LECITHINASE
LECITHINASES
LECITHINS
LECKY
LECTERN
LECTERNS
LECTIN
LECTINS
LECTION
LECTIONARIES
LECTIONARY
LECTIONS
LECTISTERNIA

LECTISTERNIUM
LECTOR
LECTORATE
LECTORATES
LECTORS
LECTORSHIP
LECTORSHIPS
LECTOTYPE
LECTOTYPES
LECTRESS
LECTRESSES
LECTURE
LECTURED
LECTURER
LECTURERS
LECTURES
LECTURESHIP
LECTURESHIPS
LECTURING
LECTURN
LECTURNS
LECYTHI
LECYTHIDACEOUS
LECYTHIS
LECYTHUS
LED
LEDDEN
LEDDENS
LEDERHOSEN
LEDGE
LEDGED
LEDGER
LEDGERED
LEDGERING
LEDGERS
LEDGES
LEDGIER
LEDGIEST
LEDGY
LEDUM
LEDUMS
LEE
LEEAR
LEEARS
LEEBOARD
LEEBOARDS
LEECH
LEECHCRAFT
LEECHCRAFTS
LEECHDOM
LEECHDOMS
LEECHED
LEECHEE
LEECHEES
LEECHES

LEECHING
LEECHLIKE
LEED
LEEING
LEEK
LEEKS
LEEP
LEEPED
LEEPING
LEEPS
LEER
LEERED
LEERIER
LEERIEST
LEERILY
LEERINESS
LEERING
LEERINGLY
LEERINGS
LEERS
LEERY
LEES
LEESE
LEESES
LEESING
LEET
LEETLE
LEETS
LEEWARD
LEEWARDS
LEEWAY
LEEWAYS
LEFT
LEFTE
LEFTER
LEFTEST
LEFTIE
LEFTIES
LEFTISH
LEFTISM
LEFTISMS
LEFTIST
LEFTISTS
LEFTOVER
LEFTOVERS
LEFTS
LEFTWARD
LEFTWARDLY
LEFTWARDS
LEFTWING
LEFTY
LEG
LEGACIES
LEGACY
LEGAL

LEGALESE
LEGALESES
LEGALISATION
LEGALISATIONS
LEGALISE
LEGALISED
LEGALISES
LEGALISING
LEGALISM
LEGALISMS
LEGALIST
LEGALISTIC
LEGALISTICALLY
LEGALISTS
LEGALITIES
LEGALITY
LEGALIZATION
LEGALIZATIONS
LEGALIZE
LEGALIZED
LEGALIZER
LEGALIZERS
LEGALIZES
LEGALIZING
LEGALLY
LEGALS
LEGATARIES
LEGATARY
LEGATE
LEGATED
LEGATEE
LEGATEES
LEGATES
LEGATESHIP
LEGATESHIPS
LEGATINE
LEGATING
LEGATION
LEGATIONARY
LEGATIONS
LEGATISSIMO
LEGATO
LEGATOR
LEGATORIAL
LEGATORS
LEGATOS
LEGEND
LEGENDARIES
LEGENDARILY
LEGENDARY
LEGENDIST
LEGENDISTS
LEGENDRIES
LEGENDRY
LEGENDS

LEGER
LEGERDEMAIN
LEGERDEMAINIST
LEGERDEMAINISTS
LEGERDEMAINS
LEGERING
LEGERINGS
LEGERITIES
LEGERITY
LEGERS
LEGES
LEGGE
LEGGED
LEGGER
LEGGERS
LEGGES
LEGGIER
LEGGIERO
LEGGIEST
LEGGIN
LEGGINESS
LEGGINESSES
LEGGING
LEGGINGED
LEGGINGS
LEGGINS
LEGGISM
LEGGISMS
LEGGY
LEGHORN
LEGHORNS
LEGIBILITIES
LEGIBILITY
LEGIBLE
LEGIBLENESS
LEGIBLENESSES
LEGIBLY
LEGION
LEGIONARIES
LEGIONARY
LEGIONED
LEGIONNAIRE
LEGIONNAIRES
LEGIONS
LEGISLATE
LEGISLATED
LEGISLATES
LEGISLATING
LEGISLATION
LEGISLATIONS
LEGISLATIVE
LEGISLATIVELY
LEGISLATIVES
LEGISLATOR
LEGISLATORIAL

LEGISLATORS
LEGISLATORSHIP
LEGISLATORSHIPS
LEGISLATRESS
LEGISLATRESSES
LEGISLATURE
LEGISLATURES
LEGIST
LEGISTS
LEGIT
LEGITIM
LEGITIMACIES
LEGITIMACY
LEGITIMATE
LEGITIMATED
LEGITIMATELY
LEGITIMATENESS
LEGITIMATES
LEGITIMATING
LEGITIMATION
LEGITIMATIONS
LEGITIMATISE
LEGITIMATISED
LEGITIMATISES
LEGITIMATISING
LEGITIMATIZE
LEGITIMATIZED
LEGITIMATIZES
LEGITIMATIZING
LEGITIMATOR
LEGITIMATORS
LEGITIMISATION
LEGITIMISATIONS
LEGITIMISE
LEGITIMISED
LEGITIMISES
LEGITIMISING
LEGITIMISM
LEGITIMISMS
LEGITIMIST
LEGITIMISTIC
LEGITIMISTS
LEGITIMIZATION
LEGITIMIZATIONS
LEGITIMIZE
LEGITIMIZED
LEGITIMIZER
LEGITIMIZERS
LEGITIMIZES
LEGITIMIZING
LEGITIMS
LEGITS
LEGLAN
LEGLANS
LEGLEN

LEGLENS	LEISHER	LEMMATA	LENES
LEGLESS	LEISHEST	LEMMATISATION	LENG
LEGLESSNESS	LEISHMANIA	LEMMATISATIONS	LENGED
LEGLESSNESSES	LEISHMANIAE	LEMMATISE	LENGER
LEGLET	LEISHMANIAL	LEMMATISED	LENGEST
LEGLETS	LEISHMANIAS	LEMMATISES	LENGING
LEGLIKE	LEISHMANIASES	LEMMATISING	LENGS
LEGLIN	LEISHMANIASIS	LEMMATIZATION	LENGTH
LEGLINS	LEISHMANIOSES	LEMMATIZATIONS	LENGTHEN
LEGMAN	LEISHMANIOSIS	LEMMATIZE	LENGTHENED
LEGMEN	LEISLER	LEMMATIZED	LENGTHENER
LEGONG	LEISLERS	LEMMATIZES	LENGTHENERS
LEGONGS	LEISTER	LEMMATIZING	LENGTHENING
LEGROOM	LEISTERED	LEMMING	LENGTHENS
LEGROOMS	LEISTERING	LEMMINGLIKE	LENGTHFUL
LEGS	LEISTERS	LEMMINGS	LENGTHIER
LEGUAAN	LEISURABLE	LEMNISCAL	LENGTHIEST
LEGUAANS	LEISURABLY	LEMNISCATE	LENGTHILY
LEGUAN	LEISURE	LEMNISCATES	LENGTHINESS
LEGUANS	LEISURED	LEMNISCI	LENGTHINESSES
LEGUME	LEISURELINESS	LEMNISCUS	LENGTHMAN
LEGUMES	LEISURELINESSES	LEMON	LENGTHMEN
LEGUMIN	LEISURELY	LEMONADE	LENGTHS
LEGUMINOUS	LEISURES	LEMONADES	LENGTHSMAN
LEGUMINS	LEISURING	LEMONED	LENGTHSMEN
LEGWARMER	LEITMOTIF	LEMONFISH	LENGTHWAYS
LEGWARMERS	LEITMOTIFS	LEMONFISHES	LENGTHWISE
LEGWEAR	LEITMOTIV	LEMONGRASS	LENGTHY
LEGWEARS	LEITMOTIVS	LEMONGRASSES	LENIENCE
LEGWORK	LEK	LEMONIER	LENIENCES
LEGWORKS	LEKE	LEMONIEST	LENIENCIES
LEHAIM	LEKGOTLA	LEMONING	LENIENCY
LEHAYIM	LEKKED	LEMONISH	LENIENT
LEHAYIMS	LEKKER	LEMONS	LENIENTLY
LEHR	LEKKERS	LEMONWOOD	LENIENTS
LEHRJAHRE	LEKKING	LEMONWOODS	LENIFIED
LEHRS	LEKKINGS	LEMONY	LENIFIES
LEHUA	LEKS	LEMPIRA	LENIFY
LEHUAS	LEKU	LEMPIRAS	LENIFYING
LEI	LEKVAR	LEMUR	LENIS
LEIDGER	LEKVARS	LEMURES	LENITIES
LEIDGERS	LEKYTHI	LEMURIAN	LENITION
LEIGER	LEKYTHOI	LEMURIANS	LENITIONS
LEIGERS	LEKYTHOS	LEMURINE	LENITIVE
LEIOTRICHIES	LEKYTHUS	LEMURINES	LENITIVELY
LEIOTRICHOUS	LEMAN	LEMUROID	LENITIVES
LEIOTRICHY	LEMANS	LEMUROIDS	LENITY
LEIPOA	LEME	LEMURS	LENO
LEIPOAS	LEMED	LEND	LENOCINIUM
LEIR	LEMEL	LENDABLE	LENOCINIUMS
LEIRED	LEMELS	LENDER	LENOS
LEIRING	LEMES	LENDERS	LENS
LEIRS	LEMING	LENDING	LENSE
LEIS	LEMMA	LENDINGS	LENSED
LEISH	LEMMAS	LENDS	LENSES

LENSING
LENSLESS
LENSMAN
LENSMEN
LENT
LENTAMENTE
LENTANDO
LENTEN
LENTI
LENTIC
LENTICEL
LENTICELLATE
LENTICELS
LENTICLE
LENTICLES
LENTICULAR
LENTICULARLY
LENTICULARS
LENTICULE
LENTICULES
LENTIFORM
LENTIGINES
LENTIGINOSE
LENTIGINOUS
LENTIGO
LENTIL
LENTILS
LENTISK
LENTISKS
LENTISSIMO
LENTIVIRUS
LENTIVIRUSES
LENTO
LENTOID
LENTOR
LENTORS
LENTOS
LENTOUS
LENVOY
LENVOYS
LEONE
LEONES
LEONINE
LEONTIASES
LEONTIASIS
LEONTOPODIA
LEONTOPODIUM
LEONTOPODIUMS
LEOPARD
LEOPARDESS
LEOPARDESSES
LEOPARDS
LEOTARD
LEOTARDED
LEOTARDS

LEP
LEPER
LEPERS
LEPID
LEPIDODENDROID
LEPIDODENDROIDS
LEPIDOLITE
LEPIDOLITES
LEPIDOMELANE
LEPIDOMELANES
LEPIDOPTERA
LEPIDOPTERAN
LEPIDOPTERANS
LEPIDOPTERIST
LEPIDOPTERISTS
LEPIDOPTEROLOGY
LEPIDOPTERON
LEPIDOPTERONS
LEPIDOPTEROUS
LEPIDOSIREN
LEPIDOSIRENS
LEPIDOTE
LEPIDOTES
LEPORID
LEPORIDAE
LEPORIDS
LEPORINE
LEPPED
LEPPING
LEPRA
LEPRAS
LEPRECHAUN
LEPRECHAUNISH
LEPRECHAUNS
LEPRECHAWN
LEPRECHAWNS
LEPROMATOUS
LEPROSARIA
LEPROSARIUM
LEPROSARIUMS
LEPROSE
LEPROSERIE
LEPROSERIES
LEPROSERY
LEPROSIES
LEPROSITIES
LEPROSITY
LEPROSY
LEPROTIC
LEPROUS
LEPROUSLY
LEPROUSNESS
LEPS
LEPT
LEPTA

LEPTIN
LEPTINS
LEPTOCEPHALI
LEPTOCEPHALIC
LEPTOCEPHALOUS
LEPTOCEPHALUS
LEPTOCERCAL
LEPTODACTYL
LEPTODACTYLOUS
LEPTODACTYLS
LEPTOKURTIC
LEPTOME
LEPTOMES
LEPTON
LEPTONIC
LEPTONS
LEPTOPHYLLOUS
LEPTORRHINE
LEPTOSOMATIC
LEPTOSOME
LEPTOSOMES
LEPTOSOMIC
LEPTOSPIRAL
LEPTOSPIRE
LEPTOSPIRES
LEPTOSPIROSES
LEPTOSPIROSIS
LEPTOTENE
LEPTOTENES
LEQUEAR
LEQUEARS
LERE
LERED
LERES
LERING
LERNAEAN
LERNEAN
LERP
LERPS
LES
LESBIAN
LESBIANISM
LESBIANISMS
LESBIANS
LESBIC
LESBO
LESBOS
LESES
LESION
LESIONED
LESIONS
LESPEDEZA
LESPEDEZAS
LESS
LESSEE

LESSEES
LESSEESHIP
LESSEESHIPS
LESSEN
LESSENED
LESSENING
LESSENS
LESSER
LESSES
LESSON
LESSONED
LESSONING
LESSONINGS
LESSONS
LESSOR
LESSORS
LEST
LESTED
LESTING
LESTS
LET
LETCH
LETCHED
LETCHES
LETCHING
LETCHINGS
LETDOWN
LETDOWNS
LETHAL
LETHALITIES
LETHALITY
LETHALLY
LETHALS
LETHARGIC
LETHARGICAL
LETHARGICALLY
LETHARGIED
LETHARGIES
LETHARGISE
LETHARGISED
LETHARGISES
LETHARGISING
LETHARGIZE
LETHARGIZED
LETHARGIZES
LETHARGIZING
LETHARGY
LETHE
LETHEAN
LETHEE
LETHEES
LETHES
LETHIED
LETHIFEROUS
LETS

LETTABLE	LEUCITIC	LEUDES	LEVANT
LETTED	LEUCITOHEDRON	LEUDS	LEVANTED
LETTER	LEUCITOHEDRONS	LEUGH	LEVANTER
LETTERBOX	LEUCO	LEUGHEN	LEVANTERS
LETTERBOXED	LEUCOBLAST	LEUKAEMIA	LEVANTINE
LETTERBOXES	LEUCOBLASTS	LEUKAEMIAS	LEVANTINES
LETTERBOXING	LEUCOCIDIN	LEUKAEMOGENESES	LEVANTING
LETTERBOXINGS	LEUCOCIDINS	LEUKAEMOGENESIS	LEVANTS
LETTERED	LEUCOCRATIC	LEUKEMIA	LEVATOR
LETTERER	LEUCOCYTE	LEUKEMIAS	LEVATORES
LETTERERS	LEUCOCYTES	LEUKEMIC	LEVATORS
LETTERFORM	LEUCOCYTHAEMIA	LEUKEMICS	LEVE
LETTERFORMS	LEUCOCYTHAEMIAS	LEUKEMOGENESES	LEVEE
LETTERHEAD	LEUCOCYTIC	LEUKEMOGENESIS	LEVEED
LETTERHEADS	LEUCOCYTOLYSES	LEUKEMOGENIC	LEVEEING
LETTERING	LEUCOCYTOLYSIS	LEUKEMOID	LEVEES
LETTERINGS	LEUCOCYTOPENIA	LEUKOBLAST	LEVEL
LETTERLESS	LEUCOCYTOPENIAS	LEUKOBLASTS	LEVELED
LETTERMAN	LEUCOCYTOSES	LEUKOCYTE	LEVELER
LETTERMEN	LEUCOCYTOSIS	LEUKOCYTES	LEVELERS
LETTERN	LEUCOCYTOTIC	LEUKOCYTIC	LEVELHEADED
LETTERNS	LEUCODEPLETED	LEUKOCYTOSES	LEVELHEADEDNESS
LETTERPRESS	LEUCODERMA	LEUKOCYTOSIS	LEVELING
LETTERPRESSES	LEUCODERMAL	LEUKOCYTOTIC	LEVELLED
LETTERS	LEUCODERMAS	LEUKODERMA	LEVELLER
LETTERSET	LEUCODERMIA	LEUKODERMAL	LEVELLERS
LETTERSPACING	LEUCODERMIAS	LEUKODERMAS	LEVELLEST
LETTERSPACINGS	LEUCODERMIC	LEUKODERMIA	LEVELLING
LETTING	LEUCOMA	LEUKODERMIC	LEVELLINGS
LETTINGS	LEUCOMAINE	LEUKODYSTROPHY	LEVELLY
LETTRE	LEUCOMAINES	LEUKOMA	LEVELNESS
LETTRES	LEUCOMAS	LEUKOMAS	LEVELNESSES
LETTUCE	LEUCOPENIA	LEUKON	LEVELS
LETTUCES	LEUCOPENIAS	LEUKONS	LEVER
LETUP	LEUCOPENIC	LEUKOPENIA	LEVERAGE
LETUPS	LEUCOPLAKIA	LEUKOPENIAS	LEVERAGED
LEU	LEUCOPLAKIAS	LEUKOPENIC	LEVERAGES
LEUCAEMIA	LEUCOPLAST	LEUKOPLAKIA	LEVERAGING
LEUCAEMIAS	LEUCOPLASTID	LEUKOPLAKIAS	LEVERED
LEUCAEMIC	LEUCOPLASTIDS	LEUKOPLAKIC	LEVERET
LEUCAEMOGENIC	LEUCOPLASTS	LEUKOPOIESES	LEVERETS
LEUCAEMOGENS	LEUCOPOIESES	LEUKOPOIESIS	LEVERING
LEUCEMIA	LEUCOPOIESIS	LEUKOPOIETIC	LEVERS
LEUCEMIAS	LEUCOPOIETIC	LEUKORRHEA	LEVIABLE
LEUCEMIC	LEUCORRHOEA	LEUKORRHEAL	LEVIATHAN
LEUCH	LEUCORRHOEAL	LEUKORRHEAS	LEVIATHANS
LEUCHAEMIA	LEUCORRHOEAS	LEUKOSES	LEVIED
LEUCHAEMIAS	LEUCORRHOEIC	LEUKOSIS	LEVIER
LEUCHEN	LEUCOSIN	LEUKOTIC	LEVIERS
LEUCIN	LEUCOSINS	LEUKOTOMIES	LEVIES
LEUCINE	LEUCOTOME	LEUKOTOMY	LEVIGABLE
LEUCINES	LEUCOTOMES	LEUKOTRIENE	LEVIGATE
LEUCINS	LEUCOTOMIES	LEUKOTRIENES	LEVIGATED
LEUCITE	LEUCOTOMY	LEV	LEVIGATES
LEUCITES	LEUD	LEVA	LEVIGATING

LEVIGATION
LEVIGATIONS
LEVIGATOR
LEVIGATORS
LEVIN
LEVINS
LEVIRATE
LEVIRATES
LEVIRATIC
LEVIRATICAL
LEVIRATION
LEVIRATIONS
LEVIS
LEVITATE
LEVITATED
LEVITATES
LEVITATING
LEVITATION
LEVITATIONAL
LEVITATIONS
LEVITATOR
LEVITATORS
LEVITE
LEVITES
LEVITIC
LEVITICAL
LEVITICALLY
LEVITIES
LEVITY
LEVO
LEVODOPA
LEVODOPAS
LEVOGYRE
LEVOROTARY
LEVOROTATORY
LEVULIN
LEVULINS
LEVULOSE
LEVULOSES
LEVY
LEVYING
LEW
LEWD
LEWDER
LEWDEST
LEWDLY
LEWDNESS
LEWDNESSES
LEWDSBIES
LEWDSBY
LEWDSTER
LEWDSTERS
LEWIS
LEWISES
LEWISIA

LEWISIAS
LEWISITE
LEWISITES
LEWISSON
LEWISSONS
LEX
LEXEME
LEXEMES
LEXEMIC
LEXES
LEXICA
LEXICAL
LEXICALISATION
LEXICALISATIONS
LEXICALISE
LEXICALISED
LEXICALISES
LEXICALISING
LEXICALITIES
LEXICALITY
LEXICALIZATION
LEXICALIZATIONS
LEXICALIZE
LEXICALIZED
LEXICALIZES
LEXICALIZING
LEXICALLY
LEXICOGRAPHER
LEXICOGRAPHERS
LEXICOGRAPHIC
LEXICOGRAPHICAL
LEXICOGRAPHIES
LEXICOGRAPHIST
LEXICOGRAPHISTS
LEXICOGRAPHY
LEXICOLOGICAL
LEXICOLOGICALLY
LEXICOLOGIES
LEXICOLOGIST
LEXICOLOGISTS
LEXICOLOGY
LEXICON
LEXICONS
LEXIGRAM
LEXIGRAMS
LEXIGRAPHIC
LEXIGRAPHICAL
LEXIGRAPHIES
LEXIGRAPHY
LEXIS
LEXISES
LEY
LEYLANDI
LEYLANDII
LEYS

LEZ
LEZES
LEZZ
LEZZA
LEZZES
LEZZIE
LEZZIES
LEZZY
LHERZOLITE
LHERZOLITES
LI
LIABILITIES
LIABILITY
LIABLE
LIABLENESS
LIAISE
LIAISED
LIAISES
LIAISING
LIAISON
LIAISONS
LIANA
LIANAS
LIANE
LIANES
LIANG
LIANGS
LIANOID
LIAR
LIARD
LIARDS
LIARS
LIART
LIATRIS
LIB
LIBANT
LIBATE
LIBATED
LIBATES
LIBATING
LIBATION
LIBATIONAL
LIBATIONARY
LIBATIONS
LIBATORY
LIBBARD
LIBBARDS
LIBBED
LIBBER
LIBBERS
LIBBING
LIBECCHIO
LIBECCHIOS
LIBECCIO
LIBECCIOS

LIBEL
LIBELANT
LIBELANTS
LIBELED
LIBELEE
LIBELEES
LIBELER
LIBELERS
LIBELING
LIBELINGS
LIBELIST
LIBELISTS
LIBELLANT
LIBELLANTS
LIBELLED
LIBELLEE
LIBELLEES
LIBELLER
LIBELLERS
LIBELLING
LIBELLINGS
LIBELLOUS
LIBELLOUSLY
LIBELOUS
LIBELS
LIBER
LIBERAL
LIBERALISATION
LIBERALISATIONS
LIBERALISE
LIBERALISED
LIBERALISER
LIBERALISERS
LIBERALISES
LIBERALISING
LIBERALISM
LIBERALISMS
LIBERALIST
LIBERALISTIC
LIBERALISTS
LIBERALITIES
LIBERALITY
LIBERALIZATION
LIBERALIZATIONS
LIBERALIZE
LIBERALIZED
LIBERALIZER
LIBERALIZERS
LIBERALIZES
LIBERALIZING
LIBERALLY
LIBERALNESS
LIBERALNESSES
LIBERALS
LIBERATE

LIBERATED	LIBRARIES	LICHEN	LICKSPITTLE
LIBERATES	LIBRARY	LICHENED	LICKSPITTLES
LIBERATING	LIBRAS	LICHENIN	LICORICE
LIBERATION	LIBRATE	LICHENING	LICORICES
LIBERATIONISM	LIBRATED	LICHENINS	LICTOR
LIBERATIONISMS	LIBRATES	LICHENISM	LICTORS
LIBERATIONIST	LIBRATING	LICHENISMS	LID
LIBERATIONISTS	LIBRATION	LICHENIST	LIDAR
LIBERATIONS	LIBRATIONAL	LICHENISTS	LIDARS
LIBERATOR	LIBRATIONS	LICHENOID	LIDDED
LIBERATORS	LIBRATORY	LICHENOLOGICAL	LIDDING
LIBERATORY	LIBRETTI	LICHENOLOGIES	LIDGER
LIBERO	LIBRETTIST	LICHENOLOGIST	LIDGERS
LIBEROS	LIBRETTISTS	LICHENOLOGISTS	LIDLESS
LIBERS	LIBRETTO	LICHENOLOGY	LIDO
LIBERTARIAN	LIBRETTOS	LICHENOSE	LIDOCAINE
LIBERTARIANISM	LIBRI	LICHENOUS	LIDOCAINES
LIBERTARIANISMS	LIBRIFORM	LICHENS	LIDOS
LIBERTARIANS	LIBS	LICHES	LIDS
LIBERTICIDAL	LICE	LICHGATE	LIE
LIBERTICIDE	LICENCE	LICHGATES	LIEBFRAUMILCH
LIBERTICIDES	LICENCED	LICHI	LIEBFRAUMILCHS
LIBERTIES	LICENCEE	LICHIS	LIED
LIBERTINAGE	LICENCEES	LICHT	LIEDER
LIBERTINAGES	LICENCER	LICHTED	LIEF
LIBERTINE	LICENCERS	LICHTER	LIEFER
LIBERTINES	LICENCES	LICHTEST	LIEFEST
LIBERTINISM	LICENCING	LICHTING	LIEFLY
LIBERTINISMS	LICENSABLE	LICHTLIED	LIEFS
LIBERTY	LICENSE	LICHTLIES	LIEGE
LIBIDINAL	LICENSED	LICHTLY	LIEGEDOM
LIBIDINALLY	LICENSEE	LICHTLYING	LIEGEDOMS
LIBIDINIST	LICENSEES	LICHTS	LIEGELESS
LIBIDINISTS	LICENSER	LICHWAKE	LIEGEMAN
LIBIDINOSITIES	LICENSERS	LICHWAKES	LIEGEMEN
LIBIDINOSITY	LICENSES	LICHWAY	LIEGER
LIBIDINOUS	LICENSING	LICHWAYS	LIEGERS
LIBIDINOUSLY	LICENSOR	LICIT	LIEGES
LIBIDINOUSNESS	LICENSORS	LICITLY	LIEN
LIBIDO	LICENSURE	LICITNESS	LIENABLE
LIBIDOS	LICENSURES	LICK	LIENAL
LIBKEN	LICENTE	LICKED	LIENS
LIBKENS	LICENTIATE	LICKER	LIENTERIC
LIBLAB	LICENTIATES	LICKERISH	LIENTERIES
LIBLABS	LICENTIATESHIP	LICKERISHLY	LIENTERY
LIBRA	LICENTIATESHIPS	LICKERISHNESS	LIER
LIBRAE	LICENTIATION	LICKERISHNESSES	LIERNE
LIBRAIRE	LICENTIOUS	LICKERS	LIERNES
LIBRAIRES	LICENTIOUSLY	LICKING	LIERS
LIBRAIRIE	LICENTIOUSNESS	LICKINGS	LIES
LIBRAIRIES	LICH	LICKPENNIES	LIEU
LIBRARIAN	LICHANOS	LICKPENNY	LIEUS
LIBRARIANS	LICHANOSES	LICKS	LIEUTENANCIES
LIBRARIANSHIP	LICHEE	LICKSPIT	LIEUTENANCY
LIBRARIANSHIPS	LICHEES	LICKSPITS	LIEUTENANT

LIEUTENANTRIES
LIEUTENANTRY
LIEUTENANTS
LIEUTENANTSHIP
LIEUTENANTSHIPS
LIEVE
LIEVER
LIEVEST
LIFE
LIFEBELT
LIFEBELTS
LIFEBLOOD
LIFEBLOODS
LIFEBOAT
LIFEBOATS
LIFEBUOY
LIFEBUOYS
LIFEFUL
LIFEGUARD
LIFEGUARDED
LIFEGUARDING
LIFEGUARDS
LIFEHOLD
LIFELESS
LIFELESSLY
LIFELESSNESS
LIFELESSNESSES
LIFELIKE
LIFELIKENESS
LIFELIKENESSES
LIFELINE
LIFELINES
LIFELONG
LIFEMANSHIP
LIFEMANSHIPS
LIFER
LIFERS
LIFESAVER
LIFESAVERS
LIFESAVING
LIFESAVINGS
LIFESOME
LIFESPAN
LIFESPANS
LIFESTYLE
LIFESTYLER
LIFESTYLERS
LIFESTYLES
LIFETIME
LIFETIMES
LIFEWAY
LIFEWAYS
LIFEWORK
LIFEWORKS
LIFT

LIFTABLE
LIFTBACK
LIFTBACKS
LIFTBOY
LIFTBOYS
LIFTED
LIFTER
LIFTERS
LIFTGATE
LIFTGATES
LIFTING
LIFTMAN
LIFTMEN
LIFTOFF
LIFTOFFS
LIFTS
LIFULL
LIG
LIGAMENT
LIGAMENTAL
LIGAMENTARY
LIGAMENTOUS
LIGAMENTS
LIGAN
LIGAND
LIGANDS
LIGANS
LIGASE
LIGASES
LIGATE
LIGATED
LIGATES
LIGATING
LIGATION
LIGATIONS
LIGATIVE
LIGATURE
LIGATURED
LIGATURES
LIGATURING
LIGER
LIGERS
LIGGE
LIGGED
LIGGEN
LIGGER
LIGGERS
LIGGES
LIGGING
LIGGINGS
LIGHT
LIGHTBULB
LIGHTBULBS
LIGHTED
LIGHTEN

LIGHTENED
LIGHTENER
LIGHTENERS
LIGHTENING
LIGHTENINGS
LIGHTENS
LIGHTER
LIGHTERAGE
LIGHTERAGES
LIGHTERED
LIGHTERING
LIGHTERMAN
LIGHTERMEN
LIGHTERS
LIGHTEST
LIGHTFACE
LIGHTFACED
LIGHTFACES
LIGHTFAST
LIGHTFASTNESS
LIGHTFASTNESSES
LIGHTFUL
LIGHTHEARTED
LIGHTHEARTEDLY
LIGHTHOUSE
LIGHTHOUSEMAN
LIGHTHOUSEMEN
LIGHTHOUSES
LIGHTING
LIGHTINGS
LIGHTISH
LIGHTLESS
LIGHTLIED
LIGHTLIES
LIGHTLY
LIGHTLYING
LIGHTNESS
LIGHTNESSES
LIGHTNING
LIGHTNINGED
LIGHTNINGS
LIGHTPLANE
LIGHTPLANES
LIGHTPROOF
LIGHTS
LIGHTSHIP
LIGHTSHIPS
LIGHTSOME
LIGHTSOMELY
LIGHTSOMENESS
LIGHTSOMENESSES
LIGHTTIGHT
LIGHTWEIGHT
LIGHTWEIGHTS
LIGHTWOOD

LIGHTWOODS
LIGNAGE
LIGNAGES
LIGNALOES
LIGNE
LIGNEOUS
LIGNES
LIGNICOLE
LIGNICOLOUS
LIGNIFICATION
LIGNIFICATIONS
LIGNIFIED
LIGNIFIES
LIGNIFORM
LIGNIFY
LIGNIFYING
LIGNIN
LIGNINS
LIGNIPERDOUS
LIGNITE
LIGNITES
LIGNITIC
LIGNIVOROUS
LIGNOCAINE
LIGNOCAINES
LIGNOCELLULOSE
LIGNOCELLULOSES
LIGNOCELLULOSIC
LIGNOSE
LIGNOSES
LIGNOSULFONATE
LIGNOSULFONATES
LIGNUM
LIGNUMS
LIGROIN
LIGROINE
LIGROINES
LIGROINS
LIGS
LIGULA
LIGULAE
LIGULAR
LIGULAS
LIGULATE
LIGULE
LIGULES
LIGULOID
LIGURE
LIGURES
LIKABILITIES
LIKABILITY
LIKABLE
LIKABLENESS
LIKABLENESSES
LIKE

LIKEABLE	LIMA	LIME	LIMITER
LIKEABLENESS	LIMACEL	LIMEADE	LIMITERS
LIKED	LIMACELS	LIMEADES	LIMITES
LIKELIER	LIMACEOUS	LIMED	LIMITING
LIKELIEST	LIMACES	LIMEKILN	LIMITINGLY
LIKELIHOOD	LIMACIFORM	LIMEKILNS	LIMITINGS
LIKELIHOODS	LIMACINE	LIMELESS	LIMITLESS
LIKELINESS	LIMACOLOGIES	LIMELIGHT	LIMITLESSLY
LIKELINESSES	LIMACOLOGIST	LIMELIGHTED	LIMITLESSNESS
LIKELY	LIMACOLOGISTS	LIMELIGHTER	LIMITLESSNESSES
LIKEN	LIMACOLOGY	LIMELIGHTERS	LIMITROPHE
LIKENED	LIMACON	LIMELIGHTING	LIMITS
LIKENESS	LIMACONS	LIMELIGHTS	LIMIVOROUS
LIKENESSES	LIMAIL	LIMELIT	LIMMA
LIKENING	LIMAILS	LIMEN	LIMMAS
LIKENS	LIMAN	LIMENS	LIMMER
LIKER	LIMANS	LIMEPIT	LIMMERS
LIKERS	LIMAS	LIMEPITS	LIMN
LIKES	LIMATION	LIMERICK	LIMNAEID
LIKEST	LIMATIONS	LIMERICKS	LIMNAEIDS
LIKEWAKE	LIMAX	LIMES	LIMNED
LIKEWAKES	LIMB	LIMESCALE	LIMNER
LIKEWALK	LIMBA	LIMESTONE	LIMNERS
LIKEWALKS	LIMBAS	LIMESTONES	LIMNETIC
LIKEWISE	LIMBATE	LIMEWASH	LIMNIC
LIKIN	LIMBEC	LIMEWASHES	LIMNING
LIKING	LIMBECK	LIMEWATER	LIMNOLOGIC
LIKINGS	LIMBECKS	LIMEWATERS	LIMNOLOGICAL
LIKINS	LIMBECS	LIMEY	LIMNOLOGICALLY
LIKUTA	LIMBED	LIMEYS	LIMNOLOGIES
LILAC	LIMBER	LIMICOLINE	LIMNOLOGIST
LILACS	LIMBERED	LIMICOLOUS	LIMNOLOGISTS
LILANGENI	LIMBERER	LIMIER	LIMNOLOGY
LILIACEOUS	LIMBEREST	LIMIEST	LIMNOPHILOUS
LILIED	LIMBERING	LIMINA	LIMNS
LILIES	LIMBERLY	LIMINAL	LIMO
LILL	LIMBERNESS	LIMINESS	LIMONENE
LILLED	LIMBERNESSES	LIMINESSES	LIMONENES
LILLING	LIMBERS	LIMING	LIMONITE
LILLIPUT	LIMBI	LIMINGS	LIMONITES
LILLIPUTIAN	LIMBIC	LIMIT	LIMONITIC
LILLIPUTIANS	LIMBIER	LIMITABLE	LIMOS
LILLIPUTS	LIMBIEST	LIMITABLENESS	LIMOSES
LILLS	LIMBING	LIMITARIAN	LIMOSIS
LILO	LIMBLESS	LIMITARIANS	LIMOUS
LILOS	LIMBMEAL	LIMITARY	LIMOUSINE
LILT	LIMBO	LIMITATION	LIMOUSINES
LILTED	LIMBOS	LIMITATIONAL	LIMP
LILTING	LIMBOUS	LIMITATIONS	LIMPA
LILTINGLY	LIMBS	LIMITATIVE	LIMPAS
LILTINGNESS	LIMBURGITE	LIMITED	LIMPED
LILTINGNESSES	LIMBURGITES	LIMITEDLY	LIMPER
LILTS	LIMBUS	LIMITEDNESS	LIMPERS
LILY	LIMBUSES	LIMITEDNESSES	LIMPEST
LILYLIKE	LIMBY	LIMITEDS	LIMPET

LIMPETS
LIMPID
LIMPIDITIES
LIMPIDITY
LIMPIDLY
LIMPIDNESS
LIMPIDNESSES
LIMPING
LIMPINGLY
LIMPINGS
LIMPKIN
LIMPKINS
LIMPLY
LIMPNESS
LIMPNESSES
LIMPS
LIMPSEY
LIMPSIER
LIMPSIEST
LIMPSY
LIMULI
LIMULOID
LIMULOIDS
LIMULUS
LIMULUSES
LIMY
LIN
LINABLE
LINAC
LINACS
LINAGE
LINAGES
LINALOL
LINALOLS
LINALOOL
LINALOOLS
LINCH
LINCHES
LINCHET
LINCHETS
LINCHPIN
LINCHPINS
LINCOMYCIN
LINCOMYCINS
LINCRUSTA
LINCRUSTAS
LINCTURE
LINCTURES
LINCTUS
LINCTUSES
LIND
LINDANE
LINDANES
LINDEN
LINDENS

LINDIES
LINDS
LINDWORM
LINDWORMS
LINDY
LINE
LINEABLE
LINEAGE
LINEAGES
LINEAL
LINEALITIES
LINEALITY
LINEALLY
LINEAMENT
LINEAMENTAL
LINEAMENTS
LINEAR
LINEARISE
LINEARISED
LINEARISES
LINEARISING
LINEARITIES
LINEARITY
LINEARIZATION
LINEARIZATIONS
LINEARIZE
LINEARIZED
LINEARIZES
LINEARIZING
LINEARLY
LINEATE
LINEATED
LINEATION
LINEATIONS
LINEBACKER
LINEBACKERS
LINEBACKING
LINEBACKINGS
LINEBRED
LINEBREEDING
LINEBREEDINGS
LINECASTER
LINECASTERS
LINECASTING
LINECASTINGS
LINECUT
LINECUTS
LINED
LINELESS
LINELIKE
LINEMAN
LINEMEN
LINEN
LINENS
LINENY

LINEOLATE
LINEOLATED
LINER
LINERBOARD
LINERBOARDS
LINERLESS
LINERS
LINES
LINESMAN
LINESMEN
LINEUP
LINEUPS
LINEY
LING
LINGA
LINGAM
LINGAMS
LINGAS
LINGCOD
LINGCODS
LINGEL
LINGELS
LINGER
LINGERED
LINGERER
LINGERERS
LINGERIE
LINGERIES
LINGERING
LINGERINGLY
LINGERINGS
LINGERS
LINGIER
LINGIEST
LINGLE
LINGLES
LINGO
LINGOES
LINGONBERRIES
LINGONBERRY
LINGOT
LINGOTS
LINGS
LINGSTER
LINGSTERS
LINGUA
LINGUAE
LINGUAL
LINGUALLY
LINGUALS
LINGUAS
LINGUIFORM
LINGUINE
LINGUINES
LINGUINI

LINGUINIS
LINGUIST
LINGUISTER
LINGUISTERS
LINGUISTIC
LINGUISTICAL
LINGUISTICALLY
LINGUISTICIAN
LINGUISTICIANS
LINGUISTICS
LINGUISTRIES
LINGUISTRY
LINGUISTS
LINGULA
LINGULAE
LINGULAR
LINGULAS
LINGULATE
LINGULATED
LINGY
LINHAY
LINHAYS
LINIER
LINIEST
LINIMENT
LINIMENTS
LININ
LINING
LININGS
LININS
LINISH
LINISHED
LINISHER
LINISHERS
LINISHES
LINISHING
LINISHINGS
LINK
LINKABLE
LINKAGE
LINKAGES
LINKBOY
LINKBOYS
LINKED
LINKER
LINKERS
LINKING
LINKMAN
LINKMEN
LINKS
LINKSMAN
LINKSMEN
LINKSTER
LINKSTERS
LINKUP

LINKUPS	LINUMS	LIPIDOPLAST	LIPPENED
LINKWORK	LINURON	LIPIDOPLASTS	LIPPENING
LINKWORKS	LINURONS	LIPIDS	LIPPENS
LINKY	LINY	LIPIN	LIPPER
LINN	LION	LIPINS	LIPPERED
LINNED	LIONCEL	LIPLESS	LIPPERING
LINNET	LIONCELLE	LIPLIKE	LIPPERS
LINNETS	LIONCELLES	LIPOCHROME	LIPPIE
LINNEY	LIONCELS	LIPOCHROMES	LIPPIER
LINNEYS	LIONEL	LIPOCYTE	LIPPIES
LINNIES	LIONELS	LIPOCYTES	LIPPIEST
LINNING	LIONESS	LIPODYSTROPHY	LIPPING
LINNS	LIONESSES	LIPOGENESES	LIPPINGS
LINNY	LIONET	LIPOGENESIS	LIPPITUDE
LINO	LIONETS	LIPOGRAM	LIPPITUDES
LINOCUT	LIONFISH	LIPOGRAMMATIC	LIPPY
LINOCUTS	LIONFISHES	LIPOGRAMMATISM	LIPREADING
LINOLEATE	LIONHEARTED	LIPOGRAMMATISMS	LIPREADINGS
LINOLEATES	LIONHEARTEDNESS	LIPOGRAMMATIST	LIPS
LINOLEIC	LIONISATION	LIPOGRAMMATISTS	LIPSTICK
LINOLENIC	LIONISATIONS	LIPOGRAMS	LIPSTICKED
LINOLEUM	LIONISE	LIPOGRAPHIES	LIPSTICKING
LINOLEUMS	LIONISED	LIPOGRAPHY	LIPSTICKS
LINOS	LIONISER	LIPOIC	LIPURIA
LINS	LIONISERS	LIPOID	LIQUABLE
LINSANG	LIONISES	LIPOIDAL	LIQUATE
LINSANGS	LIONISING	LIPOIDS	LIQUATED
LINSEED	LIONISM	LIPOLYSES	LIQUATES
LINSEEDS	LIONISMS	LIPOLYSIS	LIQUATING
LINSEY	LIONIZATION	LIPOLYTIC	LIQUATION
LINSEYS	LIONIZATIONS	LIPOMA	LIQUATIONS
LINSTOCK	LIONIZE	LIPOMAS	LIQUEFACIENT
LINSTOCKS	LIONIZED	LIPOMATA	LIQUEFACIENTS
LINT	LIONIZER	LIPOMATOSES	LIQUEFACTION
LINTEL	LIONIZERS	LIPOMATOSIS	LIQUEFACTIONS
LINTELLED	LIONIZES	LIPOMATOUS	LIQUEFACTIVE
LINTELS	LIONIZING	LIPOPHILIC	LIQUEFIABLE
LINTER	LIONLIKE	LIPOPLAST	LIQUEFIED
LINTERS	LIONLY	LIPOPLASTS	LIQUEFIER
LINTIE	LIONS	LIPOPROTEIN	LIQUEFIERS
LINTIER	LIP	LIPOPROTEINS	LIQUEFIES
LINTIES	LIPA	LIPOSOMAL	LIQUEFY
LINTIEST	LIPAEMIA	LIPOSOME	LIQUEFYING
LINTLESS	LIPAEMIC	LIPOSOMES	LIQUESCE
LINTOL	LIPARITE	LIPOSUCK	LIQUESCED
LINTOLS	LIPARITES	LIPOSUCKED	LIQUESCENCE
LINTS	LIPASE	LIPOSUCKING	LIQUESCENCES
LINTSEED	LIPASES	LIPOSUCKS	LIQUESCENCIES
LINTSEEDS	LIPECTOMIES	LIPOSUCTION	LIQUESCENCY
LINTSTOCK	LIPECTOMY	LIPOSUCTIONS	LIQUESCENT
LINTSTOCKS	LIPEMIA	LIPOTROPIC	LIQUESCES
LINTWHITE	LIPID	LIPOTROPIN	LIQUESCING
LINTWHITES	LIPIDE	LIPOTROPINS	LIQUEUR
LINTY	LIPIDES	LIPPED	LIQUEURED
LINUM	LIPIDIC	LIPPEN	LIQUEURING

LIQUEURS
LIQUID
LIQUIDAMBAR
LIQUIDAMBARS
LIQUIDATE
LIQUIDATED
LIQUIDATES
LIQUIDATING
LIQUIDATION
LIQUIDATIONS
LIQUIDATOR
LIQUIDATORS
LIQUIDISE
LIQUIDISED
LIQUIDISER
LIQUIDISERS
LIQUIDISES
LIQUIDISING
LIQUIDITIES
LIQUIDITY
LIQUIDIZE
LIQUIDIZED
LIQUIDIZER
LIQUIDIZERS
LIQUIDIZES
LIQUIDIZING
LIQUIDLY
LIQUIDNESS
LIQUIDNESSES
LIQUIDS
LIQUIDUS
LIQUIDUSES
LIQUIFIED
LIQUIFIER
LIQUIFIERS
LIQUIFIES
LIQUIFY
LIQUIFYING
LIQUOR
LIQUORED
LIQUORICE
LIQUORICES
LIQUORING
LIQUORISH
LIQUORISHLY
LIQUORISHNESS
LIQUORS
LIRA
LIRAS
LIRE
LIRI
LIRIODENDRA
LIRIODENDRON
LIRIODENDRONS
LIRIPIPE

LIRIPIPES
LIRIPOOP
LIRIPOOPS
LIRK
LIRKED
LIRKING
LIRKS
LIROT
LIROTH
LIS
LISENTE
LISK
LISKS
LISLE
LISLES
LISP
LISPED
LISPER
LISPERS
LISPING
LISPINGLY
LISPINGS
LISPOUND
LISPOUNDS
LISPS
LISPUND
LISPUNDS
LISSENCEPHALOUS
LISSES
LISSOM
LISSOME
LISSOMELY
LISSOMENESS
LISSOMENESSES
LISSOMLY
LISSOMNESS
LISSOMNESSES
LISSOTRICHOUS
LIST
LISTABLE
LISTED
LISTEE
LISTEES
LISTEL
LISTELS
LISTEN
LISTENABILITY
LISTENABLE
LISTENED
LISTENER
LISTENERS
LISTENERSHIP
LISTENERSHIPS
LISTENING
LISTENS

LISTER
LISTERIA
LISTERIAL
LISTERIAS
LISTERIC
LISTERIOSES
LISTERIOSIS
LISTERS
LISTETH
LISTFUL
LISTING
LISTINGS
LISTLESS
LISTLESSLY
LISTLESSNESS
LISTLESSNESSES
LISTS
LISTSERV
LIT
LITAI
LITANIES
LITANY
LITAS
LITCHI
LITCHIS
LITE
LITED
LITER
LITERACIES
LITERACY
LITERAL
LITERALISE
LITERALISED
LITERALISER
LITERALISERS
LITERALISES
LITERALISING
LITERALISM
LITERALISMS
LITERALIST
LITERALISTIC
LITERALISTS
LITERALITIES
LITERALITY
LITERALIZATION
LITERALIZATIONS
LITERALIZE
LITERALIZED
LITERALIZER
LITERALIZERS
LITERALIZES
LITERALIZING
LITERALLY
LITERALNESS
LITERALNESSES

LITERALS
LITERARILY
LITERARINESS
LITERARINESSES
LITERARY
LITERARYISM
LITERARYISMS
LITERATE
LITERATELY
LITERATENESS
LITERATENESSES
LITERATES
LITERATI
LITERATIM
LITERATION
LITERATIONS
LITERATO
LITERATOR
LITERATORS
LITERATURE
LITERATURED
LITERATURES
LITERATUS
LITEROSE
LITEROSITIES
LITEROSITY
LITERS
LITES
LITH
LITHARGE
LITHARGES
LITHATE
LITHATES
LITHE
LITHED
LITHELY
LITHEMIA
LITHEMIAS
LITHEMIC
LITHENESS
LITHENESSES
LITHER
LITHERLY
LITHES
LITHESOME
LITHESOMENESS
LITHESOMENESSES
LITHEST
LITHIA
LITHIAS
LITHIASES
LITHIASIS
LITHIC
LITHIFICATION
LITHIFICATIONS

LITHIFIED
LITHIFIES
LITHIFY
LITHIFYING
LITHING
LITHISTID
LITHISTIDS
LITHITE
LITHITES
LITHIUM
LITHIUMS
LITHO
LITHOCHROMATIC
LITHOCHROMATICS
LITHOCHROMIES
LITHOCHROMY
LITHOCLAST
LITHOCLASTS
LITHOCYST
LITHOCYSTS
LITHODOMOUS
LITHOED
LITHOGENOUS
LITHOGLYPH
LITHOGLYPHS
LITHOGRAPH
LITHOGRAPHED
LITHOGRAPHER
LITHOGRAPHERS
LITHOGRAPHIC
LITHOGRAPHICAL
LITHOGRAPHIES
LITHOGRAPHING
LITHOGRAPHS
LITHOGRAPHY
LITHOID
LITHOIDAL
LITHOING
LITHOLAPAXIES
LITHOLAPAXY
LITHOLATRIES
LITHOLATROUS
LITHOLATRY
LITHOLOGIC
LITHOLOGICAL
LITHOLOGICALLY
LITHOLOGIES
LITHOLOGIST
LITHOLOGISTS
LITHOLOGY
LITHOMANCIES
LITHOMANCY
LITHOMARGE
LITHOMARGES
LITHOMETEOR

LITHOMETEORS
LITHONTHRYPTIC
LITHONTHRYPTICS
LITHONTRIPTIC
LITHONTRIPTICS
LITHONTRIPTIST
LITHONTRIPTISTS
LITHONTRIPTOR
LITHONTRIPTORS
LITHOPHAGOUS
LITHOPHANE
LITHOPHANES
LITHOPHILOUS
LITHOPHYSA
LITHOPHYSAE
LITHOPHYSE
LITHOPHYSES
LITHOPHYTE
LITHOPHYTES
LITHOPHYTIC
LITHOPONE
LITHOPONES
LITHOPRINT
LITHOPRINTS
LITHOS
LITHOSOL
LITHOSOLS
LITHOSPERMUM
LITHOSPERMUMS
LITHOSPHERE
LITHOSPHERES
LITHOSPHERIC
LITHOSTATIC
LITHOTOME
LITHOTOMES
LITHOTOMIC
LITHOTOMICAL
LITHOTOMIES
LITHOTOMIST
LITHOTOMISTS
LITHOTOMOUS
LITHOTOMY
LITHOTRIPSIES
LITHOTRIPSY
LITHOTRIPTER
LITHOTRIPTERS
LITHOTRIPTIC
LITHOTRIPTICS
LITHOTRIPTIST
LITHOTRIPTISTS
LITHOTRIPTOR
LITHOTRIPTORS
LITHOTRITE
LITHOTRITES
LITHOTRITIC

LITHOTRITICS
LITHOTRITIES
LITHOTRITISE
LITHOTRITISED
LITHOTRITISES
LITHOTRITISING
LITHOTRITIST
LITHOTRITISTS
LITHOTRITIZE
LITHOTRITIZED
LITHOTRITIZES
LITHOTRITIZING
LITHOTRITOR
LITHOTRITORS
LITHOTRITY
LITHS
LITIGABLE
LITIGANT
LITIGANTS
LITIGATE
LITIGATED
LITIGATES
LITIGATING
LITIGATION
LITIGATIONS
LITIGATOR
LITIGATORS
LITIGIOUS
LITIGIOUSLY
LITIGIOUSNESS
LITIGIOUSNESSES
LITING
LITMUS
LITMUSES
LITORAL
LITOTES
LITOTIC
LITRE
LITRES
LITS
LITTEN
LITTER
LITTERATEUR
LITTERATEURS
LITTERBAG
LITTERBAGS
LITTERBUG
LITTERBUGS
LITTERED
LITTERER
LITTERERS
LITTERING
LITTERMATE
LITTERMATES
LITTERS

LITTERY
LITTLE
LITTLEANES
LITTLENECK
LITTLENECKS
LITTLENESS
LITTLENESSES
LITTLER
LITTLES
LITTLEST
LITTLEWORTH
LITTLIE
LITTLIES
LITTLIN
LITTLING
LITTLINGS
LITTLINS
LITTLISH
LITTORAL
LITTORALS
LITU
LITURGIC
LITURGICAL
LITURGICALLY
LITURGICS
LITURGIES
LITURGIOLOGIES
LITURGIOLOGIST
LITURGIOLOGISTS
LITURGIOLOGY
LITURGISM
LITURGIST
LITURGISTIC
LITURGISTS
LITURGY
LITUUS
LITUUSES
LIVABILITIES
LIVABILITY
LIVABLE
LIVABLENESS
LIVABLENESSES
LIVE
LIVEABILITIES
LIVEABILITY
LIVEABLE
LIVEABLENESS
LIVED
LIVEDO
LIVEDOS
LIVELIER
LIVELIEST
LIVELIHEAD
LIVELIHEADS
LIVELIHOOD

LIVELIHOODS
LIVELILY
LIVELINESS
LIVELINESSES
LIVELOD
LIVELODS
LIVELONG
LIVELONGS
LIVELOOD
LIVELOODS
LIVELY
LIVEN
LIVENED
LIVENER
LIVENERS
LIVENESS
LIVENESSES
LIVENING
LIVENS
LIVER
LIVERIED
LIVERIES
LIVERISH
LIVERISHNESS
LIVERISHNESSES
LIVERLESS
LIVERS
LIVERWINGS
LIVERWORT
LIVERWORTS
LIVERWURST
LIVERWURSTS
LIVERY
LIVERYMAN
LIVERYMEN
LIVES
LIVEST
LIVESTOCK
LIVESTOCKS
LIVETRAP
LIVETRAPPED
LIVETRAPPING
LIVETRAPS
LIVEWARE
LIVEWARES
LIVEYER
LIVEYERE
LIVEYERES
LIVEYERS
LIVID
LIVIDER
LIVIDEST
LIVIDITIES
LIVIDITY
LIVIDLY

LIVIDNESS
LIVIDNESSES
LIVIER
LIVIERS
LIVING
LIVINGLY
LIVINGNESS
LIVINGNESSES
LIVINGS
LIVOR
LIVORS
LIVRAISON
LIVRAISONS
LIVRE
LIVRES
LIVYER
LIVYERS
LIXIVIA
LIXIVIAL
LIXIVIATE
LIXIVIATED
LIXIVIATES
LIXIVIATING
LIXIVIATION
LIXIVIATIONS
LIXIVIOUS
LIXIVIUM
LIXIVIUMS
LIZARD
LIZARDS
LLAMA
LLAMAS
LLANERO
LLANEROS
LLANO
LLANOS
LO
LOACH
LOACHES
LOAD
LOADED
LOADEN
LOADENED
LOADENING
LOADENS
LOADER
LOADERS
LOADING
LOADINGS
LOADMASTER
LOADMASTERS
LOADS
LOADSAMONEY
LOADSAMONEYS
LOADSPACE

LOADSPACES
LOADSTAR
LOADSTARS
LOADSTONE
LOADSTONES
LOAF
LOAFED
LOAFER
LOAFERISH
LOAFERS
LOAFING
LOAFINGS
LOAFS
LOAM
LOAMED
LOAMIER
LOAMIEST
LOAMINESS
LOAMINESSES
LOAMING
LOAMLESS
LOAMS
LOAMY
LOAN
LOANABLE
LOANBACK
LOANBACKS
LOANED
LOANER
LOANERS
LOANING
LOANINGS
LOANS
LOANWORD
LOANWORDS
LOAST
LOATH
LOATHE
LOATHED
LOATHEDNESS
LOATHEDNESSES
LOATHER
LOATHERS
LOATHES
LOATHEST
LOATHFUL
LOATHFULNESS
LOATHFULNESSES
LOATHING
LOATHINGLY
LOATHINGS
LOATHLINESS
LOATHLINESSES
LOATHLY
LOATHNESS

LOATHNESSES
LOATHSOME
LOATHSOMELY
LOATHSOMENESS
LOATHSOMENESSES
LOATHY
LOAVE
LOAVED
LOAVES
LOAVING
LOB
LOBAR
LOBATE
LOBATED
LOBATELY
LOBATION
LOBATIONS
LOBBED
LOBBER
LOBBERS
LOBBIED
LOBBIES
LOBBING
LOBBY
LOBBYER
LOBBYERS
LOBBYGOW
LOBBYGOWS
LOBBYING
LOBBYINGS
LOBBYISM
LOBBYISMS
LOBBYIST
LOBBYISTS
LOBE
LOBECTOMIES
LOBECTOMY
LOBED
LOBEFIN
LOBEFINS
LOBELET
LOBELETS
LOBELIA
LOBELIAS
LOBELINE
LOBELINES
LOBES
LOBI
LOBING
LOBINGS
LOBIPED
LOBLOLLIES
LOBLOLLY
LOBO
LOBOLA

LOBOLAS
LOBOLO
LOBOLOS
LOBOS
LOBOSE
LOBOTOMIES
LOBOTOMISE
LOBOTOMISED
LOBOTOMISES
LOBOTOMISING
LOBOTOMIZE
LOBOTOMIZED
LOBOTOMIZES
LOBOTOMIZING
LOBOTOMY
LOBS
LOBSCOUSE
LOBSCOUSES
LOBSTER
LOBSTERED
LOBSTERING
LOBSTERINGS
LOBSTERLIKE
LOBSTERMAN
LOBSTERMEN
LOBSTERS
LOBSTICK
LOBSTICKS
LOBULAR
LOBULATE
LOBULATED
LOBULATION
LOBULATIONS
LOBULE
LOBULES
LOBULI
LOBULOSE
LOBULUS
LOBUS
LOBWORM
LOBWORMS
LOCA
LOCAL
LOCALE
LOCALES
LOCALISABLE
LOCALISATION
LOCALISATIONS
LOCALISE
LOCALISED
LOCALISER
LOCALISERS
LOCALISES
LOCALISING
LOCALISM

LOCALISMS
LOCALIST
LOCALISTIC
LOCALISTS
LOCALITE
LOCALITES
LOCALITIES
LOCALITY
LOCALIZABILITY
LOCALIZABLE
LOCALIZATION
LOCALIZATIONS
LOCALIZE
LOCALIZED
LOCALIZER
LOCALIZERS
LOCALIZES
LOCALIZING
LOCALLY
LOCALNESS
LOCALS
LOCATABLE
LOCATE
LOCATEABLE
LOCATED
LOCATER
LOCATERS
LOCATES
LOCATING
LOCATION
LOCATIONAL
LOCATIONALLY
LOCATIONS
LOCATIVE
LOCATIVES
LOCATOR
LOCATORS
LOCELLATE
LOCH
LOCHAN
LOCHANS
LOCHIA
LOCHIAL
LOCHS
LOCI
LOCK
LOCKABLE
LOCKAGE
LOCKAGES
LOCKAWAY
LOCKAWAYS
LOCKBOX
LOCKBOXES
LOCKDOWN
LOCKDOWNS

LOCKED
LOCKER
LOCKERS
LOCKET
LOCKETS
LOCKFAST
LOCKFUL
LOCKFULS
LOCKHOUSE
LOCKHOUSES
LOCKING
LOCKJAW
LOCKJAWS
LOCKKEEPER
LOCKKEEPERS
LOCKMAN
LOCKMEN
LOCKNUT
LOCKNUTS
LOCKOUT
LOCKOUTS
LOCKPICK
LOCKPICKS
LOCKRAM
LOCKRAMS
LOCKS
LOCKSMAN
LOCKSMEN
LOCKSMITH
LOCKSMITHERY
LOCKSMITHING
LOCKSMITHINGS
LOCKSMITHS
LOCKSTEP
LOCKSTEPS
LOCKSTITCH
LOCKSTITCHED
LOCKSTITCHES
LOCKSTITCHING
LOCKUP
LOCKUPS
LOCO
LOCOED
LOCOES
LOCOFOCO
LOCOFOCOS
LOCOING
LOCOISM
LOCOISMS
LOCOMAN
LOCOMEN
LOCOMOBILE
LOCOMOBILES
LOCOMOBILITIES
LOCOMOBILITY

LOCOMOTE
LOCOMOTED
LOCOMOTES
LOCOMOTING
LOCOMOTION
LOCOMOTIONS
LOCOMOTIVE
LOCOMOTIVELY
LOCOMOTIVENESS
LOCOMOTIVES
LOCOMOTIVITIES
LOCOMOTIVITY
LOCOMOTOR
LOCOMOTORS
LOCOMOTORY
LOCOPLANT
LOCOPLANTS
LOCOS
LOCOWEED
LOCOWEEDS
LOCULAMENT
LOCULAMENTS
LOCULAR
LOCULATE
LOCULATION
LOCULE
LOCULED
LOCULES
LOCULI
LOCULICIDAL
LOCULUS
LOCUM
LOCUMS
LOCUPLETE
LOCUS
LOCUST
LOCUSTA
LOCUSTAE
LOCUSTAL
LOCUSTED
LOCUSTING
LOCUSTS
LOCUTION
LOCUTIONARY
LOCUTIONS
LOCUTORIES
LOCUTORY
LOD
LODE
LODEN
LODENS
LODES
LODESMAN
LODESMEN
LODESTAR

LODESTARS
LODESTONE
LODESTONES
LODGE
LODGEABLE
LODGED
LODGEMENT
LODGEMENTS
LODGEPOLE
LODGEPOLES
LODGER
LODGERS
LODGES
LODGING
LODGINGS
LODGMENT
LODGMENTS
LODICULA
LODICULAE
LODICULE
LODICULES
LODS
LOERIE
LOERIES
LOESS
LOESSAL
LOESSES
LOESSIAL
LOFT
LOFTED
LOFTER
LOFTERS
LOFTIER
LOFTIEST
LOFTILY
LOFTINESS
LOFTINESSES
LOFTING
LOFTLESS
LOFTLIKE
LOFTS
LOFTSMAN
LOFTSMEN
LOFTY
LOG
LOGAGRAPHIA
LOGAN
LOGANBERRIES
LOGANBERRY
LOGANIA
LOGANIACEOUS
LOGANIAS
LOGANS
LOGAOEDIC
LOGAOEDICS

LOGARITHM
LOGARITHMIC
LOGARITHMICAL
LOGARITHMICALLY
LOGARITHMS
LOGBOARD
LOGBOARDS
LOGBOOK
LOGBOOKS
LOGE
LOGES
LOGGAT
LOGGATS
LOGGED
LOGGER
LOGGERHEAD
LOGGERHEADED
LOGGERHEADS
LOGGERS
LOGGETS
LOGGIA
LOGGIAS
LOGGIE
LOGGIER
LOGGIEST
LOGGING
LOGGINGS
LOGGY
LOGIA
LOGIC
LOGICAL
LOGICALITIES
LOGICALITY
LOGICALLY
LOGICALNESS
LOGICALNESSES
LOGICIAN
LOGICIANS
LOGICISE
LOGICISED
LOGICISES
LOGICISING
LOGICISM
LOGICISMS
LOGICIST
LOGICISTS
LOGICIZE
LOGICIZED
LOGICIZES
LOGICIZING
LOGICS
LOGIE
LOGIER
LOGIES
LOGIEST

LOGILY
LOGIN
LOGINESS
LOGINESSES
LOGINS
LOGION
LOGIONS
LOGISTIC
LOGISTICAL
LOGISTICALLY
LOGISTICIAN
LOGISTICIANS
LOGISTICS
LOGJAM
LOGJAMS
LOGJUICE
LOGJUICES
LOGLINE
LOGLINES
LOGLOG
LOGLOGS
LOGNORMAL
LOGNORMALITIES
LOGNORMALITY
LOGNORMALLY
LOGO
LOGODAEDALIC
LOGODAEDALIES
LOGODAEDALUS
LOGODAEDALUSES
LOGODAEDALY
LOGOFF
LOGOFFS
LOGOGRAM
LOGOGRAMMATIC
LOGOGRAMS
LOGOGRAPH
LOGOGRAPHER
LOGOGRAPHERS
LOGOGRAPHIC
LOGOGRAPHICAL
LOGOGRAPHICALLY
LOGOGRAPHIES
LOGOGRAPHS
LOGOGRAPHY
LOGOGRIPH
LOGOGRIPHIC
LOGOGRIPHS
LOGOI
LOGOMACH
LOGOMACHIES
LOGOMACHIST
LOGOMACHISTS
LOGOMACHS
LOGOMACHY

LOGON
LOGONS
LOGOPAEDIC
LOGOPAEDICS
LOGOPEDIC
LOGOPEDICS
LOGOPHILE
LOGOPHILES
LOGORRHEA
LOGORRHEAS
LOGORRHEIC
LOGORRHOEA
LOGORRHOEAS
LOGOS
LOGOTHETE
LOGOTHETES
LOGOTYPE
LOGOTYPES
LOGOTYPIES
LOGOTYPY
LOGOUT
LOGOUTS
LOGROLL
LOGROLLED
LOGROLLER
LOGROLLERS
LOGROLLING
LOGROLLINGS
LOGROLLS
LOGS
LOGWAY
LOGWAYS
LOGWOOD
LOGWOODS
LOGY
LOHAN
LOHANS
LOID
LOIDED
LOIDING
LOIDS
LOIN
LOINCLOTH
LOINCLOTHS
LOINS
LOIPE
LOIPEN
LOIR
LOIRS
LOITER
LOITERED
LOITERER
LOITERERS
LOITERING
LOITERINGLY

LOITERINGS
LOITERS
LOKE
LOKES
LOKSHEN
LOLIGO
LOLIGOS
LOLIUM
LOLIUMS
LOLL
LOLLAPALOOZA
LOLLAPALOOZAS
LOLLED
LOLLER
LOLLERS
LOLLIES
LOLLING
LOLLINGLY
LOLLIPOP
LOLLIPOPS
LOLLOP
LOLLOPED
LOLLOPING
LOLLOPS
LOLLS
LOLLY
LOLLYGAG
LOLLYGAGGED
LOLLYGAGGING
LOLLYGAGS
LOLLYPOP
LOLLYPOPS
LOLOG
LOLOGS
LOMA
LOMAS
LOMATA
LOME
LOMED
LOMEIN
LOMEINS
LOMENT
LOMENTA
LOMENTACEOUS
LOMENTS
LOMENTUM
LOMENTUMS
LOMES
LOMING
LOMPISH
LONE
LONELIER
LONELIEST
LONELILY
LONELINESS

LONELINESSES
LONELY
LONENESS
LONENESSES
LONER
LONERS
LONESOME
LONESOMELY
LONESOMENESS
LONESOMENESSES
LONESOMES
LONG
LONGA
LONGAEVAL
LONGAEVOUS
LONGAN
LONGANIMITIES
LONGANIMITY
LONGANIMOUS
LONGANS
LONGAS
LONGBOAT
LONGBOATS
LONGBOW
LONGBOWMAN
LONGBOWMEN
LONGBOWS
LONGCASE
LONGCLOTH
LONGCLOTHS
LONGE
LONGED
LONGEING
LONGER
LONGERON
LONGERONS
LONGERS
LONGES
LONGEST
LONGEVAL
LONGEVITIES
LONGEVITY
LONGEVOUS
LONGHAIR
LONGHAIRED
LONGHAIRS
LONGHAND
LONGHANDS
LONGHEAD
LONGHEADED
LONGHEADEDNESS
LONGHEADS
LONGHORN
LONGHORNS
LONGHOUSE

LONGHOUSES
LONGICAUDATE
LONGICORN
LONGICORNS
LONGIES
LONGING
LONGINGLY
LONGINGS
LONGINQUITIES
LONGINQUITY
LONGIPENNATE
LONGIROSTRAL
LONGISH
LONGITUDE
LONGITUDES
LONGITUDINAL
LONGITUDINALLY
LONGLEAF
LONGLEAVES
LONGLINE
LONGLINES
LONGLY
LONGNESS
LONGNESSES
LONGPRIMER
LONGPRIMERS
LONGS
LONGSHIP
LONGSHIPS
LONGSHORE
LONGSHOREMAN
LONGSHOREMEN
LONGSHORING
LONGSHORINGS
LONGSIGHTED
LONGSIGHTEDNESS
LONGSOME
LONGSOMELY
LONGSOMENESS
LONGSOMENESSES
LONGSPUR
LONGSPURS
LONGSUFFERING
LONGSUFFERINGS
LONGTIME
LONGUEUR
LONGUEURS
LONGWALL
LONGWALLS
LONGWAYS
LONGWEARING
LONGWISE
LONICERA
LONICERAS
LOO

LOOBIER
LOOBIES
LOOBIEST
LOOBILY
LOOBY
LOOED
LOOEY
LOOEYS
LOOF
LOOFA
LOOFAH
LOOFAHS
LOOFAS
LOOFFUL
LOOFFULS
LOOFS
LOOIE
LOOIES
LOOING
LOOK
LOOKALIKE
LOOKALIKES
LOOKDOWN
LOOKDOWNS
LOOKED
LOOKER
LOOKERS
LOOKING
LOOKISM
LOOKISMS
LOOKOUT
LOOKOUTS
LOOKOVER
LOOKOVERS
LOOKS
LOOKUP
LOOKUPS
LOOM
LOOMED
LOOMING
LOOMS
LOON
LOONEY
LOONEYS
LOONIE
LOONIER
LOONIES
LOONIEST
LOONINESS
LOONINESSES
LOONING
LOONINGS
LOONS
LOONY
LOOP

LOOPED
LOOPER
LOOPERS
LOOPHOLE
LOOPHOLED
LOOPHOLES
LOOPHOLING
LOOPIER
LOOPIEST
LOOPING
LOOPINGS
LOOPS
LOOPY
LOOR
LOORD
LOORDS
LOOS
LOOSE
LOOSEBOX
LOOSEBOXES
LOOSED
LOOSELY
LOOSEN
LOOSENED
LOOSENER
LOOSENERS
LOOSENESS
LOOSENESSES
LOOSENING
LOOSENS
LOOSER
LOOSES
LOOSEST
LOOSESTRIFE
LOOSESTRIFES
LOOSIES
LOOSING
LOOSINGS
LOOT
LOOTED
LOOTEN
LOOTER
LOOTERS
LOOTING
LOOTINGS
LOOTS
LOOVES
LOOYENWORK
LOOYENWORKS
LOP
LOPE
LOPED
LOPER
LOPERS
LOPES

LOPGRASS
LOPGRASSES
LOPHOBRANCH
LOPHOBRANCHES
LOPHOBRANCHIATE
LOPHOBRANCHS
LOPHODONT
LOPHOPHORATE
LOPHOPHORATES
LOPHOPHORE
LOPHOPHORES
LOPING
LOPOLITH
LOPOLITHS
LOPPED
LOPPER
LOPPERED
LOPPERING
LOPPERS
LOPPIER
LOPPIEST
LOPPING
LOPPINGS
LOPPY
LOPS
LOPSIDED
LOPSIDEDLY
LOPSIDEDNESS
LOPSIDEDNESSES
LOPSTICK
LOPSTICKS
LOQUACIOUS
LOQUACIOUSLY
LOQUACIOUSNESS
LOQUACITIES
LOQUACITY
LOQUAT
LOQUATS
LOQUITUR
LOR
LORAL
LORAN
LORANS
LORATE
LORAZEPAM
LORAZEPAMS
LORCHA
LORCHAS
LORD
LORDED
LORDING
LORDINGS
LORDKIN
LORDKINS
LORDLESS

LORDLIER
LORDLIEST
LORDLIKE
LORDLINESS
LORDLINESSES
LORDLING
LORDLINGS
LORDLY
LORDOLATRIES
LORDOLATRY
LORDOMA
LORDOMAS
LORDOSES
LORDOSIS
LORDOTIC
LORDS
LORDSHIP
LORDSHIPS
LORDY
LORE
LOREAL
LOREL
LORELS
LORES
LORETTE
LORETTES
LORGNETTE
LORGNETTES
LORGNON
LORGNONS
LORIC
LORICA
LORICAE
LORICATE
LORICATED
LORICATES
LORICATING
LORICATION
LORICATIONS
LORICS
LORIES
LORIKEET
LORIKEETS
LORIMER
LORIMERS
LORINER
LORINERS
LORING
LORINGS
LORIOT
LORIOTS
LORIS
LORISES
LORN
LORNNESS

LORNNESSES
LORRELL
LORRELLS
LORRIES
LORRY
LORY
LOS
LOSABLE
LOSABLENESS
LOSABLENESSES
LOSE
LOSED
LOSEL
LOSELS
LOSEN
LOSER
LOSERS
LOSES
LOSH
LOSING
LOSINGLY
LOSINGS
LOSS
LOSSES
LOSSIER
LOSSIEST
LOSSMAKER
LOSSMAKERS
LOSSMAKING
LOSSY
LOST
LOSTNESS
LOSTNESSES
LOT
LOTA
LOTAH
LOTAHS
LOTAS
LOTE
LOTES
LOTH
LOTHARIO
LOTHARIOS
LOTHEFULL
LOTHER
LOTHEST
LOTHFULL
LOTHNESS
LOTHSOME
LOTI
LOTIC
LOTION
LOTIONS
LOTO
LOTOS

LOTOSES
LOTS
LOTTE
LOTTED
LOTTERIES
LOTTERY
LOTTES
LOTTING
LOTTO
LOTTOS
LOTUS
LOTUSES
LOTUSLAND
LOTUSLANDS
LOU
LOUCHE
LOUCHELY
LOUD
LOUDEN
LOUDENED
LOUDENING
LOUDENS
LOUDER
LOUDEST
LOUDHAILER
LOUDHAILERS
LOUDISH
LOUDLIER
LOUDLIEST
LOUDLY
LOUDMOUTH
LOUDMOUTHED
LOUDMOUTHS
LOUDNESS
LOUDNESSES
LOUDSPEAKER
LOUDSPEAKERS
LOUED
LOUGH
LOUGHS
LOUIE
LOUIES
LOUING
LOUIS
LOUN
LOUND
LOUNDED
LOUNDER
LOUNDERED
LOUNDERING
LOUNDERINGS
LOUNDERS
LOUNDING
LOUNDS
LOUNED

LOUNGE
LOUNGED
LOUNGER
LOUNGERS
LOUNGES
LOUNGEWEAR
LOUNGEWEARS
LOUNGING
LOUNGINGLY
LOUNGINGS
LOUNGY
LOUNING
LOUNS
LOUP
LOUPE
LOUPED
LOUPEN
LOUPES
LOUPING
LOUPIT
LOUPS
LOUR
LOURE
LOURED
LOURES
LOURIE
LOURIER
LOURIES
LOURIEST
LOURING
LOURINGLY
LOURINGS
LOURS
LOURY
LOUS
LOUSE
LOUSED
LOUSER
LOUSERS
LOUSES
LOUSEWORT
LOUSEWORTS
LOUSIER
LOUSIEST
LOUSILY
LOUSINESS
LOUSINESSES
LOUSING
LOUSY
LOUT
LOUTED
LOUTING
LOUTISH
LOUTISHLY
LOUTISHNESS

LOUTISHNESSES
LOUTS
LOUVAR
LOUVARS
LOUVER
LOUVERED
LOUVERS
LOUVRE ,
LOUVRED
LOUVRES
LOVABILITIES
LOVABILITY
LOVABLE
LOVABLENESS
LOVABLENESSES
LOVABLY
LOVAGE
LOVAGES
LOVASTATIN
LOVASTATINS
LOVAT
LOVATS
LOVE
LOVEABILITY
LOVEABLE
LOVEABLENESS
LOVEABLY
LOVEBIRD
LOVEBIRDS
LOVEBITE
LOVEBITES
LOVEBUG
LOVEBUGS
LOVED
LOVELESS
LOVELESSLY
LOVELESSNESS
LOVELESSNESSES
LOVELIER
LOVELIES
LOVELIEST
LOVELIGHT
LOVELIGHTS
LOVELIHEAD
LOVELIHEADS
LOVELILY
LOVELINESS
LOVELINESSES
LOVELOCK
LOVELOCKS
LOVELORN
LOVELORNNESS
LOVELORNNESSES
LOVELY
LOVEMAKER

LOVEMAKERS
LOVEMAKING
LOVEMAKINGS
LOVER
LOVERED
LOVERLESS
LOVERLY
LOVERS
LOVES
LOVESICK
LOVESICKNESS
LOVESICKNESSES
LOVESOME
LOVESTRUCK
LOVEVINE
LOVEVINES
LOVEWORTHY
LOVEY
LOVEYS
LOVIES
LOVING
LOVINGLY
LOVINGNESS
LOVINGNESSES
LOVINGS
LOW
LOWAN
LOWANS
LOWBALL
LOWBALLED
LOWBALLING
LOWBALLINGS
LOWBALLS
LOWBORN
LOWBOY
LOWBOYS
LOWBRED
LOWBROW
LOWBROWED
LOWBROWISM
LOWBROWS
LOWDOWN
LOWDOWNS
LOWE
LOWED
LOWER
LOWERABLE
LOWERCASE
LOWERCASED
LOWERCASES
LOWERCASING
LOWERCLASSMAN
LOWERCLASSMEN
LOWERED
LOWERIER

LOWERIEST
LOWERING
LOWERINGLY
LOWERINGS
LOWERMOST
LOWERS
LOWERY
LOWES
LOWEST
LOWING
LOWINGS
LOWISH
LOWLAND
LOWLANDER
LOWLANDERS
LOWLANDS
LOWLIER
LOWLIEST
LOWLIFE
LOWLIFER
LOWLIFERS
LOWLIFES
LOWLIGHT
LOWLIGHTED
LOWLIGHTING
LOWLIGHTS
LOWLIHEAD
LOWLIHEADS
LOWLILY
LOWLINESS
LOWLINESSES
LOWLIVES
LOWLY
LOWN
LOWND
LOWNDED
LOWNDING
LOWNDS
LOWNE
LOWNED
LOWNES
LOWNESS
LOWNESSES
LOWNING
LOWNS
LOWP
LOWPED
LOWPING
LOWPS
LOWRIDER
LOWRIDERS
LOWRIE
LOWRIES
LOWRY
LOWS

LOWSE
LOWSED
LOWSENING
LOWSENINGS
LOWSER
LOWSES
LOWSEST
LOWSING
LOWSIT
LOWT
LOWTED
LOWTING
LOWTS
LOWVELD
LOWVELDS
LOX
LOXED
LOXES
LOXING
LOXODROME
LOXODROMES
LOXODROMIC
LOXODROMICAL
LOXODROMICALLY
LOXODROMICS
LOXODROMIES
LOXODROMY
LOXYGEN
LOXYGENS
LOY
LOYAL
LOYALER
LOYALEST
LOYALISM
LOYALISMS
LOYALIST
LOYALISTS
LOYALLER
LOYALLEST
LOYALLY
LOYALNESS
LOYALTIES
LOYALTY
LOYS
LOZELL
LOZELLS
LOZEN
LOZENGE
LOZENGED
LOZENGES
LOZENGY
LOZENS
LUACH
LUACHS
LUAU

LUAUS
LUBBARD
LUBBARDS
LUBBER
LUBBERLINESS
LUBBERLINESSES
LUBBERLY
LUBBERS
LUBE
LUBES
LUBFISH
LUBFISHES
LUBRA
LUBRAS
LUBRIC
LUBRICAL
LUBRICANT
LUBRICANTS
LUBRICATE
LUBRICATED
LUBRICATES
LUBRICATING
LUBRICATION
LUBRICATIONAL
LUBRICATIONS
LUBRICATIVE
LUBRICATOR
LUBRICATORS
LUBRICIOUS
LUBRICIOUSLY
LUBRICITIES
LUBRICITY
LUBRICOUS
LUBRICOUSLY
LUBRITORIA
LUBRITORIUM
LUBRITORIUMS
LUCARNE
LUCARNES
LUCE
LUCENCE
LUCENCES
LUCENCIES
LUCENCY
LUCENT
LUCENTLY
LUCERN
LUCERNE
LUCERNES
LUCERNS
LUCES
LUCID
LUCIDER
LUCIDEST
LUCIDITIES

LUCIDITY
LUCIDLY
LUCIDNESS
LUCIDNESSES
LUCIFER
LUCIFERASE
LUCIFERASES
LUCIFERIN
LUCIFERINS
LUCIFEROUS
LUCIFERS
LUCIFUGOUS
LUCIGEN
LUCIGENS
LUCK
LUCKED
LUCKEN
LUCKENBOOTH
LUCKENBOOTHS
LUCKENGOWANS
LUCKIE
LUCKIER
LUCKIES
LUCKIEST
LUCKILY
LUCKINESS
LUCKINESSES
LUCKING
LUCKLESS
LUCKLESSLY
LUCKLESSNESS
LUCKLESSNESSES
LUCKPENNIES
LUCKPENNY
LUCKS
LUCKY
LUCRATIVE
LUCRATIVELY
LUCRATIVENESS
LUCRATIVENESSES
LUCRE
LUCRES
LUCTATION
LUCTATIONS
LUCUBRATE
LUCUBRATED
LUCUBRATES
LUCUBRATING
LUCUBRATION
LUCUBRATIONS
LUCUBRATOR
LUCUBRATORS
LUCULENT
LUCULENTLY
LUCUMA

LUCUMAS
LUCUMO
LUCUMONES
LUCUMOS
LUD
LUDE
LUDERICK
LUDERICKS
LUDES
LUDIC
LUDICALLY
LUDICROUS
LUDICROUSLY
LUDICROUSNESS
LUDICROUSNESSES
LUDO
LUDOS
LUDS
LUDSHIP
LUDSHIPS
LUES
LUETIC
LUETICALLY
LUETICS
LUFF
LUFFA
LUFFAS
LUFFED
LUFFING
LUFFS
LUFTMENSCH
LUFTMENSCHEN
LUG
LUGE
LUGED
LUGEING
LUGEINGS
LUGER
LUGERS
LUGES
LUGGABLE
LUGGABLES
LUGGAGE
LUGGAGES
LUGGED
LUGGER
LUGGERS
LUGGIE
LUGGIES
LUGGING
LUGHOLE
LUGHOLES
LUGING
LUGINGS
LUGS

LUGSAIL
LUGSAILS
LUGUBRIOUS
LUGUBRIOUSLY
LUGUBRIOUSNESS
LUGWORM
LUGWORMS
LUIT
LUITEN
LUKE
LUKEWARM
LUKEWARMISH
LUKEWARMLY
LUKEWARMNESS
LUKEWARMNESSES
LUKEWARMTH
LUKEWARMTHS
LULIBUB
LULIBUBS
LULL
LULLABIED
LULLABIES
LULLABY
LULLABYING
LULLED
LULLING
LULLS
LULU
LULUS
LUM
LUMA
LUMBAGINOUS
LUMBAGO
LUMBAGOS
LUMBANG
LUMBANGS
LUMBAR
LUMBARS
LUMBER
LUMBERED
LUMBERER
LUMBERERS
LUMBERING
LUMBERINGLY
LUMBERINGNESS
LUMBERINGS
LUMBERJACK
LUMBERJACKET
LUMBERJACKETS
LUMBERJACKS
LUMBERLY
LUMBERMAN
LUMBERMEN
LUMBERS
LUMBERSOME

LUMBERSOMENESS
LUMBERYARD
LUMBERYARDS
LUMBOSACRAL
LUMBRICAL
LUMBRICALES
LUMBRICALIS
LUMBRICALISES
LUMBRICALS
LUMBRICI
LUMBRICIFORM
LUMBRICOID
LUMBRICUS
LUMBRICUSES
LUMBUS
LUMEN
LUMENAL
LUMENS
LUMINA
LUMINAIRE
LUMINAIRES
LUMINAL
LUMINANCE
LUMINANCES
LUMINANT
LUMINANTS
LUMINARIA
LUMINARIAS
LUMINARIES
LUMINARISM
LUMINARISMS
LUMINARIST
LUMINARISTS
LUMINARY
LUMINATION
LUMINATIONS
LUMINE
LUMINED
LUMINES
LUMINESCE
LUMINESCED
LUMINESCENCE
LUMINESCENCES
LUMINESCENT
LUMINESCES
LUMINESCING
LUMINIFEROUS
LUMINING
LUMINISM
LUMINISMS
LUMINIST
LUMINISTS
LUMINOSITIES
LUMINOSITY
LUMINOUS

LUMINOUSLY
LUMINOUSNESS
LUMINOUSNESSES
LUMISTEROL
LUMME
LUMMIER
LUMMIEST
LUMMOX
LUMMOXES
LUMMY
LUMP
LUMPECTOMIES
LUMPECTOMY
LUMPED
LUMPEN
LUMPENLY
LUMPENS
LUMPER
LUMPERS
LUMPFISH
LUMPFISHES
LUMPIER
LUMPIEST
LUMPILY
LUMPINESS
LUMPINESSES
LUMPING
LUMPISH
LUMPISHLY
LUMPISHNESS
LUMPISHNESSES
LUMPKIN
LUMPKINS
LUMPS
LUMPSUCKER
LUMPSUCKERS
LUMPY
LUMS
LUNA
LUNACIES
LUNACY
LUNANAUT
LUNANAUTS
LUNAR
LUNARIAN
LUNARIANS
LUNARIES
LUNARIST
LUNARISTS
LUNARNAUT
LUNARNAUTS
LUNARS
LUNARY
LUNAS
LUNATE

LUNATED	LUNGWORM	LURDANE	LUSKISH
LUNATEDS	LUNGWORMS	LURDANES	LUSKISHNESS
LUNATELY	LUNGWORT	LURDANS	LUSKISHNESSES
LUNATES	LUNGWORTS	LURDEN	LUSKS
LUNATIC	LUNGYI	LURDENS	LUST
LUNATICAL	LUNGYIS	LURE	LUSTED
LUNATICALLY	LUNIER	LURED	LUSTER
LUNATICS	LUNIES	LURER	LUSTERED
LUNATION	LUNIEST	LURERS	LUSTERING
LUNATIONS	LUNINESS	LURES	LUSTERLESS
LUNCH	LUNISOLAR	LURGI	LUSTERS
LUNCHBOX	LUNITIDAL	LURGIES	LUSTERWARE
LUNCHBOXES	LUNK	LURGIS	LUSTERWARES
LUNCHED	LUNKER	LURGY	LUSTFUL
LUNCHEON	LUNKERS	LURID	LUSTFULLY
LUNCHEONED	LUNKHEAD	LURIDER	LUSTFULNESS
LUNCHEONETTE	LUNKHEADED	LURIDEST	LUSTFULNESSES
LUNCHEONETTES	LUNKHEADS	LURIDLY	LUSTICK
LUNCHEONING	LUNKS	LURIDNESS	LUSTIER
LUNCHEONS	LUNT	LURIDNESSES	LUSTIEST
LUNCHER	LUNTED	LURING	LUSTIHEAD
LUNCHERS	LUNTING	LURK	LUSTIHEADS
LUNCHES	LUNTS	LURKED	LUSTIHOOD
LUNCHING	LUNULA	LURKER	LUSTIHOODS
LUNCHROOM	LUNULAE	LURKERS	LUSTILY
LUNCHROOMS	LUNULAR	LURKING	LUSTINESS
LUNCHTIME	LUNULATE	LURKINGS	LUSTINESSES
LUNCHTIMES	LUNULATED	LURKS	LUSTING
LUNE	LUNULE	LURRIES	LUSTIQUE
LUNES	LUNULES	LURRY	LUSTLESS
LUNET	LUNY	LURS	LUSTRA
LUNETS	LUNYIE	LURVE	LUSTRAL
LUNETTE	LUNYIES	LURVES	LUSTRATE
LUNETTES	LUPANAR	LUSCIOUS	LUSTRATED
LUNG	LUPANARS	LUSCIOUSLY	LUSTRATES
LUNGAN	LUPIN	LUSCIOUSNESS	LUSTRATING
LUNGANS	LUPINE	LUSCIOUSNESSES	LUSTRATION
LUNGE	LUPINES	LUSER	LUSTRATIONS
LUNGED	LUPINS	LUSERS	LUSTRATIVE
LUNGEE	LUPOUS	LUSH	LUSTRE
LUNGEES	LUPPEN	LUSHED	LUSTRED
LUNGEING	LUPULIN	LUSHER	LUSTRELESS
LUNGER	LUPULINE	LUSHERS	LUSTRES
LUNGERS	LUPULINIC	LUSHES	LUSTREWARE
LUNGES	LUPULINS	LUSHEST	LUSTREWARES
LUNGFISH	LUPUS	LUSHIER	LUSTRINE
LUNGFISHES	LUPUSES	LUSHIEST	LUSTRINES
LUNGFUL	LUR	LUSHING	LUSTRING
LUNGFULS	LURCH	LUSHLY	LUSTRINGS
LUNGI	LURCHED	LUSHNESS	LUSTROUS
LUNGIE	LURCHER	LUSHNESSES	LUSTROUSLY
LUNGIES	LURCHERS	LUSHY	LUSTROUSNESS
LUNGING	LURCHES	LUSK	LUSTROUSNESSES
LUNGIS	LURCHING	LUSKED	LUSTRUM
LUNGS	LURDAN	LUSKING	LUSTRUMS

LUSTS
LUSTY
LUSUS
LUSUSES
LUTANIST
LUTANISTS
LUTE
LUTEA
LUTEAL
LUTECIUM
LUTECIUMS
LUTED
LUTEFISK
LUTEFISKS
LUTEIN
LUTEINISATION
LUTEINISATIONS
LUTEINISE
LUTEINISED
LUTEINISES
LUTEINISING
LUTEINIZATION
LUTEINIZATIONS
LUTEINIZE
LUTEINIZED
LUTEINIZES
LUTEINIZING
LUTEINS
LUTENIST
LUTENISTS
LUTEOLIN
LUTEOLINS
LUTEOLOUS
LUTEOTROPHIC
LUTEOTROPHIN
LUTEOTROPHINS
LUTEOTROPIC
LUTEOTROPIN
LUTEOTROPINS
LUTEOUS
LUTER
LUTERS
LUTES
LUTESCENT
LUTESTRING
LUTESTRINGS
LUTETIUM
LUTETIUMS
LUTEUM
LUTHERN
LUTHERNS
LUTHIER
LUTHIERS
LUTING
LUTINGS

LUTIST
LUTISTS
LUTITE
LUTITES
LUTTEN
LUTZ
LUTZES
LUV
LUVS
LUVVIE
LUVVIES
LUVVY
LUX
LUXATE
LUXATED
LUXATES
LUXATING
LUXATION
LUXATIONS
LUXE
LUXES
LUXMETER
LUXMETERS
LUXULIANITE
LUXULIANITES
LUXULLIANITE
LUXULLIANITES
LUXULYANITE
LUXULYANITES
LUXURIANCE
LUXURIANCES
LUXURIANCIES
LUXURIANCY
LUXURIANT
LUXURIANTLY
LUXURIATE
LUXURIATED
LUXURIATES
LUXURIATING
LUXURIATION
LUXURIATIONS
LUXURIES
LUXURIOUS
LUXURIOUSLY
LUXURIOUSNESS
LUXURIOUSNESSES
LUXURIST
LUXURISTS
LUXURY
LUZ
LUZERN
LUZERNS
LUZZES
LWEI
LWEIS

LYAM
LYAMS
LYARD
LYART
LYASE
LYASES
LYCANTHROPE
LYCANTHROPES
LYCANTHROPIC
LYCANTHROPIES
LYCANTHROPIST
LYCANTHROPISTS
LYCANTHROPY
LYCEA
LYCEE
LYCEES
LYCEUM
LYCEUMS
LYCH
LYCHEE
LYCHEES
LYCHES
LYCHGATE
LYCHGATES
LYCHNIDES
LYCHNIS
LYCHNISES
LYCHNOSCOPE
LYCHNOSCOPES
LYCOPENE
LYCOPENES
LYCOPOD
LYCOPODIUM
LYCOPODIUMS
LYCOPODS
LYDDITE
LYDDITES
LYE
LYES
LYFULL
LYING
LYINGLY
LYINGS
LYKEWAKE
LYKEWAKES
LYKEWALK
LYKEWALKS
LYM
LYME
LYMES
LYMITER
LYMITERS
LYMPH
LYMPHAD
LYMPHADENITIS

LYMPHADENITISES
LYMPHADENOPATHY
LYMPHADS
LYMPHANGIAL
LYMPHANGIOGRAM
LYMPHANGIOGRAMS
LYMPHANGITIC
LYMPHANGITIDES
LYMPHANGITIS
LYMPHANGITISES
LYMPHATIC
LYMPHATICALLY
LYMPHATICS
LYMPHOADENOMA
LYMPHOADENOMAS
LYMPHOBLAST
LYMPHOBLASTIC
LYMPHOBLASTS
LYMPHOCYTE
LYMPHOCYTES
LYMPHOCYTIC
LYMPHOCYTOPENIA
LYMPHOCYTOSES
LYMPHOCYTOSIS
LYMPHOCYTOTIC
LYMPHOGRAM
LYMPHOGRAMS
LYMPHOGRANULOMA
LYMPHOGRAPHIC
LYMPHOGRAPHIES
LYMPHOGRAPHY
LYMPHOID
LYMPHOKINE
LYMPHOKINES
LYMPHOMA
LYMPHOMAS
LYMPHOMATA
LYMPHOMATOID
LYMPHOMATOSES
LYMPHOMATOSIS
LYMPHOMATOUS
LYMPHOPENIA
LYMPHOPOIESES
LYMPHOPOIESIS
LYMPHOPOIETIC
LYMPHOSARCOMA
LYMPHOSARCOMAS
LYMPHOSARCOMATA
LYMPHOTROPHIC
LYMPHS
LYMS
LYNAGE
LYNAGES
LYNCEAN
LYNCH

LYNCHED
LYNCHER
LYNCHERS
LYNCHES
LYNCHET
LYNCHETS
LYNCHING
LYNCHINGS
LYNCHPIN
LYNCHPINS
LYNE
LYNES
LYNX
LYNXES
LYNXLIKE
LYOLYSIS
LYOMEROUS
LYONNAISE
LYOPHIL
LYOPHILE
LYOPHILED
LYOPHILIC
LYOPHILISATION
LYOPHILISATIONS
LYOPHILISE
LYOPHILISED
LYOPHILISES
LYOPHILISING
LYOPHILIZATION
LYOPHILIZATIONS
LYOPHILIZE
LYOPHILIZED
LYOPHILIZER
LYOPHILIZERS
LYOPHILIZES
LYOPHILIZING
LYOPHOBE
LYOPHOBIC
LYOSORPTION
LYRA
LYRAS
LYRATE
LYRATED
LYRATELY
LYRE
LYREBIRD
LYREBIRDS
LYRES
LYRIC
LYRICAL
LYRICALLY
LYRICALNESS
LYRICALNESSES
LYRICISE
LYRICISED

LYRICISES
LYRICISING
LYRICISM
LYRICISMS
LYRICIST
LYRICISTS
LYRICIZE
LYRICIZED
LYRICIZES
LYRICIZING
LYRICON
LYRICONS
LYRICS
LYRIFORM
LYRISM
LYRISMS
LYRIST
LYRISTS
LYSATE
LYSATES
LYSE
LYSED
LYSERGIC
LYSERGIDE
LYSERGIDES
LYSES
LYSIGENIC
LYSIGENOUS
LYSIMETER
LYSIMETERS
LYSIMETRIC
LYSIN
LYSINE
LYSINES
LYSING
LYSINS
LYSIS
LYSOGEN
LYSOGENIC
LYSOGENICITIES
LYSOGENICITY
LYSOGENIES
LYSOGENISE
LYSOGENISED
LYSOGENISES
LYSOGENISING
LYSOGENIZATION
LYSOGENIZATIONS
LYSOGENIZE
LYSOGENIZED
LYSOGENIZES
LYSOGENIZING
LYSOGENS
LYSOGENY
LYSOL

LYSOLECITHIN
LYSOLECITHINS
LYSOLS
LYSOSOMAL
LYSOSOME
LYSOSOMES
LYSOZYME
LYSOZYMES
LYSSA
LYSSAS
LYTE
LYTED
LYTES
LYTHE
LYTHES
LYTHRACEOUS
LYTIC
LYTICALLY
LYTING
LYTTA
LYTTAE
LYTTAS

M

MA	MACARIZE	MACH	MACHMETERS
MAA	MACARIZED	MACHAIR	MACHO
MAAED	MACARIZES	MACHAIRODONT	MACHOS
MAAING	MACARIZING	MACHAIRODONTS	MACHREE
MAAR	MACARONI	MACHAIRS	MACHREES
MAARE	MACARONIC	MACHAN	MACHS
MAARS	MACARONICALLY	MACHANS	MACHTPOLITIK
MAAS	MACARONICS	MACHE	MACHZOR
MAATJES	MACARONIES	MACHER	MACHZORIM
MABE	MACARONIS	MACHERS	MACHZORS
MABELA	MACAROON	MACHES	MACING
MABES	MACAROONS	MACHETE	MACINTOSH
MAC	MACASSAR	MACHETES	MACINTOSHES
MACABER	MACASSARS	MACHICOLATE	MACK
MACABERESQUE	MACAW	MACHICOLATED	MACKEREL
MACABRE	MACAWS	MACHICOLATES	MACKERELS
MACABRELY	MACCABAW	MACHICOLATING	MACKINAW
MACACO	MACCABAWS	MACHICOLATION	MACKINAWS
MACACOS	MACCABOY	MACHICOLATIONS	MACKINTOSH
MACADAM	MACCABOYS	MACHINABILITIES	MACKINTOSHES
MACADAMIA	MACCARONI	MACHINABILITY	MACKLE
MACADAMIAS	MACCARONIES	MACHINABLE	MACKLED
MACADAMISATION	MACCARONIS	MACHINATE	MACKLES
MACADAMISATIONS	MACCHIA	MACHINATED	MACKLING
MACADAMISE	MACCHIATO	MACHINATES	MACKS
MACADAMISED	MACCHIE	MACHINATING	MACLE
MACADAMISER	MACCOBOY	MACHINATION	MACLED
MACADAMISERS	MACCOBOYS	MACHINATIONS	MACLES
MACADAMISES	MACE	MACHINATOR	MACON
MACADAMISING	MACEBEARER	MACHINATORS	MACONOCHIE
MACADAMIZATION	MACEBEARERS	MACHINE	MACONOCHIES
MACADAMIZATIONS	MACED	MACHINEABILITY	MACONS
MACADAMIZE	MACEDOINE	MACHINEABLE	MACOYA
MACADAMIZED	MACEDOINES	MACHINED	MACOYAS
MACADAMIZER	MACER	MACHINEGUN	MACRAME
MACADAMIZERS	MACERAL	MACHINEGUNNED	MACRAMES
MACADAMIZES	MACERALS	MACHINEGUNNING	MACRAMI
MACADAMIZING	MACERANDUBAS	MACHINEGUNS	MACRAMIS
MACADAMS	MACERATE	MACHINELESS	MACRENCEPHALIA
MACAHUBA	MACERATED	MACHINELIKE	MACRENCEPHALY
MACAHUBAS	MACERATER	MACHINEMAN	MACRO
MACALLUM	MACERATERS	MACHINEMEN	MACROAGGREGATE
MACALLUMS	MACERATES	MACHINERIES	MACROAGGREGATED
MACAQUE	MACERATING	MACHINERY	MACROAGGREGATES
MACAQUES	MACERATION	MACHINES	MACROBIAN
MACARISE	MACERATIONS	MACHINING	MACROBIOTA
MACARISED	MACERATIVE	MACHINIST	MACROBIOTE
MACARISES	MACERATOR	MACHINISTS	MACROBIOTES
MACARISING	MACERATORS	MACHISMO	MACROBIOTIC
MACARISM	MACERS	MACHISMOS	MACROBIOTICS
MACARISMS	MACES	MACHMETER	MACROCARPA

MACROCARPAS
MACROCEPHALIA
MACROCEPHALIC
MACROCEPHALIES
MACROCEPHALOUS
MACROCEPHALY
MACROCLIMATE
MACROCLIMATES
MACROCLIMATIC
MACROCODE
MACROCODES
MACROCOPIES
MACROCOPY
MACROCOSM
MACROCOSMIC
MACROCOSMICALLY
MACROCOSMS
MACROCYCLE
MACROCYCLES
MACROCYCLIC
MACROCYST
MACROCYSTS
MACROCYTE
MACROCYTES
MACROCYTIC
MACROCYTOSES
MACROCYTOSIS
MACRODACTYL
MACRODACTYLIC
MACRODACTYLIES
MACRODACTYLOUS
MACRODACTYLY
MACRODIAGONAL
MACRODIAGONALS
MACRODOME
MACRODOMES
MACROECONOMIC
MACROECONOMICS
MACROEVOLUTION
MACROEVOLUTIONS
MACROFAUNA
MACROFLORA
MACROFOSSIL
MACROFOSSILS
MACROGAMETE
MACROGAMETES
MACROGLIA
MACROGLOBULIN
MACROGLOBULINS
MACROGRAPH
MACROGRAPHIC
MACROGRAPHS
MACROLOGIES
MACROLOGY
MACROMERE
MACROMERES

MACROMOLECULAR
MACROMOLECULE
MACROMOLECULES
MACRON
MACRONS
MACRONUCLEAR
MACRONUCLEI
MACRONUCLEUS
MACRONUTRIENT
MACRONUTRIENTS
MACROPHAGE
MACROPHAGES
MACROPHAGIC
MACROPHAGOUS
MACROPHOTOGRAPH
MACROPHYSICS
MACROPHYTE
MACROPHYTES
MACROPHYTIC
MACROPINAKOID
MACROPINAKOIDS
MACROPOD
MACROPODS
MACROPRISM
MACROPRISMS
MACROPSIA
MACROPTEROUS
MACROS
MACROSCALE
MACROSCALES
MACROSCOPIC
MACROSCOPICALLY
MACROSOCIOLOGY
MACROSPORANGIA
MACROSPORANGIUM
MACROSPORE
MACROSPORES
MACROSTRUCTURAL
MACROSTRUCTURE
MACROSTRUCTURES
MACROTOUS
MACROZAMIA
MACROZAMIAS
MACRURAL
MACRURAN
MACRURANS
MACRUROID
MACRUROUS
MACS
MACTATION
MACTATIONS
MACULA
MACULAE
MACULAR
MACULAS
MACULATE

MACULATED
MACULATES
MACULATING
MACULATION
MACULATIONS
MACULATURE
MACULATURES
MACULE
MACULED
MACULES
MACULING
MACULOSE
MACUMBA
MACUMBAS
MAD
MADAFU
MADAM
MADAME
MADAMED
MADAMES
MADAMING
MADAMS
MADAROSES
MADAROSIS
MADBRAIN
MADBRAINED
MADCAP
MADCAPS
MADDED
MADDEN
MADDENED
MADDENING
MADDENINGLY
MADDENINGNESS
MADDENS
MADDER
MADDERS
MADDEST
MADDING
MADDINGLY
MADDISH
MADDOCK
MADDOCKS
MADE
MADEFACTION
MADEFACTIONS
MADEFIED
MADEFIES
MADEFY
MADEFYING
MADEIRA
MADEIRAS
MADELEINE
MADELEINES
MADEMOISELLE
MADEMOISELLES

MADERISATION
MADERISATIONS
MADERISE
MADERISED
MADERISES
MADERISING
MADERIZATION
MADERIZATIONS
MADERIZE
MADERIZED
MADERIZES
MADERIZING
MADGE
MADGES
MADHOUSE
MADHOUSES
MADID
MADISON
MADISONS
MADLING
MADLINGS
MADLY
MADMAN
MADMEN
MADNESS
MADNESSES
MADONNA
MADONNAISH
MADONNAS
MADONNAWISE
MADOQUA
MADOQUAS
MADRAS
MADRASA
MADRASAH
MADRASAHS
MADRASAS
MADRASES
MADRASSA
MADRASSAH
MADRASSAHS
MADRASSAS
MADRE
MADREPORAL
MADREPORE
MADREPORES
MADREPORIAN
MADREPORIANS
MADREPORIC
MADREPORITE
MADREPORITES
MADREPORITIC
MADRES
MADRIGAL
MADRIGALESQUE
MADRIGALIAN

MADRIGALIST
MADRIGALISTS
MADRIGALS
MADRILENE
MADRILENES
MADRONA
MADRONAS
MADRONE
MADRONES
MADRONO
MADRONOS
MADS
MADURO
MADUROS
MADWOMAN
MADWOMEN
MADWORT
MADWORTS
MADZOON
MADZOONS
MAE
MAELID
MAELIDS
MAELSTROM
MAELSTROMS
MAENAD
MAENADES
MAENADIC
MAENADICALLY
MAENADISM
MAENADS
MAES
MAESTOSO
MAESTOSOS
MAESTRI
MAESTRO
MAESTROS
MAFFIA
MAFFIAS
MAFFICK
MAFFICKED
MAFFICKER
MAFFICKERS
MAFFICKING
MAFFICKINGS
MAFFICKS
MAFFLED
MAFFLIN
MAFFLING
MAFFLINGS
MAFFLINS
MAFIA
MAFIAS
MAFIC
MAFICS
MAFIOSI

MAFIOSO
MAFIOSOS
MAFTED
MAFTIR
MAFTIRS
MAG
MAGAININ
MAGAININS
MAGALOG
MAGALOGS
MAGALOGUE
MAGALOGUES
MAGAZINE
MAGAZINES
MAGAZINIST
MAGAZINISTS
MAGDALEN
MAGDALENE
MAGDALENES
MAGDALENS
MAGE
MAGENTA
MAGENTAS
MAGES
MAGESHIP
MAGESHIPS
MAGG
MAGGED
MAGGIE
MAGGIES
MAGGING
MAGGOT
MAGGOTIER
MAGGOTIEST
MAGGOTORIUM
MAGGOTS
MAGGOTY
MAGGS
MAGHRIBI
MAGI
MAGIAN
MAGIANISM
MAGIANISMS
MAGIANS
MAGIC
MAGICAL
MAGICALLY
MAGICIAN
MAGICIANS
MAGICKED
MAGICKING
MAGICS
MAGILP
MAGILPS
MAGISM
MAGISMS

MAGISTER
MAGISTERIAL
MAGISTERIALLY
MAGISTERIALNESS
MAGISTERIES
MAGISTERIUM
MAGISTERIUMS
MAGISTERS
MAGISTERY
MAGISTRACIES
MAGISTRACY
MAGISTRAL
MAGISTRALITIES
MAGISTRALITY
MAGISTRALLY
MAGISTRALS
MAGISTRAND
MAGISTRANDS
MAGISTRATE
MAGISTRATES
MAGISTRATESHIP
MAGISTRATIC
MAGISTRATICAL
MAGISTRATICALLY
MAGISTRATURE
MAGISTRATURES
MAGLEV
MAGLEVS
MAGMA
MAGMAS
MAGMATA
MAGMATIC
MAGMATISM
MAGNALIUM
MAGNALIUMS
MAGNANIMITIES
MAGNANIMITY
MAGNANIMOUS
MAGNANIMOUSLY
MAGNANIMOUSNESS
MAGNATE
MAGNATES
MAGNATESHIP
MAGNES
MAGNESES
MAGNESIA
MAGNESIAL
MAGNESIAN
MAGNESIAS
MAGNESIC
MAGNESITE
MAGNESITES
MAGNESIUM
MAGNESIUMS
MAGNESSTONE
MAGNESSTONES

MAGNET
MAGNETAR
MAGNETARS
MAGNETIC
MAGNETICAL
MAGNETICALLY
MAGNETICIAN
MAGNETICIANS
MAGNETICS
MAGNETISABLE
MAGNETISATION
MAGNETISATIONS
MAGNETISE
MAGNETISED
MAGNETISER
MAGNETISERS
MAGNETISES
MAGNETISING
MAGNETISM
MAGNETISMS
MAGNETIST
MAGNETISTS
MAGNETITE
MAGNETITES
MAGNETITIC
MAGNETIZABLE
MAGNETIZATION
MAGNETIZATIONS
MAGNETIZE
MAGNETIZED
MAGNETIZER
MAGNETIZERS
MAGNETIZES
MAGNETIZING
MAGNETO
MAGNETOCHEMICAL
MAGNETOELECTRIC
MAGNETOGRAPH
MAGNETOGRAPHS
MAGNETOMETER
MAGNETOMETERS
MAGNETOMETRIC
MAGNETOMETRIES
MAGNETOMETRY
MAGNETOMOTIVE
MAGNETON
MAGNETONS
MAGNETOPAUSE
MAGNETOPAUSES
MAGNETOS
MAGNETOSPHERE
MAGNETOSPHERES
MAGNETOSPHERIC
MAGNETOSTATIC
MAGNETOSTATICS
MAGNETRON

MAGNETRONS	MAHARANEE	MAIDENLY	MAILMERGE
MAGNETS	MAHARANEES	MAIDENS	MAILMERGED
MAGNIFIABLE	MAHARANI	MAIDENWEED	MAILMERGES
MAGNIFIC	MAHARANIS	MAIDENWEEDS	MAILMERGING
MAGNIFICAL	MAHARISHI	MAIDHOOD	MAILPOUCH
MAGNIFICALLY	MAHARISHIS	MAIDHOODS	MAILPOUCHES
MAGNIFICAT	MAHATMA	MAIDING	MAILROOM
MAGNIFICATION	MAHATMAISM	MAIDISH	MAILROOMS
MAGNIFICATIONS	MAHATMAISMS	MAIDISHNESS	MAILS
MAGNIFICATS	MAHATMAS	MAIDISM	MAILSACK
MAGNIFICENCE	MAHEWU	MAIDISMS	MAILSACKS
MAGNIFICENCES	MAHIMAHI	MAIDLESS	MAILSHOT
MAGNIFICENT	MAHJONG	MAIDS	MAILSHOTS
MAGNIFICENTLY	MAHJONGG	MAIDSERVANT	MAILSHOTTED
MAGNIFICENTNESS	MAHJONGGS	MAIDSERVANTS	MAILSHOTTING
MAGNIFICO	MAHJONGS	MAIEUTIC	MAILVAN
MAGNIFICOES	MAHLSTICK	MAIEUTICAL	MAILVANS
MAGNIFICOS	MAHLSTICKS	MAIEUTICS	MAIM
MAGNIFIED	MAHMAL	MAIGRE	MAIMAI
MAGNIFIER	MAHMALS	MAIGRES	MAIMAIS
MAGNIFIERS	MAHOE	MAIHEM	MAIMED
MAGNIFIES	MAHOES	MAIHEMS	MAIMEDNESS
MAGNIFY	MAHOGANIES	MAIK	MAIMEDNESSES
MAGNIFYING	MAHOGANY	MAIKO	MAIMER
MAGNILOQUENCE	MAHONIA	MAIKOS	MAIMERS
MAGNILOQUENCES	MAHONIAS	MAIKS	MAIMING
MAGNILOQUENT	MAHOUT	MAIL	MAIMINGS
MAGNILOQUENTLY	MAHOUTS	MAILABILITIES	MAIMS
MAGNITUDE	MAHSEER	MAILABILITY	MAIN
MAGNITUDES	MAHSEERS	MAILABLE	MAINBOOM
MAGNITUDINOUS	MAHSIR	MAILBAG	MAINBOOMS
MAGNOLIA	MAHSIRS	MAILBAGS	MAINBRACE
MAGNOLIACEOUS	MAHUA	MAILBOX	MAINBRACES
MAGNOLIAS	MAHUANG	MAILBOXES	MAINDOOR
MAGNON	MAHUANGS	MAILCAR	MAINDOORS
MAGNONS	MAHUAS	MAILCARS	MAINED
MAGNOX	MAHWA	MAILCOACH	MAINER
MAGNOXES	MAHWAS	MAILCOACHES	MAINEST
MAGNUM	MAHZOR	MAILE	MAINFRAME
MAGNUMS	MAHZORIM	MAILED	MAINFRAMES
MAGNUS	MAHZORS	MAILER	MAINING
MAGOT	MAID	MAILERS	MAINLAND
MAGOTS	MAIDAN	MAILES	MAINLANDER
MAGPIE	MAIDANS	MAILGRAM	MAINLANDERS
MAGPIES	MAIDED	MAILGRAMMED	MAINLANDS
MAGS	MAIDEN	MAILGRAMMING	MAINLINE
MAGSMAN	MAIDENHAIR	MAILGRAMS	MAINLINED
MAGSMEN	MAIDENHAIRS	MAILING	MAINLINER
MAGUEY	MAIDENHEAD	MAILINGS	MAINLINERS
MAGUEYS	MAIDENHEADS	MAILL	MAINLINES
MAGUS	MAIDENHOOD	MAILLESS	MAINLINING
MAGYAR	MAIDENHOODS	MAILLOT	MAINLININGS
MAHARAJA	MAIDENISH	MAILLOTS	MAINLY
MAHARAJAH	MAIDENLIKE	MAILLS	MAINMAST
MAHARAJAHS	MAIDENLINESS	MAILMAN	MAINMASTS
MAHARAJAS	MAIDENLINESSES	MAILMEN	MAINOR

MAINORS
MAINOUR
MAINOURS
MAINPERNOR
MAINPERNORS
MAINPRISE
MAINPRISES
MAINS
MAINSAIL
MAINSAILS
MAINSHEET
MAINSHEETS
MAINSPRING
MAINSPRINGS
MAINSTAY
MAINSTAYS
MAINSTREAM
MAINSTREAMED
MAINSTREAMING
MAINSTREAMS
MAINSTREETING
MAINSTREETINGS
MAINTAIN
MAINTAINABILITY
MAINTAINABLE
MAINTAINED
MAINTAINER
MAINTAINERS
MAINTAINING
MAINTAINS
MAINTENANCE
MAINTENANCED
MAINTENANCES
MAINTENANCING
MAINTOP
MAINTOPMAST
MAINTOPMASTS
MAINTOPS
MAINTOPSAIL
MAINTOPSAILS
MAINYARD
MAINYARDS
MAIOLICA
MAIOLICAS
MAIR
MAIRE
MAIRES
MAIRS
MAISE
MAISES
MAISONETTE
MAISONETTES
MAISONNETTE
MAISONNETTES
MAIST
MAISTER

MAISTERDOME
MAISTERDOMES
MAISTERED
MAISTERING
MAISTERS
MAISTRIES
MAISTRING
MAISTRINGS
MAISTRY
MAISTS
MAIZE
MAIZES
MAJAGUA
MAJAGUAS
MAJESTIC
MAJESTICAL
MAJESTICALLY
MAJESTICALNESS
MAJESTICNESS
MAJESTICNESSES
MAJESTIES
MAJESTY
MAJLIS
MAJLISES
MAJOLICA
MAJOLICAS
MAJOLICAWARE
MAJOLICAWARES
MAJOR
MAJORAT
MAJORATS
MAJORDOMO
MAJORDOMOS
MAJORED
MAJORETTE
MAJORETTES
MAJORETTING
MAJORETTINGS
MAJORING
MAJORITAIRE
MAJORITAIRES
MAJORITARIAN
MAJORITARIANISM
MAJORITARIANS
MAJORITIES
MAJORITY
MAJORLY
MAJORS
MAJORSHIP
MAJORSHIPS
MAJUSCULAR
MAJUSCULE
MAJUSCULES
MAK
MAKABLE
MAKAR

MAKARS
MAKE
MAKEABLE
MAKEBATE
MAKEBATES
MAKEFAST
MAKEFASTS
MAKELESS
MAKEOVER
MAKEOVERS
MAKER
MAKEREADIES
MAKEREADY
MAKERS
MAKES
MAKESHIFT
MAKESHIFTS
MAKEUP
MAKEUPS
MAKEWEIGHT
MAKEWEIGHTS
MAKIMONO
MAKIMONOS
MAKING
MAKINGS
MAKIT
MAKO
MAKOMAKO
MAKOMAKOS
MAKOS
MAKS
MAKUNOUCHI
MAKUNOUCHIS
MAKUTA
MAKUTU
MAKUTUS
MAL
MALA
MALABSORPTION
MALABSORPTIONS
MALACCA
MALACCAS
MALACHITE
MALACHITES
MALACIA
MALACIAS
MALACOLOGICAL
MALACOLOGICALLY
MALACOLOGIES
MALACOLOGIST
MALACOLOGISTS
MALACOLOGY
MALACOPHILIES
MALACOPHILOUS
MALACOPHILY
MALACOPHYLLOUS

MALACOPTERYGIAN
MALACOSTRACAN
MALACOSTRACANS
MALACOSTRACOUS
MALADAPTATION
MALADAPTATIONS
MALADAPTED
MALADAPTIVE
MALADAPTIVELY
MALADDRESS
MALADDRESSES
MALADIES
MALADJUSTED
MALADJUSTIVE
MALADJUSTMENT
MALADJUSTMENTS
MALADMINISTER
MALADMINISTERED
MALADMINISTERS
MALADROIT
MALADROITLY
MALADROITNESS
MALADROITNESSES
MALADY
MALAGUENA
MALAGUENAS
MALAGUETTA
MALAGUETTAS
MALAISE
MALAISES
MALAKATOONE
MALAKATOONES
MALAM
MALAMS
MALAMUTE
MALAMUTES
MALANDER
MALANDERS
MALANGA
MALANGAS
MALAPERT
MALAPERTLY
MALAPERTNESS
MALAPERTNESSES
MALAPERTS
MALAPPORTIONED
MALAPPROPRIATE
MALAPPROPRIATED
MALAPPROPRIATES
MALAPROP
MALAPROPIAN
MALAPROPISM
MALAPROPISMS
MALAPROPIST
MALAPROPISTS
MALAPROPOS

MALAPROPS	MALEDICTORY	MALICED	MALLARD
MALAR	MALEDICTS	MALICES	MALLARDS
MALARIA	MALEFACTION	MALICHO	MALLEABILITIES
MALARIAL	MALEFACTIONS	MALICHOS	MALLEABILITY
MALARIAN	MALEFACTOR	MALICING	MALLEABLE
MALARIAS	MALEFACTORS	MALICIOUS	MALLEABLENESS
MALARIOLOGIES	MALEFACTORY	MALICIOUSLY	MALLEABLENESSES
MALARIOLOGIST	MALEFACTRESS	MALICIOUSNESS	MALLEABLY
MALARIOLOGISTS	MALEFACTRESSES	MALICIOUSNESSES	MALLEATE
MALARIOLOGY	MALEFFECT	MALIGN	MALLEATED
MALARIOUS	MALEFFECTS	MALIGNANCE	MALLEATES
MALARKEY	MALEFIC	MALIGNANCES	MALLEATING
MALARKEYS	MALEFICALLY	MALIGNANCIES	MALLEATION
MALARKIES	MALEFICE	MALIGNANCY	MALLEATIONS
MALARKY	MALEFICENCE	MALIGNANT	MALLECHO
MALAROMA	MALEFICENCES	MALIGNANTLY	MALLECHOS
MALAROMAS	MALEFICENT	MALIGNANTS	MALLED
MALARS	MALEFICES	MALIGNED	MALLEE
MALAS	MALEFICIAL	MALIGNER	MALLEES
MALASSIMILATION	MALEIC	MALIGNERS	MALLEI
MALATE	MALEMIUT	MALIGNING	MALLEIFORM
MALATES	MALEMIUTS	MALIGNITIES	MALLEMAROKING
MALATHION	MALEMUTE	MALIGNITY	MALLEMAROKINGS
MALATHIONS	MALEMUTES	MALIGNLY	MALLEMUCK
MALAX	MALENESS	MALIGNMENT	MALLEMUCKS
MALAXAGE	MALENESSES	MALIGNMENTS	MALLENDER
MALAXAGES	MALENGINE	MALIGNS	MALLENDERS
MALAXATE	MALENGINES	MALIHINI	MALLEOLAR
MALAXATED	MALENTENDU	MALIHINIS	MALLEOLI
MALAXATES	MALENTENDUS	MALIK	MALLEOLUS
MALAXATING	MALES	MALIKS	MALLEOLUSES
MALAXATION	MALEVOLENCE	MALIMPRINTED	MALLET
MALAXATIONS	MALEVOLENCES	MALIMPRINTING	MALLETS
MALAXATOR	MALEVOLENT	MALINE	MALLEUS
MALAXATORS	MALEVOLENTLY	MALINES	MALLEUSES
MALAXED	MALFEASANCE	MALINGER	MALLING
MALAXES	MALFEASANCES	MALINGERED	MALLOPHAGOUS
MALAXING	MALFEASANT	MALINGERER	MALLOW
MALCONFORMATION	MALFEASANTS	MALINGERERS	MALLOWPUFF
MALCONTENT	MALFED	MALINGERIES	MALLOWPUFFS
MALCONTENTED	MALFORMATION	MALINGERING	MALLOWS
MALCONTENTEDLY	MALFORMATIONS	MALINGERS	MALLS
MALCONTENTS	MALFORMED	MALINGERY	MALM
MALDEPLOYMENT	MALFUNCTION	MALIS	MALMAG
MALDEPLOYMENTS	MALFUNCTIONED	MALISM	MALMAGS
MALDISTRIBUTION	MALFUNCTIONING	MALISMS	MALMIER
MALE	MALFUNCTIONINGS	MALISON	MALMIEST
MALEATE	MALFUNCTIONS	MALISONS	MALMS
MALEATES	MALGRADO	MALIST	MALMSEY
MALEDICENT	MALGRE	MALKIN	MALMSEYS
MALEDICT	MALGRED	MALKINS	MALMSTONE
MALEDICTED	MALGRES	MALL	MALMSTONES
MALEDICTING	MALGRING	MALLAM	MALMY
MALEDICTION	MALI	MALLAMS	MALNOURISHED
MALEDICTIONS	MALIC	MALLANDER	MALNUTRITION
MALEDICTIVE	MALICE	MALLANDERS	MALNUTRITIONS

MALOCCLUDED
MALOCCLUSION
MALOCCLUSIONS
MALODOR
MALODOROUS
MALODOROUSLY
MALODOROUSNESS
MALODORS
MALODOUR
MALODOURS
MALOLACTIC
MALONATE
MALONATES
MALONIC
MALONYLUREA
MALOTI
MALPIGHIACEOUS
MALPOSED
MALPOSITION
MALPOSITIONS
MALPRACTICE
MALPRACTICES
MALPRACTITIONER
MALPRESENTATION
MALS
MALSTICK
MALSTICKS
MALT
MALTALENT
MALTALENTS
MALTASE
MALTASES
MALTED
MALTEDS
MALTHA
MALTHAS
MALTIER
MALTIEST
MALTINESS
MALTING
MALTINGS
MALTMAN
MALTMEN
MALTOL
MALTOLS
MALTOSE
MALTOSES
MALTREAT
MALTREATED
MALTREATER
MALTREATERS
MALTREATING
MALTREATMENT
MALTREATMENTS
MALTREATS
MALTS

MALTSTER
MALTSTERS
MALTWORM
MALTWORMS
MALTY
MALVA
MALVACEOUS
MALVAS
MALVASIA
MALVASIAN
MALVASIAS
MALVERSATION
MALVERSATIONS
MALVESIE
MALVESIES
MALVOISIE
MALVOISIES
MALWA
MAM
MAMA
MAMAGUY
MAMAGUYED
MAMAGUYING
MAMAGUYS
MAMALIGA
MAMALIGAS
MAMAS
MAMBA
MAMBAS
MAMBO
MAMBOED
MAMBOES
MAMBOING
MAMBOS
MAMEE
MAMEES
MAMELON
MAMELONS
MAMELUCO
MAMELUCOS
MAMELUKE
MAMELUKES
MAMEY
MAMEYES
MAMEYS
MAMIE
MAMIES
MAMILLA
MAMILLAE
MAMILLAR
MAMILLARY
MAMILLATE
MAMILLATED
MAMILLATION
MAMILLATIONS
MAMILLIFORM

MAMLUK
MAMLUKS
MAMMA
MAMMAE
MAMMAL
MAMMALIAN
MAMMALIANS
MAMMALIFEROUS
MAMMALLIKE
MAMMALOGICAL
MAMMALOGIES
MAMMALOGIST
MAMMALOGISTS
MAMMALOGY
MAMMALS
MAMMARY
MAMMAS
MAMMATE
MAMMATI
MAMMATUS
MAMMECTOMIES
MAMMECTOMY
MAMMEE
MAMMEES
MAMMER
MAMMERED
MAMMERING
MAMMERS
MAMMET
MAMMETRIES
MAMMETRY
MAMMETS
MAMMEY
MAMMEYS
MAMMIE
MAMMIES
MAMMIFER
MAMMIFEROUS
MAMMIFERS
MAMMIFORM
MAMMILLA
MAMMILLAE
MAMMILLARIA
MAMMILLARIAS
MAMMILLARY
MAMMILLATE
MAMMILLATED
MAMMITIDES
MAMMITIS
MAMMOCK
MAMMOCKED
MAMMOCKING
MAMMOCKS
MAMMOGENIC
MAMMOGRAM
MAMMOGRAMS

MAMMOGRAPH
MAMMOGRAPHIC
MAMMOGRAPHIES
MAMMOGRAPHS
MAMMOGRAPHY
MAMMON
MAMMONISH
MAMMONISM
MAMMONISMS
MAMMONIST
MAMMONISTIC
MAMMONISTS
MAMMONITE
MAMMONITES
MAMMONS
MAMMOPLASTIES
MAMMOPLASTY
MAMMOTH
MAMMOTHS
MAMMY
MAMPARA
MAMPARAS
MAMPOER
MAMS
MAMSELLE
MAMSELLES
MAMZER
MAMZERIM
MAMZERS
MAN
MANA
MANACLE
MANACLED
MANACLES
MANACLING
MANAGE
MANAGEABILITIES
MANAGEABILITY
MANAGEABLE
MANAGEABLENESS
MANAGEABLY
MANAGED
MANAGEMENT
MANAGEMENTAL
MANAGEMENTS
MANAGER
MANAGERESS
MANAGERESSES
MANAGERIAL
MANAGERIALISM
MANAGERIALISMS
MANAGERIALIST
MANAGERIALISTS
MANAGERIALLY
MANAGERS
MANAGERSHIP

MANAGERSHIPS
MANAGES
MANAGING
MANAIA
MANAIAS
MANAKIN
MANAKINS
MANANA
MANANAS
MANAS
MANAT
MANATEE
MANATEES
MANATI
MANATIS
MANATOID
MANCALA
MANCALAS
MANCANDO
MANCHE
MANCHES
MANCHESTER
MANCHESTERS
MANCHET
MANCHETS
MANCHINEEL
MANCHINEELS
MANCIPATE
MANCIPATED
MANCIPATES
MANCIPATING
MANCIPATION
MANCIPATIONS
MANCIPATORY
MANCIPLE
MANCIPLES
MANCUS
MANCUSES
MAND
MANDALA
MANDALAS
MANDALIC
MANDAMUS
MANDAMUSED
MANDAMUSES
MANDAMUSING
MANDARIN
MANDARINATE
MANDARINATES
MANDARINE
MANDARINES
MANDARINIC
MANDARINISM
MANDARINISMS
MANDARINS
MANDATARIES

MANDATARY
MANDATE
MANDATED
MANDATES
MANDATING
MANDATOR
MANDATORIES
MANDATORILY
MANDATORS
MANDATORY
MANDI
MANDIBLE
MANDIBLES
MANDIBULAR
MANDIBULATE
MANDIBULATED
MANDILION
MANDILIONS
MANDIOC
MANDIOCA
MANDIOCAS
MANDIOCCA
MANDIOCCAS
MANDIOCS
MANDIR
MANDIRA
MANDIRAS
MANDIRS
MANDIS
MANDOLA
MANDOLAS
MANDOLIN
MANDOLINE
MANDOLINES
MANDOLINIST
MANDOLINISTS
MANDOLINS
MANDOM
MANDOMS
MANDORA
MANDORAS
MANDORLA
MANDORLAS
MANDRAGORA
MANDRAGORAS
MANDRAKE
MANDRAKES
MANDREL
MANDRELS
MANDRIL
MANDRILL
MANDRILLS
MANDRILS
MANDUCABLE
MANDUCATE
MANDUCATED

MANDUCATES
MANDUCATING
MANDUCATION
MANDUCATIONS
MANDUCATORY
MANDYLION
MANDYLIONS
MANE
MANED
MANEGE
MANEGED
MANEGES
MANEGING
MANEH
MANEHS
MANELESS
MANENT
MANES
MANET
MANEUVER
MANEUVERABILITY
MANEUVERABLE
MANEUVERED
MANEUVERER
MANEUVERERS
MANEUVERING
MANEUVERINGS
MANEUVERS
MANFUL
MANFULLY
MANFULNESS
MANFULNESSES
MANG
MANGA
MANGABEIRA
MANGABEIRAS
MANGABEY
MANGABEYS
MANGABIES
MANGABY
MANGAL
MANGALS
MANGALSUTRA
MANGALSUTRAS
MANGANATE
MANGANATES
MANGANESE
MANGANESES
MANGANESIAN
MANGANIC
MANGANIFEROUS
MANGANITE
MANGANITES
MANGANOUS
MANGAS
MANGE

MANGED
MANGEL
MANGELS
MANGELWURZEL
MANGELWURZELS
MANGER
MANGERS
MANGES
MANGETOUT
MANGETOUTS
MANGEY
MANGIER
MANGIEST
MANGILY
MANGINESS
MANGINESSES
MANGING
MANGLE
MANGLED
MANGLER
MANGLERS
MANGLES
MANGLING
MANGO
MANGOES
MANGOLD
MANGOLDS
MANGOLDWURZEL
MANGOLDWURZELS
MANGONEL
MANGONELS
MANGOS
MANGOSTAN
MANGOSTANS
MANGOSTEEN
MANGOSTEENS
MANGOUSTE
MANGOUSTES
MANGROVE
MANGROVES
MANGS
MANGULATE
MANGULATED
MANGULATES
MANGULATING
MANGULATION
MANGY
MANHANDLE
MANHANDLED
MANHANDLES
MANHANDLING
MANHATTAN
MANHATTANS
MANHOLE
MANHOLES
MANHOOD

MANHOODS	MANIHOCS	MANMADE	MANOMETRY
MANHUNT	MANIHOT	MANNA	MANOR
MANHUNTER	MANIHOTS	MANNAN	MANORIAL
MANHUNTERS	MANIKIN	MANNANS	MANORIALISM
MANHUNTS	MANIKINS	MANNAS	MANORIALISMS
MANI	MANILA	MANNED	MANORS
MANIA	MANILAS	MANNEQUIN	MANOS
MANIAC	MANILLA	MANNEQUINS	MANOSCOPIC
MANIACAL	MANILLAS	MANNER	MANOSCOPY
MANIACALLY	MANILLE	MANNERED	MANPACK
MANIACS	MANILLES	MANNERISM	MANPACKS
MANIAS	MANIOC	MANNERISMS	MANPOWER
MANIC	MANIOCA	MANNERIST	MANPOWERS
MANICALLY	MANIOCAS	MANNERISTIC	MANQUE
MANICOTTI	MANIOCS	MANNERISTICAL	MANRED
MANICS	MANIPLE	MANNERISTICALLY	MANREDS
MANICURE	MANIPLES	MANNERISTS	MANRENT
MANICURED	MANIPLIES	MANNERLESS	MANRENTS
MANICURES	MANIPULABILITY	MANNERLESSNESS	MANRIDER
MANICURING	MANIPULABLE	MANNERLINESS	MANRIDERS
MANICURIST	MANIPULAR	MANNERLINESSES	MANRIDING
MANICURISTS	MANIPULARS	MANNERLY	MANROPE
MANIES	MANIPULATABLE	MANNERS	MANROPES
MANIFEST	MANIPULATE	MANNIFEROUS	MANS
MANIFESTABLE	MANIPULATED	MANNIKIN	MANSARD
MANIFESTANT	MANIPULATES	MANNIKINS	MANSARDED
MANIFESTANTS	MANIPULATING	MANNING	MANSARDS
MANIFESTATION	MANIPULATION	MANNISH	MANSE
MANIFESTATIONAL	MANIPULATIONS	MANNISHLY	MANSERVANT
MANIFESTATIONS	MANIPULATIVE	MANNISHNESS	MANSES
MANIFESTATIVE	MANIPULATIVELY	MANNISHNESSES	MANSHIFT
MANIFESTED	MANIPULATOR	MANNITE	MANSHIFTS
MANIFESTER	MANIPULATORS	MANNITES	MANSION
MANIFESTERS	MANIPULATORY	MANNITIC	MANSIONARIES
MANIFESTIBLE	MANIS	MANNITOL	MANSIONARY
MANIFESTING	MANITO	MANNITOLS	MANSIONS
MANIFESTLY	MANITOS	MANNOSE	MANSLAUGHTER
MANIFESTNESS	MANITOU	MANNOSES	MANSLAUGHTERS
MANIFESTNESSES	MANITOUS	MANO	MANSLAYER
MANIFESTO	MANITU	MANOAO	MANSLAYERS
MANIFESTOED	MANITUS	MANOAOS	MANSONRIES
MANIFESTOES	MANJACK	MANOEUVRABILITY	MANSONRY
MANIFESTOING	MANJACKS	MANOEUVRABLE	MANSUETE
MANIFESTOS	MANKIER	MANOEUVRE	MANSUETUDE
MANIFESTS	MANKIEST	MANOEUVRED	MANSUETUDES
MANIFOLD	MANKIND	MANOEUVRER	MANSWORN
MANIFOLDED	MANKINDS	MANOEUVRERS	MANTA
MANIFOLDER	MANKY	MANOEUVRES	MANTAS
MANIFOLDERS	MANLESS	MANOEUVRING	MANTEAU
MANIFOLDING	MANLIER	MANOEUVRINGS	MANTEAUS
MANIFOLDLY	MANLIEST	MANOMETER	MANTEAUX
MANIFOLDNESS	MANLIKE	MANOMETERS	MANTEEL
MANIFOLDNESSES	MANLILY	MANOMETRIC	MANTEELS
MANIFOLDS	MANLINESS	MANOMETRICAL	MANTEL
MANIFORM	MANLINESSES	MANOMETRICALLY	MANTELET
MANIHOC	MANLY	MANOMETRIES	MANTELETS

MANTELLETTA
MANTELLETTAS
MANTELPIECE
MANTELPIECES
MANTELS
MANTELSHELF
MANTELSHELVES
MANTELTREE
MANTELTREES
MANTES
MANTIC
MANTICALLY
MANTICORA
MANTICORAS
MANTICORE
MANTICORES
MANTID
MANTIDS
MANTIES
MANTILLA
MANTILLAS
MANTIS
MANTISES
MANTISSA
MANTISSAS
MANTLE
MANTLED
MANTLES
MANTLET
MANTLETREE
MANTLETREES
MANTLETS
MANTLING
MANTLINGS
MANTO
MANTOES
MANTOS
MANTRA
MANTRAM
MANTRAMS
MANTRAP
MANTRAPS
MANTRAS
MANTRIC
MANTUA
MANTUAS
MANTY
MANUAL
MANUALLY
MANUALS
MANUARY
MANUBRIA
MANUBRIAL
MANUBRIUM
MANUBRIUMS
MANUFACTORIES

MANUFACTORY
MANUFACTURABLE
MANUFACTURAL
MANUFACTURE
MANUFACTURED
MANUFACTURER
MANUFACTURERS
MANUFACTURES
MANUFACTURING
MANUFACTURINGS
MANUHIRI
MANUHIRIS
MANUKA
MANUKAS
MANUL
MANULS
MANUMEA
MANUMEAS
MANUMISSION
MANUMISSIONS
MANUMIT
MANUMITS
MANUMITTED
MANUMITTER
MANUMITTERS
MANUMITTING
MANURANCE
MANURANCES
MANURE
MANURED
MANURER
MANURERS
MANURES
MANURIAL
MANURING
MANURINGS
MANUS
MANUSCRIPT
MANUSCRIPTS
MANUWHIRI
MANWARD
MANWARDS
MANWISE
MANY
MANYATA
MANYATAS
MANYATTA
MANYATTAS
MANYFOLD
MANYPLIES
MANZANILLA
MANZANILLAS
MANZANITA
MANZANITAS
MANZELLO
MANZELLOS

MAOMAO
MAOMAOS
MAORMOR
MAORMORS
MAP
MAPAU
MAPAUS
MAPLE
MAPLES
MAPLESS
MAPLIKE
MAPMAKER
MAPMAKERS
MAPMAKING
MAPMAKINGS
MAPOU
MAPOUS
MAPPABLE
MAPPED
MAPPEMOND
MAPPEMONDS
MAPPER
MAPPERIES
MAPPERS
MAPPERY
MAPPING
MAPPINGS
MAPPIST
MAPPISTS
MAPS
MAPSTICK
MAPSTICKS
MAPWISE
MAQUETTE
MAQUETTES
MAQUI
MAQUILADORA
MAQUILADORAS
MAQUILLAGE
MAQUILLAGES
MAQUIS
MAQUISARD
MAQUISARDS
MAR
MARA
MARABI
MARABOU
MARABOUS
MARABOUT
MARABOUTS
MARABUNTA
MARABUNTAS
MARACA
MARACAS
MARAE
MARAES

MARAGING
MARAGINGS
MARAH
MARAHS
MARANTA
MARANTAS
MARARI
MARARIS
MARAS
MARASCA
MARASCAS
MARASCHINO
MARASCHINOS
MARASMIC
MARASMUS
MARASMUSES
MARATHON
MARATHONER
MARATHONERS
MARATHONING
MARATHONINGS
MARATHONS
MARAUD
MARAUDED
MARAUDER
MARAUDERS
MARAUDING
MARAUDS
MARAVEDI
MARAVEDIS
MARBLE
MARBLED
MARBLEISE
MARBLEISED
MARBLEISES
MARBLEISING
MARBLEIZE
MARBLEIZED
MARBLEIZES
MARBLEIZING
MARBLER
MARBLERS
MARBLES
MARBLEWOOD
MARBLEWOODS
MARBLIER
MARBLIEST
MARBLING
MARBLINGS
MARBLY
MARC
MARCANTANT
MARCANTANTS
MARCASITE
MARCASITES
MARCASITICAL

MARCATISSIMO
MARCATO
MARCEL
MARCELLA
MARCELLAS
MARCELLED
MARCELLER
MARCELLERS
MARCELLING
MARCELS
MARCESCENCE
MARCESCENT
MARCESCIBLE
MARCH
MARCHANTIA
MARCHANTIAS
MARCHED
MARCHEN
MARCHER
MARCHERS
MARCHES
MARCHESA
MARCHESAS
MARCHESE
MARCHESES
MARCHESI
MARCHING
MARCHIONESS
MARCHIONESSES
MARCHLAND
MARCHLANDS
MARCHLIKE
MARCHMAN
MARCHMEN
MARCHPANE
MARCHPANES
MARCONI
MARCONIED
MARCONIGRAM
MARCONIGRAMS
MARCONIGRAPH
MARCONIGRAPHED
MARCONIGRAPHING
MARCONIGRAPHS
MARCONIING
MARCONIS
MARCS
MARD
MARDIED
MARDIER
MARDIES
MARDIEST
MARDY
MARDYING
MARE
MAREMMA

MAREMMAS
MAREMME
MARENGO
MARES
MARESCHAL
MARESCHALS
MARG
MARGARIC
MARGARIN
MARGARINE
MARGARINES
MARGARINS
MARGARITA
MARGARITAS
MARGARITE
MARGARITES
MARGARITIC
MARGARITIFEROUS
MARGAY
MARGAYS
MARGE
MARGENT
MARGENTED
MARGENTING
MARGENTS
MARGES
MARGIN
MARGINAL
MARGINALIA
MARGINALISATION
MARGINALISE
MARGINALISED
MARGINALISES
MARGINALISING
MARGINALISM
MARGINALISMS
MARGINALIST
MARGINALISTS
MARGINALITIES
MARGINALITY
MARGINALIZATION
MARGINALIZE
MARGINALIZED
MARGINALIZES
MARGINALIZING
MARGINALLY
MARGINALS
MARGINATE
MARGINATED
MARGINATES
MARGINATING
MARGINATION
MARGINATIONS
MARGINED
MARGINING
MARGINS

MARGOSA
MARGOSAS
MARGRAVATE
MARGRAVATES
MARGRAVE
MARGRAVES
MARGRAVIAL
MARGRAVIATE
MARGRAVIATES
MARGRAVINE
MARGRAVINES
MARGS
MARGUERITE
MARGUERITES
MARIA
MARIACHI
MARIACHIS
MARIALITE
MARIALITES
MARICULTURE
MARICULTURES
MARICULTURIST
MARICULTURISTS
MARID
MARIDS
MARIES
MARIGOLD
MARIGOLDS
MARIGRAM
MARIGRAMS
MARIGRAPH
MARIGRAPHS
MARIHUANA
MARIHUANAS
MARIJUANA
MARIJUANAS
MARIMBA
MARIMBAPHONE
MARIMBAPHONES
MARIMBAS
MARIMBIST
MARIMBISTS
MARINA
MARINADE
MARINADED
MARINADES
MARINADING
MARINARA
MARINARAS
MARINAS
MARINATE
MARINATED
MARINATES
MARINATING
MARINATION
MARINATIONS

MARINE
MARINER
MARINERA
MARINERAS
MARINERS
MARINES
MARINIERE
MARIONBERRIES
MARIONBERRY
MARIONETTE
MARIONETTES
MARIPOSA
MARIPOSAS
MARISCHAL
MARISCHALLED
MARISCHALLING
MARISCHALS
MARISH
MARISHES
MARITAGE
MARITAGES
MARITAL
MARITALLY
MARITIME
MARIVAUDAGE
MARIVAUDAGES
MARJORAM
MARJORAMS
MARK
MARKA
MARKAS
MARKDOWN
MARKDOWNS
MARKED
MARKEDLY
MARKEDNESS
MARKEDNESSES
MARKER
MARKERS
MARKET
MARKETABILITIES
MARKETABILITY
MARKETABLE
MARKETABLENESS
MARKETABLY
MARKETED
MARKETEER
MARKETEERS
MARKETER
MARKETERS
MARKETING
MARKETINGS
MARKETISATION
MARKETISATIONS
MARKETIZATION
MARKETIZATIONS

MARKETPLACE	MARMARISES	MARQUESSES	MARSALAS
MARKETPLACES	MARMARISING	MARQUETERIE	MARSE
MARKETS	MARMARIZE	MARQUETERIES	MARSEILLE
MARKHOOR	MARMARIZED	MARQUETRIES	MARSEILLES
MARKHOORS	MARMARIZES	MARQUETRY	MARSES
MARKHOR	MARMARIZING	MARQUIS	MARSH
MARKHORS	MARMAROSES	MARQUISATE	MARSHAL
MARKING	MARMAROSIS	MARQUISATES	MARSHALCIES
MARKINGS	MARMELISE	MARQUISE	MARSHALCY
MARKKA	MARMELISED	MARQUISES	MARSHALED
MARKKAA	MARMELISES	MARQUISETTE	MARSHALER
MARKKAS	MARMELISING	MARQUISETTES	MARSHALERS
MARKMAN	MARMELIZE	MARRAM	MARSHALING
MARKMEN	MARMELIZED	MARRAMS	MARSHALL
MARKS	MARMELIZES	MARRANO	MARSHALLED
MARKSMAN	MARMELIZING	MARRANOS	MARSHALLER
MARKSMANSHIP	MARMITE	MARRED	MARSHALLERS
MARKSMANSHIPS	MARMITES	MARRELS	MARSHALLING
MARKSMEN	MARMOREAL	MARRER	MARSHALLINGS
MARKSWOMAN	MARMOREALLY	MARRERS	MARSHALS
MARKSWOMEN	MARMOREAN	MARRI	MARSHALSHIP
MARKUP	MARMOSE	MARRIAGE	MARSHALSHIPS
MARKUPS	MARMOSES	MARRIAGEABILITY	MARSHBUCK
MARL	MARMOSET	MARRIAGEABLE	MARSHBUCKS
MARLACIOUS	MARMOSETS	MARRIAGES	MARSHES
MARLE	MARMOT	MARRIED	MARSHIER
MARLED	MARMOTS	MARRIEDS	MARSHIEST
MARLES	MARMS	MARRIER	MARSHINESS
MARLIER	MAROCAIN	MARRIERS	MARSHINESSES
MARLIEST	MAROCAINS	MARRIES	MARSHLAND
MARLIN	MARON	MARRING	MARSHLANDER
MARLINE	MARONS	MARRIS	MARSHLANDERS
MARLINES	MAROON	MARRON	MARSHLANDS
MARLINESPIKE	MAROONED	MARRONS	MARSHLIKE
MARLINESPIKES	MAROONER	MARROW	MARSHLOCKS
MARLING	MAROONERS	MARROWBONE	MARSHLOCKSES
MARLINGS	MAROONING	MARROWBONES	MARSHMALLOW
MARLINGSPIKE	MAROONINGS	MARROWED	MARSHMALLOWS
MARLINGSPIKES	MAROONS	MARROWFAT	MARSHMALLOWY
MARLINS	MAROQUIN	MARROWFATS	MARSHWORT
MARLINSPIKE	MAROQUINS	MARROWING	MARSHWORTS
MARLINSPIKES	MAROR	MARROWISH	MARSHY
MARLITE	MARORS	MARROWLESS	MARSIPOBRANCH
MARLITES	MARPLOT	MARROWS	MARSIPOBRANCHES
MARLITIC	MARPLOTS	MARROWSKIED	MARSIPOBRANCHS
MARLS	MARPRELATE	MARROWSKIES	MARSPORT
MARLSTONE	MARPRELATED	MARROWSKY	MARSPORTS
MARLSTONES	MARPRELATES	MARROWSKYING	MARSQUAKE
MARLY	MARPRELATING	MARROWY	MARSQUAKES
MARM	MARQUE	MARRUM	MARSUPIA
MARMALADE	MARQUEE	MARRUMS	MARSUPIAL
MARMALADES	MARQUEES	MARRY	MARSUPIALIAN
MARMALISE	MARQUES	MARRYING	MARSUPIALS
MARMALIZE	MARQUESS	MARRYINGS	MARSUPIAN
MARMARISE	MARQUESSATE	MARS	MARSUPIANS
MARMARISED	MARQUESSATES	MARSALA	

MARSUPIUM
MARSUPIUMS
MART
MARTAGON
MARTAGONS
MARTED
MARTEL
MARTELLANDO
MARTELLATO
MARTELLED
MARTELLING
MARTELLO
MARTELLOS
MARTELS
MARTEN
MARTENS
MARTENSITE
MARTENSITES
MARTENSITIC
MARTENSITICALLY
MARTEXT
MARTEXTS
MARTIAL
MARTIALISM
MARTIALISMS
MARTIALIST
MARTIALISTS
MARTIALLY
MARTIALNESS
MARTIALNESSES
MARTIAN
MARTIANS
MARTIN
MARTINET
MARTINETISH
MARTINETISM
MARTINETISMS
MARTINETS
MARTING
MARTINGALE
MARTINGALES
MARTINI
MARTINIS
MARTINS
MARTLET
MARTLETS
MARTS
MARTYR
MARTYRDOM
MARTYRDOMS
MARTYRED
MARTYRIA
MARTYRIES
MARTYRING
MARTYRISATION
MARTYRISATIONS

MARTYRISE
MARTYRISED
MARTYRISES
MARTYRISING
MARTYRIUM
MARTYRIZATION
MARTYRIZATIONS
MARTYRIZE
MARTYRIZED
MARTYRIZES
MARTYRIZING
MARTYRLY
MARTYROLOGIC
MARTYROLOGICAL
MARTYROLOGIES
MARTYROLOGIST
MARTYROLOGISTS
MARTYROLOGY
MARTYRS
MARTYRY
MARVEL
MARVELED
MARVELING
MARVELLED
MARVELLING
MARVELLOUS
MARVELLOUSLY
MARVELLOUSNESS
MARVELOUS
MARVELOUSLY
MARVELOUSNESS
MARVELOUSNESSES
MARVELS
MARVER
MARVERED
MARVERING
MARVERS
MARVY
MARXISANT
MARY
MARYBUD
MARYBUDS
MARYJANE
MARYJANES
MARZIPAN
MARZIPANS
MAS
MASA
MASALA
MASALAS
MASAS
MASCARA
MASCARAED
MASCARAING
MASCARAS
MASCARON

MASCARONS
MASCARPONE
MASCARPONES
MASCLE
MASCLED
MASCLES
MASCON
MASCONS
MASCOT
MASCOTS
MASCULINE
MASCULINELY
MASCULINENESS
MASCULINENESSES
MASCULINES
MASCULINISATION
MASCULINISE
MASCULINISED
MASCULINISES
MASCULINISING
MASCULINIST
MASCULINISTS
MASCULINITIES
MASCULINITY
MASCULINIZATION
MASCULINIZE
MASCULINIZED
MASCULINIZES
MASCULINIZING
MASCULIST
MASCULISTS
MASCULY
MASE
MASED
MASER
MASERS
MASES
MASH
MASHALLAH
MASHED
MASHER
MASHERS
MASHES
MASHIACH
MASHIE
MASHIER
MASHIES
MASHIEST
MASHING
MASHINGS
MASHLAM
MASHLAMS
MASHLIM
MASHLIMS
MASHLIN
MASHLINS

MASHLOCH
MASHLOCHS
MASHLUM
MASHLUMS
MASHMAN
MASHMEN
MASHUA
MASHUAS
MASHUP
MASHY
MASING
MASJID
MASJIDS
MASK
MASKABLE
MASKALLONGE
MASKALLONGES
MASKALONGE
MASKALONGES
MASKANONGE
MASKANONGES
MASKED
MASKEG
MASKEGS
MASKER
MASKERS
MASKING
MASKINGS
MASKINONGE
MASKINONGES
MASKIROVKA
MASKIROVKAS
MASKLIKE
MASKS
MASLIN
MASLINS
MASOCHISM
MASOCHISMS
MASOCHIST
MASOCHISTIC
MASOCHISTICALLY
MASOCHISTS
MASON
MASONED
MASONIC
MASONICALLY
MASONING
MASONRIED
MASONRIES
MASONRY
MASONS
MASOOLAH
MASOOLAHS
MASQUE
MASQUER
MASQUERADE

MASQUERADED
MASQUERADER
MASQUERADERS
MASQUERADES
MASQUERADING
MASQUERS
MASQUES
MASS
MASSA
MASSACRE
MASSACRED
MASSACRER
MASSACRERS
MASSACRES
MASSACRING
MASSAGE
MASSAGED
MASSAGER
MASSAGERS
MASSAGES
MASSAGING
MASSAGIST
MASSAGISTS
MASSARANDUBA
MASSARANDUBAS
MASSAS
MASSASAUGA
MASSASAUGAS
MASSCULT
MASSCULTS
MASSE
MASSED
MASSEDLY
MASSERANDUBA
MASSERANDUBAS
MASSES
MASSETER
MASSETERIC
MASSETERS
MASSEUR
MASSEURS
MASSEUSE
MASSEUSES
MASSICOT
MASSICOTS
MASSIER
MASSIEST
MASSIF
MASSIFS
MASSINESS
MASSINESSES
MASSING
MASSIVE
MASSIVELY
MASSIVENESS
MASSIVENESSES

MASSLESS
MASSOOLA
MASSOOLAS
MASSOTHERAPIST
MASSOTHERAPISTS
MASSOTHERAPY
MASSPRIEST
MASSPRIESTS
MASSY
MASSYMORE
MASSYMORES
MAST
MASTABA
MASTABAH
MASTABAHS
MASTABAS
MASTECTOMIES
MASTECTOMY
MASTED
MASTER
MASTERATE
MASTERATES
MASTERCLASS
MASTERCLASSES
MASTERDOM
MASTERDOMS
MASTERED
MASTERFUL
MASTERFULLY
MASTERFULNESS
MASTERFULNESSES
MASTERHOOD
MASTERHOODS
MASTERIES
MASTERING
MASTERINGS
MASTERLESS
MASTERLINESS
MASTERLINESSES
MASTERLY
MASTERMIND
MASTERMINDED
MASTERMINDING
MASTERMINDS
MASTERPIECE
MASTERPIECES
MASTERS
MASTERSHIP
MASTERSHIPS
MASTERSINGER
MASTERSINGERS
MASTERSTROKE
MASTERSTROKES
MASTERWORK
MASTERWORKS
MASTERWORT

MASTERWORTS
MASTERY
MASTFUL
MASTHEAD
MASTHEADED
MASTHEADING
MASTHEADS
MASTHOUSE
MASTHOUSES
MASTIC
MASTICABLE
MASTICATE
MASTICATED
MASTICATES
MASTICATING
MASTICATION
MASTICATIONS
MASTICATOR
MASTICATORIES
MASTICATORS
MASTICATORY
MASTICH
MASTICHE
MASTICHES
MASTICHS
MASTICOT
MASTICOTS
MASTICS
MASTIER
MASTIEST
MASTIFF
MASTIFFS
MASTIGOPHORAN
MASTIGOPHORANS
MASTIGOPHORE
MASTIGOPHORES
MASTIGOPHORIC
MASTIGOPHOROUS
MASTING
MASTITIC
MASTITIDES
MASTITIS
MASTITISES
MASTIX
MASTIXES
MASTLESS
MASTLIKE
MASTODON
MASTODONIC
MASTODONS
MASTODONT
MASTODONTIC
MASTODONTS
MASTODYNIA
MASTODYNIAS
MASTOID

MASTOIDAL
MASTOIDECTOMIES
MASTOIDECTOMY
MASTOIDITIS
MASTOIDITISES
MASTOIDS
MASTS
MASTURBATE
MASTURBATED
MASTURBATES
MASTURBATING
MASTURBATION
MASTURBATIONS
MASTURBATOR
MASTURBATORS
MASTURBATORY
MASTY
MASU
MASULA
MASULAS
MASURIUM
MASURIUMS
MASUS
MAT
MATACHIN
MATACHINA
MATACHINAS
MATACHINI
MATADOR
MATADORA
MATADORAS
MATADORE
MATADORES
MATADORS
MATAGOURI
MATAGOURIS
MATAI
MATAIS
MATAMATA
MATAMATAS
MATAMBALA
MATCH
MATCHABLE
MATCHBOARD
MATCHBOARDING
MATCHBOARDINGS
MATCHBOARDS
MATCHBOOK
MATCHBOOKS
MATCHBOX
MATCHBOXES
MATCHED
MATCHER
MATCHERS
MATCHES
MATCHET

MATCHETS
MATCHING
MATCHLESS
MATCHLESSLY
MATCHLESSNESS
MATCHLESSNESSES
MATCHLOCK
MATCHLOCKS
MATCHMAKER
MATCHMAKERS
MATCHMAKING
MATCHMAKINGS
MATCHMARK
MATCHMARKED
MATCHMARKING
MATCHMARKS
MATCHPLAY
MATCHSTICK
MATCHSTICKS
MATCHUP
MATCHUPS
MATCHWOOD
MATCHWOODS
MATE
MATED
MATELASSE
MATELASSES
MATELESS
MATELLASSE
MATELLASSES
MATELOT
MATELOTE
MATELOTES
MATELOTS
MATELOTTE
MATELOTTES
MATER
MATERFAMILIAS
MATERFAMILIASES
MATERIAL
MATERIALISATION
MATERIALISE
MATERIALISED
MATERIALISER
MATERIALISERS
MATERIALISES
MATERIALISING
MATERIALISM
MATERIALISMS
MATERIALIST
MATERIALISTIC
MATERIALISTICAL
MATERIALISTS
MATERIALITIES
MATERIALITY
MATERIALIZATION

MATERIALIZE
MATERIALIZED
MATERIALIZER
MATERIALIZERS
MATERIALIZES
MATERIALIZING
MATERIALLY
MATERIALNESS
MATERIALNESSES
MATERIALS
MATERIEL
MATERIELS
MATERNAL
MATERNALISM
MATERNALISTIC
MATERNALLY
MATERNITIES
MATERNITY
MATERS
MATES
MATESHIP
MATESHIPS
MATEY
MATEYNESS
MATEYNESSES
MATEYS
MATFELON
MATFELONS
MATGRASS
MATGRASSES
MATH
MATHEMATIC
MATHEMATICAL
MATHEMATICALLY
MATHEMATICIAN
MATHEMATICIANS
MATHEMATICISE
MATHEMATICISED
MATHEMATICISES
MATHEMATICISING
MATHEMATICISM
MATHEMATICISMS
MATHEMATICIZE
MATHEMATICIZED
MATHEMATICIZES
MATHEMATICIZING
MATHEMATICS
MATHEMATISATION
MATHEMATISE
MATHEMATISED
MATHEMATISES
MATHEMATISING
MATHEMATIZATION
MATHEMATIZE
MATHEMATIZED
MATHEMATIZES

MATHEMATIZING
MATHESES
MATHESIS
MATHS
MATICO
MATICOS
MATIER
MATIES
MATIEST
MATILDA
MATILDAS
MATILY
MATIN
MATINAL
MATINEE
MATINEES
MATINESS
MATINESSES
MATING
MATINGS
MATINS
MATIPO
MATIPOS
MATJES
MATLESS
MATLO
MATLOS
MATLOW
MATLOWS
MATOKE
MATOKES
MATOOKE
MATOOKES
MATRASS
MATRASSES
MATRES
MATRESFAMILIAS
MATRIARCH
MATRIARCHAL
MATRIARCHALISM
MATRIARCHALISMS
MATRIARCHATE
MATRIARCHATES
MATRIARCHIC
MATRIARCHICAL
MATRIARCHICALLY
MATRIARCHIES
MATRIARCHS
MATRIARCHY
MATRIC
MATRICE
MATRICES
MATRICIDAL
MATRICIDE
MATRICIDES
MATRICLINOUS

MATRICS
MATRICULA
MATRICULANT
MATRICULANTS
MATRICULAR
MATRICULAS
MATRICULATE
MATRICULATED
MATRICULATES
MATRICULATING
MATRICULATION
MATRICULATIONS
MATRICULATOR
MATRICULATORS
MATRICULATORY
MATRIFOCAL
MATRIFOCALITIES
MATRIFOCALITY
MATRILINEAL
MATRILINEALLY
MATRILINEAR
MATRILINIES
MATRILINY
MATRILOCAL
MATRILOCALITY
MATRILOCALLY
MATRIMONIAL
MATRIMONIALLY
MATRIMONIES
MATRIMONY
MATRIOSHKA
MATRIX
MATRIXES
MATROCLINAL
MATROCLINIC
MATROCLINIES
MATROCLINOUS
MATROCLINY
MATRON
MATRONAGE
MATRONAGES
MATRONAL
MATRONHOOD
MATRONHOODS
MATRONISE
MATRONISED
MATRONISES
MATRONISING
MATRONIZE
MATRONIZED
MATRONIZES
MATRONIZING
MATRONLINESS
MATRONLY
MATRONS
MATRONSHIP

MATRONSHIPS
MATRONYMIC
MATRONYMICS
MATROSS
MATROSSES
MATRYOSHKA
MATRYOSHKAS
MATS
MATSAH
MATSAHS
MATSURI
MATSURIS
MATT
MATTAMORE
MATTAMORES
MATTE
MATTED
MATTEDLY
MATTER
MATTERED
MATTERFUL
MATTERING
MATTERLESS
MATTERS
MATTERY
MATTES
MATTIE
MATTIES
MATTIFIED
MATTIFIES
MATTIFY
MATTIFYING
MATTIN
MATTING
MATTINGS
MATTINS
MATTOCK
MATTOCKS
MATTOID
MATTOIDS
MATTRASS
MATTRASSES
MATTRESS
MATTRESSES
MATTS
MATURABLE
MATURATE
MATURATED
MATURATES
MATURATING
MATURATION
MATURATIONAL
MATURATIONS
MATURATIVE
MATURE
MATURED

MATURELY
MATURENESS
MATURENESSES
MATURER
MATURES
MATUREST
MATURING
MATURITIES
MATURITY
MATUTINAL
MATUTINALLY
MATUTINE
MATWEED
MATWEEDS
MATY
MATZA
MATZAH
MATZAHS
MATZAS
MATZO
MATZOH
MATZOHS
MATZOON
MATZOONS
MATZOS
MATZOT
MATZOTH
MAUBIES
MAUBY
MAUD
MAUDLIN
MAUDLINISM
MAUDLINISMS
MAUDLINLY
MAUDLINNESS
MAUDS
MAUGER
MAUGRE
MAUGRED
MAUGRES
MAUGRING
MAUL
MAULED
MAULER
MAULERS
MAULGRE
MAULGRED
MAULGRES
MAULGRING
MAULING
MAULS
MAULSTICK
MAULSTICKS
MAULVI
MAULVIS
MAUMET

MAUMETRIES
MAUMETRY
MAUMETS
MAUN
MAUND
MAUNDED
MAUNDER
MAUNDERED
MAUNDERER
MAUNDERERS
MAUNDERING
MAUNDERINGS
MAUNDERS
MAUNDIES
MAUNDING
MAUNDS
MAUNDY
MAUNGIER
MAUNGIEST
MAUNGY
MAUNNA
MAURI
MAURIKIGUSARIS
MAURIS
MAUSOLEA
MAUSOLEAN
MAUSOLEANS
MAUSOLEUM
MAUSOLEUMS
MAUT
MAUTHER
MAUTHERS
MAUTS
MAUVAIS
MAUVAISE
MAUVE
MAUVEIN
MAUVEINE
MAUVEINES
MAUVEINS
MAUVER
MAUVES
MAUVEST
MAUVIN
MAUVINE
MAUVINES
MAUVINS
MAVEN
MAVENS
MAVERICK
MAVERICKED
MAVERICKING
MAVERICKS
MAVIE
MAVIES
MAVIN

MAVINS
MAVIS
MAVISES
MAVOURNEEN
MAVOURNEENS
MAVOURNIN
MAW
MAWBOUND
MAWED
MAWGER
MAWING
MAWK
MAWKIER
MAWKIEST
MAWKIN
MAWKINS
MAWKISH
MAWKISHLY
MAWKISHNESS
MAWKISHNESSES
MAWKS
MAWKY
MAWMET
MAWMETRIES
MAWMETRY
MAWMETS
MAWN
MAWPUS
MAWPUSES
MAWR
MAWRS
MAWS
MAWSEED
MAWSEEDS
MAWSIE
MAWSIES
MAWTHER
MAWTHERS
MAX
MAXES
MAXI
MAXICOAT
MAXICOATS
MAXILLA
MAXILLAE
MAXILLAR
MAXILLARIES
MAXILLARY
MAXILLAS
MAXILLIPED
MAXILLIPEDARY
MAXILLIPEDE
MAXILLIPEDES
MAXILLIPEDS
MAXILLOFACIAL
MAXILLULA

MAXILLULAE	MAYDAYS	MAZERS	MEALERS
MAXIM	MAYED	MAZES	MEALIE
MAXIMA	MAYEST	MAZEY	MEALIER
MAXIMAL	MAYFLIES	MAZHBI	MEALIES
MAXIMALIST	MAYFLOWER	MAZHBIS	MEALIEST
MAXIMALISTS	MAYFLOWERS	MAZIER	MEALINESS
MAXIMALLY	MAYFLY	MAZIEST	MEALINESSES
MAXIMALS	MAYHAP	MAZILY	MEALING
MAXIMAPHILIES	MAYHEM	MAZINESS	MEALLESS
MAXIMAPHILY	MAYHEMS	MAZINESSES	MEALS
MAXIMATION	MAYING	MAZING	MEALTIME
MAXIMATIONS	MAYINGS	MAZOURKA	MEALTIMES
MAXIMIN	MAYO	MAZOURKAS	MEALWORM
MAXIMINS	MAYONNAISE	MAZOUT	MEALWORMS
MAXIMISATION	MAYONNAISES	MAZOUTS	MEALY
MAXIMISATIONS	MAYOR	MAZUMA	MEALYBUG
MAXIMISE	MAYORAL	MAZUMAS	MEALYBUGS
MAXIMISED	MAYORALTIES	MAZURKA	MEALYMOUTHED
MAXIMISER	MAYORALTY	MAZURKAS	MEAN
MAXIMISERS	MAYORESS	MAZUT	MEANDER
MAXIMISES	MAYORESSES	MAZUTS	MEANDERED
MAXIMISING	MAYORS	MAZY	MEANDERER
MAXIMIST	MAYORSHIP	MAZZARD	MEANDERERS
MAXIMISTS	MAYORSHIPS	MAZZARDS	MEANDERING
MAXIMITE	MAYOS	MBAQANGA	MEANDERINGLY
MAXIMITES	MAYPOLE	MBAQANGAS	MEANDERS
MAXIMIZATION	MAYPOLES	MBIRA	MEANDRIAN
MAXIMIZATIONS	MAYPOP	MBIRAS	MEANDROUS
MAXIMIZE	MAYPOPS	ME	MEANE
MAXIMIZED	MAYS	MEACOCK	MEANED
MAXIMIZER	MAYST	MEACOCKS	MEANER
MAXIMIZERS	MAYSTER	MEAD	MEANERS
MAXIMIZES	MAYSTERDOME	MEADOW	MEANES
MAXIMIZING	MAYSTERDOMES	MEADOWLAND	MEANEST
MAXIMS	MAYSTERS	MEADOWLANDS	MEANIE
MAXIMUM	MAYVIN	MEADOWLARK	MEANIES
MAXIMUMS	MAYVINS	MEADOWLARKS	MEANING
MAXIMUS	MAYWEED	MEADOWS	MEANINGFUL
MAXIS	MAYWEEDS	MEADOWSWEET	MEANINGFULLY
MAXISINGLE	MAZAEDIA	MEADOWSWEETS	MEANINGFULNESS
MAXISINGLES	MAZAEDIUM	MEADOWY	MEANINGLESS
MAXIXE	MAZARD	MEADS	MEANINGLESSLY
MAXIXES	MAZARDS	MEAGER	MEANINGLESSNESS
MAXWELL	MAZARINADE	MEAGERLY	MEANINGLY
MAXWELLS	MAZARINADES	MEAGERNESS	MEANINGS
MAY	MAZARINE	MEAGERNESSES	MEANLY
MAYA	MAZARINES	MEAGRE	MEANNESS
MAYAN	MAZE	MEAGRELY	MEANNESSES
MAYAPPLE	MAZED	MEAGRENESS	MEANS
MAYAPPLES	MAZEDLY	MEAGRENESSES	MEANT
MAYAS	MAZEFUL	MEAGRER	MEANTIME
MAYBE	MAZELIKE	MEAGRES	MEANTIMES
MAYBES	MAZELTOV	MEAGREST	MEANWHILE
MAYBUSH	MAZEMENT	MEAL	MEANWHILES
MAYBUSHES	MAZEMENTS	MEALED	MEANY
MAYDAY	MAZER	MEALER	MEARE

MEARES
MEARING
MEASE
MEASED
MEASES
MEASING
MEASLE
MEASLED
MEASLES
MEASLIER
MEASLIEST
MEASLINESS
MEASLINESSES
MEASLING
MEASLY
MEASURABILITIES
MEASURABILITY
MEASURABLE
MEASURABLENESS
MEASURABLY
MEASURE
MEASURED
MEASUREDLY
MEASUREDNESS
MEASURELESS
MEASURELESSLY
MEASURELESSNESS
MEASUREMENT
MEASUREMENTS
MEASURER
MEASURERS
MEASURES
MEASURING
MEASURINGS
MEAT
MEATAL
MEATAXE
MEATAXES
MEATBALL
MEATBALLS
MEATED
MEATH
MEATHE
MEATHEAD
MEATHEADS
MEATHES
MEATHS
MEATIER
MEATIEST
MEATILY
MEATINESS
MEATINESSES
MEATLESS
MEATLOAF
MEATLOAVES
MEATMAN

MEATMEN
MEATPACKING
MEATPACKINGS
MEATS
MEATSCREEN
MEATSCREENS
MEATSPACE
MEATSPACES
MEATUS
MEATUSES
MEATY
MEAWES
MEAZEL
MEAZELS
MEBOS
MEBOSES
MECAMYLAMINE
MECAMYLAMINES
MECCA
MECCAS
MECHANIC
MECHANICAL
MECHANICALISM
MECHANICALLY
MECHANICALNESS
MECHANICALS
MECHANICIAN
MECHANICIANS
MECHANICS
MECHANISATION
MECHANISATIONS
MECHANISE
MECHANISED
MECHANISER
MECHANISERS
MECHANISES
MECHANISING
MECHANISM
MECHANISMS
MECHANIST
MECHANISTIC
MECHANISTICALLY
MECHANISTS
MECHANIZABLE
MECHANIZATION
MECHANIZATIONS
MECHANIZE
MECHANIZED
MECHANIZER
MECHANIZERS
MECHANIZES
MECHANIZING
MECHANOCHEMICAL
MECHANOMORPHISM
MECHANORECEPTOR
MECHANOTHERAPY

MECHATRONIC
MECHATRONICS
MECK
MECKS
MECLIZINE
MECLIZINES
MECONATE
MECONATES
MECONIC
MECONIN
MECONINS
MECONIUM
MECONIUMS
MECONOPSES
MECONOPSIS
MED
MEDACCA
MEDACCAS
MEDAEWARTS
MEDAILLON
MEDAILLONS
MEDAKA
MEDAKAS
MEDAL
MEDALED
MEDALET
MEDALETS
MEDALING
MEDALIST
MEDALISTS
MEDALLED
MEDALLIC
MEDALLING
MEDALLION
MEDALLIONED
MEDALLIONING
MEDALLIONS
MEDALLIST
MEDALLISTS
MEDALS
MEDCINAL
MEDDLE
MEDDLED
MEDDLER
MEDDLERS
MEDDLES
MEDDLESOME
MEDDLESOMELY
MEDDLESOMENESS
MEDDLING
MEDDLINGLY
MEDDLINGS
MEDEVAC
MEDEVACKED
MEDEVACKING
MEDEVACS

MEDFLIES
MEDFLY
MEDIA
MEDIACIES
MEDIACY
MEDIAD
MEDIAE
MEDIAEVAL
MEDIAEVALISM
MEDIAEVALISMS
MEDIAEVALIST
MEDIAEVALISTIC
MEDIAEVALISTS
MEDIAEVALLY
MEDIAEVALS
MEDIAGENIC
MEDIAL
MEDIALLY
MEDIALS
MEDIAN
MEDIANLY
MEDIANS
MEDIANT
MEDIANTS
MEDIAS
MEDIASTINA
MEDIASTINAL
MEDIASTINUM
MEDIATE
MEDIATED
MEDIATELY
MEDIATENESS
MEDIATENESSES
MEDIATES
MEDIATING
MEDIATION
MEDIATIONAL
MEDIATIONS
MEDIATISATION
MEDIATISATIONS
MEDIATISE
MEDIATISED
MEDIATISES
MEDIATISING
MEDIATIVE
MEDIATIZATION
MEDIATIZATIONS
MEDIATIZE
MEDIATIZED
MEDIATIZES
MEDIATIZING
MEDIATOR
MEDIATORIAL
MEDIATORIALLY
MEDIATORS
MEDIATORSHIP

MEDIATORSHIPS	MEDICK	MEDRESSEHS	MEG
MEDIATORY	MEDICKS	MEDULLA	MEGA
MEDIATRESS	MEDICO	MEDULLAE	MEGABAR
MEDIATRESSES	MEDICOLEGAL	MEDULLAR	MEGABARS
MEDIATRICES	MEDICOS	MEDULLARY	MEGABIT
MEDIATRIX	MEDICS	MEDULLAS	MEGABITS
MEDIATRIXES	MEDIEVAL	MEDULLATE	MEGABUCK
MEDIC	MEDIEVALISM	MEDULLATED	MEGABUCKS
MEDICABLE	MEDIEVALISMS	MEDULLOBLASTOMA	MEGABYTE
MEDICABLY	MEDIEVALIST	MEDUSA	MEGABYTES
MEDICAID	MEDIEVALISTIC	MEDUSAE	MEGACEPHALIC
MEDICAIDS	MEDIEVALISTS	MEDUSAL	MEGACEPHALOUS
MEDICAL	MEDIEVALLY	MEDUSAN	MEGACEPHALY
MEDICALISATION	MEDIEVALS	MEDUSANS	MEGACITIES
MEDICALISATIONS	MEDII	MEDUSAS	MEGACITY
MEDICALISE	MEDINA	MEDUSIFORM	MEGACORPORATION
MEDICALISED	MEDINAS	MEDUSOID	MEGACURIE
MEDICALISES	MEDIOCRACIES	MEDUSOIDS	MEGACURIES
MEDICALISING	MEDIOCRACY	MEED	MEGACYCLE
MEDICALIZATION	MEDIOCRE	MEEDS	MEGACYCLES
MEDICALIZATIONS	MEDIOCRITIES	MEEK	MEGADEAL
MEDICALIZE	MEDIOCRITY	MEEKEN	MEGADEALS
MEDICALIZED	MEDITATE	MEEKENED	MEGADEATH
MEDICALIZES	MEDITATED	MEEKENING	MEGADEATHS
MEDICALIZING	MEDITATES	MEEKENS	MEGADOSE
MEDICALLY	MEDITATING	MEEKER	MEGADOSES
MEDICALS	MEDITATION	MEEKEST	MEGADYNE
MEDICAMENT	MEDITATIONS	MEEKLY	MEGADYNES
MEDICAMENTAL	MEDITATIVE	MEEKNESS	MEGAFARAD
MEDICAMENTALLY	MEDITATIVELY	MEEKNESSES	MEGAFARADS
MEDICAMENTARY	MEDITATIVENESS	MEEMIE	MEGAFAUNA
MEDICAMENTED	MEDITATOR	MEEMIES	MEGAFAUNAE
MEDICAMENTING	MEDITATORS	MEER	MEGAFAUNAL
MEDICAMENTOUS	MEDITERRANEAN	MEERCAT	MEGAFAUNAS
MEDICAMENTS	MEDIUM	MEERCATS	MEGAFLOP
MEDICARE	MEDIUMISTIC	MEERED	MEGAFLOPS
MEDICARES	MEDIUMS	MEERING	MEGAFLORA
MEDICASTER	MEDIUMSHIP	MEERKAT	MEGAFLORAE
MEDICASTERS	MEDIUMSHIPS	MEERKATS	MEGAFLORAS
MEDICATE	MEDIUS	MEERS	MEGAFOG
MEDICATED	MEDIUSES	MEERSCHAUM	MEGAFOGS
MEDICATES	MEDIVAC	MEERSCHAUMS	MEGAGAMETE
MEDICATING	MEDIVACING	MEET	MEGAGAMETES
MEDICATION	MEDIVACKED	MEETER	MEGAGAMETOPHYTE
MEDICATIONS	MEDIVACS	MEETERS	MEGAGAUSS
MEDICATIVE	MEDLAR	MEETEST	MEGAGAUSSES
MEDICINABLE	MEDLARS	MEETING	MEGAHERBIVORE
MEDICINAL	MEDLE	MEETINGHOUSE	MEGAHERBIVORES
MEDICINALLY	MEDLED	MEETINGHOUSES	MEGAHERTZ
MEDICINALS	MEDLES	MEETINGS	MEGAHERTZES
MEDICINE	MEDLEY	MEETLY	MEGAHIT
MEDICINED	MEDLEYS	MEETNESS	MEGAHITS
MEDICINER	MEDLING	MEETNESSES	MEGAJOULE
MEDICINERS	MEDRESE	MEETS	MEGAJOULES
MEDICINES	MEDRESES	MEFLOQUINE	MEGAKARYOCYTE
MEDICINING	MEDRESSEH	MEFLOQUINES	MEGAKARYOCYTES

MEGAKARYOCYTIC
MEGALITH
MEGALITHIC
MEGALITHS
MEGALOBLAST
MEGALOBLASTIC
MEGALOBLASTS
MEGALOCARDIA
MEGALOCEPHALIC
MEGALOCEPHALOUS
MEGALOCEPHALY
MEGALOMANIA
MEGALOMANIAC
MEGALOMANIACAL
MEGALOMANIACS
MEGALOMANIAS
MEGALOMANIC
MEGALOPOLIS
MEGALOPOLISES
MEGALOPOLITAN
MEGALOPOLITANS
MEGALOPS
MEGALOPSES
MEGALOSAUR
MEGALOSAURIAN
MEGALOSAURIANS
MEGALOSAURS
MEGALOSAURUS
MEGALOSAURUSES
MEGANEWTON
MEGANEWTONS
MEGAPARSEC
MEGAPARSECS
MEGAPHONE
MEGAPHONED
MEGAPHONES
MEGAPHONIC
MEGAPHONICALLY
MEGAPHONING
MEGAPHYLL
MEGAPHYLLS
MEGAPLEX
MEGAPLEXES
MEGAPOD
MEGAPODE
MEGAPODES
MEGAPODS
MEGAPROJECT
MEGAPROJECTS
MEGARA
MEGARAD
MEGARADS
MEGARON
MEGARONS
MEGASCOPE
MEGASCOPES

MEGASCOPIC
MEGASCOPICALLY
MEGASPORANGIA
MEGASPORANGIUM
MEGASPORE
MEGASPORES
MEGASPORIC
MEGASPOROPHYLL
MEGASPOROPHYLLS
MEGASS
MEGASSE
MEGASSES
MEGASTAR
MEGASTARS
MEGASTORE
MEGASTORES
MEGASTRUCTURE
MEGASTRUCTURES
MEGATECHNOLOGY
MEGATHERE
MEGATHERES
MEGATHERIAN
MEGATON
MEGATONIC
MEGATONNAGE
MEGATONNAGES
MEGATONS
MEGAVERTEBRATE
MEGAVERTEBRATES
MEGAVITAMIN
MEGAVITAMINS
MEGAVOLT
MEGAVOLTS
MEGAWATT
MEGAWATTS
MEGILLAH
MEGILLAHS
MEGILLOTH
MEGILP
MEGILPH
MEGILPHS
MEGILPS
MEGOHM
MEGOHMS
MEGRIM
MEGRIMS
MEGS
MEHNDI
MEIBOMIAN
MEIKLE
MEIN
MEINED
MEINEY
MEINEYS
MEINIE
MEINIES

MEINING
MEINS
MEINT
MEINY
MEIOCYTE
MEIOCYTES
MEIOFAUNA
MEIOFAUNAL
MEIONITE
MEIONITES
MEIOSES
MEIOSIS
MEIOSPORE
MEIOSPORES
MEIOTIC
MEIOTICALLY
MEISHI
MEISHIS
MEISTER
MEISTERS
MEITH
MEITHS
MEITNERIUM
MEITNERIUMS
MEJLIS
MEJLISES
MEKOMETER
MEKOMETERS
MEL
MELA
MELACONITE
MELACONITES
MELALEUCA
MELALEUCAS
MELAMDIM
MELAMED
MELAMINE
MELAMINES
MELAMPODE
MELAMPODES
MELANAEMIA
MELANAEMIAS
MELANCHOLIA
MELANCHOLIAC
MELANCHOLIACS
MELANCHOLIAS
MELANCHOLIC
MELANCHOLICALLY
MELANCHOLICS
MELANCHOLIES
MELANCHOLILY
MELANCHOLINESS
MELANCHOLIOUS
MELANCHOLY
MELANGE
MELANGES

MELANIAN
MELANIC
MELANICS
MELANIN
MELANINS
MELANISM
MELANISMS
MELANIST
MELANISTIC
MELANISTS
MELANITE
MELANITES
MELANITIC
MELANIZATION
MELANIZATIONS
MELANIZE
MELANIZED
MELANIZES
MELANIZING
MELANO
MELANOBLAST
MELANOBLASTS
MELANOCHROI
MELANOCHROIC
MELANOCHROOUS
MELANOCYTE
MELANOCYTES
MELANOGENESES
MELANOGENESIS
MELANOID
MELANOIDS
MELANOMA
MELANOMAS
MELANOMATA
MELANOPHORE
MELANOPHORES
MELANOS
MELANOSES
MELANOSIS
MELANOSITY
MELANOSOME
MELANOSOMES
MELANOTIC
MELANOTROPIN
MELANOTROPINS
MELANOUS
MELANTERITE
MELANTERITES
MELANURIA
MELANURIAS
MELANURIC
MELAPHYRE
MELAPHYRES
MELAS
MELASTOMACEOUS
MELATONIN

MELATONINS
MELD
MELDED
MELDER
MELDERS
MELDING
MELDS
MELEE
MELEES
MELIACEOUS
MELIC
MELICK
MELICKS
MELICOTTON
MELICOTTONS
MELICS
MELIK
MELIKS
MELILITE
MELILITES
MELILOT
MELILOTS
MELINITE
MELINITES
MELIORABLE
MELIORATE
MELIORATED
MELIORATES
MELIORATING
MELIORATION
MELIORATIONS
MELIORATIVE
MELIORATOR
MELIORATORS
MELIORISM
MELIORISMS
MELIORIST
MELIORISTIC
MELIORISTS
MELIORITIES
MELIORITY
MELIPHAGOUS
MELISMA
MELISMAS
MELISMATA
MELISMATIC
MELL
MELLAY
MELLAYS
MELLED
MELLIFEROUS
MELLIFIC
MELLIFICATION
MELLIFICATIONS
MELLIFLUENCE
MELLIFLUENCES

MELLIFLUENT
MELLIFLUENTLY
MELLIFLUOUS
MELLIFLUOUSLY
MELLIFLUOUSNESS
MELLING
MELLIPHAGOUS
MELLITE
MELLITES
MELLITIC
MELLIVOROUS
MELLOPHONE
MELLOPHONES
MELLOTRON
MELLOTRONS
MELLOW
MELLOWED
MELLOWER
MELLOWEST
MELLOWING
MELLOWLY
MELLOWNESS
MELLOWNESSES
MELLOWS
MELLOWSPEAK
MELLOWSPEAKS
MELLOWY
MELLS
MELOCOTON
MELOCOTONS
MELOCOTOON
MELOCOTOONS
MELODEON
MELODEONS
MELODIA
MELODIAS
MELODIC
MELODICA
MELODICALLY
MELODICAS
MELODICS
MELODIES
MELODION
MELODIONS
MELODIOUS
MELODIOUSLY
MELODIOUSNESS
MELODIOUSNESSES
MELODISE
MELODISED
MELODISER
MELODISERS
MELODISES
MELODISING
MELODIST
MELODISTS

MELODIZE
MELODIZED
MELODIZER
MELODIZERS
MELODIZES
MELODIZING
MELODRAMA
MELODRAMAS
MELODRAMATIC
MELODRAMATICS
MELODRAMATISE
MELODRAMATISED
MELODRAMATISES
MELODRAMATISING
MELODRAMATIST
MELODRAMATISTS
MELODRAMATIZE
MELODRAMATIZED
MELODRAMATIZES
MELODRAMATIZING
MELODRAME
MELODRAMES
MELODY
MELOID
MELOIDS
MELOMANIA
MELOMANIAC
MELOMANIACS
MELOMANIAS
MELOMANIC
MELON
MELONS
MELPHALAN
MELPHALANS
MELS
MELT
MELTABILITIES
MELTABILITY
MELTABLE
MELTAGE
MELTAGES
MELTDOWN
MELTDOWNS
MELTED
MELTEMI
MELTER
MELTERS
MELTIER
MELTIEST
MELTING
MELTINGLY
MELTINGNESS
MELTINGNESSES
MELTINGS
MELTITH
MELTITHS

MELTON
MELTONS
MELTS
MELTWATER
MELTWATERS
MELTY
MELUNGEON
MELUNGEONS
MEM
MEMBER
MEMBERED
MEMBERLESS
MEMBERLESSNESS
MEMBERS
MEMBERSHIP
MEMBERSHIPS
MEMBRAL
MEMBRANACEOUS
MEMBRANE
MEMBRANED
MEMBRANEOUS
MEMBRANES
MEMBRANOUS
MEMBRANOUSLY
MEME
MEMENTO
MEMENTOES
MEMENTOS
MEMES
MEMO
MEMOIR
MEMOIRISM
MEMOIRISMS
MEMOIRIST
MEMOIRISTS
MEMOIRS
MEMORABILE
MEMORABILIA
MEMORABILITIES
MEMORABILITY
MEMORABLE
MEMORABLENESS
MEMORABLENESSES
MEMORABLY
MEMORANDA
MEMORANDUM
MEMORANDUMS
MEMORATIVE
MEMORIAL
MEMORIALISATION
MEMORIALISE
MEMORIALISED
MEMORIALISER
MEMORIALISERS
MEMORIALISES
MEMORIALISING

MEMORIALIST
MEMORIALISTS
MEMORIALIZATION
MEMORIALIZE
MEMORIALIZED
MEMORIALIZER
MEMORIALIZERS
MEMORIALIZES
MEMORIALIZING
MEMORIALLY
MEMORIALS
MEMORIES
MEMORISABLE
MEMORISATION
MEMORISATIONS
MEMORISE
MEMORISED
MEMORISER
MEMORISERS
MEMORISES
MEMORISING
MEMORITER
MEMORIZABLE
MEMORIZATION
MEMORIZATIONS
MEMORIZE
MEMORIZED
MEMORIZER
MEMORIZERS
MEMORIZES
MEMORIZING
MEMORY
MEMOS
MEMS
MEMSAHIB
MEMSAHIBS
MEN
MENACE
MENACED
MENACER
MENACERS
MENACES
MENACING
MENACINGLY
MENAD
MENADIONE
MENADIONES
MENADS
MENAGE
MENAGED
MENAGERIE
MENAGERIES
MENAGES
MENAGING
MENAQUINONE
MENARCHE

MENARCHEAL
MENARCHES
MENARCHIAL
MENAZON
MENAZONS
MEND
MENDABLE
MENDACIOUS
MENDACIOUSLY
MENDACIOUSNESS
MENDACITIES
MENDACITY
MENDED
MENDELEVIUM
MENDELEVIUMS
MENDER
MENDERS
MENDICANCIES
MENDICANCY
MENDICANT
MENDICANTS
MENDICITIES
MENDICITY
MENDIGO
MENDIGOS
MENDING
MENDINGS
MENDS
MENE
MENED
MENEER
MENEERS
MENES
MENFOLK
MENFOLKS
MENG
MENGE
MENGED
MENGES
MENGING
MENGS
MENHADEN
MENHADENS
MENHIR
MENHIRS
MENIAL
MENIALLY
MENIALS
MENILITE
MENING
MENINGEAL
MENINGES
MENINGIOMA
MENINGIOMAS
MENINGIOMATA
MENINGITIC

MENINGITIDES
MENINGITIS
MENINGITISES
MENINGOCELE
MENINGOCELES
MENINGOCOCCAL
MENINGOCOCCI
MENINGOCOCCIC
MENINGOCOCCUS
MENINX
MENISCAL
MENISCECTOMIES
MENISCECTOMY
MENISCI
MENISCOID
MENISCUS
MENISCUSES
MENISPERMACEOUS
MENISPERMUM
MENISPERMUMS
MENO
MENOLOGIES
MENOLOGY
MENOMINEE
MENOMINEES
MENOMINI
MENOMINIS
MENOPAUSAL
MENOPAUSE
MENOPAUSES
MENOPAUSIC
MENOPOME
MENOPOMES
MENORAH
MENORAHS
MENORRHAGIA
MENORRHAGIAS
MENORRHAGIC
MENORRHEA
MENORRHEAS
MENORRHOEA
MENORRHOEAS
MENSA
MENSAE
MENSAL
MENSAS
MENSCH
MENSCHEN
MENSCHES
MENSE
MENSED
MENSEFUL
MENSELESS
MENSERVANTS
MENSES
MENSH

MENSHED
MENSHES
MENSHING
MENSING
MENSTRUA
MENSTRUAL
MENSTRUALLY
MENSTRUATE
MENSTRUATED
MENSTRUATES
MENSTRUATING
MENSTRUATION
MENSTRUATIONS
MENSTRUOUS
MENSTRUUM
MENSTRUUMS
MENSUAL
MENSURABILITIES
MENSURABILITY
MENSURABLE
MENSURAL
MENSURATION
MENSURATIONAL
MENSURATIONS
MENSURATIVE
MENSWEAR
MENSWEARS
MENT
MENTA
MENTAL
MENTALISM
MENTALISMS
MENTALIST
MENTALISTIC
MENTALISTICALLY
MENTALISTS
MENTALITIES
MENTALITY
MENTALLY
MENTATION
MENTATIONS
MENTEE
MENTEES
MENTHACEOUS
MENTHENE
MENTHENES
MENTHOL
MENTHOLATED
MENTHOLS
MENTICIDE
MENTICIDES
MENTION
MENTIONABLE
MENTIONED
MENTIONER
MENTIONERS

MENTIONING
MENTIONS
MENTO
MENTONNIERE
MENTONNIERES
MENTOR
MENTORED
MENTORIAL
MENTORING
MENTORINGS
MENTORS
MENTORSHIP
MENTORSHIPS
MENTOS
MENTUM
MENU
MENUISIER
MENUISIERS
MENURA
MENURAS
MENUS
MENYIE
MENYIES
MEOU
MEOUED
MEOUING
MEOUS
MEOW
MEOWED
MEOWING
MEOWS
MEPACRINE
MEPACRINES
MEPERIDINE
MEPERIDINES
MEPHITIC
MEPHITICAL
MEPHITICALLY
MEPHITIS
MEPHITISES
MEPHITISM
MEPHITISMS
MEPROBAMATE
MEPROBAMATES
MERANTI
MERBROMIN
MERBROMINS
MERC
MERCANTILE
MERCANTILISM
MERCANTILISMS
MERCANTILIST
MERCANTILISTIC
MERCANTILISTS
MERCAPTAN
MERCAPTANS

MERCAPTIDE
MERCAPTIDES
MERCAPTO
MERCAPTOPURINE
MERCAPTOPURINES
MERCAT
MERCATS
MERCENARIES
MERCENARILY
MERCENARINESS
MERCENARINESSES
MERCENARISM
MERCENARISMS
MERCENARY
MERCER
MERCERIES
MERCERISATION
MERCERISATIONS
MERCERISE
MERCERISED
MERCERISER
MERCERISERS
MERCERISES
MERCERISING
MERCERIZATION
MERCERIZATIONS
MERCERIZE
MERCERIZED
MERCERIZER
MERCERIZERS
MERCERIZES
MERCERIZING
MERCERS
MERCERY
MERCHANDISE
MERCHANDISED
MERCHANDISER
MERCHANDISERS
MERCHANDISES
MERCHANDISING
MERCHANDISINGS
MERCHANDIZE
MERCHANDIZED
MERCHANDIZER
MERCHANDIZERS
MERCHANDIZES
MERCHANDIZING
MERCHANDIZINGS
MERCHANT
MERCHANTABILITY
MERCHANTABLE
MERCHANTED
MERCHANTING
MERCHANTINGS
MERCHANTLIKE
MERCHANTMAN

MERCHANTMEN
MERCHANTRIES
MERCHANTRY
MERCHANTS
MERCHET
MERCHETS
MERCHILD
MERCHILDREN
MERCIABLE
MERCIES
MERCIFIDE
MERCIFIED
MERCIFIES
MERCIFUL
MERCIFULLY
MERCIFULNESS
MERCIFULNESSES
MERCIFY
MERCIFYING
MERCILESS
MERCILESSLY
MERCILESSNESS
MERCILESSNESSES
MERCS
MERCURATE
MERCURATED
MERCURATES
MERCURATING
MERCURATION
MERCURATIONS
MERCURIAL
MERCURIALISE
MERCURIALISED
MERCURIALISES
MERCURIALISING
MERCURIALISM
MERCURIALISMS
MERCURIALIST
MERCURIALISTS
MERCURIALITY
MERCURIALIZE
MERCURIALIZED
MERCURIALIZES
MERCURIALIZING
MERCURIALLY
MERCURIALNESS
MERCURIALNESSES
MERCURIALS
MERCURIC
MERCURIES
MERCURISE
MERCURISED
MERCURISES
MERCURISING
MERCURIZE
MERCURIZED

MERCURIZES
MERCURIZING
MERCUROUS
MERCURY
MERCY
MERDE
MERDES
MERDIVOROUS
MERE
MERED
MEREL
MERELL
MERELLS
MERELS
MERELY
MERENGUE
MERENGUES
MEREOLOGICAL
MEREOLOGY
MERER
MERES
MERESMAN
MERESMEN
MEREST
MERESTONE
MERESTONES
MERETRICIOUS
MERETRICIOUSLY
MERFOLK
MERFOLKS
MERGANSER
MERGANSERS
MERGE
MERGED
MERGENCE
MERGENCES
MERGER
MERGERS
MERGES
MERGING
MERI
MERICARP
MERICARPS
MERIDIAN
MERIDIANS
MERIDIONAL
MERIDIONALITIES
MERIDIONALITY
MERIDIONALLY
MERIDIONALS
MERIL
MERILS
MERIMAKE
MERIMAKES
MERING
MERINGS

MERINGUE
MERINGUES
MERINO
MERINOS
MERIS
MERISES
MERISIS
MERISM
MERISMS
MERISTEM
MERISTEMATIC
MERISTEMS
MERISTIC
MERISTICALLY
MERIT
MERITED
MERITING
MERITLESS
MERITOCRACIES
MERITOCRACY
MERITOCRAT
MERITOCRATIC
MERITOCRATS
MERITORIOUS
MERITORIOUSLY
MERITORIOUSNESS
MERITS
MERK
MERKIN
MERKINS
MERKS
MERL
MERLE
MERLES
MERLIN
MERLING
MERLINGS
MERLINS
MERLON
MERLONS
MERLOT
MERLOTS
MERLS
MERMAID
MERMAIDEN
MERMAIDENS
MERMAIDS
MERMAN
MERMEN
MEROBLASTIC
MEROBLASTICALLY
MEROCRINE
MEROGENESES
MEROGENESIS
MEROGENETIC
MEROGONIES

MEROGONY
MEROISTIC
MEROME
MEROMES
MEROMORPHIC
MEROMYOSIN
MEROMYOSINS
MERONYM
MERONYMIES
MERONYMS
MERONYMY
MEROPIA
MEROPIAS
MEROPIC
MEROPIDAN
MEROPIDANS
MEROPLANKTON
MEROSOME
MEROSOMES
MEROZOITE
MEROZOITES
MERPEOPLE
MERPEOPLES
MERRIER
MERRIES
MERRIEST
MERRILY
MERRIMENT
MERRIMENTS
MERRINESS
MERRINESSES
MERRY
MERRYMAKER
MERRYMAKERS
MERRYMAKING
MERRYMAKINGS
MERRYMAN
MERRYMEN
MERRYTHOUGHT
MERRYTHOUGHTS
MERSALYL
MERSALYLS
MERSE
MERSES
MERSION
MERSIONS
MERVEILLEUSE
MERVEILLEUSES
MERVEILLEUX
MERVEILLEUXES
MERYCISM
MERYCISMS
MES
MESA
MESAIL
MESAILS

MESAL
MESALLIANCE
MESALLIANCES
MESALLY
MESARAIC
MESARCH
MESAS
MESATICEPHALIC
MESATICEPHALIES
MESATICEPHALOUS
MESATICEPHALY
MESCAL
MESCALIN
MESCALINE
MESCALINES
MESCALINS
MESCALISM
MESCALISMS
MESCALS
MESCLUM
MESCLUMS
MESCLUN
MESCLUNS
MESDAMES
MESDEMOISELLES
MESE
MESEEMED
MESEEMETH
MESEEMS
MESEL
MESELED
MESELS
MESENCEPHALA
MESENCEPHALIC
MESENCEPHALON
MESENCEPHALONS
MESENCHYMAL
MESENCHYMATOUS
MESENCHYME
MESENCHYMES
MESENTERA
MESENTERIAL
MESENTERIC
MESENTERIES
MESENTERITIS
MESENTERON
MESENTERONIC
MESENTERY
MESES
MESETA
MESETAS
MESH
MESHED
MESHES
MESHIER
MESHIEST

MESHING
MESHINGS
MESHUGA
MESHUGAAS
MESHUGAASEN
MESHUGAH
MESHUGGA
MESHUGGAH
MESHUGGE
MESHUGGENAH
MESHUGGENAHS
MESHUGGENEH
MESHUGGENEHS
MESHUGGENER
MESHUGGENERS
MESHWORK
MESHWORKS
MESHY
MESIAD
MESIAL
MESIALLY
MESIAN
MESIC
MESICALLY
MESITYLENE
MESMERIC
MESMERICAL
MESMERICALLY
MESMERISATION
MESMERISATIONS
MESMERISE
MESMERISED
MESMERISER
MESMERISERS
MESMERISES
MESMERISING
MESMERISM
MESMERISMS
MESMERIST
MESMERISTS
MESMERIZATION
MESMERIZATIONS
MESMERIZE
MESMERIZED
MESMERIZER
MESMERIZERS
MESMERIZES
MESMERIZING
MESNALTIES
MESNALTY
MESNE
MESNES
MESOAMERICAN
MESOBENTHOS
MESOBLAST
MESOBLASTIC

MESOBLASTS
MESOCARP
MESOCARPS
MESOCEPHALIC
MESOCEPHALICS
MESOCEPHALIES
MESOCEPHALISM
MESOCEPHALISMS
MESOCEPHALOUS
MESOCEPHALY
MESOCRATIC
MESOCYCLONE
MESOCYCLONES
MESODERM
MESODERMAL
MESODERMIC
MESODERMS
MESOGASTRIC
MESOGASTRIUM
MESOGASTRIUMS
MESOGLEA
MESOGLEAS
MESOGLOEA
MESOGLOEAS
MESOGNATHISM
MESOGNATHOUS
MESOGNATHY
MESOHIPPUS
MESOHIPPUSES
MESOKURTIC
MESOLITE
MESOLITES
MESOMERE
MESOMERES
MESOMERISM
MESOMERISMS
MESOMORPH
MESOMORPHIC
MESOMORPHIES
MESOMORPHISM
MESOMORPHOUS
MESOMORPHS
MESOMORPHY
MESON
MESONEPHRIC
MESONEPHROI
MESONEPHROS
MESONEPHROSES
MESONIC
MESONS
MESOPAUSE
MESOPAUSES
MESOPELAGIC
MESOPHILE
MESOPHILES
MESOPHILIC

MESOPHYL
MESOPHYLL
MESOPHYLLIC
MESOPHYLLOUS
MESOPHYLLS
MESOPHYLS
MESOPHYTE
MESOPHYTES
MESOPHYTIC
MESOSCALE
MESOSCAPHE
MESOSCAPHES
MESOSOME
MESOSOMES
MESOSPHERE
MESOSPHERES
MESOSPHERIC
MESOTHELIA
MESOTHELIAL
MESOTHELIOMA
MESOTHELIOMAS
MESOTHELIOMATA
MESOTHELIUM
MESOTHELIUMS
MESOTHORACES
MESOTHORACIC
MESOTHORAX
MESOTHORAXES
MESOTHORIUM
MESOTHORIUMS
MESOTRON
MESOTRONS
MESOTROPHIC
MESPRISE
MESPRISES
MESPRIZE
MESPRIZES
MESQUIN
MESQUINE
MESQUINERIE
MESQUINERIES
MESQUIT
MESQUITE
MESQUITES
MESQUITS
MESS
MESSAGE
MESSAGED
MESSAGES
MESSAGING
MESSAGINGS
MESSALINE
MESSALINES
MESSAN
MESSANS
MESSED

MESSEIGNEURS
MESSENGER
MESSENGERED
MESSENGERING
MESSENGERS
MESSES
MESSIAH
MESSIAHS
MESSIAHSHIP
MESSIAHSHIPS
MESSIANIC
MESSIANICALLY
MESSIANISM
MESSIANISMS
MESSIAS
MESSIASES
MESSIER
MESSIEST
MESSIEURS
MESSILY
MESSINESS
MESSINESSES
MESSING
MESSMAN
MESSMATE
MESSMATES
MESSMEN
MESSUAGE
MESSUAGES
MESSY
MESTEE
MESTEES
MESTER
MESTERS
MESTESO
MESTESOES
MESTESOS
MESTINO
MESTINOES
MESTINOS
MESTIZA
MESTIZAS
MESTIZO
MESTIZOES
MESTIZOS
MESTO
MESTOM
MESTOME
MESTOMES
MESTOMS
MESTRANOL
MESTRANOLS
MET
META
METABASES
METABASIS

METABATIC
METABOLIC
METABOLICALLY
METABOLISABLE
METABOLISE
METABOLISED
METABOLISES
METABOLISING
METABOLISM
METABOLISMS
METABOLITE
METABOLITES
METABOLIZABLE
METABOLIZE
METABOLIZED
METABOLIZES
METABOLIZING
METABOLOME
METABOLOMICS
METABOLY
METACARPAL
METACARPALS
METACARPI
METACARPUS
METACENTER
METACENTERS
METACENTRE
METACENTRES
METACENTRIC
METACENTRICS
METACERCARIA
METACERCARIAE
METACERCARIAL
METACHROMATIC
METACHROMATISM
METACHRONISM
METACHRONISMS
METACHROSES
METACHROSIS
METACINNABARITE
METACOGNITION
METACOMPUTER
METAETHICAL
METAETHICS
METAFEMALE
METAFEMALES
METAFICTION
METAFICTIONAL
METAFICTIONIST
METAFICTIONISTS
METAFICTIONS
METAGALACTIC
METAGALAXIES
METAGALAXY
METAGE
METAGENESES

METAGENESIS
METAGENETIC
METAGENETICALLY
METAGENIC
METAGES
METAGNATHISM
METAGNATHOUS
METAGRABOLISED
METAGRABOLISES
METAGRABOLISING
METAGRABOLIZE
METAGRABOLIZED
METAGRABOLIZES
METAGRABOLIZING
METAGROBOLISE
METAGROBOLISED
METAGROBOLISES
METAGROBOLISING
METAGROBOLIZE
METAGROBOLIZED
METAGROBOLIZES
METAGROBOLIZING
METAIRIE
METAIRIES
METAL
METALANGUAGE
METALANGUAGES
METALDEHYDE
METALDEHYDES
METALED
METALEPSES
METALEPSIS
METALEPTIC
METALEPTICAL
METALING
METALINGUISTIC
METALINGUISTICS
METALISE
METALISED
METALISES
METALISING
METALIST
METALISTS
METALIZATION
METALIZATIONS
METALIZE
METALIZED
METALIZES
METALIZING
METALLED
METALLIC
METALLICALLY
METALLICS
METALLIDING
METALLIDINGS
METALLIFEROUS

METALLINE
METALLING
METALLINGS
METALLISATION
METALLISATIONS
METALLISE
METALLISED
METALLISES
METALLISING
METALLIST
METALLISTS
METALLIZATION
METALLIZATIONS
METALLIZE
METALLIZED
METALLIZES
METALLIZING
METALLOCENE
METALLOCENES
METALLOGENETIC
METALLOGENIC
METALLOGENIES
METALLOGENY
METALLOGRAPHER
METALLOGRAPHERS
METALLOGRAPHIC
METALLOGRAPHIES
METALLOGRAPHIST
METALLOGRAPHY
METALLOID
METALLOIDAL
METALLOIDS
METALLOPHONE
METALLOPHONES
METALLURGIC
METALLURGICAL
METALLURGICALLY
METALLURGIES
METALLURGIST
METALLURGISTS
METALLURGY
METALLY
METALMARK
METALMARKS
METALS
METALSMITH
METALSMITHS
METALWARE
METALWARES
METALWORK
METALWORKER
METALWORKERS
METALWORKING
METALWORKINGS
METALWORKS
METAMALE

METAMALES
METAMATHEMATICS
METAMER
METAMERAL
METAMERE
METAMERES
METAMERIC
METAMERICALLY
METAMERISM
METAMERISMS
METAMERS
METAMICT
METAMICTISATION
METAMICTIZATION
METAMORPHIC
METAMORPHICALLY
METAMORPHISM
METAMORPHISMS
METAMORPHIST
METAMORPHISTS
METAMORPHOSE
METAMORPHOSED
METAMORPHOSES
METAMORPHOSING
METAMORPHOSIS
METAMORPHOUS
METANALYSES
METANALYSIS
METANEPHRIC
METANEPHROI
METANEPHROS
METANOIA
METANOIAS
METAPELET
METAPHASE
METAPHASES
METAPHOR
METAPHORIC
METAPHORICAL
METAPHORICALLY
METAPHORIST
METAPHORISTS
METAPHORS
METAPHOSPHATE
METAPHOSPHATES
METAPHOSPHORIC
METAPHRASE
METAPHRASED
METAPHRASES
METAPHRASING
METAPHRASIS
METAPHRAST
METAPHRASTIC
METAPHRASTICAL
METAPHRASTS
METAPHYSIC

METAPHYSICAL
METAPHYSICALLY
METAPHYSICIAN
METAPHYSICIANS
METAPHYSICISE
METAPHYSICISED
METAPHYSICISES
METAPHYSICISING
METAPHYSICIST
METAPHYSICISTS
METAPHYSICIZE
METAPHYSICIZED
METAPHYSICIZES
METAPHYSICIZING
METAPHYSICS
METAPLASES
METAPLASIA
METAPLASIAS
METAPLASIS
METAPLASM
METAPLASMIC
METAPLASMS
METAPLASTIC
METAPLOT
METAPOLITICAL
METAPOLITICS
METAPSYCHIC
METAPSYCHICAL
METAPSYCHICS
METAPSYCHOLOGY
METARCHON
METARCHONS
METASEQUOIA
METASEQUOIAS
METASILICATE
METASILICATES
METASILICIC
METASOMA
METASOMAS
METASOMATIC
METASOMATICALLY
METASOMATISM
METASOMATISMS
METASOMATOSIS
METASTABILITIES
METASTABILITY
METASTABLE
METASTABLES
METASTABLY
METASTASES
METASTASIS
METASTASISE
METASTASISED
METASTASISES
METASTASISING
METASTASIZE

METASTASIZED	METEMPIRICIST	METESTROUS	METHODISES
METASTASIZES	METEMPIRICISTS	METESTRUS	METHODISING
METASTASIZING	METEMPIRICS	METESTRUSES	METHODISM
METASTATIC	METEMPSYCHOSES	METEWAND	METHODISMS
METASTATICALLY	METEMPSYCHOSIS	METEWANDS	METHODIST
METATARSAL	METEMPSYCHOSIST	METEYARD	METHODISTIC
METATARSALS	METENCEPHALA	METEYARDS	METHODISTS
METATARSI	METENCEPHALIC	METH	METHODIZATION
METATARSUS	METENCEPHALON	METHACRYLATE	METHODIZE
METATE	METENCEPHALONS	METHACRYLATES	METHODIZED
METATES	METEOR	METHACRYLIC	METHODIZER
METATHEORETICAL	METEORIC	METHADON	METHODIZERS
METATHEORIES	METEORICALLY	METHADONE	METHODIZES
METATHEORY	METEORISM	METHADONES	METHODIZING
METATHERIAN	METEORISMS	METHADONS	METHODOLOGICAL
METATHERIANS	METEORIST	METHAEMOGLOBIN	METHODOLOGIES
METATHESES	METEORISTS	METHAMPHETAMINE	METHODOLOGIST
METATHESIS	METEORITAL	METHANAL	METHODOLOGISTS
METATHESISE	METEORITE	METHANALS	METHODOLOGY
METATHESISED	METEORITES	METHANATION	METHODS
METATHESISES	METEORITIC	METHANATIONS	METHOMANIA
METATHESISING	METEORITICAL	METHANE	METHOMANIAS
METATHESIZE	METEORITICIST	METHANES	METHOS
METATHESIZED	METEORITICISTS	METHANOIC	METHOTREXATE
METATHESIZES	METEORITICS	METHANOL	METHOTREXATES
METATHESIZING	METEOROGRAM	METHANOLS	METHOUGHT
METATHETIC	METEOROGRAMS	METHANOMETER	METHOXIDE
METATHETICAL	METEOROGRAPH	METHANOMETERS	METHOXIDES
METATHETICALLY	METEOROGRAPHIC	METHAQUALONE	METHOXY
METATHORACES	METEOROGRAPHS	METHAQUALONES	METHOXYBENZENE
METATHORACIC	METEOROID	METHEDRINE	METHOXYCHLOR
METATHORAX	METEOROIDAL	METHEDRINES	METHOXYCHLORS
METATHORAXES	METEOROIDS	METHEGLIN	METHOXYFLURANE
METAXYLEM	METEOROLITE	METHEGLINS	METHOXYFLURANES
METAXYLEMS	METEOROLITES	METHEMOGLOBIN	METHOXYL
METAYAGE	METEOROLOGIC	METHEMOGLOBINS	METHS
METAYAGES	METEOROLOGICAL	METHENAMINE	METHYL
METAYER	METEOROLOGIES	METHENAMINES	METHYLAL
METAYERS	METEOROLOGIST	METHICILLIN	METHYLALS
METAZOA	METEOROLOGISTS	METHICILLINS	METHYLAMINE
METAZOAL	METEOROLOGY	METHINK	METHYLAMINES
METAZOAN	METEOROUS	METHINKETH	METHYLASE
METAZOANS	METEORS	METHINKS	METHYLASES
METAZOIC	METEPA	METHIONINE	METHYLATE
METAZOON	METEPAS	METHIONINES	METHYLATED
METCAST	METER	METHO	METHYLATES
METCASTS	METERAGE	METHOD	METHYLATING
METE	METERAGES	METHODIC	METHYLATION
METECDYSES	METERED	METHODICAL	METHYLATIONS
METECDYSIS	METERING	METHODICALLY	METHYLATOR
METED	METERS	METHODICALNESS	METHYLATORS
METEMPIRIC	METERSTICK	METHODISATION	METHYLCELLULOSE
METEMPIRICAL	METERSTICKS	METHODISE	METHYLDOPA
METEMPIRICALLY	METES	METHODISED	METHYLDOPAS
METEMPIRICISM	METESTICK	METHODISER	METHYLENE
METEMPIRICISMS	METESTICKS	METHODISERS	METHYLENES

METHYLIC
METHYLMERCURIES
METHYLMERCURY
METHYLPHENIDATE
METHYLPHENOL
METHYLS
METHYLTHIONINE
METHYLXANTHINE
METHYLXANTHINES
METHYSERGIDE
METHYSERGIDES
METHYSES
METHYSIS
METHYSTIC
METIC
METICAIS
METICAL
METICALS
METICS
METICULOSITIES
METICULOSITY
METICULOUS
METICULOUSLY
METICULOUSNESS
METIER
METIERS
METIF
METIFS
METING
METIS
METISSE
METISSES
METOESTROUS
METOESTRUS
METOL
METOLS
METONYM
METONYMIC
METONYMICAL
METONYMICALLY
METONYMIES
METONYMS
METONYMY
METOPAE
METOPE
METOPES
METOPIC
METOPISM
METOPISMS
METOPON
METOPONS
METOPOSCOPIC
METOPOSCOPICAL
METOPOSCOPIES
METOPOSCOPIST
METOPOSCOPISTS

METOPOSCOPY
METOPRYL
METOPRYLS
METRALGIA
METRE
METRED
METRES
METRIC
METRICAL
METRICALLY
METRICATE
METRICATED
METRICATES
METRICATING
METRICATION
METRICATIONS
METRICIAN
METRICIANS
METRICISE
METRICISED
METRICISES
METRICISING
METRICIST
METRICISTS
METRICIZE
METRICIZED
METRICIZES
METRICIZING
METRICS
METRIFICATION
METRIFICATIONS
METRIFIED
METRIFIER
METRIFIERS
METRIFIES
METRIFY
METRIFYING
METRING
METRIST
METRISTS
METRITIS
METRITISES
METRO
METROLOGIC
METROLOGICAL
METROLOGICALLY
METROLOGIES
METROLOGIST
METROLOGISTS
METROLOGY
METROMANIA
METROMANIAS
METRONIDAZOLE
METRONIDAZOLES
METRONOME
METRONOMES

METRONOMIC
METRONOMICAL
METRONOMICALLY
METRONYMIC
METRONYMICS
METROPLEX
METROPLEXES
METROPOLIS
METROPOLISES
METROPOLITAN
METROPOLITANATE
METROPOLITANISE
METROPOLITANISM
METROPOLITANIST
METROPOLITANIZE
METROPOLITANS
METROPOLITICAL
METRORRHAGIA
METRORRHAGIAS
METROS
METROSTYLE
METROSTYLES
METS
METTLE
METTLED
METTLES
METTLESOME
METTLESOMENESS
METUMP
METUMPS
MEU
MEUNIERE
MEUS
MEUSE
MEUSED
MEUSES
MEUSING
MEVE
MEVED
MEVES
MEVING
MEVROU
MEVROUS
MEW
MEWED
MEWING
MEWL
MEWLED
MEWLER
MEWLERS
MEWLING
MEWLS
MEWS
MEWSED
MEWSES
MEWSING

MEYNT
MEZAIL
MEZAILS
MEZCAL
MEZCALINE
MEZCALS
MEZE
MEZEREON
MEZEREONS
MEZEREUM
MEZEREUMS
MEZES
MEZQUIT
MEZQUITE
MEZQUITES
MEZQUITS
MEZUZA
MEZUZAH
MEZUZAHS
MEZUZAS
MEZUZOT
MEZUZOTH
MEZZ
MEZZANINE
MEZZANINES
MEZZE
MEZZES
MEZZO
MEZZOS
MEZZOTINT
MEZZOTINTED
MEZZOTINTER
MEZZOTINTERS
MEZZOTINTING
MEZZOTINTO
MEZZOTINTOS
MEZZOTINTS
MGANGA
MGANGAS
MHO
MHORR
MHORRS
MHOS
MI
MIAOU
MIAOUED
MIAOUING
MIAOUS
MIAOW
MIAOWED
MIAOWING
MIAOWS
MIAROLITIC
MIASM
MIASMA
MIASMAL

MIASMAS
MIASMATA
MIASMATIC
MIASMATICAL
MIASMATOUS
MIASMIC
MIASMICALLY
MIASMOUS
MIASMS
MIAUL
MIAULED
MIAULING
MIAULS
MIB
MIBS
MICA
MICACEOUS
MICAS
MICATE
MICATED
MICATES
MICATING
MICAWBER
MICAWBERS
MICE
MICELL
MICELLA
MICELLAE
MICELLAR
MICELLAS
MICELLE
MICELLES
MICELLS
MICH
MICHE
MICHED
MICHER
MICHERS
MICHES
MICHIGAN
MICHIGANS
MICHING
MICHINGS
MICHT
MICK
MICKERIES
MICKERY
MICKEY
MICKEYED
MICKEYING
MICKEYS
MICKIES
MICKLE
MICKLER
MICKLES
MICKLEST

MICKS
MICKY
MICO
MICOS
MICRA
MICRIFIED
MICRIFIES
MICRIFY.
MICRIFYING
MICRO
MICROAEROPHILE
MICROAEROPHILES
MICROAEROPHILIC
MICROAMPERE
MICROAMPERES
MICROANALYSES
MICROANALYSIS
MICROANALYST
MICROANALYSTS
MICROANALYTIC
MICROANALYTICAL
MICROANATOMICAL
MICROANATOMIES
MICROANATOMY
MICROBALANCE
MICROBALANCES
MICROBAR
MICROBAROGRAPH
MICROBAROGRAPHS
MICROBARS
MICROBE
MICROBEAM
MICROBEAMS
MICROBES
MICROBIAL
MICROBIAN
MICROBIC
MICROBIOLOGIC
MICROBIOLOGICAL
MICROBIOLOGIES
MICROBIOLOGIST
MICROBIOLOGISTS
MICROBIOLOGY
MICROBIOTA
MICROBREW
MICROBREWER
MICROBREWERIES
MICROBREWERS
MICROBREWERY
MICROBREWING
MICROBREWINGS
MICROBREWS
MICROBUBBLES
MICROBURST
MICROBURSTS
MICROBUS

MICROBUSES
MICROBUSSES
MICROCAPSULE
MICROCAPSULES
MICROCAR
MICROCARD
MICROCARDS
MICROCARS
MICROCASSETTE
MICROCASSETTES
MICROCELEBRITY
MICROCEPHAL
MICROCEPHALIC
MICROCEPHALICS
MICROCEPHALIES
MICROCEPHALOUS
MICROCEPHALS
MICROCEPHALY
MICROCHEMICAL
MICROCHEMISTRY
MICROCHIP
MICROCHIPS
MICROCIRCUIT
MICROCIRCUITRY
MICROCIRCUITS
MICROCLIMATE
MICROCLIMATES
MICROCLIMATIC
MICROCLINE
MICROCLINES
MICROCOCCAL
MICROCOCCI
MICROCOCCUS
MICROCODE
MICROCODES
MICROCOMPONENT
MICROCOMPONENTS
MICROCOMPUTER
MICROCOMPUTERS
MICROCOMPUTING
MICROCOMPUTINGS
MICROCOPIED
MICROCOPIES
MICROCOPY
MICROCOPYING
MICROCOPYINGS
MICROCOSM
MICROCOSMIC
MICROCOSMICAL
MICROCOSMICALLY
MICROCOSMOS
MICROCOSMOSES
MICROCOSMS
MICROCRACK
MICROCRACKED
MICROCRACKING

MICROCRACKINGS
MICROCRACKS
MICROCRYSTAL
MICROCRYSTALS
MICROCULTURAL
MICROCULTURE
MICROCULTURES
MICROCURIE
MICROCURIES
MICROCYTE
MICROCYTES
MICROCYTIC
MICRODETECTION
MICRODETECTIONS
MICRODETECTOR
MICRODETECTORS
MICRODISSECTION
MICRODONT
MICRODONTOUS
MICRODOT
MICRODOTS
MICROEARTHQUAKE
MICROECONOMIC
MICROECONOMICS
MICROELECTRODE
MICROELECTRODES
MICROELECTRONIC
MICROELEMENT
MICROELEMENTS
MICROEVOLUTION
MICROEVOLUTIONS
MICROFARAD
MICROFARADS
MICROFAUNA
MICROFAUNAE
MICROFAUNAL
MICROFAUNAS
MICROFELSITIC
MICROFIBER
MICROFIBERS
MICROFIBRE
MICROFIBRES
MICROFIBRIL
MICROFIBRILLAR
MICROFIBRILS
MICROFICHE
MICROFICHES
MICROFILAMENT
MICROFILAMENTS
MICROFILARIA
MICROFILARIAE
MICROFILARIAL
MICROFILARIAS
MICROFILING
MICROFILINGS
MICROFILM

MICROFILMABLE
MICROFILMED
MICROFILMER
MICROFILMERS
MICROFILMING
MICROFILMS
MICROFLOPPIES
MICROFLOPPY
MICROFLORA
MICROFLORAE
MICROFLORAL
MICROFLORAS
MICROFORM
MICROFORMS
MICROFOSSIL
MICROFOSSILS
MICROFUNGI
MICROFUNGUS
MICROGAMETE
MICROGAMETES
MICROGAMETOCYTE
MICROGLIA
MICROGLIAS
MICROGRAM
MICROGRAMS
MICROGRANITE
MICROGRANITES
MICROGRANITIC
MICROGRAPH
MICROGRAPHED
MICROGRAPHER
MICROGRAPHERS
MICROGRAPHIC
MICROGRAPHICS
MICROGRAPHIES
MICROGRAPHING
MICROGRAPHS
MICROGRAPHY
MICROGRAVITIES
MICROGRAVITY
MICROGROOVE
MICROGROOVES
MICROHABITAT
MICROHABITATS
MICROHM
MICROHMS
MICROIMAGE
MICROIMAGES
MICROINCH
MICROINCHES
MICROINJECT
MICROINJECTED
MICROINJECTING
MICROINJECTION
MICROINJECTIONS
MICROINJECTS

MICROLIGHT
MICROLIGHTING
MICROLIGHTINGS
MICROLIGHTS
MICROLITE
MICROLITER
MICROLITERS
MICROLITES
MICROLITH
MICROLITHIC
MICROLITHS
MICROLITIC
MICROLOGIC
MICROLOGICAL
MICROLOGICALLY
MICROLOGIES
MICROLOGIST
MICROLOGISTS
MICROLOGY
MICROLUCES
MICROLUX
MICROLUXES
MICROMANAGE
MICROMANAGED
MICROMANAGEMENT
MICROMANAGER
MICROMANAGERS
MICROMANAGES
MICROMANAGING
MICROMARKETING
MICROMERE
MICROMERES
MICROMESH
MICROMESHES
MICROMETEORITE
MICROMETEORITES
MICROMETEORITIC
MICROMETEOROID
MICROMETEOROIDS
MICROMETER
MICROMETERS
MICROMETHOD
MICROMETHODS
MICROMETRE
MICROMETRES
MICROMETRIC
MICROMETRICAL
MICROMETRIES
MICROMETRY
MICROMHO
MICROMHOS
MICROMICROCURIE
MICROMICROFARAD
MICROMILLIMETRE
MICROMINI
MICROMINIATURE

MICROMINIS
MICROMOLAR
MICROMOLE
MICROMOLES
MICROMORPHOLOGY
MICRON
MICRONEEDLE
MICRONEEDLES
MICRONIZE
MICRONIZED
MICRONIZES
MICRONIZING
MICRONS
MICRONUCLEI
MICRONUCLEUS
MICRONUCLEUSES
MICRONUTRIENT
MICRONUTRIENTS
MICROORGANISM
MICROORGANISMS
MICROPARASITE
MICROPARASITES
MICROPARASITIC
MICROPARASITISM
MICROPARTICLE
MICROPARTICLES
MICROPAYMENT
MICROPEGMATITE
MICROPEGMATITES
MICROPEGMATITIC
MICROPHAGE
MICROPHAGES
MICROPHAGOUS
MICROPHONE
MICROPHONES
MICROPHONIC
MICROPHONICS
MICROPHOTOGRAPH
MICROPHOTOMETER
MICROPHOTOMETRY
MICROPHYLL
MICROPHYLLOUS
MICROPHYLLS
MICROPHYSICAL
MICROPHYSICALLY
MICROPHYSICS
MICROPHYTE
MICROPHYTES
MICROPHYTIC
MICROPIPET
MICROPIPETS
MICROPIPETTE
MICROPIPETTES
MICROPLANKTON
MICROPLANKTONS
MICROPOLIS

MICROPOLISES
MICROPORE
MICROPORES
MICROPOROSITIES
MICROPOROSITY
MICROPOROUS
MICROPOWER
MICROPRINT
MICROPRINTED
MICROPRINTING
MICROPRINTINGS
MICROPRINTS
MICROPRISM
MICROPRISMS
MICROPROBE
MICROPROBES
MICROPROCESSING
MICROPROCESSOR
MICROPROCESSORS
MICROPROGRAM
MICROPROGRAMS
MICROPROJECTION
MICROPROJECTOR
MICROPROJECTORS
MICROPSIA
MICROPSIAS
MICROPTEROUS
MICROPUBLISHER
MICROPUBLISHERS
MICROPUBLISHING
MICROPULSATION
MICROPULSATIONS
MICROPUMP
MICROPUMPS
MICROPUNCTURE
MICROPUNCTURES
MICROPYLAR
MICROPYLE
MICROPYLES
MICROPYROMETER
MICROPYROMETERS
MICROQUAKE
MICROQUAKES
MICRORADIOGRAPH
MICROREADER
MICROREADERS
MICROS
MICROSATELLITE
MICROSCALE
MICROSCALES
MICROSCOPE
MICROSCOPES
MICROSCOPIC
MICROSCOPICAL
MICROSCOPICALLY
MICROSCOPIES

MICROSCOPIST
MICROSCOPISTS
MICROSCOPY
MICROSECOND
MICROSECONDS
MICROSEISM
MICROSEISMIC
MICROSEISMICAL
MICROSEISMICITY
MICROSEISMS
MICROSITE
MICROSITES
MICROSKIRT
MICROSKIRTS
MICROSLEEP
MICROSLEEPS
MICROSMATIC
MICROSOMAL
MICROSOME
MICROSOMES
MICROSPECIES
MICROSPHERE
MICROSPHERES
MICROSPHERICAL
MICROSPORANGIA
MICROSPORANGIUM
MICROSPORE
MICROSPORES
MICROSPORIC
MICROSPOROCYTE
MICROSPOROCYTES
MICROSPOROPHYLL
MICROSPOROUS
MICROSTATE
MICROSTATES
MICROSTOMATOUS
MICROSTOMOUS
MICROSTRUCTURAL
MICROSTRUCTURE
MICROSTRUCTURES
MICROSURGEON
MICROSURGEONS
MICROSURGERIES
MICROSURGERY
MICROSURGICAL
MICROSWITCH
MICROSWITCHES
MICROTECHNIC
MICROTECHNICS
MICROTECHNIQUE
MICROTECHNIQUES
MICROTECHNOLOGY
MICROTOME
MICROTOMES
MICROTOMIC
MICROTOMICAL

MICROTOMIES
MICROTOMIST
MICROTOMISTS
MICROTOMY
MICROTONAL
MICROTONALITIES
MICROTONALITY
MICROTONALLY
MICROTONE
MICROTONES
MICROTUBULAR
MICROTUBULE
MICROTUBULES
MICROTUNNELLING
MICROVASCULAR
MICROVILLAR
MICROVILLI
MICROVILLOUS
MICROVILLUS
MICROVOLT
MICROVOLTS
MICROWATT
MICROWATTS
MICROWAVABLE
MICROWAVE
MICROWAVEABLE
MICROWAVED
MICROWAVES
MICROWAVING
MICROWIRE
MICROWIRES
MICROWORLD
MICROWORLDS
MICROWRITER
MICROWRITERS
MICRURGIES
MICRURGY
MICTION
MICTIONS
MICTURATE
MICTURATED
MICTURATES
MICTURATING
MICTURITION
MICTURITIONS
MID
MIDAIR
MIDAIRS
MIDBRAIN
MIDBRAINS
MIDCOURSE
MIDCULT
MIDCULTS
MIDDAY
MIDDAYS
MIDDELMANNETJIE

MIDDEN
MIDDENS
MIDDENSTEAD
MIDDENSTEADS
MIDDEST
MIDDIES
MIDDLE
MIDDLEBREAKER
MIDDLEBREAKERS
MIDDLEBROW
MIDDLEBROWED
MIDDLEBROWISM
MIDDLEBROWS
MIDDLEBUSTER
MIDDLEBUSTERS
MIDDLED
MIDDLEMAN
MIDDLEMEN
MIDDLEMOST
MIDDLER
MIDDLERS
MIDDLES
MIDDLEWEIGHT
MIDDLEWEIGHTS
MIDDLING
MIDDLINGLY
MIDDLINGS
MIDDORSAL
MIDDY
MIDFIELD
MIDFIELDER
MIDFIELDERS
MIDFIELDS
MIDGE
MIDGES
MIDGET
MIDGETS
MIDGIES
MIDGUT
MIDGUTS
MIDGY
MIDI
MIDINETTE
MIDINETTES
MIDIRON
MIDIRONS
MIDIS
MIDLAND
MIDLANDS
MIDLATITUDE
MIDLATITUDES
MIDLEG
MIDLEGS
MIDLIFE
MIDLINE
MIDLINES

MIDLITTORAL
MIDLITTORALS
MIDLIVES
MIDMONTH
MIDMONTHS
MIDMOST
MIDMOSTS
MIDNIGHT
MIDNIGHTLY
MIDNIGHTS
MIDNOON
MIDNOONS
MIDPOINT
MIDPOINTS
MIDRANGE
MIDRANGES
MIDRASH
MIDRASHIC
MIDRASHIM
MIDRASHOTH
MIDRIB
MIDRIBS
MIDRIFF
MIDRIFFS
MIDS
MIDSAGITTAL
MIDSECTION
MIDSECTIONS
MIDSHIP
MIDSHIPMAN
MIDSHIPMATE
MIDSHIPMATES
MIDSHIPMEN
MIDSHIPS
MIDSIZE
MIDSIZED
MIDSOLE
MIDSOLES
MIDSPACE
MIDSPACES
MIDST
MIDSTORIES
MIDSTORY
MIDSTREAM
MIDSTREAMS
MIDSTS
MIDSUMMER
MIDSUMMERS
MIDTERM
MIDTERMS
MIDTOWN
MIDTOWNS
MIDWATCH
MIDWATCHES
MIDWAY
MIDWAYS

MIDWEEK
MIDWEEKLY
MIDWEEKS
MIDWIFE
MIDWIFED
MIDWIFERIES
MIDWIFERY
MIDWIFES
MIDWIFING
MIDWINTER
MIDWINTERS
MIDWIVE
MIDWIVED
MIDWIVES
MIDWIVING
MIDYEAR
MIDYEARS
MIELIE
MIELIES
MIEN
MIENS
MIEVE
MIEVED
MIEVES
MIEVING
MIFEPRISTONE
MIFEPRISTONES
MIFF
MIFFED
MIFFIER
MIFFIEST
MIFFILY
MIFFINESS
MIFFINESSES
MIFFING
MIFFS
MIFFY
MIFTY
MIG
MIGG
MIGGLE
MIGGLES
MIGGS
MIGHT
MIGHTEST
MIGHTFUL
MIGHTIER
MIGHTIEST
MIGHTILY
MIGHTINESS
MIGHTINESSES
MIGHTS
MIGHTST
MIGHTY
MIGMATITE
MIGMATITES

MIGNON
MIGNONETTE
MIGNONETTES
MIGNONNE
MIGNONS
MIGRAINE
MIGRAINES
MIGRAINEUR
MIGRAINEURS
MIGRAINOUS
MIGRANT
MIGRANTS
MIGRATE
MIGRATED
MIGRATES
MIGRATING
MIGRATION
MIGRATIONAL
MIGRATIONIST
MIGRATIONISTS
MIGRATIONS
MIGRATOR
MIGRATORS
MIGRATORY
MIGS
MIHI
MIHRAB
MIHRABS
MIJNHEER
MIJNHEERS
MIKADO
MIKADOS
MIKE
MIKED
MIKES
MIKING
MIKRA
MIKRON
MIKRONS
MIKVAH
MIKVAHS
MIKVEH
MIKVEHS
MIKVOTH
MIL
MILADI
MILADIES
MILADIS
MILADY
MILAGE
MILAGES
MILAH
MILAHS
MILATAINMENT
MILATAINMENTS
MILCH

MILCHIG
MILCHIK
MILD
MILDEN
MILDENED
MILDENING
MILDENS
MILDER
MILDEST
MILDEW
MILDEWED
MILDEWING
MILDEWS
MILDEWY
MILDLY
MILDNESS
MILDNESSES
MILDS
MILE
MILEAGE
MILEAGES
MILEOMETER
MILEOMETERS
MILEPOST
MILEPOSTS
MILER
MILERS
MILES
MILESIMO
MILESIMOS
MILESTONE
MILESTONES
MILFOIL
MILFOILS
MILIA
MILIARIA
MILIARIAL
MILIARIAS
MILIARY
MILIEU
MILIEUS
MILIEUX
MILITANCE
MILITANCES
MILITANCIES
MILITANCY
MILITANT
MILITANTLY
MILITANTNESS
MILITANTNESSES
MILITANTS
MILITAR
MILITARIA
MILITARIES
MILITARILY
MILITARISATION

MILITARISATIONS
MILITARISE
MILITARISED
MILITARISES
MILITARISING
MILITARISM
MILITARISMS
MILITARIST
MILITARISTIC
MILITARISTS
MILITARIZATION
MILITARIZATIONS
MILITARIZE
MILITARIZED
MILITARIZES
MILITARIZING
MILITARY
MILITATE
MILITATED
MILITATES
MILITATING
MILITATION
MILITATIONS
MILITIA
MILITIAMAN
MILITIAMEN
MILITIAS
MILIUM
MILK
MILKED
MILKEN
MILKER
MILKERS
MILKFISH
MILKFISHES
MILKIER
MILKIEST
MILKILY
MILKINESS
MILKINESSES
MILKING
MILKINGS
MILKLESS
MILKLIKE
MILKMAID
MILKMAIDS
MILKMAN
MILKMEN
MILKO
MILKOS
MILKS
MILKSHED
MILKSHEDS
MILKSOP
MILKSOPISM
MILKSOPPING

MILKSOPPY
MILKSOPS
MILKTOAST
MILKTOASTS
MILKWEED
MILKWEEDS
MILKWOOD
MILKWOODS
MILKWORT
MILKWORTS
MILKY
MILL
MILLABLE
MILLAGE
MILLAGES
MILLBOARD
MILLBOARDS
MILLCAKE
MILLCAKES
MILLDAM
MILLDAMS
MILLE
MILLED
MILLEFEUILLE
MILLEFEUILLES
MILLEFIORI
MILLEFIORIS
MILLEFLEUR
MILLEFLEURS
MILLENARIAN
MILLENARIANISM
MILLENARIANISMS
MILLENARIANS
MILLENARIES
MILLENARISM
MILLENARISMS
MILLENARY
MILLENNIA
MILLENNIAL
MILLENNIALISM
MILLENNIALISMS
MILLENNIALIST
MILLENNIALISTS
MILLENNIALLY
MILLENNIANISM
MILLENNIANISMS
MILLENNIARISM
MILLENNIARISMS
MILLENNIUM
MILLENNIUMS
MILLEPED
MILLEPEDE
MILLEPEDES
MILLEPEDS
MILLEPORE
MILLEPORES

MILLER
MILLERITE
MILLERITES
MILLERS
MILLES
MILLESIMAL
MILLESIMALLY
MILLESIMALS
MILLET
MILLETS
MILLIAMPERE
MILLIAMPERES
MILLIARD
MILLIARDS
MILLIARE
MILLIARES
MILLIARIES
MILLIARY
MILLIBAR
MILLIBARS
MILLICURIE
MILLICURIES
MILLIDEGREE
MILLIDEGREES
MILLIEME
MILLIEMES
MILLIER
MILLIERS
MILLIGAL
MILLIGALS
MILLIGRAM
MILLIGRAMME
MILLIGRAMMES
MILLIGRAMS
MILLIHENRIES
MILLIHENRY
MILLIHENRYS
MILLILAMBERT
MILLILAMBERTS
MILLILITER
MILLILITERS
MILLILITRE
MILLILITRES
MILLILUCES
MILLILUX
MILLILUXES
MILLIME
MILLIMES
MILLIMETER
MILLIMETERS
MILLIMETRE
MILLIMETRES
MILLIMHO
MILLIMHOS
MILLIMICRON
MILLIMICRONS

MILLIMOLAR
MILLIMOLE
MILLIMOLES
MILLINE
MILLINER
MILLINERIES
MILLINERS
MILLINERY
MILLINES
MILLING
MILLINGS
MILLIOHM
MILLIOHMS
MILLION
MILLIONAIRE
MILLIONAIRES
MILLIONAIRESS
MILLIONAIRESSES
MILLIONARY
MILLIONFOLD
MILLIONNAIRE
MILLIONNAIRES
MILLIONNAIRESS
MILLIONS
MILLIONTH
MILLIONTHS
MILLIOSMOL
MILLIOSMOLS
MILLIPED
MILLIPEDE
MILLIPEDES
MILLIPEDS
MILLIPROBE
MILLIPROBES
MILLIRADIAN
MILLIRADIANS
MILLIREM
MILLIREMS
MILLIROENTGEN
MILLIROENTGENS
MILLISECOND
MILLISECONDS
MILLISIEVERT
MILLISIEVERTS
MILLIVOLT
MILLIVOLTS
MILLIWATT
MILLIWATTS
MILLOCRACIES
MILLOCRACY
MILLOCRAT
MILLOCRATS
MILLPOND
MILLPONDS
MILLRACE
MILLRACES

MILLRIND
MILLRINDS
MILLRUN
MILLRUNS
MILLS
MILLSCALE
MILLSCALES
MILLSTONE
MILLSTONES
MILLSTREAM
MILLSTREAMS
MILLTAIL
MILLTAILS
MILLWHEEL
MILLWHEELS
MILLWORK
MILLWORKS
MILLWRIGHT
MILLWRIGHTS
MILNEB
MILNEBS
MILO
MILOMETER
MILOMETERS
MILOR
MILORD
MILORDS
MILORS
MILOS
MILPA
MILPAS
MILQUETOAST
MILQUETOASTS
MILREIS
MILS
MILSEY
MILSEYS
MILT
MILTED
MILTER
MILTERS
MILTIER
MILTIEST
MILTING
MILTONIA
MILTONIAS
MILTS
MILTY
MILTZ
MILTZES
MILVINE
MIM
MIMBAR
MIMBARS
MIME
MIMED

MIMEO
MIMEOED
MIMEOGRAPH
MIMEOGRAPHED
MIMEOGRAPHING
MIMEOGRAPHS
MIMEOING
MIMEOS
MIMER
MIMERS
MIMES
MIMESES
MIMESIS
MIMESISES
MIMESTER
MIMESTERS
MIMETIC
MIMETICAL
MIMETICALLY
MIMETITE
MIMETITES
MIMIC
MIMICAL
MIMICKED
MIMICKER
MIMICKERS
MIMICKING
MIMICRIES
MIMICRY
MIMICS
MIMING
MIMMER
MIMMEST
MIMMICK
MIMMICKED
MIMMICKING
MIMMICKS
MIMOGRAPHER
MIMOGRAPHERS
MIMOGRAPHIES
MIMOGRAPHY
MIMOSA
MIMOSACEOUS
MIMOSAS
MIMSEY
MIMSIER
MIMSIEST
MIMSY
MIMULUS
MIMULUSES
MINA
MINABLE
MINACIOUS
MINACIOUSLY
MINACITIES
MINACITY

MINAE
MINAH
MINAHS
MINAR
MINARET
MINARETED
MINARETS
MINARS
MINAS
MINATORIAL
MINATORIALLY
MINATORILY
MINATORY
MINAUDERIE
MINAUDERIES
MINAUDIERE
MINAUDIERES
MINBAR
MINBARS
MINCE
MINCED
MINCEMEAT
MINCEMEATS
MINCER
MINCERS
MINCES
MINCEUR
MINCIER
MINCIEST
MINCING
MINCINGLY
MINCINGS
MINCY
MIND
MINDBLOWER
MINDBLOWERS
MINDED
MINDEDNESS
MINDEDNESSES
MINDER
MINDERS
MINDFUCK
MINDFUCKS
MINDFUL
MINDFULLY
MINDFULNESS
MINDFULNESSES
MINDING
MINDINGS
MINDLESS
MINDLESSLY
MINDLESSNESS
MINDLESSNESSES
MINDS
MINDSET
MINDSETS

MINDSHARE
MINDSHARED
MINDSHARES
MINDSHARING
MINE
MINEABLE
MINED
MINEFIELD
MINEFIELDS
MINEHUNTER
MINEHUNTERS
MINELAYER
MINELAYERS
MINEOLA
MINEOLAS
MINER
MINERAL
MINERALISATION
MINERALISATIONS
MINERALISE
MINERALISED
MINERALISER
MINERALISERS
MINERALISES
MINERALISING
MINERALIST
MINERALISTS
MINERALIZABLE
MINERALIZATION
MINERALIZATIONS
MINERALIZE
MINERALIZED
MINERALIZER
MINERALIZERS
MINERALIZES
MINERALIZING
MINERALOGIC
MINERALOGICAL
MINERALOGICALLY
MINERALOGIES
MINERALOGISE
MINERALOGISED
MINERALOGISES
MINERALOGISING
MINERALOGIST
MINERALOGISTS
MINERALOGIZE
MINERALOGIZED
MINERALOGIZES
MINERALOGIZING
MINERALOGY
MINERALS
MINERS
MINES
MINESTONE
MINESTONES

MINESTRONE
MINESTRONES
MINESWEEPER
MINESWEEPERS
MINESWEEPING
MINESWEEPINGS
MINETTE
MINETTES
MINEVER
MINEVERS
MING
MINGE
MINGED
MINGER
MINGERS
MINGES
MINGIER
MINGIEST
MINGIMINGI
MINGIMINGIS
MINGIN
MINGINESS
MINGINESSES
MINGING
MINGLE
MINGLED
MINGLEMENT
MINGLEMENTS
MINGLER
MINGLERS
MINGLES
MINGLING
MINGLINGLY
MINGLINGS
MINGS
MINGY
MINI
MINIATE
MINIATED
MINIATES
MINIATING
MINIATION
MINIATIONS
MINIATURE
MINIATURED
MINIATURES
MINIATURING
MINIATURISATION
MINIATURISE
MINIATURISED
MINIATURISES
MINIATURISING
MINIATURIST
MINIATURISTIC
MINIATURISTS
MINIATURIZATION

MINIATURIZE
MINIATURIZED
MINIATURIZES
MINIATURIZING
MINIBAR
MINIBARS
MINIBIKE
MINIBIKER
MINIBIKERS
MINIBIKES
MINIBREAK
MINIBREAKS
MINIBUDGET
MINIBUDGETS
MINIBUS
MINIBUSES
MINIBUSSES
MINICAB
MINICABBING
MINICABBINGS
MINICABS
MINICAM
MINICAMP
MINICAMPS
MINICAMS
MINICAR
MINICARS
MINICOM
MINICOMPUTER
MINICOMPUTERS
MINICOMS
MINICOURSE
MINICOURSES
MINIDISC
MINIDISCS
MINIDISH
MINIDISHES
MINIDISK
MINIDISKS
MINIDRESS
MINIDRESSES
MINIER
MINIEST
MINIFICATION
MINIFICATIONS
MINIFIED
MINIFIES
MINIFLOPPIES
MINIFLOPPY
MINIFY
MINIFYING
MINIKIN
MINIKINS
MINILAB
MINILABS
MINIM

MINIMA
MINIMAL
MINIMALISM
MINIMALISMS
MINIMALIST
MINIMALISTS
MINIMALLY
MINIMALS
MINIMAX
MINIMAXED
MINIMAXES
MINIMAXING
MINIMENT
MINIMENTS
MINIMILL
MINIMILLS
MINIMISATION
MINIMISATIONS
MINIMISE
MINIMISED
MINIMISER
MINIMISERS
MINIMISES
MINIMISING
MINIMISM
MINIMISMS
MINIMIST
MINIMISTS
MINIMIZATION
MINIMIZATIONS
MINIMIZE
MINIMIZED
MINIMIZER
MINIMIZERS
MINIMIZES
MINIMIZING
MINIMS
MINIMUM
MINIMUMS
MINIMUS
MINIMUSES
MINING
MININGS
MINION
MINIONS
MINIPARK
MINIPARKS
MINIPILL
MINIPILLS
MINIRUGBIES
MINIRUGBY
MINIS
MINISCHOOL
MINISCHOOLS
MINISCULE
MINISCULES

MINISERIES
MINISH
MINISHED
MINISHES
MINISHING
MINISKI
MINISKIRT
MINISKIRTED
MINISKIRTS
MINISKIS
MINISTATE
MINISTATES
MINISTER
MINISTERED
MINISTERIA
MINISTERIAL
MINISTERIALIST
MINISTERIALISTS
MINISTERIALLY
MINISTERING
MINISTERIUM
MINISTERS
MINISTERSHIP
MINISTERSHIPS
MINISTRANT
MINISTRANTS
MINISTRATION
MINISTRATIONS
MINISTRATIVE
MINISTRESS
MINISTRESSES
MINISTRIES
MINISTROKE
MINISTROKES
MINISTRY
MINIUM
MINIUMS
MINIVAN
MINIVANS
MINIVER
MINIVERS
MINIVET
MINIVETS
MINIVOLLEY
MINIVOLLEYS
MINK
MINKE
MINKES
MINKS
MINNEOLA
MINNEOLAS
MINNESINGER
MINNESINGERS
MINNICK
MINNICKED
MINNICKING

MINNICKS
MINNIE
MINNIES
MINNOCK
MINNOCKED
MINNOCKING
MINNOCKS
MINNOW
MINNOWS
MINNY
MINO
MINOR
MINORCA
MINORCAS
MINORED
MINORING
MINORITAIRE
MINORITAIRES
MINORITIES
MINORITY
MINORS
MINORSHIP
MINORSHIPS
MINOS
MINOXIDIL
MINOXIDILS
MINSHUKU
MINSHUKUS
MINSTER
MINSTERS
MINSTREL
MINSTRELS
MINSTRELSIES
MINSTRELSY
MINT
MINTAGE
MINTAGES
MINTED
MINTER
MINTERS
MINTIER
MINTIEST
MINTING
MINTS
MINTY
MINUEND
MINUENDS
MINUET
MINUETS
MINUS
MINUSCULAR
MINUSCULE
MINUSCULES
MINUSES
MINUTE
MINUTED

MINUTELY
MINUTEMAN
MINUTEMEN
MINUTENESS
MINUTENESSES
MINUTER
MINUTES
MINUTEST
MINUTIA
MINUTIAE
MINUTIAL
MINUTING
MINUTIOSE
MINX
MINXES
MINXISH
MINY
MINYAN
MINYANIM
MINYANS
MIOMBO
MIOMBOS
MIOSES
MIOSIS
MIOTIC
MIOTICS
MIQUELET
MIQUELETS
MIR
MIRABELLE
MIRABELLES
MIRABILIA
MIRABILIS
MIRABILISES
MIRABLE
MIRACIDIA
MIRACIDIAL
MIRACIDIUM
MIRACLE
MIRACLES
MIRACULOUS
MIRACULOUSLY
MIRACULOUSNESS
MIRADOR
MIRADORS
MIRAGE
MIRAGES
MIRBANE
MIRBANES
MIRE
MIRED
MIREPOIX
MIRES
MIREX
MIREXES
MIRI

MIRIER
MIRIEST
MIRIFIC
MIRIFICAL
MIRIFICALLY
MIRIN
MIRINESS
MIRINESSES
MIRING
MIRINS
MIRITI
MIRITIS
MIRK
MIRKER
MIRKEST
MIRKIER
MIRKIEST
MIRKILY
MIRKINESS
MIRKS
MIRKY
MIRLIER
MIRLIEST
MIRLIGOES
MIRLITON
MIRLITONS
MIRLY
MIRO
MIROMIRO
MIROMIROS
MIRROR
MIRRORED
MIRRORING
MIRRORLIKE
MIRRORS
MIRRORWISE
MIRS
MIRTH
MIRTHFUL
MIRTHFULLY
MIRTHFULNESS
MIRTHFULNESSES
MIRTHLESS
MIRTHLESSLY
MIRTHLESSNESS
MIRTHLESSNESSES
MIRTHS
MIRV
MIRVED
MIRVING
MIRVS
MIRY
MIRZA
MIRZAS
MIS
MISACCEPTATION

MISACCEPTATIONS
MISACT
MISACTED
MISACTING
MISACTS
MISADAPT
MISADAPTED
MISADAPTING
MISADAPTS
MISADD
MISADDED
MISADDING
MISADDRESS
MISADDRESSED
MISADDRESSES
MISADDRESSING
MISADDS
MISADJUST
MISADJUSTED
MISADJUSTING
MISADJUSTS
MISADVENTURE
MISADVENTURED
MISADVENTURER
MISADVENTURERS
MISADVENTURES
MISADVENTURING
MISADVENTUROUS
MISADVERTENCE
MISADVERTENCES
MISADVISE
MISADVISED
MISADVISEDLY
MISADVISEDNESS
MISADVISES
MISADVISING
MISAGENT
MISAGENTS
MISAIM
MISAIMED
MISAIMING
MISAIMS
MISALIGN
MISALIGNED
MISALIGNING
MISALIGNMENT
MISALIGNMENTS
MISALIGNS
MISALLEGE
MISALLEGED
MISALLEGES
MISALLEGING
MISALLIANCE
MISALLIANCES
MISALLIED
MISALLIES

MISALLOCATE
MISALLOCATED
MISALLOCATES
MISALLOCATING
MISALLOCATION
MISALLOCATIONS
MISALLOT
MISALLOTMENT
MISALLOTMENTS
MISALLOTS
MISALLOTTED
MISALLOTTING
MISALLY
MISALLYING
MISALTER
MISALTERED
MISALTERING
MISALTERS
MISANALYSES
MISANALYSIS
MISANDRIES
MISANDRIST
MISANDRISTS
MISANDROUS
MISANDRY
MISANTHROPE
MISANTHROPES
MISANTHROPIC
MISANTHROPICAL
MISANTHROPIES
MISANTHROPIST
MISANTHROPISTS
MISANTHROPOS
MISANTHROPOSES
MISANTHROPY
MISAPPELLATION
MISAPPELLATIONS
MISAPPLICATION
MISAPPLICATIONS
MISAPPLIED
MISAPPLIES
MISAPPLY
MISAPPLYING
MISAPPRAISAL
MISAPPRAISALS
MISAPPRAISE
MISAPPRAISED
MISAPPRAISES
MISAPPRAISING
MISAPPRECIATE
MISAPPRECIATED
MISAPPRECIATES
MISAPPRECIATING
MISAPPRECIATION
MISAPPRECIATIVE
MISAPPREHEND

MISAPPREHENDED
MISAPPREHENDING
MISAPPREHENDS
MISAPPREHENSION
MISAPPREHENSIVE
MISAPPROPRIATE
MISAPPROPRIATED
MISAPPROPRIATES
MISARRANGE
MISARRANGED
MISARRANGEMENT
MISARRANGEMENTS
MISARRANGES
MISARRANGING
MISARRAY
MISARRAYS
MISARTICULATE
MISARTICULATED
MISARTICULATES
MISARTICULATING
MISASSAY
MISASSAYED
MISASSAYING
MISASSAYS
MISASSEMBLE
MISASSEMBLED
MISASSEMBLES
MISASSEMBLING
MISASSIGN
MISASSIGNED
MISASSIGNING
MISASSIGNS
MISASSOCIATE
MISASSOCIATED
MISASSOCIATES
MISASSOCIATING
MISASSOCIATION
MISASSOCIATIONS
MISASSUMPTION
MISASSUMPTIONS
MISATE
MISATONE
MISATONED
MISATONES
MISATONING
MISATTRIBUTE
MISATTRIBUTED
MISATTRIBUTES
MISATTRIBUTING
MISATTRIBUTION
MISATTRIBUTIONS
MISAUNTER
MISAUNTERS
MISAVER
MISAVERRED
MISAVERRING

MISAVERS
MISAVISED
MISAWARD
MISAWARDED
MISAWARDING
MISAWARDS
MISBALANCE
MISBALANCED
MISBALANCES
MISBALANCING
MISBECAME
MISBECOME
MISBECOMES
MISBECOMING
MISBECOMINGNESS
MISBEGAN
MISBEGIN
MISBEGINNING
MISBEGINS
MISBEGOT
MISBEGOTTEN
MISBEGUN
MISBEHAVE
MISBEHAVED
MISBEHAVER
MISBEHAVERS
MISBEHAVES
MISBEHAVING
MISBEHAVIOR
MISBEHAVIORS
MISBEHAVIOUR
MISBEHAVIOURS
MISBELIEF
MISBELIEFS
MISBELIEVE
MISBELIEVED
MISBELIEVER
MISBELIEVERS
MISBELIEVES
MISBELIEVING
MISBESEEM
MISBESEEMED
MISBESEEMING
MISBESEEMS
MISBESTOW
MISBESTOWAL
MISBESTOWALS
MISBESTOWED
MISBESTOWING
MISBESTOWS
MISBIAS
MISBIASED
MISBIASES
MISBIASING
MISBIASSED
MISBIASSES

MISBIASSING
MISBILL
MISBILLED
MISBILLING
MISBILLS
MISBIND
MISBINDING
MISBINDS
MISBIRTH
MISBIRTHS
MISBORN
MISBOUND
MISBRAND
MISBRANDED
MISBRANDING
MISBRANDS
MISBUILD
MISBUILDING
MISBUILDS
MISBUILT
MISBUTTON
MISBUTTONED
MISBUTTONING
MISBUTTONS
MISCALCULATE
MISCALCULATED
MISCALCULATES
MISCALCULATING
MISCALCULATION
MISCALCULATIONS
MISCALCULATOR
MISCALCULATORS
MISCALL
MISCALLED
MISCALLER
MISCALLERS
MISCALLING
MISCALLS
MISCANTHUS
MISCANTHUSES
MISCAPTION
MISCAPTIONED
MISCAPTIONING
MISCAPTIONS
MISCARRIAGE
MISCARRIAGES
MISCARRIED
MISCARRIES
MISCARRY
MISCARRYING
MISCAST
MISCASTING
MISCASTS
MISCATALOG
MISCATALOGED
MISCATALOGING

MISCATALOGS
MISCATEGORISE
MISCATEGORISED
MISCATEGORISES
MISCATEGORISING
MISCATEGORIZE
MISCATEGORIZED
MISCATEGORIZES
MISCATEGORIZING
MISCEGEN
MISCEGENATE
MISCEGENATED
MISCEGENATES
MISCEGENATING
MISCEGENATION
MISCEGENATIONAL
MISCEGENATIONS
MISCEGENATOR
MISCEGENATORS
MISCEGENE
MISCEGENES
MISCEGENETIC
MISCEGENIST
MISCEGENISTS
MISCEGENS
MISCEGINE
MISCEGINES
MISCELLANARIAN
MISCELLANARIANS
MISCELLANEA
MISCELLANEOUS
MISCELLANEOUSLY
MISCELLANIES
MISCELLANIST
MISCELLANISTS
MISCELLANY
MISCH
MISCHALLENGE
MISCHALLENGES
MISCHANCE
MISCHANCED
MISCHANCEFUL
MISCHANCES
MISCHANCING
MISCHANCY
MISCHANNEL
MISCHANNELED
MISCHANNELING
MISCHANNELLED
MISCHANNELLING
MISCHANNELS
MISCHANTER
MISCHANTERS
MISCHARACTERISE
MISCHARACTERIZE
MISCHARGE

MISCHARGED
MISCHARGES
MISCHARGING
MISCHIEF
MISCHIEFED
MISCHIEFING
MISCHIEFS
MISCHIEVOUS
MISCHIEVOUSLY
MISCHIEVOUSNESS
MISCHMETAL
MISCHMETALS
MISCHOICE
MISCHOICES
MISCHOOSE
MISCHOOSES
MISCHOOSING
MISCHOOSINGS
MISCHOSE
MISCHOSEN
MISCIBILITIES
MISCIBILITY
MISCIBLE
MISCITATION
MISCITATIONS
MISCITE
MISCITED
MISCITES
MISCITING
MISCLAIM
MISCLAIMED
MISCLAIMING
MISCLAIMS
MISCLASS
MISCLASSED
MISCLASSES
MISCLASSIFIED
MISCLASSIFIES
MISCLASSIFY
MISCLASSIFYING
MISCLASSING
MISCODE
MISCODED
MISCODES
MISCODING
MISCOIN
MISCOINED
MISCOINING
MISCOINS
MISCOLOR
MISCOLORED
MISCOLORING
MISCOLORS
MISCOLOUR
MISCOLOURED
MISCOLOURING

MISCOLOURS
MISCOMPREHEND
MISCOMPREHENDED
MISCOMPREHENDS
MISCOMPUTATION
MISCOMPUTATIONS
MISCOMPUTE
MISCOMPUTED
MISCOMPUTES
MISCOMPUTING
MISCONCEIT
MISCONCEITED
MISCONCEITING
MISCONCEITS
MISCONCEIVE
MISCONCEIVED
MISCONCEIVER
MISCONCEIVERS
MISCONCEIVES
MISCONCEIVING
MISCONCEPTION
MISCONCEPTIONS
MISCONDUCT
MISCONDUCTED
MISCONDUCTING
MISCONDUCTS
MISCONJECTURE
MISCONJECTURED
MISCONJECTURES
MISCONJECTURING
MISCONNECT
MISCONNECTED
MISCONNECTING
MISCONNECTION
MISCONNECTIONS
MISCONNECTS
MISCONSTER
MISCONSTERED
MISCONSTERING
MISCONSTERS
MISCONSTRUCT
MISCONSTRUCTED
MISCONSTRUCTING
MISCONSTRUCTION
MISCONSTRUCTS
MISCONSTRUE
MISCONSTRUED
MISCONSTRUES
MISCONSTRUING
MISCONTENT
MISCONTENTED
MISCONTENTING
MISCONTENTMENT
MISCONTENTMENTS
MISCONTENTS
MISCOOK

MISCOOKED
MISCOOKING
MISCOOKS
MISCOPIED
MISCOPIES
MISCOPY
MISCOPYING
MISCORRECT
MISCORRECTED
MISCORRECTING
MISCORRECTION
MISCORRECTIONS
MISCORRECTS
MISCORRELATION
MISCORRELATIONS
MISCOUNSEL
MISCOUNSELLED
MISCOUNSELLING
MISCOUNSELS
MISCOUNT
MISCOUNTED
MISCOUNTING
MISCOUNTS
MISCREANCE
MISCREANCES
MISCREANCIES
MISCREANCY
MISCREANT
MISCREANTS
MISCREATE
MISCREATED
MISCREATES
MISCREATING
MISCREATION
MISCREATIONS
MISCREATIVE
MISCREATOR
MISCREATORS
MISCREAUNCE
MISCREAUNCES
MISCREDIT
MISCREDITED
MISCREDITING
MISCREDITS
MISCREED
MISCREEDS
MISCUE
MISCUED
MISCUEING
MISCUES
MISCUING
MISCUT
MISCUTS
MISCUTTING
MISDATE
MISDATED

MISDATES
MISDATING
MISDEAL
MISDEALER
MISDEALERS
MISDEALING
MISDEALS
MISDEALT
MISDEED
MISDEEDS
MISDEEM
MISDEEMED
MISDEEMFUL
MISDEEMING
MISDEEMINGS
MISDEEMS
MISDEFINE
MISDEFINED
MISDEFINES
MISDEFINING
MISDEMEAN
MISDEMEANANT
MISDEMEANANTS
MISDEMEANED
MISDEMEANING
MISDEMEANOR
MISDEMEANORS
MISDEMEANOUR
MISDEMEANOURS
MISDEMEANS
MISDEMPT
MISDESCRIBE
MISDESCRIBED
MISDESCRIBES
MISDESCRIBING
MISDESCRIPTION
MISDESCRIPTIONS
MISDESERT
MISDESERTS
MISDEVELOP
MISDEVELOPED
MISDEVELOPING
MISDEVELOPS
MISDEVOTION
MISDEVOTIONS
MISDIAGNOSE
MISDIAGNOSED
MISDIAGNOSES
MISDIAGNOSING
MISDIAGNOSIS
MISDIAL
MISDIALED
MISDIALING
MISDIALLED
MISDIALLING
MISDIALS

MISDID
MISDIET
MISDIETS
MISDIGHT
MISDIRECT
MISDIRECTED
MISDIRECTING
MISDIRECTION
MISDIRECTIONS
MISDIRECTS
MISDISTRIBUTION
MISDIVISION
MISDIVISIONS
MISDO
MISDOER
MISDOERS
MISDOES
MISDOING
MISDOINGS
MISDONE
MISDONNE
MISDOUBT
MISDOUBTED
MISDOUBTFUL
MISDOUBTING
MISDOUBTS
MISDRAW
MISDRAWING
MISDRAWINGS
MISDRAWN
MISDRAWS
MISDREAD
MISDREADS
MISDREW
MISDRIVE
MISDRIVEN
MISDRIVES
MISDRIVING
MISDROVE
MISE
MISEASE
MISEASES
MISEAT
MISEATEN
MISEATING
MISEATS
MISEDIT
MISEDITED
MISEDITING
MISEDITS
MISEDUCATE
MISEDUCATED
MISEDUCATES
MISEDUCATING
MISEDUCATION
MISEDUCATIONS

MISEMPHASES
MISEMPHASIS
MISEMPHASIZE
MISEMPHASIZED
MISEMPHASIZES
MISEMPHASIZING
MISEMPLOY
MISEMPLOYED
MISEMPLOYING
MISEMPLOYMENT
MISEMPLOYMENTS
MISEMPLOYS
MISENROL
MISENROLL
MISENROLLED
MISENROLLING
MISENROLLS
MISENROLS
MISENTER
MISENTERED
MISENTERING
MISENTERS
MISENTREAT
MISENTREATED
MISENTREATING
MISENTREATS
MISENTRIES
MISENTRY
MISER
MISERABILISM
MISERABILIST
MISERABILISTS
MISERABLE
MISERABLENESS
MISERABLENESSES
MISERABLES
MISERABLISM
MISERABLIST
MISERABLISTS
MISERABLY
MISERE
MISERERE
MISERERES
MISERES
MISERICORD
MISERICORDE
MISERICORDES
MISERICORDS
MISERIES
MISERLIER
MISERLIEST
MISERLINESS
MISERLINESSES
MISERLY
MISERS
MISERY

MISES
MISESTEEM
MISESTEEMED
MISESTEEMING
MISESTEEMS
MISESTIMATE
MISESTIMATED
MISESTIMATES
MISESTIMATING
MISESTIMATION
MISESTIMATIONS
MISEVALUATE
MISEVALUATED
MISEVALUATES
MISEVALUATING
MISEVALUATION
MISEVALUATIONS
MISEVENT
MISEVENTS
MISFAITH
MISFAITHS
MISFALL
MISFALLEN
MISFALLING
MISFALLS
MISFALNE
MISFARE
MISFARED
MISFARES
MISFARING
MISFARINGS
MISFEASANCE
MISFEASANCES
MISFEASOR
MISFEASORS
MISFEATURE
MISFEATURED
MISFEATURES
MISFEATURING
MISFED
MISFEED
MISFEEDING
MISFEEDS
MISFEIGN
MISFEIGNED
MISFEIGNING
MISFEIGNS
MISFELL
MISFIELD
MISFIELDED
MISFIELDING
MISFIELDS
MISFILE
MISFILED
MISFILES
MISFILING

MISFIRE
MISFIRED
MISFIRES
MISFIRING
MISFIT
MISFITS
MISFITTED
MISFITTING
MISFOCUS
MISFOCUSED
MISFOCUSES
MISFOCUSING
MISFOCUSSED
MISFOCUSSES
MISFOCUSSING
MISFORM
MISFORMATION
MISFORMATIONS
MISFORMED
MISFORMING
MISFORMS
MISFORTUNE
MISFORTUNED
MISFORTUNES
MISFRAME
MISFRAMED
MISFRAMES
MISFRAMING
MISFUNCTION
MISFUNCTIONED
MISFUNCTIONING
MISFUNCTIONS
MISGAUGE
MISGAUGED
MISGAUGES
MISGAUGING
MISGAVE
MISGIVE
MISGIVEN
MISGIVES
MISGIVING
MISGIVINGS
MISGO
MISGOES
MISGOING
MISGONE
MISGOTTEN
MISGOVERN
MISGOVERNAUNCE
MISGOVERNAUNCES
MISGOVERNED
MISGOVERNING
MISGOVERNMENT
MISGOVERNMENTS
MISGOVERNOR
MISGOVERNORS

MISGOVERNS
MISGRADE
MISGRADED
MISGRADES
MISGRADING
MISGRAFF
MISGRAFT
MISGRAFTED
MISGRAFTING
MISGRAFTS
MISGREW
MISGROW
MISGROWING
MISGROWN
MISGROWS
MISGROWTH
MISGROWTHS
MISGUESS
MISGUESSED
MISGUESSES
MISGUESSING
MISGUGGLE
MISGUGGLED
MISGUGGLES
MISGUGGLING
MISGUIDANCE
MISGUIDANCES
MISGUIDE
MISGUIDED
MISGUIDEDLY
MISGUIDEDNESS
MISGUIDEDNESSES
MISGUIDER
MISGUIDERS
MISGUIDES
MISGUIDING
MISHALLOWED
MISHANDLE
MISHANDLED
MISHANDLES
MISHANDLING
MISHANTER
MISHANTERS
MISHAP
MISHAPPED
MISHAPPEN
MISHAPPENED
MISHAPPENING
MISHAPPENS
MISHAPPING
MISHAPS
MISHAPT
MISHEAR
MISHEARD
MISHEARING
MISHEARS

MISHEGAAS
MISHEGAASEN
MISHGUGGLED
MISHGUGGLES
MISHGUGGLING
MISHIT
MISHITS
MISHITTING
MISHMASH
MISHMASHES
MISHMEE
MISHMEES
MISHMI
MISHMIS
MISHMOSH
MISHMOSHES
MISIDENTIFIED
MISIDENTIFIES
MISIDENTIFY
MISIDENTIFYING
MISIMPRESSION
MISIMPRESSIONS
MISIMPROVE
MISIMPROVED
MISIMPROVEMENT
MISIMPROVEMENTS
MISIMPROVES
MISIMPROVING
MISINFER
MISINFERRED
MISINFERRING
MISINFERS
MISINFORM
MISINFORMANT
MISINFORMANTS
MISINFORMATION
MISINFORMATIONS
MISINFORMED
MISINFORMER
MISINFORMERS
MISINFORMING
MISINFORMS
MISINSTRUCT
MISINSTRUCTED
MISINSTRUCTING
MISINSTRUCTION
MISINSTRUCTIONS
MISINSTRUCTS
MISINTELLIGENCE
MISINTEND
MISINTENDED
MISINTENDING
MISINTENDS
MISINTER
MISINTERPRET
MISINTERPRETED

MISINTERPRETER
MISINTERPRETERS
MISINTERPRETING
MISINTERPRETS
MISINTERRED
MISINTERRING
MISINTERS
MISJOIN
MISJOINDER
MISJOINDERS
MISJOINED
MISJOINING
MISJOINS
MISJUDGE
MISJUDGED
MISJUDGEMENT
MISJUDGEMENTS
MISJUDGER
MISJUDGERS
MISJUDGES
MISJUDGING
MISJUDGMENT
MISJUDGMENTS
MISKAL
MISKALS
MISKEEP
MISKEEPING
MISKEEPS
MISKEN
MISKENNED
MISKENNING
MISKENS
MISKENT
MISKEPT
MISKEY
MISKEYED
MISKEYING
MISKEYS
MISKICK
MISKICKED
MISKICKING
MISKICKS
MISKNEW
MISKNOW
MISKNOWING
MISKNOWLEDGE
MISKNOWLEDGES
MISKNOWN
MISKNOWS
MISLABEL
MISLABELED
MISLABELING
MISLABELLED
MISLABELLING
MISLABELS
MISLABOR

MISLABORED
MISLABORING
MISLABORS
MISLAID
MISLAIN
MISLAY
MISLAYER
MISLAYERS
MISLAYING
MISLAYS
MISLEAD
MISLEADER
MISLEADERS
MISLEADING
MISLEADINGLY
MISLEADS
MISLEARED
MISLEARN
MISLEARNED
MISLEARNING
MISLEARNS
MISLEARNT
MISLED
MISLEEKE
MISLEEKED
MISLEEKES
MISLEEKING
MISLETOE
MISLETOES
MISLIE
MISLIES
MISLIGHT
MISLIGHTED
MISLIGHTING
MISLIGHTS
MISLIKE
MISLIKED
MISLIKER
MISLIKERS
MISLIKES
MISLIKING
MISLIKINGS
MISLIPPEN
MISLIPPENED
MISLIPPENING
MISLIPPENS
MISLIT
MISLIVE
MISLIVED
MISLIVES
MISLIVING
MISLOCATE
MISLOCATED
MISLOCATES
MISLOCATING
MISLOCATION

MISLOCATIONS
MISLODGE
MISLODGED
MISLODGES
MISLODGING
MISLUCK
MISLUCKED
MISLUCKING
MISLUCKS
MISLYING
MISMADE
MISMAKE
MISMAKES
MISMAKING
MISMANAGE
MISMANAGED
MISMANAGEMENT
MISMANAGEMENTS
MISMANAGER
MISMANAGERS
MISMANAGES
MISMANAGING
MISMANNERS
MISMARK
MISMARKED
MISMARKING
MISMARKS
MISMARRIAGE
MISMARRIAGES
MISMARRIED
MISMARRIES
MISMARRY
MISMARRYING
MISMATCH
MISMATCHED
MISMATCHES
MISMATCHING
MISMATCHMENT
MISMATCHMENTS
MISMATE
MISMATED
MISMATES
MISMATING
MISMEASURE
MISMEASURED
MISMEASUREMENT
MISMEASUREMENTS
MISMEASURES
MISMEASURING
MISMEET
MISMEETING
MISMEETS
MISMET
MISMETRE
MISMETRED
MISMETRES

MISMETRING
MISMOVE
MISMOVED
MISMOVES
MISMOVING
MISNAME
MISNAMED
MISNAMES
MISNAMING
MISNOMER
MISNOMERED
MISNOMERING
MISNOMERS
MISNUMBER
MISNUMBERED
MISNUMBERING
MISNUMBERS
MISO
MISOBSERVANCE
MISOBSERVANCES
MISOBSERVE
MISOBSERVED
MISOBSERVES
MISOBSERVING
MISOCAPNIC
MISOCLERE
MISOGAMIES
MISOGAMIST
MISOGAMISTS
MISOGAMY
MISOGYNIC
MISOGYNIES
MISOGYNIST
MISOGYNISTIC
MISOGYNISTICAL
MISOGYNISTS
MISOGYNOUS
MISOGYNY
MISOLOGIES
MISOLOGIST
MISOLOGISTS
MISOLOGY
MISONEISM
MISONEISMS
MISONEIST
MISONEISTIC
MISONEISTS
MISORDER
MISORDERED
MISORDERING
MISORDERS
MISORIENT
MISORIENTATION
MISORIENTATIONS
MISORIENTED
MISORIENTING

MISORIENTS
MISOS
MISPACKAGE
MISPACKAGED
MISPACKAGES
MISPACKAGING
MISPAGE
MISPAGED
MISPAGES
MISPAGING
MISPAINT
MISPAINTED
MISPAINTING
MISPAINTS
MISPARSE
MISPARSED
MISPARSES
MISPARSING
MISPART
MISPARTED
MISPARTING
MISPARTS
MISPATCH
MISPATCHED
MISPATCHES
MISPATCHING
MISPEN
MISPENNED
MISPENNING
MISPENS
MISPERCEIVE
MISPERCEIVED
MISPERCEIVES
MISPERCEIVING
MISPERCEPTION
MISPERCEPTIONS
MISPERSUADE
MISPERSUADED
MISPERSUADES
MISPERSUADING
MISPERSUASION
MISPERSUASIONS
MISPHRASE
MISPHRASED
MISPHRASES
MISPHRASING
MISPICKEL
MISPICKELS
MISPLACE
MISPLACED
MISPLACEMENT
MISPLACEMENTS
MISPLACES
MISPLACING
MISPLAN
MISPLANNED

MISPLANNING
MISPLANS
MISPLANT
MISPLANTED
MISPLANTING
MISPLANTS
MISPLAY
MISPLAYED
MISPLAYING
MISPLAYS
MISPLEAD
MISPLEADED
MISPLEADING
MISPLEADINGS
MISPLEADS
MISPLEASE
MISPLEASED
MISPLEASES
MISPLEASING
MISPLED
MISPOINT
MISPOINTED
MISPOINTING
MISPOINTS
MISPOISE
MISPOISED
MISPOISES
MISPOISING
MISPOSITION
MISPOSITIONED
MISPOSITIONING
MISPOSITIONS
MISPRAISE
MISPRAISED
MISPRAISES
MISPRAISING
MISPRICE
MISPRICED
MISPRICES
MISPRICING
MISPRINCIPLED
MISPRINT
MISPRINTED
MISPRINTING
MISPRINTS
MISPRISE
MISPRISED
MISPRISES
MISPRISING
MISPRISION
MISPRISIONS
MISPRIZE
MISPRIZED
MISPRIZES
MISPRIZING
MISPROGRAM

MISPROGRAMED
MISPROGRAMING
MISPROGRAMMED
MISPROGRAMMING
MISPROGRAMS
MISPRONOUNCE
MISPRONOUNCED
MISPRONOUNCES
MISPRONOUNCING
MISPROPORTION
MISPROPORTIONED
MISPROPORTIONS
MISPROUD
MISPUNCTUATE
MISPUNCTUATED
MISPUNCTUATES
MISPUNCTUATING
MISPUNCTUATION
MISPUNCTUATIONS
MISQUOTATION
MISQUOTATIONS
MISQUOTE
MISQUOTED
MISQUOTES
MISQUOTING
MISRAISE
MISRAISED
MISRAISES
MISRAISING
MISRATE
MISRATED
MISRATES
MISRATING
MISREAD
MISREADING
MISREADINGS
MISREADS
MISRECKON
MISRECKONED
MISRECKONING
MISRECKONINGS
MISRECKONS
MISRECOGNISE
MISRECOGNISED
MISRECOGNISES
MISRECOGNISING
MISRECOGNIZE
MISRECOGNIZED
MISRECOGNIZES
MISRECOGNIZING
MISRECOLLECTION
MISRECORD
MISRECORDED
MISRECORDING
MISRECORDS
MISREFER

MISREFERENCE
MISREFERENCES
MISREFERRED
MISREFERRING
MISREFERS
MISREGARD
MISREGARDS
MISREGISTER
MISREGISTERED
MISREGISTERING
MISREGISTERS
MISREGISTRATION
MISRELATE
MISRELATED
MISRELATES
MISRELATING
MISRELATION
MISRELATIONS
MISRELIED
MISRELIES
MISRELY
MISRELYING
MISREMEMBER
MISREMEMBERED
MISREMEMBERING
MISREMEMBERS
MISRENDER
MISRENDERED
MISRENDERING
MISRENDERS
MISREPORT
MISREPORTED
MISREPORTER
MISREPORTERS
MISREPORTING
MISREPORTS
MISREPRESENT
MISREPRESENTED
MISREPRESENTER
MISREPRESENTERS
MISREPRESENTING
MISREPRESENTS
MISRHYMED
MISROUTE
MISROUTED
MISROUTEING
MISROUTES
MISROUTING
MISRULE
MISRULED
MISRULES
MISRULING
MISS
MISSA
MISSABLE
MISSAE

MISSAID
MISSAL
MISSALS
MISSAW
MISSAY
MISSAYING
MISSAYINGS
MISSAYS
MISSEAT
MISSEATED
MISSEATING
MISSEATS
MISSED
MISSEE
MISSEEING
MISSEEM
MISSEEMED
MISSEEMING
MISSEEMINGS
MISSEEMS
MISSEEN
MISSEES
MISSEL
MISSELS
MISSEND
MISSENDING
MISSENDS
MISSENSE
MISSENSES
MISSENT
MISSES
MISSET
MISSETS
MISSETTING
MISSHAPE
MISSHAPED
MISSHAPEN
MISSHAPENLY
MISSHAPENNESS
MISSHAPENNESSES
MISSHAPES
MISSHAPING
MISSHEATHED
MISSHOD
MISSHOOD
MISSHOODS
MISSIER
MISSIES
MISSIEST
MISSILE
MISSILEER
MISSILEERS
MISSILEMAN
MISSILEMEN
MISSILERIES
MISSILERY

MISSILES
MISSILRIES
MISSILRY
MISSING
MISSINGLY
MISSIOLOGIES
MISSIOLOGY
MISSION
MISSIONARIES
MISSIONARISE
MISSIONARISED
MISSIONARISES
MISSIONARISING
MISSIONARIZE
MISSIONARIZED
MISSIONARIZES
MISSIONARIZING
MISSIONARY
MISSIONED
MISSIONER
MISSIONERS
MISSIONING
MISSIONISE
MISSIONISED
MISSIONISES
MISSIONISING
MISSIONIZATION
MISSIONIZATIONS
MISSIONIZE
MISSIONIZED
MISSIONIZER
MISSIONIZERS
MISSIONIZES
MISSIONIZING
MISSIONS
MISSIS
MISSISES
MISSISH
MISSISHNESS
MISSISHNESSES
MISSIVE
MISSIVES
MISSORT
MISSORTED
MISSORTING
MISSORTS
MISSOUND
MISSOUNDED
MISSOUNDING
MISSOUNDS
MISSOUT
MISSOUTS
MISSPACE
MISSPACED
MISSPACES
MISSPACING

MISSPEAK	MISSY	MISTHROWN	MISTREAT
MISSPEAKING	MIST	MISTHROWS	MISTREATED
MISSPEAKS	MISTAKABLE	MISTICO	MISTREATING
MISSPELL	MISTAKABLY	MISTICOS	MISTREATMENT
MISSPELLED	MISTAKE	MISTIER	MISTREATMENTS
MISSPELLING	MISTAKEABLE	MISTIEST	MISTREATS
MISSPELLINGS	MISTAKEABLY	MISTIGRIS	MISTRESS
MISSPELLS	MISTAKEN	MISTIGRISES	MISTRESSED
MISSPELT	MISTAKENLY	MISTILY	MISTRESSES
MISSPEND	MISTAKENNESS	MISTIME	MISTRESSING
MISSPENDER	MISTAKENNESSES	MISTIMED	MISTRESSLESS
MISSPENDERS	MISTAKER	MISTIMES	MISTRESSLY
MISSPENDING	MISTAKERS	MISTIMING	MISTRIAL
MISSPENDS	MISTAKES	MISTINESS	MISTRIALS
MISSPENT	MISTAKING	MISTINESSES	MISTRUST
MISSPOKE	MISTAKINGS	MISTING	MISTRUSTED
MISSPOKEN	MISTAL	MISTINGS	MISTRUSTER
MISSTART	MISTALS	MISTITLE	MISTRUSTERS
MISSTARTED	MISTAUGHT	MISTITLED	MISTRUSTFUL
MISSTARTING	MISTBOW	MISTITLES	MISTRUSTFULLY
MISSTARTS	MISTBOWS	MISTITLING	MISTRUSTFULNESS
MISSTATE	MISTEACH	MISTLE	MISTRUSTING
MISSTATED	MISTEACHES	MISTLED	MISTRUSTINGLY
MISSTATEMENT	MISTEACHING	MISTLES	MISTRUSTLESS
MISSTATEMENTS	MISTED	MISTLETOE	MISTRUSTS
MISSTATES	MISTELL	MISTLETOES	MISTRUTH
MISSTATING	MISTELLING	MISTLING	MISTRUTHS
MISSTEER	MISTELLS	MISTOLD	MISTRYST
MISSTEERED	MISTEMPER	MISTOOK	MISTRYSTED
MISSTEERING	MISTEMPERED	MISTOUCH	MISTRYSTING
MISSTEERS	MISTEMPERING	MISTOUCHED	MISTRYSTS
MISSTEP	MISTEMPERS	MISTOUCHES	MISTS
MISSTEPPED	MISTEND	MISTOUCHING	MISTUNE
MISSTEPPING	MISTENDED	MISTRACE	MISTUNED
MISSTEPS	MISTENDING	MISTRACED	MISTUNES
MISSTOP	MISTENDS	MISTRACES	MISTUNING
MISSTOPPED	MISTER	MISTRACING	MISTUTOR
MISSTOPPING	MISTERED	MISTRAIN	MISTUTORED
MISSTOPS	MISTERIES	MISTRAINED	MISTUTORING
MISSTRICKEN	MISTERING	MISTRAINING	MISTUTORS
MISSTRIKE	MISTERM	MISTRAINS	MISTY
MISSTRIKES	MISTERMED	MISTRAL	MISTYPE
MISSTRIKING	MISTERMING	MISTRALS	MISTYPED
MISSTRUCK	MISTERMS	MISTRANSCRIBE	MISTYPES
MISSTYLE	MISTERS	MISTRANSCRIBED	MISTYPING
MISSTYLED	MISTERY	MISTRANSCRIBES	MISUNDERSTAND
MISSTYLES	MISTEUK	MISTRANSCRIBING	MISUNDERSTANDS
MISSTYLING	MISTFUL	MISTRANSLATE	MISUNDERSTOOD
MISSUIT	MISTHINK	MISTRANSLATED	MISUNION
MISSUITED	MISTHINKING	MISTRANSLATES	MISUNIONS
MISSUITING	MISTHINKS	MISTRANSLATING	MISUSAGE
MISSUITS	MISTHOUGHT	MISTRANSLATION	MISUSAGES
MISSUMMATION	MISTHOUGHTS	MISTRANSLATIONS	MISUSE
MISSUMMATIONS	MISTHREW	MISTRAYNED	MISUSED
MISSUS	MISTHROW	MISTREADING	MISUSER
MISSUSES	MISTHROWING	MISTREADINGS	MISUSERS

MISUSES
MISUSING
MISUST
MISUTILIZATION
MISUTILIZATIONS
MISVALUE
MISVALUED
MISVALUES
MISVALUING
MISVENTURE
MISVENTURES
MISVENTUROUS
MISVOCALIZATION
MISWANDRED
MISWEEN
MISWEENED
MISWEENING
MISWEENS
MISWEND
MISWENDING
MISWENDS
MISWENT
MISWORD
MISWORDED
MISWORDING
MISWORDINGS
MISWORDS
MISWORSHIP
MISWORSHIPPED
MISWORSHIPPING
MISWORSHIPS
MISWRIT
MISWRITE
MISWRITES
MISWRITING
MISWRITTEN
MISWROTE
MISYOKE
MISYOKED
MISYOKES
MISYOKING
MITCH
MITCHED
MITCHES
MITCHING
MITE
MITER
MITERED
MITERER
MITERERS
MITERING
MITERS
MITERWORT
MITERWORTS
MITES
MITHER

MITHERED
MITHERING
MITHERS
MITHRADATIC
MITHRIDATE
MITHRIDATES
MITHRIDATIC
MITHRIDATISE
MITHRIDATISED
MITHRIDATISES
MITHRIDATISING
MITHRIDATISM
MITHRIDATISMS
MITHRIDATIZE
MITHRIDATIZED
MITHRIDATIZES
MITHRIDATIZING
MITICIDAL
MITICIDE
MITICIDES
MITIER
MITIEST
MITIGABLE
MITIGANT
MITIGATE
MITIGATED
MITIGATES
MITIGATING
MITIGATION
MITIGATIONS
MITIGATIVE
MITIGATIVES
MITIGATOR
MITIGATORS
MITIGATORY
MITIS
MITISES
MITOCHONDRIA
MITOCHONDRIAL
MITOCHONDRION
MITOGEN
MITOGENETIC
MITOGENIC
MITOGENICITIES
MITOGENICITY
MITOGENS
MITOMYCIN
MITOMYCINS
MITOSES
MITOSIS
MITOTIC
MITOTICALLY
MITRAILLE
MITRAILLES
MITRAILLEUR
MITRAILLEURS

MITRAILLEUSE
MITRAILLEUSES
MITRAL
MITRE
MITRED
MITRES
MITREWORT
MITREWORTS
MITRIFORM
MITRING
MITSVAH
MITSVAHS
MITSVOTH
MITT
MITTEN
MITTENED
MITTENS
MITTIMUS
MITTIMUSES
MITTS
MITY
MITZVAH
MITZVAHS
MITZVOTH
MIURUS
MIURUSES
MIX
MIXABILITY
MIXABLE
MIXDOWN
MIXDOWNS
MIXED
MIXEDLY
MIXEDNESS
MIXEDNESSES
MIXEN
MIXENS
MIXER
MIXERS
MIXES
MIXIBLE
MIXIER
MIXIEST
MIXING
MIXMASTER
MIXOBARBARIC
MIXOLOGIES
MIXOLOGIST
MIXOLOGISTS
MIXOLOGY
MIXOLYDIAN
MIXOTROPHIC
MIXT
MIXTE
MIXTER
MIXTEST

MIXTION
MIXTIONS
MIXTURE
MIXTURES
MIXUP
MIXUPS
MIXY
MIZ
MIZEN
MIZENMAST
MIZENMASTS
MIZENS
MIZMAZE
MIZMAZES
MIZUNA
MIZZ
MIZZEN
MIZZENMAST
MIZZENMASTS
MIZZENS
MIZZES
MIZZLE
MIZZLED
MIZZLES
MIZZLIER
MIZZLIEST
MIZZLING
MIZZLINGS
MIZZLY
MIZZONITE
MIZZONITES
MM
MNA
MNAS
MNEME
MNEMES
MNEMIC
MNEMON
MNEMONIC
MNEMONICAL
MNEMONICALLY
MNEMONICS
MNEMONIST
MNEMONISTS
MNEMONS
MNEMOTECHNIC
MNEMOTECHNICS
MNEMOTECHNIST
MNEMOTECHNISTS
MO
MOA
MOAI
MOAN
MOANED
MOANER
MOANERS

MOANFUL
MOANFULLY
MOANING
MOANINGLY
MOANS
MOAS
MOAT
MOATED
MOATING
MOATLIKE
MOATS
MOB
MOBBED
MOBBER
MOBBERS
MOBBIE
MOBBIES
MOBBING
MOBBINGS
MOBBISH
MOBBLE
MOBBLED
MOBBLES
MOBBLING
MOBBY
MOBCAP
MOBCAPS
MOBE
MOBES
MOBIE
MOBIES
MOBILE
MOBILES
MOBILISABILITY
MOBILISABLE
MOBILISATION
MOBILISATIONS
MOBILISE
MOBILISED
MOBILISER
MOBILISERS
MOBILISES
MOBILISING
MOBILITIES
MOBILITY
MOBILIZABLE
MOBILIZATION
MOBILIZATIONS
MOBILIZE
MOBILIZED
MOBILIZER
MOBILIZERS
MOBILIZES
MOBILIZING
MOBLE
MOBLED

MOBLES
MOBLING
MOBLOG
MOBOCRACIES
MOBOCRACY
MOBOCRAT
MOBOCRATIC
MOBOCRATICAL
MOBOCRATS
MOBS
MOBSMAN
MOBSMEN
MOBSTER
MOBSTERS
MOBY
MOC
MOCASSIN
MOCASSINS
MOCCASIN
MOCCASINS
MOCH
MOCHA
MOCHAS
MOCHELL
MOCHELLS
MOCHIE
MOCHIER
MOCHIEST
MOCHILA
MOCHILAS
MOCHINESS
MOCHINESSES
MOCHS
MOCHY
MOCK
MOCKABLE
MOCKADO
MOCKADOES
MOCKAGE
MOCKAGES
MOCKED
MOCKER
MOCKERIES
MOCKERNUT
MOCKERNUTS
MOCKERS
MOCKERY
MOCKING
MOCKINGBIRD
MOCKINGBIRDS
MOCKINGLY
MOCKINGS
MOCKNEY
MOCKNEYS
MOCKS
MOCKUMENTARIES

MOCKUMENTARY
MOCKUP
MOCKUPS
MOCOCK
MOCOCKS
MOCS
MOCUCK
MOCUCKS
MOCUDDUM
MOCUDDUMS
MOD
MODAL
MODALISM
MODALISMS
MODALIST
MODALISTIC
MODALISTS
MODALITIES
MODALITY
MODALLY
MODALS
MODE
MODEL
MODELED
MODELER
MODELERS
MODELING
MODELINGS
MODELIST
MODELISTS
MODELLED
MODELLER
MODELLERS
MODELLI
MODELLING
MODELLINGS
MODELLO
MODELLOS
MODELS
MODEM
MODEMED
MODEMING
MODEMS
MODENA
MODENAS
MODER
MODERATE
MODERATED
MODERATELY
MODERATENESS
MODERATENESSES
MODERATES
MODERATING
MODERATION
MODERATIONS
MODERATISM

MODERATISMS
MODERATO
MODERATOR
MODERATORS
MODERATORSHIP
MODERATORSHIPS
MODERATOS
MODERATRICES
MODERATRIX
MODERATRIXES
MODERN
MODERNE
MODERNER
MODERNEST
MODERNISATION
MODERNISATIONS
MODERNISE
MODERNISED
MODERNISER
MODERNISERS
MODERNISES
MODERNISING
MODERNISM
MODERNISMS
MODERNIST
MODERNISTIC
MODERNISTICALLY
MODERNISTS
MODERNITIES
MODERNITY
MODERNIZATION
MODERNIZATIONS
MODERNIZE
MODERNIZED
MODERNIZER
MODERNIZERS
MODERNIZES
MODERNIZING
MODERNLY
MODERNNESS
MODERNNESSES
MODERNS
MODERS
MODES
MODEST
MODESTER
MODESTEST
MODESTIES
MODESTLY
MODESTY
MODGE
MODGED
MODGES
MODGING
MODI
MODICA

MODICUM
MODICUMS
MODIFIABILITIES
MODIFIABILITY
MODIFIABLE
MODIFIABLENESS
MODIFICATION
MODIFICATIONS
MODIFICATIVE
MODIFICATORY
MODIFIED
MODIFIER
MODIFIERS
MODIFIES
MODIFY
MODIFYING
MODII
MODILLION
MODILLIONS
MODIOLAR
MODIOLI
MODIOLUS
MODIOLUSES
MODISH
MODISHLY
MODISHNESS
MODISHNESSES
MODIST
MODISTE
MODISTES
MODISTS
MODIUS
MODIWORT
MODIWORTS
MODS
MODULABILITIES
MODULABILITY
MODULAR
MODULARISED
MODULARITIES
MODULARITY
MODULARIZED
MODULARLY
MODULATE
MODULATED
MODULATES
MODULATING
MODULATION
MODULATIONS
MODULATIVE
MODULATOR
MODULATORS
MODULATORY
MODULE
MODULES
MODULI

MODULO
MODULUS
MODUS
MOE
MOELLON
MOELLONS
MOER
MOES
MOFETTE
MOFETTES
MOFFETTE
MOFFETTES
MOFFIE
MOFFIES
MOFO
MOFOS
MOFUSSIL
MOFUSSILS
MOG
MOGGAN
MOGGANS
MOGGED
MOGGIE
MOGGIES
MOGGING
MOGGY
MOGS
MOGUL
MOGULED
MOGULS
MOHAIR
MOHAIRS
MOHALIM
MOHAWK
MOHAWKS
MOHEL
MOHELIM
MOHELS
MOHICAN
MOHICANS
MOHR
MOHRS
MOHUR
MOHURS
MOI
MOIDER
MOIDERED
MOIDERING
MOIDERS
MOIDORE
MOIDORES
MOIETIES
MOIETY
MOIL
MOILED
MOILER

MOILERS
MOILING
MOILINGLY
MOILS
MOINEAU
MOINEAUS
MOIRA
MOIRAI
MOIRE
MOIRES
MOISER
MOISERS
MOIST
MOISTED
MOISTEN
MOISTENED
MOISTENER
MOISTENERS
MOISTENING
MOISTENS
MOISTER
MOISTEST
MOISTFUL
MOISTIFIED
MOISTIFIES
MOISTIFY
MOISTIFYING
MOISTING
MOISTLY
MOISTNESS
MOISTNESSES
MOISTS
MOISTURE
MOISTURELESS
MOISTURES
MOISTURISE
MOISTURISED
MOISTURISER
MOISTURISERS
MOISTURISES
MOISTURISING
MOISTURIZE
MOISTURIZED
MOISTURIZER
MOISTURIZERS
MOISTURIZES
MOISTURIZING
MOIT
MOITHER
MOITHERED
MOITHERING
MOITHERS
MOITS
MOJARRA
MOJARRAS
MOJO

MOJOES
MOJOS
MOKADDAM
MOKADDAMS
MOKE
MOKES
MOKI
MOKIHI
MOKIHIS
MOKIS
MOKO
MOKOPUNA
MOKOPUNAS
MOKORO
MOKOROS
MOKOS
MOKSHA
MOL
MOLA
MOLAL
MOLALITIES
MOLALITY
MOLAR
MOLARITIES
MOLARITY
MOLARS
MOLAS
MOLASSE
MOLASSES
MOLASSESES
MOLD
MOLDABILITY
MOLDABLE
MOLDAVITE
MOLDBOARD
MOLDBOARDS
MOLDED
MOLDER
MOLDERED
MOLDERING
MOLDERS
MOLDIER
MOLDIEST
MOLDINESS
MOLDINESSES
MOLDING
MOLDINGS
MOLDS
MOLDWARP
MOLDWARPS
MOLDY
MOLE
MOLECAST
MOLECASTS
MOLECATCHER
MOLECATCHERS

MOLECULAR
MOLECULARITIES
MOLECULARITY
MOLECULARLY
MOLECULE
MOLECULES
MOLEHILL
MOLEHILLS
MOLEHUNT
MOLEHUNTER
MOLEHUNTERS
MOLEHUNTS
MOLENDINAR
MOLENDINARIES
MOLENDINARS
MOLENDINARY
MOLERAT
MOLERATS
MOLES
MOLESKIN
MOLESKINS
MOLEST
MOLESTATION
MOLESTATIONS
MOLESTED
MOLESTER
MOLESTERS
MOLESTFUL
MOLESTING
MOLESTS
MOLIES
MOLIMEN
MOLIMENS
MOLIMINOUS
MOLINE
MOLINES
MOLINET
MOLINETS
MOLL
MOLLA
MOLLAH
MOLLAHS
MOLLAS
MOLLESCENCE
MOLLESCENT
MOLLIE
MOLLIES
MOLLIFIABLE
MOLLIFICATION
MOLLIFICATIONS
MOLLIFIED
MOLLIFIER
MOLLIFIERS
MOLLIFIES
MOLLIFY
MOLLIFYING

MOLLITIES
MOLLITIOUS
MOLLS
MOLLUSC
MOLLUSCAN
MOLLUSCICIDAL
MOLLUSCICIDE
MOLLUSCICIDES
MOLLUSCOID
MOLLUSCOIDAL
MOLLUSCOIDS
MOLLUSCOUS
MOLLUSCS
MOLLUSK
MOLLUSKAN
MOLLUSKS
MOLLY
MOLLYCODDLE
MOLLYCODDLED
MOLLYCODDLER
MOLLYCODDLERS
MOLLYCODDLES
MOLLYCODDLING
MOLLYHAWK
MOLLYHAWKS
MOLLYMAWK
MOLLYMAWKS
MOLOCH
MOLOCHISE
MOLOCHISED
MOLOCHISES
MOLOCHISING
MOLOCHIZE
MOLOCHIZED
MOLOCHIZES
MOLOCHIZING
MOLOCHS
MOLOSSI
MOLOSSUS
MOLS
MOLT
MOLTED
MOLTEN
MOLTENLY
MOLTER
MOLTERS
MOLTING
MOLTO
MOLTS
MOLY
MOLYBDATE
MOLYBDATES
MOLYBDENITE
MOLYBDENITES
MOLYBDENOSES
MOLYBDENOSIS

MOLYBDENOUS
MOLYBDENUM
MOLYBDENUMS
MOLYBDIC
MOLYBDOSES
MOLYBDOSIS
MOLYBDOUS
MOM
MOME
MOMENT
MOMENTA
MOMENTANEOUS
MOMENTANY
MOMENTARILY
MOMENTARINESS
MOMENTARINESSES
MOMENTARY
MOMENTLY
MOMENTO
MOMENTOES
MOMENTOS
MOMENTOUS
MOMENTOUSLY
MOMENTOUSNESS
MOMENTOUSNESSES
MOMENTS
MOMENTUM
MOMENTUMS
MOMES
MOMI
MOMISM
MOMISMS
MOMMA
MOMMAS
MOMMET
MOMMETS
MOMMIES
MOMMY
MOMS
MOMSER
MOMSERS
MOMUS
MOMUSES
MOMZER
MOMZERIM
MOMZERS
MON
MONA
MONACHAL
MONACHISM
MONACHISMS
MONACHIST
MONACHISTS
MONACID
MONACIDIC
MONACIDS

MONACT
MONACTINAL
MONACTINE
MONAD
MONADAL
MONADELPHOUS
MONADES
MONADIC
MONADICAL
MONADICALLY
MONADIFORM
MONADISM
MONADISMS
MONADISTIC
MONADNOCK
MONADNOCKS
MONADOLOGIES
MONADOLOGY
MONADS
MONAL
MONALS
MONANDRIES
MONANDROUS
MONANDRY
MONANTHOUS
MONARCH
MONARCHAL
MONARCHALLY
MONARCHIAL
MONARCHIC
MONARCHICAL
MONARCHICALLY
MONARCHIES
MONARCHISE
MONARCHISED
MONARCHISES
MONARCHISING
MONARCHISM
MONARCHISMS
MONARCHIST
MONARCHISTIC
MONARCHISTS
MONARCHIZE
MONARCHIZED
MONARCHIZES
MONARCHIZING
MONARCHS
MONARCHY
MONARDA
MONARDAS
MONAS
MONASES
MONASTERIAL
MONASTERIES
MONASTERY
MONASTIC

MONASTICAL
MONASTICALLY
MONASTICISM
MONASTICISMS
MONASTICS
MONATOMIC
MONAUL
MONAULS
MONAURAL
MONAURALLY
MONAXIAL
MONAXON
MONAXONIC
MONAXONS
MONAZITE
MONAZITES
MONCHIQUITE
MONCHIQUITES
MONDAIN
MONDAINE
MONDAINES
MONDAINS
MONDE
MONDEGREEN
MONDEGREENS
MONDES
MONDIAL
MONDO
MONDOS
MONECIAN
MONECIOUS
MONECIOUSLY
MONELLIN
MONELLINS
MONEME
MONEMES
MONER
MONERA
MONERAN
MONERANS
MONERGISM
MONERGISMS
MONERON
MONESTROUS
MONETARILY
MONETARISM
MONETARISMS
MONETARIST
MONETARISTS
MONETARY
MONETH
MONETHS
MONETISATION
MONETISATIONS
MONETISE
MONETISED

MONETISES
MONETISING
MONETIZATION
MONETIZATIONS
MONETIZE
MONETIZED
MONETIZES
MONETIZING
MONEY
MONEYBAG
MONEYBAGS
MONEYCHANGER
MONEYCHANGERS
MONEYED
MONEYER
MONEYERS
MONEYGRUBBING
MONEYGRUBBINGS
MONEYLENDER
MONEYLENDERS
MONEYLENDING
MONEYLENDINGS
MONEYLESS
MONEYMAKER
MONEYMAKERS
MONEYMAKING
MONEYMAKINGS
MONEYMAN
MONEYMEN
MONEYS
MONEYSPINNING
MONEYWORT
MONEYWORTS
MONG
MONGCORN
MONGCORNS
MONGED
MONGEESE
MONGER
MONGERED
MONGERIES
MONGERING
MONGERINGS
MONGERS
MONGERY
MONGO
MONGOE
MONGOES
MONGOL
MONGOLIAN
MONGOLISM
MONGOLISMS
MONGOLOID
MONGOLOIDS
MONGOLS
MONGOOSE

MONGOOSES
MONGOS
MONGREL
MONGRELISATION
MONGRELISE
MONGRELISED
MONGRELISER
MONGRELISERS
MONGRELISES
MONGRELISING
MONGRELISM
MONGRELISMS
MONGRELIZATION
MONGRELIZATIONS
MONGRELIZE
MONGRELIZED
MONGRELIZER
MONGRELIZES
MONGRELIZING
MONGRELLY
MONGRELS
MONGS
MONGST
MONIAL
MONIALS
MONICKER
MONICKERS
MONIE
MONIED
MONIES
MONIKER
MONIKERS
MONILIA
MONILIAL
MONILIAS
MONILIASES
MONILIASIS
MONILIFORM
MONIMENT
MONIMENTS
MONIPLIES
MONISH
MONISHED
MONISHES
MONISHING
MONISM
MONISMS
MONIST
MONISTIC
MONISTICAL
MONISTICALLY
MONISTS
MONITION
MONITIONS
MONITIVE
MONITOR

MONITORED
MONITORIAL
MONITORIALLY
MONITORIES
MONITORING
MONITORS
MONITORSHIP
MONITORSHIPS
MONITORY
MONITRESS
MONITRESSES
MONK
MONKERIES
MONKERY
MONKEY
MONKEYED
MONKEYING
MONKEYISH
MONKEYISM
MONKEYISMS
MONKEYPOD
MONKEYPODS
MONKEYPOT
MONKEYPOTS
MONKEYS
MONKEYSHINE
MONKEYSHINES
MONKFISH
MONKFISHES
MONKHOOD
MONKHOODS
MONKISH
MONKISHLY
MONKISHNESS
MONKS
MONKSHOOD
MONKSHOODS
MONO
MONOACID
MONOACIDIC
MONOACIDS
MONOAMINE
MONOAMINERGIC
MONOAMINES
MONOATOMIC
MONOBASIC
MONOBLEPSES
MONOBLEPSIS
MONOBROW
MONOCARBOXYLIC
MONOCARDIAN
MONOCARP
MONOCARPELLARY
MONOCARPIC
MONOCARPOUS
MONOCARPS

MONOCEROS
MONOCEROSES
MONOCEROUS
MONOCHASIA
MONOCHASIAL
MONOCHASIUM
MONOCHLAMYDEOUS
MONOCHLORIDE
MONOCHLORIDES
MONOCHORD
MONOCHORDS
MONOCHROIC
MONOCHROICS
MONOCHROMASIES
MONOCHROMASY
MONOCHROMAT
MONOCHROMATE
MONOCHROMATES
MONOCHROMATIC
MONOCHROMATICS
MONOCHROMATISM
MONOCHROMATISMS
MONOCHROMATOR
MONOCHROMATORS
MONOCHROMATS
MONOCHROME
MONOCHROMES
MONOCHROMIC
MONOCHROMICAL
MONOCHROMIES
MONOCHROMIST
MONOCHROMISTS
MONOCHROMY
MONOCLE
MONOCLED
MONOCLES
MONOCLINAL
MONOCLINALLY
MONOCLINE
MONOCLINES
MONOCLINIC
MONOCLINISM
MONOCLINOUS
MONOCLONAL
MONOCLONALS
MONOCOQUE
MONOCOQUES
MONOCOT
MONOCOTS
MONOCOTYLEDON
MONOCOTYLEDONS
MONOCRACIES
MONOCRACY
MONOCRAT
MONOCRATIC
MONOCRATS

MONOCRYSTAL
MONOCRYSTALLINE
MONOCRYSTALS
MONOCULAR
MONOCULARLY
MONOCULARS
MONOCULOUS
MONOCULTURAL
MONOCULTURE
MONOCULTURES
MONOCYCLE
MONOCYCLES
MONOCYCLIC
MONOCYTE
MONOCYTES
MONOCYTIC
MONOCYTOID
MONODACTYLOUS
MONODELPHIAN
MONODELPHIC
MONODELPHOUS
MONODIC
MONODICAL
MONODICALLY
MONODIES
MONODISPERSE
MONODIST
MONODISTS
MONODONT
MONODRAMA
MONODRAMAS
MONODRAMATIC
MONODY
MONOECIES
MONOECIOUS
MONOECIOUSLY
MONOECISM
MONOECISMS
MONOECY
MONOESTER
MONOESTERS
MONOFIL
MONOFILAMENT
MONOFILAMENTS
MONOFILS
MONOFUEL
MONOFUELS
MONOGAMIC
MONOGAMIES
MONOGAMIST
MONOGAMISTIC
MONOGAMISTS
MONOGAMOUS
MONOGAMOUSLY
MONOGAMOUSNESS
MONOGAMY

MONOGASTRIC
MONOGENEAN
MONOGENEANS
MONOGENESES
MONOGENESIS
MONOGENETIC
MONOGENIC
MONOGENICALLY
MONOGENIES
MONOGENISM
MONOGENISMS
MONOGENIST
MONOGENISTIC
MONOGENISTS
MONOGENOUS
MONOGENY
MONOGERM
MONOGLOT
MONOGLOTS
MONOGLYCERIDE
MONOGLYCERIDES
MONOGONIES
MONOGONY
MONOGRAM
MONOGRAMED
MONOGRAMING
MONOGRAMMATIC
MONOGRAMMED
MONOGRAMMER
MONOGRAMMERS
MONOGRAMMING
MONOGRAMS
MONOGRAPH
MONOGRAPHED
MONOGRAPHER
MONOGRAPHERS
MONOGRAPHIC
MONOGRAPHICAL
MONOGRAPHICALLY
MONOGRAPHIES
MONOGRAPHING
MONOGRAPHIST
MONOGRAPHISTS
MONOGRAPHS
MONOGRAPHY
MONOGYNIAN
MONOGYNIES
MONOGYNIST
MONOGYNISTS
MONOGYNOUS
MONOGYNY
MONOHULL
MONOHULLS
MONOHYBRID
MONOHYBRIDS
MONOHYDRATE

MONOHYDRATED
MONOHYDRATES
MONOHYDRIC
MONOHYDROXY
MONOICOUS
MONOICOUSLY
MONOKINI
MONOKINIS
MONOLATER
MONOLATERS
MONOLATRIES
MONOLATRIST
MONOLATRISTS
MONOLATROUS
MONOLATRY
MONOLAYER
MONOLAYERS
MONOLINGUAL
MONOLINGUALISM
MONOLINGUALISMS
MONOLINGUALS
MONOLINGUIST
MONOLINGUISTS
MONOLITH
MONOLITHIC
MONOLITHICALLY
MONOLITHS
MONOLOG
MONOLOGIC
MONOLOGICAL
MONOLOGIES
MONOLOGISE
MONOLOGISED
MONOLOGISES
MONOLOGISING
MONOLOGIST
MONOLOGISTS
MONOLOGIZE
MONOLOGIZED
MONOLOGIZES
MONOLOGIZING
MONOLOGS
MONOLOGUE
MONOLOGUES
MONOLOGUISE
MONOLOGUISED
MONOLOGUISES
MONOLOGUISING
MONOLOGUIST
MONOLOGUISTS
MONOLOGUIZE
MONOLOGUIZED
MONOLOGUIZES
MONOLOGUIZING
MONOLOGY
MONOMACHIA

MONOMACHIAS
MONOMACHIES
MONOMACHY
MONOMANIA
MONOMANIAC
MONOMANIACAL
MONOMANIACALLY
MONOMANIACS
MONOMANIAS
MONOMARK
MONOMARKS
MONOMER
MONOMERIC
MONOMEROUS
MONOMERS
MONOMETALLIC
MONOMETALLISM
MONOMETALLISMS
MONOMETALLIST
MONOMETALLISTS
MONOMETER
MONOMETERS
MONOMETRIC
MONOMETRICAL
MONOMETRICALLY
MONOMIAL
MONOMIALS
MONOMODE
MONOMOLECULAR
MONOMOLECULARLY
MONOMORPHEMIC
MONOMORPHIC
MONOMORPHISM
MONOMORPHISMS
MONOMORPHOUS
MONOMYARIAN
MONONUCLEAR
MONONUCLEARS
MONONUCLEATE
MONONUCLEATED
MONONUCLEOSES
MONONUCLEOSIS
MONONUCLEOTIDE
MONONUCLEOTIDES
MONONYM
MONONYMOUS
MONONYMS
MONOPETALOUS
MONOPHAGIES
MONOPHAGOUS
MONOPHAGY
MONOPHASE
MONOPHASIC
MONOPHOBIA
MONOPHOBIAS
MONOPHOBIC

MONOPHOBICS
MONOPHONIC
MONOPHONICALLY
MONOPHONIES
MONOPHONY
MONOPHTHONG
MONOPHTHONGAL
MONOPHTHONGISE
MONOPHTHONGISED
MONOPHTHONGISES
MONOPHTHONGIZE
MONOPHTHONGIZED
MONOPHTHONGIZES
MONOPHTHONGS
MONOPHYLETIC
MONOPHYLIES
MONOPHYLLOUS
MONOPHYLY
MONOPHYODONT
MONOPHYODONTS
MONOPHYSITE
MONOPHYSITES
MONOPHYSITIC
MONOPHYSITISM
MONOPHYSITISMS
MONOPITCH
MONOPLANE
MONOPLANES
MONOPLEGIA
MONOPLEGIAS
MONOPLEGIC
MONOPLOID
MONOPLOIDS
MONOPOD
MONOPODE
MONOPODES
MONOPODIA
MONOPODIAL
MONOPODIALLY
MONOPODIES
MONOPODIUM
MONOPODS
MONOPODY
MONOPOLE
MONOPOLES
MONOPOLIES
MONOPOLISATION
MONOPOLISATIONS
MONOPOLISE
MONOPOLISED
MONOPOLISER
MONOPOLISERS
MONOPOLISES
MONOPOLISING
MONOPOLISM
MONOPOLIST

MONOPOLISTIC
MONOPOLISTS
MONOPOLIZATION
MONOPOLIZATIONS
MONOPOLIZE
MONOPOLIZED
MONOPOLIZER
MONOPOLIZERS
MONOPOLIZES
MONOPOLIZING
MONOPOLY
MONOPRIONIDIAN
MONOPROPELLANT
MONOPROPELLANTS
MONOPSONIES
MONOPSONIST
MONOPSONISTIC
MONOPSONISTS
MONOPSONY
MONOPTERA
MONOPTERAL
MONOPTEROI
MONOPTERON
MONOPTEROS
MONOPTEROSES
MONOPTOTE
MONOPTOTES
MONOPULSE
MONOPULSES
MONORAIL
MONORAILS
MONORCHID
MONORCHIDISM
MONORCHIDISMS
MONORCHIDS
MONORCHISM
MONORCHISMS
MONORHINAL
MONORHINE
MONORHYME
MONORHYMED
MONORHYMES
MONOS
MONOSACCHARIDE
MONOSACCHARIDES
MONOSEMOUS
MONOSEMY
MONOSEPALOUS
MONOSES
MONOSIES
MONOSIS
MONOSKI
MONOSKIER
MONOSKIERS
MONOSKIING
MONOSKIS

MONOSODIUM
MONOSOME
MONOSOMES
MONOSOMIC
MONOSOMICS
MONOSOMIES
MONOSOMY
MONOSPECIFIC
MONOSPECIFICITY
MONOSPERMAL
MONOSPERMOUS
MONOSTABLE
MONOSTELE
MONOSTELES
MONOSTELIC
MONOSTELIES
MONOSTELY
MONOSTICH
MONOSTICHIC
MONOSTICHOUS
MONOSTICHS
MONOSTOME
MONOSTOMES
MONOSTOMOUS
MONOSTROPHE
MONOSTROPHES
MONOSTROPHIC
MONOSTROPHICS
MONOSTYLAR
MONOSTYLE
MONOSTYLOUS
MONOSY
MONOSYLLABIC
MONOSYLLABICITY
MONOSYLLABISM
MONOSYLLABISMS
MONOSYLLABLE
MONOSYLLABLES
MONOSYMMETRIC
MONOSYMMETRICAL
MONOSYMMETRY
MONOSYNAPTIC
MONOTELEPHONE
MONOTELEPHONES
MONOTERPENE
MONOTERPENES
MONOTHALAMIC
MONOTHALAMOUS
MONOTHECAL
MONOTHECOUS
MONOTHEISM
MONOTHEISMS
MONOTHEIST
MONOTHEISTIC
MONOTHEISTICAL
MONOTHEISTS

MONOTHELETE	MONOXIDES	MONTERO	MOOD
MONOTHELETES	MONOXYLON	MONTEROS	MOODIED
MONOTHELETIC	MONOXYLONS	MONTES	MOODIER
MONOTHELETICAL	MONOXYLOUS	MONTGOLFIER	MOODIES
MONOTHELETISM	MONOZYGOTIC	MONTGOLFIERS	MOODIEST
MONOTHELETISMS	MONS	MONTH	MOODILY
MONOTHELISM	MONSEIGNEUR	MONTHLIES	MOODINESS
MONOTHELISMS	MONSIEUR	MONTHLING	MOODINESSES
MONOTHELITE	MONSIGNOR	MONTHLINGS	MOODS
MONOTHELITES	MONSIGNORI	MONTHLONG	MOODY
MONOTHELITISM	MONSIGNORIAL	MONTHLY	MOODYING
MONOTHELITISMS	MONSIGNORS	MONTHS	MOOED
MONOTINT	MONSOON	MONTICELLITE	MOOI
MONOTINTS	MONSOONAL	MONTICELLITES	MOOING
MONOTOCOUS	MONSOONS	MONTICLE	MOOK
MONOTONE	MONSTER	MONTICLES	MOOKS
MONOTONED	MONSTERA	MONTICOLOUS	MOOKTAR
MONOTONES	MONSTERAS	MONTICULATE	MOOKTARS
MONOTONIC	MONSTERING	MONTICULE	MOOL
MONOTONICALLY	MONSTERS	MONTICULES	MOOLA
MONOTONICITIES	MONSTRANCE	MONTICULOUS	MOOLAH
MONOTONICITY	MONSTRANCES	MONTICULUS	MOOLAHS
MONOTONIES	MONSTROSITIES	MONTICULUSES	MOOLAS
MONOTONING	MONSTROSITY	MONTIES	MOOLED
MONOTONISE	MONSTROUS	MONTMORILLONITE	MOOLEY
MONOTONISED	MONSTROUSLY	MONTRE	MOOLEYS
MONOTONISES	MONSTROUSNESS	MONTRES	MOOLI
MONOTONISING	MONSTROUSNESSES	MONTURE	MOOLIES
MONOTONIZE	MONSTRUOSITIES	MONTURES	MOOLING
MONOTONIZED	MONSTRUOSITY	MONTY	MOOLIS
MONOTONIZES	MONSTRUOUS	MONUMENT	MOOLOO
MONOTONIZING	MONTADALE	MONUMENTAL	MOOLOOS
MONOTONOUS	MONTADALES	MONUMENTALITIES	MOOLS
MONOTONOUSLY	MONTAGE	MONUMENTALITY	MOOLVI
MONOTONOUSNESS	MONTAGED	MONUMENTALIZE	MOOLVIE
MONOTONY	MONTAGES	MONUMENTALIZED	MOOLVIES
MONOTREMATOUS	MONTAGING	MONUMENTALIZES	MOOLVIS
MONOTREME	MONTAGNARD	MONUMENTALIZING	MOOLY
MONOTREMES	MONTAGNARDS	MONUMENTALLY	MOON
MONOTRICHIC	MONTANE	MONUMENTED	MOONBEAM
MONOTRICHOUS	MONTANES	MONUMENTING	MOONBEAMS
MONOTROCH	MONTANT	MONUMENTS	MOONBLIND
MONOTROCHS	MONTANTO	MONURON	MOONBOW
MONOTYPE	MONTANTOS	MONURONS	MOONBOWS
MONOTYPES	MONTANTS	MONY	MOONCALF
MONOTYPIC	MONTARIA	MONYPLIES	MOONCALVES
MONOUNSATURATE	MONTARIAS	MONZONITE	MOONDUST
MONOUNSATURATED	MONTBRETIA	MONZONITES	MOONDUSTS
MONOUNSATURATES	MONTBRETIAS	MONZONITIC	MOONED
MONOVALENCE	MONTE	MOO	MOONER
MONOVALENCES	MONTEITH	MOOCH	MOONERS
MONOVALENCIES	MONTEITHS	MOOCHED	MOONEYE
MONOVALENCY	MONTELIMAR	MOOCHER	MOONEYES
MONOVALENT	MONTELIMARS	MOOCHERS	MOONFACE
MONOVULAR	MONTEM	MOOCHES	MOONFACED
MONOXIDE	MONTEMS	MOOCHING	MOONFACES

MOONFISH
MOONFISHES
MOONFLOWER
MOONFLOWERS
MOONIER
MOONIES
MOONIEST
MOONILY
MOONINESS
MOONING
MOONISH
MOONISHLY
MOONLESS
MOONLET
MOONLETS
MOONLIGHT
MOONLIGHTED
MOONLIGHTER
MOONLIGHTERS
MOONLIGHTING
MOONLIGHTINGS
MOONLIGHTS
MOONLIKE
MOONLIT
MOONPHASE
MOONPHASES
MOONPORT
MOONPORTS
MOONQUAKE
MOONQUAKES
MOONRAKER
MOONRAKERS
MOONRAKING
MOONRAKINGS
MOONRISE
MOONRISES
MOONROCK
MOONROCKS
MOONROOF
MOONROOFS
MOONS
MOONSAIL
MOONSAILS
MOONSCAPE
MOONSCAPES
MOONSEED
MOONSEEDS
MOONSET
MOONSETS
MOONSHEE
MOONSHEES
MOONSHINE
MOONSHINER
MOONSHINERS
MOONSHINES
MOONSHINY

MOONSHOT
MOONSHOTS
MOONSTONE
MOONSTONES
MOONSTRICKEN
MOONSTRIKE
MOONSTRIKES
MOONSTRUCK
MOONWALK
MOONWALKED
MOONWALKER
MOONWALKERS
MOONWALKING
MOONWALKS
MOONWARD
MOONWORT
MOONWORTS
MOONY
MOOP
MOOPED
MOOPING
MOOPS
MOOR
MOORAGE
MOORAGES
MOORBURN
MOORBURNING
MOORBUZZARDS
MOORCOCK
MOORCOCKS
MOORED
MOORFOWL
MOORFOWLS
MOORHEN
MOORHENS
MOORIER
MOORIEST
MOORILL
MOORILLS
MOORING
MOORINGS
MOORISH
MOORLAND
MOORLANDS
MOORLOG
MOORLOGS
MOORMAN
MOORMEN
MOORS
MOORVA
MOORVAS
MOORWORT
MOORWORTS
MOORY
MOOS
MOOSE

MOOSEYARD
MOOSEYARDS
MOOT
MOOTABLE
MOOTED
MOOTER
MOOTERS
MOOTEST
MOOTING
MOOTINGS
MOOTMAN
MOOTMEN
MOOTS
MOOVE
MOOVED
MOOVES
MOOVING
MOP
MOPANE
MOPANES
MOPANI
MOPANIS
MOPBOARD
MOPBOARDS
MOPE
MOPED
MOPEDS
MOPEHAWK
MOPEHAWKS
MOPER
MOPERIES
MOPERS
MOPERY
MOPES
MOPEY
MOPHEAD
MOPHEADS
MOPIER
MOPIEST
MOPING
MOPINGLY
MOPISH
MOPISHLY
MOPISHNESS
MOPISHNESSES
MOPOKE
MOPOKES
MOPPED
MOPPER
MOPPERS
MOPPET
MOPPETS
MOPPIER
MOPPIEST
MOPPING
MOPPY

MOPS
MOPSIES
MOPSTICK
MOPSTICKS
MOPSY
MOPUS
MOPUSES
MOPY
MOQUETTE
MOQUETTES
MOR
MORA
MORACEOUS
MORAE
MORAINAL
MORAINE
MORAINES
MORAINIC
MORAL
MORALE
MORALES
MORALISATION
MORALISATIONS
MORALISE
MORALISED
MORALISER
MORALISERS
MORALISES
MORALISING
MORALISM
MORALISMS
MORALIST
MORALISTIC
MORALISTICALLY
MORALISTS
MORALITIES
MORALITY
MORALIZATION
MORALIZATIONS
MORALIZE
MORALIZED
MORALIZER
MORALIZERS
MORALIZES
MORALIZING
MORALL
MORALLED
MORALLER
MORALLERS
MORALLING
MORALLS
MORALLY
MORALS
MORAS
MORASS
MORASSES

MORASSY
MORAT
MORATORIA
MORATORIUM
MORATORIUMS
MORATORY
MORATS
MORAY
MORAYS
MORBID
MORBIDER
MORBIDEST
MORBIDEZZA
MORBIDEZZAS
MORBIDITIES
MORBIDITY
MORBIDLY
MORBIDNESS
MORBIDNESSES
MORBIFEROUS
MORBIFIC
MORBIFICALLY
MORBILLI
MORBILLIFORM
MORBILLIVIRUS
MORBILLIVIRUSES
MORBILLOUS
MORBUS
MORBUSES
MORCEAU
MORCEAUX
MORCHA
MORCHAS
MORDACIOUS
MORDACIOUSLY
MORDACIOUSNESS
MORDACITIES
MORDACITY
MORDANCIES
MORDANCY
MORDANT
MORDANTED
MORDANTING
MORDANTLY
MORDANTS
MORDENT
MORDENTS
MORE
MOREEN
MOREENS
MOREISH
MOREL
MORELLE
MORELLES
MORELLO
MORELLOS

MORELS
MORENDO
MOREOVER
MOREPORK
MOREPORKS
MORES
MORESQUE
MORESQUES
MORGAN
MORGANATIC
MORGANATICALLY
MORGANITE
MORGANITES
MORGANS
MORGAY
MORGAYS
MORGEN
MORGENS
MORGENSTERN
MORGENSTERNS
MORGUE
MORGUES
MORIA
MORIAS
MORIBUND
MORIBUNDITIES
MORIBUNDITY
MORIBUNDLY
MORICHE
MORICHES
MORIGERATE
MORIGERATION
MORIGERATIONS
MORIGEROUS
MORION
MORIONS
MORISCO
MORISCOES
MORISCOS
MORISH
MORKIN
MORKINS
MORLING
MORLINGS
MORMAOR
MORMAORS
MORN
MORNAY
MORNAYS
MORNE
MORNED
MORNES
MORNING
MORNINGS
MORNS
MOROCCO

MOROCCOS
MORON
MORONIC
MORONICALLY
MORONISM
MORONISMS
MORONITIES
MORONITY
MORONS
MOROSE
MOROSELY
MOROSENESS
MOROSENESSES
MOROSER
MOROSEST
MOROSITIES
MOROSITY
MORPH
MORPHACTIN
MORPHACTINS
MORPHALLAXES
MORPHALLAXIS
MORPHEAN
MORPHED
MORPHEME
MORPHEMES
MORPHEMIC
MORPHEMICALLY
MORPHEMICS
MORPHETIC
MORPHEW
MORPHEWS
MORPHIA
MORPHIAS
MORPHIC
MORPHIN
MORPHINE
MORPHINES
MORPHING
MORPHINGS
MORPHINISM
MORPHINISMS
MORPHINOMANIA
MORPHINOMANIAC
MORPHINOMANIACS
MORPHINOMANIAS
MORPHINS
MORPHO
MORPHOGEN
MORPHOGENESES
MORPHOGENESIS
MORPHOGENETIC
MORPHOGENIC
MORPHOGENIES
MORPHOGENS
MORPHOGENY

MORPHOGRAPHER
MORPHOGRAPHERS
MORPHOGRAPHIES
MORPHOGRAPHY
MORPHOLOGIC
MORPHOLOGICAL
MORPHOLOGICALLY
MORPHOLOGIES
MORPHOLOGIST
MORPHOLOGISTS
MORPHOLOGY
MORPHOMETRIC
MORPHOMETRICS
MORPHOMETRIES
MORPHOMETRY
MORPHOPHONEME
MORPHOPHONEMES
MORPHOPHONEMIC
MORPHOPHONEMICS
MORPHOS
MORPHOSES
MORPHOSIS
MORPHOTIC
MORPHOTROPIC
MORPHOTROPIES
MORPHOTROPY
MORPHS
MORRA
MORRAS
MORRELL
MORRELLS
MORRHUA
MORRHUAS
MORRICE
MORRICES
MORRION
MORRIONS
MORRIS
MORRISED
MORRISES
MORRISING
MORRO
MORROS
MORROW
MORROWS
MORS
MORSAL
MORSE
MORSEL
MORSELED
MORSELING
MORSELLED
MORSELLING
MORSELS
MORSES
MORSURE

MORSURES
MORT
MORTADELLA
MORTADELLAS
MORTAL
MORTALISE
MORTALISED
MORTALISES
MORTALISING
MORTALITIES
MORTALITY
MORTALIZE
MORTALIZED
MORTALIZES
MORTALIZING
MORTALLY
MORTALS
MORTAR
MORTARBOARD
MORTARBOARDS
MORTARED
MORTARING
MORTARLESS
MORTARS
MORTARY
MORTBELL
MORTBELLS
MORTCLOTH
MORTCLOTHS
MORTGAGE
MORTGAGEABLE
MORTGAGED
MORTGAGEE
MORTGAGEES
MORTGAGER
MORTGAGERS
MORTGAGES
MORTGAGING
MORTGAGOR
MORTGAGORS
MORTICE
MORTICED
MORTICER
MORTICERS
MORTICES
MORTICIAN
MORTICIANS
MORTICING
MORTIFEROUS
MORTIFEROUSNESS
MORTIFIC
MORTIFICATION
MORTIFICATIONS
MORTIFIED
MORTIFIER
MORTIFIERS

MORTIFIES
MORTIFY
MORTIFYING
MORTIFYINGLY
MORTIFYINGS
MORTISE
MORTISED
MORTISER
MORTISERS
MORTISES
MORTISING
MORTLING
MORTLINGS
MORTMAIN
MORTMAINS
MORTS
MORTSAFE
MORTSAFES
MORTUARIES
MORTUARY
MORULA
MORULAE
MORULAR
MORULAS
MORULATION
MORULATIONS
MORWONG
MORWONGS
MORYAH
MOS
MOSAIC
MOSAICALLY
MOSAICISM
MOSAICISMS
MOSAICIST
MOSAICISTS
MOSAICKED
MOSAICKING
MOSAICLIKE
MOSAICS
MOSASAUR
MOSASAURI
MOSASAURIAN
MOSASAURS
MOSASAURUS
MOSBOLLETJIE
MOSBOLLETJIES
MOSCHATE
MOSCHATEL
MOSCHATELS
MOSCHIFEROUS
MOSE
MOSED
MOSES
MOSEY
MOSEYED

MOSEYING
MOSEYS
MOSH
MOSHAV
MOSHAVIM
MOSHED
MOSHES
MOSHING
MOSHINGS
MOSHPIT
MOSHPITS
MOSING
MOSK
MOSKONFYT
MOSKONFYTS
MOSKS
MOSLINGS
MOSOMORPHOUS
MOSQUE
MOSQUES
MOSQUITO
MOSQUITOES
MOSQUITOEY
MOSQUITOS
MOSS
MOSSBACK
MOSSBACKED
MOSSBACKS
MOSSBLUITERS
MOSSBUNKER
MOSSBUNKERS
MOSSED
MOSSER
MOSSERS
MOSSES
MOSSIE
MOSSIER
MOSSIES
MOSSIEST
MOSSINESS
MOSSINESSES
MOSSING
MOSSLAND
MOSSLANDS
MOSSLIKE
MOSSO
MOSSPLANT
MOSSPLANTS
MOSSTROOPER
MOSSTROOPERS
MOSSY
MOST
MOSTE
MOSTEST
MOSTESTS
MOSTLY

MOSTS
MOSTWHAT
MOT
MOTE
MOTED
MOTEL
MOTELIER
MOTELIERS
MOTELS
MOTEN
MOTES
MOTET
MOTETS
MOTETT
MOTETTIST
MOTETTISTS
MOTETTS
MOTEY
MOTH
MOTHBALL
MOTHBALLED
MOTHBALLING
MOTHBALLS
MOTHED
MOTHER
MOTHERBOARD
MOTHERBOARDS
MOTHERCRAFT
MOTHERCRAFTS
MOTHERED
MOTHERESE
MOTHERFUCKER
MOTHERFUCKERS
MOTHERFUCKING
MOTHERHOOD
MOTHERHOODS
MOTHERHOUSE
MOTHERHOUSES
MOTHERING
MOTHERINGS
MOTHERLAND
MOTHERLANDS
MOTHERLESS
MOTHERLESSNESS
MOTHERLINESS
MOTHERLINESSES
MOTHERLY
MOTHERS
MOTHERWORT
MOTHERWORTS
MOTHERY
MOTHIER
MOTHIEST
MOTHLIKE
MOTHPROOF
MOTHPROOFED

MOTHPROOFER	MOTOCROSS	MOTORIZATION	MOUCHES
MOTHPROOFERS	MOTOCROSSES	MOTORIZATIONS	MOUCHING
MOTHPROOFING	MOTONEURON	MOTORIZE	MOUCHOIR
MOTHPROOFS	MOTONEURONAL	MOTORIZED	MOUCHOIRS
MOTHS	MOTONEURONS	MOTORIZES	MOUDIEWART
MOTHY	MOTOR	MOTORIZING	MOUDIEWARTS
MOTIER	MOTORABLE	MOTORLESS	MOUDIEWORT
MOTIEST	MOTORAIL	MOTORMAN	MOUDIEWORTS
MOTIF	MOTORAILS	MOTORMEN	MOUDIWART
MOTIFIC	MOTORBICYCLE	MOTORMOUTH	MOUDIWARTS
MOTIFS	MOTORBICYCLES	MOTORMOUTHS	MOUDIWORT
MOTILE	MOTORBIKE	MOTORS	MOUDIWORTS
MOTILES	MOTORBIKED	MOTORTRUCK	MOUE
MOTILITIES	MOTORBIKES	MOTORTRUCKS	MOUES
MOTILITY	MOTORBIKING	MOTORWAY	MOUFFLON
MOTION	MOTORBOAT	MOTORWAYS	MOUFFLONS
MOTIONAL	MOTORBOATER	MOTORY	MOUFLON
MOTIONED	MOTORBOATERS	MOTOSCAFI	MOUFLONS
MOTIONER	MOTORBOATING	MOTOSCAFO	MOUGHT
MOTIONERS	MOTORBOATINGS	MOTS	MOUILLE
MOTIONING	MOTORBOATS	MOTSER	MOUJIK
MOTIONIST	MOTORBUS	MOTSERS	MOUJIKS
MOTIONISTS	MOTORBUSES	MOTT	MOULAGE
MOTIONLESS	MOTORBUSSES	MOTTE	MOULAGES
MOTIONLESSLY	MOTORCADE	MOTTES	MOULD
MOTIONLESSNESS	MOTORCADED	MOTTIER	MOULDABILITY
MOTIONS	MOTORCADES	MOTTIES	MOULDABLE
MOTIVATE	MOTORCADING	MOTTIEST	MOULDBOARD
MOTIVATED	MOTORCAR	MOTTLE	MOULDBOARDS
MOTIVATES	MOTORCARS	MOTTLED	MOULDED
MOTIVATING	MOTORCOACH	MOTTLER	MOULDER
MOTIVATION	MOTORCOACHES	MOTTLERS	MOULDERED
MOTIVATIONAL	MOTORCYCLE	MOTTLES	MOULDERING
MOTIVATIONALLY	MOTORCYCLED	MOTTLING	MOULDERS
MOTIVATIONS	MOTORCYCLES	MOTTLINGS	MOULDIER
MOTIVATIVE	MOTORCYCLING	MOTTO	MOULDIEST
MOTIVATOR	MOTORCYCLIST	MOTTOED	MOULDINESS
MOTIVATORS	MOTORCYCLISTS	MOTTOES	MOULDINESSES
MOTIVE	MOTORDOM	MOTTOS	MOULDING
MOTIVED	MOTORDOMS	MOTTS	MOULDINGS
MOTIVELESS	MOTORED	MOTTY	MOULDS
MOTIVELESSLY	MOTORIAL	MOTU	MOULDWARP
MOTIVELESSNESS	MOTORIC	MOTUCA	MOULDWARPS
MOTIVES	MOTORICALLY	MOTUCAS	MOULDY
MOTIVIC	MOTORING	MOTUS	MOULDYWARP
MOTIVING	MOTORINGS	MOTZA	MOULDYWARPS
MOTIVITIES	MOTORISATION	MOTZAS	MOULIN
MOTIVITY	MOTORISATIONS	MOU	MOULINET
MOTLEY	MOTORISE	MOUCH	MOULINETS
MOTLEYER	MOTORISED	MOUCHARABIES	MOULINS
MOTLEYEST	MOTORISES	MOUCHARABY	MOULS
MOTLEYS	MOTORISING	MOUCHARD	MOULT
MOTLIER	MOTORIST	MOUCHARDS	MOULTED
MOTLIEST	MOTORISTS	MOUCHED	MOULTEN
MOTMOT	MOTORIUM	MOUCHER	MOULTER
MOTMOTS	MOTORIUMS	MOUCHERS	MOULTERS

MOULTING
MOULTINGS
MOULTS
MOUND
MOUNDED
MOUNDING
MOUNDS
MOUNSEER
MOUNSEERS
MOUNT
MOUNTABLE
MOUNTAIN
MOUNTAINED
MOUNTAINEER
MOUNTAINEERED
MOUNTAINEERING
MOUNTAINEERINGS
MOUNTAINEERS
MOUNTAINOUS
MOUNTAINOUSLY
MOUNTAINOUSNESS
MOUNTAINS
MOUNTAINSIDE
MOUNTAINSIDES
MOUNTAINTOP
MOUNTAINTOPS
MOUNTAINY
MOUNTANT
MOUNTANTS
MOUNTEBANK
MOUNTEBANKED
MOUNTEBANKERIES
MOUNTEBANKERY
MOUNTEBANKING
MOUNTEBANKINGS
MOUNTEBANKISM
MOUNTEBANKISMS
MOUNTEBANKS
MOUNTED
MOUNTENANCE
MOUNTENANCES
MOUNTENAUNCE
MOUNTENAUNCES
MOUNTER
MOUNTERS
MOUNTING
MOUNTINGS
MOUNTS
MOUP
MOUPED
MOUPING
MOUPS
MOURN
MOURNED
MOURNER
MOURNERS

MOURNFUL
MOURNFULLER
MOURNFULLEST
MOURNFULLY
MOURNFULNESS
MOURNFULNESSES
MOURNING
MOURNINGLY
MOURNINGS
MOURNIVAL
MOURNIVALS
MOURNS
MOUS
MOUSAKA
MOUSAKAS
MOUSE
MOUSEBIRD
MOUSEBIRDS
MOUSED
MOUSEKIN
MOUSEKINS
MOUSELIKE
MOUSEPIECE
MOUSEPIECES
MOUSER
MOUSERIES
MOUSERS
MOUSERY
MOUSES
MOUSETAIL
MOUSETAILS
MOUSETRAP
MOUSETRAPPED
MOUSETRAPPING
MOUSETRAPS
MOUSEY
MOUSIE
MOUSIER
MOUSIES
MOUSIEST
MOUSILY
MOUSINESS
MOUSINESSES
MOUSING
MOUSINGS
MOUSLE
MOUSLED
MOUSLES
MOUSLING
MOUSME
MOUSMEE
MOUSMEES
MOUSMES
MOUSQUETAIRE
MOUSQUETAIRES
MOUSSAKA

MOUSSAKAS
MOUSSE
MOUSSED
MOUSSELINE
MOUSSELINES
MOUSSES
MOUSSING
MOUST
MOUSTACHE
MOUSTACHED
MOUSTACHES
MOUSTACHIAL
MOUSTACHIO
MOUSTACHIOS
MOUSTED
MOUSTING
MOUSTS
MOUSY
MOUTAN
MOUTANS
MOUTER
MOUTERED
MOUTERER
MOUTERERS
MOUTERING
MOUTERS
MOUTH
MOUTHABLE
MOUTHBREATHER
MOUTHBREATHERS
MOUTHBREEDER
MOUTHBREEDERS
MOUTHBROODER
MOUTHBROODERS
MOUTHED
MOUTHER
MOUTHERS
MOUTHFEEL
MOUTHFEELS
MOUTHFUL
MOUTHFULS
MOUTHIER
MOUTHIEST
MOUTHILY
MOUTHING
MOUTHLESS
MOUTHLIKE
MOUTHPART
MOUTHPARTS
MOUTHPIECE
MOUTHPIECES
MOUTHS
MOUTHWASH
MOUTHWASHES
MOUTHWATERING
MOUTHWATERINGLY

MOUTHY
MOUTON
MOUTONS
MOUVEMENTE
MOVABILITIES
MOVABILITY
MOVABLE
MOVABLENESS
MOVABLENESSES
MOVABLES
MOVABLY
MOVE
MOVEABILITIES
MOVEABILITY
MOVEABLE
MOVEABLENESS
MOVEABLENESSES
MOVEABLES
MOVEABLY
MOVED
MOVELESS
MOVELESSLY
MOVELESSNESS
MOVELESSNESSES
MOVEMENT
MOVEMENTS
MOVER
MOVERS
MOVES
MOVIE
MOVIEDOM
MOVIEDOMS
MOVIEGOER
MOVIEGOERS
MOVIEGOING
MOVIEGOINGS
MOVIELAND
MOVIELANDS
MOVIEMAKER
MOVIEMAKERS
MOVIEMAKING
MOVIEMAKINGS
MOVIEOLA
MOVIEOLAS
MOVIES
MOVING
MOVINGLY
MOVIOLA
MOVIOLAS
MOW
MOWA
MOWAS
MOWBURN
MOWBURNED
MOWBURNING
MOWBURNS

MOWBURNT
MOWDIE
MOWDIES
MOWDIEWART
MOWDIEWARTS
MOWDIEWORT
MOWDIEWORTS
MOWDIWARTS
MOWDIWORTS
MOWED
MOWER
MOWERS
MOWING
MOWINGS
MOWN
MOWRA
MOWRAS
MOWS
MOXA
MOXAS
MOXIBUSTION
MOXIBUSTIONS
MOXIE
MOXIES
MOY
MOYA
MOYAS
MOYGASHEL
MOYGASHELS
MOYITIES
MOYITY
MOYL
MOYLE
MOYLED
MOYLES
MOYLING
MOYLS
MOYS
MOZ
MOZE
MOZED
MOZES
MOZETTA
MOZETTAS
MOZETTE
MOZING
MOZO
MOZOS
MOZZ
MOZZARELLA
MOZZARELLAS
MOZZES
MOZZETTA
MOZZETTAS
MOZZETTE
MOZZIE

MOZZIES
MOZZLE
MOZZLES
MPRET
MPRETS
MRIDAMGAM
MRIDAMGAMS
MRIDANG
MRIDANGA
MRIDANGAM
MRIDANGAMS
MRIDANGAS
MRIDANGS
MU
MUCATE
MUCATES
MUCEDINOUS
MUCH
MUCHACHO
MUCHACHOS
MUCHEL
MUCHELL
MUCHELLS
MUCHELS
MUCHES
MUCHLY
MUCHNESS
MUCHNESSES
MUCIC
MUCID
MUCIDITIES
MUCIDITY
MUCIDNESS
MUCIFEROUS
MUCIGEN
MUCIGENS
MUCILAGE
MUCILAGES
MUCILAGINOUS
MUCILAGINOUSLY
MUCIN
MUCINOID
MUCINOUS
MUCINS
MUCK
MUCKAMUCK
MUCKAMUCKED
MUCKAMUCKING
MUCKAMUCKS
MUCKED
MUCKENDER
MUCKENDERS
MUCKER
MUCKERED
MUCKERING
MUCKERISH

MUCKERS
MUCKHEAP
MUCKHEAPS
MUCKIER
MUCKIEST
MUCKILY
MUCKINESS
MUCKINESSES
MUCKING
MUCKLE
MUCKLES
MUCKLUCK
MUCKLUCKS
MUCKRAKE
MUCKRAKED
MUCKRAKER
MUCKRAKERS
MUCKRAKES
MUCKRAKING
MUCKS
MUCKSPREAD
MUCKSPREADER
MUCKSPREADERS
MUCKSPREADING
MUCKSPREADS
MUCKSWEAT
MUCKSWEATS
MUCKWORM
MUCKWORMS
MUCKY
MUCLUC
MUCLUCS
MUCOCUTANEOUS
MUCOID
MUCOIDAL
MUCOIDS
MUCOLYTIC
MUCOMEMBRANOUS
MUCOPEPTIDE
MUCOPEPTIDES
MUCOPROTEIN
MUCOPROTEINS
MUCOPURULENT
MUCOR
MUCORS
MUCOSA
MUCOSAE
MUCOSAL
MUCOSANGUINEOUS
MUCOSAS
MUCOSE
MUCOSITIES
MUCOSITY
MUCOUS
MUCOVISCIDOSES
MUCOVISCIDOSIS

MUCRO
MUCRONATE
MUCRONATED
MUCRONATION
MUCRONATIONS
MUCRONES
MUCROS
MUCULENT
MUCUS
MUCUSES
MUD
MUDBATH
MUDBATHS
MUDCAP
MUDCAPPED
MUDCAPPING
MUDCAPS
MUDCAT
MUDCATS
MUDDED
MUDDER
MUDDERS
MUDDIED
MUDDIER
MUDDIES
MUDDIEST
MUDDILY
MUDDINESS
MUDDINESSES
MUDDING
MUDDLE
MUDDLED
MUDDLEDNESS
MUDDLEHEAD
MUDDLEHEADED
MUDDLEHEADEDLY
MUDDLEHEADS
MUDDLEMENT
MUDDLER
MUDDLERS
MUDDLES
MUDDLING
MUDDLINGLY
MUDDLY
MUDDY
MUDDYING
MUDEJAR
MUDEJARES
MUDFISH
MUDFISHES
MUDFLAP
MUDFLAPS
MUDFLAT
MUDFLATS
MUDFLOW
MUDFLOWS

MUDGE
MUDGED
MUDGER
MUDGERS
MUDGES
MUDGING
MUDGUARD
MUDGUARDS
MUDHOLE
MUDHOLES
MUDHOOK
MUDHOOKS
MUDIR
MUDIRIA
MUDIRIAS
MUDIRIEH
MUDIRIEHS
MUDIRS
MUDLARK
MUDLARKED
MUDLARKING
MUDLARKS
MUDLOGGER
MUDLOGGERS
MUDLOGGING
MUDLOGGINGS
MUDPACK
MUDPACKS
MUDPUPPIES
MUDPUPPY
MUDRA
MUDRAS
MUDROCK
MUDROCKS
MUDROOM
MUDROOMS
MUDS
MUDSCOW
MUDSCOWS
MUDSILL
MUDSILLS
MUDSKIPPER
MUDSKIPPERS
MUDSLIDE
MUDSLIDES
MUDSLINGER
MUDSLINGERS
MUDSLINGING
MUDSLINGINGS
MUDSTONE
MUDSTONES
MUDWORT
MUDWORTS
MUEDDIN
MUEDDINS
MUENSTER

MUENSTERS
MUESLI
MUESLIS
MUEZZIN
MUEZZINS
MUFF
MUFFED
MUFFETTEES
MUFFIN
MUFFINEER
MUFFINEERS
MUFFING
MUFFINS
MUFFISH
MUFFLE
MUFFLED
MUFFLER
MUFFLERED
MUFFLERS
MUFFLES
MUFFLING
MUFFS
MUFLON
MUFLONS
MUFTI
MUFTIS
MUG
MUGEARITE
MUGEARITES
MUGFUL
MUGFULS
MUGG
MUGGA
MUGGAR
MUGGARS
MUGGED
MUGGEE
MUGGEES
MUGGER
MUGGERS
MUGGIER
MUGGIEST
MUGGILY
MUGGINESS
MUGGINESSES
MUGGING
MUGGINGS
MUGGINS
MUGGINSES
MUGGISH
MUGGS
MUGGUR
MUGGURS
MUGGY
MUGS
MUGSHOT

MUGSHOTS
MUGWORT
MUGWORTS
MUGWUMP
MUGWUMPERIES
MUGWUMPERY
MUGWUMPISH
MUGWUMPISM
MUGWUMPS
MUHLIES
MUHLY
MUID
MUIDS
MUIL
MUILS
MUIR
MUIRBURN
MUIRBURNS
MUIRS
MUIST
MUISTED
MUISTING
MUISTS
MUJAHEDDIN
MUJAHEDEEN
MUJAHEDIN
MUJAHIDEEN
MUJAHIDIN
MUJIK
MUJIKS
MUKHTAR
MUKHTARS
MUKLUK
MUKLUKS
MUKTUK
MUKTUKS
MULATTA
MULATTAS
MULATTO
MULATTOES
MULATTOS
MULATTRESS
MULATTRESSES
MULBERRIES
MULBERRY
MULCH
MULCHED
MULCHES
MULCHING
MULCT
MULCTED
MULCTING
MULCTS
MULE
MULED
MULES

MULESED
MULESES
MULESING
MULETA
MULETAS
MULETEER
MULETEERS
MULEY
MULEYS
MULGA
MULGAS
MULIEBRITIES
MULIEBRITY
MULING
MULISH
MULISHLY
MULISHNESS
MULISHNESSES
MULL
MULLA
MULLAH
MULLAHISM
MULLAHISMS
MULLAHS
MULLARKIES
MULLARKY
MULLAS
MULLED
MULLEIN
MULLEINS
MULLEN
MULLENS
MULLER
MULLERED
MULLERS
MULLET
MULLETS
MULLEY
MULLEYS
MULLIGAN
MULLIGANS
MULLIGATAWNIES
MULLIGATAWNY
MULLIGRUBS
MULLING
MULLION
MULLIONED
MULLIONING
MULLIONS
MULLITE
MULLITES
MULLOCK
MULLOCKS
MULLOCKY
MULLOWAY
MULLOWAYS

MULLS
MULMUL
MULMULL
MULMULLS
MULMULS
MULSE
MULSES
MULSH
MULSHED
MULSHES
MULSHING
MULTANGULAR
MULTANIMOUS
MULTARTICULATE
MULTEITIES
MULTEITY
MULTIACCESS
MULTIAGE
MULTIAGENCY
MULTIANGULAR
MULTIARMED
MULTIARTICULATE
MULTIATOM
MULTIAUTHOR
MULTIAXIAL
MULTIBAND
MULTIBANK
MULTIBARREL
MULTIBARRELED
MULTIBILLION
MULTIBLADED
MULTIBRANCHED
MULTIBUILDING
MULTICAMERATE
MULTICAMPUS
MULTICAPITATE
MULTICAR
MULTICARBON
MULTICAULINE
MULTICAUSAL
MULTICELL
MULTICELLED
MULTICELLULAR
MULTICENTER
MULTICENTRAL
MULTICENTRIC
MULTICHAIN
MULTICHAMBERED
MULTICHANNEL
MULTICHARACTER
MULTICIDAL
MULTICIDE
MULTICIDES
MULTICIPITAL
MULTICITY
MULTICLIENT

MULTICOATED
MULTICOLOR
MULTICOLORED
MULTICOLORS
MULTICOLOUR
MULTICOLOURED
MULTICOLOURS
MULTICOLUMN
MULTICOMPONENT
MULTICONDUCTOR
MULTICOPY
MULTICOSTATE
MULTICOUNTY
MULTICOURSE
MULTICULTURAL
MULTICURIE
MULTICURRENCIES
MULTICURRENCY
MULTICUSPID
MULTICUSPIDATE
MULTICUSPIDS
MULTICYCLE
MULTICYCLES
MULTIDENTATE
MULTIDIALECTAL
MULTIDIGITATE
MULTIDISCIPLINE
MULTIDIVISIONAL
MULTIDOMAIN
MULTIDRUG
MULTIELECTRODE
MULTIELEMENT
MULTIEMPLOYER
MULTIEMPLOYERS
MULTIENGINE
MULTIENZYME
MULTIETHNIC
MULTIETHNICS
MULTIFACED
MULTIFACETED
MULTIFACTOR
MULTIFACTORIAL
MULTIFAMILY
MULTIFARIOUS
MULTIFARIOUSLY
MULTIFID
MULTIFIDLY
MULTIFIDOUS
MULTIFIL
MULTIFILAMENT
MULTIFILAMENTS
MULTIFILS
MULTIFLASH
MULTIFLORA
MULTIFLOROUS
MULTIFOCAL

MULTIFOIL
MULTIFOILS
MULTIFOLD
MULTIFOLIATE
MULTIFOLIOLATE
MULTIFORM
MULTIFORMITIES
MULTIFORMITY
MULTIFORMS
MULTIFREQUENCY
MULTIFUNCTION
MULTIFUNCTIONAL
MULTIGENIC
MULTIGERM
MULTIGRADE
MULTIGRAIN
MULTIGRAVIDA
MULTIGRAVIDAE
MULTIGRAVIDAS
MULTIGRID
MULTIGROUP
MULTIGYM
MULTIGYMS
MULTIHEADED
MULTIHOSPITAL
MULTIHUED
MULTIHULL
MULTIHULLS
MULTIJET
MULTIJUGATE
MULTIJUGOUS
MULTILANE
MULTILATERAL
MULTILATERALISM
MULTILATERALIST
MULTILATERALLY
MULTILAYER
MULTILAYERED
MULTILEVEL
MULTILEVELED
MULTILINE
MULTILINEAL
MULTILINEAR
MULTILINGUAL
MULTILINGUALISM
MULTILINGUALLY
MULTILINGUIST
MULTILINGUISTS
MULTILOBATE
MULTILOBED
MULTILOBULAR
MULTILOBULATE
MULTILOCATIONAL
MULTILOCULAR
MULTILOCULATE
MULTILOQUENCE

MULTILOQUENCES
MULTILOQUENT
MULTILOQUIES
MULTILOQUOUS
MULTILOQUY
MULTIMANNED
MULTIMEDIA
MULTIMEDIAS
MULTIMEGATON
MULTIMEGAWATT
MULTIMEGAWATTS
MULTIMEMBER
MULTIMETALLIC
MULTIMETER
MULTIMETERS
MULTIMETRIC
MULTIMETRICAL
MULTIMILLENNIAL
MULTIMILLION
MULTIMODAL
MULTIMODE
MULTIMOLECULAR
MULTINATION
MULTINATIONAL
MULTINATIONALS
MULTINOMIAL
MULTINOMIALS
MULTINOMINAL
MULTINUCLEAR
MULTINUCLEATE
MULTINUCLEATED
MULTINUCLEOLATE
MULTIORGASMIC
MULTIPACK
MULTIPACKS
MULTIPAGE
MULTIPANED
MULTIPARA
MULTIPARAE
MULTIPARAMETER
MULTIPARAS
MULTIPARITIES
MULTIPARITY
MULTIPAROUS
MULTIPART
MULTIPARTICLE
MULTIPARTITE
MULTIPARTY
MULTIPARTYISM
MULTIPARTYISMS
MULTIPATH
MULTIPED
MULTIPEDE
MULTIPEDES
MULTIPEDS
MULTIPHASE

MULTIPHASIC
MULTIPHOTON
MULTIPICTURE
MULTIPIECE
MULTIPION
MULTIPISTON
MULTIPLANE
MULTIPLANES
MULTIPLANT
MULTIPLAYER
MULTIPLE
MULTIPLES
MULTIPLET
MULTIPLETS
MULTIPLEX
MULTIPLEXED
MULTIPLEXER
MULTIPLEXERS
MULTIPLEXES
MULTIPLEXING
MULTIPLEXOR
MULTIPLEXORS
MULTIPLIABLE
MULTIPLICABLE
MULTIPLICAND
MULTIPLICANDS
MULTIPLICATE
MULTIPLICATES
MULTIPLICATION
MULTIPLICATIONS
MULTIPLICATIVE
MULTIPLICATOR
MULTIPLICATORS
MULTIPLICITIES
MULTIPLICITY
MULTIPLIED
MULTIPLIER
MULTIPLIERS
MULTIPLIES
MULTIPLY
MULTIPLYING
MULTIPOLAR
MULTIPOLARITIES
MULTIPOLARITY
MULTIPOLE
MULTIPOTENT
MULTIPOTENTIAL
MULTIPOWER
MULTIPRESENCE
MULTIPRESENCES
MULTIPRESENT
MULTIPROBLEM
MULTIPROCESSING
MULTIPROCESSOR
MULTIPROCESSORS
MULTIPRODUCT

MULTIPRONGED
MULTIPURPOSE
MULTIRACIAL
MULTIRACIALISM
MULTIRACIALISMS
MULTIRAMIFIED
MULTIRANGE
MULTIREGIONAL
MULTIRELIGIOUS
MULTIROLE
MULTIROLES
MULTIROOM
MULTISCIENCE
MULTISCIENCES
MULTISCREEN
MULTISENSE
MULTISENSORY
MULTISEPTATE
MULTISERIAL
MULTISERIATE
MULTISERVICE
MULTISIDED
MULTISITE
MULTISIZE
MULTISKILL
MULTISKILLED
MULTISKILLING
MULTISKILLINGS
MULTISKILLS
MULTISONANT
MULTISOURCE
MULTISPECIES
MULTISPECTRAL
MULTISPEED
MULTISPIRAL
MULTISPORT
MULTISTAGE
MULTISTATE
MULTISTEMMED
MULTISTEP
MULTISTOREY
MULTISTOREYS
MULTISTORIED
MULTISTORY
MULTISTRANDED
MULTISTRIKE
MULTISTRIKES
MULTISULCATE
MULTISYLLABIC
MULTISYSTEM
MULTITALENTED
MULTITASK
MULTITASKED
MULTITASKING
MULTITASKINGS
MULTITASKS

MULTITERMINAL
MULTITHREADING
MULTITHREADINGS
MULTITIERED
MULTITON
MULTITONE
MULTITOWERED
MULTITRACK
MULTITRILLION
MULTITUDE
MULTITUDES
MULTITUDINARY
MULTITUDINOUS
MULTITUDINOUSLY
MULTIUNION
MULTIUNIT
MULTIUSE
MULTIUSER
MULTIVALENCE
MULTIVALENCES
MULTIVALENCIES
MULTIVALENCY
MULTIVALENT
MULTIVALENTS
MULTIVARIABLE
MULTIVARIATE
MULTIVARIOUS
MULTIVERSITIES
MULTIVERSITY
MULTIVIBRATOR
MULTIVIBRATORS
MULTIVIOUS
MULTIVITAMIN
MULTIVITAMINS
MULTIVOCAL
MULTIVOCALS
MULTIVOLTINE
MULTIVOLUME
MULTIWALL
MULTIWARHEAD
MULTIWAVELENGTH
MULTIWINDOW
MULTIWINDOWS
MULTIYEAR
MULTOCULAR
MULTUM
MULTUMS
MULTUNGULATE
MULTUNGULATES
MULTURE
MULTURED
MULTURER
MULTURERS
MULTURES
MULTURING
MUM

MUMBLE
MUMBLED
MUMBLEMENT
MUMBLEMENTS
MUMBLER
MUMBLERS
MUMBLES
MUMBLETYPEG
MUMBLING
MUMBLINGLY
MUMBLINGS
MUMBLY
MUMBO
MUMCHANCE
MUMCHANCES
MUMM
MUMMED
MUMMER
MUMMERIES
MUMMERS
MUMMERY
MUMMIA
MUMMIAS
MUMMICHOG
MUMMICHOGS
MUMMIED
MUMMIES
MUMMIFICATION
MUMMIFICATIONS
MUMMIFIED
MUMMIFIES
MUMMIFORM
MUMMIFY
MUMMIFYING
MUMMING
MUMMINGS
MUMMOCK
MUMMOCKS
MUMMS
MUMMY
MUMMYING
MUMP
MUMPED
MUMPER
MUMPERS
MUMPING
MUMPISH
MUMPISHLY
MUMPISHNESS
MUMPISHNESSES
MUMPS
MUMPSIMUS
MUMPSIMUSES
MUMS
MUMSIER
MUMSIEST

MUMSY
MUMU
MUMUS
MUN
MUNCH
MUNCHED
MUNCHER
MUNCHERS
MUNCHES
MUNCHIES
MUNCHING
MUNCHKIN
MUNCHKINS
MUNDANE
MUNDANELY
MUNDANENESS
MUNDANENESSES
MUNDANER
MUNDANEST
MUNDANITIES
MUNDANITY
MUNDIC
MUNDICS
MUNDIFICATION
MUNDIFICATIONS
MUNDIFICATIVE
MUNDIFIED
MUNDIFIES
MUNDIFY
MUNDIFYING
MUNDUNGO
MUNDUNGOS
MUNDUNGUS
MUNDUNGUSES
MUNG
MUNGA
MUNGAS
MUNGCORN
MUNGCORNS
MUNGO
MUNGOOSE
MUNGOOSES
MUNGOS
MUNI
MUNICIPAL
MUNICIPALISE
MUNICIPALISED
MUNICIPALISES
MUNICIPALISING
MUNICIPALISM
MUNICIPALISMS
MUNICIPALIST
MUNICIPALISTS
MUNICIPALITIES
MUNICIPALITY
MUNICIPALIZE

MUNICIPALIZED
MUNICIPALIZES
MUNICIPALIZING
MUNICIPALLY
MUNICIPALS
MUNIFICENCE
MUNIFICENCES
MUNIFICENT
MUNIFICENTLY
MUNIFICENTNESS
MUNIFIED
MUNIFIENCE
MUNIFIENCES
MUNIFIES
MUNIFY
MUNIFYING
MUNIMENT
MUNIMENTS
MUNIS
MUNITE
MUNITED
MUNITES
MUNITING
MUNITION
MUNITIONED
MUNITIONEER
MUNITIONEERS
MUNITIONER
MUNITIONERS
MUNITIONETTE
MUNITIONETTES
MUNITIONING
MUNITIONS
MUNNION
MUNNIONS
MUNS
MUNSHI
MUNSHIS
MUNSTER
MUNSTERS
MUNT
MUNTER
MUNTERS
MUNTIN
MUNTING
MUNTINGS
MUNTINS
MUNTJAC
MUNTJACS
MUNTJAK
MUNTJAKS
MUNTS
MUNTU
MUNTUS
MUON
MUONIC

MUONIUM
MUONIUMS
MUONS
MUPPET
MUPPETS
MUQADDAM
MUQADDAMS
MURA
MURAENA
MURAENAS
MURAENID
MURAENIDS
MURAGE
MURAGES
MURAL
MURALIST
MURALISTS
MURALS
MURAS
MURDABAD
MURDABADED
MURDABADING
MURDABADS
MURDER
MURDERED
MURDEREE
MURDEREES
MURDERER
MURDERERS
MURDERESS
MURDERESSES
MURDERING
MURDEROUS
MURDEROUSLY
MURDEROUSNESS
MURDEROUSNESSES
MURDERS
MURE
MURED
MUREIN
MUREINS
MURENA
MURENAS
MURES
MUREX
MUREXES
MURGEON
MURGEONED
MURGEONING
MURGEONS
MURIATE
MURIATED
MURIATES
MURIATIC
MURICATE
MURICATED

MURICES
MURID
MURIDS
MURIFORM
MURINE
MURINES
MURING
MURK
MURKER
MURKEST
MURKIER
MURKIEST
MURKILY
MURKINESS
MURKINESSES
MURKISH
MURKLY
MURKS
MURKSOME
MURKY
MURL
MURLAIN
MURLAINS
MURLAN
MURLANS
MURLED
MURLIER
MURLIEST
MURLIN
MURLING
MURLINS
MURLS
MURLY
MURMUR
MURMURATION
MURMURATIONS
MURMURED
MURMURER
MURMURERS
MURMURING
MURMURINGLY
MURMURINGS
MURMUROUS
MURMUROUSLY
MURMURS
MURPHIES
MURPHY
MURR
MURRA
MURRAGH
MURRAGHS
MURRAIN
MURRAINED
MURRAINS
MURRAM
MURRAMS

MURRAS
MURRAY
MURRAYS
MURRE
MURREE
MURREES
MURRELET
MURRELETS
MURREN
MURRENS
MURRES
MURREY
MURREYS
MURRHA
MURRHAS
MURRHINE
MURRI
MURRIES
MURRIN
MURRINE
MURRINS
MURRION
MURRIONS
MURRIS
MURRS
MURRY
MURTHER
MURTHERED
MURTHERER
MURTHERERS
MURTHERING
MURTHERS
MURTI
MURTIS
MURVA
MURVAS
MUS
MUSACEOUS
MUSANG
MUSANGS
MUSAR
MUSARS
MUSCA
MUSCADEL
MUSCADELLE
MUSCADELLES
MUSCADELS
MUSCADET
MUSCADETS
MUSCADIN
MUSCADINE
MUSCADINES
MUSCADINS
MUSCAE
MUSCARDINE
MUSCARDINES

MUSCARINE
MUSCARINES
MUSCARINIC
MUSCAT
MUSCATEL
MUSCATELS
MUSCATORIUM
MUSCATS
MUSCAVADO
MUSCAVADOS
MUSCID
MUSCIDS
MUSCLE
MUSCLED
MUSCLEMAN
MUSCLEMEN
MUSCLES
MUSCLIER
MUSCLIEST
MUSCLING
MUSCLINGS
MUSCLY
MUSCOID
MUSCOLOGIES
MUSCOLOGY
MUSCONE
MUSCONES
MUSCOSE
MUSCOVADO
MUSCOVADOS
MUSCOVITE
MUSCOVITES
MUSCULAR
MUSCULARITIES
MUSCULARITY
MUSCULARLY
MUSCULATION
MUSCULATIONS
MUSCULATURE
MUSCULATURES
MUSCULOSKELETAL
MUSCULOUS
MUSE
MUSED
MUSEFUL
MUSEFULLY
MUSEOLOGICAL
MUSEOLOGIES
MUSEOLOGIST
MUSEOLOGISTS
MUSEOLOGY
MUSER
MUSERS
MUSES
MUSET
MUSETS

MUSETTE
MUSETTES
MUSEUM
MUSEUMS
MUSH
MUSHA
MUSHED
MUSHER
MUSHERS
MUSHES
MUSHIER
MUSHIEST
MUSHILY
MUSHINESS
MUSHINESSES
MUSHING
MUSHMOUTH
MUSHMOUTHS
MUSHROOM
MUSHROOMED
MUSHROOMER
MUSHROOMERS
MUSHROOMING
MUSHROOMS
MUSHY
MUSIC
MUSICAL
MUSICALE
MUSICALES
MUSICALISE
MUSICALISED
MUSICALISES
MUSICALISING
MUSICALITIES
MUSICALITY
MUSICALIZATION
MUSICALIZATIONS
MUSICALIZE
MUSICALIZED
MUSICALIZES
MUSICALIZING
MUSICALLY
MUSICALNESS
MUSICALNESSES
MUSICALS
MUSICASSETTE
MUSICASSETTES
MUSICIAN
MUSICIANER
MUSICIANERS
MUSICIANLY
MUSICIANS
MUSICIANSHIP
MUSICIANSHIPS
MUSICKED
MUSICKER

MUSICKERS
MUSICKING
MUSICOLOGICAL
MUSICOLOGICALLY
MUSICOLOGIES
MUSICOLOGIST
MUSICOLOGISTS
MUSICOLOGY
MUSICOTHERAPIES
MUSICOTHERAPY
MUSICS
MUSIMON
MUSIMONS
MUSING
MUSINGLY
MUSINGS
MUSIT
MUSITS
MUSIVE
MUSJID
MUSJIDS
MUSK
MUSKED
MUSKEG
MUSKEGS
MUSKELLUNGE
MUSKELLUNGES
MUSKET
MUSKETEER
MUSKETEERS
MUSKETOON
MUSKETOONS
MUSKETRIES
MUSKETRY
MUSKETS
MUSKIE
MUSKIER
MUSKIES
MUSKIEST
MUSKILY
MUSKINESS
MUSKINESSES
MUSKING
MUSKIT
MUSKITS
MUSKLE
MUSKLES
MUSKMELON
MUSKMELONS
MUSKONE
MUSKONES
MUSKRAT
MUSKRATS
MUSKS
MUSKY
MUSLIN

MUSLINED
MUSLINET
MUSLINETS
MUSLINS
MUSMON
MUSMONS
MUSO
MUSOS
MUSPIKE
MUSPIKES
MUSQUASH
MUSQUASHES
MUSQUETOON
MUSQUETOONS
MUSROL
MUSROLS
MUSS
MUSSE
MUSSED
MUSSEL
MUSSELCRACKER
MUSSELCRACKERS
MUSSELLED
MUSSELS
MUSSES
MUSSIER
MUSSIEST
MUSSILY
MUSSINESS
MUSSINESSES
MUSSING
MUSSITATE
MUSSITATED
MUSSITATES
MUSSITATING
MUSSITATION
MUSSITATIONS
MUSSY
MUST
MUSTACHE
MUSTACHED
MUSTACHES
MUSTACHIO
MUSTACHIOED
MUSTACHIOS
MUSTANG
MUSTANGS
MUSTARD
MUSTARDS
MUSTARDY
MUSTED
MUSTEE
MUSTEES
MUSTELINE
MUSTELINES
MUSTER

MUSTERED
MUSTERER
MUSTERERS
MUSTERING
MUSTERS
MUSTH
MUSTHS
MUSTIER
MUSTIEST
MUSTILY
MUSTINESS
MUSTINESSES
MUSTING
MUSTS
MUSTY
MUT
MUTABILITIES
MUTABILITY
MUTABLE
MUTABLENESS
MUTABLENESSES
MUTABLY
MUTAGEN
MUTAGENESES
MUTAGENESIS
MUTAGENIC
MUTAGENICALLY
MUTAGENICITIES
MUTAGENICITY
MUTAGENISE
MUTAGENISED
MUTAGENISES
MUTAGENISING
MUTAGENIZE
MUTAGENIZED
MUTAGENIZES
MUTAGENIZING
MUTAGENS
MUTANDA
MUTANDUM
MUTANT
MUTANTS
MUTASE
MUTASES
MUTATE
MUTATED
MUTATES
MUTATING
MUTATION
MUTATIONAL
MUTATIONALLY
MUTATIONIST
MUTATIONISTS
MUTATIONS
MUTATIVE
MUTATORY

MUTCH
MUTCHED
MUTCHES
MUTCHING
MUTCHKIN
MUTCHKINS
MUTE
MUTED
MUTEDLY
MUTELY
MUTENESS
MUTENESSES
MUTER
MUTES
MUTESSARIF
MUTESSARIFAT
MUTESSARIFATS
MUTESSARIFS
MUTEST
MUTI
MUTICATE
MUTICOUS
MUTILATE
MUTILATED
MUTILATES
MUTILATING
MUTILATION
MUTILATIONS
MUTILATIVE
MUTILATOR
MUTILATORS
MUTINE
MUTINED
MUTINEER
MUTINEERED
MUTINEERING
MUTINEERS
MUTINES
MUTING
MUTINIED
MUTINIES
MUTINING
MUTINOUS
MUTINOUSLY
MUTINOUSNESS
MUTINOUSNESSES
MUTINY
MUTINYING
MUTIS
MUTISM
MUTISMS
MUTON
MUTONS
MUTOSCOPE
MUTOSCOPES
MUTS

MUTT
MUTTER
MUTTERATION
MUTTERATIONS
MUTTERED
MUTTERER
MUTTERERS
MUTTERING
MUTTERINGLY
MUTTERINGS
MUTTERS
MUTTON
MUTTONCHOPS
MUTTONFISH
MUTTONFISHES
MUTTONHEAD
MUTTONHEADED
MUTTONHEADS
MUTTONS
MUTTONY
MUTTS
MUTUAL
MUTUALISATION
MUTUALISATIONS
MUTUALISE
MUTUALISED
MUTUALISES
MUTUALISING
MUTUALISM
MUTUALISMS
MUTUALIST
MUTUALISTIC
MUTUALISTS
MUTUALITIES
MUTUALITY
MUTUALIZATION
MUTUALIZATIONS
MUTUALIZE
MUTUALIZED
MUTUALIZES
MUTUALIZING
MUTUALLY
MUTUALNESS
MUTUALS
MUTUCA
MUTUCAS
MUTUEL
MUTUELS
MUTULAR
MUTULE
MUTULES
MUTUUM
MUTUUMS
MUUMUU
MUUMUUS
MUX

MUXED	MYCETOMA	MYELENCEPHALIC	MYLONITISES
MUXES	MYCETOMAS	MYELENCEPHALON	MYLONITISING
MUXING	MYCETOMATA	MYELENCEPHALONS	MYLONITIZATION
MUZAKY	MYCETOMATOUS	MYELENCEPHALOUS	MYLONITIZATIONS
MUZHIK	MYCETOPHAGOUS	MYELIN	MYLONITIZE
MUZHIKS	MYCETOZOAN	MYELINATED	MYLONITIZED
MUZJIK	MYCETOZOANS	MYELINE	MYLONITIZES
MUZJIKS	MYCOBACTERIA	MYELINES	MYLONITIZING
MUZZ	MYCOBACTERIAL	MYELINIC	MYNA
MUZZED	MYCOBACTERIUM	MYELINS	MYNAH
MUZZES	MYCOBIONT	MYELITIDES	MYNAHS
MUZZIER	MYCOBIONTS	MYELITIS	MYNAS
MUZZIEST	MYCODOMATIUM	MYELITISES	MYNHEER
MUZZILY	MYCOFLORA	MYELOBLAST	MYNHEERS
MUZZINESS	MYCOFLORAE	MYELOBLASTIC	MYOBLAST
MUZZINESSES	MYCOFLORAS	MYELOBLASTS	MYOBLASTIC
MUZZING	MYCOLOGIC	MYELOCYTE	MYOBLASTS
MUZZLE	MYCOLOGICAL	MYELOCYTES	MYOCARDIA
MUZZLED	MYCOLOGICALLY	MYELOCYTIC	MYOCARDIAL
MUZZLER	MYCOLOGIES	MYELOFIBROSES	MYOCARDIOGRAPH
MUZZLERS	MYCOLOGIST	MYELOFIBROSIS	MYOCARDIOGRAPHS
MUZZLES	MYCOLOGISTS	MYELOFIBROTIC	MYOCARDIOPATHY
MUZZLING	MYCOLOGY	MYELOGENOUS	MYOCARDITIS
MUZZY	MYCOPHAGIES	MYELOGRAM	MYOCARDITISES
MVULE	MYCOPHAGIST	MYELOGRAMS	MYOCARDIUM
MVULES	MYCOPHAGISTS	MYELOGRAPHY	MYOCARDIUMS
MWALIMU	MYCOPHAGOUS	MYELOID	MYOCLONIC
MWALIMUS	MYCOPHAGY	MYELOMA	MYOCLONUS
MY	MYCOPHILE	MYELOMAS	MYOCLONUSES
MYAL	MYCOPHILES	MYELOMATA	MYOELECTRIC
MYALGIA	MYCOPLASMA	MYELOMATOID	MYOELECTRICAL
MYALGIAS	MYCOPLASMAL	MYELOMATOUS	MYOFIBRIL
MYALGIC	MYCOPLASMAS	MYELON	MYOFIBRILLAR
MYALISM	MYCOPLASMATA	MYELONS	MYOFIBRILS
MYALISMS	MYCOPLASMOSIS	MYELOPATHIC	MYOFILAMENT
MYALIST	MYCORHIZA	MYELOPATHIES	MYOFILAMENTS
MYALISTS	MYCORHIZAL	MYELOPATHY	MYOGEN
MYALL	MYCORHIZAS	MYGALE	MYOGENIC
MYALLS	MYCORRHIZA	MYGALES	MYOGENS
MYASES	MYCORRHIZAE	MYIASES	MYOGLOBIN
MYASIS	MYCORRHIZAL	MYIASIS	MYOGLOBINS
MYASTHENIA	MYCORRHIZAS	MYIOPHILOUS	MYOGRAM
MYASTHENIAS	MYCOSES	MYIOPHILY	MYOGRAMS
MYASTHENIC	MYCOSIS	MYLODON	MYOGRAPH
MYASTHENICS	MYCOTIC	MYLODONS	MYOGRAPHIC
MYCELE	MYCOTOXICOSES	MYLODONT	MYOGRAPHICAL
MYCELES	MYCOTOXICOSIS	MYLODONTS	MYOGRAPHICALLY
MYCELIA	MYCOTOXIN	MYLOHYOID	MYOGRAPHIES
MYCELIAL	MYCOTOXINS	MYLOHYOIDS	MYOGRAPHIST
MYCELIAN	MYCOTOXOLOGY	MYLONITE	MYOGRAPHISTS
MYCELIUM	MYCOTROPHIC	MYLONITES	MYOGRAPHS
MYCELLA	MYDRIASES	MYLONITIC	MYOGRAPHY
MYCELOID	MYDRIASIS	MYLONITISATION	MYOID
MYCETES	MYDRIATIC	MYLONITISATIONS	MYOINOSITOL
MYCETOLOGIES	MYDRIATICS	MYLONITISE	MYOINOSITOLS
MYCETOLOGY	MYELENCEPHALA	MYLONITISED	MYOLOGIC

MYOLOGICAL
MYOLOGIES
MYOLOGIST
MYOLOGISTS
MYOLOGY
MYOMA
MYOMANCIES
MYOMANCY
MYOMANTIC
MYOMAS
MYOMATA
MYOMATOUS
MYOMECTOMIES
MYOMECTOMY
MYONEURAL
MYOPATHIC
MYOPATHIES
MYOPATHY
MYOPE
MYOPES
MYOPHILOUS
MYOPHILY
MYOPIA
MYOPIAS
MYOPIC
MYOPICALLY
MYOPICS
MYOPIES
MYOPS
MYOPSES
MYOPY
MYOSCOPE
MYOSCOPES
MYOSES
MYOSIN
MYOSINS
MYOSIS
MYOSITIS
MYOSITISES
MYOSOTE
MYOSOTES
MYOSOTIS
MYOSOTISES
MYOTIC
MYOTICS
MYOTOME
MYOTOMES
MYOTONIA
MYOTONIAS
MYOTONIC
MYOTUBE
MYOTUBES
MYRBANE
MYRBANES
MYRIAD
MYRIADFOLD

MYRIADFOLDS
MYRIADS
MYRIADTH
MYRIADTHS
MYRIAPOD
MYRIAPODAN
MYRIAPODOUS
MYRIAPODS
MYRICA
MYRICAS
MYRINGA
MYRINGAS
MYRINGITIS
MYRINGITISES
MYRINGOSCOPE
MYRINGOSCOPES
MYRINGOTOMIES
MYRINGOTOMY
MYRIOPOD
MYRIOPODS
MYRIORAMA
MYRIORAMAS
MYRIOSCOPE
MYRIOSCOPES
MYRISTIC
MYRISTICIVOROUS
MYRMECOCHORE
MYRMECOCHORES
MYRMECOCHOROUS
MYRMECOCHORY
MYRMECOID
MYRMECOLOGIC
MYRMECOLOGICAL
MYRMECOLOGIES
MYRMECOLOGIST
MYRMECOLOGISTS
MYRMECOLOGY
MYRMECOPHAGOUS
MYRMECOPHILE
MYRMECOPHILES
MYRMECOPHILIES
MYRMECOPHILOUS
MYRMECOPHILY
MYRMIDON
MYRMIDONIAN
MYRMIDONS
MYROBALAN
MYROBALANS
MYRRH
MYRRHIC
MYRRHINE
MYRRHOL
MYRRHOLS
MYRRHS
MYRTACEOUS
MYRTLE

MYRTLES
MYSELF
MYSID
MYSIDS
MYSOPHOBIA
MYSOPHOBIAS
MYSOST
MYSOSTS
MYSTAGOG
MYSTAGOGIC
MYSTAGOGICAL
MYSTAGOGICALLY
MYSTAGOGIES
MYSTAGOGS
MYSTAGOGUE
MYSTAGOGUES
MYSTAGOGUS
MYSTAGOGUSES
MYSTAGOGY
MYSTERIES
MYSTERIOUS
MYSTERIOUSLY
MYSTERIOUSNESS
MYSTERY
MYSTIC
MYSTICAL
MYSTICALLY
MYSTICALNESS
MYSTICALNESSES
MYSTICISM
MYSTICISMS
MYSTICLY
MYSTICS
MYSTIFICATION
MYSTIFICATIONS
MYSTIFIED
MYSTIFIER
MYSTIFIERS
MYSTIFIES
MYSTIFY
MYSTIFYING
MYSTIFYINGLY
MYSTIQUE
MYSTIQUES
MYTH
MYTHI
MYTHIC
MYTHICAL
MYTHICALLY
MYTHICISATION
MYTHICISE
MYTHICISED
MYTHICISER
MYTHICISERS
MYTHICISES
MYTHICISING

MYTHICISM
MYTHICISMS
MYTHICIST
MYTHICISTS
MYTHICIZATION
MYTHICIZE
MYTHICIZED
MYTHICIZER
MYTHICIZERS
MYTHICIZES
MYTHICIZING
MYTHIER
MYTHIEST
MYTHISE
MYTHISED
MYTHISES
MYTHISING
MYTHISM
MYTHISMS
MYTHIST
MYTHISTS
MYTHIZE
MYTHIZED
MYTHIZES
MYTHIZING
MYTHMAKER
MYTHMAKERS
MYTHMAKING
MYTHMAKINGS
MYTHOGENESES
MYTHOGENESIS
MYTHOGRAPHER
MYTHOGRAPHERS
MYTHOGRAPHIES
MYTHOGRAPHY
MYTHOI
MYTHOLOGER
MYTHOLOGERS
MYTHOLOGIAN
MYTHOLOGIANS
MYTHOLOGIC
MYTHOLOGICAL
MYTHOLOGICALLY
MYTHOLOGIES
MYTHOLOGISATION
MYTHOLOGISE
MYTHOLOGISED
MYTHOLOGISER
MYTHOLOGISERS
MYTHOLOGISES
MYTHOLOGISING
MYTHOLOGIST
MYTHOLOGISTS
MYTHOLOGIZATION
MYTHOLOGIZE
MYTHOLOGIZED

MYTHOLOGIZER
MYTHOLOGIZERS
MYTHOLOGIZES
MYTHOLOGIZING
MYTHOLOGY
MYTHOMANE
MYTHOMANES
MYTHOMANIA
MYTHOMANIAC
MYTHOMANIACS
MYTHOMANIAS
MYTHOPOEIA
MYTHOPOEIAS
MYTHOPOEIC
MYTHOPOEISM
MYTHOPOEIST
MYTHOPOEISTS
MYTHOPOESIS
MYTHOPOET
MYTHOPOETIC
MYTHOPOETICAL
MYTHOPOETS
MYTHOS
MYTHS
MYTHUS
MYTHY
MYTILIFORM
MYTILOID
MYXEDEMA
MYXEDEMAS
MYXEDEMATOUS
MYXEDEMIC
MYXO
MYXOCYTE
MYXOCYTES
MYXOEDEMA
MYXOEDEMAS
MYXOEDEMATOUS
MYXOEDEMIC
MYXOID
MYXOMA
MYXOMAS
MYXOMATA
MYXOMATOSES
MYXOMATOSIS
MYXOMATOUS
MYXOMYCETE
MYXOMYCETES
MYXOMYCETOUS
MYXOVIRAL
MYXOVIRUS
MYXOVIRUSES
MZEE
MZEES
MZUNGU
MZUNGUS

N

NA
NAAM
NAAMS
NAAN
NAANS
NAARTJE
NAARTJES
NAARTJIE
NAARTJIES
NAB
NABBED
NABBER
NABBERS
NABBING
NABE
NABES
NABIS
NABK
NABKS
NABLA
NABLAS
NABOB
NABOBERIES
NABOBERY
NABOBESS
NABOBESSES
NABOBISH
NABOBISM
NABOBISMS
NABOBS
NABS
NACARAT
NACARATS
NACELLE
NACELLES
NACH
NACHAS
NACHE
NACHES
NACHO
NACHOS
NACHTMAAL
NACHTMAALS
NACKET
NACKETS
NACRE
NACRED
NACREOUS
NACRES
NACRITE
NACRITES

NACROUS
NADA
NADAS
NADIR
NADIRAL
NADIRS
NADORS
NADS
NAE
NAEBODIES
NAEBODY
NAETHING
NAETHINGS
NAEVE
NAEVES
NAEVI
NAEVOID
NAEVUS
NAFF
NAFFER
NAFFEST
NAFFING
NAFFLY
NAFFNESS
NAFFNESSES
NAFFS
NAG
NAGA
NAGANA
NAGANAS
NAGAPIE
NAGAPIES
NAGARI
NAGARIS
NAGAS
NAGGED
NAGGER
NAGGERS
NAGGIER
NAGGIEST
NAGGING
NAGGINGLY
NAGGY
NAGMAAL
NAGMAALS
NAGOR
NAGORS
NAGS
NAH
NAHAL
NAHALS

NAIAD
NAIADES
NAIADS
NAIANT
NAIF
NAIFER
NAIFEST
NAIFLY
NAIFNESS
NAIFS
NAIK
NAIKS
NAIL
NAILBITER
NAILBITERS
NAILBRUSH
NAILBRUSHES
NAILED
NAILER
NAILERIES
NAILERS
NAILERY
NAILFILE
NAILFILES
NAILFOLD
NAILFOLDS
NAILHEAD
NAILHEADS
NAILING
NAILINGS
NAILLESS
NAILS
NAILSET
NAILSETS
NAIN
NAINSELL
NAINSELLS
NAINSOOK
NAINSOOKS
NAIRA
NAIRAS
NAISSANT
NAIVE
NAIVELY
NAIVENESS
NAIVENESSES
NAIVER
NAIVES
NAIVEST
NAIVETE
NAIVETES

NAIVETIES
NAIVETY
NAIVIST
NAKED
NAKEDER
NAKEDEST
NAKEDLY
NAKEDNESS
NAKEDNESSES
NAKER
NAKERS
NAKFA
NAKFAS
NALA
NALAS
NALED
NALEDS
NALLA
NALLAH
NALLAHS
NALLAS
NALORPHINE
NALORPHINES
NALOXONE
NALOXONES
NALTREXONE
NALTREXONES
NAM
NAMABLE
NAMASKAR
NAMASKARS
NAMASTE
NAMASTES
NAME
NAMEABLE
NAMECHECK
NAMECHECKED
NAMECHECKING
NAMECHECKS
NAMED
NAMELESS
NAMELESSLY
NAMELESSNESS
NAMELESSNESSES
NAMELY
NAMEPLATE
NAMEPLATES
NAMER
NAMERS
NAMES
NAMESAKE

NAMESAKES	NANOMETRES	NAPIFORM	NARCOCATHARSES
NAMETAG	NANOOK	NAPKIN	NARCOCATHARSIS
NAMETAGS	NANOOKS	NAPKINS	NARCOHYPNOSES
NAMETAPE	NANOPHYSICS	NAPLESS	NARCOHYPNOSIS
NAMETAPES	NANOPLANKTON	NAPOLEON	NARCOLEPSIES
NAMEWORTHY	NANOPLANKTONS	NAPOLEONITE	NARCOLEPSY
NAMING	NANOSECOND	NAPOLEONITES	NARCOLEPTIC
NAMINGS	NANOSECONDS	NAPOLEONS	NARCOLEPTICS
NAMS	NANOTECHNOLOGY	NAPOO	NARCOS
NAN	NANOTESLA	NAPOOED	NARCOSE
NANA	NANOTESLAS	NAPOOING	NARCOSES
NANAS	NANOWATT	NAPOOS	NARCOSIS
NANCE	NANOWATTS	NAPPA	NARCOSYNTHESES
NANCES	NANOWORLD	NAPPAS	NARCOSYNTHESIS
NANCIES	NANOWORLDS	NAPPE	NARCOTERRORISM
NANCY	NANS	NAPPED	NARCOTERRORISMS
NANDIN	NAOI	NAPPER	NARCOTIC
NANDINA	NAOS	NAPPERS	NARCOTICALLY
NANDINAS	NAOSES	NAPPES	NARCOTICS
NANDINE	NAP	NAPPIE	NARCOTINE
NANDINES	NAPA	NAPPIER	NARCOTINES
NANDINS	NAPALM	NAPPIES	NARCOTISATION
NANDOO	NAPALMED	NAPPIEST	NARCOTISATIONS
NANDOOS	NAPALMING	NAPPINESS	NARCOTISE
NANDROLONE	NAPALMS	NAPPINESSES	NARCOTISED
NANDU	NAPAS	NAPPING	NARCOTISES
NANDUS	NAPE	NAPPY	NARCOTISING
NANE	NAPERIES	NAPRAPATHIES	NARCOTISM
NANISATION	NAPERY	NAPRAPATHY	NARCOTISMS
NANISATIONS	NAPES	NAPRON	NARCOTIST
NANISM	NAPHTHA	NAPRONS	NARCOTISTS
NANISMS	NAPHTHALENE	NAPS	NARCOTIZATION
NANIZATION	NAPHTHALENES	NARAS	NARCOTIZATIONS
NANIZATIONS	NAPHTHALIC	NARASES	NARCOTIZE
NANKEEN	NAPHTHALIN	NARC	NARCOTIZED
NANKEENS	NAPHTHALINE	NARCEEN	NARCOTIZES
NANKIN	NAPHTHALISE	NARCEENS	NARCOTIZING
NANKINS	NAPHTHALISED	NARCEIN	NARCS
NANNA	NAPHTHALISES	NARCEINE	NARD
NANNAS	NAPHTHALISING	NARCEINES	NARDED
NANNIE	NAPHTHALIZE	NARCEINS	NARDINE
NANNIED	NAPHTHALIZED	NARCISM	NARDING
NANNIES	NAPHTHALIZES	NARCISMS	NARDOO
NANNOPLANKTON	NAPHTHALIZING	NARCISSI	NARDOOS
NANNOPLANKTONS	NAPHTHAS	NARCISSISM	NARDS
NANNY	NAPHTHENE	NARCISSISMS	NARE
NANNYGAI	NAPHTHENES	NARCISSIST	NARES
NANNYGAIS	NAPHTHENIC	NARCISSISTIC	NARGHILE
NANNYGHAIS	NAPHTHOL	NARCISSISTS	NARGHILES
NANNYING	NAPHTHOLS	NARCISSUS	NARGHILIES
NANNYISH	NAPHTHYL	NARCISSUSES	NARGHILLIES
NANOGRAM	NAPHTHYLAMINE	NARCIST	NARGHILLY
NANOGRAMS	NAPHTHYLAMINES	NARCISTS	NARGHILY
NANOMETER	NAPHTHYLS	NARCO	NARGILE
NANOMETERS	NAPHTOL	NARCOANALYSES	NARGILEH
NANOMETRE	NAPHTOLS	NARCOANALYSIS	NARGILEHS

NARGILES	NARROWNESSES	NASTIC	NATIONALIZES
NARGILIES	NARROWS	NASTIER	NATIONALIZING
NARGILLIES	NARTHEX	NASTIES	NATIONALLY
NARGILY	NARTHEXES	NASTIEST	NATIONALS
NARIAL	NARTJIE	NASTILY	NATIONHOOD
NARIC	NARTJIES	NASTINESS	NATIONHOODS
NARICORN	NARWAL	NASTINESSES	NATIONLESS
NARICORNS	NARWALS	NASTURTIUM	NATIONS
NARINE	NARWHAL	NASTURTIUMS	NATIONWIDE
NARIS	NARWHALE	NASTY	NATIS
NARK	NARWHALES	NASUTE	NATIVE
NARKED	NARWHALS	NASUTES	NATIVELY
NARKIER	NARY	NAT	NATIVENESS
NARKIEST	NAS	NATAL	NATIVENESSES
NARKING	NASAL	NATALITIAL	NATIVES
NARKS	NASALISATION	NATALITIES	NATIVISM
NARKY	NASALISATIONS	NATALITY	NATIVISMS
NARQUOIS	NASALISE	NATANT	NATIVIST
NARRAS	NASALISED	NATANTLY	NATIVISTIC
NARRASES	NASALISES	NATATION	NATIVISTS
NARRATABLE	NASALISING	NATATIONAL	NATIVITIES
NARRATE	NASALITIES	NATATIONALLY	NATIVITY
NARRATED	NASALITY	NATATIONS	NATRIUM
NARRATER	NASALIZATION	NATATORIA	NATRIUMS
NARRATERS	NASALIZATIONS	NATATORIAL	NATRIURESES
NARRATES	NASALIZE	NATATORIUM	NATRIURESIS
NARRATING	NASALIZED	NATATORIUMS	NATRIURETIC
NARRATION	NASALIZES	NATATORY	NATRIURETICS
NARRATIONAL	NASALIZING	NATCH	NATROLITE
NARRATIONS	NASALLY	NATCHES	NATROLITES
NARRATIVE	NASALS	NATES	NATRON
NARRATIVELY	NASARD	NATHELESS	NATRONS
NARRATIVES	NASARDS	NATHELESSE	NATS
NARRATOLOGICAL	NASCENCE	NATHEMO	NATTER
NARRATOLOGIES	NASCENCES	NATHEMORE	NATTERED
NARRATOLOGIST	NASCENCIES	NATHLESS	NATTERER
NARRATOLOGISTS	NASCENCY	NATIFORM	NATTERERS
NARRATOLOGY	NASCENT	NATION	NATTERING
NARRATOR	NASEBERRIES	NATIONAL	NATTERJACK
NARRATORS	NASEBERRY	NATIONALISATION	NATTERJACKS
NARRATORY	NASHGAB	NATIONALISE	NATTERS
NARRE	NASHGABS	NATIONALISED	NATTERY
NARROW	NASHI	NATIONALISES	NATTIER
NARROWBAND	NASHIS	NATIONALISING	NATTIEST
NARROWCAST	NASIAL	NATIONALISM	NATTILY
NARROWCASTED	NASION	NATIONALISMS	NATTINESS
NARROWCASTING	NASIONS	NATIONALIST	NATTINESSES
NARROWCASTINGS	NASOFRONTAL	NATIONALISTIC	NATTY
NARROWCASTS	NASOGASTRIC	NATIONALISTS	NATURA
NARROWED	NASOLACRYMAL	NATIONALITIES	NATURAE
NARROWER	NASOPHARYNGEAL	NATIONALITY	NATURAL
NARROWEST	NASOPHARYNGES	NATIONALIZATION	NATURALISATION
NARROWING	NASOPHARYNX	NATIONALIZE	NATURALISATIONS
NARROWINGS	NASOPHARYNXES	NATIONALIZED	NATURALISE
NARROWLY	NASTALIK	NATIONALIZER	NATURALISED
NARROWNESS	NASTALIKS	NATIONALIZERS	NATURALISES

653

NATURALISING	NAUSEAS	NAVICULAS	NEANDERTAL
NATURALISM	NAUSEATE	NAVIES	NEANDERTALER
NATURALISMS	NAUSEATED	NAVIGABILITIES	NEANDERTALERS
NATURALIST	NAUSEATES	NAVIGABILITY	NEANDERTALS
NATURALISTIC	NAUSEATING	NAVIGABLE	NEANDERTHAL
NATURALISTS	NAUSEATINGLY	NAVIGABLENESS	NEANDERTHALER
NATURALIZATION	NAUSEATION	NAVIGABLENESSES	NEANDERTHALERS
NATURALIZATIONS	NAUSEATIVE	NAVIGABLY	NEANDERTHALOID
NATURALIZE	NAUSEOUS	NAVIGATE	NEANDERTHALS
NATURALIZED	NAUSEOUSLY	NAVIGATED	NEANIC
NATURALIZES	NAUSEOUSNESS	NAVIGATES	NEAP
NATURALIZING	NAUSEOUSNESSES	NAVIGATING	NEAPED
NATURALLY	NAUTCH	NAVIGATION	NEAPING
NATURALNESS	NAUTCHES	NAVIGATIONAL	NEAPOLITAN
NATURALNESSES	NAUTIC	NAVIGATIONALLY	NEAPOLITANS
NATURALS	NAUTICAL	NAVIGATIONS	NEAPS
NATURE	NAUTICALLY	NAVIGATOR	NEAR
NATURED	NAUTICS	NAVIGATORS	NEARBY
NATURES	NAUTILI	NAVVIED	NEARED
NATURING	NAUTILOID	NAVVIES	NEARER
NATURISM	NAUTILOIDS	NAVVY	NEAREST
NATURISMS	NAUTILUS	NAVVYING	NEARING
NATURIST	NAUTILUSES	NAVY	NEARLIER
NATURISTIC	NAVAID	NAW	NEARLIEST
NATURISTS	NAVAIDS	NAWAB	NEARLY
NATUROPATH	NAVAL	NAWABS	NEARNESS
NATUROPATHIC	NAVALISM	NAY	NEARNESSES
NATUROPATHIES	NAVALISMS	NAYS	NEARS
NATUROPATHS	NAVALLY	NAYSAYER	NEARSHORE
NATUROPATHY	NAVAR	NAYSAYERS	NEARSIDE
NAUCH	NAVARCH	NAYTHLES	NEARSIDES
NAUCHES	NAVARCHIES	NAYWARD	NEARSIGHTED
NAUGHT	NAVARCHS	NAYWARDS	NEARSIGHTEDLY
NAUGHTIER	NAVARCHY	NAYWORD	NEARSIGHTEDNESS
NAUGHTIES	NAVARHO	NAYWORDS	NEARTHROSES
NAUGHTIEST	NAVARHOS	NAZE	NEARTHROSIS
NAUGHTILY	NAVARIN	NAZES	NEAT
NAUGHTINESS	NAVARINS	NAZI	NEATEN
NAUGHTINESSES	NAVARS	NAZIFICATION	NEATENED
NAUGHTS	NAVE	NAZIFICATIONS	NEATENING
NAUGHTY	NAVEL	NAZIFIED	NEATENS
NAUMACHIA	NAVELS	NAZIFIES	NEATER
NAUMACHIAE	NAVELWORT	NAZIFY	NEATEST
NAUMACHIAS	NAVELWORTS	NAZIFYING	NEATH
NAUMACHIES	NAVES	NAZIR	NEATHERD
NAUMACHY	NAVETTE	NAZIRS	NEATHERDS
NAUNT	NAVETTES	NAZIS	NEATLY
NAUNTS	NAVEW	NE	NEATNESS
NAUPLIAL	NAVEWS	NEAFE	NEATNESSES
NAUPLII	NAVICERT	NEAFES	NEATS
NAUPLIIFORM	NAVICERTS	NEAFFE	NEB
NAUPLIOID	NAVICULA	NEAFFES	NEBBED
NAUPLIUS	NAVICULAR	NEAL	NEBBICH
NAUSEA	NAVICULARE	NEALED	NEBBICHS
NAUSEANT	NAVICULARES	NEALING	NEBBING
NAUSEANTS	NAVICULARS	NEALS	NEBBISH

NEBBISHE
NEBBISHER
NEBBISHERS
NEBBISHES
NEBBISHY
NEBBUK
NEBBUKS
NEBECK
NEBECKS
NEBEK
NEBEKS
NEBEL
NEBELS
NEBENKERN
NEBENKERNS
NEBISH
NEBISHES
NEBRIS
NEBRISES
NEBS
NEBUCHADNEZZAR
NEBUCHADNEZZARS
NEBULA
NEBULAE
NEBULAR
NEBULAS
NEBULE
NEBULES
NEBULISATION
NEBULISATIONS
NEBULISE
NEBULISED
NEBULISER
NEBULISERS
NEBULISES
NEBULISING
NEBULIUM
NEBULIUMS
NEBULIZATION
NEBULIZATIONS
NEBULIZE
NEBULIZED
NEBULIZER
NEBULIZERS
NEBULIZES
NEBULIZING
NEBULOSE
NEBULOSITIES
NEBULOSITY
NEBULOUS
NEBULOUSLY
NEBULOUSNESS
NEBULOUSNESSES
NEBULY
NECESSAIRE
NECESSAIRES

NECESSARIAN
NECESSARIANISM
NECESSARIANISMS
NECESSARIANS
NECESSARIES
NECESSARILY
NECESSARINESS
NECESSARINESSES
NECESSARY
NECESSITARIAN
NECESSITARIANS
NECESSITATE
NECESSITATED
NECESSITATES
NECESSITATING
NECESSITATION
NECESSITATIONS
NECESSITATIVE
NECESSITIED
NECESSITIES
NECESSITOUS
NECESSITOUSLY
NECESSITOUSNESS
NECESSITY
NECK
NECKATEE
NECKATEES
NECKBAND
NECKBANDS
NECKBEEF
NECKBEEFS
NECKCLOTH
NECKCLOTHS
NECKED
NECKER
NECKERCHIEF
NECKERCHIEFS
NECKERCHIEVES
NECKERS
NECKGEAR
NECKGEARS
NECKING
NECKINGS
NECKLACE
NECKLACED
NECKLACES
NECKLACING
NECKLACINGS
NECKLESS
NECKLET
NECKLETS
NECKLIKE
NECKLINE
NECKLINES
NECKPIECE
NECKPIECES

NECKS
NECKTIE
NECKTIES
NECKVERSE
NECKVERSES
NECKWEAR
NECKWEARS
NECKWEED
NECKWEEDS
NECROBIOSES
NECROBIOSIS
NECROBIOTIC
NECROGRAPHER
NECROGRAPHERS
NECROLATERS
NECROLATRIES
NECROLATRY
NECROLOGIC
NECROLOGICAL
NECROLOGIES
NECROLOGIST
NECROLOGISTS
NECROLOGY
NECROMANCER
NECROMANCERS
NECROMANCIES
NECROMANCY
NECROMANIA
NECROMANIAC
NECROMANIACS
NECROMANTIC
NECROMANTICAL
NECROMANTICALLY
NECROPHAGOUS
NECROPHIL
NECROPHILE
NECROPHILES
NECROPHILIA
NECROPHILIAC
NECROPHILIACS
NECROPHILIAS
NECROPHILIC
NECROPHILIES
NECROPHILISM
NECROPHILISMS
NECROPHILOUS
NECROPHILS
NECROPHILY
NECROPHOBE
NECROPHOBES
NECROPHOBIA
NECROPHOBIAS
NECROPHOBIC
NECROPHOROUS
NECROPOLEIS
NECROPOLES

NECROPOLI
NECROPOLIS
NECROPOLISES
NECROPSIED
NECROPSIES
NECROPSY
NECROPSYING
NECROSCOPIC
NECROSCOPICAL
NECROSCOPIES
NECROSCOPY
NECROSE
NECROSED
NECROSES
NECROSING
NECROSIS
NECROTIC
NECROTISE
NECROTISED
NECROTISES
NECROTISING
NECROTIZE
NECROTIZED
NECROTIZES
NECROTIZING
NECROTOMIES
NECROTOMY
NECROTROPH
NECROTROPHIC
NECROTROPHS
NECTAR
NECTAREAL
NECTAREAN
NECTARED
NECTAREOUS
NECTAREOUSNESS
NECTARIAL
NECTARIES
NECTARIFEROUS
NECTARINE
NECTARINES
NECTARIVOROUS
NECTAROUS
NECTARS
NECTARY
NECTOCALYCES
NECTOCALYX
NED
NEDDIES
NEDDY
NEDS
NEE
NEED
NEEDCESSITIES
NEEDCESSITY
NEEDED

NEEDER
NEEDERS
NEEDFIRE
NEEDFIRES
NEEDFUL
NEEDFULLY
NEEDFULNESS
NEEDFULNESSES
NEEDFULS
NEEDIER
NEEDIEST
NEEDILY
NEEDINESS
NEEDINESSES
NEEDING
NEEDLE
NEEDLECORD
NEEDLECORDS
NEEDLECRAFT
NEEDLECRAFTS
NEEDLED
NEEDLEFISH
NEEDLEFISHES
NEEDLEFUL
NEEDLEFULS
NEEDLELIKE
NEEDLEPOINT
NEEDLEPOINTS
NEEDLER
NEEDLERS
NEEDLES
NEEDLESS
NEEDLESSLY
NEEDLESSNESS
NEEDLESSNESSES
NEEDLESTICK
NEEDLEWOMAN
NEEDLEWOMEN
NEEDLEWORK
NEEDLEWORKER
NEEDLEWORKERS
NEEDLEWORKS
NEEDLIER
NEEDLIEST
NEEDLING
NEEDLINGS
NEEDLY
NEEDMENT
NEEDMENTS
NEEDS
NEEDY
NEELD
NEELDS
NEELE
NEELES
NEEM

NEEMB
NEEMBS
NEEMS
NEEP
NEEPS
NEESBERRIES
NEESBERRY
NEESE
NEESED
NEESES
NEESING
NEEZE
NEEZED
NEEZES
NEEZING
NEF
NEFANDOUS
NEFARIOUS
NEFARIOUSLY
NEFARIOUSNESS
NEFARIOUSNESSES
NEFAST
NEFS
NEGATE
NEGATED
NEGATER
NEGATERS
NEGATES
NEGATING
NEGATION
NEGATIONAL
NEGATIONIST
NEGATIONISTS
NEGATIONS
NEGATIVE
NEGATIVED
NEGATIVELY
NEGATIVENESS
NEGATIVENESSES
NEGATIVES
NEGATIVING
NEGATIVISM
NEGATIVISMS
NEGATIVIST
NEGATIVISTIC
NEGATIVISTS
NEGATIVITIES
NEGATIVITY
NEGATON
NEGATONS
NEGATOR
NEGATORS
NEGATORY
NEGATRON
NEGATRONS
NEGLECT

NEGLECTABLE
NEGLECTED
NEGLECTEDNESS
NEGLECTEDNESSES
NEGLECTER
NEGLECTERS
NEGLECTFUL
NEGLECTFULLY
NEGLECTFULNESS
NEGLECTING
NEGLECTINGLY
NEGLECTION
NEGLECTIONS
NEGLECTIVE
NEGLECTOR
NEGLECTORS
NEGLECTS
NEGLIGE
NEGLIGEABLE
NEGLIGEE
NEGLIGEES
NEGLIGENCE
NEGLIGENCES
NEGLIGENT
NEGLIGENTLY
NEGLIGES
NEGLIGIBILITIES
NEGLIGIBILITY
NEGLIGIBLE
NEGLIGIBLENESS
NEGLIGIBLY
NEGOCIANT
NEGOCIANTS
NEGOTIABILITIES
NEGOTIABILITY
NEGOTIABLE
NEGOTIANT
NEGOTIANTS
NEGOTIATE
NEGOTIATED
NEGOTIATES
NEGOTIATING
NEGOTIATION
NEGOTIATIONS
NEGOTIATOR
NEGOTIATORS
NEGOTIATORY
NEGOTIATRESS
NEGOTIATRESSES
NEGOTIATRIX
NEGOTIATRIXES
NEGRESS
NEGRESSES
NEGRITUDE
NEGRITUDES
NEGRO

NEGROES
NEGROHEAD
NEGROHEADS
NEGROID
NEGROIDAL
NEGROIDS
NEGROISM
NEGROISMS
NEGRONI
NEGRONIS
NEGROPHIL
NEGROPHILE
NEGROPHILES
NEGROPHILISM
NEGROPHILISMS
NEGROPHILIST
NEGROPHILISTS
NEGROPHILS
NEGROPHOBE
NEGROPHOBES
NEGROPHOBIA
NEGROPHOBIAS
NEGUS
NEGUSES
NEIF
NEIFS
NEIGH
NEIGHBOR
NEIGHBORED
NEIGHBORHOOD
NEIGHBORHOODS
NEIGHBORING
NEIGHBORLESS
NEIGHBORLINESS
NEIGHBORLY
NEIGHBORS
NEIGHBOUR
NEIGHBOURED
NEIGHBOURHOOD
NEIGHBOURHOODS
NEIGHBOURING
NEIGHBOURLESS
NEIGHBOURLINESS
NEIGHBOURLY
NEIGHBOURS
NEIGHED
NEIGHING
NEIGHS
NEINEI
NEINEIS
NEIST
NEITHER
NEIVE
NEIVES
NEK
NEKS

NEKTON
NEKTONIC
NEKTONS
NELIES
NELIS
NELLIE
NELLIES
NELLY
NELSON
NELSONS
NELUMBIUM
NELUMBIUMS
NELUMBO
NELUMBOS
NEMA
NEMAS
NEMATHELMINTH
NEMATHELMINTHIC
NEMATHELMINTHS
NEMATIC
NEMATICIDAL
NEMATICIDE
NEMATICIDES
NEMATOBLAST
NEMATOBLASTS
NEMATOCIDAL
NEMATOCIDE
NEMATOCIDES
NEMATOCYST
NEMATOCYSTIC
NEMATOCYSTS
NEMATODE
NEMATODES
NEMATODIRIASES
NEMATODIRIASIS
NEMATODIRUS
NEMATODIRUSES
NEMATOID
NEMATOLOGICAL
NEMATOLOGIES
NEMATOLOGIST
NEMATOLOGISTS
NEMATOLOGY
NEMATOPHORE
NEMATOPHORES
NEMERTEAN
NEMERTEANS
NEMERTIAN
NEMERTIANS
NEMERTINE
NEMERTINES
NEMESES
NEMESIA
NEMESIAS
NEMESIS
NEMN

NEMNED
NEMNING
NEMNS
NEMOPHILA
NEMOPHILAS
NEMORAL
NEMOROUS
NEMPT
NENE
NENES
NENNIGAI
NENNIGAIS
NENUPHAR
NENUPHARS
NEOANTHROPIC
NEOARSPHENAMINE
NEOBLAST
NEOBLASTS
NEOCLASSIC
NEOCLASSICAL
NEOCLASSICISM
NEOCLASSICISMS
NEOCLASSICIST
NEOCLASSICISTS
NEOCOLONIAL
NEOCOLONIALISM
NEOCOLONIALISMS
NEOCOLONIALIST
NEOCOLONIALISTS
NEOCONSERVATISM
NEOCONSERVATIVE
NEOCORTEX
NEOCORTEXES
NEOCORTICAL
NEOCORTICES
NEODYMIUM
NEODYMIUMS
NEOGENESES
NEOGENESIS
NEOGENETIC
NEOGOTHIC
NEOGRAMMARIAN
NEOGRAMMARIANS
NEOLIBERAL
NEOLIBERALISM
NEOLIBERALISMS
NEOLIBERALS
NEOLITH
NEOLITHIC
NEOLITHS
NEOLOGIAN
NEOLOGIANS
NEOLOGIC
NEOLOGICAL
NEOLOGICALLY
NEOLOGIES

NEOLOGISE
NEOLOGISED
NEOLOGISES
NEOLOGISING
NEOLOGISM
NEOLOGISMS
NEOLOGIST
NEOLOGISTIC
NEOLOGISTICAL
NEOLOGISTICALLY
NEOLOGISTS
NEOLOGIZE
NEOLOGIZED
NEOLOGIZES
NEOLOGIZING
NEOLOGY
NEOMORPH
NEOMORPHS
NEOMYCIN
NEOMYCINS
NEON
NEONATAL
NEONATALLY
NEONATE
NEONATES
NEONATICIDE
NEONATICIDES
NEONATOLOGIES
NEONATOLOGIST
NEONATOLOGISTS
NEONATOLOGY
NEONED
NEONOMIAN
NEONOMIANISM
NEONOMIANISMS
NEONOMIANS
NEONS
NEOORTHODOX
NEOORTHODOXIES
NEOORTHODOXY
NEOPAGAN
NEOPAGANISE
NEOPAGANISED
NEOPAGANISES
NEOPAGANISING
NEOPAGANISM
NEOPAGANISMS
NEOPAGANIZE
NEOPAGANIZED
NEOPAGANIZES
NEOPAGANIZING
NEOPAGANS
NEOPHILE
NEOPHILES
NEOPHILIA
NEOPHILIAC

NEOPHILIACS
NEOPHILIAS
NEOPHOBE
NEOPHOBES
NEOPHOBIA
NEOPHOBIAS
NEOPHOBIC
NEOPHYTE
NEOPHYTES
NEOPHYTIC
NEOPILINA
NEOPILINAS
NEOPLASIA
NEOPLASIAS
NEOPLASM
NEOPLASMS
NEOPLASTIC
NEOPLASTICISM
NEOPLASTICISMS
NEOPLASTICIST
NEOPLASTICISTS
NEOPLASTIES
NEOPLASTY
NEOPRENE
NEOPRENES
NEOREALISM
NEOREALISMS
NEOREALIST
NEOREALISTIC
NEOREALISTS
NEOSTIGMINE
NEOSTIGMINES
NEOTEINIA
NEOTEINIAS
NEOTENIC
NEOTENIES
NEOTENOUS
NEOTENY
NEOTERIC
NEOTERICAL
NEOTERICALLY
NEOTERICALS
NEOTERICS
NEOTERISE
NEOTERISED
NEOTERISES
NEOTERISING
NEOTERISM
NEOTERISMS
NEOTERIST
NEOTERISTS
NEOTERIZE
NEOTERIZED
NEOTERIZES
NEOTERIZING
NEOTOXIN

NEOTOXINS
NEOTROPICS
NEOTYPE
NEOTYPES
NEOVITALISM
NEOVITALISMS
NEOVITALIST
NEOVITALISTS
NEP
NEPENTHE
NEPENTHEAN
NEPENTHES
NEPER
NEPERS
NEPETA
NEPETAS
NEPHALISM
NEPHALISMS
NEPHALIST
NEPHALISTS
NEPHELINE
NEPHELINES
NEPHELINIC
NEPHELINITE
NEPHELINITES
NEPHELINITIC
NEPHELITE
NEPHELITES
NEPHELOMETER
NEPHELOMETERS
NEPHELOMETRIC
NEPHELOMETRIES
NEPHELOMETRY
NEPHEW
NEPHEWS
NEPHOGRAM
NEPHOGRAMS
NEPHOGRAPH
NEPHOGRAPHS
NEPHOLOGIC
NEPHOLOGICAL
NEPHOLOGIES
NEPHOLOGIST
NEPHOLOGISTS
NEPHOLOGY
NEPHOSCOPE
NEPHOSCOPES
NEPHRALGIA
NEPHRALGIAS
NEPHRALGIC
NEPHRALGIES
NEPHRALGY
NEPHRECTOMIES
NEPHRECTOMIZE
NEPHRECTOMIZED
NEPHRECTOMIZES

NEPHRECTOMIZING
NEPHRECTOMY
NEPHRIC
NEPHRIDIA
NEPHRIDIAL
NEPHRIDIUM
NEPHRISM
NEPHRISMS
NEPHRITE
NEPHRITES
NEPHRITIC
NEPHRITICAL
NEPHRITICS
NEPHRITIDES
NEPHRITIS
NEPHRITISES
NEPHROBLASTOMA
NEPHROID
NEPHROLEPIS
NEPHROLEPISES
NEPHROLOGICAL
NEPHROLOGIES
NEPHROLOGIST
NEPHROLOGISTS
NEPHROLOGY
NEPHRON
NEPHRONS
NEPHROPATHIC
NEPHROPATHIES
NEPHROPATHY
NEPHROPEXIES
NEPHROPEXY
NEPHROPTOSES
NEPHROPTOSIS
NEPHROSCOPE
NEPHROSCOPES
NEPHROSCOPIES
NEPHROSCOPY
NEPHROSES
NEPHROSIS
NEPHROSTOME
NEPHROSTOMES
NEPHROTIC
NEPHROTICS
NEPHROTOMIES
NEPHROTOMY
NEPHROTOXIC
NEPHROTOXICITY
NEPIONIC
NEPIT
NEPITS
NEPOTIC
NEPOTISM
NEPOTISMS
NEPOTIST
NEPOTISTIC

NEPOTISTS
NEPS
NEPTUNIUM
NEPTUNIUMS
NERAL
NERALS
NERD
NERDIER
NERDIEST
NERDISH
NERDS
NERDY
NEREID
NEREIDES
NEREIDS
NEREIS
NERINE
NERINES
NERITE
NERITES
NERITIC
NERK
NERKA
NERKAS
NERKS
NEROL
NEROLI
NEROLIS
NEROLS
NERTS
NERTZ
NERVAL
NERVATE
NERVATION
NERVATIONS
NERVATURE
NERVATURES
NERVE
NERVED
NERVELESS
NERVELESSLY
NERVELESSNESS
NERVELESSNESSES
NERVELET
NERVELETS
NERVER
NERVERS
NERVES
NERVIER
NERVIEST
NERVILY
NERVINE
NERVINES
NERVINESS
NERVINESSES
NERVING

NERVINGS
NERVOSITIES
NERVOSITY
NERVOUS
NERVOUSLY
NERVOUSNESS
NERVOUSNESSES
NERVULAR
NERVULE
NERVULES
NERVURATION
NERVURATIONS
NERVURE
NERVURES
NERVY
NESCIENCE
NESCIENCES
NESCIENT
NESCIENTS
NESH
NESHER
NESHEST
NESHNESS
NESHNESSES
NESS
NESSELRODE
NESSELRODES
NESSES
NEST
NESTABLE
NESTED
NESTER
NESTERS
NESTFUL
NESTFULS
NESTING
NESTINGS
NESTLE
NESTLED
NESTLER
NESTLERS
NESTLES
NESTLIKE
NESTLING
NESTLINGS
NESTOR
NESTORS
NESTS
NET
NETBALL
NETBALLER
NETBALLERS
NETBALLS
NETE
NETES
NETFUL

NETFULS	NETWORKING	NEUROBIOLOGISTS	NEUROLINGUISTS
NETHEAD	NETWORKINGS	NEUROBIOLOGY	NEUROLOGIC
NETHEADED	NETWORKS	NEUROBLAST	NEUROLOGICAL
NETHEADS	NEUK	NEUROBLASTOMA	NEUROLOGICALLY
NETHELESS	NEUKS	NEUROBLASTOMAS	NEUROLOGIES
NETHER	NEUM	NEUROBLASTOMATA	NEUROLOGIST
NETHERLINGS	NEUMATIC	NEUROBLASTS	NEUROLOGISTS
NETHERMORE	NEUME	NEUROCHEMICAL	NEUROLOGY
NETHERMOST	NEUMES	NEUROCHEMICALS	NEUROLYSES
NETHERSTOCK	NEUMIC	NEUROCHEMIST	NEUROLYSIS
NETHERSTOCKS	NEUMS	NEUROCHEMISTRY	NEUROMA
NETHERWARD	NEURAL	NEUROCHEMISTS	NEUROMAS
NETHERWARDS	NEURALGIA	NEUROCHIP	NEUROMATA
NETHERWORLD	NEURALGIAS	NEUROCHIPS	NEUROMATOUS
NETHERWORLDS	NEURALGIC	NEUROCOELE	NEUROMUSCULAR
NETIQUETTE	NEURALLY	NEUROCOELES	NEURON
NETIQUETTES	NEURAMINIDASE	NEUROCOMPUTER	NEURONAL
NETIZEN	NEURAMINIDASES	NEUROCOMPUTERS	NEURONE
NETIZENS	NEURASTHENIA	NEUROCOMPUTING	NEURONES
NETLESS	NEURASTHENIAC	NEUROCOMPUTINGS	NEURONIC
NETLIKE	NEURASTHENIACS	NEUROENDOCRINE	NEURONS
NETMINDER	NEURASTHENIAS	NEUROETHOLOGIES	NEUROPATH
NETMINDERS	NEURASTHENIC	NEUROETHOLOGY	NEUROPATHIC
NETOP	NEURASTHENICS	NEUROFIBRIL	NEUROPATHICAL
NETOPS	NEURATION	NEUROFIBRILAR	NEUROPATHICALLY
NETS	NEURATIONS	NEUROFIBRILLAR	NEUROPATHIES
NETSUKE	NEURAXON	NEUROFIBRILLARY	NEUROPATHIST
NETSUKES	NEURAXONS	NEUROFIBRILS	NEUROPATHISTS
NETT	NEURECTOMIES	NEUROFIBROMA	NEUROPATHOLOGIC
NETTABLE	NEURECTOMY	NEUROFIBROMAS	NEUROPATHOLOGY
NETTED	NEURILEMMA	NEUROFIBROMATA	NEUROPATHS
NETTER	NEURILEMMAL	NEUROGENESES	NEUROPATHY
NETTERS	NEURILEMMAS	NEUROGENESIS	NEUROPEPTIDE
NETTIE	NEURILITIES	NEUROGENIC	NEUROPEPTIDES
NETTIER	NEURILITY	NEUROGENICALLY	NEUROPHYSIOLOGY
NETTIES	NEURINE	NEUROGLIA	NEUROPIL
NETTIEST	NEURINES	NEUROGLIAL	NEUROPILS
NETTING	NEURISM	NEUROGLIAS	NEUROPLASM
NETTINGS	NEURISMS	NEUROGRAM	NEUROPLASMS
NETTLE	NEURITE	NEUROGRAMS	NEUROPSYCHIATRY
NETTLED	NEURITES	NEUROHORMONAL	NEUROPSYCHOLOGY
NETTLELIKE	NEURITIC	NEUROHORMONE	NEUROPTERA
NETTLER	NEURITICS	NEUROHORMONES	NEUROPTERAN
NETTLERS	NEURITIDES	NEUROHUMOR	NEUROPTERANS
NETTLES	NEURITIS	NEUROHUMORAL	NEUROPTERIST
NETTLESOME	NEURITISES	NEUROHUMORS	NEUROPTERISTS
NETTLIER	NEUROACTIVE	NEUROHYPNOLOGY	NEUROPTERON
NETTLIEST	NEUROANATOMIC	NEUROHYPOPHYSES	NEUROPTERONS
NETTLING	NEUROANATOMICAL	NEUROHYPOPHYSIS	NEUROPTEROUS
NETTLY	NEUROANATOMIES	NEUROID	NEURORADIOLOGY
NETTS	NEUROANATOMIST	NEUROLEMMA	NEUROSAL
NETTY	NEUROANATOMISTS	NEUROLEMMAS	NEUROSCIENCE
NETWORK	NEUROANATOMY	NEUROLEPTIC	NEUROSCIENCES
NETWORKED	NEUROBIOLOGICAL	NEUROLEPTICS	NEUROSCIENTIFIC
NETWORKER	NEUROBIOLOGIES	NEUROLINGUIST	NEUROSCIENTIST
NETWORKERS	NEUROBIOLOGIST	NEUROLINGUISTIC	NEUROSCIENTISTS

NEUROSECRETION	NEUTRALISM	NEWELL	NEWSHOUNDS
NEUROSECRETIONS	NEUTRALISMS	NEWELLED	NEWSIE
NEUROSECRETORY	NEUTRALIST	NEWELLS	NEWSIER
NEUROSENSORY	NEUTRALISTIC	NEWELS	NEWSIES
NEUROSES	NEUTRALISTS	NEWER	NEWSIEST
NEUROSIS	NEUTRALITIES	NEWEST	NEWSINESS
NEUROSPORA	NEUTRALITY	NEWFANGLE	NEWSINESSES
NEUROSPORAS	NEUTRALIZATION	NEWFANGLED	NEWSING
NEUROSURGEON	NEUTRALIZATIONS	NEWFANGLEDLY	NEWSLESS
NEUROSURGEONS	NEUTRALIZE	NEWFANGLEDNESS	NEWSLETTER
NEUROSURGERIES	NEUTRALIZED	NEWFANGLENESS	NEWSLETTERS
NEUROSURGERY	NEUTRALIZER	NEWFANGLENESSES	NEWSMAGAZINE
NEUROSURGICAL	NEUTRALIZERS	NEWFOUND	NEWSMAGAZINES
NEUROSURGICALLY	NEUTRALIZES	NEWIE	NEWSMAN
NEUROTIC	NEUTRALIZING	NEWIES	NEWSMEN
NEUROTICALLY	NEUTRALLY	NEWING	NEWSMONGER
NEUROTICISM	NEUTRALNESS	NEWISH	NEWSMONGERS
NEUROTICISMS	NEUTRALNESSES	NEWISHLY	NEWSPAPER
NEUROTICS	NEUTRALS	NEWISHNESS	NEWSPAPERDOM
NEUROTOMIES	NEUTRETTO	NEWISHNESSES	NEWSPAPERDOMS
NEUROTOMIST	NEUTRETTOS	NEWLY	NEWSPAPERED
NEUROTOMISTS	NEUTRINO	NEWLYWED	NEWSPAPERING
NEUROTOMY	NEUTRINOLESS	NEWLYWEDS	NEWSPAPERISM
NEUROTOXIC	NEUTRINOS	NEWMARKET	NEWSPAPERISMS
NEUROTOXICITIES	NEUTRON	NEWMARKETS	NEWSPAPERMAN
NEUROTOXICITY	NEUTRONIC	NEWMOWN	NEWSPAPERMEN
NEUROTOXIN	NEUTRONS	NEWNESS	NEWSPAPERS
NEUROTOXINS	NEUTROPENIA	NEWNESSES	NEWSPAPERWOMAN
NEUROTROPHIC	NEUTROPHIL	NEWS	NEWSPAPERWOMEN
NEUROTROPHIES	NEUTROPHILE	NEWSAGENCIES	NEWSPEAK
NEUROTROPHY	NEUTROPHILES	NEWSAGENCY	NEWSPEAKS
NEUROTROPIC	NEUTROPHILIC	NEWSAGENT	NEWSPEOPLE
NEUROVASCULAR	NEUTROPHILS	NEWSAGENTS	NEWSPERSON
NEURULA	NEVE	NEWSBOY	NEWSPERSONS
NEURULAE	NEVEL	NEWSBOYS	NEWSPRINT
NEURULAS	NEVELLED	NEWSBREAK	NEWSPRINTS
NEURULATION	NEVELLING	NEWSBREAKS	NEWSREADER
NEURULATIONS	NEVELS	NEWSCAST	NEWSREADERS
NEURYPNOLOGIES	NEVER	NEWSCASTER	NEWSREEL
NEURYPNOLOGY	NEVERMORE	NEWSCASTERS	NEWSREELS
NEUSTON	NEVERTHELESS	NEWSCASTING	NEWSROOM
NEUSTONIC	NEVERTHEMORE	NEWSCASTINGS	NEWSROOMS
NEUSTONS	NEVES	NEWSCASTS	NEWSSTAND
NEUTER	NEVI	NEWSDEALER	NEWSSTANDS
NEUTERED	NEVOID	NEWSDEALERS	NEWSTRADE
NEUTERING	NEVUS	NEWSED	NEWSTRADES
NEUTERS	NEW	NEWSES	NEWSWEEKLIES
NEUTRAL	NEWBIE	NEWSFLASH	NEWSWEEKLY
NEUTRALISATION	NEWBIES	NEWSFLASHES	NEWSWIRE
NEUTRALISATIONS	NEWBORN	NEWSGIRL	NEWSWIRES
NEUTRALISE	NEWBORNS	NEWSGIRLS	NEWSWOMAN
NEUTRALISED	NEWCOME	NEWSGROUP	NEWSWOMEN
NEUTRALISER	NEWCOMER	NEWSGROUPS	NEWSWORTHINESS
NEUTRALISERS	NEWCOMERS	NEWSHAWK	NEWSWORTHY
NEUTRALISES	NEWED	NEWSHAWKS	NEWSWRITING
NEUTRALISING	NEWEL	NEWSHOUND	NEWSWRITINGS

NEWSY	NICE	NICKNAME	NIDDERLING
NEWT	NICEISH	NICKNAMED	NIDDERLINGS
NEWTON	NICELY	NICKNAMER	NIDDICK
NEWTONS	NICENESS	NICKNAMERS	NIDDICKS
NEWTS	NICENESSES	NICKNAMES	NIDE
NEXT	NICER	NICKNAMING	NIDED
NEXTDOOR	NICEST	NICKPOINT	NIDERING
NEXTLY	NICETIES	NICKPOINTS	NIDERINGS
NEXTNESS	NICETY	NICKS	NIDERLING
NEXTNESSES	NICHE	NICKSTICK	NIDERLINGS
NEXTS	NICHED	NICKSTICKS	NIDES
NEXUS	NICHER	NICKUM	NIDGET
NEXUSES	NICHERED	NICKUMPOOP	NIDGETS
NGAI	NICHERING	NICKUMPOOPS	NIDI
NGAIO	NICHERS	NICKUMS	NIDICOLOUS
NGAIOS	NICHES	NICOL	NIDIFICATE
NGANA	NICHING	NICOLS	NIDIFICATED
NGANAS	NICHT	NICOMPOOP	NIDIFICATES
NGARARA	NICHTS	NICOMPOOPS	NIDIFICATING
NGARARAS	NICISH	NICOTIAN	NIDIFICATION
NGATI	NICK	NICOTIANA	NIDIFICATIONS
NGOMA	NICKAR	NICOTIANAS	NIDIFIED
NGOMAS	NICKARS	NICOTIANS	NIDIFIES
NGULTRUM	NICKED	NICOTIN	NIDIFUGOUS
NGULTRUMS	NICKEL	NICOTINAMIDE	NIDIFY
NGWEE	NICKELED	NICOTINAMIDES	NIDIFYING
NGWEES	NICKELIC	NICOTINE	NIDING
NHANDU	NICKELIFEROUS	NICOTINED	NIDINGS
NHANDUS	NICKELINE	NICOTINES	NIDOR
NIACIN	NICKELINES	NICOTINIC	NIDOROUS
NIACINAMIDE	NICKELING	NICOTINISM	NIDORS
NIACINAMIDES	NICKELISE	NICOTINISMS	NIDS
NIACINS	NICKELISED	NICOTINS	NIDULATION
NIAISERIE	NICKELISES	NICROSILAL	NIDULATIONS
NIAISERIES	NICKELISING	NICROSILALS	NIDUS
NIALAMIDE	NICKELIZE	NICTATE	NIDUSES
NIALAMIDES	NICKELIZED	NICTATED	NIE
NIB	NICKELIZES	NICTATES	NIECE
NIBBED	NICKELIZING	NICTATING	NIECES
NIBBING	NICKELLED	NICTATION	NIED
NIBBLE	NICKELLING	NICTATIONS	NIEF
NIBBLED	NICKELODEON	NICTITATE	NIEFS
NIBBLER	NICKELODEONS	NICTITATED	NIELLATED
NIBBLERS	NICKELOUS	NICTITATES	NIELLI
NIBBLES	NICKELS	NICTITATING	NIELLIST
NIBBLING	NICKER	NICTITATION	NIELLISTS
NIBBLINGLY	NICKERED	NICTITATIONS	NIELLO
NIBBLINGS	NICKERING	NID	NIELLOED
NIBLICK	NICKERS	NIDAL	NIELLOING
NIBLICKS	NICKING	NIDAMENTA	NIELLOS
NIBLIKE	NICKLE	NIDAMENTAL	NIES
NIBS	NICKLED	NIDAMENTUM	NIEVE
NICAD	NICKLES	NIDATION	NIEVEFUL
NICADS	NICKLING	NIDATIONS	NIEVEFULS
NICCOLITE	NICKNACK	NIDDERING	NIEVES
NICCOLITES	NICKNACKS	NIDDERINGS	NIFE

NIFEDIPINE
NIFEDIPINES
NIFES
NIFF
NIFFED
NIFFER
NIFFERED
NIFFERING
NIFFERS
NIFFIER
NIFFIEST
NIFFING
NIFFNAFF
NIFFNAFFED
NIFFNAFFING
NIFFNAFFS
NIFFS
NIFFY
NIFTIER
NIFTIES
NIFTIEST
NIFTILY
NIFTINESS
NIFTINESSES
NIFTY
NIGELLA
NIGELLAS
NIGER
NIGERS
NIGGARD
NIGGARDED
NIGGARDING
NIGGARDISE
NIGGARDISES
NIGGARDIZE
NIGGARDIZES
NIGGARDLINESS
NIGGARDLINESSES
NIGGARDLY
NIGGARDS
NIGGER
NIGGERDOM
NIGGERDOMS
NIGGERED
NIGGERHEAD
NIGGERHEADS
NIGGERING
NIGGERISH
NIGGERISM
NIGGERISMS
NIGGERLING
NIGGERLINGS
NIGGERS
NIGGERY
NIGGLE
NIGGLED

NIGGLER
NIGGLERS
NIGGLES
NIGGLIER
NIGGLIEST
NIGGLING
NIGGLINGLY
NIGGLINGS
NIGGLY
NIGH
NIGHED
NIGHER
NIGHEST
NIGHING
NIGHLY
NIGHNESS
NIGHNESSES
NIGHS
NIGHT
NIGHTBIRD
NIGHTBIRDS
NIGHTBLIND
NIGHTBLINDNESS
NIGHTCAP
NIGHTCAPS
NIGHTCLASS
NIGHTCLASSES
NIGHTCLOTHES
NIGHTCLUB
NIGHTCLUBBED
NIGHTCLUBBER
NIGHTCLUBBERS
NIGHTCLUBBING
NIGHTCLUBBINGS
NIGHTCLUBS
NIGHTDRESS
NIGHTDRESSES
NIGHTED
NIGHTFALL
NIGHTFALLS
NIGHTFARING
NIGHTFIRE
NIGHTFIRES
NIGHTGEAR
NIGHTGEARS
NIGHTGLOW
NIGHTGLOWS
NIGHTGOWN
NIGHTGOWNS
NIGHTHAWK
NIGHTHAWKS
NIGHTIE
NIGHTIES
NIGHTINGALE
NIGHTINGALES
NIGHTJAR

NIGHTJARS
NIGHTLESS
NIGHTLIFE
NIGHTLIFES
NIGHTLIKE
NIGHTLONG
NIGHTLY
NIGHTMARE
NIGHTMARES
NIGHTMARISH
NIGHTMARISHLY
NIGHTMARISHNESS
NIGHTMARY
NIGHTPIECE
NIGHTPIECES
NIGHTRIDER
NIGHTRIDERS
NIGHTRIDING
NIGHTS
NIGHTSCOPE
NIGHTSCOPES
NIGHTSHADE
NIGHTSHADES
NIGHTSHIRT
NIGHTSHIRTS
NIGHTSIDE
NIGHTSIDES
NIGHTSPOT
NIGHTSPOTS
NIGHTSTAND
NIGHTSTANDS
NIGHTSTICK
NIGHTSTICKS
NIGHTTIME
NIGHTTIMES
NIGHTWALKER
NIGHTWALKERS
NIGHTWARD
NIGHTWEAR
NIGHTWEARS
NIGHTY
NIGRESCENCE
NIGRESCENCES
NIGRESCENT
NIGRICANT
NIGRIFIED
NIGRIFIES
NIGRIFY
NIGRIFYING
NIGRITUDE
NIGRITUDES
NIGROMANCIES
NIGROMANCY
NIGROSIN
NIGROSINE
NIGROSINES

NIGROSINS
NIHIL
NIHILISM
NIHILISMS
NIHILIST
NIHILISTIC
NIHILISTS
NIHILITIES
NIHILITY
NIHILS
NIHONGA
NIHONGAS
NIKAU
NIKAUS
NIKETHAMIDE
NIKETHAMIDES
NIL
NILGAI
NILGAIS
NILGAU
NILGAUS
NILGHAI
NILGHAIS
NILGHAU
NILGHAUS
NILL
NILLED
NILLING
NILLS
NILPOTENT
NILS
NIM
NIMB
NIMBED
NIMBI
NIMBLE
NIMBLENESS
NIMBLENESSES
NIMBLER
NIMBLESSE
NIMBLESSES
NIMBLEST
NIMBLEWIT
NIMBLEWITS
NIMBLEWITTED
NIMBLY
NIMBOSTRATI
NIMBOSTRATUS
NIMBS
NIMBUS
NIMBUSED
NIMBUSES
NIMBYISM
NIMBYISMS
NIMIETIES
NIMIETY

NIMIOUS
NIMMED
NIMMER
NIMMERS
NIMMING
NIMONIC
NIMPS
NIMROD
NIMRODS
NIMS
NINCOM
NINCOMPOOP
NINCOMPOOPERIES
NINCOMPOOPERY
NINCOMPOOPS
NINCOMS
NINCUM
NINCUMS
NINE
NINEBARK
NINEBARKS
NINEFOLD
NINEHOLES
NINEPENCE
NINEPENCES
NINEPENNIES
NINEPENNY
NINEPIN
NINEPINS
NINES
NINESCORE
NINESCORES
NINETEEN
NINETEENS
NINETEENTH
NINETEENTHLY
NINETEENTHS
NINETIES
NINETIETH
NINETIETHS
NINETY
NINHYDRIN
NINHYDRINS
NINJA
NINJAS
NINJITSU
NINJITSUS
NINJUTSU
NINJUTSUS
NINNIES
NINNY
NINNYHAMMER
NINNYHAMMERS
NINNYISH
NINON
NINONS

NINTH
NINTHLY
NINTHS
NIOBATE
NIOBATES
NIOBIC
NIOBITE
NIOBITES
NIOBIUM
NIOBIUMS
NIOBOUS
NIP
NIPA
NIPAS
NIPCHEESE
NIPCHEESES
NIPPED
NIPPER
NIPPERED
NIPPERING
NIPPERKIN
NIPPERKINS
NIPPERS
NIPPIER
NIPPIEST
NIPPILY
NIPPINESS
NIPPINESSES
NIPPING
NIPPINGLY
NIPPLE
NIPPLED
NIPPLES
NIPPLEWORT
NIPPLEWORTS
NIPPLING
NIPPY
NIPS
NIPTER
NIPTERS
NIRAMIAI
NIRAMIAIS
NIRL
NIRLED
NIRLIE
NIRLIER
NIRLIEST
NIRLING
NIRLIT
NIRLS
NIRLY
NIRVANA
NIRVANAS
NIRVANIC
NIS
NISBERRIES

NISBERRY
NISEI
NISEIS
NISGUL
NISGULS
NISH
NISI
NISSE
NISSES
NISUS
NIT
NITCHIE
NITCHIES
NITE
NITER
NITERIE
NITERIES
NITERS
NITERY
NITES
NITHER
NITHING
NITHINGS
NITID
NITINOL
NITINOLS
NITON
NITONS
NITPICK
NITPICKED
NITPICKER
NITPICKERS
NITPICKIER
NITPICKIEST
NITPICKING
NITPICKS
NITPICKY
NITRAMINE
NITRANILINE
NITRANILINES
NITRATE
NITRATED
NITRATES
NITRATINE
NITRATINES
NITRATING
NITRATION
NITRATIONS
NITRATOR
NITRATORS
NITRAZEPAM
NITRAZEPAMS
NITRE
NITRES
NITRIC
NITRID

NITRIDE
NITRIDED
NITRIDES
NITRIDING
NITRIDINGS
NITRIDS
NITRIFIABLE
NITRIFICATION
NITRIFICATIONS
NITRIFIED
NITRIFIER
NITRIFIERS
NITRIFIES
NITRIFY
NITRIFYING
NITRIL
NITRILE
NITRILES
NITRILS
NITRITE
NITRITES
NITRO
NITROBACTERIA
NITROBACTERIUM
NITROBENZENE
NITROBENZENES
NITROCELLULOSE
NITROCELLULOSES
NITROCHLOROFORM
NITROCOTTON
NITROCOTTONS
NITROFURAN
NITROFURANS
NITROGEN
NITROGENASE
NITROGENASES
NITROGENISATION
NITROGENISE
NITROGENISED
NITROGENISES
NITROGENISING
NITROGENIZATION
NITROGENIZE
NITROGENIZED
NITROGENIZES
NITROGENIZING
NITROGENOUS
NITROGENS
NITROGLYCERIN
NITROGLYCERINE
NITROGLYCERINES
NITROGLYCERINS
NITROLIC
NITROMETER
NITROMETERS
NITROMETHANE

NITROMETHANES
NITROMETRIC
NITROPARAFFIN
NITROPARAFFINS
NITROPHILOUS
NITROS
NITROSAMINE
NITROSAMINES
NITROSATION
NITROSATIONS
NITROSO
NITROSYL
NITROSYLS
NITROTOLUENE
NITROTOLUENES
NITROUS
NITROXYL
NITROXYLS
NITRY
NITRYL
NITRYLS
NITS
NITTIER
NITTIEST
NITTY
NITWIT
NITWITS
NITWITTED
NITWITTEDNESS
NITWITTEDNESSES
NITWITTERIES
NITWITTERY
NIVAL
NIVATION
NIVATIONS
NIVEOUS
NIX
NIXE
NIXED
NIXER
NIXERS
NIXES
NIXIE
NIXIES
NIXING
NIXY
NIZAM
NIZAMATE
NIZAMATES
NIZAMS
NKOSI
NO
NOAH
NOAHS
NOB
NOBBIER

NOBBIEST
NOBBILY
NOBBINESS
NOBBINESSES
NOBBLE
NOBBLED
NOBBLER
NOBBLERS
NOBBLES
NOBBLING
NOBBUT
NOBBY
NOBELIUM
NOBELIUMS
NOBILESSE
NOBILESSES
NOBILIARY
NOBILITATE
NOBILITATED
NOBILITATES
NOBILITATING
NOBILITATION
NOBILITATIONS
NOBILITIES
NOBILITY
NOBLE
NOBLEMAN
NOBLEMEN
NOBLENESS
NOBLENESSES
NOBLER
NOBLES
NOBLESSE
NOBLESSES
NOBLEST
NOBLEWOMAN
NOBLEWOMEN
NOBLY
NOBODIES
NOBODY
NOBS
NOCAKE
NOCAKES
NOCENT
NOCENTLY
NOCENTS
NOCHEL
NOCHELLED
NOCHELLING
NOCHELS
NOCICEPTIVE
NOCICEPTOR
NOCICEPTORS
NOCIRECEPTOR
NOCIRECEPTORS
NOCK

NOCKED
NOCKET
NOCKETS
NOCKING
NOCKS
NOCTAMBULATION
NOCTAMBULATIONS
NOCTAMBULISM
NOCTAMBULISMS
NOCTAMBULIST
NOCTAMBULISTS
NOCTILIO
NOCTILIOS
NOCTILUCA
NOCTILUCAE
NOCTILUCENCE
NOCTILUCENCES
NOCTILUCENT
NOCTILUCOUS
NOCTIVAGANT
NOCTIVAGATION
NOCTIVAGATIONS
NOCTIVAGOUS
NOCTUA
NOCTUARIES
NOCTUARY
NOCTUAS
NOCTUID
NOCTUIDS
NOCTULE
NOCTULES
NOCTUOID
NOCTURN
NOCTURNAL
NOCTURNALITIES
NOCTURNALITY
NOCTURNALLY
NOCTURNALS
NOCTURNE
NOCTURNES
NOCTURNS
NOCUOUS
NOCUOUSLY
NOCUOUSNESS
NOCUOUSNESSES
NOD
NODAL
NODALISE
NODALISED
NODALISES
NODALISING
NODALITIES
NODALITY
NODALIZE
NODALIZED
NODALIZES

NODALIZING
NODALLY
NODATED
NODATION
NODATIONS
NODDED
NODDER
NODDERS
NODDIES
NODDING
NODDINGLY
NODDINGS
NODDLE
NODDLED
NODDLES
NODDLING
NODDY
NODE
NODES
NODI
NODICAL
NODOSE
NODOSITIES
NODOSITY
NODOUS
NODS
NODULAR
NODULATED
NODULATION
NODULATIONS
NODULE
NODULED
NODULES
NODULOSE
NODULOUS
NODUS
NOEL
NOELS
NOEMATICAL
NOEMATICALLY
NOES
NOESES
NOESIS
NOESISES
NOETIC
NOG
NOGAKU
NOGG
NOGGED
NOGGIN
NOGGING
NOGGINGS
NOGGINS
NOGGS
NOGS
NOH

NOHOW	NOMADIC	NOMINALIZE	NONABSORBABLE
NOHOWISH	NOMADICALLY	NOMINALIZED	NONABSORBENT
NOIL	NOMADIES	NOMINALIZES	NONABSORPTIVE
NOILS	NOMADISATION	NOMINALIZING	NONABSTRACT
NOILY	NOMADISATIONS	NOMINALLY	NONACADEMIC
NOINT	NOMADISE	NOMINALS	NONACADEMICS
NOINTED	NOMADISED	NOMINATE	NONACCEPTANCE
NOINTER	NOMADISES	NOMINATED	NONACCEPTANCES
NOINTING	NOMADISING	NOMINATELY	NONACCIDENTAL
NOINTS	NOMADISM	NOMINATES	NONACCOUNTABLE
NOIR	NOMADISMS	NOMINATING	NONACCREDITED
NOIRISH	NOMADIZATION	NOMINATION	NONACCRUAL
NOIRS	NOMADIZATIONS	NOMINATIONS	NONACHIEVEMENT
NOISE	NOMADIZE	NOMINATIVAL	NONACHIEVEMENTS
NOISED	NOMADIZED	NOMINATIVALLY	NONACID
NOISEFUL	NOMADIZES	NOMINATIVE	NONACIDIC
NOISELESS	NOMADIZING	NOMINATIVELY	NONACIDS
NOISELESSLY	NOMADS	NOMINATIVES	NONACQUISITIVE
NOISELESSNESS	NOMADY	NOMINATOR	NONACTING
NOISELESSNESSES	NOMARCH	NOMINATORS	NONACTION
NOISEMAKER	NOMARCHIES	NOMINEE	NONACTIONS
NOISEMAKERS	NOMARCHS	NOMINEES	NONACTIVATED
NOISEMAKING	NOMARCHY	NOMISM	NONACTOR
NOISEMAKINGS	NOMAS	NOMISMS	NONACTORS
NOISENIK	NOMBLES	NOMISTIC	NONADAPTIVE
NOISENIKS	NOMBRIL	NOMOCRACIES	NONADDICT
NOISEOME	NOMBRILS	NOMOCRACY	NONADDICTIVE
NOISEOMELY	NOME	NOMOGENIES	NONADDICTS
NOISEOMENESS	NOMEN	NOMOGENY	NONADDITIVE
NOISES	NOMENCLATIVE	NOMOGRAM	NONADDITIVITIES
NOISETTE	NOMENCLATOR	NOMOGRAMS	NONADDITIVITY
NOISETTES	NOMENCLATORIAL	NOMOGRAPH	NONADHESIVE
NOISIER	NOMENCLATORS	NOMOGRAPHER	NONADIABATIC
NOISIEST	NOMENCLATURAL	NOMOGRAPHERS	NONADJACENT
NOISILY	NOMENCLATURE	NOMOGRAPHIC	NONADMIRER
NOISINESS	NOMENCLATURES	NOMOGRAPHICAL	NONADMIRERS
NOISINESSES	NOMENKLATURA	NOMOGRAPHICALLY	NONADMISSION
NOISING	NOMENKLATURAS	NOMOGRAPHIES	NONADMISSIONS
NOISOME	NOMES	NOMOGRAPHS	NONADULT
NOISOMELY	NOMIC	NOMOGRAPHY	NONADULTS
NOISOMENESS	NOMINA	NOMOI	NONAESTHETIC
NOISOMENESSES	NOMINABLE	NOMOLOGICAL	NONAFFILIATED
NOISY	NOMINAL	NOMOLOGICALLY	NONAFFLUENT
NOLE	NOMINALISATION	NOMOLOGIES	NONAGE
NOLES	NOMINALISATIONS	NOMOLOGIST	NONAGED
NOLITION	NOMINALISE	NOMOLOGISTS	NONAGENARIAN
NOLITIONS	NOMINALISED	NOMOLOGY	NONAGENARIANS
NOLL	NOMINALISES	NOMOS	NONAGES
NOLLS	NOMINALISING	NOMOTHETE	NONAGESIMAL
NOLO	NOMINALISM	NOMOTHETES	NONAGESIMALS
NOLOS	NOMINALISMS	NOMOTHETIC	NONAGGRESSION
NOM	NOMINALIST	NOMOTHETICAL	NONAGGRESSIONS
NOMA	NOMINALISTIC	NOMS	NONAGGRESSIVE
NOMAD	NOMINALISTS	NON	NONAGON
NOMADE	NOMINALIZATION	NONA	NONAGONAL
NOMADES	NOMINALIZATIONS	NONABRASIVE	NONAGONS

NONAGRICULTURAL
NONALCOHOLIC
NONALIGNED
NONALIGNMENT
NONALIGNMENTS
NONALLELIC
NONALLERGENIC
NONALLERGIC
NONALPHABETIC
NONALUMINUM
NONAMBIGUOUS
NONANALYTIC
NONANATOMIC
NONANE
NONANES
NONANIMAL
NONANOIC
NONANSWER
NONANSWERS
NONANTAGONISTIC
NONANTIBIOTIC
NONANTIBIOTICS
NONANTIGENIC
NONAPPEARANCE
NONAPPEARANCES
NONAQUATIC
NONAQUEOUS
NONARABLE
NONARBITRARY
NONARCHITECT
NONARCHITECTS
NONARCHITECTURE
NONARGUMENT
NONARGUMENTS
NONARISTOCRATIC
NONAROMATIC
NONAROMATICS
NONART
NONARTIST
NONARTISTIC
NONARTISTS
NONARTS
NONARY
NONAS
NONASCETIC
NONASPIRIN
NONASSERTIVE
NONASSOCIATED
NONASTRONOMICAL
NONATHLETE
NONATHLETES
NONATHLETIC
NONATOMIC
NONATTACHED
NONATTACHMENT
NONATTACHMENTS

NONATTENDANCE
NONATTENDANCES
NONATTENDER
NONATTENDERS
NONATTRIBUTABLE
NONATTRIBUTIVE
NONAUDITORY
NONAUTHOR
NONAUTHORS
NONAUTOMATED
NONAUTOMATIC
NONAUTOMOTIVE
NONAUTONOMOUS
NONAVAILABILITY
NONBACTERIAL
NONBANK
NONBANKING
NONBANKS
NONBARBITURATE
NONBARBITURATES
NONBASIC
NONBEARING
NONBEHAVIORAL
NONBEING
NONBEINGS
NONBELIEF
NONBELIEFS
NONBELIEVER
NONBELIEVERS
NONBELLIGERENCY
NONBELLIGERENT
NONBELLIGERENTS
NONBETTING
NONBINARY
NONBINDING
NONBIOGRAPHICAL
NONBIOLOGICAL
NONBIOLOGICALLY
NONBIOLOGIST
NONBIOLOGISTS
NONBITING
NONBLACK
NONBLACKS
NONBODIES
NONBODY
NONBONDED
NONBONDING
NONBOOK
NONBOOKS
NONBOTANIST
NONBOTANISTS
NONBRAND
NONBREAKABLE
NONBREATHING
NONBREEDER
NONBREEDERS

NONBREEDING
NONBROADCAST
NONBUILDING
NONBURNABLE
NONBUSINESS
NONBUYING
NONCABINET
NONCAKING
NONCALLABLE
NONCALORIC
NONCAMPUS
NONCANCELABLE
NONCANCEROUS
NONCANDIDACIES
NONCANDIDACY
NONCANDIDATE
NONCANDIDATES
NONCAPITAL
NONCAPITALIST
NONCAPITALISTS
NONCARBONATED
NONCARCINOGEN
NONCARCINOGENIC
NONCARCINOGENS
NONCARDIAC
NONCAREER
NONCARNIVOROUS
NONCARRIER
NONCARRIERS
NONCASH
NONCASUAL
NONCAUSAL
NONCE
NONCELEBRATION
NONCELEBRATIONS
NONCELEBRITIES
NONCELEBRITY
NONCELESTIAL
NONCELLULAR
NONCELLULOSIC
NONCENTRAL
NONCEREBRAL
NONCEREBRALLY
NONCERTIFICATED
NONCERTIFIED
NONCES
NONCHALANCE
NONCHALANCES
NONCHALANT
NONCHALANTLY
NONCHARACTER
NONCHARACTERS
NONCHARGEABLE
NONCHARISMATIC
NONCHARISMATICS
NONCHAUVINIST

NONCHEMICAL
NONCHEMICALS
NONCHROMOSOMAL
NONCHURCH
NONCHURCHGOER
NONCHURCHGOERS
NONCIRCULAR
NONCIRCULATING
NONCITIZEN
NONCITIZENS
NONCLAIM
NONCLAIMS
NONCLANDESTINE
NONCLASS
NONCLASSES
NONCLASSIC
NONCLASSICAL
NONCLASSIFIED
NONCLASSROOM
NONCLERICAL
NONCLING
NONCLINICAL
NONCLOGGING
NONCOAGULATING
NONCOAGULATION
NONCOERCIVE
NONCOGNITIVE
NONCOGNITIVISM
NONCOHERENT
NONCOINCIDENCE
NONCOINCIDENCES
NONCOITAL
NONCOKING
NONCOLA
NONCOLLECTOR
NONCOLLECTORS
NONCOLLEGE
NONCOLLEGIATE
NONCOLLINEAR
NONCOLOR
NONCOLORED
NONCOLORFAST
NONCOLORS
NONCOM
NONCOMBAT
NONCOMBATANT
NONCOMBATANTS
NONCOMBATIVE
NONCOMBINING
NONCOMBUSTIBLE
NONCOMMERCIAL
NONCOMMISSIONED
NONCOMMITMENT
NONCOMMITMENTS
NONCOMMITTAL
NONCOMMITTALLY

NONCOMMITTED
NONCOMMUNICANT
NONCOMMUNICANTS
NONCOMMUNIST
NONCOMMUNISTS
NONCOMMUNITY
NONCOMMUTATIVE
NONCOMPARABLE
NONCOMPATIBLE
NONCOMPETITION
NONCOMPETITIVE
NONCOMPETITOR
NONCOMPETITORS
NONCOMPLEX
NONCOMPLIANCE
NONCOMPLIANCES
NONCOMPLICATED
NONCOMPLYING
NONCOMPOSER
NONCOMPOSERS
NONCOMPOUND
NONCOMPRESSIBLE
NONCOMPUTER
NONCOMPUTERIZED
NONCOMS
NONCONCEPTUAL
NONCONCERN
NONCONCERNS
NONCONCILIATORY
NONCONCLUSION
NONCONCLUSIONS
NONCONCLUSIVE
NONCONCLUSIVELY
NONCONCUR
NONCONCURRED
NONCONCURRENCE
NONCONCURRENCES
NONCONCURRENT
NONCONCURRING
NONCONCURS
NONCONDENSABLE
NONCONDITIONED
NONCONDUCTING
NONCONDUCTION
NONCONDUCTIVE
NONCONDUCTOR
NONCONDUCTORS
NONCONFERENCE
NONCONFIDENCE
NONCONFIDENCES
NONCONFIDENTIAL
NONCONFLICTING
NONCONFORM
NONCONFORMANCE
NONCONFORMANCES
NONCONFORMED

NONCONFORMER
NONCONFORMERS
NONCONFORMING
NONCONFORMISM
NONCONFORMISMS
NONCONFORMIST
NONCONFORMISTS
NONCONFORMITIES
NONCONFORMITY
NONCONFORMS
NONCONGENITAL
NONCONGENITALLY
NONCONGRUENT
NONCONJUGATED
NONCONNECTION
NONCONNECTIONS
NONCONNECTIVE
NONCONSCIOUS
NONCONSECUTIVE
NONCONSENSUAL
NONCONSENTING
NONCONSERVATION
NONCONSERVATIVE
NONCONSOLIDATED
NONCONSTANT
NONCONSTRAINING
NONCONSTRUCTION
NONCONSTRUCTIVE
NONCONSUMER
NONCONSUMERS
NONCONSUMING
NONCONSUMPTION
NONCONSUMPTIONS
NONCONSUMPTIVE
NONCONTACT
NONCONTAGIOUS
NONCONTEMPORARY
NONCONTIGUOUS
NONCONTINGENT
NONCONTINUOUS
NONCONTRACT
NONCONTRACTUAL
NONCONTRIBUTING
NONCONTRIBUTORY
NONCONTROLLABLE
NONCONTROLLED
NONCONTROLLING
NONCONVENTIONAL
NONCONVERGENT
NONCONVERSANT
NONCONVERTIBLE
NONCOOPERATION
NONCOOPERATIONS
NONCOOPERATIVE
NONCOOPERATOR
NONCOOPERATORS

NONCOPLANAR
NONCORPORATE
NONCORRELATION
NONCORRELATIONS
NONCORRODIBLE
NONCORRODING
NONCORROSIVE
NONCOUNTRY
NONCOUNTY
NONCOVERAGE
NONCOVERAGES
NONCREATIVE
NONCREATIVITIES
NONCREATIVITY
NONCREDENTIALED
NONCREDIT
NONCRIME
NONCRIMES
NONCRIMINAL
NONCRIMINALS
NONCRISES
NONCRISIS
NONCRITICAL
NONCROSSOVER
NONCRUSHABLE
NONCRYSTALLINE
NONCULINARY
NONCULTIVATED
NONCULTIVATION
NONCULTIVATIONS
NONCULTURAL
NONCUMULATIVE
NONCURRENT
NONCUSTODIAL
NONCUSTOMER
NONCUSTOMERS
NONCYCLIC
NONCYCLICAL
NONDAIRY
NONDANCE
NONDANCER
NONDANCERS
NONDANCES
NONDECEPTIVE
NONDECIDUOUS
NONDECISION
NONDECISIONS
NONDECREASING
NONDEDUCTIBLE
NONDEDUCTIVE
NONDEFENSE
NONDEFERRABLE
NONDEFORMING
NONDEGENERATE
NONDEGRADABLE
NONDEGREE

NONDELEGATE
NONDELEGATES
NONDELIBERATE
NONDELINQUENT
NONDELINQUENTS
NONDELIVERIES
NONDELIVERY
NONDEMANDING
NONDEMOCRATIC
NONDEMONSTRABLE
NONDEPARTMENTAL
NONDEPENDENCE
NONDEPENDENCY
NONDEPENDENT
NONDEPENDENTS
NONDEPLETABLE
NONDEPLETING
NONDEPOSITION
NONDEPOSITIONS
NONDEPRESSED
NONDERIVATIVE
NONDESCRIPT
NONDESCRIPTIVE
NONDESCRIPTLY
NONDESCRIPTNESS
NONDESCRIPTS
NONDESERT
NONDESTRUCTIVE
NONDETACHABLE
NONDETONATING
NONDEVELOPMENT
NONDEVELOPMENTS
NONDEVIANT
NONDIABETIC
NONDIABETICS
NONDIALYZABLE
NONDIAPAUSING
NONDICTATORIAL
NONDIDACTIC
NONDIFFUSIBLE
NONDIFFUSING
NONDIMENSIONAL
NONDIPLOMATIC
NONDIRECTED
NONDIRECTIONAL
NONDIRECTIVE
NONDISABLED
NONDISCIPLINARY
NONDISCLOSURE
NONDISCLOSURES
NONDISCOUNT
NONDISCURSIVE
NONDISJUNCTION
NONDISJUNCTIONS
NONDISPERSIVE
NONDISRUPTIVE

NONDISTINCTIVE
NONDIVERSIFIED
NONDIVIDING
NONDIVISIBLE
NONDOCTOR
NONDOCTORS
NONDOCTRINAIRE
NONDOCTRINAL
NONDOCUMENTARY
NONDOGMATIC
NONDOLLAR
NONDOMESTIC
NONDOMESTICATED
NONDOMICILED
NONDOMINANT
NONDORMANT
NONDRAMATIC
NONDRINKER
NONDRINKERS
NONDRINKING
NONDRIP
NONDRIVER
NONDRIVERS
NONDRUG
NONDURABLE
NONE
NONEARNING
NONECONOMIC
NONECONOMIST
NONECONOMISTS
NONEDIBLE
NONEDITORIAL
NONEDUCATION
NONEDUCATIONAL
NONEFFECTIVE
NONEFFECTIVES
NONEGO
NONEGOS
NONELASTIC
NONELECT
NONELECTED
NONELECTION
NONELECTIONS
NONELECTIVE
NONELECTRIC
NONELECTRICAL
NONELECTROLYTE
NONELECTROLYTES
NONELECTRONIC
NONELEMENTARY
NONELIGIBLE
NONELITE
NONEMERGENCIES
NONEMERGENCY
NONEMOTIONAL
NONEMPHATIC

NONEMPIRICAL
NONEMPLOYEE
NONEMPLOYEES
NONEMPLOYMENT
NONEMPLOYMENTS
NONEMPTY
NONENCAPSULATED
NONENDING
NONENERGY
NONENFORCEMENT
NONENFORCEMENTS
NONENGAGEMENT
NONENGAGEMENTS
NONENGINEERING
NONENTITIES
NONENTITY
NONENTRIES
NONENTRY
NONENZYMATIC
NONENZYMIC
NONEQUAL
NONEQUALS
NONEQUILIBRIA
NONEQUILIBRIUM
NONEQUILIBRIUMS
NONEQUIVALENCE
NONEQUIVALENCES
NONEQUIVALENT
NONEROTIC
NONES
NONESSENTIAL
NONESSENTIALS
NONESTABLISHED
NONESTERIFIED
NONESUCH
NONESUCHES
NONET
NONETHELESS
NONETHICAL
NONETHNIC
NONETS
NONETTE
NONETTES
NONETTI
NONETTO
NONETTOS
NONEVALUATIVE
NONEVENT
NONEVENTS
NONEVIDENCE
NONEVIDENCES
NONEXCHANGEABLE
NONEXCLUSIVE
NONEXECUTIVE
NONEXECUTIVES
NONEXEMPT

NONEXISTENCE
NONEXISTENCES
NONEXISTENT
NONEXISTENTIAL
NONEXOTIC
NONEXPENDABLE
NONEXPERIMENTAL
NONEXPERT
NONEXPERTS
NONEXPLANATORY
NONEXPLOITATION
NONEXPLOITATIVE
NONEXPLOITIVE
NONEXPLOSIVE
NONEXPOSED
NONEXTANT
NONFACT
NONFACTOR
NONFACTORS
NONFACTS
NONFACTUAL
NONFACULTY
NONFADING
NONFAMILIAL
NONFAMILIES
NONFAMILY
NONFAN
NONFANS
NONFARM
NONFARMER
NONFARMERS
NONFAT
NONFATAL
NONFATTENING
NONFATTY
NONFEASANCE
NONFEASANCES
NONFEDERAL
NONFEDERATED
NONFEMINIST
NONFEMINISTS
NONFERROUS
NONFICTION
NONFICTIONAL
NONFICTIONALLY
NONFICTIONS
NONFICTITIOUS
NONFIGURATIVE
NONFILAMENTOUS
NONFILTERABLE
NONFINAL
NONFINANCIAL
NONFINITE
NONFISSIONABLE
NONFLAMMABILITY
NONFLAMMABLE

NONFLEXIBLE
NONFLOWERING
NONFLUENCIES
NONFLUENCY
NONFLUID
NONFLUIDS
NONFLUORESCENT
NONFLYING
NONFOCAL
NONFOOD
NONFORFEITABLE
NONFORFEITURE
NONFORFEITURES
NONFORMAL
NONFORMATION
NONFOSSIL
NONFREEZING
NONFRIVOLOUS
NONFROZEN
NONFUEL
NONFULFILLMENT
NONFULFILLMENTS
NONFULFILMENT
NONFUNCTIONAL
NONFUNCTIONING
NONFUSIBLE
NONG
NONGAME
NONGASEOUS
NONGAY
NONGAYS
NONGENETIC
NONGENITAL
NONGEOMETRICAL
NONGHETTO
NONGLAMOROUS
NONGLARE
NONGOLFER
NONGOLFERS
NONGONOCOCCAL
NONGOVERNMENT
NONGOVERNMENTAL
NONGRADED
NONGRADUATE
NONGRADUATES
NONGRAMMATICAL
NONGRANULAR
NONGREASY
NONGREEN
NONGREGARIOUS
NONGROWING
NONGROWTH
NONGS
NONGUEST
NONGUESTS
NONGUILT

NONGUILTS
NONHABITABLE
NONHALOGENATED
NONHANDICAPPED
NONHAPPENING
NONHAPPENINGS
NONHARDY
NONHARMONIC
NONHAZARDOUS
NONHEME
NONHEMOLYTIC
NONHEREDITARY
NONHERITABLE
NONHERO
NONHEROES
NONHIERARCHICAL
NONHISTONE
NONHISTORICAL
NONHOME
NONHOMOGENEOUS
NONHOMOLOGOUS
NONHOMOSEXUAL
NONHOMOSEXUALS
NONHORMONAL
NONHOSPITAL
NONHOSPITALIZED
NONHOSTILE
NONHOUSING
NONHUMAN
NONHUNTER
NONHUNTERS
NONHUNTING
NONHYGROSCOPIC
NONHYSTERICAL
NONIDEAL
NONIDENTICAL
NONIDENTITIES
NONIDENTITY
NONIDEOLOGICAL
NONIDIOMATIC
NONILLION
NONILLIONS
NONILLIONTH
NONILLIONTHS
NONIMAGE
NONIMITATIVE
NONIMMIGRANT
NONIMMIGRANTS
NONIMMUNE
NONIMPACT
NONIMPLICATION
NONIMPLICATIONS
NONIMPORTATION
NONIMPORTATIONS
NONINCLUSION
NONINCLUSIONS

NONINCREASING
NONINCUMBENT
NONINCUMBENTS
NONINDEPENDENCE
NONINDEPENDENT
NONINDICTABLE
NONINDIGENOUS
NONINDIVIDUAL
NONINDUCTIVE
NONINDUSTRIAL
NONINDUSTRY
NONINFECTED
NONINFECTIOUS
NONINFECTIVE
NONINFESTED
NONINFLAMMABLE
NONINFLAMMATORY
NONINFLATIONARY
NONINFLECTED
NONINFLECTIONAL
NONINFLUENCE
NONINFLUENCES
NONINFORMATION
NONINFORMATIONS
NONINFORMATIVE
NONINFRINGEMENT
NONINHERENT
NONINHERITABLE
NONINITIAL
NONINITIATE
NONINITIATES
NONINJURIOUS
NONINJURY
NONINSECT
NONINSECTICIDAL
NONINSECTS
NONINSTALLMENT
NONINSTALLMENTS
NONINSTINCTIVE
NONINSTRUMENTAL
NONINSURANCE
NONINSURED
NONINTEGRAL
NONINTEGRATED
NONINTELLECTUAL
NONINTERACTING
NONINTERACTIVE
NONINTERCOURSE
NONINTERCOURSES
NONINTEREST
NONINTERFERENCE
NONINTERSECTING
NONINTERVENTION
NONINTIMIDATING
NONINTOXICANT
NONINTOXICANTS

NONINTOXICATING
NONINTRUSIVE
NONINTUITIVE
NONINVASIVE
NONINVOLVED
NONINVOLVEMENT
NONINVOLVEMENTS
NONIONIC
NONIONIZING
NONIRON
NONIRRADIATED
NONIRRIGATED
NONIRRITANT
NONIRRITANTS
NONIRRITATING
NONISSUE
NONISSUES
NONJOINDER
NONJOINDERS
NONJOINER
NONJOINERS
NONJUDGEMENTAL
NONJUDGMENTAL
NONJUDICIAL
NONJURING
NONJUROR
NONJURORS
NONJURY
NONJUSTICIABLE
NONKOSHER
NONLABOR
NONLAMINATED
NONLANDOWNER
NONLANDOWNERS
NONLANGUAGE
NONLANGUAGES
NONLAWYER
NONLAWYERS
NONLEADED
NONLEAFY
NONLEAGUE
NONLEGAL
NONLEGUME
NONLEGUMES
NONLEGUMINOUS
NONLETHAL
NONLEXICAL
NONLIBRARIAN
NONLIBRARIANS
NONLIBRARY
NONLIFE
NONLINEAL
NONLINEAR
NONLINEARITIES
NONLINEARITY
NONLINGUISTIC

NONLIQUID
NONLIQUIDS
NONLITERAL
NONLITERARY
NONLITERATE
NONLITERATES
NONLITURGICAL
NONLIVES
NONLIVING
NONLOCAL
NONLOCALS
NONLOGICAL
NONLUMINOUS
NONMAGNETIC
NONMAINSTREAM
NONMAJOR
NONMAJORS
NONMALIGNANT
NONMALLEABLE
NONMAN
NONMANAGEMENT
NONMANAGERIAL
NONMANUAL
NONMARITAL
NONMARITIME
NONMARKET
NONMARRIED
NONMATERIAL
NONMATERNAL
NONMATHEMATICAL
NONMATRICULATED
NONMEANINGFUL
NONMEASURABLE
NONMEAT
NONMECHANICAL
NONMECHANISTIC
NONMEDICAL
NONMEDICINAL
NONMEETING
NONMEETINGS
NONMELODIC
NONMEMBER
NONMEMBERS
NONMEMBERSHIP
NONMEMBERSHIPS
NONMEN
NONMENTAL
NONMERCURIAL
NONMETAL
NONMETALLIC
NONMETALS
NONMETAMERIC
NONMETAPHORICAL
NONMETRIC
NONMETRICAL
NONMETRO

NONMETROPOLITAN
NONMICROBIAL
NONMIGRANT
NONMIGRATORY
NONMILITANT
NONMILITANTS
NONMILITARY
NONMIMETIC
NONMINISTERIAL
NONMINORITIES
NONMINORITY
NONMOBILE
NONMODAL
NONMOLECULAR
NONMONETARIST
NONMONETARISTS
NONMONETARY
NONMONEY
NONMONOGAMOUS
NONMORAL
NONMOTILE
NONMOTILITIES
NONMOTILITY
NONMOTORIZED
NONMOUNTAINOUS
NONMOVING
NONMUNICIPAL
NONMUSIC
NONMUSICAL
NONMUSICALS
NONMUSICIAN
NONMUSICIANS
NONMUSICS
NONMUTANT
NONMUTANTS
NONMYELINATED
NONMYSTICAL
NONMYTHICAL
NONNARRATIVE
NONNATIONAL
NONNATIONALS
NONNATIVE
NONNATIVES
NONNATURAL
NONNAVAL
NONNECESSITIES
NONNECESSITY
NONNEGATIVE
NONNEGLIGENT
NONNEGOTIABLE
NONNEGOTIABLES
NONNETWORK
NONNEWS
NONNIES
NONNITROGENOUS
NONNORMATIVE

NONNOVEL
NONNOVELS
NONNUCLEAR
NONNUCLEATED
NONNUMERICAL
NONNUTRITIOUS
NONNUTRITIVE
NONNY
NONOBESE
NONOBJECTIVE
NONOBJECTIVISM
NONOBJECTIVISMS
NONOBJECTIVIST
NONOBJECTIVISTS
NONOBJECTIVITY
NONOBLIGATORY
NONOBSCENE
NONOBSERVANCE
NONOBSERVANCES
NONOBSERVANT
NONOBVIOUS
NONOCCUPATIONAL
NONOCCURRENCE
NONOCCURRENCES
NONOFFICIAL
NONOFFICIALS
NONOHMIC
NONOILY
NONOPERABLE
NONOPERATIC
NONOPERATING
NONOPERATIONAL
NONOPERATIVE
NONOPTIMAL
NONORGANIC
NONORGASMIC
NONORTHODOX
NONOSTENSIVE
NONOVERLAPPING
NONOWNER
NONOWNERS
NONOXIDIZING
NONPAGAN
NONPAGANS
NONPAID
NONPAPAL
NONPAR
NONPARALLEL
NONPARAMETRIC
NONPARASITIC
NONPAREIL
NONPAREILS
NONPARENTAL
NONPAROCHIAL
NONPAROUS
NONPARTICIPANT

NONPARTICIPANTS
NONPARTISAN
NONPARTISANSHIP
NONPARTIZAN
NONPARTIZANSHIP
NONPARTY
NONPASSERINE
NONPASSIVE
NONPAST
NONPASTS
NONPATERNAL
NONPATHOGENIC
NONPAYING
NONPAYMENT
NONPAYMENTS
NONPEAK
NONPERFORMANCE
NONPERFORMANCES
NONPERFORMER
NONPERFORMERS
NONPERFORMING
NONPERISHABLE
NONPERISHABLES
NONPERMANENT
NONPERMANENTLY
NONPERMEABLE
NONPERMISSIVE
NONPERSISTENT
NONPERSON
NONPERSONAL
NONPERSONS
NONPETROLEUM
NONPHILOSOPHER
NONPHILOSOPHERS
NONPHONEMIC
NONPHONETIC
NONPHOSPHATE
NONPHOTOGRAPHIC
NONPHYSICAL
NONPHYSICIAN
NONPHYSICIANS
NONPLANAR
NONPLASTIC
NONPLASTICS
NONPLAY
NONPLAYING
NONPLAYS
NONPLUS
NONPLUSED
NONPLUSES
NONPLUSING
NONPLUSSED
NONPLUSSES
NONPLUSSING
NONPOETIC
NONPOINT

NONPOISONOUS
NONPOLAR
NONPOLARIZABLE
NONPOLICE
NONPOLITICAL
NONPOLITICALLY
NONPOLITICIAN
NONPOLITICIANS
NONPOLLUTING
NONPOOR
NONPOROUS
NONPOSSESSION
NONPOSSESSIONS
NONPRACTICAL
NONPRACTICING
NONPRACTISING
NONPRECIOUS
NONPREDATORY
NONPREDICTABLE
NONPREGNANT
NONPREJUDICIAL
NONPRESCRIPTION
NONPRESCRIPTIVE
NONPRESERVABLE
NONPRESERVATION
NONPRINT
NONPROBLEM
NONPROBLEMS
NONPRODUCING
NONPRODUCTIVE
NONPRODUCTIVITY
NONPROFESSIONAL
NONPROFESSORIAL
NONPROFIT
NONPROFITS
NONPROGRAM
NONPROGRAMMER
NONPROGRAMMERS
NONPROGRESSIVE
NONPROPORTIONAL
NONPROPRIETARY
NONPROS
NONPROSSED
NONPROSSES
NONPROSSING
NONPROTECTIVE
NONPROTEIN
NONPSYCHIATRIC
NONPSYCHIATRIST
NONPSYCHOTIC
NONPUBLIC
NONPUNISHABLE
NONPUNITIVE
NONPURPOSIVE
NONQUANTIFIABLE
NONQUANTITATIVE

NONQUOTA
NONRACIAL
NONRACIALLY
NONRADICAL
NONRADIOACTIVE
NONRAILROAD
NONRANDOM
NONRANDOMNESS
NONRANDOMNESSES
NONRATED
NONRATIONAL
NONREACTIVE
NONREACTOR
NONREACTORS
NONREADER
NONREADERS
NONREADING
NONREALISTIC
NONRECEIPT
NONRECEIPTS
NONRECIPROCAL
NONRECOGNITION
NONRECOGNITIONS
NONRECOMBINANT
NONRECOMBINANTS
NONRECOURSE
NONRECOVERABLE
NONRECURRENT
NONRECURRING
NONRECYCLABLE
NONRECYCLABLES
NONREDUCING
NONREDUNDANT
NONREFILLABLE
NONREFLECTING
NONREFLECTIVE
NONREFLEXIVE
NONREFUNDABLE
NONREGIMENTED
NONREGISTERED
NONREGULATED
NONREGULATION
NONRELATIVE
NONRELATIVES
NONRELATIVISTIC
NONRELEVANT
NONRELIGIOUS
NONRENEWABLE
NONRENEWAL
NONREPAYABLE
NONREPRODUCTIVE
NONRESIDENCE
NONRESIDENCES
NONRESIDENCIES
NONRESIDENCY
NONRESIDENT

NONRESIDENTIAL
NONRESIDENTS
NONRESISTANCE
NONRESISTANCES
NONRESISTANT
NONRESISTANTS
NONRESONANT
NONRESPONDENT
NONRESPONDENTS
NONRESPONDER
NONRESPONDERS
NONRESPONSE
NONRESPONSES
NONRESPONSIVE
NONRESTRICTED
NONRESTRICTIVE
NONRETRACTILE
NONRETROACTIVE
NONRETURN
NONRETURNABLE
NONRETURNABLES
NONREUSABLE
NONREVERSIBLE
NONRHOTIC
NONRHOTICITY
NONRIGID
NONRIOTER
NONRIOTERS
NONRIOTING
NONRIVAL
NONRIVALS
NONROTATING
NONROUTINE
NONROYAL
NONRUBBER
NONRULING
NONRUMINANT
NONRUMINANTS
NONRURAL
NONSALABLE
NONSALINE
NONSAPONIFIABLE
NONSCHEDULED
NONSCHOOL
NONSCIENCE
NONSCIENCES
NONSCIENTIFIC
NONSCIENTIST
NONSCIENTISTS
NONSEASONAL
NONSECRETOR
NONSECRETORS
NONSECRETORY
NONSECTARIAN
NONSECULAR
NONSECURE

NONSEDIMENTABLE
NONSEGREGATED
NONSEGREGATION
NONSEGREGATIONS
NONSELECTED
NONSELECTIVE
NONSELF
NONSELVES
NONSENSATIONAL
NONSENSE
NONSENSES
NONSENSICAL
NONSENSICALITY
NONSENSICALLY
NONSENSICALNESS
NONSENSITIVE
NONSENSUOUS
NONSENTENCE
NONSENTENCES
NONSEPTATE
NONSEQUENTIAL
NONSERIOUS
NONSEXIST
NONSEXUAL
NONSHRINK
NONSHRINKABLE
NONSIGNER
NONSIGNERS
NONSIGNIFICANT
NONSIMULTANEOUS
NONSINKABLE
NONSKATER
NONSKATERS
NONSKED
NONSKEDS
NONSKELETAL
NONSKID
NONSKIER
NONSKIERS
NONSKILLED
NONSLIP
NONSMOKER
NONSMOKERS
NONSMOKING
NONSOCIAL
NONSOCIALIST
NONSOCIALISTS
NONSOLAR
NONSOLID
NONSOLIDS
NONSOLUBLE
NONSOLUTION
NONSOLUTIONS
NONSPATIAL
NONSPEAKER
NONSPEAKERS

NONSPEAKING
NONSPECIALIST
NONSPECIALISTS
NONSPECIFIC
NONSPECIFICALLY
NONSPECTACULAR
NONSPECULAR
NONSPECULATIVE
NONSPEECH
NONSPHERICAL
NONSPIRITUAL
NONSPORTING
NONSTAINABLE
NONSTAINING
NONSTANDARD
NONSTARTER
NONSTARTERS
NONSTATIONARY
NONSTATISTICAL
NONSTATIVE
NONSTATIVES
NONSTEADY
NONSTELLAR
NONSTEROID
NONSTEROIDAL
NONSTEROIDS
NONSTICK
NONSTOP
NONSTORIES
NONSTORY
NONSTRATEGIC
NONSTRIATED
NONSTRUCTURAL
NONSTRUCTURED
NONSTUDENT
NONSTUDENTS
NONSTYLE
NONSTYLES
NONSUBJECT
NONSUBJECTIVE
NONSUBJECTS
NONSUBSCRIBER
NONSUBSCRIBERS
NONSUBSIDIZED
NONSUCCESS
NONSUCCESSES
NONSUCH
NONSUCHES
NONSUGAR
NONSUGARS
NONSUGGESTIVE
NONSUGGESTIVELY
NONSUIT
NONSUITED
NONSUITING
NONSUITS

NONSULPHUROUS
NONSUPERVISORY
NONSUPPORT
NONSUPPORTS
NONSUPPRESSION
NONSURGICAL
NONSUSTAINING
NONSWIMMER
NONSWIMMERS
NONSYLLABIC
NONSYMBOLIC
NONSYMMETRIC
NONSYMMETRICAL
NONSYNCHRONOUS
NONSYSTEM
NONSYSTEMATIC
NONSYSTEMIC
NONSYSTEMS
NONTARGET
NONTARIFF
NONTAX
NONTAXABLE
NONTAXES
NONTEACHING
NONTECHNICAL
NONTEMPORAL
NONTENURED
NONTERMINAL
NONTERMINALS
NONTERMINATING
NONTERRITORIAL
NONTHEATRICAL
NONTHEIST
NONTHEISTIC
NONTHEISTS
NONTHEOLOGICAL
NONTHEORETICAL
NONTHERAPEUTIC
NONTHERMAL
NONTHINKING
NONTHREATENING
NONTIDAL
NONTITLE
NONTOBACCO
NONTONAL
NONTOTALITARIAN
NONTOXIC
NONTRADITIONAL
NONTRANSFERABLE
NONTRANSITIVE
NONTREATMENT
NONTREATMENTS
NONTRIVIAL
NONTROPICAL
NONTRUMP
NONTRUTH

NONTRUTHS
NONTURBULENT
NONTYPICAL
NONUNANIMOUS
NONUNIFORM
NONUNIFORMITIES
NONUNIFORMITY
NONUNION
NONUNIONISM
NONUNIONIST
NONUNIONISTS
NONUNIONIZED
NONUNIONS
NONUNIQUE
NONUNIQUENESS
NONUNIQUENESSES
NONUNIVERSAL
NONUNIVERSITY
NONUPLE
NONUPLES
NONUPLET
NONUPLETS
NONURBAN
NONURGENT
NONUSAGE
NONUSE
NONUSER
NONUSERS
NONUSES
NONUSING
NONUTILITARIAN
NONUTILITIES
NONUTILITY
NONUTOPIAN
NONVALID
NONVALIDITIES
NONVALIDITY
NONVANISHING
NONVASCULAR
NONVECTOR
NONVECTORS
NONVEGETARIAN
NONVEGETARIANS
NONVENOMOUS
NONVERBAL
NONVERBALLY
NONVERIFIABLE
NONVETERAN
NONVETERANS
NONVIABLE
NONVIEWER
NONVIEWERS
NONVINTAGE
NONVIOLENCE
NONVIOLENCES
NONVIOLENT

NONVIOLENTLY
NONVIRAL
NONVIRGIN
NONVIRGINS
NONVISCOUS
NONVISUAL
NONVOCAL
NONVOCATIONAL
NONVOLATILE
NONVOLCANIC
NONVOLUNTARY
NONVOTER
NONVOTERS
NONVOTING
NONWAR
NONWARS
NONWHITE
NONWHITES
NONWINNING
NONWOODY
NONWORD
NONWORDS
NONWORK
NONWORKER
NONWORKERS
NONWORKING
NONWOVEN
NONWOVENS
NONWRITER
NONWRITERS
NONYELLOWING
NONYL
NONYLS
NONZERO
NOO
NOODGE
NOODGED
NOODGES
NOODGING
NOODLE
NOODLED
NOODLEDOM
NOODLEDOMS
NOODLES
NOODLING
NOOGENESES
NOOGENESIS
NOOK
NOOKIE
NOOKIER
NOOKIES
NOOKIEST
NOOKLIKE
NOOKS
NOOKY
NOOLOGIES

NOOLOGY
NOOMETRIES
NOOMETRY
NOON
NOONDAY
NOONDAYS
NOONED
NOONER
NOONERS
NOONING
NOONINGS
NOONS
NOONTIDE
NOONTIDES
NOONTIME
NOONTIMES
NOOP
NOOPS
NOOSE
NOOSED
NOOSER
NOOSERS
NOOSES
NOOSING
NOOSPHERE
NOOSPHERES
NOOTROPICS
NOPAL
NOPALS
NOPE
NOR
NORADRENALIN
NORADRENALINE
NORADRENALINES
NORADRENALINS
NORADRENERGIC
NORDIC
NOREPINEPHRINE
NOREPINEPHRINES
NORETHINDRONE
NORETHINDRONES
NORETHISTERONE
NORETHISTERONES
NORI
NORIA
NORIAS
NORIMON
NORIMONS
NORIS
NORITE
NORITES
NORITIC
NORK
NORKS
NORLAND
NORLANDS

NORM
NORMA
NORMAL
NORMALCIES
NORMALCY
NORMALISATION
NORMALISATIONS
NORMALISE
NORMALISED
NORMALISES
NORMALISING
NORMALITIES
NORMALITY
NORMALIZABLE
NORMALIZATION
NORMALIZATIONS
NORMALIZE
NORMALIZED
NORMALIZER
NORMALIZERS
NORMALIZES
NORMALIZING
NORMALLY
NORMALS
NORMAN
NORMANDE
NORMANS
NORMAS
NORMATIVE
NORMATIVELY
NORMATIVENESS
NORMATIVENESSES
NORMED
NORMLESS
NORMOTENSIVE
NORMOTENSIVES
NORMOTHERMIA
NORMOTHERMIAS
NORMOTHERMIC
NORMS
NORSEL
NORSELLED
NORSELLER
NORSELLERS
NORSELLING
NORSELS
NORTENA
NORTENAS
NORTENO
NORTENOS
NORTH
NORTHBOUND
NORTHCOUNTRYMAN
NORTHCOUNTRYMEN
NORTHEAST
NORTHEASTER

NORTHEASTERLIES
NORTHEASTERLY
NORTHEASTERN
NORTHEASTERS
NORTHEASTS
NORTHEASTWARD
NORTHEASTWARDLY
NORTHEASTWARDS
NORTHED
NORTHER
NORTHERED
NORTHERING
NORTHERLIES
NORTHERLINESS
NORTHERLINESSES
NORTHERLY
NORTHERMOST
NORTHERN
NORTHERNER
NORTHERNERS
NORTHERNISE
NORTHERNISED
NORTHERNISES
NORTHERNISING
NORTHERNISM
NORTHERNISMS
NORTHERNIZE
NORTHERNIZED
NORTHERNIZES
NORTHERNIZING
NORTHERNMOST
NORTHERNS
NORTHERS
NORTHING
NORTHINGS
NORTHLAND
NORTHLANDS
NORTHMOST
NORTHS
NORTHWARD
NORTHWARDLY
NORTHWARDS
NORTHWEST
NORTHWESTER
NORTHWESTERLIES
NORTHWESTERLY
NORTHWESTERN
NORTHWESTERS
NORTHWESTS
NORTHWESTWARD
NORTHWESTWARDLY
NORTHWESTWARDS
NORTRIPTYLINE
NORTRIPTYLINES
NORWARD
NORWARDS

NOS
NOSE
NOSEAN
NOSEANS
NOSEBAG
NOSEBAGS
NOSEBAND
NOSEBANDED
NOSEBANDS
NOSEBLEED
NOSEBLEEDING
NOSEBLEEDINGS
NOSEBLEEDS
NOSED
NOSEDIVE
NOSEDIVED
NOSEDIVES
NOSEDIVING
NOSEGAY
NOSEGAYS
NOSEGUARD
NOSEGUARDS
NOSELESS
NOSELIKE
NOSELITE
NOSELITES
NOSEPIECE
NOSEPIECES
NOSER
NOSERS
NOSES
NOSEWHEEL
NOSEWHEELS
NOSEY
NOSEYS
NOSH
NOSHED
NOSHER
NOSHERIE
NOSHERIES
NOSHERS
NOSHERY
NOSHES
NOSHING
NOSIER
NOSIES
NOSIEST
NOSILY
NOSINESS
NOSINESSES
NOSING
NOSINGS
NOSOCOMIAL
NOSODE
NOSODES
NOSOGRAPHER

NOSOGRAPHERS
NOSOGRAPHIC
NOSOGRAPHIES
NOSOGRAPHY
NOSOLOGIC
NOSOLOGICAL
NOSOLOGICALLY
NOSOLOGIES
NOSOLOGIST
NOSOLOGISTS
NOSOLOGY
NOSOPHOBIA
NOSOPHOBIAS
NOSTALGIA
NOSTALGIAS
NOSTALGIC
NOSTALGICALLY
NOSTALGICS
NOSTALGIST
NOSTALGISTS
NOSTOC
NOSTOCS
NOSTOI
NOSTOLOGIC
NOSTOLOGICAL
NOSTOLOGIES
NOSTOLOGY
NOSTOMANIA
NOSTOMANIAS
NOSTOPATHIES
NOSTOPATHY
NOSTOS
NOSTRADAMIC
NOSTRIL
NOSTRILS
NOSTRO
NOSTRUM
NOSTRUMS
NOSY
NOT
NOTA
NOTABILIA
NOTABILITIES
NOTABILITY
NOTABLE
NOTABLENESS
NOTABLENESSES
NOTABLES
NOTABLY
NOTAEUM
NOTAEUMS
NOTAL
NOTANDA
NOTANDUM
NOTAPHILIC
NOTAPHILIES

NOTAPHILISM
NOTAPHILISMS
NOTAPHILIST
NOTAPHILISTS
NOTAPHILY
NOTARIAL
NOTARIALLY
NOTARIES
NOTARISE
NOTARISED
NOTARISES
NOTARISING
NOTARIZATION
NOTARIZATIONS
NOTARIZE
NOTARIZED
NOTARIZES
NOTARIZING
NOTARY
NOTARYSHIP
NOTARYSHIPS
NOTATE
NOTATED
NOTATES
NOTATING
NOTATION
NOTATIONAL
NOTATIONS
NOTCH
NOTCHBACK
NOTCHBACKS
NOTCHED
NOTCHEL
NOTCHELLED
NOTCHELLING
NOTCHELS
NOTCHER
NOTCHERS
NOTCHES
NOTCHIER
NOTCHIEST
NOTCHING
NOTCHINGS
NOTCHY
NOTE
NOTEBOOK
NOTEBOOKS
NOTECASE
NOTECASES
NOTED
NOTEDLY
NOTEDNESS
NOTEDNESSES
NOTELESS
NOTELET
NOTELETS

NOTEPAD
NOTEPADS
NOTEPAPER
NOTEPAPERS
NOTER
NOTERS
NOTES
NOTEWORTHILY
NOTEWORTHINESS
NOTEWORTHY
NOTHER
NOTHING
NOTHINGARIAN
NOTHINGARIANISM
NOTHINGARIANS
NOTHINGISM
NOTHINGISMS
NOTHINGNESS
NOTHINGNESSES
NOTHINGS
NOTICE
NOTICEABILITY
NOTICEABLE
NOTICEABLY
NOTICED
NOTICER
NOTICERS
NOTICES
NOTICING
NOTIFIABLE
NOTIFICATION
NOTIFICATIONS
NOTIFIED
NOTIFIER
NOTIFIERS
NOTIFIES
NOTIFY
NOTIFYING
NOTING
NOTION
NOTIONAL
NOTIONALIST
NOTIONALISTS
NOTIONALITIES
NOTIONALITY
NOTIONALLY
NOTIONIST
NOTIONISTS
NOTIONS
NOTITIA
NOTITIAE
NOTITIAS
NOTOCHORD
NOTOCHORDAL
NOTOCHORDS
NOTODONTID

NOTODONTIDS
NOTONECTAL
NOTORIETIES
NOTORIETY
NOTORIOUS
NOTORIOUSLY
NOTORIOUSNESS
NOTORIOUSNESSES
NOTORNIS
NOTORNISES
NOTOTHERIUM
NOTOTHERIUMS
NOTOUNGULATE
NOTOUNGULATES
NOTOUR
NOTS
NOTT
NOTTURNI
NOTTURNO
NOTUM
NOTUNGULATE
NOTUNGULATES
NOTWITHSTANDING
NOUGAT
NOUGATS
NOUGHT
NOUGHTIES
NOUGHTS
NOUL
NOULD
NOULDE
NOULE
NOULES
NOULS
NOUMENA
NOUMENAL
NOUMENALISM
NOUMENALIST
NOUMENALISTS
NOUMENALITY
NOUMENALLY
NOUMENON
NOUN
NOUNAL
NOUNALLY
NOUNIER
NOUNIEST
NOUNLESS
NOUNS
NOUNY
NOUP
NOUPS
NOURICE
NOURICES
NOURISH
NOURISHABLE

NOURISHED
NOURISHER
NOURISHERS
NOURISHES
NOURISHING
NOURISHINGLY
NOURISHMENT
NOURISHMENTS
NOURITURE
NOURITURES
NOURRITURE
NOURRITURES
NOURSLE
NOURSLED
NOURSLES
NOURSLING
NOUS
NOUSELL
NOUSELLED
NOUSELLING
NOUSELLS
NOUSES
NOUSLE
NOUSLED
NOUSLES
NOUSLING
NOUT
NOUVEAU
NOUVEAUX
NOUVELLE
NOUVELLES
NOVA
NOVACULITE
NOVACULITES
NOVAE
NOVALIA
NOVALIKE
NOVAS
NOVATION
NOVATIONS
NOVEL
NOVELDOM
NOVELDOMS
NOVELESE
NOVELESES
NOVELETTE
NOVELETTES
NOVELETTISH
NOVELETTIST
NOVELETTISTS
NOVELISATION
NOVELISATIONS
NOVELISE
NOVELISED
NOVELISER
NOVELISERS

NOVELISES
NOVELISH
NOVELISING
NOVELISM
NOVELISMS
NOVELIST
NOVELISTIC
NOVELISTICALLY
NOVELISTS
NOVELIZATION
NOVELIZATIONS
NOVELIZE
NOVELIZED
NOVELIZER
NOVELIZERS
NOVELIZES
NOVELIZING
NOVELLA
NOVELLAE
NOVELLAS
NOVELLE
NOVELLY
NOVELS
NOVELTIES
NOVELTY
NOVEMDECILLION
NOVEMDECILLIONS
NOVENA
NOVENAE
NOVENARIES
NOVENARY
NOVENAS
NOVENNIAL
NOVERCAL
NOVERINT
NOVERINTS
NOVICE
NOVICEHOOD
NOVICEHOODS
NOVICES
NOVICESHIP
NOVICESHIPS
NOVICIATE
NOVICIATES
NOVITIATE
NOVITIATES
NOVITIES
NOVITY
NOVOBIOCIN
NOVOBIOCINS
NOVOCAINE
NOVOCAINES
NOVOCENTENARIES
NOVOCENTENARY
NOVODAMUS
NOVODAMUSES

NOVUM
NOVUMS
NOW
NOWADAYS
NOWAY
NOWAYS
NOWCASTING
NOWCASTINGS
NOWED
NOWHENCE
NOWHERE
NOWHERES
NOWHITHER
NOWISE
NOWL
NOWLS
NOWN
NOWNESS
NOWNESSES
NOWS
NOWT
NOWTIER
NOWTIEST
NOWTS
NOWTY
NOWY
NOX
NOXAL
NOXES
NOXIOUS
NOXIOUSLY
NOXIOUSNESS
NOXIOUSNESSES
NOY
NOYADE
NOYADES
NOYANCE
NOYANCES
NOYAU
NOYAUS
NOYED
NOYES
NOYESES
NOYING
NOYOUS
NOYS
NOYSOME
NOZZER
NOZZERS
NOZZLE
NOZZLES
NTH
NU
NUANCE
NUANCED
NUANCES

NUANCING
NUB
NUBBED
NUBBIER
NUBBIEST
NUBBIN
NUBBING
NUBBINS
NUBBLE
NUBBLED
NUBBLES
NUBBLIER
NUBBLIEST
NUBBLING
NUBBLY
NUBBY
NUBECULA
NUBECULAE
NUBIA
NUBIAS
NUBIFEROUS
NUBIFORM
NUBIGENOUS
NUBILE
NUBILITIES
NUBILITY
NUBILOSE
NUBILOUS
NUBS
NUCELLAR
NUCELLI
NUCELLUS
NUCHA
NUCHAE
NUCHAL
NUCHALS
NUCIFEROUS
NUCIVOROUS
NUCLEAL
NUCLEAR
NUCLEARISATION
NUCLEARISATIONS
NUCLEARISE
NUCLEARISED
NUCLEARISES
NUCLEARISING
NUCLEARIZATION
NUCLEARIZATIONS
NUCLEARIZE
NUCLEARIZED
NUCLEARIZES
NUCLEARIZING
NUCLEASE
NUCLEASES
NUCLEATE
NUCLEATED

NUCLEATES
NUCLEATING
NUCLEATION
NUCLEATIONS
NUCLEATOR
NUCLEATORS
NUCLEI
NUCLEIC
NUCLEIDE
NUCLEIDES
NUCLEIN
NUCLEINS
NUCLEOCAPSID
NUCLEOCAPSIDS
NUCLEOID
NUCLEOIDS
NUCLEOLAR
NUCLEOLATE
NUCLEOLATED
NUCLEOLE
NUCLEOLES
NUCLEOLI
NUCLEOLUS
NUCLEON
NUCLEONIC
NUCLEONICALLY
NUCLEONICS
NUCLEONS
NUCLEOPHILE
NUCLEOPHILES
NUCLEOPHILIC
NUCLEOPHILICITY
NUCLEOPLASM
NUCLEOPLASMATIC
NUCLEOPLASMIC
NUCLEOPLASMS
NUCLEOPROTEIN
NUCLEOPROTEINS
NUCLEOSIDE
NUCLEOSIDES
NUCLEOSOMAL
NUCLEOSOME
NUCLEOSOMES
NUCLEOSYNTHESES
NUCLEOSYNTHESIS
NUCLEOSYNTHETIC
NUCLEOTIDASE
NUCLEOTIDASES
NUCLEOTIDE
NUCLEOTIDES
NUCLEUS
NUCLEUSES
NUCLIDE
NUCLIDES
NUCLIDIC
NUCULE

NUCULES	NUISANCER	NUMBFISHES	NUMISMATICS
NUDATION	NUISANCERS	NUMBING	NUMISMATIST
NUDATIONS	NUISANCES	NUMBINGLY	NUMISMATISTS
NUDDY	NUKE	NUMBLES	NUMISMATOLOGIES
NUDE	NUKED	NUMBLY	NUMISMATOLOGIST
NUDELY	NUKES	NUMBNESS	NUMISMATOLOGY
NUDENESS	NUKING	NUMBNESSES	NUMMARY
NUDENESSES	NULL	NUMBS	NUMMULAR
NUDER	NULLA	NUMBSKULL	NUMMULARY
NUDES	NULLAH	NUMBSKULLS	NUMMULATED
NUDEST	NULLAHS	NUMDAH	NUMMULATION
NUDGE	NULLAS	NUMDAHS	NUMMULATIONS
NUDGED	NULLED	NUMEN	NUMMULINE
NUDGER	NULLIFICATION	NUMERABILITIES	NUMMULITE
NUDGERS	NULLIFICATIONS	NUMERABILITY	NUMMULITES
NUDGES	NULLIFIDIAN	NUMERABLE	NUMMULITIC
NUDGING	NULLIFIDIANS	NUMERABLY	NUMNAH
NUDIBRANCH	NULLIFIED	NUMERACIES	NUMNAHS
NUDIBRANCHIATE	NULLIFIER	NUMERACY	NUMPTIES
NUDIBRANCHIATES	NULLIFIERS	NUMERAIRE	NUMPTY
NUDIBRANCHS	NULLIFIES	NUMERAIRES	NUMSKULL
NUDICAUDATE	NULLIFY	NUMERAL	NUMSKULLED
NUDICAUL	NULLIFYING	NUMERALLY	NUMSKULLS
NUDICAULOUS	NULLING	NUMERALS	NUN
NUDIE	NULLINGS	NUMERARY	NUNATAK
NUDIES	NULLIPARA	NUMERATE	NUNATAKER
NUDISM	NULLIPARAE	NUMERATED	NUNATAKS
NUDISMS	NULLIPARAS	NUMERATES	NUNCHAKU
NUDIST	NULLIPARITIES	NUMERATING	NUNCHAKUS
NUDISTS	NULLIPARITY	NUMERATION	NUNCHEON
NUDITIES	NULLIPAROUS	NUMERATIONS	NUNCHEONS
NUDITY	NULLIPORE	NUMERATIVE	NUNCIATURE
NUDNICK	NULLIPORES	NUMERATOR	NUNCIATURES
NUDNICKS	NULLITIES	NUMERATORS	NUNCIO
NUDNIK	NULLITY	NUMERIC	NUNCIOS
NUDNIKS	NULLNESS	NUMERICAL	NUNCLE
NUDZH	NULLNESSES	NUMERICALLY	NUNCLES
NUDZHED	NULLS	NUMERICS	NUNCUPATE
NUDZHES	NUMB	NUMEROLOGICAL	NUNCUPATED
NUDZHING	NUMBAT	NUMEROLOGIES	NUNCUPATES
NUFF	NUMBATS	NUMEROLOGIST	NUNCUPATING
NUFFIN	NUMBED	NUMEROLOGISTS	NUNCUPATION
NUFFINS	NUMBER	NUMEROLOGY	NUNCUPATIONS
NUFFS	NUMBERABLE	NUMEROSITIES	NUNCUPATIVE
NUGAE	NUMBERED	NUMEROSITY	NUNCUPATORY
NUGATORINESS	NUMBERER	NUMEROUS	NUNDINAL
NUGATORINESSES	NUMBERERS	NUMEROUSLY	NUNDINE
NUGATORY	NUMBERING	NUMEROUSNESS	NUNDINES
NUGGAR	NUMBERLESS	NUMEROUSNESSES	NUNHOOD
NUGGARS	NUMBERLESSLY	NUMINA	NUNHOODS
NUGGET	NUMBERLESSNESS	NUMINOUS	NUNLIKE
NUGGETS	NUMBERPLATE	NUMINOUSES	NUNNATION
NUGGETTED	NUMBERPLATES	NUMINOUSNESS	NUNNATIONS
NUGGETTING	NUMBERS	NUMINOUSNESSES	NUNNERIES
NUGGETY	NUMBEST	NUMISMATIC	NUNNERY
NUISANCE	NUMBFISH	NUMISMATICALLY	NUNNISH

NUNNISHNESS
NUNNISHNESSES
NUNNY
NUNS
NUNSHIP
NUNSHIPS
NUPTIAL
NUPTIALITIES
NUPTIALITY
NUPTIALLY
NUPTIALS
NUR
NURAGHE
NURAGHI
NURAGHIC
NURD
NURDIER
NURDIEST
NURDISH
NURDLE
NURDLED
NURDLES
NURDLING
NURDS
NURDY
NURHAG
NURHAGS
NURL
NURLED
NURLING
NURLS
NURR
NURRS
NURS
NURSE
NURSED
NURSEHOUND
NURSEHOUNDS
NURSELIKE
NURSELING
NURSELINGS
NURSEMAID
NURSEMAIDED
NURSEMAIDING
NURSEMAIDS
NURSER
NURSERIES
NURSERS
NURSERY
NURSERYMAID
NURSERYMAIDS
NURSERYMAN
NURSERYMEN
NURSES
NURSING
NURSINGS

NURSLE
NURSLED
NURSLES
NURSLING
NURSLINGS
NURTURABLE
NURTURAL
NURTURANCE
NURTURANCES
NURTURANT
NURTURE
NURTURED
NURTURER
NURTURERS
NURTURES
NURTURING
NUS
NUT
NUTANT
NUTARIAN
NUTARIANS
NUTATE
NUTATED
NUTATES
NUTATING
NUTATION
NUTATIONAL
NUTATIONS
NUTBROWN
NUTBUTTER
NUTBUTTERS
NUTCASE
NUTCASES
NUTCRACKER
NUTCRACKERS
NUTGALL
NUTGALLS
NUTGRASS
NUTGRASSES
NUTHATCH
NUTHATCHES
NUTHOUSE
NUTHOUSES
NUTJOBBER
NUTJOBBERS
NUTLET
NUTLETS
NUTLIKE
NUTMEAL
NUTMEALS
NUTMEAT
NUTMEATS
NUTMEG
NUTMEGGED
NUTMEGGING
NUTMEGGY

NUTMEGS
NUTPECKER
NUTPECKERS
NUTPICK
NUTPICKS
NUTRACEUTICAL
NUTRACEUTICALS
NUTRIA
NUTRIAS
NUTRIENT
NUTRIENTS
NUTRIMENT
NUTRIMENTAL
NUTRIMENTS
NUTRITION
NUTRITIONAL
NUTRITIONALLY
NUTRITIONARY
NUTRITIONIST
NUTRITIONISTS
NUTRITIONS
NUTRITIOUS
NUTRITIOUSLY
NUTRITIOUSNESS
NUTRITIVE
NUTRITIVELY
NUTRITIVES
NUTS
NUTSEDGE
NUTSEDGES
NUTSHELL
NUTSHELLS
NUTSIER
NUTSIEST
NUTSO
NUTSOS
NUTSY
NUTTED
NUTTER
NUTTERIES
NUTTERS
NUTTERY
NUTTIER
NUTTIEST
NUTTILY
NUTTINESS
NUTTINESSES
NUTTING
NUTTINGS
NUTTY
NUTWOOD
NUTWOODS
NUZZER
NUZZERS
NUZZLE
NUZZLED

NUZZLER
NUZZLERS
NUZZLES
NUZZLING
NY
NYAFF
NYAFFED
NYAFFING
NYAFFS
NYALA
NYALAS
NYANZA
NYANZAS
NYAS
NYASES
NYBBLE
NYBBLES
NYCHTHEMERAL
NYCHTHEMERON
NYCHTHEMERONS
NYCTAGINACEOUS
NYCTALOPES
NYCTALOPIA
NYCTALOPIAS
NYCTALOPIC
NYCTALOPS
NYCTANTHOUS
NYCTINASTIC
NYCTINASTIES
NYCTINASTY
NYCTITROPIC
NYCTITROPISM
NYCTITROPISMS
NYCTOPHOBIA
NYCTOPHOBIAS
NYCTOPHOBIC
NYE
NYED
NYES
NYING
NYLGHAI
NYLGHAIS
NYLGHAU
NYLGHAUS
NYLON
NYLONS
NYMPH
NYMPHA
NYMPHAE
NYMPHAEA
NYMPHAEACEOUS
NYMPHAEUM
NYMPHAEUMS
NYMPHAL
NYMPHALID
NYMPHALIDS

NYMPHEAN
NYMPHET
NYMPHETS
NYMPHETTE
NYMPHETTES
NYMPHIC
NYMPHICAL
NYMPHISH
NYMPHLIKE
NYMPHLY
NYMPHO
NYMPHOLEPSIES
NYMPHOLEPSY
NYMPHOLEPT
NYMPHOLEPTIC
NYMPHOLEPTS
NYMPHOMANIA
NYMPHOMANIAC
NYMPHOMANIACAL
NYMPHOMANIACS
NYMPHOMANIAS
NYMPHOS
NYMPHS
NYS
NYSSA
NYSSAS
NYSTAGMIC
NYSTAGMOID
NYSTAGMUS
NYSTAGMUSES
NYSTATIN
NYSTATINS

O

OAF
OAFISH
OAFISHLY
OAFISHNESS
OAFISHNESSES
OAFS
OAK
OAKEN
OAKENSHAW
OAKENSHAWS
OAKER
OAKERS
OAKIER
OAKIES
OAKIEST
OAKLEAF
OAKLEAVES
OAKLIKE
OAKLING
OAKLINGS
OAKMOSS
OAKMOSSES
OAKS
OAKUM
OAKUMS
OAKY
OANSHAGH
OANSHAGHS
OAR
OARAGE
OARAGES
OARED
OARFISH
OARFISHES
OARIER
OARIEST
OARING
OARLESS
OARLIKE
OARLOCK
OARLOCKS
OARS
OARSMAN
OARSMANSHIP
OARSMANSHIPS
OARSMEN
OARSWOMAN
OARSWOMEN
OARWEED
OARWEEDS
OARY

OASES
OASIS
OAST
OASTHOUSE
OASTHOUSES
OASTS
OAT
OATCAKE
OATCAKES
OATEN
OATER
OATERS
OATH
OATHABLE
OATHS
OATLIKE
OATMEAL
OATMEALS
OATS
OAVES
OB
OBA
OBANG
OBANGS
OBAS
OBBLIGATI
OBBLIGATO
OBBLIGATOS
OBCOMPRESSED
OBCONIC
OBCONICAL
OBCORDATE
OBDURACIES
OBDURACY
OBDURATE
OBDURATED
OBDURATELY
OBDURATENESS
OBDURATENESSES
OBDURATES
OBDURATING
OBDURATION
OBDURATIONS
OBDURE
OBDURED
OBDURES
OBDURING
OBE
OBEAH
OBEAHED
OBEAHING

OBEAHISM
OBEAHISMS
OBEAHS
OBECHE
OBECHES
OBEDIENCE
OBEDIENCES
OBEDIENT
OBEDIENTIAL
OBEDIENTIARIES
OBEDIENTIARY
OBEDIENTLY
OBEISANCE
OBEISANCES
OBEISANT
OBEISANTLY
OBEISM
OBEISMS
OBELI
OBELIA
OBELIAS
OBELION
OBELISCAL
OBELISE
OBELISED
OBELISES
OBELISING
OBELISK
OBELISKOID
OBELISKS
OBELISM
OBELISMS
OBELIZE
OBELIZED
OBELIZES
OBELIZING
OBELUS
OBES
OBESE
OBESELY
OBESENESS
OBESENESSES
OBESER
OBESEST
OBESITIES
OBESITY
OBEY
OBEYABLE
OBEYED
OBEYER
OBEYERS

OBEYING
OBEYS
OBFUSCATE
OBFUSCATED
OBFUSCATES
OBFUSCATING
OBFUSCATION
OBFUSCATIONS
OBFUSCATORY
OBI
OBIA
OBIAS
OBIED
OBIING
OBIISM
OBIISMS
OBIIT
OBIS
OBIT
OBITAL
OBITER
OBITS
OBITUAL
OBITUARIES
OBITUARIST
OBITUARISTS
OBITUARY
OBJECT
OBJECTED
OBJECTIFICATION
OBJECTIFIED
OBJECTIFIES
OBJECTIFY
OBJECTIFYING
OBJECTING
OBJECTION
OBJECTIONABLE
OBJECTIONABLY
OBJECTIONS
OBJECTIVAL
OBJECTIVATE
OBJECTIVATED
OBJECTIVATES
OBJECTIVATING
OBJECTIVATION
OBJECTIVATIONS
OBJECTIVE
OBJECTIVELY
OBJECTIVENESS
OBJECTIVENESSES
OBJECTIVES

OBJECTIVISE
OBJECTIVISED
OBJECTIVISES
OBJECTIVISING
OBJECTIVISM
OBJECTIVISMS
OBJECTIVIST
OBJECTIVISTIC
OBJECTIVISTS
OBJECTIVITIES
OBJECTIVITY
OBJECTIVIZE
OBJECTIVIZED
OBJECTIVIZES
OBJECTIVIZING
OBJECTLESS
OBJECTLESSNESS
OBJECTOR
OBJECTORS
OBJECTS
OBJET
OBJETS
OBJURATION
OBJURATIONS
OBJURE
OBJURED
OBJURES
OBJURGATE
OBJURGATED
OBJURGATES
OBJURGATING
OBJURGATION
OBJURGATIONS
OBJURGATIVE
OBJURGATOR
OBJURGATORS
OBJURGATORY
OBJURING
OBLANCEOLATE
OBLAST
OBLASTI
OBLASTS
OBLATE
OBLATELY
OBLATENESS
OBLATENESSES
OBLATES
OBLATION
OBLATIONAL
OBLATIONS
OBLATORY
OBLIGABLE
OBLIGANT
OBLIGANTS
OBLIGATE
OBLIGATED

OBLIGATELY
OBLIGATES
OBLIGATI
OBLIGATING
OBLIGATION
OBLIGATIONAL
OBLIGATIONS
OBLIGATIVE
OBLIGATO
OBLIGATOR
OBLIGATORILY
OBLIGATORINESS
OBLIGATORS
OBLIGATORY
OBLIGATOS
OBLIGE
OBLIGED
OBLIGEE
OBLIGEES
OBLIGEMENT
OBLIGEMENTS
OBLIGER
OBLIGERS
OBLIGES
OBLIGING
OBLIGINGLY
OBLIGINGNESS
OBLIGINGNESSES
OBLIGOR
OBLIGORS
OBLIQUATION
OBLIQUATIONS
OBLIQUE
OBLIQUED
OBLIQUELY
OBLIQUENESS
OBLIQUENESSES
OBLIQUER
OBLIQUES
OBLIQUEST
OBLIQUID
OBLIQUING
OBLIQUITIES
OBLIQUITOUS
OBLIQUITY
OBLITERATE
OBLITERATED
OBLITERATES
OBLITERATING
OBLITERATION
OBLITERATIONS
OBLITERATIVE
OBLITERATOR
OBLITERATORS
OBLIVION
OBLIVIONS

OBLIVIOUS
OBLIVIOUSLY
OBLIVIOUSNESS
OBLIVIOUSNESSES
OBLIVISCENCE
OBLIVISCENCES
OBLONG
OBLONGLY
OBLONGS
OBLOQUIES
OBLOQUY
OBMUTESCENCE
OBMUTESCENCES
OBMUTESCENT
OBNOXIOUS
OBNOXIOUSLY
OBNOXIOUSNESS
OBNOXIOUSNESSES
OBNUBILATE
OBNUBILATED
OBNUBILATES
OBNUBILATING
OBNUBILATION
OBNUBILATIONS
OBO
OBOE
OBOES
OBOIST
OBOISTS
OBOL
OBOLARY
OBOLE
OBOLES
OBOLI
OBOLS
OBOLUS
OBOS
OBOVATE
OBOVATELY
OBOVOID
OBREPTION
OBREPTIONS
OBREPTITIOUS
OBS
OBSCENE
OBSCENELY
OBSCENENESS
OBSCENENESSES
OBSCENER
OBSCENEST
OBSCENITIES
OBSCENITY
OBSCURANT
OBSCURANTIC
OBSCURANTISM
OBSCURANTISMS

OBSCURANTIST
OBSCURANTISTS
OBSCURANTS
OBSCURATION
OBSCURATIONS
OBSCURE
OBSCURED
OBSCURELY
OBSCUREMENT
OBSCUREMENTS
OBSCURENESS
OBSCURENESSES
OBSCURER
OBSCURERS
OBSCURES
OBSCUREST
OBSCURING
OBSCURITIES
OBSCURITY
OBSECRATE
OBSECRATED
OBSECRATES
OBSECRATING
OBSECRATION
OBSECRATIONS
OBSEQUENT
OBSEQUIAL
OBSEQUIE
OBSEQUIES
OBSEQUIOUS
OBSEQUIOUSLY
OBSEQUIOUSNESS
OBSEQUY
OBSERVABILITIES
OBSERVABILITY
OBSERVABLE
OBSERVABLENESS
OBSERVABLES
OBSERVABLY
OBSERVANCE
OBSERVANCES
OBSERVANCIES
OBSERVANCY
OBSERVANT
OBSERVANTLY
OBSERVANTS
OBSERVATION
OBSERVATIONAL
OBSERVATIONALLY
OBSERVATIONS
OBSERVATIVE
OBSERVATOR
OBSERVATORIES
OBSERVATORS
OBSERVATORY
OBSERVE

OBSERVED	OBSOLETISMS	OBTAINING	OBTURATORS
OBSERVER	OBSTACLE	OBTAINMENT	OBTUSE
OBSERVERS	OBSTACLES	OBTAINMENTS	OBTUSELY
OBSERVES	OBSTETRIC	OBTAINS	OBTUSENESS
OBSERVING	OBSTETRICAL	OBTECT	OBTUSENESSES
OBSERVINGLY	OBSTETRICALLY	OBTECTED	OBTUSER
OBSESS	OBSTETRICIAN	OBTEMPER	OBTUSEST
OBSESSED	OBSTETRICIANS	OBTEMPERATE	OBTUSITIES
OBSESSES	OBSTETRICS	OBTEMPERATED	OBTUSITY
OBSESSING	OBSTINACIES	OBTEMPERATES	OBUMBRATE
OBSESSION	OBSTINACY	OBTEMPERATING	OBUMBRATED
OBSESSIONAL	OBSTINATE	OBTEMPERED	OBUMBRATES
OBSESSIONALLY	OBSTINATELY	OBTEMPERING	OBUMBRATING
OBSESSIONIST	OBSTINATENESS	OBTEMPERS	OBUMBRATION
OBSESSIONISTS	OBSTINATENESSES	OBTEND	OBUMBRATIONS
OBSESSIONS	OBSTIPATION	OBTENDED	OBVENTION
OBSESSIVE	OBSTIPATIONS	OBTENDING	OBVENTIONS
OBSESSIVELY	OBSTREPERATE	OBTENDS	OBVERSE
OBSESSIVENESS	OBSTREPERATED	OBTENTION	OBVERSELY
OBSESSIVENESSES	OBSTREPERATES	OBTENTIONS	OBVERSES
OBSESSIVES	OBSTREPERATING	OBTEST	OBVERSION
OBSESSOR	OBSTREPEROUS	OBTESTATION	OBVERSIONS
OBSESSORS	OBSTREPEROUSLY	OBTESTATIONS	OBVERT
OBSIDIAN	OBSTRICTION	OBTESTED	OBVERTED
OBSIDIANS	OBSTRICTIONS	OBTESTING	OBVERTING
OBSIDIONAL	OBSTROPALOUS	OBTESTS	OBVERTS
OBSIDIONARY	OBSTROPULOUS	OBTRUDE	OBVIABLE
OBSIGN	OBSTRUCT	OBTRUDED	OBVIATE
OBSIGNATE	OBSTRUCTED	OBTRUDER	OBVIATED
OBSIGNATED	OBSTRUCTER	OBTRUDERS	OBVIATES
OBSIGNATES	OBSTRUCTERS	OBTRUDES	OBVIATING
OBSIGNATING	OBSTRUCTING	OBTRUDING	OBVIATION
OBSIGNATION	OBSTRUCTION	OBTRUDINGS	OBVIATIONS
OBSIGNATIONS	OBSTRUCTIONAL	OBTRUNCATE	OBVIATOR
OBSIGNATORY	OBSTRUCTIONALLY	OBTRUNCATED	OBVIATORS
OBSIGNED	OBSTRUCTIONISM	OBTRUNCATES	OBVIOUS
OBSIGNING	OBSTRUCTIONISMS	OBTRUNCATING	OBVIOUSLY
OBSIGNS	OBSTRUCTIONIST	OBTRUSION	OBVIOUSNESS
OBSOLESCE	OBSTRUCTIONISTS	OBTRUSIONS	OBVIOUSNESSES
OBSOLESCED	OBSTRUCTIONS	OBTRUSIVE	OBVOLUTE
OBSOLESCENCE	OBSTRUCTIVE	OBTRUSIVELY	OBVOLUTED
OBSOLESCENCES	OBSTRUCTIVELY	OBTRUSIVENESS	OBVOLUTION
OBSOLESCENT	OBSTRUCTIVENESS	OBTRUSIVENESSES	OBVOLUTIONS
OBSOLESCENTLY	OBSTRUCTIVES	OBTUND	OBVOLUTIVE
OBSOLESCES	OBSTRUCTOR	OBTUNDED	OBVOLVENT
OBSOLESCING	OBSTRUCTORS	OBTUNDENT	OCA
OBSOLETE	OBSTRUCTS	OBTUNDENTS	OCARINA
OBSOLETED	OBSTRUENT	OBTUNDING	OCARINAS
OBSOLETELY	OBSTRUENTS	OBTUNDS	OCAS
OBSOLETENESS	OBTAIN	OBTURATE	OCCAM
OBSOLETENESSES	OBTAINABILITIES	OBTURATED	OCCAMIES
OBSOLETES	OBTAINABILITY	OBTURATES	OCCAMS
OBSOLETING	OBTAINABLE	OBTURATING	OCCAMY
OBSOLETION	OBTAINED	OBTURATION	OCCASION
OBSOLETIONS	OBTAINER	OBTURATIONS	OCCASIONAL
OBSOLETISM	OBTAINERS	OBTURATOR	OCCASIONALISM

OCCASIONALISMS
OCCASIONALIST
OCCASIONALISTS
OCCASIONALITIES
OCCASIONALITY
OCCASIONALLY
OCCASIONED
OCCASIONER
OCCASIONERS
OCCASIONING
OCCASIONS
OCCIDENT
OCCIDENTAL
OCCIDENTALISE
OCCIDENTALISED
OCCIDENTALISES
OCCIDENTALISING
OCCIDENTALIZE
OCCIDENTALIZED
OCCIDENTALIZES
OCCIDENTALIZING
OCCIDENTALLY
OCCIDENTALS
OCCIDENTS
OCCIPITA
OCCIPITAL
OCCIPITALLY
OCCIPITALS
OCCIPUT
OCCIPUTS
OCCLUDE
OCCLUDED
OCCLUDENT
OCCLUDENTS
OCCLUDER
OCCLUDERS
OCCLUDES
OCCLUDING
OCCLUSAL
OCCLUSION
OCCLUSIONS
OCCLUSIVE
OCCLUSIVENESS
OCCLUSIVES
OCCLUSOR
OCCLUSORS
OCCULT
OCCULTATION
OCCULTATIONS
OCCULTED
OCCULTER
OCCULTERS
OCCULTING
OCCULTISM
OCCULTISMS
OCCULTIST

OCCULTISTS
OCCULTLY
OCCULTNESS
OCCULTNESSES
OCCULTS
OCCUPANCE
OCCUPANCES
OCCUPANCIES
OCCUPANCY
OCCUPANT
OCCUPANTS
OCCUPATE
OCCUPATED
OCCUPATES
OCCUPATING
OCCUPATION
OCCUPATIONAL
OCCUPATIONALLY
OCCUPATIONS
OCCUPATIVE
OCCUPIED
OCCUPIER
OCCUPIERS
OCCUPIES
OCCUPY
OCCUPYING
OCCUR
OCCURRED
OCCURRENCE
OCCURRENCES
OCCURRENT
OCCURRENTS
OCCURRING
OCCURS
OCEAN
OCEANARIA
OCEANARIUM
OCEANARIUMS
OCEANAUT
OCEANAUTS
OCEANFRONT
OCEANFRONTS
OCEANGOING
OCEANIC
OCEANID
OCEANIDES
OCEANIDS
OCEANOGRAPHER
OCEANOGRAPHERS
OCEANOGRAPHIC
OCEANOGRAPHICAL
OCEANOGRAPHIES
OCEANOGRAPHY
OCEANOLOGICAL
OCEANOLOGIES
OCEANOLOGIST

OCEANOLOGISTS
OCEANOLOGY
OCEANS
OCELLAR
OCELLATE
OCELLATED
OCELLATION
OCELLATIONS
OCELLI
OCELLUS
OCELOID
OCELOT
OCELOTS
OCH
OCHE
OCHER
OCHERED
OCHERING
OCHEROUS
OCHERS
OCHERY
OCHES
OCHIDORE
OCHIDORES
OCHLOCRACIES
OCHLOCRACY
OCHLOCRAT
OCHLOCRATIC
OCHLOCRATICAL
OCHLOCRATICALLY
OCHLOCRATS
OCHLOPHOBIA
OCHLOPHOBIAC
OCHLOPHOBIACS
OCHLOPHOBIAS
OCHLOPHOBIC
OCHONE
OCHRACEOUS
OCHRE
OCHREA
OCHREAE
OCHREATE
OCHRED
OCHREOUS
OCHRES
OCHREY
OCHRING
OCHROID
OCHROLEUCOUS
OCHROUS
OCHRY
OCICAT
OCICATS
OCKER
OCKERISM
OCKERISMS

OCKERS
OCKODOLS
OCOTILLO
OCOTILLOS
OCREA
OCREAE
OCREATE
OCTA
OCTACHORD
OCTACHORDAL
OCTACHORDS
OCTAD
OCTADIC
OCTADS
OCTAGON
OCTAGONAL
OCTAGONALLY
OCTAGONS
OCTAHEDRA
OCTAHEDRAL
OCTAHEDRALLY
OCTAHEDRITE
OCTAHEDRITES
OCTAHEDRON
OCTAHEDRONS
OCTAL
OCTALS
OCTAMEROUS
OCTAMETER
OCTAMETERS
OCTAN
OCTANDRIAN
OCTANDROUS
OCTANE
OCTANEDIOIC
OCTANES
OCTANGLE
OCTANGLES
OCTANGULAR
OCTANOL
OCTANOLS
OCTANS
OCTANT
OCTANTAL
OCTANTS
OCTAPEPTIDE
OCTAPEPTIDES
OCTAPLA
OCTAPLAS
OCTAPLOID
OCTAPLOIDIES
OCTAPLOIDS
OCTAPLOIDY
OCTAPODIC
OCTAPODIES
OCTAPODY

OCTARCHIES
OCTARCHY
OCTAROON
OCTAROONS
OCTAS
OCTASTICH
OCTASTICHON
OCTASTICHONS
OCTASTICHS
OCTASTROPHIC
OCTASTYLE
OCTASTYLES
OCTAVAL
OCTAVALENT
OCTAVE
OCTAVES
OCTAVO
OCTAVOS
OCTENNIAL
OCTENNIALLY
OCTET
OCTETS
OCTETT
OCTETTE
OCTETTES
OCTETTS
OCTILLION
OCTILLIONS
OCTILLIONTH
OCTILLIONTHS
OCTINGENARIES
OCTINGENTENARY
OCTOCENTENARIES
OCTOCENTENARY
OCTODECILLION
OCTODECILLIONS
OCTODECIMO
OCTODECIMOS
OCTOFID
OCTOGENARIAN
OCTOGENARIANS
OCTOGENARIES
OCTOGENARY
OCTOGYNOUS
OCTOHEDRA
OCTOHEDRON
OCTOHEDRONS
OCTONARIAN
OCTONARIANS
OCTONARIES
OCTONARII
OCTONARIUS
OCTONARY
OCTONOCULAR
OCTOPETALOUS
OCTOPI

OCTOPLOID
OCTOPLOIDS
OCTOPOD
OCTOPODES
OCTOPODOUS
OCTOPODS
OCTOPUS
OCTOPUSES
OCTOPUSH
OCTOPUSHER
OCTOPUSHERS
OCTOPUSHES
OCTOROON
OCTOROONS
OCTOSEPALOUS
OCTOSTICHOUS
OCTOSTYLE
OCTOSTYLES
OCTOSYLLABIC
OCTOSYLLABICS
OCTOSYLLABLE
OCTOSYLLABLES
OCTOTHORP
OCTOTHORPS
OCTROI
OCTROIS
OCTUOR
OCTUORS
OCTUPLE
OCTUPLED
OCTUPLES
OCTUPLET
OCTUPLETS
OCTUPLEX
OCTUPLICATE
OCTUPLICATES
OCTUPLING
OCTUPLY
OCTYL
OCTYLS
OCULAR
OCULARIST
OCULARISTS
OCULARLY
OCULARS
OCULATE
OCULATED
OCULI
OCULIST
OCULISTS
OCULOMOTOR
OCULUS
OD
ODA
ODAL
ODALIQUE

ODALIQUES
ODALISK
ODALISKS
ODALISQUE
ODALISQUES
ODALLER
ODALLERS
ODALS
ODAS
ODD
ODDBALL
ODDBALLS
ODDER
ODDEST
ODDISH
ODDITIES
ODDITY
ODDLY
ODDMENT
ODDMENTS
ODDNESS
ODDNESSES
ODDS
ODDSMAKER
ODDSMAKERS
ODDSMAN
ODDSMEN
ODE
ODEA
ODEON
ODEONS
ODES
ODEUM
ODEUMS
ODIC
ODIOUS
ODIOUSLY
ODIOUSNESS
ODIOUSNESSES
ODISM
ODISMS
ODIST
ODISTS
ODIUM
ODIUMS
ODOGRAPH
ODOGRAPHS
ODOMETER
ODOMETERS
ODOMETRIES
ODOMETRY
ODONATE
ODONATES
ODONATIST
ODONATISTS
ODONATOLOGIES

ODONATOLOGIST
ODONATOLOGISTS
ODONATOLOGY
ODONTALGIA
ODONTALGIAS
ODONTALGIC
ODONTALGIES
ODONTALGY
ODONTIC
ODONTIST
ODONTISTS
ODONTOBLAST
ODONTOBLASTIC
ODONTOBLASTS
ODONTOCETE
ODONTOCETES
ODONTOGENIC
ODONTOGENIES
ODONTOGENY
ODONTOGLOSSUM
ODONTOGLOSSUMS
ODONTOGRAPH
ODONTOGRAPHIES
ODONTOGRAPHS
ODONTOGRAPHY
ODONTOID
ODONTOIDS
ODONTOLITE
ODONTOLITES
ODONTOLOGIC
ODONTOLOGICAL
ODONTOLOGIES
ODONTOLOGIST
ODONTOLOGISTS
ODONTOLOGY
ODONTOMA
ODONTOMAS
ODONTOMATA
ODONTOPHOBIA
ODONTOPHOBIAS
ODONTOPHORAL
ODONTOPHORE
ODONTOPHORES
ODONTOPHOROUS
ODONTORHYNCHOUS
ODONTORNITHES
ODONTOSTOMATOUS
ODOR
ODORANT
ODORANTS
ODORATE
ODORED
ODORFUL
ODORIFEROUS
ODORIFEROUSLY
ODORIFEROUSNESS

ODORIMETRIES
ODORIMETRY
ODORIPHORE
ODORIPHORES
ODORIZE
ODORIZED
ODORIZES
ODORIZING
ODORLESS
ODOROUS
ODOROUSLY
ODOROUSNESS
ODOROUSNESSES
ODORS
ODOUR
ODOURED
ODOURFUL
ODOURLESS
ODOURS
ODS
ODSO
ODSOS
ODYL
ODYLE
ODYLES
ODYLISM
ODYLISMS
ODYLS
ODYSSEY
ODYSSEYS
ODZOOKS
OE
OECIST
OECISTS
OECOLOGICAL
OECOLOGICALLY
OECOLOGIES
OECOLOGIST
OECOLOGISTS
OECOLOGY
OECUMENIC
OECUMENICAL
OECUMENICALLY
OEDEMA
OEDEMAS
OEDEMATA
OEDEMATOSE
OEDEMATOUS
OEDIPAL
OEDIPALLY
OEDIPEAN
OEDOMETER
OEDOMETERS
OEDOMETRIC
OEDOMETRICALLY
OEILLADE

OEILLADES
OENANTHIC
OENOLOGICAL
OENOLOGIES
OENOLOGIST
OENOLOGISTS
OENOLOGY
OENOMANCIES
OENOMANCY
OENOMANIA
OENOMANIAS
OENOMEL
OENOMELS
OENOMETER
OENOMETERS
OENOPHIL
OENOPHILE
OENOPHILES
OENOPHILIES
OENOPHILIST
OENOPHILISTS
OENOPHILS
OENOPHILY
OENOTHERA
OENOTHERAS
OERLIKON
OERLIKONS
OERSTED
OERSTEDS
OES
OESOPHAGEAL
OESOPHAGI
OESOPHAGOSCOPE
OESOPHAGOSCOPES
OESOPHAGOSCOPIC
OESOPHAGOSCOPY
OESOPHAGUS
OESTRADIOL
OESTRADIOLS
OESTRAL
OESTRIN
OESTRINS
OESTRIOL
OESTRIOLS
OESTROGEN
OESTROGENIC
OESTROGENICALLY
OESTROGENS
OESTRONE
OESTRONES
OESTROUS
OESTRUM
OESTRUMS
OESTRUS
OESTRUSES
OEUVRE

OEUVRES
OF
OFAY
OFAYS
OFF
OFFAL
OFFALS
OFFBEAT
OFFBEATS
OFFCAST
OFFCASTS
OFFCUT
OFFCUTS
OFFED
OFFENCE
OFFENCEFUL
OFFENCELESS
OFFENCES
OFFEND
OFFENDED
OFFENDEDLY
OFFENDER
OFFENDERS
OFFENDING
OFFENDRESS
OFFENDRESSES
OFFENDS
OFFENSE
OFFENSELESS
OFFENSES
OFFENSIVE
OFFENSIVELY
OFFENSIVENESS
OFFENSIVENESSES
OFFENSIVES
OFFER
OFFERABLE
OFFERED
OFFEREE
OFFEREES
OFFERER
OFFERERS
OFFERING
OFFERINGS
OFFEROR
OFFERORS
OFFERS
OFFERTORIES
OFFERTORY
OFFHAND
OFFHANDED
OFFHANDEDLY
OFFHANDEDNESS
OFFHANDEDNESSES
OFFICE
OFFICEHOLDER

OFFICEHOLDERS
OFFICER
OFFICERED
OFFICERING
OFFICERS
OFFICES
OFFICIAL
OFFICIALDOM
OFFICIALDOMS
OFFICIALESE
OFFICIALESES
OFFICIALISM
OFFICIALISMS
OFFICIALITIES
OFFICIALITY
OFFICIALLY
OFFICIALS
OFFICIALTIES
OFFICIALTY
OFFICIANT
OFFICIANTS
OFFICIARIES
OFFICIARY
OFFICIATE
OFFICIATED
OFFICIATES
OFFICIATING
OFFICIATION
OFFICIATIONS
OFFICIATOR
OFFICIATORS
OFFICINAL
OFFICINALLY
OFFICINALS
OFFICIOUS
OFFICIOUSLY
OFFICIOUSNESS
OFFICIOUSNESSES
OFFING
OFFINGS
OFFISH
OFFISHLY
OFFISHNESS
OFFISHNESSES
OFFKEY
OFFLINE
OFFLOAD
OFFLOADED
OFFLOADING
OFFLOADS
OFFPEAK
OFFPRINT
OFFPRINTED
OFFPRINTING
OFFPRINTS
OFFPUT

OFFPUTS
OFFRAMP
OFFRAMPS
OFFS
OFFSADDLE
OFFSADDLED
OFFSADDLES
OFFSADDLING
OFFSCOURING
OFFSCOURINGS
OFFSCREEN
OFFSCUM
OFFSCUMS
OFFSEASON
OFFSEASONS
OFFSET
OFFSETABLE
OFFSETS
OFFSETTING
OFFSHOOT
OFFSHOOTS
OFFSHORE
OFFSIDE
OFFSIDER
OFFSIDERS
OFFSIDES
OFFSPRING
OFFSPRINGS
OFFSTAGE
OFFSTAGES
OFFTAKE
OFFTAKES
OFFTRACK
OFLAG
OFLAGS
OFT
OFTEN
OFTENER
OFTENEST
OFTENNESS
OFTENNESSES
OFTENTIMES
OFTER
OFTEST
OFTTIMES
OGAM
OGAMIC
OGAMS
OGDOAD
OGDOADS
OGEE
OGEES
OGGIN
OGGINS
OGHAM
OGHAMIC

OGHAMIST
OGHAMISTS
OGHAMS
OGIVAL
OGIVE
OGIVES
OGLE
OGLED
OGLER
OGLERS
OGLES
OGLING
OGLINGS
OGMIC
OGRE
OGREISH
OGREISM
OGREISMS
OGRES
OGRESS
OGRESSES
OGRISH
OGRISHLY
OGRISM
OGRISMS
OH
OHED
OHIA
OHIAS
OHING
OHM
OHMAGE
OHMAGES
OHMIC
OHMICALLY
OHMMETER
OHMMETERS
OHMS
OHO
OHONE
OHOS
OHS
OI
OIDIA
OIDIUM
OIK
OIKIST
OIKISTS
OIKS
OIL
OILBIRD
OILBIRDS
OILCAMP
OILCAMPS
OILCAN
OILCANS

OILCLOTH
OILCLOTHS
OILCUP
OILCUPS
OILED
OILER
OILERIES
OILERS
OILERY
OILFIELD
OILFIELDS
OILFIRED
OILGAS
OILGASES
OILHOLE
OILHOLES
OILIER
OILIEST
OILILY
OILINESS
OILINESSES
OILING
OILLET
OILLETS
OILMAN
OILMEN
OILNUT
OILNUTS
OILPAPER
OILPAPERS
OILPROOF
OILS
OILSEED
OILSEEDS
OILSKIN
OILSKINS
OILSTONE
OILSTONES
OILTIGHT
OILWAY
OILWAYS
OILY
OINK
OINKED
OINKING
OINKS
OINOLOGIES
OINOLOGY
OINOMEL
OINOMELS
OINT
OINTED
OINTING
OINTMENT
OINTMENTS
OINTS

OITICICA
OITICICAS
OJIME
OJIMES
OKA
OKAPI
OKAPIS
OKAS
OKAY
OKAYED
OKAYING
OKAYS
OKE
OKEH
OKEHS
OKES
OKEYDOKE
OKEYDOKEY
OKIMONO
OKIMONOS
OKRA
OKRAS
OKTA
OKTAS
OLD
OLDEN
OLDENED
OLDENING
OLDENS
OLDER
OLDEST
OLDFANGLED
OLDIE
OLDIES
OLDISH
OLDNESS
OLDNESSES
OLDS
OLDSQUAW
OLDSQUAWS
OLDSTER
OLDSTERS
OLDSTYLE
OLDSTYLES
OLDWIFE
OLDWIVES
OLDY
OLE
OLEA
OLEACEOUS
OLEAGINOUS
OLEAGINOUSLY
OLEAGINOUSNESS
OLEANDER
OLEANDERS
OLEANDOMYCIN

OLEANDOMYCINS
OLEARIA
OLEARIAS
OLEASTER
OLEASTERS
OLEATE
OLEATES
OLECRANAL
OLECRANON
OLECRANONS
OLEFIANT
OLEFIN
OLEFINE
OLEFINES
OLEFINIC
OLEFINS
OLEIC
OLEIFEROUS
OLEIN
OLEINE
OLEINES
OLEINS
OLENT
OLEO
OLEOGRAPH
OLEOGRAPHIC
OLEOGRAPHIES
OLEOGRAPHS
OLEOGRAPHY
OLEOMARGARIN
OLEOMARGARINE
OLEOMARGARINES
OLEOMARGARINS
OLEOPHILIC
OLEORESIN
OLEORESINOUS
OLEORESINS
OLEOS
OLERACEOUS
OLES
OLEUM
OLEUMS
OLFACT
OLFACTED
OLFACTIBLE
OLFACTING
OLFACTION
OLFACTIONS
OLFACTIVE
OLFACTOLOGIES
OLFACTOLOGIST
OLFACTOLOGISTS
OLFACTOLOGY
OLFACTOMETER
OLFACTOMETERS
OLFACTOMETRIES

OLFACTOMETRY
OLFACTORIES
OLFACTORY
OLFACTRONICS
OLFACTS
OLIBANUM
OLIBANUMS
OLID
OLIGAEMIA
OLIGAEMIAS
OLIGAEMIC
OLIGARCH
OLIGARCHAL
OLIGARCHIC
OLIGARCHICAL
OLIGARCHICALLY
OLIGARCHIES
OLIGARCHS
OLIGARCHY
OLIGEMIA
OLIGEMIC
OLIGIST
OLIGISTS
OLIGOCHAETE
OLIGOCHAETES
OLIGOCHROME
OLIGOCHROMES
OLIGOCLASE
OLIGOCLASES
OLIGOCYTHAEMIA
OLIGOCYTHAEMIAS
OLIGODENDROCYTE
OLIGODENDROGLIA
OLIGOMER
OLIGOMERIC
OLIGOMERIZATION
OLIGOMEROUS
OLIGOMERS
OLIGONUCLEOTIDE
OLIGOPEPTIDE
OLIGOPEPTIDES
OLIGOPHAGIES
OLIGOPHAGOUS
OLIGOPHAGY
OLIGOPOLIES
OLIGOPOLISTIC
OLIGOPOLY
OLIGOPSONIES
OLIGOPSONISTIC
OLIGOPSONY
OLIGOSACCHARIDE
OLIGOSPERMIA
OLIGOTROPHIC
OLIGOTROPHIES
OLIGOTROPHY
OLIGURESIS

OLIGURETIC
OLIGURIA
OLIGURIAS
OLIO
OLIOS
OLIPHANT
OLIPHANTS
OLITORIES
OLITORY
OLIVACEOUS
OLIVARY
OLIVE
OLIVENITE
OLIVENITES
OLIVER
OLIVERS
OLIVES
OLIVET
OLIVETS
OLIVINE
OLIVINES
OLIVINIC
OLIVINITIC
OLLA
OLLAMH
OLLAMHS
OLLAS
OLLAV
OLLAVS
OLLER
OLLIE
OLM
OLMS
OLOGIES
OLOGIST
OLOGISTS
OLOGOAN
OLOGOANED
OLOGOANING
OLOGOANS
OLOGY
OLOLIUQUI
OLOLIUQUIS
OLOROSO
OLOROSOS
OLPAE
OLPE
OLPES
OLYCOOK
OLYCOOKS
OLYKOEK
OLYKOEKS
OLYMPIAD
OLYMPIADS
OLYMPICS
OM

OMADHAUN
OMADHAUNS
OMASA
OMASAL
OMASUM
OMBER
OMBERS
OMBRE
OMBRELLA
OMBRELLAS
OMBRES
OMBROGENOUS
OMBROMETER
OMBROMETERS
OMBROPHIL
OMBROPHILE
OMBROPHILES
OMBROPHILOUS
OMBROPHILS
OMBROPHOBE
OMBROPHOBES
OMBROPHOBOUS
OMBU
OMBUDSMAN
OMBUDSMANSHIP
OMBUDSMANSHIPS
OMBUDSMEN
OMBUS
OMEGA
OMEGAS
OMELET
OMELETS
OMELETTE
OMELETTES
OMEN
OMENED
OMENING
OMENS
OMENTA
OMENTAL
OMENTUM
OMENTUMS
OMER
OMERS
OMERTA
OMERTAS
OMICRON
OMICRONS
OMIGOD
OMIKRON
OMIKRONS
OMINOUS
OMINOUSLY
OMINOUSNESS
OMINOUSNESSES
OMISSIBLE

OMISSION
OMISSIONS
OMISSIVE
OMISSIVENESS
OMISSIVENESSES
OMIT
OMITS
OMITTANCE
OMITTANCES
OMITTED
OMITTER
OMITTERS
OMITTING
OMLAH
OMLAHS
OMMATEA
OMMATEUM
OMMATIDIA
OMMATIDIAL
OMMATIDIUM
OMMATOPHORE
OMMATOPHORES
OMMATOPHOROUS
OMNEITIES
OMNEITY
OMNIANA
OMNIARCH
OMNIARCHS
OMNIBENEVOLENCE
OMNIBENEVOLENT
OMNIBUS
OMNIBUSES
OMNICOMPETENCE
OMNICOMPETENCES
OMNICOMPETENT
OMNIDIRECTIONAL
OMNIETIES
OMNIETY
OMNIFARIOUS
OMNIFARIOUSLY
OMNIFARIOUSNESS
OMNIFEROUS
OMNIFIC
OMNIFICENCE
OMNIFICENT
OMNIFIED
OMNIFIES
OMNIFORM
OMNIFORMITIES
OMNIFORMITY
OMNIFY
OMNIFYING
OMNIGENOUS
OMNIMODE
OMNIPARITIES
OMNIPARITY

OMNIPAROUS
OMNIPATIENT
OMNIPOTENCE
OMNIPOTENCES
OMNIPOTENCIES
OMNIPOTENCY
OMNIPOTENT
OMNIPOTENTLY
OMNIPOTENTS
OMNIPRESENCE
OMNIPRESENCES
OMNIPRESENT
OMNIRANGE
OMNIRANGES
OMNISCIENCE
OMNISCIENCES
OMNISCIENT
OMNISCIENTLY
OMNIUM
OMNIUMS
OMNIVORA
OMNIVORE
OMNIVORES
OMNIVORIES
OMNIVOROUS
OMNIVOROUSLY
OMNIVOROUSNESS
OMNIVORY
OMOHYOID
OMOHYOIDS
OMOPHAGIA
OMOPHAGIAS
OMOPHAGIC
OMOPHAGIES
OMOPHAGOUS
OMOPHAGY
OMOPHORIA
OMOPHORION
OMOPLATE
OMOPLATES
OMOPLATOSCOPIES
OMOPLATOSCOPY
OMPHACITE
OMPHACITES
OMPHALI
OMPHALIC
OMPHALOID
OMPHALOMANCIES
OMPHALOMANCY
OMPHALOS
OMPHALOSKEPSES
OMPHALOSKEPSIS
OMRAH
OMRAHS
OMS
ON

ONAGER
ONAGERS
ONAGRACEOUS
ONAGRI
ONANISM
ONANISMS
ONANIST
ONANISTIC
ONANISTS
ONBEAT
ONBEATS
ONBOARD
ONCE
ONCER
ONCERS
ONCES
ONCHOCERCIASES
ONCHOCERCIASIS
ONCIDIUM
ONCIDIUMS
ONCOGEN
ONCOGENE
ONCOGENES
ONCOGENESES
ONCOGENESIS
ONCOGENETICIST
ONCOGENETICISTS
ONCOGENIC
ONCOGENICITIES
ONCOGENICITY
ONCOGENOUS
ONCOGENS
ONCOLOGIC
ONCOLOGICAL
ONCOLOGIES
ONCOLOGIST
ONCOLOGISTS
ONCOLOGY
ONCOLYSES
ONCOLYSIS
ONCOLYTIC
ONCOLYTICS
ONCOME
ONCOMES
ONCOMETER
ONCOMETERS
ONCOMICE
ONCOMING
ONCOMINGS
ONCOMOUSE
ONCORNAVIRUS
ONCORNAVIRUSES
ONCOST
ONCOSTMAN
ONCOSTMEN
ONCOSTS

ONCOTOMIES
ONCOTOMY
ONCUS
ONDATRA
ONDATRAS
ONDINE
ONDINES
ONDING
ONDINGS
ONDOGRAM
ONDOGRAMS
ONDOGRAPH
ONDOGRAPHS
ONE
ONEFOLD
ONEIRIC
ONEIRICALLY
ONEIROCRITIC
ONEIROCRITICAL
ONEIROCRITICISM
ONEIROCRITICS
ONEIRODYNIA
ONEIRODYNIAS
ONEIROLOGIES
ONEIROLOGY
ONEIROMANCER
ONEIROMANCERS
ONEIROMANCIES
ONEIROMANCY
ONEIROSCOPIES
ONEIROSCOPIST
ONEIROSCOPISTS
ONEIROSCOPY
ONELY
ONENESS
ONENESSES
ONER
ONERIER
ONERIEST
ONEROUS
ONEROUSLY
ONEROUSNESS
ONEROUSNESSES
ONERS
ONERY
ONES
ONESELF
ONETIME
ONEYER
ONEYERS
ONEYRE
ONEYRES
ONFALL
ONFALLS
ONFLOW
ONFLOWS

ONGOING
ONGOINGNESS
ONGOINGNESSES
ONGOINGS
ONIE
ONION
ONIONED
ONIONIER
ONIONIEST
ONIONING
ONIONS
ONIONSKIN
ONIONSKINS
ONIONY
ONIRIC
ONISCOID
ONIUM
ONKUS
ONLIEST
ONLINE
ONLINER
ONLINERS
ONLOOKER
ONLOOKERS
ONLOOKING
ONLY
ONNED
ONNING
ONOCENTAUR
ONOCENTAURS
ONOMASIOLOGY
ONOMASTIC
ONOMASTICALLY
ONOMASTICIAN
ONOMASTICIANS
ONOMASTICON
ONOMASTICONS
ONOMASTICS
ONOMATOLOGIES
ONOMATOLOGIST
ONOMATOLOGISTS
ONOMATOLOGY
ONOMATOPOEIA
ONOMATOPOEIAS
ONOMATOPOEIC
ONOMATOPOESES
ONOMATOPOESIS
ONOMATOPOETIC
ONOMATOPOIESES
ONOMATOPOIESIS
ONRUSH
ONRUSHES
ONRUSHING
ONS
ONSET
ONSETS

ONSETTER
ONSETTERS
ONSETTING
ONSETTINGS
ONSHORE
ONSIDE
ONSIDES
ONSLAUGHT
ONSLAUGHTS
ONST
ONSTAGE
ONSTEAD
ONSTEADS
ONSTREAM
ONTIC
ONTICALLY
ONTO
ONTOGENESES
ONTOGENESIS
ONTOGENETIC
ONTOGENETICALLY
ONTOGENIC
ONTOGENICALLY
ONTOGENIES
ONTOGENY
ONTOLOGIC
ONTOLOGICAL
ONTOLOGICALLY
ONTOLOGIES
ONTOLOGIST
ONTOLOGISTS
ONTOLOGY
ONUS
ONUSES
ONWARD
ONWARDLY
ONWARDS
ONY
ONYCHA
ONYCHAS
ONYCHIA
ONYCHIAS
ONYCHITE
ONYCHITES
ONYCHITIS
ONYCHITISES
ONYCHIUM
ONYCHIUMS
ONYCHOCRYPTOSES
ONYCHOCRYPTOSIS
ONYCHOMANCIES
ONYCHOMANCY
ONYCHOPHAGIES
ONYCHOPHAGIST
ONYCHOPHAGISTS
ONYCHOPHAGY

ONYCHOPHORAN
ONYCHOPHORANS
ONYMOUS
ONYX
ONYXES
OO
OOBIT
OOBITS
OOCYST
OOCYSTS
OOCYTE
OOCYTES
OODLES
OODLINS
OOF
OOFS
OOFTISH
OOFTISHES
OOFY
OOGAMETE
OOGAMETES
OOGAMIES
OOGAMOUS
OOGAMY
OOGENESES
OOGENESIS
OOGENETIC
OOGENIES
OOGENY
OOGONIA
OOGONIAL
OOGONIUM
OOGONIUMS
OOH
OOHED
OOHING
OOHS
OOIDAL
OOLACHAN
OOLACHANS
OOLAKAN
OOLAKANS
OOLITE
OOLITES
OOLITH
OOLITHS
OOLITIC
OOLOGIC
OOLOGICAL
OOLOGIES
OOLOGIST
OOLOGISTS
OOLOGY
OOLONG
OOLONGS
OOM

OOMIAC
OOMIACK
OOMIACKS
OOMIACS
OOMIAK
OOMIAKS
OOMPAH
OOMPAHED
OOMPAHING
OOMPAHS
OOMPH
OOMPHS
OOMS
OOMYCETE
OON
OONS
OONT
OONTS
OOP
OOPED
OOPHORECTOMIES
OOPHORECTOMISE
OOPHORECTOMISED
OOPHORECTOMISES
OOPHORECTOMIZE
OOPHORECTOMIZED
OOPHORECTOMIZES
OOPHORECTOMY
OOPHORITIC
OOPHORITIS
OOPHORITISES
OOPHORON
OOPHORONS
OOPHYTE
OOPHYTES
OOPHYTIC
OOPING
OOPS
OOR
OORALI
OORALIS
OORIAL
OORIALS
OORIE
OORIER
OORIEST
OOS
OOSE
OOSES
OOSIER
OOSIEST
OOSPERM
OOSPERMS
OOSPHERE
OOSPHERES
OOSPORE

OOSPORES
OOSPORIC
OOSPOROUS
OOSY
OOT
OOTHECA
OOTHECAE
OOTHECAL
OOTID
OOTIDS
OOTS
OOZE
OOZED
OOZES
OOZIER
OOZIEST
OOZILY
OOZINESS
OOZINESSES
OOZING
OOZY
OP
OPACIFIED
OPACIFIES
OPACIFY
OPACIFYING
OPACITIES
OPACITY
OPACOUS
OPAH
OPAHS
OPAL
OPALED
OPALESCE
OPALESCED
OPALESCENCE
OPALESCENCES
OPALESCENT
OPALESCENTLY
OPALESCES
OPALESCING
OPALINE
OPALINES
OPALISED
OPALIZED
OPALS
OPAQUE
OPAQUED
OPAQUELY
OPAQUENESS
OPAQUENESSES
OPAQUER
OPAQUES
OPAQUEST
OPAQUING
OPCODE

OPCODES
OPE
OPED
OPEIDOSCOPE
OPEIDOSCOPES
OPEN
OPENABILITIES
OPENABILITY
OPENABLE
OPENCAST
OPENED
OPENER
OPENERS
OPENEST
OPENHANDED
OPENHANDEDLY
OPENHANDEDNESS
OPENHEARTED
OPENHEARTEDLY
OPENHEARTEDNESS
OPENING
OPENINGS
OPENLY
OPENMOUTHED
OPENMOUTHEDLY
OPENMOUTHEDNESS
OPENNESS
OPENNESSES
OPENS
OPENWORK
OPENWORKS
OPEPE
OPEPES
OPERA
OPERABILITIES
OPERABILITY
OPERABLE
OPERABLY
OPERAGOER
OPERAGOERS
OPERAGOING
OPERAGOINGS
OPERAND
OPERANDS
OPERANT
OPERANTLY
OPERANTS
OPERAS
OPERATE
OPERATED
OPERATES
OPERATIC
OPERATICALLY
OPERATICS
OPERATING
OPERATION

OPERATIONAL
OPERATIONALISM
OPERATIONALISMS
OPERATIONALIST
OPERATIONALISTS
OPERATIONALLY
OPERATIONISM
OPERATIONISMS
OPERATIONIST
OPERATIONISTS
OPERATIONS
OPERATISE
OPERATISED
OPERATISES
OPERATISING
OPERATIVE
OPERATIVELY
OPERATIVENESS
OPERATIVENESSES
OPERATIVES
OPERATIVITY
OPERATIZE
OPERATIZED
OPERATIZES
OPERATIZING
OPERATOR
OPERATORLESS
OPERATORS
OPERCELE
OPERCELES
OPERCULA
OPERCULAR
OPERCULARS
OPERCULATE
OPERCULATED
OPERCULE
OPERCULES
OPERCULUM
OPERCULUMS
OPERETTA
OPERETTAS
OPERETTIST
OPERETTISTS
OPERON
OPERONS
OPEROSE
OPEROSELY
OPEROSENESS
OPEROSENESSES
OPEROSITIES
OPEROSITY
OPES
OPHICALCITE
OPHICALCITES
OPHICLEIDE
OPHICLEIDES

OPHIDIAN
OPHIDIANS
OPHIDIARIUM
OPHIDIARIUMS
OPHIOLATER
OPHIOLATERS
OPHIOLATRIES
OPHIOLATROUS
OPHIOLATRY
OPHIOLITE
OPHIOLITES
OPHIOLITIC
OPHIOLOGIC
OPHIOLOGICAL
OPHIOLOGIES
OPHIOLOGIST
OPHIOLOGISTS
OPHIOLOGY
OPHIOMORPH
OPHIOMORPHIC
OPHIOMORPHOUS
OPHIOMORPHS
OPHIOPHAGOUS
OPHIOPHILIST
OPHIOPHILISTS
OPHITE
OPHITES
OPHITIC
OPHIURA
OPHIURAN
OPHIURANS
OPHIURAS
OPHIURID
OPHIURIDS
OPHIUROID
OPHIUROIDS
OPHTHALMIA
OPHTHALMIAS
OPHTHALMIC
OPHTHALMIST
OPHTHALMISTS
OPHTHALMITIS
OPHTHALMITISES
OPHTHALMOLOGIC
OPHTHALMOLOGIES
OPHTHALMOLOGIST
OPHTHALMOLOGY
OPHTHALMOMETER
OPHTHALMOMETERS
OPHTHALMOMETRY
OPHTHALMOPHOBIA
OPHTHALMOPLEGIA
OPHTHALMOSCOPE
OPHTHALMOSCOPES
OPHTHALMOSCOPIC
OPHTHALMOSCOPY

OPIATE
OPIATED
OPIATES
OPIATING
OPIFICER
OPIFICERS
OPINABLE
OPINE
OPINED
OPINES
OPING
OPINICUS
OPINICUSES
OPINING
OPINION
OPINIONATED
OPINIONATEDLY
OPINIONATEDNESS
OPINIONATELY
OPINIONATIVE
OPINIONATIVELY
OPINIONATOR
OPINIONATORS
OPINIONED
OPINIONIST
OPINIONISTS
OPINIONS
OPIOID
OPIOIDS
OPISOMETER
OPISOMETERS
OPISTHOBRANCH
OPISTHOBRANCHS
OPISTHOCOELIAN
OPISTHOCOELOUS
OPISTHODOMOS
OPISTHOGLOSSAL
OPISTHOGNATHISM
OPISTHOGNATHOUS
OPISTHOGRAPH
OPISTHOGRAPHIC
OPISTHOGRAPHIES
OPISTHOGRAPHS
OPISTHOGRAPHY
OPISTHOSOMA
OPISTHOSOMAS
OPISTHOTONIC
OPISTHOTONOS
OPISTHOTONOSES
OPIUM
OPIUMISM
OPIUMISMS
OPIUMS
OPOBALSAM
OPOBALSAMS
OPODELDOC

OPODELDOCS
OPOPANAX
OPOPANAXES
OPORICE
OPORICES
OPOSSUM
OPOSSUMS
OPOTHERAPIES
OPOTHERAPY
OPPIDAN
OPPIDANS
OPPIGNERATE
OPPIGNERATED
OPPIGNERATES
OPPIGNERATING
OPPIGNORATE
OPPIGNORATED
OPPIGNORATES
OPPIGNORATING
OPPIGNORATION
OPPIGNORATIONS
OPPILANT
OPPILATE
OPPILATED
OPPILATES
OPPILATING
OPPILATION
OPPILATIONS
OPPILATIVE
OPPO
OPPONENCIES
OPPONENCY
OPPONENT
OPPONENTS
OPPORTUNE
OPPORTUNELY
OPPORTUNENESS
OPPORTUNENESSES
OPPORTUNISM
OPPORTUNISMS
OPPORTUNIST
OPPORTUNISTIC
OPPORTUNISTS
OPPORTUNITIES
OPPORTUNITY
OPPOS
OPPOSABILITIES
OPPOSABILITY
OPPOSABLE
OPPOSABLY
OPPOSE
OPPOSED
OPPOSELESS
OPPOSER
OPPOSERS
OPPOSES

OPPOSING
OPPOSINGLY
OPPOSITE
OPPOSITELY
OPPOSITENESS
OPPOSITENESSES
OPPOSITES
OPPOSITION
OPPOSITIONAL
OPPOSITIONIST
OPPOSITIONISTS
OPPOSITIONLESS
OPPOSITIONS
OPPOSITIVE
OPPRESS
OPPRESSED
OPPRESSES
OPPRESSING
OPPRESSINGLY
OPPRESSION
OPPRESSIONS
OPPRESSIVE
OPPRESSIVELY
OPPRESSIVENESS
OPPRESSOR
OPPRESSORS
OPPROBRIOUS
OPPROBRIOUSLY
OPPROBRIOUSNESS
OPPROBRIUM
OPPROBRIUMS
OPPUGN
OPPUGNANCIES
OPPUGNANCY
OPPUGNANT
OPPUGNANTLY
OPPUGNANTS
OPPUGNED
OPPUGNER
OPPUGNERS
OPPUGNING
OPPUGNS
OPS
OPSIMATH
OPSIMATHIES
OPSIMATHS
OPSIMATHY
OPSIN
OPSINS
OPSIOMETER
OPSIOMETERS
OPSITBANK
OPSITBANKS
OPSOMANIA
OPSOMANIAC
OPSOMANIACS

OPSOMANIAS
OPSONIC
OPSONIFICATION
OPSONIFICATIONS
OPSONIFIED
OPSONIFIES
OPSONIFY
OPSONIFYING
OPSONIN
OPSONINS
OPSONISATION
OPSONISATIONS
OPSONISE
OPSONISED
OPSONISES
OPSONISING
OPSONIUM
OPSONIUMS
OPSONIZATION
OPSONIZATIONS
OPSONIZE
OPSONIZED
OPSONIZES
OPSONIZING
OPT
OPTANT
OPTANTS
OPTATIVE
OPTATIVELY
OPTATIVES
OPTED
OPTER
OPTERS
OPTIC
OPTICAL
OPTICALLY
OPTICIAN
OPTICIANS
OPTICIST
OPTICISTS
OPTICS
OPTIMA
OPTIMAL
OPTIMALISATION
OPTIMALISATIONS
OPTIMALISE
OPTIMALISED
OPTIMALISES
OPTIMALISING
OPTIMALITIES
OPTIMALITY
OPTIMALIZATION
OPTIMALIZATIONS
OPTIMALIZE
OPTIMALIZED
OPTIMALIZES

OPTIMALIZING	OPTOMETRY	ORALLY	ORBICULARES
OPTIMALLY	OPTOPHONE	ORALS	ORBICULARIS
OPTIMATE	OPTOPHONES	ORANG	ORBICULARITY
OPTIMATES	OPTRONICS	ORANGE	ORBICULARLY
OPTIME	OPTS	ORANGEADE	ORBICULATE
OPTIMES	OPULENCE	ORANGEADES	ORBICULATED
OPTIMISATION	OPULENCES	ORANGER	ORBIER
OPTIMISATIONS	OPULENCIES	ORANGERIE	ORBIEST
OPTIMISE	OPULENCY	ORANGERIES	ORBING
OPTIMISED	OPULENT	ORANGERY	ORBIT
OPTIMISES	OPULENTLY	ORANGES	ORBITA
OPTIMISING	OPULUS	ORANGEST	ORBITAL
OPTIMISM	OPULUSES	ORANGEWOOD	ORBITALLY
OPTIMISMS	OPUNTIA	ORANGEWOODS	ORBITALS
OPTIMIST	OPUNTIAS	ORANGEY	ORBITAS
OPTIMISTIC	OPUS	ORANGIER	ORBITED
OPTIMISTICAL	OPUSCLE	ORANGIEST	ORBITER
OPTIMISTICALLY	OPUSCLES	ORANGISH	ORBITERS
OPTIMISTS	OPUSCULA	ORANGS	ORBITIES
OPTIMIZATION	OPUSCULAR	ORANGUTAN	ORBITING
OPTIMIZATIONS	OPUSCULE	ORANGUTANS	ORBITS
OPTIMIZE	OPUSCULES	ORANGY	ORBITY
OPTIMIZED	OPUSCULUM	ORANT	ORBS
OPTIMIZER	OPUSES	ORANTS	ORBY
OPTIMIZERS	OQUASSA	ORARIA	ORC
OPTIMIZES	OQUASSAS	ORARIAN	ORCA
OPTIMIZING	OR	ORARIANS	ORCAS
OPTIMUM	ORA	ORARION	ORCEIN
OPTIMUMS	ORACH	ORARIONS	ORCEINS
OPTING	ORACHE	ORARIUM	ORCHARD
OPTION	ORACHES	ORARIUMS	ORCHARDING
OPTIONAL	ORACIES	ORATE	ORCHARDINGS
OPTIONALITIES	ORACLE	ORATED	ORCHARDIST
OPTIONALITY	ORACLED	ORATES	ORCHARDISTS
OPTIONALLY	ORACLES	ORATING	ORCHARDMAN
OPTIONALS	ORACLING	ORATION	ORCHARDMEN
OPTIONED	ORACULAR	ORATIONS	ORCHARDS
OPTIONEE	ORACULARITIES	ORATOR	ORCHAT
OPTIONEES	ORACULARITY	ORATORIAL	ORCHATS
OPTIONING	ORACULARLY	ORATORIAN	ORCHEL
OPTIONS	ORACULARNESS	ORATORIANS	ORCHELLA
OPTOACOUSTIC	ORACULARNESSES	ORATORICAL	ORCHELLAS
OPTOELECTRONIC	ORACULOUS	ORATORICALLY	ORCHELS
OPTOELECTRONICS	ORACULOUSLY	ORATORIES	ORCHESES
OPTOKINETIC	ORACULOUSNESS	ORATORIO	ORCHESIS
OPTOLOGIES	ORACULOUSNESSES	ORATORIOS	ORCHESOGRAPHIES
OPTOLOGIST	ORACY	ORATORS	ORCHESOGRAPHY
OPTOLOGISTS	ORAD	ORATORY	ORCHESTIC
OPTOLOGY	ORAGIOUS	ORATRESS	ORCHESTICS
OPTOMETER	ORAL	ORATRESSES	ORCHESTRA
OPTOMETERS	ORALISM	ORATRICES	ORCHESTRAL
OPTOMETRIC	ORALISMS	ORATRIX	ORCHESTRALIST
OPTOMETRICAL	ORALIST	ORATRIXES	ORCHESTRALISTS
OPTOMETRIES	ORALISTS	ORB	ORCHESTRALLY
OPTOMETRIST	ORALITIES	ORBED	ORCHESTRAS
OPTOMETRISTS	ORALITY	ORBICULAR	ORCHESTRATE

ORCHESTRATED
ORCHESTRATER
ORCHESTRATERS
ORCHESTRATES
ORCHESTRATING
ORCHESTRATION
ORCHESTRATIONAL
ORCHESTRATIONS
ORCHESTRATOR
ORCHESTRATORS
ORCHESTRIC
ORCHESTRINA
ORCHESTRINAS
ORCHESTRION
ORCHESTRIONS
ORCHID
ORCHIDACEOUS
ORCHIDECTOMIES
ORCHIDECTOMY
ORCHIDEOUS
ORCHIDIST
ORCHIDISTS
ORCHIDLIKE
ORCHIDOLOGIES
ORCHIDOLOGIST
ORCHIDOLOGISTS
ORCHIDOLOGY
ORCHIDOMANIA
ORCHIDOMANIAC
ORCHIDOMANIACS
ORCHIDOMANIAS
ORCHIDS
ORCHIECTOMIES
ORCHIECTOMY
ORCHIL
ORCHILLA
ORCHILLAS
ORCHILS
ORCHIS
ORCHISES
ORCHITIC
ORCHITIS
ORCHITISES
ORCIN
ORCINE
ORCINES
ORCINOL
ORCINOLS
ORCINS
ORCS
ORD
ORDAIN
ORDAINABLE
ORDAINED
ORDAINER
ORDAINERS

ORDAINING
ORDAINMENT
ORDAINMENTS
ORDAINS
ORDALIAN
ORDALIUM
ORDALIUMS
ORDEAL
ORDEALS
ORDER
ORDERABLE
ORDERED
ORDERER
ORDERERS
ORDERING
ORDERINGS
ORDERLESS
ORDERLIES
ORDERLINESS
ORDERLINESSES
ORDERLY
ORDERS
ORDINAIRE
ORDINAIRES
ORDINAL
ORDINALS
ORDINANCE
ORDINANCES
ORDINAND
ORDINANDS
ORDINANT
ORDINANTS
ORDINAR
ORDINARIER
ORDINARIES
ORDINARIEST
ORDINARILY
ORDINARINESS
ORDINARINESSES
ORDINARS
ORDINARY
ORDINATE
ORDINATED
ORDINATELY
ORDINATES
ORDINATING
ORDINATION
ORDINATIONS
ORDINEE
ORDINEES
ORDINES
ORDNANCE
ORDNANCES
ORDO
ORDONNANCE
ORDONNANCES

ORDOS
ORDS
ORDURE
ORDURES
ORDUROUS
ORE
OREAD
OREADES
OREADS
ORECROWED
ORECROWES
ORECROWING
ORECTIC
ORECTIVE
OREGANO
OREGANOS
OREIDE
OREIDES
OREOGRAPHIC
OREOGRAPHICAL
OREOGRAPHIES
OREOGRAPHY
OREOLOGIES
OREOLOGIST
OREOLOGISTS
OREOLOGY
OREPEARCH
OREPEARCHED
OREPEARCHES
OREPEARCHING
ORES
ORESTUNCK
OREWEED
OREWEEDS
OREXIS
OREXISES
ORF
ORFE
ORFES
ORFRAY
ORFRAYS
ORFS
ORGAN
ORGANA
ORGANDIE
ORGANDIES
ORGANDY
ORGANELLE
ORGANELLES
ORGANIC
ORGANICAL
ORGANICALLY
ORGANICISM
ORGANICISMS
ORGANICIST
ORGANICISTIC

ORGANICISTS
ORGANICITIES
ORGANICITY
ORGANICS
ORGANISABILITY
ORGANISABLE
ORGANISATION
ORGANISATIONAL
ORGANISATIONS
ORGANISE
ORGANISED
ORGANISER
ORGANISERS
ORGANISES
ORGANISING
ORGANISM
ORGANISMAL
ORGANISMALLY
ORGANISMIC
ORGANISMICALLY
ORGANISMS
ORGANIST
ORGANISTRUM
ORGANISTRUMS
ORGANISTS
ORGANITIES
ORGANITY
ORGANIZABILITY
ORGANIZABLE
ORGANIZATION
ORGANIZATIONAL
ORGANIZATIONS
ORGANIZE
ORGANIZED
ORGANIZER
ORGANIZERS
ORGANIZES
ORGANIZING
ORGANOCHLORINE
ORGANOCHLORINES
ORGANOGENESES
ORGANOGENESIS
ORGANOGENETIC
ORGANOGENIES
ORGANOGENY
ORGANOGRAM
ORGANOGRAMS
ORGANOGRAPHIC
ORGANOGRAPHICAL
ORGANOGRAPHIES
ORGANOGRAPHIST
ORGANOGRAPHISTS
ORGANOGRAPHY
ORGANOLEPTIC
ORGANOLOGICAL
ORGANOLOGIES

ORGANOLOGIST
ORGANOLOGISTS
ORGANOLOGY
ORGANOMERCURIAL
ORGANOMETALLIC
ORGANOMETALLICS
ORGANON
ORGANONS
ORGANOPHOSPHATE
ORGANOTHERAPIES
ORGANOTHERAPY
ORGANOTIN
ORGANS
ORGANUM
ORGANUMS
ORGANZA
ORGANZAS
ORGANZINE
ORGANZINES
ORGASM
ORGASMED
ORGASMIC
ORGASMING
ORGASMS
ORGASTIC
ORGEAT
ORGEATS
ORGIA
ORGIAC
ORGIAS
ORGIAST
ORGIASTIC
ORGIASTICALLY
ORGIASTS
ORGIC
ORGIES
ORGILLOUS
ORGONE
ORGONES
ORGUE
ORGUES
ORGULOUS
ORGY
ORIBATID
ORIBATIDS
ORIBI
ORIBIS
ORICALCHE
ORICALCHES
ORICHALC
ORICHALCEOUS
ORICHALCS
ORIEL
ORIELLED
ORIELS
ORIENCIES

ORIENCY
ORIENT
ORIENTAL
ORIENTALISE
ORIENTALISED
ORIENTALISES
ORIENTALISING
ORIENTALISM
ORIENTALISMS
ORIENTALIST
ORIENTALISTS
ORIENTALITIES
ORIENTALITY
ORIENTALIZE
ORIENTALIZED
ORIENTALIZES
ORIENTALIZING
ORIENTALLY
ORIENTALS
ORIENTATE
ORIENTATED
ORIENTATES
ORIENTATING
ORIENTATION
ORIENTATIONAL
ORIENTATIONALLY
ORIENTATIONS
ORIENTATOR
ORIENTATORS
ORIENTED
ORIENTEER
ORIENTEERED
ORIENTEERING
ORIENTEERINGS
ORIENTEERS
ORIENTING
ORIENTS
ORIFEX
ORIFEXES
ORIFICE
ORIFICES
ORIFICIAL
ORIFLAMME
ORIFLAMMES
ORIGAMI
ORIGAMIS
ORIGAN
ORIGANE
ORIGANES
ORIGANS
ORIGANUM
ORIGANUMS
ORIGIN
ORIGINAL
ORIGINALITIES
ORIGINALITY

ORIGINALLY
ORIGINALS
ORIGINATE
ORIGINATED
ORIGINATES
ORIGINATING
ORIGINATION
ORIGINATIONS
ORIGINATIVE
ORIGINATIVELY
ORIGINATOR
ORIGINATORS
ORIGINS
ORILLION
ORILLIONS
ORINASAL
ORINASALLY
ORINASALS
ORIOLE
ORIOLES
ORISHA
ORISHAS
ORISMOLOGICAL
ORISMOLOGIES
ORISMOLOGY
ORISON
ORISONS
ORIXA
ORIXAS
ORLE
ORLEANS
ORLEANSES
ORLES
ORLOP
ORLOPS
ORMER
ORMERS
ORMOLU
ORMOLUS
ORNAMENT
ORNAMENTAL
ORNAMENTALLY
ORNAMENTALS
ORNAMENTATION
ORNAMENTATIONS
ORNAMENTED
ORNAMENTER
ORNAMENTERS
ORNAMENTING
ORNAMENTIST
ORNAMENTISTS
ORNAMENTS
ORNATE
ORNATELY
ORNATENESS
ORNATENESSES

ORNATER
ORNATEST
ORNERIER
ORNERIEST
ORNERINESS
ORNERINESSES
ORNERY
ORNIS
ORNISES
ORNITHES
ORNITHIC
ORNITHICHNITE
ORNITHICHNITES
ORNITHINE
ORNITHINES
ORNITHISCHIAN
ORNITHISCHIANS
ORNITHODELPHIAN
ORNITHODELPHIC
ORNITHODELPHOUS
ORNITHOGALUM
ORNITHOGALUMS
ORNITHOID
ORNITHOLOGIC
ORNITHOLOGICAL
ORNITHOLOGIES
ORNITHOLOGIST
ORNITHOLOGISTS
ORNITHOLOGY
ORNITHOMANCIES
ORNITHOMANCY
ORNITHOMANTIC
ORNITHOMORPH
ORNITHOMORPHIC
ORNITHOMORPHS
ORNITHOPHILIES
ORNITHOPHILOUS
ORNITHOPHILY
ORNITHOPHOBIA
ORNITHOPHOBIAS
ORNITHOPOD
ORNITHOPODS
ORNITHOPTER
ORNITHOPTERS
ORNITHORHYNCHUS
ORNITHOSAUR
ORNITHOSAURS
ORNITHOSCOPIES
ORNITHOSCOPY
ORNITHOSES
ORNITHOSIS
OROBANCHACEOUS
OROGEN
OROGENESES
OROGENESIS
OROGENETIC

OROGENETICALLY
OROGENIC
OROGENICALLY
OROGENIES
OROGENS
OROGENY
OROGRAPHER
OROGRAPHERS
OROGRAPHIC
OROGRAPHICAL
OROGRAPHICALLY
OROGRAPHIES
OROGRAPHY
OROIDE
OROIDES
OROLOGICAL
OROLOGICALLY
OROLOGIES
OROLOGIST
OROLOGISTS
OROLOGY
OROMETER
OROMETERS
ORONASAL
OROPESA
OROPESAS
OROPHARYNGEAL
OROPHARYNGES
OROPHARYNX
OROPHARYNXES
OROROTUNDITIES
OROROTUNDITY
OROTUND
OROTUNDITIES
OROTUNDITY
ORPHAN
ORPHANAGE
ORPHANAGES
ORPHANED
ORPHANHOOD
ORPHANHOODS
ORPHANING
ORPHANISM
ORPHANISMS
ORPHANS
ORPHARION
ORPHARIONS
ORPHEOREON
ORPHEOREONS
ORPHIC
ORPHICAL
ORPHICALLY
ORPHREY
ORPHREYS
ORPIMENT
ORPIMENTS

ORPIN
ORPINE
ORPINES
ORPINS
ORRA
ORRAMAN
ORRAMEN
ORRERIES
ORRERY
ORRICE
ORRICES
ORRIS
ORRISES
ORRISROOT
ORRISROOTS
ORS
ORSEILLE
ORSEILLES
ORSELLIC
ORT
ORTANIQUE
ORTANIQUES
ORTHIAN
ORTHICON
ORTHICONS
ORTHO
ORTHOAXES
ORTHOAXIS
ORTHOBORATE
ORTHOBORATES
ORTHOBORIC
ORTHOCAINE
ORTHOCAINES
ORTHOCENTER
ORTHOCENTERS
ORTHOCENTRE
ORTHOCENTRES
ORTHOCEPHALIC
ORTHOCEPHALOUS
ORTHOCEPHALY
ORTHOCHROMATIC
ORTHOCHROMATISM
ORTHOCLASE
ORTHOCLASES
ORTHOCOUSINS
ORTHODIAGONAL
ORTHODIAGONALS
ORTHODONTIA
ORTHODONTIAS
ORTHODONTIC
ORTHODONTICALLY
ORTHODONTICS
ORTHODONTIST
ORTHODONTISTS
ORTHODOX
ORTHODOXES

ORTHODOXIES
ORTHODOXLY
ORTHODOXY
ORTHODROMIC
ORTHODROMICS
ORTHODROMIES
ORTHODROMY
ORTHOEPIC
ORTHOEPICAL
ORTHOEPICALLY
ORTHOEPIES
ORTHOEPIST
ORTHOEPISTS
ORTHOEPY
ORTHOGENESES
ORTHOGENESIS
ORTHOGENETIC
ORTHOGENIC
ORTHOGENICALLY
ORTHOGENICS
ORTHOGNATHIC
ORTHOGNATHISM
ORTHOGNATHISMS
ORTHOGNATHOUS
ORTHOGNATHY
ORTHOGONAL
ORTHOGONALITIES
ORTHOGONALITY
ORTHOGONALIZE
ORTHOGONALIZED
ORTHOGONALIZES
ORTHOGONALIZING
ORTHOGONALLY
ORTHOGRADE
ORTHOGRAPH
ORTHOGRAPHER
ORTHOGRAPHERS
ORTHOGRAPHIC
ORTHOGRAPHICAL
ORTHOGRAPHIES
ORTHOGRAPHIST
ORTHOGRAPHISTS
ORTHOGRAPHS
ORTHOGRAPHY
ORTHOHYDROGEN
ORTHOMOLECULAR
ORTHOMORPHIC
ORTHOMORPHISM
ORTHONORMAL
ORTHOPAEDIC
ORTHOPAEDICAL
ORTHOPAEDICS
ORTHOPAEDIES
ORTHOPAEDIST
ORTHOPAEDISTS
ORTHOPAEDY

ORTHOPEDIA
ORTHOPEDIAS
ORTHOPEDIC
ORTHOPEDICAL
ORTHOPEDICALLY
ORTHOPEDICS
ORTHOPEDIES
ORTHOPEDIST
ORTHOPEDISTS
ORTHOPEDY
ORTHOPHOSPHATE
ORTHOPHOSPHATES
ORTHOPHOSPHORIC
ORTHOPHYRE
ORTHOPHYRES
ORTHOPHYRIC
ORTHOPINAKOID
ORTHOPINAKOIDS
ORTHOPNOEA
ORTHOPNOEAS
ORTHOPOD
ORTHOPODS
ORTHOPRAXES
ORTHOPRAXIES
ORTHOPRAXIS
ORTHOPRAXY
ORTHOPRISM
ORTHOPRISMS
ORTHOPSYCHIATRY
ORTHOPTER
ORTHOPTERA
ORTHOPTERAN
ORTHOPTERANS
ORTHOPTERIST
ORTHOPTERISTS
ORTHOPTEROID
ORTHOPTEROIDS
ORTHOPTEROLOGY
ORTHOPTERON
ORTHOPTEROUS
ORTHOPTERS
ORTHOPTIC
ORTHOPTICS
ORTHOPTIST
ORTHOPTISTS
ORTHOPYROXENE
ORTHOPYROXENES
ORTHORHOMBIC
ORTHOS
ORTHOSCOPE
ORTHOSCOPES
ORTHOSCOPIC
ORTHOSES
ORTHOSILICATE
ORTHOSILICATES
ORTHOSIS

ORTHOSTATIC
ORTHOSTICHIES
ORTHOSTICHOUS
ORTHOSTICHY
ORTHOTIC
ORTHOTICS
ORTHOTIST
ORTHOTISTS
ORTHOTONE
ORTHOTONES
ORTHOTONESES
ORTHOTONESIS
ORTHOTONIC
ORTHOTOPIC
ORTHOTROPIC
ORTHOTROPIES
ORTHOTROPISM
ORTHOTROPISMS
ORTHOTROPOUS
ORTHOTROPY
ORTHROS
ORTHROSES
ORTOLAN
ORTOLANS
ORTS
ORVAL
ORVALS
ORYCTOLOGIES
ORYCTOLOGY
ORYX
ORYXES
ORZO
ORZOS
OS
OSAR
OSCAR
OSCARS
OSCHEAL
OSCILLATE
OSCILLATED
OSCILLATES
OSCILLATING
OSCILLATION
OSCILLATIONAL
OSCILLATIONS
OSCILLATIVE
OSCILLATOR
OSCILLATORS
OSCILLATORY
OSCILLOGRAM
OSCILLOGRAMS
OSCILLOGRAPH
OSCILLOGRAPHIC
OSCILLOGRAPHIES
OSCILLOGRAPHS
OSCILLOGRAPHY

OSCILLOSCOPE
OSCILLOSCOPES
OSCILLOSCOPIC
OSCINE
OSCINES
OSCININE
OSCITANCE
OSCITANCES
OSCITANCIES
OSCITANCY
OSCITANT
OSCITANTLY
OSCITATE
OSCITATED
OSCITATES
OSCITATING
OSCITATION
OSCITATIONS
OSCULA
OSCULANT
OSCULAR
OSCULATE
OSCULATED
OSCULATES
OSCULATING
OSCULATION
OSCULATIONS
OSCULATORIES
OSCULATORY
OSCULE
OSCULES
OSCULUM
OSE
OSES
OSHAC
OSHACS
OSIER
OSIERED
OSIERIES
OSIERS
OSIERY
OSMATE
OSMATES
OSMATIC
OSMETERIA
OSMETERIUM
OSMIATE
OSMIATES
OSMIC
OSMICS
OSMIDROSES
OSMIDROSIS
OSMIOUS
OSMIRIDIUM
OSMIRIDIUMS
OSMIUM

OSMIUMS
OSMOL
OSMOLAL
OSMOLALITIES
OSMOLALITY
OSMOLAR
OSMOLARITIES
OSMOLARITY
OSMOLE
OSMOLES
OSMOLS
OSMOMETER
OSMOMETERS
OSMOMETRIC
OSMOMETRICALLY
OSMOMETRIES
OSMOMETRY
OSMOREGULATION
OSMOREGULATIONS
OSMOREGULATORY
OSMOSE
OSMOSED
OSMOSES
OSMOSING
OSMOSIS
OSMOTIC
OSMOTICALLY
OSMOUS
OSMUND
OSMUNDA
OSMUNDAS
OSMUNDS
OSNABURG
OSNABURGS
OSPREY
OSPREYS
OSSA
OSSARIUM
OSSARIUMS
OSSEIN
OSSEINS
OSSELET
OSSELETS
OSSEOUS
OSSEOUSLY
OSSETER
OSSETERS
OSSIA
OSSICLE
OSSICLES
OSSICULAR
OSSIFEROUS
OSSIFIC
OSSIFICATION
OSSIFICATIONS
OSSIFIED

OSSIFIER
OSSIFIERS
OSSIFIES
OSSIFRAGA
OSSIFRAGAS
OSSIFRAGE
OSSIFRAGES
OSSIFY
OSSIFYING
OSSIVOROUS
OSSUARIES
OSSUARY
OSTEAL
OSTEICHTHYAN
OSTEICHTHYANS
OSTEITIC
OSTEITIDES
OSTEITIS
OSTEITISES
OSTENSIBILITIES
OSTENSIBILITY
OSTENSIBLE
OSTENSIBLY
OSTENSIVE
OSTENSIVELY
OSTENSORIA
OSTENSORIES
OSTENSORIUM
OSTENSORY
OSTENT
OSTENTATION
OSTENTATIONS
OSTENTATIOUS
OSTENTATIOUSLY
OSTENTS
OSTEOARTHRITIC
OSTEOARTHRITICS
OSTEOARTHRITIS
OSTEOARTHROSES
OSTEOARTHROSIS
OSTEOBLAST
OSTEOBLASTIC
OSTEOBLASTS
OSTEOCLASES
OSTEOCLASIS
OSTEOCLAST
OSTEOCLASTIC
OSTEOCLASTS
OSTEOCOLLA
OSTEOCOLLAS
OSTEOCYTE
OSTEOCYTES
OSTEODERM
OSTEODERMAL
OSTEODERMATOUS
OSTEODERMIC

695

OSTEODERMS
OSTEOFIBROSIS
OSTEOGEN
OSTEOGENESES
OSTEOGENESIS
OSTEOGENETIC
OSTEOGENIC
OSTEOGENIES
OSTEOGENOUS
OSTEOGENS
OSTEOGENY
OSTEOGRAPHIES
OSTEOGRAPHY
OSTEOID
OSTEOIDS
OSTEOLOGICAL
OSTEOLOGICALLY
OSTEOLOGIES
OSTEOLOGIST
OSTEOLOGISTS
OSTEOLOGY
OSTEOMA
OSTEOMALACIA
OSTEOMALACIAL
OSTEOMALACIAS
OSTEOMALACIC
OSTEOMAS
OSTEOMATA
OSTEOMYELITIS
OSTEOMYELITISES
OSTEOPATH
OSTEOPATHIC
OSTEOPATHICALLY
OSTEOPATHIES
OSTEOPATHIST
OSTEOPATHISTS
OSTEOPATHS
OSTEOPATHY
OSTEOPETROSES
OSTEOPETROSIS
OSTEOPHYTE
OSTEOPHYTES
OSTEOPHYTIC
OSTEOPLASTIC
OSTEOPLASTIES
OSTEOPLASTY
OSTEOPOROSES
OSTEOPOROSIS
OSTEOPOROTIC
OSTEOSARCOMA
OSTEOSARCOMAS
OSTEOSARCOMATA
OSTEOSES
OSTEOSIS
OSTEOSISES
OSTEOTOME

OSTEOTOMES
OSTEOTOMIES
OSTEOTOMY
OSTIA
OSTIAL
OSTIARIES
OSTIARY
OSTIATE
OSTINATO
OSTINATOS
OSTIOLAR
OSTIOLATE
OSTIOLE
OSTIOLES
OSTIUM
OSTLER
OSTLERESS
OSTLERESSES
OSTLERS
OSTMARK
OSTMARKS
OSTOMIES
OSTOMY
OSTOSES
OSTOSIS
OSTOSISES
OSTRACA
OSTRACEAN
OSTRACEOUS
OSTRACISABLE
OSTRACISE
OSTRACISED
OSTRACISER
OSTRACISERS
OSTRACISES
OSTRACISING
OSTRACISM
OSTRACISMS
OSTRACIZABLE
OSTRACIZE
OSTRACIZED
OSTRACIZER
OSTRACIZERS
OSTRACIZES
OSTRACIZING
OSTRACOD
OSTRACODAN
OSTRACODE
OSTRACODERM
OSTRACODERMS
OSTRACODES
OSTRACODOUS
OSTRACODS
OSTRACON
OSTRACONS
OSTRAKA

OSTRAKON
OSTREACEOUS
OSTREGER
OSTREGERS
OSTREICULTURE
OSTREICULTURES
OSTREICULTURIST
OSTREOPHAGE
OSTREOPHAGES
OSTREOPHAGIES
OSTREOPHAGOUS
OSTRICH
OSTRICHES
OSTRICHISM
OSTRICHISMS
OSTRICHLIKE
OTAKU
OTALGIA
OTALGIAS
OTALGIC
OTALGIES
OTALGY
OTARIES
OTARINE
OTARY
OTHER
OTHERGATES
OTHERGUESS
OTHERNESS
OTHERNESSES
OTHERS
OTHERWHERE
OTHERWHILE
OTHERWHILES
OTHERWISE
OTHERWORLD
OTHERWORLDISH
OTHERWORLDLY
OTHERWORLDS
OTIC
OTIOSE
OTIOSELY
OTIOSENESS
OTIOSENESSES
OTIOSITIES
OTIOSITY
OTITIC
OTITIDES
OTITIS
OTITISES
OTOCYST
OTOCYSTIC
OTOCYSTS
OTOLARYNGOLOGY
OTOLITH
OTOLITHIC

OTOLITHS
OTOLOGICAL
OTOLOGIES
OTOLOGIST
OTOLOGISTS
OTOLOGY
OTORRHOEA
OTORRHOEAS
OTOSCLEROSES
OTOSCLEROSIS
OTOSCOPE
OTOSCOPES
OTOSCOPIC
OTOSCOPICALLY
OTOSCOPIES
OTOSCOPY
OTOTOXIC
OTOTOXICITIES
OTOTOXICITY
OTTAR
OTTARS
OTTAVA
OTTAVAS
OTTAVINO
OTTAVINOS
OTTER
OTTERED
OTTERING
OTTERS
OTTO
OTTOMAN
OTTOMANS
OTTOS
OTTRELITE
OTTRELITES
OU
OUABAIN
OUABAINS
OUAKARI
OUAKARIS
OUANANICHE
OUANANICHES
OUBAAS
OUBAASES
OUBIT
OUBITS
OUBLIETTE
OUBLIETTES
OUCH
OUCHED
OUCHES
OUCHING
OUCHT
OUCHTS
OUD
OUDS

OUGHLIED
OUGHLIES
OUGHLY
OUGHLYING
OUGHT
OUGHTED
OUGHTING
OUGHTNESS
OUGHTNESSES
OUGHTS
OUGLIE
OUGLIED
OUGLIEING
OUGLIES
OUGUIYA
OUGUIYAS
OUIJA
OUIJAS
OUISTITI
OUISTITIS
OUK
OUKS
OULACHON
OULACHONS
OULAKAN
OULAKANS
OULD
OULDER
OULDEST
OULK
OULKS
OULONG
OULONGS
OUMA
OUMAS
OUNCE
OUNCES
OUNDY
OUP
OUPA
OUPAS
OUPED
OUPH
OUPHE
OUPHES
OUPHS
OUPING
OUPS
OUR
OURALI
OURALIS
OURANG
OURANGS
OURARI
OURARIS
OUREBI

OUREBIS
OURIE
OURIER
OURIEST
OURN
OUROBOROS
OUROBOROSES
OUROLOGIES
OUROLOGY
OUROSCOPIES
OUROSCOPY
OURS
OURSELF
OURSELVES
OUSEL
OUSELS
OUST
OUSTED
OUSTER
OUSTERS
OUSTING
OUSTITI
OUSTITIS
OUSTS
OUT
OUTACHIEVE
OUTACHIEVED
OUTACHIEVES
OUTACHIEVING
OUTACT
OUTACTED
OUTACTING
OUTACTS
OUTADD
OUTADDED
OUTADDING
OUTADDS
OUTAGE
OUTAGES
OUTARGUE
OUTARGUED
OUTARGUES
OUTARGUING
OUTASIGHT
OUTASK
OUTASKED
OUTASKING
OUTASKS
OUTATE
OUTBACK
OUTBACKER
OUTBACKERS
OUTBACKS
OUTBAKE
OUTBAKED
OUTBAKES

OUTBAKING
OUTBALANCE
OUTBALANCED
OUTBALANCES
OUTBALANCING
OUTBAR
OUTBARGAIN
OUTBARGAINED
OUTBARGAINING
OUTBARGAINS
OUTBARK
OUTBARKED
OUTBARKING
OUTBARKS
OUTBARRED
OUTBARRING
OUTBARS
OUTBAWL
OUTBAWLED
OUTBAWLING
OUTBAWLS
OUTBEAM
OUTBEAMED
OUTBEAMING
OUTBEAMS
OUTBEG
OUTBEGGED
OUTBEGGING
OUTBEGS
OUTBID
OUTBIDDEN
OUTBIDDING
OUTBIDS
OUTBITCH
OUTBITCHED
OUTBITCHES
OUTBITCHING
OUTBLAZE
OUTBLAZED
OUTBLAZES
OUTBLAZING
OUTBLEAT
OUTBLEATED
OUTBLEATING
OUTBLEATS
OUTBLESS
OUTBLESSED
OUTBLESSES
OUTBLESSING
OUTBLOOM
OUTBLOOMED
OUTBLOOMING
OUTBLOOMS
OUTBLUFF
OUTBLUFFED
OUTBLUFFING

OUTBLUFFS
OUTBLUSH
OUTBLUSHED
OUTBLUSHES
OUTBLUSHING
OUTBLUSTER
OUTBLUSTERED
OUTBLUSTERING
OUTBLUSTERS
OUTBOARD
OUTBOARDS
OUTBOAST
OUTBOASTED
OUTBOASTING
OUTBOASTS
OUTBOUGHT
OUTBOUND
OUTBOUNDS
OUTBOX
OUTBOXED
OUTBOXES
OUTBOXING
OUTBRAG
OUTBRAGGED
OUTBRAGGING
OUTBRAGS
OUTBRAVE
OUTBRAVED
OUTBRAVES
OUTBRAVING
OUTBRAWL
OUTBRAWLED
OUTBRAWLING
OUTBRAWLS
OUTBREAK
OUTBREAKING
OUTBREAKS
OUTBREATHE
OUTBREATHED
OUTBREATHES
OUTBREATHING
OUTBRED
OUTBREED
OUTBREEDING
OUTBREEDINGS
OUTBREEDS
OUTBRIBE
OUTBRIBED
OUTBRIBES
OUTBRIBING
OUTBROKE
OUTBROKEN
OUTBUILD
OUTBUILDING
OUTBUILDINGS
OUTBUILDS

OUTBUILT
OUTBULK
OUTBULKED
OUTBULKING
OUTBULKS
OUTBULLIED
OUTBULLIES
OUTBULLY
OUTBULLYING
OUTBURN
OUTBURNED
OUTBURNING
OUTBURNS
OUTBURNT
OUTBURST
OUTBURSTING
OUTBURSTS
OUTBUY
OUTBUYING
OUTBUYS
OUTBY
OUTBYE
OUTCAPER
OUTCAPERED
OUTCAPERING
OUTCAPERS
OUTCAST
OUTCASTE
OUTCASTED
OUTCASTES
OUTCASTING
OUTCASTS
OUTCATCH
OUTCATCHES
OUTCATCHING
OUTCAUGHT
OUTCAVIL
OUTCAVILED
OUTCAVILING
OUTCAVILLED
OUTCAVILLING
OUTCAVILS
OUTCHARGE
OUTCHARGED
OUTCHARGES
OUTCHARGING
OUTCHARM
OUTCHARMED
OUTCHARMING
OUTCHARMS
OUTCHEAT
OUTCHEATED
OUTCHEATING
OUTCHEATS
OUTCHID
OUTCHIDDEN

OUTCHIDE
OUTCHIDED
OUTCHIDES
OUTCHIDING
OUTCLASS
OUTCLASSED
OUTCLASSES
OUTCLASSING
OUTCLIMB
OUTCLIMBED
OUTCLIMBING
OUTCLIMBS
OUTCLOMB
OUTCOACH
OUTCOACHED
OUTCOACHES
OUTCOACHING
OUTCOME
OUTCOMES
OUTCOMPETE
OUTCOMPETED
OUTCOMPETES
OUTCOMPETING
OUTCOOK
OUTCOOKED
OUTCOOKING
OUTCOOKS
OUTCOUNT
OUTCOUNTED
OUTCOUNTING
OUTCOUNTS
OUTCRAFTIED
OUTCRAFTIES
OUTCRAFTY
OUTCRAFTYING
OUTCRAWL
OUTCRAWLED
OUTCRAWLING
OUTCRAWLS
OUTCRIED
OUTCRIES
OUTCROP
OUTCROPPED
OUTCROPPING
OUTCROPPINGS
OUTCROPS
OUTCROSS
OUTCROSSED
OUTCROSSES
OUTCROSSING
OUTCROSSINGS
OUTCROW
OUTCROWED
OUTCROWING
OUTCROWS
OUTCRY

OUTCRYING
OUTCURSE
OUTCURSED
OUTCURSES
OUTCURSING
OUTCURVE
OUTCURVES
OUTDACIOUS
OUTDANCE
OUTDANCED
OUTDANCES
OUTDANCING
OUTDARE
OUTDARED
OUTDARES
OUTDARING
OUTDATE
OUTDATED
OUTDATEDLY
OUTDATEDNESS
OUTDATEDNESSES
OUTDATES
OUTDATING
OUTDAZZLE
OUTDAZZLED
OUTDAZZLES
OUTDAZZLING
OUTDEBATE
OUTDEBATED
OUTDEBATES
OUTDEBATING
OUTDELIVER
OUTDELIVERED
OUTDELIVERING
OUTDELIVERS
OUTDESIGN
OUTDESIGNED
OUTDESIGNING
OUTDESIGNS
OUTDID
OUTDISTANCE
OUTDISTANCED
OUTDISTANCES
OUTDISTANCING
OUTDO
OUTDODGE
OUTDODGED
OUTDODGES
OUTDODGING
OUTDOER
OUTDOERS
OUTDOES
OUTDOING
OUTDONE
OUTDOOR
OUTDOORS

OUTDOORSMAN
OUTDOORSMANSHIP
OUTDOORSMEN
OUTDOORSY
OUTDRAG
OUTDRAGGED
OUTDRAGGING
OUTDRAGS
OUTDRANK
OUTDRAW
OUTDRAWING
OUTDRAWN
OUTDRAWS
OUTDREAM
OUTDREAMED
OUTDREAMING
OUTDREAMS
OUTDREAMT
OUTDRESS
OUTDRESSED
OUTDRESSES
OUTDRESSING
OUTDREW
OUTDRINK
OUTDRINKING
OUTDRINKS
OUTDRIVE
OUTDRIVEN
OUTDRIVES
OUTDRIVING
OUTDROP
OUTDROPPED
OUTDROPPING
OUTDROPS
OUTDROVE
OUTDRUNK
OUTDUEL
OUTDUELED
OUTDUELING
OUTDUELLED
OUTDUELLING
OUTDUELS
OUTDURE
OUTDURED
OUTDURES
OUTDURING
OUTDWELL
OUTDWELLED
OUTDWELLING
OUTDWELLS
OUTDWELT
OUTEARN
OUTEARNED
OUTEARNING
OUTEARNS
OUTEAT

OUTEATEN
OUTEATING
OUTEATS
OUTECHO
OUTECHOED
OUTECHOES
OUTECHOING
OUTED
OUTEDGE
OUTEDGES
OUTER
OUTERCOAT
OUTERCOATS
OUTERCOURSE
OUTERMOST
OUTERS
OUTERWEAR
OUTERWEARS
OUTFABLE
OUTFABLED
OUTFABLES
OUTFABLING
OUTFACE
OUTFACED
OUTFACES
OUTFACING
OUTFALL
OUTFALLS
OUTFANGTHIEF
OUTFAST
OUTFASTED
OUTFASTING
OUTFASTS
OUTFAWN
OUTFAWNED
OUTFAWNING
OUTFAWNS
OUTFEAST
OUTFEASTED
OUTFEASTING
OUTFEASTS
OUTFEEL
OUTFEELING
OUTFEELS
OUTFELT
OUTFIELD
OUTFIELDER
OUTFIELDERS
OUTFIELDS
OUTFIGHT
OUTFIGHTING
OUTFIGHTS
OUTFIGURE
OUTFIGURED
OUTFIGURES
OUTFIGURING

OUTFIND
OUTFINDING
OUTFINDS
OUTFIRE
OUTFIRED
OUTFIRES
OUTFIRING
OUTFISH
OUTFISHED
OUTFISHES
OUTFISHING
OUTFIT
OUTFITS
OUTFITTED
OUTFITTER
OUTFITTERS
OUTFITTING
OUTFITTINGS
OUTFLANK
OUTFLANKED
OUTFLANKING
OUTFLANKS
OUTFLASH
OUTFLASHED
OUTFLASHES
OUTFLASHING
OUTFLEW
OUTFLIES
OUTFLING
OUTFLINGS
OUTFLOW
OUTFLOWED
OUTFLOWING
OUTFLOWINGS
OUTFLOWN
OUTFLOWS
OUTFLUSH
OUTFLUSHED
OUTFLUSHES
OUTFLUSHING
OUTFLY
OUTFLYING
OUTFOOL
OUTFOOLED
OUTFOOLING
OUTFOOLS
OUTFOOT
OUTFOOTED
OUTFOOTING
OUTFOOTS
OUTFOUGHT
OUTFOUND
OUTFOX
OUTFOXED
OUTFOXES
OUTFOXING

OUTFROWN
OUTFROWNED
OUTFROWNING
OUTFROWNS
OUTFUMBLE
OUTFUMBLED
OUTFUMBLES
OUTFUMBLING
OUTGAIN
OUTGAINED
OUTGAINING
OUTGAINS
OUTGAS
OUTGASES
OUTGASSED
OUTGASSES
OUTGASSING
OUTGASSINGS
OUTGATE
OUTGATES
OUTGAVE
OUTGENERAL
OUTGENERALED
OUTGENERALING
OUTGENERALLED
OUTGENERALLING
OUTGENERALS
OUTGIVE
OUTGIVEN
OUTGIVES
OUTGIVING
OUTGIVINGS
OUTGLARE
OUTGLARED
OUTGLARES
OUTGLARING
OUTGLITTER
OUTGLITTERED
OUTGLITTERING
OUTGLITTERS
OUTGLOW
OUTGLOWED
OUTGLOWING
OUTGLOWS
OUTGNAW
OUTGNAWED
OUTGNAWING
OUTGNAWN
OUTGNAWS
OUTGO
OUTGOER
OUTGOERS
OUTGOES
OUTGOING
OUTGOINGNESS
OUTGOINGNESSES

OUTGOINGS
OUTGONE
OUTGREW
OUTGRIN
OUTGRINNED
OUTGRINNING
OUTGRINS
OUTGROSS
OUTGROSSED
OUTGROSSES
OUTGROSSING
OUTGROUP
OUTGROUPS
OUTGROW
OUTGROWING
OUTGROWN
OUTGROWS
OUTGROWTH
OUTGROWTHS
OUTGUARD
OUTGUARDS
OUTGUESS
OUTGUESSED
OUTGUESSES
OUTGUESSING
OUTGUIDE
OUTGUIDED
OUTGUIDES
OUTGUIDING
OUTGUN
OUTGUNNED
OUTGUNNING
OUTGUNS
OUTGUSH
OUTGUSHED
OUTGUSHES
OUTGUSHING
OUTHAUL
OUTHAULER
OUTHAULERS
OUTHAULS
OUTHEAR
OUTHEARD
OUTHEARING
OUTHEARS
OUTHER
OUTHIRE
OUTHIRED
OUTHIRES
OUTHIRING
OUTHIT
OUTHITS
OUTHITTING
OUTHOMER
OUTHOMERED
OUTHOMERING

OUTHOMERS
OUTHOUSE
OUTHOUSES
OUTHOWL
OUTHOWLED
OUTHOWLING
OUTHOWLS
OUTHUMOR
OUTHUMORED
OUTHUMORING
OUTHUMORS
OUTHUNT
OUTHUNTED
OUTHUNTING
OUTHUNTS
OUTHUSTLE
OUTHUSTLED
OUTHUSTLES
OUTHUSTLING
OUTHYRE
OUTHYRED
OUTHYRES
OUTHYRING
OUTING
OUTINGS
OUTINTRIGUE
OUTINTRIGUED
OUTINTRIGUES
OUTINTRIGUING
OUTJEST
OUTJESTED
OUTJESTING
OUTJESTS
OUTJET
OUTJETS
OUTJETTING
OUTJETTINGS
OUTJINX
OUTJINXED
OUTJINXES
OUTJINXING
OUTJOCKEY
OUTJOCKEYED
OUTJOCKEYING
OUTJOCKEYS
OUTJUMP
OUTJUMPED
OUTJUMPING
OUTJUMPS
OUTJUT
OUTJUTS
OUTJUTTED
OUTJUTTING
OUTJUTTINGS
OUTKEEP
OUTKEEPING

OUTKEEPS
OUTKEPT
OUTKICK
OUTKICKED
OUTKICKING
OUTKICKS
OUTKILL
OUTKILLED
OUTKILLING
OUTKILLS
OUTKISS
OUTKISSED
OUTKISSES
OUTKISSING
OUTLAID
OUTLAIN
OUTLAND
OUTLANDER
OUTLANDERS
OUTLANDISH
OUTLANDISHLY
OUTLANDISHNESS
OUTLANDS
OUTLASH
OUTLASHES
OUTLAST
OUTLASTED
OUTLASTING
OUTLASTS
OUTLAUGH
OUTLAUGHED
OUTLAUGHING
OUTLAUGHS
OUTLAUNCE
OUTLAUNCED
OUTLAUNCES
OUTLAUNCH
OUTLAUNCHED
OUTLAUNCHES
OUTLAUNCHING
OUTLAUNCING
OUTLAW
OUTLAWED
OUTLAWING
OUTLAWRIES
OUTLAWRY
OUTLAWS
OUTLAY
OUTLAYING
OUTLAYS
OUTLEAP
OUTLEAPED
OUTLEAPING
OUTLEAPS
OUTLEAPT
OUTLEARN

OUTLEARNED
OUTLEARNING
OUTLEARNS
OUTLEARNT
OUTLER
OUTLERS
OUTLET
OUTLETS
OUTLIE
OUTLIED
OUTLIER
OUTLIERS
OUTLIES
OUTLINE
OUTLINEAR
OUTLINED
OUTLINER
OUTLINERS
OUTLINES
OUTLINING
OUTLIVE
OUTLIVED
OUTLIVER
OUTLIVERS
OUTLIVES
OUTLIVING
OUTLODGING
OUTLODGINGS
OUTLOOK
OUTLOOKED
OUTLOOKING
OUTLOOKS
OUTLOVE
OUTLOVED
OUTLOVES
OUTLOVING
OUTLUSTRE
OUTLUSTRED
OUTLUSTRES
OUTLUSTRING
OUTLYING
OUTMAN
OUTMANEUVER
OUTMANEUVERED
OUTMANEUVERING
OUTMANEUVERS
OUTMANIPULATE
OUTMANIPULATED
OUTMANIPULATES
OUTMANIPULATING
OUTMANNED
OUTMANNING
OUTMANOEUVRE
OUTMANOEUVRED
OUTMANOEUVRES
OUTMANOEUVRING

OUTMANS
OUTMANTLE
OUTMANTLED
OUTMANTLES
OUTMANTLING
OUTMARCH
OUTMARCHED
OUTMARCHES
OUTMARCHING
OUTMARRIAGE
OUTMARRIAGES
OUTMATCH
OUTMATCHED
OUTMATCHES
OUTMATCHING
OUTMEASURE
OUTMEASURED
OUTMEASURES
OUTMEASURING
OUTMODE
OUTMODED
OUTMODEDLY
OUTMODEDNESS
OUTMODES
OUTMODING
OUTMOST
OUTMOVE
OUTMOVED
OUTMOVES
OUTMOVING
OUTMUSCLE
OUTMUSCLED
OUTMUSCLES
OUTMUSCLING
OUTNAME
OUTNAMED
OUTNAMES
OUTNAMING
OUTNESS
OUTNESSES
OUTNIGHT
OUTNIGHTED
OUTNIGHTING
OUTNIGHTS
OUTNUMBER
OUTNUMBERED
OUTNUMBERING
OUTNUMBERS
OUTORGANIZE
OUTORGANIZED
OUTORGANIZES
OUTORGANIZING
OUTPACE
OUTPACED
OUTPACES
OUTPACING

OUTPAINT
OUTPAINTED
OUTPAINTING
OUTPAINTS
OUTPART
OUTPARTS
OUTPASS
OUTPASSED
OUTPASSES
OUTPASSING
OUTPASSION
OUTPASSIONED
OUTPASSIONING
OUTPASSIONS
OUTPATIENT
OUTPATIENTS
OUTPEEP
OUTPEEPED
OUTPEEPING
OUTPEEPS
OUTPEER
OUTPEERED
OUTPEERING
OUTPEERS
OUTPERFORM
OUTPERFORMED
OUTPERFORMING
OUTPERFORMS
OUTPITCH
OUTPITCHED
OUTPITCHES
OUTPITCHING
OUTPITIED
OUTPITIES
OUTPITY
OUTPITYING
OUTPLACE
OUTPLACED
OUTPLACEMENT
OUTPLACEMENTS
OUTPLACER
OUTPLACERS
OUTPLACES
OUTPLACING
OUTPLAN
OUTPLANNED
OUTPLANNING
OUTPLANS
OUTPLAY
OUTPLAYED
OUTPLAYING
OUTPLAYS
OUTPLOD
OUTPLODDED
OUTPLODDING
OUTPLODS

OUTPLOT
OUTPLOTS
OUTPLOTTED
OUTPLOTTING
OUTPOINT
OUTPOINTED
OUTPOINTING
OUTPOINTS
OUTPOLITICK
OUTPOLITICKED
OUTPOLITICKING
OUTPOLITICKS
OUTPOLL
OUTPOLLED
OUTPOLLING
OUTPOLLS
OUTPOPULATE
OUTPOPULATED
OUTPOPULATES
OUTPOPULATING
OUTPORT
OUTPORTER
OUTPORTERS
OUTPORTS
OUTPOST
OUTPOSTS
OUTPOUR
OUTPOURED
OUTPOURER
OUTPOURERS
OUTPOURING
OUTPOURINGS
OUTPOURS
OUTPOWER
OUTPOWERED
OUTPOWERING
OUTPOWERS
OUTPRAY
OUTPRAYED
OUTPRAYING
OUTPRAYS
OUTPREACH
OUTPREACHED
OUTPREACHES
OUTPREACHING
OUTPREEN
OUTPREENED
OUTPREENING
OUTPREENS
OUTPRESS
OUTPRESSED
OUTPRESSES
OUTPRESSING
OUTPRICE
OUTPRICED
OUTPRICES

OUTPRICING
OUTPRIZE
OUTPRIZED
OUTPRIZES
OUTPRIZING
OUTPRODUCE
OUTPRODUCED
OUTPRODUCES
OUTPRODUCING
OUTPROMISE
OUTPROMISED
OUTPROMISES
OUTPROMISING
OUTPULL
OUTPULLED
OUTPULLING
OUTPULLS
OUTPUNCH
OUTPUNCHED
OUTPUNCHES
OUTPUNCHING
OUTPUSH
OUTPUSHED
OUTPUSHES
OUTPUSHING
OUTPUTS
OUTPUTTED
OUTPUTTING
OUTQUARTERS
OUTQUOTE
OUTQUOTED
OUTQUOTES
OUTQUOTING
OUTRACE
OUTRACED
OUTRACES
OUTRACING
OUTRAGE
OUTRAGED
OUTRAGEOUS
OUTRAGEOUSLY
OUTRAGEOUSNESS
OUTRAGES
OUTRAGING
OUTRAIGNED
OUTRAIGNES
OUTRAIGNING
OUTRAISE
OUTRAISED
OUTRAISES
OUTRAISING
OUTRAN
OUTRANCE
OUTRANCES
OUTRANG

OUTRANGE
OUTRANGED
OUTRANGES
OUTRANGING
OUTRANK
OUTRANKED
OUTRANKING
OUTRANKS
OUTRATE
OUTRATED
OUTRATES
OUTRATING
OUTRAVE
OUTRAVED
OUTRAVES
OUTRAVING
OUTRE
OUTREACH
OUTREACHED
OUTREACHES
OUTREACHING
OUTREAD
OUTREADING
OUTREADS
OUTREBOUND
OUTREBOUNDED
OUTREBOUNDING
OUTREBOUNDS
OUTRECUIDANCE
OUTRECUIDANCES
OUTRED
OUTREDDED
OUTREDDEN
OUTREDDENED
OUTREDDENING
OUTREDDENS
OUTREDDING
OUTREDS
OUTREIGN
OUTREIGNED
OUTREIGNING
OUTREIGNS
OUTRELIEF
OUTRELIEFS
OUTREMER
OUTREMERS
OUTREPRODUCE
OUTREPRODUCED
OUTREPRODUCES
OUTREPRODUCING
OUTRIDDEN
OUTRIDE
OUTRIDER
OUTRIDERS
OUTRIDES
OUTRIDING

OUTRIGGER
OUTRIGGERS
OUTRIGHT
OUTRIGHTLY
OUTRING
OUTRINGING
OUTRINGS
OUTRIVAL
OUTRIVALED
OUTRIVALING
OUTRIVALLED
OUTRIVALLING
OUTRIVALS
OUTRO
OUTROAR
OUTROARED
OUTROARING
OUTROARS
OUTROCK
OUTROCKED
OUTROCKING
OUTROCKS
OUTRODE
OUTROLL
OUTROLLED
OUTROLLING
OUTROLLS
OUTROOP
OUTROOPER
OUTROOPERS
OUTROOPS
OUTROOT
OUTROOTED
OUTROOTING
OUTROOTS
OUTROPE
OUTROPER
OUTROPERS
OUTROPES
OUTROS
OUTROW
OUTROWED
OUTROWING
OUTROWS
OUTRUN
OUTRUNG
OUTRUNNER
OUTRUNNERS
OUTRUNNING
OUTRUNS
OUTRUSH
OUTRUSHED
OUTRUSHES
OUTRUSHING
OUTS
OUTSAIL

OUTSAILED
OUTSAILING
OUTSAILS
OUTSANG
OUTSAT
OUTSAVOR
OUTSAVORED
OUTSAVORING
OUTSAVORS
OUTSAW
OUTSCHEME
OUTSCHEMED
OUTSCHEMES
OUTSCHEMING
OUTSCOLD
OUTSCOLDED
OUTSCOLDING
OUTSCOLDS
OUTSCOOP
OUTSCOOPED
OUTSCOOPING
OUTSCOOPS
OUTSCORE
OUTSCORED
OUTSCORES
OUTSCORING
OUTSCORN
OUTSCORNED
OUTSCORNING
OUTSCORNS
OUTSEE
OUTSEEING
OUTSEEN
OUTSEES
OUTSELL
OUTSELLING
OUTSELLS
OUTSERT
OUTSERTS
OUTSERVE
OUTSERVED
OUTSERVES
OUTSERVING
OUTSET
OUTSETS
OUTSETTING
OUTSETTINGS
OUTSETTLEMENT
OUTSETTLEMENTS
OUTSHAME
OUTSHAMED
OUTSHAMES
OUTSHAMING
OUTSHINE
OUTSHINED
OUTSHINES

OUTSHINING
OUTSHONE
OUTSHOOT
OUTSHOOTING
OUTSHOOTS
OUTSHOT
OUTSHOTS
OUTSHOUT
OUTSHOUTED
OUTSHOUTING
OUTSHOUTS
OUTSIDE
OUTSIDER
OUTSIDERNESS
OUTSIDERNESSES
OUTSIDERS
OUTSIDES
OUTSIGHT
OUTSIGHTS
OUTSIN
OUTSING
OUTSINGING
OUTSINGS
OUTSINNED
OUTSINNING
OUTSINS
OUTSIT
OUTSITS
OUTSITTING
OUTSIZE
OUTSIZED
OUTSIZES
OUTSKATE
OUTSKATED
OUTSKATES
OUTSKATING
OUTSKIRT
OUTSKIRTS
OUTSLEEP
OUTSLEEPING
OUTSLEEPS
OUTSLEPT
OUTSLICK
OUTSLICKED
OUTSLICKING
OUTSLICKS
OUTSMART
OUTSMARTED
OUTSMARTING
OUTSMARTS
OUTSMILE
OUTSMILED
OUTSMILES
OUTSMILING
OUTSMOKE
OUTSMOKED

OUTSMOKES
OUTSMOKING
OUTSNORE
OUTSNORED
OUTSNORES
OUTSNORING
OUTSOAR
OUTSOARED
OUTSOARING
OUTSOARS
OUTSOLD
OUTSOLE
OUTSOLES
OUTSOURCE
OUTSOURCED
OUTSOURCES
OUTSOURCING
OUTSOURCINGS
OUTSPAN
OUTSPANNED
OUTSPANNING
OUTSPANS
OUTSPARKLE
OUTSPARKLED
OUTSPARKLES
OUTSPARKLING
OUTSPEAK
OUTSPEAKING
OUTSPEAKS
OUTSPECKLE
OUTSPECKLES
OUTSPED
OUTSPEED
OUTSPEEDED
OUTSPEEDING
OUTSPEEDS
OUTSPELL
OUTSPELLED
OUTSPELLING
OUTSPELLS
OUTSPELT
OUTSPEND
OUTSPENDING
OUTSPENDS
OUTSPENT
OUTSPOKE
OUTSPOKEN
OUTSPOKENESS
OUTSPOKENLY
OUTSPOKENNESS
OUTSPOKENNESSES
OUTSPORT
OUTSPORTED
OUTSPORTING
OUTSPORTS
OUTSPRANG

OUTSPREAD
OUTSPREADING
OUTSPREADS
OUTSPRING
OUTSPRINGING
OUTSPRINGS
OUTSPRINT
OUTSPRINTED
OUTSPRINTING
OUTSPRINTS
OUTSPRUNG
OUTSTAND
OUTSTANDING
OUTSTANDINGLY
OUTSTANDS
OUTSTARE
OUTSTARED
OUTSTARES
OUTSTARING
OUTSTART
OUTSTARTED
OUTSTARTING
OUTSTARTS
OUTSTATE
OUTSTATED
OUTSTATES
OUTSTATING
OUTSTATION
OUTSTATIONS
OUTSTAY
OUTSTAYED
OUTSTAYING
OUTSTAYS
OUTSTEER
OUTSTEERED
OUTSTEERING
OUTSTEERS
OUTSTEP
OUTSTEPPED
OUTSTEPPING
OUTSTEPS
OUTSTOOD
OUTSTRAIN
OUTSTRAINED
OUTSTRAINING
OUTSTRAINS
OUTSTRETCH
OUTSTRETCHED
OUTSTRETCHES
OUTSTRETCHING
OUTSTRIDDEN
OUTSTRIDE
OUTSTRIDES
OUTSTRIDING
OUTSTRIKE
OUTSTRIKES

OUTSTRIKING
OUTSTRIP
OUTSTRIPPED
OUTSTRIPPING
OUTSTRIPS
OUTSTRODE
OUTSTRUCK
OUTSTUDIED
OUTSTUDIES
OUTSTUDY
OUTSTUDYING
OUTSTUNT
OUTSTUNTED
OUTSTUNTING
OUTSTUNTS
OUTSULK
OUTSULKED
OUTSULKING
OUTSULKS
OUTSUM
OUTSUMMED
OUTSUMMING
OUTSUMS
OUTSUNG
OUTSWAM
OUTSWARE
OUTSWEAR
OUTSWEARING
OUTSWEARS
OUTSWEETEN
OUTSWEETENED
OUTSWEETENING
OUTSWEETENS
OUTSWELL
OUTSWELLED
OUTSWELLING
OUTSWELLS
OUTSWIM
OUTSWIMMING
OUTSWIMS
OUTSWING
OUTSWINGER
OUTSWINGERS
OUTSWINGS
OUTSWOLLEN
OUTSWORE
OUTSWORN
OUTSWUM
OUTTAKE
OUTTAKEN
OUTTAKES
OUTTAKING
OUTTALK
OUTTALKED
OUTTALKING
OUTTALKS

OUTTASK
OUTTASKED
OUTTASKING
OUTTASKS
OUTTELL
OUTTELLING
OUTTELLS
OUTTHANK
OUTTHANKED
OUTTHANKING
OUTTHANKS
OUTTHINK
OUTTHINKING
OUTTHINKS
OUTTHOUGHT
OUTTHREW
OUTTHROB
OUTTHROBBED
OUTTHROBBING
OUTTHROBS
OUTTHROW
OUTTHROWING
OUTTHROWN
OUTTHROWS
OUTTOLD
OUTTONGUE
OUTTONGUED
OUTTONGUES
OUTTONGUING
OUTTOOK
OUTTOP
OUTTOPPED
OUTTOPPING
OUTTOPS
OUTTOWER
OUTTOWERED
OUTTOWERING
OUTTOWERS
OUTTRADE
OUTTRADED
OUTTRADES
OUTTRADING
OUTTRAVEL
OUTTRAVELED
OUTTRAVELING
OUTTRAVELLED
OUTTRAVELLING
OUTTRAVELS
OUTTRICK
OUTTRICKED
OUTTRICKING
OUTTRICKS
OUTTROT
OUTTROTS
OUTTROTTED
OUTTROTTING

OUTTRUMP
OUTTRUMPED
OUTTRUMPING
OUTTRUMPS
OUTTURN
OUTTURNS
OUTVALUE
OUTVALUED
OUTVALUES
OUTVALUING
OUTVAUNT
OUTVAUNTED
OUTVAUNTING
OUTVAUNTS
OUTVENOM
OUTVENOMED
OUTVENOMING
OUTVENOMS
OUTVIE
OUTVIED
OUTVIES
OUTVILLAIN
OUTVILLAINED
OUTVILLAINING
OUTVILLAINS
OUTVOICE
OUTVOICED
OUTVOICES
OUTVOICING
OUTVOTE
OUTVOTED
OUTVOTER
OUTVOTERS
OUTVOTES
OUTVOTING
OUTVYING
OUTWAIT
OUTWAITED
OUTWAITING
OUTWAITS
OUTWALK
OUTWALKED
OUTWALKING
OUTWALKS
OUTWAR
OUTWARD
OUTWARDLY
OUTWARDNESS
OUTWARDNESSES
OUTWARDS
OUTWARRED
OUTWARRING
OUTWARS
OUTWASH
OUTWASHES
OUTWASTE

OUTWASTED
OUTWASTES
OUTWASTING
OUTWATCH
OUTWATCHED
OUTWATCHES
OUTWATCHING
OUTWEAR
OUTWEARIED
OUTWEARIES
OUTWEARING
OUTWEARS
OUTWEARY
OUTWEARYING
OUTWEED
OUTWEEDED
OUTWEEDING
OUTWEEDS
OUTWEEP
OUTWEEPING
OUTWEEPS
OUTWEIGH
OUTWEIGHED
OUTWEIGHING
OUTWEIGHS
OUTWELL
OUTWELLED
OUTWELLING
OUTWELLS
OUTWENT
OUTWEPT
OUTWHIRL
OUTWHIRLED
OUTWHIRLING
OUTWHIRLS
OUTWICK
OUTWICKED
OUTWICKING
OUTWICKS
OUTWILE
OUTWILED
OUTWILES
OUTWILING
OUTWILL
OUTWILLED
OUTWILLING
OUTWILLS
OUTWIN
OUTWIND
OUTWINDED
OUTWINDING
OUTWINDS
OUTWING
OUTWINGED
OUTWINGING
OUTWINGS

OUTWINNING
OUTWINS
OUTWISH
OUTWISHED
OUTWISHES
OUTWISHING
OUTWIT
OUTWITH
OUTWITS
OUTWITTED
OUTWITTING
OUTWON
OUTWORE
OUTWORK
OUTWORKED
OUTWORKER
OUTWORKERS
OUTWORKING
OUTWORKS
OUTWORN
OUTWORTH
OUTWORTHED
OUTWORTHING
OUTWORTHS
OUTWOUND
OUTWREST
OUTWRESTED
OUTWRESTING
OUTWRESTLE
OUTWRESTLED
OUTWRESTLES
OUTWRESTLING
OUTWRESTS
OUTWRIT
OUTWRITE
OUTWRITES
OUTWRITING
OUTWRITTEN
OUTWROTE
OUTWROUGHT
OUTYELL
OUTYELLED
OUTYELLING
OUTYELLS
OUTYELP
OUTYELPED
OUTYELPING
OUTYELPS
OUTYIELD
OUTYIELDED
OUTYIELDING
OUTYIELDS
OUVERT
OUVERTE
OUVIRANDRA
OUVIRANDRAS

OUVRAGE
OUVRAGES
OUVRIER
OUVRIERE
OUVRIERES
OUVRIERS
OUZEL
OUZELS
OUZO
OUZOS
OVA
OVAL
OVALBUMIN
OVALBUMINS
OVALITIES
OVALITY
OVALLY
OVALNESS
OVALNESSES
OVALS
OVARIAL
OVARIAN
OVARIECTOMIES
OVARIECTOMIZED
OVARIECTOMY
OVARIES
OVARIOLE
OVARIOLES
OVARIOTOMIES
OVARIOTOMIST
OVARIOTOMISTS
OVARIOTOMY
OVARIOUS
OVARITIDES
OVARITIS
OVARITISES
OVARY
OVATE
OVATED
OVATELY
OVATES
OVATING
OVATION
OVATIONAL
OVATIONS
OVATOR
OVATORS
OVEL
OVELS
OVEN
OVENABLE
OVENBIRD
OVENBIRDS
OVENED
OVENING
OVENLIKE

OVENPROOF
OVENS
OVENWARE
OVENWARES
OVENWOOD
OVENWOODS
OVER
OVERABLE
OVERABOUND
OVERABOUNDED
OVERABOUNDING
OVERABOUNDS
OVERABSTRACT
OVERABUNDANCE
OVERABUNDANCES
OVERABUNDANT
OVERACCENTUATE
OVERACCENTUATED
OVERACCENTUATES
OVERACHIEVE
OVERACHIEVED
OVERACHIEVEMENT
OVERACHIEVER
OVERACHIEVERS
OVERACHIEVES
OVERACHIEVING
OVERACT
OVERACTED
OVERACTING
OVERACTION
OVERACTIONS
OVERACTIVE
OVERACTIVITIES
OVERACTIVITY
OVERACTS
OVERADJUSTMENT
OVERADJUSTMENTS
OVERADORNED
OVERADVANCE
OVERADVANCED
OVERADVANCES
OVERADVANCING
OVERADVERTISE
OVERADVERTISED
OVERADVERTISES
OVERADVERTISING
OVERAFFECT
OVERAFFECTED
OVERAFFECTING
OVERAFFECTS
OVERAGE
OVERAGED
OVERAGES
OVERAGGRESSIVE
OVERALERT
OVERALL

OVERALLED
OVERALLS
OVERAMBITIOUS
OVERAMBITIOUSLY
OVERAMPLIFIED
OVERANALYSE
OVERANALYSED
OVERANALYSES
OVERANALYSING
OVERANALYSIS
OVERANALYTICAL
OVERANALYZE
OVERANALYZED
OVERANALYZES
OVERANALYZING
OVERANGRILY
OVERANGRY
OVERANIMATED
OVERANIMATEDLY
OVERANIMATION
OVERANXIETIES
OVERANXIETY
OVERANXIOUS
OVERAPPLICATION
OVERAPT
OVERARCH
OVERARCHED
OVERARCHES
OVERARCHING
OVERARM
OVERAROUSAL
OVERAROUSALS
OVERARRANGE
OVERARRANGED
OVERARRANGES
OVERARRANGING
OVERARTICULATE
OVERARTICULATED
OVERARTICULATES
OVERASSERT
OVERASSERTED
OVERASSERTING
OVERASSERTION
OVERASSERTIONS
OVERASSERTIVE
OVERASSERTIVELY
OVERASSERTS
OVERASSESSMENT
OVERASSESSMENTS
OVERASSURED
OVERASSUREDNESS
OVERATE
OVERATTACHED
OVERATTENTION
OVERATTENTIONS
OVERATTENTIVE

OVERATTENTIVELY
OVERAWE
OVERAWED
OVERAWES
OVERAWING
OVERBAKE
OVERBAKED
OVERBAKES
OVERBAKING
OVERBALANCE
OVERBALANCED
OVERBALANCES
OVERBALANCING
OVERBEAR
OVERBEARING
OVERBEARINGLY
OVERBEARINGNESS
OVERBEARS
OVERBEAT
OVERBEATEN
OVERBEATING
OVERBEATS
OVERBED
OVERBEJEWELED
OVERBET
OVERBETS
OVERBETTED
OVERBETTING
OVERBID
OVERBIDDEN
OVERBIDDER
OVERBIDDERS
OVERBIDDING
OVERBIDDINGS
OVERBIDS
OVERBIG
OVERBILL
OVERBILLED
OVERBILLING
OVERBILLS
OVERBITE
OVERBITES
OVERBLANKET
OVERBLANKETS
OVERBLEACH
OVERBLEACHED
OVERBLEACHES
OVERBLEACHING
OVERBLEW
OVERBLOUSE
OVERBLOUSES
OVERBLOW
OVERBLOWING
OVERBLOWN
OVERBLOWS
OVERBOARD

OVERBOIL
OVERBOILED
OVERBOILING
OVERBOILS
OVERBOLD
OVERBOLDLY
OVERBOOK
OVERBOOKED
OVERBOOKING
OVERBOOKS
OVERBOOT
OVERBOOTS
OVERBORE
OVERBORN
OVERBORNE
OVERBORROW
OVERBORROWED
OVERBORROWING
OVERBORROWS
OVERBOUGHT
OVERBOUND
OVERBOUNDED
OVERBOUNDING
OVERBOUNDS
OVERBRAVE
OVERBRAVERY
OVERBREATHING
OVERBREATHINGS
OVERBRED
OVERBRIDGE
OVERBRIDGED
OVERBRIDGES
OVERBRIDGING
OVERBRIEF
OVERBRIGHT
OVERBRIM
OVERBRIMMED
OVERBRIMMING
OVERBRIMS
OVERBROAD
OVERBROW
OVERBROWED
OVERBROWING
OVERBROWS
OVERBROWSE
OVERBROWSED
OVERBROWSES
OVERBROWSING
OVERBRUTAL
OVERBUILD
OVERBUILDING
OVERBUILDS
OVERBUILT
OVERBULK
OVERBULKED
OVERBULKING

OVERBULKS
OVERBULKY
OVERBURDEN
OVERBURDENED
OVERBURDENING
OVERBURDENS
OVERBURDENSOME
OVERBURN
OVERBURNED
OVERBURNING
OVERBURNS
OVERBURNT
OVERBURTHEN
OVERBURTHENED
OVERBURTHENING
OVERBURTHENS
OVERBUSIED
OVERBUSIES
OVERBUSY
OVERBUSYING
OVERBUY
OVERBUYING
OVERBUYS
OVERBY
OVERCALL
OVERCALLED
OVERCALLING
OVERCALLS
OVERCAME
OVERCANOPIED
OVERCANOPIES
OVERCANOPY
OVERCANOPYING
OVERCAPACITIES
OVERCAPACITY
OVERCAPITALISE
OVERCAPITALISED
OVERCAPITALISES
OVERCAPITALIZE
OVERCAPITALIZED
OVERCAPITALIZES
OVERCAREFUL
OVERCARRIED
OVERCARRIES
OVERCARRY
OVERCARRYING
OVERCAST
OVERCASTED
OVERCASTING
OVERCASTINGS
OVERCASTS
OVERCASUAL
OVERCASUALLY
OVERCATCH
OVERCATCHES
OVERCATCHING

OVERCAUGHT
OVERCAUTION
OVERCAUTIONS
OVERCAUTIOUS
OVERCENTRALIZE
OVERCENTRALIZED
OVERCENTRALIZES
OVERCEREBRAL
OVERCHARGE
OVERCHARGED
OVERCHARGES
OVERCHARGING
OVERCHECK
OVERCHECKS
OVERCHILL
OVERCHILLED
OVERCHILLING
OVERCHILLS
OVERCIVIL
OVERCIVILISE
OVERCIVILISED
OVERCIVILISES
OVERCIVILISING
OVERCIVILITY
OVERCIVILIZE
OVERCIVILIZED
OVERCIVILIZES
OVERCIVILIZING
OVERCLAD
OVERCLAIM
OVERCLAIMED
OVERCLAIMING
OVERCLAIMS
OVERCLASSIFIED
OVERCLASSIFIES
OVERCLASSIFY
OVERCLASSIFYING
OVERCLEAN
OVERCLEANED
OVERCLEANING
OVERCLEANS
OVERCLEAR
OVERCLEARED
OVERCLEARING
OVERCLEARS
OVERCLOUD
OVERCLOUDED
OVERCLOUDING
OVERCLOUDS
OVERCLOY
OVERCLOYED
OVERCLOYING
OVERCLOYS
OVERCOACH
OVERCOACHED
OVERCOACHES

OVERCOACHING
OVERCOAT
OVERCOATING
OVERCOATINGS
OVERCOATS
OVERCOLD
OVERCOLOUR
OVERCOLOURED
OVERCOLOURING
OVERCOLOURS
OVERCOME
OVERCOMER
OVERCOMERS
OVERCOMES
OVERCOMING
OVERCOMMIT
OVERCOMMITMENT
OVERCOMMITMENTS
OVERCOMMITS
OVERCOMMITTED
OVERCOMMITTING
OVERCOMMON
OVERCOMMUNICATE
OVERCOMPENSATE
OVERCOMPENSATED
OVERCOMPENSATES
OVERCOMPETITIVE
OVERCOMPLACENCY
OVERCOMPLACENT
OVERCOMPLEX
OVERCOMPLIANCE
OVERCOMPLIANCES
OVERCOMPLICATE
OVERCOMPLICATED
OVERCOMPLICATES
OVERCOMPRESS
OVERCOMPRESSED
OVERCOMPRESSES
OVERCOMPRESSING
OVERCONCERN
OVERCONCERNED
OVERCONCERNING
OVERCONCERNS
OVERCONFIDENCE
OVERCONFIDENCES
OVERCONFIDENT
OVERCONFIDENTLY
OVERCONSCIOUS
OVERCONSIDERATE
OVERCONSTRUCT
OVERCONSTRUCTED
OVERCONSTRUCTS
OVERCONSUME
OVERCONSUMED
OVERCONSUMES
OVERCONSUMING

OVERCONSUMPTION
OVERCONTROL
OVERCONTROLLED
OVERCONTROLLING
OVERCONTROLS
OVERCOOK
OVERCOOKED
OVERCOOKING
OVERCOOKS
OVERCOOL
OVERCOOLED
OVERCOOLING
OVERCOOLS
OVERCORRECT
OVERCORRECTED
OVERCORRECTING
OVERCORRECTION
OVERCORRECTIONS
OVERCORRECTS
OVERCOSTLY
OVERCOUNT
OVERCOUNTED
OVERCOUNTING
OVERCOUNTS
OVERCOVER
OVERCOVERED
OVERCOVERING
OVERCOVERS
OVERCOY
OVERCRAM
OVERCRAMMED
OVERCRAMMING
OVERCRAMS
OVERCRAW
OVERCRAWED
OVERCRAWING
OVERCRAWS
OVERCREDULITIES
OVERCREDULITY
OVERCREDULOUS
OVERCRITICAL
OVERCRITICISE
OVERCRITICISED
OVERCRITICISES
OVERCRITICISING
OVERCRITICIZE
OVERCRITICIZED
OVERCRITICIZES
OVERCRITICIZING
OVERCROP
OVERCROPPED
OVERCROPPING
OVERCROPS
OVERCROW
OVERCROWD
OVERCROWDED

OVERCROWDING
OVERCROWDINGS
OVERCROWDS
OVERCROWED
OVERCROWING
OVERCROWS
OVERCULTIVATE
OVERCULTIVATED
OVERCULTIVATES
OVERCULTIVATING
OVERCULTIVATION
OVERCURE
OVERCURED
OVERCURES
OVERCURING
OVERCURIOSITY
OVERCURIOUS
OVERCUT
OVERCUTS
OVERCUTTING
OVERDARE
OVERDARED
OVERDARES
OVERDARING
OVERDATED
OVERDEAR
OVERDECK
OVERDECKED
OVERDECKING
OVERDECKS
OVERDECORATE
OVERDECORATED
OVERDECORATES
OVERDECORATING
OVERDECORATION
OVERDECORATIONS
OVERDEFENSIVE
OVERDEFENSIVELY
OVERDEFERENTIAL
OVERDELIBERATE
OVERDELICATE
OVERDELICATELY
OVERDEMANDING
OVERDEPENDENCE
OVERDEPENDENCES
OVERDEPENDENT
OVERDESIGN
OVERDESIGNED
OVERDESIGNING
OVERDESIGNS
OVERDESIROUS
OVERDETAILED
OVERDETERMINED
OVERDEVELOP
OVERDEVELOPED
OVERDEVELOPING

OVERDEVELOPMENT
OVERDEVELOPS
OVERDEVIATE
OVERDEVIATED
OVERDEVIATES
OVERDEVIATING
OVERDID
OVERDIGHT
OVERDILIGENT
OVERDILIGENTLY
OVERDILUTE
OVERDILUTED
OVERDILUTES
OVERDILUTING
OVERDIRECT
OVERDIRECTED
OVERDIRECTING
OVERDIRECTS
OVERDISCOUNT
OVERDISCOUNTED
OVERDISCOUNTING
OVERDISCOUNTS
OVERDISTANT
OVERDIVERSIFIED
OVERDIVERSIFIES
OVERDIVERSIFY
OVERDIVERSITIES
OVERDIVERSITY
OVERDO
OVERDOCUMENT
OVERDOCUMENTED
OVERDOCUMENTING
OVERDOCUMENTS
OVERDOER
OVERDOERS
OVERDOES
OVERDOG
OVERDOGS
OVERDOING
OVERDOMINANCE
OVERDOMINANCES
OVERDOMINANT
OVERDONE
OVERDOSAGE
OVERDOSAGES
OVERDOSE
OVERDOSED
OVERDOSES
OVERDOSING
OVERDRAFT
OVERDRAFTS
OVERDRAMATIC
OVERDRAMATISE
OVERDRAMATISED
OVERDRAMATISES
OVERDRAMATISING

OVERDRAMATIZE
OVERDRAMATIZED
OVERDRAMATIZES
OVERDRAMATIZING
OVERDRANK
OVERDRAUGHT
OVERDRAUGHTS
OVERDRAW
OVERDRAWING
OVERDRAWN
OVERDRAWS
OVERDRESS
OVERDRESSED
OVERDRESSES
OVERDRESSING
OVERDREW
OVERDRIED
OVERDRIES
OVERDRINK
OVERDRINKING
OVERDRINKS
OVERDRIVE
OVERDRIVEN
OVERDRIVES
OVERDRIVING
OVERDROVE
OVERDRUNK
OVERDRY
OVERDRYING
OVERDUB
OVERDUBBED
OVERDUBBING
OVERDUBS
OVERDUE
OVERDUST
OVERDUSTED
OVERDUSTING
OVERDUSTS
OVERDYE
OVERDYED
OVERDYEING
OVERDYES
OVEREAGER
OVEREAGERNESS
OVEREAGERNESSES
OVEREARNEST
OVEREASY
OVEREAT
OVEREATEN
OVEREATER
OVEREATERS
OVEREATING
OVEREATS
OVERED
OVEREDIT
OVEREDITED

OVEREDITING
OVEREDITS
OVEREDUCATE
OVEREDUCATED
OVEREDUCATES
OVEREDUCATING
OVEREDUCATION
OVEREDUCATIONS
OVEREFFUSIVE
OVEREFFUSIVELY
OVERELABORATE
OVERELABORATED
OVERELABORATES
OVERELABORATING
OVERELABORATION
OVERELATE
OVERELATED
OVERELATES
OVERELATING
OVERELATION
OVEREMBELLISH
OVEREMBELLISHED
OVEREMBELLISHES
OVEREMBROIDER
OVEREMBROIDERED
OVEREMBROIDERS
OVEREMBROIDERY
OVEREMOTE
OVEREMOTED
OVEREMOTES
OVEREMOTING
OVEREMOTIONAL
OVEREMPHASES
OVEREMPHASIS
OVEREMPHASISE
OVEREMPHASISED
OVEREMPHASISES
OVEREMPHASISING
OVEREMPHASIZE
OVEREMPHASIZED
OVEREMPHASIZES
OVEREMPHASIZING
OVEREMPHATIC
OVEREMULATION
OVEREMULATIONS
OVERENAMORED
OVERENCOURAGE
OVERENCOURAGED
OVERENCOURAGES
OVERENCOURAGING
OVERENERGETIC
OVERENGINEER
OVERENGINEERED
OVERENGINEERING
OVERENGINEERS
OVERENROLLED

OVERENTERTAINED
OVERENTHUSIASM
OVERENTHUSIASMS
OVEREQUIPPED
OVERESTIMATE
OVERESTIMATED
OVERESTIMATES
OVERESTIMATING
OVERESTIMATION
OVERESTIMATIONS
OVEREVALUATION
OVEREVALUATIONS
OVEREXACTING
OVEREXAGGERATE
OVEREXAGGERATED
OVEREXAGGERATES
OVEREXCITABLE
OVEREXCITABLY
OVEREXCITE
OVEREXCITED
OVEREXCITES
OVEREXCITING
OVEREXERCISE
OVEREXERCISED
OVEREXERCISES
OVEREXERCISING
OVEREXERT
OVEREXERTED
OVEREXERTING
OVEREXERTION
OVEREXERTIONS
OVEREXERTS
OVEREXPAND
OVEREXPANDED
OVEREXPANDING
OVEREXPANDS
OVEREXPANSION
OVEREXPANSIONS
OVEREXPECTANT
OVEREXPECTATION
OVEREXPENDITURE
OVEREXPLAIN
OVEREXPLAINED
OVEREXPLAINING
OVEREXPLAINS
OVEREXPLICIT
OVEREXPLOIT
OVEREXPLOITED
OVEREXPLOITING
OVEREXPLOITS
OVEREXPOSE
OVEREXPOSED
OVEREXPOSES
OVEREXPOSING
OVEREXPOSURE
OVEREXPOSURES

OVEREXPRESSIVE
OVEREXTEND
OVEREXTENDED
OVEREXTENDING
OVEREXTENDS
OVEREXTENSION
OVEREXTENSIONS
OVEREXTRACTION
OVEREXTRACTIONS
OVEREXTRAVAGANT
OVEREXUBERANT
OVEREYE
OVEREYED
OVEREYEING
OVEREYES
OVEREYING
OVERFACILE
OVERFALL
OVERFALLEN
OVERFALLING
OVERFALLS
OVERFAMILIAR
OVERFAMILIARITY
OVERFANCIFUL
OVERFANCIFULLY
OVERFAR
OVERFAST
OVERFASTIDIOUS
OVERFAT
OVERFATIGUE
OVERFATIGUED
OVERFATIGUES
OVERFAVOR
OVERFAVORED
OVERFAVORING
OVERFAVORS
OVERFEAR
OVERFEARED
OVERFEARFUL
OVERFEARFULLY
OVERFEARFULNESS
OVERFEARING
OVERFEARS
OVERFED
OVERFEED
OVERFEEDING
OVERFEEDS
OVERFELL
OVERFERTILIZE
OVERFERTILIZED
OVERFERTILIZES
OVERFERTILIZING
OVERFILL
OVERFILLED
OVERFILLING
OVERFILLS

OVERFINE
OVERFINENESS
OVERFINENESSES
OVERFINISHED
OVERFISH
OVERFISHED
OVERFISHES
OVERFISHING
OVERFLEW
OVERFLIES
OVERFLIGHT
OVERFLIGHTS
OVERFLOURISH
OVERFLOURISHED
OVERFLOURISHES
OVERFLOURISHING
OVERFLOW
OVERFLOWED
OVERFLOWING
OVERFLOWINGLY
OVERFLOWINGS
OVERFLOWN
OVERFLOWS
OVERFLUSH
OVERFLUSHES
OVERFLY
OVERFLYING
OVERFOCUS
OVERFOCUSED
OVERFOCUSES
OVERFOCUSING
OVERFOCUSSED
OVERFOCUSSES
OVERFOCUSSING
OVERFOLD
OVERFOLDED
OVERFOLDING
OVERFOLDS
OVERFOND
OVERFONDLY
OVERFONDNESS
OVERFONDNESSES
OVERFORWARD
OVERFORWARDNESS
OVERFOUL
OVERFRAGILE
OVERFRAGILITY
OVERFRAUGHT
OVERFREE
OVERFREEDOM
OVERFREEDOMS
OVERFREELY
OVERFREIGHT
OVERFREIGHTING
OVERFREIGHTS
OVERFULFILL

OVERFULFILLED
OVERFULFILLING
OVERFULFILLS
OVERFULL
OVERFULLNESS
OVERFULLNESSES
OVERFULNESS
OVERFULNESSES
OVERFUND
OVERFUNDED
OVERFUNDING
OVERFUNDINGS
OVERFUNDS
OVERFURNISH
OVERFURNISHED
OVERFURNISHES
OVERFURNISHING
OVERFUSSY
OVERGALL
OVERGALLED
OVERGALLING
OVERGALLS
OVERGANG
OVERGANGING
OVERGANGS
OVERGARMENT
OVERGARMENTS
OVERGAVE
OVERGEAR
OVERGEARED
OVERGEARING
OVERGEARS
OVERGENERALISE
OVERGENERALISED
OVERGENERALISES
OVERGENERALIZE
OVERGENERALIZED
OVERGENERALIZES
OVERGENEROSITY
OVERGENEROUS
OVERGENEROUSLY
OVERGET
OVERGETS
OVERGETTING
OVERGILD
OVERGILDED
OVERGILDING
OVERGILDS
OVERGILT
OVERGIRD
OVERGIRDED
OVERGIRDING
OVERGIRDS
OVERGIRT
OVERGIVE
OVERGIVEN

OVERGIVES
OVERGIVING
OVERGLAD
OVERGLAMORIZE
OVERGLAMORIZED
OVERGLAMORIZES
OVERGLAMORIZING
OVERGLANCE
OVERGLANCED
OVERGLANCES
OVERGLANCING
OVERGLAZE
OVERGLAZED
OVERGLAZES
OVERGLAZING
OVERGLOOM
OVERGLOOMED
OVERGLOOMING
OVERGLOOMS
OVERGO
OVERGOAD
OVERGOADED
OVERGOADING
OVERGOADS
OVERGOES
OVERGOING
OVERGOINGS
OVERGONE
OVERGORGE
OVERGORGED
OVERGORGES
OVERGORGING
OVERGOT
OVERGOVERN
OVERGOVERNED
OVERGOVERNING
OVERGOVERNS
OVERGRAIN
OVERGRAINED
OVERGRAINER
OVERGRAINERS
OVERGRAINING
OVERGRAINS
OVERGRASS
OVERGRASSED
OVERGRASSES
OVERGRASSING
OVERGRAZE
OVERGRAZED
OVERGRAZES
OVERGRAZING
OVERGRAZINGS
OVERGREAT
OVERGREEDY
OVERGREEN
OVERGREENED

OVERGREENING
OVERGREENS
OVERGREW
OVERGROUND
OVERGROW
OVERGROWING
OVERGROWN
OVERGROWS
OVERGROWTH
OVERGROWTHS
OVERHAILE
OVERHAILED
OVERHAILES
OVERHAILING
OVERHAIR
OVERHAIRS
OVERHALE
OVERHALED
OVERHALES
OVERHALING
OVERHAND
OVERHANDED
OVERHANDING
OVERHANDLE
OVERHANDLED
OVERHANDLES
OVERHANDLING
OVERHANDS
OVERHANG
OVERHANGING
OVERHANGS
OVERHAPPY
OVERHARD
OVERHARVEST
OVERHARVESTED
OVERHARVESTING
OVERHARVESTS
OVERHASTE
OVERHASTES
OVERHASTILY
OVERHASTINESS
OVERHASTINESSES
OVERHASTY
OVERHATE
OVERHATED
OVERHATES
OVERHATING
OVERHAUL
OVERHAULED
OVERHAULING
OVERHAULS
OVERHEAD
OVERHEADS
OVERHEAP
OVERHEAPED
OVERHEAPING

OVERHEAPS
OVERHEAR
OVERHEARD
OVERHEARING
OVERHEARS
OVERHEAT
OVERHEATED
OVERHEATING
OVERHEATINGS
OVERHEATS
OVERHELD
OVERHENT
OVERHENTING
OVERHENTS
OVERHIGH
OVERHIT
OVERHITS
OVERHITTING
OVERHOLD
OVERHOLDING
OVERHOLDS
OVERHOLY
OVERHOMOGENIZE
OVERHOMOGENIZED
OVERHOMOGENIZES
OVERHOPE
OVERHOPED
OVERHOPES
OVERHOPING
OVERHOT
OVERHUNG
OVERHUNT
OVERHUNTED
OVERHUNTING
OVERHUNTINGS
OVERHUNTS
OVERHURRIED
OVERHURRIEDNESS
OVERHYPE
OVERHYPED
OVERHYPES
OVERHYPING
OVERIDEALISE
OVERIDEALISED
OVERIDEALISES
OVERIDEALISING
OVERIDEALISTIC
OVERIDEALIZE
OVERIDEALIZED
OVERIDEALIZES
OVERIDEALIZING
OVERIDENTIFIED
OVERIDENTIFIES
OVERIDENTIFY
OVERIDENTIFYING
OVERIDLE

OVERIMAGINATIVE
OVERIMPRESS
OVERIMPRESSED
OVERIMPRESSES
OVERIMPRESSING
OVERINCLINE
OVERINCLINED
OVERINCLINES
OVERINCLINING
OVERINDULGE
OVERINDULGED
OVERINDULGENCE
OVERINDULGENCES
OVERINDULGENT
OVERINDULGES
OVERINDULGING
OVERINFLATE
OVERINFLATED
OVERINFLATES
OVERINFLATING
OVERINFLATION
OVERINFLATIONS
OVERINFLUENCE
OVERINFLUENCED
OVERINFLUENCES
OVERINFLUENCING
OVERINFLUENTIAL
OVERINFORM
OVERINFORMED
OVERINFORMING
OVERINFORMS
OVERING
OVERINGENIOUS
OVERINGENUITIES
OVERINGENUITY
OVERINKED
OVERINSISTENCE
OVERINSISTENT
OVERINSISTENTLY
OVERINSURANCE
OVERINSURANCES
OVERINSURE
OVERINSURED
OVERINSURES
OVERINSURING
OVERINTENSE
OVERINTENSELY
OVERINTENSITIES
OVERINTENSITY
OVERINTEREST
OVERINTERESTED
OVERINVEST
OVERINVESTED
OVERINVESTING
OVERINVESTMENT
OVERINVESTMENTS

OVERINVESTS
OVERISSUANCE
OVERISSUANCES
OVERISSUE
OVERISSUED
OVERISSUES
OVERISSUING
OVERJOY
OVERJOYED
OVERJOYING
OVERJOYS
OVERJUMP
OVERJUMPED
OVERJUMPING
OVERJUMPS
OVERJUST
OVERKEEN
OVERKEEP
OVERKEEPING
OVERKEEPS
OVERKEPT
OVERKEST
OVERKILL
OVERKILLED
OVERKILLING
OVERKILLS
OVERKIND
OVERKINDNESS
OVERKINDNESSES
OVERKING
OVERKINGS
OVERKNEE
OVERLABOR
OVERLABORED
OVERLABORING
OVERLABORS
OVERLABOUR
OVERLABOURED
OVERLABOURING
OVERLABOURS
OVERLADE
OVERLADED
OVERLADEN
OVERLADES
OVERLADING
OVERLAID
OVERLAIN
OVERLAND
OVERLANDED
OVERLANDER
OVERLANDERS
OVERLANDING
OVERLANDS
OVERLAP
OVERLAPPED
OVERLAPPING

OVERLAPS
OVERLARD
OVERLARDED
OVERLARDING
OVERLARDS
OVERLARGE
OVERLATE
OVERLAUNCH
OVERLAUNCHED
OVERLAUNCHES
OVERLAUNCHING
OVERLAVISH
OVERLAX
OVERLAY
OVERLAYING
OVERLAYINGS
OVERLAYS
OVERLEAF
OVERLEAP
OVERLEAPED
OVERLEAPING
OVERLEAPS
OVERLEAPT
OVERLEARN
OVERLEARNED
OVERLEARNING
OVERLEARNS
OVERLEATHER
OVERLEATHERS
OVERLEAVEN
OVERLEAVENED
OVERLEAVENING
OVERLEAVENS
OVERLEND
OVERLENDING
OVERLENDS
OVERLENGTH
OVERLENGTHEN
OVERLENGTHENED
OVERLENGTHENING
OVERLENGTHENS
OVERLENGTHS
OVERLENT
OVERLET
OVERLETS
OVERLETTING
OVERLEWD
OVERLIE
OVERLIER
OVERLIERS
OVERLIES
OVERLIGHT
OVERLIGHTED
OVERLIGHTING
OVERLIGHTS
OVERLIT

OVERLITERAL
OVERLITERARY
OVERLIVE
OVERLIVED
OVERLIVES
OVERLIVING
OVERLOAD
OVERLOADED
OVERLOADING
OVERLOADS
OVERLOCK
OVERLOCKED
OVERLOCKER
OVERLOCKERS
OVERLOCKING
OVERLOCKINGS
OVERLOCKS
OVERLONG
OVERLOOK
OVERLOOKED
OVERLOOKER
OVERLOOKERS
OVERLOOKING
OVERLOOKS
OVERLORD
OVERLORDED
OVERLORDING
OVERLORDS
OVERLORDSHIP
OVERLORDSHIPS
OVERLOUD
OVERLOVE
OVERLOVED
OVERLOVES
OVERLOVING
OVERLUSH
OVERLUSTY
OVERLY
OVERLYING
OVERMAGNIFIED
OVERMAGNIFIES
OVERMAGNIFY
OVERMAGNIFYING
OVERMAN
OVERMANAGE
OVERMANAGED
OVERMANAGES
OVERMANAGING
OVERMANNED
OVERMANNERED
OVERMANNING
OVERMANS
OVERMANTEL
OVERMANTELS
OVERMANY
OVERMAST

OVERMASTED
OVERMASTER
OVERMASTERED
OVERMASTERING
OVERMASTERS
OVERMASTING
OVERMASTS
OVERMATCH
OVERMATCHED
OVERMATCHES
OVERMATCHING
OVERMATTER
OVERMATTERS
OVERMATURE
OVERMATURITIES
OVERMATURITY
OVERMEASURE
OVERMEASURED
OVERMEASURES
OVERMEASURING
OVERMEDICATE
OVERMEDICATED
OVERMEDICATES
OVERMEDICATING
OVERMEDICATION
OVERMEDICATIONS
OVERMEEK
OVERMELT
OVERMELTED
OVERMELTING
OVERMELTS
OVERMEN
OVERMERRY
OVERMIGHTY
OVERMILD
OVERMILK
OVERMILKED
OVERMILKING
OVERMILKS
OVERMINE
OVERMINED
OVERMINES
OVERMINING
OVERMIX
OVERMIXED
OVERMIXES
OVERMIXING
OVERMODEST
OVERMODESTLY
OVERMODIFIED
OVERMODIFIES
OVERMODIFY
OVERMODIFYING
OVERMOUNT
OVERMOUNTED
OVERMOUNTING

OVERMOUNTS
OVERMUCH
OVERMUCHES
OVERMULTIPLIED
OVERMULTIPLIES
OVERMULTIPLY
OVERMULTIPLYING
OVERMULTITUDE
OVERMULTITUDED
OVERMULTITUDES
OVERMULTITUDING
OVERMUSCLED
OVERNAME
OVERNAMED
OVERNAMES
OVERNAMING
OVERNEAR
OVERNEAT
OVERNET
OVERNETS
OVERNETTED
OVERNETTING
OVERNEW
OVERNICE
OVERNICELY
OVERNICENESS
OVERNICENESSES
OVERNIGHT
OVERNIGHTED
OVERNIGHTER
OVERNIGHTERS
OVERNIGHTING
OVERNIGHTS
OVERNOURISH
OVERNOURISHED
OVERNOURISHES
OVERNOURISHING
OVERNUTRITION
OVERNUTRITIONS
OVEROBVIOUS
OVEROFFICE
OVEROFFICED
OVEROFFICES
OVEROFFICING
OVEROPERATE
OVEROPERATED
OVEROPERATES
OVEROPERATING
OVEROPINIONATED
OVEROPTIMISM
OVEROPTIMISMS
OVEROPTIMIST
OVEROPTIMISTIC
OVEROPTIMISTS
OVERORCHESTRATE
OVERORGANIZE

OVERORGANIZED
OVERORGANIZES
OVERORGANIZING
OVERORNAMENT
OVERORNAMENTED
OVERORNAMENTING
OVERORNAMENTS
OVERPACKAGE
OVERPACKAGED
OVERPACKAGES
OVERPACKAGING
OVERPAGE
OVERPAID
OVERPAINT
OVERPAINTED
OVERPAINTING
OVERPAINTS
OVERPART
OVERPARTED
OVERPARTICULAR
OVERPARTING
OVERPARTS
OVERPASS
OVERPASSED
OVERPASSES
OVERPASSING
OVERPAST
OVERPAY
OVERPAYING
OVERPAYMENT
OVERPAYMENTS
OVERPAYS
OVERPEDAL
OVERPEDALED
OVERPEDALING
OVERPEDALLED
OVERPEDALLING
OVERPEDALS
OVERPEER
OVERPEERED
OVERPEERING
OVERPEERS
OVERPEOPLE
OVERPEOPLED
OVERPEOPLES
OVERPEOPLING
OVERPERCH
OVERPERCHED
OVERPERCHES
OVERPERCHING
OVERPERSUADE
OVERPERSUADED
OVERPERSUADES
OVERPERSUADING
OVERPERSUASION
OVERPERSUASIONS

OVERPERT
OVERPESSIMISTIC
OVERPICTURE
OVERPICTURED
OVERPICTURES
OVERPICTURING
OVERPITCH
OVERPITCHED
OVERPITCHES
OVERPITCHING
OVERPLACED
OVERPLAID
OVERPLAIDED
OVERPLAIDS
OVERPLAN
OVERPLANNED
OVERPLANNING
OVERPLANS
OVERPLANT
OVERPLANTED
OVERPLANTING
OVERPLANTS
OVERPLAST
OVERPLAY
OVERPLAYED
OVERPLAYING
OVERPLAYS
OVERPLIED
OVERPLIES
OVERPLOT
OVERPLOTS
OVERPLOTTED
OVERPLOTTING
OVERPLUS
OVERPLUSES
OVERPLUSSES
OVERPLY
OVERPLYING
OVERPOISE
OVERPOISED
OVERPOISES
OVERPOISING
OVERPOPULATE
OVERPOPULATED
OVERPOPULATES
OVERPOPULATING
OVERPOPULATION
OVERPOPULATIONS
OVERPOST
OVERPOSTED
OVERPOSTING
OVERPOSTS
OVERPOTENT
OVERPOWER
OVERPOWERED
OVERPOWERFUL

OVERPOWERING
OVERPOWERINGLY
OVERPOWERS
OVERPRAISE
OVERPRAISED
OVERPRAISES
OVERPRAISING
OVERPRECISE
OVERPREPARATION
OVERPREPARE
OVERPREPARED
OVERPREPARES
OVERPREPARING
OVERPRESCRIBE
OVERPRESCRIBED
OVERPRESCRIBES
OVERPRESCRIBING
OVERPRESS
OVERPRESSED
OVERPRESSES
OVERPRESSING
OVERPRESSURE
OVERPRESSURES
OVERPRICE
OVERPRICED
OVERPRICES
OVERPRICING
OVERPRINT
OVERPRINTED
OVERPRINTING
OVERPRINTS
OVERPRIVILEGED
OVERPRIZE
OVERPRIZED
OVERPRIZES
OVERPRIZING
OVERPROCESS
OVERPROCESSED
OVERPROCESSES
OVERPROCESSING
OVERPRODUCE
OVERPRODUCED
OVERPRODUCES
OVERPRODUCING
OVERPRODUCTION
OVERPRODUCTIONS
OVERPROGRAM
OVERPROGRAMED
OVERPROGRAMING
OVERPROGRAMMED
OVERPROGRAMMING
OVERPROGRAMS
OVERPROMINENCE
OVERPROMINENT
OVERPROMINENTLY
OVERPROMISE

OVERPROMISED
OVERPROMISES
OVERPROMISING
OVERPROMOTE
OVERPROMOTED
OVERPROMOTES
OVERPROMOTING
OVERPROMPT
OVERPROMPTLY
OVERPROOF
OVERPROPORTION
OVERPROPORTIONS
OVERPROTECT
OVERPROTECTED
OVERPROTECTING
OVERPROTECTION
OVERPROTECTIONS
OVERPROTECTIVE
OVERPROTECTS
OVERPROUD
OVERPUBLICISE
OVERPUBLICISED
OVERPUBLICISES
OVERPUBLICISING
OVERPUBLICIZE
OVERPUBLICIZED
OVERPUBLICIZES
OVERPUBLICIZING
OVERPUMP
OVERPUMPED
OVERPUMPING
OVERPUMPS
OVERQUALIFIED
OVERRACK
OVERRACKED
OVERRACKING
OVERRACKS
OVERRAKE
OVERRAKED
OVERRAKES
OVERRAKING
OVERRAN
OVERRANK
OVERRASH
OVERRASHLY
OVERRASHNESS
OVERRASHNESSES
OVERRATE
OVERRATED
OVERRATES
OVERRATING
OVERRAUGHT
OVERREACH
OVERREACHED
OVERREACHER
OVERREACHERS

OVERREACHES
OVERREACHING
OVERREACT
OVERREACTED
OVERREACTING
OVERREACTION
OVERREACTIONS
OVERREACTS
OVERREAD
OVERREADING
OVERREADS
OVERRECKON
OVERRECKONED
OVERRECKONING
OVERRECKONS
OVERRED
OVERREDDED
OVERREDDING
OVERREDS
OVERREFINE
OVERREFINED
OVERREFINEMENT
OVERREFINEMENTS
OVERREFINES
OVERREFINING
OVERREGULATE
OVERREGULATED
OVERREGULATES
OVERREGULATING
OVERREGULATION
OVERREGULATIONS
OVERRELIANCE
OVERRELIANCES
OVERREN
OVERRENNING
OVERRENS
OVERREPORT
OVERREPORTED
OVERREPORTING
OVERREPORTS
OVERREPRESENTED
OVERRESPOND
OVERRESPONDED
OVERRESPONDING
OVERRESPONDS
OVERRESTRICT
OVERRESTRICTED
OVERRESTRICTING
OVERRESTRICTION
OVERRESTRICTS
OVERRICH
OVERRIDDEN
OVERRIDE
OVERRIDER
OVERRIDERS
OVERRIDES

OVERRIDING
OVERRIFE
OVERRIGHTEOUS
OVERRIGHTEOUSLY
OVERRIGID
OVERRIPE
OVERRIPEN
OVERRIPENED
OVERRIPENESS
OVERRIPENESSES
OVERRIPENING
OVERRIPENS
OVERROAST
OVERROASTED
OVERROASTING
OVERROASTS
OVERRODE
OVERROMANTICISE
OVERROMANTICIZE
OVERRUDE
OVERRUFF
OVERRUFFED
OVERRUFFING
OVERRUFFS
OVERRULE
OVERRULED
OVERRULER
OVERRULERS
OVERRULES
OVERRULING
OVERRULINGS
OVERRUN
OVERRUNNER
OVERRUNNERS
OVERRUNNING
OVERRUNS
OVERS
OVERSAD
OVERSAIL
OVERSAILED
OVERSAILING
OVERSAILS
OVERSALE
OVERSALES
OVERSALT
OVERSALTED
OVERSALTING
OVERSALTS
OVERSANGUINE
OVERSATURATE
OVERSATURATED
OVERSATURATES
OVERSATURATING
OVERSATURATION
OVERSATURATIONS
OVERSAUCE

OVERSAUCED
OVERSAUCES
OVERSAUCING
OVERSAVE
OVERSAVED
OVERSAVES
OVERSAVING
OVERSAW
OVERSCALE
OVERSCALED
OVERSCEPTICAL
OVERSCEPTICALLY
OVERSCORE
OVERSCORED
OVERSCORES
OVERSCORING
OVERSCRUPULOUS
OVERSCUTCHED
OVERSEA
OVERSEAS
OVERSECRETION
OVERSECRETIONS
OVERSEE
OVERSEED
OVERSEEDED
OVERSEEDING
OVERSEEDS
OVERSEEING
OVERSEEN
OVERSEER
OVERSEERS
OVERSEES
OVERSELL
OVERSELLING
OVERSELLS
OVERSENSITIVE
OVERSENSITIVITY
OVERSERIOUS
OVERSERIOUSLY
OVERSERVICE
OVERSERVICED
OVERSERVICES
OVERSERVICING
OVERSET
OVERSETS
OVERSETTING
OVERSEVERE
OVERSEVERELY
OVERSEW
OVERSEWED
OVERSEWING
OVERSEWN
OVERSEWS
OVERSEXED
OVERSHADE
OVERSHADED

OVERSHADES
OVERSHADING
OVERSHADOW
OVERSHADOWED
OVERSHADOWING
OVERSHADOWS
OVERSHARP
OVERSHARPLY
OVERSHINE
OVERSHINES
OVERSHINING
OVERSHIRT
OVERSHIRTS
OVERSHOE
OVERSHOES
OVERSHONE
OVERSHOOT
OVERSHOOTING
OVERSHOOTS
OVERSHOT
OVERSHOTS
OVERSHOWER
OVERSHOWERED
OVERSHOWERING
OVERSHOWERS
OVERSICK
OVERSIDE
OVERSIDES
OVERSIGHT
OVERSIGHTS
OVERSIMPLE
OVERSIMPLIFIED
OVERSIMPLIFIES
OVERSIMPLIFY
OVERSIMPLIFYING
OVERSIMPLISTIC
OVERSIMPLY
OVERSIZE
OVERSIZED
OVERSIZES
OVERSIZING
OVERSKIP
OVERSKIPPED
OVERSKIPPING
OVERSKIPS
OVERSKIRT
OVERSKIRTS
OVERSLAUGH
OVERSLAUGHED
OVERSLAUGHING
OVERSLAUGHS
OVERSLEEP
OVERSLEEPING
OVERSLEEPS
OVERSLEEVE
OVERSLEEVES

OVERSLEPT
OVERSLIP
OVERSLIPPED
OVERSLIPPING
OVERSLIPS
OVERSLIPT
OVERSLOW
OVERSMAN
OVERSMART
OVERSMARTLY
OVERSMEN
OVERSMOKE
OVERSMOKED
OVERSMOKES
OVERSMOKING
OVERSOAK
OVERSOAKED
OVERSOAKING
OVERSOAKS
OVERSOFT
OVERSOLD
OVERSOLICITOUS
OVERSOON
OVERSOUL
OVERSOULS
OVERSOW
OVERSOWED
OVERSOWING
OVERSOWN
OVERSOWS
OVERSPARING
OVERSPECIALISE
OVERSPECIALISED
OVERSPECIALISES
OVERSPECIALIZE
OVERSPECIALIZED
OVERSPECIALIZES
OVERSPECULATE
OVERSPECULATED
OVERSPECULATES
OVERSPECULATING
OVERSPECULATION
OVERSPEND
OVERSPENDER
OVERSPENDERS
OVERSPENDING
OVERSPENDS
OVERSPENT
OVERSPILL
OVERSPILLED
OVERSPILLING
OVERSPILLS
OVERSPILT
OVERSPIN
OVERSPINS
OVERSPREAD

OVERSPREADING
OVERSPREADS
OVERSTABILITIES
OVERSTABILITY
OVERSTAFF
OVERSTAFFED
OVERSTAFFING
OVERSTAFFS
OVERSTAIN
OVERSTAINED
OVERSTAINING
OVERSTAINS
OVERSTAND
OVERSTANDING
OVERSTANDS
OVERSTANK
OVERSTARE
OVERSTARED
OVERSTARES
OVERSTARING
OVERSTATE
OVERSTATED
OVERSTATEMENT
OVERSTATEMENTS
OVERSTATES
OVERSTATING
OVERSTAY
OVERSTAYED
OVERSTAYER
OVERSTAYERS
OVERSTAYING
OVERSTAYS
OVERSTEER
OVERSTEERED
OVERSTEERING
OVERSTEERS
OVERSTEP
OVERSTEPPED
OVERSTEPPING
OVERSTEPS
OVERSTIMULATE
OVERSTIMULATED
OVERSTIMULATES
OVERSTIMULATING
OVERSTIMULATION
OVERSTINK
OVERSTINKING
OVERSTINKS
OVERSTIR
OVERSTIRRED
OVERSTIRRING
OVERSTIRS
OVERSTOCK
OVERSTOCKED
OVERSTOCKING
OVERSTOCKS

OVERSTOOD
OVERSTORIES
OVERSTORY
OVERSTRAIN
OVERSTRAINED
OVERSTRAINING
OVERSTRAINS
OVERSTRESS
OVERSTRESSED
OVERSTRESSES
OVERSTRESSING
OVERSTRETCH
OVERSTRETCHED
OVERSTRETCHES
OVERSTRETCHING
OVERSTREW
OVERSTREWED
OVERSTREWING
OVERSTREWN
OVERSTREWS
OVERSTRICT
OVERSTRIDDEN
OVERSTRIDE
OVERSTRIDES
OVERSTRIDING
OVERSTRIKE
OVERSTRIKES
OVERSTRIKING
OVERSTRODE
OVERSTRONG
OVERSTROOKE
OVERSTRUCK
OVERSTRUCTURED
OVERSTRUNG
OVERSTUDIED
OVERSTUDIES
OVERSTUDY
OVERSTUDYING
OVERSTUFF
OVERSTUFFED
OVERSTUFFING
OVERSTUFFS
OVERSTUNK
OVERSUBSCRIBE
OVERSUBSCRIBED
OVERSUBSCRIBES
OVERSUBSCRIBING
OVERSUBTLE
OVERSUBTLETIES
OVERSUBTLETY
OVERSUDS
OVERSUDSED
OVERSUDSES
OVERSUDSING
OVERSUP
OVERSUPPED

OVERSUPPING
OVERSUPPLIED
OVERSUPPLIES
OVERSUPPLY
OVERSUPPLYING
OVERSUPS
OVERSURE
OVERSUSCEPTIBLE
OVERSUSPICIOUS
OVERSWAM
OVERSWAY
OVERSWAYED
OVERSWAYING
OVERSWAYS
OVERSWEAR
OVERSWEARING
OVERSWEARS
OVERSWEET
OVERSWEETEN
OVERSWEETENED
OVERSWEETENING
OVERSWEETENS
OVERSWEETNESS
OVERSWEETNESSES
OVERSWELL
OVERSWELLED
OVERSWELLING
OVERSWELLS
OVERSWIM
OVERSWIMMING
OVERSWIMS
OVERSWING
OVERSWINGING
OVERSWINGS
OVERSWOLLEN
OVERSWORE
OVERSWORN
OVERSWUM
OVERSWUNG
OVERSYSTEMATIC
OVERT
OVERTAKE
OVERTAKEN
OVERTAKES
OVERTAKING
OVERTALK
OVERTALKATIVE
OVERTALKED
OVERTALKING
OVERTALKS
OVERTAME
OVERTART
OVERTASK
OVERTASKED
OVERTASKING
OVERTASKS

OVERTAX
OVERTAXATION
OVERTAXATIONS
OVERTAXED
OVERTAXES
OVERTAXING
OVERTECHNICAL
OVERTEDIOUS
OVERTEEM
OVERTEEMED
OVERTEEMING
OVERTEEMS
OVERTHIN
OVERTHINK
OVERTHINKING
OVERTHINKS
OVERTHOUGHT
OVERTHREW
OVERTHROW
OVERTHROWER
OVERTHROWERS
OVERTHROWING
OVERTHROWN
OVERTHROWS
OVERTHRUST
OVERTHRUSTS
OVERTHWART
OVERTHWARTED
OVERTHWARTING
OVERTHWARTS
OVERTIGHTEN
OVERTIGHTENED
OVERTIGHTENING
OVERTIGHTENS
OVERTIME
OVERTIMED
OVERTIMELY
OVERTIMER
OVERTIMERS
OVERTIMES
OVERTIMING
OVERTIP
OVERTIPPED
OVERTIPPING
OVERTIPS
OVERTIRE
OVERTIRED
OVERTIRES
OVERTIRING
OVERTLY
OVERTNESS
OVERTNESSES
OVERTOIL
OVERTOILED
OVERTOILING
OVERTOILS

OVERTONE
OVERTONES
OVERTOOK
OVERTOP
OVERTOPPED
OVERTOPPING
OVERTOPS
OVERTOWER
OVERTOWERED
OVERTOWERING
OVERTOWERS
OVERTRADE
OVERTRADED
OVERTRADES
OVERTRADING
OVERTRAIN
OVERTRAINED
OVERTRAINING
OVERTRAINS
OVERTREAT
OVERTREATED
OVERTREATING
OVERTREATMENT
OVERTREATMENTS
OVERTREATS
OVERTRICK
OVERTRICKS
OVERTRIM
OVERTRIMMED
OVERTRIMMING
OVERTRIMS
OVERTRIP
OVERTRIPPED
OVERTRIPPING
OVERTRIPS
OVERTRUMP
OVERTRUMPED
OVERTRUMPING
OVERTRUMPS
OVERTRUST
OVERTRUSTED
OVERTRUSTING
OVERTRUSTS
OVERTURE
OVERTURED
OVERTURES
OVERTURING
OVERTURN
OVERTURNED
OVERTURNER
OVERTURNERS
OVERTURNING
OVERTURNS
OVERTYPE
OVERTYPED
OVERTYPES

OVERTYPING
OVERURGE
OVERURGED
OVERURGES
OVERURGING
OVERUSE
OVERUSED
OVERUSES
OVERUSING
OVERUTILIZATION
OVERUTILIZE
OVERUTILIZED
OVERUTILIZES
OVERUTILIZING
OVERVALUATION
OVERVALUATIONS
OVERVALUE
OVERVALUED
OVERVALUES
OVERVALUING
OVERVEIL
OVERVEILED
OVERVEILING
OVERVEILS
OVERVIEW
OVERVIEWS
OVERVIOLENT
OVERVIVID
OVERVOLTAGE
OVERVOLTAGES
OVERVOTE
OVERVOTED
OVERVOTES
OVERVOTING
OVERWARM
OVERWARMED
OVERWARMING
OVERWARMS
OVERWARY
OVERWASH
OVERWASHES
OVERWATCH
OVERWATCHED
OVERWATCHES
OVERWATCHING
OVERWATER
OVERWATERED
OVERWATERING
OVERWATERS
OVERWEAK
OVERWEAR
OVERWEARIED
OVERWEARIES
OVERWEARING
OVERWEARS
OVERWEARY

OVERWEARYING
OVERWEATHER
OVERWEATHERED
OVERWEATHERING
OVERWEATHERS
OVERWEEN
OVERWEENED
OVERWEENING
OVERWEENINGLY
OVERWEENINGNESS
OVERWEENINGS
OVERWEENS
OVERWEIGH
OVERWEIGHED
OVERWEIGHING
OVERWEIGHS
OVERWEIGHT
OVERWEIGHTED
OVERWEIGHTING
OVERWEIGHTS
OVERWENT
OVERWET
OVERWETS
OVERWETTED
OVERWETTING
OVERWHELM
OVERWHELMED
OVERWHELMING
OVERWHELMINGLY
OVERWHELMINGS
OVERWHELMS
OVERWIDE
OVERWILLING
OVERWILLINGNESS
OVERWILY
OVERWIND
OVERWINDING
OVERWINDS
OVERWING
OVERWINGED
OVERWINGING
OVERWINGS
OVERWINTER
OVERWINTERED
OVERWINTERING
OVERWINTERS
OVERWISE
OVERWISELY
OVERWITHHELD
OVERWITHHOLD
OVERWITHHOLDING
OVERWITHHOLDS
OVERWORD
OVERWORDS
OVERWORE
OVERWORK

OVERWORKED	OVIPOSITS	OWLETS	OXBOW
OVERWORKING	OVIRAPTOR	OWLIER	OXBOWS
OVERWORKS	OVIRAPTORS	OWLIEST	OXCART
OVERWORN	OVISAC	OWLING	OXCARTS
OVERWOUND	OVISACS	OWLISH	OXEN
OVERWREST	OVIST	OWLISHLY	OXER
OVERWRESTED	OVISTS	OWLISHNESS	OXERS
OVERWRESTING	OVOID	OWLISHNESSES	OXES
OVERWRESTLE	OVOIDAL	OWLLIKE	OXEYE
OVERWRESTLED	OVOIDS	OWLS	OXEYES
OVERWRESTLES	OVOLI	OWLY	OXFORD
OVERWRESTLING	OVOLO	OWN	OXFORDS
OVERWRESTS	OVOLOS	OWNABLE	OXGANG
OVERWRITE	OVONIC	OWNED	OXGANGS
OVERWRITES	OVONICS	OWNER	OXGATE
OVERWRITING	OVOTESTES	OWNERLESS	OXGATES
OVERWRITTEN	OVOTESTIS	OWNERS	OXHEAD
OVERWROTE	OVOVIVIPARITY	OWNERSHIP	OXHEADS
OVERWROUGHT	OVOVIVIPAROUS	OWNERSHIPS	OXHEART
OVERYEAR	OVOVIVIPAROUSLY	OWNING	OXHEARTS
OVERYEARED	OVULAR	OWNS	OXHIDE
OVERYEARING	OVULARY	OWRE	OXHIDES
OVERYEARS	OVULATE	OWRECOME	OXID
OVERZEAL	OVULATED	OWRECOMES	OXIDABLE
OVERZEALOUS	OVULATES	OWRELAY	OXIDANT
OVERZEALOUSLY	OVULATING	OWRELAYS	OXIDANTS
OVERZEALOUSNESS	OVULATION	OWRES	OXIDASE
OVERZEALS	OVULATIONS	OWREWORD	OXIDASES
OVIBOS	OVULATORY	OWREWORDS	OXIDASIC
OVIBOSES	OVULE	OWRIE	OXIDATE
OVIBOVINE	OVULES	OWRIER	OXIDATED
OVICIDAL	OVULIFEROUS	OWRIEST	OXIDATES
OVICIDE	OVUM	OWSE	OXIDATING
OVICIDES	OW	OWSEN	OXIDATION
OVIDUCAL	OWCHE	OWT	OXIDATIONAL
OVIDUCT	OWCHES	OWTS	OXIDATIONS
OVIDUCTAL	OWE	OX	OXIDATIVE
OVIDUCTS	OWED	OXACILLIN	OXIDATIVELY
OVIFEROUS	OWELTIES	OXACILLINS	OXIDE
OVIFORM	OWELTY	OXALACETATE	OXIDES
OVIGEROUS	OWER	OXALACETATES	OXIDIC
OVINE	OWERBY	OXALATE	OXIDIMETRIC
OVINES	OWERLOUP	OXALATED	OXIDIMETRY
OVIPARA	OWERLOUPEN	OXALATES	OXIDISABLE
OVIPARITIES	OWERLOUPING	OXALATING	OXIDISATION
OVIPARITY	OWERLOUPIT	OXALIC	OXIDISE
OVIPAROUS	OWERLOUPS	OXALIS	OXIDISED
OVIPAROUSLY	OWES	OXALISES	OXIDISER
OVIPOSIT	OWING	OXALOACETATE	OXIDISERS
OVIPOSITED	OWL	OXALOACETATES	OXIDISES
OVIPOSITING	OWLED	OXAZEPAM	OXIDISING
OVIPOSITION	OWLER	OXAZEPAMS	OXIDIZABLE
OVIPOSITIONAL	OWLERIES	OXAZINE	OXIDIZATION
OVIPOSITIONS	OWLERS	OXAZINES	OXIDIZE
OVIPOSITOR	OWLERY	OXBLOOD	OXIDIZED
OVIPOSITORS	OWLET	OXBLOODS	OXIDIZER

OXIDIZERS
OXIDIZES
OXIDIZING
OXIDOREDUCTASE
OXIDOREDUCTASES
OXIDS
OXIM
OXIME
OXIMES
OXIMETER
OXIMETERS
OXIMS
OXLAND
OXLANDS
OXLIP
OXLIPS
OXO
OXONIUM
OXONIUMS
OXPECKER
OXPECKERS
OXSLIP
OXSLIPS
OXTAIL
OXTAILS
OXTER
OXTERED
OXTERING
OXTERS
OXTONGUE
OXTONGUES
OXY
OXYACETYLENE
OXYACID
OXYACIDS
OXYCEPHALIC
OXYCEPHALOUS
OXYCEPHALY
OXYGEN
OXYGENATE
OXYGENATED
OXYGENATES
OXYGENATING
OXYGENATION
OXYGENATIONS
OXYGENATOR
OXYGENATORS
OXYGENIC
OXYGENISE
OXYGENISED
OXYGENISER
OXYGENISERS
OXYGENISES
OXYGENISING
OXYGENIZE
OXYGENIZED

OXYGENIZER
OXYGENIZERS
OXYGENIZES
OXYGENIZING
OXYGENLESS
OXYGENOUS
OXYGENS
OXYHAEMOGLOBIN
OXYHAEMOGLOBINS
OXYHEMOGLOBIN
OXYHEMOGLOBINS
OXYHYDROGEN
OXYMEL
OXYMELS
OXYMORA
OXYMORON
OXYMORONIC
OXYMORONICALLY
OXYMORONS
OXYNTIC
OXYPHENBUTAZONE
OXYPHIL
OXYPHILE
OXYPHILES
OXYPHILIC
OXYPHILS
OXYRHYNCHUS
OXYRHYNCHUSES
OXYSALT
OXYSALTS
OXYSOME
OXYSOMES
OXYSULPHIDE
OXYTETRACYCLINE
OXYTOCIC
OXYTOCICS
OXYTOCIN
OXYTOCINS
OXYTONE
OXYTONES
OXYURIASES
OXYURIASIS
OY
OYE
OYER
OYERS
OYES
OYESES
OYESSES
OYEZ
OYEZES
OYS
OYSTER
OYSTERCATCHER
OYSTERCATCHERS
OYSTERED

OYSTERER
OYSTERERS
OYSTERING
OYSTERINGS
OYSTERMAN
OYSTERMEN
OYSTERS
OYSTRIGE
OYSTRIGES
OZAENA
OZAENAS
OZEKI
OZEKIS
OZOCERITE
OZOCERITES
OZOKERITE
OZOKERITES
OZONATE
OZONATED
OZONATES
OZONATING
OZONATION
OZONATIONS
OZONE
OZONES
OZONIC
OZONIDE
OZONIDES
OZONIFEROUS
OZONISATION
OZONISATIONS
OZONISE
OZONISED
OZONISER
OZONISERS
OZONISES
OZONISING
OZONIZATION
OZONIZATIONS
OZONIZE
OZONIZED
OZONIZER
OZONIZERS
OZONIZES
OZONIZING
OZONOLYSIS
OZONOSPHERE
OZONOSPHERES
OZONOUS
OZZIE

P

PA
PAAL
PAALS
PABLUM
PABLUMS
PABOUCHE
PABOUCHES
PABULAR
PABULOUS
PABULUM
PABULUMS
PAC
PACA
PACABLE
PACAS
PACATION
PACATIONS
PACE
PACED
PACEMAKER
PACEMAKERS
PACEMAKING
PACEMAKINGS
PACER
PACERS
PACES
PACESETTER
PACESETTERS
PACESETTING
PACEWAY
PACEWAYS
PACEY
PACHA
PACHADOM
PACHADOMS
PACHAK
PACHAKS
PACHALIC
PACHALICS
PACHAS
PACHINKO
PACHINKOS
PACHISI
PACHISIS
PACHOULI
PACHOULIS
PACHUCO
PACHUCOS
PACHYCARPOUS
PACHYDACTYL
PACHYDACTYLOUS

PACHYDERM
PACHYDERMAL
PACHYDERMATOUS
PACHYDERMIA
PACHYDERMIAS
PACHYDERMIC
PACHYDERMOUS
PACHYDERMS
PACHYMENINGITIS
PACHYMETER
PACHYMETERS
PACHYSANDRA
PACHYSANDRAS
PACHYTENE
PACHYTENES
PACIER
PACIEST
PACIFIABLE
PACIFIC
PACIFICAL
PACIFICALLY
PACIFICATE
PACIFICATED
PACIFICATES
PACIFICATING
PACIFICATION
PACIFICATIONS
PACIFICATOR
PACIFICATORS
PACIFICATORY
PACIFICISM
PACIFICISMS
PACIFICIST
PACIFICISTS
PACIFIED
PACIFIER
PACIFIERS
PACIFIES
PACIFISM
PACIFISMS
PACIFIST
PACIFISTIC
PACIFISTICALLY
PACIFISTS
PACIFY
PACIFYING
PACING
PACK
PACKABILITIES
PACKABILITY
PACKABLE

PACKAGE
PACKAGED
PACKAGER
PACKAGERS
PACKAGES
PACKAGING
PACKAGINGS
PACKBOARD
PACKBOARDS
PACKED
PACKER
PACKERS
PACKET
PACKETED
PACKETING
PACKETS
PACKETTED
PACKETTING
PACKFONG
PACKFONGS
PACKFRAME
PACKFRAMES
PACKHORSE
PACKHORSES
PACKING
PACKINGHOUSE
PACKINGHOUSES
PACKINGS
PACKLY
PACKMAN
PACKMEN
PACKNESS
PACKNESSES
PACKS
PACKSACK
PACKSACKS
PACKSADDLE
PACKSADDLES
PACKSHEET
PACKSHEETS
PACKSTAFF
PACKSTAFFS
PACKTHREAD
PACKTHREADS
PACKWAX
PACKWAXES
PACKWAY
PACKWAYS
PACLITAXEL
PACLITAXELS
PACO

PACOS
PACS
PACT
PACTA
PACTION
PACTIONAL
PACTIONED
PACTIONING
PACTIONS
PACTS
PACTUM
PACY
PAD
PADANG
PADANGS
PADAUK
PADAUKS
PADDED
PADDER
PADDERS
PADDIES
PADDING
PADDINGS
PADDLE
PADDLEBALL
PADDLEBALLS
PADDLEBOARD
PADDLEBOARDS
PADDLEBOAT
PADDLEBOATS
PADDLED
PADDLEFISH
PADDLEFISHES
PADDLER
PADDLERS
PADDLES
PADDLING
PADDLINGS
PADDOCK
PADDOCKED
PADDOCKING
PADDOCKS
PADDY
PADDYMELON
PADDYMELONS
PADDYWACK
PADDYWACKS
PADDYWHACK
PADDYWHACKS
PADELLA
PADELLAS

PADEMELON	PAEDIATRIST	PAGANISE	PAH
PADEMELONS	PAEDIATRISTS	PAGANISED	PAHLAVI
PADERERO	PAEDIATRY	PAGANISER	PAHLAVIS
PADEREROES	PAEDOBAPTISM	PAGANISERS	PAHOEHOE
PADEREROS	PAEDOBAPTISMS	PAGANISES	PAHOEHOES
PADI	PAEDOBAPTIST	PAGANISH	PAHS
PADIS	PAEDOBAPTISTS	PAGANISING	PAID
PADISHAH	PAEDODONTIC	PAGANISM	PAIDEUTIC
PADISHAHS	PAEDODONTICS	PAGANISMS	PAIDEUTICS
PADKOS	PAEDOGENESES	PAGANIST	PAIDLE
PADLE	PAEDOGENESIS	PAGANISTIC	PAIDLES
PADLES	PAEDOGENETIC	PAGANISTICALLY	PAIGLE
PADLOCK	PAEDOGENIC	PAGANISTS	PAIGLES
PADLOCKED	PAEDOLOGICAL	PAGANIZATION	PAIK
PADLOCKING	PAEDOLOGIES	PAGANIZATIONS	PAIKED
PADLOCKS	PAEDOLOGIST	PAGANIZE	PAIKING
PADMA	PAEDOLOGISTS	PAGANIZED	PAIKS
PADMAS	PAEDOLOGY	PAGANIZER	PAIL
PADNAG	PAEDOMORPHIC	PAGANIZERS	PAILFUL
PADNAGS	PAEDOMORPHISM	PAGANIZES	PAILFULS
PADOUK	PAEDOMORPHISMS	PAGANIZING	PAILLARD
PADOUKS	PAEDOMORPHOSES	PAGANS	PAILLARDS
PADRE	PAEDOMORPHOSIS	PAGE	PAILLASSE
PADRES	PAEDOPHILE	PAGEANT	PAILLASSES
PADRI	PAEDOPHILES	PAGEANTRIES	PAILLETTE
PADRONE	PAEDOPHILIA	PAGEANTRY	PAILLETTES
PADRONES	PAEDOPHILIAC	PAGEANTS	PAILLON
PADRONI	PAEDOPHILIACS	PAGEBOY	PAILLONS
PADS	PAEDOPHILIAS	PAGEBOYS	PAILS
PADSAW	PAEDOPHILIC	PAGED	PAILSFUL
PADSAWS	PAEDOPHILICS	PAGEHOOD	PAIN
PADSHAH	PAEDOTRIBE	PAGEHOODS	PAINCH
PADSHAHS	PAEDOTRIBES	PAGER	PAINCHES
PADUASOY	PAEDOTROPHIES	PAGERS	PAINED
PADUASOYS	PAEDOTROPHY	PAGES	PAINFUL
PADYMELON	PAELLA	PAGINAL	PAINFULLER
PADYMELONS	PAELLAS	PAGINATE	PAINFULLEST
PAEAN	PAENULA	PAGINATED	PAINFULLY
PAEANISM	PAENULAE	PAGINATES	PAINFULNESS
PAEANISMS	PAENULAS	PAGINATING	PAINFULNESSES
PAEANS	PAEON	PAGINATION	PAINIM
PAEDAGOGIC	PAEONIC	PAGINATIONS	PAINIMS
PAEDAGOGUE	PAEONICS	PAGING	PAINING
PAEDAGOGUES	PAEONIES	PAGINGS	PAINKILLER
PAEDERAST	PAEONS	PAGLE	PAINKILLERS
PAEDERASTIC	PAEONY	PAGLES	PAINKILLING
PAEDERASTICALLY	PAESAN	PAGOD	PAINLESS
PAEDERASTS	PAESANI	PAGODA	PAINLESSLY
PAEDERASTY	PAESANO	PAGODAS	PAINLESSNESS
PAEDEUTIC	PAESANOS	PAGODS	PAINLESSNESSES
PAEDEUTICS	PAESANS	PAGRI	PAINS
PAEDIATRIC	PAGAN	PAGRIS	PAINSTAKER
PAEDIATRICIAN	PAGANDOM	PAGURIAN	PAINSTAKERS
PAEDIATRICIANS	PAGANDOMS	PAGURIANS	PAINSTAKING
PAEDIATRICS	PAGANISATION	PAGURID	PAINSTAKINGLY
PAEDIATRIES	PAGANISATIONS	PAGURIDS	PAINSTAKINGNESS

PAINSTAKINGS
PAINT
PAINTABLE
PAINTBALL
PAINTBALLS
PAINTBOX
PAINTBOXES
PAINTBRUSH
PAINTBRUSHES
PAINTED
PAINTER
PAINTERLINESS
PAINTERLINESSES
PAINTERLY
PAINTERS
PAINTIER
PAINTIEST
PAINTINESS
PAINTINESSES
PAINTING
PAINTINGS
PAINTRESS
PAINTRESSES
PAINTS
PAINTURE
PAINTURES
PAINTWORK
PAINTWORKS
PAINTY
PAIOCK
PAIOCKE
PAIOCKES
PAIOCKS
PAIR
PAIRE
PAIRED
PAIRER
PAIRES
PAIREST
PAIRIAL
PAIRIALS
PAIRING
PAIRINGS
PAIRS
PAIRWISE
PAIS
PAISA
PAISAN
PAISANA
PAISANAS
PAISANO
PAISANOS
PAISANS
PAISAS
PAISE
PAISLEY

PAISLEYS
PAITRICK
PAITRICKS
PAJAMA
PAJAMAED
PAJAMAS
PAJOCK
PAJOCKE
PAJOCKES
PAJOCKS
PAKAHI
PAKAHIS
PAKAPOO
PAKAPOOS
PAKEHA
PAKEHAS
PAKFONG
PAKFONGS
PAKIHI
PAKIHIS
PAKIRIKIRI
PAKKA
PAKOKO
PAKOKOS
PAKORA
PAKORAS
PAKTHONG
PAKTHONGS
PAKTONG
PAKTONGS
PAL
PALABRA
PALABRAS
PALACE
PALACED
PALACES
PALADIN
PALADINS
PALAEANTHROPIC
PALAEBIOLOGIES
PALAEBIOLOGIST
PALAEBIOLOGISTS
PALAEBIOLOGY
PALAEETHNOLOGY
PALAEOANTHROPIC
PALAEOBIOLOGIC
PALAEOBIOLOGIES
PALAEOBIOLOGIST
PALAEOBIOLOGY
PALAEOBOTANIC
PALAEOBOTANICAL
PALAEOBOTANIES
PALAEOBOTANIST
PALAEOBOTANISTS
PALAEOBOTANY
PALAEOCLIMATE

PALAEOCLIMATES
PALAEOCLIMATIC
PALAEOCRYSTIC
PALAEOCURRENT
PALAEOCURRENTS
PALAEOECOLOGIC
PALAEOECOLOGIES
PALAEOECOLOGIST
PALAEOECOLOGY
PALAEOETHNOLOGY
PALAEOGAEA
PALAEOGAEAS
PALAEOGEOGRAPHY
PALAEOGRAPHER
PALAEOGRAPHERS
PALAEOGRAPHIC
PALAEOGRAPHICAL
PALAEOGRAPHIES
PALAEOGRAPHIST
PALAEOGRAPHISTS
PALAEOGRAPHY
PALAEOLIMNOLOGY
PALAEOLITH
PALAEOLITHS
PALAEOMAGNETIC
PALAEOMAGNETISM
PALAEONTOGRAPHY
PALAEONTOLOGIES
PALAEONTOLOGIST
PALAEONTOLOGY
PALAEOPATHOLOGY
PALAEOPEDOLOGY
PALAEOPHYTOLOGY
PALAEOTYPE
PALAEOTYPES
PALAEOTYPIC
PALAEOZOOLOGIES
PALAEOZOOLOGIST
PALAEOZOOLOGY
PALAESTRA
PALAESTRAE
PALAESTRAL
PALAESTRAS
PALAESTRIC
PALAESTRICAL
PALAFITTE
PALAFITTES
PALAGI
PALAGIS
PALAGONITE
PALAGONITES
PALAIS
PALAMA
PALAMAE
PALAMATE
PALAMINO

PALAMINOS
PALAMPORE
PALAMPORES
PALANKEEN
PALANKEENS
PALANQUIN
PALANQUINS
PALAS
PALASES
PALATABILITIES
PALATABILITY
PALATABLE
PALATABLENESS
PALATABLENESSES
PALATABLY
PALATAL
PALATALISATION
PALATALISATIONS
PALATALISE
PALATALISED
PALATALISES
PALATALISING
PALATALIZATION
PALATALIZATIONS
PALATALIZE
PALATALIZED
PALATALIZES
PALATALIZING
PALATALLY
PALATALS
PALATE
PALATED
PALATES
PALATIAL
PALATIALLY
PALATIALNESS
PALATIALNESSES
PALATINATE
PALATINATES
PALATINE
PALATINES
PALATING
PALAVER
PALAVERED
PALAVERER
PALAVERERS
PALAVERING
PALAVERS
PALAY
PALAYS
PALAZZI
PALAZZO
PALAZZOS
PALE
PALEA
PALEACEOUS

PALEAE
PALEAL
PALEBUCK
PALEBUCKS
PALED
PALEFACE
PALEFACES
PALELY
PALEMPORE
PALEMPORES
PALENESS
PALENESSES
PALEOBIOLOGIC
PALEOBIOLOGICAL
PALEOBIOLOGIES
PALEOBIOLOGIST
PALEOBIOLOGISTS
PALEOBIOLOGY
PALEOBOTANIC
PALEOBOTANICAL
PALEOBOTANIES
PALEOBOTANIST
PALEOBOTANISTS
PALEOBOTANY
PALEOECOLOGIC
PALEOECOLOGICAL
PALEOECOLOGIES
PALEOECOLOGIST
PALEOECOLOGISTS
PALEOECOLOGY
PALEOGEOGRAPHIC
PALEOGEOGRAPHY
PALEOGRAPHER
PALEOGRAPHERS
PALEOGRAPHIC
PALEOGRAPHICAL
PALEOGRAPHIES
PALEOGRAPHY
PALEOMAGNETIC
PALEOMAGNETISM
PALEOMAGNETISMS
PALEOMAGNETIST
PALEOMAGNETISTS
PALEONTOLOGIC
PALEONTOLOGICAL
PALEONTOLOGIES
PALEONTOLOGIST
PALEONTOLOGISTS
PALEONTOLOGY
PALEOPATHOLOGY
PALEOSOL
PALEOSOLS
PALEOZOOLOGICAL
PALEOZOOLOGIES
PALEOZOOLOGIST
PALEOZOOLOGISTS

PALEOZOOLOGY
PALER
PALES
PALEST
PALESTRA
PALESTRAE
PALESTRAS
PALET
PALETOT
PALETOTS
PALETS
PALETTE
PALETTES
PALEWAYS
PALEWISE
PALFRENIER
PALFRENIERS
PALFREY
PALFREYED
PALFREYS
PALIER
PALIEST
PALIFICATION
PALIFICATIONS
PALIFORM
PALIKAR
PALIKARS
PALILALIA
PALILALIAS
PALILLOGIES
PALILLOGY
PALIMONIES
PALIMONY
PALIMPSEST
PALIMPSESTS
PALINDROME
PALINDROMES
PALINDROMIC
PALINDROMICAL
PALINDROMIST
PALINDROMISTS
PALING
PALINGENESES
PALINGENESIA
PALINGENESIAS
PALINGENESIES
PALINGENESIS
PALINGENESIST
PALINGENESISTS
PALINGENESY
PALINGENETIC
PALINGENETICAL
PALINGS
PALINKA
PALINODE
PALINODES

PALINODIES
PALINODY
PALINOPIA
PALINOPSIA
PALISADE
PALISADED
PALISADES
PALISADING
PALISADO
PALISADOED
PALISADOES
PALISADOING
PALISANDER
PALISANDERS
PALISH
PALKEE
PALKEES
PALKI
PALKIS
PALL
PALLA
PALLADIA
PALLADIC
PALLADIOUS
PALLADIUM
PALLADIUMS
PALLADOUS
PALLAE
PALLAH
PALLAHS
PALLBEARER
PALLBEARERS
PALLED
PALLESCENCE
PALLESCENCES
PALLESCENT
PALLET
PALLETED
PALLETISATION
PALLETISATIONS
PALLETISE
PALLETISED
PALLETISER
PALLETISERS
PALLETISES
PALLETISING
PALLETIZATION
PALLETIZATIONS
PALLETIZE
PALLETIZED
PALLETIZER
PALLETIZERS
PALLETIZES
PALLETIZING
PALLETS
PALLETTE

PALLETTES
PALLIA
PALLIAL
PALLIAMENT
PALLIAMENTS
PALLIARD
PALLIARDS
PALLIASSE
PALLIASSES
PALLIATE
PALLIATED
PALLIATES
PALLIATING
PALLIATION
PALLIATIONS
PALLIATIVE
PALLIATIVELY
PALLIATIVES
PALLIATOR
PALLIATORS
PALLIATORY
PALLID
PALLIDER
PALLIDEST
PALLIDITIES
PALLIDITY
PALLIDLY
PALLIDNESS
PALLIDNESSES
PALLIER
PALLIEST
PALLING
PALLIUM
PALLIUMS
PALLONE
PALLONES
PALLOR
PALLORS
PALLS
PALLY
PALM
PALMACEOUS
PALMAR
PALMARIAN
PALMARY
PALMATE
PALMATED
PALMATELY
PALMATIFID
PALMATION
PALMATIONS
PALMATIPARTITE
PALMATISECT
PALMCORDER
PALMCORDERS
PALMED

PALMER
PALMERS
PALMERWORM
PALMERWORMS
PALMETTE
PALMETTES
PALMETTO
PALMETTOES
PALMETTOS
PALMFUL
PALMFULS
PALMHOUSE
PALMHOUSES
PALMIE
PALMIER
PALMIES
PALMIEST
PALMIET
PALMIETS
PALMIFICATION
PALMIFICATIONS
PALMING
PALMIPED
PALMIPEDE
PALMIPEDES
PALMIPEDS
PALMIST
PALMISTRIES
PALMISTRY
PALMISTS
PALMITATE
PALMITATES
PALMITIC
PALMITIN
PALMITINS
PALMLIKE
PALMS
PALMTOP
PALMTOPS
PALMY
PALMYRA
PALMYRAS
PALOLO
PALOLOS
PALOMINO
PALOMINOS
PALOOKA
PALOOKAS
PALOVERDE
PALOVERDES
PALP
PALPABILITIES
PALPABILITY
PALPABLE
PALPABLENESS
PALPABLENESSES

PALPABLY
PALPAL
PALPATE
PALPATED
PALPATES
PALPATING
PALPATION
PALPATIONS
PALPATOR
PALPATORS
PALPEBRA
PALPEBRAE
PALPEBRAL
PALPEBRATE
PALPEBRATED
PALPEBRATES
PALPEBRATING
PALPED
PALPI
PALPING
PALPITANT
PALPITATE
PALPITATED
PALPITATES
PALPITATING
PALPITATION
PALPITATIONS
PALPS
PALPUS
PALS
PALSGRAVE
PALSGRAVES
PALSGRAVINE
PALSGRAVINES
PALSHIP
PALSHIPS
PALSIED
PALSIER
PALSIES
PALSIEST
PALSTAFF
PALSTAFFS
PALSTAVE
PALSTAVES
PALSY
PALSYING
PALTER
PALTERED
PALTERER
PALTERERS
PALTERING
PALTERS
PALTRIER
PALTRIEST
PALTRILY
PALTRINESS

PALTRINESSES
PALTRY
PALUDAL
PALUDAMENT
PALUDAMENTA
PALUDAMENTS
PALUDAMENTUM
PALUDAMENTUMS
PALUDIC
PALUDICOLOUS
PALUDINAL
PALUDINE
PALUDINOUS
PALUDISM
PALUDISMS
PALUDOSE
PALUDOUS
PALUSTRAL
PALUSTRIAN
PALUSTRINE
PALY
PALYNOLOGIC
PALYNOLOGICAL
PALYNOLOGICALLY
PALYNOLOGIES
PALYNOLOGIST
PALYNOLOGISTS
PALYNOLOGY
PAM
PAMPA
PAMPAS
PAMPASES
PAMPEAN
PAMPEANS
PAMPELMOOSE
PAMPELMOOSES
PAMPELMOUSE
PAMPELMOUSES
PAMPER
PAMPERED
PAMPEREDNESS
PAMPEREDNESSES
PAMPERER
PAMPERERS
PAMPERING
PAMPERO
PAMPEROS
PAMPERS
PAMPHLET
PAMPHLETEER
PAMPHLETEERED
PAMPHLETEERING
PAMPHLETEERINGS
PAMPHLETEERS
PAMPHLETS
PAMPHREY

PAMPHREYS
PAMPOEN
PAMPOENS
PAMPOOTIE
PAMPOOTIES
PAMS
PAN
PANACEA
PANACEAN
PANACEAS
PANACHAEA
PANACHAEAS
PANACHE
PANACHES
PANADA
PANADAS
PANAESTHESIA
PANAESTHESIAS
PANAESTHETISM
PANAESTHETISMS
PANAMA
PANAMAS
PANARIES
PANARITIUM
PANARITIUMS
PANARTHRITIS
PANARTHRITISES
PANARY
PANATELA
PANATELAS
PANATELLA
PANATELLAS
PANAX
PANAXES
PANBROIL
PANBROILED
PANBROILING
PANBROILS
PANCAKE
PANCAKED
PANCAKES
PANCAKING
PANCE
PANCES
PANCETTA
PANCETTAS
PANCHAX
PANCHAXES
PANCHAYAT
PANCHAYATS
PANCHEON
PANCHEONS
PANCHION
PANCHIONS
PANCHROMATIC
PANCHROMATISM

PANCHROMATISMS
PANCOSMIC
PANCOSMISM
PANCOSMISMS
PANCRATIA
PANCRATIAN
PANCRATIAST
PANCRATIASTS
PANCRATIC
PANCRATIST
PANCRATISTS
PANCRATIUM
PANCRATIUMS
PANCREAS
PANCREASES
PANCREATECTOMY
PANCREATIC
PANCREATIN
PANCREATINS
PANCREATITIDES
PANCREATITIS
PANCREATITISES
PANCREOZYMIN
PANCREOZYMINS
PANCYTOPENIA
PANCYTOPENIAS
PAND
PANDA
PANDAEMONIUM
PANDAEMONIUMS
PANDANACEOUS
PANDANI
PANDANUS
PANDANUSES
PANDAR
PANDARED
PANDARING
PANDARS
PANDAS
PANDATION
PANDATIONS
PANDECT
PANDECTIST
PANDECTISTS
PANDECTS
PANDEMIA
PANDEMIAN
PANDEMIAS
PANDEMIC
PANDEMICS
PANDEMONIAC
PANDEMONIACAL
PANDEMONIAN
PANDEMONIC
PANDEMONIUM
PANDEMONIUMS

PANDER
PANDERED
PANDERER
PANDERERS
PANDERESS
PANDERESSES
PANDERING
PANDERISM
PANDERISMS
PANDERLY
PANDERMITE
PANDERMITES
PANDEROUS
PANDERS
PANDICULATION
PANDICULATIONS
PANDIED
PANDIES
PANDIT
PANDITS
PANDOOR
PANDOORS
PANDORA
PANDORAS
PANDORE
PANDORES
PANDOUR
PANDOURS
PANDOWDIES
PANDOWDY
PANDS
PANDURA
PANDURAS
PANDURATE
PANDURATED
PANDURIFORM
PANDY
PANDYING
PANE
PANED
PANEER
PANEGOISM
PANEGOISMS
PANEGYRIC
PANEGYRICA
PANEGYRICAL
PANEGYRICALLY
PANEGYRICON
PANEGYRICS
PANEGYRIES
PANEGYRISE
PANEGYRISED
PANEGYRISES
PANEGYRISING
PANEGYRIST
PANEGYRISTS

PANEGYRIZE
PANEGYRIZED
PANEGYRIZES
PANEGYRIZING
PANEGYRY
PANEITIES
PANEITY
PANEL
PANELED
PANELING
PANELINGS
PANELIST
PANELISTS
PANELLED
PANELLING
PANELLINGS
PANELLIST
PANELLISTS
PANELS
PANENTHEISM
PANENTHEISMS
PANENTHEIST
PANENTHEISTS
PANES
PANESTHESIA
PANESTHESIAS
PANETELA
PANETELAS
PANETTONE
PANETTONES
PANETTONI
PANFISH
PANFISHES
PANFRIED
PANFRIES
PANFRY
PANFRYING
PANFUL
PANFULS
PANG
PANGA
PANGAMIC
PANGAMIES
PANGAMY
PANGAS
PANGED
PANGEN
PANGENE
PANGENES
PANGENESES
PANGENESIS
PANGENETIC
PANGENETICALLY
PANGENS
PANGING
PANGLESS

PANGOLIN
PANGOLINS
PANGRAM
PANGRAMMATIST
PANGRAMMATISTS
PANGRAMS
PANGS
PANHANDLE
PANHANDLED
PANHANDLER
PANHANDLERS
PANHANDLES
PANHANDLING
PANHARMONICON
PANHARMONICONS
PANHELLENIC
PANHELLENION
PANHELLENIONS
PANHELLENIUM
PANHELLENIUMS
PANHUMAN
PANIC
PANICK
PANICKED
PANICKIER
PANICKIEST
PANICKING
PANICKS
PANICKY
PANICLE
PANICLED
PANICLES
PANICMONGER
PANICMONGERING
PANICMONGERS
PANICS
PANICULATE
PANICULATED
PANICULATELY
PANICUM
PANICUMS
PANIDIOMORPHIC
PANIER
PANIERS
PANIFICATION
PANIFICATIONS
PANIM
PANIMS
PANING
PANISC
PANISCS
PANISK
PANISKS
PANISLAM
PANISLAMIC
PANISLAMISM

PANISLAMISMS
PANISLAMIST
PANISLAMISTS
PANISLAMS
PANJANDARUMS
PANJANDRA
PANJANDRUM
PANJANDRUMS
PANLEUCOPENIA
PANLEUCOPENIAS
PANLEUKOPENIA
PANLEUKOPENIAS
PANLOGISM
PANLOGISMS
PANMICTIC
PANMIXES
PANMIXIA
PANMIXIAS
PANMIXIS
PANMIXISES
PANNAGE
PANNAGES
PANNE
PANNED
PANNELLED
PANNES
PANNICK
PANNICKS
PANNICLE
PANNICLES
PANNICULUS
PANNICULUSES
PANNIER
PANNIERED
PANNIERS
PANNIKEL
PANNIKELL
PANNIKELLS
PANNIKELS
PANNIKIN
PANNIKINS
PANNING
PANNINGS
PANNOSE
PANNUS
PANNUSES
PANOCHA
PANOCHAS
PANOCHE
PANOCHES
PANOISTIC
PANOMPHAEAN
PANOPHOBIA
PANOPHOBIAS
PANOPHTHALMIA
PANOPHTHALMIAS

PANOPHTHALMITIS
PANOPLIED
PANOPLIES
PANOPLY
PANOPTIC
PANOPTICAL
PANOPTICALLY
PANOPTICON
PANOPTICONS
PANORAMA
PANORAMAS
PANORAMIC
PANORAMICALLY
PANPHARMACON
PANPHARMACONS
PANPIPE
PANPIPES
PANPSYCHISM
PANPSYCHISMS
PANPSYCHIST
PANPSYCHISTIC
PANPSYCHISTS
PANRADIOMETER
PANRADIOMETERS
PANS
PANSEXUAL
PANSEXUALISM
PANSEXUALISMS
PANSEXUALIST
PANSEXUALISTS
PANSEXUALITIES
PANSEXUALITY
PANSIED
PANSIES
PANSOPHIC
PANSOPHICAL
PANSOPHICALLY
PANSOPHIES
PANSOPHISM
PANSOPHISMS
PANSOPHIST
PANSOPHISTS
PANSOPHY
PANSPERMATISM
PANSPERMATISMS
PANSPERMATIST
PANSPERMATISTS
PANSPERMIA
PANSPERMIAS
PANSPERMIC
PANSPERMIES
PANSPERMISM
PANSPERMISMS
PANSPERMIST
PANSPERMISTS
PANSPERMY

PANSY
PANT
PANTABLE
PANTABLES
PANTAGAMIES
PANTAGAMY
PANTAGRAPH
PANTAGRAPHS
PANTALEON
PANTALEONS
PANTALETS
PANTALETTED
PANTALETTES
PANTALON
PANTALONES
PANTALONS
PANTALOON
PANTALOONED
PANTALOONERIES
PANTALOONERY
PANTALOONS
PANTDRESS
PANTDRESSES
PANTECHNICON
PANTECHNICONS
PANTED
PANTER
PANTERS
PANTHEISM
PANTHEISMS
PANTHEIST
PANTHEISTIC
PANTHEISTICAL
PANTHEISTICALLY
PANTHEISTS
PANTHENOL
PANTHENOLS
PANTHEOLOGIES
PANTHEOLOGIST
PANTHEOLOGISTS
PANTHEOLOGY
PANTHEON
PANTHEONS
PANTHER
PANTHERESS
PANTHERESSES
PANTHERINE
PANTHERISH
PANTHERS
PANTIE
PANTIES
PANTIHOSE
PANTILE
PANTILED
PANTILES

PANTILING
PANTILINGS
PANTINE
PANTINES
PANTING
PANTINGLY
PANTINGS
PANTISOCRACIES
PANTISOCRACY
PANTISOCRAT
PANTISOCRATIC
PANTISOCRATICAL
PANTISOCRATIST
PANTISOCRATISTS
PANTISOCRATS
PANTLER
PANTLERS
PANTO
PANTOFFLE
PANTOFFLES
PANTOFLE
PANTOFLES
PANTOGRAPH
PANTOGRAPHER
PANTOGRAPHERS
PANTOGRAPHIC
PANTOGRAPHICAL
PANTOGRAPHIES
PANTOGRAPHS
PANTOGRAPHY
PANTOMIME
PANTOMIMED
PANTOMIMES
PANTOMIMIC
PANTOMIMICAL
PANTOMIMICALLY
PANTOMIMING
PANTOMIMIST
PANTOMIMISTS
PANTON
PANTONS
PANTOPHAGIES
PANTOPHAGIST
PANTOPHAGISTS
PANTOPHAGOUS
PANTOPHAGY
PANTOPHOBIA
PANTOPHOBIAS
PANTOPRAGMATIC
PANTOPRAGMATICS
PANTOS
PANTOSCOPE
PANTOSCOPES
PANTOSCOPIC
PANTOTHENATE
PANTOTHENATES

PANTOTHENIC
PANTOUFLE
PANTOUFLES
PANTOUM
PANTOUMS
PANTRIES
PANTROPIC
PANTROPICAL
PANTRY
PANTRYMAID
PANTRYMAIDS
PANTRYMAN
PANTRYMEN
PANTS
PANTSUIT
PANTSUITED
PANTSUITS
PANTUN
PANTUNS
PANTY
PANTYHOSE
PANTYWAIST
PANTYWAISTS
PANZER
PANZERS
PANZOOTIC
PAOLI
PAOLO
PAP
PAPA
PAPABLE
PAPACIES
PAPACY
PAPAIN
PAPAINS
PAPAL
PAPALISE
PAPALISED
PAPALISES
PAPALISING
PAPALISM
PAPALISMS
PAPALIST
PAPALISTS
PAPALIZE
PAPALIZED
PAPALIZES
PAPALIZING
PAPALLY
PAPAPRELATIST
PAPAPRELATISTS
PAPARAZZI
PAPARAZZO
PAPAS
PAPAVERACEOUS
PAPAVERINE

PAPAVERINES
PAPAVEROUS
PAPAW
PAPAWS
PAPAYA
PAPAYAN
PAPAYAS
PAPE
PAPER
PAPERBACK
PAPERBACKED
PAPERBACKER
PAPERBACKERS
PAPERBACKING
PAPERBACKS
PAPERBARK
PAPERBARKS
PAPERBOARD
PAPERBOARDS
PAPERBOUND
PAPERBOUNDS
PAPERBOY
PAPERBOYS
PAPERCLIP
PAPERCLIPS
PAPERED
PAPERER
PAPERERS
PAPERGIRL
PAPERGIRLS
PAPERHANGER
PAPERHANGERS
PAPERHANGING
PAPERHANGINGS
PAPERIER
PAPERIEST
PAPERINESS
PAPERINESSES
PAPERING
PAPERINGS
PAPERKNIFE
PAPERKNIVES
PAPERLESS
PAPERMAKER
PAPERMAKERS
PAPERMAKING
PAPERMAKINGS
PAPERS
PAPERWARE
PAPERWARES
PAPERWEIGHT
PAPERWEIGHTS
PAPERWORK
PAPERWORKS
PAPERY
PAPES

PAPETERIE
PAPETERIES
PAPHIAN
PAPHIANS
PAPILIO
PAPILIONACEOUS
PAPILIOS
PAPILLA
PAPILLAE
PAPILLAR
PAPILLARY
PAPILLATE
PAPILLATED
PAPILLIFEROUS
PAPILLIFORM
PAPILLITIS
PAPILLITISES
PAPILLOMA
PAPILLOMAS
PAPILLOMATA
PAPILLOMATOSIS
PAPILLOMATOUS
PAPILLOMAVIRUS
PAPILLON
PAPILLONS
PAPILLOSE
PAPILLOTE
PAPILLOTES
PAPILLOUS
PAPILLULATE
PAPILLULE
PAPILLULES
PAPISH
PAPISHER
PAPISHERS
PAPISHES
PAPISM
PAPISMS
PAPIST
PAPISTIC
PAPISTICAL
PAPISTICALLY
PAPISTRIES
PAPISTRY
PAPISTS
PAPOOSE
PAPOOSES
PAPOVAVIRUS
PAPOVAVIRUSES
PAPPADOM
PAPPADOMS
PAPPED
PAPPI
PAPPIER
PAPPIES
PAPPIEST

PAPPING
PAPPOOSE
PAPPOOSES
PAPPOSE
PAPPOUS
PAPPUS
PAPPUSES
PAPPY
PAPRICA
PAPRICAS
PAPRIKA
PAPRIKAS
PAPS
PAPULA
PAPULAE
PAPULAR
PAPULATION
PAPULATIONS
PAPULE
PAPULES
PAPULIFEROUS
PAPULOSE
PAPULOUS
PAPYRACEOUS
PAPYRAL
PAPYRI
PAPYRIAN
PAPYRINE
PAPYROLOGICAL
PAPYROLOGIES
PAPYROLOGIST
PAPYROLOGISTS
PAPYROLOGY
PAPYRUS
PAPYRUSES
PAR
PARA
PARABAPTISM
PARABAPTISMS
PARABASES
PARABASIS
PARABEMA
PARABEMATA
PARABEMATIC
PARABIOSES
PARABIOSIS
PARABIOTIC
PARABIOTICALLY
PARABLAST
PARABLASTIC
PARABLASTS
PARABLE
PARABLED
PARABLEPSES
PARABLEPSIES
PARABLEPSIS

PARABLEPSY
PARABLEPTIC
PARABLES
PARABLING
PARABOLA
PARABOLANUS
PARABOLANUSES
PARABOLAS
PARABOLE
PARABOLES
PARABOLIC
PARABOLICAL
PARABOLICALLY
PARABOLISATION
PARABOLISATIONS
PARABOLISE
PARABOLISED
PARABOLISES
PARABOLISING
PARABOLIST
PARABOLISTS
PARABOLIZATION
PARABOLIZATIONS
PARABOLIZE
PARABOLIZED
PARABOLIZES
PARABOLIZING
PARABOLOID
PARABOLOIDAL
PARABOLOIDS
PARABRAKE
PARABRAKES
PARACASEIN
PARACENTESES
PARACENTESIS
PARACETAMOL
PARACETAMOLS
PARACHOR
PARACHORS
PARACHRONISM
PARACHRONISMS
PARACHUTE
PARACHUTED
PARACHUTES
PARACHUTIC
PARACHUTING
PARACHUTIST
PARACHUTISTS
PARACLETE
PARACLETES
PARACME
PARACMES
PARACROSTIC
PARACROSTICS
PARACUSES
PARACUSIS

PARACYANOGEN
PARACYANOGENS
PARADE
PARADED
PARADER
PARADERS
PARADES
PARADIDDLE
PARADIDDLES
PARADIGM
PARADIGMATIC
PARADIGMATICAL
PARADIGMS
PARADING
PARADISAIC
PARADISAICAL
PARADISAICALLY
PARADISAL
PARADISE
PARADISEAN
PARADISES
PARADISIAC
PARADISIACAL
PARADISIACALLY
PARADISIAL
PARADISIAN
PARADISIC
PARADISICAL
PARADOCTOR
PARADOCTORS
PARADOR
PARADORES
PARADORS
PARADOS
PARADOSES
PARADOX
PARADOXAL
PARADOXER
PARADOXERS
PARADOXES
PARADOXICAL
PARADOXICALITY
PARADOXICALLY
PARADOXICALNESS
PARADOXIDIAN
PARADOXIES
PARADOXIST
PARADOXISTS
PARADOXOLOGIES
PARADOXOLOGY
PARADOXURE
PARADOXURES
PARADOXURINE
PARADOXY
PARADROP
PARADROPPED

PARADROPPING
PARADROPS
PARAENESES
PARAENESIS
PARAENETIC
PARAENETICAL
PARAESTHESIA
PARAESTHESIAS
PARAESTHETIC
PARAFFIN
PARAFFINE
PARAFFINED
PARAFFINES
PARAFFINIC
PARAFFINING
PARAFFINOID
PARAFFINS
PARAFFINY
PARAFFLE
PARAFFLES
PARAFLE
PARAFLES
PARAFOIL
PARAFOILS
PARAFORM
PARAFORMS
PARAGE
PARAGENESES
PARAGENESIA
PARAGENESIAS
PARAGENESIS
PARAGENETIC
PARAGENETICALLY
PARAGES
PARAGLIDER
PARAGLIDERS
PARAGLIDING
PARAGLIDINGS
PARAGLOSSA
PARAGLOSSAE
PARAGLOSSAL
PARAGLOSSATE
PARAGNATHISM
PARAGNATHISMS
PARAGNATHOUS
PARAGNOSES
PARAGNOSIS
PARAGOGE
PARAGOGES
PARAGOGIC
PARAGOGICAL
PARAGOGICALLY
PARAGOGUE
PARAGOGUES
PARAGON
PARAGONED

PARAGONING
PARAGONITE
PARAGONITES
PARAGONS
PARAGRAM
PARAGRAMMATIST
PARAGRAMMATISTS
PARAGRAMS
PARAGRAPH
PARAGRAPHED
PARAGRAPHER
PARAGRAPHERS
PARAGRAPHIA
PARAGRAPHIAS
PARAGRAPHIC
PARAGRAPHICAL
PARAGRAPHICALLY
PARAGRAPHING
PARAGRAPHIST
PARAGRAPHISTS
PARAGRAPHS
PARAHELIOTROPIC
PARAHYDROGEN
PARAINFLUENZA
PARAINFLUENZAS
PARAJOURNALISM
PARAJOURNALISMS
PARAKEELYA
PARAKEELYAS
PARAKEET
PARAKEETS
PARAKELIA
PARAKELIAS
PARAKITE
PARAKITES
PARAKITING
PARAKITINGS
PARALALIA
PARALALIAS
PARALANGUAGE
PARALANGUAGES
PARALDEHYDE
PARALDEHYDES
PARALEGAL
PARALEGALS
PARALEIPOMENA
PARALEIPOMENON
PARALEIPSES
PARALEIPSIS
PARALEXIA
PARALEXIAS
PARALEXIC
PARALIMNION
PARALIMNIONS
PARALINGUISTIC
PARALINGUISTICS

PARALIPOMENA
PARALIPOMENON
PARALIPSES
PARALIPSIS
PARALLACTIC
PARALLACTICAL
PARALLACTICALLY
PARALLAX
PARALLAXES
PARALLEL
PARALLELED
PARALLELEPIPED
PARALLELEPIPEDA
PARALLELEPIPEDS
PARALLELING
PARALLELINGS
PARALLELISE
PARALLELISED
PARALLELISES
PARALLELISING
PARALLELISM
PARALLELISMS
PARALLELIST
PARALLELISTIC
PARALLELISTS
PARALLELIZE
PARALLELIZED
PARALLELIZES
PARALLELIZING
PARALLELLED
PARALLELLING
PARALLELLY
PARALLELOGRAM
PARALLELOGRAMS
PARALLELOPIPED
PARALLELOPIPEDA
PARALLELOPIPEDS
PARALLELS
PARALLELWISE
PARALOGIA
PARALOGIAS
PARALOGIES
PARALOGISE
PARALOGISED
PARALOGISES
PARALOGISING
PARALOGISM
PARALOGISMS
PARALOGIST
PARALOGISTIC
PARALOGISTICAL
PARALOGISTS
PARALOGIZE
PARALOGIZED
PARALOGIZES
PARALOGIZING

PARALOGY
PARALYMPIC
PARALYMPICS
PARALYSATION
PARALYSATIONS
PARALYSE
PARALYSED
PARALYSER
PARALYSERS
PARALYSES
PARALYSING
PARALYSIS
PARALYTIC
PARALYTICALLY
PARALYTICS
PARALYZATION
PARALYZATIONS
PARALYZE
PARALYZED
PARALYZER
PARALYZERS
PARALYZES
PARALYZING
PARALYZINGLY
PARAMAECIA
PARAMAECIUM
PARAMAGNET
PARAMAGNETIC
PARAMAGNETISM
PARAMAGNETISMS
PARAMAGNETS
PARAMASTOID
PARAMASTOIDS
PARAMATTA
PARAMATTAS
PARAMECIA
PARAMECIUM
PARAMECIUMS
PARAMEDIC
PARAMEDICAL
PARAMEDICALS
PARAMEDICO
PARAMEDICOS
PARAMEDICS
PARAMENSTRUA
PARAMENSTRUUM
PARAMENSTRUUMS
PARAMENT
PARAMENTA
PARAMENTS
PARAMESE
PARAMESES
PARAMETER
PARAMETERIZE
PARAMETERIZED
PARAMETERIZES

PARAMETERIZING
PARAMETERS
PARAMETRAL
PARAMETRIC
PARAMETRICAL
PARAMETRICALLY
PARAMETRIZATION
PARAMETRIZE
PARAMETRIZED
PARAMETRIZES
PARAMETRIZING
PARAMILITARIES
PARAMILITARY
PARAMNESIA
PARAMNESIAS
PARAMO
PARAMOECIA
PARAMOECIUM
PARAMORPH
PARAMORPHIC
PARAMORPHINE
PARAMORPHISM
PARAMORPHISMS
PARAMORPHOUS
PARAMORPHS
PARAMOS
PARAMOUNCIES
PARAMOUNCY
PARAMOUNT
PARAMOUNTCIES
PARAMOUNTCY
PARAMOUNTLY
PARAMOUNTS
PARAMOUR
PARAMOURS
PARAMYLUM
PARAMYLUMS
PARAMYXOVIRUS
PARAMYXOVIRUSES
PARANEPHRIC
PARANEPHROS
PARANEPHROSES
PARANETE
PARANETES
PARANG
PARANGS
PARANOEA
PARANOEAS
PARANOEIC
PARANOEICS
PARANOIA
PARANOIAC
PARANOIACS
PARANOIAS
PARANOIC
PARANOICALLY

PARANOICS
PARANOID
PARANOIDAL
PARANOIDS
PARANORMAL
PARANORMALITIES
PARANORMALITY
PARANORMALLY
PARANORMALS
PARANTHELIA
PARANTHELION
PARANTHROPUS
PARANTHROPUSES
PARANYM
PARANYMPH
PARANYMPHS
PARANYMS
PARAPARESES
PARAPARESIS
PARAPARETIC
PARAPENTE
PARAPENTES
PARAPENTING
PARAPENTINGS
PARAPET
PARAPETED
PARAPETS
PARAPH
PARAPHASIA
PARAPHASIAS
PARAPHASIC
PARAPHED
PARAPHERNALIA
PARAPHILIA
PARAPHILIAC
PARAPHILIACS
PARAPHILIAS
PARAPHIMOSES
PARAPHIMOSIS
PARAPHING
PARAPHONIA
PARAPHONIAS
PARAPHONIC
PARAPHRASABLE
PARAPHRASE
PARAPHRASED
PARAPHRASER
PARAPHRASERS
PARAPHRASES
PARAPHRASING
PARAPHRAST
PARAPHRASTIC
PARAPHRASTICAL
PARAPHRASTS
PARAPHRAXES
PARAPHRAXIAS

PARAPHRAXIS
PARAPHRENIA
PARAPHRENIAS
PARAPHS
PARAPHYSATE
PARAPHYSES
PARAPHYSIS
PARAPINEAL
PARAPLEGIA
PARAPLEGIAS
PARAPLEGIC
PARAPLEGICS
PARAPODIA
PARAPODIAL
PARAPODIUM
PARAPOPHYSES
PARAPOPHYSIAL
PARAPOPHYSIS
PARAPRAXES
PARAPRAXIS
PARAPSYCHIC
PARAPSYCHICAL
PARAPSYCHISM
PARAPSYCHISMS
PARAPSYCHOLOGY
PARAPSYCHOSES
PARAPSYCHOSIS
PARAQUADRATE
PARAQUADRATES
PARAQUAT
PARAQUATS
PARAQUET
PARAQUETS
PARAQUITO
PARAQUITOS
PARARHYME
PARARHYMES
PARAROSANILINE
PARAROSANILINES
PARARTHRIA
PARARTHRIAS
PARAS
PARASAILING
PARASAILINGS
PARASANG
PARASANGS
PARASCENDER
PARASCENDERS
PARASCENDING
PARASCENDINGS
PARASCENIA
PARASCENIUM
PARASCEVE
PARASCEVES
PARASCIENCE
PARASCIENCES

PARASELENAE
PARASELENE
PARASELENIC
PARASEXUAL
PARASEXUALITIES
PARASEXUALITY
PARASHAH
PARASHIOTH
PARASHOTH
PARASITAEMIA
PARASITAEMIAS
PARASITE
PARASITES
PARASITIC
PARASITICAL
PARASITICALLY
PARASITICALNESS
PARASITICIDAL
PARASITICIDE
PARASITICIDES
PARASITISE
PARASITISED
PARASITISES
PARASITISING
PARASITISM
PARASITISMS
PARASITIZATION
PARASITIZATIONS
PARASITIZE
PARASITIZED
PARASITIZES
PARASITIZING
PARASITOID
PARASITOIDS
PARASITOLOGIC
PARASITOLOGICAL
PARASITOLOGIES
PARASITOLOGIST
PARASITOLOGISTS
PARASITOLOGY
PARASITOSES
PARASITOSIS
PARASKIED
PARASKIER
PARASKIERS
PARASKIING
PARASKIS
PARASOL
PARASOLS
PARASPHENOID
PARASPHENOIDS
PARASTATAL
PARASTATALLY
PARASTATALS
PARASTICHIES
PARASTICHOUS

PARASTICHY
PARASUICIDE
PARASUICIDES
PARASYMBIONT
PARASYMBIONTIC
PARASYMBIONTS
PARASYMBIOSES
PARASYMBIOSIS
PARASYMBIOTIC
PARASYMPATHETIC
PARASYNAPSES
PARASYNAPSIS
PARASYNAPTIC
PARASYNTHESES
PARASYNTHESIS
PARASYNTHETA
PARASYNTHETIC
PARASYNTHETON
PARATACTIC
PARATACTICAL
PARATACTICALLY
PARATAXES
PARATAXIS
PARATHA
PARATHAS
PARATHESES
PARATHESIS
PARATHION
PARATHIONS
PARATHORMONE
PARATHORMONES
PARATHYROID
PARATHYROIDS
PARATONIC
PARATROOP
PARATROOPER
PARATROOPERS
PARATROOPS
PARATYPHOID
PARATYPHOIDS
PARAVAIL
PARAVANE
PARAVANES
PARAVANT
PARAVAUNT
PARAWALKER
PARAWALKERS
PARAWING
PARAWINGS
PARAXIAL
PARAXIALLY
PARAZOA
PARAZOAN
PARAZOANS
PARAZOON
PARBOIL

PARBOILED
PARBOILING
PARBOILS
PARBREAK
PARBREAKED
PARBREAKING
PARBREAKS
PARBUCKLE
PARBUCKLED
PARBUCKLES
PARBUCKLING
PARCEL
PARCELED
PARCELING
PARCELLED
PARCELLING
PARCELS
PARCELWISE
PARCENARIES
PARCENARY
PARCENER
PARCENERS
PARCH
PARCHED
PARCHEDLY
PARCHEDNESS
PARCHEDNESSES
PARCHEESI
PARCHEESIS
PARCHES
PARCHESI
PARCHESIS
PARCHING
PARCHISI
PARCHISIS
PARCHMENT
PARCHMENTISE
PARCHMENTISED
PARCHMENTISES
PARCHMENTISING
PARCHMENTIZE
PARCHMENTIZED
PARCHMENTIZES
PARCHMENTIZING
PARCHMENTS
PARCHMENTY
PARCIMONIES
PARCIMONY
PARCLOSE
PARCLOSES
PARD
PARDAH
PARDAHS
PARDAL
PARDALE
PARDALES

PARDALIS
PARDALISES
PARDALOTE
PARDALOTES
PARDALS
PARDED
PARDEE
PARDI
PARDIE
PARDINE
PARDNER
PARDNERS
PARDON
PARDONABLE
PARDONABLENESS
PARDONABLY
PARDONED
PARDONER
PARDONERS
PARDONING
PARDONINGS
PARDONLESS
PARDONS
PARDS
PARDY
PARE
PARECIOUS
PARECISM
PARECISMS
PARED
PAREGORIC
PAREGORICS
PAREIRA
PAREIRAS
PARELLA
PARELLAS
PARELLE
PARELLES
PARENCEPHALON
PARENCHYMA
PARENCHYMAL
PARENCHYMAS
PARENCHYMATA
PARENCHYMATOUS
PARENESES
PARENESIS
PARENT
PARENTAGE
PARENTAGES
PARENTAL
PARENTALLY
PARENTED
PARENTERAL
PARENTERALLY
PARENTHESES
PARENTHESIS

PARENTHESISE
PARENTHESISED
PARENTHESISES
PARENTHESISING
PARENTHESIZE
PARENTHESIZED
PARENTHESIZES
PARENTHESIZING
PARENTHETIC
PARENTHETICAL
PARENTHETICALLY
PARENTHOOD
PARENTHOODS
PARENTING
PARENTINGS
PARENTLESS
PARENTS
PAREO
PAREOS
PARER
PARERGA
PARERGON
PARERS
PARES
PARESES
PARESIS
PARESTHESIA
PARESTHESIAS
PARESTHETIC
PARETIC
PARETICS
PAREU
PAREUS
PAREV
PAREVE
PARFAIT
PARFAITS
PARFLECHE
PARFLECHES
PARFLESH
PARFLESHES
PARFOCAL
PARFOCALITIES
PARFOCALITY
PARFOCALIZE
PARFOCALIZED
PARFOCALIZES
PARFOCALIZING
PARGANA
PARGANAS
PARGASITE
PARGASITES
PARGE
PARGED
PARGES
PARGET

PARGETED
PARGETER
PARGETERS
PARGETING
PARGETINGS
PARGETS
PARGETTED
PARGETTING
PARGETTINGS
PARGING
PARGINGS
PARGO
PARGOS
PARGYLINE
PARGYLINES
PARHELIA
PARHELIACAL
PARHELIC
PARHELION
PARHYPATE
PARHYPATES
PARIAH
PARIAHS
PARIAL
PARIALS
PARIAN
PARIANS
PARIES
PARIETAL
PARIETALS
PARIETES
PARING
PARINGS
PARIPINNATE
PARIS
PARISCHAN
PARISCHANES
PARISCHANS
PARISES
PARISH
PARISHEN
PARISHENS
PARISHES
PARISHIONER
PARISHIONERS
PARISON
PARISONS
PARISYLLABIC
PARITIES
PARITOR
PARITORS
PARITY
PARK
PARKA
PARKADE
PARKADES

PARKAS
PARKED
PARKEE
PARKEES
PARKER
PARKERS
PARKETTE
PARKETTES
PARKI
PARKIE
PARKIER
PARKIES
PARKIEST
PARKIN
PARKING
PARKINGS
PARKINS
PARKINSONIAN
PARKINSONISM
PARKINSONISMS
PARKIS
PARKISH
PARKLAND
PARKLANDS
PARKLEAVES
PARKLIKE
PARKLY
PARKS
PARKWARD
PARKWARDS
PARKWAY
PARKWAYS
PARKY
PARLANCE
PARLANCES
PARLANDO
PARLANTE
PARLAY
PARLAYED
PARLAYING
PARLAYS
PARLE
PARLED
PARLEMENT
PARLEMENTS
PARLES
PARLEY
PARLEYED
PARLEYER
PARLEYERS
PARLEYING
PARLEYS
PARLEYVOO
PARLEYVOOED
PARLEYVOOING
PARLEYVOOS

PARLIAMENT
PARLIAMENTARIAN
PARLIAMENTARILY
PARLIAMENTARISM
PARLIAMENTARY
PARLIAMENTING
PARLIAMENTINGS
PARLIAMENTS
PARLIES
PARLING
PARLOR
PARLORS
PARLOUR
PARLOURS
PARLOUS
PARLOUSLY
PARLOUSNESS
PARLY
PARMACITIE
PARMACITIES
PARMIGIANA
PARMIGIANO
PAROCCIPITAL
PAROCHIAL
PAROCHIALISE
PAROCHIALISED
PAROCHIALISES
PAROCHIALISING
PAROCHIALISM
PAROCHIALISMS
PAROCHIALITIES
PAROCHIALITY
PAROCHIALIZE
PAROCHIALIZED
PAROCHIALIZES
PAROCHIALIZING
PAROCHIALLY
PAROCHIN
PAROCHINE
PAROCHINES
PAROCHINS
PARODIC
PARODICAL
PARODIED
PARODIES
PARODIST
PARODISTIC
PARODISTS
PARODOI
PARODOS
PARODY
PARODYING
PAROECIOUS
PAROEMIA
PAROEMIAC
PAROEMIACS

PAROEMIAL
PAROEMIAS
PAROEMIOGRAPHER
PAROEMIOGRAPHY
PAROEMIOLOGIES
PAROEMIOLOGY
PAROICOUS
PAROL
PAROLABLE
PAROLE
PAROLED
PAROLEE
PAROLEES
PAROLES
PAROLING
PAROLS
PARONOMASIA
PARONOMASIAS
PARONOMASIES
PARONOMASTIC
PARONOMASTICAL
PARONOMASY
PARONYCHIA
PARONYCHIAL
PARONYCHIAS
PARONYM
PARONYMIC
PARONYMICALLY
PARONYMIES
PARONYMOUS
PARONYMOUSLY
PARONYMS
PARONYMY
PAROQUET
PAROQUETS
PAROSMIA
PAROSMIAS
PAROTIC
PAROTID
PAROTIDITIC
PAROTIDITIS
PAROTIDITISES
PAROTIDS
PAROTIS
PAROTISES
PAROTITIC
PAROTITIS
PAROTITISES
PAROTOID
PAROTOIDS
PAROUS
PAROUSIA
PAROUSIAS
PAROXETINE
PAROXETINES
PAROXYSM

PAROXYSMAL
PAROXYSMALLY
PAROXYSMIC
PAROXYSMICALLY
PAROXYSMS
PAROXYTONE
PAROXYTONES
PAROXYTONIC
PAROXYTONICALLY
PARP
PARPANE
PARPANES
PARPED
PARPEN
PARPEND
PARPENDS
PARPENS
PARPENT
PARPENTS
PARPING
PARPOINT
PARPOINTS
PARPS
PARQUET
PARQUETED
PARQUETING
PARQUETRIES
PARQUETRY
PARQUETS
PARQUETTED
PARQUETTING
PARR
PARRA
PARRAKEET
PARRAKEETS
PARRAL
PARRALS
PARRAMATTA
PARRAMATTAS
PARRAS
PARRED
PARREL
PARRELS
PARRHESIA
PARRHESIAS
PARRICIDAL
PARRICIDE
PARRICIDES
PARRIDGE
PARRIDGES
PARRIED
PARRIES
PARRING
PARRITCH
PARRITCHES
PARROCK

PARROCKED
PARROCKING
PARROCKS
PARROKET
PARROKETS
PARROQUET
PARROQUETS
PARROT
PARROTED
PARROTER
PARROTERS
PARROTFISH
PARROTFISHES
PARROTING
PARROTRIES
PARROTRY
PARROTS
PARROTY
PARRS
PARRY
PARRYING
PARS
PARSABLE
PARSE
PARSEC
PARSECS
PARSED
PARSER
PARSERS
PARSES
PARSIMONIES
PARSIMONIOUS
PARSIMONIOUSLY
PARSIMONY
PARSING
PARSINGS
PARSLEY
PARSLEYED
PARSLEYS
PARSLIED
PARSNEP
PARSNEPS
PARSNIP
PARSNIPS
PARSON
PARSONAGE
PARSONAGES
PARSONIC
PARSONICAL
PARSONISH
PARSONS
PART
PARTAKE
PARTAKEN
PARTAKER
PARTAKERS

PARTAKES
PARTAKING
PARTAKINGS
PARTAN
PARTANS
PARTED
PARTER
PARTERRE
PARTERRES
PARTERS
PARTHENOCARPIC
PARTHENOCARPIES
PARTHENOCARPOUS
PARTHENOCARPY
PARTHENOGENESES
PARTHENOGENESIS
PARTHENOGENETIC
PARTHENOSPORE
PARTHENOSPORES
PARTI
PARTIAL
PARTIALISE
PARTIALISED
PARTIALISES
PARTIALISING
PARTIALISM
PARTIALISMS
PARTIALIST
PARTIALISTS
PARTIALITIES
PARTIALITY
PARTIALIZE
PARTIALIZED
PARTIALIZES
PARTIALIZING
PARTIALLY
PARTIALNESS
PARTIALS
PARTIBILITIES
PARTIBILITY
PARTIBLE
PARTICIPABLE
PARTICIPANT
PARTICIPANTLY
PARTICIPANTS
PARTICIPATE
PARTICIPATED
PARTICIPATES
PARTICIPATING
PARTICIPATION
PARTICIPATIONAL
PARTICIPATIONS
PARTICIPATIVE
PARTICIPATOR
PARTICIPATORS
PARTICIPATORY

PARTICIPIAL
PARTICIPIALLY
PARTICIPLE
PARTICIPLES
PARTICLE
PARTICLEBOARD
PARTICLEBOARDS
PARTICLES
PARTICULAR
PARTICULARISE
PARTICULARISED
PARTICULARISER
PARTICULARISERS
PARTICULARISES
PARTICULARISING
PARTICULARISM
PARTICULARISMS
PARTICULARIST
PARTICULARISTIC
PARTICULARISTS
PARTICULARITIES
PARTICULARITY
PARTICULARIZE
PARTICULARIZED
PARTICULARIZER
PARTICULARIZERS
PARTICULARIZES
PARTICULARIZING
PARTICULARLY
PARTICULARNESS
PARTICULARS
PARTICULATE
PARTICULATES
PARTIED
PARTIER
PARTIERS
PARTIES
PARTIM
PARTING
PARTINGS
PARTIS
PARTISAN
PARTISANLY
PARTISANS
PARTISANSHIP
PARTISANSHIPS
PARTITA
PARTITAS
PARTITE
PARTITION
PARTITIONED
PARTITIONER
PARTITIONERS
PARTITIONING
PARTITIONIST
PARTITIONISTS

PARTITIONMENT
PARTITIONMENTS
PARTITIONS
PARTITIVE
PARTITIVELY
PARTITIVES
PARTITURA
PARTITURAS
PARTIZAN
PARTIZANS
PARTIZANSHIP
PARTLET
PARTLETS
PARTLY
PARTNER
PARTNERED
PARTNERING
PARTNERLESS
PARTNERS
PARTNERSHIP
PARTNERSHIPS
PARTON
PARTONS
PARTOOK
PARTRIDGE
PARTRIDGEBERRY
PARTRIDGES
PARTS
PARTURE
PARTURES
PARTURIENCY
PARTURIENT
PARTURIENTS
PARTURIFACIENT
PARTURITION
PARTURITIONS
PARTWAY
PARTWORK
PARTWORKS
PARTY
PARTYER
PARTYERS
PARTYGOER
PARTYGOERS
PARTYING
PARTYISM
PARTYISMS
PARULIDES
PARULIS
PARULISES
PARURA
PARURAS
PARURE
PARURES
PARVANIMITIES
PARVANIMITY

PARVE
PARVENU
PARVENUE
PARVENUES
PARVENUS
PARVIFOLIATE
PARVIS
PARVISE
PARVISES
PARVO
PARVOLIN
PARVOLINS
PARVOS
PARVOVIRUS
PARVOVIRUSES
PAS
PASCAL
PASCALS
PASCHAL
PASCHALS
PASCUAL
PASE
PASEAR
PASEARED
PASEARING
PASEARS
PASELA
PASELAS
PASEO
PASEOS
PASES
PASH
PASHA
PASHADOM
PASHADOMS
PASHALIC
PASHALICS
PASHALIK
PASHALIKS
PASHAS
PASHED
PASHES
PASHIM
PASHIMS
PASHING
PASHKA
PASHKAS
PASHM
PASHMINA
PASHMINAS
PASHMS
PASIGRAPHIC
PASIGRAPHICAL
PASIGRAPHIES
PASIGRAPHY
PASPALUM

PASPALUMS
PASPIES
PASPY
PASQUEFLOWER
PASQUEFLOWERS
PASQUIL
PASQUILANT
PASQUILANTS
PASQUILER
PASQUILERS
PASQUILLED
PASQUILLER
PASQUILLERS
PASQUILLING
PASQUILS
PASQUINADE
PASQUINADED
PASQUINADER
PASQUINADERS
PASQUINADES
PASQUINADING
PASS
PASSABLE
PASSABLENESS
PASSABLENESSES
PASSABLY
PASSACAGLIA
PASSACAGLIAS
PASSADE
PASSADES
PASSADO
PASSADOES
PASSADOS
PASSAGE
PASSAGED
PASSAGER
PASSAGERS
PASSAGES
PASSAGEWAY
PASSAGEWAYS
PASSAGEWORK
PASSAGEWORKS
PASSAGING
PASSAMENT
PASSAMENTED
PASSAMENTING
PASSAMENTS
PASSAMEZZO
PASSAMEZZOS
PASSANT
PASSATA
PASSATAS
PASSBAND
PASSBANDS
PASSBOOK
PASSBOOKS

PASSE
PASSED
PASSEE
PASSEL
PASSELS
PASSEMEASURE
PASSEMEASURES
PASSEMENT
PASSEMENTED
PASSEMENTERIE
PASSEMENTERIES
PASSEMENTING
PASSEMENTS
PASSENGER
PASSENGERS
PASSEPIED
PASSEPIEDS
PASSER
PASSERBY
PASSERINE
PASSERINES
PASSERS
PASSERSBY
PASSES
PASSIBILITIES
PASSIBILITY
PASSIBLE
PASSIBLENESS
PASSIBLENESSES
PASSIBLY
PASSIFLORA
PASSIFLORACEOUS
PASSIFLORAS
PASSIM
PASSIMETER
PASSIMETERS
PASSING
PASSINGS
PASSION
PASSIONAL
PASSIONALS
PASSIONARIES
PASSIONARY
PASSIONATE
PASSIONATED
PASSIONATELY
PASSIONATENESS
PASSIONATES
PASSIONATING
PASSIONED
PASSIONFLOWER
PASSIONFLOWERS
PASSIONING
PASSIONLESS
PASSIONLESSLY
PASSIONLESSNESS

PASSIONS
PASSIVATE
PASSIVATED
PASSIVATES
PASSIVATING
PASSIVATION
PASSIVATIONS
PASSIVE
PASSIVELY
PASSIVENESS
PASSIVENESSES
PASSIVES
PASSIVISM
PASSIVISMS
PASSIVIST
PASSIVISTS
PASSIVITIES
PASSIVITY
PASSKEY
PASSKEYS
PASSLESS
PASSMAN
PASSMEN
PASSMENT
PASSMENTED
PASSMENTING
PASSMENTS
PASSOUT
PASSOUTS
PASSOVER
PASSOVERS
PASSPORT
PASSPORTS
PASSUS
PASSUSES
PASSWORD
PASSWORDS
PAST
PASTA
PASTANCE
PASTANCES
PASTAS
PASTE
PASTEBOARD
PASTEBOARDS
PASTED
PASTEDOWN
PASTEDOWNS
PASTEL
PASTELIST
PASTELISTS
PASTELLIST
PASTELLISTS
PASTELS
PASTER
PASTERN

PASTERNS
PASTERS
PASTES
PASTEUP
PASTEUPS
PASTEURELLA
PASTEURELLAE
PASTEURELLAS
PASTEURISATION
PASTEURISATIONS
PASTEURISE
PASTEURISED
PASTEURISER
PASTEURISERS
PASTEURISES
PASTEURISING
PASTEURISM
PASTEURISMS
PASTEURIZATION
PASTEURIZATIONS
PASTEURIZE
PASTEURIZED
PASTEURIZER
PASTEURIZERS
PASTEURIZES
PASTEURIZING
PASTICCI
PASTICCIO
PASTICCIOS
PASTICHE
PASTICHES
PASTICHEUR
PASTICHEURS
PASTIE
PASTIER
PASTIES
PASTIEST
PASTIL
PASTILLE
PASTILLES
PASTILS
PASTILY
PASTIME
PASTIMES
PASTINA
PASTINAS
PASTINESS
PASTINESSES
PASTING
PASTINGS
PASTIS
PASTISES
PASTITSIO
PASTITSIOS
PASTLESS
PASTMASTER

PASTMASTERS
PASTNESS
PASTNESSES
PASTOR
PASTORAL
PASTORALE
PASTORALES
PASTORALI
PASTORALISM
PASTORALISMS
PASTORALIST
PASTORALISTS
PASTORALLY
PASTORALNESS
PASTORALNESSES
PASTORALS
PASTORATE
PASTORATES
PASTORED
PASTORING
PASTORLY
PASTORS
PASTORSHIP
PASTORSHIPS
PASTOURELLE
PASTOURELLES
PASTRAMI
PASTRAMIS
PASTRIES
PASTROMI
PASTROMIS
PASTRY
PASTRYCOOK
PASTRYCOOKS
PASTS
PASTURABLE
PASTURAGE
PASTURAGES
PASTURAL
PASTURE
PASTURED
PASTURELAND
PASTURELANDS
PASTURELESS
PASTURER
PASTURERS
PASTURES
PASTURING
PASTY
PAT
PATACA
PATACAS
PATAGIA
PATAGIAL
PATAGIUM
PATAKA

PATAKAS
PATAMAR
PATAMARS
PATAPHYSICS
PATBALL
PATBALLS
PATCH
PATCHABLE
PATCHBOARD
PATCHBOARDS
PATCHCOCKES
PATCHED
PATCHER
PATCHERIES
PATCHERS
PATCHERY
PATCHES
PATCHIER
PATCHIEST
PATCHILY
PATCHINESS
PATCHINESSES
PATCHING
PATCHINGS
PATCHOCKES
PATCHOULI
PATCHOULIES
PATCHOULIS
PATCHOULY
PATCHWORK
PATCHWORKS
PATCHY
PATE
PATED
PATELLA
PATELLAE
PATELLAR
PATELLAS
PATELLATE
PATELLECTOMIES
PATELLECTOMY
PATELLIFORM
PATEN
PATENCIES
PATENCY
PATENS
PATENT
PATENTABILITIES
PATENTABILITY
PATENTABLE
PATENTED
PATENTEE
PATENTEES
PATENTING
PATENTLY
PATENTOR

PATENTORS
PATENTS
PATER
PATERA
PATERAE
PATERCOVE
PATERCOVES
PATERERO
PATEREROES
PATEREROS
PATERFAMILIAS
PATERFAMILIASES
PATERNAL
PATERNALISM
PATERNALISMS
PATERNALIST
PATERNALISTIC
PATERNALISTS
PATERNALLY
PATERNITIES
PATERNITY
PATERNOSTER
PATERNOSTERS
PATERS
PATES
PATH
PATHBREAKING
PATHED
PATHETIC
PATHETICAL
PATHETICALLY
PATHETICS
PATHFINDER
PATHFINDERS
PATHFINDING
PATHFINDINGS
PATHIC
PATHICS
PATHING
PATHLESS
PATHLESSNESS
PATHLESSNESSES
PATHOBIOLOGIES
PATHOBIOLOGY
PATHOGEN
PATHOGENE
PATHOGENES
PATHOGENESES
PATHOGENESIS
PATHOGENETIC
PATHOGENIC
PATHOGENICALLY
PATHOGENICITIES
PATHOGENICITY
PATHOGENIES
PATHOGENOUS

PATHOGENS
PATHOGENY
PATHOGNOMIES
PATHOGNOMONIC
PATHOGNOMY
PATHOGRAPHIES
PATHOGRAPHY
PATHOLOGIC
PATHOLOGICAL
PATHOLOGICALLY
PATHOLOGIES
PATHOLOGISE
PATHOLOGIST
PATHOLOGISTS
PATHOLOGIZE
PATHOLOGIZED
PATHOLOGIZES
PATHOLOGIZING
PATHOLOGY
PATHOPHOBIA
PATHOPHOBIAS
PATHOPHYSIOLOGY
PATHOS
PATHOSES
PATHS
PATHWAY
PATHWAYS
PATIBLE
PATIBULARY
PATIENCE
PATIENCES
PATIENT
PATIENTED
PATIENTER
PATIENTEST
PATIENTING
PATIENTLY
PATIENTS
PATIN
PATINA
PATINAE
PATINAS
PATINATE
PATINATED
PATINATES
PATINATING
PATINATION
PATINATIONS
PATINE
PATINED
PATINES
PATINING
PATINIZE
PATINIZED
PATINIZES
PATINIZING

PATINS
PATIO
PATIOS
PATISSERIE
PATISSERIES
PATISSIER
PATISSIERS
PATLY
PATNESS
PATNESSES
PATOIS
PATONCE
PATRESFAMILIAS
PATRIAL
PATRIALISATION
PATRIALISATIONS
PATRIALISE
PATRIALISED
PATRIALISES
PATRIALISING
PATRIALISM
PATRIALISMS
PATRIALITIES
PATRIALITY
PATRIALIZATION
PATRIALIZATIONS
PATRIALIZE
PATRIALIZED
PATRIALIZES
PATRIALIZING
PATRIALS
PATRIARCH
PATRIARCHAL
PATRIARCHALISM
PATRIARCHALISMS
PATRIARCHALLY
PATRIARCHALNESS
PATRIARCHATE
PATRIARCHATES
PATRIARCHIES
PATRIARCHISM
PATRIARCHISMS
PATRIARCHS
PATRIARCHY
PATRIATE
PATRIATED
PATRIATES
PATRIATING
PATRIATION
PATRIATIONS
PATRICIAN
PATRICIANLY
PATRICIANS
PATRICIATE
PATRICIATES
PATRICIDAL

PATRICIDE
PATRICIDES
PATRICK
PATRICKS
PATRICLINOUS
PATRICO
PATRICOES
PATRIFOCAL
PATRIFOCALITIES
PATRIFOCALITY
PATRILINEAGE
PATRILINEAGES
PATRILINEAL
PATRILINEALLY
PATRILINEAR
PATRILINEARLY
PATRILINIES
PATRILINY
PATRILOCAL
PATRILOCALLY
PATRIMONIAL
PATRIMONIALLY
PATRIMONIES
PATRIMONY
PATRIOT
PATRIOTIC
PATRIOTICALLY
PATRIOTISM
PATRIOTISMS
PATRIOTS
PATRISTIC
PATRISTICAL
PATRISTICALLY
PATRISTICALNESS
PATRISTICISM
PATRISTICISMS
PATRISTICS
PATROCLINAL
PATROCLINALLY
PATROCLINIC
PATROCLINIES
PATROCLINOUS
PATROCLINY
PATROL
PATROLLED
PATROLLER
PATROLLERS
PATROLLING
PATROLMAN
PATROLMEN
PATROLOGICAL
PATROLOGICALLY
PATROLOGIES
PATROLOGIST
PATROLOGISTS
PATROLOGY

PATROLS
PATROLWOMAN
PATROLWOMEN
PATRON
PATRONAGE
PATRONAGED
PATRONAGES
PATRONAGING
PATRONAL
PATRONESS
PATRONESSES
PATRONISE
PATRONISED
PATRONISER
PATRONISERS
PATRONISES
PATRONISING
PATRONISINGLY
PATRONIZATION
PATRONIZATIONS
PATRONIZE
PATRONIZED
PATRONIZER
PATRONIZERS
PATRONIZES
PATRONIZING
PATRONIZINGLY
PATRONLESS
PATRONLY
PATRONNE
PATRONNES
PATRONS
PATRONYMIC
PATRONYMICS
PATROON
PATROONS
PATROONSHIP
PATROONSHIPS
PATS
PATSIES
PATSY
PATTAMAR
PATTAMARS
PATTE
PATTED
PATTEE
PATTEN
PATTENED
PATTENING
PATTENS
PATTER
PATTERED
PATTERER
PATTERERS
PATTERING
PATTERN

PATTERNED
PATTERNING
PATTERNINGS
PATTERNLESS
PATTERNS
PATTERS
PATTES
PATTIE
PATTIES
PATTING
PATTLE
PATTLES
PATTY
PATTYPAN
PATTYPANS
PATU
PATULENT
PATULIN
PATULINS
PATULOUS
PATULOUSLY
PATULOUSNESS
PATUS
PATUTUKI
PATUTUKIS
PATY
PATZER
PATZERS
PAUA
PAUAS
PAUCAL
PAUCALS
PAUCILOQUENT
PAUCITIES
PAUCITY
PAUGHTIER
PAUGHTIEST
PAUGHTY
PAUL
PAULDRON
PAULDRONS
PAULIN
PAULINS
PAULOWNIA
PAULOWNIAS
PAULS
PAUNCE
PAUNCES
PAUNCH
PAUNCHED
PAUNCHES
PAUNCHIER
PAUNCHIEST
PAUNCHINESS
PAUNCHINESSES
PAUNCHING

PAUNCHY
PAUPER
PAUPERED
PAUPERESS
PAUPERESSES
PAUPERING
PAUPERISATION
PAUPERISATIONS
PAUPERISE
PAUPERISED
PAUPERISES
PAUPERISING
PAUPERISM
PAUPERISMS
PAUPERIZATION
PAUPERIZATIONS
PAUPERIZE
PAUPERIZED
PAUPERIZES
PAUPERIZING
PAUPERS
PAUPIETTE
PAUPIETTES
PAUROPOD
PAUROPODAN
PAUROPODS
PAUSAL
PAUSE
PAUSED
PAUSEFUL
PAUSEFULLY
PAUSELESS
PAUSELESSLY
PAUSER
PAUSERS
PAUSES
PAUSING
PAUSINGLY
PAUSINGS
PAV
PAVAGE
PAVAGES
PAVAN
PAVANE
PAVANES
PAVANS
PAVE
PAVED
PAVEED
PAVEMENT
PAVEMENTED
PAVEMENTING
PAVEMENTS
PAVEN
PAVENS
PAVER

PAVERS
PAVES
PAVID
PAVILION
PAVILIONED
PAVILIONING
PAVILIONS
PAVILLON
PAVILLONS
PAVIN
PAVING
PAVINGS
PAVINS
PAVIOR
PAVIORS
PAVIOUR
PAVIOURS
PAVIS
PAVISE
PAVISER
PAVISERS
PAVISES
PAVLOVA
PAVLOVAS
PAVONAZZO
PAVONAZZOS
PAVONE
PAVONES
PAVONIAN
PAVONINE
PAVS
PAW
PAWA
PAWAS
PAWAW
PAWAWED
PAWAWING
PAWAWS
PAWED
PAWER
PAWERS
PAWING
PAWK
PAWKIER
PAWKIEST
PAWKILY
PAWKINESS
PAWKINESSES
PAWKS
PAWKY
PAWL
PAWLS
PAWN
PAWNABLE
PAWNAGE
PAWNAGES

PAWNBROKER
PAWNBROKERS
PAWNBROKING
PAWNBROKINGS
PAWNCE
PAWNCES
PAWNED
PAWNEE
PAWNEES
PAWNER
PAWNERS
PAWNING
PAWNOR
PAWNORS
PAWNS
PAWNSHOP
PAWNSHOPS
PAWNTICKET
PAWNTICKETS
PAWPAW
PAWPAWS
PAWS
PAX
PAXES
PAXIUBA
PAXIUBAS
PAXWAX
PAXWAXES
PAY
PAYABLE
PAYABLES
PAYABLY
PAYBACK
PAYBACKS
PAYCHECK
PAYCHECKS
PAYDAY
PAYDAYS
PAYED
PAYEE
PAYEES
PAYER
PAYERS
PAYFONE
PAYFONES
PAYGRADE
PAYGRADES
PAYING
PAYINGS
PAYLOAD
PAYLOADS
PAYMASTER
PAYMASTERS
PAYMENT
PAYMENTS
PAYNIM

PAYNIMRIES
PAYNIMRY
PAYNIMS
PAYOFF
PAYOFFS
PAYOLA
PAYOLAS
PAYOR
PAYORS
PAYOUT
PAYOUTS
PAYPHONE
PAYPHONES
PAYROLL
PAYROLLS
PAYS
PAYSAGE
PAYSAGES
PAYSAGIST
PAYSAGISTS
PAYSD
PAYSLIP
PAYSLIPS
PAZAZZ
PAZAZZES
PAZZAZZ
PE
PEA
PEABERRIES
PEABERRY
PEACE
PEACEABLE
PEACEABLENESS
PEACEABLENESSES
PEACEABLY
PEACED
PEACEFUL
PEACEFULLER
PEACEFULLEST
PEACEFULLY
PEACEFULNESS
PEACEFULNESSES
PEACEKEEPER
PEACEKEEPERS
PEACEKEEPING
PEACEKEEPINGS
PEACELESS
PEACELESSNESS
PEACELESSNESSES
PEACEMAKER
PEACEMAKERS
PEACEMAKING
PEACEMAKINGS
PEACENIK
PEACENIKS
PEACES

PEACETIME
PEACETIMES
PEACH
PEACHED
PEACHER
PEACHERINO
PEACHERINOS
PEACHERS
PEACHES
PEACHIER
PEACHIEST
PEACHILY
PEACHINESS
PEACHING
PEACHY
PEACING
PEACOAT
PEACOATS
PEACOCK
PEACOCKED
PEACOCKERIES
PEACOCKERY
PEACOCKIER
PEACOCKIEST
PEACOCKING
PEACOCKISH
PEACOCKS
PEACOCKY
PEACOD
PEACODS
PEAFOWL
PEAFOWLS
PEAG
PEAGE
PEAGES
PEAGS
PEAHEN
PEAHENS
PEAK
PEAKED
PEAKEDNESS
PEAKEDNESSES
PEAKIER
PEAKIEST
PEAKING
PEAKISH
PEAKLESS
PEAKLIKE
PEAKS
PEAKY
PEAL
PEALED
PEALIKE
PEALING
PEALS
PEAN

PEANED
PEANING
PEANS
PEANUT
PEANUTS
PEAPOD
PEAPODS
PEAR
PEARCE
PEARCED
PEARCES
PEARCING
PEARE
PEARES
PEARL
PEARLASH
PEARLASHES
PEARLED
PEARLER
PEARLERS
PEARLESCENCE
PEARLESCENCES
PEARLESCENT
PEARLIER
PEARLIES
PEARLIEST
PEARLIN
PEARLINESS
PEARLINESSES
PEARLING
PEARLINGS
PEARLINS
PEARLISED
PEARLITE
PEARLITES
PEARLITIC
PEARLIZED
PEARLS
PEARLWORT
PEARLWORTS
PEARLY
PEARMAIN
PEARMAINS
PEARMONGER
PEARMONGERS
PEARS
PEARST
PEART
PEARTER
PEARTEST
PEARTLY
PEARTNESS
PEAS
PEASANT
PEASANTRIES
PEASANTRY

PEASANTS
PEASANTY
PEASCOD
PEASCODS
PEASE
PEASECOD
PEASECODS
PEASED
PEASEN
PEASES
PEASEWEEPS
PEASHOOTER
PEASHOOTERS
PEASING
PEASON
PEASOUPER
PEASOUPERS
PEAT
PEATARIES
PEATARY
PEATERIES
PEATERY
PEATIER
PEATIEST
PEATLAND
PEATLANDS
PEATMAN
PEATMEN
PEATS
PEATSHIP
PEATSHIPS
PEATY
PEAVEY
PEAVEYS
PEAVIES
PEAVY
PEAZE
PEAZED
PEAZES
PEAZING
PEBA
PEBAS
PEBBLE
PEBBLED
PEBBLEDASH
PEBBLEDASHED
PEBBLEDASHES
PEBBLEDASHING
PEBBLES
PEBBLIER
PEBBLIEST
PEBBLING
PEBBLINGS
PEBBLY
PEBRINE
PEBRINES

PEC
PECAN
PECANS
PECCABILITIES
PECCABILITY
PECCABLE
PECCADILLO
PECCADILLOES
PECCADILLOS
PECCANCIES
PECCANCY
PECCANT
PECCANTLY
PECCARIES
PECCARY
PECCAVI
PECCAVIS
PECH
PECHAN
PECHANS
PECHED
PECHING
PECHS
PECK
PECKE
PECKED
PECKER
PECKERS
PECKERWOOD
PECKERWOODS
PECKES
PECKIER
PECKIEST
PECKING
PECKINGS
PECKISH
PECKISHNESS
PECKISHNESSES
PECKS
PECKY
PECORINI
PECORINO
PECORINOS
PECS
PECTASE
PECTASES
PECTATE
PECTATES
PECTEN
PECTENS
PECTIC
PECTIN
PECTINACEOUS
PECTINAL
PECTINATE
PECTINATED

PECTINATELY
PECTINATION
PECTINATIONS
PECTINEAL
PECTINES
PECTINESTERASE
PECTINESTERASES
PECTINOUS
PECTINOUSLY
PECTINS
PECTISABLE
PECTISABLY
PECTISATION
PECTISATIONS
PECTISE
PECTISED
PECTISES
PECTISING
PECTIZATION
PECTIZATIONS
PECTIZE
PECTIZED
PECTIZES
PECTIZING
PECTOLITE
PECTOLITES
PECTORAL
PECTORALLY
PECTORALS
PECTORILOQUIES
PECTORILOQUY
PECTOSE
PECTOSES
PECULATE
PECULATED
PECULATES
PECULATING
PECULATION
PECULATIONS
PECULATOR
PECULATORS
PECULIA
PECULIAR
PECULIARISE
PECULIARISED
PECULIARISES
PECULIARISING
PECULIARITIES
PECULIARITY
PECULIARIZE
PECULIARIZED
PECULIARIZES
PECULIARIZING
PECULIARLY
PECULIARS
PECULIUM

PECUNIARILY
PECUNIARY
PECUNIOUS
PED
PEDAGOG
PEDAGOGIC
PEDAGOGICAL
PEDAGOGICALLY
PEDAGOGICS
PEDAGOGIES
PEDAGOGISM
PEDAGOGISMS
PEDAGOGS
PEDAGOGUE
PEDAGOGUED
PEDAGOGUERIES
PEDAGOGUERY
PEDAGOGUES
PEDAGOGUING
PEDAGOGUISH
PEDAGOGUISHNESS
PEDAGOGUISM
PEDAGOGUISMS
PEDAGOGY
PEDAL
PEDALED
PEDALFER
PEDALFERS
PEDALIER
PEDALIERS
PEDALING
PEDALLED
PEDALLER
PEDALLERS
PEDALLING
PEDALLINGS
PEDALO
PEDALOES
PEDALOS
PEDALS
PEDANT
PEDANTIC
PEDANTICAL
PEDANTICALLY
PEDANTICISE
PEDANTICISED
PEDANTICISES
PEDANTICISING
PEDANTICISM
PEDANTICISMS
PEDANTICIZE
PEDANTICIZED
PEDANTICIZES
PEDANTICIZING
PEDANTISE
PEDANTISED

PEDANTISES
PEDANTISING
PEDANTISM
PEDANTISMS
PEDANTIZE
PEDANTIZED
PEDANTIZES
PEDANTIZING
PEDANTOCRACIES
PEDANTOCRACY
PEDANTOCRAT
PEDANTOCRATIC
PEDANTOCRATS
PEDANTRIES
PEDANTRY
PEDANTS
PEDATE
PEDATELY
PEDATIFID
PEDDER
PEDDERS
PEDDLE
PEDDLED
PEDDLER
PEDDLERIES
PEDDLERS
PEDDLERY
PEDDLES
PEDDLING
PEDDLINGS
PEDERAST
PEDERASTIC
PEDERASTIES
PEDERASTS
PEDERASTY
PEDERERO
PEDEREROES
PEDEREROS
PEDES
PEDESES
PEDESIS
PEDESTAL
PEDESTALED
PEDESTALING
PEDESTALLED
PEDESTALLING
PEDESTALS
PEDESTRIAN
PEDESTRIANISE
PEDESTRIANISED
PEDESTRIANISES
PEDESTRIANISING
PEDESTRIANISM
PEDESTRIANISMS
PEDESTRIANIZE
PEDESTRIANIZED

PEDESTRIANIZES
PEDESTRIANIZING
PEDESTRIANS
PEDETENTOUS
PEDETIC
PEDIATRIC
PEDIATRICIAN
PEDIATRICIANS
PEDIATRICS
PEDIATRIST
PEDIATRISTS
PEDICAB
PEDICABS
PEDICEL
PEDICELLARIA
PEDICELLARIAE
PEDICELLATE
PEDICELS
PEDICLE
PEDICLED
PEDICLES
PEDICULAR
PEDICULATE
PEDICULATED
PEDICULATES
PEDICULATION
PEDICULATIONS
PEDICULI
PEDICULOSES
PEDICULOSIS
PEDICULOUS
PEDICULUS
PEDICURE
PEDICURED
PEDICURES
PEDICURING
PEDICURIST
PEDICURISTS
PEDIFORM
PEDIGREE
PEDIGREED
PEDIGREES
PEDIMENT
PEDIMENTAL
PEDIMENTED
PEDIMENTS
PEDIPALP
PEDIPALPI
PEDIPALPS
PEDIPALPUS
PEDLAR
PEDLARIES
PEDLARS
PEDLARY
PEDLER
PEDLERIES

PEDLERS
PEDLERY
PEDOCAL
PEDOCALIC
PEDOCALS
PEDOGENESES
PEDOGENESIS
PEDOGENETIC
PEDOGENIC
PEDOLOGIC
PEDOLOGICAL
PEDOLOGIES
PEDOLOGIST
PEDOLOGISTS
PEDOLOGY
PEDOMETER
PEDOMETERS
PEDOPHILE
PEDOPHILES
PEDOPHILIA
PEDOPHILIAC
PEDOPHILIACS
PEDOPHILIAS
PEDOPHILIC
PEDRAIL
PEDRAILS
PEDRERO
PEDREROES
PEDREROS
PEDRO
PEDROS
PEDS
PEDUNCLE
PEDUNCLED
PEDUNCLES
PEDUNCULAR
PEDUNCULATE
PEDUNCULATED
PEDUNCULATION
PEDUNCULATIONS
PEE
PEEBEEN
PEEBEENS
PEECE
PEECES
PEED
PEEING
PEEK
PEEKABO
PEEKABOO
PEEKABOOS
PEEKABOS
PEEKED
PEEKING
PEEKS
PEEL

PEELABLE
PEELED
PEELER
PEELERS
PEELGARLIC
PEELGARLICS
PEELING
PEELINGS
PEELS
PEEN
PEENED
PEENGE
PEENGED
PEENGEING
PEENGES
PEENGING
PEENING
PEENS
PEEOY
PEEOYS
PEEP
PEEPE
PEEPED
PEEPER
PEEPERS
PEEPES
PEEPHOLE
PEEPHOLES
PEEPING
PEEPS
PEEPSHOW
PEEPSHOWS
PEEPUL
PEEPULS
PEER
PEERAGE
PEERAGES
PEERED
PEERESS
PEERESSES
PEERIE
PEERIER
PEERIES
PEERIEST
PEERING
PEERLESS
PEERLESSLY
PEERLESSNESS
PEERLESSNESSES
PEERS
PEERY
PEES
PEESWEEP
PEESWEEPS
PEETWEET
PEETWEETS

PEEVE
PEEVED
PEEVER
PEEVERS
PEEVES
PEEVING
PEEVISH
PEEVISHLY
PEEVISHNESS
PEEVISHNESSES
PEEWEE
PEEWEES
PEEWIT
PEEWITS
PEG
PEGASUS
PEGASUSES
PEGBOARD
PEGBOARDS
PEGBOX
PEGBOXES
PEGGED
PEGGIES
PEGGING
PEGGINGS
PEGGY
PEGH
PEGHED
PEGHING
PEGHS
PEGLESS
PEGLIKE
PEGMATITE
PEGMATITES
PEGMATITIC
PEGS
PEH
PEHS
PEIGNOIR
PEIGNOIRS
PEIN
PEINCT
PEINCTED
PEINCTING
PEINCTS
PEINED
PEINING
PEINS
PEIRASTIC
PEIRASTICALLY
PEISE
PEISED
PEISES
PEISHWA
PEISHWAH
PEISHWAHS

PEISHWAS
PEISING
PEIZE
PEIZED
PEIZES
PEIZING
PEJORATE
PEJORATED
PEJORATES
PEJORATING
PEJORATION
PEJORATIONS
PEJORATIVE
PEJORATIVELY
PEJORATIVES
PEKAN
PEKANS
PEKE
PEKES
PEKIN
PEKINS
PEKOE
PEKOES
PELA
PELAGE
PELAGES
PELAGIAL
PELAGIAN
PELAGIANS
PELAGIC
PELARGONIC
PELARGONIUM
PELARGONIUMS
PELAS
PELE
PELECYPOD
PELECYPODS
PELERINE
PELERINES
PELES
PELF
PELFS
PELHAM
PELHAMS
PELICAN
PELICANS
PELISSE
PELISSES
PELITE
PELITES
PELITIC
PELL
PELLACH
PELLACHS
PELLACK
PELLACKS

PELLAGRA
PELLAGRAS
PELLAGRIN
PELLAGRINS
PELLAGROUS
PELLET
PELLETAL
PELLETED
PELLETIFIED
PELLETIFIES
PELLETIFY
PELLETIFYING
PELLETING
PELLETISATION
PELLETISATIONS
PELLETISE
PELLETISED
PELLETISES
PELLETISING
PELLETIZATION
PELLETIZATIONS
PELLETIZE
PELLETIZED
PELLETIZER
PELLETIZERS
PELLETIZES
PELLETIZING
PELLETS
PELLICLE
PELLICLES
PELLICULAR
PELLITORIES
PELLITORY
PELLMELL
PELLMELLS
PELLOCK
PELLOCKS
PELLS
PELLUCID
PELLUCIDITIES
PELLUCIDITY
PELLUCIDLY
PELLUCIDNESS
PELLUCIDNESSES
PELLUM
PELMA
PELMANISM
PELMANISMS
PELMAS
PELMATIC
PELMET
PELMETS
PELOID
PELOIDS
PELOLOGIES
PELOLOGY

PELON
PELORIA
PELORIAN
PELORIAS
PELORIC
PELORIES
PELORISED
PELORISM
PELORISMS
PELORIZED
PELORUS
PELORUSES
PELORY
PELOTA
PELOTAS
PELOTHERAPIES
PELOTHERAPY
PELOTON
PELOTONS
PELT
PELTA
PELTAE
PELTAS
PELTAST
PELTASTS
PELTATE
PELTATELY
PELTATION
PELTATIONS
PELTED
PELTER
PELTERED
PELTERING
PELTERS
PELTING
PELTINGLY
PELTINGS
PELTMONGER
PELTMONGERS
PELTRIES
PELTRY
PELTS
PELVES
PELVIC
PELVICS
PELVIFORM
PELVIMETER
PELVIMETERS
PELVIMETRIES
PELVIMETRY
PELVIS
PELVISES
PELYCOSAUR
PELYCOSAURS
PEMBINA
PEMBINAS

PEMBROKE
PEMBROKES
PEMICAN
PEMICANS
PEMMICAN
PEMMICANS
PEMOLINE
PEMOLINES
PEMPHIGOID
PEMPHIGOUS
PEMPHIGUS
PEMPHIGUSES
PEMPHIX
PEMPHIXES
PEN
PENAL
PENALISATION
PENALISATIONS
PENALISE
PENALISED
PENALISES
PENALISING
PENALITIES
PENALITY
PENALIZATION
PENALIZATIONS
PENALIZE
PENALIZED
PENALIZES
PENALIZING
PENALLY
PENALTIES
PENALTY
PENANCE
PENANCED
PENANCES
PENANCING
PENANG
PENANGS
PENANNULAR
PENATES
PENCE
PENCEL
PENCELS
PENCES
PENCHANT
PENCHANTS
PENCIL
PENCILED
PENCILER
PENCILERS
PENCILING
PENCILINGS
PENCILLED
PENCILLER
PENCILLERS

PENCILLING
PENCILLINGS
PENCILS
PENCRAFT
PENCRAFTS
PEND
PENDANT
PENDANTS
PENDED
PENDENCIES
PENDENCY
PENDENT
PENDENTIVE
PENDENTIVES
PENDENTLY
PENDENTS
PENDICLE
PENDICLER
PENDICLERS
PENDICLES
PENDING
PENDRAGON
PENDRAGONS
PENDRAGONSHIP
PENDRAGONSHIPS
PENDS
PENDULAR
PENDULATE
PENDULATED
PENDULATES
PENDULATING
PENDULE
PENDULES
PENDULINE
PENDULOSITIES
PENDULOSITY
PENDULOUS
PENDULOUSLY
PENDULOUSNESS
PENDULOUSNESSES
PENDULUM
PENDULUMS
PENE
PENED
PENELOPISED
PENELOPISES
PENELOPISING
PENELOPIZE
PENELOPIZED
PENELOPIZES
PENELOPIZING
PENEPLAIN
PENEPLAINS
PENEPLANATION
PENEPLANATIONS
PENEPLANE

PENEPLANES
PENES
PENETRABILITIES
PENETRABILITY
PENETRABLE
PENETRABLENESS
PENETRABLY
PENETRALIA
PENETRALIAN
PENETRANCE
PENETRANCES
PENETRANCIES
PENETRANCY
PENETRANT
PENETRANTS
PENETRATE
PENETRATED
PENETRATES
PENETRATING
PENETRATINGLY
PENETRATION
PENETRATIONS
PENETRATIVE
PENETRATIVELY
PENETRATIVENESS
PENETRATOR
PENETRATORS
PENETROMETER
PENETROMETERS
PENFOLD
PENFOLDS
PENFUL
PENFULS
PENGO
PENGOS
PENGUIN
PENGUINERIES
PENGUINERY
PENGUINRIES
PENGUINRY
PENGUINS
PENHOLDER
PENHOLDERS
PENI
PENIAL
PENICIL
PENICILLAMINE
PENICILLAMINES
PENICILLATE
PENICILLATELY
PENICILLATION
PENICILLATIONS
PENICILLIA
PENICILLIFORM
PENICILLIN
PENICILLINASE

PENICILLINASES
PENICILLINS
PENICILLIUM
PENICILLIUMS
PENICILS
PENIE
PENIES
PENILE
PENILL
PENILLION
PENING
PENINSULA
PENINSULAR
PENINSULARITIES
PENINSULARITY
PENINSULAS
PENINSULATE
PENINSULATED
PENINSULATES
PENINSULATING
PENIS
PENISES
PENISTONE
PENISTONES
PENITENCE
PENITENCES
PENITENCIES
PENITENCY
PENITENT
PENITENTIAL
PENITENTIALLY
PENITENTIALS
PENITENTIARIES
PENITENTIARY
PENITENTLY
PENITENTS
PENK
PENKNIFE
PENKNIVES
PENKS
PENLIGHT
PENLIGHTS
PENLITE
PENLITES
PENMAN
PENMANSHIP
PENMANSHIPS
PENMEN
PENNA
PENNACEOUS
PENNAE
PENNAL
PENNALISM
PENNALISMS
PENNALS
PENNAME

PENNAMES
PENNANT
PENNANTS
PENNATE
PENNATED
PENNATULA
PENNATULACEOUS
PENNATULAE
PENNATULAS
PENNE
PENNED
PENNEECH
PENNEECHS
PENNEECK
PENNEECKS
PENNER
PENNERS
PENNES
PENNI
PENNIA
PENNIED
PENNIES
PENNIFORM
PENNILESS
PENNILESSLY
PENNILESSNESS
PENNILESSNESSES
PENNILL
PENNILLION
PENNINE
PENNINES
PENNING
PENNINITE
PENNINITES
PENNIS
PENNON
PENNONCEL
PENNONCELLE
PENNONCELLES
PENNONCELS
PENNONED
PENNONS
PENNY
PENNYBOY
PENNYBOYS
PENNYCRESS
PENNYCRESSES
PENNYFEE
PENNYFEES
PENNYLAND
PENNYLANDS
PENNYROYAL
PENNYROYALS
PENNYWEIGHT
PENNYWEIGHTS
PENNYWHISTLE

PENNYWHISTLES
PENNYWINKLE
PENNYWINKLES
PENNYWORT
PENNYWORTH
PENNYWORTHS
PENNYWORTS
PENOCHE
PENOCHES
PENOLOGICAL
PENOLOGICALLY
PENOLOGIES
PENOLOGIST
PENOLOGISTS
PENOLOGY
PENONCEL
PENONCELLES
PENONCELS
PENPOINT
PENPOINTS
PENPUSHER
PENPUSHERS
PENPUSHING
PENS
PENSEE
PENSEES
PENSEL
PENSELS
PENSIEROSO
PENSIL
PENSILE
PENSILENESS
PENSILENESSES
PENSILITIES
PENSILITY
PENSILS
PENSION
PENSIONABLE
PENSIONARIES
PENSIONARY
PENSIONE
PENSIONED
PENSIONEER
PENSIONEERS
PENSIONER
PENSIONERS
PENSIONES
PENSIONING
PENSIONLESS
PENSIONNAT
PENSIONNATS
PENSIONS
PENSIVE
PENSIVELY
PENSIVENESS
PENSIVENESSES

PENSTEMON
PENSTEMONS
PENSTER
PENSTERS
PENSTOCK
PENSTOCKS
PENSUM
PENSUMS
PENT
PENTACHORD
PENTACHORDS
PENTACLE
PENTACLES
PENTACRINOID
PENTACRINOIDS
PENTACT
PENTACTINAL
PENTACTS
PENTACYCLIC
PENTAD
PENTADACTYL
PENTADACTYLE
PENTADACTYLES
PENTADACTYLIC
PENTADACTYLIES
PENTADACTYLISM
PENTADACTYLISMS
PENTADACTYLOUS
PENTADACTYLS
PENTADACTYLY
PENTADELPHOUS
PENTADIC
PENTADS
PENTAGON
PENTAGONAL
PENTAGONALLY
PENTAGONALS
PENTAGONS
PENTAGRAM
PENTAGRAMS
PENTAGRAPH
PENTAGRAPHS
PENTAGYNIAN
PENTAGYNOUS
PENTAHEDRA
PENTAHEDRAL
PENTAHEDRON
PENTAHEDRONS
PENTALOGIES
PENTALOGY
PENTALPHA
PENTALPHAS
PENTAMERIES
PENTAMERISM
PENTAMERISMS
PENTAMEROUS

PENTAMERY
PENTAMETER
PENTAMETERS
PENTAMIDINE
PENTAMIDINES
PENTANDRIAN
PENTANDROUS
PENTANE
PENTANES
PENTANGLE
PENTANGLES
PENTANGULAR
PENTANOIC
PENTANOL
PENTANOLS
PENTAPEPTIDE
PENTAPEPTIDES
PENTAPLOID
PENTAPLOIDIES
PENTAPLOIDS
PENTAPLOIDY
PENTAPODIC
PENTAPODIES
PENTAPODY
PENTAPOLIS
PENTAPOLISES
PENTAPOLITAN
PENTAPRISM
PENTAPRISMS
PENTAQUINE
PENTARCH
PENTARCHICAL
PENTARCHICALLY
PENTARCHIES
PENTARCHS
PENTARCHY
PENTASTICH
PENTASTICHES
PENTASTICHOUS
PENTASTICHS
PENTASTYLE
PENTASTYLES
PENTASYLLABIC
PENTATEUCHAL
PENTATHLA
PENTATHLETE
PENTATHLETES
PENTATHLON
PENTATHLONS
PENTATHLUM
PENTATHLUMS
PENTATOMIC
PENTATONIC
PENTAVALENT
PENTAZOCINE
PENTAZOCINES

PENTECONTER
PENTECONTERS
PENTEL
PENTELS
PENTENE
PENTENES
PENTETERIC
PENTHEMIMER
PENTHEMIMERAL
PENTHEMIMERS
PENTHIA
PENTHIAS
PENTHOUSE
PENTHOUSED
PENTHOUSES
PENTHOUSING
PENTICE
PENTICED
PENTICES
PENTICING
PENTIMENTI
PENTIMENTO
PENTISE
PENTISED
PENTISES
PENTISING
PENTITI
PENTITO
PENTLANDITE
PENTLANDITES
PENTOBARBITAL
PENTOBARBITALS
PENTOBARBITONE
PENTOBARBITONES
PENTODE
PENTODES
PENTOMIC
PENTOSAN
PENTOSANE
PENTOSANES
PENTOSANS
PENTOSE
PENTOSES
PENTOXIDE
PENTOXIDES
PENTROOF
PENTROOFS
PENTS
PENTSTEMON
PENTSTEMONS
PENTYL
PENTYLENE
PENTYLENES
PENTYLS
PENUCHE
PENUCHES

PENUCHI
PENUCHIS
PENUCHLE
PENUCHLES
PENUCKLE
PENUCKLES
PENULT
PENULTIMA
PENULTIMAS
PENULTIMATE
PENULTIMATELY
PENULTIMATES
PENULTS
PENUMBRA
PENUMBRAE
PENUMBRAL
PENUMBRAS
PENUMBROUS
PENURIES
PENURIOUS
PENURIOUSLY
PENURIOUSNESS
PENURIOUSNESSES
PENURY
PENWOMAN
PENWOMEN
PEON
PEONAGE
PEONAGES
PEONES
PEONIES
PEONISM
PEONISMS
PEONS
PEONY
PEOPLE
PEOPLED
PEOPLEHOOD
PEOPLEHOODS
PEOPLELESS
PEOPLER
PEOPLERS
PEOPLES
PEOPLING
PEP
PEPERINO
PEPERINOS
PEPEROMIA
PEPEROMIAS
PEPERONI
PEPERONIS
PEPFUL
PEPINO
PEPINOS
PEPLA
PEPLOS

PEPLOSES
PEPLUM
PEPLUMED
PEPLUMS
PEPLUS
PEPLUSES
PEPO
PEPONIDA
PEPONIDAS
PEPONIUM
PEPONIUMS
PEPOS
PEPPED
PEPPER
PEPPERBOX
PEPPERBOXES
PEPPERCORN
PEPPERCORNS
PEPPERCORNY
PEPPERED
PEPPERER
PEPPERERS
PEPPERGRASS
PEPPERGRASSES
PEPPERIDGE
PEPPERIDGES
PEPPERIER
PEPPERIEST
PEPPERINESS
PEPPERINESSES
PEPPERING
PEPPERINGS
PEPPERMILL
PEPPERMILLS
PEPPERMINT
PEPPERMINTS
PEPPERMINTY
PEPPERONI
PEPPERONIS
PEPPERS
PEPPERTREE
PEPPERTREES
PEPPERWORT
PEPPERWORTS
PEPPERY
PEPPIER
PEPPIEST
PEPPILY
PEPPINESS
PEPPINESSES
PEPPING
PEPPY
PEPS
PEPSIN
PEPSINATE
PEPSINATED

PEPSINATES
PEPSINATING
PEPSINE
PEPSINES
PEPSINOGEN
PEPSINOGENS
PEPSINS
PEPTIC
PEPTICITIES
PEPTICITY
PEPTICS
PEPTID
PEPTIDASE
PEPTIDASES
PEPTIDE
PEPTIDES
PEPTIDIC
PEPTIDOGLYCAN
PEPTIDOGLYCANS
PEPTIDS
PEPTISABLE
PEPTISATION
PEPTISATIONS
PEPTISE
PEPTISED
PEPTISER
PEPTISERS
PEPTISES
PEPTISING
PEPTIZABLE
PEPTIZATION
PEPTIZATIONS
PEPTIZE
PEPTIZED
PEPTIZER
PEPTIZERS
PEPTIZES
PEPTIZING
PEPTONE
PEPTONES
PEPTONIC
PEPTONISATION
PEPTONISATIONS
PEPTONISE
PEPTONISED
PEPTONISER
PEPTONISERS
PEPTONISES
PEPTONISING
PEPTONIZATION
PEPTONIZATIONS
PEPTONIZE
PEPTONIZED
PEPTONIZER
PEPTONIZERS
PEPTONIZES

PEPTONIZING
PER
PERACID
PERACIDITY
PERACIDS
PERACUTE
PERADVENTURE
PERADVENTURES
PERAEA
PERAEON
PERAEONS
PERAEOPOD
PERAEOPODS
PERAI
PERAIS
PERAMBULATE
PERAMBULATED
PERAMBULATES
PERAMBULATING
PERAMBULATION
PERAMBULATIONS
PERAMBULATOR
PERAMBULATORS
PERAMBULATORY
PERBORATE
PERBORATES
PERCALE
PERCALES
PERCALINE
PERCALINES
PERCASE
PERCE
PERCEABLE
PERCEANT
PERCED
PERCEIVABILITY
PERCEIVABLE
PERCEIVABLY
PERCEIVE
PERCEIVED
PERCEIVER
PERCEIVERS
PERCEIVES
PERCEIVING
PERCEIVINGS
PERCEN
PERCENT
PERCENTAGE
PERCENTAGES
PERCENTAL
PERCENTILE
PERCENTILES
PERCENTS
PERCEPT
PERCEPTIBILITY
PERCEPTIBLE

PERCEPTIBLY
PERCEPTION
PERCEPTIONAL
PERCEPTIONS
PERCEPTIVE
PERCEPTIVELY
PERCEPTIVENESS
PERCEPTIVITIES
PERCEPTIVITY
PERCEPTS
PERCEPTUAL
PERCEPTUALLY
PERCES
PERCH
PERCHANCE
PERCHED
PERCHER
PERCHERIES
PERCHERON
PERCHERONS
PERCHERS
PERCHERY
PERCHES
PERCHING
PERCHINGS
PERCHLORATE
PERCHLORATES
PERCHLORIC
PERCHLORIDE
PERCHLORIDES
PERCHLOROETHENE
PERCIFORM
PERCINE
PERCING
PERCIPIENCE
PERCIPIENCES
PERCIPIENCIES
PERCIPIENCY
PERCIPIENT
PERCIPIENTLY
PERCIPIENTS
PERCOCT
PERCOID
PERCOIDEAN
PERCOIDEANS
PERCOIDS
PERCOLABLE
PERCOLATE
PERCOLATED
PERCOLATES
PERCOLATING
PERCOLATION
PERCOLATIONS
PERCOLATIVE
PERCOLATOR
PERCOLATORS

PERCOLIN
PERCOLINS
PERCURRENT
PERCURSORY
PERCUSS
PERCUSSANT
PERCUSSED
PERCUSSES
PERCUSSING
PERCUSSION
PERCUSSIONAL
PERCUSSIONIST
PERCUSSIONISTS
PERCUSSIONS
PERCUSSIVE
PERCUSSIVELY
PERCUSSIVENESS
PERCUSSOR
PERCUSSORS
PERCUTANEOUS
PERCUTANEOUSLY
PERCUTIENT
PERCUTIENTS
PERDENDO
PERDENDOSI
PERDIE
PERDITION
PERDITIONABLE
PERDITIONS
PERDU
PERDUE
PERDUELLION
PERDUELLIONS
PERDUES
PERDURABILITIES
PERDURABILITY
PERDURABLE
PERDURABLY
PERDURANCE
PERDURANCES
PERDURATION
PERDURATIONS
PERDURE
PERDURED
PERDURES
PERDURING
PERDUS
PERDY
PERE
PEREA
PEREGAL
PEREGALS
PEREGRIN
PEREGRINATE
PEREGRINATED
PEREGRINATES

PEREGRINATING
PEREGRINATION
PEREGRINATIONS
PEREGRINATOR
PEREGRINATORS
PEREGRINATORY
PEREGRINE
PEREGRINES
PEREGRINITIES
PEREGRINITY
PEREGRINS
PEREIA
PEREION
PEREIOPOD
PEREIOPODS
PEREIRA
PEREIRAS
PEREMPTORILY
PEREMPTORINESS
PEREMPTORY
PERENNATE
PERENNATED
PERENNATES
PERENNATING
PERENNATION
PERENNATIONS
PERENNIAL
PERENNIALITIES
PERENNIALITY
PERENNIALLY
PERENNIALS
PERENNIBRANCH
PERENNIBRANCHS
PERENNITIES
PERENNITY
PERENTIE
PERENTIES
PERENTY
PEREON
PEREOPOD
PEREOPODS
PERES
PERESTROIKA
PERESTROIKAS
PERFAY
PERFECT
PERFECTA
PERFECTAS
PERFECTATION
PERFECTATIONS
PERFECTED
PERFECTER
PERFECTERS
PERFECTEST
PERFECTI
PERFECTIBILIAN

PERFECTIBILIANS
PERFECTIBILISM
PERFECTIBILISMS
PERFECTIBILIST
PERFECTIBILISTS
PERFECTIBILITY
PERFECTIBLE
PERFECTING
PERFECTION
PERFECTIONATE
PERFECTIONATED
PERFECTIONATES
PERFECTIONATING
PERFECTIONISM
PERFECTIONISMS
PERFECTIONIST
PERFECTIONISTIC
PERFECTIONISTS
PERFECTIONS
PERFECTIVE
PERFECTIVELY
PERFECTIVENESS
PERFECTIVES
PERFECTIVITIES
PERFECTIVITY
PERFECTLY
PERFECTNESS
PERFECTNESSES
PERFECTO
PERFECTOR
PERFECTORS
PERFECTOS
PERFECTS
PERFED
PERFERVID
PERFERVIDITIES
PERFERVIDITY
PERFERVIDLY
PERFERVIDNESS
PERFERVIDNESSES
PERFERVOR
PERFERVORS
PERFERVOUR
PERFERVOURS
PERFET
PERFICIENT
PERFIDIES
PERFIDIOUS
PERFIDIOUSLY
PERFIDIOUSNESS
PERFIDY
PERFIN
PERFING
PERFINS
PERFLUOROCARBON
PERFOLIATE

PERFOLIATION
PERFOLIATIONS
PERFORABLE
PERFORANS
PERFORANSES
PERFORANT
PERFORATE
PERFORATED
PERFORATES
PERFORATING
PERFORATION
PERFORATIONS
PERFORATIVE
PERFORATOR
PERFORATORS
PERFORATORY
PERFORATUS
PERFORATUSES
PERFORCE
PERFORM
PERFORMABILITY
PERFORMABLE
PERFORMANCE
PERFORMANCES
PERFORMATIVE
PERFORMATIVELY
PERFORMATIVES
PERFORMATORY
PERFORMED
PERFORMER
PERFORMERS
PERFORMING
PERFORMINGS
PERFORMS
PERFS
PERFUME
PERFUMED
PERFUMELESS
PERFUMER
PERFUMERIES
PERFUMERS
PERFUMERY
PERFUMES
PERFUMIER
PERFUMIERS
PERFUMING
PERFUMY
PERFUNCTORILY
PERFUNCTORINESS
PERFUNCTORY
PERFUSATE
PERFUSATES
PERFUSE
PERFUSED
PERFUSES
PERFUSING

PERFUSION
PERFUSIONIST
PERFUSIONISTS
PERFUSIONS
PERFUSIVE
PERGAMENEOUS
PERGAMENTACEOUS
PERGOLA
PERGOLAS
PERGUNNAH
PERGUNNAHS
PERHAPS
PERHAPSES
PERI
PERIAGUA
PERIAGUAS
PERIAKTOI
PERIAKTOS
PERIANTH
PERIANTHS
PERIAPT
PERIAPTS
PERIASTRON
PERIASTRONS
PERIBLAST
PERIBLASTS
PERIBLEM
PERIBLEMS
PERIBOLI
PERIBOLOI
PERIBOLOS
PERIBOLUS
PERICARDIA
PERICARDIAC
PERICARDIAL
PERICARDIAN
PERICARDITIC
PERICARDITIS
PERICARDITISES
PERICARDIUM
PERICARDIUMS
PERICARP
PERICARPIAL
PERICARPIC
PERICARPS
PERICENTER
PERICENTERS
PERICENTRAL
PERICENTRALLY
PERICENTRE
PERICENTRES
PERICENTRIC
PERICHAETIA
PERICHAETIAL
PERICHAETIUM
PERICHONDRAL

PERICHONDRIA
PERICHONDRIAL
PERICHONDRIUM
PERICHORESES
PERICHORESIS
PERICHYLOUS
PERICLASE
PERICLASES
PERICLASTIC
PERICLINAL
PERICLINE
PERICLINES
PERICLITATE
PERICLITATED
PERICLITATES
PERICLITATING
PERICON
PERICONES
PERICOPAE
PERICOPE
PERICOPES
PERICOPIC
PERICRANIA
PERICRANIAL
PERICRANIES
PERICRANIUM
PERICRANIUMS
PERICULOUS
PERICYCLE
PERICYCLES
PERICYCLIC
PERICYNTHION
PERICYNTHIONS
PERIDERM
PERIDERMAL
PERIDERMIC
PERIDERMS
PERIDESMIA
PERIDESMIUM
PERIDIA
PERIDIAL
PERIDINIA
PERIDINIAN
PERIDINIANS
PERIDINIUM
PERIDINIUMS
PERIDIUM
PERIDIUMS
PERIDOT
PERIDOTE
PERIDOTES
PERIDOTIC
PERIDOTITE
PERIDOTITES
PERIDOTITIC
PERIDOTS

PERIDROME
PERIDROMES
PERIEGESES
PERIEGESIS
PERIGASTRIC
PERIGASTRITIS
PERIGASTRITISES
PERIGEAL
PERIGEAN
PERIGEE
PERIGEES
PERIGENESES
PERIGENESIS
PERIGLACIAL
PERIGON
PERIGONE
PERIGONES
PERIGONIA
PERIGONIAL
PERIGONIUM
PERIGONS
PERIGYNIES
PERIGYNOUS
PERIGYNY
PERIHELIA
PERIHELIAL
PERIHELION
PERIHEPATIC
PERIHEPATITIS
PERIHEPATITISES
PERIKARYA
PERIKARYAL
PERIKARYON
PERIL
PERILED
PERILING
PERILLA
PERILLAS
PERILLED
PERILLING
PERILOUS
PERILOUSLY
PERILOUSNESS
PERILOUSNESSES
PERILS
PERILUNE
PERILUNES
PERILYMPH
PERILYMPHS
PERIMETER
PERIMETERS
PERIMETRAL
PERIMETRIC
PERIMETRICAL
PERIMETRICALLY
PERIMETRIES

PERIMETRY
PERIMORPH
PERIMORPHIC
PERIMORPHISM
PERIMORPHOUS
PERIMORPHS
PERIMYSIA
PERIMYSIUM
PERIMYSIUMS
PERINAEUM
PERINAEUMS
PERINATAL
PERINATALLY
PERINEA
PERINEAL
PERINEPHRIA
PERINEPHRIC
PERINEPHRITIS
PERINEPHRITISES
PERINEPHRIUM
PERINEUM
PERINEUMS
PERINEURAL
PERINEURALLY
PERINEURIA
PERINEURIAL
PERINEURITIC
PERINEURITIS
PERINEURITISES
PERINEURIUM
PERINEURIUMS
PERIOD
PERIODATE
PERIODATES
PERIODED
PERIODIC
PERIODICAL
PERIODICALIST
PERIODICALISTS
PERIODICALLY
PERIODICALS
PERIODICITIES
PERIODICITY
PERIODID
PERIODIDS
PERIODING
PERIODISATION
PERIODISATIONS
PERIODIZATION
PERIODIZATIONS
PERIODONTAL
PERIODONTALLY
PERIODONTIA
PERIODONTIAS
PERIODONTIC
PERIODONTICALLY

PERIODONTICS
PERIODONTIST
PERIODONTISTS
PERIODONTITIS
PERIODONTITISES
PERIODONTOLOGY
PERIODS
PERIONYCHIA
PERIONYCHIUM
PERIOST
PERIOSTEA
PERIOSTEAL
PERIOSTEUM
PERIOSTITIC
PERIOSTITIS
PERIOSTITISES
PERIOSTRACUM
PERIOSTRACUMS
PERIOSTS
PERIOTIC
PERIOTICS
PERIPATETIC
PERIPATETICAL
PERIPATETICALLY
PERIPATETICISM
PERIPATETICISMS
PERIPATETICS
PERIPATUS
PERIPATUSES
PERIPETEIA
PERIPETEIAN
PERIPETEIAS
PERIPETIA
PERIPETIAN
PERIPETIAS
PERIPETIES
PERIPETY
PERIPHERAL
PERIPHERALITIES
PERIPHERALITY
PERIPHERALLY
PERIPHERALS
PERIPHERIC
PERIPHERICAL
PERIPHERIES
PERIPHERY
PERIPHONIC
PERIPHRASE
PERIPHRASED
PERIPHRASES
PERIPHRASING
PERIPHRASIS
PERIPHRASTIC
PERIPHRASTICAL
PERIPHYTIC
PERIPHYTON

PERIPHYTONS
PERIPLAST
PERIPLASTS
PERIPLUS
PERIPLUSES
PERIPROCT
PERIPROCTS
PERIPTER
PERIPTERAL
PERIPTERIES
PERIPTERS
PERIPTERY
PERIQUE
PERIQUES
PERIS
PERISARC
PERISARCAL
PERISARCOUS
PERISARCS
PERISCIAN
PERISCIANS
PERISCOPE
PERISCOPES
PERISCOPIC
PERISCOPICALLY
PERISELENIUM
PERISH
PERISHABILITIES
PERISHABILITY
PERISHABLE
PERISHABLENESS
PERISHABLES
PERISHABLY
PERISHED
PERISHER
PERISHERS
PERISHES
PERISHING
PERISHINGLY
PERISPERM
PERISPERMAL
PERISPERMIC
PERISPERMS
PERISPOMENON
PERISPOMENONS
PERISSODACTYL
PERISSODACTYLE
PERISSODACTYLES
PERISSODACTYLIC
PERISSODACTYLS
PERISSOLOGIES
PERISSOLOGY
PERISSOSYLLABIC
PERISTALITH
PERISTALITHS
PERISTALSES

PERISTALSIS
PERISTALTIC
PERISTALTICALLY
PERISTERITE
PERISTERITES
PERISTERONIC
PERISTOMAL
PERISTOMATIC
PERISTOME
PERISTOMES
PERISTOMIAL
PERISTREPHIC
PERISTYLAR
PERISTYLE
PERISTYLES
PERITECTIC
PERITHECIA
PERITHECIAL
PERITHECIUM
PERITI
PERITONAEA
PERITONAEAL
PERITONAEUM
PERITONAEUMS
PERITONEA
PERITONEAL
PERITONEALLY
PERITONEOSCOPY
PERITONEUM
PERITONEUMS
PERITONITIC
PERITONITIS
PERITONITISES
PERITRACK
PERITRACKS
PERITRICH
PERITRICHA
PERITRICHOUS
PERITRICHOUSLY
PERITUS
PERITYPHLITIS
PERITYPHLITISES
PERIVITELLINE
PERIWIG
PERIWIGGED
PERIWIGGING
PERIWIGS
PERIWINKLE
PERIWINKLES
PERJINK
PERJINKETY
PERJINKITIES
PERJINKITY
PERJURE
PERJURED
PERJURER

PERJURERS
PERJURES
PERJURIES
PERJURING
PERJURIOUS
PERJURIOUSLY
PERJUROUS
PERJURY
PERK
PERKED
PERKIER
PERKIEST
PERKILY
PERKIN
PERKINESS
PERKINESSES
PERKING
PERKINS
PERKISH
PERKS
PERKY
PERLEMOEN
PERLEMOENS
PERLITE
PERLITES
PERLITIC
PERLOCUTION
PERLOCUTIONARY
PERLOCUTIONS
PERLOUS
PERLUSTRATE
PERLUSTRATED
PERLUSTRATES
PERLUSTRATING
PERLUSTRATION
PERLUSTRATIONS
PERM
PERMACULTURE
PERMACULTURES
PERMAFROST
PERMAFROSTS
PERMALLOY
PERMALLOYS
PERMANENCE
PERMANENCES
PERMANENCIES
PERMANENCY
PERMANENT
PERMANENTLY
PERMANENTNESS
PERMANENTNESSES
PERMANENTS
PERMANGANATE
PERMANGANATES
PERMANGANIC
PERMEABILITIES

PERMEABILITY
PERMEABLE
PERMEABLENESS
PERMEABLY
PERMEAMETER
PERMEAMETERS
PERMEANCE
PERMEANCES
PERMEANT
PERMEASE
PERMEASES
PERMEATE
PERMEATED
PERMEATES
PERMEATING
PERMEATION
PERMEATIONS
PERMEATIVE
PERMED
PERMETHRIN
PERMETHRINS
PERMIE
PERMILLAGE
PERMILLAGES
PERMING
PERMISSIBILITY
PERMISSIBLE
PERMISSIBLENESS
PERMISSIBLY
PERMISSION
PERMISSIONS
PERMISSIVE
PERMISSIVELY
PERMISSIVENESS
PERMIT
PERMITS
PERMITTANCE
PERMITTANCES
PERMITTED
PERMITTEE
PERMITTEES
PERMITTER
PERMITTERS
PERMITTING
PERMITTIVITIES
PERMITTIVITY
PERMS
PERMUTABILITIES
PERMUTABILITY
PERMUTABLE
PERMUTABLENESS
PERMUTABLY
PERMUTATE
PERMUTATED
PERMUTATES
PERMUTATING

PERMUTATION
PERMUTATIONAL
PERMUTATIONS
PERMUTE
PERMUTED
PERMUTES
PERMUTING
PERN
PERNANCIES
PERNANCY
PERNICIOUS
PERNICIOUSLY
PERNICIOUSNESS
PERNICKETINESS
PERNICKETY
PERNIO
PERNIOS
PERNOCTATE
PERNOCTATED
PERNOCTATES
PERNOCTATING
PERNOCTATION
PERNOCTATIONS
PERNS
PERONE
PERONEAL
PERONES
PERONEUS
PERONEUSES
PERORAL
PERORALLY
PERORATE
PERORATED
PERORATES
PERORATING
PERORATION
PERORATIONAL
PERORATIONS
PEROVSKIA
PEROVSKIAS
PEROVSKITE
PEROVSKITES
PEROXID
PEROXIDASE
PEROXIDASES
PEROXIDATION
PEROXIDATIONS
PEROXIDE
PEROXIDED
PEROXIDES
PEROXIDIC
PEROXIDING
PEROXIDISE
PEROXIDISED
PEROXIDISES
PEROXIDISING

PEROXIDIZE
PEROXIDIZED
PEROXIDIZES
PEROXIDIZING
PEROXIDS
PEROXISOMAL
PEROXISOME
PEROXISOMES
PEROXY
PEROXYSULPHURIC
PERPEND
PERPENDED
PERPENDICULAR
PERPENDICULARLY
PERPENDICULARS
PERPENDING
PERPENDS
PERPENT
PERPENTS
PERPETRABLE
PERPETRATE
PERPETRATED
PERPETRATES
PERPETRATING
PERPETRATION
PERPETRATIONS
PERPETRATOR
PERPETRATORS
PERPETUABLE
PERPETUAL
PERPETUALISM
PERPETUALISMS
PERPETUALIST
PERPETUALISTS
PERPETUALITIES
PERPETUALITY
PERPETUALLY
PERPETUALS
PERPETUANCE
PERPETUANCES
PERPETUATE
PERPETUATED
PERPETUATES
PERPETUATING
PERPETUATION
PERPETUATIONS
PERPETUATOR
PERPETUATORS
PERPETUITIES
PERPETUITY
PERPHENAZINE
PERPHENAZINES
PERPLEX
PERPLEXED
PERPLEXEDLY
PERPLEXEDNESS

PERPLEXEDNESSES
PERPLEXES
PERPLEXING
PERPLEXINGLY
PERPLEXITIES
PERPLEXITY
PERQUISITE
PERQUISITES
PERQUISITION
PERQUISITIONS
PERQUISITOR
PERQUISITORS
PERRADIAL
PERRADII
PERRADIUS
PERRIER
PERRIERS
PERRIES
PERRON
PERRONS
PERRUQUE
PERRUQUES
PERRUQUIER
PERRUQUIERS
PERRY
PERSALT
PERSALTS
PERSANT
PERSAUNT
PERSCRUTATION
PERSCRUTATIONS
PERSE
PERSECUTE
PERSECUTED
PERSECUTEE
PERSECUTEES
PERSECUTES
PERSECUTING
PERSECUTION
PERSECUTIONS
PERSECUTIVE
PERSECUTOR
PERSECUTORS
PERSECUTORY
PERSEITIES
PERSEITY
PERSELINE
PERSELINES
PERSES
PERSEVERANCE
PERSEVERANCES
PERSEVERANT
PERSEVERATE
PERSEVERATED
PERSEVERATES
PERSEVERATING

PERSEVERATION
PERSEVERATIONS
PERSEVERATIVE
PERSEVERATOR
PERSEVERATORS
PERSEVERE
PERSEVERED
PERSEVERES
PERSEVERING
PERSEVERINGLY
PERSICARIA
PERSICARIAS
PERSICO
PERSICOS
PERSICOT
PERSICOTS
PERSIENNE
PERSIENNES
PERSIFLAGE
PERSIFLAGES
PERSIFLEUR
PERSIFLEURS
PERSIMMON
PERSIMMONS
PERSING
PERSIST
PERSISTED
PERSISTENCE
PERSISTENCES
PERSISTENCIES
PERSISTENCY
PERSISTENT
PERSISTENTLY
PERSISTENTS
PERSISTER
PERSISTERS
PERSISTING
PERSISTINGLY
PERSISTIVE
PERSISTS
PERSNICKETINESS
PERSNICKETY
PERSON
PERSONA
PERSONABLE
PERSONABLENESS
PERSONABLY
PERSONAE
PERSONAGE
PERSONAGES
PERSONAL
PERSONALIA
PERSONALISATION
PERSONALISE
PERSONALISED
PERSONALISES

PERSONALISING
PERSONALISM
PERSONALISMS
PERSONALIST
PERSONALISTIC
PERSONALISTS
PERSONALITIES
PERSONALITY
PERSONALIZATION
PERSONALIZE
PERSONALIZED
PERSONALIZES
PERSONALIZING
PERSONALLY
PERSONALS
PERSONALTIES
PERSONALTY
PERSONAS
PERSONATE
PERSONATED
PERSONATES
PERSONATING
PERSONATINGS
PERSONATION
PERSONATIONS
PERSONATIVE
PERSONATOR
PERSONATORS
PERSONHOOD
PERSONHOODS
PERSONIFIABLE
PERSONIFICATION
PERSONIFIED
PERSONIFIER
PERSONIFIERS
PERSONIFIES
PERSONIFY
PERSONIFYING
PERSONISE
PERSONISED
PERSONISES
PERSONISING
PERSONIZE
PERSONIZED
PERSONIZES
PERSONIZING
PERSONNED
PERSONNEL
PERSONNELS
PERSONPOWER
PERSONPOWERS
PERSONS
PERSPECTIVAL
PERSPECTIVE
PERSPECTIVELY
PERSPECTIVES

PERSPECTIVISM
PERSPECTIVISMS
PERSPECTIVIST
PERSPECTIVISTS
PERSPICACIOUS
PERSPICACIOUSLY
PERSPICACITIES
PERSPICACITY
PERSPICUITIES
PERSPICUITY
PERSPICUOUS
PERSPICUOUSLY
PERSPICUOUSNESS
PERSPIRABLE
PERSPIRATE
PERSPIRATED
PERSPIRATES
PERSPIRATING
PERSPIRATION
PERSPIRATIONS
PERSPIRATORY
PERSPIRE
PERSPIRED
PERSPIRES
PERSPIRING
PERSPIRINGLY
PERSPIRY
PERST
PERSTRINGE
PERSTRINGED
PERSTRINGES
PERSTRINGING
PERSUADABILITY
PERSUADABLE
PERSUADABLY
PERSUADE
PERSUADED
PERSUADER
PERSUADERS
PERSUADES
PERSUADING
PERSUASIBILITY
PERSUASIBLE
PERSUASION
PERSUASIONS
PERSUASIVE
PERSUASIVELY
PERSUASIVENESS
PERSUASIVES
PERSUASORY
PERSUE
PERSUED
PERSUES
PERSUING
PERSULFURIC
PERSULPHATE

PERSULPHATES
PERSULPHURIC
PERSWADE
PERSWADED
PERSWADES
PERSWADING
PERT
PERTAIN
PERTAINED
PERTAINING
PERTAINS
PERTAKE
PERTAKEN
PERTAKES
PERTAKING
PERTER
PERTEST
PERTHITE
PERTHITES
PERTHITIC
PERTINACIOUS
PERTINACIOUSLY
PERTINACITIES
PERTINACITY
PERTINENCE
PERTINENCES
PERTINENCIES
PERTINENCY
PERTINENT
PERTINENTLY
PERTINENTS
PERTLY
PERTNESS
PERTNESSES
PERTOOK
PERTS
PERTURB
PERTURBABILITY
PERTURBABLE
PERTURBABLY
PERTURBANCE
PERTURBANCES
PERTURBANT
PERTURBANTS
PERTURBATE
PERTURBATED
PERTURBATES
PERTURBATING
PERTURBATION
PERTURBATIONAL
PERTURBATIONS
PERTURBATIVE
PERTURBATOR
PERTURBATORIES
PERTURBATORS
PERTURBATORY

PERTURBED
PERTURBEDLY
PERTURBER
PERTURBERS
PERTURBING
PERTURBINGLY
PERTURBS
PERTUSATE
PERTUSE
PERTUSED
PERTUSION
PERTUSIONS
PERTUSSAL
PERTUSSIS
PERTUSSISES
PERUKE
PERUKED
PERUKES
PERUSAL
PERUSALS
PERUSE
PERUSED
PERUSER
PERUSERS
PERUSES
PERUSING
PERV
PERVADE
PERVADED
PERVADER
PERVADERS
PERVADES
PERVADING
PERVASION
PERVASIONS
PERVASIVE
PERVASIVELY
PERVASIVENESS
PERVASIVENESSES
PERVE
PERVED
PERVERSE
PERVERSELY
PERVERSENESS
PERVERSENESSES
PERVERSER
PERVERSEST
PERVERSION
PERVERSIONS
PERVERSITIES
PERVERSITY
PERVERSIVE
PERVERT
PERVERTED
PERVERTEDLY
PERVERTEDNESS

PERVERTEDNESSES
PERVERTER
PERVERTERS
PERVERTIBLE
PERVERTING
PERVERTS
PERVES
PERVIATE
PERVIATED
PERVIATES
PERVIATING
PERVICACIES
PERVICACIOUS
PERVICACITIES
PERVICACITY
PERVICACY
PERVING
PERVIOUS
PERVIOUSLY
PERVIOUSNESS
PERVIOUSNESSES
PERVS
PES
PESADE
PESADES
PESANT
PESANTE
PESANTS
PESAUNT
PESAUNTS
PESETA
PESETAS
PESEWA
PESEWAS
PESHWA
PESHWAS
PESKIER
PESKIEST
PESKILY
PESKINESS
PESKY
PESO
PESOS
PESSARIES
PESSARY
PESSIMA
PESSIMAL
PESSIMISM
PESSIMISMS
PESSIMIST
PESSIMISTIC
PESSIMISTICAL
PESSIMISTICALLY
PESSIMISTS
PESSIMUM
PEST

PESTER
PESTERED
PESTERER
PESTERERS
PESTERING
PESTERINGLY
PESTERMENT
PESTERMENTS
PESTEROUS
PESTERS
PESTFUL
PESTHOLE
PESTHOLES
PESTHOUSE
PESTHOUSES
PESTICIDAL
PESTICIDE
PESTICIDES
PESTIER
PESTIEST
PESTIFEROUS
PESTIFEROUSLY
PESTIFEROUSNESS
PESTILENCE
PESTILENCES
PESTILENT
PESTILENTIAL
PESTILENTIALLY
PESTILENTLY
PESTLE
PESTLED
PESTLES
PESTLING
PESTO
PESTOLOGICAL
PESTOLOGIES
PESTOLOGIST
PESTOLOGISTS
PESTOLOGY
PESTOS
PESTS
PESTY
PET
PETAL
PETALED
PETALIFEROUS
PETALINE
PETALISM
PETALISMS
PETALLED
PETALLIKE
PETALODIC
PETALODIES
PETALODY
PETALOID
PETALOMANIA

PETALOMANIAS
PETALOUS
PETALS
PETANQUE
PETANQUES
PETAR
PETARA
PETARAS
PETARD
PETARDS
PETARIES
PETARS
PETARY
PETASOS
PETASOSES
PETASUS
PETASUSES
PETAURINE
PETAURIST
PETAURISTS
PETCHARIES
PETCHARY
PETCOCK
PETCOCKS
PETECHIA
PETECHIAE
PETECHIAL
PETER
PETERED
PETERING
PETERMAN
PETERMEN
PETERS
PETERSHAM
PETERSHAMS
PETHER
PETHERS
PETHIDINE
PETHIDINES
PETILLANT
PETIOLAR
PETIOLATE
PETIOLATED
PETIOLE
PETIOLED
PETIOLES
PETIOLULE
PETIOLULES
PETIT
PETITE
PETITENESS
PETITENESSES
PETITES
PETITIO
PETITION
PETITIONARY

PETITIONED
PETITIONER
PETITIONERS
PETITIONING
PETITIONINGS
PETITIONIST
PETITIONISTS
PETITIONS
PETITORY
PETNAP
PETNAPPED
PETNAPPING
PETNAPS
PETRALE
PETRALES
PETRARIES
PETRARY
PETRE
PETREL
PETRELS
PETRES
PETRIFACTION
PETRIFACTIONS
PETRIFACTIVE
PETRIFIC
PETRIFICATION
PETRIFICATIONS
PETRIFIED
PETRIFIER
PETRIFIERS
PETRIFIES
PETRIFY
PETRIFYING
PETRISSAGE
PETRISSAGES
PETROCHEMICAL
PETROCHEMICALLY
PETROCHEMICALS
PETROCHEMISTRY
PETROCURRENCIES
PETROCURRENCY
PETRODOLLAR
PETRODOLLARS
PETRODROMES
PETROGENESES
PETROGENESIS
PETROGENETIC
PETROGLYPH
PETROGLYPHIC
PETROGLYPHIES
PETROGLYPHS
PETROGLYPHY
PETROGRAM
PETROGRAMS
PETROGRAPHER
PETROGRAPHERS

PETROGRAPHIC
PETROGRAPHICAL
PETROGRAPHIES
PETROGRAPHY
PETROL
PETROLAGE
PETROLAGES
PETROLATUM
PETROLATUMS
PETROLEOUS
PETROLEUM
PETROLEUMS
PETROLEUR
PETROLEURS
PETROLEUSE
PETROLEUSES
PETROLHEAD
PETROLHEADS
PETROLIC
PETROLIFEROUS
PETROLLED
PETROLLING
PETROLOGIC
PETROLOGICAL
PETROLOGICALLY
PETROLOGIES
PETROLOGIST
PETROLOGISTS
PETROLOGY
PETROLS
PETROMONEY
PETROMONEYS
PETRONEL
PETRONELLA
PETRONELLAS
PETRONELS
PETROPHYSICAL
PETROPHYSICIST
PETROPHYSICISTS
PETROPHYSICS
PETROSAL
PETROSALS
PETROUS
PETS
PETSAI
PETSAIS
PETTED
PETTEDLY
PETTEDNESS
PETTEDNESSES
PETTER
PETTERS
PETTI
PETTICHAPS
PETTICHAPSES
PETTICOAT

PETTICOATED
PETTICOATS
PETTIER
PETTIES
PETTIEST
PETTIFOG
PETTIFOGGED
PETTIFOGGER
PETTIFOGGERIES
PETTIFOGGERS
PETTIFOGGERY
PETTIFOGGING
PETTIFOGGINGS
PETTIFOGS
PETTILY
PETTINESS
PETTINESSES
PETTING
PETTINGS
PETTISH
PETTISHLY
PETTISHNESS
PETTISHNESSES
PETTITOES
PETTLE
PETTLED
PETTLES
PETTLING
PETTO
PETTY
PETULANCE
PETULANCES
PETULANCIES
PETULANCY
PETULANT
PETULANTLY
PETUNIA
PETUNIAS
PETUNTSE
PETUNTSES
PETUNTZE
PETUNTZES
PEW
PEWEE
PEWEES
PEWHOLDER
PEWHOLDERS
PEWIT
PEWITS
PEWS
PEWTER
PEWTERER
PEWTERERS
PEWTERS
PEYOTE
PEYOTES

PEYOTISM
PEYOTISMS
PEYOTIST
PEYOTISTS
PEYOTL
PEYOTLS
PEYSE
PEYSED
PEYSES
PEYSING
PEYTRAL
PEYTRALS
PEYTREL
PEYTRELS
PEZANT
PEZANTS
PEZIZOID
PFENNIG
PFENNIGE
PFENNIGS
PFENNING
PFENNINGS
PFFT
PFUI
PH
PHACELIA
PHACELIAS
PHACOID
PHACOIDAL
PHACOLITE
PHACOLITES
PHACOLITH
PHACOLITHS
PHAEIC
PHAEISM
PHAEISMS
PHAELONIONS
PHAENOGAM
PHAENOGAMIC
PHAENOGAMOUS
PHAENOGAMS
PHAENOLOGIES
PHAENOLOGY
PHAENOMENA
PHAENOMENON
PHAENOTYPE
PHAENOTYPED
PHAENOTYPES
PHAENOTYPING
PHAEOMELANIN
PHAEOMELANINS
PHAETON
PHAETONS
PHAGE
PHAGEDAENA
PHAGEDAENAS

PHAGEDAENIC
PHAGEDENA
PHAGEDENAS
PHAGEDENIC
PHAGES
PHAGOCYTE
PHAGOCYTES
PHAGOCYTIC
PHAGOCYTICAL
PHAGOCYTISM
PHAGOCYTISMS
PHAGOCYTIZE
PHAGOCYTIZED
PHAGOCYTIZES
PHAGOCYTIZING
PHAGOCYTOSE
PHAGOCYTOSED
PHAGOCYTOSES
PHAGOCYTOSING
PHAGOCYTOSIS
PHAGOCYTOTIC
PHAGOMANIA
PHAGOMANIAC
PHAGOMANIACS
PHAGOPHOBIA
PHAGOPHOBIAS
PHALANGAL
PHALANGE
PHALANGEAL
PHALANGER
PHALANGERS
PHALANGES
PHALANGID
PHALANGIDS
PHALANGIST
PHALANGISTS
PHALANSTERIAN
PHALANSTERIES
PHALANSTERISM
PHALANSTERISMS
PHALANSTERIST
PHALANSTERISTS
PHALANSTERY
PHALANX
PHALANXES
PHALAROPE
PHALAROPES
PHALLI
PHALLIC
PHALLICALLY
PHALLICISM
PHALLICISMS
PHALLICIST
PHALLICISTS
PHALLIN
PHALLINS

PHALLISM
PHALLISMS
PHALLIST
PHALLISTS
PHALLOCENTRIC
PHALLOCENTRISM
PHALLOCENTRIST
PHALLOCENTRISTS
PHALLOCRAT
PHALLOCRATIC
PHALLOCRATS
PHALLOID
PHALLOIDIN
PHALLOIDINS
PHALLUS
PHALLUSES
PHANEROGAM
PHANEROGAMIC
PHANEROGAMOUS
PHANEROGAMS
PHANEROPHYTE
PHANEROPHYTES
PHANG
PHANGED
PHANGING
PHANGS
PHANSIGAR
PHANSIGARS
PHANTASIAST
PHANTASIASTS
PHANTASIED
PHANTASIES
PHANTASIM
PHANTASIME
PHANTASIMES
PHANTASIMS
PHANTASM
PHANTASMA
PHANTASMAGORIA
PHANTASMAGORIAL
PHANTASMAGORIAS
PHANTASMAGORIC
PHANTASMAGORIES
PHANTASMAGORY
PHANTASMAL
PHANTASMALIAN
PHANTASMALITIES
PHANTASMALITY
PHANTASMALLY
PHANTASMATA
PHANTASMIC
PHANTASMICAL
PHANTASMICALLY
PHANTASMS
PHANTAST
PHANTASTIC

PHANTASTICS
PHANTASTRIES
PHANTASTRY
PHANTASTS
PHANTASY
PHANTASYING
PHANTOM
PHANTOMATIC
PHANTOMISH
PHANTOMLIKE
PHANTOMS
PHANTOMY
PHANTOSME
PHANTOSMES
PHARAOH
PHARAOHS
PHARAONIC
PHARE
PHARES
PHARISAIC
PHARISAICAL
PHARISAICALLY
PHARISAICALNESS
PHARISAISM
PHARISAISMS
PHARISEE
PHARISEEISM
PHARISEEISMS
PHARISEES
PHARMACEUTIC
PHARMACEUTICAL
PHARMACEUTICALS
PHARMACEUTICS
PHARMACEUTIST
PHARMACEUTISTS
PHARMACIES
PHARMACIST
PHARMACISTS
PHARMACODYNAMIC
PHARMACOGNOSIES
PHARMACOGNOSIST
PHARMACOGNOSTIC
PHARMACOGNOSY
PHARMACOKINETIC
PHARMACOLOGIC
PHARMACOLOGICAL
PHARMACOLOGIES
PHARMACOLOGIST
PHARMACOLOGISTS
PHARMACOLOGY
PHARMACOPEIA
PHARMACOPEIAL
PHARMACOPEIAS
PHARMACOPOEIA
PHARMACOPOEIAL
PHARMACOPOEIAN

PHARMACOPOEIAS
PHARMACOPOEIC
PHARMACOPOEIST
PHARMACOPOEISTS
PHARMACOPOLIST
PHARMACOPOLISTS
PHARMACOTHERAPY
PHARMACY
PHARMED
PHARMER
PHARMERS
PHARMING
PHARMS
PHAROS
PHAROSES
PHARYNGAL
PHARYNGEAL
PHARYNGES
PHARYNGITIC
PHARYNGITIDES
PHARYNGITIS
PHARYNGITISES
PHARYNGOLOGICAL
PHARYNGOLOGIES
PHARYNGOLOGIST
PHARYNGOLOGISTS
PHARYNGOLOGY
PHARYNGOSCOPE
PHARYNGOSCOPES
PHARYNGOSCOPIC
PHARYNGOSCOPIES
PHARYNGOSCOPY
PHARYNGOTOMIES
PHARYNGOTOMY
PHARYNX
PHARYNXES
PHASCOGALE
PHASCOGALES
PHASE
PHASEAL
PHASED
PHASEDOWN
PHASEDOWNS
PHASELESS
PHASEOLIN
PHASEOLINS
PHASEOUT
PHASEOUTS
PHASES
PHASIC
PHASING
PHASINGS
PHASIS
PHASMID
PHASMIDS
PHASOR

PHASORS
PHAT
PHATIC
PHATICALLY
PHATTER
PHATTEST
PHEASANT
PHEASANTRIES
PHEASANTRY
PHEASANTS
PHEAZAR
PHEAZARS
PHEER
PHEERE
PHEERES
PHEERS
PHEESE
PHEESED
PHEESES
PHEESING
PHEEZE
PHEEZED
PHEEZES
PHEEZING
PHELLEM
PHELLEMS
PHELLODERM
PHELLODERMAL
PHELLODERMS
PHELLOGEN
PHELLOGENETIC
PHELLOGENIC
PHELLOGENS
PHELLOID
PHELLOPLASTIC
PHELLOPLASTICS
PHELONIA
PHELONION
PHELONIONS
PHENACAINE
PHENACAINES
PHENACETIN
PHENACETINS
PHENACITE
PHENACITES
PHENAKISM
PHENAKISMS
PHENAKISTOSCOPE
PHENAKITE
PHENAKITES
PHENANTHRENE
PHENANTHRENES
PHENATE
PHENATES
PHENAZIN
PHENAZINE

PHENAZINES
PHENAZINS
PHENCYCLIDINE
PHENCYCLIDINES
PHENE
PHENES
PHENETIC
PHENETICIST
PHENETICISTS
PHENETICS
PHENETIDINE
PHENETOL
PHENETOLE
PHENETOLS
PHENFORMIN
PHENGITE
PHENGITES
PHENGOPHOBIA
PHENGOPHOBIAS
PHENIC
PHENIX
PHENIXES
PHENMETRAZINE
PHENMETRAZINES
PHENOBARBITAL
PHENOBARBITALS
PHENOBARBITONE
PHENOBARBITONES
PHENOCOPIES
PHENOCOPY
PHENOCRYST
PHENOCRYSTIC
PHENOCRYSTS
PHENOGAM
PHENOGAMS
PHENOL
PHENOLATE
PHENOLATED
PHENOLATES
PHENOLATING
PHENOLIC
PHENOLICS
PHENOLOGICAL
PHENOLOGICALLY
PHENOLOGIES
PHENOLOGIST
PHENOLOGISTS
PHENOLOGY
PHENOLPHTHALEIN
PHENOLS
PHENOM
PHENOMENA
PHENOMENAL
PHENOMENALISE
PHENOMENALISED
PHENOMENALISES

PHENOMENALISING
PHENOMENALISM
PHENOMENALISMS
PHENOMENALIST
PHENOMENALISTIC
PHENOMENALISTS
PHENOMENALITIES
PHENOMENALITY
PHENOMENALIZE
PHENOMENALIZED
PHENOMENALIZES
PHENOMENALIZING
PHENOMENALLY
PHENOMENAS
PHENOMENISE
PHENOMENISED
PHENOMENISES
PHENOMENISING
PHENOMENISM
PHENOMENISMS
PHENOMENIST
PHENOMENISTS
PHENOMENIZE
PHENOMENIZED
PHENOMENIZES
PHENOMENIZING
PHENOMENOLOGIES
PHENOMENOLOGIST
PHENOMENOLOGY
PHENOMENON
PHENOMENONS
PHENOMS
PHENOTHIAZINE
PHENOTHIAZINES
PHENOTYPE
PHENOTYPED
PHENOTYPES
PHENOTYPIC
PHENOTYPICAL
PHENOTYPICALLY
PHENOTYPING
PHENOXIDE
PHENOXIDES
PHENOXY
PHENTOLAMINE
PHENTOLAMINES
PHENYL
PHENYLALANIN
PHENYLALANINE
PHENYLALANINES
PHENYLALANINS
PHENYLAMINE
PHENYLBUTAZONE
PHENYLBUTAZONES
PHENYLEPHRINE
PHENYLEPHRINES

PHENYLIC
PHENYLKETONURIA
PHENYLKETONURIC
PHENYLMETHYL
PHENYLS
PHENYLTHIOUREA
PHENYLTHIOUREAS
PHENYTOIN
PHENYTOINS
PHEON
PHEONS
PHEROMONAL
PHEROMONE
PHEROMONES
PHESE
PHESED
PHESES
PHESING
PHEW
PHI
PHIAL
PHIALIFORM
PHIALLED
PHIALLING
PHIALS
PHILABEG
PHILABEGS
PHILADELPHUS
PHILADELPHUSES
PHILAMOT
PHILAMOTS
PHILANDER
PHILANDERED
PHILANDERER
PHILANDERERS
PHILANDERING
PHILANDERS
PHILANTHROPE
PHILANTHROPES
PHILANTHROPIC
PHILANTHROPICAL
PHILANTHROPIES
PHILANTHROPIST
PHILANTHROPISTS
PHILANTHROPOID
PHILANTHROPOIDS
PHILANTHROPY
PHILATELIC
PHILATELICALLY
PHILATELIES
PHILATELIST
PHILATELISTS
PHILATELY
PHILHARMONIC
PHILHARMONICS
PHILHELLENE

PHILHELLENES
PHILHELLENIC
PHILHELLENISM
PHILHELLENISMS
PHILHELLENIST
PHILHELLENISTS
PHILHORSE
PHILHORSES
PHILIBEG
PHILIBEGS
PHILIPPIC
PHILIPPICS
PHILIPPINA
PHILIPPINAS
PHILIPPINE
PHILIPPINES
PHILISTIA
PHILISTINE
PHILISTINES
PHILISTINISM
PHILISTINISMS
PHILLABEG
PHILLABEGS
PHILLIBEG
PHILLIBEGS
PHILLIPSITE
PHILLIPSITES
PHILLUMENIES
PHILLUMENIST
PHILLUMENISTS
PHILLUMENY
PHILODENDRA
PHILODENDRON
PHILODENDRONS
PHILOGYNIES
PHILOGYNIST
PHILOGYNISTS
PHILOGYNOUS
PHILOGYNY
PHILOLOGER
PHILOLOGERS
PHILOLOGIAN
PHILOLOGIANS
PHILOLOGIC
PHILOLOGICAL
PHILOLOGICALLY
PHILOLOGIES
PHILOLOGIST
PHILOLOGISTS
PHILOLOGUE
PHILOLOGUES
PHILOLOGY
PHILOMATH
PHILOMATHIC
PHILOMATHICAL
PHILOMATHIES

PHILOMATHS
PHILOMATHY
PHILOMEL
PHILOMELA
PHILOMELAS
PHILOMELS
PHILOMOT
PHILOMOTS
PHILOPENA
PHILOPENAS
PHILOPOENA
PHILOPOENAS
PHILOSOPHASTER
PHILOSOPHASTERS
PHILOSOPHE
PHILOSOPHER
PHILOSOPHERESS
PHILOSOPHERS
PHILOSOPHES
PHILOSOPHESS
PHILOSOPHESSES
PHILOSOPHIC
PHILOSOPHICAL
PHILOSOPHICALLY
PHILOSOPHIES
PHILOSOPHISE
PHILOSOPHISED
PHILOSOPHISER
PHILOSOPHISERS
PHILOSOPHISES
PHILOSOPHISING
PHILOSOPHISM
PHILOSOPHISMS
PHILOSOPHIST
PHILOSOPHISTIC
PHILOSOPHISTS
PHILOSOPHIZE
PHILOSOPHIZED
PHILOSOPHIZER
PHILOSOPHIZERS
PHILOSOPHIZES
PHILOSOPHIZING
PHILOSOPHY
PHILOXENIA
PHILOXENIAS
PHILTER
PHILTERED
PHILTERING
PHILTERS
PHILTRA
PHILTRE
PHILTRED
PHILTRES
PHILTRING
PHILTRUM
PHIMOSES

PHIMOSIS
PHIMOTIC
PHINNOCK
PHINNOCKS
PHIS
PHISNOMIES
PHISNOMY
PHIZ
PHIZES
PHIZOG
PHIZOGS
PHIZZES
PHLEBECTOMIES
PHLEBECTOMY
PHLEBITIC
PHLEBITIDES
PHLEBITIS
PHLEBITISES
PHLEBOGRAM
PHLEBOGRAMS
PHLEBOGRAPHIC
PHLEBOGRAPHIES
PHLEBOGRAPHY
PHLEBOLITE
PHLEBOLITES
PHLEBOLOGIES
PHLEBOLOGY
PHLEBOSCLEROSES
PHLEBOSCLEROSIS
PHLEBOSCLEROTIC
PHLEBOTOMIC
PHLEBOTOMICAL
PHLEBOTOMICALLY
PHLEBOTOMIES
PHLEBOTOMISE
PHLEBOTOMISED
PHLEBOTOMISES
PHLEBOTOMISING
PHLEBOTOMIST
PHLEBOTOMISTS
PHLEBOTOMIZE
PHLEBOTOMIZED
PHLEBOTOMIZES
PHLEBOTOMIZING
PHLEBOTOMY
PHLEGM
PHLEGMAGOGUE
PHLEGMAGOGUES
PHLEGMASIA
PHLEGMASIAS
PHLEGMATIC
PHLEGMATICAL
PHLEGMATICALLY
PHLEGMATICNESS
PHLEGMIER
PHLEGMIEST

PHLEGMON
PHLEGMONIC
PHLEGMONOID
PHLEGMONOUS
PHLEGMONS
PHLEGMS
PHLEGMY
PHLOEM
PHLOEMS
PHLOGISTIC
PHLOGISTICATE
PHLOGISTICATED
PHLOGISTICATES
PHLOGISTICATING
PHLOGISTON
PHLOGISTONS
PHLOGOPITE
PHLOGOPITES
PHLOMIS
PHLOMISES
PHLOX
PHLOXES
PHLYCTAENA
PHLYCTAENAE
PHLYCTENA
PHLYCTENAE
PHO
PHOBIA
PHOBIAS
PHOBIC
PHOBICS
PHOBISM
PHOBISMS
PHOBIST
PHOBISTS
PHOCA
PHOCAE
PHOCAS
PHOCINE
PHOCOMELIA
PHOCOMELIAS
PHOCOMELIC
PHOCOMELY
PHOEBE
PHOEBES
PHOEBUS
PHOEBUSES
PHOENIX
PHOENIXES
PHOENIXISM
PHOENIXISMS
PHOENIXLIKE
PHOH
PHOHS
PHOLADES
PHOLAS

PHOLIDOSES
PHOLIDOSIS
PHON
PHONAL
PHONASTHENIA
PHONASTHENIAS
PHONATE
PHONATED
PHONATES
PHONATING
PHONATION
PHONATIONS
PHONATORY
PHONAUTOGRAPH
PHONAUTOGRAPHIC
PHONAUTOGRAPHS
PHONE
PHONECARD
PHONECARDS
PHONED
PHONEMATIC
PHONEMATICALLY
PHONEME
PHONEMES
PHONEMIC
PHONEMICALLY
PHONEMICISATION
PHONEMICISE
PHONEMICISED
PHONEMICISES
PHONEMICISING
PHONEMICIST
PHONEMICISTS
PHONEMICIZATION
PHONEMICIZE
PHONEMICIZED
PHONEMICIZES
PHONEMICIZING
PHONEMICS
PHONENDOSCOPE
PHONENDOSCOPES
PHONER
PHONERS
PHONES
PHONETIC
PHONETICAL
PHONETICALLY
PHONETICIAN
PHONETICIANS
PHONETICISATION
PHONETICISE
PHONETICISED
PHONETICISES
PHONETICISING
PHONETICISM
PHONETICISMS

PHONETICIST
PHONETICISTS
PHONETICIZATION
PHONETICIZE
PHONETICIZED
PHONETICIZES
PHONETICIZING
PHONETICS
PHONETISATION
PHONETISATIONS
PHONETISE
PHONETISED
PHONETISES
PHONETISING
PHONETISM
PHONETISMS
PHONETIST
PHONETISTS
PHONETIZATION
PHONETIZATIONS
PHONETIZE
PHONETIZED
PHONETIZES
PHONETIZING
PHONEY
PHONEYED
PHONEYING
PHONEYNESS
PHONEYNESSES
PHONEYS
PHONIC
PHONICALLY
PHONICS
PHONIED
PHONIER
PHONIES
PHONIEST
PHONILY
PHONINESS
PHONINESSES
PHONING
PHONMETER
PHONMETERS
PHONO
PHONOCAMPTIC
PHONOCAMPTICS
PHONOCARDIOGRAM
PHONOCHEMICAL
PHONOCHEMICALLY
PHONOCHEMISTRY
PHONOCHEMISTS
PHONOFIDDLE
PHONOFIDDLES
PHONOGRAM
PHONOGRAMIC
PHONOGRAMICALLY

PHONOGRAMMIC
PHONOGRAMS
PHONOGRAPH
PHONOGRAPHER
PHONOGRAPHERS
PHONOGRAPHIC
PHONOGRAPHIES
PHONOGRAPHIST
PHONOGRAPHISTS
PHONOGRAPHS
PHONOGRAPHY
PHONOLITE
PHONOLITES
PHONOLITIC
PHONOLOGIC
PHONOLOGICAL
PHONOLOGICALLY
PHONOLOGIES
PHONOLOGIST
PHONOLOGISTS
PHONOLOGY
PHONOMETER
PHONOMETERS
PHONOMETRIC
PHONOMETRICAL
PHONON
PHONONS
PHONOPHOBIA
PHONOPHOBIAS
PHONOPHORE
PHONOPHORES
PHONOPORE
PHONOPORES
PHONOS
PHONOSCOPE
PHONOSCOPES
PHONOSCOPIC
PHONOSCOPICALLY
PHONOTACTIC
PHONOTACTICS
PHONOTYPE
PHONOTYPED
PHONOTYPER
PHONOTYPERS
PHONOTYPES
PHONOTYPIC
PHONOTYPICAL
PHONOTYPICALLY
PHONOTYPIES
PHONOTYPING
PHONOTYPIST
PHONOTYPISTS
PHONOTYPY
PHONS
PHONY
PHONYING

PHOOEY
PHORATE
PHORATES
PHORESY
PHORETICALLY
PHORMINGES
PHORMINX
PHORMIUM
PHORMIUMS
PHORONID
PHORONIDS
PHOS
PHOSGENE
PHOSGENES
PHOSGENITE
PHOSPHATASE
PHOSPHATASES
PHOSPHATE
PHOSPHATED
PHOSPHATES
PHOSPHATIC
PHOSPHATIDE
PHOSPHATIDES
PHOSPHATIDIC
PHOSPHATIDYL
PHOSPHATIDYLS
PHOSPHATING
PHOSPHATISATION
PHOSPHATISE
PHOSPHATISED
PHOSPHATISES
PHOSPHATISING
PHOSPHATIZATION
PHOSPHATIZE
PHOSPHATIZED
PHOSPHATIZES
PHOSPHATIZING
PHOSPHATURIA
PHOSPHATURIAS
PHOSPHATURIC
PHOSPHENE
PHOSPHENES
PHOSPHID
PHOSPHIDE
PHOSPHIDES
PHOSPHIDS
PHOSPHIN
PHOSPHINE
PHOSPHINES
PHOSPHINS
PHOSPHITE
PHOSPHITES
PHOSPHOCREATIN
PHOSPHOCREATINE
PHOSPHOKINASE
PHOSPHOKINASES

PHOSPHOLIPASE
PHOSPHOLIPASES
PHOSPHOLIPID
PHOSPHOLIPIDS
PHOSPHONIC
PHOSPHONIUM
PHOSPHONIUMS
PHOSPHOPROTEIN
PHOSPHOPROTEINS
PHOSPHOR
PHOSPHORATE
PHOSPHORATED
PHOSPHORATES
PHOSPHORATING
PHOSPHORE
PHOSPHORES
PHOSPHORESCE
PHOSPHORESCED
PHOSPHORESCENCE
PHOSPHORESCENT
PHOSPHORESCES
PHOSPHORESCING
PHOSPHORET
PHOSPHORETS
PHOSPHORETTED
PHOSPHORIC
PHOSPHORISE
PHOSPHORISED
PHOSPHORISES
PHOSPHORISING
PHOSPHORISM
PHOSPHORISMS
PHOSPHORITE
PHOSPHORITES
PHOSPHORITIC
PHOSPHORIZE
PHOSPHORIZED
PHOSPHORIZES
PHOSPHORIZING
PHOSPHOROLYSES
PHOSPHOROLYSIS
PHOSPHOROLYTIC
PHOSPHOROSCOPE
PHOSPHOROSCOPES
PHOSPHOROSCOPIC
PHOSPHOROUS
PHOSPHORS
PHOSPHORUS
PHOSPHORUSES
PHOSPHORYL
PHOSPHORYLASE
PHOSPHORYLASES
PHOSPHORYLATE
PHOSPHORYLATED
PHOSPHORYLATES
PHOSPHORYLATING

PHOSPHORYLATION
PHOSPHORYLATIVE
PHOSPHORYLS
PHOSPHURET
PHOSPHURETS
PHOSPHURETTED
PHOSSY
PHOT
PHOTIC
PHOTICALLY
PHOTICS
PHOTINIA
PHOTINIAS
PHOTISM
PHOTISMS
PHOTO
PHOTOACTINIC
PHOTOACTIVE
PHOTOAUTOTROPH
PHOTOAUTOTROPHS
PHOTOBATHIC
PHOTOBIOLOGIC
PHOTOBIOLOGICAL
PHOTOBIOLOGIES
PHOTOBIOLOGIST
PHOTOBIOLOGISTS
PHOTOBIOLOGY
PHOTOCATALYSES
PHOTOCATALYSIS
PHOTOCATALYTIC
PHOTOCATHODE
PHOTOCATHODES
PHOTOCELL
PHOTOCELLS
PHOTOCHEMICAL
PHOTOCHEMICALLY
PHOTOCHEMIST
PHOTOCHEMISTRY
PHOTOCHEMISTS
PHOTOCHROMIC
PHOTOCHROMICS
PHOTOCHROMIES
PHOTOCHROMISM
PHOTOCHROMISMS
PHOTOCHROMY
PHOTOCOMPOSE
PHOTOCOMPOSED
PHOTOCOMPOSER
PHOTOCOMPOSERS
PHOTOCOMPOSES
PHOTOCOMPOSING
PHOTOCONDUCTING
PHOTOCONDUCTION
PHOTOCONDUCTIVE
PHOTOCONDUCTOR
PHOTOCONDUCTORS

PHOTOCONDUCTS
PHOTOCOPIABLE
PHOTOCOPIED
PHOTOCOPIER
PHOTOCOPIERS
PHOTOCOPIES
PHOTOCOPY
PHOTOCOPYING
PHOTOCOPYINGS
PHOTOCURRENT
PHOTOCURRENTS
PHOTODEGRADABLE
PHOTODETECTOR
PHOTODETECTORS
PHOTODIODE
PHOTODIODES
PHOTODISSOCIATE
PHOTODUPLICATE
PHOTODUPLICATED
PHOTODUPLICATES
PHOTODYNAMIC
PHOTODYNAMICS
PHOTOED
PHOTOELASTIC
PHOTOELASTICITY
PHOTOELECTRIC
PHOTOELECTRICAL
PHOTOELECTRODE
PHOTOELECTRODES
PHOTOELECTRON
PHOTOELECTRONIC
PHOTOELECTRONS
PHOTOEMISSION
PHOTOEMISSIONS
PHOTOEMISSIVE
PHOTOENGRAVE
PHOTOENGRAVED
PHOTOENGRAVER
PHOTOENGRAVERS
PHOTOENGRAVES
PHOTOENGRAVING
PHOTOENGRAVINGS
PHOTOEXCITATION
PHOTOEXCITED
PHOTOFINISHER
PHOTOFINISHERS
PHOTOFINISHING
PHOTOFINISHINGS
PHOTOFISSION
PHOTOFISSIONS
PHOTOFIT
PHOTOFITS
PHOTOFLASH
PHOTOFLASHES
PHOTOFLOOD
PHOTOFLOODS

PHOTOFLUOROGRAM
PHOTOG
PHOTOGELATIN
PHOTOGEN
PHOTOGENE
PHOTOGENES
PHOTOGENIC
PHOTOGENICALLY
PHOTOGENIES
PHOTOGENS
PHOTOGENY
PHOTOGEOLOGIC
PHOTOGEOLOGICAL
PHOTOGEOLOGIES
PHOTOGEOLOGIST
PHOTOGEOLOGISTS
PHOTOGEOLOGY
PHOTOGLYPH
PHOTOGLYPHIC
PHOTOGLYPHIES
PHOTOGLYPHS
PHOTOGLYPHY
PHOTOGRAM
PHOTOGRAMMETRIC
PHOTOGRAMMETRY
PHOTOGRAMS
PHOTOGRAPH
PHOTOGRAPHED
PHOTOGRAPHER
PHOTOGRAPHERS
PHOTOGRAPHIC
PHOTOGRAPHICAL
PHOTOGRAPHIES
PHOTOGRAPHING
PHOTOGRAPHIST
PHOTOGRAPHISTS
PHOTOGRAPHS
PHOTOGRAPHY
PHOTOGRAVURE
PHOTOGRAVURES
PHOTOGS
PHOTOINDUCED
PHOTOINDUCTION
PHOTOINDUCTIONS
PHOTOINDUCTIVE
PHOTOING
PHOTOIONIZATION
PHOTOIONIZE
PHOTOIONIZED
PHOTOIONIZES
PHOTOIONIZING
PHOTOJOURNALISM
PHOTOJOURNALIST
PHOTOKINESES
PHOTOKINESIS
PHOTOKINETIC

PHOTOLITHO
PHOTOLITHOGRAPH
PHOTOLUMINESCE
PHOTOLUMINESCED
PHOTOLUMINESCES
PHOTOLYSE
PHOTOLYSED
PHOTOLYSES
PHOTOLYSING
PHOTOLYSIS
PHOTOLYTIC
PHOTOLYTICALLY
PHOTOLYZABLE
PHOTOLYZE
PHOTOLYZED
PHOTOLYZES
PHOTOLYZING
PHOTOMACROGRAPH
PHOTOMAP
PHOTOMAPPED
PHOTOMAPPING
PHOTOMAPS
PHOTOMASK
PHOTOMASKS
PHOTOMECHANICAL
PHOTOMETER
PHOTOMETERS
PHOTOMETRIC
PHOTOMETRICALLY
PHOTOMETRIES
PHOTOMETRIST
PHOTOMETRISTS
PHOTOMETRY
PHOTOMICROGRAPH
PHOTOMONTAGE
PHOTOMONTAGES
PHOTOMOSAIC
PHOTOMOSAICS
PHOTOMULTIPLIER
PHOTOMURAL
PHOTOMURALS
PHOTON
PHOTONASTIC
PHOTONASTIES
PHOTONASTY
PHOTONEGATIVE
PHOTONEUTRON
PHOTONEUTRONS
PHOTONIC
PHOTONICS
PHOTONOVEL
PHOTONOVELS
PHOTONUCLEAR
PHOTOOXIDATION
PHOTOOXIDATIONS

PHOTOOXIDATIVE
PHOTOOXIDIZE
PHOTOOXIDIZED
PHOTOOXIDIZES
PHOTOOXIDIZING
PHOTOPERIOD
PHOTOPERIODIC
PHOTOPERIODISM
PHOTOPERIODISMS
PHOTOPERIODS
PHOTOPHASE
PHOTOPHASES
PHOTOPHIL
PHOTOPHILIC
PHOTOPHILIES
PHOTOPHILOUS
PHOTOPHILS
PHOTOPHILY
PHOTOPHOBE
PHOTOPHOBES
PHOTOPHOBIA
PHOTOPHOBIAS
PHOTOPHOBIC
PHOTOPHONE
PHOTOPHONES
PHOTOPHONIC
PHOTOPHONIES
PHOTOPHONY
PHOTOPHORE
PHOTOPHORES
PHOTOPHORESES
PHOTOPHORESIS
PHOTOPIA
PHOTOPIAS
PHOTOPIC
PHOTOPLAY
PHOTOPLAYS
PHOTOPOLYMER
PHOTOPOLYMERS
PHOTOPOSITIVE
PHOTOPRODUCT
PHOTOPRODUCTION
PHOTOPRODUCTS
PHOTOPSIA
PHOTOPSIAS
PHOTOPSIES
PHOTOPSY
PHOTOREACTION
PHOTOREACTIONS
PHOTOREALISM
PHOTOREALISMS
PHOTOREALIST
PHOTOREALISTIC
PHOTOREALISTS
PHOTORECEPTION
PHOTORECEPTIONS

PHOTORECEPTIVE
PHOTORECEPTOR
PHOTORECEPTORS
PHOTOREDUCE
PHOTOREDUCED
PHOTOREDUCES
PHOTOREDUCING
PHOTOREDUCTION
PHOTOREDUCTIONS
PHOTOREFRACTIVE
PHOTORESIST
PHOTORESISTS
PHOTOS
PHOTOSENSITISE
PHOTOSENSITISED
PHOTOSENSITISER
PHOTOSENSITISES
PHOTOSENSITIVE
PHOTOSENSITIZE
PHOTOSENSITIZED
PHOTOSENSITIZER
PHOTOSENSITIZES
PHOTOSET
PHOTOSETS
PHOTOSETTER
PHOTOSETTERS
PHOTOSETTING
PHOTOSETTINGS
PHOTOSPHERE
PHOTOSPHERES
PHOTOSPHERIC
PHOTOSTAT
PHOTOSTATED
PHOTOSTATIC
PHOTOSTATING
PHOTOSTATS
PHOTOSTATTED
PHOTOSTATTING
PHOTOSYNTHATE
PHOTOSYNTHATES
PHOTOSYNTHESES
PHOTOSYNTHESIS
PHOTOSYNTHESISE
PHOTOSYNTHESIZE
PHOTOSYNTHETIC
PHOTOSYSTEM
PHOTOSYSTEMS
PHOTOTACTIC
PHOTOTACTICALLY
PHOTOTAXES
PHOTOTAXIS
PHOTOTAXY
PHOTOTELEGRAPH
PHOTOTELEGRAPHS
PHOTOTELEGRAPHY
PHOTOTHERAPIES

PHOTOTHERAPY
PHOTOTHERMAL
PHOTOTHERMALLY
PHOTOTHERMIC
PHOTOTONIC
PHOTOTONUS
PHOTOTOPOGRAPHY
PHOTOTOXIC
PHOTOTOXICITIES
PHOTOTOXICITY
PHOTOTRANSISTOR
PHOTOTROPE
PHOTOTROPES
PHOTOTROPH
PHOTOTROPHIC
PHOTOTROPHS
PHOTOTROPIC
PHOTOTROPICALLY
PHOTOTROPIES
PHOTOTROPISM
PHOTOTROPISMS
PHOTOTROPY
PHOTOTUBE
PHOTOTUBES
PHOTOTYPE
PHOTOTYPED
PHOTOTYPES
PHOTOTYPESET
PHOTOTYPESETS
PHOTOTYPESETTER
PHOTOTYPIC
PHOTOTYPICALLY
PHOTOTYPIES
PHOTOTYPING
PHOTOTYPOGRAPHY
PHOTOTYPY
PHOTOVOLTAIC
PHOTOVOLTAICS
PHOTOXYLOGRAPHY
PHOTOZINCOGRAPH
PHOTS
PHPHT
PHRAGMOPLAST
PHRAGMOPLASTS
PHRASAL
PHRASALLY
PHRASE
PHRASED
PHRASELESS
PHRASEMAKER
PHRASEMAKERS
PHRASEMAKING
PHRASEMAKINGS
PHRASEMAN
PHRASEMEN
PHRASEMONGER

PHRASEMONGERING
PHRASEMONGERS
PHRASEOGRAM
PHRASEOGRAMS
PHRASEOGRAPH
PHRASEOGRAPHIC
PHRASEOGRAPHS
PHRASEOGRAPHY
PHRASEOLOGIC
PHRASEOLOGICAL
PHRASEOLOGIES
PHRASEOLOGIST
PHRASEOLOGISTS
PHRASEOLOGY
PHRASER
PHRASERS
PHRASES
PHRASIER
PHRASIEST
PHRASING
PHRASINGS
PHRASY
PHRATRAL
PHRATRIC
PHRATRIES
PHRATRY
PHREAK
PHREAKING
PHREAKINGS
PHREAKS
PHREATIC
PHREATOPHYTE
PHREATOPHYTES
PHREATOPHYTIC
PHRENESES
PHRENESIAC
PHRENESIS
PHRENETIC
PHRENETICAL
PHRENETICALLY
PHRENETICNESS
PHRENETICS
PHRENIC
PHRENISM
PHRENISMS
PHRENITIC
PHRENITIS
PHRENITISES
PHRENOLOGIC
PHRENOLOGICAL
PHRENOLOGICALLY
PHRENOLOGIES
PHRENOLOGISE
PHRENOLOGISED
PHRENOLOGISES
PHRENOLOGISING

PHRENOLOGIST
PHRENOLOGISTS
PHRENOLOGIZE
PHRENOLOGIZED
PHRENOLOGIZES
PHRENOLOGIZING
PHRENOLOGY
PHRENSICAL
PHRENSIED
PHRENSIES
PHRENSY
PHRENSYING
PHRENTICK
PHRONTISTERIES
PHRONTISTERY
PHRYGANA
PHS
PHT
PHTHALATE
PHTHALATES
PHTHALEIN
PHTHALEINS
PHTHALIC
PHTHALIN
PHTHALINS
PHTHALOCYANIN
PHTHALOCYANINE
PHTHALOCYANINES
PHTHALOCYANINS
PHTHIRIASES
PHTHIRIASIS
PHTHISES
PHTHISIC
PHTHISICAL
PHTHISICKY
PHTHISICS
PHTHISIS
PHUT
PHUTS
PHUTTED
PHUTTING
PHYCOBILIN
PHYCOBILINS
PHYCOBIONT
PHYCOCYAN
PHYCOCYANIN
PHYCOCYANINS
PHYCOCYANS
PHYCOERYTHRIN
PHYCOERYTHRINS
PHYCOLOGICAL
PHYCOLOGIES
PHYCOLOGIST
PHYCOLOGISTS
PHYCOLOGY
PHYCOMYCETE

PHYCOMYCETES
PHYCOMYCETOUS
PHYCOPHAEIN
PHYCOPHAEINS
PHYCOXANTHIN
PHYCOXANTHINS
PHYLA
PHYLACTERIC
PHYLACTERICAL
PHYLACTERIES
PHYLACTERY
PHYLAE
PHYLAR
PHYLARCH
PHYLARCHIES
PHYLARCHS
PHYLARCHY
PHYLAXIS
PHYLAXISES
PHYLE
PHYLESES
PHYLESIS
PHYLESISES
PHYLETIC
PHYLETICALLY
PHYLIC
PHYLLARIES
PHYLLARY
PHYLLID
PHYLLIDS
PHYLLITE
PHYLLITES
PHYLLITIC
PHYLLO
PHYLLOCLAD
PHYLLOCLADE
PHYLLOCLADES
PHYLLOCLADS
PHYLLODE
PHYLLODES
PHYLLODIA
PHYLLODIAL
PHYLLODIES
PHYLLODIUM
PHYLLODY
PHYLLOID
PHYLLOIDS
PHYLLOMANIA
PHYLLOMANIAS
PHYLLOME
PHYLLOMES
PHYLLOMIC
PHYLLOPHAGOUS
PHYLLOPLANE
PHYLLOPLANES
PHYLLOPOD

PHYLLOPODS
PHYLLOQUINONE
PHYLLOQUINONES
PHYLLOS
PHYLLOSILICATE
PHYLLOSILICATES
PHYLLOSPHERE
PHYLLOSPHERES
PHYLLOTACTIC
PHYLLOTACTICAL
PHYLLOTAXES
PHYLLOTAXIES
PHYLLOTAXIS
PHYLLOTAXY
PHYLLOXERA
PHYLLOXERAE
PHYLLOXERAS
PHYLOGENESES
PHYLOGENESIS
PHYLOGENETIC
PHYLOGENIC
PHYLOGENICALLY
PHYLOGENIES
PHYLOGENY
PHYLON
PHYLUM
PHYSALIA
PHYSALIAS
PHYSALIS
PHYSALISES
PHYSED
PHYSEDS
PHYSES
PHYSETER
PHYSETERS
PHYSHARMONICA
PHYSHARMONICAS
PHYSIATRIC
PHYSIATRICAL
PHYSIATRICALLY
PHYSIATRICS
PHYSIATRIST
PHYSIATRISTS
PHYSIC
PHYSICAL
PHYSICALISM
PHYSICALISMS
PHYSICALIST
PHYSICALISTIC
PHYSICALISTS
PHYSICALITIES
PHYSICALITY
PHYSICALLY
PHYSICALNESS
PHYSICALNESSES
PHYSICALS

PHYSICIAN
PHYSICIANCIES
PHYSICIANCY
PHYSICIANER
PHYSICIANERS
PHYSICIANS
PHYSICIANSHIP
PHYSICIANSHIPS
PHYSICISM
PHYSICISMS
PHYSICIST
PHYSICISTS
PHYSICKED
PHYSICKING
PHYSICKY
PHYSICOCHEMICAL
PHYSICS
PHYSIO
PHYSIOCRACIES
PHYSIOCRACY
PHYSIOCRAT
PHYSIOCRATIC
PHYSIOCRATS
PHYSIOGNOMIC
PHYSIOGNOMICAL
PHYSIOGNOMIES
PHYSIOGNOMIST
PHYSIOGNOMISTS
PHYSIOGNOMY
PHYSIOGRAPHER
PHYSIOGRAPHERS
PHYSIOGRAPHIC
PHYSIOGRAPHICAL
PHYSIOGRAPHIES
PHYSIOGRAPHY
PHYSIOLATER
PHYSIOLATERS
PHYSIOLATRIES
PHYSIOLATRY
PHYSIOLOGIC
PHYSIOLOGICAL
PHYSIOLOGICALLY
PHYSIOLOGIES
PHYSIOLOGIST
PHYSIOLOGISTS
PHYSIOLOGUS
PHYSIOLOGUSES
PHYSIOLOGY
PHYSIOPATHOLOGY
PHYSIOS
PHYSIOTHERAPIES
PHYSIOTHERAPIST
PHYSIOTHERAPY
PHYSIQUE
PHYSIQUES
PHYSIS

PHYSITHEISM
PHYSITHEISMS
PHYSITHEISTIC
PHYSOCLISTOUS
PHYSOSTIGMIN
PHYSOSTIGMINE
PHYSOSTIGMINES
PHYSOSTOMOUS
PHYTANE
PHYTANES
PHYTOALEXIN
PHYTOALEXINS
PHYTOBENTHOS
PHYTOBENTHOSES
PHYTOCHEMICAL
PHYTOCHEMICALLY
PHYTOCHEMICALS
PHYTOCHEMIST
PHYTOCHEMISTRY
PHYTOCHEMISTS
PHYTOCHROME
PHYTOCHROMES
PHYTOFLAGELLATE
PHYTOGENESES
PHYTOGENESIS
PHYTOGENETIC
PHYTOGENETICAL
PHYTOGENIC
PHYTOGENIES
PHYTOGENY
PHYTOGEOGRAPHER
PHYTOGEOGRAPHIC
PHYTOGEOGRAPHY
PHYTOGRAPHER
PHYTOGRAPHERS
PHYTOGRAPHIC
PHYTOGRAPHIES
PHYTOGRAPHY
PHYTOHORMONE
PHYTOHORMONES
PHYTOID
PHYTOL
PHYTOLOGICAL
PHYTOLOGICALLY
PHYTOLOGIES
PHYTOLOGIST
PHYTOLOGISTS
PHYTOLOGY
PHYTOLS
PHYTON
PHYTONADIONE
PHYTONADIONES
PHYTONIC
PHYTONS
PHYTOPATHOGEN
PHYTOPATHOGENIC

PHYTOPATHOGENS
PHYTOPATHOLOGY
PHYTOPHAGIC
PHYTOPHAGOUS
PHYTOPHAGOUSLY
PHYTOPHAGY
PHYTOPLANKTER
PHYTOPLANKTERS
PHYTOPLANKTON
PHYTOPLANKTONIC
PHYTOPLANKTONS
PHYTOSES
PHYTOSIS
PHYTOSOCIOLOGY
PHYTOSTEROL
PHYTOSTEROLS
PHYTOTOMIES
PHYTOTOMIST
PHYTOTOMISTS
PHYTOTOMY
PHYTOTOXIC
PHYTOTOXICITIES
PHYTOTOXICITY
PHYTOTOXIN
PHYTOTOXINS
PHYTOTRON
PHYTOTRONS
PI
PIA
PIACEVOLE
PIACULAR
PIACULARITIES
PIACULARITY
PIAFFE
PIAFFED
PIAFFER
PIAFFERS
PIAFFES
PIAFFING
PIAL
PIAN
PIANETTE
PIANETTES
PIANIC
PIANINO
PIANINOS
PIANISM
PIANISMS
PIANISSIMI
PIANISSIMO
PIANISSIMOS
PIANISSISSIMO
PIANIST
PIANISTE
PIANISTES
PIANISTIC

PIANISTICALLY
PIANISTS
PIANO
PIANOFORTE
PIANOFORTES
PIANOLIST
PIANOLISTS
PIANOS
PIANS
PIARIST
PIARISTS
PIAS
PIASABA
PIASABAS
PIASAVA
PIASAVAS
PIASSABA
PIASSABAS
PIASSAVA
PIASSAVAS
PIASTER
PIASTERS
PIASTRE
PIASTRES
PIAZZA
PIAZZAS
PIAZZE
PIAZZIAN
PIBAL
PIBALS
PIBROCH
PIBROCHS
PIC
PICA
PICACHO
PICACHOS
PICADOR
PICADORES
PICADORS
PICAL
PICAMAR
PICAMARS
PICANINNIES
PICANINNY
PICARA
PICARAS
PICARESQUE
PICARESQUES
PICARIAN
PICARIANS
PICARO
PICAROON
PICAROONED
PICAROONING
PICAROONS
PICAROS

PICAS
PICAYUNE
PICAYUNES
PICAYUNISH
PICAYUNISHLY
PICAYUNISHNESS
PICCADELLS
PICCADILL
PICCADILLIES
PICCADILLO
PICCADILLOES
PICCADILLS
PICCADILLY
PICCALILLI
PICCALILLIS
PICCANIN
PICCANINNIES
PICCANINNY
PICCANINS
PICCIES
PICCOLO
PICCOLOIST
PICCOLOISTS
PICCOLOS
PICCY
PICE
PICENE
PICENES
PICEOUS
PICHICIAGO
PICHICIAGOS
PICHICIEGO
PICHICIEGOS
PICHURIM
PICHURIMS
PICIFORM
PICINE
PICK
PICKABACK
PICKABACKED
PICKABACKING
PICKABACKS
PICKABILITY
PICKABLE
PICKABLENESS
PICKADELLS
PICKADIL
PICKADILL
PICKADILLIES
PICKADILLO
PICKADILLOES
PICKADILLS
PICKADILLY
PICKADILS
PICKANINNIES
PICKANINNY

PICKAPACK
PICKAPACKS
PICKAROON
PICKAROONS
PICKAX
PICKAXE
PICKAXED
PICKAXES
PICKAXING
PICKBACK
PICKBACKS
PICKED
PICKEDNESS
PICKEDNESSES
PICKEER
PICKEERED
PICKEERER
PICKEERERS
PICKEERING
PICKEERS
PICKELHAUBE
PICKELHAUBES
PICKER
PICKEREL
PICKERELS
PICKERELWEED
PICKERELWEEDS
PICKERIES
PICKERS
PICKERY
PICKET
PICKETBOAT
PICKETBOATS
PICKETED
PICKETER
PICKETERS
PICKETING
PICKETS
PICKIER
PICKIEST
PICKILY
PICKIN
PICKINESS
PICKING
PICKINGS
PICKINS
PICKLE
PICKLED
PICKLER
PICKLERS
PICKLES
PICKLING
PICKLOCK
PICKLOCKS
PICKMAW
PICKMAWS

PICKOFF
PICKOFFS
PICKPOCKET
PICKPOCKETS
PICKPROOF
PICKS
PICKTHANK
PICKTHANKS
PICKUP
PICKUPS
PICKWICK
PICKWICKS
PICKY
PICLORAM
PICLORAMS
PICNIC
PICNICKED
PICNICKER
PICNICKERS
PICNICKING
PICNICKY
PICNICS
PICOCURIE
PICOCURIES
PICOFARAD
PICOFARADS
PICOGRAM
PICOGRAMS
PICOLIN
PICOLINE
PICOLINES
PICOLINIC
PICOLINS
PICOMOLE
PICOMOLES
PICONG
PICONGS
PICORNAVIRUS
PICORNAVIRUSES
PICOSECOND
PICOSECONDS
PICOT
PICOTE
PICOTED
PICOTEE
PICOTEES
PICOTING
PICOTITE
PICOTITES
PICOTS
PICQUET
PICQUETED
PICQUETING
PICQUETS
PICRA
PICRAS

PICRATE
PICRATED
PICRATES
PICRIC
PICRITE
PICRITES
PICRITIC
PICROCARMINE
PICROCARMINES
PICROTOXIN
PICROTOXINS
PICS
PICTARNIE
PICTARNIES
PICTOGRAM
PICTOGRAMS
PICTOGRAPH
PICTOGRAPHIC
PICTOGRAPHIES
PICTOGRAPHS
PICTOGRAPHY
PICTORIAL
PICTORIALISM
PICTORIALISMS
PICTORIALIST
PICTORIALISTS
PICTORIALIZE
PICTORIALIZED
PICTORIALIZES
PICTORIALIZING
PICTORIALLY
PICTORIALNESS
PICTORIALNESSES
PICTORIALS
PICTORICAL
PICTORICALLY
PICTURAL
PICTURALS
PICTURE
PICTURED
PICTUREGOER
PICTUREGOERS
PICTUREGOING
PICTUREPHONE
PICTUREPHONES
PICTURES
PICTURESQUE
PICTURESQUELY
PICTURESQUENESS
PICTURING
PICTURIZATION
PICTURIZATIONS
PICTURIZE
PICTURIZED
PICTURIZES
PICTURIZING

PICUL
PICULS
PIDDLE
PIDDLED
PIDDLER
PIDDLERS
PIDDLES
PIDDLING
PIDDLINGLY
PIDDLY
PIDDOCK
PIDDOCKS
PIDGEON
PIDGEONS
PIDGIN
PIDGINISATION
PIDGINISATIONS
PIDGINIZATION
PIDGINIZATIONS
PIDGINIZE
PIDGINIZED
PIDGINIZES
PIDGINIZING
PIDGINS
PIE
PIEBALD
PIEBALDS
PIECE
PIECED
PIECELESS
PIECEMEAL
PIECEMEALED
PIECEMEALING
PIECEMEALS
PIECEN
PIECENED
PIECENER
PIECENERS
PIECENING
PIECENS
PIECER
PIECERS
PIECES
PIECEWISE
PIECEWORK
PIECEWORKER
PIECEWORKERS
PIECEWORKS
PIECING
PIECINGS
PIECRUST
PIECRUSTS
PIED
PIEDFORT
PIEDFORTS
PIEDISH

PIEDISHES
PIEDMONT
PIEDMONTITE
PIEDMONTITES
PIEDMONTS
PIEDNESS
PIEDNESSES
PIEFORT
PIEFORTS
PIEING
PIEMAN
PIEMEN
PIEMONTITE
PIEND
PIENDS
PIEPLANT
PIEPLANTS
PIEPOWDER
PIEPOWDERS
PIER
PIERAGE
PIERAGES
PIERCE
PIERCEABLE
PIERCED
PIERCER
PIERCERS
PIERCES
PIERCING
PIERCINGLY
PIERCINGNESS
PIERCINGNESSES
PIERCINGS
PIERID
PIERIDINE
PIERIDS
PIERIS
PIEROGI
PIEROGIES
PIERRETTE
PIERRETTES
PIERROT
PIERROTS
PIERS
PIERST
PIERT
PIES
PIET
PIETA
PIETAS
PIETIES
PIETISM
PIETISMS
PIETIST
PIETISTIC
PIETISTICAL

PIETISTICALLY
PIETISTS
PIETS
PIETY
PIEZO
PIEZOCHEMISTRY
PIEZOELECTRIC
PIEZOMAGNETIC
PIEZOMAGNETISM
PIEZOMAGNETISMS
PIEZOMETER
PIEZOMETERS
PIEZOMETRIC
PIEZOMETRICALLY
PIEZOMETRY
PIFFERARI
PIFFERARO
PIFFERO
PIFFEROS
PIFFLE
PIFFLED
PIFFLER
PIFFLERS
PIFFLES
PIFFLING
PIG
PIGBOAT
PIGBOATS
PIGEON
PIGEONED
PIGEONHOLE
PIGEONHOLED
PIGEONHOLER
PIGEONHOLERS
PIGEONHOLES
PIGEONHOLING
PIGEONING
PIGEONITE
PIGEONITES
PIGEONRIES
PIGEONRY
PIGEONS
PIGEONWING
PIGEONWINGS
PIGFACE
PIGFACED
PIGFACES
PIGFEED
PIGFEEDS
PIGFISH
PIGFISHES
PIGGED
PIGGERIES
PIGGERY
PIGGIE
PIGGIER

PIGGIES
PIGGIEST
PIGGIN
PIGGING
PIGGINGS
PIGGINS
PIGGISH
PIGGISHLY
PIGGISHNESS
PIGGISHNESSES
PIGGY
PIGGYBACK
PIGGYBACKED
PIGGYBACKING
PIGGYBACKS
PIGHEADED
PIGHEADEDLY
PIGHEADEDNESS
PIGHEADEDNESSES
PIGHT
PIGHTED
PIGHTING
PIGHTLE
PIGHTLES
PIGHTS
PIGLET
PIGLETS
PIGLIKE
PIGLING
PIGLINGS
PIGMAEAN
PIGMEAN
PIGMEAT
PIGMEATS
PIGMENT
PIGMENTAL
PIGMENTARY
PIGMENTATION
PIGMENTATIONS
PIGMENTED
PIGMENTING
PIGMENTS
PIGMIES
PIGMOID
PIGMY
PIGNERATE
PIGNERATED
PIGNERATES
PIGNERATING
PIGNOLI
PIGNOLIA
PIGNOLIAS
PIGNOLIS
PIGNORA
PIGNORATE
PIGNORATED

PIGNORATES	PIKES	PILFER	PILLARLESS
PIGNORATING	PIKESTAFF	PILFERABLE	PILLARS
PIGNORATION	PIKESTAFFS	PILFERAGE	PILLAU
PIGNORATIONS	PIKESTAVES	PILFERAGES	PILLAUS
PIGNUS	PIKI	PILFERED	PILLBOX
PIGNUT	PIKING	PILFERER	PILLBOXES
PIGNUTS	PIKIS	PILFERERS	PILLED
PIGOUT	PIKUL	PILFERIES	PILLHEAD
PIGOUTS	PIKULS	PILFERING	PILLHEADS
PIGPEN	PILA	PILFERINGLY	PILLICOCK
PIGPENS	PILAF	PILFERINGS	PILLICOCKS
PIGS	PILAFF	PILFERPROOF	PILLIE
PIGSCONCE	PILAFFS	PILFERS	PILLIES
PIGSCONCES	PILAFS	PILFERY	PILLING
PIGSKIN	PILAO	PILGARLIC	PILLINGS
PIGSKINS	PILAOS	PILGARLICK	PILLION
PIGSNEY	PILAR	PILGARLICKS	PILLIONED
PIGSNEYS	PILASTER	PILGARLICKY	PILLIONING
PIGSNIE	PILASTERED	PILGARLICS	PILLIONIST
PIGSNIES	PILASTERS	PILGRIM	PILLIONISTS
PIGSNY	PILAU	PILGRIMAGE	PILLIONS
PIGSTICK	PILAUS	PILGRIMAGED	PILLIWINKS
PIGSTICKED	PILAW	PILGRIMAGER	PILLOCK
PIGSTICKER	PILAWS	PILGRIMAGERS	PILLOCKS
PIGSTICKERS	PILCH	PILGRIMAGES	PILLORIED
PIGSTICKING	PILCHARD	PILGRIMAGING	PILLORIES
PIGSTICKS	PILCHARDS	PILGRIMER	PILLORISE
PIGSTIES	PILCHER	PILGRIMERS	PILLORISED
PIGSTUCK	PILCHERS	PILGRIMISE	PILLORISES
PIGSTY	PILCHES	PILGRIMISED	PILLORISING
PIGSWILL	PILCORN	PILGRIMISES	PILLORIZE
PIGSWILLS	PILCORNS	PILGRIMISING	PILLORIZED
PIGTAIL	PILCROW	PILGRIMIZE	PILLORIZES
PIGTAILED	PILCROWS	PILGRIMIZED	PILLORIZING
PIGTAILS	PILE	PILGRIMIZES	PILLORY
PIGWASH	PILEA	PILGRIMIZING	PILLORYING
PIGWASHES	PILEAS	PILGRIMS	PILLOW
PIGWEED	PILEATE	PILHORSES	PILLOWCASE
PIGWEEDS	PILEATED	PILI	PILLOWCASES
PIING	PILED	PILIFEROUS	PILLOWED
PIKA	PILEI	PILIFORM	PILLOWING
PIKAKE	PILELESS	PILING	PILLOWS
PIKAKES	PILEORHIZA	PILINGS	PILLOWSLIP
PIKAS	PILEORHIZAS	PILIS	PILLOWSLIPS
PIKAU	PILEOUS	PILL	PILLOWY
PIKAUS	PILER	PILLAGE	PILLS
PIKE	PILERS	PILLAGED	PILLWORM
PIKED	PILES	PILLAGER	PILLWORMS
PIKELET	PILEUM	PILLAGERS	PILLWORT
PIKELETS	PILEUP	PILLAGES	PILLWORTS
PIKEMAN	PILEUPS	PILLAGING	PILNIEWINKS
PIKEMEN	PILEUS	PILLAR	PILOCARPIN
PIKEPERCH	PILEWORK	PILLARED	PILOCARPINE
PIKEPERCHES	PILEWORKS	PILLARING	PILOCARPINES
PIKER	PILEWORT	PILLARIST	PILOCARPINS
PIKERS	PILEWORTS	PILLARISTS	PILOMOTOR

PILOSE
PILOSITIES
PILOSITY
PILOT
PILOTAGE
PILOTAGES
PILOTED
PILOTHOUSE
PILOTHOUSES
PILOTING
PILOTINGS
PILOTIS
PILOTLESS
PILOTMAN
PILOTMEN
PILOTS
PILOUS
PILOW
PILOWS
PILSENER
PILSENERS
PILSNER
PILSNERS
PILULA
PILULAR
PILULAS
PILULE
PILULES
PILUM
PILUS
PILY
PIMA
PIMAS
PIMENT
PIMENTO
PIMENTOS
PIMENTS
PIMIENTO
PIMIENTOS
PIMP
PIMPED
PIMPERNEL
PIMPERNELS
PIMPING
PIMPLE
PIMPLED
PIMPLES
PIMPLIER
PIMPLIEST
PIMPLINESS
PIMPLY
PIMPMOBILE
PIMPMOBILES
PIMPS
PIN
PINA

PINACEOUS
PINACOID
PINACOIDAL
PINACOIDS
PINACOTHECA
PINACOTHECAE
PINAFORE
PINAFORED
PINAFORES
PINAKOID
PINAKOIDAL
PINAKOIDS
PINAKOTHEK
PINAKOTHEKS
PINANG
PINANGS
PINAS
PINASTER
PINASTERS
PINATA
PINATAS
PINBALL
PINBALLS
PINBONE
PINBONES
PINCASE
PINCASES
PINCER
PINCERED
PINCERING
PINCERLIKE
PINCERS
PINCH
PINCHBECK
PINCHBECKS
PINCHBUG
PINCHBUGS
PINCHCOCK
PINCHCOCKS
PINCHCOMMONS
PINCHCOMMONSES
PINCHECK
PINCHECKS
PINCHED
PINCHER
PINCHERS
PINCHES
PINCHFIST
PINCHFISTS
PINCHGUT
PINCHGUTS
PINCHING
PINCHINGLY
PINCHINGS
PINCHPENNIES
PINCHPENNY

PINCHPOINT
PINCHPOINTS
PINCUSHION
PINCUSHIONS
PINDAN
PINDANS
PINDAREE
PINDAREES
PINDARI
PINDARIS
PINDER
PINDERS
PINDLING
PINDOWN
PINDOWNS
PINE
PINEAL
PINEALECTOMIES
PINEALECTOMIZE
PINEALECTOMIZED
PINEALECTOMIZES
PINEALECTOMY
PINEALS
PINEAPPLE
PINEAPPLES
PINECONE
PINECONES
PINED
PINEDROPS
PINELAND
PINELANDS
PINELIKE
PINENE
PINENES
PINERIES
PINERY
PINES
PINESAP
PINESAPS
PINETA
PINETUM
PINEWOOD
PINEWOODS
PINEY
PINFALL
PINFALLS
PINFEATHER
PINFEATHERS
PINFISH
PINFISHES
PINFOLD
PINFOLDED
PINFOLDING
PINFOLDS
PING
PINGAO

PINGED
PINGER
PINGERS
PINGING
PINGLE
PINGLED
PINGLER
PINGLERS
PINGLES
PINGLING
PINGO
PINGOES
PINGOS
PINGRASS
PINGRASSES
PINGS
PINGUEFIED
PINGUEFIES
PINGUEFY
PINGUEFYING
PINGUID
PINGUIDITIES
PINGUIDITY
PINGUIN
PINGUINS
PINGUITUDE
PINGUITUDES
PINHEAD
PINHEADED
PINHEADEDNESS
PINHEADEDNESSES
PINHEADS
PINHOLE
PINHOLES
PINHOOKER
PINHOOKERS
PINIER
PINIES
PINIEST
PINING
PINION
PINIONED
PINIONING
PINIONS
PINITE
PINITES
PINITOL
PINITOLS
PINK
PINKED
PINKEN
PINKENED
PINKENING
PINKENS
PINKER
PINKERS

PINKERTON
PINKERTONS
PINKEST
PINKEY
PINKEYE
PINKEYES
PINKEYS
PINKIE
PINKIER
PINKIES
PINKIEST
PINKINESS
PINKINESSES
PINKING
PINKINGS
PINKISH
PINKISHNESS
PINKISHNESSES
PINKLY
PINKNESS
PINKNESSES
PINKO
PINKOES
PINKOS
PINKROOT
PINKROOTS
PINKS
PINKY
PINNA
PINNACE
PINNACES
PINNACLE
PINNACLED
PINNACLES
PINNACLING
PINNAE
PINNAL
PINNAS
PINNATE
PINNATED
PINNATELY
PINNATIFID
PINNATIFIDLY
PINNATIFIDNESS
PINNATION
PINNATIONS
PINNATIPARTITE
PINNATIPED
PINNATISECT
PINNED
PINNER
PINNERS
PINNET
PINNETS
PINNIE
PINNIES

PINNIEWINKLES
PINNING
PINNINGS
PINNIPED
PINNIPEDE
PINNIPEDES
PINNIPEDIAN
PINNIPEDIANS
PINNIPEDS
PINNOCK
PINNOCKS
PINNOED
PINNULA
PINNULAE
PINNULAR
PINNULAS
PINNULATE
PINNULATED
PINNULE
PINNULES
PINNY
PINNYWINKLES
PINOCHLE
PINOCHLES
PINOCLE
PINOCLES
PINOCYTIC
PINOCYTOSES
PINOCYTOSIS
PINOCYTOTIC
PINOCYTOTICALLY
PINOLE
PINOLES
PINON
PINONES
PINONS
PINOT
PINOTAGE
PINOTAGES
PINOTS
PINPOINT
PINPOINTED
PINPOINTING
PINPOINTS
PINPRICK
PINPRICKED
PINPRICKING
PINPRICKS
PINS
PINSCHER
PINSCHERS
PINSETTER
PINSETTERS
PINSPOTTER
PINSPOTTERS
PINSTRIPE

PINSTRIPES
PINSWELL
PINSWELLS
PINT
PINTA
PINTABLE
PINTABLES
PINTADA
PINTADAS
PINTADERA
PINTADERAS
PINTADO
PINTADOES
PINTADOS
PINTAIL
PINTAILED
PINTAILS
PINTANO
PINTANOS
PINTAS
PINTLE
PINTLES
PINTO
PINTOES
PINTOS
PINTS
PINTSIZE
PINUP
PINUPS
PINWALE
PINWALES
PINWEED
PINWEEDS
PINWHEEL
PINWHEELED
PINWHEELING
PINWHEELS
PINWORK
PINWORKS
PINWORM
PINWORMS
PINXIT
PINY
PINYIN
PINYON
PINYONS
PIOLET
PIOLETS
PION
PIONED
PIONEER
PIONEERED
PIONEERING
PIONEERS
PIONER
PIONERS

PIONEY
PIONEYS
PIONIC
PIONIES
PIONING
PIONINGS
PIONS
PIONY
PIOPIO
PIOPIOS
PIOSITIES
PIOSITY
PIOTED
PIOUS
PIOUSLY
PIOUSNESS
PIOUSNESSES
PIOY
PIOYE
PIOYES
PIOYS
PIP
PIPA
PIPAGE
PIPAGES
PIPAL
PIPALS
PIPAS
PIPE
PIPEAGE
PIPEAGES
PIPECLAY
PIPECLAYED
PIPECLAYING
PIPECLAYS
PIPED
PIPEFISH
PIPEFISHES
PIPEFITTER
PIPEFITTERS
PIPEFITTING
PIPEFUL
PIPEFULS
PIPELESS
PIPELIKE
PIPELINE
PIPELINED
PIPELINES
PIPELINING
PIPELININGS
PIPER
PIPERACEOUS
PIPERAZINE
PIPERAZINES
PIPERIC
PIPERIDINE

PIPERIDINES
PIPERINE
PIPERINES
PIPERONAL
PIPERONALS
PIPERS
PIPES
PIPESTEM
PIPESTEMS
PIPESTONE
PIPESTONES
PIPET
PIPETS
PIPETTE
PIPETTED
PIPETTES
PIPETTING
PIPEWORK
PIPEWORKS
PIPEWORT
PIPEWORTS
PIPI
PIPIER
PIPIEST
PIPINESS
PIPINESSES
PIPING
PIPINGLY
PIPINGS
PIPIS
PIPISTRELLE
PIPISTRELLES
PIPIT
PIPITS
PIPIWHARAUROA
PIPIWHARAUROAS
PIPKIN
PIPKINS
PIPLESS
PIPPED
PIPPIER
PIPPIEST
PIPPIN
PIPPING
PIPPINS
PIPPY
PIPS
PIPSISSEWA
PIPSISSEWAS
PIPSQUEAK
PIPSQUEAKS
PIPUL
PIPULS
PIPY
PIQUANCE
PIQUANCES

PIQUANCIES
PIQUANCY
PIQUANT
PIQUANTLY
PIQUANTNESS
PIQUANTNESSES
PIQUE
PIQUED
PIQUES
PIQUET
PIQUETED
PIQUETING
PIQUETS
PIQUING
PIR
PIRACIES
PIRACY
PIRAGUA
PIRAGUAS
PIRAI
PIRAIS
PIRANA
PIRANAS
PIRANHA
PIRANHAS
PIRARUCU
PIRARUCUS
PIRATE
PIRATED
PIRATES
PIRATIC
PIRATICAL
PIRATICALLY
PIRATING
PIRAYA
PIRAYAS
PIRIFORM
PIRIPIRI
PIRIPIRIS
PIRL
PIRLICUE
PIRLICUED
PIRLICUES
PIRLICUING
PIRLS
PIRN
PIRNIE
PIRNIES
PIRNIT
PIRNS
PIROG
PIROGEN
PIROGHI
PIROGI
PIROGIES
PIROGUE

PIROGUES
PIROJKI
PIROPLASM
PIROPLASMA
PIROPLASMATA
PIROPLASMS
PIROQUE
PIROQUES
PIROSHKI
PIROUETTE
PIROUETTED
PIROUETTER
PIROUETTERS
PIROUETTES
PIROUETTING
PIROZHKI
PIROZHOK
PIRS
PIS
PISCARIES
PISCARY
PISCATOR
PISCATORIAL
PISCATORIALLY
PISCATORS
PISCATORY
PISCATRIX
PISCATRIXES
PISCICOLOUS
PISCICULTURAL
PISCICULTURALLY
PISCICULTURE
PISCICULTURES
PISCICULTURIST
PISCICULTURISTS
PISCIFAUNA
PISCIFAUNAS
PISCIFORM
PISCINA
PISCINAE
PISCINAL
PISCINAS
PISCINE
PISCINES
PISCIVOROUS
PISCO
PISCOS
PISE
PISES
PISH
PISHED
PISHES
PISHING
PISHOGE
PISHOGES
PISHOGUE

PISHOGUES
PISIFORM
PISIFORMS
PISKIES
PISKY
PISMIRE
PISMIRES
PISO
PISOLITE
PISOLITES
PISOLITHS
PISOLITIC
PISOS
PISS
PISSANT
PISSANTS
PISSASPHALT
PISSASPHALTS
PISSED
PISSER
PISSERS
PISSES
PISSHEAD
PISSHEADS
PISSING
PISSOIR
PISSOIRS
PISTACHE
PISTACHES
PISTACHIO
PISTACHIOS
PISTAREEN
PISTAREENS
PISTE
PISTES
PISTIL
PISTILLARY
PISTILLATE
PISTILLODE
PISTILLODES
PISTILS
PISTOL
PISTOLE
PISTOLED
PISTOLEER
PISTOLEERS
PISTOLES
PISTOLET
PISTOLETS
PISTOLING
PISTOLLED
PISTOLLING
PISTOLS
PISTON
PISTONS
PIT

PITA
PITAPAT
PITAPATS
PITAPATTED
PITAPATTING
PITARA
PITARAH
PITARAHS
PITARAS
PITAS
PITCH
PITCHBEND
PITCHBENDS
PITCHBLENDE
PITCHBLENDES
PITCHED
PITCHER
PITCHERFUL
PITCHERFULS
PITCHERS
PITCHERSFUL
PITCHES
PITCHFORK
PITCHFORKED
PITCHFORKING
PITCHFORKS
PITCHIER
PITCHIEST
PITCHILY
PITCHINESS
PITCHINESSES
PITCHING
PITCHINGS
PITCHMAN
PITCHMEN
PITCHOMETER
PITCHOMETERS
PITCHOUT
PITCHOUTS
PITCHPERSON
PITCHPERSONS
PITCHPINE
PITCHPINES
PITCHPIPE
PITCHPIPES
PITCHPOLE
PITCHPOLED
PITCHPOLES
PITCHPOLING
PITCHSTONE
PITCHSTONES
PITCHWOMAN
PITCHWOMEN
PITCHY
PITEOUS
PITEOUSLY

PITEOUSNESS
PITEOUSNESSES
PITFALL
PITFALLS
PITH
PITHBALL
PITHBALLS
PITHEAD
PITHEADS
PITHECANTHROPI
PITHECANTHROPUS
PITHECOID
PITHED
PITHFUL
PITHIER
PITHIEST
PITHILY
PITHINESS
PITHINESSES
PITHING
PITHLESS
PITHLIKE
PITHOI
PITHOS
PITHS
PITHY
PITIABLE
PITIABLENESS
PITIABLENESSES
PITIABLY
PITIED
PITIER
PITIERS
PITIES
PITIFUL
PITIFULLER
PITIFULLEST
PITIFULLY
PITIFULNESS
PITIFULNESSES
PITILESS
PITILESSLY
PITILESSNESS
PITILESSNESSES
PITMAN
PITMANS
PITMEN
PITON
PITONS
PITPROP
PITPROPS
PITS
PITSAW
PITSAWS
PITTA
PITTANCE

PITTANCES
PITTAS
PITTED
PITTEN
PITTER
PITTERED
PITTERING
PITTERS
PITTING
PITTINGS
PITTITE
PITTITES
PITTOSPORUM
PITTOSPORUMS
PITUITA ·
PITUITARIES
PITUITARY
PITUITAS
PITUITE
PITUITES
PITUITRIN
PITUITRINS
PITURI
PITURIS
PITY
PITYING
PITYINGLY
PITYRIASES
PITYRIASIS
PITYROID
PITYROSPORUM
PITYROSPORUMS
PIU
PIUM
PIUMS
PIUPIU
PIUPIUS
PIVOT
PIVOTABLE
PIVOTAL
PIVOTALLY
PIVOTED
PIVOTER
PIVOTERS
PIVOTING
PIVOTINGS
PIVOTMAN
PIVOTMEN
PIVOTS
PIWAKAWAKA
PIWAKAWAKAS
PIX
PIXEL
PIXELATION
PIXELATIONS
PIXELLATED

PIXELS
PIXES
PIXIE
PIXIEISH
PIXIES
PIXILATED
PIXILATION
PIXILATIONS
PIXILLATED
PIXILLATION
PIXILLATIONS
PIXINESS
PIXINESSES
PIXY
PIXYISH
PIZAZZ
PIZAZZES
PIZAZZY
PIZE
PIZED
PIZES
PIZING
PIZZA
PIZZAIOLA
PIZZALIKE
PIZZAS
PIZZAZZ
PIZZERIA
PIZZERIAS
PIZZICATI
PIZZICATO
PIZZICATOS
PIZZLE
PIZZLES
PLAAS
PLAASES
PLACABILITIES
PLACABILITY
PLACABLE
PLACABLENESS
PLACABLENESSES
PLACABLY
PLACARD
PLACARDED
PLACARDING
PLACARDS
PLACATE
PLACATED
PLACATER
PLACATERS
PLACATES
PLACATING
PLACATINGLY
PLACATION
PLACATIONS
PLACATIVE

PLACATORY
PLACCAT
PLACCATE
PLACCATES
PLACCATS
PLACE
PLACEABLE
PLACEBO
PLACEBOES
PLACEBOS
PLACED
PLACEHOLDER
PLACEHOLDERS
PLACEKICK
PLACEKICKED
PLACEKICKER
PLACEKICKERS
PLACEKICKING
PLACEKICKS
PLACELESS
PLACELESSLY
PLACEMAN
PLACEMEN
PLACEMENT
PLACEMENTS
PLACENTA
PLACENTAE
PLACENTAL
PLACENTALS
PLACENTAS
PLACENTATE
PLACENTATION
PLACENTATIONS
PLACENTIFORM
PLACENTOLOGIES
PLACENTOLOGY
PLACER
PLACERS
PLACES
PLACET
PLACETS
PLACID
PLACIDER
PLACIDEST
PLACIDITIES
PLACIDITY
PLACIDLY
PLACIDNESS
PLACIDNESSES
PLACING
PLACINGS
PLACIT
PLACITA
PLACITORY
PLACITS
PLACITUM

PLACK
PLACKET
PLACKETS
PLACKLESS
PLACKS
PLACODERM
PLACODERMS
PLACOID
PLACOIDS
PLAFOND
PLAFONDS
PLAGAL
PLAGE
PLAGES
PLAGIARIES
PLAGIARISE
PLAGIARISED
PLAGIARISER
PLAGIARISERS
PLAGIARISES
PLAGIARISING
PLAGIARISM
PLAGIARISMS
PLAGIARIST
PLAGIARISTIC
PLAGIARISTS
PLAGIARIZE
PLAGIARIZED
PLAGIARIZER
PLAGIARIZERS
PLAGIARIZES
PLAGIARIZING
PLAGIARY
PLAGIOCEPHALIES
PLAGIOCEPHALY
PLAGIOCLASE
PLAGIOCLASES
PLAGIOCLASTIC
PLAGIOCLIMATIC
PLAGIOCLIMAX
PLAGIOCLIMAXES
PLAGIOSTOMATOUS
PLAGIOSTOME
PLAGIOSTOMES
PLAGIOSTOMOUS
PLAGIOTROPIC
PLAGIOTROPISM
PLAGIOTROPISMS
PLAGIOTROPOUS
PLAGIUM
PLAGIUMS
PLAGUE
PLAGUED
PLAGUER
PLAGUERS
PLAGUES

PLAGUESOME
PLAGUEY
PLAGUIER
PLAGUIEST
PLAGUILY
PLAGUING
PLAGUY
PLAICE
PLAICES
PLAID
PLAIDED
PLAIDING
PLAIDINGS
PLAIDMAN
PLAIDMEN
PLAIDS
PLAIN
PLAINANT
PLAINANTS
PLAINCHANT
PLAINCHANTS
PLAINCLOTHES
PLAINCLOTHESMAN
PLAINCLOTHESMEN
PLAINED
PLAINER
PLAINEST
PLAINFUL
PLAINING
PLAININGS
PLAINISH
PLAINLY
PLAINNESS
PLAINNESSES
PLAINS
PLAINSMAN
PLAINSMEN
PLAINSONG
PLAINSONGS
PLAINSPOKEN
PLAINSPOKENNESS
PLAINSTANES
PLAINSTONES
PLAINT
PLAINTEXT
PLAINTEXTS
PLAINTFUL
PLAINTIFF
PLAINTIFFS
PLAINTIVE
PLAINTIVELY
PLAINTIVENESS
PLAINTIVENESSES
PLAINTLESS
PLAINTS
PLAINWORK

PLAINWORKS
PLAISTER
PLAISTERED
PLAISTERING
PLAISTERS
PLAIT
PLAITED
PLAITER
PLAITERS
PLAITING
PLAITINGS
PLAITS
PLAN
PLANAR
PLANARIA
PLANARIAN
PLANARIANS
PLANARIAS
PLANARITIES
PLANARITY
PLANATE
PLANATION
PLANATIONS
PLANCH
PLANCHE
PLANCHED
PLANCHES
PLANCHET
PLANCHETS
PLANCHETTE
PLANCHETTES
PLANCHING
PLANE
PLANED
PLANELOAD
PLANELOADS
PLANENESS
PLANER
PLANERS
PLANES
PLANET
PLANETARIA
PLANETARIES
PLANETARIUM
PLANETARIUMS
PLANETARY
PLANETESIMAL
PLANETESIMALS
PLANETIC
PLANETICAL
PLANETLIKE
PLANETOID
PLANETOIDAL
PLANETOIDS
PLANETOLOGICAL
PLANETOLOGIES

PLANETOLOGIST
PLANETOLOGISTS
PLANETOLOGY
PLANETS
PLANETWIDE
PLANFORM
PLANFORMS
PLANGENCIES
PLANGENCY
PLANGENT
PLANGENTLY
PLANIGRAPH
PLANIGRAPHS
PLANIMETER
PLANIMETERS
PLANIMETRIC
PLANIMETRICAL
PLANIMETRICALLY
PLANIMETRIES
PLANIMETRY
PLANING
PLANISH
PLANISHED
PLANISHER
PLANISHERS
PLANISHES
PLANISHING
PLANISPHERE
PLANISPHERES
PLANISPHERIC
PLANK
PLANKED
PLANKING
PLANKINGS
PLANKS
PLANKTER
PLANKTERS
PLANKTON
PLANKTONIC
PLANKTONS
PLANLESS
PLANLESSLY
PLANLESSNESS
PLANLESSNESSES
PLANNED
PLANNER
PLANNERS
PLANNING
PLANNINGS
PLANOBLAST
PLANOBLASTS
PLANOGAMETE
PLANOGAMETES
PLANOGRAPHIC
PLANOGRAPHIES
PLANOGRAPHY

PLANOMETER
PLANOMETERS
PLANOMETRIC
PLANOMETRICALLY
PLANOMETRY
PLANOSOL
PLANOSOLS
PLANS
PLANT
PLANTA
PLANTABLE
PLANTAGE
PLANTAGES
PLANTAGINACEOUS
PLANTAIN
PLANTAINS
PLANTAR
PLANTAS
PLANTATION
PLANTATIONS
PLANTED
PLANTER
PLANTERS
PLANTIGRADE
PLANTIGRADES
PLANTING
PLANTINGS
PLANTLESS
PLANTLET
PLANTLETS
PLANTLIKE
PLANTLING
PLANTLINGS
PLANTOCRACIES
PLANTOCRACY
PLANTS
PLANTSMAN
PLANTSMEN
PLANTSWOMAN
PLANTSWOMEN
PLANTULE
PLANTULES
PLANULA
PLANULAE
PLANULAR
PLANULIFORM
PLANULOID
PLANURIA
PLANURIAS
PLANURIES
PLANURY
PLANXTIES
PLANXTY
PLAP
PLAPPED
PLAPPING

PLAPS
PLAQUE
PLAQUES
PLAQUETTE
PLAQUETTES
PLASH
PLASHED
PLASHER
PLASHERS
PLASHES
PLASHET
PLASHETS
PLASHIER
PLASHIEST
PLASHING
PLASHINGS
PLASHY
PLASM
PLASMA
PLASMAGEL
PLASMAGELS
PLASMAGENE
PLASMAGENES
PLASMAGENIC
PLASMAGENICALLY
PLASMALEMMA
PLASMALEMMAS
PLASMAPHERESES
PLASMAPHERESIS
PLASMAS
PLASMASOL
PLASMASOLS
PLASMATIC
PLASMATICAL
PLASMIC
PLASMID
PLASMIDS
PLASMIN
PLASMINOGEN
PLASMINOGENS
PLASMINS
PLASMODESM
PLASMODESMA
PLASMODESMAS
PLASMODESMATA
PLASMODESMIC
PLASMODESMS
PLASMODIA
PLASMODIAL
PLASMODIUM
PLASMOGAMIES
PLASMOGAMY
PLASMOID
PLASMOIDS
PLASMOLYSE
PLASMOLYSED

PLASMOLYSES
PLASMOLYSING
PLASMOLYSIS
PLASMOLYTIC
PLASMOLYTICALLY
PLASMOLYZE
PLASMOLYZED
PLASMOLYZES
PLASMOLYZING
PLASMON
PLASMONS
PLASMOSOMA
PLASMOSOME
PLASMOSOMES
PLASMS
PLAST
PLASTE
PLASTER
PLASTERBOARD
PLASTERBOARDS
PLASTERED
PLASTERER
PLASTERERS
PLASTERINESS
PLASTERINESSES
PLASTERING
PLASTERINGS
PLASTERS
PLASTERSTONE
PLASTERSTONES
PLASTERWORK
PLASTERWORKS
PLASTERY
PLASTIC
PLASTICALLY
PLASTICENE
PLASTICENES
PLASTICINE
PLASTICINES
PLASTICISATION
PLASTICISE
PLASTICISED
PLASTICISER
PLASTICISERS
PLASTICISES
PLASTICISING
PLASTICITIES
PLASTICITY
PLASTICIZATION
PLASTICIZATIONS
PLASTICIZE
PLASTICIZED
PLASTICIZER
PLASTICIZERS
PLASTICIZES
PLASTICIZING

PLASTICKY
PLASTICS
PLASTID
PLASTIDIAL
PLASTIDS
PLASTIDULE
PLASTIDULES
PLASTILINA
PLASTILINAS
PLASTIQUE
PLASTIQUES
PLASTISOL
PLASTISOLS
PLASTOCYANIN
PLASTOCYANINS
PLASTOGAMIES
PLASTOGAMY
PLASTOMETER
PLASTOMETERS
PLASTOMETRIC
PLASTOMETRY
PLASTOQUINONE
PLASTOQUINONES
PLASTRAL
PLASTRON
PLASTRONS
PLASTRUM
PLASTRUMS
PLAT
PLATAN
PLATANACEOUS
PLATANE
PLATANES
PLATANNA
PLATANNAS
PLATANS
PLATBAND
PLATBANDS
PLATE
PLATEASM
PLATEASMS
PLATEAU
PLATEAUED
PLATEAUING
PLATEAUS
PLATEAUX
PLATED
PLATEFUL
PLATEFULS
PLATEGLASS
PLATELAYER
PLATELAYERS
PLATELAYING
PLATELET
PLATELETS
PLATELIKE

PLATEMAKER
PLATEMAKERS
PLATEMAKING
PLATEMAKINGS
PLATEMAN
PLATEMARK
PLATEMARKS
PLATEMEN
PLATEN
PLATENS
PLATER
PLATERESQUE
PLATERS
PLATES
PLATESFUL
PLATFORM
PLATFORMED
PLATFORMING
PLATFORMINGS
PLATFORMS
PLATIER
PLATIES
PLATIEST
PLATINA
PLATINAS
PLATING
PLATINGS
PLATINIC
PLATINIFEROUS
PLATINIRIDIUM
PLATINIRIDIUMS
PLATINISATION
PLATINISATIONS
PLATINISE
PLATINISED
PLATINISER
PLATINISERS
PLATINISES
PLATINISING
PLATINIZATION
PLATINIZATIONS
PLATINIZE
PLATINIZED
PLATINIZER
PLATINIZERS
PLATINIZES
PLATINIZING
PLATINOCYANIC
PLATINOCYANIDE
PLATINOCYANIDES
PLATINOID
PLATINOIDS
PLATINOTYPE
PLATINOTYPES
PLATINOUS
PLATINUM

PLATINUMS
PLATITUDE
PLATITUDES
PLATITUDINAL
PLATITUDINARIAN
PLATITUDINISE
PLATITUDINISED
PLATITUDINISER
PLATITUDINISERS
PLATITUDINISES
PLATITUDINISING
PLATITUDINIZE
PLATITUDINIZED
PLATITUDINIZER
PLATITUDINIZERS
PLATITUDINIZES
PLATITUDINIZING
PLATITUDINOUS
PLATITUDINOUSLY
PLATONIC
PLATONICALLY
PLATONICS
PLATOON
PLATOONED
PLATOONING
PLATOONS
PLATS
PLATTED
PLATTELAND
PLATTELANDS
PLATTER
PLATTERFUL
PLATTERFULS
PLATTERS
PLATTERSFUL
PLATTING
PLATTINGS
PLATY
PLATYCEPHALIC
PLATYCEPHALOUS
PLATYFISH
PLATYFISHES
PLATYHELMINTH
PLATYHELMINTHIC
PLATYHELMINTHS
PLATYKURTIC
PLATYKURTICALLY
PLATYPI
PLATYPUS
PLATYPUSES
PLATYRRHINE
PLATYRRHINES
PLATYRRHINIAN
PLATYRRHINIANS
PLATYS
PLATYSMA

PLATYSMAS
PLAUDIT
PLAUDITE
PLAUDITORY
PLAUDITS
PLAUSIBILITIES
PLAUSIBILITY
PLAUSIBLE
PLAUSIBLENESS
PLAUSIBLENESSES
PLAUSIBLY
PLAUSIVE
PLAUSTRAL
PLAY
PLAYA
PLAYABILITIES
PLAYABILITY
PLAYABLE
PLAYACT
PLAYACTED
PLAYACTING
PLAYACTINGS
PLAYACTS
PLAYAS
PLAYBACK
PLAYBACKS
PLAYBILL
PLAYBILLS
PLAYBOOK
PLAYBOOKS
PLAYBOY
PLAYBOYS
PLAYBUS
PLAYBUSES
PLAYBUSSES
PLAYDATE
PLAYDATES
PLAYDAY
PLAYDAYS
PLAYDOWN
PLAYDOWNS
PLAYED
PLAYER
PLAYERS
PLAYFELLOW
PLAYFELLOWS
PLAYFIELD
PLAYFIELDS
PLAYFUL
PLAYFULLY
PLAYFULNESS
PLAYFULNESSES
PLAYGIRL
PLAYGIRLS
PLAYGOER
PLAYGOERS

PLAYGROUND
PLAYGROUNDS
PLAYGROUP
PLAYGROUPS
PLAYHOUSE
PLAYHOUSES
PLAYING
PLAYLAND
PLAYLANDS
PLAYLEADER
PLAYLEADERS
PLAYLESS
PLAYLET
PLAYLETS
PLAYLIKE
PLAYLIST
PLAYLISTS
PLAYMAKER
PLAYMAKERS
PLAYMAKING
PLAYMAKINGS
PLAYMATE
PLAYMATES
PLAYOFF
PLAYOFFS
PLAYPEN
PLAYPENS
PLAYROOM
PLAYROOMS
PLAYS
PLAYSCHOOL
PLAYSCHOOLS
PLAYSOME
PLAYSUIT
PLAYSUITS
PLAYTHING
PLAYTHINGS
PLAYTIME
PLAYTIMES
PLAYWEAR
PLAYWRIGHT
PLAYWRIGHTING
PLAYWRIGHTINGS
PLAYWRIGHTS
PLAYWRITING
PLAYWRITINGS
PLAZA
PLAZAS
PLEA
PLEACH
PLEACHED
PLEACHES
PLEACHING
PLEAD
PLEADABLE
PLEADED

PLEADER
PLEADERS
PLEADING
PLEADINGLY
PLEADINGS
PLEADS
PLEAED
PLEAING
PLEAS
PLEASABLE
PLEASABLY
PLEASANCE
PLEASANCES
PLEASANT
PLEASANTER
PLEASANTEST
PLEASANTLY
PLEASANTNESS
PLEASANTNESSES
PLEASANTRIES
PLEASANTRY
PLEASE
PLEASED
PLEASEDLY
PLEASEMAN
PLEASEMEN
PLEASER
PLEASERS
PLEASES
PLEASETH
PLEASING
PLEASINGLY
PLEASINGNESS
PLEASINGNESSES
PLEASINGS
PLEASURABILITY
PLEASURABLE
PLEASURABLENESS
PLEASURABLY
PLEASURE
PLEASURED
PLEASUREFUL
PLEASURELESS
PLEASURER
PLEASURERS
PLEASURES
PLEASURING
PLEAT
PLEATED
PLEATER
PLEATERS
PLEATING
PLEATLESS
PLEATS
PLEB
PLEBBIER

PLEBBIEST
PLEBBY
PLEBE
PLEBEAN
PLEBEIAN
PLEBEIANISE
PLEBEIANISED
PLEBEIANISES
PLEBEIANISING
PLEBEIANISM
PLEBEIANISMS
PLEBEIANIZE
PLEBEIANIZED
PLEBEIANIZES
PLEBEIANIZING
PLEBEIANLY
PLEBEIANS
PLEBES
PLEBIFICATION
PLEBIFICATIONS
PLEBIFIED
PLEBIFIES
PLEBIFY
PLEBIFYING
PLEBISCITARY
PLEBISCITE
PLEBISCITES
PLEBS
PLECOPTERAN
PLECOPTERANS
PLECOPTEROUS
PLECTOGNATH
PLECTOGNATHIC
PLECTOGNATHOUS
PLECTOGNATHS
PLECTOPTEROUS
PLECTRA
PLECTRE
PLECTRES
PLECTRON
PLECTRONS
PLECTRUM
PLECTRUMS
PLED
PLEDGABLE
PLEDGE
PLEDGEABLE
PLEDGED
PLEDGEE
PLEDGEES
PLEDGEOR
PLEDGEORS
PLEDGER
PLEDGERS
PLEDGES
PLEDGET

PLEDGETS
PLEDGING
PLEDGOR
PLEDGORS
PLEIAD
PLEIADES
PLEIADS
PLEINAIRISM
PLEINAIRISMS
PLEINAIRIST
PLEINAIRISTS
PLEIOCHASIA
PLEIOCHASIUM
PLEIOMERIES
PLEIOMEROUS
PLEIOMERY
PLEIOTROPIC
PLEIOTROPIES
PLEIOTROPISM
PLEIOTROPISMS
PLEIOTROPY
PLENA
PLENARIES
PLENARILY
PLENARTIES
PLENARTY
PLENARY
PLENCH
PLENCHES
PLENILUNAR
PLENILUNE
PLENILUNES
PLENIPO
PLENIPOES
PLENIPOS
PLENIPOTENCE
PLENIPOTENCES
PLENIPOTENCIES
PLENIPOTENCY
PLENIPOTENT
PLENIPOTENTIAL
PLENIPOTENTIARY
PLENISH
PLENISHED
PLENISHER
PLENISHERS
PLENISHES
PLENISHING
PLENISHINGS
PLENISHMENT
PLENISHMENTS
PLENISM
PLENISMS
PLENIST
PLENISTS
PLENITUDE

PLENITUDES
PLENITUDINOUS
PLENTEOUS
PLENTEOUSLY
PLENTEOUSNESS
PLENTEOUSNESSES
PLENTIES
PLENTIFUL
PLENTIFULLY
PLENTIFULNESS
PLENTIFULNESSES
PLENTITUDE
PLENTITUDES
PLENTY
PLENUM
PLENUMS
PLEOCHROIC
PLEOCHROISM
PLEOCHROISMS
PLEOMORPHIC
PLEOMORPHIES
PLEOMORPHISM
PLEOMORPHISMS
PLEOMORPHOUS
PLEOMORPHY
PLEON
PLEONASM
PLEONASMS
PLEONAST
PLEONASTE
PLEONASTES
PLEONASTIC
PLEONASTICAL
PLEONASTICALLY
PLEONASTS
PLEONECTIC
PLEONEXIA
PLEONEXIAS
PLEONS
PLEOPOD
PLEOPODS
PLERION
PLERIONS
PLEROCERCOID
PLEROCERCOIDS
PLEROMA
PLEROMAS
PLEROMATIC
PLEROME
PLEROMES
PLEROPHORIA
PLEROPHORIAS
PLEROPHORIES
PLEROPHORY
PLESH
PLESHES

PLESIOSAUR
PLESIOSAURIAN
PLESIOSAURS
PLESSIMETER
PLESSIMETERS
PLESSIMETRIC
PLESSIMETRIES
PLESSIMETRY
PLESSOR
PLESSORS
PLETHORA
PLETHORAS
PLETHORIC
PLETHORICAL
PLETHORICALLY
PLETHYSMOGRAM
PLETHYSMOGRAMS
PLETHYSMOGRAPH
PLETHYSMOGRAPHS
PLETHYSMOGRAPHY
PLEUCH
PLEUCHED
PLEUCHING
PLEUCHS
PLEUGH
PLEUGHED
PLEUGHING
PLEUGHS
PLEURA
PLEURAE
PLEURAL
PLEURAPOPHYSES
PLEURAPOPHYSIS
PLEURAS
PLEURISIES
PLEURISY
PLEURITIC
PLEURITICAL
PLEURITICS
PLEURITIS
PLEURITISES
PLEUROCARPOUS
PLEUROCENTESIS
PLEURODONT
PLEURODONTS
PLEURODYNIA
PLEURODYNIAS
PLEURON
PLEUROPNEUMONIA
PLEUROTOMIES
PLEUROTOMY
PLEUSTON
PLEUSTONIC
PLEUSTONS
PLEW
PLEWS

PLEXAL
PLEXIFORM
PLEXIGLASS
PLEXIGLASSES
PLEXIMETER
PLEXIMETERS
PLEXIMETRIC
PLEXIMETRIES
PLEXIMETRY
PLEXOR
PLEXORS
PLEXURE
PLEXURES
PLEXUS
PLEXUSES
PLIABILITIES
PLIABILITY
PLIABLE
PLIABLENESS
PLIABLENESSES
PLIABLY
PLIANCIES
PLIANCY
PLIANT
PLIANTLY
PLIANTNESS
PLIANTNESSES
PLICA
PLICAE
PLICAL
PLICATE
PLICATED
PLICATELY
PLICATENESS
PLICATES
PLICATING
PLICATION
PLICATIONS
PLICATURE
PLICATURES
PLIE
PLIED
PLIER
PLIERS
PLIES
PLIGHT
PLIGHTED
PLIGHTER
PLIGHTERS
PLIGHTFUL
PLIGHTING
PLIGHTS
PLIM
PLIMMED
PLIMMING
PLIMS

PLIMSOL
PLIMSOLE
PLIMSOLES
PLIMSOLL
PLIMSOLLS
PLIMSOLS
PLING
PLINGS
PLINK
PLINKED
PLINKER
PLINKERS
PLINKING
PLINKS
PLINTH
PLINTHS
PLIOSAUR
PLIOSAURS
PLIOTRON
PLIOTRONS
PLISKIE
PLISKIES
PLISKY
PLISSE
PLISSES
PLOAT
PLOATED
PLOATING
PLOATS
PLOD
PLODDED
PLODDER
PLODDERS
PLODDING
PLODDINGLY
PLODDINGNESS
PLODDINGS
PLODGE
PLODGED
PLODGER
PLODGERS
PLODGES
PLODGING
PLODS
PLOIDIES
PLOIDY
PLONG
PLONGD
PLONGE
PLONGED
PLONGES
PLONGING
PLONGS
PLONK
PLONKED
PLONKER

PLONKERS	PLOUGHER	PLOWSTAFFS	PLUMBAGINACEOUS
PLONKIER	PLOUGHERS	PLOWTER	PLUMBAGINOUS
PLONKIEST	PLOUGHGATE	PLOWTERED	PLUMBAGO
PLONKING	PLOUGHGATES	PLOWTERING	PLUMBAGOS
PLONKINGS	PLOUGHING	PLOWTERS	PLUMBATE
PLONKO	PLOUGHINGS	PLOY	PLUMBATES
PLONKOS	PLOUGHLAND	PLOYED	PLUMBED
PLONKS	PLOUGHLANDS	PLOYING	PLUMBEOUS
PLONKY	PLOUGHMAN	PLOYS	PLUMBER
PLOOK	PLOUGHMANSHIP	PLU	PLUMBERIES
PLOOKIE	PLOUGHMEN	PLUCK	PLUMBERS
PLOOKIER	PLOUGHS	PLUCKED	PLUMBERY
PLOOKIEST	PLOUGHSHARE	PLUCKER	PLUMBIC
PLOOKINESS	PLOUGHSHARES	PLUCKERS	PLUMBIFEROUS
PLOOKS	PLOUGHSTAFF	PLUCKIER	PLUMBING
PLOOKY	PLOUGHSTAFFS	PLUCKIEST	PLUMBINGS
PLOP	PLOUGHTAIL	PLUCKILY	PLUMBISM
PLOPPED	PLOUGHTAILS	PLUCKINESS	PLUMBISMS
PLOPPING	PLOUGHWISE	PLUCKINESSES	PLUMBISOLVENCY
PLOPS	PLOUGHWRIGHT	PLUCKING	PLUMBISOLVENT
PLOSION	PLOUGHWRIGHTS	PLUCKS	PLUMBITE
PLOSIONS	PLOUK	PLUCKY	PLUMBITES
PLOSIVE	PLOUKIE	PLUE	PLUMBLESS
PLOSIVES	PLOUKIER	PLUES	PLUMBOSOLVENCY
PLOT	PLOUKIEST	PLUFF	PLUMBOSOLVENT
PLOTFUL	PLOUKINESS	PLUFFED	PLUMBOUS
PLOTLESS	PLOUKS	PLUFFIER	PLUMBS
PLOTLESSNESS	PLOUKY	PLUFFIEST	PLUMBUM
PLOTLESSNESSES	PLOUTER	PLUFFING	PLUMBUMS
PLOTLINE	PLOUTERED	PLUFFS	PLUMCOT
PLOTLINES	PLOUTERING	PLUFFY	PLUMCOTS
PLOTS	PLOUTERS	PLUG	PLUMDAMAS
PLOTTAGE	PLOVER	PLUGBOARD	PLUMDAMASES
PLOTTAGES	PLOVERS	PLUGBOARDS	PLUME
PLOTTED	PLOVERY	PLUGGED	PLUMED
PLOTTER	PLOW	PLUGGER	PLUMELESS
PLOTTERED	PLOWABLE	PLUGGERS	PLUMELET
PLOTTERING	PLOWBACK	PLUGGING	PLUMELETS
PLOTTERS	PLOWBACKS	PLUGGINGS	PLUMELIKE
PLOTTIE	PLOWBOY	PLUGHOLE	PLUMERIA
PLOTTIER	PLOWBOYS	PLUGHOLES	PLUMERIAS
PLOTTIES	PLOWED	PLUGLESS	PLUMERIES
PLOTTIEST	PLOWER	PLUGOLA	PLUMERY
PLOTTING	PLOWERS	PLUGOLAS	PLUMES
PLOTTINGLY	PLOWHEAD	PLUGS	PLUMIER
PLOTTINGS	PLOWHEADS	PLUGUGLIES	PLUMIEST
PLOTTY	PLOWING	PLUGUGLY	PLUMIGEROUS
PLOTZ	PLOWLAND	PLUM	PLUMING
PLOTZED	PLOWLANDS	PLUMAGE	PLUMIPED
PLOTZES	PLOWMAN	PLUMAGED	PLUMIPEDS
PLOTZING	PLOWMANSHIP	PLUMAGES	PLUMIST
PLOUGH	PLOWMEN	PLUMASSIER	PLUMISTS
PLOUGHABLE	PLOWS	PLUMASSIERS	PLUMLIKE
PLOUGHBOY	PLOWSHARE	PLUMATE	PLUMMET
PLOUGHBOYS	PLOWSHARES	PLUMB	PLUMMETED
PLOUGHED	PLOWSTAFF	PLUMBABLE	PLUMMETING

PLUMMETS
PLUMMIER
PLUMMIEST
PLUMMY
PLUMOSE
PLUMOSELY
PLUMOSENESS
PLUMOSITY
PLUMOUS
PLUMP
PLUMPED
PLUMPEN
PLUMPENED
PLUMPENING
PLUMPENS
PLUMPER
PLUMPERS
PLUMPEST
PLUMPIE
PLUMPIER
PLUMPIEST
PLUMPING
PLUMPISH
PLUMPLY
PLUMPNESS
PLUMPNESSES
PLUMPS
PLUMPY
PLUMS
PLUMULA
PLUMULACEOUS
PLUMULAE
PLUMULAR
PLUMULARIAN
PLUMULARIANS
PLUMULATE
PLUMULE
PLUMULES
PLUMULOSE
PLUMY
PLUNDER
PLUNDERABLE
PLUNDERAGE
PLUNDERAGES
PLUNDERED
PLUNDERER
PLUNDERERS
PLUNDERING
PLUNDEROUS
PLUNDERS
PLUNGE
PLUNGED
PLUNGER
PLUNGERS
PLUNGES
PLUNGING

PLUNGINGS
PLUNK
PLUNKED
PLUNKER
PLUNKERS
PLUNKING
PLUNKS
PLUPERFECT
PLUPERFECTS
PLURAL
PLURALISATION
PLURALISATIONS
PLURALISE
PLURALISED
PLURALISER
PLURALISERS
PLURALISES
PLURALISING
PLURALISM
PLURALISMS
PLURALIST
PLURALISTIC
PLURALISTICALLY
PLURALISTS
PLURALITIES
PLURALITY
PLURALIZATION
PLURALIZATIONS
PLURALIZE
PLURALIZED
PLURALIZER
PLURALIZERS
PLURALIZES
PLURALIZING
PLURALLY
PLURALS
PLURILITERAL
PLURILOCULAR
PLURIPARA
PLURIPARAE
PLURIPARAS
PLURIPOTENT
PLURIPRESENCE
PLURIPRESENCES
PLURISERIAL
PLURISERIATE
PLURISIE
PLURISIES
PLURRY
PLUS
PLUSAGE
PLUSAGES
PLUSED
PLUSES
PLUSH
PLUSHER

PLUSHES
PLUSHEST
PLUSHIER
PLUSHIEST
PLUSHILY
PLUSHINESS
PLUSHINESSES
PLUSHLY
PLUSHNESS
PLUSHNESSES
PLUSHY
PLUSING
PLUSSAGE
PLUSSAGES
PLUSSED
PLUSSES
PLUSSING
PLUTEAL
PLUTEI
PLUTEUS
PLUTEUSES
PLUTOCRACIES
PLUTOCRACY
PLUTOCRAT
PLUTOCRATIC
PLUTOCRATICAL
PLUTOCRATICALLY
PLUTOCRATS
PLUTOLATRIES
PLUTOLATRY
PLUTOLOGIES
PLUTOLOGIST
PLUTOLOGISTS
PLUTOLOGY
PLUTON
PLUTONIAN
PLUTONIC
PLUTONIUM
PLUTONIUMS
PLUTONOMIES
PLUTONOMIST
PLUTONOMISTS
PLUTONOMY
PLUTONS
PLUVIAL
PLUVIALS
PLUVIAN
PLUVIOMETER
PLUVIOMETERS
PLUVIOMETRIC
PLUVIOMETRICAL
PLUVIOMETRY
PLUVIOSE
PLUVIOUS
PLY
PLYER

PLYERS
PLYING
PLYINGLY
PLYOMETRIC
PLYOMETRICS
PLYWOOD
PLYWOODS
PNEUMA
PNEUMAS
PNEUMATHODE
PNEUMATHODES
PNEUMATIC
PNEUMATICAL
PNEUMATICALLY
PNEUMATICITIES
PNEUMATICITY
PNEUMATICS
PNEUMATOLOGICAL
PNEUMATOLOGIES
PNEUMATOLOGIST
PNEUMATOLOGISTS
PNEUMATOLOGY
PNEUMATOLYSES
PNEUMATOLYSIS
PNEUMATOLYTIC
PNEUMATOMETER
PNEUMATOMETERS
PNEUMATOMETRY
PNEUMATOPHORE
PNEUMATOPHORES
PNEUMECTOMIES
PNEUMECTOMY
PNEUMOBACILLARY
PNEUMOBACILLI
PNEUMOBACILLUS
PNEUMOCOCCAL
PNEUMOCOCCI
PNEUMOCOCCUS
PNEUMOCONIOSES
PNEUMOCONIOSIS
PNEUMOCONIOTIC
PNEUMOCONIOTICS
PNEUMOCYSTIS
PNEUMODYNAMICS
PNEUMOGASTRIC
PNEUMOGASTRICS
PNEUMOGRAM
PNEUMOGRAMS
PNEUMOGRAPH
PNEUMOGRAPHS
PNEUMOKONIOSES
PNEUMOKONIOSIS
PNEUMONECTOMIES
PNEUMONECTOMY
PNEUMONIA
PNEUMONIAS

PNEUMONIC
PNEUMONICS
PNEUMONITIS
PNEUMONITISES
PNEUMOTHORACES
PNEUMOTHORAX
PNEUMOTHORAXES
PO
POA
POACEOUS
POACH
POACHED
POACHER
POACHERS
POACHES
POACHIER
POACHIEST
POACHINESS
POACHINESSES
POACHING
POACHINGS
POACHY
POAKA
POAKAS
POAKE
POAKES
POAS
POCHARD
POCHARDS
POCHAY
POCHAYS
POCHETTE
POCHETTES
POCHOIR
POCHOIRS
POCK
POCKARD
POCKARDS
POCKED
POCKET
POCKETABLE
POCKETBOOK
POCKETBOOKS
POCKETED
POCKETER
POCKETERS
POCKETFUL
POCKETFULS
POCKETING
POCKETKNIFE
POCKETKNIVES
POCKETLESS
POCKETPHONE
POCKETPHONES
POCKETS
POCKETSFUL

POCKIER
POCKIES
POCKIEST
POCKILY
POCKING
POCKMANKIES
POCKMANKY
POCKMANTIE
POCKMANTIES
POCKMARK
POCKMARKED
POCKMARKING
POCKMARKS
POCKPIT
POCKPITS
POCKPITTED
POCKS
POCKY
POCO
POCOCURANTE
POCOCURANTEISM
POCOCURANTEISMS
POCOCURANTES
POCOCURANTISM
POCOCURANTISMS
POCOCURANTIST
POCOCURANTISTS
POCOSIN
POCOSINS
POCULIFORM
POD
PODAGRA
PODAGRAL
PODAGRAS
PODAGRIC
PODAGRICAL
PODAGROUS
PODAL
PODALIC
PODARGUS
PODARGUSES
PODDED
PODDIED
PODDIER
PODDIES
PODDIEST
PODDING
PODDLE
PODDLED
PODDLER
PODDLERS
PODDLES
PODDLING
PODDY
PODDYING
PODESTA

PODESTAS
PODEX
PODEXES
PODGE
PODGES
PODGIER
PODGIEST
PODGINESS
PODGINESSES
PODGY
PODIA
PODIAL
PODIATRIC
PODIATRIES
PODIATRIST
PODIATRISTS
PODIATRY
PODITE
PODITES
PODITIC
PODIUM
PODIUMS
PODLEY
PODLEYS
PODLIKE
PODOCARP
PODOCARPS
PODOCONIOSES
PODOCONIOSIS
PODOLOGIES
PODOLOGIST
PODOLOGISTS
PODOLOGY
PODOMERE
PODOMERES
PODOPHTHALMOUS
PODOPHYLIN
PODOPHYLLI
PODOPHYLLIN
PODOPHYLLINS
PODOPHYLLUM
PODOPHYLLUMS
PODOUS
PODS
PODSOL
PODSOLIC
PODSOLISATION
PODSOLISE
PODSOLISED
PODSOLISES
PODSOLISING
PODSOLIZATION
PODSOLIZATIONS
PODSOLIZE
PODSOLIZED

PODSOLIZES
PODSOLIZING
PODSOLS
PODZOL
PODZOLIC
PODZOLISATION
PODZOLISE
PODZOLISED
PODZOLISES
PODZOLISING
PODZOLIZATION
PODZOLIZATIONS
PODZOLIZE
PODZOLIZED
PODZOLIZES
PODZOLIZING
PODZOLS
POECHORE
POECHORES
POEM
POEMATIC
POEMS
POENOLOGIES
POENOLOGY
POEP
POEPS
POESIED
POESIES
POESY
POESYING
POET
POETASTER
POETASTERIES
POETASTERING
POETASTERINGS
POETASTERS
POETASTERY
POETASTRIES
POETASTRY
POETESS
POETESSES
POETIC
POETICAL
POETICALLY
POETICALNESS
POETICALNESSES
POETICALS
POETICISE
POETICISED
POETICISES
POETICISING
POETICISM
POETICISMS
POETICIZE
POETICIZED
POETICIZES

POETICIZING
POETICS
POETICULE
POETICULES
POETISE
POETISED
POETISER
POETISERS
POETISES
POETISING
POETIZE
POETIZED
POETIZER
POETIZERS
POETIZES
POETIZING
POETLESS
POETLIKE
POETRESSE
POETRESSES
POETRIES
POETRY
POETS
POETSHIP
POETSHIPS
POFFLE
POFFLES
POGEY
POGEYS
POGGE
POGGES
POGIES
POGO
POGOED
POGOER
POGOERS
POGOING
POGONIA
POGONIAS
POGONIP
POGONIPS
POGONOPHORAN
POGONOPHORANS
POGONOTOMIES
POGONOTOMY
POGOS
POGROM
POGROMED
POGROMING
POGROMIST
POGROMISTS
POGROMS
POGY
POH
POHIRI
POHIRIS

POHUTUKAWA
POHUTUKAWAS
POI
POIGNADO
POIGNADOES
POIGNANCE
POIGNANCES
POIGNANCIES
POIGNANCY
POIGNANT
POIGNANTLY
POIKILITIC
POIKILOCYTE
POIKILOCYTES
POIKILOTHERM
POIKILOTHERMAL
POIKILOTHERMIC
POIKILOTHERMIES
POIKILOTHERMISM
POIKILOTHERMS
POIKILOTHERMY
POILU
POILUS
POINADO
POINADOES
POINCIANA
POINCIANAS
POIND
POINDED
POINDER
POINDERS
POINDING
POINDINGS
POINDS
POINSETTIA
POINSETTIAS
POINT
POINTE
POINTED
POINTEDLY
POINTEDNESS
POINTEDNESSES
POINTEL
POINTELLE
POINTELLES
POINTELS
POINTER
POINTERS
POINTES
POINTIER
POINTIEST
POINTILLE
POINTILLISM
POINTILLISME
POINTILLISMES
POINTILLISMS

POINTILLIST
POINTILLISTE
POINTILLISTES
POINTILLISTIC
POINTILLISTS
POINTING
POINTINGS
POINTLESS
POINTLESSLY
POINTLESSNESS
POINTLESSNESSES
POINTMAN
POINTMEN
POINTS
POINTSMAN
POINTSMEN
POINTY
POIS
POISE
POISED
POISER
POISERS
POISES
POISHA
POISING
POISON
POISONABLE
POISONED
POISONER
POISONERS
POISONING
POISONOUS
POISONOUSLY
POISONOUSNESS
POISONOUSNESSES
POISONS
POISONWOOD
POISONWOODS
POISSON
POISSONS
POITIN
POITREL
POITRELS
POITRINE
POITRINES
POKAL
POKALS
POKE
POKEBERRIES
POKEBERRY
POKED
POKEFUL
POKEFULS
POKELOGAN
POKELOGANS
POKER

POKERISH
POKERISHLY
POKEROOT
POKEROOTS
POKERS
POKERWORK
POKES
POKEWEED
POKEWEEDS
POKEY
POKEYS
POKIE
POKIER
POKIES
POKIEST
POKILY
POKINESS
POKINESSES
POKING
POKY
POL
POLACCA
POLACCAS
POLACRE
POLACRES
POLAR
POLARIMETER
POLARIMETERS
POLARIMETRIC
POLARIMETRIES
POLARIMETRY
POLARISABLE
POLARISATION
POLARISATIONS
POLARISCOPE
POLARISCOPES
POLARISCOPIC
POLARISE
POLARISED
POLARISER
POLARISERS
POLARISES
POLARISING
POLARITIES
POLARITY
POLARIZABILITY
POLARIZABLE
POLARIZATION
POLARIZATIONS
POLARIZE
POLARIZED
POLARIZER
POLARIZERS
POLARIZES
POLARIZING
POLAROGRAM

POLAROGRAMS
POLAROGRAPH
POLAROGRAPHIC
POLAROGRAPHIES
POLAROGRAPHS
POLAROGRAPHY
POLARON
POLARONS
POLARS
POLDER
POLDERED
POLDERING
POLDERS
POLE
POLEAX
POLEAXE
POLEAXED
POLEAXES
POLEAXING
POLECAT
POLECATS
POLED
POLEIS
POLELESS
POLEMARCH
POLEMARCHES
POLEMARCHS
POLEMIC
POLEMICAL
POLEMICALLY
POLEMICIST
POLEMICISTS
POLEMICIZE
POLEMICIZED
POLEMICIZES
POLEMICIZING
POLEMICS
POLEMISE
POLEMISED
POLEMISES
POLEMISING
POLEMIST
POLEMISTS
POLEMIZE
POLEMIZED
POLEMIZES
POLEMIZING
POLEMONIACEOUS
POLEMONIUM
POLEMONIUMS
POLENTA
POLENTAS
POLER
POLERS
POLES
POLESTAR

POLESTARS
POLEWARD
POLEY
POLEYN
POLEYNS
POLEYS
POLIANITE
POLIANITES
POLICE
POLICED
POLICEMAN
POLICEMEN
POLICES
POLICEWOMAN
POLICEWOMEN
POLICIES
POLICING
POLICY
POLICYHOLDER
POLICYHOLDERS
POLING
POLINGS
POLIO
POLIOMYELITIDES
POLIOMYELITIS
POLIOMYELITISES
POLIORCETIC
POLIORCETICS
POLIOS
POLIOVIRUS
POLIOVIRUSES
POLIS
POLISH
POLISHABLE
POLISHED
POLISHER
POLISHERS
POLISHES
POLISHING
POLISHINGS
POLISHMENT
POLISHMENTS
POLITBURO
POLITBUROS
POLITE
POLITELY
POLITENESS
POLITENESSES
POLITER
POLITESSE
POLITESSES
POLITEST
POLITIC
POLITICAL
POLITICALIZE
POLITICALIZED

POLITICALIZES
POLITICALIZING
POLITICALLY
POLITICASTER
POLITICASTERS
POLITICIAN
POLITICIANS
POLITICISATION
POLITICISATIONS
POLITICISE
POLITICISED
POLITICISES
POLITICISING
POLITICIZATION
POLITICIZATIONS
POLITICIZE
POLITICIZED
POLITICIZES
POLITICIZING
POLITICK
POLITICKED
POLITICKER
POLITICKERS
POLITICKING
POLITICKINGS
POLITICKS
POLITICLY
POLITICO
POLITICOES
POLITICOS
POLITICS
POLITIES
POLITIQUE
POLITIQUES
POLITY
POLJE
POLJES
POLK
POLKA
POLKAED
POLKAING
POLKAS
POLKED
POLKING
POLKS
POLL
POLLACK
POLLACKS
POLLAN
POLLANS
POLLARD
POLLARDED
POLLARDING
POLLARDS
POLLED
POLLEE

POLLEES
POLLEN
POLLENED
POLLENIFEROUS
POLLENING
POLLENIZER
POLLENIZERS
POLLENOSES
POLLENOSIS
POLLENS
POLLENT
POLLER
POLLERS
POLLEX
POLLICAL
POLLICES
POLLICIE
POLLICIES
POLLICITATION
POLLICITATIONS
POLLICY
POLLIES
POLLINATE
POLLINATED
POLLINATES
POLLINATING
POLLINATION
POLLINATIONS
POLLINATOR
POLLINATORS
POLLING
POLLINGS
POLLINIA
POLLINIC
POLLINIFEROUS
POLLINIUM
POLLINIZER
POLLINIZERS
POLLINOSES
POLLINOSIS
POLLIST
POLLISTS
POLLIWIG
POLLIWIGS
POLLIWOG
POLLIWOGS
POLLMAN
POLLMEN
POLLOCK
POLLOCKS
POLLS
POLLSTER
POLLSTERS
POLLUCITE
POLLUSION
POLLUSIONS

POLLUTANT
POLLUTANTS
POLLUTE
POLLUTED
POLLUTEDLY
POLLUTEDNESS
POLLUTEDNESSES
POLLUTER
POLLUTERS
POLLUTES
POLLUTING
POLLUTION
POLLUTIONS
POLLUTIVE
POLLY
POLLYANNA
POLLYANNAISH
POLLYANNAISM
POLLYANNAISMS
POLLYANNAS
POLLYANNISH
POLLYWIG
POLLYWIGS
POLLYWOG
POLLYWOGS
POLO
POLOIDAL
POLOIST
POLOISTS
POLONAISE
POLONAISES
POLONIE
POLONIES
POLONISE
POLONISED
POLONISES
POLONISING
POLONISM
POLONISMS
POLONIUM
POLONIUMS
POLONIZE
POLONIZED
POLONIZES
POLONIZING
POLONY
POLOS
POLS
POLT
POLTED
POLTERGEIST
POLTERGEISTS
POLTFEET
POLTFOOT
POLTING
POLTROON

POLTROONERIES
POLTROONERY
POLTROONS
POLTS
POLVERINE
POLVERINES
POLY
POLYACID
POLYACRYLAMIDE
POLYACRYLAMIDES
POLYACT
POLYACTINAL
POLYACTINE
POLYADELPHOUS
POLYADIC
POLYADICALLY
POLYALCOHOL
POLYALCOHOLS
POLYAMIDE
POLYAMIDES
POLYAMINE
POLYAMINES
POLYANDRIES
POLYANDROUS
POLYANDRY
POLYANTHA
POLYANTHAS
POLYANTHI
POLYANTHUS
POLYANTHUSES
POLYARCH
POLYARCHIES
POLYARCHY
POLYATOMIC
POLYAXIAL
POLYAXIALS
POLYAXON
POLYAXONIC
POLYAXONS
POLYBASIC
POLYBASITE
POLYBRID
POLYBRIDS
POLYBUTADIENE
POLYBUTADIENES
POLYCARBONATE
POLYCARBONATES
POLYCARBOXYLATE
POLYCARBOXYLIC
POLYCARPELLARY
POLYCARPIC
POLYCARPOUS
POLYCARPY
POLYCENTRIC
POLYCENTRISM
POLYCENTRISMS

POLYCHAETE
POLYCHAETES
POLYCHAETOUS
POLYCHASIA
POLYCHASIUM
POLYCHLORINATED
POLYCHLOROPRENE
POLYCHOTOMIES
POLYCHOTOMOUS
POLYCHOTOMY
POLYCHREST
POLYCHRESTS
POLYCHROIC
POLYCHROISM
POLYCHROISMS
POLYCHROMATIC
POLYCHROMATISM
POLYCHROME
POLYCHROMED
POLYCHROMES
POLYCHROMIC
POLYCHROMIES
POLYCHROMING
POLYCHROMOUS
POLYCHROMY
POLYCISTRONIC
POLYCLINIC
POLYCLINICS
POLYCLONAL
POLYCONIC
POLYCOT
POLYCOTS
POLYCOTTON
POLYCOTTONS
POLYCOTYLEDON
POLYCOTYLEDONS
POLYCROTIC
POLYCROTISM
POLYCROTISMS
POLYCRYSTAL
POLYCRYSTALLINE
POLYCRYSTALS
POLYCULTURE
POLYCULTURES
POLYCYCLIC
POLYCYCLICALLY
POLYCYCLICS
POLYCYSTIC
POLYCYTHAEMIA
POLYCYTHAEMIAS
POLYCYTHEMIA
POLYCYTHEMIAS
POLYCYTHEMIC
POLYDACTYL
POLYDACTYLIES
POLYDACTYLISM

POLYDACTYLISMS
POLYDACTYLOUS
POLYDACTYLS
POLYDACTYLY
POLYDAEMONISM
POLYDAEMONISMS
POLYDEMIC
POLYDEMICALLY
POLYDEMONISM
POLYDEMONISMS
POLYDIPSIA
POLYDIPSIAS
POLYDIPSIC
POLYDISPERSE
POLYDISPERSITY
POLYELECTROLYTE
POLYEMBRYONATE
POLYEMBRYONIC
POLYEMBRYONIES
POLYEMBRYONY
POLYENE
POLYENES
POLYENIC
POLYESTER
POLYESTERS
POLYESTROUS
POLYETHENE
POLYETHENES
POLYETHYLENE
POLYETHYLENES
POLYGALA
POLYGALACEOUS
POLYGALAS
POLYGAM
POLYGAMIC
POLYGAMIES
POLYGAMIST
POLYGAMISTS
POLYGAMIZE
POLYGAMIZED
POLYGAMIZES
POLYGAMIZING
POLYGAMOUS
POLYGAMOUSLY
POLYGAMS
POLYGAMY
POLYGENE
POLYGENES
POLYGENESES
POLYGENESIS
POLYGENETIC
POLYGENETICALLY
POLYGENIC
POLYGENIES
POLYGENISM
POLYGENISMS

POLYGENIST
POLYGENISTS
POLYGENOUS
POLYGENY
POLYGLOT
POLYGLOTISM
POLYGLOTISMS
POLYGLOTS
POLYGLOTT
POLYGLOTTAL
POLYGLOTTIC
POLYGLOTTISM
POLYGLOTTISMS
POLYGLOTTOUS
POLYGLOTTS
POLYGON
POLYGONACEOUS
POLYGONAL
POLYGONALLY
POLYGONATUM
POLYGONATUMS
POLYGONIES
POLYGONS
POLYGONUM
POLYGONUMS
POLYGONY
POLYGRAPH
POLYGRAPHER
POLYGRAPHERS
POLYGRAPHIC
POLYGRAPHICALLY
POLYGRAPHIES
POLYGRAPHIST
POLYGRAPHISTS
POLYGRAPHS
POLYGRAPHY
POLYGYNIAN
POLYGYNIES
POLYGYNIST
POLYGYNISTS
POLYGYNOUS
POLYGYNOUSLY
POLYGYNY
POLYHALITE
POLYHALITES
POLYHEDRA
POLYHEDRAL
POLYHEDRIC
POLYHEDRON
POLYHEDRONS
POLYHEDROSES
POLYHEDROSIS
POLYHISTOR
POLYHISTORIAN
POLYHISTORIANS
POLYHISTORIC

POLYHISTORIES
POLYHISTORS
POLYHISTORY
POLYHYBRID
POLYHYBRIDS
POLYHYDRIC
POLYHYDROXY
POLYISOPRENE
POLYISOPRENES
POLYLEMMA
POLYLEMMAS
POLYLYSINE
POLYLYSINES
POLYMASTIA
POLYMASTIAS
POLYMASTIC
POLYMASTIES
POLYMASTISM
POLYMASTISMS
POLYMASTY
POLYMATH
POLYMATHIC
POLYMATHIES
POLYMATHS
POLYMATHY
POLYMER
POLYMERASE
POLYMERASES
POLYMERIC
POLYMERIDE
POLYMERIDES
POLYMERIES
POLYMERISATION
POLYMERISATIONS
POLYMERISE
POLYMERISED
POLYMERISES
POLYMERISING
POLYMERISM
POLYMERISMS
POLYMERIZATION
POLYMERIZATIONS
POLYMERIZE
POLYMERIZED
POLYMERIZES
POLYMERIZING
POLYMEROUS
POLYMERS
POLYMERY
POLYMORPH
POLYMORPHIC
POLYMORPHICALLY
POLYMORPHISM
POLYMORPHISMS
POLYMORPHOUS
POLYMORPHOUSLY

POLYMORPHS
POLYMYOSITIS
POLYMYOSITISES
POLYMYXIN
POLYMYXINS
POLYNEURITIS
POLYNEURITISES
POLYNIA
POLYNIAS
POLYNOMIAL
POLYNOMIALISM
POLYNOMIALISMS
POLYNOMIALS
POLYNUCLEAR
POLYNUCLEATE
POLYNUCLEOTIDE
POLYNUCLEOTIDES
POLYNYA
POLYNYAS
POLYNYI
POLYOLEFIN
POLYOLEFINS
POLYOMA
POLYOMAS
POLYOMINO
POLYOMINOS
POLYONYM
POLYONYMIC
POLYONYMIES
POLYONYMOUS
POLYONYMS
POLYONYMY
POLYP
POLYPARIA
POLYPARIES
POLYPARIUM
POLYPARY
POLYPE
POLYPEPTIDE
POLYPEPTIDES
POLYPEPTIDIC
POLYPES
POLYPETALOUS
POLYPHAGIA
POLYPHAGIAS
POLYPHAGIES
POLYPHAGOUS
POLYPHAGY
POLYPHARMACIES
POLYPHARMACY
POLYPHASE
POLYPHASIC
POLYPHENOL
POLYPHENOLIC
POLYPHENOLS
POLYPHLOESBOEAN

POLYPHLOISBIC
POLYPHON
POLYPHONE
POLYPHONES
POLYPHONIC
POLYPHONICALLY
POLYPHONIES
POLYPHONIST
POLYPHONISTS
POLYPHONOUS
POLYPHONOUSLY
POLYPHONS
POLYPHONY
POLYPHOSPHORIC
POLYPHYLETIC
POLYPHYLLOUS
POLYPHYODONT
POLYPI
POLYPIDE
POLYPIDES
POLYPIDOM
POLYPIDOMS
POLYPINE
POLYPITE
POLYPITES
POLYPLOID
POLYPLOIDAL
POLYPLOIDIC
POLYPLOIDIES
POLYPLOIDS
POLYPLOIDY
POLYPNEA
POLYPNEAS
POLYPOD
POLYPODIES
POLYPODOUS
POLYPODS
POLYPODY
POLYPOID
POLYPORE
POLYPORES
POLYPOSES
POLYPOSIS
POLYPOUS
POLYPROPENE
POLYPROPENES
POLYPROPYLENE
POLYPROPYLENES
POLYPROTODONT
POLYPROTODONTS
POLYPS
POLYPTYCH
POLYPTYCHS
POLYPUS
POLYPUSES
POLYRHYTHM

POLYRHYTHMIC
POLYRHYTHMS
POLYRIBOSOMAL
POLYRIBOSOME
POLYRIBOSOMES
POLYS
POLYSACCHARIDE
POLYSACCHARIDES
POLYSACCHAROSE
POLYSACCHAROSES
POLYSEMANT
POLYSEMANTS
POLYSEME
POLYSEMES
POLYSEMIES
POLYSEMOUS
POLYSEMY
POLYSEPALOUS
POLYSILOXANE
POLYSILOXANES
POLYSOME
POLYSOMES
POLYSOMIC
POLYSOMIES
POLYSOMY
POLYSORBATE
POLYSORBATES
POLYSTICHOUS
POLYSTYLAR
POLYSTYLE
POLYSTYRENE
POLYSTYRENES
POLYSULFIDE
POLYSULFIDES
POLYSULPHIDE
POLYSULPHIDES
POLYSYLLABIC
POLYSYLLABICAL
POLYSYLLABICISM
POLYSYLLABISM
POLYSYLLABISMS
POLYSYLLABLE
POLYSYLLABLES
POLYSYLLOGISM
POLYSYLLOGISMS
POLYSYNAPTIC
POLYSYNDETON
POLYSYNDETONS
POLYSYNTHESES
POLYSYNTHESIS
POLYSYNTHESISM
POLYSYNTHETIC
POLYSYNTHETICAL
POLYSYNTHETISM
POLYSYNTHETISMS
POLYTECHNIC

POLYTECHNICAL
POLYTECHNICS
POLYTENE
POLYTENIES
POLYTENY
POLYTHALAMOUS
POLYTHEISM
POLYTHEISMS
POLYTHEIST
POLYTHEISTIC
POLYTHEISTICAL
POLYTHEISTS
POLYTHENE
POLYTHENES
POLYTOCOUS
POLYTONAL
POLYTONALISM
POLYTONALIST
POLYTONALISTS
POLYTONALITIES
POLYTONALITY
POLYTONALLY
POLYTROPHIC
POLYTROPHICALLY
POLYTUNNEL
POLYTUNNELS
POLYTYPE
POLYTYPES
POLYTYPIC
POLYTYPICAL
POLYTYPICALLY
POLYUNSATURATED
POLYURETHAN
POLYURETHANE
POLYURETHANES
POLYURETHANS
POLYURIA
POLYURIAS
POLYURIC
POLYVALENCE
POLYVALENCES
POLYVALENCY
POLYVALENT
POLYVINYL
POLYVINYLIDENE
POLYVINYLS
POLYWATER
POLYWATERS
POLYZOA
POLYZOAN
POLYZOANS
POLYZOARIA
POLYZOARIAL
POLYZOARIES
POLYZOARIUM
POLYZOARY

POLYZOIC
POLYZONAL
POLYZOOID
POLYZOON
POM
POMACE
POMACEOUS
POMACES
POMADE
POMADED
POMADES
POMADING
POMANDER
POMANDERS
POMATO
POMATOES
POMATUM
POMATUMS
POMBE
POMBES
POME
POMEGRANATE
POMEGRANATES
POMELO
POMELOS
POMEROY
POMEROYS
POMES
POMFRET
POMFRETS
POMICULTURE
POMICULTURES
POMIFEROUS
POMMEE
POMMEL
POMMELE
POMMELED
POMMELING
POMMELLED
POMMELLING
POMMELS
POMMETTY
POMMIE
POMMIES
POMMY
POMOERIUM
POMOERIUMS
POMOLOGICAL
POMOLOGICALLY
POMOLOGIES
POMOLOGIST
POMOLOGISTS
POMOLOGY
POMP
POMPADOUR
POMPADOURED

POMPADOURS
POMPANO
POMPANOS
POMPELMOOSE
POMPELMOOSES
POMPELMOUS
POMPELMOUSE
POMPELMOUSES
POMPELO
POMPELOS
POMPEY
POMPEYED
POMPEYING
POMPEYS
POMPHOLYGOUS
POMPHOLYX
POMPHOLYXES
POMPIER
POMPILID
POMPILIDS
POMPION
POMPIONS
POMPOM
POMPOMS
POMPON
POMPONS
POMPOON
POMPOONS
POMPOSITIES
POMPOSITY
POMPOUS
POMPOUSLY
POMPOUSNESS
POMPOUSNESSES
POMPS
POMROY
POMROYS
POMS
POMWATER
POMWATERS
PONCE
PONCEAU
PONCEAUS
PONCEAUX
PONCED
PONCES
PONCEY
PONCHO
PONCHOS
PONCIER
PONCIEST
PONCING
PONCY
POND
PONDAGE
PONDAGES

PONDED
PONDER
PONDERABILITIES
PONDERABILITY
PONDERABLE
PONDERABLES
PONDERABLY
PONDERAL
PONDERANCE
PONDERANCES
PONDERANCIES
PONDERANCY
PONDERATE
PONDERATED
PONDERATES
PONDERATING
PONDERATION
PONDERATIONS
PONDERED
PONDERER
PONDERERS
PONDERING
PONDERINGLY
PONDERMENT
PONDERMENTS
PONDEROSA
PONDEROSAS
PONDEROSITIES
PONDEROSITY
PONDEROUS
PONDEROUSLY
PONDEROUSNESS
PONDEROUSNESSES
PONDERS
PONDING
PONDOK
PONDOKKIE
PONDOKKIES
PONDOKS
PONDS
PONDWEED
PONDWEEDS
PONE
PONENT
PONEROLOGIES
PONEROLOGY
PONES
PONEY
PONEYS
PONG
PONGA
PONGAS
PONGED
PONGEE
PONGEES
PONGID

PONGIDS
PONGIER
PONGIEST
PONGING
PONGO
PONGOES
PONGOS
PONGS
PONGY
PONIARD
PONIARDED
PONIARDING
PONIARDS
PONIED
PONIES
PONK
PONKED
PONKING
PONKS
PONS
PONT
PONTAGE
PONTAGES
PONTAL
PONTES
PONTIANAC
PONTIANACS
PONTIANAK
PONTIANAKS
PONTIC
PONTICELLO
PONTICELLOS
PONTIE
PONTIES
PONTIFEX
PONTIFF
PONTIFFS
PONTIFIC
PONTIFICAL
PONTIFICALITIES
PONTIFICALITY
PONTIFICALLY
PONTIFICALS
PONTIFICATE
PONTIFICATED
PONTIFICATES
PONTIFICATING
PONTIFICATION
PONTIFICATIONS
PONTIFICATOR
PONTIFICATORS
PONTIFICE
PONTIFICES
PONTIFIED
PONTIFIES
PONTIFY

PONTIFYING
PONTIL
PONTILE
PONTILES
PONTILS
PONTINE
PONTLEVIS
PONTLEVISES
PONTON
PONTONEER
PONTONEERS
PONTONIER
PONTONIERS
PONTONNIER
PONTONNIERS
PONTONS
PONTOON
PONTOONED
PONTOONER
PONTOONERS
PONTOONING
PONTOONS
PONTS
PONTY
PONY
PONYING
PONYSKIN
PONYSKINS
PONYTAIL
PONYTAILED
PONYTAILS
POO
POOCH
POOCHED
POOCHES
POOCHING
POOD
POODLE
POODLES
POODS
POOED
POOF
POOFIER
POOFIEST
POOFS
POOFTAH
POOFTAHS
POOFTER
POOFTERS
POOFY
POOGYE
POOGYEES
POOGYES
POOH
POOHED
POOHING

POOHS
POOING
POOJA
POOJAH
POOJAHS
POOJAS
POOK
POOKA
POOKAS
POOKING
POOKIT
POOKS
POOL
POOLED
POOLHALL
POOLHALLS
POOLING
POOLROOM
POOLROOMS
POOLS
POOLSIDE
POOLSIDES
POON
POONAC
POONACS
POONCE
POONCED
POONCES
POONCING
POONS
POONTANG
POONTANGS
POOP
POOPED
POOPING
POOPS
POOR
POORER
POOREST
POORHOUSE
POORHOUSES
POORI
POORIS
POORISH
POORLIER
POORLIEST
POORLY
POORNESS
POORNESSES
POORT
POORTITH
POORTITHS
POORTS
POORWILL
POORWILLS
POOS

POOT
POOTED
POOTER
POOTERS
POOTING
POOTLE
POOTLED
POOTLER
POOTLERS
POOTLES
POOTLING
POOTS
POOVE
POOVERIES
POOVERY
POOVES
POOVIER
POOVIEST
POOVY
POP
POPADUM
POPADUMS
POPCORN
POPCORNS
POPE
POPEDOM
POPEDOMS
POPEHOOD
POPEHOODS
POPELESS
POPELIKE
POPELING
POPELINGS
POPERIES
POPERIN
POPERINS
POPERY
POPES
POPESEYE
POPESEYES
POPESHIP
POPESHIPS
POPETTE
POPETTES
POPEYED
POPGUN
POPGUNS
POPINJAY
POPINJAYS
POPISH
POPISHLY
POPJOY
POPJOYED
POPJOYING
POPJOYS
POPLAR

POPLARS
POPLIN
POPLINETTE
POPLINETTES
POPLINS
POPLITEAL
POPLITIC
POPMOBILITY
POPOVER
POPOVERS
POPPA
POPPADOM
POPPADOMS
POPPADUM
POPPADUMS
POPPAS
POPPED
POPPER
POPPERING
POPPERINGS
POPPERS
POPPET
POPPETS
POPPIED
POPPIER
POPPIES
POPPIEST
POPPING
POPPISH
POPPIT
POPPITS
POPPLE
POPPLED
POPPLES
POPPLIER
POPPLIEST
POPPLING
POPPLY
POPPY
POPPYCOCK
POPPYCOCKS
POPPYHEAD
POPPYHEADS
POPRIN
POPRINS
POPS
POPSIE
POPSIES
POPSTER
POPSTERS
POPSY
POPULACE
POPULACES
POPULAR
POPULARISATION
POPULARISATIONS

POPULARISE
POPULARISED
POPULARISER
POPULARISERS
POPULARISES
POPULARISING
POPULARITIES
POPULARITY
POPULARIZATION
POPULARIZATIONS
POPULARIZE
POPULARIZED
POPULARIZER
POPULARIZERS
POPULARIZES
POPULARIZING
POPULARLY
POPULARS
POPULATE
POPULATED
POPULATES
POPULATING
POPULATION
POPULATIONAL
POPULATIONS
POPULISM
POPULISMS
POPULIST
POPULISTIC
POPULISTS
POPULOUS
POPULOUSLY
POPULOUSNESS
POPULOUSNESSES
PORAE
PORAL
PORANGI
PORBEAGLE
PORBEAGLES
PORCELAIN
PORCELAINEOUS
PORCELAINISE
PORCELAINISED
PORCELAINISES
PORCELAINISING
PORCELAINIZE
PORCELAINIZED
PORCELAINIZES
PORCELAINIZING
PORCELAINLIKE
PORCELAINOUS
PORCELAINS
PORCELANEOUS
PORCELLANEOUS
PORCELLANISED
PORCELLANISES

PORCELLANISING
PORCELLANITE
PORCELLANITES
PORCELLANIZE
PORCELLANIZED
PORCELLANIZES
PORCELLANIZING
PORCELLANOUS
PORCH
PORCHES
PORCINE
PORCINI
PORCINO
PORCPISCES
PORCUPINE
PORCUPINES
PORCUPINISH
PORCUPINY
PORE
PORED
PORER
PORERS
PORES
PORGE
PORGED
PORGES
PORGIE
PORGIES
PORGING
PORGY
PORIER
PORIEST
PORIFER
PORIFERAL
PORIFERAN
PORIFERANS
PORIFEROUS
PORIFERS
PORINA
PORINAS
PORINESS
PORINESSES
PORING
PORISM
PORISMATIC
PORISMATICAL
PORISMS
PORISTIC
PORISTICAL
PORK
PORKER
PORKERS
PORKIER
PORKIES
PORKIEST
PORKILY

PORKINESS
PORKLING
PORKLINGS
PORKPIE
PORKPIES
PORKS
PORKWOOD
PORKWOODS
PORKY
PORLOCKING
PORLOCKINGS
PORN
PORNIER
PORNIEST
PORNO
PORNOCRACIES
PORNOCRACY
PORNOGRAPHER
PORNOGRAPHERS
PORNOGRAPHIC
PORNOGRAPHIES
PORNOGRAPHY
PORNOMAG
PORNOMAGS
PORNOS
PORNOTOPIA
PORNOTOPIAN
PORNOTOPIAS
PORNS
PORNY
POROGAMIC
POROGAMIES
POROGAMY
POROMERIC
POROMERICS
POROSCOPE
POROSCOPES
POROSCOPIC
POROSCOPIES
POROSCOPY
POROSE
POROSES
POROSIS
POROSITIES
POROSITY
POROUS
POROUSLY
POROUSNESS
POROUSNESSES
PORPENTINE
PORPENTINES
PORPESS
PORPESSE
PORPESSES
PORPHYRIA
PORPHYRIAS

PORPHYRIES
PORPHYRIN
PORPHYRINS
PORPHYRIO
PORPHYRIOS
PORPHYRITE
PORPHYRITES
PORPHYRITIC
PORPHYROGENITE
PORPHYROGENITES
PORPHYROID
PORPHYROIDS
PORPHYROPSIN
PORPHYROPSINS
PORPHYROUS
PORPHYRY
PORPOISE
PORPOISED
PORPOISES
PORPOISING
PORPORATE
PORRACEOUS
PORRECT
PORRECTED
PORRECTING
PORRECTION
PORRECTIONS
PORRECTS
PORRENGER
PORRENGERS
PORRIDGE
PORRIDGES
PORRIDGY
PORRIGINOUS
PORRIGO
PORRIGOS
PORRINGER
PORRINGERS
PORT
PORTA
PORTABELLA
PORTABELLAS
PORTABELLO
PORTABELLOS
PORTABILITIES
PORTABILITY
PORTABLE
PORTABLES
PORTABLY
PORTAGE
PORTAGED
PORTAGES
PORTAGING
PORTAGUE
PORTAGUES
PORTAL

PORTALED
PORTALS
PORTAMENTI
PORTAMENTO
PORTANCE
PORTANCES
PORTAPACK
PORTAPACKS
PORTAPAK
PORTAPAKS
PORTAS
PORTASES
PORTATE
PORTATILE
PORTATIVE
PORTATIVES
PORTCULLIS
PORTCULLISED
PORTCULLISES
PORTCULLISING
PORTED
PORTEND
PORTENDED
PORTENDING
PORTENDS
PORTENT
PORTENTOUS
PORTENTOUSLY
PORTENTOUSNESS
PORTENTS
PORTEOUS
PORTEOUSES
PORTER
PORTERAGE
PORTERAGES
PORTERED
PORTERESS
PORTERESSES
PORTERHOUSE
PORTERHOUSES
PORTERING
PORTERLY
PORTERS
PORTESS
PORTESSE
PORTESSES
PORTFIRE
PORTFIRES
PORTFOLIO
PORTFOLIOS
PORTHOLE
PORTHOLES
PORTHORS
PORTHORSES
PORTHOS
PORTHOSES

PORTHOUSE
PORTHOUSES
PORTICO
PORTICOED
PORTICOES
PORTICOS
PORTIER
PORTIERE
PORTIERED
PORTIERES
PORTIERING
PORTIEST
PORTIGUE
PORTIGUES
PORTING
PORTION
PORTIONED
PORTIONER
PORTIONERS
PORTIONING
PORTIONIST
PORTIONISTS
PORTIONLESS
PORTIONS
PORTLAND
PORTLANDS
PORTLAST
PORTLASTS
PORTLESS
PORTLIER
PORTLIEST
PORTLINESS
PORTLINESSES
PORTLY
PORTMAN
PORTMANTEAU
PORTMANTEAUS
PORTMANTEAUX
PORTMANTLE
PORTMANTLES
PORTMANTUA
PORTMANTUAS
PORTMEN
PORTOBELLO
PORTOBELLOS
PORTOISE
PORTOISES
PORTOLAN
PORTOLANI
PORTOLANO
PORTOLANOS
PORTOLANS
PORTOUS
PORTOUSES
PORTRAIT
PORTRAITED

PORTRAITING
PORTRAITIST
PORTRAITISTS
PORTRAITS
PORTRAITURE
PORTRAITURES
PORTRAY
PORTRAYABLE
PORTRAYAL
PORTRAYALS
PORTRAYED
PORTRAYER
PORTRAYERS
PORTRAYING
PORTRAYS
PORTREEVE
PORTREEVES
PORTRESS
PORTRESSES
PORTS
PORTULACA
PORTULACACEOUS
PORTULACAS
PORTULAN
PORTULANS
PORTY
PORWIGGLE
PORWIGGLES
PORY
POS
POSADA
POSADAS
POSAUNE
POSAUNES
POSE
POSEABLE
POSED
POSER
POSERISH
POSERISHNESS
POSERS
POSES
POSEUR
POSEURS
POSEUSE
POSEUSES
POSEY
POSH
POSHED
POSHER
POSHES
POSHEST
POSHING
POSHLY
POSHNESS
POSHNESSES

POSHO
POSHOS
POSHTEEN
POSHTEENS
POSIER
POSIES
POSIEST
POSIGRADE
POSING
POSINGLY
POSINGS
POSIT
POSITED
POSITIF
POSITIFS
POSITING
POSITION
POSITIONAL
POSITIONALLY
POSITIONED
POSITIONING
POSITIONS
POSITIVE
POSITIVELY
POSITIVENESS
POSITIVENESSES
POSITIVER
POSITIVES
POSITIVEST
POSITIVISM
POSITIVISMS
POSITIVIST
POSITIVISTIC
POSITIVISTS
POSITIVITIES
POSITIVITY
POSITON
POSITONS
POSITRON
POSITRONIUM
POSITRONIUMS
POSITRONS
POSITS
POSNET
POSNETS
POSOLOGICAL
POSOLOGIES
POSOLOGY
POSS
POSSE
POSSED
POSSER
POSSERS
POSSES
POSSESS
POSSESSABLE

POSSESSED
POSSESSEDLY
POSSESSEDNESS
POSSESSEDNESSES
POSSESSES
POSSESSING
POSSESSION
POSSESSIONAL
POSSESSIONARY
POSSESSIONATE
POSSESSIONATES
POSSESSIONED
POSSESSIONLESS
POSSESSIONS
POSSESSIVE
POSSESSIVELY
POSSESSIVENESS
POSSESSIVES
POSSESSOR
POSSESSORS
POSSESSORSHIP
POSSESSORSHIPS
POSSESSORY
POSSET
POSSETED
POSSETING
POSSETS
POSSIBILISM
POSSIBILISMS
POSSIBILIST
POSSIBILISTS
POSSIBILITIES
POSSIBILITY
POSSIBLE
POSSIBLER
POSSIBLES
POSSIBLEST
POSSIBLY
POSSIE
POSSIES
POSSING
POSSUM
POSSUMED
POSSUMING
POSSUMS
POST
POSTABORTION
POSTACCIDENT
POSTADOLESCENT
POSTAGE
POSTAGES
POSTAL
POSTALLY
POSTALS
POSTAMPUTATION
POSTANAL

POSTAPOCALYPTIC
POSTARREST
POSTATOMIC
POSTATTACK
POSTAXIAL
POSTBAG
POSTBAGS
POSTBASE
POSTBELLUM
POSTBIBLICAL
POSTBOURGEOIS
POSTBOX
POSTBOXES
POSTBOY
POSTBOYS
POSTBURN
POSTBUS
POSTBUSES
POSTBUSSES
POSTCAPITALIST
POSTCARD
POSTCARDED
POSTCARDING
POSTCARDLIKE
POSTCARDS
POSTCAVA
POSTCAVAE
POSTCAVAL
POSTCAVAS
POSTCLASSIC
POSTCLASSICAL
POSTCODE
POSTCODED
POSTCODES
POSTCODING
POSTCOITAL
POSTCOLLEGE
POSTCOLLEGIATE
POSTCOLONIAL
POSTCONCEPTION
POSTCONCERT
POSTCONQUEST
POSTCONSONANTAL
POSTCONVENTION
POSTCOPULATORY
POSTCORONARY
POSTCOUP
POSTCRANIAL
POSTCRANIALLY
POSTCRASH
POSTCRISIS
POSTDATE
POSTDATED
POSTDATES
POSTDATING
POSTDEADLINE

POSTDEBATE
POSTDEBUTANTE
POSTDELIVERY
POSTDEPRESSION
POSTDEVALUATION
POSTDIAGNOSTIC
POSTDIGESTIVE
POSTDILUVIAL
POSTDILUVIALLY
POSTDILUVIAN
POSTDILUVIANS
POSTDIVE
POSTDIVESTITURE
POSTDIVORCE
POSTDOC
POSTDOCS
POSTDOCTORAL
POSTDOCTORATE
POSTDRUG
POSTED
POSTEDITING
POSTEEN
POSTEENS
POSTELECTION
POSTEMBRYONAL
POSTEMBRYONIC
POSTEMERGENCE
POSTEMERGENCY
POSTEPILEPTIC
POSTER
POSTERED
POSTERING
POSTERIOR
POSTERIORITIES
POSTERIORITY
POSTERIORLY
POSTERIORS
POSTERISATION
POSTERISATIONS
POSTERITIES
POSTERITY
POSTERIZATION
POSTERIZATIONS
POSTERN
POSTERNS
POSTEROLATERAL
POSTERS
POSTERUPTIVE
POSTEXERCISE
POSTEXILIAN
POSTEXILIC
POSTEXPERIENCE
POSTEXPOSURE
POSTFACE
POSTFACES
POSTFAULT

POSTFEMINISM
POSTFEMINISMS
POSTFEMINIST
POSTFEMINISTS
POSTFIRE
POSTFIX
POSTFIXED
POSTFIXES
POSTFIXING
POSTFLIGHT
POSTFORM
POSTFORMED
POSTFORMING
POSTFORMS
POSTFRACTURE
POSTFREEZE
POSTGAME
POSTGANGLIONIC
POSTGLACIAL
POSTGRADUATE
POSTGRADUATES
POSTGRADUATION
POSTHARVEST
POSTHASTE
POSTHASTES
POSTHEAT
POSTHEATS
POSTHEMORRHAGIC
POSTHOLDER
POSTHOLDERS
POSTHOLE
POSTHOLES
POSTHOLIDAY
POSTHOLOCAUST
POSTHORSE
POSTHORSES
POSTHOSPITAL
POSTHOUSE
POSTHOUSES
POSTHUMOUS
POSTHUMOUSLY
POSTHUMOUSNESS
POSTHYPNOTIC
POSTICAL
POSTICALLY
POSTICHE
POSTICHES
POSTICOUS
POSTIE
POSTIES
POSTIL
POSTILED
POSTILING
POSTILION
POSTILIONS
POSTILLATE

POSTILLATED
POSTILLATES
POSTILLATING
POSTILLATION
POSTILLATIONS
POSTILLATOR
POSTILLATORS
POSTILLED
POSTILLER
POSTILLERS
POSTILLING
POSTILLION
POSTILLIONS
POSTILS
POSTIMPACT
POSTIMPERIAL
POSTIN
POSTINAUGURAL
POSTINDUSTRIAL
POSTINFECTION
POSTING
POSTINGS
POSTINJECTION
POSTINOCULATION
POSTINS
POSTIQUE
POSTIQUES
POSTIRRADIATION
POSTISCHEMIC
POSTISOLATION
POSTLANDING
POSTLAPSARIAN
POSTLAUNCH
POSTLIBERATION
POSTLIMINARY
POSTLIMINIA
POSTLIMINIARY
POSTLIMINIES
POSTLIMINIOUS
POSTLIMINIUM
POSTLIMINOUS
POSTLIMINY
POSTLITERATE
POSTLUDE
POSTLUDES
POSTMAN
POSTMARITAL
POSTMARK
POSTMARKED
POSTMARKING
POSTMARKS
POSTMASTECTOMY
POSTMASTER
POSTMASTERS
POSTMASTERSHIP
POSTMASTERSHIPS

POSTMATING
POSTMEDIEVAL
POSTMEN
POSTMENOPAUSAL
POSTMENSTRUAL
POSTMERIDIAN
POSTMIDNIGHT
POSTMILLENARIAN
POSTMILLENNIAL
POSTMISTRESS
POSTMISTRESSES
POSTMODERN
POSTMODERNISM
POSTMODERNISMS
POSTMODERNIST
POSTMODERNISTS
POSTMORTEM
POSTMORTEMS
POSTNASAL
POSTNATAL
POSTNATALLY
POSTNATI
POSTNEONATAL
POSTNUPTIAL
POSTOCULAR
POSTOPERATIVE
POSTOPERATIVELY
POSTORAL
POSTORBITAL
POSTORGASMIC
POSTPAID
POSTPARTUM
POSTPERSON
POSTPERSONS
POSTPITUITARY
POSTPOLLINATION
POSTPONABLE
POSTPONE
POSTPONED
POSTPONEMENT
POSTPONEMENTS
POSTPONENCE
POSTPONENCES
POSTPONER
POSTPONERS
POSTPONES
POSTPONING
POSTPOSE
POSTPOSED
POSTPOSES
POSTPOSING
POSTPOSITION
POSTPOSITIONAL
POSTPOSITIONS
POSTPOSITIVE
POSTPOSITIVELY

POSTPOSITIVES
POSTPRANDIAL
POSTPRIMARY
POSTPRISON
POSTPRODUCTION
POSTPRODUCTIONS
POSTPUBERTY
POSTPUBESCENT
POSTRACE
POSTRECESSION
POSTRETIREMENT
POSTRIDER
POSTRIDERS
POSTRIOT
POSTROMANTIC
POSTS
POSTSCENIUM
POSTSCENIUMS
POSTSCRIPT
POSTSCRIPTS
POSTSEASON
POSTSEASONAL
POSTSEASONALLY
POSTSEASONS
POSTSECONDARY
POSTSHOW
POSTSTIMULATION
POSTSTIMULATORY
POSTSTIMULUS
POSTSTRIKE
POSTSURGICAL
POSTSYNAPTIC
POSTSYNC
POSTSYNCED
POSTSYNCING
POSTSYNCS
POSTTAX
POSTTEEN
POSTTENSION
POSTTENSIONED
POSTTENSIONING
POSTTENSIONS
POSTTEST
POSTTESTS
POSTTRANSFUSION
POSTTRAUMATIC
POSTTREATMENT
POSTTRIAL
POSTULANCIES
POSTULANCY
POSTULANT
POSTULANTS
POSTULANTSHIP
POSTULATA
POSTULATE
POSTULATED

POSTULATES
POSTULATING
POSTULATION
POSTULATIONAL
POSTULATIONALLY
POSTULATIONS
POSTULATOR
POSTULATORS
POSTULATORY
POSTULATUM
POSTURAL
POSTURE
POSTURED
POSTURER
POSTURERS
POSTURES
POSTURING
POSTURISE
POSTURISED
POSTURISES
POSTURISING
POSTURIST
POSTURISTS
POSTURIZE
POSTURIZED
POSTURIZES
POSTURIZING
POSTVACCINAL
POSTVACCINATION
POSTVAGOTOMY
POSTVASECTOMY
POSTVIRAL
POSTVOCALIC
POSTWAR
POSTWEANING
POSTWOMAN
POSTWOMEN
POSTWORKSHOP
POSY
POT
POTABILITIES
POTABILITY
POTABLE
POTABLENESS
POTABLENESSES
POTABLES
POTAE
POTAES
POTAGE
POTAGER
POTAGERS
POTAGES
POTAMIC
POTAMOGETON
POTAMOGETONS
POTAMOLOGICAL

POTAMOLOGIES
POTAMOLOGIST
POTAMOLOGISTS
POTAMOLOGY
POTASH
POTASHED
POTASHES
POTASHING
POTASS
POTASSA
POTASSAS
POTASSES
POTASSIC
POTASSIUM
POTASSIUMS
POTATION
POTATIONS
POTATO
POTATOES
POTATORY
POTBELLIED
POTBELLIES
POTBELLY
POTBOIL
POTBOILED
POTBOILER
POTBOILERS
POTBOILING
POTBOILS
POTBOY
POTBOYS
POTCH
POTCHE
POTCHED
POTCHER
POTCHERS
POTCHES
POTCHING
POTE
POTED
POTEEN
POTEENS
POTENCE
POTENCES
POTENCIES
POTENCY
POTENT
POTENTATE
POTENTATES
POTENTIAL
POTENTIALITIES
POTENTIALITY
POTENTIALLY
POTENTIALS
POTENTIARIES
POTENTIARY

POTENTIATE
POTENTIATED
POTENTIATES
POTENTIATING
POTENTIATION
POTENTIATIONS
POTENTIATOR
POTENTIATORS
POTENTILLA
POTENTILLAS
POTENTIOMETER
POTENTIOMETERS
POTENTIOMETRIC
POTENTIOMETRY
POTENTISE
POTENTISED
POTENTISES
POTENTISING
POTENTIZE
POTENTIZED
POTENTIZES
POTENTIZING
POTENTLY
POTENTNESS
POTENTS
POTES
POTFUL
POTFULS
POTGUN
POTGUNS
POTHEAD
POTHEADS
POTHECARIES
POTHECARY
POTHEEN
POTHEENS
POTHER
POTHERB
POTHERBS
POTHERED
POTHERING
POTHERS
POTHERY
POTHOLE
POTHOLED
POTHOLER
POTHOLERS
POTHOLES
POTHOLING
POTHOLINGS
POTHOOK
POTHOOKS
POTHOUSE
POTHOUSES
POTHUNTER
POTHUNTERS

POTHUNTING	POTTAGES	POUFFS	POUNDAGE
POTHUNTINGS	POTTED	POUFING	POUNDAGES
POTICARIES	POTTEEN	POUFS	POUNDAL
POTICARY	POTTEENS	POUFTAH	POUNDALS
POTICHE	POTTER	POUFTAHS	POUNDED
POTICHES	POTTERED	POUFTER	POUNDER
POTICHOMANIA	POTTERER	POUFTERS	POUNDERS
POTICHOMANIAS	POTTERERS	POUK	POUNDING
POTIN	POTTERIES	POUKE	POUNDS
POTING	POTTERING	POUKES	POUPE
POTINS	POTTERINGLY	POUKING	POUPED
POTION	POTTERINGS	POUKIT	POUPES
POTIONS	POTTERS	POUKS	POUPING
POTLACH	POTTERY	POULAINE	POUPT
POTLACHE	POTTIER	POULAINES	POUR
POTLACHES	POTTIES	POULARD	POURABLE
POTLATCH	POTTIEST	POULARDE	POURBOIRE
POTLATCHED	POTTINESS	POULARDES	POURBOIRES
POTLATCHES	POTTINESSES	POULARDS	POURED
POTLATCHING	POTTING	POULDER	POURER
POTLIKE	POTTINGAR	POULDERS	POURERS
POTLINE	POTTINGARS	POULDRE	POURIE
POTLINES	POTTINGER	POULDRES	POURIES
POTLUCK	POTTINGERS	POULDRON	POURING
POTLUCKS	POTTLE	POULDRONS	POURINGLY
POTMAN	POTTLES	POULE	POURINGS
POTMEN	POTTO	POULES	POURPARLER
POTOMETER	POTTOS	POULP	POURPARLERS
POTOMETERS	POTTS	POULPE	POURPOINT
POTOO	POTTY	POULPES	POURPOINTS
POTOOS	POTTYMOUTH	POULPS	POURS
POTOROO	POTTYMOUTHS	POULT	POURSEW
POTOROOS	POTWALLER	POULTER	POURSEWED
POTPIE	POTWALLERS	POULTERER	POURSEWING
POTPIES	POTZER	POULTERERS	POURSEWS
POTPOURRI	POTZERS	POULTERS	POURSUE
POTPOURRIS	POUCH	POULTICE	POURSUED
POTS	POUCHED	POULTICED	POURSUES
POTSHARD	POUCHES	POULTICES	POURSUING
POTSHARDS	POUCHFUL	POULTICING	POURSUIT
POTSHARE	POUCHFULS	POULTRIES	POURSUITS
POTSHARES	POUCHIER	POULTROONES	POURSUITTS
POTSHERD	POUCHIEST	POULTRY	POURTRAHED
POTSHERDS	POUCHING	POULTRYMAN	POURTRAICT
POTSHOP	POUCHY	POULTRYMEN	POURTRAICTS
POTSHOPS	POUDER	POULTS	POURTRAY
POTSHOT	POUDERS	POUNCE	POURTRAYD
POTSHOTS	POUDRE	POUNCED	POURTRAYED
POTSHOTTING	POUDRES	POUNCER	POURTRAYING
POTSIE	POUF	POUNCERS	POURTRAYS
POTSIES	POUFED	POUNCES	POUSOWDIE
POTSTONE	POUFF	POUNCET	POUSOWDIES
POTSTONES	POUFFE	POUNCETS	POUSSE
POTSY	POUFFED	POUNCHING	POUSSES
POTT	POUFFES	POUNCING	POUSSETTE
POTTAGE	POUFFING	POUND	POUSSETTED

POUSSETTES
POUSSETTING
POUSSIE
POUSSIES
POUSSIN
POUSSINS
POUT
POUTED
POUTER
POUTERS
POUTFUL
POUTHER
POUTHERED
POUTHERING
POUTHERS
POUTIER
POUTIEST
POUTINE
POUTINES
POUTING
POUTINGLY
POUTINGS
POUTS
POUTY
POVERTIES
POVERTY
POW
POWAN
POWANS
POWDER
POWDERED
POWDERER
POWDERERS
POWDERIER
POWDERIEST
POWDERING
POWDERLESS
POWDERLIKE
POWDERS
POWDERY
POWELLISED
POWELLISES
POWELLISING
POWELLITE
POWELLITES
POWELLIZE
POWELLIZED
POWELLIZES
POWELLIZING
POWER
POWERBOAT
POWERBOATED
POWERBOATER
POWERBOATERS
POWERBOATING
POWERBOATS

POWERED
POWERFUL
POWERFULLY
POWERFULNESS
POWERFULNESSES
POWERHOUSE
POWERHOUSES
POWERING
POWERLESS
POWERLESSLY
POWERLESSNESS
POWERLESSNESSES
POWERLIFTING
POWERLIFTINGS
POWERPLAY
POWERPLAYS
POWERS
POWERTRAIN
POWERTRAINS
POWFAGGED
POWHIRI
POWHIRIS
POWIN
POWINS
POWN
POWND
POWNDED
POWNDING
POWNDS
POWNEY
POWNEYS
POWNIE
POWNIES
POWNS
POWNY
POWRE
POWRED
POWRES
POWRING
POWS
POWSOWDIES
POWSOWDY
POWTER
POWTERED
POWTERING
POWTERS
POWWAW
POWWOW
POWWOWED
POWWOWING
POWWOWS
POX
POXED
POXES
POXIER
POXIEST

POXING
POXVIRUS
POXVIRUSES
POXY
POYNANT
POYNT
POYNTED
POYNTING
POYNTS
POYOU
POYOUS
POYSE
POYSED
POYSES
POYSING
POYSON
POYSONED
POYSONING
POYSONS
POZ
POZZ
POZZIES
POZZOLAN
POZZOLANA
POZZOLANAS
POZZOLANIC
POZZOLANS
POZZUOLANA
POZZUOLANAS
POZZY
PRAAM
PRAAMS
PRABBLE
PRABBLES
PRACHARAK
PRACHARAKS
PRACTIC
PRACTICABILITY
PRACTICABLE
PRACTICABLENESS
PRACTICABLY
PRACTICAL
PRACTICALISM
PRACTICALISMS
PRACTICALIST
PRACTICALISTS
PRACTICALITIES
PRACTICALITY
PRACTICALLY
PRACTICALNESS
PRACTICALNESSES
PRACTICALS
PRACTICE
PRACTICED
PRACTICER
PRACTICERS

PRACTICES
PRACTICIAN
PRACTICIANS
PRACTICING
PRACTICK
PRACTICKS
PRACTICS
PRACTICUM
PRACTICUMS
PRACTIQUE
PRACTIQUES
PRACTISANT
PRACTISANTS
PRACTISE
PRACTISED
PRACTISER
PRACTISERS
PRACTISES
PRACTISING
PRACTITIONER
PRACTITIONERS
PRACTIVE
PRACTOLOL
PRACTOLOLS
PRAD
PRADS
PRAEAMBLE
PRAEAMBLES
PRAECAVA
PRAECAVAE
PRAECIPE
PRAECIPES
PRAECOCES
PRAECOCIAL
PRAECORDIAL
PRAEDIAL
PRAEDIALITY
PRAEDIALS
PRAEFECT
PRAEFECTORIAL
PRAEFECTS
PRAELECT
PRAELECTED
PRAELECTING
PRAELECTS
PRAELUDIA
PRAELUDIUM
PRAEMUNIRE
PRAEMUNIRES
PRAENOMEN
PRAENOMENS
PRAENOMINA
PRAENOMINAL
PRAENOMINALLY
PRAEPOSTOR
PRAEPOSTORS

PRAESES
PRAESIDIA
PRAESIDIUM
PRAESIDIUMS
PRAETOR
PRAETORIAL
PRAETORIAN
PRAETORIANS
PRAETORIUM
PRAETORIUMS
PRAETORS
PRAETORSHIP
PRAETORSHIPS
PRAGMATIC
PRAGMATICAL
PRAGMATICALITY
PRAGMATICALLY
PRAGMATICALNESS
PRAGMATICISM
PRAGMATICISMS
PRAGMATICIST
PRAGMATICISTS
PRAGMATICS
PRAGMATISATION
PRAGMATISATIONS
PRAGMATISE
PRAGMATISED
PRAGMATISER
PRAGMATISERS
PRAGMATISES
PRAGMATISING
PRAGMATISM
PRAGMATISMS
PRAGMATIST
PRAGMATISTIC
PRAGMATISTS
PRAGMATIZATION
PRAGMATIZATIONS
PRAGMATIZE
PRAGMATIZED
PRAGMATIZER
PRAGMATIZERS
PRAGMATIZES
PRAGMATIZING
PRAHU
PRAHUS
PRAIRIE
PRAIRIED
PRAIRIES
PRAISE
PRAISEACH
PRAISEACHS
PRAISED
PRAISEFUL
PRAISELESS
PRAISER

PRAISERS
PRAISES
PRAISEWORTHILY
PRAISEWORTHY
PRAISING
PRAISINGLY
PRAISINGS
PRAJNA
PRALINE
PRALINES
PRALLTRILLER
PRALLTRILLERS
PRAM
PRAMS
PRANA
PRANAS
PRANAYAMA
PRANAYAMAS
PRANCE
PRANCED
PRANCER
PRANCERS
PRANCES
PRANCING
PRANCINGLY
PRANCINGS
PRANCK
PRANCKE
PRANCKED
PRANCKES
PRANCKING
PRANCKS
PRANDIAL
PRANDIALLY
PRANG
PRANGED
PRANGING
PRANGS
PRANK
PRANKED
PRANKFUL
PRANKIER
PRANKIEST
PRANKING
PRANKINGLY
PRANKINGS
PRANKISH
PRANKISHLY
PRANKISHNESS
PRANKISHNESSES
PRANKLE
PRANKLED
PRANKLES
PRANKLING
PRANKS
PRANKSOME

PRANKSTER
PRANKSTERS
PRANKY
PRAO
PRAOS
PRASE
PRASEODYMIUM
PRASEODYMIUMS
PRASES
PRAT
PRATE
PRATED
PRATER
PRATERS
PRATES
PRATFALL
PRATFALLEN
PRATFALLING
PRATFALLS
PRATFELL
PRATIE
PRATIES
PRATINCOLE
PRATINCOLES
PRATING
PRATINGLY
PRATINGS
PRATIQUE
PRATIQUES
PRATS
PRATT
PRATTED
PRATTING
PRATTLE
PRATTLEBOXES
PRATTLED
PRATTLEMENT
PRATTLEMENTS
PRATTLER
PRATTLERS
PRATTLES
PRATTLING
PRATTLINGLY
PRATTS
PRATY
PRAU
PRAUNCE
PRAUNCED
PRAUNCES
PRAUNCING
PRAUS
PRAVITIES
PRAVITY
PRAWLE
PRAWLES
PRAWLIN

PRAWLINS
PRAWN
PRAWNED
PRAWNER
PRAWNERS
PRAWNING
PRAWNS
PRAXEOLOGICAL
PRAXEOLOGIES
PRAXEOLOGY
PRAXES
PRAXINOSCOPE
PRAXINOSCOPES
PRAXIS
PRAXISES
PRAY
PRAYED
PRAYER
PRAYERFUL
PRAYERFULLY
PRAYERFULNESS
PRAYERFULNESSES
PRAYERLESS
PRAYERLESSLY
PRAYERLESSNESS
PRAYERS
PRAYING
PRAYINGLY
PRAYINGS
PRAYS
PRE
PREABSORB
PREABSORBED
PREABSORBING
PREABSORBS
PREACCEPT
PREACCEPTED
PREACCEPTING
PREACCEPTS
PREACCUSTOM
PREACCUSTOMED
PREACCUSTOMING
PREACCUSTOMS
PREACE
PREACED
PREACES
PREACH
PREACHABLE
PREACHED
PREACHER
PREACHERS
PREACHERSHIP
PREACHERSHIPS
PREACHES
PREACHIER
PREACHIEST

PREACHIFIED
PREACHIFIES
PREACHIFY
PREACHIFYING
PREACHILY
PREACHINESS
PREACHINESSES
PREACHING
PREACHINGLY
PREACHINGS
PREACHMENT
PREACHMENTS
PREACHY
PREACING
PREACQUAINT
PREACQUAINTANCE
PREACQUAINTED
PREACQUAINTING
PREACQUAINTS
PREACQUISITION
PREACQUISITIONS
PREACT
PREACTED
PREACTING
PREACTS
PREADAMIC
PREADAMITE
PREADAMITES
PREADAPT
PREADAPTATION
PREADAPTATIONS
PREADAPTED
PREADAPTING
PREADAPTIVE
PREADAPTS
PREADDRESS
PREADDRESSED
PREADDRESSES
PREADDRESSING
PREADJUST
PREADJUSTED
PREADJUSTING
PREADJUSTS
PREADMISSION
PREADMISSIONS
PREADMIT
PREADMITS
PREADMITTED
PREADMITTING
PREADMONISH
PREADMONISHED
PREADMONISHES
PREADMONISHING
PREADMONITION
PREADMONITIONS
PREADOLESCENCE

PREADOLESCENCES
PREADOLESCENT
PREADOLESCENTS
PREADOPT
PREADOPTED
PREADOPTING
PREADOPTS
PREADULT
PREADVERTISE
PREADVERTISED
PREADVERTISES
PREADVERTISING
PREAGED
PREAGRICULTURAL
PREALLOT
PREALLOTS
PREALLOTTED
PREALLOTTING
PREAMBLE
PREAMBLED
PREAMBLES
PREAMBLING
PREAMBULARY
PREAMBULATE
PREAMBULATED
PREAMBULATES
PREAMBULATING
PREAMBULATORY
PREAMP
PREAMPLIFIER
PREAMPLIFIERS
PREAMPS
PREANAL
PREANESTHETIC
PREANNOUNCE
PREANNOUNCED
PREANNOUNCES
PREANNOUNCING
PREANTIQUITIES
PREANTIQUITY
PREAPPEARANCE
PREAPPEARANCES
PREAPPLICATION
PREAPPLICATIONS
PREAPPOINT
PREAPPOINTED
PREAPPOINTING
PREAPPOINTS
PREAPPROVE
PREAPPROVED
PREAPPROVES
PREAPPROVING
PREARM
PREARMED
PREARMING
PREARMS

PREARRANGE
PREARRANGED
PREARRANGEMENT
PREARRANGEMENTS
PREARRANGES
PREARRANGING
PREASCERTAIN
PREASCERTAINED
PREASCERTAINING
PREASCERTAINS
PREASE
PREASED
PREASES
PREASING
PREASSE
PREASSED
PREASSEMBLE
PREASSEMBLED
PREASSEMBLES
PREASSEMBLING
PREASSEMBLY
PREASSES
PREASSIGN
PREASSIGNED
PREASSIGNING
PREASSIGNS
PREASSING
PREASSUMPTION
PREASSUMPTIONS
PREASSURANCE
PREASSURANCES
PREATOMIC
PREATTUNE
PREATTUNED
PREATTUNES
PREATTUNING
PREAUDIENCE
PREAUDIENCES
PREAUDIT
PREAUDITS
PREAVER
PREAVERRED
PREAVERRING
PREAVERS
PREAXIAL
PREAXIALLY
PREBAKE
PREBAKED
PREBAKES
PREBAKING
PREBASAL
PREBATTLE
PREBEND
PREBENDAL
PREBENDARIES
PREBENDARY

PREBENDS
PREBIBLICAL
PREBILL
PREBILLED
PREBILLING
PREBILLS
PREBIND
PREBINDING
PREBINDS
PREBIOLOGIC
PREBIOLOGICAL
PREBIOTIC
PREBLESS
PREBLESSED
PREBLESSES
PREBLESSING
PREBOIL
PREBOILED
PREBOILING
PREBOILS
PREBOOK
PREBOOKED
PREBOOKING
PREBOOKS
PREBOOM
PREBORN
PREBOUND
PREBREAKFAST
PREBUTTAL
PREBUTTALS
PRECALCULI
PRECALCULUS
PRECALCULUSES
PRECANCEL
PRECANCELED
PRECANCELING
PRECANCELLATION
PRECANCELLED
PRECANCELLING
PRECANCELS
PRECANCEROUS
PRECAPITALIST
PRECAPITALISTIC
PRECARIOUS
PRECARIOUSLY
PRECARIOUSNESS
PRECAST
PRECASTING
PRECASTS
PRECATIVE
PRECATORY
PRECAUTION
PRECAUTIONAL
PRECAUTIONARY
PRECAUTIONED
PRECAUTIONING

PRECAUTIONS
PRECAUTIOUS
PRECAVA
PRECAVAE
PRECAVAL
PRECEDE
PRECEDED
PRECEDENCE
PRECEDENCES
PRECEDENCIES
PRECEDENCY
PRECEDENT
PRECEDENTED
PRECEDENTIAL
PRECEDENTIALLY
PRECEDENTLY
PRECEDENTS
PRECEDES
PRECEDING
PRECEESE
PRECENSOR
PRECENSORED
PRECENSORING
PRECENSORS
PRECENT
PRECENTED
PRECENTING
PRECENTOR
PRECENTORIAL
PRECENTORS
PRECENTORSHIP
PRECENTORSHIPS
PRECENTRESS
PRECENTRESSES
PRECENTRIX
PRECENTRIXES
PRECENTS
PRECEPIT
PRECEPITS
PRECEPT
PRECEPTIAL
PRECEPTIVE
PRECEPTIVELY
PRECEPTOR
PRECEPTORAL
PRECEPTORATE
PRECEPTORATES
PRECEPTORIAL
PRECEPTORIALLY
PRECEPTORIALS
PRECEPTORIES
PRECEPTORS
PRECEPTORSHIP
PRECEPTORSHIPS
PRECEPTORY
PRECEPTRESS

PRECEPTRESSES
PRECEPTS
PRECESS
PRECESSED
PRECESSES
PRECESSING
PRECESSION
PRECESSIONAL
PRECESSIONALLY
PRECESSIONS
PRECHECK
PRECHECKED
PRECHECKING
PRECHECKS
PRECHILL
PRECHILLED
PRECHILLING
PRECHILLS
PRECHRISTIAN
PRECIEUSE
PRECIEUSES
PRECIEUX
PRECINCT
PRECINCTS
PRECIOSITIES
PRECIOSITY
PRECIOUS
PRECIOUSES
PRECIOUSLY
PRECIOUSNESS
PRECIOUSNESSES
PRECIPE
PRECIPES
PRECIPICE
PRECIPICED
PRECIPICES
PRECIPITABILITY
PRECIPITABLE
PRECIPITABLY
PRECIPITANCE
PRECIPITANCES
PRECIPITANCIES
PRECIPITANCY
PRECIPITANT
PRECIPITANTLY
PRECIPITANTNESS
PRECIPITANTS
PRECIPITATE
PRECIPITATED
PRECIPITATELY
PRECIPITATENESS
PRECIPITATES
PRECIPITATING
PRECIPITATION
PRECIPITATIONS
PRECIPITATIVE

PRECIPITATOR
PRECIPITATORS
PRECIPITIN
PRECIPITINOGEN
PRECIPITINOGENS
PRECIPITINS
PRECIPITOUS
PRECIPITOUSLY
PRECIPITOUSNESS
PRECIS
PRECISE
PRECISED
PRECISELY
PRECISENESS
PRECISENESSES
PRECISER
PRECISES
PRECISEST
PRECISIAN
PRECISIANISM
PRECISIANISMS
PRECISIANIST
PRECISIANISTS
PRECISIANS
PRECISING
PRECISION
PRECISIONISM
PRECISIONIST
PRECISIONISTS
PRECISIONS
PRECISIVE
PRECITED
PRECIVILISATION
PRECIVILIZATION
PRECLASSICAL
PRECLEAN
PRECLEANED
PRECLEANING
PRECLEANS
PRECLEAR
PRECLEARANCE
PRECLEARANCES
PRECLEARED
PRECLEARING
PRECLEARS
PRECLINICAL
PRECLINICALLY
PRECLUDABLE
PRECLUDE
PRECLUDED
PRECLUDES
PRECLUDING
PRECLUSION
PRECLUSIONS
PRECLUSIVE
PRECLUSIVELY

PRECOCIAL
PRECOCIALS
PRECOCIOUS
PRECOCIOUSLY
PRECOCIOUSNESS
PRECOCITIES
PRECOCITY
PRECODE
PRECODED
PRECODES
PRECODING
PRECOGITATE
PRECOGITATED
PRECOGITATES
PRECOGITATING
PRECOGITATION
PRECOGITATIONS
PRECOGNISANT
PRECOGNISE
PRECOGNISED
PRECOGNISES
PRECOGNISING
PRECOGNITION
PRECOGNITIONS
PRECOGNITIVE
PRECOGNIZANT
PRECOGNIZE
PRECOGNIZED
PRECOGNIZES
PRECOGNIZING
PRECOGNOSCE
PRECOGNOSCED
PRECOGNOSCES
PRECOGNOSCING
PRECOITAL
PRECOLLEGE
PRECOLLEGIATE
PRECOLONIAL
PRECOMBUSTION
PRECOMBUSTIONS
PRECOMMITMENT
PRECOMMITMENTS
PRECOMPETITIVE
PRECOMPOSE
PRECOMPOSED
PRECOMPOSES
PRECOMPOSING
PRECOMPUTE
PRECOMPUTED
PRECOMPUTER
PRECOMPUTES
PRECOMPUTING
PRECONCEIT
PRECONCEITS
PRECONCEIVE
PRECONCEIVED

PRECONCEIVES	PRECONSULTED	PREDACITIES	PREDESTINATES
PRECONCEIVING	PRECONSULTING	PREDACITY	PREDESTINATING
PRECONCEPTION	PRECONSULTS	PREDATE	PREDESTINATION
PRECONCEPTIONS	PRECONSUME	PREDATED	PREDESTINATIONS
PRECONCERT	PRECONSUMED	PREDATES	PREDESTINATIVE
PRECONCERTED	PRECONSUMES	PREDATING	PREDESTINATOR
PRECONCERTEDLY	PRECONSUMING	PREDATION	PREDESTINATORS
PRECONCERTING	PRECONTACT	PREDATIONS	PREDESTINE
PRECONCERTS	PRECONTRACT	PREDATIVE	PREDESTINED
PRECONCESSION	PRECONTRACTED	PREDATOR	PREDESTINES
PRECONCESSIONS	PRECONTRACTING	PREDATORILY	PREDESTINIES
PRECONCILIAR	PRECONTRACTS	PREDATORINESS	PREDESTINING
PRECONDEMN	PRECONTRIVE	PREDATORINESSES	PREDESTINY
PRECONDEMNATION	PRECONTRIVED	PREDATORS	PREDETERMINABLE
PRECONDEMNED	PRECONTRIVES	PREDATORY	PREDETERMINATE
PRECONDEMNING	PRECONTRIVING	PREDAWN	PREDETERMINE
PRECONDEMNS	PRECONVENTION	PREDAWNS	PREDETERMINED
PRECONDITION	PRECONVICTION	PREDECEASE	PREDETERMINER
PRECONDITIONED	PRECONVICTIONS	PREDECEASED	PREDETERMINERS
PRECONDITIONING	PRECOOK	PREDECEASES	PREDETERMINES
PRECONDITIONS	PRECOOKED	PREDECEASING	PREDETERMINING
PRECONISATION	PRECOOKING	PREDECESSOR	PREDETERMINISM
PRECONISATIONS	PRECOOKS	PREDECESSORS	PREDETERMINISMS
PRECONISE	PRECOOL	PREDEFINE	PREDEVALUATION
PRECONISED	PRECOOLED	PREDEFINED	PREDEVELOP
PRECONISES	PRECOOLING	PREDEFINES	PREDEVELOPED
PRECONISING	PRECOOLS	PREDEFINING	PREDEVELOPING
PRECONIZATION	PRECOPULATORY	PREDEFINITION	PREDEVELOPMENT
PRECONIZATIONS	PRECORDIAL	PREDEFINITIONS	PREDEVELOPMENTS
PRECONIZE	PRECOUP	PREDELIVERY	PREDEVELOPS
PRECONIZED	PRECRASH	PREDELLA	PREDEVOTE
PRECONIZES	PRECREASE	PREDELLAS	PREDIABETES
PRECONIZING	PRECREASED	PREDELLE	PREDIABETESES
PRECONJECTURE	PRECREASES	PREDENTATE	PREDIABETIC
PRECONJECTURED	PRECREASING	PREDEPARTURE	PREDIABETICS
PRECONJECTURES	PRECRISIS	PREDEPOSIT	PREDIAL
PRECONJECTURING	PRECRITICAL	PREDEPOSITED	PREDIALITY
PRECONNECTED	PRECURE	PREDEPOSITING	PREDIALLY
PRECONNECTING	PRECURED	PREDEPOSITS	PREDIALS
PRECONNECTION	PRECURES	PREDESIGN	PREDICABILITIES
PRECONNECTIONS	PRECURING	PREDESIGNATE	PREDICABILITY
PRECONNECTS	PRECURRER	PREDESIGNATED	PREDICABLE
PRECONQUEST	PRECURRERS	PREDESIGNATES	PREDICABLENESS
PRECONSCIOUS	PRECURSE	PREDESIGNATING	PREDICABLES
PRECONSCIOUSES	PRECURSES	PREDESIGNATION	PREDICAMENT
PRECONSCIOUSLY	PRECURSIVE	PREDESIGNATIONS	PREDICAMENTAL
PRECONSIDERED	PRECURSOR	PREDESIGNATORY	PREDICAMENTS
PRECONSIDERING	PRECURSORS	PREDESIGNED	PREDICANT
PRECONSIDERS	PRECURSORY	PREDESIGNING	PREDICANTS
PRECONSONANTAL	PRECUT	PREDESIGNS	PREDICATE
PRECONSTRUCT	PRECUTS	PREDESTINABLE	PREDICATED
PRECONSTRUCTED	PRECUTTING	PREDESTINABLY	PREDICATES
PRECONSTRUCTING	PREDACEOUS	PREDESTINARIAN	PREDICATING
PRECONSTRUCTION	PREDACEOUSNESS	PREDESTINARIANS	PREDICATION
PRECONSTRUCTS	PREDACIOUS	PREDESTINATE	PREDICATIONS
PRECONSULTATION	PREDACIOUSNESS	PREDESTINATED	PREDICATIVE

PREDICATIVELY
PREDICATOR
PREDICATORS
PREDICATORY
PREDICT
PREDICTABILITY
PREDICTABLE
PREDICTABLENESS
PREDICTABLY
PREDICTED
PREDICTER
PREDICTERS
PREDICTING
PREDICTION
PREDICTIONS
PREDICTIVE
PREDICTIVELY
PREDICTOR
PREDICTORS
PREDICTS
PREDIED
PREDIES
PREDIGEST
PREDIGESTED
PREDIGESTING
PREDIGESTION
PREDIGESTIONS
PREDIGESTS
PREDIKANT
PREDIKANTS
PREDILECT
PREDILECTED
PREDILECTION
PREDILECTIONS
PREDINNER
PREDISCHARGE
PREDISCOVERIES
PREDISCOVERY
PREDISPOSAL
PREDISPOSALS
PREDISPOSE
PREDISPOSED
PREDISPOSES
PREDISPOSING
PREDISPOSITION
PREDISPOSITIONS
PREDISSOLVE
PREDISSOLVED
PREDISSOLVES
PREDISSOLVING
PREDISTINGUISH
PREDIVE
PREDIVIDE
PREDIVIDED
PREDIVIDES
PREDIVIDING

PREDNISOLONE
PREDNISOLONES
PREDNISONE
PREDNISONES
PREDOCTORAL
PREDOMINANCE
PREDOMINANCES
PREDOMINANCIES
PREDOMINANCY
PREDOMINANT
PREDOMINANTLY
PREDOMINATE
PREDOMINATED
PREDOMINATELY
PREDOMINATES
PREDOMINATING
PREDOMINATION
PREDOMINATIONS
PREDOMINATOR
PREDOMINATORS
PREDOOM
PREDOOMED
PREDOOMING
PREDOOMS
PREDRILL
PREDRILLED
PREDRILLING
PREDRILLS
PREDUSK
PREDUSKS
PREDY
PREDYING
PREDYNASTIC
PREE
PREECLAMPSIA
PREECLAMPSIAS
PREECLAMPTIC
PREED
PREEDIT
PREEDITED
PREEDITING
PREEDITS
PREEING
PREELECT
PREELECTED
PREELECTING
PREELECTION
PREELECTRIC
PREELECTS
PREEMBARGO
PREEMERGENCE
PREEMERGENT
PREEMIE
PREEMIES
PREEMINENCE
PREEMINENCES

PREEMINENT
PREEMINENTLY
PREEMPLOYMENT
PREEMPT
PREEMPTED
PREEMPTING
PREEMPTION
PREEMPTIONS
PREEMPTIVE
PREEMPTIVELY
PREEMPTOR
PREEMPTORS
PREEMPTS
PREEN
PREENACT
PREENACTED
PREENACTING
PREENACTS
PREENED
PREENER
PREENERS
PREENING
PREENROLLMENT
PREENS
PREERECT
PREERECTED
PREERECTING
PREERECTS
PREES
PREESTABLISH
PREESTABLISHED
PREESTABLISHES
PREESTABLISHING
PREETHICAL
PREEVE
PREEVED
PREEVES
PREEVING
PREEXILIC
PREEXIST
PREEXISTED
PREEXISTENCE
PREEXISTENCES
PREEXISTENT
PREEXISTING
PREEXISTS
PREEXPERIMENT
PREFAB
PREFABBED
PREFABBING
PREFABRICATE
PREFABRICATED
PREFABRICATES
PREFABRICATING
PREFABRICATION
PREFABRICATIONS

PREFABRICATOR
PREFABRICATORS
PREFABS
PREFACE
PREFACED
PREFACER
PREFACERS
PREFACES
PREFACIAL
PREFACING
PREFADE
PREFADED
PREFADES
PREFADING
PREFARD
PREFASCIST
PREFATORIAL
PREFATORIALLY
PREFATORILY
PREFATORY
PREFECT
PREFECTORIAL
PREFECTS
PREFECTSHIP
PREFECTSHIPS
PREFECTURAL
PREFECTURE
PREFECTURES
PREFER
PREFERABILITIES
PREFERABILITY
PREFERABLE
PREFERABLENESS
PREFERABLY
PREFERENCE
PREFERENCES
PREFERENTIAL
PREFERENTIALISM
PREFERENTIALIST
PREFERENTIALITY
PREFERENTIALLY
PREFERMENT
PREFERMENTS
PREFERRABLE
PREFERRED
PREFERRER
PREFERRERS
PREFERRING
PREFERS
PREFEUDAL
PREFIGHT
PREFIGURATE
PREFIGURATED
PREFIGURATES
PREFIGURATING
PREFIGURATION

PREFIGURATIONS
PREFIGURATIVE
PREFIGURATIVELY
PREFIGURE
PREFIGURED
PREFIGUREMENT
PREFIGUREMENTS
PREFIGURES
PREFIGURING
PREFILE
PREFILED
PREFILES
PREFILING
PREFILLED
PREFINANCE
PREFINANCED
PREFINANCES
PREFINANCING
PREFIRE
PREFIRED
PREFIRES
PREFIRING
PREFIX
PREFIXABLE
PREFIXAL
PREFIXALLY
PREFIXED
PREFIXES
PREFIXING
PREFIXION
PREFIXIONS
PREFIXTURE
PREFIXTURES
PREFLAME
PREFLIGHT
PREFLORATION
PREFLORATIONS
PREFOCUS
PREFOCUSED
PREFOCUSES
PREFOCUSING
PREFOCUSSED
PREFOCUSSES
PREFOCUSSING
PREFOLIATION
PREFOLIATIONS
PREFORM
PREFORMAT
PREFORMATION
PREFORMATIONISM
PREFORMATIONIST
PREFORMATIONS
PREFORMATIVE
PREFORMATS
PREFORMATTED
PREFORMATTING

PREFORMED
PREFORMING
PREFORMS
PREFORMULATE
PREFORMULATED
PREFORMULATES
PREFORMULATING
PREFRANK
PREFRANKED
PREFRANKING
PREFRANKS
PREFREEZE
PREFREEZES
PREFREEZING
PREFRESHMAN
PREFRONTAL
PREFRONTALS
PREFROZE
PREFROZEN
PREFULGENT
PREGAME
PREGANGLIONIC
PREGENITAL
PREGGERS
PREGGY
PREGLACIAL
PREGLACIALLY
PREGNABILITIES
PREGNABILITY
PREGNABLE
PREGNANCE
PREGNANCES
PREGNANCIES
PREGNANCY
PREGNANT
PREGNANTLY
PREGNENOLONE
PREGNENOLONES
PREGUSTATION
PREGUSTATIONS
PREHALLUCES
PREHALLUX
PREHARDEN
PREHARDENED
PREHARDENING
PREHARDENS
PREHARVEST
PREHEADACHE
PREHEAT
PREHEATED
PREHEATER
PREHEATERS
PREHEATING
PREHEATS
PREHEMINENCE
PREHEMINENCES

PREHEND
PREHENDED
PREHENDING
PREHENDS
PREHENSIBLE
PREHENSILE
PREHENSILITIES
PREHENSILITY
PREHENSION
PREHENSIONS
PREHENSIVE
PREHENSOR
PREHENSORIAL
PREHENSORS
PREHENSORY
PREHIRING
PREHISTORIAN
PREHISTORIANS
PREHISTORIC
PREHISTORICAL
PREHISTORICALLY
PREHISTORIES
PREHISTORY
PREHNITE
PREHNITES
PREHOLIDAY
PREHOMINID
PREHOMINIDS
PREHUMAN
PREHUMANS
PREIF
PREIFE
PREIFES
PREIFS
PREIGNITION
PREIGNITIONS
PREIMPLANTATION
PREINAUGURAL
PREINDICATE
PREINDICATED
PREINDICATES
PREINDICATING
PREINDICATOR
PREINDICATORS
PREINDUCTION
PREINDUSTRIAL
PREINFORM
PREINFORMED
PREINFORMING
PREINFORMS
PREINSTRUCT
PREINSTRUCTED
PREINSTRUCTING
PREINSTRUCTION
PREINSTRUCTIONS
PREINSTRUCTS

PREINTERVIEW
PREINTERVIEWED
PREINTERVIEWING
PREINTERVIEWS
PREINVASION
PREJINK
PREJUDGE
PREJUDGED
PREJUDGEMENT
PREJUDGEMENTS
PREJUDGER
PREJUDGERS
PREJUDGES
PREJUDGING
PREJUDGMENT
PREJUDGMENTS
PREJUDICANT
PREJUDICATE
PREJUDICATED
PREJUDICATES
PREJUDICATING
PREJUDICATION
PREJUDICATIONS
PREJUDICATIVE
PREJUDICE
PREJUDICED
PREJUDICES
PREJUDICIAL
PREJUDICIALLY
PREJUDICIALNESS
PREJUDICING
PREJUDIZE
PREJUDIZES
PREKINDERGARTEN
PRELACIES
PRELACY
PRELAPSARIAN
PRELATE
PRELATES
PRELATESHIP
PRELATESHIPS
PRELATESS
PRELATESSES
PRELATIAL
PRELATIC
PRELATICAL
PRELATICALLY
PRELATIES
PRELATION
PRELATIONS
PRELATISE
PRELATISED
PRELATISES
PRELATISH
PRELATISING
PRELATISM

PRELATISMS
PRELATIST
PRELATISTS
PRELATIZE
PRELATIZED
PRELATIZES
PRELATIZING
PRELATURE
PRELATURES
PRELATY
PRELAUNCH
PRELECT
PRELECTED
PRELECTING
PRELECTION
PRELECTIONS
PRELECTOR
PRELECTORS
PRELECTS
PRELEGAL
PRELEXICAL
PRELEXICALLY
PRELIBATION
PRELIBATIONS
PRELIFE
PRELIM
PRELIMINARIES
PRELIMINARILY
PRELIMINARY
PRELIMIT
PRELIMITED
PRELIMITING
PRELIMITS
PRELIMS
PRELINGUAL
PRELINGUALLY
PRELITERACY
PRELITERARY
PRELITERATE
PRELITERATES
PRELIVES
PRELOCATE
PRELOCATED
PRELOCATES
PRELOCATING
PRELOCATION
PRELOCATIONS
PRELOGICAL
PRELOVED
PRELUDE
PRELUDED
PRELUDER
PRELUDERS
PRELUDES
PRELUDI
PRELUDIAL

PRELUDING
PRELUDIO
PRELUDIOUS
PRELUNCH
PRELUNCHEON
PRELUSION
PRELUSIONS
PRELUSIVE
PRELUSIVELY
PRELUSORILY
PRELUSORY
PREMADE
PREMALIGNANT
PREMAN
PREMANDIBULAR
PREMANDIBULARS
PREMANUFACTURE
PREMANUFACTURED
PREMANUFACTURES
PREMARITAL
PREMARITALLY
PREMARKET
PREMARKETING
PREMARRIAGE
PREMATURE
PREMATURELY
PREMATURENESS
PREMATURENESSES
PREMATURES
PREMATURITIES
PREMATURITY
PREMAXILLA
PREMAXILLAE
PREMAXILLARIES
PREMAXILLARY
PREMAXILLAS
PREMEAL
PREMEASURE
PREMEASURED
PREMEASURES
PREMEASURING
PREMED
PREMEDIC
PREMEDICAL
PREMEDICALLY
PREMEDICATE
PREMEDICATED
PREMEDICATES
PREMEDICATING
PREMEDICATION
PREMEDICATIONS
PREMEDICS
PREMEDIEVAL
PREMEDITATE
PREMEDITATED
PREMEDITATEDLY

PREMEDITATES
PREMEDITATING
PREMEDITATION
PREMEDITATIONS
PREMEDITATIVE
PREMEDITATOR
PREMEDITATORS
PREMEDS
PREMEET
PREMEIOTIC
PREMEN
PREMENOPAUSAL
PREMENSTRUAL
PREMENSTRUALLY
PREMERGER
PREMIA
PREMIE
PREMIER
PREMIERE
PREMIERED
PREMIERES
PREMIERING
PREMIERS
PREMIERSHIP
PREMIERSHIPS
PREMIES
PREMIGRATION
PREMILLENARIAN
PREMILLENARIANS
PREMILLENNIAL
PREMILLENNIALLY
PREMISE
PREMISED
PREMISES
PREMISING
PREMISS
PREMISSES
PREMIUM
PREMIUMS
PREMIX
PREMIXED
PREMIXES
PREMIXING
PREMIXT
PREMODERN
PREMODIFICATION
PREMODIFIED
PREMODIFIES
PREMODIFY
PREMODIFYING
PREMOISTEN
PREMOISTENED
PREMOISTENING
PREMOISTENS
PREMOLAR
PREMOLARS

PREMOLD
PREMOLDED
PREMOLDING
PREMOLDS
PREMOLT
PREMONISH
PREMONISHED
PREMONISHES
PREMONISHING
PREMONISHMENT
PREMONISHMENTS
PREMONITION
PREMONITIONS
PREMONITIVE
PREMONITOR
PREMONITORILY
PREMONITORS
PREMONITORY
PREMORAL
PREMORSE
PREMOSAIC
PREMOTION
PREMOTIONS
PREMOVE
PREMOVED
PREMOVEMENT
PREMOVEMENTS
PREMOVES
PREMOVING
PREMUNE
PREMUNITION
PREMUNITIONS
PREMY
PREMYCOTIC
PRENAME
PRENAMES
PRENASAL
PRENASALS
PRENATAL
PRENATALLY
PRENATALS
PRENEGOTIATE
PRENEGOTIATED
PRENEGOTIATES
PRENEGOTIATING
PRENEGOTIATION
PRENEGOTIATIONS
PRENOMEN
PRENOMENS
PRENOMINA
PRENOMINAL
PRENOMINALLY
PRENOMINATE
PRENOMINATED
PRENOMINATES
PRENOMINATING

PRENOMINATION
PRENOMINATIONS
PRENOON
PRENOTIFICATION
PRENOTIFIED
PRENOTIFIES
PRENOTIFY
PRENOTIFYING
PRENOTION
PRENOTIONS
PRENT
PRENTED
PRENTICE
PRENTICED
PRENTICES
PRENTICESHIP
PRENTICESHIPS
PRENTICING
PRENTING
PRENTS
PRENUBILE
PRENUMBER
PRENUMBERED
PRENUMBERING
PRENUMBERS
PRENUP
PRENUPS
PRENUPTIAL
PRENZIE
PREOCCUPANCIES
PREOCCUPANCY
PREOCCUPANT
PREOCCUPANTS
PREOCCUPATE
PREOCCUPATED
PREOCCUPATES
PREOCCUPATING
PREOCCUPATION
PREOCCUPATIONS
PREOCCUPIED
PREOCCUPIES
PREOCCUPY
PREOCCUPYING
PREOCULAR
PREOPENING
PREOPERATIONAL
PREOPERATIVE
PREOPERATIVELY
PREOPTION
PREOPTIONS
PREORAL
PREORDAIN
PREORDAINED
PREORDAINING
PREORDAINMENT
PREORDAINMENTS

PREORDAINS
PREORDER
PREORDERED
PREORDERING
PREORDERS
PREORDINANCE
PREORDINANCES
PREORDINATION
PREORDINATIONS
PREOVULATORY
PREP
PREPACK
PREPACKAGE
PREPACKAGED
PREPACKAGES
PREPACKAGING
PREPACKED
PREPACKING
PREPACKS
PREPAID
PREPALATAL
PREPARATION
PREPARATIONS
PREPARATIVE
PREPARATIVELY
PREPARATIVES
PREPARATOR
PREPARATORILY
PREPARATORS
PREPARATORY
PREPARE
PREPARED
PREPAREDLY
PREPAREDNESS
PREPAREDNESSES
PREPARER
PREPARERS
PREPARES
PREPARING
PREPASTE
PREPASTED
PREPASTES
PREPASTING
PREPAY
PREPAYABLE
PREPAYING
PREPAYMENT
PREPAYMENTS
PREPAYS
PREPENSE
PREPENSED
PREPENSELY
PREPENSES
PREPENSING
PREPENSIVE
PREPERFORMANCE

PREPILL
PREPLACE
PREPLACED
PREPLACES
PREPLACING
PREPLAN
PREPLANNED
PREPLANNING
PREPLANS
PREPLANT
PREPLANTING
PREPOLLENCE
PREPOLLENCES
PREPOLLENCIES
PREPOLLENCY
PREPOLLENT
PREPOLLEX
PREPOLLICES
PREPONDERANCE
PREPONDERANCES
PREPONDERANCIES
PREPONDERANCY
PREPONDERANT
PREPONDERANTLY
PREPONDERATE
PREPONDERATED
PREPONDERATELY
PREPONDERATES
PREPONDERATING
PREPONDERATION
PREPONDERATIONS
PREPONE
PREPONED
PREPONES
PREPONING
PREPORTION
PREPORTIONED
PREPORTIONING
PREPORTIONS
PREPOSE
PREPOSED
PREPOSES
PREPOSING
PREPOSITION
PREPOSITIONAL
PREPOSITIONALLY
PREPOSITIONS
PREPOSITIVE
PREPOSITIVELY
PREPOSITIVES
PREPOSITOR
PREPOSITORS
PREPOSSESS
PREPOSSESSED
PREPOSSESSES
PREPOSSESSING

PREPOSSESSINGLY
PREPOSSESSION
PREPOSSESSIONS
PREPOSTEROUS
PREPOSTEROUSLY
PREPOSTOR
PREPOSTORS
PREPOTENCE
PREPOTENCES
PREPOTENCIES
PREPOTENCY
PREPOTENT
PREPOTENTLY
PREPPED
PREPPIE
PREPPIER
PREPPIES
PREPPIEST
PREPPILY
PREPPINESS
PREPPINESSES
PREPPING
PREPPY
PREPRANDIAL
PREPREG
PREPREGS
PREPREPARED
PREPRESIDENTIAL
PREPRICE
PREPRICED
PREPRICES
PREPRICING
PREPRIMARIES
PREPRIMARY
PREPRINT
PREPRINTED
PREPRINTING
PREPRINTS
PREPROCESS
PREPROCESSED
PREPROCESSES
PREPROCESSING
PREPROCESSOR
PREPROCESSORS
PREPRODUCTION
PREPRODUCTIONS
PREPROFESSIONAL
PREPROGRAM
PREPROGRAMED
PREPROGRAMING
PREPROGRAMMED
PREPROGRAMMING
PREPROGRAMS
PREPS
PREPSYCHEDELIC
PREPUBERAL

PREPUBERTAL
PREPUBERTIES
PREPUBERTY
PREPUBESCENCE
PREPUBESCENCES
PREPUBESCENT
PREPUBESCENTS
PREPUBLICATION
PREPUBLICATIONS
PREPUCE
PREPUCES
PREPUNCH
PREPUNCHED
PREPUNCHES
PREPUNCHING
PREPUNCTUAL
PREPUPAL
PREPURCHASE
PREPURCHASED
PREPURCHASES
PREPURCHASING
PREPUTIAL
PREQUALIFIED
PREQUALIFIES
PREQUALIFY
PREQUALIFYING
PREQUEL
PREQUELS
PRERACE
PREREADING
PREREADINGS
PRERECESSION
PRERECORD
PRERECORDED
PRERECORDING
PRERECORDS
PREREGISTER
PREREGISTERED
PREREGISTERING
PREREGISTERS
PREREGISTRATION
PREREHEARSAL
PRERELEASE
PRERELEASED
PRERELEASES
PRERELEASING
PRERENAL
PREREQUIRE
PREREQUIRED
PREREQUIRES
PREREQUIRING
PREREQUISITE
PREREQUISITES
PRERETIREMENT
PRERETURN
PREREVIEW

PREREVISIONIST
PREREVOLUTION
PRERINSE
PRERINSES
PRERIOT
PREROCK
PREROGATIVE
PREROGATIVED
PREROGATIVELY
PREROGATIVES
PREROMANTIC
PREROSIONS
PRERUPT
PRESA
PRESAGE
PRESAGED
PRESAGEFUL
PRESAGEFULLY
PRESAGEMENT
PRESAGEMENTS
PRESAGER
PRESAGERS
PRESAGES
PRESAGING
PRESALE
PRESANCTIFIED
PRESANCTIFIES
PRESANCTIFY
PRESANCTIFYING
PRESBYACOUSES
PRESBYACOUSIS
PRESBYACUSES
PRESBYACUSIS
PRESBYCOUSES
PRESBYCOUSIS
PRESBYCUSES
PRESBYCUSIS
PRESBYOPE
PRESBYOPES
PRESBYOPIA
PRESBYOPIAS
PRESBYOPIC
PRESBYOPICS
PRESBYOPIES
PRESBYOPY
PRESBYTE
PRESBYTER
PRESBYTERAL
PRESBYTERATE
PRESBYTERATES
PRESBYTERIAL
PRESBYTERIALLY
PRESBYTERIALS
PRESBYTERIAN
PRESBYTERIANISE
PRESBYTERIANISM

PRESBYTERIANIZE
PRESBYTERIANS
PRESBYTERIES
PRESBYTERS
PRESBYTERSHIP
PRESBYTERSHIPS
PRESBYTERY
PRESBYTES
PRESBYTIC
PRESBYTISM
PRESBYTISMS
PRESCHEDULE
PRESCHEDULED
PRESCHEDULES
PRESCHEDULING
PRESCHOOL
PRESCHOOLER
PRESCHOOLERS
PRESCHOOLS
PRESCIENCE
PRESCIENCES
PRESCIENT
PRESCIENTIFIC
PRESCIENTLY
PRESCIND
PRESCINDED
PRESCINDENT
PRESCINDING
PRESCINDS
PRESCIOUS
PRESCISSION
PRESCISSIONS
PRESCORE
PRESCORED
PRESCORES
PRESCORING
PRESCREEN
PRESCREENED
PRESCREENING
PRESCREENS
PRESCRIBE
PRESCRIBED
PRESCRIBER
PRESCRIBERS
PRESCRIBES
PRESCRIBING
PRESCRIPT
PRESCRIPTIBLE
PRESCRIPTION
PRESCRIPTIONS
PRESCRIPTIVE
PRESCRIPTIVELY
PRESCRIPTIVISM
PRESCRIPTIVISMS
PRESCRIPTIVIST
PRESCRIPTIVISTS

PRESCRIPTS
PRESCUTA
PRESCUTUM
PRESE
PRESEASON
PRESEASONAL
PRESEASONALLY
PRESELECT
PRESELECTED
PRESELECTING
PRESELECTION
PRESELECTIONS
PRESELECTOR
PRESELECTORS
PRESELECTS
PRESELL
PRESELLING
PRESELLS
PRESENCE
PRESENCES
PRESENILE
PRESENILITY
PRESENSION
PRESENSIONS
PRESENT
PRESENTABILITY
PRESENTABLE
PRESENTABLENESS
PRESENTABLY
PRESENTATION
PRESENTATIONAL
PRESENTATIONISM
PRESENTATIONIST
PRESENTATIONS
PRESENTATIVE
PRESENTED
PRESENTEE
PRESENTEEISM
PRESENTEES
PRESENTENCE
PRESENTENCED
PRESENTENCES
PRESENTENCING
PRESENTER
PRESENTERS
PRESENTIAL
PRESENTIALITIES
PRESENTIALITY
PRESENTIALLY
PRESENTIENT
PRESENTIMENT
PRESENTIMENTAL
PRESENTIMENTS
PRESENTING
PRESENTISM
PRESENTISMS

PRESENTIST
PRESENTIVE
PRESENTIVENESS
PRESENTLY
PRESENTMENT
PRESENTMENTS
PRESENTNESS
PRESENTNESSES
PRESENTS
PRESERVABILITY
PRESERVABLE
PRESERVABLY
PRESERVATION
PRESERVATIONIST
PRESERVATIONS
PRESERVATIVE
PRESERVATIVES
PRESERVATORIES
PRESERVATORY
PRESERVE
PRESERVED
PRESERVER
PRESERVERS
PRESERVES
PRESERVICE
PRESERVING
PRESES
PRESET
PRESETS
PRESETTING
PRESETTLEMENT
PRESHAPE
PRESHAPED
PRESHAPES
PRESHAPING
PRESHOW
PRESHOWED
PRESHOWING
PRESHOWN
PRESHOWS
PRESHRANK
PRESHRINK
PRESHRINKING
PRESHRINKS
PRESHRUNK
PRESHRUNKEN
PRESIDE
PRESIDED
PRESIDENCIES
PRESIDENCY
PRESIDENT
PRESIDENTESS
PRESIDENTESSES
PRESIDENTIAL
PRESIDENTIALLY
PRESIDENTS

PRESIDENTSHIP
PRESIDENTSHIPS
PRESIDER
PRESIDERS
PRESIDES
PRESIDIA
PRESIDIAL
PRESIDIARY
PRESIDING
PRESIDIO
PRESIDIOS
PRESIDIUM
PRESIDIUMS
PRESIFT
PRESIFTED
PRESIFTING
PRESIFTS
PRESIGNIFIED
PRESIGNIFIES
PRESIGNIFY
PRESIGNIFYING
PRESLAUGHTER
PRESLEEP
PRESLICE
PRESLICED
PRESLICES
PRESLICING
PRESOAK
PRESOAKED
PRESOAKING
PRESOAKS
PRESOLD
PRESONG
PRESORT
PRESORTED
PRESORTING
PRESORTS
PRESPECIFIED
PRESPECIFIES
PRESPECIFY
PRESPECIFYING
PRESPLIT
PRESS
PRESSBOARD
PRESSBOARDS
PRESSED
PRESSER
PRESSERS
PRESSES
PRESSFAT
PRESSFATS
PRESSFUL
PRESSFULS
PRESSIE
PRESSIES
PRESSING

PRESSINGLY
PRESSINGNESS
PRESSINGS
PRESSION
PRESSIONS
PRESSMAN
PRESSMARK
PRESSMARKS
PRESSMEN
PRESSOR
PRESSORS
PRESSROOM
PRESSROOMS
PRESSRUN
PRESSRUNS
PRESSURE
PRESSURED
PRESSURELESS
PRESSURES
PRESSURING
PRESSURISATION
PRESSURISATIONS
PRESSURISE
PRESSURISED
PRESSURISER
PRESSURISERS
PRESSURISES
PRESSURISING
PRESSURIZATION
PRESSURIZATIONS
PRESSURIZE
PRESSURIZED
PRESSURIZER
PRESSURIZERS
PRESSURIZES
PRESSURIZING
PRESSWOMAN
PRESSWOMEN
PRESSWORK
PRESSWORKS
PREST
PRESTAMP
PRESTAMPED
PRESTAMPING
PRESTAMPS
PRESTATION
PRESTATIONS
PRESTED
PRESTER
PRESTERILIZE
PRESTERILIZED
PRESTERILIZES
PRESTERILIZING
PRESTERNA
PRESTERNUM
PRESTERNUMS

PRESTERS
PRESTIDIGITATOR
PRESTIGE
PRESTIGEFUL
PRESTIGES
PRESTIGIATOR
PRESTIGIATORS
PRESTIGIOUS
PRESTIGIOUSLY
PRESTIGIOUSNESS
PRESTING
PRESTISSIMO
PRESTISSIMOS
PRESTO
PRESTORAGE
PRESTOS
PRESTRESS
PRESTRESSED
PRESTRESSES
PRESTRESSING
PRESTRICTION
PRESTRICTIONS
PRESTRIKE
PRESTRUCTURE
PRESTRUCTURED
PRESTRUCTURES
PRESTRUCTURING
PRESTS
PRESUMABLE
PRESUMABLY
PRESUME
PRESUMED
PRESUMEDLY
PRESUMER
PRESUMERS
PRESUMES
PRESUMING
PRESUMINGLY
PRESUMMIT
PRESUMPTION
PRESUMPTIONS
PRESUMPTIVE
PRESUMPTIVELY
PRESUMPTIVENESS
PRESUMPTUOUS
PRESUMPTUOUSLY
PRESUPPOSE
PRESUPPOSED
PRESUPPOSES
PRESUPPOSING
PRESUPPOSITION
PRESUPPOSITIONS
PRESURGERY
PRESURGICAL
PRESURGICALLY
PRESURMISE

PRESURMISES
PRESWEETEN
PRESWEETENED
PRESWEETENING
PRESWEETENS
PRESYMPTOMATIC
PRESYNAPTIC
PRESYNAPTICALLY
PRETAPE
PRETAPED
PRETAPES
PRETAPING
PRETASTE
PRETASTED
PRETASTES
PRETASTING
PRETAX
PRETEEN
PRETEENS
PRETELEVISION
PRETENCE
PRETENCELESS
PRETENCES
PRETEND
PRETENDANT
PRETENDANTS
PRETENDED
PRETENDEDLY
PRETENDENT
PRETENDENTS
PRETENDER
PRETENDERS
PRETENDERSHIP
PRETENDERSHIPS
PRETENDING
PRETENDINGLY
PRETENDS
PRETENSE
PRETENSES
PRETENSION
PRETENSIONED
PRETENSIONING
PRETENSIONLESS
PRETENSIONS
PRETENSIVE
PRETENSIVELY
PRETENTIOUS
PRETENTIOUSLY
PRETENTIOUSNESS
PRETERHUMAN
PRETERIST
PRETERISTS
PRETERIT
PRETERITE
PRETERITENESS
PRETERITENESSES

PRETERITES
PRETERITION
PRETERITIONS
PRETERITIVE
PRETERITS
PRETERM
PRETERMINAL
PRETERMINATION
PRETERMINATIONS
PRETERMISSION
PRETERMISSIONS
PRETERMIT
PRETERMITS
PRETERMITTED
PRETERMITTER
PRETERMITTERS
PRETERMITTING
PRETERNATURAL
PRETERNATURALLY
PRETERPERFECT
PRETERPERFECTS
PRETEST
PRETESTED
PRETESTING
PRETESTS
PRETEXT
PRETEXTED
PRETEXTING
PRETEXTS
PRETHEATER
PRETONIC
PRETONICALLY
PRETOR
PRETORIAL
PRETORIAN
PRETORIANS
PRETORS
PRETORSHIP
PRETOURNAMENT
PRETRAIN
PRETRAINED
PRETRAINING
PRETRAINS
PRETRAVEL
PRETREAT
PRETREATED
PRETREATING
PRETREATMENT
PRETREATMENTS
PRETREATS
PRETRIAL
PRETRIALS
PRETRIM
PRETRIMMED
PRETRIMMING
PRETRIMS

PRETTIED
PRETTIER
PRETTIES
PRETTIEST
PRETTIFICATION
PRETTIFICATIONS
PRETTIFIED
PRETTIFIER
PRETTIFIERS
PRETTIFIES
PRETTIFY
PRETTIFYING
PRETTILY
PRETTINESS
PRETTINESSES
PRETTY
PRETTYING
PRETTYISH
PRETTYISM
PRETTYISMS
PRETYPE
PRETYPED
PRETYPES
PRETYPING
PRETZEL
PRETZELS
PREUNIFICATION
PREUNION
PREUNIONS
PREUNITE
PREUNITED
PREUNITES
PREUNITING
PREUNIVERSITY
PREVAIL
PREVAILED
PREVAILER
PREVAILERS
PREVAILING
PREVAILINGLY
PREVAILMENT
PREVAILMENTS
PREVAILS
PREVALENCE
PREVALENCES
PREVALENCIES
PREVALENCY
PREVALENT
PREVALENTLY
PREVALENTNESS
PREVALENTS
PREVARICATE
PREVARICATED
PREVARICATES
PREVARICATING
PREVARICATION

PREVARICATIONS
PREVARICATOR
PREVARICATORS
PREVE
PREVED
PREVENANCIES
PREVENANCY
PREVENE
PREVENED
PREVENES
PREVENIENCE
PREVENIENCES
PREVENIENT
PREVENIENTLY
PREVENING
PREVENT
PREVENTABILITY
PREVENTABLE
PREVENTABLY
PREVENTATIVE
PREVENTATIVES
PREVENTED
PREVENTER
PREVENTERS
PREVENTIBILITY
PREVENTIBLE
PREVENTIBLY
PREVENTING
PREVENTION
PREVENTIONS
PREVENTIVE
PREVENTIVELY
PREVENTIVENESS
PREVENTIVES
PREVENTS
PREVERB
PREVERBAL
PREVERBS
PREVES
PREVIABLE
PREVIEW
PREVIEWED
PREVIEWER
PREVIEWERS
PREVIEWING
PREVIEWS
PREVING
PREVIOUS
PREVIOUSLY
PREVIOUSNESS
PREVIOUSNESSES
PREVISE
PREVISED
PREVISES
PREVISING
PREVISION

PREVISIONAL	PRIAPIC	PRIDING	PRIMA
PREVISIONARY	PRIAPISM	PRIED	PRIMACIES
PREVISIONED	PRIAPISMS	PRIEDIEU	PRIMACY
PREVISIONING	PRIAPUS	PRIEDIEUS	PRIMAEVAL
PREVISIONS	PRIAPUSES	PRIEDIEUX	PRIMAEVALLY
PREVISOR	PRIBBLE	PRIEF	PRIMAGE
PREVISORS	PRIBBLES	PRIEFE	PRIMAGES
PREVOCALIC	PRICE	PRIEFES	PRIMAL
PREVOCALICALLY	PRICED	PRIEFS	PRIMALITIES
PREVOCATIONAL	PRICELESS	PRIER	PRIMALITY
PREVUE	PRICELESSLY	PRIERS	PRIMALLY
PREVUED	PRICELESSNESS	PRIES	PRIMAQUINE
PREVUES	PRICELESSNESSES	PRIEST	PRIMARIES
PREVUING	PRICER	PRIESTCRAFT	PRIMARILY
PREWAR	PRICERS	PRIESTCRAFTS	PRIMARINESS
PREWARM	PRICES	PRIESTED	PRIMARINESSES
PREWARMED	PRICEY	PRIESTESS	PRIMARY
PREWARMING	PRICIER	PRIESTESSES	PRIMAS
PREWARMS	PRICIEST	PRIESTHOOD	PRIMATAL
PREWARN	PRICINESS	PRIESTHOODS	PRIMATALS
PREWARNED	PRICINESSES	PRIESTING	PRIMATE
PREWARNING	PRICING	PRIESTLIER	PRIMATES
PREWARNS	PRICK	PRIESTLIEST	PRIMATESHIP
PREWASH	PRICKED	PRIESTLIKE	PRIMATESHIPS
PREWASHED	PRICKER	PRIESTLINESS	PRIMATIAL
PREWASHES	PRICKERS	PRIESTLINESSES	PRIMATIC
PREWASHING	PRICKET	PRIESTLING	PRIMATICAL
PREWEANING	PRICKETS	PRIESTLINGS	PRIMATOLOGICAL
PREWORK	PRICKIER	PRIESTLY	PRIMATOLOGIES
PREWRAP	PRICKIEST	PRIESTS	PRIMATOLOGIST
PREWRAPPED	PRICKING	PRIESTSHIP	PRIMATOLOGISTS
PREWRAPPING	PRICKINGS	PRIESTSHIPS	PRIMATOLOGY
PREWRAPS	PRICKLE	PRIEVE	PRIME
PREWRITING	PRICKLED	PRIEVED	PRIMED
PREWRITINGS	PRICKLES	PRIEVES	PRIMELY
PREWYN	PRICKLIER	PRIEVING	PRIMENESS
PREWYNS	PRICKLIEST	PRIG	PRIMENESSES
PREX	PRICKLINESS	PRIGGED	PRIMER
PREXES	PRICKLINESSES	PRIGGER	PRIMERO
PREXIES	PRICKLING	PRIGGERIES	PRIMEROS
PREXY	PRICKLINGS	PRIGGERS	PRIMERS
PREY	PRICKLY	PRIGGERY	PRIMES
PREYED	PRICKS	PRIGGING	PRIMETIME
PREYER	PRICKWOOD	PRIGGINGS	PRIMEUR
PREYERS	PRICKWOODS	PRIGGISH	PRIMEURS
PREYFUL	PRICKY	PRIGGISHLY	PRIMEVAL
PREYING	PRICY	PRIGGISHNESS	PRIMEVALLY
PREYS	PRIDE	PRIGGISHNESSES	PRIMI
PREZ	PRIDED	PRIGGISM	PRIMIGENIAL
PREZES	PRIDEFUL	PRIGGISMS	PRIMIGRAVIDA
PREZZIE	PRIDEFULLY	PRIGS	PRIMIGRAVIDAE
PREZZIES	PRIDEFULNESS	PRILL	PRIMIGRAVIDAS
PRIAL	PRIDEFULNESSES	PRILLED	PRIMINE
PRIALS	PRIDELESS	PRILLING	PRIMINES
PRIAPEAN	PRIDES	PRILLS	PRIMING
PRIAPI	PRIDIAN	PRIM	PRIMINGS

PRIMIPARA
PRIMIPARAE
PRIMIPARAS
PRIMIPARITIES
PRIMIPARITY
PRIMIPAROUS
PRIMITIAE
PRIMITIAL
PRIMITIAS
PRIMITIVE
PRIMITIVELY
PRIMITIVENESS
PRIMITIVENESSES
PRIMITIVES
PRIMITIVISM
PRIMITIVISMS
PRIMITIVIST
PRIMITIVISTIC
PRIMITIVISTS
PRIMITIVITIES
PRIMITIVITY
PRIMLY
PRIMMED
PRIMMER
PRIMMERS
PRIMMEST
PRIMMING
PRIMNESS
PRIMNESSES
PRIMO
PRIMOGENIAL
PRIMOGENIT
PRIMOGENITAL
PRIMOGENITARY
PRIMOGENITIVE
PRIMOGENITIVES
PRIMOGENITOR
PRIMOGENITORS
PRIMOGENITRIX
PRIMOGENITRIXES
PRIMOGENITS
PRIMOGENITURE
PRIMOGENITURES
PRIMORDIA
PRIMORDIAL
PRIMORDIALISM
PRIMORDIALISMS
PRIMORDIALITIES
PRIMORDIALITY
PRIMORDIALLY
PRIMORDIALS
PRIMORDIUM
PRIMOS
PRIMP
PRIMPED
PRIMPING

PRIMPS
PRIMROSE
PRIMROSED
PRIMROSES
PRIMROSING
PRIMROSY
PRIMS
PRIMSIE
PRIMSIER
PRIMSIEST
PRIMULA
PRIMULACEOUS
PRIMULAS
PRIMULINE
PRIMULINES
PRIMUS
PRIMUSES
PRIMY
PRINCE
PRINCED
PRINCEDOM
PRINCEDOMS
PRINCEHOOD
PRINCEHOODS
PRINCEKIN
PRINCEKINS
PRINCELET
PRINCELETS
PRINCELIER
PRINCELIEST
PRINCELIKE
PRINCELINESS
PRINCELINESSES
PRINCELING
PRINCELINGS
PRINCELY
PRINCES
PRINCESHIP
PRINCESHIPS
PRINCESS
PRINCESSE
PRINCESSES
PRINCESSLY
PRINCIFIED
PRINCING
PRINCIPAL
PRINCIPALITIES
PRINCIPALITY
PRINCIPALLY
PRINCIPALNESS
PRINCIPALNESSES
PRINCIPALS
PRINCIPALSHIP
PRINCIPALSHIPS
PRINCIPATE
PRINCIPATES

PRINCIPE
PRINCIPI
PRINCIPIA
PRINCIPIAL
PRINCIPIUM
PRINCIPLE
PRINCIPLED
PRINCIPLES
PRINCIPLING
PRINCOCK
PRINCOCKS
PRINCOX
PRINCOXES
PRINK
PRINKED
PRINKER
PRINKERS
PRINKING
PRINKS
PRINT
PRINTABILITIES
PRINTABILITY
PRINTABLE
PRINTABLENESS
PRINTED
PRINTER
PRINTERIES
PRINTERS
PRINTERY
PRINTHEAD
PRINTHEADS
PRINTING
PRINTINGS
PRINTLESS
PRINTMAKER
PRINTMAKERS
PRINTMAKING
PRINTMAKINGS
PRINTOUT
PRINTOUTS
PRINTS
PRINTWHEEL
PRINTWHEELS
PRINTWORKS
PRION
PRIONS
PRIOR
PRIORATE
PRIORATES
PRIORESS
PRIORESSES
PRIORIES
PRIORITIES
PRIORITISATION
PRIORITISATIONS
PRIORITISE

PRIORITISED
PRIORITISES
PRIORITISING
PRIORITIZATION
PRIORITIZATIONS
PRIORITIZE
PRIORITIZED
PRIORITIZES
PRIORITIZING
PRIORITY
PRIORLY
PRIORS
PRIORSHIP
PRIORSHIPS
PRIORY
PRISAGE
PRISAGES
PRISE
PRISED
PRISER
PRISERE
PRISERES
PRISERS
PRISES
PRISING
PRISM
PRISMATIC
PRISMATICAL
PRISMATICALLY
PRISMATOID
PRISMATOIDAL
PRISMATOIDS
PRISMOID
PRISMOIDAL
PRISMOIDS
PRISMS
PRISMY
PRISON
PRISONED
PRISONER
PRISONERS
PRISONING
PRISONMENT
PRISONMENTS
PRISONOUS
PRISONS
PRISS
PRISSED
PRISSES
PRISSIER
PRISSIES
PRISSIEST
PRISSILY
PRISSINESS
PRISSINESSES
PRISSING

PRISSY
PRISTANE
PRISTANES
PRISTINE
PRISTINELY
PRITHEE
PRIVACIES
PRIVACY
PRIVADO
PRIVADOES
PRIVADOS
PRIVATDOCENT
PRIVATDOCENTS
PRIVATDOZENT
PRIVATDOZENTS
PRIVATE
PRIVATEER
PRIVATEERED
PRIVATEERING
PRIVATEERINGS
PRIVATEERS
PRIVATEERSMAN
PRIVATEERSMEN
PRIVATELY
PRIVATENESS
PRIVATENESSES
PRIVATER
PRIVATES
PRIVATEST
PRIVATION
PRIVATIONS
PRIVATISATION
PRIVATISATIONS
PRIVATISE
PRIVATISED
PRIVATISER
PRIVATISERS
PRIVATISES
PRIVATISING
PRIVATISM
PRIVATISMS
PRIVATIVE
PRIVATIVELY
PRIVATIVES
PRIVATIZATION
PRIVATIZATIONS
PRIVATIZE
PRIVATIZED
PRIVATIZER
PRIVATIZERS
PRIVATIZES
PRIVATIZING
PRIVET
PRIVETS
PRIVIER
PRIVIES

PRIVIEST
PRIVILEGE
PRIVILEGED
PRIVILEGES
PRIVILEGING
PRIVILY
PRIVITIES
PRIVITY
PRIVY
PRIZABLE
PRIZE
PRIZED
PRIZEFIGHT
PRIZEFIGHTER
PRIZEFIGHTERS
PRIZEFIGHTING
PRIZEFIGHTINGS
PRIZEFIGHTS
PRIZEMAN
PRIZEMEN
PRIZER
PRIZERS
PRIZES
PRIZEWINNER
PRIZEWINNERS
PRIZEWINNING
PRIZEWOMAN
PRIZEWOMEN
PRIZING
PRO
PROA
PROABOLITION
PROABOLITIONIST
PROABORTION
PROACTION
PROACTIVE
PROAIRESES
PROAIRESIS
PROAMENDMENT
PROANNEXATION
PROAPPROVAL
PROARBITRATION
PROAS
PROAUTOMATION
PROB
PROBABILIORISM
PROBABILIORISMS
PROBABILIORIST
PROBABILIORISTS
PROBABILISM
PROBABILISMS
PROBABILIST
PROBABILISTIC
PROBABILISTS
PROBABILITIES
PROBABILITY

PROBABLE
PROBABLES
PROBABLY
PROBALL
PROBAND
PROBANDS
PROBANG
PROBANGS
PROBATE
PROBATED
PROBATES
PROBATING
PROBATION
PROBATIONAL
PROBATIONALLY
PROBATIONARIES
PROBATIONARY
PROBATIONER
PROBATIONERS
PROBATIONERSHIP
PROBATIONS
PROBATIVE
PROBATIVELY
PROBATORY
PROBE
PROBEABLE
PROBED
PROBENECID
PROBENECIDS
PROBER
PROBERS
PROBES
PROBIBLICAL
PROBIBLICALLY
PROBING
PROBIOTIC
PROBIOTICS
PROBIT
PROBITIES
PROBITS
PROBITY
PROBLEM
PROBLEMATIC
PROBLEMATICAL
PROBLEMATICALLY
PROBLEMATICS
PROBLEMIST
PROBLEMISTS
PROBLEMS
PROBOSCIDEAN
PROBOSCIDEANS
PROBOSCIDES
PROBOSCIDIAN
PROBOSCIDIANS
PROBOSCIS
PROBOSCISES

PROBOULEUTIC
PROBS
PROBUSINESS
PROCACIOUS
PROCACITIES
PROCACITY
PROCAINE
PROCAINES
PROCAMBIA
PROCAMBIAL
PROCAMBIUM
PROCAMBIUMS
PROCAPITALIST
PROCAPITALISTIC
PROCAPITALISTS
PROCARBAZINE
PROCARBAZINES
PROCARP
PROCARPS
PROCARYON
PROCARYONS
PROCARYOTE
PROCARYOTES
PROCARYOTIC
PROCATHEDRAL
PROCATHEDRALS
PROCEDURAL
PROCEDURALLY
PROCEDURALS
PROCEDURE
PROCEDURES
PROCEED
PROCEEDED
PROCEEDER
PROCEEDERS
PROCEEDING
PROCEEDINGS
PROCEEDS
PROCELEUSMATIC
PROCELEUSMATICS
PROCELLARIAN
PROCEPHALIC
PROCERCOID
PROCERCOIDS
PROCEREBRA
PROCEREBRAL
PROCEREBRUM
PROCEREBRUMS
PROCERITIES
PROCERITY
PROCESS
PROCESSABILITY
PROCESSABLE
PROCESSED
PROCESSES
PROCESSIBILITY

PROCESSIBLE
PROCESSING
PROCESSION
PROCESSIONAL
PROCESSIONALIST
PROCESSIONALLY
PROCESSIONALS
PROCESSIONARY
PROCESSIONED
PROCESSIONER
PROCESSIONERS
PROCESSIONING
PROCESSIONINGS
PROCESSIONS
PROCESSOR
PROCESSORS
PROCESSUAL
PROCHAIN
PROCHEIN
PROCHRONISM
PROCHRONISMS
PROCHURCH
PROCIDENCE
PROCIDENCES
PROCIDENT
PROCINCT
PROCINCTS
PROCLAIM
PROCLAIMANT
PROCLAIMANTS
PROCLAIMED
PROCLAIMER
PROCLAIMERS
PROCLAIMING
PROCLAIMS
PROCLAMATION
PROCLAMATIONS
PROCLAMATORY
PROCLERICAL
PROCLISES
PROCLISIS
PROCLITIC
PROCLITICS
PROCLIVE
PROCLIVITIES
PROCLIVITY
PROCOELOUS
PROCONSCRIPTION
PROCONSERVATION
PROCONSUL
PROCONSULAR
PROCONSULATE
PROCONSULATES
PROCONSULS
PROCONSULSHIP
PROCONSULSHIPS

PROCRASTINATE
PROCRASTINATED
PROCRASTINATES
PROCRASTINATING
PROCRASTINATION
PROCRASTINATIVE
PROCRASTINATOR
PROCRASTINATORS
PROCRASTINATORY
PROCREANT
PROCREANTS
PROCREATE
PROCREATED
PROCREATES
PROCREATING
PROCREATION
PROCREATIONAL
PROCREATIONS
PROCREATIVE
PROCREATIVENESS
PROCREATOR
PROCREATORS
PROCRUSTEAN
PROCRYPSES
PROCRYPSIS
PROCRYPTIC
PROCRYPTICALLY
PROCTAL
PROCTALGIA
PROCTALGIAS
PROCTITIS
PROCTITISES
PROCTODAEA
PROCTODAEAL
PROCTODAEUM
PROCTODAEUMS
PROCTOLOGIC
PROCTOLOGICAL
PROCTOLOGIES
PROCTOLOGIST
PROCTOLOGISTS
PROCTOLOGY
PROCTOR
PROCTORAGE
PROCTORAGES
PROCTORED
PROCTORIAL
PROCTORIALLY
PROCTORING
PROCTORISE
PROCTORISED
PROCTORISES
PROCTORISING
PROCTORIZE
PROCTORIZED
PROCTORIZES

PROCTORIZING
PROCTORS
PROCTORSHIP
PROCTORSHIPS
PROCTOSCOPE
PROCTOSCOPES
PROCTOSCOPIC
PROCTOSCOPIES
PROCTOSCOPY
PROCUMBENT
PROCURABILITY
PROCURABLE
PROCURACIES
PROCURACY
PROCURAL
PROCURALS
PROCURANCE
PROCURANCES
PROCURATION
PROCURATIONS
PROCURATOR
PROCURATORIAL
PROCURATORIES
PROCURATORS
PROCURATORSHIP
PROCURATORSHIPS
PROCURATORY
PROCURE
PROCURED
PROCUREMENT
PROCUREMENTS
PROCURER
PROCURERS
PROCURES
PROCURESS
PROCURESSES
PROCUREUR
PROCUREURS
PROCURING
PROD
PRODDED
PRODDER
PRODDERS
PRODDING
PRODEMOCRATIC
PRODIGAL
PRODIGALISE
PRODIGALISED
PRODIGALISES
PRODIGALISING
PRODIGALITIES
PRODIGALITY
PRODIGALIZE
PRODIGALIZED
PRODIGALIZES
PRODIGALIZING

PRODIGALLY
PRODIGALS
PRODIGIES
PRODIGIOSITIES
PRODIGIOSITY
PRODIGIOUS
PRODIGIOUSLY
PRODIGIOUSNESS
PRODIGY
PRODISARMAMENT
PRODISSOLUTION
PRODITOR
PRODITORIOUS
PRODITORS
PRODITORY
PRODNOSE
PRODNOSED
PRODNOSES
PRODNOSING
PRODROMAL
PRODROMATA
PRODROME
PRODROMES
PRODROMI
PRODROMIC
PRODROMUS
PRODRUG
PRODS
PRODUCE
PRODUCED
PRODUCEMENT
PRODUCEMENTS
PRODUCER
PRODUCERS
PRODUCES
PRODUCIBILITIES
PRODUCIBILITY
PRODUCIBLE
PRODUCING
PRODUCT
PRODUCTIBILITY
PRODUCTILE
PRODUCTION
PRODUCTIONAL
PRODUCTIONS
PRODUCTIVE
PRODUCTIVELY
PRODUCTIVENESS
PRODUCTIVITIES
PRODUCTIVITY
PRODUCTS
PROEM
PROEMBRYO
PROEMBRYOS
PROEMIAL
PROEMS

PROENFORCEMENT
PROENZYME
PROENZYMES
PROESTRUS
PROESTRUSES
PROETTE
PROETTES
PROF
PROFACE
PROFANATION
PROFANATIONS
PROFANATORY
PROFANE
PROFANED
PROFANELY
PROFANENESS
PROFANENESSES
PROFANER
PROFANERS
PROFANES
PROFANING
PROFANITIES
PROFANITY
PROFASCIST
PROFASCISTS
PROFECTITIOUS
PROFEDERATION
PROFEMINIST
PROFEMINISTS
PROFESS
PROFESSED
PROFESSEDLY
PROFESSES
PROFESSING
PROFESSION
PROFESSIONAL
PROFESSIONALISE
PROFESSIONALISM
PROFESSIONALIST
PROFESSIONALIZE
PROFESSIONALLY
PROFESSIONALS
PROFESSIONS
PROFESSOR
PROFESSORATE
PROFESSORATES
PROFESSORESS
PROFESSORESSES
PROFESSORIAL
PROFESSORIALLY
PROFESSORIAT
PROFESSORIATE
PROFESSORIATES
PROFESSORIATS
PROFESSORS
PROFESSORSHIP

PROFESSORSHIPS
PROFFER
PROFFERED
PROFFERER
PROFFERERS
PROFFERING
PROFFERS
PROFICIENCE
PROFICIENCES
PROFICIENCIES
PROFICIENCY
PROFICIENT
PROFICIENTLY
PROFICIENTS
PROFILE
PROFILED
PROFILER
PROFILERS
PROFILES
PROFILING
PROFILINGS
PROFILIST
PROFILISTS
PROFIT
PROFITABILITIES
PROFITABILITY
PROFITABLE
PROFITABLENESS
PROFITABLY
PROFITED
PROFITEER
PROFITEERED
PROFITEERING
PROFITEERINGS
PROFITEERS
PROFITER
PROFITEROLE
PROFITEROLES
PROFITERS
PROFITING
PROFITINGS
PROFITLESS
PROFITLESSLY
PROFITS
PROFITWISE
PROFLIGACIES
PROFLIGACY
PROFLIGATE
PROFLIGATELY
PROFLIGATES
PROFLUENCE
PROFLUENCES
PROFLUENT
PROFOREIGN
PROFORMA
PROFORMAS

PROFOUND
PROFOUNDER
PROFOUNDEST
PROFOUNDLY
PROFOUNDNESS
PROFOUNDNESSES
PROFOUNDS
PROFS
PROFULGENT
PROFUNDITIES
PROFUNDITY
PROFUSE
PROFUSELY
PROFUSENESS
PROFUSENESSES
PROFUSER
PROFUSERS
PROFUSION
PROFUSIONS
PROG
PROGENIES
PROGENITIVE
PROGENITIVELY
PROGENITIVENESS
PROGENITOR
PROGENITORIAL
PROGENITORS
PROGENITORSHIP
PROGENITORSHIPS
PROGENITRESS
PROGENITRESSES
PROGENITRICES
PROGENITRIX
PROGENITRIXES
PROGENITURE
PROGENITURES
PROGENY
PROGERIA
PROGERIAS
PROGESTATIONAL
PROGESTERONE
PROGESTERONES
PROGESTIN
PROGESTINS
PROGESTOGEN
PROGESTOGENIC
PROGESTOGENS
PROGGED
PROGGER
PROGGERS
PROGGING
PROGGINS
PROGGINSES
PROGLOTTIC
PROGLOTTICALLY
PROGLOTTID

PROGLOTTIDEAN
PROGLOTTIDES
PROGLOTTIDS
PROGLOTTIS
PROGNATHIC
PROGNATHISM
PROGNATHISMS
PROGNATHOUS
PROGNOSE
PROGNOSED
PROGNOSES
PROGNOSING
PROGNOSIS
PROGNOSTIC
PROGNOSTICATE
PROGNOSTICATED
PROGNOSTICATES
PROGNOSTICATING
PROGNOSTICATION
PROGNOSTICATIVE
PROGNOSTICATOR
PROGNOSTICATORS
PROGNOSTICS
PROGRADATION
PROGRADATIONS
PROGRADE
PROGRADED
PROGRADES
PROGRADING
PROGRAM
PROGRAMABILITY
PROGRAMABLE
PROGRAMED
PROGRAMER
PROGRAMERS
PROGRAMING
PROGRAMINGS
PROGRAMMABILITY
PROGRAMMABLE
PROGRAMMABLES
PROGRAMMATIC
PROGRAMME
PROGRAMMED
PROGRAMMER
PROGRAMMERS
PROGRAMMES
PROGRAMMING
PROGRAMMINGS
PROGRAMS
PROGRESS
PROGRESSED
PROGRESSES
PROGRESSING
PROGRESSION
PROGRESSIONAL
PROGRESSIONALLY

PROGRESSIONARY
PROGRESSIONISM
PROGRESSIONISMS
PROGRESSIONIST
PROGRESSIONISTS
PROGRESSIONS
PROGRESSISM
PROGRESSISMS
PROGRESSIST
PROGRESSISTS
PROGRESSIVE
PROGRESSIVELY
PROGRESSIVENESS
PROGRESSIVES
PROGRESSIVISM
PROGRESSIVISMS
PROGRESSIVIST
PROGRESSIVISTIC
PROGRESSIVISTS
PROGRESSIVITIES
PROGRESSIVITY
PROGS
PROGYMNASIA
PROGYMNASIUM
PROGYMNASIUMS
PROHIBIT
PROHIBITED
PROHIBITER
PROHIBITERS
PROHIBITING
PROHIBITION
PROHIBITIONARY
PROHIBITIONISM
PROHIBITIONISMS
PROHIBITIONIST
PROHIBITIONISTS
PROHIBITIONS
PROHIBITIVE
PROHIBITIVELY
PROHIBITIVENESS
PROHIBITOR
PROHIBITORS
PROHIBITORY
PROHIBITS
PROIGN
PROIGNED
PROIGNING
PROIGNS
PROIMMIGRATION
PROIN
PROINDUSTRY
PROINE
PROINED
PROINES
PROINING
PROINS

PROINSULIN
PROINSULINS
PROINTEGRATION
PROINTERVENTION
PROINVESTMENT
PROIRRIGATION
PROJECT
PROJECTABLE
PROJECTED
PROJECTILE
PROJECTILES
PROJECTING
PROJECTINGS
PROJECTION
PROJECTIONAL
PROJECTIONIST
PROJECTIONISTS
PROJECTIONS
PROJECTISATION
PROJECTISATIONS
PROJECTIVE
PROJECTIVELY
PROJECTIVITIES
PROJECTIVITY
PROJECTIZATION
PROJECTIZATIONS
PROJECTMENT
PROJECTMENTS
PROJECTOR
PROJECTORS
PROJECTS
PROJECTURE
PROJECTURES
PROJET
PROJETS
PROKARYON
PROKARYONS
PROKARYOT
PROKARYOTE
PROKARYOTES
PROKARYOTIC
PROKARYOTS
PROKE
PROKED
PROKER
PROKERS
PROKES
PROKING
PROLABOR
PROLABOUR
PROLACTIN
PROLACTINS
PROLAMIN
PROLAMINE
PROLAMINES
PROLAMINS

PROLAN
PROLANS
PROLAPSE
PROLAPSED
PROLAPSES
PROLAPSING
PROLAPSUS
PROLAPSUSES
PROLATE
PROLATED
PROLATELY
PROLATENESS
PROLATENESSES
PROLATES
PROLATING
PROLATION
PROLATIONS
PROLATIVE
PROLE
PROLED
PROLEG
PROLEGOMENA
PROLEGOMENAL
PROLEGOMENARY
PROLEGOMENON
PROLEGOMENOUS
PROLEGS
PROLEPSES
PROLEPSIS
PROLEPTIC
PROLEPTICAL
PROLEPTICALLY
PROLER
PROLERS
PROLES
PROLETARIAN
PROLETARIANISE
PROLETARIANISED
PROLETARIANISES
PROLETARIANISM
PROLETARIANISMS
PROLETARIANIZE
PROLETARIANIZED
PROLETARIANIZES
PROLETARIANNESS
PROLETARIANS
PROLETARIAT
PROLETARIATE
PROLETARIATES
PROLETARIATS
PROLETARIES
PROLETARY
PROLICIDAL
PROLICIDE
PROLICIDES
PROLIFERATE

PROLIFERATED
PROLIFERATES
PROLIFERATING
PROLIFERATION
PROLIFERATIONS
PROLIFERATIVE
PROLIFEROUS
PROLIFEROUSLY
PROLIFIC
PROLIFICACIES
PROLIFICACY
PROLIFICAL
PROLIFICALLY
PROLIFICATION
PROLIFICATIONS
PROLIFICITIES
PROLIFICITY
PROLIFICNESS
PROLIFICNESSES
PROLINE
PROLINES
PROLING
PROLIX
PROLIXIOUS
PROLIXITIES
PROLIXITY
PROLIXLY
PROLIXNESS
PROLIXNESSES
PROLL
PROLLED
PROLLER
PROLLERS
PROLLING
PROLLS
PROLOCUTION
PROLOCUTIONS
PROLOCUTOR
PROLOCUTORS
PROLOCUTORSHIP
PROLOCUTORSHIPS
PROLOCUTRIX
PROLOCUTRIXES
PROLOG
PROLOGED
PROLOGING
PROLOGISE
PROLOGISED
PROLOGISES
PROLOGISING
PROLOGIZE
PROLOGIZED
PROLOGIZES
PROLOGIZING
PROLOGS
PROLOGUE

PROLOGUED
PROLOGUES
PROLOGUING
PROLOGUISE
PROLOGUISED
PROLOGUISES
PROLOGUISING
PROLOGUIZE
PROLOGUIZED
PROLOGUIZES
PROLOGUIZING
PROLONG
PROLONGABLE
PROLONGATE
PROLONGATED
PROLONGATES
PROLONGATING
PROLONGATION
PROLONGATIONS
PROLONGE
PROLONGED
PROLONGER
PROLONGERS
PROLONGES
PROLONGING
PROLONGMENT
PROLONGMENTS
PROLONGS
PROLUSION
PROLUSIONS
PROLUSORY
PROM
PROMACHOS
PROMACHOSES
PROMENADE
PROMENADED
PROMENADER
PROMENADERS
PROMENADES
PROMENADING
PROMETAL
PROMETALS
PROMETHAZINE
PROMETHAZINES
PROMETHEUM
PROMETHEUMS
PROMETHIUM
PROMETHIUMS
PROMILITARY
PROMIMENTLY
PROMINE
PROMINENCE
PROMINENCES
PROMINENCIES
PROMINENCY
PROMINENT

PROMINENTLY
PROMINENTNESS
PROMINES
PROMINORITY
PROMISCUITIES
PROMISCUITY
PROMISCUOUS
PROMISCUOUSLY
PROMISCUOUSNESS
PROMISE
PROMISED
PROMISEE
PROMISEES
PROMISEFUL
PROMISELESS
PROMISER
PROMISERS
PROMISES
PROMISING
PROMISINGLY
PROMISOR
PROMISORS
PROMISSIVE
PROMISSOR
PROMISSORILY
PROMISSORS
PROMISSORY
PROMMER
PROMMERS
PROMO
PROMODERN
PROMODERNISM
PROMODERNIST
PROMODERNISTIC
PROMONARCHIST
PROMONARCHISTS
PROMONTORIES
PROMONTORY
PROMOS
PROMOTABILITIES
PROMOTABILITY
PROMOTABLE
PROMOTE
PROMOTED
PROMOTER
PROMOTERS
PROMOTES
PROMOTING
PROMOTION
PROMOTIONAL
PROMOTIONS
PROMOTIVE
PROMOTIVENESS
PROMOTIVENESSES
PROMOTOR
PROMOTORS

PROMPT
PROMPTBOOK
PROMPTBOOKS
PROMPTED
PROMPTER
PROMPTERS
PROMPTEST
PROMPTING
PROMPTINGS
PROMPTITUDE
PROMPTITUDES
PROMPTLY
PROMPTNESS
PROMPTNESSES
PROMPTS
PROMPTUARIES
PROMPTUARY
PROMPTURE
PROMPTURES
PROMS
PROMULGATE
PROMULGATED
PROMULGATES
PROMULGATING
PROMULGATION
PROMULGATIONS
PROMULGATOR
PROMULGATORS
PROMULGE
PROMULGED
PROMULGES
PROMULGING
PROMUSCES
PROMUSCIDATE
PROMUSCIDES
PROMUSCIS
PROMYCELIA
PROMYCELIAL
PROMYCELIUM
PRONAOI
PRONAOS
PRONATE
PRONATED
PRONATES
PRONATING
PRONATION
PRONATIONALIST
PRONATIONALISTS
PRONATIONS
PRONATOR
PRONATORES
PRONATORS
PRONE
PRONELY
PRONENESS
PRONENESSES

PRONEPHRA
PRONEPHRIC
PRONEPHROI
PRONEPHROS
PRONEPHROSES
PRONER
PRONES
PRONEST
PRONEUR
PRONEURS
PRONG
PRONGBUCK
PRONGBUCKS
PRONGED
PRONGHORN
PRONGHORNS
PRONGING
PRONGS
PRONK
PRONKED
PRONKING
PRONKS
PRONOMINAL
PRONOMINALISE
PRONOMINALISED
PRONOMINALISES
PRONOMINALISING
PRONOMINALIZE
PRONOMINALIZED
PRONOMINALIZES
PRONOMINALIZING
PRONOMINALLY
PRONOTA
PRONOTAL
PRONOTUM
PRONOTUMS
PRONOUN
PRONOUNCE
PRONOUNCEABLE
PRONOUNCED
PRONOUNCEDLY
PRONOUNCEMENT
PRONOUNCEMENTS
PRONOUNCER
PRONOUNCERS
PRONOUNCES
PRONOUNCING
PRONOUNCINGS
PRONOUNS
PRONTO
PRONUCLEAR
PRONUCLEARIST
PRONUCLEARISTS
PRONUCLEI
PRONUCLEUS
PRONUCLEUSES

PRONUNCIAMENTO
PRONUNCIAMENTOS
PRONUNCIATION
PRONUNCIATIONAL
PRONUNCIATIONS
PRONUNCIO
PRONUNCIOS
PROO
PROOEMION
PROOEMIONS
PROOEMIUM
PROOEMIUMS
PROOF
PROOFED
PROOFER
PROOFERS
PROOFING
PROOFINGS
PROOFLESS
PROOFREAD
PROOFREADER
PROOFREADERS
PROOFREADING
PROOFREADINGS
PROOFREADS
PROOFROOM
PROOFROOMS
PROOFS
PROOTIC
PROOTICS
PROP
PROPAEDEUTIC
PROPAEDEUTICAL
PROPAEDEUTICS
PROPAGABILITY
PROPAGABLE
PROPAGABLENESS
PROPAGANDA
PROPAGANDAS
PROPAGANDISE
PROPAGANDISED
PROPAGANDISES
PROPAGANDISING
PROPAGANDISM
PROPAGANDISMS
PROPAGANDIST
PROPAGANDISTIC
PROPAGANDISTS
PROPAGANDIZE
PROPAGANDIZED
PROPAGANDIZER
PROPAGANDIZERS
PROPAGANDIZES
PROPAGANDIZING
PROPAGATE
PROPAGATED

PROPAGATES
PROPAGATING
PROPAGATION
PROPAGATIONAL
PROPAGATIONALLY
PROPAGATIONS
PROPAGATIVE
PROPAGATOR
PROPAGATORS
PROPAGE
PROPAGED
PROPAGES
PROPAGING
PROPAGULA
PROPAGULE
PROPAGULES
PROPAGULUM
PROPAGULUMS
PROPALE
PROPALED
PROPALES
PROPALING
PROPANE
PROPANEDIOIC
PROPANES
PROPANOIC
PROPANOL
PROPANOLS
PROPANONE
PROPAROXYTONE
PROPAROXYTONES
PROPEL
PROPELLANT
PROPELLANTS
PROPELLED
PROPELLENT
PROPELLENTS
PROPELLER
PROPELLERS
PROPELLING
PROPELLOR
PROPELLORS
PROPELMENT
PROPELMENTS
PROPELS
PROPEND
PROPENDED
PROPENDENT
PROPENDING
PROPENDS
PROPENE
PROPENES
PROPENOL
PROPENOLS
PROPENSE
PROPENSELY

PROPENSENESS
PROPENSENESSES
PROPENSION
PROPENSIONS
PROPENSITIES
PROPENSITY
PROPENSIVE
PROPENYL
PROPER
PROPERDIN
PROPERDINS
PROPERER
PROPEREST
PROPERISPOMENON
PROPERLY
PROPERNESS
PROPERNESSES
PROPERS
PROPERTIED
PROPERTIES
PROPERTY
PROPERTYING
PROPERTYLESS
PROPHAGE
PROPHAGES
PROPHASE
PROPHASES
PROPHASIC
PROPHECIES
PROPHECY
PROPHESIABILITY
PROPHESIABLE
PROPHESIED
PROPHESIER
PROPHESIERS
PROPHESIES
PROPHESY
PROPHESYING
PROPHESYINGS
PROPHET
PROPHETESS
PROPHETESSES
PROPHETHOOD
PROPHETHOODS
PROPHETIC
PROPHETICAL
PROPHETICALLY
PROPHETICISM
PROPHETICISMS
PROPHETISM
PROPHETISMS
PROPHETS
PROPHETSHIP
PROPHETSHIPS
PROPHYLACTIC
PROPHYLACTICS

PROPHYLAXES
PROPHYLAXIS
PROPHYLL
PROPHYLLS
PROPINE
PROPINED
PROPINES
PROPINING
PROPINQUITIES
PROPINQUITY
PROPIONATE
PROPIONATES
PROPIONIC
PROPITIABLE
PROPITIATE
PROPITIATED
PROPITIATES
PROPITIATING
PROPITIATION
PROPITIATIONS
PROPITIATIOUS
PROPITIATIVE
PROPITIATOR
PROPITIATORIES
PROPITIATORILY
PROPITIATORS
PROPITIATORY
PROPITIOUS
PROPITIOUSLY
PROPITIOUSNESS
PROPJET
PROPJETS
PROPLASTID
PROPLASTIDS
PROPMAN
PROPMEN
PROPODEON
PROPODEONS
PROPODEUM
PROPODEUMS
PROPOLIS
PROPOLISES
PROPONE
PROPONED
PROPONENT
PROPONENTS
PROPONES
PROPONING
PROPORTION
PROPORTIONABLE
PROPORTIONABLY
PROPORTIONAL
PROPORTIONALITY
PROPORTIONALLY
PROPORTIONALS
PROPORTIONATE

PROPORTIONATED
PROPORTIONATELY
PROPORTIONATES
PROPORTIONATING
PROPORTIONED
PROPORTIONING
PROPORTIONINGS
PROPORTIONLESS
PROPORTIONMENT
PROPORTIONMENTS
PROPORTIONS
PROPOSABLE
PROPOSAL
PROPOSALS
PROPOSE
PROPOSED
PROPOSER
PROPOSERS
PROPOSES
PROPOSING
PROPOSITA
PROPOSITAE
PROPOSITI
PROPOSITION
PROPOSITIONAL
PROPOSITIONALLY
PROPOSITIONED
PROPOSITIONING
PROPOSITIONS
PROPOSITUS
PROPOUND
PROPOUNDED
PROPOUNDER
PROPOUNDERS
PROPOUNDING
PROPOUNDS
PROPOXYPHENE
PROPOXYPHENES
PROPPANT
PROPPANTS
PROPPED
PROPPING
PROPRAETOR
PROPRAETORIAL
PROPRAETORIAN
PROPRAETORS
PROPRANOLOL
PROPRANOLOLS
PROPRETOR
PROPRETORS
PROPRIETARIES
PROPRIETARILY
PROPRIETARINESS
PROPRIETARY
PROPRIETIES
PROPRIETOR

PROPRIETORIAL
PROPRIETORIALLY
PROPRIETORS
PROPRIETORSHIP
PROPRIETORSHIPS
PROPRIETRESS
PROPRIETRESSES
PROPRIETRICES
PROPRIETRIX
PROPRIETRIXES
PROPRIETY
PROPRIOCEPTION
PROPRIOCEPTIONS
PROPRIOCEPTIVE
PROPRIOCEPTOR
PROPRIOCEPTORS
PROPRIUM
PROPRIUMS
PROPROCTOR
PROPROCTORS
PROPS
PROPTOSES
PROPTOSIS
PROPUGNATION
PROPUGNATIONS
PROPULSION
PROPULSIONS
PROPULSIVE
PROPULSOR
PROPULSORS
PROPULSORY
PROPYL
PROPYLA
PROPYLAEA
PROPYLAEUM
PROPYLAMINE
PROPYLAMINES
PROPYLENE
PROPYLENES
PROPYLIC
PROPYLITE
PROPYLITES
PROPYLITISATION
PROPYLITISE
PROPYLITISED
PROPYLITISES
PROPYLITISING
PROPYLITIZATION
PROPYLITIZE
PROPYLITIZED
PROPYLITIZES
PROPYLITIZING
PROPYLON
PROPYLONS
PROPYLS
PRORATABLE

PRORATE
PRORATED
PRORATES
PRORATING
PRORATION
PRORATIONS
PRORE
PRORECTOR
PRORECTORS
PROREFORM
PRORES
PRORESTORATION
PROREVISION
PROROGATE
PROROGATED
PROROGATES
PROROGATING
PROROGATION
PROROGATIONS
PROROGUE
PROROGUED
PROROGUES
PROROGUING
PROS
PROSAIC
PROSAICAL
PROSAICALLY
PROSAICALNESS
PROSAICALNESSES
PROSAICISM
PROSAICISMS
PROSAICNESS
PROSAICNESSES
PROSAISM
PROSAISMS
PROSAIST
PROSAISTS
PROSATEUR
PROSATEURS
PROSAUROPOD
PROSAUROPODS
PROSCENIA
PROSCENIUM
PROSCENIUMS
PROSCIUTTI
PROSCIUTTO
PROSCIUTTOS
PROSCRIBE
PROSCRIBED
PROSCRIBER
PROSCRIBERS
PROSCRIBES
PROSCRIBING
PROSCRIPT
PROSCRIPTION
PROSCRIPTIONS

PROSCRIPTIVE
PROSCRIPTIVELY
PROSCRIPTS
PROSE
PROSECT
PROSECTED
PROSECTING
PROSECTOR
PROSECTORIAL
PROSECTORS
PROSECTORSHIP
PROSECTORSHIPS
PROSECTS
PROSECUTABLE
PROSECUTE
PROSECUTED
PROSECUTES
PROSECUTING
PROSECUTION
PROSECUTIONS
PROSECUTOR
PROSECUTORIAL
PROSECUTORS
PROSECUTRICES
PROSECUTRIX
PROSECUTRIXES
PROSED
PROSELIKE
PROSELYISATIONS
PROSELYTE
PROSELYTED
PROSELYTES
PROSELYTIC
PROSELYTICALLY
PROSELYTING
PROSELYTISATION
PROSELYTISE
PROSELYTISED
PROSELYTISER
PROSELYTISERS
PROSELYTISES
PROSELYTISING
PROSELYTISM
PROSELYTISMS
PROSELYTIZATION
PROSELYTIZE
PROSELYTIZED
PROSELYTIZER
PROSELYTIZERS
PROSELYTIZES
PROSELYTIZING
PROSEMAN
PROSEMEN
PROSEMINAR
PROSEMINARS
PROSENCEPHALA

PROSENCEPHALIC
PROSENCEPHALON
PROSENCHYMA
PROSENCHYMAS
PROSENCHYMATA
PROSENCHYMATOUS
PROSER
PROSERS
PROSES
PROSEUCHA
PROSEUCHAE
PROSEUCHE
PROSIER
PROSIEST
PROSIFIED
PROSIFIES
PROSIFY
PROSIFYING
PROSILIENCIES
PROSILIENCY
PROSILIENT
PROSILY
PROSIMIAN
PROSIMIANS
PROSINESS
PROSINESSES
PROSING
PROSINGS
PROSIT
PROSLAMBANOMENE
PROSLAVERY
PROSO
PROSOBRANCH
PROSOBRANCHS
PROSODIAL
PROSODIAN
PROSODIANS
PROSODIC
PROSODICAL
PROSODICALLY
PROSODIES
PROSODIST
PROSODISTS
PROSODY
PROSOMA
PROSOMAL
PROSOMAS
PROSOMATA
PROSOPAGNOSIA
PROSOPAGNOSIAS
PROSOPOGRAPHER
PROSOPOGRAPHERS
PROSOPOGRAPHIC
PROSOPOGRAPHIES
PROSOPOGRAPHY
PROSOPON

PROSOPONS
PROSOPOPEIA
PROSOPOPEIAL
PROSOPOPEIAS
PROSOPOPOEIA
PROSOPOPOEIAL
PROSOPOPOEIAS
PROSOS
PROSPECT
PROSPECTED
PROSPECTING
PROSPECTINGS
PROSPECTION
PROSPECTIONS
PROSPECTIVE
PROSPECTIVELY
PROSPECTIVENESS
PROSPECTIVES
PROSPECTLESS
PROSPECTOR
PROSPECTORS
PROSPECTS
PROSPECTUS
PROSPECTUSES
PROSPER
PROSPERED
PROSPERING
PROSPERITIES
PROSPERITY
PROSPEROUS
PROSPEROUSLY
PROSPEROUSNESS
PROSPERS
PROSS
PROSSES
PROSSIE
PROSSIES
PROST
PROSTACYCLIN
PROSTACYCLINS
PROSTAGLANDIN
PROSTAGLANDINS
PROSTANTHERA
PROSTANTHERAS
PROSTATE
PROSTATECTOMIES
PROSTATECTOMY
PROSTATES
PROSTATIC
PROSTATISM
PROSTATISMS
PROSTATITIS
PROSTATITISES
PROSTERNA
PROSTERNUM
PROSTERNUMS

PROSTHESES
PROSTHESIS
PROSTHETIC
PROSTHETICALLY
PROSTHETICS
PROSTHETIST
PROSTHETISTS
PROSTHODONTIA
PROSTHODONTIAS
PROSTHODONTICS
PROSTHODONTIST
PROSTHODONTISTS
PROSTIE
PROSTIES
PROSTITUTE
PROSTITUTED
PROSTITUTES
PROSTITUTING
PROSTITUTION
PROSTITUTIONS
PROSTITUTOR
PROSTITUTORS
PROSTOMIA
PROSTOMIAL
PROSTOMIUM
PROSTOMIUMS
PROSTRATE
PROSTRATED
PROSTRATES
PROSTRATING
PROSTRATION
PROSTRATIONS
PROSTYLE
PROSTYLES
PROSUPERVISION
PROSURRENDER
PROSY
PROSYLLOGISM
PROSYLLOGISMS
PROSYNDICALISM
PROSYNDICALIST
PROSYNDICALISTS
PROTACTINIUM
PROTACTINIUMS
PROTAGONISM
PROTAGONIST
PROTAGONISTS
PROTAMIN
PROTAMINE
PROTAMINES
PROTAMINS
PROTANDRIES
PROTANDROUS
PROTANDRY
PROTANOMALIES
PROTANOMALOUS

PROTANOMALY
PROTANOPE
PROTANOPES
PROTANOPIA
PROTANOPIAS
PROTANOPIC
PROTASES
PROTASIS
PROTATIC
PROTEA
PROTEACEOUS
PROTEAN
PROTEANS
PROTEAS
PROTEASE
PROTEASES
PROTECT
PROTECTANT
PROTECTANTS
PROTECTED
PROTECTING
PROTECTINGLY
PROTECTION
PROTECTIONISM
PROTECTIONISMS
PROTECTIONIST
PROTECTIONISTS
PROTECTIONS
PROTECTIVE
PROTECTIVELY
PROTECTIVENESS
PROTECTIVES
PROTECTOR
PROTECTORAL
PROTECTORATE
PROTECTORATES
PROTECTORIAL
PROTECTORIES
PROTECTORLESS
PROTECTORS
PROTECTORSHIP
PROTECTORSHIPS
PROTECTORY
PROTECTRESS
PROTECTRESSES
PROTECTRICES
PROTECTRIX
PROTECTRIXES
PROTECTS
PROTEGE
PROTEGEE
PROTEGEES
PROTEGES
PROTEI
PROTEID
PROTEIDE

PROTEIDES
PROTEIDS
PROTEIFORM
PROTEIN
PROTEINACEOUS
PROTEINASE
PROTEINASES
PROTEINIC
PROTEINOUS
PROTEINS
PROTEINURIA
PROTEINURIAS
PROTEND
PROTENDED
PROTENDING
PROTENDS
PROTENSE
PROTENSES
PROTENSION
PROTENSIONS
PROTENSITIES
PROTENSITY
PROTENSIVE
PROTENSIVELY
PROTEOCLASTIC
PROTEOGLYCAN
PROTEOGLYCANS
PROTEOLYSE
PROTEOLYSED
PROTEOLYSES
PROTEOLYSING
PROTEOLYSIS
PROTEOLYTIC
PROTEOLYTICALLY
PROTEOME
PROTEOMES
PROTEOMICS
PROTEOSE
PROTEOSES
PROTERANDRIES
PROTERANDROUS
PROTERANDRY
PROTEROGYNIES
PROTEROGYNOUS
PROTEROGYNY
PROTERVITIES
PROTERVITY
PROTEST
PROTESTANT
PROTESTANTS
PROTESTATION
PROTESTATIONS
PROTESTED
PROTESTER
PROTESTERS
PROTESTING

PROTESTINGLY
PROTESTOR
PROTESTORS
PROTESTS
PROTEUS
PROTEUSES
PROTHALAMIA
PROTHALAMION
PROTHALAMIUM
PROTHALLI
PROTHALLIA
PROTHALLIAL
PROTHALLIC
PROTHALLIUM
PROTHALLOID
PROTHALLUS
PROTHALLUSES
PROTHESES
PROTHESIS
PROTHETIC
PROTHETICALLY
PROTHONOTARIAL
PROTHONOTARIAT
PROTHONOTARIATS
PROTHONOTARIES
PROTHONOTARY
PROTHORACES
PROTHORACIC
PROTHORAX
PROTHORAXES
PROTHROMBIN
PROTHROMBINS
PROTHYL
PROTHYLES
PROTHYLS
PROTIST
PROTISTAN
PROTISTANS
PROTISTIC
PROTISTOLOGIES
PROTISTOLOGIST
PROTISTOLOGISTS
PROTISTOLOGY
PROTISTS
PROTIUM
PROTIUMS
PROTOACTINIUM
PROTOACTINIUMS
PROTOAVIS
PROTOAVISES
PROTOCHORDATE
PROTOCHORDATES
PROTOCOCCAL
PROTOCOL
PROTOCOLED
PROTOCOLIC

PROTOCOLING
PROTOCOLISE
PROTOCOLISED
PROTOCOLISES
PROTOCOLISING
PROTOCOLIST
PROTOCOLISTS
PROTOCOLIZE
PROTOCOLIZED
PROTOCOLIZES
PROTOCOLIZING
PROTOCOLLED
PROTOCOLLING
PROTOCOLS
PROTOCTIST
PROTOCTISTA
PROTOCTISTS
PROTODERM
PROTODERMS
PROTOGALAXIES
PROTOGALAXY
PROTOGENIC
PROTOGINE
PROTOGINES
PROTOGYNIES
PROTOGYNOUS
PROTOGYNY
PROTOHISTORIAN
PROTOHISTORIANS
PROTOHISTORIC
PROTOHISTORIES
PROTOHISTORY
PROTOHUMAN
PROTOHUMANS
PROTOLANGUAGE
PROTOLANGUAGES
PROTOLITHIC
PROTOMARTYR
PROTOMARTYRS
PROTOMORPHIC
PROTON
PROTONATE
PROTONATED
PROTONATES
PROTONATING
PROTONATION
PROTONATIONS
PROTONEMA
PROTONEMAL
PROTONEMATA
PROTONEMATAL
PROTONIC
PROTONOTARIAL
PROTONOTARIAT
PROTONOTARIATS
PROTONOTARIES

PROTONOTARY
PROTONS
PROTOPATHIC
PROTOPATHIES
PROTOPATHY
PROTOPHILIC
PROTOPHILICALLY
PROTOPHLOEM
PROTOPHLOEMS
PROTOPHYTE
PROTOPHYTES
PROTOPHYTIC
PROTOPLANET
PROTOPLANETARY
PROTOPLANETS
PROTOPLASM
PROTOPLASMAL
PROTOPLASMATIC
PROTOPLASMIC
PROTOPLASMS
PROTOPLAST
PROTOPLASTIC
PROTOPLASTS
PROTOPOD
PROTOPODS
PROTOPORPHYRIN
PROTOPORPHYRINS
PROTORE
PROTORES
PROTOSPATAIRES
PROTOSPATHAIRE
PROTOSPATHAIRES
PROTOSPATHARIUS
PROTOSTAR
PROTOSTARS
PROTOSTELE
PROTOSTELES
PROTOSTELIC
PROTOSTOME
PROTOSTOMES
PROTOTHERIAN
PROTOTHERIANS
PROTOTROPH
PROTOTROPHIC
PROTOTROPHIES
PROTOTROPHS
PROTOTROPHY
PROTOTYPAL
PROTOTYPE
PROTOTYPED
PROTOTYPES
PROTOTYPIC
PROTOTYPICAL
PROTOTYPICALLY
PROTOTYPING
PROTOXID

PROTOXIDE
PROTOXIDES
PROTOXIDS
PROTOXYLEM
PROTOXYLEMS
PROTOZOA
PROTOZOAL
PROTOZOAN
PROTOZOANS
PROTOZOIC
PROTOZOOLOGICAL
PROTOZOOLOGIES
PROTOZOOLOGIST
PROTOZOOLOGISTS
PROTOZOOLOGY
PROTOZOON
PROTRACT
PROTRACTED
PROTRACTEDLY
PROTRACTEDNESS
PROTRACTIBLE
PROTRACTILE
PROTRACTING
PROTRACTION
PROTRACTIONS
PROTRACTIVE
PROTRACTOR
PROTRACTORS
PROTRACTS
PROTREPTIC
PROTREPTICAL
PROTREPTICS
PROTRUDABLE
PROTRUDE
PROTRUDED
PROTRUDENT
PROTRUDES
PROTRUDING
PROTRUSIBLE
PROTRUSILE
PROTRUSION
PROTRUSIONS
PROTRUSIVE
PROTRUSIVELY
PROTRUSIVENESS
PROTUBERANCE
PROTUBERANCES
PROTUBERANCIES
PROTUBERANCY
PROTUBERANT
PROTUBERANTLY
PROTUBERATE
PROTUBERATED
PROTUBERATES
PROTUBERATING
PROTUBERATION

PROTUBERATIONS
PROTYL
PROTYLE
PROTYLES
PROTYLS
PROUD
PROUDER
PROUDEST
PROUDFUL
PROUDHEARTED
PROUDISH
PROUDLY
PROUDNESS
PROUDNESSES
PROUL
PROULED
PROULER
PROULERS
PROULING
PROULS
PROUNION
PROUNIVERSITY
PROUSTITE
PROUSTITES
PROVABILITY
PROVABLE
PROVABLENESS
PROVABLENESSES
PROVABLY
PROVAND
PROVANDS
PROVANT
PROVASCULAR
PROVE
PROVEABLE
PROVEABLY
PROVECTION
PROVECTIONS
PROVED
PROVEDITOR
PROVEDITORE
PROVEDITORES
PROVEDITORS
PROVEDOR
PROVEDORE
PROVEDORES
PROVEDORS
PROVEN
PROVENANCE
PROVENANCES
PROVEND
PROVENDER
PROVENDERED
PROVENDERING
PROVENDERS
PROVENDS

PROVENIENCE
PROVENIENCES
PROVENLY
PROVENTRICULAR
PROVENTRICULI
PROVENTRICULUS
PROVER
PROVERB
PROVERBED
PROVERBIAL
PROVERBIALISE
PROVERBIALISED
PROVERBIALISES
PROVERBIALISING
PROVERBIALISM
PROVERBIALISMS
PROVERBIALIST
PROVERBIALISTS
PROVERBIALIZE
PROVERBIALIZED
PROVERBIALIZES
PROVERBIALIZING
PROVERBIALLY
PROVERBING
PROVERBS
PROVERS
PROVES
PROVIANT
PROVIANTS
PROVIDABLE
PROVIDE
PROVIDED
PROVIDENCE
PROVIDENCES
PROVIDENT
PROVIDENTIAL
PROVIDENTIALLY
PROVIDENTLY
PROVIDER
PROVIDERS
PROVIDES
PROVIDING
PROVIDOR
PROVIDORS
PROVINCE
PROVINCES
PROVINCEWIDE
PROVINCIAL
PROVINCIALISE
PROVINCIALISED
PROVINCIALISES
PROVINCIALISING
PROVINCIALISM
PROVINCIALISMS
PROVINCIALIST
PROVINCIALISTS

PROVINCIALITIES
PROVINCIALITY
PROVINCIALIZE
PROVINCIALIZED
PROVINCIALIZES
PROVINCIALIZING
PROVINCIALLY
PROVINCIALS
PROVINE
PROVINED
PROVINES
PROVING
PROVINGS
PROVINING
PROVIRAL
PROVIRUS
PROVIRUSES
PROVISION
PROVISIONAL
PROVISIONALLY
PROVISIONALS
PROVISIONARIES
PROVISIONARILY
PROVISIONARY
PROVISIONED
PROVISIONER
PROVISIONERS
PROVISIONING
PROVISIONS
PROVISO
PROVISOES
PROVISOR
PROVISORILY
PROVISORS
PROVISORY
PROVISOS
PROVITAMIN
PROVITAMINS
PROVOCABLE
PROVOCANT
PROVOCANTS
PROVOCATEUR
PROVOCATEURS
PROVOCATION
PROVOCATIONS
PROVOCATIVE
PROVOCATIVELY
PROVOCATIVENESS
PROVOCATIVES
PROVOCATOR
PROVOCATORS
PROVOCATORY
PROVOKABLE
PROVOKE
PROVOKED
PROVOKEMENT

PROVOKEMENTS
PROVOKER
PROVOKERS
PROVOKES
PROVOKING
PROVOKINGLY
PROVOLONE
PROVOLONES
PROVOST
PROVOSTRIES
PROVOSTRY
PROVOSTS
PROVOSTSHIP
PROVOSTSHIPS
PROW
PROWAR
PROWER
PROWESS
PROWESSED
PROWESSES
PROWEST
PROWL
PROWLED
PROWLER
PROWLERS
PROWLING
PROWLINGLY
PROWLINGS
PROWLS
PROWS
PROXEMIC
PROXEMICS
PROXIES
PROXIMAL
PROXIMALLY
PROXIMATE
PROXIMATELY
PROXIMATENESS
PROXIMATENESSES
PROXIMATION
PROXIMATIONS
PROXIMITIES
PROXIMITY
PROXIMO
PROXY
PROYN
PROYNE
PROYNED
PROYNES
PROYNING
PROYNS
PROZYMITE
PROZYMITES
PRUDE
PRUDENCE
PRUDENCES

PRUDENT
PRUDENTIAL
PRUDENTIALISM
PRUDENTIALISMS
PRUDENTIALIST
PRUDENTIALISTS
PRUDENTIALITIES
PRUDENTIALITY
PRUDENTIALLY
PRUDENTIALS
PRUDENTLY
PRUDERIES
PRUDERY
PRUDISH
PRUDISHLY
PRUDISHNESS
PRUDISHNESSES
PRUH
PRUINA
PRUINAS
PRUINE
PRUINES
PRUINOSE
PRUNABLE
PRUNE
PRUNED
PRUNELLA
PRUNELLAS
PRUNELLE
PRUNELLES
PRUNELLO
PRUNELLOS
PRUNER
PRUNERS
PRUNES
PRUNING
PRUNINGS
PRUNT
PRUNTED
PRUNTS
PRUNUS
PRUNUSES
PRURIENCE
PRURIENCES
PRURIENCIES
PRURIENCY
PRURIENT
PRURIENTLY
PRURIGINOUS
PRURIGO
PRURIGOS
PRURITIC
PRURITUS
PRURITUSES
PRUSIK

PRUSIKED
PRUSIKING
PRUSIKS
PRUSSIANISE
PRUSSIANISED
PRUSSIANISES
PRUSSIANISING
PRUSSIANIZATION
PRUSSIANIZE
PRUSSIANIZED
PRUSSIANIZES
PRUSSIANIZING
PRUSSIATE
PRUSSIATES
PRUSSIC
PRUTA
PRUTAH
PRUTOT
PRUTOTH
PRY
PRYER
PRYERS
PRYING
PRYINGLY
PRYINGS
PRYS
PRYSE
PRYSED
PRYSES
PRYSING
PRYTANEA
PRYTANEUM
PRYTHEE
PSALIGRAPHIES
PSALM
PSALMBOOK
PSALMBOOKS
PSALMED
PSALMIC
PSALMING
PSALMIST
PSALMISTS
PSALMODIC
PSALMODICAL
PSALMODIES
PSALMODISE
PSALMODISED
PSALMODISES
PSALMODISING
PSALMODIST
PSALMODISTS
PSALMODIZE
PSALMODIZED
PSALMODIZES
PSALMODIZING
PSALMODY

PSALMS
PSALTER
PSALTERIA
PSALTERIAN
PSALTERIES
PSALTERIUM
PSALTERS
PSALTERY
PSALTRESS
PSALTRESSES
PSALTRIES
PSALTRY
PSAMMITE
PSAMMITES
PSAMMITIC
PSAMMON
PSAMMONS
PSAMMOPHIL
PSAMMOPHILE
PSAMMOPHILES
PSAMMOPHILOUS
PSAMMOPHILS
PSAMMOPHYTE
PSAMMOPHYTES
PSAMMOPHYTIC
PSCHENT
PSCHENTS
PSELLISM
PSELLISMS
PSELLISMUS
PSELLISMUSES
PSEPHISM
PSEPHISMS
PSEPHITE
PSEPHITES
PSEPHITIC
PSEPHOANALYSES
PSEPHOLOGICAL
PSEPHOLOGICALLY
PSEPHOLOGIES
PSEPHOLOGIST
PSEPHOLOGISTS
PSEPHOLOGY
PSEUD
PSEUDAESTHESIA
PSEUDAESTHESIAS
PSEUDARTHRITIC
PSEUDARTHROSES
PSEUDARTHROSIS
PSEUDAXES
PSEUDAXIS
PSEUDEPIGRAPH
PSEUDEPIGRAPHA
PSEUDEPIGRAPHIC
PSEUDEPIGRAPHON
PSEUDEPIGRAPHS

PSEUDEPIGRAPHY
PSEUDERIES
PSEUDERY
PSEUDIMAGINES
PSEUDIMAGO
PSEUDIMAGOS
PSEUDISH
PSEUDO
PSEUDOACID
PSEUDOACIDS
PSEUDOALLELE
PSEUDOALLELES
PSEUDOANTIQUE
PSEUDOARCHAIC
PSEUDOARTHRITIC
PSEUDOARTHROSES
PSEUDOARTHROSIS
PSEUDOARTISTIC
PSEUDOBULB
PSEUDOBULBS
PSEUDOCARP
PSEUDOCARPOUS
PSEUDOCARPS
PSEUDOCLASSIC
PSEUDOCLASSICAL
PSEUDOCLASSICS
PSEUDOCODE
PSEUDOCODES
PSEUDOCOEL
PSEUDOCOELOMATE
PSEUDOCOELS
PSEUDOCYESES
PSEUDOCYESIS
PSEUDOEPHEDRINE
PSEUDOGRAPH
PSEUDOGRAPHIES
PSEUDOGRAPHS
PSEUDOGRAPHY
PSEUDOHISTORIC
PSEUDOLITERARY
PSEUDOLOGIA
PSEUDOLOGIAS
PSEUDOLOGIES
PSEUDOLOGUE
PSEUDOLOGUES
PSEUDOLOGY
PSEUDOMARTYR
PSEUDOMARTYRS
PSEUDOMEDICAL
PSEUDOMEDIEVAL
PSEUDOMEMBRANE
PSEUDOMEMBRANES
PSEUDOMODERN
PSEUDOMONAD
PSEUDOMONADES
PSEUDOMONADS

PSEUDOMONAS
PSEUDOMORPH
PSEUDOMORPHIC
PSEUDOMORPHISM
PSEUDOMORPHISMS
PSEUDOMORPHOUS
PSEUDOMORPHS
PSEUDOMUTUALITY
PSEUDOMYTHICAL
PSEUDONYM
PSEUDONYMITIES
PSEUDONYMITY
PSEUDONYMOUS
PSEUDONYMOUSLY
PSEUDONYMS
PSEUDOPATRIOTIC
PSEUDOPOD
PSEUDOPODAL
PSEUDOPODIA
PSEUDOPODIAL
PSEUDOPODIUM
PSEUDOPODS
PSEUDOPREGNANCY
PSEUDOPREGNANT
PSEUDORANDOM
PSEUDOS
PSEUDOSCALAR
PSEUDOSCALARS
PSEUDOSCHOLARLY
PSEUDOSCIENCE
PSEUDOSCIENCES
PSEUDOSCIENTIST
PSEUDOSCOPE
PSEUDOSCOPES
PSEUDOSCORPION
PSEUDOSCORPIONS
PSEUDOSOLUTION
PSEUDOSOLUTIONS
PSEUDOSYMMETRY
PSEUDOVECTOR
PSEUDOVECTORS
PSEUDS
PSHAW
PSHAWED
PSHAWING
PSHAWS
PSI
PSILANTHROPIC
PSILANTHROPIES
PSILANTHROPISM
PSILANTHROPISMS
PSILANTHROPIST
PSILANTHROPISTS
PSILANTHROPY
PSILOCIN
PSILOCINS

PSILOCYBIN
PSILOCYBINS
PSILOMELANE
PSILOMELANES
PSILOPHYTE
PSILOPHYTES
PSILOPHYTIC
PSILOSES
PSILOSIS
PSILOTIC
PSION
PSIONIC
PSIONICS
PSIONS
PSIS
PSITTACINE
PSITTACINES
PSITTACOSES
PSITTACOSIS
PSITTACOTIC
PSOAE
PSOAI
PSOAS
PSOASES
PSOATIC
PSOCID
PSOCIDS
PSORA
PSORALEA
PSORALEAS
PSORALEN
PSORALENS
PSORAS
PSORIASES
PSORIASIS
PSORIATIC
PSORIATICS
PSORIC
PSST
PST
PSYCH
PSYCHAGOGUE
PSYCHAGOGUES
PSYCHASTHENIA
PSYCHASTHENIAS
PSYCHASTHENIC
PSYCHASTHENICS
PSYCHE
PSYCHED
PSYCHEDELIA
PSYCHEDELIAS
PSYCHEDELIC
PSYCHEDELICALLY
PSYCHEDELICS
PSYCHES
PSYCHIATER

PSYCHIATERS
PSYCHIATRIC
PSYCHIATRICAL
PSYCHIATRICALLY
PSYCHIATRIES
PSYCHIATRIST
PSYCHIATRISTS
PSYCHIATRY
PSYCHIC
PSYCHICAL
PSYCHICALLY
PSYCHICISM
PSYCHICISMS
PSYCHICIST
PSYCHICISTS
PSYCHICS
PSYCHING
PSYCHISM
PSYCHISMS
PSYCHIST
PSYCHISTS
PSYCHO
PSYCHOACOUSTIC
PSYCHOACOUSTICS
PSYCHOACTIVE
PSYCHOANALYSE
PSYCHOANALYSED
PSYCHOANALYSER
PSYCHOANALYSERS
PSYCHOANALYSES
PSYCHOANALYSING
PSYCHOANALYSIS
PSYCHOANALYST
PSYCHOANALYSTS
PSYCHOANALYTIC
PSYCHOANALYZE
PSYCHOANALYZED
PSYCHOANALYZER
PSYCHOANALYZERS
PSYCHOANALYZES
PSYCHOANALYZING
PSYCHOBABBLE
PSYCHOBABBLER
PSYCHOBABBLERS
PSYCHOBABBLES
PSYCHOBILLY
PSYCHOBIOGRAPHY
PSYCHOBIOLOGIC
PSYCHOBIOLOGIES
PSYCHOBIOLOGIST
PSYCHOBIOLOGY
PSYCHOCHEMICAL
PSYCHOCHEMICALS
PSYCHOCHEMISTRY
PSYCHODELIA
PSYCHODELIAS

PSYCHODELIC
PSYCHODELICALLY
PSYCHODRAMA
PSYCHODRAMAS
PSYCHODRAMATIC
PSYCHODYNAMIC
PSYCHODYNAMICS
PSYCHOGALVANIC
PSYCHOGAS
PSYCHOGASES
PSYCHOGENESES
PSYCHOGENESIS
PSYCHOGENETIC
PSYCHOGENETICAL
PSYCHOGENETICS
PSYCHOGENIC
PSYCHOGENICALLY
PSYCHOGERIATRIC
PSYCHOGNOSIS
PSYCHOGNOSTIC
PSYCHOGONIES
PSYCHOGONY
PSYCHOGRAM
PSYCHOGRAMS
PSYCHOGRAPH
PSYCHOGRAPHIC
PSYCHOGRAPHICAL
PSYCHOGRAPHICS
PSYCHOGRAPHIES
PSYCHOGRAPHS
PSYCHOGRAPHY
PSYCHOHISTORIAN
PSYCHOHISTORIES
PSYCHOHISTORY
PSYCHOID
PSYCHOIDS
PSYCHOKINESES
PSYCHOKINESIS
PSYCHOKINETIC
PSYCHOLINGUIST
PSYCHOLINGUISTS
PSYCHOLOGIC
PSYCHOLOGICAL
PSYCHOLOGICALLY
PSYCHOLOGIES
PSYCHOLOGISE
PSYCHOLOGISED
PSYCHOLOGISES
PSYCHOLOGISING
PSYCHOLOGISM
PSYCHOLOGISMS
PSYCHOLOGIST
PSYCHOLOGISTIC
PSYCHOLOGISTS
PSYCHOLOGIZE
PSYCHOLOGIZED

PSYCHOLOGIZES
PSYCHOLOGIZING
PSYCHOLOGY
PSYCHOMACHIA
PSYCHOMACHY
PSYCHOMETER
PSYCHOMETERS
PSYCHOMETRIC
PSYCHOMETRICAL
PSYCHOMETRICIAN
PSYCHOMETRICS
PSYCHOMETRIES
PSYCHOMETRIST
PSYCHOMETRISTS
PSYCHOMETRY
PSYCHOMOTOR
PSYCHONEUROSES
PSYCHONEUROSIS
PSYCHONEUROTIC
PSYCHONEUROTICS
PSYCHONOMIC
PSYCHONOMICS
PSYCHOPATH
PSYCHOPATHIC
PSYCHOPATHICS
PSYCHOPATHIES
PSYCHOPATHIST
PSYCHOPATHISTS
PSYCHOPATHOLOGY
PSYCHOPATHS
PSYCHOPATHY
PSYCHOPHILIES
PSYCHOPHILY
PSYCHOPHYSICAL
PSYCHOPHYSICIST
PSYCHOPHYSICS
PSYCHOPOMP
PSYCHOPOMPS
PSYCHOS
PSYCHOSES
PSYCHOSEXUAL
PSYCHOSEXUALITY
PSYCHOSEXUALLY
PSYCHOSIS
PSYCHOSOCIAL
PSYCHOSOCIALLY
PSYCHOSOMATIC
PSYCHOSOMATICS
PSYCHOSOMIMETIC
PSYCHOSURGEON
PSYCHOSURGEONS
PSYCHOSURGERIES
PSYCHOSURGERY
PSYCHOSURGICAL
PSYCHOSYNTHESES
PSYCHOSYNTHESIS

PSYCHOTECHNICS
PSYCHOTHERAPIES
PSYCHOTHERAPIST
PSYCHOTHERAPY
PSYCHOTIC
PSYCHOTICALLY
PSYCHOTICISM
PSYCHOTICISMS
PSYCHOTICS
PSYCHOTOMIMETIC
PSYCHOTOXIC
PSYCHOTROPIC
PSYCHOTROPICS
PSYCHROMETER
PSYCHROMETERS
PSYCHROMETRIC
PSYCHROMETRICAL
PSYCHROMETRIES
PSYCHROMETRY
PSYCHROPHILIC
PSYCHS
PSYLLA
PSYLLAS
PSYLLID
PSYLLIDS
PSYLLIUM
PSYLLIUMS
PSYOP
PSYOPS
PSYWAR
PSYWARS
PTARMIC
PTARMICS
PTARMIGAN
PTARMIGANS
PTERANODON
PTERANODONS
PTERIA
PTERIDINE
PTERIDINES
PTERIDOLOGICAL
PTERIDOLOGIES
PTERIDOLOGIST
PTERIDOLOGISTS
PTERIDOLOGY
PTERIDOMANIA
PTERIDOMANIAS
PTERIDOPHILIST
PTERIDOPHILISTS
PTERIDOPHYTE
PTERIDOPHYTES
PTERIDOPHYTIC
PTERIDOPHYTOUS
PTERIDOSPERM
PTERIDOSPERMS
PTERIN

PTERINS
PTERION
PTERODACTYL
PTERODACTYLE
PTERODACTYLES
PTERODACTYLS
PTEROPOD
PTEROPODS
PTEROSAUR
PTEROSAURIAN
PTEROSAURIANS
PTEROSAURS
PTERYGIA
PTERYGIAL
PTERYGIALS
PTERYGIUM
PTERYGIUMS
PTERYGOID
PTERYGOIDS
PTERYLA
PTERYLAE
PTERYLOGRAPHIC
PTERYLOGRAPHIES
PTERYLOGRAPHY
PTERYLOSES
PTERYLOSIS
PTILOSES
PTILOSIS
PTISAN
PTISANS
PTOCHOCRACIES
PTOCHOCRACY
PTOMAIN
PTOMAINE
PTOMAINES
PTOMAINS
PTOSES
PTOSIS
PTOTIC
PTYALAGOGIC
PTYALAGOGUE
PTYALAGOGUES
PTYALIN
PTYALINS
PTYALISE
PTYALISED
PTYALISES
PTYALISING
PTYALISM
PTYALISMS
PTYALIZE
PTYALIZED
PTYALIZES
PTYALIZING
PTYXES
PTYXIS

PTYXISES
PUB
PUBBED
PUBBER
PUBBERS
PUBBING
PUBE
PUBERAL
PUBERTAL
PUBERTIES
PUBERTY
PUBERULENT
PUBERULOUS
PUBES
PUBESCENCE
PUBESCENCES
PUBESCENT
PUBIC
PUBIS
PUBISES
PUBLIC
PUBLICALLY
PUBLICAN
PUBLICANS
PUBLICATION
PUBLICATIONS
PUBLICISE
PUBLICISED
PUBLICISES
PUBLICISING
PUBLICIST
PUBLICISTS
PUBLICITIES
PUBLICITY
PUBLICIZE
PUBLICIZED
PUBLICIZES
PUBLICIZING
PUBLICLY
PUBLICNESS
PUBLICNESSES
PUBLICS
PUBLISH
PUBLISHABLE
PUBLISHED
PUBLISHER
PUBLISHERS
PUBLISHES
PUBLISHING
PUBLISHINGS
PUBLISHMENT
PUBLISHMENTS
PUBS
PUCAN
PUCANS
PUCCINIACEOUS

PUCCOON
PUCCOONS
PUCE
PUCELAGE
PUCELAGES
PUCELLE
PUCELLES
PUCER
PUCES
PUCEST
PUCK
PUCKA
PUCKED
PUCKER
PUCKERED
PUCKERER
PUCKERERS
PUCKERIER
PUCKERIEST
PUCKERING
PUCKEROOD
PUCKEROOING
PUCKEROOS
PUCKERS
PUCKERY
PUCKFIST
PUCKFISTS
PUCKING
PUCKISH
PUCKISHLY
PUCKISHNESS
PUCKISHNESSES
PUCKLE
PUCKLES
PUCKS
PUD
PUDDEN
PUDDENING
PUDDENINGS
PUDDENS
PUDDER
PUDDERED
PUDDERING
PUDDERS
PUDDIES
PUDDING
PUDDINGS
PUDDINGY
PUDDLE
PUDDLED
PUDDLER
PUDDLERS
PUDDLES
PUDDLIER
PUDDLIEST
PUDDLING

PUDDLINGS
PUDDLY
PUDDOCK
PUDDOCKS
PUDDY
PUDENCIES
PUDENCY
PUDENDA
PUDENDAL
PUDENDOUS
PUDENDUM
PUDENT
PUDGE
PUDGES
PUDGIER
PUDGIEST
PUDGILY
PUDGINESS
PUDGINESSES
PUDGY
PUDIBUND
PUDIBUNDITIES
PUDIBUNDITY
PUDIC
PUDICITIES
PUDICITY
PUDOR
PUDORS
PUDS
PUDSEY
PUDSIER
PUDSIEST
PUDSY
PUDU
PUDUS
PUEBLO
PUEBLOS
PUER
PUERED
PUERILE
PUERILELY
PUERILISM
PUERILISMS
PUERILITIES
PUERILITY
PUERING
PUERPERAL
PUERPERALLY
PUERPERIA
PUERPERIUM
PUERPERIUMS
PUERS
PUFF
PUFFBALL
PUFFBALLS
PUFFBIRD

PUFFBIRDS
PUFFED
PUFFER
PUFFERIES
PUFFERS
PUFFERY
PUFFIER
PUFFIEST
PUFFILY
PUFFIN
PUFFINESS
PUFFINESSES
PUFFING
PUFFINGLY
PUFFINGS
PUFFINS
PUFFS
PUFFY
PUFTALOON
PUFTALOONS
PUG
PUGAREE
PUGAREES
PUGGAREE
PUGGAREES
PUGGED
PUGGERIES
PUGGERY
PUGGIE
PUGGIER
PUGGIES
PUGGIEST
PUGGING
PUGGINGS
PUGGISH
PUGGLE
PUGGLED
PUGGLES
PUGGLING
PUGGREE
PUGGREES
PUGGRIES
PUGGRY
PUGGY
PUGH
PUGIL
PUGILISM
PUGILISMS
PUGILIST
PUGILISTIC
PUGILISTICAL
PUGILISTICALLY
PUGILISTS
PUGILS
PUGMARK
PUGMARKS

PUGNACIOUS
PUGNACIOUSLY
PUGNACIOUSNESS
PUGNACITIES
PUGNACITY
PUGREE
PUGREES
PUGS
PUH
PUHA
PUHAS
PUIR
PUIRER
PUIREST
PUIRTITH
PUISNE
PUISNES
PUISNY
PUISSANCE
PUISSANCES
PUISSANT
PUISSANTLY
PUISSAUNCE
PUISSAUNCES
PUISSAUNT
PUJA
PUJAH
PUJAHS
PUJAS
PUKATEA
PUKATEAS
PUKE
PUKED
PUKEKO
PUKEKOS
PUKER
PUKERS
PUKES
PUKING
PUKKA
PUKU
PUKUS
PUL
PULA
PULAS
PULCHRITUDE
PULCHRITUDES
PULCHRITUDINOUS
PULDRON
PULDRONS
PULE
PULED
PULER
PULERS
PULES
PULI

PULICENE
PULICIDE
PULICIDES
PULIER
PULIEST
PULIK
PULING
PULINGLY
PULINGS
PULIS
PULK
PULKA
PULKAS
PULKHA
PULKHAS
PULKS
PULL
PULLBACK
PULLBACKS
PULLED
PULLER
PULLERS
PULLET
PULLETS
PULLEY
PULLEYS
PULLI
PULLING
PULLMAN
PULLMANS
PULLORUM
PULLOUT
PULLOUTS
PULLOVER
PULLOVERS
PULLS
PULLULATE
PULLULATED
PULLULATES
PULLULATING
PULLULATION
PULLULATIONS
PULLUP
PULLUPS
PULLUS
PULLUSES
PULMO
PULMOBRANCHIATE
PULMOBRANCHS
PULMONARY
PULMONATE
PULMONATES
PULMONES
PULMONIC
PULMONICS
PULMOTOR

PULMOTORS
PULP
PULPAL
PULPALLY
PULPBOARD
PULPBOARDS
PULPED
PULPER
PULPERS
PULPIER
PULPIEST
PULPIFIED
PULPIFIES
PULPIFY
PULPIFYING
PULPILY
PULPINESS
PULPINESSES
PULPING
PULPIT
PULPITAL
PULPITED
PULPITEER
PULPITEERS
PULPITER
PULPITERS
PULPITRIES
PULPITRY
PULPITS
PULPITUM
PULPITUMS
PULPLESS
PULPMILL
PULPMILLS
PULPOUS
PULPS
PULPSTONE
PULPSTONES
PULPWOOD
PULPWOODS
PULPY
PULQUE
PULQUES
PULS
PULSANT
PULSAR
PULSARS
PULSATANCE
PULSATANCES
PULSATE
PULSATED
PULSATES
PULSATILE
PULSATILITY
PULSATILLA
PULSATILLAS

PULSATING
PULSATION
PULSATIONS
PULSATIVE
PULSATIVELY
PULSATIVENESS
PULSATOR
PULSATORS
PULSATORY
PULSE
PULSED
PULSEJET
PULSEJETS
PULSELESS
PULSELESSNESS
PULSELESSNESSES
PULSER
PULSERS
PULSES
PULSIDGE
PULSIDGES
PULSIFIC
PULSIMETER
PULSIMETERS
PULSING
PULSION
PULSIONS
PULSOJET
PULSOJETS
PULSOMETER
PULSOMETERS
PULTACEOUS
PULTAN
PULTANS
PULTON
PULTONS
PULTOON
PULTOONS
PULTRUSION
PULTRUSIONS
PULTUN
PULTUNS
PULTURE
PULTURES
PULU
PULUS
PULVER
PULVERABLE
PULVERATION
PULVERATIONS
PULVERED
PULVERINE
PULVERINES
PULVERING
PULVERISABLE
PULVERISATION

PULVERISATIONS
PULVERISE
PULVERISED
PULVERISER
PULVERISERS
PULVERISES
PULVERISING
PULVERIZABLE
PULVERIZATION
PULVERIZATIONS
PULVERIZE
PULVERIZED
PULVERIZER
PULVERIZERS
PULVERIZES
PULVERIZING
PULVEROUS
PULVERS
PULVERULENCE
PULVERULENCES
PULVERULENT
PULVIL
PULVILIO
PULVILIOS
PULVILLAR
PULVILLE
PULVILLED
PULVILLES
PULVILLI
PULVILLIFORM
PULVILLING
PULVILLIO
PULVILLIOS
PULVILLUS
PULVILS
PULVINAR
PULVINARS
PULVINATE
PULVINATED
PULVINI
PULVINULE
PULVINULES
PULVINUS
PULWAR
PULWARS
PULY
PUMA
PUMAS
PUMELO
PUMELOS
PUMICATE
PUMICATED
PUMICATES
PUMICATING
PUMICE
PUMICED

PUMICEOUS
PUMICER
PUMICERS
PUMICES
PUMICING
PUMICITE
PUMICITES
PUMIE
PUMIES
PUMMEL
PUMMELED
PUMMELING
PUMMELLED
PUMMELLING
PUMMELO
PUMMELOS
PUMMELS
PUMP
PUMPED
PUMPER
PUMPERNICKEL
PUMPERNICKELS
PUMPERS
PUMPHOOD
PUMPHOODS
PUMPING
PUMPION
PUMPIONS
PUMPKIN
PUMPKINS
PUMPKINSEED
PUMPKINSEEDS
PUMPLESS
PUMPLIKE
PUMPS
PUMY
PUN
PUNA
PUNALUA
PUNALUAN
PUNALUAS
PUNAS
PUNCE
PUNCED
PUNCES
PUNCH
PUNCHBAG
PUNCHBAGS
PUNCHBALL
PUNCHBALLS
PUNCHBOARD
PUNCHBOARDS
PUNCHBOWL
PUNCHBOWLS
PUNCHED
PUNCHEON

PUNCHEONS
PUNCHER
PUNCHERS
PUNCHES
PUNCHIER
PUNCHIEST
PUNCHILY
PUNCHINELLO
PUNCHINELLOS
PUNCHINESS
PUNCHING
PUNCHINGBAG
PUNCHINGBAGS
PUNCHLESS
PUNCHY
PUNCING
PUNCTA
PUNCTATE
PUNCTATED
PUNCTATION
PUNCTATIONS
PUNCTATOR
PUNCTATORS
PUNCTILIO
PUNCTILIOS
PUNCTILIOUS
PUNCTILIOUSLY
PUNCTILIOUSNESS
PUNCTO
PUNCTOS
PUNCTUAL
PUNCTUALIST
PUNCTUALISTS
PUNCTUALITIES
PUNCTUALITY
PUNCTUALLY
PUNCTUATE
PUNCTUATED
PUNCTUATES
PUNCTUATING
PUNCTUATION
PUNCTUATIONIST
PUNCTUATIONISTS
PUNCTUATIONS
PUNCTUATIVE
PUNCTUATOR
PUNCTUATORS
PUNCTULATE
PUNCTULATED
PUNCTULATION
PUNCTULATIONS
PUNCTULE
PUNCTULES
PUNCTUM
PUNCTURABILITY
PUNCTURABLE

PUNCTURATION
PUNCTURATIONS
PUNCTURE
PUNCTURED
PUNCTURER
PUNCTURERS
PUNCTURES
PUNCTURING
PUNDIGRION
PUNDIGRIONS
PUNDIT
PUNDITIC
PUNDITRIES
PUNDITRY
PUNDITS
PUNDONOR
PUNDONORES
PUNG
PUNGA
PUNGAS
PUNGENCE
PUNGENCES
PUNGENCIES
PUNGENCY
PUNGENT
PUNGENTLY
PUNGLE
PUNGLED
PUNGLES
PUNGLING
PUNGS
PUNICACEOUS
PUNIER
PUNIEST
PUNILY
PUNINESS
PUNINESSES
PUNISH
PUNISHABILITIES
PUNISHABILITY
PUNISHABLE
PUNISHED
PUNISHER
PUNISHERS
PUNISHES
PUNISHING
PUNISHINGLY
PUNISHMENT
PUNISHMENTS
PUNITION
PUNITIONS
PUNITIVE
PUNITIVELY
PUNITIVENESS
PUNITIVENESSES
PUNITORY

PUNK	PUPARIUM	PUR	PURGED
PUNKA	PUPAS	PURANA	PURGER
PUNKAH	PUPATE	PURANAS	PURGERS
PUNKAHS	PUPATED	PURANIC	PURGES
PUNKAS	PUPATES	PURBLIND	PURGING
PUNKER	PUPATING	PURBLINDLY	PURGINGS
PUNKERS	PUPATION	PURBLINDNESS	PURI
PUNKEST	PUPATIONS	PURBLINDNESSES	PURIFICATION
PUNKEY	PUPFISH	PURCHASABILITY	PURIFICATIONS
PUNKEYS	PUPFISHES	PURCHASABLE	PURIFICATIVE
PUNKIE	PUPIGEROUS	PURCHASE	PURIFICATOR
PUNKIER	PUPIL	PURCHASED	PURIFICATORS
PUNKIES	PUPILABILITIES	PURCHASER	PURIFICATORY
PUNKIEST	PUPILABILITY	PURCHASERS	PURIFIED
PUNKIN	PUPILAGE	PURCHASES	PURIFIER
PUNKINESS	PUPILAGES	PURCHASING	PURIFIERS
PUNKINESSES	PUPILAR	PURDA	PURIFIES
PUNKINS	PUPILARITY	PURDAH	PURIFY
PUNKISH	PUPILARY	PURDAHED	PURIFYING
PUNKS	PUPILLAGE	PURDAHS	PURIM
PUNKY	PUPILLAGES	PURDAS	PURIMS
PUNNED	PUPILLAR	PURDONIUM	PURIN
PUNNER	PUPILLARITIES	PURDONIUMS	PURINE
PUNNERS	PUPILLARITY	PURE	PURINES
PUNNET	PUPILLARY	PUREBLOOD	PURING
PUNNETS	PUPILLATE	PUREBLOODS	PURINS
PUNNIER	PUPILS	PUREBRED	PURIRI
PUNNIEST	PUPILSHIP	PUREBREDS	PURIRIS
PUNNING	PUPILSHIPS	PURED	PURIS
PUNNINGLY	PUPIPAROUS	PUREE	PURISM
PUNNINGS	PUPPED	PUREED	PURISMS
PUNNY	PUPPET	PUREEING	PURIST
PUNS	PUPPETEER	PUREES	PURISTIC
PUNSTER	PUPPETEERS	PURELY	PURISTICAL
PUNSTERS	PUPPETLIKE	PURENESS	PURISTICALLY
PUNT	PUPPETRIES	PURENESSES	PURISTS
PUNTED	PUPPETRY	PURER	PURITAN
PUNTEE	PUPPETS	PURES	PURITANIC
PUNTEES	PUPPIED	PUREST	PURITANICAL
PUNTER	PUPPIES	PURFLE	PURITANICALLY
PUNTERS	PUPPING	PURFLED	PURITANICALNESS
PUNTIES	PUPPODUM	PURFLES	PURITANISE
PUNTING	PUPPODUMS	PURFLING	PURITANISED
PUNTO	PUPPY	PURFLINGS	PURITANISES
PUNTOS	PUPPYDOM	PURFLY	PURITANISING
PUNTS	PUPPYDOMS	PURGATION	PURITANISM
PUNTSMAN	PUPPYHOOD	PURGATIONS	PURITANISMS
PUNTSMEN	PUPPYHOODS	PURGATIVE	PURITANIZE
PUNTY	PUPPYING	PURGATIVELY	PURITANIZED
PUNY	PUPPYISH	PURGATIVES	PURITANIZES
PUP	PUPPYISM	PURGATORIAL	PURITANIZING
PUPA	PUPPYISMS	PURGATORIALLY	PURITANS
PUPAE	PUPPYLIKE	PURGATORIAN	PURITIES
PUPAL	PUPS	PURGATORIES	PURITY
PUPARIA	PUPUNHA	PURGATORY	PURL
PUPARIAL	PUPUNHAS	PURGE	PURLED

PURLER	PURPOSIVE	PURSUERS	PUSHILY
PURLERS	PURPOSIVELY	PURSUES	PUSHINESS
PURLICUE	PURPOSIVENESS	PURSUING	PUSHINESSES
PURLICUED	PURPOSIVENESSES	PURSUINGLY	PUSHING
PURLICUES	PURPRESTURE	PURSUINGS	PUSHINGLY
PURLICUING	PURPRESTURES	PURSUIT	PUSHINGNESS
PURLIEU	PURPURA	PURSUITS	PUSHOVER
PURLIEUS	PURPURAS	PURSUIVANT	PUSHOVERS
PURLIN	PURPURE	PURSUIVANTS	PUSHPIN
PURLINE	PURPUREAL	PURSY	PUSHPINS
PURLINES	PURPURES	PURTENANCE	PUSHROD
PURLING	PURPURIC	PURTENANCES	PUSHRODS
PURLINGS	PURPURIN	PURTIER	PUSHUP
PURLINS	PURPURINS	PURTIEST	PUSHUPS
PURLOIN	PURPY	PURTRAID	PUSHY
PURLOINED	PURR	PURTRAYD	PUSILLANIMITIES
PURLOINER	PURRED	PURTY	PUSILLANIMITY
PURLOINERS	PURRING	PURULENCE	PUSILLANIMOUS
PURLOINING	PURRINGLY	PURULENCES	PUSILLANIMOUSLY
PURLOINS	PURRINGS	PURULENCIES	PUSLE
PURLS	PURRS	PURULENCY	PUSLED
PUROMYCIN	PURS	PURULENT	PUSLES
PUROMYCINS	PURSE	PURULENTLY	PUSLEY
PURPIE	PURSED	PURVEY	PUSLEYS
PURPIES	PURSEFUL	PURVEYANCE	PUSLIKE
PURPLE	PURSEFULS	PURVEYANCES	PUSLING
PURPLED	PURSELIKE	PURVEYED	PUSS
PURPLEHEART	PURSER	PURVEYING	PUSSEL
PURPLEHEARTS	PURSERS	PURVEYOR	PUSSELS
PURPLENESS	PURSERSHIP	PURVEYORS	PUSSER
PURPLER	PURSERSHIPS	PURVEYS	PUSSERS
PURPLES	PURSES	PURVIEW	PUSSES
PURPLEST	PURSEW	PURVIEWS	PUSSIER
PURPLIER	PURSEWED	PUS	PUSSIES
PURPLIEST	PURSEWING	PUSCHKINIA	PUSSIEST
PURPLING	PURSEWS	PUSCHKINIAS	PUSSLEY
PURPLISH	PURSIER	PUSES	PUSSLEYS
PURPLISHNESS	PURSIEST	PUSH	PUSSLIES
PURPLY	PURSILY	PUSHBALL	PUSSLIKE
PURPORT	PURSINESS	PUSHBALLS	PUSSLY
PURPORTED	PURSINESSES	PUSHCART	PUSSY
PURPORTEDLY	PURSING	PUSHCARTS	PUSSYCAT
PURPORTING	PURSLAIN	PUSHCHAIR	PUSSYCATS
PURPORTLESS	PURSLAINS	PUSHCHAIRS	PUSSYFOOT
PURPORTS	PURSLANE	PUSHDOWN	PUSSYFOOTED
PURPOSE	PURSLANES	PUSHDOWNS	PUSSYFOOTER
PURPOSED	PURSUABLE	PUSHED	PUSSYFOOTERS
PURPOSEFUL	PURSUAL	PUSHER	PUSSYFOOTING
PURPOSEFULLY	PURSUALS	PUSHERS	PUSSYFOOTS
PURPOSEFULNESS	PURSUANCE	PUSHES	PUSSYTOES
PURPOSELESS	PURSUANCES	PUSHFUL	PUSTULANT
PURPOSELESSLY	PURSUANT	PUSHFULLY	PUSTULANTS
PURPOSELESSNESS	PURSUANTLY	PUSHFULNESS	PUSTULAR
PURPOSELY	PURSUE	PUSHFULNESSES	PUSTULATE
PURPOSES	PURSUED	PUSHIER	PUSTULATED
PURPOSING	PURSUER	PUSHIEST	PUSTULATES

PUSTULATING
PUSTULATION
PUSTULATIONS
PUSTULE
PUSTULED
PUSTULES
PUSTULOUS
PUT
PUTAMEN
PUTAMINA
PUTANGITANGI
PUTANGITANGIS
PUTATIVE
PUTATIVELY
PUTCHEON
PUTCHEONS
PUTCHER
PUTCHERS
PUTCHOCK
PUTCHOCKS
PUTCHUK
PUTCHUKS
PUTEAL
PUTEALS
PUTELI
PUTELIS
PUTID
PUTLOCK
PUTLOCKS
PUTLOG
PUTLOGS
PUTOFF
PUTOFFS
PUTOIS
PUTON
PUTONS
PUTOUT
PUTOUTS
PUTREFACIENT
PUTREFACTION
PUTREFACTIONS
PUTREFACTIVE
PUTREFIABLE
PUTREFICATION
PUTREFIED
PUTREFIER
PUTREFIERS
PUTREFIES
PUTREFY
PUTREFYING
PUTRESCENCE
PUTRESCENCES
PUTRESCENT
PUTRESCIBILITY
PUTRESCIBLE
PUTRESCIBLES

PUTRESCIBLY
PUTRESCINE
PUTRESCINES
PUTRID
PUTRIDER
PUTRIDEST
PUTRIDITIES
PUTRIDITY
PUTRIDLY
PUTRIDNESS
PUTRIDNESSES
PUTS
PUTSCH
PUTSCHES
PUTSCHIST
PUTSCHISTS
PUTT
PUTTED
PUTTEE
PUTTEES
PUTTEN
PUTTER
PUTTERED
PUTTERER
PUTTERERS
PUTTERING
PUTTERS
PUTTI
PUTTIE
PUTTIED
PUTTIER
PUTTIERS
PUTTIES
PUTTING
PUTTINGS
PUTTO
PUTTOCK
PUTTOCKS
PUTTS
PUTTY
PUTTYING
PUTTYLESS
PUTTYLIKE
PUTTYROOT
PUTTYROOTS
PUTURE
PUTURES
PUTZ
PUTZED
PUTZES
PUTZING
PUY
PUYS
PUZEL
PUZELS
PUZZEL

PUZZELS
PUZZLE
PUZZLED
PUZZLEDOM
PUZZLEDOMS
PUZZLEHEADED
PUZZLEMENT
PUZZLEMENTS
PUZZLER
PUZZLERS
PUZZLES
PUZZLING
PUZZLINGLY
PUZZOLANA
PUZZOLANAS
PYA
PYAEMIA
PYAEMIAS
PYAEMIC
PYAS
PYAT
PYATS
PYCNIC
PYCNIDIA
PYCNIDIAL
PYCNIDIOSPORE
PYCNIDIOSPORES
PYCNIDIUM
PYCNITE
PYCNITES
PYCNOCONIDIA
PYCNOCONIDIUM
PYCNODYSOSTOSES
PYCNODYSOSTOSIS
PYCNOGONID
PYCNOGONIDS
PYCNOGONOID
PYCNOMETER
PYCNOMETERS
PYCNOMETRIC
PYCNOMETRICALLY
PYCNON
PYCNONS
PYCNOSES
PYCNOSIS
PYCNOSPORE
PYCNOSPORES
PYCNOSTYLE
PYCNOSTYLES
PYCNOTIC
PYE
PYEBALD
PYEBALDS
PYEING
PYELITIC
PYELITIS

PYELITISES
PYELOGRAM
PYELOGRAMS
PYELOGRAPHIC
PYELOGRAPHIES
PYELOGRAPHY
PYELONEPHRITIC
PYELONEPHRITIS
PYEMIA
PYEMIAS
PYEMIC
PYENGADU
PYENGADUS
PYES
PYET
PYETS
PYGAL
PYGALS
PYGARG
PYGARGS
PYGIDIA
PYGIDIAL
PYGIDIUM
PYGIDIUMS
PYGMAEAN
PYGMEAN
PYGMIES
PYGMOID
PYGMY
PYGMYISH
PYGMYISM
PYGMYISMS
PYGOSTYLE
PYGOSTYLES
PYIC
PYIN
PYINKADO
PYINKADOS
PYINS
PYJAMA
PYJAMAED
PYJAMAS
PYKNIC
PYKNICS
PYKNODYSOSTOSES
PYKNODYSOSTOSIS
PYKNOMETER
PYKNOMETERS
PYKNOSES
PYKNOSIS
PYKNOSOME
PYKNOSOMES
PYKNOTIC
PYLON
PYLONS
PYLORECTOMIES

PYLORECTOMY
PYLORI
PYLORIC
PYLORUS
PYLORUSES
PYNE
PYNED
PYNES
PYNING
PYODERMA
PYODERMAS
PYOGENESES
PYOGENESIS
PYOGENIC
PYOID
PYONER
PYONERS
PYONINGS
PYORRHEA
PYORRHEAL
PYORRHEAS
PYORRHEIC
PYORRHOEA
PYORRHOEAL
PYORRHOEAS
PYORRHOEIC
PYOSES
PYOSIS
PYOT
PYOTS
PYRACANTH
PYRACANTHA
PYRACANTHAS
PYRACANTHS
PYRAL
PYRALID
PYRALIDS
PYRALIS
PYRALISES
PYRAMID
PYRAMIDAL
PYRAMIDALLY
PYRAMIDED
PYRAMIDES
PYRAMIDIA
PYRAMIDIC
PYRAMIDICAL
PYRAMIDICALLY
PYRAMIDING
PYRAMIDION
PYRAMIDIONS
PYRAMIDIST
PYRAMIDISTS
PYRAMIDOLOGIES
PYRAMIDOLOGIST
PYRAMIDOLOGISTS

PYRAMIDOLOGY
PYRAMIDON
PYRAMIDONS
PYRAMIDS
PYRAMIS
PYRAMISES
PYRAN
PYRANOID
PYRANOMETER
PYRANOMETERS
PYRANOMETRIC
PYRANOSE
PYRANOSES
PYRANOSIDE
PYRANOSIDES
PYRANS
PYRARGYRITE
PYRARGYRITES
PYRAZOLE
PYRE
PYRENE
PYRENEITE
PYRENEITES
PYRENES
PYRENOCARP
PYRENOCARPS
PYRENOID
PYRENOIDS
PYRENOMYCETOUS
PYRES
PYRETHRIN
PYRETHRINS
PYRETHROID
PYRETHROIDS
PYRETHRUM
PYRETHRUMS
PYRETIC
PYRETOLOGIES
PYRETOLOGY
PYRETOTHERAPIES
PYRETOTHERAPY
PYREXIA
PYREXIAL
PYREXIAS
PYREXIC
PYRGEOMETER
PYRGEOMETERS
PYRHELIOMETER
PYRHELIOMETERS
PYRHELIOMETRIC
PYRIC
PYRIDIC
PYRIDINE
PYRIDINES
PYRIDOXAL
PYRIDOXALS

PYRIDOXAMINE
PYRIDOXAMINES
PYRIDOXIN
PYRIDOXINE
PYRIDOXINES
PYRIDOXINS
PYRIFORM
PYRIMETHAMINE
PYRIMETHAMINES
PYRIMIDINE
PYRIMIDINES
PYRITE
PYRITES
PYRITHIAMINE
PYRITHIAMINES
PYRITIC
PYRITICAL
PYRITIFEROUS
PYRITISE
PYRITISED
PYRITISES
PYRITISING
PYRITIZE
PYRITIZED
PYRITIZES
PYRITIZING
PYRITOHEDRA
PYRITOHEDRAL
PYRITOHEDRON
PYRITOUS
PYRO
PYROBALLOGIES
PYROBALLOGY
PYROCATECHIN
PYROCATECHOL
PYROCATECHOLS
PYROCHEMICAL
PYROCHEMICALLY
PYROCLAST
PYROCLASTIC
PYROCLASTICS
PYROCLASTS
PYROELECTRIC
PYROELECTRICITY
PYROELECTRICS
PYROGALLATE
PYROGALLATES
PYROGALLIC
PYROGALLOL
PYROGALLOLS
PYROGEN
PYROGENETIC
PYROGENIC
PYROGENICITIES
PYROGENICITY
PYROGENOUS

PYROGENS
PYROGNOSTIC
PYROGNOSTICS
PYROGRAPHER
PYROGRAPHERS
PYROGRAPHIC
PYROGRAPHICALLY
PYROGRAPHIES
PYROGRAPHY
PYROGRAVURE
PYROGRAVURES
PYROKINESES
PYROKINESIS
PYROLA
PYROLAS
PYROLATER
PYROLATERS
PYROLATRIES
PYROLATRY
PYROLIGNEOUS
PYROLIGNIC
PYROLIZE
PYROLIZED
PYROLIZES
PYROLIZING
PYROLOGIES
PYROLOGY
PYROLUSITE
PYROLUSITES
PYROLYSATE
PYROLYSATES
PYROLYSE
PYROLYSED
PYROLYSER
PYROLYSERS
PYROLYSES
PYROLYSING
PYROLYSIS
PYROLYTIC
PYROLYTICALLY
PYROLYZABLE
PYROLYZATE
PYROLYZATES
PYROLYZE
PYROLYZED
PYROLYZER
PYROLYZERS
PYROLYZES
PYROLYZING
PYROMAGNETIC
PYROMANCER
PYROMANCERS
PYROMANCIES
PYROMANCY
PYROMANIA
PYROMANIAC

PYROMANIACAL
PYROMANIACS
PYROMANIAS
PYROMANTIC
PYROMANTICALLY
PYROMERIDES
PYROMETALLURGY
PYROMETER
PYROMETERS
PYROMETRIC
PYROMETRICAL
PYROMETRICALLY
PYROMETRIES
PYROMETRY
PYROMORPHITE
PYROMORPHITES
PYRONE
PYRONES
PYRONINE
PYRONINES
PYRONINOPHILIC
PYROPE
PYROPES
PYROPHOBIA
PYROPHOBIAS
PYROPHOBIC
PYROPHOBICS
PYROPHONE
PYROPHONES
PYROPHORIC
PYROPHOROUS
PYROPHORUS
PYROPHORUSES
PYROPHOSPHATE
PYROPHOSPHATES
PYROPHOSPHORIC
PYROPHOTOGRAPH
PYROPHOTOGRAPHS
PYROPHOTOGRAPHY
PYROPHOTOMETER
PYROPHOTOMETERS
PYROPHOTOMETRIC
PYROPHOTOMETRY
PYROPHYLLITE
PYROPHYLLITES
PYROPUS
PYROPUSES
PYROS
PYROSCOPE
PYROSCOPES
PYROSES
PYROSIS
PYROSISES
PYROSOME
PYROSOMES
PYROSTAT

PYROSTATIC
PYROSTATS
PYROSULPHATE
PYROSULPHATES
PYROSULPHURIC
PYROTARTRATE
PYROTARTRATES
PYROTECHNIC
PYROTECHNICAL
PYROTECHNICALLY
PYROTECHNICIAN
PYROTECHNICIANS
PYROTECHNICS
PYROTECHNIES
PYROTECHNIST
PYROTECHNISTS
PYROTECHNY
PYROXENE
PYROXENES
PYROXENIC
PYROXENITE
PYROXENITES
PYROXENITIC
PYROXENOID
PYROXENOIDS
PYROXYLE
PYROXYLES
PYROXYLIC
PYROXYLIN
PYROXYLINE
PYROXYLINES
PYROXYLINS
PYRRHIC
PYRRHICIST
PYRRHICISTS
PYRRHICS
PYRRHOTINE
PYRRHOTINES
PYRRHOTITE
PYRRHOTITES
PYRRHOUS
PYRRHULOXIA
PYRRHULOXIAS
PYRROL
PYRROLE
PYRROLES
PYRROLIC
PYRROLIDINE
PYRROLIDINES
PYRROLS
PYRUVATE
PYRUVATES
PYRUVIC
PYTHIUM
PYTHIUMS
PYTHOGENIC

PYTHON
PYTHONESS
PYTHONESSES
PYTHONIC
PYTHONOMORPH
PYTHONOMORPHS
PYTHONS
PYURIA
PYURIAS
PYX
PYXED
PYXES
PYXIDES
PYXIDIA
PYXIDIUM
PYXIE
PYXIES
PYXING
PYXIS
PZAZZ
PZAZZES

Q

QABALAH
QABALAHS
QADI
QADIS
QAID
QAIDS
QAIMAQAM
QAIMAQAMS
QALAMDAN
QALAMDANS
QANAT
QANATS
QASIDA
QASIDAS
QAT
QATS
QAWWAL
QAWWALI
QAWWALIS
QAWWALS
QI
QIBLA
QIBLAS
QIGONG
QIGONGS
QINDAR
QINDARKA
QINDARS
QINGHAOSU
QINGHAOSUS
QINTAR
QINTARS
QIS
QIVIUT
QIVIUTS
QOPH
QOPHS
QORMA
QORMAS
QUA
QUAALUDE
QUAALUDES
QUACK
QUACKED
QUACKER
QUACKERIES
QUACKERS
QUACKERY
QUACKING
QUACKISH
QUACKISM

QUACKISMS
QUACKLE
QUACKLED
QUACKLES
QUACKLING
QUACKS
QUACKSALVER
QUACKSALVERS
QUACKSALVING
QUAD
QUADDED
QUADDIES
QUADDING
QUADDY
QUADPLEX
QUADPLEXES
QUADRAGENARIAN
QUADRAGENARIANS
QUADRAGESIMAL
QUADRANGLE
QUADRANGLES
QUADRANGULAR
QUADRANGULARLY
QUADRANS
QUADRANT
QUADRANTAL
QUADRANTES
QUADRANTS
QUADRAPHONIC
QUADRAPHONICS
QUADRAPHONIES
QUADRAPHONY
QUADRAPLEGIA
QUADRAPLEGIAS
QUADRAPLEGIC
QUADRAPLEGICS
QUADRAT
QUADRATE
QUADRATED
QUADRATES
QUADRATIC
QUADRATICAL
QUADRATICALLY
QUADRATICS
QUADRATING
QUADRATRIX
QUADRATRIXES
QUADRATS
QUADRATURA
QUADRATURE
QUADRATURES

QUADRATUS
QUADRATUSES
QUADRELLA
QUADRELLAS
QUADRENNIA
QUADRENNIAL
QUADRENNIALLY
QUADRENNIALS
QUADRENNIUM
QUADRENNIUMS
QUADRIC
QUADRICEPS
QUADRICEPSES
QUADRICIPITAL
QUADRICONE
QUADRICONES
QUADRICS
QUADRIENNIAL
QUADRIENNIUM
QUADRIFARIOUS
QUADRIFID
QUADRIFOLIATE
QUADRIFORM
QUADRIGA
QUADRIGAE
QUADRIGAS
QUADRIGEMINAL
QUADRIGEMINATE
QUADRIGEMINOUS
QUADRILATERAL
QUADRILATERALS
QUADRILINGUAL
QUADRILITERAL
QUADRILITERALS
QUADRILLE
QUADRILLED
QUADRILLER
QUADRILLERS
QUADRILLES
QUADRILLING
QUADRILLION
QUADRILLIONS
QUADRILLIONTH
QUADRILLIONTHS
QUADRILOCULAR
QUADRINGENARIES
QUADRINOMIAL
QUADRINOMIALS
QUADRIPARTITE
QUADRIPARTITION
QUADRIPHONIC

QUADRIPHONICS
QUADRIPLEGIA
QUADRIPLEGIAS
QUADRIPLEGIC
QUADRIPLEGICS
QUADRIPOLE
QUADRIPOLES
QUADRIREME
QUADRIREMES
QUADRISECT
QUADRISECTED
QUADRISECTING
QUADRISECTION
QUADRISECTIONS
QUADRISECTS
QUADRISYLLABIC
QUADRISYLLABLE
QUADRISYLLABLES
QUADRIVALENCE
QUADRIVALENCES
QUADRIVALENCY
QUADRIVALENT
QUADRIVALENTS
QUADRIVIA
QUADRIVIAL
QUADRIVIALLY
QUADRIVIUM
QUADRIVIUMS
QUADROON
QUADROONS
QUADROPHONIC
QUADROPHONICS
QUADROPHONIES
QUADROPHONY
QUADRUMAN
QUADRUMANE
QUADRUMANES
QUADRUMANOUS
QUADRUMANS
QUADRUMVIR
QUADRUMVIRATE
QUADRUMVIRATES
QUADRUMVIRS
QUADRUPED
QUADRUPEDAL
QUADRUPEDS
QUADRUPLE
QUADRUPLED
QUADRUPLES
QUADRUPLET
QUADRUPLETS

QUADRUPLEX
QUADRUPLEXED
QUADRUPLEXES
QUADRUPLEXING
QUADRUPLICATE
QUADRUPLICATED
QUADRUPLICATES
QUADRUPLICATING
QUADRUPLICATION
QUADRUPLICITIES
QUADRUPLICITY
QUADRUPLIES
QUADRUPLING
QUADRUPLY
QUADRUPOLE
QUADRUPOLES
QUADS
QUAERE
QUAERED
QUAEREING
QUAERES
QUAERITUR
QUAESITUM
QUAESITUMS
QUAESTIONARIES
QUAESTIONARY
QUAESTOR
QUAESTORIAL
QUAESTORS
QUAESTORSHIP
QUAESTORSHIPS
QUAESTUARIES
QUAESTUARY
QUAFF
QUAFFABLE
QUAFFABLY
QUAFFED
QUAFFER
QUAFFERS
QUAFFING
QUAFFS
QUAG
QUAGGA
QUAGGAS
QUAGGIER
QUAGGIEST
QUAGGINESS
QUAGGINESSES
QUAGGY
QUAGMIRE
QUAGMIRED
QUAGMIRES
QUAGMIRIER
QUAGMIRIEST
QUAGMIRING
QUAGMIRY

QUAGS
QUAHAUG
QUAHAUGS
QUAHOG
QUAHOGS
QUAI
QUAICH
QUAICHES
QUAICHS
QUAIGH
QUAIGHS
QUAIL
QUAILED
QUAILING
QUAILINGS
QUAILS
QUAINT
QUAINTER
QUAINTEST
QUAINTLY
QUAINTNESS
QUAINTNESSES
QUAIR
QUAIRS
QUAIS
QUAKE
QUAKED
QUAKER
QUAKERS
QUAKES
QUAKIER
QUAKIEST
QUAKILY
QUAKINESS
QUAKINESSES
QUAKING
QUAKINGLY
QUAKINGS
QUAKY
QUALE
QUALIA
QUALIFIABLE
QUALIFICATION
QUALIFICATIONS
QUALIFICATIVE
QUALIFICATIVES
QUALIFICATOR
QUALIFICATORS
QUALIFICATORY
QUALIFIED
QUALIFIEDLY
QUALIFIER
QUALIFIERS
QUALIFIES
QUALIFY
QUALIFYING

QUALIFYINGS
QUALITATIVE
QUALITATIVELY
QUALITIED
QUALITIES
QUALITY
QUALM
QUALMIER
QUALMIEST
QUALMING
QUALMISH
QUALMISHLY
QUALMISHNESS
QUALMISHNESSES
QUALMLESS
QUALMS
QUALMY
QUAMASH
QUAMASHES
QUANDANG
QUANDANGS
QUANDARIES
QUANDARY
QUANDONG
QUANDONGS
QUANGO
QUANGOCRACIES
QUANGOCRACY
QUANGOS
QUANNET
QUANNETS
QUANT
QUANTA
QUANTAL
QUANTED
QUANTIC
QUANTICAL
QUANTICS
QUANTIFIABLE
QUANTIFICATION
QUANTIFICATIONS
QUANTIFIED
QUANTIFIER
QUANTIFIERS
QUANTIFIES
QUANTIFY
QUANTIFYING
QUANTILE
QUANTILES
QUANTING
QUANTISATION
QUANTISATIONS
QUANTISE
QUANTISED
QUANTISES
QUANTISING

QUANTITATE
QUANTITATED
QUANTITATES
QUANTITATING
QUANTITATION
QUANTITATIONS
QUANTITATIVE
QUANTITATIVELY
QUANTITIES
QUANTITIVE
QUANTITIVELY
QUANTITY
QUANTIVALENCE
QUANTIVALENCES
QUANTIVALENT
QUANTIZATION
QUANTIZATIONS
QUANTIZE
QUANTIZED
QUANTIZER
QUANTIZERS
QUANTIZES
QUANTIZING
QUANTOMETER
QUANTOMETERS
QUANTONG
QUANTONGS
QUANTS
QUANTUM
QUAQUAVERSAL
QUAQUAVERSALLY
QUARANTINE
QUARANTINED
QUARANTINES
QUARANTINING
QUARE
QUARENDEN
QUARENDENS
QUARENDER
QUARENDERS
QUARER
QUAREST
QUARK
QUARKS
QUARREL
QUARRELED
QUARRELER
QUARRELERS
QUARRELING
QUARRELLED
QUARRELLER
QUARRELLERS
QUARRELLING
QUARRELLINGS
QUARRELLOUS
QUARRELS

QUARRELSOME
QUARRELSOMELY
QUARRELSOMENESS
QUARRENDER
QUARRENDERS
QUARRIABLE
QUARRIAN
QUARRIANS
QUARRIED
QUARRIER
QUARRIERS
QUARRIES
QUARRINGTON
QUARRINGTONS
QUARRION
QUARRIONS
QUARRY
QUARRYING
QUARRYINGS
QUARRYMAN
QUARRYMASTER
QUARRYMASTERS
QUARRYMEN
QUART
QUARTAN
QUARTANS
QUARTATION
QUARTATIONS
QUARTE
QUARTER
QUARTERAGE
QUARTERAGES
QUARTERBACK
QUARTERBACKED
QUARTERBACKING
QUARTERBACKS
QUARTERDECK
QUARTERDECKER
QUARTERDECKERS
QUARTERDECKS
QUARTERED
QUARTERFINAL
QUARTERFINALIST
QUARTERFINALS
QUARTERING
QUARTERINGS
QUARTERLIES
QUARTERLIGHT
QUARTERLIGHTS
QUARTERLY
QUARTERMASTER
QUARTERMASTERS
QUARTERMISTRESS
QUARTERN
QUARTERNS
QUARTEROON

QUARTEROONS
QUARTERS
QUARTERSAW
QUARTERSAWED
QUARTERSAWING
QUARTERSAWN
QUARTERSAWS
QUARTERSTAFF
QUARTERSTAFFS
QUARTERSTAVES
QUARTES
QUARTET
QUARTETS
QUARTETT
QUARTETTE
QUARTETTES
QUARTETTI
QUARTETTO
QUARTETTS
QUARTIC
QUARTICS
QUARTIER
QUARTIERS
QUARTILE
QUARTILES
QUARTO
QUARTODECIMAN
QUARTODECIMANS
QUARTOS
QUARTS
QUARTZ
QUARTZES
QUARTZIER
QUARTZIEST
QUARTZIFEROUS
QUARTZITE
QUARTZITES
QUARTZITIC
QUARTZOSE
QUARTZY
QUASAR
QUASARS
QUASH
QUASHED
QUASHEE
QUASHEES
QUASHER
QUASHERS
QUASHES
QUASHIE
QUASHIES
QUASHING
QUASI
QUASICRYSTAL
QUASICRYSTALS
QUASIPARTICLE

QUASIPARTICLES
QUASIPERIODIC
QUASS
QUASSES
QUASSIA
QUASSIAS
QUASSIN
QUASSINS
QUAT
QUATCH
QUATCHED
QUATCHES
QUATCHING
QUATE
QUATERCENTENARY
QUATERNARIES
QUATERNARY
QUATERNATE
QUATERNION
QUATERNIONIST
QUATERNIONISTS
QUATERNIONS
QUATERNITIES
QUATERNITY
QUATORZAIN
QUATORZAINS
QUATORZE
QUATORZES
QUATRAIN
QUATRAINS
QUATRE
QUATREFEUILLE
QUATREFEUILLES
QUATREFOIL
QUATREFOILS
QUATRES
QUATS
QUATTROCENTISM
QUATTROCENTISMS
QUATTROCENTIST
QUATTROCENTISTS
QUATTROCENTO
QUATTROCENTOS
QUAVER
QUAVERED
QUAVERER
QUAVERERS
QUAVERIER
QUAVERIEST
QUAVERING
QUAVERINGLY
QUAVERINGS
QUAVEROUS
QUAVEROUSLY
QUAVERS
QUAVERY

QUAY
QUAYAGE
QUAYAGES
QUAYD
QUAYLIKE
QUAYS
QUAYSIDE
QUAYSIDES
QUAZZIER
QUAZZIEST
QUAZZILY
QUAZZINESS
QUAZZY
QUEACH
QUEACHES
QUEACHIER
QUEACHIEST
QUEACHY
QUEAN
QUEANS
QUEASIER
QUEASIEST
QUEASILY
QUEASINESS
QUEASINESSES
QUEASY
QUEAZIER
QUEAZIEST
QUEAZY
QUEBRACHO
QUEBRACHOS
QUEECHIER
QUEECHIEST
QUEECHY
QUEEN
QUEENCAKE
QUEENCAKES
QUEENCRAFT
QUEENCRAFTS
QUEENDOM
QUEENDOMS
QUEENED
QUEENHOOD
QUEENHOODS
QUEENIE
QUEENIER
QUEENIES
QUEENIEST
QUEENING
QUEENINGS
QUEENITE
QUEENITES
QUEENLESS
QUEENLET
QUEENLETS
QUEENLIER

QUEENLIEST
QUEENLINESS
QUEENLINESSES
QUEENLY
QUEENS
QUEENSHIP
QUEENSHIPS
QUEENSIDE
QUEENSIDES
QUEENY
QUEER
QUEERCORE
QUEERCORES
QUEERDOM
QUEERDOMS
QUEERED
QUEERER
QUEEREST
QUEERING
QUEERISH
QUEERITIES
QUEERITY
QUEERLY
QUEERNESS
QUEERNESSES
QUEERS
QUEEST
QUEESTS
QUEINT
QUELCH
QUELCHED
QUELCHES
QUELCHING
QUELEA
QUELEAS
QUELL
QUELLED
QUELLER
QUELLERS
QUELLING
QUELLS
QUELQUECHOSE
QUELQUECHOSES
QUEME
QUEMED
QUEMES
QUEMING
QUENA
QUENAS
QUENCH
QUENCHABLE
QUENCHED
QUENCHER
QUENCHERS
QUENCHES
QUENCHING

QUENCHINGS
QUENCHLESS
QUENCHLESSLY
QUENELLE
QUENELLES
QUEP
QUERCETIC
QUERCETIN
QUERCETINS
QUERCETUM
QUERCETUMS
QUERCINE
QUERCITIN
QUERCITRON
QUERCITRONS
QUERIDA
QUERIDAS
QUERIED
QUERIER
QUERIERS
QUERIES
QUERIMONIES
QUERIMONIOUS
QUERIMONIOUSLY
QUERIMONY
QUERIST
QUERISTS
QUERN
QUERNS
QUERNSTONE
QUERNSTONES
QUERSPRUNG
QUERSPRUNGS
QUERULOUS
QUERULOUSLY
QUERULOUSNESS
QUERULOUSNESSES
QUERY
QUERYING
QUERYINGLY
QUERYINGS
QUESADILLA
QUESADILLAS
QUEST
QUESTANT
QUESTANTS
QUESTED
QUESTER
QUESTERS
QUESTING
QUESTINGLY
QUESTINGS
QUESTION
QUESTIONABILITY
QUESTIONABLE
QUESTIONABLY

QUESTIONARIES
QUESTIONARY
QUESTIONED
QUESTIONEE
QUESTIONEES
QUESTIONER
QUESTIONERS
QUESTIONING
QUESTIONINGLY
QUESTIONINGS
QUESTIONIST
QUESTIONISTS
QUESTIONLESS
QUESTIONLESSLY
QUESTIONNAIRE
QUESTIONNAIRES
QUESTIONS
QUESTOR
QUESTORIAL
QUESTORS
QUESTORSHIP
QUESTORSHIPS
QUESTRIST
QUESTRISTS
QUESTS
QUETCH
QUETCHED
QUETCHES
QUETCHING
QUETHE
QUETHES
QUETHING
QUETSCH
QUETSCHES
QUETZAL
QUETZALES
QUETZALS
QUEUE
QUEUED
QUEUEING
QUEUEINGS
QUEUER
QUEUERS
QUEUES
QUEUING
QUEUINGS
QUEY
QUEYN
QUEYNIE
QUEYNIES
QUEYNS
QUEYS
QUEZAL
QUEZALES
QUEZALS
QUIBBLE

QUIBBLED
QUIBBLER
QUIBBLERS
QUIBBLES
QUIBBLING
QUIBBLINGLY
QUIBBLINGS
QUIBLIN
QUIBLINS
QUICH
QUICHE
QUICHED
QUICHES
QUICHING
QUICK
QUICKBEAM
QUICKBEAMS
QUICKEN
QUICKENED
QUICKENER
QUICKENERS
QUICKENING
QUICKENINGS
QUICKENS
QUICKER
QUICKEST
QUICKIE
QUICKIES
QUICKLIME
QUICKLIMES
QUICKLY
QUICKNESS
QUICKNESSES
QUICKS
QUICKSAND
QUICKSANDS
QUICKSET
QUICKSETS
QUICKSILVER
QUICKSILVERED
QUICKSILVERING
QUICKSILVERINGS
QUICKSILVERISH
QUICKSILVERS
QUICKSILVERY
QUICKSTEP
QUICKSTEPPED
QUICKSTEPPING
QUICKSTEPS
QUICKTHORN
QUICKTHORNS
QUID
QUIDAM
QUIDAMS
QUIDDANIES
QUIDDANY

QUIDDIT
QUIDDITATIVE
QUIDDITCH
QUIDDITIES
QUIDDITS
QUIDDITY
QUIDDLE
QUIDDLED
QUIDDLER
QUIDDLERS
QUIDDLES
QUIDDLING
QUIDNUNC
QUIDNUNCS
QUIDS
QUIESCE
QUIESCED
QUIESCENCE
QUIESCENCES
QUIESCENCIES
QUIESCENCY
QUIESCENT
QUIESCENTLY
QUIESCES
QUIESCING
QUIET
QUIETED
QUIETEN
QUIETENED
QUIETENING
QUIETENINGS
QUIETENS
QUIETER
QUIETERS
QUIETEST
QUIETING
QUIETINGS
QUIETISM
QUIETISMS
QUIETIST
QUIETISTIC
QUIETISTS
QUIETIVE
QUIETIVES
QUIETLY
QUIETNESS
QUIETNESSES
QUIETS
QUIETSOME
QUIETUDE
QUIETUDES
QUIETUS
QUIETUSES
QUIFF
QUIFFS
QUIGHT

QUIGHTED
QUIGHTING
QUIGHTS
QUILL
QUILLAI
QUILLAIA
QUILLAIAS
QUILLAIS
QUILLAJA
QUILLAJAS
QUILLBACK
QUILLBACKS
QUILLED
QUILLET
QUILLETS
QUILLING
QUILLINGS
QUILLMAN
QUILLMEN
QUILLON
QUILLONS
QUILLS
QUILLWORK
QUILLWORKS
QUILLWORT
QUILLWORTS
QUILT
QUILTED
QUILTER
QUILTERS
QUILTING
QUILTINGS
QUILTS
QUIM
QUIMS
QUIN
QUINA
QUINACRINE
QUINACRINES
QUINAQUINA
QUINAQUINAS
QUINARIES
QUINARY
QUINAS
QUINATE
QUINCE
QUINCENTENARIES
QUINCENTENARY
QUINCENTENNIAL
QUINCENTENNIALS
QUINCES
QUINCHE
QUINCHED
QUINCHES
QUINCHING
QUINCUNCIAL

QUINCUNCIALLY
QUINCUNX
QUINCUNXES
QUINCUNXIAL
QUINDECAGON
QUINDECAGONS
QUINDECAPLET
QUINDECAPLETS
QUINDECENNIAL
QUINDECENNIALS
QUINDECILLION
QUINDECILLIONS
QUINE
QUINELA
QUINELAS
QUINELLA
QUINELLAS
QUINES
QUINGENTENARIES
QUINGENTENARY
QUINIC
QUINIDINE
QUINIDINES
QUINIE
QUINIELA
QUINIELAS
QUINIES
QUININ
QUININA
QUININAS
QUININE
QUININES
QUININS
QUINNAT
QUINNATS
QUINOA
QUINOAS
QUINOID
QUINOIDAL
QUINOIDS
QUINOL
QUINOLIN
QUINOLINE
QUINOLINES
QUINOLINS
QUINOLONE
QUINOLONES
QUINOLS
QUINONE
QUINONES
QUINONOID
QUINQUAGENARIAN
QUINQUAGESIMAL
QUINQUECOSTATE
QUINQUEFARIOUS
QUINQUEFOLIATE

QUINQUENNIA
QUINQUENNIAD
QUINQUENNIADS
QUINQUENNIAL
QUINQUENNIALLY
QUINQUENNIALS
QUINQUENNIUM
QUINQUENNIUMS
QUINQUEPARTITE
QUINQUEREME
QUINQUEREMES
QUINQUEVALENCE
QUINQUEVALENCES
QUINQUEVALENCY
QUINQUEVALENT
QUINQUINA
QUINQUINAS
QUINQUIVALENT
QUINS
QUINSIED
QUINSIES
QUINSY
QUINT
QUINTA
QUINTAIN
QUINTAINS
QUINTAL
QUINTALS
QUINTAN
QUINTANS
QUINTAR
QUINTARS
QUINTAS
QUINTE
QUINTES
QUINTESSENCE
QUINTESSENCES
QUINTESSENTIAL
QUINTET
QUINTETS
QUINTETT
QUINTETTE
QUINTETTES
QUINTETTI
QUINTETTO
QUINTETTS
QUINTIC
QUINTICS
QUINTILE
QUINTILES
QUINTILLION
QUINTILLIONS
QUINTILLIONTH
QUINTILLIONTHS
QUINTIN
QUINTINS

QUINTROON
QUINTROONS
QUINTS
QUINTUPLE
QUINTUPLED
QUINTUPLES
QUINTUPLET
QUINTUPLETS
QUINTUPLICATE
QUINTUPLICATED
QUINTUPLICATES
QUINTUPLICATING
QUINTUPLICATION
QUINTUPLING
QUINZE
QUINZES
QUIP
QUIPO
QUIPOS
QUIPPED
QUIPPER
QUIPPERS
QUIPPING
QUIPPISH
QUIPPU
QUIPPUS
QUIPS
QUIPSTER
QUIPSTERS
QUIPU
QUIPUS
QUIRE
QUIRED
QUIRES
QUIRING
QUIRISTER
QUIRISTERS
QUIRK
QUIRKED
QUIRKIER
QUIRKIEST
QUIRKILY
QUIRKINESS
QUIRKINESSES
QUIRKING
QUIRKISH
QUIRKS
QUIRKY
QUIRT
QUIRTED
QUIRTING
QUIRTS
QUISLING
QUISLINGISM
QUISLINGISMS
QUISLINGS

QUIST
QUISTS
QUIT
QUITCH
QUITCHED
QUITCHES
QUITCHING
QUITCLAIM
QUITCLAIMED
QUITCLAIMING
QUITCLAIMS
QUITE
QUITED
QUITES
QUITING
QUITRENT
QUITRENTS
QUITS
QUITTAL
QUITTALS
QUITTANCE
QUITTANCED
QUITTANCES
QUITTANCING
QUITTED
QUITTER
QUITTERS
QUITTING
QUITTOR
QUITTORS
QUIVER
QUIVERED
QUIVERER
QUIVERERS
QUIVERFUL
QUIVERFULS
QUIVERIER
QUIVERIEST
QUIVERING
QUIVERINGLY
QUIVERINGS
QUIVERISH
QUIVERS
QUIVERY
QUIXOTE
QUIXOTES
QUIXOTIC
QUIXOTICAL
QUIXOTICALLY
QUIXOTISM
QUIXOTISMS
QUIXOTRIES
QUIXOTRY
QUIZ
QUIZMASTER
QUIZMASTERS

QUIZZED
QUIZZER
QUIZZERIES
QUIZZERS
QUIZZERY
QUIZZES
QUIZZICAL
QUIZZICALITIES
QUIZZICALITY
QUIZZICALLY
QUIZZIFICATION
QUIZZIFICATIONS
QUIZZIFIED
QUIZZIFIES
QUIZZIFY
QUIZZIFYING
QUIZZINESS
QUIZZINESSES
QUIZZING
QUIZZINGS
QUOAD
QUOD
QUODDED
QUODDING
QUODLIBET
QUODLIBETARIAN
QUODLIBETARIANS
QUODLIBETIC
QUODLIBETICAL
QUODLIBETICALLY
QUODLIBETS
QUODLIN
QUODLINS
QUODS
QUOHOG
QUOHOGS
QUOIF
QUOIFED
QUOIFING
QUOIFS
QUOIN
QUOINED
QUOINING
QUOINS
QUOIST
QUOISTS
QUOIT
QUOITED
QUOITER
QUOITERS
QUOITING
QUOITS
QUOKKA
QUOKKAS
QUOLL
QUOLLS

QUOMODO
QUOMODOS
QUONDAM
QUONK
QUONKED
QUONKING
QUONKS
QUOOKE
QUOP
QUOPPED
QUOPPING
QUOPS
QUORATE
QUORUM
QUORUMS
QUOTA
QUOTABILITIES
QUOTABILITY
QUOTABLE
QUOTABLENESS
QUOTABLENESSES
QUOTABLY
QUOTAS
QUOTATION
QUOTATIONS
QUOTATIOUS
QUOTATIVE
QUOTATIVES
QUOTE
QUOTED
QUOTER
QUOTERS
QUOTES
QUOTEWORTHY
QUOTH
QUOTHA
QUOTIDIAN
QUOTIDIANS
QUOTIENT
QUOTIENTS
QUOTING
QUOTITION
QUOTITIONS
QUOTUM
QUOTUMS
QURSH
QURSHES
QURUSH
QURUSHES
QUYTE
QUYTED
QUYTES
QUYTING
QWERTIES
QWERTY
QWERTYS

R

RABANNA
RABANNAS
RABAT
RABATINE
RABATINES
RABATMENT
RABATMENTS
RABATO
RABATOES
RABATOS
RABATS
RABATTE
RABATTED
RABATTEMENT
RABATTEMENTS
RABATTES
RABATTING
RABATTINGS
RABBET
RABBETED
RABBETING
RABBETS
RABBI
RABBIES
RABBIN
RABBINATE
RABBINATES
RABBINIC
RABBINICAL
RABBINICALLY
RABBINICS
RABBINISM
RABBINISMS
RABBINIST
RABBINISTIC
RABBINISTS
RABBINITE
RABBINITES
RABBINS
RABBIS
RABBIT
RABBITBRUSH
RABBITBRUSHES
RABBITED
RABBITER
RABBITERS
RABBITFISH
RABBITFISHES
RABBITING
RABBITO
RABBITOH

RABBITOHS
RABBITOS
RABBITRIES
RABBITRY
RABBITS
RABBITY
RABBLE
RABBLED
RABBLEMENT
RABBLEMENTS
RABBLER
RABBLERS
RABBLES
RABBLING
RABBLINGS
RABBONI
RABBONIS
RABI
RABIC
RABID
RABIDER
RABIDEST
RABIDITIES
RABIDITY
RABIDLY
RABIDNESS
RABIDNESSES
RABIES
RABIETIC
RABIS
RACA
RACAHOUT
RACAHOUTS
RACCAHOUT
RACCAHOUTS
RACCOON
RACCOONS
RACE
RACECARD
RACECARDS
RACECOURSE
RACECOURSES
RACED
RACEGOER
RACEGOERS
RACEGOING
RACEGOINGS
RACEHORSE
RACEHORSES
RACEMATE
RACEMATES

RACEMATION
RACEMATIONS
RACEME
RACEMED
RACEMES
RACEMIC
RACEMISATION
RACEMISATIONS
RACEMISE
RACEMISED
RACEMISES
RACEMISING
RACEMISM
RACEMISMS
RACEMIZATION
RACEMIZATIONS
RACEMIZE
RACEMIZED
RACEMIZES
RACEMIZING
RACEMOID
RACEMOSE
RACEMOSELY
RACEMOUS
RACEMOUSLY
RACEPATH
RACEPATHS
RACER
RACERS
RACES
RACETRACK
RACETRACKER
RACETRACKERS
RACETRACKS
RACEWALKER
RACEWALKERS
RACEWALKING
RACEWALKINGS
RACEWAY
RACEWAYS
RACH
RACHE
RACHES
RACHET
RACHETS
RACHIAL
RACHIDES
RACHIDIAL
RACHIDIAN
RACHILLA
RACHILLAE

RACHILLAS
RACHIOTOMIES
RACHIOTOMY
RACHIS
RACHISCHISES
RACHISCHISIS
RACHISES
RACHITIC
RACHITIDES
RACHITIS
RACHITISES
RACIAL
RACIALISE
RACIALISM
RACIALISMS
RACIALIST
RACIALISTIC
RACIALISTS
RACIALIZE
RACIALLY
RACIATION
RACIATIONS
RACIER
RACIEST
RACILY
RACINESS
RACINESSES
RACING
RACINGS
RACISM
RACISMS
RACIST
RACISTS
RACK
RACKABONES
RACKED
RACKER
RACKERS
RACKET
RACKETED
RACKETEER
RACKETEERED
RACKETEERING
RACKETEERINGS
RACKETEERS
RACKETER
RACKETERS
RACKETIER
RACKETIEST
RACKETING
RACKETRIES

RACKETRY
RACKETS
RACKETT
RACKETTS
RACKETY
RACKFUL
RACKFULS
RACKING
RACKINGLY
RACKINGS
RACKLE
RACKS
RACKWORK
RACKWORKS
RACLETTE
RACLETTES
RACLOIR
RACLOIRS
RACON
RACONS
RACONTEUR
RACONTEURING
RACONTEURINGS
RACONTEURS
RACONTEUSE
RACONTEUSES
RACOON
RACOONS
RACQUET
RACQUETBALL
RACQUETBALLS
RACQUETED
RACQUETING
RACQUETS
RACY
RAD
RADAR
RADARS
RADARSCOPE
RADARSCOPES
RADDED
RADDER
RADDEST
RADDING
RADDLE
RADDLED
RADDLEMAN
RADDLEMEN
RADDLES
RADDLING
RADDOCKE
RADDOCKES
RADE
RADGE
RADGER
RADGES

RADGEST
RADIABLE
RADIAL
RADIALE
RADIALIA
RADIALISATION
RADIALISATIONS
RADIALISE
RADIALISED
RADIALISES
RADIALISING
RADIALITIES
RADIALITY
RADIALIZATION
RADIALIZATIONS
RADIALIZE
RADIALIZED
RADIALIZES
RADIALIZING
RADIALLY
RADIALS
RADIAN
RADIANCE
RADIANCES
RADIANCIES
RADIANCY
RADIANS
RADIANT
RADIANTLY
RADIANTS
RADIATA
RADIATAS
RADIATE
RADIATED
RADIATELY
RADIATES
RADIATING
RADIATION
RADIATIONAL
RADIATIONLESS
RADIATIONS
RADIATIVE
RADIATOR
RADIATORS
RADIATORY
RADICAL
RADICALISATION
RADICALISATIONS
RADICALISE
RADICALISED
RADICALISES
RADICALISING
RADICALISM
RADICALISMS
RADICALISTIC
RADICALITIES

RADICALITY
RADICALIZATION
RADICALIZATIONS
RADICALIZE
RADICALIZED
RADICALIZES
RADICALIZING
RADICALLY
RADICALNESS
RADICALNESSES
RADICALS
RADICAND
RADICANDS
RADICANT
RADICATE
RADICATED
RADICATES
RADICATING
RADICATION
RADICATIONS
RADICCHIO
RADICCHIOS
RADICEL
RADICELS
RADICES
RADICICOLOUS
RADICIFORM
RADICIVOROUS
RADICLE
RADICLES
RADICULAR
RADICULE
RADICULES
RADICULOSE
RADIESTHESIA
RADIESTHESIAS
RADIESTHESIST
RADIESTHESISTS
RADIESTHETIC
RADII
RADIO
RADIOACTIVATE
RADIOACTIVATED
RADIOACTIVATES
RADIOACTIVATING
RADIOACTIVATION
RADIOACTIVE
RADIOACTIVELY
RADIOACTIVITIES
RADIOACTIVITY
RADIOAUTOGRAPH
RADIOAUTOGRAPHS
RADIOAUTOGRAPHY
RADIOBIOLOGIC
RADIOBIOLOGICAL
RADIOBIOLOGIES

RADIOBIOLOGIST
RADIOBIOLOGISTS
RADIOBIOLOGY
RADIOCARBON
RADIOCARBONS
RADIOCHEMICAL
RADIOCHEMICALLY
RADIOCHEMIST
RADIOCHEMISTRY
RADIOCHEMISTS
RADIOECOLOGIES
RADIOECOLOGY
RADIOED
RADIOELEMENT
RADIOELEMENTS
RADIOGENIC
RADIOGONIOMETER
RADIOGRAM
RADIOGRAMS
RADIOGRAPH
RADIOGRAPHED
RADIOGRAPHER
RADIOGRAPHERS
RADIOGRAPHIC
RADIOGRAPHIES
RADIOGRAPHING
RADIOGRAPHS
RADIOGRAPHY
RADIOING
RADIOISOTOPE
RADIOISOTOPES
RADIOISOTOPIC
RADIOLABEL
RADIOLABELED
RADIOLABELING
RADIOLABELLED
RADIOLABELLING
RADIOLABELS
RADIOLARIAN
RADIOLARIANS
RADIOLOCATION
RADIOLOCATIONAL
RADIOLOCATIONS
RADIOLOGIC
RADIOLOGICAL
RADIOLOGICALLY
RADIOLOGIES
RADIOLOGIST
RADIOLOGISTS
RADIOLOGY
RADIOLUCENCIES
RADIOLUCENCY
RADIOLUCENT
RADIOLYSES
RADIOLYSIS
RADIOLYTIC

RADIOMAN
RADIOMEN
RADIOMETER
RADIOMETERS
RADIOMETRIC
RADIOMETRICALLY
RADIOMETRIES
RADIOMETRY
RADIOMICROMETER
RADIOMIMETIC
RADIONICS
RADIONUCLIDE
RADIONUCLIDES
RADIOPACITY
RADIOPAGER
RADIOPAGERS
RADIOPAGING
RADIOPAGINGS
RADIOPAQUE
RADIOPAQUELY
RADIOPHONE
RADIOPHONES
RADIOPHONIC
RADIOPHONICALLY
RADIOPHONICS
RADIOPHONIES
RADIOPHONIST
RADIOPHONISTS
RADIOPHONY
RADIOPHOTO
RADIOPHOTOS
RADIOPROTECTION
RADIOPROTECTIVE
RADIORESISTANT
RADIOS
RADIOSCOPE
RADIOSCOPES
RADIOSCOPIC
RADIOSCOPICALLY
RADIOSCOPIES
RADIOSCOPY
RADIOSENSITISE
RADIOSENSITISED
RADIOSENSITISES
RADIOSENSITIVE
RADIOSENSITIZE
RADIOSENSITIZED
RADIOSENSITIZES
RADIOSONDE
RADIOSONDES
RADIOSTRONTIUM
RADIOSTRONTIUMS
RADIOTELEGRAM
RADIOTELEGRAMS
RADIOTELEGRAPH
RADIOTELEGRAPHS

RADIOTELEGRAPHY
RADIOTELEMETER
RADIOTELEMETERS
RADIOTELEMETRIC
RADIOTELEMETRY
RADIOTELEPHONE
RADIOTELEPHONES
RADIOTELEPHONIC
RADIOTELEPHONY
RADIOTELETYPE
RADIOTELETYPES
RADIOTHERAPIES
RADIOTHERAPIST
RADIOTHERAPISTS
RADIOTHERAPY
RADIOTHERMY
RADIOTHON
RADIOTHONS
RADIOTHORIUM
RADIOTHORIUMS
RADIOTOXIC
RADIOTRACER
RADIOTRACERS
RADISH
RADISHES
RADIUM
RADIUMS
RADIUS
RADIUSES
RADIX
RADIXES
RADOME
RADOMES
RADON
RADONS
RADS
RADULA
RADULAE
RADULAR
RADULAS
RADULATE
RADULIFORM
RADWASTE
RADWASTES
RAFALE
RAFALES
RAFF
RAFFIA
RAFFIAS
RAFFINATE
RAFFINATES
RAFFINOSE
RAFFINOSES
RAFFISH
RAFFISHLY
RAFFISHNESS

RAFFISHNESSES
RAFFLE
RAFFLED
RAFFLER
RAFFLERS
RAFFLES
RAFFLESIA
RAFFLESIAS
RAFFLING
RAFFS
RAFT
RAFTED
RAFTER
RAFTERED
RAFTERING
RAFTERINGS
RAFTERS
RAFTING
RAFTMAN
RAFTMEN
RAFTS
RAFTSMAN
RAFTSMEN
RAG
RAGA
RAGAMUFFIN
RAGAMUFFINS
RAGAS
RAGBAG
RAGBAGS
RAGBOLT
RAGBOLTS
RAGDE
RAGE
RAGED
RAGEE
RAGEES
RAGEFUL
RAGER
RAGERS
RAGES
RAGG
RAGGA
RAGGAMUFFIN
RAGGAMUFFINS
RAGGAS
RAGGED
RAGGEDER
RAGGEDEST
RAGGEDLY
RAGGEDNESS
RAGGEDNESSES
RAGGEDY
RAGGEE
RAGGEES
RAGGERIES

RAGGERY
RAGGIER
RAGGIES
RAGGIEST
RAGGING
RAGGINGS
RAGGLE
RAGGLED
RAGGLES
RAGGLING
RAGGS
RAGGY
RAGHEAD
RAGHEADS
RAGI
RAGING
RAGINGLY
RAGINGS
RAGINI
RAGINIS
RAGIS
RAGLAN
RAGLANS
RAGMAN
RAGMANS
RAGMATICAL
RAGMEN
RAGMENT
RAGMENTS
RAGOUT
RAGOUTED
RAGOUTING
RAGOUTS
RAGPICKER
RAGPICKERS
RAGS
RAGSTONE
RAGSTONES
RAGTAG
RAGTAGS
RAGTIME
RAGTIMER
RAGTIMERS
RAGTIMES
RAGTOP
RAGTOPS
RAGULED
RAGULY
RAGWEED
RAGWEEDS
RAGWHEEL
RAGWHEELS
RAGWORK
RAGWORKS
RAGWORM
RAGWORMS

RAGWORT
RAGWORTS
RAH
RAHED
RAHING
RAHS
RAHUI
RAHUIS
RAI
RAIA
RAIAS
RAID
RAIDED
RAIDER
RAIDERS
RAIDING
RAIDS
RAIK
RAIKED
RAIKING
RAIKS
RAIL
RAILBED
RAILBEDS
RAILBIRD
RAILBIRDS
RAILBUS
RAILBUSES
RAILBUSSES
RAILCAR
RAILCARD
RAILCARDS
RAILCARS
RAILE
RAILED
RAILER
RAILERS
RAILES
RAILHEAD
RAILHEADS
RAILING
RAILINGLY
RAILINGS
RAILLERIES
RAILLERY
RAILLESS
RAILLIES
RAILLY
RAILMAN
RAILMEN
RAILROAD
RAILROADED
RAILROADER
RAILROADERS
RAILROADING
RAILROADINGS

RAILROADS
RAILS
RAILWAY
RAILWAYMAN
RAILWAYMEN
RAILWAYS
RAILWOMAN
RAILWOMEN
RAIMENT
RAIMENTS
RAIN
RAINBAND
RAINBANDS
RAINBIRD
RAINBIRDS
RAINBOW
RAINBOWED
RAINBOWLIKE
RAINBOWS
RAINBOWY
RAINCHECK
RAINCHECKS
RAINCOAT
RAINCOATS
RAINDATE
RAINDATES
RAINDROP
RAINDROPS
RAINE
RAINED
RAINES
RAINFALL
RAINFALLS
RAINFOREST
RAINFORESTS
RAINIER
RAINIEST
RAINILY
RAININESS
RAININESSES
RAINING
RAINLESS
RAINMAKER
RAINMAKERS
RAINMAKING
RAINMAKINGS
RAINOUT
RAINOUTS
RAINPROOF
RAINPROOFED
RAINPROOFING
RAINPROOFS
RAINS
RAINSPOUT
RAINSPOUTS
RAINSQUALL

RAINSQUALLS
RAINSTORM
RAINSTORMS
RAINTIGHT
RAINWASH
RAINWASHED
RAINWASHES
RAINWASHING
RAINWATER
RAINWATERS
RAINWEAR
RAINWEARS
RAINY
RAIRD
RAIRDS
RAIS
RAISABLE
RAISE
RAISEABLE
RAISED
RAISER
RAISERS
RAISES
RAISIN
RAISING
RAISINGS
RAISINS
RAISINY
RAISONNE
RAISONNEUR
RAISONNEURS
RAIT
RAITA
RAITAS
RAITED
RAITING
RAITS
RAIYAT
RAIYATS
RAIYATWARI
RAIYATWARIS
RAJ
RAJA
RAJAH
RAJAHS
RAJAHSHIP
RAJAHSHIPS
RAJAS
RAJASHIP
RAJASHIPS
RAJES
RAJPRAMUKH
RAJPRAMUKHS
RAKE
RAKED
RAKEE

RAKEES
RAKEHELL
RAKEHELLS
RAKEHELLY
RAKEOFF
RAKEOFFS
RAKER
RAKERIES
RAKERS
RAKERY
RAKES
RAKESHAME
RAKESHAMES
RAKI
RAKING
RAKINGS
RAKIS
RAKISH
RAKISHLY
RAKISHNESS
RAKISHNESSES
RAKSHAS
RAKSHASA
RAKSHASAS
RAKSHASES
RAKU
RAKUS
RALE
RALES
RALLENTANDO
RALLENTANDOS
RALLIED
RALLIER
RALLIERS
RALLIES
RALLINE
RALLY
RALLYCROSS
RALLYE
RALLYES
RALLYING
RALLYINGLY
RALLYINGS
RALLYIST
RALLYISTS
RALPH
RALPHED
RALPHING
RALPHS
RAM
RAMAKIN
RAMAKINS
RAMAL
RAMAPITHECINE
RAMAPITHECINES
RAMATE

RAMBLE
RAMBLED
RAMBLER
RAMBLERS
RAMBLES
RAMBLING
RAMBLINGLY
RAMBLINGS
RAMBOUILLET
RAMBOUILLETS
RAMBUNCTIOUS
RAMBUNCTIOUSLY
RAMBUTAN
RAMBUTANS
RAMCAT
RAMCATS
RAMEAL
RAMEE
RAMEES
RAMEKIN
RAMEKINS
RAMEN
RAMENS
RAMENTA
RAMENTACEOUS
RAMENTUM
RAMEOUS
RAMEQUIN
RAMEQUINS
RAMET
RAMETS
RAMFEEZLED
RAMFEEZLES
RAMFEEZLING
RAMGUNSHOCH
RAMI
RAMIE
RAMIES
RAMIFICATION
RAMIFICATIONS
RAMIFIED
RAMIFIES
RAMIFORM
RAMIFY
RAMIFYING
RAMILIE
RAMILIES
RAMILLIE
RAMILLIES
RAMIN
RAMINS
RAMIS
RAMJET
RAMJETS
RAMMED
RAMMEL

RAMMER
RAMMERS
RAMMIER
RAMMIES
RAMMIEST
RAMMING
RAMMISH
RAMMISHLY
RAMMISHNESS
RAMMLE
RAMMY
RAMOSE
RAMOSELY
RAMOSITIES
RAMOSITY
RAMOUS
RAMOUSLY
RAMP
RAMPACIOUS
RAMPAGE
RAMPAGED
RAMPAGEOUS
RAMPAGEOUSLY
RAMPAGEOUSNESS
RAMPAGER
RAMPAGERS
RAMPAGES
RAMPAGING
RAMPAGINGS
RAMPALLIAN
RAMPALLIANS
RAMPANCIES
RAMPANCY
RAMPANT
RAMPANTLY
RAMPART
RAMPARTED
RAMPARTING
RAMPARTS
RAMPAUGE
RAMPAUGED
RAMPAUGES
RAMPAUGING
RAMPED
RAMPER
RAMPERS
RAMPICK
RAMPICKED
RAMPICKS
RAMPIKE
RAMPIKES
RAMPING
RAMPINGS
RAMPION
RAMPIONS
RAMPIRE

RAMPIRED
RAMPIRES
RAMPOLE
RAMPOLES
RAMPS
RAMPSMAN
RAMPSMEN
RAMROD
RAMRODDED
RAMRODDING
RAMRODS
RAMS
RAMSHACKLE
RAMSHORN
RAMSHORNS
RAMSON
RAMSONS
RAMSTAM
RAMTIL
RAMTILS
RAMULAR
RAMULI
RAMULOSE
RAMULOUS
RAMULUS
RAMUS
RAN
RANA
RANARIAN
RANARIUM
RANARIUMS
RANAS
RANCE
RANCED
RANCEL
RANCELS
RANCES
RANCH
RANCHED
RANCHER
RANCHERIA
RANCHERIAS
RANCHERIE
RANCHERIES
RANCHERO
RANCHEROS
RANCHERS
RANCHES
RANCHING
RANCHINGS
RANCHMAN
RANCHMEN
RANCHO
RANCHOS
RANCID
RANCIDER

RANCIDEST
RANCIDITIES
RANCIDITY
RANCIDLY
RANCIDNESS
RANCIDNESSES
RANCING
RANCOR
RANCORED
RANCOROUS
RANCOROUSLY
RANCOROUSNESS
RANCORS
RANCOUR
RANCOURS
RAND
RANDAN
RANDANS
RANDED
RANDEM
RANDEMS
RANDIE
RANDIER
RANDIES
RANDIEST
RANDILY
RANDINESS
RANDING
RANDLORD
RANDLORDS
RANDOM
RANDOMISATION
RANDOMISATIONS
RANDOMISE
RANDOMISED
RANDOMISER
RANDOMISERS
RANDOMISES
RANDOMISING
RANDOMIZATION
RANDOMIZATIONS
RANDOMIZE
RANDOMIZED
RANDOMIZER
RANDOMIZERS
RANDOMIZES
RANDOMIZING
RANDOMLY
RANDOMNESS
RANDOMNESSES
RANDOMS
RANDOMWISE
RANDON
RANDONS
RANDS
RANDY

RANEE
RANEES
RANG
RANGATIRA
RANGATIRAS
RANGATIRATANGA
RANGATIRATANGAS
RANGE
RANGED
RANGEFINDER
RANGEFINDERS
RANGEFINDING
RANGEFINDINGS
RANGELAND
RANGELANDS
RANGER
RANGERS
RANGERSHIP
RANGERSHIPS
RANGES
RANGI
RANGIER
RANGIEST
RANGILY
RANGINESS
RANGINESSES
RANGING
RANGIORA
RANGIORAS
RANGOLI
RANGOLIS
RANGY
RANI
RANID
RANIDS
RANIFORM
RANINE
RANIS
RANIVOROUS
RANK
RANKE
RANKED
RANKER
RANKERS
RANKES
RANKEST
RANKING
RANKINGS
RANKISH
RANKLE
RANKLED
RANKLES
RANKLING
RANKLY
RANKNESS
RANKNESSES

RANKS
RANKSHIFT
RANKSHIFTED
RANKSHIFTING
RANKSHIFTS
RANPIKE
RANPIKES
RANSACK
RANSACKED
RANSACKER
RANSACKERS
RANSACKING
RANSACKS
RANSEL
RANSELS
RANSHACKLE
RANSHACKLED
RANSHACKLES
RANSHACKLING
RANSHAKLE
RANSHAKLED
RANSHAKLES
RANSHAKLING
RANSOM
RANSOMABLE
RANSOMED
RANSOMER
RANSOMERS
RANSOMING
RANSOMLESS
RANSOMS
RANT
RANTED
RANTER
RANTERISM
RANTERISMS
RANTERS
RANTING
RANTINGLY
RANTINGS
RANTIPOLE
RANTIPOLED
RANTIPOLES
RANTIPOLING
RANTS
RANULA
RANULAS
RANUNCULACEOUS
RANUNCULI
RANUNCULUS
RANUNCULUSES
RANZEL
RANZELMAN
RANZELMEN
RANZELS
RAOULIA

RAOULIAS
RAP
RAPACIOUS
RAPACIOUSLY
RAPACIOUSNESS
RAPACIOUSNESSES
RAPACITIES
RAPACITY
RAPE
RAPED
RAPER
RAPERS
RAPES
RAPESEED
RAPESEEDS
RAPHAE
RAPHANIA
RAPHANIAS
RAPHE
RAPHES
RAPHIA
RAPHIAS
RAPHIDE
RAPHIDES
RAPHIS
RAPID
RAPIDER
RAPIDEST
RAPIDITIES
RAPIDITY
RAPIDLY
RAPIDNESS
RAPIDNESSES
RAPIDS
RAPIER
RAPIERED
RAPIERLIKE
RAPIERS
RAPINE
RAPINES
RAPING
RAPINI
RAPIST
RAPISTS
RAPLOCH
RAPLOCHS
RAPPAREE
RAPPAREES
RAPPE
RAPPED
RAPPEE
RAPPEES
RAPPEL
RAPPELED
RAPPELING
RAPPELLED

RAPPELLING
RAPPELLINGS
RAPPELS
RAPPEN
RAPPER
RAPPERS
RAPPING
RAPPINGS
RAPPINI
RAPPORT
RAPPORTAGE
RAPPORTAGES
RAPPORTEUR
RAPPORTEURS
RAPPORTS
RAPPROCHEMENT
RAPPROCHEMENTS
RAPS
RAPSCALLION
RAPSCALLIONS
RAPT
RAPTATORIAL
RAPTLY
RAPTNESS
RAPTNESSES
RAPTOR
RAPTORIAL
RAPTORS
RAPTURE
RAPTURED
RAPTURELESS
RAPTURES
RAPTURING
RAPTURISE
RAPTURISED
RAPTURISES
RAPTURISING
RAPTURIST
RAPTURISTS
RAPTURIZE
RAPTURIZED
RAPTURIZES
RAPTURIZING
RAPTUROUS
RAPTUROUSLY
RAPTUROUSNESS
RAPTUROUSNESSES
RARE
RAREBIT
RAREBITS
RARED
RAREE
RAREFACTION
RAREFACTIONAL
RAREFACTIONS
RAREFACTIVE

RAREFIABLE
RAREFICATION
RAREFICATIONAL
RAREFICATIONS
RAREFIED
RAREFIER
RAREFIERS
RAREFIES
RAREFY
RAREFYING
RARELY
RARENESS
RARENESSES
RARER
RARERIPE
RARERIPES
RARES
RAREST
RARIFIED
RARIFIES
RARIFY
RARIFYING
RARING
RARITIES
RARITY
RAS
RASBORA
RASBORAS
RASCAILLE
RASCAILLES
RASCAL
RASCALDOM
RASCALDOMS
RASCALISM
RASCALISMS
RASCALITIES
RASCALITY
RASCALLIEST
RASCALLION
RASCALLIONS
RASCALLY
RASCALS
RASCASSE
RASCASSES
RASCHEL
RASCHELS
RASE
RASED
RASER
RASERS
RASES
RASH
RASHED
RASHER
RASHERS
RASHES

RASHEST
RASHING
RASHLIKE
RASHLY
RASHNESS
RASHNESSES
RASING
RASORIAL
RASP
RASPATORIES
RASPATORY
RASPBERRIES
RASPBERRY
RASPED
RASPER
RASPERS
RASPIER
RASPIEST
RASPING
RASPINGLY
RASPINGS
RASPISH
RASPS
RASPY
RASSE
RASSES
RASSLE
RASSLED
RASSLES
RASSLING
RAST
RASTA
RASTAFARI
RASTAFARIAN
RASTAFARIANS
RASTER
RASTERISE
RASTERISED
RASTERISES
RASTERISING
RASTERIZE
RASTERIZED
RASTERIZES
RASTERIZING
RASTERS
RASTRUM
RASTRUMS
RASURE
RASURES
RAT
RATA
RATABILITIES
RATABILITY
RATABLE
RATABLENESS
RATABLY

RATAFEE
RATAFEES
RATAFIA
RATAFIAS
RATAL
RATALS
RATAN
RATANIES
RATANS
RATANY
RATAPLAN
RATAPLANNED
RATAPLANNING
RATAPLANS
RATAS
RATATAT
RATATATS
RATATOUILLE
RATATOUILLES
RATBAG
RATBAGGERY
RATBAGS
RATBITE
RATBITES
RATCH
RATCHED
RATCHES
RATCHET
RATCHETED
RATCHETING
RATCHETS
RATCHING
RATE
RATEABILITIES
RATEABILITY
RATEABLE
RATEABLENESS
RATEABLY
RATED
RATEEN
RATEL
RATELS
RATEMETER
RATEMETERS
RATEPAYER
RATEPAYERS
RATER
RATERS
RATES
RATFINK
RATFINKS
RATFISH
RATFISHES
RATH
RATHA
RATHAS

RATHE
RATHER
RATHEREST
RATHERIPE
RATHERIPES
RATHERISH
RATHEST
RATHOLE
RATHOLES
RATHOUSE
RATHOUSES
RATHRIPE
RATHRIPES
RATHS
RATHSKELLER
RATHSKELLERS
RATICIDE
RATICIDES
RATIFIABLE
RATIFIABLY
RATIFICATION
RATIFICATIONS
RATIFIED
RATIFIER
RATIFIERS
RATIFIES
RATIFY
RATIFYING
RATINE
RATINES
RATING
RATINGS
RATIO
RATIOCINATE
RATIOCINATED
RATIOCINATES
RATIOCINATING
RATIOCINATION
RATIOCINATIONS
RATIOCINATIVE
RATIOCINATOR
RATIOCINATORS
RATIOCINATORY
RATION
RATIONAL
RATIONALE
RATIONALES
RATIONALISATION
RATIONALISE
RATIONALISED
RATIONALISER
RATIONALISERS
RATIONALISES
RATIONALISING
RATIONALISM
RATIONALISMS

RATIONALIST
RATIONALISTIC
RATIONALISTS
RATIONALITIES
RATIONALITY
RATIONALIZABLE
RATIONALIZATION
RATIONALIZE
RATIONALIZED
RATIONALIZER
RATIONALIZERS
RATIONALIZES
RATIONALIZING
RATIONALLY
RATIONALNESS
RATIONALNESSES
RATIONALS
RATIONED
RATIONING
RATIONS
RATIOS
RATITE
RATITES
RATLIKE
RATLIN
RATLINE
RATLINES
RATLING
RATLINGS
RATLINS
RATO
RATOO
RATOON
RATOONED
RATOONER
RATOONERS
RATOONING
RATOONS
RATOOS
RATOS
RATPACK
RATPACKS
RATPROOF
RATS
RATSBANE
RATSBANES
RATTAIL
RATTAILS
RATTAN
RATTANS
RATTED
RATTEEN
RATTEENS
RATTEN
RATTENED
RATTENER

RATTENERS
RATTENING
RATTENINGS
RATTENS
RATTER
RATTERIES
RATTERS
RATTERY
RATTIER
RATTIEST
RATTILY
RATTINESS
RATTING
RATTINGS
RATTISH
RATTLE
RATTLEBAG
RATTLEBAGS
RATTLEBOX
RATTLEBOXES
RATTLEBRAIN
RATTLEBRAINED
RATTLEBRAINS
RATTLED
RATTLEHEAD
RATTLEHEADS
RATTLEPATE
RATTLEPATES
RATTLER
RATTLERS
RATTLES
RATTLESNAKE
RATTLESNAKES
RATTLETRAP
RATTLETRAPS
RATTLIER
RATTLIEST
RATTLIN
RATTLINE
RATTLINES
RATTLING
RATTLINGLY
RATTLINGS
RATTLINS
RATTLY
RATTON
RATTONS
RATTOON
RATTOONED
RATTOONING
RATTOONS
RATTRAP
RATTRAPS
RATTY
RATU
RATUS

RAUCID
RAUCITIES
RAUCITY
RAUCLE
RAUCLER
RAUCLEST
RAUCOUS
RAUCOUSLY
RAUCOUSNESS
RAUCOUSNESSES
RAUGHT
RAUN
RAUNCH
RAUNCHED
RAUNCHES
RAUNCHIER
RAUNCHIEST
RAUNCHILY
RAUNCHINESS
RAUNCHINESSES
RAUNCHING
RAUNCHY
RAUNGE
RAUNGED
RAUNGES
RAUNGING
RAUNS
RAUPATU
RAUPO
RAURIKI
RAURIKIS
RAUWOLFIA
RAUWOLFIAS
RAVAGE
RAVAGED
RAVAGEMENT
RAVAGEMENTS
RAVAGER
RAVAGERS
RAVAGES
RAVAGING
RAVE
RAVED
RAVEL
RAVELED
RAVELER
RAVELERS
RAVELIN
RAVELING
RAVELINGS
RAVELINS
RAVELLED
RAVELLER
RAVELLERS
RAVELLING
RAVELLINGS

RAVELLY
RAVELMENT
RAVELMENTS
RAVELS
RAVEN
RAVENED
RAVENER
RAVENERS
RAVENING
RAVENINGLY
RAVENINGS
RAVENOUS
RAVENOUSLY
RAVENOUSNESS
RAVENOUSNESSES
RAVENS
RAVER
RAVERS
RAVES
RAVIGOTE
RAVIGOTES
RAVIN
RAVINE
RAVINED
RAVINES
RAVING
RAVINGLY
RAVINGS
RAVINING
RAVINS
RAVIOLI
RAVIOLIS
RAVISH
RAVISHED
RAVISHER
RAVISHERS
RAVISHES
RAVISHING
RAVISHINGLY
RAVISHMENT
RAVISHMENTS
RAW
RAWARU
RAWARUS
RAWBONE
RAWBONED
RAWER
RAWEST
RAWHEAD
RAWHEADS
RAWHIDE
RAWHIDED
RAWHIDES
RAWHIDING
RAWIN
RAWING

RAWINGS
RAWINS
RAWINSONDE
RAWINSONDES
RAWISH
RAWLY
RAWN
RAWNESS
RAWNESSES
RAWNS
RAWS
RAX
RAXED
RAXES
RAXING
RAY
RAYA
RAYAH
RAYAHS
RAYAS
RAYED
RAYGRASS
RAYGRASSES
RAYING
RAYLE
RAYLED
RAYLES
RAYLESS
RAYLESSLY
RAYLESSNESS
RAYLESSNESSES
RAYLET
RAYLETS
RAYLIKE
RAYLING
RAYNE
RAYNES
RAYON
RAYONS
RAYS
RAZE
RAZED
RAZEE
RAZEED
RAZEEING
RAZEES
RAZER
RAZERS
RAZES
RAZING
RAZMATAZ
RAZMATAZES
RAZOO
RAZOOS
RAZOR
RAZORABLE

RAZORBACK
RAZORBACKS
RAZORBILL
RAZORBILLS
RAZORED
RAZORING
RAZORS
RAZURE
RAZURES
RAZZ
RAZZAMATAZZ
RAZZAMATAZZES
RAZZED
RAZZES
RAZZIA
RAZZIAS
RAZZING
RAZZLE
RAZZLES
RAZZMATAZZ
RAZZMATAZZES
RE
REABSORB
REABSORBED
REABSORBING
REABSORBS
REABSORPTION
REABSORPTIONS
REACCEDE
REACCEDED
REACCEDES
REACCEDING
REACCELERATE
REACCELERATED
REACCELERATES
REACCELERATING
REACCENT
REACCENTED
REACCENTING
REACCENTS
REACCEPT
REACCEPTANCE
REACCEPTANCES
REACCEPTED
REACCEPTING
REACCEPTS
REACCESSION
REACCESSIONS
REACCLAIM
REACCLAIMED
REACCLAIMING
REACCLAIMS
REACCLIMATISE
REACCLIMATISED
REACCLIMATISES
REACCLIMATISING

REACCLIMATIZE
REACCLIMATIZED
REACCLIMATIZES
REACCLIMATIZING
REACCOMMODATE
REACCOMMODATED
REACCOMMODATES
REACCOMMODATING
REACCOMMODATION
REACCREDIT
REACCREDITATION
REACCREDITED
REACCREDITING
REACCREDITS
REACCUSE
REACCUSED
REACCUSES
REACCUSING
REACCUSTOM
REACCUSTOMED
REACCUSTOMING
REACCUSTOMS
REACH
REACHABLE
REACHED
REACHER
REACHERS
REACHES
REACHING
REACHLESS
REACIDIFICATION
REACIDIFIED
REACIDIFIES
REACIDIFY
REACIDIFYING
REACQUAINT
REACQUAINTANCE
REACQUAINTANCES
REACQUAINTED
REACQUAINTING
REACQUAINTS
REACQUIRE
REACQUIRED
REACQUIRES
REACQUIRING
REACQUISITION
REACQUISITIONS
REACT
REACTANCE
REACTANCES
REACTANT
REACTANTS
REACTED
REACTING
REACTION
REACTIONAL

REACTIONARIES
REACTIONARISM
REACTIONARISMS
REACTIONARIST
REACTIONARISTS
REACTIONARY
REACTIONARYISM
REACTIONARYISMS
REACTIONISM
REACTIONIST
REACTIONISTS
REACTIONS
REACTIVATE
REACTIVATED
REACTIVATES
REACTIVATING
REACTIVATION
REACTIVATIONS
REACTIVE
REACTIVELY
REACTIVENESS
REACTIVENESSES
REACTIVITIES
REACTIVITY
REACTOR
REACTORS
REACTS
REACTUATE
REACTUATED
REACTUATES
REACTUATING
READ
READABILITIES
READABILITY
READABLE
READABLENESS
READABLENESSES
READABLY
READAPT
READAPTATION
READAPTATIONS
READAPTED
READAPTING
READAPTS
READD
READDED
READDICT
READDICTED
READDICTING
READDICTS
READDING
READDRESS
READDRESSED
READDRESSES
READDRESSING
READDS

READER
READERLY
READERS
READERSHIP
READERSHIPS
READIED
READIER
READIES
READIEST
READILY
READINESS
READINESSES
READING
READINGS
READJOURN
READJOURNED
READJOURNING
READJOURNMENT
READJOURNMENTS
READJOURNS
READJUST
READJUSTABILITY
READJUSTABLE
READJUSTED
READJUSTER
READJUSTERS
READJUSTING
READJUSTMENT
READJUSTMENTS
READJUSTS
READMISSION
READMISSIONS
READMIT
READMITS
READMITTANCE
READMITTANCES
READMITTED
READMITTING
READOPT
READOPTED
READOPTING
READOPTION
READOPTIONS
READOPTS
READORN
READORNED
READORNING
READORNS
READOUT
READOUTS
READS
READVANCE
READVANCED
READVANCES
READVANCING
READVERTISE

READVERTISED
READVERTISEMENT
READVERTISES
READVERTISING
READVISE
READVISED
READVISES
READVISING
READY
READYING
READYMADE
READYMADES
REAEDIFIED
REAEDIFIES
REAEDIFY
REAEDIFYE
REAEDIFYED
REAEDIFYES
REAEDIFYING
REAFFIRM
REAFFIRMATION
REAFFIRMATIONS
REAFFIRMED
REAFFIRMING
REAFFIRMS
REAFFIX
REAFFIXED
REAFFIXES
REAFFIXING
REAFFOREST
REAFFORESTATION
REAFFORESTED
REAFFORESTING
REAFFORESTS
REAGENCIES
REAGENCY
REAGENT
REAGENTS
REAGGREGATE
REAGGREGATED
REAGGREGATES
REAGGREGATING
REAGGREGATION
REAGGREGATIONS
REAGIN
REAGINIC
REAGINS
REAK
REAKED
REAKING
REAKS
REAL
REALER
REALES
REALEST
REALGAR

REALGARS
REALIA
REALIGN
REALIGNED
REALIGNING
REALIGNMENT
REALIGNMENTS
REALIGNS
REALISABILITIES
REALISABILITY
REALISABLE
REALISABLY
REALISATION
REALISATIONS
REALISE
REALISED
REALISER
REALISERS
REALISES
REALISING
REALISM
REALISMS
REALIST
REALISTIC
REALISTICALLY
REALISTS
REALITIES
REALITY
REALIZABILITIES
REALIZABILITY
REALIZABLE
REALIZABLY
REALIZATION
REALIZATIONS
REALIZE
REALIZED
REALIZER
REALIZERS
REALIZES
REALIZING
REALLIE
REALLIED
REALLIES
REALLOCATE
REALLOCATED
REALLOCATES
REALLOCATING
REALLOCATION
REALLOCATIONS
REALLOT
REALLOTMENT
REALLOTMENTS
REALLOTS
REALLOTTED
REALLOTTING
REALLY

REALLYING
REALM
REALMLESS
REALMS
REALNESS
REALNESSES
REALO
REALOS
REALPOLITIK
REALPOLITIKER
REALPOLITIKERS
REALPOLITIKS
REALS
REALTER
REALTERATION
REALTERATIONS
REALTERED
REALTERING
REALTERS
REALTIE
REALTIES
REALTIME
REALTOR
REALTORS
REALTY
REAM
REAME
REAMED
REAMEND
REAMENDED
REAMENDING
REAMENDMENT
REAMENDMENTS
REAMENDS
REAMER
REAMERS
REAMES
REAMIER
REAMIEST
REAMING
REAMS
REAMY
REAN
REANALYSE
REANALYSED
REANALYSES
REANALYSING
REANALYSIS
REANALYZE
REANALYZED
REANALYZES
REANALYZING
REANIMATE
REANIMATED
REANIMATES
REANIMATING

REANIMATION
REANIMATIONS
REANNEX
REANNEXATION
REANNEXATIONS
REANNEXED
REANNEXES
REANNEXING
REANOINT
REANOINTED
REANOINTING
REANOINTS
REANS
REANSWER
REANSWERED
REANSWERING
REANSWERS
REAP
REAPABLE
REAPED
REAPER
REAPERS
REAPHOOK
REAPHOOKS
REAPING
REAPPAREL
REAPPARELLED
REAPPARELLING
REAPPARELS
REAPPEAR
REAPPEARANCE
REAPPEARANCES
REAPPEARED
REAPPEARING
REAPPEARS
REAPPLICATION
REAPPLICATIONS
REAPPLIED
REAPPLIES
REAPPLY
REAPPLYING
REAPPOINT
REAPPOINTED
REAPPOINTING
REAPPOINTMENT
REAPPOINTMENTS
REAPPOINTS
REAPPORTION
REAPPORTIONED
REAPPORTIONING
REAPPORTIONMENT
REAPPORTIONS
REAPPRAISAL
REAPPRAISALS
REAPPRAISE
REAPPRAISED

REAPPRAISEMENT
REAPPRAISEMENTS
REAPPRAISER
REAPPRAISERS
REAPPRAISES
REAPPRAISING
REAPPROPRIATE
REAPPROPRIATED
REAPPROPRIATES
REAPPROPRIATING
REAPPROVE
REAPPROVED
REAPPROVES
REAPPROVING
REAPS
REAR
REARED
REARER
REARERS
REARGUARD
REARGUARDS
REARGUE
REARGUED
REARGUES
REARGUING
REARGUMENT
REARGUMENTS
REARHORSE
REARHORSES
REARING
REARISE
REARISEN
REARISES
REARISING
REARLY
REARM
REARMAMENT
REARMAMENTS
REARMED
REARMICE
REARMING
REARMOST
REARMOUSE
REARMS
REAROSE
REAROUSAL
REAROUSALS
REAROUSE
REAROUSED
REAROUSES
REAROUSING
REARRANGE
REARRANGED
REARRANGEMENT
REARRANGEMENTS
REARRANGER

REARRANGERS
REARRANGES
REARRANGING
REARREST
REARRESTED
REARRESTING
REARRESTS
REARS
REARTICULATE
REARTICULATED
REARTICULATES
REARTICULATING
REARWARD
REARWARDS
REASCEND
REASCENDED
REASCENDING
REASCENDS
REASCENSION
REASCENSIONS
REASCENT
REASCENTS
REASON
REASONABILITIES
REASONABILITY
REASONABLE
REASONABLENESS
REASONABLY
REASONED
REASONEDLY
REASONER
REASONERS
REASONING
REASONINGS
REASONLESS
REASONLESSLY
REASONS
REASSAIL
REASSAILED
REASSAILING
REASSAILS
REASSEMBLAGE
REASSEMBLAGES
REASSEMBLE
REASSEMBLED
REASSEMBLES
REASSEMBLIES
REASSEMBLING
REASSEMBLY
REASSERT
REASSERTED
REASSERTING
REASSERTION
REASSERTIONS
REASSERTS
REASSESS

REASSESSED
REASSESSES
REASSESSING
REASSESSMENT
REASSESSMENTS
REASSIGN
REASSIGNED
REASSIGNING
REASSIGNMENT
REASSIGNMENTS
REASSIGNS
REASSIMILATE
REASSIMILATED
REASSIMILATES
REASSIMILATING
REASSIMILATION
REASSIMILATIONS
REASSORT
REASSORTED
REASSORTING
REASSORTS
REASSUME
REASSUMED
REASSUMES
REASSUMING
REASSUMPTION
REASSUMPTIONS
REASSURANCE
REASSURANCES
REASSURE
REASSURED
REASSURER
REASSURERS
REASSURES
REASSURING
REASSURINGLY
REAST
REASTED
REASTIER
REASTIEST
REASTINESS
REASTINESSES
REASTING
REASTS
REASTY
REATA
REATAS
REATE
REATES
REATTACH
REATTACHED
REATTACHES
REATTACHING
REATTACHMENT
REATTACHMENTS
REATTACK

REATTACKED
REATTACKING
REATTACKS
REATTAIN
REATTAINED
REATTAINING
REATTAINMENT
REATTAINMENTS
REATTAINS
REATTEMPT
REATTEMPTED
REATTEMPTING
REATTEMPTS
REATTRIBUTE
REATTRIBUTED
REATTRIBUTES
REATTRIBUTING
REATTRIBUTION
REATTRIBUTIONS
REAUTHORIZATION
REAUTHORIZE
REAUTHORIZED
REAUTHORIZES
REAUTHORIZING
REAVAIL
REAVAILED
REAVAILING
REAVAILS
REAVE
REAVED
REAVER
REAVERS
REAVES
REAVING
REAVOW
REAVOWED
REAVOWING
REAVOWS
REAWAKE
REAWAKED
REAWAKEN
REAWAKENED
REAWAKENING
REAWAKENINGS
REAWAKENS
REAWAKES
REAWAKING
REAWOKE
REAWOKEN
REB
REBACK
REBACKED
REBACKING
REBACKS
REBADGE
REBADGED

REBADGES
REBADGING
REBAIT
REBAITED
REBAITING
REBAITS
REBALANCE
REBALANCED
REBALANCES
REBALANCING
REBAPTISE
REBAPTISED
REBAPTISES
REBAPTISING
REBAPTISM
REBAPTISMS
REBAPTIZE
REBAPTIZED
REBAPTIZES
REBAPTIZING
REBAR
REBARBATIVE
REBARBATIVELY
REBARS
REBATABLE
REBATE
REBATEABLE
REBATED
REBATEMENT
REBATEMENTS
REBATER
REBATERS
REBATES
REBATING
REBATO
REBATOES
REBATOS
REBBE
REBBES
REBBETZIN
REBBETZINS
REBEC
REBECK
REBECKS
REBECS
REBEGAN
REBEGIN
REBEGINNING
REBEGINS
REBEGUN
REBEL
REBELDOM
REBELDOMS
REBELLED
REBELLER
REBELLERS

REBELLING
REBELLION
REBELLIONS
REBELLIOUS
REBELLIOUSLY
REBELLIOUSNESS
REBELLOW
REBELLOWED
REBELLOWING
REBELLOWS
REBELS
REBID
REBIDDABLE
REBIDDEN
REBIDDING
REBIDS
REBILL
REBILLED
REBILLING
REBILLS
REBIND
REBINDING
REBINDS
REBIRTH
REBIRTHING
REBIRTHINGS
REBIRTHS
REBIT
REBITE
REBITES
REBITING
REBITTEN
REBLEND
REBLENDED
REBLENDING
REBLENDS
REBLOOM
REBLOOMED
REBLOOMING
REBLOOMS
REBLOSSOM
REBLOSSOMED
REBLOSSOMING
REBLOSSOMS
REBOANT
REBOARD
REBOARDED
REBOARDING
REBOARDS
REBOATION
REBOATIONS
REBODIED
REBODIES
REBODY
REBODYING
REBOIL

REBOILED
REBOILING
REBOILS
REBOOK
REBOOKED
REBOOKING
REBOOKS
REBOOT
REBOOTED
REBOOTING
REBOOTS
REBOP
REBOPS
REBORE
REBORED
REBORES
REBORING
REBORN
REBORROW
REBORROWED
REBORROWING
REBORROWS
REBOTTLE
REBOTTLED
REBOTTLES
REBOTTLING
REBOUGHT
REBOUND
REBOUNDED
REBOUNDER
REBOUNDERS
REBOUNDING
REBOUNDS
REBOZO
REBOZOS
REBRACE
REBRACED
REBRACES
REBRACING
REBRANCH
REBRANCHED
REBRANCHES
REBRANCHING
REBRAND
REBRANDED
REBRANDER
REBRANDERS
REBRANDING
REBRED
REBREED
REBREEDING
REBREEDS
REBROADCAST
REBROADCASTED
REBROADCASTING
REBROADCASTS

REBS
REBUFF
REBUFFED
REBUFFING
REBUFFS
REBUILD
REBUILDED
REBUILDING
REBUILDS
REBUILT
REBUKABLE
REBUKE
REBUKED
REBUKEFUL
REBUKEFULLY
REBUKER
REBUKERS
REBUKES
REBUKING
REBUKINGLY
REBURIAL
REBURIALS
REBURIED
REBURIES
REBURY
REBURYING
REBUS
REBUSES
REBUT
REBUTMENT
REBUTMENTS
REBUTS
REBUTTABLE
REBUTTAL
REBUTTALS
REBUTTED
REBUTTER
REBUTTERS
REBUTTING
REBUTTON
REBUTTONED
REBUTTONING
REBUTTONS
REBUY
REBUYING
REBUYS
REC
RECAL
RECALCITRANCE
RECALCITRANCES
RECALCITRANCIES
RECALCITRANCY
RECALCITRANT
RECALCITRANTS
RECALCITRATE
RECALCITRATED

RECALCITRATES
RECALCITRATING
RECALCITRATION
RECALCITRATIONS
RECALCULATE
RECALCULATED
RECALCULATES
RECALCULATING
RECALCULATION
RECALCULATIONS
RECALESCE
RECALESCED
RECALESCENCE
RECALESCENCES
RECALESCENT
RECALESCES
RECALESCING
RECALIBRATE
RECALIBRATED
RECALIBRATES
RECALIBRATING
RECALIBRATION
RECALIBRATIONS
RECALL
RECALLABILITIES
RECALLABILITY
RECALLABLE
RECALLED
RECALLER
RECALLERS
RECALLING
RECALLMENT
RECALLMENTS
RECALLS
RECALMENT
RECALMENTS
RECALS
RECAMIER
RECAMIERS
RECANALIZATION
RECANALIZATIONS
RECANALIZE
RECANALIZED
RECANALIZES
RECANALIZING
RECANE
RECANED
RECANES
RECANING
RECANT
RECANTATION
RECANTATIONS
RECANTED
RECANTER
RECANTERS
RECANTING

RECANTS
RECAP
RECAPITALISE
RECAPITALISED
RECAPITALISES
RECAPITALISING
RECAPITALIZE
RECAPITALIZED
RECAPITALIZES
RECAPITALIZING
RECAPITULATE
RECAPITULATED
RECAPITULATES
RECAPITULATING
RECAPITULATION
RECAPITULATIONS
RECAPITULATIVE
RECAPITULATORY
RECAPPABLE
RECAPPED
RECAPPING
RECAPS
RECAPTION
RECAPTIONS
RECAPTOR
RECAPTORS
RECAPTURE
RECAPTURED
RECAPTURER
RECAPTURERS
RECAPTURES
RECAPTURING
RECARRIED
RECARRIES
RECARRY
RECARRYING
RECAST
RECASTING
RECASTS
RECATCH
RECATCHES
RECATCHING
RECAUGHT
RECAUTION
RECAUTIONED
RECAUTIONING
RECAUTIONS
RECCE
RECCED
RECCEED
RECCEING
RECCES
RECCIED
RECCIES
RECCO
RECCOS

RECCY
RECCYING
RECEDE
RECEDED
RECEDES
RECEDING
RECEIPT
RECEIPTED
RECEIPTING
RECEIPTOR
RECEIPTORS
RECEIPTS
RECEIVABILITIES
RECEIVABILITY
RECEIVABLE
RECEIVABLENESS
RECEIVABLES
RECEIVAL
RECEIVALS
RECEIVE
RECEIVED
RECEIVER
RECEIVERS
RECEIVERSHIP
RECEIVERSHIPS
RECEIVES
RECEIVING
RECEIVINGS
RECENCIES
RECENCY
RECENSE
RECENSED
RECENSES
RECENSING
RECENSION
RECENSIONS
RECENT
RECENTER
RECENTEST
RECENTLY
RECENTNESS
RECENTNESSES
RECENTRE
RECENTRED
RECENTRES
RECENTRIFUGE
RECENTRIFUGED
RECENTRIFUGES
RECENTRIFUGING
RECENTRING
RECEPT
RECEPTACLE
RECEPTACLES
RECEPTACULA
RECEPTACULAR
RECEPTACULUM

RECEPTIBILITIES
RECEPTIBILITY
RECEPTIBLE
RECEPTION
RECEPTIONIST
RECEPTIONISTS
RECEPTIONS
RECEPTIVE
RECEPTIVELY
RECEPTIVENESS
RECEPTIVENESSES
RECEPTIVITIES
RECEPTIVITY
RECEPTOR
RECEPTORS
RECEPTS
RECERTIFICATION
RECERTIFIED
RECERTIFIES
RECERTIFY
RECERTIFYING
RECESS
RECESSED
RECESSES
RECESSING
RECESSION
RECESSIONAL
RECESSIONALS
RECESSIONARY
RECESSIONS
RECESSIVE
RECESSIVELY
RECESSIVENESS
RECESSIVENESSES
RECESSIVES
RECHALLENGE
RECHALLENGED
RECHALLENGES
RECHALLENGING
RECHANGE
RECHANGED
RECHANGES
RECHANGING
RECHANNEL
RECHANNELED
RECHANNELING
RECHANNELLED
RECHANNELLING
RECHANNELS
RECHARGE
RECHARGEABLE
RECHARGED
RECHARGER
RECHARGERS
RECHARGES
RECHARGING

RECHART
RECHARTED
RECHARTER
RECHARTERED
RECHARTERING
RECHARTERS
RECHARTING
RECHARTS
RECHATE
RECHATES
RECHAUFFE
RECHAUFFES
RECHEAT
RECHEATED
RECHEATING
RECHEATS
RECHECK
RECHECKED
RECHECKING
RECHECKS
RECHERCHE
RECHEW
RECHEWED
RECHEWING
RECHEWS
RECHIE
RECHLESSE
RECHOOSE
RECHOOSES
RECHOOSING
RECHOREOGRAPH
RECHOREOGRAPHED
RECHOREOGRAPHS
RECHOSE
RECHOSEN
RECHRISTEN
RECHRISTENED
RECHRISTENING
RECHRISTENS
RECHROMATOGRAPH
RECIDIVISM
RECIDIVISMS
RECIDIVIST
RECIDIVISTIC
RECIDIVISTS
RECIDIVOUS
RECIDIVOUSLY
RECIPE
RECIPES
RECIPIENCE
RECIPIENCES
RECIPIENCIES
RECIPIENCY
RECIPIENT
RECIPIENTS
RECIPROCAL

RECIPROCALITIES
RECIPROCALITY
RECIPROCALLY
RECIPROCALS
RECIPROCANT
RECIPROCANTS
RECIPROCATE
RECIPROCATED
RECIPROCATES
RECIPROCATING
RECIPROCATION
RECIPROCATIONS
RECIPROCATIVE
RECIPROCATOR
RECIPROCATORILY
RECIPROCATORS
RECIPROCATORY
RECIPROCITIES
RECIPROCITY
RECIRCLE
RECIRCLED
RECIRCLES
RECIRCLING
RECIRCULATE
RECIRCULATED
RECIRCULATES
RECIRCULATING
RECIRCULATION
RECIRCULATIONS
RECISION
RECISIONS
RECIT
RECITABILITY
RECITABLE
RECITAL
RECITALIST
RECITALISTS
RECITALS
RECITATION
RECITATIONIST
RECITATIONISTS
RECITATIONS
RECITATIVE
RECITATIVES
RECITATIVI
RECITATIVO
RECITATIVOS
RECITE
RECITED
RECITER
RECITERS
RECITES
RECITING
RECITS
RECK
RECKAN

RECKED
RECKING
RECKLESS
RECKLESSLY
RECKLESSNESS
RECKLESSNESSES
RECKLING
RECKLINGS
RECKON
RECKONED
RECKONER
RECKONERS
RECKONING
RECKONINGS
RECKONS
RECKS
RECLAD
RECLAIM
RECLAIMABLE
RECLAIMABLY
RECLAIMANT
RECLAIMANTS
RECLAIMED
RECLAIMER
RECLAIMERS
RECLAIMING
RECLAIMS
RECLAMATION
RECLAMATIONS
RECLAME
RECLAMES
RECLASP
RECLASPED
RECLASPING
RECLASPS
RECLASSIFIED
RECLASSIFIES
RECLASSIFY
RECLASSIFYING
RECLEAN
RECLEANED
RECLEANING
RECLEANS
RECLIMB
RECLIMBED
RECLIMBING
RECLIMBS
RECLINABLE
RECLINATE
RECLINATION
RECLINATIONS
RECLINE
RECLINED
RECLINER
RECLINERS
RECLINES

RECLINING
RECLOSABLE
RECLOSE
RECLOSED
RECLOSES
RECLOSING
RECLOTHE
RECLOTHED
RECLOTHES
RECLOTHING
RECLUSE
RECLUSELY
RECLUSENESS
RECLUSENESSES
RECLUSES
RECLUSION
RECLUSIONS
RECLUSIVE
RECLUSIVELY
RECLUSIVENESS
RECLUSIVENESSES
RECLUSORIES
RECLUSORY
RECOAL
RECOALED
RECOALING
RECOALS
RECOCK
RECOCKED
RECOCKING
RECOCKS
RECODE
RECODED
RECODES
RECODIFICATION
RECODIFICATIONS
RECODIFIED
RECODIFIES
RECODIFY
RECODIFYING
RECODING
RECOGNISABILITY
RECOGNISABLE
RECOGNISABLY
RECOGNISANCE
RECOGNISANCES
RECOGNISANT
RECOGNISE
RECOGNISED
RECOGNISEE
RECOGNISEES
RECOGNISER
RECOGNISERS
RECOGNISES
RECOGNISING
RECOGNISOR

RECOGNISORS
RECOGNITION
RECOGNITIONS
RECOGNITIVE
RECOGNITORY
RECOGNIZABILITY
RECOGNIZABLE
RECOGNIZABLY
RECOGNIZANCE
RECOGNIZANCES
RECOGNIZANT
RECOGNIZANTLY
RECOGNIZE
RECOGNIZED
RECOGNIZEE
RECOGNIZEES
RECOGNIZER
RECOGNIZERS
RECOGNIZES
RECOGNIZING
RECOGNIZOR
RECOGNIZORS
RECOIL
RECOILED
RECOILER
RECOILERS
RECOILING
RECOILLESS
RECOILS
RECOIN
RECOINAGE
RECOINAGES
RECOINED
RECOINING
RECOINS
RECOLLECT
RECOLLECTED
RECOLLECTEDLY
RECOLLECTEDNESS
RECOLLECTING
RECOLLECTION
RECOLLECTIONS
RECOLLECTIVE
RECOLLECTIVELY
RECOLLECTS
RECOLLET
RECOLLETS
RECOLONISATION
RECOLONISATIONS
RECOLONISE
RECOLONISED
RECOLONISES
RECOLONISING
RECOLONIZATION
RECOLONIZATIONS
RECOLONIZE

RECOLONIZED
RECOLONIZES
RECOLONIZING
RECOLOR
RECOLORED
RECOLORING
RECOLORS
RECOLOUR
RECOLOURED
RECOLOURING
RECOLOURS
RECOMB
RECOMBED
RECOMBINANT
RECOMBINANTS
RECOMBINATION
RECOMBINATIONAL
RECOMBINATIONS
RECOMBINE
RECOMBINED
RECOMBINES
RECOMBING
RECOMBINING
RECOMBS
RECOMFORT
RECOMFORTED
RECOMFORTING
RECOMFORTLESS
RECOMFORTS
RECOMFORTURE
RECOMFORTURES
RECOMMENCE
RECOMMENCED
RECOMMENCEMENT
RECOMMENCEMENTS
RECOMMENCES
RECOMMENCING
RECOMMEND
RECOMMENDABLE
RECOMMENDABLY
RECOMMENDATION
RECOMMENDATIONS
RECOMMENDATORY
RECOMMENDED
RECOMMENDER
RECOMMENDERS
RECOMMENDING
RECOMMENDS
RECOMMISSION
RECOMMISSIONED
RECOMMISSIONING
RECOMMISSIONS
RECOMMIT
RECOMMITMENT
RECOMMITMENTS
RECOMMITS

RECOMMITTAL
RECOMMITTALS
RECOMMITTED
RECOMMITTING
RECOMPACT
RECOMPACTED
RECOMPACTING
RECOMPACTS
RECOMPARE
RECOMPARED
RECOMPARES
RECOMPARING
RECOMPARISON
RECOMPARISONS
RECOMPENCE
RECOMPENCES
RECOMPENSABLE
RECOMPENSE
RECOMPENSED
RECOMPENSER
RECOMPENSERS
RECOMPENSES
RECOMPENSING
RECOMPILATION
RECOMPILATIONS
RECOMPILE
RECOMPILED
RECOMPILES
RECOMPILING
RECOMPOSE
RECOMPOSED
RECOMPOSES
RECOMPOSING
RECOMPOSITION
RECOMPOSITIONS
RECOMPOUND
RECOMPOUNDED
RECOMPOUNDING
RECOMPOUNDS
RECOMPRESS
RECOMPRESSED
RECOMPRESSES
RECOMPRESSING
RECOMPRESSION
RECOMPRESSIONS
RECOMPUTATION
RECOMPUTATIONS
RECOMPUTE
RECOMPUTED
RECOMPUTES
RECOMPUTING
RECON
RECONCEIVE
RECONCEIVED
RECONCEIVES
RECONCEIVING

RECONCENTRATE
RECONCENTRATED
RECONCENTRATES
RECONCENTRATING
RECONCENTRATION
RECONCEPTION
RECONCEPTIONS
RECONCEPTUALIZE
RECONCILABILITY
RECONCILABLE
RECONCILABLY
RECONCILE
RECONCILED
RECONCILEMENT
RECONCILEMENTS
RECONCILER
RECONCILERS
RECONCILES
RECONCILIATION
RECONCILIATIONS
RECONCILIATORY
RECONCILING
RECONDENSATION
RECONDENSATIONS
RECONDENSE
RECONDENSED
RECONDENSES
RECONDENSING
RECONDITE
RECONDITELY
RECONDITENESS
RECONDITENESSES
RECONDITION
RECONDITIONED
RECONDITIONING
RECONDITIONS
RECONFIGURATION
RECONFIGURE
RECONFIGURED
RECONFIGURES
RECONFIGURING
RECONFIRM
RECONFIRMATION
RECONFIRMATIONS
RECONFIRMED
RECONFIRMING
RECONFIRMS
RECONNAISSANCE
RECONNAISSANCES
RECONNECT
RECONNECTED
RECONNECTING
RECONNECTION
RECONNECTIONS
RECONNECTS
RECONNOISSANCE

RECONNOISSANCES
RECONNOITER
RECONNOITERED
RECONNOITERER
RECONNOITERERS
RECONNOITERING
RECONNOITERS
RECONNOITRE
RECONNOITRED
RECONNOITRER
RECONNOITRERS
RECONNOITRES
RECONNOITRING
RECONQUER
RECONQUERED
RECONQUERING
RECONQUERS
RECONQUEST
RECONQUESTS
RECONS
RECONSECRATE
RECONSECRATED
RECONSECRATES
RECONSECRATING
RECONSECRATION
RECONSECRATIONS
RECONSIDER
RECONSIDERATION
RECONSIDERED
RECONSIDERING
RECONSIDERS
RECONSIGN
RECONSIGNED
RECONSIGNING
RECONSIGNMENT
RECONSIGNMENTS
RECONSIGNS
RECONSOLIDATE
RECONSOLIDATED
RECONSOLIDATES
RECONSOLIDATING
RECONSOLIDATION
RECONSTITUENT
RECONSTITUENTS
RECONSTITUTABLE
RECONSTITUTE
RECONSTITUTED
RECONSTITUTES
RECONSTITUTING
RECONSTITUTION
RECONSTITUTIONS
RECONSTRUCT
RECONSTRUCTED
RECONSTRUCTIBLE
RECONSTRUCTING
RECONSTRUCTION

RECONSTRUCTIONS
RECONSTRUCTIVE
RECONSTRUCTOR
RECONSTRUCTORS
RECONSTRUCTS
RECONTACT
RECONTACTED
RECONTACTING
RECONTACTS
RECONTAMINATE
RECONTAMINATED
RECONTAMINATES
RECONTAMINATING
RECONTAMINATION
RECONTEST
RECONTESTED
RECONTESTING
RECONTESTS
RECONTEXTUALIZE
RECONTINUE
RECONTINUED
RECONTINUES
RECONTINUING
RECONTOUR
RECONTOURED
RECONTOURING
RECONTOURS
RECONVALESCENCE
RECONVENE
RECONVENED
RECONVENES
RECONVENING
RECONVERSION
RECONVERSIONS
RECONVERT
RECONVERTED
RECONVERTING
RECONVERTS
RECONVEY
RECONVEYANCE
RECONVEYANCES
RECONVEYED
RECONVEYING
RECONVEYS
RECONVICT
RECONVICTED
RECONVICTING
RECONVICTION
RECONVICTIONS
RECONVICTS
RECONVINCE
RECONVINCED
RECONVINCES
RECONVINCING
RECOOK
RECOOKED

RECOOKING
RECOOKS
RECOPIED
RECOPIES
RECOPY
RECOPYING
RECORD
RECORDABLE
RECORDATION
RECORDATIONS
RECORDED
RECORDER
RECORDERS
RECORDERSHIP
RECORDERSHIPS
RECORDING
RECORDINGS
RECORDIST
RECORDISTS
RECORDS
RECORK
RECORKED
RECORKING
RECORKS
RECOUNT
RECOUNTAL
RECOUNTALS
RECOUNTED
RECOUNTER
RECOUNTERS
RECOUNTING
RECOUNTMENT
RECOUNTMENTS
RECOUNTS
RECOUP
RECOUPABLE
RECOUPE
RECOUPED
RECOUPING
RECOUPLE
RECOUPLED
RECOUPLES
RECOUPLING
RECOUPMENT
RECOUPMENTS
RECOUPS
RECOURE
RECOURED
RECOURES
RECOURING
RECOURSE
RECOURSED
RECOURSES
RECOURSING
RECOVER
RECOVERABILITY

RECOVERABLE
RECOVERABLENESS
RECOVERED
RECOVEREE
RECOVEREES
RECOVERER
RECOVERERS
RECOVERIES
RECOVERING
RECOVEROR
RECOVERORS
RECOVERS
RECOVERY
RECOWER
RECOWERED
RECOWERING
RECOWERS
RECOYLE
RECOYLED
RECOYLES
RECOYLING
RECRATE
RECRATED
RECRATES
RECRATING
RECREANCE
RECREANCES
RECREANCIES
RECREANCY
RECREANT
RECREANTLY
RECREANTS
RECREATE
RECREATED
RECREATES
RECREATING
RECREATION
RECREATIONAL
RECREATIONIST
RECREATIONISTS
RECREATIONS
RECREATIVE
RECREATIVELY
RECREATIVENESS
RECREATOR
RECREATORS
RECREMENT
RECREMENTAL
RECREMENTITIAL
RECREMENTITIOUS
RECREMENTS
RECRIMINATE
RECRIMINATED
RECRIMINATES
RECRIMINATING
RECRIMINATION

RECRIMINATIONS
RECRIMINATIVE
RECRIMINATOR
RECRIMINATORS
RECRIMINATORY
RECROSS
RECROSSED
RECROSSES
RECROSSING
RECROWN
RECROWNED
RECROWNING
RECROWNS
RECRUDESCE
RECRUDESCED
RECRUDESCENCE
RECRUDESCENCES
RECRUDESCENCIES
RECRUDESCENCY
RECRUDESCENT
RECRUDESCES
RECRUDESCING
RECRUIT
RECRUITABILITY
RECRUITABLE
RECRUITAL
RECRUITALS
RECRUITED
RECRUITER
RECRUITERS
RECRUITING
RECRUITMENT
RECRUITMENTS
RECRUITS
RECRYSTALLISE
RECRYSTALLISED
RECRYSTALLISES
RECRYSTALLISING
RECRYSTALLIZE
RECRYSTALLIZED
RECRYSTALLIZES
RECRYSTALLIZING
RECS
RECTA
RECTAL
RECTALLY
RECTANGLE
RECTANGLED
RECTANGLES
RECTANGULAR
RECTANGULARITY
RECTANGULARLY
RECTI
RECTIFIABILITY
RECTIFIABLE
RECTIFICATION

RECTIFICATIONS
RECTIFIED
RECTIFIER
RECTIFIERS
RECTIFIES
RECTIFY
RECTIFYING
RECTILINEAL
RECTILINEALLY
RECTILINEAR
RECTILINEARITY
RECTILINEARLY
RECTION
RECTIONS
RECTIPETALIES
RECTIPETALITIES
RECTIPETALITY
RECTIROSTRAL
RECTISERIAL
RECTITIC
RECTITIS
RECTITISES
RECTITUDE
RECTITUDES
RECTITUDINOUS
RECTO
RECTOCELE
RECTOCELES
RECTOR
RECTORAL
RECTORATE
RECTORATES
RECTORESS
RECTORESSES
RECTORIAL
RECTORIALS
RECTORIES
RECTORS
RECTORSHIP
RECTORSHIPS
RECTORY
RECTOS
RECTRESS
RECTRESSES
RECTRICES
RECTRICIAL
RECTRIX
RECTUM
RECTUMS
RECTUS
RECUILE
RECUILED
RECUILES
RECUILING
RECULE
RECULED

RECULES
RECULING
RECULTIVATE
RECULTIVATED
RECULTIVATES
RECULTIVATING
RECUMBENCE
RECUMBENCES
RECUMBENCIES
RECUMBENCY
RECUMBENT
RECUMBENTLY
RECUPERABLE
RECUPERATE
RECUPERATED
RECUPERATES
RECUPERATING
RECUPERATION
RECUPERATIONS
RECUPERATIVE
RECUPERATOR
RECUPERATORS
RECUPERATORY
RECUR
RECURE
RECURED
RECURELESS
RECURES
RECURING
RECURRED
RECURRENCE
RECURRENCES
RECURRENCIES
RECURRENCY
RECURRENT
RECURRENTLY
RECURRING
RECURRINGLY
RECURS
RECURSION
RECURSIONS
RECURSIVE
RECURSIVELY
RECURSIVENESS
RECURSIVENESSES
RECURVATE
RECURVE
RECURVED
RECURVES
RECURVING
RECURVIROSTRAL
RECUSAL
RECUSALS
RECUSANCE
RECUSANCES
RECUSANCIES

RECUSANCY
RECUSANT
RECUSANTS
RECUSATION
RECUSATIONS
RECUSE
RECUSED
RECUSES
RECUSING
RECUT
RECUTS
RECUTTING
RECYCLABLE
RECYCLABLES
RECYCLATE
RECYCLATES
RECYCLE
RECYCLEABILITY
RECYCLEABLE
RECYCLED
RECYCLER
RECYCLERS
RECYCLES
RECYCLING
RECYCLIST
RECYCLISTS
RED
REDACT
REDACTED
REDACTING
REDACTION
REDACTIONAL
REDACTIONS
REDACTOR
REDACTORIAL
REDACTORS
REDACTS
REDAMAGE
REDAMAGED
REDAMAGES
REDAMAGING
REDAN
REDANS
REDARGUE
REDARGUED
REDARGUES
REDARGUING
REDATE
REDATED
REDATES
REDATING
REDBACK
REDBACKS
REDBAIT
REDBAITED
REDBAITING

REDBAITS
REDBAY
REDBAYS
REDBELLIES
REDBELLY
REDBIRD
REDBIRDS
REDBONE
REDBONES
REDBREAST
REDBREASTS
REDBRICK
REDBRICKS
REDBUD
REDBUDS
REDBUG
REDBUGS
REDCAP
REDCAPS
REDCOAT
REDCOATS
REDCURRANT
REDCURRANTS
REDD
REDDED
REDDEN
REDDENDA
REDDENDO
REDDENDOS
REDDENDUM
REDDENED
REDDENING
REDDENS
REDDER
REDDERS
REDDEST
REDDIER
REDDIEST
REDDING
REDDINGS
REDDISH
REDDISHLY
REDDISHNESS
REDDISHNESSES
REDDLE
REDDLED
REDDLEMAN
REDDLEMEN
REDDLES
REDDLING
REDDS
REDDY
REDE
REDEAL
REDEALING
REDEALS

REDEALT
REDEAR
REDEARS
REDECIDE
REDECIDED
REDECIDES
REDECIDING
REDECORATE
REDECORATED
REDECORATES
REDECORATING
REDECORATION
REDECORATIONS
REDECORATOR
REDECORATORS
REDECRAFT
REDECRAFTS
REDED
REDEDICATE
REDEDICATED
REDEDICATES
REDEDICATING
REDEDICATION
REDEDICATIONS
REDEEM
REDEEMABILITIES
REDEEMABILITY
REDEEMABLE
REDEEMABLENESS
REDEEMABLY
REDEEMED
REDEEMER
REDEEMERS
REDEEMING
REDEEMLESS
REDEEMS
REDEFEAT
REDEFEATED
REDEFEATING
REDEFEATS
REDEFECT
REDEFECTED
REDEFECTING
REDEFECTS
REDEFIED
REDEFIES
REDEFINE
REDEFINED
REDEFINES
REDEFINING
REDEFINITION
REDEFINITIONS
REDEFY
REDEFYING
REDELESS
REDELIBERATION

REDELIBERATIONS
REDELIVER
REDELIVERANCE
REDELIVERANCES
REDELIVERED
REDELIVERER
REDELIVERERS
REDELIVERIES
REDELIVERING
REDELIVERS
REDELIVERY
REDEMAND
REDEMANDED
REDEMANDING
REDEMANDS
REDEMONSTRATE
REDEMONSTRATED
REDEMONSTRATES
REDEMONSTRATING
REDEMONSTRATION
REDEMPTIBLE
REDEMPTION
REDEMPTIONAL
REDEMPTIONALLY
REDEMPTIONER
REDEMPTIONERS
REDEMPTIONS
REDEMPTIVE
REDEMPTIVELY
REDEMPTIVENESS
REDEMPTORY
REDENIED
REDENIES
REDENY
REDENYING
REDEPLOY
REDEPLOYED
REDEPLOYING
REDEPLOYMENT
REDEPLOYMENTS
REDEPLOYS
REDEPOSIT
REDEPOSITED
REDEPOSITING
REDEPOSITS
REDES
REDESCEND
REDESCENDED
REDESCENDING
REDESCENDS
REDESCRIBE
REDESCRIBED
REDESCRIBES
REDESCRIBING
REDESCRIPTION
REDESCRIPTIONS

REDESIGN
REDESIGNED
REDESIGNING
REDESIGNS
REDETERMINATION
REDETERMINE
REDETERMINED
REDETERMINES
REDETERMINING
REDEVELOP
REDEVELOPED
REDEVELOPER
REDEVELOPERS
REDEVELOPING
REDEVELOPMENT
REDEVELOPMENTS
REDEVELOPS
REDEYE
REDEYES
REDFIN
REDFINS
REDFISH
REDFISHES
REDFOOT
REDHANDED
REDHEAD
REDHEADED
REDHEADS
REDHORSE
REDHORSES
REDIA
REDIAE
REDIAL
REDIALED
REDIALING
REDIALLED
REDIALLING
REDIALS
REDIAS
REDID
REDIGEST
REDIGESTED
REDIGESTING
REDIGESTION
REDIGESTIONS
REDIGESTS
REDING
REDINGOTE
REDINGOTES
REDINTEGRATE
REDINTEGRATED
REDINTEGRATES
REDINTEGRATING
REDINTEGRATION
REDINTEGRATIONS
REDINTEGRATIVE

REDIP
REDIPPED
REDIPPING
REDIPS
REDIPT
REDIRECT
REDIRECTED
REDIRECTING
REDIRECTION
REDIRECTIONS
REDIRECTS
REDISBURSE
REDISBURSED
REDISBURSES
REDISBURSING
REDISCOUNT
REDISCOUNTABLE
REDISCOUNTED
REDISCOUNTING
REDISCOUNTS
REDISCOVER
REDISCOVERED
REDISCOVERER
REDISCOVERERS
REDISCOVERIES
REDISCOVERING
REDISCOVERS
REDISCOVERY
REDISCUSS
REDISCUSSED
REDISCUSSES
REDISCUSSING
REDISPLAY
REDISPLAYED
REDISPLAYING
REDISPLAYS
REDISPOSE
REDISPOSED
REDISPOSES
REDISPOSING
REDISPOSITION
REDISPOSITIONS
REDISSOLUTION
REDISSOLUTIONS
REDISSOLVE
REDISSOLVED
REDISSOLVES
REDISSOLVING
REDISTIL
REDISTILL
REDISTILLATION
REDISTILLATIONS
REDISTILLED
REDISTILLING
REDISTILLS
REDISTILS

REDISTRIBUTE
REDISTRIBUTED
REDISTRIBUTES
REDISTRIBUTING
REDISTRIBUTION
REDISTRIBUTIONS
REDISTRIBUTIVE
REDISTRICT
REDISTRICTED
REDISTRICTING
REDISTRICTS
REDIVIDE
REDIVIDED
REDIVIDES
REDIVIDING
REDIVISION
REDIVISIONS
REDIVIVUS
REDLEG
REDLEGS
REDLINE
REDLINED
REDLINES
REDLINING
REDLY
REDNECK
REDNECKED
REDNECKS
REDNESS
REDNESSES
REDO
REDOCK
REDOCKED
REDOCKING
REDOCKS
REDOES
REDOING
REDOLENCE
REDOLENCES
REDOLENCIES
REDOLENCY
REDOLENT
REDOLENTLY
REDON
REDONE
REDONNED
REDONNING
REDONS
REDOS
REDOUBLE
REDOUBLED
REDOUBLEMENT
REDOUBLEMENTS
REDOUBLES
REDOUBLING
REDOUBT

REDOUBTABLE
REDOUBTABLENESS
REDOUBTABLY
REDOUBTED
REDOUBTING
REDOUBTS
REDOUND
REDOUNDED
REDOUNDING
REDOUNDINGS
REDOUNDS
REDOUT
REDOUTS
REDOWA
REDOWAS
REDOX
REDOXES
REDPOLL
REDPOLLS
REDRAFT
REDRAFTED
REDRAFTING
REDRAFTS
REDRAW
REDRAWER
REDRAWERS
REDRAWING
REDRAWN
REDRAWS
REDREAM
REDREAMED
REDREAMING
REDREAMS
REDREAMT
REDRESS
REDRESSABILITY
REDRESSABLE
REDRESSED
REDRESSER
REDRESSERS
REDRESSES
REDRESSIBILITY
REDRESSIBLE
REDRESSING
REDRESSIVE
REDRESSOR
REDRESSORS
REDREW
REDRIED
REDRIES
REDRILL
REDRILLED
REDRILLING
REDRILLS
REDRIVE
REDRIVEN

REDRIVES
REDRIVING
REDROOT
REDROOTS
REDROVE
REDRUTHITE
REDRUTHITES
REDRY
REDRYING
REDS
REDSEAR
REDSHANK
REDSHANKS
REDSHARE
REDSHIFT
REDSHIFTED
REDSHIFTS
REDSHIRE
REDSHIRT
REDSHIRTED
REDSHIRTING
REDSHIRTS
REDSHORT
REDSKIN
REDSKINS
REDSTART
REDSTARTS
REDSTREAK
REDSTREAKS
REDTAIL
REDTAILS
REDTOP
REDTOPS
REDUB
REDUBBED
REDUBBING
REDUBS
REDUCE
REDUCED
REDUCER
REDUCERS
REDUCES
REDUCIBILITIES
REDUCIBILITY
REDUCIBLE
REDUCIBLENESS
REDUCIBLENESSES
REDUCIBLY
REDUCING
REDUCTANT
REDUCTANTS
REDUCTASE
REDUCTASES
REDUCTION
REDUCTIONAL
REDUCTIONISM

REDUCTIONISMS
REDUCTIONIST
REDUCTIONISTIC
REDUCTIONISTS
REDUCTIONS
REDUCTIVE
REDUCTIVELY
REDUCTIVENESS
REDUCTIVENESSES
REDUCTOR
REDUCTORS
REDUIT
REDUITS
REDUNDANCE
REDUNDANCES
REDUNDANCIES
REDUNDANCY
REDUNDANT
REDUNDANTLY
REDUPLICATE
REDUPLICATED
REDUPLICATES
REDUPLICATING
REDUPLICATION
REDUPLICATIONS
REDUPLICATIVE
REDUPLICATIVELY
REDUVIID
REDUVIIDS
REDUX
REDWARE
REDWARES
REDWATER
REDWATERS
REDWING
REDWINGS
REDWOOD
REDWOODS
REDYE
REDYED
REDYEING
REDYES
REDYING
REE
REEARN
REEARNED
REEARNING
REEARNS
REEBOK
REEBOKS
REECH
REECHED
REECHES
REECHIE
REECHIER
REECHIEST

REECHING
REECHO
REECHOED
REECHOES
REECHOING
REECHY
REED
REEDBED
REEDBEDS
REEDBIRD
REEDBIRDS
REEDBUCK
REEDBUCKS
REEDE
REEDED
REEDEN
REEDER
REEDERS
REEDES
REEDIER
REEDIEST
REEDIFIED
REEDIFIES
REEDIFY
REEDIFYING
REEDILY
REEDINESS
REEDINESSES
REEDING
REEDINGS
REEDIT
REEDITED
REEDITING
REEDITION
REEDITIONS
REEDITS
REEDLIKE
REEDLING
REEDLINGS
REEDMACE
REEDMACES
REEDMAN
REEDMEN
REEDS
REEDSMAN
REEDSMEN
REEDSTOP
REEDSTOPS
REEDUCATE
REEDUCATED
REEDUCATES
REEDUCATING
REEDUCATION
REEDUCATIONS
REEDUCATIVE
REEDY

REEF
REEFABLE
REEFED
REEFER
REEFERS
REEFIER
REEFIEST
REEFING
REEFINGS
REEFS
REEFY
REEJECT
REEJECTED
REEJECTING
REEJECTS
REEK
REEKED
REEKER
REEKERS
REEKIE
REEKIER
REEKIEST
REEKING
REEKINGLY
REEKS
REEKY
REEL
REELABLE
REELECT
REELECTED
REELECTING
REELECTION
REELECTIONS
REELECTS
REELED
REELER
REELERS
REELIGIBILITIES
REELIGIBILITY
REELIGIBLE
REELING
REELINGLY
REELINGS
REELMAN
REELMEN
REELS
REEMBARK
REEMBARKED
REEMBARKING
REEMBARKS
REEMBODIED
REEMBODIES
REEMBODY
REEMBODYING
REEMBROIDER
REEMBROIDERED

REEMBROIDERING
REEMBROIDERS
REEMERGE
REEMERGED
REEMERGENCE
REEMERGENCES
REEMERGES
REEMERGING
REEMISSION
REEMISSIONS
REEMIT
REEMITS
REEMITTED
REEMITTING
REEMPHASES
REEMPHASIS
REEMPHASIZE
REEMPHASIZED
REEMPHASIZES
REEMPHASIZING
REEMPLOY
REEMPLOYED
REEMPLOYING
REEMPLOYMENT
REEMPLOYMENTS
REEMPLOYS
REEN
REENACT
REENACTED
REENACTING
REENACTMENT
REENACTMENTS
REENACTS
REENCOUNTER
REENCOUNTERED
REENCOUNTERING
REENCOUNTERS
REENDOW
REENDOWED
REENDOWING
REENDOWS
REENERGIZE
REENERGIZED
REENERGIZES
REENERGIZING
REENFORCE
REENFORCED
REENFORCES
REENFORCING
REENGAGE
REENGAGED
REENGAGEMENT
REENGAGEMENTS
REENGAGES
REENGAGING
REENGINEER

REENGINEERED
REENGINEERING
REENGINEERS
REENGRAVE
REENGRAVED
REENGRAVES
REENGRAVING
REENJOY
REENJOYED
REENJOYING
REENJOYS
REENLIST
REENLISTED
REENLISTING
REENLISTMENT
REENLISTMENTS
REENLISTS
REENROLL
REENROLLED
REENROLLING
REENROLLS
REENS
REENTER
REENTERED
REENTERING
REENTERS
REENTHRONE
REENTHRONED
REENTHRONES
REENTHRONING
REENTRANCE
REENTRANCES
REENTRANT
REENTRANTS
REENTRIES
REENTRY
REEQUIP
REEQUIPMENT
REEQUIPMENTS
REEQUIPPED
REEQUIPPING
REEQUIPS
REERECT
REERECTED
REERECTING
REERECTS
REES
REESCALATE
REESCALATED
REESCALATES
REESCALATING
REESCALATION
REESCALATIONS
REEST
REESTABLISH
REESTABLISHED

REESTABLISHES
REESTABLISHING
REESTABLISHMENT
REESTED
REESTIER
REESTIEST
REESTIMATE
REESTIMATED
REESTIMATES
REESTIMATING
REESTING
REESTS
REESTY
REEVALUATE
REEVALUATED
REEVALUATES
REEVALUATING
REEVALUATION
REEVALUATIONS
REEVE
REEVED
REEVES
REEVING
REEVOKE
REEVOKED
REEVOKES
REEVOKING
REEXAMINATION
REEXAMINATIONS
REEXAMINE
REEXAMINED
REEXAMINES
REEXAMINING
REEXPEL
REEXPELLED
REEXPELLING
REEXPELS
REEXPERIENCE
REEXPERIENCED
REEXPERIENCES
REEXPERIENCING
REEXPLORE
REEXPLORED
REEXPLORES
REEXPLORING
REEXPORT
REEXPORTATION
REEXPORTATIONS
REEXPORTED
REEXPORTING
REEXPORTS
REEXPOSE
REEXPOSED
REEXPOSES
REEXPOSING
REEXPOSURE

REEXPOSURES
REEXPRESS
REEXPRESSED
REEXPRESSES
REEXPRESSING
REF
REFACE
REFACED
REFACES
REFACING
REFALL
REFALLEN
REFALLING
REFALLS
REFASHION
REFASHIONED
REFASHIONING
REFASHIONMENT
REFASHIONMENTS
REFASHIONS
REFASTEN
REFASTENED
REFASTENING
REFASTENS
REFECT
REFECTED
REFECTING
REFECTION
REFECTIONER
REFECTIONERS
REFECTIONS
REFECTORIAN
REFECTORIANS
REFECTORIES
REFECTORY
REFECTS
REFED
REFEED
REFEEDING
REFEEDS
REFEEL
REFEELING
REFEELS
REFEL
REFELL
REFELLED
REFELLING
REFELS
REFELT
REFENCE
REFENCED
REFENCES
REFENCING
REFER
REFERABLE
REFEREE

REFEREED
REFEREEING
REFEREES
REFERENCE
REFERENCED
REFERENCER
REFERENCERS
REFERENCES
REFERENCING
REFERENDA
REFERENDARIES
REFERENDARY
REFERENDUM
REFERENDUMS
REFERENT
REFERENTIAL
REFERENTIALITY
REFERENTIALLY
REFERENTS
REFERRABLE
REFERRAL
REFERRALS
REFERRED
REFERRER
REFERRERS
REFERRIBLE
REFERRING
REFERS
REFFED
REFFING
REFFO
REFFOS
REFIGHT
REFIGHTING
REFIGHTS
REFIGURE
REFIGURED
REFIGURES
REFIGURING
REFILE
REFILED
REFILES
REFILING
REFILL
REFILLABLE
REFILLED
REFILLING
REFILLS
REFILM
REFILMED
REFILMING
REFILMS
REFILTER
REFILTERED
REFILTERING
REFILTERS

REFINABILITY
REFINABLE
REFINABLY
REFINANCE
REFINANCED
REFINANCES
REFINANCING
REFINANCINGS
REFIND
REFINDING
REFINDS
REFINE
REFINED
REFINEDLY
REFINEDNESS
REFINEDNESSES
REFINEMENT
REFINEMENTS
REFINER
REFINERIES
REFINERS
REFINERY
REFINES
REFINING
REFININGS
REFINISH
REFINISHED
REFINISHER
REFINISHERS
REFINISHES
REFINISHING
REFIRE
REFIRED
REFIRES
REFIRING
REFIT
REFITMENT
REFITMENTS
REFITS
REFITTED
REFITTING
REFITTINGS
REFIX
REFIXED
REFIXES
REFIXING
REFLAG
REFLAGGED
REFLAGGING
REFLAGS
REFLATE
REFLATED
REFLATES
REFLATING
REFLATION
REFLATIONARY

REFLATIONS
REFLECT
REFLECTANCE
REFLECTANCES
REFLECTED
REFLECTER
REFLECTERS
REFLECTING
REFLECTINGLY
REFLECTION
REFLECTIONAL
REFLECTIONLESS
REFLECTIONS
REFLECTIVE
REFLECTIVELY
REFLECTIVENESS
REFLECTIVITIES
REFLECTIVITY
REFLECTOGRAM
REFLECTOGRAMS
REFLECTOGRAPH
REFLECTOGRAPHS
REFLECTOGRAPHY
REFLECTOMETER
REFLECTOMETERS
REFLECTOMETRIES
REFLECTOMETRY
REFLECTOR
REFLECTORIZE
REFLECTORIZED
REFLECTORIZES
REFLECTORIZING
REFLECTORS
REFLECTS
REFLET
REFLETS
REFLEW
REFLEX
REFLEXED
REFLEXES
REFLEXIBILITIES
REFLEXIBILITY
REFLEXIBLE
REFLEXING
REFLEXION
REFLEXIONAL
REFLEXIONALLY
REFLEXIONS
REFLEXIVE
REFLEXIVELY
REFLEXIVENESS
REFLEXIVENESSES
REFLEXIVES
REFLEXIVITIES
REFLEXIVITY
REFLEXLY

REFLEXOLOGICAL
REFLEXOLOGIES
REFLEXOLOGIST
REFLEXOLOGISTS
REFLEXOLOGY
REFLIES
REFLOAT
REFLOATED
REFLOATING
REFLOATS
REFLOOD
REFLOODED
REFLOODING
REFLOODS
REFLOW
REFLOWED
REFLOWER
REFLOWERED
REFLOWERING
REFLOWERINGS
REFLOWERS
REFLOWING
REFLOWINGS
REFLOWN
REFLOWS
REFLUENCE
REFLUENCES
REFLUENT
REFLUX
REFLUXED
REFLUXES
REFLUXING
REFLY
REFLYING
REFOCILLATE
REFOCILLATED
REFOCILLATES
REFOCILLATING
REFOCILLATION
REFOCILLATIONS
REFOCUS
REFOCUSED
REFOCUSES
REFOCUSING
REFOCUSSED
REFOCUSSES
REFOCUSSING
REFOLD
REFOLDED
REFOLDING
REFOLDS
REFOOT
REFOOTED
REFOOTING
REFOOTS
REFOREST

REFORESTATION
REFORESTATIONS
REFORESTED
REFORESTING
REFORESTS
REFORGE
REFORGED
REFORGES
REFORGING
REFORM
REFORMABILITIES
REFORMABILITY
REFORMABLE
REFORMADE
REFORMADES
REFORMADO
REFORMADOES
REFORMADOS
REFORMAT
REFORMATE
REFORMATES
REFORMATION
REFORMATIONAL
REFORMATIONIST
REFORMATIONISTS
REFORMATIONS
REFORMATIVE
REFORMATORIES
REFORMATORY
REFORMATS
REFORMATTED
REFORMATTING
REFORMED
REFORMER
REFORMERS
REFORMING
REFORMISM
REFORMISMS
REFORMIST
REFORMISTS
REFORMS
REFORMULATE
REFORMULATED
REFORMULATES
REFORMULATING
REFORMULATION
REFORMULATIONS
REFORTIFICATION
REFORTIFIED
REFORTIFIES
REFORTIFY
REFORTIFYING
REFOUGHT
REFOUND
REFOUNDATION
REFOUNDATIONS

REFOUNDED
REFOUNDER
REFOUNDERS
REFOUNDING
REFOUNDS
REFRACT
REFRACTABLE
REFRACTARIES
REFRACTARY
REFRACTED
REFRACTILE
REFRACTING
REFRACTION
REFRACTIONS
REFRACTIVE
REFRACTIVELY
REFRACTIVENESS
REFRACTIVITIES
REFRACTIVITY
REFRACTOMETER
REFRACTOMETERS
REFRACTOMETRIC
REFRACTOMETRIES
REFRACTOMETRY
REFRACTOR
REFRACTORIES
REFRACTORILY
REFRACTORINESS
REFRACTORS
REFRACTORY
REFRACTS
REFRACTURE
REFRACTURES
REFRAIN
REFRAINED
REFRAINER
REFRAINERS
REFRAINING
REFRAINMENT
REFRAINMENTS
REFRAINS
REFRAME
REFRAMED
REFRAMES
REFRAMING
REFRANGIBILITY
REFRANGIBLE
REFRANGIBLENESS
REFREEZE
REFREEZES
REFREEZING
REFRESH
REFRESHED
REFRESHEN
REFRESHENED
REFRESHENER

REFRESHENERS
REFRESHENING
REFRESHENS
REFRESHER
REFRESHERS
REFRESHES
REFRESHFUL
REFRESHFULLY
REFRESHING
REFRESHINGLY
REFRESHMENT
REFRESHMENTS
REFRIED
REFRIES
REFRIGERANT
REFRIGERANTS
REFRIGERATE
REFRIGERATED
REFRIGERATES
REFRIGERATING
REFRIGERATION
REFRIGERATIONS
REFRIGERATIVE
REFRIGERATOR
REFRIGERATORIES
REFRIGERATORS
REFRIGERATORY
REFRINGE
REFRINGED
REFRINGENCE
REFRINGENCIES
REFRINGENCY
REFRINGENT
REFRINGENTLY
REFRINGES
REFRINGING
REFRONT
REFRONTED
REFRONTING
REFRONTS
REFROZE
REFROZEN
REFRY
REFRYING
REFS
REFT
REFUEL
REFUELABLE
REFUELED
REFUELING
REFUELLABLE
REFUELLED
REFUELLING
REFUELS
REFUGE
REFUGED

REFUGEE
REFUGEEISM
REFUGEEISMS
REFUGEES
REFUGES
REFUGIA
REFUGING
REFUGIUM
REFULGENCE
REFULGENCES
REFULGENCIES
REFULGENCY
REFULGENT
REFULGENTLY
REFUND
REFUNDABILITIES
REFUNDABILITY
REFUNDABLE
REFUNDED
REFUNDER
REFUNDERS
REFUNDING
REFUNDMENT
REFUNDMENTS
REFUNDS
REFURBISH
REFURBISHED
REFURBISHER
REFURBISHERS
REFURBISHES
REFURBISHING
REFURBISHINGS
REFURBISHMENT
REFURBISHMENTS
REFURNISH
REFURNISHED
REFURNISHES
REFURNISHING
REFUSABLE
REFUSAL
REFUSALS
REFUSE
REFUSED
REFUSENIK
REFUSENIKS
REFUSER
REFUSERS
REFUSES
REFUSING
REFUSION
REFUSIONS
REFUSNIK
REFUSNIKS
REFUTABILITY
REFUTABLE
REFUTABLY

REFUTAL
REFUTALS
REFUTATION
REFUTATIONS
REFUTE
REFUTED
REFUTER
REFUTERS
REFUTES
REFUTING
REG
REGAIN
REGAINABLE
REGAINED
REGAINER
REGAINERS
REGAINING
REGAINMENT
REGAINMENTS
REGAINS
REGAL
REGALE
REGALED
REGALEMENT
REGALEMENTS
REGALER
REGALERS
REGALES
REGALIA
REGALIAN
REGALIAS
REGALING
REGALISM
REGALISMS
REGALIST
REGALISTS
REGALITIES
REGALITY
REGALLY
REGALS
REGALVANISE
REGALVANISED
REGALVANISES
REGALVANISING
REGALVANIZE
REGALVANIZED
REGALVANIZES
REGALVANIZING
REGAR
REGARD
REGARDABLE
REGARDANT
REGARDED
REGARDER
REGARDERS
REGARDFUL

REGARDFULLY
REGARDFULNESS
REGARDFULNESSES
REGARDING
REGARDLESS
REGARDLESSLY
REGARDLESSNESS
REGARDS
REGARS
REGATHER
REGATHERED
REGATHERING
REGATHERS
REGATTA
REGATTAS
REGAUGE
REGAUGED
REGAUGES
REGAUGING
REGAVE
REGEAR
REGEARED
REGEARING
REGEARS
REGELATE
REGELATED
REGELATES
REGELATING
REGELATION
REGELATIONS
REGENCE
REGENCES
REGENCIES
REGENCY
REGENERABLE
REGENERACIES
REGENERACY
REGENERATE
REGENERATED
REGENERATELY
REGENERATENESS
REGENERATES
REGENERATING
REGENERATION
REGENERATIONS
REGENERATIVE
REGENERATIVELY
REGENERATOR
REGENERATORS
REGENERATORY
REGENESES
REGENESIS
REGENT
REGENTAL
REGENTS
REGENTSHIP

REGENTSHIPS
REGERMINATE
REGERMINATED
REGERMINATES
REGERMINATING
REGERMINATION
REGERMINATIONS
REGES
REGEST
REGESTS
REGGAE
REGGAES
REGGO
REGGOS
REGICIDAL
REGICIDE
REGICIDES
REGIE
REGIES
REGILD
REGILDED
REGILDING
REGILDS
REGILT
REGIME
REGIMEN
REGIMENS
REGIMENT
REGIMENTAL
REGIMENTALLY
REGIMENTALS
REGIMENTATION
REGIMENTATIONS
REGIMENTED
REGIMENTING
REGIMENTS
REGIMES
REGIMINAL
REGINA
REGINAE
REGINAL
REGINAS
REGION
REGIONAL
REGIONALISATION
REGIONALISE
REGIONALISED
REGIONALISES
REGIONALISING
REGIONALISM
REGIONALISMS
REGIONALIST
REGIONALISTIC
REGIONALISTS
REGIONALIZATION
REGIONALIZE

REGIONALIZED
REGIONALIZES
REGIONALIZING
REGIONALLY
REGIONALS
REGIONARY
REGIONS
REGISSEUR
REGISSEURS
REGISTER
REGISTERABLE
REGISTERED
REGISTERER
REGISTERERS
REGISTERING
REGISTERS
REGISTRABLE
REGISTRANT
REGISTRANTS
REGISTRAR
REGISTRARIES
REGISTRARS
REGISTRARSHIP
REGISTRARSHIPS
REGISTRARY
REGISTRATION
REGISTRATIONAL
REGISTRATIONS
REGISTRIES
REGISTRY
REGIUS
REGIVE
REGIVEN
REGIVES
REGIVING
REGLAZE
REGLAZED
REGLAZES
REGLAZING
REGLET
REGLETS
REGLOSS
REGLOSSED
REGLOSSES
REGLOSSING
REGLOW
REGLOWED
REGLOWING
REGLOWS
REGLUE
REGLUED
REGLUES
REGLUING
REGMA
REGMAKER
REGMAKERS

REGMATA
REGNA
REGNAL
REGNANCIES
REGNANCY
REGNANT
REGNUM
REGO
REGOLITH
REGOLITHS
REGORGE
REGORGED
REGORGES
REGORGING
REGOS
REGOSOL
REGOSOLS
REGRADE
REGRADED
REGRADES
REGRADING
REGRAFT
REGRAFTED
REGRAFTING
REGRAFTS
REGRANT
REGRANTED
REGRANTING
REGRANTS
REGRATE
REGRATED
REGRATER
REGRATERS
REGRATES
REGRATING
REGRATINGS
REGRATOR
REGRATORS
REGREDE
REGREDED
REGREDES
REGREDIENCE
REGREDIENCES
REGREDING
REGREEN
REGREENED
REGREENING
REGREENS
REGREET
REGREETED
REGREETING
REGREETS
REGRESS
REGRESSED
REGRESSES
REGRESSING

REGRESSION
REGRESSIONS
REGRESSIVE
REGRESSIVELY
REGRESSIVENESS
REGRESSIVITIES
REGRESSIVITY
REGRESSOR
REGRESSORS
REGRET
REGRETFUL
REGRETFULLY
REGRETFULNESS
REGRETFULNESSES
REGRETS
REGRETTABLE
REGRETTABLY
REGRETTED
REGRETTER
REGRETTERS
REGRETTING
REGREW
REGRIND
REGRINDING
REGRINDS
REGROOM
REGROOMED
REGROOMING
REGROOMS
REGROOVE
REGROOVED
REGROOVES
REGROOVING
REGROUND
REGROUP
REGROUPED
REGROUPING
REGROUPS
REGROW
REGROWING
REGROWN
REGROWS
REGROWTH
REGROWTHS
REGS
REGUERDON
REGUERDONED
REGUERDONING
REGUERDONS
REGULA
REGULABILITY
REGULABLE
REGULABLY
REGULAE
REGULAR
REGULARISATION

REGULARISATIONS
REGULARISE
REGULARISED
REGULARISES
REGULARISING
REGULARITIES
REGULARITY
REGULARIZATION
REGULARIZATIONS
REGULARIZE
REGULARIZED
REGULARIZES
REGULARIZING
REGULARLY
REGULARS
REGULATE
REGULATED
REGULATES
REGULATING
REGULATION
REGULATIONS
REGULATIVE
REGULATIVELY
REGULATIVENESS
REGULATOR
REGULATORS
REGULATORY
REGULI
REGULINE
REGULISE
REGULISED
REGULISES
REGULISING
REGULIZE
REGULIZED
REGULIZES
REGULIZING
REGULO
REGULOS
REGULUS
REGULUSES
REGUR
REGURGITANT
REGURGITANTS
REGURGITATE
REGURGITATED
REGURGITATES
REGURGITATING
REGURGITATION
REGURGITATIONS
REGURS
REH
REHAB
REHABBED
REHABBER
REHABBERS

REHABBING
REHABILITANT
REHABILITANTS
REHABILITATE
REHABILITATED
REHABILITATES
REHABILITATING
REHABILITATION
REHABILITATIONS
REHABILITATIVE
REHABILITATOR
REHABILITATORS
REHABS
REHAMMER
REHAMMERED
REHAMMERING
REHAMMERS
REHANDLE
REHANDLED
REHANDLES
REHANDLING
REHANDLINGS
REHANG
REHANGED
REHANGING
REHANGS
REHARDEN
REHARDENED
REHARDENING
REHARDENS
REHARNESS
REHARNESSED
REHARNESSES
REHARNESSING
REHASH
REHASHED
REHASHES
REHASHING
REHEAR
REHEARD
REHEARING
REHEARINGS
REHEARS
REHEARSAL
REHEARSALS
REHEARSE
REHEARSED
REHEARSER
REHEARSERS
REHEARSES
REHEARSING
REHEARSINGS
REHEAT
REHEATED
REHEATER
REHEATERS

REHEATING
REHEATINGS
REHEATS
REHEEL
REHEELED
REHEELING
REHEELS
REHEM
REHEMMED
REHEMMING
REHEMS
REHINGE
REHINGED
REHINGES
REHINGING
REHIRE
REHIRED
REHIRES
REHIRING
REHOBOAM
REHOBOAMS
REHOSPITALIZE
REHOSPITALIZED
REHOSPITALIZES
REHOSPITALIZING
REHOUSE
REHOUSED
REHOUSES
REHOUSING
REHOUSINGS
REHS
REHUMANISE
REHUMANISED
REHUMANISES
REHUMANISING
REHUMANIZE
REHUMANIZED
REHUMANIZES
REHUMANIZING
REHUNG
REHYDRATABLE
REHYDRATE
REHYDRATED
REHYDRATES
REHYDRATING
REHYDRATION
REHYDRATIONS
REHYPNOTIZE
REHYPNOTIZED
REHYPNOTIZES
REHYPNOTIZING
REI
REICHSMARK
REICHSMARKS
REIDENTIFIED
REIDENTIFIES

REIDENTIFY
REIDENTIFYING
REIF
REIFICATION
REIFICATIONS
REIFICATORY
REIFIED
REIFIER
REIFIERS
REIFIES
REIFS
REIFY
REIFYING
REIGN
REIGNED
REIGNING
REIGNITE
REIGNITED
REIGNITES
REIGNITING
REIGNITION
REIGNITIONS
REIGNS
REIK
REIKI
REIKIS
REIKS
REILLUME
REILLUMED
REILLUMES
REILLUMINE
REILLUMINED
REILLUMINES
REILLUMING
REILLUMINING
REIMAGE
REIMAGED
REIMAGES
REIMAGINE
REIMAGINED
REIMAGINES
REIMAGING
REIMAGINING
REIMBURSABLE
REIMBURSE
REIMBURSED
REIMBURSEMENT
REIMBURSEMENTS
REIMBURSER
REIMBURSERS
REIMBURSES
REIMBURSING
REIMMERSE
REIMMERSED
REIMMERSES
REIMMERSING

REIMPLANT
REIMPLANTATION
REIMPLANTATIONS
REIMPLANTED
REIMPLANTING
REIMPLANTS
REIMPORT
REIMPORTATION
REIMPORTATIONS
REIMPORTED
REIMPORTER
REIMPORTERS
REIMPORTING
REIMPORTS
REIMPOSE
REIMPOSED
REIMPOSES
REIMPOSING
REIMPOSITION
REIMPOSITIONS
REIMPRESSION
REIMPRESSIONS
REIMPRISON
REIMPRISONED
REIMPRISONING
REIMPRISONMENT
REIMPRISONS
REIN
REINCARNATE
REINCARNATED
REINCARNATES
REINCARNATING
REINCARNATION
REINCARNATIONS
REINCITE
REINCITED
REINCITES
REINCITING
REINCORPORATE
REINCORPORATED
REINCORPORATES
REINCORPORATING
REINCORPORATION
REINCREASE
REINCREASED
REINCREASES
REINCREASING
REINCUR
REINCURRED
REINCURRING
REINCURS
REINDEER
REINDEERS
REINDEX
REINDEXED
REINDEXES

REINDEXING
REINDICT
REINDICTED
REINDICTING
REINDICTMENT
REINDICTMENTS
REINDICTS
REINDUCE
REINDUCED
REINDUCES
REINDUCING
REINDUCT
REINDUCTED
REINDUCTING
REINDUCTION
REINDUCTIONS
REINDUCTS
REINDUSTRIALISE
REINDUSTRIALIZE
REINED
REINETTE
REINETTES
REINFECT
REINFECTED
REINFECTING
REINFECTION
REINFECTIONS
REINFECTS
REINFEST
REINFESTATION
REINFESTATIONS
REINFESTED
REINFESTING
REINFESTS
REINFLAME
REINFLAMED
REINFLAMES
REINFLAMING
REINFLAMMATION
REINFLATE
REINFLATED
REINFLATES
REINFLATING
REINFLATION
REINFLATIONS
REINFORCE
REINFORCEABLE
REINFORCED
REINFORCEMENT
REINFORCEMENTS
REINFORCER
REINFORCERS
REINFORCES
REINFORCING
REINFORM
REINFORMED

REINFORMING
REINFORMS
REINFUND
REINFUNDED
REINFUNDING
REINFUNDS
REINFUSE
REINFUSED
REINFUSES
REINFUSING
REINFUSION
REINFUSIONS
REINHABIT
REINHABITED
REINHABITING
REINHABITS
REINING
REINITIATE
REINITIATED
REINITIATES
REINITIATING
REINJECT
REINJECTED
REINJECTING
REINJECTION
REINJECTIONS
REINJECTS
REINJURE
REINJURED
REINJURES
REINJURIES
REINJURING
REINJURY
REINK
REINKED
REINKING
REINKS
REINLESS
REINNERVATE
REINNERVATED
REINNERVATES
REINNERVATING
REINNERVATION
REINNERVATIONS
REINOCULATE
REINOCULATED
REINOCULATES
REINOCULATING
REINOCULATION
REINOCULATIONS
REINS
REINSERT
REINSERTED
REINSERTING
REINSERTION
REINSERTIONS

REINSERTS
REINSMAN
REINSMEN
REINSPECT
REINSPECTED
REINSPECTING
REINSPECTION
REINSPECTIONS
REINSPECTS
REINSPIRE
REINSPIRED
REINSPIRES
REINSPIRING
REINSPIRIT
REINSPIRITED
REINSPIRITING
REINSPIRITS
REINSTAL
REINSTALED
REINSTALING
REINSTALL
REINSTALLATION
REINSTALLATIONS
REINSTALLED
REINSTALLING
REINSTALLS
REINSTALMENT
REINSTALMENTS
REINSTALS
REINSTATE
REINSTATED
REINSTATEMENT
REINSTATEMENTS
REINSTATES
REINSTATING
REINSTATION
REINSTATIONS
REINSTATOR
REINSTATORS
REINSTITUTE
REINSTITUTED
REINSTITUTES
REINSTITUTING
REINSTRUCT
REINSTRUCTED
REINSTRUCTING
REINSTRUCTION
REINSTRUCTIONS
REINSTRUCTS
REINSURANCE
REINSURANCES
REINSURE
REINSURED
REINSURER
REINSURERS
REINSURES

REINSURING
REINTEGRATE
REINTEGRATED
REINTEGRATES
REINTEGRATING
REINTEGRATION
REINTEGRATIONS
REINTEGRATIVE
REINTER
REINTERMENT
REINTERMENTS
REINTERPRET
REINTERPRETED
REINTERPRETING
REINTERPRETS
REINTERRED
REINTERRING
REINTERROGATE
REINTERROGATED
REINTERROGATES
REINTERROGATING
REINTERROGATION
REINTERS
REINTERVIEW
REINTERVIEWED
REINTERVIEWING
REINTERVIEWS
REINTRODUCE
REINTRODUCED
REINTRODUCES
REINTRODUCING
REINTRODUCTION
REINTRODUCTIONS
REINVADE
REINVADED
REINVADES
REINVADING
REINVASION
REINVASIONS
REINVENT
REINVENTED
REINVENTING
REINVENTION
REINVENTIONS
REINVENTS
REINVEST
REINVESTED
REINVESTIGATE
REINVESTIGATED
REINVESTIGATES
REINVESTIGATING
REINVESTIGATION
REINVESTING
REINVESTMENT
REINVESTMENTS
REINVESTS

REINVIGORATE
REINVIGORATED
REINVIGORATES
REINVIGORATING
REINVIGORATION
REINVIGORATIONS
REINVIGORATOR
REINVIGORATORS
REINVITE
REINVITED
REINVITES
REINVITING
REINVOKE
REINVOKED
REINVOKES
REINVOKING
REINVOLVE
REINVOLVED
REINVOLVEMENT
REINVOLVEMENTS
REINVOLVES
REINVOLVING
REIOYNDURES
REIRD
REIRDS
REIS
REISES
REISSUABLE
REISSUE
REISSUED
REISSUER
REISSUERS
REISSUES
REISSUING
REIST
REISTAFEL
REISTAFELS
REISTED
REISTING
REISTS
REITBOK
REITBOKS
REITER
REITERANCE
REITERANCES
REITERANT
REITERATE
REITERATED
REITERATEDLY
REITERATES
REITERATING
REITERATION
REITERATIONS
REITERATIVE
REITERATIVELY
REITERATIVES

REITERS
REIVE
REIVED
REIVER
REIVERS
REIVES
REIVING
REJACKET
REJACKETED
REJACKETING
REJACKETS
REJECT
REJECTABLE
REJECTAMENTA
REJECTED
REJECTEE
REJECTEES
REJECTER
REJECTERS
REJECTIBLE
REJECTING
REJECTINGLY
REJECTION
REJECTIONIST
REJECTIONISTS
REJECTIONS
REJECTIVE
REJECTOR
REJECTORS
REJECTS
REJIG
REJIGGED
REJIGGER
REJIGGERED
REJIGGERING
REJIGGERS
REJIGGING
REJIGS
REJOICE
REJOICED
REJOICEFUL
REJOICEMENT
REJOICEMENTS
REJOICER
REJOICERS
REJOICES
REJOICING
REJOICINGLY
REJOICINGS
REJOIN
REJOINDER
REJOINDERS
REJOINDURE
REJOINDURES
REJOINED
REJOINING

REJOINS
REJON
REJONEADOR
REJONEADORA
REJONEADORAS
REJONEADORES
REJONEO
REJONEOS
REJONES
REJOURN
REJOURNED
REJOURNING
REJOURNS
REJUDGE
REJUDGED
REJUDGES
REJUDGING
REJUGGLE
REJUGGLED
REJUGGLES
REJUGGLING
REJUVENATE
REJUVENATED
REJUVENATES
REJUVENATING
REJUVENATION
REJUVENATIONS
REJUVENATOR
REJUVENATORS
REJUVENESCE
REJUVENESCED
REJUVENESCENCE
REJUVENESCENCES
REJUVENESCENT
REJUVENESCES
REJUVENESCING
REJUVENISED
REJUVENISES
REJUVENISING
REJUVENIZE
REJUVENIZED
REJUVENIZES
REJUVENIZING
REKE
REKED
REKES
REKEY
REKEYBOARD
REKEYBOARDED
REKEYBOARDING
REKEYBOARDS
REKEYED
REKEYING
REKEYS
REKINDLE
REKINDLED

REKINDLES
REKINDLING
REKING
REKNIT
REKNITS
REKNITTED
REKNITTING
RELABEL
RELABELED
RELABELING
RELABELLED
RELABELLING
RELABELS
RELACE
RELACED
RELACES
RELACHE
RELACHES
RELACING
RELACQUER
RELACQUERED
RELACQUERING
RELACQUERS
RELAID
RELANDSCAPE
RELANDSCAPED
RELANDSCAPES
RELANDSCAPING
RELAPSE
RELAPSED
RELAPSER
RELAPSERS
RELAPSES
RELAPSING
RELATA
RELATABLE
RELATE
RELATED
RELATEDLY
RELATEDNESS
RELATEDNESSES
RELATER
RELATERS
RELATES
RELATING
RELATION
RELATIONAL
RELATIONALLY
RELATIONISM
RELATIONISMS
RELATIONIST
RELATIONISTS
RELATIONLESS
RELATIONS
RELATIONSHIP
RELATIONSHIPS

RELATIVAL
RELATIVE
RELATIVELY
RELATIVENESS
RELATIVENESSES
RELATIVES
RELATIVISATION
RELATIVISE
RELATIVISED
RELATIVISES
RELATIVISING
RELATIVISM
RELATIVISMS
RELATIVIST
RELATIVISTIC
RELATIVISTS
RELATIVITIES
RELATIVITIST
RELATIVITISTS
RELATIVITY
RELATIVIZATION
RELATIVIZE
RELATIVIZED
RELATIVIZES
RELATIVIZING
RELATOR
RELATORS
RELATUM
RELAUNCH
RELAUNCHED
RELAUNCHES
RELAUNCHING
RELAX
RELAXABILITY
RELAXABLE
RELAXANT
RELAXANTS
RELAXATION
RELAXATIONS
RELAXATIVE
RELAXED
RELAXEDLY
RELAXEDNESS
RELAXEDNESSES
RELAXER
RELAXERS
RELAXES
RELAXIN
RELAXING
RELAXINS
RELAY
RELAYED
RELAYING
RELAYS
RELEARN
RELEARNED

RELEARNING
RELEARNS
RELEARNT
RELEASABLE
RELEASE
RELEASED
RELEASEE
RELEASEES
RELEASEMENT
RELEASEMENTS
RELEASER
RELEASERS
RELEASES
RELEASING
RELEASOR
RELEASORS
RELEGABLE
RELEGATABLE
RELEGATE
RELEGATED
RELEGATES
RELEGATING
RELEGATION
RELEGATIONS
RELEND
RELENDING
RELENDS
RELENT
RELENTED
RELENTING
RELENTINGS
RELENTLESS
RELENTLESSLY
RELENTLESSNESS
RELENTMENT
RELENTMENTS
RELENTS
RELET
RELETS
RELETTER
RELETTERED
RELETTERING
RELETTERS
RELETTING
RELEVANCE
RELEVANCES
RELEVANCIES
RELEVANCY
RELEVANT
RELEVANTLY
RELEVE
RELEVES
RELIABILITIES
RELIABILITY
RELIABLE
RELIABLENESS

RELIABLENESSES
RELIABLES
RELIABLY
RELIANCE
RELIANCES
RELIANT
RELIANTLY
RELIC
RELICENSE
RELICENSED
RELICENSES
RELICENSING
RELICENSURE
RELICENSURES
RELICS
RELICT
RELICTION
RELICTIONS
RELICTS
RELIDE
RELIE
RELIED
RELIEF
RELIEFLESS
RELIEFS
RELIER
RELIERS
RELIES
RELIEVABLE
RELIEVE
RELIEVED
RELIEVEDLY
RELIEVER
RELIEVERS
RELIEVES
RELIEVING
RELIEVO
RELIEVOS
RELIGHT
RELIGHTED
RELIGHTING
RELIGHTS
RELIGIEUSE
RELIGIEUSES
RELIGIEUX
RELIGION
RELIGIONARIES
RELIGIONARY
RELIGIONER
RELIGIONERS
RELIGIONISE
RELIGIONISED
RELIGIONISES
RELIGIONISING
RELIGIONISM
RELIGIONISMS

RELIGIONIST
RELIGIONISTS
RELIGIONIZE
RELIGIONIZED
RELIGIONIZES
RELIGIONIZING
RELIGIONLESS
RELIGIONS
RELIGIOSE
RELIGIOSELY
RELIGIOSITIES
RELIGIOSITY
RELIGIOSO
RELIGIOUS
RELIGIOUSES
RELIGIOUSLY
RELIGIOUSNESS
RELIGIOUSNESSES
RELINE
RELINED
RELINES
RELINING
RELINK
RELINKED
RELINKING
RELINKS
RELINQUISH
RELINQUISHED
RELINQUISHER
RELINQUISHERS
RELINQUISHES
RELINQUISHING
RELINQUISHMENT
RELINQUISHMENTS
RELIQUAIRE
RELIQUAIRES
RELIQUARIES
RELIQUARY
RELIQUE
RELIQUEFIED
RELIQUEFIES
RELIQUEFY
RELIQUEFYING
RELIQUES
RELIQUIAE
RELISH
RELISHABLE
RELISHED
RELISHES
RELISHING
RELIST
RELISTED
RELISTING
RELISTS
RELIT
RELIVABLE

RELIVE
RELIVED
RELIVER
RELIVERED
RELIVERING
RELIVERS
RELIVES
RELIVING
RELLIES
RELLISH
RELLISHED
RELLISHES
RELLISHING
RELOAD
RELOADED
RELOADER
RELOADERS
RELOADING
RELOADS
RELOAN
RELOANED
RELOANING
RELOANS
RELOCATABLE
RELOCATE
RELOCATED
RELOCATEE
RELOCATEES
RELOCATES
RELOCATING
RELOCATION
RELOCATIONS
RELOCK
RELOCKED
RELOCKING
RELOCKS
RELOOK
RELOOKED
RELOOKING
RELOOKS
RELUBRICATE
RELUBRICATED
RELUBRICATES
RELUBRICATING
RELUBRICATION
RELUBRICATIONS
RELUCENT
RELUCT
RELUCTANCE
RELUCTANCES
RELUCTANCIES
RELUCTANCY
RELUCTANT
RELUCTANTLY
RELUCTATE
RELUCTATED

RELUCTATES
RELUCTATING
RELUCTATION
RELUCTATIONS
RELUCTED
RELUCTING
RELUCTIVITIES
RELUCTIVITY
RELUCTS
RELUME
RELUMED
RELUMES
RELUMINE
RELUMINED
RELUMINES
RELUMING
RELUMINING
RELY
RELYING
REM
REMADE
REMADES
REMAIL
REMAILED
REMAILING
REMAILS
REMAIN
REMAINDER
REMAINDERED
REMAINDERING
REMAINDERMAN
REMAINDERMEN
REMAINDERS
REMAINED
REMAINING
REMAINS
REMAKE
REMAKER
REMAKERS
REMAKES
REMAKING
REMAN
REMAND
REMANDED
REMANDING
REMANDMENT
REMANDMENTS
REMANDS
REMANENCE
REMANENCES
REMANENCIES
REMANENCY
REMANENT
REMANENTS
REMANET
REMANETS

REMANIE
REMANIES
REMANNED
REMANNING
REMANS
REMANUFACTURE
REMANUFACTURED
REMANUFACTURER
REMANUFACTURERS
REMANUFACTURES
REMANUFACTURING
REMAP
REMAPPED
REMAPPING
REMAPS
REMARK
REMARKABILITY
REMARKABLE
REMARKABLENESS
REMARKABLES
REMARKABLY
REMARKED
REMARKER
REMARKERS
REMARKET
REMARKETED
REMARKETING
REMARKETS
REMARKING
REMARKS
REMARQUE
REMARQUED
REMARQUES
REMARRIAGE
REMARRIAGES
REMARRIED
REMARRIES
REMARRY
REMARRYING
REMASTER
REMASTERED
REMASTERING
REMASTERS
REMATCH
REMATCHED
REMATCHES
REMATCHING
REMATE
REMATED
REMATERIALIZE
REMATERIALIZED
REMATERIALIZES
REMATERIALIZING
REMATES
REMATING
REMBLAI

REMBLAIS
REMBLE
REMBLED
REMBLES
REMBLING
REMEAD
REMEADED
REMEADING
REMEADS
REMEASURE
REMEASURED
REMEASUREMENT
REMEASUREMENTS
REMEASURES
REMEASURING
REMEDE
REMEDED
REMEDES
REMEDIABILITIES
REMEDIABILITY
REMEDIABLE
REMEDIABLY
REMEDIAL
REMEDIALLY
REMEDIAT
REMEDIATE
REMEDIATED
REMEDIATES
REMEDIATING
REMEDIATION
REMEDIATIONS
REMEDIED
REMEDIES
REMEDILESS
REMEDILESSLY
REMEDILESSNESS
REMEDING
REMEDY
REMEDYING
REMEET
REMEETING
REMEETS
REMEID
REMEIDED
REMEIDING
REMEIDS
REMELT
REMELTED
REMELTING
REMELTS
REMEMBER
REMEMBERABILITY
REMEMBERABLE
REMEMBERABLY
REMEMBERED
REMEMBERER

REMEMBERERS
REMEMBERING
REMEMBERS
REMEMBRANCE
REMEMBRANCER
REMEMBRANCERS
REMEMBRANCES
REMEN
REMEND
REMENDED
REMENDING
REMENDS
REMENS
REMERCIED
REMERCIES
REMERCY
REMERCYING
REMERGE
REMERGED
REMERGES
REMERGING
REMET
REMEX
REMIGATE
REMIGATED
REMIGATES
REMIGATING
REMIGATION
REMIGATIONS
REMIGES
REMIGIAL
REMIGRATE
REMIGRATED
REMIGRATES
REMIGRATING
REMIGRATION
REMIGRATIONS
REMILITARISE
REMILITARISED
REMILITARISES
REMILITARISING
REMILITARIZE
REMILITARIZED
REMILITARIZES
REMILITARIZING
REMIND
REMINDED
REMINDER
REMINDERS
REMINDFUL
REMINDING
REMINDS
REMINERALISE
REMINERALISED
REMINERALISES
REMINERALISING

REMINERALIZE
REMINERALIZED
REMINERALIZES
REMINERALIZING
REMINISCE
REMINISCED
REMINISCENCE
REMINISCENCES
REMINISCENT
REMINISCENTIAL
REMINISCENTLY
REMINISCENTS
REMINISCER
REMINISCERS
REMINISCES
REMINISCING
REMINT
REMINTED
REMINTING
REMINTS
REMISE
REMISED
REMISES
REMISING
REMISS
REMISSIBILITIES
REMISSIBILITY
REMISSIBLE
REMISSIBLENESS
REMISSIBLY
REMISSION
REMISSIONS
REMISSIVE
REMISSIVELY
REMISSIVENESS
REMISSLY
REMISSNESS
REMISSNESSES
REMISSORY
REMIT
REMITMENT
REMITMENTS
REMITS
REMITTABLE
REMITTAL
REMITTALS
REMITTANCE
REMITTANCES
REMITTED
REMITTEE
REMITTEES
REMITTENCE
REMITTENCY
REMITTENT
REMITTENTLY
REMITTER

REMITTERS
REMITTING
REMITTOR
REMITTORS
REMIX
REMIXED
REMIXES
REMIXING
REMIXT
REMNANT
REMNANTS
REMOBILIZATION
REMOBILIZATIONS
REMOBILIZE
REMOBILIZED
REMOBILIZES
REMOBILIZING
REMODEL
REMODELED
REMODELING
REMODELLED
REMODELLER
REMODELLERS
REMODELLING
REMODELS
REMODIFICATION
REMODIFICATIONS
REMODIFIED
REMODIFIER
REMODIFIERS
REMODIFIES
REMODIFY
REMODIFYING
REMODULATE
REMODULATED
REMODULATES
REMODULATING
REMODULATION
REMOISTEN
REMOISTENED
REMOISTENING
REMOISTENS
REMOLADE
REMOLADES
REMOLD
REMOLDED
REMOLDING
REMOLDS
REMONETISATION
REMONETISATIONS
REMONETISE
REMONETISED
REMONETISES
REMONETISING
REMONETIZATION
REMONETIZATIONS

REMONETIZE
REMONETIZED
REMONETIZES
REMONETIZING
REMONSTRANCE
REMONSTRANCES
REMONSTRANT
REMONSTRANTLY
REMONSTRANTS
REMONSTRATE
REMONSTRATED
REMONSTRATES
REMONSTRATING
REMONSTRATINGLY
REMONSTRATION
REMONSTRATIONS
REMONSTRATIVE
REMONSTRATIVELY
REMONSTRATOR
REMONSTRATORS
REMONSTRATORY
REMONTANT
REMONTANTS
REMONTOIR
REMONTOIRE
REMONTOIRES
REMONTOIRS
REMORA
REMORALISATION
REMORALISATIONS
REMORALISE
REMORALISED
REMORALISES
REMORALISING
REMORALIZATION
REMORALIZATIONS
REMORALIZE
REMORALIZED
REMORALIZES
REMORALIZING
REMORAS
REMORID
REMORSE
REMORSEFUL
REMORSEFULLY
REMORSEFULNESS
REMORSELESS
REMORSELESSLY
REMORSELESSNESS
REMORSES
REMORTGAGE
REMORTGAGED
REMORTGAGES
REMORTGAGING
REMOTE
REMOTELY

REMOTENESS
REMOTENESSES
REMOTER
REMOTES
REMOTEST
REMOTION
REMOTIONS
REMOTIVATE
REMOTIVATED
REMOTIVATES
REMOTIVATING
REMOTIVATION
REMOTIVATIONS
REMOUD
REMOULADE
REMOULADES
REMOULD
REMOULDED
REMOULDING
REMOULDS
REMOUNT
REMOUNTED
REMOUNTING
REMOUNTS
REMOVABILITIES
REMOVABILITY
REMOVABLE
REMOVABLENESS
REMOVABLENESSES
REMOVABLY
REMOVAL
REMOVALIST
REMOVALISTS
REMOVALS
REMOVE
REMOVEABLE
REMOVED
REMOVEDNESS
REMOVEDNESSES
REMOVER
REMOVERS
REMOVES
REMOVING
REMS
REMUAGE
REMUAGES
REMUDA
REMUDAS
REMUEUR
REMUEURS
REMUNERABILITY
REMUNERABLE
REMUNERABLY
REMUNERATE
REMUNERATED
REMUNERATES

REMUNERATING
REMUNERATION
REMUNERATIONS
REMUNERATIVE
REMUNERATIVELY
REMUNERATOR
REMUNERATORS
REMUNERATORY
REMURMUR
REMURMURED
REMURMURING
REMURMURS
REMYTHOLOGIZE
REMYTHOLOGIZED
REMYTHOLOGIZES
REMYTHOLOGIZING
REN
RENAGUE
RENAGUED
RENAGUES
RENAGUING
RENAIL
RENAILED
RENAILING
RENAILS
RENAISSANCE
RENAISSANCES
RENAL
RENAME
RENAMED
RENAMES
RENAMING
RENASCENCE
RENASCENCES
RENASCENT
RENATIONALIZE
RENATIONALIZED
RENATIONALIZES
RENATIONALIZING
RENATURATION
RENATURATIONS
RENATURE
RENATURED
RENATURES
RENATURING
RENAY
RENAYED
RENAYING
RENAYS
RENCONTRE
RENCONTRES
RENCOUNTER
RENCOUNTERED
RENCOUNTERING
RENCOUNTERS
REND

RENDED
RENDER
RENDERABLE
RENDERED
RENDERER
RENDERERS
RENDERING
RENDERINGS
RENDERS
RENDEZVOUS
RENDEZVOUSED
RENDEZVOUSES
RENDEZVOUSING
RENDIBLE
RENDING
RENDITION
RENDITIONS
RENDS
RENDZINA
RENDZINAS
RENEGADE
RENEGADED
RENEGADES
RENEGADING
RENEGADO
RENEGADOES
RENEGADOS
RENEGATE
RENEGATES
RENEGATION
RENEGATIONS
RENEGE
RENEGED
RENEGER
RENEGERS
RENEGES
RENEGING
RENEGOTIABLE
RENEGOTIATE
RENEGOTIATED
RENEGOTIATES
RENEGOTIATING
RENEGOTIATION
RENEGOTIATIONS
RENEGUE
RENEGUED
RENEGUER
RENEGUERS
RENEGUES
RENEGUING
RENEST
RENESTED
RENESTING
RENESTS
RENEW
RENEWABILITIES

RENEWABILITY
RENEWABLE
RENEWABLES
RENEWABLY
RENEWAL
RENEWALS
RENEWED
RENEWEDNESS
RENEWEDNESSES
RENEWER
RENEWERS
RENEWING
RENEWINGS
RENEWS
RENEY
RENEYED
RENEYING
RENEYS
RENFIERST
RENFORCE
RENFORCED
RENFORCES
RENFORCING
RENFORST
RENGA
RENGAS
RENIED
RENIES
RENIFORM
RENIG
RENIGGED
RENIGGING
RENIGS
RENIN
RENINS
RENITENCE
RENITENCIES
RENITENCY
RENITENT
RENITENTLY
RENK
RENKER
RENKEST
RENKLY
RENKNESS
RENMINBI
RENMINBIS
RENNASE
RENNASES
RENNE
RENNED
RENNES
RENNET
RENNETS
RENNIN
RENNING

RENNINGS
RENNINS
RENOGRAM
RENOGRAMS
RENOGRAPHIC
RENOGRAPHIES
RENOGRAPHY
RENOMINATE
RENOMINATED
RENOMINATES
RENOMINATING
RENOMINATION
RENOMINATIONS
RENORMALISATION
RENORMALISE
RENORMALISED
RENORMALISES
RENORMALISING
RENORMALIZATION
RENORMALIZE
RENORMALIZED
RENORMALIZES
RENORMALIZING
RENOTIFICATION
RENOTIFICATIONS
RENOTIFIED
RENOTIFIER
RENOTIFIERS
RENOTIFIES
RENOTIFY
RENOTIFYING
RENOUNCE
RENOUNCEABLE
RENOUNCED
RENOUNCEMENT
RENOUNCEMENTS
RENOUNCER
RENOUNCERS
RENOUNCES
RENOUNCING
RENOVASCULAR
RENOVATE
RENOVATED
RENOVATES
RENOVATING
RENOVATION
RENOVATIONS
RENOVATIVE
RENOVATOR
RENOVATORS
RENOWN
RENOWNED
RENOWNER
RENOWNERS
RENOWNING
RENOWNS

RENS
RENSSELAERITE
RENSSELAERITES
RENT
RENTABILITIES
RENTABILITY
RENTABLE
RENTAL
RENTALLER
RENTALLERS
RENTALS
RENTE
RENTED
RENTER
RENTERS
RENTES
RENTIER
RENTIERS
RENTING
RENTS
RENUMBER
RENUMBERED
RENUMBERING
RENUMBERS
RENUNCIATION
RENUNCIATIONS
RENUNCIATIVE
RENUNCIATORY
RENVERSE
RENVERSED
RENVERSEMENT
RENVERSEMENTS
RENVERSES
RENVERSING
RENVERST
RENVOI
RENVOIS
RENVOY
RENVOYS
RENY
RENYING
REO
REOBJECT
REOBJECTED
REOBJECTING
REOBJECTS
REOBSERVE
REOBSERVED
REOBSERVES
REOBSERVING
REOBTAIN
REOBTAINABLE
REOBTAINED
REOBTAINING
REOBTAINS
REOCCUPATION

REOCCUPATIONS
REOCCUPIED
REOCCUPIES
REOCCUPY
REOCCUPYING
REOCCUR
REOCCURRED
REOCCURRENCE
REOCCURRENCES
REOCCURRING
REOCCURS
REOFFEND
REOFFENDED
REOFFENDING
REOFFENDS
REOFFER
REOFFERED
REOFFERING
REOFFERS
REOIL
REOILED
REOILING
REOILS
REOPEN
REOPENED
REOPENER
REOPENERS
REOPENING
REOPENS
REOPERATE
REOPERATED
REOPERATES
REOPERATING
REOPERATION
REOPERATIONS
REOPPOSE
REOPPOSED
REOPPOSES
REOPPOSING
REORCHESTRATE
REORCHESTRATED
REORCHESTRATES
REORCHESTRATING
REORCHESTRATION
REORDAIN
REORDAINED
REORDAINING
REORDAINS
REORDER
REORDERED
REORDERING
REORDERS
REORDINATION
REORDINATIONS
REORGANISATION
REORGANISATIONS

REORGANISE
REORGANISED
REORGANISER
REORGANISERS
REORGANISES
REORGANISING
REORGANIZATION
REORGANIZATIONS
REORGANIZE
REORGANIZED
REORGANIZER
REORGANIZERS
REORGANIZES
REORGANIZING
REORIENT
REORIENTATE
REORIENTATED
REORIENTATES
REORIENTATING
REORIENTATION
REORIENTATIONS
REORIENTED
REORIENTING
REORIENTS
REOUTFIT
REOUTFITS
REOUTFITTED
REOUTFITTING
REOVIRUS
REOVIRUSES
REOXIDATION
REOXIDATIONS
REOXIDIZE
REOXIDIZED
REOXIDIZES
REOXIDIZING
REP
REPACIFIED
REPACIFIES
REPACIFY
REPACIFYING
REPACK
REPACKAGE
REPACKAGED
REPACKAGER
REPACKAGERS
REPACKAGES
REPACKAGING
REPACKED
REPACKING
REPACKS
REPAGINATE
REPAGINATED
REPAGINATES
REPAGINATING
REPAGINATION

REPAGINATIONS
REPAID
REPAINT
REPAINTED
REPAINTING
REPAINTINGS
REPAINTS
REPAIR
REPAIRABILITIES
REPAIRABILITY
REPAIRABLE
REPAIRED
REPAIRER
REPAIRERS
REPAIRING
REPAIRMAN
REPAIRMEN
REPAIRS
REPAND
REPANDLY
REPANEL
REPANELED
REPANELING
REPANELLED
REPANELLING
REPANELS
REPAPER
REPAPERED
REPAPERING
REPAPERS
REPARABILITIES
REPARABILITY
REPARABLE
REPARABLY
REPARATION
REPARATIONS
REPARATIVE
REPARATORY
REPARK
REPARKED
REPARKING
REPARKS
REPARTEE
REPARTEED
REPARTEEING
REPARTEES
REPARTITION
REPARTITIONED
REPARTITIONING
REPARTITIONS
REPASS
REPASSAGE
REPASSAGES
REPASSED
REPASSES
REPASSING

REPAST
REPASTED
REPASTING
REPASTS
REPASTURE
REPASTURES
REPATCH
REPATCHED
REPATCHES
REPATCHING
REPATRIATE
REPATRIATED
REPATRIATES
REPATRIATING
REPATRIATION
REPATRIATIONS
REPATRIATOR
REPATRIATORS
REPATTERN
REPATTERNED
REPATTERNING
REPATTERNS
REPAVE
REPAVED
REPAVES
REPAVING
REPAY
REPAYABLE
REPAYING
REPAYMENT
REPAYMENTS
REPAYS
REPEAL
REPEALABLE
REPEALED
REPEALER
REPEALERS
REPEALING
REPEALS
REPEAT
REPEATABILITIES
REPEATABILITY
REPEATABLE
REPEATED
REPEATEDLY
REPEATER
REPEATERS
REPEATING
REPEATINGS
REPEATS
REPECHAGE
REPECHAGES
REPEG
REPEGGED
REPEGGING
REPEGS

REPEL
REPELLANCE
REPELLANCES
REPELLANCIES
REPELLANCY
REPELLANT
REPELLANTLY
REPELLANTS
REPELLED
REPELLENCE
REPELLENCES
REPELLENCIES
REPELLENCY
REPELLENT
REPELLENTLY
REPELLENTS
REPELLER
REPELLERS
REPELLING
REPELLINGLY
REPELS
REPENT
REPENTANCE
REPENTANCES
REPENTANT
REPENTANTLY
REPENTANTS
REPENTED
REPENTER
REPENTERS
REPENTING
REPENTINGLY
REPENTS
REPEOPLE
REPEOPLED
REPEOPLES
REPEOPLING
REPERCUSS
REPERCUSSED
REPERCUSSES
REPERCUSSING
REPERCUSSION
REPERCUSSIONS
REPERCUSSIVE
REPERK
REPERKED
REPERKING
REPERKS
REPERTOIRE
REPERTOIRES
REPERTORIAL
REPERTORIALLY
REPERTORIES
REPERTORY
REPERUSAL
REPERUSALS

REPERUSE
REPERUSED
REPERUSES
REPERUSING
REPESSED
REPETEND
REPETENDS
REPETITEUR
REPETITEURS
REPETITEUSE
REPETITEUSES
REPETITION
REPETITIONAL
REPETITIONARY
REPETITIONS
REPETITIOUS
REPETITIOUSLY
REPETITIOUSNESS
REPETITIVE
REPETITIVELY
REPETITIVENESS
REPHOTOGRAPH
REPHOTOGRAPHED
REPHOTOGRAPHING
REPHOTOGRAPHS
REPHRASE
REPHRASED
REPHRASES
REPHRASING
REPIN
REPINE
REPINED
REPINEMENT
REPINEMENTS
REPINER
REPINERS
REPINES
REPINING
REPININGLY
REPININGS
REPINNED
REPINNING
REPINS
REPIQUE
REPIQUED
REPIQUES
REPIQUING
REPLA
REPLACE
REPLACEABILITY
REPLACEABLE
REPLACED
REPLACEMENT
REPLACEMENTS
REPLACER
REPLACERS

REPLACES
REPLACING
REPLAN
REPLANNED
REPLANNING
REPLANS
REPLANT
REPLANTATION
REPLANTATIONS
REPLANTED
REPLANTING
REPLANTS
REPLASTER
REPLASTERED
REPLASTERING
REPLASTERS
REPLATE
REPLATED
REPLATES
REPLATING
REPLAY
REPLAYED
REPLAYING
REPLAYS
REPLEAD
REPLEADED
REPLEADER
REPLEADERS
REPLEADING
REPLEADS
REPLED
REPLEDGE
REPLEDGED
REPLEDGES
REPLEDGING
REPLENISH
REPLENISHABLE
REPLENISHED
REPLENISHER
REPLENISHERS
REPLENISHES
REPLENISHING
REPLENISHMENT
REPLENISHMENTS
REPLETE
REPLETED
REPLETELY
REPLETENESS
REPLETENESSES
REPLETES
REPLETING
REPLETION
REPLETIONS
REPLEVIABLE
REPLEVIED
REPLEVIES

REPLEVIN
REPLEVINED
REPLEVINING
REPLEVINS
REPLEVISABLE
REPLEVY
REPLEVYING
REPLICA
REPLICABILITIES
REPLICABILITY
REPLICABLE
REPLICAS
REPLICASE
REPLICASES
REPLICATE
REPLICATED
REPLICATES
REPLICATING
REPLICATION
REPLICATIONS
REPLICATIVE
REPLICATOR
REPLICATORS
REPLICON
REPLICONS
REPLIED
REPLIER
REPLIERS
REPLIES
REPLOT
REPLOTS
REPLOTTED
REPLOTTING
REPLUM
REPLUMB
REPLUMBED
REPLUMBING
REPLUMBS
REPLUNGE
REPLUNGED
REPLUNGES
REPLUNGING
REPLY
REPLYING
REPO
REPOINT
REPOINTED
REPOINTING
REPOINTS
REPOLARIZATION
REPOLARIZATIONS
REPOLARIZE
REPOLARIZED
REPOLARIZES
REPOLARIZING
REPOLISH

REPOLISHED
REPOLISHES
REPOLISHING
REPOLL
REPOLLED
REPOLLING
REPOLLS
REPOMAN
REPOMEN
REPONE
REPONED
REPONES
REPONING
REPOPULARIZE
REPOPULARIZED
REPOPULARIZES
REPOPULARIZING
REPOPULATE
REPOPULATED
REPOPULATES
REPOPULATING
REPOPULATION
REPOPULATIONS
REPORT
REPORTABLE
REPORTAGE
REPORTAGES
REPORTED
REPORTEDLY
REPORTER
REPORTERS
REPORTING
REPORTINGLY
REPORTINGS
REPORTORIAL
REPORTORIALLY
REPORTS
REPOS
REPOSAL
REPOSALL
REPOSALLS
REPOSALS
REPOSE
REPOSED
REPOSEDLY
REPOSEDNESS
REPOSEDNESSES
REPOSEFUL
REPOSEFULLY
REPOSEFULNESS
REPOSEFULNESSES
REPOSER
REPOSERS
REPOSES
REPOSING
REPOSIT

REPOSITED
REPOSITING
REPOSITION
REPOSITIONED
REPOSITIONING
REPOSITIONS
REPOSITOR
REPOSITORIES
REPOSITORS
REPOSITORY
REPOSITS
REPOSSESS
REPOSSESSED
REPOSSESSES
REPOSSESSING
REPOSSESSION
REPOSSESSIONS
REPOSSESSOR
REPOSSESSORS
REPOST
REPOSTED
REPOSTING
REPOSTS
REPOSURE
REPOSURES
REPOT
REPOTS
REPOTTED
REPOTTING
REPOTTINGS
REPOUR
REPOURED
REPOURING
REPOURS
REPOUSSAGE
REPOUSSAGES
REPOUSSE
REPOUSSES
REPOUSSOIR
REPOUSSOIRS
REPOWER
REPOWERED
REPOWERING
REPOWERS
REPP
REPPED
REPPING
REPPINGS
REPPS
REPREEVE
REPREEVED
REPREEVES
REPREEVING
REPREHEND
REPREHENDABLE
REPREHENDED

REPREHENDER
REPREHENDERS
REPREHENDING
REPREHENDS
REPREHENSIBLE
REPREHENSIBLY
REPREHENSION
REPREHENSIONS
REPREHENSIVE
REPREHENSIVELY
REPREHENSORY
REPRESENT
REPRESENTABLE
REPRESENTAMEN
REPRESENTAMENS
REPRESENTANT
REPRESENTANTS
REPRESENTATION
REPRESENTATIONS
REPRESENTATIVE
REPRESENTATIVES
REPRESENTED
REPRESENTEE
REPRESENTEES
REPRESENTER
REPRESENTERS
REPRESENTING
REPRESENTMENT
REPRESENTMENTS
REPRESENTOR
REPRESENTORS
REPRESENTS
REPRESS
REPRESSED
REPRESSER
REPRESSERS
REPRESSES
REPRESSIBILITY
REPRESSIBLE
REPRESSIBLY
REPRESSING
REPRESSION
REPRESSIONIST
REPRESSIONS
REPRESSIVE
REPRESSIVELY
REPRESSIVENESS
REPRESSOR
REPRESSORS
REPRESSURIZE
REPRESSURIZED
REPRESSURIZES
REPRESSURIZING
REPRICE
REPRICED
REPRICES

REPRICING
REPRIEFE
REPRIEFES
REPRIEVABLE
REPRIEVAL
REPRIEVALS
REPRIEVE
REPRIEVED
REPRIEVER
REPRIEVERS
REPRIEVES
REPRIEVING
REPRIMAND
REPRIMANDED
REPRIMANDING
REPRIMANDS
REPRIME
REPRIMED
REPRIMES
REPRIMING
REPRINT
REPRINTED
REPRINTER
REPRINTERS
REPRINTING
REPRINTS
REPRISAL
REPRISALS
REPRISE
REPRISED
REPRISES
REPRISING
REPRISTINATE
REPRISTINATED
REPRISTINATES
REPRISTINATING
REPRISTINATION
REPRISTINATIONS
REPRIVATISATION
REPRIVATISE
REPRIVATISED
REPRIVATISES
REPRIVATISING
REPRIVATIZATION
REPRIVATIZE
REPRIVATIZED
REPRIVATIZES
REPRIVATIZING
REPRIVE
REPRIVED
REPRIVES
REPRIVING
REPRIZE
REPRIZED
REPRIZES
REPRIZING

REPRO
REPROACH
REPROACHABILITY
REPROACHABLE
REPROACHABLY
REPROACHED
REPROACHER
REPROACHERS
REPROACHES
REPROACHFUL
REPROACHFULLY
REPROACHFULNESS
REPROACHING
REPROACHINGLY
REPROACHLESS
REPROBACIES
REPROBACY
REPROBANCE
REPROBANCES
REPROBATE
REPROBATED
REPROBATENESS
REPROBATER
REPROBATERS
REPROBATES
REPROBATING
REPROBATION
REPROBATIONARY
REPROBATIONS
REPROBATIVE
REPROBATIVELY
REPROBATOR
REPROBATORS
REPROBATORY
REPROBE
REPROBED
REPROBES
REPROBING
REPROCESS
REPROCESSED
REPROCESSES
REPROCESSING
REPRODUCE
REPRODUCED
REPRODUCER
REPRODUCERS
REPRODUCES
REPRODUCIBILITY
REPRODUCIBLE
REPRODUCIBLES
REPRODUCIBLY
REPRODUCING
REPRODUCTION
REPRODUCTIONS
REPRODUCTIVE
REPRODUCTIVELY

REPRODUCTIVES
REPRODUCTIVITY
REPROGRAM
REPROGRAMABLE
REPROGRAMED
REPROGRAMER
REPROGRAMERS
REPROGRAMING
REPROGRAMMABLE
REPROGRAMME
REPROGRAMMED
REPROGRAMMES
REPROGRAMMING
REPROGRAMS
REPROGRAPHER
REPROGRAPHERS
REPROGRAPHIC
REPROGRAPHICS
REPROGRAPHIES
REPROGRAPHY
REPROOF
REPROOFED
REPROOFING
REPROOFS
REPROS
REPROVABILITY
REPROVABLE
REPROVAL
REPROVALS
REPROVE
REPROVED
REPROVER
REPROVERS
REPROVES
REPROVING
REPROVINGLY
REPROVINGS
REPROVISION
REPROVISIONED
REPROVISIONING
REPROVISIONS
REPRYVE
REPRYVED
REPRYVES
REPRYVING
REPS
REPTANT
REPTATION
REPTATIONS
REPTILE
REPTILES
REPTILIAN
REPTILIANLY
REPTILIANS
REPTILIFEROUS
REPTILIOUS

REPTILOID
REPUBLIC
REPUBLICAN
REPUBLICANISE
REPUBLICANISED
REPUBLICANISES
REPUBLICANISING
REPUBLICANISM
REPUBLICANISMS
REPUBLICANIZE
REPUBLICANIZED
REPUBLICANIZES
REPUBLICANIZING
REPUBLICANS
REPUBLICATION
REPUBLICATIONS
REPUBLICS
REPUBLISH
REPUBLISHED
REPUBLISHER
REPUBLISHERS
REPUBLISHES
REPUBLISHING
REPUDIABLE
REPUDIATE
REPUDIATED
REPUDIATES
REPUDIATING
REPUDIATION
REPUDIATIONIST
REPUDIATIONISTS
REPUDIATIONS
REPUDIATIVE
REPUDIATOR
REPUDIATORS
REPUGN
REPUGNANCE
REPUGNANCES
REPUGNANCIES
REPUGNANCY
REPUGNANT
REPUGNANTLY
REPUGNED
REPUGNING
REPUGNS
REPULP
REPULPED
REPULPING
REPULPS
REPULSE
REPULSED
REPULSER
REPULSERS
REPULSES
REPULSING
REPULSION

REPULSIONS
REPULSIVE
REPULSIVELY
REPULSIVENESS
REPULSIVENESSES
REPUMP
REPUMPED
REPUMPING
REPUMPS
REPUNCTUATION
REPUNCTUATIONS
REPUNIT
REPUNITS
REPURCHASE
REPURCHASED
REPURCHASES
REPURCHASING
REPURE
REPURED
REPURES
REPURIFIED
REPURIFIES
REPURIFY
REPURIFYING
REPURING
REPURSUE
REPURSUED
REPURSUES
REPURSUING
REPUTABILITIES
REPUTABILITY
REPUTABLE
REPUTABLY
REPUTATION
REPUTATIONAL
REPUTATIONLESS
REPUTATIONS
REPUTATIVE
REPUTATIVELY
REPUTE
REPUTED
REPUTEDLY
REPUTELESS
REPUTES
REPUTING
REPUTINGS
REQUERE
REQUERED
REQUERES
REQUERING
REQUEST
REQUESTED
REQUESTER
REQUESTERS
REQUESTING
REQUESTOR

REQUESTORS
REQUESTS
REQUICKEN
REQUICKENED
REQUICKENING
REQUICKENS
REQUIEM
REQUIEMS
REQUIESCAT
REQUIESCATS
REQUIGHT
REQUIGHTED
REQUIGHTING
REQUIGHTS
REQUIN
REQUINS
REQUIRABLE
REQUIRE
REQUIRED
REQUIREMENT
REQUIREMENTS
REQUIRER
REQUIRERS
REQUIRES
REQUIRING
REQUIRINGS
REQUISITE
REQUISITELY
REQUISITENESS
REQUISITENESSES
REQUISITES
REQUISITION
REQUISITIONARY
REQUISITIONED
REQUISITIONING
REQUISITIONIST
REQUISITIONISTS
REQUISITIONS
REQUISITOR
REQUISITORS
REQUISITORY
REQUIT
REQUITABLE
REQUITAL
REQUITALS
REQUITE
REQUITED
REQUITEFUL
REQUITELESS
REQUITEMENT
REQUITEMENTS
REQUITER
REQUITERS
REQUITES
REQUITING
REQUITS

REQUITTED
REQUITTING
REQUOTE
REQUOTED
REQUOTES
REQUOTING
REQUOYLE
REQUOYLED
REQUOYLES
REQUOYLING
RERACK
RERACKED
RERACKING
RERACKS
RERADIATE
RERADIATED
RERADIATES
RERADIATING
RERADIATION
RERADIATIONS
RERAIL
RERAILED
RERAILING
RERAILS
RERAISE
RERAISED
RERAISES
RERAISING
RERAN
REREAD
REREADING
REREADINGS
REREADS
REREBRACE
REREBRACES
RERECORD
RERECORDED
RERECORDER
RERECORDERS
RERECORDING
RERECORDINGS
RERECORDS
REREDORSES
REREDORTER
REREDORTERS
REREDOS
REREDOSES
REREDOSSE
REREDOSSES
REREGISTER
REREGISTERED
REREGISTERING
REREGISTERS
REREGISTRATION
REREGISTRATIONS
REREGULATE

REREGULATED
REREGULATES
REREGULATING
REREGULATION
REREGULATIONS
RERELEASE
RERELEASED
RERELEASES
RERELEASING
REREMICE
REREMIND
REREMINDED
REREMINDING
REREMINDS
REREMOUSE
REREPEAT
REREPEATED
REREPEATING
REREPEATS
REREVIEW
REREVIEWED
REREVIEWING
REREVIEWS
REREVISE
REREVISED
REREVISES
REREVISING
REREWARD
REREWARDS
RERIG
RERIGGED
RERIGGING
RERIGS
RERISE
RERISEN
RERISES
RERISING
REROLL
REROLLED
REROLLER
REROLLERS
REROLLING
REROLLS
REROOF
REROOFED
REROOFING
REROOFS
REROSE
REROUTE
REROUTED
REROUTEING
REROUTES
REROUTING
RERUN
RERUNNING
RERUNS

RES
RESADDLE
RESADDLED
RESADDLES
RESADDLING
RESAID
RESAIL
RESAILED
RESAILING
RESAILS
RESALABLE
RESALE
RESALEABILITY
RESALEABLE
RESALES
RESALGAR
RESALGARS
RESALUTE
RESALUTED
RESALUTES
RESALUTING
RESAMPLE
RESAMPLED
RESAMPLES
RESAMPLING
RESAT
RESAW
RESAWED
RESAWING
RESAWN
RESAWS
RESAY
RESAYING
RESAYS
RESCALE
RESCALED
RESCALES
RESCALING
RESCHEDULE
RESCHEDULED
RESCHEDULES
RESCHEDULING
RESCHEDULINGS
RESCHOOL
RESCHOOLED
RESCHOOLING
RESCHOOLS
RESCIND
RESCINDABILITY
RESCINDABLE
RESCINDED
RESCINDER
RESCINDERS
RESCINDING
RESCINDMENT
RESCINDMENTS

RESCINDS
RESCISSIBILITY
RESCISSIBLE
RESCISSION
RESCISSIONS
RESCISSORY
RESCORE
RESCORED
RESCORES
RESCORING
RESCREEN
RESCREENED
RESCREENING
RESCREENS
RESCRIPT
RESCRIPTED
RESCRIPTING
RESCRIPTS
RESCUABLE
RESCUE
RESCUED
RESCUER
RESCUERS
RESCUES
RESCUING
RESCULPT
RESCULPTED
RESCULPTING
RESCULPTS
RESEAL
RESEALABLE
RESEALED
RESEALING
RESEALS
RESEARCH
RESEARCHABLE
RESEARCHED
RESEARCHER
RESEARCHERS
RESEARCHES
RESEARCHFUL
RESEARCHING
RESEARCHIST
RESEARCHISTS
RESEASON
RESEASONED
RESEASONING
RESEASONS
RESEAT
RESEATED
RESEATING
RESEATS
RESEAU
RESEAUS
RESEAUX
RESECT

RESECTABILITIES
RESECTABILITY
RESECTABLE
RESECTED
RESECTING
RESECTION
RESECTIONAL
RESECTIONS
RESECTS
RESECURE
RESECURED
RESECURES
RESECURING
RESEDA
RESEDAS
RESEE
RESEED
RESEEDED
RESEEDING
RESEEDS
RESEEING
RESEEK
RESEEKING
RESEEKS
RESEEN
RESEES
RESEGREGATE
RESEGREGATED
RESEGREGATES
RESEGREGATING
RESEGREGATION
RESEGREGATIONS
RESEIZE
RESEIZED
RESEIZES
RESEIZING
RESELECT
RESELECTED
RESELECTING
RESELECTION
RESELECTIONS
RESELECTS
RESELL
RESELLER
RESELLERS
RESELLING
RESELLS
RESEMBLANCE
RESEMBLANCES
RESEMBLANT
RESEMBLE
RESEMBLED
RESEMBLER
RESEMBLERS
RESEMBLES
RESEMBLING

RESEND
RESENDING
RESENDS
RESENSITIZE
RESENSITIZED
RESENSITIZES
RESENSITIZING
RESENT
RESENTED
RESENTENCE
RESENTENCED
RESENTENCES
RESENTENCING
RESENTER
RESENTERS
RESENTFUL
RESENTFULLY
RESENTFULNESS
RESENTFULNESSES
RESENTING
RESENTINGLY
RESENTIVE
RESENTMENT
RESENTMENTS
RESENTS
RESERPINE
RESERPINES
RESERVABLE
RESERVATION
RESERVATIONIST
RESERVATIONISTS
RESERVATIONS
RESERVATORIES
RESERVATORY
RESERVE
RESERVED
RESERVEDLY
RESERVEDNESS
RESERVEDNESSES
RESERVER
RESERVERS
RESERVES
RESERVICE
RESERVICED
RESERVICES
RESERVICING
RESERVING
RESERVIST
RESERVISTS
RESERVOIR
RESERVOIRED
RESERVOIRING
RESERVOIRS
RESES
RESET
RESETS

RESETTABLE
RESETTED
RESETTER
RESETTERS
RESETTING
RESETTLE
RESETTLED
RESETTLEMENT
RESETTLEMENTS
RESETTLES
RESETTLING
RESEW
RESEWED
RESEWING
RESEWN
RESEWS
RESH
RESHAPE
RESHAPED
RESHAPER
RESHAPERS
RESHAPES
RESHAPING
RESHARPEN
RESHARPENED
RESHARPENER
RESHARPENERS
RESHARPENING
RESHARPENS
RESHAVE
RESHAVED
RESHAVEN
RESHAVES
RESHAVING
RESHES
RESHINE
RESHINED
RESHINES
RESHINGLE
RESHINGLED
RESHINGLES
RESHINGLING
RESHINING
RESHIP
RESHIPMENT
RESHIPMENTS
RESHIPPED
RESHIPPING
RESHIPS
RESHOD
RESHOE
RESHOEING
RESHOES
RESHONE
RESHOOT
RESHOOTING

RESHOOTS
RESHOT
RESHOW
RESHOWED
RESHOWING
RESHOWN
RESHOWS
RESHUFFLE
RESHUFFLED
RESHUFFLES
RESHUFFLING
RESIANCE
RESIANCES
RESIANT
RESIANTS
RESID
RESIDE
RESIDED
RESIDENCE
RESIDENCES
RESIDENCIES
RESIDENCY
RESIDENT
RESIDENTER
RESIDENTERS
RESIDENTIAL
RESIDENTIALLY
RESIDENTIARIES
RESIDENTIARY
RESIDENTS
RESIDENTSHIP
RESIDENTSHIPS
RESIDER
RESIDERS
RESIDES
RESIDING
RESIDS
RESIDUA
RESIDUAL
RESIDUALLY
RESIDUALS
RESIDUARY
RESIDUE
RESIDUES
RESIDUOUS
RESIDUUM
RESIDUUMS
RESIFT
RESIFTED
RESIFTING
RESIFTS
RESIGHT
RESIGHTED
RESIGHTING
RESIGHTS
RESIGN

RESIGNATION
RESIGNATIONS
RESIGNED
RESIGNEDLY
RESIGNEDNESS
RESIGNEDNESSES
RESIGNER
RESIGNERS
RESIGNING
RESIGNMENT
RESIGNMENTS
RESIGNS
RESILE
RESILED
RESILEMENT
RESILES
RESILIENCE
RESILIENCES
RESILIENCIES
RESILIENCY
RESILIENT
RESILIENTLY
RESILING
RESILVER
RESILVERED
RESILVERING
RESILVERS
RESIMBURSEMENT
RESIN
RESINATA
RESINATAS
RESINATE
RESINATED
RESINATES
RESINATING
RESINED
RESINER
RESINERS
RESINIFEROUS
RESINIFICATION
RESINIFICATIONS
RESINIFIED
RESINIFIES
RESINIFY
RESINIFYING
RESINING
RESINISE
RESINISED
RESINISES
RESINISING
RESINIZE
RESINIZED
RESINIZES
RESINIZING
RESINOID
RESINOIDS

RESINOSES
RESINOSIS
RESINOUS
RESINOUSLY
RESINOUSNESS
RESINS
RESINY
RESIPISCENCE
RESIPISCENCES
RESIPISCENCIES
RESIPISCENCY
RESIPISCENT
RESIST
RESISTANCE
RESISTANCES
RESISTANT
RESISTANTS
RESISTED
RESISTENT
RESISTENTS
RESISTER
RESISTERS
RESISTIBILITIES
RESISTIBILITY
RESISTIBLE
RESISTIBLY
RESISTING
RESISTINGLY
RESISTIVE
RESISTIVELY
RESISTIVENESS
RESISTIVENESSES
RESISTIVITIES
RESISTIVITY
RESISTLESS
RESISTLESSLY
RESISTLESSNESS
RESISTOR
RESISTORS
RESISTS
RESIT
RESITE
RESITED
RESITES
RESITING
RESITS
RESITTING
RESITTINGS
RESIZE
RESIZED
RESIZES
RESIZING
RESKETCH
RESKETCHED
RESKETCHES
RESKETCHING

RESKEW
RESKEWED
RESKEWING
RESKEWS
RESKILL
RESKILLED
RESKILLING
RESKILLINGS
RESKILLS
RESKUE
RESKUED
RESKUES
RESKUING
RESLATE
RESLATED
RESLATES
RESLATING
RESMELT
RESMELTED
RESMELTING
RESMELTS
RESMOOTH
RESMOOTHED
RESMOOTHING
RESMOOTHS
RESNATRON
RESNATRONS
RESOAK
RESOAKED
RESOAKING
RESOAKS
RESOCIALIZATION
RESOCIALIZE
RESOCIALIZED
RESOCIALIZES
RESOCIALIZING
RESOD
RESODDED
RESODDING
RESODS
RESOJET
RESOJETS
RESOLD
RESOLDER
RESOLDERED
RESOLDERING
RESOLDERS
RESOLE
RESOLED
RESOLES
RESOLIDIFIED
RESOLIDIFIES
RESOLIDIFY
RESOLIDIFYING
RESOLING
RESOLUBILITY

RESOLUBLE
RESOLUBLENESS
RESOLUTE
RESOLUTELY
RESOLUTENESS
RESOLUTENESSES
RESOLUTER
RESOLUTES
RESOLUTEST
RESOLUTION
RESOLUTIONER
RESOLUTIONERS
RESOLUTIONIST
RESOLUTIONISTS
RESOLUTIONS
RESOLUTIVE
RESOLVABILITIES
RESOLVABILITY
RESOLVABLE
RESOLVABLENESS
RESOLVE
RESOLVED
RESOLVEDLY
RESOLVEDNESS
RESOLVEDNESSES
RESOLVENT
RESOLVENTS
RESOLVER
RESOLVERS
RESOLVES
RESOLVING
RESONANCE
RESONANCES
RESONANT
RESONANTLY
RESONANTS
RESONATE
RESONATED
RESONATES
RESONATING
RESONATION
RESONATIONS
RESONATOR
RESONATORS
RESORB
RESORBED
RESORBENCE
RESORBENCES
RESORBENT
RESORBING
RESORBS
RESORCIN
RESORCINAL
RESORCINOL
RESORCINOLS
RESORCINS

RESORPTION
RESORPTIONS
RESORPTIVE
RESORT
RESORTED
RESORTER
RESORTERS
RESORTING
RESORTS
RESOUGHT
RESOUND
RESOUNDED
RESOUNDING
RESOUNDINGLY
RESOUNDS
RESOURCE
RESOURCED
RESOURCEFUL
RESOURCEFULLY
RESOURCEFULNESS
RESOURCELESS
RESOURCES
RESOURCING
RESOW
RESOWED
RESOWING
RESOWN
RESOWS
RESPACE
RESPACED
RESPACES
RESPACING
RESPADE
RESPADED
RESPADES
RESPADING
RESPEAK
RESPEAKING
RESPEAKS
RESPECT
RESPECTABILISE
RESPECTABILISED
RESPECTABILISES
RESPECTABILITY
RESPECTABILIZE
RESPECTABILIZED
RESPECTABILIZES
RESPECTABLE
RESPECTABLENESS
RESPECTABLES
RESPECTABLY
RESPECTANT
RESPECTED
RESPECTER
RESPECTERS
RESPECTFUL

RESPECTFULLY
RESPECTFULNESS
RESPECTING
RESPECTIVE
RESPECTIVELY
RESPECTIVENESS
RESPECTLESS
RESPECTS
RESPELL
RESPELLED
RESPELLING
RESPELLINGS
RESPELLS
RESPELT
RESPIRABILITY
RESPIRABLE
RESPIRATION
RESPIRATIONAL
RESPIRATIONALLY
RESPIRATIONS
RESPIRATOR
RESPIRATORS
RESPIRATORY
RESPIRE
RESPIRED
RESPIRES
RESPIRING
RESPIRITUALIZE
RESPIRITUALIZED
RESPIRITUALIZES
RESPIROMETER
RESPIROMETERS
RESPIROMETRIC
RESPIROMETRIES
RESPIROMETRY
RESPITE
RESPITED
RESPITELESS
RESPITES
RESPITING
RESPLEND
RESPLENDED
RESPLENDENCE
RESPLENDENCES
RESPLENDENCIES
RESPLENDENCY
RESPLENDENT
RESPLENDENTLY
RESPLENDING
RESPLENDS
RESPLICE
RESPLICED
RESPLICES
RESPLICING
RESPLIT
RESPLITS

RESPLITTING
RESPOKE
RESPOKEN
RESPOND
RESPONDED
RESPONDENCE
RESPONDENCES
RESPONDENCIES
RESPONDENCY
RESPONDENT
RESPONDENTIA
RESPONDENTIAS
RESPONDENTS
RESPONDER
RESPONDERS
RESPONDING
RESPONDS
RESPONSA
RESPONSE
RESPONSELESS
RESPONSER
RESPONSERS
RESPONSES
RESPONSIBILITY
RESPONSIBLE
RESPONSIBLENESS
RESPONSIBLY
RESPONSIONS
RESPONSIVE
RESPONSIVELY
RESPONSIVENESS
RESPONSOR
RESPONSORIAL
RESPONSORIALS
RESPONSORIES
RESPONSORS
RESPONSORY
RESPONSUM
RESPONSUMS
RESPOT
RESPOTS
RESPOTTED
RESPOTTING
RESPRANG
RESPRAY
RESPRAYED
RESPRAYING
RESPRAYS
RESPREAD
RESPREADING
RESPREADS
RESPRING
RESPRINGING
RESPRINGS
RESPROUT
RESPROUTED

RESPROUTING
RESPROUTS
RESPRUNG
RESSALDAR
RESSALDARS
RESSENTIMENT
RESSENTIMENTS
REST
RESTABILIZE
RESTABILIZED
RESTABILIZES
RESTABILIZING
RESTACK
RESTACKED
RESTACKING
RESTACKS
RESTAFF
RESTAFFED
RESTAFFING
RESTAFFS
RESTAGE
RESTAGED
RESTAGES
RESTAGING
RESTAMP
RESTAMPED
RESTAMPING
RESTAMPS
RESTART
RESTARTABLE
RESTARTED
RESTARTER
RESTARTERS
RESTARTING
RESTARTS
RESTATE
RESTATED
RESTATEMENT
RESTATEMENTS
RESTATES
RESTATING
RESTAURANT
RESTAURANTEUR
RESTAURANTEURS
RESTAURANTS
RESTAURATEUR
RESTAURATEURS
RESTAURATION
RESTAURATIONS
RESTED
RESTEM
RESTEMMED
RESTEMMING
RESTEMS
RESTER
RESTERS

RESTFUL
RESTFULLER
RESTFULLEST
RESTFULLY
RESTFULNESS
RESTFULNESSES
RESTHARROW
RESTHARROWS
RESTIER
RESTIEST
RESTIFF
RESTIFORM
RESTIMULATE
RESTIMULATED
RESTIMULATES
RESTIMULATING
RESTIMULATION
RESTIMULATIONS
RESTING
RESTINGS
RESTITCH
RESTITCHED
RESTITCHES
RESTITCHING
RESTITUTE
RESTITUTED
RESTITUTES
RESTITUTING
RESTITUTION
RESTITUTIONISM
RESTITUTIONISMS
RESTITUTIONIST
RESTITUTIONISTS
RESTITUTIONS
RESTITUTIVE
RESTITUTOR
RESTITUTORS
RESTITUTORY
RESTIVE
RESTIVELY
RESTIVENESS
RESTIVENESSES
RESTLESS
RESTLESSLY
RESTLESSNESS
RESTLESSNESSES
RESTO
RESTOCK
RESTOCKED
RESTOCKING
RESTOCKS
RESTOKE
RESTOKED
RESTOKES
RESTOKING
RESTORABLE

RESTORABLENESS
RESTORAL
RESTORALS
RESTORATION
RESTORATIONISM
RESTORATIONISMS
RESTORATIONIST
RESTORATIONISTS
RESTORATIONS
RESTORATIVE
RESTORATIVELY
RESTORATIVES
RESTORE
RESTORED
RESTORER
RESTORERS
RESTORES
RESTORING
RESTOS
RESTRAIGHTEN
RESTRAIGHTENED
RESTRAIGHTENING
RESTRAIGHTENS
RESTRAIN
RESTRAINABLE
RESTRAINED
RESTRAINEDLY
RESTRAINEDNESS
RESTRAINER
RESTRAINERS
RESTRAINING
RESTRAININGS
RESTRAINS
RESTRAINT
RESTRAINTS
RESTRENGTHEN
RESTRENGTHENED
RESTRENGTHENING
RESTRENGTHENS
RESTRESS
RESTRESSED
RESTRESSES
RESTRESSING
RESTRICKEN
RESTRICT
RESTRICTED
RESTRICTEDLY
RESTRICTEDNESS
RESTRICTING
RESTRICTION
RESTRICTIONISM
RESTRICTIONISMS
RESTRICTIONIST
RESTRICTIONISTS
RESTRICTIONS
RESTRICTIVE

RESTRICTIVELY
RESTRICTIVENESS
RESTRICTIVES
RESTRICTS
RESTRIKE
RESTRIKES
RESTRIKING
RESTRING
RESTRINGE
RESTRINGED
RESTRINGEING
RESTRINGENT
RESTRINGENTS
RESTRINGES
RESTRINGING
RESTRINGS
RESTRIVE
RESTRIVEN
RESTRIVES
RESTRIVING
RESTROOM
RESTROOMS
RESTROVE
RESTRUCK
RESTRUCTURE
RESTRUCTURED
RESTRUCTURES
RESTRUCTURING
RESTRUCTURINGS
RESTRUNG
RESTS
RESTUDIED
RESTUDIES
RESTUDY
RESTUDYING
RESTUFF
RESTUFFED
RESTUFFING
RESTUFFS
RESTY
RESTYLE
RESTYLED
RESTYLES
RESTYLING
RESUBMISSION
RESUBMISSIONS
RESUBMIT
RESUBMITS
RESUBMITTED
RESUBMITTING
RESUBSCRIBE
RESUBSCRIBED
RESUBSCRIBER
RESUBSCRIBERS
RESUBSCRIBES
RESUBSCRIBING

RESUBSCRIPTION
RESUBSCRIPTIONS
RESULT
RESULTANT
RESULTANTLY
RESULTANTS
RESULTATIVE
RESULTED
RESULTFUL
RESULTING
RESULTLESS
RESULTLESSNESS
RESULTS
RESUMABLE
RESUME
RESUMED
RESUMER
RESUMERS
RESUMES
RESUMING
RESUMMON
RESUMMONED
RESUMMONING
RESUMMONS
RESUMPTION
RESUMPTIONS
RESUMPTIVE
RESUMPTIVELY
RESUPINATE
RESUPINATION
RESUPINATIONS
RESUPINE
RESUPPLIED
RESUPPLIES
RESUPPLY
RESUPPLYING
RESURFACE
RESURFACED
RESURFACER
RESURFACERS
RESURFACES
RESURFACING
RESURGE
RESURGED
RESURGENCE
RESURGENCES
RESURGENT
RESURGES
RESURGING
RESURRECT
RESURRECTED
RESURRECTING
RESURRECTION
RESURRECTIONAL
RESURRECTIONARY
RESURRECTIONISE

RESURRECTIONISM
RESURRECTIONIST
RESURRECTIONIZE
RESURRECTIONS
RESURRECTIVE
RESURRECTOR
RESURRECTORS
RESURRECTS
RESURVEY
RESURVEYED
RESURVEYING
RESURVEYS
RESUSCITABLE
RESUSCITANT
RESUSCITANTS
RESUSCITATE
RESUSCITATED
RESUSCITATES
RESUSCITATING
RESUSCITATION
RESUSCITATIONS
RESUSCITATIVE
RESUSCITATOR
RESUSCITATORS
RESYNCHRONISE
RESYNCHRONISED
RESYNCHRONISES
RESYNCHRONISING
RESYNCHRONIZE
RESYNCHRONIZED
RESYNCHRONIZES
RESYNCHRONIZING
RESYNTHESES
RESYNTHESIS
RESYNTHESIZE
RESYNTHESIZED
RESYNTHESIZES
RESYNTHESIZING
RESYSTEMATIZE
RESYSTEMATIZED
RESYSTEMATIZES
RESYSTEMATIZING
RET
RETABLE
RETABLES
RETACK
RETACKED
RETACKING
RETACKLE
RETACKLED
RETACKLES
RETACKLING
RETACKS
RETAG
RETAGGED
RETAGGING

RETAGS
RETAIL
RETAILED
RETAILER
RETAILERS
RETAILING
RETAILINGS
RETAILMENT
RETAILMENTS
RETAILOR
RETAILORED
RETAILORING
RETAILORS
RETAILS
RETAIN
RETAINABLE
RETAINED
RETAINER
RETAINERS
RETAINERSHIP
RETAINERSHIPS
RETAINING
RETAINMENT
RETAINMENTS
RETAINS
RETAKE
RETAKEN
RETAKER
RETAKERS
RETAKES
RETAKING
RETAKINGS
RETALIATE
RETALIATED
RETALIATES
RETALIATING
RETALIATION
RETALIATIONIST
RETALIATIONISTS
RETALIATIONS
RETALIATIVE
RETALIATOR
RETALIATORS
RETALIATORY
RETAMA
RETAMAS
RETAPE
RETAPED
RETAPES
RETAPING
RETARD
RETARDANT
RETARDANTS
RETARDATE
RETARDATES
RETARDATION

RETARDATIONS
RETARDATIVE
RETARDATORY
RETARDED
RETARDER
RETARDERS
RETARDING
RETARDMENT
RETARDMENTS
RETARDS
RETARGET
RETARGETED
RETARGETING
RETARGETS
RETASTE
RETASTED
RETASTES
RETASTING
RETAUGHT
RETAX
RETAXED
RETAXES
RETAXING
RETCH
RETCHED
RETCHES
RETCHING
RETCHLESS
RETE
RETEACH
RETEACHES
RETEACHING
RETEAM
RETEAMED
RETEAMING
RETEAMS
RETEAR
RETEARING
RETEARS
RETELL
RETELLER
RETELLERS
RETELLING
RETELLINGS
RETELLS
RETEM
RETEMPER
RETEMPERED
RETEMPERING
RETEMPERS
RETEMS
RETENE
RETENES
RETENTION
RETENTIONIST
RETENTIONISTS

RETENTIONS
RETENTIVE
RETENTIVELY
RETENTIVENESS
RETENTIVENESSES
RETENTIVITIES
RETENTIVITY
RETES
RETEST
RETESTED
RETESTIFIED
RETESTIFIES
RETESTIFY
RETESTIFYING
RETESTING
RETESTS
RETEXTURE
RETEXTURED
RETEXTURES
RETEXTURING
RETHINK
RETHINKER
RETHINKERS
RETHINKING
RETHINKS
RETHOUGHT
RETHREAD
RETHREADED
RETHREADING
RETHREADS
RETIA
RETIAL
RETIARII
RETIARIUS
RETIARIUSES
RETIARY
RETICELLA
RETICELLAS
RETICENCE
RETICENCES
RETICENCIES
RETICENCY
RETICENT
RETICENTLY
RETICLE
RETICLES
RETICULA
RETICULAR
RETICULARLY
RETICULARY
RETICULATE
RETICULATED
RETICULATELY
RETICULATES
RETICULATING
RETICULATION

RETICULATIONS
RETICULE
RETICULES
RETICULOCYTE
RETICULOCYTES
RETICULUM
RETICULUMS
RETIE
RETIED
RETIES
RETIFORM
RETIGHTEN
RETIGHTENED
RETIGHTENING
RETIGHTENS
RETILE
RETILED
RETILES
RETILING
RETIME
RETIMED
RETIMES
RETIMING
RETINA
RETINACULA
RETINACULAR
RETINACULUM
RETINAE
RETINAL
RETINALITE
RETINALITES
RETINALS
RETINAS
RETINE
RETINENE
RETINENES
RETINES
RETINISPORA
RETINISPORAS
RETINITE
RETINITES
RETINITIDES
RETINITIS
RETINITISES
RETINOBLASTOMA
RETINOBLASTOMAS
RETINOID
RETINOIDS
RETINOL
RETINOLS
RETINOPATHIES
RETINOPATHY
RETINOSCOPE
RETINOSCOPES
RETINOSCOPIC
RETINOSCOPIES

RETINOSCOPIST
RETINOSCOPISTS
RETINOSCOPY
RETINOSPORA
RETINOSPORAS
RETINOTECTAL
RETINT
RETINTED
RETINTING
RETINTS
RETINUE
RETINUED
RETINUES
RETINULA
RETINULAE
RETINULAR
RETINULAS
RETIRACIES
RETIRACY
RETIRAL
RETIRALS
RETIRANT
RETIRANTS
RETIRE
RETIRED
RETIREDLY
RETIREDNESS
RETIREDNESSES
RETIREE
RETIREES
RETIREMENT
RETIREMENTS
RETIRER
RETIRERS
RETIRES
RETIRING
RETIRINGLY
RETIRINGNESS
RETIRINGNESSES
RETITLE
RETITLED
RETITLES
RETITLING
RETOLD
RETOOK
RETOOL
RETOOLED
RETOOLING
RETOOLS
RETORE
RETORN
RETORSION
RETORSIONS
RETORT
RETORTED
RETORTER

RETORTERS
RETORTING
RETORTION
RETORTIONS
RETORTIVE
RETORTS
RETOUCH
RETOUCHABILITY
RETOUCHABLE
RETOUCHED
RETOUCHER
RETOUCHERS
RETOUCHES
RETOUCHING
RETOUR
RETOURED
RETOURING
RETOURS
RETRACE
RETRACEABILITY
RETRACEABLE
RETRACEABLY
RETRACED
RETRACEMENT
RETRACER
RETRACERS
RETRACES
RETRACING
RETRACINGS
RETRACK
RETRACKED
RETRACKING
RETRACKS
RETRACT
RETRACTABILITY
RETRACTABLE
RETRACTABLY
RETRACTATION
RETRACTATIONS
RETRACTED
RETRACTIBILITY
RETRACTIBLE
RETRACTILE
RETRACTILITIES
RETRACTILITY
RETRACTING
RETRACTION
RETRACTIONS
RETRACTIVE
RETRACTIVELY
RETRACTOR
RETRACTORS
RETRACTS
RETRAICT
RETRAICTS
RETRAIN

RETRAINABLE
RETRAINED
RETRAINING
RETRAINS
RETRAIT
RETRAITE
RETRAITES
RETRAITS
RETRAITT
RETRAITTS
RETRAL
RETRALLY
RETRANSFER
RETRANSFERRED
RETRANSFERRING
RETRANSFERS
RETRANSFORM
RETRANSFORMED
RETRANSFORMING
RETRANSFORMS
RETRANSLATE
RETRANSLATED
RETRANSLATES
RETRANSLATING
RETRANSLATION
RETRANSLATIONS
RETRANSMISSION
RETRANSMISSIONS
RETRANSMIT
RETRANSMITS
RETRANSMITTED
RETRANSMITTING
RETRATE
RETRATED
RETRATES
RETRATING
RETREAD
RETREADED
RETREADING
RETREADS
RETREAT
RETREATANT
RETREATANTS
RETREATED
RETREATER
RETREATERS
RETREATING
RETREATS
RETREE
RETREES
RETRENCH
RETRENCHABILITY
RETRENCHABLE
RETRENCHABLY
RETRENCHED
RETRENCHES

RETRENCHING
RETRENCHMENT
RETRENCHMENTS
RETRIAL
RETRIALS
RETRIBUTE
RETRIBUTED
RETRIBUTES
RETRIBUTING
RETRIBUTION
RETRIBUTIONS
RETRIBUTIVE
RETRIBUTIVELY
RETRIBUTOR
RETRIBUTORS
RETRIBUTORY
RETRIED
RETRIES
RETRIEVABILITY
RETRIEVABLE
RETRIEVABLENESS
RETRIEVABLY
RETRIEVAL
RETRIEVALS
RETRIEVE
RETRIEVED
RETRIEVEMENT
RETRIEVEMENTS
RETRIEVER
RETRIEVERS
RETRIEVES
RETRIEVING
RETRIEVINGS
RETRIM
RETRIMMED
RETRIMMING
RETRIMS
RETRO
RETROACT
RETROACTED
RETROACTING
RETROACTION
RETROACTIONS
RETROACTIVE
RETROACTIVELY
RETROACTIVENESS
RETROACTIVITIES
RETROACTIVITY
RETROACTS
RETROBULBAR
RETROCEDE
RETROCEDED
RETROCEDENCE
RETROCEDENT
RETROCEDES
RETROCEDING

RETROCESSION
RETROCESSIONS
RETROCHOIR
RETROCHOIRS
RETROCOGNITION
RETROCOGNITIONS
RETROD
RETRODDEN
RETRODICT
RETRODICTED
RETRODICTING
RETRODICTION
RETRODICTIONS
RETRODICTIVE
RETRODICTS
RETROFIRE
RETROFIRED
RETROFIRES
RETROFIRING
RETROFIT
RETROFITS
RETROFITTED
RETROFITTING
RETROFITTINGS
RETROFLECTED
RETROFLECTION
RETROFLECTIONS
RETROFLEX
RETROFLEXED
RETROFLEXION
RETROFLEXIONS
RETROGRADATION
RETROGRADATIONS
RETROGRADE
RETROGRADED
RETROGRADELY
RETROGRADES
RETROGRADING
RETROGRESS
RETROGRESSED
RETROGRESSES
RETROGRESSING
RETROGRESSION
RETROGRESSIONAL
RETROGRESSIONS
RETROGRESSIVE
RETROGRESSIVELY
RETROJECT
RETROJECTED
RETROJECTING
RETROJECTION
RETROJECTIONS
RETROJECTS
RETROLENTAL
RETROMINGENCIES
RETROMINGENCY

RETROMINGENT
RETROMINGENTS
RETROPACK
RETROPACKS
RETROPERITONEAL
RETROPHILIA
RETROPHILIAC
RETROPHILIACS
RETROPHILIAS
RETROPULSION
RETROPULSIONS
RETROPULSIVE
RETROREFLECTION
RETROREFLECTIVE
RETROREFLECTOR
RETROREFLECTORS
RETROROCKET
RETROROCKETS
RETRORSE
RETRORSELY
RETROS
RETROSPECT
RETROSPECTED
RETROSPECTING
RETROSPECTION
RETROSPECTIONS
RETROSPECTIVE
RETROSPECTIVELY
RETROSPECTIVES
RETROSPECTS
RETROUSSAGE
RETROUSSAGES
RETROUSSE
RETROVERSE
RETROVERSELY
RETROVERSION
RETROVERSIONS
RETROVERT
RETROVERTED
RETROVERTING
RETROVERTS
RETROVIRAL
RETROVIRUS
RETROVIRUSES
RETRY
RETRYING
RETS
RETSINA
RETSINAS
RETTED
RETTERIES
RETTERY
RETTING
RETUND
RETUNDED
RETUNDING

RETUNDS
RETUNE
RETUNED
RETUNES
RETUNING
RETURF
RETURFED
RETURFING
RETURFS
RETURN
RETURNABILITY
RETURNABLE
RETURNABLES
RETURNED
RETURNEE
RETURNEES
RETURNER
RETURNERS
RETURNIK
RETURNIKS
RETURNING
RETURNLESS
RETURNS
RETUSE
RETWIST
RETWISTED
RETWISTING
RETWISTS
RETYING
RETYPE
RETYPED
RETYPES
RETYPING
REUNIFICATION
REUNIFICATIONS
REUNIFIED
REUNIFIES
REUNIFY
REUNIFYING
REUNION
REUNIONISM
REUNIONISMS
REUNIONIST
REUNIONISTIC
REUNIONISTS
REUNIONS
REUNITABLE
REUNITE
REUNITED
REUNITER
REUNITERS
REUNITES
REUNITING
REUPHOLSTER
REUPHOLSTERED
REUPHOLSTERING

REUPHOLSTERS
REURGE
REURGED
REURGES
REURGING
REUSABILITIES
REUSABILITY
REUSABLE
REUSABLENESS
REUSABLENESSES
REUSABLY
REUSE
REUSED
REUSES
REUSING
REUTILISATION
REUTILISATIONS
REUTILISE
REUTILISED
REUTILISER
REUTILISERS
REUTILISES
REUTILISING
REUTILIZATION
REUTILIZATIONS
REUTILIZE
REUTILIZED
REUTILIZES
REUTILIZING
REUTTER
REUTTERED
REUTTERING
REUTTERS
REV
REVACCINATE
REVACCINATED
REVACCINATES
REVACCINATING
REVACCINATION
REVACCINATIONS
REVALENTA
REVALENTAS
REVALIDATE
REVALIDATED
REVALIDATES
REVALIDATING
REVALIDATION
REVALIDATIONS
REVALORISATION
REVALORISATIONS
REVALORISE
REVALORISED
REVALORISES
REVALORISING
REVALORIZATION
REVALORIZATIONS

REVALORIZE
REVALORIZED
REVALORIZES
REVALORIZING
REVALUATE
REVALUATED
REVALUATES
REVALUATING
REVALUATION
REVALUATIONS
REVALUE
REVALUED
REVALUES
REVALUING
REVAMP
REVAMPED
REVAMPER
REVAMPERS
REVAMPING
REVAMPINGS
REVAMPS
REVANCHE
REVANCHES
REVANCHISM
REVANCHISMS
REVANCHIST
REVANCHISTS
REVARNISH
REVARNISHED
REVARNISHES
REVARNISHING
REVARNISHINGS
REVEAL
REVEALABILITY
REVEALABLE
REVEALED
REVEALER
REVEALERS
REVEALING
REVEALINGLY
REVEALINGNESS
REVEALINGS
REVEALMENT
REVEALMENTS
REVEALS
REVEGETATE
REVEGETATED
REVEGETATES
REVEGETATING
REVEGETATION
REVEGETATIONS
REVEHENT
REVEILLE
REVEILLES
REVEL
REVELATION

REVELATIONAL
REVELATIONIST
REVELATIONISTS
REVELATIONS
REVELATIVE
REVELATOR
REVELATORS
REVELATORY
REVELED
REVELER
REVELERS
REVELING
REVELLED
REVELLER
REVELLERS
REVELLING
REVELLINGS
REVELMENT
REVELMENTS
REVELRIES
REVELRY
REVELS
REVENANT
REVENANTS
REVENDICATE
REVENDICATED
REVENDICATES
REVENDICATING
REVENDICATION
REVENDICATIONS
REVENGE
REVENGED
REVENGEFUL
REVENGEFULLY
REVENGEFULNESS
REVENGELESS
REVENGEMENT
REVENGEMENTS
REVENGER
REVENGERS
REVENGES
REVENGING
REVENGINGLY
REVENGINGS
REVENGIVE
REVENUAL
REVENUE
REVENUED
REVENUER
REVENUERS
REVENUES
REVERABLE
REVERB
REVERBED
REVERBERANT
REVERBERANTLY

REVERBERATE
REVERBERATED
REVERBERATES
REVERBERATING
REVERBERATION
REVERBERATIONS
REVERBERATIVE
REVERBERATOR
REVERBERATORIES
REVERBERATORS
REVERBERATORY
REVERBING
REVERBS
REVERE
REVERED
REVERENCE
REVERENCED
REVERENCER
REVERENCERS
REVERENCES
REVERENCING
REVEREND
REVERENDS
REVERENT
REVERENTIAL
REVERENTIALLY
REVERENTLY
REVERENTNESS
REVERER
REVERERS
REVERES
REVERIE
REVERIES
REVERIFICATION
REVERIFICATIONS
REVERIFIED
REVERIFIER
REVERIFIERS
REVERIFIES
REVERIFY
REVERIFYING
REVERING
REVERIST
REVERISTS
REVERS
REVERSAL
REVERSALS
REVERSE
REVERSED
REVERSEDLY
REVERSELESS
REVERSELY
REVERSER
REVERSERS
REVERSES
REVERSI

REVERSIBILITIES
REVERSIBILITY
REVERSIBLE
REVERSIBLES
REVERSIBLY
REVERSING
REVERSINGS
REVERSION
REVERSIONAL
REVERSIONALLY
REVERSIONARIES
REVERSIONARY
REVERSIONER
REVERSIONERS
REVERSIONS
REVERSIS
REVERSISES
REVERSO
REVERSOS
REVERT
REVERTANT
REVERTANTS
REVERTED
REVERTER
REVERTERS
REVERTIBLE
REVERTING
REVERTIVE
REVERTS
REVERY
REVEST
REVESTED
REVESTIARIES
REVESTIARY
REVESTING
REVESTRIES
REVESTRY
REVESTS
REVET
REVETMENT
REVETMENTS
REVETS
REVETTED
REVETTING
REVEUR
REVEURS
REVEUSE
REVEUSES
REVICTUAL
REVICTUALED
REVICTUALING
REVICTUALLED
REVICTUALLING
REVICTUALS
REVIE
REVIED

REVIES
REVIEW
REVIEWABLE
REVIEWAL
REVIEWALS
REVIEWED
REVIEWER
REVIEWERS
REVIEWING
REVIEWS
REVILE
REVILED
REVILEMENT
REVILEMENTS
REVILER
REVILERS
REVILES
REVILING
REVILINGLY
REVILINGS
REVINDICATE
REVINDICATED
REVINDICATES
REVINDICATING
REVINDICATION
REVINDICATIONS
REVIOLATE
REVIOLATED
REVIOLATES
REVIOLATING
REVIOLATION
REVIOLATIONS
REVISABLE
REVISAL
REVISALS
REVISE
REVISED
REVISER
REVISERS
REVISES
REVISING
REVISION
REVISIONAL
REVISIONARY
REVISIONISM
REVISIONISMS
REVISIONIST
REVISIONISTS
REVISIONS
REVISIT
REVISITANT
REVISITANTS
REVISITATION
REVISITATIONS
REVISITED
REVISITING

REVISITS
REVISOR
REVISORS
REVISORY
REVISUALIZATION
REVITALISATION
REVITALISATIONS
REVITALISE
REVITALISED
REVITALISES
REVITALISING
REVITALIZATION
REVITALIZATIONS
REVITALIZE
REVITALIZED
REVITALIZES
REVITALIZING
REVIVABILITIES
REVIVABILITY
REVIVABLE
REVIVABLY
REVIVAL
REVIVALISM
REVIVALISMS
REVIVALIST
REVIVALISTIC
REVIVALISTS
REVIVALS
REVIVE
REVIVED
REVIVEMENT
REVIVEMENTS
REVIVER
REVIVERS
REVIVES
REVIVESCENCE
REVIVESCENCES
REVIVESCENCIES
REVIVESCENCY
REVIVESCENT
REVIVIFICATION
REVIVIFICATIONS
REVIVIFIED
REVIVIFIES
REVIVIFY
REVIVIFYING
REVIVING
REVIVINGLY
REVIVINGS
REVIVISCENCE
REVIVISCENCES
REVIVISCENCIES
REVIVISCENCY
REVIVISCENT
REVIVOR
REVIVORS

REVOCABILITIES
REVOCABILITY
REVOCABLE
REVOCABLENESS
REVOCABLENESSES
REVOCABLY
REVOCATION
REVOCATIONS
REVOCATORY
REVOICE
REVOICED
REVOICES
REVOICING
REVOKABILITY
REVOKABLE
REVOKABLY
REVOKE
REVOKED
REVOKEMENT
REVOKEMENTS
REVOKER
REVOKERS
REVOKES
REVOKING
REVOLT
REVOLTED
REVOLTER
REVOLTERS
REVOLTING
REVOLTINGLY
REVOLTS
REVOLUTE
REVOLUTION
REVOLUTIONAL
REVOLUTIONARIES
REVOLUTIONARILY
REVOLUTIONARY
REVOLUTIONER
REVOLUTIONERS
REVOLUTIONISE
REVOLUTIONISED
REVOLUTIONISER
REVOLUTIONISERS
REVOLUTIONISES
REVOLUTIONISING
REVOLUTIONISM
REVOLUTIONISMS
REVOLUTIONIST
REVOLUTIONISTS
REVOLUTIONIZE
REVOLUTIONIZED
REVOLUTIONIZER
REVOLUTIONIZERS
REVOLUTIONIZES
REVOLUTIONIZING
REVOLUTIONS

REVOLVABILITY
REVOLVABLE
REVOLVABLY
REVOLVE
REVOLVED
REVOLVENCIES
REVOLVENCY
REVOLVER
REVOLVERS
REVOLVES
REVOLVING
REVOLVINGLY
REVOLVINGS
REVOTE
REVOTED
REVOTES
REVOTING
REVS
REVUE
REVUES
REVUIST
REVUISTS
REVULSED
REVULSION
REVULSIONARY
REVULSIONS
REVULSIVE
REVULSIVELY
REVULSIVENESS
REVULSIVES
REVVED
REVVING
REVYING
REW
REWAKE
REWAKED
REWAKEN
REWAKENED
REWAKENING
REWAKENS
REWAKES
REWAKING
REWAN
REWARD
REWARDABLE
REWARDABLENESS
REWARDED
REWARDER
REWARDERS
REWARDFUL
REWARDING
REWARDINGLY
REWARDLESS
REWARDS
REWAREWA
REWAREWAS

REWARM
REWARMED
REWARMING
REWARMS
REWASH
REWASHED
REWASHES
REWASHING
REWAX
REWAXED
REWAXES
REWAXING
REWEAVE
REWEAVED
REWEAVES
REWEAVING
REWED
REWEDDED
REWEDDING
REWEDS
REWEIGH
REWEIGHED
REWEIGHING
REWEIGHS
REWELD
REWELDED
REWELDING
REWELDS
REWET
REWETS
REWETTED
REWETTING
REWIDEN
REWIDENED
REWIDENING
REWIDENS
REWIN
REWIND
REWINDED
REWINDER
REWINDERS
REWINDING
REWINDS
REWINNING
REWINS
REWIRABILITY
REWIRABLE
REWIRE
REWIRED
REWIRER
REWIRERS
REWIRES
REWIRING
REWIRINGS
REWOKE
REWOKEN

REWON
REWORD
REWORDED
REWORDING
REWORDS
REWORK
REWORKED
REWORKING
REWORKS
REWOUND
REWOVE
REWOVEN
REWRAP
REWRAPPED
REWRAPPING
REWRAPS
REWRAPT
REWRITE
REWRITER
REWRITERS
REWRITES
REWRITING
REWRITTEN
REWROTE
REWROUGHT
REWS
REWTH
REWTHS
REX
REXES
REYNARD
REYNARDS
REZ
REZONE
REZONED
REZONES
REZONING
REZZES
RHABDOCOELE
RHABDOCOELES
RHABDOID
RHABDOIDS
RHABDOLITH
RHABDOLITHS
RHABDOM
RHABDOMANCER
RHABDOMANCERS
RHABDOMANCIES
RHABDOMANCY
RHABDOMANTIST
RHABDOMANTISTS
RHABDOME
RHABDOMERE
RHABDOMERES
RHABDOMES
RHABDOMS

RHABDOMYOMA
RHABDOMYOMAS
RHABDOMYOMATA
RHABDOSPHERE
RHABDOSPHERES
RHABDOVIRUS
RHABDOVIRUSES
RHABDUS
RHABDUSES
RHACHIAL
RHACHIDES
RHACHIDIAL
RHACHILLA
RHACHILLAS
RHACHIS
RHACHISES
RHACHITIS
RHACHITISES
RHADAMANTHINE
RHAGADES
RHAGADIFORM
RHAMNACEOUS
RHAMNOSE
RHAMNOSES
RHAMNUS
RHAMNUSES
RHAMPHOID
RHAMPHOTHECA
RHAMPHOTHECAE
RHAPHAE
RHAPHE
RHAPHES
RHAPHIDE
RHAPHIDES
RHAPHIS
RHAPONTIC
RHAPONTICS
RHAPSODE
RHAPSODES
RHAPSODIC
RHAPSODICAL
RHAPSODICALLY
RHAPSODIES
RHAPSODISE
RHAPSODISED
RHAPSODISES
RHAPSODISING
RHAPSODIST
RHAPSODISTIC
RHAPSODISTS
RHAPSODIZE
RHAPSODIZED
RHAPSODIZES
RHAPSODIZING
RHAPSODY
RHATANIES

RHATANY
RHEA
RHEAS
RHEBOK
RHEBOKS
RHEMATIC
RHEME
RHEMES
RHENIUM
RHENIUMS
RHEOBASE
RHEOBASES
RHEOCHORD
RHEOCHORDS
RHEOCORD
RHEOCORDS
RHEOLOGIC
RHEOLOGICAL
RHEOLOGICALLY
RHEOLOGIES
RHEOLOGIST
RHEOLOGISTS
RHEOLOGY
RHEOMETER
RHEOMETERS
RHEOMETRIC
RHEOMETRICAL
RHEOMETRICALLY
RHEOMETRY
RHEOMORPHIC
RHEOMORPHICALLY
RHEOMORPHISM
RHEOPHIL
RHEORECEPTOR
RHEORECEPTORS
RHEOSTAT
RHEOSTATIC
RHEOSTATS
RHEOTACTIC
RHEOTACTICALLY
RHEOTAXES
RHEOTAXIS
RHEOTOME
RHEOTOMES
RHEOTROPE
RHEOTROPES
RHEOTROPIC
RHEOTROPISM
RHEOTROPISMS
RHESUS
RHESUSES
RHETOR
RHETORIC
RHETORICAL
RHETORICALLY
RHETORICIAN

RHETORICIANS
RHETORICS
RHETORISE
RHETORISED
RHETORISES
RHETORISING
RHETORIZE
RHETORIZED
RHETORIZES
RHETORIZING
RHETORS
RHEUM
RHEUMATEESES
RHEUMATIC
RHEUMATICAL
RHEUMATICALLY
RHEUMATICKY
RHEUMATICS
RHEUMATISE
RHEUMATISES
RHEUMATISM
RHEUMATISMAL
RHEUMATISMS
RHEUMATIZ
RHEUMATIZE
RHEUMATIZES
RHEUMATOID
RHEUMATOIDALLY
RHEUMATOLOGICAL
RHEUMATOLOGIES
RHEUMATOLOGIST
RHEUMATOLOGISTS
RHEUMATOLOGY
RHEUMED
RHEUMIC
RHEUMIER
RHEUMIEST
RHEUMS
RHEUMY
RHEXES
RHEXIS
RHEXISES
RHIES
RHIGOLENE
RHIME
RHIMES
RHINAL
RHINE
RHINENCEPHALA
RHINENCEPHALIC
RHINENCEPHALON
RHINENCEPHALONS
RHINES
RHINESTONE
RHINESTONED
RHINESTONES

RHINITIC
RHINITIDES
RHINITIS
RHINITISES
RHINO
RHINOCERI
RHINOCERICAL
RHINOCEROS
RHINOCEROSES
RHINOCEROT
RHINOCEROTE
RHINOCEROTES
RHINOCEROTIC
RHINOLALIA
RHINOLALIAS
RHINOLITH
RHINOLITHS
RHINOLOGICAL
RHINOLOGIES
RHINOLOGIST
RHINOLOGISTS
RHINOLOGY
RHINOPHYMA
RHINOPHYMAS
RHINOPLASTIC
RHINOPLASTIES
RHINOPLASTY
RHINORRHAGIA
RHINORRHAGIAS
RHINORRHOEA
RHINORRHOEAL
RHINORRHOEAS
RHINOS
RHINOSCLEROMA
RHINOSCLEROMAS
RHINOSCOPE
RHINOSCOPES
RHINOSCOPIC
RHINOSCOPIES
RHINOSCOPY
RHINOTHECA
RHINOTHECAE
RHINOVIRUS
RHINOVIRUSES
RHIPIDATE
RHIPIDION
RHIPIDIONS
RHIPIDIUM
RHIPIDIUMS
RHIZANTHOUS
RHIZIC
RHIZINE
RHIZINES
RHIZOBIA
RHIZOBIAL
RHIZOBIUM

RHIZOCARP
RHIZOCARPIC
RHIZOCARPOUS
RHIZOCARPS
RHIZOCAUL
RHIZOCAULS
RHIZOCEPHALAN
RHIZOCEPHALANS
RHIZOCEPHALOUS
RHIZOCTONIA
RHIZOCTONIAS
RHIZOGENETIC
RHIZOGENIC
RHIZOGENOUS
RHIZOID
RHIZOIDAL
RHIZOIDS
RHIZOMA
RHIZOMATA
RHIZOMATOUS
RHIZOME
RHIZOMES
RHIZOMIC
RHIZOMORPH
RHIZOMORPHOUS
RHIZOMORPHS
RHIZOPHAGOUS
RHIZOPHILOUS
RHIZOPHORE
RHIZOPHORES
RHIZOPI
RHIZOPLANE
RHIZOPLANES
RHIZOPOD
RHIZOPODAN
RHIZOPODANS
RHIZOPODOUS
RHIZOPODS
RHIZOPUS
RHIZOPUSES
RHIZOSPHERE
RHIZOSPHERES
RHIZOTOMIES
RHIZOTOMY
RHO
RHODAMIN
RHODAMINE
RHODAMINES
RHODAMINS
RHODANATE
RHODANATES
RHODANIC
RHODANISE
RHODANISED
RHODANISES
RHODANISING

RHODANIZE
RHODANIZED
RHODANIZES
RHODANIZING
RHODIC
RHODIE
RHODIES
RHODINAL
RHODIUM
RHODIUMS
RHODOCHROSITE
RHODOCHROSITES
RHODODAPHNE
RHODODAPHNES
RHODODENDRON
RHODODENDRONS
RHODOLITE
RHODOLITES
RHODOMONTADE
RHODOMONTADED
RHODOMONTADES
RHODOMONTADING
RHODONITE
RHODONITES
RHODOPHANE
RHODOPHANES
RHODOPSIN
RHODOPSINS
RHODORA
RHODORAS
RHODOUS
RHODY
RHOEADINE
RHOEADINES
RHOICISSUS
RHOICISSUSES
RHOMB
RHOMBENCEPHALA
RHOMBENCEPHALON
RHOMBENPORPHYR
RHOMBENPORPHYRS
RHOMBENPORPHYRY
RHOMBI
RHOMBIC
RHOMBOHEDRA
RHOMBOHEDRAL
RHOMBOHEDRON
RHOMBOHEDRONS
RHOMBOI
RHOMBOID
RHOMBOIDAL
RHOMBOIDEI
RHOMBOIDES
RHOMBOIDEUS
RHOMBOIDS
RHOMBOS

RHOMBPORPHYRIES
RHOMBPORPHYRY
RHOMBS
RHOMBUS
RHOMBUSES
RHONCHAL
RHONCHI
RHONCHIAL
RHONCHUS
RHONE
RHONES
RHOPALIC
RHOPALISM
RHOPALISMS
RHOPALOCERAL
RHOPALOCEROUS
RHOS
RHOTACISE
RHOTACISED
RHOTACISES
RHOTACISING
RHOTACISM
RHOTACISMS
RHOTACIST
RHOTACISTIC
RHOTACISTS
RHOTACIZE
RHOTACIZED
RHOTACIZES
RHOTACIZING
RHOTIC
RHOTICALLY
RHOTICITY
RHUBARB
RHUBARBED
RHUBARBING
RHUBARBINGS
RHUBARBS
RHUBARBY
RHUMB
RHUMBA
RHUMBAED
RHUMBAING
RHUMBAS
RHUMBATRON
RHUMBATRONS
RHUMBS
RHUS
RHUSES
RHY
RHYME
RHYMED
RHYMELESS
RHYMER
RHYMERS
RHYMES

873

RHYMESTER
RHYMESTERS
RHYMING
RHYMIST
RHYMISTS
RHYNCHOCOEL
RHYNCHOCOELS
RHYNCHODONT
RHYNCHOPHORE
RHYNCHOPHORES
RHYNCHOPHOROUS
RHYNE
RHYNES
RHYOLITE
RHYOLITES
RHYOLITIC
RHYPAROGRAPHER
RHYPAROGRAPHERS
RHYPAROGRAPHIC
RHYPAROGRAPHIES
RHYPAROGRAPHY
RHYTA
RHYTHM
RHYTHMAL
RHYTHMED
RHYTHMI
RHYTHMIC
RHYTHMICAL
RHYTHMICALLY
RHYTHMICITIES
RHYTHMICITY
RHYTHMICS
RHYTHMISE
RHYTHMISED
RHYTHMISES
RHYTHMISING
RHYTHMIST
RHYTHMISTS
RHYTHMIZATION
RHYTHMIZATIONS
RHYTHMIZE
RHYTHMIZED
RHYTHMIZES
RHYTHMIZING
RHYTHMLESS
RHYTHMOMETER
RHYTHMOMETERS
RHYTHMOPOEIA
RHYTHMOPOEIAS
RHYTHMS
RHYTHMUS
RHYTHMUSES
RHYTIDECTOMIES
RHYTIDECTOMY
RHYTIDOME
RHYTIDOMES

RHYTINA
RHYTINAS
RHYTON
RHYTONS
RIA
RIAL
RIALS
RIALTO
RIALTOS
RIANCIES
RIANCY
RIANT
RIANTLY
RIAS
RIATA
RIATAS
RIB
RIBALD
RIBALDLY
RIBALDRIES
RIBALDRY
RIBALDS
RIBAND
RIBANDS
RIBATTUTA
RIBATTUTAS
RIBAUD
RIBAUDRED
RIBAUDRIES
RIBAUDRY
RIBAUDS
RIBAVIRIN
RIBAVIRINS
RIBBAND
RIBBANDS
RIBBED
RIBBER
RIBBERS
RIBBIER
RIBBIEST
RIBBING
RIBBINGS
RIBBON
RIBBONED
RIBBONFISH
RIBBONFISHES
RIBBONING
RIBBONLIKE
RIBBONRIES
RIBBONRY
RIBBONS
RIBBONWOOD
RIBBONWOODS
RIBBONY
RIBBY
RIBCAGE

RIBCAGES
RIBES
RIBGRASS
RIBGRASSES
RIBIBE
RIBIBES
RIBIBLE
RIBIBLES
RIBIER
RIBIERS
RIBLESS
RIBLET
RIBLETS
RIBLIKE
RIBOFLAVIN
RIBOFLAVINE
RIBOFLAVINS
RIBONUCLEASE
RIBONUCLEASES
RIBONUCLEIC
RIBONUCLEOSIDE
RIBONUCLEOSIDES
RIBONUCLEOTIDE
RIBONUCLEOTIDES
RIBOSE
RIBOSES
RIBOSOMAL
RIBOSOME
RIBOSOMES
RIBOZYME
RIBOZYMES
RIBS
RIBSTON
RIBSTONE
RIBSTONES
RIBSTONS
RIBWORK
RIBWORKS
RIBWORT
RIBWORTS
RICE
RICEBIRD
RICEBIRDS
RICED
RICER
RICERCAR
RICERCARE
RICERCARES
RICERCARI
RICERCARS
RICERCATA
RICERCATAS
RICERS
RICES
RICEY
RICH

RICHED
RICHEN
RICHENED
RICHENING
RICHENS
RICHER
RICHES
RICHESSE
RICHESSES
RICHEST
RICHING
RICHLY
RICHNESS
RICHNESSES
RICHT
RICHTED
RICHTER
RICHTEST
RICHTING
RICHTS
RICHWEED
RICHWEEDS
RICIER
RICIEST
RICIN
RICING
RICINOLEIC
RICINS
RICINUS
RICINUSES
RICK
RICKBURNERS
RICKED
RICKER
RICKERS
RICKETIER
RICKETIEST
RICKETILY
RICKETINESS
RICKETINESSES
RICKETS
RICKETTIER
RICKETTIEST
RICKETTSIA
RICKETTSIAE
RICKETTSIAL
RICKETTSIAS
RICKETTY
RICKETY
RICKEY
RICKEYS
RICKING
RICKLE
RICKLES
RICKLY
RICKRACK

RICKRACKS
RICKS
RICKSHA
RICKSHAS
RICKSHAW
RICKSHAWS
RICKSTAND
RICKSTANDS
RICKSTICK
RICKSTICKS
RICKYARD
RICKYARDS
RICOCHET
RICOCHETED
RICOCHETING
RICOCHETS
RICOCHETTED
RICOCHETTING
RICOTTA
RICOTTAS
RICRAC
RICRACS
RICTAL
RICTUS
RICTUSES
RICY
RID
RIDABILITIES
RIDABILITY
RIDABLE
RIDDANCE
RIDDANCES
RIDDED
RIDDEN
RIDDER
RIDDERS
RIDDING
RIDDLE
RIDDLED
RIDDLER
RIDDLERS
RIDDLES
RIDDLING
RIDDLINGLY
RIDDLINGS
RIDE
RIDEABLE
RIDENT
RIDER
RIDERED
RIDERLESS
RIDERS
RIDERSHIP
RIDERSHIPS
RIDES
RIDGE

RIDGEBACK
RIDGEBACKS
RIDGED
RIDGEL
RIDGELIKE
RIDGELINE
RIDGELINES
RIDGELING
RIDGELINGS
RIDGELS
RIDGEPOLE
RIDGEPOLES
RIDGER
RIDGERS
RIDGES
RIDGETREE
RIDGETREES
RIDGEWAY
RIDGEWAYS
RIDGIER
RIDGIEST
RIDGIL
RIDGILS
RIDGING
RIDGINGS
RIDGLING
RIDGLINGS
RIDGY
RIDICULE
RIDICULED
RIDICULER
RIDICULERS
RIDICULES
RIDICULING
RIDICULOUS
RIDICULOUSLY
RIDICULOUSNESS
RIDING
RIDINGS
RIDLEY
RIDLEYS
RIDOTTO
RIDOTTOS
RIDS
RIEBECKITE
RIEBECKITES
RIEL
RIELS
RIEM
RIEMPIE
RIEMPIES
RIEMS
RIESLING
RIESLINGS
RIEVE
RIEVER

RIEVERS
RIEVES
RIEVING
RIF
RIFACIMENTI
RIFACIMENTO
RIFAMPICIN
RIFAMPICINS
RIFAMPIN
RIFAMPINS
RIFE
RIFELY
RIFENESS
RIFENESSES
RIFER
RIFEST
RIFF
RIFFED
RIFFING
RIFFLE
RIFFLED
RIFFLER
RIFFLERS
RIFFLES
RIFFLING
RIFFOLA
RIFFRAFF
RIFFRAFFS
RIFFS
RIFLE
RIFLEBIRD
RIFLEBIRDS
RIFLED
RIFLEMAN
RIFLEMEN
RIFLER
RIFLERIES
RIFLERS
RIFLERY
RIFLES
RIFLING
RIFLINGS
RIFS
RIFT
RIFTE
RIFTED
RIFTIER
RIFTIEST
RIFTING
RIFTLESS
RIFTS
RIFTY
RIG
RIGADOON
RIGADOONS
RIGAMAROLE

RIGAMAROLES
RIGATONI
RIGATONIS
RIGAUDON
RIGAUDONS
RIGG
RIGGALD
RIGGALDS
RIGGED
RIGGER
RIGGERS
RIGGING
RIGGINGS
RIGGISH
RIGGS
RIGHT
RIGHTABLE
RIGHTABLENESS
RIGHTABLY
RIGHTED
RIGHTEN
RIGHTENED
RIGHTENING
RIGHTENS
RIGHTEOUS
RIGHTEOUSLY
RIGHTEOUSNESS
RIGHTEOUSNESSES
RIGHTER
RIGHTERS
RIGHTEST
RIGHTFUL
RIGHTFULLY
RIGHTFULNESS
RIGHTFULNESSES
RIGHTIES
RIGHTING
RIGHTINGS
RIGHTISH
RIGHTISM
RIGHTISMS
RIGHTIST
RIGHTISTS
RIGHTLESS
RIGHTLY
RIGHTMOST
RIGHTNESS
RIGHTNESSES
RIGHTO
RIGHTOS
RIGHTS
RIGHTSIZE
RIGHTSIZED
RIGHTSIZES
RIGHTSIZING
RIGHTWARD

RIGHTWARDS
RIGHTY
RIGID
RIGIDER
RIGIDEST
RIGIDIFICATION
RIGIDIFICATIONS
RIGIDIFIED
RIGIDIFIES
RIGIDIFY
RIGIDIFYING
RIGIDISE
RIGIDISED
RIGIDISES
RIGIDISING
RIGIDITIES
RIGIDITY
RIGIDIZE
RIGIDIZED
RIGIDIZES
RIGIDIZING
RIGIDLY
RIGIDNESS
RIGIDNESSES
RIGIDS
RIGLIN
RIGLING
RIGLINGS
RIGLINS
RIGMAROLE
RIGMAROLES
RIGOL
RIGOLL
RIGOLLS
RIGOLS
RIGOR
RIGORISM
RIGORISMS
RIGORIST
RIGORISTIC
RIGORISTS
RIGOROUS
RIGOROUSLY
RIGOROUSNESS
RIGOROUSNESSES
RIGORS
RIGOUR
RIGOURS
RIGOUT
RIGOUTS
RIGS
RIGSDALER
RIGSDALERS
RIGWIDDIE
RIGWIDDIES
RIGWOODIE

RIGWOODIES
RIJKSDAALER
RIJKSDAALERS
RIJSTAFEL
RIJSTAFELS
RIJSTTAFEL
RIJSTTAFELS
RIKISHA
RIKISHAS
RIKISHI
RIKSHAW
RIKSHAWS
RILE
RILED
RILES
RILEY
RILIER
RILIEST
RILIEVI
RILIEVO
RILING
RILL
RILLE
RILLED
RILLES
RILLET
RILLETS
RILLETTES
RILLING
RILLMARK
RILLMARKS
RILLS
RIM
RIMA
RIMAE
RIMAYE
RIMAYES
RIME
RIMED
RIMELESS
RIMELESSNESS
RIMER
RIMERS
RIMES
RIMESTER
RIMESTERS
RIMFIRE
RIMFIRES
RIMIER
RIMIEST
RIMINESS
RIMINESSES
RIMING
RIMLAND
RIMLANDS
RIMLESS

RIMMED
RIMMER
RIMMERS
RIMMING
RIMMINGS
RIMOSE
RIMOSELY
RIMOSITIES
RIMOSITY
RIMOUS
RIMPLE
RIMPLED
RIMPLES
RIMPLING
RIMROCK
RIMROCKS
RIMS
RIMU
RIMUS
RIMY
RIN
RIND
RINDED
RINDERPEST
RINDERPESTS
RINDIER
RINDIEST
RINDING
RINDLESS
RINDS
RINDY
RINE
RINES
RINFORZANDO
RING
RINGBARK
RINGBARKED
RINGBARKING
RINGBARKS
RINGBIT
RINGBITS
RINGBOLT
RINGBOLTS
RINGBONE
RINGBONES
RINGDOVE
RINGDOVES
RINGED
RINGENT
RINGER
RINGERS
RINGGIT
RINGGITS
RINGHALS
RINGHALSES
RINGING

RINGINGLY
RINGINGS
RINGLEADER
RINGLEADERS
RINGLESS
RINGLET
RINGLETED
RINGLETS
RINGLIKE
RINGMAN
RINGMASTER
RINGMASTERS
RINGMEN
RINGNECK
RINGNECKS
RINGS
RINGSIDE
RINGSIDER
RINGSIDERS
RINGSIDES
RINGSTAND
RINGSTANDS
RINGSTER
RINGSTERS
RINGSTRAKED
RINGTAIL
RINGTAILS
RINGTAW
RINGTAWS
RINGTOSS
RINGTOSSES
RINGWAY
RINGWAYS
RINGWISE
RINGWOMB
RINGWORK
RINGWORKS
RINGWORM
RINGWORMS
RINK
RINKED
RINKHALS
RINKHALSES
RINKING
RINKS
RINNING
RINS
RINSABILITIES
RINSABILITY
RINSABLE
RINSE
RINSEABLE
RINSED
RINSER
RINSERS
RINSES

RINSIBILITIES
RINSIBILITY
RINSIBLE
RINSING
RINSINGS
RINTHEREOUT
RINTHEREOUTS
RIOJA
RIOJAS
RIOT
RIOTED
RIOTER
RIOTERS
RIOTING
RIOTINGS
RIOTISE
RIOTISES
RIOTIZE
RIOTIZES
RIOTOUS
RIOTOUSLY
RIOTOUSNESS
RIOTOUSNESSES
RIOTRIES
RIOTRY
RIOTS
RIP
RIPARIAL
RIPARIAN
RIPARIANS
RIPCORD
RIPCORDS
RIPE
RIPECK
RIPECKS
RIPED
RIPELY
RIPEN
RIPENED
RIPENER
RIPENERS
RIPENESS
RIPENESSES
RIPENING
RIPENS
RIPER
RIPERS
RIPES
RIPEST
RIPIDOLITE
RIPIDOLITES
RIPIENI
RIPIENIST
RIPIENISTS
RIPIENO
RIPIENOS

RIPING
RIPOFF
RIPOFFS
RIPOST
RIPOSTE
RIPOSTED
RIPOSTES
RIPOSTING
RIPOSTS
RIPP
RIPPABLE
RIPPED
RIPPER
RIPPERS
RIPPIER
RIPPIERS
RIPPING
RIPPINGLY
RIPPLE
RIPPLED
RIPPLER
RIPPLERS
RIPPLES
RIPPLET
RIPPLETS
RIPPLIER
RIPPLIEST
RIPPLING
RIPPLINGLY
RIPPLINGS
RIPPLY
RIPPS
RIPRAP
RIPRAPPED
RIPRAPPING
RIPRAPS
RIPS
RIPSAW
RIPSAWS
RIPSNORTER
RIPSNORTERS
RIPSNORTING
RIPSTOP
RIPSTOPS
RIPT
RIPTIDE
RIPTIDES
RIRORIRO
RIRORIROS
RISALDAR
RISALDARS
RISE
RISEN
RISER
RISERS
RISES

RISHI
RISHIS
RISIBILITIES
RISIBILITY
RISIBLE
RISIBLES
RISIBLY
RISING
RISINGS
RISK
RISKED
RISKER
RISKERS
RISKFUL
RISKIER
RISKIEST
RISKILY
RISKINESS
RISKINESSES
RISKING
RISKLESS
RISKS
RISKY
RISOLUTO
RISORGIMENTO
RISORGIMENTOS
RISOTTO
RISOTTOS
RISP
RISPED
RISPETTI
RISPETTO
RISPING
RISPINGS
RISPS
RISQUE
RISQUES
RISSOLE
RISSOLES
RISUS
RISUSES
RIT
RITARD
RITARDANDO
RITARDANDOS
RITARDS
RITE
RITELESS
RITENUTO
RITENUTOS
RITES
RITORNEL
RITORNELL
RITORNELLE
RITORNELLES
RITORNELLI

RITORNELLO
RITORNELLOS
RITORNELLS
RITORNELS
RITOURNELLE
RITOURNELLES
RITS
RITT
RITTED
RITTER
RITTERS
RITTING
RITTS
RITUAL
RITUALISATION
RITUALISATIONS
RITUALISE
RITUALISED
RITUALISES
RITUALISING
RITUALISM
RITUALISMS
RITUALIST
RITUALISTIC
RITUALISTICALLY
RITUALISTS
RITUALIZATION
RITUALIZATIONS
RITUALIZE
RITUALIZED
RITUALIZES
RITUALIZING
RITUALLY
RITUALS
RITZ
RITZES
RITZIER
RITZIEST
RITZILY
RITZINESS
RITZINESSES
RITZY
RIVA
RIVAGE
RIVAGES
RIVAL
RIVALED
RIVALESS
RIVALESSES
RIVALING
RIVALISE
RIVALISED
RIVALISES
RIVALISING
RIVALITIES
RIVALITY

RIVALIZE
RIVALIZED
RIVALIZES
RIVALIZING
RIVALLED
RIVALLESS
RIVALLING
RIVALRIES
RIVALROUS
RIVALRY
RIVALS
RIVALSHIP
RIVALSHIPS
RIVAS
RIVE
RIVED
RIVEL
RIVELLED
RIVELLING
RIVELS
RIVEN
RIVER
RIVERAIN
RIVERAINS
RIVERBANK
RIVERBANKS
RIVERBED
RIVERBEDS
RIVERBOAT
RIVERBOATS
RIVERCRAFT
RIVERCRAFTS
RIVERED
RIVERET
RIVERETS
RIVERFRONT
RIVERFRONTS
RIVERINE
RIVERLESS
RIVERLIKE
RIVERMAN
RIVERMEN
RIVERS
RIVERSCAPE
RIVERSCAPES
RIVERSIDE
RIVERSIDES
RIVERWARD
RIVERWARDS
RIVERWAY
RIVERWAYS
RIVERWEED
RIVERWEEDS
RIVERWORTHINESS
RIVERWORTHY
RIVERY

RIVES
RIVET
RIVETED
RIVETER
RIVETERS
RIVETING
RIVETINGLY
RIVETINGS
RIVETS
RIVETTED
RIVETTING
RIVIERA
RIVIERAS
RIVIERE
RIVIERES
RIVING
RIVLIN
RIVLINS
RIVO
RIVOS
RIVULET
RIVULETS
RIVULOSE
RIYAL
RIYALS
RIZ
RIZA
RIZARD
RIZARDS
RIZAS
RIZZAR
RIZZARED
RIZZARING
RIZZARS
RIZZART
RIZZARTS
RIZZER
RIZZERED
RIZZERING
RIZZERS
RIZZOR
RIZZORED
RIZZORING
RIZZORS
ROACH
ROACHED
ROACHES
ROACHING
ROAD
ROADABILITIES
ROADABILITY
ROADBED
ROADBEDS
ROADBLOCK
ROADBLOCKED
ROADBLOCKING

ROADBLOCKS
ROADCRAFT
ROADCRAFTS
ROADEO
ROADEOS
ROADHEADER
ROADHEADERS
ROADHOLDING
ROADHOLDINGS
ROADHOUSE
ROADHOUSES
ROADIE
ROADIES
ROADING
ROADINGS
ROADKILL
ROADKILLS
ROADLESS
ROADMAN
ROADMEN
ROADROLLER
ROADROLLERS
ROADRUNNER
ROADRUNNERS
ROADS
ROADSHOW
ROADSHOWS
ROADSIDE
ROADSIDES
ROADSMAN
ROADSMEN
ROADSTEAD
ROADSTEADS
ROADSTER
ROADSTERS
ROADWAY
ROADWAYS
ROADWORK
ROADWORKS
ROADWORTHINESS
ROADWORTHY
ROAM
ROAMED
ROAMER
ROAMERS
ROAMING
ROAMINGS
ROAMS
ROAN
ROANS
ROAR
ROARED
ROARER
ROARERS
ROARIE
ROARIER

ROARIEST
ROARING
ROARINGLY
ROARINGS
ROARMING
ROARS
ROARY
ROAST
ROASTED
ROASTER
ROASTERS
ROASTING
ROASTINGS
ROASTS
ROATE
ROATED
ROATES
ROATING
ROB
ROBALO
ROBALOS
ROBAND
ROBANDS
ROBBED
ROBBER
ROBBERIES
ROBBERS
ROBBERY
ROBBIN
ROBBING
ROBBINS
ROBE
ROBED
ROBERDSMAN
ROBERDSMEN
ROBERTSMAN
ROBERTSMEN
ROBES
ROBIN
ROBING
ROBINGS
ROBINIA
ROBINIAS
ROBINS
ROBLE
ROBLES
ROBORANT
ROBORANTS
ROBORATING
ROBOT
ROBOTIC
ROBOTICALLY
ROBOTICS
ROBOTISE
ROBOTISED
ROBOTISES

ROBOTISING
ROBOTISM
ROBOTISMS
ROBOTIZATION
ROBOTIZATIONS
ROBOTIZE
ROBOTIZED
ROBOTIZES
ROBOTIZING
ROBOTRIES
ROBOTRY
ROBOTS
ROBS
ROBURITE
ROBURITES
ROBUST
ROBUSTA
ROBUSTAS
ROBUSTER
ROBUSTEST
ROBUSTIOUS
ROBUSTIOUSLY
ROBUSTIOUSNESS
ROBUSTLY
ROBUSTNESS
ROBUSTNESSES
ROC
ROCAILLE
ROCAILLES
ROCAMBOLE
ROCAMBOLES
ROCH
ROCHES
ROCHET
ROCHETS
ROCK
ROCKABIES
ROCKABILLIES
ROCKABILLY
ROCKABY
ROCKABYE
ROCKABYES
ROCKAWAY
ROCKAWAYS
ROCKBOUND
ROCKCRESS
ROCKCRESSES
ROCKED
ROCKER
ROCKERIES
ROCKERS
ROCKERY
ROCKET
ROCKETED
ROCKETEER
ROCKETEERS

ROCKETER
ROCKETERS
ROCKETING
ROCKETRIES
ROCKETRY
ROCKETS
ROCKFALL
ROCKFALLS
ROCKFISH
ROCKFISHES
ROCKHOPPER
ROCKHOPPERS
ROCKHOUNDING
ROCKHOUNDINGS
ROCKIER
ROCKIERS
ROCKIEST
ROCKILY
ROCKINESS
ROCKINESSES
ROCKING
ROCKINGS
ROCKLAY
ROCKLAYS
ROCKLESS
ROCKLIKE
ROCKLING
ROCKLINGS
ROCKOON
ROCKOONS
ROCKROSE
ROCKROSES
ROCKS
ROCKSHAFT
ROCKSHAFTS
ROCKSTEADIES
ROCKSTEADY
ROCKWATER
ROCKWATERS
ROCKWEED
ROCKWEEDS
ROCKWORK
ROCKWORKS
ROCKY
ROCOCO
ROCOCOS
ROCQUET
ROCQUETS
ROCS
ROD
RODDED
RODDING
RODDINGS
RODE
RODED
RODENT

RODENTICIDE
RODENTICIDES
RODENTS
RODEO
RODEOED
RODEOING
RODEOS
RODES
RODEWAY
RODEWAYS
RODFISHER
RODFISHERS
RODFISHING
RODFISHINGS
RODGERSIA
RODGERSIAS
RODING
RODINGS
RODLESS
RODLIKE
RODMAN
RODMEN
RODOMONTADE
RODOMONTADED
RODOMONTADER
RODOMONTADERS
RODOMONTADES
RODOMONTADING
RODS
RODSMAN
RODSMEN
RODSTER
RODSTERS
ROE
ROEBUCK
ROEBUCKS
ROED
ROEMER
ROEMERS
ROENTGEN
ROENTGENISATION
ROENTGENISE
ROENTGENISED
ROENTGENISES
ROENTGENISING
ROENTGENIZATION
ROENTGENIZE
ROENTGENIZED
ROENTGENIZES
ROENTGENIZING
ROENTGENOGRAM
ROENTGENOGRAMS
ROENTGENOGRAPH
ROENTGENOGRAPHS
ROENTGENOGRAPHY
ROENTGENOLOGIC

ROENTGENOLOGIES
ROENTGENOLOGIST
ROENTGENOLOGY
ROENTGENOPAQUE
ROENTGENOSCOPE
ROENTGENOSCOPES
ROENTGENOSCOPIC
ROENTGENOSCOPY
ROENTGENS
ROES
ROESTONE
ROESTONES
ROGALLO
ROGALLOS
ROGATION
ROGATIONS
ROGATORY
ROGER
ROGERED
ROGERING
ROGERINGS
ROGERS
ROGNON
ROGNONS
ROGUE
ROGUED
ROGUEING
ROGUERIES
ROGUERY
ROGUES
ROGUESHIP
ROGUESHIPS
ROGUING
ROGUISH
ROGUISHLY
ROGUISHNESS
ROGUISHNESSES
ROGUY
ROIL
ROILED
ROILIER
ROILIEST
ROILING
ROILS
ROILY
ROIN
ROINED
ROINING
ROINISH
ROINS
ROIST
ROISTED
ROISTER
ROISTERED
ROISTERER
ROISTERERS

ROISTERING
ROISTERINGS
ROISTEROUS
ROISTEROUSLY
ROISTERS
ROISTING
ROISTS
ROJAK
ROJAKS
ROJI
ROJIS
ROK
ROKE
ROKED
ROKELAY
ROKELAYS
ROKER
ROKERS
ROKES
ROKIER
ROKIEST
ROKING
ROKKAKU
ROKS
ROKY
ROLAG
ROLAGS
ROLAMITE
ROLAMITES
ROLE
ROLES
ROLF
ROLFED
ROLFER
ROLFERS
ROLFING
ROLFINGS
ROLFS
ROLL
ROLLABLE
ROLLAWAY
ROLLBACK
ROLLBACKS
ROLLBAR
ROLLBARS
ROLLCOLLAR
ROLLCOLLARS
ROLLED
ROLLER
ROLLERBALL
ROLLERBALLS
ROLLERBLADE
ROLLERBLADED
ROLLERBLADER
ROLLERBLADERS
ROLLERBLADES

ROLLERBLADING
ROLLERBLADINGS
ROLLERCOASTER
ROLLERCOASTERED
ROLLERCOASTERS
ROLLERS
ROLLICK
ROLLICKED
ROLLICKING
ROLLICKINGS
ROLLICKS
ROLLICKY
ROLLING
ROLLINGS
ROLLMOP
ROLLMOPS
ROLLNECK
ROLLNECKS
ROLLOCK
ROLLOCKING
ROLLOCKINGS
ROLLOCKS
ROLLOUT
ROLLOUTS
ROLLOVER
ROLLOVERS
ROLLS
ROLLTOP
ROLLWAY
ROLLWAYS
ROM
ROMA
ROMAGE
ROMAGES
ROMAIKA
ROMAIKAS
ROMAINE
ROMAINES
ROMAJI
ROMAL
ROMALS
ROMAN
ROMANCE
ROMANCED
ROMANCER
ROMANCERS
ROMANCES
ROMANCICAL
ROMANCING
ROMANCINGS
ROMANICITE
ROMANISE
ROMANISED
ROMANISES
ROMANISING
ROMANIZATION

ROMANIZATIONS
ROMANIZE
ROMANIZED
ROMANIZES
ROMANIZING
ROMANO
ROMANOS
ROMANS
ROMANTIC
ROMANTICAL
ROMANTICALITIES
ROMANTICALITY
ROMANTICALLY
ROMANTICISATION
ROMANTICISE
ROMANTICISED
ROMANTICISES
ROMANTICISING
ROMANTICISM
ROMANTICISMS
ROMANTICIST
ROMANTICISTS
ROMANTICIZATION
ROMANTICIZE
ROMANTICIZED
ROMANTICIZES
ROMANTICIZING
ROMANTICS
ROMANZA
ROMANZAS
ROMAS
ROMAUNT
ROMAUNTS
ROMCOM
ROMCOMS
ROMELDALE
ROMELDALES
ROMEO
ROMEOS
ROMNEYA
ROMNEYAS
ROMP
ROMPED
ROMPER
ROMPERS
ROMPING
ROMPINGLY
ROMPISH
ROMPISHLY
ROMPISHNESS
ROMPISHNESSES
ROMPS
ROMS
RONCADOR
RONCADORS
RONCHIAL

RONDACHE
RONDACHES
RONDAVEL
RONDAVELS
RONDE
RONDEAU
RONDEAUX
RONDEL
RONDELET
RONDELETS
RONDELLE
RONDELLES
RONDELS
RONDES
RONDINO
RONDINOS
RONDO
RONDOLETTO
RONDOLETTOS
RONDOS
RONDURE
RONDURES
RONE
RONEO
RONEOED
RONEOING
RONEOS
RONEPIPE
RONEPIPES
RONES
RONG
RONGGENG
RONGGENGS
RONIN
RONINS
RONION
RONIONS
RONNE
RONNEL
RONNELS
RONNING
RONT
RONTE
RONTES
RONTGEN
RONTGENISATION
RONTGENISE
RONTGENISED
RONTGENISES
RONTGENISING
RONTGENIZATION
RONTGENIZE
RONTGENIZED
RONTGENIZES
RONTGENIZING
RONTGENOGRAM

RONTGENOGRAMS
RONTGENOGRAPH
RONTGENOGRAPHS
RONTGENOGRAPHY
RONTGENOLOGICAL
RONTGENOLOGIES
RONTGENOLOGIST
RONTGENOLOGISTS
RONTGENOLOGY
RONTGENOPAQUE
RONTGENOSCOPE
RONTGENOSCOPES
RONTGENOSCOPIC
RONTGENOSCOPIES
RONTGENOSCOPY
RONTGENOTHERAPY
RONTGENS
RONTS
RONYON
RONYONS
ROO
ROOD
ROODS
ROOF
ROOFED
ROOFER
ROOFERS
ROOFIER
ROOFIEST
ROOFING
ROOFINGS
ROOFLESS
ROOFLESSNESS
ROOFLESSNESSES
ROOFLIKE
ROOFLINE
ROOFLINES
ROOFS
ROOFSCAPE
ROOFSCAPES
ROOFTOP
ROOFTOPS
ROOFTREE
ROOFTREES
ROOFY
ROOIBOS
ROOIKAT
ROOIKATS
ROOINEK
ROOINEKS
ROOK
ROOKED
ROOKERIES
ROOKERY
ROOKIE
ROOKIER

ROOKIES
ROOKIEST
ROOKING
ROOKISH
ROOKS
ROOKY
ROOM
ROOMED
ROOMER
ROOMERS
ROOMETTE
ROOMETTES
ROOMFUL
ROOMFULS
ROOMIE
ROOMIER
ROOMIES
ROOMIEST
ROOMILY
ROOMINESS
ROOMINESSES
ROOMING
ROOMMATE
ROOMMATES
ROOMS
ROOMSOME
ROOMY
ROON
ROONS
ROOP
ROOPED
ROOPIER
ROOPIEST
ROOPING
ROOPIT
ROOPS
ROOPY
ROORBACH
ROORBACHS
ROORBACK
ROORBACKS
ROOS
ROOSA
ROOSAS
ROOSE
ROOSED
ROOSER
ROOSERS
ROOSES
ROOSING
ROOST
ROOSTED
ROOSTER
ROOSTERS
ROOSTING
ROOSTS

ROOT
ROOTAGE
ROOTAGES
ROOTED
ROOTEDLY
ROOTEDNESS
ROOTEDNESSES
ROOTER
ROOTERS
ROOTHOLD
ROOTHOLDS
ROOTIER
ROOTIES
ROOTIEST
ROOTINESS
ROOTING
ROOTINGS
ROOTLE
ROOTLED
ROOTLES
ROOTLESS
ROOTLESSNESS
ROOTLESSNESSES
ROOTLET
ROOTLETS
ROOTLIKE
ROOTLING
ROOTS
ROOTSERVER
ROOTSERVERS
ROOTSIER
ROOTSIEST
ROOTSINESS
ROOTSINESSES
ROOTSTALK
ROOTSTALKS
ROOTSTOCK
ROOTSTOCKS
ROOTSY
ROOTY
ROPABLE
ROPE
ROPEABLE
ROPED
ROPEDANCER
ROPEDANCERS
ROPEDANCING
ROPEDANCINGS
ROPELIKE
ROPER
ROPERIES
ROPERS
ROPERY
ROPES
ROPEWALK
ROPEWALKER

ROPEWALKERS
ROPEWALKS
ROPEWAY
ROPEWAYS
ROPEWORK
ROPEWORKS
ROPEY
ROPIER
ROPIEST
ROPILY
ROPINESS
ROPINESSES
ROPING
ROPINGS
ROPY
ROQUE
ROQUELAURE
ROQUELAURES
ROQUES
ROQUET
ROQUETED
ROQUETING
ROQUETS
ROQUETTE
ROQUETTES
RORAL
RORE
RORES
RORIC
RORID
RORIE
RORIER
RORIEST
RORQUAL
RORQUALS
RORT
RORTED
RORTER
RORTERS
RORTIER
RORTIEST
RORTING
RORTS
RORTY
RORY
ROSACE
ROSACEA
ROSACEAS
ROSACEOUS
ROSACES
ROSAKER
ROSAKERS
ROSALIA
ROSALIAS
ROSANILIN
ROSANILINE

ROSANILINES
ROSARIA
ROSARIAN
ROSARIANS
ROSARIES
ROSARIUM
ROSARIUMS
ROSARY
ROSBIF
ROSBIFS
ROSCID
ROSCOE
ROSCOES
ROSE
ROSEAL
ROSEATE
ROSEATELY
ROSEBAY
ROSEBAYS
ROSEBOWL
ROSEBOWLS
ROSEBUD
ROSEBUDS
ROSEBUSH
ROSEBUSHES
ROSED
ROSEFINCH
ROSEFINCHES
ROSEFISH
ROSEFISHES
ROSEHIP
ROSEHIPS
ROSELESS
ROSELIKE
ROSELLA
ROSELLAS
ROSELLE
ROSELLES
ROSEMALING
ROSEMALINGS
ROSEMARIES
ROSEMARY
ROSEOLA
ROSEOLAR
ROSEOLAS
ROSERIES
ROSEROOT
ROSEROOTS
ROSERY
ROSES
ROSESLUG
ROSESLUGS
ROSET
ROSETED
ROSETING
ROSETS

ROSETTE
ROSETTED
ROSETTES
ROSETTY
ROSETY
ROSEWATER
ROSEWATERS
ROSEWOOD
ROSEWOODS
ROSIED
ROSIER
ROSIERE
ROSIERES
ROSIERS
ROSIES
ROSIEST
ROSILY
ROSIN
ROSINATE
ROSINATES
ROSINED
ROSINER
ROSINERS
ROSINESS
ROSINESSES
ROSING
ROSINING
ROSINOL
ROSINOLS
ROSINOUS
ROSINS
ROSINWEED
ROSINWEEDS
ROSINY
ROSIT
ROSITED
ROSITING
ROSITS
ROSMARINE
ROSMARINES
ROSOGLIO
ROSOGLIOS
ROSOLIO
ROSOLIOS
ROSSER
ROSSERS
ROST
ROSTED
ROSTELLA
ROSTELLAR
ROSTELLATE
ROSTELLUM
ROSTELLUMS
ROSTER
ROSTERED
ROSTERING

ROSTERINGS
ROSTERS
ROSTING
ROSTRA
ROSTRAL
ROSTRALLY
ROSTRATE
ROSTRATED
ROSTROCARINATE
ROSTROCARINATES
ROSTRUM
ROSTRUMS
ROSTS
ROSULA
ROSULAS
ROSULATE
ROSY
ROSYING
ROT
ROTA
ROTACHUTE
ROTACHUTES
ROTAL
ROTAMETER
ROTAMETERS
ROTAN
ROTANS
ROTAPLANE
ROTAPLANES
ROTARIES
ROTARY
ROTAS
ROTATABLE
ROTATE
ROTATED
ROTATES
ROTATING
ROTATION
ROTATIONAL
ROTATIONS
ROTATIVE
ROTATIVELY
ROTATOR
ROTATORES
ROTATORS
ROTATORY
ROTAVATE
ROTAVATED
ROTAVATES
ROTAVATING
ROTAVATOR
ROTAVATORS
ROTAVIRUS
ROTAVIRUSES
ROTCH
ROTCHE

ROTCHES
ROTCHIE
ROTCHIES
ROTE
ROTED
ROTENONE
ROTENONES
ROTES
ROTGRASS
ROTGRASSES
ROTGUT
ROTGUTS
ROTHER
ROTHERS
ROTI
ROTIFER
ROTIFERAL
ROTIFEROUS
ROTIFERS
ROTIFORM
ROTING
ROTIS
ROTISSERIE
ROTISSERIES
ROTL
ROTLS
ROTO
ROTOGRAPH
ROTOGRAPHED
ROTOGRAPHING
ROTOGRAPHS
ROTOGRAVURE
ROTOGRAVURES
ROTOLO
ROTOLOS
ROTON
ROTONS
ROTOR
ROTORCRAFT
ROTORCRAFTS
ROTORS
ROTOS
ROTOTILL
ROTOTILLED
ROTOTILLER
ROTOTILLERS
ROTOTILLING
ROTOTILLS
ROTOVATE
ROTOVATED
ROTOVATES
ROTOVATING
ROTOVATOR
ROTOVATORS
ROTS
ROTTAN

ROTTANS
ROTTE
ROTTED
ROTTEN
ROTTENER
ROTTENEST
ROTTENLY
ROTTENNESS
ROTTENNESSES
ROTTENS
ROTTENSTONE
ROTTENSTONED
ROTTENSTONES
ROTTENSTONING
ROTTER
ROTTERS
ROTTES
ROTTING
ROTTWEILER
ROTTWEILERS
ROTULA
ROTULAS
ROTUND
ROTUNDA
ROTUNDAS
ROTUNDATE
ROTUNDED
ROTUNDER
ROTUNDEST
ROTUNDING
ROTUNDITIES
ROTUNDITY
ROTUNDLY
ROTUNDNESS
ROTUNDNESSES
ROTUNDS
ROTURIER
ROTURIERS
ROUBLE
ROUBLES
ROUCHE
ROUCHES
ROUCOU
ROUCOUS
ROUE
ROUEN
ROUENS
ROUES
ROUGE
ROUGED
ROUGES
ROUGH
ROUGHAGE
ROUGHAGES
ROUGHCAST
ROUGHCASTED

ROUGHCASTER
ROUGHCASTERS
ROUGHCASTING
ROUGHCASTS
ROUGHDRIED
ROUGHDRIES
ROUGHDRY
ROUGHDRYING
ROUGHED
ROUGHEN
ROUGHENED
ROUGHENING
ROUGHENS
ROUGHER
ROUGHERS
ROUGHEST
ROUGHHEW
ROUGHHEWED
ROUGHHEWING
ROUGHHEWN
ROUGHHEWS
ROUGHHOUSE
ROUGHHOUSED
ROUGHHOUSES
ROUGHHOUSING
ROUGHIE
ROUGHIES
ROUGHING
ROUGHISH
ROUGHLEG
ROUGHLEGS
ROUGHLY
ROUGHNECK
ROUGHNECKED
ROUGHNECKING
ROUGHNECKS
ROUGHNESS
ROUGHNESSES
ROUGHRIDER
ROUGHRIDERS
ROUGHS
ROUGHSHOD
ROUGHT
ROUGHY
ROUGING
ROUILLE
ROUILLES
ROUL
ROULADE
ROULADES
ROULE
ROULEAU
ROULEAUS
ROULEAUX
ROULES
ROULETTE

ROULETTED
ROULETTES
ROULETTING
ROULS
ROUM
ROUMING
ROUMINGS
ROUMS
ROUNCE
ROUNCES
ROUNCEVAL
ROUNCEVALS
ROUNCIES
ROUNCY
ROUND
ROUNDABOUT
ROUNDABOUTATION
ROUNDABOUTED
ROUNDABOUTEDLY
ROUNDABOUTING
ROUNDABOUTLY
ROUNDABOUTNESS
ROUNDABOUTS
ROUNDARCH
ROUNDARCHED
ROUNDED
ROUNDEDLY
ROUNDEDNESS
ROUNDEDNESSES
ROUNDEL
ROUNDELAY
ROUNDELAYS
ROUNDELS
ROUNDER
ROUNDERS
ROUNDEST
ROUNDHAND
ROUNDHANDS
ROUNDHEADED
ROUNDHEADEDNESS
ROUNDHOUSE
ROUNDHOUSES
ROUNDING
ROUNDINGS
ROUNDISH
ROUNDLE
ROUNDLES
ROUNDLET
ROUNDLETS
ROUNDLY
ROUNDNESS
ROUNDNESSES
ROUNDS
ROUNDSMAN
ROUNDSMEN
ROUNDTABLE

ROUNDTABLES
ROUNDTRIPPER
ROUNDTRIPPERS
ROUNDTRIPPING
ROUNDUP
ROUNDUPS
ROUNDURE
ROUNDURES
ROUNDWOOD
ROUNDWOODS
ROUNDWORM
ROUNDWORMS
ROUP
ROUPED
ROUPET
ROUPIER
ROUPIEST
ROUPILY
ROUPING
ROUPIT
ROUPS
ROUPY
ROUSANT
ROUSE
ROUSEABOUT
ROUSEABOUTS
ROUSED
ROUSEDLY
ROUSEDNESS
ROUSEMENT
ROUSEMENTS
ROUSER
ROUSERS
ROUSES
ROUSING
ROUSINGLY
ROUSSEAU
ROUSSEAUS
ROUSSETTE
ROUSSETTES
ROUST
ROUSTABOUT
ROUSTABOUTS
ROUSTED
ROUSTER
ROUSTERS
ROUSTING
ROUSTS
ROUT
ROUTE
ROUTED
ROUTEING
ROUTEMAN
ROUTEMARCH
ROUTEMARCHED
ROUTEMARCHES

ROUTEMARCHING	ROWDIER	ROYALISTS	RUBBER
ROUTEMEN	ROWDIES	ROYALIZE	RUBBERED
ROUTER	ROWDIEST	ROYALIZED	RUBBERIER
ROUTERS	ROWDILY	ROYALIZES	RUBBERIEST
ROUTES	ROWDINESS	ROYALIZING	RUBBERING
ROUTEWAY	ROWDINESSES	ROYALLER	RUBBERISE
ROUTEWAYS	ROWDY	ROYALLEST	RUBBERISED
ROUTH	ROWDYDOW	ROYALLY	RUBBERISES
ROUTHIE	ROWDYDOWS	ROYALS	RUBBERISING
ROUTHIER	ROWDYISH	ROYALTIES	RUBBERIZE
ROUTHIEST	ROWDYISM	ROYALTY	RUBBERIZED
ROUTHS	ROWDYISMS	ROYNE	RUBBERIZES
ROUTINE	ROWED	ROYNED	RUBBERIZING
ROUTINEER	ROWEL	ROYNES	RUBBERLIKE
ROUTINEERS	ROWELED	ROYNING	RUBBERNECK
ROUTINELY	ROWELING	ROYNISH	RUBBERNECKED
ROUTINES	ROWELLED	ROYST	RUBBERNECKER
ROUTING	ROWELLING	ROYSTED	RUBBERNECKERS
ROUTINGS	ROWELS	ROYSTER	RUBBERNECKING
ROUTINISE	ROWEN	ROYSTERED	RUBBERNECKS
ROUTINISED	ROWENS	ROYSTERER	RUBBERS
ROUTINISES	ROWER	ROYSTERERS	RUBBERWEAR
ROUTINISING	ROWERS	ROYSTERING	RUBBERWEARS
ROUTINISM	ROWING	ROYSTEROUS	RUBBERY
ROUTINISMS	ROWINGS	ROYSTERS	RUBBET
ROUTINIST	ROWLOCK	ROYSTING	RUBBIDIES
ROUTINISTS	ROWLOCKS	ROYSTS	RUBBIDY
ROUTINIZATION	ROWME	ROZELLE	RUBBIES
ROUTINIZATIONS	ROWMES	ROZELLES	RUBBING
ROUTINIZE	ROWND	ROZET	RUBBINGS
ROUTINIZED	ROWNDED	ROZETED	RUBBISH
ROUTINIZES	ROWNDELL	ROZETING	RUBBISHED
ROUTINIZING	ROWNDELLS	ROZETS	RUBBISHES
ROUTOUS	ROWNDING	ROZIT	RUBBISHING
ROUTOUSLY	ROWNDS	ROZITED	RUBBISHLY
ROUTS	ROWOVER	ROZITING	RUBBISHY
ROUX	ROWOVERS	ROZITS	RUBBIT
ROVE	ROWS	ROZZER	RUBBITIES
ROVED	ROWT	ROZZERS	RUBBITY
ROVEN	ROWTED	RUANA	RUBBLE
ROVER	ROWTH	RUANAS	RUBBLED
ROVERS	ROWTHS	RUB	RUBBLES
ROVES	ROWTING	RUBABOO	RUBBLEWORK
ROVING	ROWTS	RUBABOOS	RUBBLIER
ROVINGLY	ROYAL	RUBACE	RUBBLIEST
ROVINGS	ROYALET	RUBACES	RUBBLINESS
ROW	ROYALETS	RUBAI	RUBBLING
ROWABLE	ROYALISE	RUBAIYAT	RUBBLY
ROWAN	ROYALISED	RUBASSE	RUBBY
ROWANBERRIES	ROYALISES	RUBASSES	RUBDOWN
ROWANBERRY	ROYALISING	RUBATI	RUBDOWNS
ROWANS	ROYALISM	RUBATO	RUBE
ROWBOAT	ROYALISMS	RUBATOS	RUBEFACIENT
ROWBOATS	ROYALIST	RUBBABOO	RUBEFACIENTS
ROWDEDOW	ROYALISTIC	RUBBABOOS	RUBEFACTION
ROWDEDOWS	ROYALISTICALLY	RUBBED	RUBEFACTIONS

RUBEFIED
RUBEFIES
RUBEFY
RUBEFYING
RUBELLA
RUBELLAN
RUBELLANS
RUBELLAS
RUBELLITE
RUBELLITES
RUBEOLA
RUBEOLAR
RUBEOLAS
RUBES
RUBESCENCE
RUBESCENT
RUBESCENTLY
RUBIACEOUS
RUBICELLE
RUBICELLES
RUBICON
RUBICONED
RUBICONING
RUBICONS
RUBICUND
RUBICUNDITIES
RUBICUNDITY
RUBIDIC
RUBIDIUM
RUBIDIUMS
RUBIED
RUBIER
RUBIES
RUBIEST
RUBIFIED
RUBIFIES
RUBIFY
RUBIFYING
RUBIGINOSE
RUBIGINOUS
RUBIGO
RUBIGOS
RUBIN
RUBINE
RUBINEOUS
RUBINES
RUBINS
RUBIOUS
RUBLE
RUBLES
RUBOFF
RUBOFFS
RUBOUT
RUBOUTS
RUBRIC
RUBRICAL

RUBRICALLY
RUBRICATE
RUBRICATED
RUBRICATES
RUBRICATING
RUBRICATION
RUBRICATIONS
RUBRICATOR
RUBRICATORS
RUBRICIAN
RUBRICIANS
RUBRICS
RUBS
RUBSTONE
RUBSTONES
RUBUS
RUBY
RUBYING
RUBYLIKE
RUBYTHROAT
RUBYTHROATS
RUC
RUCHE
RUCHED
RUCHES
RUCHING
RUCHINGS
RUCK
RUCKED
RUCKING
RUCKLE
RUCKLED
RUCKLES
RUCKLING
RUCKMAN
RUCKS
RUCKSACK
RUCKSACKS
RUCKSEAT
RUCKSEATS
RUCKUS
RUCKUSES
RUCOLA
RUCOLAS
RUCS
RUCTATION
RUCTATIONS
RUCTION
RUCTIONS
RUCTIOUS
RUD
RUDACEOUS
RUDAS
RUDASES
RUDBECKIA
RUDBECKIAS

RUDD
RUDDED
RUDDER
RUDDERHEAD
RUDDERHEADS
RUDDERLESS
RUDDERPOST
RUDDERPOSTS
RUDDERS
RUDDERSTOCK
RUDDERSTOCKS
RUDDIED
RUDDIER
RUDDIES
RUDDIEST
RUDDILY
RUDDINESS
RUDDINESSES
RUDDING
RUDDLE
RUDDLED
RUDDLEMAN
RUDDLEMEN
RUDDLES
RUDDLING
RUDDOCK
RUDDOCKS
RUDDS
RUDDY
RUDDYING
RUDE
RUDELY
RUDENESS
RUDENESSES
RUDER
RUDERAL
RUDERALS
RUDERIES
RUDERY
RUDES
RUDESBIES
RUDESBY
RUDEST
RUDIE
RUDIES
RUDIMENT
RUDIMENTAL
RUDIMENTALLY
RUDIMENTARILY
RUDIMENTARINESS
RUDIMENTARY
RUDIMENTS
RUDISH
RUDS
RUE
RUED

RUEFUL
RUEFULLY
RUEFULNESS
RUEFULNESSES
RUEING
RUEINGS
RUELLE
RUELLES
RUELLIA
RUELLIAS
RUER
RUERS
RUES
RUFESCENCE
RUFESCENT
RUFF
RUFFE
RUFFED
RUFFES
RUFFIAN
RUFFIANED
RUFFIANING
RUFFIANISH
RUFFIANISM
RUFFIANISMS
RUFFIANLY
RUFFIANS
RUFFIN
RUFFING
RUFFINS
RUFFLE
RUFFLED
RUFFLER
RUFFLERS
RUFFLES
RUFFLIER
RUFFLIEST
RUFFLIKE
RUFFLING
RUFFLINGS
RUFFLY
RUFFS
RUFIYAA
RUFIYAAS
RUFOUS
RUG
RUGA
RUGAE
RUGAL
RUGATE
RUGBIES
RUGBY
RUGELACH
RUGGED
RUGGEDER
RUGGEDEST

RUGGEDISE
RUGGEDISED
RUGGEDISES
RUGGEDISING
RUGGEDIZATION
RUGGEDIZATIONS
RUGGEDIZE
RUGGEDIZED
RUGGEDIZES
RUGGEDIZING
RUGGEDLY
RUGGEDNESS
RUGGEDNESSES
RUGGELACH
RUGGER
RUGGERS
RUGGIER
RUGGIEST
RUGGING
RUGGINGS
RUGGY
RUGLIKE
RUGOLA
RUGOLAS
RUGOSA
RUGOSAS
RUGOSE
RUGOSELY
RUGOSITIES
RUGOSITY
RUGOUS
RUGS
RUGULOSE
RUIN
RUINABLE
RUINATE
RUINATED
RUINATES
RUINATING
RUINATION
RUINATIONS
RUINED
RUINER
RUINERS
RUING
RUINGS
RUINING
RUININGS
RUINOUS
RUINOUSLY
RUINOUSNESS
RUINOUSNESSES
RUINS
RUKH
RUKHS
RULABLE

RULE
RULED
RULELESS
RULER
RULERED
RULERING
RULERS
RULERSHIP
RULERSHIPS
RULES
RULESSE
RULIER
RULIEST
RULING
RULINGS
RULLION
RULLIONS
RULLOCK
RULLOCKS
RULY
RUM
RUMAKI
RUMAKIS
RUMAL
RUMALS
RUMBA
RUMBAED
RUMBAING
RUMBAS
RUMBELOW
RUMBELOWS
RUMBLE
RUMBLED
RUMBLEDETHUMP
RUMBLEDETHUMPS
RUMBLEGUMPTION
RUMBLEGUMPTIONS
RUMBLER
RUMBLERS
RUMBLES
RUMBLIER
RUMBLIEST
RUMBLING
RUMBLINGLY
RUMBLINGS
RUMBLY
RUMBO
RUMBOS
RUMBULLION
RUMBULLIONS
RUMBUSTICAL
RUMBUSTIOUS
RUMBUSTIOUSLY
RUMBUSTIOUSNESS
RUME
RUMELGUMPTIONS

RUMEN
RUMENS
RUMES
RUMFUSTIAN
RUMFUSTIANS
RUMGUMPTION
RUMGUMPTIONS
RUMINA
RUMINAL
RUMINANT
RUMINANTLY
RUMINANTS
RUMINATE
RUMINATED
RUMINATES
RUMINATING
RUMINATINGLY
RUMINATION
RUMINATIONS
RUMINATIVE
RUMINATIVELY
RUMINATOR
RUMINATORS
RUMKIN
RUMKINS
RUMLEGUMPTIONS
RUMLY
RUMMAGE
RUMMAGED
RUMMAGER
RUMMAGERS
RUMMAGES
RUMMAGING
RUMMELGUMPTIONS
RUMMER
RUMMERS
RUMMEST
RUMMIER
RUMMIES
RUMMIEST
RUMMILY
RUMMINESS
RUMMINESSES
RUMMISH
RUMMLEGUMPTION
RUMMLEGUMPTIONS
RUMMY
RUMNESS
RUMNESSES
RUMOR
RUMORED
RUMORING
RUMORMONGER
RUMORMONGERING
RUMORMONGERINGS
RUMORMONGERS

RUMOROUS
RUMORS
RUMOUR
RUMOURED
RUMOURER
RUMOURERS
RUMOURING
RUMOURS
RUMP
RUMPED
RUMPIES
RUMPING
RUMPLE
RUMPLED
RUMPLES
RUMPLESS
RUMPLIER
RUMPLIEST
RUMPLING
RUMPLY
RUMPS
RUMPUS
RUMPUSES
RUMPY
RUMRUNNER
RUMRUNNERS
RUMS
RUN
RUNABOUT
RUNABOUTS
RUNAGATE
RUNAGATES
RUNANGA
RUNANGAS
RUNAROUND
RUNAROUNDS
RUNAWAY
RUNAWAYS
RUNBACK
RUNBACKS
RUNCH
RUNCHES
RUNCIBLE
RUNCINATE
RUND
RUNDALE
RUNDALES
RUNDLE
RUNDLED
RUNDLES
RUNDLET
RUNDLETS
RUNDOWN
RUNDOWNS
RUNDS
RUNE

RUNECRAFT
RUNECRAFTS
RUNED
RUNELIKE
RUNES
RUNFLAT
RUNG
RUNGLESS
RUNGS
RUNIC
RUNKLE
RUNKLED
RUNKLES
RUNKLING
RUNLESS
RUNLET
RUNLETS
RUNNABLE
RUNNEL
RUNNELS
RUNNER
RUNNERS
RUNNET
RUNNETS
RUNNIER
RUNNIEST
RUNNING
RUNNINGLY
RUNNINGS
RUNNION
RUNNIONS
RUNNY
RUNOFF
RUNOFFS
RUNOUT
RUNOUTS
RUNOVER
RUNOVERS
RUNRIG
RUNRIGS
RUNROUND
RUNROUNDS
RUNS
RUNT
RUNTED
RUNTIER
RUNTIEST
RUNTINESS
RUNTINESSES
RUNTISH
RUNTS
RUNTY
RUNWAY
RUNWAYS
RUPEE
RUPEES

RUPESTRIAN
RUPIA
RUPIAH
RUPIAHS
RUPIAS
RUPICOLINE
RUPICOLOUS
RUPTURABILITY
RUPTURABLE
RUPTURE
RUPTURED
RUPTURES
RUPTUREWORT
RUPTUREWORTS
RUPTURING
RURAL
RURALISATION
RURALISATIONS
RURALISE
RURALISED
RURALISES
RURALISING
RURALISM
RURALISMS
RURALIST
RURALISTS
RURALITE
RURALITES
RURALITIES
RURALITY
RURALIZATION
RURALIZATIONS
RURALIZE
RURALIZED
RURALIZES
RURALIZING
RURALLY
RURALNESS
RURALNESSES
RURALS
RURBAN
RURIDECANAL
RURP
RURPS
RURU
RURUS
RUSA
RUSALKA
RUSALKAS
RUSAS
RUSCUS
RUSCUSES
RUSE
RUSES
RUSH
RUSHED

RUSHEE
RUSHEES
RUSHEN
RUSHER
RUSHERS
RUSHES
RUSHIER
RUSHIEST
RUSHINESS
RUSHINESSES
RUSHING
RUSHINGS
RUSHLIGHT
RUSHLIGHTS
RUSHLIKE
RUSHY
RUSINE
RUSK
RUSKS
RUSMA
RUSMAS
RUSSEL
RUSSELS
RUSSET
RUSSETED
RUSSETING
RUSSETINGS
RUSSETS
RUSSETTING
RUSSETTINGS
RUSSETY
RUSSIA
RUSSIAS
RUSSIFIED
RUSSIFIES
RUSSIFY
RUSSIFYING
RUSSULA
RUSSULAE
RUSSULAS
RUST
RUSTABLE
RUSTBUCKET
RUSTBUCKETS
RUSTED
RUSTIC
RUSTICAL
RUSTICALLY
RUSTICALS
RUSTICANA
RUSTICATE
RUSTICATED
RUSTICATES
RUSTICATING
RUSTICATION
RUSTICATIONS

RUSTICATOR
RUSTICATORS
RUSTICIAL
RUSTICISE
RUSTICISED
RUSTICISES
RUSTICISING
RUSTICISM
RUSTICISMS
RUSTICITIES
RUSTICITY
RUSTICIZE
RUSTICIZED
RUSTICIZES
RUSTICIZING
RUSTICLY
RUSTICS
RUSTICWORK
RUSTIER
RUSTIEST
RUSTILY
RUSTINESS
RUSTINESSES
RUSTING
RUSTINGS
RUSTLE
RUSTLED
RUSTLER
RUSTLERS
RUSTLES
RUSTLESS
RUSTLING
RUSTLINGLY
RUSTLINGS
RUSTPROOF
RUSTRE
RUSTRED
RUSTRES
RUSTS
RUSTY
RUT
RUTABAGA
RUTABAGAS
RUTACEOUS
RUTH
RUTHENIC
RUTHENIOUS
RUTHENIUM
RUTHENIUMS
RUTHERFORD
RUTHERFORDIUM
RUTHERFORDIUMS
RUTHERFORDS
RUTHFUL
RUTHFULLY
RUTHFULNESS

RUTHFULNESSES
RUTHLESS
RUTHLESSLY
RUTHLESSNESS
RUTHLESSNESSES
RUTHS
RUTILANT
RUTILATED
RUTILE
RUTILES
RUTIN
RUTINS
RUTS
RUTTED
RUTTER
RUTTERS
RUTTIER
RUTTIEST
RUTTILY
RUTTINESS
RUTTING
RUTTINGS
RUTTISH
RUTTISHLY
RUTTISHNESS
RUTTISHNESSES
RUTTY
RYA
RYAL
RYALS
RYAS
RYBAT
RYBATS
RYBAUDRYE
RYBAUDRYES
RYBAULDS
RYE
RYEBREAD
RYEBREADS
RYEFLOUR
RYEFLOURS
RYEGRASS
RYEGRASSES
RYEPECK
RYEPECKS
RYES
RYFE
RYKE
RYKED
RYKES
RYKING
RYMME
RYMMED
RYMMES
RYMMING
RYND

RYNDS
RYOKAN
RYOKANS
RYOT
RYOTS
RYOTWARI
RYOTWARIS
RYPE
RYPECK
RYPECKS
RYPER

S

SAB
SABADILLA
SABADILLAS
SABATON
SABATONS
SABAYON
SABAYONS
SABBAT
SABBATARIAN
SABBATH
SABBATHS
SABBATIC
SABBATICAL
SABBATICALS
SABBATICS
SABBATINE
SABBATISE
SABBATISED
SABBATISES
SABBATISING
SABBATISM
SABBATISMS
SABBATIZE
SABBATIZED
SABBATIZES
SABBATIZING
SABBATS
SABBED
SABBING
SABE
SABED
SABEING
SABELLA
SABELLAS
SABER
SABERED
SABERING
SABERMETRICIAN
SABERMETRICIANS
SABERMETRICS
SABERS
SABES
SABIN
SABINE
SABINES
SABINS
SABIR
SABIRS
SABKHA
SABKHAH
SABKHAHS
SABKHAS

SABKHAT
SABKHATS
SABLE
SABLED
SABLEFISH
SABLEFISHES
SABLES
SABLING
SABOT
SABOTAGE
SABOTAGED
SABOTAGES
SABOTAGING
SABOTEUR
SABOTEURS
SABOTIER
SABOTIERS
SABOTS
SABRA
SABRAS
SABRE
SABRED
SABRES
SABRETACHE
SABRETACHES
SABREUR
SABREURS
SABRING
SABS
SABULINE
SABULOSE
SABULOSITY
SABULOUS
SABURRA
SABURRAL
SABURRAS
SABURRATION
SABURRATIONS
SAC
SACAHUISTA
SACAHUISTAS
SACAHUISTE
SACAHUISTES
SACATON
SACATONS
SACBUT
SACBUTS
SACCADE
SACCADES
SACCADIC
SACCADICALLY
SACCATE

SACCHARASE
SACCHARASES
SACCHARATE
SACCHARATED
SACCHARATES
SACCHARIC
SACCHARIDE
SACCHARIDES
SACCHARIFEROUS
SACCHARIFIED
SACCHARIFIES
SACCHARIFY
SACCHARIFYING
SACCHARIMETER
SACCHARIMETERS
SACCHARIMETRIES
SACCHARIMETRY
SACCHARIN
SACCHARINE
SACCHARINELY
SACCHARINENESS
SACCHARINES
SACCHARINITIES
SACCHARINITY
SACCHARINS
SACCHARISATION
SACCHARISATIONS
SACCHARISE
SACCHARISED
SACCHARISES
SACCHARISING
SACCHARIZATION
SACCHARIZATIONS
SACCHARIZE
SACCHARIZED
SACCHARIZES
SACCHARIZING
SACCHAROID
SACCHAROIDAL
SACCHAROIDS
SACCHAROMETER
SACCHAROMETERS
SACCHAROMYCES
SACCHAROMYCETES
SACCHAROSE
SACCHAROSES
SACCHARUM
SACCHARUMS
SACCIFORM
SACCOI
SACCOS
SACCOSES

SACCULAR
SACCULATE
SACCULATED
SACCULATION
SACCULATIONS
SACCULE
SACCULES
SACCULI
SACCULIFORM
SACCULUS
SACELLA
SACELLUM
SACERDOTAL
SACERDOTALISE
SACERDOTALISED
SACERDOTALISES
SACERDOTALISING
SACERDOTALISM
SACERDOTALISMS
SACERDOTALIST
SACERDOTALISTS
SACERDOTALIZE
SACERDOTALIZED
SACERDOTALIZES
SACERDOTALIZING
SACERDOTALLY
SACHEM
SACHEMDOM
SACHEMDOMS
SACHEMIC
SACHEMS
SACHEMSHIP
SACHEMSHIPS
SACHET
SACHETED
SACHETS
SACK
SACKABILITY
SACKABLE
SACKAGE
SACKAGES
SACKBUT
SACKBUTS
SACKCLOTH
SACKCLOTHS
SACKED
SACKER
SACKERS
SACKFUL
SACKFULS
SACKING
SACKINGS

SACKLESS
SACKLIKE
SACKS
SACKSFUL
SACLESS
SACLIKE
SACQUE
SACQUES
SACRA
SACRAL
SACRALGIA
SACRALGIAS
SACRALISATION
SACRALISATIONS
SACRALISE
SACRALISED
SACRALISES
SACRALISING
SACRALIZATION
SACRALIZATIONS
SACRALIZE
SACRALIZED
SACRALIZES
SACRALIZING
SACRALS
SACRAMENT
SACRAMENTAL
SACRAMENTALISM
SACRAMENTALISMS
SACRAMENTALIST
SACRAMENTALISTS
SACRAMENTALITY
SACRAMENTALLY
SACRAMENTALNESS
SACRAMENTALS
SACRAMENTARIAN
SACRAMENTARIANS
SACRAMENTARIES
SACRAMENTARY
SACRAMENTED
SACRAMENTING
SACRAMENTS
SACRARIA
SACRARIUM
SACRED
SACREDLY
SACREDNESS
SACREDNESSES
SACRIFICE
SACRIFICEABLE
SACRIFICED
SACRIFICER
SACRIFICERS
SACRIFICES
SACRIFICIAL
SACRIFICIALLY
SACRIFICING

SACRIFIDE
SACRIFIED
SACRIFIES
SACRIFY
SACRIFYING
SACRILEGE
SACRILEGES
SACRILEGIOUS
SACRILEGIOUSLY
SACRILEGIST
SACRILEGISTS
SACRING
SACRINGS
SACRIST
SACRISTAN
SACRISTANS
SACRISTIES
SACRISTS
SACRISTY
SACROCOCCYGEAL
SACROCOSTAL
SACROCOSTALS
SACROILIAC
SACROILIACS
SACROILIITIS
SACROILIITISES
SACROSANCT
SACROSANCTITIES
SACROSANCTITY
SACROSANCTNESS
SACRUM
SACRUMS
SACS
SAD
SADDEN
SADDENED
SADDENING
SADDENS
SADDER
SADDEST
SADDHU
SADDHUS
SADDISH
SADDLE
SADDLEBACK
SADDLEBACKED
SADDLEBACKS
SADDLEBAG
SADDLEBAGS
SADDLEBILL
SADDLEBILLS
SADDLEBOW
SADDLEBOWS
SADDLEBRED
SADDLEBREDS
SADDLECLOTH
SADDLECLOTHS

SADDLED
SADDLELESS
SADDLER
SADDLERIES
SADDLEROOM
SADDLEROOMS
SADDLERS
SADDLERY
SADDLES
SADDLETREE
SADDLETREES
SADDLING
SADDO
SADDOS
SADE
SADES
SADHANA
SADHE
SADHES
SADHU
SADHUS
SADI
SADIRON
SADIRONS
SADIS
SADISM
SADISMS
SADIST
SADISTIC
SADISTICALLY
SADISTS
SADLY
SADNESS
SADNESSES
SADO
SADOMASOCHISM
SADOMASOCHISMS
SADOMASOCHIST
SADOMASOCHISTIC
SADOMASOCHISTS
SADZA
SADZAS
SAE
SAECULUM
SAECULUMS
SAETER
SAETERS
SAFARI
SAFARIED
SAFARIING
SAFARIS
SAFARIST
SAFARISTS
SAFE
SAFECRACKER
SAFECRACKERS
SAFECRACKING

SAFECRACKINGS
SAFED
SAFEGUARD
SAFEGUARDED
SAFEGUARDING
SAFEGUARDS
SAFEKEEPING
SAFEKEEPINGS
SAFELIGHT
SAFELIGHTS
SAFELY
SAFENESS
SAFENESSES
SAFER
SAFES
SAFEST
SAFETIED
SAFETIES
SAFETY
SAFETYING
SAFETYMAN
SAFETYMEN
SAFFIAN
SAFFIANS
SAFFLOWER
SAFFLOWERS
SAFFRON
SAFFRONED
SAFFRONS
SAFFRONY
SAFING
SAFRANIN
SAFRANINE
SAFRANINES
SAFRANINS
SAFROL
SAFROLE
SAFROLES
SAFROLS
SAFRONAL
SAFRONALS
SAFT
SAFTER
SAFTEST
SAFTNESS
SAG
SAGA
SAGACIOUS
SAGACIOUSLY
SAGACIOUSNESS
SAGACIOUSNESSES
SAGACITIES
SAGACITY
SAGAMAN
SAGAMEN
SAGAMORE
SAGAMORES

SAGANASH
SAGANASHES
SAGAPENUM
SAGAPENUMS
SAGAS
SAGATHIES
SAGATHY
SAGBUT
SAGBUTS
SAGE
SAGEBRUSH
SAGEBRUSHES
SAGELY
SAGENE
SAGENES
SAGENESS
SAGENESSES
SAGENITE
SAGENITES
SAGENITIC
SAGER
SAGES
SAGEST
SAGGAR
SAGGARD
SAGGARDS
SAGGARED
SAGGARING
SAGGARS
SAGGED
SAGGER
SAGGERED
SAGGERING
SAGGERS
SAGGIER
SAGGIEST
SAGGING
SAGGINGS
SAGGY
SAGIER
SAGIEST
SAGINATE
SAGINATED
SAGINATES
SAGINATING
SAGINATION
SAGINATIONS
SAGITTA
SAGITTAL
SAGITTALLY
SAGITTARIAN
SAGITTARIANS
SAGITTARIES
SAGITTARY
SAGITTAS
SAGITTATE
SAGITTIFORM

SAGO
SAGOIN
SAGOINS
SAGOS
SAGOUIN
SAGOUINS
SAGS
SAGUARO
SAGUAROS
SAGUIN
SAGUINS
SAGUM
SAGY
SAHEB
SAHEBS
SAHIB
SAHIBA
SAHIBAH
SAHIBAHS
SAHIBAS
SAHIBS
SAHIWAL
SAHIWALS
SAHUARO
SAHUAROS
SAI
SAIBLING
SAIBLINGS
SAIC
SAICE
SAICES
SAICK
SAICKS
SAICS
SAID
SAIDEST
SAIDS
SAIDST
SAIGA
SAIGAS
SAIKEI
SAIKEIS
SAIKLESS
SAIL
SAILABLE
SAILBOARD
SAILBOARDER
SAILBOARDERS
SAILBOARDING
SAILBOARDINGS
SAILBOARDS
SAILBOAT
SAILBOATER
SAILBOATERS
SAILBOATING
SAILBOATINGS
SAILBOATS

SAILCLOTH
SAILCLOTHS
SAILED
SAILER
SAILERS
SAILFISH
SAILFISHES
SAILING
SAILINGS
SAILLESS
SAILOR
SAILORING
SAILORINGS
SAILORLESS
SAILORLIKE
SAILORLY
SAILORS
SAILPLANE
SAILPLANED
SAILPLANER
SAILPLANERS
SAILPLANES
SAILPLANING
SAILROOM
SAILROOMS
SAILS
SAIM
SAIMIN
SAIMINS
SAIMIRI
SAIMIRIS
SAIMS
SAIN
SAINE
SAINED
SAINFOIN
SAINFOINS
SAINING
SAINS
SAINT
SAINTDOM
SAINTDOMS
SAINTED
SAINTESS
SAINTESSES
SAINTFOIN
SAINTFOINS
SAINTHOOD
SAINTHOODS
SAINTING
SAINTISH
SAINTISM
SAINTISMS
SAINTLESS
SAINTLIER
SAINTLIEST
SAINTLIKE

SAINTLILY
SAINTLINESS
SAINTLINESSES
SAINTLING
SAINTLINGS
SAINTLY
SAINTPAULIA
SAINTPAULIAS
SAINTS
SAINTSHIP
SAINTSHIPS
SAIQUE
SAIQUES
SAIR
SAIRED
SAIRER
SAIREST
SAIRING
SAIRS
SAIS
SAIST
SAITH
SAITHE
SAITHES
SAITHS
SAIYID
SAIYIDS
SAJOU
SAJOUS
SAKAI
SAKAIS
SAKE
SAKER
SAKERET
SAKERETS
SAKERS
SAKES
SAKI
SAKIA
SAKIAS
SAKIEH
SAKIEHS
SAKIS
SAKIYEH
SAKIYEHS
SAKKOI
SAKKOS
SAKKOSES
SAKSAUL
SAKSAULS
SAL
SALAAM
SALAAMED
SALAAMING
SALAAMS
SALABILITIES
SALABILITY

SALABLE
SALABLENESS
SALABLENESSES
SALABLY
SALACIOUS
SALACIOUSLY
SALACIOUSNESS
SALACIOUSNESSES
SALACITIES
SALACITY
SALAD
SALADANG
SALADANGS
SALADE
SALADES
SALADING
SALADINGS
SALADS
SALAL
SALALS
SALAMANDER
SALAMANDERS
SALAMANDRIAN
SALAMANDRINE
SALAMANDROID
SALAMANDROIDS
SALAMI
SALAMIS
SALAMON
SALAMONS
SALANGANE
SALANGANES
SALARIAT
SALARIATS
SALARIED
SALARIES
SALARY
SALARYING
SALARYMAN
SALARYMEN
SALBAND
SALBANDS
SALBUTAMOL
SALBUTAMOLS
SALCHOW
SALCHOWS
SALE
SALEABILITIES
SALEABILITY
SALEABLE
SALEABLENESS
SALEABLENESSES
SALEABLY
SALEP
SALEPS
SALERATUS
SALERATUSES

SALERING
SALERINGS
SALEROOM
SALEROOMS
SALES
SALESCLERK
SALESCLERKS
SALESGIRL
SALESGIRLS
SALESLADIES
SALESLADY
SALESMAN
SALESMANSHIP
SALESMANSHIPS
SALESMEN
SALESPEOPLE
SALESPERSON
SALESPERSONS
SALESROOM
SALESROOMS
SALESWOMAN
SALESWOMEN
SALET
SALETS
SALEWD
SALEYARD
SALEYARDS
SALFERN
SALFERNS
SALIAUNCE
SALIAUNCES
SALIC
SALICACEOUS
SALICES
SALICET
SALICETA
SALICETS
SALICETUM
SALICETUMS
SALICIN
SALICINE
SALICINES
SALICINS
SALICIONAL
SALICIONALS
SALICORNIA
SALICORNIAS
SALICYLAMIDE
SALICYLAMIDES
SALICYLATE
SALICYLATED
SALICYLATES
SALICYLATING
SALICYLIC
SALICYLISM
SALICYLISMS
SALIENCE

SALIENCES
SALIENCIES
SALIENCY
SALIENT
SALIENTIAN
SALIENTIANS
SALIENTLY
SALIENTS
SALIFEROUS
SALIFIABLE
SALIFICATION
SALIFICATIONS
SALIFIED
SALIFIES
SALIFY
SALIFYING
SALIGOT
SALIGOTS
SALIMETER
SALIMETERS
SALIMETRIC
SALIMETRICALLY
SALIMETRY
SALINA
SALINAS
SALINE
SALINES
SALINITIES
SALINITY
SALINIZATION
SALINIZATIONS
SALINIZE
SALINIZED
SALINIZES
SALINIZING
SALINOMETER
SALINOMETERS
SALINOMETRIC
SALINOMETRY
SALIVA
SALIVAL
SALIVARY
SALIVAS
SALIVATE
SALIVATED
SALIVATES
SALIVATING
SALIVATION
SALIVATIONS
SALIVATOR
SALIVATORS
SALIX
SALL
SALLAD
SALLADS
SALLAL
SALLALS

SALLE
SALLEE
SALLEES
SALLENDERS
SALLES
SALLET
SALLETS
SALLIED
SALLIER
SALLIERS
SALLIES
SALLOW
SALLOWED
SALLOWER
SALLOWEST
SALLOWING
SALLOWISH
SALLOWLY
SALLOWNESS
SALLOWNESSES
SALLOWS
SALLOWY
SALLY
SALLYING
SALLYPORT
SALLYPORTS
SALMAGUNDI
SALMAGUNDIES
SALMAGUNDIS
SALMAGUNDY
SALMANASER
SALMANASERS
SALMANAZAR
SALMANAZARS
SALMI
SALMIS
SALMON
SALMONBERRIES
SALMONBERRY
SALMONELLA
SALMONELLAE
SALMONELLAS
SALMONELLOSES
SALMONELLOSIS
SALMONET
SALMONETS
SALMONID
SALMONIDS
SALMONOID
SALMONOIDS
SALMONS
SALOL
SALOLS
SALOMETER
SALOMETERS
SALON
SALONS

SALOON
SALOONS
SALOOP
SALOOPS
SALOP
SALOPETTES
SALOPIAN
SALOPS
SALP
SALPA
SALPAE
SALPAS
SALPIAN
SALPIANS
SALPICON
SALPICONS
SALPID
SALPIDS
SALPIFORM
SALPIGLOSSES
SALPIGLOSSIS
SALPIGLOSSISES
SALPINGECTOMIES
SALPINGECTOMY
SALPINGES
SALPINGIAN
SALPINGITIC
SALPINGITIS
SALPINGITISES
SALPINX
SALPINXES
SALPS
SALS
SALSA
SALSAED
SALSAING
SALSAS
SALSE
SALSES
SALSIFIES
SALSIFY
SALSILLA
SALSILLAS
SALSOLACEOUS
SALSUGINOUS
SALT
SALTANDO
SALTANT
SALTANTS
SALTARELLI
SALTARELLO
SALTARELLOS
SALTATE
SALTATED
SALTATES
SALTATING
SALTATION

SALTATIONISM
SALTATIONISMS
SALTATIONIST
SALTATIONISTS
SALTATIONS
SALTATO
SALTATORIAL
SALTATORIOUS
SALTATORY
SALTBOX
SALTBOXES
SALTBUSH
SALTBUSHES
SALTCAT
SALTCATS
SALTCELLAR
SALTCELLARS
SALTCHUCK
SALTCHUCKER
SALTCHUCKERS
SALTCHUCKS
SALTED
SALTER
SALTERN
SALTERNS
SALTERS
SALTEST
SALTFISH
SALTFISHES
SALTIE
SALTIER
SALTIERS
SALTIES
SALTIEST
SALTIGRADE
SALTIGRADES
SALTILY
SALTIMBANCO
SALTIMBANCOS
SALTIMBOCCA
SALTIMBOCCAS
SALTINE
SALTINES
SALTINESS
SALTINESSES
SALTING
SALTINGS
SALTIRE
SALTIRES
SALTIREWISE
SALTISH
SALTISHLY
SALTISHNESS
SALTISHNESSES
SALTLESS
SALTLIKE
SALTLY

SALTNESS
SALTNESSES
SALTO
SALTOED
SALTOING
SALTOS
SALTPAN
SALTPANS
SALTPETER
SALTPETERS
SALTPETRE
SALTPETREMAN
SALTPETREMEN
SALTPETRES
SALTS
SALTSHAKER
SALTSHAKERS
SALTUS
SALTUSES
SALTWATER
SALTWORK
SALTWORKS
SALTWORT
SALTWORTS
SALTY
SALUBRIOUS
SALUBRIOUSLY
SALUBRIOUSNESS
SALUBRITIES
SALUBRITY
SALUE
SALUED
SALUES
SALUING
SALUKI
SALUKIS
SALUTARILY
SALUTARINESS
SALUTARINESSES
SALUTARY
SALUTATION
SALUTATIONAL
SALUTATIONS
SALUTATORIAN
SALUTATORIANS
SALUTATORIES
SALUTATORILY
SALUTATORY
SALUTE
SALUTED
SALUTER
SALUTERS
SALUTES
SALUTIFEROUS
SALUTING
SALVABILITIES
SALVABILITY

SALVABLE
SALVABLENESS
SALVABLY
SALVAGE
SALVAGEABILITY
SALVAGEABLE
SALVAGED
SALVAGEE
SALVAGEES
SALVAGER
SALVAGERS
SALVAGES
SALVAGING
SALVARSAN
SALVARSANS
SALVATION
SALVATIONAL
SALVATIONISM
SALVATIONISMS
SALVATIONIST
SALVATIONISTS
SALVATIONS
SALVATORIES
SALVATORY
SALVE
SALVED
SALVER
SALVERFORM
SALVERS
SALVES
SALVETE
SALVETES
SALVIA
SALVIAS
SALVIFIC
SALVIFICAL
SALVIFICALLY
SALVING
SALVINGS
SALVINIACEOUS
SALVO
SALVOED
SALVOES
SALVOING
SALVOR
SALVORS
SALVOS
SAM
SAMA
SAMAAN
SAMAANS
SAMADHI
SAMADHIS
SAMAN
SAMANS
SAMARA
SAMARAS

SAMARIFORM	SAMITIS	SANCTA	SANDBAG
SAMARITAN	SAMIZDAT	SANCTIFIABLE	SANDBAGGED
SAMARITANS	SAMIZDATS	SANCTIFICATION	SANDBAGGER
SAMARIUM	SAMLET	SANCTIFICATIONS	SANDBAGGERS
SAMARIUMS	SAMLETS	SANCTIFIED	SANDBAGGING
SAMARSKITE	SAMLOR	SANCTIFIEDLY	SANDBAGS
SAMARSKITES	SAMLORS	SANCTIFIER	SANDBANK
SAMAS	SAMMED	SANCTIFIERS	SANDBANKS
SAMBA	SAMMIES	SANCTIFIES	SANDBAR
SAMBAED	SAMMING	SANCTIFY	SANDBARS
SAMBAING	SAMMY	SANCTIFYING	SANDBLAST
SAMBAL	SAMNITIS	SANCTIFYINGLY	SANDBLASTED
SAMBALS	SAMNITISES	SANCTIFYINGS	SANDBLASTER
SAMBAR	SAMOSA	SANCTIMONIES	SANDBLASTERS
SAMBARS	SAMOSAS	SANCTIMONIOUS	SANDBLASTING
SAMBAS	SAMOVAR	SANCTIMONIOUSLY	SANDBLASTINGS
SAMBHAR	SAMOVARS	SANCTIMONY	SANDBLASTS
SAMBHARS	SAMP	SANCTION	SANDBOX
SAMBHUR	SAMPAN	SANCTIONABLE	SANDBOXES
SAMBHURS	SAMPANS	SANCTIONED	SANDBOY
SAMBO	SAMPHIRE	SANCTIONEER	SANDBOYS
SAMBOS	SAMPHIRES	SANCTIONEERS	SANDBUR
SAMBUCA	SAMPI	SANCTIONER	SANDBURR
SAMBUCAS	SAMPIRE	SANCTIONERS	SANDBURRS
SAMBUKE	SAMPIRES	SANCTIONING	SANDBURS
SAMBUKES	SAMPIS	SANCTIONLESS	SANDCASTLE
SAMBUR	SAMPLE	SANCTIONS	SANDCASTLES
SAMBURS	SAMPLED	SANCTITIES	SANDDAB
SAME	SAMPLER	SANCTITUDE	SANDDABS
SAMECH	SAMPLERIES	SANCTITUDES	SANDED
SAMECHS	SAMPLERS	SANCTITY	SANDEK
SAMEK	SAMPLERY	SANCTORUM	SANDEKS
SAMEKH	SAMPLES	SANCTUARIES	SANDER
SAMEKHS	SAMPLING	SANCTUARISE	SANDERLING
SAMEKS	SAMPLINGS	SANCTUARISED	SANDERLINGS
SAMEL	SAMPS	SANCTUARISES	SANDERS
SAMELY	SAMS	SANCTUARISING	SANDERSES
SAMEN	SAMSARA	SANCTUARIZE	SANDERSWOOD
SAMENESS	SAMSARAS	SANCTUARIZED	SANDERSWOODS
SAMENESSES	SAMSHOO	SANCTUARIZES	SANDFISH
SAMES	SAMSHOOS	SANCTUARIZING	SANDFISHES
SAMEY	SAMSHU	SANCTUARY	SANDFLIES
SAMFOO	SAMSHUS	SANCTUM	SANDFLY
SAMFOOS	SAMURAI	SANCTUMS	SANDGLASS
SAMFU	SAMURAIS	SAND	SANDGLASSES
SAMFUS	SAN	SANDAL	SANDGROPER
SAMIEL	SANATIVE	SANDALED	SANDGROPERS
SAMIELS	SANATORIA	SANDALING	SANDGROUSE
SAMIER	SANATORIUM	SANDALLED	SANDGROUSES
SAMIEST	SANATORIUMS	SANDALLING	SANDHEAP
SAMISEN	SANATORY	SANDALS	SANDHEAPS
SAMISENS	SANBENITO	SANDALWOOD	SANDHI
SAMITE	SANBENITOS	SANDALWOODS	SANDHILL
SAMITES	SANCAI	SANDARAC	SANDHILLS
SAMITHI	SANCAIS	SANDARACH	SANDHIS
SAMITHIS	SANCHO	SANDARACHS	SANDHOG
SAMITI	SANCHOS	SANDARACS	SANDHOGS

SANDIER	SANDY	SANGUINOLENCY	SANNIE
SANDIEST	SANE	SANGUINOLENT	SANNIES
SANDINESS	SANED	SANGUIVOROUS	SANNOP
SANDINESSES	SANELY	SANICLE	SANNOPS
SANDING	SANENESS	SANICLES	SANNUP
SANDINGS	SANENESSES	SANIDINE	SANNUPS
SANDIVER	SANER	SANIDINES	SANNYASI
SANDIVERS	SANES	SANIES	SANNYASIN
SANDLIKE	SANEST	SANIFIED	SANNYASINS
SANDLING	SANG	SANIFIES	SANNYASIS
SANDLINGS	SANGA	SANIFY	SANPAN
SANDLOT	SANGAR	SANIFYING	SANPANS
SANDLOTS	SANGAREE	SANING	SANPRO
SANDLOTTER	SANGAREES	SANIOUS	SANS
SANDLOTTERS	SANGARS	SANITARIA	SANSA
SANDMAN	SANGAS	SANITARIAN	SANSAR
SANDMEN	SANGER	SANITARIANISM	SANSARS
SANDPAINTING	SANGERS	SANITARIANISMS	SANSAS
SANDPAINTINGS	SANGFROID	SANITARIANS	SANSCULOTTE
SANDPAPER	SANGFROIDS	SANITARIES	SANSCULOTTERIE
SANDPAPERED	SANGH	SANITARILY	SANSCULOTTERIES
SANDPAPERING	SANGHAT	SANITARINESS	SANSCULOTTES
SANDPAPERS	SANGHATS	SANITARIST	SANSCULOTTIC
SANDPAPERY	SANGHS	SANITARISTS	SANSCULOTTIDES
SANDPEEP	SANGLIER	SANITARIUM	SANSCULOTTISH
SANDPEEPS	SANGLIERS	SANITARIUMS	SANSCULOTTISM
SANDPILE	SANGO	SANITARY	SANSCULOTTISMS
SANDPILES	SANGOMA	SANITATE	SANSCULOTTIST
SANDPIPER	SANGOMAS	SANITATED	SANSCULOTTISTS
SANDPIPERS	SANGRIA	SANITATES	SANSEI
SANDPIT	SANGRIAS	SANITATING	SANSEIS
SANDPITS	SANGS	SANITATION	SANSERIF
SANDPUMP	SANGUIFEROUS	SANITATIONIST	SANSERIFS
SANDPUMPS	SANGUIFICATION	SANITATIONISTS	SANSEVIERIA
SANDS	SANGUIFICATIONS	SANITATIONS	SANSEVIERIAS
SANDSHOE	SANGUIFIED	SANITIES	SANT
SANDSHOES	SANGUIFIES	SANITISATION	SANTAL
SANDSOAP	SANGUIFY	SANITISATIONS	SANTALACEOUS
SANDSOAPS	SANGUIFYING	SANITISE	SANTALIC
SANDSPOUT	SANGUINARIA	SANITISED	SANTALIN
SANDSPOUTS	SANGUINARIAS	SANITISES	SANTALINS
SANDSPUR	SANGUINARILY	SANITISING	SANTALOL
SANDSPURS	SANGUINARINESS	SANITIZATION	SANTALOLS
SANDSTONE	SANGUINARY	SANITIZATIONS	SANTALS
SANDSTONES	SANGUINE	SANITIZE	SANTIMI
SANDSTORM	SANGUINED	SANITIZED	SANTIMS
SANDSTORMS	SANGUINELY	SANITIZES	SANTIR
SANDSUCKER	SANGUINENESS	SANITIZING	SANTIRS
SANDSUCKERS	SANGUINENESSES	SANITORIA	SANTO
SANDWICH	SANGUINEOUS	SANITORIUM	SANTOL
SANDWICHED	SANGUINEOUSLY	SANITORIUMS	SANTOLINA
SANDWICHES	SANGUINEOUSNESS	SANITY	SANTOLINAS
SANDWICHING	SANGUINES	SANJAK	SANTOLS
SANDWORM	SANGUINING	SANJAKS	SANTON
SANDWORMS	SANGUINITIES	SANK	SANTONICA
SANDWORT	SANGUINITY	SANKO	SANTONICAS
SANDWORTS	SANGUINIVOROUS	SANKOS	SANTONIN

SANTONINS
SANTONS
SANTOS
SANTOUR
SANTOURS
SANTS
SANTUR
SANTURS
SAOUARI
SAOUARIS
SAP
SAPAJOU
SAPAJOUS
SAPAN
SAPANS
SAPANWOOD
SAPANWOODS
SAPEGO
SAPEGOES
SAPELE
SAPELES
SAPFUL
SAPHEAD
SAPHEADED
SAPHEADS
SAPHENA
SAPHENAE
SAPHENAS
SAPHENOUS
SAPID
SAPIDITIES
SAPIDITY
SAPIDLESS
SAPIDNESS
SAPIDNESSES
SAPIENCE
SAPIENCES
SAPIENCIES
SAPIENCY
SAPIENS
SAPIENT
SAPIENTIAL
SAPIENTIALLY
SAPIENTLY
SAPINDACEOUS
SAPLESS
SAPLESSNESS
SAPLESSNESSES
SAPLING
SAPLINGS
SAPODILLA
SAPODILLAS
SAPOGENIN
SAPOGENINS
SAPONACEOUS
SAPONACEOUSNESS
SAPONARIA

SAPONARIAS
SAPONIFIABLE
SAPONIFICATION
SAPONIFICATIONS
SAPONIFIED
SAPONIFIER
SAPONIFIERS
SAPONIFIES
SAPONIFY
SAPONIFYING
SAPONIN
SAPONINE
SAPONINES
SAPONINS
SAPONITE
SAPONITES
SAPOR
SAPORIFIC
SAPOROUS
SAPORS
SAPOTA
SAPOTACEOUS
SAPOTAS
SAPOTE
SAPOTES
SAPOUR
SAPOURS
SAPPAN
SAPPANS
SAPPANWOOD
SAPPANWOODS
SAPPED
SAPPER
SAPPERMENT
SAPPERS
SAPPHIC
SAPPHICS
SAPPHIRE
SAPPHIRED
SAPPHIRES
SAPPHIRINE
SAPPHIRINES
SAPPHISM
SAPPHISMS
SAPPHIST
SAPPHISTS
SAPPIER
SAPPIEST
SAPPILY
SAPPINESS
SAPPINESSES
SAPPING
SAPPLE
SAPPLED
SAPPLES
SAPPLING
SAPPY

SAPRAEMIA
SAPRAEMIAS
SAPRAEMIC
SAPREMIA
SAPREMIAS
SAPREMIC
SAPROBE
SAPROBES
SAPROBIC
SAPROBIONT
SAPROBIONTS
SAPROBIOTIC
SAPROGENIC
SAPROGENICITIES
SAPROGENICITY
SAPROGENOUS
SAPROLEGNIA
SAPROLEGNIAS
SAPROLITE
SAPROLITES
SAPROLITIC
SAPROPEL
SAPROPELIC
SAPROPELITE
SAPROPELITES
SAPROPELS
SAPROPHAGOUS
SAPROPHYTE
SAPROPHYTES
SAPROPHYTIC
SAPROPHYTICALLY
SAPROPHYTISM
SAPROPHYTISMS
SAPROTROPH
SAPROTROPHIC
SAPROTROPHS
SAPROZOIC
SAPS
SAPSAGO
SAPSAGOS
SAPSUCKER
SAPSUCKERS
SAPUCAIA
SAPUCAIAS
SAPWOOD
SAPWOODS
SAR
SARABAND
SARABANDE
SARABANDES
SARABANDS
SARAFAN
SARAFANS
SARAN
SARANGI
SARANGIS
SARANS

SARAPE
SARAPES
SARBACANE
SARBACANES
SARCASM
SARCASMS
SARCASTIC
SARCASTICALLY
SARCENCHYMES
SARCENET
SARCENETS
SARCOCARP
SARCOCARPS
SARCOCOLLA
SARCOCOLLAS
SARCOCYSTIS
SARCOCYSTISES
SARCODE
SARCODES
SARCODIC
SARCOID
SARCOIDOSES
SARCOIDOSIS
SARCOIDS
SARCOLEMMA
SARCOLEMMAL
SARCOLEMMAS
SARCOLEMMATA
SARCOLOGIES
SARCOLOGY
SARCOMA
SARCOMAS
SARCOMATA
SARCOMATOID
SARCOMATOSES
SARCOMATOSIS
SARCOMATOUS
SARCOMERE
SARCOMERES
SARCONET
SARCONETS
SARCOPHAGAL
SARCOPHAGI
SARCOPHAGOUS
SARCOPHAGUS
SARCOPHAGUSES
SARCOPLASM
SARCOPLASMIC
SARCOPLASMS
SARCOPTIC
SARCOSOMAL
SARCOSOME
SARCOSOMES
SARCOUS
SARD
SARDANA
SARDANAS

SARDAR
SARDARS
SARDEL
SARDELLE
SARDELLES
SARDELS
SARDINE
SARDINES
SARDIUS
SARDIUSES
SARDONIAN
SARDONIC
SARDONICAL
SARDONICALLY
SARDONICISM
SARDONICISMS
SARDONYX
SARDONYXES
SARDS
SARED
SAREE
SAREES
SARGASSO
SARGASSOS
SARGASSUM
SARGASSUMS
SARGE
SARGES
SARGO
SARGOS
SARGOSES
SARGUS
SARGUSES
SARI
SARIN
SARING
SARINS
SARIS
SARK
SARKIER
SARKIEST
SARKING
SARKINGS
SARKS
SARKY
SARMENT
SARMENTA
SARMENTACEOUS
SARMENTOSE
SARMENTOUS
SARMENTS
SARMENTUM
SARMIE
SARMIES
SARNEY
SARNEYS
SARNIE

SARNIES
SAROD
SARODE
SARODES
SARODIST
SARODISTS
SARODS
SARONG
SARONGS
SARONIC
SAROS
SAROSES
SARPANCH
SARPANCHES
SARRACENIA
SARRACENIACEOUS
SARRACENIAS
SARRASIN
SARRASINS
SARRAZIN
SARRAZINS
SARRUSOPHONE
SARRUSOPHONES
SARS
SARSAPARILLA
SARSAPARILLAS
SARSAR
SARSARS
SARSDEN
SARSDENS
SARSEN
SARSENET
SARSENETS
SARSENS
SARSNET
SARSNETS
SARTOR
SARTORIAL
SARTORIALLY
SARTORIAN
SARTORII
SARTORIUS
SARTORIUSES
SARTORS
SARUS
SARUSES
SASARARA
SASARARAS
SASER
SASERS
SASH
SASHAY
SASHAYED
SASHAYING
SASHAYS
SASHED
SASHES

SASHIMI
SASHIMIS
SASHING
SASIN
SASINE
SASINES
SASINS
SASKATOON
SASKATOONS
SASQUATCH
SASQUATCHES
SASS
SASSABIES
SASSABY
SASSAFRAS
SASSAFRASES
SASSARARA
SASSARARAS
SASSE
SASSED
SASSES
SASSIER
SASSIES
SASSIEST
SASSILY
SASSINESS
SASSING
SASSOLIN
SASSOLINS
SASSOLITE
SASSOLITES
SASSWOOD
SASSWOODS
SASSY
SASTRA
SASTRAS
SASTRUGA
SASTRUGI
SAT
SATAI
SATAIS
SATANG
SATANGS
SATANIC
SATANICAL
SATANICALLY
SATANICALNESS
SATANICALNESSES
SATANISM
SATANISMS
SATANIST
SATANISTS
SATANITIES
SATANITY
SATANOLOGIES
SATANOLOGY
SATANOPHANIES

SATANOPHANY
SATANOPHOBIA
SATANOPHOBIAS
SATARA
SATARAS
SATAY
SATAYS
SATCHEL
SATCHELFUL
SATCHELFULS
SATCHELLED
SATCHELS
SATCHELSFUL
SATE
SATED
SATEDNESS
SATEDNESSES
SATEEN
SATEENS
SATELESS
SATELLES
SATELLITE
SATELLITED
SATELLITES
SATELLITIC
SATELLITING
SATELLITISE
SATELLITISED
SATELLITISES
SATELLITISING
SATELLITIUM
SATELLITIUMS
SATELLITIZE
SATELLITIZED
SATELLITIZES
SATELLITIZING
SATEM
SATES
SATI
SATIABILITIES
SATIABILITY
SATIABLE
SATIABLY
SATIATE
SATIATED
SATIATES
SATIATING
SATIATION
SATIATIONS
SATIETIES
SATIETY
SATIN
SATINED
SATINET
SATINETS
SATINETTA
SATINETTAS

SATINETTE
SATINETTES
SATINFLOWER
SATINFLOWERS
SATING
SATINING
SATINPOD
SATINPODS
SATINS
SATINWOOD
SATINWOODS
SATINY
SATIRE
SATIRES
SATIRIC
SATIRICAL
SATIRICALLY
SATIRICALNESS
SATIRICALNESSES
SATIRISATION
SATIRISATIONS
SATIRISE
SATIRISED
SATIRISER
SATIRISERS
SATIRISES
SATIRISING
SATIRIST
SATIRISTS
SATIRIZABLE
SATIRIZATION
SATIRIZE
SATIRIZED
SATIRIZER
SATIRIZERS
SATIRIZES
SATIRIZING
SATIS
SATISFACTION
SATISFACTIONS
SATISFACTORILY
SATISFACTORY
SATISFIABLE
SATISFICE
SATISFICED
SATISFICER
SATISFICERS
SATISFICES
SATISFICING
SATISFICINGS
SATISFIED
SATISFIER
SATISFIERS
SATISFIES
SATISFY
SATISFYING
SATISFYINGLY

SATIVE
SATORI
SATORIS
SATRAP
SATRAPAL
SATRAPIES
SATRAPS
SATRAPY
SATSUMA
SATSUMAS
SATURABILITY
SATURABLE
SATURABLY
SATURANT
SATURANTS
SATURATE
SATURATED
SATURATER
SATURATERS
SATURATES
SATURATING
SATURATION
SATURATIONS
SATURATOR
SATURATORS
SATURNALIA
SATURNALIAN
SATURNALIANLY
SATURNALIAS
SATURNIC
SATURNIID
SATURNIIDS
SATURNINE
SATURNINELY
SATURNINITY
SATURNISM
SATURNISMS
SATURNIST
SATURNISTS
SATYAGRAHA
SATYAGRAHAS
SATYAGRAHI
SATYAGRAHIS
SATYR
SATYRA
SATYRAL
SATYRALS
SATYRAS
SATYRESQUE
SATYRESS
SATYRESSES
SATYRIASES
SATYRIASIS
SATYRIC
SATYRICAL
SATYRID
SATYRIDS

SATYRISK
SATYRISKS
SATYRS
SAU
SAUBA
SAUBAS
SAUCE
SAUCEBOAT
SAUCEBOATS
SAUCEBOX
SAUCEBOXES
SAUCED
SAUCELESS
SAUCEPAN
SAUCEPANS
SAUCER
SAUCERFUL
SAUCERFULS
SAUCERLESS
SAUCERLIKE
SAUCERS
SAUCES
SAUCH
SAUCHS
SAUCIER
SAUCIEST
SAUCILY
SAUCINESS
SAUCINESSES
SAUCING
SAUCISSE
SAUCISSES
SAUCISSON
SAUCISSONS
SAUCY
SAUERBRATEN
SAUERBRATENS
SAUERKRAUT
SAUERKRAUTS
SAUFGARD
SAUFGARDS
SAUGER
SAUGERS
SAUGH
SAUGHS
SAUGHY
SAUL
SAULGE
SAULGES
SAULIE
SAULIES
SAULS
SAULT
SAULTS
SAUNA
SAUNAS
SAUNT

SAUNTED
SAUNTER
SAUNTERED
SAUNTERER
SAUNTERERS
SAUNTERING
SAUNTERINGLY
SAUNTERINGS
SAUNTERS
SAUNTING
SAUNTS
SAUREL
SAURELS
SAURIAN
SAURIANS
SAURIES
SAURISCHIAN
SAURISCHIANS
SAUROGNATHOUS
SAUROID
SAUROPOD
SAUROPODOUS
SAUROPODS
SAUROPSIDAN
SAUROPSIDANS
SAUROPTERYGIAN
SAURY
SAUSAGE
SAUSAGES
SAUSSURITE
SAUSSURITES
SAUSSURITIC
SAUT
SAUTE
SAUTED
SAUTEED
SAUTEEING
SAUTEES
SAUTEING
SAUTERNE
SAUTERNES
SAUTES
SAUTING
SAUTOIR
SAUTOIRE
SAUTOIRES
SAUTOIRS
SAUTS
SAV
SAVABLE
SAVABLENESS
SAVABLENESSES
SAVAGE
SAVAGED
SAVAGEDOM
SAVAGEDOMS
SAVAGELY

SAVAGENESS	SAVORIER	SAWDUSTED	SAXOPHONIST
SAVAGENESSES	SAVORIES	SAWDUSTING	SAXOPHONISTS
SAVAGER	SAVORIEST	SAWDUSTS	SAXTUBA
SAVAGERIES	SAVORILY	SAWDUSTY	SAXTUBAS
SAVAGERY	SAVORINESS	SAWED	SAY
SAVAGES	SAVORINESSES	SAWER	SAYABLE
SAVAGEST	SAVORING	SAWERS	SAYED
SAVAGING	SAVORLESS	SAWFISH	SAYER
SAVAGISM	SAVOROUS	SAWFISHES	SAYERS
SAVAGISMS	SAVORS	SAWFLIES	SAYEST
SAVANNA	SAVORY	SAWFLY	SAYID
SAVANNAH	SAVOUR	SAWHORSE	SAYIDS
SAVANNAHS	SAVOURED	SAWHORSES	SAYING
SAVANNAS	SAVOURER	SAWING	SAYINGS
SAVANT	SAVOURERS	SAWINGS	SAYNE
SAVANTE	SAVOURIER	SAWLIKE	SAYON
SAVANTES	SAVOURIES	SAWLOG	SAYONARA
SAVANTS	SAVOURIEST	SAWLOGS	SAYONARAS
SAVARIN	SAVOURILY	SAWMILL	SAYONS
SAVARINS	SAVOURINESS	SAWMILLS	SAYS
SAVATE	SAVOURINESSES	SAWN	SAYST
SAVATES	SAVOURING	SAWNEY	SAYYID
SAVE	SAVOURLESS	SAWNEYS	SAYYIDS
SAVEABLE	SAVOURLY	SAWPIT	SAZ
SAVEABLENESS	SAVOURS	SAWPITS	SAZERAC
SAVEABLY	SAVOURY	SAWS	SAZERACS
SAVED	SAVOY	SAWSHARK	SAZES
SAVEGARD	SAVOYARD	SAWSHARKS	SAZHEN
SAVEGARDED	SAVOYARDS	SAWTEETH	SAZHENS
SAVEGARDING	SAVOYS	SAWTIMBER	SAZZES
SAVEGARDS	SAVS	SAWTIMBERS	SBIRRI
SAVELOY	SAVVEY	SAWTOOTH	SBIRRO
SAVELOYS	SAVVEYED	SAWYER	SCAB
SAVER	SAVVEYING	SAWYERS	SCABBARD
SAVERS	SAVVEYS	SAX	SCABBARDED
SAVES	SAVVIED	SAXATILE	SCABBARDING
SAVEY	SAVVIER	SAXAUL	SCABBARDLESS
SAVEYED	SAVVIES	SAXAULS	SCABBARDS
SAVEYING	SAVVIEST	SAXES	SCABBED
SAVEYS	SAVVY	SAXHORN	SCABBEDNESS
SAVIN	SAVVYING	SAXHORNS	SCABBEDNESSES
SAVINE	SAW	SAXICAVOUS	SCABBIER
SAVINES	SAWAH	SAXICOLE	SCABBIEST
SAVING	SAWAHS	SAXICOLINE	SCABBILY
SAVINGLY	SAWBILL	SAXICOLOUS	SCABBINESS
SAVINGNESS	SAWBILLS	SAXIFRAGACEOUS	SCABBINESSES
SAVINGNESSES	SAWBLADE	SAXIFRAGE	SCABBING
SAVINGS	SAWBLADES	SAXIFRAGES	SCABBLE
SAVINS	SAWBONES	SAXITOXIN	SCABBLED
SAVIOR	SAWBONESES	SAXITOXINS	SCABBLES
SAVIORS	SAWBUCK	SAXONIES	SCABBLING
SAVIOUR	SAWBUCKS	SAXONITE	SCABBY
SAVIOURS	SAWDER	SAXONITES	SCABERULOUS
SAVOR	SAWDERED	SAXONY	SCABIES
SAVORED	SAWDERING	SAXOPHONE	SCABIETIC
SAVORER	SAWDERS	SAXOPHONES	SCABIOSA
SAVORERS	SAWDUST	SAXOPHONIC	SCABIOSAS

SCABIOUS
SCABIOUSES
SCABLAND
SCABLANDS
SCABLIKE
SCABRID
SCABRIDITIES
SCABRIDITY
SCABROUS
SCABROUSLY
SCABROUSNESS
SCABROUSNESSES
SCABS
SCAD
SCADS
SCAFF
SCAFFIE
SCAFFIES
SCAFFOLAGE
SCAFFOLAGES
SCAFFOLD
SCAFFOLDAGE
SCAFFOLDAGES
SCAFFOLDED
SCAFFOLDER
SCAFFOLDERS
SCAFFOLDING
SCAFFOLDINGS
SCAFFOLDS
SCAFFS
SCAG
SCAGGED
SCAGGING
SCAGLIA
SCAGLIAS
SCAGLIOLA
SCAGLIOLAS
SCAGS
SCAIL
SCAILED
SCAILING
SCAILS
SCAITH
SCAITHED
SCAITHING
SCAITHLESS
SCAITHS
SCALA
SCALABILITIES
SCALABILITY
SCALABLE
SCALABLENESS
SCALABLY
SCALADE
SCALADES
SCALADO
SCALADOS

SCALAE
SCALAGE
SCALAGES
SCALAR
SCALARE
SCALARES
SCALARIFORM
SCALARIFORMLY
SCALARS
SCALAWAG
SCALAWAGS
SCALD
SCALDBERRIES
SCALDBERRY
SCALDED
SCALDER
SCALDERS
SCALDFISH
SCALDFISHES
SCALDHEAD
SCALDHEADS
SCALDIC
SCALDING
SCALDINGS
SCALDINI
SCALDINO
SCALDS
SCALDSHIP
SCALDSHIPS
SCALE
SCALEBOARD
SCALEBOARDS
SCALED
SCALELESS
SCALELIKE
SCALENE
SCALENI
SCALENOHEDRA
SCALENOHEDRON
SCALENOHEDRONS
SCALENUS
SCALEPAN
SCALEPANS
SCALER
SCALERS
SCALES
SCALEUP
SCALEUPS
SCALEWORK
SCALEWORKS
SCALIER
SCALIEST
SCALINESS
SCALINESSES
SCALING
SCALINGS
SCALL

SCALLAWAG
SCALLAWAGS
SCALLED
SCALLIES
SCALLION
SCALLIONS
SCALLOP
SCALLOPED
SCALLOPER
SCALLOPERS
SCALLOPING
SCALLOPINI
SCALLOPINIS
SCALLOPS
SCALLS
SCALLY
SCALLYWAG
SCALLYWAGS
SCALOGRAM
SCALOGRAMS
SCALOPPINE
SCALOPPINES
SCALOPPINI
SCALP
SCALPED
SCALPEL
SCALPELLIC
SCALPELLIFORM
SCALPELS
SCALPER
SCALPERS
SCALPING
SCALPINGS
SCALPINS
SCALPLESS
SCALPRIFORM
SCALPRUM
SCALPRUMS
SCALPS
SCALY
SCAM
SCAMBLE
SCAMBLED
SCAMBLER
SCAMBLERS
SCAMBLES
SCAMBLING
SCAMBLINGLY
SCAMBLINGS
SCAMEL
SCAMELS
SCAMMED
SCAMMER
SCAMMERS
SCAMMING
SCAMMONIATE
SCAMMONIES

SCAMMONY
SCAMP
SCAMPED
SCAMPER
SCAMPERED
SCAMPERER
SCAMPERERS
SCAMPERING
SCAMPERS
SCAMPI
SCAMPIES
SCAMPING
SCAMPINGS
SCAMPIS
SCAMPISH
SCAMPISHLY
SCAMPISHNESS
SCAMPISHNESSES
SCAMPS
SCAMS
SCAMSTER
SCAMSTERS
SCAMTO
SCAN
SCAND
SCANDAL
SCANDALED
SCANDALING
SCANDALISATION
SCANDALISATIONS
SCANDALISE
SCANDALISED
SCANDALISER
SCANDALISERS
SCANDALISES
SCANDALISING
SCANDALIZATION
SCANDALIZATIONS
SCANDALIZE
SCANDALIZED
SCANDALIZER
SCANDALIZERS
SCANDALIZES
SCANDALIZING
SCANDALLED
SCANDALLING
SCANDALMONGER
SCANDALMONGERS
SCANDALOUS
SCANDALOUSLY
SCANDALOUSNESS
SCANDALS
SCANDENT
SCANDIA
SCANDIAS
SCANDIC
SCANDIUM

SCANDIUMS	SCAPHOCEPHALI	SCARCELY	SCARLESS
SCANNABLE	SCAPHOCEPHALIC	SCARCEMENT	SCARLET
SCANNED	SCAPHOCEPHALIES	SCARCEMENTS	SCARLETED
SCANNER	SCAPHOCEPHALOUS	SCARCENESS	SCARLETING
SCANNERS	SCAPHOCEPHALUS	SCARCENESSES	SCARLETS
SCANNING	SCAPHOCEPHALY	SCARCER	SCARMOGE
SCANNINGS	SCAPHOID	SCARCEST	SCARMOGES
SCANS	SCAPHOIDS	SCARCITIES	SCARP
SCANSION	SCAPHOPOD	SCARCITY	SCARPA
SCANSIONS	SCAPHOPODS	SCARE	SCARPAED
SCANSORIAL	SCAPI	SCARECROW	SCARPAING
SCANT	SCAPIGEROUS	SCARECROWS	SCARPAS
SCANTED	SCAPING	SCARED	SCARPED
SCANTER	SCAPOLITE	SCAREDER	SCARPER
SCANTEST	SCAPOLITES	SCAREDEST	SCARPERED
SCANTIER	SCAPOSE	SCAREHEAD	SCARPERING
SCANTIES	SCAPPLE	SCAREHEADS	SCARPERS
SCANTIEST	SCAPPLED	SCAREMONGER	SCARPETTI
SCANTILY	SCAPPLES	SCAREMONGERING	SCARPETTO
SCANTINESS	SCAPPLING	SCAREMONGERINGS	SCARPH
SCANTINESSES	SCAPULA	SCAREMONGERS	SCARPHED
SCANTING	SCAPULAE	SCARER	SCARPHING
SCANTITIES	SCAPULAR	SCARERS	SCARPHS
SCANTITY	SCAPULARIES	SCARES	SCARPINES
SCANTLE	SCAPULARS	SCAREY	SCARPING
SCANTLED	SCAPULARY	SCARF	SCARPINGS
SCANTLES	SCAPULAS	SCARFED	SCARPS
SCANTLING	SCAPULATED	SCARFING	SCARRE
SCANTLINGS	SCAPULIMANCIES	SCARFINGS	SCARRED
SCANTLY	SCAPULIMANCY	SCARFISH	SCARRES
SCANTNESS	SCAPULIMANTIC	SCARFISHES	SCARRIER
SCANTNESSES	SCAPULOMANCIES	SCARFPIN	SCARRIEST
SCANTS	SCAPULOMANCY	SCARFPINS	SCARRING
SCANTY	SCAPULOMANTIC	SCARFS	SCARRINGS
SCAPA	SCAPUS	SCARFSKIN	SCARRY
SCAPAED	SCAR	SCARFSKINS	SCARS
SCAPAING	SCARAB	SCARFWISE	SCART
SCAPAS	SCARABAEAN	SCARIER	SCARTED
SCAPE	SCARABAEANS	SCARIEST	SCARTH
SCAPED	SCARABAEI	SCARIFICATION	SCARTHS
SCAPEGALLOWS	SCARABAEID	SCARIFICATIONS	SCARTING
SCAPEGALLOWSES	SCARABAEIDS	SCARIFICATOR	SCARTS
SCAPEGOAT	SCARABAEIST	SCARIFICATORS	SCARVES
SCAPEGOATED	SCARABAEISTS	SCARIFIED	SCARY
SCAPEGOATING	SCARABAEOID	SCARIFIER	SCAT
SCAPEGOATINGS	SCARABAEOIDS	SCARIFIERS	SCATBACK
SCAPEGOATISM	SCARABAEUS	SCARIFIES	SCATBACKS
SCAPEGOATISMS	SCARABAEUSES	SCARIFY	SCATCH
SCAPEGOATS	SCARABEE	SCARIFYING	SCATCHES
SCAPEGRACE	SCARABEES	SCARIFYINGLY	SCATH
SCAPEGRACES	SCARABOID	SCARILY	SCATHE
SCAPELESS	SCARABOIDS	SCARING	SCATHED
SCAPEMENT	SCARABS	SCARIOSE	SCATHEFUL
SCAPEMENTS	SCARAMOUCH	SCARIOUS	SCATHEFULNESS
SCAPES	SCARAMOUCHE	SCARLATINA	SCATHEFULNESSES
SCAPEWHEEL	SCARAMOUCHES	SCARLATINAL	SCATHELESS
SCAPEWHEELS	SCARCE	SCARLATINAS	SCATHES

SCATHING
SCATHINGLY
SCATHS
SCATOLE
SCATOLES
SCATOLOGIC
SCATOLOGICAL
SCATOLOGICALLY
SCATOLOGIES
SCATOLOGIST
SCATOLOGISTS
SCATOLOGY
SCATOPHAGIES
SCATOPHAGOUS
SCATOPHAGY
SCATS
SCATT
SCATTED
SCATTER
SCATTERABLE
SCATTERATION
SCATTERATIONS
SCATTERBRAIN
SCATTERBRAINED
SCATTERBRAINS
SCATTERED
SCATTEREDLY
SCATTERER
SCATTERERS
SCATTERGOOD
SCATTERGOODS
SCATTERGRAM
SCATTERGRAMS
SCATTERGUN
SCATTERGUNS
SCATTERING
SCATTERINGLY
SCATTERINGS
SCATTERLING
SCATTERLINGS
SCATTERMOUCH
SCATTERMOUCHES
SCATTERS
SCATTERSHOT
SCATTERY
SCATTIER
SCATTIEST
SCATTILY
SCATTINESS
SCATTINESSES
SCATTING
SCATTINGS
SCATTS
SCATTY
SCATURIENT
SCAUD
SCAUDED

SCAUDING
SCAUDS
SCAUP
SCAUPED
SCAUPER
SCAUPERS
SCAUPING
SCAUPS
SCAUR
SCAURED
SCAURIES
SCAURING
SCAURS
SCAURY
SCAVAGE
SCAVAGER
SCAVAGERS
SCAVAGES
SCAVENGE
SCAVENGED
SCAVENGER
SCAVENGERED
SCAVENGERIES
SCAVENGERING
SCAVENGERINGS
SCAVENGERS
SCAVENGERY
SCAVENGES
SCAVENGING
SCAVENGINGS
SCAW
SCAWS
SCAWTITE
SCAWTITES
SCAZON
SCAZONS
SCAZONTES
SCAZONTIC
SCAZONTICS
SCEAT
SCEATT
SCEATTAS
SCEDULE
SCEDULED
SCEDULES
SCEDULING
SCELERAT
SCELERATE
SCELERATES
SCELERATS
SCENA
SCENARIES
SCENARIO
SCENARIOS
SCENARISATION
SCENARISATIONS
SCENARISE

SCENARISED
SCENARISES
SCENARISING
SCENARIST
SCENARISTS
SCENARIZATION
SCENARIZATIONS
SCENARIZE
SCENARIZED
SCENARIZES
SCENARIZING
SCENARY
SCENAS
SCEND
SCENDED
SCENDING
SCENDS
SCENE
SCENED
SCENEMAN
SCENEMEN
SCENERIES
SCENERY
SCENES
SCENESHIFTER
SCENESHIFTERS
SCENIC
SCENICAL
SCENICALLY
SCENING
SCENOGRAPHER
SCENOGRAPHERS
SCENOGRAPHIC
SCENOGRAPHICAL
SCENOGRAPHIES
SCENOGRAPHY
SCENT
SCENTED
SCENTFUL
SCENTING
SCENTINGS
SCENTLESS
SCENTS
SCEPSIS
SCEPSISES
SCEPTER
SCEPTERED
SCEPTERING
SCEPTERLESS
SCEPTERS
SCEPTIC
SCEPTICAL
SCEPTICALLY
SCEPTICISM
SCEPTICISMS
SCEPTICS
SCEPTRAL

SCEPTRE
SCEPTRED
SCEPTRELESS
SCEPTRES
SCEPTRING
SCEPTRY
SCERNE
SCERNED
SCERNES
SCERNING
SCEUOPHYLACIUM
SCEUOPHYLAX
SCEUOPHYLAXES
SCHADENFREUDE
SCHADENFREUDES
SCHALSTEIN
SCHALSTEINS
SCHANSE
SCHANSES
SCHANTZE
SCHANTZES
SCHANZE
SCHANZES
SCHAPPE
SCHAPPED
SCHAPPEING
SCHAPPES
SCHAPSKA
SCHAPSKAS
SCHAV
SCHAVS
SCHECHITA
SCHECHITAH
SCHECHITAHS
SCHECHITAS
SCHECKLATONS
SCHEDULAR
SCHEDULE
SCHEDULED
SCHEDULER
SCHEDULERS
SCHEDULES
SCHEDULING
SCHEELITE
SCHEELITES
SCHEFFLERA
SCHEFFLERAS
SCHELLUM
SCHELLUMS
SCHELM
SCHELMS
SCHEMA
SCHEMAS
SCHEMATA
SCHEMATIC
SCHEMATICAL
SCHEMATICALLY

SCHEMATICS
SCHEMATISATION
SCHEMATISATIONS
SCHEMATISE
SCHEMATISED
SCHEMATISES
SCHEMATISING
SCHEMATISM
SCHEMATISMS
SCHEMATIST
SCHEMATISTS
SCHEMATIZATION
SCHEMATIZATIONS
SCHEMATIZE
SCHEMATIZED
SCHEMATIZES
SCHEMATIZING
SCHEME
SCHEMED
SCHEMER
SCHEMERS
SCHEMES
SCHEMING
SCHEMINGLY
SCHEMINGS
SCHEMOZZLE
SCHEMOZZLED
SCHEMOZZLES
SCHEMOZZLING
SCHERZANDI
SCHERZANDO
SCHERZANDOS
SCHERZI
SCHERZO
SCHERZOS
SCHIAVONE
SCHIAVONES
SCHIEDAM
SCHIEDAMS
SCHILLER
SCHILLERISATION
SCHILLERISE
SCHILLERISED
SCHILLERISES
SCHILLERISING
SCHILLERIZATION
SCHILLERIZE
SCHILLERIZED
SCHILLERIZES
SCHILLERIZING
SCHILLERS
SCHILLING
SCHILLINGS
SCHIMMEL
SCHIMMELS
SCHINDYLESES
SCHINDYLESIS

SCHINDYLETIC
SCHIPPERKE
SCHIPPERKES
SCHISM
SCHISMA
SCHISMAS
SCHISMATIC
SCHISMATICAL
SCHISMATICALLY
SCHISMATICALS
SCHISMATICS
SCHISMATISE
SCHISMATISED
SCHISMATISES
SCHISMATISING
SCHISMATIZE
SCHISMATIZED
SCHISMATIZES
SCHISMATIZING
SCHISMS
SCHIST
SCHISTOSE
SCHISTOSITIES
SCHISTOSITY
SCHISTOSOMAL
SCHISTOSOME
SCHISTOSOMES
SCHISTOSOMIASES
SCHISTOSOMIASIS
SCHISTOUS
SCHISTS
SCHIZAEACEOUS
SCHIZANTHUS
SCHIZANTHUSES
SCHIZIER
SCHIZIEST
SCHIZO
SCHIZOCARP
SCHIZOCARPIC
SCHIZOCARPOUS
SCHIZOCARPS
SCHIZOGENESES
SCHIZOGENESIS
SCHIZOGENETIC
SCHIZOGENIC
SCHIZOGNATHOUS
SCHIZOGONIC
SCHIZOGONIES
SCHIZOGONOUS
SCHIZOGONY
SCHIZOID
SCHIZOIDAL
SCHIZOIDS
SCHIZOMYCETE
SCHIZOMYCETES
SCHIZOMYCETIC
SCHIZOMYCETOUS

SCHIZONT
SCHIZONTS
SCHIZOPHRENE
SCHIZOPHRENES
SCHIZOPHRENETIC
SCHIZOPHRENIA
SCHIZOPHRENIAS
SCHIZOPHRENIC
SCHIZOPHRENICS
SCHIZOPHYCEOUS
SCHIZOPHYTE
SCHIZOPHYTES
SCHIZOPHYTIC
SCHIZOPOD
SCHIZOPODAL
SCHIZOPODOUS
SCHIZOPODS
SCHIZOS
SCHIZOTHYMIA
SCHIZOTHYMIAS
SCHIZOTHYMIC
SCHIZY
SCHIZZIER
SCHIZZIEST
SCHIZZY
SCHLAGER
SCHLAGERS
SCHLEMIEL
SCHLEMIELS
SCHLEMIHL
SCHLEMIHLS
SCHLEP
SCHLEPP
SCHLEPPED
SCHLEPPER
SCHLEPPERS
SCHLEPPIER
SCHLEPPIEST
SCHLEPPING
SCHLEPPS
SCHLEPPY
SCHLEPS
SCHLICH
SCHLICHS
SCHLIERE
SCHLIEREN
SCHLIERIC
SCHLIMAZEL
SCHLIMAZELS
SCHLOCK
SCHLOCKER
SCHLOCKERS
SCHLOCKIER
SCHLOCKIEST
SCHLOCKS
SCHLOCKY
SCHLONG

SCHLONGS
SCHLOSS
SCHLOSSES
SCHLUB
SCHLUMBERGERA
SCHLUMBERGERAS
SCHLUMP
SCHLUMPED
SCHLUMPING
SCHLUMPS
SCHMALTZ
SCHMALTZES
SCHMALTZIER
SCHMALTZIEST
SCHMALTZY
SCHMALZ
SCHMALZES
SCHMALZIER
SCHMALZIEST
SCHMALZY
SCHMEAR
SCHMEARS
SCHMECK
SCHMECKS
SCHMEER
SCHMEERED
SCHMEERING
SCHMEERS
SCHMELZ
SCHMELZE
SCHMELZES
SCHMO
SCHMOCK
SCHMOCKS
SCHMOE
SCHMOES
SCHMOOS
SCHMOOSE
SCHMOOSED
SCHMOOSES
SCHMOOSING
SCHMOOZ
SCHMOOZE
SCHMOOZED
SCHMOOZES
SCHMOOZING
SCHMOS
SCHMUCK
SCHMUCKS
SCHMUTTER
SCHMUTTERS
SCHNAPPER
SCHNAPPERS
SCHNAPPS
SCHNAPPSES
SCHNAPS
SCHNAPSES

SCHNAUZER
SCHNAUZERS
SCHNECKE
SCHNECKEN
SCHNELL
SCHNITZEL
SCHNITZELS
SCHNOOK
SCHNOOKS
SCHNORKEL
SCHNORKELED
SCHNORKELING
SCHNORKELLED
SCHNORKELLER
SCHNORKELLERS
SCHNORKELLING
SCHNORKELS
SCHNORKLE
SCHNORKLED
SCHNORKLES
SCHNORKLING
SCHNORR
SCHNORRED
SCHNORRER
SCHNORRERS
SCHNORRING
SCHNORRS
SCHNOZ
SCHNOZZ
SCHNOZZES
SCHNOZZLE
SCHNOZZLES
SCHOLAR
SCHOLARCH
SCHOLARCHS
SCHOLARLIER
SCHOLARLIEST
SCHOLARLINESS
SCHOLARLINESSES
SCHOLARLY
SCHOLARS
SCHOLARSHIP
SCHOLARSHIPS
SCHOLASTIC
SCHOLASTICAL
SCHOLASTICALLY
SCHOLASTICATE
SCHOLASTICATES
SCHOLASTICISM
SCHOLASTICISMS
SCHOLASTICS
SCHOLIA
SCHOLIAST
SCHOLIASTIC
SCHOLIASTS
SCHOLION
SCHOLIUM

SCHOLIUMS
SCHOOL
SCHOOLBAG
SCHOOLBAGS
SCHOOLBOOK
SCHOOLBOOKS
SCHOOLBOY
SCHOOLBOYISH
SCHOOLBOYS
SCHOOLCHILD
SCHOOLCHILDREN
SCHOOLCRAFT
SCHOOLCRAFTS
SCHOOLDAY
SCHOOLDAYS
SCHOOLE
SCHOOLED
SCHOOLERIES
SCHOOLERY
SCHOOLES
SCHOOLFELLOW
SCHOOLFELLOWS
SCHOOLGIRL
SCHOOLGIRLISH
SCHOOLGIRLS
SCHOOLGOING
SCHOOLGOINGS
SCHOOLHOUSE
SCHOOLHOUSES
SCHOOLIE
SCHOOLIES
SCHOOLING
SCHOOLINGS
SCHOOLKID
SCHOOLKIDS
SCHOOLMAID
SCHOOLMAIDS
SCHOOLMAN
SCHOOLMARM
SCHOOLMARMISH
SCHOOLMARMS
SCHOOLMASTER
SCHOOLMASTERED
SCHOOLMASTERING
SCHOOLMASTERISH
SCHOOLMASTERLY
SCHOOLMASTERS
SCHOOLMATE
SCHOOLMATES
SCHOOLMEN
SCHOOLMISTRESS
SCHOOLMISTRESSY
SCHOOLROOM
SCHOOLROOMS
SCHOOLS
SCHOOLTEACHER
SCHOOLTEACHERS

SCHOOLTEACHING
SCHOOLTEACHINGS
SCHOOLTIDE
SCHOOLTIDES
SCHOOLTIME
SCHOOLTIMES
SCHOOLWARD
SCHOOLWARDS
SCHOOLWORK
SCHOOLWORKS
SCHOONER
SCHOONERS
SCHORL
SCHORLACEOUS
SCHORLOMITE
SCHORLOMITES
SCHORLS
SCHOTTISCHE
SCHOTTISCHES
SCHOUT
SCHOUTS
SCHRECKLICH
SCHRIK
SCHRIKS
SCHROD
SCHRODS
SCHTICK
SCHTICKS
SCHTIK
SCHTIKS
SCHTOOK
SCHTOOKS
SCHTOOM
SCHTUCK
SCHTUCKS
SCHUBS
SCHUIT
SCHUITS
SCHUL
SCHULN
SCHULS
SCHUSS
SCHUSSBOOMER
SCHUSSBOOMERS
SCHUSSED
SCHUSSER
SCHUSSERS
SCHUSSES
SCHUSSING
SCHUTZSTAFFEL
SCHUTZSTAFFELS
SCHUYT
SCHUYTS
SCHWA
SCHWARMEREI
SCHWARMEREIS
SCHWARMERISCH

SCHWARZLOT
SCHWARZLOTS
SCHWAS
SCIAENID
SCIAENIDS
SCIAENOID
SCIAENOIDS
SCIAMACHIES
SCIAMACHY
SCIARID
SCIARIDS
SCIATIC
SCIATICA
SCIATICAL
SCIATICAS
SCIATICS
SCIENCE
SCIENCED
SCIENCES
SCIENT
SCIENTER
SCIENTIAL
SCIENTIFIC
SCIENTIFICAL
SCIENTIFICALLY
SCIENTISE
SCIENTISED
SCIENTISES
SCIENTISING
SCIENTISM
SCIENTISMS
SCIENTIST
SCIENTISTIC
SCIENTISTS
SCIENTIZE
SCIENTIZED
SCIENTIZES
SCIENTIZING
SCILICET
SCILLA
SCILLAS
SCIMETAR
SCIMETARS
SCIMITAR
SCIMITARS
SCIMITER
SCIMITERS
SCINCOID
SCINCOIDIAN
SCINCOIDIANS
SCINCOIDS
SCINDAPSUS
SCINDAPSUSES
SCINTIGRAM
SCINTIGRAMS
SCINTIGRAPHIC
SCINTIGRAPHIES

SCINTIGRAPHY
SCINTILLA
SCINTILLAE
SCINTILLANT
SCINTILLANTLY
SCINTILLAS
SCINTILLASCOPE
SCINTILLASCOPES
SCINTILLATE
SCINTILLATED
SCINTILLATES
SCINTILLATING
SCINTILLATINGLY
SCINTILLATION
SCINTILLATIONS
SCINTILLATOR
SCINTILLATORS
SCINTILLISCANS
SCINTILLOMETER
SCINTILLOMETERS
SCINTILLON
SCINTILLONS
SCINTILLOSCOPE
SCINTILLOSCOPES
SCINTISCAN
SCINTISCANNER
SCINTISCANNERS
SCINTISCANS
SCIOLISM
SCIOLISMS
SCIOLIST
SCIOLISTIC
SCIOLISTS
SCIOLOUS
SCIOLTO
SCIOMACHIES
SCIOMACHY
SCIOMANCER
SCIOMANCERS
SCIOMANCY
SCIOMANTIC
SCIOMANTICALLY
SCION
SCIONS
SCIOPHYTE
SCIOPHYTES
SCIOPHYTIC
SCIOSOPHIES
SCIOSOPHY
SCIROC
SCIROCCO
SCIROCCOS
SCIROCS
SCIRRHI
SCIRRHOID
SCIRRHOSITY
SCIRRHOUS

SCIRRHUS
SCIRRHUSES
SCISSEL
SCISSELS
SCISSIL
SCISSILE
SCISSILS
SCISSION
SCISSIONS
SCISSIPARITIES
SCISSIPARITY
SCISSOR
SCISSORED
SCISSORER
SCISSORERS
SCISSORING
SCISSORS
SCISSORTAIL
SCISSORTAILS
SCISSORWISE
SCISSURE
SCISSURES
SCITAMINEOUS
SCIURID
SCIURIDS
SCIURINE
SCIURINES
SCIUROID
SCLAFF
SCLAFFED
SCLAFFER
SCLAFFERS
SCLAFFING
SCLAFFS
SCLATE
SCLATED
SCLATES
SCLATING
SCLAUNDER
SCLAUNDERS
SCLAVE
SCLAVES
SCLERA
SCLERAE
SCLERAL
SCLERAS
SCLERE
SCLEREID
SCLEREIDE
SCLEREIDES
SCLEREIDS
SCLEREMA
SCLEREMAS
SCLERENCHYMA
SCLERENCHYMAS
SCLERENCHYMATA
SCLERES

SCLERIASES
SCLERIASIS
SCLERITE
SCLERITES
SCLERITIC
SCLERITIS
SCLERITISES
SCLEROCAULIES
SCLEROCAULY
SCLERODERM
SCLERODERMA
SCLERODERMAS
SCLERODERMATA
SCLERODERMATOUS
SCLERODERMIA
SCLERODERMIAS
SCLERODERMIC
SCLERODERMITE
SCLERODERMITES
SCLERODERMOUS
SCLERODERMS
SCLEROID
SCLEROMA
SCLEROMALACIA
SCLEROMALACIAS
SCLEROMAS
SCLEROMATA
SCLEROMETER
SCLEROMETERS
SCLEROMETRIC
SCLEROPHYLL
SCLEROPHYLLIES
SCLEROPHYLLOUS
SCLEROPHYLLS
SCLEROPHYLLY
SCLEROPROTEIN
SCLEROPROTEINS
SCLEROSAL
SCLEROSE
SCLEROSED
SCLEROSES
SCLEROSING
SCLEROSIS
SCLEROTAL
SCLEROTALS
SCLEROTIA
SCLEROTIAL
SCLEROTIC
SCLEROTICS
SCLEROTIN
SCLEROTINS
SCLEROTIOID
SCLEROTISATION
SCLEROTISE
SCLEROTISED
SCLEROTISES
SCLEROTISING

SCLEROTITIS
SCLEROTITISES
SCLEROTIUM
SCLEROTIZATION
SCLEROTIZATIONS
SCLEROTIZE
SCLEROTIZED
SCLEROTIZES
SCLEROTIZING
SCLEROTOMIES
SCLEROTOMY
SCLEROUS
SCLIFF
SCLIFFS
SCLIM
SCLIMMED
SCLIMMING
SCLIMS
SCODIER
SCODIEST
SCODY
SCOFF
SCOFFED
SCOFFER
SCOFFERS
SCOFFING
SCOFFINGLY
SCOFFINGS
SCOFFLAW
SCOFFLAWS
SCOFFS
SCOG
SCOGGED
SCOGGING
SCOGS
SCOINSON
SCOINSONS
SCOLD
SCOLDABLE
SCOLDED
SCOLDER
SCOLDERS
SCOLDING
SCOLDINGLY
SCOLDINGS
SCOLDS
SCOLECES
SCOLECID
SCOLECIDS
SCOLECIFORM
SCOLECITE
SCOLECITES
SCOLECOID
SCOLEX
SCOLIA
SCOLICES
SCOLIOMA

SCOLIOMAS
SCOLION
SCOLIOSES
SCOLIOSIS
SCOLIOTIC
SCOLLOP
SCOLLOPED
SCOLLOPING
SCOLLOPS
SCOLOPACEOUS
SCOLOPENDRA
SCOLOPENDRAS
SCOLOPENDRID
SCOLOPENDRIDS
SCOLOPENDRIFORM
SCOLOPENDRINE
SCOLOPENDRIUM
SCOLOPENDRIUMS
SCOLYTID
SCOLYTIDS
SCOLYTOID
SCOLYTOIDS
SCOMBRID
SCOMBRIDS
SCOMBROID
SCOMBROIDS
SCOMFISH
SCOMFISHED
SCOMFISHES
SCOMFISHING
SCONCE
SCONCED
SCONCES
SCONCHEON
SCONCHEONS
SCONCING
SCONE
SCONES
SCONTION
SCONTIONS
SCOOBIES
SCOOBY
SCOOG
SCOOGED
SCOOGING
SCOOGS
SCOOP
SCOOPED
SCOOPER
SCOOPERS
SCOOPFUL
SCOOPFULS
SCOOPING
SCOOPINGS
SCOOPS
SCOOPSFUL
SCOOSH

SCOOSHED
SCOOSHER
SCOOSHERS
SCOOSHES
SCOOSHIER
SCOOSHIEST
SCOOSHING
SCOOSHY
SCOOT
SCOOTED
SCOOTER
SCOOTERIST
SCOOTERISTS
SCOOTERS
SCOOTING
SCOOTS
SCOP
SCOPA
SCOPAE
SCOPAS
SCOPATE
SCOPE
SCOPED
SCOPELID
SCOPELIDS
SCOPELOID
SCOPELOIDS
SCOPES
SCOPING
SCOPOLAMINE
SCOPOLAMINES
SCOPOLINE
SCOPOPHILIA
SCOPOPHILIAC
SCOPOPHILIACS
SCOPOPHILIAS
SCOPOPHILIC
SCOPOPHOBIA
SCOPOPHOBIAS
SCOPS
SCOPTOPHILIA
SCOPTOPHILIAS
SCOPTOPHOBIA
SCOPTOPHOBIAS
SCOPULA
SCOPULAE
SCOPULAS
SCOPULATE
SCORBUTIC
SCORBUTICALLY
SCORCH
SCORCHED
SCORCHER
SCORCHERS
SCORCHES
SCORCHING
SCORCHINGLY

SCORCHINGNESS
SCORCHINGNESSES
SCORCHINGS
SCORDATO
SCORDATURA
SCORDATURAS
SCORE
SCOREBOARD
SCOREBOARDS
SCORECARD
SCORECARDS
SCORED
SCOREKEEPER
SCOREKEEPERS
SCORELESS
SCORELINE
SCORELINES
SCOREPAD
SCOREPADS
SCORER
SCORERS
SCORES
SCORESHEET
SCORESHEETS
SCORIA
SCORIAC
SCORIACEOUS
SCORIAE
SCORIFICATION
SCORIFICATIONS
SCORIFIED
SCORIFIER
SCORIFIERS
SCORIFIES
SCORIFY
SCORIFYING
SCORING
SCORINGS
SCORIOUS
SCORN
SCORNED
SCORNER
SCORNERS
SCORNFUL
SCORNFULLY
SCORNFULNESS
SCORNFULNESSES
SCORNING
SCORNINGS
SCORNS
SCORODITE
SCORODITES
SCORPAENID
SCORPAENIDS
SCORPAENOID
SCORPAENOIDS
SCORPER

SCORPERS
SCORPIOID
SCORPIOIDS
SCORPION
SCORPIONIC
SCORPIONS
SCORRENDO
SCORSE
SCORSED
SCORSER
SCORSERS
SCORSES
SCORSING
SCORZONERA
SCORZONERAS
SCOT
SCOTCH
SCOTCHED
SCOTCHES
SCOTCHING
SCOTER
SCOTERS
SCOTIA
SCOTIAS
SCOTODINIA
SCOTODINIAS
SCOTOMA
SCOTOMAS
SCOTOMATA
SCOTOMATOUS
SCOTOMETER
SCOTOMETERS
SCOTOMIA
SCOTOMIAS
SCOTOMIES
SCOTOMY
SCOTOPIA
SCOTOPIAS
SCOTOPIC
SCOTS
SCOTTIE
SCOTTIES
SCOUG
SCOUGED
SCOUGING
SCOUGS
SCOUNDREL
SCOUNDRELLY
SCOUNDRELS
SCOUP
SCOUPED
SCOUPING
SCOUPS
SCOUR
SCOURED
SCOURER
SCOURERS

SCOURGE
SCOURGED
SCOURGER
SCOURGERS
SCOURGES
SCOURGING
SCOURIE
SCOURIES
SCOURING
SCOURINGS
SCOURS
SCOURSE
SCOURSED
SCOURSES
SCOURSING
SCOUSE
SCOUSER
SCOUSERS
SCOUSES
SCOUT
SCOUTCRAFT
SCOUTCRAFTS
SCOUTED
SCOUTER
SCOUTERS
SCOUTH
SCOUTHER
SCOUTHERED
SCOUTHERING
SCOUTHERINGS
SCOUTHERS
SCOUTHERY
SCOUTHS
SCOUTING
SCOUTINGS
SCOUTMASTER
SCOUTMASTERS
SCOUTS
SCOW
SCOWDER
SCOWDERED
SCOWDERING
SCOWDERINGS
SCOWDERS
SCOWED
SCOWING
SCOWL
SCOWLED
SCOWLER
SCOWLERS
SCOWLING
SCOWLINGLY
SCOWLS
SCOWP
SCOWPED
SCOWPING
SCOWPS

SCOWRER
SCOWRERS
SCOWRIE
SCOWRIES
SCOWS
SCOWTH
SCOWTHER
SCOWTHERED
SCOWTHERING
SCOWTHERS
SCOWTHS
SCOZZA
SCOZZAS
SCRAB
SCRABBED
SCRABBING
SCRABBLE
SCRABBLED
SCRABBLER
SCRABBLERS
SCRABBLES
SCRABBLIER
SCRABBLIEST
SCRABBLING
SCRABBLY
SCRABS
SCRAE
SCRAES
SCRAG
SCRAGGED
SCRAGGEDNESS
SCRAGGEDNESSES
SCRAGGIER
SCRAGGIEST
SCRAGGILY
SCRAGGINESS
SCRAGGINESSES
SCRAGGING
SCRAGGLIER
SCRAGGLIEST
SCRAGGLING
SCRAGGLY
SCRAGGY
SCRAGS
SCRAICH
SCRAICHED
SCRAICHING
SCRAICHS
SCRAIGH
SCRAIGHED
SCRAIGHING
SCRAIGHS
SCRAM
SCRAMB
SCRAMBED
SCRAMBING
SCRAMBLE

SCRAMBLED
SCRAMBLER
SCRAMBLERS
SCRAMBLES
SCRAMBLING
SCRAMBLINGLY
SCRAMBLINGS
SCRAMBS
SCRAMJET
SCRAMJETS
SCRAMMED
SCRAMMING
SCRAMS
SCRAN
SCRANCH
SCRANCHED
SCRANCHES
SCRANCHING
SCRANNEL
SCRANNELS
SCRANNIER
SCRANNIEST
SCRANNY
SCRANS
SCRAP
SCRAPABILITY
SCRAPABLE
SCRAPABLY
SCRAPBOOK
SCRAPBOOKS
SCRAPE
SCRAPED
SCRAPEGOODS
SCRAPEGUT
SCRAPEGUTS
SCRAPEPENNIES
SCRAPEPENNY
SCRAPER
SCRAPERBOARD
SCRAPERBOARDS
SCRAPERS
SCRAPES
SCRAPHEAP
SCRAPHEAPS
SCRAPIE
SCRAPIES
SCRAPING
SCRAPINGS
SCRAPPAGE
SCRAPPAGES
SCRAPPED
SCRAPPER
SCRAPPERS
SCRAPPIER
SCRAPPIEST
SCRAPPILY
SCRAPPINESS

SCRAPPINESSES
SCRAPPING
SCRAPPLE
SCRAPPLES
SCRAPPY
SCRAPS
SCRAPYARD
SCRAPYARDS
SCRAT
SCRATCH
SCRATCHBACK
SCRATCHBACKS
SCRATCHBOARD
SCRATCHBOARDS
SCRATCHBUILD
SCRATCHBUILDER
SCRATCHBUILDERS
SCRATCHBUILDING
SCRATCHBUILDS
SCRATCHBUILT
SCRATCHCARD
SCRATCHCARDS
SCRATCHED
SCRATCHER
SCRATCHERS
SCRATCHES
SCRATCHIE
SCRATCHIER
SCRATCHIES
SCRATCHIEST
SCRATCHILY
SCRATCHINESS
SCRATCHINESSES
SCRATCHING
SCRATCHINGLY
SCRATCHINGS
SCRATCHLESS
SCRATCHPLATE
SCRATCHPLATES
SCRATCHY
SCRATS
SCRATTED
SCRATTING
SCRATTLE
SCRATTLED
SCRATTLES
SCRATTLING
SCRAUCH
SCRAUCHED
SCRAUCHING
SCRAUCHS
SCRAUGH
SCRAUGHED
SCRAUGHING
SCRAUGHS
SCRAW
SCRAWL

907

SCRAWLED
SCRAWLER
SCRAWLERS
SCRAWLIER
SCRAWLIEST
SCRAWLING
SCRAWLINGLY
SCRAWLINGS
SCRAWLS
SCRAWLY
SCRAWM
SCRAWMED
SCRAWMING
SCRAWMS
SCRAWNIER
SCRAWNIEST
SCRAWNILY
SCRAWNINESS
SCRAWNINESSES
SCRAWNY
SCRAWP
SCRAWPED
SCRAWPER
SCRAWPERS
SCRAWPING
SCRAWS
SCRAY
SCRAYE
SCRAYES
SCRAYS
SCREAK
SCREAKED
SCREAKIER
SCREAKIEST
SCREAKING
SCREAKS
SCREAKY
SCREAM
SCREAMED
SCREAMER
SCREAMERS
SCREAMING
SCREAMINGLY
SCREAMS
SCREE
SCREECH
SCREECHED
SCREECHER
SCREECHERS
SCREECHES
SCREECHIER
SCREECHIEST
SCREECHING
SCREECHY
SCREED
SCREEDED
SCREEDER

SCREEDERS
SCREEDING
SCREEDINGS
SCREEDS
SCREEN
SCREENABLE
SCREENAGER
SCREENAGERS
SCREENCRAFT
SCREENCRAFTS
SCREENED
SCREENER
SCREENERS
SCREENFUL
SCREENFULS
SCREENING
SCREENINGS
SCREENLAND
SCREENLANDS
SCREENLIKE
SCREENPLAY
SCREENPLAYS
SCREENS
SCREENSAVER
SCREENSAVERS
SCREENWRITER
SCREENWRITERS
SCREES
SCREET
SCREETED
SCREETERS
SCREETING
SCREETS
SCREEVE
SCREEVED
SCREEVER
SCREEVERS
SCREEVES
SCREEVING
SCREEVINGS
SCREICH
SCREICHED
SCREICHES
SCREICHING
SCREICHS
SCREIGH
SCREIGHED
SCREIGHING
SCREIGHS
SCREW
SCREWBALL
SCREWBALLS
SCREWBEAN
SCREWBEANS
SCREWDRIVER
SCREWDRIVERS
SCREWED

SCREWER
SCREWERS
SCREWIER
SCREWIEST
SCREWINESS
SCREWINESSES
SCREWING
SCREWINGS
SCREWLIKE
SCREWS
SCREWTOP
SCREWTOPS
SCREWUP
SCREWUPS
SCREWWORM
SCREWWORMS
SCREWY
SCRIBABLE
SCRIBACIOUS
SCRIBACIOUSNESS
SCRIBAL
SCRIBBLE
SCRIBBLED
SCRIBBLEMENT
SCRIBBLEMENTS
SCRIBBLER
SCRIBBLERS
SCRIBBLES
SCRIBBLIER
SCRIBBLIEST
SCRIBBLING
SCRIBBLINGLY
SCRIBBLINGS
SCRIBBLY
SCRIBE
SCRIBED
SCRIBER
SCRIBERS
SCRIBES
SCRIBING
SCRIBINGS
SCRIBISM
SCRIBISMS
SCRIECH
SCRIECHED
SCRIECHING
SCRIECHS
SCRIED
SCRIENE
SCRIENES
SCRIES
SCRIEVE
SCRIEVEBOARD
SCRIEVEBOARDS
SCRIEVED
SCRIEVES
SCRIEVING

SCRIGGLE
SCRIGGLED
SCRIGGLES
SCRIGGLIER
SCRIGGLIEST
SCRIGGLING
SCRIGGLY
SCRIKE
SCRIKED
SCRIKES
SCRIKING
SCRIM
SCRIMMAGE
SCRIMMAGED
SCRIMMAGER
SCRIMMAGERS
SCRIMMAGES
SCRIMMAGING
SCRIMP
SCRIMPED
SCRIMPER
SCRIMPERS
SCRIMPIER
SCRIMPIEST
SCRIMPILY
SCRIMPINESS
SCRIMPINESSES
SCRIMPING
SCRIMPIT
SCRIMPLY
SCRIMPNESS
SCRIMPNESSES
SCRIMPS
SCRIMPY
SCRIMS
SCRIMSHANDER
SCRIMSHANDERED
SCRIMSHANDERING
SCRIMSHANDERS
SCRIMSHANDIED
SCRIMSHANDIES
SCRIMSHANDY
SCRIMSHANDYING
SCRIMSHANK
SCRIMSHANKED
SCRIMSHANKING
SCRIMSHANKS
SCRIMSHAW
SCRIMSHAWED
SCRIMSHAWING
SCRIMSHAWS
SCRIMSHONERS
SCRIMURE
SCRIMURES
SCRINE
SCRINES
SCRIP

SCRIPOPHILE
SCRIPOPHILES
SCRIPOPHILIES
SCRIPOPHILIST
SCRIPOPHILISTS
SCRIPOPHILY
SCRIPPAGE
SCRIPPAGES
SCRIPS
SCRIPT
SCRIPTED
SCRIPTER
SCRIPTERS
SCRIPTING
SCRIPTORIA
SCRIPTORIAL
SCRIPTORIUM
SCRIPTORIUMS
SCRIPTORY
SCRIPTS
SCRIPTURAL
SCRIPTURALISM
SCRIPTURALISMS
SCRIPTURALIST
SCRIPTURALISTS
SCRIPTURALLY
SCRIPTURE
SCRIPTURES
SCRIPTURISM
SCRIPTURISMS
SCRIPTURIST
SCRIPTURISTS
SCRIPTWRITER
SCRIPTWRITERS
SCRIPTWRITING
SCRITCH
SCRITCHED
SCRITCHES
SCRITCHING
SCRIVE
SCRIVEBOARD
SCRIVEBOARDS
SCRIVED
SCRIVENER
SCRIVENERS
SCRIVENERSHIP
SCRIVENERSHIPS
SCRIVENING
SCRIVENINGS
SCRIVES
SCRIVING
SCROBE
SCROBES
SCROBICULAR
SCROBICULATE
SCROBICULATED
SCROBICULE

SCROBICULES
SCROD
SCRODDLED
SCRODS
SCROFULA
SCROFULAS
SCROFULOUS
SCROFULOUSLY
SCROFULOUSNESS
SCROG
SCROGGIE
SCROGGIER
SCROGGIEST
SCROGGIN
SCROGGINS
SCROGGY
SCROGS
SCROLL
SCROLLABLE
SCROLLED
SCROLLING
SCROLLS
SCROLLWISE
SCROLLWORK
SCROLLWORKS
SCROME
SCROMED
SCROMES
SCROMING
SCROOCH
SCROOCHED
SCROOCHES
SCROOCHING
SCROOGE
SCROOGED
SCROOGES
SCROOGING
SCROOP
SCROOPED
SCROOPING
SCROOPS
SCROOTCH
SCROOTCHED
SCROOTCHES
SCROOTCHING
SCROPHULARIA
SCROPHULARIAS
SCRORP
SCRORPS
SCROTA
SCROTAL
SCROTUM
SCROTUMS
SCROUGE
SCROUGED
SCROUGER
SCROUGERS

SCROUGES
SCROUGING
SCROUNGE
SCROUNGED
SCROUNGER
SCROUNGERS
SCROUNGES
SCROUNGIER
SCROUNGIEST
SCROUNGING
SCROUNGINGS
SCROUNGY
SCROW
SCROWDGE
SCROWDGED
SCROWDGES
SCROWDGING
SCROWL
SCROWLE
SCROWLED
SCROWLES
SCROWLING
SCROWLS
SCROWS
SCROYLE
SCROYLES
SCRUB
SCRUBBABLE
SCRUBBED
SCRUBBER
SCRUBBERS
SCRUBBIER
SCRUBBIEST
SCRUBBILY
SCRUBBINESS
SCRUBBING
SCRUBBINGS
SCRUBBY
SCRUBLAND
SCRUBLANDS
SCRUBS
SCRUBWOMAN
SCRUBWOMEN
SCRUFF
SCRUFFIER
SCRUFFIEST
SCRUFFILY
SCRUFFINESS
SCRUFFINESSES
SCRUFFS
SCRUFFY
SCRUM
SCRUMDOWN
SCRUMDOWNS
SCRUMMAGE
SCRUMMAGED
SCRUMMAGER

SCRUMMAGERS
SCRUMMAGES
SCRUMMAGING
SCRUMMED
SCRUMMIER
SCRUMMIEST
SCRUMMING
SCRUMMY
SCRUMP
SCRUMPED
SCRUMPIES
SCRUMPING
SCRUMPLE
SCRUMPLED
SCRUMPLES
SCRUMPLING
SCRUMPOX
SCRUMPOXES
SCRUMPS
SCRUMPTIOUS
SCRUMPTIOUSLY
SCRUMPTIOUSNESS
SCRUMPY
SCRUMS
SCRUNCH
SCRUNCHED
SCRUNCHEON
SCRUNCHEONS
SCRUNCHES
SCRUNCHIE
SCRUNCHIER
SCRUNCHIES
SCRUNCHIEST
SCRUNCHING
SCRUNCHION
SCRUNCHIONS
SCRUNCHY
SCRUNT
SCRUNTIER
SCRUNTIEST
SCRUNTS
SCRUNTY
SCRUPLE
SCRUPLED
SCRUPLELESS
SCRUPLELESSLY
SCRUPLELESSNESS
SCRUPLER
SCRUPLERS
SCRUPLES
SCRUPLING
SCRUPULOSITIES
SCRUPULOSITY
SCRUPULOUS
SCRUPULOUSLY
SCRUPULOUSNESS
SCRUTABILITY

SCRUTABLE
SCRUTATOR
SCRUTATORS
SCRUTINEER
SCRUTINEERS
SCRUTINIES
SCRUTINISE
SCRUTINISED
SCRUTINISER
SCRUTINISERS
SCRUTINISES
SCRUTINISING
SCRUTINISINGLY
SCRUTINIZE
SCRUTINIZED
SCRUTINIZER
SCRUTINIZERS
SCRUTINIZES
SCRUTINIZING
SCRUTINIZINGLY
SCRUTINOUS
SCRUTINOUSLY
SCRUTINY
SCRUTO
SCRUTOIRE
SCRUTOIRES
SCRUTOS
SCRUZE
SCRUZED
SCRUZES
SCRUZING
SCRY
SCRYDE
SCRYER
SCRYERS
SCRYING
SCRYINGS
SCRYNE
SCRYNES
SCUBA
SCUBAS
SCUCHIN
SCUCHINS
SCUCHIONS
SCUD
SCUDDALER
SCUDDALERS
SCUDDED
SCUDDER
SCUDDERS
SCUDDING
SCUDDLE
SCUDDLED
SCUDDLES
SCUDDLING
SCUDI
SCUDLER

SCUDLERS
SCUDO
SCUDS
SCUFF
SCUFFED
SCUFFING
SCUFFLE
SCUFFLED
SCUFFLER
SCUFFLERS
SCUFFLES
SCUFFLING
SCUFFS
SCUFT
SCUFTS
SCUG
SCUGGED
SCUGGING
SCUGS
SCUL
SCULDUDDERIES
SCULDUDDERY
SCULDUDDRIES
SCULDUDDRY
SCULDUGGERIES
SCULDUGGERY
SCULK
SCULKED
SCULKER
SCULKERS
SCULKING
SCULKS
SCULL
SCULLE
SCULLED
SCULLER
SCULLERIES
SCULLERS
SCULLERY
SCULLES
SCULLING
SCULLINGS
SCULLION
SCULLIONS
SCULLS
SCULP
SCULPED
SCULPIN
SCULPING
SCULPINS
SCULPS
SCULPSIT
SCULPT
SCULPTED
SCULPTING
SCULPTOR
SCULPTORS

SCULPTRESS
SCULPTRESSES
SCULPTS
SCULPTURAL
SCULPTURALLY
SCULPTURE
SCULPTURED
SCULPTURES
SCULPTURESQUE
SCULPTURESQUELY
SCULPTURING
SCULPTURINGS
SCULS
SCUM
SCUMBAG
SCUMBAGS
SCUMBER
SCUMBERED
SCUMBERING
SCUMBERS
SCUMBLE
SCUMBLED
SCUMBLES
SCUMBLING
SCUMBLINGS
SCUMFISH
SCUMFISHED
SCUMFISHES
SCUMFISHING
SCUMLIKE
SCUMMED
SCUMMER
SCUMMERS
SCUMMIER
SCUMMIEST
SCUMMING
SCUMMINGS
SCUMMY
SCUMS
SCUNCHEON
SCUNCHEONS
SCUNGE
SCUNGED
SCUNGES
SCUNGIER
SCUNGIEST
SCUNGILLI
SCUNGILLIS
SCUNGING
SCUNGY
SCUNNER
SCUNNERED
SCUNNERING
SCUNNERS
SCUP
SCUPPAUG
SCUPPAUGS

SCUPPER
SCUPPERED
SCUPPERING
SCUPPERNONG
SCUPPERNONGS
SCUPPERS
SCUPS
SCUR
SCURF
SCURFIER
SCURFIEST
SCURFINESS
SCURFINESSES
SCURFS
SCURFY
SCURRED
SCURRIED
SCURRIER
SCURRIERS
SCURRIES
SCURRIL
SCURRILE
SCURRILITIES
SCURRILITY
SCURRILOUS
SCURRILOUSLY
SCURRILOUSNESS
SCURRING
SCURRIOUR
SCURRIOURS
SCURRY
SCURRYING
SCURS
SCURVIER
SCURVIES
SCURVIEST
SCURVILY
SCURVINESS
SCURVINESSES
SCURVY
SCUSE
SCUSED
SCUSES
SCUSING
SCUT
SCUTA
SCUTAGE
SCUTAGES
SCUTAL
SCUTATE
SCUTATION
SCUTCH
SCUTCHED
SCUTCHEON
SCUTCHEONLESS
SCUTCHEONS
SCUTCHER

SCUTCHERS	SCYTHELIKE	SEADOG	SEALYHAM
SCUTCHES	SCYTHEMAN	SEADOGS	SEALYHAMS
SCUTCHING	SCYTHEMEN	SEADROME	SEAM
SCUTCHINGS	SCYTHER	SEADROMES	SEAMAID
SCUTE	SCYTHERS	SEAFARER	SEAMAIDS
SCUTELLA	SCYTHES	SEAFARERS	SEAMAN
SCUTELLAR	SCYTHING	SEAFARING	SEAMANLIKE
SCUTELLATE	SDAINE	SEAFARINGS	SEAMANLY
SCUTELLATED	SDAINED	SEAFLOOR	SEAMANSHIP
SCUTELLATION	SDAINES	SEAFLOORS	SEAMANSHIPS
SCUTELLATIONS	SDAINING	SEAFOLK	SEAMARK
SCUTELLUM	SDAYN	SEAFOLKS	SEAMARKS
SCUTES	SDAYNED	SEAFOOD	SEAME
SCUTIFORM	SDAYNING	SEAFOODS	SEAMED
SCUTIGER	SDAYNS	SEAFOWL	SEAMEN
SCUTIGERS	SDEIGN	SEAFOWLS	SEAMER
SCUTS	SDEIGNE	SEAFRONT	SEAMERS
SCUTTER	SDEIGNED	SEAFRONTS	SEAMES
SCUTTERED	SDEIGNES	SEAGIRT	SEAMIER
SCUTTERING	SDEIGNFULL	SEAGOING	SEAMIEST
SCUTTERS	SDEIGNING	SEAGULL	SEAMINESS
SCUTTLE	SDEIGNS	SEAGULLS	SEAMINESSES
SCUTTLEBUTT	SDEIN	SEAHAWK	SEAMING
SCUTTLEBUTTS	SDEINED	SEAHAWKS	SEAMLESS
SCUTTLED	SDEINING	SEAHOG	SEAMLESSLY
SCUTTLEFUL	SDEINS	SEAHOGS	SEAMLESSNESS
SCUTTLEFULS	SDRUCCIOLA	SEAHORSE	SEAMLESSNESSES
SCUTTLER	SEA	SEAHORSES	SEAMLIKE
SCUTTLERS	SEABAG	SEAHOUND	SEAMOUNT
SCUTTLES	SEABAGS	SEAHOUNDS	SEAMOUNTS
SCUTTLING	SEABANK	SEAKALE	SEAMS
SCUTUM	SEABANKS	SEAKALES	SEAMSET
SCUZZ	SEABEACH	SEAL	SEAMSETS
SCUZZBALL	SEABEACHES	SEALABLE	SEAMSTER
SCUZZBALLS	SEABED	SEALANT	SEAMSTERS
SCUZZES	SEABEDS	SEALANTS	SEAMSTRESS
SCUZZIER	SEABIRD	SEALCH	SEAMSTRESSES
SCUZZIEST	SEABIRDS	SEALCHS	SEAMSTRESSIES
SCUZZY	SEABLITE	SEALED	SEAMSTRESSY
SCYBALA	SEABLITES	SEALER	SEAMY
SCYBALOUS	SEABOARD	SEALERIES	SEAN
SCYBALUM	SEABOARDS	SEALERS	SEANCE
SCYE	SEABOOT	SEALERY	SEANCES
SCYES	SEABOOTS	SEALGH	SEANED
SCYPHATE	SEABORGIUM	SEALGHS	SEANING
SCYPHI	SEABORGIUMS	SEALINE	SEANNACHIE
SCYPHIFORM	SEABORNE	SEALINES	SEANNACHIES
SCYPHISTOMA	SEABOTTLE	SEALING	SEANS
SCYPHISTOMAE	SEABOTTLES	SEALINGS	SEAPIECE
SCYPHISTOMAS	SEACOAST	SEALLIKE	SEAPIECES
SCYPHOZOAN	SEACOASTS	SEALPOINT	SEAPLANE
SCYPHOZOANS	SEACOCK	SEALPOINTS	SEAPLANES
SCYPHUS	SEACOCKS	SEALS	SEAPORT
SCYTALE	SEACRAFT	SEALSKIN	SEAPORTS
SCYTALES	SEACRAFTS	SEALSKINS	SEAQUAKE
SCYTHE	SEACUNNIES	SEALWAX	SEAQUAKES
SCYTHED	SEACUNNY	SEALWAXES	SEAQUARIA

SEAQUARIUM
SEAQUARIUMS
SEAR
SEARAT
SEARATS
SEARCE
SEARCED
SEARCES
SEARCH
SEARCHABLE
SEARCHED
SEARCHER
SEARCHERS
SEARCHES
SEARCHING
SEARCHINGLY
SEARCHINGNESS
SEARCHINGNESSES
SEARCHLESS
SEARCHLIGHT
SEARCHLIGHTS
SEARCING
SEARE
SEARED
SEAREDNESS
SEAREDNESSES
SEARER
SEAREST
SEARING
SEARINGLY
SEARINGS
SEARNESS
SEARNESSES
SEAROBIN
SEAROBINS
SEARS
SEAS
SEASCAPE
SEASCAPES
SEASCOUT
SEASCOUTS
SEASE
SEASED
SEASES
SEASHELL
SEASHELLS
SEASHORE
SEASHORES
SEASICK
SEASICKER
SEASICKEST
SEASICKNESS
SEASICKNESSES
SEASIDE
SEASIDES
SEASING
SEASON

SEASONABLE
SEASONABLENESS
SEASONABLY
SEASONAL
SEASONALITIES
SEASONALITY
SEASONALLY
SEASONALNESS
SEASONED
SEASONER
SEASONERS
SEASONING
SEASONINGS
SEASONLESS
SEASONS
SEASPEAK
SEASPEAKS
SEASTRAND
SEASTRANDS
SEASURE
SEASURES
SEAT
SEATED
SEATER
SEATERS
SEATING
SEATINGS
SEATLESS
SEATMATE
SEATMATES
SEATRAIN
SEATRAINS
SEATS
SEATWORK
SEATWORKS
SEAWALL
SEAWALLS
SEAWAN
SEAWANS
SEAWANT
SEAWANTS
SEAWARD
SEAWARDLY
SEAWARDS
SEAWARE
SEAWARES
SEAWATER
SEAWATERS
SEAWAY
SEAWAYS
SEAWEED
SEAWEEDS
SEAWIFE
SEAWIVES
SEAWOMAN
SEAWOMEN
SEAWORM

SEAWORMS
SEAWORTHINESS
SEAWORTHINESSES
SEAWORTHY
SEAZE
SEAZED
SEAZES
SEAZING
SEBACEOUS
SEBACIC
SEBASIC
SEBATE
SEBATES
SEBESTEN
SEBESTENS
SEBIFEROUS
SEBIFIC
SEBORRHEA
SEBORRHEAL
SEBORRHEAS
SEBORRHEIC
SEBORRHOEA
SEBORRHOEAL
SEBORRHOEAS
SEBORRHOEIC
SEBUM
SEBUMS
SEBUNDIES
SEBUNDY
SEC
SECALOSE
SECALOSES
SECANT
SECANTLY
SECANTS
SECATEUR
SECATEURS
SECCO
SECCOS
SECEDE
SECEDED
SECEDER
SECEDERS
SECEDES
SECEDING
SECERN
SECERNED
SECERNENT
SECERNENTS
SECERNING
SECERNMENT
SECERNMENTS
SECERNS
SECESH
SECESHER
SECESHERS
SECESHES

SECESSION
SECESSIONAL
SECESSIONISM
SECESSIONISMS
SECESSIONIST
SECESSIONISTS
SECESSIONS
SECH
SECKEL
SECKELS
SECKLE
SECKLES
SECLUDE
SECLUDED
SECLUDEDLY
SECLUDEDNESS
SECLUDEDNESSES
SECLUDES
SECLUDING
SECLUSION
SECLUSIONIST
SECLUSIONISTS
SECLUSIONS
SECLUSIVE
SECLUSIVELY
SECLUSIVENESS
SECLUSIVENESSES
SECO
SECOBARBITAL
SECOBARBITALS
SECODONT
SECODONTS
SECOND
SECONDARIES
SECONDARILY
SECONDARINESS
SECONDARINESSES
SECONDARY
SECONDE
SECONDED
SECONDEE
SECONDEES
SECONDER
SECONDERS
SECONDES
SECONDHAND
SECONDI
SECONDING
SECONDLY
SECONDMENT
SECONDMENTS
SECONDO
SECONDS
SECPAR
SECPARS
SECRECIES
SECRECY

SECRET
SECRETA
SECRETAGE
SECRETAGES
SECRETAGOGIC
SECRETAGOGUE
SECRETAGOGUES
SECRETAIRE
SECRETAIRES
SECRETARIAL
SECRETARIAT
SECRETARIATE
SECRETARIATES
SECRETARIATS
SECRETARIES
SECRETARY
SECRETARYSHIP
SECRETARYSHIPS
SECRETE
SECRETED
SECRETER
SECRETES
SECRETEST
SECRETIN
SECRETING
SECRETINS
SECRETION
SECRETIONAL
SECRETIONARY
SECRETIONS
SECRETIVE
SECRETIVELY
SECRETIVENESS
SECRETIVENESSES
SECRETLY
SECRETNESS
SECRETNESSES
SECRETOR
SECRETORS
SECRETORY
SECRETS
SECS
SECT
SECTARIAL
SECTARIAN
SECTARIANISE
SECTARIANISED
SECTARIANISES
SECTARIANISING
SECTARIANISM
SECTARIANISMS
SECTARIANIZE
SECTARIANIZED
SECTARIANIZES
SECTARIANIZING
SECTARIANS
SECTARIES

SECTARY
SECTATOR
SECTATORS
SECTILE
SECTILITIES
SECTILITY
SECTION
SECTIONAL
SECTIONALISE
SECTIONALISED
SECTIONALISES
SECTIONALISING
SECTIONALISM
SECTIONALISMS
SECTIONALIST
SECTIONALISTS
SECTIONALIZE
SECTIONALIZED
SECTIONALIZES
SECTIONALIZING
SECTIONALLY
SECTIONALS
SECTIONED
SECTIONING
SECTIONISATION
SECTIONISATIONS
SECTIONISE
SECTIONISED
SECTIONISES
SECTIONISING
SECTIONIZATION
SECTIONIZATIONS
SECTIONIZE
SECTIONIZED
SECTIONIZES
SECTIONIZING
SECTIONS
SECTOR
SECTORAL
SECTORED
SECTORIAL
SECTORIALS
SECTORING
SECTORISATION
SECTORISATIONS
SECTORISE
SECTORISED
SECTORISES
SECTORISING
SECTORIZATION
SECTORIZATIONS
SECTORIZE
SECTORIZED
SECTORIZES
SECTORIZING
SECTORS
SECTS

SECULAR
SECULARISATION
SECULARISATIONS
SECULARISE
SECULARISED
SECULARISER
SECULARISERS
SECULARISES
SECULARISING
SECULARISM
SECULARISMS
SECULARIST
SECULARISTIC
SECULARISTS
SECULARITIES
SECULARITY
SECULARIZATION
SECULARIZATIONS
SECULARIZE
SECULARIZED
SECULARIZER
SECULARIZERS
SECULARIZES
SECULARIZING
SECULARLY
SECULARS
SECULUM
SECULUMS
SECUND
SECUNDINE
SECUNDINES
SECUNDLY
SECUNDOGENITURE
SECUNDUM
SECURABLE
SECURANCE
SECURANCES
SECURE
SECURED
SECURELY
SECUREMENT
SECUREMENTS
SECURENESS
SECURENESSES
SECURER
SECURERS
SECURES
SECUREST
SECURIFORM
SECURING
SECURITAN
SECURITANS
SECURITIES
SECURITISATION
SECURITISATIONS
SECURITISE
SECURITISED

SECURITISES
SECURITISING
SECURITIZATION
SECURITIZATIONS
SECURITIZE
SECURITIZED
SECURITIZES
SECURITIZING
SECURITY
SECUROCRAT
SECUROCRATIC
SECUROCRATS
SECY
SED
SEDAN
SEDANS
SEDARIM
SEDATE
SEDATED
SEDATELY
SEDATENESS
SEDATENESSES
SEDATER
SEDATES
SEDATEST
SEDATING
SEDATION
SEDATIONS
SEDATIVE
SEDATIVES
SEDENT
SEDENTARILY
SEDENTARINESS
SEDENTARINESSES
SEDENTARY
SEDER
SEDERS
SEDERUNT
SEDERUNTS
SEDES
SEDGE
SEDGED
SEDGELAND
SEDGELANDS
SEDGES
SEDGIER
SEDGIEST
SEDGY
SEDIGITATED
SEDILE
SEDILIA
SEDILIUM
SEDIMENT
SEDIMENTABLE
SEDIMENTARILY
SEDIMENTARY
SEDIMENTATION

SEDIMENTATIONS
SEDIMENTED
SEDIMENTING
SEDIMENTOLOGIC
SEDIMENTOLOGIES
SEDIMENTOLOGIST
SEDIMENTOLOGY
SEDIMENTOUS
SEDIMENTS
SEDITION
SEDITIONARIES
SEDITIONARY
SEDITIONS
SEDITIOUS
SEDITIOUSLY
SEDITIOUSNESS
SEDITIOUSNESSES
SEDUCE
SEDUCEABLE
SEDUCED
SEDUCEMENT
SEDUCEMENTS
SEDUCER
SEDUCERS
SEDUCES
SEDUCIBLE
SEDUCING
SEDUCINGLY
SEDUCINGS
SEDUCIVE
SEDUCTION
SEDUCTIONS
SEDUCTIVE
SEDUCTIVELY
SEDUCTIVENESS
SEDUCTIVENESSES
SEDUCTOR
SEDUCTORS
SEDUCTRESS
SEDUCTRESSES
SEDULITIES
SEDULITY
SEDULOUS
SEDULOUSLY
SEDULOUSNESS
SEDULOUSNESSES
SEDUM
SEDUMS
SEE
SEEABLE
SEECATCH
SEECATCHIE
SEED
SEEDBED
SEEDBEDS
SEEDBOX
SEEDBOXES

SEEDCAKE
SEEDCAKES
SEEDCASE
SEEDCASES
SEEDEATER
SEEDEATERS
SEEDED
SEEDER
SEEDERS
SEEDIER
SEEDIEST
SEEDILY
SEEDINESS
SEEDINESSES
SEEDING
SEEDINGS
SEEDLESS
SEEDLIKE
SEEDLING
SEEDLINGS
SEEDLIP
SEEDLIPS
SEEDMAN
SEEDMEN
SEEDNESS
SEEDNESSES
SEEDPOD
SEEDPODS
SEEDS
SEEDSMAN
SEEDSMEN
SEEDTIME
SEEDTIMES
SEEDY
SEEING
SEEINGS
SEEK
SEEKER
SEEKERS
SEEKING
SEEKS
SEEL
SEELD
SEELED
SEELIE
SEELIER
SEELIEST
SEELING
SEELINGS
SEELS
SEELY
SEEM
SEEMED
SEEMELESSE
SEEMER
SEEMERS
SEEMING

SEEMINGLY
SEEMINGNESS
SEEMINGNESSES
SEEMINGS
SEEMLESS
SEEMLIER
SEEMLIEST
SEEMLIHEAD
SEEMLIHEADS
SEEMLIHED
SEEMLIHEDS
SEEMLINESS
SEEMLINESSES
SEEMLY
SEEMLYHED
SEEMLYHEDS
SEEMS
SEEN
SEEP
SEEPAGE
SEEPAGES
SEEPED
SEEPIER
SEEPIEST
SEEPING
SEEPS
SEEPY
SEER
SEERESS
SEERESSES
SEERS
SEERSUCKER
SEERSUCKERS
SEES
SEESAW
SEESAWED
SEESAWING
SEESAWS
SEETHE
SEETHED
SEETHER
SEETHERS
SEETHES
SEETHING
SEETHINGLY
SEETHINGS
SEEWING
SEFER
SEFERS
SEG
SEGAR
SEGARS
SEGETAL
SEGGAR
SEGGARS
SEGHOL
SEGHOLATE

SEGHOLATES
SEGHOLS
SEGMENT
SEGMENTAL
SEGMENTALLY
SEGMENTARY
SEGMENTATE
SEGMENTATION
SEGMENTATIONS
SEGMENTED
SEGMENTING
SEGMENTS
SEGNI
SEGNO
SEGNOS
SEGO
SEGOL
SEGOLATE
SEGOLATES
SEGOLS
SEGOS
SEGREANT
SEGREGABLE
SEGREGANT
SEGREGANTS
SEGREGATE
SEGREGATED
SEGREGATES
SEGREGATING
SEGREGATION
SEGREGATIONAL
SEGREGATIONALLY
SEGREGATIONIST
SEGREGATIONISTS
SEGREGATIONS
SEGREGATIVE
SEGREGATOR
SEGREGATORS
SEGS
SEGUE
SEGUED
SEGUEING
SEGUES
SEGUIDILLA
SEGUIDILLAS
SEI
SEICENTO
SEICENTOS
SEICHE
SEICHES
SEIDEL
SEIDELS
SEIF
SEIFS
SEIGNEUR
SEIGNEURIAL
SEIGNEURIE

SEIGNEURIES
SEIGNEURS
SEIGNEURY
SEIGNIOR
SEIGNIORAGE
SEIGNIORAGES
SEIGNIORALTIES
SEIGNIORALTY
SEIGNIORIAL
SEIGNIORIES
SEIGNIORS
SEIGNIORSHIP
SEIGNIORSHIPS
SEIGNIORY
SEIGNORAGE
SEIGNORAGES
SEIGNORAL
SEIGNORIAL
SEIGNORIES
SEIGNORY
SEIK
SEIKER
SEIKEST
SEIL
SEILED
SEILING
SEILS
SEINE
SEINED
SEINER
SEINERS
SEINES
SEINING
SEININGS
SEIR
SEIRS
SEIS
SEISABLE
SEISE
SEISED
SEISER
SEISERS
SEISES
SEISIN
SEISING
SEISINGS
SEISINS
SEISM
SEISMAL
SEISMIC
SEISMICAL
SEISMICALLY
SEISMICITIES
SEISMICITY
SEISMISM
SEISMISMS
SEISMOGRAM

SEISMOGRAMS
SEISMOGRAPH
SEISMOGRAPHER
SEISMOGRAPHERS
SEISMOGRAPHIC
SEISMOGRAPHICAL
SEISMOGRAPHIES
SEISMOGRAPHS
SEISMOGRAPHY
SEISMOLOGIC
SEISMOLOGICAL
SEISMOLOGICALLY
SEISMOLOGIES
SEISMOLOGIST
SEISMOLOGISTS
SEISMOLOGY
SEISMOMETER
SEISMOMETERS
SEISMOMETRIC
SEISMOMETRICAL
SEISMOMETRIES
SEISMOMETRY
SEISMONASTIC
SEISMONASTIES
SEISMONASTY
SEISMOSCOPE
SEISMOSCOPES
SEISMOSCOPIC
SEISMS
SEISOR
SEISORS
SEISURE
SEISURES
SEITEN
SEITENS
SEITIES
SEITY
SEIZABLE
SEIZE
SEIZED
SEIZER
SEIZERS
SEIZES
SEIZIN
SEIZING
SEIZINGS
SEIZINS
SEIZOR
SEIZORS
SEIZURE
SEIZURES
SEJANT
SEJEANT
SEKOS
SEKOSES
SEKT
SEKTS

SEL
SELACHIAN
SELACHIANS
SELADANG
SELADANGS
SELAGINELLA
SELAGINELLAS
SELAH
SELAHS
SELAMLIK
SELAMLIKS
SELCOUTH
SELD
SELDOM
SELDOMLY
SELDOMNESS
SELDOMNESSES
SELDSEEN
SELDSHOWN
SELE
SELECT
SELECTA
SELECTABLE
SELECTAS
SELECTED
SELECTEE
SELECTEES
SELECTING
SELECTION
SELECTIONIST
SELECTIONISTS
SELECTIONS
SELECTIVE
SELECTIVELY
SELECTIVENESS
SELECTIVENESSES
SELECTIVITIES
SELECTIVITY
SELECTLY
SELECTMAN
SELECTMEN
SELECTNESS
SELECTNESSES
SELECTOR
SELECTORATE
SELECTORIAL
SELECTORS
SELECTS
SELEGILINE
SELEGILINES
SELENATE
SELENATES
SELENIAN
SELENIC
SELENIDE
SELENIDES
SELENIFEROUS

SELENIOUS
SELENITE
SELENITES
SELENITIC
SELENIUM
SELENIUMS
SELENOCENTRIC
SELENODONT
SELENODONTS
SELENOGRAPH
SELENOGRAPHER
SELENOGRAPHERS
SELENOGRAPHIC
SELENOGRAPHICAL
SELENOGRAPHIES
SELENOGRAPHIST
SELENOGRAPHISTS
SELENOGRAPHS
SELENOGRAPHY
SELENOLOGICAL
SELENOLOGIES
SELENOLOGIST
SELENOLOGISTS
SELENOLOGY
SELENOUS
SELES
SELF
SELFDOM
SELFDOMS
SELFED
SELFHEAL
SELFHEALS
SELFHOOD
SELFHOODS
SELFING
SELFINGS
SELFISH
SELFISHLY
SELFISHNESS
SELFISHNESSES
SELFISM
SELFISMS
SELFIST
SELFISTS
SELFLESS
SELFLESSLY
SELFLESSNESS
SELFLESSNESSES
SELFNESS
SELFNESSES
SELFS
SELFSAME
SELFSAMENESS
SELFSAMENESSES
SELFWARD
SELICTAR
SELICTARS

SELKIE
SELKIES
SELL
SELLA
SELLABLE
SELLAE
SELLAS
SELLE
SELLENOGRAPHIST
SELLER
SELLERS
SELLES
SELLING
SELLOTAPE
SELLOTAPED
SELLOTAPES
SELLOTAPING
SELLOUT
SELLOUTS
SELLS
SELS
SELSYN
SELSYNS
SELTZER
SELTZERS
SELTZOGENE
SELTZOGENES
SELVA
SELVAGE
SELVAGED
SELVAGEE
SELVAGEES
SELVAGES
SELVAGING
SELVAS
SELVEDGE
SELVEDGED
SELVEDGES
SELVEDGING
SELVES
SEMANTEME
SEMANTEMES
SEMANTIC
SEMANTICAL
SEMANTICALLY
SEMANTICIST
SEMANTICISTS
SEMANTICS
SEMANTIDE
SEMANTIDES
SEMANTRA
SEMANTRON
SEMAPHORE
SEMAPHORED
SEMAPHORES
SEMAPHORIC
SEMAPHORICAL

SEMAPHORICALLY
SEMAPHORING
SEMASIOLOGICAL
SEMASIOLOGIES
SEMASIOLOGIST
SEMASIOLOGISTS
SEMASIOLOGY
SEMATIC
SEMATOLOGICAL
SEMATOLOGICALLY
SEMATOLOGY
SEMBLABLE
SEMBLABLES
SEMBLABLY
SEMBLANCE
SEMBLANCES
SEMBLANT
SEMBLANTS
SEMBLATIVE
SEMBLE
SEMBLED
SEMBLES
SEMBLING
SEME
SEMEE
SEMEED
SEMEIA
SEMEIOLOGIC
SEMEIOLOGICAL
SEMEIOLOGICALLY
SEMEIOLOGIES
SEMEIOLOGIST
SEMEIOLOGISTS
SEMEIOLOGY
SEMEION
SEMEIOTIC
SEMEIOTICIAN
SEMEIOTICIANS
SEMEIOTICS
SEMELPARITY
SEMELPAROUS
SEMELPAROUSLY
SEMEME
SEMEMES
SEMEMIC
SEMEN
SEMENS
SEMES
SEMESTER
SEMESTERS
SEMESTRAL
SEMESTRIAL
SEMI
SEMIABSTRACT
SEMIABSTRACTION
SEMIACTIVE
SEMIACTIVELY

SEMIANGLE
SEMIANGLES
SEMIANGULAR
SEMIANIMATED
SEMIANNUAL
SEMIANNUALLY
SEMIAQUATIC
SEMIARBOREAL
SEMIARID
SEMIARIDITIES
SEMIARIDITY
SEMIAUTOMATIC
SEMIAUTOMATICS
SEMIAUTONOMOUS
SEMIBALD
SEMIBLIND
SEMIBOLD
SEMIBOLDS
SEMIBREVE
SEMIBREVES
SEMIBULL
SEMIBULLS
SEMICARBAZIDE
SEMICARBAZIDES
SEMICARBAZONE
SEMICARBAZONES
SEMICENTENNIAL
SEMICENTENNIALS
SEMICHORUS
SEMICHORUSES
SEMICIRCLE
SEMICIRCLED
SEMICIRCLES
SEMICIRCULAR
SEMICIRCULARLY
SEMICIRQUE
SEMICIRQUES
SEMICIVILISED
SEMICIVILIZED
SEMICLASSIC
SEMICLASSICAL
SEMICLASSICALLY
SEMICLASSICS
SEMICOLON
SEMICOLONIAL
SEMICOLONIALISM
SEMICOLONIES
SEMICOLONS
SEMICOLONY
SEMICOMA
SEMICOMAS
SEMICOMATOSE
SEMICOMICAL
SEMICOMMERCIAL
SEMICONDUCTING
SEMICONDUCTION
SEMICONDUCTOR

SEMICONDUCTORS
SEMICONSCIOUS
SEMICONSCIOUSLY
SEMICRYSTALLINE
SEMICYLINDER
SEMICYLINDERS
SEMICYLINDRICAL
SEMIDAILY
SEMIDARKNESS
SEMIDARKNESSES
SEMIDEAF
SEMIDEIFIED
SEMIDEIFIES
SEMIDEIFY
SEMIDEIFYING
SEMIDEPENDENCE
SEMIDEPENDENT
SEMIDEPONENT
SEMIDEPONENTS
SEMIDESERT
SEMIDESERTS
SEMIDETACHED
SEMIDIAMETER
SEMIDIAMETERS
SEMIDIRECT
SEMIDIRECTLY
SEMIDIRECTNESS
SEMIDIURNAL
SEMIDIVINE
SEMIDOCUMENTARY
SEMIDOME
SEMIDOMED
SEMIDOMES
SEMIDOMINANT
SEMIDRY
SEMIDRYING
SEMIDWARF
SEMIDWARFS
SEMIDWARVES
SEMIE
SEMIELLIPTICAL
SEMIEMPIRICAL
SEMIERECT
SEMIES
SEMIEVERGREEN
SEMIEXPOSED
SEMIFEUDAL
SEMIFICTIONAL
SEMIFINAL
SEMIFINALIST
SEMIFINALISTS
SEMIFINALS
SEMIFINISHED
SEMIFIT
SEMIFITTED
SEMIFLEXIBLE
SEMIFLUID

SEMIFLUIDIC
SEMIFLUIDITY
SEMIFLUIDS
SEMIFORMAL
SEMIFORMED
SEMIFREDDO
SEMIFREDDOS
SEMIFRIABLE
SEMIGALA
SEMIGLOBULAR
SEMIGLOSS
SEMIGROUP
SEMIGROUPS
SEMIHARD
SEMIHIGH
SEMIHOBO
SEMIHOBOES
SEMIHOBOS
SEMILEGENDARY
SEMILETHAL
SEMILETHALS
SEMILIQUID
SEMILIQUIDS
SEMILITERATE
SEMILITERATES
SEMILOG
SEMILOGARITHMIC
SEMILUCENT
SEMILUNAR
SEMILUNATE
SEMILUNE
SEMILUNES
SEMILUSTROUS
SEMIMANUFACTURE
SEMIMAT
SEMIMATT
SEMIMATTE
SEMIMATURE
SEMIMATURITY
SEMIMENSTRUAL
SEMIMETAL
SEMIMETALLIC
SEMIMETALS
SEMIMICRO
SEMIMOIST
SEMIMONASTIC
SEMIMONTHLIES
SEMIMONTHLY
SEMIMOUNTAINOUS
SEMIMUTE
SEMIMYSTICAL
SEMIMYTHICAL
SEMINA
SEMINAL
SEMINALITIES
SEMINALITY
SEMINALLY

SEMINAR
SEMINARIAL
SEMINARIAN
SEMINARIANS
SEMINARIES
SEMINARIST
SEMINARISTS
SEMINARS
SEMINARY
SEMINATE
SEMINATED
SEMINATES
SEMINATING
SEMINATION
SEMINATIONS
SEMINATURAL
SEMINIFEROUS
SEMINOMA
SEMINOMAD
SEMINOMADIC
SEMINOMADS
SEMINOMAS
SEMINORMAL
SEMINORMALITY
SEMINORMALLY
SEMINUDE
SEMINUDITIES
SEMINUDITY
SEMIOCHEMICAL
SEMIOCHEMICALS
SEMIOFFICIAL
SEMIOFFICIALLY
SEMIOLOGIC
SEMIOLOGICAL
SEMIOLOGICALLY
SEMIOLOGIES
SEMIOLOGIST
SEMIOLOGISTS
SEMIOLOGY
SEMIOPAQUE
SEMIORGANISED
SEMIORGANIZED
SEMIORIENTAL
SEMIOSES
SEMIOSIS
SEMIOTIC
SEMIOTICIAN
SEMIOTICIANS
SEMIOTICIST
SEMIOTICISTS
SEMIOTICS
SEMIOVIPAROUS
SEMIPAGAN
SEMIPAGANS
SEMIPALMATE
SEMIPALMATED
SEMIPALMATION

SEMIPALMATIONS
SEMIPARALYSED
SEMIPARALYSES
SEMIPARALYSIS
SEMIPARALYTIC
SEMIPARALYTICS
SEMIPARASITE
SEMIPARASITES
SEMIPARASITIC
SEMIPARASITISM
SEMIPED
SEMIPEDS
SEMIPELLUCID
SEMIPERIMETER
SEMIPERIMETERS
SEMIPERMANENT
SEMIPERMEABLE
SEMIPETRIFIED
SEMIPLASTIC
SEMIPLASTICITY
SEMIPLUME
SEMIPLUMES
SEMIPOLAR
SEMIPOLITICAL
SEMIPOPULAR
SEMIPORCELAIN
SEMIPORCELAINS
SEMIPORNOGRAPHY
SEMIPOROSITY
SEMIPOROUS
SEMIPOSTAL
SEMIPOSTALS
SEMIPRECIOUS
SEMIPRIMITIVE
SEMIPRIVATE
SEMIPRO
SEMIPROS
SEMIPUBLIC
SEMIPURPOSIVE
SEMIPURPOSIVELY
SEMIQUAVER
SEMIQUAVERS
SEMIRAW
SEMIREBELLIOUS
SEMIREFINED
SEMIREFINEMENT
SEMIRELIGIOUS
SEMIRESOLUTE
SEMIRESOLUTELY
SEMIRESPECTABLE
SEMIRESPECTABLY
SEMIRETIRED
SEMIRETIREMENT
SEMIRETIREMENTS
SEMIRIGID
SEMIROUND
SEMIRURAL

SEMIS
SEMISACRED
SEMISATIRICAL
SEMISATIRICALLY
SEMISECRET
SEMISEDENTARY
SEMISERIOUS
SEMISERIOUSLY
SEMISERIOUSNESS
SEMISES
SEMISHRUBBY
SEMISKILLED
SEMISOCIALISTIC
SEMISOFT
SEMISOLID
SEMISOLIDS
SEMISOLUS
SEMISOLUSES
SEMISUBMERSIBLE
SEMISUBURBAN
SEMISUCCESFULLY
SEMISUCCESSFUL
SEMISWEET
SEMISYNTHETIC
SEMITAR
SEMITARS
SEMITAUR
SEMITAURS
SEMITERETE
SEMITERRESTRIAL
SEMITIST
SEMITISTS
SEMITONAL
SEMITONALLY
SEMITONE
SEMITONES
SEMITONIC
SEMITONICALLY
SEMITRADITIONAL
SEMITRAILER
SEMITRAILERS
SEMITRAINED
SEMITRANSLUCENT
SEMITRANSPARENT
SEMITROPIC
SEMITROPICAL
SEMITROPICS
SEMITRUTHFUL
SEMITRUTHFULLY
SEMIURBAN
SEMIVITREOUS
SEMIVOCAL
SEMIVOCALIC
SEMIVOLUNTARILY
SEMIVOLUNTARY
SEMIVOWEL
SEMIVOWELS

SEMIWEEKLIES
SEMIWEEKLY
SEMIWILD
SEMIWORKS
SEMIYEARLY
SEMMIT
SEMMITS
SEMOLINA
SEMOLINAS
SEMPER
SEMPERVIVUM
SEMPERVIVUMS
SEMPITERNAL
SEMPITERNALLY
SEMPITERNITIES
SEMPITERNITY
SEMPITERNUM
SEMPITERNUMS
SEMPLE
SEMPLER
SEMPLEST
SEMPLICE
SEMPRE
SEMPSTER
SEMPSTERING
SEMPSTERINGS
SEMPSTERS
SEMPSTRESS
SEMPSTRESSES
SEMPSTRESSING
SEMPSTRESSINGS
SEMSEM
SEMSEMS
SEMUNCIA
SEMUNCIAE
SEMUNCIAL
SEMUNCIAS
SEN
SENA
SENARIES
SENARII
SENARIUS
SENARMONTITE
SENARY
SENAS
SENATE
SENATES
SENATOR
SENATORIAL
SENATORIALLY
SENATORIAN
SENATORS
SENATORSHIP
SENATORSHIPS
SEND
SENDABLE
SENDAL

SENDALS
SENDED
SENDER
SENDERS
SENDING
SENDINGS
SENDOFF
SENDOFFS
SENDS
SENDUP
SENDUPS
SENE
SENECA
SENECAS
SENECIO
SENECIOS
SENECTITUDE
SENECTITUDES
SENEGA
SENEGAS
SENESCENCE
SENESCENCES
SENESCENT
SENESCHAL
SENESCHALS
SENESCHALSHIP
SENESCHALSHIPS
SENGI
SENGREEN
SENGREENS
SENHOR
SENHORA
SENHORAS
SENHORES
SENHORITA
SENHORITAS
SENHORS
SENILE
SENILELY
SENILES
SENILITIES
SENILITY
SENIOR
SENIORITIES
SENIORITY
SENIORS
SENITI
SENNA
SENNACHIE
SENNACHIES
SENNAS
SENNET
SENNETS
SENNIGHT
SENNIGHTS
SENNIT
SENNITS

SENOPIA
SENOPIAS
SENOR
SENORA
SENORAS
SENORES
SENORITA
SENORITAS
SENORS
SENRYU
SENS
SENSA
SENSATE
SENSATED
SENSATELY
SENSATES
SENSATING
SENSATION
SENSATIONAL
SENSATIONALISE
SENSATIONALISED
SENSATIONALISES
SENSATIONALISM
SENSATIONALISMS
SENSATIONALIST
SENSATIONALISTS
SENSATIONALIZE
SENSATIONALIZED
SENSATIONALIZES
SENSATIONALLY
SENSATIONISM
SENSATIONISMS
SENSATIONIST
SENSATIONISTS
SENSATIONLESS
SENSATIONLESSLY
SENSATIONS
SENSE
SENSED
SENSEFUL
SENSELESS
SENSELESSLY
SENSELESSNESS
SENSELESSNESSES
SENSES
SENSIBILIA
SENSIBILITIES
SENSIBILITY
SENSIBLE
SENSIBLENESS
SENSIBLENESSES
SENSIBLER
SENSIBLES
SENSIBLEST
SENSIBLY
SENSILE
SENSILLA

SENSILLAE
SENSILLUM
SENSING
SENSINGS
SENSISM
SENSISMS
SENSIST
SENSISTS
SENSITISATION
SENSITISATIONS
SENSITISE
SENSITISED
SENSITISER
SENSITISERS
SENSITISES
SENSITISING
SENSITIVE
SENSITIVELY
SENSITIVENESS
SENSITIVENESSES
SENSITIVES
SENSITIVITIES
SENSITIVITY
SENSITIZATION
SENSITIZATIONS
SENSITIZE
SENSITIZED
SENSITIZER
SENSITIZERS
SENSITIZES
SENSITIZING
SENSITOMETER
SENSITOMETERS
SENSITOMETRIC
SENSITOMETRIES
SENSITOMETRY
SENSOMOTOR
SENSOR
SENSORIA
SENSORIAL
SENSORIALLY
SENSORILY
SENSORIMOTOR
SENSORINEURAL
SENSORIUM
SENSORIUMS
SENSORS
SENSORY
SENSUAL
SENSUALISATION
SENSUALISATIONS
SENSUALISE
SENSUALISED
SENSUALISES
SENSUALISING
SENSUALISM
SENSUALISMS

SENSUALIST
SENSUALISTIC
SENSUALISTS
SENSUALITIES
SENSUALITY
SENSUALIZATION
SENSUALIZATIONS
SENSUALIZE
SENSUALIZED
SENSUALIZES
SENSUALIZING
SENSUALLY
SENSUALNESS
SENSUALNESSES
SENSUM
SENSUOSITIES
SENSUOSITY
SENSUOUS
SENSUOUSLY
SENSUOUSNESS
SENSUOUSNESSES
SENT
SENTE
SENTED
SENTENCE
SENTENCED
SENTENCER
SENTENCERS
SENTENCES
SENTENCING
SENTENTIA
SENTENTIAE
SENTENTIAL
SENTENTIALLY
SENTENTIOUS
SENTENTIOUSLY
SENTENTIOUSNESS
SENTI
SENTIENCE
SENTIENCES
SENTIENCIES
SENTIENCY
SENTIENT
SENTIENTLY
SENTIENTS
SENTIMENT
SENTIMENTAL
SENTIMENTALISE
SENTIMENTALISED
SENTIMENTALISES
SENTIMENTALISM
SENTIMENTALISMS
SENTIMENTALIST
SENTIMENTALISTS
SENTIMENTALITY
SENTIMENTALIZE
SENTIMENTALIZED

SENTIMENTALIZES
SENTIMENTALLY
SENTIMENTS
SENTIMO
SENTIMOS
SENTINEL
SENTINELED
SENTINELING
SENTINELLED
SENTINELLING
SENTINELS
SENTING
SENTRIES
SENTRY
SENTS
SENVIES
SENVY
SENZA
SEPAD
SEPADDED
SEPADDING
SEPADS
SEPAL
SEPALED
SEPALINE
SEPALLED
SEPALODIES
SEPALODY
SEPALOID
SEPALOUS
SEPALS
SEPARABILITIES
SEPARABILITY
SEPARABLE
SEPARABLENESS
SEPARABLENESSES
SEPARABLY
SEPARATA
SEPARATE
SEPARATED
SEPARATELY
SEPARATENESS
SEPARATENESSES
SEPARATES
SEPARATING
SEPARATION
SEPARATIONISM
SEPARATIONISMS
SEPARATIONIST
SEPARATIONISTS
SEPARATIONS
SEPARATISM
SEPARATISMS
SEPARATIST
SEPARATISTIC
SEPARATISTS
SEPARATIVE

SEPARATIVELY
SEPARATIVENESS
SEPARATOR
SEPARATORIES
SEPARATORS
SEPARATORY
SEPARATRICES
SEPARATRIX
SEPARATUM
SEPARATUMS
SEPHEN
SEPHENS
SEPIA
SEPIAS
SEPIC
SEPIMENT
SEPIMENTS
SEPIOLITE
SEPIOLITES
SEPIOST
SEPIOSTAIRE
SEPIOSTAIRES
SEPIOSTS
SEPIUM
SEPIUMS
SEPMAG
SEPOY
SEPOYS
SEPPUKU
SEPPUKUS
SEPS
SEPSES
SEPSIS
SEPT
SEPTA
SEPTAL
SEPTARIA
SEPTARIAN
SEPTARIUM
SEPTATE
SEPTATION
SEPTATIONS
SEPTAVALENCY
SEPTAVALENT
SEPTEMFID
SEPTEMVIR
SEPTEMVIRATE
SEPTEMVIRATES
SEPTEMVIRI
SEPTEMVIRS
SEPTENARIES
SEPTENARII
SEPTENARIUS
SEPTENARY
SEPTENDECILLION
SEPTENNATE
SEPTENNATES

SEPTENNIA
SEPTENNIAL
SEPTENNIALLY
SEPTENNIUM
SEPTENNIUMS
SEPTENTRIAL
SEPTENTRION
SEPTENTRIONAL
SEPTENTRIONALLY
SEPTENTRIONES
SEPTENTRIONS
SEPTET
SEPTETS
SEPTETTE
SEPTETTES
SEPTIC
SEPTICAEMIA
SEPTICAEMIAS
SEPTICAEMIC
SEPTICAL
SEPTICALLY
SEPTICEMIA
SEPTICEMIAS
SEPTICEMIC
SEPTICIDAL
SEPTICIDALLY
SEPTICITIES
SEPTICITY
SEPTICS
SEPTIFEROUS
SEPTIFORM
SEPTIFRAGAL
SEPTILATERAL
SEPTILLION
SEPTILLIONS
SEPTILLIONTH
SEPTILLIONTHS
SEPTIMAL
SEPTIME
SEPTIMES
SEPTIMOLE
SEPTIMOLES
SEPTIVALENT
SEPTLEVA
SEPTLEVAS
SEPTS
SEPTUAGENARIAN
SEPTUAGENARIANS
SEPTUAGENARIES
SEPTUAGENARY
SEPTUM
SEPTUMS
SEPTUOR
SEPTUORS
SEPTUPLE
SEPTUPLED
SEPTUPLES

SEPTUPLET
SEPTUPLETS
SEPTUPLICATE
SEPTUPLICATES
SEPTUPLING
SEPULCHER
SEPULCHERED
SEPULCHERING
SEPULCHERS
SEPULCHRAL
SEPULCHRALLY
SEPULCHRE
SEPULCHRED
SEPULCHRES
SEPULCHRING
SEPULCHROUS
SEPULTURAL
SEPULTURE
SEPULTURED
SEPULTURES
SEPULTURING
SEQUACIOUS
SEQUACIOUSLY
SEQUACIOUSNESS
SEQUACITIES
SEQUACITY
SEQUEL
SEQUELA
SEQUELAE
SEQUELS
SEQUENCE
SEQUENCED
SEQUENCER
SEQUENCERS
SEQUENCES
SEQUENCIES
SEQUENCING
SEQUENCINGS
SEQUENCY
SEQUENT
SEQUENTIAL
SEQUENTIALITIES
SEQUENTIALITY
SEQUENTIALLY
SEQUENTLY
SEQUENTS
SEQUESTER
SEQUESTERED
SEQUESTERING
SEQUESTERS
SEQUESTRA
SEQUESTRABLE
SEQUESTRAL
SEQUESTRANT
SEQUESTRANTS
SEQUESTRATE
SEQUESTRATED

SEQUESTRATES
SEQUESTRATING
SEQUESTRATION
SEQUESTRATIONS
SEQUESTRATOR
SEQUESTRATORS
SEQUESTRUM
SEQUESTRUMS
SEQUIN
SEQUINED
SEQUINNED
SEQUINS
SEQUITUR
SEQUITURS
SEQUOIA
SEQUOIAS
SER
SERA
SERAC
SERACS
SERAFILE
SERAFILES
SERAFIN
SERAFINS
SERAGLIO
SERAGLIOS
SERAI
SERAIL
SERAILS
SERAIS
SERAL
SERANG
SERANGS
SERAPE
SERAPES
SERAPH
SERAPHIC
SERAPHICAL
SERAPHICALLY
SERAPHIM
SERAPHIMS
SERAPHIN
SERAPHINE
SERAPHINES
SERAPHINS
SERAPHS
SERASKIER
SERASKIERATE
SERASKIERATES
SERASKIERS
SERDAB
SERDABS
SERE
SERED
SEREIN
SEREINS
SERENADE

SERENADED
SERENADER
SERENADERS
SERENADES
SERENADING
SERENATA
SERENATAS
SERENATE
SERENATES
SERENDIPITIES
SERENDIPITIST
SERENDIPITISTS
SERENDIPITOUS
SERENDIPITOUSLY
SERENDIPITY
SERENE
SERENED
SERENELY
SERENENESS
SERENENESSES
SERENER
SERENES
SERENEST
SERENING
SERENITIES
SERENITY
SERER
SERES
SEREST
SERF
SERFAGE
SERFAGES
SERFDOM
SERFDOMS
SERFHOOD
SERFHOODS
SERFISH
SERFLIKE
SERFS
SERFSHIP
SERFSHIPS
SERGE
SERGEANCIES
SERGEANCY
SERGEANT
SERGEANTIES
SERGEANTS
SERGEANTSHIP
SERGEANTSHIPS
SERGEANTY
SERGES
SERGING
SERGINGS
SERIAL
SERIALISATION
SERIALISATIONS
SERIALISE

SERIALISED
SERIALISES
SERIALISING
SERIALISM
SERIALISMS
SERIALIST
SERIALISTS
SERIALITIES
SERIALITY
SERIALIZATION
SERIALIZATIONS
SERIALIZE
SERIALIZED
SERIALIZES
SERIALIZING
SERIALLY
SERIALS
SERIATE
SERIATED
SERIATELY
SERIATES
SERIATIM
SERIATING
SERIATION
SERIATIONS
SERIC
SERICEOUS
SERICICULTURE
SERICICULTURES
SERICICULTURIST
SERICIN
SERICINS
SERICITE
SERICITES
SERICITIC
SERICITISATION
SERICITISATIONS
SERICITIZATION
SERICITIZATIONS
SERICON
SERICONS
SERICTERIA
SERICTERIUM
SERICULTURAL
SERICULTURE
SERICULTURES
SERICULTURIST
SERICULTURISTS
SERIEMA
SERIEMAS
SERIES
SERIF
SERIFED
SERIFFED
SERIFS
SERIGRAPH
SERIGRAPHER

SERIGRAPHERS
SERIGRAPHIC
SERIGRAPHIES
SERIGRAPHS
SERIGRAPHY
SERIN
SERINE
SERINES
SERINETTE
SERINETTES
SERING
SERINGA
SERINGAS
SERINS
SERIOCOMIC
SERIOCOMICAL
SERIOCOMICALLY
SERIOUS
SERIOUSLY
SERIOUSNESS
SERIOUSNESSES
SERIPH
SERIPHS
SERJEANCIES
SERJEANCY
SERJEANT
SERJEANTIES
SERJEANTRIES
SERJEANTRY
SERJEANTS
SERJEANTSHIP
SERJEANTSHIPS
SERJEANTY
SERK
SERKALI
SERKALIS
SERKS
SERMON
SERMONED
SERMONEER
SERMONEERS
SERMONER
SERMONERS
SERMONET
SERMONETS
SERMONETTE
SERMONETTES
SERMONIC
SERMONICAL
SERMONING
SERMONINGS
SERMONISE
SERMONISED
SERMONISER
SERMONISERS
SERMONISES
SERMONISING

SERMONIZE
SERMONIZED
SERMONIZER
SERMONIZERS
SERMONIZES
SERMONIZING
SERMONS
SEROCONVERSION
SEROCONVERSIONS
SEROCONVERT
SEROCONVERTED
SEROCONVERTING
SEROCONVERTS
SERODIAGNOSES
SERODIAGNOSIS
SERODIAGNOSTIC
SEROLOGIC
SEROLOGICAL
SEROLOGICALLY
SEROLOGIES
SEROLOGIST
SEROLOGISTS
SEROLOGY
SERON
SERONEGATIVE
SERONEGATIVITY
SERONS
SEROON
SEROONS
SEROPOSITIVE
SEROPOSITIVITY
SEROPURULENT
SEROPUS
SEROPUSES
SEROSA
SEROSAE
SEROSAL
SEROSAS
SEROSITIES
SEROSITY
SEROTAXONOMIES
SEROTAXONOMY
SEROTHERAPIES
SEROTHERAPY
SEROTINAL
SEROTINE
SEROTINES
SEROTINOUS
SEROTONERGIC
SEROTONIN
SEROTONINERGIC
SEROTONINS
SEROTYPE
SEROTYPED
SEROTYPES
SEROTYPING
SEROTYPINGS

SEROUS
SEROUSNESS
SEROW
SEROWS
SERPENT
SERPENTIFORM
SERPENTINE
SERPENTINED
SERPENTINELY
SERPENTINES
SERPENTINIC
SERPENTINING
SERPENTININGLY
SERPENTININGS
SERPENTINISE
SERPENTINISED
SERPENTINISES
SERPENTINISING
SERPENTINITE
SERPENTINITES
SERPENTINIZE
SERPENTINIZED
SERPENTINIZES
SERPENTINIZING
SERPENTINOUS
SERPENTISE
SERPENTISED
SERPENTISES
SERPENTISING
SERPENTIZE
SERPENTIZED
SERPENTIZES
SERPENTIZING
SERPENTLIKE
SERPENTRIES
SERPENTRY
SERPENTS
SERPIGINES
SERPIGINOUS
SERPIGINOUSLY
SERPIGO
SERPIGOES
SERPIGOS
SERPULA
SERPULAE
SERPULID
SERPULIDS
SERPULITE
SERPULITES
SERR
SERRA
SERRADELLA
SERRADELLAS
SERRADILLA
SERRADILLAS
SERRAE
SERRAN

SERRANID
SERRANIDS
SERRANO
SERRANOID
SERRANOIDS
SERRANOS
SERRANS
SERRAS
SERRASALMO
SERRASALMOS
SERRATE
SERRATED
SERRATES
SERRATI
SERRATING
SERRATION
SERRATIONS
SERRATIROSTRAL
SERRATULATE
SERRATURE
SERRATURES
SERRATUS
SERRATUSES
SERRE
SERRED
SERREFILE
SERREFILES
SERRES
SERRICORN
SERRIED
SERRIEDLY
SERRIEDNESS
SERRIEDNESSES
SERRIES
SERRIFORM
SERRING
SERRS
SERRULATE
SERRULATED
SERRULATION
SERRULATIONS
SERRY
SERRYING
SERS
SERTULARIAN
SERTULARIANS
SERUEWE
SERUEWED
SERUEWES
SERUEWING
SERUM
SERUMAL
SERUMS
SERVABLE
SERVAL
SERVALS
SERVANT

SERVANTED
SERVANTHOOD
SERVANTHOODS
SERVANTING
SERVANTLESS
SERVANTRIES
SERVANTRY
SERVANTS
SERVANTSHIP
SERVANTSHIPS
SERVE
SERVEABILITY
SERVEABLE
SERVED
SERVER
SERVERIES
SERVERS
SERVERY
SERVES
SERVEWE
SERVEWED
SERVEWES
SERVEWING
SERVICE
SERVICEABILITY
SERVICEABLE
SERVICEABLENESS
SERVICEABLY
SERVICEBERRIES
SERVICEBERRY
SERVICED
SERVICELESS
SERVICEMAN
SERVICEMEN
SERVICER
SERVICERS
SERVICES
SERVICEWOMAN
SERVICEWOMEN
SERVICING
SERVIENT
SERVIETTE
SERVIETTES
SERVILE
SERVILELY
SERVILENESS
SERVILENESSES
SERVILES
SERVILISM
SERVILISMS
SERVILITIES
SERVILITY
SERVING
SERVINGS
SERVITOR
SERVITORIAL
SERVITORS

SERVITORSHIP
SERVITORSHIPS
SERVITRESS
SERVITRESSES
SERVITUDE
SERVITUDES
SERVO
SERVOCONTROL
SERVOCONTROLS
SERVOMECHANICAL
SERVOMECHANISM
SERVOMECHANISMS
SERVOMOTOR
SERVOMOTORS
SERVOS
SERVQUAL
SERVQUALS
SESAME
SESAMES
SESAMOID
SESAMOIDS
SESE
SESELI
SESELIS
SESEY
SESH
SESQUIALTER
SESQUIALTERA
SESQUIALTERAS
SESQUICARBONATE
SESQUICENTENARY
SESQUIOXIDE
SESQUIOXIDES
SESQUIPEDAL
SESQUIPEDALIAN
SESQUIPEDALITY
SESQUIPLICATE
SESQUISULPHIDE
SESQUISULPHIDES
SESQUITERPENE
SESQUITERPENES
SESQUITERTIA
SESQUITERTIAS
SESS
SESSA
SESSES
SESSILE
SESSILITY
SESSION
SESSIONAL
SESSIONALLY
SESSIONS
SESSPOOL
SESSPOOLS
SESTERCE
SESTERCES
SESTERTIA

SESTERTIUM
SESTERTIUS
SESTERTIUSES
SESTET
SESTETS
SESTETT
SESTETTE
SESTETTES
SESTETTO
SESTETTOS
SESTETTS
SESTINA
SESTINAS
SESTINE
SESTINES
SESTON
SESTONS
SET
SETA
SETACEOUS
SETACEOUSLY
SETAE
SETAL
SETBACK
SETBACKS
SETENANT
SETENANTS
SETIFEROUS
SETIFORM
SETIGEROUS
SETLINE
SETLINES
SETNESS
SETNESSES
SETOFF
SETOFFS
SETON
SETONS
SETOSE
SETOUS
SETOUT
SETOUTS
SETS
SETSCREW
SETSCREWS
SETT
SETTEE
SETTEES
SETTER
SETTERED
SETTERING
SETTERS
SETTERWORT
SETTERWORTS
SETTING
SETTINGS
SETTLE

SETTLEABLE
SETTLED
SETTLEDNESS
SETTLEDNESSES
SETTLEMENT
SETTLEMENTS
SETTLER
SETTLERS
SETTLES
SETTLING
SETTLINGS
SETTLOR
SETTLORS
SETTS
SETUALE
SETUALES
SETULE
SETULES
SETULOSE
SETULOUS
SETUP
SETUPS
SETWALL
SETWALLS
SEVEN
SEVENFOLD
SEVENPENCE
SEVENPENCES
SEVENPENNIES
SEVENPENNY
SEVENS
SEVENTEEN
SEVENTEENS
SEVENTEENTH
SEVENTEENTHLY
SEVENTEENTHS
SEVENTH
SEVENTHLY
SEVENTHS
SEVENTIES
SEVENTIETH
SEVENTIETHS
SEVENTY
SEVER
SEVERABILITIES
SEVERABILITY
SEVERABLE
SEVERAL
SEVERALFOLD
SEVERALLY
SEVERALS
SEVERALTIES
SEVERALTY
SEVERANCE
SEVERANCES
SEVERE
SEVERED

SEVERELY
SEVERENESS
SEVERENESSES
SEVERER
SEVEREST
SEVERIES
SEVERING
SEVERITIES
SEVERITY
SEVERS
SEVERY
SEVICHE
SEVICHES
SEVRUGA
SEVRUGAS
SEW
SEWABILITIES
SEWABILITY
SEWABLE
SEWAGE
SEWAGES
SEWAN
SEWANS
SEWAR
SEWARS
SEWED
SEWEL
SEWELLEL
SEWELLELS
SEWELS
SEWEN
SEWENS
SEWER
SEWERAGE
SEWERAGES
SEWERED
SEWERING
SEWERINGS
SEWERS
SEWIN
SEWING
SEWINGS
SEWINS
SEWN
SEWS
SEX
SEXAGENARIAN
SEXAGENARIANS
SEXAGENARIES
SEXAGENARY
SEXAGESIMAL
SEXAGESIMALLY
SEXAGESIMALS
SEXANGULAR
SEXANGULARLY
SEXAVALENCY
SEXAVALENT

SEXCENTENARIES
SEXCENTENARY
SEXCENTENARYS
SEXDECILLION
SEXDECILLIONS
SEXED
SEXENNIAL
SEXENNIALLY
SEXENNIALS
SEXER
SEXERCISE
SEXERS
SEXES
SEXFID
SEXFOIL
SEXFOILS
SEXIER
SEXIEST
SEXILY
SEXINESS
SEXINESSES
SEXING
SEXISM
SEXISMS
SEXIST
SEXISTS
SEXIVALENT
SEXLESS
SEXLESSLY
SEXLESSNESS
SEXLESSNESSES
SEXLINKED
SEXLOCULAR
SEXOLOGICAL
SEXOLOGIES
SEXOLOGIST
SEXOLOGISTS
SEXOLOGY
SEXPARTITE
SEXPERT
SEXPERTS
SEXPLOITATION
SEXPLOITATIONS
SEXPOT
SEXPOTS
SEXT
SEXTAIN
SEXTAINS
SEXTAN
SEXTANS
SEXTANSES
SEXTANT
SEXTANTAL
SEXTANTS
SEXTARII
SEXTARIUS
SEXTET

SEXTETS
SEXTETT
SEXTETTE
SEXTETTES
SEXTETTS
SEXTILE
SEXTILES
SEXTILLION
SEXTILLIONS
SEXTILLIONTH
SEXTILLIONTHS
SEXTO
SEXTODECIMO
SEXTODECIMOS
SEXTOLET
SEXTOLETS
SEXTON
SEXTONESS
SEXTONESSES
SEXTONS
SEXTONSHIP
SEXTONSHIPS
SEXTOS
SEXTS
SEXTUOR
SEXTUORS
SEXTUPLE
SEXTUPLED
SEXTUPLES
SEXTUPLET
SEXTUPLETS
SEXTUPLICATE
SEXTUPLICATED
SEXTUPLICATES
SEXTUPLICATING
SEXTUPLING
SEXTUPLY
SEXUAL
SEXUALISATION
SEXUALISATIONS
SEXUALISE
SEXUALISED
SEXUALISES
SEXUALISING
SEXUALISM
SEXUALISMS
SEXUALIST
SEXUALISTS
SEXUALITIES
SEXUALITY
SEXUALIZATION
SEXUALIZATIONS
SEXUALIZE
SEXUALIZED
SEXUALIZES
SEXUALIZING
SEXUALLY

SEXVALENT
SEXY
SEY
SEYEN
SEYENS
SEYS
SEYSURE
SEYSURES
SEZ
SFERICS
SFORZANDI
SFORZANDO
SFORZANDOS
SFORZATI
SFORZATO
SFORZATOS
SFUMATO
SFUMATOS
SGRAFFITI
SGRAFFITO
SH
SHA
SHABBIER
SHABBIEST
SHABBILY
SHABBINESS
SHABBINESSES
SHABBLE
SHABBLES
SHABBY
SHABRACK
SHABRACKS
SHABRACQUE
SHABRACQUES
SHACK
SHACKED
SHACKING
SHACKLE
SHACKLEBONE
SHACKLEBONES
SHACKLED
SHACKLER
SHACKLERS
SHACKLES
SHACKLING
SHACKO
SHACKOES
SHACKOS
SHACKS
SHAD
SHADBERRIES
SHADBERRY
SHADBLOW
SHADBLOWS
SHADBUSH
SHADBUSHES
SHADCHAN

SHADCHANIM
SHADCHANS
SHADDOCK
SHADDOCKS
SHADE
SHADED
SHADELESS
SHADER
SHADERS
SHADES
SHADFLIES
SHADFLY
SHADIER
SHADIEST
SHADILY
SHADINESS
SHADINESSES
SHADING
SHADINGS
SHADOOF
SHADOOFS
SHADOW
SHADOWBOX
SHADOWBOXED
SHADOWBOXES
SHADOWBOXING
SHADOWCAST
SHADOWCASTING
SHADOWCASTINGS
SHADOWCASTS
SHADOWED
SHADOWER
SHADOWERS
SHADOWGRAPH
SHADOWGRAPHIES
SHADOWGRAPHS
SHADOWGRAPHY
SHADOWIER
SHADOWIEST
SHADOWILY
SHADOWINESS
SHADOWINESSES
SHADOWING
SHADOWINGS
SHADOWLESS
SHADOWLIKE
SHADOWS
SHADOWY
SHADRACH
SHADRACHS
SHADS
SHADUF
SHADUFS
SHADY
SHAFT
SHAFTED
SHAFTER

SHAFTERS
SHAFTING
SHAFTINGS
SHAFTLESS
SHAFTS
SHAG
SHAGBARK
SHAGBARKS
SHAGGABLE
SHAGGABLENESS
SHAGGED
SHAGGEDNESS
SHAGGEDNESSES
SHAGGER
SHAGGERS
SHAGGIER
SHAGGIEST
SHAGGILY
SHAGGINESS
SHAGGINESSES
SHAGGING
SHAGGY
SHAGGYMANE
SHAGGYMANES
SHAGPILE
SHAGREEN
SHAGREENED
SHAGREENS
SHAGROON
SHAGROONS
SHAGS
SHAGTASTIC
SHAGTASTICALLY
SHAH
SHAHADA
SHAHDOM
SHAHDOMS
SHAHS
SHAHTOOSH
SHAIKH
SHAIKHS
SHAIRD
SHAIRDS
SHAIRN
SHAIRNS
SHAITAN
SHAITANS
SHAKABLE
SHAKE
SHAKEABLE
SHAKED
SHAKEDOWN
SHAKEDOWNS
SHAKEN
SHAKEOUT
SHAKEOUTS
SHAKER

SHAKERS
SHAKES
SHAKEUP
SHAKEUPS
SHAKIER
SHAKIEST
SHAKILY
SHAKINESS
SHAKINESSES
SHAKING
SHAKINGS
SHAKO
SHAKOES
SHAKOS
SHAKT
SHAKUDO
SHAKUDOS
SHAKUHACHI
SHAKUHACHIS
SHAKY
SHALE
SHALED
SHALES
SHALEY
SHALIER
SHALIEST
SHALING
SHALL
SHALLI
SHALLIS
SHALLON
SHALLONS
SHALLOON
SHALLOONS
SHALLOP
SHALLOPS
SHALLOT
SHALLOTS
SHALLOW
SHALLOWED
SHALLOWER
SHALLOWEST
SHALLOWING
SHALLOWINGS
SHALLOWLY
SHALLOWNESS
SHALLOWNESSES
SHALLOWS
SHALM
SHALMS
SHALOM
SHALOMS
SHALOT
SHALOTS
SHALT
SHALWAR
SHALWARS

SHALY
SHAM
SHAMA
SHAMABLE
SHAMAN
SHAMANIC
SHAMANISM
SHAMANISMS
SHAMANIST
SHAMANISTIC
SHAMANISTS
SHAMANS
SHAMAS
SHAMATEUR
SHAMATEURISM
SHAMATEURISMS
SHAMATEURS
SHAMBA
SHAMBAS
SHAMBLE
SHAMBLED
SHAMBLES
SHAMBLIER
SHAMBLIEST
SHAMBLING
SHAMBLINGS
SHAMBLY
SHAMBOLIC
SHAME
SHAMEABLE
SHAMED
SHAMEFACED
SHAMEFACEDLY
SHAMEFACEDNESS
SHAMEFAST
SHAMEFASTNESS
SHAMEFASTNESSES
SHAMEFUL
SHAMEFULLY
SHAMEFULNESS
SHAMEFULNESSES
SHAMELESS
SHAMELESSLY
SHAMELESSNESS
SHAMELESSNESSES
SHAMER
SHAMERS
SHAMES
SHAMEWORTHY
SHAMIANA
SHAMIANAH
SHAMIANAHS
SHAMIANAS
SHAMINA
SHAMING
SHAMISEN
SHAMISENS

SHAMIYANAHS
SHAMMAS
SHAMMASH
SHAMMASHIM
SHAMMASIM
SHAMMED
SHAMMER
SHAMMERS
SHAMMES
SHAMMIED
SHAMMIES
SHAMMING
SHAMMOS
SHAMMOSIM
SHAMMY
SHAMMYING
SHAMOIS
SHAMOS
SHAMOSIM
SHAMOY
SHAMOYED
SHAMOYING
SHAMOYS
SHAMPOO
SHAMPOOED
SHAMPOOER
SHAMPOOERS
SHAMPOOING
SHAMPOOS
SHAMROCK
SHAMROCKS
SHAMS
SHAMUS
SHAMUSES
SHAN
SHANACHIE
SHANACHIES
SHAND
SHANDIES
SHANDRIES
SHANDRY
SHANDRYDAN
SHANDRYDANS
SHANDS
SHANDY
SHANDYGAFF
SHANDYGAFFS
SHANGHAI
SHANGHAIED
SHANGHAIER
SHANGHAIERS
SHANGHAIING
SHANGHAIS
SHANK
SHANKBONE
SHANKBONES
SHANKED

SHANKING
SHANKPIECE
SHANKPIECES
SHANKS
SHANNIES
SHANNY
SHANS
SHANTEY
SHANTEYS
SHANTI
SHANTIES
SHANTIH
SHANTIHS
SHANTIS
SHANTUNG
SHANTUNGS
SHANTY
SHANTYMAN
SHANTYMEN
SHANTYTOWN
SHANTYTOWNS
SHAPABLE
SHAPE
SHAPEABLE
SHAPED
SHAPELESS
SHAPELESSLY
SHAPELESSNESS
SHAPELESSNESSES
SHAPELIER
SHAPELIEST
SHAPELINESS
SHAPELINESSES
SHAPELY
SHAPEN
SHAPER
SHAPERS
SHAPES
SHAPEUP
SHAPEUPS
SHAPING
SHAPINGS
SHAPS
SHARABLE
SHARAWADGI
SHARAWADGIS
SHARAWAGGI
SHARAWAGGIS
SHARD
SHARDED
SHARDS
SHARE
SHAREABILITIES
SHAREABILITY
SHAREABLE
SHARECROP
SHARECROPPED

SHARECROPPER
SHARECROPPERS
SHARECROPPING
SHARECROPS
SHARED
SHAREFARMER
SHAREFARMERS
SHAREHOLDER
SHAREHOLDERS
SHAREHOLDING
SHAREHOLDINGS
SHAREMAN
SHAREMEN
SHAREMILKER
SHAREMILKERS
SHARER
SHARERS
SHARES
SHARESMAN
SHARESMEN
SHAREWARE
SHAREWARES
SHARIA
SHARIAS
SHARIAT
SHARIATS
SHARIF
SHARIFIAN
SHARIFS
SHARING
SHARINGS
SHARK
SHARKED
SHARKER
SHARKERS
SHARKING
SHARKINGS
SHARKLIKE
SHARKS
SHARKSKIN
SHARKSKINS
SHARKSUCKER
SHARKSUCKERS
SHARN
SHARNIER
SHARNIEST
SHARNS
SHARNY
SHARON
SHARP
SHARPBENDER
SHARPBENDERS
SHARPED
SHARPEN
SHARPENED
SHARPENER
SHARPENERS

SHARPENING
SHARPENS
SHARPER
SHARPERS
SHARPEST
SHARPIE
SHARPIES
SHARPING
SHARPINGS
SHARPISH
SHARPLY
SHARPNESS
SHARPNESSES
SHARPS
SHARPSHOOTER
SHARPSHOOTERS
SHARPSHOOTING
SHARPSHOOTINGS
SHARPY
SHASH
SHASHED
SHASHES
SHASHING
SHASHLICK
SHASHLICKS
SHASHLIK
SHASHLIKS
SHASLIK
SHASLIKS
SHASTER
SHASTERS
SHASTRA
SHASTRAS
SHAT
SHATTER
SHATTERED
SHATTERER
SHATTERERS
SHATTERING
SHATTERINGLY
SHATTERPROOF
SHATTERS
SHATTERY
SHAUCHLE
SHAUCHLED
SHAUCHLES
SHAUCHLIER
SHAUCHLIEST
SHAUCHLING
SHAUCHLY
SHAUGH
SHAUGHS
SHAUL
SHAULED
SHAULING
SHAULS
SHAVABLE

SHAVE
SHAVEABLE
SHAVED
SHAVELING
SHAVELINGS
SHAVEN
SHAVER
SHAVERS
SHAVES
SHAVETAIL
SHAVETAILS
SHAVIE
SHAVIES
SHAVING
SHAVINGS
SHAW
SHAWED
SHAWING
SHAWL
SHAWLED
SHAWLEY
SHAWLEYS
SHAWLIE
SHAWLIES
SHAWLING
SHAWLINGS
SHAWLLESS
SHAWLS
SHAWM
SHAWMS
SHAWN
SHAWS
SHAY
SHAYA
SHAYAS
SHAYS
SHCHI
SHCHIS
SHE
SHEA
SHEADING
SHEADINGS
SHEAF
SHEAFED
SHEAFIER
SHEAFIEST
SHEAFING
SHEAFLIKE
SHEAFS
SHEAFY
SHEAL
SHEALED
SHEALING
SHEALINGS
SHEALS
SHEAR
SHEARED

SHEARER
SHEARERS
SHEARING
SHEARINGS
SHEARLEG
SHEARLEGS
SHEARLING
SHEARLINGS
SHEARMAN
SHEARMEN
SHEARS
SHEARWATER
SHEARWATERS
SHEAS
SHEATFISH
SHEATFISHES
SHEATH
SHEATHBILL
SHEATHBILLS
SHEATHE
SHEATHED
SHEATHER
SHEATHERS
SHEATHES
SHEATHFISH
SHEATHFISHES
SHEATHIER
SHEATHIEST
SHEATHING
SHEATHINGS
SHEATHLESS
SHEATHS
SHEATHY
SHEAVE
SHEAVED
SHEAVES
SHEAVING
SHEBANG
SHEBANGS
SHEBEAN
SHEBEANS
SHEBEEN
SHEBEENED
SHEBEENER
SHEBEENERS
SHEBEENING
SHEBEENINGS
SHEBEENS
SHECHITA
SHECHITAH
SHECHITAHS
SHECHITAS
SHECKLATON
SHECKLATONS
SHED
SHEDABLE
SHEDDABLE

SHEDDED
SHEDDER
SHEDDERS
SHEDDING
SHEDDINGS
SHEDLIKE
SHEDLOAD
SHEDLOADS
SHEDS
SHEEL
SHEELED
SHEELING
SHEELS
SHEEN
SHEENED
SHEENEY
SHEENEYS
SHEENFUL
SHEENIE
SHEENIER
SHEENIES
SHEENIEST
SHEENING
SHEENS
SHEENY
SHEEP
SHEEPBERRIES
SHEEPBERRY
SHEEPCOT
SHEEPCOTE
SHEEPCOTES
SHEEPCOTS
SHEEPDOG
SHEEPDOGS
SHEEPFOLD
SHEEPFOLDS
SHEEPHERDER
SHEEPHERDERS
SHEEPHERDING
SHEEPHERDINGS
SHEEPIER
SHEEPIEST
SHEEPISH
SHEEPISHLY
SHEEPISHNESS
SHEEPISHNESSES
SHEEPLIKE
SHEEPMAN
SHEEPMEN
SHEEPO
SHEEPOS
SHEEPSHANK
SHEEPSHANKS
SHEEPSHEAD
SHEEPSHEADS
SHEEPSHEARER
SHEEPSHEARERS

SHEEPSHEARING
SHEEPSHEARINGS
SHEEPSKIN
SHEEPSKINS
SHEEPTRACK
SHEEPTRACKS
SHEEPWALK
SHEEPWALKS
SHEEPY
SHEER
SHEERED
SHEERER
SHEEREST
SHEERING
SHEERLEG
SHEERLEGS
SHEERLY
SHEERNESS
SHEERNESSES
SHEERS
SHEESH
SHEET
SHEETED
SHEETER
SHEETERS
SHEETFED
SHEETIER
SHEETIEST
SHEETING
SHEETINGS
SHEETLIKE
SHEETS
SHEETY
SHEEVE
SHEEVES
SHEGETZ
SHEHITA
SHEHITAH
SHEHITAHS
SHEHITAS
SHEIK
SHEIKDOM
SHEIKDOMS
SHEIKH
SHEIKHA
SHEIKHAS
SHEIKHDOM
SHEIKHDOMS
SHEIKHS
SHEIKS
SHEILA
SHEILAS
SHEILING
SHEILINGS
SHEITAN
SHEITANS
SHEKEL

SHEKELS
SHELDDUCK
SHELDDUCKS
SHELDRAKE
SHELDRAKES
SHELDUCK
SHELDUCKS
SHELF
SHELFED
SHELFFUL
SHELFFULS
SHELFIER
SHELFIEST
SHELFING
SHELFLIKE
SHELFROOM
SHELFROOMS
SHELFS
SHELFTALKER
SHELFTALKERS
SHELFY
SHELL
SHELLAC
SHELLACK
SHELLACKED
SHELLACKER
SHELLACKERS
SHELLACKING
SHELLACKINGS
SHELLACKS
SHELLACS
SHELLBACK
SHELLBACKS
SHELLBARK
SHELLBARKS
SHELLBOUND
SHELLCRACKER
SHELLCRACKERS
SHELLDRAKE
SHELLDRAKES
SHELLDUCK
SHELLDUCKS
SHELLED
SHELLER
SHELLERS
SHELLFIRE
SHELLFIRES
SHELLFISH
SHELLFISHERIES
SHELLFISHERY
SHELLFISHES
SHELLFUL
SHELLFULS
SHELLIER
SHELLIEST
SHELLINESS
SHELLINESSES

SHELLING
SHELLINGS
SHELLPROOF
SHELLS
SHELLSHOCK
SHELLSHOCKED
SHELLSHOCKS
SHELLWORK
SHELLWORKS
SHELLY
SHELLYCOAT
SHELLYCOATS
SHELTA
SHELTAS
SHELTER
SHELTERBELT
SHELTERBELTS
SHELTERED
SHELTERER
SHELTERERS
SHELTERING
SHELTERINGS
SHELTERLESS
SHELTERS
SHELTERY
SHELTIE
SHELTIES
SHELTY
SHELVE
SHELVED
SHELVER
SHELVERS
SHELVES
SHELVIER
SHELVIEST
SHELVING
SHELVINGS
SHELVY
SHEMOZZLE
SHEMOZZLED
SHEMOZZLES
SHEMOZZLING
SHENANIGAN
SHENANIGANS
SHEND
SHENDING
SHENDS
SHENT
SHEOL
SHEOLS
SHEPHERD
SHEPHERDED
SHEPHERDESS
SHEPHERDESSES
SHEPHERDING
SHEPHERDLESS
SHEPHERDLING

SHEPHERDLINGS
SHEPHERDS
SHEQALIM
SHEQEL
SHERANG
SHERANGS
SHERARDISATION
SHERARDISE
SHERARDISED
SHERARDISES
SHERARDISING
SHERARDIZATION
SHERARDIZE
SHERARDIZED
SHERARDIZES
SHERARDIZING
SHERBERT
SHERBERTS
SHERBET
SHERBETS
SHERD
SHERDS
SHERE
SHEREEF
SHEREEFIAN
SHEREEFS
SHERGOTTITE
SHERGOTTITES
SHERIA
SHERIAS
SHERIAT
SHERIATS
SHERIF
SHERIFF
SHERIFFALTIES
SHERIFFALTY
SHERIFFDOM
SHERIFFDOMS
SHERIFFS
SHERIFFSHIP
SHERIFFSHIPS
SHERIFIAN
SHERIFS
SHERLOCK
SHERLOCKS
SHEROOT
SHEROOTS
SHERPA
SHERPAS
SHERRIES
SHERRIS
SHERRISES
SHERRY
SHERWANI
SHERWANIS
SHES
SHET

SHETLAND
SHETLANDS
SHETS
SHETTING
SHEUCH
SHEUCHED
SHEUCHING
SHEUCHS
SHEUGH
SHEUGHED
SHEUGHING
SHEUGHS
SHEVA
SHEVAS
SHEW
SHEWBREAD
SHEWBREADS
SHEWED
SHEWEL
SHEWELS
SHEWER
SHEWERS
SHEWING
SHEWN
SHEWS
SHH
SHIAI
SHIAIS
SHIATSU
SHIATSUS
SHIATZU
SHIATZUS
SHIBAH
SHIBAHS
SHIBBOLETH
SHIBBOLETHS
SHIBUICHI
SHIBUICHIS
SHICKER
SHICKERED
SHICKERS
SHICKSA
SHICKSAS
SHIDDER
SHIDDERS
SHIDDUCH
SHIDDUCHIM
SHIED
SHIEL
SHIELD
SHIELDED
SHIELDER
SHIELDERS
SHIELDING
SHIELDINGS
SHIELDLESS
SHIELDLIKE

SHIELDLING
SHIELDLINGS
SHIELDRAKE
SHIELDRAKES
SHIELDS
SHIELDUCKS
SHIELDWALL
SHIELDWALLS
SHIELED
SHIELING
SHIELINGS
SHIELS
SHIER
SHIERS
SHIES
SHIEST
SHIFT
SHIFTABLE
SHIFTED
SHIFTER
SHIFTERS
SHIFTIER
SHIFTIEST
SHIFTILY
SHIFTINESS
SHIFTINESSES
SHIFTING
SHIFTINGS
SHIFTLESS
SHIFTLESSLY
SHIFTLESSNESS
SHIFTLESSNESSES
SHIFTS
SHIFTWORK
SHIFTY
SHIGELLA
SHIGELLAE
SHIGELLAS
SHIGELLOSES
SHIGELLOSIS
SHIITAKE
SHIITAKES
SHIKAR
SHIKAREE
SHIKAREES
SHIKARI
SHIKARIS
SHIKARRED
SHIKARRING
SHIKARS
SHIKKER
SHIKKERS
SHIKSA
SHIKSAS
SHIKSE
SHIKSES
SHILINGI

SHILL
SHILLABER
SHILLABERS
SHILLALA
SHILLALAH
SHILLALAHS
SHILLALAS
SHILLED
SHILLELAGH
SHILLELAGHS
SHILLING
SHILLINGLESS
SHILLINGS
SHILLINGSWORTH
SHILLINGSWORTHS
SHILLS
SHILLYSHALLIED
SHILLYSHALLIER
SHILLYSHALLIERS
SHILLYSHALLIES
SHILLYSHALLY
SHILLYSHALLYING
SHILPIT
SHILY
SHIM
SHIMAAL
SHIMAALS
SHIMMED
SHIMMER
SHIMMERED
SHIMMERING
SHIMMERINGLY
SHIMMERINGS
SHIMMERS
SHIMMERY
SHIMMEY
SHIMMEYS
SHIMMIED
SHIMMIES
SHIMMING
SHIMMY
SHIMMYING
SHIMOZZLE
SHIMOZZLES
SHIMS
SHIN
SHINBONE
SHINBONES
SHINDIES
SHINDIG
SHINDIGS
SHINDY
SHINDYS
SHINE
SHINED
SHINELESS
SHINER

SHINERS
SHINES
SHINESS
SHINESSES
SHINGLE
SHINGLED
SHINGLER
SHINGLERS
SHINGLES
SHINGLIER
SHINGLIEST
SHINGLING
SHINGLINGS
SHINGLY
SHINIER
SHINIES
SHINIEST
SHINILY
SHININESS
SHININESSES
SHINING
SHININGLY
SHININGNESS
SHININGNESSES
SHINJU
SHINKIN
SHINKINS
SHINLEAF
SHINLEAFS
SHINLEAVES
SHINNE
SHINNED
SHINNERIES
SHINNERY
SHINNEY
SHINNEYED
SHINNEYING
SHINNEYS
SHINNIED
SHINNIES
SHINNING
SHINNY
SHINNYING
SHINPLASTER
SHINPLASTERS
SHINS
SHINSPLINTS
SHINTAIDO
SHINTIED
SHINTIES
SHINTY
SHINTYING
SHINY
SHIP
SHIPBOARD
SHIPBOARDS

SHIPBORNE
SHIPBROKER
SHIPBROKERS
SHIPBUILDER
SHIPBUILDERS
SHIPBUILDING
SHIPBUILDINGS
SHIPFITTER
SHIPFITTERS
SHIPFUL
SHIPFULS
SHIPLAP
SHIPLAPPED
SHIPLAPPING
SHIPLAPS
SHIPLESS
SHIPLOAD
SHIPLOADS
SHIPMAN
SHIPMASTER
SHIPMASTERS
SHIPMATE
SHIPMATES
SHIPMEN
SHIPMENT
SHIPMENTS
SHIPOWNER
SHIPOWNERS
SHIPPABLE
SHIPPED
SHIPPEN
SHIPPENS
SHIPPER
SHIPPERS
SHIPPIE
SHIPPIES
SHIPPING
SHIPPINGS
SHIPPO
SHIPPON
SHIPPONS
SHIPPOS
SHIPPOUND
SHIPPOUNDS
SHIPS
SHIPSHAPE
SHIPSIDE
SHIPSIDES
SHIPWAY
SHIPWAYS
SHIPWORM
SHIPWORMS
SHIPWRECK
SHIPWRECKED
SHIPWRECKING
SHIPWRECKS
SHIPWRIGHT

SHIPWRIGHTS	SHIRTWAISTS	SHIVS	SHNOOK
SHIPYARD	SHIRTY	SHIVVED	SHNOOKS
SHIPYARDS	SHISH	SHIVVING	SHOAL
SHIR	SHIST	SHKOTZIM	SHOALED
SHIRALEE	SHISTS	SHLEMIEHL	SHOALER
SHIRALEES	SHIT	SHLEMIEHLS	SHOALEST
SHIRE	SHITAKE	SHLEMIEL	SHOALIER
SHIRED	SHITAKES	SHLEMIELS	SHOALIEST
SHIREMAN	SHITE	SHLEMOZZLE	SHOALINESS
SHIREMEN	SHITED	SHLEMOZZLED	SHOALING
SHIRES	SHITES	SHLEMOZZLES	SHOALINGS
SHIRING	SHITHEAD	SHLEMOZZLING	SHOALNESS
SHIRK	SHITHEADS	SHLEP	SHOALNESSES
SHIRKED	SHITHOLE	SHLEPP	SHOALS
SHIRKER	SHITHOLES	SHLEPPED	SHOALWISE
SHIRKERS	SHITING	SHLEPPER	SHOALY
SHIRKING	SHITS	SHLEPPERS	SHOAT
SHIRKS	SHITTAH	SHLEPPING	SHOATS
SHIRR	SHITTAHS	SHLEPPS	SHOCHET
SHIRRA	SHITTED	SHLEPS	SHOCHETIM
SHIRRALEE	SHITTIER	SHLIMAZEL	SHOCHETS
SHIRRALEES	SHITTIEST	SHLIMAZELS	SHOCK
SHIRRAS	SHITTILY	SHLOCK	SHOCKABILITIES
SHIRRED	SHITTIM	SHLOCKS	SHOCKABILITY
SHIRRING	SHITTIMS	SHLOSHIM	SHOCKABLE
SHIRRINGS	SHITTIMWOOD	SHLOSHIMS	SHOCKED
SHIRRS	SHITTIMWOODS	SHLUMP	SHOCKER
SHIRS	SHITTINESS	SHLUMPED	SHOCKERS
SHIRT	SHITTINESSES	SHLUMPING	SHOCKHEADED
SHIRTBAND	SHITTING	SHLUMPS	SHOCKING
SHIRTBANDS	SHITTY	SHLUMPY	SHOCKINGLY
SHIRTDRESS	SHIUR	SHMALTZ	SHOCKINGNESS
SHIRTDRESSES	SHIURIM	SHMALTZES	SHOCKINGNESSES
SHIRTED	SHIV	SHMALTZIER	SHOCKPROOF
SHIRTFRONT	SHIVA	SHMALTZIEST	SHOCKS
SHIRTFRONTS	SHIVAH	SHMALTZY	SHOCKSTALL
SHIRTIER	SHIVAHS	SHMATTE	SHOCKSTALLS
SHIRTIEST	SHIVAREE	SHMATTES	SHOD
SHIRTILY	SHIVAREED	SHMEAR	SHODDEN
SHIRTINESS	SHIVAREEING	SHMEARS	SHODDIER
SHIRTINESSES	SHIVAREES	SHMEK	SHODDIES
SHIRTING	SHIVAS	SHMEKS	SHODDIEST
SHIRTINGS	SHIVE	SHMO	SHODDILY
SHIRTLESS	SHIVER	SHMOCK	SHODDINESS
SHIRTLIFTER	SHIVERED	SHMOCKS	SHODDINESSES
SHIRTLIFTERS	SHIVERER	SHMOES	SHODDY
SHIRTMAKER	SHIVERERS	SHMOOSE	SHODER
SHIRTMAKERS	SHIVERIER	SHMOOSED	SHODERS
SHIRTS	SHIVERIEST	SHMOOSES	SHOE
SHIRTSLEEVE	SHIVERING	SHMOOSING	SHOEBILL
SHIRTSLEEVED	SHIVERINGLY	SHMOOZE	SHOEBILLS
SHIRTSLEEVES	SHIVERINGS	SHMOOZED	SHOEBLACK
SHIRTTAIL	SHIVERS	SHMOOZES	SHOEBLACKS
SHIRTTAILS	SHIVERY	SHMOOZING	SHOED
SHIRTWAIST	SHIVES	SHMUCK	SHOEHORN
SHIRTWAISTER	SHIVOO	SHMUCKS	SHOEHORNED
SHIRTWAISTERS	SHIVOOS	SHNAPS	SHOEHORNING

929

SHOEHORNS
SHOEING
SHOEINGS
SHOELACE
SHOELACES
SHOELESS
SHOEMAKER
SHOEMAKERS
SHOEMAKING
SHOEMAKINGS
SHOEPAC
SHOEPACK
SHOEPACKS
SHOEPACS
SHOER
SHOERS
SHOES
SHOESHINE
SHOESHINES
SHOESTRING
SHOESTRINGS
SHOETREE
SHOETREES
SHOFAR
SHOFARS
SHOFROTH
SHOG
SHOGGED
SHOGGING
SHOGGLE
SHOGGLED
SHOGGLES
SHOGGLIER
SHOGGLIEST
SHOGGLING
SHOGGLY
SHOGI
SHOGIS
SHOGS
SHOGUN
SHOGUNAL
SHOGUNATE
SHOGUNATES
SHOGUNS
SHOJI
SHOJIS
SHOLA
SHOLAS
SHOLOM
SHOLOMS
SHONE
SHONEEN
SHONEENS
SHONKIER
SHONKIEST
SHONKY
SHOO

SHOOED
SHOOFLIES
SHOOFLY
SHOOGIE
SHOOGIED
SHOOGIEING
SHOOGIES
SHOOGLE
SHOOGLED
SHOOGLES
SHOOGLIER
SHOOGLIEST
SHOOGLING
SHOOGLY
SHOOING
SHOOK
SHOOKS
SHOOL
SHOOLE
SHOOLED
SHOOLES
SHOOLING
SHOOLS
SHOON
SHOORA
SHOOS
SHOOT
SHOOTABLE
SHOOTER
SHOOTERS
SHOOTING
SHOOTINGS
SHOOTIST
SHOOTISTS
SHOOTOUT
SHOOTOUTS
SHOOTS
SHOP
SHOPAHOLIC
SHOPAHOLICS
SHOPBOARD
SHOPBOARDS
SHOPBOY
SHOPBOYS
SHOPBREAKER
SHOPBREAKERS
SHOPBREAKING
SHOPBREAKINGS
SHOPE
SHOPFRONT
SHOPFRONTS
SHOPFUL
SHOPFULS
SHOPGIRL
SHOPGIRLS
SHOPHAR
SHOPHARS

SHOPHROTH
SHOPKEEPER
SHOPKEEPERS
SHOPKEEPING
SHOPKEEPINGS
SHOPLIFT
SHOPLIFTED
SHOPLIFTER
SHOPLIFTERS
SHOPLIFTING
SHOPLIFTS
SHOPMAN
SHOPMEN
SHOPPE
SHOPPED
SHOPPER
SHOPPERS
SHOPPES
SHOPPIER
SHOPPIEST
SHOPPING
SHOPPINGS
SHOPPY
SHOPS
SHOPSOILED
SHOPTALK
SHOPTALKS
SHOPWALKER
SHOPWALKERS
SHOPWALKING
SHOPWINDOW
SHOPWINDOWS
SHOPWORN
SHORAN
SHORANS
SHORE
SHOREBIRD
SHOREBIRDS
SHORED
SHOREFRONT
SHOREFRONTS
SHORELESS
SHORELINE
SHORELINES
SHOREMAN
SHOREMEN
SHORER
SHORERS
SHORES
SHORESIDE
SHORESMAN
SHORESMEN
SHOREWARD
SHOREWARDS
SHOREWEED
SHOREWEEDS
SHORING

SHORINGS
SHORL
SHORLS
SHORN
SHORT
SHORTAGE
SHORTAGES
SHORTARM
SHORTBREAD
SHORTBREADS
SHORTCAKE
SHORTCAKES
SHORTCHANGE
SHORTCHANGED
SHORTCHANGER
SHORTCHANGERS
SHORTCHANGES
SHORTCHANGING
SHORTCOMING
SHORTCOMINGS
SHORTCRUST
SHORTCUT
SHORTCUTS
SHORTCUTTING
SHORTED
SHORTEN
SHORTENED
SHORTENER
SHORTENERS
SHORTENING
SHORTENINGS
SHORTENS
SHORTER
SHORTEST
SHORTFALL
SHORTFALLS
SHORTGOWN
SHORTGOWNS
SHORTHAIR
SHORTHAIRED
SHORTHAIRS
SHORTHAND
SHORTHANDED
SHORTHANDS
SHORTHOLD
SHORTHORN
SHORTHORNS
SHORTIA
SHORTIAS
SHORTIE
SHORTIES
SHORTING
SHORTISH
SHORTLIST
SHORTLISTS
SHORTLY
SHORTNESS

SHORTNESSES
SHORTS
SHORTSIGHTED
SHORTSIGHTEDLY
SHORTSTOP
SHORTSTOPS
SHORTSWORD
SHORTSWORDS
SHORTWAVE
SHORTWAVES
SHORTY
SHOT
SHOTE
SHOTES
SHOTFIRER
SHOTFIRERS
SHOTGUN
SHOTGUNNED
SHOTGUNNER
SHOTGUNNERS
SHOTGUNNING
SHOTGUNS
SHOTHOLE
SHOTHOLES
SHOTMAKER
SHOTMAKERS
SHOTMAKING
SHOTMAKINGS
SHOTPROOF
SHOTPUT
SHOTPUTS
SHOTS
SHOTT
SHOTTE
SHOTTED
SHOTTEN
SHOTTES
SHOTTING
SHOTTLE
SHOTTLES
SHOTTS
SHOUGH
SHOUGHS
SHOULD
SHOULDER
SHOULDERED
SHOULDERING
SHOULDERINGS
SHOULDERS
SHOULDEST
SHOULDST
SHOUSE
SHOUSES
SHOUT
SHOUTED
SHOUTER
SHOUTERS

SHOUTHER
SHOUTHERED
SHOUTHERING
SHOUTHERS
SHOUTIER
SHOUTIEST
SHOUTILY
SHOUTINESS
SHOUTING
SHOUTINGLY
SHOUTINGS
SHOUTLINE
SHOUTLINES
SHOUTS
SHOUTY
SHOVE
SHOVED
SHOVEL
SHOVELBOARD
SHOVELBOARDS
SHOVELED
SHOVELER
SHOVELERS
SHOVELFUL
SHOVELFULS
SHOVELHEAD
SHOVELHEADS
SHOVELING
SHOVELLED
SHOVELLER
SHOVELLERS
SHOVELLING
SHOVELNOSE
SHOVELNOSES
SHOVELS
SHOVELSFUL
SHOVER
SHOVERS
SHOVES
SHOVING
SHOW
SHOWABLE
SHOWBIZ
SHOWBIZZES
SHOWBIZZY
SHOWBOAT
SHOWBOATED
SHOWBOATER
SHOWBOATERS
SHOWBOATING
SHOWBOATS
SHOWBOX
SHOWBOXES
SHOWBREAD
SHOWBREADS
SHOWCASE
SHOWCASED

SHOWCASES
SHOWCASING
SHOWD
SHOWDED
SHOWDING
SHOWDOWN
SHOWDOWNS
SHOWDS
SHOWED
SHOWER
SHOWERED
SHOWERER
SHOWERERS
SHOWERFUL
SHOWERHEAD
SHOWERHEADS
SHOWERIER
SHOWERIEST
SHOWERINESS
SHOWERINESSES
SHOWERING
SHOWERINGS
SHOWERLESS
SHOWERPROOF
SHOWERPROOFED
SHOWERPROOFING
SHOWERPROOFS
SHOWERS
SHOWERY
SHOWGHE
SHOWGHES
SHOWGIRL
SHOWGIRLS
SHOWGROUND
SHOWGROUNDS
SHOWIER
SHOWIEST
SHOWILY
SHOWINESS
SHOWINESSES
SHOWING
SHOWINGS
SHOWJUMPER
SHOWJUMPERS
SHOWJUMPING
SHOWJUMPINGS
SHOWMAN
SHOWMANLY
SHOWMANSHIP
SHOWMANSHIPS
SHOWMEN
SHOWN
SHOWOFF
SHOWOFFS
SHOWPIECE
SHOWPIECES
SHOWPLACE

SHOWPLACES
SHOWRING
SHOWRINGS
SHOWROOM
SHOWROOMS
SHOWS
SHOWSTOPPER
SHOWSTOPPERS
SHOWSTOPPING
SHOWY
SHOWYARD
SHOWYARDS
SHOYU
SHOYUS
SHRADDHA
SHRADDHAS
SHRANK
SHRAPNEL
SHRAPNELS
SHRED
SHREDDED
SHREDDER
SHREDDERS
SHREDDIER
SHREDDIEST
SHREDDING
SHREDDINGS
SHREDDY
SHREDLESS
SHREDS
SHREEK
SHREEKED
SHREEKING
SHREEKS
SHREIK
SHREIKED
SHREIKING
SHREIKS
SHREW
SHREWD
SHREWDER
SHREWDEST
SHREWDIE
SHREWDIES
SHREWDLY
SHREWDNESS
SHREWDNESSES
SHREWED
SHREWING
SHREWISH
SHREWISHLY
SHREWISHNESS
SHREWISHNESSES
SHREWLIKE
SHREWMICE
SHREWMOUSE
SHREWS

SHRI
SHRIECH
SHRIECHED
SHRIECHES
SHRIECHING
SHRIEK
SHRIEKED
SHRIEKER
SHRIEKERS
SHRIEKIER
SHRIEKIEST
SHRIEKING
SHRIEKINGLY
SHRIEKINGS
SHRIEKS
SHRIEKY
SHRIEVAL
SHRIEVALTIES
SHRIEVALTY
SHRIEVE
SHRIEVED
SHRIEVES
SHRIEVING
SHRIFT
SHRIFTS
SHRIGHT
SHRIGHTS
SHRIKE
SHRIKED
SHRIKES
SHRIKING
SHRILL
SHRILLED
SHRILLER
SHRILLEST
SHRILLIER
SHRILLIEST
SHRILLING
SHRILLINGS
SHRILLNESS
SHRILLNESSES
SHRILLS
SHRILLY
SHRIMP
SHRIMPED
SHRIMPER
SHRIMPERS
SHRIMPIER
SHRIMPIEST
SHRIMPING
SHRIMPINGS
SHRIMPLIKE
SHRIMPS
SHRIMPY
SHRINAL
SHRINE
SHRINED

SHRINELIKE
SHRINES
SHRINING
SHRINK
SHRINKABLE
SHRINKAGE
SHRINKAGES
SHRINKER
SHRINKERS
SHRINKING
SHRINKINGLY
SHRINKPACK
SHRINKPACKS
SHRINKS
SHRIS
SHRITCH
SHRITCHED
SHRITCHES
SHRITCHING
SHRIVE
SHRIVED
SHRIVEL
SHRIVELED
SHRIVELING
SHRIVELLED
SHRIVELLING
SHRIVELS
SHRIVEN
SHRIVER
SHRIVERS
SHRIVES
SHRIVING
SHRIVINGS
SHROFF
SHROFFAGE
SHROFFAGES
SHROFFED
SHROFFING
SHROFFS
SHROUD
SHROUDED
SHROUDIER
SHROUDIEST
SHROUDING
SHROUDINGS
SHROUDLESS
SHROUDS
SHROUDY
SHROVE
SHROVED
SHROVES
SHROVING
SHROW
SHROWD
SHROWED
SHROWING
SHROWS

SHRUB
SHRUBBED
SHRUBBERIED
SHRUBBERIES
SHRUBBERY
SHRUBBIER
SHRUBBIEST
SHRUBBINESS
SHRUBBINESSES
SHRUBBING
SHRUBBY
SHRUBLESS
SHRUBLIKE
SHRUBS
SHRUG
SHRUGGED
SHRUGGING
SHRUGS
SHRUNK
SHRUNKEN
SHTCHI
SHTCHIS
SHTETEL
SHTETELACH
SHTETELS
SHTETL
SHTETLACH
SHTETLS
SHTICK
SHTICKS
SHTIK
SHTIKS
SHTOOK
SHTOOKS
SHTOOM
SHTUCK
SHTUCKS
SHTUM
SHTUMM
SHTUP
SHTUPPED
SHTUPPING
SHTUPS
SHUBUNKIN
SHUBUNKINS
SHUCK
SHUCKED
SHUCKER
SHUCKERS
SHUCKING
SHUCKINGS
SHUCKS
SHUDDER
SHUDDERED
SHUDDERING
SHUDDERINGLY
SHUDDERINGS

SHUDDERS
SHUDDERSOME
SHUDDERY
SHUFFLE
SHUFFLEBOARD
SHUFFLEBOARDS
SHUFFLED
SHUFFLER
SHUFFLERS
SHUFFLES
SHUFFLING
SHUFFLINGLY
SHUFFLINGS
SHUFTI
SHUFTIES
SHUFTIS
SHUFTY
SHUGGIES
SHUGGY
SHUL
SHULE
SHULED
SHULES
SHULING
SHULN
SHULS
SHUN
SHUNAMITISM
SHUNAMITISMS
SHUNLESS
SHUNNABLE
SHUNNED
SHUNNER
SHUNNERS
SHUNNING
SHUNPIKE
SHUNPIKED
SHUNPIKER
SHUNPIKERS
SHUNPIKES
SHUNPIKING
SHUNPIKINGS
SHUNS
SHUNT
SHUNTED
SHUNTER
SHUNTERS
SHUNTING
SHUNTINGS
SHUNTS
SHURA
SHURAS
SHUSH
SHUSHED
SHUSHES
SHUSHING
SHUT

SHUTDOWN
SHUTDOWNS
SHUTE
SHUTED
SHUTES
SHUTEYE
SHUTEYES
SHUTING
SHUTOFF
SHUTOFFS
SHUTOUT
SHUTOUTS
SHUTS
SHUTTER
SHUTTERBUG
SHUTTERBUGS
SHUTTERED
SHUTTERING
SHUTTERINGS
SHUTTERLESS
SHUTTERS
SHUTTING
SHUTTLE
SHUTTLECOCK
SHUTTLECOCKED
SHUTTLECOCKING
SHUTTLECOCKS
SHUTTLED
SHUTTLELESS
SHUTTLES
SHUTTLEWISE
SHUTTLING
SHWA
SHWANPAN
SHWANPANS
SHWAS
SHY
SHYER
SHYERS
SHYEST
SHYING
SHYISH
SHYLOCK
SHYLOCKED
SHYLOCKING
SHYLOCKS
SHYLY
SHYNESS
SHYNESSES
SHYPOO
SHYPOOS
SHYSTER
SHYSTERS
SI
SIAL
SIALAGOGIC
SIALAGOGUE

SIALAGOGUES
SIALIC
SIALID
SIALIDAN
SIALIDANS
SIALIDS
SIALOGOGIC
SIALOGOGUE
SIALOGOGUES
SIALOGRAM
SIALOGRAMS
SIALOGRAPHIES
SIALOGRAPHY
SIALOID
SIALOLITH
SIALOLITHS
SIALON
SIALONS
SIALORRHOEA
SIALORRHOEAS
SIALS
SIAMANG
SIAMANGS
SIAMESE
SIAMESED
SIAMESES
SIAMESING
SIAMEZE
SIAMEZED
SIAMEZES
SIAMEZING
SIB
SIBB
SIBBS
SIBILANCE
SIBILANCES
SIBILANCIES
SIBILANCY
SIBILANT
SIBILANTLY
SIBILANTS
SIBILATE
SIBILATED
SIBILATES
SIBILATING
SIBILATION
SIBILATIONS
SIBILATOR
SIBILATORS
SIBILATORY
SIBILOUS
SIBLING
SIBLINGS
SIBS
SIBSHIP
SIBSHIPS
SIBYL

SIBYLIC
SIBYLLIC
SIBYLLINE
SIBYLS
SIC
SICCAN
SICCAR
SICCATIVE
SICCATIVES
SICCED
SICCING
SICCITIES
SICCITY
SICE
SICES
SICH
SICHT
SICHTED
SICHTING
SICHTS
SICILIANA
SICILIANE
SICILIANO
SICILIANOS
SICILIENNE
SICILIENNES
SICK
SICKBAY
SICKBAYS
SICKBED
SICKBEDS
SICKED
SICKEE
SICKEES
SICKEN
SICKENED
SICKENER
SICKENERS
SICKENING
SICKENINGLY
SICKENINGS
SICKENS
SICKER
SICKERLY
SICKERNESS
SICKERNESSES
SICKEST
SICKIE
SICKIES
SICKING
SICKISH
SICKISHLY
SICKISHNESS
SICKISHNESSES
SICKLE
SICKLEBILL
SICKLEBILLS

SICKLED
SICKLEMAN
SICKLEMEN
SICKLEMIA
SICKLEMIAS
SICKLES
SICKLIED
SICKLIER
SICKLIES
SICKLIEST
SICKLILY
SICKLINESS
SICKLINESSES
SICKLING
SICKLY
SICKLYING
SICKNESS
SICKNESSES
SICKNURSE
SICKNURSES
SICKNURSING
SICKNURSINGS
SICKO
SICKOS
SICKOUT
SICKOUTS
SICKROOM
SICKROOMS
SICKS
SICLIKE
SICS
SIDA
SIDALCEA
SIDALCEAS
SIDAS
SIDDHA
SIDDHAS
SIDDHI
SIDDHIS
SIDDUR
SIDDURIM
SIDDURS
SIDE
SIDEARM
SIDEARMS
SIDEBAND
SIDEBANDS
SIDEBAR
SIDEBARS
SIDEBOARD
SIDEBOARDS
SIDEBONES
SIDEBURNED
SIDEBURNS
SIDECAR
SIDECARS
SIDED

SIDEDNESS	SIDEROSES	SIDEWINDER	SIFFLED
SIDEDNESSES	SIDEROSIS	SIDEWINDERS	SIFFLES
SIDEDRESS	SIDEROSTAT	SIDEWISE	SIFFLEUR
SIDEDRESSES	SIDEROSTATIC	SIDHA	SIFFLEURS
SIDEFOOT	SIDEROSTATS	SIDHAS	SIFFLEUSE
SIDEFOOTED	SIDEROTIC	SIDHE	SIFFLEUSES
SIDEFOOTING	SIDERS	SIDING	SIFFLING
SIDEFOOTS	SIDES	SIDINGS	SIFT
SIDEHILL	SIDESADDLE	SIDLE	SIFTED
SIDEHILLS	SIDESADDLES	SIDLED	SIFTER
SIDEKICK	SIDESHOOT	SIDLER	SIFTERS
SIDEKICKS	SIDESHOOTS	SIDLERS	SIFTING
SIDELEVERS	SIDESHOW	SIDLES	SIFTINGLY
SIDELIGHT	SIDESHOWS	SIDLING	SIFTINGS
SIDELIGHTS	SIDESLIP	SIECLE	SIFTS
SIDELINE	SIDESLIPPED	SIECLES	SIGANID
SIDELINED	SIDESLIPPING	SIEGE	SIGANIDS
SIDELINER	SIDESLIPS	SIEGECRAFT	SIGH
SIDELINERS	SIDESMAN	SIEGECRAFTS	SIGHED
SIDELINES	SIDESMEN	SIEGED	SIGHER
SIDELING	SIDESPIN	SIEGER	SIGHERS
SIDELINING	SIDESPINS	SIEGERS	SIGHFUL
SIDELOCK	SIDESPLITTING	SIEGES	SIGHING
SIDELOCKS	SIDESPLITTINGLY	SIEGEWORKS	SIGHINGLY
SIDELONG	SIDESTEP	SIEGING	SIGHLESS
SIDEMAN	SIDESTEPPED	SIELD	SIGHLIKE
SIDEMEN	SIDESTEPPER	SIEMENS	SIGHS
SIDENOTE	SIDESTEPPERS	SIEN	SIGHT
SIDENOTES	SIDESTEPPING	SIENITE	SIGHTABLE
SIDEPATH	SIDESTEPS	SIENITES	SIGHTED
SIDEPATHS	SIDESTREAM	SIENNA	SIGHTER
SIDEPIECE	SIDESTREET	SIENNAS	SIGHTERS
SIDEPIECES	SIDESTREETS	SIENS	SIGHTING
SIDER	SIDESTROKE	SIENT	SIGHTINGS
SIDERAL	SIDESTROKES	SIENTS	SIGHTLESS
SIDERATE	SIDESWIPE	SIEROZEM	SIGHTLESSLY
SIDERATED	SIDESWIPED	SIEROZEMS	SIGHTLESSNESS
SIDERATES	SIDESWIPER	SIERRA	SIGHTLESSNESSES
SIDERATING	SIDESWIPERS	SIERRAN	SIGHTLIER
SIDERATION	SIDESWIPES	SIERRAS	SIGHTLIEST
SIDERATIONS	SIDESWIPING	SIES	SIGHTLINE
SIDEREAL	SIDETRACK	SIESTA	SIGHTLINES
SIDEREALLY	SIDETRACKED	SIESTAS	SIGHTLINESS
SIDERITE	SIDETRACKING	SIETH	SIGHTLINESSES
SIDERITES	SIDETRACKS	SIETHS	SIGHTLY
SIDERITIC	SIDEWALK	SIEUR	SIGHTS
SIDEROAD	SIDEWALKS	SIEURS	SIGHTSAW
SIDEROADS	SIDEWALL	SIEVE	SIGHTSCREEN
SIDEROLITE	SIDEWALLS	SIEVED	SIGHTSCREENS
SIDEROLITES	SIDEWARD	SIEVELIKE	SIGHTSEE
SIDEROPENIA	SIDEWARDS	SIEVERT	SIGHTSEEING
SIDEROPENIAS	SIDEWAY	SIEVERTS	SIGHTSEEINGS
SIDEROPHILE	SIDEWAYS	SIEVES	SIGHTSEEN
SIDEROPHILES	SIDEWHEEL	SIEVING	SIGHTSEER
SIDEROPHILIC	SIDEWHEELER	SIFAKA	SIGHTSEERS
SIDEROPHILIN	SIDEWHEELERS	SIFAKAS	SIGHTSEES
SIDEROPHILINS	SIDEWHEELS	SIFFLE	SIGHTSMAN

SIGHTSMEN
SIGHTWORTHY
SIGIL
SIGILLARIAN
SIGILLARIANS
SIGILLARID
SIGILLARIDS
SIGILLARY
SIGILLATE
SIGILLATION
SIGILLATIONS
SIGILS
SIGISBEI
SIGISBEO
SIGLA
SIGLAS
SIGLOI
SIGLOS
SIGMA
SIGMAS
SIGMATE
SIGMATED
SIGMATES
SIGMATIC
SIGMATING
SIGMATION
SIGMATIONS
SIGMATISM
SIGMATISMS
SIGMATRON
SIGMATRONS
SIGMOID
SIGMOIDAL
SIGMOIDALLY
SIGMOIDECTOMIES
SIGMOIDECTOMY
SIGMOIDOSCOPE
SIGMOIDOSCOPES
SIGMOIDOSCOPIC
SIGMOIDOSCOPIES
SIGMOIDOSCOPY
SIGMOIDS
SIGN
SIGNABLE
SIGNAGE
SIGNAGES
SIGNAL
SIGNALED
SIGNALER
SIGNALERS
SIGNALING
SIGNALINGS
SIGNALISE
SIGNALISED
SIGNALISES
SIGNALISING
SIGNALIZATION

SIGNALIZATIONS
SIGNALIZE
SIGNALIZED
SIGNALIZES
SIGNALIZING
SIGNALLED
SIGNALLER
SIGNALLERS
SIGNALLING
SIGNALLINGS
SIGNALLY
SIGNALMAN
SIGNALMEN
SIGNALMENT
SIGNALMENTS
SIGNALS
SIGNARIES
SIGNARY
SIGNATORIES
SIGNATORY
SIGNATURE
SIGNATURES
SIGNBOARD
SIGNBOARDS
SIGNED
SIGNEE
SIGNEES
SIGNER
SIGNERS
SIGNET
SIGNETED
SIGNETING
SIGNETS
SIGNEUR
SIGNEURIE
SIGNEURIES
SIGNIEUR
SIGNIEURS
SIGNIFIABLE
SIGNIFICANCE
SIGNIFICANCES
SIGNIFICANCIES
SIGNIFICANCY
SIGNIFICANT
SIGNIFICANTLY
SIGNIFICANTS
SIGNIFICATE
SIGNIFICATES
SIGNIFICATION
SIGNIFICATIONS
SIGNIFICATIVE
SIGNIFICATIVELY
SIGNIFICATOR
SIGNIFICATORS
SIGNIFICATORY
SIGNIFICS
SIGNIFIED

SIGNIFIEDS
SIGNIFIER
SIGNIFIERS
SIGNIFIES
SIGNIFY
SIGNIFYING
SIGNIFYINGS
SIGNING
SIGNINGS
SIGNIOR
SIGNIORI
SIGNIORIES
SIGNIORS
SIGNIORY
SIGNLESS
SIGNOR
SIGNORA
SIGNORAS
SIGNORE
SIGNORES
SIGNORI
SIGNORIA
SIGNORIAL
SIGNORIAS
SIGNORIES
SIGNORINA
SIGNORINAS
SIGNORINE
SIGNORINI
SIGNORINO
SIGNORS
SIGNORY
SIGNPOST
SIGNPOSTED
SIGNPOSTING
SIGNPOSTS
SIGNS
SIJO
SIJOS
SIK
SIKA
SIKAS
SIKE
SIKER
SIKES
SIKORSKIES
SIKORSKY
SILAGE
SILAGED
SILAGEING
SILAGES
SILAGING
SILANE
SILANES
SILASTIC
SILASTICS
SILD

SILDS
SILE
SILED
SILEN
SILENCE
SILENCED
SILENCER
SILENCERS
SILENCES
SILENCING
SILENE
SILENES
SILENI
SILENS
SILENT
SILENTER
SILENTEST
SILENTIARIES
SILENTIARY
SILENTLY
SILENTNESS
SILENTNESSES
SILENTS
SILENUS
SILER
SILERS
SILES
SILESIA
SILESIAS
SILEX
SILEXES
SILHOUETTE
SILHOUETTED
SILHOUETTES
SILHOUETTING
SILHOUETTIST
SILHOUETTISTS
SILICA
SILICAS
SILICATE
SILICATED
SILICATES
SILICATING
SILICEOUS
SILICIC
SILICICOLOUS
SILICIDE
SILICIDES
SILICIFEROUS
SILICIFICATION
SILICIFICATIONS
SILICIFIED
SILICIFIES
SILICIFY
SILICIFYING
SILICIOUS
SILICIUM

SILICIUMS
SILICLE
SILICLES
SILICON
SILICONE
SILICONES
SILICONIZED
SILICONS
SILICOSES
SILICOSIS
SILICOTIC
SILICOTICS
SILICULA
SILICULAE
SILICULAS
SILICULE
SILICULES
SILICULOSE
SILING
SILIQUA
SILIQUACEOUS
SILIQUAE
SILIQUAS
SILIQUE
SILIQUES
SILIQUOSE
SILIQUOUS
SILK
SILKALENE
SILKALENES
SILKALINE
SILKALINES
SILKED
SILKEN
SILKENED
SILKENING
SILKENS
SILKGROWER
SILKGROWERS
SILKIE
SILKIER
SILKIES
SILKIEST
SILKILY
SILKINESS
SILKINESSES
SILKING
SILKLIKE
SILKOLINE
SILKOLINES
SILKS
SILKSCREEN
SILKSCREENS
SILKTAIL
SILKTAILS
SILKWEED
SILKWEEDS

SILKWORM
SILKWORMS
SILKY
SILL
SILLABUB
SILLABUBS
SILLADAR
SILLADARS
SILLER
SILLERS
SILLIBUB
SILLIBUBS
SILLIER
SILLIES
SILLIEST
SILLILY
SILLIMANITE
SILLIMANITES
SILLINESS
SILLINESSES
SILLOCK
SILLOCKS
SILLS
SILLY
SILO
SILOED
SILOING
SILOS
SILOXANE
SILOXANES
SILPHIA
SILPHIUM
SILPHIUMS
SILT
SILTATION
SILTATIONS
SILTED
SILTIER
SILTIEST
SILTING
SILTS
SILTSTONE
SILTSTONES
SILTY
SILURID
SILURIDS
SILURIST
SILURISTS
SILUROID
SILUROIDS
SILVA
SILVAE
SILVAN
SILVANS
SILVAS
SILVATIC
SILVER

SILVERBACK
SILVERBACKS
SILVERBERRIES
SILVERBERRY
SILVERBILL
SILVERBILLS
SILVERED
SILVERER
SILVERERS
SILVEREYE
SILVEREYES
SILVERFISH
SILVERFISHES
SILVERHORN
SILVERHORNS
SILVERIER
SILVERIEST
SILVERINESS
SILVERINESSES
SILVERING
SILVERINGS
SILVERISE
SILVERISED
SILVERISES
SILVERISING
SILVERIZE
SILVERIZED
SILVERIZES
SILVERIZING
SILVERLING
SILVERLINGS
SILVERLY
SILVERN
SILVERPOINT
SILVERPOINTS
SILVERS
SILVERSIDE
SILVERSIDES
SILVERSIDESES
SILVERSKIN
SILVERSKINS
SILVERSMITH
SILVERSMITHING
SILVERSMITHINGS
SILVERSMITHS
SILVERTAIL
SILVERTAILS
SILVERWARE
SILVERWARES
SILVERWEED
SILVERWEEDS
SILVERY
SILVESTRIAN
SILVEX
SILVEXES
SILVICAL
SILVICS

SILVICULTURAL
SILVICULTURALLY
SILVICULTURE
SILVICULTURES
SILVICULTURIST
SILVICULTURISTS
SIM
SIMA
SIMAR
SIMAROUBA
SIMAROUBACEOUS
SIMAROUBAS
SIMARRE
SIMARRES
SIMARS
SIMARUBA
SIMARUBACEOUS
SIMARUBAS
SIMAS
SIMATIC
SIMAZINE
SIMAZINES
SIMBA
SIMBAS
SIMI
SIMIAL
SIMIAN
SIMIANS
SIMILAR
SIMILARITIES
SIMILARITY
SIMILARLY
SIMILATIVE
SIMILE
SIMILES
SIMILISE
SIMILISED
SIMILISES
SIMILISING
SIMILITUDE
SIMILITUDES
SIMILIZE
SIMILIZED
SIMILIZES
SIMILIZING
SIMILLIMUM
SIMILLIMUMS
SIMILOR
SIMILORS
SIMIOID
SIMIOUS
SIMIS
SIMITAR
SIMITARS
SIMKIN
SIMKINS
SIMLIN

SIMLINS
SIMMER
SIMMERED
SIMMERING
SIMMERS
SIMNEL
SIMNELS
SIMOLEON
SIMOLEONS
SIMONIAC
SIMONIACAL
SIMONIACALLY
SIMONIACS
SIMONIES
SIMONIOUS
SIMONIST
SIMONISTS
SIMONIZE
SIMONIZED
SIMONIZES
SIMONIZING
SIMONY
SIMOOM
SIMOOMS
SIMOON
SIMOONS
SIMORG
SIMORGS
SIMP
SIMPAI
SIMPAIS
SIMPATICO
SIMPER
SIMPERED
SIMPERER
SIMPERERS
SIMPERING
SIMPERINGLY
SIMPERS
SIMPKIN
SIMPKINS
SIMPLE
SIMPLED
SIMPLEMINDED
SIMPLEMINDEDLY
SIMPLENESS
SIMPLENESSES
SIMPLER
SIMPLERS
SIMPLES
SIMPLESSE
SIMPLESSES
SIMPLEST
SIMPLETON
SIMPLETONS
SIMPLEX
SIMPLEXES

SIMPLICES
SIMPLICIA
SIMPLICIAL
SIMPLICIALLY
SIMPLICIDENTATE
SIMPLICITER
SIMPLICITIES
SIMPLICITY
SIMPLIFICATION
SIMPLIFICATIONS
SIMPLIFICATIVE
SIMPLIFICATOR
SIMPLIFICATORS
SIMPLIFIED
SIMPLIFIER
SIMPLIFIERS
SIMPLIFIES
SIMPLIFY
SIMPLIFYING
SIMPLING
SIMPLINGS
SIMPLISM
SIMPLISMS
SIMPLIST
SIMPLISTE
SIMPLISTIC
SIMPLISTICALLY
SIMPLISTS
SIMPLY
SIMPS
SIMS
SIMSIM
SIMSIMS
SIMUL
SIMULACRA
SIMULACRE
SIMULACRES
SIMULACRUM
SIMULACRUMS
SIMULANT
SIMULANTS
SIMULAR
SIMULARS
SIMULATE
SIMULATED
SIMULATES
SIMULATING
SIMULATION
SIMULATIONS
SIMULATIVE
SIMULATIVELY
SIMULATOR
SIMULATORS
SIMULATORY
SIMULCAST
SIMULCASTED
SIMULCASTING

SIMULCASTS
SIMULIUM
SIMULIUMS
SIMULS
SIMULTANEITIES
SIMULTANEITY
SIMULTANEOUS
SIMULTANEOUSES
SIMULTANEOUSLY
SIMURG
SIMURGH
SIMURGHS
SIMURGS
SIN
SINANTHROPIC
SINANTHROPUS
SINANTHROPUSES
SINAPISM
SINAPISMS
SINARCHISM
SINARCHISMS
SINARCHIST
SINARCHISTS
SINARQUISM
SINARQUISMS
SINARQUIST
SINARQUISTS
SINCE
SINCERE
SINCERELY
SINCERENESS
SINCERENESSES
SINCERER
SINCEREST
SINCERITIES
SINCERITY
SINCIPITA
SINCIPITAL
SINCIPUT
SINCIPUTS
SIND
SINDED
SINDING
SINDINGS
SINDON
SINDONOLOGIES
SINDONOLOGIST
SINDONOLOGISTS
SINDONOLOGY
SINDONOPHANIES
SINDONS
SINDS
SINE
SINECURE
SINECURES
SINECURISM
SINECURISMS

SINECURIST
SINECURISTS
SINED
SINES
SINEW
SINEWED
SINEWIER
SINEWIEST
SINEWINESS
SINEWING
SINEWLESS
SINEWS
SINEWY
SINFONIA
SINFONIAS
SINFONIE
SINFONIETTA
SINFONIETTAS
SINFUL
SINFULLY
SINFULNESS
SINFULNESSES
SING
SINGABLE
SINGABLENESS
SINGABLENESSES
SINGALONG
SINGALONGS
SINGE
SINGED
SINGEING
SINGER
SINGERS
SINGES
SINGING
SINGINGLY
SINGINGS
SINGLE
SINGLED
SINGLEDOM
SINGLEHOOD
SINGLEHOODS
SINGLENESS
SINGLENESSES
SINGLES
SINGLESTICK
SINGLESTICKS
SINGLET
SINGLETON
SINGLETONS
SINGLETREE
SINGLETREES
SINGLETS
SINGLING
SINGLINGS
SINGLY
SINGS

SINGSONG	SINISTRORSAL	SINTERING	SIPHUNCLES
SINGSONGED	SINISTRORSALLY	SINTERS	SIPING
SINGSONGING	SINISTRORSE	SINTERY	SIPPED
SINGSONGS	SINISTRORSELY	SINUATE	SIPPER
SINGSONGY	SINISTROUS	SINUATED	SIPPERS
SINGSPIEL	SINISTROUSLY	SINUATELY	SIPPET
SINGSPIELS	SINK	SINUATES	SIPPETS
SINGULAR	SINKABLE	SINUATING	SIPPING
SINGULARISATION	SINKAGE	SINUATION	SIPPLE
SINGULARISE	SINKAGES	SINUATIONS	SIPPLED
SINGULARISED	SINKER	SINUITIS	SIPPLES
SINGULARISES	SINKERS	SINUITISES	SIPPLING
SINGULARISING	SINKHOLE	SINUOSE	SIPS
SINGULARISM	SINKHOLES	SINUOSITIES	SIPUNCULID
SINGULARISMS	SINKIER	SINUOSITY	SIPUNCULIDS
SINGULARIST	SINKIEST	SINUOUS	SIPUNCULOID
SINGULARISTS	SINKING	SINUOUSLY	SIPUNCULOIDS
SINGULARITIES	SINKINGS	SINUOUSNESS	SIR
SINGULARITY	SINKS	SINUOUSNESSES	SIRCAR
SINGULARIZATION	SINKY	SINUPALLIAL	SIRCARS
SINGULARIZE	SINLESS	SINUPALLIATE	SIRDAR
SINGULARIZED	SINLESSLY	SINUS	SIRDARS
SINGULARIZES	SINLESSNESS	SINUSES	SIRE
SINGULARIZING	SINLESSNESSES	SINUSITIS	SIRED
SINGULARLY	SINNED	SINUSITISES	SIREE
SINGULARNESS	SINNER	SINUSOID	SIREES
SINGULARS	SINNERED	SINUSOIDAL	SIREN
SINGULARY	SINNERING	SINUSOIDALLY	SIRENIAN
SINGULT	SINNERS	SINUSOIDS	SIRENIANS
SINGULTS	SINNET	SIP	SIRENIC
SINGULTUS	SINNETS	SIPE	SIRENISE
SINGULTUSES	SINNING	SIPED	SIRENISED
SINH	SINNINGIA	SIPES	SIRENISES
SINHS	SINNINGIAS	SIPHON	SIRENISING
SINICAL	SINOATRIAL	SIPHONAGE	SIRENIZE
SINICISE	SINOLOGICAL	SIPHONAGES	SIRENIZED
SINICISED	SINOLOGIES	SIPHONAL	SIRENIZES
SINICISES	SINOLOGIST	SIPHONATE	SIRENIZING
SINICISING	SINOLOGISTS	SIPHONED	SIRENS
SINICIZE	SINOLOGUE	SIPHONET	SIRES
SINICIZED	SINOLOGUES	SIPHONETS	SIRGANG
SINICIZES	SINOLOGY	SIPHONIC	SIRGANGS
SINICIZING	SINOPIA	SIPHONING	SIRI
SINING	SINOPIAS	SIPHONOGAM	SIRIASES
SINISTER	SINOPIE	SIPHONOGAMIES	SIRIASIS
SINISTERITIES	SINOPIS	SIPHONOGAMS	SIRIH
SINISTERITY	SINOPISES	SIPHONOGAMY	SIRIHS
SINISTERLY	SINOPITE	SIPHONOPHORAN	SIRING
SINISTERNESS	SINOPITES	SIPHONOPHORANS	SIRIS
SINISTERNESSES	SINS	SIPHONOPHORE	SIRKAR
SINISTERWISE	SINSEMILLA	SIPHONOPHORES	SIRKARS
SINISTRAL	SINSEMILLAS	SIPHONOPHOROUS	SIRLOIN
SINISTRALITIES	SINSYNE	SIPHONOSTELE	SIRLOINS
SINISTRALITY	SINTER	SIPHONOSTELES	SIRNAME
SINISTRALLY	SINTERABILITIES	SIPHONOSTELIC	SIRNAMED
SINISTRALS	SINTERABILITY	SIPHONS	SIRNAMES
SINISTRODEXTRAL	SINTERED	SIPHUNCLE	SIRNAMING

SIROC	SISTERLINESS	SITTEN	SIXTEENMOS
SIROCCO	SISTERLINESSES	SITTER	SIXTEENS
SIROCCOS	SISTERLY	SITTERS	SIXTEENTH
SIROCS	SISTERS	SITTINE	SIXTEENTHLY
SIRONISE	SISTING	SITTING	SIXTEENTHS
SIRONISED	SISTRA	SITTINGS	SIXTES
SIRONISES	SISTROID	SITUATE	SIXTH
SIRONISING	SISTRUM	SITUATED	SIXTHLY
SIRONIZE	SISTRUMS	SITUATES	SIXTHS
SIRONIZED	SISTS	SITUATING	SIXTIES
SIRONIZES	SIT	SITUATION	SIXTIETH
SIRONIZING	SITAR	SITUATIONAL	SIXTIETHS
SIROSET	SITARIST	SITUATIONALLY	SIXTY
SIRRA	SITARISTS	SITUATIONISM	SIXTYISH
SIRRAH	SITARS	SITUATIONISMS	SIZABLE
SIRRAHS	SITATUNGA	SITUATIONS	SIZABLENESS
SIRRAS	SITATUNGAS	SITULA	SIZABLENESSES
SIRRED	SITCOM	SITULAE	SIZABLY
SIRREE	SITCOMS	SITUP	SIZAR
SIRREES	SITE	SITUPS	SIZARS
SIRRING	SITED	SITUS	SIZARSHIP
SIRS	SITELLA	SITUSES	SIZARSHIPS
SIRUP	SITELLAS	SITUTUNGA	SIZE
SIRUPED	SITES	SITUTUNGAS	SIZEABLE
SIRUPING	SITFAST	SITZ	SIZEABLENESS
SIRUPS	SITFASTS	SITZKRIEG	SIZEABLY
SIRUPY	SITH	SITZKRIEGS	SIZED
SIRVENTE	SITHE	SITZMARK	SIZEISM
SIRVENTES	SITHED	SITZMARKS	SIZEISMS
SIS	SITHEE	SIVER	SIZEIST
SISAL	SITHEN	SIVERS	SIZEISTS
SISALS	SITHENCE	SIWASH	SIZEL
SISERARIES	SITHENS	SIWASHED	SIZELS
SISERARY	SITHES	SIWASHES	SIZER
SISES	SITHING	SIWASHING	SIZERS
SISKIN	SITING	SIX	SIZES
SISKINS	SITIOLOGIES	SIXAIN	SIZIER
SISS	SITIOLOGY	SIXAINE	SIZIEST
SISSERARIES	SITIOPHOBIA	SIXAINES	SIZINESS
SISSES	SITIOPHOBIAS	SIXAINS	SIZINESSES
SISSIER	SITKA	SIXER	SIZING
SISSIES	SITKAMER	SIXERS	SIZINGS
SISSIEST	SITKAMERS	SIXES	SIZISM
SISSIFIED	SITKAS	SIXFOLD	SIZISMS
SISSOO	SITOLOGIES	SIXMO	SIZIST
SISSOOS	SITOLOGY	SIXMOS	SIZISTS
SISSY	SITOPHOBIA	SIXPENCE	SIZY
SISSYISH	SITOPHOBIAS	SIXPENCES	SIZZLE
SIST	SITOSTEROL	SIXPENNIES	SIZZLED
SISTED	SITOSTEROLS	SIXPENNY	SIZZLER
SISTER	SITREP	SIXSCORE	SIZZLERS
SISTERED	SITREPS	SIXSCORES	SIZZLES
SISTERHOOD	SITS	SIXTE	SIZZLING
SISTERHOODS	SITTAR	SIXTEEN	SIZZLINGLY
SISTERING	SITTARS	SIXTEENER	SIZZLINGS
SISTERLESS	SITTELLA	SIXTEENERS	SJAMBOK
SISTERLIKE	SITTELLAS	SIXTEENMO	SJAMBOKED

SJAMBOKING
SJAMBOKKED
SJAMBOKKING
SJAMBOKS
SKA
SKAG
SKAGS
SKAIL
SKAILED
SKAILING
SKAILS
SKAITH
SKAITHED
SKAITHING
SKAITHLESS
SKAITHS
SKALD
SKALDIC
SKALDS
SKALDSHIP
SKALDSHIPS
SKANK
SKANKED
SKANKING
SKANKINGS
SKANKS
SKANKY
SKART
SKARTH
SKARTHS
SKARTS
SKAS
SKAT
SKATE
SKATEBOARD
SKATEBOARDED
SKATEBOARDER
SKATEBOARDERS
SKATEBOARDING
SKATEBOARDINGS
SKATEBOARDS
SKATED
SKATEPARK
SKATEPARKS
SKATER
SKATERS
SKATES
SKATING
SKATINGS
SKATOL
SKATOLE
SKATOLES
SKATOLS
SKATS
SKATT
SKATTS
SKAW

SKAWS
SKEAN
SKEANE
SKEANES
SKEANS
SKEAR
SKEARED
SKEARIER
SKEARIEST
SKEARING
SKEARS
SKEARY
SKEDADDLE
SKEDADDLED
SKEDADDLER
SKEDADDLERS
SKEDADDLES
SKEDADDLING
SKEE
SKEECHAN
SKEECHANS
SKEED
SKEEING
SKEELIER
SKEELIEST
SKEELY
SKEEN
SKEENS
SKEER
SKEERED
SKEERIER
SKEERIEST
SKEERING
SKEERS
SKEERY
SKEES
SKEESICKS
SKEET
SKEETER
SKEETERS
SKEETS
SKEG
SKEGG
SKEGGER
SKEGGERS
SKEGGS
SKEGS
SKEIGH
SKEIGHER
SKEIGHEST
SKEIN
SKEINED
SKEINING
SKEINS
SKELDER
SKELDERED
SKELDERING

SKELDERS
SKELETAL
SKELETALLY
SKELETOGENOUS
SKELETON
SKELETONIC
SKELETONISE
SKELETONISED
SKELETONISES
SKELETONISING
SKELETONIZE
SKELETONIZED
SKELETONIZER
SKELETONIZERS
SKELETONIZES
SKELETONIZING
SKELETONS
SKELF
SKELFS
SKELL
SKELLIE
SKELLIED
SKELLIER
SKELLIES
SKELLIEST
SKELLOCH
SKELLOCHED
SKELLOCHING
SKELLOCHS
SKELLS
SKELLUM
SKELLUMS
SKELLY
SKELLYING
SKELM
SKELMS
SKELP
SKELPED
SKELPING
SKELPINGS
SKELPIT
SKELPS
SKELTER
SKELTERED
SKELTERING
SKELTERS
SKELUM
SKELUMS
SKEN
SKENE
SKENES
SKENNED
SKENNING
SKENS
SKEO
SKEOS
SKEP

SKEPFUL
SKEPFULS
SKEPPED
SKEPPING
SKEPS
SKEPSIS
SKEPSISES
SKEPTIC
SKEPTICAL
SKEPTICALLY
SKEPTICALNESS
SKEPTICISM
SKEPTICISMS
SKEPTICS
SKER
SKERRED
SKERRICK
SKERRICKS
SKERRIES
SKERRING
SKERRY
SKERS
SKET
SKETCH
SKETCHABILITIES
SKETCHABILITY
SKETCHABLE
SKETCHBOOK
SKETCHBOOKS
SKETCHED
SKETCHER
SKETCHERS
SKETCHES
SKETCHIER
SKETCHIEST
SKETCHILY
SKETCHINESS
SKETCHINESSES
SKETCHING
SKETCHY
SKETS
SKETTED
SKETTING
SKEUOMORPH
SKEUOMORPHIC
SKEUOMORPHISM
SKEUOMORPHISMS
SKEUOMORPHS
SKEW
SKEWBACK
SKEWBACKED
SKEWBACKS
SKEWBALD
SKEWBALDS
SKEWED
SKEWER
SKEWERED

SKEWERING
SKEWERS
SKEWEST
SKEWING
SKEWNESS
SKEWNESSES
SKEWS
SKEWWHIFF
SKI
SKIABLE
SKIAGRAM
SKIAGRAMS
SKIAGRAPH
SKIAGRAPHS
SKIAMACHIES
SKIAMACHY
SKIASCOPE
SKIASCOPES
SKIASCOPIC
SKIASCOPICALLY
SKIASCOPIES
SKIASCOPY
SKIATRON
SKIATRONS
SKIBOB
SKIBOBBED
SKIBOBBER
SKIBOBBERS
SKIBOBBING
SKIBOBBINGS
SKIBOBS
SKID
SKIDDED
SKIDDER
SKIDDERS
SKIDDIER
SKIDDIEST
SKIDDING
SKIDDOO
SKIDDOOED
SKIDDOOING
SKIDDOOS
SKIDDY
SKIDLID
SKIDLIDS
SKIDOO
SKIDOOED
SKIDOOING
SKIDOOS
SKIDPAN
SKIDPANS
SKIDPROOF
SKIDS
SKIDWAY
SKIDWAYS
SKIED
SKIER

SKIERS
SKIES
SKIEY
SKIEYER
SKIEYEST
SKIFF
SKIFFED
SKIFFING
SKIFFLE
SKIFFLED
SKIFFLES
SKIFFLING
SKIFFS
SKIING
SKIINGS
SKIJORER
SKIJORERS
SKIJORING
SKIJORINGS
SKIKJORING
SKIKJORINGS
SKILFUL
SKILFULLY
SKILFULNESS
SKILFULNESSES
SKILL
SKILLCENTRE
SKILLCENTRES
SKILLED
SKILLESS
SKILLESSNESS
SKILLESSNESSES
SKILLET
SKILLETS
SKILLFUL
SKILLFULLY
SKILLFULNESS
SKILLFULNESSES
SKILLIER
SKILLIES
SKILLIEST
SKILLIGALEE
SKILLIGALEES
SKILLIGOLEE
SKILLIGOLEES
SKILLING
SKILLINGS
SKILLION
SKILLIONS
SKILLS
SKILLY
SKIM
SKIMBOARD
SKIMBOARDS
SKIMMED
SKIMMER
SKIMMERS

SKIMMIA
SKIMMIAS
SKIMMING
SKIMMINGLY
SKIMMINGS
SKIMMINGTON
SKIMMINGTONS
SKIMO
SKIMOBILE
SKIMOBILES
SKIMOS
SKIMP
SKIMPED
SKIMPIER
SKIMPIEST
SKIMPILY
SKIMPINESS
SKIMPINESSES
SKIMPING
SKIMPINGLY
SKIMPS
SKIMPY
SKIMS
SKIN
SKINCARE
SKINCARES
SKINFLICK
SKINFLICKS
SKINFLINT
SKINFLINTS
SKINFLINTY
SKINFOOD
SKINFOODS
SKINFUL
SKINFULS
SKINHEAD
SKINHEADS
SKINK
SKINKED
SKINKER
SKINKERS
SKINKING
SKINKS
SKINLESS
SKINLIKE
SKINNED
SKINNER
SKINNERS
SKINNIER
SKINNIEST
SKINNINESS
SKINNINESSES
SKINNING
SKINNY
SKINS
SKINT
SKINTER

SKINTEST
SKINTIGHT
SKIO
SKIORING
SKIORINGS
SKIOS
SKIP
SKIPJACK
SKIPJACKS
SKIPLANE
SKIPLANES
SKIPPABLE
SKIPPED
SKIPPER
SKIPPERED
SKIPPERING
SKIPPERINGS
SKIPPERS
SKIPPET
SKIPPETS
SKIPPIER
SKIPPIEST
SKIPPING
SKIPPINGLY
SKIPPINGS
SKIPPY
SKIPS
SKIRL
SKIRLED
SKIRLING
SKIRLINGS
SKIRLS
SKIRMISH
SKIRMISHED
SKIRMISHER
SKIRMISHERS
SKIRMISHES
SKIRMISHING
SKIRMISHINGS
SKIRR
SKIRRED
SKIRRET
SKIRRETS
SKIRRING
SKIRRS
SKIRT
SKIRTED
SKIRTER
SKIRTERS
SKIRTING
SKIRTINGS
SKIRTLESS
SKIRTS
SKIS
SKIT
SKITCH
SKITCHED

SKITCHES	SKOALS	SKRIMSHANKER	SKUTTERUDITE
SKITCHING	SKOFF	SKRIMSHANKERS	SKUTTERUDITES
SKITE	SKOFFED	SKRIMSHANKING	SKUTTLE
SKITED	SKOFFING	SKRIMSHANKS	SKUTTLED
SKITES	SKOFFS	SKRUMP	SKUTTLES
SKITING	SKOKIAAN	SKRUMPED	SKUTTLING
SKITS	SKOKIAANS	SKRUMPING	SKY
SKITTER	SKOL	SKRUMPS	SKYBORN
SKITTERED	SKOLIA	SKRY	SKYBORNE
SKITTERIER	SKOLION	SKRYER	SKYBOX
SKITTERIEST	SKOLLIE	SKRYERS	SKYBOXES
SKITTERING	SKOLLIES	SKRYING	SKYCAP
SKITTERS	SKOLLY	SKUA	SKYCAPS
SKITTERY	SKOOKUM	SKUAS	SKYCLAD
SKITTISH	SKOOL	SKUDLER	SKYDIVE
SKITTISHLY	SKOOLS	SKUDLERS	SKYDIVED
SKITTISHNESS	SKOOSH	SKUG	SKYDIVER
SKITTISHNESSES	SKOOSHED	SKUGGED	SKYDIVERS
SKITTLE	SKOOSHES	SKUGGING	SKYDIVES
SKITTLED	SKOOSHING	SKUGS	SKYDIVING
SKITTLES	SKOSH	SKULDUDDERIES	SKYDIVINGS
SKITTLING	SKOSHES	SKULDUDDERY	SKYDOVE
SKIVE	SKRAN	SKULDUGGERIES	SKYED
SKIVED	SKRANS	SKULDUGGERY	SKYER
SKIVER	SKREEGH	SKULK	SKYERS
SKIVERED	SKREEGHED	SKULKED	SKYEY
SKIVERING	SKREEGHING	SKULKER	SKYHOOK
SKIVERS	SKREEGHS	SKULKERS	SKYHOOKS
SKIVES	SKREEN	SKULKING	SKYIER
SKIVIE	SKREENS	SKULKINGLY	SKYIEST
SKIVIER	SKREIGH	SKULKINGS	SKYING
SKIVIEST	SKREIGHED	SKULKS	SKYISH
SKIVING	SKREIGHING	SKULL	SKYJACK
SKIVINGS	SKREIGHS	SKULLCAP	SKYJACKED
SKIVVIED	SKRIECH	SKULLCAPS	SKYJACKER
SKIVVIES	SKRIECHED	SKULLDUGGERIES	SKYJACKERS
SKIVVY	SKRIECHING	SKULLDUGGERY	SKYJACKING
SKIVVYING	SKRIECHS	SKULLED	SKYJACKINGS
SKIVY	SKRIED	SKULLS	SKYJACKS
SKIWEAR	SKRIEGH	SKULPIN	SKYLAB
SKLATE	SKRIEGHED	SKULPINS	SKYLABS
SKLATED	SKRIEGHING	SKUMMER	SKYLARK
SKLATES	SKRIEGHS	SKUMMERED	SKYLARKED
SKLATING	SKRIES	SKUMMERING	SKYLARKER
SKLENT	SKRIK	SKUMMERS	SKYLARKERS
SKLENTED	SKRIKE	SKUNK	SKYLARKING
SKLENTING	SKRIKS	SKUNKBIRD	SKYLARKINGS
SKLENTS	SKRIMMAGE	SKUNKBIRDS	SKYLARKS
SKLIFF	SKRIMMAGED	SKUNKED	SKYLIGHT
SKLIFFS	SKRIMMAGES	SKUNKING	SKYLIGHTED
SKLIM	SKRIMMAGING	SKUNKS	SKYLIGHTS
SKLIMMED	SKRIMP	SKUNKWEED	SKYLIKE
SKLIMMING	SKRIMPED	SKUNKWEEDS	SKYLINE
SKLIMS	SKRIMPING	SKURRIED	SKYLINES
SKOAL	SKRIMPS	SKURRIES	SKYLIT
SKOALED	SKRIMSHANK	SKURRY	SKYMAN
SKOALING	SKRIMSHANKED	SKURRYING	SKYMEN

SKYPHOI	SLACKEN	SLAMMER	SLAPHEAD
SKYPHOS	SLACKENED	SLAMMERKIN	SLAPHEADS
SKYR	SLACKENING	SLAMMERKINS	SLAPJACK
SKYRE	SLACKENINGS	SLAMMERS	SLAPJACKS
SKYRED	SLACKENS	SLAMMING	SLAPPED
SKYRES	SLACKER	SLAMMINGS	SLAPPER
SKYRING	SLACKERS	SLAMS	SLAPPERS
SKYROCKET	SLACKEST	SLANDER	SLAPPING
SKYROCKETED	SLACKING	SLANDERED	SLAPS
SKYROCKETING	SLACKLY	SLANDERER	SLAPSHOT
SKYROCKETS	SLACKNESS	SLANDERERS	SLAPSHOTS
SKYRS	SLACKNESSES	SLANDERING	SLAPSTICK
SKYSAIL	SLACKS	SLANDEROUS	SLAPSTICKS
SKYSAILS	SLADANG	SLANDEROUSLY	SLART
SKYSCAPE	SLADANGS	SLANDEROUSNESS	SLARTED
SKYSCAPES	SLADE	SLANDERS	SLARTING
SKYSCRAPER	SLADES	SLANE	SLARTS
SKYSCRAPERS	SLAE	SLANES	SLASH
SKYTE	SLAES	SLANG	SLASHED
SKYTED	SLAG	SLANGED	SLASHER
SKYTES	SLAGGED	SLANGER	SLASHERS
SKYTING	SLAGGIER	SLANGERS	SLASHES
SKYWALK	SLAGGIEST	SLANGIER	SLASHING
SKYWALKS	SLAGGING	SLANGIEST	SLASHINGLY
SKYWARD	SLAGGINGS	SLANGILY	SLASHINGS
SKYWARDS	SLAGGY	SLANGINESS	SLAT
SKYWAY	SLAGS	SLANGINESSES	SLATCH
SKYWAYS	SLAID	SLANGING	SLATCHES
SKYWRITE	SLAIN	SLANGINGLY	SLATE
SKYWRITER	SLAINTE	SLANGINGS	SLATED
SKYWRITERS	SLAIRGED	SLANGISH	SLATELIKE
SKYWRITES	SLAIRGING	SLANGS	SLATER
SKYWRITING	SLAIRGS	SLANGUAGE	SLATERS
SKYWRITINGS	SLAISTER	SLANGUAGES	SLATES
SKYWRITTEN	SLAISTERED	SLANGULAR	SLATEY
SKYWROTE	SLAISTERIES	SLANGY	SLATHER
SLAB	SLAISTERING	SLANK	SLATHERED
SLABBED	SLAISTERS	SLANT	SLATHERING
SLABBER	SLAISTERY	SLANTED	SLATHERS
SLABBERED	SLAKABLE	SLANTENDICULAR	SLATIER
SLABBERER	SLAKE	SLANTER	SLATIEST
SLABBERERS	SLAKEABILITY	SLANTERS	SLATINESS
SLABBERING	SLAKEABLE	SLANTINDICULAR	SLATINESSES
SLABBERS	SLAKED	SLANTING	SLATING
SLABBERY	SLAKELESS	SLANTINGLY	SLATINGS
SLABBIER	SLAKER	SLANTINGWAYS	SLATS
SLABBIEST	SLAKERS	SLANTLY	SLATTED
SLABBINESS	SLAKES	SLANTS	SLATTER
SLABBINESSES	SLAKING	SLANTWAYS	SLATTERED
SLABBING	SLALOM	SLANTWISE	SLATTERING
SLABBY	SLALOMED	SLANTY	SLATTERN
SLABLIKE	SLALOMING	SLAP	SLATTERNLINESS
SLABS	SLALOMS	SLAPDASH	SLATTERNLY
SLABSTONE	SLAM	SLAPDASHES	SLATTERNS
SLABSTONES	SLAMMAKIN	SLAPHAPPIER	SLATTERS
SLACK	SLAMMAKINS	SLAPHAPPIEST	SLATTERY
SLACKED	SLAMMED	SLAPHAPPY	SLATTING

SLATTINGS
SLATY
SLAUGHTER
SLAUGHTERABLE
SLAUGHTERED
SLAUGHTERER
SLAUGHTERERS
SLAUGHTERHOUSE
SLAUGHTERHOUSES
SLAUGHTERIES
SLAUGHTERING
SLAUGHTERMAN
SLAUGHTERMEN
SLAUGHTEROUS
SLAUGHTEROUSLY
SLAUGHTERS
SLAUGHTERY
SLAVE
SLAVED
SLAVEHOLDER
SLAVEHOLDERS
SLAVEHOLDING
SLAVEHOLDINGS
SLAVER
SLAVERED
SLAVERER
SLAVERERS
SLAVERIES
SLAVERING
SLAVERINGLY
SLAVERS
SLAVERY
SLAVES
SLAVEY
SLAVEYS
SLAVING
SLAVISH
SLAVISHLY
SLAVISHNESS
SLAVISHNESSES
SLAVOCRACIES
SLAVOCRACY
SLAVOCRAT
SLAVOCRATS
SLAW
SLAWS
SLAY
SLAYED
SLAYER
SLAYERS
SLAYING
SLAYS
SLEAVE
SLEAVED
SLEAVES
SLEAVING
SLEAZE

SLEAZEBAG
SLEAZEBAGS
SLEAZEBALL
SLEAZEBALLS
SLEAZES
SLEAZIER
SLEAZIEST
SLEAZILY
SLEAZINESS
SLEAZINESSES
SLEAZO
SLEAZY
SLED
SLEDDED
SLEDDER
SLEDDERS
SLEDDING
SLEDDINGS
SLEDED
SLEDGE
SLEDGED
SLEDGEHAMMER
SLEDGEHAMMERED
SLEDGEHAMMERING
SLEDGEHAMMERS
SLEDGER
SLEDGERS
SLEDGES
SLEDGING
SLEDGINGS
SLEDING
SLEDS
SLEE
SLEECH
SLEECHES
SLEECHIER
SLEECHIEST
SLEECHY
SLEEK
SLEEKED
SLEEKEN
SLEEKENED
SLEEKENING
SLEEKENS
SLEEKER
SLEEKERS
SLEEKEST
SLEEKIER
SLEEKIEST
SLEEKING
SLEEKINGS
SLEEKIT
SLEEKLY
SLEEKNESS
SLEEKNESSES
SLEEKS
SLEEKSTONE

SLEEKSTONES
SLEEKY
SLEEP
SLEEPER
SLEEPERS
SLEEPERY
SLEEPIER
SLEEPIEST
SLEEPILY
SLEEPINESS
SLEEPINESSES
SLEEPING
SLEEPINGS
SLEEPLESS
SLEEPLESSLY
SLEEPLESSNESS
SLEEPLESSNESSES
SLEEPLIKE
SLEEPOUT
SLEEPOUTS
SLEEPOVER
SLEEPOVERS
SLEEPRY
SLEEPS
SLEEPSUIT
SLEEPSUITS
SLEEPWALK
SLEEPWALKED
SLEEPWALKER
SLEEPWALKERS
SLEEPWALKING
SLEEPWALKINGS
SLEEPWALKS
SLEEPWEAR
SLEEPY
SLEEPYHEAD
SLEEPYHEADED
SLEEPYHEADS
SLEER
SLEEST
SLEET
SLEETED
SLEETIER
SLEETIEST
SLEETINESS
SLEETINESSES
SLEETING
SLEETS
SLEETY
SLEEVE
SLEEVED
SLEEVEEN
SLEEVEENS
SLEEVEHAND
SLEEVEHANDS
SLEEVELESS
SLEEVELET

SLEEVELETS
SLEEVELIKE
SLEEVER
SLEEVERS
SLEEVES
SLEEVING
SLEEVINGS
SLEEZIER
SLEEZIEST
SLEEZY
SLEIDED
SLEIGH
SLEIGHED
SLEIGHER
SLEIGHERS
SLEIGHING
SLEIGHINGS
SLEIGHS
SLEIGHT
SLEIGHTS
SLENDER
SLENDERER
SLENDEREST
SLENDERISE
SLENDERISED
SLENDERISES
SLENDERISING
SLENDERIZE
SLENDERIZED
SLENDERIZES
SLENDERIZING
SLENDERLY
SLENDERNESS
SLENDERNESSES
SLENTER
SLENTERS
SLEPT
SLEUTH
SLEUTHED
SLEUTHHOUND
SLEUTHHOUNDS
SLEUTHING
SLEUTHS
SLEW
SLEWED
SLEWING
SLEWS
SLEY
SLEYS
SLICE
SLICEABLE
SLICED
SLICER
SLICERS
SLICES
SLICING
SLICINGS

SLICK
SLICKED
SLICKEN
SLICKENED
SLICKENING
SLICKENS
SLICKENSIDE
SLICKENSIDED
SLICKENSIDES
SLICKER
SLICKERED
SLICKERS
SLICKEST
SLICKING
SLICKINGS
SLICKLY
SLICKNESS
SLICKNESSES
SLICKROCK
SLICKROCKS
SLICKS
SLICKSTONE
SLICKSTONES
SLID
SLIDABLE
SLIDDEN
SLIDDER
SLIDDERED
SLIDDERING
SLIDDERS
SLIDDERY
SLIDE
SLIDED
SLIDER
SLIDERS
SLIDES
SLIDEWAY
SLIDEWAYS
SLIDING
SLIDINGLY
SLIDINGS
SLIER
SLIEST
SLIGHT
SLIGHTED
SLIGHTER
SLIGHTEST
SLIGHTING
SLIGHTINGLY
SLIGHTISH
SLIGHTLY
SLIGHTNESS
SLIGHTNESSES
SLIGHTS
SLILY
SLIM
SLIMDOWN

SLIMDOWNS
SLIME
SLIMEBALL
SLIMEBALLS
SLIMED
SLIMES
SLIMIER
SLIMIEST
SLIMILY
SLIMINESS
SLIMINESSES
SLIMING
SLIMLINE
SLIMLY
SLIMMED
SLIMMER
SLIMMERS
SLIMMEST
SLIMMING
SLIMMINGS
SLIMMISH
SLIMNASTICS
SLIMNESS
SLIMNESSES
SLIMPSIER
SLIMPSIEST
SLIMPSY
SLIMS
SLIMSIER
SLIMSIEST
SLIMSY
SLIMY
SLING
SLINGBACK
SLINGBACKS
SLINGER
SLINGERS
SLINGING
SLINGS
SLINGSHOT
SLINGSHOTS
SLINGSTONE
SLINGSTONES
SLINK
SLINKED
SLINKER
SLINKERS
SLINKIER
SLINKIEST
SLINKILY
SLINKINESS
SLINKINESSES
SLINKING
SLINKS
SLINKSKIN
SLINKSKINS
SLINKWEED

SLINKWEEDS
SLINKY
SLINTER
SLINTERS
SLIOTAR
SLIOTARS
SLIP
SLIPCASE
SLIPCASED
SLIPCASES
SLIPCOVER
SLIPCOVERS
SLIPE
SLIPED
SLIPES
SLIPFORM
SLIPFORMED
SLIPFORMING
SLIPFORMS
SLIPING
SLIPKNOT
SLIPKNOTS
SLIPLESS
SLIPNOOSE
SLIPNOOSES
SLIPOUT
SLIPOUTS
SLIPOVER
SLIPOVERS
SLIPPAGE
SLIPPAGES
SLIPPED
SLIPPER
SLIPPERED
SLIPPERIER
SLIPPERIEST
SLIPPERILY
SLIPPERINESS
SLIPPERINESSES
SLIPPERING
SLIPPERS
SLIPPERWORT
SLIPPERWORTS
SLIPPERY
SLIPPIER
SLIPPIEST
SLIPPINESS
SLIPPINESSES
SLIPPING
SLIPPY
SLIPRAIL
SLIPRAILS
SLIPS
SLIPSHEET
SLIPSHEETED
SLIPSHEETING
SLIPSHEETS

SLIPSHOD
SLIPSHODDINESS
SLIPSHODNESS
SLIPSLOP
SLIPSLOPS
SLIPSOLE
SLIPSOLES
SLIPSTREAM
SLIPSTREAMED
SLIPSTREAMING
SLIPSTREAMS
SLIPT
SLIPUP
SLIPUPS
SLIPWARE
SLIPWARES
SLIPWAY
SLIPWAYS
SLISH
SLISHES
SLIT
SLITHER
SLITHERED
SLITHERIER
SLITHERIEST
SLITHERING
SLITHERS
SLITHERY
SLITLESS
SLITS
SLITTED
SLITTER
SLITTERS
SLITTING
SLIVE
SLIVED
SLIVEN
SLIVER
SLIVERED
SLIVERER
SLIVERERS
SLIVERING
SLIVERS
SLIVES
SLIVING
SLIVOVIC
SLIVOVICA
SLIVOVICAS
SLIVOVICES
SLIVOVITZ
SLIVOVITZES
SLIVOWITZ
SLIVOWITZES
SLOAN
SLOANS
SLOB
SLOBBER

SLOBBERED
SLOBBERER
SLOBBERERS
SLOBBERIER
SLOBBERIEST
SLOBBERING
SLOBBERS
SLOBBERY
SLOBBIER
SLOBBIEST
SLOBBISH
SLOBBISHNESS
SLOBBISHNESSES
SLOBBY
SLOBLAND
SLOBLANDS
SLOBS
SLOCKDOLAGERS
SLOCKDOLIGERS
SLOCKDOLOGERS
SLOCKEN
SLOCKENED
SLOCKENING
SLOCKENS
SLOE
SLOEBUSH
SLOEBUSHES
SLOES
SLOETHORN
SLOETHORNS
SLOETREE
SLOETREES
SLOG
SLOGAN
SLOGANEER
SLOGANEERED
SLOGANEERING
SLOGANEERINGS
SLOGANEERS
SLOGANISE
SLOGANISED
SLOGANISES
SLOGANISING
SLOGANISINGS
SLOGANIZE
SLOGANIZED
SLOGANIZES
SLOGANIZING
SLOGANIZINGS
SLOGANS
SLOGGED
SLOGGER
SLOGGERS
SLOGGING
SLOGS
SLOID
SLOIDS

SLOJD
SLOJDS
SLOKEN
SLOKENED
SLOKENING
SLOKENS
SLOMMOCK
SLOMMOCKED
SLOMMOCKING
SLOMMOCKS
SLOOM
SLOOMED
SLOOMIER
SLOOMIEST
SLOOMING
SLOOMS
SLOOMY
SLOOP
SLOOPS
SLOOSH
SLOOSHED
SLOOSHES
SLOOSHING
SLOOT
SLOOTS
SLOP
SLOPE
SLOPED
SLOPER
SLOPERS
SLOPES
SLOPEWISE
SLOPIER
SLOPIEST
SLOPING
SLOPINGLY
SLOPINGNESS
SLOPPED
SLOPPIER
SLOPPIEST
SLOPPILY
SLOPPINESS
SLOPPINESSES
SLOPPING
SLOPPY
SLOPS
SLOPWORK
SLOPWORKER
SLOPWORKERS
SLOPWORKS
SLOPY
SLORM
SLORMED
SLORMING
SLORMS
SLOSH
SLOSHED

SLOSHES
SLOSHIER
SLOSHIEST
SLOSHING
SLOSHINGS
SLOSHY
SLOT
SLOTBACK
SLOTBACKS
SLOTH
SLOTHED
SLOTHFUL
SLOTHFULLY
SLOTHFULNESS
SLOTHFULNESSES
SLOTHING
SLOTHS
SLOTS
SLOTTED
SLOTTER
SLOTTERS
SLOTTING
SLOUCH
SLOUCHED
SLOUCHER
SLOUCHERS
SLOUCHES
SLOUCHIER
SLOUCHIEST
SLOUCHILY
SLOUCHINESS
SLOUCHINESSES
SLOUCHING
SLOUCHINGLY
SLOUCHY
SLOUGH
SLOUGHED
SLOUGHIER
SLOUGHIEST
SLOUGHING
SLOUGHS
SLOUGHY
SLOVE
SLOVEN
SLOVENLIER
SLOVENLIEST
SLOVENLIKE
SLOVENLINESS
SLOVENLINESSES
SLOVENLY
SLOVENRIES
SLOVENRY
SLOVENS
SLOW
SLOWBACK
SLOWBACKS
SLOWCOACH

SLOWCOACHES
SLOWDOWN
SLOWDOWNS
SLOWED
SLOWER
SLOWEST
SLOWING
SLOWINGS
SLOWISH
SLOWLY
SLOWNESS
SLOWNESSES
SLOWPOKE
SLOWPOKES
SLOWS
SLOWWORM
SLOWWORMS
SLOYD
SLOYDS
SLUB
SLUBB
SLUBBED
SLUBBER
SLUBBERED
SLUBBERING
SLUBBERINGLY
SLUBBERINGS
SLUBBERS
SLUBBIER
SLUBBIEST
SLUBBING
SLUBBINGS
SLUBBS
SLUBBY
SLUBS
SLUDGE
SLUDGES
SLUDGIER
SLUDGIEST
SLUDGY
SLUE
SLUED
SLUEING
SLUES
SLUFF
SLUFFED
SLUFFING
SLUFFS
SLUG
SLUGABED
SLUGABEDS
SLUGFEST
SLUGFESTS
SLUGGABED
SLUGGABEDS
SLUGGARD
SLUGGARDISE

SLUGGARDISED
SLUGGARDISES
SLUGGARDISING
SLUGGARDIZE
SLUGGARDIZED
SLUGGARDIZES
SLUGGARDIZING
SLUGGARDLINESS
SLUGGARDLY
SLUGGARDNESS
SLUGGARDNESSES
SLUGGARDRY
SLUGGARDS
SLUGGED
SLUGGER
SLUGGERS
SLUGGING
SLUGGISH
SLUGGISHLY
SLUGGISHNESS
SLUGGISHNESSES
SLUGHORN
SLUGHORNE
SLUGHORNES
SLUGHORNS
SLUGS
SLUICE
SLUICED
SLUICEGATE
SLUICEGATES
SLUICELIKE
SLUICES
SLUICEWAY
SLUICEWAYS
SLUICIER
SLUICIEST
SLUICING
SLUICY
SLUING
SLUIT
SLUITS
SLUM
SLUMBER
SLUMBERED
SLUMBERER
SLUMBERERS
SLUMBERFUL
SLUMBERING
SLUMBERINGLY
SLUMBERINGS
SLUMBERLAND
SLUMBERLANDS
SLUMBERLESS
SLUMBEROUS
SLUMBEROUSLY
SLUMBEROUSNESS
SLUMBERS

SLUMBERSOME
SLUMBERY
SLUMBROUS
SLUMBROUSLY
SLUMBRY
SLUMGULLION
SLUMGULLIONS
SLUMGUM
SLUMGUMS
SLUMISM
SLUMISMS
SLUMLORD
SLUMLORDS
SLUMMED
SLUMMER
SLUMMERS
SLUMMIER
SLUMMIEST
SLUMMING
SLUMMINGS
SLUMMOCK
SLUMMOCKED
SLUMMOCKING
SLUMMOCKS
SLUMMY
SLUMP
SLUMPED
SLUMPFLATION
SLUMPFLATIONARY
SLUMPFLATIONS
SLUMPIER
SLUMPIEST
SLUMPING
SLUMPS
SLUMPY
SLUMS
SLUNG
SLUNGSHOT
SLUNGSHOTS
SLUNK
SLUR
SLURB
SLURBAN
SLURBS
SLURP
SLURPED
SLURPER
SLURPERS
SLURPING
SLURPS
SLURRED
SLURRIED
SLURRIES
SLURRING
SLURRY
SLURRYING
SLURS

SLUSE
SLUSES
SLUSH
SLUSHED
SLUSHES
SLUSHIER
SLUSHIES
SLUSHIEST
SLUSHILY
SLUSHINESS
SLUSHINESSES
SLUSHING
SLUSHY
SLUT
SLUTCH
SLUTCHIER
SLUTCHIEST
SLUTCHY
SLUTS
SLUTTERIES
SLUTTERY
SLUTTIER
SLUTTIEST
SLUTTISH
SLUTTISHLY
SLUTTISHNESS
SLUTTISHNESSES
SLUTTY
SLY
SLYBOOTS
SLYER
SLYEST
SLYISH
SLYLY
SLYNESS
SLYNESSES
SLYPE
SLYPES
SMA
SMACK
SMACKED
SMACKER
SMACKERS
SMACKHEAD
SMACKHEADED
SMACKHEADS
SMACKING
SMACKINGS
SMACKS
SMAIK
SMAIKS
SMALL
SMALLAGE
SMALLAGES
SMALLBOY
SMALLBOYS
SMALLCLOTHES

SMALLED
SMALLER
SMALLEST
SMALLHOLDER
SMALLHOLDERS
SMALLHOLDING
SMALLHOLDINGS
SMALLING
SMALLISH
SMALLMOUTH
SMALLMOUTHS
SMALLNESS
SMALLNESSES
SMALLPOX
SMALLPOXES
SMALLS
SMALLSAT
SMALLSATS
SMALLSWORD
SMALLSWORDS
SMALM
SMALMED
SMALMILY
SMALMINESS
SMALMINESSES
SMALMING
SMALMS
SMALMY
SMALT
SMALTI
SMALTINE
SMALTINES
SMALTITE
SMALTITES
SMALTO
SMALTOS
SMALTS
SMARAGD
SMARAGDE
SMARAGDES
SMARAGDINE
SMARAGDITE
SMARAGDITES
SMARAGDS
SMARM
SMARMED
SMARMIER
SMARMIEST
SMARMILY
SMARMINESS
SMARMINESSES
SMARMING
SMARMS
SMARMY
SMART
SMARTARSE
SMARTARSED

SMARTARSEDNESS
SMARTARSES
SMARTASS
SMARTASSES
SMARTED
SMARTEN
SMARTENED
SMARTENING
SMARTENS
SMARTER
SMARTEST
SMARTIE
SMARTIES
SMARTING
SMARTISH
SMARTLY
SMARTMOUTH
SMARTMOUTHED
SMARTMOUTHING
SMARTMOUTHS
SMARTNESS
SMARTNESSES
SMARTS
SMARTWEED
SMARTWEEDS
SMARTY
SMARTYPANTS
SMASH
SMASHABILITY
SMASHABLE
SMASHED
SMASHER
SMASHEROO
SMASHEROOS
SMASHERS
SMASHES
SMASHING
SMASHINGLY
SMASHINGS
SMASHUP
SMASHUPS
SMATCH
SMATCHED
SMATCHES
SMATCHING
SMATTER
SMATTERED
SMATTERER
SMATTERERS
SMATTERING
SMATTERINGLY
SMATTERINGS
SMATTERS
SMAZE
SMAZES
SMEAR
SMEARCASE

SMEARCASES
SMEARED
SMEARER
SMEARERS
SMEARIER
SMEARIEST
SMEARILY
SMEARINESS
SMEARINESSES
SMEARING
SMEARS
SMEARY
SMEATH
SMEATHS
SMECTIC
SMECTITE
SMECTITES
SMECTITIC
SMEDDUM
SMEDDUMS
SMEE
SMEECH
SMEECHED
SMEECHES
SMEECHING
SMEEK
SMEEKED
SMEEKING
SMEEKS
SMEES
SMEETH
SMEETHS
SMEGMA
SMEGMAS
SMELL
SMELLED
SMELLER
SMELLERS
SMELLIER
SMELLIES
SMELLIEST
SMELLINESS
SMELLINESSES
SMELLING
SMELLINGS
SMELLS
SMELLY
SMELT
SMELTED
SMELTER
SMELTERIES
SMELTERS
SMELTERY
SMELTING
SMELTINGS
SMELTS
SMERK

SMERKED
SMERKING
SMERKS
SMEUSE
SMEUSES
SMEW
SMEWS
SMICKER
SMICKERED
SMICKERING
SMICKERINGS
SMICKERS
SMICKET
SMICKETS
SMICKLY
SMIDDIED
SMIDDIES
SMIDDY
SMIDDYING
SMIDGE
SMIDGEN
SMIDGENS
SMIDGEON
SMIDGEONS
SMIDGES
SMIDGIN
SMIDGINS
SMIERCASE
SMIERCASES
SMIFLIGATE
SMIFLIGATED
SMIFLIGATES
SMIFLIGATING
SMIGHT
SMIGHTING
SMIGHTS
SMILACACEOUS
SMILAX
SMILAXES
SMILE
SMILED
SMILEFUL
SMILELESS
SMILER
SMILERS
SMILES
SMILET
SMILETS
SMILEY
SMILEYS
SMILING
SMILINGLY
SMILINGNESS
SMILINGNESSES
SMILINGS
SMILODON
SMILODONS

SMIR
SMIRCH
SMIRCHED
SMIRCHER
SMIRCHERS
SMIRCHES
SMIRCHING
SMIRK
SMIRKED
SMIRKER
SMIRKERS
SMIRKIER
SMIRKIEST
SMIRKING
SMIRKINGLY
SMIRKS
SMIRKY
SMIRR
SMIRRED
SMIRRIER
SMIRRIEST
SMIRRING
SMIRRS
SMIRRY
SMIRS
SMIT
SMITE
SMITER
SMITERS
SMITES
SMITH
SMITHCRAFT
SMITHCRAFTS
SMITHED
SMITHEREEN
SMITHEREENED
SMITHEREENING
SMITHEREENS
SMITHERIES
SMITHERS
SMITHERY
SMITHIED
SMITHIES
SMITHING
SMITHS
SMITHSONITE
SMITHSONITES
SMITHY
SMITHYING
SMITING
SMITS
SMITTED
SMITTEN
SMITTING
SMITTLE
SMOCK
SMOCKED

SMOCKING	SMOKO	SMORBROD	SMUDGERS
SMOCKINGS	SMOKOS	SMORBRODS	SMUDGES
SMOCKLIKE	SMOKY	SMORE	SMUDGIER
SMOCKS	SMOLDER	SMORED	SMUDGIEST
SMOG	SMOLDERED	SMORES	SMUDGILY
SMOGGIER	SMOLDERING	SMORGASBORD	SMUDGINESS
SMOGGIEST	SMOLDERS	SMORGASBORDS	SMUDGINESSES
SMOGGY	SMOLT	SMORING	SMUDGING
SMOGLESS	SMOLTS	SMORREBROD	SMUDGY
SMOGS	SMOOCH	SMORREBRODS	SMUG
SMOILE	SMOOCHED	SMORZANDO	SMUGGED
SMOILED	SMOOCHES	SMORZATO	SMUGGER
SMOILES	SMOOCHING	SMOTE	SMUGGERY
SMOILING	SMOOCHY	SMOTHER	SMUGGEST
SMOKABLE	SMOODGE	SMOTHERED	SMUGGING
SMOKE	SMOODGED	SMOTHERER	SMUGGISH
SMOKEABLE	SMOODGES	SMOTHERERS	SMUGGLE
SMOKEBOARD	SMOODGING	SMOTHERINESS	SMUGGLED
SMOKEBOARDS	SMOOGE	SMOTHERINESSES	SMUGGLER
SMOKEBUSH	SMOOGED	SMOTHERING	SMUGGLERS
SMOKEBUSHES	SMOOGES	SMOTHERINGLY	SMUGGLES
SMOKED	SMOOGING	SMOTHERINGS	SMUGGLING
SMOKEHO	SMOOR	SMOTHERS	SMUGGLINGS
SMOKEHOOD	SMOORED	SMOTHERY	SMUGLY
SMOKEHOODS	SMOORING	SMOUCH	SMUGNESS
SMOKEHOS	SMOORS	SMOUCHED	SMUGNESSES
SMOKEHOUSE	SMOOT	SMOUCHES	SMUGS
SMOKEHOUSES	SMOOTED	SMOUCHING	SMUR
SMOKEJACK	SMOOTH	SMOULDER	SMURRED
SMOKEJACKS	SMOOTHABLE	SMOULDERED	SMURRIER
SMOKELESS	SMOOTHBORE	SMOULDERING	SMURRIEST
SMOKELESSLY	SMOOTHBORED	SMOULDERINGS	SMURRING
SMOKELESSNESS	SMOOTHBORES	SMOULDERS	SMURRY
SMOKELESSNESSES	SMOOTHED	SMOULDRY	SMURS
SMOKELIKE	SMOOTHEN	SMOUSE	SMUT
SMOKEPOT	SMOOTHENED	SMOUSED	SMUTCH
SMOKEPOTS	SMOOTHENING	SMOUSER	SMUTCHED
SMOKEPROOF	SMOOTHENS	SMOUSERS	SMUTCHES
SMOKER	SMOOTHER	SMOUSES	SMUTCHIER
SMOKERS	SMOOTHERS	SMOUSING	SMUTCHIEST
SMOKES	SMOOTHES	SMOUT	SMUTCHING
SMOKESCREEN	SMOOTHEST	SMOUTED	SMUTCHY
SMOKESCREENS	SMOOTHIE	SMOUTING	SMUTS
SMOKESTACK	SMOOTHIES	SMOUTS	SMUTTED
SMOKESTACKS	SMOOTHING	SMOWT	SMUTTIER
SMOKETIGHT	SMOOTHINGLY	SMOWTS	SMUTTIEST
SMOKETREE	SMOOTHINGS	SMOYLE	SMUTTILY
SMOKETREES	SMOOTHISH	SMOYLED	SMUTTINESS
SMOKEY	SMOOTHLY	SMOYLES	SMUTTINESSES
SMOKIER	SMOOTHNESS	SMOYLING	SMUTTING
SMOKIES	SMOOTHNESSES	SMRITI	SMUTTY
SMOKIEST	SMOOTHPATE	SMRITIS	SMYTRIE
SMOKILY	SMOOTHPATES	SMUDGE	SMYTRIES
SMOKINESS	SMOOTHS	SMUDGED	SNAB
SMOKINESSES	SMOOTHY	SMUDGEDLY	SNABBLE
SMOKING	SMOOTING	SMUDGELESS	SNABBLED
SMOKINGS	SMOOTS	SMUDGER	SNABBLES

SNABBLING
SNABS
SNACK
SNACKED
SNACKETTE
SNACKETTES
SNACKING
SNACKS
SNAFFLE
SNAFFLED
SNAFFLES
SNAFFLING
SNAFU
SNAFUED
SNAFUES
SNAFUING
SNAFUS
SNAG
SNAGGED
SNAGGIER
SNAGGIEST
SNAGGING
SNAGGLETEETH
SNAGGLETOOTH
SNAGGLETOOTHED
SNAGGY
SNAGLIKE
SNAGS
SNAIL
SNAILED
SNAILERIES
SNAILERY
SNAILFISH
SNAILFISHES
SNAILIER
SNAILIEST
SNAILING
SNAILLIKE
SNAILS
SNAILY
SNAKE
SNAKEBIRD
SNAKEBIRDS
SNAKEBIT
SNAKEBITE
SNAKEBITES
SNAKEBITTEN
SNAKED
SNAKEHEAD
SNAKEHEADS
SNAKELIKE
SNAKEMOUTH
SNAKEMOUTHS
SNAKEROOT
SNAKEROOTS
SNAKES
SNAKESKIN

SNAKESKINS
SNAKESTONE
SNAKESTONES
SNAKEWEED
SNAKEWEEDS
SNAKEWISE
SNAKEWOOD
SNAKEWOODS
SNAKEY
SNAKIER
SNAKIEST
SNAKILY
SNAKINESS
SNAKINESSES
SNAKING
SNAKISH
SNAKISHNESS
SNAKISHNESSES
SNAKY
SNAP
SNAPBACK
SNAPBACKS
SNAPDRAGON
SNAPDRAGONS
SNAPHANCE
SNAPHANCES
SNAPHAUNCE
SNAPHAUNCES
SNAPHAUNCHES
SNAPLESS
SNAPLINK
SNAPLINKS
SNAPPABILITY
SNAPPABLE
SNAPPED
SNAPPER
SNAPPERED
SNAPPERING
SNAPPERS
SNAPPIER
SNAPPIEST
SNAPPILY
SNAPPINESS
SNAPPINESSES
SNAPPING
SNAPPINGLY
SNAPPINGS
SNAPPISH
SNAPPISHLY
SNAPPISHNESS
SNAPPISHNESSES
SNAPPY
SNAPS
SNAPSHOOTER
SNAPSHOOTERS
SNAPSHOOTING
SNAPSHOOTINGS

SNAPSHOT
SNAPSHOTS
SNAPSHOTTED
SNAPSHOTTING
SNAPTIN
SNAPTINS
SNAPWEED
SNAPWEEDS
SNAR
SNARE
SNARED
SNARELESS
SNARER
SNARERS
SNARES
SNARF
SNARFED
SNARFING
SNARFS
SNARIER
SNARIEST
SNARING
SNARINGS
SNARK
SNARKIER
SNARKIEST
SNARKS
SNARKY
SNARL
SNARLED
SNARLER
SNARLERS
SNARLIER
SNARLIEST
SNARLING
SNARLINGLY
SNARLINGS
SNARLS
SNARLY
SNARRED
SNARRING
SNARS
SNARY
SNASH
SNASHED
SNASHES
SNASHING
SNASTE
SNASTES
SNATCH
SNATCHED
SNATCHER
SNATCHERS
SNATCHES
SNATCHIER
SNATCHIEST
SNATCHILY

SNATCHING
SNATCHINGLY
SNATCHY
SNATH
SNATHE
SNATHES
SNATHS
SNAW
SNAWED
SNAWING
SNAWS
SNAZZIER
SNAZZIEST
SNAZZILY
SNAZZINESS
SNAZZY
SNEAD
SNEADS
SNEAK
SNEAKED
SNEAKER
SNEAKERED
SNEAKERS
SNEAKEUP
SNEAKEUPS
SNEAKIER
SNEAKIEST
SNEAKILY
SNEAKINESS
SNEAKINESSES
SNEAKING
SNEAKINGLY
SNEAKINGNESS
SNEAKISH
SNEAKISHLY
SNEAKISHNESS
SNEAKISHNESSES
SNEAKS
SNEAKSBIES
SNEAKSBY
SNEAKY
SNEAP
SNEAPED
SNEAPING
SNEAPS
SNEATH
SNEATHS
SNEB
SNEBBE
SNEBBED
SNEBBES
SNEBBING
SNEBS
SNECK
SNECKED
SNECKING
SNECKS

SNED	SNICKED	SNIFTIEST	SNIPS
SNEDDED	SNICKER	SNIFTING	SNIPY
SNEDDING	SNICKERED	SNIFTS	SNIRT
SNEDS	SNICKERER	SNIFTY	SNIRTLE
SNEE	SNICKERERS	SNIG	SNIRTLED
SNEED	SNICKERING	SNIGGED	SNIRTLES
SNEEING	SNICKERS	SNIGGER	SNIRTLING
SNEER	SNICKERSNEE	SNIGGERED	SNIRTS
SNEERED	SNICKERSNEED	SNIGGERER	SNIT
SNEERER	SNICKERSNEEING	SNIGGERERS	SNITCH
SNEERERS	SNICKERSNEES	SNIGGERING	SNITCHED
SNEERFUL	SNICKERY	SNIGGERINGLY	SNITCHER
SNEERIER	SNICKET	SNIGGERINGS	SNITCHERS
SNEERIEST	SNICKETS	SNIGGERS	SNITCHES
SNEERING	SNICKING	SNIGGING	SNITCHIER
SNEERINGLY	SNICKS	SNIGGLE	SNITCHIEST
SNEERINGS	SNIDE	SNIGGLED	SNITCHING
SNEERS	SNIDELY	SNIGGLER	SNITCHY
SNEERY	SNIDENESS	SNIGGLERS	SNITS
SNEES	SNIDENESSES	SNIGGLES	SNIVEL
SNEESH	SNIDER	SNIGGLING	SNIVELED
SNEESHAN	SNIDES	SNIGGLINGS	SNIVELER
SNEESHANS	SNIDEST	SNIGS	SNIVELERS
SNEESHES	SNIDEY	SNIP	SNIVELING
SNEESHIN	SNIES	SNIPE	SNIVELLED
SNEESHING	SNIFF	SNIPED	SNIVELLER
SNEESHINGS	SNIFFED	SNIPEFISH	SNIVELLERS
SNEESHINS	SNIFFER	SNIPEFISHES	SNIVELLING
SNEEZE	SNIFFERS	SNIPELIKE	SNIVELLY
SNEEZED	SNIFFIER	SNIPER	SNIVELS
SNEEZELESS	SNIFFIEST	SNIPERS	SNOB
SNEEZER	SNIFFILY	SNIPERSCOPE	SNOBBERIES
SNEEZERS	SNIFFINESS	SNIPERSCOPES	SNOBBERY
SNEEZES	SNIFFINESSES	SNIPES	SNOBBIER
SNEEZEWEED	SNIFFING	SNIPIER	SNOBBIEST
SNEEZEWEEDS	SNIFFINGLY	SNIPIEST	SNOBBILY
SNEEZEWOOD	SNIFFINGS	SNIPING	SNOBBISH
SNEEZEWOODS	SNIFFISH	SNIPINGS	SNOBBISHLY
SNEEZEWORT	SNIFFISHLY	SNIPPED	SNOBBISHNESS
SNEEZEWORTS	SNIFFISHNESS	SNIPPER	SNOBBISHNESSES
SNEEZIER	SNIFFISHNESSES	SNIPPERS	SNOBBISM
SNEEZIEST	SNIFFLE	SNIPPERSNAPPER	SNOBBISMS
SNEEZING	SNIFFLED	SNIPPERSNAPPERS	SNOBBOCRACIES
SNEEZINGS	SNIFFLER	SNIPPET	SNOBBY
SNEEZY	SNIFFLERS	SNIPPETIER	SNOBLING
SNELL	SNIFFLES	SNIPPETIEST	SNOBLINGS
SNELLED	SNIFFLING	SNIPPETINESS	SNOBOCRACIES
SNELLER	SNIFFLY	SNIPPETINESSES	SNOBOCRACY
SNELLEST	SNIFFS	SNIPPETS	SNOBOGRAPHER
SNELLING	SNIFFY	SNIPPETY	SNOBOGRAPHERS
SNELLS	SNIFT	SNIPPIER	SNOBOGRAPHIES
SNELLY	SNIFTED	SNIPPIEST	SNOBOGRAPHY
SNIB	SNIFTER	SNIPPILY	SNOBS
SNIBBED	SNIFTERED	SNIPPINESS	SNOD
SNIBBING	SNIFTERING	SNIPPING	SNODDED
SNIBS	SNIFTERS	SNIPPINGS	SNODDER
SNICK	SNIFTIER	SNIPPY	SNODDEST

SNODDING
SNODDIT
SNODS
SNOEK
SNOEKS
SNOEP
SNOG
SNOGGED
SNOGGING
SNOGS
SNOKE
SNOKED
SNOKES
SNOKING
SNOLLYGOSTER
SNOLLYGOSTERS
SNOOD
SNOODED
SNOODING
SNOODS
SNOOK
SNOOKED
SNOOKER
SNOOKERED
SNOOKERING
SNOOKERS
SNOOKING
SNOOKS
SNOOL
SNOOLED
SNOOLING
SNOOLS
SNOOP
SNOOPED
SNOOPER
SNOOPERS
SNOOPERSCOPE
SNOOPERSCOPES
SNOOPIER
SNOOPIEST
SNOOPILY
SNOOPING
SNOOPS
SNOOPY
SNOOT
SNOOTED
SNOOTFUL
SNOOTFULS
SNOOTIER
SNOOTIEST
SNOOTILY
SNOOTINESS
SNOOTINESSES
SNOOTING
SNOOTS
SNOOTY
SNOOZE

SNOOZED
SNOOZER
SNOOZERS
SNOOZES
SNOOZIER
SNOOZIEST
SNOOZING
SNOOZLE
SNOOZLED
SNOOZLES
SNOOZLING
SNOOZY
SNORE
SNORED
SNORER
SNORERS
SNORES
SNORING
SNORINGS
SNORKEL
SNORKELED
SNORKELER
SNORKELERS
SNORKELING
SNORKELLED
SNORKELLING
SNORKELLINGS
SNORKELS
SNORKLER
SNORKLERS
SNORT
SNORTED
SNORTER
SNORTERS
SNORTIER
SNORTIEST
SNORTING
SNORTINGLY
SNORTINGS
SNORTS
SNORTY
SNOT
SNOTS
SNOTTED
SNOTTER
SNOTTERED
SNOTTERIES
SNOTTERING
SNOTTERS
SNOTTERY
SNOTTIE
SNOTTIER
SNOTTIES
SNOTTIEST
SNOTTILY
SNOTTINESS
SNOTTINESSES

SNOTTING
SNOTTY
SNOUT
SNOUTED
SNOUTIER
SNOUTIEST
SNOUTING
SNOUTISH
SNOUTLESS
SNOUTLESSNESS
SNOUTLIKE
SNOUTS
SNOUTY
SNOW
SNOWBALL
SNOWBALLED
SNOWBALLING
SNOWBALLS
SNOWBANK
SNOWBANKS
SNOWBELL
SNOWBELLS
SNOWBELT
SNOWBELTS
SNOWBERRIES
SNOWBERRY
SNOWBIRD
SNOWBIRDS
SNOWBLINK
SNOWBLINKS
SNOWBLOWER
SNOWBLOWERS
SNOWBOARD
SNOWBOARDER
SNOWBOARDERS
SNOWBOARDING
SNOWBOARDINGS
SNOWBOARDS
SNOWBOOT
SNOWBOOTS
SNOWBOUND
SNOWBRUSH
SNOWBRUSHES
SNOWBUSH
SNOWBUSHES
SNOWCAP
SNOWCAPPED
SNOWCAPS
SNOWDRIFT
SNOWDRIFTS
SNOWDROP
SNOWDROPS
SNOWED
SNOWFALL
SNOWFALLS
SNOWFIELD
SNOWFIELDS

SNOWFLAKE
SNOWFLAKES
SNOWFLECK
SNOWFLECKS
SNOWFLICK
SNOWFLICKS
SNOWIER
SNOWIEST
SNOWILY
SNOWINESS
SNOWINESSES
SNOWING
SNOWISH
SNOWK
SNOWKED
SNOWKING
SNOWKS
SNOWLAND
SNOWLANDS
SNOWLESS
SNOWLIKE
SNOWLINE
SNOWLINES
SNOWMAKER
SNOWMAKERS
SNOWMAKING
SNOWMAN
SNOWMELT
SNOWMELTS
SNOWMEN
SNOWMOBILE
SNOWMOBILER
SNOWMOBILERS
SNOWMOBILES
SNOWMOBILING
SNOWMOBILINGS
SNOWMOBILIST
SNOWMOBILISTS
SNOWMOLD
SNOWMOLDS
SNOWPACK
SNOWPACKS
SNOWPLOUGH
SNOWPLOUGHED
SNOWPLOUGHING
SNOWPLOUGHS
SNOWPLOW
SNOWPLOWED
SNOWPLOWING
SNOWPLOWS
SNOWS
SNOWSCAPE
SNOWSCAPES
SNOWSHED
SNOWSHEDS
SNOWSHOE
SNOWSHOED

SNOWSHOEING	SNUFFLIER	SOAPERS	SOBERIZE
SNOWSHOER	SNUFFLIEST	SOAPIE	SOBERIZED
SNOWSHOERS	SNUFFLING	SOAPIER	SOBERIZES
SNOWSHOES	SNUFFLINGS	SOAPIES	SOBERIZING
SNOWSLIDE	SNUFFLY	SOAPIEST	SOBERLY
SNOWSLIDES	SNUFFS	SOAPILY	SOBERNESS
SNOWSLIP	SNUFFY	SOAPINESS	SOBERNESSES
SNOWSLIPS	SNUG	SOAPINESSES	SOBERS
SNOWSTORM	SNUGGED	SOAPING	SOBERSIDED
SNOWSTORMS	SNUGGER	SOAPLAND	SOBERSIDEDNESS
SNOWSUIT	SNUGGERIES	SOAPLANDS	SOBERSIDES
SNOWSUITS	SNUGGERY	SOAPLESS	SOBFUL
SNOWSURFING	SNUGGEST	SOAPLIKE	SOBOLE
SNOWSURFINGS	SNUGGIES	SOAPOLALLIE	SOBOLES
SNOWTUBING	SNUGGING	SOAPOLALLIES	SOBOLIFEROUS
SNOWY	SNUGGLE	SOAPROOT	SOBRIETIES
SNUB	SNUGGLED	SOAPROOTS	SOBRIETY
SNUBBE	SNUGGLES	SOAPS	SOBRIQUET
SNUBBED	SNUGGLING	SOAPSTONE	SOBRIQUETS
SNUBBER	SNUGLY	SOAPSTONES	SOBS
SNUBBERS	SNUGNESS	SOAPSUDS	SOC
SNUBBES	SNUGNESSES	SOAPSUDSY	SOCA
SNUBBIER	SNUGS	SOAPWORT	SOCAGE
SNUBBIEST	SNUSH	SOAPWORTS	SOCAGER
SNUBBINESS	SNUSHED	SOAPY	SOCAGERS
SNUBBINESSES	SNUSHES	SOAR	SOCAGES
SNUBBING	SNUSHING	SOARAWAY	SOCAS
SNUBBINGLY	SNUZZLE	SOARE	SOCCAGE
SNUBBINGS	SNUZZLED	SOARED	SOCCAGES
SNUBBISH	SNUZZLES	SOARER	SOCCER
SNUBBY	SNUZZLING	SOARERS	SOCCERS
SNUBNESS	SNY	SOARES	SOCDOLAGER
SNUBNESSES	SNYE	SOARING	SOCDOLAGERS
SNUBS	SNYES	SOARINGLY	SOCDOLIGERS
SNUCK	SO	SOARINGS	SOCDOLOGERS
SNUDGE	SOAK	SOARS	SOCIABILITIES
SNUDGED	SOAKAGE	SOAVE	SOCIABILITY
SNUDGES	SOAKAGES	SOAVES	SOCIABLE
SNUDGING	SOAKAWAY	SOB	SOCIABLENESS
SNUFF	SOAKAWAYS	SOBA	SOCIABLENESSES
SNUFFBOX	SOAKED	SOBBED	SOCIABLES
SNUFFBOXES	SOAKEN	SOBBER	SOCIABLY
SNUFFED	SOAKER	SOBBERS	SOCIAL
SNUFFER	SOAKERS	SOBBING	SOCIALISABILITY
SNUFFERS	SOAKING	SOBBINGLY	SOCIALISABLE
SNUFFIER	SOAKINGLY	SOBBINGS	SOCIALISATION
SNUFFIEST	SOAKINGS	SOBEIT	SOCIALISATIONS
SNUFFILY	SOAKS	SOBER	SOCIALISE
SNUFFINESS	SOAP	SOBERED	SOCIALISED
SNUFFINESSES	SOAPBARK	SOBERER	SOCIALISER
SNUFFING	SOAPBARKS	SOBEREST	SOCIALISERS
SNUFFINGS	SOAPBERRIES	SOBERING	SOCIALISES
SNUFFLE	SOAPBERRY	SOBERINGLY	SOCIALISING
SNUFFLED	SOAPBOX	SOBERISE	SOCIALISM
SNUFFLER	SOAPBOXES	SOBERISED	SOCIALISMS
SNUFFLERS	SOAPED	SOBERISES	SOCIALIST
SNUFFLES	SOAPER	SOBERISING	SOCIALISTIC

SOCIALISTICALLY
SOCIALISTS
SOCIALITE
SOCIALITES
SOCIALITIES
SOCIALITY
SOCIALIZABLE
SOCIALIZATION
SOCIALIZATIONS
SOCIALIZE
SOCIALIZED
SOCIALIZER
SOCIALIZERS
SOCIALIZES
SOCIALIZING
SOCIALLY
SOCIALNESS
SOCIALNESSES
SOCIALS
SOCIATE
SOCIATES
SOCIATION
SOCIATIONS
SOCIATIVE
SOCIETAL
SOCIETALLY
SOCIETIES
SOCIETY
SOCIOBIOLOGICAL
SOCIOBIOLOGIES
SOCIOBIOLOGIST
SOCIOBIOLOGISTS
SOCIOBIOLOGY
SOCIOCULTURAL
SOCIOCULTURALLY
SOCIOECONOMIC
SOCIOGRAM
SOCIOGRAMS
SOCIOHISTORICAL
SOCIOLECT
SOCIOLECTS
SOCIOLINGUIST
SOCIOLINGUISTIC
SOCIOLINGUISTS
SOCIOLOGESE
SOCIOLOGESES
SOCIOLOGIC
SOCIOLOGICAL
SOCIOLOGICALLY
SOCIOLOGIES
SOCIOLOGISM
SOCIOLOGISMS
SOCIOLOGIST
SOCIOLOGISTIC
SOCIOLOGISTS
SOCIOLOGY
SOCIOMETRIC

SOCIOMETRIES
SOCIOMETRIST
SOCIOMETRISTS
SOCIOMETRY
SOCIOPATH
SOCIOPATHIC
SOCIOPATHIES
SOCIOPATHS
SOCIOPATHY
SOCIOPOLITICAL
SOCIORELIGIOUS
SOCIOSEXUAL
SOCK
SOCKDOLAGER
SOCKDOLAGERS
SOCKDOLIGERS
SOCKDOLOGER
SOCKDOLOGERS
SOCKED
SOCKET
SOCKETED
SOCKETING
SOCKETS
SOCKETTE
SOCKETTES
SOCKEYE
SOCKEYES
SOCKING
SOCKLESS
SOCKMAN
SOCKMEN
SOCKO
SOCKS
SOCLE
SOCLES
SOCMAN
SOCMEN
SOCS
SOD
SODA
SODAIC
SODAIN
SODAINE
SODALESS
SODALIST
SODALISTS
SODALITE
SODALITES
SODALITIES
SODALITY
SODAMIDE
SODAMIDES
SODAS
SODBUSTER
SODBUSTERS
SODDED
SODDEN

SODDENED
SODDENING
SODDENLY
SODDENNESS
SODDENNESSES
SODDENS
SODDIER
SODDIES
SODDIEST
SODDING
SODDY
SODGER
SODGERED
SODGERING
SODGERS
SODIC
SODIUM
SODIUMS
SODOM
SODOMIES
SODOMISE
SODOMISED
SODOMISES
SODOMISING
SODOMIST
SODOMISTS
SODOMITE
SODOMITES
SODOMITIC
SODOMITICAL
SODOMITICALLY
SODOMIZE
SODOMIZED
SODOMIZES
SODOMIZING
SODOMS
SODOMY
SODS
SOEVER
SOFA
SOFAR
SOFARS
SOFAS
SOFFIONI
SOFFIT
SOFFITS
SOFT
SOFTA
SOFTAS
SOFTBACK
SOFTBACKS
SOFTBALL
SOFTBALLER
SOFTBALLERS
SOFTBALLS
SOFTBOUND
SOFTCOVER

SOFTCOVERS
SOFTED
SOFTEN
SOFTENED
SOFTENER
SOFTENERS
SOFTENING
SOFTENINGS
SOFTENS
SOFTER
SOFTEST
SOFTHEAD
SOFTHEADED
SOFTHEADEDLY
SOFTHEADEDNESS
SOFTHEADS
SOFTHEARTED
SOFTHEARTEDLY
SOFTHEARTEDNESS
SOFTIE
SOFTIES
SOFTING
SOFTISH
SOFTLINER
SOFTLINERS
SOFTLING
SOFTLINGS
SOFTLY
SOFTNESS
SOFTNESSES
SOFTPASTE
SOFTS
SOFTSHELL
SOFTSHELLS
SOFTWARE
SOFTWARES
SOFTWOOD
SOFTWOODS
SOFTY
SOG
SOGDOLAGERS
SOGDOLIGERS
SOGDOLOGERS
SOGER
SOGERS
SOGGED
SOGGIER
SOGGIEST
SOGGILY
SOGGINESS
SOGGINESSES
SOGGING
SOGGINGS
SOGGY
SOGS
SOH
SOHO

SOHS
SOIGNE
SOIGNEE
SOIL
SOILAGE
SOILAGES
SOILBORNE
SOILED
SOILIER
SOILIEST
SOILINESS
SOILINESSES
SOILING
SOILINGS
SOILLESS
SOILS
SOILURE
SOILURES
SOILY
SOIREE
SOIREES
SOJA
SOJAS
SOJOURN
SOJOURNED
SOJOURNER
SOJOURNERS
SOJOURNING
SOJOURNINGS
SOJOURNMENT
SOJOURNMENTS
SOJOURNS
SOKAH
SOKAHS
SOKAIYA
SOKE
SOKEMAN
SOKEMANRIES
SOKEMANRY
SOKEMEN
SOKEN
SOKENS
SOKES
SOKOL
SOKOLS
SOL
SOLA
SOLACE
SOLACED
SOLACEMENT
SOLACEMENTS
SOLACER
SOLACERS
SOLACES
SOLACING
SOLACIOUS
SOLAH

SOLAHS
SOLAN
SOLANACEOUS
SOLAND
SOLANDER
SOLANDERS
SOLANDS
SOLANIN
SOLANINE
SOLANINES
SOLANINS
SOLANO
SOLANOS
SOLANS
SOLANUM
SOLANUMS
SOLAR
SOLARIA
SOLARIMETER
SOLARIMETERS
SOLARISATION
SOLARISATIONS
SOLARISE
SOLARISED
SOLARISES
SOLARISING
SOLARISM
SOLARISMS
SOLARIST
SOLARISTS
SOLARIUM
SOLARIUMS
SOLARIZATION
SOLARIZATIONS
SOLARIZE
SOLARIZED
SOLARIZES
SOLARIZING
SOLARS
SOLAS
SOLATE
SOLATED
SOLATES
SOLATIA
SOLATING
SOLATION
SOLATIONS
SOLATIUM
SOLD
SOLDADO
SOLDADOS
SOLDAN
SOLDANS
SOLDATESQUE
SOLDE
SOLDER
SOLDERABILITIES

SOLDERABILITY
SOLDERABLE
SOLDERED
SOLDERER
SOLDERERS
SOLDERING
SOLDERINGS
SOLDERS
SOLDES
SOLDI
SOLDIER
SOLDIERED
SOLDIERIES
SOLDIERING
SOLDIERINGS
SOLDIERLIKE
SOLDIERLINESS
SOLDIERLINESSES
SOLDIERLY
SOLDIERS
SOLDIERSHIP
SOLDIERSHIPS
SOLDIERY
SOLDO
SOLDS
SOLE
SOLECISE
SOLECISED
SOLECISES
SOLECISING
SOLECISM
SOLECISMS
SOLECIST
SOLECISTIC
SOLECISTICAL
SOLECISTICALLY
SOLECISTS
SOLECIZE
SOLECIZED
SOLECIZES
SOLECIZING
SOLED
SOLEI
SOLEIN
SOLELESS
SOLELY
SOLEMN
SOLEMNER
SOLEMNESS
SOLEMNESSES
SOLEMNEST
SOLEMNIFICATION
SOLEMNIFIED
SOLEMNIFIES
SOLEMNIFY
SOLEMNIFYING
SOLEMNISATION

SOLEMNISATIONS
SOLEMNISE
SOLEMNISED
SOLEMNISER
SOLEMNISERS
SOLEMNISES
SOLEMNISING
SOLEMNITIES
SOLEMNITY
SOLEMNIZATION
SOLEMNIZATIONS
SOLEMNIZE
SOLEMNIZED
SOLEMNIZER
SOLEMNIZERS
SOLEMNIZES
SOLEMNIZING
SOLEMNLY
SOLEMNNESS
SOLEMNNESSES
SOLENESS
SOLENESSES
SOLENETTE
SOLENETTES
SOLENODON
SOLENODONS
SOLENOID
SOLENOIDAL
SOLENOIDALLY
SOLENOIDS
SOLEPLATE
SOLEPLATES
SOLER
SOLERA
SOLERAS
SOLERET
SOLERETS
SOLERS
SOLES
SOLEUS
SOLEUSES
SOLFATARA
SOLFATARAS
SOLFATARIC
SOLFEGE
SOLFEGES
SOLFEGGI
SOLFEGGIO
SOLFEGGIOS
SOLFERINO
SOLFERINOS
SOLGEL
SOLI
SOLICIT
SOLICITANT
SOLICITANTS
SOLICITATION

SOLICITATIONS
SOLICITED
SOLICITIES
SOLICITING
SOLICITINGS
SOLICITOR
SOLICITORS
SOLICITORSHIP
SOLICITORSHIPS
SOLICITOUS
SOLICITOUSLY
SOLICITOUSNESS
SOLICITS
SOLICITUDE
SOLICITUDES
SOLICITY
SOLID
SOLIDAGO
SOLIDAGOS
SOLIDARE
SOLIDARES
SOLIDARISM
SOLIDARISMS
SOLIDARIST
SOLIDARISTIC
SOLIDARISTS
SOLIDARITIES
SOLIDARITY
SOLIDARY
SOLIDATE
SOLIDATED
SOLIDATES
SOLIDATING
SOLIDER
SOLIDEST
SOLIDI
SOLIDIFIABLE
SOLIDIFICATION
SOLIDIFICATIONS
SOLIDIFIED
SOLIDIFIER
SOLIDIFIERS
SOLIDIFIES
SOLIDIFY
SOLIDIFYING
SOLIDISH
SOLIDISM
SOLIDISMS
SOLIDIST
SOLIDISTS
SOLIDITIES
SOLIDITY
SOLIDLY
SOLIDNESS
SOLIDNESSES
SOLIDS
SOLIDUM

SOLIDUMS
SOLIDUNGULATE
SOLIDUNGULOUS
SOLIDUS
SOLIFIDIAN
SOLIFIDIANISM
SOLIFIDIANISMS
SOLIFIDIANS
SOLIFLUCTION
SOLIFLUCTIONS
SOLIFLUXION
SOLIFLUXIONS
SOLILOQUIES
SOLILOQUISE
SOLILOQUISED
SOLILOQUISER
SOLILOQUISERS
SOLILOQUISES
SOLILOQUISING
SOLILOQUIST
SOLILOQUISTS
SOLILOQUIZE
SOLILOQUIZED
SOLILOQUIZER
SOLILOQUIZERS
SOLILOQUIZES
SOLILOQUIZING
SOLILOQUY
SOLING
SOLION
SOLIONS
SOLIPED
SOLIPEDOUS
SOLIPEDS
SOLIPSISM
SOLIPSISMS
SOLIPSIST
SOLIPSISTIC
SOLIPSISTICALLY
SOLIPSISTS
SOLIQUID
SOLIQUIDS
SOLITAIRE
SOLITAIRES
SOLITARIAN
SOLITARIANS
SOLITARIES
SOLITARILY
SOLITARINESS
SOLITARINESSES
SOLITARY
SOLITO
SOLITON
SOLITONS
SOLITUDE
SOLITUDES
SOLITUDINARIAN

SOLITUDINARIANS
SOLITUDINOUS
SOLIVAGANT
SOLIVAGANTS
SOLIVE
SOLIVES
SOLLAR
SOLLARS
SOLLER
SOLLERET
SOLLERETS
SOLLERS
SOLLICKER
SOLLICKERS
SOLMISATION
SOLMISATIONS
SOLMIZATION
SOLMIZATIONS
SOLO
SOLOED
SOLOING
SOLOIST
SOLOISTS
SOLON
SOLONCHAK
SOLONCHAKS
SOLONETS
SOLONETSES
SOLONETZ
SOLONETZES
SOLONETZIC
SOLONISATION
SOLONISATIONS
SOLONIZATION
SOLONIZATIONS
SOLONS
SOLOS
SOLPUGID
SOLPUGIDS
SOLS
SOLSTICE
SOLSTICES
SOLSTITIAL
SOLSTITIALLY
SOLUBILISATION
SOLUBILISATIONS
SOLUBILISE
SOLUBILISED
SOLUBILISES
SOLUBILISING
SOLUBILITIES
SOLUBILITY
SOLUBILIZATION
SOLUBILIZATIONS
SOLUBILIZE
SOLUBILIZED
SOLUBILIZES

SOLUBILIZING
SOLUBLE
SOLUBLENESS
SOLUBLES
SOLUBLY
SOLUM
SOLUMS
SOLUS
SOLUTE
SOLUTES
SOLUTION
SOLUTIONAL
SOLUTIONED
SOLUTIONING
SOLUTIONIST
SOLUTIONISTS
SOLUTIONS
SOLUTIVE
SOLVABILITIES
SOLVABILITY
SOLVABLE
SOLVABLENESS
SOLVATE
SOLVATED
SOLVATES
SOLVATING
SOLVATION
SOLVATIONS
SOLVE
SOLVED
SOLVENCIES
SOLVENCY
SOLVENT
SOLVENTLESS
SOLVENTLY
SOLVENTS
SOLVER
SOLVERS
SOLVES
SOLVING
SOLVOLYSES
SOLVOLYSIS
SOLVOLYTIC
SOMA
SOMAESTHESIA
SOMAESTHESIS
SOMAESTHETIC
SOMAN
SOMANS
SOMAS
SOMASCOPE
SOMASCOPES
SOMATA
SOMATIC
SOMATICALLY
SOMATISM
SOMATISMS

SOMATIST
SOMATISTS
SOMATOGENIC
SOMATOLOGIC
SOMATOLOGICAL
SOMATOLOGICALLY
SOMATOLOGIES
SOMATOLOGIST
SOMATOLOGISTS
SOMATOLOGY
SOMATOMEDIN
SOMATOMEDINS
SOMATOPLASM
SOMATOPLASMS
SOMATOPLASTIC
SOMATOPLEURAL
SOMATOPLEURE
SOMATOPLEURES
SOMATOPLEURIC
SOMATOSENSORY
SOMATOSTATIN
SOMATOSTATINS
SOMATOTONIA
SOMATOTONIAS
SOMATOTONIC
SOMATOTROPHIC
SOMATOTROPHIN
SOMATOTROPHINS
SOMATOTROPIC
SOMATOTROPIN
SOMATOTROPINS
SOMATOTYPE
SOMATOTYPED
SOMATOTYPES
SOMATOTYPING
SOMBER
SOMBERED
SOMBERER
SOMBEREST
SOMBERING
SOMBERLY
SOMBERNESS
SOMBERNESSES
SOMBERS
SOMBRE
SOMBRED
SOMBRELY
SOMBRENESS
SOMBRENESSES
SOMBRER
SOMBRERITE
SOMBRERITES
SOMBRERO
SOMBREROS
SOMBRES
SOMBREST
SOMBRING

SOMBROUS
SOME
SOMEBODIES
SOMEBODY
SOMEDAY
SOMEDEAL
SOMEDELE
SOMEGATE
SOMEHOW
SOMEONE
SOMEONES
SOMEPLACE
SOMERSAULT
SOMERSAULTED
SOMERSAULTING
SOMERSAULTS
SOMERSET
SOMERSETED
SOMERSETING
SOMERSETS
SOMERSETTED
SOMERSETTING
SOMESTHESIA
SOMESTHESIS
SOMESTHETIC
SOMETHING
SOMETHINGS
SOMETIME
SOMETIMES
SOMEWAY
SOMEWAYS
SOMEWHAT
SOMEWHATS
SOMEWHEN
SOMEWHENCE
SOMEWHERE
SOMEWHERES
SOMEWHILE
SOMEWHILES
SOMEWHITHER
SOMEWHY
SOMEWISE
SOMITAL
SOMITE
SOMITES
SOMITIC
SOMMELIER
SOMMELIERS
SOMNAMBULANCE
SOMNAMBULANCES
SOMNAMBULANT
SOMNAMBULANTS
SOMNAMBULAR
SOMNAMBULARY
SOMNAMBULATE
SOMNAMBULATED
SOMNAMBULATES

SOMNAMBULATING
SOMNAMBULATION
SOMNAMBULATIONS
SOMNAMBULATOR
SOMNAMBULATORS
SOMNAMBULE
SOMNAMBULES
SOMNAMBULIC
SOMNAMBULISM
SOMNAMBULISMS
SOMNAMBULIST
SOMNAMBULISTIC
SOMNAMBULISTS
SOMNIAL
SOMNIATE
SOMNIATED
SOMNIATES
SOMNIATING
SOMNIATIVE
SOMNIATORY
SOMNIFACIENT
SOMNIFACIENTS
SOMNIFEROUS
SOMNIFEROUSLY
SOMNIFIC
SOMNILOQIES
SOMNILOQUENCE
SOMNILOQUENCES
SOMNILOQUIES
SOMNILOQUISE
SOMNILOQUISED
SOMNILOQUISES
SOMNILOQUISING
SOMNILOQUISM
SOMNILOQUISMS
SOMNILOQUIST
SOMNILOQUISTIC
SOMNILOQUISTS
SOMNILOQUIZE
SOMNILOQUIZED
SOMNILOQUIZES
SOMNILOQUIZING
SOMNILOQUOUS
SOMNILOQUY
SOMNOLENCE
SOMNOLENCES
SOMNOLENCIES
SOMNOLENCY
SOMNOLENT
SOMNOLENTLY
SOMNOLESCENT
SOMY
SON
SONANCE
SONANCES
SONANCIES
SONANCY

SONANT
SONANTAL
SONANTIC
SONANTS
SONAR
SONARMAN
SONARMEN
SONARS
SONATA
SONATAS
SONATINA
SONATINAS
SONATINE
SONCE
SONCES
SONDAGE
SONDAGES
SONDE
SONDELI
SONDELIS
SONDER
SONDERS
SONDES
SONE
SONERI
SONERIS
SONES
SONG
SONGBIRD
SONGBIRDS
SONGBOOK
SONGBOOKS
SONGCRAFT
SONGCRAFTS
SONGFEST
SONGFESTS
SONGFUL
SONGFULLY
SONGFULNESS
SONGFULNESSES
SONGKOK
SONGKOKS
SONGLESS
SONGLESSLY
SONGLIKE
SONGMAN
SONGMEN
SONGOLOLO
SONGOLOLOS
SONGS
SONGSMITH
SONGSMITHS
SONGSTER
SONGSTERS
SONGSTRESS
SONGSTRESSES
SONGWRITER

SONGWRITERS
SONGWRITING
SONGWRITINGS
SONHOOD
SONHOODS
SONIC
SONICALLY
SONICATE
SONICATED
SONICATES
SONICATING
SONICATION
SONICATIONS
SONICS
SONIFEROUS
SONLESS
SONLIKE
SONLY
SONNE
SONNES
SONNET
SONNETARY
SONNETED
SONNETEER
SONNETEERING
SONNETEERINGS
SONNETEERS
SONNETING
SONNETISE
SONNETISED
SONNETISES
SONNETISING
SONNETIZE
SONNETIZED
SONNETIZES
SONNETIZING
SONNETS
SONNETTED
SONNETTING
SONNIES
SONNY
SONOBUOY
SONOBUOYS
SONOFABITCH
SONOGRAM
SONOGRAMS
SONOGRAPH
SONOGRAPHER
SONOGRAPHERS
SONOGRAPHIES
SONOGRAPHS
SONOGRAPHY
SONOMETER
SONOMETERS
SONORANT
SONORANTS
SONORITIES

SONORITY
SONOROUS
SONOROUSLY
SONOROUSNESS
SONOROUSNESSES
SONOVOX
SONOVOXES
SONS
SONSE
SONSES
SONSHIP
SONSHIPS
SONSIE
SONSIER
SONSIEST
SONSY
SONTAG
SONTAGS
SONTIES
SOOCHONG
SOOCHONGS
SOOEY
SOOGEE
SOOGEED
SOOGEEING
SOOGEES
SOOGIE
SOOGIED
SOOGIEING
SOOGIES
SOOJEY
SOOJEYS
SOOK
SOOKED
SOOKING
SOOKS
SOOL
SOOLE
SOOLED
SOOLER
SOOLERS
SOOLES
SOOLING
SOOLS
SOOM
SOOMED
SOOMING
SOOMS
SOON
SOONER
SOONERS
SOONEST
SOOP
SOOPED
SOOPING
SOOPINGS
SOOPS

SOOPSTAKE
SOOT
SOOTE
SOOTED
SOOTERKIN
SOOTERKINS
SOOTES
SOOTFLAKE
SOOTFLAKES
SOOTH
SOOTHE
SOOTHED
SOOTHER
SOOTHERED
SOOTHERING
SOOTHERS
SOOTHES
SOOTHEST
SOOTHFAST
SOOTHFASTLY
SOOTHFASTNESS
SOOTHFASTNESSES
SOOTHFUL
SOOTHING
SOOTHINGLY
SOOTHINGNESS
SOOTHINGNESSES
SOOTHINGS
SOOTHLICH
SOOTHLY
SOOTHS
SOOTHSAID
SOOTHSAY
SOOTHSAYER
SOOTHSAYERS
SOOTHSAYING
SOOTHSAYINGS
SOOTHSAYS
SOOTIER
SOOTIEST
SOOTILY
SOOTINESS
SOOTINESSES
SOOTING
SOOTLESS
SOOTS
SOOTY
SOP
SOPAIPILLA
SOPAIPILLAS
SOPAPILLA
SOPAPILLAS
SOPH
SOPHERIC
SOPHERIM
SOPHIES
SOPHISM

SOPHISMS
SOPHIST
SOPHISTER
SOPHISTERS
SOPHISTIC
SOPHISTICAL
SOPHISTICALLY
SOPHISTICATE
SOPHISTICATED
SOPHISTICATEDLY
SOPHISTICATES
SOPHISTICATING
SOPHISTICATION
SOPHISTICATIONS
SOPHISTICATOR
SOPHISTICATORS
SOPHISTRIES
SOPHISTRY
SOPHISTS
SOPHOMORE
SOPHOMORES
SOPHOMORIC
SOPHOMORICAL
SOPHS
SOPHY
SOPITE
SOPITED
SOPITES
SOPITING
SOPOR
SOPORIFEROUS
SOPORIFEROUSLY
SOPORIFIC
SOPORIFICALLY
SOPORIFICS
SOPOROSE
SOPOROUS
SOPORS
SOPPED
SOPPIER
SOPPIEST
SOPPILY
SOPPINESS
SOPPINESSES
SOPPING
SOPPINGS
SOPPY
SOPRA
SOPRANI
SOPRANINI
SOPRANINO
SOPRANINOS
SOPRANIST
SOPRANISTS
SOPRANO
SOPRANOS
SOPS

SORA
SORAGE
SORAGES
SORAL
SORAS
SORB
SORBABILITIES
SORBABILITY
SORBABLE
SORBARIA
SORBARIAS
SORBATE
SORBATES
SORBED
SORBEFACIENT
SORBEFACIENTS
SORBENT
SORBENTS
SORBET
SORBETS
SORBIC
SORBING
SORBITE
SORBITES
SORBITIC
SORBITISATION
SORBITISATIONS
SORBITISE
SORBITISED
SORBITISES
SORBITISING
SORBITIZATION
SORBITIZATIONS
SORBITIZE
SORBITIZED
SORBITIZES
SORBITIZING
SORBITOL
SORBITOLS
SORBO
SORBOSE
SORBOSES
SORBS
SORBUS
SORBUSES
SORCERER
SORCERERS
SORCERESS
SORCERESSES
SORCERIES
SORCEROUS
SORCERY
SORD
SORDA
SORDAMENTE
SORDES
SORDID

SORDIDER
SORDIDEST
SORDIDLY
SORDIDNESS
SORDIDNESSES
SORDINE
SORDINES
SORDINI
SORDINO
SORDO
SORDOR
SORDORS
SORDS
SORE
SORED
SOREDIA
SOREDIAL
SOREDIATE
SOREDIUM
SOREE
SOREES
SOREHEAD
SOREHEADED
SOREHEADEDLY
SOREHEADEDNESS
SOREHEADS
SOREHON
SOREHONS
SOREL
SORELL
SORELLS
SORELS
SORELY
SORENESS
SORENESSES
SORER
SORES
SOREST
SOREX
SOREXES
SORGHO
SORGHOS
SORGHUM
SORGHUMS
SORGO
SORGOS
SORI
SORICIDENT
SORICINE
SORICOID
SORING
SORINGS
SORITES
SORITIC
SORITICAL
SORN
SORNED

SORNER
SORNERS
SORNING
SORNINGS
SORNS
SOROBAN
SOROBANS
SOROCHE
SOROCHES
SORORAL
SORORATE
SORORATES
SORORIAL
SORORIALLY
SORORICIDAL
SORORICIDE
SORORICIDES
SORORISE
SORORISED
SORORISES
SORORISING
SORORITIES
SORORITY
SORORIZE
SORORIZED
SORORIZES
SORORIZING
SOROSES
SOROSIS
SOROSISES
SORPTION
SORPTIONS
SORPTIVE
SORRA
SORRAS
SORREL
SORRELS
SORRIER
SORRIEST
SORRILY
SORRINESS
SORRINESSES
SORROW
SORROWED
SORROWER
SORROWERS
SORROWFUL
SORROWFULLY
SORROWFULNESS
SORROWFULNESSES
SORROWING
SORROWINGS
SORROWLESS
SORROWS
SORRY
SORRYISH
SORT

SORTABLE
SORTABLY
SORTAL
SORTALS
SORTANCE
SORTANCES
SORTATION
SORTATIONS
SORTED
SORTER
SORTERS
SORTES
SORTIE
SORTIED
SORTIEING
SORTIES
SORTILEGE
SORTILEGER
SORTILEGERS
SORTILEGES
SORTILEGIES
SORTILEGY
SORTING
SORTINGS
SORTITION
SORTITIONS
SORTMENT
SORTMENTS
SORTS
SORUS
SOS
SOSATIE
SOSATIES
SOSS
SOSSED
SOSSES
SOSSING
SOSSINGS
SOSTENUTO
SOSTENUTOS
SOT
SOTERIAL
SOTERIOLOGIC
SOTERIOLOGICAL
SOTERIOLOGIES
SOTERIOLOGY
SOTH
SOTHS
SOTOL
SOTOLS
SOTS
SOTTED
SOTTING
SOTTINGS
SOTTISH
SOTTISHLY
SOTTISHNESS

959

SOTTISHNESSES
SOTTISIER
SOTTISIERS
SOU
SOUARI
SOUARIS
SOUBISE
SOUBISES
SOUBRETTE
SOUBRETTES
SOUBRETTISH
SOUBRETTISHNESS
SOUBRIQUET
SOUBRIQUETS
SOUCAR
SOUCARS
SOUCE
SOUCED
SOUCES
SOUCHONG
SOUCHONGS
SOUCING
SOUCT
SOUDAN
SOUDANS
SOUFFLE
SOUFFLED
SOUFFLEED
SOUFFLES
SOUGH
SOUGHED
SOUGHING
SOUGHS
SOUGHT
SOUK
SOUKED
SOUKING
SOUKOUS
SOUKOUSES
SOUKS
SOUL
SOULDAN
SOULDANS
SOULDIER
SOULDIERED
SOULDIERING
SOULDIERS
SOULED
SOULFUL
SOULFULLY
SOULFULNESS
SOULFULNESSES
SOULLESS
SOULLESSLY
SOULLESSNESS
SOULLESSNESSES
SOULLIKE

SOULS
SOUM
SOUMED
SOUMING
SOUMINGS
SOUMS
SOUND
SOUNDABLE
SOUNDALIKE
SOUNDALIKES
SOUNDBITE
SOUNDBITES
SOUNDBOARD
SOUNDBOARDS
SOUNDBOX
SOUNDBOXES
SOUNDCARD
SOUNDCARDS
SOUNDED
SOUNDER
SOUNDERS
SOUNDEST
SOUNDING
SOUNDINGLY
SOUNDINGS
SOUNDLESS
SOUNDLESSLY
SOUNDLESSNESS
SOUNDLY
SOUNDMAN
SOUNDMEN
SOUNDNESS
SOUNDNESSES
SOUNDPOST
SOUNDPOSTS
SOUNDPROOF
SOUNDPROOFED
SOUNDPROOFING
SOUNDPROOFINGS
SOUNDPROOFS
SOUNDS
SOUNDSCAPE
SOUNDSCAPES
SOUNDSTAGE
SOUNDSTAGES
SOUNDTRACK
SOUNDTRACKS
SOUP
SOUPCON
SOUPCONS
SOUPED
SOUPER
SOUPERS
SOUPFIN
SOUPFINS
SOUPIER
SOUPIEST

SOUPING
SOUPLE
SOUPLED
SOUPLES
SOUPLING
SOUPS
SOUPSPOON
SOUPSPOONS
SOUPY
SOUR
SOURBALL
SOURBALLS
SOURCE
SOURCEBOOK
SOURCEBOOKS
SOURCED
SOURCELESS
SOURCES
SOURCING
SOURCINGS
SOURDELINE
SOURDELINES
SOURDINE
SOURDINES
SOURDOUGH
SOURDOUGHS
SOURED
SOURER
SOUREST
SOURING
SOURINGS
SOURISH
SOURISHLY
SOURLY
SOURNESS
SOURNESSES
SOUROCK
SOUROCKS
SOURPUSS
SOURPUSSES
SOURS
SOURSE
SOURSES
SOURSOP
SOURSOPS
SOURWOOD
SOURWOODS
SOUS
SOUSAPHONE
SOUSAPHONES
SOUSAPHONIST
SOUSAPHONISTS
SOUSE
SOUSED
SOUSES
SOUSING
SOUSINGS

SOUSLIK
SOUSLIKS
SOUT
SOUTACHE
SOUTACHES
SOUTANE
SOUTANES
SOUTAR
SOUTARS
SOUTENEUR
SOUTENEURS
SOUTER
SOUTERLY
SOUTERRAIN
SOUTERRAINS
SOUTERS
SOUTH
SOUTHBOUND
SOUTHEAST
SOUTHEASTER
SOUTHEASTERLIES
SOUTHEASTERLY
SOUTHEASTERN
SOUTHEASTERS
SOUTHEASTS
SOUTHEASTWARD
SOUTHEASTWARDS
SOUTHED
SOUTHER
SOUTHERED
SOUTHERING
SOUTHERLIES
SOUTHERLINESS
SOUTHERLINESSES
SOUTHERLY
SOUTHERMOST
SOUTHERN
SOUTHERNER
SOUTHERNERS
SOUTHERNISE
SOUTHERNISED
SOUTHERNISES
SOUTHERNISING
SOUTHERNISM
SOUTHERNISMS
SOUTHERNIZE
SOUTHERNIZED
SOUTHERNIZES
SOUTHERNIZING
SOUTHERNLY
SOUTHERNMOST
SOUTHERNNESS
SOUTHERNNESSES
SOUTHERNS
SOUTHERNWOOD
SOUTHERNWOODS
SOUTHERS

SOUTHING
SOUTHINGS
SOUTHLAND
SOUTHLANDER
SOUTHLANDERS
SOUTHLANDS
SOUTHMOST
SOUTHPAW
SOUTHPAWS
SOUTHRON
SOUTHRONS
SOUTHS
SOUTHSAY
SOUTHSAYING
SOUTHSAYS
SOUTHWARD
SOUTHWARDLY
SOUTHWARDS
SOUTHWEST
SOUTHWESTER
SOUTHWESTERLIES
SOUTHWESTERLY
SOUTHWESTERN
SOUTHWESTERS
SOUTHWESTS
SOUTHWESTWARD
SOUTHWESTWARDLY
SOUTHWESTWARDS
SOUTS
SOUVENIR
SOUVENIRED
SOUVENIRING
SOUVENIRS
SOUVLAKI
SOUVLAKIA
SOUVLAKIAS
SOUVLAKIS
SOV
SOVENANCE
SOVENANCES
SOVEREIGN
SOVEREIGNLY
SOVEREIGNS
SOVEREIGNTIES
SOVEREIGNTIST
SOVEREIGNTISTS
SOVEREIGNTY
SOVIET
SOVIETIC
SOVIETISATION
SOVIETISE
SOVIETISED
SOVIETISES
SOVIETISING
SOVIETISM
SOVIETISMS
SOVIETIST

SOVIETISTIC
SOVIETISTS
SOVIETIZATION
SOVIETIZATIONS
SOVIETIZE
SOVIETIZED
SOVIETIZES
SOVIETIZING
SOVIETOLOGICAL
SOVIETOLOGIST
SOVIETOLOGISTS
SOVIETS
SOVKHOZ
SOVKHOZES
SOVKHOZY
SOVRAN
SOVRANLY
SOVRANS
SOVRANTIES
SOVRANTY
SOVS
SOW
SOWABLE
SOWANS
SOWAR
SOWARREE
SOWARREES
SOWARRIES
SOWARRY
SOWARS
SOWBACK
SOWBACKS
SOWBELLIES
SOWBELLY
SOWBREAD
SOWBREADS
SOWCAR
SOWCARS
SOWCE
SOWCED
SOWCES
SOWCING
SOWED
SOWENS
SOWER
SOWERS
SOWF
SOWFED
SOWFF
SOWFFED
SOWFFING
SOWFFS
SOWFING
SOWFS
SOWING
SOWINGS
SOWL

SOWLE
SOWLED
SOWLES
SOWLING
SOWLS
SOWM
SOWMED
SOWMING
SOWMS
SOWN
SOWND
SOWNDED
SOWNDING
SOWNDS
SOWNE
SOWNES
SOWP
SOWPS
SOWS
SOWSE
SOWSED
SOWSES
SOWSING
SOWSSE
SOWSSED
SOWSSES
SOWSSING
SOWTER
SOWTERS
SOWTH
SOWTHED
SOWTHING
SOWTHS
SOX
SOY
SOYA
SOYAS
SOYBEAN
SOYBEANS
SOYLE
SOYLES
SOYMILK
SOYMILKS
SOYS
SOYUZ
SOYUZES
SOZIN
SOZINE
SOZINES
SOZINS
SOZZLE
SOZZLED
SOZZLES
SOZZLIER
SOZZLIEST
SOZZLING
SOZZLY

SPA
SPACE
SPACEBAND
SPACEBANDS
SPACEBORNE
SPACECRAFT
SPACECRAFTS
SPACED
SPACEFARING
SPACEFARINGS
SPACEFLIGHT
SPACEFLIGHTS
SPACELAB
SPACELABS
SPACELESS
SPACEMAN
SPACEMEN
SPACEPLANE
SPACEPLANES
SPACEPORT
SPACEPORTS
SPACER
SPACERS
SPACES
SPACESHIP
SPACESHIPS
SPACESUIT
SPACESUITS
SPACEWALK
SPACEWALKED
SPACEWALKER
SPACEWALKERS
SPACEWALKING
SPACEWALKS
SPACEWARD
SPACEWOMAN
SPACEWOMEN
SPACEY
SPACIAL
SPACIER
SPACIEST
SPACING
SPACINGS
SPACIOUS
SPACIOUSLY
SPACIOUSNESS
SPACIOUSNESSES
SPACKLE
SPACKLED
SPACKLES
SPACKLING
SPACY
SPADASSIN
SPADASSINS
SPADE
SPADED
SPADEFISH

SPADEFISHES	SPAGHETTIS	SPAMMIE	SPANIOLISED
SPADEFUL	SPAGIRIC	SPAMMIER	SPANIOLISES
SPADEFULS	SPAGIRICS	SPAMMIEST	SPANIOLISING
SPADELIKE	SPAGIRIST	SPAMMING	SPANIOLIZE
SPADEMAN	SPAGIRISTS	SPAMMINGS	SPANIOLIZED
SPADEMEN	SPAGS	SPAMMY	SPANIOLIZES
SPADER	SPAGYRIC	SPAMS	SPANIOLIZING
SPADERS	SPAGYRICAL	SPAN	SPANK
SPADES	SPAGYRICALLY	SPANAEMIA	SPANKED
SPADESMAN	SPAGYRICS	SPANAEMIAS	SPANKER
SPADESMEN	SPAGYRIST	SPANAEMIC	SPANKERS
SPADEWORK	SPAGYRISTS	SPANAKOPITA	SPANKING
SPADEWORKS	SPAHEE	SPANAKOPITAS	SPANKINGLY
SPADGER	SPAHEES	SPANCEL	SPANKINGS
SPADGERS	SPAHI	SPANCELED	SPANKS
SPADICEOUS	SPAHIS	SPANCELING	SPANLESS
SPADICES	SPAIL	SPANCELLED	SPANNED
SPADICIFLORAL	SPAILS	SPANCELLING	SPANNER
SPADILLE	SPAIN	SPANCELS	SPANNERS
SPADILLES	SPAINED	SPANDEX	SPANNING
SPADILLIO	SPAING	SPANDEXES	SPANOKOPITA
SPADILLIOS	SPAINGS	SPANDREL	SPANOKOPITAS
SPADILLO	SPAINING	SPANDRELS	SPANS
SPADILLOS	SPAINS	SPANDRIL	SPANSPEK
SPADING	SPAIRGE	SPANDRILS	SPANSPEKS
SPADIX	SPAIRGED	SPANE	SPANSULE
SPADIXES	SPAIRGES	SPANED	SPANSULES
SPADO	SPAIRGING	SPANES	SPANWORM
SPADOES	SPAIT	SPANG	SPANWORMS
SPADONES	SPAITS	SPANGED	SPAR
SPADOS	SPAKE	SPANGHEW	SPARABLE
SPADROON	SPALD	SPANGHEWED	SPARABLES
SPADROONS	SPALDS	SPANGHEWING	SPARAGMATIC
SPAE	SPALE	SPANGHEWS	SPARAGRASS
SPAED	SPALES	SPANGING	SPARAGRASSES
SPAEING	SPALL	SPANGLE	SPARAXIS
SPAEINGS	SPALLABLE	SPANGLED	SPARAXISES
SPAEMAN	SPALLATION	SPANGLER	SPARD
SPAEMEN	SPALLATIONS	SPANGLERS	SPARE
SPAER	SPALLE	SPANGLES	SPAREABLE
SPAERS	SPALLED	SPANGLET	SPARED
SPAES	SPALLER	SPANGLETS	SPARELESS
SPAETZLE	SPALLERS	SPANGLIER	SPARELY
SPAETZLES	SPALLES	SPANGLIEST	SPARENESS
SPAEWIFE	SPALLING	SPANGLING	SPARENESSES
SPAEWIVES	SPALLINGS	SPANGLINGS	SPARER
SPAG	SPALLS	SPANGLY	SPARERIB
SPAGERIC	SPALPEEN	SPANGS	SPARERIBS
SPAGERICS	SPALPEENS	SPANIEL	SPARERS
SPAGERIST	SPALT	SPANIELLED	SPARES
SPAGERISTS	SPALTED	SPANIELLING	SPAREST
SPAGGED	SPALTING	SPANIELS	SPARGANIUM
SPAGGING	SPALTS	SPANING	SPARGANIUMS
SPAGHETTI	SPAM	SPANIOLATE	SPARGE
SPAGHETTILIKE	SPAMMED	SPANIOLATED	SPARGED
SPAGHETTINI	SPAMMER	SPANIOLATES	SPARGER
SPAGHETTINIS	SPAMMERS	SPANIOLATING	SPARGERS

SPARGES	SPARRINGS	SPATCHCOCKS	SPAWLED
SPARGING	SPARROW	SPATE	SPAWLING
SPARID	SPARROWFART	SPATES	SPAWLS
SPARIDS	SPARROWGRASS	SPATFALL	SPAWN
SPARING	SPARROWHAWK	SPATFALLS	SPAWNED
SPARINGLY	SPARROWHAWKS	SPATHACEOUS	SPAWNER
SPARINGNESS	SPARROWLIKE	SPATHAL	SPAWNERS
SPARINGNESSES	SPARROWS	SPATHE	SPAWNIER
SPARK	SPARRY	SPATHED	SPAWNIEST
SPARKE	SPARS	SPATHES	SPAWNING
SPARKED	SPARSE	SPATHIC	SPAWNINGS
SPARKER	SPARSEDLY	SPATHIPHYLLUM	SPAWNS
SPARKERS	SPARSELY	SPATHIPHYLLUMS	SPAWNY
SPARKES	SPARSENESS	SPATHOSE	SPAWS
SPARKIE	SPARSENESSES	SPATHULATE	SPAY
SPARKIER	SPARSER	SPATIAL	SPAYAD
SPARKIES	SPARSEST	SPATIALITIES	SPAYADS
SPARKIEST	SPARSITIES	SPATIALITY	SPAYD
SPARKILY	SPARSITY	SPATIALLY	SPAYDS
SPARKING	SPART	SPATIOTEMPORAL	SPAYED
SPARKISH	SPARTAN	SPATLESE	SPAYING
SPARKISHLY	SPARTANS	SPATLESEN	SPAYS
SPARKLE	SPARTEINE	SPATLESES	SPAZ
SPARKLED	SPARTEINES	SPATS	SPAZZ
SPARKLER	SPARTERIE	SPATTED	SPAZZED
SPARKLERS	SPARTERIES	SPATTEE	SPAZZES
SPARKLES	SPARTH	SPATTEES	SPAZZING
SPARKLESS	SPARTHE	SPATTER	SPEAK
SPARKLESSLY	SPARTHES	SPATTERDASH	SPEAKABLE
SPARKLET	SPARTHS	SPATTERDASHES	SPEAKEASIES
SPARKLETS	SPARTS	SPATTERDOCK	SPEAKEASY
SPARKLIER	SPAS	SPATTERDOCKS	SPEAKER
SPARKLIES	SPASM	SPATTERED	SPEAKERINE
SPARKLIEST	SPASMATIC	SPATTERING	SPEAKERINES
SPARKLING	SPASMATICAL	SPATTERS	SPEAKERPHONE
SPARKLINGLY	SPASMED	SPATTERWORK	SPEAKERPHONES
SPARKLINGS	SPASMIC	SPATTERWORKS	SPEAKERS
SPARKLY	SPASMING	SPATTING	SPEAKERSHIP
SPARKPLUG	SPASMODIC	SPATULA	SPEAKERSHIPS
SPARKPLUGGED	SPASMODICAL	SPATULAR	SPEAKING
SPARKPLUGGING	SPASMODICALLY	SPATULAS	SPEAKINGLY
SPARKPLUGS	SPASMODIST	SPATULATE	SPEAKINGS
SPARKS	SPASMODISTS	SPATULE	SPEAKOUT
SPARKY	SPASMOLYTIC	SPATULES	SPEAKOUTS
SPARLIKE	SPASMOLYTICS	SPATZLE	SPEAKS
SPARLING	SPASMS	SPAUL	SPEAL
SPARLINGS	SPASTIC	SPAULD	SPEALS
SPAROID	SPASTICALLY	SPAULDS	SPEAN
SPAROIDS	SPASTICITIES	SPAULS	SPEANED
SPARRE	SPASTICITY	SPAVIE	SPEANING
SPARRED	SPASTICS	SPAVIES	SPEANS
SPARRER	SPAT	SPAVIET	SPEAR
SPARRERS	SPATANGOID	SPAVIN	SPEARED
SPARRES	SPATANGOIDS	SPAVINED	SPEARER
SPARRIER	SPATCHCOCK	SPAVINS	SPEARERS
SPARRIEST	SPATCHCOCKED	SPAW	SPEARFISH
SPARRING	SPATCHCOCKING	SPAWL	SPEARFISHED

SPEARFISHES
SPEARFISHING
SPEARGUN
SPEARGUNS
SPEARHEAD
SPEARHEADED
SPEARHEADING
SPEARHEADS
SPEARIER
SPEARIEST
SPEARING
SPEARMAN
SPEARMEN
SPEARMINT
SPEARMINTS
SPEARS
SPEARWORT
SPEARWORTS
SPEARY
SPEAT
SPEATS
SPEC
SPECCED
SPECCIES
SPECCING
SPECCY
SPECIAL
SPECIALER
SPECIALEST
SPECIALISATION
SPECIALISATIONS
SPECIALISE
SPECIALISED
SPECIALISER
SPECIALISERS
SPECIALISES
SPECIALISING
SPECIALISM
SPECIALISMS
SPECIALIST
SPECIALISTIC
SPECIALISTS
SPECIALITIES
SPECIALITY
SPECIALIZATION
SPECIALIZATIONS
SPECIALIZE
SPECIALIZED
SPECIALIZER
SPECIALIZERS
SPECIALIZES
SPECIALIZING
SPECIALLED
SPECIALLING
SPECIALLY
SPECIALNESS
SPECIALNESSES

SPECIALOGUE
SPECIALOGUES
SPECIALS
SPECIALTIES
SPECIALTY
SPECIATE
SPECIATED
SPECIATES
SPECIATING
SPECIATION
SPECIATIONAL
SPECIATIONS
SPECIE
SPECIES
SPECIESISM
SPECIESISMS
SPECIESIST
SPECIESISTS
SPECIFIABLE
SPECIFIC
SPECIFICAL
SPECIFICALLY
SPECIFICATE
SPECIFICATED
SPECIFICATES
SPECIFICATING
SPECIFICATION
SPECIFICATIONS
SPECIFICATIVE
SPECIFICATIVELY
SPECIFICITIES
SPECIFICITY
SPECIFICS
SPECIFIED
SPECIFIER
SPECIFIERS
SPECIFIES
SPECIFY
SPECIFYING
SPECIMEN
SPECIMENS
SPECIOCIDE
SPECIOCIDES
SPECIOSITIES
SPECIOSITY
SPECIOUS
SPECIOUSLY
SPECIOUSNESS
SPECIOUSNESSES
SPECK
SPECKED
SPECKIER
SPECKIEST
SPECKING
SPECKLE
SPECKLED
SPECKLEDNESS

SPECKLEDNESSES
SPECKLES
SPECKLESS
SPECKLING
SPECKS
SPECKSIONEER
SPECKSIONEERS
SPECKTIONEER
SPECKTIONEERS
SPECKY
SPECS
SPECTACLE
SPECTACLED
SPECTACLES
SPECTACULAR
SPECTACULARITY
SPECTACULARLY
SPECTACULARS
SPECTATE
SPECTATED
SPECTATES
SPECTATING
SPECTATOR
SPECTATORIAL
SPECTATORS
SPECTATORSHIP
SPECTATORSHIPS
SPECTATRESS
SPECTATRESSES
SPECTATRICES
SPECTATRIX
SPECTATRIXES
SPECTER
SPECTERS
SPECTINOMYCIN
SPECTINOMYCINS
SPECTRA
SPECTRAL
SPECTRALITIES
SPECTRALITY
SPECTRALLY
SPECTRALNESS
SPECTRE
SPECTRES
SPECTRIN
SPECTROGRAM
SPECTROGRAMS
SPECTROGRAPH
SPECTROGRAPHIC
SPECTROGRAPHIES
SPECTROGRAPHS
SPECTROGRAPHY
SPECTROLOGICAL
SPECTROLOGIES
SPECTROLOGY
SPECTROMETER
SPECTROMETERS

SPECTROMETRIC
SPECTROMETRIES
SPECTROMETRY
SPECTROSCOPE
SPECTROSCOPES
SPECTROSCOPIC
SPECTROSCOPICAL
SPECTROSCOPIES
SPECTROSCOPIST
SPECTROSCOPISTS
SPECTROSCOPY
SPECTRUM
SPECTRUMS
SPECULA
SPECULAR
SPECULARITIES
SPECULARITY
SPECULARLY
SPECULATE
SPECULATED
SPECULATES
SPECULATING
SPECULATION
SPECULATIONS
SPECULATIST
SPECULATISTS
SPECULATIVE
SPECULATIVELY
SPECULATIVENESS
SPECULATOR
SPECULATORS
SPECULATORY
SPECULATRICES
SPECULATRIX
SPECULATRIXES
SPECULUM
SPECULUMS
SPED
SPEECH
SPEECHCRAFT
SPEECHCRAFTS
SPEECHED
SPEECHES
SPEECHFUL
SPEECHFULNESS
SPEECHFULNESSES
SPEECHIFICATION
SPEECHIFIED
SPEECHIFIER
SPEECHIFIERS
SPEECHIFIES
SPEECHIFY
SPEECHIFYING
SPEECHING
SPEECHLESS
SPEECHLESSLY
SPEECHLESSNESS

SPEECHMAKER	SPEERINGS	SPELLBINDING	SPERMACETI
SPEECHMAKERS	SPEERS	SPELLBINDINGLY	SPERMACETIS
SPEECHMAKING	SPEIL	SPELLBINDS	SPERMADUCT
SPEECHMAKINGS	SPEILED	SPELLBOUND	SPERMADUCTS
SPEECHWRITER	SPEILING	SPELLCHECK	SPERMAGONIA
SPEECHWRITERS	SPEILS	SPELLCHECKER	SPERMAGONIUM
SPEED	SPEIR	SPELLCHECKERS	SPERMAPHYTE
SPEEDBALL	SPEIRED	SPELLCHECKS	SPERMAPHYTES
SPEEDBALLED	SPEIRING	SPELLDOWN	SPERMAPHYTIC
SPEEDBALLING	SPEIRINGS	SPELLDOWNS	SPERMARIA
SPEEDBALLINGS	SPEIRS	SPELLED	SPERMARIES
SPEEDBALLS	SPEISE	SPELLER	SPERMARIUM
SPEEDBOAT	SPEISES	SPELLERS	SPERMARY
SPEEDBOATING	SPEISS	SPELLFUL	SPERMATHECA
SPEEDBOATINGS	SPEISSES	SPELLICAN	SPERMATHECAE
SPEEDBOATS	SPEK	SPELLICANS	SPERMATHECAL
SPEEDED	SPEKBOOM	SPELLING	SPERMATHECAS
SPEEDER	SPEKBOOMS	SPELLINGLY	SPERMATIA
SPEEDERS	SPEKS	SPELLINGS	SPERMATIAL
SPEEDFREAK	SPELAEAN	SPELLS	SPERMATIC
SPEEDFREAKISH	SPELAEOLOGICAL	SPELLSTOPT	SPERMATICAL
SPEEDFREAKS	SPELAEOLOGIES	SPELT	SPERMATICALLY
SPEEDFUL	SPELAEOLOGIST	SPELTER	SPERMATICS
SPEEDFULLY	SPELAEOLOGISTS	SPELTERS	SPERMATID
SPEEDIER	SPELAEOLOGY	SPELTS	SPERMATIDS
SPEEDIEST	SPELAEOTHEM	SPELTZ	SPERMATIUM
SPEEDILY	SPELAEOTHEMS	SPELTZES	SPERMATOBLAST
SPEEDINESS	SPELD	SPELUNK	SPERMATOBLASTIC
SPEEDINESSES	SPELDED	SPELUNKED	SPERMATOBLASTS
SPEEDING	SPELDER	SPELUNKER	SPERMATOCELE
SPEEDINGS	SPELDERED	SPELUNKERS	SPERMATOCELES
SPEEDLESS	SPELDERING	SPELUNKING	SPERMATOCIDAL
SPEEDO	SPELDERS	SPELUNKINGS	SPERMATOCIDE
SPEEDOMETER	SPELDIN	SPELUNKS	SPERMATOCIDES
SPEEDOMETERS	SPELDING	SPENCE	SPERMATOCYTE
SPEEDOS	SPELDINGS	SPENCER	SPERMATOCYTES
SPEEDS	SPELDINS	SPENCERS	SPERMATOGENESES
SPEEDSKATING	SPELDRING	SPENCES	SPERMATOGENESIS
SPEEDSKATINGS	SPELDRINGS	SPEND	SPERMATOGENETIC
SPEEDSTER	SPELDRINS	SPENDABLE	SPERMATOGENIC
SPEEDSTERS	SPELDS	SPENDALL	SPERMATOGENIES
SPEEDUP	SPELEAN	SPENDALLS	SPERMATOGENOUS
SPEEDUPS	SPELEOLOGICAL	SPENDER	SPERMATOGENY
SPEEDWAY	SPELEOLOGIES	SPENDERS	SPERMATOGONIA
SPEEDWAYS	SPELEOLOGIST	SPENDING	SPERMATOGONIAL
SPEEDWELL	SPELEOLOGISTS	SPENDINGS	SPERMATOGONIUM
SPEEDWELLS	SPELEOLOGY	SPENDS	SPERMATOPHORAL
SPEEDY	SPELEOTHEM	SPENDTHRIFT	SPERMATOPHORE
SPEEL	SPELEOTHEMS	SPENDTHRIFTS	SPERMATOPHORES
SPEELED	SPELEOTHERAPY	SPENSE	SPERMATOPHORIC
SPEELER	SPELK	SPENSES	SPERMATOPHYTE
SPEELERS	SPELKS	SPENT	SPERMATOPHYTES
SPEELING	SPELL	SPEOS	SPERMATOPHYTIC
SPEELS	SPELLABLE	SPEOSES	SPERMATORRHEA
SPEER	SPELLBIND	SPERLING	SPERMATORRHEAS
SPEERED	SPELLBINDER	SPERLINGS	SPERMATORRHOEA
SPEERING	SPELLBINDERS	SPERM	SPERMATORRHOEAS

SPERMATOTHECA
SPERMATOZOA
SPERMATOZOAL
SPERMATOZOAN
SPERMATOZOANS
SPERMATOZOIC
SPERMATOZOID
SPERMATOZOIDS
SPERMATOZOON
SPERMIC
SPERMICIDAL
SPERMICIDE
SPERMICIDES
SPERMIDUCT
SPERMIDUCTS
SPERMINE
SPERMINES
SPERMIOGENESES
SPERMIOGENESIS
SPERMIOGENETIC
SPERMOGONE
SPERMOGONES
SPERMOGONIA
SPERMOGONIUM
SPERMOPHILE
SPERMOPHILES
SPERMOPHYTE
SPERMOPHYTES
SPERMOPHYTIC
SPERMOUS
SPERMS
SPERRE
SPERRED
SPERRES
SPERRING
SPERRYLITE
SPERRYLITES
SPERSE
SPERSED
SPERSES
SPERSING
SPERST
SPERTHE
SPERTHES
SPESSARTINE
SPESSARTINES
SPESSARTITE
SPESSARTITES
SPET
SPETCH
SPETCHES
SPETS
SPETSNAZ
SPETSNAZES
SPETTING
SPETZNAZ
SPETZNAZES

SPEUG
SPEUGS
SPEW
SPEWED
SPEWER
SPEWERS
SPEWIER
SPEWIEST
SPEWINESS
SPEWINESSES
SPEWING
SPEWS
SPEWY
SPHACELATE
SPHACELATED
SPHACELATES
SPHACELATING
SPHACELATION
SPHACELATIONS
SPHACELUS
SPHACELUSES
SPHAER
SPHAERE
SPHAERES
SPHAERIDIA
SPHAERIDIUM
SPHAERITES
SPHAEROCRYSTALS
SPHAEROSIDERITE
SPHAERS
SPHAGNICOLOUS
SPHAGNOLOGIES
SPHAGNOLOGIST
SPHAGNOLOGISTS
SPHAGNOLOGY
SPHAGNOUS
SPHAGNUM
SPHAGNUMS
SPHAIREE
SPHAIRISTIKE
SPHAIRISTIKES
SPHALERITE
SPHALERITES
SPHEAR
SPHEARE
SPHEARES
SPHEARS
SPHENDONE
SPHENDONES
SPHENE
SPHENES
SPHENIC
SPHENODON
SPHENODONS
SPHENODONT
SPHENOGRAM

SPHENOGRAMS
SPHENOID
SPHENOIDAL
SPHENOIDS
SPHENOPSID
SPHENOPSIDS
SPHERAL
SPHERE
SPHERED
SPHERELESS
SPHERELIKE
SPHERES
SPHERIC
SPHERICAL
SPHERICALITIES
SPHERICALITY
SPHERICALLY
SPHERICALNESS
SPHERICALNESSES
SPHERICITIES
SPHERICITY
SPHERICS
SPHERIER
SPHERIEST
SPHERING
SPHERISTERION
SPHERISTERIONS
SPHEROCYTE
SPHEROCYTES
SPHEROCYTOSES
SPHEROCYTOSIS
SPHEROID
SPHEROIDAL
SPHEROIDALLY
SPHEROIDICALLY
SPHEROIDICITIES
SPHEROIDICITY
SPHEROIDISATION
SPHEROIDISE
SPHEROIDISED
SPHEROIDISES
SPHEROIDISING
SPHEROIDIZATION
SPHEROIDIZE
SPHEROIDIZED
SPHEROIDIZES
SPHEROIDIZING
SPHEROIDS
SPHEROMETER
SPHEROMETERS
SPHEROPLAST
SPHEROPLASTS
SPHERULAR
SPHERULE
SPHERULES
SPHERULITE
SPHERULITES

SPHERULITIC
SPHERY
SPHINCTER
SPHINCTERAL
SPHINCTERIAL
SPHINCTERIC
SPHINCTERS
SPHINGES
SPHINGID
SPHINGIDS
SPHINGOMYELIN
SPHINGOMYELINS
SPHINGOSINE
SPHINGOSINES
SPHINX
SPHINXES
SPHINXLIKE
SPHRAGISTIC
SPHRAGISTICS
SPHYGMIC
SPHYGMOGRAM
SPHYGMOGRAMS
SPHYGMOGRAPH
SPHYGMOGRAPHIC
SPHYGMOGRAPHIES
SPHYGMOGRAPHS
SPHYGMOGRAPHY
SPHYGMOID
SPHYGMOLOGIES
SPHYGMOLOGY
SPHYGMOMETER
SPHYGMOMETERS
SPHYGMOPHONE
SPHYGMOPHONES
SPHYGMOSCOPE
SPHYGMOSCOPES
SPHYGMUS
SPHYGMUSES
SPIAL
SPIALS
SPIC
SPICA
SPICAE
SPICAS
SPICATE
SPICATED
SPICCATO
SPICCATOS
SPICE
SPICEBERRIES
SPICEBERRY
SPICEBUSH
SPICEBUSHES
SPICED
SPICELESS
SPICER
SPICERIES

SPICERS
SPICERY
SPICES
SPICEY
SPICIER
SPICIEST
SPICILEGE
SPICILEGES
SPICILY
SPICINESS
SPICINESSES
SPICING
SPICK
SPICKER
SPICKEST
SPICKNEL
SPICKNELS
SPICKS
SPICS
SPICULA
SPICULAE
SPICULAR
SPICULATE
SPICULATION
SPICULATIONS
SPICULE
SPICULES
SPICULUM
SPICY
SPIDE
SPIDER
SPIDERIER
SPIDERIEST
SPIDERISH
SPIDERLIKE
SPIDERMAN
SPIDERMEN
SPIDERS
SPIDERWEB
SPIDERWEBS
SPIDERWOOD
SPIDERWORK
SPIDERWORKS
SPIDERWORT
SPIDERWORTS
SPIDERY
SPIE
SPIED
SPIEGEL
SPIEGELEISEN
SPIEGELEISENS
SPIEGELS
SPIEL
SPIELED
SPIELER
SPIELERS
SPIELING

SPIELS
SPIER
SPIERED
SPIERING
SPIERS
SPIES
SPIF
SPIFF
SPIFFED
SPIFFIER
SPIFFIEST
SPIFFILY
SPIFFINESS
SPIFFINESSES
SPIFFING
SPIFFLICATE
SPIFFLICATED
SPIFFLICATES
SPIFFLICATING
SPIFFLICATION
SPIFFLICATIONS
SPIFFS
SPIFFY
SPIFLICATE
SPIFLICATED
SPIFLICATES
SPIFLICATING
SPIFLICATION
SPIFLICATIONS
SPIFS
SPIGHT
SPIGHTED
SPIGHTING
SPIGHTS
SPIGNEL
SPIGNELS
SPIGOT
SPIGOTS
SPIK
SPIKE
SPIKED
SPIKEFISH
SPIKEFISHES
SPIKELET
SPIKELETS
SPIKELIKE
SPIKENARD
SPIKENARDS
SPIKER
SPIKERIES
SPIKERS
SPIKERY
SPIKES
SPIKEY
SPIKIER
SPIKIEST
SPIKILY

SPIKINESS
SPIKINESSES
SPIKING
SPIKS
SPIKY
SPILE
SPILED
SPILES
SPILIKIN
SPILIKINS
SPILING
SPILINGS
SPILITE
SPILITES
SPILITIC
SPILL
SPILLABLE
SPILLAGE
SPILLAGES
SPILLED
SPILLER
SPILLERS
SPILLIKIN
SPILLIKINS
SPILLING
SPILLINGS
SPILLOVER
SPILLOVERS
SPILLS
SPILLWAY
SPILLWAYS
SPILOSITE
SPILOSITES
SPILT
SPILTH
SPILTHS
SPIN
SPINA
SPINACENE
SPINACENES
SPINACEOUS
SPINACH
SPINACHES
SPINACHLIKE
SPINACHY
SPINAE
SPINAGE
SPINAGES
SPINAL
SPINALLY
SPINALS
SPINAR
SPINARS
SPINAS
SPINATE
SPINDLE
SPINDLED

SPINDLELEGGED
SPINDLELEGS
SPINDLER
SPINDLERS
SPINDLES
SPINDLESHANKED
SPINDLESHANKS
SPINDLIER
SPINDLIEST
SPINDLING
SPINDLINGS
SPINDLY
SPINDRIFT
SPINDRIFTS
SPINE
SPINED
SPINEL
SPINELESS
SPINELESSLY
SPINELESSNESS
SPINELESSNESSES
SPINELIKE
SPINELLE
SPINELLES
SPINELS
SPINES
SPINESCENCE
SPINESCENCES
SPINESCENT
SPINET
SPINETS
SPINETTE
SPINETTES
SPINIER
SPINIEST
SPINIFEROUS
SPINIFEX
SPINIFEXES
SPINIFORM
SPINIGEROUS
SPINIGRADE
SPININESS
SPININESSES
SPINK
SPINKS
SPINLESS
SPINNAKER
SPINNAKERS
SPINNER
SPINNERET
SPINNERETS
SPINNERETTE
SPINNERETTES
SPINNERIES
SPINNERS
SPINNERULE
SPINNERULES

SPINNERY
SPINNET
SPINNETS
SPINNEY
SPINNEYS
SPINNIES
SPINNING
SPINNINGS
SPINNY
SPINODE
SPINODES
SPINOFF
SPINOFFS
SPINOR
SPINORS
SPINOSE
SPINOSELY
SPINOSITIES
SPINOSITY
SPINOUS
SPINOUT
SPINOUTS
SPINS
SPINSTER
SPINSTERDOM
SPINSTERDOMS
SPINSTERHOOD
SPINSTERHOODS
SPINSTERIAL
SPINSTERIAN
SPINSTERISH
SPINSTERLY
SPINSTERS
SPINSTERSHIP
SPINSTERSHIPS
SPINSTRESS
SPINSTRESSES
SPINTEXT
SPINTEXTS
SPINTHARISCOPE
SPINTHARISCOPES
SPINTO
SPINTOS
SPINULA
SPINULAE
SPINULATE
SPINULE
SPINULES
SPINULESCENT
SPINULIFEROUS
SPINULOSE
SPINULOUS
SPINY
SPIRACLE
SPIRACLES
SPIRACULA
SPIRACULAR

SPIRACULATE
SPIRACULUM
SPIRAEA
SPIRAEAS
SPIRAL
SPIRALED
SPIRALIFORM
SPIRALING
SPIRALISM
SPIRALISMS
SPIRALIST
SPIRALISTS
SPIRALITIES
SPIRALITY
SPIRALLED
SPIRALLING
SPIRALLY
SPIRALS
SPIRANT
SPIRANTS
SPIRASTER
SPIRASTERS
SPIRATED
SPIRATION
SPIRATIONS
SPIRE
SPIREA
SPIREAS
SPIRED
SPIRELESS
SPIRELET
SPIRELETS
SPIREM
SPIREME
SPIREMES
SPIREMS
SPIRES
SPIREWISE
SPIRIC
SPIRICS
SPIRIER
SPIRIEST
SPIRIFEROUS
SPIRILLA
SPIRILLAR
SPIRILLOSES
SPIRILLOSIS
SPIRILLUM
SPIRING
SPIRIT
SPIRITED
SPIRITEDLY
SPIRITEDNESS
SPIRITEDNESSES
SPIRITFUL
SPIRITING
SPIRITINGS

SPIRITISM
SPIRITISMS
SPIRITIST
SPIRITISTIC
SPIRITISTS
SPIRITLESS
SPIRITLESSLY
SPIRITLESSNESS
SPIRITOSO
SPIRITOUS
SPIRITOUSNESS
SPIRITOUSNESSES
SPIRITS
SPIRITUAL
SPIRITUALISE
SPIRITUALISED
SPIRITUALISER
SPIRITUALISERS
SPIRITUALISES
SPIRITUALISING
SPIRITUALISM
SPIRITUALISMS
SPIRITUALIST
SPIRITUALISTIC
SPIRITUALISTS
SPIRITUALITIES
SPIRITUALITY
SPIRITUALIZE
SPIRITUALIZED
SPIRITUALIZER
SPIRITUALIZERS
SPIRITUALIZES
SPIRITUALIZING
SPIRITUALLY
SPIRITUALNESS
SPIRITUALNESSES
SPIRITUALS
SPIRITUALTIES
SPIRITUALTY
SPIRITUEL
SPIRITUELLE
SPIRITUOSITIES
SPIRITUOSITY
SPIRITUOUS
SPIRITUOUSNESS
SPIRITUS
SPIRITUSES
SPIRITY
SPIRKETTING
SPIRKETTINGS
SPIRLING
SPIRLINGS
SPIROCHAETAEMIA
SPIROCHAETE
SPIROCHAETES
SPIROCHAETOSES
SPIROCHAETOSIS

SPIROCHETAL
SPIROCHETE
SPIROCHETES
SPIROCHETOSES
SPIROCHETOSIS
SPIROGRAM
SPIROGRAMS
SPIROGRAPH
SPIROGRAPHIC
SPIROGRAPHIES
SPIROGRAPHS
SPIROGRAPHY
SPIROGYRA
SPIROGYRAS
SPIROID
SPIROMETER
SPIROMETERS
SPIROMETRIC
SPIROMETRIES
SPIROMETRY
SPIRONOLACTONE
SPIRONOLACTONES
SPIROPHORE
SPIROPHORES
SPIRT
SPIRTED
SPIRTING
SPIRTLE
SPIRTLES
SPIRTS
SPIRULA
SPIRULAE
SPIRULAS
SPIRULINA
SPIRULINAS
SPIRY
SPISSITUDE
SPISSITUDES
SPIT
SPITAL
SPITALS
SPITBALL
SPITBALLS
SPITCHCOCK
SPITCHCOCKED
SPITCHCOCKING
SPITCHCOCKS
SPITCHER
SPITE
SPITED
SPITEFUL
SPITEFULLER
SPITEFULLEST
SPITEFULLY
SPITEFULNESS
SPITEFULNESSES
SPITES

SPITFIRE	SPLATCHES	SPLENECTOMY	SPLODGE
SPITFIRES	SPLATCHING	SPLENETIC	SPLODGED
SPITING	SPLATS	SPLENETICAL	SPLODGES
SPITS	SPLATTED	SPLENETICALLY	SPLODGIER
SPITSTICKER	SPLATTER	SPLENETICS	SPLODGIEST
SPITSTICKERS	SPLATTERED	SPLENIA	SPLODGILY
SPITTED	SPLATTERING	SPLENIAL	SPLODGINESS
SPITTEN	SPLATTERPUNK	SPLENIC	SPLODGINESSES
SPITTER	SPLATTERPUNKS	SPLENII	SPLODGING
SPITTERS	SPLATTERPUNKY	SPLENISATION	SPLODGY
SPITTING	SPLATTERS	SPLENISATIONS	SPLOOSH
SPITTINGS	SPLATTING	SPLENITIS	SPLOOSHED
SPITTLE	SPLATTINGS	SPLENITISES	SPLOOSHES
SPITTLEBUG	SPLAY	SPLENIUM	SPLOOSHING
SPITTLEBUGS	SPLAYED	SPLENIUMS	SPLORE
SPITTLES	SPLAYFEET	SPLENIUS	SPLORES
SPITTOON	SPLAYFOOT	SPLENIUSES	SPLOSH
SPITTOONS	SPLAYFOOTED	SPLENIZATION	SPLOSHED
SPITZ	SPLAYFOOTEDLY	SPLENIZATIONS	SPLOSHES
SPITZES	SPLAYING	SPLENOMEGALIES	SPLOSHING
SPIV	SPLAYS	SPLENOMEGALY	SPLOTCH
SPIVS	SPLEEN	SPLENT	SPLOTCHED
SPIVVERIES	SPLEENFUL	SPLENTS	SPLOTCHES
SPIVVERY	SPLEENFULLY	SPLEUCHAN	SPLOTCHIER
SPIVVIER	SPLEENIER	SPLEUCHANS	SPLOTCHIEST
SPIVVIEST	SPLEENIEST	SPLICE	SPLOTCHILY
SPIVVY	SPLEENISH	SPLICED	SPLOTCHINESS
SPLAKE	SPLEENLESS	SPLICER	SPLOTCHINESSES
SPLAKES	SPLEENS	SPLICERS	SPLOTCHING
SPLANCHNIC	SPLEENSTONE	SPLICES	SPLOTCHY
SPLANCHNOCELE	SPLEENSTONES	SPLICING	SPLURGE
SPLANCHNOCELES	SPLEENWORT	SPLIFF	SPLURGED
SPLANCHNOLOGIES	SPLEENWORTS	SPLIFFS	SPLURGER
SPLANCHNOLOGY	SPLEENY	SPLINE	SPLURGERS
SPLASH	SPLENATIVE	SPLINED	SPLURGES
SPLASHBACK	SPLENDENT	SPLINES	SPLURGIER
SPLASHBACKS	SPLENDID	SPLINING	SPLURGIEST
SPLASHBOARD	SPLENDIDER	SPLINT	SPLURGING
SPLASHBOARDS	SPLENDIDEST	SPLINTED	SPLURGY
SPLASHDOWN	SPLENDIDIOUS	SPLINTER	SPLUTTER
SPLASHDOWNS	SPLENDIDLY	SPLINTERED	SPLUTTERED
SPLASHED	SPLENDIDNESS	SPLINTERIER	SPLUTTERER
SPLASHER	SPLENDIDNESSES	SPLINTERIEST	SPLUTTERERS
SPLASHERS	SPLENDIDOUS	SPLINTERING	SPLUTTERING
SPLASHES	SPLENDIFEROUS	SPLINTERS	SPLUTTERINGLY
SPLASHIER	SPLENDIFEROUSLY	SPLINTERY	SPLUTTERINGS
SPLASHIEST	SPLENDOR	SPLINTING	SPLUTTERS
SPLASHILY	SPLENDOROUS	SPLINTLIKE	SPLUTTERY
SPLASHINESS	SPLENDORS	SPLINTS	SPODE
SPLASHINESSES	SPLENDOUR	SPLINTWOOD	SPODES
SPLASHING	SPLENDOURS	SPLINTWOODS	SPODIUM
SPLASHINGS	SPLENDROUS	SPLIT	SPODIUMS
SPLASHPROOF	SPLENECTOMIES	SPLITS	SPODOGRAM
SPLASHY	SPLENECTOMIZE	SPLITTED	SPODOGRAMS
SPLAT	SPLENECTOMIZED	SPLITTER	SPODOMANCIES
SPLATCH	SPLENECTOMIZES	SPLITTERS	SPODOMANCY
SPLATCHED	SPLENECTOMIZING	SPLITTING	SPODOMANTIC

SPODUMENE
SPODUMENES
SPOFFISH
SPOFFY
SPOIL
SPOILABLE
SPOILAGE
SPOILAGES
SPOILED
SPOILER
SPOILERS
SPOILFIVE
SPOILFIVES
SPOILFUL
SPOILING
SPOILS
SPOILSMAN
SPOILSMEN
SPOILSPORT
SPOILSPORTS
SPOILT
SPOKE
SPOKED
SPOKEN
SPOKES
SPOKESHAVE
SPOKESHAVES
SPOKESMAN
SPOKESMANSHIP
SPOKESMANSHIPS
SPOKESMEN
SPOKESPEOPLE
SPOKESPERSON
SPOKESPERSONS
SPOKESWOMAN
SPOKESWOMEN
SPOKEWISE
SPOKING
SPOLIATE
SPOLIATED
SPOLIATES
SPOLIATING
SPOLIATION
SPOLIATIONS
SPOLIATIVE
SPOLIATOR
SPOLIATORS
SPOLIATORY
SPONDAIC
SPONDAICAL
SPONDAICS
SPONDEE
SPONDEES
SPONDOOLICKS
SPONDULICKS
SPONDULIX
SPONDYL

SPONDYLITIC
SPONDYLITICS
SPONDYLITIS
SPONDYLITISES
SPONDYLOLYSES
SPONDYLOLYSIS
SPONDYLOSES
SPONDYLOSIS
SPONDYLOUS
SPONDYLS
SPONGE
SPONGEABLE
SPONGEBAG
SPONGEBAGS
SPONGED
SPONGELIKE
SPONGEOUS
SPONGER
SPONGERS
SPONGES
SPONGEWARE
SPONGEWARES
SPONGEWOOD
SPONGEWOODS
SPONGICOLOUS
SPONGIER
SPONGIEST
SPONGIFORM
SPONGILY
SPONGIN
SPONGINESS
SPONGINESSES
SPONGING
SPONGINS
SPONGIOBLAST
SPONGIOBLASTIC
SPONGIOBLASTS
SPONGIOSE
SPONGIOUS
SPONGOID
SPONGOLOGIES
SPONGOLOGIST
SPONGOLOGISTS
SPONGOLOGY
SPONGY
SPONSAL
SPONSALIA
SPONSIBLE
SPONSING
SPONSINGS
SPONSION
SPONSIONAL
SPONSIONS
SPONSON
SPONSONS
SPONSOR
SPONSORED

SPONSORIAL
SPONSORING
SPONSORS
SPONSORSHIP
SPONSORSHIPS
SPONTANEITIES
SPONTANEITY
SPONTANEOUS
SPONTANEOUSLY
SPONTANEOUSNESS
SPONTOON
SPONTOONS
SPOOF
SPOOFED
SPOOFER
SPOOFERIES
SPOOFERS
SPOOFERY
SPOOFING
SPOOFS
SPOOFY
SPOOK
SPOOKED
SPOOKERIES
SPOOKERY
SPOOKIER
SPOOKIEST
SPOOKILY
SPOOKINESS
SPOOKINESSES
SPOOKING
SPOOKISH
SPOOKS
SPOOKY
SPOOL
SPOOLED
SPOOLER
SPOOLERS
SPOOLING
SPOOLINGS
SPOOLS
SPOOM
SPOOMED
SPOOMING
SPOOMS
SPOON
SPOONBAIT
SPOONBAITS
SPOONBILL
SPOONBILLS
SPOONDRIFT
SPOONDRIFTS
SPOONED
SPOONERISM
SPOONERISMS
SPOONEY
SPOONEYS

SPOONFED
SPOONFUL
SPOONFULS
SPOONHOOKS
SPOONIER
SPOONIES
SPOONIEST
SPOONILY
SPOONING
SPOONS
SPOONSFUL
SPOONWAYS
SPOONWISE
SPOONY
SPOOR
SPOORED
SPOORER
SPOORERS
SPOORING
SPOORS
SPOOT
SPOOTS
SPORADIC
SPORADICAL
SPORADICALLY
SPORADICALNESS
SPORAL
SPORANGIA
SPORANGIAL
SPORANGIOLA
SPORANGIOLE
SPORANGIOLES
SPORANGIOLUM
SPORANGIOPHORE
SPORANGIOPHORES
SPORANGIOSPORE
SPORANGIOSPORES
SPORANGIUM
SPORE
SPORED
SPORES
SPORICIDAL
SPORICIDE
SPORICIDES
SPORIDESM
SPORIDESMS
SPORIDIA
SPORIDIAL
SPORIDIUM
SPORING
SPOROCARP
SPOROCARPS
SPOROCYST
SPOROCYSTIC
SPOROCYSTS
SPOROCYTE
SPOROCYTES

SPOROGENESES	SPORTIF	SPOTLIGHTS	SPRAICKLES
SPOROGENESIS	SPORTILY	SPOTLIT	SPRAICKLING
SPOROGENIC	SPORTINESS	SPOTS	SPRAID
SPOROGENIES	SPORTINESSES	SPOTTABLE	SPRAIN
SPOROGENOUS	SPORTING	SPOTTED	SPRAINED
SPOROGENY	SPORTINGLY	SPOTTEDNESS	SPRAINING
SPOROGONIA	SPORTIVE	SPOTTEDNESSES	SPRAINS
SPOROGONIAL	SPORTIVELY	SPOTTER	SPRAINT
SPOROGONIC	SPORTIVENESS	SPOTTERS	SPRAINTS
SPOROGONIES	SPORTIVENESSES	SPOTTIE	SPRANG
SPOROGONIUM	SPORTLESS	SPOTTIER	SPRANGLE
SPOROGONY	SPORTS	SPOTTIES	SPRANGLED
SPOROID	SPORTSCAST	SPOTTIEST	SPRANGLES
SPOROPHORE	SPORTSCASTER	SPOTTILY	SPRANGLING
SPOROPHORES	SPORTSCASTERS	SPOTTINESS	SPRANGS
SPOROPHORIC	SPORTSCASTS	SPOTTINESSES	SPRAT
SPOROPHOROUS	SPORTSMAN	SPOTTING	SPRATS
SPOROPHYL	SPORTSMANLIKE	SPOTTINGS	SPRATTLE
SPOROPHYLL	SPORTSMANLY	SPOTTY	SPRATTLED
SPOROPHYLLS	SPORTSMANSHIP	SPOUSAGE	SPRATTLES
SPOROPHYLS	SPORTSMANSHIPS	SPOUSAGES	SPRATTLING
SPOROPHYTE	SPORTSMEN	SPOUSAL	SPRAUCHLE
SPOROPHYTES	SPORTSPEOPLE	SPOUSALLY	SPRAUCHLED
SPOROPHYTIC	SPORTSPERSON	SPOUSALS	SPRAUCHLES
SPOROPOLLENIN	SPORTSPERSONS	SPOUSE	SPRAUCHLING
SPOROPOLLENINS	SPORTSWEAR	SPOUSED	SPRAUNCIER
SPOROTRICHOSES	SPORTSWEARS	SPOUSELESS	SPRAUNCIEST
SPOROTRICHOSIS	SPORTSWOMAN	SPOUSES	SPRAUNCY
SPOROZOA	SPORTSWOMEN	SPOUSING	SPRAWL
SPOROZOAN	SPORTSWRITER	SPOUT	SPRAWLED
SPOROZOANS	SPORTSWRITERS	SPOUTED	SPRAWLER
SPOROZOITE	SPORTSWRITING	SPOUTER	SPRAWLERS
SPOROZOITES	SPORTSWRITINGS	SPOUTERS	SPRAWLIER
SPOROZOON	SPORTY	SPOUTIER	SPRAWLIEST
SPORRAN	SPORULAR	SPOUTING	SPRAWLING
SPORRANS	SPORULATE	SPOUTINGS	SPRAWLS
SPORT	SPORULATED	SPOUTLESS	SPRAWLY
SPORTABILITIES	SPORULATES	SPOUTS	SPRAY
SPORTABILITY	SPORULATING	SPOUTY	SPRAYED
SPORTABLE	SPORULATION	SPRACHGEFUHL	SPRAYER
SPORTANCE	SPORULATIONS	SPRACHGEFUHLS	SPRAYERS
SPORTANCES	SPORULATIVE	SPRACK	SPRAYEY
SPORTCASTER	SPORULE	SPRACKLE	SPRAYIER
SPORTCASTERS	SPORULES	SPRACKLED	SPRAYIEST
SPORTED	SPOSH	SPRACKLES	SPRAYING
SPORTER	SPOSHES	SPRACKLING	SPRAYS
SPORTERS	SPOSHIER	SPRAD	SPREAD
SPORTFISHERMAN	SPOSHIEST	SPRADDLE	SPREADABILITIES
SPORTFISHERMEN	SPOSHY	SPRADDLED	SPREADABILITY
SPORTFISHING	SPOT	SPRADDLES	SPREADABLE
SPORTFISHINGS	SPOTLESS	SPRADDLING	SPREADER
SPORTFUL	SPOTLESSLY	SPRAG	SPREADERS
SPORTFULLY	SPOTLESSNESS	SPRAGGED	SPREADING
SPORTFULNESS	SPOTLESSNESSES	SPRAGGING	SPREADINGLY
SPORTFULNESSES	SPOTLIGHT	SPRAGS	SPREADINGS
SPORTIER	SPOTLIGHTED	SPRAICKLED	SPREADS
SPORTIEST	SPOTLIGHTING		SPREADSHEET

SPREADSHEETS	SPRIGHTFUL	SPRINGTIME	SPRUCENESS
SPREAGH	SPRIGHTFULLY	SPRINGTIMES	SPRUCENESSES
SPREAGHERIES	SPRIGHTFULNESS	SPRINGWATER	SPRUCER
SPREAGHERY	SPRIGHTING	SPRINGWATERS	SPRUCES
SPREAGHS	SPRIGHTLESS	SPRINGWOOD	SPRUCEST
SPREATHE	SPRIGHTLIER	SPRINGWOODS	SPRUCIER
SPREATHED	SPRIGHTLIEST	SPRINGWORT	SPRUCIEST
SPREATHES	SPRIGHTLINESS	SPRINGWORTS	SPRUCING
SPREATHING	SPRIGHTLINESSES	SPRINGY	SPRUCY
SPREAZE	SPRIGHTLY	SPRINKLE	SPRUE
SPREAZED	SPRIGHTS	SPRINKLED	SPRUES
SPREAZES	SPRIGS	SPRINKLER	SPRUG
SPREAZING	SPRING	SPRINKLERED	SPRUGS
SPRECHERIES	SPRINGAL	SPRINKLERS	SPRUIK
SPRECHERY	SPRINGALD	SPRINKLES	SPRUIKED
SPRECHGESANG	SPRINGALDS	SPRINKLING	SPRUIKER
SPRECHGESANGS	SPRINGALS	SPRINKLINGS	SPRUIKERS
SPRECHSTIMME	SPRINGBOARD	SPRINT	SPRUIKING
SPRECHSTIMMES	SPRINGBOARDS	SPRINTED	SPRUIKS
SPRECKLED	SPRINGBOK	SPRINTER	SPRUIT
SPRED	SPRINGBOKS	SPRINTERS	SPRUITS
SPREDD	SPRINGBUCK	SPRINTING	SPRUNG
SPREDDE	SPRINGBUCKS	SPRINTINGS	SPRUSH
SPREDDEN	SPRINGE	SPRINTS	SPRUSHED
SPREDDES	SPRINGED	SPRIT	SPRUSHES
SPREDDING	SPRINGEING	SPRITE	SPRUSHING
SPREDDS	SPRINGER	SPRITEFUL	SPRY
SPREDS	SPRINGERS	SPRITELIER	SPRYER
SPREE	SPRINGES	SPRITELIEST	SPRYEST
SPREED	SPRINGHAAS	SPRITELY	SPRYLY
SPREEING	SPRINGHALT	SPRITES	SPRYNESS
SPREES	SPRINGHALTS	SPRITS	SPRYNESSES
SPREETHE	SPRINGHASE	SPRITSAIL	SPUD
SPREETHED	SPRINGHEAD	SPRITSAILS	SPUDDED
SPREETHES	SPRINGHEADS	SPRITZ	SPUDDER
SPREETHING	SPRINGHOUSE	SPRITZED	SPUDDERS
SPREEZE	SPRINGHOUSES	SPRITZER	SPUDDIER
SPREEZED	SPRINGIER	SPRITZERS	SPUDDIEST
SPREEZES	SPRINGIEST	SPRITZES	SPUDDING
SPREEZING	SPRINGILY	SPRITZIG	SPUDDINGS
SPREKELIA	SPRINGINESS	SPRITZIGS	SPUDDLE
SPREKELIAS	SPRINGINESSES	SPRITZING	SPUDDLES
SPRENT	SPRINGING	SPROCKET	SPUDDY
SPREW	SPRINGINGS	SPROCKETS	SPUDS
SPREWS	SPRINGKEEPER	SPROD	SPUE
SPRIER	SPRINGKEEPERS	SPRODS	SPUED
SPRIEST	SPRINGLE	SPROG	SPUEING
SPRIG	SPRINGLES	SPROGS	SPUER
SPRIGGED	SPRINGLESS	SPRONG	SPUERS
SPRIGGER	SPRINGLET	SPROUT	SPUES
SPRIGGERS	SPRINGLETS	SPROUTED	SPUG
SPRIGGIER	SPRINGLIKE	SPROUTING	SPUGGIES
SPRIGGIEST	SPRINGS	SPROUTINGS	SPUGGY
SPRIGGING	SPRINGTAIL	SPROUTS	SPUGS
SPRIGGY	SPRINGTAILS	SPRUCE	SPUILZIE
SPRIGHT	SPRINGTIDE	SPRUCED	SPUILZIED
SPRIGHTED	SPRINGTIDES	SPRUCELY	SPUILZIEING

SPUILZIES
SPUING
SPULE
SPULEBANES
SPULEBLADES
SPULEBONES
SPULES
SPULYE
SPULYED
SPULYEING
SPULYES
SPULYIE
SPULYIED
SPULYIEING
SPULYIES
SPULZIE
SPULZIED
SPULZIEING
SPULZIES
SPUMANTE
SPUMANTES
SPUME
SPUMED
SPUMES
SPUMESCENCE
SPUMESCENCES
SPUMESCENT
SPUMIER
SPUMIEST
SPUMING
SPUMONE
SPUMONES
SPUMONI
SPUMONIS
SPUMOUS
SPUMY
SPUN
SPUNBONDED
SPUNGE
SPUNGES
SPUNK
SPUNKED
SPUNKIE
SPUNKIER
SPUNKIES
SPUNKIEST
SPUNKILY
SPUNKINESS
SPUNKINESSES
SPUNKING
SPUNKS
SPUNKY
SPUNYARN
SPUNYARNS
SPUR
SPURGALL
SPURGALLED

SPURGALLING
SPURGALLS
SPURGE
SPURGES
SPURIAE
SPURIOSITIES
SPURIOSITY
SPURIOUS
SPURIOUSLY
SPURIOUSNESS
SPURIOUSNESSES
SPURLESS
SPURLING
SPURLINGS
SPURN
SPURNE
SPURNED
SPURNER
SPURNERS
SPURNES
SPURNING
SPURNINGS
SPURNS
SPURRED
SPURRER
SPURRERS
SPURREY
SPURREYS
SPURRIER
SPURRIERS
SPURRIES
SPURRIEST
SPURRING
SPURRINGS
SPURRY
SPURS
SPURT
SPURTED
SPURTING
SPURTLE
SPURTLES
SPURTS
SPURWAY
SPURWAYS
SPUTA
SPUTNIK
SPUTNIKS
SPUTTER
SPUTTERED
SPUTTERER
SPUTTERERS
SPUTTERING
SPUTTERINGLY
SPUTTERINGS
SPUTTERS
SPUTTERY
SPUTUM

SPY
SPYAL
SPYALS
SPYGLASS
SPYGLASSES
SPYHOLE
SPYHOLES
SPYING
SPYINGS
SPYMASTER
SPYMASTERS
SPYPLANE
SPYPLANES
SPYRE
SPYRES
SQUAB
SQUABASH
SQUABASHED
SQUABASHER
SQUABASHERS
SQUABASHES
SQUABASHING
SQUABBED
SQUABBER
SQUABBEST
SQUABBIER
SQUABBIEST
SQUABBING
SQUABBISH
SQUABBLE
SQUABBLED
SQUABBLER
SQUABBLERS
SQUABBLES
SQUABBLING
SQUABBY
SQUABS
SQUACCO
SQUACCOS
SQUAD
SQUADDED
SQUADDIE
SQUADDIES
SQUADDING
SQUADDY
SQUADRON
SQUADRONAL
SQUADRONE
SQUADRONED
SQUADRONES
SQUADRONING
SQUADRONS
SQUADS
SQUAIL
SQUAILED
SQUAILER
SQUAILERS

SQUAILING
SQUAILINGS
SQUAILS
SQUALENE
SQUALENES
SQUALID
SQUALIDER
SQUALIDEST
SQUALIDITIES
SQUALIDITY
SQUALIDLY
SQUALIDNESS
SQUALIDNESSES
SQUALL
SQUALLED
SQUALLER
SQUALLERS
SQUALLIER
SQUALLIEST
SQUALLING
SQUALLINGS
SQUALLISH
SQUALLISHNESS
SQUALLS
SQUALLY
SQUALOID
SQUALOR
SQUALORS
SQUAMA
SQUAMAE
SQUAMATE
SQUAMATION
SQUAMATIONS
SQUAME
SQUAMELLA
SQUAMELLAS
SQUAMES
SQUAMIFORM
SQUAMOSAL
SQUAMOSALS
SQUAMOSE
SQUAMOSELY
SQUAMOSENESS
SQUAMOSITIES
SQUAMOSITY
SQUAMOUS
SQUAMOUSLY
SQUAMOUSNESS
SQUAMULA
SQUAMULAS
SQUAMULE
SQUAMULES
SQUAMULOSE
SQUANDER
SQUANDERED
SQUANDERER
SQUANDERERS

SQUANDERING
SQUANDERINGLY
SQUANDERINGS
SQUANDERMANIA
SQUANDERMANIAS
SQUANDERS
SQUARE
SQUARED
SQUAREHEAD
SQUAREHEADS
SQUARELY
SQUARENESS
SQUARENESSES
SQUARER
SQUARERS
SQUARES
SQUAREST
SQUAREWISE
SQUARIAL
SQUARIALS
SQUARING
SQUARINGS
SQUARISH
SQUARISHLY
SQUARISHNESS
SQUARISHNESSES
SQUARROSE
SQUARSON
SQUARSONAGE
SQUARSONAGES
SQUARSONS
SQUASH
SQUASHABLE
SQUASHED
SQUASHER
SQUASHERS
SQUASHES
SQUASHIER
SQUASHIEST
SQUASHILY
SQUASHINESS
SQUASHINESSES
SQUASHING
SQUASHY
SQUAT
SQUATLY
SQUATNESS
SQUATNESSES
SQUATS
SQUATTED
SQUATTER
SQUATTERED
SQUATTERING
SQUATTERS
SQUATTEST
SQUATTIER
SQUATTIEST

SQUATTINESS
SQUATTINESSES
SQUATTING
SQUATTLE
SQUATTLED
SQUATTLES
SQUATTLING
SQUATTOCRACIES
SQUATTOCRACY
SQUATTY
SQUAW
SQUAWFISH
SQUAWFISHES
SQUAWK
SQUAWKED
SQUAWKER
SQUAWKERS
SQUAWKIER
SQUAWKIEST
SQUAWKING
SQUAWKINGS
SQUAWKS
SQUAWKY
SQUAWMAN
SQUAWMEN
SQUAWROOT
SQUAWROOTS
SQUAWS
SQUEAK
SQUEAKED
SQUEAKER
SQUEAKERIES
SQUEAKERS
SQUEAKERY
SQUEAKIER
SQUEAKIEST
SQUEAKILY
SQUEAKINESS
SQUEAKINESSES
SQUEAKING
SQUEAKINGLY
SQUEAKINGS
SQUEAKS
SQUEAKY
SQUEAL
SQUEALED
SQUEALER
SQUEALERS
SQUEALING
SQUEALINGS
SQUEALS
SQUEAMISH
SQUEAMISHLY
SQUEAMISHNESS
SQUEAMISHNESSES
SQUEEGEE
SQUEEGEED

SQUEEGEEING
SQUEEGEES
SQUEEZABILITIES
SQUEEZABILITY
SQUEEZABLE
SQUEEZE
SQUEEZED
SQUEEZER
SQUEEZERS
SQUEEZES
SQUEEZIER
SQUEEZIEST
SQUEEZING
SQUEEZINGS
SQUEEZY
SQUEG
SQUEGGED
SQUEGGER
SQUEGGERS
SQUEGGING
SQUEGGINGS
SQUEGS
SQUELCH
SQUELCHED
SQUELCHER
SQUELCHERS
SQUELCHES
SQUELCHIER
SQUELCHIEST
SQUELCHING
SQUELCHINGS
SQUELCHY
SQUETEAGUE
SQUETEAGUES
SQUIB
SQUIBBED
SQUIBBING
SQUIBBINGS
SQUIBS
SQUID
SQUIDDED
SQUIDDING
SQUIDGE
SQUIDGED
SQUIDGES
SQUIDGIER
SQUIDGIEST
SQUIDGING
SQUIDGY
SQUIDS
SQUIER
SQUIERS
SQUIFF
SQUIFFED
SQUIFFER
SQUIFFERS
SQUIFFIER

SQUIFFIEST
SQUIFFY
SQUIGGLE
SQUIGGLED
SQUIGGLER
SQUIGGLERS
SQUIGGLES
SQUIGGLIER
SQUIGGLIEST
SQUIGGLING
SQUIGGLY
SQUILGEE
SQUILGEED
SQUILGEEING
SQUILGEES
SQUILL
SQUILLA
SQUILLAE
SQUILLAS
SQUILLION
SQUILLIONS
SQUILLS
SQUINANCIES
SQUINANCY
SQUINCH
SQUINCHED
SQUINCHES
SQUINCHING
SQUINIED
SQUINIES
SQUINNIED
SQUINNIER
SQUINNIES
SQUINNIEST
SQUINNY
SQUINNYING
SQUINT
SQUINTED
SQUINTER
SQUINTERS
SQUINTEST
SQUINTIER
SQUINTIEST
SQUINTING
SQUINTINGLY
SQUINTINGS
SQUINTS
SQUINTY
SQUINY
SQUINYING
SQUIRAGE
SQUIRAGES
SQUIRALITIES
SQUIRALITY
SQUIRALTIES
SQUIRALTY
SQUIRARCH

SQUIRARCHAL
SQUIRARCHICAL
SQUIRARCHIES
SQUIRARCHS
SQUIRARCHY
SQUIRE
SQUIREAGE
SQUIREAGES
SQUIREARCH
SQUIREARCHAL
SQUIREARCHICAL
SQUIREARCHIES
SQUIREARCHS
SQUIREARCHY
SQUIRED
SQUIREDOM
SQUIREDOMS
SQUIREEN
SQUIREENS
SQUIREHOOD
SQUIREHOODS
SQUIRELIKE
SQUIRELING
SQUIRELINGS
SQUIRELY
SQUIRES
SQUIRESHIP
SQUIRESHIPS
SQUIRESS
SQUIRESSES
SQUIRING
SQUIRISH
SQUIRM
SQUIRMED
SQUIRMER
SQUIRMERS
SQUIRMIER
SQUIRMIEST
SQUIRMING
SQUIRMINGLY
SQUIRMS
SQUIRMY
SQUIRR
SQUIRRED
SQUIRREL
SQUIRRELED
SQUIRRELFISH
SQUIRRELFISHES
SQUIRRELING
SQUIRRELLED
SQUIRRELLING
SQUIRRELLY
SQUIRRELS
SQUIRRELY
SQUIRRING
SQUIRRS
SQUIRT

SQUIRTED
SQUIRTER
SQUIRTERS
SQUIRTING
SQUIRTINGS
SQUIRTS
SQUISH
SQUISHED
SQUISHES
SQUISHIER
SQUISHIEST
SQUISHINESS
SQUISHINESSES
SQUISHING
SQUISHY
SQUIT
SQUITCH
SQUITCHES
SQUITS
SQUIZ
SQUIZZES
SQUOOSH
SQUOOSHED
SQUOOSHES
SQUOOSHIER
SQUOOSHIEST
SQUOOSHING
SQUOOSHY
SQUUSH
SQUUSHED
SQUUSHES
SQUUSHING
SRADDHA
SRADDHAS
SRADHA
SRADHAS
SRI
SRIS
ST
STAB
STABBED
STABBER
STABBERS
STABBING
STABBINGLY
STABBINGS
STABILATE
STABILATES
STABILE
STABILES
STABILISATION
STABILISATIONS
STABILISATOR
STABILISATORS
STABILISE
STABILISED
STABILISER

STABILISERS
STABILISES
STABILISING
STABILITIES
STABILITY
STABILIZATION
STABILIZATIONS
STABILIZATOR
STABILIZATORS
STABILIZE
STABILIZED
STABILIZER
STABILIZERS
STABILIZES
STABILIZING
STABLE
STABLEBOY
STABLEBOYS
STABLED
STABLEMAN
STABLEMATE
STABLEMATES
STABLEMEN
STABLENESS
STABLENESSES
STABLER
STABLERS
STABLES
STABLEST
STABLING
STABLINGS
STABLISH
STABLISHED
STABLISHES
STABLISHING
STABLISHMENT
STABLISHMENTS
STABLY
STABS
STACCATI
STACCATISSIMO
STACCATO
STACCATOS
STACHYS
STACHYSES
STACK
STACKABLE
STACKED
STACKER
STACKERS
STACKET
STACKETS
STACKING
STACKINGS
STACKROOM
STACKROOMS
STACKS

STACKUP
STACKUPS
STACKYARD
STACKYARDS
STACTE
STACTES
STACTOMETER
STACTOMETERS
STADDA
STADDAS
STADDLE
STADDLES
STADDLESTONE
STADDLESTONES
STADE
STADES
STADHOLDER
STADHOLDERATE
STADHOLDERATES
STADHOLDERS
STADHOLDERSHIP
STADHOLDERSHIPS
STADIA
STADIAL
STADIALS
STADIAS
STADIOMETER
STADIOMETERS
STADIOMETRIC
STADIUM
STADIUMS
STADTHOLDER
STADTHOLDERATE
STADTHOLDERATES
STADTHOLDERS
STADTHOLDERSHIP
STAFF
STAFFAGE
STAFFAGES
STAFFED
STAFFER
STAFFERS
STAFFING
STAFFMAN
STAFFMEN
STAFFROOM
STAFFROOMS
STAFFS
STAG
STAGE
STAGEABLE
STAGECOACH
STAGECOACHES
STAGECOACHING
STAGECOACHINGS
STAGECOACHMAN
STAGECOACHMEN

STAGECRAFT
STAGECRAFTS
STAGED
STAGEFUL
STAGEFULS
STAGEHAND
STAGEHANDS
STAGELIKE
STAGER
STAGERIES
STAGERS
STAGERY
STAGES
STAGESTRUCK
STAGEY
STAGFLATION
STAGFLATIONARY
STAGFLATIONS
STAGGARD
STAGGARDS
STAGGART
STAGGARTS
STAGGED
STAGGER
STAGGERBUSH
STAGGERBUSHES
STAGGERED
STAGGERER
STAGGERERS
STAGGERING
STAGGERINGLY
STAGGERINGS
STAGGERS
STAGGERY
STAGGIE
STAGGIER
STAGGIES
STAGGIEST
STAGGING
STAGGY
STAGHORN
STAGHORNS
STAGHOUND
STAGHOUNDS
STAGIER
STAGIEST
STAGILY
STAGINESS
STAGINESSES
STAGING
STAGINGS
STAGNANCE
STAGNANCIES
STAGNANCY
STAGNANT
STAGNANTLY
STAGNATE

STAGNATED
STAGNATES
STAGNATING
STAGNATION
STAGNATIONS
STAGS
STAGY
STAID
STAIDER
STAIDEST
STAIDLY
STAIDNESS
STAIDNESSES
STAIG
STAIGS
STAIN
STAINABILITIES
STAINABILITY
STAINABLE
STAINED
STAINER
STAINERS
STAINING
STAININGS
STAINLESS
STAINLESSES
STAINLESSLY
STAINLESSNESS
STAINLESSNESSES
STAINPROOF
STAINS
STAIR
STAIRCASE
STAIRCASED
STAIRCASES
STAIRCASING
STAIRCASINGS
STAIRED
STAIRFOOT
STAIRFOOTS
STAIRHEAD
STAIRHEADS
STAIRLIFT
STAIRLIFTS
STAIRS
STAIRWAY
STAIRWAYS
STAIRWELL
STAIRWELLS
STAIRWISE
STAIRWORK
STAIRWORKS
STAITH
STAITHE
STAITHES
STAITHS
STAKE

STAKED
STAKEHOLDER
STAKEHOLDERS
STAKEOUT
STAKEOUTS
STAKES
STAKHANOVISM
STAKHANOVISMS
STAKHANOVITE
STAKHANOVITES
STAKING
STAKTOMETER
STAKTOMETERS
STALACTIC
STALACTICAL
STALACTIFORM
STALACTITAL
STALACTITE
STALACTITED
STALACTITES
STALACTITIC
STALACTITICAL
STALACTITICALLY
STALACTITIFORM
STALACTITIOUS
STALAG
STALAGMITE
STALAGMITES
STALAGMITIC
STALAGMITICAL
STALAGMITICALLY
STALAGMOMETER
STALAGMOMETERS
STALAGMOMETRIES
STALAGMOMETRY
STALAGS
STALE
STALED
STALELY
STALEMATE
STALEMATED
STALEMATES
STALEMATING
STALENESS
STALENESSES
STALER
STALES
STALEST
STALING
STALK
STALKED
STALKER
STALKERS
STALKIER
STALKIEST
STALKILY
STALKINESS

STALKING
STALKINGS
STALKLESS
STALKLIKE
STALKO
STALKOES
STALKS
STALKY
STALL
STALLAGE
STALLAGES
STALLED
STALLENGER
STALLENGERS
STALLHOLDER
STALLHOLDERS
STALLING
STALLINGER
STALLINGERS
STALLINGS
STALLION
STALLIONS
STALLMAN
STALLMASTER
STALLMASTERS
STALLMEN
STALLS
STALWART
STALWARTLY
STALWARTNESS
STALWARTNESSES
STALWARTS
STALWORTH
STALWORTHS
STAMEN
STAMENED
STAMENS
STAMINA
STAMINAL
STAMINAS
STAMINATE
STAMINEAL
STAMINEOUS
STAMINIFEROUS
STAMINODE
STAMINODES
STAMINODIA
STAMINODIES
STAMINODIUM
STAMINODY
STAMINOID
STAMMEL
STAMMELS
STAMMER
STAMMERED
STAMMERER
STAMMERERS

STAMMERING
STAMMERINGLY
STAMMERINGS
STAMMERS
STAMNOI
STAMNOS
STAMP
STAMPED
STAMPEDE
STAMPEDED
STAMPEDER
STAMPEDERS
STAMPEDES
STAMPEDING
STAMPEDO
STAMPEDOED
STAMPEDOING
STAMPEDOS
STAMPER
STAMPERS
STAMPING
STAMPINGS
STAMPLESS
STAMPS
STANCE
STANCES
STANCH
STANCHABLE
STANCHED
STANCHEL
STANCHELLED
STANCHELLING
STANCHELS
STANCHER
STANCHERED
STANCHERING
STANCHERS
STANCHES
STANCHEST
STANCHING
STANCHINGS
STANCHION
STANCHIONED
STANCHIONING
STANCHIONS
STANCHLESS
STANCHLY
STANCHNESS
STANCHNESSES
STANCK
STAND
STANDARD
STANDARDBRED
STANDARDBREDS
STANDARDISATION
STANDARDISE
STANDARDISED

STANDARDISER
STANDARDISERS
STANDARDISES
STANDARDISING
STANDARDIZATION
STANDARDIZE
STANDARDIZED
STANDARDIZER
STANDARDIZERS
STANDARDIZES
STANDARDIZING
STANDARDLESS
STANDARDLY
STANDARDS
STANDAWAY
STANDBY
STANDBYS
STANDEE
STANDEES
STANDEN
STANDER
STANDERS
STANDFAST
STANDFASTS
STANDFIRST
STANDFIRSTS
STANDGALE
STANDGALES
STANDING
STANDINGS
STANDISH
STANDISHES
STANDOFF
STANDOFFISH
STANDOFFISHLY
STANDOFFISHNESS
STANDOFFS
STANDOUT
STANDOUTS
STANDOVER
STANDOVERS
STANDPAT
STANDPATTER
STANDPATTERS
STANDPATTISM
STANDPATTISMS
STANDPIPE
STANDPIPES
STANDPOINT
STANDPOINTS
STANDS
STANDSTILL
STANDSTILLS
STANDUP
STANE
STANED
STANES

STANG
STANGED
STANGING
STANGS
STANHOPE
STANHOPES
STANIEL
STANIELS
STANINE
STANINES
STANING
STANK
STANKED
STANKING
STANKS
STANNARIES
STANNARY
STANNATE
STANNATES
STANNATOR
STANNATORS
STANNEL
STANNELS
STANNIC
STANNIFEROUS
STANNITE
STANNITES
STANNOTYPE
STANNOTYPES
STANNOUS
STANNUM
STANNUMS
STANYEL
STANYELS
STANZA
STANZAED
STANZAIC
STANZAS
STANZE
STANZES
STANZO
STANZOES
STANZOS
STAP
STAPEDECTOMIES
STAPEDECTOMY
STAPEDES
STAPEDIAL
STAPEDII
STAPEDIUS
STAPEDIUSES
STAPELIA
STAPELIAS
STAPES
STAPH
STAPHS
STAPHYLINE

STAPHYLINID
STAPHYLINIDS
STAPHYLITIS
STAPHYLITISES
STAPHYLOCOCCAL
STAPHYLOCOCCI
STAPHYLOCOCCIC
STAPHYLOCOCCUS
STAPHYLOMA
STAPHYLOMAS
STAPHYLOMATA
STAPHYLOPLASIES
STAPHYLOPLASTIC
STAPHYLOPLASTY
STAPHYLORRHAPHY
STAPLE
STAPLED
STAPLER
STAPLERS
STAPLES
STAPLING
STAPPED
STAPPING
STAPPLE
STAPPLES
STAPS
STAR
STARAGEN
STARAGENS
STARBOARD
STARBOARDED
STARBOARDING
STARBOARDS
STARBURST
STARBURSTS
STARCH
STARCHED
STARCHEDLY
STARCHEDNESS
STARCHEDNESSES
STARCHER
STARCHERS
STARCHES
STARCHIER
STARCHIEST
STARCHILY
STARCHINESS
STARCHINESSES
STARCHING
STARCHLIKE
STARCHY
STARDOM
STARDOMS
STARDRIFT
STARDRIFTS
STARDUST
STARDUSTS

STARE
STARED
STARER
STARERS
STARES
STARETS
STARETSES
STARETZ
STARETZES
STARFISH
STARFISHED
STARFISHES
STARFLOWER
STARFLOWERS
STARFRUIT
STARFRUITS
STARFUCKER
STARFUCKERS
STARFUCKING
STARFUCKINGS
STARGAZE
STARGAZED
STARGAZER
STARGAZERS
STARGAZES
STARGAZING
STARGAZINGS
STARING
STARINGLY
STARINGS
STARK
STARKED
STARKEN
STARKENED
STARKENING
STARKENS
STARKER
STARKERS
STARKEST
STARKING
STARKLY
STARKNESS
STARKNESSES
STARKS
STARLESS
STARLET
STARLETS
STARLIGHT
STARLIGHTED
STARLIGHTEDNESS
STARLIGHTS
STARLIKE
STARLING
STARLINGS
STARLIT
STARMONGER
STARMONGERS

STARN
STARNED
STARNIE
STARNIES
STARNING
STARNOSE
STARNOSES
STARNS
STAROSTA
STAROSTAS
STAROSTIES
STAROSTY
STARR
STARRED
STARRIER
STARRIEST
STARRILY
STARRINESS
STARRINESSES
STARRING
STARRINGS
STARRS
STARRY
STARS
STARSHINE
STARSHINES
STARSHIP
STARSHIPS
STARSPOT
STARSPOTS
STARSTONE
STARSTONES
STARSTRUCK
START
STARTED
STARTER
STARTERS
STARTFUL
STARTING
STARTINGLY
STARTINGS
STARTISH
STARTLE
STARTLED
STARTLEMENT
STARTLEMENTS
STARTLER
STARTLERS
STARTLES
STARTLING
STARTLINGLY
STARTLINGS
STARTLISH
STARTLY
STARTS
STARTSY
STARTUP

STARTUPS
STARVATION
STARVATIONS
STARVE
STARVED
STARVELING
STARVELINGS
STARVER
STARVERS
STARVES
STARVING
STARVINGS
STARWORT
STARWORTS
STASES
STASH
STASHED
STASHES
STASHIE
STASHIES
STASHING
STASIDION
STASIDIONS
STASIES
STASIMA
STASIMON
STASIMORPHIES
STASIMORPHY
STASIS
STAT
STATABLE
STATAL
STATANT
STATE
STATEABLE
STATECRAFT
STATECRAFTS
STATED
STATEDLY
STATEHOOD
STATEHOODS
STATEHOUSE
STATEHOUSES
STATELESS
STATELESSNESS
STATELESSNESSES
STATELET
STATELETS
STATELIER
STATELIEST
STATELILY
STATELINESS
STATELINESSES
STATELY
STATEMENT
STATEMENTED
STATEMENTING

STATEMENTINGS
STATEMENTS
STATER
STATEROOM
STATEROOMS
STATERS
STATES
STATESIDE
STATESMAN
STATESMANLIKE
STATESMANLY
STATESMANSHIP
STATESMANSHIPS
STATESMEN
STATESPEOPLE
STATESPERSON
STATESPERSONS
STATESWOMAN
STATESWOMEN
STATEWIDE
STATIC
STATICAL
STATICALLY
STATICE
STATICES
STATICKY
STATICS
STATIM
STATIN
STATING
STATION
STATIONAL
STATIONARIES
STATIONARILY
STATIONARINESS
STATIONARITY
STATIONARY
STATIONED
STATIONER
STATIONERIES
STATIONERS
STATIONERY
STATIONING
STATIONMASTER
STATIONMASTERS
STATIONS
STATISM
STATISMS
STATIST
STATISTIC
STATISTICAL
STATISTICALLY
STATISTICIAN
STATISTICIANS
STATISTICS
STATISTS
STATIVE

STATIVES
STATOBLAST
STATOBLASTS
STATOCYST
STATOCYSTS
STATOLATRY
STATOLITH
STATOLITHIC
STATOLITHS
STATOR
STATORS
STATOSCOPE
STATOSCOPES
STATS
STATUA
STATUARIES
STATUARY
STATUAS
STATUE
STATUED
STATUES
STATUESQUE
STATUESQUELY
STATUESQUENESS
STATUETTE
STATUETTES
STATURE
STATURED
STATURES
STATUS
STATUSES
STATUSY
STATUTABLE
STATUTABLY
STATUTE
STATUTES
STATUTORILY
STATUTORY
STAUMREL
STAUMRELS
STAUN
STAUNCH
STAUNCHABLE
STAUNCHED
STAUNCHER
STAUNCHERS
STAUNCHES
STAUNCHEST
STAUNCHING
STAUNCHINGS
STAUNCHLESS
STAUNCHLY
STAUNCHNESS
STAUNCHNESSES
STAUNED
STAUNING
STAUNS

STAUROLITE
STAUROLITES
STAUROLITIC
STAUROSCOPE
STAUROSCOPES
STAUROSCOPIC
STAVE
STAVED
STAVES
STAVESACRE
STAVESACRES
STAVING
STAW
STAWED
STAWING
STAWS
STAY
STAYAWAY
STAYAWAYS
STAYED
STAYER
STAYERS
STAYING
STAYLESS
STAYMAKER
STAYMAKERS
STAYNE
STAYNED
STAYNES
STAYNING
STAYRE
STAYRES
STAYS
STAYSAIL
STAYSAILS
STEAD
STEADED
STEADFAST
STEADFASTLY
STEADFASTNESS
STEADFASTNESSES
STEADICAM
STEADICAMS
STEADIED
STEADIER
STEADIERS
STEADIES
STEADIEST
STEADILY
STEADINESS
STEADINESSES
STEADING
STEADINGS
STEADS
STEADY
STEADYING
STEAK

STEAKHOUSE
STEAKHOUSES
STEAKS
STEAL
STEALABLE
STEALAGE
STEALAGES
STEALE
STEALED
STEALER
STEALERS
STEALES
STEALING
STEALINGLY
STEALINGS
STEALS
STEALT
STEALTH
STEALTHED
STEALTHFUL
STEALTHFULLY
STEALTHFULNESS
STEALTHIER
STEALTHIEST
STEALTHILY
STEALTHINESS
STEALTHINESSES
STEALTHING
STEALTHINGS
STEALTHS
STEALTHY
STEAM
STEAMBOAT
STEAMBOATS
STEAMED
STEAMER
STEAMERED
STEAMERING
STEAMERS
STEAMFITTER
STEAMFITTERS
STEAMIE
STEAMIER
STEAMIES
STEAMIEST
STEAMILY
STEAMINESS
STEAMINESSES
STEAMING
STEAMINGS
STEAMROLL
STEAMROLLED
STEAMROLLER
STEAMROLLERED
STEAMROLLERING
STEAMROLLERS
STEAMROLLING

STEAMROLLS
STEAMS
STEAMSHIP
STEAMSHIPS
STEAMTIGHT
STEAMTIGHTNESS
STEAMY
STEAN
STEANE
STEANED
STEANES
STEANING
STEANINGS
STEANS
STEAPSIN
STEAPSINS
STEAR
STEARAGE
STEARAGES
STEARATE
STEARATES
STEARD
STEARE
STEARED
STEARES
STEARIC
STEARIN
STEARINE
STEARINES
STEARING
STEARINS
STEAROPTENE
STEAROPTENES
STEARS
STEARSMAN
STEARSMATE
STEARSMATES
STEARSMEN
STEATITE
STEATITES
STEATITIC
STEATOCELE
STEATOCELES
STEATOLYSIS
STEATOMA
STEATOMAS
STEATOMATOUS
STEATOPYGA
STEATOPYGIA
STEATOPYGIAS
STEATOPYGIC
STEATOPYGOUS
STEATORRHEA
STEATORRHEAS
STEATORRHOEA
STEATORRHOEAS
STEATOSES

STEATOSIS
STED
STEDD
STEDDE
STEDDED
STEDDES
STEDDIED
STEDDIES
STEDDING
STEDDS
STEDDY
STEDDYING
STEDE
STEDED
STEDES
STEDFAST
STEDFASTLY
STEDFASTNESS
STEDING
STEDS
STEED
STEEDED
STEEDIED
STEEDIES
STEEDING
STEEDS
STEEDY
STEEDYING
STEEK
STEEKED
STEEKING
STEEKIT
STEEKS
STEEL
STEELBOW
STEELBOWS
STEELD
STEELED
STEELHEAD
STEELHEADS
STEELIE
STEELIER
STEELIES
STEELIEST
STEELINESS
STEELINESSES
STEELING
STEELINGS
STEELMAKER
STEELMAKERS
STEELMAKING
STEELMAKINGS
STEELMAN
STEELMEN
STEELS
STEELWARE
STEELWARES

STEELWORK
STEELWORKER
STEELWORKERS
STEELWORKING
STEELWORKINGS
STEELWORKS
STEELY
STEELYARD
STEELYARDS
STEEM
STEEMED
STEEMING
STEEMS
STEEN
STEENBOK
STEENBOKS
STEENBRAS
STEENBRASES
STEENED
STEENING
STEENINGS
STEENKIRK
STEENKIRKS
STEENS
STEEP
STEEPED
STEEPEDOWNE
STEEPEN
STEEPENED
STEEPENING
STEEPENS
STEEPER
STEEPERS
STEEPEST
STEEPEUP
STEEPIER
STEEPIEST
STEEPINESS
STEEPINESSES
STEEPING
STEEPISH
STEEPLE
STEEPLEBUSH
STEEPLEBUSHES
STEEPLECHASE
STEEPLECHASED
STEEPLECHASER
STEEPLECHASERS
STEEPLECHASES
STEEPLECHASING
STEEPLECHASINGS
STEEPLED
STEEPLEJACK
STEEPLEJACKS
STEEPLES
STEEPLY
STEEPNESS

STEEPNESSES
STEEPS
STEEPUP
STEEPY
STEER
STEERABLE
STEERAGE
STEERAGES
STEERAGEWAY
STEERAGEWAYS
STEERED
STEERER
STEERERS
STEERIES
STEERING
STEERINGS
STEERLING
STEERLINGS
STEERS
STEERSMAN
STEERSMATE
STEERSMATES
STEERSMEN
STEERY
STEEVE
STEEVED
STEEVELY
STEEVER
STEEVES
STEEVEST
STEEVING
STEEVINGS
STEGANOGRAM
STEGANOGRAMS
STEGANOGRAPH
STEGANOGRAPHER
STEGANOGRAPHERS
STEGANOGRAPHIC
STEGANOGRAPHIES
STEGANOGRAPHIST
STEGANOGRAPHS
STEGANOGRAPHY
STEGANOPOD
STEGANOPODOUS
STEGANOPODS
STEGNOSES
STEGNOSIS
STEGNOTIC
STEGOCARPOUS
STEGOCEPHALIAN
STEGOCEPHALIANS
STEGOCEPHALOUS
STEGODON
STEGODONS
STEGODONT
STEGODONTS
STEGOMYIA

STEGOMYIAS
STEGOPHILIST
STEGOPHILISTS
STEGOSAUR
STEGOSAURIAN
STEGOSAURS
STEGOSAURUS
STEGOSAURUSES
STEIL
STEILS
STEIN
STEINBOCK
STEINBOCKS
STEINBOK
STEINBOKS
STEINED
STEINING
STEININGS
STEINKIRK
STEINKIRKS
STEINS
STELA
STELAE
STELAI
STELAR
STELE
STELENE
STELES
STELIC
STELL
STELLA
STELLAR
STELLARATOR
STELLARATORS
STELLAS
STELLATE
STELLATED
STELLATELY
STELLED
STELLERID
STELLERIDAN
STELLERIDANS
STELLERIDS
STELLIFEROUS
STELLIFIED
STELLIFIES
STELLIFORM
STELLIFY
STELLIFYING
STELLIFYINGS
STELLING
STELLION
STELLIONATE
STELLIONATES
STELLIONS
STELLS
STELLULAR

STELLULARLY
STELLULATE
STEM
STEMBOK
STEMBOKS
STEMBUCK
STEMBUCKS
STEME
STEMED
STEMES
STEMHEAD
STEMHEADS
STEMING
STEMLESS
STEMLET
STEMLETS
STEMLIKE
STEMMA
STEMMAS
STEMMATA
STEMMATIC
STEMMATOUS
STEMME
STEMMED
STEMMER
STEMMERIES
STEMMERS
STEMMERY
STEMMES
STEMMIER
STEMMIEST
STEMMING
STEMMINGS
STEMMY
STEMPEL
STEMPELS
STEMPLE
STEMPLES
STEMS
STEMSON
STEMSONS
STEMWARE
STEMWARES
STEMWINDER
STEMWINDERS
STEN
STENCH
STENCHED
STENCHES
STENCHFUL
STENCHIER
STENCHIEST
STENCHING
STENCHY
STENCIL
STENCILED
STENCILER

STENCILERS
STENCILING
STENCILLED
STENCILLER
STENCILLERS
STENCILLING
STENCILLINGS
STENCILS
STEND
STENDED
STENDING
STENDS
STENGAH
STENGAHS
STENLOCK
STENLOCKS
STENNED
STENNING
STENO
STENOBATHIC
STENOCARDIA
STENOCARDIAS
STENOCHROME
STENOCHROMES
STENOCHROMIES
STENOCHROMY
STENOGRAPH
STENOGRAPHED
STENOGRAPHER
STENOGRAPHERS
STENOGRAPHIC
STENOGRAPHICAL
STENOGRAPHIES
STENOGRAPHING
STENOGRAPHIST
STENOGRAPHISTS
STENOGRAPHS
STENOGRAPHY
STENOHALINE
STENOKIES
STENOKY
STENOPAEIC
STENOPAIC
STENOPETALOUS
STENOPHAGOUS
STENOPHAGY
STENOPHYLLOUS
STENOS
STENOSED
STENOSES
STENOSIS
STENOTHERM
STENOTHERMAL
STENOTHERMS
STENOTIC
STENOTOPIC
STENOTROPIC

STENOTYPE
STENOTYPED
STENOTYPER
STENOTYPERS
STENOTYPES
STENOTYPIC
STENOTYPIES
STENOTYPING
STENOTYPIST
STENOTYPISTS
STENOTYPY
STENS
STENT
STENTED
STENTING
STENTMASTER
STENTMASTERS
STENTOR
STENTORIAN
STENTORS
STENTOUR
STENTOURS
STENTS
STEP
STEPBAIRN
STEPBAIRNS
STEPBROTHER
STEPBROTHERS
STEPCHILD
STEPCHILDREN
STEPDAME
STEPDAMES
STEPDANCER
STEPDANCERS
STEPDANCING
STEPDANCINGS
STEPDAUGHTER
STEPDAUGHTERS
STEPFAMILIES
STEPFAMILY
STEPFATHER
STEPFATHERS
STEPHANE
STEPHANES
STEPHANITE
STEPHANITES
STEPHANOTIS
STEPHANOTISES
STEPLADDER
STEPLADDERS
STEPLIKE
STEPMOTHER
STEPMOTHERLY
STEPMOTHERS
STEPNEY
STEPNEYS
STEPPARENT

STEPPARENTING
STEPPARENTINGS
STEPPARENTS
STEPPE
STEPPED
STEPPER
STEPPERS
STEPPES
STEPPING
STEPS
STEPSISTER
STEPSISTERS
STEPSON
STEPSONS
STEPT
STEPWISE
STERADIAN
STERADIANS
STERCORACEOUS
STERCORAL
STERCORANISM
STERCORANISMS
STERCORANIST
STERCORANISTS
STERCORARIOUS
STERCORARY
STERCORATE
STERCORATED
STERCORATES
STERCORATING
STERCORICOLOUS
STERCULIA
STERCULIACEOUS
STERCULIAS
STERE
STEREO
STEREOACUITIES
STEREOACUITY
STEREOBATE
STEREOBATES
STEREOBATIC
STEREOBLIND
STEREOCARD
STEREOCARDS
STEREOCHEMICAL
STEREOCHEMISTRY
STEREOCHROMATIC
STEREOCHROME
STEREOCHROMED
STEREOCHROMES
STEREOCHROMIES
STEREOCHROMING
STEREOCHROMY
STEREOED
STEREOGNOSES
STEREOGNOSIS
STEREOGRAM

STEREOGRAMS
STEREOGRAPH
STEREOGRAPHED
STEREOGRAPHIC
STEREOGRAPHICAL
STEREOGRAPHIES
STEREOGRAPHING
STEREOGRAPHS
STEREOGRAPHY
STEREOING
STEREOISOMER
STEREOISOMERIC
STEREOISOMERISM
STEREOISOMERS
STEREOISOMETRIC
STEREOLOGICAL
STEREOLOGICALLY
STEREOLOGIES
STEREOLOGY
STEREOME
STEREOMES
STEREOMETER
STEREOMETERS
STEREOMETRIC
STEREOMETRICAL
STEREOMETRIES
STEREOMETRY
STEREOPHONIC
STEREOPHONIES
STEREOPHONY
STEREOPSES
STEREOPSIS
STEREOPTICON
STEREOPTICONS
STEREOPTICS
STEREOREGULAR
STEREOS
STEREOSCOPE
STEREOSCOPES
STEREOSCOPIC
STEREOSCOPICAL
STEREOSCOPIES
STEREOSCOPIST
STEREOSCOPISTS
STEREOSCOPY
STEREOSONIC
STEREOSPECIFIC
STEREOTACTIC
STEREOTACTICAL
STEREOTAXES
STEREOTAXIA
STEREOTAXIAS
STEREOTAXIC
STEREOTAXICALLY
STEREOTAXIS
STEREOTOMIES
STEREOTOMY

STEREOTROPIC
STEREOTROPISM
STEREOTROPISMS
STEREOTYPE
STEREOTYPED
STEREOTYPER
STEREOTYPERS
STEREOTYPES
STEREOTYPIC
STEREOTYPICAL
STEREOTYPICALLY
STEREOTYPIES
STEREOTYPING
STEREOTYPINGS
STEREOTYPIST
STEREOTYPISTS
STEREOTYPY
STEREOVISION
STERES
STERIC
STERICAL
STERICALLY
STERIGMA
STERIGMAS
STERIGMATA
STERILANT
STERILANTS
STERILE
STERILELY
STERILISABLE
STERILISATION
STERILISATIONS
STERILISE
STERILISED
STERILISER
STERILISERS
STERILISES
STERILISING
STERILITIES
STERILITY
STERILIZABLE
STERILIZATION
STERILIZATIONS
STERILIZE
STERILIZED
STERILIZER
STERILIZERS
STERILIZES
STERILIZING
STERLET
STERLETS
STERLING
STERLINGLY
STERLINGNESS
STERLINGNESSES
STERLINGS
STERN

STERNA
STERNAGE
STERNAGES
STERNAL
STERNALGIA
STERNALGIAS
STERNALGIC
STERNBOARD
STERNBOARDS
STERNEBRA
STERNEBRAE
STERNED
STERNER
STERNEST
STERNFAST
STERNFASTS
STERNFOREMOST
STERNING
STERNITE
STERNITES
STERNITIC
STERNLY
STERNMOST
STERNNESS
STERNNESSES
STERNOCOSTAL
STERNOTRIBE
STERNPORT
STERNPORTS
STERNPOST
STERNPOSTS
STERNS
STERNSHEETS
STERNSON
STERNSONS
STERNUM
STERNUMS
STERNUTATION
STERNUTATIONS
STERNUTATIVE
STERNUTATIVES
STERNUTATOR
STERNUTATORIES
STERNUTATORS
STERNUTATORY
STERNWARD
STERNWARDS
STERNWAY
STERNWAYS
STERNWORKS
STEROID
STEROIDAL
STEROIDOGENESES
STEROIDOGENESIS
STEROIDOGENIC
STEROIDS
STEROL

STEROLS
STERTOR
STERTOROUS
STERTOROUSLY
STERTOROUSNESS
STERTORS
STERVE
STERVED
STERVES
STERVING
STET
STETHOSCOPE
STETHOSCOPES
STETHOSCOPIC
STETHOSCOPIES
STETHOSCOPIST
STETHOSCOPISTS
STETHOSCOPY
STETS
STETSON
STETSONS
STETTED
STETTING
STEVEDORE
STEVEDORED
STEVEDORES
STEVEDORING
STEVEN
STEVENGRAPH
STEVENGRAPHS
STEVENS
STEW
STEWARD
STEWARDED
STEWARDESS
STEWARDESSES
STEWARDING
STEWARDRIES
STEWARDRY
STEWARDS
STEWARDSHIP
STEWARDSHIPS
STEWARTRIES
STEWARTRY
STEWBUM
STEWBUMS
STEWED
STEWER
STEWERS
STEWIER
STEWIEST
STEWING
STEWINGS
STEWPAN
STEWPANS
STEWPOND
STEWPONDS

STEWPOT	STICKABILITY	STICKWORKS	STIGMATA
STEWPOTS	STICKBALL	STICKY	STIGMATIC
STEWS	STICKBALLS	STICKYBEAK	STIGMATICAL
STEWY	STICKED	STICKYBEAKED	STIGMATICALLY
STEY	STICKER	STICKYBEAKING	STIGMATICS
STEYER	STICKERED	STICKYBEAKS	STIGMATIFEROUS
STEYEST	STICKERING	STICKYING	STIGMATISATION
STHENIA	STICKERS	STICTION	STIGMATISATIONS
STHENIAS	STICKFUL	STICTIONS	STIGMATISE
STHENIC	STICKFULS	STIDDIE	STIGMATISED
STIACCIATO	STICKHANDLE	STIDDIED	STIGMATISER
STIACCIATOS	STICKHANDLED	STIDDIEING	STIGMATISERS
STIBBLE	STICKHANDLER	STIDDIES	STIGMATISES
STIBBLER	STICKHANDLERS	STIE	STIGMATISING
STIBBLERS	STICKHANDLES	STIED	STIGMATISM
STIBBLES	STICKHANDLING	STIES	STIGMATISMS
STIBIAL	STICKIED	STIEVE	STIGMATIST
STIBIALISM	STICKIER	STIEVELY	STIGMATISTS
STIBIALISMS	STICKIES	STIEVER	STIGMATIZATION
STIBINE	STICKIEST	STIEVEST	STIGMATIZATIONS
STIBINES	STICKILY	STIFF	STIGMATIZE
STIBIUM	STICKINESS	STIFFED	STIGMATIZED
STIBIUMS	STICKINESSES	STIFFEN	STIGMATIZER
STIBNITE	STICKING	STIFFENED	STIGMATIZERS
STIBNITES	STICKINGS	STIFFENER	STIGMATIZES
STICCADO	STICKIT	STIFFENERS	STIGMATIZING
STICCADOES	STICKJAW	STIFFENING	STIGMATOPHILIA
STICCADOS	STICKJAWS	STIFFENINGS	STIGMATOPHILIAS
STICCATO	STICKLE	STIFFENS	STIGMATOSE
STICCATOES	STICKLEADER	STIFFER	STIGME
STICCATOS	STICKLEADERS	STIFFEST	STIGMES
STICH	STICKLEBACK	STIFFIE	STILB
STICHARIA	STICKLEBACKS	STIFFIES	STILBENE
STICHARION	STICKLED	STIFFING	STILBENES
STICHARIONS	STICKLER	STIFFISH	STILBESTROL
STICHERA	STICKLERS	STIFFLY	STILBESTROLS
STICHERON	STICKLES	STIFFNESS	STILBITE
STICHIC	STICKLIKE	STIFFNESSES	STILBITES
STICHICALLY	STICKLING	STIFFS	STILBOESTROL
STICHIDIA	STICKMAN	STIFFWARE	STILBOESTROLS
STICHIDIUM	STICKMEN	STIFFWARES	STILBS
STICHOI	STICKOUT	STIFFY	STILE
STICHOLOGIES	STICKOUTS	STIFLE	STILED
STICHOLOGY	STICKPIN	STIFLED	STILES
STICHOMETRIC	STICKPINS	STIFLER	STILET
STICHOMETRICAL	STICKS	STIFLERS	STILETS
STICHOMETRIES	STICKSEED	STIFLES	STILETTO
STICHOMETRY	STICKSEEDS	STIFLING	STILETTOED
STICHOMYTHIA	STICKTIGHT	STIFLINGLY	STILETTOEING
STICHOMYTHIAS	STICKTIGHTS	STIFLINGS	STILETTOES
STICHOMYTHIC	STICKUM	STIGMA	STILETTOING
STICHOMYTHIES	STICKUMS	STIGMAL	STILETTOS
STICHOMYTHY	STICKUP	STIGMARIAN	STILING
STICHOS	STICKUPS	STIGMARIANS	STILL
STICHS	STICKWEED	STIGMAS	STILLAGE
STICK	STICKWEEDS	STIGMASTEROL	STILLAGES
STICKABILITIES	STICKWORK	STIGMASTEROLS	STILLATORIES

983

STILLATORY
STILLBIRTH
STILLBIRTHS
STILLBORN
STILLBORNS
STILLED
STILLER
STILLERS
STILLEST
STILLHOUSE
STILLHOUSES
STILLICIDE
STILLICIDES
STILLIER
STILLIEST
STILLIFORM
STILLING
STILLINGS
STILLION
STILLIONS
STILLMAN
STILLMEN
STILLNESS
STILLNESSES
STILLROOM
STILLROOMS
STILLS
STILLY
STILPNOSIDERITE
STILT
STILTBIRD
STILTBIRDS
STILTED
STILTEDLY
STILTEDNESS
STILTEDNESSES
STILTER
STILTERS
STILTIER
STILTIEST
STILTINESS
STILTINESSES
STILTING
STILTINGS
STILTISH
STILTS
STILTY
STIM
STIME
STIMED
STIMES
STIMIE
STIMIED
STIMIES
STIMING
STIMPMETER
STIMPMETERS

STIMS
STIMULABLE
STIMULANCIES
STIMULANCY
STIMULANT
STIMULANTS
STIMULATE
STIMULATED
STIMULATER
STIMULATERS
STIMULATES
STIMULATING
STIMULATINGLY
STIMULATION
STIMULATIONS
STIMULATIVE
STIMULATIVES
STIMULATOR
STIMULATORS
STIMULATORY
STIMULI
STIMULUS
STIMY
STIMYING
STING
STINGAREE
STINGAREES
STINGBULL
STINGBULLS
STINGED
STINGER
STINGERS
STINGFISH
STINGFISHES
STINGIER
STINGIES
STINGIEST
STINGILY
STINGINESS
STINGINESSES
STINGING
STINGINGLY
STINGINGNESS
STINGINGS
STINGLESS
STINGO
STINGOS
STINGRAY
STINGRAYS
STINGS
STINGY
STINK
STINKARD
STINKARDS
STINKBUG
STINKBUGS
STINKER

STINKERS
STINKHORN
STINKHORNS
STINKIER
STINKIEST
STINKING
STINKINGLY
STINKINGNESS
STINKINGS
STINKO
STINKPOT
STINKPOTS
STINKS
STINKSTONE
STINKSTONES
STINKWEED
STINKWEEDS
STINKWOOD
STINKWOODS
STINKY
STINT
STINTED
STINTEDLY
STINTEDNESS
STINTEDNESSES
STINTER
STINTERS
STINTIER
STINTIEST
STINTING
STINTINGLY
STINTINGS
STINTLESS
STINTS
STINTY
STIPA
STIPAS
STIPE
STIPED
STIPEL
STIPELLATE
STIPELS
STIPEND
STIPENDIARIES
STIPENDIARY
STIPENDIATE
STIPENDIATED
STIPENDIATES
STIPENDIATING
STIPENDS
STIPES
STIPIFORM
STIPITATE
STIPITES
STIPITIFORM
STIPPLE
STIPPLED

STIPPLER
STIPPLERS
STIPPLES
STIPPLING
STIPPLINGS
STIPULABLE
STIPULACEOUS
STIPULAR
STIPULARY
STIPULATE
STIPULATED
STIPULATES
STIPULATING
STIPULATION
STIPULATIONS
STIPULATOR
STIPULATORS
STIPULATORY
STIPULE
STIPULED
STIPULES
STIR
STIRABOUT
STIRABOUTS
STIRE
STIRED
STIRES
STIRING
STIRK
STIRKS
STIRLESS
STIRP
STIRPES
STIRPICULTURE
STIRPICULTURES
STIRPS
STIRRA
STIRRABILITY
STIRRABLE
STIRRAH
STIRRAHS
STIRRAS
STIRRE
STIRRED
STIRRER
STIRRERS
STIRRES
STIRRING
STIRRINGLY
STIRRINGS
STIRRUP
STIRRUPS
STIRS
STISHIE
STISHIES
STITCH
STITCHCRAFT

STITCHCRAFTS
STITCHED
STITCHER
STITCHERIES
STITCHERS
STITCHERY
STITCHES
STITCHING
STITCHINGS
STITCHWORK
STITCHWORKS
STITCHWORT
STITCHWORTS
STITHIED
STITHIES
STITHY
STITHYING
STIVE
STIVED
STIVER
STIVERS
STIVES
STIVIER
STIVIEST
STIVING
STIVY
STOA
STOAE
STOAI
STOAS
STOAT
STOATS
STOB
STOBBED
STOBBING
STOBS
STOCCADO
STOCCADOS
STOCCATA
STOCCATAS
STOCHASTIC
STOCHASTICALLY
STOCIOUS
STOCK
STOCKADE
STOCKADED
STOCKADES
STOCKADING
STOCKBREEDER
STOCKBREEDERS
STOCKBREEDING
STOCKBREEDINGS
STOCKBROKER
STOCKBROKERAGE
STOCKBROKERAGES
STOCKBROKERS
STOCKBROKING

STOCKBROKINGS
STOCKCAR
STOCKCARS
STOCKED
STOCKER
STOCKERS
STOCKFISH
STOCKFISHES
STOCKHOLDER
STOCKHOLDERS
STOCKHOLDING
STOCKHOLDINGS
STOCKHORN
STOCKHORNS
STOCKHORSE
STOCKHORSES
STOCKIER
STOCKIEST
STOCKILY
STOCKINESS
STOCKINESSES
STOCKINET
STOCKINETS
STOCKINETTE
STOCKINETTES
STOCKING
STOCKINGED
STOCKINGER
STOCKINGERS
STOCKINGLESS
STOCKINGS
STOCKISH
STOCKISHLY
STOCKISHNESS
STOCKIST
STOCKISTS
STOCKJOBBER
STOCKJOBBERIES
STOCKJOBBERS
STOCKJOBBERY
STOCKJOBBING
STOCKJOBBINGS
STOCKKEEPER
STOCKKEEPERS
STOCKLESS
STOCKLIST
STOCKLISTS
STOCKLOCK
STOCKLOCKS
STOCKMAN
STOCKMEN
STOCKPILE
STOCKPILED
STOCKPILER
STOCKPILERS
STOCKPILES
STOCKPILING

STOCKPILINGS
STOCKPOT
STOCKPOTS
STOCKPUNISHT
STOCKROOM
STOCKROOMS
STOCKROUTE
STOCKROUTES
STOCKS
STOCKTAKE
STOCKTAKEN
STOCKTAKES
STOCKTAKING
STOCKTAKINGS
STOCKWORK
STOCKWORKS
STOCKY
STOCKYARD
STOCKYARDS
STODGE
STODGED
STODGER
STODGERS
STODGES
STODGIER
STODGIEST
STODGILY
STODGINESS
STODGINESSES
STODGING
STODGY
STOECHIOLOGICAL
STOECHIOLOGIES
STOECHIOLOGY
STOECHIOMETRIC
STOECHIOMETRIES
STOECHIOMETRY
STOEP
STOEPS
STOGEY
STOGEYS
STOGIE
STOGIES
STOGY
STOIC
STOICAL
STOICALLY
STOICALNESS
STOICALNESSES
STOICHEIOLOGIES
STOICHEIOLOGY
STOICHEIOMETRIC
STOICHEIOMETRY
STOICHIOLOGICAL
STOICHIOLOGIES
STOICHIOLOGY
STOICHIOMETRIC

STOICHIOMETRIES
STOICHIOMETRY
STOICISM
STOICISMS
STOICS
STOIT
STOITED
STOITER
STOITERED
STOITERING
STOITERS
STOITING
STOITS
STOKE
STOKED
STOKEHOLD
STOKEHOLDS
STOKEHOLE
STOKEHOLES
STOKER
STOKERS
STOKES
STOKESIA
STOKESIAS
STOKING
STOKVEL
STOKVELS
STOLE
STOLED
STOLEN
STOLENWISE
STOLES
STOLID
STOLIDER
STOLIDEST
STOLIDITIES
STOLIDITY
STOLIDLY
STOLIDNESS
STOLIDNESSES
STOLLEN
STOLLENS
STOLN
STOLON
STOLONIC
STOLONIFEROUS
STOLONS
STOLPORT
STOLPORTS
STOMA
STOMACH
STOMACHACHE
STOMACHACHES
STOMACHAL
STOMACHED
STOMACHER
STOMACHERS

STOMACHFUL
STOMACHFULNESS
STOMACHFULS
STOMACHIC
STOMACHICAL
STOMACHICS
STOMACHING
STOMACHLESS
STOMACHOUS
STOMACHS
STOMACHY
STOMACK
STOMACKS
STOMAL
STOMAS
STOMATA
STOMATAL
STOMATE
STOMATES
STOMATIC
STOMATITIC
STOMATITIDES
STOMATITIS
STOMATITISES
STOMATODAEUM
STOMATOGASTRIC
STOMATOLOGICAL
STOMATOLOGIES
STOMATOLOGY
STOMATOPLASTIES
STOMATOPLASTY
STOMATOPOD
STOMATOPODS
STOMATOUS
STOMIUM
STOMODAEA
STOMODAEAL
STOMODAEUM
STOMODAEUMS
STOMODEA
STOMODEAL
STOMODEUM
STOMODEUMS
STOMP
STOMPED
STOMPER
STOMPERS
STOMPIE
STOMPIES
STOMPING
STOMPS
STONABLE
STOND
STONDS
STONE
STONEABLE
STONEBOAT

STONEBOATS
STONEBORER
STONEBORERS
STONEBRASH
STONEBRASHES
STONEBREAK
STONEBREAKS
STONECAST
STONECASTS
STONECHAT
STONECHATS
STONECROP
STONECROPS
STONECUTTER
STONECUTTERS
STONECUTTING
STONECUTTINGS
STONED
STONEFISH
STONEFISHES
STONEFLIES
STONEFLY
STONEGROUND
STONEHAND
STONEHANDS
STONEHORSE
STONEHORSES
STONELESS
STONELESSNESS
STONELIKE
STONEMASON
STONEMASONRIES
STONEMASONRY
STONEMASONS
STONEN
STONER
STONERAG
STONERAGS
STONERAW
STONERAWS
STONERN
STONERS
STONES
STONESHOT
STONESHOTS
STONEWALL
STONEWALLED
STONEWALLER
STONEWALLERS
STONEWALLING
STONEWALLINGS
STONEWALLS
STONEWARE
STONEWARES
STONEWASHED
STONEWORK
STONEWORKER

STONEWORKERS
STONEWORKS
STONEWORT
STONEWORTS
STONEY
STONG
STONIED
STONIER
STONIES
STONIEST
STONILY
STONINESS
STONINESSES
STONING
STONINGS
STONISH
STONISHED
STONISHES
STONISHING
STONK
STONKED
STONKER
STONKERED
STONKERING
STONKERS
STONKING
STONKS
STONN
STONNE
STONNED
STONNES
STONNING
STONNS
STONY
STONYHEARTED
STONYING
STOOD
STOODEN
STOOGE
STOOGED
STOOGES
STOOGING
STOOK
STOOKED
STOOKER
STOOKERS
STOOKIE
STOOKIES
STOOKING
STOOKS
STOOL
STOOLBALL
STOOLBALLS
STOOLED
STOOLIE
STOOLIES
STOOLING

STOOLS
STOOP
STOOPBALL
STOOPBALLS
STOOPE
STOOPED
STOOPER
STOOPERS
STOOPES
STOOPING
STOOPINGLY
STOOPS
STOOR
STOORS
STOOSHIE
STOOSHIES
STOP
STOPBANK
STOPBANKS
STOPCOCK
STOPCOCKS
STOPE
STOPED
STOPER
STOPERS
STOPES
STOPGAP
STOPGAPS
STOPING
STOPINGS
STOPLESS
STOPLIGHT
STOPLIGHTS
STOPOFF
STOPOFFS
STOPOVER
STOPOVERS
STOPPABLE
STOPPAGE
STOPPAGES
STOPPED
STOPPER
STOPPERED
STOPPERING
STOPPERS
STOPPING
STOPPINGS
STOPPLE
STOPPLED
STOPPLES
STOPPLING
STOPS
STOPT
STOPWATCH
STOPWATCHES
STORABLE
STORABLES

STORAGE
STORAGES
STORAX
STORAXES
STORE
STORED
STOREFRONT
STOREFRONTS
STOREHOUSE
STOREHOUSES
STOREKEEPER
STOREKEEPERS
STOREKEEPING
STOREKEEPINGS
STOREMAN
STOREMEN
STORER
STOREROOM
STOREROOMS
STORERS
STORES
STORESHIP
STORESHIPS
STOREWIDE
STOREY
STOREYED
STOREYS
STORGE
STORGES
STORIATED
STORIED
STORIES
STORIETTE
STORIETTES
STORING
STORIOLOGIES
STORIOLOGIST
STORIOLOGISTS
STORIOLOGY
STORK
STORKS
STORKSBILL
STORKSBILLS
STORM
STORMBIRD
STORMBIRDS
STORMBOUND
STORMED
STORMER
STORMERS
STORMFUL
STORMFULLY
STORMFULNESS
STORMFULNESSES
STORMIER
STORMIEST
STORMILY

STORMINESS
STORMINESSES
STORMING
STORMINGS
STORMLESS
STORMLIKE
STORMPROOF
STORMS
STORMY
STORNELLI
STORNELLO
STORY
STORYBOARD
STORYBOARDED
STORYBOARDING
STORYBOARDS
STORYBOOK
STORYBOOKS
STORYETTE
STORYETTES
STORYING
STORYINGS
STORYLINE
STORYLINES
STORYTELLER
STORYTELLERS
STORYTELLING
STORYTELLINGS
STOSS
STOSSES
STOT
STOTIN
STOTINKA
STOTINKI
STOTIOUS
STOTS
STOTTED
STOTTER
STOTTERED
STOTTERING
STOTTERS
STOTTIE
STOTTIES
STOTTING
STOUN
STOUND
STOUNDED
STOUNDING
STOUNDS
STOUNING
STOUNS
STOUP
STOUPS
STOUR
STOURE
STOURES
STOURIE

STOURIER
STOURIEST
STOURS
STOURY
STOUSH
STOUSHED
STOUSHES
STOUSHIE
STOUSHIES
STOUSHING
STOUT
STOUTEN
STOUTENED
STOUTENING
STOUTENS
STOUTER
STOUTEST
STOUTH
STOUTHEARTED
STOUTHEARTEDLY
STOUTHERIES
STOUTHRIEF
STOUTHRIEFS
STOUTHRIES
STOUTHS
STOUTISH
STOUTLY
STOUTNESS
STOUTNESSES
STOUTS
STOVAINE
STOVAINES
STOVE
STOVED
STOVEPIPE
STOVEPIPES
STOVER
STOVERS
STOVES
STOVETOP
STOVETOPS
STOVIES
STOVING
STOVINGS
STOW
STOWABLE
STOWAGE
STOWAGES
STOWAWAY
STOWAWAYS
STOWDOWN
STOWDOWNS
STOWED
STOWER
STOWERS
STOWING
STOWINGS

STOWLINS
STOWN
STOWND
STOWNDED
STOWNDING
STOWNDS
STOWNLINS
STOWP
STOWPS
STOWRE
STOWRES
STOWS
STRABISM
STRABISMAL
STRABISMIC
STRABISMICAL
STRABISMOMETER
STRABISMOMETERS
STRABISMS
STRABISMUS
STRABISMUSES
STRABOMETER
STRABOMETERS
STRABOTOMIES
STRABOTOMY
STRACCHINI
STRACCHINO
STRAD
STRADDLE
STRADDLEBACK
STRADDLED
STRADDLER
STRADDLERS
STRADDLES
STRADDLING
STRADIOT
STRADIOTS
STRADS
STRAE
STRAES
STRAFE
STRAFED
STRAFER
STRAFERS
STRAFES
STRAFF
STRAFFED
STRAFFING
STRAFFS
STRAFING
STRAG
STRAGGLE
STRAGGLED
STRAGGLER
STRAGGLERS
STRAGGLES
STRAGGLIER

STRAGGLIEST
STRAGGLING
STRAGGLINGLY
STRAGGLINGS
STRAGGLY
STRAGS
STRAICHT
STRAICHTER
STRAICHTEST
STRAIGHT
STRAIGHTAWAY
STRAIGHTAWAYS
STRAIGHTBRED
STRAIGHTBREDS
STRAIGHTED
STRAIGHTEDGE
STRAIGHTEDGED
STRAIGHTEDGES
STRAIGHTEN
STRAIGHTENED
STRAIGHTENER
STRAIGHTENERS
STRAIGHTENING
STRAIGHTENS
STRAIGHTER
STRAIGHTEST
STRAIGHTFORTH
STRAIGHTFORWARD
STRAIGHTING
STRAIGHTISH
STRAIGHTJACKET
STRAIGHTJACKETS
STRAIGHTLACED
STRAIGHTLY
STRAIGHTNESS
STRAIGHTNESSES
STRAIGHTS
STRAIGHTWAY
STRAIGHTWAYS
STRAIK
STRAIKED
STRAIKING
STRAIKS
STRAIN
STRAINED
STRAINEDLY
STRAINER
STRAINERS
STRAINING
STRAININGS
STRAINS
STRAINT
STRAINTS
STRAIT
STRAITED
STRAITEN
STRAITENED

STRAITENING
STRAITENS
STRAITER
STRAITEST
STRAITING
STRAITJACKET
STRAITJACKETED
STRAITJACKETING
STRAITJACKETS
STRAITLACED
STRAITLACEDLY
STRAITLACEDNESS
STRAITLY
STRAITNESS
STRAITNESSES
STRAITS
STRAITWAISTCOAT
STRAKE
STRAKED
STRAKES
STRAMACON
STRAMACONS
STRAMASH
STRAMASHED
STRAMASHES
STRAMASHING
STRAMAZON
STRAMAZONS
STRAMINEOUS
STRAMMEL
STRAMMELS
STRAMONIES
STRAMONIUM
STRAMONIUMS
STRAMONY
STRAMP
STRAMPED
STRAMPING
STRAMPS
STRAND
STRANDED
STRANDEDNESS
STRANDEDNESSES
STRANDER
STRANDERS
STRANDFLAT
STRANDFLATS
STRANDING
STRANDLINE
STRANDLINES
STRANDS
STRANDWOLF
STRANDWOLVES
STRANG
STRANGE
STRANGELY
STRANGENESS

STRANGENESSES
STRANGER
STRANGERED
STRANGERING
STRANGERS
STRANGEST
STRANGLE
STRANGLED
STRANGLEHOLD
STRANGLEHOLDS
STRANGLEMENT
STRANGLEMENTS
STRANGLER
STRANGLERS
STRANGLES
STRANGLING
STRANGULATE
STRANGULATED
STRANGULATES
STRANGULATING
STRANGULATION
STRANGULATIONS
STRANGURIES
STRANGURY
STRAP
STRAPHANG
STRAPHANGER
STRAPHANGERS
STRAPHANGING
STRAPHANGS
STRAPHUNG
STRAPLESS
STRAPLESSES
STRAPLINE
STRAPLINES
STRAPONTIN
STRAPONTINS
STRAPPADO
STRAPPADOED
STRAPPADOES
STRAPPADOING
STRAPPADOS
STRAPPED
STRAPPER
STRAPPERS
STRAPPIER
STRAPPIEST
STRAPPING
STRAPPINGS
STRAPPY
STRAPS
STRAPWORT
STRAPWORTS
STRASS
STRASSES
STRATA
STRATAGEM

STRATAGEMS
STRATAL
STRATAS
STRATEGETIC
STRATEGETICAL
STRATEGIC
STRATEGICAL
STRATEGICALLY
STRATEGICS
STRATEGIES
STRATEGIST
STRATEGISTS
STRATEGIZE
STRATEGIZED
STRATEGIZES
STRATEGIZING
STRATEGY
STRATH
STRATHS
STRATHSPEY
STRATHSPEYS
STRATI
STRATICULATE
STRATICULATION
STRATICULATIONS
STRATIFICATION
STRATIFICATIONS
STRATIFIED
STRATIFIES
STRATIFORM
STRATIFY
STRATIFYING
STRATIGRAPHER
STRATIGRAPHERS
STRATIGRAPHIC
STRATIGRAPHICAL
STRATIGRAPHIES
STRATIGRAPHIST
STRATIGRAPHISTS
STRATIGRAPHY
STRATOCRACIES
STRATOCRACY
STRATOCRAT
STRATOCRATIC
STRATOCRATS
STRATOCUMULI
STRATOCUMULUS
STRATONIC
STRATOPAUSE
STRATOPAUSES
STRATOSE
STRATOSPHERE
STRATOSPHERES
STRATOSPHERIC
STRATOSPHERICAL
STRATOTANKER
STRATOTANKERS

STRATOUS
STRATOVOLCANO
STRATOVOLCANOES
STRATOVOLCANOS
STRATUM
STRATUMS
STRATUS
STRAUCHT
STRAUCHTED
STRAUCHTER
STRAUCHTEST
STRAUCHTING
STRAUCHTS
STRAUGHT
STRAUGHTED
STRAUGHTER
STRAUGHTEST
STRAUGHTING
STRAUGHTS
STRAUNGE
STRAVAGE
STRAVAGED
STRAVAGES
STRAVAGING
STRAVAIG
STRAVAIGED
STRAVAIGER
STRAVAIGERS
STRAVAIGING
STRAVAIGS
STRAW
STRAWBERRIES
STRAWBERRY
STRAWBOARD
STRAWBOARDS
STRAWED
STRAWEN
STRAWFLOWER
STRAWFLOWERS
STRAWHAT
STRAWIER
STRAWIEST
STRAWING
STRAWLESS
STRAWLIKE
STRAWN
STRAWS
STRAWWEIGHT
STRAWWEIGHTS
STRAWWORM
STRAWWORMS
STRAWY
STRAY
STRAYED
STRAYER
STRAYERS
STRAYING

STRAYINGS
STRAYLING
STRAYLINGS
STRAYS
STRAYVE
STRAYVED
STRAYVES
STRAYVING
STREAK
STREAKED
STREAKER
STREAKERS
STREAKIER
STREAKIEST
STREAKILY
STREAKINESS
STREAKINESSES
STREAKING
STREAKINGS
STREAKLIKE
STREAKS
STREAKY
STREAM
STREAMBED
STREAMBEDS
STREAMED
STREAMER
STREAMERED
STREAMERS
STREAMIER
STREAMIEST
STREAMINESS
STREAMINESSES
STREAMING
STREAMINGLY
STREAMINGS
STREAMLESS
STREAMLET
STREAMLETS
STREAMLIKE
STREAMLINE
STREAMLINED
STREAMLINER
STREAMLINERS
STREAMLINES
STREAMLING
STREAMLINGS
STREAMLINING
STREAMS
STREAMSIDE
STREAMSIDES
STREAMY
STREEK
STREEKED
STREEKER
STREEKERS
STREEKING

STREEKS
STREEL
STREELED
STREELING
STREELS
STREET
STREETAGE
STREETAGES
STREETBOY
STREETBOYS
STREETCAR
STREETCARS
STREETED
STREETFUL
STREETFULS
STREETIER
STREETIEST
STREETING
STREETKEEPER
STREETKEEPERS
STREETLAMP
STREETLAMPS
STREETLIGHT
STREETLIGHTS
STREETROOM
STREETROOMS
STREETS
STREETSCAPE
STREETSCAPES
STREETSMART
STREETWALKER
STREETWALKERS
STREETWALKING
STREETWALKINGS
STREETWARD
STREETWARDS
STREETWEAR
STREETWISE
STREETY
STREIGHT
STREIGHTS
STREIGNE
STREIGNED
STREIGNES
STREIGNING
STRELITZ
STRELITZES
STRELITZI
STRELITZIA
STRELITZIAS
STRENE
STRENES
STRENGTH
STRENGTHEN
STRENGTHENED
STRENGTHENER
STRENGTHENERS

STRENGTHENING
STRENGTHENINGS
STRENGTHENS
STRENGTHFUL
STRENGTHLESS
STRENGTHS
STRENUITIES
STRENUITY
STRENUOSITIES
STRENUOSITY
STRENUOUS
STRENUOUSLY
STRENUOUSNESS
STRENUOUSNESSES
STREP
STREPENT
STREPEROUS
STREPHOSYMBOLIA
STREPITANT
STREPITATION
STREPITATIONS
STREPITOSO
STREPITOUS
STREPS
STREPSIPTEROUS
STREPTOBACILLI
STREPTOBACILLUS
STREPTOCARPUS
STREPTOCARPUSES
STREPTOCOCCAL
STREPTOCOCCI
STREPTOCOCCIC
STREPTOCOCCUS
STREPTOKINASE
STREPTOKINASES
STREPTOLYSIN
STREPTOLYSINS
STREPTOMYCES
STREPTOMYCETE
STREPTOMYCETES
STREPTOMYCIN
STREPTOMYCINS
STREPTOSOLEN
STREPTOSOLENS
STREPTOTHRICIN
STREPTOTHRICINS
STRESS
STRESSBUSTER
STRESSBUSTERS
STRESSBUSTING
STRESSED
STRESSES
STRESSFUL
STRESSFULLY
STRESSFULNESS
STRESSING
STRESSLESS

STRESSLESSNESS
STRESSOR
STRESSORS
STRETCH
STRETCHABILITY
STRETCHABLE
STRETCHED
STRETCHER
STRETCHERED
STRETCHERING
STRETCHERS
STRETCHES
STRETCHIER
STRETCHIEST
STRETCHINESS
STRETCHING
STRETCHLESS
STRETCHMARKS
STRETCHY
STRETTA
STRETTAS
STRETTE
STRETTI
STRETTO
STRETTOS
STREUSEL
STREUSELS
STREW
STREWAGE
STREWAGES
STREWED
STREWER
STREWERS
STREWING
STREWINGS
STREWMENT
STREWMENTS
STREWN
STREWS
STREWTH
STRIA
STRIAE
STRIATA
STRIATE
STRIATED
STRIATES
STRIATING
STRIATION
STRIATIONS
STRIATUM
STRIATUMS
STRIATURE
STRIATURES
STRICH
STRICHES
STRICK
STRICKEN

STRICKENLY
STRICKLE
STRICKLED
STRICKLES
STRICKLING
STRICKS
STRICT
STRICTER
STRICTEST
STRICTION
STRICTISH
STRICTLY
STRICTNESS
STRICTNESSES
STRICTURE
STRICTURED
STRICTURES
STRIDDEN
STRIDDLE
STRIDDLED
STRIDDLES
STRIDDLING
STRIDE
STRIDELEGS
STRIDENCE
STRIDENCES
STRIDENCIES
STRIDENCY
STRIDENT
STRIDENTLY
STRIDER
STRIDERS
STRIDES
STRIDEWAYS
STRIDING
STRIDLING
STRIDOR
STRIDORS
STRIDULANCE
STRIDULANT
STRIDULANTLY
STRIDULATE
STRIDULATED
STRIDULATES
STRIDULATING
STRIDULATION
STRIDULATIONS
STRIDULATOR
STRIDULATORS
STRIDULATORY
STRIDULOUS
STRIDULOUSLY
STRIDULOUSNESS
STRIFE
STRIFEFUL
STRIFELESS
STRIFES

STRIFT
STRIFTS
STRIG
STRIGA
STRIGAE
STRIGATE
STRIGGED
STRIGGING
STRIGIFORM
STRIGIL
STRIGILS
STRIGINE
STRIGOSE
STRIGS
STRIKE
STRIKEBOUND
STRIKEBREAKER
STRIKEBREAKERS
STRIKEBREAKING
STRIKEBREAKINGS
STRIKELESS
STRIKELESSNESS
STRIKEOUT
STRIKEOUTS
STRIKEOVER
STRIKEOVERS
STRIKER
STRIKERS
STRIKES
STRIKING
STRIKINGLY
STRIKINGNESS
STRIKINGNESSES
STRIKINGS
STRING
STRINGBOARD
STRINGBOARDS
STRINGCOURSE
STRINGCOURSES
STRINGED
STRINGENCIES
STRINGENCY
STRINGENDO
STRINGENT
STRINGENTLY
STRINGENTNESS
STRINGENTNESSES
STRINGER
STRINGERS
STRINGHALT
STRINGHALTED
STRINGHALTS
STRINGIER
STRINGIEST
STRINGILY
STRINGINESS
STRINGINESSES

STRINGING
STRINGINGS
STRINGLESS
STRINGLIKE
STRINGPIECE
STRINGPIECES
STRINGS
STRINGY
STRINGYBARK
STRINGYBARKS
STRINKLE
STRINKLED
STRINKLES
STRINKLING
STRINKLINGS
STRIP
STRIPAGRAM
STRIPAGRAMS
STRIPE
STRIPED
STRIPELESS
STRIPER
STRIPERS
STRIPES
STRIPEY
STRIPIER
STRIPIEST
STRIPINESS
STRIPINESSES
STRIPING
STRIPINGS
STRIPLING
STRIPLINGS
STRIPPABLE
STRIPPED
STRIPPER
STRIPPERGRAM
STRIPPERGRAMS
STRIPPERS
STRIPPING
STRIPPINGS
STRIPS
STRIPT
STRIPTEASE
STRIPTEASER
STRIPTEASERS
STRIPTEASES
STRIPY
STRIVE
STRIVED
STRIVEN
STRIVER
STRIVERS
STRIVES
STRIVING
STRIVINGLY
STRIVINGS

STROAM
STROAMED
STROAMING
STROAMS
STROBE
STROBED
STROBES
STROBIC
STROBIL
STROBILA
STROBILACEOUS
STROBILAE
STROBILATE
STROBILATED
STROBILATES
STROBILATING
STROBILATION
STROBILATIONS
STROBILE
STROBILES
STROBILI
STROBILIFORM
STROBILINE
STROBILISATION
STROBILISATIONS
STROBILIZATION
STROBILIZATIONS
STROBILOID
STROBILS
STROBILUS
STROBILUSES
STROBING
STROBINGS
STROBOSCOPE
STROBOSCOPES
STROBOSCOPIC
STROBOSCOPICAL
STROBOTRON
STROBOTRONS
STRODDLE
STRODDLED
STRODDLES
STRODDLING
STRODE
STRODLE
STRODLED
STRODLES
STRODLING
STROGANOFF
STROGANOFFS
STROKE
STROKED
STROKEN
STROKEPLAY
STROKER
STROKERS
STROKES

STROKING
STROKINGS
STROLL
STROLLED
STROLLER
STROLLERS
STROLLING
STROLLINGS
STROLLS
STROMA
STROMAL
STROMATA
STROMATIC
STROMATOLITE
STROMATOLITES
STROMATOLITIC
STROMATOUS
STROMB
STROMBS
STROMBULIFEROUS
STROMBULIFORM
STROMBUS
STROMBUSES
STROND
STRONDS
STRONG
STRONGARM
STRONGARMED
STRONGARMING
STRONGARMS
STRONGBOX
STRONGBOXES
STRONGER
STRONGEST
STRONGHOLD
STRONGHOLDS
STRONGISH
STRONGLY
STRONGMAN
STRONGMEN
STRONGNESS
STRONGPOINT
STRONGPOINTS
STRONGROOM
STRONGROOMS
STRONGYL
STRONGYLE
STRONGYLES
STRONGYLOID
STRONGYLOIDOSES
STRONGYLOIDOSIS
STRONGYLOIDS
STRONGYLOSES
STRONGYLOSIS
STRONGYLS
STRONTIA
STRONTIAN

STRONTIANITE
STRONTIANITES
STRONTIANS
STRONTIAS
STRONTIC
STRONTIUM
STRONTIUMS
STROOK
STROOKE
STROOKEN
STROOKES
STROP
STROPHANTHIN
STROPHANTHINS
STROPHANTHUS
STROPHANTHUSES
STROPHE
STROPHES
STROPHIC
STROPHICAL
STROPHIOLATE
STROPHIOLATED
STROPHIOLE
STROPHIOLES
STROPPED
STROPPER
STROPPERS
STROPPIER
STROPPIEST
STROPPILY
STROPPINESS
STROPPING
STROPPY
STROPS
STROSSERS
STROUD
STROUDING
STROUDINGS
STROUDS
STROUP
STROUPACH
STROUPACHS
STROUPAN
STROUPANS
STROUPS
STROUT
STROUTED
STROUTING
STROUTS
STROVE
STROW
STROWED
STROWER
STROWERS
STROWING
STROWINGS
STROWN

STROWS
STROY
STROYED
STROYER
STROYERS
STROYING
STROYS
STRUCK
STRUCKEN
STRUCTURAL
STRUCTURALISM
STRUCTURALISMS
STRUCTURALIST
STRUCTURALISTS
STRUCTURALIZE
STRUCTURALIZED
STRUCTURALIZES
STRUCTURALIZING
STRUCTURALLY
STRUCTURATION
STRUCTURATIONS
STRUCTURE
STRUCTURED
STRUCTURELESS
STRUCTURES
STRUCTURING
STRUDEL
STRUDELS
STRUGGLE
STRUGGLED
STRUGGLER
STRUGGLERS
STRUGGLES
STRUGGLING
STRUGGLINGLY
STRUGGLINGS
STRUM
STRUMA
STRUMAE
STRUMAS
STRUMATIC
STRUMITIS
STRUMITISES
STRUMMED
STRUMMEL
STRUMMELS
STRUMMER
STRUMMERS
STRUMMING
STRUMOSE
STRUMOUS
STRUMPET
STRUMPETED
STRUMPETING
STRUMPETS
STRUMS
STRUNG

STRUNT
STRUNTED
STRUNTING
STRUNTS
STRUT
STRUTHIOID
STRUTHIOIDS
STRUTHIOUS
STRUTS
STRUTTED
STRUTTER
STRUTTERS
STRUTTING
STRUTTINGLY
STRUTTINGS
STRYCHNIA
STRYCHNIAS
STRYCHNIC
STRYCHNINE
STRYCHNINED
STRYCHNINES
STRYCHNINING
STRYCHNINISM
STRYCHNINISMS
STRYCHNISM
STRYCHNISMS
STUB
STUBBED
STUBBIE
STUBBIER
STUBBIES
STUBBIEST
STUBBILY
STUBBINESS
STUBBINESSES
STUBBING
STUBBLE
STUBBLED
STUBBLES
STUBBLIER
STUBBLIEST
STUBBLY
STUBBORN
STUBBORNED
STUBBORNER
STUBBORNEST
STUBBORNING
STUBBORNLY
STUBBORNNESS
STUBBORNNESSES
STUBBORNS
STUBBY
STUBS
STUCCO
STUCCOED
STUCCOER
STUCCOERS

STUCCOES
STUCCOING
STUCCOS
STUCCOWORK
STUCCOWORKS
STUCK
STUCKS
STUD
STUDBOOK
STUDBOOKS
STUDDED
STUDDEN
STUDDIE
STUDDIES
STUDDING
STUDDINGS
STUDDINGSAIL
STUDDINGSAILS
STUDDLE
STUDDLES
STUDENT
STUDENTRIES
STUDENTRY
STUDENTS
STUDENTSHIP
STUDENTSHIPS
STUDENTY
STUDFARM
STUDFARMS
STUDFISH
STUDFISHES
STUDHORSE
STUDHORSES
STUDIED
STUDIEDLY
STUDIEDNESS
STUDIEDNESSES
STUDIER
STUDIERS
STUDIES
STUDIO
STUDIOS
STUDIOUS
STUDIOUSLY
STUDIOUSNESS
STUDIOUSNESSES
STUDLIER
STUDLIEST
STUDLY
STUDS
STUDWORK
STUDWORKS
STUDY
STUDYING
STUFF
STUFFED
STUFFER

STUFFERS
STUFFIER
STUFFIEST
STUFFILY
STUFFINESS
STUFFINESSES
STUFFING
STUFFINGS
STUFFLESS
STUFFS
STUFFY
STUGGIER
STUGGIEST
STUGGY
STUIVER
STUIVERS
STULL
STULLS
STULM
STULMS
STULTIFICATION
STULTIFICATIONS
STULTIFIED
STULTIFIER
STULTIFIERS
STULTIFIES
STULTIFY
STULTIFYING
STUM
STUMBLE
STUMBLEBUM
STUMBLEBUMS
STUMBLED
STUMBLER
STUMBLERS
STUMBLES
STUMBLIER
STUMBLIEST
STUMBLING
STUMBLINGLY
STUMBLY
STUMER
STUMERS
STUMM
STUMMED
STUMMEL
STUMMELS
STUMMING
STUMP
STUMPAGE
STUMPAGES
STUMPED
STUMPER
STUMPERS
STUMPIER
STUMPIES
STUMPIEST

STUMPILY
STUMPINESS
STUMPINESSES
STUMPING
STUMPS
STUMPWORK
STUMPY
STUMS
STUN
STUNG
STUNK
STUNKARD
STUNNED
STUNNER
STUNNERS
STUNNING
STUNNINGLY
STUNNINGS
STUNS
STUNSAIL
STUNSAILS
STUNT
STUNTED
STUNTEDNESS
STUNTEDNESSES
STUNTING
STUNTMAN
STUNTMEN
STUNTS
STUNTWOMAN
STUNTWOMEN
STUPA
STUPAS
STUPE
STUPED
STUPEFACIENT
STUPEFACIENTS
STUPEFACTION
STUPEFACTIONS
STUPEFACTIVE
STUPEFIED
STUPEFIER
STUPEFIERS
STUPEFIES
STUPEFY
STUPEFYING
STUPEFYINGLY
STUPENDIOUS
STUPENDOUS
STUPENDOUSLY
STUPENDOUSNESS
STUPENT
STUPES
STUPID
STUPIDER
STUPIDEST
STUPIDITIES

STUPIDITY
STUPIDLY
STUPIDNESS
STUPIDNESSES
STUPIDS
STUPING
STUPOR
STUPOROUS
STUPORS
STUPRATE
STUPRATED
STUPRATES
STUPRATING
STUPRATION
STUPRATIONS
STURDIED
STURDIER
STURDIES
STURDIEST
STURDILY
STURDINESS
STURDINESSES
STURDY
STURE
STURGEON
STURGEONS
STURMER
STURMERS
STURNINE
STURNOID
STURNUS
STURNUSES
STURT
STURTED
STURTING
STURTS
STUSHIE
STUSHIES
STUTTER
STUTTERED
STUTTERER
STUTTERERS
STUTTERING
STUTTERINGLY
STUTTERINGS
STUTTERS
STY
STYE
STYED
STYES
STYGIAN
STYING
STYLAR
STYLATE
STYLE
STYLEBOOK
STYLEBOOKS

STYLED
STYLELESS
STYLELESSNESS
STYLELESSNESSES
STYLER
STYLERS
STYLES
STYLET
STYLETS
STYLI
STYLIE
STYLIFEROUS
STYLIFORM
STYLING
STYLINGS
STYLISATION
STYLISATIONS
STYLISE
STYLISED
STYLISER
STYLISERS
STYLISES
STYLISH
STYLISHLY
STYLISHNESS
STYLISHNESSES
STYLISING
STYLIST
STYLISTIC
STYLISTICALLY
STYLISTICS
STYLISTS
STYLITE
STYLITES
STYLITIC
STYLIZATION
STYLIZATIONS
STYLIZE
STYLIZED
STYLIZER
STYLIZERS
STYLIZES
STYLIZING
STYLO
STYLOBATE
STYLOBATES
STYLOGRAPH
STYLOGRAPHIC
STYLOGRAPHICAL
STYLOGRAPHIES
STYLOGRAPHS
STYLOGRAPHY
STYLOID
STYLOIDS
STYLOLITE
STYLOLITES
STYLOLITIC

STYLOMETRIES
STYLOMETRY
STYLOPES
STYLOPHONE
STYLOPHONES
STYLOPISE
STYLOPISED
STYLOPISES
STYLOPISING
STYLOPIZE
STYLOPIZED
STYLOPIZES
STYLOPIZING
STYLOPODIA
STYLOPODIUM
STYLOPS
STYLOS
STYLOSTIXIS
STYLUS
STYLUSES
STYME
STYMED
STYMES
STYMIE
STYMIED
STYMIEING
STYMIES
STYMING
STYMY
STYMYING
STYPSIS
STYPSISES
STYPTIC
STYPTICAL
STYPTICITIES
STYPTICITY
STYPTICS
STYRACACEOUS
STYRAX
STYRAXES
STYRE
STYRED
STYRENE
STYRENES
STYRES
STYRING
STYROFOAM
STYROFOAMS
STYTE
STYTED
STYTES
STYTING
SUABILITIES
SUABILITY
SUABLE
SUABLY
SUASIBLE

SUASION
SUASIONS
SUASIVE
SUASIVELY
SUASIVENESS
SUASIVENESSES
SUASORY
SUAVE
SUAVELY
SUAVENESS
SUAVENESSES
SUAVEOLENT
SUAVER
SUAVEST
SUAVITIES
SUAVITY
SUB
SUBA
SUBABBOT
SUBABBOTS
SUBABDOMINAL
SUBACETATE
SUBACETATES
SUBACID
SUBACIDITIES
SUBACIDITY
SUBACIDLY
SUBACIDNESS
SUBACIDNESSES
SUBACRID
SUBACT
SUBACTED
SUBACTING
SUBACTION
SUBACTIONS
SUBACTS
SUBACUTE
SUBACUTELY
SUBADAR
SUBADARS
SUBADOLESCENT
SUBADOLESCENTS
SUBADULT
SUBADULTS
SUBAERIAL
SUBAERIALLY
SUBAFFLUENT
SUBAGENCIES
SUBAGENCY
SUBAGENT
SUBAGENTS
SUBAGGREGATE
SUBAGGREGATES
SUBAGGREGATION
SUBAGGREGATIONS
SUBAH
SUBAHDAR

SUBAHDARIES
SUBAHDARS
SUBAHDARY
SUBAHS
SUBAHSHIP
SUBAHSHIPS
SUBALAR
SUBALLIANCE
SUBALLIANCES
SUBALLOCATION
SUBALLOCATIONS
SUBALPINE
SUBALTERN
SUBALTERNANT
SUBALTERNANTS
SUBALTERNATE
SUBALTERNATES
SUBALTERNATION
SUBALTERNATIONS
SUBALTERNITIES
SUBALTERNITY
SUBALTERNS
SUBANGULAR
SUBANTARCTIC
SUBAPICAL
SUBAPOSTOLIC
SUBAPPEARANCE
SUBAPPEARANCES
SUBAQUA
SUBAQUATIC
SUBAQUEOUS
SUBARACHNOID
SUBARACHNOIDAL
SUBARBOREAL
SUBARBORESCENT
SUBARCTIC
SUBARCTICS
SUBARCUATE
SUBARCUATION
SUBARCUATIONS
SUBAREA
SUBAREAS
SUBARID
SUBARRATION
SUBARRATIONS
SUBARRHATION
SUBARRHATIONS
SUBARTICLE
SUBARTICLES
SUBAS
SUBASSEMBLE
SUBASSEMBLED
SUBASSEMBLES
SUBASSEMBLIES
SUBASSEMBLING
SUBASSEMBLY
SUBASSOCIATION

SUBASSOCIATIONS
SUBASTRAL
SUBATMOSPHERIC
SUBATOM
SUBATOMIC
SUBATOMICS
SUBATOMS
SUBATTORNEY
SUBATTORNIES
SUBAUDIBLE
SUBAUDIO
SUBAUDITION
SUBAUDITIONS
SUBAURAL
SUBAURICULAR
SUBAVERAGE
SUBAXIAL
SUBAXILLARY
SUBBASAL
SUBBASE
SUBBASEMENT
SUBBASEMENTS
SUBBASES
SUBBASIN
SUBBASINS
SUBBASS
SUBBASSES
SUBBED
SUBBIE
SUBBIES
SUBBING
SUBBINGS
SUBBITUMINOUS
SUBBLOCK
SUBBLOCKS
SUBBRANCH
SUBBRANCHES
SUBBREED
SUBBREEDS
SUBBUREAU
SUBBUREAUS
SUBBUREAUX
SUBBY
SUBCABINET
SUBCABINETS
SUBCALIBER
SUBCALIBRE
SUBCANTOR
SUBCANTORS
SUBCAPSULAR
SUBCARDINAL
SUBCARDINALS
SUBCARRIER
SUBCARRIERS
SUBCASTE
SUBCASTES
SUBCATEGORIES

SUBCATEGORIZE
SUBCATEGORIZED
SUBCATEGORIZES
SUBCATEGORIZING
SUBCATEGORY
SUBCAUDAL
SUBCAUSE
SUBCAUSES
SUBCAVITIES
SUBCAVITY
SUBCEILING
SUBCEILINGS
SUBCELESTIAL
SUBCELESTIALS
SUBCELL
SUBCELLAR
SUBCELLARS
SUBCELLS
SUBCELLULAR
SUBCENTER
SUBCENTERS
SUBCENTRAL
SUBCENTRALLY
SUBCEPTION
SUBCEPTIONS
SUBCHANTER
SUBCHANTERS
SUBCHAPTER
SUBCHAPTERS
SUBCHARTER
SUBCHARTERS
SUBCHASER
SUBCHASERS
SUBCHELATE
SUBCHIEF
SUBCHIEFS
SUBCHLORIDE
SUBCHLORIDES
SUBCHORD
SUBCHORDS
SUBCIRCUIT
SUBCIRCUITS
SUBCIVILIZATION
SUBCIVILIZED
SUBCLAIM
SUBCLAIMS
SUBCLAN
SUBCLANS
SUBCLASS
SUBCLASSED
SUBCLASSES
SUBCLASSIFIED
SUBCLASSIFIES
SUBCLASSIFY
SUBCLASSIFYING
SUBCLASSING
SUBCLAUSE

SUBCLAUSES
SUBCLAVIAN
SUBCLAVIANS
SUBCLAVICULAR
SUBCLERK
SUBCLERKS
SUBCLIMACTIC
SUBCLIMATE
SUBCLIMATES
SUBCLIMAX
SUBCLIMAXES
SUBCLINICAL
SUBCLINICALLY
SUBCLUSTER
SUBCLUSTERED
SUBCLUSTERING
SUBCLUSTERS
SUBCODE
SUBCODES
SUBCOLLECTION
SUBCOLLECTIONS
SUBCOLLEGE
SUBCOLLEGIATE
SUBCOLONIES
SUBCOLONY
SUBCOMMANDER
SUBCOMMANDERS
SUBCOMMISSION
SUBCOMMISSIONED
SUBCOMMISSIONER
SUBCOMMISSIONS
SUBCOMMITTEE
SUBCOMMITTEES
SUBCOMMUNITIES
SUBCOMMUNITY
SUBCOMPACT
SUBCOMPACTS
SUBCOMPONENT
SUBCOMPONENTS
SUBCONSCIOUS
SUBCONSCIOUSES
SUBCONSCIOUSLY
SUBCONTIGUOUS
SUBCONTINENT
SUBCONTINENTAL
SUBCONTINENTS
SUBCONTINUOUS
SUBCONTRACT
SUBCONTRACTED
SUBCONTRACTING
SUBCONTRACTINGS
SUBCONTRACTOR
SUBCONTRACTORS
SUBCONTRACTS
SUBCONTRAOCTAVE
SUBCONTRARIES
SUBCONTRARIETY

SUBCONTRARY
SUBCOOL
SUBCOOLED
SUBCOOLING
SUBCOOLS
SUBCORDATE
SUBCORIACEOUS
SUBCORTEX
SUBCORTEXES
SUBCORTICAL
SUBCORTICES
SUBCOSTA
SUBCOSTAE
SUBCOSTAL
SUBCOSTALS
SUBCOUNCIL
SUBCOUNCILS
SUBCOUNTIES
SUBCOUNTY
SUBCRANIAL
SUBCRITICAL
SUBCRUST
SUBCRUSTAL
SUBCRUSTS
SUBCULT
SUBCULTS
SUBCULTURAL
SUBCULTURALLY
SUBCULTURE
SUBCULTURED
SUBCULTURES
SUBCULTURING
SUBCURATIVE
SUBCURATOR
SUBCURATORS
SUBCUTANEOUS
SUBCUTANEOUSLY
SUBCUTES
SUBCUTIS
SUBCUTISES
SUBDEACON
SUBDEACONATE
SUBDEACONATES
SUBDEACONRIES
SUBDEACONRY
SUBDEACONS
SUBDEACONSHIP
SUBDEACONSHIPS
SUBDEAN
SUBDEANERIES
SUBDEANERY
SUBDEANS
SUBDEB
SUBDEBS
SUBDEBUTANTE
SUBDEBUTANTES
SUBDECANAL

SUBDECISION
SUBDECISIONS
SUBDEFINITION
SUBDEFINITIONS
SUBDELIRIA
SUBDELIRIOUS
SUBDELIRIUM
SUBDELIRIUMS
SUBDEPARTMENT
SUBDEPARTMENTAL
SUBDEPARTMENTS
SUBDEPOT
SUBDEPOTS
SUBDERMAL
SUBDERMALLY
SUBDEVELOPMENT
SUBDEVELOPMENTS
SUBDEW
SUBDEWED
SUBDEWING
SUBDEWS
SUBDIACONAL
SUBDIACONATE
SUBDIACONATES
SUBDIALECT
SUBDIALECTS
SUBDIRECTOR
SUBDIRECTORS
SUBDISCIPLINE
SUBDISCIPLINES
SUBDISTINCTION
SUBDISTINCTIONS
SUBDISTRICT
SUBDISTRICTS
SUBDIVIDABLE
SUBDIVIDE
SUBDIVIDED
SUBDIVIDER
SUBDIVIDERS
SUBDIVIDES
SUBDIVIDING
SUBDIVISIBLE
SUBDIVISION
SUBDIVISIONAL
SUBDIVISIONS
SUBDIVISIVE
SUBDOLOUS
SUBDOMINANT
SUBDOMINANTS
SUBDORSAL
SUBDUABLE
SUBDUABLY
SUBDUAL
SUBDUALS
SUBDUCE
SUBDUCED
SUBDUCES

SUBDUCING
SUBDUCT
SUBDUCTED
SUBDUCTING
SUBDUCTION
SUBDUCTIONS
SUBDUCTS
SUBDUE
SUBDUED
SUBDUEDLY
SUBDUEDNESS
SUBDUEDNESSES
SUBDUEMENT
SUBDUEMENTS
SUBDUER
SUBDUERS
SUBDUES
SUBDUING
SUBDUPLE
SUBDUPLICATE
SUBDURAL
SUBECHO
SUBECHOES
SUBECONOMIC
SUBECONOMIES
SUBECONOMY
SUBEDAR
SUBEDARS
SUBEDIT
SUBEDITED
SUBEDITING
SUBEDITOR
SUBEDITORIAL
SUBEDITORS
SUBEDITORSHIP
SUBEDITORSHIPS
SUBEDITS
SUBELEMENT
SUBELEMENTAL
SUBELEMENTS
SUBEMPLOYED
SUBEMPLOYMENT
SUBEMPLOYMENTS
SUBENTIRE
SUBENTRIES
SUBENTRY
SUBEPIDERMAL
SUBEPOCH
SUBEPOCHS
SUBEQUAL
SUBEQUATORIAL
SUBER
SUBERATE
SUBERATES
SUBERECT
SUBEREOUS
SUBERIC

SUBERIN
SUBERINS
SUBERISATION
SUBERISATIONS
SUBERISE
SUBERISED
SUBERISES
SUBERISING
SUBERIZATION
SUBERIZATIONS
SUBERIZE
SUBERIZED
SUBERIZES
SUBERIZING
SUBEROSE
SUBEROUS
SUBERS
SUBFACTORIAL
SUBFACTORIALS
SUBFAMILIES
SUBFAMILY
SUBFERTILE
SUBFERTILITIES
SUBFERTILITY
SUBFEU
SUBFEUDATION
SUBFEUDATIONS
SUBFEUDATORY
SUBFEUED
SUBFEUING
SUBFEUS
SUBFIELD
SUBFIELDS
SUBFILE
SUBFILES
SUBFIX
SUBFIXES
SUBFLOOR
SUBFLOORS
SUBFLUID
SUBFOREMAN
SUBFOREMEN
SUBFOSSIL
SUBFOSSILS
SUBFRACTION
SUBFRACTIONAL
SUBFRACTIONS
SUBFRAME
SUBFRAMES
SUBFREEZING
SUBFUNCTION
SUBFUNCTIONS
SUBFUSC
SUBFUSCOUS
SUBFUSCS
SUBFUSK
SUBFUSKS

SUBGENERA
SUBGENERATION
SUBGENERATIONS
SUBGENERIC
SUBGENERICALLY
SUBGENITAL
SUBGENRE
SUBGENRES
SUBGENUS
SUBGENUSES
SUBGLACIAL
SUBGLACIALLY
SUBGLOBOSE
SUBGLOBULAR
SUBGLOTTAL
SUBGLOTTALLY
SUBGOAL
SUBGOALS
SUBGOVERNMENT
SUBGOVERNMENTS
SUBGRADE
SUBGRADES
SUBGRAPH
SUBGRAPHS
SUBGROUP
SUBGROUPS
SUBGUM
SUBGUMS
SUBHA
SUBHARMONIC
SUBHARMONICS
SUBHASTATION
SUBHASTATIONS
SUBHEAD
SUBHEADING
SUBHEADINGS
SUBHEADS
SUBHEDRAL
SUBHUMAN
SUBHUMANS
SUBHUMID
SUBIDEA
SUBIDEAS
SUBIMAGINAL
SUBIMAGINES
SUBIMAGO
SUBIMAGOES
SUBIMAGOS
SUBINCISE
SUBINCISED
SUBINCISES
SUBINCISING
SUBINCISION
SUBINCISIONS
SUBINDEX
SUBINDEXES
SUBINDICATE

SUBINDICATED
SUBINDICATES
SUBINDICATING
SUBINDICATION
SUBINDICATIONS
SUBINDICATIVE
SUBINDICES
SUBINDUSTRIES
SUBINDUSTRY
SUBINFEUDATE
SUBINFEUDATED
SUBINFEUDATES
SUBINFEUDATING
SUBINFEUDATION
SUBINFEUDATIONS
SUBINFEUDATORY
SUBINHIBITORY
SUBINSINUATION
SUBINSINUATIONS
SUBINSPECTOR
SUBINSPECTORS
SUBINTELLECTION
SUBINTELLIGENCE
SUBINTELLIGITUR
SUBINTERVAL
SUBINTERVALS
SUBINTRANT
SUBINTRODUCE
SUBINTRODUCED
SUBINTRODUCES
SUBINTRODUCING
SUBINVOLUTION
SUBINVOLUTIONS
SUBIRRIGATE
SUBIRRIGATED
SUBIRRIGATES
SUBIRRIGATING
SUBIRRIGATION
SUBIRRIGATIONS
SUBITANEOUS
SUBITEM
SUBITEMS
SUBITISE
SUBITISED
SUBITISES
SUBITISING
SUBITIZE
SUBITIZED
SUBITIZES
SUBITIZING
SUBITO
SUBJACENCIES
SUBJACENCY
SUBJACENT
SUBJACENTLY
SUBJECT
SUBJECTABILITY

SUBJECTABLE
SUBJECTED
SUBJECTIFIED
SUBJECTIFIES
SUBJECTIFY
SUBJECTIFYING
SUBJECTING
SUBJECTION
SUBJECTIONS
SUBJECTIVE
SUBJECTIVELY
SUBJECTIVENESS
SUBJECTIVES
SUBJECTIVISE
SUBJECTIVISED
SUBJECTIVISES
SUBJECTIVISING
SUBJECTIVISM
SUBJECTIVISMS
SUBJECTIVIST
SUBJECTIVISTIC
SUBJECTIVISTS
SUBJECTIVITIES
SUBJECTIVITY
SUBJECTIVIZE
SUBJECTIVIZED
SUBJECTIVIZES
SUBJECTIVIZING
SUBJECTLESS
SUBJECTS
SUBJECTSHIP
SUBJECTSHIPS
SUBJOIN
SUBJOINDER
SUBJOINDERS
SUBJOINED
SUBJOINING
SUBJOINS
SUBJUGABILITY
SUBJUGABLE
SUBJUGATE
SUBJUGATED
SUBJUGATES
SUBJUGATING
SUBJUGATION
SUBJUGATIONS
SUBJUGATOR
SUBJUGATORS
SUBJUNCTION
SUBJUNCTIONS
SUBJUNCTIVE
SUBJUNCTIVELY
SUBJUNCTIVES
SUBKINGDOM
SUBKINGDOMS
SUBLANCEOLATE
SUBLANGUAGE

SUBLANGUAGES
SUBLAPSARIAN
SUBLAPSARIANISM
SUBLAPSARIANS
SUBLATE
SUBLATED
SUBLATES
SUBLATING
SUBLATION
SUBLATIONS
SUBLEASE
SUBLEASED
SUBLEASES
SUBLEASING
SUBLESSEE
SUBLESSEES
SUBLESSOR
SUBLESSORS
SUBLET
SUBLETHAL
SUBLETHALLY
SUBLETS
SUBLETTER
SUBLETTERS
SUBLETTING
SUBLETTINGS
SUBLEVEL
SUBLEVELS
SUBLIBRARIAN
SUBLIBRARIANS
SUBLICENSE
SUBLICENSED
SUBLICENSES
SUBLICENSING
SUBLIEUTENANCY
SUBLIEUTENANT
SUBLIEUTENANTS
SUBLIMABLE
SUBLIMATE
SUBLIMATED
SUBLIMATES
SUBLIMATING
SUBLIMATION
SUBLIMATIONS
SUBLIME
SUBLIMED
SUBLIMELY
SUBLIMENESS
SUBLIMENESSES
SUBLIMER
SUBLIMERS
SUBLIMES
SUBLIMEST
SUBLIMINAL
SUBLIMINALLY
SUBLIMINALS
SUBLIMING

SUBLIMINGS
SUBLIMISE
SUBLIMISED
SUBLIMISES
SUBLIMISING
SUBLIMITIES
SUBLIMITY
SUBLIMIZE
SUBLIMIZED
SUBLIMIZES
SUBLIMIZING
SUBLINE
SUBLINEAR
SUBLINEATION
SUBLINEATIONS
SUBLINES
SUBLINGUAL
SUBLITERACIES
SUBLITERACY
SUBLITERARY
SUBLITERATE
SUBLITERATES
SUBLITERATURE
SUBLITERATURES
SUBLITTORAL
SUBLITTORALS
SUBLOT
SUBLOTS
SUBLUNAR
SUBLUNARY
SUBLUNATE
SUBLUXATE
SUBLUXATED
SUBLUXATES
SUBLUXATING
SUBLUXATION
SUBLUXATIONS
SUBMAN
SUBMANAGER
SUBMANAGERS
SUBMANDIBULAR
SUBMANDIBULARS
SUBMARGINAL
SUBMARGINALLY
SUBMARINE
SUBMARINED
SUBMARINER
SUBMARINERS
SUBMARINES
SUBMARINING
SUBMARKET
SUBMARKETS
SUBMATRICES
SUBMATRIX
SUBMATRIXES
SUBMAXILLARIES
SUBMAXILLARY

SUBMAXIMAL
SUBMEDIANT
SUBMEDIANTS
SUBMEMBER
SUBMEMBERS
SUBMEN
SUBMENTA
SUBMENTAL
SUBMENTUM
SUBMENU
SUBMENUS
SUBMERGE
SUBMERGED
SUBMERGEMENT
SUBMERGEMENTS
SUBMERGENCE
SUBMERGENCES
SUBMERGES
SUBMERGIBILITY
SUBMERGIBLE
SUBMERGIBLES
SUBMERGING
SUBMERSE
SUBMERSED
SUBMERSES
SUBMERSIBILITY
SUBMERSIBLE
SUBMERSIBLES
SUBMERSING
SUBMERSION
SUBMERSIONS
SUBMETACENTRIC
SUBMETACENTRICS
SUBMICROGRAM
SUBMICRON
SUBMICRONS
SUBMICROSCOPIC
SUBMILLIMETER
SUBMINIATURE
SUBMINIATURES
SUBMINIATURISE
SUBMINIATURISED
SUBMINIATURISES
SUBMINIATURIZE
SUBMINIATURIZED
SUBMINIATURIZES
SUBMINIMAL
SUBMINISTER
SUBMINISTERS
SUBMISS
SUBMISSIBLE
SUBMISSION
SUBMISSIONS
SUBMISSIVE
SUBMISSIVELY
SUBMISSIVENESS
SUBMISSLY

SUBMISSNESS
SUBMISSNESSES
SUBMIT
SUBMITS
SUBMITTABILITY
SUBMITTABLE
SUBMITTAL
SUBMITTALS
SUBMITTED
SUBMITTER
SUBMITTERS
SUBMITTING
SUBMITTINGS
SUBMOLECULAR
SUBMOLECULE
SUBMOLECULES
SUBMONTANE
SUBMONTANELY
SUBMUCOSA
SUBMUCOSAE
SUBMUCOSAL
SUBMUCOSAS
SUBMUCOUS
SUBMULTIPLE
SUBMULTIPLES
SUBMUNITION
SUBMUNITIONS
SUBNASAL
SUBNASCENT
SUBNATIONAL
SUBNATURAL
SUBNET
SUBNETS
SUBNETWORK
SUBNETWORKED
SUBNETWORKING
SUBNETWORKS
SUBNEURAL
SUBNICHE
SUBNICHES
SUBNIVEAL
SUBNIVEAN
SUBNODAL
SUBNORMAL
SUBNORMALITIES
SUBNORMALITY
SUBNORMALLY
SUBNORMALS
SUBNUCLEAR
SUBOCCIPITAL
SUBOCEANIC
SUBOCTAVE
SUBOCTAVES
SUBOCTUPLE
SUBOCULAR
SUBOFFICE
SUBOFFICER

SUBOFFICERS
SUBOFFICES
SUBOFFICIAL
SUBOFFICIALS
SUBOPERCULA
SUBOPERCULAR
SUBOPERCULUM
SUBOPTIC
SUBOPTIMAL
SUBOPTIMIZATION
SUBOPTIMIZE
SUBOPTIMIZED
SUBOPTIMIZES
SUBOPTIMIZING
SUBOPTIMUM
SUBORAL
SUBORBICULAR
SUBORBITAL
SUBORDER
SUBORDERS
SUBORDINAL
SUBORDINANCIES
SUBORDINANCY
SUBORDINARIES
SUBORDINARY
SUBORDINATE
SUBORDINATED
SUBORDINATELY
SUBORDINATENESS
SUBORDINATES
SUBORDINATING
SUBORDINATION
SUBORDINATIONS
SUBORDINATIVE
SUBORDINATOR
SUBORDINATORS
SUBORGANIZATION
SUBORN
SUBORNATION
SUBORNATIONS
SUBORNATIVE
SUBORNED
SUBORNER
SUBORNERS
SUBORNING
SUBORNS
SUBOVAL
SUBOVATE
SUBOXIDE
SUBOXIDES
SUBPANATION
SUBPANATIONS
SUBPANEL
SUBPANELS
SUBPAR
SUBPARAGRAPH
SUBPARAGRAPHS

SUBPARALLEL
SUBPART
SUBPARTITION
SUBPARTITIONING
SUBPARTITIONS
SUBPARTS
SUBPATTERN
SUBPATTERNS
SUBPENA
SUBPENAED
SUBPENAING
SUBPENAS
SUBPERIOD
SUBPERIODS
SUBPHASE
SUBPHASES
SUBPHRENIC
SUBPHYLA
SUBPHYLAR
SUBPHYLUM
SUBPLOT
SUBPLOTS
SUBPOENA
SUBPOENAED
SUBPOENAING
SUBPOENAS
SUBPOLAR
SUBPOPULATION
SUBPOPULATIONS
SUBPOTENCIES
SUBPOTENCY
SUBPOTENT
SUBPREFECT
SUBPREFECTS
SUBPREFECTURE
SUBPREFECTURES
SUBPRIMATE
SUBPRIMATES
SUBPRINCIPAL
SUBPRINCIPALS
SUBPRIOR
SUBPRIORESS
SUBPRIORESSES
SUBPRIORS
SUBPROBLEM
SUBPROBLEMS
SUBPROCESS
SUBPROCESSES
SUBPRODUCT
SUBPRODUCTS
SUBPROFESSIONAL
SUBPROGRAM
SUBPROGRAMS
SUBPROJECT
SUBPROJECTS
SUBPROLETARIAT
SUBPROLETARIATS

SUBPROVINCE
SUBPROVINCES
SUBPUBIC
SUBRACE
SUBRACES
SUBRATIONAL
SUBREFERENCE
SUBREFERENCES
SUBREGION
SUBREGIONAL
SUBREGIONS
SUBRENT
SUBRENTS
SUBREPTION
SUBREPTIONS
SUBREPTITIOUS
SUBREPTITIOUSLY
SUBREPTIVE
SUBRING
SUBRINGS
SUBROGATE
SUBROGATED
SUBROGATES
SUBROGATING
SUBROGATION
SUBROGATIONS
SUBROUTINE
SUBROUTINES
SUBRULE
SUBRULES
SUBS
SUBSACRAL
SUBSALE
SUBSALES
SUBSAMPLE
SUBSAMPLED
SUBSAMPLES
SUBSAMPLING
SUBSATELLITE
SUBSATELLITES
SUBSATURATED
SUBSATURATION
SUBSATURATIONS
SUBSCALE
SUBSCALES
SUBSCAPULAR
SUBSCAPULARS
SUBSCHEDULE
SUBSCHEDULES
SUBSCHEMA
SUBSCHEMATA
SUBSCIENCE
SUBSCIENCES
SUBSCRIBABLE
SUBSCRIBE
SUBSCRIBED
SUBSCRIBER

SUBSCRIBERS
SUBSCRIBES
SUBSCRIBING
SUBSCRIBINGS
SUBSCRIPT
SUBSCRIPTION
SUBSCRIPTIONS
SUBSCRIPTIVE
SUBSCRIPTS
SUBSEA
SUBSECIVE
SUBSECRETARIES
SUBSECRETARY
SUBSECT
SUBSECTION
SUBSECTIONS
SUBSECTOR
SUBSECTORS
SUBSECTS
SUBSEGMENT
SUBSEGMENTS
SUBSEIZURE
SUBSEIZURES
SUBSELLIA
SUBSELLIUM
SUBSELLIUMS
SUBSENSE
SUBSENSES
SUBSENSIBLE
SUBSENTENCE
SUBSENTENCES
SUBSEQUENCE
SUBSEQUENCES
SUBSEQUENT
SUBSEQUENTIAL
SUBSEQUENTLY
SUBSEQUENTNESS
SUBSEQUENTS
SUBSERE
SUBSERES
SUBSERIES
SUBSERVE
SUBSERVED
SUBSERVES
SUBSERVIENCE
SUBSERVIENCES
SUBSERVIENCIES
SUBSERVIENCY
SUBSERVIENT
SUBSERVIENTLY
SUBSERVIENTS
SUBSERVING
SUBSESSILE
SUBSET
SUBSETS
SUBSHAFT
SUBSHAFTS

SUBSHELL
SUBSHELLS
SUBSHRUB
SUBSHRUBBY
SUBSHRUBS
SUBSIDE
SUBSIDED
SUBSIDENCE
SUBSIDENCES
SUBSIDENCIES
SUBSIDENCY
SUBSIDER
SUBSIDERS
SUBSIDES
SUBSIDIARIES
SUBSIDIARILY
SUBSIDIARINESS
SUBSIDIARITIES
SUBSIDIARITY
SUBSIDIARY
SUBSIDIES
SUBSIDING
SUBSIDISABLE
SUBSIDISATION
SUBSIDISATIONS
SUBSIDISE
SUBSIDISED
SUBSIDISER
SUBSIDISERS
SUBSIDISES
SUBSIDISING
SUBSIDIZABLE
SUBSIDIZATION
SUBSIDIZATIONS
SUBSIDIZE
SUBSIDIZED
SUBSIDIZER
SUBSIDIZERS
SUBSIDIZES
SUBSIDIZING
SUBSIDY
SUBSIST
SUBSISTED
SUBSISTENCE
SUBSISTENCES
SUBSISTENT
SUBSISTENTIAL
SUBSISTER
SUBSISTERS
SUBSISTING
SUBSISTS
SUBSITE
SUBSITES
SUBSIZAR
SUBSIZARS
SUBSKILL
SUBSKILLS

SUBSOCIAL
SUBSOCIALLY
SUBSOCIETIES
SUBSOCIETY
SUBSOIL
SUBSOILED
SUBSOILER
SUBSOILERS
SUBSOILING
SUBSOILINGS
SUBSOILS
SUBSOLAR
SUBSONG
SUBSONGS
SUBSONIC
SUBSONICALLY
SUBSPACE
SUBSPACES
SUBSPECIALIST
SUBSPECIALISTS
SUBSPECIALITIES
SUBSPECIALITY
SUBSPECIALIZE
SUBSPECIALIZED
SUBSPECIALIZES
SUBSPECIALIZING
SUBSPECIALTIES
SUBSPECIALTY
SUBSPECIES
SUBSPECIFIC
SUBSPECIFICALLY
SUBSPINOUS
SUBSPONTANEOUS
SUBSTAGE
SUBSTAGES
SUBSTANCE
SUBSTANCELESS
SUBSTANCES
SUBSTANDARD
SUBSTANTIAL
SUBSTANTIALISE
SUBSTANTIALISED
SUBSTANTIALISES
SUBSTANTIALISM
SUBSTANTIALISMS
SUBSTANTIALIST
SUBSTANTIALISTS
SUBSTANTIALITY
SUBSTANTIALIZE
SUBSTANTIALIZED
SUBSTANTIALIZES
SUBSTANTIALLY
SUBSTANTIALNESS
SUBSTANTIALS
SUBSTANTIATE
SUBSTANTIATED
SUBSTANTIATES

SUBSTANTIATING
SUBSTANTIATION
SUBSTANTIATIONS
SUBSTANTIATIVE
SUBSTANTIATOR
SUBSTANTIATORS
SUBSTANTIVAL
SUBSTANTIVALLY
SUBSTANTIVE
SUBSTANTIVELY
SUBSTANTIVENESS
SUBSTANTIVES
SUBSTANTIVISE
SUBSTANTIVISED
SUBSTANTIVISES
SUBSTANTIVISING
SUBSTANTIVITIES
SUBSTANTIVITY
SUBSTANTIVIZE
SUBSTANTIVIZED
SUBSTANTIVIZES
SUBSTANTIVIZING
SUBSTATE
SUBSTATES
SUBSTATION
SUBSTATIONS
SUBSTELLAR
SUBSTERNAL
SUBSTITUENT
SUBSTITUENTS
SUBSTITUTABLE
SUBSTITUTE
SUBSTITUTED
SUBSTITUTES
SUBSTITUTING
SUBSTITUTION
SUBSTITUTIONAL
SUBSTITUTIONARY
SUBSTITUTIONS
SUBSTITUTIVE
SUBSTITUTIVELY
SUBSTITUTIVITY
SUBSTRACT
SUBSTRACTED
SUBSTRACTING
SUBSTRACTION
SUBSTRACTIONS
SUBSTRACTOR
SUBSTRACTORS
SUBSTRACTS
SUBSTRATA
SUBSTRATAL
SUBSTRATE
SUBSTRATES
SUBSTRATIVE
SUBSTRATOSPHERE
SUBSTRATUM

SUBSTRUCT
SUBSTRUCTED
SUBSTRUCTING
SUBSTRUCTION
SUBSTRUCTIONS
SUBSTRUCTS
SUBSTRUCTURAL
SUBSTRUCTURE
SUBSTRUCTURES
SUBSTYLAR
SUBSTYLE
SUBSTYLES
SUBSULTIVE
SUBSULTORILY
SUBSULTORY
SUBSULTUS
SUBSULTUSES
SUBSUMABLE
SUBSUME
SUBSUMED
SUBSUMES
SUBSUMING
SUBSUMPTION
SUBSUMPTIONS
SUBSUMPTIVE
SUBSURFACE
SUBSURFACES
SUBSYSTEM
SUBSYSTEMS
SUBTACK
SUBTACKS
SUBTACKSMAN
SUBTACKSMEN
SUBTANGENT
SUBTANGENTS
SUBTASK
SUBTASKS
SUBTAXA
SUBTAXON
SUBTAXONS
SUBTEEN
SUBTEENS
SUBTEMPERATE
SUBTENANCIES
SUBTENANCY
SUBTENANT
SUBTENANTS
SUBTEND
SUBTENDED
SUBTENDING
SUBTENDS
SUBTENSE
SUBTENSES
SUBTENURE
SUBTENURES
SUBTERFUGE
SUBTERFUGES

SUBTERMINAL
SUBTERNATURAL
SUBTERRAIN
SUBTERRAINS
SUBTERRANE
SUBTERRANEAN
SUBTERRANEANLY
SUBTERRANEANS
SUBTERRANEOUS
SUBTERRANEOUSLY
SUBTERRANES
SUBTERRENE
SUBTERRENES
SUBTERRESTRIAL
SUBTERRESTRIALS
SUBTEST
SUBTESTS
SUBTEXT
SUBTEXTS
SUBTEXTUAL
SUBTHEME
SUBTHEMES
SUBTHERAPEUTIC
SUBTHRESHOLD
SUBTIDAL
SUBTIL
SUBTILE
SUBTILELY
SUBTILENESS
SUBTILENESSES
SUBTILER
SUBTILEST
SUBTILIN
SUBTILINS
SUBTILISATION
SUBTILISATIONS
SUBTILISE
SUBTILISED
SUBTILISER
SUBTILISERS
SUBTILISES
SUBTILISIN
SUBTILISING
SUBTILISINS
SUBTILITIES
SUBTILITY
SUBTILIZATION
SUBTILIZATIONS
SUBTILIZE
SUBTILIZED
SUBTILIZER
SUBTILIZERS
SUBTILIZES
SUBTILIZING
SUBTILTIES
SUBTILTY
SUBTITLE

SUBTITLED
SUBTITLES
SUBTITLING
SUBTITULAR
SUBTLE
SUBTLENESS
SUBTLENESSES
SUBTLER
SUBTLEST
SUBTLETIES
SUBTLETY
SUBTLY
SUBTONE
SUBTONES
SUBTONIC
SUBTONICS
SUBTOPIA
SUBTOPIAN
SUBTOPIAS
SUBTOPIC
SUBTOPICS
SUBTORRID
SUBTOTAL
SUBTOTALED
SUBTOTALING
SUBTOTALLED
SUBTOTALLING
SUBTOTALLY
SUBTOTALS
SUBTRACT
SUBTRACTED
SUBTRACTER
SUBTRACTERS
SUBTRACTING
SUBTRACTION
SUBTRACTIONS
SUBTRACTIVE
SUBTRACTOR
SUBTRACTORS
SUBTRACTS
SUBTRAHEND
SUBTRAHENDS
SUBTREASURER
SUBTREASURERS
SUBTREASURIES
SUBTREASURY
SUBTREND
SUBTRENDS
SUBTRIANGULAR
SUBTRIBE
SUBTRIBES
SUBTRIPLICATE
SUBTRIST
SUBTROPIC
SUBTROPICAL
SUBTROPICALLY
SUBTROPICS

SUBTRUDE
SUBTRUDED
SUBTRUDES
SUBTRUDING
SUBTUNIC
SUBTUNICS
SUBTYPE
SUBTYPES
SUBTYPICAL
SUBUCULA
SUBUCULAS
SUBULATE
SUBULATES
SUBUMBRELLA
SUBUMBRELLAR
SUBUMBRELLAS
SUBUNGULATE
SUBUNGULATES
SUBUNIT
SUBUNITS
SUBURB
SUBURBAN
SUBURBANISATION
SUBURBANISE
SUBURBANISED
SUBURBANISES
SUBURBANISING
SUBURBANISM
SUBURBANISMS
SUBURBANITE
SUBURBANITES
SUBURBANITIES
SUBURBANITY
SUBURBANIZATION
SUBURBANIZE
SUBURBANIZED
SUBURBANIZES
SUBURBANIZING
SUBURBANS
SUBURBED
SUBURBIA
SUBURBIAS
SUBURBICARIAN
SUBURBS
SUBURSINE
SUBVARIETIES
SUBVARIETY
SUBVASSAL
SUBVASSALS
SUBVENE
SUBVENED
SUBVENES
SUBVENING
SUBVENTION
SUBVENTIONARY
SUBVENTIONS
SUBVERSAL

SUBVERSALS
SUBVERSE
SUBVERSED
SUBVERSES
SUBVERSING
SUBVERSION
SUBVERSIONARIES
SUBVERSIONARY
SUBVERSIONS
SUBVERSIVE
SUBVERSIVELY
SUBVERSIVENESS
SUBVERSIVES
SUBVERST
SUBVERT
SUBVERTEBRAL
SUBVERTED
SUBVERTER
SUBVERTERS
SUBVERTICAL
SUBVERTING
SUBVERTS
SUBVICAR
SUBVICARS
SUBVIRAL
SUBVISIBLE
SUBVISUAL
SUBVITREOUS
SUBVOCAL
SUBVOCALIZATION
SUBVOCALIZE
SUBVOCALIZED
SUBVOCALIZES
SUBVOCALIZING
SUBVOCALLY
SUBWARDEN
SUBWARDENS
SUBWAY
SUBWAYED
SUBWAYING
SUBWAYS
SUBWOOFER
SUBWOOFERS
SUBWORLD
SUBWORLDS
SUBWRITER
SUBWRITERS
SUBZERO
SUBZONAL
SUBZONE
SUBZONES
SUCCADE
SUCCADES
SUCCAH
SUCCAHS
SUCCEDANEA
SUCCEDANEOUS

SUCCEDANEUM
SUCCEDANEUMS
SUCCEDENT
SUCCEED
SUCCEEDABILITY
SUCCEEDABLE
SUCCEEDED
SUCCEEDER
SUCCEEDERS
SUCCEEDING
SUCCEEDINGLY
SUCCEEDS
SUCCENTOR
SUCCENTORS
SUCCENTORSHIP
SUCCENTORSHIPS
SUCCES
SUCCESS
SUCCESSANTLY
SUCCESSES
SUCCESSFUL
SUCCESSFULLY
SUCCESSFULNESS
SUCCESSION
SUCCESSIONAL
SUCCESSIONALLY
SUCCESSIONIST
SUCCESSIONISTS
SUCCESSIONLESS
SUCCESSIONS
SUCCESSIVE
SUCCESSIVELY
SUCCESSIVENESS
SUCCESSLESS
SUCCESSLESSLY
SUCCESSLESSNESS
SUCCESSOR
SUCCESSORAL
SUCCESSORS
SUCCESSORSHIP
SUCCESSORSHIPS
SUCCI
SUCCINATE
SUCCINATES
SUCCINCT
SUCCINCTER
SUCCINCTEST
SUCCINCTLY
SUCCINCTNESS
SUCCINCTNESSES
SUCCINCTORIA
SUCCINCTORIES
SUCCINCTORIUM
SUCCINCTORY
SUCCINIC
SUCCINITE
SUCCINITES

SUCCINYL
SUCCINYLCHOLINE
SUCCINYLS
SUCCISE
SUCCOR
SUCCORABLE
SUCCORED
SUCCORER
SUCCORERS
SUCCORIES
SUCCORING
SUCCORLESS
SUCCORS
SUCCORY
SUCCOS
SUCCOSE
SUCCOT
SUCCOTASH
SUCCOTASHES
SUCCOTH
SUCCOUR
SUCCOURABLE
SUCCOURED
SUCCOURER
SUCCOURERS
SUCCOURING
SUCCOURLESS
SUCCOURS
SUCCOUS
SUCCUBA
SUCCUBAE
SUCCUBAS
SUCCUBI
SUCCUBINE
SUCCUBOUS
SUCCUBUS
SUCCUBUSES
SUCCULENCE
SUCCULENCES
SUCCULENCIES
SUCCULENCY
SUCCULENT
SUCCULENTLY
SUCCULENTS
SUCCUMB
SUCCUMBED
SUCCUMBER
SUCCUMBERS
SUCCUMBING
SUCCUMBS
SUCCURSAL
SUCCURSALE
SUCCURSALES
SUCCURSALS
SUCCUS
SUCCUSS
SUCCUSSATION

SUCCUSSATIONS
SUCCUSSED
SUCCUSSES
SUCCUSSING
SUCCUSSION
SUCCUSSIONS
SUCCUSSIVE
SUCH
SUCHLIKE
SUCHNESS
SUCHNESSES
SUCHWISE
SUCK
SUCKED
SUCKEN
SUCKENER
SUCKENERS
SUCKENS
SUCKER
SUCKERED
SUCKERFISH
SUCKERFISHES
SUCKERING
SUCKERS
SUCKET
SUCKETS
SUCKFISH
SUCKFISHES
SUCKING
SUCKINGS
SUCKLE
SUCKLED
SUCKLER
SUCKLERS
SUCKLES
SUCKLESS
SUCKLING
SUCKLINGS
SUCKS
SUCRALFATE
SUCRALFATES
SUCRASE
SUCRASES
SUCRE
SUCRES
SUCRIER
SUCRIERS
SUCROSE
SUCROSES
SUCTION
SUCTIONAL
SUCTIONED
SUCTIONING
SUCTIONS
SUCTORIAL
SUCTORIAN
SUCTORIANS

SUCURUJU
SUCURUJUS
SUD
SUDAMEN
SUDAMINA
SUDAMINAL
SUDARIA
SUDARIES
SUDARIUM
SUDARY
SUDATE
SUDATED
SUDATES
SUDATING
SUDATION
SUDATIONS
SUDATORIA
SUDATORIES
SUDATORIUM
SUDATORIUMS
SUDATORY
SUDD
SUDDEN
SUDDENLY
SUDDENNESS
SUDDENNESSES
SUDDENS
SUDDENTIES
SUDDENTY
SUDDER
SUDDERS
SUDDS
SUDOR
SUDORAL
SUDORIFEROUS
SUDORIFIC
SUDORIFICS
SUDORIPAROUS
SUDOROUS
SUDORS
SUDS
SUDSED
SUDSER
SUDSERS
SUDSES
SUDSIER
SUDSIEST
SUDSING
SUDSLESS
SUDSY
SUE
SUEABILITIES
SUEABILITY
SUEABLE
SUED
SUEDE
SUEDED

SUEDES
SUEDETTE
SUEDETTES
SUEDING
SUENT
SUER
SUERS
SUES
SUET
SUETIER
SUETIEST
SUETS
SUETTIER
SUETTIEST
SUETTY
SUETY
SUFFARI
SUFFARIS
SUFFECT
SUFFER
SUFFERABLE
SUFFERABLENESS
SUFFERABLY
SUFFERANCE
SUFFERANCES
SUFFERED
SUFFERER
SUFFERERS
SUFFERING
SUFFERINGLY
SUFFERINGS
SUFFERS
SUFFETE
SUFFETES
SUFFICE
SUFFICED
SUFFICER
SUFFICERS
SUFFICES
SUFFICIENCE
SUFFICIENCES
SUFFICIENCIES
SUFFICIENCY
SUFFICIENT
SUFFICIENTLY
SUFFICIENTS
SUFFICING
SUFFICINGNESS
SUFFICINGNESSES
SUFFIGANCE
SUFFIGANCES
SUFFISANCE
SUFFISANCES
SUFFIX
SUFFIXAL
SUFFIXATION
SUFFIXATIONS

SUFFIXED
SUFFIXES
SUFFIXING
SUFFIXION
SUFFIXIONS
SUFFLATE
SUFFLATED
SUFFLATES
SUFFLATING
SUFFLATION
SUFFLATIONS
SUFFOCATE
SUFFOCATED
SUFFOCATES
SUFFOCATING
SUFFOCATINGLY
SUFFOCATINGS
SUFFOCATION
SUFFOCATIONS
SUFFOCATIVE
SUFFRAGAN
SUFFRAGANS
SUFFRAGANSHIP
SUFFRAGANSHIPS
SUFFRAGE
SUFFRAGES
SUFFRAGETTE
SUFFRAGETTES
SUFFRAGETTISM
SUFFRAGETTISMS
SUFFRAGISM
SUFFRAGISMS
SUFFRAGIST
SUFFRAGISTS
SUFFRUTESCENT
SUFFRUTICOSE
SUFFUMIGATE
SUFFUMIGATED
SUFFUMIGATES
SUFFUMIGATING
SUFFUMIGATION
SUFFUMIGATIONS
SUFFUSE
SUFFUSED
SUFFUSES
SUFFUSING
SUFFUSION
SUFFUSIONS
SUFFUSIVE
SUGAN
SUGANS
SUGAR
SUGARALLIE
SUGARALLIES
SUGARALLY
SUGARBERRIES
SUGARBERRY

SUGARCANE
SUGARCANES
SUGARCOAT
SUGARCOATED
SUGARCOATING
SUGARCOATS
SUGARED
SUGARHOUSE
SUGARHOUSES
SUGARIER
SUGARIEST
SUGARINESS
SUGARINESSES
SUGARING
SUGARINGS
SUGARLESS
SUGARLOAF
SUGARLOAVES
SUGARPLUM
SUGARPLUMS
SUGARS
SUGARY
SUGGED
SUGGEST
SUGGESTED
SUGGESTER
SUGGESTERS
SUGGESTIBILITY
SUGGESTIBLE
SUGGESTIBLENESS
SUGGESTIBLY
SUGGESTING
SUGGESTION
SUGGESTIONISE
SUGGESTIONISED
SUGGESTIONISES
SUGGESTIONISING
SUGGESTIONISM
SUGGESTIONISMS
SUGGESTIONIST
SUGGESTIONISTS
SUGGESTIONIZE
SUGGESTIONIZED
SUGGESTIONIZES
SUGGESTIONIZING
SUGGESTIONS
SUGGESTIVE
SUGGESTIVELY
SUGGESTIVENESS
SUGGESTS
SUGGING
SUGGINGS
SUGH
SUGHED
SUGHING
SUGHS
SUGS

SUI
SUICIDAL
SUICIDALLY
SUICIDE
SUICIDED
SUICIDES
SUICIDING
SUICIDOLOGIES
SUICIDOLOGIST
SUICIDOLOGISTS
SUICIDOLOGY
SUID
SUIDIAN
SUIDIANS
SUIDS
SUILLINE
SUING
SUINGS
SUINT
SUINTS
SUIT
SUITABILITIES
SUITABILITY
SUITABLE
SUITABLENESS
SUITABLENESSES
SUITABLY
SUITCASE
SUITCASES
SUITE
SUITED
SUITER
SUITERS
SUITES
SUITING
SUITINGS
SUITLIKE
SUITOR
SUITORED
SUITORING
SUITORS
SUITRESS
SUITRESSES
SUITS
SUIVANTE
SUIVANTES
SUIVEZ
SUJEE
SUJEES
SUK
SUKH
SUKHS
SUKIYAKI
SUKIYAKIS
SUKKAH
SUKKAHS
SUKKOS

SUKKOT
SUKKOTH
SUKS
SULCAL
SULCALISE
SULCALISED
SULCALISES
SULCALISING
SULCALIZE
SULCALIZED
SULCALIZES
SULCALIZING
SULCATE
SULCATED
SULCATION
SULCATIONS
SULCI
SULCUS
SULDAN
SULDANS
SULFA
SULFACETAMIDE
SULFACETAMIDES
SULFADIAZINE
SULFADIAZINES
SULFADIMIDINE
SULFADOXINE
SULFADOXINES
SULFAMETHAZINE
SULFANILAMIDE
SULFANILAMIDES
SULFAS
SULFATASE
SULFATASES
SULFATE
SULFATED
SULFATES
SULFATHIAZOLE
SULFATHIAZOLES
SULFATIC
SULFATING
SULFATION
SULFATIONS
SULFHYDRYL
SULFHYDRYLS
SULFID
SULFIDE
SULFIDES
SULFIDS
SULFINPYRAZONE
SULFINPYRAZONES
SULFINYL
SULFINYLS
SULFITE
SULFITES
SULFITIC
SULFO

SULFONAMIDE
SULFONAMIDES
SULFONATE
SULFONATED
SULFONATES
SULFONATING
SULFONATION
SULFONATIONS
SULFONE
SULFONES
SULFONIC
SULFONIUM
SULFONIUMS
SULFONYL
SULFONYLS
SULFONYLUREA
SULFONYLUREAS
SULFOXIDE
SULFOXIDES
SULFUR
SULFURATE
SULFURATED
SULFURATES
SULFURATING
SULFURED
SULFURET
SULFURETED
SULFURETING
SULFURETS
SULFURETTED
SULFURETTING
SULFURIC
SULFURING
SULFURISATION
SULFURIZE
SULFURIZED
SULFURIZES
SULFURIZING
SULFUROUS
SULFUROUSLY
SULFUROUSNESS
SULFUROUSNESSES
SULFURS
SULFURY
SULFURYL
SULFURYLS
SULK
SULKED
SULKER
SULKERS
SULKIER
SULKIES
SULKIEST
SULKILY
SULKINESS
SULKINESSES
SULKING

SULKS
SULKY
SULLAGE
SULLAGES
SULLEN
SULLENED
SULLENER
SULLENEST
SULLENING
SULLENLY
SULLENNESS
SULLENNESSES
SULLENS
SULLIABLE
SULLIED
SULLIES
SULLY
SULLYING
SULPHA
SULPHACETAMIDE
SULPHACETAMIDES
SULPHADIAZINE
SULPHADIAZINES
SULPHADIMIDINE
SULPHANILAMIDE
SULPHANILAMIDES
SULPHAS
SULPHATASE
SULPHATASES
SULPHATE
SULPHATED
SULPHATES
SULPHATHIAZOLE
SULPHATHIAZOLES
SULPHATIC
SULPHATING
SULPHATION
SULPHATIONS
SULPHHYDRYL
SULPHHYDRYLS
SULPHID
SULPHIDE
SULPHIDES
SULPHIDS
SULPHINPYRAZONE
SULPHINYL
SULPHINYLS
SULPHISOXAZOLE
SULPHITE
SULPHITES
SULPHITIC
SULPHONAMIDE
SULPHONAMIDES
SULPHONATE
SULPHONATED
SULPHONATES
SULPHONATING

SULPHONATION
SULPHONATIONS
SULPHONE
SULPHONES
SULPHONIC
SULPHONIUM
SULPHONIUMS
SULPHONMETHANE
SULPHONYL
SULPHONYLUREA
SULPHONYLUREAS
SULPHUR
SULPHURATE
SULPHURATED
SULPHURATES
SULPHURATING
SULPHURATION
SULPHURATIONS
SULPHURATOR
SULPHURATORS
SULPHURED
SULPHUREOUS
SULPHUREOUSLY
SULPHUREOUSNESS
SULPHURET
SULPHURETED
SULPHURETING
SULPHURETS
SULPHURETTED
SULPHURETTING
SULPHURIC
SULPHURING
SULPHURISATION
SULPHURISATIONS
SULPHURISE
SULPHURISED
SULPHURISES
SULPHURISING
SULPHURIZATION
SULPHURIZATIONS
SULPHURIZE
SULPHURIZED
SULPHURIZES
SULPHURIZING
SULPHUROUS
SULPHUROUSLY
SULPHUROUSNESS
SULPHURS
SULPHURWORT
SULPHURWORTS
SULPHURY
SULPHURYL
SULTAN
SULTANA
SULTANAS
SULTANATE
SULTANATES

SULTANESS
SULTANESSES
SULTANIC
SULTANS
SULTANSHIP
SULTANSHIPS
SULTRIER
SULTRIEST
SULTRILY
SULTRINESS
SULTRINESSES
SULTRY
SULU
SULUS
SUM
SUMAC
SUMACH
SUMACHS
SUMACS
SUMATRA
SUMATRAS
SUMLESS
SUMMA
SUMMABILITIES
SUMMABILITY
SUMMABLE
SUMMAE
SUMMAND
SUMMANDS
SUMMAR
SUMMARIES
SUMMARILY
SUMMARINESS
SUMMARINESSES
SUMMARISABLE
SUMMARISATION
SUMMARISE
SUMMARISED
SUMMARISER
SUMMARISERS
SUMMARISES
SUMMARISING
SUMMARIST
SUMMARISTS
SUMMARIZABLE
SUMMARIZATION
SUMMARIZATIONS
SUMMARIZE
SUMMARIZED
SUMMARIZER
SUMMARIZERS
SUMMARIZES
SUMMARIZING
SUMMARY
SUMMAS
SUMMAT
SUMMATE

SUMMATED
SUMMATES
SUMMATING
SUMMATION
SUMMATIONAL
SUMMATIONS
SUMMATIVE
SUMMATS
SUMMED
SUMMER
SUMMERED
SUMMERHOUSE
SUMMERHOUSES
SUMMERIER
SUMMERIEST
SUMMERINESS
SUMMERING
SUMMERINGS
SUMMERLESS
SUMMERLIKE
SUMMERLONG
SUMMERLY
SUMMERS
SUMMERSAULT
SUMMERSAULTED
SUMMERSAULTING
SUMMERSAULTS
SUMMERSET
SUMMERSETS
SUMMERSETTED
SUMMERSETTING
SUMMERTIDE
SUMMERTIDES
SUMMERTIME
SUMMERTIMES
SUMMERWEIGHT
SUMMERWOOD
SUMMERWOODS
SUMMERY
SUMMING
SUMMINGS
SUMMIST
SUMMISTS
SUMMIT
SUMMITAL
SUMMITED
SUMMITEER
SUMMITEERS
SUMMITING
SUMMITLESS
SUMMITRIES
SUMMITRY
SUMMITS
SUMMON
SUMMONABLE
SUMMONED
SUMMONER

SUMMONERS
SUMMONING
SUMMONS
SUMMONSED
SUMMONSES
SUMMONSING
SUMO
SUMOS
SUMOTORI
SUMOTORIS
SUMP
SUMPH
SUMPHISH
SUMPHISHNESS
SUMPHISHNESSES
SUMPHS
SUMPIT
SUMPITAN
SUMPITANS
SUMPITS
SUMPS
SUMPSIMUS
SUMPSIMUSES
SUMPTER
SUMPTERS
SUMPTUARY
SUMPTUOSITIES
SUMPTUOSITY
SUMPTUOUS
SUMPTUOUSLY
SUMPTUOUSNESS
SUMPTUOUSNESSES
SUMPWEED
SUMPWEEDS
SUMS
SUN
SUNBACK
SUNBAKE
SUNBAKED
SUNBAKES
SUNBAKING
SUNBATH
SUNBATHE
SUNBATHED
SUNBATHER
SUNBATHERS
SUNBATHES
SUNBATHING
SUNBATHINGS
SUNBATHS
SUNBEAM
SUNBEAMED
SUNBEAMS
SUNBEAMY
SUNBEAT
SUNBEATEN
SUNBED

SUNBEDS
SUNBELT
SUNBELTS
SUNBERRIES
SUNBERRY
SUNBIRD
SUNBIRDS
SUNBLIND
SUNBLINDS
SUNBLOCK
SUNBLOCKS
SUNBONNET
SUNBONNETED
SUNBONNETS
SUNBOW
SUNBOWS
SUNBRIGHT
SUNBURN
SUNBURNED
SUNBURNING
SUNBURNS
SUNBURNT
SUNBURST
SUNBURSTS
SUNCHOKE
SUNCHOKES
SUNDAE
SUNDAES
SUNDARI
SUNDARIS
SUNDECK
SUNDECKS
SUNDER
SUNDERABLE
SUNDERANCE
SUNDERANCES
SUNDERED
SUNDERER
SUNDERERS
SUNDERING
SUNDERINGS
SUNDERMENT
SUNDERMENTS
SUNDERS
SUNDEW
SUNDEWS
SUNDIAL
SUNDIALS
SUNDOG
SUNDOGS
SUNDOWN
SUNDOWNER
SUNDOWNERS
SUNDOWNS
SUNDRA
SUNDRAS
SUNDRENCHED

SUNDRESS
SUNDRESSES
SUNDRI
SUNDRIES
SUNDRIS
SUNDROPS
SUNDRY
SUNFAST
SUNFISH
SUNFISHES
SUNFLOWER
SUNFLOWERS
SUNG
SUNGAR
SUNGARS
SUNGLASS
SUNGLASSES
SUNGLOW
SUNGLOWS
SUNGREBE
SUNGREBES
SUNHAT
SUNHATS
SUNK
SUNKEN
SUNKET
SUNKETS
SUNKIE
SUNKIES
SUNKS
SUNLAMP
SUNLAMPS
SUNLAND
SUNLANDS
SUNLESS
SUNLESSLY
SUNLESSNESS
SUNLESSNESSES
SUNLIGHT
SUNLIGHTS
SUNLIKE
SUNLIT
SUNLOUNGER
SUNLOUNGERS
SUNN
SUNNA
SUNNAH
SUNNAHS
SUNNAS
SUNNED
SUNNIER
SUNNIES
SUNNIEST
SUNNILY
SUNNINESS
SUNNINESSES
SUNNING

SUNNS
SUNNY
SUNPORCH
SUNPORCHES
SUNPROOF
SUNRAY
SUNRAYS
SUNRISE
SUNRISES
SUNRISING
SUNRISINGS
SUNROOF
SUNROOFS
SUNROOM
SUNROOMS
SUNS
SUNSCALD
SUNSCALDS
SUNSCREEN
SUNSCREENING
SUNSCREENS
SUNSEEKER
SUNSEEKERS
SUNSET
SUNSETS
SUNSETTING
SUNSETTINGS
SUNSHADE
SUNSHADES
SUNSHINE
SUNSHINES
SUNSHINY
SUNSPOT
SUNSPOTS
SUNSPOTTED
SUNSTAR
SUNSTARS
SUNSTONE
SUNSTONES
SUNSTROKE
SUNSTROKES
SUNSTRUCK
SUNSUIT
SUNSUITS
SUNTAN
SUNTANNED
SUNTANS
SUNTRAP
SUNTRAPS
SUNUP
SUNUPS
SUNWARD
SUNWARDS
SUNWISE
SUNWORSHIPPER
SUNWORSHIPPERS
SUOVETAURILIA

SUP
SUPAWN
SUPAWNS
SUPE
SUPER
SUPERABILITY
SUPERABLE
SUPERABLENESS
SUPERABLENESSES
SUPERABLY
SUPERABOUND
SUPERABOUNDED
SUPERABOUNDING
SUPERABOUNDS
SUPERABSORBENT
SUPERABSORBENTS
SUPERABUNDANCE
SUPERABUNDANCES
SUPERABUNDANT
SUPERABUNDANTLY
SUPERACHIEVER
SUPERACHIEVERS
SUPERACTIVE
SUPERACTIVITIES
SUPERACTIVITY
SUPERACUTE
SUPERADD
SUPERADDED
SUPERADDING
SUPERADDITION
SUPERADDITIONAL
SUPERADDITIONS
SUPERADDS
SUPERAGENCIES
SUPERAGENCY
SUPERAGENT
SUPERAGENTS
SUPERALLOY
SUPERALLOYS
SUPERALTAR
SUPERALTARS
SUPERALTERN
SUPERALTERNS
SUPERAMBITIOUS
SUPERANNUABLE
SUPERANNUATE
SUPERANNUATED
SUPERANNUATES
SUPERANNUATING
SUPERANNUATION
SUPERANNUATIONS
SUPERATE
SUPERATED
SUPERATES
SUPERATHLETE
SUPERATHLETES
SUPERATING

SUPERATION
SUPERATIONS
SUPERB
SUPERBAD
SUPERBANK
SUPERBANKS
SUPERBAZAAR
SUPERBAZAARS
SUPERBAZAR
SUPERBAZARS
SUPERBER
SUPERBEST
SUPERBIKE
SUPERBIKES
SUPERBITCH
SUPERBITCHES
SUPERBITIES
SUPERBITY
SUPERBLOCK
SUPERBLOCKS
SUPERBLY
SUPERBNESS
SUPERBNESSES
SUPERBOARD
SUPERBOARDS
SUPERBOLD
SUPERBOMB
SUPERBOMBER
SUPERBOMBERS
SUPERBOMBS
SUPERBRAIN
SUPERBRAINS
SUPERBRAT
SUPERBRATS
SUPERBRIGHT
SUPERBUG
SUPERBUGS
SUPERBUREAUCRAT
SUPERCABINET
SUPERCABINETS
SUPERCALENDER
SUPERCALENDERED
SUPERCALENDERS
SUPERCAR
SUPERCARGO
SUPERCARGOES
SUPERCARGOS
SUPERCARGOSHIP
SUPERCARGOSHIPS
SUPERCARRIER
SUPERCARRIERS
SUPERCARS
SUPERCAUTIOUS
SUPERCEDE
SUPERCEDED
SUPERCEDES
SUPERCEDING

SUPERCELESTIAL
SUPERCENTER
SUPERCENTERS
SUPERCHARGE
SUPERCHARGED
SUPERCHARGER
SUPERCHARGERS
SUPERCHARGES
SUPERCHARGING
SUPERCHERIE
SUPERCHERIES
SUPERCHIC
SUPERCHURCH
SUPERCHURCHES
SUPERCILIARIES
SUPERCILIARY
SUPERCILIOUS
SUPERCILIOUSLY
SUPERCITIES
SUPERCITY
SUPERCIVILIZED
SUPERCLASS
SUPERCLASSES
SUPERCLEAN
SUPERCLUB
SUPERCLUBS
SUPERCLUSTER
SUPERCLUSTERS
SUPERCOIL
SUPERCOILED
SUPERCOILING
SUPERCOILS
SUPERCOLD
SUPERCOLLIDER
SUPERCOLLIDERS
SUPERCOLOSSAL
SUPERCOLUMNAR
SUPERCOMPLEX
SUPERCOMPUTER
SUPERCOMPUTERS
SUPERCONDUCT
SUPERCONDUCTED
SUPERCONDUCTING
SUPERCONDUCTION
SUPERCONDUCTIVE
SUPERCONDUCTOR
SUPERCONDUCTORS
SUPERCONDUCTS
SUPERCONFIDENCE
SUPERCONFIDENT
SUPERCONFORMITY
SUPERCONGESTED
SUPERCONTINENT
SUPERCONTINENTS
SUPERCONVENIENT
SUPERCOOL
SUPERCOOLED

SUPERCOOLING
SUPERCOOLS
SUPERCOP
SUPERCOPS
SUPERCRIMINAL
SUPERCRIMINALS
SUPERCRITICAL
SUPERCURIOUS
SUPERCURRENT
SUPERCURRENTS
SUPERCUTE
SUPERCYNICAL
SUPERDAINTY
SUPERDEFICIT
SUPERDEFICITS
SUPERDELUXE
SUPERDENSE
SUPERDEVOTION
SUPERDIFFICULT
SUPERDIPLOMACY
SUPERDIPLOMAT
SUPERDIPLOMATIC
SUPERDIPLOMATS
SUPERDOMINANT
SUPERDOMINANTS
SUPERDOSE
SUPERDOSES
SUPERED
SUPEREFFECTIVE
SUPEREFFICIENCY
SUPEREFFICIENT
SUPEREGO
SUPEREGOIST
SUPEREGOISTS
SUPEREGOS
SUPERELASTIC
SUPERELEVATE
SUPERELEVATED
SUPERELEVATES
SUPERELEVATING
SUPERELEVATION
SUPERELEVATIONS
SUPERELITE
SUPEREMINENCE
SUPEREMINENCES
SUPEREMINENT
SUPEREMINENTLY
SUPEREROGANT
SUPEREROGATE
SUPEREROGATED
SUPEREROGATES
SUPEREROGATING
SUPEREROGATION
SUPEREROGATIONS
SUPEREROGATIVE
SUPEREROGATOR
SUPEREROGATORS

SUPEREROGATORY
SUPERESSENTIAL
SUPERETTE
SUPERETTES
SUPEREVIDENT
SUPEREXALT
SUPEREXALTATION
SUPEREXALTED
SUPEREXALTING
SUPEREXALTS
SUPEREXCELLENCE
SUPEREXCELLENT
SUPEREXCITED
SUPEREXPENSIVE
SUPEREXPRESS
SUPEREXPRESSES
SUPEREXPRESSIVE
SUPERFAMILIES
SUPERFAMILY
SUPERFAN
SUPERFANS
SUPERFARM
SUPERFARMS
SUPERFAST
SUPERFATTED
SUPERFECTA
SUPERFECTAS
SUPERFEMALE
SUPERFEMALES
SUPERFETATE
SUPERFETATED
SUPERFETATES
SUPERFETATING
SUPERFETATION
SUPERFETATIONS
SUPERFICIAL
SUPERFICIALISE
SUPERFICIALISED
SUPERFICIALISES
SUPERFICIALITY
SUPERFICIALIZE
SUPERFICIALIZED
SUPERFICIALIZES
SUPERFICIALLY
SUPERFICIALNESS
SUPERFICIALS
SUPERFICIES
SUPERFINE
SUPERFINENESS
SUPERFINENESSES
SUPERFINITE
SUPERFIRM
SUPERFIRMS
SUPERFIT
SUPERFIX
SUPERFIXES
SUPERFLACK

SUPERFLACKS
SUPERFLUID
SUPERFLUIDITIES
SUPERFLUIDITY
SUPERFLUIDS
SUPERFLUITIES
SUPERFLUITY
SUPERFLUOUS
SUPERFLUOUSLY
SUPERFLUOUSNESS
SUPERFLUX
SUPERFLUXES
SUPERFOETATION
SUPERFOETATIONS
SUPERFRONTAL
SUPERFRONTALS
SUPERFUND
SUPERFUNDS
SUPERFUSE
SUPERFUSED
SUPERFUSES
SUPERFUSING
SUPERFUSION
SUPERFUSIONS
SUPERGENE
SUPERGENEROSITY
SUPERGENEROUS
SUPERGENES
SUPERGIANT
SUPERGIANTS
SUPERGLACIAL
SUPERGLUE
SUPERGLUED
SUPERGLUES
SUPERGLUING
SUPERGOOD
SUPERGOVERNMENT
SUPERGRAPHICS
SUPERGRASS
SUPERGRASSES
SUPERGRAVITIES
SUPERGRAVITY
SUPERGROUP
SUPERGROUPS
SUPERGROWTH
SUPERGROWTHS
SUPERGUN
SUPERGUNS
SUPERHARDEN
SUPERHARDENED
SUPERHARDENING
SUPERHARDENS
SUPERHEAT
SUPERHEATED
SUPERHEATER
SUPERHEATERS
SUPERHEATING

SUPERHEATS
SUPERHEAVIES
SUPERHEAVY
SUPERHELICAL
SUPERHELICES
SUPERHELIX
SUPERHELIXES
SUPERHERO
SUPERHEROES
SUPERHEROINE
SUPERHEROINES
SUPERHET
SUPERHETERODYNE
SUPERHETS
SUPERHIGH
SUPERHIGHWAY
SUPERHIGHWAYS
SUPERHIT
SUPERHITS
SUPERHIVE
SUPERHIVES
SUPERHOT
SUPERHUMAN
SUPERHUMANISE
SUPERHUMANISED
SUPERHUMANISES
SUPERHUMANISING
SUPERHUMANITIES
SUPERHUMANITY
SUPERHUMANIZE
SUPERHUMANIZED
SUPERHUMANIZES
SUPERHUMANIZING
SUPERHUMANLY
SUPERHUMANNESS
SUPERHUMERAL
SUPERHUMERALS
SUPERHYPE
SUPERHYPED
SUPERHYPES
SUPERHYPING
SUPERIGNORANT
SUPERIGNORANTLY
SUPERIMPORTANT
SUPERIMPOSABLE
SUPERIMPOSE
SUPERIMPOSED
SUPERIMPOSES
SUPERIMPOSING
SUPERIMPOSITION
SUPERINCUMBENCE
SUPERINCUMBENCY
SUPERINCUMBENT
SUPERINDIVIDUAL
SUPERINDUCE
SUPERINDUCED
SUPERINDUCEMENT

SUPERINDUCES
SUPERINDUCING
SUPERINDUCTION
SUPERINDUCTIONS
SUPERINFECT
SUPERINFECTED
SUPERINFECTING
SUPERINFECTION
SUPERINFECTIONS
SUPERINFECTS
SUPERING
SUPERINSIST
SUPERINSISTED
SUPERINSISTING
SUPERINSISTS
SUPERINSULATED
SUPERINTEND
SUPERINTENDED
SUPERINTENDENCE
SUPERINTENDENCY
SUPERINTENDENT
SUPERINTENDENTS
SUPERINTENDING
SUPERINTENDS
SUPERINTENSITY
SUPERIOR
SUPERIORESS
SUPERIORESSES
SUPERIORITIES
SUPERIORITY
SUPERIORLY
SUPERIORS
SUPERIORSHIP
SUPERIORSHIPS
SUPERJACENT
SUPERJET
SUPERJETS
SUPERJOCK
SUPERJOCKS
SUPERJUMBO
SUPERJUMBOS
SUPERKINGDOM
SUPERKINGDOMS
SUPERLAIN
SUPERLARGE
SUPERLATIVE
SUPERLATIVELY
SUPERLATIVENESS
SUPERLATIVES
SUPERLAWYER
SUPERLAWYERS
SUPERLAY
SUPERLIE
SUPERLIES
SUPERLIGHT
SUPERLINER
SUPERLINERS

SUPERLOAD
SUPERLOADED
SUPERLOADS
SUPERLOBBYIST
SUPERLOBBYISTS
SUPERLOGICAL
SUPERLOGICALLY
SUPERLOO
SUPERLOOS
SUPERLOYALIST
SUPERLOYALISTS
SUPERLUCKY
SUPERLUMINAL
SUPERLUNAR
SUPERLUNARY
SUPERLUXURIOUS
SUPERLUXURY
SUPERLYING
SUPERMACHO
SUPERMAJORITIES
SUPERMAJORITY
SUPERMALE
SUPERMALES
SUPERMAN
SUPERMARKET
SUPERMARKETS
SUPERMART
SUPERMARTS
SUPERMASCULINE
SUPERMASSIVE
SUPERMAX
SUPERMEMBRANE
SUPERMEMBRANES
SUPERMEN
SUPERMICRO
SUPERMICROS
SUPERMILITANT
SUPERMILITANTS
SUPERMIND
SUPERMINDS
SUPERMINI
SUPERMINIS
SUPERMINISTER
SUPERMINISTERS
SUPERMODEL
SUPERMODELS
SUPERMODERN
SUPERMOM
SUPERMOMS
SUPERMUNDANE
SUPERNACULAR
SUPERNACULUM
SUPERNAL
SUPERNALLY
SUPERNATANT
SUPERNATANTS
SUPERNATATION

SUPERNATATIONS
SUPERNATION
SUPERNATIONAL
SUPERNATIONALLY
SUPERNATIONS
SUPERNATURAL
SUPERNATURALISE
SUPERNATURALISM
SUPERNATURALIST
SUPERNATURALIZE
SUPERNATURALLY
SUPERNATURALS
SUPERNATURE
SUPERNATURES
SUPERNEGLIGENT
SUPERNORMAL
SUPERNORMALITY
SUPERNORMALLY
SUPERNOVA
SUPERNOVAE
SUPERNOVAS
SUPERNUMERARIES
SUPERNUMERARY
SUPERNURSE
SUPERNURSES
SUPERNUTRITION
SUPERNUTRITIONS
SUPEROBLIGATION
SUPEROCTAVE
SUPEROCTAVES
SUPEROFFICIOUS
SUPEROPTIMIST
SUPEROPTIMISTIC
SUPEROPTIMISTS
SUPERORDER
SUPERORDERS
SUPERORDINAL
SUPERORDINARY
SUPERORDINATE
SUPERORDINATED
SUPERORDINATES
SUPERORDINATING
SUPERORDINATION
SUPERORGANIC
SUPERORGANICISM
SUPERORGANICIST
SUPERORGANISM
SUPERORGANISMS
SUPERORGASM
SUPERORGASMS
SUPEROVULATE
SUPEROVULATED
SUPEROVULATES
SUPEROVULATING
SUPEROVULATION
SUPEROVULATIONS
SUPEROXIDE

SUPEROXIDES
SUPERPARASITISM
SUPERPATRIOT
SUPERPATRIOTIC
SUPERPATRIOTISM
SUPERPATRIOTS
SUPERPERSON
SUPERPERSONAL
SUPERPERSONS
SUPERPHENOMENA
SUPERPHENOMENON
SUPERPHOSPHATE
SUPERPHOSPHATES
SUPERPHYLA
SUPERPHYLUM
SUPERPHYSICAL
SUPERPIMP
SUPERPIMPS
SUPERPLANE
SUPERPLANES
SUPERPLASTIC
SUPERPLASTICITY
SUPERPLASTICS
SUPERPLAYER
SUPERPLAYERS
SUPERPLUS
SUPERPLUSES
SUPERPOLITE
SUPERPOLYMER
SUPERPOLYMERS
SUPERPORT
SUPERPORTS
SUPERPOSABLE
SUPERPOSE
SUPERPOSED
SUPERPOSES
SUPERPOSING
SUPERPOSITION
SUPERPOSITIONS
SUPERPOWER
SUPERPOWERED
SUPERPOWERFUL
SUPERPOWERS
SUPERPRAISE
SUPERPRAISED
SUPERPRAISES
SUPERPRAISING
SUPERPRECISE
SUPERPREMIUM
SUPERPREMIUMS
SUPERPREPARED
SUPERPRO
SUPERPROFIT
SUPERPROFITS
SUPERPROS
SUPERPURE
SUPERQUALITY

SUPERRACE
SUPERRACES
SUPERREAL
SUPERREALISM
SUPERREALISMS
SUPERREALIST
SUPERREALISTS
SUPERREFINE
SUPERREFINED
SUPERREFINES
SUPERREFINING
SUPERREGIONAL
SUPERREGIONALS
SUPERRELIANCE
SUPERRICH
SUPERRIGHTEOUS
SUPERROAD
SUPERROADS
SUPERROMANTIC
SUPERS
SUPERSACRED
SUPERSAFE
SUPERSAFETIES
SUPERSAFETY
SUPERSALE
SUPERSALES
SUPERSALESMAN
SUPERSALESMEN
SUPERSALT
SUPERSALTS
SUPERSARCASTIC
SUPERSATURATE
SUPERSATURATED
SUPERSATURATES
SUPERSATURATING
SUPERSATURATION
SUPERSAVER
SUPERSAVERS
SUPERSCALAR
SUPERSCALE
SUPERSCHOOL
SUPERSCHOOLS
SUPERSCOUT
SUPERSCOUTS
SUPERSCREEN
SUPERSCREENS
SUPERSCRIBE
SUPERSCRIBED
SUPERSCRIBES
SUPERSCRIBING
SUPERSCRIPT
SUPERSCRIPTION
SUPERSCRIPTIONS
SUPERSCRIPTS
SUPERSECRECIES
SUPERSECRECY
SUPERSECRET

SUPERSEDABLE
SUPERSEDE
SUPERSEDEAS
SUPERSEDEASES
SUPERSEDED
SUPERSEDENCE
SUPERSEDENCES
SUPERSEDER
SUPERSEDERE
SUPERSEDERES
SUPERSEDERS
SUPERSEDES
SUPERSEDING
SUPERSEDURE
SUPERSEDURES
SUPERSELL
SUPERSELLER
SUPERSELLERS
SUPERSELLS
SUPERSENSIBLE
SUPERSENSIBLY
SUPERSENSITIVE
SUPERSENSORY
SUPERSENSUAL
SUPERSESSION
SUPERSESSIONS
SUPERSEVERE
SUPERSEVERELY
SUPERSEX
SUPERSEXES
SUPERSEXUALITY
SUPERSHARP
SUPERSHOW
SUPERSHOWS
SUPERSIMPLICITY
SUPERSINGER
SUPERSINGERS
SUPERSIZE
SUPERSIZED
SUPERSLEUTH
SUPERSLEUTHS
SUPERSLICK
SUPERSMART
SUPERSMOOTH
SUPERSOFT
SUPERSONIC
SUPERSONICALLY
SUPERSONICS
SUPERSOUND
SUPERSOUNDS
SUPERSPECIAL
SUPERSPECIALISE
SUPERSPECIALIST
SUPERSPECIALIZE
SUPERSPECIALS
SUPERSPECIES
SUPERSPECTACLE

SUPERSPECTACLES
SUPERSPEED
SUPERSPEEDS
SUPERSPIES
SUPERSPY
SUPERSTAR
SUPERSTARDOM
SUPERSTARDOMS
SUPERSTARS
SUPERSTATE
SUPERSTATES
SUPERSTATION
SUPERSTATIONS
SUPERSTIMULATE
SUPERSTIMULATED
SUPERSTIMULATES
SUPERSTITION
SUPERSTITIONS
SUPERSTITIOUS
SUPERSTITIOUSLY
SUPERSTOCK
SUPERSTOCKS
SUPERSTORE
SUPERSTORES
SUPERSTRATA
SUPERSTRATUM
SUPERSTRATUMS
SUPERSTRENGTH
SUPERSTRENGTHS
SUPERSTRICT
SUPERSTRICTLY
SUPERSTRICTNESS
SUPERSTRIKE
SUPERSTRIKES
SUPERSTRING
SUPERSTRINGS
SUPERSTRONG
SUPERSTRUCT
SUPERSTRUCTED
SUPERSTRUCTING
SUPERSTRUCTION
SUPERSTRUCTIONS
SUPERSTRUCTIVE
SUPERSTRUCTS
SUPERSTRUCTURAL
SUPERSTRUCTURE
SUPERSTRUCTURES
SUPERSTUD
SUPERSTUDS
SUPERSTYLISH
SUPERSTYLISHLY
SUPERSUBTILE
SUPERSUBTLE
SUPERSUBTLETIES
SUPERSUBTLETY
SUPERSURGEON
SUPERSURGEONS

SUPERSWEET
SUPERSYMMETRIC
SUPERSYMMETRIES
SUPERSYMMETRY
SUPERSYSTEM
SUPERSYSTEMS
SUPERTANKER
SUPERTANKERS
SUPERTAX
SUPERTAXES
SUPERTEACHER
SUPERTEACHERS
SUPERTENSION
SUPERTERRANEAN
SUPERTERRIFIC
SUPERTHICK
SUPERTHIN
SUPERTHOROUGH
SUPERTHRILLER
SUPERTHRILLERS
SUPERTIGHT
SUPERTITLE
SUPERTITLES
SUPERTONIC
SUPERTONICS
SUPERTWIST
SUPERTWISTS
SUPERVENE
SUPERVENED
SUPERVENES
SUPERVENIENCE
SUPERVENIENCES
SUPERVENIENT
SUPERVENING
SUPERVENTION
SUPERVENTIONS
SUPERVIGILANT
SUPERVIRILE
SUPERVIRTUOSI
SUPERVIRTUOSO
SUPERVIRTUOSOS
SUPERVIRULENT
SUPERVISAL
SUPERVISALS
SUPERVISE
SUPERVISED
SUPERVISEE
SUPERVISEES
SUPERVISES
SUPERVISING
SUPERVISION
SUPERVISIONS
SUPERVISOR
SUPERVISORS
SUPERVISORSHIP
SUPERVISORSHIPS
SUPERVISORY

SUPERVOLUTE
SUPERWAIF
SUPERWAIFS
SUPERWAVE
SUPERWAVES
SUPERWEAPON
SUPERWEAPONS
SUPERWEED
SUPERWEEDS
SUPERWIDE
SUPERWIFE
SUPERWIVES
SUPERWOMAN
SUPERWOMEN
SUPES
SUPINATE
SUPINATED
SUPINATES
SUPINATING
SUPINATION
SUPINATIONS
SUPINATOR
SUPINATORS
SUPINE
SUPINELY
SUPINENESS
SUPINENESSES
SUPINES
SUPLEX
SUPLEXES
SUPPAWN
SUPPAWNS
SUPPEAGO
SUPPEAGOES
SUPPED
SUPPEDANEA
SUPPEDANEUM
SUPPER
SUPPERED
SUPPERING
SUPPERLESS
SUPPERS
SUPPERTIME
SUPPERTIMES
SUPPING
SUPPLANT
SUPPLANTATION
SUPPLANTATIONS
SUPPLANTED
SUPPLANTER
SUPPLANTERS
SUPPLANTING
SUPPLANTS
SUPPLE
SUPPLED
SUPPLEJACK
SUPPLEJACKS

SUPPLELY
SUPPLEMENT
SUPPLEMENTAL
SUPPLEMENTALLY
SUPPLEMENTALS
SUPPLEMENTARIES
SUPPLEMENTARILY
SUPPLEMENTARY
SUPPLEMENTATION
SUPPLEMENTED
SUPPLEMENTER
SUPPLEMENTERS
SUPPLEMENTING
SUPPLEMENTS
SUPPLENESS
SUPPLENESSES
SUPPLER
SUPPLES
SUPPLEST
SUPPLETION
SUPPLETIONS
SUPPLETIVE
SUPPLETIVES
SUPPLETORILY
SUPPLETORY
SUPPLIABILITY
SUPPLIABLE
SUPPLIAL
SUPPLIALS
SUPPLIANCE
SUPPLIANCES
SUPPLIANT
SUPPLIANTLY
SUPPLIANTS
SUPPLICANT
SUPPLICANTS
SUPPLICAT
SUPPLICATE
SUPPLICATED
SUPPLICATES
SUPPLICATING
SUPPLICATINGLY
SUPPLICATION
SUPPLICATIONS
SUPPLICATORY
SUPPLICATS
SUPPLICAVIT
SUPPLICAVITS
SUPPLIED
SUPPLIER
SUPPLIERS
SUPPLIES
SUPPLING
SUPPLY
SUPPLYING
SUPPLYMENT
SUPPLYMENTS

SUPPORT
SUPPORTABILITY
SUPPORTABLE
SUPPORTABLENESS
SUPPORTABLY
SUPPORTANCE
SUPPORTANCES
SUPPORTED
SUPPORTER
SUPPORTERS
SUPPORTING
SUPPORTINGS
SUPPORTIVE
SUPPORTIVELY
SUPPORTIVENESS
SUPPORTLESS
SUPPORTMENT
SUPPORTMENTS
SUPPORTRESS
SUPPORTRESSES
SUPPORTS
SUPPORTURE
SUPPORTURES
SUPPOSABLE
SUPPOSABLY
SUPPOSAL
SUPPOSALS
SUPPOSE
SUPPOSED
SUPPOSEDLY
SUPPOSER
SUPPOSERS
SUPPOSES
SUPPOSING
SUPPOSINGS
SUPPOSITION
SUPPOSITIONAL
SUPPOSITIONALLY
SUPPOSITIONARY
SUPPOSITIONLESS
SUPPOSITIONS
SUPPOSITIOUS
SUPPOSITIOUSLY
SUPPOSITITIOUS
SUPPOSITIVE
SUPPOSITIVELY
SUPPOSITIVES
SUPPOSITORIES
SUPPOSITORY
SUPPRESS
SUPPRESSANT
SUPPRESSANTS
SUPPRESSED
SUPPRESSEDLY
SUPPRESSER
SUPPRESSERS
SUPPRESSES

SUPPRESSIBILITY
SUPPRESSIBLE
SUPPRESSING
SUPPRESSION
SUPPRESSIONS
SUPPRESSIVE
SUPPRESSIVENESS
SUPPRESSOR
SUPPRESSORS
SUPPURATE
SUPPURATED
SUPPURATES
SUPPURATING
SUPPURATION
SUPPURATIONS
SUPPURATIVE
SUPPURATIVES
SUPRA
SUPRACHIASMIC
SUPRACILIARY
SUPRACOSTAL
SUPRACRUSTAL
SUPRAGLOTTAL
SUPRAGLOTTALLY
SUPRALAPSARIAN
SUPRALAPSARIANS
SUPRALIMINAL
SUPRALIMINALLY
SUPRALUNAR
SUPRAMAXILLARY
SUPRAMOLECULAR
SUPRAMOLECULE
SUPRAMOLECULES
SUPRAMUNDANE
SUPRANATIONAL
SUPRANATIONALLY
SUPRAOPTIC
SUPRAORBITAL
SUPRAPUBIC
SUPRARATIONAL
SUPRARENAL
SUPRARENALS
SUPRASEGMENTAL
SUPRASENSIBLE
SUPRATEMPORAL
SUPRAVITAL
SUPRAVITALLY
SUPREMACIES
SUPREMACISM
SUPREMACISMS
SUPREMACIST
SUPREMACISTS
SUPREMACY
SUPREMATISM
SUPREMATISMS
SUPREMATIST
SUPREMATISTS

SUPREME
SUPREMELY
SUPREMENESS
SUPREMENESSES
SUPREMER
SUPREMES
SUPREMEST
SUPREMITIES
SUPREMITY
SUPREMO
SUPREMOS
SUPS
SUQ
SUQS
SUR
SURA
SURADDITION
SURADDITIONS
SURAH
SURAHS
SURAL
SURAMIN
SURAMINS
SURANCE
SURANCES
SURAS
SURAT
SURATS
SURBAHAR
SURBAHARS
SURBASE
SURBASED
SURBASEMENT
SURBASEMENTS
SURBASES
SURBATE
SURBATED
SURBATES
SURBATING
SURBED
SURBEDDED
SURBEDDING
SURBEDS
SURBET
SURCEASE
SURCEASED
SURCEASES
SURCEASING
SURCHARGE
SURCHARGED
SURCHARGEMENT
SURCHARGEMENTS
SURCHARGER
SURCHARGERS
SURCHARGES
SURCHARGING
SURCINGLE

SURCINGLED
SURCINGLES
SURCINGLING
SURCOAT
SURCOATS
SURCULI
SURCULOSE
SURCULUS
SURCULUSES
SURD
SURDITIES
SURDITY
SURDS
SURE
SURED
SUREFIRE
SUREFOOTED
SUREFOOTEDLY
SUREFOOTEDNESS
SURELY
SURENESS
SURENESSES
SURER
SURES
SUREST
SURETIED
SURETIES
SURETY
SURETYING
SURETYSHIP
SURETYSHIPS
SURF
SURFABLE
SURFACE
SURFACED
SURFACELESS
SURFACELESSNESS
SURFACEMAN
SURFACEMEN
SURFACER
SURFACERS
SURFACES
SURFACING
SURFACINGS
SURFACTANT
SURFACTANTS
SURFBIRD
SURFBIRDS
SURFBOARD
SURFBOARDED
SURFBOARDER
SURFBOARDERS
SURFBOARDING
SURFBOARDINGS
SURFBOARDS
SURFBOAT
SURFBOATS

SURFCASTER
SURFCASTERS
SURFCASTING
SURFCASTINGS
SURFED
SURFEIT
SURFEITED
SURFEITER
SURFEITERS
SURFEITING
SURFEITINGS
SURFEITS
SURFER
SURFERS
SURFFISH
SURFFISHES
SURFICIAL
SURFIE
SURFIER
SURFIES
SURFIEST
SURFING
SURFINGS
SURFLIKE
SURFMAN
SURFMEN
SURFPERCH
SURFPERCHES
SURFRIDER
SURFRIDERS
SURFS
SURFY
SURGE
SURGED
SURGEFUL
SURGELESS
SURGENT
SURGEON
SURGEONCIES
SURGEONCY
SURGEONFISH
SURGEONFISHES
SURGEONS
SURGEONSHIP
SURGEONSHIPS
SURGER
SURGERIES
SURGERS
SURGERY
SURGES
SURGICAL
SURGICALLY
SURGIER
SURGIEST
SURGING
SURGINGS
SURGY

SURICATE
SURICATES
SURIMI
SURING
SURJECTION
SURJECTIONS
SURJECTIVE
SURLIER
SURLIEST
SURLILY
SURLINESS
SURLINESSES
SURLOIN
SURLOINS
SURLY
SURMASTER
SURMASTERS
SURMISABLE
SURMISAL
SURMISALS
SURMISE
SURMISED
SURMISER
SURMISERS
SURMISES
SURMISING
SURMISINGS
SURMISTRESS
SURMISTRESSES
SURMOUNT
SURMOUNTABLE
SURMOUNTED
SURMOUNTER
SURMOUNTERS
SURMOUNTING
SURMOUNTINGS
SURMOUNTS
SURMULLET
SURMULLETS
SURNAME
SURNAMED
SURNAMER
SURNAMERS
SURNAMES
SURNAMING
SURNOMINAL
SURPASS
SURPASSABLE
SURPASSED
SURPASSES
SURPASSING
SURPASSINGLY
SURPASSINGNESS
SURPLICE
SURPLICED
SURPLICES
SURPLUS

SURPLUSAGE
SURPLUSAGES
SURPLUSES
SURPRINT
SURPRINTED
SURPRINTING
SURPRINTS
SURPRISAL
SURPRISALS
SURPRISE
SURPRISED
SURPRISEDLY
SURPRISER
SURPRISERS
SURPRISES
SURPRISING
SURPRISINGLY
SURPRISINGNESS
SURPRISINGS
SURPRIZE
SURPRIZED
SURPRIZES
SURPRIZING
SURQUEDIES
SURQUEDRIES
SURQUEDRY
SURQUEDY
SURRA
SURRAS
SURREAL
SURREALISM
SURREALISMS
SURREALIST
SURREALISTIC
SURREALISTS
SURREALLY
SURREBUT
SURREBUTS
SURREBUTTAL
SURREBUTTALS
SURREBUTTED
SURREBUTTER
SURREBUTTERS
SURREBUTTING
SURREINED
SURREJOIN
SURREJOINDER
SURREJOINDERS
SURREJOINED
SURREJOINING
SURREJOINS
SURRENDER
SURRENDERED
SURRENDEREE
SURRENDEREES
SURRENDERER
SURRENDERERS

SURRENDERING
SURRENDEROR
SURRENDERORS
SURRENDERS
SURRENDRIES
SURRENDRY
SURREPTITIOUS
SURREPTITIOUSLY
SURREY
SURREYS
SURROGACIES
SURROGACY
SURROGATE
SURROGATED
SURROGATES
SURROGATESHIP
SURROGATESHIPS
SURROGATING
SURROGATION
SURROGATIONS
SURROGATUM
SURROGATUMS
SURROUND
SURROUNDED
SURROUNDING
SURROUNDINGS
SURROUNDS
SURROYAL
SURROYALS
SURTARBRAND
SURTARBRANDS
SURTAX
SURTAXED
SURTAXES
SURTAXING
SURTITLE
SURTITLES
SURTOUT
SURTOUTS
SURTURBRAND
SURTURBRANDS
SURUCUCU
SURUCUCUS
SURVEIL
SURVEILLANCE
SURVEILLANCES
SURVEILLANT
SURVEILLANTS
SURVEILLE
SURVEILLED
SURVEILLES
SURVEILLING
SURVEILS
SURVEW
SURVEWED
SURVEWES
SURVEWING

SURVEWS
SURVEY
SURVEYABLE
SURVEYAL
SURVEYALS
SURVEYANCE
SURVEYANCES
SURVEYED
SURVEYING
SURVEYINGS
SURVEYOR
SURVEYORS
SURVEYORSHIP
SURVEYORSHIPS
SURVEYS
SURVIEW
SURVIEWED
SURVIEWING
SURVIEWS
SURVIVABILITIES
SURVIVABILITY
SURVIVABLE
SURVIVAL
SURVIVALISM
SURVIVALISMS
SURVIVALIST
SURVIVALISTS
SURVIVALS
SURVIVANCE
SURVIVANCES
SURVIVE
SURVIVED
SURVIVER
SURVIVERS
SURVIVES
SURVIVING
SURVIVOR
SURVIVORS
SURVIVORSHIP
SURVIVORSHIPS
SUS
SUSCEPTANCE
SUSCEPTANCES
SUSCEPTIBILITY
SUSCEPTIBLE
SUSCEPTIBLENESS
SUSCEPTIBLY
SUSCEPTIVE
SUSCEPTIVENESS
SUSCEPTIVITIES
SUSCEPTIVITY
SUSCEPTOR
SUSCEPTORS
SUSCIPIENT
SUSCIPIENTS
SUSCITATE
SUSCITATED

SUSCITATES
SUSCITATING
SUSCITATION
SUSCITATIONS
SUSES
SUSHI
SUSHIS
SUSLIK
SUSLIKS
SUSPECT
SUSPECTABLE
SUSPECTED
SUSPECTEDLY
SUSPECTEDNESS
SUSPECTEDNESSES
SUSPECTER
SUSPECTERS
SUSPECTFUL
SUSPECTING
SUSPECTLESS
SUSPECTS
SUSPENCE
SUSPEND
SUSPENDED
SUSPENDER
SUSPENDERED
SUSPENDERS
SUSPENDIBILITY
SUSPENDIBLE
SUSPENDING
SUSPENDS
SUSPENS
SUSPENSE
SUSPENSEFUL
SUSPENSEFULLY
SUSPENSEFULNESS
SUSPENSELESS
SUSPENSER
SUSPENSERS
SUSPENSES
SUSPENSIBILITY
SUSPENSIBLE
SUSPENSION
SUSPENSIONS
SUSPENSIVE
SUSPENSIVELY
SUSPENSIVENESS
SUSPENSOID
SUSPENSOIDS
SUSPENSOR
SUSPENSORIA
SUSPENSORIAL
SUSPENSORIES
SUSPENSORIUM
SUSPENSORS
SUSPENSORY
SUSPERCOLLATE

SUSPERCOLLATED
SUSPERCOLLATES
SUSPERCOLLATING
SUSPICION
SUSPICIONAL
SUSPICIONED
SUSPICIONING
SUSPICIONLESS
SUSPICIONS
SUSPICIOUS
SUSPICIOUSLY
SUSPICIOUSNESS
SUSPIRATION
SUSPIRATIONS
SUSPIRE
SUSPIRED
SUSPIRES
SUSPIRING
SUSPIRIOUS
SUSS
SUSSARARAS
SUSSED
SUSSES
SUSSING
SUSSO
SUSSOS
SUSTAIN
SUSTAINABILITY
SUSTAINABLE
SUSTAINED
SUSTAINEDLY
SUSTAINER
SUSTAINERS
SUSTAINING
SUSTAININGLY
SUSTAININGS
SUSTAINMENT
SUSTAINMENTS
SUSTAINS
SUSTENANCE
SUSTENANCES
SUSTENTACULA
SUSTENTACULAR
SUSTENTACULUM
SUSTENTATE
SUSTENTATED
SUSTENTATES
SUSTENTATING
SUSTENTATION
SUSTENTATIONS
SUSTENTATIVE
SUSTENTATOR
SUSTENTATORS
SUSTENTION
SUSTENTIONS
SUSTENTIVE
SUSTINENT

SUSU
SUSURRANT
SUSURRATE
SUSURRATED
SUSURRATES
SUSURRATING
SUSURRATION
SUSURRATIONS
SUSURROUS
SUSURRUS
SUSURRUSES
SUSUS
SUTILE
SUTLER
SUTLERIES
SUTLERS
SUTLERSHIP
SUTLERY
SUTOR
SUTORIAL
SUTORIAN
SUTORS
SUTRA
SUTRAS
SUTTA
SUTTAS
SUTTEE
SUTTEEISM
SUTTEEISMS
SUTTEES
SUTTLE
SUTTLED
SUTTLES
SUTTLETIE
SUTTLETIES
SUTTLING
SUTTLY
SUTURAL
SUTURALLY
SUTURATION
SUTURATIONS
SUTURE
SUTURED
SUTURES
SUTURING
SUZERAIN
SUZERAINS
SUZERAINTIES
SUZERAINTY
SVARABHAKTI
SVARABHAKTIS
SVARAJ
SVARAJES
SVASTIKA
SVASTIKAS
SVEDBERG
SVEDBERGS

SVELTE
SVELTELY
SVELTENESS
SVELTENESSES
SVELTER
SVELTEST
SWAB
SWABBED
SWABBER
SWABBERS
SWABBIE
SWABBIES
SWABBING
SWABBY
SWABS
SWACK
SWACKED
SWAD
SWADDIE
SWADDIES
SWADDLE
SWADDLED
SWADDLER
SWADDLERS
SWADDLES
SWADDLING
SWADDY
SWADS
SWAG
SWAGE
SWAGED
SWAGER
SWAGERS
SWAGES
SWAGGED
SWAGGER
SWAGGERED
SWAGGERER
SWAGGERERS
SWAGGERING
SWAGGERINGLY
SWAGGERINGS
SWAGGERS
SWAGGIE
SWAGGIES
SWAGGING
SWAGING
SWAGMAN
SWAGMEN
SWAGS
SWAGSHOP
SWAGSHOPS
SWAGSMAN
SWAGSMEN
SWAIL
SWAILS
SWAIN

SWAINING
SWAININGS
SWAINISH
SWAINISHNESS
SWAINISHNESSES
SWAINS
SWALE
SWALED
SWALES
SWALIER
SWALIEST
SWALING
SWALINGS
SWALLET
SWALLETS
SWALLOW
SWALLOWABLE
SWALLOWED
SWALLOWER
SWALLOWERS
SWALLOWING
SWALLOWS
SWALLOWTAIL
SWALLOWTAILS
SWALLOWWORT
SWALLOWWORTS
SWALY
SWAM
SWAMI
SWAMIES
SWAMIS
SWAMP
SWAMPED
SWAMPER
SWAMPERS
SWAMPIER
SWAMPIEST
SWAMPINESS
SWAMPINESSES
SWAMPING
SWAMPISH
SWAMPLAND
SWAMPLANDS
SWAMPLESS
SWAMPS
SWAMPY
SWAMY
SWAN
SWANG
SWANHERD
SWANHERDS
SWANK
SWANKED
SWANKER
SWANKERS
SWANKEST
SWANKEY

SWANKEYS
SWANKIE
SWANKIER
SWANKIES
SWANKIEST
SWANKILY
SWANKINESS
SWANKINESSES
SWANKING
SWANKPOT
SWANKPOTS
SWANKS
SWANKY
SWANLIKE
SWANNED
SWANNERIES
SWANNERY
SWANNIE
SWANNIER
SWANNIEST
SWANNING
SWANNINGS
SWANNY
SWANPAN
SWANPANS
SWANS
SWANSDOWN
SWANSDOWNS
SWANSKIN
SWANSKINS
SWAP
SWAPPED
SWAPPER
SWAPPERS
SWAPPING
SWAPPINGS
SWAPS
SWAPT
SWAPTION
SWAPTIONS
SWARAJ
SWARAJES
SWARAJISM
SWARAJISMS
SWARAJIST
SWARAJISTS
SWARD
SWARDED
SWARDIER
SWARDIEST
SWARDING
SWARDS
SWARDY
SWARE
SWARF
SWARFED
SWARFING

SWARFS
SWARM
SWARMED
SWARMER
SWARMERS
SWARMING
SWARMINGS
SWARMS
SWART
SWARTH
SWARTHIER
SWARTHIEST
SWARTHILY
SWARTHINESS
SWARTHINESSES
SWARTHNESS
SWARTHS
SWARTHY
SWARTNESS
SWARTNESSES
SWARTY
SWARVE
SWARVED
SWARVES
SWARVING
SWASH
SWASHBUCKLE
SWASHBUCKLED
SWASHBUCKLER
SWASHBUCKLERS
SWASHBUCKLES
SWASHBUCKLING
SWASHED
SWASHER
SWASHERS
SWASHES
SWASHIER
SWASHIEST
SWASHING
SWASHINGS
SWASHWORK
SWASHWORKS
SWASHY
SWASTICA
SWASTICAS
SWASTIKA
SWASTIKAS
SWAT
SWATCH
SWATCHBOOK
SWATCHBOOKS
SWATCHES
SWATH
SWATHABLE
SWATHE
SWATHEABLE
SWATHED

SWATHER
SWATHERS
SWATHES
SWATHIER
SWATHIEST
SWATHING
SWATHS
SWATHY
SWATS
SWATTED
SWATTER
SWATTERED
SWATTERING
SWATTERS
SWATTING
SWATTINGS
SWAY
SWAYABLE
SWAYBACK
SWAYBACKED
SWAYBACKS
SWAYED
SWAYER
SWAYERS
SWAYFUL
SWAYING
SWAYINGS
SWAYL
SWAYLED
SWAYLING
SWAYLINGS
SWAYLS
SWAYS
SWAZZLE
SWAZZLES
SWEAL
SWEALED
SWEALING
SWEALINGS
SWEALS
SWEAR
SWEARD
SWEARDS
SWEARER
SWEARERS
SWEARING
SWEARINGS
SWEARS
SWEARWORD
SWEARWORDS
SWEAT
SWEATBAND
SWEATBANDS
SWEATBOX
SWEATBOXES
SWEATED
SWEATER

SWEATERDRESS
SWEATERDRESSES
SWEATERS
SWEATIER
SWEATIEST
SWEATILY
SWEATINESS
SWEATINESSES
SWEATING
SWEATINGS
SWEATLESS
SWEATPANTS
SWEATS
SWEATSHIRT
SWEATSHIRTS
SWEATSHOP
SWEATSHOPS
SWEATSUIT
SWEATSUITS
SWEATY
SWEDE
SWEDES
SWEE
SWEED
SWEEING
SWEEL
SWEELED
SWEELING
SWEELS
SWEENEY
SWEENEYS
SWEENIES
SWEENY
SWEEP
SWEEPBACK
SWEEPBACKS
SWEEPER
SWEEPERS
SWEEPIER
SWEEPIEST
SWEEPING
SWEEPINGLY
SWEEPINGNESS
SWEEPINGNESSES
SWEEPINGS
SWEEPO
SWEEPOS
SWEEPS
SWEEPSTAKE
SWEEPSTAKES
SWEEPY
SWEER
SWEERED
SWEERER
SWEEREST
SWEERING
SWEERNESS

SWEERS
SWEERT
SWEES
SWEET
SWEETBREAD
SWEETBREADS
SWEETBRIAR
SWEETBRIARS
SWEETBRIER
SWEETBRIERS
SWEETCORN
SWEETCORNS
SWEETED
SWEETEN
SWEETENED
SWEETENER
SWEETENERS
SWEETENING
SWEETENINGS
SWEETENS
SWEETER
SWEETEST
SWEETFISH
SWEETFISHES
SWEETHEART
SWEETHEARTED
SWEETHEARTING
SWEETHEARTS
SWEETIE
SWEETIES
SWEETIEWIFE
SWEETIEWIVES
SWEETING
SWEETINGS
SWEETISH
SWEETISHLY
SWEETISHNESS
SWEETISHNESSES
SWEETLY
SWEETMAN
SWEETMEAL
SWEETMEAT
SWEETMEATS
SWEETMEN
SWEETNESS
SWEETNESSES
SWEETPEA
SWEETPEAS
SWEETS
SWEETSHOP
SWEETSHOPS
SWEETSOP
SWEETSOPS
SWEETWATER
SWEETWATERS
SWEETWOOD
SWEETWOODS

SWEETY
SWEIR
SWEIRED
SWEIRER
SWEIREST
SWEIRING
SWEIRNESS
SWEIRNESSES
SWEIRS
SWEIRT
SWELCHIE
SWELCHIES
SWELL
SWELLDOM
SWELLDOMS
SWELLED
SWELLER
SWELLERS
SWELLEST
SWELLFISH
SWELLFISHES
SWELLHEAD
SWELLHEADED
SWELLHEADEDNESS
SWELLHEADS
SWELLING
SWELLINGLY
SWELLINGS
SWELLISH
SWELLS
SWELT
SWELTED
SWELTER
SWELTERED
SWELTERING
SWELTERINGLY
SWELTERINGS
SWELTERS
SWELTING
SWELTRIER
SWELTRIEST
SWELTRY
SWELTS
SWEPT
SWEPTBACK
SWEPTWING
SWERF
SWERFED
SWERFING
SWERFS
SWERVABLE
SWERVE
SWERVED
SWERVELESS
SWERVER
SWERVERS
SWERVES

SWERVING
SWERVINGS
SWEVEN
SWEVENS
SWEY
SWEYED
SWEYING
SWEYS
SWIDDEN
SWIDDENS
SWIES
SWIFT
SWIFTED
SWIFTER
SWIFTERS
SWIFTEST
SWIFTIE
SWIFTIES
SWIFTING
SWIFTLET
SWIFTLETS
SWIFTLY
SWIFTNESS
SWIFTNESSES
SWIFTS
SWIFTY
SWIG
SWIGGED
SWIGGER
SWIGGERS
SWIGGING
SWIGS
SWILER
SWILERS
SWILL
SWILLED
SWILLER
SWILLERS
SWILLING
SWILLINGS
SWILLS
SWIM
SWIMFEEDER
SWIMFEEDERS
SWIMMABLE
SWIMMER
SWIMMERET
SWIMMERETS
SWIMMERS
SWIMMIER
SWIMMIEST
SWIMMILY
SWIMMING
SWIMMINGLY
SWIMMINGNESS
SWIMMINGNESSES
SWIMMINGS

SWIMMY
SWIMS
SWIMSUIT
SWIMSUITS
SWIMWEAR
SWIMWEARS
SWINDGE
SWINDGED
SWINDGES
SWINDGING
SWINDLE
SWINDLED
SWINDLER
SWINDLERS
SWINDLES
SWINDLING
SWINDLINGS
SWINE
SWINEHERD
SWINEHERDS
SWINEHOOD
SWINEHOODS
SWINELIKE
SWINEPOX
SWINEPOXES
SWINERIES
SWINERY
SWINES
SWINESTONE
SWINESTONES
SWING
SWINGBEAT
SWINGBEATS
SWINGBOAT
SWINGBOATS
SWINGBY
SWINGBYS
SWINGE
SWINGED
SWINGEING
SWINGEINGLY
SWINGER
SWINGERS
SWINGES
SWINGIER
SWINGIEST
SWINGING
SWINGINGEST
SWINGINGLY
SWINGINGS
SWINGISM
SWINGISMS
SWINGLE
SWINGLED
SWINGLES
SWINGLETREE
SWINGLETREES

SWINGLING
SWINGLINGS
SWINGMAN
SWINGMEN
SWINGOMETER
SWINGOMETERS
SWINGS
SWINGTREE
SWINGTREES
SWINGY
SWINISH
SWINISHLY
SWINISHNESS
SWINISHNESSES
SWINK
SWINKED
SWINKER
SWINKERS
SWINKING
SWINKS
SWINNEY
SWINNEYS
SWIPE
SWIPED
SWIPER
SWIPERS
SWIPES
SWIPEY
SWIPING
SWIPLE
SWIPLES
SWIPPLE
SWIPPLES
SWIRE
SWIRES
SWIRL
SWIRLED
SWIRLIER
SWIRLIEST
SWIRLING
SWIRLINGLY
SWIRLS
SWIRLY
SWISH
SWISHED
SWISHER
SWISHERS
SWISHES
SWISHEST
SWISHIER
SWISHIEST
SWISHING
SWISHINGLY
SWISHINGS
SWISHY
SWISS
SWISSES

SWISSING
SWISSINGS
SWITCH
SWITCHABLE
SWITCHBACK
SWITCHBACKED
SWITCHBACKING
SWITCHBACKS
SWITCHBLADE
SWITCHBLADES
SWITCHBOARD
SWITCHBOARDS
SWITCHED
SWITCHEL
SWITCHELS
SWITCHER
SWITCHEROO
SWITCHEROOS
SWITCHERS
SWITCHES
SWITCHGEAR
SWITCHGEARS
SWITCHGIRL
SWITCHGIRLS
SWITCHGRASS
SWITCHGRASSES
SWITCHIER
SWITCHIEST
SWITCHING
SWITCHINGS
SWITCHLIKE
SWITCHMAN
SWITCHMEN
SWITCHY
SWITCHYARD
SWITCHYARDS
SWITH
SWITHE
SWITHER
SWITHERED
SWITHERING
SWITHERS
SWITHLY
SWITS
SWITSES
SWIVE
SWIVED
SWIVEL
SWIVELBLOCKS
SWIVELED
SWIVELING
SWIVELLED
SWIVELLING
SWIVELS
SWIVES
SWIVET
SWIVETS

SWIVING
SWIZ
SWIZES
SWIZZ
SWIZZED
SWIZZES
SWIZZING
SWIZZLE
SWIZZLED
SWIZZLER
SWIZZLERS
SWIZZLES
SWIZZLING
SWOB
SWOBBED
SWOBBER
SWOBBERS
SWOBBING
SWOBS
SWOFFING
SWOLLEN
SWOLLENLY
SWOLLENNESS
SWOLN
SWONE
SWONES
SWOON
SWOONED
SWOONER
SWOONERS
SWOONING
SWOONINGLY
SWOONINGS
SWOONS
SWOOP
SWOOPED
SWOOPER
SWOOPERS
SWOOPING
SWOOPS
SWOOPSTAKE
SWOOSH
SWOOSHED
SWOOSHES
SWOOSHING
SWOP
SWOPPED
SWOPPER
SWOPPERS
SWOPPING
SWOPPINGS
SWOPS
SWOPT
SWORD
SWORDBEARER
SWORDBEARERS
SWORDBILL

SWORDBILLS
SWORDCRAFT
SWORDCRAFTS
SWORDED
SWORDER
SWORDERS
SWORDFISH
SWORDFISHES
SWORDING
SWORDLESS
SWORDLIKE
SWORDMAN
SWORDMEN
SWORDPLAY
SWORDPLAYER
SWORDPLAYERS
SWORDPLAYS
SWORDPROOF
SWORDS
SWORDSMAN
SWORDSMANSHIP
SWORDSMANSHIPS
SWORDSMEN
SWORDSTICK
SWORDSTICKS
SWORDTAIL
SWORDTAILS
SWORE
SWORN
SWOT
SWOTS
SWOTTED
SWOTTER
SWOTTERS
SWOTTIER
SWOTTIEST
SWOTTING
SWOTTINGS
SWOTTY
SWOUN
SWOUND
SWOUNDED
SWOUNDING
SWOUNDS
SWOUNE
SWOUNED
SWOUNES
SWOUNING
SWOUNS
SWOWND
SWOWNDS
SWOWNE
SWOWNES
SWOZZLE
SWOZZLES
SWUM
SWUNG

SWY
SYBARITE
SYBARITES
SYBARITIC
SYBARITICAL
SYBARITICALLY
SYBARITISH
SYBARITISM
SYBARITISMS
SYBBE
SYBBES
SYBIL
SYBILS
SYBO
SYBOE
SYBOES
SYBOTIC
SYBOTISM
SYBOTISMS
SYBOW
SYBOWS
SYCAMINE
SYCAMINES
SYCAMORE
SYCAMORES
SYCE
SYCEE
SYCEES
SYCES
SYCOMORE
SYCOMORES
SYCONIA
SYCONIUM
SYCOPHANCIES
SYCOPHANCY
SYCOPHANT
SYCOPHANTIC
SYCOPHANTICAL
SYCOPHANTICALLY
SYCOPHANTISE
SYCOPHANTISED
SYCOPHANTISES
SYCOPHANTISH
SYCOPHANTISHLY
SYCOPHANTISING
SYCOPHANTISM
SYCOPHANTISMS
SYCOPHANTIZE
SYCOPHANTIZED
SYCOPHANTIZES
SYCOPHANTIZING
SYCOPHANTLY
SYCOPHANTRIES
SYCOPHANTRY
SYCOPHANTS
SYCOSES
SYCOSIS

SYE
SYED
SYEING
SYEN
SYENITE
SYENITES
SYENITIC
SYENS
SYES
SYKE
SYKER
SYKES
SYLI
SYLIS
SYLLABARIA
SYLLABARIES
SYLLABARIUM
SYLLABARY
SYLLABI
SYLLABIC
SYLLABICAL
SYLLABICALLY
SYLLABICATE
SYLLABICATED
SYLLABICATES
SYLLABICATING
SYLLABICATION
SYLLABICATIONS
SYLLABICITIES
SYLLABICITY
SYLLABICS
SYLLABIFICATION
SYLLABIFIED
SYLLABIFIES
SYLLABIFY
SYLLABIFYING
SYLLABISE
SYLLABISED
SYLLABISES
SYLLABISING
SYLLABISM
SYLLABISMS
SYLLABIZE
SYLLABIZED
SYLLABIZES
SYLLABIZING
SYLLABLE
SYLLABLED
SYLLABLES
SYLLABLING
SYLLABOGRAM
SYLLABOGRAMS
SYLLABOGRAPHY
SYLLABUB
SYLLABUBS
SYLLABUS
SYLLABUSES

SYLLEPSES
SYLLEPSIS
SYLLEPTIC
SYLLEPTICAL
SYLLEPTICALLY
SYLLOGISATION
SYLLOGISATIONS
SYLLOGISE
SYLLOGISED
SYLLOGISER
SYLLOGISERS
SYLLOGISES
SYLLOGISING
SYLLOGISM
SYLLOGISMS
SYLLOGIST
SYLLOGISTIC
SYLLOGISTICAL
SYLLOGISTICALLY
SYLLOGISTICS
SYLLOGISTS
SYLLOGIZATION
SYLLOGIZATIONS
SYLLOGIZE
SYLLOGIZED
SYLLOGIZER
SYLLOGIZERS
SYLLOGIZES
SYLLOGIZING
SYLPH
SYLPHIC
SYLPHID
SYLPHIDE
SYLPHIDES
SYLPHIDINE
SYLPHIDS
SYLPHIER
SYLPHIEST
SYLPHINE
SYLPHISH
SYLPHLIKE
SYLPHS
SYLPHY
SYLVA
SYLVAE
SYLVAN
SYLVANER
SYLVANERS
SYLVANITE
SYLVANITES
SYLVANS
SYLVAS
SYLVATIC
SYLVESTRAL
SYLVESTRIAN
SYLVIA
SYLVIAS

SYLVICULTURAL
SYLVICULTURE
SYLVICULTURES
SYLVIINE
SYLVIN
SYLVINE
SYLVINES
SYLVINITE
SYLVINITES
SYLVINS
SYLVITE
SYLVITES
SYMAR
SYMARS
SYMBION
SYMBIONS
SYMBIONT
SYMBIONTIC
SYMBIONTICALLY
SYMBIONTS
SYMBIOSES
SYMBIOSIS
SYMBIOT
SYMBIOTE
SYMBIOTES
SYMBIOTIC
SYMBIOTICAL
SYMBIOTICALLY
SYMBIOTS
SYMBOL
SYMBOLE
SYMBOLED
SYMBOLES
SYMBOLIC
SYMBOLICAL
SYMBOLICALLY
SYMBOLICALNESS
SYMBOLICS
SYMBOLING
SYMBOLISATION
SYMBOLISATIONS
SYMBOLISE
SYMBOLISED
SYMBOLISER
SYMBOLISERS
SYMBOLISES
SYMBOLISING
SYMBOLISM
SYMBOLISMS
SYMBOLIST
SYMBOLISTIC
SYMBOLISTICAL
SYMBOLISTICALLY
SYMBOLISTS
SYMBOLIZATION
SYMBOLIZATIONS
SYMBOLIZE

SYMBOLIZED
SYMBOLIZER
SYMBOLIZERS
SYMBOLIZES
SYMBOLIZING
SYMBOLLED
SYMBOLLING
SYMBOLOGICAL
SYMBOLOGIES
SYMBOLOGIST
SYMBOLOGISTS
SYMBOLOGRAPHIES
SYMBOLOGRAPHY
SYMBOLOGY
SYMBOLOLATRIES
SYMBOLOLATRY
SYMBOLOLOGIES
SYMBOLOLOGY
SYMBOLS
SYMITAR
SYMITARE
SYMITARES
SYMITARS
SYMMETALISM
SYMMETALISMS
SYMMETALLIC
SYMMETALLISM
SYMMETALLISMS
SYMMETRAL
SYMMETRIAN
SYMMETRIANS
SYMMETRIC
SYMMETRICAL
SYMMETRICALLY
SYMMETRICALNESS
SYMMETRIES
SYMMETRISATION
SYMMETRISATIONS
SYMMETRISE
SYMMETRISED
SYMMETRISES
SYMMETRISING
SYMMETRIZATION
SYMMETRIZATIONS
SYMMETRIZE
SYMMETRIZED
SYMMETRIZES
SYMMETRIZING
SYMMETROPHOBIA
SYMMETROPHOBIAS
SYMMETRY
SYMPATHECTOMIES
SYMPATHECTOMY
SYMPATHETIC
SYMPATHETICAL
SYMPATHETICALLY
SYMPATHETICS

SYMPATHIES
SYMPATHIN
SYMPATHINS
SYMPATHIQUE
SYMPATHISE
SYMPATHISED
SYMPATHISER
SYMPATHISERS
SYMPATHISES
SYMPATHISING
SYMPATHIZE
SYMPATHIZED
SYMPATHIZER
SYMPATHIZERS
SYMPATHIZES
SYMPATHIZING
SYMPATHOLYTIC
SYMPATHOLYTICS
SYMPATHOMIMETIC
SYMPATHY
SYMPATRIC
SYMPATRICALLY
SYMPATRIES
SYMPATRY
SYMPETALIES
SYMPETALOUS
SYMPETALY
SYMPHILE
SYMPHILES
SYMPHILIES
SYMPHILISM
SYMPHILISMS
SYMPHILOUS
SYMPHILY
SYMPHONIC
SYMPHONICALLY
SYMPHONIES
SYMPHONION
SYMPHONIONS
SYMPHONIOUS
SYMPHONIOUSLY
SYMPHONIST
SYMPHONISTS
SYMPHONY
SYMPHYLOUS
SYMPHYSEAL
SYMPHYSEOTOMIES
SYMPHYSEOTOMY
SYMPHYSES
SYMPHYSIAL
SYMPHYSIOTOMIES
SYMPHYSIOTOMY
SYMPHYSIS
SYMPHYSTIC
SYMPHYTIC
SYMPIESOMETER
SYMPIESOMETERS

SYMPLAST
SYMPLASTIC
SYMPLASTS
SYMPLOCE
SYMPLOCES
SYMPODIA
SYMPODIAL
SYMPODIALLY
SYMPODIUM
SYMPOSIA
SYMPOSIAC
SYMPOSIACS
SYMPOSIAL
SYMPOSIARCH
SYMPOSIARCHS
SYMPOSIAST
SYMPOSIASTS
SYMPOSIUM
SYMPOSIUMS
SYMPTOM
SYMPTOMATIC
SYMPTOMATICAL
SYMPTOMATICALLY
SYMPTOMATISE
SYMPTOMATISED
SYMPTOMATISES
SYMPTOMATISING
SYMPTOMATIZE
SYMPTOMATIZED
SYMPTOMATIZES
SYMPTOMATIZING
SYMPTOMATOLOGIC
SYMPTOMATOLOGY
SYMPTOMLESS
SYMPTOMOLOGICAL
SYMPTOMOLOGIES
SYMPTOMOLOGY
SYMPTOMS
SYMPTOSES
SYMPTOSIS
SYMPTOTIC
SYN
SYNADELPHITE
SYNADELPHITES
SYNAERESES
SYNAERESIS
SYNAESTHESES
SYNAESTHESIA
SYNAESTHESIAS
SYNAESTHESIS
SYNAESTHETIC
SYNAGOG
SYNAGOGAL
SYNAGOGICAL
SYNAGOGS
SYNAGOGUE
SYNAGOGUES

SYNALEPHA
SYNALEPHAS
SYNALLAGMATIC
SYNALOEPHA
SYNALOEPHAS
SYNANDRIA
SYNANDRIUM
SYNANDROUS
SYNANGIA
SYNANGIUM
SYNANON
SYNANONS
SYNANTHEROUS
SYNANTHESES
SYNANTHESIS
SYNANTHETIC
SYNANTHIC
SYNANTHIES
SYNANTHOUS
SYNANTHY
SYNAPHEA
SYNAPHEAS
SYNAPHEIA
SYNAPHEIAS
SYNAPOSEMATIC
SYNAPOSEMATISM
SYNAPOSEMATISMS
SYNAPSE
SYNAPSED
SYNAPSES
SYNAPSID
SYNAPSIDS
SYNAPSING
SYNAPSIS
SYNAPTASE
SYNAPTASES
SYNAPTE
SYNAPTES
SYNAPTIC
SYNAPTICAL
SYNAPTICALLY
SYNAPTOSOMAL
SYNAPTOSOME
SYNAPTOSOMES
SYNARCHIES
SYNARCHY
SYNARTHRODIAL
SYNARTHRODIALLY
SYNARTHROSES
SYNARTHROSIS
SYNASTRIES
SYNASTRY
SYNAXARIA
SYNAXARION
SYNAXES
SYNAXIS
SYNC

SYNCARP
SYNCARPIES
SYNCARPOUS
SYNCARPS
SYNCARPY
SYNCED
SYNCH
SYNCHED
SYNCHING
SYNCHONDROSES
SYNCHONDROSIS
SYNCHORESES
SYNCHORESIS
SYNCHRO
SYNCHROFLASH
SYNCHROFLASHES
SYNCHROMESH
SYNCHROMESHES
SYNCHRONAL
SYNCHRONEITIES
SYNCHRONEITY
SYNCHRONIC
SYNCHRONICAL
SYNCHRONICALLY
SYNCHRONICITIES
SYNCHRONICITY
SYNCHRONIES
SYNCHRONISATION
SYNCHRONISE
SYNCHRONISED
SYNCHRONISER
SYNCHRONISERS
SYNCHRONISES
SYNCHRONISING
SYNCHRONISM
SYNCHRONISMS
SYNCHRONISTIC
SYNCHRONISTICAL
SYNCHRONIZATION
SYNCHRONIZE
SYNCHRONIZED
SYNCHRONIZER
SYNCHRONIZERS
SYNCHRONIZES
SYNCHRONIZING
SYNCHRONOLOGIES
SYNCHRONOLOGY
SYNCHRONOSCOPE
SYNCHRONOSCOPES
SYNCHRONOUS
SYNCHRONOUSLY
SYNCHRONOUSNESS
SYNCHRONY
SYNCHROS
SYNCHROSCOPE
SYNCHROSCOPES
SYNCHROTRON

SYNCHROTRONS
SYNCHS
SYNCHYSES
SYNCHYSIS
SYNCING
SYNCLASTIC
SYNCLINAL
SYNCLINALS
SYNCLINE
SYNCLINES
SYNCLINORIA
SYNCLINORIUM
SYNCOM
SYNCOMS
SYNCOPAL
SYNCOPATE
SYNCOPATED
SYNCOPATES
SYNCOPATING
SYNCOPATION
SYNCOPATIONS
SYNCOPATIVE
SYNCOPATOR
SYNCOPATORS
SYNCOPE
SYNCOPES
SYNCOPIC
SYNCOPTIC
SYNCRETIC
SYNCRETISATION
SYNCRETISE
SYNCRETISED
SYNCRETISES
SYNCRETISING
SYNCRETISM
SYNCRETISMS
SYNCRETIST
SYNCRETISTIC
SYNCRETISTS
SYNCRETIZATION
SYNCRETIZE
SYNCRETIZED
SYNCRETIZES
SYNCRETIZING
SYNCRISES
SYNCRISIS
SYNCS
SYNCYTIA
SYNCYTIAL
SYNCYTIUM
SYND
SYNDACTYL
SYNDACTYLIES
SYNDACTYLISM
SYNDACTYLISMS
SYNDACTYLOUS
SYNDACTYLS

SYNDACTYLY
SYNDED
SYNDERESES
SYNDERESIS
SYNDESES
SYNDESIS
SYNDESISES
SYNDESMOSES
SYNDESMOSIS
SYNDESMOTIC
SYNDET
SYNDETIC
SYNDETICAL
SYNDETICALLY
SYNDETON
SYNDETONS
SYNDETS
SYNDIC
SYNDICAL
SYNDICALISM
SYNDICALISMS
SYNDICALIST
SYNDICALISTIC
SYNDICALISTS
SYNDICATE
SYNDICATED
SYNDICATES
SYNDICATING
SYNDICATION
SYNDICATIONS
SYNDICATOR
SYNDICATORS
SYNDICS
SYNDICSHIP
SYNDING
SYNDINGS
SYNDIOTACTIC
SYNDROME
SYNDROMES
SYNDROMIC
SYNDS
SYNDYASMIAN
SYNE
SYNECDOCHE
SYNECDOCHES
SYNECDOCHIC
SYNECDOCHICAL
SYNECDOCHICALLY
SYNECDOCHISM
SYNECDOCHISMS
SYNECHIA
SYNECHIAS
SYNECIOUS
SYNECOLOGIC
SYNECOLOGICAL
SYNECOLOGICALLY
SYNECOLOGIES

SYNECOLOGIST
SYNECOLOGISTS
SYNECOLOGY
SYNECPHONESES
SYNECPHONESIS
SYNECTIC
SYNECTICALLY
SYNECTICS
SYNED
SYNEDRIA
SYNEDRIAL
SYNEDRION
SYNEDRIUM
SYNEIDESES
SYNEIDESIS
SYNERESES
SYNERESIS
SYNERGETIC
SYNERGETICALLY
SYNERGIA
SYNERGIAS
SYNERGIC
SYNERGICALLY
SYNERGID
SYNERGIDS
SYNERGIES
SYNERGISE
SYNERGISED
SYNERGISES
SYNERGISING
SYNERGISM
SYNERGISMS
SYNERGIST
SYNERGISTIC
SYNERGISTICALLY
SYNERGISTS
SYNERGIZE
SYNERGIZED
SYNERGIZES
SYNERGIZING
SYNERGY
SYNES
SYNESES
SYNESIS
SYNESISES
SYNESTHESIA
SYNESTHESIAS
SYNESTHETIC
SYNFUEL
SYNFUELS
SYNGAMIC
SYNGAMIES
SYNGAMOUS
SYNGAMY
SYNGAS
SYNGASES
SYNGASSES

SYNGENEIC
SYNGENESES
SYNGENESIOUS
SYNGENESIS
SYNGENETIC
SYNGNATHOUS
SYNGRAPH
SYNGRAPHS
SYNING
SYNIZESES
SYNIZESIS
SYNKARYON
SYNKARYONIC
SYNKARYONS
SYNOD
SYNODAL
SYNODALS
SYNODIC
SYNODICAL
SYNODICALLY
SYNODS
SYNODSMAN
SYNODSMEN
SYNOECETE
SYNOECETES
SYNOECIOSES
SYNOECIOSIS
SYNOECIOUS
SYNOECISE
SYNOECISED
SYNOECISES
SYNOECISING
SYNOECISM
SYNOECISMS
SYNOECIZE
SYNOECIZED
SYNOECIZES
SYNOECIZING
SYNOECOLOGIES
SYNOECOLOGY
SYNOEKETE
SYNOEKETES
SYNOICOUS
SYNONYM
SYNONYMATIC
SYNONYME
SYNONYMES
SYNONYMIC
SYNONYMICAL
SYNONYMICON
SYNONYMICONS
SYNONYMIES
SYNONYMISE
SYNONYMISED
SYNONYMISES
SYNONYMISING
SYNONYMIST

SYNONYMISTS
SYNONYMITIES
SYNONYMITY
SYNONYMIZE
SYNONYMIZED
SYNONYMIZES
SYNONYMIZING
SYNONYMOUS
SYNONYMOUSLY
SYNONYMOUSNESS
SYNONYMS
SYNONYMY
SYNOPSES
SYNOPSIS
SYNOPSISE
SYNOPSISED
SYNOPSISES
SYNOPSISING
SYNOPSIZE
SYNOPSIZED
SYNOPSIZES
SYNOPSIZING
SYNOPTIC
SYNOPTICAL
SYNOPTICALLY
SYNOPTICS
SYNOPTIST
SYNOPTISTIC
SYNOPTISTS
SYNOSTOSES
SYNOSTOSIS
SYNOVIA
SYNOVIAL
SYNOVIALLY
SYNOVIAS
SYNOVITIC
SYNOVITIS
SYNOVITISES
SYNROC
SYNROCS
SYNSEPALOUS
SYNTACTIC
SYNTACTICAL
SYNTACTICALLY
SYNTACTICS
SYNTAGM
SYNTAGMA
SYNTAGMAS
SYNTAGMATA
SYNTAGMATIC
SYNTAGMATITE
SYNTAGMATITES
SYNTAGMIC
SYNTAGMS
SYNTAN
SYNTANS
SYNTAX

SYNTAXES
SYNTECTIC
SYNTECTICAL
SYNTENOSES
SYNTENOSIS
SYNTERESES
SYNTERESIS
SYNTEXIS
SYNTEXISES
SYNTH
SYNTHESES
SYNTHESIS
SYNTHESISATION
SYNTHESISE
SYNTHESISED
SYNTHESISER
SYNTHESISERS
SYNTHESISES
SYNTHESISING
SYNTHESIST
SYNTHESISTS
SYNTHESIZATION
SYNTHESIZATIONS
SYNTHESIZE
SYNTHESIZED
SYNTHESIZER
SYNTHESIZERS
SYNTHESIZES
SYNTHESIZING
SYNTHESPIAN
SYNTHESPIANS
SYNTHETASE
SYNTHETASES
SYNTHETIC
SYNTHETICAL
SYNTHETICALLY
SYNTHETICISM
SYNTHETICISMS
SYNTHETICS
SYNTHETISATION
SYNTHETISE
SYNTHETISED
SYNTHETISER
SYNTHETISERS
SYNTHETISES
SYNTHETISING
SYNTHETISM
SYNTHETIST
SYNTHETISTS
SYNTHETIZATION
SYNTHETIZE
SYNTHETIZED
SYNTHETIZER
SYNTHETIZERS
SYNTHETIZES
SYNTHETIZING
SYNTHON

SYNTHONS
SYNTHRONI
SYNTHRONUS
SYNTHS
SYNTONIC
SYNTONICALLY
SYNTONIES
SYNTONIN
SYNTONINS
SYNTONISE
SYNTONISED
SYNTONISES
SYNTONISING
SYNTONIZE
SYNTONIZED
SYNTONIZES
SYNTONIZING
SYNTONOUS
SYNTONY
SYNURA
SYNURAE
SYPE
SYPED
SYPES
SYPH
SYPHER
SYPHERED
SYPHERING
SYPHERS
SYPHILIS
SYPHILISATION
SYPHILISATIONS
SYPHILISE
SYPHILISED
SYPHILISES
SYPHILISING
SYPHILITIC
SYPHILITICALLY
SYPHILITICS
SYPHILIZATION
SYPHILIZATIONS
SYPHILIZE
SYPHILIZED
SYPHILIZES
SYPHILIZING
SYPHILOID
SYPHILOLOGIES
SYPHILOLOGIST
SYPHILOLOGISTS
SYPHILOLOGY
SYPHILOMA
SYPHILOMAS
SYPHILOMATA
SYPHILOPHOBIA
SYPHILOPHOBIAS
SYPHON
SYPHONED

SYPHONING
SYPHONS
SYPHS
SYPING
SYRAH
SYRAHS
SYREN
SYRENS
SYRINGA
SYRINGAS
SYRINGE
SYRINGEAL
SYRINGED
SYRINGES
SYRINGING
SYRINGITIS
SYRINGITISES
SYRINGOMYELIA
SYRINGOMYELIAS
SYRINGOMYELIC
SYRINGOTOMIES
SYRINGOTOMY
SYRINX
SYRINXES
SYRPHIAN
SYRPHIANS
SYRPHID
SYRPHIDS
SYRTES
SYRTIS
SYRUP
SYRUPED
SYRUPIER
SYRUPIEST
SYRUPING
SYRUPS
SYRUPY
SYSOP
SYSOPS
SYSSARCOSES
SYSSARCOSIS
SYSSARCOTIC
SYSSITIA
SYSSITIAS
SYSTALTIC
SYSTEM
SYSTEMATIC
SYSTEMATICAL
SYSTEMATICALLY
SYSTEMATICIAN
SYSTEMATICIANS
SYSTEMATICNESS
SYSTEMATICS
SYSTEMATISATION
SYSTEMATISE
SYSTEMATISED
SYSTEMATISER

SYSTEMATISERS
SYSTEMATISES
SYSTEMATISING
SYSTEMATISM
SYSTEMATISMS
SYSTEMATIST
SYSTEMATISTS
SYSTEMATIZATION
SYSTEMATIZE
SYSTEMATIZED
SYSTEMATIZER
SYSTEMATIZERS
SYSTEMATIZES
SYSTEMATIZING
SYSTEMATOLOGIES
SYSTEMATOLOGY
SYSTEMED
SYSTEMIC
SYSTEMICALLY
SYSTEMICS
SYSTEMISATION
SYSTEMISATIONS
SYSTEMISE
SYSTEMISED
SYSTEMISER
SYSTEMISERS
SYSTEMISES
SYSTEMISING
SYSTEMIZATION
SYSTEMIZATIONS
SYSTEMIZE
SYSTEMIZED
SYSTEMIZER
SYSTEMIZERS
SYSTEMIZES
SYSTEMIZING
SYSTEMLESS
SYSTEMS
SYSTOLE
SYSTOLES
SYSTOLIC
SYSTYLE
SYSTYLES
SYTHE
SYTHES
SYVER
SYVERS
SYZYGAL
SYZYGETIC
SYZYGETICALLY
SYZYGIAL
SYZYGIES
SYZYGY

T

TA
TAAL
TAATA
TAATAS
TAB
TABANID
TABANIDS
TABARD
TABARDED
TABARDS
TABARET
TABARETS
TABASHEER
TABASHEERS
TABASHIR
TABASHIRS
TABBED
TABBIED
TABBIES
TABBINET
TABBINETS
TABBING
TABBIS
TABBISES
TABBOULEH
TABBOULEHS
TABBOULI
TABBY
TABBYHOOD
TABBYHOODS
TABBYING
TABEFACTION
TABEFACTIONS
TABEFIED
TABEFIES
TABEFY
TABEFYING
TABELLION
TABELLIONS
TABER
TABERD
TABERDAR
TABERDARS
TABERDS
TABERED
TABERING
TABERNACLE
TABERNACLED
TABERNACLES
TABERNACLING
TABERNACULAR
TABERS

TABES
TABESCENCE
TABESCENCES
TABESCENT
TABETIC
TABETICS
TABI
TABID
TABINET
TABINETS
TABIS
TABLA
TABLANETTE
TABLANETTES
TABLAS
TABLATURE
TABLATURES
TABLE
TABLEAU
TABLEAUS
TABLEAUX
TABLECLOTH
TABLECLOTHS
TABLED
TABLEFUL
TABLEFULS
TABLELAND
TABLELANDS
TABLELESS
TABLELESSNESS
TABLEMATE
TABLEMATES
TABLES
TABLESFUL
TABLESPOON
TABLESPOONFUL
TABLESPOONFULS
TABLESPOONS
TABLESPOONSFUL
TABLET
TABLETED
TABLETING
TABLETOP
TABLETOPPED
TABLETOPS
TABLETS
TABLETTED
TABLETTING
TABLEWARE
TABLEWARES
TABLEWISE
TABLIER

TABLIERS
TABLING
TABLINGS
TABLOID
TABLOIDS
TABLOIDY
TABOGGAN
TABOGGANED
TABOGGANING
TABOGGANS
TABOO
TABOOED
TABOOING
TABOOLEY
TABOOLEYS
TABOOS
TABOPARESES
TABOPARESIS
TABOR
TABORED
TABORER
TABORERS
TABORET
TABORETS
TABORIN
TABORINE
TABORINES
TABORING
TABORINS
TABORS
TABOULI
TABOULIS
TABOUR
TABOURED
TABOURER
TABOURERS
TABOURET
TABOURETS
TABOURIN
TABOURING
TABOURINS
TABOURS
TABRERE
TABRERES
TABRET
TABRETS
TABS
TABU
TABUED
TABUING
TABULA
TABULABLE

TABULAE
TABULAR
TABULARISATION
TABULARISATIONS
TABULARISE
TABULARISED
TABULARISEES
TABULARISES
TABULARISING
TABULARIZATION
TABULARIZATIONS
TABULARIZE
TABULARIZED
TABULARIZEES
TABULARIZES
TABULARIZING
TABULARLY
TABULATE
TABULATED
TABULATES
TABULATING
TABULATION
TABULATIONS
TABULATOR
TABULATORS
TABULATORY
TABULI
TABULIS
TABUN
TABUNS
TABUS
TACAHOUT
TACAHOUTS
TACAMAHAC
TACAMAHACS
TACAN
TACANS
TACE
TACES
TACET
TACETED
TACETING
TACETS
TACH
TACHE
TACHEOMETER
TACHEOMETERS
TACHEOMETRIC
TACHEOMETRICAL
TACHEOMETRIES
TACHEOMETRY
TACHES

TACHINA
TACHINID
TACHINIDS
TACHISM
TACHISME
TACHISMES
TACHISMS
TACHIST
TACHISTE
TACHISTES
TACHISTOSCOPE
TACHISTOSCOPES
TACHISTOSCOPIC
TACHISTS
TACHO
TACHOGRAM
TACHOGRAMS
TACHOGRAPH
TACHOGRAPHS
TACHOMETER
TACHOMETERS
TACHOMETRIC
TACHOMETRICAL
TACHOMETRICALLY
TACHOMETRIES
TACHOMETRY
TACHOS
TACHS
TACHYARRHYTHMIA
TACHYCARDIA
TACHYCARDIAC
TACHYCARDIAS
TACHYGRAPH
TACHYGRAPHER
TACHYGRAPHERS
TACHYGRAPHIC
TACHYGRAPHICAL
TACHYGRAPHIES
TACHYGRAPHIST
TACHYGRAPHISTS
TACHYGRAPHS
TACHYGRAPHY
TACHYLITE
TACHYLITES
TACHYLITIC
TACHYLYTE
TACHYLYTES
TACHYLYTIC
TACHYMETER
TACHYMETERS
TACHYMETRIC
TACHYMETRICAL
TACHYMETRICALLY
TACHYMETRIES
TACHYMETRY
TACHYON
TACHYONS

TACHYPHASIA
TACHYPHASIAS
TACHYPHRASIA
TACHYPHRASIAS
TACHYPHYLAXIS
TACHYPNEA
TACHYPNEAS
TACHYPNOEA
TACHYPNOEAS
TACIT
TACITLY
TACITNESS
TACITNESSES
TACITURN
TACITURNITIES
TACITURNITY
TACITURNLY
TACK
TACKBOARD
TACKBOARDS
TACKED
TACKER
TACKERS
TACKET
TACKETS
TACKETY
TACKEY
TACKIER
TACKIES
TACKIEST
TACKIFIED
TACKIFIER
TACKIFIERS
TACKIFIES
TACKIFY
TACKIFYING
TACKILY
TACKINESS
TACKINESSES
TACKING
TACKINGS
TACKLE
TACKLED
TACKLER
TACKLERS
TACKLES
TACKLESS
TACKLING
TACKLINGS
TACKS
TACKSMAN
TACKSMEN
TACKY
TACMAHACK
TACMAHACKS
TACNODE
TACNODES

TACO
TACONITE
TACONITES
TACOS
TACT
TACTFUL
TACTFULLY
TACTFULNESS
TACTFULNESSES
TACTIC
TACTICAL
TACTICALLY
TACTICIAN
TACTICIANS
TACTICITIES
TACTICITY
TACTICS
TACTILE
TACTILELY
TACTILIST
TACTILISTS
TACTILITIES
TACTILITY
TACTION
TACTIONS
TACTISM
TACTISMS
TACTLESS
TACTLESSLY
TACTLESSNESS
TACTLESSNESSES
TACTS
TACTUAL
TACTUALITIES
TACTUALITY
TACTUALLY
TAD
TADDIE
TADDIES
TADPOLE
TADPOLES
TADS
TADVANCE
TAE
TAED
TAEDIUM
TAEDIUMS
TAEING
TAEL
TAELS
TAENIA
TAENIACIDE
TAENIACIDES
TAENIAE
TAENIAFUGE
TAENIAFUGES
TAENIAS

TAENIASES
TAENIASIS
TAENIATE
TAENIOID
TAES
TAFFAREL
TAFFARELS
TAFFEREL
TAFFERELS
TAFFETA
TAFFETAS
TAFFETASES
TAFFETIES
TAFFETIZED
TAFFETY
TAFFIA
TAFFIAS
TAFFIES
TAFFRAIL
TAFFRAILS
TAFFY
TAFIA
TAFIAS
TAG
TAGALONG
TAGALONGS
TAGAREEN
TAGAREENS
TAGBOARD
TAGBOARDS
TAGETES
TAGGED
TAGGEE
TAGGEES
TAGGER
TAGGERS
TAGGIER
TAGGIEST
TAGGING
TAGGINGS
TAGGY
TAGHAIRM
TAGHAIRMS
TAGINE
TAGLIARINI
TAGLIARINIS
TAGLIATELLE
TAGLIATELLES
TAGLIKE
TAGLIONI
TAGLIONIS
TAGMA
TAGMATA
TAGMEME
TAGMEMES
TAGMEMIC
TAGMEMICS

TAGRAG
TAGRAGS
TAGS
TAGUAN
TAGUANS
TAHA
TAHAS
TAHINA
TAHINAS
TAHINI
TAHINIS
TAHR
TAHRS
TAHSIL
TAHSILDAR
TAHSILDARS
TAHSILS
TAI
TAIAHA
TAIAHAS
TAIG
TAIGA
TAIGAS
TAIGLACH
TAIGLE
TAIGLED
TAIGLES
TAIGLING
TAIGS
TAIHOA
TAIKONAUT
TAIKONAUTS
TAIL
TAILARD
TAILARDS
TAILBACK
TAILBACKS
TAILBOARD
TAILBOARDS
TAILBONE
TAILBONES
TAILCOAT
TAILCOATED
TAILCOATS
TAILED
TAILENDER
TAILENDERS
TAILER
TAILERON
TAILERONS
TAILERS
TAILFAN
TAILFANS
TAILFLIES
TAILFLY
TAILGATE
TAILGATED

TAILGATER
TAILGATERS
TAILGATES
TAILGATING
TAILING
TAILINGS
TAILLAMP
TAILLAMPS
TAILLE
TAILLES
TAILLESS
TAILLESSLY
TAILLESSNESS
TAILLEUR
TAILLEURS
TAILLIE
TAILLIES
TAILLIGHT
TAILLIGHTS
TAILLIKE
TAILOR
TAILORBIRD
TAILORBIRDS
TAILORED
TAILORESS
TAILORESSES
TAILORING
TAILORINGS
TAILORMADE
TAILORMAKE
TAILORMAKES
TAILORMAKING
TAILORS
TAILPIECE
TAILPIECES
TAILPIPE
TAILPIPED
TAILPIPES
TAILPIPING
TAILPLANE
TAILPLANES
TAILRACE
TAILRACES
TAILS
TAILSKID
TAILSKIDS
TAILSLIDE
TAILSLIDES
TAILSPIN
TAILSPINS
TAILSTOCK
TAILSTOCKS
TAILWATER
TAILWATERS
TAILWHEEL
TAILWHEELS
TAILWIND

TAILWINDS
TAILYE
TAILYES
TAILZIE
TAILZIES
TAIN
TAINS
TAINT
TAINTED
TAINTING
TAINTLESS
TAINTLESSLY
TAINTS
TAINTURE
TAINTURES
TAIPAN
TAIPANS
TAIRA
TAIRAS
TAIS
TAISCH
TAISCHES
TAISH
TAISHES
TAIT
TAITS
TAIVER
TAIVERED
TAIVERING
TAIVERS
TAIVERT
TAJ
TAJES
TAJINE
TAJINES
TAK
TAKA
TAKABLE
TAKAHE
TAKAHES
TAKAMAKA
TAKAMAKAS
TAKAS
TAKE
TAKEABLE
TAKEAWAY
TAKEAWAYS
TAKEDOWN
TAKEDOWNS
TAKEN
TAKEOFF
TAKEOFFS
TAKEOUT
TAKEOUTS
TAKEOVER
TAKEOVERS
TAKER

TAKERS
TAKES
TAKEUP
TAKEUPS
TAKHI
TAKHIS
TAKI
TAKIER
TAKIEST
TAKIN
TAKING
TAKINGLY
TAKINGNESS
TAKINGNESSES
TAKINGS
TAKINS
TAKIS
TAKKIES
TAKS
TAKY
TALA
TALAK
TALAKS
TALANT
TALANTS
TALAPOIN
TALAPOINS
TALAQ
TALAQS
TALAR
TALARIA
TALARS
TALAS
TALAUNT
TALAUNTS
TALAYOT
TALAYOTS
TALBOT
TALBOTS
TALBOTYPE
TALBOTYPES
TALC
TALCED
TALCIER
TALCIEST
TALCING
TALCKED
TALCKIER
TALCKIEST
TALCKING
TALCKY
TALCOSE
TALCOUS
TALCS
TALCUM
TALCUMS
TALCY

TALE
TALEA
TALEAE
TALEBEARER
TALEBEARERS
TALEBEARING
TALEBEARINGS
TALEFUL
TALEGALLA
TALEGALLAS
TALENT
TALENTED
TALENTLESS
TALENTS
TALER
TALERS
TALES
TALESMAN
TALESMEN
TALEYSIM
TALI
TALIGRADE
TALION
TALIONIC
TALIONS
TALIPAT
TALIPATS
TALIPED
TALIPEDS
TALIPES
TALIPOT
TALIPOTS
TALISMAN
TALISMANIC
TALISMANICAL
TALISMANICALLY
TALISMANS
TALK
TALKABILITIES
TALKABILITY
TALKABLE
TALKATHON
TALKATHONS
TALKATIVE
TALKATIVELY
TALKATIVENESS
TALKATIVENESSES
TALKBACK
TALKBACKS
TALKBOX
TALKBOXES
TALKED
TALKER
TALKERS
TALKFEST
TALKFESTS
TALKIE

TALKIER
TALKIES
TALKIEST
TALKINESS
TALKINESSES
TALKING
TALKINGS
TALKS
TALKY
TALL
TALLAGE
TALLAGED
TALLAGES
TALLAGING
TALLAISIM
TALLAISM
TALLAT
TALLATS
TALLBOY
TALLBOYS
TALLENT
TALLENTS
TALLER
TALLEST
TALLET
TALLETS
TALLIABLE
TALLIATE
TALLIATED
TALLIATES
TALLIATING
TALLIED
TALLIER
TALLIERS
TALLIES
TALLIS
TALLISES
TALLISH
TALLISIM
TALLIT
TALLITES
TALLITH
TALLITHES
TALLITHIM
TALLITHS
TALLITIM
TALLITOT
TALLITOTH
TALLNESS
TALLNESSES
TALLOL
TALLOLS
TALLOT
TALLOTS
TALLOW
TALLOWED
TALLOWING

TALLOWISH
TALLOWS
TALLOWY
TALLY
TALLYHO
TALLYHOED
TALLYHOING
TALLYHOS
TALLYING
TALLYMAN
TALLYMEN
TALLYSHOP
TALLYSHOPS
TALLYWOMAN
TALLYWOMEN
TALMA
TALMAS
TALMUD
TALMUDIC
TALMUDISM
TALMUDISMS
TALMUDS
TALON
TALONED
TALONS
TALOOKA
TALOOKAS
TALPA
TALPAE
TALPAS
TALUK
TALUKA
TALUKAS
TALUKDAR
TALUKDARS
TALUKS
TALUS
TALUSES
TALWEG
TALWEGS
TAM
TAMABILITIES
TAMABILITY
TAMABLE
TAMABLENESS
TAMABLENESSES
TAMAL
TAMALE
TAMALES
TAMALS
TAMANDU
TAMANDUA
TAMANDUAS
TAMANDUS
TAMANOIR
TAMANOIRS
TAMANU

TAMANUS
TAMARA
TAMARACK
TAMARACKS
TAMARAO
TAMARAOS
TAMARAS
TAMARAU
TAMARAUS
TAMARI
TAMARILLO
TAMARILLOS
TAMARIN
TAMARIND
TAMARINDS
TAMARINS
TAMARIS
TAMARISK
TAMARISKS
TAMASHA
TAMASHAS
TAMBAC
TAMBACS
TAMBAK
TAMBAKS
TAMBALA
TAMBALAS
TAMBER
TAMBERS
TAMBOUR
TAMBOURA
TAMBOURAS
TAMBOURED
TAMBOURER
TAMBOURERS
TAMBOURIN
TAMBOURINE
TAMBOURINES
TAMBOURING
TAMBOURINIST
TAMBOURINISTS
TAMBOURINS
TAMBOURS
TAMBUR
TAMBURA
TAMBURAS
TAMBURIN
TAMBURINS
TAMBURS
TAME
TAMEABILITIES
TAMEABILITY
TAMEABLE
TAMEABLENESS
TAMEABLENESSES
TAMED
TAMEIN

TAMEINS	TAMWORTH	TANGIE	TANKER
TAMELESS	TAMWORTHS	TANGIER	TANKERS
TAMELESSNESS	TAN	TANGIES	TANKFUL
TAMELESSNESSES	TANA	TANGIEST	TANKFULS
TAMELY	TANADAR	TANGING	TANKIA
TAMENESS	TANADARS	TANGIS	TANKIAS
TAMENESSES	TANAGER	TANGLE	TANKIES
TAMER	TANAGERS	TANGLED	TANKING
TAMERS	TANAGRA	TANGLEFOOT	TANKINGS
TAMES	TANAGRAS	TANGLEFOOTS	TANKINI
TAMEST	TANAGRINE	TANGLEMENT	TANKINIS
TAMIN	TANAISTE	TANGLEMENTS	TANKLESS
TAMINE	TANAISTES	TANGLER	TANKLESSNESS
TAMINES	TANALISED	TANGLERS	TANKLIKE
TAMING	TANALIZED	TANGLES	TANKS
TAMINGS	TANAS	TANGLESOME	TANKSHIP
TAMINS	TANBARK	TANGLEWEED	TANKSHIPS
TAMIS	TANBARKS	TANGLEWEEDS	TANKY
TAMISE	TANDEM	TANGLIER	TANLING
TAMISES	TANDEMS	TANGLIEST	TANLINGS
TAMMAR	TANDEMWISE	TANGLING	TANNA
TAMMARS	TANDOOR	TANGLINGLY	TANNABLE
TAMMIE	TANDOORI	TANGLINGS	TANNAGE
TAMMIED	TANDOORIS	TANGLY	TANNAGES
TAMMIES	TANDOORS	TANGO	TANNAH
TAMMY	TANE	TANGOED	TANNAHS
TAMMYING	TANG	TANGOES	TANNAS
TAMOXIFEN	TANGA	TANGOING	TANNATE
TAMOXIFENS	TANGAS	TANGOIST	TANNATES
TAMP	TANGED	TANGOISTS	TANNED
TAMPALA	TANGELO	TANGOS	TANNER
TAMPALAS	TANGELOS	TANGRAM	TANNERIES
TAMPAN	TANGENCE	TANGRAMS	TANNERS
TAMPANS	TANGENCES	TANGS	TANNERY
TAMPED	TANGENCIES	TANGUN	TANNEST
TAMPER	TANGENCY	TANGUNS	TANNIC
TAMPERED	TANGENT	TANGY	TANNIE
TAMPERER	TANGENTALLY	TANH	TANNIN
TAMPERERS	TANGENTIAL	TANHS	TANNING
TAMPERING	TANGENTIALITIES	TANIST	TANNINGS
TAMPERINGS	TANGENTIALITY	TANISTRIES	TANNINS
TAMPERPROOF	TANGENTIALLY	TANISTRY	TANNISH
TAMPERS	TANGENTS	TANISTS	TANNOY
TAMPING	TANGERINE	TANIWHA	TANNOYED
TAMPINGS	TANGERINES	TANIWHAS	TANNOYING
TAMPION	TANGHIN	TANK	TANNOYS
TAMPIONS	TANGHININ	TANKA	TANREC
TAMPON	TANGHININS	TANKAGE	TANRECS
TAMPONADE	TANGHINS	TANKAGES	TANS
TAMPONADES	TANGI	TANKARD	TANSIES
TAMPONAGE	TANGIBILITIES	TANKARDS	TANSY
TAMPONAGES	TANGIBILITY	TANKAS	TANTALATE
TAMPONED	TANGIBLE	TANKBUSTER	TANTALATES
TAMPONING	TANGIBLENESS	TANKBUSTERS	TANTALIC
TAMPONS	TANGIBLENESSES	TANKBUSTING	TANTALISATION
TAMPS	TANGIBLES	TANKBUSTINGS	TANTALISATIONS
TAMS	TANGIBLY	TANKED	TANTALISE

TANTALISED
TANTALISER
TANTALISERS
TANTALISES
TANTALISING
TANTALISINGLY
TANTALISINGS
TANTALISM
TANTALISMS
TANTALITE
TANTALITES
TANTALIZATION
TANTALIZATIONS
TANTALIZE
TANTALIZED
TANTALIZER
TANTALIZERS
TANTALIZES
TANTALIZING
TANTALIZINGLY
TANTALIZINGS
TANTALOUS
TANTALUM
TANTALUMS
TANTALUS
TANTALUSES
TANTAMOUNT
TANTARA
TANTARARA
TANTARARAS
TANTARAS
TANTI
TANTIVIES
TANTIVY
TANTO
TANTONIES
TANTONY
TANTRA
TANTRAS
TANTRIC
TANTRUM
TANTRUMS
TANUKI
TANUKIS
TANYARD
TANYARDS
TANZANITE
TANZANITES
TAO
TAOISEACH
TAOISEACHS
TAONGA
TAONGAS
TAOS
TAP
TAPA
TAPACOLO

TAPACOLOS
TAPACULO
TAPACULOS
TAPADERA
TAPADERAS
TAPADERO
TAPADEROS
TAPALO
TAPALOS
TAPAS
TAPE
TAPEABLE
TAPED
TAPELESS
TAPELIKE
TAPELINE
TAPELINES
TAPEN
TAPENADE
TAPENADES
TAPER
TAPERED
TAPERER
TAPERERS
TAPERING
TAPERINGLY
TAPERINGS
TAPERNESS
TAPERNESSES
TAPERS
TAPERSTICK
TAPERSTICKS
TAPERWISE
TAPES
TAPESCRIPT
TAPESCRIPTS
TAPESTRIED
TAPESTRIES
TAPESTRY
TAPESTRYING
TAPET
TAPETA
TAPETAL
TAPETI
TAPETIS
TAPETS
TAPETUM
TAPEWORM
TAPEWORMS
TAPHEPHOBIA
TAPHEPHOBIAS
TAPHEPHOBIC
TAPHOLE
TAPHOLES
TAPHONOMIC
TAPHONOMICAL
TAPHONOMICALLY

TAPHONOMIES
TAPHONOMIST
TAPHONOMISTS
TAPHONOMY
TAPHOPHOBIA
TAPHOPHOBIAS
TAPHOUSE
TAPHOUSES
TAPHROGENESES
TAPHROGENESIS
TAPING
TAPIOCA
TAPIOCAS
TAPIR
TAPIROID
TAPIRS
TAPIS
TAPISES
TAPIST
TAPISTS
TAPLASH
TAPLASHES
TAPOTEMENT
TAPOTEMENTS
TAPPA
TAPPABLE
TAPPAS
TAPPED
TAPPER
TAPPERS
TAPPET
TAPPETS
TAPPICE
TAPPICED
TAPPICES
TAPPICING
TAPPING
TAPPINGS
TAPPIT
TAPROOM
TAPROOMS
TAPROOT
TAPROOTED
TAPROOTEDNESS
TAPROOTS
TAPS
TAPSALTEERIE
TAPSALTEERIES
TAPSIETEERIES
TAPSMAN
TAPSMEN
TAPSTER
TAPSTERS
TAPSTRESS
TAPSTRESSES
TAPSTRY
TAPU

TAPUED
TAPUES
TAPUING
TAPUS
TAQUERIA
TAQUERIAS
TAR
TARA
TARADIDDLE
TARADIDDLES
TARAIRE
TARAIRES
TARAKIHI
TARAKIHIS
TARAMA
TARAMAS
TARAMASALATA
TARAMASALATAS
TARAND
TARANDS
TARANTARA
TARANTARAED
TARANTARAING
TARANTARAS
TARANTAS
TARANTASES
TARANTASS
TARANTASSES
TARANTELLA
TARANTELLAS
TARANTISM
TARANTISMS
TARANTULA
TARANTULAE
TARANTULAS
TARAS
TARATANTARA
TARATANTARAED
TARATANTARAING
TARATANTARAS
TARAXACUM
TARAXACUMS
TARBOGGIN
TARBOGGINED
TARBOGGINING
TARBOGGINS
TARBOOSH
TARBOOSHES
TARBOUCHE
TARBOUCHES
TARBOUSH
TARBOUSHES
TARBOY
TARBOYS
TARBUSH
TARBUSHES
TARCEL

TARCELS
TARDIED
TARDIER
TARDIES
TARDIEST
TARDIGRADE
TARDIGRADES
TARDILY
TARDINESS
TARDINESSES
TARDIVE
TARDO
TARDY
TARDYING
TARDYON
TARDYONS
TARE
TARED
TARES
TARGE
TARGED
TARGES
TARGET
TARGETABLE
TARGETED
TARGETEER
TARGETEERS
TARGETING
TARGETITIS
TARGETLESS
TARGETLESSNESS
TARGETS
TARGING
TARIFF
TARIFFED
TARIFFICATION
TARIFFICATIONS
TARIFFING
TARIFFLESS
TARIFFS
TARING
TARINGS
TARLATAN
TARLATANS
TARLETAN
TARLETANS
TARMAC
TARMACADAM
TARMACADAMS
TARMACKED
TARMACKING
TARMACS
TARN
TARNAL
TARNALLY
TARNATION
TARNATIONS

TARNISH
TARNISHABLE
TARNISHED
TARNISHER
TARNISHERS
TARNISHES
TARNISHING
TARNS
TARO
TAROC
TAROCS
TAROK
TAROKS
TAROS
TAROT
TAROTS
TARP
TARPAN
TARPANS
TARPAPER
TARPAPERS
TARPAULIN
TARPAULING
TARPAULINGS
TARPAULINS
TARPON
TARPONS
TARPS
TARRADIDDLE
TARRADIDDLES
TARRAGON
TARRAGONS
TARRAS
TARRASES
TARRE
TARRED
TARRES
TARRIANCE
TARRIANCES
TARRIED
TARRIER
TARRIERS
TARRIES
TARRIEST
TARRINESS
TARRINESSES
TARRING
TARRINGS
TARROCK
TARROCKS
TARROW
TARROWED
TARROWING
TARROWS
TARRY
TARRYING
TARS

TARSAL
TARSALGIA
TARSALGIAS
TARSALS
TARSEAL
TARSEALS
TARSEL
TARSELS
TARSI
TARSIA
TARSIAS
TARSIER
TARSIERS
TARSIOID
TARSIPED
TARSIPEDS
TARSOMETATARSAL
TARSOMETATARSI
TARSOMETATARSUS
TARSUS
TART
TARTAN
TARTANA
TARTANALIA
TARTANALIAS
TARTANAS
TARTANE
TARTANED
TARTANES
TARTANRIES
TARTANRY
TARTANS
TARTAR
TARTARE
TARTAREOUS
TARTARES
TARTARIC
TARTARISATION
TARTARISATIONS
TARTARISE
TARTARISED
TARTARISES
TARTARISING
TARTARIZATION
TARTARIZATIONS
TARTARIZE
TARTARIZED
TARTARIZES
TARTARIZING
TARTARLY
TARTAROUS
TARTARS
TARTED
TARTER
TARTEST
TARTIER
TARTIEST

TARTINE
TARTINES
TARTINESS
TARTINESSES
TARTING
TARTISH
TARTISHLY
TARTLET
TARTLETS
TARTLY
TARTNESS
TARTNESSES
TARTRATE
TARTRATED
TARTRATES
TARTRAZINE
TARTRAZINES
TARTS
TARTUFE
TARTUFES
TARTUFFE
TARTUFFES
TARTY
TARWEED
TARWEEDS
TARWHINE
TARWHINES
TARZAN
TARZANS
TAS
TASAR
TASARS
TASEOMETER
TASEOMETERS
TASER
TASERED
TASERING
TASERS
TASH
TASHED
TASHES
TASHING
TASIMETER
TASIMETERS
TASIMETRIC
TASIMETRY
TASK
TASKED
TASKER
TASKERS
TASKING
TASKINGS
TASKLESS
TASKLESSNESS
TASKMASTER
TASKMASTERS
TASKMISTRESS

TASKMISTRESSES
TASKS
TASKWORK
TASKWORKS
TASLET
TASLETS
TASS
TASSE
TASSEL
TASSELED
TASSELING
TASSELL
TASSELLED
TASSELLING
TASSELLINGS
TASSELLS
TASSELLY
TASSELS
TASSES
TASSET
TASSETS
TASSIE
TASSIES
TASSWAGE
TASTABLE
TASTE
TASTED
TASTEFUL
TASTEFULLY
TASTEFULNESS
TASTEFULNESSES
TASTELESS
TASTELESSLY
TASTELESSNESS
TASTELESSNESSES
TASTEMAKER
TASTEMAKERS
TASTER
TASTERS
TASTES
TASTEVIN
TASTEVINS
TASTIER
TASTIEST
TASTILY
TASTINESS
TASTINESSES
TASTING
TASTINGS
TASTY
TAT
TATAHASH
TATAHASHES
TATAMI
TATAMIS
TATAR
TATARS

TATE
TATER
TATERS
TATES
TATH
TATHED
TATHING
TATHS
TATIE
TATIES
TATLER
TATLERS
TATOU
TATOUAY
TATOUAYS
TATOUS
TATPURUSHA
TATPURUSHAS
TATS
TATT
TATTED
TATTER
TATTERDEMALION
TATTERDEMALIONS
TATTERDEMALLION
TATTERED
TATTERING
TATTERS
TATTERSALL
TATTERSALLS
TATTERY
TATTIE
TATTIER
TATTIES
TATTIEST
TATTILY
TATTINESS
TATTINESSES
TATTING
TATTINGS
TATTLE
TATTLED
TATTLER
TATTLERS
TATTLES
TATTLETALE
TATTLETALES
TATTLING
TATTLINGLY
TATTLINGS
TATTOO
TATTOOED
TATTOOER
TATTOOERS
TATTOOING
TATTOOIST
TATTOOISTS

TATTOOS
TATTOW
TATTOWED
TATTOWING
TATTOWS
TATTS
TATTY
TATU
TATUED
TATUING
TATUS
TAU
TAUBE
TAUBES
TAUGHT
TAUHINU
TAUHINUS
TAUIWI
TAULD
TAUNT
TAUNTED
TAUNTER
TAUNTERS
TAUNTING
TAUNTINGLY
TAUNTINGS
TAUNTS
TAUON
TAUONS
TAUPATA
TAUPATAS
TAUPE
TAUPES
TAUPIE
TAUPIES
TAUREAN
TAURIC
TAURIFORM
TAURINE
TAURINES
TAUROBOLIA
TAUROBOLIUM
TAUROMACHIAN
TAUROMACHIES
TAUROMACHY
TAUROMORPHOUS
TAUS
TAUT
TAUTAUG
TAUTAUGS
TAUTED
TAUTEN
TAUTENED
TAUTENING
TAUTENS
TAUTER
TAUTEST

TAUTING
TAUTIT
TAUTLY
TAUTNESS
TAUTNESSES
TAUTOCHRONE
TAUTOCHRONES
TAUTOCHRONISM
TAUTOCHRONISMS
TAUTOCHRONOUS
TAUTOG
TAUTOGS
TAUTOLOGIC
TAUTOLOGICAL
TAUTOLOGICALLY
TAUTOLOGIES
TAUTOLOGISE
TAUTOLOGISED
TAUTOLOGISES
TAUTOLOGISING
TAUTOLOGISM
TAUTOLOGISMS
TAUTOLOGIST
TAUTOLOGISTS
TAUTOLOGIZE
TAUTOLOGIZED
TAUTOLOGIZES
TAUTOLOGIZING
TAUTOLOGOUS
TAUTOLOGOUSLY
TAUTOLOGY
TAUTOMER
TAUTOMERIC
TAUTOMERISM
TAUTOMERISMS
TAUTOMERS
TAUTOMETRIC
TAUTOMETRICAL
TAUTONYM
TAUTONYMIC
TAUTONYMIES
TAUTONYMOUS
TAUTONYMS
TAUTONYMY
TAUTOPHONIC
TAUTOPHONICAL
TAUTOPHONIES
TAUTOPHONY
TAUTS
TAV
TAVA
TAVAH
TAVAHS
TAVAS
TAVER
TAVERED
TAVERING

TAVERN	TAWTS	TAXITIC	TEABREAD
TAVERNA	TAX	TAXIWAY	TEABREADS
TAVERNAS	TAXA	TAXIWAYS	TEACAKE
TAVERNER	TAXABILITIES	TAXLESS	TEACAKES
TAVERNERS	TAXABILITY	TAXMAN	TEACART
TAVERNS	TAXABLE	TAXMEN	TEACARTS
TAVERS	TAXABLENESS	TAXOL	TEACH
TAVERT	TAXABLES	TAXOLS	TEACHABILITIES
TAVS	TAXABLY	TAXON	TEACHABILITY
TAW	TAXACEOUS	TAXONOMER	TEACHABLE
TAWA	TAXAMETER	TAXONOMERS	TEACHABLENESS
TAWAI	TAXAMETERS	TAXONOMIC	TEACHABLENESSES
TAWAIS	TAXATION	TAXONOMICAL	TEACHABLY
TAWAS	TAXATIONAL	TAXONOMICALLY	TEACHER
TAWDRIER	TAXATIONS	TAXONOMIES	TEACHERLESS
TAWDRIES	TAXATIVE	TAXONOMIST	TEACHERLY
TAWDRIEST	TAXED	TAXONOMISTS	TEACHERS
TAWDRILY	TAXEME	TAXONOMY	TEACHERSHIP
TAWDRINESS	TAXEMES	TAXONS	TEACHERSHIPS
TAWDRINESSES	TAXEMIC	TAXOR	TEACHES
TAWDRY	TAXER	TAXORS	TEACHIE
TAWED	TAXERS	TAXPAID	TEACHING
TAWER	TAXES	TAXPAYER	TEACHINGS
TAWERIES	TAXI	TAXPAYERS	TEACHLESS
TAWERS	TAXIARCH	TAXPAYING	TEACUP
TAWERY	TAXIARCHS	TAXUS	TEACUPFUL
TAWHAI	TAXICAB	TAXWISE	TEACUPFULS
TAWHAIS	TAXICABS	TAXYING	TEACUPS
TAWHIRI	TAXIDERMAL	TAY	TEACUPSFUL
TAWHIRIS	TAXIDERMIC	TAYASSUID	TEAD
TAWIE	TAXIDERMIES	TAYASSUIDS	TEADE
TAWIER	TAXIDERMISE	TAYBERRIES	TEADES
TAWIEST	TAXIDERMISED	TAYBERRY	TEADS
TAWING	TAXIDERMISES	TAYRA	TEAED
TAWINGS	TAXIDERMISING	TAYRAS	TEAGLE
TAWNEY	TAXIDERMIST	TAYS	TEAGLED
TAWNEYS	TAXIDERMISTS	TAZZA	TEAGLES
TAWNIER	TAXIDERMIZE	TAZZAS	TEAGLING
TAWNIES	TAXIDERMIZED	TAZZE	TEAHOUSE
TAWNIEST	TAXIDERMIZES	TCHICK	TEAHOUSES
TAWNILY	TAXIDERMIZING	TCHICKED	TEAING
TAWNINESS	TAXIDERMY	TCHICKING	TEAK
TAWNINESSES	TAXIED	TCHICKS	TEAKETTLE
TAWNY	TAXIES	TCHOTCHKE	TEAKETTLES
TAWPIE	TAXIING	TCHOTCHKES	TEAKS
TAWPIES	TAXIMAN	TCHOUKBALL	TEAKWOOD
TAWS	TAXIMEN	TCHOUKBALLS	TEAKWOODS
TAWSE	TAXIMETER	TE	TEAL
TAWSED	TAXIMETERS	TEA	TEALIKE
TAWSES	TAXING	TEABERRIES	TEALS
TAWSING	TAXINGLY	TEABERRY	TEAM
TAWT	TAXINGS	TEABOARD	TEAMAKER
TAWTED	TAXIPLANE	TEABOARDS	TEAMAKERS
TAWTIE	TAXIPLANES	TEABOWL	TEAMED
TAWTIER	TAXIS	TEABOWLS	TEAMER
TAWTIEST	TAXITE	TEABOX	TEAMERS
TAWTING	TAXITES	TEABOXES	TEAMING

TEAMINGS	TEASELINGS	TECHNICAL	TECHNOMANIA
TEAMMATE	TEASELLED	TECHNICALITIES	TECHNOMANIAC
TEAMMATES	TEASELLER	TECHNICALITY	TECHNOMANIACS
TEAMS	TEASELLERS	TECHNICALIZE	TECHNOMANIAS
TEAMSTER	TEASELLING	TECHNICALIZED	TECHNOMUSIC
TEAMSTERS	TEASELLINGS	TECHNICALIZES	TECHNOMUSICS
TEAMWISE	TEASELS	TECHNICALIZING	TECHNOPHILE
TEAMWORK	TEASER	TECHNICALLY	TECHNOPHILES
TEAMWORKS	TEASERS	TECHNICALNESS	TECHNOPHOBE
TEAPOT	TEASES	TECHNICALNESSES	TECHNOPHOBES
TEAPOTS	TEASHOP	TECHNICALS	TECHNOPHOBIA
TEAPOY	TEASHOPS	TECHNICIAN	TECHNOPHOBIAS
TEAPOYS	TEASING	TECHNICIANS	TECHNOPHOBIC
TEAR	TEASINGLY	TECHNICISE	TECHNOPHOBICS
TEARABLE	TEASINGS	TECHNICISED	TECHNOPOLE
TEARAWAY	TEASPOON	TECHNICISES	TECHNOPOLES
TEARAWAYS	TEASPOONFUL	TECHNICISING	TECHNOPOLIS
TEARDOWN	TEASPOONFULS	TECHNICISM	TECHNOPOLISES
TEARDOWNS	TEASPOONS	TECHNICISMS	TECHNOPOLITAN
TEARDROP	TEASPOONSFUL	TECHNICIST	TECHNOPOLITANS
TEARDROPS	TEAT	TECHNICISTS	TECHNOPOP
TEARED	TEATED	TECHNICIZE	TECHNOPOPS
TEARER	TEATIME	TECHNICIZED	TECHNOS
TEARERS	TEATIMES	TECHNICIZES	TECHNOSPEAK
TEARFUL	TEATS	TECHNICIZING	TECHNOSPEAKS
TEARFULLY	TEAWARE	TECHNICOLOUR	TECHNOSTRESS
TEARFULNESS	TEAWARES	TECHNICOLOURED	TECHNOSTRESSES
TEARFULNESSES	TEAZE	TECHNICS	TECHNOSTRUCTURE
TEARGAS	TEAZED	TECHNIKON	TECHS
TEARGASES	TEAZEL	TECHNIKONS	TECHY
TEARGASSED	TEAZELED	TECHNIQUE	TECKEL
TEARGASSES	TEAZELING	TECHNIQUES	TECKELS
TEARGASSING	TEAZELLED	TECHNO	TECS
TEARIER	TEAZELLING	TECHNOBABBLE	TECTA
TEARIEST	TEAZELS	TECHNOBABBLES	TECTAL
TEARILY	TEAZES	TECHNOCRACIES	TECTIBRANCH
TEARING	TEAZING	TECHNOCRACY	TECTIBRANCHIATE
TEARJERKER	TEAZLE	TECHNOCRAT	TECTIBRANCHS
TEARJERKERS	TEAZLED	TECHNOCRATIC	TECTIFORM
TEARLESS	TEAZLES	TECHNOCRATS	TECTITE
TEAROOM	TEAZLING	TECHNOFEAR	TECTITES
TEAROOMS	TEBBAD	TECHNOFEARS	TECTONIC
TEARS	TEBBADS	TECHNOGRAPHIES	TECTONICALLY
TEARSHEET	TEC	TECHNOGRAPHY	TECTONICS
TEARSHEETS	TECH	TECHNOJUNKIE	TECTONISM
TEARSTAIN	TECHED	TECHNOJUNKIES	TECTONISMS
TEARSTAINED	TECHIE	TECHNOLOGIC	TECTORIAL
TEARSTAINS	TECHIER	TECHNOLOGICAL	TECTRICES
TEARY	TECHIES	TECHNOLOGICALLY	TECTRICIAL
TEAS	TECHIEST	TECHNOLOGIES	TECTRIX
TEASE	TECHILY	TECHNOLOGIST	TECTUM
TEASED	TECHINESS	TECHNOLOGISTS	TED
TEASEL	TECHINESSES	TECHNOLOGIZE	TEDDED
TEASELED	TECHNETIUM	TECHNOLOGIZED	TEDDER
TEASELER	TECHNETIUMS	TECHNOLOGIZES	TEDDERS
TEASELERS	TECHNETRONIC	TECHNOLOGIZING	TEDDIE
TEASELING	TECHNIC	TECHNOLOGY	TEDDIES

TEDDING
TEDDY
TEDESCA
TEDESCHE
TEDESCHI
TEDESCO
TEDIER
TEDIEST
TEDIOSITIES
TEDIOSITY
TEDIOUS
TEDIOUSLY
TEDIOUSNESS
TEDIOUSNESSES
TEDIOUSOME
TEDISOME
TEDIUM
TEDIUMS
TEDS
TEDY
TEE
TEED
TEEING
TEEL
TEELS
TEEM
TEEMED
TEEMER
TEEMERS
TEEMFUL
TEEMING
TEEMINGLY
TEEMINGNESS
TEEMINGNESSES
TEEMLESS
TEEMS
TEEN
TEENAGE
TEENAGED
TEENAGER
TEENAGERS
TEEND
TEENDED
TEENDING
TEENDS
TEENE
TEENED
TEENER
TEENERS
TEENES
TEENFUL
TEENIER
TEENIEST
TEENING
TEENS
TEENSIER
TEENSIEST

TEENSY
TEENTIER
TEENTIEST
TEENTSIER
TEENTSIEST
TEENTSY
TEENTY
TEENY
TEENYBOP
TEENYBOPPER
TEENYBOPPERS
TEEPEE
TEEPEES
TEER
TEERED
TEERING
TEERS
TEES
TEETER
TEETERBOARD
TEETERBOARDS
TEETERED
TEETERING
TEETERS
TEETH
TEETHE
TEETHED
TEETHER
TEETHERS
TEETHES
TEETHING
TEETHINGS
TEETHRIDGE
TEETHRIDGES
TEETOTAL
TEETOTALED
TEETOTALER
TEETOTALERS
TEETOTALING
TEETOTALISM
TEETOTALISMS
TEETOTALIST
TEETOTALISTS
TEETOTALLED
TEETOTALLER
TEETOTALLERS
TEETOTALLING
TEETOTALLY
TEETOTALS
TEETOTUM
TEETOTUMS
TEF
TEFF
TEFFS
TEFILLAH
TEFILLIN
TEFS

TEG
TEGG
TEGGS
TEGMEN
TEGMENTA
TEGMENTAL
TEGMENTUM
TEGMINA
TEGMINAL
TEGS
TEGU
TEGUA
TEGUAS
TEGUEXIN
TEGUEXINS
TEGULA
TEGULAE
TEGULAR
TEGULARLY
TEGULATED
TEGUMEN
TEGUMENT
TEGUMENTAL
TEGUMENTARY
TEGUMENTS
TEGUMINA
TEGUS
TEHR
TEHRS
TEICHOPSIA
TEICHOPSIAS
TEIGLACH
TEIID
TEIIDS
TEIL
TEILS
TEIND
TEINDED
TEINDING
TEINDS
TEINOSCOPE
TEINOSCOPES
TEKNONYMIES
TEKNONYMOUS
TEKNONYMY
TEKTITE
TEKTITES
TEKTITIC
TEL
TELA
TELAE
TELAESTHESIA
TELAESTHESIAS
TELAESTHETIC
TELAMON
TELAMONES
TELAMONS

TELANGIECTASES
TELANGIECTASIA
TELANGIECTASIAS
TELANGIECTASIS
TELANGIECTATIC
TELARY
TELAUTOGRAPHIC
TELAUTOGRAPHIES
TELAUTOGRAPHY
TELCO
TELCOS
TELD
TELE
TELEARCHICS
TELEBANKING
TELEBANKINGS
TELEBRIDGE
TELEBRIDGES
TELECAMERA
TELECAMERAS
TELECAST
TELECASTED
TELECASTER
TELECASTERS
TELECASTING
TELECASTS
TELECHIR
TELECHIRIC
TELECHIRS
TELECINE
TELECINES
TELECOM
TELECOMMAND
TELECOMMANDS
TELECOMMUTE
TELECOMMUTED
TELECOMMUTER
TELECOMMUTERS
TELECOMMUTES
TELECOMMUTING
TELECOMMUTINGS
TELECOMS
TELECONFERENCE
TELECONFERENCES
TELECONNECTION
TELECONNECTIONS
TELECONTROL
TELECONTROLS
TELECONVERTER
TELECONVERTERS
TELECOTTAGE
TELECOTTAGES
TELECOTTAGING
TELECOTTAGINGS
TELECOURSE
TELECOURSES
TELEDILDONICS

TELEDU
TELEDUS
TELEFACSIMILE
TELEFACSIMILES
TELEFAX
TELEFAXED
TELEFAXES
TELEFAXING
TELEFERIQUE
TELEFERIQUES
TELEFILM
TELEFILMS
TELEGA
TELEGAS
TELEGENIC
TELEGENICALLY
TELEGNOSES
TELEGNOSIS
TELEGNOSTIC
TELEGONIC
TELEGONIES
TELEGONOUS
TELEGONY
TELEGRAM
TELEGRAMMATIC
TELEGRAMMED
TELEGRAMMIC
TELEGRAMMING
TELEGRAMS
TELEGRAPH
TELEGRAPHED
TELEGRAPHER
TELEGRAPHERS
TELEGRAPHESE
TELEGRAPHESES
TELEGRAPHIC
TELEGRAPHICALLY
TELEGRAPHIES
TELEGRAPHING
TELEGRAPHIST
TELEGRAPHISTS
TELEGRAPHS
TELEGRAPHY
TELEJOURNALISM
TELEJOURNALISMS
TELEJOURNALIST
TELEJOURNALISTS
TELEKINESES
TELEKINESIS
TELEKINETIC
TELEKINETICALLY
TELEMAN
TELEMARK
TELEMARKED
TELEMARKETER
TELEMARKETERS
TELEMARKETING

TELEMARKETINGS
TELEMARKING
TELEMARKS
TELEMATIC
TELEMATICS
TELEMEDICINE
TELEMEN
TELEMETER
TELEMETERED
TELEMETERING
TELEMETERS
TELEMETRIC
TELEMETRICAL
TELEMETRICALLY
TELEMETRIES
TELEMETRY
TELENCEPHALA
TELENCEPHALIC
TELENCEPHALON
TELENCEPHALONS
TELEOLOGIC
TELEOLOGICAL
TELEOLOGICALLY
TELEOLOGIES
TELEOLOGISM
TELEOLOGISMS
TELEOLOGIST
TELEOLOGISTS
TELEOLOGY
TELEONOMIC
TELEONOMIES
TELEONOMY
TELEOSAUR
TELEOSAURIAN
TELEOSAURIANS
TELEOSAURS
TELEOST
TELEOSTEAN
TELEOSTEANS
TELEOSTOME
TELEOSTOMES
TELEOSTOMOUS
TELEOSTS
TELEPATH
TELEPATHED
TELEPATHIC
TELEPATHICALLY
TELEPATHIES
TELEPATHING
TELEPATHISE
TELEPATHISED
TELEPATHISES
TELEPATHISING
TELEPATHIST
TELEPATHISTS
TELEPATHIZE
TELEPATHIZED

TELEPATHIZES
TELEPATHIZING
TELEPATHS
TELEPATHY
TELEPHEME
TELEPHEMES
TELEPHERIQUE
TELEPHERIQUES
TELEPHONE
TELEPHONED
TELEPHONER
TELEPHONERS
TELEPHONES
TELEPHONIC
TELEPHONICALLY
TELEPHONIES
TELEPHONING
TELEPHONIST
TELEPHONISTS
TELEPHONY
TELEPHOTO
TELEPHOTOGRAPH
TELEPHOTOGRAPHS
TELEPHOTOGRAPHY
TELEPHOTOS
TELEPLAY
TELEPLAYS
TELEPOINT
TELEPOINTS
TELEPORT
TELEPORTATION
TELEPORTATIONS
TELEPORTED
TELEPORTING
TELEPORTS
TELEPRESENCE
TELEPRESENCES
TELEPRINTER
TELEPRINTERS
TELEPROCESSING
TELEPROCESSINGS
TELEPROMPTER
TELEPROMPTERS
TELERAN
TELERANS
TELERECORD
TELERECORDED
TELERECORDING
TELERECORDINGS
TELERECORDS
TELERGIC
TELERGICALLY
TELERGIES
TELERGY
TELES
TELESALE
TELESALES

TELESCIENCE
TELESCIENCES
TELESCOPE
TELESCOPED
TELESCOPES
TELESCOPIC
TELESCOPICAL
TELESCOPICALLY
TELESCOPIES
TELESCOPIFORM
TELESCOPING
TELESCOPIST
TELESCOPISTS
TELESCOPY
TELESCREEN
TELESCREENS
TELESELLING
TELESELLINGS
TELESEME
TELESEMES
TELESERVICES
TELESES
TELESHOPPING
TELESHOPPINGS
TELESIS
TELESM
TELESMATIC
TELESMATICAL
TELESMATICALLY
TELESMS
TELESOFTWARE
TELESOFTWARES
TELESTEREOSCOPE
TELESTHESIA
TELESTHESIAS
TELESTHETIC
TELESTIC
TELESTICH
TELESTICHS
TELESTICS
TELETEX
TELETEXES
TELETEXT
TELETEXTS
TELETHON
TELETHONS
TELETRON
TELETRONS
TELETYPESETTING
TELETYPEWRITER
TELETYPEWRITERS
TELEUTOSPORE
TELEUTOSPORES
TELEUTOSPORIC
TELEVANGELICAL
TELEVANGELISM
TELEVANGELISMS

TELEVANGELIST
TELEVANGELISTS
TELEVERITE
TELEVERITES
TELEVIEW
TELEVIEWED
TELEVIEWER
TELEVIEWERS
TELEVIEWING
TELEVIEWS
TELEVISE
TELEVISED
TELEVISER
TELEVISERS
TELEVISES
TELEVISING
TELEVISION
TELEVISIONAL
TELEVISIONALLY
TELEVISIONARY
TELEVISIONS
TELEVISOR
TELEVISORS
TELEVISUAL
TELEVISUALLY
TELEWORKER
TELEWORKERS
TELEWORKING
TELEWORKINGS
TELEWRITER
TELEWRITERS
TELEX
TELEXED
TELEXES
TELEXING
TELFER
TELFERAGE
TELFERAGES
TELFERED
TELFERIC
TELFERING
TELFERS
TELFORD
TELFORDS
TELIA
TELIAL
TELIC
TELICALLY
TELIOSPORE
TELIOSPORES
TELIUM
TELL
TELLABLE
TELLAR
TELLARED
TELLARING
TELLARS

TELLEN
TELLENS
TELLER
TELLERED
TELLERING
TELLERS
TELLERSHIP
TELLERSHIPS
TELLIES
TELLIN
TELLING
TELLINGLY
TELLINGS
TELLINOID
TELLINS
TELLS
TELLTALE
TELLTALES
TELLURAL
TELLURATE
TELLURATES
TELLURETTED
TELLURIAN
TELLURIANS
TELLURIC
TELLURIDE
TELLURIDES
TELLURION
TELLURIONS
TELLURISE
TELLURISED
TELLURISES
TELLURISING
TELLURITE
TELLURITES
TELLURIUM
TELLURIUMS
TELLURIZE
TELLURIZED
TELLURIZES
TELLURIZING
TELLUROMETER
TELLUROMETERS
TELLUROUS
TELLUS
TELLUSES
TELLY
TELLYS
TELNET
TELNETS
TELOCENTRIC
TELOCENTRICS
TELOI
TELOME
TELOMERE
TELOMERES
TELOMERISATION

TELOMERIZATION
TELOMES
TELOMIC
TELOPHASE
TELOPHASES
TELOPHASIC
TELOS
TELOSES
TELOTAXES
TELOTAXIS
TELPHER
TELPHERAGE
TELPHERAGES
TELPHERED
TELPHERIC
TELPHERING
TELPHERLINE
TELPHERLINES
TELPHERMAN
TELPHERMEN
TELPHERS
TELPHERWAY
TELPHERWAYS
TELS
TELSON
TELSONIC
TELSONS
TELT
TEMAZEPAM
TEMAZEPAMS
TEMBLOR
TEMBLORES
TEMBLORS
TEME
TEMED
TEMENE
TEMENOS
TEMERARIOUS
TEMERARIOUSLY
TEMERARIOUSNESS
TEMERITIES
TEMERITY
TEMEROUS
TEMEROUSLY
TEMES
TEMP
TEMPED
TEMPEH
TEMPEHS
TEMPER
TEMPERA
TEMPERABILITIES
TEMPERABILITY
TEMPERABLE
TEMPERALITIE
TEMPERALITIES
TEMPERAMENT

TEMPERAMENTAL
TEMPERAMENTALLY
TEMPERAMENTFUL
TEMPERAMENTS
TEMPERANCE
TEMPERANCES
TEMPERAS
TEMPERATE
TEMPERATED
TEMPERATELY
TEMPERATENESS
TEMPERATENESSES
TEMPERATES
TEMPERATING
TEMPERATIVE
TEMPERATURE
TEMPERATURES
TEMPERED
TEMPERER
TEMPERERS
TEMPERING
TEMPERINGS
TEMPERS
TEMPEST
TEMPESTED
TEMPESTING
TEMPESTIVE
TEMPESTS
TEMPESTUOUS
TEMPESTUOUSLY
TEMPESTUOUSNESS
TEMPI
TEMPING
TEMPLAR
TEMPLARS
TEMPLATE
TEMPLATES
TEMPLE
TEMPLED
TEMPLES
TEMPLET
TEMPLETS
TEMPO
TEMPOLABILE
TEMPORAL
TEMPORALITIES
TEMPORALITY
TEMPORALIZE
TEMPORALIZED
TEMPORALIZES
TEMPORALIZING
TEMPORALLY
TEMPORALNESS
TEMPORALNESSES
TEMPORALS
TEMPORALTIES
TEMPORALTY

TEMPORANEOUS
TEMPORARIES
TEMPORARILY
TEMPORARINESS
TEMPORARINESSES
TEMPORARY
TEMPORE
TEMPORISATION
TEMPORISATIONS
TEMPORISE
TEMPORISED
TEMPORISER
TEMPORISERS
TEMPORISES
TEMPORISING
TEMPORISINGLY
TEMPORISINGS
TEMPORIZATION
TEMPORIZATIONS
TEMPORIZE
TEMPORIZED
TEMPORIZER
TEMPORIZERS
TEMPORIZES
TEMPORIZING
TEMPORIZINGLY
TEMPORIZINGS
TEMPOS
TEMPS
TEMPT
TEMPTABILITIES
TEMPTABILITY
TEMPTABLE
TEMPTABLENESS
TEMPTABLENESSES
TEMPTATION
TEMPTATIONS
TEMPTATIOUS
TEMPTED
TEMPTER
TEMPTERS
TEMPTING
TEMPTINGLY
TEMPTINGNESS
TEMPTINGNESSES
TEMPTINGS
TEMPTRESS
TEMPTRESSES
TEMPTS
TEMPURA
TEMPURAS
TEMS
TEMSE
TEMSED
TEMSES
TEMSING
TEMULENCE

TEMULENCES
TEMULENCIES
TEMULENCY
TEMULENT
TEMULENTLY
TEN
TENABILITIES
TENABILITY
TENABLE
TENABLENESS
TENABLENESSES
TENABLY
TENACE
TENACES
TENACIOUS
TENACIOUSLY
TENACIOUSNESS
TENACIOUSNESSES
TENACITIES
TENACITY
TENACULA
TENACULUM
TENACULUMS
TENAIL
TENAILLE
TENAILLES
TENAILLON
TENAILLONS
TENAILS
TENANCIES
TENANCY
TENANT
TENANTABLE
TENANTED
TENANTING
TENANTLESS
TENANTRIES
TENANTRY
TENANTS
TENANTSHIP
TENANTSHIPS
TENCH
TENCHES
TEND
TENDANCE
TENDANCES
TENDED
TENDENCE
TENDENCES
TENDENCIALLY
TENDENCIES
TENDENCIOUS
TENDENCIOUSLY
TENDENCIOUSNESS
TENDENCY
TENDENTIAL
TENDENTIALLY

TENDENTIOUS
TENDENTIOUSLY
TENDENTIOUSNESS
TENDENZ
TENDENZEN
TENDER
TENDERABLE
TENDERED
TENDERER
TENDERERS
TENDEREST
TENDERFEET
TENDERFOOT
TENDERFOOTS
TENDERHEARTED
TENDERHEARTEDLY
TENDERING
TENDERINGS
TENDERISATION
TENDERISE
TENDERISED
TENDERISER
TENDERISERS
TENDERISES
TENDERISING
TENDERIZATION
TENDERIZATIONS
TENDERIZE
TENDERIZED
TENDERIZER
TENDERIZERS
TENDERIZES
TENDERIZING
TENDERLING
TENDERLINGS
TENDERLOIN
TENDERLOINS
TENDERLY
TENDERNESS
TENDERNESSES
TENDEROMETER
TENDEROMETERS
TENDERS
TENDING
TENDINITIS
TENDINITISES
TENDINOUS
TENDON
TENDONITIS
TENDONITISES
TENDONS
TENDOVAGINITIS
TENDRE
TENDRES
TENDRESSE
TENDRESSES
TENDRIL

TENDRILED
TENDRILLAR
TENDRILLED
TENDRILLOUS
TENDRILOUS
TENDRILS
TENDRON
TENDRONS
TENDS
TENE
TENEBRAE
TENEBRIFIC
TENEBRIO
TENEBRIONID
TENEBRIONIDS
TENEBRIOS
TENEBRIOUS
TENEBRIOUSNESS
TENEBRISM
TENEBRISMS
TENEBRIST
TENEBRISTS
TENEBRITIES
TENEBRITY
TENEBROSE
TENEBROSITIES
TENEBROSITY
TENEBROUS
TENEBROUSNESS
TENEMENT
TENEMENTAL
TENEMENTARY
TENEMENTED
TENEMENTS
TENENDUM
TENENDUMS
TENES
TENESMIC
TENESMUS
TENESMUSES
TENET
TENETS
TENFOLD
TENFOLDS
TENGE
TENIA
TENIACIDE
TENIACIDES
TENIAE
TENIAFUGE
TENIAFUGES
TENIAS
TENIASES
TENIASIS
TENIOID
TENNANTITE
TENNANTITES

TENNE
TENNER
TENNERS
TENNES
TENNIES
TENNIS
TENNISES
TENNIST
TENNISTS
TENNO
TENNOS
TENNY
TENON
TENONED
TENONER
TENONERS
TENONING
TENONS
TENOR
TENORIST
TENORISTS
TENORITE
TENORITES
TENORLESS
TENOROON
TENOROONS
TENORRHAPHIES
TENORRHAPHY
TENORS
TENOSYNOVITIS
TENOSYNOVITISES
TENOTOMIES
TENOTOMIST
TENOTOMISTS
TENOTOMY
TENOUR
TENOURS
TENOVAGINITIS
TENOVAGINITISES
TENPENCE
TENPENCES
TENPENNY
TENPIN
TENPINS
TENPOUNDER
TENPOUNDERS
TENREC
TENRECS
TENS
TENSE
TENSED
TENSELESS
TENSELY
TENSENESS
TENSENESSES
TENSER
TENSES

TENSEST
TENSIBILITIES
TENSIBILITY
TENSIBLE
TENSIBLENESS
TENSIBLY
TENSILE
TENSILELY
TENSILENESS
TENSILITIES
TENSILITY
TENSIMETER
TENSIMETERS
TENSING
TENSIOMETER
TENSIOMETERS
TENSIOMETRIC
TENSIOMETRIES
TENSIOMETRY
TENSION
TENSIONAL
TENSIONALLY
TENSIONED
TENSIONER
TENSIONERS
TENSIONING
TENSIONLESS
TENSIONS
TENSITIES
TENSITY
TENSIVE
TENSON
TENSONS
TENSOR
TENSORIAL
TENSORS
TENT
TENTACLE
TENTACLED
TENTACLES
TENTACULA
TENTACULAR
TENTACULATE
TENTACULIFEROUS
TENTACULITE
TENTACULITES
TENTACULOID
TENTACULUM
TENTAGE
TENTAGES
TENTATION
TENTATIONS
TENTATIVE
TENTATIVELY
TENTATIVENESS
TENTATIVENESSES
TENTATIVES

TENTED
TENTER
TENTERED
TENTERHOOK
TENTERHOOKS
TENTERING
TENTERS
TENTFUL
TENTFULS
TENTH
TENTHLY
TENTHS
TENTIE
TENTIER
TENTIEST
TENTIGINOUS
TENTIGO
TENTIGOS
TENTING
TENTINGS
TENTLESS
TENTLIKE
TENTORIA
TENTORIAL
TENTORIUM
TENTORIUMS
TENTS
TENTWISE
TENTY
TENUE
TENUES
TENUIOUS
TENUIROSTRAL
TENUIS
TENUITIES
TENUITY
TENUOUS
TENUOUSLY
TENUOUSNESS
TENUOUSNESSES
TENURABLE
TENURE
TENURED
TENURES
TENURIAL
TENURIALLY
TENUTI
TENUTO
TENUTOS
TENZON
TENZONS
TEOCALLI
TEOCALLIS
TEOPAN
TEOPANS
TEOSINTE
TEOSINTES

TEPA
TEPAL
TEPALS
TEPAS
TEPEE
TEPEES
TEPEFACTION
TEPEFACTIONS
TEPEFIED
TEPEFIES
TEPEFY
TEPEFYING
TEPHIGRAM
TEPHIGRAMS
TEPHILLAH
TEPHILLIN
TEPHRA
TEPHRAS
TEPHRITE
TEPHRITES
TEPHRITIC
TEPHROITE
TEPHROITES
TEPHROMANCIES
TEPHROMANCY
TEPID
TEPIDARIA
TEPIDARIUM
TEPIDER
TEPIDEST
TEPIDITIES
TEPIDITY
TEPIDLY
TEPIDNESS
TEPIDNESSES
TEPOY
TEPOYS
TEQUILA
TEQUILAS
TEQUILLA
TEQUILLAS
TERAFLOP
TERAGLIN
TERAGLINS
TERAI
TERAIS
TERAKIHI
TERAKIHIS
TERAOHM
TERAOHMS
TERAPH
TERAPHIM
TERAPHIMS
TERAS
TERATA
TERATISM
TERATISMS

TERATOCARCINOMA
TERATOGEN
TERATOGENESES
TERATOGENESIS
TERATOGENIC
TERATOGENICITY
TERATOGENIES
TERATOGENS
TERATOGENY
TERATOID
TERATOLOGIC
TERATOLOGICAL
TERATOLOGIES
TERATOLOGIST
TERATOLOGISTS
TERATOLOGY
TERATOMA
TERATOMAS
TERATOMATA
TERATOMATOUS
TERATOPHOBIA
TERATOPHOBIC
TERAWATT
TERAWATTS
TERBIA
TERBIAS
TERBIC
TERBIUM
TERBIUMS
TERCE
TERCEL
TERCELET
TERCELETS
TERCELS
TERCENTENARIES
TERCENTENARY
TERCENTENNIAL
TERCENTENNIALS
TERCES
TERCET
TERCETS
TERCIO
TERCIOS
TEREBENE
TEREBENES
TEREBIC
TEREBINTH
TEREBINTHINE
TEREBINTHS
TEREBRA
TEREBRAE
TEREBRANT
TEREBRANTS
TEREBRAS
TEREBRATE
TEREBRATED
TEREBRATES

TEREBRATING
TEREBRATION
TEREBRATIONS
TEREBRATULA
TEREBRATULAE
TEREBRATULAS
TEREDINES
TEREDO
TEREDOS
TEREFA
TEREFAH
TEREK
TEREKS
TEREPHTHALATE
TEREPHTHALATES
TEREPHTHALIC
TERES
TERETE
TERETES
TERF
TERFE
TERFES
TERFS
TERGA
TERGAL
TERGITE
TERGITES
TERGIVERSANT
TERGIVERSANTS
TERGIVERSATE
TERGIVERSATED
TERGIVERSATES
TERGIVERSATING
TERGIVERSATION
TERGIVERSATIONS
TERGIVERSATOR
TERGIVERSATORS
TERGIVERSATORY
TERGUM
TERIYAKI
TERIYAKIS
TERM
TERMAGANCIES
TERMAGANCY
TERMAGANT
TERMAGANTLY
TERMAGANTS
TERMED
TERMER
TERMERS
TERMINABILITIES
TERMINABILITY
TERMINABLE
TERMINABLENESS
TERMINABLY
TERMINAL
TERMINALLY

TERMINALS
TERMINATE
TERMINATED
TERMINATES
TERMINATING
TERMINATION
TERMINATIONAL
TERMINATIONS
TERMINATIVE
TERMINATIVELY
TERMINATOR
TERMINATORS
TERMINATORY
TERMINER
TERMINERS
TERMING
TERMINI
TERMINISM
TERMINISMS
TERMINIST
TERMINISTS
TERMINOLOGICAL
TERMINOLOGIES
TERMINOLOGIST
TERMINOLOGISTS
TERMINOLOGY
TERMINUS
TERMINUSES
TERMITARIA
TERMITARIES
TERMITARIUM
TERMITARIUMS
TERMITARY
TERMITE
TERMITES
TERMITIC
TERMLESS
TERMLIES
TERMLY
TERMOR
TERMORS
TERMS
TERMTIME
TERMTIMES
TERN
TERNAL
TERNARIES
TERNARY
TERNATE
TERNATELY
TERNE
TERNED
TERNEPLATE
TERNEPLATES
TERNES
TERNING
TERNION

TERNIONS
TERNS
TEROTECHNOLOGY
TERPENE
TERPENELESS
TERPENES
TERPENIC
TERPENOID
TERPENOIDS
TERPINEOL
TERPINEOLS
TERPINOL
TERPINOLS
TERPOLYMER
TERPOLYMERS
TERPSICHOREAL
TERPSICHOREAN
TERRA
TERRACE
TERRACED
TERRACELESS
TERRACES
TERRACETTE
TERRACETTES
TERRACING
TERRACINGS
TERRACOTTA
TERRACOTTAS
TERRAE
TERRAFORM
TERRAFORMED
TERRAFORMING
TERRAFORMINGS
TERRAFORMS
TERRAIN
TERRAINS
TERRAMARA
TERRAMARE
TERRAMARES
TERRANE
TERRANES
TERRAPIN
TERRAPINS
TERRAQUEOUS
TERRARIA
TERRARIUM
TERRARIUMS
TERRAS
TERRASES
TERRAZZO
TERRAZZOS
TERREEN
TERREENS
TERRELLA
TERRELLAS
TERREMOTIVE
TERRENE

TERRENELY
TERRENES
TERREPLEIN
TERREPLEINS
TERRESTRIAL
TERRESTRIALLY
TERRESTRIALNESS
TERRESTRIALS
TERRET
TERRETS
TERRIBILITIES
TERRIBILITY
TERRIBLE
TERRIBLENESS
TERRIBLENESSES
TERRIBLES
TERRIBLY
TERRICOLE
TERRICOLES
TERRICOLOUS
TERRIER
TERRIERS
TERRIES
TERRIFIC
TERRIFICALLY
TERRIFIED
TERRIFIER
TERRIFIERS
TERRIFIES
TERRIFY
TERRIFYING
TERRIFYINGLY
TERRIGENOUS
TERRINE
TERRINES
TERRIT
TERRITORIAL
TERRITORIALISE
TERRITORIALISED
TERRITORIALISES
TERRITORIALISM
TERRITORIALISMS
TERRITORIALIST
TERRITORIALISTS
TERRITORIALITY
TERRITORIALIZE
TERRITORIALIZED
TERRITORIALIZES
TERRITORIALLY
TERRITORIALS
TERRITORIED
TERRITORIES
TERRITORY
TERRITS
TERROIR
TERROIRS
TERROR

TERRORFUL
TERRORISATION
TERRORISATIONS
TERRORISE
TERRORISED
TERRORISER
TERRORISERS
TERRORISES
TERRORISING
TERRORISM
TERRORISMS
TERRORIST
TERRORISTIC
TERRORISTS
TERRORIZATION
TERRORIZATIONS
TERRORIZE
TERRORIZED
TERRORIZER
TERRORIZERS
TERRORIZES
TERRORIZING
TERRORLESS
TERRORS
TERRY
TERSANCTUS
TERSANCTUSES
TERSE
TERSELY
TERSENESS
TERSENESSES
TERSER
TERSEST
TERSION
TERSIONS
TERTIA
TERTIAL
TERTIALS
TERTIAN
TERTIANS
TERTIARIES
TERTIARY
TERTIAS
TERTIUM
TERTIUS
TERTIUSES
TERTS
TERVALENCY
TERVALENT
TERZETTA
TERZETTAS
TERZETTI
TERZETTO
TERZETTOS
TES
TESCHENITE
TESCHENITES

TESLA
TESLAS
TESSARAGLOT
TESSELLA
TESSELLAE
TESSELLAR
TESSELLATE
TESSELLATED
TESSELLATES
TESSELLATING
TESSELLATION
TESSELLATIONS
TESSERA
TESSERACT
TESSERACTS
TESSERAE
TESSERAL
TESSITURA
TESSITURAS
TEST
TESTA
TESTABILITIES
TESTABILITY
TESTABLE
TESTACEOUS
TESTACIES
TESTACY
TESTAE
TESTAMENT
TESTAMENTAL
TESTAMENTAR
TESTAMENTARILY
TESTAMENTARY
TESTAMENTS
TESTAMUR
TESTAMURS
TESTATE
TESTATES
TESTATION
TESTATIONS
TESTATOR
TESTATORS
TESTATRICES
TESTATRIX
TESTATRIXES
TESTATUM
TESTATUMS
TESTCROSS
TESTCROSSED
TESTCROSSES
TESTCROSSING
TESTE
TESTED
TESTEE
TESTEES
TESTER
TESTERN

TESTERNED
TESTERNING
TESTERNS
TESTERS
TESTES
TESTICLE
TESTICLES
TESTICULAR
TESTICULATE
TESTICULATED
TESTIER
TESTIEST
TESTIFICATE
TESTIFICATES
TESTIFICATION
TESTIFICATIONS
TESTIFICATOR
TESTIFICATORS
TESTIFICATORY
TESTIFIED
TESTIFIER
TESTIFIERS
TESTIFIES
TESTIFY
TESTIFYING
TESTILY
TESTIMONIAL
TESTIMONIALISE
TESTIMONIALISED
TESTIMONIALISES
TESTIMONIALIZE
TESTIMONIALIZED
TESTIMONIALIZES
TESTIMONIALS
TESTIMONIED
TESTIMONIES
TESTIMONY
TESTIMONYING
TESTINESS
TESTINESSES
TESTING
TESTINGS
TESTIS
TESTON
TESTONS
TESTOON
TESTOONS
TESTOSTERONE
TESTOSTERONES
TESTRIL
TESTRILL
TESTRILLS
TESTRILS
TESTS
TESTUDINAL
TESTUDINARY
TESTUDINEOUS

TESTUDINES
TESTUDO
TESTUDOS
TESTY
TET
TETANAL
TETANIC
TETANICALLY
TETANICS
TETANIES
TETANISATION
TETANISATIONS
TETANISE
TETANISED
TETANISES
TETANISING
TETANIZATION
TETANIZATIONS
TETANIZE
TETANIZED
TETANIZES
TETANIZING
TETANOID
TETANUS
TETANUSES
TETANY
TETARTOHEDRAL
TETARTOHEDRALLY
TETARTOHEDRISM
TETCHED
TETCHIER
TETCHIEST
TETCHILY
TETCHINESS
TETCHINESSES
TETCHY
TETE
TETES
TETH
TETHER
TETHERBALL
TETHERBALLS
TETHERED
TETHERING
TETHERS
TETHS
TETOTUM
TETOTUMS
TETRA
TETRABASIC
TETRABASICITIES
TETRABASICITY
TETRABRACH
TETRABRACHS
TETRABRANCHIATE
TETRACAINE
TETRACAINES

TETRACHLORIDE
TETRACHLORIDES
TETRACHORD
TETRACHORDAL
TETRACHORDS
TETRACHOTOMIES
TETRACHOTOMOUS
TETRACHOTOMY
TETRACID
TETRACIDS
TETRACT
TETRACTINAL
TETRACTINE
TETRACTS
TETRACYCLIC
TETRACYCLINE
TETRACYCLINES
TETRAD
TETRADACTYL
TETRADACTYLIES
TETRADACTYLOUS
TETRADACTYLS
TETRADACTYLY
TETRADIC
TETRADITE
TETRADITES
TETRADRACHM
TETRADRACHMS
TETRADS
TETRADYMITE
TETRADYMITES
TETRADYNAMOUS
TETRAETHYL
TETRAFLUORIDE
TETRAFLUORIDES
TETRAGON
TETRAGONAL
TETRAGONALLY
TETRAGONALNESS
TETRAGONOUS
TETRAGONS
TETRAGRAM
TETRAGRAMMATON
TETRAGRAMMATONS
TETRAGRAMS
TETRAGYNIAN
TETRAGYNOUS
TETRAHEDRA
TETRAHEDRAL
TETRAHEDRALLY
TETRAHEDRITE
TETRAHEDRITES
TETRAHEDRON
TETRAHEDRONS
TETRAHYDROFURAN
TETRAHYMENA
TETRAHYMENAS

TETRALOGIES
TETRALOGY
TETRAMER
TETRAMERAL
TETRAMERIC
TETRAMERISM
TETRAMERISMS
TETRAMEROUS
TETRAMERS
TETRAMETER
TETRAMETERS
TETRAMETHYLLEAD
TETRAMORPHIC
TETRANDRIAN
TETRANDROUS
TETRAPLA
TETRAPLAS
TETRAPLEGIA
TETRAPLEGIAS
TETRAPLEGIC
TETRAPLOID
TETRAPLOIDIES
TETRAPLOIDS
TETRAPLOIDY
TETRAPOD
TETRAPODIC
TETRAPODIES
TETRAPODOUS
TETRAPODS
TETRAPODY
TETRAPOLIS
TETRAPOLISES
TETRAPOLITAN
TETRAPTERAN
TETRAPTEROUS
TETRAPTOTE
TETRAPTOTES
TETRAPYRROLE
TETRAPYRROLES
TETRARCH
TETRARCHATE
TETRARCHATES
TETRARCHIC
TETRARCHICAL
TETRARCHIES
TETRARCHS
TETRARCHY
TETRAS
TETRASEMIC
TETRASPORANGIA
TETRASPORANGIUM
TETRASPORE
TETRASPORES
TETRASPORIC
TETRASPOROUS
TETRASTICH
TETRASTICHAL

TETRASTICHIC
TETRASTICHOUS
TETRASTICHS
TETRASTYLE
TETRASTYLES
TETRASYLLABIC
TETRASYLLABICAL
TETRASYLLABLE
TETRASYLLABLES
TETRATHEISM
TETRATHEISMS
TETRATHLON
TETRATHLONS
TETRATOMIC
TETRAVALENCY
TETRAVALENT
TETRAVALENTS
TETRAXON
TETRAXONS
TETRAZOLIUM
TETRAZOLIUMS
TETRAZZINI
TETRODE
TETRODES
TETRODOTOXIN
TETRODOTOXINS
TETRONAL
TETRONALS
TETROTOXIN
TETROTOXINS
TETROXID
TETROXIDE
TETROXIDES
TETROXIDS
TETRYL
TETRYLS
TETS
TETTER
TETTERED
TETTERING
TETTEROUS
TETTERS
TETTIX
TETTIXES
TEUCH
TEUCHAT
TEUCHATS
TEUCHER
TEUCHEST
TEUCHTER
TEUCHTERS
TEUGH
TEUGHER
TEUGHEST
TEUGHLY
TEUTONIZE
TEUTONIZED

TEUTONIZES
TEUTONIZING
TEW
TEWART
TEWARTS
TEWED
TEWEL
TEWELS
TEWHIT
TEWHITS
TEWING
TEWIT
TEWITS
TEWS
TEXAS
TEXASES
TEXT
TEXTBOOK
TEXTBOOKISH
TEXTBOOKS
TEXTER
TEXTERS
TEXTILE
TEXTILES
TEXTLESS
TEXTORIAL
TEXTPHONE
TEXTPHONES
TEXTS
TEXTUAL
TEXTUALISM
TEXTUALISMS
TEXTUALIST
TEXTUALISTS
TEXTUALLY
TEXTUARIES
TEXTUARY
TEXTURAL
TEXTURALLY
TEXTURE
TEXTURED
TEXTURELESS
TEXTURES
TEXTURING
TEXTURISE
TEXTURISED
TEXTURISES
TEXTURISING
TEXTURIZE
TEXTURIZED
TEXTURIZES
TEXTURIZING
THACK
THACKED
THACKING
THACKS
THAE

THAGI
THAGIS
THAIM
THAIRM
THAIRMS
THALAMENCEPHALA
THALAMI
THALAMIC
THALAMICALLY
THALAMIFLORAL
THALAMUS
THALASSAEMIA
THALASSAEMIAS
THALASSAEMIC
THALASSEMIA
THALASSEMIAS
THALASSEMIC
THALASSEMICS
THALASSIAN
THALASSIANS
THALASSIC
THALASSOCRACIES
THALASSOCRACY
THALASSOCRAT
THALASSOCRATS
THALASSOGRAPHER
THALASSOGRAPHIC
THALASSOGRAPHY
THALASSOTHERAPY
THALATTOCRACIES
THALATTOCRACY
THALER
THALERS
THALI
THALIAN
THALICTRUM
THALICTRUMS
THALIDOMIDE
THALIDOMIDES
THALLI
THALLIC
THALLIFORM
THALLINE
THALLIUM
THALLIUMS
THALLOID
THALLOPHYTE
THALLOPHYTES
THALLOPHYTIC
THALLOUS
THALLUS
THALLUSES
THALWEG
THALWEGS
THAN
THANA
THANADAR

THANADARS
THANAGE
THANAGES
THANAH
THANAHS
THANAS
THANATISM
THANATISMS
THANATIST
THANATISTS
THANATOGNOMONIC
THANATOGRAPHIES
THANATOGRAPHY
THANATOID
THANATOLOGICAL
THANATOLOGIES
THANATOLOGIST
THANATOLOGISTS
THANATOLOGY
THANATOPHOBIA
THANATOPHOBIAS
THANATOPSES
THANATOPSIS
THANATOS
THANATOSES
THANATOSIS
THANE
THANEDOM
THANEDOMS
THANEHOOD
THANEHOODS
THANES
THANESHIP
THANESHIPS
THANGKA
THANGKAS
THANK
THANKED
THANKEE
THANKER
THANKERS
THANKFUL
THANKFULLER
THANKFULLEST
THANKFULLY
THANKFULNESS
THANKFULNESSES
THANKING
THANKINGS
THANKLESS
THANKLESSLY
THANKLESSNESS
THANKLESSNESSES
THANKS
THANKSGIVER
THANKSGIVERS
THANKSGIVING

THANKSGIVINGS
THANKWORTHILY
THANKWORTHINESS
THANKWORTHY
THANKYOU
THANKYOUS
THANNA
THANNAH
THANNAHS
THANNAS
THANS
THAR
THARBOROUGH
THARBOROUGHS
THARM
THARMS
THARS
THAT
THATAWAY
THATCH
THATCHED
THATCHER
THATCHERS
THATCHES
THATCHIER
THATCHIEST
THATCHING
THATCHINGS
THATCHLESS
THATCHT
THATCHY
THATNESS
THATNESSES
THAUMASITE
THAUMASITES
THAUMATIN
THAUMATINS
THAUMATOGENIES
THAUMATOGENY
THAUMATOGRAPHY
THAUMATOLATRIES
THAUMATOLATRY
THAUMATOLOGIES
THAUMATOLOGY
THAUMATROPE
THAUMATROPES
THAUMATROPICAL
THAUMATURGE
THAUMATURGES
THAUMATURGIC
THAUMATURGICAL
THAUMATURGICS
THAUMATURGIES
THAUMATURGISM
THAUMATURGISMS
THAUMATURGIST
THAUMATURGISTS

THAUMATURGUS
THAUMATURGUSES
THAUMATURGY
THAW
THAWED
THAWER
THAWERS
THAWIER
THAWIEST
THAWING
THAWINGS
THAWLESS
THAWS
THAWY
THE
THEACEOUS
THEANDRIC
THEANTHROPIC
THEANTHROPIES
THEANTHROPISM
THEANTHROPISMS
THEANTHROPIST
THEANTHROPISTS
THEANTHROPY
THEARCHIC
THEARCHIES
THEARCHY
THEATER
THEATERGOER
THEATERGOERS
THEATERGOING
THEATERGOINGS
THEATERS
THEATRAL
THEATRE
THEATRES
THEATRIC
THEATRICAL
THEATRICALISE
THEATRICALISED
THEATRICALISES
THEATRICALISING
THEATRICALISM
THEATRICALISMS
THEATRICALITIES
THEATRICALITY
THEATRICALIZE
THEATRICALIZED
THEATRICALIZES
THEATRICALIZING
THEATRICALLY
THEATRICALNESS
THEATRICALS
THEATRICISE
THEATRICISED
THEATRICISES
THEATRICISING

THEATRICISM
THEATRICISMS
THEATRICIZE
THEATRICIZED
THEATRICIZES
THEATRICIZING
THEATRICS
THEATROMANIA
THEATROMANIAS
THEATROPHONE
THEATROPHONES
THEAVE
THEAVES
THEBAINE
THEBAINES
THEBE
THECA
THECAE
THECAL
THECATE
THECODONT
THECODONTS
THEE
THEED
THEEING
THEEK
THEEKED
THEEKING
THEEKS
THEELIN
THEELINS
THEELOL
THEELOLS
THEES
THEFT
THEFTBOOTS
THEFTLESS
THEFTS
THEFTUOUS
THEFTUOUSLY
THEGITHER
THEGN
THEGNLY
THEGNS
THEIC
THEICS
THEIN
THEINE
THEINES
THEINS
THEIR
THEIRS
THEIRSELVES
THEISM
THEISMS
THEIST
THEISTIC

THEISTICAL
THEISTICALLY
THEISTS
THELEMENT
THELEMENTS
THELF
THELITIS
THELITISES
THELVES
THELYTOKIES
THELYTOKOUS
THELYTOKY
THEM
THEMA
THEMATA
THEMATIC
THEMATICALLY
THEMATICS
THEMATISATION
THEMATISATIONS
THEMATIZATION
THEMATIZATIONS
THEME
THEMED
THEMELESS
THEMES
THEMING
THEMSELF
THEMSELVES
THEN
THENABOUT
THENABOUTS
THENAGE
THENAGES
THENAL
THENAR
THENARDITE
THENARS
THENCE
THENCEFORTH
THENCEFORWARD
THENCEFORWARDS
THENS
THEOBROMINE
THEOBROMINES
THEOCENTRIC
THEOCENTRICISM
THEOCENTRICISMS
THEOCENTRICITY
THEOCENTRISM
THEOCENTRISMS
THEOCRACIES
THEOCRACY
THEOCRASIES
THEOCRASY
THEOCRAT
THEOCRATIC

THEOCRATICAL
THEOCRATICALLY
THEOCRATS
THEODICEAN
THEODICEANS
THEODICIES
THEODICY
THEODOLITE
THEODOLITES
THEODOLITIC
THEOGONIC
THEOGONICAL
THEOGONIES
THEOGONIST
THEOGONISTS
THEOGONY
THEOLOG
THEOLOGASTER
THEOLOGASTERS
THEOLOGATE
THEOLOGATES
THEOLOGER
THEOLOGERS
THEOLOGIAN
THEOLOGIANS
THEOLOGIC
THEOLOGICAL
THEOLOGICALLY
THEOLOGIES
THEOLOGISATION
THEOLOGISE
THEOLOGISED
THEOLOGISER
THEOLOGISERS
THEOLOGISES
THEOLOGISING
THEOLOGIST
THEOLOGISTS
THEOLOGIZATION
THEOLOGIZE
THEOLOGIZED
THEOLOGIZER
THEOLOGIZERS
THEOLOGIZES
THEOLOGIZING
THEOLOGOUMENA
THEOLOGOUMENON
THEOLOGS
THEOLOGUE
THEOLOGUES
THEOLOGY
THEOMACHIES
THEOMACHIST
THEOMACHISTS
THEOMACHY
THEOMANCIES
THEOMANCY

THEOMANIA	THEORIQUES	THERAPEUTISTS	THERIOMORPHISM
THEOMANIAC	THEORISATION	THERAPIES	THERIOMORPHISMS
THEOMANIACS	THEORISATIONS	THERAPIST	THERIOMORPHOSES
THEOMANIAS	THEORISE	THERAPISTS	THERIOMORPHOSIS
THEOMANTIC	THEORISED	THERAPSID	THERIOMORPHOUS
THEOMORPHIC	THEORISER	THERAPSIDS	THERIOMORPHS
THEOMORPHISM	THEORISERS	THERAPY	THERM
THEOMORPHISMS	THEORISES	THERBLIG	THERMAE
THEONOMIES	THEORISING	THERBLIGS	THERMAESTHESIA
THEONOMOUS	THEORIST	THERE	THERMAL
THEONOMY	THEORISTS	THEREABOUT	THERMALISATION
THEOPATHETIC	THEORIZATION	THEREABOUTS	THERMALISATIONS
THEOPATHIC	THEORIZATIONS	THEREAFTER	THERMALISE
THEOPATHIES	THEORIZE	THEREAGAINST	THERMALISED
THEOPATHY	THEORIZED	THEREAMONG	THERMALISES
THEOPHAGIES	THEORIZER	THEREANENT	THERMALISING
THEOPHAGOUS	THEORIZERS	THEREAT	THERMALIZATION
THEOPHAGY	THEORIZES	THEREAWAY	THERMALIZATIONS
THEOPHANIC	THEORIZING	THEREBESIDE	THERMALIZE
THEOPHANIES	THEORY	THEREBY	THERMALIZED
THEOPHANOUS	THEOSOPH	THEREFOR	THERMALIZES
THEOPHANY	THEOSOPHER	THEREFORE	THERMALIZING
THEOPHOBIA	THEOSOPHERS	THEREFROM	THERMALLY
THEOPHOBIAC	THEOSOPHIC	THEREIN	THERMALS
THEOPHOBIACS	THEOSOPHICAL	THEREINAFTER	THERME
THEOPHOBIAS	THEOSOPHICALLY	THEREINBEFORE	THERMEL
THEOPHOBIST	THEOSOPHIES	THEREINTO	THERMELS
THEOPHOBISTS	THEOSOPHISE	THEREMIN	THERMES
THEOPHORIC	THEOSOPHISED	THEREMINS	THERMESTHESIA
THEOPHYLLINE	THEOSOPHISES	THERENESS	THERMETTE
THEOPHYLLINES	THEOSOPHISING	THERENESSES	THERMETTES
THEOPNEUST	THEOSOPHISM	THEREOF	THERMIC
THEOPNEUSTIC	THEOSOPHISMS	THEREON	THERMICAL
THEOPNEUSTIES	THEOSOPHIST	THEREOUT	THERMICALLY
THEOPNEUSTY	THEOSOPHISTICAL	THERES	THERMIDOR
THEORBIST	THEOSOPHISTS	THERETHROUGH	THERMION
THEORBISTS	THEOSOPHIZE	THERETO	THERMIONIC
THEORBO	THEOSOPHIZED	THERETOFORE	THERMIONICS
THEORBOS	THEOSOPHIZES	THEREUNDER	THERMIONS
THEOREM	THEOSOPHIZING	THEREUNTO	THERMISTOR
THEOREMATIC	THEOSOPHS	THEREUPON	THERMISTORS
THEOREMATICAL	THEOSOPHY	THEREWITH	THERMITE
THEOREMATICALLY	THEOTECHNIC	THEREWITHAL	THERMITES
THEOREMATIST	THEOTECHNIES	THEREWITHIN	THERMOBALANCE
THEOREMATISTS	THEOTECHNY	THERIAC	THERMOBALANCES
THEOREMIC	THEOTOKOI	THERIACA	THERMOBAROGRAPH
THEOREMS	THEOTOKOS	THERIACAL	THERMOBAROMETER
THEORETIC	THEOW	THERIACAS	THERMOCHEMICAL
THEORETICAL	THEOWS	THERIACS	THERMOCHEMIST
THEORETICALLY	THERALITE	THERIAN	THERMOCHEMISTRY
THEORETICIAN	THERALITES	THERIANS	THERMOCHEMISTS
THEORETICIANS	THERAPEUSES	THERIANTHROPIC	THERMOCHROMIC
THEORETICS	THERAPEUSIS	THERIANTHROPISM	THERMOCHROMISM
THEORIC	THERAPEUTIC	THERIOLATRIES	THERMOCHROMY
THEORICS	THERAPEUTICALLY	THERIOLATRY	THERMOCLINE
THEORIES	THERAPEUTICS	THERIOMORPH	THERMOCLINES
THEORIQUE	THERAPEUTIST	THERIOMORPHIC	THERMOCOUPLE

THERMOCOUPLES	THERMOPHILOUS	THEROLOGY	THIASUSES
THERMODURIC	THERMOPHILS	THEROPHYTE	THIAZIDE
THERMODYNAMIC	THERMOPHYLLOUS	THEROPHYTES	THIAZIDES
THERMODYNAMICAL	THERMOPILE	THEROPHYTIC	THIAZIN
THERMODYNAMICS	THERMOPILES	THEROPOD	THIAZINE
THERMOELECTRIC	THERMOPLASTIC	THEROPODAN	THIAZINES
THERMOELECTRON	THERMOPLASTICS	THEROPODANS	THIAZINS
THERMOELECTRONS	THERMORECEPTOR	THEROPODS	THIAZOL
THERMOELEMENT	THERMORECEPTORS	THERSITICAL	THIAZOLE
THERMOELEMENTS	THERMOREGULATE	THESAURAL	THIAZOLES
THERMOFORM	THERMOREGULATED	THESAURI	THIAZOLS
THERMOFORMABLE	THERMOREGULATES	THESAURUS	THIBET
THERMOFORMED	THERMOREGULATOR	THESAURUSES	THIBETS
THERMOFORMING	THERMOREMANENCE	THESE	THIBLE
THERMOFORMS	THERMOREMANENT	THESES	THIBLES
THERMOGENESES	THERMOS	THESIS	THICK
THERMOGENESIS	THERMOSCOPE	THESMOTHETE	THICKED
THERMOGENETIC	THERMOSCOPES	THESMOTHETES	THICKEN
THERMOGENIC	THERMOSCOPIC	THESPIAN	THICKENED
THERMOGENOUS	THERMOSCOPICAL	THESPIANS	THICKENER
THERMOGRAM	THERMOSES	THETA	THICKENERS
THERMOGRAMS	THERMOSET	THETAS	THICKENING
THERMOGRAPH	THERMOSETS	THETCH	THICKENINGS
THERMOGRAPHER	THERMOSETTING	THETCHED	THICKENS
THERMOGRAPHERS	THERMOSIPHON	THETCHES	THICKER
THERMOGRAPHIC	THERMOSIPHONS	THETCHING	THICKEST
THERMOGRAPHIES	THERMOSPHERE	THETE	THICKET
THERMOGRAPHS	THERMOSPHERES	THETES	THICKETED
THERMOGRAPHY	THERMOSPHERIC	THETHER	THICKETS
THERMOHALINE	THERMOSTABILITY	THETIC	THICKETY
THERMOJUNCTION	THERMOSTABLE	THETICAL	THICKHEAD
THERMOJUNCTIONS	THERMOSTAT	THETICALLY	THICKHEADED
THERMOLABILE	THERMOSTATED	THEURGIC	THICKHEADEDNESS
THERMOLABILITY	THERMOSTATIC	THEURGICAL	THICKHEADS
THERMOLOGIES	THERMOSTATICS	THEURGICALLY	THICKIE
THERMOLOGY	THERMOSTATING	THEURGIES	THICKIES
THERMOLYSES	THERMOSTATS	THEURGIST	THICKING
THERMOLYSIS	THERMOSTATTED	THEURGISTS	THICKISH
THERMOLYTIC	THERMOSTATTING	THEURGY	THICKLEAF
THERMOMAGNETIC	THERMOTACTIC	THEW	THICKLEAVES
THERMOMETER	THERMOTAXES	THEWED	THICKLY
THERMOMETERS	THERMOTAXIC	THEWES	THICKNESS
THERMOMETRIC	THERMOTAXIS	THEWIER	THICKNESSES
THERMOMETRICAL	THERMOTENSILE	THEWIEST	THICKO
THERMOMETRIES	THERMOTHERAPIES	THEWLESS	THICKOES
THERMOMETRY	THERMOTHERAPY	THEWS	THICKOS
THERMOMOTOR	THERMOTIC	THEWY	THICKS
THERMOMOTORS	THERMOTICAL	THEY	THICKSET
THERMONASTIES	THERMOTICS	THIABENDAZOLE	THICKSETS
THERMONASTY	THERMOTOLERANT	THIABENDAZOLES	THICKSKIN
THERMONUCLEAR	THERMOTROPIC	THIAMIN	THICKSKINS
THERMOPERIODIC	THERMOTROPICS	THIAMINASE	THICKY
THERMOPERIODISM	THERMOTROPISM	THIAMINASES	THIEF
THERMOPHIL	THERMOTROPISMS	THIAMINE	THIEVE
THERMOPHILE	THERMS	THIAMINES	THIEVED
THERMOPHILES	THEROID	THIAMINS	THIEVERIES
THERMOPHILIC	THEROLOGIES	THIASUS	THIEVERY

THIEVES
THIEVING
THIEVINGS
THIEVISH
THIEVISHLY
THIEVISHNESS
THIEVISHNESSES
THIG
THIGGER
THIGGERS
THIGGING
THIGGINGS
THIGGIT
THIGH
THIGHBONE
THIGHBONES
THIGHED
THIGHS
THIGMOTACTIC
THIGMOTAXES
THIGMOTAXIS
THIGMOTROPIC
THIGMOTROPISM
THIGMOTROPISMS
THIGS
THILK
THILL
THILLER
THILLERS
THILLS
THIMBLE
THIMBLEBERRIES
THIMBLEBERRY
THIMBLED
THIMBLEFUL
THIMBLEFULS
THIMBLERIG
THIMBLERIGGED
THIMBLERIGGER
THIMBLERIGGERS
THIMBLERIGGING
THIMBLERIGGINGS
THIMBLERIGS
THIMBLES
THIMBLESFUL
THIMBLEWEED
THIMBLEWEEDS
THIMBLEWIT
THIMBLEWITS
THIMBLEWITTED
THIMBLING
THIMEROSAL
THIMEROSALS
THIN
THINCLAD
THINCLADS
THINDOWN

THINDOWNS
THINE
THING
THINGAMABOB
THINGAMABOBS
THINGAMAJIG
THINGAMAJIGS
THINGAMIES
THINGAMY
THINGAMYBOB
THINGAMYBOBS
THINGAMYJIG
THINGAMYJIGS
THINGHOOD
THINGHOODS
THINGIER
THINGIES
THINGIEST
THINGINESS
THINGINESSES
THINGLINESS
THINGLINESSES
THINGNESS
THINGNESSES
THINGS
THINGUMABOB
THINGUMABOBS
THINGUMAJIG
THINGUMAJIGS
THINGUMBOB
THINGUMBOBS
THINGUMMIES
THINGUMMY
THINGUMMYBOB
THINGUMMYBOBS
THINGUMMYJIG
THINGUMMYJIGS
THINGY
THINK
THINKABLE
THINKABLENESS
THINKABLENESSES
THINKABLY
THINKER
THINKERS
THINKING
THINKINGLY
THINKINGNESS
THINKINGNESSES
THINKINGS
THINKPIECE
THINKPIECES
THINKS
THINLY
THINNED
THINNER
THINNERS

THINNESS
THINNESSES
THINNEST
THINNING
THINNINGS
THINNISH
THINS
THIO
THIOALCOHOL
THIOALCOHOLS
THIOBACILLI
THIOBACILLUS
THIOBARBITURATE
THIOCARBAMIDE
THIOCARBAMIDES
THIOCYANATE
THIOCYANATES
THIOCYANIC
THIODIGLYCOL
THIODIGLYCOLS
THIOFURAN
THIOL
THIOLIC
THIOLS
THIONATE
THIONATES
THIONIC
THIONIN
THIONINE
THIONINES
THIONINS
THIONYL
THIONYLS
THIOPENTAL
THIOPENTALS
THIOPENTONE
THIOPENTONES
THIOPHEN
THIOPHENE
THIOPHENES
THIOPHENS
THIOPHIL
THIORIDAZINE
THIORIDAZINES
THIOSINAMINE
THIOSULFATE
THIOSULFATES
THIOSULPHATE
THIOSULPHATES
THIOSULPHURIC
THIOTEPA
THIOTEPAS
THIOURACIL
THIOURACILS
THIOUREA
THIOUREAS
THIR

THIRAM
THIRAMS
THIRD
THIRDBOROUGH
THIRDBOROUGHS
THIRDED
THIRDHAND
THIRDING
THIRDINGS
THIRDLY
THIRDS
THIRDSMAN
THIRDSMEN
THIRDSTREAM
THIRL
THIRLAGE
THIRLAGES
THIRLED
THIRLING
THIRLS
THIRST
THIRSTED
THIRSTER
THIRSTERS
THIRSTFUL
THIRSTIER
THIRSTIEST
THIRSTILY
THIRSTINESS
THIRSTINESSES
THIRSTING
THIRSTLESS
THIRSTS
THIRSTY
THIRTEEN
THIRTEENS
THIRTEENTH
THIRTEENTHLY
THIRTEENTHS
THIRTIES
THIRTIETH
THIRTIETHS
THIRTY
THIRTYFOLD
THIRTYISH
THIRTYSOMETHING
THIS
THISNESS
THISNESSES
THISTLE
THISTLEDOWN
THISTLEDOWNS
THISTLES
THISTLIER
THISTLIEST
THISTLY
THITHER

THITHERTO
THITHERWARD
THITHERWARDS
THIVEL
THIVELS
THIXOTROPE
THIXOTROPES
THIXOTROPIC
THIXOTROPIES
THIXOTROPY
THLIPSES
THLIPSIS
THO
THOFT
THOFTS
THOLE
THOLED
THOLEIITE
THOLEIITES
THOLEIITIC
THOLEPIN
THOLEPINS
THOLES
THOLI
THOLING
THOLOBATE
THOLOBATES
THOLOI
THOLOS
THOLUS
THON
THONDER
THONG
THONGED
THONGS
THORACAL
THORACENTESES
THORACENTESIS
THORACES
THORACIC
THORACICALLY
THORACOCENTESES
THORACOCENTESIS
THORACOPLASTIES
THORACOPLASTY
THORACOSCOPE
THORACOSCOPES
THORACOSTOMIES
THORACOSTOMY
THORACOTOMIES
THORACOTOMY
THORAX
THORAXES
THORIA
THORIANITE
THORIANITES
THORIAS

THORIC
THORITE
THORITES
THORIUM
THORIUMS
THORN
THORNBACK
THORNBACKS
THORNBILL
THORNBILLS
THORNBUSH
THORNBUSHES
THORNED
THORNHEDGE
THORNHEDGES
THORNIER
THORNIEST
THORNILY
THORNINESS
THORNINESSES
THORNING
THORNLESS
THORNLIKE
THORNPROOFS
THORNS
THORNSET
THORNTREE
THORNTREES
THORNY
THORO
THORON
THORONS
THOROUGH
THOROUGHBASS
THOROUGHBASSES
THOROUGHBRACE
THOROUGHBRACED
THOROUGHBRACES
THOROUGHBRED
THOROUGHBREDS
THOROUGHER
THOROUGHEST
THOROUGHFARE
THOROUGHFARES
THOROUGHGOING
THOROUGHGOINGLY
THOROUGHLY
THOROUGHNESS
THOROUGHNESSES
THOROUGHPACED
THOROUGHPIN
THOROUGHPINS
THOROUGHS
THOROUGHWAX
THOROUGHWAXES
THOROUGHWORT
THOROUGHWORTS

THORP
THORPE
THORPES
THORPS
THOSE
THOTHER
THOU
THOUED
THOUGH
THOUGHT
THOUGHTCAST
THOUGHTCASTS
THOUGHTED
THOUGHTEN
THOUGHTFUL
THOUGHTFULLY
THOUGHTFULNESS
THOUGHTLESS
THOUGHTLESSLY
THOUGHTLESSNESS
THOUGHTS
THOUGHTWAY
THOUGHTWAYS
THOUING
THOUS
THOUSAND
THOUSANDFOLD
THOUSANDFOLDS
THOUSANDS
THOUSANDTH
THOUSANDTHS
THOWEL
THOWELS
THOWL
THOWLESS
THOWLS
THRAE
THRAIPED
THRAIPING
THRAIPINGS
THRAIPS
THRALDOM
THRALDOMS
THRALL
THRALLDOM
THRALLDOMS
THRALLED
THRALLING
THRALLS
THRANG
THRANGED
THRANGING
THRANGS
THRAPPLE
THRAPPLED
THRAPPLES
THRAPPLING

THRASH
THRASHED
THRASHER
THRASHERS
THRASHES
THRASHING
THRASHINGS
THRASONIC
THRASONICAL
THRASONICALLY
THRAVE
THRAVES
THRAW
THRAWARD
THRAWART
THRAWED
THRAWING
THRAWN
THRAWNLY
THRAWS
THREAD
THREADBARE
THREADBARENESS
THREADED
THREADEN
THREADER
THREADERS
THREADFIN
THREADFINS
THREADIER
THREADIEST
THREADINESS
THREADINESSES
THREADING
THREADLESS
THREADLIKE
THREADMAKER
THREADMAKERS
THREADS
THREADWORM
THREADWORMS
THREADY
THREAP
THREAPED
THREAPER
THREAPERS
THREAPING
THREAPIT
THREAPS
THREAT
THREATED
THREATEN
THREATENED
THREATENER
THREATENERS
THREATENING
THREATENINGLY

THREATENINGS	THRESHOLD	THRIVING	THROMBOSIS
THREATENS	THRESHOLDS	THRIVINGLY	THROMBOTIC
THREATFUL	THRETTIES	THRIVINGNESS	THROMBOXANE
THREATING	THRETTY	THRIVINGNESSES	THROMBOXANES
THREATS	THREW	THRIVINGS	THROMBUS
THREAVE	THRICE	THRO	THRONE
THREAVES	THRID	THROAT	THRONED
THREE	THRIDACE	THROATED	THRONELESS
THREEFOLD	THRIDACES	THROATIER	THRONES
THREEFOLDNESS	THRIDDED	THROATIEST	THRONG
THREEFOLDNESSES	THRIDDING	THROATILY	THRONGED
THREENESS	THRIDS	THROATINESS	THRONGFUL
THREENESSES	THRIFT	THROATINESSES	THRONGING
THREEP	THRIFTIER	THROATING	THRONGINGS
THREEPED	THRIFTIEST	THROATLASH	THRONGS
THREEPENCE	THRIFTILY	THROATLASHES	THRONING
THREEPENCES	THRIFTINESS	THROATLATCH	THRONNER
THREEPENNIES	THRIFTINESSES	THROATLATCHES	THROPPLE
THREEPENNY	THRIFTLESS	THROATS	THROPPLED
THREEPENNYWORTH	THRIFTLESSLY	THROATWORT	THROPPLES
THREEPER	THRIFTLESSNESS	THROATWORTS	THROPPLING
THREEPING	THRIFTS	THROATY	THROSTLE
THREEPINGS	THRIFTY	THROB	THROSTLES
THREEPIT	THRILL	THROBBED	THROTTLE
THREEPS	THRILLANT	THROBBER	THROTTLEABLE
THREES	THRILLED	THROBBERS	THROTTLED
THREESCORE	THRILLER	THROBBING	THROTTLEHOLD
THREESCORES	THRILLERS	THROBBINGLY	THROTTLEHOLDS
THREESOME	THRILLIER	THROBBINGS	THROTTLER
THREESOMES	THRILLIEST	THROBLESS	THROTTLERS
THREMMATOLOGIES	THRILLING	THROBS	THROTTLES
THREMMATOLOGY	THRILLINGLY	THROE	THROTTLING
THRENE	THRILLINGNESS	THROED	THROTTLINGS
THRENES	THRILLINGNESSES	THROEING	THROUGH
THRENETIC	THRILLS	THROES	THROUGHFARE
THRENETICAL	THRILLY	THROMBI	THROUGHFARES
THRENODE	THRIMSA	THROMBIN	THROUGHGAUNS
THRENODES	THRIMSAS	THROMBINS	THROUGHITHER
THRENODIAL	THRIP	THROMBOCYTE	THROUGHLY
THRENODIC	THRIPS	THROMBOCYTES	THROUGHOTHER
THRENODIES	THRIPSES	THROMBOCYTIC	THROUGHOUT
THRENODIST	THRISSEL	THROMBOEMBOLIC	THROUGHPUT
THRENODISTS	THRISSELS	THROMBOEMBOLISM	THROUGHPUTS
THRENODY	THRIST	THROMBOGEN	THROUGHWAY
THRENOS	THRISTED	THROMBOKINASE	THROUGHWAYS
THRENOSES	THRISTING	THROMBOKINASES	THROVE
THREONINE	THRISTLE	THROMBOLYTIC	THROW
THREONINES	THRISTLES	THROMBOLYTICS	THROWAWAY
THRESH	THRISTS	THROMBOPHILIA	THROWAWAYS
THRESHED	THRISTY	THROMBOPHILIAS	THROWBACK
THRESHEL	THRIVE	THROMBOPLASTIC	THROWBACKS
THRESHELS	THRIVED	THROMBOPLASTIN	THROWE
THRESHER	THRIVELESS	THROMBOPLASTINS	THROWER
THRESHERS	THRIVEN	THROMBOSE	THROWERS
THRESHES	THRIVER	THROMBOSED	THROWES
THRESHING	THRIVERS	THROMBOSES	THROWING
THRESHINGS	THRIVES	THROMBOSING	THROWINGS

THROWN
THROWS
THROWSTER
THROWSTERS
THRU
THRUM
THRUMMED
THRUMMER
THRUMMERS
THRUMMIER
THRUMMIEST
THRUMMING
THRUMMINGLY
THRUMMINGS
THRUMMY
THRUMS
THRUPENNY
THRUPPENCE
THRUPPENCES
THRUPPENNIES
THRUPPENNY
THRUPUT
THRUPUTS
THRUSH
THRUSHES
THRUST
THRUSTED
THRUSTER
THRUSTERS
THRUSTFUL
THRUSTING
THRUSTINGS
THRUSTOR
THRUSTORS
THRUSTS
THRUTCH
THRUTCHED
THRUTCHES
THRUTCHING
THRUWAY
THRUWAYS
THRYMSA
THRYMSAS
THUD
THUDDED
THUDDING
THUDDINGLY
THUDS
THUG
THUGGEE
THUGGEES
THUGGERIES
THUGGERY
THUGGISH
THUGGISM
THUGGISMS
THUGGO

THUGGOS
THUGS
THUJA
THUJAS
THULIA
THULIAS
THULITE
THULITES
THULIUM
THULIUMS
THUMB
THUMBED
THUMBHOLE
THUMBHOLES
THUMBIER
THUMBIEST
THUMBIKINS
THUMBING
THUMBKIN
THUMBKINS
THUMBLESS
THUMBLIKE
THUMBLING
THUMBLINGS
THUMBNAIL
THUMBNAILS
THUMBNUT
THUMBNUTS
THUMBPIECE
THUMBPIECES
THUMBPOT
THUMBPOTS
THUMBPRINT
THUMBPRINTS
THUMBS
THUMBSCREW
THUMBSCREWS
THUMBSTALL
THUMBSTALLS
THUMBTACK
THUMBTACKED
THUMBTACKING
THUMBTACKS
THUMBWHEEL
THUMBWHEELS
THUMBY
THUMP
THUMPED
THUMPER
THUMPERS
THUMPING
THUMPINGLY
THUMPS
THUNBERGIA
THUNBERGIAS
THUNDER
THUNDERBIRD

THUNDERBIRDS
THUNDERBOLT
THUNDERBOLTS
THUNDERBOX
THUNDERBOXES
THUNDERCLAP
THUNDERCLAPS
THUNDERCLOUD
THUNDERCLOUDS
THUNDERED
THUNDERER
THUNDERERS
THUNDERFLASH
THUNDERFLASHES
THUNDERHEAD
THUNDERHEADS
THUNDERIER
THUNDERIEST
THUNDERING
THUNDERINGLY
THUNDERINGS.
THUNDERLESS
THUNDEROUS
THUNDEROUSLY
THUNDEROUSNESS
THUNDERS
THUNDERSHOWER
THUNDERSHOWERS
THUNDERSTONE
THUNDERSTONES
THUNDERSTORM
THUNDERSTORMS
THUNDERSTRICKEN
THUNDERSTRIKE
THUNDERSTRIKES
THUNDERSTRIKING
THUNDERSTROKE
THUNDERSTROKES
THUNDERSTRUCK
THUNDERY
THUNDROUS
THUNK
THUNKED
THUNKING
THUNKS
THURIBLE
THURIBLES
THURIFER
THURIFEROUS
THURIFERS
THURIFICATION
THURIFICATIONS
THURIFIED
THURIFIES
THURIFY
THURIFYING
THURL

THURLS
THUS
THUSES
THUSLY
THUSNESS
THUSNESSES
THUSWISE
THUYA
THUYAS
THWACK
THWACKED
THWACKER
THWACKERS
THWACKING
THWACKINGS
THWACKS
THWAITE
THWAITES
THWART
THWARTED
THWARTEDLY
THWARTER
THWARTERS
THWARTING
THWARTINGLY
THWARTINGS
THWARTLY
THWARTS
THWARTSHIP
THWARTSHIPS
THWARTWAYS
THWARTWISE
THY
THYINE
THYLACINE
THYLACINES
THYLAKOID
THYLAKOIDS
THYLOSE
THYLOSES
THYLOSIS
THYME
THYMECTOMIES
THYMECTOMIZE
THYMECTOMIZED
THYMECTOMIZES
THYMECTOMIZING
THYMECTOMY
THYMELAEACEOUS
THYMES
THYMEY
THYMI
THYMIC
THYMIDINE
THYMIDINES
THYMIDYLIC
THYMIER

THYMIEST
THYMINE
THYMINES
THYMOCYTE
THYMOCYTES
THYMOL
THYMOLS
THYMOSIN
THYMOSINS
THYMUS
THYMUSES
THYMY
THYRATRON
THYRATRONS
THYREOID
THYREOIDS
THYRISTOR
THYRISTORS
THYROCALCITONIN
THYROGLOBULIN
THYROGLOBULINS
THYROID
THYROIDAL
THYROIDECTOMIES
THYROIDECTOMY
THYROIDITIS
THYROIDITISES
THYROIDS
THYROTOXICOSES
THYROTOXICOSIS
THYROTROPHIC
THYROTROPHIN
THYROTROPHINS
THYROTROPIC
THYROTROPIN
THYROTROPINS
THYROXIN
THYROXINE
THYROXINES
THYROXINS
THYRSE
THYRSES
THYRSI
THYRSOID
THYRSOIDAL
THYRSUS
THYSANOPTEROUS
THYSANURAN
THYSANURANS
THYSANUROUS
THYSELF
TI
TIAR
TIARA
TIARAED
TIARAS
TIARS

TIBIA
TIBIAE
TIBIAL
TIBIAS
TIBIOFIBULA
TIBIOFIBULAE
TIBIOFIBULAS
TIBIOTARSI
TIBIOTARSUS
TIBIOTARSUSES
TIBOUCHINA
TIBOUCHINAS
TIC
TICAL
TICALS
TICCA
TICE
TICED
TICES
TICH
TICHES
TICHIER
TICHIEST
TICHORRHINE
TICHY
TICING
TICK
TICKED
TICKEN
TICKENS
TICKER
TICKERS
TICKET
TICKETED
TICKETING
TICKETLESS
TICKETS
TICKETTYBOO
TICKEY
TICKEYS
TICKIES
TICKING
TICKINGS
TICKLACE
TICKLACES
TICKLE
TICKLED
TICKLER
TICKLERS
TICKLES
TICKLIER
TICKLIEST
TICKLING
TICKLINGS
TICKLISH
TICKLISHLY
TICKLISHNESS

TICKLISHNESSES
TICKLY
TICKS
TICKSEED
TICKSEEDS
TICKTACK
TICKTACKED
TICKTACKING
TICKTACKS
TICKTACKTOE
TICKTACKTOES
TICKTOCK
TICKTOCKED
TICKTOCKING
TICKTOCKS
TICKY
TICS
TICTAC
TICTACKED
TICTACKING
TICTACS
TICTOC
TICTOCKED
TICTOCKING
TICTOCS
TID
TIDAL
TIDALLY
TIDBIT
TIDBITS
TIDDIER
TIDDIES
TIDDIEST
TIDDLE
TIDDLED
TIDDLEDYWINK
TIDDLEDYWINKS
TIDDLER
TIDDLERS
TIDDLES
TIDDLEY
TIDDLEYS
TIDDLEYWINK
TIDDLEYWINKS
TIDDLIER
TIDDLIES
TIDDLIEST
TIDDLING
TIDDLY
TIDDLYWINK
TIDDLYWINKS
TIDDY
TIDE
TIDED
TIDELAND
TIDELANDS
TIDELESS

TIDELIKE
TIDEMARK
TIDEMARKS
TIDEMILL
TIDEMILLS
TIDERIP
TIDERIPS
TIDES
TIDESMAN
TIDESMEN
TIDEWAITER
TIDEWAITERS
TIDEWATER
TIDEWATERS
TIDEWAVE
TIDEWAVES
TIDEWAY
TIDEWAYS
TIDIED
TIDIER
TIDIERS
TIDIES
TIDIEST
TIDILY
TIDINESS
TIDINESSES
TIDING
TIDINGS
TIDIVATE
TIDIVATED
TIDIVATES
TIDIVATING
TIDIVATION
TIDIVATIONS
TIDS
TIDY
TIDYING
TIDYTIPS
TIE
TIEBACK
TIEBACKS
TIEBREAKER
TIEBREAKERS
TIECLASP
TIECLASPS
TIED
TIEING
TIELESS
TIEMANNITE
TIEMANNITES
TIEPIN
TIEPINS
TIER
TIERCE
TIERCED
TIERCEL
TIERCELET

TIERCELETS	TIGHTASSEDNESS	TILBURY	TIMARIOT
TIERCELS	TIGHTASSES	TILDE	TIMARIOTS
TIERCERON	TIGHTEN	TILDES	TIMBAL
TIERCERONS	TIGHTENED	TILE	TIMBALE
TIERCES	TIGHTENER	TILED	TIMBALES
TIERCET	TIGHTENERS	TILEFISH	TIMBALS
TIERCETS	TIGHTENING	TILEFISHES	TIMBER
TIERED	TIGHTENS	TILELIKE	TIMBERDOODLE
TIERING	TIGHTER	TILER	TIMBERDOODLES
TIEROD	TIGHTEST	TILERIES	TIMBERED
TIERODS	TIGHTFISTED	TILERS	TIMBERHEAD
TIERS	TIGHTFISTEDNESS	TILERY	TIMBERHEADS
TIES	TIGHTISH	TILES	TIMBERING
TIETAC	TIGHTISHLY	TILIACEOUS	TIMBERINGS
TIETACK	TIGHTKNIT	TILING	TIMBERLAND
TIETACKS	TIGHTLY	TILINGS	TIMBERLANDS
TIETACS	TIGHTNESS	TILL	TIMBERLINE
TIFF	TIGHTNESSES	TILLABLE	TIMBERLINES
TIFFANIES	TIGHTROPE	TILLAGE	TIMBERMAN
TIFFANY	TIGHTROPES	TILLAGES	TIMBERMEN
TIFFED	TIGHTS	TILLANDSIA	TIMBERS
TIFFIN	TIGHTWAD	TILLANDSIAS	TIMBERWORK
TIFFINED	TIGHTWADS	TILLED	TIMBERWORKS
TIFFING	TIGHTWIRE	TILLER	TIMBERYARD
TIFFINGS	TIGHTWIRES	TILLERED	TIMBERYARDS
TIFFINING	TIGLIC	TILLERING	TIMBO
TIFFINS	TIGLON	TILLERLESS	TIMBOS
TIFFS	TIGLONS	TILLERMAN	TIMBRAL
TIFOSI	TIGON	TILLERMEN	TIMBRE
TIFOSO	TIGONS	TILLERS	TIMBREL
TIFT	TIGRESS	TILLICUM	TIMBRELLED
TIFTED	TIGRESSES	TILLICUMS	TIMBRELS
TIFTING	TIGRIDIA	TILLIER	TIMBRES
TIFTS	TIGRIDIAE	TILLIEST	TIMBROLOGIES
TIG	TIGRINE	TILLING	TIMBROLOGIST
TIGE	TIGRISH	TILLINGS	TIMBROLOGISTS
TIGER	TIGRISHLY	TILLITE	TIMBROLOGY
TIGEREYE	TIGRISHNESS	TILLITES	TIMBROMANIA
TIGEREYES	TIGRISHNESSES	TILLS	TIMBROMANIAC
TIGERISH	TIGROID	TILLY	TIMBROMANIACS
TIGERISHLY	TIGS	TILS	TIMBROMANIAS
TIGERISHNESS	TIKA	TILT	TIMBROPHILIES
TIGERISHNESSES	TIKANGA	TILTABLE	TIMBROPHILIST
TIGERISM	TIKAS	TILTED	TIMBROPHILISTS
TIGERISMS	TIKE	TILTER	TIMBROPHILY
TIGERLIKE	TIKES	TILTERS	TIME
TIGERLY	TIKI	TILTH	TIMECARD
TIGERS	TIKIS	TILTHS	TIMECARDS
TIGERY	TIKKA	TILTING	TIMED
TIGES	TIKOLOSHE	TILTINGS	TIMEFRAME
TIGGED	TIKOLOSHES	TILTMETER	TIMEFRAMES
TIGGING	TIL	TILTMETERS	TIMEKEEPER
TIGGYWINKLE	TILAK	TILTS	TIMEKEEPERS
TIGGYWINKLES	TILAKS	TILTYARD	TIMEKEEPING
TIGHT	TILAPIA	TILTYARDS	TIMEKEEPINGS
TIGHTASS	TILAPIAS	TIMARAU	TIMELESS
TIGHTASSED	TILBURIES	TIMARAUS	TIMELESSLY

TIMELESSNESS
TIMELESSNESSES
TIMELIER
TIMELIEST
TIMELINE
TIMELINES
TIMELINESS
TIMELINESSES
TIMELY
TIMENOGUY
TIMENOGUYS
TIMEOUS
TIMEOUSLY
TIMEOUT
TIMEOUTS
TIMEPIECE
TIMEPIECES
TIMEPLEASER
TIMEPLEASERS
TIMER
TIMERS
TIMES
TIMESAVER
TIMESAVERS
TIMESAVING
TIMESCALE
TIMESCALES
TIMESERVER
TIMESERVERS
TIMESERVING
TIMESERVINGS
TIMETABLE
TIMETABLED
TIMETABLES
TIMETABLING
TIMEWORK
TIMEWORKER
TIMEWORKERS
TIMEWORKS
TIMEWORN
TIMID
TIMIDER
TIMIDEST
TIMIDITIES
TIMIDITY
TIMIDLY
TIMIDNESS
TIMIDNESSES
TIMING
TIMINGS
TIMIST
TIMISTS
TIMOCRACIES
TIMOCRACY
TIMOCRATIC
TIMOCRATICAL
TIMOLOL

TIMOLOLS
TIMON
TIMONEER
TIMONEERS
TIMONS
TIMOROUS
TIMOROUSLY
TIMOROUSNESS
TIMOROUSNESSES
TIMORSOME
TIMOTHIES
TIMOTHY
TIMOUS
TIMOUSLY
TIMPANA
TIMPANI
TIMPANIST
TIMPANISTS
TIMPANO
TIMPANUM
TIMPANUMS
TIMPS
TIN
TINAJA
TINAJAS
TINAMOU
TINAMOUS
TINCAL
TINCALS
TINCHEL
TINCHELS
TINCT
TINCTED
TINCTING
TINCTORIAL
TINCTORIALLY
TINCTS
TINCTURE
TINCTURED
TINCTURES
TINCTURING
TIND
TINDAL
TINDALS
TINDED
TINDER
TINDERBOX
TINDERBOXES
TINDERS
TINDERY
TINDING
TINDS
TINE
TINEA
TINEAL
TINEAS
TINED

TINEID
TINEIDS
TINES
TINFOIL
TINFOILS
TINFUL
TINFULS
TING
TINGE
TINGED
TINGEING
TINGES
TINGING
TINGLE
TINGLED
TINGLER
TINGLERS
TINGLES
TINGLIER
TINGLIEST
TINGLING
TINGLINGLY
TINGLINGS
TINGLISH
TINGLY
TINGS
TINGUAITE
TINGUAITES
TINHORN
TINHORNS
TINIER
TINIES
TINIEST
TINILY
TININESS
TININESSES
TINING
TINK
TINKED
TINKER
TINKERED
TINKERER
TINKERERS
TINKERING
TINKERINGS
TINKERS
TINKING
TINKLE
TINKLED
TINKLER
TINKLERS
TINKLES
TINKLIER
TINKLIEST
TINKLING
TINKLINGLY
TINKLINGS

TINKLY
TINKS
TINLIKE
TINMAN
TINMEN
TINNED
TINNER
TINNERS
TINNIE
TINNIER
TINNIES
TINNIEST
TINNILY
TINNINESS
TINNINESSES
TINNING
TINNINGS
TINNITUS
TINNITUSES
TINNY
TINPLATE
TINPLATED
TINPLATES
TINPLATING
TINPOT
TINPOTS
TINS
TINSEL
TINSELED
TINSELING
TINSELLED
TINSELLING
TINSELLY
TINSELRIES
TINSELRY
TINSELS
TINSEY
TINSEYS
TINSMITH
TINSMITHING
TINSMITHINGS
TINSMITHS
TINSNIPS
TINSTONE
TINSTONES
TINT
TINTACK
TINTACKS
TINTED
TINTER
TINTERS
TINTIER
TINTIEST
TINTINESS
TINTINESSES
TINTING
TINTINGS

TINTINNABULA	TIPSIER	TIRITI	TITANOTHERES
TINTINNABULANT	TIPSIEST	TIRL	TITANOUS
TINTINNABULAR	TIPSIFIED	TIRLED	TITANS
TINTINNABULARY	TIPSIFIES	TIRLING	TITARAKURA
TINTINNABULATE	TIPSIFY	TIRLS	TITARAKURAS
TINTINNABULATED	TIPSIFYING	TIRO	TITBIT
TINTINNABULATES	TIPSILY	TIROCINIUM	TITBITS
TINTINNABULOUS	TIPSINESS	TIROCINIUMS	TITCH
TINTINNABULUM	TIPSINESSES	TIROES	TITCHES
TINTLESS	TIPSTAFF	TIRONIC	TITCHIER
TINTOMETER	TIPSTAFFS	TIROS	TITCHIEST
TINTOMETERS	TIPSTAVES	TIRR	TITCHY
TINTOMETRICAL	TIPSTER	TIRRED	TITE
TINTOMETRICALLY	TIPSTERS	TIRRING	TITELY
TINTOMETRY	TIPSTOCK	TIRRIT	TITER
TINTS	TIPSTOCKS	TIRRITS	TITERS
TINTY	TIPSY	TIRRIVEE	TITFER
TINTYPE	TIPT	TIRRIVEES	TITFERS
TINTYPES	TIPTOE	TIRRIVIE	TITHABLE
TINWARE	TIPTOED	TIRRIVIES	TITHE
TINWARES	TIPTOEING	TIRRS	TITHED
TINWORK	TIPTOES	TIS	TITHER
TINWORKS	TIPTOP	TISANE	TITHERS
TINY	TIPTOPS	TISANES	TITHES
TIP	TIPULA	TISICK	TITHING
TIPCART	TIPULAS	TISICKS	TITHINGMAN
TIPCARTS	TIPUNA	TISSUAL	TITHINGMEN
TIPCAT	TIRADE	TISSUE	TITHINGS
TIPCATS	TIRADES	TISSUED	TITHONIA
TIPI	TIRAILLEUR	TISSUES	TITHONIAS
TIPIS	TIRAILLEURS	TISSUEY	TITI
TIPLESS	TIRAMISU	TISSUING	TITIAN
TIPOFF	TIRAMISUS	TISSULAR	TITIANS
TIPOFFS	TIRASSE	TISWAS	TITILLATE
TIPPABLE	TIRASSES	TISWASES	TITILLATED
TIPPED	TIRE	TIT	TITILLATES
TIPPEE	TIRED	TITAN	TITILLATING
TIPPER	TIREDER	TITANATE	TITILLATINGLY
TIPPERS	TIREDEST	TITANATES	TITILLATION
TIPPET	TIREDLY	TITANESS	TITILLATIONS
TIPPETS	TIREDNESS	TITANESSES	TITILLATIVE
TIPPIER	TIREDNESSES	TITANIA	TITILLATOR
TIPPIEST	TIRELESS	TITANIAS	TITILLATORS
TIPPING	TIRELESSLY	TITANIC	TITIPOUNAMU
TIPPINGS	TIRELESSNESS	TITANICALLY	TITIS
TIPPLE	TIRELESSNESSES	TITANIFEROUS	TITIVATE
TIPPLED	TIRELING	TITANIS	TITIVATED
TIPPLER	TIRELINGS	TITANISES	TITIVATES
TIPPLERS	TIRES	TITANISM	TITIVATING
TIPPLES	TIRESOME	TITANISMS	TITIVATION
TIPPLING	TIRESOMELY	TITANITE	TITIVATIONS
TIPPY	TIRESOMENESS	TITANITES	TITIVATOR
TIPPYTOE	TIRESOMENESSES	TITANIUM	TITIVATORS
TIPPYTOED	TIREWOMAN	TITANIUMS	TITLARK
TIPPYTOEING	TIREWOMEN	TITANOSAUR	TITLARKS
TIPPYTOES	TIRING	TITANOSAURS	TITLE
TIPS	TIRINGS	TITANOTHERE	TITLED

TITLEHOLDER	TITTLEBATS	TOADFISH	TOBOGGANIST
TITLEHOLDERS	TITTLED	TOADFISHES	TOBOGGANISTS
TITLEHOLDING	TITTLES	TOADFLAX	TOBOGGANS
TITLELESS	TITTLING	TOADFLAXES	TOBOGGIN
TITLER	TITTUP	TOADGRASS	TOBOGGINED
TITLERS	TITTUPED	TOADGRASSES	TOBOGGINING
TITLES	TITTUPING	TOADIED	TOBOGGINS
TITLING	TITTUPPED	TOADIES	TOBY
TITLINGS	TITTUPPING	TOADISH	TOC
TITLIST	TITTUPPY	TOADLESS	TOCCATA
TITLISTS	TITTUPS	TOADLIKE	TOCCATAS
TITMAN	TITTUPY	TOADRUSH	TOCCATE
TITMEN	TITTY	TOADRUSHES	TOCCATELLA
TITMICE	TITUBANCIES	TOADS	TOCCATELLAS
TITMOSE	TITUBANCY	TOADSTONE	TOCCATINA
TITMOUSE	TITUBANT	TOADSTONES	TOCCATINAS
TITOKI	TITUBATE	TOADSTOOL	TOCHER
TITOKIS	TITUBATED	TOADSTOOLS	TOCHERED
TITRABLE	TITUBATES	TOADY	TOCHERING
TITRANT	TITUBATING	TOADYING	TOCHERLESS
TITRANTS	TITUBATION	TOADYISH	TOCHERS
TITRATABLE	TITUBATIONS	TOADYISM	TOCK
TITRATE	TITULAR	TOADYISMS	TOCKED
TITRATED	TITULARIES	TOAST	TOCKIER
TITRATES	TITULARITIES	TOASTED	TOCKIEST
TITRATING	TITULARITY	TOASTER	TOCKING
TITRATION	TITULARLY	TOASTERS	TOCKLEY
TITRATIONS	TITULARS	TOASTIE	TOCKS
TITRATOR	TITULARY	TOASTIER	TOCKY
TITRATORS	TITULE	TOASTIES	TOCO
TITRE	TITULED	TOASTIEST	TOCOLOGIES
TITRES	TITULES	TOASTING	TOCOLOGY
TITRIMETRIC	TITULING	TOASTINGS	TOCOPHEROL
TITS	TITULUS	TOASTMASTER	TOCOPHEROLS
TITTED	TITUP	TOASTMASTERS	TOCOS
TITTER	TITUPED	TOASTMISTRESS	TOCS
TITTERED	TITUPING	TOASTMISTRESSES	TOCSIN
TITTERER	TITUPPED	TOASTS	TOCSINS
TITTERERS	TITUPPING	TOASTY	TOD
TITTERING	TITUPS	TOAZE	TODAY
TITTERINGLY	TITUPY	TOAZED	TODAYS
TITTERINGS	TIVY	TOAZES	TODDE
TITTERS	TIX	TOAZING	TODDED
TITTIE	TIZWAS	TOBACCANALIANS	TODDES
TITTIES	TIZWASES	TOBACCO	TODDIES
TITTING	TIZZ	TOBACCOES	TODDING
TITTISH	TIZZES	TOBACCOLESS	TODDLE
TITTIVATE	TIZZIES	TOBACCONIST	TODDLED
TITTIVATED	TIZZY	TOBACCONISTS	TODDLER
TITTIVATES	TJANTING	TOBACCOS	TODDLERHOOD
TITTIVATING	TJANTINGS	TOBIES	TODDLERHOODS
TITTIVATION	TMESES	TOBOGGAN	TODDLERS
TITTIVATIONS	TMESIS	TOBOGGANED	TODDLES
TITTIVATOR	TO	TOBOGGANER	TODDLING
TITTIVATORS	TOAD	TOBOGGANERS	TODDY
TITTLE	TOADEATER	TOBOGGANING	TODIES
TITTLEBAT	TOADEATERS	TOBOGGANINGS	TODS

TODY	TOGE	TOINGS	TOLE
TOE	TOGED	TOISE	TOLED
TOEA	TOGES	TOISEACH	TOLEDO
TOEAS	TOGETHER	TOISEACHS	TOLEDOS
TOECAP	TOGETHERNESS	TOISECH	TOLERABILITIES
TOECAPS	TOGETHERNESSES	TOISECHS	TOLERABILITY
TOECLIP	TOGGED	TOISES	TOLERABLE
TOECLIPS	TOGGER	TOISON	TOLERABLENESS
TOED	TOGGERIES	TOISONS	TOLERABLY
TOEHOLD	TOGGERS	TOIT	TOLERANCE
TOEHOLDS	TOGGERY	TOITED	TOLERANCES
TOEIER	TOGGING	TOITING	TOLERANT
TOEIEST	TOGGLE	TOITOI	TOLERANTLY
TOEING	TOGGLED	TOITOIS	TOLERATE
TOELESS	TOGGLER	TOITS	TOLERATED
TOELIKE	TOGGLERS	TOKAMAK	TOLERATES
TOENAIL	TOGGLES	TOKAMAKS	TOLERATING
TOENAILED	TOGGLING	TOKAY	TOLERATION
TOENAILING	TOGS	TOKAYS	TOLERATIONISM
TOENAILS	TOGUE	TOKE	TOLERATIONISMS
TOEPIECE	TOGUES	TOKED	TOLERATIONIST
TOEPIECES	TOHEROA	TOKEN	TOLERATIONISTS
TOEPLATE	TOHEROAS	TOKENED	TOLERATIONS
TOEPLATES	TOHO	TOKENING	TOLERATIVE
TOERAG	TOHOS	TOKENISM	TOLERATOR
TOERAGGER	TOHUNGA	TOKENISMS	TOLERATORS
TOERAGGERS	TOHUNGAS	TOKENISTIC	TOLES
TOERAGS	TOIL	TOKENS	TOLEWARE
TOES	TOILE	TOKER	TOLEWARES
TOESHOE	TOILED	TOKERS	TOLIDIN
TOESHOES	TOILER	TOKES	TOLIDINE
TOETOE	TOILERS	TOKING	TOLIDINES
TOETOES	TOILES	TOKO	TOLIDINS
TOEY	TOILET	TOKOLOGIES	TOLING
TOFF	TOILETED	TOKOLOGY	TOLINGS
TOFFEE	TOILETING	TOKOLOSHE	TOLL
TOFFEES	TOILETRIES	TOKOLOSHES	TOLLABLE
TOFFIER	TOILETRY	TOKOMAK	TOLLAGE
TOFFIES	TOILETS	TOKOMAKS	TOLLAGES
TOFFIEST	TOILETTE	TOKONOMA	TOLLBAR
TOFFISH	TOILETTES	TOKONOMAS	TOLLBARS
TOFFISHNESS	TOILFUL	TOKOS	TOLLBOOTH
TOFFISHNESSES	TOILFULLY	TOKOTOKO	TOLLBOOTHS
TOFFS	TOILINET	TOLA	TOLLBRIDGE
TOFFY	TOILINETS	TOLAN	TOLLBRIDGES
TOFORE	TOILINETTE	TOLANE	TOLLDISH
TOFT	TOILINETTES	TOLANES	TOLLDISHES
TOFTS	TOILING	TOLANS	TOLLED
TOFU	TOILINGS	TOLAR	TOLLER
TOFUS	TOILLESS	TOLARJI	TOLLERS
TOG	TOILS	TOLARS	TOLLGATE
TOGA	TOILSOME	TOLAS	TOLLGATES
TOGAE	TOILSOMELY	TOLBOOTH	TOLLHOUSE
TOGAED	TOILSOMENESS	TOLBOOTHS	TOLLHOUSES
TOGAS	TOILSOMENESSES	TOLBUTAMIDE	TOLLIE
TOGATE	TOILWORN	TOLBUTAMIDES	TOLLIES
TOGATED	TOING	TOLD	TOLLING

TOLLINGS	TOMB	TOMMYROT	TONETTES
TOLLMAN	TOMBAC	TOMMYROTS	TONEY
TOLLMEN	TOMBACK	TOMO	TONG
TOLLS	TOMBACKS	TOMOGRAM	TONGA
TOLLWAY	TOMBACS	TOMOGRAMS	TONGAS
TOLLWAYS	TOMBAK	TOMOGRAPH	TONGED
TOLLY	TOMBAKS	TOMOGRAPHIC	TONGER
TOLSEL	TOMBAL	TOMOGRAPHIES	TONGERS
TOLSELS	TOMBED	TOMOGRAPHS	TONGING
TOLSEY	TOMBIC	TOMOGRAPHY	TONGMAN
TOLSEYS	TOMBING	TOMOMETRICAL	TONGMEN
TOLT	TOMBLESS	TOMORROW	TONGS
TOLTER	TOMBLIKE	TOMORROWS	TONGSTER
TOLTERED	TOMBOC	TOMPION	TONGSTERS
TOLTERING	TOMBOCS	TOMPIONS	TONGUE
TOLTERS	TOMBOLA	TOMPON	TONGUED
TOLTS	TOMBOLAS	TOMPONED	TONGUELESS
TOLU	TOMBOLO	TOMPONING	TONGUELET
TOLUATE	TOMBOLOS	TOMPONS	TONGUELETS
TOLUATES	TOMBOY	TOMS	TONGUELIKE
TOLUENE	TOMBOYISH	TOMTIT	TONGUES
TOLUENES	TOMBOYISHLY	TOMTITS	TONGUESTER
TOLUIC	TOMBOYISHNESS	TON	TONGUESTERS
TOLUID	TOMBOYISHNESSES	TONAL	TONGUING
TOLUIDE	TOMBOYS	TONALITE	TONGUINGS
TOLUIDES	TOMBS	TONALITES	TONIC
TOLUIDIN	TOMBSTONE	TONALITIES	TONICALLY
TOLUIDINE	TOMBSTONES	TONALITIVE	TONICITIES
TOLUIDINES	TOMCAT	TONALITY	TONICITY
TOLUIDINS	TOMCATS	TONALLY	TONICS
TOLUIDS	TOMCATTED	TONANT	TONIER
TOLUOL	TOMCATTING	TONDI	TONIES
TOLUOLE	TOMCOD	TONDINI	TONIEST
TOLUOLES	TOMCODS	TONDINO	TONIGHT
TOLUOLS	TOME	TONDINOS	TONIGHTS
TOLUS	TOMENTA	TONDO	TONING
TOLUYL	TOMENTOSE	TONDOS	TONINGS
TOLUYLS	TOMENTOUS	TONE	TONISH
TOLYL	TOMENTUM	TONEARM	TONISHLY
TOLYLS	TOMES	TONEARMS	TONISHNESS
TOLZEY	TOMFOOL	TONED	TONISHNESSES
TOLZEYS	TOMFOOLED	TONELESS	TONITE
TOM	TOMFOOLERIES	TONELESSLY	TONITES
TOMAHAWK	TOMFOOLERY	TONELESSNESS	TONK
TOMAHAWKED	TOMFOOLING	TONELESSNESSES	TONKA
TOMAHAWKING	TOMFOOLISH	TONEME	TONKED
TOMAHAWKS	TOMFOOLISHNESS	TONEMES	TONKER
TOMALLEY	TOMFOOLS	TONEMIC	TONKERS
TOMALLEYS	TOMIA	TONEPAD	TONKING
TOMAN	TOMIAL	TONEPADS	TONKS
TOMANS	TOMIUM	TONER	TONLET
TOMATILLO	TOMMED	TONERS	TONLETS
TOMATILLOES	TOMMIED	TONES	TONNAG
TOMATILLOS	TOMMIES	TONETIC	TONNAGE
TOMATO	TOMMING	TONETICALLY	TONNAGES
TOMATOES	TOMMY	TONETICS	TONNAGS
TOMATOEY	TOMMYING	TONETTE	TONNE

TONNEAU
TONNEAUS
TONNEAUX
TONNELL
TONNELLS
TONNER
TONNERS
TONNES
TONNISH
TONNISHLY
TONNISHNESS
TONNISHNESSES
TONOMETER
TONOMETERS
TONOMETRIC
TONOMETRIES
TONOMETRY
TONOPLAST
TONOPLASTS
TONS
TONSIL
TONSILAR
TONSILITIS
TONSILITISES
TONSILLAR
TONSILLARY
TONSILLECTOMIES
TONSILLECTOMY
TONSILLITIC
TONSILLITIS
TONSILLITISES
TONSILLOTOMIES
TONSILLOTOMY
TONSILS
TONSOR
TONSORIAL
TONSORS
TONSURE
TONSURED
TONSURES
TONSURING
TONTINE
TONTINER
TONTINERS
TONTINES
TONUS
TONUSES
TONY
TOO
TOOART
TOOARTS
TOOK
TOOL
TOOLBAG
TOOLBAGS
TOOLBAR
TOOLBARS

TOOLBOX
TOOLBOXES
TOOLED
TOOLER
TOOLERS
TOOLHEAD
TOOLHEADS
TOOLHOLDER
TOOLHOLDERS
TOOLHOUSE
TOOLHOUSES
TOOLING
TOOLINGS
TOOLKIT
TOOLKITS
TOOLLESS
TOOLMAKER
TOOLMAKERS
TOOLMAKING
TOOLMAKINGS
TOOLMAN
TOOLMEN
TOOLPUSHER
TOOLPUSHERS
TOOLROOM
TOOLROOMS
TOOLS
TOOLSHED
TOOLSHEDS
TOOM
TOOMED
TOOMER
TOOMEST
TOOMING
TOOMS
TOON
TOONIE
TOONIES
TOONS
TOORIE
TOORIES
TOOSHIE
TOOT
TOOTED
TOOTER
TOOTERS
TOOTH
TOOTHACHE
TOOTHACHES
TOOTHBRUSH
TOOTHBRUSHES
TOOTHBRUSHING
TOOTHBRUSHINGS
TOOTHCOMB
TOOTHCOMBS
TOOTHED
TOOTHFUL

TOOTHFULS
TOOTHIER
TOOTHIEST
TOOTHILY
TOOTHINESS
TOOTHINESSES
TOOTHING
TOOTHLESS
TOOTHLIKE
TOOTHPASTE
TOOTHPASTES
TOOTHPICK
TOOTHPICKS
TOOTHS
TOOTHSHELL
TOOTHSHELLS
TOOTHSOME
TOOTHSOMELY
TOOTHSOMENESS
TOOTHSOMENESSES
TOOTHWASH
TOOTHWASHES
TOOTHWORT
TOOTHWORTS
TOOTHY
TOOTING
TOOTLE
TOOTLED
TOOTLER
TOOTLERS
TOOTLES
TOOTLING
TOOTS
TOOTSED
TOOTSES
TOOTSIE
TOOTSIES
TOOTSING
TOOTSY
TOP
TOPAGNOSIA
TOPAGNOSIS
TOPALGIA
TOPARCH
TOPARCHIES
TOPARCHS
TOPARCHY
TOPAZ
TOPAZES
TOPAZINE
TOPAZOLITE
TOPAZOLITES
TOPCOAT
TOPCOATS
TOPCROSS
TOPCROSSES
TOPDRESSING

TOPDRESSINGS
TOPE
TOPECTOMIES
TOPECTOMY
TOPED
TOPEE
TOPEES
TOPEK
TOPEKS
TOPER
TOPERS
TOPES
TOPFLIGHT
TOPFUL
TOPFULL
TOPGALLANT
TOPGALLANTS
TOPH
TOPHACEOUS
TOPHE
TOPHEAVINESS
TOPHES
TOPHI
TOPHS
TOPHUS
TOPI
TOPIARIAN
TOPIARIES
TOPIARIST
TOPIARISTS
TOPIARY
TOPIC
TOPICAL
TOPICALITIES
TOPICALITY
TOPICALLY
TOPICS
TOPING
TOPIS
TOPKICK
TOPKICKS
TOPKNOT
TOPKNOTS
TOPKNOTTED
TOPLESS
TOPLESSNESS
TOPLESSNESSES
TOPLINE
TOPLINED
TOPLINER
TOPLINERS
TOPLINES
TOPLINING
TOPLOFTICAL
TOPLOFTIER
TOPLOFTIEST
TOPLOFTILY

TOPLOFTINESS
TOPLOFTINESSES
TOPLOFTY
TOPMAKER
TOPMAKERS
TOPMAKING
TOPMAKINGS
TOPMAN
TOPMAST
TOPMASTS
TOPMEN
TOPMINNOW
TOPMINNOWS
TOPMOST
TOPNOTCH
TOPNOTCHER
TOPNOTCHERS
TOPO
TOPOCENTRIC
TOPOCHEMICAL
TOPOCHEMISTRY
TOPOGRAPHER
TOPOGRAPHERS
TOPOGRAPHIC
TOPOGRAPHICAL
TOPOGRAPHICALLY
TOPOGRAPHIES
TOPOGRAPHY
TOPOI
TOPOLOGIC
TOPOLOGICAL
TOPOLOGICALLY
TOPOLOGIES
TOPOLOGIST
TOPOLOGISTS
TOPOLOGY
TOPONYM
TOPONYMAL
TOPONYMIC
TOPONYMICAL
TOPONYMICS
TOPONYMIES
TOPONYMIST
TOPONYMISTS
TOPONYMS
TOPONYMY
TOPOPHILIA
TOPOPHILIAS
TOPOS
TOPOTYPE
TOPOTYPES
TOPPED
TOPPER
TOPPERS
TOPPING
TOPPINGLY
TOPPINGS

TOPPLE
TOPPLED
TOPPLES
TOPPLING
TOPS
TOPSAIL
TOPSAILS
TOPSIDE
TOPSIDER
TOPSIDERS
TOPSIDES
TOPSMAN
TOPSMEN
TOPSOIL
TOPSOILED
TOPSOILING
TOPSOILINGS
TOPSOILS
TOPSPIN
TOPSPINS
TOPSTITCH
TOPSTITCHED
TOPSTITCHES
TOPSTITCHING
TOPSTONE
TOPSTONES
TOPWORK
TOPWORKED
TOPWORKING
TOPWORKS
TOQUE
TOQUES
TOQUET
TOQUETS
TOQUILLA
TOQUILLAS
TOR
TORA
TORAH
TORAHS
TORAN
TORANA
TORANAS
TORANS
TORAS
TORBANITE
TORBANITES
TORBERNITE
TORBERNITES
TORC
TORCH
TORCHBEARER
TORCHBEARERS
TORCHED
TORCHER
TORCHERE
TORCHERES

TORCHERS
TORCHES
TORCHIER
TORCHIERE
TORCHIERES
TORCHIERS
TORCHIEST
TORCHING
TORCHINGS
TORCHLIGHT
TORCHLIGHTS
TORCHLIKE
TORCHON
TORCHONS
TORCHWOOD
TORCHWOODS
TORCHY
TORCS
TORCULAR
TORCULARS
TORDION
TORDIONS
TORE
TOREADOR
TOREADORS
TORERO
TOREROS
TORES
TOREUTIC
TOREUTICS
TORGOCH
TORGOCHS
TORI
TORIC
TORIES
TORII
TORMENT
TORMENTA
TORMENTED
TORMENTEDLY
TORMENTER
TORMENTERS
TORMENTIL
TORMENTILS
TORMENTING
TORMENTINGLY
TORMENTINGS
TORMENTOR
TORMENTORS
TORMENTS
TORMENTUM
TORMENTUMS
TORMINA
TORMINAL
TORMINOUS
TORN
TORNADE

TORNADES
TORNADIC
TORNADO
TORNADOES
TORNADOS
TORNILLO
TORNILLOS
TORO
TOROID
TOROIDAL
TOROIDALLY
TOROIDS
TOROS
TOROSE
TOROSITIES
TOROSITY
TOROT
TOROTH
TOROUS
TORPEDINOUS
TORPEDO
TORPEDOED
TORPEDOER
TORPEDOERS
TORPEDOES
TORPEDOING
TORPEDOIST
TORPEDOISTS
TORPEDOS
TORPEFIED
TORPEFIES
TORPEFY
TORPEFYING
TORPESCENCE
TORPESCENCES
TORPESCENT
TORPID
TORPIDITIES
TORPIDITY
TORPIDLY
TORPIDNESS
TORPIDNESSES
TORPIDS
TORPITUDE
TORPITUDES
TORPOR
TORPORIFIC
TORPORS
TORQUATE
TORQUATED
TORQUE
TORQUED
TORQUER
TORQUERS
TORQUES
TORQUESES
TORQUING

TORR
TORREFACTION
TORREFACTIONS
TORREFIED
TORREFIES
TORREFY
TORREFYING
TORRENT
TORRENTIAL
TORRENTIALITIES
TORRENTIALITY
TORRENTIALLY
TORRENTS
TORRENTUOUS
TORRET
TORRETS
TORRID
TORRIDER
TORRIDEST
TORRIDITIES
TORRIDITY
TORRIDLY
TORRIDNESS
TORRIDNESSES
TORRIFIED
TORRIFIES
TORRIFY
TORRIFYING
TORRS
TORS
TORSADE
TORSADES
TORSE
TORSEL
TORSELS
TORSES
TORSI
TORSIBILITIES
TORSIBILITY
TORSIOGRAPH
TORSIOGRAPHS
TORSION
TORSIONAL
TORSIONALLY
TORSIONS
TORSIVE
TORSK
TORSKS
TORSO
TORSOS
TORT
TORTE
TORTELLINI
TORTELLINIS
TORTEN
TORTES
TORTFEASOR

TORTFEASORS
TORTICOLLAR
TORTICOLLIS
TORTICOLLISES
TORTILE
TORTILITIES
TORTILITY
TORTILLA
TORTILLAS
TORTILLON
TORTILLONS
TORTIOUS
TORTIOUSLY
TORTIVE
TORTOISE
TORTOISES
TORTOISESHELL
TORTOISESHELLS
TORTONI
TORTONIS
TORTRICES
TORTRICID
TORTRICIDS
TORTRIX
TORTRIXES
TORTS
TORTUOSITIES
TORTUOSITY
TORTUOUS
TORTUOUSLY
TORTUOUSNESS
TORTUOUSNESSES
TORTURE
TORTURED
TORTUREDLY
TORTURER
TORTURERS
TORTURES
TORTURESOME
TORTURING
TORTURINGLY
TORTURINGS
TORTUROUS
TORTUROUSLY
TORULA
TORULAE
TORULAS
TORULI
TORULIN
TORULINS
TORULOSE
TORULOSES
TORULOSIS
TORULUS
TORUS
TORY
TOSA

TOSAS
TOSE
TOSED
TOSES
TOSH
TOSHACH
TOSHACHS
TOSHED
TOSHER
TOSHERS
TOSHES
TOSHIER
TOSHIEST
TOSHING
TOSHY
TOSING
TOSS
TOSSED
TOSSEN
TOSSER
TOSSERS
TOSSES
TOSSICATED
TOSSIER
TOSSIEST
TOSSILY
TOSSING
TOSSINGS
TOSSPOT
TOSSPOTS
TOSSUP
TOSSUPS
TOSSY
TOST
TOSTADA
TOSTADAS
TOSTADO
TOSTADOS
TOSTICATED
TOSTICATION
TOSTICATIONS
TOT
TOTABLE
TOTAL
TOTALED
TOTALING
TOTALISATION
TOTALISATIONS
TOTALISATOR
TOTALISATORS
TOTALISE
TOTALISED
TOTALISER
TOTALISERS
TOTALISES
TOTALISING
TOTALISM

TOTALISMS
TOTALIST
TOTALISTIC
TOTALISTS
TOTALITARIAN
TOTALITARIANISM
TOTALITARIANIZE
TOTALITARIANS
TOTALITIES
TOTALITY
TOTALIZATION
TOTALIZATIONS
TOTALIZATOR
TOTALIZATORS
TOTALIZE
TOTALIZED
TOTALIZER
TOTALIZERS
TOTALIZES
TOTALIZING
TOTALLED
TOTALLING
TOTALLY
TOTALS
TOTANUS
TOTANUSES
TOTAQUINE
TOTAQUINES
TOTARA
TOTARAS
TOTE
TOTED
TOTEM
TOTEMIC
TOTEMICALLY
TOTEMISM
TOTEMISMS
TOTEMIST
TOTEMISTIC
TOTEMISTS
TOTEMITE
TOTEMITES
TOTEMS
TOTER
TOTERS
TOTES
TOTHER
TOTIENT
TOTIENTS
TOTING
TOTIPALMATE
TOTIPALMATION
TOTIPALMATIONS
TOTIPOTENCIES
TOTIPOTENCY
TOTIPOTENT
TOTITIVE

TOTITIVES
TOTS
TOTTED
TOTTER
TOTTERED
TOTTERER
TOTTERERS
TOTTERING
TOTTERINGLY
TOTTERINGS
TOTTERS
TOTTERY
TOTTIE
TOTTIER
TOTTIES
TOTTIEST
TOTTING
TOTTINGS
TOTTY
TOUCAN
TOUCANET
TOUCANETS
TOUCANS
TOUCH
TOUCHABLE
TOUCHABLENESS
TOUCHABLENESSES
TOUCHBACK
TOUCHBACKS
TOUCHDOWN
TOUCHDOWNS
TOUCHE
TOUCHED
TOUCHER
TOUCHERS
TOUCHES
TOUCHHOLE
TOUCHHOLES
TOUCHIER
TOUCHIEST
TOUCHILY
TOUCHINESS
TOUCHINESSES
TOUCHING
TOUCHINGLY
TOUCHINGNESS
TOUCHINGNESSES
TOUCHINGS
TOUCHLESS
TOUCHLINE
TOUCHLINES
TOUCHMARK
TOUCHMARKS
TOUCHPAPER
TOUCHPAPERS
TOUCHSTONE
TOUCHSTONES

TOUCHTONE
TOUCHUP
TOUCHUPS
TOUCHWOOD
TOUCHWOODS
TOUCHY
TOUGH
TOUGHED
TOUGHEN
TOUGHENED
TOUGHENER
TOUGHENERS
TOUGHENING
TOUGHENINGS
TOUGHENS
TOUGHER
TOUGHEST
TOUGHIE
TOUGHIES
TOUGHING
TOUGHISH
TOUGHLY
TOUGHNESS
TOUGHNESSES
TOUGHS
TOUGHY
TOUK
TOUKED
TOUKING
TOUKS
TOUN
TOUNS
TOUPEE
TOUPEES
TOUPET
TOUPETS
TOUR
TOURACO
TOURACOS
TOURBILLION
TOURBILLIONS
TOURBILLON
TOURBILLONS
TOURED
TOURER
TOURERS
TOURIE
TOURIES
TOURING
TOURINGS
TOURISM
TOURISMS
TOURIST
TOURISTIC
TOURISTICALLY
TOURISTS
TOURISTY

TOURMALINE
TOURMALINES
TOURMALINIC
TOURNAMENT
TOURNAMENTS
TOURNEDOS
TOURNEY
TOURNEYED
TOURNEYER
TOURNEYERS
TOURNEYING
TOURNEYS
TOURNIQUET
TOURNIQUETS
TOURNURE
TOURNURES
TOURS
TOURTIERE
TOURTIERES
TOUSE
TOUSED
TOUSER
TOUSERS
TOUSES
TOUSIER
TOUSIEST
TOUSING
TOUSINGS
TOUSLE
TOUSLED
TOUSLES
TOUSLING
TOUSTIE
TOUSTIER
TOUSTIEST
TOUSY
TOUT
TOUTED
TOUTER
TOUTERS
TOUTIE
TOUTIER
TOUTIEST
TOUTING
TOUTS
TOUZE
TOUZED
TOUZES
TOUZIER
TOUZIEST
TOUZING
TOUZLE
TOUZLED
TOUZLES
TOUZLING
TOUZY
TOVARICH

TOVARICHES
TOVARISCH
TOVARISCHES
TOVARISH
TOVARISHES
TOW
TOWABLE
TOWAGE
TOWAGES
TOWAI
TOWARD
TOWARDLINESS
TOWARDLINESSES
TOWARDLY
TOWARDNESS
TOWARDNESSES
TOWARDS
TOWAWAY
TOWAWAYS
TOWBAR
TOWBARS
TOWBOAT
TOWBOATS
TOWED
TOWEL
TOWELED
TOWELETTE
TOWELETTES
TOWELHEAD
TOWELHEADS
TOWELING
TOWELINGS
TOWELLED
TOWELLING
TOWELLINGS
TOWELS
TOWER
TOWERED
TOWERIER
TOWERIEST
TOWERING
TOWERINGLY
TOWERLESS
TOWERLIKE
TOWERS
TOWERY
TOWHEAD
TOWHEADED
TOWHEADS
TOWHEE
TOWHEES
TOWIE
TOWIER
TOWIES
TOWIEST
TOWING
TOWINGS

TOWKAY
TOWKAYS
TOWLINE
TOWLINES
TOWMON
TOWMOND
TOWMONDS
TOWMONS
TOWMONT
TOWMONTS
TOWN
TOWNEE
TOWNEES
TOWNFOLK
TOWNHALL
TOWNHOME
TOWNHOMES
TOWNHOUSE
TOWNHOUSES
TOWNIE
TOWNIER
TOWNIES
TOWNIEST
TOWNISH
TOWNLAND
TOWNLANDS
TOWNLESS
TOWNLET
TOWNLETS
TOWNLIER
TOWNLIEST
TOWNLING
TOWNLINGS
TOWNLY
TOWNS
TOWNSCAPE
TOWNSCAPED
TOWNSCAPES
TOWNSCAPING
TOWNSCAPINGS
TOWNSFOLK
TOWNSFOLKS
TOWNSHIP
TOWNSHIPS
TOWNSKIP
TOWNSKIPS
TOWNSMAN
TOWNSMEN
TOWNSPEOPLE
TOWNSPEOPLES
TOWNSWOMAN
TOWNSWOMEN
TOWNWEAR
TOWNY
TOWPATH
TOWPATHS
TOWROPE

TOWROPES
TOWS
TOWSE
TOWSED
TOWSER
TOWSERS
TOWSES
TOWSIER
TOWSIEST
TOWSING
TOWSY
TOWT
TOWTED
TOWTING
TOWTS
TOWY
TOWZE
TOWZED
TOWZES
TOWZIER
TOWZIEST
TOWZING
TOWZY
TOXAEMIA
TOXAEMIAS
TOXAEMIC
TOXALBUMIN
TOXALBUMINS
TOXAPHENE
TOXAPHENES
TOXEMIA
TOXEMIAS
TOXEMIC
TOXIC
TOXICAL
TOXICALLY
TOXICANT
TOXICANTS
TOXICATION
TOXICATIONS
TOXICITIES
TOXICITY
TOXICOGENIC
TOXICOLOGIC
TOXICOLOGICAL
TOXICOLOGICALLY
TOXICOLOGIES
TOXICOLOGIST
TOXICOLOGISTS
TOXICOLOGY
TOXICOMANIA
TOXICOMANIAS
TOXICOPHAGOUS
TOXICOPHOBIA
TOXICOPHOBIAS
TOXICOSES
TOXICOSIS

TOXICS
TOXIGENIC
TOXIGENICITIES
TOXIGENICITY
TOXIN
TOXINE
TOXINES
TOXINS
TOXIPHAGOUS
TOXIPHOBIA
TOXIPHOBIAC
TOXIPHOBIACS
TOXIPHOBIAS
TOXOCARA
TOXOCARAS
TOXOCARIASES
TOXOCARIASIS
TOXOID
TOXOIDS
TOXOPHILIES
TOXOPHILITE
TOXOPHILITES
TOXOPHILITIC
TOXOPHILY
TOXOPLASMA
TOXOPLASMAS
TOXOPLASMIC
TOXOPLASMOSES
TOXOPLASMOSIS
TOY
TOYED
TOYER
TOYERS
TOYING
TOYINGS
TOYISH
TOYISHLY
TOYISHNESS
TOYISHNESSES
TOYLESOME
TOYLESS
TOYLIKE
TOYLSOM
TOYMAN
TOYMEN
TOYO
TOYON
TOYONS
TOYOS
TOYS
TOYSHOP
TOYSHOPS
TOYSOME
TOYTOWN
TOYWOMAN
TOYWOMEN
TOZE

TOZED
TOZES
TOZIE
TOZIES
TOZING
TRABEATE
TRABEATED
TRABEATION
TRABEATIONS
TRABECULA
TRABECULAE
TRABECULAR
TRABECULAS
TRABECULATE
TRABECULATED
TRABS
TRACASSERIE
TRACASSERIES
TRACE
TRACEABILITIES
TRACEABILITY
TRACEABLE
TRACEABLENESS
TRACEABLENESSES
TRACEABLY
TRACED
TRACELESS
TRACELESSLY
TRACER
TRACERIED
TRACERIES
TRACERS
TRACERY
TRACES
TRACHEA
TRACHEAE
TRACHEAL
TRACHEARIAN
TRACHEARIANS
TRACHEARIES
TRACHEARY
TRACHEAS
TRACHEATE
TRACHEATED
TRACHEID
TRACHEIDAL
TRACHEIDE
TRACHEIDES
TRACHEIDS
TRACHEITIS
TRACHEITISES
TRACHELATE
TRACHEOLAR
TRACHEOLE
TRACHEOLES
TRACHEOPHYTE
TRACHEOPHYTES

TRACHEOSCOPIES	TRACKWALKER	TRADES	TRADUCTIVE
TRACHEOSCOPY	TRACKWALKERS	TRADESCANTIA	TRAFFIC
TRACHEOSTOMIES	TRACKWAY	TRADESCANTIAS	TRAFFICABILITY
TRACHEOSTOMY	TRACKWAYS	TRADESFOLK	TRAFFICABLE
TRACHEOTOMIES	TRACT	TRADESFOLKS	TRAFFICATOR
TRACHEOTOMY	TRACTABILITIES	TRADESMAN	TRAFFICATORS
TRACHINUS	TRACTABILITY	TRADESMANLIKE	TRAFFICKED
TRACHINUSES	TRACTABLE	TRADESMEN	TRAFFICKER
TRACHITIS	TRACTABLENESS	TRADESPEOPLE	TRAFFICKERS
TRACHITISES	TRACTABLENESSES	TRADESPEOPLES	TRAFFICKING
TRACHLE	TRACTABLY	TRADESWOMAN	TRAFFICKINGS
TRACHLED	TRACTARIAN	TRADESWOMEN	TRAFFICKLESS
TRACHLES	TRACTARIANS	TRADING	TRAFFICKY
TRACHLING	TRACTATE	TRADINGS	TRAFFICLESS
TRACHOMA	TRACTATES	TRADITION	TRAFFICS
TRACHOMAS	TRACTATOR	TRADITIONAL	TRAGACANTH
TRACHOMATOUS	TRACTATORS	TRADITIONALISM	TRAGACANTHS
TRACHYPTERUS	TRACTED	TRADITIONALISMS	TRAGAL
TRACHYPTERUSES	TRACTILE	TRADITIONALIST	TRAGEDIAN
TRACHYTE	TRACTILITIES	TRADITIONALISTS	TRAGEDIANS
TRACHYTES	TRACTILITY	TRADITIONALITY	TRAGEDIENNE
TRACHYTIC	TRACTING	TRADITIONALIZE	TRAGEDIENNES
TRACHYTOID	TRACTION	TRADITIONALIZED	TRAGEDIES
TRACING	TRACTIONAL	TRADITIONALIZES	TRAGEDY
TRACINGS	TRACTIONS	TRADITIONALLY	TRAGELAPH
TRACK	TRACTIVE	TRADITIONARILY	TRAGELAPHINE
TRACKABLE	TRACTOR	TRADITIONARY	TRAGELAPHS
TRACKAGE	TRACTORATION	TRADITIONER	TRAGI
TRACKAGES	TRACTORATIONS	TRADITIONERS	TRAGIC
TRACKBALL	TRACTORFEED	TRADITIONIST	TRAGICAL
TRACKBALLS	TRACTORS	TRADITIONISTS	TRAGICALLY
TRACKED	TRACTRICES	TRADITIONLESS	TRAGICALNESS
TRACKER	TRACTRIX	TRADITIONS	TRAGICALNESSES
TRACKERBALL	TRACTS	TRADITIVE	TRAGICOMEDIES
TRACKERBALLS	TRACTUS	TRADITOR	TRAGICOMEDY
TRACKERS	TRACTUSES	TRADITORES	TRAGICOMIC
TRACKING	TRAD	TRADITORS	TRAGICOMICAL
TRACKINGS	TRADABLE	TRADS	TRAGICOMICALLY
TRACKLAYER	TRADE	TRADUCE	TRAGICS
TRACKLAYERS	TRADEABLE	TRADUCED	TRAGOPAN
TRACKLAYING	TRADECRAFT	TRADUCEMENT	TRAGOPANS
TRACKLAYINGS	TRADECRAFTS	TRADUCEMENTS	TRAGULE
TRACKLEMENT	TRADED	TRADUCER	TRAGULES
TRACKLEMENTS	TRADEFUL	TRADUCERS	TRAGULINE
TRACKLESS	TRADELESS	TRADUCES	TRAGUS
TRACKLESSLY	TRADEMARK	TRADUCIAN	TRAHISON
TRACKLESSNESS	TRADEMARKED	TRADUCIANISM	TRAHISONS
TRACKLESSNESSES	TRADEMARKING	TRADUCIANIST	TRAIK
TRACKMAN	TRADEMARKS	TRADUCIANISTIC	TRAIKED
TRACKMEN	TRADENAME	TRADUCIANISTS	TRAIKING
TRACKROAD	TRADENAMES	TRADUCIANS	TRAIKIT
TRACKROADS	TRADEOFF	TRADUCIBLE	TRAIKS
TRACKS	TRADEOFFS	TRADUCING	TRAIL
TRACKSIDE	TRADER	TRADUCINGLY	TRAILABLE
TRACKSIDES	TRADERS	TRADUCINGS	TRAILBASTON
TRACKSUIT	TRADERSHIP	TRADUCTION	TRAILBASTONS
TRACKSUITS	TRADERSHIPS	TRADUCTIONS	TRAILBLAZER

TRAILBLAZERS	TRAITORESS	TRAMONTANAS	TRANKUMS
TRAILBLAZING	TRAITORESSES	TRAMONTANE	TRANNIE
TRAILBREAKER	TRAITORHOOD	TRAMONTANES	TRANNIES
TRAILBREAKERS	TRAITORHOODS	TRAMP	TRANNY
TRAILED	TRAITORISM	TRAMPED	TRANQ
TRAILER	TRAITORISMS	TRAMPER	TRANQS
TRAILERABLE	TRAITORLY	TRAMPERS	TRANQUIL
TRAILERED	TRAITOROUS	TRAMPET	TRANQUILER
TRAILERING	TRAITOROUSLY	TRAMPETS	TRANQUILEST
TRAILERINGS	TRAITOROUSNESS	TRAMPETTE	TRANQUILITIES
TRAILERIST	TRAITORS	TRAMPETTES	TRANQUILITY
TRAILERISTS	TRAITORSHIP	TRAMPING	TRANQUILIZATION
TRAILERITE	TRAITORSHIPS	TRAMPINGS	TRANQUILIZE
TRAILERITES	TRAITRESS	TRAMPISH	TRANQUILIZED
TRAILERS	TRAITRESSES	TRAMPLE	TRANQUILIZER
TRAILHEAD	TRAITS	TRAMPLED	TRANQUILIZERS
TRAILHEADS	TRAJECT	TRAMPLER	TRANQUILIZES
TRAILING	TRAJECTED	TRAMPLERS	TRANQUILIZING
TRAILINGLY	TRAJECTILE	TRAMPLES	TRANQUILIZINGLY
TRAILLESS	TRAJECTING	TRAMPLING	TRANQUILLER
TRAILS	TRAJECTION	TRAMPLINGS	TRANQUILLEST
TRAILSIDE	TRAJECTIONS	TRAMPOLIN	TRANQUILLISE
TRAIN	TRAJECTORIES	TRAMPOLINE	TRANQUILLISED
TRAINABILITIES	TRAJECTORY	TRAMPOLINED	TRANQUILLISER
TRAINABILITY	TRAJECTS	TRAMPOLINER	TRANQUILLISERS
TRAINABLE	TRALATICIOUS	TRAMPOLINERS	TRANQUILLISES
TRAINBAND	TRALATITIOUS	TRAMPOLINES	TRANQUILLISING
TRAINBANDS	TRAM	TRAMPOLINING	TRANQUILLITIES
TRAINBEARER	TRAMCAR	TRAMPOLININGS	TRANQUILLITY
TRAINBEARERS	TRAMCARS	TRAMPOLINIST	TRANQUILLIZE
TRAINED	TRAMEL	TRAMPOLINISTS	TRANQUILLIZED
TRAINEE	TRAMELED	TRAMPOLINS	TRANQUILLIZER
TRAINEES	TRAMELING	TRAMPS	TRANQUILLIZERS
TRAINEESHIP	TRAMELL	TRAMROAD	TRANQUILLIZES
TRAINEESHIPS	TRAMELLED	TRAMROADS	TRANQUILLIZING
TRAINER	TRAMELLING	TRAMS	TRANQUILLY
TRAINERS	TRAMELLS	TRAMWAY	TRANQUILNESS
TRAINFUL	TRAMELS	TRAMWAYS	TRANQUILNESSES
TRAINFULS	TRAMLESS	TRANCE	TRANS
TRAINING	TRAMLINE	TRANCED	TRANSACT
TRAININGS	TRAMLINED	TRANCEDLY	TRANSACTED
TRAINLESS	TRAMLINES	TRANCELIKE	TRANSACTING
TRAINLOAD	TRAMMED	TRANCES	TRANSACTINIDE
TRAINLOADS	TRAMMEL	TRANCHE	TRANSACTINIDES
TRAINMAN	TRAMMELED	TRANCHES	TRANSACTION
TRAINMEN	TRAMMELER	TRANCHET	TRANSACTIONAL
TRAINS	TRAMMELERS	TRANCHETS	TRANSACTIONALLY
TRAINSPOTTERISH	TRAMMELING	TRANCING	TRANSACTIONS
TRAINWAY	TRAMMELLED	TRANECT	TRANSACTOR
TRAINWAYS	TRAMMELLER	TRANECTS	TRANSACTORS
TRAIPSE	TRAMMELLERS	TRANGAM	TRANSACTS
TRAIPSED	TRAMMELLING	TRANGAMS	TRANSALPINE
TRAIPSES	TRAMMELS	TRANGLE	TRANSALPINES
TRAIPSING	TRAMMIE	TRANGLES	TRANSAMINASE
TRAIPSINGS	TRAMMIES	TRANK	TRANSAMINASES
TRAIT	TRAMMING	TRANKS	TRANSAMINATION
TRAITOR	TRAMONTANA	TRANKUM	TRANSAMINATIONS

TRANSANDEAN
TRANSANDINE
TRANSATLANTIC
TRANSAXLE
TRANSAXLES
TRANSCALENCIES
TRANSCALENCY
TRANSCALENT
TRANSCAUCASIAN
TRANSCEIVER
TRANSCEIVERS
TRANSCEND
TRANSCENDED
TRANSCENDENCE
TRANSCENDENCES
TRANSCENDENCIES
TRANSCENDENCY
TRANSCENDENT
TRANSCENDENTAL
TRANSCENDENTALS
TRANSCENDENTLY
TRANSCENDENTS
TRANSCENDING
TRANSCENDINGLY
TRANSCENDS
TRANSCRIPTIONAL
TRANSCRIPTIONS
TRANSCRIPTIVE
TRANSCRIPTIVELY
TRANSCRIPTS
TRANSCULTURAL
TRANSCURRENT
TRANSCURRENTLY
TRANSCUTANEOUS
TRANSDERMAL
TRANSDUCE
TRANSDUCED
TRANSDUCER
TRANSDUCERS
TRANSDUCES
TRANSDUCING
TRANSDUCTANT
TRANSDUCTANTS
TRANSDUCTION
TRANSDUCTIONAL
TRANSDUCTIONS

TRANSDUCTOR
TRANSDUCTORS
TRANSE
TRANSECT
TRANSECTED
TRANSECTING
TRANSECTION
TRANSECTIONS
TRANSECTS
TRANSENNA
TRANSENNAS
TRANSEPT
TRANSEPTAL
TRANSEPTATE
TRANSEPTS
TRANSES
TRANSEUNT
TRANSEXUAL
TRANSEXUALISM
TRANSEXUALITY
TRANSEXUALLY
TRANSEXUALS
TRANSFARD
TRANSFECT
TRANSFECTED
TRANSFECTING
TRANSFECTION
TRANSFECTIONS
TRANSFECTS
TRANSFER
TRANSFERABILITY
TRANSFERABLE
TRANSFERAL
TRANSFERALS
TRANSFERASE
TRANSFERASES
TRANSFEREE
TRANSFEREES
TRANSFERENCE
TRANSFERENCES
TRANSFERENTIAL
TRANSFEROR
TRANSFERORS
TRANSFERRABLE
TRANSFERRAL
TRANSFERRALS
TRANSFERRED
TRANSFERRER
TRANSFERRERS
TRANSFERRIBLE
TRANSFERRIN
TRANSFERRING
TRANSFERRINS
TRANSFERS
TRANSFIGURATION
TRANSFIGURE
TRANSFIGURED

TRANSFIGUREMENT
TRANSFIGURES
TRANSFIGURING
TRANSFINITE
TRANSFIX
TRANSFIXED
TRANSFIXES
TRANSFIXING
TRANSFIXION
TRANSFIXIONS
TRANSFIXT
TRANSFORM
TRANSFORMABLE
TRANSFORMATION
TRANSFORMATIONS
TRANSFORMATIVE
TRANSFORMED
TRANSFORMER
TRANSFORMERS
TRANSFORMING
TRANSFORMINGS
TRANSFORMISM
TRANSFORMISMS
TRANSFORMIST
TRANSFORMISTIC
TRANSFORMISTS
TRANSFORMS
TRANSFUSABLE
TRANSFUSE
TRANSFUSED
TRANSFUSER
TRANSFUSERS
TRANSFUSES
TRANSFUSIBLE
TRANSFUSING
TRANSFUSION
TRANSFUSIONAL
TRANSFUSIONIST
TRANSFUSIONISTS
TRANSFUSIONS
TRANSFUSIVE
TRANSFUSIVELY
TRANSGENDER
TRANSGENDERED
TRANSGENDERS
TRANSGENE
TRANSGENESES
TRANSGENESIS
TRANSGENIC
TRANSGENICS
TRANSGRESS
TRANSGRESSED
TRANSGRESSES
TRANSGRESSING
TRANSGRESSION
TRANSGRESSIONAL
TRANSGRESSIONS

TRANSGRESSIVE
TRANSGRESSIVELY
TRANSGRESSOR
TRANSGRESSORS
TRANSHIP
TRANSHIPMENT
TRANSHIPMENTS
TRANSHIPPED
TRANSHIPPER
TRANSHIPPERS
TRANSHIPPING
TRANSHIPPINGS
TRANSHIPS
TRANSHISTORICAL
TRANSHUMANCE
TRANSHUMANCES
TRANSHUMANT
TRANSHUMANTS
TRANSHUME
TRANSHUMED
TRANSHUMES
TRANSHUMING
TRANSIENCE
TRANSIENCES
TRANSIENCIES
TRANSIENCY
TRANSIENT
TRANSIENTLY
TRANSIENTNESS
TRANSIENTNESSES
TRANSIENTS
TRANSILIENCE
TRANSILIENCIES
TRANSILIENCY
TRANSILIENT
TRANSILLUMINATE
TRANSIRE
TRANSIRES
TRANSISTHMIAN
TRANSISTOR
TRANSISTORISE
TRANSISTORISED
TRANSISTORISES
TRANSISTORISING
TRANSISTORIZE
TRANSISTORIZED
TRANSISTORIZES
TRANSISTORIZING
TRANSISTORS
TRANSIT
TRANSITABLE
TRANSITED
TRANSITING
TRANSITION
TRANSITIONAL
TRANSITIONALLY
TRANSITIONALS

TRANSITIONARY
TRANSITIONS
TRANSITIVE
TRANSITIVELY
TRANSITIVENESS
TRANSITIVES
TRANSITIVITIES
TRANSITIVITY
TRANSITORILY
TRANSITORINESS
TRANSITORY
TRANSITS
TRANSLATABILITY
TRANSLATABLE
TRANSLATE
TRANSLATED
TRANSLATES
TRANSLATING
TRANSLATION
TRANSLATIONAL
TRANSLATIONALLY
TRANSLATIONS
TRANSLATIVE
TRANSLATIVES
TRANSLATOR
TRANSLATORIAL
TRANSLATORS
TRANSLATORY
TRANSLEITHAN
TRANSLITERATE
TRANSLITERATED
TRANSLITERATES
TRANSLITERATING
TRANSLITERATION
TRANSLITERATOR
TRANSLITERATORS
TRANSLOCATE
TRANSLOCATED
TRANSLOCATES
TRANSLOCATING
TRANSLOCATION
TRANSLOCATIONS
TRANSLUCENCE
TRANSLUCENCES
TRANSLUCENCIES
TRANSLUCENCY
TRANSLUCENT
TRANSLUCENTLY
TRANSLUCID
TRANSLUCIDITIES
TRANSLUCIDITY
TRANSLUNAR
TRANSLUNARY
TRANSMANCHE
TRANSMARINE
TRANSMEMBRANE
TRANSMEW

TRANSMEWED
TRANSMEWING
TRANSMEWS
TRANSMIGRANT
TRANSMIGRANTS
TRANSMIGRATE
TRANSMIGRATED
TRANSMIGRATES
TRANSMIGRATING
TRANSMIGRATION
TRANSMIGRATIONS
TRANSMIGRATIVE
TRANSMIGRATOR
TRANSMIGRATORS
TRANSMIGRATORY
TRANSMISSIBLE
TRANSMISSION
TRANSMISSIONAL
TRANSMISSIONS
TRANSMISSIVE
TRANSMISSIVELY
TRANSMISSIVITY
TRANSMISSOMETER
TRANSMIT
TRANSMITS
TRANSMITTABLE
TRANSMITTAL
TRANSMITTALS
TRANSMITTANCE
TRANSMITTANCES
TRANSMITTANCY
TRANSMITTED
TRANSMITTER
TRANSMITTERS
TRANSMITTIBLE
TRANSMITTING
TRANSMITTIVITY
TRANSMOGRIFIED
TRANSMOGRIFIES
TRANSMOGRIFY
TRANSMOGRIFYING
TRANSMONTANE
TRANSMONTANES
TRANSMOUNTAIN
TRANSMOVE
TRANSMOVED
TRANSMOVES
TRANSMOVING
TRANSMUNDANE
TRANSMUTABILITY
TRANSMUTABLE
TRANSMUTABLY
TRANSMUTATION
TRANSMUTATIONAL
TRANSMUTATIONS
TRANSMUTATIVE
TRANSMUTE

TRANSMUTED
TRANSMUTER
TRANSMUTERS
TRANSMUTES
TRANSMUTING
TRANSNATIONAL
TRANSNATURAL
TRANSOCEANIC
TRANSOM
TRANSOMED
TRANSOMS
TRANSONIC
TRANSONICS
TRANSPACIFIC
TRANSPADANE
TRANSPARENCE
TRANSPARENCES
TRANSPARENCIES
TRANSPARENCY
TRANSPARENT
TRANSPARENTIZE
TRANSPARENTIZED
TRANSPARENTIZES
TRANSPARENTLY
TRANSPARENTNESS
TRANSPERSONAL
TRANSPICUOUS
TRANSPICUOUSLY
TRANSPIERCE
TRANSPIERCED
TRANSPIERCES
TRANSPIERCING
TRANSPIRABLE
TRANSPIRATION
TRANSPIRATIONAL
TRANSPIRATIONS
TRANSPIRATORY
TRANSPIRE
TRANSPIRED
TRANSPIRES
TRANSPIRING
TRANSPLACENTAL
TRANSPLANT
TRANSPLANTABLE
TRANSPLANTATION
TRANSPLANTED
TRANSPLANTER
TRANSPLANTERS
TRANSPLANTING
TRANSPLANTINGS
TRANSPLANTS
TRANSPOLAR
TRANSPONDER
TRANSPONDERS
TRANSPONDOR
TRANSPONDORS
TRANSPONTINE

TRANSPORT
TRANSPORTABLE
TRANSPORTAL
TRANSPORTALS
TRANSPORTANCE
TRANSPORTANCES
TRANSPORTATION
TRANSPORTATIONS
TRANSPORTED
TRANSPORTEDLY
TRANSPORTEDNESS
TRANSPORTER
TRANSPORTERS
TRANSPORTING
TRANSPORTINGLY
TRANSPORTINGS
TRANSPORTIVE
TRANSPORTS
TRANSPOSABILITY
TRANSPOSABLE
TRANSPOSAL
TRANSPOSALS
TRANSPOSE
TRANSPOSED
TRANSPOSER
TRANSPOSERS
TRANSPOSES
TRANSPOSING
TRANSPOSINGS
TRANSPOSITION
TRANSPOSITIONAL
TRANSPOSITIONS
TRANSPOSITIVE
TRANSPOSON
TRANSPOSONS
TRANSPUTER
TRANSPUTERS
TRANSSEXUAL
TRANSSEXUALISM
TRANSSEXUALISMS
TRANSSEXUALITY
TRANSSEXUALS
TRANSSHAPE
TRANSSHAPED
TRANSSHAPES
TRANSSHAPING
TRANSSHIP
TRANSSHIPMENT
TRANSSHIPMENTS
TRANSSHIPPED
TRANSSHIPPER
TRANSSHIPPERS
TRANSSHIPPING
TRANSSHIPPINGS
TRANSSHIPS
TRANSSONIC
TRANSTHORACIC

TRANSUBSTANTIAL	TRANSVESTITE	TRAPNESTS	TRAUMATA
TRANSUDATE	TRANSVESTITES	TRAPPEAN	TRAUMATIC
TRANSUDATES	TRANSVESTITISM	TRAPPED	TRAUMATICALLY
TRANSUDATION	TRANSVESTITISMS	TRAPPER	TRAUMATISATION
TRANSUDATIONS	TRANSVESTS	TRAPPERS	TRAUMATISATIONS
TRANSUDATORY	TRANT	TRAPPIER	TRAUMATISE
TRANSUDE	TRANTED	TRAPPIEST	TRAUMATISED
TRANSUDED	TRANTER	TRAPPINESS	TRAUMATISES
TRANSUDES	TRANTERS	TRAPPINESSES	TRAUMATISING
TRANSUDING	TRANTING	TRAPPING	TRAUMATISM
TRANSUME	TRANTS	TRAPPINGS	TRAUMATISMS
TRANSUMED	TRAP	TRAPPOSE	TRAUMATIZATION
TRANSUMES	TRAPAN	TRAPPOUS	TRAUMATIZATIONS
TRANSUMING	TRAPANNED	TRAPPY	TRAUMATIZE
TRANSUMPT	TRAPANNER	TRAPROCK	TRAUMATIZED
TRANSUMPTION	TRAPANNERS	TRAPROCKS	TRAUMATIZES
TRANSUMPTIONS	TRAPANNING	TRAPS	TRAUMATIZING
TRANSUMPTIVE	TRAPANS	TRAPSHOOTER	TRAUMATOLOGICAL
TRANSUMPTS	TRAPBALL	TRAPSHOOTERS	TRAUMATOLOGIES
TRANSURANIAN	TRAPBALLS	TRAPSHOOTING	TRAUMATOLOGY
TRANSURANIC	TRAPDOOR	TRAPSHOOTINGS	TRAUMATONASTIES
TRANSURANICS	TRAPDOORS	TRAPT	TRAVAIL
TRANSURANIUM	TRAPE	TRAPUNTO	TRAVAILED
TRANSVALUATE	TRAPED	TRAPUNTOS	TRAVAILING
TRANSVALUATED	TRAPES	TRASH	TRAVAILS
TRANSVALUATES	TRAPESED	TRASHCAN	TRAVE
TRANSVALUATING	TRAPESES	TRASHCANS	TRAVEL
TRANSVALUATION	TRAPESING	TRASHED	TRAVELATOR
TRANSVALUATIONS	TRAPESINGS	TRASHERIES	TRAVELATORS
TRANSVALUE	TRAPEZE	TRASHERY	TRAVELED
TRANSVALUED	TRAPEZED	TRASHES	TRAVELER
TRANSVALUER	TRAPEZES	TRASHIER	TRAVELERS
TRANSVALUERS	TRAPEZIA	TRASHIEST	TRAVELING
TRANSVALUES	TRAPEZIAL	TRASHILY	TRAVELINGS
TRANSVALUING	TRAPEZIFORM	TRASHINESS	TRAVELLED
TRANSVERSAL	TRAPEZII	TRASHINESSES	TRAVELLER
TRANSVERSALITY	TRAPEZING	TRASHING	TRAVELLERS
TRANSVERSALLY	TRAPEZIST	TRASHMAN	TRAVELLING
TRANSVERSALS	TRAPEZISTS	TRASHMEN	TRAVELLINGS
TRANSVERSE	TRAPEZIUM	TRASHTRIE	TRAVELOG
TRANSVERSED	TRAPEZIUMS	TRASHTRIES	TRAVELOGS
TRANSVERSELY	TRAPEZIUS	TRASHY	TRAVELOGUE
TRANSVERSENESS	TRAPEZIUSES	TRASS	TRAVELOGUES
TRANSVERSES	TRAPEZOHEDRA	TRASSES	TRAVELS
TRANSVERSING	TRAPEZOHEDRAL	TRAT	TRAVERSABLE
TRANSVERSION	TRAPEZOHEDRON	TRATS	TRAVERSAL
TRANSVERSIONS	TRAPEZOHEDRONS	TRATT	TRAVERSALS
TRANSVERTER	TRAPEZOID	TRATTORIA	TRAVERSE
TRANSVERTERS	TRAPEZOIDAL	TRATTORIAS	TRAVERSED
TRANSVEST	TRAPEZOIDS	TRATTORIE	TRAVERSER
TRANSVESTED	TRAPING	TRATTS	TRAVERSERS
TRANSVESTIC	TRAPLIKE	TRAUCHLE	TRAVERSES
TRANSVESTING	TRAPLINE	TRAUCHLED	TRAVERSING
TRANSVESTISM	TRAPLINES	TRAUCHLES	TRAVERSINGS
TRANSVESTISMS	TRAPNEST	TRAUCHLING	TRAVERTIN
TRANSVESTIST	TRAPNESTED	TRAUMA	TRAVERTINE
TRANSVESTISTS	TRAPNESTING	TRAUMAS	TRAVERTINES

TRAVERTINS
TRAVES
TRAVESTIED
TRAVESTIES
TRAVESTY
TRAVESTYING
TRAVIS
TRAVISES
TRAVOIS
TRAVOISE
TRAVOISES
TRAVOLATOR
TRAVOLATORS
TRAWL
TRAWLED
TRAWLER
TRAWLERMAN
TRAWLERMEN
TRAWLERS
TRAWLEY
TRAWLEYS
TRAWLING
TRAWLINGS
TRAWLNET
TRAWLNETS
TRAWLS
TRAY
TRAYBIT
TRAYBITS
TRAYFUL
TRAYFULS
TRAYMOBILE
TRAYMOBILES
TRAYNE
TRAYNED
TRAYNES
TRAYNING
TRAYS
TREACHER
TREACHERER
TREACHERERS
TREACHERIES
TREACHEROUS
TREACHEROUSLY
TREACHEROUSNESS
TREACHERS
TREACHERY
TREACHETOUR
TREACHETOURS
TREACHOUR
TREACHOURS
TREACLE
TREACLED
TREACLES
TREACLIER
TREACLIEST
TREACLINESS

TREACLINESSES
TREACLING
TREACLY
TREAD
TREADED
TREADER
TREADERS
TREADING
TREADINGS
TREADLE
TREADLED
TREADLER
TREADLERS
TREADLES
TREADLESS
TREADLING
TREADLINGS
TREADMILL
TREADMILLS
TREADS
TREADWHEEL
TREADWHEELS
TREAGUE
TREAGUES
TREASON
TREASONABLE
TREASONABLENESS
TREASONABLY
TREASONOUS
TREASONS
TREASURABLE
TREASURE
TREASURED
TREASURELESS
TREASURER
TREASURERS
TREASURERSHIP
TREASURERSHIPS
TREASURES
TREASURIES
TREASURING
TREASURY
TREAT
TREATABILITIES
TREATABILITY
TREATABLE
TREATED
TREATER
TREATERS
TREATIES
TREATING
TREATINGS
TREATISE
TREATISES
TREATMENT
TREATMENTS
TREATS

TREATY
TREATYLESS
TREBLE
TREBLED
TREBLENESS
TREBLENESSES
TREBLES
TREBLING
TREBLY
TREBUCHET
TREBUCHETS
TREBUCKET
TREBUCKETS
TRECENTIST
TRECENTISTS
TRECENTO
TRECENTOS
TRECK
TRECKED
TRECKING
TRECKS
TREDDLE
TREDDLED
TREDDLES
TREDDLING
TREDECILLION
TREDECILLIONS
TREDILLE
TREDILLES
TREDRILLE
TREDRILLES
TREE
TREED
TREEHOPPER
TREEHOPPERS
TREEING
TREELAWN
TREELAWNS
TREELESS
TREELESSNESS
TREELESSNESSES
TREELIKE
TREEN
TREENAIL
TREENAILS
TREENS
TREENWARE
TREENWARES
TREES
TREESHIP
TREESHIPS
TREETOP
TREETOPS
TREEWARE
TREEWAX
TREEWAXES
TREF

TREFA
TREFAH
TREFOIL
TREFOILED
TREFOILS
TREGETOUR
TREGETOURS
TREHALA
TREHALAS
TREHALOSE
TREHALOSES
TREIF
TREIFA
TREILLAGE
TREILLAGED
TREILLAGES
TREILLE
TREILLES
TREK
TREKKED
TREKKER
TREKKERS
TREKKING
TREKS
TREKSCHUIT
TREKSCHUITS
TRELLIS
TRELLISED
TRELLISES
TRELLISING
TRELLISWORK
TRELLISWORKS
TREMA
TREMAS
TREMATIC
TREMATODE
TREMATODES
TREMATOID
TREMATOIDS
TREMBLANT
TREMBLE
TREMBLED
TREMBLEMENT
TREMBLEMENTS
TREMBLER
TREMBLERS
TREMBLES
TREMBLIER
TREMBLIEST
TREMBLING
TREMBLINGLY
TREMBLINGS
TREMBLY
TREMENDOUS
TREMENDOUSLY
TREMENDOUSNESS
TREMIE

TREMIES	TRENDINESS	TRESSED	TRIADELPHOUS
TREMOLANDI	TRENDINESSES	TRESSEL	TRIADIC
TREMOLANDO	TRENDING	TRESSELS	TRIADICALLY
TREMOLANDOS	TRENDS	TRESSES	TRIADICS
TREMOLANT	TRENDSETTER	TRESSIER	TRIADISM
TREMOLANTS	TRENDSETTERS	TRESSIEST	TRIADISMS
TREMOLITE	TRENDSETTING	TRESSING	TRIADIST
TREMOLITES	TRENDSETTINGS	TRESSOUR	TRIADISTS
TREMOLITIC	TRENDY	TRESSOURS	TRIADS
TREMOLO	TRENDYISM	TRESSURE	TRIAGE
TREMOLOS	TRENDYISMS	TRESSURED	TRIAGED
TREMOR	TRENISE	TRESSURES	TRIAGES
TREMORED	TRENISES	TRESSY	TRIAGING
TREMORING	TRENTAL	TREST	TRIAL
TREMORLESS	TRENTALS	TRESTLE	TRIALISM
TREMOROUS	TREPAN	TRESTLES	TRIALISMS
TREMOROUSNESS	TREPANATION	TRESTLETREE	TRIALIST
TREMORS	TREPANATIONS	TRESTLETREES	TRIALISTS
TREMULANT	TREPANG	TRESTLEWORK	TRIALITIES
TREMULANTS	TREPANGS	TRESTLEWORKS	TRIALITY
TREMULATE	TREPANNED	TRESTS	TRIALLED
TREMULATED	TREPANNER	TRET	TRIALLING
TREMULATES	TREPANNERS	TRETINOIN	TRIALLIST
TREMULATING	TREPANNING	TRETINOINS	TRIALLISTS
TREMULOUS	TREPANNINGS	TRETS	TRIALOGUE
TREMULOUSLY	TREPANS	TREVALLIES	TRIALOGUES
TREMULOUSNESS	TREPHINATION	TREVALLY	TRIALS
TREMULOUSNESSES	TREPHINATIONS	TREVET	TRIAMCINOLONE
TRENAIL	TREPHINE	TREVETS	TRIAMCINOLONES
TRENAILS	TREPHINED	TREVIS	TRIANDRIAN
TRENCH	TREPHINER	TREVISES	TRIANDROUS
TRENCHANCIES	TREPHINERS	TREVISS	TRIANGLE
TRENCHANCY	TREPHINES	TREVISSES	TRIANGLED
TRENCHAND	TREPHINING	TREW	TRIANGLES
TRENCHANT	TREPHININGS	TREWS	TRIANGULAR
TRENCHANTLY	TREPID	TREWSMAN	TRIANGULARITIES
TRENCHARD	TREPIDANT	TREWSMEN	TRIANGULARITY
TRENCHARDS	TREPIDATION	TREY	TRIANGULARLY
TRENCHED	TREPIDATIONS	TREYBIT	TRIANGULATE
TRENCHER	TREPIDATORY	TREYBITS	TRIANGULATED
TRENCHERMAN	TREPONEMA	TREYS	TRIANGULATELY
TRENCHERMEN	TREPONEMAL	TREZ	TRIANGULATES
TRENCHERS	TREPONEMAS	TREZES	TRIANGULATING
TRENCHES	TREPONEMATA	TRIABLE	TRIANGULATION
TRENCHING	TREPONEMATOSES	TRIABLENESS	TRIANGULATIONS
TREND	TREPONEMATOSIS	TRIAC	TRIAPSAL
TRENDED	TREPONEMATOUS	TRIACETATE	TRIAPSIDAL
TRENDIER	TREPONEME	TRIACETATES	TRIARCH
TRENDIES	TREPONEMES	TRIACID	TRIARCHIES
TRENDIEST	TRES	TRIACIDS	TRIARCHS
TRENDIFIED	TRESPASS	TRIACONTER	TRIARCHY
TRENDIFIER	TRESPASSED	TRIACONTERS	TRIATHLETE
TRENDIFIERS	TRESPASSER	TRIACS	TRIATHLETES
TRENDIFIES	TRESPASSERS	TRIACT	TRIATHLON
TRENDIFY	TRESPASSES	TRIACTINAL	TRIATHLONS
TRENDIFYING	TRESPASSING	TRIACTINE	TRIATIC
TRENDILY	TRESS	TRIAD	TRIATICS

TRIATOMIC	TRIBROMOMETHANE	TRICHINIASES	TRICHOMONIASES
TRIATOMICALLY	TRIBULATE	TRICHINIASIS	TRICHOMONIASIS
TRIAXIAL	TRIBULATED	TRICHINISATION	TRICHOPHYTON
TRIAXIALITIES	TRIBULATES	TRICHINISATIONS	TRICHOPHYTONS
TRIAXIALITY	TRIBULATING	TRICHINISE	TRICHOPHYTOSES
TRIAXIALS	TRIBULATION	TRICHINISED	TRICHOPHYTOSIS
TRIAXON	TRIBULATIONS	TRICHINISES	TRICHOPTERAN
TRIAXONS	TRIBUNAL	TRICHINISING	TRICHOPTERANS
TRIAZIN	TRIBUNALS	TRICHINIZATION	TRICHOPTERISTS
TRIAZINE	TRIBUNARY	TRICHINIZATIONS	TRICHOPTEROUS
TRIAZINES	TRIBUNATE	TRICHINIZE	TRICHORD
TRIAZINS	TRIBUNATES	TRICHINIZED	TRICHORDS
TRIAZOLE	TRIBUNE	TRICHINIZES	TRICHOSES
TRIAZOLES	TRIBUNES	TRICHINIZING	TRICHOSIS
TRIAZOLIC	TRIBUNESHIP	TRICHINOSE	TRICHOTHECENE
TRIBACHIAL	TRIBUNESHIPS	TRICHINOSED	TRICHOTHECENES
TRIBADE	TRIBUNICIAL	TRICHINOSES	TRICHOTOMIC
TRIBADES	TRIBUNICIAN	TRICHINOSING	TRICHOTOMIES
TRIBADIC	TRIBUNITIAL	TRICHINOSIS	TRICHOTOMISE
TRIBADIES	TRIBUNITIAN	TRICHINOTIC	TRICHOTOMISED
TRIBADISM	TRIBUTARIES	TRICHINOUS	TRICHOTOMISES
TRIBADISMS	TRIBUTARILY	TRICHITE	TRICHOTOMISING
TRIBADY	TRIBUTARINESS	TRICHITES	TRICHOTOMIZE
TRIBAL	TRIBUTARINESSES	TRICHITIC	TRICHOTOMIZED
TRIBALISM	TRIBUTARY	TRICHLORFON	TRICHOTOMIZES
TRIBALISMS	TRIBUTE	TRICHLORFONS	TRICHOTOMIZING
TRIBALIST	TRIBUTER	TRICHLORIDE	TRICHOTOMOUS
TRIBALISTIC	TRIBUTERS	TRICHLORIDES	TRICHOTOMOUSLY
TRIBALISTS	TRIBUTES	TRICHLOROACETIC	TRICHOTOMY
TRIBALLY	TRICAMERAL	TRICHLOROETHANE	TRICHROIC
TRIBASIC	TRICAR	TRICHLORPHON	TRICHROISM
TRIBBLE	TRICARBOXYLIC	TRICHLORPHONS	TRICHROISMS
TRIBBLES	TRICARPELLARY	TRICHOBACTERIA	TRICHROMAT
TRIBE	TRICARS	TRICHOCYST	TRICHROMATIC
TRIBELESS	TRICE	TRICHOCYSTIC	TRICHROMATISM
TRIBES	TRICED	TRICHOCYSTS	TRICHROMATISMS
TRIBESMAN	TRICENTENARIES	TRICHOGYNE	TRICHROMATS
TRIBESMEN	TRICENTENARY	TRICHOGYNES	TRICHROME
TRIBESPEOPLE	TRICENTENNIAL	TRICHOGYNIAL	TRICHROMIC
TRIBESWOMAN	TRICENTENNIALS	TRICHOGYNIC	TRICHROMICS
TRIBESWOMEN	TRICEPHALOUS	TRICHOID	TRICHRONOUS
TRIBLET	TRICEPS	TRICHOLOGICAL	TRICHURIASIS
TRIBLETS	TRICEPSES	TRICHOLOGIES	TRICING
TRIBOELECTRIC	TRICERATOPS	TRICHOLOGIST	TRICK
TRIBOLOGICAL	TRICERATOPSES	TRICHOLOGISTS	TRICKED
TRIBOLOGIES	TRICERION	TRICHOLOGY	TRICKER
TRIBOLOGIST	TRICERIONS	TRICHOME	TRICKERIES
TRIBOLOGISTS	TRICES	TRICHOMES	TRICKERS
TRIBOLOGY	TRICHIASES	TRICHOMIC	TRICKERY
TRIBOMETER	TRICHIASIS	TRICHOMONA	TRICKIE
TRIBOMETERS	TRICHINA	TRICHOMONACIDAL	TRICKIER
TRIBRACH	TRICHINAE	TRICHOMONACIDE	TRICKIEST
TRIBRACHIAL	TRICHINAL	TRICHOMONACIDES	TRICKILY
TRIBRACHIC	TRICHINAS	TRICHOMONAD	TRICKINESS
TRIBRACHS	TRICHINELLA	TRICHOMONADAL	TRICKINESSES
TRIBROMOETHANE	TRICHINELLAE	TRICHOMONADS	TRICKING
TRIBROMOETHANOL	TRICHINELLAS	TRICHOMONAL	TRICKINGS

TRICKISH
TRICKISHLY
TRICKISHNESS
TRICKISHNESSES
TRICKLE
TRICKLED
TRICKLES
TRICKLESS
TRICKLET
TRICKLETS
TRICKLIER
TRICKLIEST
TRICKLING
TRICKLINGLY
TRICKLINGS
TRICKLY
TRICKS
TRICKSIER
TRICKSIEST
TRICKSINESS
TRICKSINESSES
TRICKSOME
TRICKSTER
TRICKSTERING
TRICKSTERINGS
TRICKSTERS
TRICKSY
TRICKTRACK
TRICKY
TRICLAD
TRICLADS
TRICLINIA
TRICLINIC
TRICLINIUM
TRICOLETTE
TRICOLETTES
TRICOLOR
TRICOLORED
TRICOLORS
TRICOLOUR
TRICOLOURED
TRICOLOURS
TRICONSONANTAL
TRICONSONANTIC
TRICORN
TRICORNE
TRICORNERED
TRICORNES
TRICORNS
TRICORPORATE
TRICORPORATED
TRICOSTATE
TRICOT
TRICOTEUSE
TRICOTEUSES
TRICOTINE
TRICOTINES

TRICOTS
TRICROTIC
TRICROTISM
TRICROTISMS
TRICROTOUS
TRICTRAC
TRICTRACS
TRICUSPID
TRICUSPIDAL
TRICUSPIDATE
TRICUSPIDS
TRICYCLE
TRICYCLED
TRICYCLER
TRICYCLERS
TRICYCLES
TRICYCLIC
TRICYCLICS
TRICYCLING
TRICYCLINGS
TRICYCLIST
TRICYCLISTS
TRIDACNA
TRIDACNAS
TRIDACTYL
TRIDACTYLOUS
TRIDARN
TRIDARNS
TRIDE
TRIDENT
TRIDENTAL
TRIDENTATE
TRIDENTED
TRIDENTS
TRIDIMENSIONAL
TRIDOMINIUM
TRIDUAN
TRIDUUM
TRIDUUMS
TRIDYMITE
TRIDYMITES
TRIE
TRIECIOUS
TRIED
TRIELLA
TRIELLAS
TRIENE
TRIENES
TRIENNIA
TRIENNIAL
TRIENNIALLY
TRIENNIALS
TRIENNIUM
TRIENNIUMS
TRIENS
TRIENTES
TRIER

TRIERARCH
TRIERARCHAL
TRIERARCHIES
TRIERARCHS
TRIERARCHY
TRIERS
TRIES
TRIETERIC
TRIETHYL
TRIETHYLAMINE
TRIETHYLAMINES
TRIFACIAL
TRIFARIOUS
TRIFECTA
TRIFECTAS
TRIFF
TRIFFER
TRIFFEST
TRIFFIC
TRIFFID
TRIFFIDS
TRIFFIDY
TRIFID
TRIFLE
TRIFLED
TRIFLER
TRIFLERS
TRIFLES
TRIFLING
TRIFLINGLY
TRIFLINGNESS
TRIFLINGNESSES
TRIFLINGS
TRIFLUOPERAZINE
TRIFLURALIN
TRIFLURALINS
TRIFOCAL
TRIFOCALS
TRIFOLD
TRIFOLIATE
TRIFOLIATED
TRIFOLIES
TRIFOLIOLATE
TRIFOLIUM
TRIFOLIUMS
TRIFOLY
TRIFORIA
TRIFORIAL
TRIFORIUM
TRIFORM
TRIFORMED
TRIFURCATE
TRIFURCATED
TRIFURCATES
TRIFURCATING
TRIFURCATION
TRIFURCATIONS

TRIG
TRIGAMIES
TRIGAMIST
TRIGAMISTS
TRIGAMOUS
TRIGAMY
TRIGEMINAL
TRIGEMINALS
TRIGGED
TRIGGER
TRIGGERED
TRIGGERFISH
TRIGGERFISHES
TRIGGERING
TRIGGERLESS
TRIGGERMAN
TRIGGERMEN
TRIGGERS
TRIGGEST
TRIGGING
TRIGLOT
TRIGLOTS
TRIGLY
TRIGLYCERIDE
TRIGLYCERIDES
TRIGLYPH
TRIGLYPHIC
TRIGLYPHICAL
TRIGLYPHS
TRIGNESS
TRIGNESSES
TRIGO
TRIGON
TRIGONAL
TRIGONALLY
TRIGONIC
TRIGONOMETER
TRIGONOMETERS
TRIGONOMETRIC
TRIGONOMETRICAL
TRIGONOMETRIES
TRIGONOMETRY
TRIGONOUS
TRIGONS
TRIGOS
TRIGRAM
TRIGRAMMATIC
TRIGRAMMIC
TRIGRAMS
TRIGRAPH
TRIGRAPHIC
TRIGRAPHS
TRIGS
TRIGYNIAN
TRIGYNOUS
TRIHALOMETHANE
TRIHALOMETHANES

TRIHEDRA
TRIHEDRAL
TRIHEDRALS
TRIHEDRON
TRIHEDRONS
TRIHYBRID
TRIHYBRIDS
TRIHYDRATE
TRIHYDRATED
TRIHYDRATES
TRIHYDRATING
TRIHYDRIC
TRIHYDROXY
TRIIODOMETHANE
TRIJET
TRIJETS
TRIKE
TRIKES
TRILATERAL
TRILATERALISM
TRILATERALISMS
TRILATERALIST
TRILATERALISTS
TRILATERALLY
TRILATERALS
TRILATERATION
TRILATERATIONS
TRILBIES
TRILBY
TRILBYS
TRILD
TRILEMMA
TRILEMMAS
TRILINEAR
TRILINEATE
TRILINGUAL
TRILINGUALISM
TRILINGUALISMS
TRILINGUALLY
TRILITERAL
TRILITERALISM
TRILITERALISMS
TRILITERALS
TRILITH
TRILITHIC
TRILITHON
TRILITHONS
TRILITHS
TRILL
TRILLED
TRILLER
TRILLERS
TRILLING
TRILLINGS
TRILLION
TRILLIONAIRE
TRILLIONS

TRILLIONTH
TRILLIONTHS
TRILLIUM
TRILLIUMS
TRILLO
TRILLOES
TRILLS
TRILOBAL
TRILOBATE
TRILOBATED
TRILOBE
TRILOBED
TRILOBES
TRILOBITE
TRILOBITES
TRILOBITIC
TRILOCULAR
TRILOGIES
TRILOGY
TRIM
TRIMARAN
TRIMARANS
TRIMER
TRIMERIC
TRIMEROUS
TRIMERS
TRIMESTER
TRIMESTERS
TRIMESTRAL
TRIMESTRALLY
TRIMESTRIAL
TRIMETER
TRIMETERS
TRIMETHADIONE
TRIMETHOPRIM
TRIMETHOPRIMS
TRIMETHYL
TRIMETHYLAMINE
TRIMETHYLAMINES
TRIMETHYLENE
TRIMETHYLENES
TRIMETRIC
TRIMETRICAL
TRIMETROGON
TRIMETROGONS
TRIMLY
TRIMMED
TRIMMER
TRIMMERS
TRIMMEST
TRIMMING
TRIMMINGLY
TRIMMINGS
TRIMNESS
TRIMNESSES
TRIMOLECULAR
TRIMONOECIOUS

TRIMONTHLY
TRIMORPH
TRIMORPHIC
TRIMORPHISM
TRIMORPHISMS
TRIMORPHOUS
TRIMORPHS
TRIMOTOR
TRIMOTORS
TRIMS
TRIMTAB
TRIMTABS
TRIN
TRINACRIAN
TRINACRIFORM
TRINAL
TRINARY
TRINDLE
TRINDLED
TRINDLES
TRINDLING
TRINE
TRINED
TRINES
TRINGLE
TRINGLES
TRINING
TRINISCOPE
TRINISCOPES
TRINITARIAN
TRINITIES
TRINITRATE
TRINITRATES
TRINITRIN
TRINITRINS
TRINITROBENZENE
TRINITROCRESOL
TRINITROPHENOL
TRINITROPHENOLS
TRINITROTOLUENE
TRINITROTOLUOL
TRINITROTOLUOLS
TRINITY
TRINKET
TRINKETED
TRINKETER
TRINKETERS
TRINKETING
TRINKETINGS
TRINKETRIES
TRINKETRY
TRINKETS
TRINKUM
TRINKUMS
TRINOCULAR
TRINODAL
TRINOMIAL

TRINOMIALISM
TRINOMIALISMS
TRINOMIALIST
TRINOMIALISTS
TRINOMIALLY
TRINOMIALS
TRINS
TRINUCLEOTIDE
TRINUCLEOTIDES
TRIO
TRIODE
TRIODES
TRIOECIOUS
TRIOL
TRIOLEIN
TRIOLET
TRIOLETS
TRIOLS
TRIONES
TRIONYM
TRIONYMAL
TRIONYMS
TRIOR
TRIORS
TRIOS
TRIOSE
TRIOSES
TRIOXID
TRIOXIDE
TRIOXIDES
TRIOXIDS
TRIOXYGEN
TRIP
TRIPACK
TRIPACKS
TRIPALMITIN
TRIPART
TRIPARTISM
TRIPARTISMS
TRIPARTITE
TRIPARTITELY
TRIPARTITION
TRIPARTITIONS
TRIPE
TRIPEDAL
TRIPEHOUND
TRIPEHOUNDS
TRIPERIES
TRIPERSONAL
TRIPERSONALISM
TRIPERSONALISMS
TRIPERSONALIST
TRIPERSONALISTS
TRIPERSONALITY
TRIPERY
TRIPES
TRIPETALOUS

TRIPEY	TRIPODAL	TRIQUETRAL	TRISTESSES
TRIPHAMMER	TRIPODIC	TRIQUETRAS	TRISTEZA
TRIPHAMMERS	TRIPODIES	TRIQUETROUS	TRISTEZAS
TRIPHASE	TRIPODS	TRIQUETROUSLY	TRISTFUL
TRIPHENYLAMINE	TRIPODY	TRIQUETRUM	TRISTFULLY
TRIPHENYLAMINES	TRIPOLI	TRIRADIAL	TRISTFULNESS
TRIPHIBIOUS	TRIPOLIS	TRIRADIATE	TRISTFULNESSES
TRIPHONE	TRIPOS	TRIRADIATELY	TRISTICH
TRIPHONES	TRIPOSES	TRIRADIATION	TRISTICHIC
TRIPHOSPHATE	TRIPPANT	TRIREME	TRISTICHOUS
TRIPHOSPHATES	TRIPPED	TRIREMES	TRISTICHS
TRIPHTHONG	TRIPPER	TRISACCHARIDE	TRISTIMULUS
TRIPHTHONGAL	TRIPPERISH	TRISACCHARIDES	TRISUBSTITUTED
TRIPHTHONGS	TRIPPERS	TRISAGION	TRISUL
TRIPHYLITE	TRIPPERY	TRISAGIONS	TRISULA
TRIPHYLLOUS	TRIPPET	TRISCELE	TRISULAS
TRIPIER	TRIPPETS	TRISCELES	TRISULCATE
TRIPIEST	TRIPPIER	TRISECT	TRISULFIDE
TRIPINNATE	TRIPPIEST	TRISECTED	TRISULFIDES
TRIPINNATELY	TRIPPING	TRISECTING	TRISULPHIDE
TRIPITAKA	TRIPPINGLY	TRISECTION	TRISULPHIDES
TRIPITAKAS	TRIPPINGS	TRISECTIONS	TRISULS
TRIPLANE	TRIPPLE	TRISECTOR	TRISYLLABIC
TRIPLANES	TRIPPLED	TRISECTORS	TRISYLLABICAL
TRIPLE	TRIPPLER	TRISECTRICES	TRISYLLABICALLY
TRIPLED	TRIPPLERS	TRISECTRIX	TRISYLLABLE
TRIPLENESS	TRIPPLES	TRISECTS	TRISYLLABLES
TRIPLENESSES	TRIPPLING	TRISEME	TRITAGONIST
TRIPLES	TRIPPY	TRISEMES	TRITAGONISTS
TRIPLET	TRIPS	TRISEMIC	TRITANOPIA
TRIPLETAIL	TRIPSES	TRISERIAL	TRITANOPIAS
TRIPLETAILS	TRIPSIS	TRISHAW	TRITANOPIC
TRIPLETS	TRIPTANE	TRISHAWS	TRITE
TRIPLEX	TRIPTANES	TRISKELE	TRITELY
TRIPLEXES	TRIPTEROUS	TRISKELES	TRITENESS
TRIPLICATE	TRIPTOTE	TRISKELIA	TRITENESSES
TRIPLICATED	TRIPTOTES	TRISKELION	TRITER
TRIPLICATES	TRIPTYCA	TRISKELIONS	TRITERNATE
TRIPLICATING	TRIPTYCAS	TRISMIC	TRITES
TRIPLICATION	TRIPTYCH	TRISMUS	TRITEST
TRIPLICATIONS	TRIPTYCHS	TRISMUSES	TRITHEISM
TRIPLICITIES	TRIPTYQUE	TRISOCTAHEDRA	TRITHEISMS
TRIPLICITY	TRIPTYQUES	TRISOCTAHEDRAL	TRITHEIST
TRIPLIED	TRIPUDIA	TRISOCTAHEDRON	TRITHEISTIC
TRIPLIES	TRIPUDIARY	TRISOCTAHEDRONS	TRITHEISTICAL
TRIPLING	TRIPUDIATE	TRISOME	TRITHEISTS
TRIPLINGS	TRIPUDIATED	TRISOMES	TRITHING
TRIPLITE	TRIPUDIATES	TRISOMIC	TRITHINGS
TRIPLITES	TRIPUDIATING	TRISOMICS	TRITHIONATE
TRIPLOBLASTIC	TRIPUDIATION	TRISOMIES	TRITHIONATES
TRIPLOID	TRIPUDIATIONS	TRISOMY	TRITHIONIC
TRIPLOIDIES	TRIPUDIUM	TRIST	TRITIATE
TRIPLOIDS	TRIPUDIUMS	TRISTATE	TRITIATED
TRIPLOIDY	TRIPWIRE	TRISTE	TRITIATES
TRIPLY	TRIPWIRES	TRISTEARIN	TRITIATING
TRIPLYING	TRIPY	TRISTEARINS	TRITIATION
TRIPOD	TRIQUETRA	TRISTESSE	TRITIATIONS

TRITICAL
TRITICALE
TRITICALES
TRITICALLY
TRITICALNESS
TRITICALNESSES
TRITICEOUS
TRITICISM
TRITICISMS
TRITICUM
TRITICUMS
TRITIDE
TRITIDES
TRITIUM
TRITIUMS
TRITOMA
TRITOMAS
TRITON
TRITONE
TRITONES
TRITONIA
TRITONIAS
TRITONS
TRITUBERCULAR
TRITUBERCULATE
TRITUBERCULIES
TRITUBERCULISM
TRITUBERCULISMS
TRITUBERCULY
TRITURABLE
TRITURATE
TRITURATED
TRITURATES
TRITURATING
TRITURATION
TRITURATIONS
TRITURATOR
TRITURATORS
TRIUMPH
TRIUMPHAL
TRIUMPHALISM
TRIUMPHALISMS
TRIUMPHALIST
TRIUMPHALISTS
TRIUMPHALS
TRIUMPHANT
TRIUMPHANTLY
TRIUMPHED
TRIUMPHER
TRIUMPHERIES
TRIUMPHERS
TRIUMPHERY
TRIUMPHING
TRIUMPHINGS
TRIUMPHS
TRIUMVIR
TRIUMVIRAL

TRIUMVIRATE
TRIUMVIRATES
TRIUMVIRI
TRIUMVIRIES
TRIUMVIRS
TRIUMVIRY
TRIUNE
TRIUNES
TRIUNITIES
TRIUNITY
TRIVALENCE
TRIVALENCES
TRIVALENCIES
TRIVALENCY
TRIVALENT
TRIVALVE
TRIVALVED
TRIVALVES
TRIVALVULAR
TRIVET
TRIVETS
TRIVIA
TRIVIAL
TRIVIALISATION
TRIVIALISATIONS
TRIVIALISE
TRIVIALISED
TRIVIALISES
TRIVIALISING
TRIVIALISM
TRIVIALISMS
TRIVIALIST
TRIVIALISTS
TRIVIALITIES
TRIVIALITY
TRIVIALIZATION
TRIVIALIZATIONS
TRIVIALIZE
TRIVIALIZED
TRIVIALIZES
TRIVIALIZING
TRIVIALLY
TRIVIALNESS
TRIVIALNESSES
TRIVIUM
TRIVIUMS
TRIWEEKLIES
TRIWEEKLY
TRIZONAL
TRIZONE
TRIZONES
TROAD
TROADE
TROADES
TROADS
TROAK
TROAKED

TROAKING
TROAKS
TROAT
TROATED
TROATING
TROATS
TROCAR
TROCARS
TROCHAIC
TROCHAICALLY
TROCHAICS
TROCHAL
TROCHANTER
TROCHANTERAL
TROCHANTERIC
TROCHANTERS
TROCHAR
TROCHARS
TROCHE
TROCHEAMETER
TROCHEAMETERS
TROCHEE
TROCHEES
TROCHELMINTH
TROCHELMINTHS
TROCHES
TROCHI
TROCHIL
TROCHILI
TROCHILIC
TROCHILS
TROCHILUS
TROCHILUSES
TROCHISCUS
TROCHISCUSES
TROCHISK
TROCHISKS
TROCHITE
TROCHITES
TROCHLEA
TROCHLEAE
TROCHLEAR
TROCHLEARS
TROCHLEAS
TROCHOID
TROCHOIDAL
TROCHOIDALLY
TROCHOIDS
TROCHOMETER
TROCHOMETERS
TROCHOPHORE
TROCHOPHORES
TROCHOSPHERE
TROCHOSPHERES
TROCHOTRON
TROCHOTRONS
TROCHUS

TROCHUSES
TROCK
TROCKED
TROCKEN
TROCKING
TROCKS
TROCTOLITE
TROCTOLITES
TROD
TRODDEN
TRODE
TRODES
TRODS
TROELIE
TROELIES
TROELY
TROFFER
TROFFERS
TROG
TROGGED
TROGGING
TROGGS
TROGLODYTE
TROGLODYTES
TROGLODYTIC
TROGLODYTICAL
TROGLODYTISM
TROGLODYTISMS
TROGON
TROGONS
TROGS
TROIKA
TROIKAS
TROILISM
TROILISMS
TROILIST
TROILISTS
TROILITE
TROILITES
TROILUS
TROILUSES
TROIS
TROKE
TROKED
TROKES
TROKING
TROLAND
TROLANDS
TROLL
TROLLED
TROLLER
TROLLERS
TROLLEY
TROLLEYBUS
TROLLEYBUSES
TROLLEYBUSSES
TROLLEYED

TROLLEYING	TROOPIALS	TROPICALIZATION	TROTLINE
TROLLEYS	TROOPING	TROPICALIZE	TROTLINES
TROLLIED	TROOPS	TROPICALIZED	TROTS
TROLLIES	TROOPSHIP	TROPICALIZES	TROTTED
TROLLING	TROOPSHIPS	TROPICALIZING	TROTTER
TROLLINGS	TROOSTITE	TROPICALLY	TROTTERS
TROLLIUS	TROOZ	TROPICBIRD	TROTTING
TROLLIUSES	TROP	TROPICBIRDS	TROTTINGS
TROLLOP	TROPAEOLA	TROPICS	TROTTOIR
TROLLOPED	TROPAEOLIN	TROPIN	TROTTOIRS
TROLLOPEE	TROPAEOLINS	TROPINE	TROTYL
TROLLOPEES	TROPAEOLUM	TROPINES	TROTYLS
TROLLOPING	TROPAEOLUMS	TROPING	TROUBADOUR
TROLLOPISH	TROPARIA	TROPINS	TROUBADOURS
TROLLOPS	TROPARION	TROPISM	TROUBLE
TROLLOPY	TROPE	TROPISMATIC	TROUBLED
TROLLS	TROPED	TROPISMS	TROUBLEDLY
TROLLY	TROPES	TROPIST	TROUBLEFREE
TROLLYING	TROPHALLACTIC	TROPISTIC	TROUBLEMAKER
TROMBICULID	TROPHALLAXES	TROPISTS	TROUBLEMAKERS
TROMBICULIDS	TROPHALLAXIS	TROPOCOLLAGEN	TROUBLEMAKING
TROMBIDIASIS	TROPHESIAL	TROPOCOLLAGENS	TROUBLEMAKINGS
TROMBONE	TROPHESIES	TROPOLOGIC	TROUBLER
TROMBONES	TROPHESY	TROPOLOGICAL	TROUBLERS
TROMBONIST	TROPHI	TROPOLOGICALLY	TROUBLES
TROMBONISTS	TROPHIC	TROPOLOGIES	TROUBLESHOOT
TROMINO	TROPHICALLY	TROPOLOGY	TROUBLESHOOTER
TROMINOES	TROPHIED	TROPOMYOSIN	TROUBLESHOOTERS
TROMINOS	TROPHIES	TROPOMYOSINS	TROUBLESHOOTING
TROMMEL	TROPHOBIOSES	TROPONIN	TROUBLESHOOTS
TROMMELS	TROPHOBIOSIS	TROPONINS	TROUBLESHOT
TROMOMETER	TROPHOBIOTIC	TROPOPAUSE	TROUBLESOME
TROMOMETERS	TROPHOBLAST	TROPOPAUSES	TROUBLESOMELY
TROMOMETRIC	TROPHOBLASTIC	TROPOPHILOUS	TROUBLESOMENESS
TROMP	TROPHOBLASTS	TROPOPHYTE	TROUBLING
TROMPE	TROPHOLOGIES	TROPOPHYTES	TROUBLINGS
TROMPED	TROPHOLOGY	TROPOPHYTIC	TROUBLOUS
TROMPES	TROPHONEUROSES	TROPOSCATTER	TROUBLOUSLY
TROMPING	TROPHONEUROSIS	TROPOSCATTERS	TROUBLOUSNESS
TROMPS	TROPHOPLASM	TROPOSPHERE	TROUBLOUSNESSES
TRON	TROPHOPLASMS	TROPOSPHERES	TROUCH
TRONA	TROPHOTAXIS	TROPOSPHERIC	TROUGH
TRONAS	TROPHOTROPIC	TROPOTAXES	TROUGHLIKE
TRONC	TROPHOTROPISM	TROPOTAXIS	TROUGHS
TRONCS	TROPHOTROPISMS	TROPPO	TROULE
TRONE	TROPHOZOITE	TROSSERS	TROULED
TRONES	TROPHOZOITES	TROT	TROULES
TRONK	TROPHY	TROTH	TROULING
TRONKS	TROPHYING	TROTHED	TROUNCE
TRONS	TROPIC	TROTHFUL	TROUNCED
TROOLIE	TROPICAL	TROTHING	TROUNCER
TROOLIES	TROPICALISATION	TROTHLESS	TROUNCERS
TROOP	TROPICALISE	TROTHPLIGHT	TROUNCES
TROOPED	TROPICALISED	TROTHPLIGHTED	TROUNCING
TROOPER	TROPICALISES	TROTHPLIGHTING	TROUNCINGS
TROOPERS	TROPICALISING	TROTHPLIGHTS	TROUPE
TROOPIAL	TROPICALITY	TROTHS	TROUPED

TROUPER
TROUPERS
TROUPES
TROUPIAL
TROUPIALS
TROUPING
TROUSE
TROUSER
TROUSERED
TROUSERING
TROUSERINGS
TROUSERLESS
TROUSERS
TROUSES
TROUSSEAU
TROUSSEAUS
TROUSSEAUX
TROUT
TROUTER
TROUTERS
TROUTFUL
TROUTIER
TROUTIEST
TROUTING
TROUTINGS
TROUTLESS
TROUTLET
TROUTLETS
TROUTLING
TROUTLINGS
TROUTS
TROUTSTONE
TROUTSTONES
TROUTY
TROUVAILLE
TROUVAILLES
TROUVERE
TROUVERES
TROUVEUR
TROUVEURS
TROVE
TROVER
TROVERS
TROVES
TROW
TROWED
TROWEL
TROWELED
TROWELER
TROWELERS
TROWELING
TROWELLED
TROWELLER
TROWELLERS
TROWELLING
TROWELS
TROWING

TROWS
TROWSERS
TROWTH
TROWTHS
TROY
TROYS
TRUANCIES
TRUANCY
TRUANT
TRUANTED
TRUANTING
TRUANTRIES
TRUANTRY
TRUANTS
TRUANTSHIP
TRUANTSHIPS
TRUCAGE
TRUCAGES
TRUCE
TRUCED
TRUCELESS
TRUCES
TRUCHMAN
TRUCHMANS
TRUCHMEN
TRUCIAL
TRUCING
TRUCK
TRUCKAGE
TRUCKAGES
TRUCKED
TRUCKER
TRUCKERS
TRUCKFUL
TRUCKFULS
TRUCKIE
TRUCKIES
TRUCKING
TRUCKINGS
TRUCKLE
TRUCKLED
TRUCKLER
TRUCKLERS
TRUCKLES
TRUCKLINE
TRUCKLINES
TRUCKLING
TRUCKLINGS
TRUCKLOAD
TRUCKLOADS
TRUCKMAN
TRUCKMASTER
TRUCKMASTERS
TRUCKMEN
TRUCKS
TRUCULENCE
TRUCULENCES

TRUCULENCIES
TRUCULENCY
TRUCULENT
TRUCULENTLY
TRUDGE
TRUDGED
TRUDGEN
TRUDGENS
TRUDGEON
TRUDGEONS
TRUDGER
TRUDGERS
TRUDGES
TRUDGING
TRUDGINGS
TRUE
TRUEBLUE
TRUEBLUES
TRUEBORN
TRUEBRED
TRUED
TRUEHEARTED
TRUEHEARTEDNESS
TRUEING
TRUELOVE
TRUELOVES
TRUEMAN
TRUEMEN
TRUENESS
TRUENESSES
TRUEPENNIES
TRUEPENNY
TRUER
TRUES
TRUEST
TRUFFE
TRUFFES
TRUFFLE
TRUFFLED
TRUFFLES
TRUFFLING
TRUFFLINGS
TRUG
TRUGO
TRUGS
TRUING
TRUISM
TRUISMS
TRUISTIC
TRULL
TRULLS
TRULY
TRUMEAU
TRUMEAUX
TRUMP
TRUMPED
TRUMPERIES

TRUMPERY
TRUMPET
TRUMPETED
TRUMPETER
TRUMPETERS
TRUMPETING
TRUMPETINGS
TRUMPETLIKE
TRUMPETS
TRUMPETWEED
TRUMPETWEEDS
TRUMPING
TRUMPINGS
TRUMPLESS
TRUMPLESSNESS
TRUMPS
TRUNCAL
TRUNCATE
TRUNCATED
TRUNCATELY
TRUNCATES
TRUNCATING
TRUNCATION
TRUNCATIONS
TRUNCHEON
TRUNCHEONED
TRUNCHEONER
TRUNCHEONERS
TRUNCHEONING
TRUNCHEONS
TRUNDLE
TRUNDLED
TRUNDLER
TRUNDLERS
TRUNDLES
TRUNDLING
TRUNK
TRUNKED
TRUNKFISH
TRUNKFISHES
TRUNKFUL
TRUNKFULS
TRUNKING
TRUNKINGS
TRUNKLESS
TRUNKLESSNESS
TRUNKS
TRUNKSLEEVE
TRUNKSLEEVES
TRUNNEL
TRUNNELS
TRUNNION
TRUNNIONED
TRUNNIONS
TRUQUAGE
TRUQUAGES
TRUQUEUR

TRUQUEURS	TRUTHLESS	TSADDIKIM	TSKTSKS
TRUSS	TRUTHLESSNESS	TSADDIKS	TSOORIS
TRUSSED	TRUTHLESSNESSES	TSADDIQ	TSORES
TRUSSER	TRUTHLIKE	TSADDIQIM	TSORIS
TRUSSERS	TRUTHS	TSADDIQS	TSORRISS
TRUSSES	TRUTHY	TSADE	TSOTSI
TRUSSING	TRY	TSADES	TSOTSIS
TRUSSINGS	TRYE	TSADI	TSOTSITAAL
TRUST	TRYER	TSADIS	TSOURIS
TRUSTABILITIES	TRYERS	TSAMBA	TSOURISES
TRUSTABILITY	TRYING	TSAMBAS	TSUBA
TRUSTABLE	TRYINGLY	TSANTSA	TSUBAS
TRUSTAFARIAN	TRYINGNESS	TSAR	TSUNAMI
TRUSTBUSTER	TRYINGS	TSARDOM	TSUNAMIC
TRUSTBUSTERS	TRYMA	TSARDOMS	TSUNAMIS
TRUSTBUSTING	TRYMATA	TSAREVICH	TSURIS
TRUSTED	TRYOUT	TSAREVICHES	TSURISES
TRUSTEE	TRYOUTS	TSAREVITCH	TSUTSUGAMUSHI
TRUSTEED	TRYP	TSAREVITCHES	TSUTSUGAMUSHIS
TRUSTEEING	TRYPAFLAVINE	TSAREVNA	TSUTSUMU
TRUSTEES	TRYPAFLAVINES	TSAREVNAS	TSUTSUMUS
TRUSTEESHIP	TRYPAN	TSARINA	TUAN
TRUSTEESHIPS	TRYPANOCIDAL	TSARINAS	TUANS
TRUSTER	TRYPANOCIDE	TSARISM	TUART
TRUSTERS	TRYPANOCIDES	TSARISMS	TUARTS
TRUSTFUL	TRYPANOSOMAL	TSARIST	TUATARA
TRUSTFULLY	TRYPANOSOME	TSARISTS	TUATARAS
TRUSTFULNESS	TRYPANOSOMES	TSARITSA	TUATERA
TRUSTFULNESSES	TRYPANOSOMIASES	TSARITSAS	TUATERAS
TRUSTIER	TRYPANOSOMIASIS	TSARITZA	TUATH
TRUSTIES	TRYPANOSOMIC	TSARITZAS	TUATHS
TRUSTIEST	TRYPARSAMIDE	TSARS	TUATUA
TRUSTILY	TRYPARSAMIDES	TSCHERNOSEM	TUB
TRUSTINESS	TRYPS	TSCHERNOSEMS	TUBA
TRUSTINESSES	TRYPSIN	TSESAREVICH	TUBAE
TRUSTING	TRYPSINOGEN	TSESAREVICHES	TUBAGE
TRUSTINGLY	TRYPSINOGENS	TSESAREVITCH	TUBAGES
TRUSTINGNESS	TRYPSINS	TSESAREVITCHES	TUBAIST
TRUSTINGNESSES	TRYPTAMINE	TSESAREVNA	TUBAISTS
TRUSTLESS	TRYPTAMINES	TSESAREVNAS	TUBAL
TRUSTLESSLY	TRYPTIC	TSESAREWICHES	TUBAR
TRUSTLESSNESS	TRYPTOPHAN	TSESAREWITCHES	TUBAS
TRUSTLESSNESSES	TRYPTOPHANE	TSESSEBE	TUBATE
TRUSTOR	TRYPTOPHANES	TSESSEBES	TUBBABLE
TRUSTORS	TRYPTOPHANS	TSETSE	TUBBED
TRUSTS	TRYSAIL	TSETSES	TUBBER
TRUSTWORTHILY	TRYSAILS	TSIGANE	TUBBERS
TRUSTWORTHINESS	TRYST	TSIGANES	TUBBIER
TRUSTWORTHY	TRYSTE	TSIMMES	TUBBIEST
TRUSTY	TRYSTED	TSITSITH	TUBBINESS
TRUTH	TRYSTER	TSK	TUBBINESSES
TRUTHFUL	TRYSTERS	TSKED	TUBBING
TRUTHFULLY	TRYSTES	TSKING	TUBBINGS
TRUTHFULNESS	TRYSTING	TSKS	TUBBISH
TRUTHFULNESSES	TRYSTS	TSKTSK	TUBBY
TRUTHIER	TRYWORKS	TSKTSKED	TUBE
TRUTHIEST	TSADDIK	TSKTSKING	TUBECTOMIES

TUBECTOMY
TUBED
TUBEFUL
TUBEFULS
TUBELESS
TUBELIKE
TUBENOSE
TUBENOSES
TUBER
TUBERACEOUS
TUBERCLE
TUBERCLED
TUBERCLES
TUBERCULA
TUBERCULAR
TUBERCULARLY
TUBERCULARS
TUBERCULATE
TUBERCULATED
TUBERCULATELY
TUBERCULATION
TUBERCULATIONS
TUBERCULE
TUBERCULES
TUBERCULIN
TUBERCULINS
TUBERCULISATION
TUBERCULISE
TUBERCULISED
TUBERCULISES
TUBERCULISING
TUBERCULIZATION
TUBERCULIZE
TUBERCULIZED
TUBERCULIZES
TUBERCULIZING
TUBERCULOID
TUBERCULOMA
TUBERCULOMAS
TUBERCULOMATA
TUBERCULOSE
TUBERCULOSED
TUBERCULOSES
TUBERCULOSIS
TUBERCULOUS
TUBERCULOUSLY
TUBERCULUM
TUBERIFEROUS
TUBERIFORM
TUBEROID
TUBEROSE
TUBEROSES
TUBEROSITIES
TUBEROSITY
TUBEROUS
TUBERS
TUBES

TUBEWORK
TUBEWORKS
TUBFAST
TUBFASTS
TUBFISH
TUBFISHES
TUBFUL
TUBFULS
TUBICOLAR
TUBICOLE
TUBICOLES
TUBICOLOUS
TUBIFEX
TUBIFEXES
TUBIFICID
TUBIFICIDS
TUBIFLOROUS
TUBIFORM
TUBING
TUBINGS
TUBIST
TUBISTS
TUBLIKE
TUBOCURARINE
TUBOCURARINES
TUBOPLASTIES
TUBOPLASTY
TUBS
TUBULAR
TUBULARIAN
TUBULARIANS
TUBULARITIES
TUBULARITY
TUBULARLY
TUBULATE
TUBULATED
TUBULATES
TUBULATING
TUBULATION
TUBULATIONS
TUBULATOR
TUBULATORS
TUBULATURE
TUBULATURES
TUBULE
TUBULES
TUBULIFLORAL
TUBULIFLOROUS
TUBULIN
TUBULINS
TUBULOSE
TUBULOUS
TUBULOUSLY
TUBULURE
TUBULURES
TUCHUN
TUCHUNS

TUCK
TUCKAHOE
TUCKAHOES
TUCKED
TUCKER
TUCKERBAG
TUCKERBAGS
TUCKERBOX
TUCKERBOXES
TUCKERED
TUCKERING
TUCKERS
TUCKET
TUCKETS
TUCKING
TUCKS
TUCKSHOP
TUCKSHOPS
TUCOTUCO
TUCOTUCOS
TUCUTUCO
TUCUTUCOS
TUCUTUCU
TUCUTUCUS
TUFA
TUFACEOUS
TUFAS
TUFF
TUFFACEOUS
TUFFE
TUFFES
TUFFET
TUFFETS
TUFFS
TUFFTAFFETAS
TUFFTAFFETIES
TUFOLI
TUFT
TUFTAFFETA
TUFTAFFETAS
TUFTAFFETIES
TUFTAFFETY
TUFTED
TUFTER
TUFTERS
TUFTIER
TUFTIEST
TUFTILY
TUFTING
TUFTINGS
TUFTS
TUFTY
TUG
TUGBOAT
TUGBOATS
TUGGED
TUGGER

TUGGERS
TUGGING
TUGGINGLY
TUGGINGS
TUGHRA
TUGHRAS
TUGHRIK
TUGHRIKS
TUGLESS
TUGRA
TUGRAS
TUGRIK
TUGRIKS
TUGS
TUI
TUILLE
TUILLES
TUILLETTE
TUILLETTES
TUILYIE
TUILYIED
TUILYIEING
TUILYIES
TUILZIE
TUILZIED
TUILZIEING
TUILZIES
TUINA
TUINAS
TUIS
TUISM
TUISMS
TUITION
TUITIONAL
TUITIONARY
TUITIONS
TUKTOO
TUKTOOS
TUKTU
TUKTUS
TULADI
TULADIS
TULARAEMIA
TULARAEMIAS
TULARAEMIC
TULAREMIA
TULAREMIAS
TULAREMIC
TULBAN
TULBANS
TULCHAN
TULCHANS
TULE
TULES
TULIP
TULIPANT
TULIPANTS

TULIPOMANIA
TULIPOMANIAS
TULIPS
TULIPWOOD
TULIPWOODS
TULLE
TULLES
TULLIBEE
TULLIBEES
TULWAR
TULWARS
TUM
TUMATAKURU
TUMATAKURUS
TUMBLE
TUMBLEBUG
TUMBLEBUGS
TUMBLED
TUMBLEDOWN
TUMBLEHOME
TUMBLER
TUMBLERFUL
TUMBLERFULS
TUMBLERS
TUMBLERSFUL
TUMBLES
TUMBLEWEED
TUMBLEWEEDS
TUMBLING
TUMBLINGS
TUMBREL
TUMBRELS
TUMBRIL
TUMBRILS
TUMEFACIENT
TUMEFACTION
TUMEFACTIONS
TUMEFIED
TUMEFIES
TUMEFY
TUMEFYING
TUMESCE
TUMESCED
TUMESCENCE
TUMESCENCES
TUMESCENT
TUMESCES
TUMESCING
TUMID
TUMIDITIES
TUMIDITY
TUMIDLY
TUMIDNESS
TUMIDNESSES
TUMMIES
TUMMLER
TUMMLERS

TUMMY
TUMOR
TUMORAL
TUMORGENIC
TUMORGENICITIES
TUMORGENICITY
TUMORIGENESES
TUMORIGENESIS
TUMORIGENIC
TUMORIGENICITY
TUMORLIKE
TUMOROUS
TUMORS
TUMOUR
TUMOURS
TUMP
TUMPED
TUMPHIES
TUMPHY
TUMPIER
TUMPIEST
TUMPING
TUMPLINE
TUMPLINES
TUMPS
TUMPY
TUMS
TUMSHIE
TUMSHIES
TUMULAR
TUMULARY
TUMULI
TUMULOSE
TUMULOSITY
TUMULOUS
TUMULT
TUMULTED
TUMULTING
TUMULTS
TUMULTUARY
TUMULTUATE
TUMULTUATED
TUMULTUATES
TUMULTUATING
TUMULTUATION
TUMULTUATIONS
TUMULTUOUS
TUMULTUOUSLY
TUMULTUOUSNESS
TUMULUS
TUMULUSES
TUN
TUNA
TUNABILITIES
TUNABILITY
TUNABLE
TUNABLENESS

TUNABLENESSES
TUNABLY
TUNAS
TUNBELLIED
TUNBELLIES
TUNBELLY
TUND
TUNDED
TUNDING
TUNDISH
TUNDISHES
TUNDRA
TUNDRAS
TUNDS
TUNDUN
TUNDUNS
TUNE
TUNEABLE
TUNEABLY
TUNED
TUNEFUL
TUNEFULLY
TUNEFULNESS
TUNEFULNESSES
TUNELESS
TUNELESSLY
TUNELESSNESS
TUNER
TUNERS
TUNES
TUNESMITH
TUNESMITHS
TUNEUP
TUNEUPS
TUNG
TUNGS
TUNGSTATE
TUNGSTATES
TUNGSTEN
TUNGSTENS
TUNGSTIC
TUNGSTITE
TUNGSTOUS
TUNIC
TUNICA
TUNICAE
TUNICAS
TUNICATE
TUNICATED
TUNICATES
TUNICIN
TUNICINS
TUNICKED
TUNICLE
TUNICLES
TUNICS
TUNIER

TUNIEST
TUNING
TUNINGS
TUNNAGE
TUNNAGES
TUNNED
TUNNEL
TUNNELED
TUNNELER
TUNNELERS
TUNNELING
TUNNELLED
TUNNELLER
TUNNELLERS
TUNNELLIKE
TUNNELLING
TUNNELLINGS
TUNNELS
TUNNIES
TUNNING
TUNNINGS
TUNNY
TUNS
TUNY
TUP
TUPEK
TUPEKS
TUPELO
TUPELOS
TUPIK
TUPIKS
TUPPED
TUPPENCE
TUPPENCES
TUPPENNIES
TUPPENNY
TUPPING
TUPS
TUPTOWING
TUPUNA
TUQUE
TUQUES
TURACIN
TURACINS
TURACO
TURACOS
TURACOU
TURACOUS
TURACOVERDIN
TURACOVERDINS
TURANGAWAEWAE
TURBAN
TURBAND
TURBANDS
TURBANED
TURBANNED
TURBANS

TURBANT
TURBANTS
TURBARIES
TURBARY
TURBELLARIAN
TURBELLARIANS
TURBETH
TURBETHS
TURBID
TURBIDIMETER
TURBIDIMETERS
TURBIDIMETRIC
TURBIDIMETRIES
TURBIDIMETRY
TURBIDITE
TURBIDITES
TURBIDITIES
TURBIDITY
TURBIDLY
TURBIDNESS
TURBIDNESSES
TURBINAL
TURBINALS
TURBINATE
TURBINATED
TURBINATES
TURBINATION
TURBINE
TURBINED
TURBINES
TURBIT
TURBITH
TURBITHS
TURBITS
TURBO
TURBOCAR
TURBOCARS
TURBOCHARGED
TURBOCHARGER
TURBOCHARGERS
TURBOCHARGING
TURBOCHARGINGS
TURBOELECTRIC
TURBOFAN
TURBOFANS
TURBOGENERATOR
TURBOGENERATORS
TURBOJET
TURBOJETS
TURBOMACHINERY
TURBOND
TURBONDS
TURBOPROP
TURBOPROPS
TURBOS
TURBOSHAFT
TURBOSHAFTS

TURBOT
TURBOTS
TURBULATOR
TURBULATORS
TURBULENCE
TURBULENCES
TURBULENCIES
TURBULENCY
TURBULENT
TURBULENTLY
TURCOPOLE
TURCOPOLES
TURCOPOLIER
TURCOPOLIERS
TURD
TURDINE
TURDION
TURDIONS
TURDOID
TURDS
TUREEN
TUREENS
TURF
TURFED
TURFEN
TURFIER
TURFIEST
TURFINESS
TURFINESSES
TURFING
TURFINGS
TURFITE
TURFITES
TURFLESS
TURFLIKE
TURFMAN
TURFMEN
TURFS
TURFSKI
TURFSKIING
TURFSKIINGS
TURFSKIS
TURFY
TURGENCIES
TURGENCY
TURGENT
TURGENTLY
TURGESCENCE
TURGESCENCES
TURGESCENCIES
TURGESCENCY
TURGESCENT
TURGID
TURGIDER
TURGIDEST
TURGIDITIES
TURGIDITY

TURGIDLY
TURGIDNESS
TURGIDNESSES
TURGITE
TURGITES
TURGOR
TURGORS
TURION
TURIONS
TURISTA
TURISTAS
TURK
TURKEY
TURKEYS
TURKIES
TURKIESES
TURKIS
TURKISES
TURKOIS
TURKOISES
TURKS
TURLOUGH
TURLOUGHS
TURM
TURME
TURMERIC
TURMERICS
TURMES
TURMOIL
TURMOILED
TURMOILING
TURMOILS
TURMS
TURN
TURNABLE
TURNABOUT
TURNABOUTS
TURNAGAIN
TURNAGAINS
TURNAROUND
TURNAROUNDS
TURNBACK
TURNBACKS
TURNBROACH
TURNBROACHES
TURNBUCKLE
TURNBUCKLES
TURNCOAT
TURNCOATS
TURNCOCK
TURNCOCKS
TURNDOWN
TURNDOWNS
TURNDUN
TURNDUNS
TURNED
TURNER

TURNERIES
TURNERS
TURNERY
TURNHALL
TURNHALLS
TURNING
TURNINGS
TURNIP
TURNIPED
TURNIPING
TURNIPS
TURNKEY
TURNKEYS
TURNOFF
TURNOFFS
TURNOUT
TURNOUTS
TURNOVER
TURNOVERS
TURNPIKE
TURNPIKES
TURNROUND
TURNROUNDS
TURNS
TURNSKIN
TURNSKINS
TURNSOLE
TURNSOLES
TURNSPIT
TURNSPITS
TURNSTILE
TURNSTILES
TURNSTONE
TURNSTONES
TURNTABLE
TURNTABLES
TURNUP
TURNUPS
TURNVEREIN
TURNVEREINS
TUROPHILE
TUROPHILES
TURPENTINE
TURPENTINED
TURPENTINES
TURPENTINING
TURPENTINY
TURPETH
TURPETHS
TURPITUDE
TURPITUDES
TURPS
TURQUOIS
TURQUOISE
TURQUOISES
TURRET
TURRETED

TURRETS	TUSSARS	TUTORISM	TWADDLES
TURRIBANT	TUSSEH	TUTORISMS	TWADDLIER
TURRIBANTS	TUSSEHS	TUTORIZE	TWADDLIEST
TURRICAL	TUSSER	TUTORIZED	TWADDLING
TURRICULATE	TUSSERS	TUTORIZES	TWADDLINGS
TURRICULATED	TUSSIS	TUTORIZING	TWADDLY
TURTLE	TUSSISES	TUTORS	TWAE
TURTLEBACK	TUSSIVE	TUTORSHIP	TWAES
TURTLEBACKS	TUSSLE	TUTORSHIPS	TWAFALD
TURTLED	TUSSLED	TUTOYED	TWAIN
TURTLEDOVE	TUSSLES	TUTOYER	TWAINS
TURTLEDOVES	TUSSLING	TUTOYERED	TWAITE
TURTLEHEAD	TUSSOCK	TUTOYERING	TWAITES
TURTLEHEADS	TUSSOCKS	TUTOYERS	TWAL
TURTLENECK	TUSSOCKY	TUTRESS	TWALPENNIES
TURTLENECKED	TUSSOR	TUTRESSES	TWALPENNY
TURTLENECKS	TUSSORE	TUTRICES	TWALS
TURTLER	TUSSORES	TUTRIX	TWANG
TURTLERS	TUSSORS	TUTRIXES	TWANGED
TURTLES	TUSSUCK	TUTS	TWANGER
TURTLING	TUSSUCKS	TUTSAN	TWANGERS
TURTLINGS	TUSSUR	TUTSANS	TWANGIER
TURVES	TUSSURS	TUTSED	TWANGIEST
TUSCHE	TUT	TUTSES	TWANGING
TUSCHES	TUTANIA	TUTSING	TWANGINGLY
TUSH	TUTANIAS	TUTTED	TWANGINGS
TUSHED	TUTEE	TUTTI	TWANGLE
TUSHERIES	TUTEES	TUTTIES	TWANGLED
TUSHERY	TUTELAGE	TUTTING	TWANGLER
TUSHERYS	TUTELAGES	TUTTINGS	TWANGLERS
TUSHES	TUTELAR	TUTTIS	TWANGLES
TUSHIE	TUTELARIES	TUTTY	TWANGLING
TUSHIES	TUTELARS	TUTU	TWANGLINGLY
TUSHING	TUTELARY	TUTUS	TWANGLINGS
TUSHKAR	TUTENAG	TUTWORK	TWANGS
TUSHKARS	TUTENAGS	TUTWORKER	TWANGY
TUSHKER	TUTIORISM	TUTWORKERS	TWANK
TUSHKERS	TUTIORISMS	TUTWORKMAN	TWANKAY
TUSHY	TUTIORIST	TUTWORKMEN	TWANKAYS
TUSK	TUTIORISTS	TUTWORKS	TWANKIES
TUSKAR	TUTMAN	TUX	TWANKS
TUSKARS	TUTMEN	TUXEDO	TWANKY
TUSKED	TUTOR	TUXEDOED	TWAS
TUSKER	TUTORAGE	TUXEDOES	TWASOME
TUSKERS	TUTORAGES	TUXEDOS	TWASOMES
TUSKIER	TUTORED	TUXES	TWAT
TUSKIEST	TUTORESS	TUYER	TWATS
TUSKING	TUTORESSES	TUYERE	TWATTLE
TUSKINGS	TUTORIAL	TUYERES	TWATTLED
TUSKLESS	TUTORIALLY	TUYERS	TWATTLER
TUSKLIKE	TUTORIALS	TUZZ	TWATTLERS
TUSKS	TUTORING	TUZZES	TWATTLES
TUSKY	TUTORINGS	TWA	TWATTLING
TUSSAH	TUTORISE	TWADDLE	TWATTLINGS
TUSSAHS	TUTORISED	TWADDLED	TWAY
TUSSAL	TUTORISES	TWADDLER	TWAYBLADE
TUSSAR	TUTORISING	TWADDLERS	TWAYBLADES

TWAYS
TWEAK
TWEAKED
TWEAKER
TWEAKERS
TWEAKIER
TWEAKIEST
TWEAKING
TWEAKINGS
TWEAKS
TWEAKY
TWEE
TWEED
TWEEDIER
TWEEDIEST
TWEEDINESS
TWEEDINESSES
TWEEDLE
TWEEDLED
TWEEDLEDEE
TWEEDLEDEED
TWEEDLEDEEING
TWEEDLEDEES
TWEEDLER
TWEEDLERS
TWEEDLES
TWEEDLING
TWEEDS
TWEEDY
TWEEL
TWEELED
TWEELING
TWEELS
TWEELY
TWEEN
TWEENAGER
TWEENAGERS
TWEENESS
TWEENESSES
TWEENIE
TWEENIES
TWEENY
TWEER
TWEERED
TWEERING
TWEERS
TWEEST
TWEET
TWEETED
TWEETER
TWEETERS
TWEETING
TWEETS
TWEEZE
TWEEZED
TWEEZER
TWEEZERS

TWEEZES
TWEEZING
TWELFTH
TWELFTHLY
TWELFTHS
TWELVE
TWELVEFOLD
TWELVEMO
TWELVEMONTH
TWELVEMONTHS
TWELVEMOS
TWELVES
TWENTIES
TWENTIETH
TWENTIETHS
TWENTY
TWENTYFOLD
TWENTYFOLDS
TWENTYISH
TWERP
TWERPS
TWIBIL
TWIBILL
TWIBILLS
TWIBILS
TWICE
TWICER
TWICERS
TWICHILD
TWICHILDREN
TWIDDLE
TWIDDLED
TWIDDLER
TWIDDLERS
TWIDDLES
TWIDDLIER
TWIDDLIEST
TWIDDLING
TWIDDLINGS
TWIDDLY
TWIER
TWIERS
TWIFOLD
TWIFORKED
TWIFORMED
TWIG
TWIGGED
TWIGGEN
TWIGGER
TWIGGERS
TWIGGIER
TWIGGIEST
TWIGGING
TWIGGY
TWIGHT
TWIGHTED
TWIGHTING

TWIGHTS
TWIGLESS
TWIGLIKE
TWIGLOO
TWIGLOOS
TWIGS
TWIGSOME
TWILIGHT
TWILIGHTED
TWILIGHTING
TWILIGHTS
TWILIT
TWILL
TWILLED
TWILLIES
TWILLING
TWILLINGS
TWILLS
TWILLY
TWILT
TWILTED
TWILTING
TWILTS
TWIN
TWINBERRIES
TWINBERRY
TWINBORN
TWINE
TWINED
TWINER
TWINERS
TWINES
TWINFLOWER
TWINFLOWERS
TWINGE
TWINGED
TWINGEING
TWINGES
TWINGING
TWINIER
TWINIEST
TWINIGHT
TWINING
TWININGLY
TWININGS
TWINJET
TWINJETS
TWINK
TWINKED
TWINKING
TWINKLE
TWINKLED
TWINKLER
TWINKLERS
TWINKLES
TWINKLING
TWINKLINGS

TWINKLY
TWINKS
TWINLING
TWINLINGS
TWINNED
TWINNING
TWINNINGS
TWINS
TWINSET
TWINSETS
TWINSHIP
TWINSHIPS
TWINTER
TWINTERS
TWINY
TWIRE
TWIRED
TWIRES
TWIRING
TWIRL
TWIRLED
TWIRLER
TWIRLERS
TWIRLIER
TWIRLIEST
TWIRLING
TWIRLS
TWIRLY
TWIRP
TWIRPS
TWISCAR
TWISCARS
TWIST
TWISTABILITY
TWISTABLE
TWISTED
TWISTER
TWISTERS
TWISTIER
TWISTIEST
TWISTING
TWISTINGS
TWISTOR
TWISTORS
TWISTS
TWISTY
TWIT
TWITCH
TWITCHED
TWITCHER
TWITCHERS
TWITCHES
TWITCHIER
TWITCHIEST
TWITCHILY
TWITCHING
TWITCHINGS

TWITCHY
TWITE
TWITES
TWITS
TWITTED
TWITTEN
TWITTENS
TWITTER
TWITTERED
TWITTERER
TWITTERERS
TWITTERING
TWITTERINGLY
TWITTERINGS
TWITTERS
TWITTERY
TWITTING
TWITTINGLY
TWITTINGS
TWIXT
TWIZZLE
TWIZZLED
TWIZZLES
TWIZZLING
TWO
TWOCCER
TWOCCERS
TWOCCING
TWOCCINGS
TWOCKER
TWOCKERS
TWOCKING
TWOER
TWOERS
TWOFER
TWOFERS
TWOFOLD
TWOFOLDNESS
TWOFOLDNESSES
TWOFOLDS
TWONESS
TWONESSES
TWONIE
TWONIES
TWOPENCE
TWOPENCES
TWOPENCEWORTH
TWOPENCEWORTHS
TWOPENNIES
TWOPENNY
TWOS
TWOSEATER
TWOSEATERS
TWOSOME
TWOSOMES
TWOSTROKE
TWP

TWYER
TWYERE
TWYERES
TWYERS
TWYFOLD
TYCHISM
TYCHISMS
TYCOON
TYCOONATE
TYCOONATES
TYCOONERIES
TYCOONERY
TYCOONS
TYDE
TYE
TYED
TYEE
TYEES
TYEING
TYER
TYERS
TYES
TYG
TYGS
TYING
TYKE
TYKES
TYKISH
TYLECTOMIES
TYLECTOMY
TYLER
TYLERS
TYLOPOD
TYLOPODS
TYLOSES
TYLOSIN
TYLOSINS
TYLOSIS
TYLOTE
TYLOTES
TYMBAL
TYMBALS
TYMP
TYMPAN
TYMPANA
TYMPANAL
TYMPANI
TYMPANIC
TYMPANICS
TYMPANIES
TYMPANIFORM
TYMPANIST
TYMPANISTS
TYMPANITES
TYMPANITESES
TYMPANITIC
TYMPANITIS

TYMPANITISES
TYMPANO
TYMPANS
TYMPANUM
TYMPANUMS
TYMPANY
TYMPS
TYND
TYNDALLIMETRY
TYNDE
TYNE
TYNED
TYNES
TYNING
TYPABLE
TYPAL
TYPE
TYPEABLE
TYPEBAR
TYPEBARS
TYPECASE
TYPECASES
TYPECAST
TYPECASTER
TYPECASTERS
TYPECASTING
TYPECASTS
TYPED
TYPEFACE
TYPEFACES
TYPEFOUNDER
TYPEFOUNDERS
TYPEFOUNDING
TYPEFOUNDINGS
TYPES
TYPESCRIPT
TYPESCRIPTS
TYPESET
TYPESETS
TYPESETTER
TYPESETTERS
TYPESETTING
TYPESETTINGS
TYPESTYLE
TYPESTYLES
TYPEWRITE
TYPEWRITER
TYPEWRITERS
TYPEWRITES
TYPEWRITING
TYPEWRITINGS
TYPEWRITTEN
TYPEWROTE
TYPEY
TYPHACEOUS
TYPHLITIC
TYPHLITIS

TYPHLITISES
TYPHLOLOGIES
TYPHLOLOGY
TYPHLOSOLE
TYPHLOSOLES
TYPHOGENIC
TYPHOID
TYPHOIDAL
TYPHOIDIN
TYPHOIDS
TYPHON
TYPHONIAN
TYPHONIC
TYPHONS
TYPHOON
TYPHOONS
TYPHOSE
TYPHOUS
TYPHUS
TYPHUSES
TYPIC
TYPICAL
TYPICALITIES
TYPICALITY
TYPICALLY
TYPICALNESS
TYPICALNESSES
TYPIER
TYPIEST
TYPIFICATION
TYPIFICATIONS
TYPIFIED
TYPIFIER
TYPIFIERS
TYPIFIES
TYPIFY
TYPIFYING
TYPING
TYPINGS
TYPIST
TYPISTS
TYPO
TYPOGRAPH
TYPOGRAPHED
TYPOGRAPHER
TYPOGRAPHERS
TYPOGRAPHIA
TYPOGRAPHIC
TYPOGRAPHICAL
TYPOGRAPHICALLY
TYPOGRAPHIES
TYPOGRAPHING
TYPOGRAPHIST
TYPOGRAPHISTS
TYPOGRAPHS
TYPOGRAPHY
TYPOLOGIC

TYPOLOGICAL
TYPOLOGICALLY
TYPOLOGIES
TYPOLOGIST
TYPOLOGISTS
TYPOLOGY
TYPOMANIA
TYPOMANIAS
TYPOS
TYPOTHETAE
TYPP
TYPPS
TYPTO
TYPTOED
TYPTOING
TYPTOS
TYPY
TYRAMINE
TYRAMINES
TYRAN
TYRANED
TYRANING
TYRANNE
TYRANNED
TYRANNES
TYRANNESS
TYRANNESSES
TYRANNIC
TYRANNICAL
TYRANNICALLY
TYRANNICALNESS
TYRANNICIDAL
TYRANNICIDE
TYRANNICIDES
TYRANNIES
TYRANNING
TYRANNIS
TYRANNISE
TYRANNISED
TYRANNISER
TYRANNISERS
TYRANNISES
TYRANNISING
TYRANNIZE
TYRANNIZED
TYRANNIZER
TYRANNIZERS
TYRANNIZES
TYRANNIZING
TYRANNOSAUR
TYRANNOSAURS
TYRANNOSAURUS
TYRANNOSAURUSES
TYRANNOUS
TYRANNOUSLY
TYRANNOUSNESS
TYRANNY

TYRANS
TYRANT
TYRANTED
TYRANTING
TYRANTS
TYRE
TYRED
TYRELESS
TYRES
TYRING
TYRO
TYROCIDIN
TYROCIDINE
TYROCIDINES
TYROCIDINS
TYROES
TYROGLYPHID
TYROGLYPHIDS
TYRONES
TYRONIC
TYROPITTA
TYROPITTAS
TYROS
TYROSINASE
TYROSINASES
TYROSINE
TYROSINES
TYROTHRICIN
TYROTHRICINS
TYRRANNICIDAL
TYSTIE
TYSTIES
TYTE
TYTHE
TYTHED
TYTHES
TYTHING
TYUM
TYUMS
TZADDIK
TZADDIKIM
TZADDIKS
TZADDIQ
TZADDIQIM
TZADDIQS
TZAR
TZARDOM
TZARDOMS
TZAREVNA
TZAREVNAS
TZARINA
TZARINAS
TZARISM
TZARISMS
TZARIST
TZARISTS
TZARITZA

TZARITZAS
TZARS
TZATZIKI
TZATZIKIS
TZETSE
TZETSES
TZETZE
TZETZES
TZIGANE
TZIGANES
TZIGANIES
TZIGANY
TZIMMES
TZITZIS
TZITZIT
TZITZITH
TZURIS

U

UAKARI	UGH	ULCERATE	ULOTRICHY
UAKARIS	UGHS	ULCERATED	ULPAN
UBEROUS	UGLIED	ULCERATES	ULPANIM
UBERTIES	UGLIER	ULCERATING	ULSTER
UBERTY	UGLIES	ULCERATION	ULSTERED
UBIETIES	UGLIEST	ULCERATIONS	ULSTERETTE
UBIETY	UGLIFICATION	ULCERATIVE	ULSTERETTES
UBIQUARIAN	UGLIFICATIONS	ULCERED	ULSTERS
UBIQUE	UGLIFIED	ULCERING	ULTERIOR
UBIQUINONE	UGLIFIER	ULCEROGENIC	ULTERIORLY
UBIQUINONES	UGLIFIERS	ULCEROUS	ULTIMA
UBIQUITARIAN	UGLIFIES	ULCEROUSLY	ULTIMACIES
UBIQUITARIANISM	UGLIFY	ULCEROUSNESS	ULTIMACY
UBIQUITARIANS	UGLIFYING	ULCEROUSNESSES	ULTIMAS
UBIQUITARY	UGLILY	ULCERS	ULTIMATA
UBIQUITIES	UGLINESS	ULE	ULTIMATE
UBIQUITOUS	UGLINESSES	ULEMA	ULTIMATED
UBIQUITOUSLY	UGLY	ULEMAS	ULTIMATELY
UBIQUITOUSNESS	UGLYING	ULES	ULTIMATENESS
UBIQUITY	UGS	ULEX	ULTIMATENESSES
UCKERS	UGSOME	ULEXES	ULTIMATES
UDAL	UGSOMENESS	ULEXITE	ULTIMATING
UDALLER	UGSOMENESSES	ULEXITES	ULTIMATUM
UDALLERS	UH	ULICHONS	ULTIMATUMS
UDALS	UHLAN	ULICON	ULTIMO
UDDER	UHLANS	ULICONS	ULTIMOGENITURE
UDDERED	UHURU	ULIGINOSE	ULTIMOGENITURES
UDDERFUL	UHURUS	ULIGINOUS	ULTION
UDDERLESS	UILLEAN	ULIKON	ULTIONS
UDDERS	UINTAHITE	ULIKONS	ULTRA
UDO	UINTAHITES	ULITIS	ULTRABASIC
UDOMETER	UINTAITE	ULITISES	ULTRABASICS
UDOMETERS	UINTAITES	ULLAGE	ULTRACAREFUL
UDOMETRIC	UINTATHERE	ULLAGED	ULTRACASUAL
UDOMETRIES	UINTATHERES	ULLAGES	ULTRACAUTIOUS
UDOMETRY	UITLANDER	ULLAGING	ULTRACENTRIFUGE
UDON	UITLANDERS	ULLING	ULTRACHIC
UDOS	UJAMAA	ULLINGS	ULTRACIVILIZED
UDS	UJAMAAS	ULMACEOUS	ULTRACLEAN
UEY	UKASE	ULMIN	ULTRACOLD
UEYS	UKASES	ULMINS	ULTRACOMMERCIAL
UFO	UKE	ULNA	ULTRACOMPACT
UFOLOGICAL	UKELELE	ULNAD	ULTRACOMPETENT
UFOLOGIES	UKELELES	ULNAE	ULTRACONVENIENT
UFOLOGIST	UKES	ULNAR	ULTRACOOL
UFOLOGISTS	UKULELE	ULNARE	ULTRACREPIDATE
UFOLOGY	UKULELES	ULNARIA	ULTRACREPIDATED
UFOS	ULAMA	ULNAS	ULTRACREPIDATES
UG	ULAMAS	ULOSES	ULTRACRITICAL
UGALI	ULAN	ULOSIS	ULTRADEMOCRATIC
UGGED	ULANS	ULOTRICHIES	ULTRADENSE
UGGING	ULCER	ULOTRICHOUS	ULTRADISTANCE

ULTRADISTANT
ULTRADRY
ULTRAEFFICIENT
ULTRAENERGETIC
ULTRAEXCLUSIVE
ULTRAFAMILIAR
ULTRAFAST
ULTRAFASTIDIOUS
ULTRAFEMININE
ULTRAFICHE
ULTRAFICHES
ULTRAFILTER
ULTRAFILTERED
ULTRAFILTERING
ULTRAFILTERS
ULTRAFILTRATE
ULTRAFILTRATES
ULTRAFILTRATION
ULTRAFINE
ULTRAGLAMOROUS
ULTRAHAZARDOUS
ULTRAHEAT
ULTRAHEATED
ULTRAHEATING
ULTRAHEATS
ULTRAHEAVY
ULTRAHIGH
ULTRAHIP
ULTRAHOT
ULTRAHUMAN
ULTRAISM
ULTRAISMS
ULTRAIST
ULTRAISTIC
ULTRAISTS
ULTRALARGE
ULTRALEFT
ULTRALEFTISM
ULTRALEFTISMS
ULTRALEFTIST
ULTRALEFTISTS
ULTRALIBERAL
ULTRALIBERALISM
ULTRALIBERALS
ULTRALIGHT
ULTRALIGHTS
ULTRALOW
ULTRAMAFIC
ULTRAMARATHON
ULTRAMARATHONER
ULTRAMARATHONS
ULTRAMARINE
ULTRAMARINES
ULTRAMASCULINE
ULTRAMICRO
ULTRAMICROMETER
ULTRAMICROSCOPE

ULTRAMICROSCOPY
ULTRAMICROTOME
ULTRAMICROTOMES
ULTRAMICROTOMY
ULTRAMILITANT
ULTRAMILITANTS
ULTRAMINIATURE
ULTRAMODERN
ULTRAMODERNISM
ULTRAMODERNIST
ULTRAMODERNISTS
ULTRAMONTANE
ULTRAMONTANES
ULTRAMONTANISM
ULTRAMONTANISMS
ULTRAMONTANIST
ULTRAMONTANISTS
ULTRAMUNDANE
ULTRANATIONAL
ULTRAORTHODOX
ULTRAPATRIOTIC
ULTRAPHYSICAL
ULTRAPOWERFUL
ULTRAPRACTICAL
ULTRAPRECISE
ULTRAPRECISION
ULTRAPURE
ULTRAQUIET
ULTRARADICAL
ULTRARADICALS
ULTRARAPID
ULTRARARE
ULTRARAREFIED
ULTRARATIONAL
ULTRAREALISM
ULTRAREALISMS
ULTRAREALIST
ULTRAREALISTIC
ULTRAREALISTS
ULTRARED
ULTRAREDS
ULTRAREFINED
ULTRARELIABLE
ULTRARICH
ULTRARIGHT
ULTRARIGHTIST
ULTRARIGHTISTS
ULTRAROMANTIC
ULTRAROYALIST
ULTRAROYALISTS
ULTRAS
ULTRASAFE
ULTRASECRET
ULTRASENSITIVE
ULTRASENSUAL
ULTRASERIOUS
ULTRASHARP

ULTRASHORT
ULTRASIMPLE
ULTRASLICK
ULTRASLOW
ULTRASMALL
ULTRASMART
ULTRASMOOTH
ULTRASOFT
ULTRASONIC
ULTRASONICALLY
ULTRASONICS
ULTRASONOGRAPHY
ULTRASOUND
ULTRASOUNDS
ULTRASTRUCTURAL
ULTRASTRUCTURE
ULTRASTRUCTURES
ULTRATHIN
ULTRAVACUA
ULTRAVACUUM
ULTRAVACUUMS
ULTRAVIOLENCE
ULTRAVIOLENCES
ULTRAVIOLENT
ULTRAVIOLET
ULTRAVIOLETS
ULTRAVIRILE
ULTRAVIRILITIES
ULTRAVIRILITY
ULTRAVIRUS
ULTRAVIRUSES
ULTRAWIDE
ULTRONEOUS
ULTRONEOUSLY
ULTRONEOUSNESS
ULU
ULULANT
ULULATE
ULULATED
ULULATES
ULULATING
ULULATION
ULULATIONS
ULUS
ULVA
ULVAS
ULYIE
ULYIES
ULZIE
ULZIES
UM
UMANGITE
UMANGITES
UMBEL
UMBELED
UMBELLAR
UMBELLATE

UMBELLATED
UMBELLATELY
UMBELLED
UMBELLET
UMBELLETS
UMBELLIFER
UMBELLIFEROUS
UMBELLIFERS
UMBELLULATE
UMBELLULE
UMBELLULES
UMBELS
UMBER
UMBERED
UMBERING
UMBERS
UMBERY
UMBILICAL
UMBILICALLY
UMBILICALS
UMBILICATE
UMBILICATED
UMBILICATION
UMBILICATIONS
UMBILICI
UMBILICUS
UMBILICUSES
UMBILIFORM
UMBLE
UMBLES
UMBO
UMBONAL
UMBONATE
UMBONATION
UMBONATIONS
UMBONES
UMBONIC
UMBOS
UMBRA
UMBRACULA
UMBRACULATE
UMBRACULIFORM
UMBRACULUM
UMBRAE
UMBRAGE
UMBRAGED
UMBRAGEOUS
UMBRAGEOUSLY
UMBRAGEOUSNESS
UMBRAGES
UMBRAGING
UMBRAL
UMBRAS
UMBRATED
UMBRATIC
UMBRATICAL
UMBRATILE

UMBRATILOUS	UMPTIETH	UNACQUAINTANCE	UNAGING
UMBRE	UMPTY	UNACQUAINTANCES	UNAGREEABLE
UMBREL	UMPY	UNACQUAINTED	UNAI
UMBRELLA	UMQUHILE	UNACQUITTABLE	UNAIDABLE
UMBRELLAED	UMTEENTH	UNACQUITTED	UNAIDED
UMBRELLAING	UMU	UNACTABLE	UNAIMED
UMBRELLAS	UMWELT	UNACTED	UNAIRED
UMBRELLO	UMWELTS	UNACTIONABILITY	UNAIS
UMBRELLOES	UMWHILE	UNACTIONABLE	UNAKIN
UMBRELLOS	UN	UNACTIVE	UNAKING
UMBRELS	UNABASHED	UNACTORISH	UNAKITE
UMBRERE	UNABASHEDLY	UNACTUATED	UNAKITES
UMBRERES	UNABATED	UNADAPTABLE	UNALARMED
UMBRES	UNABATEDLY	UNADAPTED	UNALIENABLE
UMBRETTE	UNABBREVIATED	UNADDRESSED	UNALIENABLY
UMBRETTES	UNABLE	UNADJOURNED	UNALIENATED
UMBRIERE	UNABOLISHED	UNADJUDICATED	UNALIGNED
UMBRIERES	UNABRADED	UNADJUSTABILITY	UNALIKE
UMBRIFEROUS	UNABRIDGED	UNADJUSTABLE	UNALIST
UMBRIL	UNABROGATED	UNADJUSTED	UNALISTS
UMBRILS	UNABSOLVED	UNADMIRED	UNALIVE
UMBROSE	UNABSORBED	UNADMIRING	UNALLAYED
UMBROUS	UNABSORBENT	UNADMITTED	UNALLEVIATED
UMFAZI	UNABUSED	UNADMONISHED	UNALLIED
UMFAZIS	UNACADEMIC	UNADOPTABLE	UNALLOCATED
UMIAC	UNACADEMICALLY	UNADOPTED	UNALLOTTED
UMIACK	UNACCENTED	UNADORED	UNALLOWABLE
UMIACKS	UNACCENTUATED	UNADORNED	UNALLOYED
UMIACS	UNACCEPTABILITY	UNADULT	UNALLURING
UMIAK	UNACCEPTABLE	UNADULTERATE	UNALTERABILITY
UMIAKS	UNACCEPTABLY	UNADULTERATED	UNALTERABLE
UMIAQ	UNACCEPTANCE	UNADULTERATEDLY	UNALTERABLENESS
UMIAQS	UNACCEPTANCES	UNADVANTAGEOUS	UNALTERABLY
UMLAUT	UNACCEPTED	UNADVENTROUS	UNALTERED
UMLAUTED	UNACCLAIMED	UNADVENTUROUS	UNALTERING
UMLAUTING	UNACCLIMATED	UNADVERTISED	UNAMAZED
UMLAUTS	UNACCLIMATISED	UNADVISABLE	UNAMBIGUOUS
UMLUNGU	UNACCLIMATIZED	UNADVISABLENESS	UNAMBIGUOUSLY
UMLUNGUS	UNACCOMMODATED	UNADVISABLY	UNAMBITIOUS
UMM	UNACCOMMODATING	UNADVISED	UNAMBITIOUSLY
UMP	UNACCOMPANIED	UNADVISEDLY	UNAMBIVALENT
UMPED	UNACCOMPLISHED	UNADVISEDNESS	UNAMBIVALENTLY
UMPH	UNACCOUNTABLE	UNADVISEDNESSES	UNAMENABLE
UMPIE	UNACCOUNTABLY	UNAESTHETIC	UNAMENDABLE
UMPIES	UNACCOUNTED	UNAFFECTED	UNAMENDED
UMPING	UNACCREDITED	UNAFFECTEDLY	UNAMERCED
UMPIRAGE	UNACCULTURATED	UNAFFECTEDNESS	UNAMIABILITIES
UMPIRAGES	UNACCUSABLE	UNAFFECTING	UNAMIABILITY
UMPIRE	UNACCUSABLY	UNAFFECTIONATE	UNAMIABLE
UMPIRED	UNACCUSED	UNAFFILIATED	UNAMIABLENESS
UMPIRES	UNACCUSTOMED	UNAFFLUENT	UNAMIABLENESSES
UMPIRESHIP	UNACCUSTOMEDLY	UNAFFORDABLE	UNAMICABILITY
UMPIRESHIPS	UNACHIEVABLE	UNAFRAID	UNAMICABLE
UMPIRING	UNACHIEVED	UNAGED	UNAMICABLENESS
UMPS	UNACHING	UNAGEING	UNAMICABLY
UMPTEEN	UNACKNOWLEDGED	UNAGGRESSIVE	UNAMORTIZED
UMPTEENTH	UNACQUAINT	UNAGILE	UNAMPLIFIED

UNAMUSABLE
UNAMUSED
UNAMUSING
UNAMUSINGLY
UNANALYSABLE
UNANALYSED
UNANALYTIC
UNANALYTICAL
UNANALYZABLE
UNANALYZED
UNANCHOR
UNANCHORED
UNANCHORING
UNANCHORS
UNANELED
UNANESTHETIZED
UNANIMATED
UNANIMITIES
UNANIMITY
UNANIMOUS
UNANIMOUSLY
UNANIMOUSNESS
UNANNEALED
UNANNOTATED
UNANNOUNCED
UNANSWERABILITY
UNANSWERABLE
UNANSWERABLY
UNANSWERED
UNANTICIPATED
UNANTICIPATEDLY
UNANXIOUS
UNAPOLOGETIC
UNAPOLOGIZING
UNAPOSTOLIC
UNAPOSTOLICAL
UNAPOSTOLICALLY
UNAPPALLED
UNAPPAREL
UNAPPARELLED
UNAPPARELLING
UNAPPARELS
UNAPPARENT
UNAPPEALABLE
UNAPPEALABLY
UNAPPEALING
UNAPPEALINGLY
UNAPPEASABLE
UNAPPEASABLY
UNAPPEASED
UNAPPETISING
UNAPPETIZING
UNAPPETIZINGLY
UNAPPLAUSIVE
UNAPPLICABLE
UNAPPLIED
UNAPPOINTED

UNAPPORTIONED
UNAPPRECIATED
UNAPPRECIATION
UNAPPRECIATIONS
UNAPPRECIATIVE
UNAPPREHENDED
UNAPPREHENSIBLE
UNAPPREHENSIVE
UNAPPRISED
UNAPPROACHABLE
UNAPPROACHABLY
UNAPPROACHED
UNAPPROPRIATE
UNAPPROPRIATED
UNAPPROVED
UNAPPROVING
UNAPPROVINGLY
UNAPT
UNAPTLY
UNAPTNESS
UNAPTNESSES
UNARGUABLE
UNARGUABLY
UNARGUED
UNARISEN
UNARM
UNARMED
UNARMING
UNARMORED
UNARMOURED
UNARMS
UNARRANGED
UNARROGANT
UNARTFUL
UNARTFULLY
UNARTICULATE
UNARTICULATED
UNARTIFICIAL
UNARTIFICIALLY
UNARTISTIC
UNARTISTLIKE
UNARY
UNASCENDABLE
UNASCENDED
UNASCENDIBLE
UNASCERTAINABLE
UNASCERTAINED
UNASHAMED
UNASHAMEDLY
UNASHAMEDNESS
UNASKED
UNASPIRATED
UNASPIRING
UNASPIRINGLY
UNASPIRINGNESS
UNASSAILABILITY
UNASSAILABLE

UNASSAILABLY
UNASSAILED
UNASSAYED
UNASSEMBLED
UNASSERTIVE
UNASSERTIVELY
UNASSESSABLE
UNASSESSED
UNASSIGNABLE
UNASSIGNED
UNASSIMILABLE
UNASSIMILATED
UNASSISTED
UNASSISTEDLY
UNASSISTING
UNASSOCIATED
UNASSORTED
UNASSUAGEABLE
UNASSUAGED
UNASSUMED
UNASSUMING
UNASSUMINGLY
UNASSUMINGNESS
UNASSURED
UNATHLETIC
UNATONABLE
UNATONED
UNATTACHED
UNATTAINABILITY
UNATTAINABLE
UNATTAINABLY
UNATTAINED
UNATTAINTED
UNATTEMPTED
UNATTENDED
UNATTENDING
UNATTENTIVE
UNATTENUATED
UNATTESTED
UNATTIRED
UNATTRACTIVE
UNATTRACTIVELY
UNATTRIBUTABLE
UNATTRIBUTED
UNATTUNED
UNAU
UNAUDITED
UNAUGMENTED
UNAUS
UNAUSPICIOUS
UNAUTHENTIC
UNAUTHENTICATED
UNAUTHENTICITY
UNAUTHORISED
UNAUTHORITATIVE
UNAUTHORIZED
UNAUTOMATED

UNAVAILABILITY
UNAVAILABLE
UNAVAILABLENESS
UNAVAILABLY
UNAVAILING
UNAVAILINGLY
UNAVAILINGNESS
UNAVENGED
UNAVERAGE
UNAVERTABLE
UNAVERTIBLE
UNAVOIDABILITY
UNAVOIDABLE
UNAVOIDABLENESS
UNAVOIDABLY
UNAVOIDED
UNAVOWED
UNAVOWEDLY
UNAWAKED
UNAWAKENED
UNAWAKENING
UNAWARDED
UNAWARE
UNAWARELY
UNAWARENESS
UNAWARENESSES
UNAWARES
UNAWED
UNAWESOME
UNBACKED
UNBAFFLED
UNBAG
UNBAGGED
UNBAGGING
UNBAGS
UNBAILABLE
UNBAITED
UNBAKED
UNBALANCE
UNBALANCED
UNBALANCES
UNBALANCING
UNBALLASTED
UNBAN
UNBANDAGE
UNBANDAGED
UNBANDAGES
UNBANDAGING
UNBANDED
UNBANKED
UNBANNED
UNBANNING
UNBANS
UNBAPTISE
UNBAPTISED
UNBAPTISES
UNBAPTISING

UNBAPTIZE	UNBEGETTING	UNBESEEMINGLY	UNBLESS
UNBAPTIZED	UNBEGGED	UNBESEEMS	UNBLESSED
UNBAPTIZES	UNBEGINNING	UNBESOUGHT	UNBLESSEDNESS
UNBAPTIZING	UNBEGOT	UNBESPEAK	UNBLESSEDNESSES
UNBAR	UNBEGOTTEN	UNBESPEAKING	UNBLESSES
UNBARBED	UNBEGUILE	UNBESPEAKS	UNBLESSING
UNBARBERED	UNBEGUILED	UNBESPOKE	UNBLEST
UNBARE	UNBEGUILES	UNBESPOKEN	UNBLIND
UNBARED	UNBEGUILING	UNBESTOWED	UNBLINDED
UNBARES	UNBEGUN	UNBETRAYED	UNBLINDFOLD
UNBARING	UNBEHOLDEN	UNBETTERABLE	UNBLINDFOLDED
UNBARK	UNBEING	UNBETTERED	UNBLINDFOLDING
UNBARKED	UNBEINGS	UNBEWAILED	UNBLINDFOLDS
UNBARKING	UNBEKNOWN	UNBIAS	UNBLINDING
UNBARKS	UNBEKNOWNST	UNBIASED	UNBLINDS
UNBARRED	UNBELIEF	UNBIASEDLY	UNBLINKING
UNBARRICADE	UNBELIEFS	UNBIASEDNESS	UNBLINKINGLY
UNBARRICADED	UNBELIEVABILITY	UNBIASEDNESSES	UNBLISSFUL
UNBARRICADES	UNBELIEVABLE	UNBIASES	UNBLOCK
UNBARRICADING	UNBELIEVABLY	UNBIASING	UNBLOCKED
UNBARRING	UNBELIEVE	UNBIASSED	UNBLOCKING
UNBARS	UNBELIEVED	UNBIASSEDLY	UNBLOCKS
UNBASED	UNBELIEVER	UNBIASSEDNESS	UNBLOODED
UNBASHFUL	UNBELIEVERS	UNBIASSEDNESSES	UNBLOODIED
UNBATED	UNBELIEVES	UNBIASSES	UNBLOODY
UNBATHED	UNBELIEVING	UNBIASSING	UNBLOTTED
UNBATTERED	UNBELIEVINGLY	UNBIBLICAL	UNBLOWED
UNBE	UNBELIEVINGNESS	UNBID	UNBLOWN
UNBEAR	UNBELLIGERENT	UNBIDDEN	UNBLUNTED
UNBEARABLE	UNBELOVED	UNBILLED	UNBLUSHING
UNBEARABLENESS	UNBELT	UNBIND	UNBLUSHINGLY
UNBEARABLY	UNBELTED	UNBINDING	UNBLUSHINGNESS
UNBEARDED	UNBELTING	UNBINDINGS	UNBOASTFUL
UNBEARED	UNBELTS	UNBINDS	UNBODIED
UNBEARING	UNBEMUSED	UNBIRTHDAY	UNBODING
UNBEARS	UNBEND	UNBIRTHDAYS	UNBOLT
UNBEATABLE	UNBENDABLE	UNBISHOP	UNBOLTED
UNBEATABLY	UNBENDED	UNBISHOPED	UNBOLTING
UNBEATEN	UNBENDING	UNBISHOPING	UNBOLTS
UNBEAUTIFUL	UNBENDINGLY	UNBISHOPS	UNBONE
UNBEAUTIFULLY	UNBENDINGNESS	UNBITT	UNBONED
UNBEAVERED	UNBENDINGNESSES	UNBITTED	UNBONES
UNBECOMING	UNBENDINGS	UNBITTEN	UNBONING
UNBECOMINGLY	UNBENDS	UNBITTER	UNBONNET
UNBECOMINGNESS	UNBENEFICED	UNBITTING	UNBONNETED
UNBECOMINGS	UNBENEFICIAL	UNBITTS	UNBONNETING
UNBED	UNBENEFITED	UNBLAMABLE	UNBONNETS
UNBEDDED	UNBENIGHTED	UNBLAMABLY	UNBOOKED
UNBEDDING	UNBENIGN	UNBLAMEABLE	UNBOOKISH
UNBEDIMMED	UNBENIGNANT	UNBLAMEABLY	UNBOOT
UNBEDINNED	UNBENIGNLY	UNBLAMED	UNBOOTED
UNBEDS	UNBENT	UNBLEACHED	UNBOOTING
UNBEEN	UNBEREFT	UNBLEMISHED	UNBOOTS
UNBEFITTING	UNBERUFEN	UNBLENCHED	UNBORE
UNBEFRIENDED	UNBESEEM	UNBLENCHING	UNBORN
UNBEGET	UNBESEEMED	UNBLENDED	UNBORNE
UNBEGETS	UNBESEEMING	UNBLENT	UNBORROWED

UNBOSOM
UNBOSOMED
UNBOSOMER
UNBOSOMERS
UNBOSOMING
UNBOSOMS
UNBOTTOMED
UNBOUGHT
UNBOUNCY
UNBOUND
UNBOUNDED
UNBOUNDEDLY
UNBOUNDEDNESS
UNBOUNDEDNESSES
UNBOWDLERIZED
UNBOWED
UNBOX
UNBOXED
UNBOXES
UNBOXING
UNBRACE
UNBRACED
UNBRACES
UNBRACING
UNBRACKETED
UNBRAID
UNBRAIDED
UNBRAIDING
UNBRAIDS
UNBRAKE
UNBRAKED
UNBRAKES
UNBRAKING
UNBRANCHED
UNBRANDED
UNBRASTE
UNBREACHABLE
UNBREACHED
UNBREAKABLE
UNBREATHABLE
UNBREATHED
UNBREATHING
UNBRED
UNBREECH
UNBREECHED
UNBREECHES
UNBREECHING
UNBRIBABLE
UNBRIDGEABLE
UNBRIDGED
UNBRIDLE
UNBRIDLED
UNBRIDLEDLY
UNBRIDLEDNESS
UNBRIDLEDNESSES
UNBRIDLES
UNBRIDLING

UNBRIEFED
UNBRIGHT
UNBRILLIANT
UNBRIZZED
UNBROKE
UNBROKEN
UNBROKENLY
UNBROKENNESS
UNBROKENNESSES
UNBROTHERLIKE
UNBROTHERLY
UNBRUISED
UNBRUSED
UNBRUSHED
UNBUCKLE
UNBUCKLED
UNBUCKLES
UNBUCKLING
UNBUDDED
UNBUDGEABLE
UNBUDGEABLY
UNBUDGETED
UNBUDGING
UNBUDGINGLY
UNBUFFERED
UNBUILD
UNBUILDABLE
UNBUILDING
UNBUILDS
UNBUILT
UNBULKY
UNBUNDLE
UNBUNDLED
UNBUNDLER
UNBUNDLERS
UNBUNDLES
UNBUNDLING
UNBUNDLINGS
UNBURDEN
UNBURDENED
UNBURDENING
UNBURDENS
UNBUREAUCRATIC
UNBURIED
UNBURIES
UNBURNABLE
UNBURNED
UNBURNISHED
UNBURNT
UNBURROW
UNBURROWED
UNBURROWING
UNBURROWS
UNBURTHEN
UNBURTHENED
UNBURTHENING
UNBURTHENS

UNBURY
UNBURYING
UNBUSINESSLIKE
UNBUSTED
UNBUSY
UNBUTTERED
UNBUTTON
UNBUTTONED
UNBUTTONING
UNBUTTONS
UNCAGE
UNCAGED
UNCAGES
UNCAGING
UNCAKE
UNCAKED
UNCAKES
UNCAKING
UNCALCIFIED
UNCALCINED
UNCALCULATED
UNCALCULATING
UNCALIBRATED
UNCALLED
UNCALLOUSED
UNCANCELED
UNCANDID
UNCANDIDLY
UNCANDIDNESS
UNCANDIDNESSES
UNCANDOUR
UNCANDOURS
UNCANNIER
UNCANNIEST
UNCANNILY
UNCANNINESS
UNCANNINESSES
UNCANNY
UNCANONIC
UNCANONICAL
UNCANONICALNESS
UNCANONISE
UNCANONISED
UNCANONISES
UNCANONISING
UNCANONIZE
UNCANONIZED
UNCANONIZES
UNCANONIZING
UNCAP
UNCAPABLE
UNCAPE
UNCAPED
UNCAPES
UNCAPING
UNCAPITALIZED
UNCAPPED

UNCAPPING
UNCAPS
UNCAPSIZABLE
UNCAPTIONED
UNCAPTURABLE
UNCAREFUL
UNCARING
UNCARPETED
UNCART
UNCARTED
UNCARTING
UNCARTS
UNCASE
UNCASED
UNCASES
UNCASHED
UNCASING
UNCASKED
UNCASTRATED
UNCATALOGED
UNCATALOGUED
UNCATCHABLE
UNCATCHY
UNCATE
UNCATEGORICAL
UNCATEGORIZABLE
UNCAUGHT
UNCAUSED
UNCE
UNCEASING
UNCEASINGLY
UNCEASINGNESS
UNCELEBRATED
UNCENSORED
UNCENSORIOUS
UNCENSURED
UNCEREBRAL
UNCEREMONIOUS
UNCEREMONIOUSLY
UNCERTAIN
UNCERTAINLY
UNCERTAINNESS
UNCERTAINNESSES
UNCERTAINTIES
UNCERTAINTY
UNCERTIFICATED
UNCERTIFIED
UNCES
UNCESSANT
UNCHAIN
UNCHAINED
UNCHAINING
UNCHAINS
UNCHALLENGEABLE
UNCHALLENGEABLY
UNCHALLENGED
UNCHALLENGING

UNCHANCIER
UNCHANCIEST
UNCHANCY
UNCHANGEABILITY
UNCHANGEABLE
UNCHANGEABLY
UNCHANGED
UNCHANGING
UNCHANGINGLY
UNCHANGINGNESS
UNCHANNELED
UNCHAPERONED
UNCHARGE
UNCHARGED
UNCHARGES
UNCHARGING
UNCHARISMATIC
UNCHARITABLE
UNCHARITABLY
UNCHARITIES
UNCHARITY
UNCHARM
UNCHARMED
UNCHARMING
UNCHARMS
UNCHARNEL
UNCHARNELLED
UNCHARNELLING
UNCHARNELS
UNCHARTED
UNCHARTERED
UNCHARY
UNCHASTE
UNCHASTELY
UNCHASTENED
UNCHASTENESS
UNCHASTENESSES
UNCHASTISABLE
UNCHASTISED
UNCHASTITIES
UNCHASTITY
UNCHASTIZED
UNCHAUVINISTIC
UNCHECK
UNCHECKABLE
UNCHECKED
UNCHECKING
UNCHECKS
UNCHEERED
UNCHEERFUL
UNCHEERFULLY
UNCHEERFULNESS
UNCHEWABLE
UNCHEWED
UNCHIC
UNCHICLY
UNCHILD

UNCHILDED
UNCHILDING
UNCHILDLIKE
UNCHILDS
UNCHIVALROUS
UNCHIVALROUSLY
UNCHLORINATED
UNCHOKE
UNCHOKED
UNCHOKES
UNCHOKING
UNCHOREOGRAPHED
UNCHOSEN
UNCHRISOM
UNCHRISTEN
UNCHRISTENED
UNCHRISTENING
UNCHRISTENS
UNCHRISTIAN
UNCHRISTIANED
UNCHRISTIANING
UNCHRISTIANISE
UNCHRISTIANISED
UNCHRISTIANISES
UNCHRISTIANIZE
UNCHRISTIANIZED
UNCHRISTIANIZES
UNCHRISTIANLIKE
UNCHRISTIANLY
UNCHRISTIANS
UNCHRONICLED
UNCHRONOLOGICAL
UNCHURCH
UNCHURCHED
UNCHURCHES
UNCHURCHING
UNCHURCHLY
UNCI
UNCIA
UNCIAE
UNCIAL
UNCIALLY
UNCIALS
UNCIFORM
UNCIFORMS
UNCILIATED
UNCINAL
UNCINARIASES
UNCINARIASIS
UNCINATE
UNCINATED
UNCINEMATIC
UNCINI
UNCINUS
UNCIPHER
UNCIPHERED
UNCIPHERING

UNCIPHERS
UNCIRCULATED
UNCIRCUMCISED
UNCIRCUMCISION
UNCIRCUMCISIONS
UNCIRCUMSCRIBED
UNCITED
UNCIVIL
UNCIVILISED
UNCIVILISEDLY
UNCIVILISEDNESS
UNCIVILITY
UNCIVILIZED
UNCIVILIZEDLY
UNCIVILIZEDNESS
UNCIVILLY
UNCIVILNESS
UNCLAD
UNCLAIMED
UNCLAMP
UNCLAMPED
UNCLAMPING
UNCLAMPS
UNCLARIFIED
UNCLARITIES
UNCLARITY
UNCLASP
UNCLASPED
UNCLASPING
UNCLASPS
UNCLASSED
UNCLASSICAL
UNCLASSIFIABLE
UNCLASSIFIED
UNCLASSY
UNCLE
UNCLEAN
UNCLEANED
UNCLEANER
UNCLEANEST
UNCLEANLINESS
UNCLEANLINESSES
UNCLEANLY
UNCLEANNESS
UNCLEANNESSES
UNCLEANSED
UNCLEAR
UNCLEARED
UNCLEARER
UNCLEAREST
UNCLEARLY
UNCLEARNESS
UNCLEARNESSES
UNCLED
UNCLENCH
UNCLENCHED
UNCLENCHES

UNCLENCHING
UNCLERICAL
UNCLES
UNCLESHIP
UNCLESHIPS
UNCLEW
UNCLEWED
UNCLEWING
UNCLEWS
UNCLICHED
UNCLIMBABLE
UNCLIMBABLENESS
UNCLINCH
UNCLINCHED
UNCLINCHES
UNCLINCHING
UNCLING
UNCLIP
UNCLIPPED
UNCLIPPING
UNCLIPS
UNCLIPT
UNCLOAK
UNCLOAKED
UNCLOAKING
UNCLOAKS
UNCLOG
UNCLOGGED
UNCLOGGING
UNCLOGS
UNCLOISTER
UNCLOISTERED
UNCLOISTERING
UNCLOISTERS
UNCLOSE
UNCLOSED
UNCLOSES
UNCLOSING
UNCLOTHE
UNCLOTHED
UNCLOTHES
UNCLOTHING
UNCLOUD
UNCLOUDED
UNCLOUDEDLY
UNCLOUDEDNESS
UNCLOUDEDNESSES
UNCLOUDING
UNCLOUDS
UNCLOUDY
UNCLOVEN
UNCLOYED
UNCLOYING
UNCLUBABLE
UNCLUBBABLE
UNCLUTCH
UNCLUTCHED

UNCLUTCHES
UNCLUTCHING
UNCLUTTER
UNCLUTTERED
UNCLUTTERING
UNCLUTTERS
UNCO
UNCOALESCE
UNCOALESCED
UNCOALESCES
UNCOALESCING
UNCOATED
UNCOATING
UNCOATINGS
UNCOCK
UNCOCKED
UNCOCKING
UNCOCKS
UNCODED
UNCODIFIED
UNCOER
UNCOERCED
UNCOERCIVE
UNCOERCIVELY
UNCOES
UNCOEST
UNCOFFIN
UNCOFFINED
UNCOFFINING
UNCOFFINS
UNCOIL
UNCOILED
UNCOILING
UNCOILS
UNCOINED
UNCOLLECTED
UNCOLLECTIBLE
UNCOLLECTIBLES
UNCOLORED
UNCOLOURED
UNCOLT
UNCOLTED
UNCOLTING
UNCOLTS
UNCOMATABLE
UNCOMBATIVE
UNCOMBED
UNCOMBINE
UNCOMBINED
UNCOMBINES
UNCOMBINING
UNCOMEATABLE
UNCOMELINESS
UNCOMELINESSES
UNCOMELY
UNCOMFORTABLE
UNCOMFORTABLY

UNCOMFORTED
UNCOMIC
UNCOMMENDABLE
UNCOMMENDABLY
UNCOMMENDED
UNCOMMERCIAL
UNCOMMITTED
UNCOMMON
UNCOMMONER
UNCOMMONEST
UNCOMMONLY
UNCOMMONNESS
UNCOMMONNESSES
UNCOMMUNICABLE
UNCOMMUNICATED
UNCOMMUNICATIVE
UNCOMMUTED
UNCOMPACTED
UNCOMPANIED
UNCOMPANIONABLE
UNCOMPANIONED
UNCOMPASSIONATE
UNCOMPELLED
UNCOMPELLING
UNCOMPENSATED
UNCOMPETITIVE
UNCOMPLACENT
UNCOMPLAINING
UNCOMPLAININGLY
UNCOMPLAISANT
UNCOMPLAISANTLY
UNCOMPLETED
UNCOMPLIANT
UNCOMPLICATED
UNCOMPLIMENTARY
UNCOMPLYING
UNCOMPOSABLE
UNCOMPOUNDED
UNCOMPREHENDED
UNCOMPREHENDING
UNCOMPREHENSIVE
UNCOMPROMISABLE
UNCOMPROMISING
UNCOMPUTERIZED
UNCONCEALABLE
UNCONCEALED
UNCONCEALING
UNCONCEDED
UNCONCEIVABLE
UNCONCEIVABLY
UNCONCEIVED
UNCONCERN
UNCONCERNED
UNCONCERNEDLY
UNCONCERNEDNESS
UNCONCERNING
UNCONCERNMENT

UNCONCERNMENTS
UNCONCERNS
UNCONCERTED
UNCONCILIATORY
UNCONCLUDED
UNCONCLUSIVE
UNCONCOCTED
UNCONDEMNED
UNCONDENSED
UNCONDITIONAL
UNCONDITIONALLY
UNCONDITIONED
UNCONDUCIVE
UNCONFEDERATED
UNCONFESSED
UNCONFIDENT
UNCONFIDENTLY
UNCONFINABLE
UNCONFINE
UNCONFINED
UNCONFINEDLY
UNCONFINES
UNCONFINING
UNCONFIRMED
UNCONFORM
UNCONFORMABLE
UNCONFORMABLY
UNCONFORMING
UNCONFORMITIES
UNCONFORMITY
UNCONFOUNDED
UNCONFUSE
UNCONFUSED
UNCONFUSEDLY
UNCONFUSES
UNCONFUSING
UNCONGEAL
UNCONGEALED
UNCONGEALING
UNCONGEALS
UNCONGENIAL
UNCONGENIALITY
UNCONJECTURED
UNCONJUGAL
UNCONJUGATED
UNCONJUNCTIVE
UNCONNECTED
UNCONNECTEDLY
UNCONNECTEDNESS
UNCONNIVING
UNCONQUERABLE
UNCONQUERABLY
UNCONQUERED
UNCONSCIENTIOUS
UNCONSCIONABLE
UNCONSCIONABLY
UNCONSCIOUS

UNCONSCIOUSES
UNCONSCIOUSLY
UNCONSCIOUSNESS
UNCONSECRATE
UNCONSECRATED
UNCONSECRATES
UNCONSECRATING
UNCONSENTANEOUS
UNCONSENTING
UNCONSIDERED
UNCONSIDERING
UNCONSOLED
UNCONSOLIDATED
UNCONSTANT
UNCONSTRAINABLE
UNCONSTRAINED
UNCONSTRAINEDLY
UNCONSTRAINT
UNCONSTRAINTS
UNCONSTRICTED
UNCONSTRUCTED
UNCONSTRUCTIVE
UNCONSUMED
UNCONSUMMATED
UNCONTAINABLE
UNCONTAMINATED
UNCONTEMNED
UNCONTEMPLATED
UNCONTEMPORARY
UNCONTENTIOUS
UNCONTESTABLE
UNCONTESTED
UNCONTRACTED
UNCONTRADICTED
UNCONTRIVED
UNCONTROLLABLE
UNCONTROLLABLY
UNCONTROLLED
UNCONTROLLEDLY
UNCONTROVERSIAL
UNCONTROVERTED
UNCONVENTIONAL
UNCONVERSABLE
UNCONVERSANT
UNCONVERTED
UNCONVERTIBLE
UNCONVICTED
UNCONVINCED
UNCONVINCING
UNCONVINCINGLY
UNCONVOYED
UNCOOKED
UNCOOL
UNCOOLED
UNCOOPERATIVE
UNCOOPERATIVELY
UNCOORDINATED

UNCOPE	UNCRATED	UNCURABLE	UNDEAFED
UNCOPED	UNCRATES	UNCURB	UNDEAFING
UNCOPES	UNCRATING	UNCURBABLE	UNDEAFS
UNCOPING	UNCRAZY	UNCURBED	UNDEALT
UNCOPYRIGHTABLE	UNCREATE	UNCURBING	UNDEAR
UNCOQUETTISH	UNCREATED	UNCURBS	UNDEBARRED
UNCORD	UNCREATEDNESS	UNCURDLED	UNDEBASED
UNCORDED	UNCREATEDNESSES	UNCURED	UNDEBATABLE
UNCORDIAL	UNCREATES	UNCURIOUS	UNDEBATABLY
UNCORDING	UNCREATING	UNCURL	UNDEBAUCHED
UNCORDS	UNCREATIVE	UNCURLED	UNDECADENT
UNCORK	UNCREDENTIALED	UNCURLING	UNDECAGON
UNCORKED	UNCREDIBLE	UNCURLS	UNDECAGONS
UNCORKING	UNCREDITABLE	UNCURRENT	UNDECAYED
UNCORKS	UNCREDITED	UNCURSE	UNDECEIVABILITY
UNCORRECTABLE	UNCRIPPLED	UNCURSED	UNDECEIVABLE
UNCORRECTED	UNCRITICAL	UNCURSES	UNDECEIVABLY
UNCORRELATED	UNCRITICALLY	UNCURSING	UNDECEIVE
UNCORROBORATED	UNCROPPED	UNCURTAILED	UNDECEIVED
UNCORRUPT	UNCROSS	UNCURTAIN	UNDECEIVER
UNCORRUPTED	UNCROSSABLE	UNCURTAINED	UNDECEIVERS
UNCORSETED	UNCROSSED	UNCURTAINING	UNDECEIVES
UNCOS	UNCROSSES	UNCURTAINS	UNDECEIVING
UNCOSTLY	UNCROSSING	UNCURVED	UNDECEIVINGLY
UNCOUNSELLED	UNCROWDED	UNCUS	UNDECENT
UNCOUNTABLE	UNCROWN	UNCUSTOMARILY	UNDECIDABILITY
UNCOUNTED	UNCROWNED	UNCUSTOMARY	UNDECIDABLE
UNCOUPLE	UNCROWNING	UNCUSTOMED	UNDECIDED
UNCOUPLED	UNCROWNS	UNCUT	UNDECIDEDLY
UNCOUPLER	UNCRUDDED	UNCUTE	UNDECIDEDNESS
UNCOUPLERS	UNCRUMPLE	UNCYNICAL	UNDECIDEDS
UNCOUPLES	UNCRUMPLED	UNCYNICALLY	UNDECILLION
UNCOUPLING	UNCRUMPLES	UNDAM	UNDECILLIONS
UNCOURAGEOUS	UNCRUMPLING	UNDAMAGED	UNDECIMAL
UNCOURTEOUS	UNCRUSHABLE	UNDAMMED	UNDECIMOLE
UNCOURTLINESS	UNCRYSTALLISED	UNDAMMING	UNDECIMOLES
UNCOURTLINESSES	UNCRYSTALLIZED	UNDAMNED	UNDECIPHERABLE
UNCOURTLY	UNCTION	UNDAMPED	UNDECIPHERED
UNCOUTH	UNCTIONLESS	UNDAMS	UNDECISIVE
UNCOUTHER	UNCTIONS	UNDANCEABLE	UNDECK
UNCOUTHEST	UNCTUOSITIES	UNDARING	UNDECKED
UNCOUTHLY	UNCTUOSITY	UNDASHED	UNDECKING
UNCOUTHNESS	UNCTUOUS	UNDATE	UNDECKS
UNCOUTHNESSES	UNCTUOUSLY	UNDATED	UNDECLARED
UNCOVENANTED	UNCTUOUSNESS	UNDAUNTABLE	UNDECLINING
UNCOVER	UNCTUOUSNESSES	UNDAUNTED	UNDECOMPOSABLE
UNCOVERED	UNCUCKOLDED	UNDAUNTEDLY	UNDECOMPOSED
UNCOVERING	UNCUFF	UNDAUNTEDNESS	UNDECORATED
UNCOVERS	UNCUFFED	UNDAUNTEDNESSES	UNDEDICATED
UNCOWL	UNCUFFING	UNDAWNING	UNDEE
UNCOWLED	UNCUFFS	UNDAZZLE	UNDEEDED
UNCOWLING	UNCULLED	UNDAZZLED	UNDEFACED
UNCOWLS	UNCULTIVABLE	UNDAZZLES	UNDEFEATED
UNCOY	UNCULTIVATABLE	UNDAZZLING	UNDEFENDED
UNCOYNED	UNCULTIVATED	UNDE	UNDEFIDE
UNCRACKED	UNCULTURED	UNDEAD	UNDEFIED
UNCRATE	UNCUMBERED	UNDEAF	UNDEFILED

UNDEFINABLE
UNDEFINED
UNDEFOLIATED
UNDEFORMED
UNDEIFIED
UNDEIFIES
UNDEIFY
UNDEIFYING
UNDELAYED
UNDELAYING
UNDELECTABLE
UNDELEGATED
UNDELIBERATE
UNDELIGHT
UNDELIGHTED
UNDELIGHTFUL
UNDELIGHTS
UNDELIVERABLE
UNDELIVERED
UNDELUDED
UNDEMANDING
UNDEMOCRATIC
UNDEMONSTRABLE
UNDEMONSTRATIVE
UNDENIABLE
UNDENIABLENESS
UNDENIABLY
UNDENIED
UNDEPENDABLE
UNDEPENDING
UNDEPLORED
UNDEPRAVED
UNDEPRECIATED
UNDEPRESSED
UNDEPRIVED
UNDER
UNDERACHIEVE
UNDERACHIEVED
UNDERACHIEVER
UNDERACHIEVERS
UNDERACHIEVES
UNDERACHIEVING
UNDERACT
UNDERACTED
UNDERACTING
UNDERACTION
UNDERACTIONS
UNDERACTIVE
UNDERACTIVITIES
UNDERACTIVITY
UNDERACTOR
UNDERACTORS
UNDERACTS
UNDERAGE
UNDERAGENT
UNDERAGENTS
UNDERAGES

UNDERARM
UNDERARMS
UNDERATE
UNDERBEAR
UNDERBEARER
UNDERBEARERS
UNDERBEARING
UNDERBEARINGS
UNDERBEARS
UNDERBELLIES
UNDERBELLY
UNDERBID
UNDERBIDDER
UNDERBIDDERS
UNDERBIDDING
UNDERBIDS
UNDERBIT
UNDERBITE
UNDERBITES
UNDERBITING
UNDERBITTEN
UNDERBLANKET
UNDERBLANKETS
UNDERBODIES
UNDERBODY
UNDERBORE
UNDERBORNE
UNDERBOSS
UNDERBOSSES
UNDERBOUGH
UNDERBOUGHS
UNDERBOUGHT
UNDERBREATH
UNDERBREATHS
UNDERBRED
UNDERBREEDING
UNDERBRIDGE
UNDERBRIDGES
UNDERBRIM
UNDERBRIMS
UNDERBRUSH
UNDERBRUSHED
UNDERBRUSHES
UNDERBRUSHING
UNDERBUD
UNDERBUDDED
UNDERBUDDING
UNDERBUDGET
UNDERBUDGETED
UNDERBUDGETING
UNDERBUDGETS
UNDERBUDS
UNDERBUILD
UNDERBUILDER
UNDERBUILDERS
UNDERBUILDING
UNDERBUILDS

UNDERBUILT
UNDERBURNT
UNDERBUSH
UNDERBUSHED
UNDERBUSHES
UNDERBUSHING
UNDERBUY
UNDERBUYING
UNDERBUYS
UNDERCAPITALISE
UNDERCAPITALIZE
UNDERCARD
UNDERCARDS
UNDERCARRIAGE
UNDERCARRIAGES
UNDERCART
UNDERCARTS
UNDERCAST
UNDERCASTS
UNDERCHARGE
UNDERCHARGED
UNDERCHARGES
UNDERCHARGING
UNDERCLAD
UNDERCLASS
UNDERCLASSES
UNDERCLASSMAN
UNDERCLASSMEN
UNDERCLAY
UNDERCLAYS
UNDERCLERK
UNDERCLERKS
UNDERCLIFF
UNDERCLIFFS
UNDERCLOTHE
UNDERCLOTHED
UNDERCLOTHES
UNDERCLOTHING
UNDERCLOTHINGS
UNDERCLUB
UNDERCLUBBED
UNDERCLUBBING
UNDERCLUBS
UNDERCOAT
UNDERCOATED
UNDERCOATING
UNDERCOATINGS
UNDERCOATS
UNDERCOOK
UNDERCOOKED
UNDERCOOKING
UNDERCOOKS
UNDERCOOL
UNDERCOOLED
UNDERCOOLING
UNDERCOOLS
UNDERCOUNT

UNDERCOUNTED
UNDERCOUNTING
UNDERCOUNTS
UNDERCOVER
UNDERCOVERT
UNDERCOVERTS
UNDERCREST
UNDERCRESTED
UNDERCRESTING
UNDERCRESTS
UNDERCROFT
UNDERCROFTS
UNDERCURRENT
UNDERCURRENTS
UNDERCUT
UNDERCUTS
UNDERCUTTING
UNDERDAKS
UNDERDAMPER
UNDERDAMPERS
UNDERDECK
UNDERDECKS
UNDERDEVELOP
UNDERDEVELOPED
UNDERDEVELOPING
UNDERDEVELOPS
UNDERDID
UNDERDO
UNDERDOER
UNDERDOERS
UNDERDOES
UNDERDOG
UNDERDOGS
UNDERDOING
UNDERDONE
UNDERDRAIN
UNDERDRAINAGE
UNDERDRAINED
UNDERDRAINING
UNDERDRAINS
UNDERDRAW
UNDERDRAWERS
UNDERDRAWING
UNDERDRAWINGS
UNDERDRAWN
UNDERDRAWS
UNDERDRESS
UNDERDRESSED
UNDERDRESSES
UNDERDRESSING
UNDERDREW
UNDERDRIVE
UNDERDRIVES
UNDEREARTH
UNDEREAT
UNDEREATEN
UNDEREATING

UNDEREATS
UNDEREDUCATED
UNDEREMPHASES
UNDEREMPHASIS
UNDEREMPHASIZE
UNDEREMPHASIZED
UNDEREMPHASIZES
UNDEREMPLOYED
UNDEREMPLOYMENT
UNDERESTIMATE
UNDERESTIMATED
UNDERESTIMATES
UNDERESTIMATING
UNDERESTIMATION
UNDEREXPOSE
UNDEREXPOSED
UNDEREXPOSES
UNDEREXPOSING
UNDEREXPOSURE
UNDEREXPOSURES
UNDERFED
UNDERFEED
UNDERFEEDING
UNDERFEEDS
UNDERFELT
UNDERFELTS
UNDERFINANCED
UNDERFINISHED
UNDERFIRE
UNDERFIRED
UNDERFIRES
UNDERFIRING
UNDERFISH
UNDERFISHED
UNDERFISHES
UNDERFISHING
UNDERFLOOR
UNDERFLOW
UNDERFLOWS
UNDERFONG
UNDERFONGED
UNDERFONGING
UNDERFONGS
UNDERFOOT
UNDERFOOTED
UNDERFOOTING
UNDERFOOTS
UNDERFULFIL
UNDERFULFILLED
UNDERFULFILLING
UNDERFULFILS
UNDERFUND
UNDERFUNDED
UNDERFUNDING
UNDERFUNDINGS
UNDERFUNDS
UNDERFUR

UNDERFURS
UNDERGARMENT
UNDERGARMENTS
UNDERGIRD
UNDERGIRDED
UNDERGIRDING
UNDERGIRDS
UNDERGIRT
UNDERGLAZE
UNDERGLAZES
UNDERGO
UNDERGOD
UNDERGODS
UNDERGOER
UNDERGOERS
UNDERGOES
UNDERGOING
UNDERGONE
UNDERGOWN
UNDERGOWNS
UNDERGRAD
UNDERGRADS
UNDERGRADUATE
UNDERGRADUATES
UNDERGRADUETTE
UNDERGRADUETTES
UNDERGROUND
UNDERGROUNDER
UNDERGROUNDERS
UNDERGROUNDS
UNDERGROVE
UNDERGROVES
UNDERGROWN
UNDERGROWTH
UNDERGROWTHS
UNDERHAND
UNDERHANDED
UNDERHANDEDLY
UNDERHANDEDNESS
UNDERHANDS
UNDERHONEST
UNDERHUNG
UNDERINFLATED
UNDERINFLATION
UNDERINFLATIONS
UNDERINSURED
UNDERINVESTMENT
UNDERJAW
UNDERJAWED
UNDERJAWS
UNDERKEEP
UNDERKEEPER
UNDERKEEPERS
UNDERKEEPING
UNDERKEEPS
UNDERKEPT
UNDERKING

UNDERKINGDOM
UNDERKINGDOMS
UNDERKINGS
UNDERLAID
UNDERLAIN
UNDERLAP
UNDERLAPPED
UNDERLAPPING
UNDERLAPS
UNDERLAY
UNDERLAYER
UNDERLAYERS
UNDERLAYING
UNDERLAYMENT
UNDERLAYMENTS
UNDERLAYS
UNDERLEAF
UNDERLEASE
UNDERLEASED
UNDERLEASES
UNDERLEASING
UNDERLEAVES
UNDERLET
UNDERLETS
UNDERLETTER
UNDERLETTERS
UNDERLETTING
UNDERLETTINGS
UNDERLIE
UNDERLIER
UNDERLIERS
UNDERLIES
UNDERLINE
UNDERLINED
UNDERLINEN
UNDERLINENS
UNDERLINES
UNDERLING
UNDERLINGS
UNDERLINING
UNDERLIP
UNDERLIPS
UNDERLIT
UNDERLOOKER
UNDERLOOKERS
UNDERLYING
UNDERLYINGLY
UNDERMAN
UNDERMANNED
UNDERMANNING
UNDERMANS
UNDERMASTED
UNDERMEANING
UNDERMEANINGS
UNDERMEN
UNDERMENTIONED
UNDERMINDE

UNDERMINDED
UNDERMINDES
UNDERMINDING
UNDERMINE
UNDERMINED
UNDERMINER
UNDERMINERS
UNDERMINES
UNDERMINING
UNDERMININGS
UNDERMOST
UNDERN
UNDERNAMED
UNDERNEATH
UNDERNEATHS
UNDERNICENESS
UNDERNICENESSES
UNDERNOTE
UNDERNOTED
UNDERNOTES
UNDERNOTING
UNDERNOURISH
UNDERNOURISHED
UNDERNOURISHES
UNDERNOURISHING
UNDERNS
UNDERNTIME
UNDERNTIMES
UNDERNUTRITION
UNDERNUTRITIONS
UNDERPAID
UNDERPAINTING
UNDERPAINTINGS
UNDERPANTS
UNDERPART
UNDERPARTS
UNDERPASS
UNDERPASSES
UNDERPASSION
UNDERPASSIONS
UNDERPAY
UNDERPAYING
UNDERPAYMENT
UNDERPAYMENTS
UNDERPAYS
UNDERPEEP
UNDERPEEPED
UNDERPEEPING
UNDERPEEPS
UNDERPEOPLED
UNDERPERFORM
UNDERPERFORMED
UNDERPERFORMING
UNDERPERFORMS
UNDERPIN
UNDERPINNED
UNDERPINNING

UNDERPINNINGS
UNDERPINS
UNDERPITCH
UNDERPLANT
UNDERPLANTED
UNDERPLANTING
UNDERPLANTS
UNDERPLAY
UNDERPLAYED
UNDERPLAYING
UNDERPLAYS
UNDERPLOT
UNDERPLOTS
UNDERPOPULATED
UNDERPOWERED
UNDERPRAISE
UNDERPRAISED
UNDERPRAISES
UNDERPRAISING
UNDERPREPARED
UNDERPRICE
UNDERPRICED
UNDERPRICES
UNDERPRICING
UNDERPRISE
UNDERPRISED
UNDERPRISES
UNDERPRISING
UNDERPRIVILEGED
UNDERPRIZE
UNDERPRIZED
UNDERPRIZES
UNDERPRIZING
UNDERPRODUCE
UNDERPRODUCED
UNDERPRODUCES
UNDERPRODUCING
UNDERPRODUCTION
UNDERPROOF
UNDERPROP
UNDERPROPPED
UNDERPROPPER
UNDERPROPPERS
UNDERPROPPING
UNDERPROPS
UNDERPUBLICIZED
UNDERQUOTE
UNDERQUOTED
UNDERQUOTES
UNDERQUOTING
UNDERRAN
UNDERRATE
UNDERRATED
UNDERRATES
UNDERRATING
UNDERREACT
UNDERREACTED

UNDERREACTING
UNDERREACTS
UNDERREPORT
UNDERREPORTED
UNDERREPORTING
UNDERREPORTS
UNDERRIPENED
UNDERRUN
UNDERRUNNING
UNDERRUNNINGS
UNDERRUNS
UNDERSAID
UNDERSATURATED
UNDERSAY
UNDERSAYES
UNDERSAYING
UNDERSAYS
UNDERSCORE
UNDERSCORED
UNDERSCORES
UNDERSCORING
UNDERSCRUB
UNDERSCRUBS
UNDERSEA
UNDERSEAL
UNDERSEALED
UNDERSEALING
UNDERSEALINGS
UNDERSEALS
UNDERSEAS
UNDERSECRETARY
UNDERSELF
UNDERSELL
UNDERSELLER
UNDERSELLERS
UNDERSELLING
UNDERSELLS
UNDERSELVES
UNDERSENSE
UNDERSENSES
UNDERSERVANT
UNDERSERVANTS
UNDERSERVED
UNDERSET
UNDERSETS
UNDERSETTING
UNDERSEXED
UNDERSHAPEN
UNDERSHERIFF
UNDERSHERIFFS
UNDERSHIRT
UNDERSHIRTED
UNDERSHIRTS
UNDERSHOOT
UNDERSHOOTING
UNDERSHOOTS
UNDERSHORTS

UNDERSHOT
UNDERSHRUB
UNDERSHRUBS
UNDERSIDE
UNDERSIDES
UNDERSIGN
UNDERSIGNED
UNDERSIGNING
UNDERSIGNS
UNDERSIZE
UNDERSIZED
UNDERSKIES
UNDERSKINKER
UNDERSKINKERS
UNDERSKIRT
UNDERSKIRTS
UNDERSKY
UNDERSLEEVE
UNDERSLEEVES
UNDERSLUNG
UNDERSOIL
UNDERSOILS
UNDERSOLD
UNDERSONG
UNDERSONGS
UNDERSPEND
UNDERSPENDING
UNDERSPENDS
UNDERSPENT
UNDERSPIN
UNDERSPINS
UNDERSTAFFED
UNDERSTAFFING
UNDERSTAFFINGS
UNDERSTAND
UNDERSTANDABLE
UNDERSTANDABLY
UNDERSTANDED
UNDERSTANDER
UNDERSTANDERS
UNDERSTANDING
UNDERSTANDINGLY
UNDERSTANDINGS
UNDERSTANDS
UNDERSTATE
UNDERSTATED
UNDERSTATEDLY
UNDERSTATEMENT
UNDERSTATEMENTS
UNDERSTATES
UNDERSTATING
UNDERSTEER
UNDERSTEERED
UNDERSTEERING
UNDERSTEERS
UNDERSTOCK
UNDERSTOCKED

UNDERSTOCKING
UNDERSTOCKS
UNDERSTOOD
UNDERSTOREY
UNDERSTOREYS
UNDERSTORIES
UNDERSTORY
UNDERSTRAPPER
UNDERSTRAPPERS
UNDERSTRAPPING
UNDERSTRATA
UNDERSTRATUM
UNDERSTRENGTH
UNDERSTUDIED
UNDERSTUDIES
UNDERSTUDY
UNDERSTUDYING
UNDERSUPPLIED
UNDERSUPPLIES
UNDERSUPPLY
UNDERSUPPLYING
UNDERSURFACE
UNDERSURFACES
UNDERTAKABLE
UNDERTAKE
UNDERTAKEN
UNDERTAKER
UNDERTAKERS
UNDERTAKES
UNDERTAKING
UNDERTAKINGS
UNDERTANE
UNDERTAX
UNDERTAXED
UNDERTAXES
UNDERTAXING
UNDERTENANCIES
UNDERTENANCY
UNDERTENANT
UNDERTENANTS
UNDERTHINGS
UNDERTHIRST
UNDERTHIRSTS
UNDERTHRUST
UNDERTHRUSTING
UNDERTHRUSTS
UNDERTIME
UNDERTIMED
UNDERTIMES
UNDERTINT
UNDERTINTS
UNDERTONE
UNDERTONED
UNDERTONES
UNDERTOOK
UNDERTOW
UNDERTOWS

UNDERTRAINED	UNDERWORKED	UNDETERMINED	UNDISGUISABLE
UNDERTRICK	UNDERWORKER	UNDETERRED	UNDISGUISED
UNDERTRICKS	UNDERWORKERS	UNDEVELOPED	UNDISGUISEDLY
UNDERTRUMP	UNDERWORKING	UNDEVIATING	UNDISHONOURED
UNDERTRUMPED	UNDERWORKS	UNDEVIATINGLY	UNDISMANTLED
UNDERTRUMPING	UNDERWORLD	UNDEVOUT	UNDISMAYED
UNDERTRUMPS	UNDERWORLDS	UNDIAGNOSABLE	UNDISORDERED
UNDERUSE	UNDERWRITE	UNDIAGNOSED	UNDISPATCHED
UNDERUSED	UNDERWRITER	UNDIALECTICAL	UNDISPENSED
UNDERUSES	UNDERWRITERS	UNDID	UNDISPOSED
UNDERUSING	UNDERWRITES	UNDIDACTIC	UNDISPUTABLE
UNDERUTILISE	UNDERWRITING	UNDIES	UNDISPUTED
UNDERUTILISED	UNDERWRITINGS	UNDIFFERENCED	UNDISPUTEDLY
UNDERUTILISES	UNDERWRITTEN	UNDIGESTED	UNDISSEMBLED
UNDERUTILISING	UNDERWROTE	UNDIGESTIBLE	UNDISSOCIATED
UNDERUTILIZE	UNDERWROUGHT	UNDIGHT	UNDISSOLVED
UNDERUTILIZED	UNDESCENDABLE	UNDIGHTING	UNDISSOLVING
UNDERUTILIZES	UNDESCENDED	UNDIGHTS	UNDISTEMPERED
UNDERUTILIZING	UNDESCENDIBLE	UNDIGNIFIED	UNDISTILLED
UNDERVALUATION	UNDESCRIBABLE	UNDIGNIFIES	UNDISTINCTIVE
UNDERVALUATIONS	UNDESCRIBED	UNDIGNIFY	UNDISTINGUISHED
UNDERVALUE	UNDESCRIED	UNDIGNIFYING	UNDISTORTED
UNDERVALUED	UNDESERT	UNDILUTED	UNDISTRACTED
UNDERVALUER	UNDESERTS	UNDIMINISHABLE	UNDISTRACTEDLY
UNDERVALUERS	UNDESERVE	UNDIMINISHED	UNDISTRACTING
UNDERVALUES	UNDESERVED	UNDIMMED	UNDISTRESSABLE
UNDERVALUING	UNDESERVEDLY	UNDINE	UNDISTRESSED
UNDERVEST	UNDESERVEDNESS	UNDINES	UNDISTRIBUTED
UNDERVESTS	UNDESERVER	UNDINISM	UNDISTURBED
UNDERVIEWER	UNDESERVERS	UNDINISMS	UNDISTURBEDLY
UNDERVIEWERS	UNDESERVES	UNDINTED	UNDISTURBING
UNDERVOICE	UNDESERVING	UNDIPLOMATIC	UNDIVERSIFIED
UNDERVOICES	UNDESERVINGLY	UNDIPPED	UNDIVERTED
UNDERWATER	UNDESIGNATED	UNDIRECTED	UNDIVERTING
UNDERWATERS	UNDESIGNED	UNDISAPPOINTING	UNDIVESTED
UNDERWAY	UNDESIGNEDLY	UNDISCERNED	UNDIVESTEDLY
UNDERWEAR	UNDESIGNEDNESS	UNDISCERNEDLY	UNDIVIDABLE
UNDERWEARS	UNDESIGNING	UNDISCERNIBLE	UNDIVIDED
UNDERWEIGHT	UNDESIRABILITY	UNDISCERNIBLY	UNDIVIDEDLY
UNDERWEIGHTS	UNDESIRABLE	UNDISCERNING	UNDIVIDEDNESS
UNDERWENT	UNDESIRABLENESS	UNDISCERNINGS	UNDIVIDEDNESSES
UNDERWHELM	UNDESIRABLES	UNDISCHARGED	UNDIVINE
UNDERWHELMED	UNDESIRABLY	UNDISCIPLINABLE	UNDIVORCED
UNDERWHELMING	UNDESIRED	UNDISCIPLINE	UNDIVULGED
UNDERWHELMS	UNDESIRING	UNDISCIPLINED	UNDO
UNDERWING	UNDESIROUS	UNDISCIPLINES	UNDOABLE
UNDERWINGS	UNDESPAIRING	UNDISCLOSED	UNDOCILE
UNDERWIRED	UNDESPAIRINGLY	UNDISCOMFITED	UNDOCK
UNDERWIRING	UNDESPOILED	UNDISCORDANT	UNDOCKED
UNDERWIRINGS	UNDESTROYED	UNDISCORDING	UNDOCKING
UNDERWIT	UNDETACHABLE	UNDISCOURAGED	UNDOCKS
UNDERWITS	UNDETACHED	UNDISCOVERABLE	UNDOCTORED
UNDERWOOD	UNDETECTABLE	UNDISCOVERABLY	UNDOCTRINAIRE
UNDERWOODS	UNDETECTED	UNDISCOVERED	UNDOCUMENTED
UNDERWOOL	UNDETERMINABLE	UNDISCUSSABLE	UNDOER
UNDERWOOLS	UNDETERMINATE	UNDISCUSSED	UNDOERS
UNDERWORK	UNDETERMINATION	UNDISCUSSIBLE	UNDOES

UNDOGMATIC
UNDOGMATICALLY
UNDOING
UNDOINGS
UNDOMESTIC
UNDOMESTICATE
UNDOMESTICATED
UNDOMESTICATES
UNDOMESTICATING
UNDONE
UNDOOMED
UNDOTTED
UNDOUBLE
UNDOUBLED
UNDOUBLES
UNDOUBLING
UNDOUBTABLE
UNDOUBTED
UNDOUBTEDLY
UNDOUBTFUL
UNDOUBTING
UNDOUBTINGLY
UNDRAINABLE
UNDRAINED
UNDRAMATIC
UNDRAMATICALLY
UNDRAMATIZED
UNDRAPE
UNDRAPED
UNDRAPES
UNDRAPING
UNDRAW
UNDRAWING
UNDRAWN
UNDRAWS
UNDREADED
UNDREADING
UNDREAMED
UNDREAMING
UNDREAMT
UNDRESS
UNDRESSED
UNDRESSES
UNDRESSING
UNDRESSINGS
UNDREST
UNDREW
UNDRIED
UNDRILLED
UNDRINKABLE
UNDRIVEABLE
UNDRIVEN
UNDROOPING
UNDROSSY
UNDROWNED
UNDRUNK
UNDUBBED

UNDUE
UNDUG
UNDULANCE
UNDULANCIES
UNDULANCY
UNDULANT
UNDULAR
UNDULATE
UNDULATED
UNDULATELY
UNDULATES
UNDULATING
UNDULATINGLY
UNDULATION
UNDULATIONIST
UNDULATIONISTS
UNDULATIONS
UNDULATOR
UNDULATORS
UNDULATORY
UNDULLED
UNDULOSE
UNDULOUS
UNDULY
UNDUPLICATED
UNDUTEOUS
UNDUTIFUL
UNDUTIFULLY
UNDUTIFULNESS
UNDUTIFULNESSES
UNDY
UNDYED
UNDYING
UNDYINGLY
UNDYINGNESS
UNDYINGNESSES
UNDYNAMIC
UNEAGER
UNEARED
UNEARMARKED
UNEARNED
UNEARTH
UNEARTHED
UNEARTHING
UNEARTHLIER
UNEARTHLIEST
UNEARTHLINESS
UNEARTHLINESSES
UNEARTHLY
UNEARTHS
UNEASE
UNEASES
UNEASIER
UNEASIEST
UNEASILY
UNEASINESS
UNEASINESSES

UNEASY
UNEATABLE
UNEATABLENESS
UNEATABLENESSES
UNEATEN
UNEATH
UNEATHES
UNECCENTRIC
UNECLIPSED
UNECOLOGICAL
UNECONOMIC
UNECONOMICAL
UNEDGE
UNEDGED
UNEDGES
UNEDGING
UNEDIBLE
UNEDIFYING
UNEDITED
UNEDUCABLE
UNEDUCATED
UNEFFACED
UNEFFECTED
UNELABORATE
UNELABORATED
UNELATED
UNELECTABLE
UNELECTED
UNELECTRIFIED
UNEMANCIPATED
UNEMANCIPATION
UNEMBARRASSED
UNEMBELLISHED
UNEMBITTERED
UNEMBODIED
UNEMOTIONAL
UNEMOTIONALLY
UNEMOTIONED
UNEMPHATIC
UNEMPHATICALLY
UNEMPIRICAL
UNEMPLOYABILITY
UNEMPLOYABLE
UNEMPLOYABLES
UNEMPLOYED
UNEMPLOYEDS
UNEMPLOYMENT
UNEMPLOYMENTS
UNEMPTIED
UNENCHANTED
UNENCLOSED
UNENCOURAGING
UNENCUMBERED
UNENDANGERED
UNENDEARED
UNENDEARING
UNENDED

UNENDING
UNENDINGLY
UNENDINGNESS
UNENDINGNESSES
UNENDORSABLE
UNENDORSED
UNENDOWED
UNENDURABLE
UNENDURABLENESS
UNENDURABLY
UNENFORCEABLE
UNENFORCED
UNENGAGED
UNENJOYABLE
UNENLARGED
UNENLIGHTENED
UNENLIGHTENING
UNENQUIRING
UNENRICHED
UNENSLAVED
UNENTAILED
UNENTERED
UNENTERPRISING
UNENTERTAINED
UNENTERTAINING
UNENTHRALLED
UNENTHUSIASTIC
UNENTITLED
UNENVIABLE
UNENVIABLY
UNENVIED
UNENVIOUS
UNENVYING
UNEQUABLE
UNEQUAL
UNEQUALED
UNEQUALLED
UNEQUALLY
UNEQUALS
UNEQUIPPED
UNEQUITABLE
UNEQUIVOCABLY
UNEQUIVOCAL
UNEQUIVOCALLY
UNEQUIVOCALNESS
UNERASABLE
UNERASED
UNEROTIC
UNERRING
UNERRINGLY
UNERRINGNESS
UNERRINGNESSES
UNESCAPABLE
UNESCORTED
UNESPIED
UNESSAYED
UNESSENCE

UNESSENCED	UNEXPERIENT	UNFAMILIAR	UNFENCED
UNESSENCES	UNEXPERT	UNFAMILIARITIES	UNFENCES
UNESSENCING	UNEXPIATED	UNFAMILIARITY	UNFENCING
UNESSENTIAL	UNEXPIRED	UNFAMILIARLY	UNFERMENTED
UNESSENTIALLY	UNEXPLAINABLE	UNFAMOUS	UNFERTILE
UNESSENTIALNESS	UNEXPLAINED	UNFANCY	UNFERTILISED
UNESSENTIALS	UNEXPLICIT	UNFANNED	UNFERTILIZED
UNESTABLISHED	UNEXPLICITNESS	UNFASHIONABLE	UNFETTER
UNESTIMATED	UNEXPLODED	UNFASHIONABLY	UNFETTERED
UNETH	UNEXPLOITED	UNFASHIONED	UNFETTERING
UNETHICAL	UNEXPLORED	UNFASTEN	UNFETTERS
UNEVADED	UNEXPOSED	UNFASTENED	UNFEUDAL
UNEVALUATED	UNEXPRESSED	UNFASTENING	UNFEUDALISE
UNEVANGELICAL	UNEXPRESSIBLE	UNFASTENS	UNFEUDALISED
UNEVEN	UNEXPRESSIVE	UNFASTIDIOUS	UNFEUDALISES
UNEVENER	UNEXPUGNABLE	UNFATHERED	UNFEUDALISING
UNEVENEST	UNEXPURGATED	UNFATHERLY	UNFEUDALIZE
UNEVENLY	UNEXTENDED	UNFATHOMABLE	UNFEUDALIZED
UNEVENNESS	UNEXTENUATED	UNFATHOMABLY	UNFEUDALIZES
UNEVENNESSES	UNEXTINCT	UNFATHOMED	UNFEUDALIZING
UNEVENTFUL	UNEXTINGUISHED	UNFATIGUED	UNFEUED
UNEVENTFULLY	UNEXTRAORDINARY	UNFAULTY	UNFIGURED
UNEVENTFULNESS	UNEXTREME	UNFAVORABLE	UNFILDE
UNEVIDENCED	UNEYED	UNFAVORABLENESS	UNFILED
UNEXACTING	UNFABLED	UNFAVORABLY	UNFILIAL
UNEXAGGERATED	UNFACT	UNFAVORED	UNFILIALLY
UNEXALTED	UNFACTS	UNFAVOREDNESS	UNFILLABLE
UNEXAMINED	UNFADABLE	UNFAVORITE	UNFILLED
UNEXAMPLED	UNFADED	UNFAVOURABLE	UNFILLETED
UNEXCAVATED	UNFADING	UNFAVOURABLY	UNFILMED
UNEXCEEDED	UNFADINGLY	UNFAVOURED	UNFILTERABLE
UNEXCELLED	UNFADINGNESS	UNFAVOUREDNESS	UNFILTERED
UNEXCEPTIONABLE	UNFADINGNESSES	UNFAZED	UNFILTRABLE
UNEXCEPTIONABLY	UNFAILING	UNFEARED	UNFINDABLE
UNEXCEPTIONAL	UNFAILINGLY	UNFEARFUL	UNFINE
UNEXCEPTIONALLY	UNFAILINGNESS	UNFEARFULLY	UNFINISHED
UNEXCITABLE	UNFAIR	UNFEARING	UNFINISHING
UNEXCITED	UNFAIRED	UNFEASIBLE	UNFINISHINGS
UNEXCITING	UNFAIRER	UNFEATHERED	UNFIRED
UNEXCLUDED	UNFAIREST	UNFEATURED	UNFIRM
UNEXCLUSIVE	UNFAIRING	UNFED	UNFISHED
UNEXCLUSIVELY	UNFAIRLY	UNFEDERATED	UNFIT
UNEXCUSED	UNFAIRNESS	UNFEED	UNFITLY
UNEXECUTED	UNFAIRNESSES	UNFEELING	UNFITNESS
UNEXEMPLIFIED	UNFAIRS	UNFEELINGLY	UNFITNESSES
UNEXERCISED	UNFAITH	UNFEELINGNESS	UNFITS
UNEXHAUSTED	UNFAITHFUL	UNFEELINGNESSES	UNFITTED
UNEXOTIC	UNFAITHFULLY	UNFEIGNED	UNFITTEDNESS
UNEXPANDED	UNFAITHFULNESS	UNFEIGNEDLY	UNFITTEDNESSES
UNEXPECTANT	UNFAITHS	UNFEIGNEDNESS	UNFITTER
UNEXPECTED	UNFAKED	UNFEIGNEDNESSES	UNFITTEST
UNEXPECTEDLY	UNFALLEN	UNFEIGNING	UNFITTING
UNEXPECTEDNESS	UNFALLIBLE	UNFELLED	UNFITTINGLY
UNEXPENDED	UNFALSIFIABLE	UNFELLOWED	UNFIX
UNEXPENSIVE	UNFALTERING	UNFELT	UNFIXED
UNEXPENSIVELY	UNFALTERINGLY	UNFEMININE	UNFIXEDNESS
UNEXPERIENCED	UNFAMED	UNFENCE	UNFIXEDNESSES

UNFIXES
UNFIXING
UNFIXITIES
UNFIXITY
UNFIXT
UNFLAGGING
UNFLAGGINGLY
UNFLAMBOYANT
UNFLAPPABILITY
UNFLAPPABLE
UNFLAPPABLENESS
UNFLAPPABLY
UNFLASHY
UNFLATTERING
UNFLATTERINGLY
UNFLAVOURED
UNFLAWED
UNFLEDGED
UNFLESH
UNFLESHED
UNFLESHES
UNFLESHING
UNFLESHLY
UNFLEXED
UNFLINCHING
UNFLINCHINGLY
UNFLOORED
UNFLUSH
UNFLUSHED
UNFLUSHES
UNFLUSHING
UNFLUSTERED
UNFLYABLE
UNFOCUSED
UNFOCUSSED
UNFOILED
UNFOLD
UNFOLDED
UNFOLDER
UNFOLDERS
UNFOLDING
UNFOLDINGS
UNFOLDMENT
UNFOLDMENTS
UNFOLDS
UNFOND
UNFOOL
UNFOOLED
UNFOOLING
UNFOOLS
UNFOOTED
UNFORBEARING
UNFORBID
UNFORBIDDEN
UNFORCEABILITY
UNFORCEABLE
UNFORCED

UNFORCEDLY
UNFORCIBLE
UNFORDABLE
UNFOREBODING
UNFOREKNOWABLE
UNFOREKNOWN
UNFORESEEABLE
UNFORESEEING
UNFORESEEN
UNFORESKINNED
UNFORESTED
UNFORETOLD
UNFOREWARNED
UNFORFEITED
UNFORGED
UNFORGETTABLE
UNFORGETTABLY
UNFORGIVABLE
UNFORGIVEN
UNFORGIVENESS
UNFORGIVENESSES
UNFORGIVING
UNFORGIVINGNESS
UNFORGOT
UNFORGOTTEN
UNFORKED
UNFORM
UNFORMAL
UNFORMALISED
UNFORMALIZED
UNFORMATTED
UNFORMED
UNFORMIDABLE
UNFORMING
UNFORMS
UNFORMULATED
UNFORSAKEN
UNFORTHCOMING
UNFORTIFIED
UNFORTUNATE
UNFORTUNATELY
UNFORTUNATENESS
UNFORTUNATES
UNFORTUNE
UNFORTUNED
UNFORTUNES
UNFOSSILIFEROUS
UNFOSSILISED
UNFOSSILIZED
UNFOSTERED
UNFOUGHT
UNFOUGHTEN
UNFOUND
UNFOUNDED
UNFOUNDEDLY
UNFOUNDEDNESS
UNFRAMED

UNFRANCHISED
UNFRANKED
UNFRAUGHT
UNFRAUGHTED
UNFRAUGHTING
UNFRAUGHTS
UNFREE
UNFREED
UNFREEDOM
UNFREEDOMS
UNFREEING
UNFREEMAN
UNFREEMEN
UNFREES
UNFREEZE
UNFREEZES
UNFREEZING
UNFREQUENT
UNFREQUENTED
UNFREQUENTLY
UNFRETTED
UNFRIEND
UNFRIENDED
UNFRIENDEDNESS
UNFRIENDLIER
UNFRIENDLIEST
UNFRIENDLILY
UNFRIENDLINESS
UNFRIENDLY
UNFRIENDS
UNFRIENDSHIP
UNFRIENDSHIPS
UNFRIGHTED
UNFRIGHTENED
UNFRIVOLOUS
UNFROCK
UNFROCKED
UNFROCKING
UNFROCKS
UNFROZE
UNFROZEN
UNFRUCTUOUS
UNFRUITFUL
UNFRUITFULLY
UNFRUITFULNESS
UNFUELLED
UNFULFILLABLE
UNFULFILLED
UNFUMED
UNFUNDED
UNFUNNY
UNFURL
UNFURLED
UNFURLING
UNFURLS
UNFURNISH
UNFURNISHED

UNFURNISHES
UNFURNISHING
UNFURRED
UNFURROWED
UNFUSED
UNFUSSIER
UNFUSSIEST
UNFUSSILY
UNFUSSINESS
UNFUSSY
UNGAG
UNGAGGED
UNGAGGING
UNGAGS
UNGAIN
UNGAINFUL
UNGAINLIER
UNGAINLIEST
UNGAINLINESS
UNGAINLINESSES
UNGAINLY
UNGAINSAID
UNGAINSAYABLE
UNGALLANT
UNGALLANTLY
UNGALLED
UNGARBLED
UNGARMENTED
UNGARNERED
UNGARNISHED
UNGARTERED
UNGATHERED
UNGAUGED
UNGEAR
UNGEARED
UNGEARING
UNGEARS
UNGENEROSITIES
UNGENEROSITY
UNGENEROUS
UNGENEROUSLY
UNGENIAL
UNGENITURED
UNGENTEEL
UNGENTEELLY
UNGENTILITIES
UNGENTILITY
UNGENTLE
UNGENTLEMANLIKE
UNGENTLEMANLY
UNGENTLENESS
UNGENTLENESSES
UNGENTLY
UNGENTRIFIED
UNGENUINE
UNGENUINENESS
UNGENUINENESSES

UNGERMANE	UNGOWNED	UNGUICULATES	UNHANGING
UNGERMINATED	UNGOWNING	UNGUIDED	UNHANGS
UNGET	UNGOWNS	UNGUIFORM	UNHAPPIED
UNGETATABLE	UNGRACED	UNGUILTY	UNHAPPIER
UNGETS	UNGRACEFUL	UNGUINOUS	UNHAPPIES
UNGETTING	UNGRACEFULLY	UNGUINOUSLY	UNHAPPIEST
UNGHOSTLY	UNGRACEFULNESS	UNGUIS	UNHAPPILY
UNGIFTED	UNGRACIOUS	UNGULA	UNHAPPINESS
UNGILD	UNGRACIOUSLY	UNGULAE	UNHAPPINESSES
UNGILDED	UNGRACIOUSNESS	UNGULAR	UNHAPPY
UNGILDING	UNGRADED	UNGULATE	UNHAPPYING
UNGILDS	UNGRAMMATIC	UNGULATES	UNHARBOUR
UNGILT	UNGRAMMATICAL	UNGULED	UNHARBOURED
UNGIMMICKY	UNGRAMMATICALLY	UNGULIGRADE	UNHARBOURING
UNGIRD	UNGRASPABLE	UNGUM	UNHARBOURS
UNGIRDED	UNGRASSED	UNGUMMED	UNHARDENED
UNGIRDING	UNGRATEFUL	UNGUMMING	UNHARDY
UNGIRDS	UNGRATEFULLY	UNGUMS	UNHARMED
UNGIRT	UNGRATEFULNESS	UNGYVE	UNHARMFUL
UNGIRTH	UNGRATIFIED	UNGYVED	UNHARMFULLY
UNGIRTHED	UNGRATIFYING	UNGYVES	UNHARMING
UNGIRTHING	UNGRATIFYINGLY	UNGYVING	UNHARMONIOUS
UNGIRTHS	UNGRAVELY	UNHABITABLE	UNHARMONIOUSLY
UNGIVING	UNGRAZED	UNHABITUATED	UNHARNESS
UNGLAD	UNGREEDY	UNHABLE	UNHARNESSED
UNGLAMORIZED	UNGROOMED	UNHACKED	UNHARNESSES
UNGLAMOROUS	UNGROUND	UNHACKNEYED	UNHARNESSING
UNGLAZED	UNGROUNDED	UNHAILED	UNHARROWED
UNGLOSSED	UNGROUNDEDLY	UNHAIR	UNHARVESTED
UNGLOVE	UNGROUNDEDNESS	UNHAIRED	UNHASP
UNGLOVED	UNGROUPED	UNHAIRING	UNHASPED
UNGLOVES	UNGROWN	UNHAIRS	UNHASPING
UNGLOVING	UNGRUDGED	UNHALLOW	UNHASPS
UNGLUE	UNGRUDGING	UNHALLOWED	UNHASTING
UNGLUED	UNGRUDGINGLY	UNHALLOWING	UNHASTY
UNGLUES	UNGUAL	UNHALLOWS	UNHAT
UNGLUING	UNGUARD	UNHALSED	UNHATCHED
UNGOD	UNGUARDED	UNHALVED	UNHATS
UNGODDED	UNGUARDEDLY	UNHAMPERED	UNHATTED
UNGODDING	UNGUARDEDNESS	UNHAND	UNHATTING
UNGODLIER	UNGUARDEDNESSES	UNHANDED	UNHATTINGS
UNGODLIEST	UNGUARDING	UNHANDICAPPED	UNHAUNTED
UNGODLIKE	UNGUARDS	UNHANDIER	UNHAZARDED
UNGODLILY	UNGUENT	UNHANDIEST	UNHAZARDOUS
UNGODLINESS	UNGUENTA	UNHANDILY	UNHEAD
UNGODLINESSES	UNGUENTARIA	UNHANDINESS	UNHEADED
UNGODLY	UNGUENTARIES	UNHANDINESSES	UNHEADING
UNGODS	UNGUENTARIUM	UNHANDING	UNHEADS
UNGORD	UNGUENTARY	UNHANDLED	UNHEAL
UNGORED	UNGUENTS	UNHANDS	UNHEALABLE
UNGORGED	UNGUENTUM	UNHANDSELED	UNHEALED
UNGOT	UNGUERDONED	UNHANDSOME	UNHEALING
UNGOTTEN	UNGUES	UNHANDSOMELY	UNHEALS
UNGOVERNABLE	UNGUESSABLE	UNHANDSOMENESS	UNHEALTH
UNGOVERNABLY	UNGUESSED	UNHANDY	UNHEALTHFUL
UNGOVERNED	UNGUICULATE	UNHANG	UNHEALTHFULLY
UNGOWN	UNGUICULATED	UNHANGED	UNHEALTHFULNESS

UNHEALTHIER
UNHEALTHIEST
UNHEALTHILY
UNHEALTHINESS
UNHEALTHINESSES
UNHEALTHY
UNHEARD
UNHEARSE
UNHEARSED
UNHEARSES
UNHEARSING
UNHEART
UNHEARTED
UNHEARTING
UNHEARTS
UNHEATED
UNHEDGED
UNHEEDED
UNHEEDEDLY
UNHEEDFUL
UNHEEDFULLY
UNHEEDILY
UNHEEDING
UNHEEDINGLY
UNHEEDY
UNHELE
UNHELED
UNHELES
UNHELING
UNHELM
UNHELMED
UNHELMETED
UNHELMING
UNHELMS
UNHELPABLE
UNHELPED
UNHELPFUL
UNHELPFULLY
UNHEPPEN
UNHERALDED
UNHEROIC
UNHEROICAL
UNHEROICALLY
UNHERST
UNHESITATING
UNHESITATINGLY
UNHEWN
UNHIDDEN
UNHIDEBOUND
UNHINDERED
UNHINGE
UNHINGED
UNHINGEMENT
UNHINGEMENTS
UNHINGES
UNHINGING

UNHIP
UNHIPLY
UNHIPNESS
UNHIPPER
UNHIPPEST
UNHIRED
UNHISTORIC
UNHISTORICAL
UNHITCH
UNHITCHED
UNHITCHES
UNHITCHING
UNHIVE
UNHIVED
UNHIVES
UNHIVING
UNHOARD
UNHOARDED
UNHOARDING
UNHOARDS
UNHOLIER
UNHOLIEST
UNHOLILY
UNHOLINESS
UNHOLINESSES
UNHOLPEN
UNHOLY
UNHOMELIKE
UNHOMELY
UNHOMOGENIZED
UNHONEST
UNHONORED
UNHONOURED
UNHOOD
UNHOODED
UNHOODING
UNHOODS
UNHOOK
UNHOOKED
UNHOOKING
UNHOOKS
UNHOOP
UNHOOPED
UNHOOPING
UNHOOPS
UNHOPED
UNHOPEFUL
UNHOPEFULLY
UNHORSE
UNHORSED
UNHORSES
UNHORSING
UNHOSPITABLE
UNHOUSE
UNHOUSED
UNHOUSELED
UNHOUSES

UNHOUSING
UNHOUZZLED
UNHUMAN
UNHUMANISE
UNHUMANISED
UNHUMANISES
UNHUMANISING
UNHUMANIZE
UNHUMANIZED
UNHUMANIZES
UNHUMANIZING
UNHUMBLED
UNHUMOROUS
UNHUNG
UNHUNTED
UNHURRIED
UNHURRIEDLY
UNHURRYING
UNHURT
UNHURTFUL
UNHURTFULLY
UNHURTFULNESS
UNHURTFULNESSES
UNHUSBANDED
UNHUSK
UNHUSKED
UNHUSKING
UNHUSKS
UNHYDROLYZED
UNHYGIENIC
UNHYPHENATED
UNHYSTERICAL
UNHYSTERICALLY
UNI
UNIALGAL
UNIAXIAL
UNIAXIALLY
UNICAMERAL
UNICAMERALISM
UNICAMERALISMS
UNICAMERALIST
UNICAMERALISTS
UNICAMERALLY
UNICELLULAR
UNICELLULARITY
UNICENTRAL
UNICITIES
UNICITY
UNICOLOR
UNICOLORATE
UNICOLOROUS
UNICOLOUR
UNICOLOURED
UNICORN
UNICORNS
UNICOSTATE
UNICYCLE

UNICYCLES
UNICYCLIST
UNICYCLISTS
UNIDEAED
UNIDEAL
UNIDEALISM
UNIDEALISMS
UNIDEALISTIC
UNIDENTIFIABLE
UNIDENTIFIED
UNIDEOLOGICAL
UNIDIMENSIONAL
UNIDIOMATIC
UNIDIOMATICALLY
UNIDIRECTIONAL
UNIFACE
UNIFACES
UNIFIABLE
UNIFIC
UNIFICATION
UNIFICATIONS
UNIFIED
UNIFIER
UNIFIERS
UNIFIES
UNIFILAR
UNIFLOROUS
UNIFOLIATE
UNIFOLIOLATE
UNIFORM
UNIFORMED
UNIFORMER
UNIFORMEST
UNIFORMING
UNIFORMITARIAN
UNIFORMITARIANS
UNIFORMITIES
UNIFORMITY
UNIFORMLY
UNIFORMNESS
UNIFORMNESSES
UNIFORMS
UNIFY
UNIFYING
UNIFYINGS
UNIGENITURE
UNIGENITURES
UNIGNORABLE
UNIJUGATE
UNILABIATE
UNILATERAL
UNILATERALISM
UNILATERALISMS
UNILATERALIST
UNILATERALISTS
UNILATERALITIES
UNILATERALITY

UNILATERALLY	UNINDICTED	UNINTERESTEDLY	UNIPOLARITIES
UNILINEAL	UNINDORSED	UNINTERESTING	UNIPOLARITY
UNILINEAR	UNINFECTED	UNINTERESTINGLY	UNIQUE
UNILINGUAL	UNINFLAMED	UNINTERESTS	UNIQUELY
UNILITERAL	UNINFLAMMABLE	UNINTERMITTED	UNIQUENESS
UNILLUMED	UNINFLATED	UNINTERMITTEDLY	UNIQUENESSES
UNILLUMINATED	UNINFLECTED	UNINTERMITTING	UNIQUER
UNILLUMINATING	UNINFLUENCED	UNINTERPRETABLE	UNIQUES
UNILLUMINED	UNINFLUENTIAL	UNINTERRUPTED	UNIQUEST
UNILLUSIONED	UNINFORCEABLE	UNINTERRUPTEDLY	UNIRAMOSE
UNILLUSTRATED	UNINFORCED	UNINTIMIDATED	UNIRAMOUS
UNILOBAR	UNINFORMATIVE	UNINTOXICATING	UNIRONED
UNILOBED	UNINFORMATIVELY	UNINTRODUCED	UNIRONICALLY
UNILOBULAR	UNINFORMED	UNINUCLEAR	UNIRRADIATED
UNILOCULAR	UNINFORMING	UNINUCLEATE	UNIRRIGATED
UNIMAGINABLE	UNINGRATIATING	UNINURED	UNIS
UNIMAGINABLY	UNINHABITABLE	UNINVENTIVE	UNISEPTATE
UNIMAGINATIVE	UNINHABITED	UNINVESTED	UNISERIAL
UNIMAGINATIVELY	UNINHIBITED	UNINVESTIGATED	UNISERIALLY
UNIMAGINED	UNINHIBITEDLY	UNINVIDIOUS	UNISERIATE
UNIMBUED	UNINHIBITEDNESS	UNINVITED	UNISERIATELY
UNIMMORTAL	UNINITIATE	UNINVITING	UNISEX
UNIMMUNIZED	UNINITIATED	UNINVITINGLY	UNISEXES
UNIMOLECULAR	UNINITIATES	UNINVITINGNESS	UNISEXUAL
UNIMPAIRED	UNINJURED	UNINVOKED	UNISEXUALITIES
UNIMPARTED	UNINOCULATED	UNINVOLVED	UNISEXUALITY
UNIMPASSIONED	UNINQUIRING	UNION	UNISEXUALLY
UNIMPEACHABLE	UNINQUISITIVE	UNIONISATION	UNISON
UNIMPEACHABLY	UNINSCRIBED	UNIONISATIONS	UNISONAL
UNIMPEACHED	UNINSPECTED	UNIONISE	UNISONALLY
UNIMPEDED	UNINSPIRED	UNIONISED	UNISONANCE
UNIMPEDEDLY	UNINSPIRING	UNIONISES	UNISONANCES
UNIMPLORED	UNINSPIRINGLY	UNIONISING	UNISONANT
UNIMPORTANCE	UNINSPIRINGNESS	UNIONISM	UNISONOUS
UNIMPORTANCES	UNINSTALL	UNIONISMS	UNISONS
UNIMPORTANT	UNINSTALLED	UNIONIST	UNISSUED
UNIMPORTUNED	UNINSTALLING	UNIONISTIC	UNIT
UNIMPOSED	UNINSTALLS	UNIONISTS	UNITAGE
UNIMPOSING	UNINSTRUCTED	UNIONIZATION	UNITAGES
UNIMPREGNATED	UNINSTRUCTIVE	UNIONIZATIONS	UNITAL
UNIMPRESSED	UNINSULATED	UNIONIZE	UNITARD
UNIMPRESSIBLE	UNINSURABLE	UNIONIZED	UNITARDS
UNIMPRESSIVE	UNINSURED	UNIONIZES	UNITARIAN
UNIMPRESSIVELY	UNINTEGRATED	UNIONIZING	UNITARIANISM
UNIMPRISONED	UNINTELLECTUAL	UNIONS	UNITARIANISMS
UNIMPROVED	UNINTELLIGENCE	UNIPARENTAL	UNITARIANS
UNIMPUGNABLE	UNINTELLIGENT	UNIPARENTALLY	UNITARILY
UNINAUGURATED	UNINTELLIGENTLY	UNIPAROUS	UNITARY
UNINCHANTED	UNINTELLIGIBLE	UNIPARTITE	UNITE
UNINCITED	UNINTELLIGIBLY	UNIPED	UNITED
UNINCLOSED	UNINTENDED	UNIPEDS	UNITEDLY
UNINCORPORATED	UNINTENDEDLY	UNIPERSONAL	UNITEDNESS
UNINCUBATED	UNINTENDEDNESS	UNIPERSONALITY	UNITEDNESSES
UNINCUMBERED	UNINTENTIONAL	UNIPLANAR	UNITER
UNINDEARED	UNINTENTIONALLY	UNIPOD	UNITERS
UNINDEMNIFIED	UNINTEREST	UNIPODS	UNITES
UNINDEXED	UNINTERESTED	UNIPOLAR	UNITHOLDER

UNITHOLDERS	UNIVERSE	UNKINGED	UNLACES
UNITIES	UNIVERSES	UNKINGING	UNLACING
UNITING	UNIVERSITARIAN	UNKINGLIER	UNLADE
UNITINGS	UNIVERSITIES	UNKINGLIEST	UNLADED
UNITION	UNIVERSITY	UNKINGLIKE	UNLADEN
UNITIONS	UNIVOCAL	UNKINGLY	UNLADES
UNITISATION	UNIVOCALLY	UNKINGS	UNLADING
UNITISATIONS	UNIVOCALS	UNKINK	UNLADINGS
UNITISE	UNIVOLTINE	UNKINKED	UNLADYLIKE
UNITISED	UNJADED	UNKINKING	UNLAID
UNITISES	UNJAUNDICED	UNKINKS	UNLAMENTED
UNITISING	UNJEALOUS	UNKISS	UNLASH
UNITIVE	UNJOINED	UNKISSED	UNLASHED
UNITIVELY	UNJOINT	UNKISSES	UNLASHES
UNITIZATION	UNJOINTED	UNKISSING	UNLASHING
UNITIZATIONS	UNJOINTING	UNKNELLED	UNLAST
UNITIZE	UNJOINTS	UNKNIGHT	UNLASTE
UNITIZED	UNJOYFUL	UNKNIGHTED	UNLATCH
UNITIZER	UNJOYOUS	UNKNIGHTING	UNLATCHED
UNITIZERS	UNJUDGED	UNKNIGHTLINESS	UNLATCHES
UNITIZES	UNJUST	UNKNIGHTLY	UNLATCHING
UNITIZING	UNJUSTER	UNKNIGHTS	UNLAUNDERED
UNITRUST	UNJUSTEST	UNKNIT	UNLAW
UNITRUSTS	UNJUSTIFIABLE	UNKNITS	UNLAWED
UNITS	UNJUSTIFIABLY	UNKNITTED	UNLAWFUL
UNITY	UNJUSTIFIED	UNKNITTING	UNLAWFULLY
UNIVALENCE	UNJUSTLY	UNKNOT	UNLAWFULNESS
UNIVALENCES	UNJUSTNESS	UNKNOTS	UNLAWFULNESSES
UNIVALENCIES	UNJUSTNESSES	UNKNOTTED	UNLAWING
UNIVALENCY	UNKED	UNKNOTTING	UNLAWS
UNIVALENT	UNKEMPT	UNKNOWABILITIES	UNLAY
UNIVALENTS	UNKEMPTLY	UNKNOWABILITY	UNLAYING
UNIVALVE	UNKEMPTNESS	UNKNOWABLE	UNLAYS
UNIVALVES	UNKEND	UNKNOWABLENESS	UNLEAD
UNIVALVULAR	UNKENNED	UNKNOWABLES	UNLEADED
UNIVARIANT	UNKENNEL	UNKNOWABLY	UNLEADING
UNIVARIATE	UNKENNELED	UNKNOWING	UNLEADS
UNIVERSAL	UNKENNELING	UNKNOWINGLY	UNLEAL
UNIVERSALISE	UNKENNELLED	UNKNOWINGNESS	UNLEARN
UNIVERSALISED	UNKENNELLING	UNKNOWINGNESSES	UNLEARNABLE
UNIVERSALISES	UNKENNELS	UNKNOWINGS	UNLEARNED
UNIVERSALISING	UNKENT	UNKNOWLEDGABLE	UNLEARNEDLY
UNIVERSALISM	UNKEPT	UNKNOWLEDGABLY	UNLEARNEDNESS
UNIVERSALISMS	UNKET	UNKNOWLEDGEABLE	UNLEARNEDNESSES
UNIVERSALIST	UNKID	UNKNOWLEDGEABLY	UNLEARNING
UNIVERSALISTIC	UNKIND	UNKNOWN	UNLEARNS
UNIVERSALISTS	UNKINDER	UNKNOWNNESS	UNLEARNT
UNIVERSALITIES	UNKINDEST	UNKNOWNNESSES	UNLEASED
UNIVERSALITY	UNKINDLED	UNKNOWNS	UNLEASH
UNIVERSALIZE	UNKINDLIER	UNKOSHER	UNLEASHED
UNIVERSALIZED	UNKINDLIEST	UNLABELED	UNLEASHES
UNIVERSALIZES	UNKINDLINESS	UNLABELLED	UNLEASHING
UNIVERSALIZING	UNKINDLINESSES	UNLABORIOUS	UNLEAVENED
UNIVERSALLY	UNKINDLY	UNLABOURED	UNLED
UNIVERSALNESS	UNKINDNESS	UNLABOURING	UNLEISURED
UNIVERSALNESSES	UNKINDNESSES	UNLACE	UNLEISURELY
UNIVERSALS	UNKING	UNLACED	UNLESS

UNLESSONED	UNLINKED	UNLOVED	UNMANLIKE
UNLET	UNLINKING	UNLOVELIER	UNMANLINESS
UNLETHAL	UNLINKS	UNLOVELIEST	UNMANLINESSES
UNLETTABLE	UNLIQUEFIED	UNLOVELINESS	UNMANLY
UNLETTED	UNLIQUIDATED	UNLOVELINESSES	UNMANNED
UNLETTERED	UNLIQUORED	UNLOVELY	UNMANNERED
UNLEVEL	UNLISTED	UNLOVERLIKE	UNMANNEREDLY
UNLEVELED	UNLISTENABLE	UNLOVES	UNMANNERLINESS
UNLEVELING	UNLISTENED	UNLOVING	UNMANNERLY
UNLEVELLED	UNLISTENING	UNLOVINGLY	UNMANNING
UNLEVELLING	UNLIT	UNLOVINGNESS	UNMANS
UNLEVELS	UNLITERARY	UNLOVINGNESSES	UNMANTLE
UNLEVIED	UNLIVABLE	UNLUBRICATED	UNMANTLED
UNLIBERATED	UNLIVE	UNLUCKIER	UNMANTLES
UNLIBIDINOUS	UNLIVEABLE	UNLUCKIEST	UNMANTLING
UNLICENSED	UNLIVED	UNLUCKILY	UNMANUFACTURED
UNLICH	UNLIVELINESS	UNLUCKINESS	UNMANURED
UNLICKED	UNLIVELINESSES	UNLUCKINESSES	UNMAPPED
UNLID	UNLIVELY	UNLUCKY	UNMARD
UNLIDDED	UNLIVES	UNLUXURIANT	UNMARKED
UNLIDDING	UNLIVING	UNLUXURIOUS	UNMARKETABLE
UNLIDS	UNLOAD	UNLYRICAL	UNMARRED
UNLIFELIKE	UNLOADED	UNMACADAMISED	UNMARRIABLE
UNLIGHTED	UNLOADER	UNMACADAMIZED	UNMARRIAGEABLE
UNLIGHTENED	UNLOADERS	UNMACHO	UNMARRIED
UNLIGHTSOME	UNLOADING	UNMADE	UNMARRIEDS
UNLIKABLE	UNLOADINGS	UNMAGNIFIED	UNMARRIES
UNLIKE	UNLOADS	UNMAIDENLY	UNMARRY
UNLIKEABLE	UNLOBED	UNMAILABLE	UNMARRYING
UNLIKELIER	UNLOCALIZED	UNMAILED	UNMASCULINE
UNLIKELIEST	UNLOCATED	UNMAIMED	UNMASK
UNLIKELIHOOD	UNLOCK	UNMAINTAINABLE	UNMASKED
UNLIKELIHOODS	UNLOCKABLE	UNMAINTAINED	UNMASKER
UNLIKELINESS	UNLOCKED	UNMAKABLE	UNMASKERS
UNLIKELINESSES	UNLOCKING	UNMAKE	UNMASKING
UNLIKELY	UNLOCKS	UNMAKER	UNMASKINGS
UNLIKENESS	UNLOGICAL	UNMAKERS	UNMASKS
UNLIKENESSES	UNLOOKED	UNMAKES	UNMASTERED
UNLIKES	UNLOOSE	UNMAKING	UNMATCHABLE
UNLIMBER	UNLOOSED	UNMAKINGS	UNMATCHED
UNLIMBERED	UNLOOSEN	UNMALICIOUS	UNMATED
UNLIMBERING	UNLOOSENED	UNMALICIOUSLY	UNMATERIAL
UNLIMBERS	UNLOOSENING	UNMALLEABILITY	UNMATERIALISED
UNLIME	UNLOOSENS	UNMALLEABLE	UNMATERIALIZED
UNLIMED	UNLOOSES	UNMAN	UNMATERNAL
UNLIMES	UNLOOSING	UNMANACLE	UNMATHEMATICAL
UNLIMING	UNLOPPED	UNMANACLED	UNMATRICULATED
UNLIMITED	UNLORD	UNMANACLES	UNMATTED
UNLIMITEDLY	UNLORDED	UNMANACLING	UNMATURED
UNLIMITEDNESS	UNLORDING	UNMANAGEABLE	UNMEANING
UNLIMITEDNESSES	UNLORDLY	UNMANAGEABLY	UNMEANINGLY
UNLINE	UNLORDS	UNMANAGED	UNMEANINGNESS
UNLINEAL	UNLOSABLE	UNMANFUL	UNMEANINGNESSES
UNLINED	UNLOST	UNMANFULLY	UNMEANT
UNLINES	UNLOVABLE	UNMANIPULATED	UNMEASURABLE
UNLINING	UNLOVE	UNMANLIER	UNMEASURABLY
UNLINK	UNLOVEABLE	UNMANLIEST	UNMEASURED

UNMEASUREDLY
UNMEASUREDNESS
UNMECHANIC
UNMECHANICAL
UNMECHANISE
UNMECHANISED
UNMECHANISES
UNMECHANISING
UNMECHANIZE
UNMECHANIZED
UNMECHANIZES
UNMECHANIZING
UNMEDIATED
UNMEDICATED
UNMEDICINABLE
UNMEDITATED
UNMEEK
UNMEET
UNMEETLY
UNMEETNESS
UNMEETNESSES
UNMELLOW
UNMELLOWED
UNMELODIOUS
UNMELODIOUSNESS
UNMELTED
UNMEMORABLE
UNMEMORABLY
UNMEMORISED
UNMEMORIZED
UNMENDED
UNMENTIONABLE
UNMENTIONABLES
UNMENTIONABLY
UNMENTIONED
UNMERCENARY
UNMERCHANTABLE
UNMERCIFUL
UNMERCIFULLY
UNMERCIFULNESS
UNMERITABLE
UNMERITED
UNMERITEDLY
UNMERITING
UNMERRY
UNMESH
UNMESHED
UNMESHES
UNMESHING
UNMET
UNMETABOLIZED
UNMETALLED
UNMETAPHORICAL
UNMETAPHYSICAL
UNMETED
UNMETHODICAL
UNMETHODISED

UNMETHODIZED
UNMETRICAL
UNMEW
UNMEWED
UNMEWING
UNMEWS
UNMILITARY
UNMILKED
UNMILLED
UNMINDED
UNMINDFUL
UNMINDFULLY
UNMINDFULNESS
UNMINDFULNESSES
UNMINED
UNMINGLE
UNMINGLED
UNMINGLES
UNMINGLING
UNMINISTERIAL
UNMIRACULOUS
UNMIRY
UNMISSABLE
UNMISSED
UNMISTAKABLE
UNMISTAKABLY
UNMISTAKEABLE
UNMISTAKEABLY
UNMISTAKEN
UNMISTRUSTFUL
UNMITER
UNMITERED
UNMITERING
UNMITERS
UNMITIGABLE
UNMITIGABLY
UNMITIGATED
UNMITIGATEDLY
UNMITIGATEDNESS
UNMITRE
UNMITRED
UNMITRES
UNMITRING
UNMIX
UNMIXABLE
UNMIXED
UNMIXEDLY
UNMIXES
UNMIXING
UNMIXT
UNMOANED
UNMODERNISED
UNMODERNIZED
UNMODIFIABLE
UNMODIFIED
UNMODISH
UNMODULATED

UNMOISTENED
UNMOLD
UNMOLDED
UNMOLDING
UNMOLDS
UNMOLESTED
UNMOLTEN
UNMONEYED
UNMONIED
UNMONITORED
UNMOOR
UNMOORED
UNMOORING
UNMOORS
UNMORAL
UNMORALISED
UNMORALISING
UNMORALITIES
UNMORALITY
UNMORALIZED
UNMORALIZING
UNMORALLY
UNMORTGAGED
UNMORTIFIED
UNMORTISED
UNMOTHERLY
UNMOTIVATED
UNMOTIVED
UNMOULD
UNMOULDED
UNMOULDING
UNMOULDS
UNMOUNT
UNMOUNTED
UNMOUNTING
UNMOUNTS
UNMOURNED
UNMOVABLE
UNMOVABLY
UNMOVEABLE
UNMOVEABLY
UNMOVED
UNMOVEDLY
UNMOVING
UNMOWN
UNMUFFLE
UNMUFFLED
UNMUFFLES
UNMUFFLING
UNMUNITIONED
UNMURMURING
UNMURMURINGLY
UNMUSICAL
UNMUSICALITY
UNMUSICALLY
UNMUSICALNESS
UNMUTILATED

UNMUZZLE
UNMUZZLED
UNMUZZLES
UNMUZZLING
UNMUZZLINGS
UNMYELINATED
UNMYSTIFIED
UNNAIL
UNNAILED
UNNAILING
UNNAILS
UNNAMABLE
UNNAMEABLE
UNNAMED
UNNANELD
UNNATIVE
UNNATURAL
UNNATURALISE
UNNATURALISED
UNNATURALISES
UNNATURALISING
UNNATURALIZE
UNNATURALIZED
UNNATURALIZES
UNNATURALIZING
UNNATURALLY
UNNATURALNESS
UNNATURALNESSES
UNNAVIGABLE
UNNAVIGATED
UNNEATH
UNNECESSARILY
UNNECESSARINESS
UNNECESSARY
UNNEEDED
UNNEEDFUL
UNNEEDFULLY
UNNEGOTIABLE
UNNEGOTIATED
UNNEIGHBOURED
UNNEIGHBOURLY
UNNERVE
UNNERVED
UNNERVES
UNNERVING
UNNERVINGLY
UNNEST
UNNESTED
UNNESTING
UNNESTS
UNNETHES
UNNETTED
UNNEUROTIC
UNNEWSWORTHY
UNNILHEPTIUM
UNNILHEXIUM
UNNILHEXIUMS

UNNILPENTIUM	UNOILED	UNPAIRED	UNPAY
UNNILPENTIUMS	UNOPEN	UNPALATABILITY	UNPAYABLE
UNNILQUADIUM	UNOPENABLE	UNPALATABLE	UNPAYING
UNNILQUADIUMS	UNOPENED	UNPALATABLY	UNPAYS
UNNOBLE	UNOPERATIVE	UNPALSIED	UNPEACEABLE
UNNOBLED	UNOPPOSED	UNPAMPERED	UNPEACEABLENESS
UNNOBLES	UNOPPRESSED	UNPANEL	UNPEACEFUL
UNNOBLING	UNOPPRESSIVE	UNPANELLED	UNPEACEFULLY
UNNOISY	UNOPPRESSIVELY	UNPANELLING	UNPEDANTIC
UNNOTED	UNORDAINED	UNPANELS	UNPEDIGREED
UNNOTEWORTHY	UNORDER	UNPANGED	UNPEELED
UNNOTICEABLE	UNORDERED	UNPANNEL	UNPEERABLE
UNNOTICEABLY	UNORDERING	UNPANNELLED	UNPEERED
UNNOTICED	UNORDERLY	UNPANNELLING	UNPEG
UNNOTICING	UNORDERS	UNPANNELS	UNPEGGED
UNNOURISHED	UNORDINARY	UNPAPER	UNPEGGING
UNNOURISHING	UNORGANISED	UNPAPERED	UNPEGS
UNNUMBERED	UNORGANIZED	UNPAPERING	UNPEN
UNNURTURED	UNORIGINAL	UNPAPERS	UNPENNED
UNOBEDIENT	UNORIGINALITIES	UNPARADISE	UNPENNIED
UNOBEYED	UNORIGINALITY	UNPARADISED	UNPENNING
UNOBJECTIONABLE	UNORIGINATE	UNPARADISES	UNPENS
UNOBJECTIONABLY	UNORIGINATED	UNPARADISING	UNPENSIONED
UNOBLIGING	UNORNAMENTAL	UNPARAGONED	UNPENT
UNOBLIGINGLY	UNORNAMENTED	UNPARALLEL	UNPEOPLE
UNOBNOXIOUS	UNORNATE	UNPARALLELED	UNPEOPLED
UNOBSCURED	UNORTHODOX	UNPARASITIZED	UNPEOPLES
UNOBSERVABLE	UNORTHODOXIES	UNPARDONABLE	UNPEOPLING
UNOBSERVANCE	UNORTHODOXLY	UNPARDONABLY	UNPEPPERED
UNOBSERVANCES	UNORTHODOXY	UNPARDONED	UNPERCEIVABLE
UNOBSERVANT	UNOSSIFIED	UNPARDONING	UNPERCEIVABLY
UNOBSERVED	UNOSTENTATIOUS	UNPARED	UNPERCEIVED
UNOBSERVEDLY	UNOVERCOME	UNPARENTAL	UNPERCEIVEDLY
UNOBSERVING	UNOVERTHROWN	UNPARENTED	UNPERCEPTIVE
UNOBSTRUCTED	UNOWED	UNPARLIAMENTARY	UNPERCH
UNOBSTRUCTIVE	UNOWNED	UNPARTED	UNPERCHED
UNOBTAINABLE	UNOXIDISED	UNPARTIAL	UNPERCHES
UNOBTAINED	UNOXIDIZED	UNPASSABLE	UNPERCHING
UNOBTRUDING	UNOXYGENATED	UNPASSABLENESS	UNPERFECT
UNOBTRUSIVE	UNPACED	UNPASSIONATE	UNPERFECTED
UNOBTRUSIVELY	UNPACIFIED	UNPASSIONED	UNPERFECTION
UNOBTRUSIVENESS	UNPACK	UNPASTEURISED	UNPERFECTIONS
UNOBVIOUS	UNPACKED	UNPASTEURIZED	UNPERFECTLY
UNOCCUPIED	UNPACKER	UNPASTORAL	UNPERFECTNESS
UNOFFENDED	UNPACKERS	UNPASTURED	UNPERFECTNESSES
UNOFFENDING	UNPACKING	UNPATENTABLE	UNPERFORATED
UNOFFENSIVE	UNPACKINGS	UNPATENTED	UNPERFORMABLE
UNOFFENSIVELY	UNPACKS	UNPATHED	UNPERFORMED
UNOFFENSIVENESS	UNPAGED	UNPATHETIC	UNPERFORMING
UNOFFERED	UNPAID	UNPATHWAYED	UNPERFUMED
UNOFFICERED	UNPAINED	UNPATRIOTIC	UNPERILOUS
UNOFFICIAL	UNPAINFUL	UNPATRIOTICALLY	UNPERISHABLE
UNOFFICIALLY	UNPAINT	UNPATRONISED	UNPERISHED
UNOFFICIOUS	UNPAINTABLE	UNPATRONIZED	UNPERISHING
UNOFFICIOUSLY	UNPAINTED	UNPATTERNED	UNPERJURED
UNOFFICIOUSNESS	UNPAINTING	UNPAVED	UNPERPETRATED
UNOFTEN	UNPAINTS	UNPAVILIONED	UNPERPLEX

UNPERPLEXED
UNPERPLEXES
UNPERPLEXING
UNPERSECUTED
UNPERSON
UNPERSONED
UNPERSONING
UNPERSONS
UNPERSUADABLE
UNPERSUADED
UNPERSUASIVE
UNPERTURBABLE
UNPERTURBABLY
UNPERTURBED
UNPERVERT
UNPERVERTED
UNPERVERTING
UNPERVERTS
UNPHILOSOPHIC
UNPHILOSOPHICAL
UNPHONETIC
UNPICK
UNPICKABLE
UNPICKED
UNPICKING
UNPICKS
UNPICTURESQUE
UNPIERCED
UNPILE
UNPILED
UNPILES
UNPILING
UNPILLARED
UNPILLOWED
UNPILOTED
UNPIN
UNPINKED
UNPINKT
UNPINNED
UNPINNING
UNPINS
UNPITIED
UNPITIFUL
UNPITIFULLY
UNPITIFULNESS
UNPITIFULNESSES
UNPITYING
UNPITYINGLY
UNPLACE
UNPLACED
UNPLACES
UNPLACING
UNPLAGUED
UNPLAINED
UNPLAIT
UNPLAITED
UNPLAITING

UNPLAITS
UNPLANKED
UNPLANNED
UNPLANTED
UNPLASTERED
UNPLAUSIBLE
UNPLAUSIBLY
UNPLAUSIVE
UNPLAYABLE
UNPLAYED
UNPLEASANT
UNPLEASANTLY
UNPLEASANTNESS
UNPLEASANTRIES
UNPLEASANTRY
UNPLEASED
UNPLEASING
UNPLEASINGLY
UNPLEASURABLE
UNPLEASURABLY
UNPLEATED
UNPLEDGED
UNPLIABLE
UNPLIABLY
UNPLIANT
UNPLOUGHED
UNPLOWED
UNPLUCKED
UNPLUG
UNPLUGGED
UNPLUGGING
UNPLUGS
UNPLUMB
UNPLUMBED
UNPLUMBING
UNPLUMBS
UNPLUME
UNPLUMED
UNPLUMES
UNPLUMING
UNPOETIC
UNPOETICAL
UNPOETICALLY
UNPOETICALNESS
UNPOINTED
UNPOISED
UNPOISON
UNPOISONED
UNPOISONING
UNPOISONS
UNPOLARISABLE
UNPOLARISED
UNPOLARIZABLE
UNPOLARIZED
UNPOLICED
UNPOLICIED
UNPOLISH

UNPOLISHABLE
UNPOLISHED
UNPOLISHES
UNPOLISHING
UNPOLITE
UNPOLITELY
UNPOLITENESS
UNPOLITENESSES
UNPOLITIC
UNPOLITICAL
UNPOLLED
UNPOLLUTED
UNPOLYMERISED
UNPOLYMERIZED
UNPOPE
UNPOPED
UNPOPES
UNPOPING
UNPOPULAR
UNPOPULARITIES
UNPOPULARITY
UNPOPULARLY
UNPOPULATED
UNPOPULOUS
UNPORTIONED
UNPOSED
UNPOSSESSED
UNPOSSESSING
UNPOSSIBLE
UNPOSTED
UNPOTABLE
UNPOTTED
UNPOWDERED
UNPRACTICABLE
UNPRACTICAL
UNPRACTICALITY
UNPRACTICALLY
UNPRACTICALNESS
UNPRACTICED
UNPRACTISED
UNPRACTISEDNESS
UNPRAISE
UNPRAISED
UNPRAISES
UNPRAISEWORTHY
UNPRAISING
UNPRAY
UNPRAYED
UNPRAYING
UNPRAYS
UNPREACH
UNPREACHED
UNPREACHES
UNPREACHING
UNPRECEDENTED
UNPRECEDENTEDLY
UNPRECISE

UNPREDICT
UNPREDICTABLE
UNPREDICTABLES
UNPREDICTABLY
UNPREDICTED
UNPREDICTING
UNPREDICTS
UNPREFERRED
UNPREGNANT
UNPREJUDICED
UNPREJUDICEDLY
UNPRELATICAL
UNPREMEDITABLE
UNPREMEDITATED
UNPREMEDITATION
UNPREOCCUPIED
UNPREPARE
UNPREPARED
UNPREPAREDLY
UNPREPAREDNESS
UNPREPARES
UNPREPARING
UNPREPOSSESSED
UNPREPOSSESSING
UNPRESCRIBED
UNPRESENTABLE
UNPRESERVED
UNPRESSED
UNPRESSURED
UNPRESSURIZED
UNPRESUMING
UNPRESUMPTUOUS
UNPRETENDING
UNPRETENDINGLY
UNPRETENTIOUS
UNPRETENTIOUSLY
UNPRETTINESS
UNPRETTINESSES
UNPRETTY
UNPREVAILING
UNPREVENTABLE
UNPREVENTED
UNPRICED
UNPRIEST
UNPRIESTED
UNPRIESTING
UNPRIESTLY
UNPRIESTS
UNPRIMED
UNPRINCELY
UNPRINCIPLED
UNPRINTABILITY
UNPRINTABLE
UNPRINTABLENESS
UNPRINTABLY
UNPRINTED
UNPRISON

UNPRISONED	UNPROTESTANTIZE	UNQUALIFIES	UNRAVELLER
UNPRISONING	UNPROTESTED	UNQUALIFY	UNRAVELLERS
UNPRISONS	UNPROTESTING	UNQUALIFYING	UNRAVELLING
UNPRIVILEGED	UNPROVABLE	UNQUALITED	UNRAVELLINGS
UNPRIZABLE	UNPROVED	UNQUALITIED	UNRAVELMENT
UNPRIZED	UNPROVEN	UNQUANTIFIABLE	UNRAVELMENTS
UNPROBED	UNPROVIDE	UNQUANTIFIED	UNRAVELS
UNPROBLEMATIC	UNPROVIDED	UNQUANTISED	UNRAVISHED
UNPROCEDURAL	UNPROVIDEDLY	UNQUANTIZED	UNRAZED
UNPROCESSED	UNPROVIDENT	UNQUARRIED	UNRAZORED
UNPROCLAIMED	UNPROVIDES	UNQUEEN	UNREACHABLE
UNPROCURABLE	UNPROVIDING	UNQUEENED	UNREACHED
UNPRODUCED	UNPROVISIONED	UNQUEENING	UNREACTIVE
UNPRODUCTIVE	UNPROVOCATIVE	UNQUEENLIER	UNREAD
UNPRODUCTIVELY	UNPROVOKE	UNQUEENLIEST	UNREADABILITY
UNPRODUCTIVITY	UNPROVOKED	UNQUEENLIKE	UNREADABLE
UNPROFANED	UNPROVOKEDLY	UNQUEENLY	UNREADABLENESS
UNPROFESSED	UNPROVOKES	UNQUEENS	UNREADABLY
UNPROFESSIONAL	UNPROVOKING	UNQUELLED	UNREADIER
UNPROFESSIONALS	UNPRUNED	UNQUENCHABLE	UNREADIEST
UNPROFITABILITY	UNPUBLICIZED	UNQUENCHABLY	UNREADILY
UNPROFITABLE	UNPUBLISHABLE	UNQUENCHED	UNREADINESS
UNPROFITABLY	UNPUBLISHED	UNQUESTIONABLE	UNREADINESSES
UNPROFITED	UNPUCKER	UNQUESTIONABLY	UNREADY
UNPROFITING	UNPUCKERED	UNQUESTIONED	UNREAL
UNPROGRAMMABLE	UNPUCKERING	UNQUESTIONING	UNREALISE
UNPROGRAMMED	UNPUCKERS	UNQUESTIONINGLY	UNREALISED
UNPROGRESSIVE	UNPULLED	UNQUICKENED	UNREALISES
UNPROGRESSIVELY	UNPUNCTUAL	UNQUIET	UNREALISING
UNPROHIBITED	UNPUNCTUALITIES	UNQUIETED	UNREALISM
UNPROJECTED	UNPUNCTUALITY	UNQUIETER	UNREALISMS
UNPROLIFIC	UNPUNCTUATED	UNQUIETEST	UNREALISTIC
UNPROMISED	UNPUNISHABLE	UNQUIETING	UNREALISTICALLY
UNPROMISING	UNPUNISHABLY	UNQUIETLY	UNREALITIES
UNPROMISINGLY	UNPUNISHED	UNQUIETNESS	UNREALITY
UNPROMPTED	UNPURCHASABLE	UNQUIETNESSES	UNREALIZABLE
UNPRONOUNCEABLE	UNPURCHASEABLE	UNQUIETS	UNREALIZE
UNPRONOUNCED	UNPURCHASED	UNQUOTABLE	UNREALIZED
UNPROP	UNPURE	UNQUOTE	UNREALIZES
UNPROPER	UNPURGED	UNQUOTED	UNREALIZING
UNPROPERLY	UNPURIFIED	UNQUOTES	UNREALLY
UNPROPERTIED	UNPURPOSED	UNQUOTING	UNREAPED
UNPROPHETIC	UNPURSE	UNRACED	UNREASON
UNPROPHETICAL	UNPURSED	UNRACKED	UNREASONABLE
UNPROPITIOUS	UNPURSES	UNRAISED	UNREASONABLY
UNPROPITIOUSLY	UNPURSING	UNRAKE	UNREASONED
UNPROPORTIONATE	UNPURSUED	UNRAKED	UNREASONING
UNPROPORTIONED	UNPURVEYED	UNRAKES	UNREASONINGLY
UNPROPOSED	UNPUTDOWNABLE	UNRAKING	UNREASONS
UNPROPPED	UNPUZZLE	UNRANKED	UNREAVE
UNPROPPING	UNPUZZLED	UNRANSOMED	UNREAVED
UNPROPS	UNPUZZLES	UNRATED	UNREAVES
UNPROSPEROUS	UNPUZZLING	UNRATIFIED	UNREAVING
UNPROSPEROUSLY	UNQUALIFIABLE	UNRAVEL	UNREBATED
UNPROTECTED	UNQUALIFIED	UNRAVELED	UNREBUKED
UNPROTECTEDNESS	UNQUALIFIEDLY	UNRAVELING	UNRECALLABLE
UNPROTESTANTISE	UNQUALIFIEDNESS	UNRAVELLED	UNRECALLED

UNRECALLING
UNRECAPTURABLE
UNRECEIPTED
UNRECEIVED
UNRECEPTIVE
UNRECIPROCATED
UNRECKED
UNRECKONABLE
UNRECKONED
UNRECLAIMABLE
UNRECLAIMABLY
UNRECLAIMED
UNRECOGNISABLE
UNRECOGNISABLY
UNRECOGNISED
UNRECOGNISING
UNRECOGNIZABLE
UNRECOGNIZABLY
UNRECOGNIZED
UNRECOGNIZING
UNRECOLLECTED
UNRECOMMENDABLE
UNRECOMMENDED
UNRECOMPENSED
UNRECONCILABLE
UNRECONCILABLY
UNRECONCILED
UNRECONCILIABLE
UNRECONSTRUCTED
UNRECORDED
UNRECOUNTED
UNRECOVERABLE
UNRECOVERABLY
UNRECOVERED
UNRECTIFIED
UNRECURING
UNRECYCLABLE
UNRED
UNREDEEMABLE
UNREDEEMED
UNREDRESSED
UNREDREST
UNREDUCED
UNREDUCIBLE
UNREDY
UNREEL
UNREELED
UNREELER
UNREELERS
UNREELING
UNREELS
UNREEVE
UNREEVED
UNREEVES
UNREEVING
UNREFINED
UNREFLECTED

UNREFLECTING
UNREFLECTINGLY
UNREFLECTIVE
UNREFLECTIVELY
UNREFORMABLE
UNREFORMED
UNREFRACTED
UNREFRESHED
UNREFRESHING
UNREFRIGERATED
UNREFUTED
UNREGARDED
UNREGARDING
UNREGENERACIES
UNREGENERACY
UNREGENERATE
UNREGENERATED
UNREGENERATELY
UNREGENERATES
UNREGIMENTED
UNREGISTERED
UNREGULATED
UNREHEARSED
UNREIN
UNREINED
UNREINFORCED
UNREINING
UNREINS
UNREJOICED
UNREJOICING
UNRELATED
UNRELATIVE
UNRELAXED
UNRELENTING
UNRELENTINGLY
UNRELENTINGNESS
UNRELENTOR
UNRELENTORS
UNRELIABILITIES
UNRELIABILITY
UNRELIABLE
UNRELIABLENESS
UNRELIEVABLE
UNRELIEVED
UNRELIEVEDLY
UNRELIGIOUS
UNRELIGIOUSLY
UNRELISHED
UNRELUCTANT
UNREMAINING
UNREMARKABLE
UNREMARKABLY
UNREMARKED
UNREMEDIED
UNREMEMBERED
UNREMEMBERING
UNREMINISCENT

UNREMITTED
UNREMITTEDLY
UNREMITTENT
UNREMITTENTLY
UNREMITTING
UNREMITTINGLY
UNREMITTINGNESS
UNREMORSEFUL
UNREMORSEFULLY
UNREMORSELESS
UNREMOVABLE
UNREMOVED
UNREMUNERATIVE
UNRENDERED
UNRENEWED
UNRENOWNED
UNRENT
UNRENTED
UNREPAID
UNREPAIR
UNREPAIRABLE
UNREPAIRED
UNREPAIRS
UNREPEALABLE
UNREPEALED
UNREPEATABLE
UNREPEATED
UNREPELLED
UNREPENTANCE
UNREPENTANCES
UNREPENTANT
UNREPENTANTLY
UNREPENTED
UNREPENTING
UNREPENTINGLY
UNREPINING
UNREPININGLY
UNREPLACEABLE
UNREPLENISHED
UNREPORTABLE
UNREPORTED
UNREPOSEFUL
UNREPOSING
UNREPRESENTED
UNREPRESSED
UNREPRIEVABLE
UNREPRIEVED
UNREPRIMANDED
UNREPROACHED
UNREPROACHFUL
UNREPROACHING
UNREPRODUCIBLE
UNREPROVABLE
UNREPROVED
UNREPROVING
UNREPUGNANT
UNREPULSABLE

UNREQUESTED
UNREQUIRED
UNREQUISITE
UNREQUITED
UNREQUITEDLY
UNRESCINDED
UNRESENTED
UNRESENTFUL
UNRESENTING
UNRESERVE
UNRESERVED
UNRESERVEDLY
UNRESERVEDNESS
UNRESERVES
UNRESISTANT
UNRESISTED
UNRESISTIBLE
UNRESISTING
UNRESISTINGLY
UNRESOLVABLE
UNRESOLVED
UNRESOLVEDNESS
UNRESPECTABLE
UNRESPECTED
UNRESPECTFUL
UNRESPECTFULLY
UNRESPECTIVE
UNRESPITED
UNRESPONSIVE
UNRESPONSIVELY
UNREST
UNRESTED
UNRESTFUL
UNRESTFULNESS
UNRESTFULNESSES
UNRESTING
UNRESTINGLY
UNRESTINGNESS
UNRESTINGNESSES
UNRESTORED
UNRESTRAINABLE
UNRESTRAINED
UNRESTRAINEDLY
UNRESTRAINT
UNRESTRAINTS
UNRESTRICTED
UNRESTRICTEDLY
UNRESTS
UNRETARDED
UNRETENTIVE
UNRETOUCHED
UNRETURNABLE
UNRETURNED
UNRETURNING
UNRETURNINGLY
UNREVEALABLE
UNREVEALED

UNREVEALING
UNREVENGED
UNREVENGEFUL
UNREVEREND
UNREVERENT
UNREVERSED
UNREVERTED
UNREVIEWABLE
UNREVIEWED
UNREVISED
UNREVOKED
UNREVOLUTIONARY
UNREWARDED
UNREWARDEDLY
UNREWARDING
UNRHETORICAL
UNRHYMED
UNRHYTHMIC
UNRHYTHMICAL
UNRHYTHMICALLY
UNRIBBED
UNRID
UNRIDABLE
UNRIDDEN
UNRIDDLE
UNRIDDLEABLE
UNRIDDLED
UNRIDDLER
UNRIDDLERS
UNRIDDLES
UNRIDDLING
UNRIDEABLE
UNRIFLED
UNRIG
UNRIGGED
UNRIGGING
UNRIGHT
UNRIGHTEOUS
UNRIGHTEOUSLY
UNRIGHTEOUSNESS
UNRIGHTFUL
UNRIGHTFULLY
UNRIGHTFULNESS
UNRIGHTS
UNRIMED
UNRINGED
UNRINSED
UNRIP
UNRIPE
UNRIPELY
UNRIPENED
UNRIPENESS
UNRIPENESSES
UNRIPER
UNRIPEST
UNRIPPED

UNRIPPING
UNRIPPINGS
UNRIPS
UNRISEN
UNRIVALED
UNRIVALLED
UNRIVEN
UNRIVET
UNRIVETED
UNRIVETING
UNRIVETS
UNROBE
UNROBED
UNROBES
UNROBING
UNROLL
UNROLLED
UNROLLING
UNROLLS
UNROMANISED
UNROMANIZED
UNROMANTIC
UNROMANTICAL
UNROMANTICALLY
UNROMANTICIZED
UNROOF
UNROOFED
UNROOFING
UNROOFS
UNROOST
UNROOSTED
UNROOSTING
UNROOSTS
UNROOT
UNROOTED
UNROOTING
UNROOTS
UNROPE
UNROPED
UNROPES
UNROPING
UNROSINED
UNROTTED
UNROTTEN
UNROUGED
UNROUGH
UNROUND
UNROUNDED
UNROUNDING
UNROUNDS
UNROUSED
UNROVE
UNROVEN
UNROYAL
UNROYALLY
UNRUBBED
UNRUDE

UNRUFFABLE
UNRUFFE
UNRUFFLE
UNRUFFLED
UNRUFFLEDNESS
UNRUFFLES
UNRUFFLING
UNRULE
UNRULED
UNRULES
UNRULIER
UNRULIEST
UNRULIMENT
UNRULIMENTS
UNRULINESS
UNRULINESSES
UNRULY
UNRUMPLED
UNRUSHED
UNRUSTED
UNS
UNSADDLE
UNSADDLED
UNSADDLES
UNSADDLING
UNSAFE
UNSAFELY
UNSAFENESS
UNSAFENESSES
UNSAFER
UNSAFEST
UNSAFETIES
UNSAFETY
UNSAID
UNSAILED
UNSAILORLIKE
UNSAINED
UNSAINT
UNSAINTED
UNSAINTING
UNSAINTLIER
UNSAINTLIEST
UNSAINTLINESS
UNSAINTLINESSES
UNSAINTLY
UNSAINTS
UNSALABILITIES
UNSALABILITY
UNSALABLE
UNSALARIED
UNSALEABILITIES
UNSALEABILITY
UNSALEABLE
UNSALTED
UNSALUTED
UNSALVAGEABLE
UNSANCTIFIED

UNSANCTIFIES
UNSANCTIFY
UNSANCTIFYING
UNSANCTIONED
UNSANDALLED
UNSANITARY
UNSAPPED
UNSASHED
UNSATABLE
UNSATED
UNSATIABLE
UNSATIATE
UNSATIATED
UNSATIATING
UNSATING
UNSATIRICAL
UNSATISFACTION
UNSATISFACTIONS
UNSATISFACTORY
UNSATISFIABLE
UNSATISFIED
UNSATISFIEDNESS
UNSATISFYING
UNSATURATE
UNSATURATED
UNSATURATES
UNSATURATION
UNSATURATIONS
UNSAVED
UNSAVORILY
UNSAVORINESS
UNSAVORY
UNSAVOURILY
UNSAVOURINESS
UNSAVOURINESSES
UNSAVOURY
UNSAWED
UNSAWN
UNSAY
UNSAYABLE
UNSAYING
UNSAYS
UNSCABBARD
UNSCABBARDED
UNSCABBARDING
UNSCABBARDS
UNSCALABLE
UNSCALE
UNSCALED
UNSCALES
UNSCALING
UNSCANNED
UNSCARRED
UNSCARY
UNSCATHED
UNSCAVENGERED
UNSCENTED

UNSCEPTRED
UNSCHEDULED
UNSCHOLARLIKE
UNSCHOLARLY
UNSCHOOLED
UNSCIENTIFIC
UNSCISSORED
UNSCORCHED
UNSCOURED
UNSCRAMBLE
UNSCRAMBLED
UNSCRAMBLER
UNSCRAMBLERS
UNSCRAMBLES
UNSCRAMBLING
UNSCRATCHED
UNSCREENED
UNSCREW
UNSCREWED
UNSCREWING
UNSCREWS
UNSCRIPTED
UNSCRIPTURAL
UNSCRIPTURALLY
UNSCRUPLED
UNSCRUPULOSITY
UNSCRUPULOUS
UNSCRUPULOUSLY
UNSCRUTINISED
UNSCRUTINIZED
UNSCULPTURED
UNSCYTHED
UNSEAL
UNSEALABLE
UNSEALED
UNSEALING
UNSEALS
UNSEAM
UNSEAMED
UNSEAMING
UNSEAMS
UNSEARCHABLE
UNSEARCHABLY
UNSEARCHED
UNSEARED
UNSEASON
UNSEASONABLE
UNSEASONABLY
UNSEASONED
UNSEASONEDNESS
UNSEASONING
UNSEASONS
UNSEAT
UNSEATED
UNSEATING
UNSEATS
UNSEAWORTHINESS

UNSEAWORTHY
UNSECLUDED
UNSECONDED
UNSECRET
UNSECTARIAN
UNSECTARIANISM
UNSECTARIANISMS
UNSECULAR
UNSECURED
UNSEDUCED
UNSEEABLE
UNSEEDED
UNSEEING
UNSEEL
UNSEELED
UNSEELIE
UNSEELING
UNSEELS
UNSEEMING
UNSEEMINGS
UNSEEMLIER
UNSEEMLIEST
UNSEEMLINESS
UNSEEMLINESSES
UNSEEMLY
UNSEEN
UNSEENS
UNSEGMENTED
UNSEGREGATED
UNSEIZABLE
UNSEIZED
UNSELDOM
UNSELECTED
UNSELECTIVE
UNSELECTIVELY
UNSELF
UNSELFCONSCIOUS
UNSELFED
UNSELFING
UNSELFISH
UNSELFISHLY
UNSELFISHNESS
UNSELFISHNESSES
UNSELFS
UNSELL
UNSELLABLE
UNSELLING
UNSELLS
UNSELVES
UNSENSATIONAL
UNSENSE
UNSENSED
UNSENSES
UNSENSIBLE
UNSENSIBLY
UNSENSING
UNSENSITISED

UNSENSITIVE
UNSENSITIZED
UNSENSUALISE
UNSENSUALISED
UNSENSUALISES
UNSENSUALISING
UNSENSUALIZE
UNSENSUALIZED
UNSENSUALIZES
UNSENSUALIZING
UNSENT
UNSENTENCED
UNSENTIMENTAL
UNSEPARABLE
UNSEPARATED
UNSEPULCHRED
UNSERIOUS
UNSERIOUSNESS
UNSERIOUSNESSES
UNSERVED
UNSERVICEABLE
UNSET
UNSETS
UNSETTING
UNSETTLE
UNSETTLED
UNSETTLEDLY
UNSETTLEDNESS
UNSETTLEDNESSES
UNSETTLEMENT
UNSETTLEMENTS
UNSETTLES
UNSETTLING
UNSETTLINGLY
UNSETTLINGS
UNSEVERED
UNSEW
UNSEWED
UNSEWING
UNSEWN
UNSEWS
UNSEX
UNSEXED
UNSEXES
UNSEXING
UNSEXIST
UNSEXUAL
UNSEXY
UNSHACKLE
UNSHACKLED
UNSHACKLES
UNSHACKLING
UNSHADED
UNSHADOW
UNSHADOWABLE
UNSHADOWED
UNSHADOWING

UNSHADOWS
UNSHAKABLE
UNSHAKABLENESS
UNSHAKABLY
UNSHAKEABLE
UNSHAKEABLENESS
UNSHAKEABLY
UNSHAKED
UNSHAKEN
UNSHAKENLY
UNSHALE
UNSHALED
UNSHALES
UNSHALING
UNSHAMED
UNSHAPE
UNSHAPED
UNSHAPELIER
UNSHAPELIEST
UNSHAPELY
UNSHAPEN
UNSHAPES
UNSHAPING
UNSHARED
UNSHARP
UNSHARPENED
UNSHAVED
UNSHAVEN
UNSHEATHE
UNSHEATHED
UNSHEATHES
UNSHEATHING
UNSHED
UNSHELL
UNSHELLED
UNSHELLING
UNSHELLS
UNSHELTERED
UNSHENT
UNSHEWN
UNSHIELDED
UNSHIFT
UNSHIFTED
UNSHIFTING
UNSHIFTS
UNSHINGLED
UNSHIP
UNSHIPPED
UNSHIPPING
UNSHIPS
UNSHOCKABLE
UNSHOCKED
UNSHOD
UNSHOE
UNSHOED
UNSHOEING
UNSHOES

UNSHOOT
UNSHOOTED
UNSHOOTING
UNSHOOTS
UNSHORN
UNSHOT
UNSHOUT
UNSHOUTED
UNSHOUTING
UNSHOUTS
UNSHOWERED
UNSHOWN
UNSHOWY
UNSHRINKABLE
UNSHRINKING
UNSHRINKINGLY
UNSHRIVED
UNSHRIVEN
UNSHROUD
UNSHROUDED
UNSHROUDING
UNSHROUDS
UNSHRUBBED
UNSHRUBD
UNSHRUNK
UNSHUNNABLE
UNSHUNNED
UNSHUT
UNSHUTS
UNSHUTTER
UNSHUTTERED
UNSHUTTERING
UNSHUTTERS
UNSHUTTING
UNSICKER
UNSICKLED
UNSIFTED
UNSIGHING
UNSIGHT
UNSIGHTED
UNSIGHTEDLY
UNSIGHTING
UNSIGHTLIER
UNSIGHTLIEST
UNSIGHTLINESS
UNSIGHTLINESSES
UNSIGHTLY
UNSIGHTS
UNSIGNED
UNSILENCED
UNSILENT
UNSINEW
UNSINEWED
UNSINEWING
UNSINEWS
UNSINFUL
UNSINKABLE

UNSISTERED
UNSISTERLINESS
UNSISTERLY
UNSISTING
UNSIZABLE
UNSIZEABLE
UNSIZED
UNSKILFUL
UNSKILFULLY
UNSKILFULNESS
UNSKILFULNESSES
UNSKILLED
UNSKILLFUL
UNSKILLFULLY
UNSKILLFULNESS
UNSKIMMED
UNSKINNED
UNSLAIN
UNSLAKABLE
UNSLAKED
UNSLEEPING
UNSLICED
UNSLING
UNSLINGING
UNSLINGS
UNSLIPPING
UNSLUICE
UNSLUICED
UNSLUICES
UNSLUICING
UNSLUMBERING
UNSLUMBROUS
UNSLUNG
UNSMART
UNSMILING
UNSMILINGLY
UNSMIRCHED
UNSMITTEN
UNSMOKED
UNSMOOTH
UNSMOOTHED
UNSMOOTHING
UNSMOOTHS
UNSMOTE
UNSMOTHERABLE
UNSNAP
UNSNAPPED
UNSNAPPING
UNSNAPS
UNSNARL
UNSNARLED
UNSNARLING
UNSNARLS
UNSNECK
UNSNECKED
UNSNECKING
UNSNECKS

UNSNUFFED
UNSOAKED
UNSOAPED
UNSOBER
UNSOCIABILITIES
UNSOCIABILITY
UNSOCIABLE
UNSOCIABLENESS
UNSOCIABLY
UNSOCIAL
UNSOCIALISED
UNSOCIALISM
UNSOCIALISMS
UNSOCIALITIES
UNSOCIALITY
UNSOCIALIZED
UNSOCIALLY
UNSOCKET
UNSOCKETED
UNSOCKETING
UNSOCKETS
UNSOD
UNSODDEN
UNSOFT
UNSOFTENED
UNSOFTENING
UNSOILED
UNSOLACED
UNSOLD
UNSOLDER
UNSOLDERED
UNSOLDERING
UNSOLDERS
UNSOLDIERLIKE
UNSOLDIERLY
UNSOLEMN
UNSOLICITED
UNSOLICITOUS
UNSOLID
UNSOLIDITIES
UNSOLIDITY
UNSOLIDLY
UNSOLVABLE
UNSOLVED
UNSONCY
UNSONSIE
UNSONSY
UNSOOTE
UNSOPHISTICATE
UNSOPHISTICATED
UNSORTED
UNSOUGHT
UNSOUL
UNSOULED
UNSOULING
UNSOULS
UNSOUND

UNSOUNDABLE
UNSOUNDED
UNSOUNDER
UNSOUNDEST
UNSOUNDLY
UNSOUNDNESS
UNSOUNDNESSES
UNSOURCED
UNSOURED
UNSOWED
UNSOWN
UNSPAR
UNSPARED
UNSPARING
UNSPARINGLY
UNSPARINGNESS
UNSPARINGNESSES
UNSPARRED
UNSPARRING
UNSPARS
UNSPEAK
UNSPEAKABLE
UNSPEAKABLENESS
UNSPEAKABLY
UNSPEAKING
UNSPEAKS
UNSPECIALISED
UNSPECIALIZED
UNSPECIFIABLE
UNSPECIFIC
UNSPECIFIED
UNSPECTACLED
UNSPECTACULAR
UNSPECULATIVE
UNSPED
UNSPELL
UNSPELLED
UNSPELLING
UNSPELLS
UNSPENT
UNSPHERE
UNSPHERED
UNSPHERES
UNSPHERING
UNSPIDE
UNSPIED
UNSPILLED
UNSPILT
UNSPIRITED
UNSPIRITUAL
UNSPIRITUALISE
UNSPIRITUALISED
UNSPIRITUALISES
UNSPIRITUALIZE
UNSPIRITUALIZED
UNSPIRITUALIZES
UNSPIRITUALLY

UNSPLINTERABLE
UNSPLIT
UNSPOILED
UNSPOILT
UNSPOKE
UNSPOKEN
UNSPORTING
UNSPORTSMANLIKE
UNSPOTTED
UNSPOTTEDNESS
UNSPOTTEDNESSES
UNSPRAYED
UNSPRINKLED
UNSPRUNG
UNSPUN
UNSQUARED
UNSTABLE
UNSTABLENESS
UNSTABLENESSES
UNSTABLER
UNSTABLEST
UNSTABLY
UNSTACK
UNSTACKED
UNSTACKING
UNSTACKS
UNSTAID
UNSTAIDNESS
UNSTAIDNESSES
UNSTAINABLE
UNSTAINED
UNSTAMPED
UNSTANCHABLE
UNSTANCHED
UNSTANDARDISED
UNSTANDARDIZED
UNSTARCH
UNSTARCHED
UNSTARCHES
UNSTARCHING
UNSTARRY
UNSTARTLING
UNSTATE
UNSTATED
UNSTATES
UNSTATESMANLIKE
UNSTATING
UNSTATUTABLE
UNSTATUTABLY
UNSTAUNCHABLE
UNSTAUNCHED
UNSTAYED
UNSTAYING
UNSTEADFAST
UNSTEADFASTLY
UNSTEADFASTNESS
UNSTEADIED

UNSTEADIER
UNSTEADIES
UNSTEADIEST
UNSTEADILY
UNSTEADINESS
UNSTEADINESSES
UNSTEADY
UNSTEADYING
UNSTEEL
UNSTEELED
UNSTEELING
UNSTEELS
UNSTEMMED
UNSTEP
UNSTEPPED
UNSTEPPING
UNSTEPS
UNSTERCORATED
UNSTERILE
UNSTERILISED
UNSTERILIZED
UNSTICK
UNSTICKING
UNSTICKS
UNSTIFLED
UNSTIGMATISED
UNSTIGMATIZED
UNSTILLED
UNSTIMULATED
UNSTINTED
UNSTINTING
UNSTINTINGLY
UNSTIRRED
UNSTITCH
UNSTITCHED
UNSTITCHES
UNSTITCHING
UNSTOCK
UNSTOCKED
UNSTOCKING
UNSTOCKINGED
UNSTOCKS
UNSTONED
UNSTOOPING
UNSTOP
UNSTOPPABLE
UNSTOPPABLY
UNSTOPPED
UNSTOPPER
UNSTOPPERED
UNSTOPPERING
UNSTOPPERS
UNSTOPPING
UNSTOPS
UNSTOW
UNSTOWED
UNSTOWING

UNSTOWS
UNSTRAINED
UNSTRAP
UNSTRAPPED
UNSTRAPPING
UNSTRAPS
UNSTRATIFIED
UNSTREAMED
UNSTRENGTHENED
UNSTRESS
UNSTRESSED
UNSTRESSES
UNSTRIATED
UNSTRING
UNSTRINGED
UNSTRINGING
UNSTRINGS
UNSTRIP
UNSTRIPED
UNSTRIPPED
UNSTRIPPING
UNSTRIPS
UNSTRUCK
UNSTRUCTURED
UNSTRUNG
UNSTUCK
UNSTUDIED
UNSTUFFED
UNSTUFFY
UNSTUFT
UNSTUNG
UNSTYLISH
UNSUBDUABLE
UNSUBDUED
UNSUBJECT
UNSUBJECTED
UNSUBLIMATED
UNSUBLIMED
UNSUBMERGED
UNSUBMISSIVE
UNSUBMITTING
UNSUBSCRIBE
UNSUBSCRIBED
UNSUBSCRIBES
UNSUBSCRIBING
UNSUBSIDISED
UNSUBSIDIZED
UNSUBSTANTIAL
UNSUBSTANTIALLY
UNSUBSTANTIATED
UNSUBTLE
UNSUBTLY
UNSUCCEEDED
UNSUCCESS
UNSUCCESSES
UNSUCCESSFUL
UNSUCCESSFULLY

UNSUCCESSIVE
UNSUCCOURED
UNSUCKED
UNSUFFERABLE
UNSUFFICIENT
UNSUIT
UNSUITABILITIES
UNSUITABILITY
UNSUITABLE
UNSUITABLENESS
UNSUITABLY
UNSUITED
UNSUITING
UNSUITS
UNSULLIED
UNSUMMED
UNSUMMERED
UNSUMMONED
UNSUNG
UNSUNK
UNSUNNED
UNSUNNY
UNSUPERFLUOUS
UNSUPERVISED
UNSUPPLE
UNSUPPLENESS
UNSUPPLENESSES
UNSUPPLIED
UNSUPPORTABLE
UNSUPPORTED
UNSUPPORTEDLY
UNSUPPOSABLE
UNSUPPRESSED
UNSURE
UNSURED
UNSURELY
UNSURER
UNSUREST
UNSURFACED
UNSURMISED
UNSURMOUNTABLE
UNSURPASSABLE
UNSURPASSABLY
UNSURPASSED
UNSURPRISED
UNSURPRISING
UNSURPRISINGLY
UNSURVEYED
UNSUSCEPTIBLE
UNSUSPECT
UNSUSPECTED
UNSUSPECTEDLY
UNSUSPECTEDNESS
UNSUSPECTING
UNSUSPECTINGLY
UNSUSPENDED
UNSUSPICION

UNSUSPICIONS	UNTAINTEDLY	UNTENABLY	UNTHREADS
UNSUSPICIOUS	UNTAINTEDNESS	UNTENANT	UNTHREATENED
UNSUSPICIOUSLY	UNTAINTEDNESSES	UNTENANTABLE	UNTHREATENING
UNSUSTAINABLE	UNTAINTING	UNTENANTED	UNTHRIFT
UNSUSTAINED	UNTAKEN	UNTENANTING	UNTHRIFTILY
UNSUSTAINING	UNTALENTED	UNTENANTS	UNTHRIFTINESS
UNSWADDLE	UNTAMABLE	UNTENDED	UNTHRIFTINESSES
UNSWADDLED	UNTAMABLENESS	UNTENDER	UNTHRIFTS
UNSWADDLES	UNTAMABLENESSES	UNTENDERED	UNTHRIFTY
UNSWADDLING	UNTAMABLY	UNTENDERLY	UNTHRIFTYHEAD
UNSWALLOWED	UNTAME	UNTENT	UNTHRIFTYHEADS
UNSWATHE	UNTAMEABLE	UNTENTED	UNTHRIFTYHEDS
UNSWATHED	UNTAMEABLENESS	UNTENTING	UNTHRONE
UNSWATHES	UNTAMEABLY	UNTENTS	UNTHRONED
UNSWATHING	UNTAMED	UNTENTY	UNTHRONES
UNSWAYABLE	UNTAMEDNESS	UNTENURED	UNTHRONING
UNSWAYED	UNTAMEDNESSES	UNTERMINATED	UNTIDIED
UNSWEAR	UNTAMES	UNTERRESTRIAL	UNTIDIER
UNSWEARING	UNTAMING	UNTERRIFIED	UNTIDIES
UNSWEARINGS	UNTANGIBLE	UNTERRIFYING	UNTIDIEST
UNSWEARS	UNTANGLE	UNTESTABLE	UNTIDILY
UNSWEET	UNTANGLED	UNTESTED	UNTIDINESS
UNSWEETENED	UNTANGLES	UNTETHER	UNTIDINESSES
UNSWEPT	UNTANGLING	UNTETHERED	UNTIDY
UNSWERVING	UNTANNED	UNTETHERING	UNTIDYING
UNSWERVINGLY	UNTAPPED	UNTETHERS	UNTIE
UNSWORE	UNTARNISHED	UNTHANKED	UNTIED
UNSWORN	UNTARRED	UNTHANKFUL	UNTIES
UNSYLLABLED	UNTASTED	UNTHANKFULLY	UNTIL
UNSYMMETRICAL	UNTASTEFUL	UNTHANKFULNESS	UNTILE
UNSYMMETRICALLY	UNTAUGHT	UNTHATCH	UNTILED
UNSYMMETRIES	UNTAX	UNTHATCHED	UNTILES
UNSYMMETRISED	UNTAXED	UNTHATCHES	UNTILING
UNSYMMETRIZED	UNTAXES	UNTHATCHING	UNTILLABLE
UNSYMMETRY	UNTAXING	UNTHAW	UNTILLED
UNSYMPATHETIC	UNTEACH	UNTHAWED	UNTILTED
UNSYMPATHIES	UNTEACHABLE	UNTHAWING	UNTIMBERED
UNSYMPATHISING	UNTEACHABLENESS	UNTHAWS	UNTIMELIER
UNSYMPATHIZING	UNTEACHES	UNTHEOLOGICAL	UNTIMELIEST
UNSYMPATHY	UNTEACHING	UNTHEORETICAL	UNTIMELINESS
UNSYNCHRONIZED	UNTEAM	UNTHICKENED	UNTIMELINESSES
UNSYSTEMATIC	UNTEAMED	UNTHINK	UNTIMELY
UNSYSTEMATICAL	UNTEAMING	UNTHINKABILITY	UNTIMEOUS
UNSYSTEMATISED	UNTEAMS	UNTHINKABLE	UNTIMEOUSLY
UNSYSTEMATIZED	UNTEARABLE	UNTHINKABLENESS	UNTIN
UNTACK	UNTECHNICAL	UNTHINKABLY	UNTINCTURED
UNTACKED	UNTELLABLE	UNTHINKING	UNTINGED
UNTACKING	UNTEMPER	UNTHINKINGLY	UNTINNED
UNTACKLE	UNTEMPERED	UNTHINKINGNESS	UNTINNING
UNTACKLED	UNTEMPERING	UNTHINKS	UNTINS
UNTACKLES	UNTEMPERS	UNTHOROUGH	UNTIPPED
UNTACKLING	UNTEMPTED	UNTHOUGHT	UNTIRABLE
UNTACKS	UNTENABILITIES	UNTHOUGHTFUL	UNTIRED
UNTACTFUL	UNTENABILITY	UNTHOUGHTFULLY	UNTIRING
UNTAGGED	UNTENABLE	UNTHREAD	UNTIRINGLY
UNTAILED	UNTENABLENESS	UNTHREADED	UNTITLED
UNTAINTED	UNTENABLENESSES	UNTHREADING	UNTO

UNTOCHERED
UNTOGETHER
UNTOILING
UNTOLD
UNTOMB
UNTOMBED
UNTOMBING
UNTOMBS
UNTONED
UNTORMENTED
UNTORN
UNTORTURED
UNTOUCHABILITY
UNTOUCHABLE
UNTOUCHABLES
UNTOUCHED
UNTOWARD
UNTOWARDLINESS
UNTOWARDLY
UNTOWARDNESS
UNTOWARDNESSES
UNTRACE
UNTRACEABLE
UNTRACED
UNTRACES
UNTRACING
UNTRACKED
UNTRACTABLE
UNTRACTABLENESS
UNTRADED
UNTRADITIONAL
UNTRADITIONALLY
UNTRAINED
UNTRAMMELED
UNTRAMMELLED
UNTRAMPLED
UNTRANQUIL
UNTRANSFERABLE
UNTRANSFERRABLE
UNTRANSFORMED
UNTRANSLATABLE
UNTRANSLATABLY
UNTRANSLATED
UNTRANSMIGRATED
UNTRANSMISSIBLE
UNTRANSMITTED
UNTRANSMUTABLE
UNTRANSMUTED
UNTRANSPARENT
UNTRAVELED
UNTRAVELLED
UNTRAVERSABLE
UNTRAVERSED
UNTREAD
UNTREADING
UNTREADS
UNTREASURE

UNTREASURED
UNTREASURES
UNTREASURING
UNTREATABLE
UNTREATED
UNTREMBLING
UNTREMBLINGLY
UNTREMENDOUS
UNTREMULOUS
UNTRENCHED
UNTRENDY
UNTRESPASSING
UNTRESSED
UNTRIDE
UNTRIED
UNTRIM
UNTRIMMED
UNTRIMMING
UNTRIMS
UNTROD
UNTRODDEN
UNTROUBLED
UNTROUBLEDLY
UNTRUE
UNTRUENESS
UNTRUENESSES
UNTRUER
UNTRUEST
UNTRUISM
UNTRUISMS
UNTRULY
UNTRUSS
UNTRUSSED
UNTRUSSER
UNTRUSSERS
UNTRUSSES
UNTRUSSING
UNTRUSSINGS
UNTRUST
UNTRUSTFUL
UNTRUSTINESS
UNTRUSTINESSES
UNTRUSTING
UNTRUSTS
UNTRUSTWORTHILY
UNTRUSTWORTHY
UNTRUSTY
UNTRUTH
UNTRUTHFUL
UNTRUTHFULLY
UNTRUTHFULNESS
UNTRUTHS
UNTUCK
UNTUCKED
UNTUCKERED
UNTUCKING
UNTUCKS

UNTUFTED
UNTUMBLED
UNTUMULTUOUS
UNTUNABLE
UNTUNABLENESS
UNTUNABLENESSES
UNTUNABLY
UNTUNE
UNTUNEABLE
UNTUNED
UNTUNEFUL
UNTUNEFULLY
UNTUNEFULNESS
UNTUNEFULNESSES
UNTUNES
UNTUNING
UNTURBID
UNTURF
UNTURFED
UNTURFING
UNTURFS
UNTURN
UNTURNABLE
UNTURNED
UNTURNING
UNTURNS
UNTUTORED
UNTWINE
UNTWINED
UNTWINES
UNTWINING
UNTWIST
UNTWISTED
UNTWISTING
UNTWISTINGS
UNTWISTS
UNTYING
UNTYINGS
UNTYPABLE
UNTYPICAL
UNTYPICALLY
UNUNITED
UNUPLIFTED
UNURGED
UNUSABLE
UNUSABLY
UNUSED
UNUSEFUL
UNUSEFULLY
UNUSEFULNESS
UNUSEFULNESSES
UNUSHERED
UNUSUAL
UNUSUALLY
UNUSUALNESS
UNUSUALNESSES
UNUTILISED

UNUTILIZED
UNUTTERABLE
UNUTTERABLENESS
UNUTTERABLES
UNUTTERABLY
UNUTTERED
UNVACCINATED
UNVAIL
UNVAILE
UNVAILED
UNVAILES
UNVAILING
UNVAILS
UNVALUABLE
UNVALUED
UNVANQUISHABLE
UNVANQUISHED
UNVARIABLE
UNVARIED
UNVARIEGATED
UNVARNISHED
UNVARYING
UNVEIL
UNVEILED
UNVEILER
UNVEILERS
UNVEILING
UNVEILINGS
UNVEILS
UNVEINED
UNVENDIBLE
UNVENERABLE
UNVENTED
UNVENTILATED
UNVERACIOUS
UNVERACITIES
UNVERACITY
UNVERBALIZED
UNVERIFIABILITY
UNVERIFIABLE
UNVERIFIED
UNVERSED
UNVETTED
UNVEXED
UNVEXT
UNVIABLE
UNVIEWED
UNVIOLATED
UNVIRTUE
UNVIRTUES
UNVIRTUOUS
UNVIRTUOUSLY
UNVISITABLE
UNVISITED
UNVISOR
UNVISORED
UNVISORING

UNVISORS
UNVITAL
UNVITIATED
UNVITRIFIABLE
UNVITRIFIED
UNVIZARD
UNVIZARDED
UNVIZARDING
UNVIZARDS
UNVOCAL
UNVOCALISED
UNVOCALIZED
UNVOICE
UNVOICED
UNVOICES
UNVOICING
UNVOICINGS
UNVOYAGEABLE
UNVULGAR
UNVULGARISE
UNVULGARISED
UNVULGARISES
UNVULGARISING
UNVULGARIZE
UNVULGARIZED
UNVULGARIZES
UNVULGARIZING
UNVULNERABLE
UNWAGED
UNWAKED
UNWAKENED
UNWALLED
UNWANDERING
UNWANING
UNWANTED
UNWARDED
UNWARE
UNWARELY
UNWARENESS
UNWARENESSES
UNWARES
UNWARIE
UNWARIER
UNWARIEST
UNWARILY
UNWARINESS
UNWARINESSES
UNWARLIKE
UNWARMED
UNWARNED
UNWARPED
UNWARRANTABLE
UNWARRANTABLY
UNWARRANTED
UNWARRANTEDLY
UNWARY
UNWASHED

UNWASHEDNESS
UNWASHEDNESSES
UNWASHEDS
UNWASHEN
UNWASTED
UNWASTING
UNWATCHABLE
UNWATCHED
UNWATCHFUL
UNWATCHFULLY
UNWATCHFULNESS
UNWATER
UNWATERED
UNWATERING
UNWATERS
UNWATERY
UNWAVERING
UNWAVERINGLY
UNWAXED
UNWAYED
UNWEAKENED
UNWEAL
UNWEALS
UNWEANED
UNWEAPON
UNWEAPONED
UNWEAPONING
UNWEAPONS
UNWEARABLE
UNWEARIABLE
UNWEARIABLY
UNWEARIED
UNWEARIEDLY
UNWEARIEDNESS
UNWEARY
UNWEARYING
UNWEARYINGLY
UNWEATHERED
UNWEAVE
UNWEAVES
UNWEAVING
UNWEBBED
UNWED
UNWEDDED
UNWEDGEABLE
UNWEEDED
UNWEENED
UNWEETING
UNWEETINGLY
UNWEIGHED
UNWEIGHING
UNWEIGHT
UNWEIGHTED
UNWEIGHTING
UNWEIGHTS
UNWELCOME
UNWELCOMED

UNWELCOMELY
UNWELCOMENESS
UNWELCOMENESSES
UNWELDED
UNWELDY
UNWELL
UNWELLNESS
UNWELLNESSES
UNWEPT
UNWET
UNWETTED
UNWHIPPED
UNWHIPT
UNWHISTLEABLE
UNWHITE
UNWHOLESOME
UNWHOLESOMELY
UNWHOLESOMENESS
UNWIELDIER
UNWIELDIEST
UNWIELDILY
UNWIELDINESS
UNWIELDINESSES
UNWIELDLILY
UNWIELDLINESS
UNWIELDLY
UNWIELDY
UNWIFELIER
UNWIFELIEST
UNWIFELIKE
UNWIFELY
UNWIGGED
UNWILFUL
UNWILL
UNWILLED
UNWILLING
UNWILLINGLY
UNWILLINGNESS
UNWILLINGNESSES
UNWILLS
UNWIND
UNWINDABLE
UNWINDER
UNWINDERS
UNWINDING
UNWINDINGS
UNWINDS
UNWINGED
UNWINKING
UNWINKINGLY
UNWINNABLE
UNWINNOWED
UNWIPED
UNWIRE
UNWIRED
UNWIRES
UNWIRING

UNWISDOM
UNWISDOMS
UNWISE
UNWISELY
UNWISENESS
UNWISENESSES
UNWISER
UNWISEST
UNWISH
UNWISHED
UNWISHES
UNWISHFUL
UNWISHING
UNWIST
UNWIT
UNWITCH
UNWITCHED
UNWITCHES
UNWITCHING
UNWITHDRAWING
UNWITHERED
UNWITHERING
UNWITHHELD
UNWITHHOLDEN
UNWITHHOLDING
UNWITHSTOOD
UNWITNESSED
UNWITS
UNWITTED
UNWITTILY
UNWITTING
UNWITTINGLY
UNWITTINGNESS
UNWITTINGNESSES
UNWITTY
UNWIVE
UNWIVED
UNWIVES
UNWIVING
UNWOMAN
UNWOMANED
UNWOMANING
UNWOMANLIER
UNWOMANLIEST
UNWOMANLINESS
UNWOMANLINESSES
UNWOMANLY
UNWOMANS
UNWON
UNWONT
UNWONTED
UNWONTEDLY
UNWONTEDNESS
UNWONTEDNESSES
UNWOODED
UNWOOED
UNWORDED

UNWORK
UNWORKABILITIES
UNWORKABILITY
UNWORKABLE
UNWORKED
UNWORKING
UNWORKMANLIKE
UNWORKS
UNWORLDLIER
UNWORLDLIEST
UNWORLDLINESS
UNWORLDLINESSES
UNWORLDLY
UNWORMED
UNWORN
UNWORRIED
UNWORSHIPFUL
UNWORSHIPPED
UNWORTH
UNWORTHIER
UNWORTHIES
UNWORTHIEST
UNWORTHILY
UNWORTHINESS
UNWORTHINESSES
UNWORTHS
UNWORTHY
UNWOUND
UNWOUNDABLE
UNWOUNDED
UNWOVE
UNWOVEN
UNWRAP
UNWRAPPED
UNWRAPPING
UNWRAPS
UNWREAKED
UNWREATHE
UNWREATHED
UNWREATHES
UNWREATHING
UNWRINKLE
UNWRINKLED
UNWRINKLES
UNWRINKLING
UNWRITE
UNWRITES
UNWRITING
UNWRITTEN
UNWROTE
UNWROUGHT
UNWRUNG
UNYEANED
UNYIELDING
UNYIELDINGLY
UNYIELDINGNESS
UNYOKE

UNYOKED
UNYOKES
UNYOKING
UNYOUNG
UNZEALOUS
UNZIP
UNZIPPED
UNZIPPING
UNZIPS
UNZONED
UP
UPADAISY
UPAITHRIC
UPAS
UPASES
UPBEAR
UPBEARER
UPBEARERS
UPBEARING
UPBEARS
UPBEAT
UPBEATS
UPBIND
UPBINDING
UPBINDS
UPBLEW
UPBLOW
UPBLOWING
UPBLOWN
UPBLOWS
UPBOIL
UPBOILED
UPBOILING
UPBOILS
UPBORE
UPBORNE
UPBOUND
UPBOUNDEN
UPBOW
UPBOWS
UPBRAID
UPBRAIDED
UPBRAIDER
UPBRAIDERS
UPBRAIDING
UPBRAIDINGLY
UPBRAIDINGS
UPBRAIDS
UPBRAST
UPBRAY
UPBRAYED
UPBRAYING
UPBRAYS
UPBREAK
UPBREAKING
UPBREAKS
UPBRING

UPBRINGING
UPBRINGINGS
UPBRINGS
UPBROKE
UPBROKEN
UPBROUGHT
UPBUILD
UPBUILDER
UPBUILDERS
UPBUILDING
UPBUILDINGS
UPBUILDS
UPBUILT
UPBUOYANCE
UPBUOYANCES
UPBURNING
UPBURST
UPBURSTING
UPBURSTS
UPBY
UPBYE
UPCAST
UPCASTING
UPCASTS
UPCATCH
UPCATCHES
UPCATCHING
UPCAUGHT
UPCHEER
UPCHEERED
UPCHEERING
UPCHEERS
UPCHUCK
UPCHUCKED
UPCHUCKING
UPCHUCKS
UPCLIMB
UPCLIMBED
UPCLIMBING
UPCLIMBS
UPCLOSE
UPCLOSED
UPCLOSES
UPCLOSING
UPCOAST
UPCOIL
UPCOILED
UPCOILING
UPCOILS
UPCOME
UPCOMES
UPCOMING
UPCOUNTRY
UPCURL
UPCURLED
UPCURLING
UPCURLS

UPCURVE
UPCURVED
UPCURVES
UPCURVING
UPDART
UPDARTED
UPDARTING
UPDARTS
UPDATE
UPDATEABLE
UPDATED
UPDATER
UPDATERS
UPDATES
UPDATING
UPDIVE
UPDIVED
UPDIVES
UPDIVING
UPDO
UPDOS
UPDOVE
UPDRAFT
UPDRAFTS
UPDRAG
UPDRAGGED
UPDRAGGING
UPDRAGS
UPDRAUGHT
UPDRAUGHTS
UPDRAW
UPDRAWING
UPDRAWN
UPDRAWS
UPDREW
UPDRIED
UPDRIES
UPDRY
UPDRYING
UPEND
UPENDED
UPENDING
UPENDS
UPFIELD
UPFILL
UPFILLED
UPFILLING
UPFILLINGS
UPFILLS
UPFLASHING
UPFLING
UPFLINGING
UPFLINGS
UPFLOW
UPFLOWED
UPFLOWING
UPFLOWS

UPFLUNG
UPFOLD
UPFOLDED
UPFOLDING
UPFOLDS
UPFOLLOW
UPFOLLOWED
UPFOLLOWING
UPFOLLOWS
UPFRONT
UPFURL
UPFURLED
UPFURLING
UPFURLS
UPGANG
UPGANGS
UPGATHER
UPGATHERED
UPGATHERING
UPGATHERS
UPGAZE
UPGAZED
UPGAZES
UPGAZING
UPGIRD
UPGIRDED
UPGIRDING
UPGIRDS
UPGIRT
UPGO
UPGOES
UPGOING
UPGOINGS
UPGONE
UPGRADABILITIES
UPGRADABILITY
UPGRADABLE
UPGRADATION
UPGRADATIONS
UPGRADE
UPGRADEABILITY
UPGRADEABLE
UPGRADED
UPGRADER
UPGRADERS
UPGRADES
UPGRADING
UPGREW
UPGROW
UPGROWING
UPGROWINGS
UPGROWN
UPGROWS
UPGROWTH
UPGROWTHS
UPGUSH
UPGUSHED

UPGUSHES
UPGUSHING
UPHAND
UPHANG
UPHANGING
UPHANGS
UPHAUD
UPHAUDING
UPHAUDS
UPHEAP
UPHEAPED
UPHEAPING
UPHEAPINGS
UPHEAPS
UPHEAVAL
UPHEAVALS
UPHEAVE
UPHEAVED
UPHEAVER
UPHEAVERS
UPHEAVES
UPHEAVING
UPHELD
UPHILD
UPHILL
UPHILLS
UPHILLWARD
UPHOARD
UPHOARDED
UPHOARDING
UPHOARDS
UPHOIST
UPHOISTED
UPHOISTING
UPHOISTS
UPHOLD
UPHOLDER
UPHOLDERS
UPHOLDING
UPHOLDINGS
UPHOLDS
UPHOLSTER
UPHOLSTERED
UPHOLSTERER
UPHOLSTERERS
UPHOLSTERIES
UPHOLSTERING
UPHOLSTERS
UPHOLSTERY
UPHOLSTRESS
UPHOLSTRESSES
UPHOORD
UPHOORDED
UPHOORDING
UPHOORDS
UPHOVE
UPHROE

UPHROES
UPHUDDEN
UPHUNG
UPHURL
UPHURLED
UPHURLING
UPHURLS
UPJET
UPJETS
UPJETTED
UPJETTING
UPKEEP
UPKEEPS
UPKNIT
UPKNITS
UPKNITTED
UPKNITTING
UPLAID
UPLAND
UPLANDER
UPLANDERS
UPLANDISH
UPLANDS
UPLAY
UPLAYING
UPLAYS
UPLEAD
UPLEADING
UPLEADS
UPLEAN
UPLEANED
UPLEANING
UPLEANS
UPLEANT
UPLEAP
UPLEAPED
UPLEAPING
UPLEAPS
UPLEAPT
UPLED
UPLIFT
UPLIFTED
UPLIFTER
UPLIFTERS
UPLIFTING
UPLIFTINGLY
UPLIFTINGS
UPLIFTS
UPLIGHT
UPLIGHTED
UPLIGHTER
UPLIGHTERS
UPLIGHTING
UPLIGHTS
UPLINK
UPLINKING
UPLINKINGS

UPLINKS
UPLIT
UPLOAD
UPLOADED
UPLOADING
UPLOADS
UPLOCK
UPLOCKED
UPLOCKING
UPLOCKS
UPLOOK
UPLOOKED
UPLOOKING
UPLOOKS
UPLYING
UPMAKE
UPMAKER
UPMAKERS
UPMAKES
UPMAKING
UPMAKINGS
UPMANSHIP
UPMANSHIPS
UPMARKET
UPMOST
UPO
UPON
UPPED
UPPER
UPPERCASE
UPPERCASED
UPPERCASES
UPPERCASING
UPPERCLASSMAN
UPPERCLASSMEN
UPPERCUT
UPPERCUTS
UPPERCUTTING
UPPERMOST
UPPERPART
UPPERPARTS
UPPERS
UPPERWORKS
UPPILE
UPPILED
UPPILES
UPPILING
UPPING
UPPINGS
UPPISH
UPPISHLY
UPPISHNESS
UPPISHNESSES
UPPITINESS
UPPITINESSES
UPPITY
UPPITYNESS

UPPITYNESSES
UPPROP
UPPROPPED
UPPROPPING
UPPROPS
UPRAISE
UPRAISED
UPRAISER
UPRAISERS
UPRAISES
UPRAISING
UPRAN
UPRATE
UPRATED
UPRATES
UPRATING
UPREACH
UPREACHED
UPREACHES
UPREACHING
UPREAR
UPREARED
UPREARING
UPREARS
UPREST
UPRESTS
UPRIGHT
UPRIGHTED
UPRIGHTEOUSLY
UPRIGHTING
UPRIGHTLY
UPRIGHTNESS
UPRIGHTNESSES
UPRIGHTS
UPRISAL
UPRISALS
UPRISE
UPRISEN
UPRISER
UPRISERS
UPRISES
UPRISING
UPRISINGS
UPRIST
UPRISTS
UPRIVER
UPRIVERS
UPROAR
UPROARED
UPROARING
UPROARIOUS
UPROARIOUSLY
UPROARIOUSNESS
UPROARS
UPROLL
UPROLLED
UPROLLING

UPROLLS
UPROOT
UPROOTAL
UPROOTALS
UPROOTED
UPROOTEDNESS
UPROOTEDNESSES
UPROOTER
UPROOTERS
UPROOTING
UPROOTINGS
UPROOTS
UPROSE
UPROUSE
UPROUSED
UPROUSES
UPROUSING
UPRUN
UPRUNNING
UPRUNS
UPRUSH
UPRUSHED
UPRUSHES
UPRUSHING
UPRYST
UPS
UPSADAISY
UPSCALE
UPSCALED
UPSCALES
UPSCALING
UPSEE
UPSEES
UPSEND
UPSENDING
UPSENDS
UPSENT
UPSET
UPSETS
UPSETTABLE
UPSETTER
UPSETTERS
UPSETTING
UPSETTINGLY
UPSETTINGNESS
UPSETTINGS
UPSEY
UPSEYS
UPSHIFT
UPSHIFTED
UPSHIFTING
UPSHIFTS
UPSHOOT
UPSHOOTING
UPSHOOTS
UPSHOT
UPSHOTS

UPSIDE
UPSIDES
UPSIES
UPSILON
UPSILONS
UPSITTING
UPSITTINGS
UPSKILL
UPSKILLED
UPSKILLING
UPSKILLS
UPSOAR
UPSOARED
UPSOARING
UPSOARS
UPSPAKE
UPSPEAK
UPSPEAKING
UPSPEAKS
UPSPEAR
UPSPEARED
UPSPEARING
UPSPEARS
UPSPOKE
UPSPOKEN
UPSPRANG
UPSPRING
UPSPRINGING
UPSPRINGS
UPSPRUNG
UPSTAGE
UPSTAGED
UPSTAGES
UPSTAGING
UPSTAIR
UPSTAIRS
UPSTAND
UPSTANDING
UPSTANDINGNESS
UPSTANDS
UPSTARE
UPSTARED
UPSTARES
UPSTARING
UPSTART
UPSTARTED
UPSTARTING
UPSTARTS
UPSTATE
UPSTATER
UPSTATERS
UPSTATES
UPSTAY
UPSTAYED
UPSTAYING
UPSTAYS
UPSTEP

UPSTEPPED
UPSTEPPING
UPSTEPS
UPSTIR
UPSTIRRED
UPSTIRRING
UPSTIRS
UPSTOOD
UPSTREAM
UPSTREAMED
UPSTREAMING
UPSTREAMS
UPSTRETCHED
UPSTROKE
UPSTROKES
UPSURGE
UPSURGED
UPSURGENCE
UPSURGENCES
UPSURGES
UPSURGING
UPSWARM
UPSWARMED
UPSWARMING
UPSWARMS
UPSWAY
UPSWAYED
UPSWAYING
UPSWAYS
UPSWEEP
UPSWEEPING
UPSWEEPS
UPSWELL
UPSWELLED
UPSWELLING
UPSWELLS
UPSWEPT
UPSWING
UPSWINGING
UPSWINGS
UPSWOLLEN
UPSWUNG
UPSY
UPTA
UPTAK
UPTAKE
UPTAKEN
UPTAKES
UPTAKING
UPTAKS
UPTALK
UPTALKED
UPTALKING
UPTALKS
UPTEAR
UPTEARING
UPTEARS

UPTER
UPTHREW
UPTHROW
UPTHROWING
UPTHROWN
UPTHROWS
UPTHRUST
UPTHRUSTING
UPTHRUSTS
UPTHUNDER
UPTHUNDERED
UPTHUNDERING
UPTHUNDERS
UPTICK
UPTICKS
UPTIE
UPTIED
UPTIES
UPTIGHT
UPTIGHTER
UPTIGHTEST
UPTIGHTNESS
UPTIGHTNESSES
UPTILT
UPTILTED
UPTILTING
UPTILTS
UPTIME
UPTIMES
UPTITLING
UPTOOK
UPTORE
UPTORN
UPTOSS
UPTOSSED
UPTOSSES
UPTOSSING
UPTOWN
UPTOWNER
UPTOWNERS
UPTOWNS
UPTRAIN
UPTRAINED
UPTRAINING
UPTRAINS
UPTREND
UPTRENDS
UPTRILLED
UPTURN
UPTURNED
UPTURNING
UPTURNINGS
UPTURNS
UPTYING
UPVALUATION
UPVALUATIONS
UPVALUE

UPVALUED
UPVALUES
UPVALUING
UPWAFT
UPWAFTED
UPWAFTING
UPWAFTS
UPWARD
UPWARDLY
UPWARDNESS
UPWARDNESSES
UPWARDS
UPWELL
UPWELLED
UPWELLING
UPWELLINGS
UPWELLS
UPWENT
UPWHIRL
UPWHIRLED
UPWHIRLING
UPWHIRLS
UPWIND
UPWINDING
UPWINDS
UPWOUND
UPWRAP
UPWRAPS
UPWROUGHT
UR
URACHI
URACHUS
URACHUSES
URACIL
URACILS
URAEI
URAEMIA
URAEMIAS
URAEMIC
URAEUS
URAEUSES
URALI
URALIS
URALITE
URALITES
URALITIC
URALITISATION
URALITISATIONS
URALITISE
URALITISED
URALITISES
URALITISING
URALITIZATION
URALITIZATIONS
URALITIZE
URALITIZED
URALITIZES

URALITIZING
URANALYSES
URANALYSIS
URANIA
URANIAN
URANIAS
URANIC
URANIDE
URANIDES
URANIN
URANINITE
URANINITES
URANINS
URANISCI
URANISCUS
URANISM
URANISMS
URANITE
URANITES
URANITIC
URANIUM
URANIUMS
URANOGRAPHER
URANOGRAPHERS
URANOGRAPHIC
URANOGRAPHICAL
URANOGRAPHIES
URANOGRAPHIST
URANOGRAPHISTS
URANOGRAPHY
URANOLOGIES
URANOLOGY
URANOMETRIES
URANOMETRY
URANOPLASTIES
URANOPLASTY
URANOUS
URANYL
URANYLIC
URANYLS
URAO
URAOS
URARE
URARES
URARI
URARIS
URASE
URASES
URATE
URATES
URATIC
URB
URBAN
URBANE
URBANELY
URBANENESS
URBANENESSES

URBANER
URBANEST
URBANISATION
URBANISATIONS
URBANISE
URBANISED
URBANISES
URBANISING
URBANISM
URBANISMS
URBANIST
URBANISTIC
URBANISTICALLY
URBANISTS
URBANITE
URBANITES
URBANITIES
URBANITY
URBANIZATION
URBANIZATIONS
URBANIZE
URBANIZED
URBANIZES
URBANIZING
URBANOLOGIES
URBANOLOGIST
URBANOLOGISTS
URBANOLOGY
URBIA
URBIAS
URBS
URCEOLATE
URCEOLI
URCEOLUS
URCEOLUSES
URCHIN
URCHINS
URD
URDE
URDEE
URDS
URDY
URE
UREA
UREAL
UREAS
UREASE
UREASES
UREDIA
UREDIAL
UREDINE
UREDINES
UREDINIA
UREDINIAL
UREDINIOSPORE
UREDINIOSPORES
UREDINIUM

UREDINOUS
UREDIOSPORE
UREDIOSPORES
UREDIUM
UREDO
UREDOS
UREDOSORI
UREDOSORUS
UREDOSPORE
UREDOSPORES
UREIC
UREIDE
UREIDES
UREMIA
UREMIAS
UREMIC
URENA
URENAS
URENT
UREOTELIC
UREOTELISM
UREOTELISMS
URES
URESES
URESIS
URETER
URETERAL
URETERIC
URETERITIS
URETERITISES
URETERS
URETHAN
URETHANE
URETHANES
URETHANS
URETHRA
URETHRAE
URETHRAL
URETHRAS
URETHRITIC
URETHRITIS
URETHRITISES
URETHROSCOPE
URETHROSCOPES
URETHROSCOPIC
URETHROSCOPIES
URETHROSCOPY
URETIC
URGE
URGED
URGENCE
URGENCES
URGENCIES
URGENCY
URGENT
URGENTLY
URGER

URGERS
URGES
URGING
URGINGLY
URGINGS
URIAL
URIALS
URIC
URICASE
URICASES
URICOSURIC
URICOTELIC
URICOTELISM
URICOTELISMS
URIDINE
URIDINES
URIDYLIC
URINAL
URINALS
URINALYSES
URINALYSIS
URINANT
URINARIES
URINARY
URINATE
URINATED
URINATES
URINATING
URINATION
URINATIONS
URINATIVE
URINATOR
URINATORS
URINE
URINED
URINEMIA
URINEMIAS
URINEMIC
URINES
URINIFEROUS
URINING
URINIPAROUS
URINOGENITAL
URINOLOGIES
URINOLOGY
URINOMETER
URINOMETERS
URINOSCOPIES
URINOSCOPY
URINOSE
URINOUS
URITE
URITES
URMAN
URMANS
URN
URNAL

URNED
URNFIELD
URNFIELDS
URNFUL
URNFULS
URNING
URNINGS
URNLIKE
URNS
UROBILIN
UROCHORD
UROCHORDAL
UROCHORDATE
UROCHORDATES
UROCHORDS
UROCHROME
UROCHROMES
URODELAN
URODELANS
URODELE
URODELES
URODELOUS
URODYNAMICS
UROGENITAL
UROGENOUS
UROGRAPHIC
UROGRAPHIES
UROGRAPHY
UROKINASE
UROKINASES
UROLAGNIA
UROLAGNIAS
UROLITH
UROLITHIASES
UROLITHIASIS
UROLITHIC
UROLITHS
UROLOGIC
UROLOGICAL
UROLOGIES
UROLOGIST
UROLOGISTS
UROLOGY
UROMERE
UROMERES
UROPOD
UROPODAL
UROPODOUS
UROPODS
UROPOIESES
UROPOIESIS
UROPYGIA
UROPYGIAL
UROPYGIUM
UROPYGIUMS
UROSCOPIC
UROSCOPIES

UROSCOPIST
UROSCOPISTS
UROSCOPY
UROSES
UROSIS
UROSOME
UROSOMES
UROSTEGE
UROSTEGES
UROSTEGITE
UROSTEGITES
UROSTHENIC
UROSTOMIES
UROSTOMY
UROSTYLE
UROSTYLES
URSA
URSAE
URSIFORM
URSINE
URSON
URSONS
URTEXT
URTEXTS
URTICA
URTICACEOUS
URTICANT
URTICANTS
URTICARIA
URTICARIAL
URTICARIAS
URTICARIOUS
URTICAS
URTICATE
URTICATED
URTICATES
URTICATING
URTICATION
URTICATIONS
URUBU
URUBUS
URUS
URUSES
URUSHIOL
URUSHIOLS
URVA
URVAS
US
USABILITIES
USABILITY
USABLE
USABLENESS
USABLENESSES
USABLY
USAGE
USAGER
USAGERS

USAGES
USANCE
USANCES
USAUNCE
USAUNCES
USE
USEABILITY
USEABLE
USEABLENESS
USEABLY
USED
USEFUL
USEFULLY
USEFULNESS
USEFULNESSES
USEFULS
USELESS
USELESSLY
USELESSNESS
USELESSNESSES
USER
USERS
USES
USHER
USHERED
USHERESS
USHERESSES
USHERETTE
USHERETTES
USHERING
USHERINGS
USHERS
USHERSHIP
USHERSHIPS
USING
USNEA
USNEAS
USQUABAE
USQUABAES
USQUE
USQUEBAE
USQUEBAES
USQUEBAUGH
USQUEBAUGHS
USQUES
USTILAGINEOUS
USTION
USTIONS
USTULATE
USTULATION
USTULATIONS
USUAL
USUALLY
USUALNESS
USUALNESSES
USUALS
USUCAPIENT

USUCAPIENTS
USUCAPION
USUCAPIONS
USUCAPT
USUCAPTED
USUCAPTIBLE
USUCAPTING
USUCAPTION
USUCAPTIONS
USUCAPTS
USUFRUCT
USUFRUCTED
USUFRUCTING
USUFRUCTS
USUFRUCTUARIES
USUFRUCTUARY
USURE
USURED
USURER
USURERS
USURES
USURESS
USURESSES
USURIES
USURING
USURIOUS
USURIOUSLY
USURIOUSNESS
USURIOUSNESSES
USUROUS
USURP
USURPATION
USURPATIONS
USURPATIVE
USURPATORY
USURPATURE
USURPATURES
USURPED
USURPEDLY
USURPER
USURPERS
USURPING
USURPINGLY
USURPINGS
USURPS
USURY
USWARD
USWARDS
UT
UTA
UTAS
UTASES
UTE
UTENSIL
UTENSILS
UTERECTOMIES
UTERECTOMY

UTERI
UTERINE
UTERITIS
UTERITISES
UTEROGESTATION
UTEROGESTATIONS
UTEROTOMIES
UTEROTOMY
UTERUS
UTERUSES
UTES
UTILE
UTILIDOR
UTILIDORS
UTILISABLE
UTILISATION
UTILISATIONS
UTILISE
UTILISED
UTILISER
UTILISERS
UTILISES
UTILISING
UTILITARIAN
UTILITARIANISE
UTILITARIANISED
UTILITARIANISES
UTILITARIANISM
UTILITARIANISMS
UTILITARIANIZE
UTILITARIANIZED
UTILITARIANIZES
UTILITARIANS
UTILITIES
UTILITY
UTILIZABLE
UTILIZATION
UTILIZATIONS
UTILIZE
UTILIZED
UTILIZER
UTILIZERS
UTILIZES
UTILIZING
UTIS
UTISES
UTMOST
UTMOSTS
UTOPIA
UTOPIAN
UTOPIANISE
UTOPIANISED
UTOPIANISER
UTOPIANISERS
UTOPIANISES
UTOPIANISING
UTOPIANISM

UTOPIANISMS
UTOPIANIZE
UTOPIANIZED
UTOPIANIZER
UTOPIANIZERS
UTOPIANIZES
UTOPIANIZING
UTOPIANS
UTOPIAS
UTOPIAST
UTOPIASTS
UTOPISM
UTOPISMS
UTOPIST
UTOPISTIC
UTOPISTS
UTRICLE
UTRICLES
UTRICULAR
UTRICULARIA
UTRICULARIAS
UTRICULATE
UTRICULI
UTRICULITIS
UTRICULUS
UTS
UTTER
UTTERABLE
UTTERABLENESS
UTTERABLENESSES
UTTERANCE
UTTERANCES
UTTERED
UTTERER
UTTERERS
UTTEREST
UTTERING
UTTERINGS
UTTERLESS
UTTERLY
UTTERMOST
UTTERMOSTS
UTTERNESS
UTTERNESSES
UTTERS
UTU
UTUS
UVA
UVAE
UVAROVITE
UVAROVITES
UVAS
UVEA
UVEAL
UVEAS
UVEITIC
UVEITIS

UVEITISES
UVEOUS
UVULA
UVULAE
UVULAR
UVULARLY
UVULARS
UVULAS
UVULITIS
UVULITISES
UXORIAL
UXORIALLY
UXORICIDAL
UXORICIDE
UXORICIDES
UXORILOCAL
UXORIOUS
UXORIOUSLY
UXORIOUSNESS
UXORIOUSNESSES

V

VAC
VACANCE
VACANCES
VACANCIES
VACANCY
VACANT
VACANTLY
VACANTNESS
VACANTNESSES
VACATABLE
VACATE
VACATED
VACATES
VACATING
VACATION
VACATIONED
VACATIONER
VACATIONERS
VACATIONING
VACATIONIST
VACATIONISTS
VACATIONLAND
VACATIONLANDS
VACATIONLESS
VACATIONS
VACATUR
VACATURS
VACCINA
VACCINAL
VACCINAS
VACCINATE
VACCINATED
VACCINATES
VACCINATING
VACCINATION
VACCINATIONS
VACCINATOR
VACCINATORS
VACCINATORY
VACCINE
VACCINEE
VACCINEES
VACCINES
VACCINIA
VACCINIAL
VACCINIAS
VACCINIUM
VACCINIUMS
VACHERIN
VACHERINS
VACILLANT
VACILLATE

VACILLATED
VACILLATES
VACILLATING
VACILLATINGLY
VACILLATION
VACILLATIONS
VACILLATOR
VACILLATORS
VACILLATORY
VACKED
VACKING
VACS
VACUA
VACUATE
VACUATED
VACUATES
VACUATING
VACUATION
VACUATIONS
VACUIST
VACUISTS
VACUITIES
VACUITY
VACUOLAR
VACUOLATE
VACUOLATED
VACUOLATION
VACUOLATIONS
VACUOLE
VACUOLES
VACUOLISATION
VACUOLISATIONS
VACUOLIZATION
VACUOLIZATIONS
VACUOUS
VACUOUSLY
VACUOUSNESS
VACUOUSNESSES
VACUUM
VACUUMED
VACUUMING
VACUUMS
VADE
VADED
VADES
VADING
VADOSE
VAE
VAES
VAG
VAGABOND
VAGABONDAGE

VAGABONDAGES
VAGABONDED
VAGABONDING
VAGABONDISE
VAGABONDISED
VAGABONDISES
VAGABONDISH
VAGABONDISING
VAGABONDISM
VAGABONDISMS
VAGABONDIZE
VAGABONDIZED
VAGABONDIZES
VAGABONDIZING
VAGABONDS
VAGAL
VAGALLY
VAGARIES
VAGARIOUS
VAGARIOUSLY
VAGARISH
VAGARY
VAGGED
VAGGING
VAGI
VAGILE
VAGILITIES
VAGILITY
VAGINA
VAGINAE
VAGINAL
VAGINALLY
VAGINANT
VAGINAS
VAGINATE
VAGINATED
VAGINECTOMIES
VAGINECTOMY
VAGINICOLINE
VAGINICOLOUS
VAGINISMUS
VAGINISMUSES
VAGINITIS
VAGINITISES
VAGINULA
VAGINULAE
VAGINULE
VAGINULES
VAGITUS
VAGITUSES
VAGOTOMIES
VAGOTOMY

VAGOTONIA
VAGOTONIAS
VAGOTONIC
VAGOTROPIC
VAGRANCIES
VAGRANCY
VAGRANT
VAGRANTLY
VAGRANTNESS
VAGRANTS
VAGROM
VAGROMS
VAGS
VAGUE
VAGUED
VAGUELY
VAGUENESS
VAGUENESSES
VAGUER
VAGUES
VAGUEST
VAGUING
VAGUS
VAHANA
VAHANAS
VAHINE
VAHINES
VAIL
VAILED
VAILING
VAILS
VAIN
VAINER
VAINESSE
VAINESSES
VAINEST
VAINGLORIED
VAINGLORIES
VAINGLORIOUS
VAINGLORIOUSLY
VAINGLORY
VAINGLORYING
VAINLY
VAINNESS
VAINNESSES
VAIR
VAIRE
VAIRIER
VAIRIEST
VAIRS
VAIRY
VAIVODE

VAIVODES
VAIVODESHIP
VAIVODESHIPS
VAKASS
VAKASSES
VAKEEL
VAKEELS
VAKIL
VAKILS
VALANCE
VALANCED
VALANCES
VALANCING
VALE
VALEDICTION
VALEDICTIONS
VALEDICTORIAN
VALEDICTORIANS
VALEDICTORIES
VALEDICTORY
VALENCE
VALENCES
VALENCIA
VALENCIAS
VALENCIES
VALENCY
VALENTINE
VALENTINES
VALERATE
VALERATES
VALERIAN
VALERIANACEOUS
VALERIANS
VALERIC
VALES
VALET
VALETA
VALETAS
VALETE
VALETED
VALETES
VALETING
VALETINGS
VALETS
VALETUDINARIAN
VALETUDINARIANS
VALETUDINARIES
VALETUDINARY
VALGOID
VALGOUS
VALGUS
VALGUSES
VALI
VALIANCE
VALIANCES
VALIANCIES
VALIANCY

VALIANT
VALIANTLY
VALIANTNESS
VALIANTNESSES
VALIANTS
VALID
VALIDATE
VALIDATED
VALIDATES
VALIDATING
VALIDATION
VALIDATIONS
VALIDATORY
VALIDER
VALIDEST
VALIDITIES
VALIDITY
VALIDLY
VALIDNESS
VALIDNESSES
VALINE
VALINES
VALIS
VALISE
VALISES
VALKYR
VALKYRIE
VALKYRIES
VALKYRS
VALLAR
VALLARY
VALLATE
VALLATION
VALLATIONS
VALLECULA
VALLECULAE
VALLECULAR
VALLECULATE
VALLEY
VALLEYS
VALLONIA
VALLONIAS
VALLUM
VALLUMS
VALONEA
VALONEAS
VALONIA
VALONIAS
VALOR
VALORISATION
VALORISATIONS
VALORISE
VALORISED
VALORISES
VALORISING
VALORIZATION
VALORIZATIONS

VALORIZE
VALORIZED
VALORIZES
VALORIZING
VALOROUS
VALOROUSLY
VALORS
VALOUR
VALOURS
VALPOLICELLA
VALPOLICELLAS
VALSE
VALSED
VALSES
VALSING
VALUABLE
VALUABLENESS
VALUABLENESSES
VALUABLES
VALUABLY
VALUATE
VALUATED
VALUATES
VALUATING
VALUATION
VALUATIONAL
VALUATIONALLY
VALUATIONS
VALUATOR
VALUATORS
VALUE
VALUED
VALUELESS
VALUELESSNESS
VALUELESSNESSES
VALUER
VALUERS
VALUES
VALUING
VALUTA
VALUTAS
VALVAL
VALVAR
VALVASSOR
VALVASSORS
VALVATE
VALVE
VALVED
VALVELESS
VALVELET
VALVELETS
VALVELIKE
VALVES
VALVING
VALVULA
VALVULAE
VALVULAR

VALVULE
VALVULES
VALVULITIS
VALVULITISES
VAMBRACE
VAMBRACED
VAMBRACES
VAMOOSE
VAMOOSED
VAMOOSES
VAMOOSING
VAMOSE
VAMOSED
VAMOSES
VAMOSING
VAMP
VAMPED
VAMPER
VAMPERS
VAMPING
VAMPINGS
VAMPIRE
VAMPIRED
VAMPIRES
VAMPIRIC
VAMPIRING
VAMPIRISE
VAMPIRISED
VAMPIRISES
VAMPIRISH
VAMPIRISING
VAMPIRISM
VAMPIRISMS
VAMPIRIZE
VAMPIRIZED
VAMPIRIZES
VAMPIRIZING
VAMPISH
VAMPLATE
VAMPLATES
VAMPS
VAN
VANADATE
VANADATES
VANADIC
VANADINITE
VANADINITES
VANADIUM
VANADIUMS
VANADOUS
VANASPATI
VANASPATIS
VANCOMYCIN
VANDA
VANDAL
VANDALIC
VANDALISE

VANDALISED
VANDALISES
VANDALISH
VANDALISING
VANDALISM
VANDALISMS
VANDALISTIC
VANDALIZATION
VANDALIZATIONS
VANDALIZE
VANDALIZED
VANDALIZES
VANDALIZING
VANDALS
VANDAS
VANDYKE
VANDYKED
VANDYKES
VANDYKING
VANE
VANED
VANELESS
VANES
VANESSA
VANESSAS
VANESSID
VANESSIDS
VANG
VANGS
VANGUARD
VANGUARDISM
VANGUARDISMS
VANGUARDIST
VANGUARDISTS
VANGUARDS
VANILLA
VANILLAS
VANILLIC
VANILLIN
VANILLINS
VANISH
VANISHED
VANISHER
VANISHERS
VANISHES
VANISHING
VANISHINGLY
VANISHINGS
VANISHMENT
VANISHMENTS
VANITAS
VANITASES
VANITIED
VANITIES
VANITORIES
VANITORY
VANITY

VANMAN
VANMEN
VANNED
VANNER
VANNERS
VANNING
VANNINGS
VANPOOL
VANPOOLING
VANPOOLINGS
VANPOOLS
VANQUISH
VANQUISHABLE
VANQUISHED
VANQUISHER
VANQUISHERS
VANQUISHES
VANQUISHING
VANQUISHMENT
VANQUISHMENTS
VANS
VANT
VANTAGE
VANTAGED
VANTAGELESS
VANTAGES
VANTAGING
VANTBRACE
VANTBRACES
VANTS
VANWARD
VAPID
VAPIDER
VAPIDEST
VAPIDITIES
VAPIDITY
VAPIDLY
VAPIDNESS
VAPIDNESSES
VAPOR
VAPORABILITY
VAPORABLE
VAPORED
VAPORER
VAPORERS
VAPORESCENCE
VAPORESCENT
VAPORETTI
VAPORETTO
VAPORETTOS
VAPORIFIC
VAPORIFORM
VAPORIMETER
VAPORIMETERS
VAPORING
VAPORINGS
VAPORISABLE

VAPORISATION
VAPORISATIONS
VAPORISE
VAPORISED
VAPORISER
VAPORISERS
VAPORISES
VAPORISH
VAPORISHNESS
VAPORISHNESSES
VAPORISING
VAPORIZABLE
VAPORIZATION
VAPORIZATIONS
VAPORIZE
VAPORIZED
VAPORIZER
VAPORIZERS
VAPORIZES
VAPORIZING
VAPORLESS
VAPOROSITIES
VAPOROSITY
VAPOROUS
VAPOROUSLY
VAPOROUSNESS
VAPOROUSNESSES
VAPORS
VAPORWARE
VAPORWARES
VAPORY
VAPOUR
VAPOURABILITY
VAPOURABLE
VAPOURED
VAPOURER
VAPOURERS
VAPOURING
VAPOURINGLY
VAPOURINGS
VAPOURISH
VAPOURISHNESS
VAPOURISHNESSES
VAPOURLESS
VAPOURS
VAPOURWARE
VAPOURWARES
VAPOURY
VAPULATE
VAPULATED
VAPULATES
VAPULATING
VAPULATION
VAPULATIONS
VAQUERO
VAQUEROS
VAR

VARA
VARACTOR
VARACTORS
VARAN
VARANS
VARAS
VARDIES
VARDY
VARE
VAREC
VARECH
VARECHS
VARECS
VARES
VAREUSE
VAREUSES
VARGUENO
VARGUENOS
VARIA
VARIABILITIES
VARIABILITY
VARIABLE
VARIABLENESS
VARIABLENESSES
VARIABLES
VARIABLY
VARIANCE
VARIANCES
VARIANT
VARIANTS
VARIATE
VARIATED
VARIATES
VARIATING
VARIATION
VARIATIONAL
VARIATIONALLY
VARIATIONIST
VARIATIONISTS
VARIATIONS
VARIATIVE
VARICELLA
VARICELLAR
VARICELLAS
VARICELLATE
VARICELLOID
VARICELLOUS
VARICES
VARICOCELE
VARICOCELES
VARICOID
VARICOLORED
VARICOLOURED
VARICOSE
VARICOSED
VARICOSIS
VARICOSITIES

VARICOSITY
VARICOTOMIES
VARICOTOMY
VARIED
VARIEDLY
VARIEDNESS
VARIEGATE
VARIEGATED
VARIEGATES
VARIEGATING
VARIEGATION
VARIEGATIONS
VARIEGATOR
VARIEGATORS
VARIER
VARIERS
VARIES
VARIETAL
VARIETALLY
VARIETALS
VARIETIES
VARIETY
VARIFOCAL
VARIFOCALS
VARIFORM
VARIFORMLY
VARIOLA
VARIOLAR
VARIOLAS
VARIOLATE
VARIOLATED
VARIOLATES
VARIOLATING
VARIOLATION
VARIOLATIONS
VARIOLATOR
VARIOLATORS
VARIOLE
VARIOLES
VARIOLISATION
VARIOLITE
VARIOLITES
VARIOLITIC
VARIOLIZATION
VARIOLOID
VARIOLOIDS
VARIOLOUS
VARIOMETER
VARIOMETERS
VARIORUM
VARIORUMS
VARIOUS
VARIOUSLY
VARIOUSNESS
VARIOUSNESSES
VARISCITE
VARISCITES

VARISIZED
VARISTOR
VARISTORS
VARITYPE
VARITYPED
VARITYPES
VARITYPING
VARITYPIST
VARITYPISTS
VARIX
VARLET
VARLETESS
VARLETESSES
VARLETRIES
VARLETRY
VARLETS
VARLETTO
VARLETTOS
VARMENT
VARMENTS
VARMINT
VARMINTS
VARNA
VARNAS
VARNISH
VARNISHED
VARNISHER
VARNISHERS
VARNISHES
VARNISHING
VARNISHINGS
VARNISHY
VAROOM
VAROOMED
VAROOMING
VAROOMS
VARROA
VARROAS
VARS
VARSAL
VARSITIES
VARSITY
VARSOVIENNE
VARSOVIENNES
VARTABED
VARTABEDS
VARUS
VARUSES
VARVE
VARVED
VARVEL
VARVELLED
VARVELS
VARVES
VARY
VARYING
VARYINGLY

VARYINGS
VAS
VASA
VASAL
VASCULA
VASCULAR
VASCULARISATION
VASCULARISE
VASCULARISED
VASCULARISES
VASCULARISING
VASCULARITIES
VASCULARITY
VASCULARIZATION
VASCULARIZE
VASCULARIZED
VASCULARIZES
VASCULARIZING
VASCULARLY
VASCULATURE
VASCULATURES
VASCULIFORM
VASCULITIDES
VASCULITIS
VASCULUM
VASCULUMS
VASE
VASECTOMIES
VASECTOMIZE
VASECTOMIZED
VASECTOMIZES
VASECTOMIZING
VASECTOMY
VASELIKE
VASES
VASIFORM
VASOACTIVE
VASOACTIVITIES
VASOACTIVITY
VASOCONSTRICTOR
VASODILATATION
VASODILATATIONS
VASODILATATORY
VASODILATION
VASODILATIONS
VASODILATOR
VASODILATORS
VASODILATORY
VASOINHIBITOR
VASOINHIBITORS
VASOINHIBITORY
VASOMOTOR
VASOPRESSIN
VASOPRESSINS
VASOPRESSOR
VASOPRESSORS
VASOSPASM

VASOSPASMS
VASOSPASTIC
VASOTOCIN
VASOTOCINS
VASOTOMIES
VASOTOMY
VASOVAGAL
VASSAIL
VASSAILS
VASSAL
VASSALAGE
VASSALAGES
VASSALESS
VASSALESSES
VASSALISE
VASSALISED
VASSALISES
VASSALISING
VASSALIZE
VASSALIZED
VASSALIZES
VASSALIZING
VASSALLED
VASSALLING
VASSALRIES
VASSALRY
VASSALS
VAST
VASTER
VASTEST
VASTIDITIES
VASTIDITY
VASTIER
VASTIEST
VASTITIES
VASTITUDE
VASTITUDES
VASTITY
VASTLY
VASTNESS
VASTNESSES
VASTS
VASTY
VAT
VATABLE
VATFUL
VATFULS
VATIC
VATICAL
VATICIDE
VATICIDES
VATICINAL
VATICINATE
VATICINATED
VATICINATES
VATICINATING
VATICINATION

VATICINATIONS	VAUNTINGLY	VECTORIZATION	VEGETARIANS
VATICINATOR	VAUNTINGS	VECTORIZATIONS	VEGETATE
VATICINATORS	VAUNTS	VECTORIZE	VEGETATED
VATICINATORY	VAUNTY	VECTORIZED	VEGETATES
VATMAN	VAURIEN	VECTORIZES	VEGETATING
VATMEN	VAURIENS	VECTORIZING	VEGETATINGS
VATS	VAUS	VECTORS	VEGETATION
VATTED	VAUT	VECTORSCOPE	VEGETATIONAL
VATTER	VAUTE	VECTORSCOPES	VEGETATIONS
VATTERS	VAUTED	VEDALIA	VEGETATIOUS
VATTING	VAUTES	VEDALIAS	VEGETATIVE
VATU	VAUTING	VEDETTE	VEGETATIVELY
VATUS	VAUTS	VEDETTES	VEGETATIVENESS
VAU	VAV	VEDUTA	VEGETE
VAUCH	VAVASOR	VEDUTE	VEGETIST
VAUDEVILLE	VAVASORIES	VEDUTISTA	VEGETISTS
VAUDEVILLEAN	VAVASORS	VEDUTISTI	VEGETIVE
VAUDEVILLEANS	VAVASORY	VEE	VEGETIVES
VAUDEVILLES	VAVASOUR	VEEJAY	VEGGED
VAUDEVILLIAN	VAVASOURS	VEEJAYS	VEGGES
VAUDEVILLIANS	VAVASSOR	VEENA	VEGGIE
VAUDEVILLIST	VAVASSORS	VEENAS	VEGGIEBURGER
VAUDEVILLISTS	VAVS	VEEP	VEGGIEBURGERS
VAUDOO	VAW	VEEPEE	VEGGIES
VAUDOOS	VAWARD	VEEPEES	VEGGING
VAUDOUX	VAWARDS	VEEPS	VEGIE
VAULT	VAWNTIE	VEER	VEGIES
VAULTAGE	VAWS	VEERED	VEGO
VAULTAGES	VAWTE	VEERIES	VEGOS
VAULTED	VAWTED	VEERING	VEHEMENCE
VAULTER	VAWTES	VEERINGLY	VEHEMENCES
VAULTERS	VAWTING	VEERINGS	VEHEMENCIES
VAULTIER	VEAL	VEERS	VEHEMENCY
VAULTIEST	VEALE	VEERY	VEHEMENT
VAULTING	VEALED	VEES	VEHEMENTLY
VAULTINGLY	VEALER	VEG	VEHICLE
VAULTINGS	VEALERS	VEGA	VEHICLES
VAULTLIKE	VEALES	VEGAN	VEHICULAR
VAULTS	VEALIER	VEGANIC	VEHM
VAULTY	VEALIEST	VEGANISM	VEHME
VAUNCE	VEALING	VEGANISMS	VEHMIC
VAUNCED	VEALS	VEGANS	VEHMIQUE
VAUNCES	VEALY	VEGAS	VEIL
VAUNCING	VECTOGRAPH	VEGEBURGER	VEILED
VAUNT	VECTOGRAPHS	VEGEBURGERS	VEILEDLY
VAUNTAGE	VECTOR	VEGELATE	VEILER
VAUNTAGES	VECTORED	VEGELATES	VEILERS
VAUNTED	VECTORIAL	VEGES	VEILIER
VAUNTER	VECTORIALLY	VEGETABLE	VEILIEST
VAUNTERIES	VECTORING	VEGETABLES	VEILING
VAUNTERS	VECTORINGS	VEGETABLY	VEILINGS
VAUNTERY	VECTORISATION	VEGETAL	VEILLESS
VAUNTFUL	VECTORISATIONS	VEGETALS	VEILLEUSE
VAUNTIE	VECTORISE	VEGETANT	VEILLEUSES
VAUNTIER	VECTORISED	VEGETARIAN	VEILLIKE
VAUNTIEST	VECTORISES	VEGETARIANISM	VEILS
VAUNTING	VECTORISING	VEGETARIANISMS	VEILY

VEIN
VEINAL
VEINED
VEINER
VEINERS
VEINIER
VEINIEST
VEINING
VEININGS
VEINLESS
VEINLET
VEINLETS
VEINLIKE
VEINOUS
VEINS
VEINSTONE
VEINSTONES
VEINSTUFF
VEINSTUFFS
VEINULE
VEINULES
VEINULET
VEINULETS
VEINY
VELA
VELAMEN
VELAMINA
VELAR
VELARIA
VELARIC
VELARISATION
VELARISATIONS
VELARISE
VELARISED
VELARISES
VELARISING
VELARIUM
VELARIZATION
VELARIZATIONS
VELARIZE
VELARIZED
VELARIZES
VELARIZING
VELARS
VELATE
VELATED
VELATURA
VELATURAS
VELD
VELDS
VELDSCHOEN
VELDSCHOENS
VELDSKOEN
VELDSKOENS
VELDT
VELDTS
VELE

VELES
VELETA
VELETAS
VELIGER
VELIGERS
VELITATION
VELITATIONS
VELITES
VELL
VELLEITIES
VELLEITY
VELLENAGE
VELLENAGES
VELLET
VELLETS
VELLICATE
VELLICATED
VELLICATES
VELLICATING
VELLICATION
VELLICATIONS
VELLICATIVE
VELLON
VELLONS
VELLS
VELLUM
VELLUMS
VELOCE
VELOCIMETER
VELOCIMETERS
VELOCIMETRIES
VELOCIMETRY
VELOCIPEDE
VELOCIPEDEAN
VELOCIPEDEANS
VELOCIPEDED
VELOCIPEDER
VELOCIPEDERS
VELOCIPEDES
VELOCIPEDIANS
VELOCIPEDING
VELOCIPEDIST
VELOCIPEDISTS
VELOCIRAPTOR
VELOCIRAPTORS
VELOCITIES
VELOCITY
VELODROME
VELODROMES
VELOUR
VELOURS
VELOUTE
VELOUTES
VELOUTINE
VELOUTINES
VELSKOEN
VELSKOENS

VELUM
VELURE
VELURED
VELURES
VELURING
VELUTINOUS
VELVERET
VELVERETS
VELVET
VELVETED
VELVETEEN
VELVETEENED
VELVETEENS
VELVETIER
VELVETIEST
VELVETINESS
VELVETINESSES
VELVETING
VELVETINGS
VELVETLIKE
VELVETS
VELVETY
VENA
VENAE
VENAL
VENALITIES
VENALITY
VENALLY
VENATIC
VENATICAL
VENATICALLY
VENATION
VENATIONAL
VENATIONS
VENATOR
VENATORIAL
VENATORS
VEND
VENDABLE
VENDACE
VENDACES
VENDAGE
VENDAGES
VENDANGE
VENDANGES
VENDED
VENDEE
VENDEES
VENDER
VENDERS
VENDETTA
VENDETTAS
VENDETTIST
VENDETTISTS
VENDEUSE
VENDEUSES
VENDIBILITIES

VENDIBILITY
VENDIBLE
VENDIBLENESS
VENDIBLENESSES
VENDIBLES
VENDIBLY
VENDING
VENDIS
VENDISES
VENDISS
VENDISSES
VENDITATION
VENDITATIONS
VENDITION
VENDITIONS
VENDOR
VENDORS
VENDS
VENDUE
VENDUES
VENEER
VENEERED
VENEERER
VENEERERS
VENEERING
VENEERINGS
VENEERS
VENEFIC
VENEFICAL
VENEFICALLY
VENEFICIOUS
VENEFICIOUSLY
VENEFICOUS
VENEFICOUSLY
VENENATE
VENENATED
VENENATES
VENENATING
VENENOSE
VENEPUNCTURE
VENEPUNCTURES
VENERABILITIES
VENERABILITY
VENERABLE
VENERABLENESS
VENERABLENESSES
VENERABLY
VENERATE
VENERATED
VENERATES
VENERATING
VENERATION
VENERATIONAL
VENERATIONS
VENERATIVENESS
VENERATOR
VENERATORS

VENEREAL
VENEREAN
VENEREANS
VENEREOLOGICAL
VENEREOLOGIES
VENEREOLOGIST
VENEREOLOGISTS
VENEREOLOGY
VENEREOUS
VENERER
VENERERS
VENERIES
VENERY
VENESECTION
VENESECTIONS
VENETIAN
VENETIANS
VENEWE
VENEWES
VENEY
VENEYS
VENGE
VENGEABLE
VENGEABLY
VENGEANCE
VENGEANCES
VENGED
VENGEFUL
VENGEFULLY
VENGEFULNESS
VENGEFULNESSES
VENGEMENT
VENGEMENTS
VENGER
VENGERS
VENGES
VENGING
VENIAL
VENIALITIES
VENIALITY
VENIALLY
VENIALNESS
VENIALNESSES
VENIDIUM
VENIDIUMS
VENIN
VENINE
VENINES
VENINS
VENIPUNCTURE
VENIPUNCTURES
VENIRE
VENIREMAN
VENIREMEN
VENIRES
VENISECTION
VENISECTIONS

VENISON
VENISONS
VENITE
VENITES
VENNEL
VENNELS
VENOGRAM
VENOGRAMS
VENOGRAPHIC
VENOGRAPHICAL
VENOGRAPHIES
VENOGRAPHY
VENOM
VENOMED
VENOMER
VENOMERS
VENOMING
VENOMLESS
VENOMOUS
VENOMOUSLY
VENOMOUSNESS
VENOMOUSNESSES
VENOMS
VENOSCLEROSIS
VENOSCLEROTIC
VENOSE
VENOSITIES
VENOSITY
VENOUS
VENOUSLY
VENOUSNESS
VENT
VENTAGE
VENTAGES
VENTAIL
VENTAILE
VENTAILES
VENTAILS
VENTANA
VENTANAS
VENTAYLE
VENTAYLES
VENTED
VENTER
VENTERS
VENTIDUCT
VENTIDUCTS
VENTIFACT
VENTIFACTS
VENTIGE
VENTIGES
VENTIL
VENTILABLE
VENTILATE
VENTILATED
VENTILATES
VENTILATING

VENTILATION
VENTILATIONS
VENTILATIVE
VENTILATOR
VENTILATORS
VENTILATORY
VENTILS
VENTING
VENTINGS
VENTLESS
VENTOSE
VENTOSITIES
VENTOSITY
VENTOUSE
VENTOUSES
VENTRAL
VENTRALLY
VENTRALS
VENTRE
VENTRED
VENTRES
VENTRICLE
VENTRICLES
VENTRICOSE
VENTRICOSITY
VENTRICOUS
VENTRICULAR
VENTRICULE
VENTRICULES
VENTRICULI
VENTRICULUS
VENTRILOQUAL
VENTRILOQUIAL
VENTRILOQUIALLY
VENTRILOQUIES
VENTRILOQUISE
VENTRILOQUISED
VENTRILOQUISES
VENTRILOQUISING
VENTRILOQUISM
VENTRILOQUISMS
VENTRILOQUIST
VENTRILOQUISTIC
VENTRILOQUISTS
VENTRILOQUIZE
VENTRILOQUIZED
VENTRILOQUIZES
VENTRILOQUIZING
VENTRILOQUOUS
VENTRILOQUY
VENTRING
VENTRINGS
VENTRIPOTENT
VENTROLATERAL
VENTROMEDIAL
VENTROUS
VENTS

VENTURE
VENTURED
VENTURER
VENTURERS
VENTURES
VENTURESOME
VENTURESOMELY
VENTURESOMENESS
VENTURI
VENTURIES
VENTURING
VENTURINGLY
VENTURINGS
VENTURIS
VENTUROUS
VENTUROUSLY
VENTUROUSNESS
VENTUROUSNESSES
VENUE
VENUES
VENULAR
VENULE
VENULES
VENULOSE
VENULOUS
VENUS
VENUSES
VENVILLE
VENVILLES
VERA
VERACIOUS
VERACIOUSLY
VERACIOUSNESS
VERACIOUSNESSES
VERACITIES
VERACITY
VERANDA
VERANDAED
VERANDAH
VERANDAHED
VERANDAHS
VERANDAS
VERAPAMIL
VERAPAMILS
VERATRIA
VERATRIAS
VERATRIDINE
VERATRIDINES
VERATRIN
VERATRINE
VERATRINES
VERATRINS
VERATRUM
VERATRUMS
VERB
VERBAL
VERBALISATION

VERBALISATIONS
VERBALISE
VERBALISED
VERBALISER
VERBALISERS
VERBALISES
VERBALISING
VERBALISM
VERBALISMS
VERBALIST
VERBALISTIC
VERBALISTS
VERBALITIES
VERBALITY
VERBALIZATION
VERBALIZATIONS
VERBALIZE
VERBALIZED
VERBALIZER
VERBALIZERS
VERBALIZES
VERBALIZING
VERBALLED
VERBALLING
VERBALLY
VERBALS
VERBARIAN
VERBARIANS
VERBASCUM
VERBASCUMS
VERBATIM
VERBENA
VERBENACEOUS
VERBENAS
VERBERATE
VERBERATED
VERBERATES
VERBERATING
VERBERATION
VERBERATIONS
VERBIAGE
VERBIAGES
VERBICIDE
VERBICIDES
VERBID
VERBIDS
VERBIFICATION
VERBIFICATIONS
VERBIFIED
VERBIFIES
VERBIFY
VERBIFYING
VERBIGERATE
VERBIGERATED
VERBIGERATES
VERBIGERATING
VERBIGERATION

VERBIGERATIONS
VERBILE
VERBILES
VERBLESS
VERBOSE
VERBOSELY
VERBOSENESS
VERBOSENESSES
VERBOSER
VERBOSEST
VERBOSITIES
VERBOSITY
VERBOTEN
VERBS
VERDANCIES
VERDANCY
VERDANT
VERDANTLY
VERDELHO
VERDELHOS
VERDERER
VERDERERS
VERDEROR
VERDERORS
VERDET
VERDETS
VERDICT
VERDICTS
VERDIGRIS
VERDIGRISED
VERDIGRISES
VERDIGRISING
VERDIN
VERDINS
VERDIT
VERDITE
VERDITER
VERDITERS
VERDITES
VERDITS
VERDOY
VERDURE
VERDURED
VERDURELESS
VERDURES
VERDUROUS
VERECUND
VERGE
VERGEBOARD
VERGEBOARDS
VERGED
VERGENCE
VERGENCES
VERGENCIES
VERGENCY
VERGER
VERGERS

VERGERSHIP
VERGERSHIPS
VERGES
VERGING
VERGLAS
VERGLASES
VERIDIC
VERIDICAL
VERIDICALITIES
VERIDICALITY
VERIDICALLY
VERIDICOUS
VERIER
VERIEST
VERIFIABILITIES
VERIFIABILITY
VERIFIABLE
VERIFIABLENESS
VERIFIABLY
VERIFICATION
VERIFICATIONS
VERIFICATIVE
VERIFICATORY
VERIFIED
VERIFIER
VERIFIERS
VERIFIES
VERIFY
VERIFYING
VERILY
VERISIMILAR
VERISIMILARLY
VERISIMILITIES
VERISIMILITUDE
VERISIMILITUDES
VERISIMILITY
VERISIMILOUS
VERISM
VERISMO
VERISMOS
VERISMS
VERIST
VERISTIC
VERISTS
VERITABLE
VERITABLENESS
VERITABLENESSES
VERITABLY
VERITAS
VERITATES
VERITE
VERITES
VERITIES
VERITY
VERJUICE
VERJUICED
VERJUICES

VERJUICING
VERKRAMP
VERKRAMPTE
VERKRAMPTES
VERLAN
VERLIG
VERLIGTE
VERLIGTES
VERMAL
VERMEIL
VERMEILED
VERMEILING
VERMEILLE
VERMEILLED
VERMEILLES
VERMEILLING
VERMEILS
VERMELL
VERMELLS
VERMES
VERMIAN
VERMICELLI
VERMICELLIS
VERMICIDAL
VERMICIDE
VERMICIDES
VERMICULAR
VERMICULARLY
VERMICULATE
VERMICULATED
VERMICULATES
VERMICULATING
VERMICULATION
VERMICULATIONS
VERMICULE
VERMICULES
VERMICULITE
VERMICULITES
VERMICULOUS
VERMICULTURE
VERMICULTURES
VERMIFORM
VERMIFUGAL
VERMIFUGE
VERMIFUGES
VERMIL
VERMILIES
VERMILION
VERMILIONED
VERMILIONING
VERMILIONS
VERMILLED
VERMILLING
VERMILLION
VERMILLIONS
VERMILS
VERMILY

VERMIN	VERNATIONS	VERSICLES	VERTICALITIES
VERMINATE	VERNICLE	VERSICOLOR	VERTICALITY
VERMINATED	VERNICLES	VERSICOLOUR	VERTICALLY
VERMINATES	VERNIER	VERSICOLOURED	VERTICALNESS
VERMINATING	VERNIERS	VERSICULAR	VERTICALNESSES
VERMINATION	VERNISSAGE	VERSIFICATION	VERTICALS
VERMINATIONS	VERNISSAGES	VERSIFICATIONS	VERTICES
VERMINED	VERNIX	VERSIFICATOR	VERTICIL
VERMINOUS	VERNIXES	VERSIFICATORS	VERTICILLASTER
VERMINOUSLY	VERONAL	VERSIFIED	VERTICILLASTERS
VERMINOUSNESS	VERONALS	VERSIFIER	VERTICILLATE
VERMINS	VERONICA	VERSIFIERS	VERTICILLATED
VERMINY	VERONICAS	VERSIFIES	VERTICILLATELY
VERMIS	VERONIQUE	VERSIFORM	VERTICILLATION
VERMIVOROUS	VERQUERE	VERSIFY	VERTICILLATIONS
VERMOULU	VERQUERES	VERSIFYING	VERTICILLIUM
VERMOUTH	VERQUIRE	VERSIN	VERTICILLIUMS
VERMOUTHS	VERQUIRES	VERSINE	VERTICILS
VERMUTH	VERRA	VERSINES	VERTICITIES
VERMUTHS	VERREL	VERSING	VERTICITY
VERNACLE	VERRELS	VERSINGS	VERTIGINES
VERNACLES	VERREY	VERSINS	VERTIGINOUS
VERNACULAR	VERRUCA	VERSION	VERTIGINOUSLY
VERNACULARISE	VERRUCAE	VERSIONAL	VERTIGINOUSNESS
VERNACULARISED	VERRUCAS	VERSIONER	VERTIGO
VERNACULARISES	VERRUCIFORM	VERSIONERS	VERTIGOES
VERNACULARISING	VERRUCOSE	VERSIONING	VERTIGOS
VERNACULARISM	VERRUCOSITY	VERSIONIST	VERTING
VERNACULARISMS	VERRUCOUS	VERSIONISTS	VERTIPORT
VERNACULARIST	VERRUGA	VERSIONS	VERTIPORTS
VERNACULARISTS	VERRUGAS	VERSLIBRIST	VERTS
VERNACULARITIES	VERRY	VERSLIBRISTE	VERTU
VERNACULARITY	VERS	VERSLIBRISTES	VERTUE
VERNACULARIZE	VERSABILITIES	VERSLIBRISTS	VERTUES
VERNACULARIZED	VERSABILITY	VERSO	VERTUOUS
VERNACULARIZES	VERSAL	VERSOS	VERTUS
VERNACULARIZING	VERSALS	VERST	VERUMONTANUM
VERNACULARLY	VERSANT	VERSTE	VERUMONTANUMS
VERNACULARS	VERSANTS	VERSTES	VERVAIN
VERNAL	VERSATILE	VERSTS	VERVAINS
VERNALISATION	VERSATILELY	VERSUS	VERVE
VERNALISATIONS	VERSATILENESS	VERSUTE	VERVEL
VERNALISE	VERSATILENESSES	VERT	VERVELLED
VERNALISED	VERSATILITIES	VERTEBRA	VERVELS
VERNALISES	VERSATILITY	VERTEBRAE	VERVEN
VERNALISING	VERSE	VERTEBRAL	VERVENS
VERNALITIES	VERSED	VERTEBRALLY	VERVES
VERNALITY	VERSELET	VERTEBRAS	VERVET
VERNALIZATION	VERSELETS	VERTEBRATE	VERVETS
VERNALIZATIONS	VERSEMAN	VERTEBRATED	VERY
VERNALIZE	VERSEMEN	VERTEBRATES	VESICA
VERNALIZED	VERSER	VERTEBRATION	VESICAE
VERNALIZES	VERSERS	VERTEBRATIONS	VESICAL
VERNALIZING	VERSES	VERTED	VESICANT
VERNALLY	VERSET	VERTEX	VESICANTS
VERNANT	VERSETS	VERTEXES	VESICATE
VERNATION	VERSICLE	VERTICAL	VESICATED

VESICATES
VESICATING
VESICATION
VESICATIONS
VESICATORIES
VESICATORY
VESICLE
VESICLES
VESICULA
VESICULAE
VESICULAR
VESICULARITIES
VESICULARITY
VESICULARLY
VESICULATE
VESICULATED
VESICULATES
VESICULATING
VESICULATION
VESICULATIONS
VESICULOSE
VESPA
VESPAS
VESPER
VESPERAL
VESPERALS
VESPERS
VESPERTILIAN
VESPERTILIONID
VESPERTILIONIDS
VESPERTILIONINE
VESPERTINAL
VESPERTINE
VESPIARIES
VESPIARY
VESPID
VESPIDS
VESPINE
VESPOID
VESSAIL
VESSAILS
VESSEL
VESSELED
VESSELS
VEST
VESTA
VESTAL
VESTALLY
VESTALS
VESTAS
VESTED
VESTEE
VESTEES
VESTIARIES
VESTIARY
VESTIBULA
VESTIBULAR

VESTIBULE
VESTIBULED
VESTIBULES
VESTIBULING
VESTIBULITIS
VESTIBULITISES
VESTIBULUM
VESTIGE
VESTIGES
VESTIGIA
VESTIGIAL
VESTIGIALLY
VESTIGIUM
VESTIMENT
VESTIMENTAL
VESTIMENTARY
VESTIMENTS
VESTING
VESTINGS
VESTITURE
VESTITURES
VESTLESS
VESTLIKE
VESTMENT
VESTMENTAL
VESTMENTED
VESTMENTS
VESTRAL
VESTRIES
VESTRY
VESTRYMAN
VESTRYMEN
VESTS
VESTURAL
VESTURE
VESTURED
VESTURER
VESTURERS
VESTURES
VESTURING
VESUVIAN
VESUVIANITE
VESUVIANITES
VESUVIANS
VET
VETCH
VETCHES
VETCHIER
VETCHIEST
VETCHLING
VETCHLINGS
VETCHY
VETER
VETERAN
VETERANS
VETERINARIAN
VETERINARIANS

VETERINARIES
VETERINARY
VETIVER
VETIVERS
VETIVERT
VETIVERTS
VETKOEK
VETKOEKS
VETO
VETOED
VETOER
VETOERS
VETOES
VETOING
VETOLESS
VETS
VETTED
VETTING
VETTURA
VETTURAS
VETTURINI
VETTURINO
VEX
VEXATION
VEXATIONS
VEXATIOUS
VEXATIOUSLY
VEXATIOUSNESS
VEXATIOUSNESSES
VEXATORY
VEXED
VEXEDLY
VEXEDNESS
VEXEDNESSES
VEXER
VEXERS
VEXES
VEXIL
VEXILLA
VEXILLAR
VEXILLARIES
VEXILLARY
VEXILLATE
VEXILLATION
VEXILLATIONS
VEXILLOLOGIC
VEXILLOLOGICAL
VEXILLOLOGIES
VEXILLOLOGIST
VEXILLOLOGISTS
VEXILLOLOGY
VEXILLUM
VEXILS
VEXING
VEXINGLY
VEXINGNESS
VEXINGNESSES

VEXINGS
VEXT
VEZIR
VEZIRS
VIA
VIABILITIES
VIABILITY
VIABLE
VIABLY
VIADUCT
VIADUCTS
VIAE
VIAL
VIALED
VIALFUL
VIALFULS
VIALING
VIALLED
VIALLING
VIALS
VIAMETER
VIAMETERS
VIAND
VIANDS
VIAS
VIATIC
VIATICA
VIATICAL
VIATICALS
VIATICUM
VIATICUMS
VIATOR
VIATORES
VIATORIAL
VIATORS
VIBE
VIBES
VIBEX
VIBEY
VIBICES
VIBIER
VIBIEST
VIBIST
VIBISTS
VIBRACULA
VIBRACULAR
VIBRACULARIA
VIBRACULARIUM
VIBRACULOID
VIBRACULUM
VIBRAHARP
VIBRAHARPIST
VIBRAHARPISTS
VIBRAHARPS
VIBRANCE
VIBRANCES
VIBRANCIES

VIBRANCY	VICARIAL	VICIOSITIES	VICTRIXES
VIBRANT	VICARIANCE	VICIOSITY	VICTROLLA
VIBRANTLY	VICARIANCES	VICIOUS	VICTROLLAS
VIBRANTS	VICARIANT	VICIOUSLY	VICTUAL
VIBRAPHONE	VICARIANTS	VICIOUSNESS	VICTUALAGE
VIBRAPHONES	VICARIATE	VICIOUSNESSES	VICTUALED
VIBRAPHONIST	VICARIATES	VICISSITUDE	VICTUALER
VIBRAPHONISTS	VICARIES	VICISSITUDES	VICTUALERS
VIBRATE	VICARIOUS	VICISSITUDINARY	VICTUALING
VIBRATED	VICARIOUSLY	VICISSITUDINOUS	VICTUALLAGE
VIBRATES	VICARIOUSNESS	VICOMTE	VICTUALLAGES
VIBRATILE	VICARIOUSNESSES	VICOMTES	VICTUALLED
VIBRATILITIES	VICARLY	VICOMTESSE	VICTUALLER
VIBRATILITY	VICARS	VICOMTESSES	VICTUALLERS
VIBRATING	VICARSHIP	VICTIM	VICTUALLESS
VIBRATINGLY	VICARSHIPS	VICTIMHOOD	VICTUALLING
VIBRATION	VICARY	VICTIMHOODS	VICTUALS
VIBRATIONAL	VICE	VICTIMISATION	VICUGNA
VIBRATIONLESS	VICED	VICTIMISATIONS	VICUGNAS
VIBRATIONS	VICEGERAL	VICTIMISE	VICUNA
VIBRATIUNCLE	VICEGERENCIES	VICTIMISED	VICUNAS
VIBRATIUNCLES	VICEGERENCY	VICTIMISER	VID
VIBRATIVE	VICEGERENT	VICTIMISERS	VIDAME
VIBRATO	VICEGERENTS	VICTIMISES	VIDAMES
VIBRATOLESS	VICELESS	VICTIMISING	VIDE
VIBRATOR	VICELIKE	VICTIMIZATION	VIDELICET
VIBRATORS	VICENARY	VICTIMIZATIONS	VIDENDA
VIBRATORY	VICENNIAL	VICTIMIZE	VIDENDUM
VIBRATOS	VICEREGAL	VICTIMIZED	VIDEO
VIBRIO	VICEREGALLY	VICTIMIZER	VIDEOCASSETTE
VIBRIOID	VICEREGENT	VICTIMIZERS	VIDEOCASSETTES
VIBRION	VICEREGENTS	VICTIMIZES	VIDEOCONFERENCE
VIBRIONIC	VICEREINE	VICTIMIZING	VIDEODISC
VIBRIONS	VICEREINES	VICTIMLESS	VIDEODISCS
VIBRIOS	VICEROY	VICTIMOLOGIES	VIDEODISK
VIBRIOSES	VICEROYALTIES	VICTIMOLOGIST	VIDEODISKS
VIBRIOSIS	VICEROYALTY	VICTIMOLOGISTS	VIDEOED
VIBRISSA	VICEROYS	VICTIMOLOGY	VIDEOFIT
VIBRISSAE	VICEROYSHIP	VICTIMS	VIDEOFITS
VIBRISSAL	VICEROYSHIPS	VICTOR	VIDEOGRAM
VIBROFLOTATION	VICES	VICTORESS	VIDEOGRAMS
VIBROFLOTATIONS	VICESIMAL	VICTORESSES	VIDEOGRAPHER
VIBROGRAPH	VICHIES	VICTORIA	VIDEOGRAPHERS
VIBROGRAPHS	VICHY	VICTORIANA	VIDEOGRAPHIES
VIBROMETER	VICHYSSOIS	VICTORIAS	VIDEOGRAPHY
VIBROMETERS	VICHYSSOISE	VICTORIES	VIDEOING
VIBRONIC	VICHYSSOISES	VICTORINE	VIDEOLAND
VIBS	VICIATE	VICTORINES	VIDEOLANDS
VIBURNUM	VICIATED	VICTORIOUS	VIDEOPHILE
VIBURNUMS	VICIATES	VICTORIOUSLY	VIDEOPHILES
VICAR	VICIATING	VICTORIOUSNESS	VIDEOPHONE
VICARAGE	VICINAGE	VICTORS	VIDEOPHONES
VICARAGES	VICINAGES	VICTORY	VIDEOPHONIC
VICARATE	VICINAL	VICTORYLESS	VIDEOS
VICARATES	VICING	VICTRESS	VIDEOTAPE
VICARESS	VICINITIES	VICTRESSES	VIDEOTAPED
VICARESSES	VICINITY	VICTRIX	VIDEOTAPES

VIDEOTAPING	VIGAS	VILELY	VILLANAGE
VIDEOTELEPHONE	VIGESIMAL	VILENESS	VILLANAGES
VIDEOTELEPHONES	VIGIA	VILENESSES	VILLANELLA
VIDEOTEX	VIGIAS	VILER	VILLANELLAS
VIDEOTEXES	VIGIL	VILEST	VILLANELLE
VIDEOTEXT	VIGILANCE	VILIACO	VILLANELLES
VIDEOTEXTS	VIGILANCES	VILIACOES	VILLANIES
VIDETTE	VIGILANT	VILIACOS	VILLANOUS
VIDETTES	VIGILANTE	VILIAGO	VILLANOUSLY
VIDICON	VIGILANTES	VILIAGOES	VILLANS
VIDICONS	VIGILANTISM	VILIAGOS	VILLANY
VIDIMUS	VIGILANTISMS	VILIFICATION	VILLAR
VIDIMUSES	VIGILANTLY	VILIFICATIONS	VILLAS
VIDS	VIGILANTNESS	VILIFIED	VILLATIC
VIDUAGE	VIGILS	VILIFIER	VILLEGGIATURA
VIDUAGES	VIGINTILLION	VILIFIERS	VILLEGGIATURAS
VIDUAL	VIGINTILLIONS	VILIFIES	VILLEIN
VIDUITIES	VIGNERON	VILIFY	VILLEINAGE
VIDUITY	VIGNERONS	VILIFYING	VILLEINAGES
VIDUOUS	VIGNETTE	VILIPEND	VILLEINS
VIE	VIGNETTED	VILIPENDED	VILLENAGE
VIED	VIGNETTER	VILIPENDER	VILLENAGES
VIELLE	VIGNETTERS	VILIPENDERS	VILLI
VIELLES	VIGNETTES	VILIPENDING	VILLIAGO
VIER	VIGNETTING	VILIPENDS	VILLIAGOES
VIERS	VIGNETTIST	VILL	VILLIAGOS
VIES	VIGNETTISTS	VILLA	VILLICATION
VIEW	VIGOR	VILLADOM	VILLICATIONS
VIEWABLE	VIGORISH	VILLADOMS	VILLIFORM
VIEWDATA	VIGORISHES	VILLAE	VILLOSE
VIEWDATAS	VIGORO	VILLAGE	VILLOSITIES
VIEWED	VIGOROS	VILLAGER	VILLOSITY
VIEWER	VIGOROSO	VILLAGERIES	VILLOUS
VIEWERS	VIGOROUS	VILLAGERS	VILLOUSLY
VIEWERSHIP	VIGOROUSLY	VILLAGERY	VILLS
VIEWERSHIPS	VIGOROUSNESS	VILLAGES	VILLUS
VIEWFINDER	VIGOROUSNESSES	VILLAGIO	VIM
VIEWFINDERS	VIGORS	VILLAGIOES	VIMANA
VIEWIER	VIGOUR	VILLAGIOS	VIMANAS
VIEWIEST	VIGOURS	VILLAGISATION	VIMEN
VIEWINESS	VIGS	VILLAGISATIONS	VIMINA
VIEWINESSES	VIHARA	VILLAGIZATION	VIMINAL
VIEWING	VIHARAS	VILLAGIZATIONS	VIMINEOUS
VIEWINGS	VIHUELA	VILLAGREE	VIMS
VIEWLESS	VIHUELAS	VILLAGREES	VIN
VIEWLESSLY	VIKING	VILLAIN	VINA
VIEWLY	VIKINGISM	VILLAINAGE	VINACEOUS
VIEWPHONE	VIKINGISMS	VILLAINAGES	VINAIGRETTE
VIEWPHONES	VIKINGS	VILLAINESS	VINAIGRETTES
VIEWPOINT	VILAYET	VILLAINESSES	VINAL
VIEWPOINTS	VILAYETS	VILLAINIES	VINALS
VIEWS	VILD	VILLAINOUS	VINAS
VIEWY	VILDE	VILLAINOUSLY	VINASSE
VIFDA	VILDLY	VILLAINOUSNESS	VINASSES
VIFDAS	VILDNESS	VILLAINS	VINBLASTINE
VIG	VILDNESSES	VILLAINY	VINBLASTINES
VIGA	VILE	VILLAN	VINCA

VINCAS
VINCIBILITIES
VINCIBILITY
VINCIBLE
VINCIBLENESS
VINCIBLY
VINCRISTINE
VINCRISTINES
VINCULA
VINCULUM
VINCULUMS
VINDALOO
VINDALOOS
VINDEMIAL
VINDEMIATE
VINDEMIATED
VINDEMIATES
VINDEMIATING
VINDICABILITIES
VINDICABILITY
VINDICABLE
VINDICATE
VINDICATED
VINDICATES
VINDICATING
VINDICATION
VINDICATIONS
VINDICATIVE
VINDICATIVENESS
VINDICATOR
VINDICATORILY
VINDICATORS
VINDICATORY
VINDICATRESS
VINDICATRESSES
VINDICTIVE
VINDICTIVELY
VINDICTIVENESS
VINE
VINEAL
VINED
VINEDRESSER
VINEDRESSERS
VINEGAR
VINEGARED
VINEGARETTE
VINEGARING
VINEGARISH
VINEGARRED
VINEGARRETTE
VINEGARRETTES
VINEGARRING
VINEGARROON
VINEGARROONS
VINEGARS
VINEGARY
VINELESS

VINELIKE
VINER
VINERIES
VINERS
VINERY
VINES
VINEW
VINEWED
VINEWING
VINEWS
VINEYARD
VINEYARDIST
VINEYARDISTS
VINEYARDS
VINIC
VINICULTURAL
VINICULTURE
VINICULTURES
VINICULTURIST
VINICULTURISTS
VINIER
VINIEST
VINIFERA
VINIFERAS
VINIFEROUS
VINIFICATION
VINIFICATIONS
VINIFICATOR
VINIFICATORS
VINIFIED
VINIFIES
VINIFY
VINIFYING
VINING
VINO
VINOLENT
VINOLOGIES
VINOLOGIST
VINOLOGISTS
VINOLOGY
VINOS
VINOSITIES
VINOSITY
VINOUS
VINOUSLY
VINS
VINT
VINTAGE
VINTAGED
VINTAGER
VINTAGERS
VINTAGES
VINTAGING
VINTAGINGS
VINTED
VINTING
VINTNER

VINTNERS
VINTRIES
VINTRY
VINTS
VINY
VINYL
VINYLCYANIDE
VINYLIC
VINYLIDENE
VINYLIDENES
VINYLS
VIOL
VIOLA
VIOLABILITIES
VIOLABILITY
VIOLABLE
VIOLABLENESS
VIOLABLENESSES
VIOLABLY
VIOLACEOUS
VIOLAS
VIOLATE
VIOLATED
VIOLATER
VIOLATERS
VIOLATES
VIOLATING
VIOLATION
VIOLATIONS
VIOLATIVE
VIOLATOR
VIOLATORS
VIOLD
VIOLENCE
VIOLENCES
VIOLENT
VIOLENTED
VIOLENTING
VIOLENTLY
VIOLENTS
VIOLER
VIOLERS
VIOLET
VIOLETS
VIOLIN
VIOLINIST
VIOLINISTIC
VIOLINISTICALLY
VIOLINISTS
VIOLINS
VIOLIST
VIOLISTS
VIOLONCELLI
VIOLONCELLIST
VIOLONCELLISTS
VIOLONCELLO
VIOLONCELLOS

VIOLONE
VIOLONES
VIOLS
VIOMYCIN
VIOMYCINS
VIPER
VIPERIFORM
VIPERINE
VIPERISH
VIPERISHLY
VIPEROUS
VIPEROUSLY
VIPERS
VIRAEMIA
VIRAEMIAS
VIRAEMIC
VIRAGINIAN
VIRAGINOUS
VIRAGO
VIRAGOES
VIRAGOISH
VIRAGOS
VIRAL
VIRALLY
VIRANDA
VIRANDAS
VIRANDO
VIRANDOS
VIRE
VIRED
VIRELAI
VIRELAIS
VIRELAY
VIRELAYS
VIREMENT
VIREMENTS
VIREMIA
VIREMIAS
VIREMIC
VIRENT
VIREO
VIREOS
VIRES
VIRESCENCE
VIRESCENCES
VIRESCENT
VIRETOT
VIRETOTS
VIRGA
VIRGAS
VIRGATE
VIRGATES
VIRGE
VIRGER
VIRGERS
VIRGES
VIRGIN

VIRGINAL
VIRGINALIST
VIRGINALISTS
VIRGINALLED
VIRGINALLING
VIRGINALLY
VIRGINALS
VIRGINED
VIRGINHOOD
VIRGINHOODS
VIRGINING
VIRGINITIES
VIRGINITY
VIRGINIUM
VIRGINIUMS
VIRGINLY
VIRGINS
VIRGULATE
VIRGULE
VIRGULES
VIRICIDAL
VIRICIDE
VIRICIDES
VIRID
VIRIDESCENCE
VIRIDESCENCES
VIRIDESCENT
VIRIDIAN
VIRIDIANS
VIRIDITE
VIRIDITES
VIRIDITIES
VIRIDITY
VIRILE
VIRILELY
VIRILESCENCE
VIRILESCENCES
VIRILESCENT
VIRILISATION
VIRILISATIONS
VIRILISED
VIRILISING
VIRILISM
VIRILISMS
VIRILITIES
VIRILITY
VIRILIZATION
VIRILIZATIONS
VIRILIZED
VIRILIZING
VIRING
VIRINO
VIRINOS
VIRION
VIRIONS
VIRL
VIRLS

VIROGENE
VIROGENES
VIROID
VIROIDS
VIROLOGIC
VIROLOGICAL
VIROLOGICALLY
VIROLOGIES
VIROLOGIST
VIROLOGISTS
VIROLOGY
VIROSE
VIROSES
VIROSIS
VIROUS
VIRTU
VIRTUAL
VIRTUALISM
VIRTUALISMS
VIRTUALIST
VIRTUALISTS
VIRTUALITIES
VIRTUALITY
VIRTUALLY
VIRTUE
VIRTUELESS
VIRTUES
VIRTUOSA
VIRTUOSAS
VIRTUOSE
VIRTUOSI
VIRTUOSIC
VIRTUOSITIES
VIRTUOSITY
VIRTUOSO
VIRTUOSOS
VIRTUOSOSHIP
VIRTUOSOSHIPS
VIRTUOUS
VIRTUOUSLY
VIRTUOUSNESS
VIRTUOUSNESSES
VIRTUS
VIRUCIDAL
VIRUCIDE
VIRUCIDES
VIRULENCE
VIRULENCES
VIRULENCIES
VIRULENCY
VIRULENT
VIRULENTLY
VIRULIFEROUS
VIRUS
VIRUSES
VIS
VISA

VISAED
VISAGE
VISAGED
VISAGES
VISAGIST
VISAGISTE
VISAGISTES
VISAGISTS
VISAING
VISARD
VISARDS
VISAS
VISCACHA
VISCACHAS
VISCACHERA
VISCACHERAS
VISCARIA
VISCARIAS
VISCERA
VISCERAL
VISCERALLY
VISCERATE
VISCERATED
VISCERATES
VISCERATING
VISCEROMOTOR
VISCEROPTOSES
VISCEROPTOSIS
VISCEROTONIA
VISCEROTONIAS
VISCEROTONIC
VISCID
VISCIDITIES
VISCIDITY
VISCIDLY
VISCIDNESS
VISCIN
VISCINS
VISCOELASTIC
VISCOELASTICITY
VISCOID
VISCOIDAL
VISCOMETER
VISCOMETERS
VISCOMETRIC
VISCOMETRICAL
VISCOMETRIES
VISCOMETRY
VISCOSE
VISCOSES
VISCOSIMETER
VISCOSIMETERS
VISCOSIMETRIC
VISCOSIMETRICAL
VISCOSIMETRIES
VISCOSIMETRY
VISCOSITIES

VISCOSITY
VISCOUNT
VISCOUNTCIES
VISCOUNTCY
VISCOUNTESS
VISCOUNTESSES
VISCOUNTIES
VISCOUNTS
VISCOUNTSHIP
VISCOUNTSHIPS
VISCOUNTY
VISCOUS
VISCOUSLY
VISCOUSNESS
VISCOUSNESSES
VISCUM
VISCUMS
VISCUS
VISE
VISED
VISEED
VISEING
VISELIKE
VISES
VISIBILITIES
VISIBILITY
VISIBLE
VISIBLENESS
VISIBLENESSES
VISIBLES
VISIBLY
VISIE
VISIED
VISIEING
VISIER
VISIERS
VISIES
VISILE
VISILES
VISING
VISIOGENIC
VISION
VISIONAL
VISIONALLY
VISIONARIES
VISIONARINESS
VISIONARINESSES
VISIONARY
VISIONED
VISIONER
VISIONERS
VISIONING
VISIONINGS
VISIONIST
VISIONISTS
VISIONLESS
VISIONS

VISIOPHONE
VISIOPHONES
VISIT
VISITABLE
VISITANT
VISITANTS
VISITATION
VISITATIONAL
VISITATIONS
VISITATIVE
VISITATOR
VISITATORIAL
VISITATORS
VISITE
VISITED
VISITEE
VISITEES
VISITER
VISITERS
VISITES
VISITING
VISITINGS
VISITOR
VISITORIAL
VISITORS
VISITRESS
VISITRESSES
VISITS
VISIVE
VISNE
VISNES
VISNOMIE
VISNOMIES
VISNOMY
VISON
VISONS
VISOR
VISORED
VISORING
VISORLESS
VISORS
VISTA
VISTAED
VISTAING
VISTAL
VISTALESS
VISTAS
VISTO
VISTOS
VISUAL
VISUALISATION
VISUALISATIONS
VISUALISE
VISUALISED
VISUALISER
VISUALISERS
VISUALISES

VISUALISING
VISUALIST
VISUALISTS
VISUALITIES
VISUALITY
VISUALIZATION
VISUALIZATIONS
VISUALIZE
VISUALIZED
VISUALIZER
VISUALIZERS
VISUALIZES
VISUALIZING
VISUALLY
VISUALS
VITA
VITACEOUS
VITAE
VITAL
VITALISATION
VITALISATIONS
VITALISE
VITALISED
VITALISER
VITALISERS
VITALISES
VITALISING
VITALISM
VITALISMS
VITALIST
VITALISTIC
VITALISTICALLY
VITALISTS
VITALITIES
VITALITY
VITALIZATION
VITALIZATIONS
VITALIZE
VITALIZED
VITALIZER
VITALIZERS
VITALIZES
VITALIZING
VITALLY
VITALNESS
VITALS
VITAMER
VITAMERS
VITAMIN
VITAMINE
VITAMINES
VITAMINIC
VITAMINISE
VITAMINISED
VITAMINISES
VITAMINISING
VITAMINIZE

VITAMINIZED
VITAMINIZES
VITAMINIZING
VITAMINS
VITAS
VITASCOPE
VITASCOPES
VITATIVE
VITATIVENESS
VITATIVENESSES
VITE
VITELLARY
VITELLI
VITELLICLE
VITELLICLES
VITELLIGENOUS
VITELLIN
VITELLINE
VITELLINES
VITELLINS
VITELLOGENESES
VITELLOGENESIS
VITELLOGENIC
VITELLUS
VITELLUSES
VITESSE
VITESSES
VITEX
VITEXES
VITIABLE
VITIATE
VITIATED
VITIATES
VITIATING
VITIATION
VITIATIONS
VITIATOR
VITIATORS
VITICETA
VITICETUM
VITICETUMS
VITICIDE
VITICIDES
VITICOLOUS
VITICULTURAL
VITICULTURALLY
VITICULTURE
VITICULTURER
VITICULTURERS
VITICULTURES
VITICULTURIST
VITICULTURISTS
VITIFEROUS
VITILIGO
VITILIGOS
VITILITIGATE
VITILITIGATED

VITILITIGATES
VITILITIGATING
VITILITIGATION
VITILITIGATIONS
VITIOSITIES
VITIOSITY
VITRAGE
VITRAGES
VITRAIL
VITRAILLED
VITRAILLISTS
VITRAIN
VITRAINS
VITRAUX
VITRECTOMIES
VITRECTOMY
VITREOSITIES
VITREOSITY
VITREOUS
VITREOUSES
VITREOUSLY
VITREOUSNESS
VITREOUSNESSES
VITRESCENCE
VITRESCENCES
VITRESCENT
VITRESCIBILITY
VITRESCIBLE
VITREUM
VITREUMS
VITRIC
VITRICS
VITRIFACTION
VITRIFACTIONS
VITRIFACTURE
VITRIFACTURES
VITRIFIABILITY
VITRIFIABLE
VITRIFICATION
VITRIFICATIONS
VITRIFIED
VITRIFIES
VITRIFORM
VITRIFY
VITRIFYING
VITRINE
VITRINES
VITRIOL
VITRIOLATE
VITRIOLATED
VITRIOLATES
VITRIOLATING
VITRIOLATION
VITRIOLATIONS
VITRIOLED
VITRIOLIC
VITRIOLING

VITRIOLISATION
VITRIOLISATIONS
VITRIOLISE
VITRIOLISED
VITRIOLISES
VITRIOLISING
VITRIOLIZATION
VITRIOLIZATIONS
VITRIOLIZE
VITRIOLIZED
VITRIOLIZES
VITRIOLIZING
VITRIOLLED
VITRIOLLING
VITRIOLS
VITTA
VITTAE
VITTATE
VITTLE
VITTLED
VITTLES
VITTLING
VITULAR
VITULINE
VITUPERABLE
VITUPERATE
VITUPERATED
VITUPERATES
VITUPERATING
VITUPERATION
VITUPERATIONS
VITUPERATIVE
VITUPERATIVELY
VITUPERATOR
VITUPERATORS
VITUPERATORY
VIVA
VIVACE
VIVACES
VIVACIOUS
VIVACIOUSLY
VIVACIOUSNESS
VIVACIOUSNESSES
VIVACISSIMO
VIVACITIES
VIVACITY
VIVAED
VIVAING
VIVAMENTE
VIVANDIER
VIVANDIERE
VIVANDIERES
VIVANDIERS
VIVARIA
VIVARIES
VIVARIUM
VIVARIUMS

VIVARY
VIVAS
VIVAT
VIVATS
VIVDA
VIVDAS
VIVE
VIVELY
VIVENCIES
VIVENCY
VIVER
VIVERRA
VIVERRAS
VIVERRID
VIVERRIDS
VIVERRINE
VIVERRINES
VIVERS
VIVES
VIVIANITE
VIVIANITES
VIVID
VIVIDER
VIVIDEST
VIVIDITIES
VIVIDITY
VIVIDLY
VIVIDNESS
VIVIDNESSES
VIVIFIC
VIVIFICATION
VIVIFICATIONS
VIVIFIED
VIVIFIER
VIVIFIERS
VIVIFIES
VIVIFY
VIVIFYING
VIVIPARA
VIVIPARIES
VIVIPARISM
VIVIPARISMS
VIVIPARITIES
VIVIPARITY
VIVIPAROUS
VIVIPAROUSLY
VIVIPAROUSNESS
VIVIPARY
VIVISECT
VIVISECTED
VIVISECTING
VIVISECTION
VIVISECTIONAL
VIVISECTIONALLY
VIVISECTIONIST
VIVISECTIONISTS
VIVISECTIONS

VIVISECTIVE
VIVISECTOR
VIVISECTORIUM
VIVISECTORIUMS
VIVISECTORS
VIVISECTS
VIVISEPULTURE
VIVISEPULTURES
VIVO
VIVRES
VIXEN
VIXENISH
VIXENISHLY
VIXENISHNESS
VIXENLY
VIXENS
VIZAMENT
VIZAMENTS
VIZARD
VIZARDED
VIZARDING
VIZARDS
VIZCACHA
VIZCACHAS
VIZIED
VIZIER
VIZIERATE
VIZIERATES
VIZIERIAL
VIZIERS
VIZIERSHIP
VIZIERSHIPS
VIZIES
VIZIR
VIZIRATE
VIZIRATES
VIZIRIAL
VIZIRS
VIZIRSHIP
VIZIRSHIPS
VIZOR
VIZORED
VIZORING
VIZORLESS
VIZORS
VIZSLA
VIZSLAS
VIZY
VIZYING
VIZZIE
VIZZIED
VIZZIEING
VIZZIES
VLEI
VLEIS
VLIES
VLY

VOAR
VOARS
VOCAB
VOCABLE
VOCABLES
VOCABLY
VOCABS
VOCABULAR
VOCABULARIAN
VOCABULARIANS
VOCABULARIED
VOCABULARIES
VOCABULARY
VOCABULIST
VOCABULISTS
VOCAL
VOCALESE
VOCALESES
VOCALIC
VOCALICALLY
VOCALICS
VOCALION
VOCALIONS
VOCALISATION
VOCALISATIONS
VOCALISE
VOCALISED
VOCALISER
VOCALISERS
VOCALISING
VOCALISM
VOCALISMS
VOCALIST
VOCALISTS
VOCALITIES
VOCALITY
VOCALIZATION
VOCALIZATIONS
VOCALIZE
VOCALIZED
VOCALIZER
VOCALIZERS
VOCALIZES
VOCALIZING
VOCALLY
VOCALNESS
VOCALNESSES
VOCALS
VOCATION
VOCATIONAL
VOCATIONALISM
VOCATIONALISMS
VOCATIONALIST
VOCATIONALISTS
VOCATIONALLY
VOCATIONS

VOCATIVE	VOGUISH	VOLARIES	VOLERIES
VOCATIVELY	VOGUISHNESS	VOLARY	VOLERY
VOCATIVES	VOGUISHNESSES	VOLATIC	VOLES
VOCES	VOICE	VOLATILE	VOLET
VOCICULTURAL	VOICED	VOLATILENESS	VOLETS
VOCIFERANCE	VOICEFUL	VOLATILENESSES	VOLING
VOCIFERANCES	VOICEFULNESS	VOLATILES	VOLITANT
VOCIFERANT	VOICEFULNESSES	VOLATILISABLE	VOLITATE
VOCIFERANTS	VOICELESS	VOLATILISATION	VOLITATED
VOCIFERATE	VOICELESSLY	VOLATILISATIONS	VOLITATES
VOCIFERATED	VOICELESSNESS	VOLATILISE	VOLITATING
VOCIFERATES	VOICELESSNESSES	VOLATILISED	VOLITATION
VOCIFERATING	VOICEPRINT	VOLATILISES	VOLITATIONAL
VOCIFERATION	VOICEPRINTS	VOLATILISING	VOLITATIONS
VOCIFERATIONS	VOICER	VOLATILITIES	VOLITIENT
VOCIFERATOR	VOICERS	VOLATILITY	VOLITION
VOCIFERATORS	VOICES	VOLATILIZABLE	VOLITIONAL
VOCIFEROSITIES	VOICING	VOLATILIZATION	VOLITIONALLY
VOCIFEROSITY	VOICINGS	VOLATILIZATIONS	VOLITIONARY
VOCIFEROUS	VOID	VOLATILIZE	VOLITIONLESS
VOCIFEROUSLY	VOIDABLE	VOLATILIZED	VOLITIONS
VOCIFEROUSNESS	VOIDABLENESS	VOLATILIZES	VOLITIVE
VOCODER	VOIDABLENESSES	VOLATILIZING	VOLITIVES
VOCODERS	VOIDANCE	VOLCANIAN	VOLITORIAL
VOCULAR	VOIDANCES	VOLCANIC	VOLK
VOCULE	VOIDED	VOLCANICALLY	VOLKS
VOCULES	VOIDEE	VOLCANICITIES	VOLKSLIED
VODKA	VOIDEES	VOLCANICITY	VOLKSLIEDER
VODKAS	VOIDER	VOLCANICS	VOLKSRAAD
VODOUN	VOIDERS	VOLCANISATION	VOLKSRAADS
VODOUNS	VOIDING	VOLCANISATIONS	VOLLEY
VODUN	VOIDINGS	VOLCANISE	VOLLEYBALL
VODUNS	VOIDNESS	VOLCANISED	VOLLEYBALLS
VOE	VOIDNESSES	VOLCANISES	VOLLEYED
VOEMA	VOIDS	VOLCANISING	VOLLEYER
VOES	VOILA	VOLCANISM	VOLLEYERS
VOETGANGER	VOILE	VOLCANISMS	VOLLEYING
VOETGANGERS	VOILES	VOLCANIST	VOLLEYS
VOETSAK	VOISINAGE	VOLCANISTS	VOLOST
VOETSEK	VOISINAGES	VOLCANIZATION	VOLOSTS
VOETSTOETS	VOITURE	VOLCANIZATIONS	VOLPINO
VOETSTOOTS	VOITURES	VOLCANIZE	VOLPINOS
VOGIE	VOITURIER	VOLCANIZED	VOLPLANE
VOGIER	VOITURIERS	VOLCANIZES	VOLPLANED
VOGIEST	VOIVODE	VOLCANIZING	VOLPLANES
VOGUE	VOIVODES	VOLCANO	VOLPLANING
VOGUED	VOIVODESHIP	VOLCANOES	VOLS
VOGUEING	VOIVODESHIPS	VOLCANOLOGIC	VOLT
VOGUEINGS	VOL	VOLCANOLOGICAL	VOLTA
VOGUER	VOLA	VOLCANOLOGIES	VOLTAGE
VOGUERS	VOLABLE	VOLCANOLOGIST	VOLTAGES
VOGUES	VOLAE	VOLCANOLOGISTS	VOLTAIC
VOGUEY	VOLAGE	VOLCANOLOGY	VOLTAISM
VOGUIER	VOLANT	VOLCANOS	VOLTAISMS
VOGUIEST	VOLANTE	VOLE	VOLTAMETER
VOGUING	VOLANTES	VOLED	VOLTAMETERS
VOGUINGS	VOLAR	VOLENS	VOLTAMETRIC

VOLTAMMETER
VOLTAMMETERS
VOLTE
VOLTES
VOLTI
VOLTIGEUR
VOLTIGEURS
VOLTINISM
VOLTINISMS
VOLTMETER
VOLTMETERS
VOLTS
VOLUBIL
VOLUBILITIES
VOLUBILITY
VOLUBLE
VOLUBLENESS
VOLUBLENESSES
VOLUBLY
VOLUCRINE
VOLUME
VOLUMED
VOLUMENOMETER
VOLUMENOMETERS
VOLUMES
VOLUMETER
VOLUMETERS
VOLUMETRIC
VOLUMETRICAL
VOLUMETRICALLY
VOLUMETRY
VOLUMINAL
VOLUMING
VOLUMINOSITIES
VOLUMINOSITY
VOLUMINOUS
VOLUMINOUSLY
VOLUMINOUSNESS
VOLUMISE
VOLUMISED
VOLUMISES
VOLUMISING
VOLUMIST
VOLUMISTS
VOLUMIZE
VOLUMIZED
VOLUMIZES
VOLUMIZING
VOLUMOMETER
VOLUMOMETERS
VOLUNTARIES
VOLUNTARILY
VOLUNTARINESS
VOLUNTARINESSES
VOLUNTARISM
VOLUNTARISMS
VOLUNTARIST

VOLUNTARISTIC
VOLUNTARISTS
VOLUNTARY
VOLUNTARYISM
VOLUNTARYISMS
VOLUNTARYIST
VOLUNTARYISTS
VOLUNTATIVE
VOLUNTEER
VOLUNTEERED
VOLUNTEERING
VOLUNTEERISM
VOLUNTEERISMS
VOLUNTEERS
VOLUPTUARIES
VOLUPTUARY
VOLUPTUOSITIES
VOLUPTUOSITY
VOLUPTUOUS
VOLUPTUOUSLY
VOLUPTUOUSNESS
VOLUSPA
VOLUSPAS
VOLUTATION
VOLUTATIONS
VOLUTE
VOLUTED
VOLUTES
VOLUTIN
VOLUTINS
VOLUTION
VOLUTIONS
VOLUTOID
VOLVA
VOLVAE
VOLVAS
VOLVATE
VOLVE
VOLVED
VOLVES
VOLVING
VOLVOX
VOLVOXES
VOLVULI
VOLVULUS
VOLVULUSES
VOMER
VOMERINE
VOMERONASAL
VOMERS
VOMICA
VOMICAE
VOMICAS
VOMIT
VOMITED
VOMITER
VOMITERS

VOMITING
VOMITINGS
VOMITIVE
VOMITIVES
VOMITO
VOMITORIA
VOMITORIES
VOMITORIUM
VOMITORIUMS
VOMITORY
VOMITOS
VOMITOUS
VOMITS
VOMITURITION
VOMITURITIONS
VOMITUS
VOMITUSES
VOODOO
VOODOOED
VOODOOING
VOODOOISM
VOODOOISMS
VOODOOIST
VOODOOISTIC
VOODOOISTS
VOODOOS
VOORKAMER
VOORKAMERS
VOORSKOT
VOORSKOTS
VOORTREKKER
VOORTREKKERS
VOR
VORACIOUS
VORACIOUSLY
VORACIOUSNESS
VORACIOUSNESSES
VORACITIES
VORACITY
VORAGINOUS
VORAGO
VORAGOES
VORANT
VORLAGE
VORLAGES
VORPAL
VORRED
VORRING
VORS
VORTEX
VORTEXES
VORTICAL
VORTICALLY
VORTICELLA
VORTICELLAE
VORTICELLAS
VORTICES

VORTICISM
VORTICISMS
VORTICIST
VORTICISTS
VORTICITIES
VORTICITY
VORTICOSE
VORTICULAR
VORTIGINOUS
VOTABLE
VOTARESS
VOTARESSES
VOTARIES
VOTARIST
VOTARISTS
VOTARY
VOTE
VOTEABLE
VOTED
VOTEEN
VOTEENS
VOTELESS
VOTER
VOTERS
VOTES
VOTING
VOTIVE
VOTIVELY
VOTIVENESS
VOTIVENESSES
VOTRESS
VOTRESSES
VOUCH
VOUCHED
VOUCHEE
VOUCHEES
VOUCHER
VOUCHERED
VOUCHERING
VOUCHERS
VOUCHES
VOUCHING
VOUCHSAFE
VOUCHSAFED
VOUCHSAFEMENT
VOUCHSAFEMENTS
VOUCHSAFES
VOUCHSAFING
VOUCHSAFINGS
VOUDOU
VOUDOUED
VOUDOUING
VOUDOUS
VOUGE
VOUGES
VOULGE
VOULGES

VOULU
VOUSSOIR
VOUSSOIRED
VOUSSOIRING
VOUSSOIRS
VOUTSAFE
VOUTSAFED
VOUTSAFES
VOUTSAFING
VOUVRAY
VOUVRAYS
VOW
VOWED
VOWEL
VOWELISATION
VOWELISE
VOWELISED
VOWELISES
VOWELISING
VOWELIZATION
VOWELIZE
VOWELIZED
VOWELIZES
VOWELIZING
VOWELLED
VOWELLESS
VOWELLING
VOWELLY
VOWELS
VOWER
VOWERS
VOWESS
VOWESSES
VOWING
VOWLESS
VOWS
VOX
VOXEL
VOXELS
VOYAGE
VOYAGEABLE
VOYAGED
VOYAGER
VOYAGERS
VOYAGES
VOYAGEUR
VOYAGEURS
VOYAGING
VOYEUR
VOYEURISM
VOYEURISMS
VOYEURISTIC
VOYEURISTICALLY
VOYEURS
VOZHD
VOZHDS
VRAIC

VRAICKER
VRAICKERS
VRAICKING
VRAICKINGS
VRAICS
VRAISEMBLANCE
VRAISEMBLANCES
VRIL
VRILS
VROOM
VROOMED
VROOMING
VROOMS
VROU
VROUS
VROUW
VROUWS
VROW
VROWS
VUG
VUGG
VUGGIER
VUGGIEST
VUGGS
VUGGY
VUGH
VUGHS
VUGHY
VUGS
VULCAN
VULCANIAN
VULCANIC
VULCANICITIES
VULCANICITY
VULCANISABLE
VULCANISATE
VULCANISATES
VULCANISATION
VULCANISATIONS
VULCANISE
VULCANISED
VULCANISER
VULCANISERS
VULCANISES
VULCANISING
VULCANISM
VULCANISMS
VULCANIST
VULCANISTS
VULCANITE
VULCANITES
VULCANIZABLE
VULCANIZATE
VULCANIZATES
VULCANIZATION
VULCANIZATIONS
VULCANIZE

VULCANIZED
VULCANIZER
VULCANIZERS
VULCANIZES
VULCANIZING
VULCANOLOGICAL
VULCANOLOGIES
VULCANOLOGIST
VULCANOLOGISTS
VULCANOLOGY
VULCANS
VULGAR
VULGARER
VULGAREST
VULGARIAN
VULGARIANS
VULGARISATION
VULGARISATIONS
VULGARISE
VULGARISED
VULGARISER
VULGARISERS
VULGARISES
VULGARISING
VULGARISM
VULGARISMS
VULGARITIES
VULGARITY
VULGARIZATION
VULGARIZATIONS
VULGARIZE
VULGARIZED
VULGARIZER
VULGARIZERS
VULGARIZES
VULGARIZING
VULGARLY
VULGARNESS
VULGARNESSES
VULGARS
VULGATE
VULGATES
VULGO
VULGUS
VULGUSES
VULN
VULNED
VULNERABILITIES
VULNERABILITY
VULNERABLE
VULNERABLENESS
VULNERABLY
VULNERARIES
VULNERARY
VULNERATE
VULNERATED
VULNERATES

VULNERATING
VULNERATION
VULNERATIONS
VULNING
VULNS
VULPECULAR
VULPICIDE
VULPICIDES
VULPINE
VULPINISM
VULPINISMS
VULPINITE
VULPINITES
VULSELLA
VULSELLUM
VULTURE
VULTURES
VULTURINE
VULTURISH
VULTURISM
VULTURISMS
VULTURN
VULTURNS
VULTUROUS
VULVA
VULVAE
VULVAL
VULVAR
VULVAS
VULVATE
VULVIFORM
VULVITIS
VULVITISES
VULVOVAGINAL
VULVOVAGINITIS
VUM
VUMMED
VUMMING
VUMS
VUTTIER
VUTTIEST
VUTTY
VYING
VYINGLY

W

WAAC	WADDS	WAFFIES	WAGGISHNESS
WAACS	WADDY	WAFFING	WAGGISHNESSES
WAB	WADDYING	WAFFLE	WAGGLE
WABAIN	WADE	WAFFLED	WAGGLED
WABAINS	WADEABLE	WAFFLER	WAGGLER
WABBIT	WADED	WAFFLERS	WAGGLERS
WABBLE	WADER	WAFFLES	WAGGLES
WABBLED	WADERS	WAFFLESTOMPER	WAGGLIER
WABBLER	WADES	WAFFLESTOMPERS	WAGGLIEST
WABBLERS	WADI	WAFFLIER	WAGGLING
WABBLES	WADIES	WAFFLIEST	WAGGLINGLY
WABBLIER	WADING	WAFFLING	WAGGLY
WABBLIEST	WADINGS	WAFFLINGS	WAGGON
WABBLING	WADIS	WAFFLY	WAGGONED
WABBLY	WADMAAL	WAFFS	WAGGONER
WABOOM	WADMAALS	WAFT	WAGGONERS
WABOOMS	WADMAL	WAFTAGE	WAGGONETTE
WABS	WADMALS	WAFTAGES	WAGGONETTES
WABSTER	WADMEL	WAFTED	WAGGONING
WABSTERS	WADMELS	WAFTER	WAGGONLESS
WACK	WADMOL	WAFTERS	WAGGONLOAD
WACKE	WADMOLL	WAFTING	WAGGONLOADS
WACKER	WADMOLLS	WAFTINGS	WAGGONS
WACKERS	WADMOLS	WAFTS	WAGHALTER
WACKES	WADS	WAFTURE	WAGHALTERS
WACKIER	WADSET	WAFTURES	WAGING
WACKIEST	WADSETS	WAG	WAGMOIRE
WACKILY	WADSETT	WAGE	WAGMOIRES
WACKINESS	WADSETTED	WAGED	WAGON
WACKINESSES	WADSETTER	WAGELESS	WAGONAGE
WACKO	WADSETTERS	WAGELESSNESS	WAGONAGES
WACKOS	WADSETTING	WAGENBOOM	WAGONED
WACKS	WADSETTS	WAGENBOOMS	WAGONER
WACKY	WADT	WAGER	WAGONERS
WAD	WADTS	WAGERED	WAGONETTE
WADABLE	WADY	WAGERER	WAGONETTES
WADD	WAE	WAGERERS	WAGONFUL
WADDED	WAEFUL	WAGERING	WAGONFULS
WADDER	WAENESS	WAGERS	WAGONING
WADDERS	WAENESSES	WAGES	WAGONLESS
WADDIE	WAES	WAGEWORKER	WAGONLOAD
WADDIED	WAESOME	WAGEWORKERS	WAGONLOADS
WADDIES	WAESUCK	WAGGA	WAGONS
WADDING	WAESUCKS	WAGGAS	WAGONWRIGHT
WADDINGS	WAFER	WAGGED	WAGONWRIGHTS
WADDLE	WAFERED	WAGGER	WAGS
WADDLED	WAFERING	WAGGERIES	WAGSOME
WADDLER	WAFERS	WAGGERS	WAGTAIL
WADDLERS	WAFERY	WAGGERY	WAGTAILS
WADDLES	WAFF	WAGGING	WAHCONDA
WADDLING	WAFFED	WAGGISH	WAHCONDAS
WADDLY	WAFFIE	WAGGISHLY	WAHINE

WAHINES	WAISTCOAT	WAKEBOARDER	WALING
WAHOO	WAISTCOATED	WAKEBOARDERS	WALIS
WAHOOS	WAISTCOATEER	WAKEBOARDING	WALISE
WAI	WAISTCOATEERS	WAKEBOARDINGS	WALISES
WAIATA	WAISTCOATING	WAKED	WALK
WAID	WAISTCOATINGS	WAKEFUL	WALKABLE
WAIDE	WAISTCOATS	WAKEFULLY	WALKABOUT
WAIF	WAISTED	WAKEFULNESS	WALKABOUTS
WAIFED	WAISTER	WAKEFULNESSES	WALKATHON
WAIFING	WAISTERS	WAKELESS	WALKATHONS
WAIFLIKE	WAISTING	WAKEMAN	WALKAWAY
WAIFS	WAISTINGS	WAKEMEN	WALKAWAYS
WAIFT	WAISTLESS	WAKEN	WALKED
WAIFTS	WAISTLINE	WAKENED	WALKER
WAIL	WAISTLINES	WAKENER	WALKERS
WAILED	WAISTS	WAKENERS	WALKING
WAILER	WAIT	WAKENING	WALKINGS
WAILERS	WAITAS	WAKENINGS	WALKINGSTICK
WAILFUL	WAITE	WAKENS	WALKINGSTICKS
WAILFULLY	WAITED	WAKER	WALKMILL
WAILING	WAITER	WAKERIFE	WALKMILLS
WAILINGLY	WAITERAGE	WAKERIFENESS	WALKOUT
WAILINGS	WAITERAGES	WAKERS	WALKOUTS
WAILS	WAITERHOOD	WAKES	WALKOVER
WAILSOME	WAITERHOODS	WAKF	WALKOVERS
WAIN	WAITERING	WAKFS	WALKS
WAINAGE	WAITERINGS	WAKIKI	WALKSHORTS
WAINAGES	WAITERS	WAKIKIS	WALKUP
WAINED	WAITES	WAKING	WALKUPS
WAINING	WAITING	WAKINGS	WALKWAY
WAINS	WAITINGLY	WALD	WALKWAYS
WAINSCOT	WAITINGS	WALDFLUTE	WALKYRIE
WAINSCOTED	WAITPERSON	WALDFLUTES	WALKYRIES
WAINSCOTING	WAITPERSONS	WALDGRAVE	WALL
WAINSCOTINGS	WAITRESS	WALDGRAVES	WALLA
WAINSCOTS	WAITRESSED	WALDGRAVINE	WALLABA
WAINSCOTTED	WAITRESSES	WALDGRAVINES	WALLABAS
WAINSCOTTING	WAITRESSING	WALDHORN	WALLABIES
WAINSCOTTINGS	WAITRESSINGS	WALDHORNS	WALLABY
WAINWRIGHT	WAITS	WALDO	WALLAH
WAINWRIGHTS	WAIVE	WALDOES	WALLAHS
WAIR	WAIVED	WALDOS	WALLAROO
WAIRED	WAIVER	WALDRAPP	WALLAROOS
WAIRING	WAIVERS	WALDRAPPS	WALLAS
WAIRS	WAIVES	WALDS	WALLBOARD
WAIRSH	WAIVING	WALDSTERBEN	WALLBOARDS
WAIRSHER	WAIVODE	WALDSTERBENS	WALLCHART
WAIRSHEST	WAIVODES	WALE	WALLCHARTS
WAIRUA	WAIWODE	WALED	WALLCLIMBER
WAIST	WAIWODES	WALER	WALLCLIMBERS
WAISTBAND	WAKA	WALERS	WALLCOVERING
WAISTBANDS	WAKANDA	WALES	WALLCOVERINGS
WAISTBELT	WAKANDAS	WALEST	WALLED
WAISTBELTS	WAKANE	WALI	WALLER
WAISTBOATS	WAKANES	WALIER	WALLERS
WAISTCLOTH	WAKAS	WALIES	WALLET
WAISTCLOTHS	WAKE	WALIEST	WALLETS

WALLEYE	WALTZING	WANDLE	WANNING
WALLEYED	WALTZINGS	WANDLIKE	WANNISH
WALLEYES	WALTZLIKE	WANDOO	WANS
WALLFISH	WALY	WANDOOS	WANT
WALLFISHES	WAMBENGER	WANDS	WANTAGE
WALLFLOWER	WAMBENGERS	WANE	WANTAGES
WALLFLOWERS	WAMBLE	WANED	WANTED
WALLIE	WAMBLED	WANES	WANTER
WALLIER	WAMBLES	WANEY	WANTERS
WALLIES	WAMBLIER	WANG	WANTHILL
WALLIEST	WAMBLIEST	WANGAN	WANTHILLS
WALLING	WAMBLINESS	WANGANS	WANTIES
WALLINGS	WAMBLINESSES	WANGLE	WANTING
WALLOP	WAMBLING	WANGLED	WANTINGS
WALLOPED	WAMBLINGLY	WANGLER	WANTON
WALLOPER	WAMBLINGS	WANGLERS	WANTONED
WALLOPERS	WAMBLY	WANGLES	WANTONER
WALLOPING	WAME	WANGLING	WANTONERS
WALLOPINGS	WAMED	WANGLINGS	WANTONEST
WALLOPS	WAMEFOU	WANGS	WANTONING
WALLOW	WAMEFOUS	WANGUN	WANTONISE
WALLOWED	WAMEFUL	WANGUNS	WANTONISED
WALLOWER	WAMEFULS	WANHOPE	WANTONISES
WALLOWERS	WAMES	WANHOPES	WANTONISING
WALLOWING	WAMMUL	WANIER	WANTONIZE
WALLOWINGS	WAMMUS	WANIEST	WANTONIZED
WALLOWS	WAMMUSES	WANIGAN	WANTONIZES
WALLPAPER	WAMPEE	WANIGANS	WANTONIZING
WALLPAPERED	WAMPEES	WANING	WANTONLY
WALLPAPERING	WAMPISH	WANINGS	WANTONNESS
WALLPAPERS	WAMPISHED	WANION	WANTONNESSES
WALLPOSTER	WAMPISHES	WANIONS	WANTONS
WALLPOSTERS	WAMPISHING	WANK	WANTS
WALLS	WAMPUM	WANKED	WANTY
WALLSEND	WAMPUMPEAG	WANKER	WANWORDY
WALLSENDS	WAMPUMPEAGS	WANKERS	WANWORTH
WALLWORT	WAMPUMS	WANKIER	WANWORTHS
WALLWORTS	WAMPUS	WANKIEST	WANY
WALLY	WAMPUSES	WANKING	WANZE
WALLYDRAG	WAMUS	WANKLE	WANZED
WALLYDRAGS	WAMUSES	WANKS	WANZES
WALLYDRAIGLE	WAN	WANKY	WANZING
WALLYDRAIGLES	WANCHANCIE	WANLE	WAP
WALNUT	WANCHANCY	WANLY	WAPENSCHAW
WALNUTS	WAND	WANNA	WAPENSCHAWS
WALNUTWOOD	WANDER	WANNABE	WAPENSHAW
WALNUTWOODS	WANDERED	WANNABEE	WAPENSHAWS
WALRUS	WANDERER	WANNABEES	WAPENTAKE
WALRUSES	WANDERERS	WANNABES	WAPENTAKES
WALTIER	WANDERING	WANNED	WAPINSCHAW
WALTIEST	WANDERINGLY	WANNEL	WAPINSCHAWS
WALTY	WANDERINGS	WANNER	WAPINSHAW
WALTZ	WANDERLUST	WANNESS	WAPINSHAWS
WALTZED	WANDERLUSTS	WANNESSES	WAPITI
WALTZER	WANDEROO	WANNEST	WAPITIS
WALTZERS	WANDEROOS	WANNIGAN	WAPPED
WALTZES	WANDERS	WANNIGANS	WAPPEND

WAPPENSCHAW
WAPPENSCHAWING
WAPPENSCHAWINGS
WAPPENSCHAWS
WAPPENSHAW
WAPPENSHAWING
WAPPENSHAWINGS
WAPPENSHAWS
WAPPER
WAPPERED
WAPPERING
WAPPERS
WAPPING
WAPS
WAQF
WAQFS
WAR
WARAGI
WARATAH
WARATAHS
WARB
WARBIER
WARBIEST
WARBLE
WARBLED
WARBLER
WARBLERS
WARBLES
WARBLING
WARBLINGLY
WARBLINGS
WARBONNET
WARBONNETS
WARBS
WARBY
WARCHALKING
WARCRAFT
WARCRAFTS
WARD
WARDCORN
WARDCORNS
WARDED
WARDEN
WARDENED
WARDENING
WARDENRIES
WARDENRY
WARDENS
WARDENSHIP
WARDENSHIPS
WARDER
WARDERED
WARDERING
WARDERS
WARDERSHIP
WARDERSHIPS
WARDIAN

WARDING
WARDINGS
WARDLESS
WARDMOTE
WARDMOTES
WARDOG
WARDOGS
WARDRESS
WARDRESSES
WARDROBE
WARDROBER
WARDROBERS
WARDROBES
WARDROOM
WARDROOMS
WARDROP
WARDROPS
WARDS
WARDSHIP
WARDSHIPS
WARE
WARED
WAREHOU
WAREHOUSE
WAREHOUSED
WAREHOUSEMAN
WAREHOUSEMEN
WAREHOUSER
WAREHOUSERS
WAREHOUSES
WAREHOUSING
WAREHOUSINGS
WARELESS
WARER
WAREROOM
WAREROOMS
WARES
WAREST
WARFARE
WARFARED
WARFARER
WARFARERS
WARFARES
WARFARIN
WARFARING
WARFARINGS
WARFARINS
WARHABLE
WARHEAD
WARHEADS
WARHORSE
WARHORSES
WARIBASHI
WARIBASHIS
WARIER
WARIEST
WARILY

WARIMENT
WARIMENTS
WARINESS
WARINESSES
WARING
WARISON
WARISONS
WARK
WARKED
WARKING
WARKS
WARLESS
WARLIKE
WARLIKENESS
WARLIKENESSES
WARLING
WARLINGS
WARLOCK
WARLOCKRIES
WARLOCKRY
WARLOCKS
WARLORD
WARLORDISM
WARLORDISMS
WARLORDS
WARM
WARMAKER
WARMAKERS
WARMAN
WARMBLOOD
WARMBLOODS
WARMED
WARMEN
WARMER
WARMERS
WARMEST
WARMHEARTED
WARMHEARTEDNESS
WARMING
WARMINGS
WARMISH
WARMLY
WARMNESS
WARMNESSES
WARMONGER
WARMONGERING
WARMONGERINGS
WARMONGERS
WARMOUTH
WARMOUTHS
WARMS
WARMTH
WARMTHS
WARMUP
WARMUPS
WARN
WARNED

WARNER
WARNERS
WARNING
WARNINGLY
WARNINGS
WARNS
WARP
WARPAGE
WARPAGES
WARPATH
WARPATHS
WARPED
WARPER
WARPERS
WARPING
WARPINGS
WARPLANE
WARPLANES
WARPOWER
WARPOWERS
WARPS
WARPWISE
WARRAGAL
WARRAGALS
WARRAGLE
WARRAGLES
WARRAGUL
WARRAGULS
WARRAN
WARRAND
WARRANDED
WARRANDICE
WARRANDICES
WARRANDING
WARRANDS
WARRANED
WARRANING
WARRANS
WARRANT
WARRANTABILITY
WARRANTABLE
WARRANTABLENESS
WARRANTABLY
WARRANTED
WARRANTEE
WARRANTEES
WARRANTER
WARRANTERS
WARRANTIES
WARRANTING
WARRANTINGS
WARRANTISE
WARRANTISES
WARRANTLESS
WARRANTOR
WARRANTORS
WARRANTS

WARRANTY	WARTY	WASHINESS	WASSUP
WARRAY	WARWOLF	WASHINESSES	WAST
WARRAYED	WARWOLVES	WASHING	WASTABLE
WARRAYING	WARWORK	WASHINGS	WASTAGE
WARRAYS	WARWORKS	WASHINGTONIA	WASTAGES
WARRE	WARWORN	WASHINGTONIAS	WASTE
WARRED	WARY	WASHINS	WASTEBASKET
WARREN	WARZONE	WASHLAND	WASTEBASKETS
WARRENER	WARZONES	WASHLANDS	WASTED
WARRENERS	WAS	WASHOUT	WASTEFUL
WARRENS	WASABI	WASHOUTS	WASTEFULLY
WARREY	WASABIS	WASHPOT	WASTEFULNESS
WARREYED	WASE	WASHPOTS	WASTEFULNESSES
WARREYING	WASEGOOSES	WASHRAG	WASTEL
WARREYS	WASES	WASHRAGS	WASTELAND
WARRIGAL	WASH	WASHROOM	WASTELANDS
WARRIGALS	WASHABILITIES	WASHROOMS	WASTELOT
WARRING	WASHABILITY	WASHSTAND	WASTELOTS
WARRIOR	WASHABLE	WASHSTANDS	WASTELS
WARRIORESS	WASHABLES	WASHTUB	WASTENESS
WARRIORESSES	WASHATERIA	WASHTUBS	WASTENESSES
WARRIORS	WASHATERIAS	WASHUP	WASTEPAPER
WARRISON	WASHAWAY	WASHUPS	WASTEPAPERS
WARRISONS	WASHAWAYS	WASHWIPE	WASTER
WARS	WASHBALL	WASHWIPES	WASTERED
WARSAW	WASHBALLS	WASHWOMAN	WASTERFUL
WARSAWS	WASHBASIN	WASHWOMEN	WASTERFULLY
WARSHIP	WASHBASINS	WASHY	WASTERFULNESS
WARSHIPS	WASHBOARD	WASM	WASTERFULNESSES
WARSLE	WASHBOARDS	WASMS	WASTERIE
WARSLED	WASHBOWL	WASP	WASTERIES
WARSLER	WASHBOWLS	WASPIE	WASTERIFES
WARSLERS	WASHCLOTH	WASPIER	WASTERING
WARSLES	WASHCLOTHS	WASPIES	WASTERS
WARSLING	WASHDAY	WASPIEST	WASTERY
WARST	WASHDAYS	WASPILY	WASTES
WARSTLE	WASHED	WASPINESS	WASTEWATER
WARSTLED	WASHEN	WASPISH	WASTEWATERS
WARSTLER	WASHER	WASPISHLY	WASTEWAY
WARSTLERS	WASHERED	WASPISHNESS	WASTEWAYS
WARSTLES	WASHERIES	WASPISHNESSES	WASTEWEIR
WARSTLING	WASHERING	WASPLIKE	WASTEWEIRS
WART	WASHERMAN	WASPNEST	WASTFULL
WARTED	WASHERMEN	WASPNESTS	WASTING
WARTHOG	WASHERS	WASPS	WASTINGLY
WARTHOGS	WASHERWOMAN	WASPY	WASTINGS
WARTIER	WASHERWOMEN	WASSAIL	WASTNESS
WARTIEST	WASHERY	WASSAILED	WASTNESSES
WARTIME	WASHES	WASSAILER	WASTREL
WARTIMES	WASHETERIA	WASSAILERS	WASTRELS
WARTLESS	WASHETERIAS	WASSAILING	WASTRIE
WARTLIKE	WASHHOUSE	WASSAILINGS	WASTRIES
WARTS	WASHHOUSES	WASSAILRIES	WASTRIFE
WARTWEED	WASHIER	WASSAILRY	WASTRIFES
WARTWEEDS	WASHIEST	WASSAILS	WASTRY
WARTWORT	WASHILY	WASSERMAN	WASTS
WARTWORTS	WASHIN	WASSERMEN	WAT

WATAP	WATERBEDS	WATERING	WATERSPOUT
WATAPE	WATERBIRD	WATERINGS	WATERSPOUTS
WATAPES	WATERBIRDS	WATERISH	WATERTHRUSH
WATAPS	WATERBORNE	WATERISHNESS	WATERTHRUSHES
WATCH	WATERBRAIN	WATERISHNESSES	WATERTIGHT
WATCHABLE	WATERBRAINS	WATERLEAF	WATERTIGHTNESS
WATCHABLES	WATERBUCK	WATERLEAFS	WATERWAY
WATCHBAND	WATERBUCKS	WATERLESS	WATERWAYS
WATCHBANDS	WATERCOLOR	WATERLESSNESS	WATERWEED
WATCHBOX	WATERCOLORIST	WATERLESSNESSES	WATERWEEDS
WATCHBOXES	WATERCOLORISTS	WATERLILIES	WATERWHEEL
WATCHCASE	WATERCOLORS	WATERLILY	WATERWHEELS
WATCHCASES	WATERCOLOUR	WATERLINE	WATERWORK
WATCHCRIES	WATERCOLOURIST	WATERLINES	WATERWORKS
WATCHCRY	WATERCOLOURISTS	WATERLOG	WATERWORN
WATCHDOG	WATERCOLOURS	WATERLOGGED	WATERY
WATCHDOGGED	WATERCOOLER	WATERLOGGING	WATERZOOI
WATCHDOGGING	WATERCOOLERS	WATERLOGS	WATERZOOIS
WATCHDOGS	WATERCOURSE	WATERLOO	WATS
WATCHED	WATERCOURSES	WATERLOOS	WATT
WATCHER	WATERCRAFT	WATERMAN	WATTAGE
WATCHERS	WATERCRAFTS	WATERMANSHIP	WATTAGES
WATCHES	WATERCRESS	WATERMANSHIPS	WATTAPE
WATCHET	WATERCRESSES	WATERMARK	WATTAPES
WATCHETS	WATERDOG	WATERMARKED	WATTER
WATCHEYE	WATERDOGS	WATERMARKING	WATTEST
WATCHEYES	WATERDRIVE	WATERMARKS	WATTHOUR
WATCHFUL	WATERDRIVES	WATERMELON	WATTHOURS
WATCHFULLY	WATERED	WATERMELONS	WATTLE
WATCHFULNESS	WATERER	WATERMEN	WATTLEBARK
WATCHFULNESSES	WATERERS	WATERPOWER	WATTLEBARKS
WATCHGLASS	WATERFALL	WATERPOWERS	WATTLEBIRD
WATCHGLASSES	WATERFALLS	WATERPOX	WATTLEBIRDS
WATCHGUARD	WATERFINDER	WATERPOXES	WATTLED
WATCHGUARDS	WATERFINDERS	WATERPROOF	WATTLES
WATCHING	WATERFLOOD	WATERPROOFED	WATTLESS
WATCHMAKER	WATERFLOODED	WATERPROOFER	WATTLEWORK
WATCHMAKERS	WATERFLOODING	WATERPROOFERS	WATTLEWORKS
WATCHMAKING	WATERFLOODINGS	WATERPROOFING	WATTLING
WATCHMAKINGS	WATERFLOODS	WATERPROOFINGS	WATTLINGS
WATCHMAN	WATERFOWL	WATERPROOFNESS	WATTMETER
WATCHMEN	WATERFOWLER	WATERPROOFS	WATTMETERS
WATCHOUT	WATERFOWLERS	WATERQUAKE	WATTS
WATCHOUTS	WATERFOWLING	WATERQUAKES	WAUCHT
WATCHSPRING	WATERFOWLINGS	WATERS	WAUCHTED
WATCHSPRINGS	WATERFOWLS	WATERSCAPE	WAUCHTING
WATCHSTRAP	WATERFRONT	WATERSCAPES	WAUCHTS
WATCHSTRAPS	WATERFRONTS	WATERSHED	WAUFF
WATCHTOWER	WATERGLASS	WATERSHEDS	WAUFFED
WATCHTOWERS	WATERGLASSES	WATERSIDE	WAUFFING
WATCHWORD	WATERHEN	WATERSIDER	WAUFFS
WATCHWORDS	WATERHENS	WATERSIDERS	WAUGH
WATE	WATERIER	WATERSIDES	WAUGHED
WATER	WATERIEST	WATERSKIING	WAUGHING
WATERAGE	WATERILY	WATERSKIINGS	WAUGHS
WATERAGES	WATERINESS	WATERSMEET	WAUGHT
WATERBED	WATERINESSES	WATERSMEETS	WAUGHTED

WAUGHTING
WAUGHTS
WAUK
WAUKED
WAUKER
WAUKERS
WAUKING
WAUKMILL
WAUKMILLS
WAUKRIFE
WAUKS
WAUL
WAULED
WAULING
WAULINGS
WAULK
WAULKED
WAULKER
WAULKERS
WAULKING
WAULKMILL
WAULKMILLS
WAULKS
WAULS
WAUR
WAURED
WAURING
WAURS
WAURST
WAVE
WAVEBAND
WAVEBANDS
WAVED
WAVEFORM
WAVEFORMS
WAVEFRONT
WAVEFRONTS
WAVEGUIDE
WAVEGUIDES
WAVELENGTH
WAVELENGTHS
WAVELESS
WAVELESSLY
WAVELET
WAVELETS
WAVELIKE
WAVELLITE
WAVELLITES
WAVEMETER
WAVEMETERS
WAVEOFF
WAVEOFFS
WAVER
WAVERED
WAVERER
WAVERERS
WAVERIER

WAVERIEST
WAVERING
WAVERINGLY
WAVERINGNESS
WAVERINGNESSES
WAVERINGS
WAVEROUS
WAVERS
WAVERY
WAVES
WAVESHAPE
WAVESHAPES
WAVESON
WAVESONS
WAVEY
WAVEYS
WAVIER
WAVIES
WAVIEST
WAVILY
WAVINESS
WAVINESSES
WAVING
WAVINGS
WAVY
WAW
WAWA
WAWAED
WAWAING
WAWAS
WAWE
WAWES
WAWL
WAWLED
WAWLING
WAWLINGS
WAWLS
WAWS
WAX
WAXBERRIES
WAXBERRY
WAXBILL
WAXBILLS
WAXCLOTH
WAXCLOTHS
WAXED
WAXEN
WAXER
WAXERS
WAXES
WAXEYE
WAXEYES
WAXIER
WAXIEST
WAXILY
WAXINESS
WAXINESSES

WAXING
WAXINGS
WAXLIKE
WAXPLANT
WAXPLANTS
WAXWEED
WAXWEEDS
WAXWING
WAXWINGS
WAXWORK
WAXWORKER
WAXWORKERS
WAXWORKS
WAXWORM
WAXWORMS
WAXY
WAY
WAYBILL
WAYBILLS
WAYBOARD
WAYBOARDS
WAYBREAD
WAYBREADS
WAYED
WAYFARE
WAYFARED
WAYFARER
WAYFARERS
WAYFARES
WAYFARING
WAYFARINGS
WAYGOING
WAYGOINGS
WAYGONE
WAYGOOSE
WAYGOOSES
WAYING
WAYLAID
WAYLAY
WAYLAYER
WAYLAYERS
WAYLAYING
WAYLAYS
WAYLEAVE
WAYLEAVES
WAYLEGGO
WAYLESS
WAYMARK
WAYMARKED
WAYMARKING
WAYMARKS
WAYMENT
WAYMENTED
WAYMENTING
WAYMENTS
WAYPOST
WAYPOSTS

WAYS
WAYSIDE
WAYSIDES
WAYWARD
WAYWARDLY
WAYWARDNESS
WAYWARDNESSES
WAYWISER
WAYWISERS
WAYWODE
WAYWODES
WAYWORN
WAYZGOOSE
WAYZGOOSES
WAZIR
WAZIRS
WAZZOCK
WE
WEAK
WEAKEN
WEAKENED
WEAKENER
WEAKENERS
WEAKENING
WEAKENS
WEAKER
WEAKEST
WEAKFISH
WEAKFISHES
WEAKHEARTED
WEAKISH
WEAKISHLY
WEAKISHNESS
WEAKLIER
WEAKLIEST
WEAKLINESS
WEAKLINESSES
WEAKLING
WEAKLINGS
WEAKLY
WEAKNESS
WEAKNESSES
WEAKSIDE
WEAKSIDES
WEAL
WEALD
WEALDS
WEALS
WEALSMAN
WEALSMEN
WEALTH
WEALTHIER
WEALTHIEST
WEALTHILY
WEALTHINESS
WEALTHINESSES
WEALTHLESS

WEALTHS	WEARISOME	WEATHERIZE	WEBMASTER
WEALTHY	WEARISOMELY	WEATHERIZED	WEBMASTERS
WEAMB	WEARISOMENESS	WEATHERIZES	WEBS
WEAMBS	WEARISOMENESSES	WEATHERIZING	WEBSITE
WEAN	WEARPROOF	WEATHERLINESS	WEBSITES
WEANED	WEARS	WEATHERLY	WEBSTER
WEANEDNESS	WEARY	WEATHERMAN	WEBSTERS
WEANEL	WEARYING	WEATHERMEN	WEBWHEEL
WEANELS	WEARYINGLY	WEATHERMOST	WEBWHEELS
WEANER	WEASAND	WEATHEROMETER	WEBWORK
WEANERS	WEASANDS	WEATHEROMETERS	WEBWORKS
WEANING	WEASEL	WEATHERPERSON	WEBWORM
WEANLING	WEASELED	WEATHERPERSONS	WEBWORMS
WEANLINGS	WEASELER	WEATHERPROOF	WECHT
WEANS	WEASELERS	WEATHERPROOFED	WECHTS
WEAPON	WEASELING	WEATHERPROOFING	WED
WEAPONED	WEASELLED	WEATHERPROOFS	WEDDED
WEAPONEER	WEASELLER	WEATHERS	WEDDER
WEAPONEERS	WEASELLERS	WEATHERWORN	WEDDERED
WEAPONING	WEASELLING	WEAVE	WEDDERING
WEAPONISE	WEASELLY	WEAVED	WEDDERS
WEAPONISED	WEASELS	WEAVER	WEDDING
WEAPONISES	WEASELY	WEAVERBIRD	WEDDINGS
WEAPONISING	WEASON	WEAVERBIRDS	WEDEL
WEAPONIZE	WEASONS	WEAVERS	WEDELED
WEAPONIZED	WEATHER	WEAVES	WEDELING
WEAPONIZES	WEATHERABILITY	WEAVING	WEDELN
WEAPONIZING	WEATHERABLE	WEAVINGS	WEDELNED
WEAPONLESS	WEATHERBOARD	WEAZAND	WEDELNING
WEAPONRIES	WEATHERBOARDED	WEAZANDS	WEDELNS
WEAPONRY	WEATHERBOARDING	WEAZEN	WEDELS
WEAPONS	WEATHERBOARDS	WEAZENED	WEDGE
WEAR	WEATHERCAST	WEAZENING	WEDGED
WEARABILITIES	WEATHERCASTER	WEAZENS	WEDGELIKE
WEARABILITY	WEATHERCASTERS	WEB	WEDGES
WEARABLE	WEATHERCASTS	WEBBED	WEDGEWISE
WEARABLES	WEATHERCLOTH	WEBBIE	WEDGIE
WEARED	WEATHERCLOTHS	WEBBIER	WEDGIER
WEARER	WEATHERCOCK	WEBBIEST	WEDGIES
WEARERS	WEATHERCOCKED	WEBBING	WEDGIEST
WEARIED	WEATHERCOCKING	WEBBINGS	WEDGING
WEARIER	WEATHERCOCKS	WEBBY	WEDGINGS
WEARIES	WEATHERED	WEBCAM	WEDGY
WEARIEST	WEATHERER	WEBCAMS	WEDLOCK
WEARIFUL	WEATHERERS	WEBCAST	WEDLOCKS
WEARIFULLY	WEATHERGIRL	WEBCASTS	WEDS
WEARIFULNESS	WEATHERGIRLS	WEBER	WEE
WEARIFULNESSES	WEATHERGLASS	WEBERS	WEED
WEARILESS	WEATHERGLASSES	WEBFED	WEEDED
WEARILESSLY	WEATHERING	WEBFEET	WEEDER
WEARILY	WEATHERINGS	WEBFOOT	WEEDERIES
WEARINESS	WEATHERISE	WEBFOOTED	WEEDERS
WEARINESSES	WEATHERISED	WEBLESS	WEEDERY
WEARING	WEATHERISES	WEBLIKE	WEEDICIDE
WEARINGLY	WEATHERISING	WEBLISH	WEEDICIDES
WEARINGS	WEATHERIZATION	WEBLOG	WEEDIER
WEARISH	WEATHERIZATIONS	WEBLOGS	WEEDIEST

WEEDILY	WEEPINESS	WEIGHING	WEIZES
WEEDINESS	WEEPING	WEIGHINGS	WEIZING
WEEDINESSES	WEEPINGLY	WEIGHMAN	WEKA
WEEDING	WEEPINGS	WEIGHMEN	WEKAS
WEEDINGS	WEEPS	WEIGHS	WELAWAY
WEEDKILLER	WEEPY	WEIGHT	WELCH
WEEDKILLERS	WEER	WEIGHTED	WELCHED
WEEDLESS	WEES	WEIGHTER	WELCHER
WEEDLIKE	WEEST	WEIGHTERS	WELCHERS
WEEDS	WEET	WEIGHTIER	WELCHES
WEEDY	WEETE	WEIGHTIEST	WELCHING
WEEING	WEETED	WEIGHTILY	WELCOME
WEEK	WEETEN	WEIGHTINESS	WELCOMED
WEEKDAY	WEETER	WEIGHTINESSES	WELCOMELY
WEEKDAYS	WEETEST	WEIGHTING	WELCOMENESS
WEEKE	WEETING	WEIGHTINGS	WELCOMENESSES
WEEKEND	WEETINGLY	WEIGHTLESS	WELCOMER
WEEKENDED	WEETLESS	WEIGHTLESSLY	WELCOMERS
WEEKENDER	WEETS	WEIGHTLESSNESS	WELCOMES
WEEKENDERS	WEEVER	WEIGHTLIFTER	WELCOMING
WEEKENDING	WEEVERS	WEIGHTLIFTERS	WELCOMINGLY
WEEKENDINGS	WEEVIL	WEIGHTLIFTING	WELD
WEEKENDS	WEEVILED	WEIGHTS	WELDABILITIES
WEEKES	WEEVILLED	WEIGHTY	WELDABILITY
WEEKLIES	WEEVILLY	WEIL	WELDABLE
WEEKLONG	WEEVILS	WEILS	WELDED
WEEKLY	WEEVILY	WEIMARANER	WELDER
WEEKNIGHT	WEEWEE	WEIMARANERS	WELDERS
WEEKNIGHTS	WEEWEED	WEINER	WELDING
WEEKS	WEEWEEING	WEINERS	WELDINGS
WEEL	WEEWEES	WEIR	WELDLESS
WEELDLESSE	WEFT	WEIRD	WELDMENT
WEELS	WEFTAGE	WEIRDED	WELDMENTS
WEEM	WEFTAGES	WEIRDER	WELDMESH
WEEMS	WEFTE	WEIRDEST	WELDMESHES
WEEN	WEFTED	WEIRDIE	WELDOR
WEENED	WEFTES	WEIRDIES	WELDORS
WEENIE	WEFTING	WEIRDING	WELDS
WEENIER	WEFTS	WEIRDLY	WELFARE
WEENIES	WEFTWISE	WEIRDNESS	WELFARES
WEENIEST	WEID	WEIRDNESSES	WELFARISM
WEENING	WEIDS	WEIRDO	WELFARISMS
WEENS	WEIGELA	WEIRDOES	WELFARIST
WEENSIER	WEIGELAS	WEIRDOS	WELFARISTIC
WEENSIEST	WEIGELIA	WEIRDS	WELFARISTS
WEENSY	WEIGELIAS	WEIRDY	WELK
WEENY	WEIGH	WEIRED	WELKE
WEEP	WEIGHABLE	WEIRING	WELKED
WEEPER	WEIGHAGE	WEIRS	WELKES
WEEPERS	WEIGHAGES	WEISE	WELKIN
WEEPHOLE	WEIGHBOARD	WEISED	WELKING
WEEPHOLES	WEIGHBOARDS	WEISENHEIMER	WELKINS
WEEPIE	WEIGHBRIDGE	WEISENHEIMERS	WELKS
WEEPIER	WEIGHBRIDGES	WEISES	WELKT
WEEPIES	WEIGHED	WEISING	WELL
WEEPIEST	WEIGHER	WEIZE	WELLADAY
WEEPILY	WEIGHERS	WEIZED	WELLADAYS

WELLANEAR
WELLAWAY
WELLAWAYS
WELLBEING
WELLBEINGS
WELLBORN
WELLCURB
WELLCURBS
WELLDOER
WELLDOERS
WELLED
WELLHEAD
WELLHEADS
WELLHOLE
WELLHOLES
WELLHOUSE
WELLHOUSES
WELLIE
WELLIES
WELLING
WELLINGS
WELLINGTON
WELLINGTONIA
WELLINGTONIAS
WELLINGTONS
WELLNESS
WELLNESSES
WELLS
WELLSITE
WELLSITES
WELLSPRING
WELLSPRINGS
WELLY
WELSH
WELSHED
WELSHER
WELSHERS
WELSHES
WELSHING
WELT
WELTANSCHAUUNG
WELTANSCHAUUNGS
WELTED
WELTER
WELTERED
WELTERING
WELTERS
WELTERWEIGHT
WELTERWEIGHTS
WELTING
WELTINGS
WELTS
WELTSCHMERZ
WELTSCHMERZES
WELWITSCHIA
WELWITSCHIAS
WEM

WEMB
WEMBS
WEMS
WEN
WENCH
WENCHED
WENCHER
WENCHERS
WENCHES
WENCHING
WEND
WENDED
WENDIGO
WENDIGOS
WENDING
WENDS
WENNIER
WENNIEST
WENNISH
WENNY
WENS
WENSLEYDALE
WENSLEYDALES
WENT
WENTLETRAP
WENTLETRAPS
WENTS
WEPT
WERE
WEREGILD
WEREGILDS
WEREWOLF
WEREWOLFERIES
WEREWOLFERY
WEREWOLFISH
WEREWOLFISM
WEREWOLFISMS
WEREWOLVES
WERGELD
WERGELDS
WERGELT
WERGELTS
WERGILD
WERGILDS
WERNERITE
WERNERITES
WERO
WERRIS
WERSH
WERSHER
WERSHEST
WERT
WERWOLF
WERWOLFISH
WERWOLVES
WESAND
WESANDS

WESKIT
WESKITS
WESSAND
WESSANDS
WEST
WESTBOUND
WESTED
WESTER
WESTERED
WESTERING
WESTERINGS
WESTERLIES
WESTERLINESS
WESTERLY
WESTERN
WESTERNER
WESTERNERS
WESTERNISATION
WESTERNISATIONS
WESTERNISE
WESTERNISED
WESTERNISES
WESTERNISING
WESTERNISM
WESTERNISMS
WESTERNIZATION
WESTERNIZATIONS
WESTERNIZE
WESTERNIZED
WESTERNIZES
WESTERNIZING
WESTERNMOST
WESTERNS
WESTERS
WESTING
WESTINGS
WESTLIN
WESTLINS
WESTMOST
WESTS
WESTWARD
WESTWARDLY
WESTWARDS
WET
WETA
WETAS
WETBACK
WETBACKS
WETHER
WETHERS
WETLAND
WETLANDS
WETLY
WETNESS
WETNESSES
WETPROOF
WETS

WETTABILITIES
WETTABILITY
WETTABLE
WETTED
WETTER
WETTERS
WETTEST
WETTIE
WETTIES
WETTING
WETTINGS
WETTISH
WETWARE
WETWARES
WEX
WEXE
WEXED
WEXES
WEXING
WEY
WEYARD
WEYS
WEYWARD
WEZAND
WEZANDS
WHA
WHACK
WHACKED
WHACKER
WHACKERS
WHACKIER
WHACKIEST
WHACKING
WHACKINGS
WHACKO
WHACKOES
WHACKOS
WHACKS
WHACKY
WHAE
WHAIKORERO
WHAISLE
WHAISLED
WHAISLES
WHAISLING
WHAIZLE
WHAIZLED
WHAIZLES
WHAIZLING
WHAKAIRO
WHAKAPAPA
WHAKAPAPAS
WHALE
WHALEBACK
WHALEBACKS
WHALEBOAT
WHALEBOATS

WHALEBONE	WHARFMASTERS	WHEECHS	WHEESH
WHALEBONES	WHARFS	WHEEDLE	WHEESHED
WHALED	WHARVE	WHEEDLED	WHEESHES
WHALELIKE	WHARVES	WHEEDLER	WHEESHING
WHALEMAN	WHAT	WHEEDLERS	WHEESHT
WHALEMEN	WHATA	WHEEDLES	WHEESHTED
WHALER	WHATABOUTS	WHEEDLESOME	WHEESHTING
WHALERIES	WHATCHAMACALLIT	WHEEDLING	WHEESHTS
WHALERS	WHATEN	WHEEDLINGLY	WHEEZE
WHALERY	WHATEVER	WHEEDLINGS	WHEEZED
WHALES	WHATNA	WHEEL	WHEEZER
WHALING	WHATNESS	WHEELBARROW	WHEEZERS
WHALINGS	WHATNESSES	WHEELBARROWED	WHEEZES
WHALLY	WHATNOT	WHEELBARROWING	WHEEZIER
WHAM	WHATNOTS	WHEELBARROWS	WHEEZIEST
WHAMMED	WHATS	WHEELBASE	WHEEZILY
WHAMMIES	WHATSHERNAME	WHEELBASES	WHEEZINESS
WHAMMING	WHATSHISNAME	WHEELCHAIR	WHEEZINESSES
WHAMMO	WHATSIS	WHEELCHAIRS	WHEEZING
WHAMMOS	WHATSISES	WHEELED	WHEEZINGS
WHAMMY	WHATSIT	WHEELER	WHEEZLE
WHAMO	WHATSITS	WHEELERS	WHEEZLED
WHAMPLE	WHATSITSNAME	WHEELHORSE	WHEEZLES
WHAMPLES	WHATSO	WHEELHORSES	WHEEZLING
WHAMS	WHATSOEVER	WHEELHOUSE	WHEEZY
WHANAU	WHATSOMEVER	WHEELHOUSES	WHEFT
WHANAUS	WHATTEN	WHEELIE	WHEFTS
WHANG	WHAUP	WHEELIER	WHELK
WHANGAM	WHAUPS	WHEELIES	WHELKED
WHANGAMS	WHAUR	WHEELIEST	WHELKIER
WHANGED	WHAURS	WHEELING	WHELKIEST
WHANGEE	WHEAL	WHEELINGS	WHELKS
WHANGEES	WHEALS	WHEELLESS	WHELKY
WHANGING	WHEAR	WHEELMAN	WHELM
WHANGS	WHEARE	WHEELMEN	WHELMED
WHAP	WHEAT	WHEELS	WHELMING
WHAPPED	WHEATEAR	WHEELSMAN	WHELMS
WHAPPER	WHEATEARS	WHEELSMEN	WHELP
WHAPPERS	WHEATEN	WHEELWORK	WHELPED
WHAPPING	WHEATENS	WHEELWORKS	WHELPING
WHAPS	WHEATFIELD	WHEELWRIGHT	WHELPS
WHARE	WHEATFIELDS	WHEELWRIGHTS	WHEMMLE
WHARENUI	WHEATGRASS	WHEELY	WHEMMLED
WHAREPUNI	WHEATIER	WHEEN	WHEMMLES
WHAREPUNIS	WHEATIEST	WHEENGE	WHEMMLING
WHARES	WHEATMEAL	WHEENGED	WHEN
WHARF	WHEATMEALS	WHEENGES	WHENAS
WHARFAGE	WHEATS	WHEENGING	WHENCE
WHARFAGES	WHEATSHEAF	WHEENS	WHENCEFORTH
WHARFED	WHEATSHEAVES	WHEEP	WHENCES
WHARFIE	WHEATWORM	WHEEPED	WHENCESOEVER
WHARFIES	WHEATWORMS	WHEEPING	WHENCEVER
WHARFING	WHEATY	WHEEPLE	WHENEVER
WHARFINGER	WHEE	WHEEPLED	WHENS
WHARFINGERS	WHEECH	WHEEPLES	WHENSOEVER
WHARFINGS	WHEECHED	WHEEPLING	WHENUA
WHARFMASTER	WHEECHING	WHEEPS	WHENWE

WHERE
WHEREABOUT
WHEREABOUTS
WHEREAFTER
WHEREAGAINST
WHEREAS
WHEREASES
WHEREAT
WHEREBY
WHEREFOR
WHEREFORE
WHEREFORES
WHEREFROM
WHEREIN
WHEREINSOEVER
WHEREINTO
WHERENESS
WHERENESSES
WHEREOF
WHEREON
WHEREOUT
WHERES
WHERESO
WHERESOEER
WHERESOEVER
WHERETHROUGH
WHERETO
WHEREUNDER
WHEREUNTIL
WHEREUNTO
WHEREUPON
WHEREVER
WHEREWITH
WHEREWITHAL
WHEREWITHALS
WHEREWITHS
WHERRET
WHERRETED
WHERRETING
WHERRETS
WHERRETTED
WHERRETTING
WHERRIED
WHERRIES
WHERRIT
WHERRITS
WHERRITTED
WHERRITTING
WHERRY
WHERRYING
WHERRYMAN
WHERRYMEN
WHERVE
WHERVES
WHET
WHETHER
WHETS

WHETSTONE
WHETSTONES
WHETTED
WHETTER
WHETTERS
WHETTING
WHEUGH
WHEUGHED
WHEUGHING
WHEUGHS
WHEW
WHEWED
WHEWELLITE
WHEWELLITES
WHEWING
WHEWS
WHEY
WHEYEY
WHEYFACE
WHEYFACED
WHEYFACES
WHEYIER
WHEYIEST
WHEYISH
WHEYISHNESS
WHEYISHNESSES
WHEYLIKE
WHEYS
WHICH
WHICHEVER
WHICHSOEVER
WHICKER
WHICKERED
WHICKERING
WHICKERS
WHID
WHIDAH
WHIDAHS
WHIDDED
WHIDDER
WHIDDERED
WHIDDERING
WHIDDERS
WHIDDING
WHIDS
WHIFF
WHIFFED
WHIFFER
WHIFFERS
WHIFFET
WHIFFETS
WHIFFIER
WHIFFIEST
WHIFFING
WHIFFINGS
WHIFFLE
WHIFFLED

WHIFFLER
WHIFFLERIES
WHIFFLERS
WHIFFLERY
WHIFFLES
WHIFFLETREE
WHIFFLETREES
WHIFFLING
WHIFFLINGS
WHIFFS
WHIFFY
WHIFT
WHIFTS
WHIG
WHIGGAMORE
WHIGGAMORES
WHIGGED
WHIGGING
WHIGMALEERIE
WHIGMALEERIES
WHIGMALEERY
WHIGS
WHILE
WHILED
WHILERE
WHILES
WHILING
WHILK
WHILLIED
WHILLIES
WHILLY
WHILLYING
WHILLYWHA
WHILLYWHAED
WHILLYWHAING
WHILLYWHAS
WHILLYWHAW
WHILLYWHAWED
WHILLYWHAWING
WHILLYWHAWS
WHILOM
WHILST
WHIM
WHIMBERRIES
WHIMBERRY
WHIMBREL
WHIMBRELS
WHIMMED
WHIMMIER
WHIMMIEST
WHIMMING
WHIMMY
WHIMPER
WHIMPERED
WHIMPERER
WHIMPERERS
WHIMPERING

WHIMPERINGLY
WHIMPERINGS
WHIMPERS
WHIMPLE
WHIMPLED
WHIMPLES
WHIMPLING
WHIMS
WHIMSEY
WHIMSEYS
WHIMSICAL
WHIMSICALITIES
WHIMSICALITY
WHIMSICALLY
WHIMSICALNESS
WHIMSICALNESSES
WHIMSIED
WHIMSIER
WHIMSIES
WHIMSIEST
WHIMSILY
WHIMSINESS
WHIMSINESSES
WHIMSY
WHIN
WHINBERRIES
WHINBERRY
WHINCHAT
WHINCHATS
WHINE
WHINED
WHINER
WHINERS
WHINES
WHINEY
WHINGE
WHINGED
WHINGEING
WHINGEINGS
WHINGER
WHINGERS
WHINGES
WHINGING
WHINIARD
WHINIARDS
WHINIER
WHINIEST
WHININESS
WHININESSES
WHINING
WHININGLY
WHININGS
WHINNIED
WHINNIER
WHINNIES
WHINNIEST
WHINNY

WHINNYING
WHINS
WHINSTONE
WHINSTONES
WHINY
WHINYARD
WHINYARDS
WHIP
WHIPBIRD
WHIPBIRDS
WHIPCAT
WHIPCATS
WHIPCORD
WHIPCORDS
WHIPCORDY
WHIPJACK
WHIPJACKS
WHIPLASH
WHIPLASHED
WHIPLASHES
WHIPLASHING
WHIPLIKE
WHIPPED
WHIPPER
WHIPPERS
WHIPPERSNAPPER
WHIPPERSNAPPERS
WHIPPET
WHIPPETING
WHIPPETINGS
WHIPPETS
WHIPPIER
WHIPPIEST
WHIPPINESS
WHIPPINESSES
WHIPPING
WHIPPINGS
WHIPPLETREE
WHIPPLETREES
WHIPPOORWILL
WHIPPOORWILLS
WHIPPY
WHIPRAY
WHIPRAYS
WHIPS
WHIPSAW
WHIPSAWED
WHIPSAWING
WHIPSAWN
WHIPSAWS
WHIPSTAFF
WHIPSTAFFS
WHIPSTALL
WHIPSTALLED
WHIPSTALLING
WHIPSTALLS
WHIPSTER

WHIPSTERS
WHIPSTITCH
WHIPSTITCHED
WHIPSTITCHES
WHIPSTITCHING
WHIPSTOCK
WHIPSTOCKS
WHIPT
WHIPTAIL
WHIPTAILED
WHIPTAILS
WHIPWORM
WHIPWORMS
WHIR
WHIRL
WHIRLABOUT
WHIRLABOUTS
WHIRLBAT
WHIRLBATS
WHIRLBLAST
WHIRLBLASTS
WHIRLED
WHIRLER
WHIRLERS
WHIRLIER
WHIRLIES
WHIRLIEST
WHIRLIGIG
WHIRLIGIGS
WHIRLING
WHIRLINGLY
WHIRLINGS
WHIRLPOOL
WHIRLPOOLS
WHIRLS
WHIRLWIND
WHIRLWINDS
WHIRLY
WHIRLYBIRD
WHIRLYBIRDS
WHIRR
WHIRRED
WHIRRET
WHIRRETED
WHIRRETING
WHIRRETS
WHIRRIED
WHIRRIES
WHIRRING
WHIRRINGS
WHIRRS
WHIRRY
WHIRRYING
WHIRS
WHIRTLE
WHIRTLES
WHISH

WHISHED
WHISHES
WHISHING
WHISHT
WHISHTED
WHISHTING
WHISHTS
WHISK
WHISKED
WHISKER
WHISKERANDO
WHISKERANDOED
WHISKERANDOS
WHISKERED
WHISKERS
WHISKERY
WHISKET
WHISKETS
WHISKEY
WHISKEYFIED
WHISKEYS
WHISKIES
WHISKIFIED
WHISKING
WHISKS
WHISKY
WHISPER
WHISPERED
WHISPERER
WHISPERERS
WHISPERING
WHISPERINGLY
WHISPERINGS
WHISPEROUSLY
WHISPERS
WHISPERY
WHISS
WHISSED
WHISSES
WHISSING
WHIST
WHISTED
WHISTING
WHISTLE
WHISTLEABLE
WHISTLED
WHISTLER
WHISTLERS
WHISTLES
WHISTLING
WHISTLINGLY
WHISTLINGS
WHISTS
WHIT
WHITE
WHITEBAIT
WHITEBAITS

WHITEBASS
WHITEBASSES
WHITEBEAM
WHITEBEAMS
WHITEBEARD
WHITEBEARDS
WHITEBOARD
WHITEBOARDS
WHITEBOYISM
WHITEBOYISMS
WHITECAP
WHITECAPS
WHITECOAT
WHITECOATS
WHITED
WHITEDAMP
WHITEFACE
WHITEFACES
WHITEFISH
WHITEFISHES
WHITEFLIES
WHITEFLY
WHITEHEAD
WHITEHEADS
WHITELY
WHITEN
WHITENED
WHITENER
WHITENERS
WHITENESS
WHITENESSES
WHITENING
WHITENINGS
WHITENS
WHITEOUT
WHITEOUTS
WHITEPOT
WHITEPOTS
WHITER
WHITES
WHITESMITH
WHITESMITHS
WHITEST
WHITETAIL
WHITETAILS
WHITETHORN
WHITETHORNS
WHITETHROAT
WHITETHROATS
WHITEWALL
WHITEWALLS
WHITEWARE
WHITEWARES
WHITEWASH
WHITEWASHED
WHITEWASHER
WHITEWASHERS

WHITEWASHES	WHITTRETS	WHOLIST	WHORED
WHITEWASHING	WHITY	WHOLISTIC	WHOREDOM
WHITEWASHINGS	WHIZ	WHOLISTS	WHOREDOMS
WHITEWING	WHIZBANG	WHOLLY	WHOREHOUSE
WHITEWINGS	WHIZBANGS	WHOM	WHOREHOUSES
WHITEWOOD	WHIZZ	WHOMBLE	WHOREMASTER
WHITEWOODS	WHIZZBANG	WHOMBLED	WHOREMASTERLY
WHITEY	WHIZZBANGS	WHOMBLES	WHOREMASTERS
WHITEYS	WHIZZED	WHOMBLING	WHOREMASTERY
WHITHER	WHIZZER	WHOMEVER	WHOREMISTRESS
WHITHERED	WHIZZERS	WHOMMLE	WHOREMISTRESSES
WHITHERING	WHIZZES	WHOMMLED	WHOREMONGER
WHITHERS	WHIZZIER	WHOMMLES	WHOREMONGERS
WHITHERSOEVER	WHIZZIEST	WHOMMLING	WHOREMONGERY
WHITHERWARD	WHIZZING	WHOMP	WHORES
WHITHERWARDS	WHIZZINGLY	WHOMPED	WHORESON
WHITIER	WHIZZINGS	WHOMPING	WHORESONS
WHITIES	WHIZZY	WHOMPS	WHORING
WHITIEST	WHO	WHOMSO	WHORISH
WHITING	WHOA	WHOMSOEVER	WHORISHLY
WHITINGS	WHODUNIT	WHOOBUB	WHORISHNESS
WHITISH	WHODUNITRIES	WHOOBUBS	WHORISHNESSES
WHITISHNESS	WHODUNITRY	WHOOF	WHORL
WHITISHNESSES	WHODUNITS	WHOOFED	WHORLBAT
WHITLEATHER	WHODUNNIT	WHOOFING	WHORLBATS
WHITLEATHERS	WHODUNNITRIES	WHOOFS	WHORLED
WHITLING	WHODUNNITRY	WHOOP	WHORLS
WHITLINGS	WHODUNNITS	WHOOPED	WHORT
WHITLOW	WHOEVER	WHOOPEE	WHORTLE
WHITLOWS	WHOLE	WHOOPEES	WHORTLEBERRIES
WHITRACK	WHOLEFOOD	WHOOPER	WHORTLEBERRY
WHITRACKS	WHOLEFOODS	WHOOPERS	WHORTLES
WHITRET	WHOLEGRAIN	WHOOPING	WHORTS
WHITRETS	WHOLEHEARTED	WHOOPINGS	WHOSE
WHITRICK	WHOLEHEARTEDLY	WHOOPLA	WHOSESOEVER
WHITRICKS	WHOLEMEAL	WHOOPLAS	WHOSEVER
WHITS	WHOLEMEALS	WHOOPS	WHOSIS
WHITSTER	WHOLENESS	WHOOPSIE	WHOSISES
WHITSTERS	WHOLENESSES	WHOOPSIES	WHOSO
WHITTAW	WHOLES	WHOOSH	WHOSOEVER
WHITTAWER	WHOLESALE	WHOOSHED	WHOT
WHITTAWERS	WHOLESALED	WHOOSHES	WHOW
WHITTAWS	WHOLESALER	WHOOSHING	WHUMMLE
WHITTER	WHOLESALERS	WHOOSIS	WHUMMLED
WHITTERED	WHOLESALES	WHOOSISES	WHUMMLES
WHITTERICK	WHOLESALING	WHOOT	WHUMMLING
WHITTERICKS	WHOLESOME	WHOOTED	WHUMP
WHITTERING	WHOLESOMELY	WHOOTING	WHUMPED
WHITTERS	WHOLESOMENESS	WHOOTS	WHUMPING
WHITTLE	WHOLESOMENESSES	WHOP	WHUMPS
WHITTLED	WHOLESOMER	WHOPPED	WHUNSTANE
WHITTLER	WHOLESOMEST	WHOPPER	WHUNSTANES
WHITTLERS	WHOLESTITCH	WHOPPERS	WHUP
WHITTLES	WHOLESTITCHES	WHOPPING	WHUPPED
WHITTLING	WHOLEWHEAT	WHOPPINGS	WHUPPING
WHITTLINGS	WHOLISM	WHOPS	WHUPS
WHITTRET	WHOLISMS	WHORE	WHY

WHYDAH
WHYDAHS
WHYDUNIT
WHYDUNITS
WHYDUNNIT
WHYDUNNITS
WHYEVER
WHYS
WIBBLE
WIBBLED
WIBBLES
WIBBLING
WICCA
WICCAN
WICCANS
WICCAS
WICE
WICH
WICHES
WICK
WICKAPE
WICKAPES
WICKED
WICKEDER
WICKEDEST
WICKEDLY
WICKEDNESS
WICKEDNESSES
WICKEDS
WICKEN
WICKENS
WICKER
WICKERED
WICKERS
WICKERWORK
WICKERWORKS
WICKET
WICKETKEEPER
WICKETKEEPERS
WICKETKEEPING
WICKETS
WICKIES
WICKING
WICKINGS
WICKIUP
WICKIUPS
WICKS
WICKTHING
WICKTHINGS
WICKY
WICKYUP
WICKYUPS
WICOPIES
WICOPY
WIDDER
WIDDERS
WIDDERSHINS

WIDDIE
WIDDIES
WIDDLE
WIDDLED
WIDDLES
WIDDLING
WIDDY
WIDE
WIDEAWAKE
WIDEAWAKES
WIDEBAND
WIDEBODY
WIDELY
WIDEMOUTHED
WIDEN
WIDENED
WIDENER
WIDENERS
WIDENESS
WIDENESSES
WIDENING
WIDENS
WIDEOUT
WIDEOUTS
WIDER
WIDERSHINS
WIDES
WIDESCREEN
WIDESPREAD
WIDEST
WIDGEON
WIDGEONS
WIDGET
WIDGETS
WIDGIE
WIDGIES
WIDISH
WIDOW
WIDOWED
WIDOWER
WIDOWERHOOD
WIDOWERHOODS
WIDOWERS
WIDOWHOOD
WIDOWHOODS
WIDOWING
WIDOWMAN
WIDOWMEN
WIDOWS
WIDTH
WIDTHS
WIDTHWAY
WIDTHWAYS
WIDTHWISE
WIEL
WIELD
WIELDABLE

WIELDED
WIELDER
WIELDERS
WIELDIER
WIELDIEST
WIELDINESS
WIELDINESSES
WIELDING
WIELDLESS
WIELDS
WIELDY
WIELS
WIENER
WIENERS
WIENERWURST
WIENERWURSTS
WIENIE
WIENIES
WIFE
WIFED
WIFEDOM
WIFEDOMS
WIFEHOOD
WIFEHOODS
WIFELESS
WIFELIER
WIFELIEST
WIFELIKE
WIFELINESS
WIFELINESSES
WIFELY
WIFES
WIFIE
WIFIES
WIFING
WIFTIER
WIFTIEST
WIFTY
WIG
WIGAN
WIGANS
WIGEON
WIGEONS
WIGGA
WIGGED
WIGGER
WIGGERIES
WIGGERY
WIGGIER
WIGGIEST
WIGGING
WIGGINGS
WIGGLE
WIGGLED
WIGGLER
WIGGLERS
WIGGLES

WIGGLIER
WIGGLIEST
WIGGLING
WIGGLY
WIGGY
WIGHT
WIGHTED
WIGHTING
WIGHTLY
WIGHTS
WIGLESS
WIGLET
WIGLETS
WIGLIKE
WIGMAKER
WIGMAKERS
WIGS
WIGWAG
WIGWAGGED
WIGWAGGER
WIGWAGGERS
WIGWAGGING
WIGWAGS
WIGWAM
WIGWAMS
WIKIUP
WIKIUPS
WILCO
WILD
WILDCAT
WILDCATS
WILDCATTED
WILDCATTER
WILDCATTERS
WILDCATTING
WILDEBEEST
WILDEBEESTS
WILDED
WILDER
WILDERED
WILDERING
WILDERMENT
WILDERMENTS
WILDERNESS
WILDERNESSES
WILDERS
WILDEST
WILDFIRE
WILDFIRES
WILDFLOWER
WILDFLOWERS
WILDFOWL
WILDFOWLER
WILDFOWLERS
WILDFOWLING
WILDFOWLINGS
WILDFOWLS

WILDGRAVE	WILLIES	WIMPISH	WINDBREAKERS
WILDGRAVES	WILLIEWAUGHT	WIMPISHLY	WINDBREAKS
WILDING	WILLIEWAUGHTS	WIMPISHNESS	WINDBURN
WILDINGS	WILLING	WIMPISHNESSES	WINDBURNED
WILDISH	WILLINGER	WIMPLE	WINDBURNING
WILDLAND	WILLINGEST	WIMPLED	WINDBURNS
WILDLANDS	WILLINGLY	WIMPLES	WINDBURNT
WILDLIFE	WILLINGNESS	WIMPLING	WINDCHEATER
WILDLIFES	WILLINGNESSES	WIMPS	WINDCHEATERS
WILDLING	WILLIWAU	WIMPY	WINDCHILL
WILDLINGS	WILLIWAUS	WIN	WINDCHILLS
WILDLY	WILLIWAW	WINCE	WINDED
WILDNESS	WILLIWAWS	WINCED	WINDER
WILDNESSES	WILLOW	WINCER	WINDERS
WILDS	WILLOWED	WINCERS	WINDFALL
WILDWOOD	WILLOWER	WINCES	WINDFALLEN
WILDWOODS	WILLOWERS	WINCEY	WINDFALLS
WILE	WILLOWHERB	WINCEYETTE	WINDFLAW
WILED	WILLOWHERBS	WINCEYETTES	WINDFLAWS
WILEFUL	WILLOWIER	WINCEYS	WINDFLOWER
WILES	WILLOWIEST	WINCH	WINDFLOWERS
WILFUL	WILLOWING	WINCHED	WINDGALL
WILFULLY	WILLOWISH	WINCHER	WINDGALLED
WILFULNESS	WILLOWLIKE	WINCHERS	WINDGALLS
WILFULNESSES	WILLOWS	WINCHES	WINDGUN
WILGA	WILLOWWARE	WINCHESTER	WINDGUNS
WILGAS	WILLOWWARES	WINCHESTERS	WINDHOVER
WILI	WILLOWY	WINCHING	WINDHOVERS
WILIER	WILLPOWER	WINCHMAN	WINDIER
WILIEST	WILLPOWERS	WINCHMEN	WINDIEST
WILILY	WILLS	WINCING	WINDIGO
WILINESS	WILLY	WINCINGS	WINDIGOS
WILINESSES	WILLYARD	WINCOPIPE	WINDILY
WILING	WILLYART	WINCOPIPES	WINDINESS
WILIS	WILLYING	WIND	WINDINESSES
WILJA	WILLYWAW	WINDABLE	WINDING
WILJAS	WILLYWAWS	WINDAC	WINDINGLY
WILL	WILT	WINDACS	WINDINGS
WILLABLE	WILTED	WINDAGE	WINDJAMMER
WILLED	WILTING	WINDAGES	WINDJAMMERS
WILLEMITE	WILTJA	WINDAS	WINDJAMMING
WILLEMITES	WILTJAS	WINDASES	WINDJAMMINGS
WILLER	WILTS	WINDBAG	WINDLASS
WILLERS	WILY	WINDBAGGERIES	WINDLASSED
WILLEST	WIMBLE	WINDBAGGERY	WINDLASSES
WILLET	WIMBLED	WINDBAGS	WINDLASSING
WILLETS	WIMBLES	WINDBILL	WINDLE
WILLEY	WIMBLING	WINDBILLS	WINDLED
WILLEYED	WIMBREL	WINDBLAST	WINDLES
WILLEYING	WIMBRELS	WINDBLASTS	WINDLESS
WILLEYS	WIMP	WINDBLOW	WINDLESSLY
WILLFUL	WIMPED	WINDBLOWN	WINDLESSNESS
WILLFULLY	WIMPIER	WINDBLOWS	WINDLESTRAE
WILLFULNESS	WIMPIEST	WINDBORNE	WINDLESTRAES
WILLFULNESSES	WIMPINESS	WINDBOUND	WINDLESTRAW
WILLIE	WIMPINESSES	WINDBREAK	WINDLESTRAWS
WILLIED	WIMPING	WINDBREAKER	WINDLING

WINDLINGS
WINDMILL
WINDMILLED
WINDMILLING
WINDMILLS
WINDOCK
WINDOCKS
WINDORE
WINDORES
WINDOW
WINDOWED
WINDOWING
WINDOWINGS
WINDOWLESS
WINDOWPANE
WINDOWPANES
WINDOWS
WINDOWSILL
WINDOWSILLS
WINDPIPE
WINDPIPES
WINDPROOF
WINDRING
WINDROSE
WINDROSES
WINDROW
WINDROWED
WINDROWER
WINDROWERS
WINDROWING
WINDROWS
WINDS
WINDSAIL
WINDSAILS
WINDSCREEN
WINDSCREENS
WINDSES
WINDSHAKE
WINDSHAKES
WINDSHIELD
WINDSHIELDS
WINDSHIP
WINDSHIPS
WINDSOCK
WINDSOCKS
WINDSTORM
WINDSTORMS
WINDSUCKER
WINDSUCKERS
WINDSURF
WINDSURFED
WINDSURFER
WINDSURFERS
WINDSURFING
WINDSURFINGS
WINDSURFS
WINDSWEPT

WINDTHROW
WINDTHROWS
WINDTIGHT
WINDUP
WINDUPS
WINDWARD
WINDWARDS
WINDWAY
WINDWAYS
WINDY
WINE
WINEBERRIES
WINEBERRY
WINEBIBBER
WINEBIBBERS
WINEBIBBING
WINEBIBBINGS
WINED
WINEGLASS
WINEGLASSES
WINEGLASSFUL
WINEGLASSFULS
WINEGROWER
WINEGROWERS
WINELESS
WINEPRESS
WINEPRESSES
WINERIES
WINERY
WINES
WINESHOP
WINESHOPS
WINESKIN
WINESKINS
WINESOP
WINESOPS
WINEY
WING
WINGBACK
WINGBACKS
WINGBEAT
WINGBEATS
WINGBOW
WINGBOWS
WINGDING
WINGDINGS
WINGE
WINGED
WINGEDLY
WINGEING
WINGER
WINGERS
WINGES
WINGIER
WINGIEST
WINGING
WINGLESS

WINGLESSNESS
WINGLESSNESSES
WINGLET
WINGLETS
WINGLIKE
WINGMAN
WINGMEN
WINGOVER
WINGOVERS
WINGS
WINGSPAN
WINGSPANS
WINGSPREAD
WINGSPREADS
WINGTIP
WINGTIPS
WINGY
WINIER
WINIEST
WINING
WINISH
WINK
WINKED
WINKER
WINKERS
WINKING
WINKINGLY
WINKINGS
WINKLE
WINKLED
WINKLER
WINKLERS
WINKLES
WINKLING
WINKS
WINLESS
WINN
WINNA
WINNABILITIES
WINNABILITY
WINNABLE
WINNARD
WINNARDS
WINNED
WINNER
WINNERS
WINNING
WINNINGLY
WINNINGNESS
WINNINGNESSES
WINNINGS
WINNLE
WINNLES
WINNOCK
WINNOCKS
WINNOW
WINNOWED

WINNOWER
WINNOWERS
WINNOWING
WINNOWINGS
WINNOWS
WINNS
WINO
WINOES
WINOS
WINS
WINSEY
WINSEYS
WINSOME
WINSOMELY
WINSOMENESS
WINSOMENESSES
WINSOMER
WINSOMEST
WINTER
WINTERBERRIES
WINTERBERRY
WINTERBOURNE
WINTERBOURNES
WINTERCRESS
WINTERCRESSES
WINTERED
WINTERER
WINTERERS
WINTERFED
WINTERFEED
WINTERFEEDING
WINTERFEEDS
WINTERGREEN
WINTERGREENS
WINTERIER
WINTERIEST
WINTERINESS
WINTERING
WINTERISATION
WINTERISATIONS
WINTERISE
WINTERISED
WINTERISES
WINTERISH
WINTERISING
WINTERIZATION
WINTERIZATIONS
WINTERIZE
WINTERIZED
WINTERIZES
WINTERIZING
WINTERKILL
WINTERKILLED
WINTERKILLING
WINTERKILLS
WINTERLESS
WINTERLINESS

WINTERLY	WIREPULLING	WISELIEST	WISTERIAS
WINTERS	WIREPULLINGS	WISELING	WISTFUL
WINTERTIDE	WIRER	WISELINGS	WISTFULLY
WINTERTIDES	WIRERS	WISELY	WISTFULNESS
WINTERTIME	WIRES	WISENESS	WISTFULNESSES
WINTERTIMES	WIRETAP	WISENESSES	WISTING
WINTERWEIGHT	WIRETAPPED	WISENHEIMER	WISTITI
WINTERY	WIRETAPPER	WISENHEIMERS	WISTITIS
WINTLE	WIRETAPPERS	WISENT	WISTLY
WINTLED	WIRETAPPING	WISENTS	WISTS
WINTLES	WIRETAPS	WISER	WIT
WINTLING	WIRETRAPPING	WISES	WITAN
WINTRIER	WIREWALKER	WISEST	WITANS
WINTRIEST	WIREWALKERS	WISEWOMAN	WITBLITS
WINTRILY	WIREWAY	WISEWOMEN	WITBLITSES
WINTRINESS	WIREWAYS	WISH	WITCH
WINTRINESSES	WIREWORK	WISHA	WITCHBROOM
WINTRY	WIREWORKER	WISHBONE	WITCHBROOMS
WINY	WIREWORKERS	WISHBONES	WITCHCRAFT
WINZE	WIREWORKING	WISHED	WITCHCRAFTS
WINZES	WIREWORKINGS	WISHER	WITCHED
WIPE	WIREWORKS	WISHERS	WITCHEN
WIPED	WIREWORM	WISHES	WITCHENS
WIPEOUT	WIREWORMS	WISHFUL	WITCHERIES
WIPEOUTS	WIREWOVE	WISHFULLY	WITCHERY
WIPER	WIRIER	WISHFULNESS	WITCHES
WIPERS	WIRIEST	WISHFULNESSES	WITCHETIES
WIPES	WIRILDA	WISHING	WITCHETTIES
WIPING	WIRILY	WISHINGS	WITCHETTY
WIPINGS	WIRINESS	WISHLESS	WITCHETY
WIPPEN	WIRINESSES	WISHT	WITCHGRASS
WIPPENS	WIRING	WISHTONWISH	WITCHGRASSES
WIRABLE	WIRINGS	WISHTONWISHES	WITCHIER
WIRE	WIRRA	WISING	WITCHIEST
WIRED	WIRRAH	WISKET	WITCHING
WIREDRAW	WIRRAHS	WISKETS	WITCHINGLY
WIREDRAWER	WIRRICOW	WISP	WITCHINGS
WIREDRAWERS	WIRRICOWS	WISPED	WITCHKNOT
WIREDRAWING	WIRY	WISPIER	WITCHKNOTS
WIREDRAWINGS	WIS	WISPIEST	WITCHLIKE
WIREDRAWN	WISARD	WISPILY	WITCHMEALS
WIREDRAWS	WISARDS	WISPINESS	WITCHWEED
WIREDREW	WISDOM	WISPINESSES	WITCHWEEDS
WIREHAIR	WISDOMS	WISPING	WITCHY
WIREHAIRED	WISE	WISPISH	WITE
WIREHAIRS	WISEACRE	WISPLIKE	WITED
WIRELESS	WISEACRES	WISPS	WITELESS
WIRELESSED	WISEASS	WISPY	WITENAGEMOT
WIRELESSES	WISEASSES	WISS	WITENAGEMOTE
WIRELESSING	WISECRACK	WISSED	WITENAGEMOTES
WIRELIKE	WISECRACKED	WISSES	WITENAGEMOTS
WIREMAN	WISECRACKER	WISSING	WITES
WIREMEN	WISECRACKERS	WIST	WITGAT
WIREPHOTO	WISECRACKING	WISTARIA	WITGATBOOM
WIREPHOTOS	WISECRACKS	WISTARIAS	WITGATBOOMS
WIREPULLER	WISED	WISTED	WITGATS
WIREPULLERS	WISELIER	WISTERIA	WITH

WITHAL
WITHDRAW
WITHDRAWABLE
WITHDRAWAL
WITHDRAWALS
WITHDRAWER
WITHDRAWERS
WITHDRAWING
WITHDRAWMENT
WITHDRAWMENTS
WITHDRAWN
WITHDRAWNNESS
WITHDRAWNNESSES
WITHDRAWS
WITHDREW
WITHE
WITHED
WITHER
WITHERED
WITHEREDNESS
WITHEREDNESSES
WITHERER
WITHERERS
WITHERING
WITHERINGLY
WITHERINGS
WITHERITE
WITHERITES
WITHERS
WITHERSHINS
WITHES
WITHHAULT
WITHHELD
WITHHOLD
WITHHOLDEN
WITHHOLDER
WITHHOLDERS
WITHHOLDING
WITHHOLDMENT
WITHHOLDMENTS
WITHHOLDS
WITHIER
WITHIES
WITHIEST
WITHIN
WITHINDOORS
WITHING
WITHINS
WITHOUT
WITHOUTDOORS
WITHOUTEN
WITHOUTS
WITHS
WITHSTAND
WITHSTANDER
WITHSTANDERS
WITHSTANDING

WITHSTANDS
WITHSTOOD
WITHWIND
WITHWINDS
WITHY
WITHYWIND
WITHYWINDS
WITING
WITLESS
WITLESSLY
WITLESSNESS
WITLESSNESSES
WITLING
WITLINGS
WITLOOF
WITLOOFS
WITNESS
WITNESSABLE
WITNESSED
WITNESSER
WITNESSERS
WITNESSES
WITNESSING
WITNEY
WITNEYS
WITS
WITTED
WITTER
WITTERED
WITTERING
WITTERS
WITTICISM
WITTICISMS
WITTIER
WITTIEST
WITTILY
WITTINESS
WITTINESSES
WITTING
WITTINGLY
WITTINGS
WITTOL
WITTOLLY
WITTOLS
WITTY
WITWALL
WITWALLS
WITWANTON
WITWANTONED
WITWANTONING
WITWANTONS
WIVE
WIVED
WIVEHOOD
WIVEHOODS
WIVER
WIVERN

WIVERNS
WIVERS
WIVES
WIVING
WIZ
WIZARD
WIZARDLY
WIZARDRIES
WIZARDRY
WIZARDS
WIZEN
WIZENED
WIZENING
WIZENS
WIZES
WIZIER
WIZIERS
WIZZEN
WIZZENS
WIZZES
WO
WOAD
WOADED
WOADS
WOADWAX
WOADWAXEN
WOADWAXENS
WOADWAXES
WOALD
WOALDS
WOBBEGONG
WOBBEGONGS
WOBBLE
WOBBLED
WOBBLER
WOBBLERS
WOBBLES
WOBBLIER
WOBBLIES
WOBBLIEST
WOBBLINESS
WOBBLINESSES
WOBBLING
WOBBLINGS
WOBBLY
WOBEGONE
WOCK
WOCKS
WODGE
WODGES
WOE
WOEBEGONE
WOEBEGONENESS
WOEBEGONENESSES
WOEFUL
WOEFULLER
WOEFULLEST

WOEFULLY
WOEFULNESS
WOEFULNESSES
WOENESS
WOENESSES
WOES
WOESOME
WOF
WOFUL
WOFULLY
WOFULNESS
WOFULNESSES
WOG
WOGGLE
WOGGLES
WOGS
WOIWODE
WOIWODES
WOK
WOKE
WOKEN
WOKKA
WOKS
WOLD
WOLDS
WOLF
WOLFBERRIES
WOLFBERRY
WOLFED
WOLFER
WOLFERS
WOLFFISH
WOLFFISHES
WOLFHOUND
WOLFHOUNDS
WOLFING
WOLFINGS
WOLFISH
WOLFISHLY
WOLFISHNESS
WOLFISHNESSES
WOLFKIN
WOLFKINS
WOLFLIKE
WOLFLING
WOLFLINGS
WOLFRAM
WOLFRAMITE
WOLFRAMITES
WOLFRAMS
WOLFS
WOLFSBANE
WOLFSBANES
WOLFSKIN
WOLFSKINS
WOLLASTONITE
WOLLASTONITES

WOLLIES	WOMBS	WONNER	WOODCUTTING
WOLLY	WOMBY	WONNERS	WOODCUTTINGS
WOLVE	WOMEN	WONNING	WOODED
WOLVED	WOMENFOLK	WONNINGS	WOODEN
WOLVER	WOMENFOLKS	WONS	WOODENED
WOLVERENE	WOMENKIND	WONT	WOODENER
WOLVERENES	WOMENKINDS	WONTED	WOODENEST
WOLVERINE	WOMENSWEAR	WONTEDLY	WOODENHEAD
WOLVERINES	WOMENSWEARS	WONTEDNESS	WOODENHEADED
WOLVERS	WOMERA	WONTEDNESSES	WOODENHEADS
WOLVES	WOMERAS	WONTING	WOODENING
WOLVING	WOMMERA	WONTLESS	WOODENLY
WOLVINGS	WOMMERAS	WONTON	WOODENNESS
WOLVISH	WOMMIT	WONTONS	WOODENNESSES
WOLVISHLY	WON	WONTS	WOODENS
WOMAN	WONDER	WOO	WOODENTOP
WOMANED	WONDERED	WOOBUT	WOODENTOPS
WOMANFULLY	WONDERER	WOOBUTS	WOODENWARE
WOMANHOOD	WONDERERS	WOOD	WOODENWARES
WOMANHOODS	WONDERFUL	WOODBIN	WOODFREE
WOMANING	WONDERFULLY	WOODBIND	WOODGROUSE
WOMANISE	WONDERFULNESS	WOODBINDS	WOODGROUSES
WOMANISED	WONDERFULNESSES	WOODBINE	WOODHEN
WOMANISER	WONDERING	WOODBINES	WOODHENS
WOMANISERS	WONDERINGLY	WOODBINS	WOODHOLE
WOMANISES	WONDERINGS	WOODBLOCK	WOODHOLES
WOMANISH	WONDERLAND	WOODBLOCKS	WOODHORSE
WOMANISHLY	WONDERLANDS	WOODBORER	WOODHORSES
WOMANISHNESS	WONDERLESS	WOODBORERS	WOODHOUSE
WOMANISHNESSES	WONDERMENT	WOODBOX	WOODHOUSES
WOMANISING	WONDERMENTS	WOODBOXES	WOODIE
WOMANIZE	WONDERMONGER	WOODBURYTYPE	WOODIER
WOMANIZED	WONDERMONGERING	WOODBURYTYPES	WOODIES
WOMANIZER	WONDERMONGERS	WOODCARVER	WOODIEST
WOMANIZERS	WONDEROUS	WOODCARVERS	WOODINESS
WOMANIZES	WONDERS	WOODCARVING	WOODINESSES
WOMANIZING	WONDERWORK	WOODCARVINGS	WOODING
WOMANKIND	WONDERWORKS	WOODCHAT	WOODLAND
WOMANKINDS	WONDRED	WOODCHATS	WOODLANDER
WOMANLESS	WONDROUS	WOODCHIP	WOODLANDERS
WOMANLIER	WONDROUSLY	WOODCHIPS	WOODLANDS
WOMANLIEST	WONDROUSNESS	WOODCHOP	WOODLARK
WOMANLIKE	WONDROUSNESSES	WOODCHOPPER	WOODLARKS
WOMANLINESS	WONGA	WOODCHOPPERS	WOODLESS
WOMANLINESSES	WONGAS	WOODCHOPS	WOODLESSNESS
WOMANLY	WONGI	WOODCHUCK	WOODLESSNESSES
WOMANPOWER	WONGIED	WOODCHUCKS	WOODLICE
WOMANPOWERS	WONGIING	WOODCOCK	WOODLORE
WOMANS	WONGIS	WOODCOCKS	WOODLORES
WOMB	WONING	WOODCRAFT	WOODLOT
WOMBAT	WONINGS	WOODCRAFTS	WOODLOTS
WOMBATS	WONK	WOODCRAFTSMAN	WOODLOUSE
WOMBED	WONKIER	WOODCRAFTSMEN	WOODMAN
WOMBIER	WONKIEST	WOODCUT	WOODMEAL
WOMBIEST	WONKS	WOODCUTS	WOODMEALS
WOMBING	WONKY	WOODCUTTER	WOODMEN
WOMBLIKE	WONNED	WOODCUTTERS	WOODMICE

WOODMOUSE
WOODNESS
WOODNESSES
WOODNOTE
WOODNOTES
WOODPECKER
WOODPECKERS
WOODPIGEON
WOODPIGEONS
WOODPILE
WOODPILES
WOODPRINT
WOODPRINTS
WOODREEVE
WOODREEVES
WOODROOF
WOODROOFS
WOODRUFF
WOODRUFFS
WOODRUSH
WOODRUSHES
WOODS
WOODSCREW
WOODSCREWS
WOODSHED
WOODSHEDDED
WOODSHEDDING
WOODSHEDDINGS
WOODSHEDS
WOODSHOCK
WOODSHOCKS
WOODSHRIKE
WOODSHRIKES
WOODSIA
WOODSIAS
WOODSIER
WOODSIEST
WOODSKIN
WOODSKINS
WOODSMAN
WOODSMEN
WOODSPITE
WOODSPITES
WOODSTONE
WOODSTONES
WOODSTOVE
WOODSTOVES
WOODSWALLOW
WOODSWALLOWS
WOODSY
WOODTHRUSH
WOODTHRUSHES
WOODWALE
WOODWALES
WOODWARD
WOODWARDS
WOODWAX

WOODWAXEN
WOODWAXENS
WOODWAXES
WOODWIND
WOODWINDS
WOODWORK
WOODWORKER
WOODWORKERS
WOODWORKING
WOODWORKINGS
WOODWORKS
WOODWORM
WOODWORMS
WOODWOSE
WOODWOSES
WOODY
WOODYARD
WOODYARDS
WOOED
WOOER
WOOERS
WOOF
WOOFED
WOOFER
WOOFERS
WOOFIER
WOOFIEST
WOOFING
WOOFS
WOOFTER
WOOFTERS
WOOFY
WOOING
WOOINGLY
WOOINGS
WOOL
WOOLD
WOOLDED
WOOLDER
WOOLDERS
WOOLDING
WOOLDINGS
WOOLDS
WOOLED
WOOLEN
WOOLENS
WOOLER
WOOLERS
WOOLFAT
WOOLFATS
WOOLFELL
WOOLFELLS
WOOLGATHERER
WOOLGATHERERS
WOOLGATHERING
WOOLGATHERINGS
WOOLGROWER

WOOLGROWERS
WOOLGROWING
WOOLHAT
WOOLHATS
WOOLIE
WOOLIER
WOOLIES
WOOLIEST
WOOLLED
WOOLLEN
WOOLLENS
WOOLLIER
WOOLLIES
WOOLLIEST
WOOLLIKE
WOOLLILY
WOOLLINESS
WOOLLINESSES
WOOLLY
WOOLLYBACK
WOOLLYBACKS
WOOLLYBUTT
WOOLLYBUTTS
WOOLLYFOOT
WOOLLYFOOTS
WOOLMAN
WOOLMEN
WOOLPACK
WOOLPACKS
WOOLS
WOOLSACK
WOOLSACKS
WOOLSEY
WOOLSEYS
WOOLSHED
WOOLSHEDS
WOOLSKIN
WOOLSKINS
WOOLSORTER
WOOLSORTERS
WOOLWARD
WOOLWORK
WOOLWORKS
WOOLY
WOOMERA
WOOMERANG
WOOMERANGS
WOOMERAS
WOON
WOONED
WOONING
WOONS
WOOPIE
WOOPIES
WOOPS
WOOPSED
WOOPSES

WOOPSING
WOORALI
WOORALIS
WOORARA
WOORARAS
WOORARI
WOORARIS
WOOS
WOOSEL
WOOSELL
WOOSELLS
WOOSELS
WOOSH
WOOSHED
WOOSHES
WOOSHING
WOOT
WOOTZ
WOOTZES
WOOZIER
WOOZIEST
WOOZILY
WOOZINESS
WOOZINESSES
WOOZY
WOP
WOPPED
WOPPING
WOPS
WORCESTER
WORCESTERBERRY
WORCESTERS
WORD
WORDAGE
WORDAGES
WORDBOOK
WORDBOOKS
WORDBOUND
WORDBREAK
WORDBREAKS
WORDED
WORDGAME
WORDGAMES
WORDIER
WORDIEST
WORDILY
WORDINESS
WORDINESSES
WORDING
WORDINGS
WORDISH
WORDISHNESS
WORDISHNESSES
WORDLESS
WORDLESSLY
WORDLESSNESS
WORDLESSNESSES

WORDLORE
WORDLORES
WORDMONGER
WORDMONGERS
WORDPLAY
WORDPLAYS
WORDS
WORDSEARCH
WORDSMITH
WORDSMITHERIES
WORDSMITHERY
WORDSMITHS
WORDY
WORE
WORK
WORKABILITIES
WORKABILITY
WORKABLE
WORKABLENESS
WORKABLENESSES
WORKADAY
WORKADAYS
WORKAHOLIC
WORKAHOLICS
WORKAHOLISM
WORKAHOLISMS
WORKAROUND
WORKBAG
WORKBAGS
WORKBASKET
WORKBASKETS
WORKBENCH
WORKBENCHES
WORKBOAT
WORKBOATS
WORKBOOK
WORKBOOKS
WORKBOX
WORKBOXES
WORKDAY
WORKDAYS
WORKED
WORKER
WORKERBOX
WORKERBOXES
WORKERIST
WORKERISTS
WORKERLESS
WORKERS
WORKFARE
WORKFARES
WORKFELLOW
WORKFELLOWS
WORKFOLK
WORKFOLKS
WORKFORCE
WORKFORCES

WORKFUL
WORKGIRL
WORKGIRLS
WORKGROUP
WORKGROUPS
WORKHORSE
WORKHORSES
WORKHOUSE
WORKHOUSES
WORKING
WORKINGMAN
WORKINGMEN
WORKINGS
WORKINGWOMAN
WORKINGWOMEN
WORKLESS
WORKLESSNESS
WORKLESSNESSES
WORKLOAD
WORKLOADS
WORKMAN
WORKMANLIKE
WORKMANLY
WORKMANSHIP
WORKMANSHIPS
WORKMASTER
WORKMASTERS
WORKMATE
WORKMATES
WORKMEN
WORKMISTRESS
WORKMISTRESSES
WORKOUT
WORKOUTS
WORKPEOPLE
WORKPIECE
WORKPIECES
WORKPLACE
WORKPLACES
WORKROOM
WORKROOMS
WORKS
WORKSHEET
WORKSHEETS
WORKSHOP
WORKSHOPPED
WORKSHOPPING
WORKSHOPS
WORKSHY
WORKSOME
WORKSTATION
WORKSTATIONS
WORKTABLE
WORKTABLES
WORKTOP
WORKTOPS
WORKUP

WORKUPS
WORKWATCHER
WORKWATCHERS
WORKWEAR
WORKWEARS
WORKWEEK
WORKWEEKS
WORKWOMAN
WORKWOMEN
WORLD
WORLDED
WORLDLIER
WORLDLIEST
WORLDLINESS
WORLDLINESSES
WORLDLING
WORLDLINGS
WORLDLY
WORLDS
WORLDSCALE
WORLDSCALES
WORLDVIEW
WORLDVIEWS
WORLDWIDE
WORM
WORMCAST
WORMCASTS
WORMED
WORMER
WORMERIES
WORMERS
WORMERY
WORMFLIES
WORMFLY
WORMHOLE
WORMHOLED
WORMHOLES
WORMIER
WORMIEST
WORMIL
WORMILS
WORMINESS
WORMING
WORMISH
WORMLIKE
WORMROOT
WORMROOTS
WORMS
WORMSEED
WORMSEEDS
WORMWOOD
WORMWOODS
WORMY
WORN
WORNNESS
WORNNESSES
WORRAL

WORRALS
WORREL
WORRELS
WORRICOW
WORRICOWS
WORRIED
WORRIEDLY
WORRIER
WORRIERS
WORRIES
WORRIMENT
WORRIMENTS
WORRISOME
WORRISOMELY
WORRISOMENESS
WORRISOMENESSES
WORRIT
WORRITED
WORRITING
WORRITS
WORRY
WORRYCOW
WORRYCOWS
WORRYGUTS
WORRYING
WORRYINGLY
WORRYINGS
WORRYWART
WORRYWARTS
WORSE
WORSED
WORSEN
WORSENED
WORSENESS
WORSENESSES
WORSENING
WORSENS
WORSER
WORSES
WORSET
WORSETS
WORSHIP
WORSHIPABLE
WORSHIPED
WORSHIPER
WORSHIPERS
WORSHIPFUL
WORSHIPFULLY
WORSHIPFULNESS
WORSHIPING
WORSHIPLESS
WORSHIPPED
WORSHIPPER
WORSHIPPERS
WORSHIPPING
WORSHIPS
WORSING

WORST	WOUNDWORT	WRAPROUNDS	WREATHIER
WORSTED	WOUNDWORTS	WRAPS	WREATHIEST
WORSTEDS	WOUNDY	WRAPT	WREATHING
WORSTING	WOURALI	WRASSE	WREATHLESS
WORSTS	WOURALIS	WRASSES	WREATHLIKE
WORT	WOVE	WRASSLE	WREATHS
WORTH	WOVEN	WRASSLED	WREATHY
WORTHED	WOVENS	WRASSLES	WRECK
WORTHFUL	WOW	WRASSLING	WRECKAGE
WORTHIED	WOWED	WRAST	WRECKAGES
WORTHIER	WOWEE	WRASTED	WRECKED
WORTHIES	WOWF	WRASTING	WRECKER
WORTHIEST	WOWFER	WRASTLE	WRECKERS
WORTHILY	WOWFEST	WRASTLED	WRECKFISH
WORTHINESS	WOWING	WRASTLES	WRECKFISHES
WORTHINESSES	WOWS	WRASTLING	WRECKFUL
WORTHING	WOWSER	WRASTS	WRECKING
WORTHLESS	WOWSERS	WRATE	WRECKINGS
WORTHLESSLY	WOX	WRATH	WRECKMASTER
WORTHLESSNESS	WOXEN	WRATHED	WRECKMASTERS
WORTHLESSNESSES	WRACK	WRATHFUL	WRECKS
WORTHS	WRACKED	WRATHFULLY	WREN
WORTHWHILE	WRACKFUL	WRATHFULNESS	WRENCH
WORTHWHILENESS	WRACKING	WRATHFULNESSES	WRENCHED
WORTHY	WRACKS	WRATHIER	WRENCHES
WORTHYING	WRAITH	WRATHIEST	WRENCHING
WORTLE	WRAITHLIKE	WRATHILY	WRENCHINGLY
WORTLES	WRAITHS	WRATHINESS	WRENCHINGS
WORTS	WRANG	WRATHINESSES	WRENS
WOS	WRANGED	WRATHING	WREST
WOSBIRD	WRANGING	WRATHLESS	WRESTED
WOSBIRDS	WRANGLE	WRATHS	WRESTER
WOST	WRANGLED	WRATHY	WRESTERS
WOT	WRANGLER	WRAWL	WRESTING
WOTCHER	WRANGLERS	WRAWLED	WRESTLE
WOTS	WRANGLERSHIP	WRAWLING	WRESTLED
WOTTED	WRANGLERSHIPS	WRAWLS	WRESTLER
WOTTEST	WRANGLES	WRAXLE	WRESTLERS
WOTTETH	WRANGLESOME	WRAXLED	WRESTLES
WOTTING	WRANGLING	WRAXLES	WRESTLING
WOUBIT	WRANGLINGS	WRAXLING	WRESTLINGS
WOUBITS	WRANGS	WRAXLINGS	WRESTS
WOULD	WRAP	WREAK	WRETCH
WOULDEST	WRAPAROUND	WREAKED	WRETCHED
WOULDS	WRAPAROUNDS	WREAKER	WRETCHEDER
WOULDST	WRAPOVER	WREAKERS	WRETCHEDEST
WOUND	WRAPOVERS	WREAKFUL	WRETCHEDLY
WOUNDABLE	WRAPPAGE	WREAKING	WRETCHEDNESS
WOUNDED	WRAPPAGES	WREAKLESS	WRETCHEDNESSES
WOUNDER	WRAPPED	WREAKS	WRETCHES
WOUNDERS	WRAPPER	WREATH	WRETHE
WOUNDILY	WRAPPERED	WREATHE	WRETHED
WOUNDING	WRAPPERING	WREATHED	WRETHES
WOUNDINGLY	WRAPPERS	WREATHEN	WRETHING
WOUNDINGS	WRAPPING	WREATHER	WRICK
WOUNDLESS	WRAPPINGS	WREATHERS	WRICKED
WOUNDS	WRAPROUND	WREATHES	WRICKING

WRICKS
WRIED
WRIER
WRIES
WRIEST
WRIGGLE
WRIGGLED
WRIGGLER
WRIGGLERS
WRIGGLES
WRIGGLIER
WRIGGLIEST
WRIGGLING
WRIGGLINGS
WRIGGLY
WRIGHT
WRIGHTS
WRING
WRINGED
WRINGER
WRINGERS
WRINGING
WRINGINGS
WRINGS
WRINKLE
WRINKLED
WRINKLELESS
WRINKLES
WRINKLIER
WRINKLIES
WRINKLIEST
WRINKLING
WRINKLY
WRIST
WRISTBAND
WRISTBANDS
WRISTIER
WRISTIEST
WRISTLET
WRISTLETS
WRISTLOCK
WRISTLOCKS
WRISTS
WRISTWATCH
WRISTWATCHES
WRISTY
WRIT
WRITABLE
WRITATIVE
WRITE
WRITER
WRITERESS
WRITERESSES
WRITERLY
WRITERS
WRITERSHIP
WRITERSHIPS

WRITES
WRITHE
WRITHED
WRITHEN
WRITHER
WRITHERS
WRITHES
WRITHING
WRITHINGLY
WRITHINGS
WRITHLED
WRITING
WRITINGS
WRITS
WRITTEN
WRIZLED
WROATH
WROATHS
WROKE
WROKEN
WRONG
WRONGDOER
WRONGDOERS
WRONGDOING
WRONGDOINGS
WRONGED
WRONGER
WRONGERS
WRONGEST
WRONGFUL
WRONGFULLY
WRONGFULNESS
WRONGFULNESSES
WRONGHEADED
WRONGHEADEDLY
WRONGHEADEDNESS
WRONGING
WRONGLY
WRONGNESS
WRONGNESSES
WRONGOUS
WRONGOUSLY
WRONGS
WROOT
WROOTED
WROOTING
WROOTS
WROTE
WROTH
WROTHFUL
WROUGHT
WRUNG
WRY
WRYBILL
WRYBILLS
WRYER
WRYEST

WRYING
WRYLY
WRYNECK
WRYNECKS
WRYNESS
WRYNESSES
WRYTHEN
WUD
WUDDED
WUDDING
WUDS
WUDU
WULFENITE
WULFENITES
WULL
WULLED
WULLING
WULLS
WUNDERKIND
WUNDERKINDER
WUNDERKINDS
WUNNER
WUNNERS
WURLEY
WURLEYS
WURLIE
WURLIES
WURST
WURSTS
WURTZITE
WURTZITES
WURZEL
WURZELS
WUS
WUSES
WUSHU
WUSHUS
WUSS
WUSSES
WUSSIER
WUSSIES
WUSSIEST
WUSSY
WUTHER
WUTHERED
WUTHERING
WUTHERS
WUZZLE
WUZZLED
WUZZLES
WUZZLING
WYANDOTTE
WYANDOTTES
WYCH
WYCHES
WYE
WYES

WYLE
WYLED
WYLES
WYLIECOAT
WYLIECOATS
WYLING
WYN
WYND
WYNDS
WYNN
WYNNS
WYNS
WYSIWYG
WYTE
WYTED
WYTES
WYTING
WYVERN
WYVERNS

X

XANTHAM
XANTHAMS
XANTHAN
XANTHANS
XANTHATE
XANTHATES
XANTHATION
XANTHATIONS
XANTHEIN
XANTHEINS
XANTHENE
XANTHENES
XANTHIC
XANTHIN
XANTHINE
XANTHINES
XANTHINS
XANTHISM
XANTHOCHROIA
XANTHOCHROIAS
XANTHOCHROIC
XANTHOCHROID
XANTHOCHROIDS
XANTHOCHROISM
XANTHOCHROISMS
XANTHOCHROMIA
XANTHOCHROMIAS
XANTHOCHROOUS
XANTHOMA
XANTHOMAS
XANTHOMATA
XANTHOMATOUS
XANTHOMELANOUS
XANTHONE
XANTHONES
XANTHOPHYL
XANTHOPHYLL
XANTHOPHYLLOUS
XANTHOPHYLLS
XANTHOPHYLS
XANTHOPSIA
XANTHOPSIAS
XANTHOPTERIN
XANTHOPTERINE
XANTHOPTERINES
XANTHOPTERINS
XANTHOUS
XANTHOXYL
XANTHOXYLS
XEBEC
XEBECS
XENARTHRAL

XENIA
XENIAL
XENIAS
XENIC
XENIUM
XENOBIOTIC
XENOBIOTICS
XENOCRYST
XENOCRYSTS
XENODIAGNOSES
XENODIAGNOSIS
XENODIAGNOSTIC
XENODOCHIUM
XENODOCHIUMS
XENOGAMIES
XENOGAMOUS
XENOGAMY
XENOGENEIC
XENOGENESES
XENOGENESIS
XENOGENETIC
XENOGENIC
XENOGENIES
XENOGENOUS
XENOGENY
XENOGLOSSIA
XENOGLOSSIAS
XENOGLOSSY
XENOGRAFT
XENOGRAFTS
XENOLITH
XENOLITHIC
XENOLITHS
XENOMANIA
XENOMANIAS
XENOMENIA
XENOMENIAS
XENOMORPHIC
XENOMORPHICALLY
XENON
XENONS
XENOPHILE
XENOPHILES
XENOPHOBE
XENOPHOBES
XENOPHOBIA
XENOPHOBIAS
XENOPHOBIC
XENOPHOBICALLY
XENOPHOBIES
XENOPHOBY
XENOPHYA

XENOPLASTIC
XENOTIME
XENOTIMES
XENOTRANSPLANT
XENOTRANSPLANTS
XENOTROPIC
XENURINE
XERAFIN
XERAFINS
XERANSES
XERANSIS
XERANTHEMUM
XERANTHEMUMS
XERANTIC
XERAPHIM
XERAPHIMS
XERARCH
XERASIA
XERASIAS
XERIC
XERICALLY
XEROCHASIES
XEROCHASY
XERODERMA
XERODERMAS
XERODERMATIC
XERODERMATOUS
XERODERMIA
XERODERMIAS
XERODERMIC
XEROGRAPHER
XEROGRAPHERS
XEROGRAPHIC
XEROGRAPHICALLY
XEROGRAPHIES
XEROGRAPHY
XEROMA
XEROMAS
XEROMATA
XEROMORPH
XEROMORPHIC
XEROMORPHOUS
XEROMORPHS
XEROPHAGIES
XEROPHAGY
XEROPHILE
XEROPHILES
XEROPHILIES
XEROPHILOUS
XEROPHILY
XEROPHTHALMIA
XEROPHTHALMIAS

XEROPHTHALMIC
XEROPHYTE
XEROPHYTES
XEROPHYTIC
XEROPHYTICALLY
XEROPHYTISM
XEROPHYTISMS
XERORADIOGRAPHY
XEROSERE
XEROSERES
XEROSES
XEROSIS
XEROSTOMA
XEROSTOMAS
XEROSTOMATA
XEROSTOMIA
XEROSTOMIAS
XEROTES
XEROTHERMIC
XEROTIC
XEROTRIPSES
XEROTRIPSIS
XEROX
XEROXED
XEROXES
XEROXING
XERUS
XERUSES
XI
XIPHIHUMERALIS
XIPHIPLASTRA
XIPHIPLASTRAL
XIPHIPLASTRALS
XIPHIPLASTRON
XIPHISTERNA
XIPHISTERNUM
XIPHISTERNUMS
XIPHOID
XIPHOIDAL
XIPHOIDS
XIPHOPAGI
XIPHOPAGIC
XIPHOPAGOUS
XIPHOPAGUS
XIPHOPAGUSES
XIPHOPHYLLOUS
XIPHOSURAN
XIPHOSURANS
XIS
XOANA
XOANON
XU

XYLAN
XYLANS
XYLEM
XYLEMS
XYLENE
XYLENES
XYLENOL
XYLENOLS
XYLIC
XYLIDIN
XYLIDINE
XYLIDINES
XYLIDINS
XYLITOL
XYLITOLS
XYLOBALSAMUM
XYLOBALSAMUMS
XYLOCARP
XYLOCARPOUS
XYLOCARPS
XYLOCHROMES
XYLOGEN
XYLOGENOUS
XYLOGENS
XYLOGRAPH
XYLOGRAPHED
XYLOGRAPHER
XYLOGRAPHERS
XYLOGRAPHIC
XYLOGRAPHICAL
XYLOGRAPHIES
XYLOGRAPHING
XYLOGRAPHS
XYLOGRAPHY
XYLOID
XYLOIDIN
XYLOIDINE
XYLOIDINES
XYLOIDINS
XYLOL
XYLOLOGIES
XYLOLOGY
XYLOLS
XYLOMA
XYLOMAS
XYLOMATA
XYLOMETER
XYLOMETERS
XYLONIC
XYLONITE
XYLONITES
XYLOPHAGAN
XYLOPHAGANS
XYLOPHAGE
XYLOPHAGES
XYLOPHAGOUS
XYLOPHILOUS

XYLOPHONE
XYLOPHONES
XYLOPHONIC
XYLOPHONIST
XYLOPHONISTS
XYLOPYROGRAPHY
XYLORIMBA
XYLORIMBAS
XYLOSE
XYLOSES
XYLOTOMIES
XYLOTOMIST
XYLOTOMISTS
XYLOTOMOUS
XYLOTOMY
XYLOTYPOGRAPHIC
XYLOTYPOGRAPHY
XYLYL
XYLYLS
XYRIDACEOUS
XYST
XYSTER
XYSTERS
XYSTI
XYSTOI
XYSTOS
XYSTOSES
XYSTS
XYSTUS
XYSTUSES

Y

YA
YABBA
YABBER
YABBERED
YABBERING
YABBERRED
YABBERRING
YABBERS
YABBIE
YABBIED
YABBIES
YABBY
YABBYING
YACCA
YACCAS
YACHT
YACHTED
YACHTER
YACHTERS
YACHTIE
YACHTIES
YACHTING
YACHTINGS
YACHTMAN
YACHTMEN
YACHTS
YACHTSMAN
YACHTSMANSHIP
YACHTSMANSHIPS
YACHTSMEN
YACHTSWOMAN
YACHTSWOMEN
YACK
YACKA
YACKAS
YACKED
YACKER
YACKERS
YACKING
YACKS
YAD
YADS
YAE
YAFF
YAFFED
YAFFING
YAFFINGALE
YAFFINGALES
YAFFLE
YAFFLES
YAFFS
YAGER

YAGERS
YAGGER
YAGGERS
YAGI
YAGIS
YAH
YAHOO
YAHOOISM
YAHOOISMS
YAHOOS
YAHRZEIT
YAHRZEITS
YAHS
YAIRD
YAIRDS
YAK
YAKHDAN
YAKHDANS
YAKIMONO
YAKIMONOS
YAKITORI
YAKITORIS
YAKKA
YAKKAS
YAKKED
YAKKER
YAKKERS
YAKKING
YAKOW
YAKOWS
YAKS
YAKUZA
YALD
YALE
YALES
YAM
YAMALKA
YAMALKAS
YAMEN
YAMENS
YAMMER
YAMMERED
YAMMERER
YAMMERERS
YAMMERING
YAMMERINGS
YAMMERS
YAMPY
YAMS
YAMULKA
YAMULKAS
YAMUN

YAMUNS
YANG
YANGS
YANK
YANKED
YANKER
YANKERS
YANKIE
YANKIES
YANKING
YANKS
YANQUI
YANQUIS
YANTRA
YANTRAS
YAOURT
YAOURTS
YAP
YAPOCK
YAPOCKS
YAPOK
YAPOKS
YAPON
YAPONS
YAPP
YAPPED
YAPPER
YAPPERS
YAPPIE
YAPPIER
YAPPIES
YAPPIEST
YAPPING
YAPPS
YAPPY
YAPS
YAPSTER
YAPSTERS
YAQONA
YAQONAS
YAR
YARBOROUGH
YARBOROUGHS
YARD
YARDAGE
YARDAGES
YARDANG
YARDANGS
YARDARM
YARDARMS
YARDBIRD
YARDBIRDS

YARDED
YARDING
YARDINGS
YARDLAND
YARDLANDS
YARDMAN
YARDMASTER
YARDMASTERS
YARDMEN
YARDS
YARDSTICK
YARDSTICKS
YARDWAND
YARDWANDS
YARDWORK
YARDWORKS
YARE
YARELY
YARER
YAREST
YARFA
YARFAS
YARK
YARMELKE
YARMELKES
YARMULKA
YARMULKAS
YARMULKE
YARMULKES
YARN
YARNED
YARNER
YARNERS
YARNING
YARNS
YARPHA
YARPHAS
YARR
YARRAMAN
YARRAMANS
YARRAMEN
YARRAN
YARRANS
YARROW
YARROWS
YARRS
YARTA
YARTAS
YARTO
YARTOS
YASHMAC
YASHMACS

YASHMAK	YAWS	YEARNER	YELLOCHS
YASHMAKS	YAWY	YEARNERS	YELLOW
YASMAK	YAY	YEARNING	YELLOWBACK
YASMAKS	YAYS	YEARNINGLY	YELLOWBACKS
YATAGAN	YBET	YEARNINGS	YELLOWBARK
YATAGANS	YBLENT	YEARNS	YELLOWBARKS
YATAGHAN	YBORE	YEARS	YELLOWBIRD
YATAGHANS	YBOUND	YEAS	YELLOWBIRDS
YATE	YBOUNDEN	YEASAYER	YELLOWCAKE
YATES	YBRENT	YEASAYERS	YELLOWCAKES
YATTER	YCLAD	YEAST	YELLOWED
YATTERED	YCLED	YEASTED	YELLOWER
YATTERING	YCLEEPE	YEASTIER	YELLOWEST
YATTERINGLY	YCLEEPED	YEASTIEST	YELLOWFIN
YATTERINGS	YCLEEPES	YEASTILY	YELLOWFINS
YATTERS	YCLEEPING	YEASTINESS	YELLOWHAMMER
YAUD	YCLEPED	YEASTINESSES	YELLOWHAMMERS
YAUDS	YCLEPT	YEASTING	YELLOWHEAD
YAULD	YCOND	YEASTLESS	YELLOWHEADS
YAUP	YDRAD	YEASTLIKE	YELLOWIER
YAUPED	YDRED	YEASTS	YELLOWIEST
YAUPER	YE	YEASTY	YELLOWING
YAUPERS	YEA	YEBO	YELLOWISH
YAUPING	YEAD	YECCH	YELLOWISHNESS
YAUPON	YEADING	YECCHS	YELLOWISHNESSES
YAUPONS	YEADS	YECH	YELLOWLEGS
YAUPS	YEAH	YECHS	YELLOWLY
YAUTIA	YEALDON	YECHY	YELLOWNESS
YAUTIAS	YEALDONS	YEDE	YELLOWNESSES
YAW	YEALING	YEDES	YELLOWS
YAWED	YEALINGS	YEDING	YELLOWTAIL
YAWEY	YEALM	YEED	YELLOWTAILS
YAWING	YEALMED	YEEDING	YELLOWTHROAT
YAWL	YEALMING	YEEDS	YELLOWTHROATS
YAWLED	YEALMS	YEELIN	YELLOWWARE
YAWLING	YEAN	YEELINS	YELLOWWARES
YAWLS	YEANED	YEGG	YELLOWWEED
YAWMETER	YEANING	YEGGMAN	YELLOWWOOD
YAWMETERS	YEANLING	YEGGMEN	YELLOWWOODS
YAWN	YEANLINGS	YEGGS	YELLOWWORT
YAWNED	YEANS	YEH	YELLOWY
YAWNER	YEAR	YELD	YELLS
YAWNERS	YEARBOOK	YELDRING	YELM
YAWNIER	YEARBOOKS	YELDRINGS	YELMED
YAWNIEST	YEARD	YELDROCK	YELMING
YAWNING	YEARDED	YELDROCKS	YELMS
YAWNINGLY	YEARDING	YELK	YELP
YAWNINGS	YEARDS	YELKS	YELPED
YAWNS	YEAREND	YELL	YELPER
YAWNY	YEARENDS	YELLED	YELPERS
YAWP	YEARLIES	YELLER	YELPING
YAWPED	YEARLING	YELLERS	YELPINGS
YAWPER	YEARLINGS	YELLING	YELPS
YAWPERS	YEARLONG	YELLINGS	YELT
YAWPING	YEARLY	YELLOCH	YELTS
YAWPINGS	YEARN	YELLOCHED	YEMMER
YAWPS	YEARNED	YELLOCHING	YEN

YENNED
YENNING
YENS
YENTA
YENTAS
YENTE
YENTES
YEOMAN
YEOMANLY
YEOMANRIES
YEOMANRY
YEOMEN
YEP
YEPS
YERBA
YERBAS
YERD
YERDED
YERDING
YERDS
YERK
YERKED
YERKING
YERKS
YERSINIA
YERSINIAE
YERSINIAS
YERSINIOSES
YERSINIOSIS
YES
YESES
YESHIVA
YESHIVAH
YESHIVAHS
YESHIVAS
YESHIVOT
YESHIVOTH
YESK
YESKED
YESKING
YESKS
YESSED
YESSES
YESSING
YEST
YESTER
YESTERDAY
YESTERDAYS
YESTEREVE
YESTEREVEN
YESTEREVENING
YESTEREVENINGS
YESTEREVENS
YESTEREVES
YESTERMORN
YESTERMORNING
YESTERMORNINGS

YESTERMORNS
YESTERN
YESTERNIGHT
YESTERNIGHTS
YESTERYEAR
YESTERYEARS
YESTREEN
YESTREENS
YESTS
YESTY
YET
YETI
YETIS
YETT
YETTIE
YETTIES
YETTS
YEUK
YEUKED
YEUKING
YEUKS
YEUKY
YEVE
YEVEN
YEVES
YEVING
YEW
YEWEN
YEWS
YEX
YEXED
YEXES
YEXING
YFERE
YGLAUNST
YGO
YGOE
YIBBLES
YICKER
YICKERED
YICKERING
YICKERS
YID
YIDS
YIELD
YIELDABLE
YIELDABLENESS
YIELDABLENESSES
YIELDED
YIELDER
YIELDERS
YIELDING
YIELDINGLY
YIELDINGNESS
YIELDINGNESSES
YIELDINGS
YIELDS

YIKE
YIKED
YIKES
YIKING
YIKKER
YIKKERED
YIKKERING
YIKKERS
YILL
YILLS
YIN
YINCE
YINS
YIP
YIPE
YIPES
YIPPED
YIPPEE
YIPPER
YIPPERS
YIPPIE
YIPPIES
YIPPING
YIPPY
YIPS
YIRD
YIRDED
YIRDING
YIRDS
YIRK
YIRKED
YIRKING
YIRKS
YIRR
YIRRED
YIRRING
YIRRS
YIRTH
YIRTHS
YITE
YITES
YITIE
YITIES
YITTEN
YLEM
YLEMS
YLIKE
YLKE
YLKES
YMOLT
YMOLTEN
YMPE
YMPES
YMPING
YMPT
YNAMBU
YNAMBUS

YO
YOB
YOBBERIES
YOBBERY
YOBBISH
YOBBISHLY
YOBBISM
YOBBISMS
YOBBO
YOBBOES
YOBBOS
YOBS
YOCK
YOCKED
YOCKING
YOCKS
YOCTOSECOND
YOCTOSECONDS
YOD
YODE
YODEL
YODELED
YODELER
YODELERS
YODELING
YODELLED
YODELLER
YODELLERS
YODELLING
YODELS
YODH
YODHS
YODLE
YODLED
YODLER
YODLERS
YODLES
YODLING
YODS
YOGA
YOGAS
YOGEE
YOGEES
YOGH
YOGHOURT
YOGHOURTS
YOGHS
YOGHURT
YOGHURTS
YOGI
YOGIC
YOGIN
YOGINI
YOGINIS
YOGINS
YOGIS
YOGISM

YOGISMS	YONDERLY	YOURN	YRAVISHED
YOGURT	YONDERS	YOURS	YRENT
YOGURTS	YONI	YOURSELF	YRIVD
YOHIMBINE	YONIC	YOURSELVES	YRNEH
YOHIMBINES	YONIS	YOURT	YRNEHS
YOICK	YONKER	YOURTS	YSAME
YOICKED	YONKERS	YOUS	YSHEND
YOICKING	YONKS	YOUSE	YSHENDING
YOICKS	YONNIE	YOUTH	YSHENDS
YOICKSED	YONNIES	YOUTHEN	YSHENT
YOICKSES	YONT	YOUTHENED	YSLAKED
YOICKSING	YOOF	YOUTHENING	YTHUNDERED
YOJAN	YOOFS	YOUTHENS	YTOST
YOJANA	YOOP	YOUTHFUL	YTTERBIA
YOJANAS	YOOPS	YOUTHFULLY	YTTERBIAS
YOJANS	YOPPER	YOUTHFULNESS	YTTERBIC
YOK	YOPPERS	YOUTHFULNESSES	YTTERBITE
YOKE	YORE	YOUTHHEAD	YTTERBIUM
YOKED	YORES	YOUTHHEADS	YTTERBIUMS
YOKEFELLOW	YORK	YOUTHHOOD	YTTRIA
YOKEFELLOWS	YORKED	YOUTHHOODS	YTTRIAS
YOKEL	YORKER	YOUTHIER	YTTRIC
YOKELESS	YORKERS	YOUTHIEST	YTTRIFEROUS
YOKELISH	YORKIE	YOUTHLESS	YTTRIOUS
YOKELS	YORKIES	YOUTHLY	YTTRIUM
YOKEMATE	YORKING	YOUTHQUAKE	YTTRIUMS
YOKEMATES	YORKS	YOUTHQUAKES	YU
YOKER	YORP	YOUTHS	YUAN
YOKERS	YOS	YOUTHSOME	YUANS
YOKES	YOU	YOUTHY	YUCA
YOKING	YOUK	YOW	YUCAS
YOKINGS	YOUKED	YOWE	YUCCA
YOKKED	YOUKING	YOWED	YUCCAS
YOKKING	YOUKS	YOWES	YUCCH
YOKOZUNA	YOUNG	YOWIE	YUCH
YOKOZUNAS	YOUNGBERRIES	YOWIES	YUCK
YOKS	YOUNGBERRY	YOWING	YUCKED
YOKUL	YOUNGER	YOWL	YUCKER
YOLD	YOUNGERS	YOWLED	YUCKERS
YOLDRING	YOUNGEST	YOWLER	YUCKIER
YOLDRINGS	YOUNGISH	YOWLERS	YUCKIEST
YOLK	YOUNGLING	YOWLEY	YUCKING
YOLKED	YOUNGLINGS	YOWLEYS	YUCKO
YOLKIER	YOUNGLY	YOWLING	YUCKS
YOLKIEST	YOUNGNESS	YOWLINGS	YUCKY
YOLKLESS	YOUNGNESSES	YOWLS	YUFT
YOLKS	YOUNGS	YOWS	YUFTS
YOLKY	YOUNGSTER	YPERITE	YUG
YOM	YOUNGSTERS	YPERITES	YUGA
YOMIM	YOUNGTH	YPIGHT	YUGARIE
YOMP	YOUNGTHLY	YPLAST	YUGARIES
YOMPED	YOUNGTHS	YPLIGHT	YUGAS
YOMPING	YOUNKER	YPSILIFORM	YUGS
YOMPS	YOUNKERS	YPSILOID	YUK
YON	YOUPON	YPSILON	YUKATA
YOND	YOUPONS	YPSILONS	YUKATAS
YONDER	YOUR	YRAPT	YUKE

YUKED
YUKES
YUKIER
YUKIEST
YUKING
YUKKED
YUKKIER
YUKKIEST
YUKKING
YUKKY
YUKO
YUKOS
YUKS
YUKY
YULAN
YULANS
YULE
YULES
YULETIDE
YULETIDES
YUM
YUMMIER
YUMMIES
YUMMIEST
YUMMO
YUMMY
YUMP
YUMPED
YUMPIE
YUMPIES
YUMPING
YUMPS
YUNX
YUNXES
YUP
YUPON
YUPONS
YUPPIE
YUPPIEDOM
YUPPIEDOMS
YUPPIES
YUPPIFICATION
YUPPIFICATIONS
YUPPIFIED
YUPPIFIES
YUPPIFY
YUPPIFYING
YUPPY
YUPS
YURT
YURTA
YURTS
YUS
YWIS
YWROKE

Z

ZABAGLIONE	ZAMANG	ZANTE	ZARNEC
ZABAGLIONES	ZAMANGS	ZANTEDESCHIA	ZARNECS
ZABAIONE	ZAMANS	ZANTEDESCHIAS	ZARNICH
ZABAIONES	ZAMARRA	ZANTES	ZARNICHS
ZABAJONE	ZAMARRAS	ZANTHOXYL	ZARZUELA
ZABAJONES	ZAMARRO	ZANTHOXYLS	ZARZUELAS
ZABETA	ZAMARROS	ZANTHOXYLUM	ZASTRUGA
ZABETAS	ZAMBO	ZANTHOXYLUMS	ZASTRUGAS
ZABRA	ZAMBOMBA	ZANY	ZASTRUGI
ZABRAS	ZAMBOMBAS	ZANYING	ZATI
ZABTIEH	ZAMBOORAK	ZANYISH	ZATIS
ZABTIEHS	ZAMBOORAKS	ZANYISM	ZAX
ZACATON	ZAMBOS	ZANYISMS	ZAXES
ZACATONS	ZAMBUCK	ZANZA	ZAYIN
ZACK	ZAMBUCKS	ZANZAS	ZAYINS
ZACKS	ZAMBUK	ZANZE	ZAZEN
ZADDICK	ZAMBUKS	ZANZES	ZAZENS
ZADDIK	ZAMIA	ZAP	ZEA
ZADDIKIM	ZAMIAS	ZAPATA	ZEAL
ZADDIKS	ZAMINDAR	ZAPATEADO	ZEALANT
ZAFFAR	ZAMINDARI	ZAPATEADOS	ZEALANTS
ZAFFARS	ZAMINDARIES	ZAPATEO	ZEALFUL
ZAFFER	ZAMINDARIS	ZAPATEOS	ZEALLESS
ZAFFERS	ZAMINDARS	ZAPOTILLA	ZEALOT
ZAFFIR	ZAMINDARY	ZAPOTILLAS	ZEALOTISM
ZAFFIRS	ZAMOUSE	ZAPPED	ZEALOTISMS
ZAFFRE	ZAMOUSES	ZAPPER	ZEALOTRIES
ZAFFRES	ZAMPOGNA	ZAPPERS	ZEALOTRY
ZAFTIG	ZAMPOGNAS	ZAPPIER	ZEALOTS
ZAG	ZAMPONE	ZAPPIEST	ZEALOUS
ZAGGED	ZAMPONI	ZAPPING	ZEALOUSLY
ZAGGING	ZAMZAWED	ZAPPY	ZEALOUSNESS
ZAGS	ZANANA	ZAPS	ZEALOUSNESSES
ZAIBATSU	ZANANAS	ZAPTIAH	ZEALS
ZAIKAI	ZANDER	ZAPTIAHS	ZEAS
ZAIKAIS	ZANDERS	ZAPTIEH	ZEATIN
ZAIRE	ZANELLA	ZAPTIEHS	ZEATINS
ZAIRES	ZANELLAS	ZARAPE	ZEBEC
ZAITECH	ZANIED	ZARAPES	ZEBECK
ZAITECHS	ZANIER	ZARATITE	ZEBECKS
ZAKAT	ZANIES	ZARATITES	ZEBECS
ZAKATS	ZANIEST	ZAREBA	ZEBRA
ZAKOUSKA	ZANILY	ZAREBAS	ZEBRAIC
ZAKOUSKI	ZANINESS	ZAREEBA	ZEBRAS
ZAKUSKA	ZANINESSES	ZAREEBAS	ZEBRASS
ZAKUSKI	ZANJA	ZARF	ZEBRASSES
ZALAMBDODONT	ZANJAS	ZARFS	ZEBRAWOOD
ZALAMBDODONTS	ZANJERO	ZARIBA	ZEBRAWOODS
ZAMAN	ZANJEROS	ZARIBAS	ZEBRINA

ZEBRINAS
ZEBRINE
ZEBRINNIES
ZEBRINNY
ZEBROID
ZEBRULA
ZEBRULAS
ZEBRULE
ZEBRULES
ZEBU
ZEBUB
ZEBUBS
ZEBUS
ZECCHIN
ZECCHINE
ZECCHINES
ZECCHINI
ZECCHINO
ZECCHINOS
ZECCHINS
ZECHIN
ZECHINS
ZED
ZEDOARIES
ZEDOARY
ZEDS
ZEE
ZEES
ZEIN
ZEINS
ZEITGEBER
ZEITGEBERS
ZEITGEIST
ZEITGEISTS
ZEK
ZEKS
ZEL
ZELANT
ZELANTS
ZELATOR
ZELATORS
ZELATRICE
ZELATRICES
ZELATRIX
ZELATRIXES
ZELKOVA
ZELKOVAS
ZELOPHOBIA
ZELOPHOBIAS
ZELOPHOBIC
ZELOPHOBICS
ZELOSO
ZELOTYPIA
ZELOTYPIAS

ZELS
ZEMINDAR
ZEMINDARI
ZEMINDARIES
ZEMINDARIS
ZEMINDARS
ZEMINDARY
ZEMSTVA
ZEMSTVO
ZEMSTVOS
ZENAIDA
ZENAIDAS
ZENANA
ZENANAS
ZENDIK
ZENDIKS
ZENITH
ZENITHAL
ZENITHS
ZEOLITE
ZEOLITES
ZEOLITIC
ZEOLITIFORM
ZEPHYR
ZEPHYRS
ZEPPELIN
ZEPPELINS
ZEPTOSECOND
ZEPTOSECONDS
ZERDA
ZERDAS
ZEREBA
ZEREBAS
ZERIBA
ZERIBAS
ZERK
ZERKS
ZERO
ZEROED
ZEROES
ZEROING
ZEROS
ZEROTH
ZERUMBET
ZERUMBETS
ZEST
ZESTED
ZESTER
ZESTERS
ZESTFUL
ZESTFULLY
ZESTFULNESS
ZESTFULNESSES
ZESTIER

ZESTIEST
ZESTING
ZESTLESS
ZESTS
ZESTY
ZETA
ZETAS
ZETETIC
ZETETICS
ZEUGLODONT
ZEUGLODONTS
ZEUGMA
ZEUGMAS
ZEUGMATIC
ZEUGMATICALLY
ZEUXITE
ZEUXITES
ZEX
ZEXES
ZEZE
ZEZES
ZHO
ZHOMO
ZHOMOS
ZHOS
ZIBELINE
ZIBELINES
ZIBELLINE
ZIBELLINES
ZIBET
ZIBETH
ZIBETHS
ZIBETS
ZIDOVUDINE
ZIDOVUDINES
ZIFF
ZIFFIUS
ZIFFIUSES
ZIFFS
ZIG
ZIGAN
ZIGANKA
ZIGANKAS
ZIGANS
ZIGGED
ZIGGING
ZIGGURAT
ZIGGURATS
ZIGS
ZIGZAG
ZIGZAGGED
ZIGZAGGEDNESS
ZIGZAGGERIES
ZIGZAGGERY

ZIGZAGGING
ZIGZAGGY
ZIGZAGS
ZIKKURAT
ZIKKURATS
ZIKURAT
ZIKURATS
ZILA
ZILAS
ZILCH
ZILCHES
ZILL
ZILLA
ZILLAH
ZILLAHS
ZILLAS
ZILLION
ZILLIONAIRE
ZILLIONAIRES
ZILLIONS
ZILLIONTH
ZILLIONTHS
ZILLS
ZIMB
ZIMBI
ZIMBIS
ZIMBS
ZIMMER
ZIMMERS
ZIMOCCA
ZIMOCCAS
ZIN
ZINC
ZINCATE
ZINCATES
ZINCED
ZINCIC
ZINCIER
ZINCIEST
ZINCIFEROUS
ZINCIFICATION
ZINCIFICATIONS
ZINCIFIED
ZINCIFIES
ZINCIFY
ZINCIFYING
ZINCING
ZINCITE
ZINCITES
ZINCKED
ZINCKENITE
ZINCKENITES
ZINCKIER
ZINCKIEST

ZINCKIFICATION	ZINKED	ZITHERS	ZOEAS
ZINCKIFICATIONS	ZINKENITE	ZITI	ZOECHROME
ZINCKIFIED	ZINKENITES	ZITIS	ZOECHROMES
ZINCKIFIES	ZINKES	ZITS	ZOECIA
ZINCKIFY	ZINKIER	ZIZ	ZOECIUM
ZINCKIFYING	ZINKIEST	ZIZANIA	ZOEFORM
ZINCKING	ZINKIFICATION	ZIZANIAS	ZOETIC
ZINCKY	ZINKIFICATIONS	ZIZEL	ZOETROPE
ZINCO	ZINKIFIED	ZIZELS	ZOETROPES
ZINCODE	ZINKIFIES	ZIZIT	ZOETROPIC
ZINCODES	ZINKIFY	ZIZITH	ZOFTIG
ZINCOGRAPH	ZINKIFYING	ZIZITHS	ZOIATRIA
ZINCOGRAPHER	ZINKING	ZIZYPHUS	ZOIATRIAS
ZINCOGRAPHERS	ZINKY	ZIZYPHUSES	ZOIATRICS
ZINCOGRAPHIC	ZINNIA	ZIZZ	ZOIC
ZINCOGRAPHICAL	ZINNIAS	ZIZZED	ZOISITE
ZINCOGRAPHIES	ZINS	ZIZZES	ZOISITES
ZINCOGRAPHS	ZINZIBERACEOUS	ZIZZING	ZOISM
ZINCOGRAPHY	ZIP	ZIZZLE	ZOISMS
ZINCOID	ZIPLESS	ZIZZLED	ZOIST
ZINCOLYSES	ZIPLOCK	ZIZZLES	ZOISTS
ZINCOS	ZIPPED	ZIZZLING	ZOMBI
ZINCOUS	ZIPPER	ZLOTE	ZOMBIE
ZINCS	ZIPPERED	ZLOTIES	ZOMBIELIKE
ZINCY	ZIPPERING	ZLOTY	ZOMBIES
ZINDABAD	ZIPPERS	ZLOTYCH	ZOMBIFICATION
ZINE	ZIPPIER	ZLOTYS	ZOMBIFICATIONS
ZINEB	ZIPPIEST	ZO	ZOMBIFIED·
ZINEBS	ZIPPING	ZOA	ZOMBIFIES
ZINES	ZIPPO	ZOAEA	ZOMBIFY
ZINFANDEL	ZIPPOS	ZOAEAE	ZOMBIFYING
ZINFANDELS	ZIPPY	ZOAEAS	ZOMBIISM
ZING	ZIPS	ZOANTHARIAN	ZOMBIISMS
ZINGANI	ZIPTOP	ZOANTHARIANS	ZOMBIS
ZINGANO	ZIRAM	ZOANTHROPIC	ZOMBORUK
ZINGARA	ZIRAMS	ZOANTHROPIES	ZOMBORUKS
ZINGARE	ZIRCALLOY	ZOANTHROPY	ZONA
ZINGARI	ZIRCALLOYS	ZOARIA	ZONAE
ZINGARO	ZIRCALOY	ZOARIAL	ZONAL
ZINGED	ZIRCALOYS	ZOARIUM	ZONALLY
ZINGEL	ZIRCON	ZOBO	ZONARY
ZINGELS	ZIRCONIA	ZOBOS	ZONATE
ZINGER	ZIRCONIAS	ZOBU	ZONATED
ZINGERS	ZIRCONIC	ZOBUS	ZONATION
ZINGIBER	ZIRCONIUM	ZOCCO	ZONATIONS
ZINGIBERACEOUS	ZIRCONIUMS	ZOCCOLO	ZONDA
ZINGIBERS	ZIRCONS	ZOCCOLOS	ZONDAS
ZINGIER	ZIT	ZOCCOS	ZONE
ZINGIEST	ZITE	ZODIAC	ZONED
ZINGING	ZITHER	ZODIACAL	ZONELESS
ZINGS	ZITHERIST	ZODIACS	ZONER
ZINGY	ZITHERISTS	ZOEA	ZONERS
ZINJANTHROPUS	ZITHERN	ZOEAE	ZONES
ZINKE	ZITHERNS	ZOEAL	ZONETIME

ZONETIMES	ZOOGEOGRAPHICAL	ZOOLOGISTS	ZOOPHAGOUS
ZONING	ZOOGEOGRAPHIES	ZOOLOGY	ZOOPHAGY
ZONINGS	ZOOGEOGRAPHY	ZOOM	ZOOPHILE
ZONK	ZOOGLEA	ZOOMAGNETIC	ZOOPHILES
ZONKED	ZOOGLEAE	ZOOMAGNETISM	ZOOPHILIA
ZONKING	ZOOGLEAL	ZOOMAGNETISMS	ZOOPHILIAS
ZONKS	ZOOGLEAS	ZOOMANCIES	ZOOPHILIC
ZONOID	ZOOGLOEA	ZOOMANCY	ZOOPHILIES
ZONULA	ZOOGLOEAE	ZOOMANIA	ZOOPHILISM
ZONULAE	ZOOGLOEAL	ZOOMANIAS	ZOOPHILISMS
ZONULAR	ZOOGLOEAS	ZOOMANTIC	ZOOPHILIST
ZONULAS	ZOOGLOEIC	ZOOMED	ZOOPHILISTS
ZONULE	ZOOGLOEOID	ZOOMETRIC	ZOOPHILOUS
ZONULES	ZOOGONIDIA	ZOOMETRICAL	ZOOPHILY
ZONULET	ZOOGONIDIUM	ZOOMETRIES	ZOOPHOBE
ZONULETS	ZOOGONIES	ZOOMETRY	ZOOPHOBES
ZONURE	ZOOGONOUS	ZOOMING	ZOOPHOBIA
ZONURES	ZOOGONY	ZOOMORPH	ZOOPHOBIAS
ZOO	ZOOGRAFT	ZOOMORPHIC	ZOOPHOBOUS
ZOOBIOTIC	ZOOGRAFTING	ZOOMORPHIES	ZOOPHORI
ZOOBLAST	ZOOGRAFTINGS	ZOOMORPHISM	ZOOPHORIC
ZOOBLASTS	ZOOGRAFTS	ZOOMORPHISMS	ZOOPHORUS
ZOOCHEMICAL	ZOOGRAPHER	ZOOMORPHS	ZOOPHYSIOLOGIES
ZOOCHEMISTRIES	ZOOGRAPHERS	ZOOMORPHY	ZOOPHYSIOLOGIST
ZOOCHEMISTRY	ZOOGRAPHIC	ZOOMS	ZOOPHYSIOLOGY
ZOOCHORE	ZOOGRAPHICAL	ZOON	ZOOPHYTE
ZOOCHORES	ZOOGRAPHIES	ZOONAL	ZOOPHYTES
ZOOCHORIES	ZOOGRAPHIST	ZOONIC	ZOOPHYTIC
ZOOCHOROUS	ZOOGRAPHISTS	ZOONITE	ZOOPHYTICAL
ZOOCHORY	ZOOGRAPHY	ZOONITES	ZOOPHYTOID
ZOOCULTURE	ZOOID	ZOONITIC	ZOOPHYTOLOGICAL
ZOOCULTURES	ZOOIDAL	ZOONOMIA	ZOOPHYTOLOGIES
ZOOCYTIA	ZOOIDS	ZOONOMIAS	ZOOPHYTOLOGIST
ZOOCYTIUM	ZOOKEEPER	ZOONOMIC	ZOOPHYTOLOGISTS
ZOODENDRIA	ZOOKEEPERS	ZOONOMIES	ZOOPHYTOLOGY
ZOODENDRIUM	ZOOKS	ZOONOMIST	ZOOPLANKTER
ZOOEA	ZOOLATER	ZOONOMISTS	ZOOPLANKTERS
ZOOEAE	ZOOLATERS	ZOONOMY	ZOOPLANKTON
ZOOEAL	ZOOLATRIA	ZOONOSES	ZOOPLANKTONIC
ZOOEAS	ZOOLATRIAS	ZOONOSIS	ZOOPLANKTONS
ZOOECIA	ZOOLATRIES	ZOONOTIC	ZOOPLASTIC
ZOOECIUM	ZOOLATROUS	ZOONS	ZOOPLASTIES
ZOOGAMETE	ZOOLATRY	ZOOPATHIES	ZOOPLASTY
ZOOGAMETES	ZOOLITE	ZOOPATHOLOGIES	ZOOPSYCHOLOGIES
ZOOGAMIES	ZOOLITES	ZOOPATHOLOGY	ZOOPSYCHOLOGY
ZOOGAMOUS	ZOOLITH	ZOOPATHY	ZOOS
ZOOGAMY	ZOOLITHIC	ZOOPERAL	ZOOSCOPIC
ZOOGENIC	ZOOLITHS	ZOOPERIES	ZOOSCOPIES
ZOOGENIES	ZOOLITIC	ZOOPERIST	ZOOSCOPY
ZOOGENOUS	ZOOLOGIC	ZOOPERISTS	ZOOSPERM
ZOOGENY	ZOOLOGICAL	ZOOPERY	ZOOSPERMATIC
ZOOGEOGRAPHER	ZOOLOGICALLY	ZOOPHAGAN	ZOOSPERMIA
ZOOGEOGRAPHERS	ZOOLOGIES	ZOOPHAGANS	ZOOSPERMIUM
ZOOGEOGRAPHIC	ZOOLOGIST	ZOOPHAGIES	ZOOSPERMS

ZOOSPORANGIA	ZOOZOOS	ZULUS	ZYGOMORPHISM
ZOOSPORANGIAL	ZOPILOTE	ZUMBOORUCKS	ZYGOMORPHISMS
ZOOSPORANGIUM	ZOPILOTES	ZUMBOORUK	ZYGOMORPHOUS
ZOOSPORE	ZOPPA	ZUMBOORUKS	ZYGOMORPHY
ZOOSPORES	ZOPPO	ZUPA	ZYGOMYCETE
ZOOSPORIC	ZORBED	ZUPAN	ZYGOMYCETES
ZOOSPOROUS	ZORBING	ZUPANS	ZYGOMYCETOUS
ZOOSTEROL	ZORBONAUT	ZUPAS	ZYGON
ZOOSTEROLS	ZORBONAUTS	ZURF	ZYGOPHYLLACEOUS
ZOOT	ZORBS	ZURFS	ZYGOPHYTE
ZOOTAXIES	ZORGITE	ZUZ	ZYGOPHYTES
ZOOTAXY	ZORGITES	ZUZIM	ZYGOPLEURAL
ZOOTECHNICAL	ZORI	ZWIEBACK	ZYGOSE
ZOOTECHNICS	ZORIL	ZWIEBACKS	ZYGOSES
ZOOTECHNIES	ZORILLA	ZWISCHENZUG	ZYGOSIS
ZOOTECHNY	ZORILLAS	ZWISCHENZUGS	ZYGOSITIES
ZOOTHAPSES	ZORILLE	ZWITTERION	ZYGOSITY
ZOOTHAPSIS	ZORILLES	ZWITTERIONIC	ZYGOSPERM
ZOOTHECIA	ZORILLO	ZWITTERIONS	ZYGOSPERMS
ZOOTHECIAL	ZORILLOS	ZYDECO	ZYGOSPHENE
ZOOTHECIUM	ZORILS	ZYDECOS	ZYGOSPHENES
ZOOTHEISM	ZORINO	ZYGA	ZYGOSPORE
ZOOTHEISMS	ZORINOS	ZYGAENID	ZYGOSPORES
ZOOTHEISTIC	ZORIS	ZYGAENOID	ZYGOSPORIC
ZOOTHERAPIES	ZORRO	ZYGAL	ZYGOTE
ZOOTHERAPY	ZORROS	ZYGANTRA	ZYGOTENE
ZOOTHOME	ZOS	ZYGANTRUM	ZYGOTENES
ZOOTHOMES	ZOSTER	ZYGANTRUMS	ZYGOTES
ZOOTIER	ZOSTERS	ZYGAPOPHYSEAL	ZYGOTIC
ZOOTIEST	ZOUAVE	ZYGAPOPHYSES	ZYGOTICALLY
ZOOTOMIC	ZOUAVES	ZYGAPOPHYSIAL	ZYLONITE
ZOOTOMICAL	ZOUK	ZYGAPOPHYSIS	ZYLONITES
ZOOTOMICALLY	ZOUKS	ZYGOBRANCH	ZYMASE
ZOOTOMIES	ZOUNDS	ZYGOBRANCHIATE	ZYMASES
ZOOTOMIST	ZOWIE	ZYGOBRANCHIATES	ZYME
ZOOTOMISTS	ZOYSIA	ZYGOBRANCHS	ZYMES
ZOOTOMY	ZOYSIAS	ZYGOCACTI	ZYMIC
ZOOTOXIC	ZUCCHETTO	ZYGOCACTUS	ZYMITE
ZOOTOXIN	ZUCCHETTOS	ZYGOCACTUSES	ZYMITES
ZOOTOXINS	ZUCCHINI	ZYGOCARDIAC	ZYMOGEN
ZOOTROPE	ZUCCHINIS	ZYGODACTYL	ZYMOGENE
ZOOTROPES	ZUCHETTA	ZYGODACTYLIC	ZYMOGENES
ZOOTROPHIC	ZUCHETTAS	ZYGODACTYLISM	ZYMOGENESIS
ZOOTROPHIES	ZUCHETTO	ZYGODACTYLISMS	ZYMOGENIC
ZOOTROPHY	ZUCHETTOS	ZYGODACTYLOUS	ZYMOGENS
ZOOTSUITER	ZUFFOLI	ZYGODACTYLS	ZYMOGRAM
ZOOTSUITERS	ZUFFOLO	ZYGODONT	ZYMOGRAMS
ZOOTY	ZUFOLI	ZYGOID	ZYMOID
ZOOTYPE	ZUFOLO	ZYGOMA	ZYMOLOGIC
ZOOTYPES	ZUGZWANG	ZYGOMAS	ZYMOLOGICAL
ZOOTYPIC	ZUGZWANGED	ZYGOMATA	ZYMOLOGIES
ZOOXANTHELLA	ZUGZWANGING	ZYGOMATIC	ZYMOLOGIST
ZOOXANTHELLAE	ZUGZWANGS	ZYGOMORPHIC	ZYMOLOGISTS
ZOOZOO	ZULU	ZYGOMORPHIES	ZYMOLOGY

ZYMOLYSES
ZYMOLYSIS
ZYMOLYTIC
ZYMOME
ZYMOMES
ZYMOMETER
ZYMOMETERS
ZYMOSAN
ZYMOSANS
ZYMOSES
ZYMOSIMETER
ZYMOSIMETERS
ZYMOSIS
ZYMOTECHNIC
ZYMOTECHNICAL
ZYMOTECHNICS
ZYMOTIC
ZYMOTICALLY
ZYMOTICS
ZYMURGIES
ZYMURGY
ZYTHUM
ZYTHUMS
ZYZZYVA
ZYZZYVAS
ZZZS

Scrabble Lists 2005

The perfect companion volume to Scrabble Words 2005

essential reference for all tournament and club players

words grouped for easy Scrabble study

help with good 2- and 3-letter words

help with words that use the 'power tiles' J, Q, X and Z

ISBN: 0-00-719020-4, 1184 pp

Collins English Dictionary

Enrich your language with Collins' comprehensive coverage of English

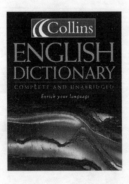

find out what the very latest buzz words mean

learn more about your language

choose the right words for every situation

discover where words come from

ISBN: 0-00-710982-2, 1888pp